# The secret of KOTA now at your Doorstep

# MATHEMATICS

## Topic Chapter Wise

# DPP *for* JEE ADVANCED

## DPP BOOKLET

## 75 + 26

**Topic-wise**     **Chapter-wise**

### Tests for Concept Checking & Speed Building

**Improves your learning by at least 20%**

- Collection of 2200 + MCQ's of all variety of questions
- Unique & innovative way of learning
- Detailed solutions to Topic-wise & Chapter-wise practice sheets
- Covers all important concepts of each topic
- As per latest pattern & syllabus

- **Corporate Office** : 45, 2nd Floor, Maharishi Dayanand Marg, Corner Market,
  Malviya Nagar, New Delhi-110017
  Tel. : 011-49842349 / 49842350

**Typeset by Disha DTP Team**

# DISHA PUBLICATION

## ALL RIGHTS RESERVED



For further information about books from DISHA,
Log on to **www.dishapublication.com** or email to **info@dishapublication.com**

# The book comprises of following two parts

# TOPIC-WISE
# DPP SHEETS
# WITH SOLUTIONS

# INDEX/SYLLABUS

# DPP - Daily Practice Problems

Name : ____________________     Date : __________

Start Time : __________     End Time : __________

## MATHEMATICS    M01

SYLLABUS : **Set Theory** : Definition of set, Representation of set, Different types of sets, Subsets, Operation on sets, Cartesian product of two sets, Venn-Diagram.

**Max. Marks : 69**     **Time : 60 min.**

### GENERAL INSTRUCTIONS

- The Daily Practice Problem Sheet contains **24** Questions divided into 4 sections.
  Section I has **13** MCQ's with ONLY 1 correct option. 2 marks for correct answer and No negative marks.
  Section II has **5** MCQ's with 1 or MORE THAN 1 correct option. 4 marks for correct answer(s) and (−1) for wrong answer.
  Section III has **1** Assertion-Reason MCQ's with ONLY 1 correct option. 3 marks for correct and (−1) mark for wrong answer.
  Section IV has **5** single digit integer answer questions. 4 marks for correct answer and (−1) for wrong answer.
- No mark will be given/ deducted if no bubble is filled. Keep a timer in front and stop immediately at the end of 60 min.
- You have to evaluate your Response Grids yourself with the help of Solution Booklet.
- The sheet follows a particular syllabus. Do not attempt the sheet before you have completed your preparation for that syllabus. Refer syllabus sheet in the starting of the book for the syllabus of all the DPP sheets.
- After completing the sheet check your answers with the solution booklet and complete the Result Grid. Finally spend time to analyse your performance and revise the areas which emerge out as weak in your evaluation.

---

## Section - I - Straight Objective Type

This section contains 13 multiple choice questions. Each question has 4 choices (a), (b), (c) and (d), out of which **ONLY ONE** is correct.

1. If A and B are non-empty subsets of a set, then $(A - B) \cup (B - A)$ equals
   (a) $(A \cap B) \cup (A \cup B)$
   (b) $(A \cup B) - (A \cap B)$
   (c) $A - (A \cap B)$
   (d) $(A \cup B) - B$

2. Let $A = \{x : x \in \mathbf{R}, |x| < 1\}$ $B = \{x : x \in \mathbf{R}, |x - 1| \geq 1\}$ and $A \cup B = \mathbf{R} - D$, then the set D is :
   (a) $\{x : 1 < x \leq 2\}$
   (b) $\{x : 1 \leq x < 2\}$
   (c) $\{x : -2 \leq x \leq 2\}$
   (d) none of these

3. If the sets A and B are defined as

$$A = \left\{(x,y) : y = \frac{1}{x}, x \neq 0, x \in \mathbf{R}\right\}; \quad B = \left\{(x,y) : y = -x, \in \mathbf{R}\right\},$$

then
   (a) $A \cap B = A$
   (b) $A \cap B = B$
   (c) $A \cap B = \phi$
   (d) none of these

4. If X and Y are two sets, then $X \cap (X \cup Y)^C$ equals
   (a) X
   (b) Y
   (c) $\phi$
   (d) none of these.

5. If A and B are any two sets, then $A \cup (A \cap B)$ is equal to
   (a) $B^C$
   (b) $A^C$
   (c) B
   (d) A

6. If sets A and B are defined as
   $A = \{(x, y) : y = e^x, x \in R\}, B = \{(x, y) : y = x, x \in R\}$ then
   (a) $B \subset A$
   (b) $A \subset B$
   (c) $A \cap B = \phi$
   (d) $A \cup B = A$

| RESPONSE GRID | 1. ⓐⓑⓒⓓ | 2. ⓐⓑⓒⓓ | 3. ⓐⓑⓒⓓ | 4. ⓐⓑⓒⓓ | 5. ⓐⓑⓒⓓ |
|---|---|---|---|---|---|
| | 6. ⓐⓑⓒⓓ | | | | |

**7.** If P, Q and R are subsets of a set A, then

$R \times (P^C \cup Q^C)^C$ equals.

(a) $(R \times P) \cap (R \times Q)$     (b) $(R \times Q) \cap (R \times P)$

(c) $(R \times P) \cup (R \times Q)$     (d) none of these

**8.** A market research group conducted a survey of 1000 consumers and reported that 720 consumers liked product A and 450 consumers liked product B. What is the least number that must have liked both products ?

(a) 170     (b) 280

(c) 220     (d) None

**9.** If $X = \{4^n - 3n - 1 / n \in \mathbf{N}\}$ and

$Y = \{9(n–1) / n \in \mathbf{N}\}$, then $X \cup Y$ is equal to

(a) X     (b) Y

(c) N     (d) $Y - \{2\}$

**10.** A survey of 500 television viewers produced the following information, 285 watch football, 195 watch hockey, 115 watch basket-ball, 45 watch football and basket ball, 70 watch football and hockey, 50 watch hockey and basket ball, 50 do not watch any of the three games. The number of viewers, who watch exactly one of the three games are

(a) 325     (b) 310

(c) 405     (d) 372

**11.** If $A = \{x \in \mathbf{R} : 0 < x < 1\}$ & $B = \{y \in \mathbf{R} : -1 < y < 1\}$, then $A \times B$ contains

(a) all point lying inside the rectangle having vertices at $(1, 1), (0, 1), (0, -1)$ and $(1, -1)$

(b) all point lying inside the rectangle having vertices at $(1, 0), (1, 1), (0, 1)$, and $(0, 0)$

(c) all point lying on the sides of the rectangle having vertices at $(1, 1), (0, 1), (0, -1)$ and $(1, -1)$

(d) none of these

**12.** If the set A has p elements, B has q elements, then the number of elements in $A \times B$ is

(a) $p + q + 1$     (b) $pq$

(c) $p^2$     (d) $p + q$

**13.** If $aN = \{ax : x \in N)$ then $3N \cap 7N =$

(a) 3N     (b) 7 N

(c) N     (d) 21 N

---

## Section - II - Multiple Correct Answer Type

This section contains 5 multiple correct answer(s) type questions. Each question has 4 choices (a), (b), (c) and (d), out of which **ONE OR MORE** is/are correct.

---

**14.** In a town of 10,000 families, it was found that 40% families buy newspaper A, 20% families buy newspaper B and 10% families buy newspaper C. 5% families buy A and B, 3% buy B and C and 4% buy A and C. If 2% families buy all the newspapers, then

(a) 3,300 families buy A only

(b) 1,400 families buy B only

(c) 4000 families buy none of A, B and C

(d) 3800 families buy A only and 1700 families buy B only

**15.** Consider the set A of all determinants of order 3 with entries 0 and 1 only. Let B be the subset of A consisting of all determinants with value 1. Let C be the subset of the set A consisting of all determinants with value 1. Then which of the following statements is/are incorrect?

(a) C is empty

(b) B has as many elements as C

(c) $A = B \cup C$

(d) B has twice as many elements as C

| RESPONSE GRID | | | | | |
|---|---|---|---|---|---|
| | **7.** ⓐⓑⓒⓓ | **8.** ⓐⓑⓒⓓ | **9.** ⓐⓑⓒⓓ | **10.** ⓐⓑⓒⓓ | **11.** ⓐⓑⓒⓓ |
| | **12.** ⓐⓑⓒⓓ | **13.** ⓐⓑⓒⓓ | **14.** ⓐⓑⓒⓓ | **15.** ⓐⓑⓒⓓ | |

*Space for Rough Work*

**16.** Let A and B two non-empty subsets of a set X such that A is not a subset of B, then which of the following statements are false ?

(a)  A is subset of the complement of B

(b)  B is a subset of A

(c)  A and B are disjoint

(d)  A and the complement of B are non-disjoint

**17.** Let A and B are two sets in a universal set U, then identify the incorrect statements from the followings.

(a)  $A - B = A' - B'$

(b)  $A - (A - B) = A \cup B$

(c)  $A - B = A' \cap B'$

(d)  $A \cup B = (A - B) \cup (B - A) \cup (A \cap B)$

**18.** Let f be a function on $\mathbf{R}$ or $\mathbf{R}$ is given by $f(x) = x^2$ and also let

$E = \{x \in \mathbf{R} : -1 \le x \le 0\}$ and $F = \{x \in \mathbf{R} : 0 \le x \le 1\}$

then which of the following are true ?

(a)  $f(E) = f(F)$

(b)  $E \cap F \subset f(E) \cap f(F)$

(c)  $E \cup F \subset f(E) \cup f(F)$

(d)  $f(E \cap F) = \{0\}$

## Section - III - Reasoning Type

This section contain 1 reasoning type question. This question has 4 choices (a), (b), (c) and (d) out of which **ONLY ONE** is correct.

**19.** **This question contains two statements: Statement-1 (Assertion) and Statement-2 (Reason) and has four alternative choices, only one of which is the correct answer. You have to select the correct choice.**

**Statement-1 :** If A and B are two non-empty sets which have 2 elements common then A × B and B × A have 4 elements common.

**Statement-2 :** If A and B have n elements common then A × B and B × A have 2n elements common.

(a)  Statement-1 is True, Statement-2 is True; Statement-2 is a correct explanation for Statement-1.

(b)  Statement-1 is True, Statement-2 is True; Statement-2 is NOT a correct explanation for Statement-1.

(c)  Statement -1 is True, Statement-2 is False.

(d)  Statement -1 is False, Statement-2 is True.

## Section - IV - Integer Type

This section contains 5 questions . The answer to each of the questions is a single digit integer. ranging from 0 to 9.

**20.** In a survey of 400 students in a school, 100 were listed as taking apple juice, 150 as taking orange juice and 75 were listed as taking both apple as well as orange juice. If $9X^2$ students were taking neither apple juice nor orange juice, then find the value of X.

**21.** Let A, B, C be finite sets. Suppose that n (A) = 10, n (B) = 15, n (C) = 20, n (A∩B) = 8 and n (B∩C) = 9. Then how many values are possible for n (A∪B∪C) ?

**22.** Suppose $A_1$, $A_2$, .......$A_{30}$, are thirty sets each with five elements and $B_1$, $B_2$,.........$B_m$ are m sets each with three elements. Let $\bigcup_{i=1}^{30} A_i = \bigcup_{j=1}^{m} B_j = S$. Assuming that each element of S belongs to exactly ten of the $A_i$'s and exactly 9 of $B_j$'s, the value of m is found to be 5Y. Find the value of Y.



*Space for Rough Work*

**23.** At a certain conference of 100 people, there are 29 Indian women and 23 Indian men. Of these Indian people, 4 are doctors and 24 are either men or doctors. There are no foreign doctors. If 8A foreigners and B women doctors are attending the conference, then find the value of A–B.

**24.** Out of 800 boys in a school, 224 played cricket, 240 played hockey and 336 played basketball. Of the total, 64 played both basketball and hockey, 40 played cricket and hockey, 80 played cricket & basketball, 24 all the three games. The number of boys who did not play any game is found to be $10(X)^4$. Find the value of X.

---

**RESPONSE GRID**   23. ⓪①②③④⑤⑥⑦⑧⑨   24. ⓪①②③④⑤⑥⑦⑧⑨

---

## DAILY PRACTICE PROBLEM DPP 01 - MATHS

| Total Questions | 24 | Total Marks | 69 |
|---|---|---|---|
| Attempted | | Correct | |
| Incorrect | | Net Score | |
| Cut-off Score | 12 | Qualifying Score | 40 |
| Success Gap = Net Score – Qualifying Score | | | |

$$\textbf{Net Score } = \sum_{i=1}^{VI}\left[(\textbf{correct}_i \times MM_i) - (In_i - NM_i)\right]$$

---

*Space for Rough Work*

# DPP - Daily Practice Problems

Name : [        ]　　　　　　　Date : [        ]

Start Time : [        ]　　　　End Time : [        ]

## MATHEMATICS　　M02

**SYLLABUS :** Relations : Definition, Domain and range, Different types of relations.

## Max. Marks : 68　　　　　　　　Time : 60 min.

### GENERAL INSTRUCTIONS

- The Daily Practice Problem Sheet contains **24** Questions divided into 5 sections.
  Section I has **12** MCQ's with ONLY 1 correct option. 2 marks for correct answer and No negative marks.
  Section II has **3** MCQ's with 1 or MORE THAN 1 correct option. 4 marks for correct answer(s) and (−1) for wrong answer.
  Section III has **1** PASSAGE with **2** MCQ's with ONLY 1 correct option. 3 marks for correct and (−1) mark for wrong answer.
  Section IV has **2** Assertion-Reason MCQ's with ONLY 1 correct option. 3 marks for correct and (−1) mark for wrong answer.
  Section V has **5** Asingle digit integer answer questions. 4 marks for correct answer and (−1) for wrong answer.
- No mark will be given/ deducted if no bubble is filled. Keep a timer in front and stop immediately at the end of 60 min.
- You have to evaluate your Response Grids yourself with the help of Solution Booklet.
- The sheet follows a particular syllabus. Do not attempt the sheet before you have completed your preparation for that syllabus. Refer syllabus sheet in the starting of the book for the syllabus of all the DPP sheets.
- After completing the sheet check your answers with the solution booklet and complete the Result Grid. Finally spend time to analyse your performance and revise the areas which emerge out as weak in your evaluation.

## Section - I - Straight Objective Type

This section contains 12 multiple choice questions. Each question has 4 choices (a), (b), (c) and (d), out of which **ONLY ONE** is correct.

**1.** Range of the relation $f(x) = \left[\dfrac{1}{ln(x^2+e)}\right] + \dfrac{1}{\sqrt{1+x^2}}$ is,

where $[*]$ denotes the greatest integer function and

$e = \underset{\alpha \to 0}{\text{Limit}}(1+\alpha)^{1/\alpha}$

(a) $\left(0, \dfrac{e+1}{e}\right) \cup \{2\}$　　　(b) $(0, 1)$

(c) $(0, 1] \cup \{2\}$　　　(d) $(0, 1) \cup \{2\}$

**2.** The range of the relation,

$f(x) = \cot^{-1}\log_{0.5}\left(x^4 - 2x^2 + 3\right)$ is

(a) $(0, \pi)$　　　(b) $\left(0, \dfrac{3\pi}{4}\right]$

(c) $\left[\dfrac{3\pi}{4}, \pi\right)$　　　(d) $\left[\dfrac{\pi}{2}, \dfrac{3\pi}{4}\right]$

**3.** The domain of the relation $y = \dfrac{1}{\log_{10}(1-x)} + \sqrt{x+2}$ is

(a) $(-3, -2)$ excluding $-2.5$
(b) $[0, 1]$ excluding $0.5$
(c) $[-2, 1)$ excluding $0$
(d) none of these

**4.** If $f(x)$ is defined on domain $[0, 1]$ then $f(2 \sin x)$ is defined on

(a) $\displaystyle\bigcup_{n \in I}\left\{\left[2n\pi, 2n\pi + \dfrac{\pi}{6}\right] \cup \left[2n\pi + \dfrac{5\pi}{6}, (2n+1)\pi\right]\right\}$

(b) $\displaystyle\bigcup_{n \in I}\left[2n\pi, 2n\pi + \dfrac{\pi}{6}\right]$

(c) $\displaystyle\bigcup_{n \in I}\left[2n\pi + \dfrac{5\pi}{6}, (2n+1)\pi\right]$

(d) None of these

| RESPONSE GRID | 1. ⓐⓑⓒⓓ | 2. ⓐⓑⓒⓓ | 3. ⓐⓑⓒⓓ | 4. ⓐⓑⓒⓓ |
|---|---|---|---|---|

**5.** Let R be a relation on $\mathbf{N} \times \mathbf{N}$ defined by
$(a, b)\, R\,(c, d) \Rightarrow ad\,(b + c) = bc\,(a+d)$. R is
(a) a partial order relation
(b) an equivalence relation
(c) an identity relation
(d) none of these

**6.** The range of the relation $f(x) = \sqrt{3x^2 - 4x + 5}$ is

(a) $\left(-\infty, \sqrt{\dfrac{11}{3}}\,\right]$ 

(b) $\left(-\infty, \sqrt{\dfrac{11}{3}}\,\right)$

(c) $\left[\sqrt{\dfrac{11}{3}}, \infty\right)$ 

(d) $\left(\sqrt{\dfrac{11}{3}}, \infty\right)$

**7.** If $f(x) = \cos^{-1}\left(\dfrac{2 - |x|}{4}\right) + [\log(3 - x)]^{-1}$, then its domain is

(a) $[-2, 6]$ 
(b) $[-6, 2) \cup (2, 3)$
(c) $[-6, 2]$ 
(d) $[-2, 2) \cup (2, 3]$

**8.** If $R_1 = \{(1, 1), (2, 2), (1, 2), (2, 1), (3, 3)\}$ and
$R_2 = \{(1, 1), (2, 2), (2, 3), (3, 2), (3, 3)\}$ are two relation in the
set $S = \{1, 2, 3\}$, the incorrect statement is :
(a) $R_1$ and $R_2$ both are equivalence relations in S.
(b) $R_1 \cap R_2$ is an equivalence relation in S.
(c) $R_1 \cup R_2$ is an equivalence relation in S.

(d) $R_1^{-1} \cap R_2^{-1}$ is an equivalence relation S.

**9.** The domain of definition of the relation $f(x) =$
$\sqrt[3]{\dfrac{2x + 1}{x^2 - 10x - 11}}$ is given by
(a) $x > 0$ 
(b) $x < 0$
(c) $x \neq -1$, $x \neq 11$ 
(d) $-\infty < x < \infty$

**10.** The domain of the relation
$f(x) = \cot^{-1}\left(\dfrac{x}{\sqrt{x^2 - [x^2]}}\right)$, $x \in R$ is

(a) $R - \{\pm\sqrt{n}, n \in N\}$
(b) All real numbers except integers
(c) R
(d) $R - \{0\}$

**11.** The range of $f(x) = \cos \dfrac{\pi[x]}{2}$ is

(a) $\{0, 1\}$ 
(b) $\{-1, 1\}$
(c) $\{-1, 0, 1\}$ 
(d) $[-1, 1]$

**12.** Range of the relation f defined by $f(x) = \left[\dfrac{1}{\sin\{x\}}\right]$ (where
[.] and {.} respectively denote the greatest integer and the
fractional part function) is
(a) I, the set of integers
(b) N, the set of natural numbers
(c) W, the set of whole numbers
(d) $\{2, 3, 4, \ldots\ldots\}$

---

## Section - II - Multiple Correct Answer Type

This section contains 3 multiple correct answer(s) type questions. Each
question has 4 choices (a), (b), (c) and (d), out of which **ONE OR MORE**
is/are correct.

---

**13.** If $l$ is a relation defined by n/m means that n is a factor of
m, then the relation '$l$' is
(a) reflexive
(b) transitive
(c) symmetric
(d) non-reflexive and symmetric.

**14.** Consider $f(x) = \left(\dfrac{2\sin x + \sin 2x}{2\cos x + \sin 2x} \cdot \dfrac{1 - \cos x}{1 - \sin x}\right)^{2/3}$ ; $x \in R$
Which of the following statements is /are correct ?
(a) Domain of f is R
(b) Range of f is R
(c) Domain of f is $R - (4n + 1)\dfrac{\pi}{2}$ , $n \in I$

(d) Domain of f is $R - (4n - 1)\dfrac{\pi}{2}$ , $n \in I$

---

<table>
<tr><td rowspan="2">RESPONSE<br>GRID</td><td>5. ⓐⓑⓒⓓ</td><td>6. ⓐⓑⓒⓓ</td><td>7. ⓐⓑⓒⓓ</td><td>8. ⓐⓑⓒⓓ</td><td>9. ⓐⓑⓒⓓ</td></tr>
<tr><td>10. ⓐⓑⓒⓓ</td><td>11. ⓐⓑⓒⓓ</td><td>12. ⓐⓑⓒⓓ</td><td>13. ⓐⓑⓒⓓ</td><td>14. ⓐⓑⓒⓓ</td></tr>
</table>

---

*Space for Rough Work*

**15.** Assume R and S (non-empty) relations in a set A. Which of the relations given below are true ?

(a)  If R and S are transitive, then $R \cup S$ is transitive.

(b)  If R and S are transitive, then $R \cap S$ is transitive.

(c)  If R and S are symmetric, then $R \cup S$ is symmetric.

(d)  If R and S are reflexive, then $R \cap S$ is reflexive.

## Section - III - Linked Comprehension Type

This section contains one paragraph. Based upon the paragraph, 3 multiple choice questions have to be answered. Each question has 4 choices (a), (b), (c) and (d), out of which **ONLY ONE** is correct.

The graph of a relation is

(i)  Symmetric with respect to the x-axis provided that whenever (a, b) is a point on the graph, so is $(a, -b)$

(ii)  Symmetric with respect to the y-axis provided that whenever (a, b) is a point on the graph, so is $(-a, b)$

(iii)  Symmetric with respect to the origin provided that whenever (a, b) is a point on the graph, so is $(-a, -b)$

(iv)  Symmetric with respect to the line $y = x$, provided that whenever (a, b) is a point on the graph, so is (b, a)

**16.** The graph of the relation $x^4 + y^3 = 1$ is symmetric with respect to

(a)  the x-axis  (b)  the y-axis

(c)  the origin  (d)  the line $y = x$

**17.** Suppose R is a relation whose graph is symmetric to both the x-axis and y-axis, and that the point $(1, 2)$ is on the graph of R. Which one of the following points is not necessarily on the graph of R?

(a)  $(-1, 2)$  (b)  $(1, -2)$

(c)  $(-1, -2)$  (d)  $(2, 1)$

## Section - IV - Reasoning Type

This section contains 2 reasoning type questions. Each question has 4 choices (a), (b), (c) and (d) out of which **ONLY ONE** is correct.

**DIRECTIONS for (Qs. 18 & 19) : Each of these questions contains two statements: Statement-1 (Assertion) and Statement-2 (Reason). Each of these questions has four alternative choices, only one of which is the correct answer. You have to select the correct choice.**

(a)  Statement-1 is True, Statement-2 is True; Statement-2 is a correct explanation for Statement-1.

(b)  Statement-1 is True, Statement-2 is True; Statement-2 is NOT a correct explanation for Statement-1.

(c)  Statement -1 is True, Statement-2 is False.

(d)  Statement -1 is False, Statement-2 is True.

**18.** If $f(x) = \dfrac{x-1}{x(x-2)}$

**Statement 1 :** The range of $f(x) = \dfrac{x-1}{x(x-2)}$ is the set of all real number.

**Statement 2 :** The range of $g(x) = \dfrac{(x-a)}{(x-c)(x-d)}$ is R if $a \in$ (c, d); a, c, d $\in$ R.

**19.**  **Statement-1:** The domain of the relation $f(x) = \sqrt{\log_2 \sin x}$ is $(4n+1)\dfrac{\pi}{2}$, $n \in$ N.

**Statement-2:** Expression under even root should be $\geq 0$.

---

| RESPONSE GRID | 15. ⓐⓑⓒⓓ | 16. ⓐⓑⓒⓓ | 17. ⓐⓑⓒⓓ | 18. ⓐⓑⓒⓓ | 19. ⓐⓑⓒⓓ |

*Space for Rough Work*

## Section - V - Integer Type

This section contains 5 questions . The answer to each of the questions is a single digit integer. ranging from 0 to 9.

**20.** The domain of the relation $f(x) = \sqrt{\log_{10}\dfrac{3-x}{x}}$ is $\left(0, \dfrac{A}{B}\right]$.

Find the value of $A - B$.

**21.** The set of all real numbers $x$ for which $\log_{2004}(\log_{2003}(\log_{2002}(\log_{2001} x)))$ is defined as $\{x \mid x > c\}$. The value of $c$ is found to be $(2000 + A)^{(2000 + B)}$.

Find the value of $A + 2B$.

**22.** Domain of $\cos^{-1}[2x^2 - 3]$, where $[\cdot]$ denotes greatest integer function, is $\left(-\sqrt{\dfrac{5}{2}}, -M\right] \cup \left[M, \sqrt{\dfrac{5}{2}}\right)$. Find the value of M.

**23.** The domain of $f(x) = \dfrac{\log_2(x+3)}{x^2 + 3x + 2}$ is $(-3, +\infty) - \{-P, -Q\}$. Find the value of $P + Q$

**24.** Let $f(x) = \dfrac{\sin x}{\sqrt{1 + \tan^2 x}} - \dfrac{\cos x}{\sqrt{1 + \cot^2 x}}$ then range of $f(x)$ is $[-A, A]$. Find the value of A.

<table>
<tr><td rowspan="3">RESPONSE GRID</td><td>20. ⓪①②③④⑤⑥⑦⑧⑨</td><td>21. ⓪①②③④⑤⑥⑦⑧⑨</td></tr>
<tr><td>22. ⓪①②③④⑤⑥⑦⑧⑨</td><td>23. ⓪①②③④⑤⑥⑦⑧⑨</td></tr>
<tr><td>24. ⓪①②③④⑤⑥⑦⑧⑨</td><td></td></tr>
</table>

## DAILY PRACTICE PROBLEM DPP 02 - MATHS

| Total Questions | 24 | Total Marks | 68 |
|---|---|---|---|
| Attempted | | Correct | |
| Incorrect | | Net Score | |
| Cut-off Score | 14 | Qualifying Score | 44 |
| Success Gap = Net Score – Qualifying Score | | | |

$$\text{Net Score} = \sum_{i=1}^{VI}\left[(\text{correct}_i \times MM_i) - (In_i - NM_i)\right]$$

# DPP - Daily Practice Problems

Name :                           Date : 

Start Time :                    End Time : 

# MATHEMATICS    M03

SYLLABUS : Logarithm and its properties

**Max. Marks : 69**           **Time : 60 min.**

## GENERAL INSTRUCTIONS

- The Daily Practice Problem Sheet contains **23** Questions divided into 6 sections.
  Section I has **8** MCQ's with ONLY 1 correct option. 2 marks for correct answer and No negative marks.
  Section II has **3** MCQ's with 1 or MORE THAN 1 correct option. 4 marks for correct answer(s) and (−1) for wrong answer.
  Section III has **1** PASSAGE with **3** MCQ's with ONLY 1 correct option. 3 marks for correct and (−1) mark for wrong answer.
  Section IV has **2** MCQ's with multiple matchings. 1 mark for the correct matching of each row & No negative marks.
  Section V has **2** Assertion-Reason MCQ's with ONLY 1 correct option. 3 marks for correct and (−1) mark for wrong answer.
  Section VI has **5** Single digit integer answer questions. 4 marks for correct answer and (−1) for wrong answer.
- No mark will be given/ deducted if no bubble is filled. Keep a timer in front and stop immediately at the end of 60 min.
- You have to evaluate your Response Grids yourself with the help of Solution Booklet.
- The sheet follows a particular syllabus. Do not attempt the sheet before you have completed your preparation for that syllabus. Refer syllabus sheet in the starting of the book for the syllabus of all the DPP sheets.
- After completing the sheet check your answers with the solution booklet and complete the Result Grid. Finally spend time to analyse your performance and revise the areas which emerge out as weak in your evaluation.

## Section - I - Straight Objective Type

This section contains 8 multiple choice questions. Each question 4 has choices (a), (b), (c) and (d), out of which **ONLY ONE** is correct.

**1.** The value of $\left(\dfrac{1}{\sqrt{27}}\right)^{2-\left(\frac{\log_5 16}{2\log_5 9}\right)}$ equals to

(a) $\dfrac{\sqrt{2}}{27}$    (b) $\dfrac{2\sqrt{2}}{27}$    (c) $\dfrac{4}{27}$    (d) $\dfrac{4\sqrt{2}}{27}$

**2.** Which of the following is / are correct ?

(a) If $x^{\log_3 x^2 + (\log_3 x)^2 - 10} = \dfrac{1}{x^2}$, then $x = 9$ or $\dfrac{1}{81}$

(b) $\dfrac{\log x + \log x^4 + \log x^9 + .... + \log x^{n^2}}{\log x + \log x^2 + \log x^3 + ........ + \log x^n} = \dfrac{2n+1}{3}$ $(x>0)$

(c) If $\log_{10} 3 = 0.477$, the number of digits in $3^{40}$ is 20

(d) all above are correct.

**3.** Solution of which of the equation is not correctly expressed

(a) If $\log_3 x \, \log_y 3 \, \log_2 y = 5$, then $x = 32$

(b) If $\log_2 x \times \log_2 \dfrac{x}{16} + 4 = 0$, then $x = 2$

(c) If $2\log_{16}(x^2 + x) - \log_4(x+1) = 2$, then $x = 16$

(d) If $y = a^{\frac{1}{1-\log_a x}}$ and $z = a^{\frac{1}{1-\log_a y}}$, then $x = a^{\frac{1}{1-\log_a z}}$

**4.** If $\dfrac{x(y+z-x)}{\log x} = \dfrac{y(z+x-y)}{\log y} = \dfrac{z(x+y-z)}{\log z}$. Then

(a) $x^y y^x = z^y y^z$      (b) $z^y y^z = x^z z^x$

(c) $x^y y^x = x^z z^x$      (d) all are correct

**5.** Which of the following is correct?

(a) If $a^2 + 4b^2 = 12ab$, then $\log(a+2b) = \dfrac{1}{2}(\log a + \log b)$

(b) If $\dfrac{\log x}{b-c} = \dfrac{\log y}{c-a} = \dfrac{\log z}{a-b}$, then $x^a . y^b . z^c = abc$

(c) $\dfrac{1}{\log_{xy} xyz} + \dfrac{1}{\log_{yz} xyz} + \dfrac{1}{\log_{zx} xyz} = 2$

(d) all are correct

---

**RESPONSE GRID**    **1.** ⓐⓑⓒⓓ    **2.** ⓐⓑⓒⓓ    **3.** ⓐⓑⓒⓓ    **4.** ⓐⓑⓒⓓ    **5.** ⓐⓑⓒⓓ

**DPP/M/03**

6. Which of the following is correct?

   (a) The value of $\dfrac{1}{\log_3 \pi} + \dfrac{1}{\log_4 \pi}$ is greater than 2

   (b) The value of $7 \log_a \dfrac{16}{15} + 5 \log_a \dfrac{25}{24} + 3 \log_a \dfrac{81}{80}$ is $\log_a 5$

   (c) $\log_7 \log_7 \sqrt{7\sqrt{7\sqrt{7}}} = 1 - 3\log_7 2$

   (d) If $A = \log_2 \log_2 \log_4 256 + 2\log_{\sqrt{2}} 2$, then A equals 5

7. Which of the following is correct?

   (a) If a, b, c, d............... are in G.P., then $\log_x a, \log_x b, \log_x c, \log_x d$ .......... are in GP

   (b) If $x^{18} = y^{21} = z^{28}$ then $3, 3\log_y x, 3\log_z y, 7\log_x z$ are in GP.

   (c) If $\log_l x, \log_m x, \log_n x$ are in arithmetic progression and $x \neq 1$, then $n^2 = (lm)^{\log_x m}$

   (d) If a, b, c are in G.P., then $\log_a x, \log_b x, \log_c x$ are in H.P.

8. Which of the following is correct ?

   (a) If $\log_{12} 27 = a$, then $\log_6 16 = \dfrac{2-a}{2+a}$

   (b) If $\log_a b = \log_b c = \log_c a$, then $a = b = c$

   (c) If $\dfrac{1}{\log_a x} + \dfrac{1}{\log_c x} = \dfrac{2}{\log_b x}$, then a, b, c are in A.P.

   (d) If $\log(3 + 4 + k) = \log 3 + \log 4 + \log k$, then the value of k is 7.

---

### Section - II - Multiple Correct Answer Type

This section contains 3 multiple correct answer(s) type questions. Each question has 4 choices (a), (b), (c) and (d), out of which **ONE OR MORE** is/are correct.

---

9. If $x^2 + 4y^2 = 12xy$, $x \in [1, 4], y \in [1, 4]$, then

   (a) the greatest value of $\log_2(x + 2y)$ is 4

   (b) the least value of $\log_2(x + 2y)$ is 3

   (c) the range of values of $\log_2(x + 2y)$ is $[2, 4]$

   (d) the number of integral values of $(x, y)$ is 2 such that $\log_2(x + 2y)$ is equal to 3

10. If $\dfrac{1}{2} \le \log_{0.1} x \le 2$ then

   (a) the maximum value of x is $\dfrac{1}{\sqrt{10}}$

   (b) x lies between $\dfrac{1}{100}$ and $\dfrac{1}{\sqrt{10}}$

   (c) x does not lie between $\dfrac{1}{100}$ and $\dfrac{1}{\sqrt{10}}$

   (d) the minimum value of x is $\dfrac{1}{100}$

11. If $x^{3/4(\log_3 x)^2 + \log_3 x - 5/4} = \sqrt{3}$ then x has
   (a) one positive integral value
   (b) one irrational value
   (c) two positive rational values
   (d) none of these

---

### Section - III - Linked Comprehension Type

This section contains one paragraph. Based upon the paragraph, 3 multiple choice questions have to be answered. Each question has 4 choices (a), (b), (c) and (d), out of which **ONLY ONE** is correct.

---

Equations of the form (i) $f(\log_a x) = 0, a > 0, a \neq 1$ and (ii) $g(\log_x A) = 0, A > 0$, then eq. (i) is equivalent to $f(t) = 0$, where $t = \log_a x$. If $t_1, t_2, t_3, ..., t_k$ are the roots of $f(t) = 0$, then $\log_a x = t_1, \log_a x = t_2, ......, \log_a x = t_k$ and eq. (ii) is equivalent to $f(y) = 0$, where $y = \log_x A$. If $y_1, y_2, y_3, ....., y_k$ are the roots of $f(y) = 0$, then $\log_x A = y_1, \log_x A = y_2, ...., \log_x A = y_k$.

On the basis of above information, answer the following questions:

12. The number of solutions of the equation
$$\dfrac{1 - 2(\log x^2)^2}{\log x - 2(\log x)^2} = 1 \text{ is}$$
   (a) 0     (b) 1     (c) 2     (d) infinite

13. The number of solutions of the equation
$$(\log_x 10)^3 - 6(\log_x 10)^2 + 11\log_x 10 - 6 = 0 \text{ is}$$
   (a) 0     (b) 1     (c) 2     (d) 3

14. The solution set of
$$(\log_5 x)^2 + \log_5 x + 1 = \dfrac{7}{\log_5 x - 1} \text{ contains}$$
   (a) $(1, 3)$     (b) $\{1\}$     (c) $\{25\}$     (d) $\{1, 25\}$

---

<table>
<tr><td rowspan="2">RESPONSE GRID</td><td>6. ⓐⓑⓒⓓ</td><td>7. ⓐⓑⓒⓓ</td><td>8. ⓐⓑⓒⓓ</td><td>9. ⓐⓑⓒⓓ</td><td>10. ⓐⓑⓒⓓ</td></tr>
<tr><td>11. ⓐⓑⓒⓓ</td><td>12. ⓐⓑⓒⓓ</td><td>13. ⓐⓑⓒⓓ</td><td>14. ⓐⓑⓒⓓ</td><td></td></tr>
</table>

---

*Space for Rough Work*

### Section - IV - Matrix-Match Type

This section contains 2 questions. It contains statements given in two columns, which have to be matched. Statements in Column I are labelled as A, B, C and D whereas statements in Column II are labelled as p, q, r and s. The answers to these questions have to be appropriately bubbled as illustrated in the following example. If the correct matches are A-p, A-r, B-p, B-s, C-r, C-s and D-q, then the correctly bubbled matrix will look like the following :

**15.**

| | Column I | | Column II |
|---|---|---|---|
| (A) | The solution set of $\log_{100}|x+y| = \dfrac{1}{2}$, $\log_{10} y - \log_{10}|x| = \log_{100} 4$ is | p. | $\{\sqrt{2}, 2\}$ |
| (B) | The solution set of $4(\log_2 x)^2 + 1 = 2\log_2 y$ and $\log_2 x^2 \ge \log_2 y$ is | q. | $\{1, 1\}$ |
| (C) | The solution set of $\log_4 x - \log_2 y = 0$ and $x^2 - 5y^2 + 4 = 0$ is | r. | $\{-10, 20\}$ |
| | | s. | $\{4, 2\}$ |
| | | t. | $\left\{\dfrac{10}{3}, \dfrac{20}{3}\right\}$ |

**16.**

| | Column I | | Column II |
|---|---|---|---|
| (A) | If $\log_{34} 5$ lies in the interval $(a, b)$, then | p. | $[10a + 10\,b] = 8$, where [.] denotes the greatest integer function |
| (B) | If $\log_{300} 4$ lies in the interval $(a, b)$, then | q. | $(10a + 10b) = 5$ where (.) denotes the least integer function |
| (C) | If $\log_{400} 3$ lies in the interval $(a, b)$, then | r. | $[6b - 3a] = 2$ where [.] denotes the greatest integer function |
| | | s. | $[10\,a + 10b] = 3$ where [.] denotes the greatest integer function |
| | | t. | $(6b - 3a) = 1$ where (.) denotes the least integer function |

### Section - V - Reasoning Type

This section contains 2 reasoning type questions. Each question has 4 choices (a), (b), (c) and (d) out of which **ONLY ONE** is correct.

**DIRECTIONS for (Qs. 17 & 18) : Each of these questions contains two statements: Statement-1 (Assertion) and Statement-2 (Reason). Each of these questions has four alternative choices, only one of which is the correct answer. You have to select the correct choice.**

(a) Statement-1 is True, Statement-2 is True; Statement-2 is a correct explanation for Statement-1.

(b) Statement-1 is True, Statement-2 is True; Statement-2 is NOT a correct explanation for Statement-1.

(c) Statement-1 is True, Statement-2 is False.

(d) Statement-1 is False, Statement-2 is True.

**17. Statement 1:** $\log_{1/5}\dfrac{4x+6}{x} \ge 0$ has no solution for $x \in \left(-\dfrac{3}{2}, -1\right)$

**Statement 2:** $2^{(y-x)}.(x+y) = 1, (x+y)^{x-y} = 2$ has only one pair of solutions.

**18. Statement 1:** $\log_a b > 0$, if $a > 1$ and $0 < b < 1$.

**Statement 2:** The number of digits in $2^{100}$ is 31.

| | |
|---|---|
| **RESPONSE GRID** | **15. A** - ⓟⓠⓡⓢⓣ; **B** - ⓟⓠⓡⓢⓣ; **C** - ⓟⓠⓡⓢⓣ; **D** - ⓟⓠⓡⓢⓣ <br> **16. A** - ⓟⓠⓡⓢⓣ; **B** - ⓟⓠⓡⓢⓣ; **C** - ⓟⓠⓡⓢⓣ; **D** - ⓟⓠⓡⓢⓣ <br> **17.** ⓐⓑⓒⓓ   **18.** ⓐⓑⓒⓓ |

*Space for Rough Work*

### Section - VI - Integer Type

This section contains 5 questions . The answer to each of the questions is a single digit integer. ranging from 0 to 9.

**19.** If $a = \log_{24} 12$, $b = \log_{36} 24$, $c = \log_{48} 36$, then $1 + abc$ is equal to $x\ a^p b^q c^r$. Find the value of $x + p + q + r$

**20.** If the value of $(0.05)^{\log_{\sqrt{20}}(0.1+0.01+0.001+\dots)}$ is $X^2$, then find the value of X.

**21.** The value of x obtained from equation $(4)^{\log_9 3} + (9)^{\log_2 4} = (10)^{\log_x 83}$ will be 2p. Find the value of p.

**22.** If sum of the roots of the equation $x + 1 = 2\log_2(2^x + 3) - 2\log_4(1980 - 2^{-x})$ is $\log_a b$, then find the value of $b - a$.

**23.** If $\log_k x \cdot \log_5 k = \log_x 5$, $k \neq 1$, then x is equal to $\dfrac{1}{a}$ or a. Find a.

| | | |
|---|---|---|
| **RESPONSE GRID** | 19. ⓪①②③④⑤⑥⑦⑧⑨ | 20. ⓪①②③④⑤⑥⑦⑧⑨ |
| | 21. ⓪①②③④⑤⑥⑦⑧⑨ | 22. ⓪①②③④⑤⑥⑦⑧⑨ |
| | 23. ⓪①②③④⑤⑥⑦⑧⑨ | |

## DAILY PRACTICE PROBLEM DPP 03 - MATHS

| Total Questions | 23 | Total Marks | 69 |
|---|---|---|---|
| Attempted | | Correct | |
| Incorrect | | Net Score | |
| Cut-off Score | 14 | Qualifying Score | 45 |
| Success Gap = Net Score – Qualifying Score | | | |

$$\text{Net Score} = \sum_{i=1}^{VI}\left[(\text{correct}_i \times MM_i) - (In_i - NM_i)\right]$$

*Space for Rough Work*

**Name :**

**Date :**

**Start Time :**

**End Time :**

# MATHEMATICS    M04

**SYLLABUS : Complex Number-1** : Integral power of iota, Algebraic operations and Equality of complex numbers, Conjugate of a complex number

## Max. Marks : 67        Time : 60 min.

### GENERAL INSTRUCTIONS

- The Daily Practice Problem Sheet contains **22** Questions divided into 5 sections.
  Section I has **8** MCQ's with ONLY 1 correct option. 2 marks for correct answer and No negative marks.
  Section II has **4** MCQ's with 1 or MORE THAN 1 correct option. 4 marks for correct answer(s) and (–1) for wrong answer.
  Section III has **1** PASSAGE with **3** MCQ's with ONLY 1 correct option. 3 marks for correct and (–1) mark for wrong answer.
  Section IV has **2** Assertion-Reason MCQ's with ONLY 1 correct option. 3 marks for correct and (–1) mark for wrong answer.
  Section V has **5** single digit integer answer questions. 4 marks for correct answer and (–1) for wrong answer.
- No mark will be given/ deducted if no bubble is filled. Keep a timer in front and stop immediately at the end of 60 min.
- You have to evaluate your Response Grids yourself with the help of Solution Booklet.
- The sheet follows a particular syllabus. Do not attempt the sheet before you have completed your preparation for that syllabus. Refer syllabus sheet in the starting of the book for the syllabus of all the DPP sheets.
- After completing the sheet check your answers with the solution booklet and complete the Result Grid. Finally spend time to analyse your performance and revise the areas which emerge out as weak in your evaluation.

## Section - I - Straight Objective Type

This section contains 8 multiple choice questions. Each question has 4 choices (a), (b), (c) and (d), out of which **ONLY ONE** is correct.

**1.** If $z = i^i$, where $i = \sqrt{-1}$, then –

(a) $z$ is purely real
(b) $z$ is purely imaginary
(c) $|z| = 1$
(d) $\arg(z) = \pi - \tan^{-1}(1/\sqrt{2})$

**2.** The value of the sum $\sum\limits_{n=1}^{13} (i^n + i^{n+1})$, where $i = \sqrt{-1}$, equals

(a) $i$       (b) $i - 1$
(c) $-i$      (d) $0$

**3.** For positive integers $n_1$, $n_2$ the value of the expression $(1+i)^{n_1} + (1+i^3)^{n_1} + (1+i^5)^{n_2} + (1+i^7)^{n_2}$, where $i = \sqrt{-1}$ is a real number if and only if

(a) $n_1 = n_2 + 1$      (b) $n_1 = n_2 - 1$
(c) $n_1 = n_2$         (d) $n_1 > 0, n_2 > 0$

**4.** If $i = \sqrt{-1}$, then $4 + 5\left(-\dfrac{1}{2} + \dfrac{i\sqrt{3}}{2}\right)^{334} + 3\left(-\dfrac{1}{2} + \dfrac{i\sqrt{3}}{2}\right)^{365}$

is equal to

(a) $1 - i\sqrt{3}$      (b) $-1 + i\sqrt{3}$
(c) $i\sqrt{3}$        (d) $-i\sqrt{3}$

**5.** The complex numbers $\sin x + i \cos 2x$ and $\cos x - i \sin 2x$ are conjugate to each other, for

(a) $x = n\pi$        (b) $x = 0$
(c) $x = (n + 1/2)\pi$   (d) no value of $x$.

| RESPONSE GRID | 1. ⓐⓑⓒⓓ | 2. ⓐⓑⓒⓓ | 3. ⓐⓑⓒⓓ | 4. ⓐⓑⓒⓓ | 5. ⓐⓑⓒⓓ |
|---|---|---|---|---|---|

**6.** If $a + ib > c + id$, then :

(a) $a > c, b > d$

(b) $a > c, b \geq d$

(c) $a > c, b = d = 0$

(d) none of these

**7.** Consider a quadratic equation $az^2 + bz + c = 0$, where $a$, $b$, $c$ are complex numbers. The condition that the equation has one purely imaginary root is

(a) $(b\overline{c} + c\overline{b})(a\overline{b} + \overline{a}b) + (c\overline{a} - a\overline{c})^2 = 0$

(b) $(b\overline{c} + c\overline{b})(c\overline{a} + a\overline{c}) + (a\overline{b} - \overline{a}b)^2 = 0$

(c) $(a\overline{b} + \overline{a}b)(c\overline{a} + \overline{c}a) + (b\overline{c} - \overline{b}c)^2 = 0$

(d) none of these

**8.** Let $z_1 = 6 + i$ and $z_2 = 4 - 3i$. Let $z$ be a complex number such that $\arg\left(\dfrac{z - z_1}{z_2 - z}\right) = \dfrac{\pi}{2}$; then $z$ satisfies

(a) $|z - (5 - i)| = 5$

(b) $|z - (5 - i)| = \sqrt{5}$

(c) $|z - (5 + i)| = 5$

(d) $|z - (5 + i)| = \sqrt{5}$

(b) $\alpha + \overline{\alpha} = 0$

(c) $\alpha + \overline{\alpha} = -1$

(d) the absolute value of the real root is 1

**10.** If $f(x)$ and $g(x)$ are two polynomials such that the polynomial $h(x) = xf(x^3) + x^2g(x^6)$ is divisible by $x^2 + x + 1$, then

(a) $f(1) = g(1)$ 　　　(b) $f(1) = -g(1)$

(c) $h(1) = 0$ 　　　(d) none of these

**11.** A complex number z satisfies the equation $|z|^2 - 2iz + 2c(1 + i) = 0$, where c is real. The values of c for which the above equation has no solution can be given by

(a) $c \in (-\infty, -1 - \sqrt{2})$

(b) $c \in [-1 - \sqrt{2}, -1 + \sqrt{2}]$

(c) $c \in (-1 + \sqrt{2}, \infty)$

(d) $c \in \mathbf{R}$

**12.** If $z_1 = a + ib$ and $z_2 = c + id$ are complex numbers such that $|z_1| = |z_2| = 1$ and $\mathrm{Re}(z_1 \overline{z}_2) = 0$, then the pair of complex numbers $\omega_1 = a + ic$ and $\omega_2 = b + id$ satisfies

(a) $|\omega_1| = 1$ 　　　(b) $|\omega_2| = 1$

(c) $\mathrm{Re}(\omega_1 \overline{\omega}_2) = 0$ 　　　(d) $\omega_1 \overline{\omega}_2 = 0$

---

## Section - II - Multiple Correct Answer Type

This section contains 4 multiple correct answer(s) type questions. Each question has 4 choices (a), (b), (c) and (d), out of which **ONE OR MORE** is/are correct.

---

**9.** If $\alpha$ is a complex constant such that $\alpha z^2 + z + \overline{\alpha} = 0$ has a real root then

(a) $\alpha + \overline{\alpha} = 1$

## Section - III - Linked Comprehension Type

This section contains one paragraph. Based upon the paragraph, 3 multiple choice questions have to be answered. Each question has 4 choices (a), (b), (c) and (d), out of which **ONLY ONE** is correct.

---

If $a\cos\alpha + b\cos\beta + \cos\gamma = 0 = a\sin\alpha + b\sin\beta + c\sin\gamma$; where $a, b, c \in R$ and $-\pi < \alpha, \beta, \gamma \leq \pi$

| | |
|---|---|
| **RESPONSE** | **6.** ⓐⓑⓒⓓ 　**7.** ⓐⓑⓒⓓ 　**8.** ⓐⓑⓒⓓ 　**9.** ⓐⓑⓒⓓ 　**10.** ⓐⓑⓒⓓ |
| **GRID** | **11.** ⓐⓑⓒⓓ 　**12.** ⓐⓑⓒⓓ |

*Space for Rough Work*

Then, let $A = e^{i\alpha}$, $B = e^{i\beta}$ and $C = e^{i\gamma}$ where $i = \sqrt{-1}$

$$aA + bB + cC = 0 \text{ and } \frac{a}{A} + \frac{b}{B} + \frac{c}{C} = 0$$

We get $(aA)^3 + (bB)^3 + (cC)^3 = 3\,abc\,ABC,$

$$\left(\frac{a}{A}\right)^3 + \left(\frac{b}{B}\right)^3 + \left(\frac{c}{C}\right)^3 = \frac{3abc}{ABC}$$

and $aBC + bCA + cAB = 0$

On the basis of above information, answer the following questions:

**13.** If $\dfrac{A}{B} + \dfrac{B}{C} + \dfrac{C}{A} = 1$, then $\Sigma \cos(\alpha - \beta)$ is equal to

(a) $-\dfrac{3}{2}$

(b) $0$

(c) $1$

(d) $\dfrac{3}{2}$

**14.** If $\sin^n \alpha + \sin^n \beta + \sin^n \gamma = \dfrac{3}{2}$

and $\cos(\alpha + \beta) + \cos(\beta + \gamma) + \cos(\gamma + \alpha) = \lambda,$ then the

value of $(n, \lambda)$ is

(a) $(3, 2)$

(b) $(2, 3)$

(c) $(2, 0)$

(d) $(3, 0)$

**15.** If $\sin \alpha + 2 \sin \beta + 3 \sin \gamma = 0$, then the value of $\alpha + \beta - \gamma$

is equal to

(a) $-2\alpha$

(b) $-2\beta$

(c) $-2\gamma$

(d) $0$

## Section - IV - Reasoning Type

This section contains 2 reasoning type questions. Each question has 4 choices (a), (b), (c) and (d) out of which **ONLY ONE** is correct.

**DIRECTIONS for (Qs. 16 & 17) :** Each of these questions contains two statements: Statement-1 (Assertion) and Statement-2 (Reason). Each of these questions has four alternative choices, only one of which is the correct answer. You have to select the correct choice.

(a) Statement-1 is True, Statement-2 is True; Statement-2 is a correct explanation for Statement-1.

(b) Statement-1 is True, Statement-2 is True; Statement-2 is NOT a correct explanation for Statement-1.

(c) Statement-1 is True, Statement-2 is False.

(d) Statement-1 is False, Statement-2 is True.

**16. Statement 1:** $\displaystyle\sum_{r=1}^{4n+11} i^r = -i, i = \sqrt{-1}$

**Statement 2:** Sum of four consecutive powers of $i$ is zero.

**17. Statement 1:** $3 + ix^2 y$ and $x^2 + y + 4i$ are conjugate numbers, then $x^2 + y^2 = 3$

**Statement 2:** If sum and product of two complex numbers is real then they are conjugate complex numbers.

## Section - V - Integer Type

This section contains 5 questions . The answer to each of the questions is a single digit integer. ranging from 0 to 9.

**18.** The polynomial $f(x) = x^4 + ax^3 + bx^2 + cx + d$ has real coefficients and $f(2i) = f(z + i) = 0$. Find the value of $(a + b + c + d)$.

<table>
<tr><td rowspan="2">**RESPONSE GRID**</td><td>13. ⓐⓑⓒⓓ</td><td>14. ⓐⓑⓒⓓ</td><td>15. ⓐⓑⓒⓓ</td><td>16. ⓐⓑⓒⓓ</td><td>17. ⓐⓑⓒⓓ</td></tr>
<tr><td colspan="5">18. ⓪①②③④⑤⑥⑦⑧⑨</td></tr>
</table>

*Space for Rough Work*

**19.** If $\left[ i^{19} + \left( \dfrac{1}{i} \right)^{25} \right]^2 = -X$, find the value of X.

**20.** If $\sum\limits_{k=0}^{100} i^k = x + iy$, then find the value of $x + y$.

**21.** Let $z = 9 + bi$ where b is non zero real and $i^2 = -1$. If the imaginary part of $z^2$ and $z^3$ are equal, then find the value of $\dfrac{b}{3}$.

**22.** Find the smallest positive integer n for which $\left( \dfrac{1+i}{1-i} \right)^n = 1$.

| RESPONSE GRID | | |
|---|---|---|
| **19.** ⓪①②③④⑤⑥⑦⑧⑨ | | **20.** ⓪①②③④⑤⑥⑦⑧⑨ |
| **21.** ⓪①②③④⑤⑥⑦⑧⑨ | | **22.** ⓪①②③④⑤⑥⑦⑧⑨ |

## DAILY PRACTICE PROBLEM DPP 04 - MATHS

| Total Questions | 22 | Total Marks | 67 |
|---|---|---|---|
| Attempted | | Correct | |
| Incorrect | | Net Score | |
| Cut-off Score | 13 | Qualifying Score | 44 |
| Success Gap = Net Score – Qualifying Score | | | |

$$\text{Net Score} = \sum_{i=\mathrm{I}}^{\mathrm{VI}} \left[ (\text{correct}_i \times MM_i) - (In_i - NM_i) \right]$$

*Space for Rough Work*

**Name :**

**Date :**

**Start Time :**

**End Time :**

# MATHEMATICS M05

SYLLABUS : Complex Number-2 : Modulus and Argument of complex numbers.

**Max. Marks : 74**

**Time : 60 min.**

## GENERAL INSTRUCTIONS

- The Daily Practice Problem Sheet contains **24** Questions divided into 6 sections.
  Section I has **8** MCQ's with ONLY 1 correct option. 2 marks for correct answer and No negative marks.
  Section II has **4** MCQ's with 1 or MORE THAN 1 correct option. 4 marks for correct answer(s) and (–1) for wrong answer.
  Section III has **1** PASSAGE with **3** MCQ's with ONLY 1 correct option. 3 marks for correct and (–1) mark for wrong answer.
  Section IV has **2** MCQ's with multiple matchings. 1 mark for the correct matching of each row & No negative marks.
  Section V has **2** Assertion-Reason MCQ's with ONLY 1 correct option. 3 marks for correct and (–1) mark for wrong answer.
  Section VI has **5** single digit integer answer questions. 4 marks for correct answer and (–1) for wrong answer.
- No mark will be given/ deducted if no bubble is filled. Keep a timer in front and stop immediately at the end of 60 min.
- You have to evaluate your Response Grids yourself with the help of Solution Booklet.
- The sheet follows a particular syllabus. Do not attempt the sheet before you have completed your preparation for that syllabus. Refer syllabus sheet in the starting of the book for the syllabus of all the DPP sheets.
- After completing the sheet check your answers with the solution booklet and complete the Result Grid. Finally spend time to analyse your performance and revise the areas which emerge out as weak in your evaluation.

## Section - I - Straight Objective Type

This section contains 8 multiple choice questions. Each question has 4 choices (a), (b), (c) and (d), out of which **ONLY ONE** is correct.

1. If a, b, c are three distinct non-zero complex number such that $|a|=|b|=|c|$ and the equation $az^2 + bz + c = 0$ has a root whose modulus is 1, then
   (a) $b^2 = ac$
   (b) $c^2 = ab$
   (c) $a^2 = bc$
   (d) None of these

2. If $|z-i| \le 2$ and $z_0 = 5 + 3i$, then the maximum value of $|iz + z_0|$ is
   (a) $2 + \sqrt{31}$
   (b) $\sqrt{31} - 2$
   (c) 7
   (d) 7

3. If $|z| = 1$ and $z \ne -1$, then $\left(\dfrac{1+z}{1+\bar{z}}\right)^4 + \left(\dfrac{1+\bar{z}}{1+z}\right)^4$ is

   (a) $2\cos 4\,(\arg z)$
   (b) $2\cos 4\left(\arg \dfrac{z}{2}\right)$
   (c) $2\sin 4\left(\arg \dfrac{z}{2}\right)$
   (d) $2\sin 4\,(\arg z)$

4. Let z and $\omega$ be two complex numbers such that $|z| \le 1$, $|\omega| \le 1$ and $|z + i\omega| = |z - i\bar{\omega}| = 2$ then z equals
   (a) 1 or i
   (b) i or $-i$
   (c) 1 or $-1$
   (d) i or $-1$

5. If $\dfrac{w - \bar{w}z}{1 - z}$ is purely real where $w = \alpha + i\beta$, $\beta \ne 0$ and $z \ne 1$, then the set of the values of z is
   (a) $\{z : |z| = 1\}$
   (b) $\{z : z = \bar{z}\}$
   (c) $\{z : z \ne 1\}$
   (d) $\{z : |z| = 1, z \ne 1\}$

| RESPONSE GRID | 1. ⓐⓑⓒⓓ | 2. ⓐⓑⓒⓓ | 3. ⓐⓑⓒⓓ | 4. ⓐⓑⓒⓓ | 5. ⓐⓑⓒⓓ |
|---|---|---|---|---|---|

**6.** Let $z$ and $\omega$ be two non zero complex numbers such that $|z| = |\omega|$ and $\text{Arg } z + \text{Arg } \omega = z$, then $z$ equals

(a) $\omega$      (b) $-\omega$      (c) $\overline{\omega}$      (d) $-\overline{\omega}$

**7.** For any two non zero complex numbers $z_1$ and $z_2$, the value

of $(|z_1| + |z_2|) \left| \dfrac{z_1}{|z_1|} + \dfrac{z_2}{|z_2|} \right|$ is

(a) less than $2(|z_1| + |z_2|)$
(b) greater than $2(|z_1| + |z_2|)$
(c) greater than or equal to $2\,(|z_1| + |z_2|)$
(d) less than or equal to $2\,(|z_1| + |z_2|)$

**8.** If $\log_{1/2} \dfrac{|z|^2 + 2|z| + 4}{2|z|^2 + 1} < 0$, then the region traced by $z$ is

(a) $|z| < 3$            (b) $1 < |z| < 3$
(c) $|z| > 1$            (d) $|z| < 2$

## Section - II - Multiple Correct Answer Type

This section contains 4 multiple correct answer(s) type questions. Each question has 4 choices (a), (b), (c) and (d), out of which **ONE OR MORE** is/are correct.

**9.** If $z$ satisfies $|z - 1| < |z + 3|$ then $\omega = 2z + 3 - i$, (where $i = \sqrt{-1}$) satisfies

(a) $|\omega - 5 - i| < |\omega + 3 + i|$

(b) $|\omega - 5| < |\omega + 3|$

(c) $\text{Im}(i\omega) > 1$

(d) $|\arg(\omega - 1)| < 1 < \pi/2$

**10.** The complex numbers satisfying $|z + 2| + |z - 2| = 8$ and $|z - 6| + |z + 6| = 12$ are

(a) $4i$            (b) $-4i$
(c) $4$             (d) $-4$

**11.** Let $z_1$ and $z_2$ be complex numbers such that $z_1 \ne z_2$ and $|z_1| = |z_2|$. If $z_1$ has positive real part and $z_2$ has negative imaginary part, then $\dfrac{z_1 + z_2}{z_1 - z_2}$ may be

(a) zero, if $a + c = b + d = 0$    (b) real and positive
(c) real and negative           (d) purely imaginary

**12.** If $z = \sqrt{20i - 21} + \sqrt{21 + 20i}$, then the principal value of argument $z$ can be

(a) $\dfrac{\pi}{4}$    (b) $\dfrac{3\pi}{4}$    (c) $-\dfrac{\pi}{4}$    (d) $-\dfrac{3\pi}{4}$

## Section - III - Linked Comprehension Type

This section contains one paragraph. Based upon the paragraph, 3 multiple choice questions have to be answered. Each question has 4 choices (a), (b), (c) and (d), out of which **ONLY ONE** is correct.

Suppose $z$ and $w$ be two complex numbers such that $|z| \le 1$, $|w| \le 1$ and $|z + iw| = |z - iw| = 2$. Use the result $|z|^2 = z\overline{z}$ and $|z + w| \le |z| + |w|$, answer the following questions

**13.** Which of the following is true about $|z|$ and $|w|$

(a) $|z| = |w| = \dfrac{1}{2}$          (b) $|z| = \dfrac{1}{2}, |w| = \dfrac{3}{4}$

(c) $|z| = |w| = \dfrac{3}{4}$          (d) $|z| = |w| = 1$

**14.** Which of the following is true for $z$ and $\omega$

(a) $\text{Re}(z) = \text{Re}(w)$      (b) $I_m(z) = I_m(w)$
(c) $\text{Re}(z) = I_m(w)$      (d) $I_m(z) = \text{Re}(w)$

**15.** Number of complex numbers $z$ satisfying the above conditions given in above passage
(a) $1$             (b) $2$
(c) $4$             (d) indeterminate

| **RESPONSE GRID** | 6. ⓐⓑⓒⓓ | 7. ⓐⓑⓒⓓ | 8. ⓐⓑⓒⓓ | 9. ⓐⓑⓒⓓ | 10. ⓐⓑⓒⓓ |
|---|---|---|---|---|---|
| | 11. ⓐⓑⓒⓓ | 12. ⓐⓑⓒⓓ | 13. ⓐⓑⓒⓓ | 14. ⓐⓑⓒⓓ | 15. ⓐⓑⓒⓓ |

## Section - IV - Matrix-Match Type

This section contains 2 questions. It contains statements given in two columns, which have to be matched. Statements in Column I are labelled as A, B, C and D whereas statements in Column II are labelled as p, q, r, s and t. The answers to these questions have to be appropriately bubbled as illustrated in the following example. If the correct matches are A-p, A-r, B-p, B-s, C-r, C-s and D-q, t; then the correctly bubbled matrix will look like the following :

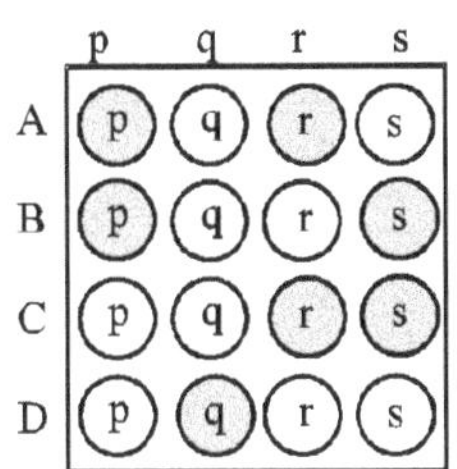

**16.**

| Column-I | Column-II |
|---|---|
| (A) If $G$ be the greatest and $L$ be the least values of $\lvert z-1 \rvert$, if $\lvert z+2+i \rvert \leq 1$; where $i = \sqrt{-1}$, then | p. $LG = 9$ |
| (B) If $G$ be the greatest and $L$ be the least values of $\lvert z+2i \rvert$, where $i = \sqrt{-1}$ if $1 \leq \lvert z-1 \rvert \leq 3$, then | q. $L+G = 6$ |
| (C) If $G$ be the greatest and $L$ be the least values of $\lvert z-2 \rvert$. If $\lvert z+i \rvert \leq 1$, where $i = \sqrt{-1}$, then | r. $\left(\sqrt{2G} - \sqrt{2L}\right)^2 = 4$ |
| | s. $LG = 4$ |
| | t. $G - L = 2$ |

**17.** Let the complex numbers $z_1$, $z_2$, and $z_3$ represent the vertices A, B and C of a triangle ABC respectively, which is inscribed in the circle of radius unity and centre at origin. The internal bisector of the angle A meets the circumcircle again at the point D, which is represented by the complex number $z_4$, and altitude from A to BC meets the circumcircle at E, given by $z_5$. Now match the entries from the following two columns:

| Column I | Column II |
|---|---|
| (A) $\arg\left(\dfrac{z_2 z_3}{z_4^2}\right)$ is equal to | p. $\pi$ |
| (B) $\arg\left(\dfrac{z_4}{z_2 - z_3}\right)$ is equal to | q. $\dfrac{\pi}{2}$ |
| (C) $\arg\left(\dfrac{z_1 z_3}{z_2 z_5}\right)$ is equal to | r. $\dfrac{\pi}{4}$ |
| (D) $\arg\left(\dfrac{z_4^2}{z_1 z_5}\right)$ is equal to | s. $0$ |
| | t. $-\dfrac{\pi}{2}$ |

## Section - V - Reasoning Type

This section contains 2 reasoning type questions. Each question has 4 choices (a), (b), (c) and (d) out of which **ONLY ONE** is correct.

**DIRECTIONS for (Qs. 18 & 19) : Each of these questions contains two statements: Statement-1 (Assertion) and Statement-2 (Reason). Each of these questions has four alternative choices, only one of which is the correct answer. You have to select the correct choice.**

(a) Statement-1 is True, Statement-2 is True; Statement-2 is a correct explanation for Statement-1.
(b) Statement-1 is True, Statement-2 is True; Statement-2 is NOT a correct explanation for Statement-1.
(c) Statement-1 is True, Statement-2 is False.
(d) Statement-1 is False, Statement-2 is True.

**18. Statement–1 :** If $\lvert z-i \rvert = 2$ and $z_0 = 5 + 3i$, then the maximum value of $\lvert iz + z_0 \rvert$ is 7
**Statement–2 :** For the complex numbers $z_1$ and $z_2$, $\lvert z_1 + z_2 \rvert \leq \lvert z_1 \rvert + \lvert z_2 \rvert$

**19. Statement 1 :** Any complex number z satisfy at least one of the two inequalities $\lvert z+1 \rvert \geq \dfrac{1}{\sqrt{2}}$ or $\lvert z^2 + 1 \rvert \geq 1$.

**Statement 2 :** There are no non-zero real numbers a and b such that $a^2 + b^2 \leq 0$.



*Space for Rough Work*

## Section - VI - Integer Type

This section contains 5 questions. The answer to each of the questions is a single digit integer ranging from 0 to 9.

**20.** If $z_1$, $z_2$ and $z_3$ are complex numbers such that

$$|z_1| = |z_2| = |z_3| = \left| \frac{1}{z_1} + \frac{1}{z_2} + \frac{1}{z_3} \right| = 1,$$

then find value of $|z_1 + z_2 + z_3|$

**21.** If the amplitude of $\sin \frac{\pi}{5} + i\left(1 - \cos \frac{\pi}{5}\right)$ is $\frac{\pi}{2p}$ then find the value of p.

**22.** For any complex number z, find the minimum value of $|z| + |z - 1|$.

**23.** If $|z| < 4$, then $|iz + 3 - 4i|$ is less than X. Find the value of X.

**24.** If $z_1$ and $z_2$ be two variable complex numbers such that $|z_1|^2 \le 169$ and $|z_2 + 3 - 4i|^2 \le 25$, then the maximum value of $|z_1 - z_2|$ is $15 + p$. Find the value of p.

| | | |
|---|---|---|
| **RESPONSE GRID** | 20. ⓪①②③④⑤⑥⑦⑧⑨ | 21. ⓪①②③④⑤⑥⑦⑧⑨ |
| | 22. ⓪①②③④⑤⑥⑦⑧⑨ | 23. ⓪①②③④⑤⑥⑦⑧⑨ |
| | 24. ⓪①②③④⑤⑥⑦⑧⑨ | |

| DAILY PRACTICE PROBLEM DPP 05 - MATHS | | | |
|---|---|---|---|
| Total Questions | 24 | Total Marks | 74 |
| Attempted | | Correct | |
| Incorrect | | Net Score | |
| Cut-off Score | 15 | Qualifying Score | 48 |
| Success Gap = Net Score – Qualifying Score | | | |

$$\textbf{Net Score} = \sum_{i=I}^{VI} \left[ (\textbf{correct}_i \times MM_i) - (In_i - NM_i) \right]$$

*Space for Rough Work*

# DPP - Daily Practice Problems

**Name :**　　　　　　　　　　　　　　　**Date :**

**Start Time :**　　　　　　　　　　　　**End Time :**

## MATHEMATICS　　M06

SYLLABUS : **Complex Number - 3** : Square root, Representation of complex numbers, Geometry of Complex numbers.

**Max. Marks : 73**　　　　　　　　　　　**Time : 60 min.**

### GENERAL INSTRUCTIONS

- The Daily Practice Problem Sheet contains **24** Questions divided into 6 sections.
  Section I has **8** MCQ's with ONLY 1 correct option. 2 marks for correct answer and No negative marks.
  Section II has **4** MCQ's with 1 or MORE THAN 1 correct option. 4 marks for correct answer(s) and (–1) for wrong answer.
  Section III has **1** PASSAGE with **3** MCQ's with ONLY 1 correct option. 3 marks for correct and (–1) mark for wrong answer.
  Section IV has **2** MCQ's with multiple matchings. 1 mark for the correct matching of each row & No negative marks.
  Section V has **2** Assertion-Reason MCQ's with ONLY 1 correct option. 3 marks for correct and (–1) mark for wrong answer.
  Section VI has **5** single digit integer answer questions. 4 marks for correct answer and (–1) for wrong answer.
- No mark will be given/ deducted if no bubble is filled. Keep a timer in front and stop immediately at the end of 60 min.
- You have to evaluate your Response Grids yourself with the help of Solution Booklet.
- The sheet follows a particular syllabus. Do not attempt the sheet before you have completed your preparation for that syllabus. Refer syllabus sheet in the starting of the book for the syllabus of all the DPP sheets.
- After completing the sheet check your answers with the solution booklet and complete the Result Grid. Finally spend time to analyse your performance and revise the areas which emerge out as weak in your evaluation.

## Section - I - Straight Objective Type

This section contains 8 multiple choice questions. Each question has 4 choices (a), (b), (c) and (d), out of which **ONLY ONE** is correct.

**1.** If a complex number $z$ lies on a circle of radius $\dfrac{1}{2}$, then the complex number $(-1 + 4z)$ lies on a circle of radius

(a) $\dfrac{1}{2}$　　　　　　　　(b) 1

(c) 2　　　　　　　　(d) 4

**2.** If A $(z_1)$ and B $(z_2)$ are two points on circle $|z| = r$ then the tangents to the circle at A and B will intersect at

(a) $\dfrac{z_1^2 + z_2^2}{z_1 + z_2}$　(b) $\dfrac{z_1 z_2}{z_1 + z_2}$　(c) $\dfrac{2z_1 z_2}{z_1 + z_2}$　(d) $\dfrac{z_1^2 + z_2^2}{2(z_1 + z_2)}$

**3.** A particle starts to travel from a point P on the curve $C_1 : |z - 3 - 4i| = 5$, where $|z|$ is maximum. From P, the particle moves through an angle $\tan^{-1}\dfrac{3}{4}$ in anticlockwise direction on $|z - 3 - 4i| = 5$ and reaches at point Q. From Q, it comes down parallel to imaginary axis by 2 units and reaches at point R. Complex number corresponding to point R in the Argand plane is –

(a) (3 + 5i)　　(b) (3 + 7i) (c) (3 + 8i)　　　(d) (3 + 9i)

**4.** The complex numbers $z_1$, $z_2$ and $z_3$ satisfying $\dfrac{z_1 - z_3}{z_2 - z_3} = \dfrac{1 - i\sqrt{3}}{2}$ are the vertices of a triangle which is

(a) of area zero　　　　　(b) right-angled isosceles

(c) equilateral　　　　　(d) obtuse-angled isosceles

**5.** The locus of z which lies in shaded region (excluding the boundaries) is best represented by

(a) $z : |z + 1| > 2$ and $|\arg(z+1)| < \pi/4$

(b) $z : |z - 1| > 2$ and $|\arg(z-1)| < \pi/4$

(c) $z : |z + 1| < 2$ and $|\arg(z+1)| < \pi/2$

(d) $z : |z - 1| < 2$ and $|\arg(z+1)| < \pi/2$

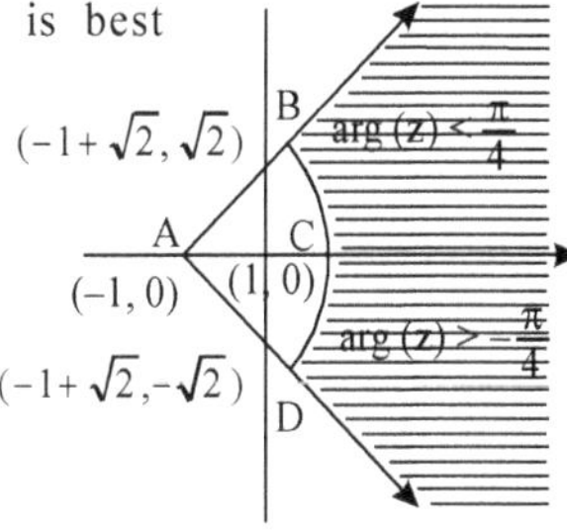


| RESPONSE GRID | 1. ⓐⓑⓒⓓ | 2. ⓐⓑⓒⓓ | 3. ⓐⓑⓒⓓ | 4. ⓐⓑⓒⓓ | 5. ⓐⓑⓒⓓ |
|---|---|---|---|---|---|

6. The locus of $z = x + iy$, which satisfies the inequality $\log_{0.3}|z-1| > \log_{0.3}|z-i|$ is given by
   (a) $x + y < 0$
   (b) $x + y > 0$
   (c) $x - y > 0$
   (d) $x - y < 0$

7. If z is a complex number, then $z^2 + \bar{z}^2 = 2$ represents
   (a) a circle
   (b) a straight line
   (c) a hyperbola
   (d) an ellipse

8. If a is a pure imaginary number and $z_0$ is a given complex number, then the equation
   $$z_0^2 + \bar{z}_0^2 + |z_0|^2 + \bar{a}z + a\bar{z} + a^2 = 0 \text{ represents}$$
   (a) a line segment
   (b) a ray
   (c) a circle
   (d) a straight line

## Section - II - Multiple Correct Answer Type

This section contains 4 multiple correct answer(s) type questions. Each question has 4 choices (a), (b), (c) and (d), out of which **ONE OR MORE** is/are correct.

9. A, B represent the complex numbers $2 - 2i$, $-6 + 2i$. P is a variable point which moves such that $\dfrac{PA}{PB} = 3$ (P is not on AB), then the locus of P is
   (a) a circle with centre $(-7, 5)$
   (b) a circle with centre $\left(-7, \dfrac{5}{2}\right)$
   (c) a circle with radius $2\sqrt{5}$
   (d) a circle with radius $\dfrac{3}{2}\sqrt{5}$

10. If $z_1, z_2, z_3, z_4$ are the vertices of a square in order, then
    (a) $z_1 + z_3 = z_2 + z_4$
    (b) $|z_1 - z_2| = |z_2 - z_3| = |z_3 - z_4| = |z_4 - z_1|$
    (c) $|z_1 - z_3| = |z_2 - z_4|$
    (d) $(z_1 - z_3)/(z_2 - z_4)$ is purely imaginary

11. $z_1, z_2, z_3, z_4$ correspond to the points A, B, C, D on a circle $|z| = 1$. If $z_1 + z_2 + z_3 + z_4 = 0$, Then ABCD is necessarily
    (a) a rectangle
    (b) a square
    (c) a rhombus
    (d) a parallelogram

12. If $\dfrac{z+1}{z+i}$ is a purely imaginary number, (where $i = \sqrt{-1}$) then $z$ lies on a
    (a) straight line
    (b) circle
    (c) circle with radius $= 1/\sqrt{2}$
    (d) circle passing through the origin

## Section - III - Linked Comprehension Type

This section contains one paragraph. Based upon the paragraph, 3 multiple choice questions have to be answered. Each question has 4 choices (a), (b), (c) and (d), out of which **ONLY ONE** is correct.

Let $f(x) = \dfrac{1}{x - i}$, where $x \in R$ and let $f(\alpha)$, $f(\beta)$, $f(\gamma)$, $f(\delta)$ be four points on the Argand plane. Now answer the following questions

13. The maximum value of $|f(\alpha) - f(\beta)|$ is
    (a) $|\alpha - \beta|$
    (b) $\left|\dfrac{1}{\alpha} - \dfrac{1}{\beta}\right|$
    (c) $1$
    (d) $2$

14. If a triangle is formed by joining the points $f(\alpha)$, $f(\beta)$, $f(\gamma)$ then maximum value of the area of triangle is
    (a) $3\sqrt{3}$
    (b) $\dfrac{3\sqrt{3}}{4}$
    (c) $\dfrac{3\sqrt{3}}{16}$
    (d) None

15. Points $f(\alpha)$, $f(\beta)$, $f(\gamma)$, $f(\delta)$ are chosen such that they form a square, the length of square is
    (a) $1/2$
    (b) $1/\sqrt{2}$
    (c) $1$
    (d) None

| **RESPONSE** | 6. ⓐⓑⓒⓓ | 7. ⓐⓑⓒⓓ | 8. ⓐⓑⓒⓓ | 9. ⓐⓑⓒⓓ | 10. ⓐⓑⓒⓓ |
| **GRID** | 11. ⓐⓑⓒⓓ | 12. ⓐⓑⓒⓓ | 13. ⓐⓑⓒⓓ | 14. ⓐⓑⓒⓓ | 15. ⓐⓑⓒⓓ |

## Section - IV - Matrix-Match Type

This section contains 2 questions. It contains statements given in two columns, which have to be matched. Statements in Column I are labelled as A, B, C and D whereas statements in Column II are labelled as p, q, r and s. The answers to these questions have to be appropriately bubbled as illustrated in the following example. If the correct matches are A-p, A-r, B-p, B-s, C-r, C-s and D-q, then the correctly bubbled matrix will look like the following :

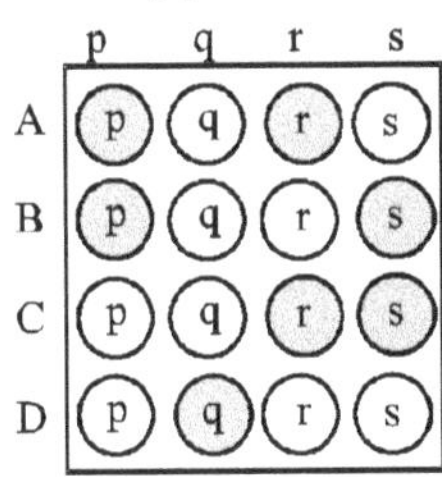

**16.**

| Column I | Column II |
|---|---|
| (A) If $z_1, z_2, z_3$ are the vertices of an equilateral triangle with $z_0$ as its nine point centre, then $z_1^2 + z_2^2 + z_3^3$ is | p. $(z_1 - z_2)^2$ $= 2(z_1 - z_3)(z_3 - z_2)$ |
| (B) If $z_1, z_2, z_3$ are the vertices A, B & C respectively of an isosceles right angled triangle with right angle at C, then | q. $3z_0^2$ |
| (C) If $z_1, z_2, z_3$ are the vertices A, B C respectively of an isosceles triangle and the angles at B and C are each equal to $\pi/6$, then | r. $(z_2 - z_3)^2$ $= 3(z_3 - z_1)(z_1 - z_2)$ |
| | s. $z_1 z_2 + z_2 z_3 + z_3 z_1$ |
| | t. $\dfrac{z_2 - z_3}{z_1 - z_3} = e^{i\pi/2}$ |

**17.**

| Column I | Column II |
|---|---|
| (A) If $\alpha$ is a complex number then the radius of the circle $\left| \dfrac{z - \alpha}{z - \overline{\alpha}} \right| = 2$ is equal to | p. $\lvert \tan \alpha \rvert$ |

(B) If arg $z = \alpha$ and $\lvert z - 1 \rvert = 1$ then $\left| \dfrac{z-2}{z} \right|$ is equal to     q. $\dfrac{2}{3} \lvert \alpha - \overline{\alpha} \rvert$

(C) Let A and B represent     r. $4\cos^2 \dfrac{\alpha}{2}$
complex numbers $z_1$ and $z_2$, which are roots of the equation $z^2 + pz + q = 0$. If $\angle AOB = \alpha \neq 0$ and OA = OB, where O is the origin then $\dfrac{p^2}{q}$ is equal to

## Section - V - Reasoning Type

This section contains 2 reasoning type questions. Each question has 4 choices (a), (b), (c) and (d) out of which **ONLY ONE** is correct.

**DIRECTIONS for (Qs. 18 & 19) : Each of these questions contains two statements: Statement-1 (Assertion) and Statement-2 (Reason). Each of these questions has four alternative choices, only one of which is the correct answer. You have to select the correct choice.**

(a) Statement-1 is True, Statement-2 is True; Statement-2 is a correct explanation for Statement-1.

(b) Statement-1 is True, Statement-2 is True; Statement-2 is NOT a correct explanation for Statement-1.

(c) Statement -1 is True, Statement-2 is False.

(d) Statement -1 is False, Statement-2 is True.

**18. Statement–1 :** Let $z_1$ and $z_2$ are two complex numbers such that $\lvert z_1 - z_2 \rvert = \lvert z_1 + z_2 \rvert$ then the orthocentre of $\Delta$ AOB is $\dfrac{z_1 + z_2}{2}$.

(where O is the origin)

**Statement–2 :** In case of right angled triangle, orthocentre is that point at which triangle is right angled.

**19. Statement-1:** Let $z$ be a complex number satisfying $\lvert z - 3 \rvert \leq \lvert z - 1 \rvert, \lvert z - 3 \rvert \leq \lvert z - 5 \rvert, \lvert z - i \rvert \leq \lvert z + i \rvert$ and $\lvert z - i \rvert \leq \lvert z - 5i \rvert$. Then the area of region in which $z$ lies is 12 sq unit.

**Statement-2:** Area of trapezium $= \dfrac{1}{2} \times$ (Sum of parallel sides) $\times$ (Distance between parallel sides)

**RESPONSE GRID**

16. A - p q r s t; B - p q r s t; C - p q r s t; D - p q r s t
17. A - p q r s t; B - p q r s t; C - p q r s t; D - p q r s t
18. a b c d    19. a b c d

## Section - VI - Integer Type

This section contains 5 questions. The answer to each of the questions is a single digit integer ranging from 0 to 9.

**20.** The equation $z\bar{z} + (4 - 3i)z + (4 + 3i)\bar{z} + 5 = 0$ represents a circle whose radius is $2\sqrt{P}$. Find the value of P.

**21.** If complex number $z_1$, $z_2$ and 0 are vertices of equilateral triangle, then find the value of $z_1^2 + z_2^2 - z_1 z_2$.

**22.** If square root of $-8 - 6i$ is $\pm (a - bi)$, find the value of $a + b$.

**23.** The area of the triangle on the Argand diagram formed by complex numbers $z$, $iz$ and $z + iz$ is $\dfrac{1}{P}|z|^2$. Find $P$.

**24.** Complex numbers $z_1$, $z_2$, $z_3$ are the vertices $A$, $B$, $C$ respectively of an isosceles right angled triangle with right angle at $C$. If $(z_1 - z_2)^2 = N(z_1 - z_3)(z_3 - z_2)$, find the value of N.

| | | |
|---|---|---|
| **RESPONSE GRID** | 20. ⓪①②③④⑤⑥⑦⑧⑨ | 21. ⓪①②③④⑤⑥⑦⑧⑨ |
| | 22. ⓪①②③④⑤⑥⑦⑧⑨ | 23. ⓪①②③④⑤⑥⑦⑧⑨ |
| | 24. ⓪①②③④⑤⑥⑦⑧⑨ | |

| DAILY PRACTICE PROBLEM DPP 06 - MATHS | | | |
|---|---|---|---|
| Total Questions | 24 | Total Marks | 73 |
| Attempted | | Correct | |
| Incorrect | | Net Score | |
| Cut-off Score | 14 | Qualifying Score | 46 |
| Success Gap = Net Score – Qualifying Score | | | |

$$\textbf{Net Score} = \sum_{i=1}^{VI}\left[(\textbf{correct}_i \times MM_i) - (In_i - NM_i)\right]$$

**Name :**

**Date :**

**Start Time :**

**End Time :**

## MATHEMATICS — M07

**SYLLABUS : Complex Number-4 :** De Moivre's theorem and Roots of unity.

**Max. Marks : 64**

**Time : 60 min.**

### GENERAL INSTRUCTIONS

- The Daily Practice Problem Sheet contains **21** Questions divided into 5 sections.
  Section I has **8** MCQ's with ONLY 1 correct option. 2 marks for correct answer and No negative marks.
  Section II has **4** MCQ's with 1 or MORE THAN 1 correct option. 4 marks for correct answer(s) and (–1) for wrong answer.
  Section III has **2** MCQ's with multiple matchings. 1 mark for the correct matching of each row & No negative marks.
  Section IV has **2** Assertion-Reason MCQ's with ONLY 1 correct option. 3 marks for correct and (–1) mark for wrong answer.
  Section V has **5** single digit integer answer questions. 4 marks for correct answer and (–1) for wrong answer.
- No mark will be given/ deducted if no bubble is filled. Keep a timer in front and stop immediately at the end of 60 min.
- You have to evaluate your Response Grids yourself with the help of Solution Booklet.
- The sheet follows a particular syllabus. Do not attempt the sheet before you have completed your preparation for that syllabus. Refer syllabus sheet in the starting of the book for the syllabus of all the DPP sheets.
- After completing the sheet check your answers with the solution booklet and complete the Result Grid. Finally spend time to analyse your performance and revise the areas which emerge out as weak in your evaluation.

## Section - I - Straight Objective Type

This section contains 8 multiple choice questions. Each question has 4 choices (a), (b), (c) and (d), out of which **ONLY ONE** is correct.

**1.** Let $z_1$ and $z_2$ be $n^{\text{th}}$ roots of unity which subtend a right angle at the origin. Then $n$ must be of the form

(a) $4k+1$      (b) $4k+2$
(c) $4k+3$      (d) $4k$

**2.** If $z = \left(\dfrac{\sqrt{3}}{2}+\dfrac{i}{2}\right)^5 + \left(\dfrac{\sqrt{3}}{2}-\dfrac{i}{2}\right)^5$, then

(a) $\mathrm{Re}(z)=0$      (b) $\mathrm{Im}(z)=0$
(c) $\mathrm{Re}(z)>0, \mathrm{Im}(z)>0$      (d) $\mathrm{Re}(z)>0, \mathrm{Im}(z)<0$

**3.** If $i=\sqrt{-1}$, then $4+5\left(-\dfrac{1}{2}+\dfrac{i\sqrt{3}}{2}\right)^{334} + 3\left(-\dfrac{1}{2}+\dfrac{i\sqrt{3}}{2}\right)^{365}$

is equal to

(a) $1-i\sqrt{3}$      (b) $-1+i\sqrt{3}$
(c) $i\sqrt{3}$      (d) $-i\sqrt{3}$

**4.** If a, b, c are distinct odd integers and $\omega$ is non real cube root of unity, then the minimum value of $|a\omega^2 + b + c\omega|$, is

(a) $0$      (b) $2\sqrt{3}$
(c) $3$      (d) $1$

**5.** If $\omega = \cos\dfrac{\pi}{n}+i\sin\dfrac{\pi}{n}$, then value of $1+\omega+\omega^2+...+\omega^{n-1}$ is

(a) $1+i$      (b) $1+i\tan(\pi/n)$
(c) $1+i\cot(\pi/2n)$      (d) None of these

| RESPONSE GRID | 1. ⓐⓑⓒⓓ | 2. ⓐⓑⓒⓓ | 3. ⓐⓑⓒⓓ | 4. ⓐⓑⓒⓓ | 5. ⓐⓑⓒⓓ |
|---|---|---|---|---|---|

**6.** If $a = \cos 2\alpha + i \sin 2\alpha$, $b = \cos 2\beta + i \sin 2\beta$, $c = \cos 2\gamma + i \sin 2\gamma$ and $d = \cos 2\delta + i \sin 2\delta$, then $\sqrt{abcd} + \dfrac{1}{\sqrt{abcd}} =$

(a) $\sqrt{2}\cos(\alpha + \beta + \gamma + \delta)$ 　　(b) $2\cos(\alpha + \beta + \gamma + \delta)$

(c) $\cos(\alpha + \beta + \gamma + \delta)$ 　　(d) None of these

**7.** If $x = \omega - \omega^2 - 2$, then the value of $x^4 + 3x^3 + 2x^2 - 11x - 6$ is

(a) 1 　　　　(b) –1 　(c) 　2

(d) none of these

**8.** If $\omega \neq 1$ and $\omega$ is a $n^{th}$ root of unity, then the value of

$1 + 4\omega + 9\omega^2 + 16\omega^3 + \dots + n^2\omega^{n-1}$ is

(a) $n\omega$ 　　　　　　(b) $n^2\omega$

(c) $n^2\omega - n^2 - 2n$ 　　(d) None of these

---

## Section - II - Multiple Correct Answer Type

This section contains 4 multiple correct answer(s) type questions. Each question has 4 choices (a), (b), (c) and (d), out of which **ONE OR MORE** is/are correct.

---

**9.** If $\omega$ is a non-real cube root of unity then the value of

$1\cdot(2 - \omega)(2 - \omega)^2 + 2\cdot(3 - \omega)(3 - \omega^2) + \dots$

$$+ (n-1)(n - \omega)(n - \omega^2) \text{ is}$$

(a) real 　　　　　　(b) $\dfrac{n^2(n-1)^2}{4} - n + 1$

(c) $\left\{\dfrac{n(n+1)}{2}\right\}^2 - n$ 　　(d) not real

**10.** The common roots of the equations

$z^3 + (1 + i)z^2 + (1 + i)z + i = 0$, (where $i = \sqrt{-1}$) and

$z^{1993} + z^{1994} + 1 = 0$ are

(a) 1 　　　　　　(b) $\omega$

(c) $\omega^2$ 　　　　(d) $\omega^{981}$

**11.** If $\cos\alpha + \cos\beta + \cos\gamma = \sin\alpha + \sin\beta + \sin\gamma = 0$, then

(a) $\cos(2\alpha) + \cos(2\beta) + \cos(2\gamma) = 0$

(b) $\sin(2\alpha) + \sin(2\beta) + \sin(2\gamma) = 0$

(c) $\cos(\beta + \gamma) + \cos(\gamma + \alpha) + \cos(\alpha + \beta) = 0$

(d) $\sin(\beta + \gamma) + \sin(\gamma + \alpha) + \sin(\alpha + \beta) = 0$

**12.** If $\alpha$ is the fifth root of unity then

(a) $\left|1 + \alpha + \alpha^2 + \alpha^3 + \alpha^4\right| = 0$

(b) $\left|1 + \alpha + \alpha^2 + \alpha^3\right| = 1$

(c) $\left|1 + \alpha + \alpha^2\right| = 2\cos\dfrac{\pi}{5}$

(d) $\left|1 + \alpha\right| = 2\cos\dfrac{\pi}{10}$

---

| RESPONSE GRID | 6. ⓐⓑⓒⓓ | 7. ⓐⓑⓒⓓ | 8. ⓐⓑⓒⓓ | 9. ⓐⓑⓒⓓ | 10. ⓐⓑⓒⓓ |
| --- | --- | --- | --- | --- | --- |
| | 11. ⓐⓑⓒⓓ | 12. ⓐⓑⓒⓓ | | | |

---

*Space for Rough Work*

## Section - III - Matrix-Match Type

This section contains 2 questions. It contains statements given in two columns, which have to be matched. Statements in Column I are labelled as A, B, C and D whereas statements in Column II are labelled as p, q, r and s. The answers to these questions have to be appropriately bubbled as illustrated in the following example. If the correct matches are A-p, A-r, B-p, B-s, C-r, C-s and D-q, then the correctly bubbled matrix will look like the following :

|   | p | q | r | s |
|---|---|---|---|---|
| A | (p) | (q) | (r) | (s) |
| B | (p) | (q) | r | (s) |
| C | p | q | (r) | (s) |
| D | (p) | (q) | r | s |

13. $\omega \ (\neq 1)$ is an $n^{th}$ roots of unity

| Column I | | Column II |
|---|---|---|
| (A) $\omega + \omega^2 + ..... + \omega^{n-1} + \omega^n$ | (p) | $-1$ |
| (B) $1 + 2\omega + ...... + n\,\omega^{n-1}$ | (q) | $\dfrac{n}{\omega - 1}$ |
| (C) $(1 - \omega)(1 - \omega^2) ..... (1 - \omega^{n-1})$ | (r) | $0$ |
| | (s) | $n$ |

14.

| Column I | | Column II |
|---|---|---|
| (A) If $\omega_1$ & $\omega_2$ are the complex cube roots of unity, then $\omega_1^4 + \omega_2^4$ is | (p) | a circle |
| (B) Locus of the point $z$ satisfying the equation $|iz - 1| + |z - i| = 2$ is | (q) | $-\dfrac{1}{\omega_1 \omega_2}$ |
| (C) If $z_1$ and $z_2$ are two $n^{th}$ roots of unity then | (r) | a straight line |

$\arg\left(\dfrac{z_1}{z_2}\right)$ is a multiple of

| | |
|---|---|
| (s) | $\dfrac{1}{\omega_1 \omega_2}$ |
| (t) | $\dfrac{2\pi}{n}$ |

## Section - IV - Reasoning Type

This section contains 2 reasoning type questions. Each question has 4 choices (a), (b), (c) and (d) out of which **ONLY ONE** is correct.

**DIRECTIONS for (Qs. 15 & 16) :** Each of these questions contains two statements: Statement-1 (Assertion) and Statement-2 (Reason). Each of these questions has four alternative choices, only one of which is the correct answer. You have to select the correct choice.

(a) Statement-1 is True, Statement-2 is True; Statement-2 is a correct explanation for Statement-1.

(b) Statement-1 is True, Statement-2 is True; Statement-2 is NOT a correct explanation for Statement-1.

(c) Statement -1 is True, Statement-2 is False.

(d) Statement -1 is False, Statement-2 is True.

15. Let $z_1, z_2, \ldots, z_n$ be the roots of $z^n = 1$, $n \in N$.
**Statement-1 :** $z_1 . z_2 \ldots z_n = (-1)^n$
**Statement-2 :** Product of the roots of the equation $a_n x^n + a_{n-1} x^{n-1} + a_{n-2} x^{n-2} + \ldots + a_1 x + a_0 = 0$, $a_n \neq 0$, is $(-1)^n . \dfrac{a_0}{a_n}$.

16. **Statement-1 :** If $\alpha = \cos\left(\dfrac{2\pi}{7}\right) + i \sin\left(\dfrac{2\pi}{7}\right)$, $p = \alpha + \alpha^2 + \alpha^4$, $q = \alpha^3 + \alpha^5 + \alpha^6$ then the equation where roots are p and q is $x^2 + x + 2 = 0$.
**Statement-2 :** If $\alpha$ is a root of $z^7 = 1$, then $1 + \alpha + \alpha^2 + \ldots\ldots\ldots + \alpha^6 = 0$.

<table>
<tr><td rowspan="4">RESPONSE GRID</td></tr>
<tr><td>13. A - (p)(q)(r)(s); B - (p)(q)(r)(s); C - (p)(q)(r)(s); D - (p)(q)(r)(s)</td></tr>
<tr><td>14. A - (p)(q)(r)(s)(t); B - (p)(q)(r)(s)(t); C - (p)(q)(r)(s)(t); D - (p)(q)(r)(s)(t)</td></tr>
<tr><td>15. (a)(b)(c)(d)　　16. (a)(b)(c)(d)</td></tr>
</table>

*Space for Rough Work*

## Section - V - Integer Type

This section contains 5 questions. The answer to each of the questions is a single digit integer ranging from 0 to 9.

**17.** Find the smallest positive integeral value of $n$ for which the complex number $\left(1+\sqrt{3}\,i\right)^{n/2}$ is real, is

**18.** Suppose that w is the imaginary $(2009)^{th}$ roots of unity. If

$$(2^{2009}-1)\sum_{r=1}^{2008}\frac{1}{2-w^r}=(a)\,(2^b)+c$$

where a, b, c $\in$ N. If the least value of $(a+b+c)$ is $251(Y)^2$, find the value of Y.

**19.** a, b, c are integers, not all simultaneously equal and $\omega$ is cube root of unity ($\omega \neq 1$), then find the minimum value of $|a + b\omega + c\omega^2|$.

**20.** If $\alpha, \beta$ are imaginary cube roots of unity, then find the value of $\alpha^4 + \beta^{28} + 1/\alpha\beta$.

**21.** If $\dfrac{1}{a+\omega}+\dfrac{1}{b+\omega}+\dfrac{1}{c+\omega}+\dfrac{1}{d+\omega}=\dfrac{1}{\omega}$, where a, b, c, d $\in$ R and $\omega$ is a cube root of unity then find the value of

$$\sum\frac{1}{a^2-a+1}.$$

| | | |
|---|---|---|
| **RESPONSE GRID** | 17. ⓪①②③④⑤⑥⑦⑧⑨ | 20. ⓪①②③④⑤⑥⑦⑧⑨ |
| | 18. ⓪①②③④⑤⑥⑦⑧⑨ | 21. ⓪①②③④⑤⑥⑦⑧⑨ |
| | 19. ⓪①②③④⑤⑥⑦⑧⑨ | |

| DAILY PRACTICE PROBLEM DPP 07 - MATHS | | | |
|---|---|---|---|
| Total Questions | 21 | Total Marks | 64 |
| Attempted | | Correct | |
| Incorrect | | Net Score | |
| Cut-off Score | 13 | Qualifying Score | 42 |
| Success Gap = Net Score – Qualifying Score | | | |

$$\text{Net Score} = \sum_{i=1}^{VI}\left[(\text{correct}_i \times MM_i)-(In_i - NM_i)\right]$$

**Name :**                                    **Date :**

**Start Time :**                              **End Time :**

# MATHEMATICS  M08

**SYLLABUS : Progressions-1 :** Arithmetic progression – Definition, nth term, Arithmetic means, Sum of finite terms.

## Max. Marks : 65                    Time : 60 min.

### GENERAL INSTRUCTIONS

- The Daily Practice Problem Sheet contains **24** Questions divided into 5 sections.
  Section I has **14** MCQ's with ONLY 1 correct option. 2 marks for correct answer and No negative marks.
  Section II has **2** MCQ's with 1 or MORE THAN 1 correct option. 4 marks for correct answer(s) and (–1) for wrong answer.
  Section III has **1** MCQ's with multiple matchings. 1 mark for the correct matching of each row & No negative marks.
  Section IV has **2** Assertion-Reason MCQ's with ONLY 1 correct option. 3 marks for correct and (–1) mark for wrong answer.
  Section V has **5** single digit integer answer questions. 4 marks for correct answer and (–1) for wrong answer.
- No mark will be given/ deducted if no bubble is filled. Keep a timer in front and stop immediately at the end of 60 min.
- You have to evaluate your Response Grids yourself with the help of Solution Booklet.
- The sheet follows a particular syllabus. Do not attempt the sheet before you have completed your preparation for that syllabus. Refer syllabus sheet in the starting of the book for the syllabus of all the DPP sheets.
- After completing the sheet check your answers with the solution booklet and complete the Result Grid. Finally spend time to analyse your performance and revise the areas which emerge out as weak in your evaluation.

## Section - I - Straight Objective Type

This section contains 14 multiple choice questions. Each question has 4 choices (a), (b), (c) and (d), out of which **ONLY ONE** is correct.

**1.** In a potato race , 8 potatoes are placed 6 metres apart on a straight line, the first being 6 metres from the basket which is also placed in the same line. A contestant starts from the basket and puts one potato at a time into the basket. Find the total distance he must run in order to finish the race.

   (a) 420           (b) 210
   (c) 432           (d) None

**2.** Consider an A.P. $a_1, a_2, a_3, \ldots$ such that $a_3 + a_5 + a_8 = 11$ and $a_4 + a_2 = -2$, then the value of $a_1 + a_6 + a_7$ is

   (a) –8           (b  5
   (c) 7            (d) 9

**3.** If for an A.P. $a_1, a_2, a_3, \ldots, a_n, \ldots$ $a_1 + a_3 + a_5 = -12$ and $a_1 a_2 a_3 = 8$ then the value of $a_2 + a_4 + a_6$ equals

   (a) –12           (b) –16
   (c) –18           (d) –21

**4.** Consider an A.P. with first term 'a' and the common difference d. Let $S_k$ denote the sum of the first K terms.

Let $\dfrac{S_{kx}}{S_x}$ is independent of x, then

   (a) $a = d/2$           (b) $a = d$
   (c) $a = 2d$           (d) None

**5.** For an increasing A.P. $a_1, a_2, \ldots, a_n$ if $a_1 + a_3 + a_5 = -12$ : $a_1 a_3 a_5 = 80$, then which of the following does not hold?

   (a) $a_1 = -10$           (b) $a_2 = -1$
   (c) $a_3 = -4$           (d) $a_5 = 2$

**RESPONSE GRID**    **1.** ⓐⓑⓒⓓ    **2.** ⓐⓑⓒⓓ    **3.** ⓐⓑⓒⓓ    **4.** ⓐⓑⓒⓓ    **5.** ⓐⓑⓒⓓ

**6.** If $a_1, a_2, a_3, \ldots\ldots, a_{2n+1}$ are in A. P. then $\dfrac{a_{2n+1} - a_1}{a_{2n+1} + a_1} +$

$\dfrac{a_{2n} - a_2}{a_{2n} + a_2} + \ldots\ldots + \dfrac{a_{n+2} - a_n}{a_{n+2} + a_n}$ is equal to

(a) $\dfrac{n(n+1)}{2} \cdot \dfrac{a_2 - a_1}{a_{n+1}}$

(b) $\dfrac{n(n+1)}{2}$

(c) $(n+1)(a_2 - a_1)$

(d) None of these

**7.** If $a_1, a_2, a_3, \ldots\ldots, a_n$ are in A.P., and

$\dfrac{1}{a_1 a_n} + \dfrac{1}{a_2 a_{n-1}} + \dfrac{1}{a_3 a_{n-2}} + \ldots\ldots + \dfrac{1}{a_n a_1}$

$= K\left(\dfrac{1}{a_1} + \dfrac{1}{a_2} + \dfrac{1}{a_3} + \ldots\ldots + \dfrac{1}{a_n}\right)$. Then K is

(a) $\dfrac{2}{a_1 + a_n}$

(b) $\dfrac{n}{a_1 + a_n}$

(c) $\dfrac{1}{a_1 + a_n}$

(d) $\dfrac{n-1}{a_1 + a_n}$

**8.** If a, b, c, d are four distinct real numbers and they are in A.P. If $2(a-b) + x(b-c)^2 + (c-a)^3 = 2(a-d) + (b-d)^2 + (c-d)^3$, then x equal to

(a) $x \geq 16$ or $x \leq -8$

(b) $x \geq -8$ or $x \leq 16$

(c) $x \geq -8$

(d) $x \leq 16$

**9.** If x, y, z be three positive numbers in A.P. then the minimum

value of $\dfrac{x+y}{2y-x} + \dfrac{y+z}{2y-z}$ is

(a) 2

(b) 4

(c) $\dfrac{1}{4}$

(d) $\dfrac{1}{2}$

**10.** The number of numbers lying between 100 and 500 that are divisible by 7 but not by 21 is

(a) 36

(b) 38

(c) 40

(d) 39

**11.** In the following two A.P.'s how many terms are identical?

2, 5, 8, 11, ........ to $60^{th}$ term

3, 5, 7, 9, .............to $50^{th}$ term

(a) 16

(b) 17

(c) 18

(d) 20

**12.** $\sqrt{2}, \sqrt{3}, \sqrt{5}$ are the following terms of an A.P.:

(a) 2nd, 3rd, and 5th

(b) 4th, 9th and 25th

(c) 4th, 6th, and 10th

(d) none of the above

**13.** Between two numbers whose sum is $2\dfrac{1}{6}$ an even number of arithmetic means are inserted, the sum of these means exceeds their number by unity. The number of the means is

(a) 12

(b) 14

(c) 6

(d) 10

**14.** If $a_r > 0$, $r \in N$ and $a_1, a_2, a_3, \ldots\ldots a_{2n}$ are in AP then

$(a_1 + a_{2n})/\left(\sqrt{a_1} + \sqrt{a_2}\right) + (a_2 + a_{2n-1})/\left(\sqrt{a_2} + \sqrt{a_3}\right) +$

$(a_3 + a_{2n-2})/\left(\sqrt{a_3} + \sqrt{a_4}\right) + \ldots\ldots + (a_n + a_{n+1})/$

$\left(\sqrt{a_n} + \sqrt{a_{n+1}}\right)$ is equal to

(a) $n-1$

(b) $n(a_1 + a_{2n})/\left(\sqrt{a_1} + \sqrt{a_{n+1}}\right)$

(c) $(n-1)/\left(\sqrt{a_1} + \sqrt{a_{n+1}}\right)$

(d) $\dfrac{(n-1)(a_1 + a_{2n})}{\sqrt{a_1} + \sqrt{a_{n+1}}}$

---

## Section - II - Multiple Correct Answer Type

This section contains 2 multiple correct answer(s) type questions. Each question has 4 choices (a), (b), (c) and (d), out of which **ONE OR MORE** is/are correct.

---

**15.** In a triangle the angles are in A.P. and lengths of two larger sides are 10 and 9 respectively, then length of the third side can be

(a) $5 + \sqrt{6}$

(b) $\dfrac{7}{10}$

(c) $5 - \sqrt{6}$

(d) $\dfrac{10}{7}$

| **RESPONSE** | 6. ⓐⓑⓒⓓ | 7. ⓐⓑⓒⓓ | 8. ⓐⓑⓒⓓ | 9. ⓐⓑⓒⓓ | 10. ⓐⓑⓒⓓ |
|---|---|---|---|---|---|
| **GRID** | 11. ⓐⓑⓒⓓ | 12. ⓐⓑⓒⓓ | 13. ⓐⓑⓒⓓ | 14. ⓐⓑⓒⓓ | 15. ⓐⓑⓒⓓ |

*Space for Rough Work*

**16.** All the terms of an A.P. are natural numbers and the sum of the first 20 terms is greater than 1072 and less than 1162. If the sixth term is 32 then

(a) first term is 12  (b) first terms is 7
(c) common difference is 4  (d) common difference is 5

$S_n = bn + cn^2$ where $b$ and $c$ are independent of $n$, then

(s) Common difference (D) = 2c

(t) Common difference (D) = (2b − 14)

## Section - III - Matrix-Match Type

This section contains 1 question. It contains statements given in two columns, which have to be matched. Statements in Column I are labelled as A, B, C and D whereas statements in Column II are labelled as p, q, r and s. The answers to these questions have to be appropriately bubbled as illustrated in the following example. If the correct matches are A-p, A-r, B-p, B-s, C-r, C-s and D-q, then the correctly bubbled matrix will look like the following :

|   | p | q | r | s |
|---|---|---|---|---|
| A | p | q | r | s |
| B | p | q | r | s |
| C | p | q | r | s |
| D | p | q | r | s |

**17.**

**Column I**

(A) If sum of $n$ terms of an AP is given by $S_n = a + bn + cn^2$ where $a$, $b$, $c$ are independent of $n$, then

(B) If sum of $n$ terms of an AP is given by $S_n = (a-1)n^3 + (b-2)n^2 + (c-3)n$, where $a$, $b$, $c$ are independent of n, then

(C) The sum of n terms of an AP is given by

**Column II**

(p) $T_n = a + b + (2n-1)c$

(q) $T_n = b + (2n-1)c$

(r) $T_n = c - a - 4n + b(2n - a)$

## Section - IV - Reasoning Type

This section contains 2 reasoning type questions. Each question has 4 choices (a), (b), (c) and (d) out of which **ONLY ONE** is correct.

**DIRECTIONS for (Qs. 18 & 19) : Each of these questions contains two statements: Statement-1 (Assertion) and Statement-2 (Reason). Each of these questions has four alternative choices, only one of which is the correct answer. You have to select the correct choice.**

(a) Statement-1 is True, Statement-2 is True; Statement-2 is a correct explanation for Statement-1.

(b) Statement-1 is True, Statement-2 is True; Statement-2 is NOT a correct explanation for Statement-1.

(c) Statement -1 is True, Statement-2 is False.

(d) Statement -1 is False, Statement-2 is True.

**18.** **Statement 1:** If $|x-1|$, 3, $|x-3|$ are first three terms of an AP, then its sixth term is 7 > third term.

**Statement 2:** $a$, $a + d$, $a + 2d$, ..... are in AP $(d \neq 0)$ then sixth term is $(a + 5d)$

**19.** **Statement 1:** The sums of $n$ terms of two arithmetic progressions are in the ration $(7n + 1) : (4n + 17)$, then the ratio of their nth terms is 7 : 4.

**Statement 2:** If $S_n = ax^2 + bx + c$, then $T_n = S_n - S_{n-1}$

| **RESPONSE GRID** | 16. (a)(b)(c)(d) |
|---|---|
| | 17. A - (p)(q)(r)(s)(t); B - (p)(q)(r)(s)(t); C - (p)(q)(r)(s)(t); D - (p)(q)(r)(s)(t) |
| | 18. (a)(b)(c)(d)   19. (a)(b)(c)(d) |

## Section - V - Integer Type

This section contains 5 questions. The answer to each of the questions is a single digit integer ranging from 0 to 9.

**20.** Along a road an odd number of stones placed at intervals of 10 m. These stones have to be assembled around the middle stone. A person can carry only one stone at a time. A man carried out the job starting with the stone in the middle, carrying stones in succession, thereby covering a distance of 4.8 km. If the number of stones is $(x + 23)$, find the value of x.

**21.** Concentric circles of radii 1, 2, 3......100 cm are drawn. The interior of the smallest circle is coloured red and the angular regions are coloured alternately green and red, so that no two adjacent regions are of the same colour. If the total area of the green regions is equal to $(1010\ P)\pi$ sq. cm, then find the value of P.

**22.** Let K is a positive integer such that $36 + K$, $300 + K$, $596 + K$ are the squares of three consecutive terms of an arithmetic progression. If $K = 37(P)^2$, then find the value of P.

**23.** An AP whose first term is unity, and in which the sum of the first half of any even numbers of terms to that of the second half of the same number of terms is in constant ratio, then the common difference d is

**24.** If a, b, c, d are distinct integers in A. P. such that $d = a^2 + b^2 + c^2$, then find the value of $a + b + c + d$

| | | |
|---|---|---|
| **RESPONSE GRID** | 20. ⓪①②③④⑤⑥⑦⑧⑨ | 21. ⓪①②③④⑤⑥⑦⑧⑨ |
| | 22. ⓪①②③④⑤⑥⑦⑧⑨ | 23. ⓪①②③④⑤⑥⑦⑧⑨ |
| | 24. ⓪①②③④⑤⑥⑦⑧⑨ | |

## DAILY PRACTICE PROBLEM DPP 08 - MATHS

| Total Questions | 24 | Total Marks | 65 |
|---|---|---|---|
| Attempted | | Correct | |
| Incorrect | | Net Score | |
| Cut-off Score | 13 | Qualifying Score | 43 |
| Success Gap = Net Score – Qualifying Score | | | |

$$\text{Net Score} = \sum_{i=1}^{VI}\left[(\text{correct}_i \times MM_i) - (In_i - NM_i)\right]$$

*Space for Rough Work*

# DPP - Daily Practice Problems

**Name :**

**Date :**

**Start Time :**

**End Time :**

# MATHEMATICS  M09

**SYLLABUS : Progressions-2 :** Geometric progression – Definition, nth term, Geometric means, Sum of finite terms, Sum of infinite terms.

## Max. Marks : 67

## Time : 60 min.

**GENERAL INSTRUCTIONS**

- The Daily Practice Problem Sheet contains **24** Questions divided into 4 sections.
  Section I has **14** MCQ's with ONLY 1 correct option. 2 marks for correct answer and No negative marks.
  Section II has **4** MCQ's with 1 or MORE THAN 1 correct option. 4 marks for correct answer(s) and (−1) for wrong answer.
  Section III has **1** Assertion-Reason MCQ's with ONLY 1 correct option. 3 marks for correct and (−1) mark for wrong answer.
  Section IV has **5** single digit integer answer questions. 4 marks for correct answer and (−1) for wrong answer.
- No mark will be given/ deducted if no bubble is filled. Keep a timer in front and stop immediately at the end of 60 min.
- You have to evaluate your Response Grids yourself with the help of Solution Booklet.
- The sheet follows a particular syllabus. Do not attempt the sheet before you have completed your preparation for that syllabus. Refer syllabus sheet in the starting of the book for the syllabus of all the DPP sheets.
- After completing the sheet check your answers with the solution booklet and complete the Result Grid. Finally spend time to analyse your performance and revise the areas which emerge out as weak in your evaluation.

## Section - I - Straight Objective Type

This section contains 14 multiple choice questions. Each question has 4 choices (a), (b), (c) and (d), out of which **ONLY ONE** is correct.

**1.** Let $a + ar_1 + ar_1^2 + \dots \infty$ and $a + ar_2 + ar_2^2 + \dots \infty$ be two infinite series of positive numbers with the same first term. The sum of the first series is $r_1$ and the sum of the second series is $r_2$. The value of $(r_1 + r_2)$ is –

(a) 1/2

(b) 1

(c) $\dfrac{\sqrt{5}+1}{2}$

(d) 2

**2.** The sum $5\sum\limits_{n=1}^{\infty} \dfrac{2^{n+2}}{4^{n-2}}$ is equal to

(a) 1372

(b) 440

(c) 320

(d) 388

**3.** If the roots of the cubic $x^3 - px^2 + qx - r = 0$ are in G.P. then

(a) $q^3 = p^3 r$

(b) $p^3 = q^3 r$

(c) $pq = r$

(d) $pr = q$

**4.** Consider a decreasing G.P. : $g_1, g_2, g_3, \dots, g_n, \dots$ such that $g_1 + g_2 + g_3 = 13$ and $g_1^2 + g_2^2 + g_3^2 = 91$ then which of the following does not hold?

(a) The greatest term of the G.P. is 9.

(b) $3g_4 = g_3$

(c) $g_1 = 1$

(d) $g_2 = 3$

**5.** The point $A(x_1, y_1)$, $B(x_2, y_2)$ and $C(x_3, y_3)$ lie on the parabola $y = 3x^2$. If $x_1, x_2, x_3$ are in A.P. and $y_1, y_2, y_3$ are in G.P. then the common ratio of the G.P. is

(a) $3 + 2\sqrt{2}$

(b) $3 + \sqrt{2}$

(c) $3 - \sqrt{2}$

(d) $3 - 2\sqrt{2}$

| RESPONSE GRID | 1. ⓐⓑⓒⓓ | 2. ⓐⓑⓒⓓ | 3. ⓐⓑⓒⓓ | 4. ⓐⓑⓒⓓ | 5. ⓐⓑⓒⓓ |

**6.** Sum of the first n terms of the series

$$\frac{1}{2} + \frac{3}{4} + \frac{7}{8} + \frac{15}{16} + \ldots\ldots\ldots \text{ is equal to}$$

(a) $2^n - n - 1$      (b) $1 - 2^{-n}$

(c) $n + 2^{-n} - 1$      (d) $2^n + 1$.

**7.** Let $\alpha, \beta$ be the roots of $x^2 - x + p = 0$ and $\gamma, \delta$ be the roots of $x^2 - 4x + q = 0$. If $\alpha, \beta, \gamma, \delta$ are in G.P., then the integral values of $p$ and $q$ respectively, are

(a) $-2, -32$      (b) $-2, 3$

(c) $-6, 3$      (d) $-6, -32$

**8.** An infinite G.P. has first term 'x' and sum '5', then x belongs to

(a) $x < -10$      (b) $-10 < x < 0$

(c) $0 < x < 10$      (d) $x > 10$

**9.** In the quadratic equation $ax^2 + bx + c = 0$, $\Delta = b^2 - 4ac$ and $\alpha + \beta, \alpha^2 + \beta^2, \alpha^3 + \beta^3$ are in G.P. where $\alpha, \beta$ are the roots of $ax^2 + bx + c = 0$, then

(a) $\Delta \neq 0$      (b) $b\Delta = 0$

(c) $c\Delta = 0$      (d) $\Delta = 0$

**10.** The sum of the first n terms of the sequence $1, (1 + 2), (1 + 2 + 2^2), \ldots\ldots, (1 + 2 + 2^2 + \ldots\ldots + 2^{k-1}), \ldots\ldots$ is of the form $2^{n+R} + S_n^2 + T_n + U$ for all $n \in N$. The value of $(R + S + T + U)$ equals

(a) $-1$      (b) $0$

(c) $1$      (d) $-2$

**11.** The sum of infinite terms of a decreasing G.P. is equal to the greatest value of the function $f(x) = x^3 + 3x - 9$ in the interval $[-2, 3]$ and the difference between the first two terms is $f'(0)$. Then the common ratio of the G.P. is :

(a) $-2/3$      (b) $4/3$

(c) $2/3$      (d) $-4/3$

**12.** Suppose $a, b, c$ are in A. P. and $a^2, b^2, c^2$ are in G. P. If $a < b < c$ and $a + b + c = \dfrac{3}{2}$, then the value of $a$ is

(a) $\dfrac{1}{2\sqrt{2}}$      (b) $\dfrac{1}{2\sqrt{3}}$

(c) $\dfrac{1}{2} - \dfrac{1}{\sqrt{3}}$      (d) $\dfrac{1}{2} - \dfrac{1}{\sqrt{2}}$

**13.** $A_r; r = 1, 2, 3, \ldots\ldots, n$ are n points on the parabola $y^2 = 4x$ in the first quadrant. If $A_r = (x_r, y_r)$, where $x_1, x_2, x_3, \ldots\ldots, x_n$ are in G. P. and $x_1 = 1$, $x_2 = 2$; then $y_n$ is equal to

(a) $-2^{\frac{n+1}{2}}$      (b) $2^{n+1}$

(c) $(\sqrt{2})^{n+1}$      (d) $2^{\frac{n}{2}}$

**14.** If a, b, c, d are in G.P., then $(a^2 + b^2 + c^2)(b^2 + c^2 + d^2)$ equal to

(a) $ab + bc + cd$      (b) $(ab + bc + cd)^2$

(c) $(ab + bc + cd)^4$      (d) None of these

## Section - II - Multiple Correct Answer Type

This section contains 4 multiple correct answer(s) type questions. Each question has 4 choices (a), (b), (c) and (d), out of which **ONE OR MORE** is/are correct.

**15.** If $b_1, b_2$ and $b_3$ ($b_1 > 0$) are three successive terms of a G.P. with common ratio r, the value of r for which the inequality $b_3 > 4b_2 - 3b_1$ holds, is given by

(a) $r > 3$      (b) $r < 1$

(c) $r = 3.5$      (d) $r = 5.2$

| **RESPONSE GRID** | 6. ⓐⓑⓒⓓ | 7. ⓐⓑⓒⓓ | 8. ⓐⓑⓒⓓ | 9. ⓐⓑⓒⓓ | 10. ⓐⓑⓒⓓ |
|---|---|---|---|---|---|
| | 11. ⓐⓑⓒⓓ | 12. ⓐⓑⓒⓓ | 13. ⓐⓑⓒⓓ | 14. ⓐⓑⓒⓓ | 15. ⓐⓑⓒⓓ |

*Space for Rough Work*

16. The first term of a geometric progression is 6 and the sum of the first n terms is 45/4 and the sum of the reciprocals of the same number of terms is 5/2. Then which of the following is / are correct ?

   (a)  The sequence is decreasing

   (b)  The value of n equals 8

   (c)  Sum of the first two terms is 9

   (d)  The sum to infinite number of terms is 12

17. If $\log_x a$, $a^{x/2}$ and $\log_b x$ are in GP, then $x$ is equal to

   (a)  $\log_a (\log_b a)$

   (b)  $\log_a (\log_e a) - \log_a (\log_e b)$

   (c)  $-\log_a (\log_e{}^b)$

   (d)  $\log a (\log_e b) - \log_a (\log_e a)$

18. The sum of squares of three distinct real numbers, which are in G. P. is $S^2$. If their sum is $\alpha S$, then $\alpha^2$ can lie in the interval

   (a)  $\left( -\infty, \dfrac{1}{3} \right)$

   (b)  $\left( \dfrac{1}{3}, 1 \right)$

   (c)  $(1, 3)$

   (d)  None of these

## Section - III - Reasoning Type

This section contains 1 reasoning type question. The question has 4 choices (a), (b), (c) and (d) out of which **ONLY ONE** is correct.

**Direction : This question contains two statements: Statement-1 (Assertion) and Statement-2 (Reason) and has four alternative choices, only one of which is the correct answer. You have to select the correct choice.**

   (a)  Statement-1 is True, Statement-2 is True; Statement-2 is a correct explanation for Statement-1.

   (b)  Statement-1 is True, Statement-2 is True; Statement-2 is NOT a correct explanation for Statement-1.

   (c)  Statement -1 is True, Statement-2 is False.

   (d)  Statement -1 is False, Statement-2 is True.

19. **Statement 1 :** 1, 2, 4, 8, ........ is a G.P. 4, 8, 16, 32 is also a  G.P. then $1 + 4, 2 + 8, 4 + 16, 8 + 32$, ........ is also a G.P.

   **Statement 2 :** Let general term of a G.P. with common ratio r be $T_{k+1}$ and general term of another G.P. with common ratio r be $T'_{k+1}$, then the series whose general term $T''_{k+1} = T_{k+1} + T'_{k+1}$ is also a G.P. with common ratio r.

<table>
<tr><td>**RESPONSE GRID**</td><td>16. ⓐⓑⓒⓓ</td><td>17. ⓐⓑⓒⓓ</td><td>18. ⓐⓑⓒⓓ</td><td>19. ⓐⓑⓒⓓ</td></tr>
</table>

*Space for Rough Work*

## Section - IV - Integer Type

This section contains 5 questions. The answer to each of the questions is a single digit integer ranging from 0 to 9.

**20.** Find the HCF of the minimum non-negative values of $a$, $b$ and $c$, given that the equation

$x^4 + ax^3 + bx^2 + cx + 1 = 0$ has only real roots.

**21.** If $\tan\left(\dfrac{\pi}{12} - x\right)$, $\tan\dfrac{\pi}{12}$, $\tan\left(\dfrac{\pi}{12} + x\right)$ in order are three consecutive terms of a G.P. then sum of all the solutions in $[0, 314]$ is $990A\pi$. The value of k is?

**22.** Find the value of $\dfrac{17}{8} - \displaystyle\sum_{r=0}^{10} \cos^3 \dfrac{\pi r}{3}$.

**23.** If $\left\{3\left(1 - \dfrac{1}{2} + \dfrac{1}{4} - \dfrac{1}{8} + .....\right)\right\}^{\log_{10} x} =$

$\left\{20\left(1 - \dfrac{1}{4} + \dfrac{1}{16} - \dfrac{1}{64} + .....\right)\right\}^{\log_x 10}$ , then x = $10^A$ or $10^{-A}$.

Find the value of A.

**24.** The third term of a G.P. is 64.

If the product of first five terms is $2^{13A + 4}$, find the value of A.



| DAILY PRACTICE PROBLEM DPP 09 - MATHS | | | |
|---|---|---|---|
| Total Questions | 24 | Total Marks | 67 |
| Attempted | | Correct | |
| Incorrect | | Net Score | |
| Cut-off Score | 13 | Qualifying Score | 44 |
| Success Gap = Net Score – Qualifying Score | | | |

$$\text{Net Score} = \sum_{i=1}^{VI}\left[(\text{correct}_i \times MM_i) - (In_i - NM_i)\right]$$

Name :                               Date :

Start Time :                      End Time :

# MATHEMATICS    M10

**SYLLABUS : Progressions-3 :** Harmonic progression, Relation among A.P., G.P. and H.P.

**Max. Marks : 72**             **Time : 60 min.**



## Section - I - Straight Objective Type

This section contains 7 multiple choice questions. Each question has 4 choices (a), (b), (c) and (d), out of which **ONLY ONE** is correct.

1. If a, b, c be in A.P.; b, c, d be in G.P. & c, d, e be in H.P., then a, c, e will be in :
   (a) A.P.         (b) G.P.
   (c) H.P.         (d) None of these

2. If a, b, c are in H.P., then a, a − c, a − b are in :
   (a) A.P.         (b) G.P.
   (c) H.P.         (d) None of these

3. If three positive numbers a , b, c are in H.P. then
   $e^{\ln(a+c)+\ln(a-2b+c)}$ simplifies to
   (a) $(a-c)^2$         (b) zero
   (c) $(a-c)$         (d) 1

4. If a, b, c are in G.P., then the equations, $ax^2 + 2bx + c = 0$ & $dx^2 + 2ex + f = 0$ have a common root, if $\dfrac{d}{a}, \dfrac{e}{b}, \dfrac{f}{c}$ are in :
   (a) A.P.         (b) GP
   (c) H.P.         (d) None

5. If the sum of the roots of the quadratic equation, $ax^2 + bx + c = 0$ is equal to sum of the squares of their reciprocals, then $\dfrac{a}{c}, \dfrac{b}{a}, \dfrac{c}{b}$ are in :
   (a) A.P.         (b) G.P.
   (c) H.P.         (d) None

**RESPONSE GRID**    1. ⓐⓑⓒⓓ    2. ⓐⓑⓒⓓ    3. ⓐⓑⓒⓓ    4. ⓐⓑⓒⓓ    5. ⓐⓑⓒⓓ

**6.** Consider the A.P. $a_1, a_2, \ldots, a_n, \ldots$ and the G.P. $b_1, b_2, \ldots, b_n, \ldots$

such that $a_1 = b_1 = 1$ ; $a_9 = b_9$ and $\sum_{r=1}^{9} a_r = 369$ then

(a) $b_6 = 27$      (b) $b_7 = 27$

(c) $b_8 = 81$      (d) $b_9 = 18$

**7.** If $p, q, r$ in H.P. and $p$ & $r$ be different having same sign then the roots of the equation $px^2 + qx + r = 0$ are

(a) real & equal      (b) real & distinct

(c) irrational      (d) imaginary

## Section - II - Multiple Correct Answer Type

This section contains 4 multiple correct answer(s) type questions. Each question has 4 choices (a), (b), (c) and (d), out of which **ONE OR MORE** is/are correct.

**8.** If three positive unequal numbers $a, b, c$, are in H.P., then

(a) $a + c > 2b$      (b) $a^2 + c^2 > 2b^2$

(c) $a^2 + c^2 > 2ac$      (d) none of these

**9.** Given four positive number in A.P. If 5 , 6 , 9 and 15 are added respectively to these numbers , we get a G.P. , then which of the following does not hold good ?

(a) The common ratio of G.P. is 3/2

(b) Common ratio of G.P. is 2/3

(c) Common difference of the A.P. is 3/2

(d) Common difference of the A.P. is 2/3

**10.** If the first and the $(2n-1)$th terms of an A.P., a G.P. and an H.P. are equal and their n-th terms are a, b and c respectively, then

(a) $a = b = c$      (b) $a > b > c$

(c) $a + c = b$      (d) $ac - b^2 = 0$

**11.** If $(m+1)$th, $(n+1)$th and $(r+1)$th terms of an A.P. are in G.P. and m, n, r are in H.P., then the ratio of the first term of the A.P. to its common difference is

(a) $-\dfrac{n}{2}$      (b) $-\dfrac{m}{2}$

(c) $r$      (d) $-\dfrac{mr}{m+r}$

## Section - III - Linked Comprehension Type

This section contains one paragraph. Based upon the paragraph, 2 multiple choice questions have to be answered. Each question has 4 choices (a), (b), (c) and (d), out of which **ONLY ONE** is correct.

If A, G and H are respectively arithmetic, geometric and harmonic means between a and b both being unequal and positive, then

$$A = \frac{a+b}{2} \Rightarrow a + b = 2A, G = \sqrt{ab} \Rightarrow ab = G^2$$

and $H = \dfrac{2ab}{a+b} \Rightarrow G^2 = AH$

**12.** If the geometric and harmonic means of two numbers are 16 and $12\dfrac{4}{5}$, then the ratio of one number to the other is

(a) $1 : 4$      (b) $2 : 3$

(c) $1 : 2$      (d) $2 : 1$

**13.** The sum of the AM and GM of two positive numbers is equal to the difference between the numbers. The numbers are in the ratio

(a) $1 : 3$      (b) $1 : 6$

(c) $9 : 1$      (d) $1 : 12$

---

**RESPONSE GRID**

6. (a)(b)(c)(d)   7. (a)(b)(c)(d)   8. (a)(b)(c)(d)   9. (a)(b)(c)(d)   10. (a)(b)(c)(d)

11. (a)(b)(c)(d)   12. (a)(b)(c)(d)   13. (a)(b)(c)(d)

*Space for Rough Work*

## Section - IV - Matrix-Match Type

This section contains 2 questions. It contains statements given in two columns, which have to be matched. Statements in Column I are labelled as A, B, C and D whereas statements in Column II are labelled as p, q, r and s. The answers to these questions have to be appropriately bubbled as illustrated in the following example. If the correct matches are A-p, A-r, B-p, B-s, C-r, C-s and D-q, then the correctly bubbled matrix will look like the following :

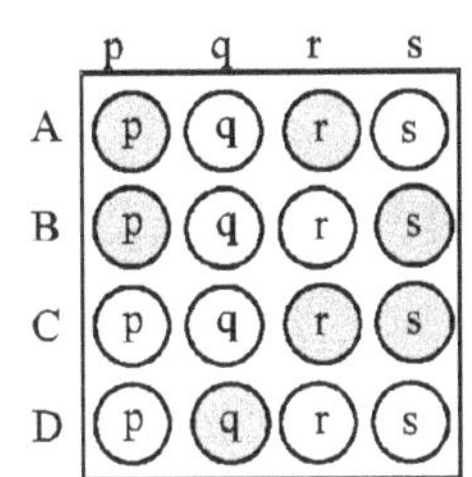

**14.**

| Column I | | Column II |
|---|---|---|
| (A) | The AM of two positive numbers a and b exceed their GM by 3/2 and the GM exceed their HM by 6/5, such that $a + b = \alpha$, $|a - b| = \beta$, then | (p) $\alpha + \beta^2 = 96$ |
| (B) | The AM of two positive numbers a and b exceed their GM by 2 and HM is one fifth of the greater of a and b, such that $a + b = \alpha$, $|a - b| = \beta$, then | (q) $\alpha + \beta^2 = 74$ |
| (C) | The HM of two positive numbers a and b is 4, their AM is A and Geometric mean G satisfy the relation $2A + G^2 = 27$. If $a + b = \alpha$, $|a - b| = \beta$, then | (r) $\alpha^2 + \beta = 234$ |
| | | (s) $\alpha^2 + \beta = 84$ |
| | | (t) $1 + \left(\dfrac{\alpha}{\beta}\right) + \left(\dfrac{\alpha}{\beta}\right)^2 + \ldots$ $+ \left(\dfrac{\alpha}{\beta}\right)^5 = 364$ |

**15.**

| Column I | | Column II |
|---|---|---|
| (A) | If a, b, c be positive numbers then $(a + b + c)\left(\dfrac{1}{a} + \dfrac{1}{b} + \dfrac{1}{c}\right)$ must be greater than or equal to | (p) 4 |
| (B) | If h be the H.M. and g be the G.M. of two positive numbers a and b such that $h : g = 4 : 5$, then $\dfrac{a}{b}$ can be equal to | (q) 9 |
| (C) | If $S = \sum\limits_{r=0}^{\infty} \dfrac{1}{2^r}$, $S_{n+1} = \sum\limits_{r=0}^{n} \dfrac{1}{2^r}$ and $S - S_{n+1} < 10^{-3}$ then n is greater than or equal to | (r) 10 |
| (D) | If $(1 + x)(1 + x^2)(1 + x^4)$ $(1 + x^8)\ldots\ldots(1 + x^{128})$ $= \sum\limits_{r=0}^{n} x^r$, then n is equal to | (s) 255 |

## Section - V - Reasoning Type

This section contains 3 reasoning type questions. Each question has 4 choices (a), (b), (c) and (d) out of which **ONLY ONE** is correct.

**DIRECTIONS for (Qs. 16 to 18) : Each of these questions contains two statements: Statement-1 (Assertion) and Statement-2 (Reason). Each of these questions has four alternative choices, only one of which is the correct answer. You have to select the correct choice.**

(a) Statement-1 is True, Statement-2 is True; Statement-2 is a correct explanation for Statement-1.

(b) Statement-1 is True, Statement-2 is True; Statement-2 is NOT a correct explanation for Statement-1.

(c) Statement -1 is True, Statement-2 is False.

(d) Statement -1 is False, Statement-2 is True.

**16. Statement-1:** For a infinite G.P. whose first term is 'a' and common ratio is r, then $S_\infty = \dfrac{a}{1-r}$ where $|r| = 1$

**Statement-2:** A, G, H are arithmetic mean, Geometric mean and harmonic mean of two positive real numbers a & b. Then A, G, H are in G.P.

**17.** **Statement-1**: If a, b, c are three positive numbers in G.P, then

$$\left(\frac{a+b+c}{3}\right)\left(\frac{3abc}{ab+bc+ca}\right) = \left(\sqrt[3]{abc}\right)^2$$

**Statement-2**: (AM) (HM)= (GM)$^2$ is true for positive numbers.

**18.** Let a, b, c and d be distinct positive real numbers in H.P.

**Statement–1** : $a + d > b + c$

**Statement–2** : $\dfrac{1}{a} + \dfrac{1}{d} = \dfrac{1}{b} + \dfrac{1}{c}$

## Section - VI - Integer Type

This section contains 5 questions. The answer to each of the questions is a single digit integer ranging from 0 to 9.

**19.** If a, b, c and d are positive integers and $a < b < c < d$ such that a, b, c are in A.P., b, c, d are in G.P. and $d - a = 30$. If the largest of these four numbers is 8P, find the value of P.

**20.** Three positive integers form the first three terms of an A.P. If the smallest number is increased by one the A.P. becomes a G.P. In original A.P. if the largest number is increased by two, the A.P. also becomes a G.P. If the smallest term of the A.P. is X, find the value of X.

**21.** Let $a_1, a_2, ....., a_{10}$ be in A, P, and $h_1, h_2, ...., h_{10}$ be in H.P. If $a_1 = h_1 = 2$ and $a_{10} = h_{10} = 3$, then find the value of $a_4 h_7$.

**22.** If $\log_{14} \sqrt{5}$, $\log_{3^x - 11} \sqrt{5}$, $\log_{3^x - \frac{61}{7}} \sqrt{5}$ are in H.P., find the sum of all possible values of x.

**23.** How many of the following statements are true?

(i) If x, y, z all greater than '1' are in G.P. then

$$\frac{1}{1+\log x}, \frac{1}{1+\log y}, \frac{1}{1+\log z} \text{ are in A.P.}$$

(ii) The digit at unit's place in the number $(13)^{1225} + (11)^{1915} - (23)^{1225}$ is equal to 1

(iii) Only one value of x satisfies the equation $\log_2 (x-1) = 2 \log_2 (x-3)$

| **RESPONSE GRID** | 17. ⓐⓑⓒⓓ 18. ⓐⓑⓒⓓ 19. ⓪①②③④⑤⑥⑦⑧⑨ |
| --- | --- |
| | 20. ⓪①②③④⑤⑥⑦⑧⑨ 21. ⓪①②③④⑤⑥⑦⑧⑨ |
| | 22. ⓪①②③④⑤⑥⑦⑧⑨ 23. ⓪①②③④⑤⑥⑦⑧⑨ |

## DAILY PRACTICE PROBLEM DPP 10 - MATHS

| Total Questions | 23 | Total Marks | 72 |
| --- | --- | --- | --- |
| Attempted | | Correct | |
| Incorrect | | Net Score | |
| Cut-off Score | 14 | Qualifying Score | 47 |
| Success Gap = Net Score – Qualifying Score | | | |

$$\text{Net Score} = \sum_{i=1}^{VI}\left[(\text{correct}_i \times MM_i) - (In_i - NM_i)\right]$$

*Space for Rough Work*

# DPP - Daily Practice Problems

**Name :**                        **Date :**

**Start Time :**                  **End Time :**

# MATHEMATICS    M11

**SYLLABUS : Progressions-4 :** Arithmetico-Geometric Progression, Sum of first n natural numbers, Sum of square of first n natural numbers, Sum of cube of first n natural numbers, Method of difference.

## Max. Marks : 63          Time : 60 min.

### GENERAL INSTRUCTIONS

- The Daily Practice Problem Sheet contains **21** Questions divided into 6 sections.
  Section I has **8** MCQ's with ONLY 1 correct option. 2 marks for correct answer and No negative marks.
  Section II has **4** MCQ's with 1 or MORE THAN 1 correct option. 4 marks for correct answer(s) and (−1) for wrong answer.
  Section III has **1** PASSAGE with **3** MCQ's with ONLY 1 correct option. 3 marks for correct and (−1) mark for wrong answer.
  Section IV has **2** MCQ's with multiple matchings. 1 mark for the correct matching of each row & No negative marks.
  Section V has **2** Assertion-Reason MCQ's with ONLY 1 correct option. 3 marks for correct and (−1) mark for wrong answer.
  Section VI has **2** single digit integer answer questions. 4 marks for correct answer and (−1) for wrong answer.
- No mark will be given/ deducted if no bubble is filled. Keep a timer in front and stop immediately at the end of 60 min.
- You have to evaluate your Response Grids yourself with the help of Solution Booklet.
- The sheet follows a particular syllabus. Do not attempt the sheet before you have completed your preparation for that syllabus. Refer syllabus sheet in the starting of the book for the syllabus of all the DPP sheets.
- After completing the sheet check your answers with the solution booklet and complete the Result Grid. Finally spend time to analyse your performance and revise the areas which emerge out as weak in your evaluation.

## Section - I - Straight Objective Type

This section contains 8 multiple choice questions. Each question has 4 choices (a), (b), (c) and (d), out of which **ONLY ONE** is correct.

**1.** If $\displaystyle\sum_{n=1}^{49} \frac{1}{\sqrt{n+\sqrt{n^2-1}}} = a+b\sqrt{2}$, then $a+b =$

   (a)  2      (b)  4      (c)  8      (d)  None

**2.** The sum $\displaystyle\sum_{r=2}^{\infty} \frac{1}{r^2-1}$ is equal to :

   (a)  1      (b)  3/4      (c)  4/3      (d)  None

**3.** If $\displaystyle\sum_{k=1}^{n}\left(\sum_{m=1}^{k} m^2\right) = an^4 + bn^3 + cn^2 + dn + e$,

then $a+b+c+d =$

   (a)  10      (b)  6      (c)  3      (d)  1

**4.** If the sum $\displaystyle\sum_{k=1}^{\infty} \frac{1}{(k+2)\sqrt{k}+k\sqrt{k+2}} = \frac{\sqrt{a}+\sqrt{b}}{\sqrt{c}}$ where a, b, c ∈

N and lie in [1, 15] then $a+b+c$ equals

   (a)  6                 (b)  8

   (c)  10              (d)  11

**5.** The sum of n terms of $1.2.3 + 2.3.4 + ....$ will be

   (a)  $\dfrac{n(n+1)(n+2)(n+3)}{4}$     (b)  $\dfrac{2n(n+1)(n+2)(n+3)}{3}$

   (c)  $\dfrac{(n+1)(n+2)(n+3)}{4}$     (d)  $\dfrac{n(n-1)(n-2)(n-3)}{4}$

| RESPONSE GRID | 1. ⓐⓑⓒⓓ | 2. ⓐⓑⓒⓓ | 3. ⓐⓑⓒⓓ | 4. ⓐⓑⓒⓓ | 5. ⓐⓑⓒⓓ |
|---|---|---|---|---|---|

**6.** ABCD is a square of length a, $a \in n$, $a > 1$. Let $L_1, L_2, L_3, ....$ be points on BC such that $BL_1 = L_1L_2 = L_2L_3 = ...... = 1$ and $M_1, M_2, M_3, ....$ be points on CD such that $CM_1 = M_1M_2 = M_2M_3 = ... = 1$. Then $\sum_{n=1}^{a-1}(AL_n^2 + L_nM_n^2)$ is equal to

(a) $(1/2)a(a-1)^2$     (b) $(1/2)a(a-1)(4a-1)$

(c) $(1/2)(a-1)(2a-1)(4a-1)$     (d) None

**7.** ABC is a right angled traingle in which $\angle B = 90°$ and BC = a. If n points $L_1, L_2, ....., L_n$ on AB are such that AB is divided in (n + 1) equal parts and $L_1M_1, L_2M_2, ...., L_nM_n$ are line segments parallel to BC and $M_1, M_2, ...., M_n$ are on AC then the sum of the lengths of $L_1M_1, L_2M_2, ...., L_nM_n$ is :

(a) a (n+ 1)/2     (b) a (n – 1)/2

(c) an/2

(d) Impossible to find from the given data

**8.** If $(1^2 - a_1) + (2^2 - a_2) + (3^2 - a_3) + .... + (n^2 - a_n) = (1/3)n(n^2 - 1)$ then $a_n$ is given by :

(a) n     (b) n+1     (c) n–1     (d) n/2

## Section - II - Multiple Correct Answer Type

This section contains 4 multiple correct answer(s) type questions. Each question has 4 choices (a), (b), (c) and (d), out of which **ONE OR MORE** is/are correct.

**9.** Let $S_n = \lim_{n \to \infty}\left(\dfrac{1}{n^6} + \dfrac{32}{n^6} + ...... + \dfrac{1}{n}\right)$ and

$T_n = \lim_{n \to \infty}\left(\dfrac{1}{n^6} + \dfrac{32}{n^6} + ...... + \dfrac{(n-1)^5}{n^6}\right)$, then which of the following is/are true?

(a) $S_n \to \dfrac{1^+}{6}$     (b) $(S_n + T_n) < \dfrac{1}{3}$

(c) $(S_n + T_n) > \dfrac{1}{3}$     (d) $T_n \to \dfrac{1^-}{6}$

**10.** Consider the series $2 + 6 + 12 + .............. + n(n + 1)$

(a) Sum of first fifty terms of series is 44200

(b) If the sum of n-terms of the series is 30 times the number of terms, then n is equal to 6

(c) Sum of first fifty terms of the series is 51800

(d) If the sum of n-terms of the series is 30 times the number of terms, then n is equal to 8

**11.** If $\sum_{r=1}^{n} r(r+1)(2r+3) = an^4 + bn^3 + cn^2 + dn + e$, then

(a) $a = 1/2$     (b) $b = 8/3$

(c) $c = 9/2$     (d) $e = 0$

**12.** If $S_1, S_2, S_3, ...., S_n$ are the sum of infinite geometric series whose first terms are 1, 2, 3, ..., n and whose common ratios are $\dfrac{1}{2}, \dfrac{1}{3}, \dfrac{1}{4}, ...., \dfrac{1}{(n+1)}$ respectively, then the value of $S_1^2 + S_2^2 + S_3^2 + ... + S_{2n-1}^2$ is equal to

(a) $\dfrac{1}{3}[n(2n+1)(4n+1) - 3]$     (b) $\dfrac{1}{3}[n(2n+1)(4n+1) + 3]$

(c) $\dfrac{1}{3}[n(2n-1)(4n+1) - 3]$     (d) $\dfrac{1}{6}[n(2n+1)(4n+1)] - 1$

## Section - III - Linked Comprehension Type

This section contains one paragraph. Based upon the paragraph, 3 multiple choice questions have to be answered. Each question has 4 choices (a), (b), (c) and (d), out of which **ONLY ONE** is correct.

Suppose a series of n terms is given by
$S_n = t_1 + t_2 + t_3 + ................. + t_n$

Then $S_{n-1} = t_1 + t_2 + t_3 + ................. + t_{n-1}, n > 1$

Subtracting we get, $S_n - S_{n-1} = t_n, n \geq 2$

Further if we put n = 1 in the first sum then $S_1 = t_1$

Thus we can write $t_n = S_n - S_{n-1}, n \geq 2$ and $t_1 = S_1$

| **RESPONSE GRID** | 6. ⓐⓑⓒⓓ | 7. ⓐⓑⓒⓓ | 8. ⓐⓑⓒⓓ | 9. ⓐⓑⓒⓓ | 10. ⓐⓑⓒⓓ |
| | 11. ⓐⓑⓒⓓ | 12. ⓐⓑⓒⓓ | | | |

The above results can be used to find the terms of any kind of series, independent of its nature, provided the sum to first n terms is given.

**13.** If sum to n terms of a series is of the form $an^2 + bn$, where a and b are constants, then the fourth term of the series is

(a) $5a + b$    (b) $7a + b$    (c) $9a + 3b$    (d) $16a + 4b$

**14.** The sum to n terms of a series is given by $\frac{1}{4} n (n + 1) (n + 2) (n + 3)$ then the nth term of the series is

(a) $n (n + 1) (n + 2)$      (b) $(n + 1) (n + 2) (n + 3)$

(c) $\frac{n(n + 1) (2n + 1)}{6}$      (d) $n(4n^2 - 1)$

**15.** If the sum to n terms of a series is given by $\frac{n(n+1)(n+2)}{6}$ then the nth term of the series is

(a) $\sum n^2$    (b) $\left(\sum n\right)^2$    (c) $\sum n$    (d) $\sum n + n$

## Section - IV - Matrix-Match Type

This section contains 2 questions. It contains statements given in two columns, which have to be matched. Statements in Column I are labelled as A, B, C and D whereas statements in Column II are labelled as p, q, r and s. The answers to these questions have to be appropriately bubbled as illustrated in the following example. If the correct matches are A-p, A-r, B-p, B-s, C-r, C-s and D-q, then the correctly bubbled matrix will look like the following :

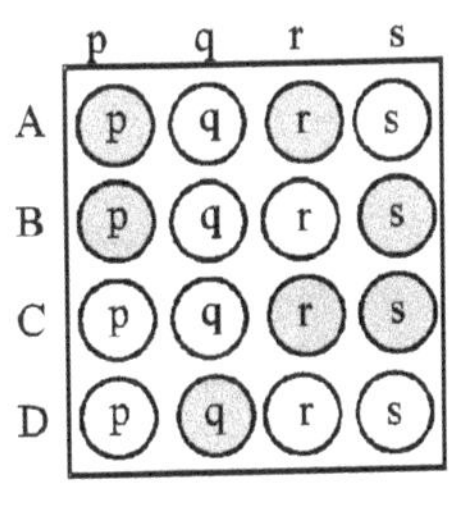

**16.**

| Column I | Column II |
|---|---|
| (A) The sum to n terms of the series $1^2 + (1^2 + 3^2) + (1^2 + 3^2 + 5^2) + \ldots$ is: | (p) $2n/n+1$ |
| (B) Sum of the series $1 + 1/(1 + 2) + 1/(1 + 2 + 3) + \ldots + 1/(1+2+\ldots+n)$ is : | (q) $446$ |
| (C) Sum to n terms of the series $1^3 + 3 . 2^3 + 3^3 + 3 . 4^3 + 5^3 + \ldots$ is (n is even) | (r) $1/6 n (n + 1) (2n^2 + 2n - 1)$ |
| (D) The sum of the following series $\frac{1^3}{1} + \frac{1^3 + 2^3}{1 + 3} + \frac{1^3 + 2^3 + 3^3}{1 + 3 + 5}.$ $+ \ldots$ upto 16 terms is | (s) $\frac{n(n^2 + 3n + 1)}{2}$ |

**17.**

| Column I | Column II |
|---|---|
| (A) Suppose that $F (n + 1) = \frac{2F(n) + 1}{2}$ for n = $1, 2, 3, \ldots$ and $F(1) = 2$. Then $F(101)$ equals | (p) $42$ |
| (B) If $a_1, a_2, a_3, \ldots a_{21}$ are in A.P. and $a_3 + a_5 + a_{11} + a_{17} + a_{19} = 10$ then the value of $\sum_{i=1}^{21} a_i$ is | (q) $1620$ |
| (C) 10th term of the sequence $S = 1 + 5 + 13 + 29 + \ldots$ is | (r) $52$ |
| (D) The sum of all two digit numbers which are not divisible by $2$ or $3$ is | (s) $2045$ |

## Section - V - Reasoning Type

This section contains 2 reasoning type questions. Each question has 4 choices (a), (b), (c) and (d) out of which **ONLY ONE** is correct.

<table>
<tr><td rowspan="3">**RESPONSE GRID**</td><td colspan="3">13. (a)(b)(c)(d)    14. (a)(b)(c)(d)    15. (a)(b)(c)(d)</td></tr>
<tr><td colspan="3">16. A - (p)(q)(r)(s); B - (p)(q)(r)(s); C - (p)(q)(r)(s); D - (p)(q)(r)(s)</td></tr>
<tr><td colspan="3">17. A - (p)(q)(r)(s); B - (p)(q)(r)(s); C - (p)(q)(r)(s); D - (p)(q)(r)(s)</td></tr>
</table>

*Space for Rough Work*

**DIRECTIONS for (Qs. 18 & 19) :** Each of these questions contains two statements: Statement-1 (Assertion) and Statement-2 (Reason). Each of these questions has four alternative choices, only one of which is the correct answer. You have to select the correct choice.

(a)  Statement-1 is True, Statement-2 is True; Statement-2 is a correct explanation for Statement-1.

(b)  Statement-1 is True, Statement-2 is True; Statement-2 is NOT a correct explanation for Statement-1.

(c)  Statement -1 is True, Statement-2 is False.

(d)  Statement -1 is False, Statement-2 is True.

18.  **Statement-1:**  The sum of all the products of the first n positive integers taken two at a time where first number is less than the second number is $\frac{1}{24}(n-1)(n+1)n(3n+2)$.

**Statement-2:** $\displaystyle\sum_{1\le i<j\le n} a_i a_j = \frac{1}{2}[(a_1+a_2+...+a_n)^2-(a_1^2+a_2^2+.....+a_n^2)]$

19.  **Statement-1 :** The sum of series $n.n+(n-1)(n+1)+(n-2)(n+2)+...+1.(2n-1)$ is $\frac{1}{6}n(n+1)(4n+1)$.

**Statement-2 :** The sum of any series $S_n$ can be given as, $S_n = \displaystyle\sum_{r=1}^{n} T_r$, where $T_r$ is the general term of the series.

## Section - VI - Integer Type

This section contains 2 questions. The answer to each of the questions is a single digit integer ranging from 0 to 9.

20.  If $S = 1+(2)(3)+4+(5)(6)+...+73+(74)(75)$, then find the value of $\dfrac{S}{9935}$.

21.  If the sum of infinite terms of series $3+5.\dfrac{1}{4}+7.\dfrac{1}{4^2}+....$ is $\dfrac{A}{B}$, find the value of B.

| RESPONSE GRID | | |
|---|---|---|
| 18. ⓐ ⓑ ⓒ ⓓ | | 20. ⓪①②③④⑤⑥⑦⑧⑨ |
| 19. ⓐ ⓑ ⓒ ⓓ | | 21. ⓪①②③④⑤⑥⑦⑧⑨ |

## DAILY PRACTICE PROBLEM DPP 11 - MATHS

| | | | |
|---|---|---|---|
| Total Questions | 21 | Total Marks | 63 |
| Attempted | | Correct | |
| Incorrect | | Net Score | |
| Cut-off Score | 13 | Qualifying Score | 41 |
| Success Gap = Net Score – Qualifying Score | | | |

$$\text{Net Score} = \sum_{i=I}^{VI}\left[(\mathbf{correct}_i \times MM_i)-(In_i - NM_i)\right]$$

*Space for Rough Work*

**Name :**

**Date :**

**Start Time :**

**End Time :**

## MATHEMATICS M12

**SYLLABUS : Quadratic Equations and Inequations-1** : Solution of quadratic equations and Nature of roots.

## Max. Marks : 61      Time : 60 min.

### GENERAL INSTRUCTIONS

- The Daily Practice Problem Sheet contains **20** Questions divided into 6 sections.
  Section I has **7** MCQ's with ONLY 1 correct option. 2 marks for correct answer and No negative marks.
  Section II has **4** MCQ's with 1 or MORE THAN 1 correct option. 4 marks for correct answer(s) and (–1) for wrong answer.
  Section III has **1** PASSAGE with **3** MCQ's with ONLY 1 correct option. 3 marks for correct and (–1) mark for wrong answer.
  Section IV has **2** MCQ's with multiple matchings. 1 mark for the correct matching of each row & No negative marks.
  Section V has **2** Assertion-Reason MCQ's with ONLY 1 correct option. 3 marks for correct and (–1) mark for wrong answer.
  Section VI has **2** single digit integer answer questions. 4 marks for correct answer and (–1) for wrong answer.
- No mark will be given/ deducted if no bubble is filled. Keep a timer in front and stop immediately at the end of 60 min.
- You have to evaluate your Response Grids yourself with the help of Solution Booklet.
- The sheet follows a particular syllabus. Do not attempt the sheet before you have completed your preparation for that syllabus. Refer syllabus sheet in the starting of the book for the syllabus of all the DPP sheets.
- After completing the sheet check your answers with the solution booklet and complete the Result Grid. Finally spend time to analyse your performance and revise the areas which emerge out as weak in your evaluation.

---

### Section - I - Straight Objective Type

This section contains 7 multiple choice questions. Each question has 4 choices (a), (b), (c) and (d), out of which **ONLY ONE** is correct.

**1.** The integral values of $m$ for which the roots of the equation

$mx^2 + (2m - 1)\, x + (m - 2) = 0$ are rational are given by the expression    [where n is integer]

(a) $n(n+2)$      (b) $n(n+1)$

(c) $n^2$      (d) None of these

**2.** If the equation $|x^2 + 4x + 3| - mx + 2m = 0$ has exactly three solutions, then the value of $m$ is equal to

(a) $-8 + 2\sqrt{15}$      (b) $-8 - 2\sqrt{15}$

(c) $3$      (d) $-\sqrt{15}$

**3.** Let $p, q \in \{1, 2, 3, 4\}$. The number of equations of the form $px^2 + qx + 1 = 0$ having real roots is

(a) 15      (b) 9

(c) 7      (d) 8

**4.** Let a, b, c be the sides of a triangle where $a \neq b \neq c$ and $\lambda \in$ R. If the roots of the equation

$x^2 + 2(a + b + c)x + 3\lambda\,(ab + bc + ca) = 0$ are real, then

(a) $\lambda < \dfrac{4}{3}$      (b) $\lambda > \dfrac{5}{3}$

(c) $\lambda \in \left(\dfrac{1}{3}, \dfrac{5}{3}\right)$      (d) $\lambda \in \left(\dfrac{4}{3}, \dfrac{5}{3}\right)$

**5.** If the roots of the equation $x^2 - 2ax + a^2 + a - 3 = 0$ are real less than 3, then

(a) $a < 2$      (b) $2 \leq a \leq 3$

(c) $3 < a \leq 4$      (d) $a > 4$

---

**RESPONSE GRID**    **1.** ⓐⓑⓒⓓ    **2.** ⓐⓑⓒⓓ    **3.** ⓐⓑⓒⓓ    **4.** ⓐⓑⓒⓓ    **5.** ⓐⓑⓒⓓ

6. If the roots of the equation, $\dfrac{1}{x+p} + \dfrac{1}{x+q} = \dfrac{1}{r}$ are equal in magnitude but opposite in sign then $p+q$ is equal to

   (a) r
   (b) $2r$
   (c) $(1/2)r$
   (d) none of these

7. If the equation $x^2 + 2(k+1)x + 9k - 5 = 0$ has only negative roots, then –

   (a) $k \le 0$
   (b) $k \ge 0$
   (c) $k \ge 6$
   (d) $k \le 6$

## Section - II - Multiple Correct Answer Type

This section contains 4 multiple correct answer(s) type questions. Each question has 4 choices (a), (b), (c) and (d), out of which **ONE OR MORE** is/are correct.

8. Let a, b, c and m $\in$ R$^+$. Possible value of m (independent of a, b and c) for which atleast one of the following equations $ax^2 + bx + cm = 0$, $bx^2 + cx + am = 0$ and $cx^2 + ax + bm = 0$ have real roots is –

   (a) 1/12
   (b) 1/8
   (c) 1/4
   (d) 1/2

9. If $a < 0$, then the root of the equation

   $x^2 - 2a|x - a| - 3a^2 = 0$ is

   (a) $a(-1-\sqrt{6})$
   (b) $a(1-\sqrt{2})$
   (c) $a(-1+\sqrt{6})$
   (d) $a(1+\sqrt{2})$

10. The equation $x^2 + a^2x + b^2 = 0$ has two roots each of which exceeds a number $c$, then

    (a) $a^4 > 4b^2$
    (b) $c^2 + a^2c + b^2 > 0$
    (c) $-a^2/2 > c$
    (d) none of these

11. If $a$, $b$, $c$ are distinct numbers in arithmetic progression, then both the roots of the quadratic equation

    $(a + 2b - 3c)\,x^2 + (b + 2c - 3a)x + (c + 2a - 3b) = 0$ are

    (a) real
    (b) positive
    (c) negative
    (d) rational

## Section - III - Linked Comprehension Type

This section contains one paragraph. Based upon the paragraph, 3 multiple choice questions have to be answered. Each question has 4 choices (a), (b), (c) and (d), out of which **ONLY ONE** is correct.

Let $y = f(x)$ be a quadratic polynomial such that

$$f\!\left(\frac{a^2 - 3}{a} + x\right) = f\!\left(\frac{a^2 - 3}{a} - x\right); \quad f\!\left(\frac{a^2 - 3}{a}\right) = -\frac{(a^2 + 3)^2}{a} \ \text{and the}$$

parabola $y^2 = \dfrac{1}{a}x$ is an equal parabola to that of $y = f(x)$.

12. The roots of the equation $y = f(x) = 0$ are

    (a) Real and distinct for all $a \ne 0$
    (b) Real and may be equal, if $a > 0$
    (c) Real and distinct only, if $a > 0$
    (d) non-real, if $a < 0$

13. If exactly one root of the equation lies in the interval $(0, 1)$, then the values of $a$ is/are

    (a) $a \in R$
    (b) $[0, 1]$
    (c) $\left[0, \dfrac{1}{2}\right)$
    (d) $\left(0, \dfrac{1}{2}\right)$

| **RESPONSE GRID** | 6. ⓐⓑⓒⓓ | 7. ⓐⓑⓒⓓ | 8. ⓐⓑⓒⓓ | 9. ⓐⓑⓒⓓ | 10. ⓐⓑⓒⓓ |
| | 11. ⓐⓑⓒⓓ | 12. ⓐⓑⓒⓓ | 13. ⓐⓑⓒⓓ | | |

**14.** Let $\alpha$, $\beta$ be the roots of the equation $y = f(x) = 0 \ \forall \ a \in R^+$. If $\lambda$ be such that $\alpha < a\lambda < \beta$ and $a \in (0,1)$, then $\lambda$ lies in

(a) $(0, 1)$

(b) $\left(0, \dfrac{1}{2}\right)$

(c) $\left(-\dfrac{6}{a^2}, 2\right)$

(d) $\left(\dfrac{6}{a^2}, 2\right)$

## Section - IV - Matrix-Match Type

This section contains 2 questions. It contains statements given in two columns, which have to be matched. Statements in Column I are labelled as A, B, C and D whereas statements in Column II are labelled as p, q, r and s. The answers to these questions have to be appropriately bubbled as illustrated in the following example. If the correct matches are A-p, A-r, B-p, B-s, C-r, C-s and D-q, then the correctly bubbled matrix will look like the following :

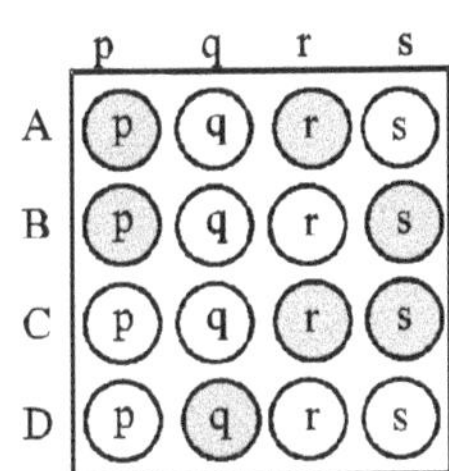

**15.** For the quadratic equation $x^2 - (k - 3) x + k = 0$ match the items in column I with items in column II.

| Column I | Column II |
|---|---|
| (A) If both roots are positive, then k exhaustively belongs to interval | (p) $\{1\} \cup [9, \infty)$ |
| (B) If both roots are negative, then k exhaustively belongs to interval | (q) $(0, 1)$ |
| (C) If both roots are equal, then k exhaustively belongs to interval | (r) $\{1, 9\}$ |
| (D) If no root lies between $(-1, 1)$, then k exhaustively belongs to interval | (s) $(9, \infty)$ |

**16.**

| Column I | Column II |
|---|---|
| (A) If a,b,c are unequal positive numbers and b is A.M of a and c then the roots of $ax^2 + 2bx + c = 0$ are | (p) of opposite signs |
| (B) If $a \in R$, then the roots of the equation $x^2 - (a + 1)x - a^2 - 4 = 0$ are | (q) rational numbers |
| (C) If a,b,c are unequal positive numbers and b is H.M of a and c, then the roots of $ax^2 + 2bx + c = 0$ are | (r) real and unequal |
| (D) If $|a \pm b| < c$ and $a = 0$ then the roots of $a^2x^2 + (b^2 + a^2 - c^2) x + b^2 = 0$ are | (s) imaginary |
| | (t) of same sign |

## Section - V - Reasoning Type

This section contains 2 reasoning type questions. Each question has 4 choices (a), (b), (c) and (d) out of which **ONLY ONE** is correct.

**DIRECTIONS for (Qs. 17 & 18) :** Each of these questions contains two statements: Statement-1 (Assertion) and Statement-2 (Reason). Each of these questions has four alternative choices, only one of which is the correct answer. You have to select the correct choice.

(a) Statement-1 is True, Statement-2 is True; Statement-2 is a correct explanation for Statement-1.

(b) Statement-1 is True, Statement-2 is True; Statement-2 is NOT a correct explanation for Statement-1.



*Space for Rough Work*

(c)    Statement -1 is True, Statement-2 is False.

(d)    Statement -1 is False, Statement-2 is True.

17.    **Statement - 1 :** For all $x \in R$, $x^2 + x + 1$ is positive.

   **Statement - 2 :** If $D < 0$, in $ax^2 + bx + c$, a have same sign for $\forall x \in R$.

18.    **Statement - 1 :** If $a > b > c$ and $a^3 + b^3 + c^3 = 3abc$, then the equation $ax^2 + bx + c = 0$ has one positive and one negative real roots.

   **Statement - 2 :** If roots are of opposite nature, then product of roots $< 0$ and |sum of roots|$\geq 0$.

## Section - VI - Integer Type

This section contains 2 questions. The answer to each of the questions is a single digit integer ranging from 0 to 9.

19.    Consider the equation $x^2 + x - n = 0$, where $n$ is an integer between 1 to 100. Find the total number of different values of '$n$' so that the equation has integral roots.

20.    If a, b, c are three distinct positive real numbers then find the number of real roots of $ax^2 + 2b|x| - c = 0$.

| RESPONSE GRID | | |
|---|---|---|
| 17. ⓐ ⓑ ⓒ ⓓ | | 19. ⓪①②③④⑤⑥⑦⑧⑨ |
| 18. ⓐ ⓑ ⓒ ⓓ | | 20. ⓪①②③④⑤⑥⑦⑧⑨ |

| DAILY PRACTICE PROBLEM DPP 12 - MATHS | | | |
|---|---|---|---|
| Total Questions | 20 | Total Marks | 61 |
| Attempted | | Correct | |
| Incorrect | | Net Score | |
| Cut-off Score | 12 | Qualifying Score | 40 |
| Success Gap = Net Score – Qualifying Score | | | |

$$\text{Net Score} = \sum_{i=I}^{VI}\left[(\text{correct}_i \times MM_i) - (In_i - NM_i)\right]$$

Name : 

Date : 

Start Time : 

End Time : 

# MATHEMATICS    M13

**SYLLABUS : Quadratic Equations and Inequations-2 : Relation between roots and coefficients.**

**Max. Marks : 65**                                     **Time : 60 min.**

### GENERAL INSTRUCTIONS

- The Daily Practice Problem Sheet contains **23** Questions divided into 5 sections.
  Section I has **11** MCQ's with ONLY 1 correct option. 2 marks for correct answer and No negative marks.
  Section II has **2** MCQ's with 1 or MORE THAN 1 correct option. 4 marks for correct answer(s) and (–1) for wrong answer.
  Section III has **1** PASSAGE with **3** MCQ's with ONLY 1 correct option. 3 marks for correct and (–1) mark for wrong answer.
  Section IV has **2** Assertion-Reason MCQ's with ONLY 1 correct option. 3 marks for correct and (–1) mark for wrong answer.
  Section V has **5** single digit integer answer questions. 4 marks for correct answer and (–1) for wrong answer.
- No mark will be given/ deducted if no bubble is filled. Keep a timer in front and stop immediately at the end of 60 min.
- You have to evaluate your Response Grids yourself with the help of Solution Booklet.
- The sheet follows a particular syllabus. Do not attempt the sheet before you have completed your preparation for that syllabus. Refer syllabus sheet in the starting of the book for the syllabus of all the DPP sheets.
- After completing the sheet check your answers with the solution booklet and complete the Result Grid. Finally spend time to analyse your performance and revise the areas which emerge out as weak in your evaluation.

## Section - I - Straight Objective Type

This section contains 11 multiple choice questions. Each question has 4 choices (a), (b), (c) and (d), out of which **ONLY ONE** is correct.

**1.** If the equation $\dfrac{ax^2 - 24x + b}{x^2 - 1} = x$, has exactly two distinct real solutions and their sum is 12 then the value of $(a - b)$ is
(a)  –5819          (b)  5854
(c)  529            (d)  –529

**2.** Suppose that $r_1 \neq r_2$ and $r_1 r_2 = 2$ ($r_1$, $r_2$ need not be real). If $r_1$ and $r_2$ are the roots of the biquadratic $x^4 - x^3 + ax^2 - 8x - 8 = 0$, then $r_1, r_2$ and a respectively are

(a)  $\dfrac{-2 \pm i\sqrt{7}}{2}, 4$          (b)  $\dfrac{-1 \pm i\sqrt{7}}{2}, -4$

(c)  $\dfrac{-2 \pm i\sqrt{7}}{2}, -4$          (d)  $\dfrac{-1 \pm i\sqrt{7}}{2}, 4$

**3.** Suppose a, b, c $\in$ I such that greatest common divisor of $x^2 + ax + b$ and $x^2 + bx + c$ is $(x + 1)$ and the least common multiple of $x^2 + ax + b$ and $x^2 + bx + c$ is $(x^3 - 4x^2 + x + 6)$. The value of $(a + b + c)$ is equal to –
(a) –6                    (b)  –4
(c) –2                    (d)  0

**4.** If $\alpha$ and $\beta$ are the roots of the equation $x^2 - p(x + 1) - q = 0$, then the value of $\dfrac{\alpha^2 + 2\alpha + 1}{\alpha^2 + 2\alpha + q} + \dfrac{\beta^2 + 2\beta + 1}{\beta^2 + 2\beta + q}$ is

(a)  2                    (b)  1
(c)  0                    (d)  None of these

**5.** If one root is square of the other root of the equation $x^2 + px + q = 0$, then the relation between p and q is
(a) $p^3 - q(3p - 1) + q^2 = 0$   (b) $p^3 - q(3p + 1) + q^2 = 0$
(c) $p^3 + q(3p - 1) + q^2 = 0$   (d) $p^3 + q(3p+1) + q^2 = 0$

**RESPONSE GRID**   1. ⓐⓑⓒⓓ   2. ⓐⓑⓒⓓ   3. ⓐⓑⓒⓓ   4. ⓐⓑⓒⓓ   5. ⓐⓑⓒⓓ

**6.** Let $a$, $b$, $c$ be real numbers, $a \neq 0$. If $\alpha$ is a root of $a^2x^2 + bx + c = 0$. $\beta$ is the root of $a^2x^2 - bx - c = 0$ and $0 < \alpha < \beta$, then the equation $a^2x^2 + 2bx + 2c = 0$ has a root $\gamma$ that always satisfies

(a) $\gamma = \dfrac{\alpha + \beta}{2}$

(b) $\gamma = \alpha + \dfrac{\beta}{2}$

(c) $\gamma = \alpha$

(d) $\alpha < \gamma < \beta$.

**7.** If $\alpha$, $\beta$ are the roots of the equation $\lambda(x^2 - x) + x + 5 = 0$ and $\lambda_1$ and $\lambda_2$ are two values of $\lambda$ for which the roots $\alpha$, $\beta$ are connected by the relation $\dfrac{\alpha}{\beta} + \dfrac{\beta}{\alpha} = \dfrac{4}{5}$, Then value of

$$\dfrac{\lambda_1}{\lambda_2} + \dfrac{\lambda_2}{\lambda_1} =$$

(a) 260        (b) 258

(c) 256        (d) 254

**8.** If $\alpha$, $\beta$ are the roots of the equation $ax^2 + bx + c = 0$ and $S_n = \alpha^n + \beta^n$, then $a\,S_{n+1} + c\,S_{n-1} =$

(a) $b\,S_n$        (b) $b^2 S_n$

(c) $2b S_n$        (d) $-b S_n$

**9.** If one root of the equation $(l - m)x^2 + lx + 1 = 0$ is double of the other and if $l$ is real then the greatest value of $m$ is $(l \neq m)$ :

(a) $\dfrac{1}{3}$        (b) $\dfrac{8}{9}$

(c) $\dfrac{9}{8}$        (d) 3

**10.** Let $\alpha_1, \alpha_2$ and $\beta_1, \beta_2$ be the roots of $ax^2 + bx + c = 0$ and $px^2 + qx + r = 0$ respectively. If the system of equations $\alpha_1 y + \alpha_2 z = 0$ and $\beta_1 y + \beta_2 z = 0$ has a nontrivial solution, then

(a) $\dfrac{b^2}{q^2} = \dfrac{ac}{pr}$        (b) $\dfrac{b}{q} = \dfrac{ac^2}{pr^2}$

(c) $\dfrac{b^2}{q} = \dfrac{ac^2}{pr}$        (d) $\dfrac{b}{q^2} = \dfrac{ac}{pr^2}$

**11.** If $\alpha$, $\beta$ are the roots of $ax^2 + bx + c = 0$, $(a \neq 0)$ and $\alpha + \delta$, $\beta + \delta$ are the roots of $Ax^2 + Bx + C = 0$, $(A \neq 0)$ for some constant $\delta$, then prove that

(a) $\dfrac{b^2 + 4a^2c^2}{a^2} = \dfrac{B^2 + 4A^2C^2}{A^2}$

(b) $\dfrac{b^2 - 4a^2c^2}{a^2} = \dfrac{B^2 - 4A^2C^2}{A^2}$

(c) $\dfrac{b^2 - 4ac}{a^2} = \dfrac{B^2 - 4AC}{A^2}$

(d) $\dfrac{b^2 - 4a^2c^2}{a^2} = \dfrac{B^2 + 4A^2C^2}{A^2}$

---

## Section - II - Multiple Correct Answer Type

This section contains 2 multiple correct answer(s) type questions. Each question has 4 choices (a), (b), (c) and (d), out of which **ONE OR MORE** is/are correct.

---



*Space for Rough Work*

**12.** The roots of $ax^2 + bx + c = 0$, where $a \neq 0$ and coefficients are real, are non-real complex and $a + c < b$. Then

(a) $4a + c > 2b$      (b) $4a + c < 2b$

(c) $a + 4c > 2b$      (d) $a + 4c < 2b$

**13.** If $c \neq 0$ and the equation $\dfrac{p}{2x} = \dfrac{a}{x+c} + \dfrac{b}{x-c}$ has two equal roots, then p can be

(a) $\left(\sqrt{a} - \sqrt{b}\right)^2$      (b) $\left(\sqrt{a} + \sqrt{b}\right)^2$

(c) $a + b$      (d) $a - b$

## Section - III - Linked Comprehension Type

This section contains one paragraph. Based upon the paragraph, 3 multiple choice questions have to be answered. Each question has 4 choices (a), (b), (c) and (d), out of which **ONLY ONE** is correct.

Let $f(x) = 4x^2 - 4ax + a^2 - 2a + 2$ be a quadratic polynomial in x, a be any real number.

**14.** If exactly one root of $f(x) = 0$ lies in $(0, 2)$, then the value of a lies in

(a) $(\sqrt{5} - 7, \sqrt{5} + 7)$      (b) $(7 - \sqrt{5}, 7 + \sqrt{5})$

(c) $(\sqrt{7} - 5, \sqrt{7} + 5)$      (d) $(5 - \sqrt{7}, 5 + \sqrt{7})$

**15.** If both roots of $f(x) = 0$ lie in $(0, 2)$, then the value of a belongs to

(a) $[1, 5 - \sqrt{7}]$      (b) $(-\infty, 5 - \sqrt{7})$

(c) $(5 + \sqrt{7}, \infty)$      (d) $(-\infty, \infty)$

**16** Find all values of a, so that 1 lies between the roots of the equation.

(a) $(3 - \sqrt{3}, 3 + \sqrt{3})$      (b) $(-3, 3)$

(c) $(\sqrt{3} - 3, \sqrt{3} + 3)$      (d) None of them

## Section - IV - Reasoning Type

This section contains 2 reasoning type questions. Each question has 4 choices (a), (b), (c) and (d) out of which **ONLY ONE** is correct.

**DIRECTIONS for (Qs. 17 & 18) : Each of these questions contains two statements: Statement-1 (Assertion) and Statement-2 (Reason). Each of these questions has four alternative choices, only one of which is the correct answer. You have to select the correct choice.**

(a) Statement-1 is True, Statement-2 is True; Statement-2 is a correct explanation for Statement-1.

(b) Statement-1 is True, Statement-2 is True; Statement-2 is NOT a correct explanation for Statement-1.

(c) Statement -1 is True, Statement-2 is False.

(d) Statement -1 is False, Statement-2 is True.

**17. Statement 1 :** If $a + b + c = 0$ and $a, b, c$ are rational, then the roots of the equation $(b + c - a)x^2 + (c + a - b)x + (a + b - c) = 0$ are rational.

**Statement 2 :** Discriminant of $(b + c - a)x^2 + (c + a - b)x + (a + b - c) = 0$ is a perfect square.

**18. Statement - 1 :** $a + b + c > 0$ and $a < 0 < b < c$, then the roots of the equation $a(x - b)(x - c) + b(x - c)(x - a) + c(x - a)(x - b) = 0$ are both negative.

**Statement - 2 :** If both roots are negative, then sum of roots $< 0$ and product of roots $> 0$

| RESPONSE GRID | 12. ⓐⓑⓒⓓ | 13. ⓐⓑⓒⓓ | 14. ⓐⓑⓒⓓ | 15. ⓐⓑⓒⓓ |
| --- | --- | --- | --- | --- |
| | 16. ⓐⓑⓒⓓ | 17. ⓐⓑⓒⓓ | 18. ⓐⓑⓒⓓ | |

## Section - V - Integer Type

This section contains 5 questions. The answer to each of the questions is a single digit integer ranging from 0 to 9.

**19.** Let $N = \alpha\alpha\alpha\alpha\alpha\alpha$ be a 6 digit number (all digit equal) and N is divisible by 924 and let $\alpha$, $\beta$ be the roots of the equation $x^2 - 11x + \lambda = 0$, then product of all possible values of $\lambda$ is found to be 112M. Find the value of M.

**20.** If the sum of the roots of the equation

$$2^{333x-2} + 2^{111x+1} = 2^{222x+2} + 1$$ is expressed in the form

$\dfrac{S_1}{S_2}$, find the value of $S_1$.

**21.** If p and q are roots of the equation $x^2 - 2x + A = 0$ and r and s be roots of the equation $x^2 - 18x + B = 0$ if $p < q < r < s$ be in A.P., then find the value of $\dfrac{A+B}{37}$.

**22.** The values of p, for which both the roots of equation $4x^2 - 20px + 25p^2 + 15p - 66 = 0$ are less than 2, belong to $(-\infty, -\beta)$. Find $\beta$.

**23.** If $\alpha$ and $\beta$ be the values of x in $m^2(x^2-x)+2mx+3 = 0$ and $m_1$ and $m_2$ be two values of m for which $\alpha$ and $\beta$ are connected by the relation $\dfrac{\alpha}{\beta} + \dfrac{\beta}{\alpha} = \dfrac{4}{3}$. If the value of $\dfrac{m_1^2}{m_2} + \dfrac{m_2^2}{m_1}$ is $\dfrac{-68}{P}$, find the value of P.

| RESPONSE GRID | | |
|---|---|---|
| 19. ⓪①②③④⑤⑥⑦⑧⑨ | | 20. ⓪①②③④⑤⑥⑦⑧⑨ |
| 21. ⓪①②③④⑤⑥⑦⑧⑨ | | 22. ⓪①②③④⑤⑥⑦⑧⑨ |
| 23. ⓪①②③④⑤⑥⑦⑧⑨ | | |

| DAILY PRACTICE PROBLEM DPP 13 - MATHS | | | |
|---|---|---|---|
| Total Questions | 23 | Total Marks | 65 |
| Attempted | | Correct | |
| Incorrect | | Net Score | |
| Cut-off Score | 13 | Qualifying Score | 42 |
| Success Gap = Net Score – Qualifying Score | | | |

$$\text{Net Score} = \sum_{i=I}^{VI}\left[(\text{correct}_i \times MM_i) - (In_i - NM_i)\right]$$

# DPP - Daily Practice Problems

Name : 

Date : 

Start Time : 

End Time : 

## MATHEMATICS  M14

**SYLLABUS : Quadratic Equations and Inequations-3 :** Condition of common roots, Solution of quadratic inequations and Miscellaneous equations.

**Max. Marks : 71**  **Time : 60 min.**

### GENERAL INSTRUCTIONS

- The Daily Practice Problem Sheet contains **24** Questions divided into 5 sections.
  Section I has **10** MCQ's with ONLY 1 correct option. 2 marks for correct answer and No negative marks.
  Section II has **4** MCQ's with 1 or MORE THAN 1 correct option. 4 marks for correct answer(s) and (–1) for wrong answer.
  Section III has **1** PASSAGE with **3** MCQ's with ONLY 1 correct option. 3 marks for correct and (–1) mark for wrong answer.
  Section IV has **2** Assertion-Reason MCQ's with ONLY 1 correct option. 3 marks for correct and (–1) mark for wrong answer.
  Section V has **5** Single digit integer answer questions. 4 marks for correct answer and (–1) for wrong answer.
- No mark will be given/ deducted if no bubble is filled. Keep a timer in front and stop immediately at the end of 60 min.
- You have to evaluate your Response Grids yourself with the help of Solution Booklet.
- The sheet follows a particular syllabus. Do not attempt the sheet before you have completed your preparation for that syllabus. Refer syllabus sheet in the starting of the book for the syllabus of all the DPP sheets.
- After completing the sheet check your answers with the solution booklet and complete the Result Grid. Finally spend time to analyse your performance and revise the areas which emerge out as weak in your evaluation.

### Section - I - Straight Objective Type

This section contains 10 multiple choice questions. Each question has 4 choices (a), (b), (c) and (d), out of which **ONLY ONE** is correct.

**1.** Solution set of the equation

$$3^{2x^2} - 2.3^{x^2+x+6} + 3^{2(x+6)} = 0 \text{ is } -$$

(a) $\{-3, 2\}$  (b) $\{6, -1\}$
(c) $\{-2, 3\}$  (d) $\{1, -6\}$

**2.** If every pair of equation among the equations
$x^2 + px + qr = 0$, $x^2 + qx + rp = 0$ and $x^2 + rx + pq = 0$ has a common root then the sum of the three common roots is –

(a) $-1/2$  (b) $0$
(c) $-1$  (d) $1$

**3.** If all the solutions 'x' of $a^{\cos x} + a^{-\cos x} = 6 \ (a > 1)$ are real, then set of values of $a$ is

(a) $[3 + 2\sqrt{2}, \infty]$  (b) $(6, 12)$

(c) $(1, 3 + 2\sqrt{2})$  (d) None of these.

**4.** The set of all values of $x$ satisfying the equation
$$x^2.2^{x+1} + 2^{|x-3|+2} = x^2 . 2^{|x-3|+4} + 2^{x-1} \text{ is}$$

(a) $[3, \infty)$  (b) $\left\{-\dfrac{1}{2}, \dfrac{1}{2}\right\} \cup [3, \infty)$

(c) $\left(-\infty, -\dfrac{1}{2}\right)$  (d) None of these

**5.** Number of solution of the equation
$$4^{\sin 2x + 2\cos^2 x} + 4^{1-\sin 2x + 2\sin^2 x} = 65 \text{ in } \left[0, \dfrac{\pi}{2}\right] \text{ is,}$$

(a) zero  (b) 1
(c) 2  (d) None of these

| RESPONSE GRID | 1. Ⓐ Ⓑ Ⓒ Ⓓ | 2. Ⓐ Ⓑ Ⓒ Ⓓ | 3. Ⓐ Ⓑ Ⓒ Ⓓ | 4. Ⓐ Ⓑ Ⓒ Ⓓ | 5. Ⓐ Ⓑ Ⓒ Ⓓ |

**6.** The largest interval for which $x^{12} - x^9 + x^4 - x + 1 > 0$ is

(a) $-4 < x \le 0$      (b) $0 < x < 1$

(c) $-100 < x < 100$      (d) $-\infty < x < \infty$

**7.** The solution set of the inequatity

$|9^x - 3^{x+1} - 15| < 2 \cdot 9^x - 3^x$ is

(a) $(-\infty, 1)$      (b) $(1, \infty)$

(c) $(-\infty, 1]$      (d) $(-\log_3 2, \infty)$

**8.** For all 'x', $x^2 + 2ax + 10 - 3a > 0$, then the interval in which 'a' lies is

(a) $a < -5$      (b) $-5 < a < 2$

(c) $a > 5$      (d) $2 < a < 5$

**9.** If a, b, c are non-zero real numbers, then two equations $2a^2x^2 - 2abx + b^2 = 0$ and $ax^2 + bx - c^2 = 0$ have

(a) no common root

(b) two common roots

(c) one common root if $a > 0$

(d) no common root if $a > 0$

**10.** The solution set of inequality $\dfrac{2x}{x^2 - 9} \le \dfrac{1}{x+2}$ is

(a) $(-\infty, -2) \cup (3, \infty)$      (b) $(-\infty, -3) \cup (-2, 3)$

(c) $(-3, 0] \cup (3, \infty)$      (d) none of these

---

## Section - II - Multiple Correct Answer Type

This section contains 4 multiple correct answer(s) type questions. Each question has 4 choices (a), (b), (c) and (d), out of which **ONE OR MORE** is/are correct.

---

**11.** Let $u : ax^2 + bx + c = 0$
$v : dx^2 + ex + f = 0$
$w : gx^2 + hx + i = 0$
are the quadratic equation in x.
Consider a quadratic equation in y as
$E : uy^2 + vy + w = 0$
Which of the following alternative(s) is/are correct –

(a) If for some value of x, say $x = x_1$, the equation $E = 0$ has one root infinite and other root a non zero finite quantity then $u = 0$ and $v = 0$ will have a common root.

(b) If for some value of x say $x = x_2$, the equation $E = 0$ has both root infinite then $u = 0$ and $v = 0$ will have a common root.

(c) If for some value of x say $x = x_3$, the equation $E = 0$ becomes an identity in y then $u = 0$, $v = 0$ and $w = 0$ must have a root, common to all of them.

(d) If for some value of x say $x = x_4$, the equation $E = 0$ has both roots real and distinct then $v = 0$ and $w = 0$ must have a common root.

**12.** If the equations $ax^3 + (a+b)x^2 + (b+c)x + c = 0$ and

$2x^3 + x^2 + 2x - 5 = 0$ have a common root, then $a + b + c$

can be equal to $(a, b, c \in R, a \ne 0)$

(a) $5a$      (b) $3b$

(c) $2c$      (d) $0$

**13.** If the reciprocal of every root of $x^3 + x^2 + ax + b = 0$ is also a root then

(a) $a = b = 1$      (b) $a = b = -1$

(c) $a = 1, b = -1$      (d) $a = -1, b = 1$

**14.** The integral value(s) of $a$ for which the equation

$(x^2 + x + 2)^2 - (a-3)(x^2 + x + 2)(x^2 + x + 1) + (a-4)$

$(x^2 + x + 1)^2 = 0$

have at least one real root is/are

(a) $5$      (b) $6$

(c) $4$      (d) $7$

---

<table>
<tr><td rowspan="2">RESPONSE<br>GRID</td><td>6. (a)(b)(c)(d)</td><td>7. (a)(b)(c)(d)</td><td>8. (a)(b)(c)(d)</td><td>9. (a)(b)(c)(d)</td><td>10. (a)(b)(c)(d)</td></tr>
<tr><td>11. (a)(b)(c)(d)</td><td>12. (a)(b)(c)(d)</td><td>13. (a)(b)(c)(d)</td><td>14. (a)(b)(c)(d)</td><td></td></tr>
</table>

*Space for Rough Work*

## Section - III - Linked Comprehension Type

This section contains one paragraph. Based upon the paragraph, 3 multiple choice questions have to be answered. Each question has 4 choices (a), (b), (c) and (d), out of which **ONLY ONE** is correct.

Let $f(x) = a_0 x^n + a_1 x^{n-1} + \ldots + a_n ; (a_0 \neq 0)$. If $f(a)$ and $f(b)$ are of opposite sign; (where $a < b$) i.e. $f(a) f(b) < 0$ then at least one or in general odd number of roots of the equation $f(x) = 0$ lie between $a$ and $b$.

15. If $0 \leq p \leq 16$, then the equation $x^3 - 12x - p = 0$ has one root in

(a) $(2, 3)$     (b) $(3, 4)$

(c) $(4, 5)$     (d) none of these

16. The equation $2\sin^2\theta\, x^2 - 3\sin\theta\, x + 1 = 0; \theta \in \left(\dfrac{\pi}{4}, \dfrac{\pi}{2}\right)$ has one root lying in the interval.

(a) $(0, 1)$     (b) $(1, 2)$

(c) $(2, 3)$     (d) $(-1, 0)$

17. If $f(x) = ax^2 + bx + c$, such that $c < 0$ and $a - 2b + 4c > 0$, then $f(x)$ has

(a) one root in the interval $\left(0, \dfrac{1}{2}\right)$

(b) one root in the interval $\left(-\dfrac{1}{2}, 0\right)$

(c) both roots are positive

(d) none of these

## Section - IV - Reasoning Type

This section contains 2 reasoning type questions. Each question has 4 choices (a), (b), (c) and (d) out of which **ONLY ONE** is correct.

**DIRECTIONS for (Qs. 18 & 19) : Each of these questions contains two statements: Statement-1 (Assertion) and Statement-2 (Reason). Each of these questions has four alternative choices, only one of which is the correct answer. You have to select the correct choice.**

(a) Statement-1 is True, Statement-2 is True; Statement-2 is a correct explanation for Statement-1.

(b) Statement-1 is True, Statement-2 is True; Statement-2 is NOT a correct explanation for Statement-1.

(c) Statement-1 is True, Statement-2 is False.

(d) Statement-1 is False, Statement-2 is True.

18. **Statement-1 :** If equations $ax^2 + bx + c = 0$, $(a, b, c \in \mathrm{R})$ and $2x^2 + 3x + 4 = 0$ have a common root, then $a : b : c = 2 : 3 : 4$.

**Statement-2 :** Roots of $2x^2 + 3x + 4 = 0$ are imaginary.

19. **Statement-1** : If $1 \leq a \leq 2$, then
$$\sqrt{a + 2\sqrt{a-1}} + \sqrt{a - 2\sqrt{a-1}} = 2$$

**Statement-2** : If $1 \leq a \leq 2$, then
$$\sqrt{a - 2\sqrt{a-1}} = \sqrt{a-1} - 1$$

| RESPONSE GRID | 15. (a)(b)(c)(d) | 16. (a)(b)(c)(d) | 17. (a)(b)(c)(d) | 18. (a)(b)(c)(d) | 19. (a)(b)(c)(d) |

*Space for Rough Work*

## Section - V - Integer Type

This section contains 5 questions. The answer to each of the questions is a single digit integer ranging from 0 to 9.

20. The equation $e^{\sin x} - e^{-\sin x} - 4 = 0$ has how many real solution ?

21. If the roots of $(5 + 2\sqrt{6})^{x^2-3} + (5 - 2\sqrt{6})^{x^2-3} = 10$ are $\pm A$ and $\pm\sqrt{A}$, then find the value of A.

22. Find the number of real solutions of the equation

$$1 + |e^x - 1| = e^x (e^x - 2)$$

23. Find the number of solutions of the equation $2^{|x^2-12|} = \sqrt{e^{|x|\log 4}}$

24. If the quadratic equations $ax^2 + 2cx + b = 0$ and $ax^2 + 2bx + c = 0$ $(b \neq c)$ have a common root, then find the value of a + 4b + 4c

**RESPONSE GRID**

20. ⓪①②③④⑤⑥⑦⑧⑨  21. ⓪①②③④⑤⑥⑦⑧⑨
22. ⓪①②③④⑤⑥⑦⑧⑨  23. ⓪①②③④⑤⑥⑦⑧⑨
24. ⓪①②③④⑤⑥⑦⑧⑨

### DAILY PRACTICE PROBLEM DPP 14 - MATHS

| Total Questions | 24 | Total Marks | 71 |
|---|---|---|---|
| Attempted | | Correct | |
| Incorrect | | Net Score | |
| Cut-off Score | 14 | Qualifying Score | 46 |
| Success Gap = Net Score – Qualifying Score | | | |

$$\text{Net Score} = \sum_{i=I}^{VI}\left[(\text{correct}_i \times MM_i) - (In_i - NM_i)\right]$$

*Space for Rough Work*

**Name :**

**Date :**

**Start Time :**

**End Time :**

## MATHEMATICS — M15

**SYLLABUS : Permutations and Combinations-1 :** Definition of permutation, Number of permutations with or without repetition, Conditional permutations, Circular permutations.

**Max. Marks : 73**  **Time : 60 min.**

### GENERAL INSTRUCTIONS

- The Daily Practice Problem Sheet contains **24** Questions divided into 6 sections.
  Section I has **8** MCQ's with ONLY 1 correct option. 2 marks for correct answer and No negative marks.
  Section II has **4** MCQ's with 1 or MORE THAN 1 correct option. 4 marks for correct answer(s) and (−1) for wrong answer.
  Section III has **1** PASSAGE with **3** MCQ's with ONLY 1 correct option. 3 marks for correct and (−1) mark for wrong answer.
  Section IV has **2** MCQ's with multiple matchings. 1 mark for the correct matching of each row & No negative marks.
  Section V has **2** Assertion-Reason MCQ's with ONLY 1 correct option. 3 marks for correct and (−1) mark for wrong answer.
  Section VI has **5** single digit integer answer questions. 4 marks for correct answer and (−1) for wrong answer.
- No mark will be given/ deducted if no bubble is filled. Keep a timer in front and stop immediately at the end of 60 min.
- You have to evaluate your Response Grids yourself with the help of Solution Booklet.
- The sheet follows a particular syllabus. Do not attempt the sheet before you have completed your preparation for that syllabus. Refer syllabus sheet in the starting of the book for the syllabus of all the DPP sheets.
- After completing the sheet check your answers with the solution booklet and complete the Result Grid. Finally spend time to analyse your performance and revise the areas which emerge out as weak in your evaluation.

### Section - I - Straight Objective Type

This section contains 8 multiple choice questions. Each question has 4 choices (a), (b), (c) and (d), out of which **ONLY ONE** is correct.

**1.** The number of positive integers n such that 2005 is a divisor of $n^2 + n + 1$ is –

(a) 0   (b) 1

(c) 2   (d) 3

**2.** Ten different letters of an alphabet are given. Words with five letters are formed from these given letters. Then the number of words which have at least one letter repeated are

(a) 69760   (b) 30240

(c) 99748   (d) none of these

**3.** The number of 6-digit numbers that can be made with the digits 0, 1, 2, 3, 4 and 5 so that even digits occupy odd places, is

(a) 24   (b) 36   (c) 48   (d) $5! - 4!$

**4.** Two 4-digits numbers are to be formed such that the sum of the number is also a 4-digit number and in no place the addition is with carrying. The number of ways of forming the numbers under above conditions is

(a) $55^4$   (b) 220   (c) $45^4$   (d) $36 \times 55^3$

**5.** A five-digit numbers divisible by 3 is to be formed using the numerals 0, 1, 2, 3, 4 and 5 without repetition. The total number of ways this can be done is

(a) 216   (b) 240

(c) 600   (d) 3125

| **RESPONSE GRID** | 1. ⓐⓑⓒⓓ | 2. ⓐⓑⓒⓓ | 3. ⓐⓑⓒⓓ | 4. ⓐⓑⓒⓓ | 5. ⓐⓑⓒⓓ |

**6.** If the LCM of p, q is $r^2 t^4 s^2$, where r, s, t are prime numbers and p, q are the positive integers then the number of ordered pair (p, q) is

(a)　252　　　(b) 254　　　(c)　225　　　(d) 224

**7.** The letters of the word COCHIN are permuted and all the permutations are arranged in an alphabetical order as in an English dictionary. The number of words that appear before the word COCHIN is

(a)　360　　　(b) 192　　　(c)　96　　　(d) 48

**8.** In a class of 10 students, there are 3 girls. In how many different ways can all the students be arranged in a row such that no two of the three girls are consecutive?

(a)　4281　　　(b) 4215　　　(c)　4018　　　(d) 3013

## Section - II - Multiple Correct Answer Type

This section contains 4 multiple correct answer(s) type questions. Each question has 4 choices (a), (b), (c) and (d), out of which **ONE OR MORE** is/are correct.

**9.** If $10! = 2^p \, 3^q \, 5^r \, 7^s$, then

(a)　$p = 7$　　　　　　　(b)　$q = 4$
(c)　$r = 2$　　　　　　　(d)　$s = 2$

**10.** Which of the following statements are correct ?

(a)　Exponent of 12 in 50 ! is 22.

(b)　The number 24 ! is divisible by $24^6$.

(c)　The number of zero's at the end of 60 ! is 14.

(d)　If $\dfrac{{}^n P_{r-1}}{a} = \dfrac{{}^n P_r}{b} = \dfrac{{}^n P_{r+1}}{c}$, then $\dfrac{b^2}{a(b+c)}$ is equal to 1.

**11.** Number of points of intersection of $n$ straight lines if $n$ satisfies ${}^{n+5} P_{n+1} = \dfrac{11(n-1)}{2} \times {}^{n+3} P_n$ is

(a)　15　　　(b)　28　　　(c)　21　　　(d)　10

**12.** The number of words which can be made from letters of the word INTERMEDIATE is

(a)　907200 if words start with $I$ and end with $E$

(b)　21600 if vowels and consonants occupy their original places

(c)　43200 if vowels and consonants occur alternatively

(d)　302400 if all the vowels occur together

## Section - III - Linked Comprehension Type

This section contains one paragraph. Based upon the paragraph, 3 multiple choice questions have to be answered. Each question has 4 choices (a), (b), (c) and (d), out of which **ONLY ONE** is correct.

From 5 novels – A, B, C, D and E and four biographies – F, G, H and I – Reena has to choose five books that she will assign over the summer to the participants in the book club she leads. Her selection will be made in accordance with the following requirements.

(i) Exactly two of the books selected must be biographies.
(ii) If B is selected, both D and G must be selected.
(iii) A cannot be selected unless F is selected.
(iv) If either C or E is selected, then the other is must.
(v) If I is selected, neither F nor H can be selected.

**13.** Which of the following could be a list of the five books that Reena selects?

(a)　A, B, D, F, H　　　　(b)　B, C, D, F, G
(c)　A, C, E, F, I　　　　(d)　A, B, D, F, G

**14.** If Reena's first two selections are F and H, which of the following must she also select?

(a)　B　　　　　　　　　(b)　C
(c)　D　　　　　　　　　(d)　G

**15.** If E is not selected, then all of the following must be selected except

(a)　A　　　　　　　　　(b)　D
(c)　F　　　　　　　　　(d)　H



*Space for Rough Work*

## Section - IV - Matrix-Match Type

This section contains 2 questions. It contains statements given in two columns, which have to be matched. Statements in Column I are labelled as A, B, C and D whereas statements in Column II are labelled as p, q, r and s. The answers to these questions have to be appropriately bubbled as illustrated in the following example. If the correct matches are A-p, A-r, B-p, B-s, C-r, C-s and D-q, then the correctly bubbled matrix will look like the following :

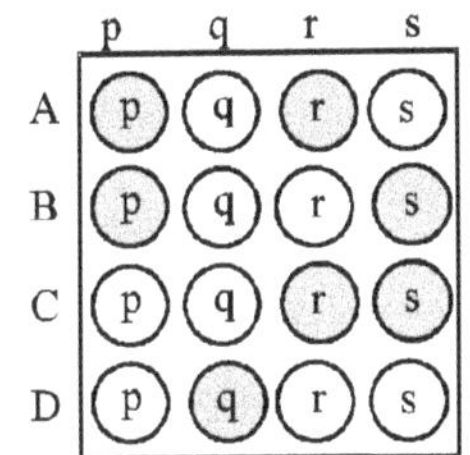

**16.**

| Column I | Column II |
|---|---|
| (A) If $\lambda$ be the number of ways in which 6 boys and 5 girls can be arranged in a line so that they are alternate, then $\lambda$ is divisible by | (p) 5! |
| (B) If $\lambda$ be the number of ways in which 6 boys and 5 girls can be seated in a row such that two girls are never together, then $\lambda$ is divisibly by | (q) 6! |
| (C) If $\lambda$ be the number of ways in which 6 boys and 5 girls can be seated around a round table if all the five girls do not sit together, then $\lambda$ is divisible by | (r) 7! |
|  | (s) 5! 6! |
|  | (t) 5! 7! |

**17.**

| Column I | Column II |
|---|---|
| (A) If $n$ be the number between 500 and 4000 can be formed with the digits 2, 3, 4, 5, 6 when repetition is not allowed, then $n$ is divisible by | (p) 2 |
| (B) If $n$ be the number of even numbers between 200 and 3000 can be formed with the digits 0, 1, 2, 3, 4 when repetitions is not allowed, then n is divisible by | (q) 3 |
| (C) If $n$ be the number of words that can be made by arranging the letters of the words ROORKEE that neither begin with R nor end with E, then n is divisible by | (r) 5 |
|  | (s) 11 |
|  | (t) 17 |

## Section - V - Reasoning Type

This section contains 2 reasoning type questions. Each question has 4 choices (a), (b), (c) and (d) out of which **ONLY ONE** is correct.

**DIRECTIONS for (Qs. 18 & 19) : Each of these questions contains two statements: Statement-1 (Assertion) and Statement-2 (Reason). Each of these questions has four alternative choices, only one of which is the correct answer. You have to select the correct choice.**

(a) Statement-1 is True, Statement-2 is True; Statement-2 is a correct explanation for Statement-1.

(b) Statement-1 is True, Statement-2 is True; Statement-2 is NOT a correct explanation for Statement-1.

(c) Statement -1 is True, Statement-2 is False.

(d) Statement -1 is False, Statement-2 is True.

**18. Statement -1:** The total number of words with letters of the word "CIVILIZATION" (all taken at a time) is 19958393.

**Statement -2:** The number of permutations of n distinct objects (taken r at a time) is $^nP_{r+1}$.

**19. Statement -1:** The number of ways of writing 1400 as a product of two positive integers is 12.

**Statement -2:** 1400 is divisible by exactly three prime numbers.

<table>
<tr><td rowspan="3">RESPONSE GRID</td><td>16. A - p q r s t; B - p q r s t; C - p q r s t; D - p q r s t</td></tr>
<tr><td>17. A - p q r s t; B - p q r s t; C - p q r s t; D - p q r s t</td></tr>
<tr><td>18. a b c d    19. a b c d</td></tr>
</table>

*Space for Rough Work*

## Section - VI - Integer Type

This section contains 5 questions. The answer to each of the questions is a single digit integer ranging from 0 to 9.

**20.** If the number of all 6 digits numbers such that (a) all the digits of each number are from the set $\{1, 2, 3, 4, 5\}$.

(b) any digit that appears in the number appeares atleast twice, are found to be $(700 P + 5)$. Find the value of P.

**21.** The number of ways in which 5 A's and 6 B's can be arranged in a row which reads the same backwards and forwards are 2X. Find X.

**22.** The number of 4 digit numbers starting with 1 and having exactly two identical digits are $(A)^3 (B)^4$. Find the value of $A + B$.

**23.** A flight of stairs has 10 steps. A person can go up the steps one at a time, two at a time, or any combination of 1's and 2's. If the total number of ways in which the person can go up the stairs are $10n^2 - 1$, find the value of n.

**24.** If different nine digit numbers that can be formed from the number 223355888 by rearranging its digits so that the odd digits occupy even positions are 10P, find the value of P.

| | | | |
|---|---|---|---|
| **RESPONSE GRID** | 20. ⓪①②③④⑤⑥⑦⑧⑨ | 21. ⓪①②③④⑤⑥⑦⑧⑨ | |
| | 22. ⓪①②③④⑤⑥⑦⑧⑨ | 23. ⓪①②③④⑤⑥⑦⑧⑨ | |
| | 24. ⓪①②③④⑤⑥⑦⑧⑨ | | |

| DAILY PRACTICE PROBLEM DPP 15 - MATHS | | | |
|---|---|---|---|
| Total Questions | 24 | Total Marks | 73 |
| Attempted | | Correct | |
| Incorrect | | Net Score | |
| Cut-off Score | 15 | Qualifying Score | 47 |
| Success Gap = Net Score – Qualifying Score | | | |

$$\text{Net Score} = \sum_{i=1}^{VI} \left[ (\text{correct}_i \times MM_i) - (In_i - NM_i) \right]$$

*Space for Rough Work*

# DPP - Daily Practice Problems



## MATHEMATICS   M16

**SYLLABUS : Permutations and Combinations-2 :** Definition of combinations, Conditional combinations, Division into groups, Derangements, Geometrical problems, Multinomial theorem, Miscellaneous problems

## Max. Marks : 75        Time : 60 min.

### GENERAL INSTRUCTIONS

- The Daily Practice Problem Sheet contains **24** Questions divided into 6 sections.
  Section I has **8** MCQ's with ONLY 1 correct option. 2 marks for correct answer and No negative marks.
  Section II has **4** MCQ's with 1 or MORE THAN 1 correct option. 4 marks for correct answer(s) and (–1) for wrong answer.
  Section III has **1** PASSAGE with **3** MCQ's with ONLY 1 correct option. 3 marks for correct and (–1) mark for wrong answer.
  Section IV has **2** MCQ's with multiple matchings. 1 mark for the correct matching of each row & No negative marks.
  Section V has **2** Assertion-Reason MCQ's with ONLY 1 correct option. 3 marks for correct and (–1) mark for wrong answer.
  Section VI has **5** single digit integer answer questions. 4 marks for correct answer and (–1) for wrong answer.
- No mark will be given/ deducted if no bubble is filled. Keep a timer in front and stop immediately at the end of 60 min.
- You have to evaluate your Response Grids yourself with the help of Solution Booklet.
- The sheet follows a particular syllabus. Do not attempt the sheet before you have completed your preparation for that syllabus. Refer syllabus sheet in the starting of the book for the syllabus of all the DPP sheets.
- After completing the sheet check your answers with the solution booklet and complete the Result Grid. Finally spend time to analyse your performance and revise the areas which emerge out as weak in your evaluation.

---

## Section - I - Straight Objective Type

This section contains 8 multiple choice questions. Each question has 4 choices (a), (b), (c) and (d), out of which **ONLY ONE** is correct.

**1** Consider the set of all triangles OPQ where O is the origin and P and Q are distinct points in the plane with non-negative integral coordinates (x, y) such that $5x + y = 99$. Number of such distinct triangles whose area is a positive integer, is
(a) 90    (b) 98    (c) 102    (d) 110

**2.** There are 3 men and 7 women taking a dance class. Number of different ways in which each man be paired with a woman partner, and the four remaining women be paired into two pairs each of two, is –
(a) 105    (b) 315    (c) 630    (d) 450

**3.** A child has a set of 96 distinct blocks. Each block is one of two material (plastic, wood), 3 sizes (small, medium, large), 4 colours (blue, green, red, yellow), and 4 shapes (circle, hexagon, square, triangle). How many blocks in the set are different from "Plastic, medium, red circle" in exactly two ways? ("The wood, medium, red, square" is such a block)
(a) 29    (b) 39    (c) 48    (d) 56

**4.** A rectangle with sides $2m - 1$ and $2n - 1$ is divided into squares of unit length by drawing parallel lines as shown in the diagram, then the number of rectangles possible with odd side lengths is

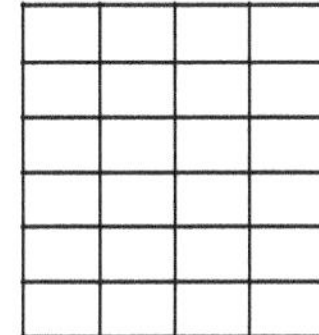

(a) $(m + n - 1)^2$      (b) $4^{m+n-1}$
(c) $m^2n^2$      (d) $m(m + 1)n(n + 1)$

**5.** ABCD is a convex quadrilateral. 3, 4, 5 and 6 points are marked on the sides AB, BC, CD and DA respectively. The number of triangles with vertices on different sides is
(a) 270    (b) 220    (c) 282    (d) 342

---

| RESPONSE GRID | 1. ⓐⓑⓒⓓ | 2. ⓐⓑⓒⓓ | 3. ⓐⓑⓒⓓ | 4. ⓐⓑⓒⓓ | 5. ⓐⓑⓒⓓ |
|---|---|---|---|---|---|

**6.** If $^{n+1}C_{r+1} : {}^{n}C_{r} : {}^{n-1}C_{r-1} = 11 : 6 : 3$, then nr =

(a)  20　　　　　　　　　　(b)  30

(c)  40　　　　　　　　　　(d)  50

**7.** A is a set containing $n$ elements. A subset $P$ of $A$ is chosen. The set $A$ is reconstructed by repacing the elements of $P$. A subset $Q$ of $A$ is again chosen. The number of ways of choosing $P$ and $Q$ so that $P \cap Q$ contains exactly two elements is

(a)  $9^{n}C_{2}$　　　　　　　　(b)  $3^{n} - {}^{n}C_{2}$

(c)  ${}^{n}C_{2}3^{n-2}$　　　　　　(d)  $4^{n} - 3^{n}$

**8.** Rajdhani express going from Bombay to Delhi stops at 5 intermediate stations . 10 passengers enter the train during the journey with ten different ticket of two classes .The number of different sets of tickets they may have is

(a)  $^{15}C_{10}$　　(b)  $^{20}C_{10}$　　(c)  $^{30}C_{10}$　　(d)  none

## Section - II - Multiple Correct Answer Type

This section contains 4 multiple correct answer(s) type questions. Each question has 4 choices (a), (b), (c) and (d), out of which **ONE OR MORE** is/are correct.

**9.** The integral value of $x$ which satisfies the inequality $^{10}C_{x-1} > 2 . {}^{10}C_{x}$ is

(a)  7　　　　　　　　　　(b)  8

(c)  9　　　　　　　　　　(d)  10

**10.** A woman has 11 close friends. Number of ways in which she can invite 5 of them to dinner, if two particular of them are not an speaking terms and will not attend together is –

(a)  $^{11}C_{5} - {}^{9}C_{3}$　　　　　(b)  $^{9}C_{5} + 2 . {}^{9}C_{4}$

(c)  $3 \, {}^{9}C_{4}$　　　　　　　(d)  None

**11.** The number of ways in which 20 identical coins be distributed in 4 persons if each person receive at least 2 coins and atmost 5 coins, are

(a)  $^{15}C_{12} - 4 . {}^{11}C_{8} + 6 . {}^{7}C_{4} - 4$　　(b)  $^{15}C_{12} - 6 . {}^{11}C_{8} + {}^{7}C_{4}$

(c)  $^{23}C_{3}$　　　　　　　　　　(d)  $^{15}C_{0}$

**12.** The number of ways of arranging the letters AAAAA, BBB, CCC, D, EE and F in a row if the letter C are separated from one another is

(a)  $^{13}C_{3} . \dfrac{12!}{5!3!2!}$　　　　(b)  $\dfrac{13!}{5!3!3!2!}$

(c)  $\dfrac{14!}{3!3!2!}$　　　　(d)  $\dfrac{15!}{5!(3!)^{2}2!} - \dfrac{13!}{5!3!2!} - \dfrac{12!}{5!3!} {}^{13}C_{2}$

## Section - III - Linked Comprehension Type

This section contains one paragraph. Based upon the paragraph, 3 multiple choice questions have to be answered. Each question has 4 choices (a), (b), (c) and (d), out of which **ONLY ONE** is correct.

Number of ways of distributing $n$ different things into $r$ different groups is $r^{n}$ when blank groups are taken into account and is $r^{n} - {}^{r}C_{1}(r-1)^{n} + {}^{r}C_{2}(r-2)^{2} - \dots + (-1)^{r-1} {}^{r}C_{r-1}$ when blank groups are not permitted.

**13.** The number of ways of posting 4 letters into 3 letter boxes is equal to

(a)  $3^{4}$　　　　　　　　　(b)  $4^{3}$

(c)  $^{4}C_{3}$　　　　　　　　(d)  $^{4}C_{3} . 4!$

**14.** 6 different balls have to be given to 3 children. Number of ways of distribution if each child gets at least one ball is

(a)  729　　　　　　　　　(b)  243

(c)  540　　　　　　　　　(d)  $^{6}C_{3} . 6!$

**15.** A function is defined from a set A containing 6 elements to a set B containing 4 elements. In how many of these functions exactly one element of the set B is not an image?

(a)  $4^{6}$　　　　　　　　　(b)  2160

(c)  729　　　　　　　　　(d)  2916

| **RESPONSE GRID** | 6. Ⓐⓑⓒⓓ | 7. Ⓐⓑⓒⓓ | 8. Ⓐⓑⓒⓓ | 9. Ⓐⓑⓒⓓ | 10. Ⓐⓑⓒⓓ |
|---|---|---|---|---|---|
| | 11. Ⓐⓑⓒⓓ | 12. Ⓐⓑⓒⓓ | 13. Ⓐⓑⓒⓓ | 14. Ⓐⓑⓒⓓ | 15. Ⓐⓑⓒⓓ |

*Space for Rough Work*

## Section - IV - Matrix-Match Type

This section contains 2 questions. It contains statements given in two columns, which have to be matched. Statements in Column I are labelled as A, B, C and D whereas statements in Column II are labelled as p, q, r and s. The answers to these questions have to be appropriately bubbled as illustrated in the following example. If the correct matches are A-p, A-r, B-p, B-s, C-r, C-s and D-q, then the correctly bubbled matrix will look like the following :

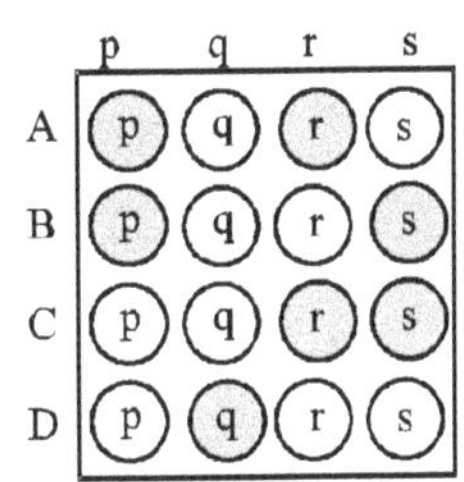

**16.**    **Column - I**         **Column - II**

(A)   The total number of three digit numbers,   (p) 54

the sum of whose digits is even is equal to

(B)   Total number of positive intergal solutions   (q) 20

of the equation $xyz = 140$ is equal to

(C)   Total number of positive intergal solutions   (r) 18

of $x + y + z \leq 10$ is equal to

(D)   If $x^3 + ax^2 + bx + c$ is divisible by $x^2 + 1$,   (s) 450

then the number of three digit numbers   (t) 120

of the form abc or bca or cab

which can be formed is equal to

**17.**    **Column - I**         **Column - II**

(A)   The maximum number of points at   (p) 120

which 5 straight lines intersect is

(B)   The number of distinct positive   (q) $2^n - 1$

divisors of $2^4$, $3^5$, $5^3$ is

(C)   Number of triangles can be drawn   (r) $^5C_2$

through 5 given points on a circle, are

(D)   The value of $\displaystyle\sum_{r=1}^{n} \frac{^nP_r}{r!}$ is   (s) $^5C_2 - 1$

                                    (t) $^5C_3$

## Section - V - Reasoning Type

This section contains 2 reasoning type questions. Each question has 4 choices (a), (b), (c) and (d) out of which **ONLY ONE** is correct.

**DIRECTIONS for (Qs. 18 & 19) : Each of these questions contains two statements: Statement-1 (Assertion) and Statement-2 (Reason). Each of these questions has four alternative choices, only one of which is the correct answer. You have to select the correct choice.**

(a)   Statement-1 is True, Statement-2 is True; Statement-2 is a correct explanation for Statement-1.

(b)   Statement-1 is True, Statement-2 is True; Statement-2 is NOT a correct explanation for Statement-1.

(c)   Statement -1 is True, Statement-2 is False.

(d)   Statement -1 is False, Statement-2 is True.

**18.**   **Statement-1 :** The number of ways of selecting 5 students from 12 students (of which six are boys and six are girls), such that in the selection there are at least three girls is $^6C_3 \ ^9C_2$.

**Statement-2 :** If a work has two independent parts, of which first part can be done in m ways and for each choice of first part, the second part can be done in n ways, then the work can be completed in m × n ways.

**19.**   **Statement-1:** The number of positive integral solutions of the equation $x_1 x_2 x_3 x_4 x_5 = 1050$ is 1875.

**Statement-2:** The total number of divisors of 1050 is 25.

---

**RESPONSE GRID**

16. A - p q r s t; B - p q r s t; C - p q r s t; D - p q r s t

17. A - p q r s t; B - p q r s t; C - p q r s t; D - p q r s t

18. a b c d     19. a b c d

*Space for Rough Work*

## Section - VI - Integer Type

This section contains 5 questions. The answer to each of the questions is a single digit integer ranging from 0 to 9.

**20.** Let $A = \{a, b, c, d, e, f\}$ and $B = \{1, 2, 3\}$ are two sets.

Let $m$ denotes the number of mappings which are into from A to B.

Let $n$ denotes the number of mappings which are injective from B to A. Find $\left(\dfrac{m + n - 9}{100}\right)$

**21.** Let the set $A = \{a, b, c, d, e\}$ and P & Q are two non empty subsets of A. If the number of ways in which P and Q can be selected so that $P \cap Q$ has at least one common element are found to be $(A)^n - (B)^n$. Find the value of $A + B - n$

**22.** Five balls of different colours are to be placed in three boxes of different size. Each box can hold all five. If the total number of ways in which we can place the balls so that no box remains empty are 75X, Find the value of X.

**23.** A student is allowed to select atmost n books from a collection of $(2n + 1)$ books. If the total number of ways in which he can select at least one book is 63, find the value of $n$.

**24.** If total number of runs scored in $n$ matches is $\left(\dfrac{n+1}{4}\right)$ $(2^{n+1} - n - 2)$ where $n > 1$, and the runs scored in the $k^{th}$ match is given by k. $2^{n+1-k}$, where $1 \leq k \leq n$. Find $n$.

| | | |
|---|---|---|
| **RESPONSE GRID** | 20. ⓪①②③④⑤⑥⑦⑧⑨ | 21. ⓪①②③④⑤⑥⑦⑧⑨ |
| | 22. ⓪①②③④⑤⑥⑦⑧⑨ | 23. ⓪①②③④⑤⑥⑦⑧⑨ |
| | 24. ⓪①②③④⑤⑥⑦⑧⑨ | |

| DAILY PRACTICE PROBLEM DPP 16 - MATHS | | | |
|---|---|---|---|
| Total Questions | 24 | Total Marks | 75 |
| Attempted | | Correct | |
| Incorrect | | Net Score | |
| Cut-off Score | 15 | Qualifying Score | 49 |
| Success Gap = Net Score – Qualifying Score | | | |

$$\textbf{Net Score} = \sum_{i=I}^{VI}\left[(\textbf{correct}_i \times MM_i) - (In_i - NM_i)\right]$$

# DPP - Daily Practice Problems

**Name :**  **Date :**

**Start Time :**  **End Time :**

## MATHEMATICS — M17

**SYLLABUS : Binomial Theorem-1 :** Expansion of binomial theorem, General term, Coefficient of any power of x, Independent term, Middle term and Greatest term & Greatest coefficient

**Max. Marks : 74**  **Time : 60 min.**

### GENERAL INSTRUCTIONS

- The Daily Practice Problem Sheet contains **24** Questions divided into 6 sections.
  Section I has **8** MCQ's with ONLY 1 correct option. 2 marks for correct answer and No negative marks.
  Section II has **4** MCQ's with 1 or MORE THAN 1 correct option. 4 marks for correct answer(s) and (–1) for wrong answer.
  Section III has **1** PASSAGE with **3** MCQ's with ONLY 1 correct option. 3 marks for correct and (–1) mark for wrong answer.
  Section IV has **2** MCQ's with multiple matchings. 1 mark for the correct matching of each row & No negative marks.
  Section V has **2** Assertion-Reason MCQ's with ONLY 1 correct option. 3 marks for correct and (–1) mark for wrong answer.
  Section VI has **5** single digit integer answer questions. 4 marks for correct answer and (–1) for wrong answer.
- No mark will be given/ deducted if no bubble is filled. Keep a timer in front and stop immediately at the end of 60 min.
- You have to evaluate your Response Grids yourself with the help of Solution Booklet.
- The sheet follows a particular syllabus. Do not attempt the sheet before you have completed your preparation for that syllabus. Refer syllabus sheet in the starting of the book for the syllabus of all the DPP sheets.
- After completing the sheet check your answers with the solution booklet and complete the Result Grid. Finally spend time to analyse your performance and revise the areas which emerge out as weak in your evaluation.

## Section - I - Straight Objective Type

This section contains 8 multiple choice questions. Each question 4 has choices (a), (b), (c) and (d), out of which **ONLY ONE** is correct.

**1.** Given that the term of the expansion $(x^{1/3} - x^{-1/2})^{15}$ which does not contain x is $5\,m$ where $m \in N$, then $m =$
(a) 1100 (b) 1010
(c) 1001 (d) none

**2.** In the binomial $(2^{1/3} + 3^{-1/3})^n$, if the ratio of the seventh term from the beginning of the expansion to the seventh term from its end is $1/6$, then $n =$
(a) 6 (b) 9 (c) 12 (d) 15

**3.** $(1+x)(1+x+x^2)(1+x+x^2+x^3)......(1+x+x^2+......+x^{100})$ when written in the ascending power of x then the highest exponent of x is –
(a) 4950 (b) 5050 (c) 5150 (d) none

**4.** The coefficient of $x^r\,(0 \le r \le n-1)$ in the expression :
$(x+2)^{n-1} + (x+2)^{n-2}.(x+1) + (x+2)^{n-3}.(x+1)^2 +......+ (x+1)^{n-1}$ is :
(a) $^nC_r(2^r - 1)$ (b) $^nC_r(2^{n-r} - 1)$
(c) $^nC_r(2^r + 1)$ (d) $^nC_r(2^{n-r} + 1)$

**5.** The remainder, when $(15^{23} + 23^{23})$ is divided by 19, is
(a) 4 (b) 15
(c) 0 (d) 18

**6.** If $(1+x)^{10} = a_0 + a_1x + a_2x^2 +............+ a_{10}x^{10}$, then
$(a_0 - a_2 + a_4 - a_6 + a_8 - a_{10})^2 + (a_1 - a_3 + a_5 - a_7 + a_9)^2$ is equal to
(a) $3^{10}$ (b) $2^{10}$
(c) $2^9$ (d) None of these

| RESPONSE GRID | 1. Ⓐ ⓑ ⓒ ⓓ | 2. Ⓐ ⓑ ⓒ ⓓ | 3. Ⓐ ⓑ ⓒ ⓓ |
| --- | --- | --- | --- |
| | 4. Ⓐ ⓑ ⓒ ⓓ | 5. Ⓐ ⓑ ⓒ ⓓ | 6. Ⓐ ⓑ ⓒ ⓓ |

**7.** The last term in the binomial expansion of $\left(\sqrt[3]{2}-\dfrac{1}{\sqrt{2}}\right)^{n}$ is $\left(\dfrac{1}{3.\sqrt[3]{9}}\right)^{\log_3 8}$. Then the $5^{th}$ term from the beginning is

(a) $^{10}C_6$              (b) $2.\,^{10}C_4$

(c) $1/2\,.\,^{10}C_4$        (d) None of these

**8.** The serial number of the term in the expansion of the binomial

$$B=\left[\exp\left(\dfrac{a}{b}\ln\left(\dfrac{x}{y^{1/c}}\right)\right)+\exp\left(\dfrac{a}{c}\ln\left(\dfrac{y}{x^{1/b}}\right)\right)\right]^{a}$$

which contains x and y to same power is [Assume that a, b, $c \in \mathbf{N}$ and $b+c+2$ divides $a\,(c+1)$]

(a) $\dfrac{a\,(c+1)}{(b+c+2)}+1$     (b) $\dfrac{a\,(c+1)}{(b+c+2)}+2$

(c) $\dfrac{a\,(c+1)}{(b+c+2)}-1$     (d) None of these

## Section - II - Multiple Correct Answer Type

This section contains 4 multiple correct answer(s) type questions. Each question has 4 choices (a), (b), (c) and (d), out of which **ONE OR MORE** is/are correct.

**9.** Which of the following statements are correct ?

(a) The term independent of x in the expansion of $\left(\dfrac{1-x}{1+x}\right)^{2}$ is 1.

(b) If $\alpha$ be a fixed natural number then number of terms in the expansion of $\left(x^{\alpha}+1+\dfrac{1}{x^{\alpha}}\right)^{n}$, $n \in N$ is $2n+1$.

(c) In the expansion of $\left(\sqrt[3]{\dfrac{x}{3}}-\sqrt{\dfrac{3}{x}}\right)^{10}$, $x>0$, the constant term is 210.

(d) The number of real negative terms in the binomial expansion of $(1+ix)^{4n-2}$, $n \in \mathbf{N}$, $x>0$ is n.

**10.** If the sum of the coefficients in the expansion of $(2+3cx+c^2x^2)^{12}$ vanishes then c equals

(a) $-2$     (b) $2$     (c) $1$     (d) $-1$

**11.** In the expansion of $\left(\sqrt[3]{4}+\dfrac{1}{\sqrt[4]{6}}\right)^{20}$

(a) the number of irrational terms $=19$

(b) middle term is irrational

(c) the number of rational term $=2$

(d) 9th term is rational

**12.** In the expansion of $(x+y+z)^{20}$

(a) coefficient of $x^7y^8z^7$ is zero

(b) total number of distinct terms is 231

(c) every term is of the form $\dfrac{20!\,x^{20-r}y^{r-k}z^{k}}{(20-r)!(r-k)!k!}$

(d) sum of coefficient is $3^{20}$

## Section - III - Linked Comprehension Type

This section contains one paragraph. Based upon the paragraph, 3 multiple choice questions have to be answered. Each question has 4 choices (a), (b), (c) and (d), out of which **ONLY ONE** is correct.

**Numerically Greatest Term in the Expansion of $(x+a)^{n}$**

Let $T_r$ and $T_{r+1}$ be $r^{th}$ and $(r+1)^{th}$ terms respectively in the expansion of bionomial $(x+a)^{n}$. Then

$$T_r = {}^nC_{r-1}\,x^{n-r+1}\,a^{r-1} \text{ and } T_{r+1} = {}^nC_r\,x^{n-r}\,a^{r}$$

$$\therefore \dfrac{T_{r+1}}{T_r} = \dfrac{n-r+1}{r}\dfrac{a}{x}$$

Now, $T_{r+1} >, =, < T_r$ According as $\left(\dfrac{n-r+1}{r}\right)\dfrac{a}{x} >, =, < 1$,

i.e. according as $\dfrac{n+1}{r}-1 >, =, < \dfrac{x}{a}$,

i.e. according as $r <, =, > \dfrac{n+1}{\frac{x}{a}+1}$.

So, if $\dfrac{n+1}{\frac{x}{a}+1}$ is an integer, say p, then

$T_{r+1} > T_r$ if $r<p$ otherwise $T_{r+1} \le T_r$

So, $T_p = T_{p+1}$ (numerically) and these are greater than any other term in the expansion.



*Space for Rough Work*

Next, if $\dfrac{n+1}{\dfrac{x}{a}+1}$ is a non-integer, suppose m be its integral part then $T_{r+1} > T_r$ if $r \le m$ and $T_{r+1} < T_r$ if $r > m$.

So, $T_{m+1}$ is the numerically greatest term among the terms of the expansion.

Again we can also write that $k^{th}$ term is numerically greatest if $T_k \ge T_{k+1}$ and $T_k \ge T_{k-1}$.

13. If $x > 0$ and the 4th term in the expansion of $\left(2 + \dfrac{3}{8}x\right)^{10}$ has maximum value, then

(a) $2 < x < 3$      (b) $3 < x < \dfrac{10}{3}$

(c) $4 < x < 5$      (d) None of these

14. If n is even positive integer, then the condition that the numerically greatest term in the expansion of $(1 + x)^n$ may have the greatest coefficient also is

(a) $\dfrac{n}{n+2} \le |x| \ge \dfrac{n+2}{n}$      (b) $\dfrac{n+1}{n} \le |x| \ge \dfrac{n}{n+1}$

(c) $\dfrac{n}{n+4} \le |x| \ge \dfrac{n+4}{n}$      (d) None of these

15. Magnitude wise the greatest term in the expansion of $(3 - 2x)^9$ when $x = 1$ is

(a) $^9C_2\, 3^7\, 2^2$      (b) $^9C_3\, 3^6\, 2^3$

(c) $^9C_4\, 3^5\, 2^4$      (d) both (b) and (c)

### Section - IV - Matrix-Match Type

This section contains 2 questions. It contains statements given in two columns, which have to be matched. Statements in Column I are labelled as A, B, C and D whereas statements in Column II are labelled as p, q, r and s. The answers to these questions have to be appropriately bubbled as illustrated in the following example. If the correct matches are A-p, A-r, B-p, B-s, C-r, C-s and D-q, then the correctly bubbled matrix will look like the following :

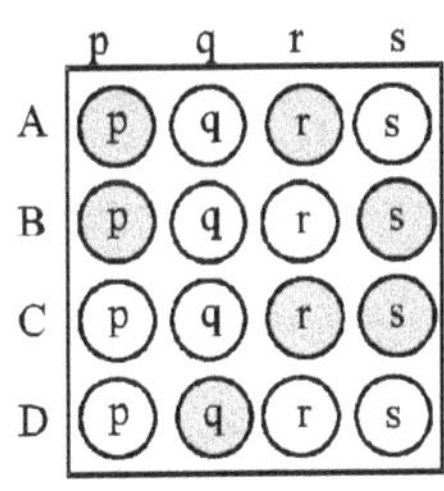

16. 

| Column I | Column II |
|---|---|
| (A) The number of integral terms in the expansion of $(\sqrt{3} + \sqrt[8]{5})^{256}$ | (p) $T_8$ |
| (B) If x is positive, the first negative term in the expansion of $(1+x)^{27/5}$ | (q) 33 |
| (C) $\dfrac{C_1}{C_0} + 2.\dfrac{C_2}{C_1} + 3.\dfrac{C_3}{C_2} + \ldots + 15\dfrac{C_{15}}{C_{14}}$ | (r) 120 |

17. 

| Column I | Column II |
|---|---|
| (A) Number of distinct terms in the expansion of $(x + y - z)^{16}$ | (p) $2^{12}$ |
| (B) Number of terms in the expansion of $(x + \sqrt{x^2 - 1})^6 + (x - \sqrt{x^2 - 1})^6$ | (q) 97 |
| (C) The number of irrational terms in $(\sqrt[8]{5} + \sqrt[6]{2})^{99}$ | (r) divisible by 4 |
| (D) The sum of numerical coefficients in the expansion of $\left(1 + \dfrac{x}{3} + \dfrac{2y}{3}\right)^{12}$ | (s) divisible by 3 |

### Section - V - Reasoning Type

This section contains 2 reasoning type questions. Each question has 4 choices (a), (b), (c) and (d) out of which **ONLY ONE** is correct.

**DIRECTIONS for (Qs. 18 & 19) :** Each of these questions contains two statements: Statement-1 (Assertion) and Statement-2 (Reason). Each of these questions has four alternative choices, only one of which is the correct answer. You have to select the correct choice.

(a) Statement-1 is True, Statement-2 is True; Statement-2 is a correct explanation for Statement-1.

(b) Statement-1 is True, Statement-2 is True; Statement-2 is NOT a correct explanation for Statement-1.

(c) Statement-1 is True, Statement-2 is False.

(d) Statement-1 is False, Statement-2 is True.



*Space for Rough Work*

**18.** **Statement-1** : If the coefficient of $x^2 y^3 z^4$ in $(x + y + z)^n$ is $A$ then the coefficient of $x^4 y^4 z$ is $\dfrac{A}{2}$.

**Statement-2** : The coefficient of $x^a y^b z^c$ in $(x + y + z)^n$ is $\dfrac{n!}{a! b! c!}$ if $a, b, c$ are non-negative integers such that $a + b + c = n$

**19.** **Statement–1** : The coefficient of $x^{203}$ in the expression $(x - 1)(x^2 - 2)(x^3 - 3) \ldots (x^{20} - 20)$ must be 13.

**Statement–2** : The coefficient of $x^8$ in the expression $(2 + x)^2 (3 + x)^3 (4 + x)^4$ is equal to 30.

## Section - VI - Integer Type

This section contains 5 questions. The answer to each of the questions is a single digit integer ranging from 0 to 9.

**20.** If $n > 3$ and $n \in N$, then $\left( {}^n C_r = C_r \right)$.

$$C_0 abc - C_1(a-1)(b-1)(c-1) + C_2(a-2)(b-2)(c-2) + \ldots + (-1)^n C_n(a-n)(b-n)(c-n) = \ .$$

**21.** Given $(1 - 2x + 5x^2 - 10x^3)(1 + x)^n = 1 + a_1 x + a_2 x^2 + \ldots$ and that $a_1^2 = 2a_2$ then find the value of n.

**22.** The greatest value of the term independent of x in the expansion of $\left( x \sin\theta + \dfrac{\cos\theta}{x} \right)^{10}$ is $\dfrac{{}^{10}C_B}{A^B}$. Find the value of $A + B$.

**23.** Coefficient of $t^{24}$ in $(1 + t^2)^{12} (1 + t^{12}) (1 + t^{24})$ is ${}^{12}C_6 + M$. Find M.

**24.** If the 3rd term in the expansion of $(x + x^t)^5$ is $10^6$ where $t = \log_{10} x$ then how many values are possible for x.

| | | |
|---|---|---|
| **RESPONSE GRID** | 18.ⓐⓑⓒⓓ  19.ⓐⓑⓒⓓ  20.⓪①②③④⑤⑥⑦⑧⑨ | |
| | 21.⓪①②③④⑤⑥⑦⑧⑨  22.⓪①②③④⑤⑥⑦⑧⑨ | |
| | 23.⓪①②③④⑤⑥⑦⑧⑨  24.⓪①②③④⑤⑥⑦⑧⑨ | |

## DAILY PRACTICE PROBLEM DPP 17 - MATHS

| Total Questions | 24 | Total Marks | 74 |
|---|---|---|---|
| Attempted | | Correct | |
| Incorrect | | Net Score | |
| Cut-off Score | 15 | Qualifying Score | 48 |
| Success Gap = Net Score – Qualifying Score | | | |

$$\text{Net Score} = \sum_{i=1}^{VI} \left[ (\text{correct}_i \times MM_i) - (In_i - NM_i) \right]$$

*Space for Rough Work*

# DPP - Daily Practice Problems

Name : [ ]          Date : [ ]

Start Time : [ ]          End Time : [ ]

## MATHEMATICS    M18

SYLLABUS : **Binomial Theorem - 2** : Properties of binomial coefficients

**Max. Marks : 74**          **Time : 60 min.**

### GENERAL INSTRUCTIONS

- The Daily Practice Problem Sheet contains **24** Questions divided into 5 sections.
  Section I has **8** MCQ's with ONLY 1 correct option. 2 marks for correct answer and No negative marks.
  Section II has **4** MCQ's with 1 or MORE THAN 1 correct option. 4 marks for correct answer(s) and (–1) for wrong answer.
  Section III has **2** MCQ's with multiple matchings. 1 mark for the correct matching of each row & No negative marks.
  Section IV has **5** Assertion-Reason MCQ's with ONLY 1 correct option. 3 marks for correct and (–1) mark for wrong answer.
  Section V has **5** Single digit integer answer questions. 4 marks for correct answer and (–1) for wrong answer.
- No mark will be given/ deducted if no bubble is filled. Keep a timer in front and stop immediately at the end of 60 min.
- You have to evaluate your Response Grids yourself with the help of Solution Booklet.
- The sheet follows a particular syllabus. Do not attempt the sheet before you have completed your preparation for that syllabus. Refer syllabus sheet in the starting of the book for the syllabus of all the DPP sheets.
- After completing the sheet check your answers with the solution booklet and complete the Result Grid. Finally spend time to analyse your performance and revise the areas which emerge out as weak in your evaluation.

---

### Section - I - Straight Objective Type

This section contains 8 multiple choice questions. Each question has 4 choices (a), (b), (c) and (d), out of which **ONLY ONE** is correct.

**1.** The value of
$$^nC_0 \cdot {}^{2n}C_n - {}^nC_1 \cdot {}^{2n-2}C_n + {}^nC_2 \cdot {}^{2n-4}C_n - \ldots \text{ is}$$
(a) $3^n$          (b) $4^n$
(c) $2^n$          (d) None of these

**2.** If $(1+x+x^2)^{25} = a_0 + a_1x + a_2x^2 + \ldots + a_{50} \cdot x^{50}$ then $a_0 + a_2 + a_4 + \ldots + a_{50}$ is :
(a) even          (b) odd & of the form 3n
(c) odd & of the form $(3n-1)$     (d) odd & of the form $(3n+1)$

**3.** The value of
$$\binom{30}{0}\binom{30}{10} - \binom{30}{1}\binom{30}{11} + \binom{30}{2}\binom{30}{12}\ldots + \binom{30}{20}\binom{30}{30} \text{ is where}$$

$$\binom{n}{r} = {}^nC_r$$

(a) $\binom{30}{10}$     (b) $\binom{30}{15}$     (c) $\binom{60}{30}$     (d) $\binom{31}{10}$

**4.** If $(1+x)^n = \displaystyle\sum_{r=0}^{n} C_r x^r$, then the value of
$$C_0 + (C_0 + C_1) + (C_0 + C_1 + C_2) + \ldots$$
$$+ (C_0 + C_1 + C_2 + \ldots + C_n) \text{ is}$$
(a) $n \cdot 2^{n-1}$          (b) $(n+2) \cdot 2^n$
(c) $2^n$          (d) $(n+2) \cdot 2^{n-1}$

**5.** If $\pi(n)$ denotes product of all binomial coefficients in $(1+x)^n$, then ratio of $\pi(2002)$ to $\pi(2001)$ is
(a) 2002     (b) $\dfrac{(2002)^{2001}}{(2001)!}$     (c) $\dfrac{(2001)^{2002}}{(2002)!}$     (d) 2001

---

| RESPONSE GRID | 1. ⓐⓑⓒⓓ | 2. ⓐⓑⓒⓓ | 3. ⓐⓑⓒⓓ | 4. ⓐⓑⓒⓓ | 5. ⓐⓑⓒⓓ |
|---|---|---|---|---|---|

**6.** If $(1+x)^n = C_0 + C_1 x + C_2 x^2 + \ldots + C_n x^n$, then

$C_0 C_r + C_1 C_{r+1} + \ldots + C_{n-r} C_n =$

(a) $\left[\dfrac{n!}{r!\,(n-r)!}\right]^2$

(b) $\dfrac{(2n)!}{(n-r)!\,(n+r)!}$

(c) $2^r$

(d) $2^{n-r}$

**7.** If $(1+x+2x^2)^{20} = a_0 + a_1 x + a_2 x^2 + \ldots + a_{40} x^{40}$ then

$a_1 + a_3 + a_5 + \ldots + a_{39} =$

(a) $2^{20} - 1$

(b) $2^{20}(2^{20} - 1)$

(c) $2^{19}(2^{20} - 1)$

(d) $2^{19}$

**8.** Let $(1+x)^{30} = a_0 + a_1 x + a_2 x^2 + \ldots + a_{30} x^{30}$,

$I : a_0 + a_3 + a_6 + \ldots + a_{30} = \dfrac{2}{3}(2^{29} + 1)$

$II : a_0 + a_1 + a_2 + \ldots + a_{30} = 2^{30}$ and

$a_0 + a_2 + a_4 + \ldots + a_{30} = 2^{29}$

then which of the following statements are correct?

(a) Only I

(b) Only II

(c) Both I and II

(d) Neither I nor II.

## Section - II - Multiple Correct Answer Type

This section contains 4 multiple correct answer(s) type questions. Each question has 4 choices (a), (b), (c) and (d), out of which **ONE OR MORE** is/are correct.

**9.** Number of values of $r$ satisfying the equation

$^{69}C_{3r-1} - {}^{69}C_{r^2-1} = {}^{69}C_{r^2-1} - {}^{69}C_{3r}$ is

(a) 1

(b) 2

(c) 3

(d) 7

**10.** If $C_r$ stands for $^nC_r$, then the sum of the series

$\dfrac{2\left(\dfrac{n}{2}\right)!\left(\dfrac{n}{2}\right)!}{n!}[C_0^2 - 2C_1^2 + 3C_2^2 - \ldots + (-1)^n(n+1)C_n^2]$,

where $n$ is an even positive integer, is not equal to

(a) 0

(b) $(-1)^{n/2}(n+1)$

(c) $(-1)^{n/2}(n+2)$

(d) $(-1)^n n$

**11.** If $C_0, C_1, C_2, \ldots, C_n$ are coefficients in the binomial expansion of $(1+x)^n$, then $C_0 C_2 + C_1 C_3 + C_2 C_4 + \ldots + C_{n-2} C_n$ is equal to

(a) $\dfrac{2n!}{(n-2)!(n+2)!}$

(b) $\dfrac{2n!}{\{(n-2)!\}^2}$

(c) $\dfrac{2n!}{\{(n+2)!\}^2}$

(d) $^{2n}C_{n-2}$

**12.** The value of $C_0^2 + 3C_1^2 + 5C_2^2 + \ldots$ to $(n+1)^{\text{th}}$ term, (given that $C_r \equiv {}^n C_r$) is

(a) $^{2n-1}C_{n-1}$

(b) $(2n+1).^{2n-1}C_n$

(c) $2(n+1).^{2n-1}C_n$

(d) $^{2n-1}C_n + (2n+1).^{2n-1}C_{n-1}$

## Section - III - Matrix-Match Type

This section contains 2 questions. It contains statements given in two columns, which have to be matched. Statements in Column I are labelled as A, B, C and D whereas statements in Column II are labelled as p, q, r and s. The answers to these questions have to be appropriately bubbled as illustrated in the following example. If the correct matches are A-p, A-r, B-p, B-s, C-r, C-s and D-q, then the correctly bubbled matrix will look like the following :

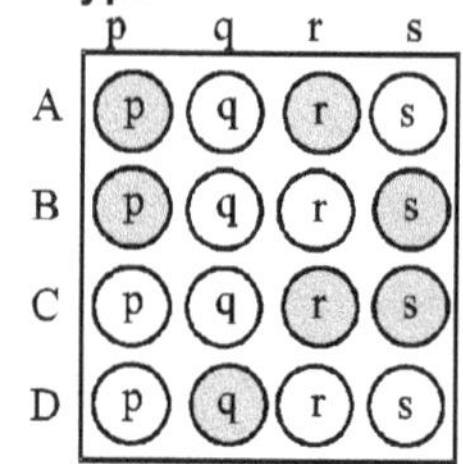

**13.** Let $(x+1)(x+2)(x+3)\ldots(x+n-1)(x+n) = A_0 + A_1 x + A_2 x^2 + \ldots + A_n x^n$

| Column I | Column II |
|---|---|
| (A) $A_0 + A_1 + A_2 + \ldots + A_n$ is equal to | (p) $(n+1)!\left(1 + \dfrac{1}{2} + \dfrac{1}{3} + \ldots + \dfrac{1}{n+1}\right)$ |
| (B) $A_0 + 2A_1 + 3A_2 + \ldots + (n+1)A_n$ is equal to | (q) $(n+1)!\left(\dfrac{1}{2} + \dfrac{1}{3} + \ldots + \dfrac{1}{n+1}\right)$ |

---

**RESPONSE GRID**

6. (a)(b)(c)(d)   7. (a)(b)(c)(d)   8. (a)(b)(c)(d)   9. (a)(b)(c)(d)

10. (a)(b)(c)(d)   11. (a)(b)(c)(d)   12. (a)(b)(c)(d)

13. A - (p)(q)(r)(s); B - (p)(q)(r)(s); C - (p)(q)(r)(s); D - (p)(q)(r)(s)

*Space for Rough Work*

(C)   $nA_0 + (n-1)A_1 +$     (r)   $(n+1)!$

    $(n-2)A_2 + \ldots\ldots + A_{n-1}$    $\left(\dfrac{1}{2} + \dfrac{2}{3} + \dfrac{3}{4} + \ldots\ldots + \dfrac{n}{n+1}\right)$

    is equal to

(D)   $A_1 + 2A_2 + 3A_3 + \ldots\ldots$    (s)   $(n+1)!$

    $\ldots\ldots + nA_n$ is equal to

**14.**     **Column I**             **Column II**

(A)   $\displaystyle\sum\sum_{0 \le i < j \le n} {}^{n}C_i$ is     (p)   $n \cdot 2^n$

    equal to

(B)   $\displaystyle\sum\sum_{0 \le i < j \le n} ({}^{n}C_i + {}^{n}C_j)$    (q)   $n(n-1)\,2^{n-3}$

    is equal to

(C)   $\displaystyle\sum\sum_{0 \le i < j \le n} i\,{}^{n}C_j$     (r)   $n \cdot 2^{n-1}$

    is equal to

## Section - IV - Reasoning Type

This section contains 5 reasoning type questions. Each question has 4 choices (a), (b), (c) and (d) out of which **ONLY ONE** is correct.

**DIRECTIONS for (Qs. 15 to 19) : Each of these questions contains two statements: Statement-1 (Assertion) and Statement-2 (Reason). Each of these questions has four alternative choices, only one of which is the correct answer. You have to select the correct choice.**

(a)   Statement-1 is True, Statement-2 is True; Statement-2 is a correct explanation for Statement-1.

(b)   Statement-1 is True, Statement-2 is True; Statement-2 is NOT a correct explanation for Statement-1.

(c)   Statement -1 is True, Statement-2 is False.

(d)   Statement -1 is False, Statement-2 is True.

**15.**   **Statement-1 :**

$$\binom{r}{r} + \binom{r+1}{r} + \binom{r+2}{r} + \ldots\ldots + \binom{n}{r} = \binom{n+r-1}{r}$$

**Statement-2 :** $\dbinom{n}{r} + \dbinom{n}{r+1} = \dbinom{n+1}{r+1}$

**16.**   **Statement 1 :** $\displaystyle\sum_{k=1}^{n} K \cdot ({}^{n}C_K)^2 = n \cdot {}^{2n-1}C_{n-1}$

    **Statement 2 :** If $2^{2003}$ is divided by 15 the remainder is 1.

**17.**   **Statement 1 :** $\displaystyle\sum\sum_{0 \le i \le j \le 10} ({}^{10}C_j)({}^{j}C_i) = 3^{10}$

    **Statement 2 :** $\displaystyle\sum_{r=1}^{n} {}^{n}C_r = 2^n - 1$

**18.**   **Statement 1 :** The value of $\displaystyle\sum_{r=1}^{15} \dfrac{r\,2^r}{(r+2)!}$ is equal to $1 - \left(\dfrac{2^{16}}{17!}\right)$

    **Statement 2 :** ${}^{n}C_r = {}^{n}C_{n-r}$.

**19.**   **Statement–1 :** ${}^{21}C_0 + {}^{21}C_1 + \ldots + {}^{21}C_{10} = 2^{20}$

    **Statement–2 :** ${}^{2n+1}C_0 + {}^{2n+1}C_1 + \ldots {}^{2n+1}C_{2n+1} = 2^{2n+1}$

    and ${}^{n}C_r = {}^{n}C_{n-r}$

---

**RESPONSE GRID**

**14. A** - (p)(q)(r)(s); **B** - (p)(q)(r)(s); **C** - (p)(q)(r)(s); **D** - (p)(q)(r)(s)

**15.** (a)(b)(c)(d)    **16.** (a)(b)(c)(d)    **17.** (a)(b)(c)(d)    **18.** (a)(b)(c)(d)

**19.** (a)(b)(c)(d)

## Section - V - Integer Type

This section contains 5 questions. The answer to each of the questions is a single digit integer ranging from 0 to 9.

**20.** If the value of $(C_0 - C_2 + C_4 - C_6 + \ldots)^2 + (C_1 - C_3 + C_5 - C_7 + \ldots)^2$ is $p^n$. Find the value of p.

**21.** Given $s_n = 1 + q + q^2 + \ldots + q^n$;

$$S_n = 1 + \frac{q+1}{2} + \left(\frac{q+1}{2}\right)^2 + \ldots + \left(\frac{q+1}{2}\right)^n, q \neq 1.$$

The value of $^{n+1}C_1 + {}^{n+1}C_2 s_1 + {}^{n+1}C_3 s_2 + \ldots + {}^{n+1}C_n s_n$

is $p^n S_n$

Find the value of p.

**22.** If $(1+x)^n = C_0 + C_1 x + C_2 x^2 + \ldots + C_n x^n$ then the sum of the products of the $C_i's$ taken two at a time, represented by

$$\sum_{0 \leq i < j \leq n} \sum C_i C_j \quad \text{is equal to } 2^{Pn-1} - \frac{(2n)!}{Q(n!)^R}. \text{ Find the}$$

value of $P + Q + R$.

**23.** Solve

$$C_0 - 2^2 C_1 + 3^2 C_2 - \ldots + (-1)^n (n+1)^2 C_n = P,$$

$n > 2$, where $C_r = {}^nC_r$. Hence find the value of P.

**24.** If $n > 3$ and $n \in N$, then where $^nC_r = C_r$ find the value of following expression.

$$C_0 abc - C_1(a-1)(b-1)(c-1) + C_2(a-2)(b-2)(c-2) + \ldots + (-1)^n C_n(a-n)(b-n)(c-n),$$

| | | |
|---|---|---|
| **RESPONSE GRID** | 20. ⓪①②③④⑤⑥⑦⑧⑨ | 21. ⓪①②③④⑤⑥⑦⑧⑨ |
| | 22. ⓪①②③④⑤⑥⑦⑧⑨ | 23. ⓪①②③④⑤⑥⑦⑧⑨ |
| | 24. ⓪①②③④⑤⑥⑦⑧⑨ | |

| DAILY PRACTICE PROBLEM DPP 18 - MATHS | | | |
|---|---|---|---|
| Total Questions | 24 | Total Marks | 74 |
| Attempted | | Correct | |
| Incorrect | | Net Score | |
| Cut-off Score | 15 | Qualifying Score | 48 |
| Success Gap = Net Score – Qualifying Score | | | |

$$\text{Net Score} = \sum_{i=1}^{VI} \left[ (\text{correct}_i \times MM_i) - (In_i - NM_i) \right]$$

*Space for Rough Work*

**Name :**

**Date :**

**Start Time :**

**End Time :**

# MATHEMATICS    M19

**SYLLABUS : Measures of Central Tendency and Dispersion-1 : Mean, Median and Mode**

**Max. Marks : 59**

**Time : 60 min.**

## GENERAL INSTRUCTIONS

- The Daily Practice Problem Sheet contains **24** Questions divided into 3 sections.

  Section I has **18** MCQ's with ONLY 1 correct option. 2 marks for correct answer and No negative marks.

  Section II has **1** Assertion-Reason MCQ's with ONLY 1 correct option. 3 marks for correct and (–1) mark for wrong answer. Section III has **5** Single digit integer answer questions. 4 marks for correct answer and (–1) for wrong answer.

- No mark will be given/ deducted if no bubble is filled. Keep a timer in front and stop immediately at the end of 60 min.

- You have to evaluate your Response Grids yourself with the help of Solution Booklet.

- The sheet follows a particular syllabus. Do not attempt the sheet before you have completed your preparation for that syllabus. Refer syllabus sheet in the starting of the book for the syllabus of all the DPP sheets.

- After completing the sheet check your answers with the solution booklet and complete the Result Grid. Finally spend time to analyse your performance and revise the areas which emerge out as weak in your evaluation.

## Section - I - Straight Objective Type

This section contains 18 multiple choice questions. Each question has 4 choices (a), (b), (c) and (d), out of which **ONLY ONE** is correct.

1. The median of a set of 9 distinct observations is 20.5. If each of the largest 4 observations of the set is increased by 2, then the median of the new set

   (a) remains the same as that of the original set

   (b) is increased by 2

   (c) is decreased by 2

   (d) is two times the original median

2. A student obtain 75%, 80% and 85% in three subjects. If the marks of an another subject is added, then his average cannot be less than

   (a) 60%  (b) 65%

   (c) 80%  (d) 90%

3. The average of n numbers $x_1, x_2, x_3, ....., x_n$ is M. If $x_n$ is replaced by x', then new average is

   (a) $M - x_n + x'$

   (b) $\dfrac{nM - x_n + x'}{n}$

   (c) $\dfrac{(n-1)M + x'}{n}$

   (d) $\dfrac{M - x_n + x'}{n}$

4. In the following frequency distribution, class limits of some of the class intervals and mid-value of a class are missing. However, the mean of the distribution is known to be 46.5,

| Class intervals | Mid-values | Frequency |
| --- | --- | --- |
| $x_1 - x_2$ | 15 | 10 |
| $x_2 - x_3$ | 30 | 40 |
| $x_3 - x_4$ | M | 30 |
| $x_4 - x_5$ | 75 | 10 |
| $x_5 - 100$ | 90 | 10 |

<table><tr><td>**RESPONSE GRID**</td><td>1. ⓐⓑⓒⓓ</td><td>2. ⓐⓑⓒⓓ</td><td>3. ⓐⓑⓒⓓ</td><td>4. ⓐⓑⓒⓓ</td></tr></table>

the values of $x_1, x_2, x_3, x_4, x_5$ respectively will be

  (a) $(0, 20, 40, 60, 80)$      (b) $(40, 50, 60, 70, 80)$

  (c) $(10, 20, 40, 70, 80)$      (d) $(0, 19.5, 39.5, 69.5, 80)$

**5.** The mean income of a group of workers is $\overline{X}$ and that of another group is $\overline{Y}$. If the number of workers in the second group is 10 times the number of workers in the first group, then the mean income of combined group is

  (a) $\dfrac{\overline{X} + 10\overline{Y}}{3}$      (b) $\dfrac{\overline{X} + 10\overline{Y}}{11}$

  (c) $\dfrac{10\overline{X} + 10\overline{Y}}{Y}$      (d) $\dfrac{X + 10\overline{Y}}{9}$

**6.** If $\overline{x}_1$ and $\overline{x}_2$ are the means of two distributions such that $\overline{x}_1 < \overline{x}_2$ and $\overline{x}$ is the mean of the combined distribution, then

  (a) $\overline{x} < \overline{x}_2$      (b) $\overline{x} > \overline{x}_2$

  (c) $\overline{x} = \dfrac{\overline{x}_1 + \overline{x}_2}{2}$      (d) $\overline{x}_1 < x < \overline{x}_2$

**7.** Let $x_1, x_2, ....., x_n$ be n observations such that $\sum x_i^2 = 400$ and $\sum x_i = 80$. Then a possible value of n among the following is

  (a) 9      (b) 12

  (c) 15      (d) 18

**8.** The mean of the values 0, 1, 2, ......, n having corresponding weight $^nC_0, {}^nC_1, {}^nC_2, ....., {}^nC_n$ respectively is

  (a) $\dfrac{2^n}{n+1}$      (b) $\dfrac{2^{n+1}}{n(n+1)}$

  (c) $\dfrac{n+1}{2}$      (d) $\dfrac{n}{2}$

**9.** If the values $1, \dfrac{1}{2}, \dfrac{1}{3}, \dfrac{1}{4}, \dfrac{1}{5}, ....., \dfrac{1}{n}$ occur with frequencies $1, 2, 3, 4, 5, ......, n$ in a distribution, then the mean is

  (a) 1      (b) n

  (c) $\dfrac{1}{n}$      (d) $\dfrac{2}{n+1}$

**10.** If the mean of the set of numbers $x_1, x_2, x_3, ......, x_n$ is $\overline{x}$ then the mean of the numbers $x_i + 2i$, $1 \le i \le n$ is

  (a) $\overline{x} + 2n$      (b) $\overline{x} + n + 1$

  (c) $\overline{x} + 2$      (d) $\overline{x} + n$

**11.** The mean of $n$ items is $\overline{x}$. If the first term is increased by 1, second by 2 and so on, then new mean is

  (a) $\overline{x} + n$      (b) $\overline{x} + \dfrac{n}{2}$

  (c) $\overline{x} + \dfrac{n+1}{2}$      (d) None of these

**12.** The arithmetic mean of the set of observation $1, 2, 3, ..., n$ is

  (a) $(n+1)/2$      (b) $(n/2+1)$

  (c) $n/2$      (d) $(n-1)/2$

**13.** The weighted A.M. of the first n natural numbers whose weights are corresponding numbers is

  (a) $\dfrac{(n+1)(2n+1)}{6}$      (b) $\dfrac{n(n+1)(2n+1)}{6}$

  (c) $\dfrac{(2n+1)}{3}$      (d) $\dfrac{(2n+1)}{6}$

**14.** Mean of n numbers $x_1, x_2, ...., x_n$, where $x_i = (i + 1)\,i$ for each $i = 1, 2, ..., n$, is

(a) $\dfrac{(n+1)(n+2)}{n}$     (b) $n + 1$

(c) $\dfrac{(n+1)(n+2)}{3}$     (d) None of these

**15.** The mode of the following data :

| Marks | 1 - 10 | 11 - 20 | 21 - 30 | 31 - 40 | 41 - 50 |
|---|---|---|---|---|---|
| Number of students | 8 | 15 | 28 | 16 | 8 |

is

(a) 25.7     (b) 25.9
(c) 25.2     (d) 25.0

**16.** If a variable takes the discrete values $\alpha + 4$, $\alpha - \dfrac{7}{2}$, $\alpha - \dfrac{5}{2}$, $\alpha - 3, \alpha - 2, \alpha + \dfrac{1}{2}, \alpha - \dfrac{1}{2}$ and $\alpha + 5$ $(\alpha > 0)$, then the median is

(a) $\alpha - \dfrac{3}{4}$     (b) $\alpha - \dfrac{1}{2}$

(c) $\alpha - 2$     (d) $\alpha + \dfrac{5}{4}$

**17.** The median of 0, 2, 2, 2, –3, 5, –1, 5, 5, -3, 6, 6, 5, 6 is

(a) 0     (b) –1.5
(c) 3.5     (d) 2

**18.** The median of the given frequency distribution is found graphically with the help of

(a) Histogram     (b) Pie Chart
(c) Frequency Curve     (d) Ogive

## Section - II - Reasoning Type

This section contains 1 reasoning type question. The question has 4 choices (a), (b), (c) and (d) out of which **ONLY ONE** is correct.

**DIRECTIONS : This question contains two statements: Statement-1 (Assertion) and Statement-2 (Reason). The question has four alternative choices, only one of which is the correct answer. You have to select the correct choice.**

(a) Statement-1 is True, Statement-2 is True; Statement-2 is a correct explanation for Statement-1.

(b) Statement-1 is True, Statement-2 is True; Statement-2 is NOT a correct explanation for Statement-1.

(c) Statement -1 is True, Statement-2 is False.

(d) Statement -1 is False, Statement-2 is True.

**19.** Let $\overline{X}_1$ and $\overline{X}_2$ are means of two distributions such that $\overline{X}_1 < \overline{X}_2$ and $\overline{X}$ is the mean of the combined distribution.

**Statement-1 :** $\overline{X}_1 < \overline{X} < \overline{X}_2$

**Statement-2 :** $\overline{X} = \dfrac{\overline{X}_1 + \overline{X}_2}{2}$

<table>
<tr><td rowspan="2">RESPONSE<br>GRID</td><td>14. ⓐⓑⓒⓓ</td><td>15. ⓐⓑⓒⓓ</td><td>16. ⓐⓑⓒⓓ</td><td>17. ⓐⓑⓒⓓ</td></tr>
<tr><td>18. ⓐⓑⓒⓓ</td><td>19. ⓐⓑⓒⓓ</td><td></td><td></td></tr>
</table>

## Section - III - Integer Type

This section contains 5 questions. The answer to each of the questions is a single digit integer ranging from 0 to 9.

**20.** In a group of students, mean weight of boys is 80 kg and mean weight of girls is 50 kg. If the mean weight of all the students together is 60 kg then the ratio of the number of boys to that of girls is X. Find the value of 4X.

**21.** Mean of the numbers 1, 2, 3, ...., n with respective weights

$$1^2 + 1, 2^2 + 2, 3^2 + 3, ..., n^2 + n \text{ is } \frac{An + B}{C}. \text{ Find } A + B + C.$$

**22.** The following data gives the distribution of height of students

| Height (in cm) | 160 | 150 | 152 | 161 | 156 | 154 | 155 |
|---|---|---|---|---|---|---|---|
| Number of students | 12 | 8 | 4 | 4 | 3 | 3 | 7 |

The median of the distribution is X. Find the value of $\dfrac{X}{31}$.

**23.** The mean weight of a group of 10 items is 28 and that of another group of n items is 35. The mean of combined group of 10 + n items is found to be 30. Find the value of n.

**24.** If the mean of the five observations x, x + 2, x + 4, x + 6, x + 8 is 11, then find the mean of the first three observation.

<table>
<tr><td rowspan="3">RESPONSE GRID</td><td>20. ⓪①②③④⑤⑥⑦⑧⑨</td><td>23. ⓪①②③④⑤⑥⑦⑧⑨</td></tr>
<tr><td>21. ⓪①②③④⑤⑥⑦⑧⑨</td><td>24. ⓪①②③④⑤⑥⑦⑧⑨</td></tr>
<tr><td>22. ⓪①②③④⑤⑥⑦⑧⑨</td><td></td></tr>
</table>

### DAILY PRACTICE PROBLEM DPP 19 - MATHS

| Total Questions | 24 | Total Marks | 59 |
|---|---|---|---|
| Attempted | | Correct | |
| Incorrect | | Net Score | |
| Cut-off Score | 10 | Qualifying Score | 32 |
| Success Gap = Net Score − Qualifying Score | | | |

$$\text{Net Score} = \sum_{i=\text{I}}^{\text{VI}} \left[ (\text{correct}_i \times MM_i) - (In_i - NM_i) \right]$$

Name : [ ]   Date : [ ]

Start Time : [ ]   End Time : [ ]

# MATHEMATICS   M20

**SYLLABUS : Measures of Central Tendency and Dispersion-2 :** Relation between mean, median & mode; mean deviation, variance and standard deviation.

**Max. Marks : 59**   **Time : 60 min.**

## GENERAL INSTRUCTIONS

- The Daily Practice Problem Sheet contains **24** Questions divided into 3 sections.

  Section I has **18** MCQ's with ONLY 1 correct option. 2 marks for correct answer and No negative marks.

  Section II has **1** Assertion-Reason MCQ's with ONLY 1 correct option. 3 marks for correct and (–1) mark for wrong answer.
  Section III has **5** single digit integer answer questions. 4 marks for correct answer and (–1) for wrong answer.

- No mark will be given/ deducted if no bubble is filled. Keep a timer in front and stop immediately at the end of 60 min.
- You have to evaluate your Response Grids yourself with the help of Solution Booklet.
- The sheet follows a particular syllabus. Do not attempt the sheet before you have completed your preparation for that syllabus. Refer syllabus sheet in the starting of the book for the syllabus of all the DPP sheets.
- After completing the sheet check your answers with the solution booklet and complete the Result Grid. Finally spend time to analyse your performance and revise the areas which emerge out as weak in your evaluation.

## Section - I - Straight Objective Type

This section contains 18 multiple choice questions. Each question 4 has choices (a), (b), (c) and (d), out of which **ONLY ONE** is correct.

1. The S.D. of a variable x is $\sigma$. The S.D. of the variate $\dfrac{ax+b}{c}$ where a, b, c are constants, is

   (a) $\left(\dfrac{a}{c}\right)\sigma$   (b) $\left|\dfrac{a}{c}\right|\sigma$

   (c) $\left(\dfrac{a^2}{c^2}\right)\sigma$   (d) None of these

2. The mean of 5 observations is 4.4 and their variance is 8.24. If three observations are 1, 2 and 6, the other two observations are

   (a) 4 and 6   (b) 4 and 9
   (c) 5 and 7   (d) 5 and 9

3. In any discrete series (when all values are not same) the relationship between M.D. about mean and S.D. is

   (a) M.D. = S.D.   (b) M.D. $\geq$ S.D.
   (c) M.D. < S.D.   (d) M.D. $\leq$ S.D.

4. Variance of the numbers 3, 7, 10, 18, 22 is equal to

   (a) 12   (b) 6.4
   (c) $\sqrt{49.2}$   (d) 49.2

5. In an experiment with 15 observations on x, the following results were available : $\Sigma x^2 = 2830$, $\Sigma x = 170$

   One observation that was 20, was found to be wrong and was replaced by the correct value 30. The corrected variance is

   (a) 8.33   (b) 78.00
   (c) 188.66   (d) 177.33

---

**RESPONSE GRID**   1. ⓐⓑⓒⓓ   2. ⓐⓑⓒⓓ   3. ⓐⓑⓒⓓ   4. ⓐⓑⓒⓓ   5. ⓐⓑⓒⓓ

**6.** If in a frequency distribution, the mean and median are 21 and 22 respectively, then its mode is approximately

(a)  22.0      (b)  20.5
(c)  25.5      (d)  24.0

**7.** For a group of 200 candidates the mean and S.D. were found to be 40 and 15 respectively. Later on it was found that the score 43 was misread as 34, then correct mean and correct S.D. is

(a)  40.045, 15.25      (b)  39.25, 14.995
(c)  40.045, 14.995      (d)  None of these

**8.** For a frequency distribution consisting of 18 observations, the mean and the standard deviation were found to be 7 and 4 respectively. But on comparison with the original data, it was found that a figure 12 was miscopied as 21 in calculations. The correct mean and standard deviation are

(a)  6.7, 2.7      (b)  6.5, 2.5
(c)  6.34, 2.34      (d)  none of these

**9.** What is the standard deviation of the following series ?

| Measurements | 0 - 10 | 10 - 20 | 20 - 30 | 30 - 40 |
|---|---|---|---|---|
| Frequency | 1 | 3 | 4 | 2 |

(a)  81      (b)  7.6
(c)  9      (d)  2.26

**10.** The mean deviation from the mean of the following data is :

| Marks | 0 - 10 | 10 - 20 | 20 - 30 | 30 - 40 | 40 - 50 |
|---|---|---|---|---|---|
| No. of Students | 5 | 8 | 15 | 16 | 6 |

(a)  10      (b)  10.22
(c)  9.86      (d)  9.44

**11.** The mean deviation from the median of the following set of observations 5, 3, 9, 12, 3, 10, 12, 21, 18, 12, 21 is

(a)  5.113      (b)  4.606
(c)  4.134      (d)  4.909

**12.** The mean and S.D. of 1, 2, 3, 4, 5, 6 is

(a)  $\dfrac{7}{2}, \sqrt{\dfrac{35}{12}}$      (b)  3, 3

(c)  $\dfrac{7}{2}, \sqrt{3}$      (d)  $3, \dfrac{35}{12}$

**13.** The mean and S.D. of the marks of 200 candidates were found to be 40 and 15 respectively. Later, it was discovered that a score of 40 was wrongly read as 50. The correct mean and S.D. respectively are

(a)  14.98, 39.95      (b)  39.95, 14.98
(c)  39.95, 224.5      (d)  None of these

**14.** Let r be the range and $S^2 = \dfrac{1}{n-1} \sum_{i=1}^{n} (x_i - \bar{x})^2$ be the S.D. of a set of observations $x_1, x_2, ..... x_n$, then

(a)  $S \le r\sqrt{\dfrac{n}{n-1}}$

(b)  $S = r\sqrt{\dfrac{n}{n-1}}$

(c)  $S \ge r\sqrt{\dfrac{n}{n-1}}$

(d)  None of these

**15.** The S.D. of the following data is nearly

| $X_i$ | 140 | 145 | 150 | 155 | 160 | 165 | 170 | 175 |
|---|---|---|---|---|---|---|---|---|
| $f_i$ | 4 | 6 | 15 | 30 | 36 | 24 | 8 | 2 |

(a) 8.64      (b) 7.26

(c) 7.05      (d) None of these

**16.** If the standard deviation of 1, 2, 3, 4, ....., 10 is $\sigma$, then the standard deviation of 11, 12, 13, 14, ..., 20 is

(a) $\sigma + 10$      (b) $10\sigma$

(c) $\sigma$      (d) None of these

**17.** If the algebraic sum of deviations of 20 observations from 30 is 20, then the mean of observations is

(a) 30      (b) 30.1

(c) 29      (d) 31

**18.** Consider any set of observations $\{x_1, x_2, x_3, ...., x_{101}\}$; it being given that $x_1 < x_2 < x_3 < ... < x_{100} < x_{101}$. Mean deviation of this set of observations from a number k is minimum when k equals

(a) $x_1$      (b) $x_{51}$

(c) $\dfrac{x_1 + x_2 + ... + x_{101}}{101}$      (d) $x_{50}$

## Section - II - Reasoning Type

This section contains 1 reasoning type question. The question has 4 choices (a), (b), (c) and (d) out of which **ONLY ONE** is correct.

**DIRECTIONS : This question contains two statements: Statement-1 (Assertion) and Statement-2 (Reason). The question has four alternative choices, only one of which is the correct answer. You have to select the correct choice.**

(a) Statement-1 is True, Statement-2 is True; Statement-2 is a correct explanation for Statement-1.

(b) Statement-1 is True, Statement-2 is True; Statement-2 is NOT a correct explanation for Statement-1.

(c) Statement -1 is True, Statement-2 is False.

(d) Statement -1 is False, Statement-2 is True.

**19.** **Statement-1 :** In a positively skewed distribution, mode is greater than the median.

**Statement-2 :** The score which occurs most frequently in a given data, is called the mode.

## Section - III - Integer Type

This section contains 5 questions. The answer to each of the questions is a single digit integer ranging from 0 to 9.

**20.** In a series of 2n observations, half of them is equal to a and remaining half is equal to –a. If the standard deviation of the observations is 2, then find the value of $|a|$.

**21.** Suppose a population A has 100 observations 101, 102, ............., 200 and another population B has 100 observations 151, 152, ................, 250. If $V_A$ and $V_B$ represent the variances of the two populations respectively, then find the value of $\dfrac{V_A}{V_B}$.



*Space for Rough Work*

**22.** The variance of the following distribution is 2M. Find M.

| $x_i$ | 2 | 3 | 11 |
|---|---|---|---|
| $f(x_i)$ | $\dfrac{1}{3}$ | $\dfrac{1}{2}$ | $\dfrac{1}{6}$ |

**23.** If the mode of a data is 18 and the mean is 24, then median is 11P. Find the value of P.

**24.** The sum of squares of deviations for 10 observations from the mean ( = 50) is 250. The coefficient of variation is X. Find $\dfrac{X}{10}$.

| **RESPONSE GRID** | **22.** ⓪①②③④⑤⑥⑦⑧⑨    **23.** ⓪①②③④⑤⑥⑦⑧⑨ <br> **24.** ⓪①②③④⑤⑥⑦⑧⑨ |
|---|---|

## DAILY PRACTICE PROBLEM DPP 20 - MATHS

| Total Questions | 24 | Total Marks | 59 |
|---|---|---|---|
| Attempted | | Correct | |
| Incorrect | | Net Score | |
| Cut-off Score | 12 | Qualifying Score | 38 |
| Success Gap = Net Score – Qualifying Score | | | |

$$\text{Net Score} = \sum_{i=1}^{VI} \left[ (\text{correct}_i \times MM_i) - (In_i - NM_i) \right]$$

# DPP - Daily Practice Problems

**Name :**

**Date :**

**Start Time :**

**End Time :**

## MATHEMATICS  M21

**SYLLABUS : Trigonometrical Ratios, Functions and Identities-1 :** Fundamental trigonometrical ratios and functions, Trigonometrical ratio of allied angles, Trigonometrical ratios of sum and difference of two and three angles.

## Max. Marks : 72

## Time : 60 min.

### GENERAL INSTRUCTIONS

- The Daily Practice Problem Sheet contains **24** Questions divided into 6 sections.
  Section I has **10** MCQ's with ONLY 1 correct option. 2 marks for correct answer and No negative marks.
  Section II has **4** MCQ's with 1 or MORE THAN 1 correct option. 4 marks for correct answer(s) and (–1) for wrong answer.
  Section III has **1** PASSAGE with **3** MCQ's with ONLY 1 correct option. 3 marks for correct and (–1) mark for wrong answer.
  Section IV has **1** MCQ's with multiple matchings. 1 mark for the correct matching of each row & No negative marks.
  Section V has **1** Assertion-Reason MCQ's with ONLY 1 correct option. 3 marks for correct and (–1) mark for wrong answer.
  Section VI has **5** single digit integer answer questions. 4 marks for correct answer and (–1) for wrong answer.
- No mark will be given/ deducted if no bubble is filled. Keep a timer in front and stop immediately at the end of 60 min.
- You have to evaluate your Response Grids yourself with the help of Solution Booklet.
- The sheet follows a particular syllabus. Do not attempt the sheet before you have completed your preparation for that syllabus. Refer syllabus sheet in the starting of the book for the syllabus of all the DPP sheets.
- After completing the sheet check your answers with the solution booklet and complete the Result Grid. Finally spend time to analyse your performance and revise the areas which emerge out as weak in your evaluation.

## Section - I - Straight Objective Type

This section contains 10 multiple choice questions. Each question has 4 choices (a), (b), (c) and (d), out of which **ONLY ONE** is correct.

**1.** The value of $(1 + \tan 1°)(1 + \tan 2°)(1 + \tan 3°) \dots (1 + \tan 44°)(1 + \tan 45°)$ is –

(a) $2^{21}$    (b) $2^{24}$    (c) $2^{23}$    (d) $2^{22}$

**2.** If $x \in (0, \pi)$ and $\cos x + \sin x = \dfrac{1}{2}$ then $\tan x$ is equal to –

(a) $\dfrac{4 - \sqrt{7}}{3}$      (b) $\dfrac{4 + \sqrt{7}}{3}$

(c) $\dfrac{-(4 + \sqrt{7})}{3}$      (d) $\dfrac{-4 + \sqrt{7}}{3}$

**3.** If $x + y = 3 - \cos 4\theta$ and $x - y = 4 \sin 2\theta$ then

(a) $x^4 + y^4 = 9$      (b) $\sqrt{x} + \sqrt{y} = 16$

(c) $x^3 + y^3 = 2(x^2 + y^2)$      (d) $\sqrt{x} + \sqrt{y} = 2$

**4.** If $\tan B = \dfrac{n \sin A \cos A}{1 - n \cos^2 A}$ then $\tan(A + B)$ equals

(a) $\dfrac{\sin A}{(1 - n)\cos A}$      (b) $\dfrac{(n - 1)\cos A}{\sin A}$

(c) $\dfrac{\sin A}{(n - 1)\cos A}$      (d) $\dfrac{\sin A}{(n + 1)\cos A}$

**5.** The set of angles between $0$ & $2\pi$ satisfying the equation $4\cos^2\theta - 2\sqrt{2}\cos\theta - 1 = 0$ is

(a) $\left\{\dfrac{\pi}{12}, \dfrac{5\pi}{12}, \dfrac{19\pi}{12}, \dfrac{23\pi}{12}\right\}$   (b) $\left\{\dfrac{\pi}{12}, \dfrac{7\pi}{12}, \dfrac{17\pi}{12}, \dfrac{23\pi}{12}\right\}$

(c) $\left\{\dfrac{5\pi}{12}, \dfrac{13\pi}{12}, \dfrac{19\pi}{12}\right\}$   (d) $\left\{\dfrac{\pi}{12}, \dfrac{7\pi}{12}, \dfrac{19\pi}{12}, \dfrac{23\pi}{12}\right\}$

<table>
<tr><td>RESPONSE GRID</td><td>1. ⓐⓑⓒⓓ</td><td>2. ⓐⓑⓒⓓ</td><td>3. ⓐⓑⓒⓓ</td><td>4. ⓐⓑⓒⓓ</td><td>5. ⓐⓑⓒⓓ</td></tr>
</table>

**6.** The value of $\cot x + \cot(60° + x) + \cot(120° + x)$ is equal to:

(a) $\cot 3x$  (b) $\tan 3x$

(c) $3\tan 3x$  (d) $\dfrac{3 - 9\tan^2 x}{3\tan x - \tan^3 x}$

**7.** If $\theta$ is eliminated from the equations $x = a\cos(\theta - \alpha)$ and $y = b\cos(\theta - \beta)$ then $\dfrac{x^2}{a^2} + \dfrac{y^2}{b^2} - \dfrac{2xy}{ab}\cos(\alpha - \beta)$ is equal to

(a) $\cos^2(\alpha - \beta)$  (b) $\sin^2(\alpha - \beta)$
(c) $\sec^2(\alpha - \beta)$  (d) $\operatorname{cosec}^2(\alpha - \beta)$

**8.** The value of
$$\left(1 + \cos\frac{\pi}{9}\right)\left(1 + \cos\frac{3\pi}{9}\right)\left(1 + \cos\frac{5\pi}{9}\right)\left(1 + \cos\frac{7\pi}{9}\right) \text{ is}$$

(a) 9/16  (b) 10/16  (c) 12/16  (d) 5/16

**9.** If $x = \sec\phi - \tan\phi$ & $y = \operatorname{cosec}\phi + \cot\phi$ then :

(a) $x = \dfrac{y - 1}{y + 1}$  (b) $y = \dfrac{1 + x}{1 - x}$

(c) $xy + x + y + 1 = 0$  (d) $xy + x - y - 1 = 0$

**10.** The value of
$$\left(1 + \cos\frac{\pi}{10}\right)\left(1 + \cos\frac{3\pi}{10}\right)\left(1 + \cos\frac{7\pi}{10}\right)\left(1 + \cos\frac{9\pi}{10}\right) \text{ is}$$

(a) $\dfrac{1}{8}$  (b) $\dfrac{1}{16}$

(c) $\dfrac{1}{32}$  (d) None of these

## Section - II - Multiple Correct Answer Type

This section contains 4 multiple correct answer(s) type questions. Each question has 4 choices (a), (b), (c) and (d), out of which **ONE OR MORE** is/are correct.

**11.** If a, b, c are the sides of triangle ABC satisfying $\log\left(1 + \dfrac{c}{a}\right) + \log a - \log b = \log 2$. Also $a(1 - x^2) + 2bx + c(1 + x^2) = 0$ has two equal roots. Then

(a) $\sin B = \dfrac{4}{5}$  (b) $\sin C = 1$

(c) $\sin A + \sin B + \sin C = \dfrac{12}{5}$  (d) $\sin A = \dfrac{4}{5}$

**12.** Choose the incorrect statement(s)?

(a) $\sin 82\dfrac{1}{2}° \cdot \cos 37\dfrac{1}{2}°$ and $\sin 127\dfrac{1}{2}° \cdot \sin 97\dfrac{1}{2}°$ have the same value.

(b) If $\tan A = \dfrac{\sqrt{3}}{4 - \sqrt{3}}$ & $\tan B = \dfrac{\sqrt{3}}{4 + \sqrt{3}}$ then $\tan(A - B)$ must be irrational.

(c) The sign of the product $\sin 2 \cdot \sin 3 \cdot \sin 5$ is positive.

(d) There exists a value of $\theta$ between $0$ & $2\pi$ which satisfies the equation $\sin^4\theta - \sin^2\theta - 1 = 0$.

**13.** If $\tan\left(\dfrac{2\pi}{3} - x\right) = \dfrac{\sin\dfrac{2\pi}{3} - \sin x}{\cos\dfrac{2\pi}{3} - \cos x}$ where $0 < x < \pi$, then the value of x is

(a) $\dfrac{\pi}{12}$  (b) $\dfrac{5\pi}{12}$  (c) $\dfrac{7\pi}{12}$  (d) $\dfrac{11\pi}{12}$

**14.** If $A + B = \dfrac{\pi}{3}$ and $\cos A + \cos B = 1$, then which of the following is /are true?

(a) $\cos(A - B) = \dfrac{1}{3}$  (b) $|\cos A - \cos B| = \sqrt{\dfrac{2}{3}}$

(c) $\cos(A - B) = -\dfrac{1}{3}$  (d) $|\cos A - \cos B| = \dfrac{1}{2\sqrt{3}}$

| RESPONSE GRID | | | | | |
|---|---|---|---|---|---|
| | 6. (a)(b)(c)(d) | 7. (a)(b)(c)(d) | 8. (a)(b)(c)(d) | 9. (a)(b)(c)(d) | 10. (a)(b)(c)(d) |
| | 11. (a)(b)(c)(d) | 12. (a)(b)(c)(d) | 13. (a)(b)(c)(d) | 14. (a)(b)(c)(d) | |

## Section - III - Linked Comprehension Type

This section contains one paragraph. Based upon the paragraph, 3 multiple choice questions have to be answered. Each question has 4 choices (a), (b), (c) and (d), out of which **ONLY ONE** is correct.

---

If $P_n = \sin^n \theta + \cos^n \theta$ where $n \in W$ (whole number) and $\theta \in R$ (real number)

**15.** If $P_1 = m$, then the value of $4(1 - P_6)$ is

   (a) $\ 3\,(m-1)^2$        (b) $\ 3\,(m^2 - 1)^2$

   (c) $\ 3\,(m+1)^2$        (d) $\ 3\,(m^2 + 1)^2$

**16.** The value of $2P_6 - 3P_4 + 10$ is

   (a) $\ 0$       (b) $\ 6$       (c) $\ 9$       (d) 15

**17.** The value of $\dfrac{P_7 - P_5}{P_5 - P_3}$ is

   (a) $\ \dfrac{P_7}{P_5}$     (b) $\ \dfrac{P_5}{P_3}$     (c) $\ \dfrac{P_3}{P_1}$     (d) $\ \dfrac{P_3}{P_5}$

---

### Section - IV - Matrix-Match Type

This section contains 1 questions. It contains statements given in two columns, which have to be matched. Statements in Column I are labelled as A, B, C and D whereas statements in Column II are labelled as p, q, r and s. The answers to these questions have to be appropriately bubbled as illustrated in the following example. If the correct matches are A-p, A-r, B-p, B-s, C-r, C-s and D-q, then the correctly bubbled matrix will look like the following :

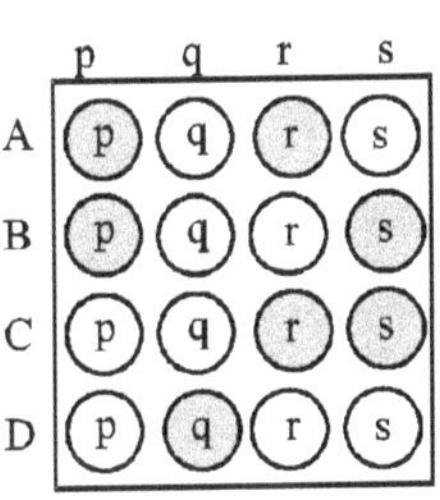

**18.**

| Column I | | Column II |
|---|---|---|
| (A) If $\theta + \phi = \dfrac{\pi}{2}$, where $\theta$ and $\phi$ are positive, then $(\sin\theta + \sin\phi)\,\sin\left(\dfrac{\pi}{4}\right)$ is always less than | | (p)   1 |
| (B) If $\sin\theta - \sin\phi = a$ and $\cos\theta + \cos\phi = b$, then $a^2 + b^2$ cannot exceed | | (q)   6 |
| (C) If $3\sin\theta + 5\cos\theta = 5$, $(\theta \neq 0)$ then the value of $5\sin\theta - 3\cos\theta$ is | | (r)   3 |
| (D) If $2\cos x + \sin x = 1$, then the value of $7\cos x + 6\sin x$ is equal to | | (s)   4 |

---

## Section - V - Reasoning Type

This section contain 1 reasoning type question. The question has 4 choices (a), (b), (c) and (d) out of which **ONLY ONE** is correct.

---

**DIRECTIONS : Each of these questions contains two statements: Statement-1 (Assertion) and Statement-2 (Reason). Each of these questions has four alternative choices, only one of which is the correct answer. You have to select the correct choice.**

(a)   Statement-1 is True, Statement-2 is True; Statement-2 is a correct explanation for Statement-1.

(b)   Statement-1 is True, Statement-2 is True; Statement-2 is NOT a correct explanation for Statement-1.

(c)   Statement -1 is True, Statement-2 is False.

(d)   Statement -1 is False, Statement-2 is True.

**19.** If $P = 2\sin 2° + 4\sin 4° + \dots\dots + 180\sin 180°$

    **Statement 1 :** $\dfrac{\sqrt{1 + \left(\dfrac{P}{90}\right)^2}}{P}$ is irrational.

    **Statement 2 :** $\tan 1°$ is irrational.

---



*Space for Rough Work*

## Section - VI - Integer Type

This section contains 5 questions. The answer to each of the questions is a single digit integer ranging from 0 to 9.

**20.** In a triangle ABC, D is on AC such that AD = BC, BD = DC, $\angle$ DBC = 2x, $\angle$ BAD = 3x, all angles in degrees, then find the value of $\dfrac{x}{2}$.

**21.** In a triangle ABC, angle B < angle C and the values of B & C satisfy the equation $2\tan x - k(1 + \tan^2 x) = 0$ where $(0 < k < 1)$. Then find the measure of angle $\dfrac{A}{10}$.

**22.** In any triangle ABC, maximum value of $\cos A \cdot \sin^2 (A/2) + \cos B \cdot \sin^2(B/2) + \cos C \cdot \sin^2(C/2)$ is $\dfrac{P}{Q}$. Find the vlue of $Q - P$.

**23.** Find the value of $\dfrac{x}{\sin 18°}$ that satisfies the relation $x = 1 - x + x^2 - x^3 + x^4 - x^5 + \ldots\ldots\ldots \infty$

**24.** Find the value of $\dfrac{3 + \cot 76° \cot 16°}{(\cot 76° + \cot 16°)\cot 44°}$.

| | | |
|---|---|---|
| **RESPONSE GRID** | **20.** ⓪①②③④⑤⑥⑦⑧⑨ | **21.** ⓪①②③④⑤⑥⑦⑧⑨ |
| | **22.** ⓪①②③④⑤⑥⑦⑧⑨ | **23.** ⓪①②③④⑤⑥⑦⑧⑨ |
| | **24.** ⓪①②③④⑤⑥⑦⑧⑨ | |

| DAILY PRACTICE PROBLEM DPP 21 - MATHS | | | |
|---|---|---|---|
| Total Questions | 24 | Total Marks | 72 |
| Attempted | | Correct | |
| Incorrect | | Net Score | |
| Cut-off Score | 14 | Qualifying Score | 47 |
| Success Gap = Net Score – Qualifying Score | | | |

$$\text{Net Score} = \sum_{i=1}^{VI}\left[(\textbf{correct}_i \times MM_i) - (In_i - NM_i)\right]$$

**Name :**

**Date :**

**Start Time :**

**End Time :**

# MATHEMATICS — M22

**SYLLABUS : Trigonometrical Ratios, Functions and Identities-2 :** Trigonometrical ratios of multiple and sub-multiple angles, Maximum & minimum values of trigonometrical functions, Conditional trigonometrical identities

## Max. Marks : 68

## Time : 60 min.

### GENERAL INSTRUCTIONS

- The Daily Practice Problem Sheet contains **23** Questions divided into 6 sections.
  Section I has **9** MCQ's with ONLY 1 correct option. 2 marks for correct answer and No negative marks.
  Section II has **2** MCQ's with 1 or MORE THAN 1 correct option. 4 marks for correct answer(s) and (−1) for wrong answer.
  Section III has **1** PASSAGE with **3** MCQ's with ONLY 1 correct option. 3 marks for correct and (−1) mark for wrong answer.
  Section IV has **2** MCQ's with multiple matchings. 1 mark for the correct matching of each row & No negative marks.
  Section V has **2** Assertion-Reason MCQ's with ONLY 1 correct option. 3 marks for correct and (−1) mark for wrong answer.
  Section VI has **5** single digit integer answer questions. 4 marks for correct answer and (−1) for wrong answer.
- No mark will be given/ deducted if no bubble is filled. Keep a timer in front and stop immediately at the end of 60 min.
- You have to evaluate your Response Grids yourself with the help of Solution Booklet.
- The sheet follows a particular syllabus. Do not attempt the sheet before you have completed your preparation for that syllabus. Refer syllabus sheet in the starting of the book for the syllabus of all the DPP sheets.
- After completing the sheet check your answers with the solution booklet and complete the Result Grid. Finally spend time to analyse your performance and revise the areas which emerge out as weak in your evaluation.

## Section - I - Straight Objective Type

This section contains 9 multiple choice questions. Each question has 4 choices (a), (b), (c) and (d), out of which **ONLY ONE** is correct.

**1.** The sum $\cos\dfrac{\pi}{9} + \cos\dfrac{2\pi}{9} + \cos\dfrac{3\pi}{9} + \ldots\ldots + \cos\dfrac{17\pi}{9}$

equals –

(a) 1/2  (b) −1/2  (c) 1  (d) −1

**2.** The maximum value of $(7\cos\theta + 24\sin\theta) \times (7\sin\theta - 24\cos\theta)$ for every $\theta \in R$.

(a) 25  (b) 625  (c) $\dfrac{625}{2}$  (d) $\dfrac{625}{4}$

**3.** The minimum value of the expression $\sin\alpha + \sin\beta + \sin\gamma$, where $\alpha, \beta, \gamma$ are real numbers satisfying $\alpha + \beta + \gamma = \pi$ is

(a) positive  (b) zero
(c) negative  (d) −3

**4.** If $A + B = \dfrac{\pi}{4}$, then maximum value of $\cos A \cos B$ is equal to

(a) $\dfrac{1}{2\sqrt{2}}$  (b) $\dfrac{1+\sqrt{2}}{2\sqrt{2}}$

(c) $\dfrac{\sqrt{2}-1}{2\sqrt{2}}$  (d) $\dfrac{1}{\sqrt{2}}$

**5.** Let $f(\theta) = \sin\theta(\sin\theta + \sin 3\theta)$. Then $f(\theta)$ is

(a) $\geq 0$, only when $\theta \geq 0$
(b) $\leq 0$, for all real $\theta$
(c) $\geq 0$, for all real $\theta$
(d) $\leq 0$, only when $\theta \leq 0$

| RESPONSE GRID | 1. ⓐⓑⓒⓓ | 2. ⓐⓑⓒⓓ | 3. ⓐⓑⓒⓓ | 4. ⓐⓑⓒⓓ | 5. ⓐⓑⓒⓓ |
|---|---|---|---|---|---|

6. If $a\,\tan\alpha + \sqrt{a^2-1}\,\tan\beta + \sqrt{a^2+1}\,\tan\gamma = 2a$, where $a$ is constant and $\alpha$, $\beta$, $\gamma$ are variable angles. Then the least value of $3\,(\tan^2\alpha + \tan^2\beta + \tan^2\gamma)$ is equal to
   (a) 4  (b) 3  (c) 2  (d) 1

7. The value of
$$\frac{\sin 8x + 7\sin 6x + 18\sin 4x + 12\sin 2x}{\sin 7x + 6\sin 5x + 12\sin 3x}$$
   is equal to
   (a) $2\cos x$  (b) $\cos x$  (c) $2\sin x$  (d) $\sin x$

8. The greatest value of $\cos(xe^{|x|} + 7x^2 - 3x)$, $x \in [-1, \infty)$ is
   (a) 0  (b) 1
   (c) $-1$  (d) None of these

9. If $\tan\theta = n\tan\phi$, then the maximum value of $\tan^2(\theta - \phi)$ is
   (a) $\dfrac{(n+1)^2}{4n}$  (b) $\dfrac{(n-1)^2}{4n}$  (c) $\dfrac{(2n+1)^2}{4n}$  (d) $\dfrac{(2n-1)^2}{4n}$

## Section - II - Multiple Correct Answer Type

This section contains 2 multiple correct answer(s) type questions. Each question has 4 choices (a), (b), (c) and (d), out of which **ONE OR MORE** is/are correct.

10. If $u = \sin^6 x + \cos^6 x$, then maximum and minimum value of $u$ which of the followings are not the
   (a) $\pm\dfrac{1}{4}$  (b) $\pm 1$  (c) $1$ and $\dfrac{1}{4}$  (d) $\dfrac{1}{4}$ and $-1$

11. If $\dfrac{\tan x}{1} = \dfrac{\tan y}{2} = \dfrac{\tan z}{3}(\neq 0)$ and $x + y + z = \pi$, then
   (a) maximum value of $\tan x + \tan y + \tan z$ is 6
   (b) minimum value of $\tan x + \tan y + \tan z$ is $-6$
   (c) $\tan x = \pm 1$, $\tan y = \pm 2$, $\tan z = \pm 3$
   (d) $\tan x + \tan y + \tan z = 0\ \ \forall x, y, z \in R$

## Section - III - Linked Comprehension Type

This section contains one paragraph. Based upon the paragraph, 3 multiple choice questions have to be answered. Each question has 4 choices (a), (b), (c) and (d), out of which **ONLY ONE** is correct.

$$\cos\alpha\,\cos 2\alpha\,\cos 2^2\alpha\,...\cos 2^{n-1}\alpha$$

$$= \begin{cases} \dfrac{\sin 2^n\alpha}{2^n\sin\alpha}, & \text{if}\quad \alpha \neq n\pi \\[3mm] \dfrac{1}{2n}, & \text{if}\quad \alpha = \dfrac{\pi}{2^n+1} \end{cases}$$

Where, $n \in I$ (Integer)

12. The value of $\cos\dfrac{2\pi}{7}\cos\dfrac{4\pi}{7}\cos\dfrac{6\pi}{7}$ is
   (a) $-1/2$  (b) $1/2$  (c) $1/4$  (d) $1/8$

13. The value of $\sin\left(\dfrac{\pi}{18}\right)\sin\left(\dfrac{5\pi}{18}\right)\sin\left(\dfrac{7\pi}{18}\right)$ is
   (a) $\dfrac{1}{16}$  (b) $\dfrac{1}{8}$  (c) $-\dfrac{1}{8}$  (d) $-1$

14. The value of $64\sqrt{3}\,\sin\dfrac{\pi}{48}\cos\dfrac{\pi}{48}\cos\dfrac{\pi}{24}\cos\dfrac{\pi}{12}\cos\dfrac{\pi}{6}$ is
   (a) 8  (b) 6  (c) 4  (d) $-1$

### Section - IV - Matrix-Match Type

This section contains 2 questions. It contains statements given in two columns, which have to be matched. Statements in Column I are labelled as A, B, C and D whereas statements in Column II are labelled as p, q, r and s. The answers to these questions have to

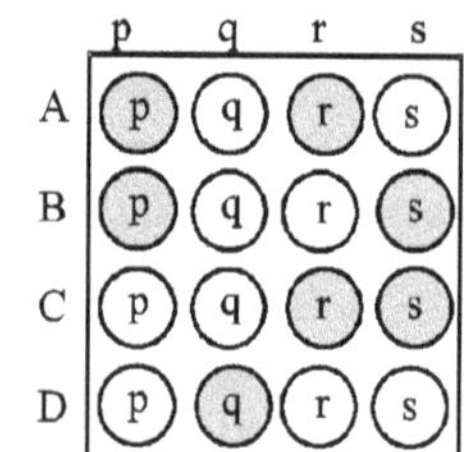

| | RESPONSE GRID | 6. ⓐⓑⓒⓓ | 7. ⓐⓑⓒⓓ | 8. ⓐⓑⓒⓓ | 9. ⓐⓑⓒⓓ | 10. ⓐⓑⓒⓓ |
| | | 11. ⓐⓑⓒⓓ | 12. ⓐⓑⓒⓓ | 13. ⓐⓑⓒⓓ | 14. ⓐⓑⓒⓓ | |

*Space for Rough Work*

be appropriately bubbled as illustrated in the following example. If the correct matches are A-p, A-r, B-p, B-s, C-r, C-s and D-q, then the correctly bubbled matrix will look like the following :

**15.**

| Column I | | Column II |
|---|---|---|
| (A) | If maximum and minimum values of $\dfrac{7+6\tan\theta-\tan^2\theta}{(1+\tan^2\theta)}$ for all real values of $\theta$ are $\lambda$ and $\mu$ respectively, then | (p) $\lambda+\mu=2$ |
| (B) | If maximum and minimum values of $5\cos\theta+3\cos\left(\theta+\dfrac{\pi}{3}\right)+3$ for all real values of $\theta$ are $\lambda$ and $\mu$ respectively, then | (q) $\lambda-\mu=6$ |
| (C) | If maximum and minimum values of $1+\sin\left(\dfrac{\pi}{4}+\theta\right)+2\cos\left(\dfrac{\pi}{4}-\theta\right)$ for all real values of $\theta$ are $\lambda$ and $\mu$ respectively, then | (r) $\lambda+\mu=6$ |
| | | (s) $\lambda-\mu=10$ |
| | | (t) $\lambda-\mu=14$ |

**16.**

| Column-I | | Column-II |
|---|---|---|
| (A) | If $f(\theta)=(\sin\theta+\csc\theta)^2+(\cos\theta+\sec\theta)^2$, then $f(\theta)$ cannot be less than | (p) $\quad$ 1 |
| (B) | If $\sin\alpha-\sin\beta=a$ and $\cos\alpha+\cos\beta=b$ then $a^2+b^2$ cannot exceed | (q) $\quad$ 2 |

| (C) | If $A+B=\dfrac{\pi}{2}$, where $A$ and $B$ are positive then $(\sin A+\sin B)\cos\dfrac{\pi}{4}$ is always less than | (r) $\quad$ 4 |
|---|---|---|
| (D) | If $2\cos x+\sin x=1$, then the value of $7\cos x+6\sin x$ is equal to | (s) $\quad$ 6 |

## Section - V - Reasoning Type

This section contains 2 reasoning type questions. Each question has 4 choices (a), (b), (c) and (d) out of which **ONLY ONE** is correct.

**DIRECTIONS for (Qs. 17 & 18) : Each of these questions contains two statements: Statement-1 (Assertion) and Statement-2 (Reason). Each of these questions has four alternative choices, only one of which is the correct answer. You have to select the correct choice.**

(a) Statement-1 is True, Statement-2 is True; Statement-2 is a correct explanation for Statement-1.

(b) Statement-1 is True, Statement-2 is True; Statement-2 is NOT a correct explanation for Statement-1.

(c) Statement-1 is True, Statement-2 is False.

(d) Statement-1 is False, Statement-2 is True.

**17. Statement-1 :** $\cos\dfrac{\pi}{7}\cos\dfrac{2\pi}{7}\cos\dfrac{4\pi}{7}=-\dfrac{1}{8}$

**Statement-2 :** $\cos\theta\cos 2\theta\cos 2^2\theta\ldots\ldots\ldots$

$\cos 2^{n-1}\theta=\dfrac{-1}{2^n}$, if $\theta=\dfrac{\pi}{2^n-1}$

**18. Statement-1:** The maximum and minimum values of the function $f(x)=\dfrac{1}{6\sin x-8\cos x+5}$ does not exist.

**Statement-2 :** The given function is an unbounded function.

## Section - VI - Integer Type

This section contains 5 questions. The answer to each of the questions is a single digit integer ranging from 0 to 9.

**19.** The value of $-\cos\dfrac{2\pi}{10}\cos\dfrac{4\pi}{10}\cos\dfrac{8\pi}{10}\cos\dfrac{16\pi}{10}$ is greater than $\dfrac{1}{2X}$. Find the value of X.

**20.** Let A, B, C be real numbers such that
(i) (sin A, cos B) lies on a unit circle centred at origin.
(ii) tan C and cot C are defined.

If the minimum value of $(\tan C - \sin A)^2 - (\cot C - \cos B)^2$ is $a + b\sqrt{2}$ where $a, b \in N$, then find the value of $a^3 + b^3 - 10$.

**21.** Given x, y $\in$ R, $x^2 + y^2 > 0$. If the maximum and minimum value of the expression $\dfrac{x^2 + y^2}{x^2 + xy + 4y^2}$ are M and m, and A denotes the average value of M and m, then find the value of 6A.

**22.** Find the maximum value of

$$4\sin^2 x + 3\cos^2 x + \sin\dfrac{x}{2} + \cos\dfrac{x}{2} - \sqrt{2}\,.$$

**23.** If $\sin x + \sin^2 x + \sin^3 x = 1$, then find the value of $\cos^6 x - 4\cos^4 x + 8\cos^2 x$.

---

| RESPONSE GRID | |
|---|---|
| 19. ⓪①②③④⑤⑥⑦⑧⑨ | 20. ⓪①②③④⑤⑥⑦⑧⑨ |
| 21. ⓪①②③④⑤⑥⑦⑧⑨ | 22. ⓪①②③④⑤⑥⑦⑧⑨ |
| 23. ⓪①②③④⑤⑥⑦⑧⑨ | |

---

### DAILY PRACTICE PROBLEM DPP 22 - MATHS

| Total Questions | 23 | Total Marks | 68 |
|---|---|---|---|
| Attempted | | Correct | |
| Incorrect | | Net Score | |
| Cut-off Score | 14 | Qualifying Score | 45 |
| Success Gap = Net Score − Qualifying Score | | | |

$$\textbf{Net Score} = \sum_{i=I}^{VI}\left[(\textbf{correct}_i \times MM_i) - (In_i - NM_i)\right]$$

**Name :**

**Date :**

**Start Time :**

**End Time :**

# MATHEMATICS    M23

**SYLLABUS : Trigonometrical Equations:** Solution of trigonometrical equations, Periodic functions

## Max. Marks : 72

## Time : 60 min.

### GENERAL INSTRUCTIONS

- The Daily Practice Problem Sheet contains **24** Questions divided into 6 sections.
  Section I has **9** MCQ's with ONLY 1 correct option. 2 marks for correct answer and No negative marks.
  Section II has **4** MCQ's with 1 or MORE THAN 1 correct option. 4 marks for correct answer(s) and (–1) for wrong answer.
  Section III has **1** PASSAGE with **3** MCQ's with ONLY 1 correct option. 3 marks for correct and (–1) mark for wrong answer.
  Section IV has **1** MCQ's with multiple matchings. 1 mark for the correct matching of each row & No negative marks.
  Section V has **2** Assertion-Reason MCQ's with ONLY 1 correct option. 3 marks for correct and (–1) mark for wrong answer.
  Section VI has **5** single digit integer answer questions. 4 marks for correct answer and (–1) for wrong answer.
- No mark will be given/ deducted if no bubble is filled. Keep a timer in front and stop immediately at the end of 60 min.
- You have to evaluate your Response Grids yourself with the help of Solution Booklet.
- The sheet follows a particular syllabus. Do not attempt the sheet before you have completed your preparation for that syllabus. Refer syllabus sheet in the starting of the book for the syllabus of all the DPP sheets.
- After completing the sheet check your answers with the solution booklet and complete the Result Grid. Finally spend time to analyse your performance and revise the areas which emerge out as weak in your evaluation.

## Section - I - Straight Objective Type

This section contains 9 multiple choice questions. Each question has 4 choices (a), (b), (c) and (d), out of which **ONLY ONE** is correct.

**1.** Given $a^2 + 2a + \mathrm{cosec}^2\left(\dfrac{\pi}{2}(a + x)\right) = 0$ then, which of the following holds good?

(a) $a = 1 \,;\, \dfrac{x}{2} \in I$      (b) $a = -1 \,;\, \dfrac{x}{2} \in I$

(c) $a \in R \,;\, x \in \phi$

(d) $a$ , $x$ are finite but not possible to find

**2.** The set of angles between $0$ & $2\pi$ satisfying the equation $4\cos^2\theta - 2\sqrt{2}\,\cos\theta - 1 = 0$ is

(a) $\left\{\dfrac{\pi}{12}, \dfrac{5\pi}{12}, \dfrac{19\pi}{12}, \dfrac{23\pi}{12}\right\}$   (b) $\left\{\dfrac{\pi}{12}, \dfrac{7\pi}{12}, \dfrac{17\pi}{12}, \dfrac{23\pi}{12}\right\}$

(c) $\left\{\dfrac{5\pi}{12}, \dfrac{13\pi}{12}, \dfrac{19\pi}{12}\right\}$   (d) $\left\{\dfrac{\pi}{12}, \dfrac{7\pi}{12}, \dfrac{19\pi}{12}, \dfrac{23\pi}{12}\right\}$

**3.** The number of solutions of $\tan(5\pi\cos\theta) = \cot(5\pi\sin\theta)$ for $\theta$ in $(0, 2\pi)$ is :

(a) 28     (b) 14     (c) 4     (d) 2

**4.** The set of values of 'a' for which the equation, $\cos 2x + a \sin x = 2a - 7$ possess a solution is :

(a) $(-\infty, 2)$   (b) $[2, 6]$    (c) $(6, \infty)$    (d) $(-\infty, \infty)$

**5.** If $x = \dfrac{n\pi}{2}$, $n \in I$; satisfies the equation $\sin\dfrac{x}{2} - \cos\dfrac{x}{2} = 1 - \sin x$ & the inequality $\left|\dfrac{x}{2} - \dfrac{\pi}{2}\right| \le \dfrac{3\pi}{4}$, then :

(a) $n = -1, 0, 3, 5$     (b) $n = 1, 2, 4, 5$

(c) $n = 0, 2, 4$          (d) $n = -1, 1, 3, 5$

| RESPONSE GRID | 1. ⓐⓑⓒⓓ | 2. ⓐⓑⓒⓓ | 3. ⓐⓑⓒⓓ | 4. ⓐⓑⓒⓓ | 5. ⓐⓑⓒⓓ |
|---|---|---|---|---|---|

**6.** The general solution of the trigonometric equation $\tan x + \tan 2x + \tan 3x = \tan x \cdot \tan 2x \cdot \tan 3x$ is

(a) $x = n\pi$

(b) $n\pi \pm \dfrac{\pi}{3}$

(c) $x = 2n\pi$

(d) $x = \dfrac{n\pi}{3}$ where $n \in I$

**7.** The number of values of $\theta$ in the interval $\left(-\dfrac{\pi}{2}, \dfrac{\pi}{2}\right)$, satisfying the equation

$(1 - \tan\theta)(1 + \tan\theta)\sec^2\theta + 2^{\tan^2\theta} = 0$ is

(a) 2

(b) 3

(c) 4

(d) None of these

**8.** In the interval $\left[-\dfrac{\pi}{2}, \dfrac{\pi}{2}\right]$, the equation $\log_{\sin\theta}(\cos 2\theta) = 2$ has

(a) no solution

(b) unique solution

(c) two solutions

(d) infinite solutions

**9.** $|\tan x + \sec x| = |\tan x| + |\sec x|$, where $x \in [0, 2\pi]$ if and only if $x$ belongs to the interval

(a) $[0, \pi]$

(b) $\left[0, \dfrac{\pi}{2}\right) \cup \left(\dfrac{\pi}{2}, \pi\right)$

(c) $\left[\pi, \dfrac{3\pi}{2}\right) \cup \left(\dfrac{3\pi}{2}, 2\pi\right]$

(d) $(\pi, 2\pi]$

## Section - II - Multiple Correct Answer Type

This section contains 4 multiple correct answer(s) type questions. Each question has 4 choices (a), (b), (c) and (d), out of which **ONE OR MORE** is/are correct.

**10.** If $\sin\theta = \sin\alpha$ then $\sin\dfrac{\theta}{3} =$

(a) $\sin\dfrac{\alpha}{3}$

(b) $\sin\left(\dfrac{\pi}{3} - \dfrac{\alpha}{3}\right)$

(c) $\sin\left(\dfrac{\pi}{3} + \dfrac{\alpha}{3}\right)$

(d) $-\sin\left(\dfrac{\pi}{3} + \dfrac{\alpha}{3}\right)$

**11.** Solution of the equation $3^{\sin 2x + 2\cos^2 x} + 3^{1 - \sin 2x + 2\sin^2 x} = 28$ is

(a) $x = n\pi$

(b) $x = (2n+1)\dfrac{\pi}{2}$

(c) $x = n\pi - \dfrac{\pi}{4}$

(d) $(2n-1)\dfrac{\pi}{6}$

**12.** $\sqrt{\cos 2x} + \sqrt{1 + \sin 2x} = 2\sqrt{\sin x + \cos x}$, if

(a) $\sin x + \cos x = 0$

(b) $x = 2n\pi$

(c) $x = n\pi - \dfrac{\pi}{4}$

(d) $x = 2n\pi \pm \cos^{-1}\left(-\dfrac{1}{5}\right)$

**13.** $\cos(x - y) - 2\sin x + 2\sin y = 3$ if $x, y \in I$; then

(a) $\sin x = \sin y$

(b) $x + y = 2n\pi, x - y = (4k + 1)\pi$

(c) $x = 2k\pi - \dfrac{\pi}{2}, y = 2n\pi + \dfrac{\pi}{2}$

(d) $\cos(x - y) = -1$

## Section - III - Linked Comprehension Type

This section contains one paragraph. Based upon the paragraph, 3 multiple choice questions have to be answered. Each question has 4 choices (a), (b), (c) and (d), out of which **ONLY ONE** is correct.

An equation of the form $f(\sin x \pm \cos x, \pm \sin x \cos x) = 0$ can be solved by changing variable.

Let $\sin x \pm \cos x = t \Rightarrow \sin^2 x + \cos^2 x \pm 2\sin x \cos x = t^2$

$\Rightarrow \pm \sin x \cos x = \left(\dfrac{t^2 - 1}{2}\right)$. Hence, reduce the given equation into $f\left(t, \dfrac{t^2 - 1}{2}\right) = 0$

**14.** If $1 - \sin 2x = \cos x - \sin x$, then $x$ is

(a) $2n\pi, 2n\pi - \dfrac{\pi}{2}, n \in I$

(b) $2n\pi + \dfrac{\pi}{3}, n\pi + \dfrac{\pi}{3}, n \in I$

---

<table>
<tr><td rowspan="2">RESPONSE<br>GRID</td><td>6. ⓐⓑⓒⓓ</td><td>7. ⓐⓑⓒⓓ</td><td>8. ⓐⓑⓒⓓ</td><td>9. ⓐⓑⓒⓓ</td><td>10. ⓐⓑⓒⓓ</td></tr>
<tr><td>11. ⓐⓑⓒⓓ</td><td>12. ⓐⓑⓒⓓ</td><td>13. ⓐⓑⓒⓓ</td><td>14. ⓐⓑⓒⓓ</td><td></td></tr>
</table>

*Space for Rough Work*

(c) $2n\pi - \dfrac{\pi}{6}, n\pi + \dfrac{\pi}{3}, n \in I$

(d) none of these

**15.** If $1 + \sin^3 x + \cos^3 x = \dfrac{3}{2} \sin 2x$, then $x$ is equal to

(a) $(2n+1)\pi, 2n\pi + \dfrac{\pi}{4}, n \in I$

(b) $(2n+1)\pi, 2n\pi - \dfrac{\pi}{2}, n \in I$

(c) $2n\pi + \dfrac{\pi}{4},\ 2n\pi + \dfrac{\pi}{2}, n \in I$

(d) none of the above

**16.** If $(\sin x + \cos x) - 2\sqrt{2}\ \sin x \cos x = 0$, then $x$ is equal to

(a) $2n\pi + \dfrac{\pi}{4}, n \in I$  (b) $2n\pi - \dfrac{\pi}{4}, n \in I$

(c) $n\pi + \dfrac{\pi}{4}, n \in I$  (d) $n\pi - \dfrac{\pi}{4}, n \in I$

### Section - IV - Matrix-Match Type

This section contains 1 question. It contains statements given in two columns, which have to be matched. Statements in Column I are labelled as A, B, C and D whereas statements in Column II are labelled as p, q, r and s. The answers to these questions have to be appropriately bubbled as illustrated in the following example. If the correct matches are A-p, A-r, B-p, B-s, C-r, C-s and D-q, then the correctly bubbled matrix will look like the following :

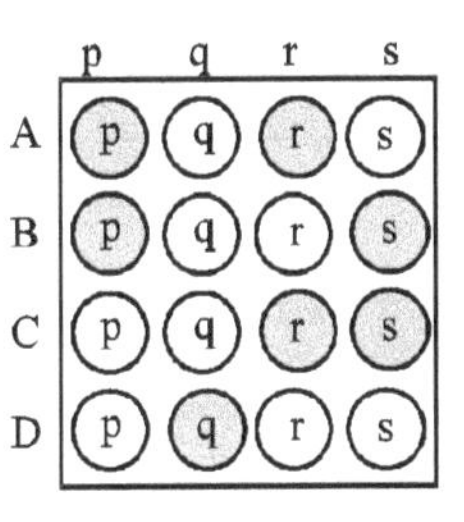

**17.**

| Column I | Column II |
|---|---|
| (A) If $\alpha, \beta$ are the solutions of $\sin x = -\dfrac{1}{2}$ in $[\,0, 2\pi]$ and $\alpha, \gamma$ are the solutions of $\cos x = -\dfrac{\sqrt{3}}{2}$ in $[\,0, 2\pi]$, then | (p) $\alpha - \beta = \pi$ |
| (B) If $\alpha, \beta$ are the solutions of $\cot x = -\sqrt{3}$ in $[\,0, 2\pi]$, and $\alpha, \gamma$ are the solutions of $\csc x = -2$ in $[\,0, 2\pi]$, then | (q) $\beta - \gamma = \pi$ |
| (C) If $\alpha, \beta$ are the solutions of $\sin x = -\dfrac{1}{2}$ in $[\,0, 2\pi]$, and $\alpha, \gamma$ are the solutions of $\tan x = \dfrac{1}{\sqrt{3}}$ in $[0, 2\pi]$, then | (r) $\alpha - \gamma = \pi$ |
| | (s) $\alpha + \beta = 3\pi$ |
| | (t) $\beta + \gamma = 2\pi$ |

### Section - V - Reasoning Type

This section contains 2 reasoning type questions. Each question has 4 choices (a), (b), (c) and (d) out of which **ONLY ONE** is correct.

**DIRECTIONS for (Qs 18 -19 ): Each of these questions contains two statements: Statement-1 (Assertion) and Statement-2 (Reason). Each of these questions has four alternative choices, only one of which is the correct answer. You have to select the correct choice.**

(a) Statement-1 is True, Statement-2 is True; Statement-2 is a correct explanation for Statement-1.

(b) Statement-1 is True, Statement-2 is True; Statement-2 is NOT a correct explanation for Statement-1.

(c) Statement -1 is True, Statement-2 is False.

(d) Statement -1 is False, Statement-2 is True.

**18. Statement-1 :** The equation $\sin(\cos x) = \cos(\sin x)$ does not possess real roots.

**Statement-2 :** If $\sin x > 0$, then $2n\pi < x < (2n+1)\pi, n \in I$.

<table>
<tr><td rowspan="3">RESPONSE GRID</td><td>15. (a)(b)(c)(d)   16. (a)(b)(c)(d)</td></tr>
<tr><td>17. A - (p)(q)(r)(s)(t); B - (p)(q)(r)(s)(t); C - (p)(q)(r)(s)(t); D - (p)(q)(r)(s)(t)</td></tr>
<tr><td>18. (a)(b)(c)(d)</td></tr>
</table>

*Space for Rough Work*

**19.** **Statement-1 :** The equation $|\sin x| + |\cos x| = \dfrac{\sqrt{3}}{2}$ has no real solution.

**Statement-2 :** For all real x, $|\sin x| + |\cos x| \le \sqrt{2}$ .

---

## Section - VI - Integer Type

This section contains 5 questions. The answer to each of the questions is a single digit integer ranging from 0 to 9.

---

**20.** Sum of all the solutions in $[0, 4\pi]$ of the equation

$\tan x + \cot x + 1 = \cos\left(x + \dfrac{\pi}{4}\right)$ is $k\pi$ then find the value of

$2k$.

**21.** Find the number of real solutions of
$\sin 3\theta = 4 \sin \theta \, \sin 2\theta \, \sin 4\theta,\ 0 \le \theta \le \pi$

**22.** If $\sin x + \sin 5x = \sin 2x + \sin 4x$ where $n \in I$ then find the value of $\dfrac{9x}{n\pi}$ .

**23.** Find the number of roots of the equation

$\cos^2 x + \dfrac{\sqrt{3}+1}{2}\sin x - \dfrac{\sqrt{3}}{4} - 1 = 0$ which lie in the interval $[-\pi, \pi]$.

**24.** Find the number of solutions of the equation
$\tan x + \sec x = 2\cos x$ lying in the interval $[0, 2\pi]$.

| | | |
|---|---|---|
| **RESPONSE GRID** | 19. ⓐ ⓑ ⓒ ⓓ | 20. ⓪①②③④⑤⑥⑦⑧⑨ |
| | 21. ⓪①②③④⑤⑥⑦⑧⑨ | 22. ⓪①②③④⑤⑥⑦⑧⑨ |
| | 23. ⓪①②③④⑤⑥⑦⑧⑨ | 24. ⓪①②③④⑤⑥⑦⑧⑨ |

| DAILY PRACTICE PROBLEM DPP 23 - MATHS | | | |
|---|---|---|---|
| Total Questions | 24 | Total Marks | 72 |
| Attempted | | Correct | |
| Incorrect | | Net Score | |
| Cut-off Score | 14 | Qualifying Score | 47 |
| Success Gap = Net Score – Qualifying Score | | | |

$$\text{Net Score} = \sum_{i=1}^{VI}\left[(\text{correct}_i \times MM_i) - (In_i - NM_i)\right]$$

---

*Space for Rough Work*

# DPP - Daily Practice Problems

Name :             Date :

Start Time :             End Time :

## MATHEMATICS    M24

**SYLLABUS : Properties of Triangles:** Relation between sides and angles, Solutions of triangles, Circle connected with triangle

## Max. Marks : 75          Time : 60 min.

### GENERAL INSTRUCTIONS

- The Daily Practice Problem Sheet contains **24** Questions divided into 6 sections.
  Section I has **8** MCQ's with ONLY 1 correct option. 2 marks for correct answer and No negative marks.
  Section II has **4** MCQ's with 1 or MORE THAN 1 correct option. 4 marks for correct answer(s) and (–1) for wrong answer.
  Section III has **1** PASSAGE with **3** MCQ's with ONLY 1 correct option. 3 marks for correct and (–1) mark for wrong answer.
  Section IV has **2** MCQ's with multiple matchings. 1 mark for the correct matching of each row & No negative marks.
  Section V has **2** Assertion-Reason MCQ's with ONLY 1 correct option. 3 marks for correct and (–1) mark for wrong answer.
  Section VI has **5** single digit integer answer questions. 4 marks for correct answer and (–1) for wrong answer.
- No mark will be given/ deducted if no bubble is filled. Keep a timer in front and stop immediately at the end of 60 min.
- You have to evaluate your Response Grids yourself with the help of Solution Booklet.
- The sheet follows a particular syllabus. Do not attempt the sheet before you have completed your preparation for that syllabus. Refer syllabus sheet in the starting of the book for the syllabus of all the DPP sheets.
- After completing the sheet check your answers with the solution booklet and complete the Result Grid. Finally spend time to analyse your performance and revise the areas which emerge out as weak in your evaluation.

## Section - I - Straight Objective Type

This section contains 8 multiple choice questions. Each question has 4 choices (a), (b), (c) and (d), out of which **ONLY ONE** is correct.

**1.** The triangle ABC, right angled at C, has median AD, BE and CF. AD lies along the line $y = x + 3$, BE lies along the line $y = 2x + 4$. If the length of the hypotenuse is 60, the area of the triangle ABC is
(a) 400 sq. unit     (b) 600 sq. unit
(c) 300 sq.unit     (d) 200 sq.unit

**2.** If x, y and z are the distances of incentre from the vertices of the triangle ABC respectively then $\dfrac{abc}{xyz}$ is equal to
(a) $\prod \tan \dfrac{A}{2}$      (b) $\sum \cot \dfrac{A}{2}$
(c) $\sum \tan \dfrac{A}{2}$      (d) $\sum \sin \dfrac{A}{2}$

**3.** If 'O' is the circumcentre of the $\Delta$ ABC and $R_1$, $R_2$ and $R_3$ are the radii of the circumcircles of triangles OBC, OCA and OAB respectively then $\dfrac{a}{R_1} + \dfrac{b}{R_2} + \dfrac{c}{R_3}$ has the value equal to:
(a) $\dfrac{abc}{2R^3}$    (b) $\dfrac{R^3}{abc}$    (c) $\dfrac{4\Delta}{R^2}$    (d) $\dfrac{\Delta}{4R^2}$

**4.** In a $\Delta ABC$, $a = a_1 = 2$ , $b = a_2$ , $c = a_3$ such that $a_{p+1} = \dfrac{5^p}{3^{2-p}} a_p \left( 2^{2-p} - \dfrac{4p-2}{5^p} a_p \right)$ where $p = 1,2$ then
(a) $r_1 = r_2$    (b) $r_3 = 2r_1$    (c) $r_2 = 2r_1$    (d) $r_2 = 3r_1$

**5.** In a triangle ABC, if tan (A/2) = 5/6 and tan (B/2) = $\dfrac{20}{37}$ , the sides a, b and c are in
(a) A.P.    (b) G.P.    (c) H.P    (d) none of these

---

**RESPONSE GRID**    1.    2.    3. ⓐⓑⓒⓓ   4. ⓐⓑⓒⓓ   5. 

**6.** The area ($\Delta$) and angle $\theta$ of a triangle are given, when the side opposite to the given angle is minimum, then the length of the remaining two sides are

(a) $\sqrt{\dfrac{2\Delta}{\sin\theta}},\sqrt{\dfrac{3\Delta}{\sin\theta}}$ 　　(b) $\sqrt{\dfrac{2\Delta}{\sin\theta}},\sqrt{\dfrac{2\Delta}{\sin\theta}}$

(c) $\sqrt{\dfrac{4\Delta}{\sin\theta}},\sqrt{\dfrac{2\Delta}{\sin\theta}}$ 　　(d) $\sqrt{\dfrac{6\Delta}{\sin\theta}},\sqrt{\dfrac{6\Delta}{\sin\theta}}$

**7.** If O is a point inside the triangle ABC such that $\angle OBC = \dfrac{A}{2}, \angle OCA = \dfrac{B}{2}, \angle OAB = \dfrac{C}{2}$ then

$$\frac{\sin(A-C/2)\sin(B-A/2)\sin(C-B/2)}{\sin A/2\,\sin B/2\,\sin C/2}$$ is equal to

(a) $\cos A/2 \cos B/2 \cos C/2$ 　(b) $\sin A \sin B \sin C$
(c) $1$ 　　　　　　　　　　　　(d) $\cos A \cos B \cos C$

**8.** The angles of a triangle ABC are in A.P. The largest angle is twice the smallest and the median to the largest side divides the angle at the vertex in the ratio 2 : 3. If the length of the median is $2\sqrt{3}$ cm, then the length of the largest side is

(a) $2\cos 42°$ 　(b) $4\sin 32°$ 　(c) $8\sin 42°$ 　(d) $8 \cos 42°$

## Section - II - Multiple Correct Answer Type

This section contains 4 multiple correct answer(s) type questions. Each question has 4 choices (a), (b), (c) and (d), out of which **ONE OR MORE** is/are correct.

**9.** Which of the following statements are correct ?
(a) With usual notations in a triangle ABC, if $r_1 = 2r_2 = 2r_3$ then $4b = 3a$
(b) If in a triangle $\sin A : \sin C = \sin(A-B) : \sin(B-C)$ then $a^2 : b^2 : c^2$ are in A.P.
(c) If $\cos A + \cos B + 2\cos C = 2$ then the sides of the $\Delta ABC$ are in A.P.
(d) In a $\Delta ABC$, a semicircle is inscribed, whose diameter lies on the side AB. Then the radius of the semicircle is $\dfrac{2\Delta}{a+b}$ where $\Delta$ is the area of the triangle ABC.

**10.** Which of the following statements are correct ?
(a) The medians of a $\Delta$ ABC are 9 cm, 12 cm and 15 cm respectively . Then the area of the triangle is 72 sq cm
(b) A point P is situated inside an angle of measure $60°$ at a distance x and y from its sides. The distance of the point P from the vertex of the given angle is $\dfrac{2}{\sqrt{3}}\sqrt{x^2+y^2+xy}$
(c) The medians of a $\Delta$ ABC are 10 cm, 15 cm and 9 cm respectively then the area of the triangle is 72 sq cm
(d) A point P is situated inside an angle of measure $60°$ at a distance x and y from its sides. The distance of the point P from the vertex of the given angle is $\dfrac{2}{3}\sqrt{x^3+y^2+xy}$

**11.** In $\Delta ABC$, internal angle bisector of $\angle A$ meets side BC in D. $DE \perp AD$ meets AC in E and AB in F, then
(a) AE is H.M of b & c 　(b) $AD = \dfrac{2bc}{b+c}\cos\dfrac{A}{2}$
(c) $EF = \dfrac{4bc}{b+c}\sin\dfrac{A}{2}$ 　(d) $\Delta AEF$ is isosceles

**12.** In a $\Delta$ ABC, if D is the mid point of BC and AD is perpendicular to AC, then
(a) $\cos A = -\dfrac{b}{c}$ 　　　(b) $\cos A \cos C = -\dfrac{2b^2}{ac}$
(c) $\cos B = \dfrac{b^2+c^2}{bc}$ 　(d) $a^2 - 3b^2 - c^2 = 0$

## Section - III - Linked Comprehension Type

This section contains one paragraph. Based upon the paragraph, 3 multiple choice questions have to be answered. Each question has 4 choices (a), (b), (c) and (d), out of which **ONLY ONE** is correct.

Consider a triangle ABC, where x , y, z are the length of perpendicular drawn from the vertices of the triangle to the opposite sides whose



*Space for Rough Work*

length are a, b, c respectively. Let the letters R, r, S, $\Delta$ denote the circumradius, inradius, semiperimeter and area of the triangle respectively.

13. If $\dfrac{bx}{c} + \dfrac{cy}{a} + \dfrac{az}{b} = \dfrac{a^2 + b^2 + c^2}{k}$, then the value of k is

    (a) R         (b) S     (c) 2R     (d) (3/2)R

14. If $\cot A + \cot B + \cot C = k\left(\dfrac{1}{x^2} + \dfrac{1}{y^2} + \dfrac{1}{z^2}\right)$, then the value of

    k is

    (a) $R^2$     (b) $rR$     (c) $\Delta$     (d) $a^2 + b^2 + c^2$

15. The value of

    $\dfrac{c\sin B + b\sin C}{x} + \dfrac{a\sin C + c\sin A}{y} + \dfrac{b\sin A + a\sin B}{z}$ is equal to

    (a) R/r     (b) S/R     (c) 2     (d) 6

### Section - IV - Matrix-Match Type

This section contains 2 questions. It contains statements given in two columns, which have to be matched. Statements in Column I are labelled as A, B, C and D whereas statements in Column II are labelled as p, q, r and s. The answers to these questions have to be appropriately bubbled as illustrated in the following example. If the correct matches are A-p, A-r, B-p, B-s, C-r, C-s and D-q, then the correctly bubbled matrix will look like the following :

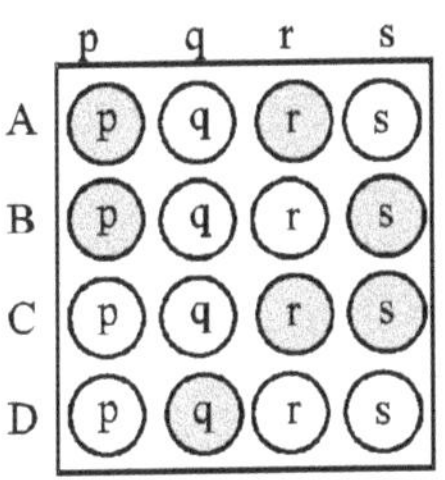

16. Match the following column I with column II. All the notations have usual meanings.

    **Column I**         **Column II**

    (A) The radius of the circle passing   (p) 3r
        through the centre of the incircle
        of $\Delta$ ABC and through the
        end points of BC is given by

    (B) If in the $\Delta$ ABC, $r_1 = 2r_2 = 3r_3$,   (q) $r^2$
        D is the mid point of BC, then
        $\cos(\angle ADC)$ is equal to

    (C) The harmonic mean of the   (r) $\dfrac{a}{2}\sec\dfrac{A}{2}$
        exradii of a triangle is equal to

    (D) If the distances of the vertices   (s) $-\dfrac{7}{25}$
        of a triangle from the nearest
        points of contact of the incircle
        with the sides be $\alpha$, $\beta$,
        $\gamma$ respectively, then $\dfrac{\alpha\beta\gamma}{\alpha + \beta + \gamma}$.

17. Match the column –

    **Column I**         **Column II**

    (A) If A, B, C are angles of acute   (p) 16
        angled triangle, then minimum
        value of $\tan^4 A + \tan^4 B + \tan^4 C$ is

    (B) If A, B, C are angles of   (q) $3\sqrt{3}$
        any $\Delta ABC$, the minimum
        value of $\left(\cot\dfrac{A}{2}\cot\dfrac{B}{2}\cot\dfrac{C}{2}\right)$ is

    (C) If A, B, C are angles of a triangle   (r) 4
        such that tan A tan C = 2 & tan B
        tan C = 18, then value of $\tan^2 C$ is

    (D) The maximum value of   (s) 27
        $1 + \sin\left(\dfrac{\pi}{4} + \theta\right) + 2\cos\left(\dfrac{\pi}{4} - \theta\right)$,
        where $\theta \in R$ is

### Section - V - Reasoning Type

This section contains 2 reasoning type questions. Each question has 4 choices (a), (b), (c) and (d) out of which **ONLY ONE** is correct.

---

**RESPONSE GRID**

13. (a)(b)(c)(d)

14. (a)(b)(c)(d)

15. (a)(b)(c)(d)

16. A - (p)(q)(r)(s); B - (p)(q)(r)(s); C - (p)(q)(r)(s); D - (p)(q)(r)(s)

17. A - (p)(q)(r)(s); B - (p)(q)(r)(s); C - (p)(q)(r)(s); D - (p)(q)(r)(s)

*Space for Rough Work*

**DIRECTIONS for (Qs 18 -19 ): Each of these questions contains two statements: Statement-1 (Assertion) and Statement-2 (Reason). Each of these questions has four alternative choices, only one of which is the correct answer. You have to select the correct choice.**

(a) Statement-1 is True, Statement-2 is True; Statement-2 is a correct explanation for Statement-1.

(b) Statement-1 is True, Statement-2 is True; Statement-2 is NOT a correct explanation for Statement-1.

(c) Statement -1 is True, Statement-2 is False.

(d) Statement -1 is False, Statement-2 is True.

18. **Statement-1 :** If the lengths of the sides of a triangle are in A.P. as well as in G.P. then R = 2r.

   **Statement-2 :** In an equilateral triangle R = 2r. Where R and r are the radius of circumcircle and incircle of the triangle respectively.

19. Let in a triangle ABC, the line joining orthocentre and circumcentre be parallel to the side BC.

   **Statement-1 :** tan A, tan B, tan C are in A.P.

   **Statement-2 :** If tan A, tan B, tan C are in A.P., then tan A tan C = 3.

## Section - VI - Integer Type

This section contains 5 questions. The answer to each of the questions is a single digit integer ranging from 0 to 9.

20. In $\triangle ABC$, a = 4 ; b = 3 ; medians AD and BE are mutually perpendicular, then find the value of $c^2$.

21. In triangle ABC, max $\{\angle A, \angle B\} = \angle C + 30°$ and

   $$\frac{R}{r} = \sqrt{3} + 1,$$ where R is the radius of the circumcircle and r is the radius of the incircle of $\triangle ABC$, then find the value of $\frac{1}{10} \angle C$ in degrees.

22. Triangle ABC is isosceles with AB = AC and BC = 65 cm. P is a point on BC such that the perpendicular distances from P of AB and AC are 24 cm and 36 cm respectively. Find the $\left(\frac{1}{2535}\right)^{th}$ part of the area of triangle ABC in sq. cm.

23. Line $\ell$ is a tangent to a unit circle S at a point P. Point A and the circle S are on the same side of $\ell$, and the distance from A to $\ell$ is 3. Two tangents from point A intersect line $\ell$ at the point B and C respectively. Find the value of (PB) (PC).

24. A triangle is inscribed in a circle. The vertices of the triangle divide the circle into three arcs of length 3, 4 and 5 units, if area of the triangle be $x$, then find the value of $\frac{\pi^2}{\sqrt{3}(1+\sqrt{3})} x$.

| RESPONSE GRID | | |
|---|---|---|
| 18. (a)(b)(c)(d) | 19. (a)(b)(c)(d) | 20. ⓪①②③④⑤⑥⑦⑧⑨ |
| 21. ⓪①②③④⑤⑥⑦⑧⑨ | | 22. ⓪①②③④⑤⑥⑦⑧⑨ |
| 23. ⓪①②③④⑤⑥⑦⑧⑨ | | 24. ⓪①②③④⑤⑥⑦⑧⑨ |

## DAILY PRACTICE PROBLEM DPP 24 - MATHS

| Total Questions | 24 | Total Marks | 75 |
|---|---|---|---|
| Attempted | | Correct | |
| Incorrect | | Net Score | |
| Cut-off Score | 15 | Qualifying Score | 49 |
| Success Gap = Net Score – Qualifying Score | | | |

$$\text{Net Score} = \sum_{i=I}^{VI} \left[ (\text{correct}_i \times MM_i) - (In_i - NM_i) \right]$$

*Space for Rough Work*

**Name :**

**Date :**

**Start Time :**

**End Time :**

# MATHEMATICS · M25

**SYLLABUS** : LIMITS

**Max. Marks : 69**

**Time : 60 min.**

## GENERAL INSTRUCTIONS

- The Daily Practice Problem Sheet contains **22** Questions divided into 6 sections.
  Section I has **7** MCQ's with ONLY 1 correct option. 2 marks for correct answer and No negative marks.
  Section II has **3** MCQ's with 1 or MORE THAN 1 correct option. 4 marks for correct answer(s) and (–1) for wrong answer.
  Section III has **1** PASSAGE with **3** MCQ's with ONLY 1 correct option. 3 marks for correct and (–1) mark for wrong answer.
  Section IV has **2** MCQ's with multiple matchings. 1 mark for the correct matching of each row & No negative marks.
  Section V has **2** Assertion-Reason MCQ's with ONLY 1 correct option. 3 marks for correct and (–1) mark for wrong answer.
  Section VI has **5** single digit integer answer questions. 4 marks for correct answer and (–1) for wrong answer.
- No mark will be given/ deducted if no bubble is filled. Keep a timer in front and stop immediately at the end of 60 min.
- You have to evaluate your Response Grids yourself with the help of Solution Booklet.
- The sheet follows a particular syllabus. Do not attempt the sheet before you have completed your preparation for that syllabus. Refer syllabus sheet in the starting of the book for the syllabus of all the DPP sheets.
- After completing the sheet check your answers with the solution booklet and complete the Result Grid. Finally spend time to analyse your performance and revise the areas which emerge out as weak in your evaluation.

## Section - I - Straight Objective Type

This section contains 7 multiple choice questions. Each question has 4 choices (a), (b), (c) and (d), out of which **ONLY ONE** is correct.

**1** Let $\lim\limits_{x \to 1} \dfrac{[x]}{x} = \ell$ and $\lim\limits_{x \to 1} \dfrac{x}{[x]} = m$ where [ ] denotes the greatest integer function, then
(a) $\ell$ exist but m does not exist
(b) m exist but $\ell$ does not exist
(c) $\ell$ and m both exist
(d) neither $\ell$ nor m exist

**2.** If m, n are positive integers then
$$\lim\limits_{x \to 0} \frac{(\cos x)^{1/m} - (\cos x)^{1/n}}{x^2} =$$
(a) $m - n$
(b) $\dfrac{1}{n} \quad \dfrac{1}{m}$
(c) $\dfrac{m - n}{2mn}$
(d) None of these

**3.** If $\lim\limits_{x \to 0} (x^{-3} \sin 3x + ax^{-2} + b)$ exists and is equal to zero then :
(a) $a = -3$ & $b = 9/2$
(b) $a = 3$ & $b = 9/2$
(c) $a = -3$ & $b = -9/2$
(d) $a = 3$ & $b = -9/2$

**4.** $\lim\limits_{n \to \infty} n\left( \left( \dfrac{n}{n+1} \right)^{\alpha} + \sin\dfrac{1}{n} - 1 \right)$ when $\alpha \in Q$, is equal to
(a) $e^{-\alpha}$
(b) $-\alpha$
(c) $e^{1-\alpha}$
(d) $e^{1+\alpha}$

**5.** Let $f : R \to R$ be such that $f(1) = 3$ and $f'(1) = 6$. Then
$$\lim\limits_{x \to 0} \left( \frac{f(1+x)}{f(1)} \right)^{1/x} \text{ equals}$$
(a) 1
(b) $e^{1/2}$
(c) $e^2$
(d) $e^3$

| RESPONSE GRID | 1. ⓐⓑⓒⓓ | 2. ⓐⓑⓒⓓ | 3. ⓐⓑⓒⓓ | 4. ⓐⓑⓒⓓ | 5. ⓐⓑⓒⓓ |
|---|---|---|---|---|---|

**6.** $\lim\limits_{h \to 0} \dfrac{f(2h+2+h^2)-f(2)}{f(h-h^2+1)-f(1)}$, given that $f'(2)=6$ and $f'(1)=4$

   (a)  does not exist      (b)  is equal to $-3/2$
   (c)  is equal to $3/2$      (d)  is equal to $3$

**7.** The value of $\lim\limits_{x \to \infty} \left( \dfrac{x^2+5x+3}{x^2+x+2} \right)^x$ is

   (a)  $e^2$    (b)  $e^3$    (c)  $e^4$    (d)  $1$

## Section - II - Multiple Correct Answer Type

This section contains 3 multiple correct answer(s) type questions. Each question has 4 choices (a), (b), (c) and (d), out of which **ONE OR MORE** is/are correct.

**8.** If $\lim\limits_{x \to 0} (1+ax+bx^2)^{2/x}=e^3$, then

   (a)  $a=3, b=0$      (b)  $a=\dfrac{3}{2}, b=1$

   (c)  $a=\dfrac{3}{2}, b=4$      (d)  $a=2, b=3$

**9.** $\lim\limits_{x \to 0} \left[ m\dfrac{\sin x}{x} \right] = $ ($m \in I$ and $[\,]$ denotes greatest integer function)

   (a)  $m$, if $m \le 0$      (b)  $m-1$, if $m>0$
   (c)  $m-1$, if $m<0$      (d)  $m$, if $m>0$

**10.** $f(x)$ be a real valued function such that

$$f(x)=\begin{cases} \dfrac{\tan^2 x}{(x^2-[x])^2}, & \text{for } x>0 \\ 1, & \text{for } x=0 \\ \sqrt{\{x\}\cot\{x\}}, & \text{for } x<0 \end{cases}$$

where, $[x]$ is the integral part and $\{x\}$ is the fractional part of $x$, then

   (a)  $\lim\limits_{x \to 0} f(x)=1$      (b)  $\lim\limits_{x \to 0^-} f(x)=\sqrt{\cot 1}$

   (c)  $\cot^{-1}\left( \lim\limits_{x \to 0^-} f(x) \right)^2 = 1$    (d)  none of these

## Section - III - Linked Comprehension Type

This section contains one paragraph. Based upon the paragraph, 3 multiple choice questions have to be answered. Each question has 4 choices (a), (b), (c) and (d), out of which **ONLY ONE** is correct.

If $\lim\limits_{x \to a} f(x) = \lim\limits_{x \to a} g(x)=0$ such that $\lim\limits_{x \to a} \dfrac{f(x)}{g(x)}$ exists, then

$$\lim\limits_{x \to a} \{1+f(x)\}^{1/g(x)} = e^{\lim\limits_{x \to a} \frac{f(x)}{g(x)}}$$

**11.** $\lim\limits_{x \to \infty} \left( 1+\dfrac{2}{x} \right)^x$

   (a)  $e^2$    (b)  $1/e^2$    (c)  $e$    (d)  $1/e$

**12.** $\lim\limits_{x \to 0} (1+\sin x)^{2\cot x}$

   (a)  $1/e^2$    (b)  $e^2$    (c)  $e$    (d)  $1/e$

**13.** $\lim\limits_{x \to 1} (\log_3 3x)^{\log_x 3}$

   (a)  $e^2$    (b)  $1/e^2$    (c)  $e$    (d)  $1/e$

## Section - IV - Matrix-Match Type

This section contains 2 questions. It contains statements given in two columns, which have to be matched. Statements in Column I are labelled as A, B, C and D whereas statements in Column II are labelled as p, q, r and s. The answers to these questions have to be appropriately bubbled as illustrated in the following example. If the correct matches are A-p, A-r, B-p, B-s, C-r, C-s and D-q, then the correctly bubbled matrix will look like the following :

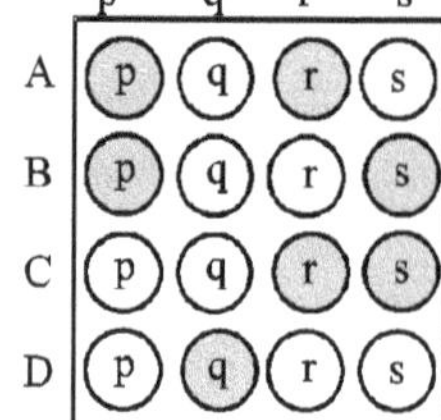



*Space for Rough Work*

**14.**

| Column I | Column II |
|---|---|
| (A) If $f(a) = 2$, $f'(a) = 1$, $g(a) = -1$, $g'(a) = 2$, then the value of $$\lim_{x \to a} \frac{g(x)f(a) - g(a)f(x)}{x - a}$$ is | (p) $(-1)^{k-1}(k-1)\pi$ |
| (B) The left-hand derivative of $f(x) = [x]\sin(\pi x)$ at $x = k$, $k$ is an integer, is | (q) 5 |
| (C) The value of $$\lim_{n \to \infty} \cos\left(\frac{x}{2}\right)\cos\left(\frac{x}{4}\right)\cos\left(\frac{x}{8}\right)\ldots\cos\left(\frac{x}{2^n}\right)$$ is | (r) $-\dfrac{3}{4}$ if n is even |
| (D) $\lim\limits_{n \to \infty} \dfrac{-3n + (-1)^n}{4n - (-1)^n}$ is | (s) $-\dfrac{3}{4}$ if n is odd |
|  | (t) $\dfrac{\sin x}{x}$ |

**15.**

| Column I | Coulmn II |
|---|---|
| (A) $\lim\limits_{x \to \infty} x\cos\dfrac{\pi}{8x} \cdot \sin\dfrac{\pi}{8x} =$ | (p) $\dfrac{\pi}{8}$ |
| (B) $\lim\limits_{x \to \infty} \dfrac{\tan[-\pi^2]x^2 - [-\pi^2]x^2}{\sin^2(x)} =$ | (q) $\dfrac{8}{\pi}$ |
| (C) $\lim\limits_{x \to \infty} \sqrt{\dfrac{2x - \sin x + \cos x}{x + \cos^2 x + \sin^2 x}} =$ | (r) $e^{\frac{n-1}{2}}$ |
| (D) $\lim\limits_{x \to \infty}\left(\dfrac{x^n - 1}{n(x-1)}\right)^{\frac{1}{x-1}} =$ | (s) 0 |
|  | (t) $\sqrt{2}$ |

## Section - V - Reasoning Type

This section contains 2 reasoning type questions. Each question has 4 choices (a), (b), (c) and (d) out of which **ONLY ONE** is correct.

**DIRECTIONS for Qs (16 -17) : Each of these questions contains two statements: Statement-1 (Assertion) and Statement-2 (Reason). Each of these questions has four alternative choices, only one of which is the correct answer. You have to select the correct choice.**

(a) Statement-1 is True, Statement-2 is True; Statement-2 is a correct explanation for Statement-1.

(b) Statement-1 is True, Statement-2 is True; Statement-2 is NOT a correct explanation for Statement-1.

(c) Statement -1 is True, Statement-2 is False.

(d) Statement -1 is False, Statement-2 is True.

**16. Statement–1 :** $\lim\limits_{x \to 0} \cos^{-1}(\cos^2 x)$ does not exist.

**Statement–2 :** $\operatorname{cosec}^{-1}x$ is well defined for $|x| \geq 1$.

**17. Statement-1 :** $\lim\limits_{x \to 0} \dfrac{\sqrt{1 - \cos 2x}}{x}$ does not exists.

**Statement-2 :** $|\sin x| = \begin{cases} \sin x, & 0 < x < \dfrac{x}{2} \\ -\sin x, & -\dfrac{\pi}{2} < x < 0 \end{cases}$

## Section - VI - Integer Type

This section contains 5 questions. The answer to each of the questions is a single digit integer ranging from 0 to 9.

**18.** For $n \in N$, let $x_n$ be defined as $\left(1 + \dfrac{1}{n}\right)^{n + x_n} = e$, then

$$\lim_{n \to \infty} x_n = \frac{A}{B}. \text{ Find the value of } A + B.$$

<table>
<tr><td rowspan="3">**RESPONSE GRID**</td><td>14. A - (p)(q)(r)(s)(t); B - (p)(q)(r)(s)(t); C - (p)(q)(r)(s)(t); D - (p)(q)(r)(s)(t)</td></tr>
<tr><td>15. A - (p)(q)(r)(s)(t); B - (p)(q)(r)(s)(t); C - (p)(q)(r)(s)(t); D - (p)(q)(r)(s)(t)</td></tr>
<tr><td>16. (a)(b)(c)(d)    17. (a)(b)(c)(d)    18. (0)(1)(2)(3)(4)(5)(6)(7)(8)(9)</td></tr>
</table>

*Space for Rough Work*

**19.** Let $\lim\limits_{n\to\infty}\left(\dfrac{1}{2n+1}+\dfrac{1}{2n+3}+\dfrac{1}{2n+5}+.....+\dfrac{1}{4n-1}\right)=\dfrac{A}{B}\log C,$ where $A,\,B,\,C\in N$ then find the value of $A+B+C.$

**20.** If $\lim\limits_{x\to\infty}\dfrac{a\,(2x^3-x^2)+b\,(x^3+5x^2-1)-c\,(3x^3+x^2)}{a\,(5x^4-x)-bx^4+c\,(4x^4+1)+2x^2+5x}=1,$ then the value of $(a+b+c)$ can be expressed in the lowest form as $\dfrac{p}{q}$. Then find the value of $\dfrac{q-p}{17}.$

**21.** Find the value of $\lim\limits_{x\to\infty}\dfrac{\cot^{-1}\left(x^{-a}\,\log_a x\right)}{\sec^{-1}\left(a^x\,\log_x a\right)}$ (given $a>1$).

**22.** Let $f\,(x)$ be a function such that $\lim\limits_{x\to0}\dfrac{f(x)}{x}=1$ and $\lim\limits_{x\to0}\dfrac{x(1+a\cos x)-b\sin x}{\{f(x)\}^3}=1,$ then find the value of $b-3a.$

---

| RESPONSE GRID | | |
|---|---|---|
| **19.** ⓪①②③④⑤⑥⑦⑧⑨ | | **20.** ⓪①②③④⑤⑥⑦⑧⑨ |
| **21.** ⓪①②③④⑤⑥⑦⑧⑨ | | **22.** ⓪①②③④⑤⑥⑦⑧⑨ |

---

| DAILY PRACTICE PROBLEM DPP 25 - MATHS | | | |
|---|---|---|---|
| Total Questions | 22 | Total Marks | 69 |
| Attempted | | Correct | |
| Incorrect | | Net Score | |
| Cut-off Score | 14 | Qualifying Score | 45 |
| Success Gap = Net Score – Qualifying Score | | | |

$$\text{Net Score}=\sum_{i=1}^{VI}\left[(\text{correct}_i\times MM_i)-(In_i-NM_i)\right]$$

---

*Space for Rough Work*

**Name :**

**Date :**

**Start Time :**

**End Time :**

## MATHEMATICS  M26

**SYLLABUS : Height and Distances :** Problems of plane figures, Problems of heights and distances of figure in three dimensions.

**Max. Marks : 58**

**Time : 60 min.**

### GENERAL INSTRUCTIONS

- The Daily Practice Problem Sheet contains **24** Questions divided into 2 sections.
  Section I has **19** MCQ's with ONLY 1 correct option. 2 marks for correct answer and No negative marks.
  Section II has **5** single digit integer answer questions. 4 marks for correct answer and (–1) for wrong answer.
- No mark will be given/ deducted if no bubble is filled. Keep a timer in front and stop immediately at the end of 60 min.
- You have to evaluate your Response Grids yourself with the help of Solution Booklet.
- The sheet follows a particular syllabus. Do not attempt the sheet before you have completed your preparation for that syllabus. Refer syllabus sheet in the starting of the book for the syllabus of all the DPP sheets.
- After completing the sheet check your answers with the solution booklet and complete the Result Grid. Finally spend time to analyse your performance and revise the areas which emerge out as weak in your evaluation.

### Section - I - Straight Objective Type

This section contains 19 multiple choice questions. Each question has 4 choices (a), (b), (c) and (d), out of which **ONLY ONE** is correct.

**1.** The angle of elevation of a stationary cloud from a point 2500m above a lake is $15°$ and the angle of depression of its reflection in the lake is $45°$. The height of cloud above the lake level is

(a) $2500\sqrt{3}$ metres     (b) $2500$ metres

(c) $500\sqrt{3}$ metres     (d) $500$ metres

**2.** ABC is a triangular park with AB = AC = 100m. A television tower stands at the midpoint of BC. The angle of elevation of the top of the tower at A, B and C are $45°$ each, then the height of the tower is

(a) $60$m     (b) $50\sqrt{2}$ m

(c) $100\sqrt{3}$ m     (d) $50$m

**3.** From the bottom of a pole of height h, the angle of elevation of the top of a tower is $\alpha$. The pole subtends an angle $\beta$ at the top of a tower. The height of the tower is

(a) $\dfrac{h\sin\alpha\cos(\alpha+\beta)}{\cos\beta}$     (b) $\dfrac{h\sin\alpha\cos(\alpha-\beta)}{\sin\beta}$

(c) $\dfrac{h\sin\alpha\sin(\alpha+\beta)}{\cos\beta}$     (d) $\dfrac{h\sin\alpha\sin(\alpha-\beta)}{\sin\beta}$

**4.** AB is a vertical pole. The end A is on the level ground, C is the middle point of AB and P is a point on the level ground. The portion CB subtends an angle $\beta$ at P. If AP = nAB, then $\tan\beta$ is equal to

(a) $\dfrac{n}{2n^2+1}$     (b) $\dfrac{n}{n^2-1}$

(c) $\dfrac{n}{n^2+1}$     (d) None of these

---

**RESPONSE GRID**    1. ⓐⓑ©ⓓ    2. ⓐⓑ©ⓓ    3. ⓐⓑ©ⓓ    4. ⓐⓑ©ⓓ

**5.** A flagstaff stands in the centre of a rectangular field whose diagonal is 1200 m, and subtends angles 15° and 45° at the mid points of the sides of the field. The height of the flagstaff is

(a) 200 m

(b) $300\sqrt{2+\sqrt{3}}$ m

(c) $300\sqrt{2-\sqrt{3}}$ m

(d) 400 m

**6.** A ladder rests against a wall at an angle $\alpha$ to the horizontal. Its foot is pulled away from the wall through a distance a, so that it slides a distance b down the wall making an angle $\beta$ with the horizontal. Then the value of a is

(a) b

(b) $b\tan\dfrac{\alpha+\beta}{2}$

(c) $b\tan\dfrac{\alpha-\beta}{2}$

(d) $b\tan\left(\dfrac{\alpha-\beta}{\alpha+\beta}\right)$

**7.** A right circular cylindrical tower of height h and radius r stands on a horizontal plane. Let A be a point in the horizontal plane and PQR be the semi-circular edge of the top of the tower such that Q is the point in it nearest to A. The angles of elevation of the points P and Q are 45° and 60° respectively. Then

(a) $\dfrac{h}{r}=\dfrac{\sqrt{3}(1+\sqrt{5})}{2}$

(b) $\dfrac{h}{r}=\dfrac{2}{\sqrt{3}\left(1+\sqrt{5}\right)}$

(c) $\dfrac{h}{r}=\dfrac{\sqrt{3}\left(1-\sqrt{5}\right)}{2}$

(d) None of these

**8.** A pole stands vertically on the centre of a square field. When $\alpha$ is the elevation of the sun its shadow just reaches the side of the square field and is at a distance x and y from the ends of that side. Then the height of the pole is

(a) $\sqrt{\dfrac{x^2+y^2}{2}}\tan\alpha$

(b) $\sqrt{\dfrac{x^2-y^2}{2}}\tan\alpha$

(c) $\dfrac{\sqrt{x^2+y^2}}{2}\tan\alpha$

(d) $\dfrac{\sqrt{x^2-y^2}}{2}\tan\alpha$

**9.** ABC is a triangular park with all sides equal. If a pillar at A subtends an angle of 45° at C, then the angle of elevation of the pillar at D, the middle point of BC, is

(a) $\tan^{-1}(\sqrt{3}/2)$

(b) $\tan^{-1}(2/\sqrt{3})$

(c) $\cot^{-1}(3)$

(d) $\tan^{-1}(3)$

**10.** A man observes a balloon in the east at an elevation of 60° and moving towards north-west direction. On walking 400 m towards the north he finds the balloon just above him. If the balloon always remains in the same horizontal plane, the height of the balloon above the man is

(a) 400 m

(b) $400\sqrt{2}$ m

(c) $400\sqrt{3}$ m

(d) none of these

**11.** A tower stands at the centre of a circular park. A and B are two points on the boundary of the park such that AB (= a) subtends an angle of 60° at the foot of the tower, and the angle of elevation of the top of the tower from A or B is 30°. The height of the tower is

(a) $a/\sqrt{3}$

(b) $a\sqrt{3}$

(c) $2a/\sqrt{3}$

(d) $2a\sqrt{3}$.

**12.** The length of the shadow of a pole inclined at 10° to the vertical towards the sun is 2.05 meters, when the elevation of the sun is 38°. The length of the pole is

(a) $\dfrac{2.05\sin 38°}{\sin 42°}$

(b) $\dfrac{2.05\sin 42°}{\sin 38°}$

(c) $\dfrac{2.05\cos 38°}{\sin 42°}$

(d) None of these

<table>
<tr><td rowspan="2">**RESPONSE GRID**</td><td>5. ⓐⓑⓒⓓ</td><td>6. ⓐⓑⓒⓓ</td><td>7. ⓐⓑⓒⓓ</td><td>8. ⓐⓑⓒⓓ</td><td>9. ⓐⓑⓒⓓ</td></tr>
<tr><td>10. ⓐⓑⓒⓓ</td><td>11. ⓐⓑⓒⓓ</td><td>12. ⓐⓑⓒⓓ</td><td></td><td></td></tr>
</table>

*Space for Rough Work*

**13.** The extremity of the shadow of a flagstaff which is 6m high and stands on the top of a pyramid on a square base, just reaches the side of the base and is distant 56 and 8 m respectively from the extremities of that side. Then the sun's altitude, if the height of the pyramid be 34 metres, is

(a)   $30°$

(b)   $60°$

(c)   $45°$

(d)   $22\dfrac{1}{2}^°$

**14.** A vertical pole PS has two marks at Q and R such that the portions PQ , PR and PS subtend angles $\alpha$, $\beta$, $\gamma$ at a point on the ground distance x from the bottom of pole P. If PQ = a, PR = b, PS = c and $\alpha + \beta + \gamma = 180°$, then $x^2 =$

(a)   $\dfrac{a^3}{a+b+c}$

(b)   $\dfrac{b^3}{a+b+c}$

(c)   $\dfrac{c^3}{a+b+c}$

(d)   $\dfrac{abc}{a+b+c}$

**15.** If two towers of heights $b_1$ and $b_2$ subtend angles $60°$ and $30°$ respectively at the midpoint of the line joining their feet then $b_1 : b_2 =$

(a)   $1:2$

(b)   $1:3$

(c)   $2:1$

(d)   $3:1$

**16.** The angle of elevation of the top C of a vertical tower CD of height h from a point A in the horizontal plane is $45°$ and from a point B at a distance a from A on the line making an angle $30°$ with AD in the vertical plane, is $60°$, then

(a)   $a = h(\sqrt{3}+1)$

(b)   $h = a(\sqrt{3}+1)$

(c)   $a = h(\sqrt{3}-1)$

(d)   $h = a(\sqrt{3}-1)$

**17.** A flagstaff of length $l$ is fixed on the top of a tower of height h. The angles of elevation of the top and bottom of the flag staff at a point on the ground are $60°$ and $30°$ respectively. Then

(a)   $l = 2h$

(b)   $2l = h$

(c)   $l = 3h$

(d)   $3l = h$

**18.** A spherical ball of diameter d subtends an angle $\alpha$ at a man's eye. When the elevation of its centre is $\beta$, the height of the centre of the ball is

(a)   $\dfrac{d}{2}\operatorname{cosec}\dfrac{\alpha}{2}\sin\beta$

(b)   $d\operatorname{cosec}\alpha\sin\dfrac{\beta}{2}$

(c)   $\dfrac{d}{2}\operatorname{cosec}\dfrac{\alpha}{2}\sin\dfrac{\beta}{2}$

(d)   $\dfrac{d}{2}\sin\dfrac{\alpha}{2}\sin\beta$

**19.** A man observes when he has climbed up $\dfrac{1}{3}$ of the length of an inclined ladder, placed against a wall, the angular depression of an object on the floor is $\alpha$ and that after he has climbed the ladder fully, the depression in $\beta$. If the inclination of the ladder to the floor is $\theta$, then $\cot\theta =$

(a)   $\dfrac{3\cot\beta - \cot\alpha}{2}$

(b)   $\dfrac{3\cot\alpha - \cot\beta}{2}$

(c)   $\dfrac{\cot\beta - \cot\alpha}{2}$

(d)   $\dfrac{\cot\alpha + \cot\beta}{2}$

## Section - II - Integer Type

This section contains 5 questions. The answer to each of the questions is a single digit integer ranging from 0 to 9.

**20.** A tower PQ stands at a point P with in the triangular park ABC such that the sides of length a, b, c of the triangle subtend equal angle at P the foot of the tower and the tower subtends angles $\alpha$, $\beta$, $\gamma$, at A, B, C respectively, then

$a^2(\cot\beta - \cot\gamma) + b^2(\cot\gamma - \cot\alpha) + c^2(\cot\alpha - \cot\beta)$ is equal to



—— *Space for Rough Work* ——

**21.** The angle of elevation of the top of a tower from a point A due south of it is $\tan^{-1} 0.6$, and that from B due east of it is $\tan^{-1} 0.75$. If h is the height of the tower, and AB = $\lambda$h, then

$$\frac{9}{41}\lambda^2 =$$

**22.** If PQ is a vertical tower subtending angles $\alpha$, $\beta$, $\gamma$ at the points A, B, C respectively on the line in the horizontal plane through the foot Q of tower and on the same side of it, then BC cot $\alpha$ – CA cot $\beta$ + AB cot $\gamma$ equals to

**23.** A vertical lamp-post of height 9 metres stands at the corner of a rectangular field. The angle of elevation of its top from the farthest corner is 30°, while from another corner, it is 45°.

If x be the area of the field then the value of $\dfrac{x}{9\sqrt{2}}$ in square meter is

**24.** Two vertical poles AL and BM of heights 20 m and 80m respectively stand apart on a horizontal plane. If A, B be the feet of the poles and AM and BL intersect at P. If height of P be z, then $\dfrac{z}{2} = \ldots\ldots$

<table>
<tr><td rowspan="2">RESPONSE GRID</td><td>21. ⓪①②③④⑤⑥⑦⑧⑨</td><td>22. ⓪①②③④⑤⑥⑦⑧⑨</td></tr>
<tr><td>23. ⓪①②③④⑤⑥⑦⑧⑨</td><td>24. ⓪①②③④⑤⑥⑦⑧⑨</td></tr>
</table>

| DAILY PRACTICE PROBLEM DPP 26 - MATHS | | | |
|---|---|---|---|
| Total Questions | 24 | Total Marks | 58 |
| Attempted | | Correct | |
| Incorrect | | Net Score | |
| Cut-off Score | 12 | Qualifying Score | 38 |
| Success Gap = Net Score – Qualifying Score | | | |

$$\text{Net Score} = \sum_{i=\text{I}}^{\text{VI}} \left[ (\text{correct}_i \times MM_i) - (In_i - NM_i) \right]$$

# DPP - Daily Practice Problems

Name : [　　　　　　　]     Date : [　　　]

Start Time : [　　　]     End Time : [　　　]

## MATHEMATICS   M27

**SYLLABUS : Mathematical Induction :** Mathematical Induction and Divisibility problems.

**Max. Marks : 68**     **Time : 60 min.**

### GENERAL INSTRUCTIONS

- The Daily Practice Problem Sheet contains **24** Questions divided into 4 sections.

  Section I has **14** MCQ's with ONLY 1 correct option. 2 marks for correct answer and No negative marks.

  Section II has **4** MCQ's with 1 or MORE THAN 1 correct option. 4 marks for correct answer(s) and (−1) for wrong answer.
  Section III has **1** MCQ's with multiple matchings. 1 mark for the correct matching of each row & No negative marks.
  Section IV has **5** single digit integer answer questions. 4 marks for correct answer and (−1) for wrong answer.
- No mark will be given/ deducted if no bubble is filled. Keep a timer in front and stop immediately at the end of 60 min.
- You have to evaluate your Response Grids yourself with the help of Solution Booklet.
- The sheet follows a particular syllabus. Do not attempt the sheet before you have completed your preparation for that syllabus. Refer syllabus sheet in the starting of the book for the syllabus of all the DPP sheets.
- After completing the sheet check your answers with the solution booklet and complete the Result Grid. Finally spend time to analyse your performance and revise the areas which emerge out as weak in your evaluation.

---

## Section - I - Straight Objective Type

This section contains 14 multiple choice questions. Each question has 4 choices (a), (b), (c) and (d), out of which **ONLY ONE** is correct.

**1.** For all natural number n,

$$\left(1+\frac{3}{1}\right)\left(1+\frac{5}{4}\right)\left(1+\frac{7}{9}\right)...\left(1+\frac{(2n+1)}{n^2}\right) =$$

(a) $2(n+1)^2$     (b) $(n+1)^2$
(c) $(n-1)^2$     (d) $(n+1)^3$

**2.** For all natural number n, $1+3+3^2+.....+3^{n-1} =$

(a) $\dfrac{(3^n-1)}{2}$     (b) $\dfrac{(3^n+1)}{2}$

(c) $\dfrac{(3^n+1)}{3}$     (d) $\dfrac{(3^n-1)}{3}$

**3.** If P(n) is a statement ($n \in N$) such that if P(k) is true, then P(k + 1) is also true for $k \in N$, then P(n) is true.

(a) for all n     (b) for all $n > 1$
(c) for all $n > 2$     (d) nothing can be said

**4.** If $n \in N$, $\left(\dfrac{n+1}{2}\right)^n \geq n!$ is true then

(a) $n > 1$     (b) $n \geq 1$
(c) $n > 2$     (d) $n \geq 2$

**5.** If $n \in N$, then the result $\dfrac{1}{n}+\dfrac{1}{n+1}+\dfrac{1}{n+2}+......+\dfrac{1}{2n-1}$

$= 1-\dfrac{1}{2}+\dfrac{1}{3}-\dfrac{1}{4}+......+\dfrac{1}{2n-1}$ holds for

(a) all $n \in N$     (b) for even values of n
(c) for odd values of n     (d) not true for any n

---

| RESPONSE GRID | 1. ⓐⓑⓒⓓ | 2. ⓐⓑⓒⓓ | 3. ⓐⓑⓒⓓ | 4. ⓐⓑⓒⓓ | 5. ⓐⓑⓒⓓ |
|---|---|---|---|---|---|

**6.** Let $T(k)$ be the statement : $1+3+5+....+(2k-1)=k^2+10$. Which of the following is correct?

(a) $T(1)$ is true

(b) $T(k)$ is true $\Rightarrow$ $T(k+1)$ is true

(c) $T(n)$ is true for all $n \in \mathbf{N}$

(d) All above are correct

**7.** Let $S(k)=1+3+5+...+(2k-1)=3+k^2$. Then which of the following is true?

(a) Principle of mathematical induction can be used to prove the formula

(b) $S(k) \Rightarrow S(k+1)$

(c) $S(k) \not\Rightarrow S(k+1)$

(d) $S(1)$ is correct

**8.** Let $P(n)$ denote the statement that $(n^2+n)$ is odd. It is seen that $P(n) \Rightarrow P(n+1)$, $P(n)$ is true for all

(a) $n>1$        (b) $n$

(c) $n>2$       (d) None of these

**9.** If $n \in N$, then $11^{n+2}+12^{2n+1}$ is divisible by

(a) 113         (b) 123

(c) 133         (d) None of these

**10.** The inequality $n! > 2^{n-1}$ is true

(a) for no $n \in N$     (b) for all $n>2$

(c) for all $n>1$      (d) for all $n \in N$

**11.** If $P(n)$ is statement such that $P(3)$ is true. Assuming $P(k)$ is true $\Rightarrow P(k+1)$ is true for all $k \geq 3$, then $P(n)$ is true.

(a) for all n       (b) for $n \geq 3$

(c) for $n \geq 4$      (d) none of these

**12.** Let $u_1 = 1, u_2 = 1$ and $u_{n+2} = u_{n+1}+u_n$, $n \geq 1$.

Then $u_n = \dfrac{1}{\sqrt{5}}\left[\left(\dfrac{1+\sqrt{5}}{2}\right)^n - \left(\dfrac{1-\sqrt{5}}{2}\right)^n\right]$ is true for

(a) $n>1$       (b) $n<-1$

(c) $n \leq -1$     (d) $n>0$

**13.** For a positive integer $n$,

Let $a(n) = 1 + \dfrac{1}{2} + \dfrac{1}{3} + \dfrac{1}{4} + ... + \dfrac{1}{(2^n)-1}$. Then

(a) $a(100) \leq 100$     (b) $a(100) > 100$

(c) $a(200) \leq 100$     (d) $50 \leq a(200) < 100$

**14.** Consider the statement, $P(n) : n^2 + n$ is an odd integer . Here $P(n) \Rightarrow P(n+1)$ for all $n \in N$. From here, we can conclude that $P(n)$ is true

(a) for all $n \in N$     (b) for $n \geq 2$

(c) for all $n \geq 3$     (d) nothing can be said.

---

## Section - II - Multiple Correct Answer Type

This section contains 4 multiple correct answer(s) type questions. Each question has 4 choices (a), (b), (c) and (d), out of which **ONE OR MORE** is/are correct.

**15.** Let $p \geq 3$ be an integer and $\alpha, \beta$ be the roots of $x^2 - (p+1)x + 1 = 0$ then using mathematical induction we found that $\alpha^n + \beta^n$.

(a) is an integer

(b) is not divisible by $p$

(c) is a irrational number

(d) is divisible by p.

| RESPONSE GRID | 6. ⓐⓑⓒⓓ | 7. ⓐⓑⓒⓓ | 8. ⓐⓑⓒⓓ | 9. ⓐⓑⓒⓓ | 10. ⓐⓑⓒⓓ |
|---|---|---|---|---|---|
| | 11. ⓐⓑⓒⓓ | 12. ⓐⓑⓒⓓ | 13. ⓐⓑⓒⓓ | 14. ⓐⓑⓒⓓ | 15. ⓐⓑⓒⓓ |

*Space for Rough Work*

16. Which of the following hold good for all positive integers $n$ ?

 (a) $\dfrac{(2n)!}{2^{2n}(n!)^2} < \dfrac{1}{(3n+1)^{1/2}}$

 (b) $\dfrac{(2n)!}{2^{2n}(n!)^2} \leq \dfrac{1}{(3n+1)^{1/2}}$

 (c) $\dfrac{(2n)!}{2^{2n}(n!)^2} > \dfrac{1}{(3n+1)^{1/2}}$

 (d) none of these

17. If $P(n) : 2+4+6+...+(2n) = n(n+1)+2, n \in N$, then $P(k) : 2+4+6+.....+2k = k(k+1)+2$ implies $P(k+1) : 2+4+6+.....+2(k+1) = (k+1)(k+2)+2$ is true for all $k \in N$. So statement is not true $P(n) : 2+4+6+.....+2n = n(n+1)+2$ for

 (a) $n \geq 1$      (b) $n \geq 2$

 (c) $n \geq 3$      (d) none of these

18. The statement $P(n) :$

 $1\times 1!+2\times 2!+3\times 3!+....+n\times n! = (n+1)!-1$ is

 (a) true for all $n = 1$

 (b) not true for any $n$

 (c) true for all $n \in N$

 (d) none of these

## Section - III - Matrix-Match Type

This section contains 1 question. It contains statements given in two columns, which have to be matched. Statements in Column I are labelled as A, B, C and D whereas statements in Column II are labelled as p, q, r and s. The answers to these questions have to be appro-priately bubbled as illustrated in the following example. If the correct matches are A-p, A-r, B-p, B-s, C-r, C-s and D-q, then the correctly bubbled matrix will look like the following :

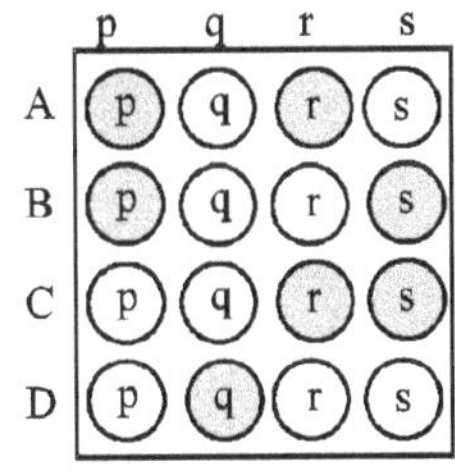

19. Match the column

| | Column I | | Column II |
|---|---|---|---|
| (A) | Let $N = 2^n(2^{n+1}-1)$ and $2^{n+1}-1$ is a prime number. If sum of all divisors of N is equal to kN, then k is equal to | (p) | 2 |
| (B) | Let $N = 2^n(2^{n+1}-1)$ and $2^{n+1}-1$ is a prime number, then sum of reciprocal of divisors of N is equal to | (q) | 1 |
| (C) | The number of positive integer x for which $x^3 - 8x^2 + 20x - 13$ is prime | (r) | 4 |
| (D) | If k is any integer and p is a prime number such that $x^2 + kx + p = 0$ has two distinct positive integer solution then $k + p + 5$ is equal to | (s) | 3 |

## Section - IV - Integer Type

This section contains 5 questions. The answer to each of the questions is a single digit integer ranging from 0 to 9.

20. Find the remainder when $2^{30}.3^{20}$ is divided by 7.



*Space for Rough Work*

**21.** If $n \in N$, then find the integer by which $\frac{1}{5}(7^{2n} + 2^{3n-3} \cdot 3^{n-1})$ is always divisible.

**22.** Find the integer by which $10^n + 3(4^{n+2}) + 5$ ($n \in N$) is divisible.

**23.** If n is a positive integer, then find the integer by which $(2 \cdot 4^{2n+1} + 3^{3n+1})$ is divisible.

**24.** Find the smallest +ve integer n for which $n! < \left(\frac{n+1}{2}\right)^n$ holds.

| RESPONSE GRID | |
|---|---|
| **21.** ⓪①②③④⑤⑥⑦⑧⑨ | **22.** ⓪①②③④⑤⑥⑦⑧⑨ |
| **23.** ⓪①②③④⑤⑥⑦⑧⑨ | **24.** ⓪①②③④⑤⑥⑦⑧⑨ |

## DAILY PRACTICE PROBLEM DPP 27 - MATHS

| Total Questions | 24 | Total Marks | 68 |
|---|---|---|---|
| Attempted | | Correct | |
| Incorrect | | Net Score | |
| Cut-off Score | 14 | Qualifying Score | 44 |
| Success Gap = Net Score – Qualifying Score | | | |

$$\text{Net Score} = \sum_{i=I}^{VI}\left[(\text{correct}_i \times MM_i) - (In_i - NM_i)\right]$$

*Space for Rough Work*

# DPP - Daily Practice Problems

**Name :**

**Date :**

**Start Time :**

**End Time :**

# MATHEMATICS M28

**SYLLABUS : Rectangular Cartesian Co-ordinates-1 :** System of co-ordinates, Distance between two points, Section formulae, Questions related to geometrical conditions

## Max. Marks : 59

## Time : 60 min.

### GENERAL INSTRUCTIONS

- The Daily Practice Problem Sheet contains **23** Questions divided into 4 sections.

  Section I has **16** MCQ's with ONLY 1 correct option. 2 marks for correct answer and No negative marks.

  Section II has **1** MCQ's with 1 or MORE THAN 1 correct option. 4 marks for correct answer(s) and (–1) for wrong answer.
  Section III has **1** Assertion-Reason MCQ's with ONLY 1 correct option. 3 marks for correct and (–1) mark for wrong answer.
  Section IV has **5** single digit integer answer questions. 4 marks for correct answer and (–1) for wrong answer.
- No mark will be given/ deducted if no bubble is filled. Keep a timer in front and stop immediately at the end of 60 min.
- You have to evaluate your Response Grids yourself with the help of Solution Booklet.
- The sheet follows a particular syllabus. Do not attempt the sheet before you have completed your preparation for that syllabus. Refer syllabus sheet in the starting of the book for the syllabus of all the DPP sheets.
- After completing the sheet check your answers with the solution booklet and complete the Result Grid. Finally spend time to analyse your performance and revise the areas which emerge out as weak in your evaluation.

## Section - I - Straight Objective Type

This section contains 16 multiple choice questions. Each question has 4 choices (a), (b), (c) and (d), out of which **ONLY ONE** is correct.

1. The number of points on the line $3x + 4y = 5$ which at a distance of $1 + \sin^2\theta$ units from the point $(2, 3)$ is

   (a) 1     (b) 2     (c) 0     (d) infinite

2. If the point $[x_1 + t(x_2 - x_1), y_1 + t(y_2 - y_1)]$ divides the join of $(x_1, y_1)$ and $(x_2, y_2)$ internally then

   (a)  $t < 0$     (b)  $0 < t < 1$
   (c)  $t > 1$     (d)  $t = 1$

3. The distance between the points $(a\cos\alpha, a\sin\alpha)$ and $(a\cos\beta, a\sin\beta)$ is

   (a)  $a\cos\dfrac{\alpha - \beta}{2}$     (b)  $2a\cos\dfrac{\alpha - \beta}{2}$

   (c)  $a\sin\dfrac{\alpha - \beta}{2}$     (d)  $2a\sin\dfrac{\alpha - \beta}{2}$

4. $\left( am_1, \dfrac{a}{m_1} \right), \left( am_2, \dfrac{a}{m_2} \right), \left( am_3, \dfrac{a}{m_3} \right)$ and

   $\left( am_1 m_2 m_3, \dfrac{a}{m_1 m_2 m_3} \right)$ are four points such that

   (a)  They are collinear
   (b)  They are equidistant from a fixed point
   (c)  They form a parallelogram
   (d)  None of these.

5. If ABCD be a square and P be any point in its plane, then $PA^2 + PC^2 =$

   (a)  $PB^2 + PD^2$

   (b)  $PB^2 - PD^2$

   (c)  $PB \cdot PD$

   (d)  $2(PB^2 + PD^2)$

| RESPONSE GRID | 1. ⓐⓑⓒⓓ | 2. ⓐⓑⓒⓓ | 3. ⓐⓑⓒⓓ | 4. ⓐⓑⓒⓓ | 5. ⓐⓑⓒⓓ |
|---|---|---|---|---|---|

**6.** Q, R and S are the points on the line joining the points P(a, x) and T (b, y) such that PQ = QR = RS = ST, then ((5a + 3b)/8, (5x + 3y)/8) is the midpoint of :

(a)  PQ

(b)  QR

(c)  RS

(d)  ST

**7.** If the midpoint of join of (x, y + 1) and (x + 1, y + 2) is (3/2, 5/2); then the midpoint of join of (x – 1, y + 1) and (x + 1, y – 1) is

(a)  (–1, –1)

(b)  (–1, 1)

(c)  (1, –1)

(d)  (1, 1)

**8.** If O be the origin and if the coordinates of any two points $Q_1$ and $Q_2$ be $(x_1, y_1)$ and $(x_2, y_2)$ respectively, then $OQ_1 . OQ_2 \cos Q_1 O Q_2 =$

(a)  $x_1 x_2 - y_1 y_2$

(b)  $x_1 y_1 - x_2 y_2$

(c)  $x_1 x_2 + y_1 y_2$

(d)  $x_1 y_1 + x_2 y_2$

**9.** P(3, 1), Q (6, 5) and R (x, y) are three points such that the angle RPQ is a right angle and the area of $\Delta RQP = 7$, then the number of such points R is

(a)  0

(b)  1

(c)  2

(d)  4

**10.** If the vertices of a traingle have integral coordinates then

(a)  the triangle must be equilateral

(b)  the triangle can never be equilateral

(c)  the triangle may or may not be equilateral

(d)  such a triangle cannot exist

**11.** ABCD is a rhombus. Its diagonals AC and BD intersect at the point M and satisfy BD = 2AC. If the coordinates of D and M are (1, 1) and (2, – 1) respectively, then the coordinates of A are

(a)  $\left(-3, -\dfrac{1}{2}\right)$

(b)  $\left(1, -\dfrac{3}{2}\right)$

(c)  $\left(\dfrac{3}{2}, -1\right)$

(d)  $\left(\dfrac{1}{2}, -3\right)$

**12.** The points $(0, 0)$, $(a, 0)$ and $\left(\dfrac{a}{2}, \dfrac{a\sqrt{3}}{2}\right)$ are vertices of

(a)  Isosceles triangle

(b)  Equilateral triangle

(c)  Scalene triangle

(d)  None of these

**13.** The number of points on x-axis which are at a distance c (c < 3) from the point (2, 3) is

(a)  2

(b)  1

(c)  Infinite

(d)  None of these

**14.** The coordinates of mid-points of the sides of a triangle are (1, 1), (2, 3) and (4, 1). The coordinates of the centroid of the triangle are

(a)  $\left(\dfrac{7}{3}, \dfrac{5}{3}\right)$

(b)  $\left(\dfrac{14}{3}, \dfrac{10}{3}\right)$

(c)  (3, 3)

(d)  None of these

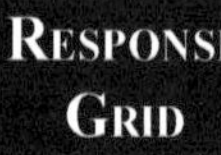

| RESPONSE GRID | 6. (a)(b)(c)(d) | 7. (a)(b)(c)(d) | 8. (a)(b)(c)(d) | 9. (a)(b)(c)(d) | 10. (a)(b)(c)(d) |
| | 11. (a)(b)(c)(d) | 12. (a)(b)(c)(d) | 13. (a)(b)(c)(d) | 14. (a)(b)(c)(d) | |

*Space for Rough Work*

15. The centre and radius of the circumcircle of the triangle whose vertices are $(-2, 3)$, $(2, -1)$, and $(4, 0)$ are

(a) $(3, 5)$; $5\sqrt{2}$

(b) $(0, 0)$; $\dfrac{5\sqrt{2}}{2}$

(c) $\left(\dfrac{1}{2}, \dfrac{3}{2}\right)$; $\dfrac{\sqrt{2}}{2}$

(d) $\left(\dfrac{3}{2}, \dfrac{5}{2}\right)$; $\dfrac{5\sqrt{2}}{2}$

16. The vertices of a traingle are $\left(ab, \dfrac{1}{ab}\right)$, $\left(bc, \dfrac{1}{bc}\right)$ and $\left(ca, \dfrac{1}{ca}\right)$. Where $a$, $b$, $c$ are the roots of the equation $x^3 - 3x^2 + 6x + 1 = 0$. The coordinates of its centroid are

(a) $(0, 1)$

(b) $(-2, 0)$

(c) $(2, -1)$

(d) $(1, 2)$

## Section - II - Multiple Correct Answer Type

This section contains 1 multiple correct answer(s) type questions. This question has 4 choices (a), (b), (c) and (d), out of which **ONE OR MORE** is/are correct.

17. If $(\alpha, \alpha^2)$ lies inside the triangle formed by the lines $2x + 3y - 1 = 0$, $x + 2y - 3 = 0$, $5x - 6y - 1 = 0$, then

(a) $2\alpha + 3\alpha^2 - 1 > 0$

(b) $\alpha + 3\alpha^2 - 3 < 0$

(c) $\alpha + 2\alpha^2 - 3 < 0$

(d) $6\alpha^2 - 5\alpha - 1 > 0$

## Section - III - Reasoning Type

This section contains 1 reasoning type question. This question has 4 choices (a), (b), (c) and (d) out of which **ONLY ONE** is correct.

**DIRECTIONS : This question contains two statements: Statement-1 (Assertion) and Statement-2 (Reason). Each of these questions has four alternative choices, only one of which is the correct answer. You have to select the correct choice.**

(a) Statement-1 is True, Statement-2 is True; Statement-2 is a correct explanation for Statement-1.

(b) Statement-1 is True, Statement-2 is True; Statement-2 is NOT a correct explanation for Statement-1.

(c) Statement -1 is True, Statement-2 is False.

(d) Statement -1 is False, Statement-2 is True.

18. Lines $L_1 : y - x = 0$ and $L_2 : 2x + y = 0$ intersect the line $L_3 : y + 2 = 0$ at P and Q, respectively. The bisector of the acute angle between $L_1$ and $L_2$ intersects $L_3$ at R.

**Statement-1:** The ratio PR : RQ equals $2\sqrt{2} : \sqrt{5}$.

**Statement-2 :** In any triangle, bisector of an angle divides the triangle into two similar triangles.

## Section - IV - Integer Type

This section contains 5 questions. The answer to each of the questions is a single digit integer ranging from 0 to 9.

| RESPONSE GRID | 15. ⓐⓑⓒⓓ | 16. ⓐⓑⓒⓓ | 17. ⓐⓑⓒⓓ | 18. ⓐⓑⓒⓓ |
|---|---|---|---|---|

*Space for Rough Work*

**19.** C is the mid-point of PQ. If P is $(4, -x)$, C is $(2, -1)$ and Q is $(-2, 4)$, then find the value of x.

**20.** The join of the points $(-3, -4)$ and $(1, -2)$ is divided by y-axis in the ratio $\lambda : 1$, Then find the value of $\lambda$.

**21.** P and Q are points on the line joining the points A $(25, 37)$ and B $(55, -21)$ such that AP = PQ = QB, then find the y-coordinate of mid point of PQ.

**22.** The extremities of a diagonal of a parallelogram are the points $(3, -4)$ and $(-6, 5)$. If third vertex is $(-2, 1)$ then find the Y–coordinates of the fourth vertex.

**23.** If P $(1, 2)$, Q $(4, 6)$, R $(5, 7)$ and S $(a, b)$ are the vertices of a parallelogram PQRS, then find the value of $\dfrac{3a}{b}$.

| | |
|---|---|
| **RESPONSE GRID** | **19.** ⓪①②③④⑤⑥⑦⑧⑨  **20.** ⓪①②③④⑤⑥⑦⑧⑨<br>**21.** ⓪①②③④⑤⑥⑦⑧⑨  **22.** ⓪①②③④⑤⑥⑦⑧⑨<br>**23.** ⓪①②③④⑤⑥⑦⑧⑨ |

## DAILY PRACTICE PROBLEM DPP 28 - MATHS

| Total Questions | 23 | Total Marks | 59 |
|---|---|---|---|
| Attempted | | Correct | |
| Incorrect | | Net Score | |
| Cut-off Score | 12 | Qualifying Score | 38 |
| Success Gap = Net Score – Qualifying Score | | | |

$$\text{Net Score } = \sum_{i=I}^{VI}\left[(\textbf{correct}_i \times MM_i) - (In_i - NM_i)\right]$$

Name : 

Date : 

Start Time : 

End Time : 

## MATHEMATICS M29

**SYLLABUS : Rectangular Cartesian Co-ordinates-2 :** Points related to triangle (Orthocentre, Circumcentre, Incentre), Area of some geometrical figures, Collinearity, Transformation of axes and locus

## Max. Marks : 70          Time : 60 min.

### GENERAL INSTRUCTIONS

- The Daily Practice Problem Sheet contains **23** Questions divided into 6 sections.
  Section I has **8** MCQ's with ONLY 1 correct option. 2 marks for correct answer and No negative marks.
  Section II has **4** MCQ's with 1 or MORE THAN 1 correct option. 4 marks for correct answer(s) and (–1) for wrong answer.
  Section III has **1** PASSAGE with **3** MCQ's with ONLY 1 correct option. 3 marks for correct and (–1) mark for wrong answer.
  Section IV has **1** MCQ's with multiple matchings. 1 mark for the correct matching of each row & No negative marks.
  Section V has **3** Assertion-Reason MCQ's with ONLY 1 correct option. 3 marks for correct and (–1) mark for wrong answer.
  Section VI has **4** single digit integer answer questions. 4 marks for correct answer and (–1) for wrong answer.
- No mark will be given/ deducted if no bubble is filled. Keep a timer in front and stop immediately at the end of 60 min.
- You have to evaluate your Response Grids yourself with the help of Solution Booklet.
- The sheet follows a particular syllabus. Do not attempt the sheet before you have completed your preparation for that syllabus. Refer syllabus sheet in the starting of the book for the syllabus of all the DPP sheets.
- After completing the sheet check your answers with the solution booklet and complete the Result Grid. Finally spend time to analyse your performance and revise the areas which emerge out as weak in your evaluation.

---

## Section - I - Straight Objective Type

This section contains 8 multiple choice questions. Each question has 4 choices (a), (b), (c) and (d), out of which **ONLY ONE** is correct.

**1.** Vertices of a triangle are $(1, \sqrt{3}), (2\cos\theta, 2\sin\theta)$ and $(2\sin\theta, -2\cos\theta)$. Then locus of orthocentre of the triangle is –

(a) $(x-1)^2 + (y-\sqrt{3})^2 = 8$   (b) $(x-2)^2 + (y-\sqrt{3})^2 = 4$

(c) $(x-1)^2 + (y-\sqrt{3})^2 = 4$   (d) None of these

**2.** Let $S = \{(x, y) + x^2 + 2xy + y^2 - 3x - 3y + 2 = 0\}$, then S –
(a) consists of two coincident lines
(b) consists of two parallel lines which are not coincident
(c) consists of two intersecting lines
(d) is a parabola

**3.** The vertices of a triangle are $\left(ab, \dfrac{1}{ab}\right)$, $\left(bc, \dfrac{1}{bc}\right)$ and $\left(ca, \dfrac{1}{ca}\right)$ where a, b, c are the roots of the equation $x^3 - 3x^2 + 6x + 1 = 0$. The coordinates of its centroid are
(a) $(0, 1)$        (b) $(-2, 0)$
(c) $(2, -1)$      (d) $(1, 2)$

**4.** The centre and radius of the circumcircle of the triangle whose vertices are $(-2, 3), (2, -1),$ and $(4, 0)$ are

(a) $(3, 5); 5\sqrt{2}$        (b) $(0, 0); \dfrac{5\sqrt{2}}{2}$

(c) $\left(\dfrac{1}{2}, \dfrac{3}{2}\right); \dfrac{\sqrt{2}}{2}$      (d) $\left(\dfrac{3}{2}, \dfrac{5}{2}\right); \dfrac{5\sqrt{2}}{2}$

---

| RESPONSE GRID | 1. ⓐⓑⓒⓓ | 2. ⓐⓑⓒⓓ | 3. ⓐⓑⓒⓓ | 4. ⓐⓑⓒⓓ |
|---|---|---|---|---|

5. Vertices of a variable triangle are $(3, 4)$, $(5\cos\theta, 5\sin\theta)$ and $(5\sin\theta, -5\cos\theta)$. Then locus of its orthocentre is
   (a) $(x+y-1)^2 + (x-y-7)^2 = 100$
   (b) $(x+y-7)^2 + (x-y-1)^2 = 100$
   (c) $(x+y-7)^2 + (x+y-1)^2 = 100$
   (d) $(x+y-7)^2 + (x-y+1)^2 = 100$

6. Locus of centroid of the triangle whose vertices are $(a\cos t, a\sin t)$, $(b\sin t, -b\cos t)$ and $(1, 0)$, where t is a parameter, is
   (a) $(3x-1)^2 + (3y)^2 = a^2 - b^2$
   (b) $(3x-1)^2 + (3y)^2 = a^2 + b^2$
   (c) $(3x+1)^2 + (3y)^2 = a^2 + b^2$
   (d) $(3x+1)^2 + (3y)^2 = a^2 - b^2$

7. Origin is the orthocentre of $\triangle ABC$ where $A = (5, -1)$, $B = (-2, 3)$ then the orthocentre of $\triangle OAB$ is
   (a) $(-4, -7)$     (b) $(3, -2)$
   (c) $(-2, 3)$     (d) $(5, -1)$

8. The vertices of a triangle are $A(x_1, x_1\tan\alpha)$, $B(x_2, x_2\tan\beta)$ and $C(x_3, x_3\tan\gamma)$. If the circumcentre of triangle $ABC$ coincides with the origin and $H(a, b)$ be its orthocentre then $\dfrac{a}{b} =$

   (a) $\dfrac{\cos\alpha + \cos\beta + \cos\gamma}{\cos\alpha.\cos\beta.\cos\gamma}$   (b) $\dfrac{\sin\alpha + \sin\beta + \sin\gamma}{\sin\alpha.\sin\beta.\sin\gamma}$

   (c) $\dfrac{\tan\alpha + \tan\beta + \tan\gamma}{\tan\alpha.\tan\beta.\tan\gamma}$   (d) $\dfrac{\sin\alpha + \sin\beta + \sin\gamma}{\cos\alpha + \cos\beta + \cos\gamma}$

## Section - II - Multiple Correct Answer Type

This section contains 4 multiple correct answer(s) type questions. Each question has 4 choices (a), (b), (c) and (d), out of which **ONE OR MORE** is/are correct.

9. A triangle $ABC$ is given where vertex $A$ is $(1, 1)$ and the orthocentre is $(2, 4)$. Also sides $AB$ and $BC$ are members of

the family of lines $ax + by + c = 0$ where $a, b, c$ are in $A.P.$, then which of the following statements are correct?
   (a) The vertex $B$ is $(1, -2)$
   (b) The vertex $C$ is $(-17, 4)$
   (c) Triangle $ABC$ is a/an obtuse angled triangle
   (d) None of these

10. If a, b, c are in A.P. and x, y, z are in G.P., then the points $(a, x)$, $(b, y)$ and $(c, z)$ are collinear if
    (a) $x^2 = yz$          (b) $z^2 = xy$
    (c) $y^2 = zx$          (d) $x = y = z$

11. If all the three vertices of an isosceles right angle triangle be integral points and length of base is also an integer, then which of the points is/are always a rational point (A point P $(x, y)$ is a rational point if both x and y are rational).
    (a) centroid          (b) incentre
    (c) circumcentre          (d) orthocentre

12. If $m_1$ and $m_2$ are the roots of the equation $x^2 - ax - a - 1 = 0$, then the area of the triangle formed by the three straight lines $y = m_1x$, $y = m_2x$ and $y = a$ $(a \neq -1)$ is

    (a) $\dfrac{a^2(a+2)}{2(a+1)}$ if $a > -1$

    (b) $\dfrac{-a^2(a+2)}{2(a+1)}$ if $-2 < a < -1$

    (c) $\dfrac{a^2(a+2)}{2(a+1)}$ if $a < -2$

    (d) $0$ for all a

## Section - III - Linked Comprehension Type

This section contains one paragraph. Based upon the paragraph, 3 multiple choice questions have to be answered. Each question has 4 choices (a), (b), (c) and (d), out of which **ONLY ONE** is correct.

| **Response Grid** | 5. ⓐⓑⓒⓓ | 6. ⓐⓑⓒⓓ | 7. ⓐⓑⓒⓓ | 8. ⓐⓑⓒⓓ | 9. ⓐⓑⓒⓓ |
| | 10. ⓐⓑⓒⓓ | 11. ⓐⓑⓒⓓ | 12. ⓐⓑⓒⓓ | | |

*Space for Rough Work*

Consider a $\triangle ABC$ whose sides AB, BC and CA are represented by the straight lines $2x + y = 0$, $x + py = q$ and $x - y = 3$ respectively. The point P is $(2, 3)$.

**13.** If P is the centroid, then $(p + q)$ equals
(a) 47     (b) 50     (c) 65     (d) 74

**14.** If P is the orthocentre, then $(p + q)$ equals
(a) 47     (b) 50     (c) 65     (d) 74

**15.** If P is the circumcentre, then $(p + q)$ equals
(a) 47     (b) 50     (c) 65     (d) 74

## Section - IV - Matrix-Match Type

This section contain 1 question. It contains statement given in two columns, which have to be matched. Statements in Column I are labelled as A, B, C and D whereas statements in Column II are labelled as p, q, r and s. The answers to these questions have to be appropriately bubbled as illustrated in the following example. If the correct matches are A-p, A-r, B-p, B-s, C-r, C-s and D-q, then the correctly bubbled matrix will look like the following :

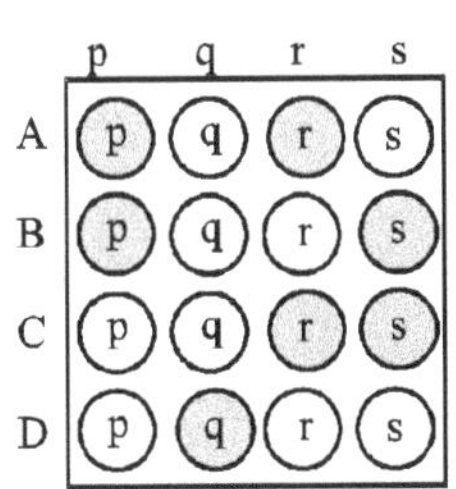

**16.**

| Column I | Column II |
|---|---|
| (A) The locus of the point $\left( ct, \dfrac{c}{t} \right)$ | (p) $\dfrac{x^2}{a^2} - \dfrac{y^2}{b^2} = 1$ |
| (B) The locus of the point $\left( \dfrac{a}{2}\left( t + \dfrac{1}{t} \right), \dfrac{a}{2}\left( t - \dfrac{1}{t} \right) \right)$ | (q) $y^2 + 4x = 4$ |
| (C) The locus of the point $(\cos^2 t, 2\sin t)$ | (r) $\sqrt{\dfrac{x}{a}} + \sqrt{\dfrac{y}{b}} = 1$ |
| (D) The locus of the point $(a\cos h\theta, b\sin h\theta)$ | (s) $xy = c^2$ |
| | (t) $x^2 - y^2 = a^2$ |

## Section - V - Reasoning Type

This section contains 3 reasoning type questions. Each question has 4 choices (a), (b), (c) and (d) out of which **ONLY ONE** is correct.

**DIRECTIONS for (Qs. 17 to 19) :** Each of these questions contains two statements: **Statement-1 (Assertion)** and **Statement-2 (Reason)**. Each of these questions has four alternative choices, only one of which is the correct answer. You have to select the correct choice.

(a) Statement-1 is True, Statement-2 is True; Statement-2 is a correct explanation for Statement-1.
(b) Statement-1 is True, Statement-2 is True; Statement-2 is NOT a correct explanation for Statement-1.
(c) Statement-1 is True, Statement-2 is False.
(d) Statement-1 is False, Statement-2 is True.

**17.** **Statement 1 :** If $y = f(x)$ be any continuous function whose graph is concave downward and always above x-axis then
$$\frac{f(\alpha) + f(\beta) + f(\gamma)}{3} < f\left( \frac{\alpha + \beta + \gamma}{3} \right)$$
**Statement 2 :** Centroid of a triangle always lie inside the triangle.

**18.** **Statement 1 :** The area of triangle formed by the points A $(2000, 2002)$, B $(2001, 2004)$, C $(2002, 2003)$ is same as area formed by P $(0, 0)$, Q $(1, 2)$, R $(2, 1)$.
**Statement 2 :** The area of triangle is constant with respect to transition of coordinate axes.

**19.** **Statement 1 :** The incentre of the triangle formed by the lines
$$x\cos\frac{\pi}{9} + y\sin\frac{\pi}{9} = \pi, \quad x\cos\frac{8\pi}{9} + y\sin\frac{8\pi}{9} = \pi,$$
$$x\cos\frac{13\pi}{9} + y\sin\frac{13\pi}{9} = \pi \text{ is } (0, 0)$$
**Statement 2 :** The point $(0, 0)$ is equidistant from the three vertices of the triangle formed by the lines
$$x\cos\frac{\pi}{9} + y\sin\frac{\pi}{9} = \pi, \quad x\cos\frac{8\pi}{9} + y\sin\frac{8\pi}{9} = \pi,$$
$$x\cos\frac{13\pi}{9} + y\sin\frac{13\pi}{9} = \pi.$$

<table>
<tr><td rowspan="3">RESPONSE GRID</td><td colspan="3">13. ⓐⓑ©ⓓ   14. ⓐⓑ©ⓓ   15. ⓐⓑ©ⓓ</td></tr>
<tr><td colspan="3">16. A - ⓟⓠⓡⓢⓣ; B - ⓟⓠⓡⓢⓣ; C - ⓟⓠⓡⓢⓣ; D - ⓟⓠⓡⓢⓣ</td></tr>
<tr><td colspan="3">17. ⓐⓑ©ⓓ   18. ⓐⓑ©ⓓ   19. ⓐⓑ©ⓓ</td></tr>
</table>

## Section - VI - Integer Type

This section contains 4 questions. The answer to each of the questions is a single digit integer ranging from 0 to 9.

**20.** The area of the triangle formed by the intersection of a line parallel to x-axis and passing through $P(h, k)$ with the lines $y = x$ and $x + y = 2$ is $4h^2$. If the locus of the point $P$ is $y = \pm Px + Q$, find the value of $P + Q$.

**21.** The area of the triangle whose vertices are $(b, c)$, $(c, a)$ and $(a, b)$ is $\Delta$ and the area of the triangle whose vertices are $(ac - b^2, ab - c^2)$, $(ab - c^2, bc - a^2)$ and $(bc - a^2, ac - b^2)$ is $\Delta'$. If $a, b, c$ represent the length of the sides of a triangle of perimeter 16 then find the value of $\dfrac{\Delta'}{32\Delta}$.

**22.** The area of a triangle is 5. Two of its vertices are $A(2, 1)$ and $B(3, -2)$. The third vertex $C$ lies on $y = x + 3$. If $C$ is $\left(\dfrac{P}{2}, \dfrac{Q}{2}\right)$ or $\left(\dfrac{-R}{2}, \dfrac{S}{2}\right)$ then find the value of $P - Q - R + S$.

**23.** The vertices of a triangle are $[at_1t_2,\ a(t_1 + t_2)]$, $[at_2t_3,\ a(t_2 + t_3)]$, $[at_3t_1,\ a(t_3 + t_1)]$. Find the orthocentre of the triangle. If $a = 1$, $t_1 + t_2 + t_3 = 2$ and $t_1t_2t_3 = 3$ then orthocentre is $H(s, t)$. Find $s + t$.

| RESPONSE GRID | | |
|---|---|---|
| 20. ⓪①②③④⑤⑥⑦⑧⑨ | | 21. ⓪①②③④⑤⑥⑦⑧⑨ |
| 22. ⓪①②③④⑤⑥⑦⑧⑨ | | 23. ⓪①②③④⑤⑥⑦⑧⑨ |

## DAILY PRACTICE PROBLEM DPP 29 - MATHS

| Total Questions | 23 | Total Marks | 70 |
|---|---|---|---|
| Attempted | | Correct | |
| Incorrect | | Net Score | |
| Cut-off Score | 13 | Qualifying Score | 44 |
| Success Gap = Net Score – Qualifying Score | | | |

$$\text{Net Score} = \sum_{i=1}^{VI}\left[(\text{correct}_i \times MM_i) - (In_i - NM_i)\right]$$

**Name :**

**Date :**

**Start Time :**

**End Time :**

## MATHEMATICS   M30

**SYLLABUS : Straight Line-1 :** Slope of line, Equation of lines in different forms, Angle between two straight lines, Bisector of angle between two lines

### Max. Marks : 73                                Time : 60 min.

**GENERAL INSTRUCTIONS**

- The Daily Practice Problem Sheet contains **24** Questions divided into 6 sections.
  Section I has **8** MCQ's with ONLY 1 correct option. 2 marks for correct answer and No negative marks.
  Section II has **4** MCQ's with 1 or MORE THAN 1 correct option. 4 marks for correct answer(s) and (–1) for wrong answer.
  Section III has **1** PASSAGE with **3** MCQ's with ONLY 1 correct option. 3 marks for correct and (–1) mark for wrong answer.
  Section IV has **1** MCQ's with multiple matchings. 1 mark for the correct matching of each row & No negative marks.
  Section V has **3** Assertion-Reason MCQ's with ONLY 1 correct option. 3 marks for correct and (–1) mark for wrong answer.
  Section VI has **5** single digit integer answer questions. 4 marks for correct answer and (–1) for wrong answer.
- No mark will be given/ deducted if no bubble is filled. Keep a timer in front and stop immediately at the end of 60 min.
- You have to evaluate your Response Grids yourself with the help of Solution Booklet.
- The sheet follows a particular syllabus. Do not attempt the sheet before you have completed your preparation for that syllabus. Refer syllabus sheet in the starting of the book for the syllabus of all the DPP sheets.
- After completing the sheet check your answers with the solution booklet and complete the Result Grid. Finally spend time to analyse your performance and revise the areas which emerge out as weak in your evaluation.

---

### Section - I - Straight Objective Type

This section contains 8 multiple choice questions. Each question has 4 choices (a), (b), (c) and (d), out of which **ONLY ONE** is correct.

---

**1.** Points A & B are in the first quadrant ; point 'O' is the origin. If the slope of OA is 1, slope of OB is 7 and OA = OB, then the slope of AB is :

(a) $-1/5$        (b) $-1/4$

(c) $-1/3$        (d) $-1/2$

**2.** The equations of the straight lines passing through the point of intersection of $x + 3y + 4 = 0$ and $3x + y + 4 = 0$ and equally inclined to the axes are

(a) $x - y + 1 = 0$ and $x + y + 2 = 0$

(b) $x - y = 0$ and $x + y + 2 = 0$

(c) $x + y = 0$ and $x - y + 2 = 0$

(d) None of these

**3.** Let $P = (-1, 0)$, $Q = (0, 0)$ and $R = (3, 3\sqrt{3})$ be three points. Then the equation of the bisector of the angle PQR is

(a) $\dfrac{\sqrt{3}}{2}x + y = 0$      (b) $x + \sqrt{3}y = 0$

(c) $\sqrt{3}x + y = 0$      (d) $x + \dfrac{\sqrt{3}}{2}y = 0$

**4.** The graph of the function $y = \cos x \cos (x + 2) - \cos^2(x+1)$ is

(a) A straight line passing through $(0, -\sin^2 1)$ with slope 2

(b) A straight line passing through origin

(c) A parabola with vertex $(1, -\sin^2 1)$

(d) A straight line passing through the point $\left(\dfrac{\pi}{2}, -\sin^2 1\right)$ and parallel to x-axis

---

**RESPONSE GRID**   **1.** ⓐⓑⓒⓓ   **2.** ⓐⓑⓒⓓ   **3.** ⓐⓑⓒⓓ   **4.** ⓐⓑⓒⓓ

5. The equation of bisector of that angle between the lines x + y + 1 = 0 and 2x − 3y − 5 = 0 which contains the point (10, − 20) is

   (a) $x(\sqrt{13} + 2\sqrt{2}) + y(\sqrt{13} - 3\sqrt{2}) + (\sqrt{13} - 5\sqrt{2}) = 0$

   (b) $x(\sqrt{13} - 2\sqrt{2}) + y(\sqrt{13} + 3\sqrt{2}) + (\sqrt{13} + 5\sqrt{2}) = 0$

   (c) $x(\sqrt{13} + 2\sqrt{2}) + y(\sqrt{13} + 3\sqrt{2}) + (\sqrt{13} + 5\sqrt{2}) = 0$

   (d) None of these

6. If one of the diagonals of a square is along the line x = 2y and one of its vertices is (3, 0), then its sides through this vertex are given by the equations

   (a) $y - 3x + 9 = 0, 3y + x - 3 = 0$

   (b) $y + 3x + 9 = 0, 3y + x - 3 = 0$

   (c) $y - 3x + 9 = 0, 3y - x + 3 = 0$

   (d) $y - 3x + 3 = 0, 3y + x + 9 = 0$

7. Consider a $\Delta$ ABC in which sides AB and AC are perpendicular to x − y − 4 = 0 and 2x − y − 5 = 0 respectively.

   Vertex A is (−2, 3) and circumcentre of the $\Delta$ ABC is $\left(\dfrac{3}{2}, \dfrac{5}{2}\right)$.

   Equation of perpendicular bisector of side AB will be
   (a) $x - y + 1 = 0$      (b) $x - y + 4 = 0$
   (c) $x - y + 2 = 0$      (d) none of these

8. The angle between the lines $(x^2 + y^2) \sin^2 \alpha$
   $= (x\cos \beta - y \sin \beta)^2$ is
   (a) $\alpha$    (b) $2\alpha$    (c) $\alpha + \beta$    (d) $2(\alpha - \beta)$

## Section - II - Multiple Correct Answer Type

This section contains 4 multiple correct answer(s) type questions. Each question has 4 choices (a), (b), (c) and (d), out of which **ONE OR MORE** is/are correct.

9. Two sides of a triangle are lines (a + b)x + (a − b)y − 2ab = 0 and (a − b) x + (a + b) y − 2ab = 0. If the triangle is isosceles

and the third side passes through point (b − a, a − b) then the equation of third side can be
   (a) $x + y = 0$      (b) $x = y + 2 (b - a)$
   (c) $x - b + a = 0$      (d) $y - a + b = 0$

10. Two straight lines u = 0 and v = 0 passes through the origin forming an angle of $\tan^{-1}(7/9)$ with each other. If the ratio of the slopes of v = 0 and u = 0 is 9/2 then their equations are
   (a) y = 3x and 3y = 2x      (b) 2y = 3x and 3y = x
   (c) y + 3x = 0 and 3y + 2x = 0 (d) 2y + 3x = 0 and 3y + x = 0

11. The equations $(b - c) x + (c - a) y + a - b = 0$, $(b^3 - c^3) x + (c^3 - a^3) y + a^3 - b^3 = 0$ will represent the same line if
   (a) b = c     (b) c = a     (c) a = b     (d) a + b + c = 0

12. Equation of a straight line passing through the point of intersection of $x - y + 1 = 0$ and $3x + y - 5 = 0$ are perpendicular to one of them is
   (a) $x + y + 3 = 0$      (b) $x + y - 3 = 0$
   (c) $x - 3y - 5 = 0$      (d) $x - 3y + 5 = 0$

## Section - III - Linked Comprehension Type

This section contains one paragraph. Based upon the paragraph, 3 multiple choice questions have to be answered. Each question has 4 choices (a), (b), (c) and (d), out of which **ONLY ONE** is correct.

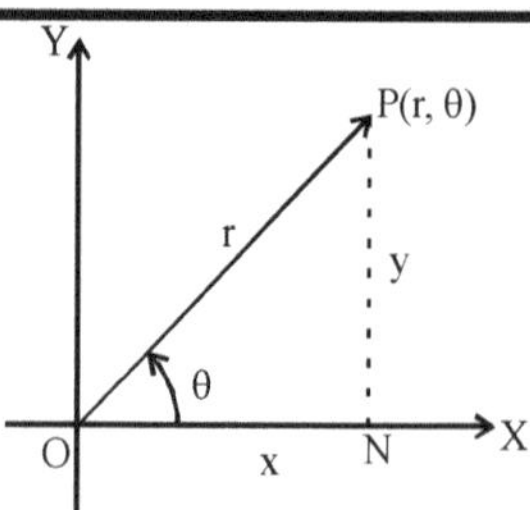


Suppose that $OX$ be a fixed straight line drawn through a fixed point $O$. The position of any point $P$ can be expressed uniquely by its distance $OP$ from $O$ and the angle that radius vector $OP$ forms with line $OX$. If $OP = r$ and $\angle XOP = \theta$ then we say $(r, \theta)$ are the polar coordinates of point $P$.

$O$ is called pole and $OX$ is the initial line. If cartesion coordinates of $P$ be $(x, y)$ as shown in figure then we have
$x = r \cos \theta$ and $y = r \sin \theta$
We know that cartesian equation of a line is
$ax + by + c = o$ or $a(r \cos \theta) + b(r \sin \theta) + c = o$

<table>
<tr><td rowspan="2">**RESPONSE GRID**</td><td>5. (a)(b)(c)(d)</td><td>6. (a)(b)(c)(d)</td><td>7. (a)(b)(c)(d)</td><td>8. (a)(b)(c)(d)</td><td>9. (a)(b)(c)(d)</td></tr>
<tr><td>10. (a)(b)(c)(d)</td><td>11. (a)(b)(c)(d)</td><td>12. (a)(b)(c)(d)</td><td></td><td></td></tr>
</table>

*Space for Rough Work*

or $-\dfrac{c}{r} = a\cos\theta + b\sin\theta$ or $\dfrac{l}{r} = a\cos\theta + b\sin\theta$,

Which is the most general equation of a straight line in polar coordinates, $l$, $a$ and $b$ being constants.

**13.** The equation of any straight line passing through the pole and making an angle $\alpha$ with the initial line is

(a) $\theta = \alpha$

(b) $r = \cos\alpha$

(c) $r = \cos(\alpha - \theta)$

(d) $r = \cos(\alpha - \theta) + \sin(\alpha - \theta)$

**14.** The equation of $a$ straight line parallel to the line

$a\cos\theta + b\sin\theta = \dfrac{l}{r}$ is

(a) $a\sin\theta + b\cos\theta = \dfrac{l'}{r}$ 　　(b) $a\sin\theta - b\cos\theta = \dfrac{l'}{r}$

(c) $a\cos\theta + b\sin\theta = \dfrac{l'}{r}$ 　　(d) $\cos\theta + \sin\theta = \dfrac{a+b}{r}$

**15.** The line perpendicular to a $a\cos\theta + b\sin\theta = \dfrac{l}{r}$ passing through pole is

(a) $a\sin\theta - b\cos\theta = \dfrac{l'}{r}$ 　　(b) $\theta = \tan^{-1}\dfrac{b}{a}$

(c) $r = a\cos\theta$ 　　(d) $r = a\sin\theta$

## Section - IV - Matrix-Match Type

This section contain 1 question. It contain statements given in two columns, which have to be matched. Statements in Column I are labelled as A, B, C and D whereas statements in Column II are labelled as p, q, r and s. The answers to these questions have to be appropriately bubbled as illustrated in the following example. If the correct matches are A-p, A-r, B-p, B-s, C-r, C-s and D-q, then the correctly bubbled matrix will look like the following :

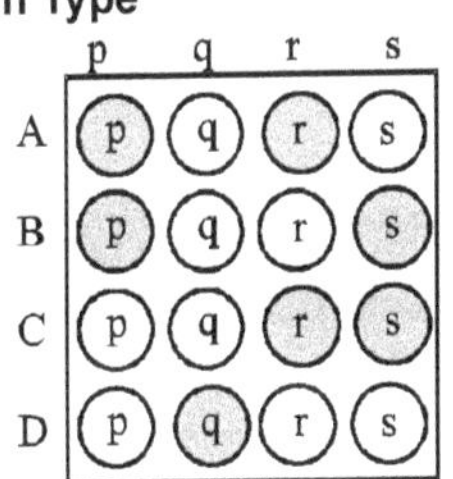

**16.**

| | Column I | | Column II |
|---|---|---|---|
| (A) | For the lines $4x+3y-6=0$ and $5x+12y+9=0$, acute angle bisector and obtuse angle bisectors represented by A and O respectively, then | p. | $A : 7x-9y-3=0$ |
| (B) | For the lines $4x-3y-6=0$ and $5x-12y+9=0$, acute angle bisector and obtuse angle bisectors represented by $A$ and $O$ respectively, then | q. | $A : 7x-9y+3=0$ |
| (C) | For the straight lines $4x-3y+6=0$ and $5x-12y-9=0$, acute angle bisector and obtuse angle bisectors represented by $A$ and $O$ respectively, then | r. | $A : 7x+9y-3=0$ |
| | | s. | $O : 9x+7y-41=0$ |
| | | t. | $O : 9x-7y-41=0$ |

## Section - V - Reasoning Type

This section contains 3 reasoning type questions. Each question has 4 choices (a), (b), (c) and (d) out of which **ONLY ONE** is correct.

**DIRECTIONS for (Qs. 17 to 19) : Each of these questions contains two statements: Statement-1 (Assertion) and Statement-2 (Reason). Each of these questions has four alternative choices, only one of which is the correct answer. You have to select the correct choice.**

(a) Statement-1 is True, Statement-2 is True; Statement-2 is a correct explanation for Statement-1.

(b) Statement-1 is True, Statement-2 is True; Statement-2 is NOT a correct explanation for Statement-1.

(c) Statement -1 is True, Statement-2 is False.

(d) Statement -1 is False, Statement-2 is True.

---

**RESPONSE GRID**

13. (a)(b)(c)(d)　14. (a)(b)(c)(d)　15. (a)(b)(c)(d)

16.A - (p)(q)(r)(s)(t); B - (p)(q)(r)(s)(t); C - (p)(q)(r)(s)(t); D - (p)(q)(r)(s)(t)

*Space for Rough Work*

**17.** **Statement-1:** The equation of the straight line which passes through the point (2, –3) and the point of the intersection of the lines $x + y + 4 = 0$ and $3x - y - 8 = 0$ is $2x - y - 7 = 0$
**Statement-2 :** Product of slopes of two perpendicular straight lines is –1.

**18.** **Statement-1 :** Consider the point A (0, 1) and B (2, 0) and P be a point on the line $4x + 3y + 9 = 0$, then coordinates of P such that $|PA - PB|$ is maximum, is $\left(-\dfrac{12}{5}, \dfrac{17}{5}\right)$

**Statement-2 :** $|PA - PB| \leq |AB|$

**19.** **Statement-1 :** The combined equation of straight lines $\ell_1, \ell_2$ is $2x^2 + 6xy + y^2 = 0$ and that of straight lines $m_1, m_2$ is $4x^2 + 18xy + y^2 = 0$. If the angle between $\ell_1$ and $m_2$ is $\alpha$ then angle between the lines $\ell_2$ and $m_1$ is $\alpha$.

**Statement-2 :** If the pairs of lines $\ell_1 \ell_2 = 0$, and $m_1 m_2 = 0$ are equally inclined then angle between $\ell_1$ and $m_2$ = angle between $\ell_2$ and $m_1$.

## Section - VI - Integer Type

This section contains 5 questions. The answer to each of the questions is a single digit integer ranging from 0 to 9.

**20.** The line $y = 3x$ bisects the angle between the lines $a^2x^2 + 2axy + y^2 = 0$. If $a = -X$ or $\dfrac{1}{X}$, then find the value of X.

**21.** If the slope of one of the lines represented by $ax^2 + 2hxy + by^2 = 0$ be the square of the other, then find the value of $\dfrac{a+b}{h} + \dfrac{8h^2}{ab}$.

**22.** One of the bisectors of the angle between the lines $a(x-1)^2 + 2h(x-1)(y-2) + b(y-2)^2 = 0$ is $x + 2y - 5 = 0$. If the other bisector passes through the point $(\alpha, \alpha - 4)$ then find the value of $\alpha$.

**23.** If $\theta_1$ and $\theta_2$ be the angles which the lines $(x^2 + y^2)(\cos^2\theta \sin^2\alpha + \sin^2\theta) = (x\tan\alpha - y\sin\theta)^2$ make with the axis of $X$, and $\theta = \dfrac{\pi}{6}$, then $\tan\theta_1 + \tan\theta_2$ $= -\dfrac{A}{B}\cos ec2\alpha$. Find the value of A– B.

**24.** Find the number of integer values of $m$, for which the $X$-coordinate of the point of intersection of the lines $3x + 4y = 9$ and $y = mx + 1$ is also an integer.

<table>
<tr><td rowspan="4">Response Grid</td><td colspan="2">17. ⓐⓑⓒⓓ   18. ⓐⓑⓒⓓ   19. ⓐⓑⓒⓓ</td></tr>
<tr><td>20. ⓪①②③④⑤⑥⑦⑧⑨</td><td>21. ⓪①②③④⑤⑥⑦⑧⑨</td></tr>
<tr><td>22. ⓪①②③④⑤⑥⑦⑧⑨</td><td>23. ⓪①②③④⑤⑥⑦⑧⑨</td></tr>
<tr><td colspan="2">24. ⓪①②③④⑤⑥⑦⑧⑨</td></tr>
</table>

## DAILY PRACTICE PROBLEM DPP 30 - MATHS

| Total Questions | 24 | Total Marks | 73 |
|---|---|---|---|
| Attempted | | Correct | |
| Incorrect | | Net Score | |
| Cut-off Score | 15 | Qualifying Score | 47 |
| Success Gap = Net Score – Qualifying Score | | | |

$$\text{Net Score} = \sum_{i=1}^{VI}\left[(\text{correct}_i \times MM_i) - (In_i - NM_i)\right]$$

*Space for Rough Work*

# DPP - Daily Practice Problems

**Name :**

**Date :**

**Start Time :**

**End Time :**

# MATHEMATICS    M31

**SYLLABUS : Straight Line-2 :** Distance between two lines, Perpendicular distance of the line from a point, Position of a point w.r.t. line, Concurrency of three lines, Foot of perpendicular, Transformation, Pedal points, Image of a point, Problems related to triangle and quadrilateral, Locus

## Max. Marks : 71                    Time : 60 min.

### GENERAL INSTRUCTIONS

- The Daily Practice Problem Sheet contains **23** Questions divided into 6 sections.
  Section I has **8** MCQ's with ONLY 1 correct option. 2 marks for correct answer and No negative marks.
  Section II has **3** MCQ's with 1 or MORE THAN 1 correct option. 4 marks for correct answer(s) and (–1) for wrong answer.
  Section III has **1** PASSAGE with **3** MCQ's with ONLY 1 correct option. 3 marks for correct and (–1) mark for wrong answer.
  Section IV has **2** MCQ's with multiple matchings. 1 mark for the correct matching of each row & No negative marks.
  Section V has **2** Assertion-Reason MCQ's with ONLY 1 correct option. 3 marks for correct and (–1) mark for wrong answer.
  Section VI has **5** single digit integer answer questions. 4 marks for correct answer and (–1) for wrong answer.
- No mark will be given/ deducted if no bubble is filled. Keep a timer in front and stop immediately at the end of 60 min.
- You have to evaluate your Response Grids yourself with the help of Solution Booklet.
- The sheet follows a particular syllabus. Do not attempt the sheet before you have completed your preparation for that syllabus. Refer syllabus sheet in the starting of the book for the syllabus of all the DPP sheets.
- After completing the sheet check your answers with the solution booklet and complete the Result Grid. Finally spend time to analyse your performance and revise the areas which emerge out as weak in your evaluation.

## Section - I - Straight Objective Type

This section contains 8 multiple choice questions. Each question has 4 choices (a), (b), (c) and (d), out of which **ONLY ONE** is correct.

**1.** A variable rectangle PQRS has its sides parallel to fixed directions. Q & S lie respectively on the lines $x = a$, $x = -a$ & P lies on the $x$ – axis . Then the locus of R is :
(a) a straight line
(b) a circle
(c) a parabola
(d) pair of straight lines

**2.** Given A(0, 0) and B(x, y) with $x \in (0, 1)$ and $y > 0$. Let the slope of the line AB equals $m_1$. Point C lies on the line $x = 1$ such that the slope of BC equals $m_2$ where $0 < m_2 < m_1$. If the area of the triangle ABC can be expressed as $(m_1 - m_2) f(x)$, then the largest possible value of $f(x)$ is
(a) 1          (b) 1/2          (c) 1/4          (d) 1/8

**3.** A line has intercepts a, b on the coordinate axes. If the axes are rotated about the origin through an angle $\alpha$ then the line has intercepts p, q on the new position of the axes respectively. Then

(a) $1/p^2 + 1/q^2 = 1/a^2 + 1/b^2$
(b) $1/p^2 - 1/q^2 = 1/a^2 - 1/b^2$
(c) $1/p^2 + 1/a^2 = 1/q^2 + 1/b^2$
(d) none

**4.** The equation $14x^2 - 4xy + 11y^2 = 60$ represents a certain locus. If the axes are rotated through an angle $\tan^{-1} 2$, without change of origin then the equation of the locus referred to new axes becomes

(a) $\dfrac{x^2}{4} + \dfrac{y^2}{5} = 1$ (b) $\dfrac{x^2}{6} + \dfrac{y^2}{4} = 1$ (c) $\dfrac{x^2}{6} - \dfrac{y^2}{4} = 1$ (d) $\dfrac{x^2}{5} - \dfrac{y^2}{4} = 1$

**5.** Three straight lines are drawn through a point P lying in the interior of the $\triangle ABC$ and parallel to its sides. The areas of the three resulting triangles with P as the vertex are $s_1, s_2$ and $s_3$. The area of the triangle in terms of $s_1, s_2$ and $s_3$ is

(a) $\sqrt{s_1 s_2 + s_2 s_3 + s_3 s_1}$   (b) $\sqrt[3]{s_1 s_2 s_3}$

(c) $\left(\sqrt{s_1} + \sqrt{s_2} + \sqrt{s_3}\right)^2$   (d) none

---

**RESPONSE GRID**    **1.** ⓐⓑⓒⓓ    **2.** ⓐⓑⓒⓓ    **3.** ⓐⓑⓒⓓ    **4.** ⓐⓑⓒⓓ    **5.** ⓐⓑⓒⓓ

**6.** Let $0 < \alpha < \dfrac{\pi}{2}$ be fixed angle. If

$P = (\cos\theta, \sin\theta)$ and $Q = (\cos(\alpha-\theta), \sin(\alpha-\theta))$, then $Q$ is obtained from $P$ by

(a) clockwise rotation around origin through an angle $\alpha$
(b) anticlockwise rotation around origin through an angle $\alpha$
(c) reflection in the line through origin with slope $\tan\alpha$
(d) reflection in the line through origin with slope $\tan(\alpha/2)$

**7.** Line $ax + by + p = 0$ makes angle $\pi/4$ with $x\cos\alpha + y\sin\alpha = p$, $p \in R^+$. If these lines and the line $x\sin\alpha - y\cos\alpha = 0$ are concurrent then -

(a) $a^2 + b^2 = 1$     (b) $a^2 + b^2 = 2$
(c) $2(a^2 + b^2) = 1$     (d) none of these

**8.** The point $(4, 1)$ undergoes the following three transformations successively.

(i) Reflection in the line $y = x$.
(ii) Translation through a distance 2 units along the positive direction of X-axis.
(iii) Rotation through an angle $\pi/4$ about the origin in the counter clockwise direction.

Then the final position of the point is given by the coordinates.

(a) $\left(\dfrac{1}{\sqrt{2}}, \dfrac{7}{\sqrt{2}}\right)$     (b) $(-\sqrt{2}, 7\sqrt{2})$

(c) $\left(-\dfrac{1}{\sqrt{2}}, \dfrac{7}{\sqrt{2}}\right)$     (d) $(\sqrt{2}, 7\sqrt{2})$

## Section - II - Multiple Correct Answer Type

This section contains 3 multiple correct answer(s) type questions. Each question has 4 choices (a), (b), (c) and (d), out of which **ONE OR MORE** is/are correct.

**9.** Let $L$ be the line $2x + y = 2$. If the axes are rotated by $45°$, then the intercept made by the line $L$ on the length of new axes are respectively

(a) $\sqrt{2}$ and 1     (b) 1 and $\sqrt{2}$
(c) $2\sqrt{2}$ and $2\sqrt{2}/3$     (d) $2\sqrt{2}/3$ and $2\sqrt{2}$

**10.** If one vertex of an equilateral triangle of side a, lies at the origin and the other lies on the line $x - \sqrt{3}\,y = 0$, the coordinates of the third vertex are

(a) $(0, a)$ (b) $(\sqrt{3}\,a/2, -a/2)$ (c) $(0, -a)$ (d) $(-\sqrt{3}\,a/2, a/2)$

**11.** If one diagonal of a square is the portion of the line $\dfrac{x}{a} + \dfrac{y}{b} = 1$ intersected by the axes, then the extremities of the other diagonal of the square are –

(a) $\left(\dfrac{a+b}{2}, \dfrac{a+b}{2}\right)$     (b) $\left(\dfrac{a-b}{2}, \dfrac{a+b}{2}\right)$

(c) $\left(\dfrac{a-b}{2}, \dfrac{b-a}{2}\right)$     (d) $\left(\dfrac{a+b}{2}, \dfrac{b-a}{2}\right)$

## Section - III - Linked Comprehension Type

This section contains one paragraph. Based upon the paragraph, 3 multiple choice questions have to be answered. Each question has 4 choices (a), (b), (c) and (d), out of which **ONLY ONE** is correct.

Let $S' = 0$ be the image or reflection of the curve $S = 0$ in line mirror $L = 0$. Suppose $P$ be any point on the curve $S = 0$ and $Q$ be the image or reflection of P in the line mirror $L = 0$, then $Q$ will lie on $S' = 0$. How to find the image or reflection of a curve? Let the given curve be $S : f(x, y) = 0$ and line mirror $L : ax + by + c = 0$.

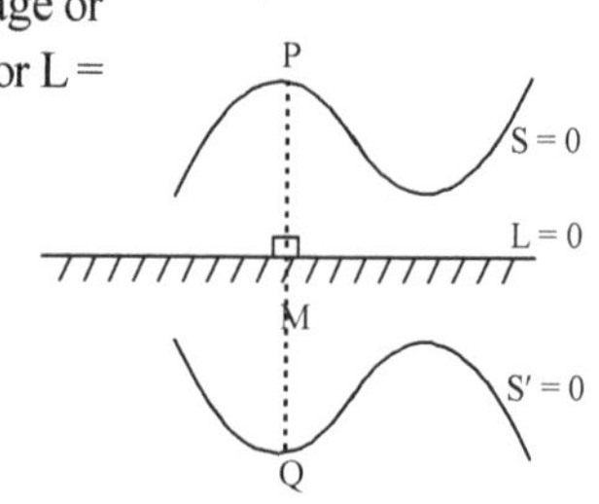


We take a point $P$ on the given curve in parametric form. Suppose $Q$ be the image or reflection of point $P$ about line mirror $L = 0$, which again contains the same parameter.

<table>
<tr><td rowspan="2">Response<br>Grid</td><td>6. ⓐⓑⓒⓓ</td><td>7. ⓐⓑⓒⓓ</td><td>8. ⓐⓑⓒⓓ</td><td>9. ⓐⓑⓒⓓ</td><td>10. ⓐⓑⓒⓓ</td></tr>
<tr><td colspan="5">11. ⓐⓑⓒⓓ</td></tr>
</table>

Let $Q = (\phi(t), \psi(t))$ where $t$ is parameter. Now let $x = \phi(t)$ and $y = \psi(t)$ Eliminating $t$, we get the equation of the reflected curve $S'$.

**On the basis of above information, answer the following questions :**

12. The image of the line $3x - y = 2$ in the line $y = x - 1$ is
 (a) $x + 3y = 2$  (b) $3x + y = 2$
 (c) $x - 3y = 2$  (d) $x + y = 2$

13. The image of the circle $x^2 + y^2 = 4$ in the line $x + y = 2$ is
 (a) $x^2 + y^2 - 2x - 2y = 0$  (b) $x^2 + y^2 - 4x - 4y + 6 = 0$
 (c) $x^2 + y^2 - 2x - 2y + 2 = 0$  (d) $x^2 + y^2 - 4x - 4y + 4 = 0$

14. The image of the parabola $x^2 = 4y$ in the line $x + y = a$ is
 (a) $(x - a)^2 = 4(a - y)$  (b) $(y - a)^2 = 4(a - x)$
 (c) $(x - a)^2 = 4(a + y)$  (d) $(y - a)^2 = 4(a + x)$

## Section - IV - Matrix-Match Type

This section contains 2 questions. It contains statements given in two columns, which have to be matched. Statements in Column I are labelled as A, B, C and D whereas statements in Column II are labelled as p, q, r and s. The answers to these questions have to be appropriately bubbled as illustrated in the following example. If the correct matches are A-p, A-r, B-p, B-s, C-r, C-s and D-q, then the correctly bubbled matrix will look like the following :

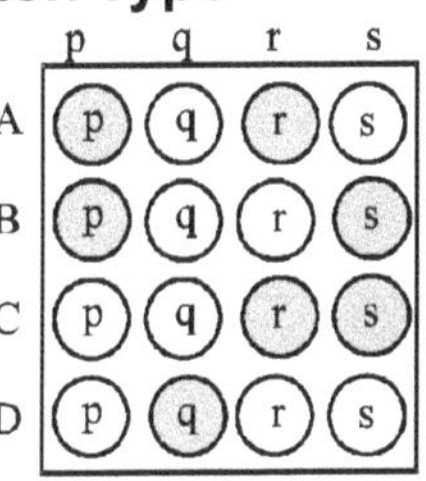

15. 

| | Column-I | | Column-II |
|---|---|---|---|
| (A) | The image of the point $(2, -3)$ with respect to $Y$-axis | p. | $(5, 0)$ |
| (B) | The image of the point $(-3, 4)$ with respect to $(1, 2)$ | q. | $(-4, 1)$ |
| (C) | The image of the point $(2, 1)$ with respect to the line $x + 1 = 0$ | r. | $(-4, -1)$ |
| (D) | The image of the point $(4, 3)$ with respect to the line $2x + y - 1 = 0$ | s. | $(-2, -3)$ |

16.

| | Column -I | | Column -II |
|---|---|---|---|
| (A) | The sides BC, CA and AB of a triangle ABC are $x + 2y = 1$, $3x + y + 5 = 0$ and $x - y + 2 = 0$. The equation of the altitude through B is | p. | $2x - y = 1$ |
| (B) | The image of the line $x - 2y = 1$ in the line $x + y = 0$ is | q. | $2x + y = 3$ |
| (C) | A right angled triangle ACB with sides AB, BC, CA in ratio 5:4:3 moves such that A and B always lie on the positive X and Y axes respectively. The locus of C is | r. | $3x - 4y = 0$ |
| (D) | A(1, 2) and B(-1, 5) are two vertices of a triangle ABC whose third vertex C lies on the line $2x + y = 2$. The locus of the centroid of the triangle is | s. | $4x + 3y = 4$ |
| | | t. | $x - 3y + 4 = 0$ |

## Section - V - Reasoning Type

This section contains 2 reasoning type questions. Each question has 4 choices (a), (b), (c) and (d) out of which **ONLY ONE** is correct.

**DIRECTIONS for (Qs. 17 & 18) :** Each of these questions contains two statements: Statement-1 (Assertion) and Statement-2 (Reason). Each of these questions has four alternative choices, only one of which is the correct answer. You have to select the correct choice.

(a) Statement-1 is True, Statement-2 is True; Statement-2 is a correct explanation for Statement-1.
(b) Statement-1 is True, Statement-2 is True; Statement-2 is NOT a correct explanation for Statement-1.
(c) Statement -1 is True, Statement-2 is False.
(d) Statement -1 is False, Statement-2 is True.

**RESPONSE GRID**

12. (a)(b)(c)(d)  13. (a)(b)(c)(d)  14. (a)(b)(c)(d)
15. A - (p)(q)(r)(s); B - (p)(q)(r)(s); C - (p)(q)(r)(s); D - (p)(q)(r)(s)
16. A - (p)(q)(r)(s)(t); B - (p)(q)(r)(s)(t); C - (p)(q)(r)(s)(t); D - (p)(q)(r)(s)(t)

*Space for Rough Work*

17. **Statement-1:** If $(a_1x + b_1y + c_1) + (a_2x + b_2y + c_2) + (a_3x + b_3y + c_3) = 0$ then lines $a_1x + b_1y + c_1 = 0$, $a_2x + b_2y + c_2 = 0$ and $a_3x + b_3y + c_3 = 0$ cannot be parallel
    **Statement-2:** If sum of three straight lines equations is identically zero then they are either concurrent or parallel.

18. **Statement-1 :** The image of $P(a, b)$ on $y = -x$ is $Q$ and the image of $Q$ on the line $y = x$ is $R$.
    **Statement-2 :** The mid-point of $PR$ is $(1, 1)$.

## Section - VI - Integer Type

This section contains 5 questions. The answer to each of the questions is a single digit integer ranging from 0 to 9.

19. If the lines $x + y + 1 = 0$ ; $4x + 3y + 4 = 0$ and $x + \alpha y + \beta = 0$, where $\alpha^2 + \beta^2 = 2$, are concurrent then find the value of $\beta$.

20. A straight line cuts the $X$-axis at point $A(1, 0)$, and $Y$-axis at point $B$, such that $\angle OAB = \alpha$ where $\left(\alpha > \dfrac{\pi}{4}\right)$. $C$ is a middle point of $AB$, if $B'$ is a mirror image of point $B$ in line $OC$ and $C'$ is a mirror image of point $C$ with respect to line $BB'$, then find the ratio of the areas of triangles $ABB'$ and $BB'C'$

21. Find the number of possible straight lines , passing through $(2, 3)$ and forming a triangle with coordinate axes, whose area is 12 sq. units

22. The distance of the point $(2, 3)$ from the line $2x - 3y + 9 = 0$ measured along a line $x - y + 1 = 0$, is $2A\sqrt{A}$ . Find A

23. If lines $x + 2y - 1 = 0$, $ax + y + 3 = 0$ and $bx - y + 2 = 0$ are concurrent and let $S$ be the curve denoting locus of $(a, b)$. Then the least distance of S from the origin is $\dfrac{A}{\sqrt{B}}$ . Find the value of A.

| RESPONSE GRID | |
|---|---|
| 17.ⓐⓑⓒⓓ 18.ⓐⓑⓒⓓ 19.⓪①②③④⑤⑥⑦⑧⑨ | |
| 20.⓪①②③④⑤⑥⑦⑧⑨ 21.⓪①②③④⑤⑥⑦⑧⑨ | |
| 22.⓪①②③④⑤⑥⑦⑧⑨ 23.⓪①②③④⑤⑥⑦⑧⑨ | |

## DAILY PRACTICE PROBLEM DPP 31 - MATHS

| Total Questions | 23 | Total Marks | 71 |
|---|---|---|---|
| Attempted | | Correct | |
| Incorrect | | Net Score | |
| Cut-off Score | 14 | Qualifying Score | 46 |
| Success Gap = Net Score – Qualifying Score | | | |

$$\text{Net Score} = \sum_{i=\text{I}}^{\text{VI}} \left[(\text{correct}_i \times MM_i) - (In_i - NM_i)\right]$$

Name : 

Date : 

Start Time : 

End Time : 

# MATHEMATICS  M32

SYLLABUS : **Circle -1** : Equation of circle, Geometrical Problems regarding circle

## Max. Marks : 73

## Time : 60 min.

**GENERAL INSTRUCTIONS**

- The Daily Practice Problem Sheet contains **24** Questions divided into 6 sections.
  Section I has **8** MCQ's with ONLY 1 correct option. 2 marks for correct answer and No negative marks.
  Section II has **4** MCQ's with 1 or MORE THAN 1 correct option. 4 marks for correct answer(s) and (–1) for wrong answer.
  Section III has **1** PASSAGE with **3** MCQ's with ONLY 1 correct option. 3 marks for correct and (–1) mark for wrong answer.
  Section IV has **2** MCQ's with multiple matchings. 1 mark for the correct matching of each row & No negative marks.
  Section V has **2** Assertion-Reason MCQ's with ONLY 1 correct option. 3 marks for correct and (–1) mark for wrong answer.
  Section VI has **5** single digit integer answer questions. 4 marks for correct answer and (–1) for wrong answer.
- No mark will be given/ deducted if no bubble is filled. Keep a timer in front and stop immediately at the end of 60 min.
- You have to evaluate your Response Grids yourself with the help of Solution Booklet.
- The sheet follows a particular syllabus. Do not attempt the sheet before you have completed your preparation for that syllabus. Refer syllabus sheet in the starting of the book for the syllabus of all the DPP sheets.
- After completing the sheet check your answers with the solution booklet and complete the Result Grid. Finally spend time to analyse your performance and revise the areas which emerge out as weak in your evaluation.

## Section - I - Straight Objective Type

This section contains 8 multiple choice questions. Each question has 4 choices (a), (b), (c) and (d), out of which **ONLY ONE** is correct.

**1.** A variable circle C has the equation $x^2 + y^2 - 2(t^2 - 3t + 1)x - 2(t^2 + 2t)y + t = 0$, where t is a parameter.
The locus of the centre of the circle is
(a) a parabola
(b) an ellipse
(c) a hyperbola
(d) pair of straight lines

**2.** If a circle of constant radius $3k$ passes through the origin 'O' and meets co-ordinate axes at A and B then the locus of the centroid of the triangle OAB is
(a) $x^2 + y^2 = (2k)^2$
(b) $x^2 + y^2 = (3k)^2$
(c) $x^2 + y^2 = (4k)^2$
(d) $x^2 + y^2 = (6k)^2$

**3.** The circle passing through the distinct points $(1, t)$, $(t, 1)$ & $(t, t)$ for all values of $'t'$, passes through the point :
(a) $(-1, -1)$
(b) $(-1, 1)$
(c) $(1, -1)$
(d) $(1, 1)$

**4.** A circle of constant radius $'a'$ passes through origin 'O' and cuts the axes of co–ordinates in points P and Q, then

the equation of the locus of the foot of perpendicular from O to PQ is :

(a) $(x^2 + y^2)\left(\dfrac{1}{x^2} + \dfrac{1}{y^2}\right) = 4a^2$

(b) $(x^2 + y^2)^2\left(\dfrac{1}{x^2} + \dfrac{1}{y^2}\right) = a^2$

(c) $(x^2 + y^2)^2\left(\dfrac{1}{x^2} + \dfrac{1}{y^2}\right) = 4a^2$

(d) $(x^2 + y^2)\left(\dfrac{1}{x^2} + \dfrac{1}{y^2}\right) = a^2$

**5.** The locus of the mid points of the chords of the circle $x^2 + y^2 - ax - by = 0$ which subtend a right angle at $\left(\dfrac{a}{2}, \dfrac{b}{2}\right)$ is

(a) $ax + by = 0$
(b) $ax + by = a^2 + b^2$

(c) $x^2 + y^2 - ax - by + \dfrac{a^2 + b^2}{8} = 0$

(d) $x^2 + y^2 - ax - by - \dfrac{a^2 + b^2}{8} = 0$

| RESPONSE GRID | 1. ⓐⓑⓒⓓ | 2. ⓐⓑⓒⓓ | 3. ⓐⓑⓒⓓ | 4. ⓐⓑⓒⓓ | 5. ⓐⓑⓒⓓ |
|---|---|---|---|---|---|

**6.** A circle lying in $1^{st}$ quadrant touches x and y axis at point P and Q respectively. BC and AD are parallel tangents to the circle with slope $-1$. If the points A and B are on the y axis while C and D are on the x-axis and the area of the figure ABCD is $900\sqrt{2}$ square units then the radius of circle is–

(a) 25                (b) 15

(c) 30                (d) None of these

**7.** The lines $2x - 3y = 5$ and $3x - 4y = 7$ are diameters of a circle of area 154 sq. units. Then the equation of this circle is

(a) $x^2 + y^2 + 2x - 2y = 62$    (b) $x^2 + y^2 + 2x - 2y = 47$

(c) $x^2 + y^2 - 2x + 2y = 47$    (d) $x^2 + y^2 - 2x + 2y = 62$

**8.** The locus of the centre of a circle, which touches externally the circle $x^2 + y^2 - 6x - 6y + 14 = 0$ and also touches the y - axis, is given by the equation :

(a) $x^2 - 6x - 10y + 14 = 0$    (b) $x^2 - 10x - 6y + 14 = 0$

(c) $y^2 - 6x - 10y + 14 = 0$    (d) $y^2 - 10x - 6y + 14 = 0$

## Section - II - Multiple Correct Answer Type

This section contains 4 multiple correct answer(s) type questions. Each question has 4 choices (a), (b), (c) and (d), out of which **ONE OR MORE** is/are correct.

**9.** The locus of the midpoint of a line segment that is drawn from a given external point P to a given circle with centre O (where O is origin) and radius r, is –

(a) radius r

(b) a circle with centre P

(c) radius $\dfrac{r}{2}$

(d) a circle with centre at the midpoint PO

**10.** Let x, y be real variable satisfying the $x^2 + y^2 + 8x - 10y - 40 = 0$. Let $a = \max \{(x+2)^2 + (y-3)^2\}$ and $b = \min \{(x+2)^2 + (y-3)^2\}$ then

(a) $a + b = 18$         (b) $a + b = 4\sqrt{2}$

(c) $a - b = 8\sqrt{2}$         (d) $a \cdot b = 73$

**11.** If $(a, 0)$ is a point on a diameter of the circle $x^2 + y^2 = 4$, then $x^2 - 4x - a^2 = 0$ has

(a) exactly one real root in $(-1, 0]$

(b) Exactly one real root in $[2, 5]$

(c) distinct roots greater than $-1$

(d) Distinct roots less than 5

**12.** The equation of a circle with centre $(4, 3)$ and touching the circle $x^2 + y^2 = 1$ is

(a) $x^2 + y^2 - 8x - 6y - 9 = 0$   (b) $x^2 + y^2 - 8x - 6y + 11 = 0$

(c) $x^2 + y^2 - 8x - 6y - 11 = 0$ (d) $x^2 + y^2 - 8x - 6y + 9 = 0$

## Section - III - Linked Comprehension Type

This section contains one paragraph. Based upon the paragraph, 3 multiple choice questions have to be answered. Each question has 4 choices (a), (b), (c) and (d), out of which **ONLY ONE** is correct.

A system of circles is said to be coaxal when every pair of the circles has the same radical axis. It follows from this definition that

(i) The centres of all circles of a coaxal system lie on one straight line, which is perpendicular to the common radical axis

(ii) Circles passing through two fixed points form a coaxal system with line joining the points as common radical axis.

(iii) The equation to a coaxal system of which two members are $S_1 = 0$ and $S_2 = 0$ is $S_1 + \lambda S_2 = 0$, $\lambda$ is parameter.

If we choose the line of centres as $x$-axis and the common radical axis as $y$-axis, then the simplest form of equation of coaxal circles is

$$x^2 + y^2 + 2gx + c = 0 \qquad ....(1)$$

where $c$ is fixed and $g$ is variable.

If $g = \pm\sqrt{c}$, $c > 0$, then the radius $g^2 - c$ vanishes and the circles become point circles. The points $(\pm\sqrt{c}, 0)$ are called the limiting points of the system of coaxal circles given by (1).

**13.** The coordinates of the limiting points of the coaxal system to which the circles $x^2 + y^2 + 4x + 2y + 5 = 0$ and $x^2 + y^2 + 2x + 4y + 7 = 0$ belong are

(a) $(0, -3), (0, 3)$        (b) $(0, 3), (-2, -1)$

(c) $(-2, -1), (0, -3)$      (d) $(2, 1), (-2, -1)$

| RESPONSE GRID | | | | | |
|---|---|---|---|---|---|
| **6.** ⓐⓑⓒⓓ | **7.** ⓐⓑⓒⓓ | **8.** ⓐⓑⓒⓓ | **9.** ⓐⓑⓒⓓ | **10.** ⓐⓑⓒⓓ |
| **11.** ⓐⓑⓒⓓ | **12.** ⓐⓑⓒⓓ | **13.** ⓐⓑⓒⓓ | | |

**14.** The equation to the circle which belongs to the coaxal system of which the limiting points are $(1, -1)$, $(2, 0)$ and which passes through the origin is

(a) $x^2 + y^2 - 4x = 0$  (b) $x^2 + y^2 + 4x = 0$

(c) $x^2 + y^2 - 4y = 0$  (d) $x^2 + y^2 + 4y = 0$

**15.** If origin be a limiting point of a coaxal system one of whose member is $x^2 + y^2 - 2\alpha x - 2\beta y + c = 0$, then the other limiting point is

(a) $\left( \dfrac{c\alpha}{\alpha^2 + \beta^2}, -\dfrac{c\beta}{\alpha^2 + \beta^2} \right)$  (b) $\left( \dfrac{c\alpha}{\alpha^2 + \beta^2}, \dfrac{c\beta}{\alpha^2 + \beta^2} \right)$

(c) $\left( \dfrac{\alpha\beta}{\alpha^2 + \beta^2}, \dfrac{c\alpha}{\alpha^2 + \beta^2} \right)$  (d) $\left( -\dfrac{c\beta}{\alpha^2 + \beta^2}, \dfrac{c\alpha}{\alpha^2 + \beta^2} \right)$

## Section - IV - Matrix-Match Type

This section contains 2 questions. It contains statements given in two columns, which have to be matched. Statements in Column I are labelled as A, B, C and D whereas statements in Column II are labelled as p, q, r and s. The answers to these questions have to be appropriately bubbled as illustrated in the following example. If the correct matches are A-p, A-r, B-p, B-s, C-r, C-s and D-q, then the correctly bubbled matrix will look like the following :

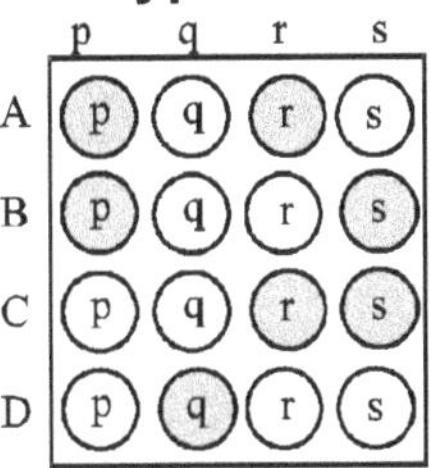

**16.**

| Column I | Column II |
|---|---|
| (A) If the shortest and largest distance from the point $(10, 7)$ to the circle $x^2 + y^2 - 4x - 2y - 20 = 0$ are $L$ and $M$ respectively, then | p. $M + L = 10$ |
| (B) If the shortest and largest distance from the point $(3, -6)$ to the circle $x^2 + y^2 - 16x - 12y - 125 = 0$ are $L$ and $M$ respectively, then | q. $M + L = 20$ |
| (C) If the shortest and largest distance from the point $(6, -6)$ to the circle $x^2 + y^2 - 4x + 6y - 12 = 0$ are $L$ and $M$ respectively, then | r. $M + L = 30$ |
| | s. $M - L = 10$ |
| | t. $M - L = 26$ |

**17.**

| Column I | Column II |
|---|---|
| (A) The largest distance between $x^2 + y^2 - 2x - 2y + 1 = 0$, $x^2 + y^2 - 10x + 4y + 20 = 0$ is $3\lambda$, then $\lambda$ is | p. 3 |
| (B) Numerical value of radius of the circle circumscribed about a square of area 200 sq. units is | q. 7 |
| (C) If a chord of the circle $x^2 + y^2 - 4x - 2y + k = 0$ is trisected at the points $\left( \dfrac{1}{3}, \dfrac{1}{3} \right)$ and $\left( \dfrac{8}{3}, \dfrac{8}{3} \right)$ and $\ell$ is the length of the chord then $\ell / \sqrt{2}$ is equal to | r. 0 |
| | s. 10 |

## Section - V - Reasoning Type

This section contains 2 reasoning type questions. Each question has 4 choices (a), (b), (c) and (d) out of which ONLY ONE is correct.

**DIRECTIONS for (Qs 18-19) :** Each of these questions contains two statements: Statement-1 (Assertion) and Statement-2 (Reason). Each of these questions has four alternative choices, only one of which is the correct answer. You have to select the correct choice.

(a) Statement-1 is True, Statement-2 is True; Statement-2 is a correct explanation for Statement-1.

(b) Statement-1 is True, Statement-2 is True; Statement-2 is NOT a correct explanation for Statement-1.

(c) Statement -1 is True, Statement-2 is False.

(d) Statement -1 is False, Statement-2 is True.



*Space for Rough Work*

**18.** **Statement - 1 :** The smallest possible radius of circle which pass through $(1, 0)$ and $(0, 1)$ is $\dfrac{1}{\sqrt{2}}$.

**Statement -2 :** Circle passes through origin.

**19.** **Statement-1** : The circle $x^2 + y^2 + 2ax + c = 0$, $x^2 + y^2 + 2by + c = 0$ touch if $\dfrac{1}{a^2} + \dfrac{1}{b^2} = \dfrac{1}{c}$

**Statement-2** : Two circles with centre $C_1, C_2$ and radii $r_1, r_2$ touch each other if $r_1 \pm r_2 = C_1C_2$

## Section - VI - Integer Type

This section contains 5 questions. The answer to each of the questions is a single digit integer ranging from 0 to 9.

**20.** The line $2x - y + 1 = 0$ is tangent to the circle at the point $(2, 5)$ and the centre of the circles lies on $x - 2y = 4$. If the radius of the circle is $A\sqrt{B}$, then find the value of $A + B$

**21.** Let $A(-4, 0)$ and $B(4, 0)$. If the number of points $C = (x, y)$ on the circle $x^2 + y^2 = 16$ is such that the area of the triangle whose vertices are A, B and C is a positive integer, are $(11P + 7)$, find the value of P.

**22.** Chord AB of the circle $x^2 + y^2 = 100$ passes through the point $(7, 1)$ and subtends an angle of $60°$ at the circumference of the circle, If $m_1$ and $m_2$ are the slopes of two such chords then the value of $m_1 m_2$, is P. Find the value of P.

**23.** The number of integral values of $\alpha$ for which the point $(\alpha - 1, \alpha + 1)$ lies in the larger segment of the circle $x^2 + y^2 - x - y - 6 = 0$ cut by the chord whose equation is $x + y - 2 = 0$ is equal to ?

**24.** Two curves $ax^2 + 2hxy + by^2 - 2gx - 2fy + c = 0$ and $a'x^2 - 2hxy + (a' + a - b)y^2 - 2g'x - 2f'y + c = 0$ intersect in four concyclic points $A$, $B$, $C$ and $D$. If $P$ be the point $\left(\dfrac{g + g'}{a + a'}, \dfrac{f + f'}{a + a'}\right)$ then $\dfrac{PA^2}{PD^2} + \dfrac{PB^2}{PD^2} + \dfrac{PC^2}{PD^2}$ is equal to

| RESPONSE GRID | | |
|---|---|---|
| 18. ⓐⓑⓒⓓ | 19. ⓐⓑⓒⓓ | 20. ⓪①②③④⑤⑥⑦⑧⑨ |
| 21. ⓪①②③④⑤⑥⑦⑧⑨ | 22. ⓪①②③④⑤⑥⑦⑧⑨ | |
| 23. ⓪①②③④⑤⑥⑦⑧⑨ | 24. ⓪①②③④⑤⑥⑦⑧⑨ | |

## DAILY PRACTICE PROBLEM DPP 32 - MATHS

| Total Questions | 24 | Total Marks | 73 |
|---|---|---|---|
| Attempted | | Correct | |
| Incorrect | | Net Score | |
| Cut-off Score | 15 | Qualifying Score | 47 |
| Success Gap = Net Score – Qualifying Score | | | |

$$\text{Net Score} = \sum_{i=I}^{VI} \left[ (\text{correct}_i \times MM_i) - (In_i - NM_i) \right]$$

**Name :**

**Date :**

**Start Time :**

**End Time :**

# MATHEMATICS  M33

**SYLLABUS : Circles-2 :** Tangent and normal to a circle

## Max. Marks : 69

## Time : 60 min.

### GENERAL INSTRUCTIONS

- The Daily Practice Problem Sheet contains **23** Questions divided into 6 sections.
  Section I has **8** MCQ's with ONLY 1 correct option. 2 marks for correct answer and No negative marks.
  Section II has **4** MCQ's with 1 or MORE THAN 1 correct option. 4 marks for correct answer(s) and (–1) for wrong answer.
  Section III has **1** PASSAGE with **3** MCQ's with ONLY 1 correct option. 3 marks for correct and (–1) mark for wrong answer.
  Section IV has **2** MCQ's with multiple matchings. 1 mark for the correct matching of each row & No negative marks.
  Section V has **2** Assertion-Reason MCQ's with ONLY 1 correct option. 3 marks for correct and (–1) mark for wrong answer.
  Section VI has **4** single digit integer answer questions. 4 marks for correct answer and (–1) for wrong answer.
- No mark will be given/ deducted if no bubble is filled. Keep a timer in front and stop immediately at the end of 60 min.
- You have to evaluate your Response Grids yourself with the help of Solution Booklet.
- The sheet follows a particular syllabus. Do not attempt the sheet before you have completed your preparation for that syllabus. Refer syllabus sheet in the starting of the book for the syllabus of all the DPP sheets.
- After completing the sheet check your answers with the solution booklet and complete the Result Grid. Finally spend time to analyse your performance and revise the areas which emerge out as weak in your evaluation.

## Section - I - Straight Objective Type

This section contains 8 multiple choice questions. Each question has 4 choices (a), (b), (c) and (d), out of which **ONLY ONE** is correct.

**1.** If the line $x \cos\theta + y \sin\theta = 2$ is a transverse common tangent to the circles $x^2 + y^2 = 4$ and $x^2 + y^2 - 6\sqrt{3}\,x - 6y + 20 = 0$, then the value of $\theta$ is :
(a) $5\pi/6$   (b) $2\pi/3$   (c) $\pi/3$   (d) $\pi/6$

**2.** Tangents are drawn to a unit circle with centre at the origin from each point on the line $2x + y = 4$. Then the equation to the locus of the middle point of the chord of contact is
(a) $2(x^2 + y^2) = x + y$   (b) $2(x^2 + y^2) = x + 2y$
(c) $4(x^2 + y^2) = 2x + y$   (d) none of these

**3.** Tangents are drawn to the circle $x^2 + y^2 = 1$ at the points where it is met by the circles,
$x^2 + y^2 - (\lambda + 6)x + (8 - 2\lambda)y - 3 = 0$. $\lambda$ being the variable. The locus of the point of intersection of these tangents is
(a) $2x - y + 10 = 0$   (b) $x + 2y - 10 = 0$
(c) $x - 2y + 10 = 0$   (d) $2x + y - 10 = 0$

**4.** Let PQ and RS be tangents at the extremities of the diameter PR of a circle of radius $r$. If PS and RQ intersect at a point $X$ on the circumference of the circle, then $2r$ equals
(a) $\sqrt{PQ \cdot RS}$   (b) $(PQ + RS)/2$
(c) $2PQ.RS/(PQ + RS)$   (d) $\sqrt{(PQ^2 + RS^2)}/2$

**5.** Tangents are drawn from $O$ (origin) to touch the circle $x^2 + y^2 + 2gx + 2fy + c = 0$ at points $P$ and $Q$. The equation of the circle circumscribing triangle $OPQ$ is
(a) $2x^2 + 2y^2 + gx + fy = 0$   (b) $x^2 + y^2 + gx + fy = 0$
(c) $x^2 + y^2 + 2gx + 2fy = 0$   (d) None of these

**6.** Tangents are drawn to the circle $x^2 + y^2 = 12$ at the points where it is met by the circle $x^2 + y^2 - 5x + 3y - 2 = 0$; the point of intersection of these tangents is

(a) $\left(6, -\dfrac{18}{5}\right)$

(b) $\left(6, \dfrac{18}{5}\right)$

(c) $\left(\dfrac{18}{5}, 6\right)$

(d) None of these.

**7.** A ray of light incident at the point $(-2, -1)$ gets reflected from the tangent at $(0, -1)$ to the circle $x^2 + y^2 = 1$. The reflected ray touches the circle. The equation of the line along which the incident ray moved, is

(a) $4x - 3y + 11 = 0$

(b) $4x + 3y + 11 = 0$

(c) $3x + 4y + 11 = 0$

(d) $4x + 3y + 7 = 0$

**8.** The range of values of $a$ such that the angle $\theta$ between the pair of tangents drawn from $(a, 0)$ to the circle $x^2 + y^2 = 1$ lies in the interval $\left(\dfrac{\pi}{3}, \pi\right)$, is

(a) $(-2, -1) \cup (1, 2)$

(b) $(-\sqrt{2}, 0) \cup (0, \sqrt{2})$

(c) $(-\sqrt{3}, -\sqrt{2})$

(d) $(-\sqrt{3}, -\sqrt{2}) \cup (\sqrt{2}, \sqrt{3})$

**9.** A point moving around circle $(x + 4)^2 + (y + 2)^2 = 25$ with centre C broke away from it either at the point A or point B on the circle and moved along a tangent to the circle passing through the point D $(3, -3)$. Then

(a) Equation of the tangents at A and B are respectively $4x + 3y = 3$ and $3x - 4y = 21$

(b) Coordinates of the points A and B are respectively $(0, 1)$ and $(-1, -6)$.

(c) Equation of the tangents at A and B are respectively $4y - 3x = 3$ and $3y + 4x = 21$

(d) Coordinates of the points A and B are respectively $(1, 0)$ and $(-6, -1)$.

**10.** The equations of the tangents drawn from the origin to the circle $x^2 + y^2 - 2rx - 2hy + h^2 = 0$, are

(a) $x = 0$

(b) $y = 0$

(c) $(h^2 - r^2)x - 2rhy = 0$

(d) $(h^2 - r^2)x + 2rhy = 0$

**11.** The tangents drawn from the origin to the circle $x^2 + y^2 - 2rx - 2hy + h^2 = 0$ are perpendicular if

(a) $h = r$

(b) $h = -r$

(c) $r^2 + h^2 = 1$

(d) $r^2 = h^2$

**12.** Tangents are drawn to the circle $x^2 + y^2 = 50$ from a point '$P$' lying on the x–axis. These tangents meet the y-axis at point '$P_1$' and '$P_2$' Possible coordinates of '$P$' so that area of triangle $PP_1P_2$ is minimum, are

(a) $(10, 0)$

(b) $(10\sqrt{2}, 0)$

(c) $(-10, 0)$

(d) $(-10\sqrt{2}, 0)$

## Section - II - Multiple Correct Answer Type

This section contains 4 multiple correct answer(s) type questions. Each question has 4 choices (a), (b), (c) and (d), out of which **ONE OR MORE** is/are correct.

## Section - III - Linked Comprehension Type

This section contains one paragraph. Based upon the paragraph, 3 multiple choice questions have to be answered. Each question has 4 choices (a), (b), (c) and (d), out of which **ONLY ONE** is correct.



*Space for Rough Work*

A ball is moving around the circle $14x^2 + 14y^2 + 216x - 69y + 432 = 0$ in clockwise direction leaves it tangentially at the point P(–3, 6). After getting reflected from a straight line L = 0 it passes through the center of the circle. The perpendicular distance of this straight line L = 0 from the point P is $\frac{11}{13}\sqrt{130}$ . You can assume that the angle of incidence is equal to the angle of reflection.

**13.** The equation of tangent to the circle at P is

   (a) $2x - y + 12 = 0$        (b) $4x + 3y - 6 = 0$

   (c) $3x - 2y + 21 = 0$      (d) $2x + 5y - 24 = 0$

**14.** Radius of the circle is

   (a) $\dfrac{165}{14}$            (b) $\dfrac{165}{46}$

   (c) $\dfrac{165}{28}$            (d) none of these

**15.** If angle between the tangent at P and the line through 'P' perpendicular to the line L = 0 is $\theta$ , then $\tan\theta$ is

   (a) 2/11            (b) 3/11

   (c) 4/11            (d) None of these

## Section - IV - Matrix-Match Type

This section contains 2 questions. It contains statements given in two columns, which have to be matched. Statements in Column I are labelled as A, B, C and D whereas statements in Column II are labelled as p, q, r and s. The answers to these questions have to be appropriately bubbled as illustrated in the following example. If the correct matches are A-p, A-r, B-p, B-s, C-r, C-s and D-q, then the correctly bubbled matrix will look like the following :

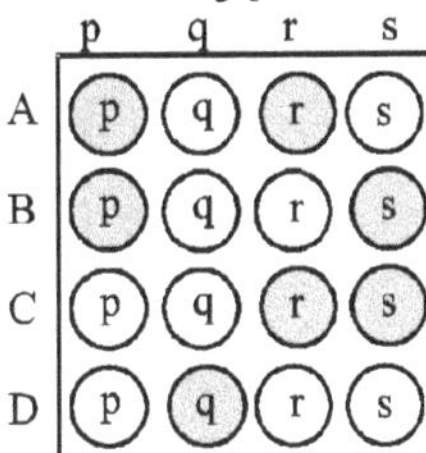

**16.**

| | Column I | Column II |
|---|---|---|
| (A) | If the straight line $y = mx \ \forall \ m \in I$ touches or lies outside the circle $x^2 + y^2 - 20y + 90 = 0$, then the value of $\lvert m \rvert$ can be | p.   0 |
| (B) | If the straight line $3x - 4y - 5k = 0$, $\forall\, k \in I$ touches or intersects the circle, $x^2 + y^2 - 4x - 8y - 5 = 0$, then the value of $\lvert k + 2 \rvert$ can be | q.   1 |
| (C) | Two circles $x^2 + y^2 + px + py - 7 = 0$ and $x^2 + y^2 - 10x + 2py + 1 = 0$ will cut orthogonally, then the value of $p$ is | r.   2 |
| | | s.   3 |
| | | t.   4 |

**17.**

| | Column I | Column II |
|---|---|---|
| (A) | If one of the diameters of the circle $x^2 + y^2 - 2x - 6y + 6 = 0$ is a chord to the circle with centre at $(2,1)$ then the radius of the circle is equal to | p.   $2 - \sqrt{3}$ |
| (B) | AB is a chord of the circle $x^2 + y^2 = 25$ and the tangents at A and B intersect at C. If $\left(2, 2\sqrt{3}\right)$ be the mid-point of AB, then the area of the quadrilateral OACB is equal to (O being origin) | q.   $2 + \sqrt{3}$ |
| | | r.   2 |
| (C) | A circle C of radius unity touches both the coordinate axes and lies in the first quadrant. If the circle $C_1$ which also touches both the axis and lies in the first quadrant, intersects C orthogonally then the radius of $C_1$ can be equal to | s.   3 |
| | | t.   $\dfrac{75}{4}$ |

## Section - V - Reasoning Type

This section contains 2 reasoning type questions. Each question has 4 choices (a), (b), (c) and (d) out of which **ONLY ONE** is correct.



*Space for Rough Work*

**DIRECTIONS for (Qs. 18 & 19) :** Each of these questions contains two statements: Statement-1 (Assertion) and Statement-2 (Reason). Each of these questions has four alternative choices, only one of which is the correct answer. You have to select the correct choice.

(a)    Statement-1 is True, Statement-2 is True; Statement-2 is a correct explanation for Statement-1.

(b)    Statement-1 is True, Statement-2 is True; Statement-2 is NOT a correct explanation for Statement-1.

(c)    Statement-1 is True, Statement-2 is False.

(d)    Statement-1 is False, Statement-2 is True.

**18.** **Statement - 1:** The line $(x-3)\cos\theta + (y-3)\sin\theta = 1$ touches a circle $(x-3)^2 + (y-3)^2 = 1$ for all values of $\theta$.

**Statement -2 :** $x\cos\theta + y\sin\theta = a$ is a tangent of circle $x^2 + y^2 = a^2$ for all values of $\theta$.

**19.** **Statement -1 :** The common tangents of the circles $x^2 + y^2 + 2x = 0$, $x^2 + y^2 - 6x = 0$ form an equilateral triangle.

**Statement -2 :** The given circles touch each other externally.

## Section - VI - Integer Type

This section contains 4 questions. The answer to each of the questions is a single digit integer ranging from 0 to 9.

**20.** Two circles of radii 4 cms & 1 cm touch each other externally and $\theta$ is the angle between their direct common tangents. If $\sin\theta = \dfrac{A}{B}$, then find the value of $B - A$.

**21.** If $p_1$ and $p_2$ are the two values of p for which two perpendicular tangents can be drawn from the origin to the circle $x^2 - 6x + y^2 - 2py + 17 = 0$, then find the value of

$$\dfrac{(p_1{}^2 + p_2{}^2)}{10}.$$

**22.** A point moving around a circle $x^2 + y^2 + 8x + 4y - 5 = 0$ with centre C broke away from it either at the point A or at the point B on the circle and moved along a tangent to the circle passing through the point D $(3, -3)$. If the area of the quadrilateral ABCD is $M^2$, find M.

**23.** If the tangent at the point P on the circle $x^2 + y^2 + 6x + 6y = 2$ meets a straight line $5x - 2y + 6 = 0$ at a point Q on the y-axis, then find the length of PQ.

<table>
<tr><td rowspan="3">RESPONSE GRID</td><td>18. ⓐⓑⓒⓓ</td><td>19. ⓐⓑⓒⓓ</td><td>20. ⓪①②③④⑤⑥⑦⑧⑨</td></tr>
<tr><td>21. ⓪①②③④⑤⑥⑦⑧⑨</td><td colspan="2">22. ⓪①②③④⑤⑥⑦⑧⑨</td></tr>
<tr><td>23. ⓪①②③④⑤⑥⑦⑧⑨</td><td></td><td></td></tr>
</table>

## DAILY PRACTICE PROBLEM DPP 33 - MATHS

| Total Questions | 23 | Total Marks | 69 |
|---|---|---|---|
| Attempted | | Correct | |
| Incorrect | | Net Score | |
| Cut-off Score | 14 | Qualifying Score | 45 |
| Success Gap = Net Score – Qualifying Score | | | |

$$\text{Net Score} = \sum_{i=1}^{VI}\left[(\mathbf{correct}_i \times MM_i) - (In_i - NM_i)\right]$$

*Space for Rough Work*

# DPP - Daily Practice Problems

**Name :**

**Date :**

**Start Time :**

**End Time :**

## MATHEMATICS M34

SYLLABUS : **Circles-3** : Chord of contact of tangent, System of circles

**Max. Marks : 68**

**Time : 60 min.**

### GENERAL INSTRUCTIONS

- The Daily Practice Problem Sheet contains **22** Questions divided into 6 sections.
  Section I has **8** MCQ's with ONLY 1 correct option. 2 marks for correct answer and No negative marks.
  Section II has **4** MCQ's with 1 or MORE THAN 1 correct option. 4 marks for correct answer(s) and (–1) for wrong answer.
  Section III has **1** PASSAGE with **3** MCQ's with ONLY 1 correct option. 3 marks for correct and (–1) mark for wrong answer.
  Section IV has **1** MCQ's with multiple matchings. 1 mark for the correct matching of each row & No negative marks.
  Section V has **1** Assertion-Reason MCQ's with ONLY 1 correct option. 3 marks for correct and (–1) mark for wrong answer.
  Section VI has **5** single digit integer answer questions. 4 marks for correct answer and (–1) for wrong answer.
- No mark will be given/ deducted if no bubble is filled. Keep a timer in front and stop immediately at the end of 60 min.
- You have to evaluate your Response Grids yourself with the help of Solution Booklet.
- The sheet follows a particular syllabus. Do not attempt the sheet before you have completed your preparation for that syllabus. Refer syllabus sheet in the starting of the book for the syllabus of all the DPP sheets.
- After completing the sheet check your answers with the solution booklet and complete the Result Grid. Finally spend time to analyse your performance and revise the areas which emerge out as weak in your evaluation.

---

## Section - I - Straight Objective Type

This section contains 8 multiple choice questions. Each question has 4 choices (a), (b), (c) and (d), out of which **ONLY ONE** is correct.

**1.** Let a and b represent the length of a right triangle's legs. If d is the diameter of a circle inscribed into the triangle, and D is the diameter of a circle superscribed on the triangle, then d + D equals

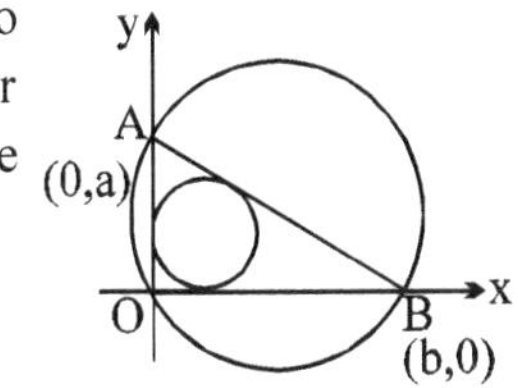

(a) $a + b$   (b) $2(a + b)$

(c) $\frac{1}{2}(a + b)$   (d) $\sqrt{a^2 + b^2}$

**2.** Three concentric circles of which the biggest is $x^2 + y^2 = 1$, have their radii in A.P. If the line $y = x + 1$ cuts all the circles in real and distinct points. The interval in which the common difference of the A.P. will lie is

(a) $\left(0, \frac{1}{4}\right)$   (b) $\left(0, \frac{1}{2\sqrt{2}}\right)$

(c) $\left(0, \frac{2 - \sqrt{2}}{4}\right)$   (d) none of these

**3.** P is a point (a, b) in the first quadrant. If the two circles which pass through P and touch both the co-ordinate axes cut at right angles, then :

(a) $a^2 - 6ab + b^2 = 0$   (b) $a^2 + 2ab - b^2 = 0$

(c) $a^2 - 4ab + b^2 = 0$   (d) $a^2 - 8ab + b^2 = 0$

**4.** The angle at which the circles $(x - 1)^2 + y^2 = 10$ and $x^2 + (y - 2)^2 = 5$ intersect is

(a) $\frac{\pi}{6}$   (b) $\frac{\pi}{4}$

(c) $\frac{\pi}{3}$   (d) $\frac{\pi}{2}$

---

| **RESPONSE GRID** | 1. ⓐⓑⓒⓓ | 2. ⓐⓑⓒⓓ | 3. ⓐⓑⓒⓓ | 4. ⓐⓑⓒⓓ |
|---|---|---|---|---|

**5.** The locus of the centers of the circles which cut the circles $x^2 + y^2 + 4x - 6y + 9 = 0$ and $x^2 + y^2 - 5x + 4y - 2 = 0$ orthogonally is :

(a) $9x + 10y - 7 = 0$       (b) $x - y + 2 = 0$

(c) $9x - 10y + 11 = 0$       (d) $9x + 10y + 7 = 0$

**6.** Let $P$ be any moving points on the circle $x^2 + y^2 - 2x = 1$. $AB$ be the chord of contact of this point with respect to the circle $x^2 + y^2 - 2x = 0$. The locus of the circumcentre of the triangle $CAB$, ($C$ centre of the circles) is

(a) $2x^2 + 2y^2 - 4x + 1 = 0$    (b) $x^2 + y^2 - 4x + 1 = 0$

(c) $x^2 + y^2 - 4x + 2 = 0$    (d) $2x^2 + 2y^2 - 4x + 3 = 0$

**7.** The chord of contact of tangents from a point P to a circle passes through Q. If $l_1$ and $l_2$ are the length of the tangents from P and Q to the circle, then PQ is equal to

(a) $\dfrac{l_1 + l_2}{2}$       (b) $\dfrac{l_1 - l_2}{2}$

(c) $\sqrt{l_1^2 + l_2^2}$       (d) $\sqrt{l_1 l_2}$

**8.** The equation of the circle described on the common chord of the circles $x^2 + y^2 + 2x = 0$ and $x^2 + y^2 + 2y = 0$ as a diameter is

(a) $x^2 + y^2 + x + y = 0$    (b) $x^2 + y^2 - x + y = 0$

(c) $x^2 + y^2 - x - y = 0$    (d) $x^2 + y^2 + x - y = 0$

## Section - II - Multiple Correct Answer Type

This section contains 4 multiple correct answer(s) type questions. Each question has 4 choices (a), (b), (c) and (d), out of which **ONE OR MORE** is/are correct.

**9.** The equation of a cricle of radius 2 touching the circles $x^2 + y^2 - 4|x| = 0$ is

(a) $x^2 + y^2 + 2\sqrt{3}y + 2 = 0$

(b) $x^2 + y^2 + 4\sqrt{3}y + 8 = 0$

(c) $x^2 + y^2 - 4\sqrt{3}y + 8 = 0$

(d) None of these.

**10.** If the equations of four circle are $(x \pm 4)^2 + (y \pm 4)^2 = 4^2$, then the radius of the smallest circle touching all the four circles is

(a) $4(\sqrt{2} + 1)$       (b) $4(\sqrt{2} - 1)$

(c) $2(\sqrt{2} - 1)$       (d) None of these

**11.** The equations of four circles are $(x \pm a)^2 + (y \pm a)^2 = a^2$. The radius of a circle touching all the four circles is

(a) $(\sqrt{2} - 1)a$       (b) $2\sqrt{2}\,a$

(c) $(\sqrt{2} + 1)\,a$       (d) $(2 + \sqrt{2})\,a$

**12.** Point M moved along the circle $(x - 4)^2 + (y - 8)^2 = 20$. At sometime it broke away from its circular path at some point moving along the tangent to the circle of the point, cuts the x-axis at the point $(-2, 0)$. The co-ordinates of the point on the circle at which the moving point broke away can be

(a) $\left(-\dfrac{3}{5}, \dfrac{46}{5}\right)$       (b) $\left(-\dfrac{2}{5}, \dfrac{44}{5}\right)$

(c) $(6, 4)$       (d) $(3, 5)$

## Section - III - Linked Comprehension Type

This section contains one paragraph. Based upon the paragraph, 3 multiple choice questions have to be answered. Each question has 4 choices (a), (b), (c) and (d), out of which **ONLY ONE** is correct.

A $(3, 7)$ and B $(6, 5)$ are two points.

C : $x^2 + y^2 - 4x - 6y - 3 = 0$ is a circle.

**13.** The chords in which the circle C cuts the members of the family S of circle passing through A and B are concurrent at–

(a) $(2, 3)$       (b) $(2, 23/3)$

(c) $(3, 23/2)$       (d) $(3, 2)$

| **RESPONSE GRID** | 5. ⓐⓑⓒⓓ | 6. ⓐⓑⓒⓓ | 7. ⓐⓑⓒⓓ | 8. ⓐⓑⓒⓓ | 9. ⓐⓑⓒⓓ |
|---|---|---|---|---|---|
| | 10. ⓐⓑⓒⓓ | 11. ⓐⓑⓒⓓ | 12. ⓐⓑⓒⓓ | 13. ⓐⓑⓒⓓ | |

*Space for Rough Work*

**14.** Equation of the member of the family of circles S that bisects the circumference of C is –

(a) $x^2 + y^2 - 5x - 1 = 0$    (b) $x^2 + y^2 - 5x + 6y - 1 = 0$

(c) $x^2 + y^2 - 5x - 6y - 1 = 0$    (d) $x^2 + y^2 + 5x - 6y - 1 = 0$

**15.** If O is the origin and P is the centre of C, then difference of the squares of the lengths of the tangents from A and B to the circle C is equal to –

(a) $(AB)^2$    (b) $(OP)^2$

(c) $|(AP)^2 - (BP)^2|$    (d) None of these

## Section - IV - Matrix-Match Type

This section contain 1 question. It contain statements given in two columns, which have to be matched. Statements in Column I are labelled as A, B, C and D whereas statements in Column II are labelled as p, q, r and s. The answers to these questions have to be appropriately bubbled as illustrated in the following example. If the correct matches are A-p, A-r, B-p, B-s, C-r, C-s and D-q, then the correctly bubbled matrix will look like the following :

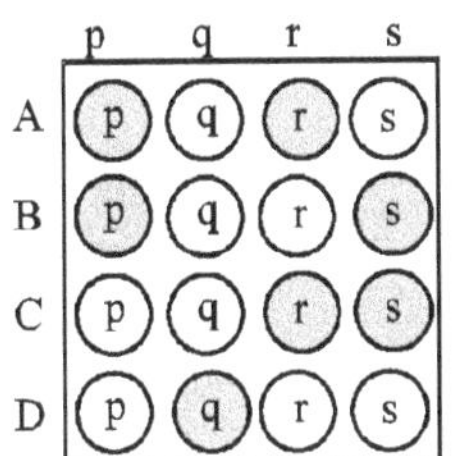

**16.** Consider two circles $C_1$ of radius a and $C_2$ of radius b (b > a) both lying in the first quadrant and touching the coordinate axes. In each of the conditions listed in column I, the ratio of b/a is given in column II.

| Column I | | Column II | |
| --- | --- | --- | --- |
| (A) | $C_1$ and $C_2$ touch each other | (p) | $2 + \sqrt{2}$ |
| (B) | $C_1$ and $C_2$ are orthogonal | (q) | 3 |
| (C) | $C_1$ and $C_2$ intersect so that the common chord is longest | (r) | $2 + \sqrt{3}$ |

(D) $C_2$ passes through the centre    (s) $3 + 2\sqrt{2}$

of $C_1$    (t) $3 - 2\sqrt{2}$

## Section - V - Reasoning Type

This section contain 1 reasoning type questions. This question has 4 choices (a), (b), (c) and (d) out of which **ONLY ONE** is correct.

**DIRECTIONS for (Qs. 17) : Each of these questions contains two statements: Statement-1 (Assertion) and Statement-2 (Reason). Each of these questions has four alternative choices, only one of which is the correct answer. You have to select the correct choice.**

(a) Statement-1 is True, Statement-2 is True; Statement-2 is a correct explanation for Statement-1.

(b) Statement-1 is True, Statement-2 is True; Statement-2 is NOT a correct explanation for Statement-1.

(c) Statement-1 is True, Statement-2 is False.

(d) Statement-1 is False, Statement-2 is True.

**17.**    **Statement 1 :** $(n \geq 3)$ for n circles the value of n for which the number of radical axes if equal to the number of radical centre is 5

     **Statement 2 :** If no two of n circle are concentric, No three of the centre are collinear then number of possible radical centres is $nc_3$

## Section - VI - Integer Type

This section contains 5 questions. The answer to each of the questions is a single digit integer ranging from 0 to 9.

**18.** Consider a circle S with centre at the origin and radius 4. Four circles A, B, C and D each with radius unity and centres (–3, 0), (–1, 0), (1, 0) and (3, 0) respectively are drawn. A chord PQ of the circle S touches the circle B and passes through the centre of the circle C. If the length of this chord can be expressed as $3\sqrt{x}$ , find x.

---

**RESPONSE GRID**

14. (a)(b)(c)(d)    15. (a)(b)(c)(d)

16. A - (p)(q)(r)(s)(t); B - (p)(q)(r)(s)(t); C - (p)(q)(r)(s)(t); D - (p)(q)(r)(s)(t)

17. (a)(b)(c)(d)    18. (0)(1)(2)(3)(4)(5)(6)(7)(8)(9)

*Space for Rough Work*

**19.** Circles A and B are externally touches to each other and to line $t$. The sum of the radii of the two circles is 12 and the radius of circle A is 3 times that of circle B. The area in between the two circles and its external tangent is

$$a\sqrt{3} - \frac{b\pi}{2} \text{ then find the value of } a - b.$$

**20.** A circle is inscribed in a triangle with sides of lengths 3, 4 and 5. A second circle, interior to the triangle, is tangent to the first circle and to both sides of the larger acute angle of the triangle. If the radius of the second circle can be expressed in the form $\dfrac{\sin k}{\cos w}$ where k and w are in degrees and lie in the interval $(0, 90°)$, find the value of $\dfrac{w}{k}$

**21.** Let $W_1$ and $W_2$ denote the circles $x^2 + y^2 + 10x - 24y - 87 = 0$ and $x^2 + y^2 - 10x - 24y + 153 = 0$ respectively. Let $m$ be the smallest positive value of 'a' for which the line $y = ax$ contains the centre of a circle that is externally tangent to $W_2$ and internally tangent to $W_1$. Given that $m = \dfrac{p}{q}$ where $p$ and $q$ are relatively prime integers, find $(p - q)$.

**22.** Equation to a system of circles is $2(x^2 + y^2) + \lambda x - (1 + \lambda^2) y - 10 = 0$. Find the number of circles belonging to the system that are orthogonal to $x^2 + y^2 + 4x + 6y + 3 = 0$.

| | | |
|---|---|---|
| **RESPONSE GRID** | 19. ⓪①②③④⑤⑥⑦⑧⑨ | 20. ⓪①②③④⑤⑥⑦⑧⑨ |
| | 21. ⓪①②③④⑤⑥⑦⑧⑨ | 22. ⓪①②③④⑤⑥⑦⑧⑨ |

## DAILY PRACTICE PROBLEM DPP 34 - MATHS

| Total Questions | 22 | Total Marks | 68 |
|---|---|---|---|
| Attempted | | Correct | |
| Incorrect | | Net Score | |
| Cut-off Score | 14 | Qualifying Score | 44 |
| Success Gap = Net Score – Qualifying Score | | | |

$$\text{Net Score} = \sum_{i=1}^{VI} \left[ (\text{correct}_i \times MM_i) - (In_i - NM_i) \right]$$

*Space for Rough Work*

Name : 

Date : 

Start Time : 

End Time : 

## MATHEMATICS  M35

SYLLABUS : Conic Sections-1 : Parabola

**Max. Marks : 74**  **Time : 60 min.**

### GENERAL INSTRUCTIONS

- The Daily Practice Problem Sheet contains **24** Questions divided into 6 sections.
  Section I has **8** MCQ's with ONLY 1 correct option. 2 marks for correct answer and No negative marks.
  Section II has **4** MCQ's with 1 or MORE THAN 1 correct option. 4 marks for correct answer(s) and (–1) for wrong answer.
  Section III has **1** PASSAGE with **3** MCQ's with ONLY 1 correct option. 3 marks for correct and (–1) mark for wrong answer.
  Section IV has **2** MCQ's with multiple matchings. 1 mark for the correct matching of each row & No negative marks.
  Section V has **2** Assertion-Reason MCQ's with ONLY 1 correct option. 3 marks for correct and (–1) mark for wrong answer.
  Section VI has **5** single digit integer answer questions. 4 marks for correct answer and (–1) for wrong answer.
- No mark will be given/ deducted if no bubble is filled. Keep a timer in front and stop immediately at the end of 60 min.
- You have to evaluate your Response Grids yourself with the help of Solution Booklet.
- The sheet follows a particular syllabus. Do not attempt the sheet before you have completed your preparation for that syllabus. Refer syllabus sheet in the starting of the book for the syllabus of all the DPP sheets.
- After completing the sheet check your answers with the solution booklet and complete the Result Grid. Finally spend time to analyse your performance and revise the areas which emerge out as weak in your evaluation.

## Section - I - Straight Objective Type

This section contains 8 multiple choice questions. Each question has 4 choices (a), (b), (c) and (d), out of which **ONLY ONE** is correct.

1. Suppose that three points on the parabola $y = x^2$ have the property that normal lines at that intersect at a common point (a, b). The sum of their x-coordinates is –

   (a)  0  (b)  $\dfrac{2b-1}{2}$

   (c)  $\dfrac{a}{2}$  (d)  $a + b$

2. Two mutually perpendicular tangents of the parabola $y^2 = 4ax$ meet the axis in $P_1$ and $P_2$. If S is the focus of the parabola then $\dfrac{1}{(SP_1)} + \dfrac{1}{(SP_2)}$ is equal to

   (a)  $\dfrac{4}{a}$  (b)  $\dfrac{2}{a}$  (c)  $\dfrac{1}{a}$  (d)  $\dfrac{1}{4a}$

3. The tangent and normal at P(t), for all real positive t, to the parabola $y^2 = 4ax$ meet the axis of the parabola in T and G respectively. Then the angle at which the tangent at P to the parabola is inclined to the tangent at P to the circle passing through the points P, T and G is

   (a)  $\cot^{-1}t$  (b)  $\cot^{-1}t^2$  (c)  $\tan^{-1}t$  (d)  $\tan^{-1}t^2$

4. Let S be the focus of $y^2 = 4x$ and a point P is moving on the curve such that it's abscissa is increasing at the rate of 4 units/sec, then the rate of increase of projection of SP on x + y = 1 when P is at (4, 4), is

   (a)  $\sqrt{2}$  (b)  $-1$

   (c)  $-\sqrt{2}$  (d)  $-\dfrac{3}{\sqrt{2}}$

5. The points of contact Q and R of tangent from the point P (2, 3) on the parabola $y^2 = 4x$ are
   (a)  (9, 6) and (1, 2)  (b)  (1, 2) and (4, 4)
   (c)  (4, 4) and (9, 6)  (d)  (9, 6) and (1/4, 1)

---

**RESPONSE GRID**  1. ⓐⓑⓒⓓ  2. ⓐⓑⓒⓓ  3. ⓐⓑⓒⓓ  4. ⓐⓑⓒⓓ  5. ⓐⓑⓒⓓ

**6.** From an external point P, pair of tangent lines are drawn to the parabola, $y^2 = 4x$. If $\theta_1$ & $\theta_2$ are the inclinations of these tangents with the axis of x such that, $\theta_1 + \theta_2 = \dfrac{\pi}{4}$, then the locus of P is :

(a)  $x - y + 1 = 0$          (b)  $x + y - 1 = 0$
(c)  $x - y - 1 = 0$          (d)  $x + y + 1 = 0$

**7.** PQ is a normal chord of the parabola $y^2 = 4ax$ at P. A being the vertex of the parabola. Through P a line is drawn parallel to AQ meeting the x–axis in R, then the length of AR is :
(a)  equal to the length of the latus rectum
(b)  equal to the focal distance of the point P
(c)  equal to twice the focal distance of the point P
(d)  equal to the distance of the point P from the directrix.

**8.** If the tangent to the parabola $y^2 = 4ax$ meets the axis in T and tangent at the vertex A in Y and the rectangle TAYG is completed, then the locus of G is
(a)  $y^2 + 2ax = 0$ (b) $y^2 + ax = 0$ (c) $x^2 + ay = 0$ (d) $x^2 + 4ay = 0$

## Section - II - Multiple Correct Answer Type

This section contains 4 multiple correct answer(s) type questions. Each question has 4 choices (a), (b), (c) and (d), out of which **ONE OR MORE** is/are correct.

**9.** A quadratic polynomial $y = f(x)$ with absolute term 3 neither touches nor intersects the abscissa axis and is symmetric about the line x = 1. The coefficient of the leading term of the polynomial is unity. A point $A(x_1, y_1)$ with abscissa $x_1 = 1$ and a point $B(x_2, y_2)$ with ordinate $y_2 = 11$ are in the first quadrant on the curve $y = f(x)$ where 'O' is the origin. Then which of the following statements are correct ?
(a)  Vertex of the quadratic polynomial is (1, 2).

(b)  The scalar product of the vectors $\overrightarrow{OA}$ and $\overrightarrow{OB}$ is 26.
(c)  The area bounded by the curve y = f(x) and a line y = 3 is 4/3.
(d)  The graph of y = f(x) represents a parabola whose focus has the co-ordinates (1, 9/4).

**10.** A variable circle passes through the point A (2, 1) and touches the x-axis. Locus of the other end of the diameter through A is a parabola. Which of the following statements are correct.

(a)  The length of the latusrectum of the parabola, is 4.
(b)  The coordinates of the foot of the directrix of the parabola, is (2, –1).
(c)  The two tangents and two normals at the extremities of the latus rectum of the parabola constitutes a quadrilateral of area equals 8.
(d)  none of these.

**11.** The parabola $x = y^2 + ay + b$ intersect the parabola $x^2 = y$ at (1, 1) at right angle.
Which of the following is/are correct –
(a)  a = 4, b = – 4          (b)  a = 2, b = – 2
(c)  Equation of the director circle for the parabola $x = y^2 + ay + b$ is 4x + 1 = 0.
(d)  Area enclosed by the parabola $x = y^2 + ay + b$ and its latusrectum is 1/6.

**12.** The line $2x - y = 1$ intersect the parabola $y^2 = 4x$ at the points A and B and the normals at A and B intersect each other at the point G. If a third normal to the parabola through G meets the parabola at C then which of the following statement(s) is/are correct.
(a)  sum of the abscissa and ordinate of the point C is – 1.
(b)  the normal at C passes through the lower end of the latus rectum of the parabola.
(c)  centroid of the triangle ABC lies at the focus of the parabola.
(d)  normal at C has the gradient – 1.

## Section - III - Linked Comprehension Type

This section contains one paragraph. Based upon the paragraph, 3 multiple choice questions have to be answered. Each question has 4 choices (a), (b), (c) and (d), out of which **ONLY ONE** is correct.

Normally, the various term you study, e.g. equation of tangent, normal, chord, focal chord, formula for focal distance etc., are derived for the parabola $y^2 = 4ax$. However, all the results with slight transformation are valid for any parabola.
Suppose we represent the equation of parabola $y^2 - 4ax = 0$ by S (x, y, a) = 0 and any equation derived for this parabola by P(x, y, a) = 0.
Now, if the given parabola is $y^2 = -4ax$, i.e. $y^2 + 4ax = 0$ we can write it S (x, y, –a) = 0. So the corresponding equation of P will be P(x, y, –a) = 0.
Similarly for $x^2 = 4ay$ can be written as S (y, x, a) and corresponding transformation is P (y, x, a) = 0 (i.e. interchange x and y).
Transformation for $x^2 = -4ay$ is P(y, x, –a) = 0.

| RESPONSE GRID | | | | | |
|---|---|---|---|---|---|
| | **6.** ⓐⓑⓒⓓ | **7.** ⓐⓑⓒⓓ | **8.** ⓐⓑⓒⓓ | **9.** ⓐⓑⓒⓓ | **10.** ⓐⓑⓒⓓ |
| | **11.** ⓐⓑⓒⓓ | **12.** ⓐⓑⓒⓓ | | | |

For example, the equation of tangent to $y^2 = 4ax$ is $y = mx + \dfrac{a}{m}$, so,

corresponding tangent to $x^2 = 4ay$ is $x = my + \dfrac{a}{m}$ and the point of

contact will be $\left( \dfrac{2a}{m}, \dfrac{a}{m^2} \right)$.

The equation of normal to $y^2 = 4ax$ is $y = mx - 2am - am^3$. The equation of normal to $x^2 = -4ay$ is $x = my + 2am + am^3$

Further, if the coordinates of vertex are not $(0, 0)$ but $(h, k)$ then we replace $x$ by $x - h$ and $y$ by $y - k$ in addition to above transformation.

**13.** The focal distance of the point $(x, y)$ on the parabola $x^2 - 8x + 16y = 0$ is

    (a) $|y - 4|$    (b) $|y - 5|$    (c) $|y - 2|$ (d) $|x - 4|$

**14.** Normals are drawn from the point $(7, 14)$ to the parabola $x^2 - 8x - 16y = 0$. The sum of the slopes of these normals is

    (a) $0$     (b) $\dfrac{3}{2}$     (c) $\dfrac{7}{3}$     (d) $-\dfrac{3}{2}$

**15.** The coordinates of the feet of normals obtained in previous problem are

    (a) $(2, 0)$     (b) $(3, 4)$     (c) $(16, 8)$ (d) $(-8, 4)$

## Section - IV - Matrix-Match Type

This section contains 2 questions. It contains statements given in two columns, which have to be matched. Statements in Column I are labelled as A, B, C and D whereas statements in Column II are labelled as p, q, r and s. The answers to these questions have to be appropriately bubbled as illustrated in the following example. If the correct matches are A-p, A-r, B-p, B-s, C-r, C-s and D-q, then the correctly bubbled matrix will look like the following

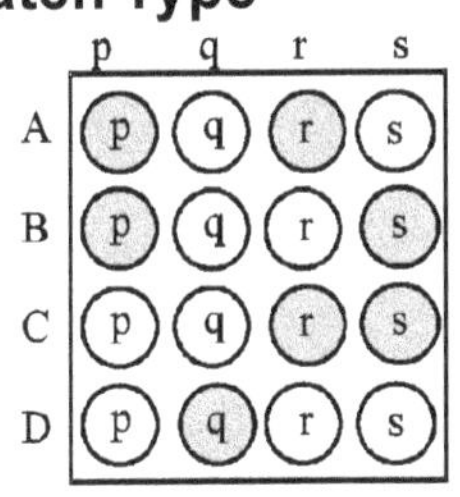

**16.**    **Column I**          **Column II**

(A)   If a parabola represented by $25(x^2 + y^2)$ $= (4x + 3y - 12)^2$, then     (p) Equation of directrix is $4x - 3y + 12 = 0$

(B)   If a parabola represented by $25(x^2 + y^2)$ $= (4x - 3y + 12)^2$, then     (q) Equation of axis of parabola is $4x + 3y = 0$

(C)   If a parabola represented by $25(x^2 + y^2)$ $= (3x - 4y + 12)^2$, then     (r) Equation of directrix is $4x + 3y = 12$

         (s) Equation of axis of parabola is $3x + 4y = 0$

         (t) Equation of directrix is $3x - 4y + 12 = 0$

**17.**    **Column I**          **Column II**

(A)   The straight line joining any point P on the parabola $y^2 = 4ax$ to the vertex and perpendicular from the focus to the tangent at P, intersect at R, then the equaiton of the locus of R is     p. $by = 2a (x - a)$

(B)   Centre of the circle is C $(0, 1)$ and radius is unity. P is the parabola $y = ax^2$. The set of values of 'a' for which they meet at a point other than the origin, is     q. $- 2 \tan \phi$

(C)   TP & TQ are tangents to the parabola, $y^2 = 4ax$ at P & Q. If the chord PQ passes through the fixed point $(- a, b)$ then the locus of T is :     r. $\left( \dfrac{1}{2}, \infty \right)$

(D)   Through the vertex O of the parabola, $y^2 = 4ax$ two chords OP & OQ are drawn and the circles on OP & OQ as diameters intersect in R. If $\theta_1$, $\theta_2$ & $\phi$ are the angles made with the axis by the tangents at P & Q on the parabola & by OR then the value of, $\cot \theta_1 + \cot \theta_2 =$     s. $2x^2 + y^2 - 2ax = 0$

## Section - V - Reasoning Type

This section contains 2 reasoning type questions. Each question has 4 choices (a), (b), (c) and (d) out of which **ONLY ONE** is correct.

<table>
<tr><td rowspan="3">**Response Grid**</td><td>13. ⓐⓑⓒⓓ    14. ⓐⓑⓒⓓ    15. ⓐⓑⓒⓓ</td></tr>
<tr><td>16. A - ⓟⓠⓡⓢⓣ B - ⓟⓠⓡⓢⓣ; C - ⓟⓠⓡⓢⓣ</td></tr>
<tr><td>17. A - ⓟⓠⓡⓢ; B - ⓟⓠⓡⓢ; C - ⓟⓠⓡⓢ; D - ⓟⓠⓡⓢ</td></tr>
</table>

*Space for Rough Work*

**DIRECTIONS for (Qs. 18 & 19) :** Each of these questions contains two statements: Statement-1 (Assertion) and Statement-2 (Reason). Each of these questions has four alternative choices, only one of which is the correct answer. You have to select the correct choice.

(a)  Statement-1 is True, Statement-2 is True; Statement-2 is a correct explanation for  Statement-1.

(b)  Statement-1 is True, Statement-2 is True; Statement-2 is NOT a correct explanation for Statement-1.

(c)  Statement -1 is True, Statement-2 is False.

(d)  Statement -1 is False, Statement-2 is True.

18.  **Statement–1:** The curve $y = \dfrac{-x^2}{2} + x + 1$ is symmetric with respect to the line $x = 1$. because

**Statement–2:** A parabola is symmetric about its axis.

19.  Tangents are drawn from the point $(-2, 5)$ to the parabola $y^2 = 8x$.

**Statement 1 :** The tangents are mutually perpendicular.

**Statement 2 :** Any point from which mutually perpendicular tangents can be drawn to the given parabola lies on $x + 2 = 0$.

## Section - VI - Integer Type

This section contains 5 questions. The answer to each of the questions is a single digit integer ranging from 0 to 9.

20.  An equilateral triangle ABC is inscribed in the parabola $y = x^2$ and one of the side of the equilateral triangle has the gradient 2. If the sum of x-coordinates of the vertices of the triangle is a rational in the form p/q where p and q are coprime, then find the value of

$\dfrac{(p+q)}{2}$

21.  A tangent is drawn to the parabola $y^2 = 4x$ at the point 'P' whose abscissa lies in the interval [1,4]. The maximum possible area of the triangle formed by the tangent at 'P' , ordinate of the point 'P' and the x-axis is equal to 4X. Find X.

22.  If the normal to a parabola $y^2 = 4ax$ at P meets the curve again in Q and if PQ and the normal at Q makes angles $\alpha$ and $\beta$ respectively with the x-axis then $\tan \alpha$ $(\tan \alpha + \tan \beta) = -N$. Find N.

23.  Tangents are drawn from the point $(-1, 2)$ on the parabola $y^2 = 4x$. The length , these tangents will intercept on the line $x = 2$ is $A\sqrt{B}$ . Find A + B.

24.  The parabola $P : y = ax^2$ where 'a' is a positive real constant, is touched by the line $L: y = mx - b$ (where $m$ is a positive constant and b is real) at the point T.

Let Q be the point of intersection of the line L and the y-axis is such that TQ = 1. If A denotes the maximum value of the region surrounded by P, L and the y-axis, find the value of $\dfrac{1}{3A}$ .

| **RESPONSE GRID** | 18. (a)(b)(c)(d)  19. (a)(b)(c)(d)  20. (0)(1)(2)(3)(4)(5)(6)(7)(8)(9) |
|---|---|
| | 21. (0)(1)(2)(3)(4)(5)(6)(7)(8)(9)  22. (0)(1)(2)(3)(4)(5)(6)(7)(8)(9) |
| | 23. (0)(1)(2)(3)(4)(5)(6)(7)(8)(9)  24. (0)(1)(2)(3)(4)(5)(6)(7)(8)(9) |

## DAILY PRACTICE PROBLEM DPP 35 - MATHS

| Total Questions | 24 | Total Marks | 74 |
|---|---|---|---|
| Attempted | | Correct | |
| Incorrect | | Net Score | |
| Cut-off Score | 15 | Qualifying Score | 49 |
| Success Gap = Net Score – Qualifying Score | | | |

$$\textbf{Net Score} = \sum_{i=I}^{VI} \Big[ (\textbf{\textit{correct}}_i \times \textbf{\textit{MM}}_i) - (\textbf{\textit{In}}_i - \textbf{\textit{NM}}_i) \Big]$$

*Space for Rough Work*

**Name :**

**Date :**

**Start Time :**

**End Time :**

## MATHEMATICS M36

SYLLABUS : Conic Sections-2 : Ellipse

## Max. Marks : 67

## Time : 60 min.

### GENERAL INSTRUCTIONS

- The Daily Practice Problem Sheet contains **22** Questions divided into 6 sections.
  Section I has **8** MCQ's with ONLY 1 correct option. 2 marks for correct answer and No negative marks.
  Section II has **4** MCQ's with 1 or MORE THAN 1 correct option. 4 marks for correct answer(s) and (–1) for wrong answer.
  Section III has **1** PASSAGE with **3** MCQ's with ONLY 1 correct option. 3 marks for correct and (–1) mark for wrong answer.
  Section IV has **1** MCQ's with multiple matchings. 1 mark for the correct matching of each row & No negative marks.
  Section V has **2** Assertion-Reason MCQ's with ONLY 1 correct option. 3 marks for correct and (–1) mark for wrong answer.
  Section VI has **4** single digit integer answer questions. 4 marks for correct answer and (–1) for wrong answer.
- No mark will be given/ deducted if no bubble is filled. Keep a timer in front and stop immediately at the end of 60 min.
- You have to evaluate your Response Grids yourself with the help of Solution Booklet.
- The sheet follows a particular syllabus. Do not attempt the sheet before you have completed your preparation for that syllabus. Refer syllabus sheet in the starting of the book for the syllabus of all the DPP sheets.
- After completing the sheet check your answers with the solution booklet and complete the Result Grid. Finally spend time to analyse your performance and revise the areas which emerge out as weak in your evaluation.

## Section - I - Straight Objective Type

This section contains 8 multiple choice questions. Each question has 4 choices (a), (b), (c) and (d), out of which **ONLY ONE** is correct.

**1.** The eccentricity of the ellipse $(x-3)^2 + (y-4)^2 = \dfrac{y^2}{9}$ is

(a) $\dfrac{\sqrt{3}}{2}$    (b) $\dfrac{1}{3}$    (c) $\dfrac{1}{3\sqrt{2}}$    (d) $\dfrac{1}{\sqrt{3}}$

**2.** The area of the rectangle formed by the perpendiculars from the centre of the standard ellipse to the tangent and normal at its point whose eccentric angle is $\pi/4$ is :

(a) $\dfrac{\left(a^2 - b^2\right) ab}{a^2 + b^2}$

(b) $\dfrac{\left(a^2 - b^2\right)}{\left(a^2 + b^2\right) ab}$

(c) $\dfrac{\left(a^2 - b^2\right)}{ab\left(a^2 + b^2\right)}$

(d) $\dfrac{a^2 + b^2}{\left(a^2 - b^2\right) ab}$

**3.** The locus of the point of intersection of two tangents to the ellipse $\dfrac{x^2}{a^2} + \dfrac{y^2}{b^2} = 1$ which are inclined at angles $\theta_1$ and $\theta_2$ with major axis such that $\theta_1 + \theta_2$ is constant, is

(a) $2xy \cot \alpha = x^2 - y^2 + b^2 - a^2$

(b) $2xy \cot \alpha = x^2 - y^2 + b^2 + a^2$

(c) $2xy \cot \alpha = x^2 - y^2 - b^2 - a^2$

(d) none of these

**4.** If a chord joining two points whose eccentric angles are $\alpha$, $\beta$ cut the major axis of the ellipse $\dfrac{x^2}{a^2} + \dfrac{y^2}{b^2} = 1$, at a distance d from the centre, then $\tan \alpha/2 . \tan \beta/2 =$

(a) $\dfrac{d+a}{d-a}$      (b) $\dfrac{d-a}{d+a}$

(c) $\dfrac{a-d}{a+d}$      (d) none of these

| RESPONSE GRID | 1. ⓐⓑⓒⓓ | 2. ⓐⓑⓒⓓ | 3. ⓐⓑⓒⓓ | 4. ⓐⓑⓒⓓ |
|---|---|---|---|---|

**5.** The eccentricity of the ellipse which meets the straight line $\dfrac{x}{7}+\dfrac{y}{2}=1$ on the axis of x and the straight line $\dfrac{x}{3}-\dfrac{y}{5}=1$ on the axis of y and whose axes lie along the axes of coordinates is

(a) $\dfrac{2\sqrt{6}}{7}$    (b) $\dfrac{3\sqrt{2}}{7}$    (c) $\dfrac{\sqrt{6}}{7}$    (d) none of these

**6.** The area of the quadrilateral formed by the tangents at the end points of latus rectum to the ellipse $\dfrac{x^2}{9}+\dfrac{y^2}{5}=1$, is

(a) 27/4 sq. units      (b) 9 sq. units
(c) 27/2 sq. units      (d) 27 sq. units

**7.** The area of the rectangle formed by the perpendiculars from the centre of ellipse $\dfrac{x^2}{a^2}+\dfrac{y^2}{b^2}=1$ to the tangent and normal at a point whose eccentric angles is $\dfrac{\pi}{4}$, is

(a) $\dfrac{(a^2-b^2)ab}{a^2+b^2}$ (b) $\dfrac{(a^2+b^2)ab}{a^2-b^2}$ (c) $\dfrac{a^2-b^2}{ab(a^2+b^2)}$ (d) $\dfrac{a^2+b^2}{ab(a^2-b^2)}$

**8.** If the line $lx+my+n=0$ cuts the ellipse $\dfrac{x^2}{a^2}+\dfrac{y^2}{b^2}=1$ in points whose eccentric angles differ by $\dfrac{\pi}{2}$, then $\dfrac{a^2l^2+b^2m^2}{n^2}=$

(a) 1      (b) 2      (c) 4      (d) $\dfrac{3}{2}$

## Section - II - Multiple Correct Answer Type

This section contains 4 multiple correct answer(s) type questions. Each question has 4 choices (a), (b), (c) and (d), out of which **ONE OR MORE** is/are correct.

**9.** An ellipse whose one focus is (4, 3) passes through (1, 2) and equation of tangent at (1, 2) is $x+y-3=0$. If the abscissa of centre of ellipse is 7, then which of the following statement is/are correct?

(a) Length of minor axis of ellipse is $12\sqrt{2}$ .

(b) Eccentricity of ellipse is $\sqrt{\dfrac{89}{125}}$ .

(c) Equation of auxiliary circle of ellipse is $(x-7)^2+(y-16)^2=250$

(d) Equation of auxiliary circle of ellipse is $(x+7)^2+(y+16)^2=250$

**10.** Extremities of the latera recta of the ellipses $\dfrac{x^2}{a^2}+\dfrac{y^2}{b^2}=1$

(a > b) having a given major axis 2a lies on
(a) $x^2=a(a-y)$      (b) $x^2=a(a+y)$
(c) $y^2=a(a+x)$      (d) $y^2=a(a-x)$

**11.** On the ellipse $4x^2+9y^2=1$, the points at which the tangents are parallel to the line $8x=9y$ are

(a) $\left(\dfrac{2}{5},\dfrac{1}{5}\right)$   (b) $\left(-\dfrac{2}{5},\dfrac{1}{5}\right)$ (c) $\left(-\dfrac{2}{5},-\dfrac{1}{5}\right)$ (d) $\left(\dfrac{2}{5},-\dfrac{1}{5}\right)$

**12.** The tangent at any point P on the standard ellipse with focii as S and S' meets the tangents at the vertices A and A' in the points V and V' then –
(a) $l\,(AV)\,l\,(A'V')=b^2$
(b) $l\,(AV)\,l\,(A'V')=a^2$
(c) $\angle\,V'SV=90°$
(d) V'S' VS is a cyclic quadrilateral

## Section - III - Linked Comprehension Type

This section contains one paragraph. Based upon the paragraph, 3 multiple choice questions have to be answered. Each question has 4 choices (a), (b), (c) and (d), out of which **ONLY ONE** is correct.

**Read the following concept carefully:**

The locus of the mid-points of parallel chords of an ellipse is called diameter of the ellipse. Two diameters are said to be conjugate

<table>
<tr><td rowspan="2">RESPONSE<br>GRID</td><td>5. (a)(b)(c)(d)</td><td>6. (a)(b)(c)(d)</td><td>7. (a)(b)(c)(d)</td><td>8. (a)(b)(c)(d)</td><td>9. (a)(b)(c)(d)</td></tr>
<tr><td>10. (a)(b)(c)(d)</td><td>11. (a)(b)(c)(d)</td><td>12. (a)(b)(c)(d)</td><td></td><td></td></tr>
</table>

*Space for Rough Work*

when bisects all chords parallel to the other. Two diameters

$$y = m_1 x \text{ and } y = m_2 x, \text{ of ellipse } \frac{x^2}{a^2} + \frac{y^2}{b^2} = 1, \text{ are conjugate}$$

if $m_1 m_2 = -\dfrac{b^2}{a^2}$.

**13.** If the eccentric angles of the end points $P$ and $Q$ of a pair of conjugate diameters be $\phi_1$ and $\phi_2$, then $\phi_1 - \phi_2$ is equal to

(a) $\pm 45°$    (b) $\pm 90°$    (c) $\pm 135°$   (d) $\pm 60°$

**14.** If $C$ is the centre of the ellipse $\dfrac{x^2}{a^2} + \dfrac{y^2}{b^2} = 1$ and $P$ and $Q$ are the end points of two conjugate diameters, then $CP^2 + CQ^2$ is equal to

(a) $\dfrac{b^4 + a^4}{a^2 + b^2}$   (b) $a^2 + b^2$   (c) $\dfrac{b^4 + a^4}{2(a^2 + b^2)}$   (d) $\dfrac{a^2 + b^2}{4}$

**15.** $C$ is the centre of the ellipse $\dfrac{x^2}{a^2} + \dfrac{y^2}{b^2} = 1$ and $P$ and $Q$ are the end points of a pair of conjugate diameters. If the tangents to the ellipse at $P$ and $Q$ meet at $R$, then the area of the quadrilateral $CPRQ$ is

(a) $4ab$     (b) $2ab$     (c) $ab$      (d) none of these

## Section - IV - Matrix-Match Type

This section contain 1 question. It contain statements given in two columns, which have to be matched. Statements in Column I are labelled as A, B, C and D whereas statements in Column II are labelled as p, q, r and s. The answers to these questions have to be appropriately bubbled as illustrated in the following example. If the correct matches

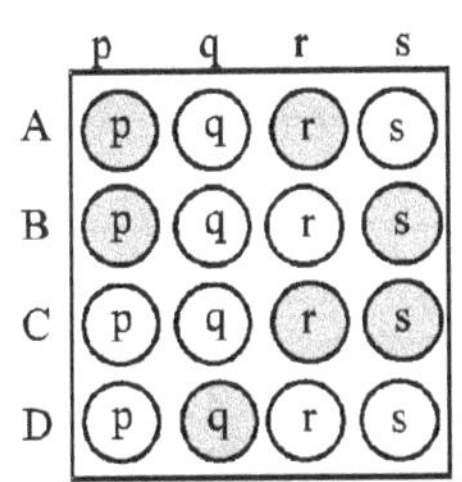

are A-p, A-r, B-p, B-s, C-r, C-s and D-q, then the correctly bubbled matrix will look like the following :

**16.** For the ellipse $\dfrac{x^2}{a^2} + \dfrac{y^2}{b^2} = 1$ $(a > b)$, match the items in column I with items in column II.

**Column I**

(A) Locus equation of point of intersection of perpendicular tangents is

(B) Locus equation of foot of perpendicular from focus upon any tangent is

(C) Locus equation of foot of perpendicular drawn from centre upon any tangent is

(D) Locus equation of mid point of segment OP where P is foot of perpendicular drawn from centre upon any tangent and O is origin is

**Column II**

(p) $(x^2 + y^2)^2 = a^2 x^2 + b^2 y^2$

(q) $4(x^2 + y^2)^2 = (a^2 x^2 + b^2 y^2)$

(r) $x^2 + y^2 = a^2$

(s) $x^2 + y^2 = a^2 + b^2$

## Section - V - Reasoning Type

This section contains 2 reasoning type questions. Each question has 4 choices (a), (b), (c) and (d) out of which **ONLY ONE** is correct.

**DIRECTIONS for (Qs. 17 & 18) : Each of these questions contains two statements: Statement-1 (Assertion) and Statement-2 (Reason). Each of these questions has four alternative choices, only one of which is the correct answer. You have to select the correct choice.**

(a) Statement-1 is True, Statement-2 is True; Statement-2 is a correct explanation for Statement-1.

(b) Statement-1 is True, Statement-2 is True; Statement-2 is NOT a correct explanation for Statement-1.

(c) Statement -1 is True, Statement-2 is False.

(d) Statement -1 is False, Statement-2 is True.

**17.** **Statement-1 :** A tangent of the ellipse $x^2 + 4y^2 = 4$ meets the ellipse $x^2 + 2y^2 = 6$ at P & Q. The angle between the tangents at P and Q of the ellipse $x^2 + 2y^2 = 6$ is $\pi/2$

**Statement-2 :** If the two tangents from point P to the ellipse $x^2/a^2 + y^2/b^2 = 1$ are at right angle, then locus of P is the circle $x^2 + y^2 = a^2 + b^2$.

**18.** **Statement-1 :** If $(5, 12)$ and $(12, 16)$ are the focii of an ellipse passing through $(0, 0)$ then the eccentricity of the ellipse is $\dfrac{\sqrt{65}}{33}$ .

**Statement-2 :** For any point P on an ellipse with foci $S_1$ and $S_2$, $S_1P + S_2P$ = Major axis of the ellipse.

## Section - VI - Integer Type

This section contains 4 questions. The answer to each of the questions is a single digit integer ranging from 0 to 9.

**19.** For an ellipse $\dfrac{x^2}{9} + \dfrac{y^2}{4} = 1$ with vertices A and A', tangent drawn at the point P in the first quadrant meets the y-axis in Q and the chord A'P meets the y-axis in M. If 'O' is the origin then find the value of $OQ^2 - MQ^2$ .

**20.** A circle has the same centre as an ellipse & passes through the foci $F_1$ & $F_2$ of the ellipse, such that the two curves intersect in 4 points. Let 'P' be any one of their point of intersection. If the major axis of the ellipse is 17 & the area of the triangle $PF_1F_2$ is 30, then the distance between the foci is 3P + 4. Find P.

**21.** Point 'O' is the centre of the ellipse with major axis AB & minor axis CD. Point F is one focus of the ellipse. If OF = 6 & the diameter of the inscribed circle of triangle OCF is 2, then the product (AB) (CD) = 13X. Find X.

**22.** A conic passing through the point A (1, 4) is such that the segment joining a point P (x, y) on the conic and the point of intersection of the normal at P with the abscissa axis is bisected by the y - axis. If the focii are (O,A) and (O, –A), then find the value of A.

| RESPONSE GRID | 18. ⓐⓑⓒⓓ | 19. ⓪①②③④⑤⑥⑦⑧⑨ |
|---|---|---|
| | 20. ⓪①②③④⑤⑥⑦⑧⑨ | 21. ⓪①②③④⑤⑥⑦⑧⑨ |
| | 22. ⓪①②③④⑤⑥⑦⑧⑨ | |

## DAILY PRACTICE PROBLEM DPP 36 - MATHS

| Total Questions | 22 | Total Marks | 67 |
|---|---|---|---|
| Attempted | | Correct | |
| Incorrect | | Net Score | |
| Cut-off Score | 14 | Qualifying Score | 46 |
| Success Gap = Net Score – Qualifying Score | | | |

$$\text{Net Score} = \sum_{i=1}^{VI} \left[ (correct_i \times MM_i) - (In_i - NM_i) \right]$$

# DPP - Daily Practice Problems

Name : 

Date : 

Start Time : 

End Time : 

## MATHEMATICS    M37

**SYLLABUS :** Conic Sections-3 : Hyperbola.

**Max. Marks : 73**

**Time : 60 min.**

### GENERAL INSTRUCTIONS

- The Daily Practice Problem Sheet contains **24** Questions divided into 6 sections.
  Section I has **8** MCQ's with ONLY 1 correct option. 2 marks for correct answer and No negative marks.
  Section II has **4** MCQ's with 1 or MORE THAN 1 correct option. 4 marks for correct answer(s) and (–1) for wrong answer.
  Section III has **1** PASSAGE with **3** MCQ's with ONLY 1 correct option. 3 marks for correct and (–1) mark for wrong answer.
  Section IV has **1** MCQ's with multiple matchings. 1 mark for the correct matching of each row & No negative marks.
  Section V has **3** Assertion-Reason MCQ's with ONLY 1 correct option. 3 marks for correct and (–1) mark for wrong answer.
  Section VI has **5** single digit integer answer questions. 4 marks for correct answer and (–1) for wrong answer.
- No mark will be given/ deducted if no bubble is filled. Keep a timer in front and stop immediately at the end of 60 min.
- You have to evaluate your Response Grids yourself with the help of Solution Booklet.
- The sheet follows a particular syllabus. Do not attempt the sheet before you have completed your preparation for that syllabus. Refer syllabus sheet in the starting of the book for the syllabus of all the DPP sheets.
- After completing the sheet check your answers with the solution booklet and complete the Result Grid. Finally spend time to analyse your performance and revise the areas which emerge out as weak in your evaluation.

## Section - I - Straight Objective Type

This section contains 8 multiple choice questions. Each question has 4 choices (a), (b), (c) and (d), out of which **ONLY ONE** is correct.

**1.** Eccentricity of the hyperbola conjugate to the hyperbola

$$\frac{x^2}{4} - \frac{y^2}{12} = 1 \text{ is}$$

(a) $\frac{2}{\sqrt{3}}$  (b) $2$  (c) $\sqrt{3}$  (d) $\frac{4}{3}$

**2.** The asymptote of the hyperbola $\dfrac{x^2}{a^2} - \dfrac{y^2}{b^2} = 1$ and any tangent to the hyperbola form a triangle whose area is $a^2\tan\lambda$ (in magnitude), then its eccentricity is :

(a) $\sec\lambda$  (b) $\csc\lambda$  (c) $\sec^2\lambda$  (d) $\csc^2\lambda$

**3.** Locus of the feet of the perpendiculars drawn from either foci on a variable tangent to the hyperbola $16y^2 - 9x^2 = 1$ is

(a) $x^2 + y^2 = 9$  (b) $x^2 + y^2 = 1/9$
(c) $x^2 + y^2 = 7/144$  (d) $x^2 + y^2 = 1/16$

**4.** Let P $(a\sec\theta, b\tan\theta)$ and Q $(a\sec\phi, b\tan\phi)$, where $\theta + \phi = \pi/2$, be two points on the hyperbola $\dfrac{x^2}{a^2} - \dfrac{y^2}{b^2} = 1$. If $(h, k)$ is the point of intersection of the normals at P and Q, then k is equal to

(a) $\dfrac{a^2 + b^2}{a}$  (b) $-\left(\dfrac{a^2 + b^2}{a}\right)$

(c) $\dfrac{a^2 + b^2}{b}$  (d) $-\left(\dfrac{a^2 + b^2}{b}\right)$

**5.** If $x = 9$ is the chord of contact of the hyperbola $x^2 - y^2 = 9$, then the equation of the corresponding pair of tangents is

(a) $9x^2 - 8y^2 + 18x - 9 = 0$  (b) $9x^2 - 8y^2 - 18x + 9 = 0$
(c) $9x^2 - 8y^2 - 18x - 9 = 0$  (d) $9x^2 - 8y^2 + 18x + 9 = 0$

<table><tr><td>**RESPONSE GRID**</td><td>1. ⓐⓑⓒⓓ</td><td>2. ⓐⓑⓒⓓ</td><td>3. ⓐⓑⓒⓓ</td><td>4. ⓐⓑⓒⓓ</td><td>5. ⓐⓑⓒⓓ</td></tr></table>

**6.** For hyperbola $\dfrac{x^2}{\cos^2\alpha} - \dfrac{y^2}{\sin^2\alpha} = 1$, which of the following remains constant with change in '$\alpha$'

(a) abscissae of vertices    (b) abscissae of foci

(c) eccentricity    (d) directrix

**7.** If a tangent at any point P on the hyperbola $\dfrac{x^2}{a^2} - \dfrac{y^2}{b^2} = 1$ meet the lines $\dfrac{x}{a} - \dfrac{y}{b} = 0$ and $\dfrac{x}{a} + \dfrac{y}{b} = 0$ in points Q and R, then

(a) P divides QR in the ratio 2 : 1

(b) P divides QR in the ratio 3 : 1

(c) P is mid point of QR

(d) none of these.

**8.** The locus of the middle points of normal chords of the rectangular hyperbola $x^2 - y^2 = a^2$ is

(a) $(y^2 - x^2)^3 = 4a^2x^2y^2$    (b) $(y^2 - x^2)^3 = 2a^2x^2y^2$

(c) $(y^2 - x^2)^3 = a^2x^2y^2$    (d) none of these

## Section - II - Multiple Correct Answer Type

This section contains 4 multiple correct answer(s) type questions. Each question has 4 choices (a), (b), (c) and (d), out of which **ONE OR MORE** is/are correct.

**9.** For the hyperbola $\dfrac{x^2}{9} + \dfrac{y^2}{3} = 1$ the incorrect statement is:

(a) the acute angle between its asymptotes is 60°

(b) its eccentricity is 4/3

(c) length of the latus rectum is 2

(d) product of the perpendicular distances from any point on the hyperbola on its asymptotes is less than the length of its latus rectum .

**10.** Equations of a common tangent to the two hyperbolas $\dfrac{x^2}{a^2} - \dfrac{y^2}{b^2} = 1$ & $\dfrac{y^2}{a^2} - \dfrac{x^2}{b^2} = 1$ is :

(a) $y = x + \sqrt{a^2 - b^2}$    (b) $y = x - \sqrt{a^2 - b^2}$

(c) $y = -x + \sqrt{a^2 - b^2}$    (d) $-x - \sqrt{a^2 - b^2}$

**11.** If the line $2x + 9y + k = 0$ is normal to the hyperbola $3x^2 - y^2 = 23$ then the value of k is

(a) 31    (b) 24    (c) −31    (d) −24

**12.** The equation $16x^2 - 3y^2 - 32x + 12y - 44 = 0$ represents a hyperbola

(a) the length of whose transverse axis is $4\sqrt{3}$

(b) the length of whose conjugate axis is 4

(c) whose centre is $(1, 2)$

(d) whose eccentricity is $\sqrt{19/3}$

## Section - III - Linked Comprehension Type

This section contains one paragraph. Based upon the paragraph, 3 multiple choice questions have to be answered. Each question has 4 choices (a), (b), (c) and (d), out of which **ONLY ONE** is correct.

The difference between the second degree curve and pair of asymptotes is constant.

If second degree curve represented by a hyperbola S = 0, then the equation of its asymptotes is $S + \lambda = 0$ where $\lambda$ is constant. Which will be a pair of straight lines, then we get $\lambda$. Then equation of asymptotes is $A = S + \lambda = 0$ and if equation of conjugate hyperbola of $S$ represented by $S_1$, then A is the arithmetic mean of $S$ and $S_1$.

**13.** The asymptotes of a hyperbola having centre at the point $(1, 2)$ are parallel to the lines $2x + 3y = 0$ and $3x + 2y = 0$. If the hyperbola passes through the point $(5, 3)$, then its equation is

(a) $(2x + 3y - 3)\,(3x + 2y - 5) = 256$

(b) $(2x + 3y - 7)\,(3x + 2y - 8) = 156$

(c) $(2x + 3y - 5)\,(3x + 2y - 3) = 252$

(d) $(2x + 3y - 8)\,(3x + 2y - 7) = 154$

| **Response** | 6. (a)(b)(c)(d) | 7. (a)(b)(c)(d) | 8. (a)(b)(c)(d) | 9. (a)(b)(c)(d) | 10. (a)(b)(c)(d) |
| **Grid** | 11. (a)(b)(c)(d) | 12. (a)(b)(c)(d) | 13. (a)(b)(c)(d) | | |

**14.** If angle between the asymptotes of hyperbola $\dfrac{x^2}{a^2} - \dfrac{y^2}{b^2} = 1$ is $\pi/3$ then the eccentricity of conjugate hyperbola is

(a) $\sqrt{2}$     (b) $2$     (c) $2/\sqrt{3}$     (d) $4/\sqrt{3}$

**15.** A hyperbola passing through origin has $3x - 4y - 1 = 0$ and $4x - 3y - 6 = 0$ as its asymptotes. Then the equation of its transverse and conjugate axes are

(a) $x - y - 5 = 0$ and $x + y + 1 = 0$
(b) $x - y = 0$ and $x + y + 5 = 0$
(c) $x + y - 5 = 0$ and $x - y - 1 = 0$
(d) $x + y - 1 = 0$ and $x - y - 5 = 0$

## Section - IV - Matrix-Match Type

This section contains 1 question. It contains statements given in two columns, which have to be matched. Statements in Column I are labelled as A, B, C and D whereas statements in Column II are labelled as p, q, r and s. The answers to these questions have to be appropriately bubbled as illustrated in the following example. If the correct matches are A-p, A-r, B-p, B-s, C-r, C-s and D-q, then the correctly bubbled matrix will look like the following :

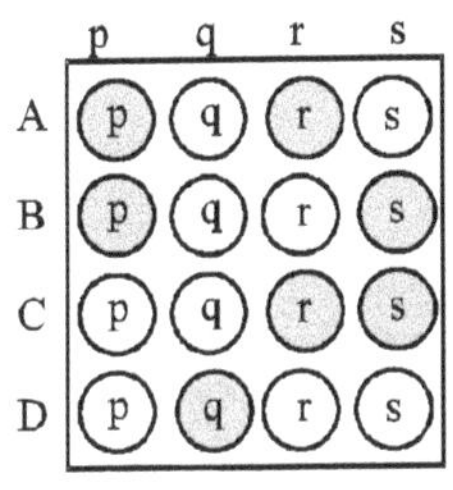

**16.**

| Column-I | Column-II |
|---|---|
| (A) Position of points $(3, 4)$ $(5, 2)$ with respect to hyperbola $x^2 - 4y^2 - 2x + 24y - 37 = 0$ | (p) $(3, 4)$ lies and inside the hyperbola |
| (B) Position of points $(3, 4)$ and $(5, 2)$ with respect to hyperbola $xy + 2x + 3y - 12 = 0$ | (q) $(5, 2)$ lies outside the hyperbola |
| (C) Position of points $(3, 4)$ $(5,2)$ with respect to hyperbola $xy = 12$ | (r). $(3, 4)$ lies and outside the hyperbola |
| | (s) $(5, 2)$ lies inside the hyperbola |
| | (t) $(3, 4)$ lies on the hyperbola |

## Section - V - Reasoning Type

This section contains 3 reasoning type questions. Each question has 4 choices (a), (b), (c) and (d) out of which **ONLY ONE** is correct.

**DIRECTIONS for (Qs. 17 – 19) : Each of these questions contains two statements: Statement-1 (Assertion) and Statement-2 (Reason). Each of these questions has four alternative choices, only one of which is the correct answer. You have to select the correct choice.**

(a) Statement-1 is True, Statement-2 is True; Statement-2 is a correct explanation for Statement-1.
(b) Statement-1 is True, Statement-2 is True; Statement-2 is NOT a correct explanation for Statement-1.
(c) Statement -1 is True, Statement-2 is False.
(d) Statement -1 is False, Statement-2 is True.

**17.** **Statement 1 :** If a circle cuts a rectangular hyperbola $xy = c^2$ in A, B, C, D and the parameters of these four points be $t_1$, $t_2$, $t_3$ and $t_4$ respectively then $t_1 t_2\, t_3\, t_4 = 1$.

**Statement 2 :** We can take $\left( ct, \dfrac{c}{t} \right), t \neq 0$ as the parametric point on the hyperbola $xy = c^2$.

**18.** **Statement–1 :** The average point of all the four intersection points of the rectangular hyperbola $xy = 1$ and circle $x^2 + y^2 = 4$ is origin $(0, 0)$.

**Statement–2 :** If a rectangular hyperbola and a circle intersect at four points, the average point of all the points of intersection is the mid point of line-joining the two centres.

**19.** **Statement–1 :** There can be infinite points from where we can draw two mutually perpendicular tangents onto the hyperbola $\dfrac{x^2}{9} - \dfrac{y^2}{16} = 1$.

**Statement–2 :** The locus of point of intersection of two mutually perpendicular tangents drawn on to the hyperbola $\dfrac{x^2}{a^2} - \dfrac{y^2}{b^2} = 1$ is its director circle whose equation is $x^2 + y^2 = a^2 - b^2$.

<table>
<tr><td rowspan="3">RESPONSE GRID</td><td colspan="3">14. ⓐⓑⓒⓓ    15. ⓐⓑⓒⓓ</td></tr>
<tr><td colspan="3">16. A - ⓟⓠⓡⓢⓣ; B - ⓟⓠⓡⓢⓣ; C - ⓟⓠⓡⓢⓣ; D - ⓟⓠⓡⓢⓣ</td></tr>
<tr><td colspan="3">17. ⓐⓑⓒⓓ    18. ⓐⓑⓒⓓ    19. ⓐⓑⓒⓓ</td></tr>
</table>

*Space for Rough Work*

## Section - VI - Integer Type

This section contains 5 questions. The answer to each of the questions is a single digit integer ranging from 0 to 9.

**20.** If the normal to the rectangular hyperbola $xy = c^2$ at the point 't' meets the curve again at '$t_1$' then find the value of $-3t^3 t_1$.

**21.** With one focus of the hyperbola $\dfrac{x^2}{9} - \dfrac{y^2}{16} = 1$ as the centre, a circle is drawn which is tangent to the hyperbola with no part of the circle being outside the hyperbola. Find the radius of the circle.

**22.** A hyperbola has one focus at the origin. Its eccentricity $= \sqrt{2}$ and one of its directrix is $x + y + 1 = 0$. The equation to its asymptotes are $x + M = 0$ and $y + N = 0$. Find the value of $M + N$.

**23.** Equation $(2 + \lambda) x^2 - 2\lambda xy + (\lambda - 1) y^2 - 4x - 2 = 0$ represents a hyperbola if $\lambda \in \left(-\infty, \dfrac{A}{B}\right) \cup \left(\dfrac{A}{B}, C\right)$. Find the value of A + B + C.

(a) $\lambda = 4$      (b) $\lambda = 1$

(c) $\lambda = 4/3$      (d) $\lambda = -1$

**24.** The lines $2x + 3y + 4 = 0$ and $3x - 2y + 5 = 0$ may be conjugate w. r. t. the hyperbola $\dfrac{x^2}{a^2} - \dfrac{y^2}{b^2} = 1$ if $a^2 + b^2 = \dfrac{P}{Q}$. Find the value of $P - Q$.

| | | |
|---|---|---|
| **RESPONSE GRID** | **20.** ⓪①②③④⑤⑥⑦⑧⑨ | **21.** ⓪①②③④⑤⑥⑦⑧⑨ |
| | **22.** ⓪①②③④⑤⑥⑦⑧⑨ | **23.** ⓪①②③④⑤⑥⑦⑧⑨ |
| | **24.** ⓪①②③④⑤⑥⑦⑧⑨ | |

## DAILY PRACTICE PROBLEM DPP 37 - MATHS

| Total Questions | 24 | Total Marks | 73 |
|---|---|---|---|
| Attempted | | Correct | |
| Incorrect | | Net Score | |
| Cut-off Score | 15 | Qualifying Score | 47 |
| Success Gap = Net Score − Qualifying Score | | | |

$$\text{Net Score } = \sum_{i=1}^{VI} \left[ (\mathbf{correct}_i \times MM_i) - (In_i - NM_i) \right]$$

# DPP - Daily Practice Problems

Name :                Date : 

Start Time :             End Time : 

# MATHEMATICS  M38

**SYLLABUS :** Conic Sections-4 : Miscellaneous.

**Max. Marks : 67**              **Time : 60 min.**

## GENERAL INSTRUCTIONS

- The Daily Practice Problem Sheet contains **22** Questions divided into 5 sections.
  Section I has **9** MCQ's with ONLY 1 correct option. 2 marks for correct answer and No negative marks.
  Section II has **4** MCQ's with 1 or MORE THAN 1 correct option. 4 marks for correct answer(s) and (−1) for wrong answer.
  Section III has **1** PASSAGE with **3** MCQ's with ONLY 1 correct option. 3 marks for correct and (−1) mark for wrong answer.
  Section IV has **2** MCQ's with multiple matchings. 1 mark for the correct matching of each row & No negative marks.
  Section V has **4** single digit integer answer questions. 4 marks for correct answer and (−1) for wrong answer.
- No mark will be given/ deducted if no bubble is filled. Keep a timer in front and stop immediately at the end of 60 min.
- You have to evaluate your Response Grids yourself with the help of Solution Booklet.
- The sheet follows a particular syllabus. Do not attempt the sheet before you have completed your preparation for that syllabus. Refer syllabus sheet in the starting of the book for the syllabus of all the DPP sheets.
- After completing the sheet check your answers with the solution booklet and complete the Result Grid. Finally spend time to analyse your performance and revise the areas which emerge out as weak in your evaluation.

## Section - I - Straight Objective Type

This section contains 9 multiple choice questions. Each question has 4 choices (a), (b), (c) and (d), out of which **ONLY ONE** is correct.

**1.** The equation $\dfrac{x^2}{1-r} - \dfrac{y^2}{1+r} = 1,\ \ r > 1$ represents

  (a) an ellipse        (b) a hyperbola
  (c) a circle          (d) none of these

**2.** Each of the four inequalties given in options defines a region in the xy plane. One of these four regions does not have the following property. For any two points $(x_1, y_1)$ and $(x_2, y_2)$ in the region, the point $\left(\dfrac{x_1 + x_2}{2}, \dfrac{y_1 + y_2}{2}\right)$ is also in the region. The inequality defining this region is

  (a) $x^2 + 2y^2 \le 1$        (b) $\text{Max}\left\{|x|, |y|\right\} \le 1$
  (c) $x^2 - y^2 \ge 1$        (d) $y^2 - x \le 0$

**3.** The curve described parametrically by $x = t^2 + t + 1$, $y = t^2 - t + 1$ represents

  (a) a pair of straight lines    (b) an ellipse
  (c) a parabola           (d) a hyperbola

**4.** The equation $2x^2 + 3y^2 - 8x - 18y + 35 = k$ represents

  (a) no locus if $k > 0$      (b) an ellipse if $k > 0$
  (c) a point if $k = 0$       (d) a hyperbola if $k > 0$

**5.** A hyperbola, having the transverse axis of length $2 \sin \theta$, is confocal with the ellipse $3x^2 + 4y^2 = 12$. Then its equation is

  (a) $x^2 \text{cosec}^2\theta - y^2 \sec^2\theta = 1$   (b) $x^2 \sec^2\theta - y^2 \text{cosec}^2\theta = 1$
  (c) $x^2 \sin^2\theta - y^2 \cos^2\theta = 1$     (d) $x^2 \cos^2\theta - y^2 \sin^2\theta = 1$

| **RESPONSE GRID** | 1. ⓐⓑⓒⓓ | 2. ⓐⓑⓒⓓ | 3. ⓐⓑⓒⓓ | 4. ⓐⓑⓒⓓ | 5. ⓐⓑⓒⓓ |
|---|---|---|---|---|---|

**6.** The line $2px + y\sqrt{1 - p^2} = 1$ $(|p| < 1)$ for different values of p, touches

(a) An ellipse of eccentricity $\dfrac{2}{\sqrt{3}}$

(b) An ellipse of eccentricity $\dfrac{\sqrt{3}}{2}$

(c) Hyperbola of eccentricity 2

(d) None of these

**7.** If the tangents drawn from a point on the hyperbola $x^2 - y^2$ $= a^2 - b^2$ to the ellipse $\dfrac{x^2}{a^2} + \dfrac{y^2}{b^2} = 1$ makes angle $\alpha$ and $\beta$ with the transverse axis of the hyperbola, then

(a) $\tan\alpha - \tan\beta = 1$　　　(b) $\tan\alpha + \tan\beta = 1$

(c) $\tan\alpha \tan\beta = 1$　　　(d) $\tan\alpha \tan\beta = -1$

**8.** A point P is taken on the right half of the hyperbola $\dfrac{x^2}{a^2} - \dfrac{y^2}{b^2} = 1$ having its foci as $S_1$ and $S_2$. If the internal angle bisector of the angle $\angle S_1 P S_2$ cuts the x-axis at the point Q $(\alpha, 0)$ then range of $\alpha$ is

(a) $[-a, a]$　　(b) $[0, a]$　　　(c) $(0, a]$　　(d) $[-a, 0)$

**9.** The area of the triangle formed by the asymptotes and any tangent to the hyperbola $x^2 - y^2 = a^2$ is

(a) $4a^2$　　　(b) $3a^2$　　(c) $2a^2$　　　(d) $a^2$

## Section - II - Multiple Correct Answer Type

This section contains 4 multiple correct answer(s) type questions. Each question has 4 choices (a), (b), (c) and (d), out of which **ONE OR MORE** is/are correct.

**10.** Consider the hyperbola $xy + x - y - 9 = 0$ and a line $x = 4$, which intersect the transverse axis at P. Then which of the following statements are correct?

(a) Equation of parabola is $9y = x^2 - 8x + 34$

(b) If tangents at P of parabola intersect hyperbola at $P'$, then area of triangle $PCP'$ (C is centre of hyperbola) is $\dfrac{1}{}$

(c) Equation of latus rectum of hyperbola which does not pass through III$^{rd}$ quadrant is $y + x + 1 = 0$

(d) Equation of latus rectum of hyperbola which does not pass through III$^{rd}$ quadrant is $x + y - 8 = 0$

**11.** The equation $(x - \alpha)^2 + (y - \beta)^2 = k\,(\ell x + my + n)^2$ represents

(a) a parabola for $k < (\ell^2 + m^2)^{-1}$

(b) an ellipse for $0 < k < (\ell^2 + m^2)^{-1}$

(c) a hyperbola for $k > (\ell^2 + m^2)^{-1}$

(d) a point circle for $k = 0$.

**12.** The line $y = x + 5$ touches

(a) the parabola $y^2 = 20x$

(b) the ellipse $9x^2 + 16y^2 = 144$

(c) the hyperbola $\dfrac{x^2}{29} - \dfrac{y^2}{4} = 1$

(d) the circle $x^2 + y^2 = 25$

**13.** A straight line touches the rectangular hyperbola $9x^2 - 9y^2$ $= 8$ and the parabola $y^2 = 32x$. The equation of the line is

(a) $9x + 3y - 8 = 0$　　　　　(b) $9x - 3y + 8 = 0$

(c) $9x + 3y + 8 = 0$　　　　　(d) $9x - 3y - 8 = 0$

## Section - III - Linked Comprehension Type

This section contains one paragraph. Based upon the paragraph, 3 multiple choice questions have to be answered. Each question has 4 choices (a), (b), (c) and (d), out of which **ONLY ONE** is correct.

From a point P three normals are drawn to the parabola $y^2 = 4x$ such that two of them make angles with the abscissa axis, the product of whose tangents is 2. Suppose the locus of the point P is a conic C. Now a circle $S = 0$ is described on the chord of the conic C as diameter passing through the point $(1, 0)$ and with gradient unity. Suppose $(a, b)$ are the coordinates of the centre of this circle. If $L_1$ and $L_2$ are the two asymptotes of the hyperbola with length of its transverse axis 2a and conjugate axis 2b (principal axes of the hyperbola along the coordinate axes) then answer the following questions.

**14.** Locus of P is a –

(a) circle　　　　　　　　　(b) parabola

(c) ellipse　　　　　　　　(d) hyperbola

| | | | | | |
|---|---|---|---|---|---|
| **RESPONSE** | **6.** ⓐⓑⓒⓓ | **7.** ⓐⓑⓒⓓ | **8.** ⓐⓑⓒⓓ | **9.** ⓐⓑⓒⓓ | **10.** ⓐⓑⓒⓓ |
| **GRID** | **11.** ⓐⓑⓒⓓ | **12.** ⓐⓑⓒⓓ | **13.** ⓐⓑⓒⓓ | **14.** ⓐⓑⓒⓓ | |

15. Radius of the circle $S = 0$ is –
    (a) 4
    (b) 5
    (c) $\sqrt{17}$
    (d) $\sqrt{23}$

16. The angle $\alpha \in (0, \pi/2)$ between the two asymptotes of the hyperbola lies in the interval –
    (a) $(0, 15°)$
    (b) $(30°, 45°)$
    (c) $(45°, 60°)$
    (d) $(60°, 75°)$

---

## Section - IV - Matrix-Match Type

This section contains 2 questions. It contains statements given in two columns, which have to be matched. Statements in Column I are labelled as A, B, C and D whereas statements in Column II are labelled as p, q, r and s. The answers to these questions have to be appropriately bubbled as illustrated in the following example. If the correct matches are A-p, A-r, B-p, B-s, C-r, C-s and D-q, then the correctly bubbled matrix will look like the following :

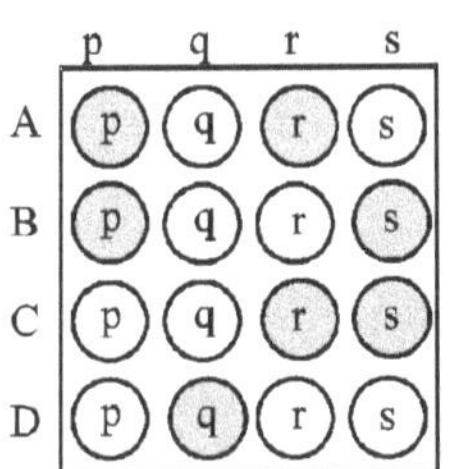

17. Match the column –

| Column I | | Column II |
|---|---|---|
| (A) The length of common chord of the parabolas $y^2 = x$ and $x^2 = y$ is | | (p) 4 |
| (B) The radius of the circle passing through the foci of the ellipse $\dfrac{x^2}{16} + \dfrac{y^2}{9} = 1$ and having its centre at $(0, 3)$ is | | (q) 3 |

(C) If one of the diameters of the circle $x^2 + y^2 - 2x - 6y + 6 = 0$ is a chord of the circle with centre $(2, 1)$, then the radius of the circle is  (r) $\sqrt{2}$

(D) If $F_1 \equiv (0, 0)$, $F_2 \equiv (1, 1)$ and $|PF_1| + |PF_2| = k$, such that the locus of P is an ellipse then k may be  (s) 1/2

18. Match the conics in **Column I** with the statements/expressions in **Column II**.

| Column I | Column II |
|---|---|
| (A) Circle | (p) The locus of the point $(h,k)$ for which the line $hx + ky = 1$ touches the circle $x^2 + y^2 = 4$ |
| (B) Parabola | (q) Points $z$ in the complex plane satisfying $|z + 2| - |z - 2| = \pm 3$ |
| (C) Ellipse | (r) Points of the conic have parametric representation $x = \sqrt{3}\left(\dfrac{1 - t^2}{1 + t^2}\right),$ $y = \dfrac{2t}{1 + t^2}$ |
| (D) Hyperbola | (s) The eccentricity of the conic lies in the interval $1 \le x < \infty$ |
| | (t) Points z in the complex plane satisfying $\mathrm{Re}\,(z + 1)^2 = |z|^2 + 1$ |



*Space for Rough Work*

### Section - V - Integer Type

This section contains 4 questions. The answer to each of the questions is a single digit integer ranging from 0 to 9.

**19.** If the eccentricity of the hyperbola $x^2 - y^2 \sec^2\alpha = 5$ is $\sqrt{3}$ times the eccentricity of the ellipse $x^2 \sec^2\alpha + y^2 = 25$, then a value of $\alpha$ is $\dfrac{A\pi}{B}$. Find $A + B$.

**20.** A normal to the parabola $y^2 = 4ax$ with slope m touches the rectangular hyperbola $x^2 - y^2 = a^2$ if $m^A + 4m^4 + 3m^B + 1 = 0$. Find value of $A + B$.

**21.** The equation of straight line which is tangent to the parabola $y^2 = 8x$ and the hyperbola $3x^2 - y^2 = 3$ is $Ax - y + 1 = 0$ and $Bx + y - 1 = 0$ respectively. Find the value of $A + B$.

**22.** If $(5, 12)$ and $(24, 7)$ are the focii of a conic passing through the origin then the eccentricity of conic is $\dfrac{\sqrt{A}}{13}$ and $\dfrac{\sqrt{B}}{38}$. Find the value of $A - B$.

| RESPONSE GRID | | |
|---|---|---|
| 19. ⓪①②③④⑤⑥⑦⑧⑨ | | 20. ⓪①②③④⑤⑥⑦⑧⑨ |
| 21. ⓪①②③④⑤⑥⑦⑧⑨ | | 22. ⓪①②③④⑤⑥⑦⑧⑨ |

| DAILY PRACTICE PROBLEM DPP 38 - MATHS | | | |
|---|---|---|---|
| Total Questions | 22 | Total Marks | 67 |
| Attempted | | Correct | |
| Incorrect | | Net Score | |
| Cut-off Score | 13 | Qualifying Score | 44 |
| Success Gap = Net Score – Qualifying Score | | | |

$$\text{Net Score} = \sum_{i=I}^{VI}\left[(\text{correct}_i \times MM_i) - (In_i - NM_i)\right]$$

# DPP - Daily Practice Problems

**Name :**                          **Date :**

**Start Time :**                    **End Time :**

## MATHEMATICS  M39

SYLLABUS : **Probability-1** : Definition of various terms, Definition of probability, Independent events, probability distribution of a random variable

**Max. Marks : 59**                          **Time : 60 min.**

### GENERAL INSTRUCTIONS

- The Daily Practice Problem Sheet contains **20** Questions divided into 6 sections.
  Section I has **7** MCQ's with ONLY 1 correct option. 2 marks for correct answer and No negative marks.
  Section II has **3** MCQ's with 1 or MORE THAN 1 correct option. 4 marks for correct answer(s) and (−1) for wrong answer.
  Section III has **1** PASSAGE with **3** MCQ's with ONLY 1 correct option. 3 marks for correct and (−1) mark for wrong answer.
  Section IV has **2** MCQ's with multiple matchings. 1 mark for the correct matching of each row & No negative marks.
  Section V has **2** Assertion-Reason MCQ's with ONLY 1 correct option. 3 marks for correct and (−1) mark for wrong answer.
  Section VI has **3** single digit integer answer questions. 4 marks for correct answer and (−1) for wrong answer.
- No mark will be given/ deducted if no bubble is filled. Keep a timer in front and stop immediately at the end of 60 min.
- You have to evaluate your Response Grids yourself with the help of Solution Booklet.
- The sheet follows a particular syllabus. Do not attempt the sheet before you have completed your preparation for that syllabus. Refer syllabus sheet in the starting of the book for the syllabus of all the DPP sheets.
- After completing the sheet check your answers with the solution booklet and complete the Result Grid. Finally spend time to analyse your performance and revise the areas which emerge out as weak in your evaluation.

## Section - I - Straight Objective Type

This section contains 7 multiple choice questions. Each question has 4 choices (a), (b), (c) and (d), out of which **ONLY ONE** is correct.

**1.** Square is selected with all their vertices belonging to point $(x_i, y_j)$ where $i, j \in (1, 2, \ldots\ldots 14, 15\}$.

If $x_{i+1} - x_i = y_{j+1} - y_j = 1$ unit, $\forall\ i, j \in (1, 2, \ldots\ldots 13, 14\}$ then probability that length of side of selected square equals to integer is

(a) $\dfrac{203}{840}$    (b) $\dfrac{229}{840}$    (c) $\dfrac{1143}{4200}$    (d) None of these

**2.** Mr. A makes a bet with Mr. B that in a single throw with two dice he will throw a total of seven before B throws four. Each of them has a pair of dice and they throw simultaneously until one of them wins, equal throws being disregarded. Probability that B wins, is –

(a) $\dfrac{1}{3}$    (b) $\dfrac{4}{11}$    (c) $\dfrac{5}{16}$    (d) $\dfrac{6}{17}$

**3.** Three boxes are labelled A, B and C and each box contains four balls numbered 1, 2, 3 and 4. The balls in each box are well mixed. A child chooses one ball at random from each of the three boxes. If a, b, and c are the numbers on the balls chosen from the boxes A, B and C respectively, the child wins a toy helicopter when a = b + c. The odds in favour of the child to receive the toy helicopter are

(a) $3 : 32$    (b) $3 : 29$    (c) $1 : 15$    (d) $5 : 59$

**4.** A man alternatively tosses a coin and throws a dice beginning with the coin. The probability that he gets head on the coin before he gets a 5 or 6 in the dice is

(a) 3/4    (b) 1/2    (c) 1/3    (d) None

**5.** An unbiased dice with faces 1, 2, 3, 4, 5 and 6 is rolled 4 times. Out of four face values obtained the probability that the minimum face value is not less than 2 and the maximum face value is not greater than 5 is

(a) $\dfrac{16}{81}$    (b) $\dfrac{1}{81}$

(c) $\dfrac{80}{81}$    (d) $\dfrac{65}{81}$

---

**1.** ⓐⓑⓒⓓ    **2.** ⓐⓑⓒⓓ    **3.** ⓐⓑⓒⓓ    **4.** ⓐⓑⓒⓓ    **5.** ⓐⓑⓒⓓ

**6.** The letters of the word SOCIETY are placed at random in a row. The probability that the three vowels come together is

(a) $\dfrac{1}{6}$  (b) $\dfrac{1}{7}$

(c) $\dfrac{2}{7}$  (d) $\dfrac{5}{6}$

**7.** A determinant is chosen at random from the set of all determinants of order 2 with elements 0 and 1 only. The probability that the value of determinant chosen is positive is

(a) $\dfrac{1}{2}$  (b) $\dfrac{1}{8}$

(c) $\dfrac{3}{16}$  (d) $\dfrac{1}{4}$

## Section - II - Multiple Correct Answer Type

This section contains 3 multiple correct answer(s) type questions. Each question has 4 choices (a), (b), (c) and (d), out of which **ONE OR MORE** is/are correct.

**8.** The probabilities that a student passes in Mathematics, Physics and Chemistry are m, p and c respectively. Of these subjects, the student has 75% chance of passing in at least one, 50% chance of passing in at least two, and 40% chance of passing in exactly two. Which of the following relations are true?

(a) $p + m + c = 19/20$  (b) $p + m + c = 27/20$
(c) $pmc = 1/10$  (d) $pmc = 1/4$

**9.** Two persons A and B, have respectively $n + 1$ and n coins, which they toss simultaneously. Then the probability that A will have more heads than B is

(a) $\dfrac{1}{2}$  (b) $> \dfrac{1}{2}$  (c) $< \dfrac{1}{2}$  (d) $> \dfrac{1}{3}$

**10.** Consider the cartesian plane and let X denotes the subset of points for which both coordinates are integers. A coin of diameter $\dfrac{1}{2}$ is tossed randomly into the plane. The probability $p$ that the coin covers a point of X satisfies

(a) $p = \dfrac{\pi}{16}$  (b) $p < \dfrac{\pi}{3}$  (c) $p > \dfrac{\pi}{30}$  (d) $p = \dfrac{1}{4}$

## Section - III - Linked Comprehension Type

This section contains one paragraph. Based upon the paragraph, 3 multiple choice questions have to be answered. Each question has 4 choices (a), (b), (c) and (d), out of which **ONLY ONE** is correct.

Consider the independent events A, B, C corresponding to a random experiment. Suppose the event $A \cup B \cup C$ represents the event of occurrence of atleast one of A, B, C and the event A.B.C represents the event of simultaneous occurrence of A, B, C. Also, the event $\overline{A}$ represents non-occurrence of A. It is given that $P(A) = a$, $P(A \cup B \cup C) = 1 - b$, $P(A \cap B \cap C) = 1 - c$ and $P(\overline{A} \cap \overline{B} \cap C) = x$. Now answer the following questions.

**11.** The probability of the event $\overline{A} \cap \overline{B} \cap \overline{C}$ is
(a) c  (b) $1 - x$  (c) b  (d) $1 - a - b - c$

**12.** The probability of occurrence of event B is

(a) $\dfrac{x}{x+b}$  (b) $\dfrac{(1-c)(x+b)}{ax}$

(c) $\dfrac{(1-a)^2 + ab}{1-a}$  (d) $\dfrac{(1-b)(x-c)}{ax}$

**13.** The probability of occurrence of event C is

(a) $\dfrac{x}{x+b}$  (b) $\dfrac{(1-c)(x+b)}{ax}$

(c) $\dfrac{(1-a)^2 + ab}{1-a}$  (d) $\dfrac{(1-b)(x-c)}{ax}$

## Section - IV - Matrix-Match Type

This section contains 2 questions. It contains statements given in two columns, which have to be matched. Statements in Column I are labelled as A, B, C and D whereas statements in Column II are labelled as p, q, r and s. The answers to these questions have to be appropriately bubbled as illustrated in the following example. If the correct matches are A-p, A-r, B-p, B-s, C-r, C-s and D-q, then the correctly bubbled matrix will look like the following :

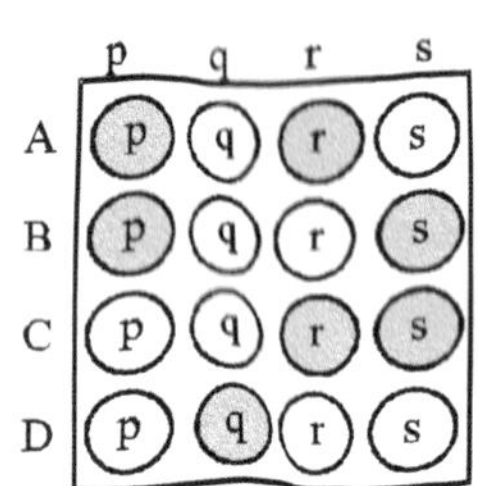



| RESPONSE GRID | | | | |
|---|---|---|---|---|
| 6. ⓐⓑⓒⓓ | 7. ⓐⓑⓒⓓ | 8. ⓐⓑⓒⓓ | 9. ⓐⓑⓒⓓ | 10. ⓐⓑⓒⓓ |
| 11. ⓐⓑⓒⓓ | 12. ⓐⓑⓒⓓ | 13. ⓐⓑⓒⓓ | | |

*Space for Rough Work*

**14.**

| Column I | | Column II |
|---|---|---|

(A) The probability that $A$, $B$, $C$ solve a problem is $\dfrac{1}{2}$, $\dfrac{1}{3}$ and $\dfrac{1}{4}$ respectively. If the probability that the problem will be solved is $\lambda$ and that the problem is solved by only one of them is $\mu$, then

p. $\lambda + \mu = \dfrac{13}{24}$

(B) The probability of hitting a target by three men is $\dfrac{1}{2}$, $\dfrac{1}{3}$ and $\dfrac{1}{4}$ respectively. If the probability that exactly two of them will hit the target is $\lambda$ and that at least two of them hit the target is $\mu$, then

q. $\lambda + \mu = \dfrac{29}{24}$

(C) A bag contains 4 white and 2 black balls. Another contains 3 white and 5 black balls. One ball is drawn from each bag. If the prabability that both are black is $\lambda$ and that both are white is $\mu$, then

r. $\lambda + \mu = \dfrac{11}{24}$

s. $\lambda - \mu = \dfrac{7}{24}$

t. $\mu - \lambda = \dfrac{1}{24}$

**15.**

| Column I | | Column II |
|---|---|---|

(A) $A$, $B$ and $C$ in order toss a coin. The first one to throw a head wins. If $p$, $q$ and $r$ are their respective chances of winning, assume that the game may continue indefinitely, then

p. $q - r = \dfrac{1}{7}$

(B) Three persons $A$, $B$ and $C$ throw a dice in succession till one gets a 'six' and wins the game. If $p$, $q$ and $r$ are their respective chances of winning, then

q. $p - r = \dfrac{3}{7}$

(C) $A$, $B$ and $C$ play a game and chances of their winning it in an attempt are $\dfrac{2}{3}, \dfrac{1}{2}$ and $\dfrac{1}{4}$ respectively. A has the first chance, followed by $B$ and then by $C$. This cycle is repeated till one of them wins the game. If $p$, $q$, $r$ are their respective chances of winning the game, then

r. $p : q = 6 : 5$

s. $p - r = \dfrac{5}{7}$

t. $p : q = 2 : 1$

## Section - V - Reasoning Type

This section contains 2 reasoning type questions. Each question has 4 choices (a), (b), (c) and (d) out of which **ONLY ONE** is correct.

**DIRECTIONS for Qs (16-17) :** Each of these questions contains two statements: Statement-1 (Assertion) and Statement-2 (Reason). Each of these questions has four alternative choices, only one of which is the correct answer. You have to select the correct choice.

(a) Statement-1 is True, Statement-2 is True; Statement-2 is a correct explanation for Statement-1.

(b) Statement-1 is True, Statement-2 is True; Statement-2 is NOT a correct explanation for Statement-1.

(c) Statement-1 is True, Statement-2 is False.

(d) Statement-1 is False, Statement-2 is True.

**16.** A fair die is rolled once.

**Statement-1 :** The probability of getting a composite number is 1/3

**Statement-2 :** There are three possibilities for the obtained number (i) the number is a prime number (ii) the number is a composite number (iii) the number is 1, and hence probability of getting a prime number = 1/3

<table>
<tr><td rowspan="2">Response Grid</td><td>14. A - ⓟⓠⓡⓢⓣ; B - ⓟⓠⓡⓢⓣ; C - ⓟⓠⓡⓢⓣ</td></tr>
<tr><td>15. A - ⓟⓠⓡⓢⓣ; B - ⓟⓠⓡⓢⓣ; C - ⓟⓠⓡⓢⓣ</td></tr>
</table>

*Space for Rough Work*

**17.** **Statement-1** : $A$ and $B$ are two candidates seeking admission in IIT. The probability that $A$ is selected is 0.5 and the probability that both $A$ and $B$ are selected is at most 0.3. Then, the probability of $B$ getting selected is 0.9

**Statement-2** : If $E_1$ and $E_2$ are the events of $A$ and $B$ selected respectively, then $P(E_1 \cap E_2) = P(E_1) \cdot P(E_2)$

## Section - VI - Integer Type

This section contains 3 questions. The answer to each of the questions is a single digit integer ranging from 0 to 9.

**18.** A and B are two independent events. The probability that both A and B occur is $\dfrac{1}{6}$ and the probability that neither of them occurs is $\dfrac{1}{3}$. The probability of occurrence of A is $\dfrac{1}{X}$. Find X.

**19.** The probability that any two different cards of a well-shuffled deck of 52 cards will be together in the deck if their suit is not considered is $\dfrac{P}{Q}$. Find the value of $Q - P$.

**20.** A five digit number is chosen at random. The probability that all the digits are distinct and digits at odd places are odd and digits at even places are even is $\dfrac{1}{15P}$. Find P.

| RESPONSE GRID | | |
|---|---|---|
| **17.** ⓐ ⓑ ⓒ ⓓ | | **18.** ⓪①②③④⑤⑥⑦⑧⑨ |
| **19.** ⓪①②③④⑤⑥⑦⑧⑨ | **20.** ⓪①②③④⑤⑥⑦⑧⑨ | |

| DAILY PRACTICE PROBLEM DPP 39 - MATHS | | | |
|---|---|---|---|
| Total Questions | 20 | Total Marks | 59 |
| Attempted | | Correct | |
| Incorrect | | Net Score | |
| Cut-off Score | 12 | Qualifying Score | 38 |
| Success Gap = Net Score – Qualifying Score | | | |

$$\text{Net Score} = \sum_{i=I}^{VI}\left[(\text{correct}_i \times MM_i) - (In_i - NM_i)\right]$$

*Space for Rough Work*

# DPP - Daily Practice Problems

Name : 

Date : 

Start Time : 

End Time : 

## MATHEMATICS  M40

SYLLABUS : **Probability-2** : Use of permutation and combinations in Probability

# Max. Marks : 70

# Time : 60 min.

## GENERAL INSTRUCTIONS

- The Daily Practice Problem Sheet contains **24** Questions divided into 4 sections.

   Section I has **12** MCQ's with ONLY 1 correct option. 2 marks for correct answer and No negative marks.

   Section II has **5** MCQ's with 1 or MORE THAN 1 correct option. 4 marks for correct answer(s) and (−1) for wrong answer.

   Section III has **2** Assertion-Reason MCQ's with ONLY 1 correct option. 3 marks for correct and (−1) mark for wrong answer.

   Section IV has **5** single digit integer answer questions. 4 marks for correct answer and (−1) for wrong answer.

- No mark will be given/ deducted if no bubble is filled. Keep a timer in front and stop immediately at the end of 60 min.

- You have to evaluate your Response Grids yourself with the help of Solution Booklet.

- The sheet follows a particular syllabus. Do not attempt the sheet before you have completed your preparation for that syllabus. Refer syllabus sheet in the starting of the book for the syllabus of all the DPP sheets.

- After completing the sheet check your answers with the solution booklet and complete the Result Grid. Finally spend time to analyse your performance and revise the areas which emerge out as weak in your evaluation.

## Section - I - Straight Objective Type

This section contains 12 multiple choice questions. Each question has 4 choices (a), (b), (c) and (d), out of which **ONLY ONE** is correct.

1. Two numbers are selected at random from $1, 2, 3, ..., 100$ and multiplied. The probability that the product thus obtained is divisible by 3, is

   (a) 0.31    (b) 0.44    (c) 0.49    (d) 0.55

2. A box contains 24 balls of which 12 are black and 12 are white. The balls are drawn at random from the box one at a time with replacement. The probability that a white ball is drawn for the 4th time on the 7th draw is

   (a) $\dfrac{5}{64}$    (b) $\dfrac{27}{32}$    (c) $\dfrac{5}{32}$    (d) $\dfrac{11}{32}$

3. An ordinary cube has 4 blank faces, one face marked 2 and another marked 3. The probability of obtaining 12 in 5 throws is :

   (a) $\dfrac{5}{2592}$    (b) $\dfrac{5}{1944}$    (c) $\dfrac{5}{1296}$    (d) $\dfrac{5}{648}$

4. A is a set containing n element. A subset P of A is chosen at random, and the set A is reconstruced by replacing the elements of P. Another subset Q of A is now chosen at random. The probability that $P \cup Q$ contains exactly r elements, $1 \le r \le n$, is

   (a) $\dfrac{{}^n C_r 3^r}{4^n}$    (b) $\dfrac{3^n}{4^n}$

   (c) $\dfrac{{}^n C_r 3^{n-r}}{4^n}$    (d) $\dfrac{{}^n C_r 3^n}{4^n}$

5. A car is parked among N cars standing in a row, but not at either end. On his return, the owner finds that exactly 'r' of the N places are still occupied. The probability that both the places neighbouring his car are empty is

   (a) $\dfrac{(r-1)!}{(N-1)!}$    (b) $\dfrac{(r-1)!(N-r)!}{(N-1)!}$

   (c) $\dfrac{(N-r)(N-r-1)}{(N+1)(N+2)}$    (d) $\dfrac{{}^{N-r}C_2}{{}^{N-1}C_2}$

**6.** Seven white balls and three black balls are randomly placed in a row. The probability that no two black balls are placed adjacently equals

(a) $\dfrac{1}{2}$      (b) $\dfrac{7}{15}$

(c) $\dfrac{2}{15}$      (d) $\dfrac{1}{3}$

**7.** Seven digits number from the numbers $1, 2, 3, 4, 5, 6, 7, 8, 9$ are written in a random order. The probability that this seven digit number is divisible by 9 is

(a) $\dfrac{2}{9}$      (b) $\dfrac{7}{36}$

(c) $\dfrac{1}{9}$      (d) $\dfrac{7}{12}$

**8.** A box contains 2-black, 4- white and 3-red balls. One ball is drawn at random from the box and kept aside . From the remaining balls in the box, another ball is drawn at random and kept beside the first. This process is repeated till all the balls are drawn from the box. The probability that balls drawn in the sequence of 2-black, 4- white and 3-red is

(a) $\dfrac{2}{9}$      (b) $\dfrac{8}{35}$

(c) $\dfrac{4}{7}$      (d) $\dfrac{1}{1260}$

**9.** If two squares are chosen at random on a chess board, the probability that they have a side in common is

(a) $\dfrac{1}{9}$      (b) $\dfrac{2}{7}$

(c) $\dfrac{1}{18}$      (d) $\dfrac{2}{9}$

**10.** A bag has 13 red, 14 green and 15 white balls, $p_1$ is the probability of drawing exactly 2 white balls when four balls are drawn. Then the number of balls of each colour are doubled. Let $p_2$ be the probability of drawing 4 white balls when 8 ball are drawn, then

(a) $p_1 = p_2$      (b) $p_1 > p_2$
(c) $p_1 < p_2$      (d) None

**11.** The probability that when 12 balls are distributed among three boxes, the first will contain three balls is,

(a) $\dfrac{2^9}{3^{12}}$      (b) $\dfrac{{}^{12}C_3.2^9}{3^{12}}$

(c) $\dfrac{{}^{12}C_3.2^{12}}{3^{12}}$      (d) None

**12.** A fair coin is tossed 2n times. The probability of getting as many heads in the first n tosses as in the last n is

(a) $\dfrac{{}^{2n}C_n}{2^{2n}}$      (b) $\dfrac{{}^{2n}C_{n-1}}{2^n}$

(c) $\dfrac{n}{2^{2n}}$      (d) None

---

## Section - II - Multiple Correct Answer Type

This section contains 5 multiple correct answer(s) type questions. Each question has 4 choices (a), (b), (c) and (d), out of which **ONE OR MORE** is/are correct.

---

**13.** Which of the following statements is /are correct :

(a) If three distinct numbers are chosen randomly from the first 100 natural numbers, then the probability that all three of them are divisible by both 2 and 3 is 4/1155

(b) 3 integers are chosen at random from the set of first 20 natural numbers. The chance that their product is a multiple of 3, is $\dfrac{194}{285}$

<table>
<tr><td rowspan="2">Response<br>Grid</td><td>6. ⓐⓑⓒⓓ</td><td>7. ⓐⓑⓒⓓ</td><td>8. ⓐⓑⓒⓓ</td><td>9. ⓐⓑⓒⓓ</td><td>10. ⓐⓑⓒⓓ</td></tr>
<tr><td>11. ⓐⓑⓒⓓ</td><td>12. ⓐⓑⓒⓓ</td><td>13. ⓐⓑⓒⓓ</td><td></td><td></td></tr>
</table>

(c) Four balls are drawn at random from a bag containing 5 white, 4 green and 3 black balls. The probability that exactly two of them are white is $\dfrac{14}{33}$

(d) Out of all the arrangements that can be made taking 5 letters at a time of the word BRILLIANT one is chosen at random. The probability that this will have 5 distinct letters is $\dfrac{252}{507}$

**14.** A fair coin is tossed $n$ times. Let $X =$ the number of times head occurs. If $P(X = 4)$, $P(X = 5)$ and $P(X = 6)$ are in AP, then the value of n can be

(a) 7        (b) 10

(c) 12       (d) 14

**15.** Let $X$ be a set containing $n$ elements. If two subsets $A$ and $B$ of $X$ are picked at random, the probability that $A$ and $B$ have the same number of elements is

(a) $\dfrac{^{2n}C_n}{2^{2n}}$        (b) $\dfrac{1}{^{2n}C_n}$

(c) $\dfrac{1.3.5...(2n-1)}{2^n \cdot n!}$        (d) $\dfrac{3^n}{4^n}$

**16.** Three six faced fair dice are thrown together. The probability that the sum of the numbers appearing on the dice is $k$ $(3 \le k \le 8)$ is

(a) $\dfrac{(k-1)(k-2)}{432}$        (b) $\dfrac{k(k-2)}{432}$

(c) $^{k-1}C_2 \times \dfrac{1}{216}$        (d) $\dfrac{k^2}{432}$

**17.** Suppose $m$ boys and $m$ girls take their seats randomly round a circle. The probability of their sitting is $\left(^{2m-1}C_m\right)^{-1}$ when

(a) no two boys sit together

(b) no two girls sit together

(c) boys and girls sit alternatively

(d) all the boys sit together

## Section - III - Reasoning Type

This section contains 2 reasoning type questions. Each question has 4 choices (a), (b), (c) and (d) out of which **ONLY ONE** is correct.

**DIRECTIONS for Qs (18-19) : Each of these questions contains two statements: Statement-1 (Assertion) and Statement-2 (Reason). Each of these questions has four alternative choices, only one of which is the correct answer. You have to select the correct choice.**

(a) Statement-1 is True, Statement-2 is True; Statement-2 is a correct explanation for Statement-1.

(b) Statement-1 is True, Statement-2 is True; Statement-2 is NOT a correct explanation for Statement-1.

(c) Statement-1 is True, Statement-2 is False.

(d) Statement-1 is False, Statement-2 is True.

**18.** **Statement-1:** Out of 5 tickets consecutively numbers, three are drawn at random, the chance that the numbers on them are in A.P. is 2/15.

**Statement-2:** Out of $(2n + 1)$ tickets consecutively numbered, three are drawn at random, the chance that the numbers on them are in A.P. is $\dfrac{3n}{4n^2 - 1}$.

**19** **Statement–1 :** Three of the six vertices of a regular hexagon are chosen at random. The probability that the triangle with these three vertices is equilateral equals to 1/10.

**Statement–2 :** A die is rolled three times. The probability of getting a large number than the previous number is 5/54.

## Section - IV - Integer Type

This section contains 5 questions. The answer to each of the questions is a single digit integer ranging from 0 to 9.

**20.** Two integers x and y are chosen (with replacement) from the set $\{0, 1, 2, ....., 10\}$. If P be the probability that $|x - y|$ is less than or equal to 5, then find the value of $\dfrac{121}{13}$P.

<table>
<tr><td rowspan="2">**RESPONSE GRID**</td><td>14. ⓐⓑⓒⓓ</td><td>15. ⓐⓑⓒⓓ</td><td>16. ⓐⓑⓒⓓ</td><td>17. ⓐⓑⓒⓓ</td><td>18. ⓐⓑⓒⓓ</td></tr>
<tr><td>19. ⓐⓑⓒⓓ</td><td colspan="4">20. ⓪①②③④⑤⑥⑦⑧⑨</td></tr>
</table>

**21.** Five persons entered the lift cabin on the ground floor of an eight floor house. Suppose that each of them independently & with equal probability can leave the cabin at any floor beginning with the first. If the probability of all 5 persons leaving at different floors is $\dfrac{^{P}C_{Q}.Q!}{P^{Q}}$. Find P – Q.

**22.** The digits of a number are $1, 2, 3, 4, 5, 6, 7, 8 \& 9$ written at random in any order. If the probability that the order is divisible by 11 is $\dfrac{X+2}{P}$, Find X.

**23.** You are given a box with 20 cards in it. 10 of these cards have the letter I printed on them. The other ten have the letter T printed on them. If you pick up 3 cards at random and keep them in the some order, the probability of making the word IIT is $\dfrac{A}{B}$. Find A.

**24.** Three faces of a fair dice are yellow, two faces are red and one face is blue. The dice is tossed three times. The probability that the colours, yellow, red, and blue appear in the first, second and third tosses respectively is $\dfrac{1}{P^{2}}$. Find P.

| RESPONSE GRID | |
|---|---|
| 21. ⓪①②③④⑤⑥⑦⑧⑨ | 22. ⓪①②③④⑤⑥⑦⑧⑨ |
| 23. ⓪①②③④⑤⑥⑦⑧⑨ | 24. ⓪①②③④⑤⑥⑦⑧⑨ |

## DAILY PRACTICE PROBLEM DPP 40 - MATHS

| Total Questions | 24 | Total Marks | 70 |
|---|---|---|---|
| Attempted | | Correct | |
| Incorrect | | Net Score | |
| Cut-off Score | 14 | Qualifying Score | 46 |
| Success Gap = Net Score – Qualifying Score | | | |

$$\textbf{Net Score} = \sum_{i=I}^{VI}\left[(\textbf{correct}_i \times MM_i) - (In_i - NM_i)\right]$$

*Space for Rough Work*

# DPP - Daily Practice Problems

**Name :**

**Date :**

**Start Time :**

**End Time :**

## MATHEMATICS    M41

SYLLABUS : **Probability-3** : Addition theorem on probability

**Max. Marks : 70**                    **Time : 60 min.**



## Section - I - Straight Objective Type

This section contains 12 multiple choice questions. Each question has 4 choices (a), (b), (c) and (d), out of which **ONLY ONE** is correct.

**1.** $P(A) = 3/7$, $P(B') = 1/2$, $P(A' \cap B') = 1/14$ then $P(A \cap B)$ is equal to (where A', B' are complement of A, B)
  (a)   1/14          (b)   3/8
  (c)   0             (d)   none of these

**2.** A fair coin is tossed until a head or five tails occur. If the probability that the coin is tossed for a maximum number of times can be expressed as a rational is $\dfrac{p}{q}$ (in the lowest form), then $(p + q)$ equals –
  (a)   17          (b)   34
  (c)   19          (d)   18

**3.** If A and B are two independent events such that $P(A) = 1/6$ and $P(B) = 1/2$, then
  (a)   $P(AB) = 1/24$      (b)   $P(A \cup B) = 1/12$
  (c)   $P(A^c B) = 1/6$      (d)   $P(A^c B^c) = 5/12$

**4.** A purse contains 4 copper and 3 silver coins and another purse contains 6 copper and 2 silver coins. One coin is drawn from any one of these two purses. The probability that it is a copper coin is
  (a)   4/7          (b)   3/4
  (c)   2/7          (d)   37/56

**5.** Two events A and B have probabilities 0.25 and 0.50 respectively. The probability that both A and B occur simultaneously is 0.14. Then the probability that neither A nor B occurs is
  (a)   0.39         (b)   0.25
  (c)   0.11         (d)   none of these

**6.** For the three events A, B, and C, P (exactly one of the events A or B occurs) = P (exactly one of the two events B or C occurs) = P(exactly one of the events C or A occurs) = p and P (all the three events occur simultaneously) = $p^2$, where $0 < p < 1/2$. Then the probability of at least one of the three events A, B and C occurring is

(a)  $\dfrac{3p + 2p^2}{2}$        (b)  $\dfrac{p + 3p^2}{4}$

(c)  $\dfrac{p + 3p^2}{2}$        (d)  $\dfrac{3p + 2p^2}{4}$

**7.** If A and B are two events such that

$P(A \cup B) = 5/6, P(A \cap B) = 1/3$ and $P(B') = 1/2,$ then

the events A and B are
(a)  dependent        (b)  independent
(c)  mutually exclusive    (d)  none

**8.** The probabilities of three events A, B and C are P(A) = 0.6, P(B) = 0.4 and P(C) = 0.5. If P(A $\cup$ B) = 0.8, P(A $\cap$ C) = 0.3, P(A $\cap$ B $\cap$ C) = 0.2 and P(A $\cup$ B $\cup$ C) $\geq$ 0.85, then

(a)  $0.2 \leq P(B \cap C) \leq 0.35$

(b)  $0.5 \leq P(B \cap C) \leq 0.85$

(c)  $0.1 \leq P(B \cap C) \leq 0.35$

(d)  None of these

**9.** Let A and B be two events such that $P(\overline{A \cup B}) = \dfrac{1}{6},$

$P(A \cap B) = \dfrac{1}{4}$ and $P(\overline{A}) = \dfrac{1}{4},$ where $\overline{A}$ stands for complement of event A. Then events A and B are
(a)  equally likely and mutually exclusive
(b)  equally likely but not independent
(c)  independent but not equally likely
(d)  mutually exclusive and independent

**10.** If A and B are two events then which of the following does not represent the probability that exactly one of them occurs?

(a)  $P(A) + P(B) - 2P(A \cap B)$

(b)  $P(A \cap B') + P(A' \cap B)$

(c)  $P(A \cup B) - P(A \cap B)$

(d)  $P(A') + P(B') - P(A' \cap B')$

**11.** Three numbers are chosen at random without replacement from 1, 2, 3,......, 10. The probability that the minimum of the chosen numbers is 4 or their maximum is 8, is
(a)  11/40          (b)  3/10
(c)  1/40          (d)  None of these

**12.** Let A, B, C be three mutually independent events. Consider the two statements $S_1$ and $S_2$
$S_1$ : A and B $\cup$ C are independent
$S_2$ : A and B $\cap$ C are independent, then
(a)  both $S_1$ and $S_2$ are true  (b)  only $S_1$ is true
(c)  only $S_2$ is true    (d)  neither $S_1$ nor $S_2$ is true

---

## Section - II - Multiple Correct Answer Type

This section contains 5 multiple correct answer(s) type questions. Each question has 4 choices (a), (b), (c) and (d), out of which **ONE OR MORE** is/are correct.

---

**13.** Identify the incorrect sentence among the following for three events A, B, and C.
(a)  P (exactly two of A, B, C occur)
$$\geq P(A \cap B) + P(B \cap C) + P(C \cap A)$$
(b)  $P(A \cup B \cup C) \leq P(A) + P(B) + P(C)$
(c)  P (exactly one of A, B, C occurs)
$$\geq P(A) + P(B) + P(C) - P(B \cap C) - P(C \cap A) - P(A \cap B)$$
(d)  P (A and at least one of B, C occur)
$$\geq P(A \cap B) + P(A \cap C)$$



*Space for Rough Work*

**14.** If $M$ and $N$ are any two events, then the probability that exactly one of them occurs is

(a) $P(M) + P(N) - 2P(M \cap N)$

(b) $P(M) + P(N) - P(M \cap N)$

(c) $P(M^c) + P(N^c) - 2P(M^c \cap N^c)$

(d) $P(M \cap N^c) + P(M^c \cap N)$

**15.** For two given events A and B, $P(A \cap B)$

(a) not less than $P(A) + P(B) - 1$

(b) not greater than $P(A) + P(B)$

(c) equal to $P(A) + P(B) - P(A \cup B)$

(d) equal to $P(A) + P(B) + P(A \cup B)$

**16.** E and F are two independent events. The probability that both E and F happen is $1/12$ and the probability that neither E nor F happens is $1/2$. Then,

(a) $P(E) = 1/3, P(F) = 1/4$

(b) $P(E) = 1/2, P(F) = 1/6$

(c) $P(E) = 1/6, P(F) = 1/2$

(d) $P(E) = 1/4, P(F) = 1/3$

**17** Three numbers are chosen at random without replacement from $\{1, 2, 3, ..., 10\}$. The probability that minimum of the chosen number is 3 or their maximum is 7, cannot exceed

(a) $\dfrac{11}{30}$

(b) $\dfrac{11}{40}$

(c) $\dfrac{11}{50}$

(d) $\dfrac{11}{60}$

## Section - III - Reasoning Type

This section contains 2 reasoning type questions. Each question has 4 choices (a), (b), (c) and (d) out of which **ONLY ONE** is correct.

**DIRECTIONS for Qs (18 -19) : Each of these questions contains two statements: Statement-1 (Assertion) and Statement-2 (Reason). Each of these questions has four alternative choices, only one of which is the correct answer. You have to select the correct choice.**

(a) Statement-1 is True, Statement-2 is True; Statement-2 is a correct explanation for Statement-1.

(b) Statement-1 is True, Statement-2 is True; Statement-2 is NOT a correct explanation for Statement-1.

(c) Statement -1 is True, Statement-2 is False.

(d) Statement -1 is False, Statement-2 is True.

**18.** **Statement-1:** A, B and C are events such that $P(A) = 0.3$, $P(B) = 0.4$, $P(C) = 0.8$, $P(A \cap B) = 0.08$, $P(A \cap C) = 0.28$, $P(A \cap B \cap C) = 0.09$ then $P(B \cap C) \in (0.23, 0.48)$.

**Statement-2:** $0.75 \le P(A \cup B \cup C) \le 1$.

**19.** **Statement-1:** If $A$ and $B$ are two events such that

$$P(A) = \frac{1}{2} \text{ and } P(B) = \frac{2}{3}, \text{ then } \frac{1}{6} \le P(A \cap B) \le \frac{1}{2}$$

**Statement-2 :** $P(A \cup B) \le \max \{P(A), P(B)\}$

and $P(A \cap B) \ge \min \{P(A), P(B)\}$

## Section - IV - Integer Type

This section contains 5 questions. The answer to each of the questions is a single digit integer ranging from 0 to 9.

**20.** A student appears for tests I, II and III. The student is successful if he passes either in test I and II or tests I and III. The probabilites of the student passing in test I, II and III are respectively $p$, $q$ and $\dfrac{1}{2}$. If the probability that the student is successful is $\dfrac{1}{2}$, then find the value of $p(1 + q)$.

| | | | | | |
|---|---|---|---|---|---|
| **RESPONSE GRID** | 14. ⓐⓑⓒⓓ | 15. ⓐⓑⓒⓓ | 16. ⓐⓑⓒⓓ | 17. ⓐⓑⓒⓓ | 18. ⓐⓑⓒⓓ |
| | 19. ⓐⓑⓒⓓ | 20. ⓪①②③④⑤⑥⑦⑧⑨ | | | |

**21.** The probability that at least one of the events A and B occurs is 3/5. If A and B occur simultaneously with probability 1/5 then $P(A') + P(B')$ is $\dfrac{M}{N}$. Find $M - N$.

**22.** Let A, B, C be three events. If the probability of occurring exactly one event out of A and B is $1 - a$, out of B and C is $1 - 2a$ and out of C and A is $1 - a$, and that of occurring three events simultaneously is $a^2$, then the probability that at least one out of A, B, C will occur is greater than $\dfrac{1}{X}$. Find X.

**23.** A and B are events such that $P(A \cup B) = \dfrac{3}{4}$, $P(A \cap B) = \dfrac{1}{4}$, $P(\overline{A}) = \dfrac{2}{3}$ then $P(\overline{A} \cap B) = \dfrac{W}{Z}$. Find $Z - W$.

**24.** From a pack of 52 cards, one card is drawn at random. The probability that it is either a King or a Queen is X. Find 26X.

<table>
<tr><td rowspan="2">RESPONSE GRID</td><td>21. ⓪①②③④⑤⑥⑦⑧⑨</td><td>22. ⓪①②③④⑤⑥⑦⑧⑨</td></tr>
<tr><td>23. ⓪①②③④⑤⑥⑦⑧⑨</td><td>24. ⓪①②③④⑤⑥⑦⑧⑨</td></tr>
</table>

## DAILY PRACTICE PROBLEM DPP 41 - MATHS

| Total Questions | 24 | Total Marks | 70 |
|---|---|---|---|
| Attempted | | Correct | |
| Incorrect | | Net Score | |
| Cut-off Score | 14 | Qualifying Score | 46 |
| Success Gap = Net Score – Qualifying Score | | | |

$$\text{Net Score} = \sum_{i=I}^{VI}\left[(\text{correct}_i \times MM_i) - (In_i - NM_i)\right]$$

*Space for Rough Work*

# DPP - Daily Practice Problems

Name :                Date :         

Start Time :             End Time :        

# MATHEMATICS  M42

**SYLLABUS : Mathematical Reasoning**

## Max. Marks : 59             Time : 60 min.

### GENERAL INSTRUCTIONS

- The Daily Practice Problem Sheet contains **24** Questions divided into 3 sections.

  Section I has **17** MCQ's with ONLY 1 correct option. 2 marks for correct answer and No negative marks.

  Section II has **4** MCQ's with 1 or MORE THAN 1 correct option. 4 marks for correct answer(s) and (–1) for wrong answer.
  Section III has **3** Assertion-Reason MCQ's with ONLY 1 correct option. 3 marks for correct and (–1) mark for wrong answer.

- No mark will be given/ deducted if no bubble is filled. Keep a timer in front and stop immediately at the end of 60 min.

- You have to evaluate your Response Grids yourself with the help of Solution Booklet.

- The sheet follows a particular syllabus. Do not attempt the sheet before you have completed your preparation for that syllabus. Refer syllabus sheet in the starting of the book for the syllabus of all the DPP sheets.

- After completing the sheet check your answers with the solution booklet and complete the Result Grid. Finally spend time to analyse your performance and revise the areas which emerge out as weak in your evaluation.

---

## Section - I - Straight Objective Type

This section contains 17 multiple choice questions. Each question has 4 choices (a), (b), (c) and (d), out of which **ONLY ONE** is correct.

**1.** If p, q, r are simple propositions with truth values T, F, T, then the truth value of $(\sim p \vee q) \wedge \sim r \Rightarrow p$ is

  (a) True          (b) False
  (c) True if r is false    (d) True if q is true

**2.** If $p \Rightarrow (q \vee r)$ is false, then the truth values of p, q, r are respectively

  (a) T, F, F          (b) F, F, F
  (c) F, T, T          (d) T, T, F

**3.** If $p \Rightarrow (\sim p \vee q)$ is false, then the truth values of p and q are respectively

  (a) F, T    (b) F, F     (c) T, T     (d) T, F

**4.** Which of the following is the inverse of the proposition : "If a number is a prime then it is odd."

  (a) If a number is not a prime then it is odd
  (b) If a number is not a prime then it is not odd
  (c) If a number is not odd then it is not a prime
  (d) If a number is not odd then it is a prime

**5.** Negation of the proposition : If we control population growth, we prosper

  (a) If we do not control population growth, we prosper
  (b) If we control population growth, we do not prosper
  (c) We control population but we do not prosper
  (d) We do not control population, but we prosper

**6.** If p and q are simple propositions, then $p \Rightarrow q$ is false when

  (a) p is true and q is true    (b) p is false and q is true
  (c) p is true and q is false    (d) Both p and q are false

---

<table>
<tr><td rowspan="2">RESPONSE<br>GRID</td><td>1. 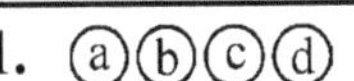</td><td>2. 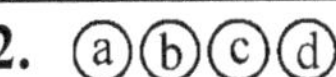</td><td>3. </td><td>4. 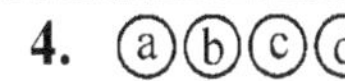</td><td>5. ⓐⓑⓒⓓ</td></tr>
<tr><td colspan="5">6. ⓐⓑⓒⓓ</td></tr>
</table>

**7.** Negation of "$2 + 3 = 5$ and $8 < 10$" is

(a) $2 + 3 \neq 5$ and $< 10$

(b) $2 + 3 = 5$ and $8 \not< 10$

(c) $2 + 3 \neq 5$ or $8 \not< 10$

(d) None of these

**8.** $(p \wedge \sim q) \wedge (\sim p \vee q)$ is

(a) A contradiction

(b) A tautology

(c) Either (a) or (b)

(d) Neither (a) nor (b)

**9.** The propositions $(p \Rightarrow \sim p) \wedge (\sim p \Rightarrow p)$ is

(a) Tautology and contradiction

(b) Neither tautology nor contradiction

(c) Contradiction

(d) Tautology

**10.** The negation of the compound propostion $p \vee (\sim p \wedge q)$

(a) $(p \wedge \sim q) \wedge \sim p$     (b) $(p \wedge \sim q) \vee \sim p$

(c) $(p \vee \sim q) \vee \sim p$     (d) None of these

**11.** The negation of the statement $(p \wedge q) \to (\sim p \vee r)$ is

(a) $(p \wedge q) \vee (p \vee \sim r)$

(b) $(p \wedge q) \vee (p \wedge \sim r)$

(c) $(p \wedge q) \wedge (p \wedge \sim r)$

(d) $p \vee q$

**12.** Negation of "Paris in France and London is in England" is

(a) Paris is in England and London is in France

(b) Paris is not in France or London is not in England

(c) Paris is in England or London is in France

(d) None of these

**13.** $\sim ((\sim p) \wedge q)$ is equal to

(a) $P \vee (\sim q)$     (b) $P \vee q$

(c) $p \wedge (\sim q)$     (d) $\sim p \wedge \sim q$

**14.** The contrapositive of $(p \vee q) \Rightarrow r$ is

(a) $r \Rightarrow (p \vee q)$     (b) $\sim r \Rightarrow (p \vee q)$

(c) $\sim r \Rightarrow \sim p \wedge \sim q$     (d) $p \Rightarrow (q \vee r)$

**15.** Let p and q stand for the statements

p : It is a cold day

q: The temperature is 5°C.

Then the meaning of $\sim (p \wedge q)$ is

(a) It is false that today is a cold day or temperature is 5°C.

(b) It is not true that today is a cold day & temperature is 5°C.

(c) Today is a cold day and temperature is 5°C.

(d) It is false that today is not a cold day or temperature is not 5°C.

**16.** Consider the statements

p : Today is Tuesday

q : It is raining

r : It is cold.

Then the meaning of $\sim q \Rightarrow (r \wedge p)$ is

(a) If today is Tuesday, then it is raining.

(b) It is not raining, then it is cold & today is Tuesday.

(c) If today is not Tuesday, then it is raining or it is cold.

(d) It is not the case that today is Tuesday or it is raining if and only if it is cold.

| RESPONSE GRID | 7. ⓐⓑⓒⓓ | 8. ⓐⓑⓒⓓ | 9. ⓐⓑⓒⓓ | 10. ⓐⓑⓒⓓ | 11. ⓐⓑⓒⓓ |
| --- | --- | --- | --- | --- | --- |
| | 12. ⓐⓑⓒⓓ | 13. ⓐⓑⓒⓓ | 14. ⓐⓑⓒⓓ | 15. ⓐⓑⓒⓓ | 16. ⓐⓑⓒⓓ |

**17.** If   p : Anil is rich,

q : Ram is poor.

Then the symbolic form of 'It is not true that Anil and Ram are both rich' is

(a)  $(\sim p) \wedge (\sim q)$          (b)  $\sim [p \wedge (-q)]$

(c)  $p \vee (\sim q)$          (d)  none of these

## Section - II - Multiple Correct Answer Type

This section contains 4 multiple correct answer(s) type questions. Each question has 4 choices (a), (b), (c) and (d), out of which **ONE OR MORE** is/are correct.

**18.** Which of the following are proposition ?

(a)  $\sqrt{3}$ is a prime

(b)  $\sqrt{2}$ is irrational

(c)  Mathematics is interesting

(d)  5 is an even integer

**19.** Which of the following is false ?

(a)  $p \Rightarrow q \equiv \sim p \Rightarrow \sim q$

(b)  $\sim (p \Rightarrow \sim q) \equiv \sim p \wedge q$

(c)  $\sim (\sim p \Rightarrow \sim q) \equiv \sim p \wedge q$

(d)  $\sim (\sim p \Leftrightarrow q) \equiv [\sim (p \Rightarrow q) \wedge \sim (q \Rightarrow p)]$

**20.** Which of the following is not a contradiction?

(a)  $(p \wedge q) \wedge \sim (p \vee q)$

(b)  $p \vee (-p \wedge q)$

(c)  $(p \Rightarrow q) \Rightarrow p$

(d)  None of these

**21.** Identity the true statement among the followings.

(a)  $p \wedge (\sim p)$ is contradiction

(b)  $(p \Rightarrow q) \Leftrightarrow (\sim q \Rightarrow \sim p)$ is a contradiction

(c)  $\sim (\sim p) \Leftrightarrow p$ is a tautology

(d)  $p \vee (\sim p) \Leftrightarrow$ is a tautology

## Section - III - Reasoning Type

This section contains 3 reasoning type questions. Each question has 4 choices (a), (b), (c) and (d) out of which **ONLY ONE** is correct.

**DIRECTIONS for Qs. (22 to 24) : Each of these questions contains two statements: Statement-1 (Assertion) and Statement-2 (Reason). Each of these questions has four alternative choices, only one of which is the correct answer. You have to select the correct choice.**

(a)   Statement-1 is True, Statement-2 is True; Statement-2 is a correct explanation for Statement-1.

(b)   Statement-1 is True, Statement-2 is True; Statement-2 is NOT a correct explanation for Statement-1.

(c)   Statement -1 is True, Statement-2 is False.

(d)   Statement -1 is False, Statement-2 is True.

| RESPONSE GRID | 17. ⓐⓑⓒⓓ | 18. ⓐⓑⓒⓓ | 19. ⓐⓑⓒⓓ | 20. ⓐⓑⓒⓓ | 21. ⓐⓑⓒⓓ |

**22.** **Statement-1 :** "Mars and Venus" revolve around the sun is a compound statement.

**Statement-2 :** Two simple statements connected by "AND" form a compound statement.

**23.** Consider the following argument :

"If it is cloudy tonight then it will rain tomorrow and if it rains tomorrow, I shall be on leave tomorrow, and the conclusion is if it is cloudy tonight then I shall be on leave tomorrow."

**Statement-1 :** The given argument is a valid argument.

**Statement-2 :** For three statements p, q and r $p \Rightarrow q$ and $q \Rightarrow r$ then $p \Rightarrow r$

**24.** **Statement-1 :** The statement $(p \vee q) \wedge \sim p$ and $\sim p \wedge q$ are logically equivalent.

**Statement-2 :** The end columns of the truth table of both statements are identical.

| RESPONSE GRID | 22. ⓪①②③④⑤⑥⑦⑧⑨ | 23. ⓪①②③④⑤⑥⑦⑧⑨ |
|---|---|---|
| | 24. ⓪①②③④⑤⑥⑦⑧⑨ | |

## DAILY PRACTICE PROBLEM DPP 42 - MATHS

| Total Questions | 24 | Total Marks | 59 |
|---|---|---|---|
| Attempted | | Correct | |
| Incorrect | | Net Score | |
| Cut-off Score | 11 | Qualifying Score | 36 |
| Success Gap = Net Score – Qualifying Score | | | |

$$\text{Net Score} = \sum_{i=1}^{VI} \left[ (\text{correct}_i \times MM_i) - (In_i - NM_i) \right]$$

# DPP - Daily Practice Problems

**Name :**

**Date :**

**Start Time :**

**End Time :**

## MATHEMATICS    M43

**SYLLABUS : Functions :** Real valued functions; into, onto and one-to-one functions; Sum, difference, product and quotient of two functions; Absolute value, Polynomial, Rational, Trigonometric, Exponential and Logarithmic functions; Composite of functions

**Max. Marks : 68**                    **Time : 60 min.**



## Section - I - Straight Objective Type

This section contains 7 multiple choice questions. Each question has 4 choices (a), (b), (c) and (d), out of which **ONLY ONE** is correct.

**1.** Consider a real valued function $f(x)$ satisfying

$2f(xy) = (f(x))^y + (f(y))^x \; \forall x, y \in R$ and $f(1) = a$ where

$a \ne 1$, then $(a-1)\sum_{i=l}^{n} f(i)$ equals

(a) $a^n$     (b) $a^{n+1}$     (c) $a^{n-1}+a$   (d) $a^{n+1}-a$

**2.** Let $f : R \to \left[0, \dfrac{\pi}{2}\right)$ defined by $f(x) = \tan^{-1}(x^2 + x + a)$, then

the set of values of $a$ for which $f$ is onto is

(a) $[0, \infty)$                  (b) $[1, 2]$

(c) $\left[\dfrac{1}{4}, \infty\right)$              (d) none of these

**3.** Let R be the set of real numbers. If $f : R \to R$ is a function defined by $f(x) = x^2$, then $f$ is :

(a) Injective but not surjective
(b) Surjective but not injective
(c) Bijective
(d) None of these.

**4.** Let $f : R \to R$ be any function. Define $g : R \to R$ by $g(x) = |f(x)|$ for all x. Then g is

(a) onto if f is onto
(b) one-one if f is one-one
(c) continuous if f is continuous
(d) differentiable if f is differentiable.

**5.** Let function $f : R \to R$ be defined by $f(x) = 2x + \sin x$ for $x \in R$, then f is

(a) one-to-one and onto
(b) one-to-one but NOT onto
(c) onto but NOT one-to-one
(d) neither one-to-one nor onto

| | | |
|---|---|---|
| **RESPONSE GRID** | **1.** (a)(b)(c)(d)    **2.** (a)(b)(c)(d)    **3.** (a)(b)(c)(d)    **4.** (a)(b)(c)(d)    **5.** (a)(b)(c)(d) | |

**6.** Let $f(x) = \sin x$ and $g(x) = \ln |x|$. If the ranges of the composition functions fog and gof are $R_1$ and $R_2$ respectively, then

   (a)  $R_1 = \{u : -1 \le u < 1\}$, $R_2 = \{v : -\infty < v < 0\}$

   (b)  $R_1 = \{u : -\infty < u < 0\}$, $R_2 = \{v : -1 \le v \le 0\}$

   (c)  $R_1 = \{u : -1 < u < 1\}$, $R_2 = \{v : -\infty < v < 0\}$

   (d)  $R_1 = \{u : -1 \le u \le 1\}$, $R_2 = \{v : -\infty < v \le 0\}$

**7.** Which of the following function is surjective but not injective?

   (a)  $f : R \to R \;\; f(x) = x^4 + 2x^3 - x^2 + 1$

   (b)  $f : R \to R \;\; f(x) = x^3 + x + 1$

   (c)  $f : R \to R^+ \;\; f(x) = \sqrt{1 + x^2}$

   (d)  $f : R \to R \;\; f(x) = x^3 + 2x^2 - x + 1$

## Section - II - Multiple Correct Answer Type

This section contains 3 multiple correct answer(s) type questions. Each question has 4 choices (a), (b), (c) and (d), out of which **ONE OR MORE** is/are correct.

**8.** Of the following functions defined from $[-1, 1]$ to $[-1, 1]$, which of the following are not bijective

   (a)  $\sin(\sin^{-1} x)$      (b)  $\dfrac{2}{\pi}\sin^{-1}(\sin x)$

   (c)  $(\operatorname{Sgn} x) / \ln(e^x)$     (d)  $x^3(\operatorname{Sgn} x)$

**9.** Let $f(x) = [x]^2 + [x+1] - 3$, where $[x] \le x$. Then

   (a)  $f(x)$ is a many - one and into function

   (b)  $f(x) = 0$ for infinite number of values of $x$

   (c)  $f(x) = 0$ for only two real values of $x$

   (d)  none of the above

**10.** Let f be the greatest integer function and g be the modulus functions, then

   (a)  $(\text{gof} - \text{fog})\left(-\dfrac{5}{3}\right) = 1$   (b)  $(f + 2g)(-1) = 1$

   (c)  $(\text{gof} - \text{fog})\left(\dfrac{5}{3}\right) = 0$   (d)  $(f + 2g)(1) = 1$

## Section - III - Linked Comprehension Type

This section contains one paragraph. Based upon the paragraph, 3 multiple choice questions have to be answered. Each question has 4 choices (a), (b), (c) and (d), out of which **ONLY ONE** is correct.

### Inverse of a Function

Let $f : X \to Y$ is a bijective function. We define a function $g : Y \to X$ such that $f(x) = y \Leftrightarrow g(y) = x$, $x \in X$, $y \in Y$  Then g is called the inverse of f, and is denoted by $f^{-1}$.

To find inverse of a function we proceed as follows :

Put $y = f(x)$

Express x as function of y, say $x = g(y)$ then inverse of $f(x)$ is $g(x)$

For example $f : R \to R$ given by $f(x) = 2x - 1$ is a bijective function, to

find its inverse, we put $y = 2x - 1 \Rightarrow x = \dfrac{1+y}{2}$

So, the desired inverse is $f^{-1}(x) = \dfrac{1+x}{2}$

The graph of a function and the graph of its inverse are symmetrical about the line $y = x$. So, they intersect when $y = x$. For example, the above the graph of the function $y = 2x - 1$

and $y = \dfrac{x+1}{2}$ given in the illustration intersect if

$2x - 1 = \dfrac{x+1}{2} \Rightarrow x = 1$

**11.** Let a function $f : R \to (-\infty, 1)$ is given by $f(x) = 1 - 2^{-x}$ then its inverse is the function

   (a)  $1 + \log_2(-x)$     (b)  $1 - \log_2(-x)$

   (c)  $\log_2(1 - x)$     (d)  $-\log_2(1 - x)$

**12.** The number of roots of the question $1 + \log_2(1 - x) = 2^{-x}$ is

   (a)  0      (b)  1      (c)  2      (d)  many

**13.** The inverse of $f(x) = x^2 + 2ax + \dfrac{1}{16}$, $x \ge -a$ is (assuming it bijective)

<table>
<tr><td rowspan="2">Response Grid</td><td>6. ⓐⓑⓒⓓ</td><td>7. ⓐⓑⓒⓓ</td><td>8. ⓐⓑⓒⓓ</td><td>9. ⓐⓑⓒⓓ</td><td>10. ⓐⓑⓒⓓ</td></tr>
<tr><td>11. ⓐⓑⓒⓓ</td><td>12. ⓐⓑⓒⓓ</td><td>13. ⓐⓑⓒⓓ</td><td></td><td></td></tr>
</table>

(a) $-\dfrac{1}{16}+\sqrt{a^2+x-\dfrac{1}{16}}$  (b) $-a+\sqrt{a^2+x-\dfrac{1}{16}}$

(c) $a-\sqrt{a^2+x-\dfrac{1}{16}}$  (d) $\dfrac{1}{16}-\sqrt{a^2+x-\dfrac{1}{16}}$

$$f(x)f\left(\dfrac{1}{x}\right)=f(x)+f\left(\dfrac{1}{x}\right)$$

and $f(3)=28$ then $f(x)$ is

(D) Let $f: R \to R$ is defined by $f(x)=2x+\sin x$, then $f(x)$ is

(s) Many-one

(t) Bijective

## Section - IV - Matrix-Match Type

This section contains 1 question. It contains statements given in two columns, which have to be matched. Statements in Column I are labelled as A, B, C and D whereas statements in Column II are labelled as p, q, r and s. The answers to these questions have to be appropriately bubbled as illustrated in the following example. If the correct matches are A-p, A-r, B-p, B-s, C-r, C-s and D-q, then the correctly bubbled matrix will look like the following :

|   | p | q | r | s |
|---|---|---|---|---|
| A | p | q | r | s |
| B | p | q | r | s |
| C | p | q | r | s |
| D | p | q | r | s |

**14.**

| Column-I | Column-II |
|---|---|
| (A) Let $f: R \to R$ satisfies $f(x+y)+f(x-y)=2f(x) f(y) \; \forall \, x,y \in R$ and $f(0) \neq 0$, then $f(x)$ is | (p) Even |
| (B) Let $f: R \to R$ is defined by $f(x)=\dfrac{e^{|x|}-e^{-x}}{e^{x}+e^{-x}}$, then $f(x)$ is | (q) Odd |
| (C) Let $f: R \to R$ be a polynomial function satisfying | (r) Into |

## Section - V - Reasoning Type

This section contains 3 reasoning type questions. Each question has 4 choices (a), (b), (c) and (d) out of which **ONLY ONE** is correct.

**DIRECTIONS for Qs. (15-17) : Each of these questions contains two statements: Statement-1 (Assertion) and Statement-2 (Reason). Each of these questions has four alternative choices, only one of which is the correct answer. You have to select the correct choice.**

(a) Statement-1 is True, Statement-2 is True; Statement-2 is a correct explanation for Statement-1.

(b) Statement-1 is True, Statement-2 is True; Statement-2 is NOT a correct explanation for Statement-1.

(c) Statement -1 is True, Statement-2 is False.

(d) Statement -1 is False, Statement-2 is True.

**15** **Statement 1 :** $f(x)=\tan^{-1}x$ is one-one function.

**Statement 2 :** If $f'(x)>0$ for all x in domain of $f(x)$ then $f(x)$ is one-one.

**16** **Statements-1:** The function $f : R \to R$ given

$f(x)=\log_{a}(x+\sqrt{x^2+1})$ for $a>0$, $a \neq 1$ is invertible.

**Statements-2:** f is many one into.

**17.** **Statements-1:** $f(x)=\begin{cases} x; & x \in Q \\ -x; & x \in Q^{C} \end{cases}$ is one to one and non-monotonic function.

**Statements-2:** Every one to one function is monotonic.

## Section - VI - Integer Type

This section contains 5 questions. The answer to each of the questions is a single digit integer ranging from 0 to 9.

**18.** Let a function f is defined as  $f: \{1, 2, 3, 4\} \to \{1, 2, 3, 4\}$. If f satisfy $f(f(x)) = f(x)$, $\forall x \in \{1, 2, 3, 4\}$, then the number of such functions is $(35 + P)$. Find the value of P.

**19.** Let $f(x) = \dfrac{\alpha x}{x + 1}, x \neq -1$ then for $\alpha = -M$, $f(f(x)) = x$. Find M.

**20.** A function $f : R \to R$, where $R$ is the set of real numbers, is defined by $f(x) = \dfrac{\alpha x^2 + 6x - 8}{\alpha + 6x - 8x^2}$. If f is onto for the interval $P < \alpha < Q$, where P and Q are constants, find the value of $\dfrac{Q}{P}$.

**21.** Let $A = \{1, 2, 3, 4, 5\}$. If $'f'$ be a bijective function from $A$ to $A$, then the number of such functions for which $f(k) \neq k$, $k = 1, 2, 3, 4, 5$, is $11P$. Find P.

**22.** If $g : D \to R$ be a function such that $g(x) = \underbrace{\ln \ln \ln \ln \ldots \ldots \ln}_{n \text{ times}}$ $[4(x^2 + x + 1) + \sin(\pi x)]$. $(n \in N)$, then find the least value of $n$ for which $g$ becomes onto.

<table>
<tr><td rowspan="3">RESPONSE GRID</td><td>18. ⓪①②③④⑤⑥⑦⑧⑨</td><td>19. ⓪①②③④⑤⑥⑦⑧⑨</td></tr>
<tr><td>20. ⓪①②③④⑤⑥⑦⑧⑨</td><td>21. ⓪①②③④⑤⑥⑦⑧⑨</td></tr>
<tr><td>22. ⓪①②③④⑤⑥⑦⑧⑨</td><td></td></tr>
</table>

## DAILY PRACTICE PROBLEM DPP 43 - MATHS

| Total Questions | 22 | Total Marks | 68 |
|---|---|---|---|
| Attempted | | Correct | |
| Incorrect | | Net Score | |
| Cut-off Score | 14 | Qualifying Score | 44 |
| Success Gap = Net Score – Qualifying Score | | | |

$$\text{Net Score} = \sum_{i=I}^{VI} \left[ (\text{correct}_i \times MM_i) - (In_i - NM_i) \right]$$

*Space for Rough Work*

**Name :**

**Date :**

**Start Time :**

**End Time :**

## MATHEMATICS  M44

**SYLLABUS :** Inverse Trigonometric Functions

**Max. Marks : 73**

**Time : 60 min.**

### GENERAL INSTRUCTIONS

- The Daily Practice Problem Sheet contains **24** Questions divided into 6 sections.
  Section I has **8** MCQ's with ONLY 1 correct option. 2 marks for correct answer and No negative marks.
  Section II has **4** MCQ's with 1 or MORE THAN 1 correct option. 4 marks for correct answer(s) and (–1) for wrong answer.
  Section III has **1** PASSAGE with **3** MCQ's with ONLY 1 correct option. 3 marks for correct and (–1) mark for wrong answer.
  Section IV has **2** MCQ's with multiple matchings. 1 mark for the correct matching of each row & No negative marks.
  Section V has **2** Assertion-Reason MCQ's with ONLY 1 correct option. 3 marks for correct and (–1) mark for wrong answer.
  Section VI has **5** single digit integer answer questions. 4 marks for correct answer and (–1) for wrong answer.
- No mark will be given/ deducted if no bubble is filled. Keep a timer in front and stop immediately at the end of 60 min.
- You have to evaluate your Response Grids yourself with the help of Solution Booklet.
- The sheet follows a particular syllabus. Do not attempt the sheet before you have completed your preparation for that syllabus. Refer syllabus sheet in the starting of the book for the syllabus of all the DPP sheets.
- After completing the sheet check your answers with the solution booklet and complete the Result Grid. Finally spend time to analyse your performance and revise the areas which emerge out as weak in your evaluation.

---

## Section - I - Straight Objective Type

This section contains 8 multiple choice questions. Each question has 4 choices (a), (b), (c) and (d), out of which **ONLY ONE** is correct.

**1.** The value of $\tan\left( \arcsin\left( -\dfrac{4}{5} \right) - \arccos\left( -\dfrac{5}{13} \right) \right)$ is equal to

(a) $\dfrac{25}{63}$  (b) $-\dfrac{3}{7}$  (c) $-\dfrac{33}{56}$  (d) $\dfrac{16}{63}$

**2.** The sum of the infinite terms of the series $\cot^{-1}\left( 1^2 + \dfrac{3}{4} \right) +$

$\cot^{-1}\left( 2^2 + \dfrac{3}{4} \right) + \cot^{-1}\left( 3^2 + \dfrac{3}{4} \right) + \ldots$ is equal to :

(a) $\tan^{-1}(1)$  (b) $\tan^{-1}(2)$  (c) $\tan^{-1}(3)$  (d) $\tan^{-1}(4)$

**3.** The value of $\tan^{-1}\left( \dfrac{1}{2} \tan 2A \right) + \tan^{-1}(\cot A) +$

$\tan^{-1}(\cot^3 A)$ for $0 < A < (\pi/4)$ is

(a) $4\tan^{-1}(1)$  (b) $2\tan^{-1}$

(2) (c) $0$  (d) none

**4.** If $x = \cos^{-1}(\cos 4)$ ; $y = \sin^{-1}(\sin 3)$ then which of the following holds ?

(a) $x - y = 1$  (b) $x + y + 1 = 0$

(c) $x + 2y = 2$  (d) $\tan(x + y) = -\tan 7$

**5.** Which of the following is the solution set of the equation $\sin^{-1}x = \cos^{-1}x + \sin^{-1}(3x - 2)$?

(a) $\left\{ \dfrac{1}{2}, 1 \right\}$  (b) $\left[ \dfrac{1}{2}, 1 \right]$

(c) $\left[ \dfrac{1}{3}, 1 \right]$  (d) $\left\{ \dfrac{1}{3}, 1 \right\}$

---

**RESPONSE GRID** 1. ⓐⓑⓒⓓ  2. ⓐⓑⓒⓓ  3. ⓐⓑⓒⓓ  4. ⓐⓑⓒⓓ  5. ⓐⓑⓒⓓ

**6.** If $f(x) = \text{cosec}^{-1}(\text{cosec}\,x)$ and $\text{cosec}(\text{cosec}^{-1}x)$ are equal functions then maximum range of values of $x$ is

(a) $\left[-\dfrac{\pi}{2}, -1\right] \cup \left[1, \dfrac{\pi}{2}\right]$

(b) $\left[-\dfrac{\pi}{2}, 0\right] \cup \left[0, \dfrac{\pi}{2}\right]$

(c) $(-\infty, -1] \cup [1, \infty)$

(d) $[-1, 0) \cup [0, 1)$

**7.** If $\sin\left[2\cos^{-1}\{\cot(2\tan^{-1}x)\}\right] = 0$, $x > 0$, then which of the following is incorrect ?

(a) $x = 1$    (b) $x = \sqrt{2} + 1$    (c) $x = \sqrt{2} - 1$    (d) $x = 3$

**8.** Which of the following value (s) of $x$ does not satisfy the equation $\sin^{-1}|\sin x| = \sqrt{\sin^{-1}|\sin x|}$ ($n$ is any integer) ?

(a) $n\pi$      (b) $n\pi + 1$    (c) $n\pi - 1$    (d) $2n\pi + 1$

## Section - II - Multiple Correct Answer Type

This section contains 4 multiple correct answer(s) type questions. Each question has 4 choices (a), (b), (c) and (d), out of which **ONE OR MORE** is/are correct.

**9.** For the equation $2x = \tan(2\tan^{-1}a) + 2\tan(\tan^{-1}a + \tan^{-1}a^3)$, which of the following is invalid?

(a) $a^2x + 2a = x$

(b) $a^2 + 2ax + 1 = 0$

(c) $a \neq 0$

(d) $a \neq -1, 1$

**10.** Identify the pair(s) of functions which are identical .

(a) $y = \tan(\cos^{-1}x)$;   $y = \dfrac{\sqrt{1 - x^2}}{x}$

(b) $y = \tan(\cot^{-1}x)$ ;   $y = \dfrac{1}{x}$

(c) $y = \sin(\arctan x)$;   $y = \dfrac{x}{\sqrt{1 + x^2}}$

(d) $y = \cos(\arctan x)$ ;   $y = \sin(\text{arc cot } x)$

**11.** If $\cos^{-1}x + \cos^{-1}y + \cos^{-1}z = \pi$, then

(a) $x^2 + y^2 + z^2 + 2xyz = 1$

(b) $2(\sin^{-1}x + \sin^{-1}y + \sin^{-1}z) = \cos^{-1}x + \cos^{-1}y + \cos^{-1}z$

(c) $xy + yz + zx = x + y + z - 1$

(d) $\left(x + \dfrac{1}{x}\right) + \left(y + \dfrac{1}{y}\right) + \left(z + \dfrac{1}{z}\right) \geq 6$

**12.** Indicate which of the following relation is true?

(a) $\tan|\tan^{-1}x| = |x|$

(b) $\cot|\cot^{-1}x| = x$

(c) $\tan^{-1}|\tan x| = x$

(d) $\sin|\sin^{-1}x| = |x|$

## Section - III - Linked Comprehension Type

This section contains one paragraph. Based upon the paragraph, 3 multiple choice questions have to be answered. Each question has 4 choices (a), (b), (c) and (d), out of which **ONLY ONE** is correct.

**Principal values for inverse trigonometric functions :**

| $x < 0$ | $x \geq 0$ |
|---|---|
| $-\dfrac{\pi}{2} \leq \sin^{-1}x < 0$ | $0 \leq \sin^{-1}x \leq \dfrac{\pi}{2}$ |
| $\dfrac{\pi}{2} < \cos^{-1}x \leq \pi$ | $0 \leq \cos^{-1}x \leq \dfrac{\pi}{2}$ |
| $-\dfrac{\pi}{2} < \tan^{-1}x < 0$ | $0 \leq \tan^{-1}x < \dfrac{\pi}{2}$ |
| $\dfrac{\pi}{2} < \cot^{-1}x < \pi$ | $0 < \cot^{-1}x \leq \dfrac{\pi}{2}$ |

$$\sin^{-1}\left(\frac{\sqrt{3}}{2}\right) = \frac{\pi}{3} \text{ not } \frac{2\pi}{3}, \quad \tan^{-1}(-\sqrt{3}) = -\frac{\pi}{3} \text{ not } \frac{2\pi}{3}$$

**On the basis of above information, answer the following questions :**

**13.** The principal value of $\sin^{-1}\left(\sin\dfrac{4\pi}{3}\right) + \cos^{-1}\left(\cos\dfrac{4\pi}{3}\right)$ is

(a) $\dfrac{8\pi}{3}$    (b) $\dfrac{4\pi}{3}$    (c) $\dfrac{2\pi}{3}$    (d) $\dfrac{\pi}{3}$

**14.** The principal value of

$$\tan^{-1}\left(\tan\left(-\frac{3\pi}{4}\right)\right) + \cot^{-1}\left(\cot\left(-\frac{3\pi}{4}\right)\right) \text{ is}$$

(a) $\dfrac{\pi}{2}$    (b) $\pi$    (c) $\dfrac{-3\pi}{2}$    (d) $0$

---

| **RESPONSE GRID** | **6.** ⓐⓑⓒⓓ | **7.** ⓐⓑⓒⓓ | **8.** ⓐⓑⓒⓓ | **9.** ⓐⓑⓒⓓ | **10.** ⓐⓑⓒⓓ |
|---|---|---|---|---|---|
| | **11.** ⓐⓑⓒⓓ | **12.** ⓐⓑⓒⓓ | **13.** ⓐⓑⓒⓓ | **14.** ⓐⓑⓒⓓ | |

*Space for Rough Work*

**15.** The value of $\sin^{-1}[\cos\{\cos^{-1}(\cos x) + \sin^{-1}(\sin x)\}]$,

where $x \in \left(\dfrac{\pi}{2}, \pi\right)$ is

(a) $\dfrac{\pi}{2}$     (b) $-\pi$     (c) $\pi$     (d) $-\dfrac{\pi}{2}$

## Section - IV - Matrix-Match Type

This section contains 2 questions. It contains statements given in two columns, which have to be matched. Statements in Column I are labelled as A, B, C and D whereas statements in Column II are labelled as p, q, r and s. The answers to these questions have to be appropriately bubbled as illustrated in the following example. If the correct matches are A-p, A-r, B-p, B-s, C-r, C-s and D-q, then the correctly bubbled matrix will look like the following :

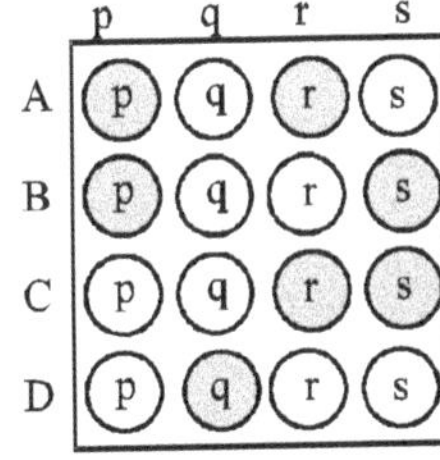

**16.**

| Column I | | Column II |
|---|---|---|

(A) If principal values of     (p) $\lambda + \mu = \dfrac{\pi}{2}$

$\sin^{-1}\left(-\dfrac{1}{2}\right) + \tan^{-1}$

$\left(\sqrt{3}\right)$ and $\cos^{-1}\left(-\dfrac{1}{2}\right)$

are $\lambda$ and $\mu$ respectively, then

(B) If principal values of     (q) $\mu - \lambda = \dfrac{\pi}{2}$

$\sin^{-1}\left(\sin\dfrac{7\pi}{6}\right)$ and

$\cos^{-1}\left\{-\sin\left(\dfrac{5\pi}{6}\right)\right\}$ are

$\lambda$ and $\mu$ respectively, then

(C) If principal values of     (r) $\lambda + \mu = -\dfrac{\pi}{6}$

$\sin^{-1}\left(-\dfrac{\sqrt{3}}{2}\right)$ and

$\sin^{-1}\left\{\cos\left(\sin^{-1}\dfrac{\sqrt{3}}{2}\right)\right\}$

are $\lambda$ and $\mu$ respectively, then

(s) $\mu - \lambda = \dfrac{5\pi}{6}$

(t) $\lambda + \mu = \dfrac{5\pi}{6}$

**17.**

| Column I | Column II |
|---|---|

(A) If $\tan^{-1}x + \tan^{-1}y + \tan^{-1}z = \pi$, then     (p) $x = y = z$

(B) If $\tan^{-1}x + \tan^{-1}y + \tan^{-1}z = \dfrac{\pi}{2}$, then     (q) $xyz \geq 3\sqrt{3}$

(C) If $\tan^{-1}x + \tan^{-1}y + \tan^{-1}z = \dfrac{\pi}{2}$, and $x + y + z = \sqrt{3}$, then     (r) $x + y + z = xyz$

(s) $xyz \leq \dfrac{1}{3\sqrt{3}}$

(t) $xy + yz + zx = 1$

## Section - V - Reasoning Type

This section contains 2 reasoning type questions. Each question has 4 choices (a), (b), (c) and (d) out of which **ONLY ONE** is correct.

**DIRECTIONS for (Qs 18 -19 ):** Each of these questions contains two statements: Statement-1 (Assertion) and Statement-2 (Reason). Each of these questions has four alternative choices, only one of which is the correct answer. You have to select the correct choice.

(a) Statement-1 is True, Statement-2 is True; Statement-2 is a correct explanation for Statement-1.

(b) Statement-1 is True, Statement-2 is True; Statement-2 is NOT a correct explanation for Statement-1.

(c) Statement -1 is True, Statement-2 is False.

(d) Statement -1 is False, Statement-2 is True.

**18.** **Statement 1 :** If $x < 0$, $\tan^{-1} x + \tan^{-1}\left(\dfrac{1}{x}\right) = \dfrac{\pi}{2}$

**Statement 2 :** $\tan^{-1} x + \cot^{-1} x = \dfrac{\pi}{2}$, $\forall x \in R$

**19.** **Statement 1 :** If $1/2 \le x \le 1$ then

$\cos^{-1} x + \cos^{-1}\left[\dfrac{x}{2} + \dfrac{\sqrt{3 - 3x^2}}{2}\right]$ is equal to $\pi/3$.

**Statement 2 :** $\sin^{-1}\left(2x\sqrt{1 - x^2}\right) = 2\sin^{-1} x$, if

$x \in \left[-1/\sqrt{2}, 1/\sqrt{2}\right]$.

## Section - VI - Integer Type

This section contains 5 questions. The answer to each of the questions is a single digit integer ranging from 0 to 9.

**20.** If $\tan\{\text{arc}\tan(2) + \text{arc}\tan(20k)\} = k$ and $k_1$, $k_2$ are two values of k then find the value of $-\dfrac{80}{19}(k_1 + k_2)$.

**21.** The number of solutions of the equation $\tan^{-1}\left(\dfrac{x}{3}\right) + \tan^{-1}\left(\dfrac{x}{2}\right) = \tan^{-1} x$.

**22.** If $x = \tan\left[\cos^{-1}\left(\dfrac{4}{5}\right) + \tan^{-1}\left(\dfrac{2}{3}\right)\right]$, then find the value of $\dfrac{12}{17}x$

**23.** Find the value of $-4x$ for which $\sin(\cot^{-1}(1 + x)) = \cos(\tan^{-1} x)$. is

**24.** If least values of $(\sin^{-1} x)^3 + (\cos^{-1} x)^3$ be $\theta$, then find the value of $\dfrac{96}{\pi^3}\theta$.

| | | |
|---|---|---|
| **RESPONSE GRID** | 18. ⓐⓑⓒⓓ  19. ⓐⓑⓒⓓ  20. ⓪①②③④⑤⑥⑦⑧⑨ | |
| | 21. ⓪①②③④⑤⑥⑦⑧⑨  22. ⓪①②③④⑤⑥⑦⑧⑨ | |
| | 23. ⓪①②③④⑤⑥⑦⑧⑨  24. ⓪①②③④⑤⑥⑦⑧⑨ | |

| DAILY PRACTICE PROBLEM DPP 44 - MATHS | | | |
|---|---|---|---|
| Total Questions | 24 | Total Marks | 73 |
| Attempted | | Correct | |
| Incorrect | | Net Score | |
| Cut-off Score | 15 | Qualifying Score | 47 |
| Success Gap = Net Score – Qualifying Score | | | |

$$\text{Net Score} = \sum_{i=I}^{VI}\left[(\text{correct}_i \times MM_i) - (In_i - NM_i)\right]$$

*Space for Rough Work*

# DPP - Daily Practice Problems

Name : 

Date : 

Start Time : 

End Time : 

## MATHEMATICS  M45

SYLLABUS : **Determinants** : Expansion of determinants, Solution of equation in the form of determinants and properties of determinants, Minors and Co-factors, Product of determinants, System of linear equations

## Max. Marks : 75  Time : 60 min.

### GENERAL INSTRUCTIONS

- The Daily Practice Problem Sheet contains **24** Questions divided into 6 sections.
  Section I has **8** MCQ's with ONLY 1 correct option. 2 marks for correct answer and No negative marks.
  Section II has **4** MCQ's with 1 or MORE THAN 1 correct option. 4 marks for correct answer(s) and (−1) for wrong answer.
  Section III has **1** PASSAGE with **3** MCQ's with ONLY 1 correct option. 3 marks for correct and (−1) mark for wrong answer.
  Section IV has **2** MCQ's with multiple matchings. 1 mark for the correct matching of each row & No negative marks.
  Section V has **2** Assertion-Reason MCQ's with ONLY 1 correct option. 3 marks for correct and (−1) mark for wrong answer.
  Section VI has **5** single digit integer answer questions. 4 marks for correct answer and (−1) for wrong answer.
- No mark will be given/ deducted if no bubble is filled. Keep a timer in front and stop immediately at the end of 60 min.
- You have to evaluate your Response Grids yourself with the help of Solution Booklet.
- The sheet follows a particular syllabus. Do not attempt the sheet before you have completed your preparation for that syllabus. Refer syllabus sheet in the starting of the book for the syllabus of all the DPP sheets.
- After completing the sheet check your answers with the solution booklet and complete the Result Grid. Finally spend time to analyse your performance and revise the areas which emerge out as weak in your evaluation.

## Section - I - Straight Objective Type

This section contains 8 multiple choice questions. Each question has 4 choices (a), (b), (c) and (d), out of which **ONLY ONE** is correct.

**1.** If $\alpha, \beta$ & $\gamma$ are real numbers, then

$$D = \begin{vmatrix} 1 & \cos(\beta-\alpha) & \cos(\gamma-\alpha) \\ \cos(\alpha-\beta) & 1 & \cos(\gamma-\beta) \\ \cos(\alpha-\gamma) & \cos(\beta-\gamma) & 1 \end{vmatrix} =$$

(a) $-1$  (b) $\cos\alpha \ \cos\beta \ \cos\gamma$
(c) $\cos\alpha + \cos\beta + \cos\gamma$  (d) zero

**2.** Let $D_1 = \begin{vmatrix} a & b & a+b \\ c & d & c+d \\ a & b & a-b \end{vmatrix}$ and $D_2 = \begin{vmatrix} a & c & a+c \\ b & d & b+d \\ a & c & a+b+c \end{vmatrix}$ then

the value of $\dfrac{D_1}{D_2}$ where $b \neq 0$ and $ad \neq bc$, is

(a) $-2$  (b) $0$  (c) $-2b$  (d) $2b$

**3.** For a non - zero, real a, b and c $\begin{vmatrix} \dfrac{a^2+b^2}{c} & c & c \\ a & \dfrac{b^2+c^2}{a} & a \\ b & b & \dfrac{c^2+a^2}{b} \end{vmatrix} = \alpha$

(a) $-4$  (b) $0$
(c) $2$  (d) $4$

**4.** If a, b, c are real then the value of determinant

$$\begin{vmatrix} a^2+1 & ab & ac \\ ab & b^2+1 & bc \\ ac & bc & c^2+1 \end{vmatrix} = 1 \ \text{if}$$

(a) $a+b+c = 0$  (b) $a+b+c = 1$
(c) $a+b+c = -1$  (d) $a = b = c = 0$

| RESPONSE GRID | 1. ⓐⓑⓒⓓ | 2. ⓐⓑⓒⓓ | 3. ⓐⓑⓒⓓ | 4. ⓐⓑⓒⓓ |
|---|---|---|---|---|

**5.** The number of positive integral solutions of the equation

$$\begin{vmatrix} x^3+1 & x^2y & x^2z \\ xy^2 & y^3+1 & y^2z \\ xz^2 & yz^2 & z^3+1 \end{vmatrix} = 11 \text{ is}$$

(a) 0     (b) 3     (c) 6     (d) 12

**6.** The determinant $\begin{vmatrix} xp+y & x & y \\ yp+z & y & z \\ 0 & xp+y & yp+z \end{vmatrix} = 0$ if

(a) x, y, z are in A.P.     (b) x, y, z are in G.P.

(c) x, y, z are in H.P.     (d) xy, yz, zx are in A.P.

**7.** The parameter, on which the value of the determinant

$$\begin{vmatrix} 1 & a & a^2 \\ \cos(p-d)x & \cos px & \cos(p+d)x \\ \sin(p-d)x & \sin px & \sin(p+d)x \end{vmatrix} \text{ does not depend upon is}$$

(a) a     (b) p     (c) d     (d) x

**8.** If $\Delta_a = \begin{vmatrix} a-1 & n & 6 \\ (a-1)^2 & 2n^2 & 4n-2 \\ (a-1)^3 & 3n^3 & 3n^2-3n \end{vmatrix}$ then $\displaystyle\sum_{a=1}^{n} \Delta_a$ is equal to

(a) 0     (b) 1     (c) $\dfrac{n(n+1)}{2}$     (d) $\dfrac{n(n-1)}{2}$

## Section - II - Multiple Correct Answer Type

This section contains 4 multiple correct answer(s) type questions. Each question has 4 choices (a), (b), (c) and (d), out of which **ONE OR MORE** is/are correct.

**9.** Consider the determinant $\begin{vmatrix} \cos(\theta+\phi) & -\sin(\theta+\phi) & \cos 2\phi \\ \sin\theta & \cos\theta & \sin\phi \\ -\cos\theta & \sin\theta & \cos\phi \end{vmatrix}$

Which of the following statement is correct regarding this determinant?

(a) Its value equal to 1, when $\phi = \dfrac{\pi}{4}$.

(b) independent of $\theta$

(c) independent of $\phi$     (d) independent of $\theta$ & $\phi$ both

**10.** The determinant $\begin{vmatrix} a & b & a\alpha+b \\ b & c & b\alpha+c \\ a\alpha+b & b\alpha+c & 0 \end{vmatrix}$ is equal to zero, if

(a) $(x-\alpha)$ is a factor of $ax^2+2bx+c$.

(b) a, b, c are in G. P.

(c) a, b, c are in H. P.

(d) $\alpha$ is a root of the equation $ax^2+bx+c=0$

**11.** The values of q lying between q = 0 and q = p/2 & satisfying

the equation : $\begin{vmatrix} 1+\sin^2\theta & \cos^2\theta & 4\sin 4\theta \\ \sin^2\theta & 1+\cos^2\theta & 4\sin 4\theta \\ \sin^2\theta & \cos^2\theta & 1+4\sin 4\theta \end{vmatrix} = 0 \text{ are}$

(a) $7\pi/24$     (b) $5\pi/24$     (c) $11\pi/24$     (d) $\pi/24$

**12.** If $\omega \neq 1$ is a cube root of unity and $x+y+z \neq 0$, then

$$\begin{vmatrix} \dfrac{x}{1+\omega} & \dfrac{y}{\omega+\omega^2} & \dfrac{z}{\omega^2+1} \\ \dfrac{y}{\omega+\omega^2} & \dfrac{z}{\omega^2+1} & \dfrac{x}{1+\omega} \\ \dfrac{z}{\omega^2+1} & \dfrac{x}{1+\omega} & \dfrac{y}{\omega+\omega^2} \end{vmatrix} = 0 \text{ if}$$

(a) $x^2+y^2+z^2=0$     (b) $x+y\omega+z\omega^2=0$

(c) $x=y=z$     (d) $x=2y=3z$

## Section - III - Linked Comprehension Type

This section contains one paragraph. Based upon the paragraph, 3 multiple choice questions have to be answered. Each question has 4 choices (a), (b), (c) and (d), out of which **ONLY ONE** is correct.

Let $\Delta(x) = \begin{vmatrix} 2x^3-3x^2 & 5x+7 & 2 \\ 4x^3-7x & 3x+2 & 1 \\ 7x^3-8x^2 & x-1 & 3 \end{vmatrix} = a_0 + a_1x + \dots + a_4x^4$

To evaluate $a_i$ we differentiate $\Delta(x)$ i times w.r.t. x and put $x=0$ or divide $\Delta(x)$ by $x^4$ put $1/x = t$, differentiate $(4-i)$ time w.r.t. x and put $t=0$

| **RESPONSE GRID** | 5. ⓐⓑⓒⓓ | 6. ⓐⓑⓒⓓ | 7. ⓐⓑⓒⓓ | 8. ⓐⓑⓒⓓ | 9. ⓐⓑⓒⓓ |
|---|---|---|---|---|---|
| | 10. ⓐⓑⓒⓓ | 11. ⓐⓑⓒⓓ | 12. ⓐⓑⓒⓓ | | |

*Space for Rough Work*

**13.** $a_1 =$
(a) 0      (b) 61      (c) 161      (d) 191

**14.** $a_3 =$
(a) −70      (b) −73      (c) −74      (d) 0

**15.** $a_4 =$
(a) 46      (b) −43      (c) 41      (d) 0

## Section - IV - Matrix-Match Type

This section contains 2 questions. It contains statements given in two columns, which have to be matched. Statements in Column I are labelled as A, B, C and D whereas statements in Column II are labelled as p, q, r and s. The answers to these questions have to be appropriately bubbled as illustrated in the following example. If the correct matches are A-p, A-r, B-p, B-s, C-r, C-s and D-q, then the correctly bubbled matrix will look like the following :

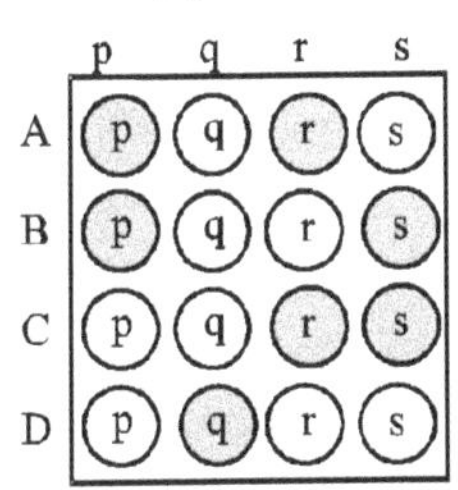

**16.** Consider the system of equation $2x + py + 6z = 8$,

$$x + 2y + qz = 5, \quad x + y + 3z = 4 \quad \text{and} \quad \Delta = \begin{vmatrix} 2 & p & 6 \\ 1 & 2 & q \\ 1 & 1 & 3 \end{vmatrix}$$

| Column I | Column II |
|---|---|
| (A) System of equation has no solution | (p) $p = 2$ |
| (B) System of equation has a unique solution | (q) $q = 3$ |
| (C) System of equation has infinitely many solutions | (r) $p \neq 2$ |
| (D) $\Delta = 0$ | (s) $q \neq 3$ |

**17.** Let $\begin{vmatrix} 1+x & x & x^2 \\ x & 1+x & x^2 \\ x^2 & x & 1+x \end{vmatrix} = ax^5 + bx^4 + cx^3 + dx^2 + ex + f$

| Column I | Column-II |
|---|---|
| (A) The value of $f$ is equal to | (p) 0 |
| (B) The value of $e$ is equal to | (q) 1 |
| (C) The value of $a + c$ is equal to | (r) −1 |
| (D) The value of $b + d$ is equal to | (s) 3 |

## Section - V - Reasoning Type

This section contains 2 reasoning type questions. Each question has 4 choices (a), (b), (c) and (d) out of which **ONLY ONE** is correct.

**DIRECTIONS for (Qs. 18 & 19) : Each of these questions contains two statements: Statement-1 (Assertion) and Statement-2 (Reason). Each of these questions has four alternative choices, only one of which is the correct answer. You have to select the correct choice.**

(a) Statement-1 is True, Statement-2 is True; Statement-2 is a correct explanation for Statement-1.

(b) Statement-1 is True, Statement-2 is True; Statement-2 is NOT a correct explanation for Statement-1.

(c) Statement-1 is True, Statement-2 is False.

(d) Statement-1 is False, Statement-2 is True.

**18.** **Statement 1 :** $\begin{vmatrix} \log a_n & \log a_{n+1} & \log a_{n+2} \\ \log a_{n+1} & \log a_{n+2} & \log a_{n+3} \\ \log a_{n+2} & \log a_{n+3} & \log a_{n+4} \end{vmatrix} = 0$ because

**Statement 2 :** $a_1, a_2, a_3$ ........... are positive numbers in G.P.

**19.** **Statement 1 :** If $\Delta(x) = \begin{vmatrix} a_{11}+x & a_{12}+x & a_{13}+x \\ a_{21}+x & a_{22}+x & a_{23}+x \\ a_{31}+x & a_{32}+x & a_{33}+x \end{vmatrix}$ then

$$A(x) = A(0) + x \sum_{k=1}^{3} \sum_{\ell=1}^{3} A_{\ell k}$$

where $A_{\ell k}$ is cofactor of the element $a_{\ell k}$ in $A(0)$.

**Statement 2 :** If $\Delta(x) = \begin{vmatrix} a_{11}(x) & a_{12}(x) & a_{13}(x) \\ a_{21}(x) & a_{22}(x) & a_{23}(x) \\ a_{31}(x) & a_{32}(x) & a_{33}(x) \end{vmatrix}$ then

$$\Delta'(x) = \begin{vmatrix} a'_{11}(x) & a_{12}(x) & a_{13}(x) \\ a_{21}(x) & a'_{22}(x) & a_{23}(x) \\ a_{31}(x) & a_{32}(x) & a'_{33}(x) \end{vmatrix}$$

## Section - VI - Integer Type

This section contains 5 questions. The answer to each of the questions is a single digit integer ranging from 0 to 9.

**20.** If $\alpha, \beta, \gamma$ are different from 1 and are the roots of $ax^3 + bx^2 + cx + d = 0$ and $(\beta - \gamma)(\gamma - \alpha)(\alpha - \beta) = 25/2$ then

$$-\frac{2\,(a+b+c+d)\,\Delta}{d} = (X)^2. , \quad \text{where } \Delta = \begin{vmatrix} \dfrac{\alpha}{1-\alpha} & \dfrac{\beta}{1-\beta} & \dfrac{\gamma}{1-\gamma} \\ \alpha & \beta & \gamma \\ \alpha^2 & \beta^2 & \gamma^2 \end{vmatrix}.$$

Find the value of X.

**21.** If $a^2 + b^2 + c^2 = -2$ and

$$f(x) = \begin{vmatrix} 1+a^2x & (1+b^2)x & (1+c^2)x \\ (1+a^2)x & 1+b^2x & (1+c^2)x \\ (1+a^2)x & (1+b^2)x & 1+c^2x \end{vmatrix}$$

then find the degree of polynomial $f(x)$.

**22.** Suppose $u$, $v$ and $w$ are twice differentiable functions of $x$ that satisfy the relations $au + bv + cw = 0$ where a, b and c are constants, not all zero. Then find the value of $\begin{vmatrix} u & v & w \\ u' & v' & w' \\ u'' & v'' & w'' \end{vmatrix}$

**23.** If $A = \begin{vmatrix} x^2+y^2+a^2 & 2ax+xy & 2ay+x^2 \\ 2ax+xy & a^2+2x^2 & 2ax+xy \\ 2ay+x^2 & 2ax+xy & x^2+y^2+a^2 \end{vmatrix}$ can be expressed as $(py^2 + qa^2 - 2ay)(2x^2 - pay - qy^2)^2$. Then find the value of $p + q$.

**24.** Find the value of the determinant

$$\begin{vmatrix} \sin^2\left(x+\dfrac{3\pi}{2}\right) & \sin^2\left(x+\dfrac{5\pi}{2}\right) & \sin^2\left(x+\dfrac{7\pi}{2}\right) \\ \sin\left(x+\dfrac{3\pi}{2}\right) & \sin\left(x+\dfrac{5\pi}{2}\right) & \sin\left(x+\dfrac{7\pi}{2}\right) \\ \sin\left(x-\dfrac{3\pi}{2}\right) & \sin\left(x-\dfrac{5\pi}{2}\right) & \sin\left(x-\dfrac{7\pi}{2}\right) \end{vmatrix}$$

| RESPONSE GRID | | |
|---|---|---|
| 20. ⓪①②③④⑤⑥⑦⑧⑨ | | 21. ⓪①②③④⑤⑥⑦⑧⑨ |
| 22. ⓪①②③④⑤⑥⑦⑧⑨ | | 23. ⓪①②③④⑤⑥⑦⑧⑨ |
| 24. ⓪①②③④⑤⑥⑦⑧⑨ | | |

## DAILY PRACTICE PROBLEM DPP 45 - MATHS

| Total Questions | 24 | Total Marks | 75 |
|---|---|---|---|
| Attempted | | Correct | |
| Incorrect | | Net Score | |
| Cut-off Score | 15 | Qualifying Score | 49 |
| Success Gap = Net Score – Qualifying Score | | | |

$$\text{Net Score} = \sum_{i=I}^{VI}\left[(\mathbf{correct}_i \times MM_i) - (In_i - NM_i)\right]$$

*Space for Rough Work*

# DPP - Daily Practice Problems

**Name :**     **Date :**

**Start Time :**    **End Time :**

## MATHEMATICS    M46

SYLLABUS : Matrices : Types of matrices, Algebra of matrices, Special types of matrices, Transpose, Adjoint and inverse of matrices, Relation between determinants and matrices, Solution of the equations

**Max. Marks : 75**    **Time : 60 min.**

### GENERAL INSTRUCTIONS

- The Daily Practice Problem Sheet contains **24** Questions divided into 6 sections.
  Section I has **8** MCQ's with ONLY 1 correct option. 2 marks for correct answer and No negative marks.
  Section II has **4** MCQ's with 1 or MORE THAN 1 correct option. 4 marks for correct answer(s) and (–1) for wrong answer.
  Section III has **1** PASSAGE with **3** MCQ's with ONLY 1 correct option. 3 marks for correct and (–1) mark for wrong answer.
  Section IV has **2** MCQ's with multiple matchings. 1 mark for the correct matching of each row & No negative marks.
  Section V has **2** Assertion-Reason MCQ's with ONLY 1 correct option. 3 marks for correct and (–1) mark for wrong answer.
  Section VI has **5** single digit integer answer questions. 4 marks for correct answer and (–1) for wrong answer.
- No mark will be given/ deducted if no bubble is filled. Keep a timer in front and stop immediately at the end of 60 min.
- You have to evaluate your Response Grids yourself with the help of Solution Booklet.
- The sheet follows a particular syllabus. Do not attempt the sheet before you have completed your preparation for that syllabus. Refer syllabus sheet in the starting of the book for the syllabus of all the DPP sheets.
- After completing the sheet check your answers with the solution booklet and complete the Result Grid. Finally spend time to analyse your performance and revise the areas which emerge out as weak in your evaluation.

---

## Section - I - Straight Objective Type

This section contains 8 multiple choice questions. Each question has 4 choices (a), (b), (c) and (d), out of which **ONLY ONE** is correct.

1. D is a $3 \times 3$ diagonal matrix. Which of the following statements is not true?
   (a) $D' = D$
   (b) $AD = DA$ for every matrix A of order 3 x 3
   (c) $D^{-1}$ if exists is a scalar matrix
   (d) none of these

2. If $A = \begin{pmatrix} 1 & a \\ 0 & 1 \end{pmatrix}$, then $A^n$ (where $n \in N$) equals

   (a) $\begin{pmatrix} 1 & na \\ 0 & 1 \end{pmatrix}$
   (b) $\begin{pmatrix} 1 & n^2a \\ 0 & 1 \end{pmatrix}$

   (c) $\begin{pmatrix} 1 & na \\ 0 & 0 \end{pmatrix}$
   (d) $\begin{pmatrix} n & na \\ 0 & n \end{pmatrix}$

3. If $A = \begin{pmatrix} a & b \\ c & d \end{pmatrix}$ satisfies the equation $x^2 - (a+d)x + k = 0$, then
   (a) $k = bc$
   (b) $k = ad$
   (c) $k = a^2 + b^2 + c^2 + d^2$
   (d) $ad - bc$

4. If A and B are non singular matrices of same order then Adj. (AB) is
   (a) Adj. (A) (Adj. B)
   (b) (Adj. B) (Adj. A)
   (c) Adj. A + Adj. B
   (d) none of these

5. A and B are two given matrices such that the order of A is $3 \times 4$, if $A'B$ and $BA'$ are both defined then
   (a) order of $B'$ is $3 \times 4$
   (b) order of $B'A$ is $4 \times 4$
   (c) order of $B'A$ is $3 \times 3$
   (d) $B'A$ is undefined

6. Given $A = \begin{bmatrix} 1 & 3 \\ 2 & 2 \end{bmatrix}$; $I = \begin{bmatrix} 1 & 0 \\ 0 & 1 \end{bmatrix}$. If $A - \lambda I$ is a singular matrix then
   (a) $\lambda \in \phi$
   (b) $\lambda^2 - 3\lambda - 4 = 0$
   (c) $\lambda^2 + 3\lambda + 4 = 0$
   (d) $\lambda^2 - 3\lambda - 6 = 0$

---

**RESPONSE GRID**    1.ⓐⓑⓒⓓ, 2.ⓐⓑⓒⓓ, 3.ⓐⓑⓒⓓ, 4.ⓐⓑⓒⓓ, 5.ⓐⓑⓒⓓ, 6.ⓐⓑⓒⓓ

7. Let $A = \begin{bmatrix} 1 & \sin\theta & 1 \\ -\sin\theta & 1 & \sin\theta \\ -1 & -\sin\theta & 1 \end{bmatrix}$, where $0 \le \theta < 2\pi$, then

   (a) Det $(A) = 0$      (b) Det $A \in (0, \infty)$
   (c) Det $(A) \in [2, 4]$      (d) Det $A \in [2, \infty)$

8. Matrix A satisfies $A^2 = 2A - I$ where I is the identity matrix then for $n \ge 2$, $A^n$ is equal to ($n \in N$)
   (a) $nA - I$      (b) $2^{n-1}A - (n-1)I$
   (c) $nA - (n-1)I$      (d) $2^{n-1}A - I$

---

## Section - II - Multiple Correct Answer Type

This section contains 4 multiple correct answer(s) type questions. Each question has 4 choices (a), (b), (c) and (d), out of which **ONE OR MORE** is/are correct.

---

9. If A is matrix such that $A^2 + A + 2I = O$, then which of the following are correct ?
   (a) A is non-singular      (b) $A \ne O$
   (c) A is symmetric      (d) $A^{-1} = -(1/2)(A + I)$
   (Where I is unit matrix of order 2 and O is null matrix of order 2 )

10. Suppose $a_1, a_2, .......$ real numbers, with $a_1 \ne 0$. If $a_1, a_2, a_3,$ ..........are in A.P. then

    (a) $A = \begin{bmatrix} a_1 & a_2 & a_3 \\ a_4 & a_5 & a_6 \\ a_5 & a_6 & a_7 \end{bmatrix}$ is singular

    (b) the system of equations $a_1x + a_2y + a_3z = 0$, $a_4x + a_5y + a_6z = 0$, $a_7x + a_8y + a_9z = 0$ has infinite number of solutions

    (c) $B = \begin{bmatrix} a_1 & ia_2 \\ ia_2 & a_1 \end{bmatrix}$ is non singular ; where $i = \sqrt{-1}$

    (d) none of these

11. Let $A = \begin{bmatrix} 1 & 2 & 2 \\ 2 & 1 & 2 \\ 2 & 2 & 1 \end{bmatrix}$, then

    (a) $A^2 - 4A - 5I_3 = 0$      (b) $A^{-1} = \dfrac{1}{5}(A - 4I_3)$
    (c) $A^3$ is not invertible      (d) $A^2$ is invertible

12. If a square matrix $A = [a_{ij}]$, $a_{ij} = i^2 - j^2$ is of even order then
    (a) A is a skew symmetric
    (b) $|A|$ is a perfect square
    (c) A is symmetric and $|A| = 0$
    (d) A is neither symmetric nor skew symmetric

---

## Section - III - Linked Comprehension Type

This section contains one paragraph. Based upon the paragraph, 3 multiple choice questions have to be answered. Each question has 4 choices (a), (b), (c) and (d), out of which **ONLY ONE** is correct.

---

Let A be a $3 \times 3$ matrix given by $A = [a_{ij}]$ such that the vector $A\vec{x}$ is orthogonal to $\vec{x}$ for every non zero $\vec{x}$ in $R^3$.

13. The matrix A is
    (a) singular and skew symmetric
    (b) non singular and symmetric
    (c) singular and symmetric
    (d) non-singular and skew symmetric

14. If $a_{13} = -2$, $a_{32} = 5$ then which of the following alternative (s) is/are correct?
    (a) $a_{23} = -5$      (b) $a_{23} = 5$
    (c) $a_{31} = -3$      (d) $a_{31} = 2$

15. Which of the following statement does not hold(s) good ?
    (a) Sum of all the elements of matrix A is zero, although matrix A cannot be uniquely determined.
    (b) Maximum number of distinct entries in matrix A is 6.
    (c) Trace of matrix A must be equal to zero.
    (d) The pair of conjugate elements of matrix A are additive inverse of each other.

---

| **RESPONSE GRID** | 7. (a)(b)(c)(d) | 8. (a)(b)(c)(d) | 9. (a)(b)(c)(d) | 10. (a)(b)(c)(d) | 11. (a)(b)(c)(d) |
|---|---|---|---|---|---|
| | 12. (a)(b)(c)(d) | 13. (a)(b)(c)(d) | 14. (a)(b)(c)(d) | 15. (a)(b)(c)(d) | |

---

*Space for Rough Work*

### Section - IV - Matrix-Match Type

This section contains 2 questions. It contains statements given in two columns, which have to be matched. Statements in Column I are labelled as A, B, C and D whereas statements in Column II are labelled as p, q, r and s. The answers to these questions have to be appropriately bubbled as illustrated in the following example. If the correct matches are A-p, A-r, B-p, B-s, C-r, C-s and D-q, then the correctly bubbled matrix will look like the following :

|   | p | q | r | s |
|---|---|---|---|---|
| A | ⬤ | q | ⬤ | s |
| B | ⬤ | q | r | ⬤ |
| C | p | q | ⬤ | ⬤ |
| D | p | ⬤ | r | s |

**16.**

| | Column I | | Column II |
|---|---|---|---|
| (A) | A is a real skew symmetric matrix such that $A^2 + I = 0$. Then | (p) | $BA - AB$ |
| (B) | A is a matrix such that $A^2 = A$. If $(I + A)^n = I + \lambda A$, then $\lambda$ equals | (q) | A is of even order |
| (C) | If for a matrix A, $A^2 = A$, and $B = I - A$, then $AB + BA + I - (I - A)^2 =$ | (r) | A |
| (D) | $\overline{A}$ is a matrix with complex entries and of complex conjugate of A. If A stands for transpose $\overline{A} = A$ and $\overline{B} = B$, then $(AB - BA)$ equals | (s) | $2^n - 1$ |

**17.**

| | Column I | | Column II |
|---|---|---|---|
| (A) | $(Adj\,A)^{-1}$ | (p) | $k^{n-1}\,(Adj\,A)$ |
| (B) | $Adj\,(A^{-1})$ | (q) | $\dfrac{A}{|A|}$ |
| (C) | $Adj\,(k\,A)$ | (r) | $|A|^{n-2}\,.\,A$ |
| (D) | $Adj\,(Adj\,A)$ | (s) | $\dfrac{adj\,(adj\,A)}{|A|^2}$ |

## Section - V - Reasoning Type

This section contains 2 reasoning type questions. Each question has 4 choices (a), (b), (c) and (d) out of which **ONLY ONE** is correct.

**DIRECTIONS for (Qs. 18 & 19) : Each of these questions contains two statements: Statement-1 (Assertion) and Statement-2 (Reason). Each of these questions has four alternative choices, only one of which is the correct answer. You have to select the correct choice.**

(a) Statement-1 is True, Statement-2 is True; Statement-2 is a correct explanation for Statement-1.

(b) Statement-1 is True, Statement-2 is True; Statement-2 is NOT a correct explanation for Statement-1.

(c) Statement -1 is True, Statement-2 is False.

(d) Statement -1 is False, Statement-2 is True.

**18.** **Statement 1 :** If A and B are two matrices such that $AB = B$ and $BA = A$, then $A^2 + B^2 = A + B$

**Statement 2 :** Matrix multiplication is associative.

**19.** **Statement-1 :** If $A = \begin{bmatrix} a & 0 & 0 \\ 0 & b & 0 \\ 0 & 0 & c \end{bmatrix}$ then $A^{-1} = \begin{bmatrix} \frac{1}{a} & 0 & 0 \\ 0 & \frac{1}{b} & 0 \\ 0 & 0 & \frac{1}{c} \end{bmatrix}$

**Statement-2 :** The inverse of a diagonal matrix is a diagonal matrix.

## Section - VI - Integer Type

This section contains 5 questions. The answer to each of the questions is a single digit integer ranging from 0 to 9.



*Space for Rough Work*

**20.** Let the matrix $A = \begin{bmatrix} 1 & 2 & 2 \\ 2 & 1 & 2 \\ 2 & 2 & 1 \end{bmatrix}$ be a zero divisor of the polynomial $f(x) = x^2 - 4x - 5$. If the sum of all the elements in the matrix $A^3$ is $3(P)^3$, find the value of P.

**21.** A is an involutary matrix given by $A = \begin{bmatrix} 0 & 1 & -1 \\ 4 & -3 & 4 \\ 3 & -3 & 4 \end{bmatrix}$ then the inverse of $\dfrac{A}{2}$ will be PA. Find the value of P.

**22.** If $A = \begin{bmatrix} 0 & 1 & 2 \\ 1 & 2 & 3 \\ 3 & a & 1 \end{bmatrix}$, $A^{-1} = \begin{bmatrix} 1/2 & -1/2 & 1/2 \\ -4 & 3 & c \\ 5/2 & -3/2 & 1/2 \end{bmatrix}$, then find the value of $a + c$.

**23.** A matrix has 12 elements. If it can have X number of possible orders, find the value of X.

**24.** Let three matrices $A = \begin{bmatrix} 2 & 1 \\ 4 & 1 \end{bmatrix}$ ; $B = \begin{bmatrix} 3 & 4 \\ 2 & 3 \end{bmatrix}$ and $C = \begin{bmatrix} 3 & -4 \\ -2 & 3 \end{bmatrix}$ then find the value of

$$t_r(A) + t_r\left(\frac{ABC}{2}\right) + t_r\left(\frac{A(BC)^2}{4}\right) + t_r\left(\frac{A(BC)^3}{8}\right) + \dots$$
$$+ \dots + \infty$$

**RESPONSE GRID**

20. ⓪①②③④⑤⑥⑦⑧⑨

21. ⓪①②③④⑤⑥⑦⑧⑨

22. ⓪①②③④⑤⑥⑦⑧⑨

23. ⓪①②③④⑤⑥⑦⑧⑨

24. ⓪①②③④⑤⑥⑦⑧⑨

| DAILY PRACTICE PROBLEM DPP 46 - MATHS | | | |
|---|---|---|---|
| Total Questions | 24 | Total Marks | 75 |
| Attempted | | Correct | |
| Incorrect | | Net Score | |
| Cut-off Score | 15 | Qualifying Score | 49 |
| Success Gap = Net Score − Qualifying Score | | | |

$$\text{Net Score} = \sum_{i=I}^{VI}\left[(\text{correct}_i \times MM_i) - (In_i - NM_i)\right]$$

# DPP - Daily Practice Problems

**Name :**

**Date :**

**Start Time :**

**End Time :**

## MATHEMATICS     M47

**SYLLABUS :** Continuity

**Max. Marks : 56**                                    **Time : 60 min.**

### GENERAL INSTRUCTIONS

- The Daily Practice Problem Sheet contains **18** Questions divided into 6 sections.
  Section I has **5** MCQ's with ONLY 1 correct option. 2 marks for correct answer and No negative marks.
  Section II has **3** MCQ's with 1 or MORE THAN 1 correct option. 4 marks for correct answer(s) and (–1) for wrong answer.
  Section III has **1** PASSAGE with **3** MCQ's with ONLY 1 correct option. 3 marks for correct and (–1) mark for wrong answer.
  Section IV has **1** MCQ's with multiple matchings. 1 mark for the correct matching of each row & No negative marks.
  Section V has **2** Assertion-Reason MCQ's with ONLY 1 correct option. 3 marks for correct and (–1) mark for wrong answer.
  Section VI has **4** single digit integer answer questions. 4 marks for correct answer and (–1) for wrong answer.
- No mark will be given/ deducted if no bubble is filled. Keep a timer in front and stop immediately at the end of 60 min.
- You have to evaluate your Response Grids yourself with the help of Solution Booklet.
- The sheet follows a particular syllabus. Do not attempt the sheet before you have completed your preparation for that syllabus. Refer syllabus sheet in the starting of the book for the syllabus of all the DPP sheets.
- After completing the sheet check your answers with the solution booklet and complete the Result Grid. Finally spend time to analyse your performance and revise the areas which emerge out as weak in your evaluation.

---

## Section - I - Straight Objective Type

This section contains 5 multiple choice questions. Each question has 4 choices (a), (b), (c) and (d), out of which **ONLY ONE** is correct.

**1.** Let $f(x)$ is a function continuous for all $x \in R$ except at $x = 0$ such that $f'(x) < 0 \ \forall \ x \in (-\infty, 0)$ and $f'(x) > 0 \ \forall \ x \in (0, \infty)$.

If $\lim_{x \to 0^+} f(x) = 3$, $\lim_{x \to 0^-} f(x) = 4$ and $f(0) = 5$, then the image of the point $(0, 1)$ about the line $\lim_{x \to 0} f(\cos^3 x - \cos^2 x)$

$= x \lim_{x \to 0} f(\sin^2 x - \sin^3 x)$ , is–

(a) $\left(\dfrac{12}{25}, \dfrac{-9}{25}\right)$
(b) $\left(\dfrac{12}{25}, \dfrac{9}{25}\right)$

(c) $\left(\dfrac{16}{25}, \dfrac{-8}{25}\right)$
(d) $\left(\dfrac{24}{25}, \dfrac{-7}{25}\right)$

**2.** If $f(x) = \begin{cases} [x], & \text{if } -3 \le x < 0 \\ 2x+1, & \text{if } 0 \le x \le 2 \end{cases}$ and $g(x) = f(|x|) + |f(x)|$, then in $[-3, 2]$

(a) $\lim_{x \to 0^+} g(x) = 2$
(b) $\lim_{x \to 0^-} g(x) = 0$

(c) $g(x)$ is discontinuous at three points
(d) None of these

**3.** Let $g(x)$ be a polynomial of degree one and $f(x)$ be defined by $f(x) = \begin{cases} g(x), x \le 0 \\ \left(\dfrac{1+x}{2+x}\right)^{\frac{1}{x}}, x > 0 \end{cases}$. If $f(x)$ is continuous satisfying $f'(1) = f(-1)$, then $g(x)$ is

(a) $(1 + \sin 1)x + 1$
(b) $(1 - \sin 1)x + 1$
(c) $(1 - \sin 1)x - 1$
(d) $(1 + \sin 1)x - 1$

**4.** The function $f(x) = [x] \cos\left(\dfrac{2x-1}{2}\right)\pi$ , $[.]$ denotes the greatest integer function, is discontinuous at

---

(a) all x
(b) all integer points
(c) no x
(d) x which is not an integer

5. If $f(x) = \lim\limits_{n \to \infty} \dfrac{x^{2n} - 1}{x^{2n} + 1}$, $x \in R$, the points where f (x) is not continuous are

(a) Only 1    (b) ±1    (c) 0, ±1    (d) 0

## Section - II - Multiple Correct Answer Type

This section contains 3 multiple correct answer(s) type questions. Each question has 4 choices (a), (b), (c) and (d), out of which **ONE OR MORE** is/are correct.

6. Let $f(x) = \sec^{-1}([1 + \sin^2 x])$ ([.]) denotes the greatest integer function. Then set of points, where $f(x)$ is not continuous is

(a) $\left\{\dfrac{n\pi}{2}, n \in I\right\}$

(b) $\left\{(2n-1)\dfrac{\pi}{2}, n \in I\right\}$

(c) $\left\{(2n+1)\dfrac{\pi}{2}, n \in I\right\}$

(d) $\{n\pi, n \in I\}$

7. Consider $f(x) = \dfrac{1}{\ln|x|}$. Which of the following alternative (s) is/are correct?

(a) Number of points of discontinuity in function is 3.

(b) $\lim\limits_{x \to 0} f(x)$ is not existent

(c) Number of inflection point(s) on the graph is 2.

(d) f (x) has two asymptotes

8. A function f is defined as follows:

$$f(x) = \begin{cases} 1 & , \text{ when } -\infty < x < 0 \\ 1 + \sin x, & \text{ when } 0 \le x < \dfrac{\pi}{2} \\ 2 + \left(x - \dfrac{\pi}{2}\right)^2 & , \text{ when } \dfrac{\pi}{2} \le x < \infty \end{cases}$$

then –
(a) f(x) is continuous at x = π/2
(b) f(x) is discontinuous at x = π/2
(c) f(x) is continuous over the whole real number
(d) f(x) is discontinuous over the whole real number

## Section - III - Linked Comprehension Type

This section contains one paragraph. Based upon the paragraph, 3 multiple choice questions have to be answered. Each question has 4 choices (a), (b), (c) and (d), out of which **ONLY ONE** is correct.

Let f (x) be a function and a be a point within or without the domain of f(x). Then we say that

(i) f (x) has an infinite discontinuity at x = a if $\lim\limits_{x \to a^-} f(x)$ or $\lim\limits_{x \to a^+} f(x)$ is infinite.

(ii) f (x) has oscillating discontinuity at x = a if $\lim\limits_{x \to a^-} f(x)$ and $\lim\limits_{x \to a^+} f(x)$ lie in a certain range but do not approach to a definite value at x = a.

(iii) f (x) has jump discontinuity at x = a if $\lim\limits_{x \to a^-} f(x)$ and $\lim\limits_{x \to a^+} f(x)$ both exist finitely but their values are unequal. We definite $\left| \lim\limits_{x \to a^-} f(x) - \lim\limits_{x \to a^+} f(x) \right| = $ jump of function at x = a.

(iv) f (x) has a removable discontinuity at x = a if $\lim\limits_{x \to a^-} f(x)$ and $\lim\limits_{x \to a^+} f(x)$ both exist finitely and their values are equal but this value is not equal to f(a). Such a function can be made continuous by redefining the function at x = a so that $\lim\limits_{x \to a^-} f(x) = \lim\limits_{x \to a^+} f(x) = f(a)$.

| RESPONSE GRID | 5. ⓐⓑ©ⓓ | 6. ⓐⓑ©ⓓ | 7. ⓐⓑ©ⓓ | 8. ⓐⓑ©ⓓ |

*Space for Rough Work*

**9.** The function $f(x) = \begin{cases} \sin\dfrac{1}{x} &, \ x \neq 0 \\ 0 &, \ x = 0 \end{cases}$ at $x = 0$

   (a)  is continuous
   (b)  has removable discontinuity
   (c)  has jump discontinuity
   (d)  has oscillating discontinuity

**10.** The function defined by

$$f(x) = \begin{cases} \dfrac{x-1}{e^{\frac{1}{x-1}}+1} &, \ x \neq 1 \\ 0 &, \ x = 1 \end{cases} \quad \text{at } x = 1$$

   (a)  is continuous
   (b)  has removable discontinuity
   (c)  has jump discontinuity
   (d)  has infinite discontinuity

**11.** The function $f(x) \begin{cases} \sin(\log e|x|),1x, & x \neq 0 \\ 1, & x = 0 \end{cases}$

   (a)  is continuous at $x = 0$
   (b)  has removable discontinuity at $x = 0$
   (c)  has jump discontinuity at $x = 0$
   (d)  has oscillating discontinuity at $x = 0$

## Section - IV - Matrix-Match Type

This section contains 1 question. It contains statements given in two columns, which have to be matched. Statements in Column I are labelled as A, B, C and D whereas statements in Column II are labelled as p, q, r and s. The answers to these questions have to be appropriately bubbled as illustrated in the following example. If the correct matches are A-p, A-r, B-p, B-s, C-r, C-s and D-q, then the correctly bubbled matrix will look like the following :

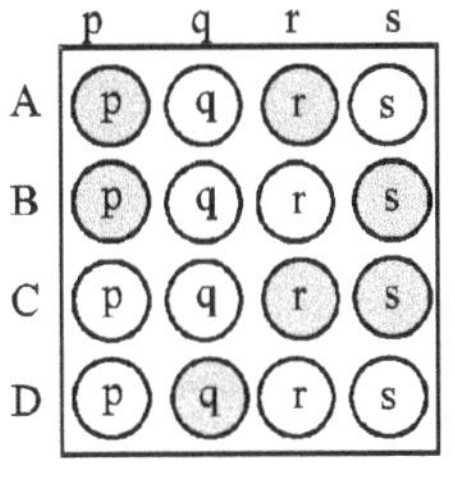

**12.**

| | Column I | Column II |
|---|---|---|

(A) If $f(x) = \begin{cases} \dfrac{a+3\cos x}{x^2}, & x < 0 \\ b\tan\left(\dfrac{\pi}{[x+3]}\right), & x \geq 0 \end{cases}$

is continuous at $x = 0$, then (where [.] denotes the greatest integer function)

  (p) $|a+b| = 0$
  (q) $|a-b| = 2$
  (r) $|a+2b| = 1$

(B) If $f(x) = \begin{cases} -2\sin x, & -\pi \leq x \leq -\dfrac{\pi}{2} \\ a\sin x + b, & -\dfrac{\pi}{2} < x < \dfrac{\pi}{2} \\ \cos x, & \dfrac{\pi}{2} \leq x \leq \pi \end{cases}$

is continuous in $[-\pi, \pi]$, then

  (s) $|a+2b| = 4$

(C) If $f(x) = \begin{cases} \left(\dfrac{3}{2}\right)^{(\cot 3x)/(\cot 2x)} &, \ 0 < x < \dfrac{\pi}{2} \\ b+3 &, \ x = \dfrac{\pi}{2} \\ (1+|\cos x|)^{\left(\frac{a|\tan x|}{b}\right)} &, \ \dfrac{\pi}{2} < x < \pi \end{cases}$

is continuous at $x = \dfrac{\pi}{2}$, then (where [.] denotes the greatest integer function)

  (t) $[a-2b] = -2$

## Section - V - Reasoning Type

This section contains 2 reasoning type questions. Each question has 4 choices (a), (b), (c) and (d) out of which **ONLY ONE** is correct.

**DIRECTIONS for Qs (13-14) :** Each of these questions contains two statements: Statement-1 (Assertion) and Statement-2 (Reason). Each of these questions has four alternative choices, only one of which is the correct answer. You have to select the correct choice.

| | | | | | |
|---|---|---|---|---|---|
| | p | q | r | s | |
| A | p | q | r | s | |
| B | p | q | r | s | |
| C | p | q | r | s | |
| D | p | q | r | s | |

**RESPONSE GRID**

9. (a)(b)(c)(d)   10. (a)(b)(c)(d)   11. (a)(b)(c)(d)

12. A - (p)(q)(r)(s)(t); B - (p)(q)(r)(s)(t); C - (p)(q)(r)(s)(t)

*Space for Rough Work*

(a) Statement-1 is True, Statement-2 is True; Statement-2 is a correct explanation for Statement-1.

(b) Statement-1 is True, Statement-2 is True; Statement-2 is NOT a correct explanation for Statement-1.

(c) Statement-1 is True, Statement-2 is False.

(d) Statement-1 is False, Statement-2 is True.

**13.** **Statement-1 :** The function $f(t) = \dfrac{1-\cos(1-\cos t)}{t^4}$ is continuous every where if $f(0) = 1/8$.

**Statement-2 :** For continuous function $f(0) = \underset{t \to 0}{Lt}\, f(t)$

**14.** **Statement 1 :** The function $f(x) = \underset{n \to \infty}{\lim} \dfrac{\log_e(1+x) - x^{2n}\sin(2x)}{1+x^{2n}}$ is discontinuous at $x = 1$.

**Statement 2 :** L.H.L. = R.H.L. $\neq f(1)$.

## Section - VI - Integer Type

This section contains 4 questions. The answer to each of the questions is a single digit integer ranging from 0 to 9.

**15.** If $f(x) = \dfrac{e^{2x} - (1+4x)^{1/2}}{\ln(1-x^2)}$ for $x \neq 0$, then the value of $f(0)$ is $-P$. Find P.

**16.** The function $f(x) = a\,[x+1] + b\,[x-1]$, where $[x]$ is the greatest integer function, then find the value of $a + b$ for which $f(x)$ is continuous at $x = 1$.

**17.** At how many points where the function $f(x) = |x-1| + |x-1| + \cos x$, [where $x \in (0, 4)$] is not continuous?

**18.** If $f(x) = \dfrac{\sin 2x + A\sin x + B\cos x}{x^3}$ is continuous at $x = 0$, then find the value of $f(0) - 4A + B$.

| RESPONSE GRID | | |
|---|---|---|
| 13. ⓐⓑⓒⓓ  14. ⓐⓑⓒⓓ | | 15. ⓪①②③④⑤⑥⑦⑧⑨ |
| 16. ⓪①②③④⑤⑥⑦⑧⑨ | | 17. ⓪①②③④⑤⑥⑦⑧⑨ |
| 18. ⓪①②③④⑤⑥⑦⑧⑨ | | |

## DAILY PRACTICE PROBLEM DPP 47 - MATHS

| Total Questions | 18 | Total Marks | 56 |
|---|---|---|---|
| Attempted | | Correct | |
| Incorrect | | Net Score | |
| Cut-off Score | 11 | Qualifying Score | 36 |
| Success Gap = Net Score – Qualifying Score | | | |

$$\text{Net Score} = \sum_{i=1}^{VI} \left[ (correct_i \times MM_i) - (In_i - NM_i) \right]$$

*Space for Rough Work*

Name : 

Date : 

Start Time : 

End Time : 

## MATHEMATICS    M48

**SYLLABUS :** Differentiability

## Max. Marks : 74        Time : 60 min.

### GENERAL INSTRUCTIONS

- The Daily Practice Problem Sheet contains **24** Questions divided into 6 sections.
  Section I has **8** MCQ's with ONLY 1 correct option. 2 marks for correct answer and No negative marks.
  Section II has **4** MCQ's with 1 or MORE THAN 1 correct option. 4 marks for correct answer(s) and (–1) for wrong answer.
  Section III has **1** PASSAGE with **3** MCQ's with ONLY 1 correct option. 3 marks for correct and (–1) mark for wrong answer.
  Section IV has **2** MCQ's with multiple matchings. 1 mark for the correct matching of each row & No negative marks.
  Section V has **2** Assertion-Reason MCQ's with ONLY 1 correct option. 3 marks for correct and (–1) mark for wrong answer.
  Section VI has **5** single digit integer answer questions. 4 marks for correct answer and (–1) for wrong answer.
- No mark will be given/ deducted if no bubble is filled. Keep a timer in front and stop immediately at the end of 60 min.
- You have to evaluate your Response Grids yourself with the help of Solution Booklet.
- The sheet follows a particular syllabus. Do not attempt the sheet before you have completed your preparation for that syllabus. Refer syllabus sheet in the starting of the book for the syllabus of all the DPP sheets.
- After completing the sheet check your answers with the solution booklet and complete the Result Grid. Finally spend time to analyse your performance and revise the areas which emerge out as weak in your evaluation.

---

### Section - I - Straight Objective Type

This section contains 8 multiple choice questions. Each question has 4 choices (a), (b), (c) and (d), out of which **ONLY ONE** is correct.

**1.** Let $f(x) = (x^2 - 3x + 2)\,|(x^3 - 6x^2 + 11x - 6)| + \left|\sin\left(x + \dfrac{\pi}{4}\right)\right|$.

The set of points at which the function $f(x)$ is not differentiable in $[0, 2\pi]$ is

(a) $\left\{1, 2, 3, \dfrac{3\pi}{4}, \dfrac{7\pi}{4}\right\}$      (b) $\{1, 2, 3\}$

(c) $\left\{3, \dfrac{3\pi}{4}, \dfrac{7\pi}{4}\right\}$      (d) $\left\{\dfrac{\pi}{4}, \dfrac{3\pi}{4}, \dfrac{5\pi}{4}\right\}$

**2.** Let f be a differentiable function on $(0, \infty)$ and suppose that $\lim\limits_{x \to \infty}(f(x) + f'(x)) = L$, where L is a finite quantity, then

(a) $\lim\limits_{x \to \infty} f(x) = 0$ and $\lim\limits_{x \to \infty} f'(x) = L$

(b) $\lim\limits_{x \to \infty} f(x) = \dfrac{L}{2}$ and $\lim\limits_{x \to \infty} f'(x) = \dfrac{L}{2}$

(c) $\lim\limits_{x \to \infty} f(x) = L$ and $\lim\limits_{x \to \infty} f'(x) = 0$

(d) nothing definite can be said

**3.** For $0 < x < \dfrac{\pi}{2}$,

let $f_1(x) = \sum\limits_{r=1}^{n} \sec\left(x + \dfrac{r\pi}{6}\right)\sec\left(x + (r-1)\dfrac{\pi}{6}\right)$

and $f_1(x) - 2f_2(x) = 2\tan\left(x + \dfrac{n\pi}{6}\right)$.

Also, $f_2(x) + f_3(x) = 0$

and $f_4(x) = \begin{cases} (\text{exp.})\,\dfrac{e^{\left(e^{x + f_2(x) + \tan x}\right)} - 1}{2\,(e^x - 1)} & ; x < 0 \\[3mm] k_1 & ; x = 0 \\[3mm] (1 + |f_2(x)|)^{\frac{k_2}{f_3(x)}} & ; x > 0 \end{cases}$

---

**RESPONSE GRID**    **1.** ⓐⓑⓒⓓ    **2.** ⓐⓑⓒⓓ    **3.** ⓐⓑⓒⓓ

$y = f_3(x)$ is –
(a) discontinuous and non-derivable at $x = \pi/4$ and $\pi/3$
(b) neither continuous nor derivable at $x = 2\pi/5$
(c) continuous and derivable in $(0, \pi/2)$
(d) continuous but not derivable at $x = 2\pi/5$

4. Let $f(x)$ be a real valued function such that $f(a) = 0$. If $g(x) = (x - a) f(x)$ is continuous but not differentiable at $x = a$ and $h(x) = (x-a)^2 f(x)$ is continuous and differentiable at $x = a$. Then $f(x)$ –
(a) must be continuous and differentiable at $x = a$
(b) must be continuous and not differentiable at $x = a$
(c) may or may not be continuous at $x = a$
(d) must be discontinuous at $x = a$

5. Let $f : R \to R$ be a function defined by $f(x) = \max\{x, x^3\}$. The set of all points where $f(x)$ is NOT differentiable is
(a) $\{-1, 1\}$  (b) $\{-1, 0\}$  (c) $\{0, 1\}$  (d) $\{-1, 0, 1\}$

6. Which of the following functions is differentiable at $x = 0$?
(a) $\cos(|x|) + |x|$ (b) $\cos(|x|) - |x|$ (c) $\sin(|x|) + |x|$ (d) $\sin(|x|) - |x|$

7. If $f(x)$ is differentiable everywhere then
(a) $|f(x)|$ is differentiable everywhere
(b) $|f|^2$ is differentiable everywhere
(c) $f|f|$ is not differentiable at some point
(d) none of these.

8. If $f(x) = \sqrt{x + 2\sqrt{2x-4}} + \sqrt{x - 2\sqrt{2x-4}}$, then $f(x)$ is differentiable on
(a) $(-\infty, \infty)$
(b) $(2, \infty) - \{4\}$
(c) $[2, \infty)$
(d) none of these

## Section - II - Multiple Correct Answer Type

This section contains 4 multiple correct answer(s) type questions. Each question has 4 choices (a), (b), (c) and (d), out of which **ONE OR MORE** is/are correct.

9. Let $f(x) = |x - 1| ([x] - [-x])$, then which of the following statement(s) is/are correct –
(where [x] denotes greatest integer function)

(a) $f(x)$ is continuous at $x = 1$
(b) $f(x)$ is derivable at $x = 1$
(c) $f(x)$ is non-derivable at $x = 1$
(d) $f(x)$ is discontinuous at $x = 1$

10. Let $f(x) = \min(x^3, x^2)$ and $g(x) = [x]^2 + \sqrt{\{x\}^2}$, where [x] denotes the greatest integer and $\{x\}$ denotes the fractional part function. Then which of the following holds –
(a) f is continuous for all x
(b) g is discontinuous for all $x \in I$
(c) f is differentiable for all $x \in (1, \infty)$
(d) g is not differentiable for all $x \in I$

11. If the function $f(x)$ defined as $f(x) = \begin{cases} -\dfrac{x^2}{2} & \text{for } x \le 0 \\ x^n \sin\dfrac{1}{x} & \text{for } x > 0 \end{cases}$

is continuous but not derivable at $x = 0$ then x cannot be
(a) $1/2$  (b) $1$  (c) $3/2$  (d) $2$

12. The function $f(x) = \begin{cases} |x - 3| & , \ x \ge 1 \\ \left(\dfrac{x^2}{4}\right) - \left(\dfrac{3x}{2}\right) + \left(\dfrac{13}{4}\right) & , \ x < 1 \end{cases}$ is :

(a) continuous at $x = 1$        (b) diff. at $x = 1$
(c) continuous at $x = 3$        (d) differentiable at $x = 3$

## Section - III - Linked Comprehension Type

This section contains one paragraph. Based upon the paragraph, 3 multiple choice questions have to be answered. Each question has 4 choices (a), (b), (c) and (d), out of which **ONLY ONE** is correct.

Let $f : R \to R$ be a differential function satisfying
$$f\left(\frac{x+y}{3}\right) = \frac{2 + f(x) + f(y)}{3}$$ for all real x and y and $f'(2) = 2$.

On the basis of above information, answer the following questions:

| | | | | | |
|---|---|---|---|---|---|
| **RESPONSE GRID** | 4. ⓐⓑⓒⓓ | 5. ⓐⓑⓒⓓ | 6. ⓐⓑⓒⓓ | 7. ⓐⓑⓒⓓ | 8. ⓐⓑⓒⓓ |
| | 9. ⓐⓑⓒⓓ | 10. ⓐⓑⓒⓓ | 11. ⓐⓑⓒⓓ | 12. ⓐⓑⓒⓓ | |

*Space for Rough Work*

13. If $g(x) = |f(|x|) - 3|$ for all $x \in R$, then for $g(x)$
    (a) one non-differentiable point
    (b) two non-differentiable point
    (c) three non-differentiable point
    (d) four non-differentiable point
14. If $x \in [-2, 3]$, then range of f(x) is
    (a) $[-2, 3]$    (b) $[-3, 4]$    (c) $[-2, 8]$    (d) $[-3, 10]$
15. The number of solutions of the equation $x^2 + (f(|x|))^2 = 9$ are
    (a) 0        (b) 2        (c) 3        (d) 5

## Section - IV - Matrix-Match Type

This section contains 2 questions. It contains statements given in two columns, which have to be matched. Statements in Column I are labelled as A, B, C and D whereas statements in Column II are labelled as p, q, r and s. The answers to these questions have to be appropriately bubbled as illustrated in the following example. If the correct matches are A-p, A-r, B-p, B-s, C-r, C-s and D-q, then the correctly bubbled matrix will look like the following:

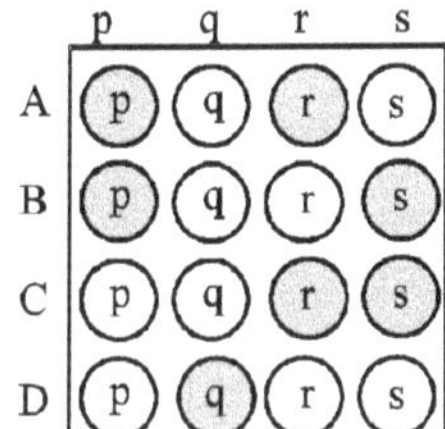

16.

| | Column I | | Column II |
|---|---|---|---|
| (A) | Let [x] denote the greatest integer less than or equal to x. If $f(x) = [x \sin \pi x]$, then $f(x)$ is | (p) | $h'(x) = 1$, for all $x > 1$ |
| (B) | Let $h(x) = \min\{x, x^2\}$, for every real number of x, Then | (q) | g is differentiable while f is not |
| (C) | Let $g(x) = x\,f(x)$, where $f(x) = \begin{cases} x \sin\dfrac{1}{x}, & x \neq 0 \\ 0, & x = 0 \end{cases}$. At $x = 0$ | (r) | continuous at all points |
| (D) | The function $f(x) = \max\{(1-x), (1+x), 2\}, x \in (-\infty, \infty)$ is | (s) | continuous at $x = 0$ |

17.

| | Column I | | Column II |
|---|---|---|---|
| (A) | The function $f(x) = \begin{cases} x^2 + 3x + a; & x \leq 1 \\ bx + 2; & x > 1 \end{cases}$ is differentiable $\forall\, x \in R$, then | (p) | $a = 3$ |
| (B) | The function $f(x) = \begin{cases} \dfrac{1}{|x|}; & |x| \geq 1 \\ ax^2 + b; & |x| < 1 \end{cases}$ is differentiable everywhere, then | (q) | $b = 5$ |
| (C) | The function $f(x) = \begin{cases} ax^2 - bx + 2; & x < 3 \\ bx^2 - 3; & x \geq 3 \end{cases}$ is differentiable everywhere then | (r) | $a = \dfrac{35}{9}$ |
| | | (s) | $b = \dfrac{3}{2}$ |
| | | (t) | $a = -\dfrac{1}{2}$ |

## Section - V - Reasoning Type

This section contains 2 reasoning type questions. Each question has 4 choices (a), (b), (c) and (d) out of which **ONLY ONE** is correct.

**DIRECTIONS for (Qs. 18 & 19) : Each of these questions contains two statements: Statement-1 (Assertion) and Statement-2 (Reason). Each of these questions has four alternative choices, only one of which is the correct answer. You have to select the correct choice.**

(a) Statement-1 is True, Statement-2 is True; Statement-2 is a correct explanation for Statement-1.
(b) Statement-1 is True, Statement-2 is True; Statement-2 is NOT a correct explanation for Statement-1.
(c) Statement-1 is True, Statement-2 is False.
(d) Statement-1 is False, Statement-2 is True.

**RESPONSE GRID**

13. (a)(b)(c)(d)    14. (a)(b)(c)(d)    15. (a)(b)(c)(d)
16. A - (p)(q)(r)(s); B - (p)(q)(r)(s); C - (p)(q)(r)(s); D - (p)(q)(r)(s)
17. A - (p)(q)(r)(s)(t); B - (p)(q)(r)(s)(t); C - (p)(q)(r)(s)(t)

*Space for Rough Work*

18. **Statement-1 :** $f(x) = x^n \sin(1/x)$ is differentiable for all real values of x ($n \geq 2$).
    **Statement-2 :** For $n \geq 2$ right hand derivative = Left hand derivative (for all real values of x).

19. **Statement-1 :** If $f(x + y) = f(x) + f(y)$, then f is either differentiable everywhere or not differentiable everywhere.
    **Statement-2 :** Any function is either differentiable everywhere or not differentiable everywhere.

## Section - VI - Integer Type

This section contains 5 questions. The answer to each of the questions is a single digit integer ranging from 0 to 9.

20. Let $f(x) = x - x^2$
    and $g(x) = \begin{cases} \max f(t), & 0 \leq t \leq x, 0 \leq x \leq 1 \\ \sin \pi x, & x > 1 \end{cases}$, then in the interval $[0, \infty)$, $g(x)$ is every where differentiable except at $x = P$. Find the value of P.

21. At how many points the function
    $f(x) = \begin{cases} [\cos x], & x \leq 1 \\ |\,2x - 3\,|\,[x - 2], & x > 1 \end{cases}$, (where [.] denotes the greatest integer function) in $[0, 2]$ is non-differentiable ?

22. Let $f(x)$ be defined in the interval $[-2, 2]$ such that
    $f(x) = \begin{cases} -1, & -2 \leq x \leq 0 \\ x - 1, & 0 < x \leq 2 \end{cases}$ and $g(x) = f(|x|) + |f(x)|$
    $g(x)$ is not differentiable at x = A in $(-2, 2)$. Find the value of A.

23. The function $f(x) = (x^2 - 1)\,|\,x^2 - 3x + 2\,| + \cos(|\,x\,|)$ is NOT differentiable at Y. Find the value of Y.

24. If $f : R \to R$ be a differentiable function such that $f(x + 2y) = f(x) + f(2y) + 4xy \,\forall\, x, y \in R$ then find the value of $f'(1) - f'(0)$.

| | |
|---|---|
| **RESPONSE GRID** | 18. ⓐⓑⓒⓓ  19. ⓐⓑⓒⓓ  20. ⓪①②③④⑤⑥⑦⑧⑨<br>21. ⓪①②③④⑤⑥⑦⑧⑨  22. ⓪①②③④⑤⑥⑦⑧⑨<br>23. ⓪①②③④⑤⑥⑦⑧⑨  24. ⓪①②③④⑤⑥⑦⑧⑨ |

### DAILY PRACTICE PROBLEM DPP 48 - MATHS

| Total Questions | 24 | Total Marks | 74 |
|---|---|---|---|
| Attempted | | Correct | |
| Incorrect | | Net Score | |
| Cut-off Score | 15 | Qualifying Score | 48 |
| Success Gap = Net Score – Qualifying Score | | | |

$$\text{Net Score} = \sum_{i=1}^{VI}\left[(\text{correct}_i \times MM_i) - (In_i - NM_i)\right]$$

**Name :**  **Date :**

**Start Time :**  **End Time :**

## MATHEMATICS  M49

**SYLLABUS : Differentiation-1 :** Derivative at a point, Standard differentiation

**Max. Marks : 67**  **Time : 60 min.**

### GENERAL INSTRUCTIONS

- The Daily Practice Problem Sheet contains **24** Questions divided into 5 sections.

  Section I has **13** MCQ's with ONLY 1 correct option. 2 marks for correct answer and No negative marks.

  Section II has **3** MCQ's with 1 or MORE THAN 1 correct option. 4 marks for correct answer(s) and (–1) for wrong answer.
  Section III has **1** MCQ's with multiple matchings. 1 mark for the correct matching of each row & No negative marks.

  Section IV has **2** Assertion-Reason MCQ's with ONLY 1 correct option. 3 marks for correct and (–1) mark for wrong answer.
  Section V has **5** single digit integer answer questions. 4 marks for correct answer and (–1) for wrong answer.

- No mark will be given/ deducted if no bubble is filled. Keep a timer in front and stop immediately at the end of 60 min.
- You have to evaluate your Response Grids yourself with the help of Solution Booklet.
- The sheet follows a particular syllabus. Do not attempt the sheet before you have completed your preparation for that syllabus. Refer syllabus sheet in the starting of the book for the syllabus of all the DPP sheets.
- After completing the sheet check your answers with the solution booklet and complete the Result Grid. Finally spend time to analyse your performance and revise the areas which emerge out as weak in your evaluation.

---

## Section - I - Straight Objective Type

This section contains 13 multiple choice questions. Each question has 4 choices (a), (b), (c) and (d), out of which **ONLY ONE** is correct.

**1.** Suppose the function $f(x) - f(2x)$ has the derivative 5 at $x = 1$ and derivative 7 at $x = 2$. The derivative of the function $f(x) - f(4x)$ at $x = 1$, has the value equal to

(a) 19   (b) 9   (c) 17   (d) 14

**2.** If $y = \dfrac{x^4 - x^2 + 1}{x^2 + \sqrt{3}x + 1}$ and $\dfrac{dy}{dx} = ax + b$ then the value of $a + b$ is equal to

(a) $\cot\dfrac{5\pi}{8}$   (b) $\cot\dfrac{5\pi}{12}$

(c) $\tan\dfrac{5\pi}{12}$   (d) $\tan\dfrac{5\pi}{8}$

**3.** If $y = (\sin x)^{\ln x} \operatorname{cosec}(e^x (a + bx))$ and $a + b = \dfrac{\pi}{2e}$ then the value of $\dfrac{dy}{dx}$ at $x = 1$ is

(a) $(\sin 1)\ln \sin 1$   (b) 0

(c) $\ln \sin 1$   (d) indeterminate

**4.** Let $f(x) = \dfrac{\tan^6 x + 9\tan^4 x - 9\tan^2 x - 1}{3\tan^3 x}$, if $f'(x) = \lambda \operatorname{cosec}^4(2x)$ then the value of $\lambda$ equals

(a) 4   (b) 9   (c) 16   (d) 64

**5.** Given $f(x) = -\dfrac{x^3}{3} + x^2 \sin 1.5\,a - x \sin a \cdot \sin 2a - 5 \arcsin(a^2 - 8a + 17)$ then :

(a) $f(x)$ is not defined at $x = \sin 8$

(b) $f'(\sin 8) > 0$

(c) $f'(x)$ is not defined at $x = \sin 8$

(d) $f'(\sin 8) < 0$

---

| **RESPONSE GRID** | **1.** ⓐⓑⓒⓓ | **2.** ⓐⓑⓒⓓ | **3.** ⓐⓑⓒⓓ | **4.** ⓐⓑⓒⓓ | **5.** ⓐⓑⓒⓓ |
|---|---|---|---|---|---|

**6.** $\dfrac{d}{dx}(\cos^{-1}x + \sin^{-1}x)$ is

(a) $\dfrac{\pi}{2}$    (b) 0    (c) $\dfrac{2}{\sqrt{1-x^2}}$    (d) None of these

**7.** If $y = |\cos x| + |\sin x|$, then $\dfrac{dy}{dx}$ at $x = \dfrac{2\pi}{3}$ is

(a) $\dfrac{1-\sqrt{3}}{2}$    (b) 0

(c) $\dfrac{1}{2}(\sqrt{3}-1)$    (d) None of these

**8.** If $y = x \tan \dfrac{x}{2}$, then $(1+\cos x)\dfrac{dy}{dx} - \sin x =$

(a) $xy$    (b) $y$    (c) 0    (d) $x$

**9.** If $y = f\left(\dfrac{2x-1}{x^2+1}\right)$ and $f'(x) = \sin x^2$, then $\dfrac{dy}{dx}$ is equal to

(a) $\sin\left(\dfrac{2x-1}{x^2+1}\right)^2 \cdot \left(\dfrac{2+2x+x^2}{(x^2+1)^2}\right)$

(b) $\sin\left(\dfrac{2x-1}{x^2+1}\right)^2 \left(\dfrac{2+2x-2x^2}{(x^2+1)^2}\right)$

(c) $\sin\left(\dfrac{2x-1}{x^2+1}\right)^2 \cdot \left(\dfrac{2+2x-x^2}{(x^2+1)^2}\right)$

(d) None of these

**10.** If $f(x) = \dfrac{1+\tan x}{1-\tan x}$, then $f'\left(\dfrac{\pi}{6}\right) =$

(a) $4+\sqrt{3}$    (b) $4+2\sqrt{3}$    (c) $4(2+\sqrt{3})$    (d) $(2+\sqrt{3})$

**11.** If $y = \dfrac{a+bx^{3/2}}{x^{5/4}}$ and $y' = 0$ at $x = 5$, then the ratio a: b is equal to

(a) $\sqrt{5}:1$    (b) $5:2$    (c) $3:5$    (d) $1:2$

**12.** If $y = \sin^{-1}\left(\dfrac{\sin \alpha \sin x}{1 - \cos \alpha \sin x}\right)$, then $y'(0) =$

(a) $\tan \alpha$    (b) $2\tan \alpha$    (c) $\sec \alpha$    (d) $\sin \alpha$

**13.** If $3f(\cos x) + 2 f(\sin x) = 5x$, then $f'(\cos x) =$

(a) $-\dfrac{5}{\cos x}$    (b) $\dfrac{5}{\cos x}$

(c) $\dfrac{-5}{\sin x}$    (d) none of these

## Section - II - Multiple Correct Answer Type

This section contains 3 multiple correct answer(s) type questions. Each question has 4 choices (a), (b), (c) and (d), out of which **ONE OR MORE** is/are correct.

**14.** Which of the following statement are correct ?

(a) If $f(x) = \dfrac{x-4}{2\sqrt{x}}$, then $f'(0)$ is does not exist.

(b) If $f(t) = \dfrac{1-t}{1+t}$, then $f'(1/t)$ is equal to $\dfrac{-2t^2}{(t+1)^2}$.

(c) If $y = \tan^{-1}\dfrac{x}{2} - \cot^{-1}\dfrac{x}{2}$, then $\dfrac{dy}{dx}$ is equal to $\dfrac{4}{4+x^2}$.

(d) If $\varphi(x) = \log_5(\log_3 x)$, then $\varphi'(e) = 1$.

**15.** Let $f(x) = x^n$, $n$ being a non-negative integer, the value of $n$ for which the equality $f'(a+b) = f'(a) + f'(b)$ is valid for all $a, b > 0$ is

(a) 0    (b) 1

(c) 2    (d) none of these

<table>
<tr><td rowspan="2">**RESPONSE GRID**</td><td>6. ⓐⓑⓒⓓ</td><td>7. ⓐⓑⓒⓓ</td><td>8. ⓐⓑⓒⓓ</td><td>9. ⓐⓑⓒⓓ</td><td>10. ⓐⓑⓒⓓ</td></tr>
<tr><td>11. ⓐⓑⓒⓓ</td><td>12. ⓐⓑⓒⓓ</td><td>13. ⓐⓑⓒⓓ</td><td>14. ⓐⓑⓒⓓ</td><td>15. ⓐⓑⓒⓓ</td></tr>
</table>

**16.** If $y = \log_2 \{\log_2 x\}$, then $\dfrac{dy}{dx}$ is equal to

(a) $\dfrac{\log_2 e}{x \log_e x}$

(b) $\dfrac{1}{x \log_e x \log_e 2}$

(c) $\dfrac{1}{\log_e (2x)^x}$

(d) none of these

## Section - III - Matrix-Match Type

This section contains 1 question. It contains statements given in two columns, which have to be matched. Statements in Column I are labelled as A, B, C and D whereas statements in Column II are labelled as p, q, r and s. The answers to these questions have to be appropriately bubbled as illustrated in the following example. If the correct matches are A-p, A-r, B-p, B-s, C-r, C-s and D-q, then the correctly bubbled matrix will look like the following :

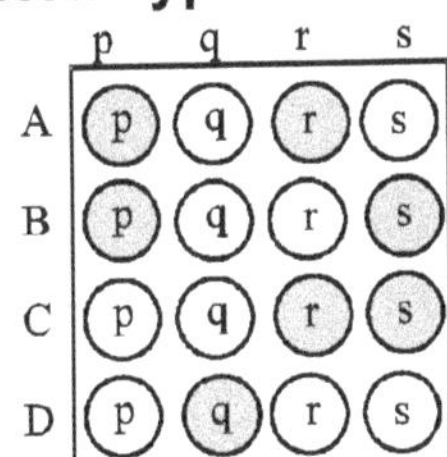

**17.**

| Column I | | Column II |
|---|---|---|

(A) $y = \sin^{-1}(3x - 4x^3)$,

then $\dfrac{dy}{dx}$ is

p. $\dfrac{3}{1+x^2}, x \in \left(-\dfrac{1}{\sqrt{3}}, \dfrac{1}{\sqrt{3}}\right)$

(B) $y = \cos^{-1}(4x^3 - 3x)$,

then $\dfrac{dy}{dx}$ is

q. $\dfrac{3}{1+x^2}, x \in \left(\dfrac{1}{\sqrt{3}}, \infty\right)$

(C) $y = \tan^{-1}\left(\dfrac{3x - x^3}{1 - 3x^2}\right)$,

then $\dfrac{dy}{dx}$ is

r. $\dfrac{3}{\sqrt{(1-x^2)}}, x \in \left(-\dfrac{1}{2}, \dfrac{1}{2}\right)$

s. $\dfrac{3}{1+x^2}, x \in \left(-\infty, -\dfrac{1}{\sqrt{3}}\right)$

t. $-\dfrac{3}{\sqrt{1-x^2}}, x \in \left(-1, -\dfrac{1}{2}\right) \cup \left(\dfrac{1}{2}, 1\right)$

## Section - IV - Reasoning Type

This section contains 2 reasoning type questions. Each question has 4 choices (a), (b), (c) and (d) out of which **ONLY ONE** is correct.

**DIRECTIONS for Qs (18 -19) :** Each of these questions contains two statements: Statement-1 (Assertion) and Statement-2 (Reason). Each of these questions has four alternative choices, only one of which is the correct answer. You have to select the correct choice.

(a) Statement-1 is True, Statement-2 is True; Statement-2 is a correct explanation for Statement-1.

(b) Statement-1 is True, Statement-2 is True; Statement-2 is NOT a correct explanation for Statement-1.

(c) Statement -1 is True, Statement-2 is False.

(d) Statement -1 is False, Statement-2 is True.

**18. Statement-1 :** For $x < 0$, $\dfrac{d}{dx}(\ln|x|) = -\dfrac{1}{x}$

**Statement-2 :** For $x < 0, |x| = -x$

**19. Statement -1 :** If $f(x) = \sin^2 x + \sin^2\left(x + \dfrac{\pi}{3}\right) + \cos x \cos\left(x + \dfrac{\pi}{3}\right)$, then $f'(x) = 0$

**Statement-2 :** Derivative of constant function is zero.

<table>
<tr><td rowspan="2">**RESPONSE GRID**</td><td>16. (a)(b)(c)(d)</td><td>17. A - (p)(q)(r)(s)(t); B - (p)(q)(r)(s)(t); C - (p)(q)(r)(s)(t)</td></tr>
<tr><td>18. (a)(b)(c)(d)</td><td>19. (a)(b)(c)(d)</td></tr>
</table>

*Space for Rough Work*

## Section - V - Integer Type

This section contains 5 questions. The answer to each of the questions is a single digit integer ranging from 0 to 9.

**20.** The graph of function $f$ contains the point P (1, 2) and Q(s, r). The equation of the secant line through P and Q is

$$y = \left(\frac{s^2 + 2s - 3}{s - 1}\right) x - 1 - s.$$ Find the value of $f'(1)$.

**21.** If $y = (1 + x^{1/4})(1 + x^{1/2})(1 - x^{1/4})$, then the value of dy/dx is $- Q$. Find the value of Q.

**22.** If $f(x) = \cos\left\{\frac{\pi}{2}[x] - x^3\right\}, -1 < x < 2$ and $[x]$ is the greatest integer less than or equal to x, then find the value of

$$f'\left(\sqrt[3]{\frac{\pi}{2}}\right).$$

**23.** If $y = 2^{\log_2(x^{2x})} - \left(\tan\frac{\pi}{4}x\right)^{\frac{4}{\pi x}}$, then find the value of

$$\frac{dy}{dx} \text{ at } x = 1.$$

**24.** If $y = \frac{1}{x}$ then find the value of $\dfrac{dy}{\sqrt{1 + y^4}} + \dfrac{dx}{\sqrt{1 + x^4}}$.

| | RESPONSE GRID | | |
|---|---|---|---|
| **20.** ⓪①②③④⑤⑥⑦⑧⑨ | | **21.** ⓪①②③④⑤⑥⑦⑧⑨ | |
| **22.** ⓪①②③④⑤⑥⑦⑧⑨ | | **23.** ⓪①②③④⑤⑥⑦⑧⑨ | |
| **24.** ⓪①②③④⑤⑥⑦⑧⑨ | | | |

## DAILY PRACTICE PROBLEM DPP 49 - MATHS

| Total Questions | 24 | Total Marks | 67 |
|---|---|---|---|
| Attempted | | Correct | |
| Incorrect | | Net Score | |
| Cut-off Score | 13 | Qualifying Score | 44 |
| Success Gap = Net Score – Qualifying Score | | | |

$$\text{Net Score} = \sum_{i=I}^{VI}\left[(\textbf{correct}_i \times MM_i) - (In_i - NM_i)\right]$$

*Space for Rough Work*

**Name :**

**Date :**

**Start Time :**

**End Time :**

# MATHEMATICS    M50

**SYLLABUS : Differentiation-2 :** Differentiation of implicit function, Parametric and Composite functions, Logarithmic differentiation, Differentiation of infinite series

## Max. Marks : 75    Time : 60 min.

### GENERAL INSTRUCTIONS

- The Daily Practice Problem Sheet contains **24** Questions divided into 6 sections.
  Section I has **8** MCQ's with ONLY 1 correct option. 2 marks for correct answer and No negative marks.
  Section II has **4** MCQ's with 1 or MORE THAN 1 correct option. 4 marks for correct answer(s) and (–1) for wrong answer.
  Section III has **1** PASSAGE with **3** MCQ's with ONLY 1 correct option. 3 marks for correct and (–1) mark for wrong answer.
  Section IV has **2** MCQ's with multiple matchings. 1 mark for the correct matching of each row & No negative marks.
  Section V has **2** Assertion-Reason MCQ's with ONLY 1 correct option. 3 marks for correct and (–1) mark for wrong answer.
  Section VI has **5** single digit integer answer questions. 4 marks for correct answer and (–1) for wrong answer.
- No mark will be given/ deducted if no bubble is filled. Keep a timer in front and stop immediately at the end of 60 min.
- You have to evaluate your Response Grids yourself with the help of Solution Booklet.
- The sheet follows a particular syllabus. Do not attempt the sheet before you have completed your preparation for that syllabus. Refer syllabus sheet in the starting of the book for the syllabus of all the DPP sheets.
- After completing the sheet check your answers with the solution booklet and complete the Result Grid. Finally spend time to analyse your performance and revise the areas which emerge out as weak in your evaluation.

## Section - I - Straight Objective Type

This section contains 8 multiple choice questions. Each question has 4 choices (a), (b), (c) and (d), out of which **ONLY ONE** is correct.

**1.** If $y = x^{(\ell n x)^{\ell n(\ell n x)}}$, then $\dfrac{d y}{d x}$ is equal to :

(a) $\dfrac{y}{x}\left(\ell n\, x^{\ell n x - 1} + 2\,\ell n\, x\, \ell n\,(\ell n\, x)\right)$

(b) $\dfrac{y}{x}\,(\ln x)^{\ln (\ln x)}\,(2 \ln (\ln x) + 1)$

(c) $\dfrac{y\, \ell n\, y}{x\, \ell n\, x}\,(2\, \ln\,(\ln x) + 1)$    (d) Both (b) and (c)

**2.** A function $f(x)$ satisfies the condition,
$f(x) = f'(x) + f''(x) + f'''(x) + \ldots\ldots \infty$ where $f(x)$ is a differentiable function indefinitely. If $f(0) = 1$, then $f(x)$ is

(a) $e^{x/2}$    (b) $e^{x}$    (c) $e^{2x}$    (d) $e^{4x}$

**3.** If $y = (\sin x)^{\tan x}$, then $\dfrac{dy}{dx}$ is equal to

(a) $(\sin x)^{\tan x}\,(1 + \sec^2 x \log \sin x)$

(b) $\tan x\,(\sin x)^{\tan x - 1}.\cos x$

(c) $(\sin x)^{\tan x}\sec^2 x \log \sin x$

(d) $\tan x\,(\sin x)^{\tan x - 1}$

**4.** If $x = e^t \cos t$, $y = e^t \sin t$ then $\left.\dfrac{d^2 y}{dx^2}\right]_{t=0} =$

(a) 0    (b) 2

(c) 2/e    (d) 1/2

**5.** If $x = 2 \ln \cot t$, $y = \tan t + \cot t$ then $1 + \dfrac{dy}{dx} . \sin 2t =$

(a) $\cos 2t$    (b) $2 \sin^2 t$

(c) $2 \cos^2 t$    (d) $\tan^2 t$

---

**RESPONSE GRID**    **1.** ⓐⓑⓒⓓ    **2.** ⓐⓑⓒⓓ    **3.** ⓐⓑⓒⓓ    **4.** ⓐⓑⓒⓓ    **5.** ⓐⓑⓒⓓ

**6.** $y = \dfrac{1}{\sqrt{a^2 - b^2}} \cos^{-1}\left[\dfrac{a\cos(x-\alpha)+b}{\theta}\right]$ where $\theta = a + b$

$\cos(x-a)$, then $\dfrac{dy}{dx} =$

(a) $\dfrac{1}{\theta}$     (b) $\dfrac{2}{\theta}$     (c) $\dfrac{1}{\theta^2}$     (d) $\dfrac{2}{\theta^2}$

**7.** If $x = f(t)\cos t - f'(t)\sin t$, $y = f(t)\sin t + f'(t)\cos t$ then

$\left(\dfrac{dx}{dt}\right)^2 + \left(\dfrac{dy}{dt}\right)^2$ is equal to

(a) $f(t) - f''(t)$     (b) $[f(t) - f''(t)]^2$     (c)

$[f(t) + f''(t)]^2$     (d) None of these

**8.** If $y = (1 + 1/x)^x$ then $\dfrac{2\sqrt{y_2(2) + 1/8}}{(\log 3/2 - 1/3)}$ is equal to

(a) 3     (b) 4     (c) 1     (d) 2

## Section - II - Multiple Correct Answer Type

This section contains 4 multiple correct answer(s) type questions. Each question has 4 choices (a), (b), (c) and (d), out of which **ONE OR MORE** is/are correct.

**9.** Which of the following statement are correct?

(a) If $y = \tan^{-1}\left(\dfrac{2^x}{1 + 2^{2x+1}}\right)$, then $\dfrac{dy}{dx}$ at $x = 0$ is $\dfrac{3}{5}\log 2$

(b) If $y = \sqrt{\sin x + \sqrt{\sin x + \sqrt{\sin x + \dots \dots \infty}}}$ then $\dfrac{dy}{dx} = \dfrac{\cos x}{2y - 1}$

(c) If $y = \tan^{-1}\left(\dfrac{2^x}{1 + 2^{2x+1}}\right)$, then $\dfrac{dy}{dx}$ at $x = 0$ is $\dfrac{2}{5}\log 2$

(d) If $y = \sqrt{\sin x + \sqrt{\sin x + \sqrt{\sin x + \dots \dots \infty}}}$ तब $\dfrac{dy}{dx} = \dfrac{\cos x}{2y + 1}$

**10.** If $y = y(x)$ and it follows the relation $e^{xy} + y\cos x = 2$, then which of the following is/are correct?

(a) $y'(0) = 0$   (b) $y''(0) = 1$    (c) $y'(0) = -1$   (d) $y''(0) = 2$

**11.** If $f(x) = \begin{vmatrix} \cos(x+\alpha) & \cos(x+\beta) & \cos(x+\gamma) \\ \sin(x+\alpha) & \sin(x+\beta) & \sin(x+\gamma) \\ \sin(\beta-\gamma) & \sin(y-\beta) & \sin(\alpha-\beta) \end{vmatrix}$ then

$f(\alpha)$, $f(\beta)$, $f(\gamma)$ are in

(a) A. P.    (b) G. P.      (c) H. P.    (d) none of these

**12.** Differential coefficient of $\sin^{-1} x$ w.r.t. $\sin^{-1}(3x - 4x^3)$ is

(a) $\dfrac{1}{3}$ if $-\dfrac{\pi}{8} < x < \dfrac{\pi}{8}$      (b) $3$ if $\dfrac{-\pi}{8} < x < \dfrac{\pi}{8}$

(c) $\dfrac{1}{3}$ if $-\dfrac{\pi}{9} < x < \dfrac{\pi}{9}$      (d) $3$ if $\dfrac{-\pi}{9} < x < \dfrac{\pi}{9}$

## Section - III - Linked Comprehension Type

This section contains one paragraph. Based upon the paragraph, 3 multiple choice questions have to be answered. Each question has 4 choices (a), (b), (c) and (d), out of which **ONLY ONE** is correct.

### USE OF DERIVATIVES FOR SUMMATION OF SERIES

Consider a series of the form $\dfrac{f_1'(x)}{f_1(x)} + \dfrac{f_2'(x)}{f_2(x)} + \dfrac{f_3'(x)}{f_3(x)} + \dots$

The sum of such a series can be obtained in the following way :

**Step 1 :** Obtain the product $f_1(x) f_2(x) \dots f_n(x)$. Let $f_1(x) f_2(x) \dots f_n(x) = g(x)$

**Step 2 :** Take log of both the sides, you get $\log f_1(x) + \log f_2(x) + \dots + \log f_n(x) = \log g(x)$

**Step 3 :** Differentiate both sides with respect to x, you get

$\dfrac{f_1'(x)}{f_1(x)} + \dfrac{f_2'(x)}{f_2(x)} + \dots + \dfrac{f_n'(x)}{f_n(x)} = \dfrac{g'(x)}{g(x)}$

The above method can be extended for the sum of infinite terms of the series provided the series is convergent.

<table>
<tr><td rowspan="2">**RESPONSE GRID**</td><td>6. ⓐⓑⓒⓓ</td><td>7. ⓐⓑⓒⓓ</td><td>8. ⓐⓑⓒⓓ</td><td>9. ⓐⓑⓒⓓ</td><td>10. ⓐⓑⓒⓓ</td></tr>
<tr><td>11. ⓐⓑⓒⓓ</td><td>12. ⓐⓑⓒⓓ</td><td></td><td></td><td></td></tr>
</table>

**13.** The value of the product $(1 + x)(1 + x^2)(1 + x^4)(1 + x^8) \ldots\ldots (1 + x^{2^{n-1}})$ is

(a) $\dfrac{1 - x^{2^n}}{1 - x}$  (b) $\dfrac{1 + x^{2^n}}{1 - x}$  (c) $(1 - x)(1 - x^{2^n})$  (d) $\dfrac{1 - x^{2^n}}{1 + x^{2^n}}$

**14.** The sum of n terms of the series

$$\frac{1}{1 + x} + \frac{2x}{1 + x^2} + \frac{4x^3}{1 + x^4} + \frac{8x^7}{1 + x^8} + \ldots\ldots$$

(a) $\dfrac{1}{1 - x} - \dfrac{2^n x^{2^n - 1}}{1 - x^{2^n}}$

(b) $\dfrac{1}{1 - x} + \dfrac{2^n x^{2^n - 1}}{1 + x^{2^n}}$

(c) $-\dfrac{1}{1 - x} - \dfrac{2^n x^{2^n - 1}}{1 - x^{2^n}}$

(d) $-2^n x^{2^{n-1}} \left[ \dfrac{1}{1 - x^{2^n}} + \dfrac{1}{1 + x^{2^n}} \right]$

**15.** The product $\cos\dfrac{x}{2}\cos\dfrac{x}{2^2}\cos\dfrac{x}{2^3}\ldots\ldots\cos\dfrac{x}{2^n}$ is

(a) $\sin x$  (b) $\dfrac{\sin x}{\sin\dfrac{x}{2^n}}$  (c) $\dfrac{\sin x}{2^n \sin\dfrac{x}{2^n}}$  (d) $2^n \cos x$

## Section - IV - Matrix-Match Type

This section contains 2 questions. It contains statements given in two columns, which have to be matched. Statements in Column I are labelled as A, B, C and D whereas statements in Column II are labelled as p, q, r and s. The answers to these questions have to be appropriately bubbled as illustrated in the following example. If the correct matches are A-p, A-r, B-p, B-s, C-r, C-s and D-q, then the correctly bubbled matrix will look like the following :

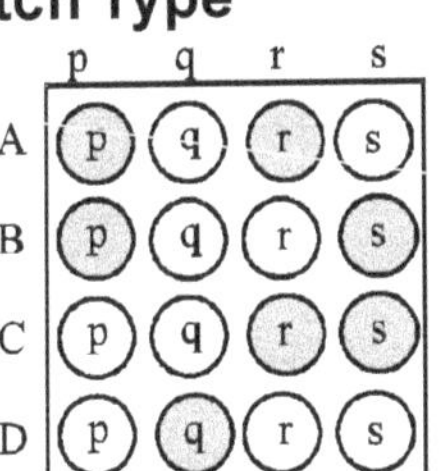

**16.** 

| Column I | Column II |
|---|---|
| (A) If $2^x + 2^y = 2^{x+y}$, then $\dfrac{dy}{dx}$ equal to | (p) $-\dfrac{y(x^{y-1} + y^{x-1}\log y)}{x(y^{x-1} + x^{y-1}\log x)}$ |

(B) If $x^y + y^x = 1$, then $\dfrac{dy}{dx}$   (q) $\dfrac{x^2 - y}{x - y^2}$

(C) If $x = a(\cos\theta + \theta\sin\theta)$   (r) $-2^{y-x}$

and $y = a(\sin\theta - \theta\cos\theta)$,

then $\dfrac{d^2 y}{dx^2}$ equals to

(D) If $x^3 + y^3 = 3xy$,   (s) $\dfrac{\sec^3\theta}{a\theta}$

then $\dfrac{dy}{dx}$ equals

**17.**

| Column-I | Column-II |
|---|---|
| (A) If $x^y = e^{x-y}$ then $\dfrac{dy}{dx} =$ | p. $\quad 2$ |
| (B) If $x = \theta - \dfrac{1}{\theta}$, $y = \theta + \dfrac{1}{\theta}$ then $\dfrac{dy}{dx} =$ | q. $\quad \dfrac{x}{y}$ |
| (C) $\dfrac{d}{dx}\left\{\cos^{-1}\left(\dfrac{4x^3}{27} - x\right)\right\} =$ | r. $\quad \dfrac{\log x}{(1 + \log x)^2}$ |
| (D) If $xy = (x + y)^n$ and $\dfrac{dy}{dx} = \dfrac{y}{x}$ then $n =$ | s. $\quad 3$ |
| | t. $\quad \dfrac{-3}{\sqrt{9 - x^2}}$ |
| | u. $\quad \dfrac{3}{\sqrt{9 - x^2}}$ |

## Section - V - Reasoning Type

This section contains 2 reasoning type questions. Each question has 4 choices (a), (b), (c) and (d) out of which **ONLY ONE** is correct.

**RESPONSE GRID**

13. (a)(b)(c)(d)   14. (a)(b)(c)(d)   15. (a)(b)(c)(d)

16. A - (p)(q)(r)(s); B - (p)(q)(r)(s); C - (p)(q)(r)(s); D - (p)(q)(r)(s)

17. A-(p)(q)(r)(s)(t)(u); B-(p)(q)(r)(s)(t)(u); C-(p)(q)(r)(s)(t)(u); D-(p)(q)(r)(s)(t)(u)

**DPP/M/50**

DIRECTIONS for Qs (18-19) : **Each of these questions contains two statements: Statement-1 (Assertion) and Statement-2 (Reason). Each of these questions has four alternative choices, only one of which is the correct answer. You have to select the correct choice.**

(a)  Statement-1 is True, Statement-2 is True; Statement-2 is a correct explanation for Statement-1.
(b)  Statement-1 is True, Statement-2 is True; Statement-2 is NOT a correct explanation for Statement-1.
(c)  Statement-1 is True, Statement-2 is False.
(d)  Statement-1 is False, Statement-2 is True.

**18.**  **Statement -1 :** Derivative of $\sin^{-1}\left(\dfrac{2x}{1+x^2}\right)$ with respect to $\cos^{-1}\left(\dfrac{1-x^2}{1+x^2}\right)$ is 1, for $0 < x < 1$.

 **Statement-2 :** $\sin^{-1}\left(\dfrac{2x}{1+x^2}\right) = \cos^{-1}\left(\dfrac{1-x^2}{1+x^2}\right)$ for $-1 \le x \le 1$

**19.**  **Statement -1 :** $\dfrac{d}{dx}\left(x^{x^x}\right) = x^{x^x} \cdot x(1 + 2\ln x)$

 **Statement-2 :** $\because \left(x^x\right)^x = x^{x^2} = e^{x^2 \ln x}$

## Section - VI - Integer Type

This section contains 5 questions. The answer to each of the questions is a single digit integer ranging from 0 to 9.

**20.**  The equation $y^2 e^{xy} = 9e^{-3} \cdot x^2$ defines y as a differentiable function of x. The value of $\dfrac{dy}{dx}$ for $x = -1$ and $y = 3$ is 5 M. Find M.

**21.**  If $y^3 - y = 2x$ then $y\left[\left(x^2 - \dfrac{1}{27}\right)\dfrac{d^2 y}{dx^2} + x\dfrac{dy}{dx}\right]^{-1}$ is equal to

**22.**  If y is a function of x and $\log(x+y) - 2xy = 0$, then find the value of y' (0).

**23.**  Let $0 < x < \pi$ and y(x) be given by $(1 + \sin x) y^3 - (\cos x) y^2 + 2(1 + \sin x) y - 2 \cos x = 0$. The derivative of y with respect to $\tan(x/2)$ at $x = \pi/2$ is $-\dfrac{A}{B}$. Find the value of A + B.

**24.**  If $y\sqrt{x^2 + 1} = \log\left\{\sqrt{x^2 + 1} - x\right\}$ then find the value of $(x^2 + 1)\dfrac{dy}{dx} + xy + 1$.

---

| **RESPONSE GRID** | 18. ⓐⓑⓒⓓ  19. ⓐⓑⓒⓓ  20. ⓪①②③④⑤⑥⑦⑧⑨ |
| --- | --- |
| | 21. ⓪①②③④⑤⑥⑦⑧⑨  22. ⓪①②③④⑤⑥⑦⑧⑨ |
| | 23. ⓪①②③④⑤⑥⑦⑧⑨  24. ⓪①②③④⑤⑥⑦⑧⑨ |

## DAILY PRACTICE PROBLEM DPP 50 - MATHS

| Total Questions | 24 | Total Marks | 75 |
| --- | --- | --- | --- |
| Attempted | | Correct | |
| Incorrect | | Net Score | |
| Cut-off Score | 15 | Qualifying Score | 49 |
| Success Gap = Net Score – Qualifying Score | | | |
| Net Score $= \sum\limits_{i=I}^{VI}\left[(correct_i \times MM_i) - (In_i - NM_i)\right]$ | | | |

**Name :**

**Date :**

**Start Time :**

**End Time :**

## MATHEMATICS — M51

SYLLABUS : **Differentiation-3** : Differentiation by substitution, Higher order derivatives

## Max. Marks : 71

## Time : 60 min.

**GENERAL INSTRUCTIONS**

- The Daily Practice Problem Sheet contains **24** Questions divided into 5 sections.

  Section I has **11** MCQ's with ONLY 1 correct option. 2 marks for correct answer and No negative marks.

  Section II has **4** MCQ's with 1 or MORE THAN 1 correct option. 4 marks for correct answer(s) and (–1) for wrong answer.

  Section III has **1** PASSAGE with **3** MCQ's with ONLY 1 correct option. 3 marks for correct and (–1) mark for wrong answer.

  Section IV has **1** MCQ's with multiple matchings. 1 mark for the correct matching of each row & No negative marks.

  Section V has **5** single digit integer answer questions. 4 marks for correct answer and (–1) for wrong answer.

- No mark will be given/ deducted if no bubble is filled. Keep a timer in front and stop immediately at the end of 60 min.

- You have to evaluate your Response Grids yourself with the help of Solution Booklet.

- The sheet follows a particular syllabus. Do not attempt the sheet before you have completed your preparation for that syllabus. Refer syllabus sheet in the starting of the book for the syllabus of all the DPP sheets.

- After completing the sheet check your answers with the solution booklet and complete the Result Grid. Finally spend time to analyse your performance and revise the areas which emerge out as weak in your evaluation.

## Section - I - Straight Objective Type

This section contains 11 multiple choice questions. Each question has 4 choices (a), (b), (c) and (d), out of which **ONLY ONE** is correct.

**1.** If $y^2 = P(x)$, a polynomial of degree 3, then $2\dfrac{d}{dx}\left(y^2\dfrac{d^2y}{dx^2}\right)$ equals

(a) $P'''(x) + P'(x)$     (b) $P''(x)P'''(x)$

(c) $P(x)P'''(x)$     (d) a constant

**2.** Let $f(x)$ be a quadratic expression which is positive for all the real values of x. If $g(x) = f(x) + f'(x) + f''(x)$, then for any real x,

(a) $g(x) < 0$     (b) $g(x) > 0$

(c) $g(x) = 0$     (d) None of these

**3.** Let $f(x) = \begin{vmatrix} x^3 & \sin x & \cos x \\ 6 & -1 & 0 \\ p & p^2 & p^3 \end{vmatrix}$ where p is a constant.

Then $\dfrac{d^3}{dx^3}(f(x))$ at $x = 0$ is

(a) $p$     (b) $p + p^2$

(c) $p + p^3$     (d) independent of p

**4.** If $x^2 + y^2 = 1$ then

(a) $yy'' - 2(y')^2 + 1 = 0$     (b) $yy'' + (y')^2 + 1 = 0$

(c) $yy'' + (y')^2 - 1 = 0$     (d) $yy'' + 2(y')^2 + 1 = 0$

**5.** Suppose the function f satisfies the equation $f(x+y) = f(x)f(y)$ for all x and y and $f(x) = 1 + xg(x)$ where $\lim_{x\to 0} g(x) = \log a$. If $f^n(x) = Kf(x)$, $f^n$ being nth derivative of f; then K =

(a) $\log a$     (b) $n\log a$

(c) $(\log a)^n$     (d) $n(\log a)^n$

**6.** If $x = e^{y + e^{y + \ldots \ldots \text{to } \infty}}$, $x > 0$ then $\dfrac{dy}{dx}$ is

(a) $\dfrac{1-x}{x}$     (b) $\dfrac{1}{x}$     (c) $\dfrac{x}{1+x}$     (d) $\dfrac{1+x}{x}$

**7.** Let $g(x)$ be the inverse of an invertible function $f(x)$ which is differentiable for all real x, then $g''(f''(x))$ equals

(a) $-\dfrac{f''(x)}{(f'(x))^3}$     (b) $\dfrac{f'(x)f''(x) - (f'(x))^3}{f'(x)}$

(c) $\dfrac{f'(x)f''(x) - (f'(x))^2}{(f'(x))^2}$     (d) none of these.

**8.** If $y^3 - y = 2x$, then $\left(x^2 - \dfrac{1}{27}\right)\dfrac{d^2y}{dx^2} + x\dfrac{dy}{dx} =$

(a) $y$     (b) $\dfrac{y}{3}$     (c) $\dfrac{y}{9}$     (d) $\dfrac{y}{27}$

**9.** If $y = e^{ax}\sin(bx+c)$, then $\dfrac{d^2y}{dx^2} - 2a\dfrac{dy}{dx} + \left(a^2 + b^2\right)y =$

(a) $0$     (b) $y$     (c) $a^2$     (d) $b^2$

**10.** If $y = \left(x + \sqrt{x^2 + 1}\right)^m$ then $(1 + x^2)y_2 + xy_1 =$

(a) $m^2 y$     (b) $my$     (c) $y$     (d) $0$

**11.** If $y = e^{\sqrt{x}} + e^{-\sqrt{x}}$ then $xy'' + y'/2 =$

(a) $y$     (b) $4y$     (c) $y/2$     (d) $y/4$

## Section - II - Multiple Correct Answer Type

This section contains 4 multiple correct answer(s) type questions. Each question has 4 choices (a), (b), (c) and (d), out of which **ONE OR MORE** is/are correct.

**12.** If $y = \sin^4 x + \cos^4 x$, then

(a) $y_n = 4^n \cos(4x + n\pi/2)$

(b) $y_n = 4^{n-1}\cos(4x + n\pi/2)$

(c) $y_n = 4^{n-1}\sin\left(\dfrac{\pi}{2}(n-1) - 4n\right)$

(d) $y_n = 4^n \sin\left(\dfrac{\pi}{2}(n-1) - 4x\right)$

**13** If $f(x) = x^3 + x^2 f'(1) + x f''(2) + f'''(3)$ for all $x \in R$, then

(a) $f(0) + f(2) = f(1)$     (b) $f(0) + f(3) = 0$

(c) $f(1) + f(3) = f(2)$     (d) None of these

**14.** Let $f(x) = x^2 + xg'(1) + g''(2)$ and $g(x) = x^2 + xf'(2) + f''(3)$, then

(a) $f'(1) = 4 + f'(2)$     (b) $g'(2) = 8 + g'(1)$

(c) $g''(2) + f''(3) = 4$     (d) None of these

**15.** If $F(x) = f(x)g(x)$ and $f'(x)g'(x) = c$, then

(a) $F' = c\left[\dfrac{f}{f'} + \dfrac{g}{g'}\right]$     (b) $\dfrac{F''}{F} = \dfrac{f''}{f} + \dfrac{g''}{g} + \dfrac{2c}{fg}$

(c) $\dfrac{F'''}{F} = \dfrac{f'''}{f} + \dfrac{g'''}{g}$     (d) $\dfrac{F'''}{F''} = \dfrac{f'''}{f''} + \dfrac{g'''}{g''}$

## Section - III - Linked Comprehension Type

This section contains one paragraph. Based upon the paragraph, 3 multiple choice questions have to be answered. Each question has 4 choices (a), (b), (c) and (d), out of which **ONLY ONE** is correct.

If $y = f(x)$ be such that it possesses a differential coefficient $f'(x)$ which is called the first derivative of $f(x)$, then $f'(x)$ being itself a function of x is capable of being differentiated further. Now if $f'(x)$ is differentiable i.e. $\underset{\delta x \to 0}{Lt}\dfrac{f'(x + \delta x) - f'(x)}{\delta x}$ exists finitely, then this limit is called the first derivative of $f'(x)$ or second derivative of $f(x)$ and is denoted by $f''(x)$. Similarly the first derivative of $f''(x)$ is called the second derivative of $f'(x)$ and third derivative of $f(x)$ and is denoted by $f'''(x)$. The nth derivative

| RESPONSE GRID | | | | | |
|---|---|---|---|---|---|
| | **6.** ⓐⓑ©ⓓ | **7.** ⓐⓑ©ⓓ | **8.** ⓐⓑ©ⓓ | **9.** ⓐⓑ©ⓓ | **10.** ⓐⓑ©ⓓ |
| | **11.** ⓐⓑ©ⓓ | **12.** ⓐⓑ©ⓓ | **13.** ⓐⓑ©ⓓ | **14.** ⓐⓑ©ⓓ | **15.** ⓐⓑ©ⓓ |

*Space for Rough Work*

of $y$ is also denoted as $y_n, \dfrac{d^n y}{dx^n}, \; D^n y, y^n, f^n(x)$.

**LEIBNITZ THEOREM**

**The nth derivative of product of two functions of $x$.**

Suppose u and v are two functions of x and all their derivatives exist; then by Leibnitz's theorem.

$$D^n(uv) = (D^n u)v + {}^nC_1(D^{n-1}u)(Dv) + {}^nC_2(D^{n-2}u)(D^n v) + \cdots$$

$$+ {}^nC_r(D^{n-r}u)(D^2 v) + \cdots + u(D^n v).$$

*Note :* When one of the two functions in the above theorem is of the form $x^m$, then we should choose it as v and the other as u because $x^m$ shall have only m differential coefficients and not more, which may be simplified.

16. If $y = \dfrac{x^2 + 1}{(x-1)(x-2)(x-3)}$ then $y_n =$

(a) $\dfrac{(-1)^n . n!}{(x-1)^{n+1}(x-2)^{n+1}(x-3)^{n+1}}$

(b) $(-1)^n\, n!\left[\dfrac{1}{(x-1)^{n+1}} + \dfrac{1}{(x-2)^{n+1}} + \dfrac{1}{(x-3)^{n+1}}\right]$

(c) $(-1)^n\, n!\left[\dfrac{1}{(x-1)^{n+1}} + \dfrac{2}{(x-2)^{n+1}} + \dfrac{3}{(x-3)^{n+1}}\right]$

(d) None of these

17. If $x^2 y_2 + xy_1 + y = 0$ then

$$x^2 y_{n+2} + (2n+1)xy_{n+1} + n^2 y_n =$$

(a) 0     (b) $y_n$     (c) $-y_n$     (d) $n\, y_n$

18. Differentiating $x^{2n}$ successively $n$ times by two different ways, the sum of the series

$$1 + \frac{n^2}{1^2} + \frac{n^2(n-1)^2}{1^2 . 2^2} + \frac{n^2(n-1)^2(n-2)^2}{1^2 . 2^2 . 3^2} + \cdots\cdots\cdots \text{ can}$$

be obtained, which is

(a) $(2n)!$    (b) $\dfrac{(2n)!}{n!}$    (c) $\dfrac{(2n)!}{(n!)^2}$    (d) $(n!)^2$

---

## Section - IV - Matrix-Match Type

This section contains 1 question. It contains statements given in two columns, which have to be matched. Statements in Column I are labelled as A, B, C and D whereas statements in Column II are labelled as p, q, r and s. The answers to these questions have to be appropriately bubbled as illustrated in the following example. If the correct matches are A-p, A-r, B-p, B-s, C-r, C-s and D-q, then the correctly bubbled matrix will look like the following :

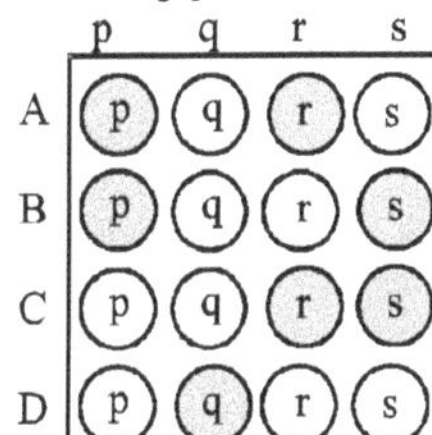

---

19.   **Column-I**            **Column-II**

(A) $\dfrac{d}{dx}\left(\sin^2 \cot^{-1}\sqrt{\dfrac{1+x}{1-x}}\right)$    p.   $\log(h(x))$

(B) If $h(x) = e^{e^x}$ then $\dfrac{h'(x)}{h(x)}$    q.   0

(C) If $f(x) = \sqrt{ax} + \dfrac{a^2}{\sqrt{ax}}$    r.   $-\dfrac{1}{2}$

     then $f'(a)$

(D) If $\sqrt{\tan y} = e^{\cos 2x}$    s.   $\sin 2y$

     $\sin x$ then $\dfrac{dy}{dx} =$

                 t.   $\sin 2y\,(\cot x - 2\sin 2x)$

<table>
<tr><td rowspan="2">Response<br>Grid</td><td>16. ⓐ ⓑ ⓒ ⓓ    17. ⓐ ⓑ ⓒ ⓓ    18. ⓐ ⓑ ⓒ ⓓ</td></tr>
<tr><td>19. A - ⓟ ⓠ ⓡ ⓢ ⓣ ; B - ⓟ ⓠ ⓡ ⓢ ⓣ ; C - ⓟ ⓠ ⓡ ⓢ ⓣ ; D - ⓟ ⓠ ⓡ ⓢ ⓣ</td></tr>
</table>

## Section - V - Integer Type

This section contains 5 questions. The answer to each of the questions is a single digit integer ranging from 0 to 9.

**20.** Let $f(x)$ be a four times differentiable function such that

$$f(2x^2 - 1) = 2xf(x) \, \forall x \in R, \text{ then find the value of } f^{iv}(0)$$

(where $f^{iv}(0)$ represents fourth derivative of $f(x)$ at $x = 0$)

**21.** If $\quad y = \sqrt{(a-x)(x-b)} - (a-b)\tan^{-1}\sqrt{\dfrac{a-x}{x-b}} \quad$ where

$0 < b < x < a$, then $\dfrac{dy}{dx} = \left(\dfrac{a-x}{x-b}\right)^{P/Q}$. Find the value of $P + Q$.

**22.** If the derivative of $\tan^{-1}\sqrt{\dfrac{1-x}{1+x}}$ with respect to $\sin^{-1} x$ is

$\dfrac{-A}{B}$. Find the value of $A + B$.

**23.** Let $z = (\cos x)^5$ and $y = \sin x$, then the value of $\dfrac{d^2 z}{dy^2}$ at

$x = \dfrac{2\pi}{9}$ is $\dfrac{P}{Q}$. Find the value of $P - Q$.

**24.** If $y = k\, e^{a \sin^{-1} x}$, then find the value of

$$(1 - x^2)\dfrac{d^2 y}{dx^2} - x\dfrac{dy}{dx} - a^2(y - 1)$$

| | | |
|---|---|---|
| **RESPONSE GRID** | **20.** ⓪①②③④⑤⑥⑦⑧⑨ | **21.** ⓪①②③④⑤⑥⑦⑧⑨ |
| | **22.** ⓪①②③④⑤⑥⑦⑧⑨ | **23.** ⓪①②③④⑤⑥⑦⑧⑨ |
| | **24.** ⓪①②③④⑤⑥⑦⑧⑨ | |

## DAILY PRACTICE PROBLEM DPP 51 - MATHS

| Total Questions | 24 | Total Marks | 71 |
|---|---|---|---|
| Attempted | | Correct | |
| Incorrect | | Net Score | |
| Cut-off Score | 14 | Qualifying Score | 46 |
| Success Gap = Net Score – Qualifying Score | | | |

$$\text{Net Score} = \sum_{i=1}^{VI}\left[(\textbf{correct}_i \times MM_i) - (In_i - NM_i)\right]$$

*Space for Rough Work*

**Name :**

**Date :**

**Start Time :**

**End Time :**

# MATHEMATICS  M52

SYLLABUS : Applications of Derivatives-1 : Geometrical Interpretation of Derivative

## Max. Marks : 64

## Time : 60 min.



## Section - I - Straight Objective Type

This section contains 16 multiple choice questions. Each question has 4 choices (a), (b), (c) and (d), out of which **ONLY ONE** is correct.

1. The radius of a right circular cylinder increases at the rate of 0.1 cm/min, and the height decreases at the rate of 0.2 cm/min. The rate of change of the volume of the cylinder, in $cm^3$/min, when the radius is 2 cm and the height is 3 cm is

   (a) $-2\pi$  (b) $-\dfrac{8\pi}{5}$  (c) $-\dfrac{3\pi}{5}$  (d) $\dfrac{2\pi}{5}$

2. Coffee is draining from a conical filter, height and diameter both 15 cm into a cylinderical coffee pot of diameter 15 cm. The rate at which coffee drains from the filter into the pot is 100 cu cm /min.

   The rate in cms/min at which the level in the pot is rising at the instant when the height of the coffee in the pot is 10 cm, is

   (a) $\dfrac{9}{16\pi}$  (b) $\dfrac{25}{9\pi}$  (c) $\dfrac{5}{3\pi}$  (d) $\dfrac{16}{9\pi}$

3. The radius of a right circular cylinder increases at a constant rate. Its altitude is a linear function of the radius and increases three times as fast as radius. When the radius is 1cm then altitude is 6 cm. When the radius is 6cm, the volume is increasing at the rate of 1cu cm/sec. When the radius is 36cm, the volume is increasing at a rate of n cu. cm/sec. The value of 'n' is equal to:

   (a) 12  (b) 22  (c) 30  (d) 33

4. A spherical iron ball 10 cm in radius is coated with a layer of ice of uniform thickness that melts at a rate of 50 $cm^3$/min. When the thickness of ice is 5 cm,then the rate at which the thickness of ice decreases is

   (a) $\dfrac{1}{36\pi}$ cm/min  (b) $\dfrac{1}{18\pi}$ cm/min

   (c) $\dfrac{1}{54\pi}$ cm/min  (d) $\dfrac{5}{6\pi}$ cm/min

5. x and y are the sides of two squares such that $y = x - x^2$. The ratio of rate of change of the area of the second square to the rate of change of area of the first square is

   (a) $x^2 - x + 1$  (b) $2x^2 + 2x - 1$
   (c) $2x^2 - 3x + 1$  (d) $x^2 + x - 1$

**6.** The volume V and depth x of water in a vessel are connected by the relation $V = 5x - \dfrac{x^2}{6}$ and the volume of water is increasing, at the rate of 5 cm$^3$/sec, when x = 2 cm. The rate at which the depth of water is increasing is

(a) $\dfrac{5}{18}$ cm / sec   (b) $\dfrac{1}{4}$ cm / sec   (c) $\dfrac{5}{16}$ cm / sec   (d) $\dfrac{15}{13}$ cm/sec

**7.** Water seeps out of a conical filter at the constant rate of 5 c.c./sec. The height of the filter is 20 cm and radius of the base is 10 cm. The rate at which the height of the water decreases when the height of the cone of water in the filter is 15 cm is

(a) $\dfrac{1}{45\pi}$ cm/sec   (b) $\dfrac{2}{45\pi}$ cm/sec

(c) $\dfrac{3}{45\pi}$ cm/sec   (d) $\dfrac{4}{45\pi}$ cm/sec

**8.** The edge of a cube is increasing at the rate of 5cm/sec. How fast is the volume of the cube increasing when the edge is 12 cm long?
(a) 432 cm$^3$/sec   (b) 2160 cm$^3$/sec
(c) 180 cm$^3$/sec   (d) 1920 cm$^3$/sec

**9.** The length of the side of a square sheet of metal is increasing at the rat of 4cm/sec. The rate at which the area of the sheet is increasing when the length of the side is 2 cm, is
(a) 16 cm$^2$/sec   (b) 8 cm$^2$/sec
(c) 32cm$^2$/sec   (d) 48 cm$^2$/sec

**10.** If by dropping a stone in a quiet lake a wave moves in circle at a speed of 3.5 cm/sec. Then the rate of increase of the area enclosed by the circular region when the radius of the circular wave is 10 cm, is $\left( \pi = \dfrac{22}{7} \right)$

(a) 220 sq. cm/sec   (b) 110 sq. cm/sec
(c) 35 sq. cm/sec   (d) 350 sq. cm/sec

**11.** If the volume of a spherical balloon is increasing at the rate of 900cm$^3$ per sec, then the rate of change of radius of balloon at instant when radius is 15 cm [ in cm/sec]

(a) $\dfrac{22}{7}$   (b) 22   (c) $\dfrac{7}{22}$   (d) $\dfrac{1}{22}$

**12.** A point on the parabola $y^2 = 18x$ at which the ordinate increases at twice the rate of the abscissa is

(a) $\left( \dfrac{-9}{8}, \dfrac{9}{2} \right)$   (b) $(2, -4)$

(c) $(2, 4)$   (d) $\left( \dfrac{9}{8}, \dfrac{9}{2} \right)$

**13.** Water is flowing into a vertical cylindrical tank at the rate of 12 cubic ft/min. If the radius of the tank is 3ft, how fast is the height of the water is rising?

(a) $\dfrac{4}{3\pi}$ ft./ min.   (b) $\dfrac{2}{3\pi}$ ft./ min.

(c) $\dfrac{3}{4\pi}$ ft./ min.   (d) None of these

**14.** Sand is pouring from a pipe at the rate of 12 cm$^3$/s. The falling sand forms a cone on the ground in such a way that the height of the cone is always one-sixth of the radius of the base. How fast is the height of the sand cone increasing when its height is 4 cm?

(a) $48\pi$ cm/sec   (b) $\dfrac{1}{48\pi}$ cm/sec

(c) $8\pi^2$ cm/sec   (d) $\dfrac{1}{8\pi}$ cm$^3$sec

**15.** A particle moves along the curve $6y = x^3 + 2$. Find the points on the curve at which the y-coordinate is changing 8 times as fast as the x-coordinate.
(a) $(7, 11)$   (b) $(4, 11)$
(c) $(4, 7)$   (d) $(4, 4)$

| RESPONSE | 6. ⓐⓑⓒⓓ | 7. ⓐⓑⓒⓓ | 8. ⓐⓑⓒⓓ | 9. ⓐⓑⓒⓓ | 10. ⓐⓑⓒⓓ |
| GRID | 11. ⓐⓑⓒⓓ | 12. ⓐⓑⓒⓓ | 13. ⓐⓑⓒⓓ | 14. ⓐⓑⓒⓓ | 15. ⓐⓑⓒⓓ |

*Space for Rough Work*

16. A balloon, which always remains spherical, has a variable diameter $\frac{3}{2}(2x+1)$. Find the rate of change of its volume with respect to x.

   (a) $27\pi(2x+1)^3$    (b) $\frac{27\pi}{8}$

   (c) $(2x+1)^2$    (d) $\frac{27\pi}{8}(2x+1)^2$

## Section - II - Multiple Correct Answer Type

This section contains 2 multiple correct answer(s) type questions. Each question has 4 choices (a), (b), (c) and (d), out of which **ONE OR MORE** is/are correct.

17. If the area of a circle increases at a uniform rate, then which of the following statements are correct ? the rate of increase of perimeter is :
   (a) the rate of increase of perimeter is directly proportional to radius
   (b) the rate of increase of area is directly proportional to radius
   (c) the rate of increase of perimeter is inversely proportional to radius
   (d) the rate of increase of area is inversely proportional to sqaure of radius

18. After t hours of instruction, a typical typing student can type $N(t) = \frac{70t^2}{30+t^2}$ words per minute (wpm). Then which of the following statements is/are corret.
   (a) The rate at which the student is improving after t hours is $\frac{4200t}{(30+t^2)^2}$
   (b) The rate at which the student improving after 5 hours is 7 wpm
   (c) The rate at which the student is improving after t hours is $\frac{42}{30-t}$
   (d) The rate at which the student improving after 5 hours is 1 wpm

## Section - III - Matrix-Match Type

This section contains 1 question. It contains statements given in two columns, which have to be matched. Statements in Column I are labelled as A, B, C and D whereas statements in Column II are labelled as p, q, r and s. The answers to these questions have to be appropriately bubbled as illustrated in the following example. If the correct matches are A-p, A-r, B-p, B-s, C-r, C-s and D-q, then the correctly bubbled matrix will look like the following :

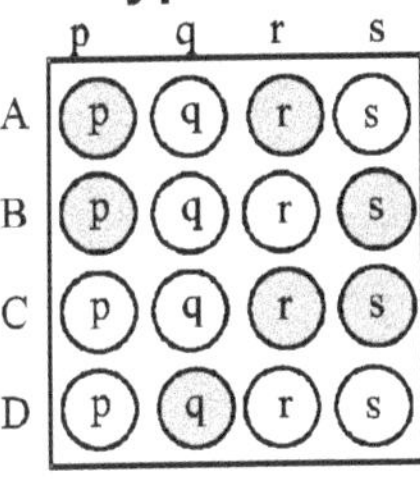

19. 

| | Column-I | | Column-II |
|---|---|---|---|
| (A) | The rate of change of the volume of a sphere (in cm$^3$/cm$^2$) with respect to its surface area when its radius is 2 cm. is | p. | $\frac{-4}{125}$ |
| (B) | The radius of an air bubble is increasing at the rate of $\frac{1}{2}$ cm/s. At what rate (in cm$^3$/ sec) is the volume of the bubble increasing when the radius is 1 cm? | q. | $v\sqrt{2-\sqrt{2}}$ |
| (C) | Two men P and Q start with velocities v at the same time from the junction of two roads inclined at 45° to each other. If they travel by different roads, the rate at which they are being separated is | r. | 1 |
| (D) | A man is moving away from a tower 41.6m high at a rate | s. | $-2\pi$ |

<table>
<tr><td rowspan="2">**RESPONSE GRID**</td><td>16. ⓐⓑ©ⓓ</td><td>17. ⓐⓑ©ⓓ</td><td>18. ⓐⓑ©ⓓ</td></tr>
<tr><td colspan="3">19. A - ⓟⓠⓡⓢⓣ; B - ⓟⓠⓡⓢⓣ; C - ⓟⓠⓡⓢⓣ; D - ⓟⓠⓡⓢⓣ</td></tr>
</table>

*Space for Rough Work*

of 2m/s. If the eye level of the man is 1.6m above the ground, then the rate (in rad s$^{-1}$) at which the angle of elevation of the top of the tower is changing when he is at a distance of 30 m from the foot of the tower is

t. $2\pi$

## Section - IV - Integer Type

This section contains 5 questions. The answer to each of the questions is a single digit integer ranging from 0 to 9.

**20.** The greatest area of the rectangular plot which can be laid out within a triangle of base 36ft. & altitude 12ft. is $3X^2$. Find X. (Assume that one side of the rectangle lies on the base of the triangle)

**21.** If 1200 sq. cm of material is available to make a box with a square base and an open top. The largest possible volume of the box (in cubic cm) is 1000M. Find the value of M.

**22.** A triangle has one side equal to 8 cm the other two sides are in the ratio 5 : 3. If the largest possible area of the triangle is 5N, then find the value of N.

**23.** A rod AB 13 ft long moves with its ends A, B on two perpendicular lines OX and OY respectively. If the end A is 12 ft from O and is slipping away at $2\frac{1}{2}$ ft/sec. then find the rate (in ft/sec) at which the end B is moving.

**24.** The length x of a rectangle is decreasing at the rate of 5 cm/minute and the width y is increasing at the rate of 4 cm/minute. When x = 8cm and y = 6cm, find the rate of change of the perimeter.

| | | |
|---|---|---|
| **RESPONSE GRID** | 20. ⓪①②③④⑤⑥⑦⑧⑨ | 21. ⓪①②③④⑤⑥⑦⑧⑨ |
| | 22. ⓪①②③④⑤⑥⑦⑧⑨ | 23. ⓪①②③④⑤⑥⑦⑧⑨ |
| | 24. ⓪①②③④⑤⑥⑦⑧⑨ | |

| DAILY PRACTICE PROBLEM DPP 52 - MATHS | | | |
|---|---|---|---|
| Total Questions | 24 | Total Marks | 64 |
| Attempted | | Correct | |
| Incorrect | | Net Score | |
| Cut-off Score | 13 | Qualifying Score | 42 |
| Success Gap = Net Score – Qualifying Score | | | |

$$\textbf{Net Score} = \sum_{i=1}^{VI}\left[(\textbf{correct}_i \times MM_i) - (In_i - NM_i)\right]$$

**Name :**

**Date :**

**Start Time :**

**End Time :**

# MATHEMATICS  M53

SYLLABUS : Applications of Derivatives-2 : Tangent and Normal

## Max. Marks : 72

## Time : 60 min.

### GENERAL INSTRUCTIONS

- The Daily Practice Problem Sheet contains **23** Questions divided into 6 sections.
  Section I has **7** MCQ's with ONLY 1 correct option. 2 marks for correct answer and No negative marks.
  Section II has **4** MCQ's with 1 or MORE THAN 1 correct option. 4 marks for correct answer(s) and (–1) for wrong answer.
  Section III has **1** PASSAGE with **3** MCQ's with ONLY 1 correct option. 3 marks for correct and (–1) mark for wrong answer.
  Section IV has **2** MCQ's with multiple matchings. 1 mark for the correct matching of each row & No negative marks.
  Section V has **2** Assertion-Reason MCQ's with ONLY 1 correct option. 3 marks for correct and (–1) mark for wrong answer.
  Section VI has **5** single digit integer answer questions. 4 marks for correct answer and (–1) for wrong answer.
- No mark will be given/ deducted if no bubble is filled. Keep a timer in front and stop immediately at the end of 60 min.
- You have to evaluate your Response Grids yourself with the help of Solution Booklet.
- The sheet follows a particular syllabus. Do not attempt the sheet before you have completed your preparation for that syllabus. Refer syllabus sheet in the starting of the book for the syllabus of all the DPP sheets.
- After completing the sheet check your answers with the solution booklet and complete the Result Grid. Finally spend time to analyse your performance and revise the areas which emerge out as weak in your evaluation.

## Section - I - Straight Objective Type

This section contains 7 multiple choice questions. Each question has 4 choices (a), (b), (c) and (d), out of which **ONLY ONE** is correct.

1. If a variable tangent to the curve $x^2 y = c^3$ makes intercepts a, b on x and y axis respectively, then the value of $a^2 b$ is

   (a) $27c^3$    (b) $\dfrac{4}{27}c^3$    (c) $\dfrac{27}{4}c^3$    (d) $\dfrac{4}{9}c^3$

2. The tangent to the graph of the function $y = f(x)$ at the point with abscissa $x = a$ forms with the x-axis an angle of $\pi/3$ and at the point with abscissa $x = b$ at an angle of $\pi/4$, then the value of the integral, $\displaystyle\int_a^b f'(x) \cdot f''(x)\,dx$ is equal to

   (a) 1    (b) 0    (c) $-\sqrt{3}$    (d) $-1$
   [ assume $f''(x)$ to be continuous ]

3. A curve is represented by the equations, $x = \sec^2 t$ and $y = \cot t$ where t is a parameter. If the tangent at the point P on the curve where $t = \pi/4$ meets the curve again at the point Q then $|PQ|$ is equal to:

   (a) $\dfrac{5\sqrt{3}}{2}$    (b) $\dfrac{5\sqrt{5}}{2}$    (c) $\dfrac{2\sqrt{5}}{3}$    (d) $\dfrac{3\sqrt{5}}{2}$

4. The x-intercept of the tangent at any arbitrary point of the curve $\dfrac{a}{x^2} + \dfrac{b}{y^2} = 1$ is proportional to:

   (a) square of the abscissa of the point of tangency
   (b) square root of the abscissa of the point of tangency
   (c) cube of the abscissa of the point of tangency
   (d) cube root of the abscissa of the point of tangency .

5. A curve $y = f(x)$ passes through the point $P(1, 1)$. The normal to the curve at P is $a(y-1) + (x-1) = 0$. If the slope of the tangent at any point on the curve is proportional to the ordinate of the point, then the equation of the curve is

   (a) $y = e^{a(x-1)}$       (b) $y = e^{a(1-x)}$
   (c) $y = e^{a/2\,(x-1)}$      (d) $e^{a/2\,(x+1)}$

---

**RESPONSE GRID**    1. ⓐⓑⓒⓓ    2. ⓐⓑⓒⓓ    3. ⓐⓑⓒⓓ    4. ⓐⓑⓒⓓ    5. ⓐⓑⓒⓓ

**6.** If OT is the perpendicular drawn from the origin to the tangent at any point t to the curve $x = a\cos^3 t$, $y = a\sin^3 t$, then OT is equal to

(a) $a\sin 2t$   (b) $\dfrac{a}{2}\sin 2t$   (c) $2a\sin 2t$   (d) $2a$

**7.** The tangent line at the point $\theta = \pi/6$ to the curve $x = a\sqrt{\cos 2\theta}\,\cos\theta$, $y = a\sqrt{\cos 2\theta}\,\sin\theta$ is

(a) parallel to the x-axis
(b) parallel to the y-axis
(c) bisector of the angle between co-ordinate axis
(d) line through the origin.

## Section - II - Multiple Correct Answer Type

This section contains 4 multiple correct answer(s) type questions. Each question has 4 choices (a), (b), (c) and (d), out of which **ONE OR MORE** is/are correct.

**8.** Consider the curve $x = 1 - 3t^2$, $y = t - 3t^3$. If tangent at point $(1 - 3t^2,\ t - 3t^3)$ the curve inclined at an angle $\theta$ with positive direction of x-axis and tangent at point $P(-2, 2)$ cuts the curve again at Q. Then which of following statements are true?

(a) The curve is symmetrical about $y = 0$.
(b) $\tan\theta + \sec\theta$ is equal to 3t.
(c) The point Q will be $(-1/3, -2/9)$.
(d) The curve is symmetrical about $x = 0$.

**9.** If the line $ax + by + c = 0$ is a normal to the curve $xy = 1$, then

(a) $a > 0, b > 0$      (b) $a > 0, b < 0$
(c) $a < 0, b > 0$      (d) $a < 0, b < 0$

**10.** In the curve $y = c\,e^{x/a}$, the

(a) subtangent is constant
(b) subnormal varies as the square of the ordinate
(c) tangent at $(x_1, y_1)$ on the curve intersects the x-axis at a distance of $(x_1 - a)$ from the origin
(d) equation of normal at the point where the curve cuts y-axis is $cy + ax = c^2$.

**11.** If at each point of the curve $y = x^3 - ax^2 + x + 1$, the tangent is inclined at a positive acute angle with positive direction of x-axis, then possible integral values of 'a' is (are)

(a) $-1$    (b) $0$    (c) $1$    (d) $2$

## Section - III - Linked Comprehension Type

This section contains 1 paragraph. Based upon the paragraph, 3 multiple choice questions have to be answered. Each question has 4 choices (a), (b), (c) and (d), out of which **ONLY ONE** is correct.

If $y = f(x)$ differentiable $\forall\ x \in R - \{0\}$ and $y = g(x)$ differentiable $\forall\ x \in R - \{0\}$ are two curves such that they pass through $(1, 1)$ and $(2, 3)$ respectively. Also tangents to the two curves where their abscissa are same intersect on y-axis and normals to the curves at the point where their abscissa are equal intersect on x-axis.

**12.** The curve $f(x)$ is –

(a) $\dfrac{2}{x} - x$      (b) $2x^2 - \dfrac{1}{x}$
(c) $\dfrac{2}{x^2} - x$      (d) None of these

**13.** The curve $g(x)$ is –

(a) $x - \dfrac{1}{x}$      (b) $x + \dfrac{2}{x}$
(c) $x^2 - \dfrac{1}{x^2}$      (d) None of these

**14.** The number of positive integral solutions of $f(x) = g(x)$ are

(a) 4      (b) 5
(c) 6      (d) None of these

## Section - IV - Matrix-Match Type

This section contains 2 questions. It contains statements given in two columns, which have to be matched. Statements in Column I are labelled as A, B, C and D whereas statements in Column II are labelled as p, q, r and s. The answers to these questions have to

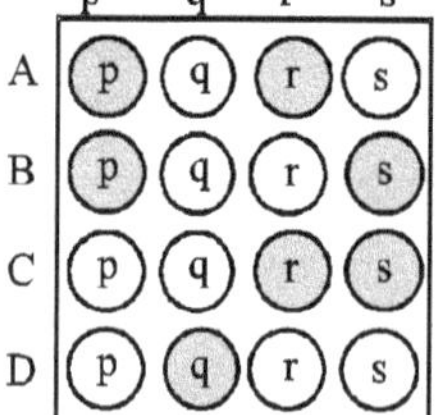

<table>
<tr><td></td><td>p</td><td>q</td><td>r</td><td>s</td></tr>
<tr><td>A</td><td>p</td><td>q</td><td>r</td><td>s</td></tr>
<tr><td>B</td><td>p</td><td>q</td><td>r</td><td>s</td></tr>
<tr><td>C</td><td>p</td><td>q</td><td>r</td><td>s</td></tr>
<tr><td>D</td><td>p</td><td>q</td><td>r</td><td>s</td></tr>
</table>

| RESPONSE GRID | | | | | |
|---|---|---|---|---|---|
| | 6. ⓐⓑⓒⓓ | 7. ⓐⓑⓒⓓ | 8. ⓐⓑⓒⓓ | 9. ⓐⓑⓒⓓ | 10. ⓐⓑⓒⓓ |
| | 11. ⓐⓑⓒⓓ | 12. ⓐⓑⓒⓓ | 13. ⓐⓑⓒⓓ | 14. ⓐⓑⓒⓓ | |

*Space for Rough Work*

be appropriately bubbled as illustrated in the following example. If the correct matches are A-p, A-r, B-p, B-s, C-r, C-s and D-q, then the correctly bubbled matrix will look like the following :

**15.**

| Column-I | | Column-II |
|---|---|---|
| (A) Equation of the tangent line to $y = b\,e^{-x/a}$ where it crosses y-axis | (p) | $a\,\sin^2\theta\mid\sec\theta\mid$ |
| (B) Subnormal length to $xy = e^2$ at $\dfrac{x}{a} + \dfrac{y}{b} = 1$ any point varies directly as | (q) | |
| (C) The length of subtangent at any point '$\theta$' on the ellipse $\dfrac{x^2}{a^2} + \dfrac{y^2}{b^2} = 1$ | (r) | Cube of ordinate |
| | (s) | Square of ordinate |

**16.**

| Column-I | | Column-II |
|---|---|---|
| (A) If the curves $y = 1 - \cos x$, $x \in (-\pi,\pi)$ and $y = \dfrac{\sqrt{3}}{2}|x| + a$ touch each other then the number of the possible values of a is equal to | (p) | 0 |
| (B) If two curves $y^2 = 4a(x - b_1)$ and $x^2 = 4a(y - b_2)$, where a is a positive constant number and $b_1$ and $b_2$ are variables, touch each other then their point of contact lies on $xy = ka^2$, where k is equal to | (q) | 2 |

| (C) The point on the parabola $y^2 = 4x$, which is nearest to the circle $x^2 + (y - 12)^2 = 1$ has the ordinate equal to | (r) | 3 |
|---|---|---|
| (D) The ordinate of the point(s) on the curve $y^3 + 3x^2 = 12y$ where the tangent is parallel to y-axis is/are | (s) | 4 |
| | (t) | –2 |

## Section - V - Reasoning Type

This section contains 2 reasoning type questions. Each question has 4 choices (a), (b), (c) and (d) out of which **ONLY ONE** is correct.

**DIRECTIONS for (Qs. 17 & 18) : Each of these questions contains two statements: Statement-1 (Assertion) and Statement-2 (Reason). Each of these questions has four alternative choices, only one of which is the correct answer. You have to select the correct choice.**

(a) Statement-1 is True, Statement-2 is True; Statement-2 is a correct explanation for Statement-1.

(b) Statement-1 is True, Statement-2 is True; Statement-2 is NOT a correct explanation for Statement-1.

(c) Statement -1 is True, Statement-2 is False.

(d) Statement -1 is False, Statement-2 is True.

**17. Statement 1 :** If length of tangent and normal at a point $(1, 2)$ on the curve $y = f(x)$ are equal then equation of tangent at $(1, 2)$ is $x - y + 1 = 0$.

**Statement 2 :** If dy/dx is finite and non-zero, then length of tangent is $y\sqrt{1 + \left(\dfrac{dx}{dy}\right)^2}$ and length of normal is $y\sqrt{1 + \left(\dfrac{dy}{dx}\right)^2}$.

**18. Statement-1 :** Equation of tangents to the curve $f(x) = x^2$ at the point where slope of tangent is equal to functional value of the curve are $4x - y - 4 = 0, y = 0$

**Statement-2:** $f'(x) = f(x)$

## Section - VI - Integer Type

This section contains 5 questions. The answer to each of the questions is a single digit integer ranging from 0 to 9.

**19.** At the point $P(a, a^n)$ on the graph of $y = x^n$ $(n \in N)$ in the first quadrant a normal is drawn. The normal intersects the y-axis at the point $(0, b)$. If $\lim_{a \to 0} b = \dfrac{1}{2}$, then find the value of $n$.

**20.** Consider the curve represented parametrically by the equation $x = t^3 - 4t^2 - 3t$ and $y = 2t^2 + 3t - 5$ where $t \in R$. If H denotes the number of point on the curve where the tangent is horizontal and V the number of point where the tangent is vertical then find the value of $H + V$.

**21.** If the point $P(a, b)$ lies on the curve $9y^2 = x^3$ such that the normal to the curve at P makes equal intercepts with the axes. Find the value of $(\dfrac{a}{4} + 3b)$.

**22.** If the normals drawn to the curve $y = x^2 - x + 1$ at the points A, B & C on the curve are concurrent at the point $P(7/2, 9/2)$ then the sum of the slopes of the three normals is $\dfrac{13}{24}$X. Find the value of X.

**23.** If the tangent at any point on the curve $x^4 + y^4 = a^4$ cuts off intercepts p and q on the co-ordinate axes then the value of $p^{-4/3} + q^{-4/3}$ is $a^{-P/Q}$. Find the value of $P + Q$.

| | | |
|---|---|---|
| **RESPONSE GRID** | 19. ⓪①②③④⑤⑥⑦⑧⑨ | 20. ⓪①②③④⑤⑥⑦⑧⑨ |
| | 21. ⓪①②③④⑤⑥⑦⑧⑨ | 22. ⓪①②③④⑤⑥⑦⑧⑨ |
| | 23. ⓪①②③④⑤⑥⑦⑧⑨ | |

| DAILY PRACTICE PROBLEM DPP 53 - MATHS | | | |
|---|---|---|---|
| Total Questions | 23 | Total Marks | 72 |
| Attempted | | Correct | |
| Incorrect | | Net Score | |
| Cut-off Score | 14 | Qualifying Score | 47 |
| Success Gap = Net Score – Qualifying Score | | | |

$$\text{Net Score} = \sum_{i=1}^{VI}\left[(correct_i \times MM_i) - (In_i - NM_i)\right]$$

**Name :**　　　　　　　　　　　　　　　　**Date :**

**Start Time :**　　　　　　　　　　　　**End Time :**

## MATHEMATICS　　M54

SYLLABUS : Applications of Derivatives-3 : Maxima and Minima

**Max. Marks : 74**　　　　　　　　　　　　　　　　**Time : 60 min.**

**GENERAL INSTRUCTIONS**

- The Daily Practice Problem Sheet contains **24** Questions divided into 6 sections.
  Section I has **8** MCQ's with ONLY 1 correct option. 2 marks for correct answer and No negative marks.
  Section II has **4** MCQ's with 1 or MORE THAN 1 correct option. 4 marks for correct answer(s) and (–1) for wrong answer.
  Section III has **1** PASSAGE with **3** MCQ's with ONLY 1 correct option. 3 marks for correct and (–1) mark for wrong answer.
  Section IV has **2** MCQ's with multiple matchings. 1 mark for the correct matching of each row & No negative marks.
  Section V has **2** Assertion-Reason MCQ's with ONLY 1 correct option. 3 marks for correct and (–1) mark for wrong answer.
  Section VI has **5** single digit integer answer questions. 4 marks for correct answer and (–1) for wrong answer.
- No mark will be given/ deducted if no bubble is filled. Keep a timer in front and stop immediately at the end of 60 min.
- You have to evaluate your Response Grids yourself with the help of Solution Booklet.
- The sheet follows a particular syllabus. Do not attempt the sheet before you have completed your preparation for that syllabus. Refer syllabus sheet in the starting of the book for the syllabus of all the DPP sheets.
- After completing the sheet check your answers with the solution booklet and complete the Result Grid. Finally spend time to analyse your performance and revise the areas which emerge out as weak in your evaluation.

## Section - I - Straight Objective Type

This section contains 8 multiple choice questions. Each question has 4 choices (a), (b), (c) and (d), out of which **ONLY ONE** is correct.

**1.** Let the function $f(x)$ be defined as follows :

$$f(x) = \begin{cases} x^3 + x^2 - 10x, & -1 \le x < 0 \\ \cos x, & 0 \le x < \dfrac{\pi}{2} \\ 1 + \sin x, & \dfrac{\pi}{2} \le x \le \pi \end{cases}$$

Then $f(x)$ has –

(a) a local minimum at $x = \pi/2$
(b) a local maximum at $x = \pi/2$
(c) absolute minimum at $x = -1$
(d) absolute maximum at $x = \pi$

**2.** Suppose $x_1$ & $x_2$ are the point of maximum and the point of minimum respectively of the function $f(x) = 2x^3 - 9ax^2 + 12$ $a^2x + 1$ respectively, then for the equality $x_1^2 = x_2$ to be true, the value of 'a' must be

(a) 0　　(b) 2　　(c) 1　　(d) 1/4

**3.** The lower corner of a leaf in a book is folded over so as to just reach the inner edge of the page. The fraction of width folded over if the area of the folded part is minimum is :

(a) 5/8　　(b) 2/3　　(c) 3/4　　(d) 4/5

**4.** The extremum values of the function

$$f(x) = \frac{1}{\sin x + 4} - \frac{1}{\cos x - 4}, \text{ where } x \in R \text{ is :}$$

(a) $\dfrac{4}{8 - \sqrt{2}}$　　(b) $\dfrac{2\sqrt{2}}{8 - \sqrt{2}}$　　(c) $\dfrac{2\sqrt{2}}{4\sqrt{2} + 1}$　　(d) $\dfrac{4\sqrt{2}}{8 + \sqrt{2}}$

**5.** A function $f$ is defined by $f$, $f(x) = |x|^m |x - 1|^n$. ($m, n \in N$) $\forall \ x \in R$. The maximum value of the function is

(a) 1　　　　　　　　　　(b) $m^n n^m$

(c) $\dfrac{m^m n^n}{(m + n)^{m+n}}$　　　　(d) $\dfrac{(mn)^{mn}}{(m + n)^{m+n}}$

| RESPONSE GRID | 1. ⓐⓑⓒⓓ | 2. ⓐⓑⓒⓓ | 3. ⓐⓑⓒⓓ | 4. ⓐⓑⓒⓓ | 5. ⓐⓑⓒⓓ |
|---|---|---|---|---|---|

**6.** If $a > b > 0$, then the maximum value of

$$\frac{ab(a^2 - b^2)\sin x \cos x}{a^2 \sin^2 x + b^2 \cos^2 x}, \quad x \in \left(0, \frac{\pi}{2}\right) \text{ is}$$

(a) $a^2 - b^2$              (b) $\dfrac{a^2 - b^2}{2}$

(c) $\dfrac{a^2 + b^2}{2}$           (d) None of these

**7.** A function $f$ such that $f'(a) = f''(a) = \dots = f^{2n}(a) = 0$ and $f$ has a local maximum value $b$ at $x = a$, if $f(x)$ is

(a) $(x - a)^{2n+2}$       b) $b - 1 - (x + 1 - a)^{2n+1}$

(c) $b - (x - a)^{2n+2}$      (d) $(x - a)^{2n+2} - b$

**8.** Let $P(x) = a_0 + a_1 x^2 + a_2 x^4 + \dots + a_n x^{2n}$ be a polynomial in a real variable $x$ with $0 < a_0 < a_1 < a_2 < \dots < a_n$. The function $P(x)$ has

(a) neither a maximum nor a minimum

(b) only one maximum

(c) only one minimum

(d) only one maximum and only one minimum

## Section - II - Multiple Correct Answer Type

This section contains 4 multiple correct answer(s) type questions. Each question has 4 choices (a), (b), (c) and (d), out of which **ONE OR MORE** is/are correct.

**9.** If $\lim\limits_{x \to a} f(x) = \lim\limits_{x \to a} [f(x)]$ (a is a finite quantity), where [ . ] denotes greatest integer function and $f(x)$ is a nonconstant continuous function, then –

(a) $\lim\limits_{x \to a} f(x)$ is an integer

(b) $\lim\limits_{x \to a} f(x)$ is non integer

(c) $f(x)$ has a local minimum at $x = a$

(d) $f(x)$ has a local maximum at $x = a$

**10.** The function $\dfrac{\sin(x+a)}{\sin(x+b)}$ has no maxima or minima if:

(a) $b - a = n\pi, \quad n \in I$       (b) $b - a = (2n+1)\pi, \, n \in I$

(c) $b - a = 2n\pi, \quad n \in I$       (d) none of these .

**11.** An extremum value of $y = \int\limits_0^x (t-1)(t-2)\, dt$ is :

(a) 5/6      (b) 2/3      (c) 1      (d) 2

**12.** Let $f(x) = \begin{cases} e^x, & 0 \le x \le 1 \\ 2 - e^{x-1}, & 1 < x \le 2 \\ x - e, & 2 < x \le 3 \end{cases}$ and $g(x) = \int\limits_0^x f(t)\, dt, \ x \in [1, 3]$

then $g(x)$ has

(a) local maxima at $x = 1 + \ln 2$

(b) local minima at $x = e$

(c) no local maxima

(d) no local minima

## Section - III - Linked Comprehension Type

This section contains 1 paragraph. Based upon the paragraph, 3 multiple choice questions have to be answered. Each question has 4 choices (a), (b), (c) and (d), out of which **ONLY ONE** is correct.

$$f(x) = 2x^3 - 3(a-3)x^2 + 6ax + a + 2$$
$$f'(x) = 6x^2 - 6(a-3)x + 6a = 6\{x^2 - (a-3)x + a\}$$

**13.** The value of 'a' for which $f(x)$ has exactly one point of local maxima and one point of local minima

(a) $(-\infty, 1) \cup (9, \infty)$      (b) $(-\infty, 1] \cup [9, \infty)$

(c) $[1, 9]$               (d) $(1, 9)$

**14.** The value of 'a' for which $f(x)$ has local minima at some negative real $x$

(a) $(-\infty, 1) \cup (9, \infty)$      (b) $(-\infty, 1] \cup [9, \infty)$

(c) $(0, 1)$             (d) $(1, 9)$

---

| **RESPONSE GRID** | 6. (a)(b)(c)(d) | 7. (a)(b)(c)(d) | 8. (a)(b)(c)(d) | 9. (a)(b)(c)(d) | 10. (a)(b)(c)(d) |
|---|---|---|---|---|---|
| | 11. (a)(b)(c)(d) | 12. (a)(b)(c)(d) | 13. (a)(b)(c)(d) | 14. (a)(b)(c)(d) | |

*Space for Rough Work*

**15.** The values of 'a' for which $f(x)$ has local maxima at some negative and local minima at positive real x

  (a)   $(-\infty,\ 0] \cup [9,\ \infty)$     (b)   $(9,\ \infty)$

  (c)   $(0, 1]$                 (d)   $(-\infty, 0)$

## Section - IV - Matrix-Match Type

This section contains 2 questions. It contains statements given in two columns, which have to be matched. Statements in Column I are labelled as A, B, C and D whereas statements in Column II are labelled as p, q, r and s. The answers to these questions have to be appropriately bubbled as illustrated in the following example. If the correct matches are A-p, A-r, B-p, B-s, C-r, C-s and D-q, then the correctly bubbled matrix will look like the following:

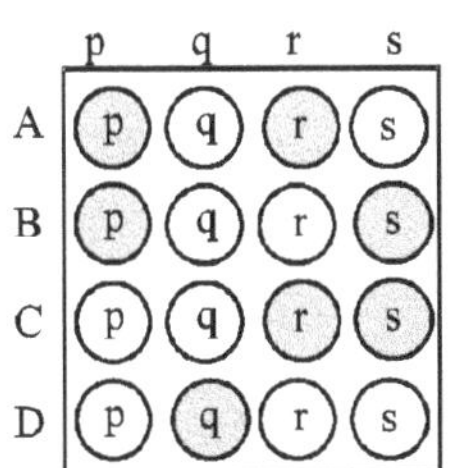

**16.**

| | Column-I | | Column-II |
|---|---|---|---|
| (A) | The minimum value of the polynomial $x(x+1)(x+2)(x+3)$ is : | p. | e |
| (B) | The minimum value of $\dfrac{\tan\left(x + \dfrac{\pi}{6}\right)}{\tan x}$ is : | q. | 0 |
| (C) | Let $f(x) = e^x \cos x$ and slope of the curve $y = f(x)$ is maximum at x = a then a equals | r. | −1 |
| (D) | Difference between the greatest and the least values of the function $f(x) = x(\ln x - 2)$ on $[1, e^2]$ is | s. | 2 |
| | | t. | 3 |

**17.** Let $f(x)$ be a real valued function defined by $f(x) = x^2 - 2|x|$

and $g(x) = \begin{cases} \text{minimum } \{f(t) : -2 \le t \le x\}, & x \in [-2, 0) \\ \text{maximum } \{f(t) : 0 \le t \le x\}, & x \in [0, 3] \end{cases}$

| | Column-I | | Column-II |
|---|---|---|---|
| (A) | $g(x)$ is not derivable at x equal to | p. | −2 |
| (B) | Number of points of local | q. | 0 |
| (C) | Absolute maximum value of $g(x)$ is equal to | r. | 1 |
| | | s. | 2 |
| | | t. | 3 |

## Section - V - Reasoning Type

This section contains 2 reasoning type questions. Each question has 4 choices (a), (b), (c) and (d) out of which **ONLY ONE** is correct.

**DIRECTIONS for (Qs. 18 & 19) : Each of these questions contains two statements: Statement-1 (Assertion) and Statement-2 (Reason). Each of these questions has four alternative choices, only one of which is the correct answer. You have to select the correct choice.**

  (a)   Statement-1 is True, Statement-2 is True; Statement-2 is a correct explanation for Statement-1.

  (b)   Statement-1 is True, Statement-2 is True; Statement-2 is NOT a correct explanation for Statement-1.

  (c)   Statement -1 is True, Statement-2 is False.

  (d)   Statement -1 is False, Statement-2 is True.

**18.** **Statement 1 :** The number 'c' in the domain of function f such that either $f'(c) = 0$ or $f'(c)$ fails to exist imply that $f(x)$ has local extremum at x = c.

  **Statement 2 :** If $f(x)$ has local extremum at x = c then either $f'(c) = 0$ or $f'(c)$ does not exist.

**19.** **Statement -1 :** For the function $f(x) = x^x$, x = 1/e is a point of local minimum.

  **Statement -2 :** $f'(x)$ changes its sign from negative to positive in neighbourhood of x = 1/e.

---

**RESPONSE GRID**

15. (a)(b)(c)(d)    16. A - (p)(q)(r)(s)(t); B - (p)(q)(r)(s)(t); C - (p)(q)(r)(s)(t); D - (p)(q)(r)(s)(t); 17. A - (p)(q)(r)(s)(t); B - (p)(q)(r)(s)(t); C - (p)(q)(r)(s)(t)

18. (a)(b)(c)(d)    19. (a)(b)(c)(d)

## Section - VI - Integer Type

This section contains 5 questions. The answer to each of the questions is a single digit integer ranging from 0 to 9.

**20.** If $f(x) = 7e^{\sin^2 x} - e^{\cos^2 x} + 2$, then find the value of $\sqrt{7f_{min} + f_{max}}$ .

**21.** Let F (x) be a cubic polynomial defined by

$$F(x) = \frac{x^3}{3} + (a-3) x^2 + x - 13.$$

If the sum of all possible inegral value(s) of 'a' for which F (x) has negative point of local minimum in the interval [1, 100] is 14 $M^2$. Find M.

**22.** A bus contractor agrees to run special buses for the employees of ABC Co. Ltd. if atleast 200 persons travel by his buses. The fare per person is to be Rs. 10 per day if 200 travel and will be decreased for everybody by 2 paise per person over 200 that travels. If 10PQ passengers will give the contractor maximum daily revenue, where P and Q are prime numbers, then find the difference of P and Q.

**23.** Let S be the set of all x such that $x^4 - 10x^2 + 9 \le 0$. If the maximum value of $f(x) = x^3 - 3x$ on S is 2N, then find the value of N.

**24.** On the interval [0, 1] the function $x^{25}(1 - x)^{75}$ takes its maximum value at the point $\dfrac{A}{B}$. Find B.

| | | |
|---|---|---|
| **RESPONSE GRID** | 20. ⓪①②③④⑤⑥⑦⑧⑨ | 21. ⓪①②③④⑤⑥⑦⑧⑨ |
| | 22. ⓪①②③④⑤⑥⑦⑧⑨ | 23. ⓪①②③④⑤⑥⑦⑧⑨ |
| | 24. ⓪①②③④⑤⑥⑦⑧⑨ | |

## DAILY PRACTICE PROBLEM DPP 54 - MATHS

| Total Questions | 24 | Total Marks | 74 |
|---|---|---|---|
| Attempted | | Correct | |
| Incorrect | | Net Score | |
| Cut-off Score | 15 | Qualifying Score | 48 |
| Success Gap = Net Score – Qualifying Score | | | |

$$\text{Net Score} = \sum_{i=1}^{VI}\left[(\text{correct}_i \times MM_i) - (In_i - NM_i)\right]$$

*Space for Rough Work*

Name :        Date :

Start Time :        End Time :

## MATHEMATICS    M55

**SYLLABUS : Applications of Derivatives-4 :** Increasing and Decreasing function

**Max. Marks : 73**        **Time : 60 min.**

### GENERAL INSTRUCTIONS

- The Daily Practice Problem Sheet contains **24** Questions divided into 5 sections.

  Section I has **10** MCQ's with ONLY 1 correct option. 2 marks for correct answer and No negative marks.

  Section II has **5** MCQ's with 1 or MORE THAN 1 correct option. 4 marks for correct answer(s) and (–1) for wrong answer.
  Section III has **2** MCQ's with multiple matchings. 1 mark for the correct matching of each row & No negative marks.

  Section IV has **2** Assertion-Reason MCQ's with ONLY 1 correct option. 3 marks for correct and (–1) mark for wrong answer.
  Section V has **5** single digit integer answer questions. 4 marks for correct answer and (–1) for wrong answer.

- No mark will be given/ deducted if no bubble is filled. Keep a timer in front and stop immediately at the end of 60 min.
- You have to evaluate your Response Grids yourself with the help of Solution Booklet.
- The sheet follows a particular syllabus. Do not attempt the sheet before you have completed your preparation for that syllabus. Refer syllabus sheet in the starting of the book for the syllabus of all the DPP sheets.
- After completing the sheet check your answers with the solution booklet and complete the Result Grid. Finally spend time to analyse your performance and revise the areas which emerge out as weak in your evaluation.

## Section - I - Straight Objective Type

This section contains 10 multiple choice questions. Each question has 4 choices (a), (b), (c) and (d), out of which **ONLY ONE** is correct.

**1.** The interval of decrease of the function

$$f(x) = x^2 \log 27 - 6x \log 27 + (3x^2 - 18x + 24)\log(x^2 - 6x + 8)$$

is   $[\text{where } \log = \log_e]$

(a)   $(3 - \sqrt{1 + 1/3e}, 2) \cup (4, 3 + \sqrt{1 + 1/3e})$

(b)   $(3 - \sqrt{1 + 1/3e},\ 3 + \sqrt{1 + 1/3e})$

(c)   $(-\infty,\ 3 - \sqrt{1 + 1/3e}) \cup (3,\ 4 + \sqrt{1 + 1/3e})$

(d)   None of these.

**2.** A function $y = f(x)$ is given by $x = \dfrac{1}{1 + t^2}$

and $y = \dfrac{1}{t(1 + t^2)}$ for all $t > 0$ then $f$ is :

(a)   increasing in $(0, 3/2)$ & decreasing in $(3/2, \infty)$

(b)   increasing in $(0, 1)$

(c)   increasing in $(0, \infty)$

(d)   decreasing in $(0, 1)$

**3.** If $f(x) = \dfrac{x}{\sin x}$ and $g(x) = \dfrac{x}{\tan x}$, where $0 < x \leq 1$, then in this interval

(a)   both f(x) and g(x) are increasing functions

(b)   both f(x) and g(x) are decreasing functions

(c)   f(x) is an increasing function

(d)   g(x) is an increasing function

**4.** If $f(x) = xe^{x(x-1)}$, then f(x) is

(a)   increasing on $[-1/2, 1]$   (b)   decreasing on R

(c)   increasing on R      (d)   decreasing on $[-1/2, 1]$

**5.** The function defined by $f(x) = (x + 2)\,e^{-x}$ is

(a)   decreasing for all x

(b)   decreasing in $(-\infty, -1)$ and increasing in $(-1, \infty)$

(c)   increasing for all x

(d)   decreasing in $(-1, \infty)$ and increasing in $(-\infty, -1)$

---

**RESPONSE GRID**   **1.** (a)(b)(c)(d)   **2.** (a)(b)(c)(d)   **3.** (a)(b)(c)(d)   **4.** (a)(b)(c)(d)   **5.** (a)(b)(c)(d)

**6.** If, a, b, c are real numbers and $a^2 + b^2 + c^2 = k$ then the

function $f(x) = \begin{vmatrix} x+a^2 & ab & ac \\ ab & x+b^2 & bc \\ ac & bc & x+c^2 \end{vmatrix}$ is

(a) increasing in $\left(-\dfrac{2k}{3}, 0\right)$

(b) increasing in $\left[-\dfrac{k}{3}, 0\right]$

(c) decreasing in $\left(-\dfrac{2k}{3}, 0\right)$

(d) decreasing in $\left(-\infty, \dfrac{2k}{3}\right) \cup (0, \infty)$

**7.** Let $f(x) = \begin{cases} xe^{ax} & ; & x \leq 0 \\ x + ax^2 - x^3 & ; & x > 0 \end{cases}$

where a is positive constant. The interval in which f'(x) is increasing is

(a) $(-\infty, \infty)$

(b) $\left(-\infty, \dfrac{-2}{a}\right) \cup \left(\dfrac{a}{3}, \infty\right)$

(c) $\left(-\dfrac{2}{a}, \dfrac{a}{3}\right)$

(d) $(0, \infty)$

**8.** The value of a for which the function $f(x) = \sin x - \cos x - ax + b$ decreases for all real values of x, is given by

(a) $a \geq \sqrt{2}$    (b) $a \geq 1$    (c) $a < \sqrt{2}$    (d) $a < 1$

**9.** If $f''(x) > 0$ and $f'(1) = 0$ such that $g(x) = f(\cot^2 x + 2\cot x + 2)$ where $0 < x < \pi$ then the interval in which g(x) is decreasing is

(a) $(0, \pi)$   (b) $\left(\dfrac{\pi}{2}, \pi\right)$   (c) $\left(\dfrac{3\pi}{4}, \pi\right)$   (d) $\left(0, \dfrac{3\pi}{4}\right)$

**10.** Let f and g be increasing and decreasing functions, respectively in $[0, \infty)$. Let $h(x) = f(g(x))$. If $h(0) = 0$, then $h(x) - h(1)$ is

(a) always zero

(b) always negative

(c) always positive

(d) strictly increasing

## Section - II - Multiple Correct Answer Type

This section contains 5 multiple correct answer(s) type questions. Each question has 4 choices (a), (b), (c) and (d), out of which **ONE OR MORE** is/are correct.

**11.** Let $h(x) = f(x) - (f(x))^2 + (f(x))^3$ for every real number x. Then

(a) h is increasing whenever f is increasing

(b) h is increasing whenever f is decreasing

(c) h is decreasing whenever f is decreasing

(d) nothing can be said in general.

**12.** The interval of increase of the function $f(x) = x - e^x + \tan(2\pi/7)$ is

(a) $(0, \infty)$   (b) $(-\infty, 0)$   (c) $(1, \infty)$   (d) $(-\infty, -1)$

**13.** If $y = 2x + \cot^{-1}x + \log\left[\sqrt{1+x^2} - x\right]$, then y

(a) Increases in $[0, \infty)$

(b) Decreases in $[0, \infty)$

(c) Neither increases nor decreases in $[0, \infty)$

(d) Increases in $(-\infty, 0]$

**14.** The function $f(x) = 2\log(x-2) - x^2 + 4x + 1$ increases in the interval

(a) $(1, 2)$   (b) $(2, 3)$   (c) $(5/2, 3)$   (d) $(2, 4)$

**15.** Let $f'(\sin x) < 0$ and $f''(\sin x) > 0 \,\forall\, x \in \left(0, \dfrac{\pi}{2}\right)$ and $g(x) = f(\sin x) + f(\cos x)$, then

(a) g(x) increases, if $x \in \left(0, \dfrac{\pi}{4}\right)$

(b) g(x) decereases, if $x \in \left(0, \dfrac{\pi}{4}\right)$

| RESPONSE GRID | | | | | |
|---|---|---|---|---|---|
| | 6. ⓐⓑⓒⓓ | 7. ⓐⓑⓒⓓ | 8. ⓐⓑⓒⓓ | 9. ⓐⓑⓒⓓ | 10. ⓐⓑⓒⓓ |
| | 11. ⓐⓑⓒⓓ | 12. ⓐⓑⓒⓓ | 13. ⓐⓑⓒⓓ | 14. ⓐⓑⓒⓓ | 15. ⓐⓑⓒⓓ |

(c)  $g(x)$ increases, if $x \in \left( \dfrac{\pi}{4}, \dfrac{\pi}{2} \right)$

(d)  $g(x)$ increases, if $x \in \left( 0, \dfrac{\pi}{2} \right)$

## Section - III - Matrix-Match Type

This section contains 2 questions. It contains statements given in two columns, which have to be matched. Statements in Column I are labelled as A, B, C and D whereas statements in Column II are labelled as p, q, r and s. The answers to these questions have to be appropriately bubbled as illustrated in the following example. If the correct matches are A-p, A-r, B-p, B-s, C-r, C-s and D-q, then the correctly bubbled matrix will look like the following :

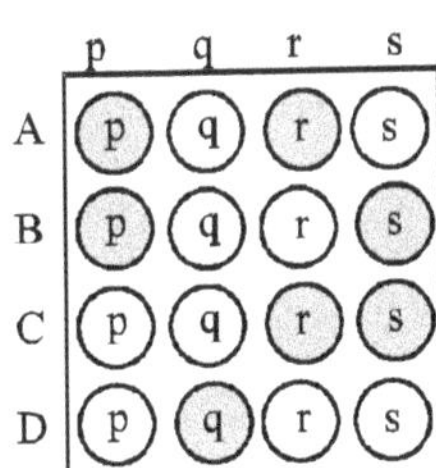

**16.**

| Column -I | Column -II |
|---|---|
| (A)  Let $f''(x) > 0 \ \forall \ x \in R$ and $g(x) = f(4-x) + f(2+x))$ then $g(x)$ increases if $x$ belongs to the interval | p.  $(-\infty, -2)$ |
| (B)  The equation $x^3 - 3x + a = 0$ will have exactly one real root if a belongs to the interval | q.  $(-\infty, -1]$ |
| (C)  If $f(x) = \cos x + a^2 x + b$ is an increasing function for all values of x, then a belongs to the interval | r.  $[0, \infty)$ |
| (D)  If $f(x) = 2e^x - ae^{-x} + (2a+1)$ $x - 3$ is increasing for all | s.  $[1, \infty)$ |

values of x, then a belongs to the interval  t.  $(2, \infty)$

**17.**

| Columns I | Column II |
|---|---|
| (A)  The function $f(x) = \dfrac{x}{(1+x^2)}$ decreases in the interval | p.  $(-\infty, -1)$ |
| (B)  The function $f(x) = \tan^{-1} x - x$ decreases in the interval | q.  $(-\infty, 0)$ |
| (C)  The function $f(x) = x - e^x + \tan\left( \dfrac{2\pi}{7} \right)$ increases in the interval | r.  $(0, \infty)$ |
| | s.  $(1, \infty)$ |
| | t.  $(-\infty, \infty)$ |

## Section - IV - Reasoning Type

This section contains 2 reasoning type questions. Each question has 4 choices (a), (b), (c) and (d) out of which **ONLY ONE** is correct.

**DIRECTIONS for (Qs. 18 & 19) :** Each of these questions contains two statements: Statement-1 (Assertion) and Statement-2 (Reason). Each of these questions has four alternative choices, only one of which is the correct answer. You have to select the correct choice.

(a)  Statement-1 is True, Statement-2 is True; Statement-2 is a correct explanation for Statement-1.

(b)  Statement-1 is True, Statement-2 is True; Statement-2 is NOT a correct explanation for Statement-1.

(c)  Statement-1 is True, Statement-2 is False.

(d)  Statement-1 is False, Statement-2 is True.

**18.**  **Statement -1:** If $f(0) = 0$, $f'(x) = \ln (x + \sqrt{1+x^2}\,)$, then $f(x)$ is positive for all $x \in R_0$

**Statement-2 :** $f(x)$ is increasing for $x > 0$ and decreasing for $x < 0$.

**19.**  **Statement -1:** $f: R \to R$ be a function such that $f(x) = x^3 + x^2 + 3x + \sin x$. Then f is one-one.

**Statement -2:** $f(x)$ is neither increasing nor decreasing.



*Space for Rough Work*

## Section - V - Integer Type

This section contains 5 questions. The answer to each of the questions is a single digit integer ranging from 0 to 9.

**20.** Let $F(x) = \begin{cases} -2x + \log_{1/2}(k^2 - 6k + 8), & -2 \le x < -1 \\ x^3 + 3x^2 + 4x + 1, & -1 \le x \le 3 \end{cases}$

If the sum of all possible positive integer(s) in the range of k such that $F(x)$ has the smallest value at $x = -1$ is 4M, find the value of M

**21.** Let $f(x)$ be a function such that $f'(x) = \log_{1/3}(\log_3(\sin x + a))$. If $f(x)$ is decreasing for all real values of $x$, then $a \in (P, \infty)$. Find the value of P.

**22.** The set of positive values of the parameter 'a' for each of which the function $f(x) = \sin 2x - 8(a+1)\sin x - (4a^2 + 8a - 14)x$ is monotonic increasing in $R$ and has no critical points are $\left(P, \sqrt{Q} - R\right)$. Find $P + Q + R$.

**23.** If $f(x) = x.e^{x(1-x)}$, then $f(x)$ is increasing on $\left[-\dfrac{P}{Q}, R\right]$. Find the value of $\dfrac{P + Q + R}{4}$.

**24.** The length of a longest interval in which the function $3\sin x - 4\sin^3 x$ is increasing, is $\dfrac{\pi}{Y}$. Find Y.

<table>
<tr><td rowspan="3">RESPONSE GRID</td><td>20. ⓪①②③④⑤⑥⑦⑧⑨</td><td>21. ⓪①②③④⑤⑥⑦⑧⑨</td></tr>
<tr><td>22. ⓪①②③④⑤⑥⑦⑧⑨</td><td>23. ⓪①②③④⑤⑥⑦⑧⑨</td></tr>
<tr><td>24. ⓪①②③④⑤⑥⑦⑧⑨</td><td></td></tr>
</table>

## DAILY PRACTICE PROBLEM DPP 55 - MATHS

| | | | |
|---|---|---|---|
| Total Questions | 24 | Total Marks | 73 |
| Attempted | | Correct | |
| Incorrect | | Net Score | |
| Cut-off Score | 15 | Qualifying Score | 47 |
| Success Gap = Net Score – Qualifying Score | | | |

$$\text{Net Score} = \sum_{i=1}^{VI}\left[(\text{correct}_i \times MM_i) - (In_i - NM_i)\right]$$

*Space for Rough Work*

Name :         Date :

Start Time :         End Time :

# MATHEMATICS    M56

**SYLLABUS : Applications of Derivatives-5 : Rolle's Theorem, Lagrange's mean value theorem**

## Max. Marks : 66        Time : 60 min.

### GENERAL INSTRUCTIONS

- The Daily Practice Problem Sheet contains **21** Questions divided into 6 sections.
  Section I has **6** MCQ's with ONLY 1 correct option. 2 marks for correct answer and No negative marks.
  Section II has **4** MCQ's with 1 or MORE THAN 1 correct option. 4 marks for correct answer(s) and (–1) for wrong answer.
  Section III has **1** PASSAGE with **3** MCQ's with ONLY 1 correct option. 3 marks for correct and (–1) mark for wrong answer.
  Section IV has **1** MCQ's with multiple matchings. 1 mark for the correct matching of each row & No negative marks.
  Section V has **2** Assertion-Reason MCQ's with ONLY 1 correct option. 3 marks for correct and (–1) mark for wrong answer.
  Section VI has **5** single digit integer answer questions. 4 marks for correct answer and (–1) for wrong answer.
- No mark will be given/ deducted if no bubble is filled. Keep a timer in front and stop immediately at the end of 60 min.
- You have to evaluate your Response Grids yourself with the help of Solution Booklet.
- The sheet follows a particular syllabus. Do not attempt the sheet before you have completed your preparation for that syllabus. Refer syllabus sheet in the starting of the book for the syllabus of all the DPP sheets.
- After completing the sheet check your answers with the solution booklet and complete the Result Grid. Finally spend time to analyse your performance and revise the areas which emerge out as weak in your evaluation.

## Section - I - Straight Objective Type

This section contains 6 multiple choice questions. Each question has 4 choices (a), (b), (c) and (d), out of which **ONLY ONE** is correct.

**1.** Let a, b, c, d are non-zero real numbers such that $6a + 4b + 3c + 3d = 0$, then the equation $ax^3 + bx^2 + cx + d = 0$ has–

(a) atleast one root in $[-2, 0]$

(b) atleast one root in $[0, 2]$

(c) atleast two root in $[-2, 2]$

(d) no root in $[-2, 2]$

**2.** Let $f(x)$ and $g(x)$ be two differentiable function in R and $f(2) = 8$, $g(2) = 0$, $f(4) = 10$ and $g(4) = 8$ then

(a) $g'(x) > 4f'(x) \ \forall x \in (2, 4)$

(b) $3g'(x) = 4f'(x)$ for at least one $x \in (2, 4)$

(c) $g(x) > f(x) \ \forall x \in (2, 4)$

(d) $g'(x) = 4f'(x)$ for at least one $x \in (2, 4)$

**3.** Let $f(x)$ and $g(x)$ are two function which are defined and differentiable for all $x \geq x_0$. If $f(x_0) = g(x_0)$ and $f'(x) > g'(x)$

for all $x > x_0$ then

(a) $f(x) < g(x)$ for some $x > x_0$

(b) $f(x) = g(x)$ for some $x > x_0$

(c) $f(x) > g(x)$ only for some $x > x_0$

(d) $f(x) > g(x)$ for all $x > x_0$

**4.** If the function $f(x) = ax^3 + bx^2 + 11x - 6$ satisfies the conditions of Rolle's theorem in $[1, 3]$ and $f'\left(2 + \dfrac{1}{\sqrt{3}}\right) = 0$, then the values of a, b are respectively

(a) $1, -6$    (b) $-2, 1$    (c) $-1, 1/2$    (d) $-1, 6$

**5.** In the Mean-Value theorem $\dfrac{f(b) - f(a)}{b - a} = f'(c)$, if $a = 0$, $b = \dfrac{1}{2}$ and $f(x) = x(x-1)(x-2)$, the value of c is

(a) $1 - \dfrac{\sqrt{15}}{6}$    (b) $1 + \sqrt{15}$    (c) $1 - \dfrac{\sqrt{21}}{6}$    (d) $1 + \sqrt{21}$

| RESPONSE GRID | 1. ⓐⓑⓒⓓ | 2. ⓐⓑⓒⓓ | 3. ⓐⓑⓒⓓ | 4. ⓐⓑⓒⓓ | 5. ⓐⓑⓒⓓ |
|---|---|---|---|---|---|

**6.** From mean value theorem $f(b) - f(a) = (b-a) f'(x_1)$, $a < x_1 < b$ if $f(x) = \dfrac{1}{2}$, then $x_1 =$

(a) $\sqrt{ab}$ (b) $\dfrac{a+b}{2}$ (c) $\dfrac{2ab}{a+b}$ (d) $\dfrac{b-a}{b+a}$

## Section - II - Multiple Correct Answer Type

This section contains 4 multiple correct answer(s) type questions. Each question has 4 choices (a), (b), (c) and (d), out of which **ONE OR MORE** is/are correct.

**7.** In which of the following cases the given equations has atleast one root in the indicated interval ?

(a) $x - \cos x = 0$ in $(0, \pi/2)$

(b) $x + \sin x = 1$ in $(0, \pi/6)$

(c) $\dfrac{a}{x-1} + \dfrac{b}{x-3} = 0$, $a, b > 0$ in $(1, 3)$

(d) $f(x) - g(x) = 0$ in $(a, b)$ where $f$ and $g$ are continuous on $[a, b]$ and $f(a) > g(a)$ and $f(b) < g(b)$

**8.** If Rolle's theorem is applicable to the function $f$ defined by

$$f(x) = \begin{cases} ax^2 + b, & |x| < 1 \\ 1, & |x| = 1 \\ \dfrac{c}{|x|}, & |x| > 1 \end{cases}$$

in the interval $[-3, 3]$, then which of the following alternative(s) is/are correct –

(a) $a + b + c = 2$  (b) $|a| + |b| + |c| = 3$

(c) $2a + 4b + 3c = 8$  (d) $4a^2 + 4b^2 + 5c^2 = 15$

**9.** Consider $f(x) = |1-x|$, $1 \leq x \leq 2$ and $g(x) = f(x) + b \sin \dfrac{\pi}{2} x$, $1 \leq x \leq 2$ then which of the following are incorrect?

(a) Rolles theorem is applicable to both $f$, $g$ and $b = 3/2$

(b) LMVT is not applicable to $f$ and Rolles theorem if applicable to $g$ with $b = 1/2$

(c) LMVT is applicable to $f$ and Rolles theorem is applicable to $g$ with $b = 1$

(d) Rolles theorem is not applicable to both $f$, $g$ for any real $b$.

**10.** Given that $f(x)$ is continuously differentiable on $a \leq x \leq b$ where $a < b, f(a) < 0$ and $f(b) > 0$, which of the following are always true?

(a) $f(x)$ is bounded on $a \leq x \leq b$.

(b) The equation $f(x) = 0$ has at least one solution in $a < x < b$.

(c) The maximum and minimum values of $f(x)$ on $a \leq x \leq b$ occur at points where $f'(c) = 0$.

(d) There is at least one point $c$ with $a < c < b$ where $f'(c) > 0$.

## Section - III - Linked Comprehension Type

This section contains 1 paragraph. Based upon the paragraph, 3 multiple choice questions have to be answered. Each question has 4 choices (a), (b), (c) and (d), out of which **ONLY ONE** is correct.

**Rolle's Theorem :** If a function $f$ with domain $[a, b]$ satisfies the following conditions

(i) $f$ is continuous in $(a, b)$

(ii) $f$ is derivable in $(a, b)$

(iii) $f(a) = f(b)$

then in the interval $(a, b)$, there exists at least one value $c$ of $x$ such that $f'(c) = 0$

**Lagrange's Theorem :** If a function $f$ with domain $[a, b]$ satisfies the following conditions

(i) $f$ is continuous in $[a, b]$

(ii) $f$ is derivable in $(a, b)$

then in the interval $(a, b)$, there exists at least one value $c$ of $x$ such that $\dfrac{f(b) - f(a)}{b - a} = f'(c)$

**11.** If $\alpha$ and $\beta$ are any two roots of equation $e^x \cos x = 1$, then the equation $e^x \sin x - 1 = 0$ has

(a) exactly one roots in $(\alpha, \beta)$

(b) exactly two roots in $(\alpha, \beta)$

(c) at least one root in $(\alpha, \beta)$

(d) no root in $(\alpha, \beta)$

| **RESPONSE GRID** | **6.** ⓐⓑ©ⓓ | **7.** ⓐⓑ©ⓓ | **8.** ⓐⓑ©ⓓ |
| --- | --- | --- | --- |
| | **9.** ⓐⓑ©ⓓ | **10.** ⓐⓑ©ⓓ | **11.** ⓐⓑ©ⓓ |

**12.** Which of the following inequalities are true?

(a)   $|\tan^{-1}x - \tan^{-1}y| \le |x-y| \;\forall\; x,y \in R$

(b)   $|\tan^{-1}x - \tan^{-1}y| \ge |x-y| \;\forall\; x,y \in R$

(c)   $|\sin x - \sin y| \le |x-y| \;\forall\; x,y \in R$

(d)   Both 'a' and 'c'

**13.** If $f'$ and $g'$ exist for all $x \in [a,b]$ and if $g'(x) \ne 0 \;\forall\; x \in (a,b)$ then for some $c \in (a,b)$, $\dfrac{f(c)-f(a)}{g(b)-g(c)} =$

(a)   $f'(c)g'(c)$

(b)   $\dfrac{f'(c)}{g'(c)}$

(c)   $f'(c) - \dfrac{1}{g'(c)}$

(d)   $\dfrac{f(a)f'(c)}{g(b)g'(c)}$

## Section - IV - Matrix-Match Type

This section contains 1 question. It contains statements given in two columns, which have to be matched. Statements in Column I are labelled as A, B, C and D whereas statements in Column II are labelled as p, q, r and s. The answers to these questions have to be appropriately bubbled as illustrated in the following example. If the correct matches are A-p, A-r, B-p, B-s, C-r, C-s and D-q, then the correctly bubbled matrix will look like the following :

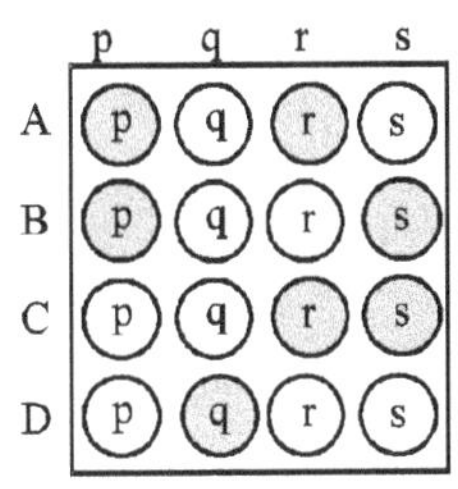

**14.**    **Column-I**          **Column-II**

(A)   The Rolle's theorem in

(p)   $f(x) = \begin{cases} \left(\dfrac{1}{2}-x\right)^2, & x > \dfrac{1}{2} \\[2mm] \left(\dfrac{1}{2}-x\right), & x \le \dfrac{1}{2} \end{cases}$

$[-1, 1]$ does not hold, then

(q)   $f(x) = |x|$

(B)   The LMVT in $[0, 1]$ does not hold, then

(r)   $f(x) = \begin{cases} 1, & 0 \le x < \dfrac{1}{2} \\[2mm] 2, & \dfrac{1}{2} \le x \le 1 \end{cases}$

(C)   The Rolle's theorem in $[0, 1]$ does not hold, then

(s)   $f(x) = \ln|x|$

(t)   $f(x) = x^2 + x + 1$

## Section - V - Reasoning Type

This section contains 2 reasoning type questions. Each question has 4 choices (a), (b), (c) and (d) out of which **ONLY ONE** is correct.

**DIRECTIONS for (Qs. 15 & 16) : Each of these questions contains two statements: Statement-1 (Assertion) and Statement-2 (Reason). Each of these questions has four alternative choices, only one of which is the correct answer. You have to select the correct choice.**

(a)   Statement-1 is True, Statement-2 is True; Statement-2 is a correct explanation for Statement-1.

(b)   Statement-1 is True, Statement-2 is True; Statement-2 is NOT a correct explanation for Statement-1.

(c)   Statement-1 is True, Statement-2 is False.

(d)   Statement-1 is False, Statement-2 is True.

**15.**   **Statement 1 :** If Rolle's theorem be applied for $f(x)$, then LMVT is also applied for $f(x)$.

**Statement 2 :** Both Rolle's theorem and LMVT cannot be applied for $f(x) = |\sin|x| | \ln\left[-\dfrac{\pi}{4},\dfrac{\pi}{4}\right]$

**16.**   **Statement 1 :** If $f(x) = x(x+3)e^{-x/2}$, then Rolle's theorem applies for $f(x)$ in $[-3, 0]$.

**Statement 2 :** LMVT is applied for $f(x) = x(x+3)e^{-x/2}$ in any interval.

<table>
<tr><td rowspan="4">RESPONSE GRID</td><td>12. ⓐⓑⓒⓓ    13. ⓐⓑⓒⓓ</td></tr>
<tr><td>14. A - ⓟⓠⓡⓢⓣ; B - ⓟⓠⓡⓢⓣ; C - ⓟⓠⓡⓢⓣ</td></tr>
<tr><td>15. ⓐⓑⓒⓓ    16. ⓐⓑⓒⓓ</td></tr>
</table>

## Section - VI - Integer Type

This section contains 5 questions. The answer to each of the questions is a single digit integer ranging from 0 to 9.

17. Suppose that $f(0) = -3$ and $f'(x) \leq 5$ for all values of x. Then find the largest value for which $f(2)$ can attain ?

18. Suppose that $f$ is differentiable for all x and that $f'(x) \leq 2$ for all x. If $f(1) = 2$ and $f(4) = 8$ then find the value of $f(2)$.

19. Let f(x) satisfy all the conditions of mean value theorem in [0, 2], If $f(0) = 0$ and $|f'(x)| \leq \dfrac{1}{2}$ for all x, in [0, 2] then $|f(x)| \leq P$. Find P.

20. The abscissa of the points of the curve $y = x^3$ in the interval $[-2, 2]$ where the slope of the tangents can be obtained by mean value theorem for the interval $[-2, 2]$, are $\pm \dfrac{A}{\sqrt{B}}$. Find the value of $A + B$.

21. The function $f(x) = x(x + 3)e^{-(1/2)x}$ satisfies all the conditions of Rolle's theorem in $[-3, 0]$. Find the value of $-c$.

<table>
<tr><td rowspan="3">RESPONSE GRID</td><td>17. ⓪①②③④⑤⑥⑦⑧⑨</td><td>18. ⓪①②③④⑤⑥⑦⑧⑨</td></tr>
<tr><td>19. ⓪①②③④⑤⑥⑦⑧⑨</td><td>20. ⓪①②③④⑤⑥⑦⑧⑨</td></tr>
<tr><td>21. ⓪①②③④⑤⑥⑦⑧⑨</td><td></td></tr>
</table>

## DAILY PRACTICE PROBLEM DPP 56 - MATHS

| Total Questions | 21 | Total Marks | 66 |
|---|---|---|---|
| Attempted | | Correct | |
| Incorrect | | Net Score | |
| Cut-off Score | 13 | Qualifying Score | 43 |
| Success Gap = Net Score − Qualifying Score | | | |

$$\textbf{Net Score} = \sum_{i=1}^{VI} \left[ (\textbf{correct}_i \times MM_i) - (In_i - NM_i) \right]$$

**Name :**

**Date :**

**Start Time :**

**End Time :**

# MATHEMATICS    M57

**SYLLABUS : Indefinite Integral-1 : Fundamental integration**

## Max. Marks : 62

## Time : 60 min.

### GENERAL INSTRUCTIONS

- The Daily Practice Problem Sheet contains **24** Questions divided into 3 sections.

  Section I has **17** MCQ's with ONLY 1 correct option. 2 marks for correct answer and No negative marks.

  Section II has **2** MCQ's with 1 or MORE THAN 1 correct option. 4 marks for correct answer(s) and (–1) for wrong answer.
  Section III has **5** single digit integer answer questions. 4 marks for correct answer and (–1) for wrong answer.
- No mark will be given/ deducted if no bubble is filled. Keep a timer in front and stop immediately at the end of 60 min.
- You have to evaluate your Response Grids yourself with the help of Solution Booklet.
- The sheet follows a particular syllabus. Do not attempt the sheet before you have completed your preparation for that syllabus. Refer syllabus sheet in the starting of the book for the syllabus of all the DPP sheets.
- After completing the sheet check your answers with the solution booklet and complete the Result Grid. Finally spend time to analyse your performance and revise the areas which emerge out as weak in your evaluation.

---

## Section - I - Straight Objective Type

This section contains 17 multiple choice questions. Each question has 4 choices (a), (b), (c) and (d), out of which **ONLY ONE** is correct.

**1.** The integral $\int\left(3x^2 \tan\dfrac{1}{x} - x\sec^2\dfrac{1}{x}\right)dx$ equals to

  (a) $x\left(\tan\dfrac{1}{x} + \sec\dfrac{1}{x}\right) + c$    (b) $x^2\tan\dfrac{1}{x} - \sec\dfrac{1}{x} + c$

  (c) $x^3\tan\dfrac{1}{x} + c$    (d) $(x^3 - 1)\tan\dfrac{1}{x} + c$

**2.** Given $f(x) = \begin{vmatrix} 0 & x^2 - \sin x & \cos x - 2 \\ \sin x - x^2 & 0 & 1 - 2x \\ 2 - \cos x & 2x - 1 & 0 \end{vmatrix}$, $\int f(x)\,dx$ is equal to

**(a)** $\dfrac{x^3}{3} - x^2\sin x + \sin 2x + C$

**(b)** $\dfrac{x^3}{3} - x^2\sin x - \cos 2x + C$

**(c)** $\dfrac{x^3}{3} - x^2\cos x - \cos 2x + C$

**(d)** none of these

**3.** $\int\left(1 + x + \dfrac{x^2}{2!} + \dfrac{x^3}{3!} + \ldots\ldots\ldots\right)dx =$

  (a) $-e^x + C$    (b) $e^x + C$    (c) $e^{-x} + C$    (d) $-e^{-x} + C$

**4.** $\int(1 + 2x + 3x^2 + 4x^3 + \ldots.)dx =$

  (a) $(1 + x)^{-1} + C$    (b) $(1 - x)^{-1} + C$

  (c) $(1 - x)^{-1} - 1 + C$    (d) None ot these

---

| RESPONSE GRID | 1. ⓐⓑⓒⓓ | 2. ⓐⓑⓒⓓ | 3. ⓐⓑⓒⓓ | 4. ⓐⓑⓒⓓ |
|---|---|---|---|---|

**5.** $\int \dfrac{\cos 2x - \cos 2\alpha}{\cos x - \cos \alpha}\, dx =$

(a) $2(\sin x + x \cos \alpha) + C$

(b) $2(\sin x + x \sin \alpha) + C$

(c) $2(-\sin x + x\cos \alpha) + C$

(d) $-2(\sin x + \sin \alpha) + C$

**6.** $\int \{1 + 2\tan x(\tan x + \sec x)\}^{1/2}\, dx$ is equal to

(a) $\log \sec x \,(\sec x - \tan x) + C$

(b) $\log \operatorname{cosec} x \,(\sec x + \tan x) + C$

(c) $\log \sec x\,(\sec x + \tan x) + C$

(d) $\log(\sec x + \tan x) + C$

**7.** $\int \log_{10} x\, dx =$

(a) $x\log_{10}x + C$

(b) $x(\log_{10} x + \log_{10} e) + C$

(c) $\log_{10}x + C$

(d) $x(\log_{10} x - \log_{10} e) + C$

**8.** $\int \tan^{-1}\left(\dfrac{\cos 2x}{1 + \sin 2x}\right) dx$ is equal to

(a) $\dfrac{\pi}{4}x - \dfrac{x^2}{2} + C$

(b) $-\dfrac{\pi}{4}x + \dfrac{x^2}{2} + C$

(c) $-x^2 + C$

(d) $x^2 + C$

**9.** If $f(0) = f'(0) = 0$ and $f''(x) = \tan^2 x$ then $f(x)$ is equal to

(a) $\log \sec x - \dfrac{1}{2}x^2$

(b) $\log \cos x + \dfrac{1}{2}x^2$

(c) $\log \sec x + \dfrac{1}{2}x^2$

(d) None

**10.** If $\int \dfrac{\sin^8 x - \cos^8 x}{1 - 2\sin^2 x \cos^2 x}\, dx = A \sin 2x + B$, then

(a) $A = -\dfrac{1}{2}$

(b) $A = \dfrac{1}{2}$

(c) $A = -1$

(d) $A = 1$

**11.** $\int \dfrac{\cos 5x + \cos 4x}{1 - 2\cos 3x}\, dx$ is equal to

(a) $\dfrac{\sin 5x}{5} - \dfrac{\sin 4x}{4} + C$

(b) $\sin x + \sin 2x + C$

(c) $\dfrac{\cos 3x}{3} - \sin x + C$

(d) $-\sin x - \dfrac{\sin 2x}{2} + C$

**12.** $\int \tan x \tan 2x \tan 3x\, dx$ is equal to

(a) $\log \sin 3x + \log \sin 2x + \log \sin x + C$

(b) $\dfrac{1}{3}\log|\sec 3x| - \dfrac{1}{2}\log|\sec 2x| - \log|\sec x| + C$

(c) $\log(\sec 3x \sec 2x \sec x) + C$

(d) None

**13.** If $0 < x < \dfrac{\pi}{2}$ then $\int \sqrt{1 + 2\tan x(\tan x + \sec x)}\, dx$ equals to

(a) $\dfrac{1}{2}\ln \sec x + C$

(b) $\ln \tan x\,(\sec x + \tan x) + C$

(c) $\ln \sec x\,(\sec x + \tan x) + C$

(d) $\dfrac{1}{2}\{\tan x\,(\sec x + \tan x)\}^{-1/2} + C$

| RESPONSE | 5. ⓐⓑⓒⓓ | 6. ⓐⓑⓒⓓ | 7. ⓐⓑⓒⓓ | 8. ⓐⓑⓒⓓ | 9. ⓐⓑⓒⓓ |
|---|---|---|---|---|---|
| GRID | 10. ⓐⓑⓒⓓ | 11. ⓐⓑⓒⓓ | 12. ⓐⓑⓒⓓ | 13. ⓐⓑⓒⓓ | |

*Space for Rough Work*

**14.** $\int \dfrac{\sin^8 x - \cos^8 x}{1 - 2\sin^2 x \cos^2 x} dx =$

(a) $\dfrac{1}{2}\sin 2x + C$

(b) $-\dfrac{1}{2}\sin 2x + C$

(c) $-\dfrac{1}{2}\sin x + C$

(d) $-\sin^2 x + C$

**15.** The value of $\int \sqrt{(1+\sin 2x)}\, dx$ is –

(a) $-\cos x + \sin x + C$

(b) $\cos x - \sin x + C$

(c) $-\cos x - \sin x + C$

(d) None of these

**16.** The value of $\int \dfrac{dx}{\sin^2 x \cos^2 x}$ is –

(a) $-\tan x - \cot x + C$

(b) $\tan x + \cot x + C$

(c) $\tan x - \cot x + C$

(d) None of these

**17.** The value of $\int \left( e^{x\log a} + e^{a\log x} + e^{a\log a} \right) dx$ is –

(a) $\dfrac{a^x}{\log a} - \dfrac{x^{a+1}}{a+1} + a^a . x + C$

(b) $\dfrac{a^x}{\log a} + \dfrac{x^{a+1}}{a+1} + a^a . x + C$

(c) $\dfrac{a^x}{\log a} + \dfrac{x^{a+1}}{a+1} - a^a . x + C$

(d) None of these

## Section - II - Multiple Correct Answer Type

This section contains 2 multiple correct answer(s) type questions. Each question has 4 choices (a), (b), (c) and (d), out of which **ONE OR MORE** is/are correct.

**18.** $\int \sqrt{\dfrac{1-x}{1+x}}\; dx$ is equal to

(a) $\sin^{-1} x + \sqrt{1-x^2} + C$

(b) $-\cos^{-1} x + \sqrt{1-x^2} + C$

(c) $\sin^{-1} x - 2\sqrt{1-x^2} + C$

(d) $2\sin^{-1} x - \sqrt{1-x^2} + C$

**19.** If $\int \dfrac{\sin x}{\sin(x-\alpha)} dx = Ax + B \ln \sin(x-\alpha) + C$, then

(a) $A = \sin \alpha$

(b) $B = \cos \alpha$

(c) $A = \cos \alpha$

(d) $B = \sin \alpha$

## Section - III - Integer Type

This section contains 5 questions. The answer to each of the questions is a single digit integer ranging from 0 to 9.

**20.** If $\int f(x)\cos x\, dx = \dfrac{1}{2} f^2(x) + C$, then $f(x)$ can be P sin x.

Find the value of P.

<table>
<tr><td rowspan="2">RESPONSE GRID</td><td>14. ⓐⓑⓒⓓ</td><td>15. ⓐⓑⓒⓓ</td><td>16. ⓐⓑⓒⓓ</td><td>17. ⓐⓑⓒⓓ</td><td>18. ⓐⓑⓒⓓ</td></tr>
<tr><td>19. ⓐⓑⓒⓓ</td><td colspan="4">20. ⓪①②③④⑤⑥⑦⑧⑨</td></tr>
</table>

*Space for Rough Work*

**21.** If $\int x^{51}(\tan^{-1}x + \cot^{-1}x)\,dx = \dfrac{x^M}{N}\,(P\tan^{-1}x + Q\cot^{-1}x) + C.$ Find the value of $\dfrac{M}{N} + P + Q.$

**22.** If $\int \dfrac{\cos 4x + 1}{\cot x - \tan x}\,dx = K\cos 4x + C,$ then find the value of $-8K.$

**23.** The value of $\int \sin^{-1}(\cos x)\,dx = \dfrac{-1}{K}\left(\dfrac{\pi}{2} - x\right)^2 + C.$ Find the value of K.

**24.** The value of $\int \left(\dfrac{4 + 3\sin x}{\cos^2 x}\right)\,dx = P\tan x + Q\sec x + C.$ Find the value of $P + Q.$

| RESPONSE GRID | | |
|---|---|---|
| 21. ⓪①②③④⑤⑥⑦⑧⑨ | | 22. ⓪①②③④⑤⑥⑦⑧⑨ |
| 23. ⓪①②③④⑤⑥⑦⑧⑨ | | 24. ⓪①②③④⑤⑥⑦⑧⑨ |

## DAILY PRACTICE PROBLEM DPP 57 - MATHS

| Total Questions | 24 | Total Marks | 62 |
|---|---|---|---|
| Attempted | | Correct | |
| Incorrect | | Net Score | |
| Cut-off Score | 12 | Qualifying Score | 40 |
| Success Gap = Net Score – Qualifying Score | | | |

$$\text{Net Score} = \sum_{i=1}^{VI}\left[(\text{correct}_i \times MM_i) - (In_i - NM_i)\right]$$

Name : [____]     Date : [____]

Start Time : [____]     End Time : [____]

# MATHEMATICS    M58

SYLLABUS : Indefinite Integral-2 : Integration by substitution

**Max. Marks : 57**     **Time : 60 min.**

## GENERAL INSTRUCTIONS

- The Daily Practice Problem Sheet contains **19** Questions divided into 6 sections.
  Section I has **6** MCQ's with ONLY 1 correct option. 2 marks for correct answer and No negative marks.
  Section II has **3** MCQ's with 1 or MORE THAN 1 correct option. 4 marks for correct answer(s) and (−1) for wrong answer.
  Section III has **1** PASSAGE with **3** MCQ's with ONLY 1 correct option. 3 marks for correct and (−1) mark for wrong answer.
  Section IV has **2** MCQ's with multiple matchings. 1 mark for the correct matching of each row & No negative marks.
  Section V has **2** Assertion-Reason MCQ's with ONLY 1 correct option. 3 marks for correct and (−1) mark for wrong answer.
  Section VI has **3** single digit integer answer questions. 4 marks for correct answer and (−1) for wrong answer.
- No mark will be given/ deducted if no bubble is filled. Keep a timer in front and stop immediately at the end of 60 min.
- You have to evaluate your Response Grids yourself with the help of Solution Booklet.
- The sheet follows a particular syllabus. Do not attempt the sheet before you have completed your preparation for that syllabus. Refer syllabus sheet in the starting of the book for the syllabus of all the DPP sheets.
- After completing the sheet check your answers with the solution booklet and complete the Result Grid. Finally spend time to analyse your performance and revise the areas which emerge out as weak in your evaluation.

## Section - I - Straight Objective Type

This section contains 6 multiple choice questions. Each question 4 has choices (a), (b), (c) and (d), out of which **ONLY ONE** is correct.

**1.** $\int \sec^2\theta \,(\sec\theta + \tan\theta)^2 \, d\theta$

(a) $\dfrac{(\sec\theta + \tan\theta)}{2}[2 + \tan\theta\,(\sec\theta + \tan\theta)] + C$

(b) $\dfrac{(\sec\theta + \tan\theta)}{3}[2 + 4\tan\theta\,(\sec\theta + \tan\theta)] + C$

(c) $\dfrac{(\sec\theta + \tan\theta)}{3}[2 + \tan\theta\,(\sec\theta + \tan\theta)] + C$

(d) $\dfrac{3(\sec\theta + \tan\theta)}{2}[2 + \tan\theta\,(\sec\theta + \tan\theta)] + C$

**2.** Let $f(x) = \dfrac{x+2}{2x+3}$, $x > 0$. If $\int\left(\dfrac{f(x)}{x^2}\right)^{1/2} dx$

$= \dfrac{1}{\sqrt{2}}\, g\!\left(\dfrac{1 + \sqrt{2f(x)}}{1 - \sqrt{2f(x)}}\right) - \sqrt{\dfrac{2}{3}}\, h\!\left(\dfrac{\sqrt{3f(x)} + \sqrt{2}}{\sqrt{3f(x)} - \sqrt{2}}\right) + C$

Where C is the constant of intergation, then

(a) $g(x) = \tan^{-1}(x), h(x) = ln\,|x|$

(b) $g(x) = ln\,|x|, h(x) = \tan^{-1}(x)$

(c) $g(x) = \tan^{-1}(x), h(x) = \tan^{-1}(x)$

(d) $g(x) = ln\,|x|, h(x) = \ell n\,|x|$

**3.** The value of the integral $\int \dfrac{\cos^3 x + \cos^5 x}{\sin^2 x + \sin^4 x} \, dx$ is

(a) $\sin x - 6\tan^{-1}(\sin x) + C$

(b) $\sin x - 2(\sin x)^{-1} + C$

(c) $\sin x - 2(\sin x)^{-1} - 6\tan^{-1}(\sin x) + C$

(d) $\sin x - 2(\sin x)^{-1} + 5\tan^{-1}(\sin x) + C$

| RESPONSE GRID | 1. ⓐⓑⓒⓓ | 2. ⓐⓑⓒⓓ | 3. ⓐⓑⓒⓓ |
|---|---|---|---|

**4.** $\int \dfrac{(x^2-1)}{(x^2+1)\sqrt{x^4+1}}\,dx$ is equal to

(a) $\sec^{-1}\left(\dfrac{x^2+1}{\sqrt{2}\,x}\right)+C$

(b) $\dfrac{1}{\sqrt{2}}\sec^{-1}\left(\dfrac{x^2+1}{\sqrt{2}\,x}\right)+C$

(c) $\dfrac{1}{\sqrt{2}}\sec^{-1}\left(\dfrac{x^2+1}{\sqrt{2}}\right)+C$

(d) None of these

**5.** $\int \dfrac{1}{a^2\cos^2 x+b^2\sin^2 x}\,dx$ is equal to

(a) $\dfrac{1}{ab}\tan^{-1}\left(\dfrac{b}{a}\tan x\right)+C$

(b) $\dfrac{1}{ab}\tan^{-1}\left(\dfrac{b}{a}\cot x\right)+C$

(c) $\dfrac{1}{ab}\cot^{-1}\left(\dfrac{b}{a}\tan x\right)+C$

(d) $-\dfrac{1}{ab}\cot^{-1}\left(\dfrac{a}{b}\cot x\right)+C$

**6.** The value of $\int \dfrac{a^x}{\sqrt{1-a^{2x}}}\,dx$ is

(a) $\dfrac{1}{\log a}\sin^{-1}(a^x)+C$

(b) $\dfrac{1}{\log a}\cos^{-1}(a^x)+C$

(c) $\dfrac{1}{\log a}\sec^{-1}(a^x)+C$

(d) None of these

## Section - II - Multiple Correct Answer Type

This section contains 3 multiple correct answer(s) type questions. Each question has 4 choices (a), (b), (c) and (d), out of which **ONE OR MORE** is/are correct.

**7.** If $I=\int \sec^2 x\,\csc^4 x\,dx=$

$K\cot^3 x+L\tan x+M\cot x+C$ then
(a) $K=-1/4$
(b) $L=2$
(c) $M=-2$
(d) None of these

**8.** If $\int \dfrac{\sin x}{\sin(x-\pi/4)}\,dx=A\left(f(x)+\log|\sin x-\cos x|\right)+C$ then

(a) $A=\sqrt{2}$
(b) $A=1/\sqrt{2}$
(c) $f(x)=\sin x$
(d) $f(x)=x$

**9.** If $\int\left(\dfrac{4e^x+6e^{-x}}{9e^x-4e^{-x}}\right)dx=Ax+B\log_e(9e^{2x}-4)+C$, then

(a) $A=3/2$

(b) $B=35/36$

(c) $C$ is indefinite

(d) $A+B=-\dfrac{19}{36}$

## Section - III - Linked Comprehension Type

This section contains one paragraph. Based upon the paragraph, 3 multiple choice questions have to be answered. Each question has 4 choices (a), (b), (c) and (d), out of which **ONLY ONE** is correct.

**Evaluation of indefinite integral with the help of specific substitution :**

In general if we have an integral of type $\int f(g(x))g'(x)dx$, we

substitute $g(x)=t \Rightarrow g'(x)dx=dt$ and the integral becomes $\int f(t)dt$.

Some of the substitution can be guessed by keen observation of the nature of given integrand. For example, we have

$\dfrac{d}{dx}\left(x+\dfrac{1}{x}\right)=1-\dfrac{1}{x^2}$. So if the integrand is of the type

$\int\left(x+\dfrac{1}{x}\right)\cdot\left(1-\dfrac{1}{x^2}\right)$, we can substitute $x+\dfrac{1}{x}=t$

Some more similar forms are given below

for integral $\int f\left(x-\dfrac{a}{x}\right)\left(1+\dfrac{a}{x^2}\right)dx$ , put $x-\dfrac{a}{x}=t$

for integral $\int f\left(x+\dfrac{a}{x}\right)\left(1-\dfrac{a}{x^2}\right)dx$ , put $x+\dfrac{a}{x}=t$

for integral $\int f\left(x^2-\dfrac{a}{x^2}\right)\left(x+\dfrac{a}{x^3}\right)dx$ , put $x^2-\dfrac{a}{x^2}=t$

for integral $\int f\left(x^2+\dfrac{a}{x^2}\right)\left(x-\dfrac{a}{x^3}\right)dx$ , put $x^2+\dfrac{a}{x^2}=t$

Many integrands can be brought into above forms by suitable reductions or transformations.

| **Response** | 4. ⓐⓑⓒⓓ | 5. ⓐⓑⓒⓓ | 6. ⓐⓑⓒⓓ |
|---|---|---|---|
| **Grid** | 7. ⓐⓑⓒⓓ | 8. ⓐⓑⓒⓓ | 9. ⓐⓑⓒⓓ |

**10.** $\displaystyle\int \frac{x^2+1}{x^4+1}\,dx =$

(a) $\dfrac{1}{\sqrt{2}}\tan^{-1}\dfrac{x^2-1}{\sqrt{2}x}+C$

(b) $\sin^{-1}\dfrac{x^2+1}{\sqrt{2}x}+C$

(c) $\dfrac{1}{2}\log\dfrac{\sqrt{2}x+1}{\sqrt{2}x-1}+c$

(d) $x^2+\dfrac{1}{x^2}+C$

**11.** $\displaystyle\int \frac{x^2-1}{(x^4+3x^2+1)\tan^{-1}\left(x+\dfrac{1}{x}\right)}\,dx =$

(a) $\tan^{-1}\left(x+\dfrac{1}{x}\right)+C$

(b) $\left(x+\dfrac{1}{x}\right)\tan^{-1}\left(x+\dfrac{1}{x}\right)+C$

(c) $\ln\left|\tan^{-1}\left(x+\dfrac{1}{x}\right)\right|+C$

(d) $\dfrac{1}{2}\ln\left|x+\dfrac{1}{x}\right|+C$

**12.** $\displaystyle\int \frac{x^4-2}{x^2\sqrt{x^4+x^2+2}}\,dx =$

(a) $\sqrt{x^2+1+\dfrac{1}{x^2}}+C$

(b) $\sqrt{x^2+1+\dfrac{2}{x^2}}+C$

(c) $\sqrt{x^2+\dfrac{1}{x^2}}+C$

(d) $\sqrt{x^2+\dfrac{2}{x^2}}+C$

---

## Section - IV - Matrix-Match Type

This section contains 2 questions. It contains statements given in two columns, which have to be matched. Statements in Column I are labelled as A, B, C and D whereas statements in Column II are labelled as p, q, r and s. The answers to these questions have to be appropriately bubbled as illustrated in the following example. If the correct matches are A-p, A-r, B-p, B-s, C-r, C-s and D-q, then the correctly bubbled matrix will look like the following :

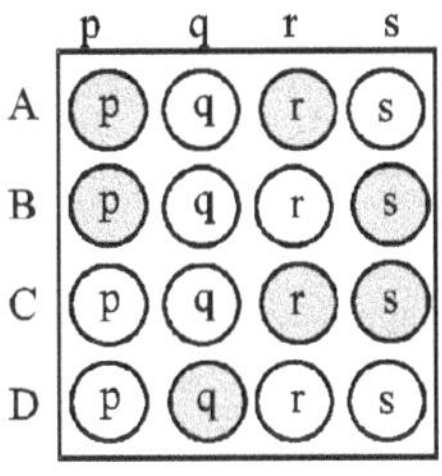

---

**13.**

| | Column-I | Column-II |
|---|---|---|
| A. | $\displaystyle\int(e^{a\log x}+e^{x\log a})\,dx$ | (p) $\dfrac{1}{\sqrt{2}}\tan^{-1}\left(\dfrac{x^2-1}{x\sqrt{2}}\right)+C$ |
| B. | $\displaystyle\int \dfrac{e^{\log\left(1+\frac{1}{x^2}\right)}}{x^2+\dfrac{1}{x^2}}\,dx$ | (q) $\dfrac{1}{4}\tan^{-1}\left(\tan x+\dfrac{1}{2}\right)+C$ |
| C. | $\displaystyle\int \dfrac{dx}{\sin^2 x+4\sin x\cos x+5\cos^2 x}$ | (r) $\dfrac{x^{a+1}}{a+1}+\dfrac{a^x}{\log a}+C$ |

**14.**

| | Column-I | Column-II |
|---|---|---|
| A. | $\displaystyle\int \dfrac{dx}{x(x^n+1)};\, n\in N$ | (p) $\displaystyle\int\dfrac{1}{(1-n)}(x^{-n}+1)^{1-1/n}+C$ |
| B. | $\displaystyle\int \dfrac{dx}{x^2(x^n+1)^{(n-1)/n}};\, n\in N$ | (q) $\ln|x|-\dfrac{1}{n}\ln|1+x^n|+C$ |
| C. | $\displaystyle\int \dfrac{dx}{x^n(1+x^n)^{1/x}};\, n\in N$ | (r) $\dfrac{(1+x^n)^{1-1/n}\cdot x^{1-n}}{(1-n)}+C$ |
| | | (s) $-\dfrac{1}{n}\ln|1+x^{-n}]+C$ |
| | | (t) $-(1+x^{-n})^{1/n}+C$ |

---

## Section - V - Reasoning Type

This section contains 2 reasoning type questions. Each question has 4 choices (a), (b), (c) and (d) out of which **ONLY ONE** is correct.

**DIRECTIONS for (Qs. 15 & 16) :** Each of these questions contains two statements: Statement-1 (Assertion) and Statement-2 (Reason). Each of these questions has four alternative choices, only one of which is the correct answer. You have to select the correct choice.

(a) Statement-1 is True, Statement-2 is True; Statement-2 is a correct explanation for Statement-1.

(b) Statement-1 is True, Statement-2 is True; Statement-2 is NOT a correct explanation for Statement-1.

(c) Statement -1 is True, Statement-2 is False.

(d) Statement -1 is False, Statement-2 is True.

---

**RESPONSE GRID**

10. (a)(b)(c)(d)   11. (a)(b)(c)(d)   12. (a)(b)(c)(d)

13. A - (p)(q)(r)(s); B - (p)(q)(r)(s); C - (p)(q)(r)(s)

14. A - (p)(q)(r)(s)(t); B - (p)(q)(r)(s)(t); C - (p)(q)(r)(s)(t)

---

*Space for Rough Work*

**15.** **Statement-1:** $\int \dfrac{x^2 - 2}{(x^4 + 5x^2 + 4)\tan^{-1}\left(\dfrac{x^2 + 2}{x}\right)} dx = \log$

$$\left|\tan^{-1}(x + 2/x)\right| + C$$

**Statement-2:** $\int \dfrac{dx}{a^2 + x^2} = \dfrac{1}{a}\tan^{-1}\dfrac{x}{a} + C$

**16.** **Statement-1:** $\int \tan 5x \, \tan 3x \, \tan 2x \, dx$

$$= \dfrac{\ln|\sec 5x|}{5} - \dfrac{\ln|\sec 3x|}{3} - \dfrac{\ln|\sec 2x|}{2} + C$$

**Statement-2:** $\tan 5x - \tan 3x - \tan 2x$

$$= \tan 5x \, \tan 3x \text{ and } 2x$$

## Section - VI - Integer Type

This section contains 3 questions. The answer to each of the questions is a single digit integer ranging from 0 to 9.

**17.** If $\int \dfrac{\sin^3 \dfrac{\theta}{2}\, d\theta}{\cos\dfrac{\theta}{2}\sqrt{\cos^3\theta + \cos^2\theta + \cos\theta}} = \tan^{-1}\sqrt{f(\theta)} + c$

then find the least value of $f(\theta)$ for allowable values of $\theta$.

**18.** If $\int \sin 4x \, e^{\tan^2 x} dx = -A\cos^4 x e^{\tan^2 x} + B,$ then find the value of A.

**19.** If $\int \dfrac{\sqrt{\cot x} - \sqrt{\tan x}}{4 + 3\sin 2x} dx = \dfrac{1}{2\sqrt{2}}\ell n\left|\dfrac{f(x) + a}{f(x) - a}\right|,$ where

$0 < x < \dfrac{\pi}{2}$ then find the value of $a$.

| | |
|---|---|
| **RESPONSE GRID** | **15.** ⓐ ⓑ ⓒ ⓓ   **16.** ⓐ ⓑ ⓒ ⓓ   **17.** ⓪ ① ② ③ ④ ⑤ ⑥ ⑦ ⑧ ⑨ <br> **18.** ⓪ ① ② ③ ④ ⑤ ⑥ ⑦ ⑧ ⑨   **19.** ⓪ ① ② ③ ④ ⑤ ⑥ ⑦ ⑧ ⑨ |

## DAILY PRACTICE PROBLEM DPP 58 - MATHS

| | | | |
|---|---|---|---|
| Total Questions | 19 | Total Marks | 57 |
| Attempted | | Correct | |
| Incorrect | | Net Score | |
| Cut-off Score | 11 | Qualifying Score | 38 |
| Success Gap = Net Score – Qualifying Score | | | |

$$\textbf{Net Score} = \sum_{i=1}^{\text{VI}}\left[(\textbf{correct}_i \times MM_i) - (In_i - NM_i)\right]$$

*Space for Rough Work*

**Name :** __________________________    **Date :** __________

**Start Time :** __________    **End Time :** __________

## MATHEMATICS    M59

**SYLLABUS : Indefinite Integral-3 :** Integration by parts, Integral of the form $\int e^x (F(x) + F'(x))$, Integral of the form $\int e^{kx}[KF(x) + F'(x)]dx$

## Max. Marks : 75    Time : 60 min.

### GENERAL INSTRUCTIONS

- The Daily Practice Problem Sheet contains **24** Questions divided into 6 sections.
  Section I has **8** MCQ's with ONLY 1 correct option. 2 marks for correct answer and No negative marks.
  Section II has **4** MCQ's with 1 or MORE THAN 1 correct option. 4 marks for correct answer(s) and (–1) for wrong answer.
  Section III has **1** PASSAGE with **3** MCQ's with ONLY 1 correct option. 3 marks for correct and (–1) mark for wrong answer.
  Section IV has **2** MCQ's with multiple matchings. 1 mark for the correct matching of each row & No negative marks.
  Section V has **2** Assertion-Reason MCQ's with ONLY 1 correct option. 3 marks for correct and (–1) mark for wrong answer.
  Section VI has **5** single digit integer answer questions. 4 marks for correct answer and (–1) for wrong answer.
- No mark will be given/ deducted if no bubble is filled. Keep a timer in front and stop immediately at the end of 60 min.
- You have to evaluate your Response Grids yourself with the help of Solution Booklet.
- The sheet follows a particular syllabus. Do not attempt the sheet before you have completed your preparation for that syllabus. Refer syllabus sheet in the starting of the book for the syllabus of all the DPP sheets.
- After completing the sheet check your answers with the solution booklet and complete the Result Grid. Finally spend time to analyse your performance and revise the areas which emerge out as weak in your evaluation.

---

### Section - I - Straight Objective Type

This section contains 8 multiple choice questions. Each question has 4 choices (a), (b), (c) and (d), out of which **ONLY ONE** is correct.

**1.** $\displaystyle \int \frac{e^x (2 - x^2)dx}{(1-x)\sqrt{1-x^2}} =$

(a) $\displaystyle \frac{e^x}{\sqrt{1-x^2}} + c$

(b) $e^x \sqrt{1-x^2} + c$

(c) $\displaystyle \frac{e^x (2-x^2)}{\sqrt{1-x^2}} + c$

(d) $\displaystyle \frac{e^x (1+x)}{\sqrt{1-x^2}} + c$

**2.** $\displaystyle \int \frac{x^2 dx}{(x\sin x + \cos x)^2} =$

(a) $\displaystyle \frac{\sin x - x\cos x}{x\sin x + \cos x} + c$

(b) $\displaystyle \frac{x\sin x - \cos x}{x\sin x + \cos x} + c$

(c) $\displaystyle \frac{\sin x + x\cos x}{x\sin x + \cos x} + c$

(d) None of these

**3.** The value of $\displaystyle \int e^x \frac{1 + n\,x^{n-1} - x^{2n}}{(1-x^n)\sqrt{1-x^{2n}}}\,dx$ (where n is a non-zero constant) is

(a) $\displaystyle \frac{e^x \sqrt{1-x^n}}{1-x^n} + C$

(b) $\displaystyle e^x \frac{\sqrt{1+x^{2n}}}{1-x^{2n}} + C$

(c) $\displaystyle e^x \frac{\sqrt{1-x^{2n}}}{1-x^n} + C$

(d) None of these

**4.** $\displaystyle \int x \tan^{-1} x\ dx =$

(a) $\displaystyle \frac{1}{2}(x^2 + 1)\tan^{-1} x - \frac{1}{2}x + C$

(b) $\displaystyle \frac{1}{2}(x^2 + 1)\tan^{-1} x + \frac{1}{2}x + C$

(c) $\displaystyle \frac{1}{2}(x^2 - 1)\tan^{-1} x - \frac{1}{2}x + C$

(d) None of these

**5.** $\displaystyle \int e^x \left[\frac{2 + \sin 2x}{1 + \cos 2x}\right]dx =$

(a) $e^x \tan x + C$

(b) $e^x \sin x + C$

(c) $e^{2x} \tan x + C$

(d) None of these

---

**RESPONSE GRID**   **1.** ⓐⓑⓒⓓ   **2.** ⓐⓑⓒⓓ   **3.** ⓐⓑⓒⓓ   **4.** ⓐⓑⓒⓓ   **5.** ⓐⓑⓒⓓ

**6.** $\int \sin 2x . \log \cos x \, dx$ is equal to

(a) $\cos^2 x \left( \dfrac{1}{2} + \log \cos x \right) + K$  (b) $\cos^2 x . \log \cos x + K$

(c) $\cos^2 x \left( \dfrac{1}{2} - \log \cos x \right) + K$  (d) None of these

**7.** If $\int \dfrac{x \tan^{-1} x}{\sqrt{1 + x^2}} \, dx = \sqrt{1 + x^2} f(x) + k \log(x + \sqrt{1 + x^2}) + C$, then

(a) $f(x) = \tan^{-1} x$, $k = -1$  (b) $f(x) = \tan^{-1} x$, $k = 1$

(c) $f(x) = 2 \tan^{-1} x$, $k = -1$  (d) $f(x) = 2 \tan^{-1} x$, $k = 1$

**8.** If $\int x \log \left( 1 + \dfrac{1}{x} \right) dx = f(x) \log(x+1) + g(x) x^2 + L(x) + C$, then

(a) $f(x) = \left( \dfrac{1}{2} \right) x^2$  (b) $g(x) = \log x$

(c) $L = 1$  (d) None of these

## Section - II - Multiple Correct Answer Type

This section contains 4 multiple correct answer(s) type questions. Each question has 4 choices (a), (b), (c) and (d), out of which **ONE OR MORE** is/are correct.

**9.** $\int e^x \left\{ \dfrac{2 \tan x}{1 + \tan x} + \cot^2 \left( x + \dfrac{\pi}{4} \right) \right\} dx$ is equal to

(a) $e^x \tan \left( \dfrac{\pi}{4} - x \right) + C$  (b) $e^x \cot \left( \dfrac{3\pi}{4} - x \right) + C$

(c) $e^x \tan \left( x - \dfrac{\pi}{4} \right) + C$  (d) $e^x \cot \left( x + \dfrac{\pi}{4} \right) + C$

**10.** If $\int \dfrac{x e^x}{\sqrt{(1 + e^x)}} dx = f(x) \sqrt{(1 + e^x)} - 2 \ln g(x) + c$, then

(a) $f(x) = x - 1$  (b) $g(x) = \dfrac{\sqrt{(1 + e^x)} - 1}{\sqrt{(1 + e^x)} + 1}$

(c) $g(x) = \dfrac{\sqrt{(1 + e^x)} + 1}{\sqrt{(1 + e^x)} - 1}$  (d) $f(x) = 2(x - 2)$

**11.** If the primitive of $\sin (\ln x)$ is $f(x) \{ \sin g(x) - \cos h(x) \} + C$ (C being the constant of integration), then

(a) $\lim\limits_{x \to 2} f(x) = 1$  (b) $\lim\limits_{x \to 1} \dfrac{g(x)}{h(x)} = 1$

(c) $g(e^3) = 3$  (d) $h(e^5) = 5$

**12.** If $\forall \, x \in [-1, 0)$, $\int \left( \cos^{-1} x + \cos^{-1} \sqrt{1 - x^2} \right) dx$

$= Ax + f(x) \sin^{-1} x - 2\sqrt{1 - x^2} + C$, then

(a) $A = \dfrac{\pi}{4}$  (b) $A = \dfrac{\pi}{2}$

(c) $f(x) = x$  (d) $f(x) = -2x$

## Section - III - Linked Comprehension Type

This section contains one paragraph. Based upon the paragraph, 3 multiple choice questions have to be answered. Each question has 4 choices (a), (b), (c) and (d), out of which **ONLY ONE** is correct.

**Evaluation of Indefinite Integral by parts integrating such that some of terms cancel, whose primitive cannot by evaluated:**

In some of the cases we can split the integrand into the sum of the two functions such that the integration of one of them by parts produces an integral which cancels the other integral.

Suppose we have an integral of the type $\int [f(x) \, h(x) + g(x)] \, dx$

Let $\int f(x) \, h(x) \, dx = I_1$ and $\int g(x) \, dx = I_2$

Integrating $I_1$ by parts we get

$I_1 = f(x) \int h(x) \, dx - \int \{ f'(x) \int h(x) \, dx \} \, dx$

Suppose $\int \{ f'(x) \int h(x) \, dx \} dx$ converts to $I_2$, then we get

$I_1 + I_2 = f(x) \int h(x) dx + C$, which is the desired integral.

In particular consider the integral of the kind

$I = \int e^x \{ f(x) + f'(x) \} \, dx = \int e^x f(x) \, dx + \int e^x \, f'(x) \, dx$

Integrating first integral by parts, we get ($e^x$ is second function)

$I = e^x f(x) - \int e^x f'(x) \, dx + \int e^x \, f'(x) \, dx = e^x f(x) + C$

| **Response Grid** | 6. Ⓐ Ⓑ Ⓒ Ⓓ | 7. Ⓐ Ⓑ Ⓒ Ⓓ | 8. Ⓐ Ⓑ Ⓒ Ⓓ | 9. Ⓐ Ⓑ Ⓒ Ⓓ | 10. Ⓐ Ⓑ Ⓒ Ⓓ |
| | 11. Ⓐ Ⓑ Ⓒ Ⓓ | 12. Ⓐ Ⓑ Ⓒ Ⓓ | | | |

**13.** $\int \dfrac{xe^x}{(1+x)^2}\, dx =$

   (a)   $xe^x + C$        (b)   $\dfrac{e^x}{(x+1)^2} + C$

   (c)   $e^x - \dfrac{1}{x+1} + C$    (d)   $\dfrac{e^x}{x+1} + C$

**14.** The integral of $\int e^{\sin x}(x\cos x - \sec x \tan x)\, dx$ is

   (a)   $xe^{\sin x} - e^{\sin x}\sec x + C$    (b)   $(x + \sec x)e^{\sin x} + C$

   (c)   $e^{\sin x}\cos x + C$    (d)   $e^{\sin x}(\cos x - \sec x) + C$

**15.** Antiderivative of $f(x) = \log(\log x) + \dfrac{1}{(\log x)^2}$ is

   (a)   $\log(\log x)$       (b)   $x\log(\log x) - \dfrac{x}{\log x}$

   (c)   $\dfrac{x}{\log x} - \log x$    (d)   $\log(\log x) - \dfrac{x}{\log x}$

**(B)**   $\int e^x(1 - \cot x + \cot^2 x)\, dx =$    q.   $\log\left| 1 - \cot\left(\dfrac{x}{2}\right)\right| + C$

**(C)**   $\int \dfrac{\sin^3 x + \cos^3 x}{\cos^2 x \sin^2 x}\, dx =$    r.   $\sec x - \csc x + C$

**(D)**   $\int \dfrac{dx}{1 - \cos x - \sin x} =$    s.   $\dfrac{2}{3}\tan^{-1}\sqrt{x} + C$

                             t.   $-e^x \cdot \cot x + C$

**17.**      **Column -I**          **Column -II**

**(A)**   $\int \dfrac{e^x}{x+2}[1 + (x+2)\log(x+2)]dx$   p.   $\sin^{-1}\left(\dfrac{2x+3}{\sqrt{17}}\right) + C$

**(B)**   $\int \sin^2 x \cos^3 x\, dx$    q.   $\dfrac{x^4}{4} - \dfrac{x^2}{2} + \dfrac{1}{2}$

                              $\log(x^2 + 1) + C$

**(C)**   $\int \dfrac{dx}{\sqrt{2 - 3x - x^2}}$    r.   $e^x \log(x+2) + C$

**(D)**   $\int \dfrac{x^5}{x^2+1}\, dx$    s.   $\dfrac{\sin^3 x}{3} - \dfrac{\sin^5 x}{5} + C$

                              t.   $\dfrac{\sin^2 x}{2} - \sin x + C$

## Section - IV - Matrix-Match Type

This section contains 2 questions. It contains statements given in two columns, which have to be matched. Statements in Column I are labelled as A, B, C and D whereas statements in Column II are labelled as p, q, r and s. The answers to these questions have to be appropriately bubbled as illustrated in the following example. If the correct matches are A-p, A-r, B-p, B-s, C-r, C-s and D-q, then the correctly bubbled matrix will look like the following :

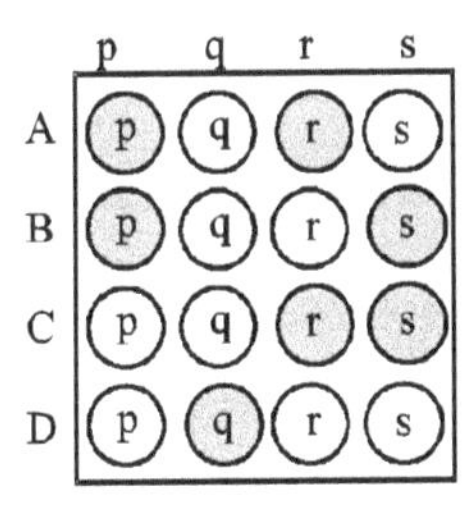

**16.**      **Column -I**          **Column -II**

**(A)**   $\int \dfrac{dx}{\sqrt{x}(x+9)} =$    p.   $\log\left| 1 - \tan\left(\dfrac{x}{2}\right)\right| + C$

## Section - V - Reasoning Type

This section contains 2 reasoning type questions. Each question has 4 choices (a), (b), (c) and (d) out of which **ONLY ONE** is correct.

**DIRECTIONS for Qs (18-19) :** Each of these questions contains two statements: **Statement-1 (Assertion)** and **Statement-2 (Reason).** Each of these questions has four alternative choices, only one of which is the correct answer. You have to select the correct choice.

(a)   Statement-1 is True, Statement-2 is True; Statement-2 is a correct explanation for Statement-1.

(b)   Statement-1 is True, Statement-2 is True; Statement-2 is NOT a correct explanation for Statement-1.

(c)   Statement -1 is True, Statement-2 is False.

(d)   Statement -1 is False, Statement-2 is True.

**18.** **Statement–1 :** $\int e^{ax}\sin bx\,dx = \dfrac{e^{ax}}{A}(a\sin bx - b\cos bx) + c.$

Then A is $\sqrt{a^2 + b^2}$

**Statement–2 :** $\int e^x\left(\dfrac{1+\sin x\cos x}{\cos^2 x}\right)dx = e^x\tan x + C$

**19.** Let $g(x)$ be an integrable function and $\int g(x)\,dx = g(x)$.

**Statement-1 :** $\int g(x)\,(f(x) - f''(x))\,dx = g(x)(f(x) - f'(x)) + C$

**Statement-2 :** $\int g(x)\,(f(x) + f'(x))\,dx = g(x)f(x) + C$

---

## Section - VI - Integer Type

This section contains 5 questions. The answer to each of the questions is a single digit integeres ranging from 0 to 9.

---

**20.** If $P = \int e^{ax}\cos bx\,dx$ and $Q = \int e^{ax}\sin bx\,dx$, without constant of integration then find the value of $e^{-2ax}(P^2 + Q^2)(a^2 + b^2)$.

**21.** If $f(x) = \int \cos^2(\ln x)\,dx =$

$\dfrac{x}{P} + \dfrac{x\cos(2\ln x) + Qx\sin(2\ln x)}{10} + C$, then find the value of P + Q.

**22.** If $l_{m,n} = \int \cos^m x\sin nx\,dx$, then

$7I_{4,3} - 4I_{3,2} = -\cos^A x\cos Bx + C$, then find the value of A + B.

**23.** If polynomials P and Q satisfies

$\int((3x-1)\cos x + (1-2x)\sin x)dx = P\cos x + Q\sin x$ (ignoring the constant of integration) then find the value of $\dfrac{P}{1+x} + \dfrac{Q}{x-1}$.

**24.** If $\int \log_e\left(\sqrt{1-x} + \sqrt{1+x}\right)dx = Ax\log_e$

$\left(\sqrt{1-x} + \sqrt{1+x}\right) + \dfrac{1}{B}(\sin^{-1}x - x) + C$, then find the value of A + B.

---

<table>
<tr><td rowspan="3">RESPONSE GRID</td><td>18. ⓐⓑⓒⓓ</td><td>19. ⓐⓑⓒⓓ</td><td>20. ⓪①②③④⑤⑥⑦⑧⑨</td></tr>
<tr><td>21. ⓪①②③④⑤⑥⑦⑧⑨</td><td colspan="2">22. ⓪①②③④⑤⑥⑦⑧⑨</td></tr>
<tr><td>23. ⓪①②③④⑤⑥⑦⑧⑨</td><td colspan="2">24. ⓪①②③④⑤⑥⑦⑧⑨</td></tr>
</table>

## DAILY PRACTICE PROBLEM DPP 59 - MATHS

| Total Questions | 24 | Total Marks | 75 |
|---|---|---|---|
| Attempted | | Correct | |
| Incorrect | | Net Score | |
| Cut-off Score | 15 | Qualifying Score | 49 |
| Success Gap = Net Score – Qualifying Score | | | |

$$\text{Net Score} = \sum_{i=I}^{VI}\left[(\text{correct}_i \times MM_i) - (In_i - NM_i)\right]$$

---

*Space for Rough Work*

# DPP - Daily Practice Problems

**Name :**

**Date :**

**Start Time :**

**End Time :**

## MATHEMATICS — M60

**SYLLABUS : Indefinite Integral-4 :** Integration of rational function by using partial fractions, Evaluation of various forms of integration

**Max. Marks : 72**

**Time : 60 min.**

### GENERAL INSTRUCTIONS

- The Daily Practice Problem Sheet contains **24** Questions divided into 6 sections.
  Section I has **9** MCQ's with ONLY 1 correct option. 2 marks for correct answer and No negative marks.
  Section II has **4** MCQ's with 1 or MORE THAN 1 correct option. 4 marks for correct answer(s) and (–1) for wrong answer.
  Section III has **1** PASSAGE with **3** MCQ's with ONLY 1 correct option. 3 marks for correct and (–1) mark for wrong answer.
  Section IV has **1** MCQ's with multiple matchings. 1 mark for the correct matching of each row & No negative marks.
  Section V has **2** Assertion-Reason MCQ's with ONLY 1 correct option. 3 marks for correct and (–1) mark for wrong answer.
  Section VI has **5** single digit integer answer questions. 4 marks for correct answer and (–1) for wrong answer.
- No mark will be given/ deducted if no bubble is filled. Keep a timer in front and stop immediately at the end of 60 min.
- You have to evaluate your Response Grids yourself with the help of Solution Booklet.
- The sheet follows a particular syllabus. Do not attempt the sheet before you have completed your preparation for that syllabus. Refer syllabus sheet in the starting of the book for the syllabus of all the DPP sheets.
- After completing the sheet check your answers with the solution booklet and complete the Result Grid. Finally spend time to analyse your performance and revise the areas which emerge out as weak in your evaluation.

## Section - I - Straight Objective Type

This section contains 9 multiple choice questions. Each question has 4 choices (a), (b), (c) and (d), out of which **ONLY ONE** is correct.

**1.** If $I_n = \int \cot^n x\, dx$, then

$$I_0 + I_1 + 2(I_2 + I_3 + \ldots\ldots I_8) + I_9 + I_{10} =$$

(a) $-\sum\limits_{k=1}^{9} \dfrac{\cot^k x}{k}$    (b) $\sum\limits_{k=1}^{9} \dfrac{\cot^k x}{k!}$    (c) $\sum\limits_{k=1}^{10} \dfrac{\cot^k x}{10}$    (d) $-\sum\limits_{k=1}^{10} k \cot^k x$

**2.** $\displaystyle\int \dfrac{e^{x-1}}{(x^2 - 5x + 4)} \cdot 2x\, dx = A\, F(x-1) + B\,(x-4) + C$, where $F(x) = \displaystyle\int \dfrac{e^x}{x}\, dx$, then A and B ordered set is

(a) $\left(-\dfrac{2}{3}, \dfrac{8}{3}\right)$   (b) $\left(-\dfrac{2}{3}, \dfrac{8e^3}{3}\right)$   (c) $\left(\dfrac{8}{3}, \dfrac{2}{3}\right)$   (d) $\left(-\dfrac{2}{3}, -\dfrac{8e^3}{3}\right)$

**3.** $\displaystyle\int \dfrac{(x-1)\,dx}{(2x+1)(x-2)(x-3)} =$

(a) $\dfrac{3}{35}\ln|2x+1| - \dfrac{1}{5}\ln|x-2| + \dfrac{2}{7}\ln|x-3| + C$

(b) $\dfrac{3}{35}\ln|2x+1| - \dfrac{1}{5}\ln|x+2| + \dfrac{2}{7}\ln|x-3| + C$

(c) $\dfrac{3}{35}\ln|2x+1| + \dfrac{1}{5}\ln|x+2| + \dfrac{2}{7}\ln|x-3| + C$

(d) None of these

**4.** $\displaystyle\int \dfrac{1}{9x^2 - 4}\, dx =$

(a) $\dfrac{1}{12}\log\left|\dfrac{3x-2}{3x+2}\right| + C$    (b) $\dfrac{1}{12}\log\left|\dfrac{x-2}{3x+2}\right| + C$

(c) $\dfrac{1}{12}\log\left|\dfrac{x-2}{x+2}\right| + C$    (d) None of these

---

**RESPONSE GRID**    **1.** Ⓐ Ⓑ Ⓒ Ⓓ    **2.** Ⓐ Ⓑ Ⓒ Ⓓ    **3.** Ⓐ Ⓑ Ⓒ Ⓓ    **4.** Ⓐ Ⓑ Ⓒ Ⓓ

**5.** $\int \dfrac{x^2+1}{x^4+1}\,dx =$

(a) $\dfrac{1}{\sqrt{2}}\tan^{-1}\left(\dfrac{x^2-1}{\sqrt{2}x}\right)+C$    (b) $\dfrac{1}{2}\tan^{-1}\left(\dfrac{x^2-1}{\sqrt{2}}\right)+C$

(c) $\dfrac{1}{\sqrt{3}}\tan^{-1}\left(\dfrac{x^2-1}{\sqrt{2}}\right)+C$    (d) None of these

**6.** The value of the integral $\int \dfrac{\cos^3 x+\cos^5 x}{\sin^2 x+\sin^4 x}\,dx$ is

(a) $\sin x - 6\tan^{-1}(\sin x)+C$
(b) $\sin x - 2(\sin x)^{-1}+C$
(c) $\sin x - 2(\sin x)^{-1}-6\tan^{-1}(\sin x)+C$
(d) $\sin x - 2(\sin x)^{-1}+5\tan^{-1}(\sin x)+C$

**7.** $\int \dfrac{1}{x^4+1+5x^2}\,dx =$

(a) $0$

(b) $\dfrac{1}{2\sqrt{7}}\tan^{-1}\left(\dfrac{x-\dfrac{1}{x}}{\sqrt{7}}\right)-\dfrac{1}{2\sqrt{3}}\tan^{-1}\left(\dfrac{x+\dfrac{1}{x}}{\sqrt{3}}\right)+C$

(c) $\dfrac{1}{2\sqrt{7}}\cot^{-1}\left(\dfrac{x-\dfrac{1}{x}}{\sqrt{7}}\right)+\dfrac{1}{2\sqrt{3}}\cot^{-1}\left(\dfrac{x+\dfrac{1}{x}}{\sqrt{3}}\right)+C$

(d) None of these

**8.** If the primitive of $f(x)=\dfrac{1}{3\sin x+\sin^3 x}$ is equal to

$\dfrac{1}{6}\log\dfrac{t-1}{t+1}+\dfrac{1}{12}\log\dfrac{2+t}{2-t}+C$ then

(a) $t=\sin x$      (b) $t=\tan\dfrac{x}{2}$

(c) $t=2\cos x$      (d) $t=\cos x$

**9.** $\int \dfrac{dx}{\sqrt[4]{1+x^4}} = \dfrac{1}{2}\left(\dfrac{1}{2}\log\dfrac{1+z}{1-z}-\tan^{-1}z\right)+C$, where

(a) $z=\dfrac{\sqrt[4]{1+x^4}}{x}$      (b) $z=\dfrac{x}{\sqrt[4]{1+x^4}}$

(c) $z=\dfrac{-\sqrt[4]{1+x^4}}{x}$      (d) None of these

## Section - II - Multiple Correct Answer Type

This section contains 4 multiple correct answer(s) type questions. Each question has 4 choices (a), (b), (c) and (d), out of which **ONE OR MORE** is/are correct.

**10.** If the primitive of $\dfrac{1}{(e^x-1)^2}$ is $f(x)-\log g(x)+C$, then which of the following is incorrect?

(a) dom $f=R$      (b) $g(x)=1-e^x$
(c) dom $f=R-\{0\}$      (d) $f(x)=1-e^{-x}$

**11.** $\int \dfrac{x^3+x}{x^4-9}\,dx = \dfrac{1}{P}f(x)+\dfrac{1}{Q}g(x)+C$

(a) $P=4, f(x)=\log_e|x^4-9|$    (b) $P=4, f(x)=\log_e|x^4+9|$

(c) $Q=12, g(x)=\log_e\left|\dfrac{x^3-3}{x^3+3}\right|$    (d) $Q=12, g(x)=\log_e\left|\dfrac{x^2-3}{x^2+3}\right|$

**12.** If $f(x)=\lim\limits_{n\to\infty} e^{x\tan(1/n)\ln(1/n)}$ and $\int \dfrac{f(x)}{\sqrt[3]{(\sin^{11}x\cos x)}}\,dx = g(x)+C$, then

(a) $g\left(\dfrac{\pi}{4}\right)=\dfrac{3}{2}$

(b) $g(x)$ is continuous for all $x$

(c) $g\left(\dfrac{\pi}{4}\right)=-\dfrac{15}{8}$

(d) $g(x)$ is non differentiable at infinitely many points

| | | | | | |
|---|---|---|---|---|---|
| **RESPONSE** | 5. ⓐⓑⓒⓓ | 6. ⓐⓑⓒⓓ | 7. ⓐⓑⓒⓓ | 8. ⓐⓑⓒⓓ | 9. ⓐⓑⓒⓓ |
| **GRID** | 10. ⓐⓑⓒⓓ | 11. ⓐⓑⓒⓓ | 12. ⓐⓑⓒⓓ | | |

**13.** The value of $\int_{0}^{x} \dfrac{x(t-|t|)^2}{(1+t^2)}\,dt$ is equal to

(a)  $4(x - \tan^{-1} x)$, if $x < 0$    (b)  $0$, if $x > 0$

(c)  $\ln(1 + x^2)$, if $x > 0$    (d)  None of the above

## Section - III - Linked Comprehension Type

This section contains one paragraph. Based upon the paragraph, 3 multiple choice questions have to be answered. Each question has 4 choices (a), (b), (c) and (d), out of which **ONLY ONE** is correct.

Repeated application of integration by parts gives us the reduction formula if the integrand is dependent of $n$, on $n \in N$.

**14.** If $I_{m-2,\,n+2} = \int \sin^{m-2} x \cos^{n+2} x\,dx$ and

$$I_{m,\,n} = -\frac{\sin^{m-1} x \cos^{n+1} x}{(n+1)} + f(m,n)\, I_{m-2,\,n+2}, \text{ then}$$

$f(2, 3)$ is equal to

(a)  $\dfrac{1}{2}$    (b)  $\dfrac{1}{3}$    (c)  $\dfrac{1}{4}$    (d)  $\dfrac{1}{5}$

**15.** If $I_n = \int x \sin^n x\,dx$ and $I_n = -\dfrac{x \sin^{n-1} x \cos x}{n} + \dfrac{\sin^n x}{n^2} + f(n)\, I_{n-2}$, then the value of $f(n)$ is equal to

(a)  $\dfrac{n-1}{n}$    (b)  $\dfrac{n-2}{n-1}$    (c)  $\dfrac{n+1}{n}$    (d)  $\dfrac{n+1}{n-1}$

**16.** If $I_n = \int e^{ax} . \sin^n x\,dx$ and $I_n = \dfrac{e^{ax} \sin^{n-1} x (a \sin x - \cos x)}{(n + a^2)}$

$- A \sin^n x + B\, I_{n-2}$, then $A + B$ is equal to

(a)  $\dfrac{a(n^2 + 1)}{n(n + a^2)}$    (b)  $\dfrac{a(n^2 - 1)}{n(n + a^2)}$    (c)  $\dfrac{a(n^2 + 1)}{n(n^2 + a^2)}$    (d)  $\dfrac{a(n^2 - 1)}{n(n^2 + a^2)}$

## Section - IV - Matrix-Match Type

This section contains 2 questions. It contains statements given in two columns, which have to be matched. Statements in Column I are labelled as A, B, C and D whereas statements in Column II are labelled as p, q, r and s. The answers to these questions have to be appropriately bubbled as illustrated in the following example. If the correct matches are A-p, A-r, B-p, B-s, C-r, C-s and D-q, then the correctly bubbled matrix will look like the following :

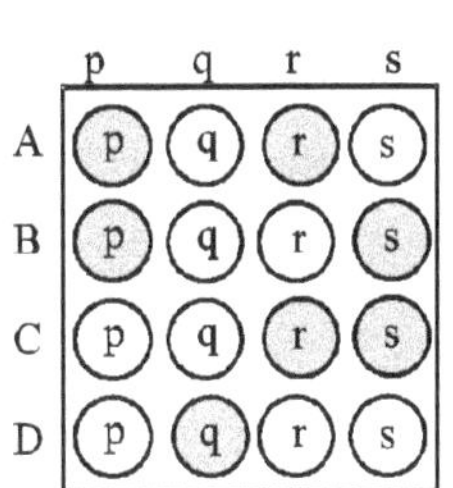

**17.**  **Column I**                  **Column II**

(A)  $\int \dfrac{dx}{e^{2x} + 1}$    p.  $\ln\left(e^x + \sqrt{(e^{2x} + 1)}\right) + C$

(B)  $\int \dfrac{e^x dx}{\sqrt{(e^{2x} + 1)}}$    q.  $x - \dfrac{1}{2}\ln(1 + e^{2x}) + \dfrac{1}{2}\left(\dfrac{1}{e^{2x} + 1}\right) + C$

(C)  $\int \dfrac{1}{(e^{2x} + 1)^2}\,dx$    r.  $-\dfrac{1}{2}\ln(1 + e^{-2x}) + C$

s.  $x + \ln\left(1 + \sqrt{(1 + e^{-2x})}\right) + C$

t.  $x - \dfrac{1}{2}\ln(1 + e^{2x}) + C$

## Section - V - Reasoning Type

This section contains 2 reasoning type questions. Each question has 4 choices (a), (b), (c) and (d) out of which **ONLY ONE** is correct.

**DIRECTIONS : Each of these questions contains two statements: Statement-1 (Assertion) and Statement-2 (Reason). Each of these questions has four alternative choices, only one of which is the correct answer. You have to select the correct choice.**

(a)  Statement-1 is True, Statement-2 is True; Statement-2 is a correct explanation for Statement-1.

| **RESPONSE GRID** | 13. ⓐⓑ©ⓓ  14. ⓐⓑ©ⓓ  15. ⓐⓑ©ⓓ  16. ⓐⓑ©ⓓ |
|---|---|
| | 17. A - ⓟⓠⓡⓢⓣ; B - ⓟⓠⓡⓢⓣ; C - ⓟⓠⓡⓢⓣ |

(b)  Statement-1 is True, Statement-2 is True; Statement-2 is NOT a correct explanation for Statement-1.

(c)  Statement -1 is True, Statement-2 is False.

(d)  Statement -1 is False, Statement-2 is True.

**18.**  **Statement–1 :** $\displaystyle\int \frac{x^{9/2}}{\sqrt{1+x^{11}}}\,dx = \frac{2}{11}\ln\left|x^{11/2}+\sqrt{1+x^{11}}\right|+C$

**Statement–2 :** $\displaystyle\int \frac{dx}{\sqrt{1+x^2}} = \ln\left|x+\sqrt{1+x^2}\right|+C$

**19.**  **Statement 1 :** If $I_n = \displaystyle\int \tan^n x\,dx$ then $5(I_4+I_6) = \tan^5 x$

**Statement 2 :** If $I_n = \displaystyle\int \tan^n x\,dx$ then $I_n - I_{n-2} = \dfrac{\tan^{n-1} x}{n}$

where $n \in N$

---

### Section - VI - Integer Type

This section contains 5 questions . The answer to each of the questions is a single digit integer ranging from 0 to 9.

**20.**  If $\displaystyle\int \frac{ax^2-b}{x\sqrt{c^2x^2-(ax^2+b)^2}}\,dx = P\sin^{-1}\left(\frac{(ax+b/x)}{c}\right)+K$ , find the value of P.

**21.**  If $\displaystyle\int\sqrt{\frac{x}{4-x^3}}\,dx = \frac{A}{B}\sin^{-1}\left(\frac{x^{3/2}}{2}\right)+C$, then find the value of A + B.

**22.**  If $\displaystyle\int \frac{dx}{2+\cos x} = \frac{A}{\sqrt{B}}\tan^{-1}\left(\frac{P}{\sqrt{Q}}\tan\frac{x}{R}\right)+C$ , then find the value of $(P+Q+R)-(A+B)$

**23.**  If $\displaystyle\int \frac{dx}{x\sqrt{5x^2-3}} = \frac{M}{\sqrt{K}}\tan^{-1}f(x)+C$, then find the vlaue of M + K.

**24.**  If $\displaystyle\int \frac{\cos^2 x + \sin 2x}{(2\cos x - \sin x)}\,dx = \frac{\cos x}{2\cos x - \sin x}$
$+ax + b\,ln\,|\,2\cos x - \sin x\,|+C$ , then find the value of $5a-10b$,

<table>
<tr><td rowspan="3">RESPONSE<br>GRID</td><td>18. ⓐⓑⓒⓓ</td><td>19. ⓐⓑⓒⓓ</td><td>20. ⓪①②③④⑤⑥⑦⑧⑨</td></tr>
<tr><td>21. ⓪①②③④⑤⑥⑦⑧⑨</td><td colspan="2">22. ⓪①②③④⑤⑥⑦⑧⑨</td></tr>
<tr><td>23. ⓪①②③④⑤⑥⑦⑧⑨</td><td colspan="2">24. ⓪①②③④⑤⑥⑦⑧⑨</td></tr>
</table>

| DAILY PRACTICE PROBLEM DPP 60 - MATHS | | | |
|---|---|---|---|
| Total Questions | 24 | Total Marks | 72 |
| Attempted | | Correct | |
| Incorrect | | Net Score | |
| Cut-off Score | 14 | Qualifying Score | 47 |
| Success Gap = Net Score – Qualifying Score | | | |

$$\text{Net Score} = \sum_{i=I}^{VI}\left[(\textbf{correct}_i \times MM_i)-(In_i - NM_i)\right]$$

**Name :**                                           **Date :**

**Start Time :**                                **End Time :**

# MATHEMATICS    M61

**SYLLABUS : Definite Integral-1 :** Fundamental Definite Integration, Definite Integration by substitution,

## Max. Marks : 74               Time : 60 min.

### GENERAL INSTRUCTIONS

- The Daily Practice Problem Sheet contains **24** Questions divided into 6 sections.

  Section I has **8** MCQ's with ONLY 1 correct option. 2 marks for correct answer and No negative marks.

  Section II has **4** MCQ's with 1 or MORE THAN 1 correct option. 4 marks for correct answer(s) and (–1) for wrong answer.

  Section III has **1** PASSAGE with **3** MCQ's with ONLY 1 correct option. 3 marks for correct and (–1) mark for wrong answer.

  Section IV has **2** MCQ's with multiple matchings. 1 mark for the correct matching of each row & No negative marks.

  Section V has **2** Assertion-Reason MCQ's with ONLY 1 correct option. 3 marks for correct and (–1) mark for wrong answer.

  Section VI has **5** single digit integer answer questions. 4 marks for correct answer and (–1) for wrong answer.
- No mark will be given/ deducted if no bubble is filled. Keep a timer in front and stop immediately at the end of 60 min.
- You have to evaluate your Response Grids yourself with the help of Solution Booklet.
- The sheet follows a particular syllabus. Do not attempt the sheet before you have completed your preparation for that syllabus. Refer syllabus sheet in the starting of the book for the syllabus of all the DPP sheets.
- After completing the sheet check your answers with the solution booklet and complete the Result Grid. Finally spend time to analyse your performance and revise the areas which emerge out as weak in your evaluation.

## Section - I - Straight Objective Type

This section contains 8 multiple choice questions. Each question has 4 choices (a), (b), (c) and (d), out of which **ONLY ONE** is correct.

**1.** The value of the definite integral, $\displaystyle\int_{1}^{\infty}(e^{x+1}+e^{3-x})^{-1}\,dx$ is

(a) $\dfrac{\pi}{4e^2}$        (b) $\dfrac{\pi}{4e}$

(c) $\dfrac{1}{e^2}\left(\dfrac{\pi}{2}-\tan^{-1}\dfrac{1}{e}\right)$    (d) $\dfrac{\pi}{2e^2}$

**2.** Let $f(x)$ be a function satisfying $f'(x)=f(x)$ with $f(0)=1$ and $g$ be the function satisfying $f(x)+g(x)=x^2$. The value of the integral $\displaystyle\int_{0}^{1} f(x)g(x)\,dx$ is

(a) $e-\dfrac{1}{2}e^2-\dfrac{5}{2}$      (b) $e-e^2-3$

(c) $\dfrac{1}{2}(e-3)$        (d) $e-\dfrac{1}{2}e^2-\dfrac{3}{2}$

**3.** $\displaystyle\int_{0}^{\infty} x^{2n+1}\cdot e^{-x^2}\,dx$ is equal to ($n\in N$).

(a) $n!$      (b) $2(n!)$     (c) $\dfrac{n!}{2}$    (d) $\dfrac{(n+1)!}{2}$

**4.** If $\displaystyle\beta+2\int_{0}^{1}x^2\,e^{-x^2}\,dx=\int_{0}^{1}e^{-x^2}\,dx$ then the value of $\beta$ is

(a) $e^{-1}$          (b) $e$

(c) $1/2e$         (d) can not be determined

**5.** Let $f(x)=\dfrac{\sin x}{x}$, then $\displaystyle\int_{0}^{\pi/2} f(x)\,f\left(\dfrac{\pi}{2}-x\right)dx=$

(a) $\dfrac{2}{\pi}\displaystyle\int_{0}^{\pi} f(x)\,dx$      (b) $\displaystyle\int_{0}^{\pi} f(x)\,dx$

(c) $\pi\displaystyle\int_{0}^{\pi} f(x)\,dx$      (d) $\dfrac{1}{\pi}\displaystyle\int_{0}^{\pi} f(x)\,dx$

| RESPONSE GRID | 1. ⓐⓑⓒⓓ | 2. ⓐⓑⓒⓓ | 3. ⓐⓑⓒⓓ | 4. ⓐⓑⓒⓓ | 5. ⓐⓑⓒⓓ |
|---|---|---|---|---|---|

**6.** $\displaystyle\int_0^{\sin^2 x} \sin^{-1}\sqrt{t}\, dt + \int_0^{\cos^2 x} \cos^{-1}\sqrt{t}\, dt$ is equal to

(a) $\pi/2$     (b) $1$     (c) $\pi/4$    (d) None of these

**7.** $\displaystyle\int_{\log \pi - \log 2}^{\log \pi} \frac{e^x dx}{1 - \cos\left(\frac{2}{3}e^x\right)}$ is equal to

(a) $\sqrt{3}$     (b) $-\sqrt{3}$     (c) $\dfrac{1}{\sqrt{3}}$     (d) $\dfrac{-1}{\sqrt{3}}$

**8.** $\displaystyle\int_0^{\pi} \frac{dx}{1 + 2^{\cos x}}$ is equal to

(a) $\pi$     (b) $0$     (c) $\pi/2$     (d) $2\pi$

## Section - II - Multiple Correct Answer Type

This section contains 4 multiple correct answer(s) type questions. Each question has 4 choices (a), (b), (c) and (d), out of which **ONE OR MORE** is/are correct.

**9.** Let $J = \displaystyle\int_{-1}^{2}\left(\cot^{-1}\frac{1}{x} + \cot^{-1} x\right) dx$ and $K = \displaystyle\int_{-2\pi}^{7\pi} \frac{\sin x}{|\sin x|}\, dx$

Then which of the following alternative(s) is/are correct –

(a) $2J + 3K = 8\pi$       (b) $4J^2 + K^2 = 26\pi^2$

(c) $2J - K = 3\pi$       (d) $\dfrac{J}{K} = \dfrac{2}{5}$

**10.** For $U_n = \displaystyle\int_0^1 x^n(2-x)^n dx$; $V_n = \displaystyle\int_0^1 x^n(1-x)^n dx$ $n \in N$, which of the following statement(s) is/are false?

(a) $U_n = 2^n V_n$       (b) $U_n = 2^{-n} V_n$

(c) $U_n = 2^{2n} V_n$       (d) $U_n = 2^{-2n} V_n$

**11.** If $a_0, a_1, a_2, a_3$ are all positive, then $4a_0 x^3 + 3a_1 x^2 + 2a_2 x + a_3 = 0$ has atleast one root in $(-1, 0)$ if

(a) $a_0 + a_2 = a_1 + a_3$     (b) $4a_0 + 2a_2 > 3a_1 + a_3$

(c) $4a_0 + 2a_2 < 3a_1 + a_3$     (d) $4a_0 + 2a_2 = 3a_1 + a_3$

**12.** If $I_n = \displaystyle\int_0^1 \frac{dx}{(1 + x^2)^n}$, $n \in N$, then which of the following statements hold good

(a) $2n\, I_{n+1} = 2^{-n} + (2n-1)\, I_n$    (b) $I_2 = \dfrac{\pi}{8} + \dfrac{1}{4}$

(c) $I_2 = \dfrac{\pi}{8} - \dfrac{1}{4}$          (d) $I_3 = \dfrac{\pi}{16} - \dfrac{5}{48}$

## Section - III - Linked Comprehension Type

This section contains one paragraph. Based upon the paragraph, 3 multiple choice questions have to be answered. Each question has 4 choices (a), (b), (c) and (d), out of which **ONLY ONE** is correct.

Let $f(a, x)$ be a function of $f(x)$ dependent on the parameter $a$ then the integral $I = \displaystyle\int_\alpha^\beta f(a,x)dx$ after evaluation will be a function of $a$,

say $F(a)$ then $I = F(a) = \displaystyle\int_\alpha^\beta f(a,x)dx$     ...(1)

Differentiating above with respect to $a$ we get $F'(a) = \displaystyle\int_\alpha^\beta \frac{\partial f(a,x)}{\partial a} dx$, ...(2)

where, $\dfrac{\partial f(a,x)}{\partial a}$ is derivative of $f(a,x)$ with respect to $a$ assuming $x$ as constant. Evaluating R.H.S. of (2) and then integrating the result so obtained we can obtain $F(a)$. Constant of integration in this process can be obtained by using suitable value of $a$.

**13.** If $\alpha$ is a parameter independent of $x$, and $\alpha \neq (2n+1)\pi$, $n \in I$, then the value of integral $\displaystyle\int_0^1 \frac{x^{\cos\alpha} - 1}{\ell n\, x} dx$, $x > 0$, $x \neq 1$, is

(a) $\ell n\, |\cos\alpha|$       (b) $\ell n(1 - \cos\alpha)$

(c) $\ell n(1 + \cos\alpha)$       (d) $1 - \cos\alpha$

| **Response** **Grid** | 6. ⓐⓑⓒⓓ | 7. ⓐⓑⓒⓓ | 8. ⓐⓑⓒⓓ | 9. ⓐⓑⓒⓓ | 10. ⓐⓑⓒⓓ |
|---|---|---|---|---|---|
| | 11. ⓐⓑⓒⓓ | 12. ⓐⓑⓒⓓ | 13. ⓐⓑⓒⓓ | | |

*Space for Rough Work*

**14.** The value of the integral $\int_0^1 \dfrac{x^{2\alpha}-1}{\ell n\, x}\,dx$, if $\alpha = \dfrac{2n-1}{2}$, is

    (a) $\log n$      (b) $2\log n$    (c) $2\log 2n$    (d) $\log 2 + \log n$

**15.** The value of the integral $\displaystyle\int_0^\infty \dfrac{e^{-ax}-e^{-bx}}{x}\,dx,\ a>0,\ b>0,$

    is equal to

    (a) $\dfrac{\ell n\, a}{\ell n\, b}$      (b) $\ell n\!\left(\dfrac{b}{a}\right)$    (c) $\ell n\, a + \ell n\, b$    (d) $e^{a/b}$

## Section - IV - Matrix-Match Type

This section contains 2 questions. It contains statements given in two columns, which have to be matched. Statements in Column I are labelled as A, B, C and D whereas statements in Column II are labelled as p, q, r and s. The answers to these questions have to be appropriately bubbled as illustrated in the following example. If the correct matches are A-p, A-r, B-p, B-s, C-r, C-s and D-q, then the correctly bubbled matrix will look like the following :

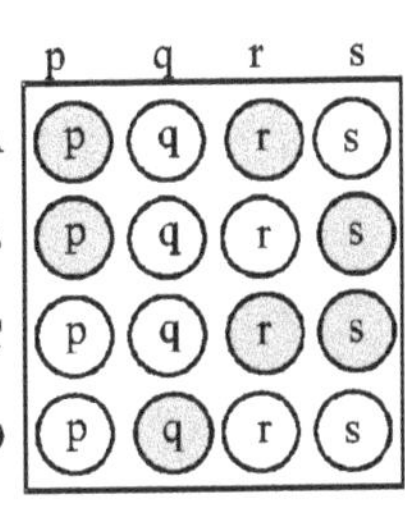

**16.** 

| Column I | Column II |
|---|---|
| (A) If $I = \displaystyle\int_0^1 \dfrac{x\,dx}{x^3+16}$ and $[.]$ represents the greatest integer function then $[I]$ is equal to | p. 0 |
| (B) If $f(\pi)=5$ and $\displaystyle\int_0^\pi \{f(x)+f''(x)\}\sin x\,dx = 2$, then $f(0)$ is equal to | q. 3 |
| (C) $\displaystyle\int_0^{\frac{\pi}{2}} \log\!\left(\dfrac{4+3\sin x}{4+3\cos x}\right)dx$ is equal to | r. $-3$ |

(D) If $x = \displaystyle\int_0^y \dfrac{dt}{\sqrt{1+9t^2}}$ and $\dfrac{d^2y}{dx^2} = a^2 y$ then 'a' is equal to

**17.** If at every point x of an interval [a, b] the inequalities $g(x) \le f(x) \le h(x)$ are fulfilled, then

$$\int_a^b g(x)\,dx \le \int_a^b f(x)\,dx \le \int_a^b h(x)\,dx,\ a<b$$

| Column I | Column II |
|---|---|
| (A) If $\mu < \displaystyle\int_0^1 \dfrac{x^7\,dx}{\sqrt[3]{(1+x^8)}} < \lambda$, then | p. $[\lambda+\mu]=2$, where $[.]$ denotes the greatest integer function. |
| (B) If $\mu < \displaystyle\int_0^1 \dfrac{dx}{\sqrt{(1+x^6)}} < \lambda$, then | q. $[\lambda+\mu]=4$, where $[.]$ denotes the greatest integer function. |
| (C) If $\mu < \displaystyle\int_0^1 \dfrac{dx}{\sqrt{(4-x^2-x^3)}} < \lambda$, then | r. $[\lambda-\mu]=0$, where $[.]$ denotes the greatest integer function. |
| | s. $[\lambda-\mu]=3$, where $[.]$ denotes the greatest integer function. |
| | t. $[\lambda+\mu]=0$, where $[.]$ denotes the greatest integer function. |

## Section - V - Reasoning Type

This section contains 2 reasoning type questions. Each question has 4 choices (a), (b), (c) and (d) out of which **ONLY ONE** is correct.

**DIRECTIONS for Qs. (18-19) :** Each of these questions contains two statements: **Statement-1 (Assertion) and Statement-2 (Reason).** Each of these questions has four alternative choices, only one of which is the correct answer. You have to select the correct choice.

(a) Statement-1 is True, Statement-2 is True; Statement-2 is a correct explanation for Statement-1.

(b) Statement-1 is True, Statement-2 is True; Statement-2 is NOT a correct explanation for Statement-1.

(c) Statement -1 is True, Statement-2 is False.

(d) Statement -1 is False, Statement-2 is True.

<table>
<tr><td rowspan="3">Response Grid</td><td>14. Ⓐ ⓑ ⓒ ⓓ    15. Ⓐ ⓑ ⓒ ⓓ</td></tr>
<tr><td>16. A - Ⓟ Ⓠ Ⓡ Ⓢ; B - Ⓟ Ⓠ Ⓡ Ⓢ; C - Ⓟ Ⓠ Ⓡ Ⓢ; D - Ⓟ Ⓠ Ⓡ Ⓢ</td></tr>
<tr><td>17. A - Ⓟ Ⓠ Ⓡ Ⓢ Ⓣ; B - Ⓟ Ⓠ Ⓡ Ⓢ Ⓣ; C - Ⓟ Ⓠ Ⓡ Ⓢ Ⓣ</td></tr>
</table>

*Space for Rough Work*

**18.** Statement–1 : $8 < \int\limits_{4}^{6} 2x\,dx < 12$ .

Statement–2 : If m is the smallest and M is the greatest vlaue of a function $f(x)$ in an interval (a, b), then for a < b,

$$m(b-a) \le \int_{a}^{b} f(x)\,dx \le m(b-a)$$

**19.** Statement–1 : $\int_{0}^{\pi/2} \dfrac{\sin x}{x}\,dx < \dfrac{\pi}{2}$

Statement–2 : $\lim\limits_{x \to 0} \dfrac{\sin x}{x} = 1$

## Section - VI - Integer Type

This section contains 5 questions. The answer to each of the questions is a single digit integer ranging from 0 to 9.

**20.** If the value of the definite integral

$$\int\limits_{-1/2}^{1/2} \left( \sin^{-1}(3x - 4x^3) - \cos^{-1}(4x^3 - 3x) \right) dx \ \ \text{is} - \dfrac{\pi}{A}.$$

Find A.

**21.** If $\int\limits_{0}^{f(x)} t^2\,dt = x \cos \pi x$ , then f' (9) is equal to $-\dfrac{1}{P}$ then find the value of P.

**22.** Let a, b and c be positive constants. The value of 'a' in terms of 'c' if the value of integral

$$\int\limits_{0}^{1} (acx^{b+1} + a^3 bx^{3b+5})\,dx \ \ \text{is independent of b equals}$$

$\sqrt{\dfrac{PC}{Q}}$, Find the value of P + Q.

**23.** Let $u = \int\limits_{0}^{1} \dfrac{ln(x+1)}{x^2+1}\,dx$ and $v = \int\limits_{0}^{\pi/2} ln(\sin 2x)\,dx$ then find the value of $\dfrac{-v}{u}$ .

**24.** If $\int\limits_{0}^{\pi/2} \dfrac{1 - \sin 2x}{(1+\sin 2x)^2}\,dx = \dfrac{a}{b}$ where a, b are relatively prime, find a + b + ab.



### DAILY PRACTICE PROBLEM DPP 61 - MATHS

| Total Questions | 24 | Total Marks | 74 |
| --- | --- | --- | --- |
| Attempted | | Correct | |
| Incorrect | | Net Score | |
| Cut-off Score | 15 | Qualifying Score | 48 |
| Success Gap = Net Score – Qualifying Score | | | |

$$\text{Net Score} = \sum_{i=\text{I}}^{\text{VI}} \left[ (\text{correct}_i \times MM_i) - (In_i - NM_i) \right]$$

**Name :**

**Date :**

**Start Time :**

**End Time :**

## MATHEMATICS     M62

**SYLLABUS : Definite Integral-2 :** Definite Integration as a limit of sum, Properties of definite integration

## Max. Marks : 74                  Time : 60 min.

### GENERAL INSTRUCTIONS

- The Daily Practice Problem Sheet contains **24** Questions divided into 6 sections.
  Section I has **8** MCQ's with ONLY 1 correct option. 2 marks for correct answer and No negative marks.
  Section II has **4** MCQ's with 1 or MORE THAN 1 correct option. 4 marks for correct answer(s) and (–1) for wrong answer.
  Section III has **1** PASSAGE with **3** MCQ's with ONLY 1 correct option. 3 marks for correct and (–1) mark for wrong answer.
  Section IV has **2** MCQ's with multiple matchings. 1 mark for the correct matching of each row & No negative marks.
  Section V has **2** Assertion-Reason MCQ's with ONLY 1 correct option. 3 marks for correct and (–1) mark for wrong answer.
  Section VI has **5** single digit integer answer questions. 4 marks for correct answer and (–1) for wrong answer.
- No mark will be given/ deducted if no bubble is filled. Keep a timer in front and stop immediately at the end of 60 min.
- You have to evaluate your Response Grids yourself with the help of Solution Booklet.
- The sheet follows a particular syllabus. Do not attempt the sheet before you have completed your preparation for that syllabus. Refer syllabus sheet in the starting of the book for the syllabus of all the DPP sheets.
- After completing the sheet check your answers with the solution booklet and complete the Result Grid. Finally spend time to analyse your performance and revise the areas which emerge out as weak in your evaluation.

---

### Section - I - Straight Objective Type

This section contains 8 multiple choice questions. Each question has 4 choices (a), (b), (c) and (d), out of which **ONLY ONE** is correct.

**1.** The value of the integral $\int_{-\pi}^{\pi} (\cos px - \sin qx)^2\, dx$ where p, q are integers, is equal to :

(a) $-\pi$    (b) $0$    (c) $\pi$    (d) $2\pi$

**2.** The value of $\displaystyle \lim_{n \to \infty} \sum_{r=1}^{r=4n} \frac{\sqrt{n}}{\sqrt{r}\left(3\sqrt{r} + 4\sqrt{n}\right)^2}$ is equal to

(a) $1/35$    (b) $1/14$    (c) $1/10$    (d) $1/5$

**3.** Let $f : R \to R$ and $g : R \to R$ be continous functions. Then the value of the integral
$\int_{-\pi/2}^{\pi/2} [f(x) + f(-x)]\,[g(x) - g(-x)]dx$ is

(a) $\pi$    (b) $1$    (c) $-1$    (d) $0$

**4.** Let $f$ be a positive function.

Let $I_1 = \int_{1-k}^{k} xf[x(1-x)]dx,\ I_2 = \int_{1-k}^{k} f[x(1-x)]dx,$ where $2k-1 > 0$. Then $\dfrac{I_1}{I_2}$ is

(a) $2$    (b) $k$    (c) $\dfrac{1}{2}$    (d) $1$

**5.** $\int_{\pi/4}^{3\pi/4} \dfrac{dx}{1 + \cos x}$ is equal to

(a) $2$    (b) $-2$    (c) $1/2$    (d) $-1/2$

---

| RESPONSE GRID | 1. ⓐⓑⓒⓓ | 2. ⓐⓑⓒⓓ | 3. ⓐⓑⓒⓓ | 4. ⓐⓑⓒⓓ | 5. ⓐⓑⓒⓓ |
|---|---|---|---|---|---|

**6.** If f is continuous and differentiable on [0, 1] with $f(0) = 0$ and $f(a) = 1$, then the minimum value of $\int_0^1 (f'(x))^2 \, dx$ is

(a) 0      (b) 1/2      (c) 2/3      (d) 1

**7.** $\displaystyle \lim_{n \to \infty} \frac{1}{n^6} \{(n+1)^5 + (n+2)^5 + \ldots\ldots + (2n)^5\}$ is equal to

(a) 0      (b) $\dfrac{21}{2}$      (c) $\dfrac{31}{2}$      (d) $\dfrac{32}{3}$

**8.** The value of $\displaystyle \int_\alpha^{\pi/2 - \alpha} \frac{d\theta}{1 + \cot^n \theta}$ , where $0 < \alpha < \pi/2,\ n > 0$ is

(a) independent of $\alpha$
(b) independent of n
(c) independent of both $\alpha$ and n
(d) none of these

## Section - II - Multiple Correct Answer Type

This section contains 4 multiple correct answer(s) type questions. Each question has 4 choices (a), (b), (c) and (d), out of which **ONE OR MORE** is/are correct.

**9.** Which of the following statements are correct ?

(a) $\displaystyle \lim_{n \to \infty} n \int_0^{\pi/2} (1 - \sqrt[n]{\sin x}) \, dx = \frac{\pi}{2} \ln 2$

(b) The value of definite integral

$\displaystyle \int_\infty^0 \frac{z e^{-z}}{\sqrt{1 - e^{-2z}}} \, dz = -\frac{\pi}{2} \ln 2$

(c) The value of definite integral

$\displaystyle \int_0^\pi \frac{x \,|\sin x|}{1 + |\cos x|} \, dx = -\pi \ln 2$

(d) The value of definite integral $\displaystyle \int_0^\pi \frac{x \,|\sin x|}{1 + |\cos x|} \, dx = \pi \ln 2$

**10.** If $f(x)$ is integrable over $[1, 2]$, then $\displaystyle \int_1^2 f(x) \, dx$ is equal to

(a) $\displaystyle \lim_{n \to \infty} \frac{1}{n} \sum_{r=1}^{n} f\left(\frac{r}{n}\right)$      (b) $\displaystyle \lim_{n \to \infty} \frac{1}{n} \sum_{r=n+1}^{2n} f\left(\frac{r}{n}\right)$

(c) $\displaystyle \lim_{n \to \infty} \frac{1}{n} \sum_{r=1}^{2n} f\left(\frac{r+n}{n}\right)$      (d) $\displaystyle \lim_{n \to \infty} \frac{1}{n} \sum_{r=1}^{2n} f\left(\frac{r}{n}\right)$

**11.** The value of the integral $\displaystyle \int_a^b \frac{|x|}{x} dx \ (a < b)$ is

(a) $b - a$      (b) $a - b$
(c) $b + a$      (d) None of the above

**12.** The integral $\displaystyle \int_0^\pi x \, f(\sin x) \, dx$ is equal to

(a) $\dfrac{\pi}{2} \displaystyle\int_0^\pi f(\sin x) \, dx$      (b) $\dfrac{\pi}{4} \displaystyle\int_0^\pi f(\sin x) \, dx$

(c) $\pi \displaystyle\int_0^{\pi/2} f(\sin x) \, dx$      (d) $\pi \displaystyle\int_0^{\pi/2} f(\cos x) \, dx$

## Section - III - Linked Comprehension Type

This section contains one paragraph. Based upon the paragraph, 3 multiple choice questions have to be answered. Each question has 4 choices (a), (b), (c) and (d), out of which **ONLY ONE** is correct.

Let f be an even function integrable every where and periodic with period 2.

Let $g(x) = \displaystyle\int_0^x f(t) dt$ and $g(1) = \alpha$

| RESPONSE GRID | | | | | |
|---|---|---|---|---|---|
| | 6. ⓐⓑ©ⓓ | 7. ⓐⓑ©ⓓ | 8. ⓐⓑ©ⓓ | 9. ⓐⓑ©ⓓ | 10. ⓐⓑ©ⓓ |
| | 11. ⓐⓑ©ⓓ | 12. ⓐⓑ©ⓓ | | | |

**13.** Function g(x) is
  (a) odd  (b) even
  (c) neither even nor odd  (d) none of these

**14.** Which of the following statement is correct for all x
  (a) $g(x+2)+g(x)=g(2)$  (b) $g(x+2)-g(x)=g(2)$
  (c) $g(x+2)-g(x)=2g(2)$  (d) none of these

**15.** The value of $\alpha$ for which g(x) be periodic with period 2
  (a) $\alpha=1$  (b) $\alpha=-1$
  (c) $\alpha=0$  (d) none of these

## Section - IV - Matrix-Match Type

This section contains 2 questions. It contains statements given in two columns, which have to be matched. Statements in Column I are labelled as A, B, C and D whereas statements in Column II are labelled as p, q, r and s. The answers to these questions have to be appropriately bubbled as illustrated in the following example. If the correct matches are A-p, A-r, B-p, B-s, C-r, C-s and D-q, then the correctly bubbled matrix will look like the following :

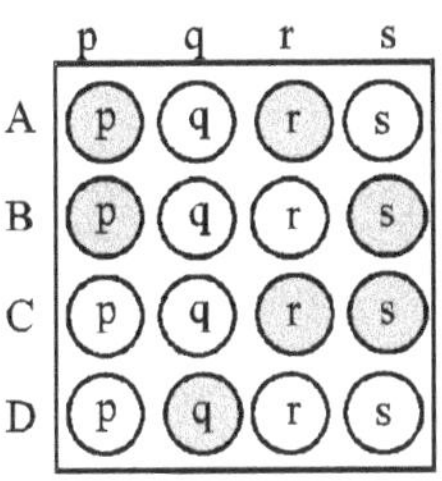

**16.** **Column I**  **Column II**

(A) $\displaystyle\int_{-4}^{-5} e^{(x+5)^2}\,dx + 3\int_{1/3}^{2/3} e^{9\left(x-\frac{2}{3}\right)^2}\,dx$  p. 0

(B) $\displaystyle\int_{-2}^{2} [x]$  q. $2\pi$

(C) $\displaystyle\int_{-1}^{3}\left(\tan^{-1}\left(\frac{x^2+1}{x}\right)+\tan^{-1}\left(\frac{x}{1+x^2}\right)\right)$  r. $-2$

(D) The greater of $\displaystyle\int_{0}^{\pi/2}\frac{\sin x}{x}\,dx$ and $\dfrac{\pi}{2}$  s. $\dfrac{\pi}{2}$

**17.** **Column-I**  **Column-II**

(A) If $\displaystyle\int_{1}^{4}|x-3|\,dx = 2a+b$, then  p. $a=3, b=3/2$

(B) If $\displaystyle\int_{-1}^{1}\frac{|x|}{x}\,dx = a-2b$, then  q. $a=1, b=\dfrac{1}{2}$

(C) If $\displaystyle\int_{0}^{2\pi}|\sin x|\,dx = 5a+b$, then  r. $a=1, b=-1$

  s. $a=2, b=-3/2$

  t. $a=\dfrac{1}{2}, b=\dfrac{3}{2}$

## Section - V - Reasoning Type

This section contains 2 reasoning type questions. Each question has 4 choices (a), (b), (c) and (d) out of which **ONLY ONE** is correct.

**DIRECTIONS for (Qs 18-19) : Each of these questions contains two statements: Statement-1 (Assertion) and Statement-2 (Reason). Each of these questions has four alternative choices, only one of which is the correct answer. You have to select the correct choice.**

(a) Statement-1 is True, Statement-2 is True; Statement-2 is a correct explanation for Statement-1.

(b) Statement-1 is True, Statement-2 is True; Statement-2 is NOT a correct explanation for Statement-1.

(c) Statement -1 is True, Statement-2 is False.

(d) Statement -1 is False, Statement-2 is True.



*Space for Rough Work*

18. **Statement 1 :** $\displaystyle\int_{0}^{10}\{x-[x]\}dx = 5$ , where $[\,.\,]$ denotes greatest integer function.

    **Statement 2 :** $\displaystyle\int_{0}^{na} f(x)dx = n\int_{0}^{a} f(x)dx$ , if $f(x+a)=f(x)$

19. **Statement 1 :** $\displaystyle\int_{-2}^{2} \log\left(\dfrac{1+x}{1-x}\right)dx = 0$

    **Statement 2 :** If $f$ is an odd function, then $\displaystyle\int_{-a}^{a} f(x)dx = 0$

---

### Section - VI - Integer Type

This section contains 5 questions. The answer to each of the questions is a single digit integer ranging from 0 to 9.

20. If $\displaystyle I = \int_{0}^{\pi/2} \ell n\,(\sin x)\ dx$ then $\displaystyle\int_{-\pi/4}^{\pi/4} \ell n\,(\sin x + \cos x)\ dx$ $= \dfrac{I}{P}$ . Find P.

21. If $\displaystyle\int_{-\pi/4}^{\pi/4} \dfrac{(\pi - 4\theta)\tan\theta}{1-\tan\theta}d\theta = \pi\,\ell n\,k - \dfrac{\pi^2}{w}$ , find the value of $(kw)$, where $k,\ w \in N$.

22. If $\displaystyle\lim_{n\to\infty}\left(\dfrac{1}{n+1}+\dfrac{1}{n+2}+...+\dfrac{1}{6n}\right) = \log A$ , then find the value of A.

23. If $\displaystyle\int_{0}^{1}\dfrac{\log(1+x)}{1+x^2}\,dx = \dfrac{A\pi}{B}\log C$ , then find the value of $A+B-C$.

24. If $\displaystyle\int_{2}^{3}\dfrac{\sqrt{x}}{\sqrt{5-x}+\sqrt{x}}dx = x$, then find the value of $4x$.

<table>
<tr><td rowspan="3">RESPONSE GRID</td><td>18. ⓐⓑⓒⓓ</td><td>19. ⓐⓑⓒⓓ</td><td>20. ⓪①②③④⑤⑥⑦⑧⑨</td></tr>
<tr><td>21. ⓪①②③④⑤⑥⑦⑧⑨</td><td colspan="2">22. ⓪①②③④⑤⑥⑦⑧⑨</td></tr>
<tr><td>23. ⓪①②③④⑤⑥⑦⑧⑨</td><td colspan="2">24. ⓪①②③④⑤⑥⑦⑧⑨</td></tr>
</table>

### DAILY PRACTICE PROBLEM DPP 62 - MATHS

| Total Questions | 24 | Total Marks | 74 |
|---|---|---|---|
| Attempted | | Correct | |
| Incorrect | | Net Score | |
| Cut-off Score | 15 | Qualifying Score | 48 |
| Success Gap = Net Score – Qualifying Score | | | |

$$\textbf{Net Score} = \sum_{i=1}^{VI}\left[(\textbf{correct}_i \times MM_i)-(In_i - NM_i)\right]$$

---

*Space for Rough Work*

**Name :**                                                                          **Date :**

**Start Time :**                                                                     **End Time :**

# MATHEMATICS     M63

**SYLLABUS : Application of Integrals :** Area of bounded region

## Max. Marks : 74                                                    Time : 60 min.

### GENERAL INSTRUCTIONS

- The Daily Practice Problem Sheet contains **24** Questions divided into 6 sections.
  Section I has **8** MCQ's with ONLY 1 correct option. 2 marks for correct answer and No negative marks.
  Section II has **4** MCQ's with 1 or MORE THAN 1 correct option. 4 marks for correct answer(s) and (–1) for wrong answer.
  Section III has **1** PASSAGE with **3** MCQ's with ONLY 1 correct option. 3 marks for correct and (–1) mark for wrong answer.
  Section IV has **2** MCQ's with multiple matchings. 1 mark for the correct matching of each row & No negative marks.
  Section V has **2** Assertion-Reason MCQ's with ONLY 1 correct option. 3 marks for correct and (–1) mark for wrong answer.
  Section VI has **5** single digit integer answer questions. 4 marks for correct answer and (–1) for wrong answer.
- No mark will be given/ deducted if no bubble is filled. Keep a timer in front and stop immediately at the end of 60 min.
- You have to evaluate your Response Grids yourself with the help of Solution Booklet.
- The sheet follows a particular syllabus. Do not attempt the sheet before you have completed your preparation for that syllabus. Refer syllabus sheet in the starting of the book for the syllabus of all the DPP sheets.
- After completing the sheet check your answers with the solution booklet and complete the Result Grid. Finally spend time to analyse your performance and revise the areas which emerge out as weak in your evaluation.

## Section - I - Straight Objective Type

This section contains 8 multiple choice questions. Each question has 4 choices (a), (b), (c) and (d), out of which **ONLY ONE** is correct.

**1.** Area bounded by the curves $y = \sin^{-1}(\sin x)$ and

$$|y| = \sqrt{\frac{\pi^2}{4} - \left(x - \frac{\pi}{2}\right)^2} \text{ is } -$$

(a) $\dfrac{\pi^2}{4}\left(\dfrac{\pi}{2}+1\right)(\text{unit})^2$     (b) $\dfrac{\pi^2}{2}\left(\dfrac{\pi}{2}+1\right)(\text{unit})^2$

(c) $\dfrac{\pi^2}{2}\left(\dfrac{\pi}{4}+1\right)(\text{unit})^2$     (d) None of these

**2.** The positive values of the parameter 'a' for which the area of the figure bounded by the curve $y = \cos ax$, $y = 0$,

$x = \dfrac{\pi}{6a}, x = \dfrac{5\pi}{6a}$ is greater than 3 are :

(a)  $\phi$                              (b)  $(0, 1/3)$
(c)  $(3, \infty)$                        (d)  none of these

**3.** If $(a, 0); a > 0$ is the point where the curve $y = \sin 2x - \sqrt{3}\sin x$ cuts the x-axis first, A is the area bounded by this part of the curve , the origin and the positive x-axis, then

(a)  $4A + 8\cos a = 7$          (b)  $4A + 8\sin a = 7$
(c)  $4A - 8\sin a = 7$          (d)  $4A - 8\cos a = 7$

**4.** Area bounded by the parabola $y = x^2 - 2x + 3$ and tangents drawn to it from the point $P(1, 0)$ is equal to

(a)  $4\sqrt{2}$ sq. units          (b)  $\dfrac{4\sqrt{2}}{3}$ sq. units

(c)  $\dfrac{8\sqrt{2}}{3}$ sq. units          (d)  $\dfrac{16}{3}\sqrt{2}$ sq. units

**5.** Area of the region which consists of all the points satisfying the conditions $|x - y| + |x + y| \le 8$ and $xy \ge 2$, is equal to

(a)  $4(7 - \ln 8)$ sq. units     (b)  $4(9 - \ln 8)$ sq. units
(c)  $2(7 - \ln 8)$ sq. units     (d)  $2(9 - \ln 8)$ sq. units

| RESPONSE GRID | 1. ⓐⓑⓒⓓ | 2. ⓐⓑⓒⓓ | 3. ⓐⓑⓒⓓ | 4. ⓐⓑⓒⓓ | 5. ⓐⓑⓒⓓ |
|---|---|---|---|---|---|

6. Find the area of the region bounded by
$y = \log_e x$ and $y = \sin^4 \pi x$.
(a) $1/8$    (b) $11/8$    (c) $3/8$    (d) $2/7$

7. A point P moves in xy plane in such a way that $[|x|] + [|y|] = 1$, where $[.]$ denotes the greatest integer function. Area of the region representing all possible positions of the point P is equal to
(a) 4 sq. units      (b) 16 sq. units
(c) $2\sqrt{2}$ sq. units      (d) 8 sq. units

8. Find the area bounded by
$|x| \le 2, |y| \le 2, 2xy \le |x+y| \le x^2 + y^2$.
(a) $12 - \pi + \log 3$      (b) $12 + \pi + \log 3$
(c) $12 - \pi - \log 3$      (d) None of these

---

## Section - II - Multiple Correct Answer Type

This section contains 4 multiple correct answer(s) type questions. Each question has 4 choices (a), (b), (c) and (d), out of which **ONE OR MORE** is/are correct.

9. A function $y = f(x)$ satisfies the condition $f'(x) \sin x + f(x) \cos x = 1$, $f(x)$ being bounded when

$x \to 0$. If $I = \displaystyle\int_0^{\pi/2} f(x)\,dx$ then

(a) $\dfrac{\pi}{2} < I < \dfrac{\pi^2}{4}$      (b) $\dfrac{\pi}{4} < I < \dfrac{\pi^2}{2}$

(c) $1 < I < \dfrac{\pi}{2}$      (d) $0 < I < 1$

10. Which of the following statements are correct ?
(a) Area bounded by the curve $y = \max\{\sin x, \cos x\}$ and x-axis, between the lines $x = \pi/4$ and $x = 2\pi$ is equal to

$\dfrac{(4\sqrt{2}-1)}{\sqrt{2}}$ sq. units.

(b) The area bounded by the curves $y = \sqrt{x},\ 2y+3 = x$ and x-axis in the $1^{st}$ quadrant is 9

(c) The area of the region bounded by $y = |x-1|$ and $y = 1$ is 1

(d) The area of the region bounded by x-axis and the curves defined by $y = \tan x,\ -\pi/3 \le x \le \pi/3$ and $y = \cot x,\ +\pi/6 \le x \le 3\pi/2$ is $\log 2$

11. For which of the following values of m, is the area of the region bounded by the curve $y = x - x^2$ and the line $y = mx$ equals $9/2$ sq unit?
(a) $-4$      (b) $-2$
(c) $2$      (d) $4$

12. The area enclosed between the curves, $x^2 = y$ and $y^2 = x$ is equal to
(a) $\dfrac{1}{3}$ sq. unit      (b) $2\displaystyle\int_0^1 (x - x^2)\,dx$
(c) area of the region $\{(x,y) : x^2 \le y \le |x|\}$
(d) $1$ sq. unit

---

## Section - III - Linked Comprehension Type

This section contains one paragraph. Based upon the paragraph, 3 multiple choice questions have to be answered. Each question has 4 choices (a), (b), (c) and (d), out of which **ONLY ONE** is correct.

---

If $x = f(y)$ and $x = g(y)$ be two functional curves, then area bounded by curves $x = f(y),\ x = g(y),\ y = c$ and $y = d$ is

given by $\displaystyle\int_c^d |(f(y) - g(y))|\,dy$, where $d > c$. In case of $g(y)$

always left of $f(y)$, required area $= \displaystyle\int_c^d (f(y) - g(y))\,dy$

13. The area bounded by $y = \ln x$, x–axis and y–axis is given by

(a) $\displaystyle\int_1^\infty \ell n\, y\, dy$    (b) $\displaystyle\int_{-\infty}^0 e^{-y} dy$    (c) $\displaystyle\int_{-\infty}^0 e^y dy$    (d) none of these

---

| **RESPONSE GRID** | 6. Ⓐ Ⓑ Ⓒ Ⓓ | 7. Ⓐ Ⓑ Ⓒ Ⓓ | 8. Ⓐ Ⓑ Ⓒ Ⓓ | 9. Ⓐ Ⓑ Ⓒ Ⓓ | 10. Ⓐ Ⓑ Ⓒ Ⓓ |
| | 11. Ⓐ Ⓑ Ⓒ Ⓓ | 12. Ⓐ Ⓑ Ⓒ Ⓓ | 13. Ⓐ Ⓑ Ⓒ Ⓓ | | |

*Space for Rough Work*

**14.** Area bounded by $y = \tan^{-1} x$, $y = \cot^{-1} x$ and $y$–axis is equal to

(a) $\ln \sqrt{2}$ sq. units

(b) $\ln 4$ sq. untis

(c) $\ln 2$ sq. units

(d) none of these

**15.** The area bounded by $y^2 = 2x + 1$ and $x - y - 1 = 0$, will be

(a) 16/9

(b) 16/3

(c) 8/3

(d) none of these

## Section - IV - Matrix-Match Type

This section contains 2 questions. It contains statements given in two columns, which have to be matched. Statements in Column I are labelled as A, B, C and D whereas statements in Column II are labelled as p, q, r and s. The answers to these questions have to be appropriately bubbled as illustrated in the following example. If the correct matches

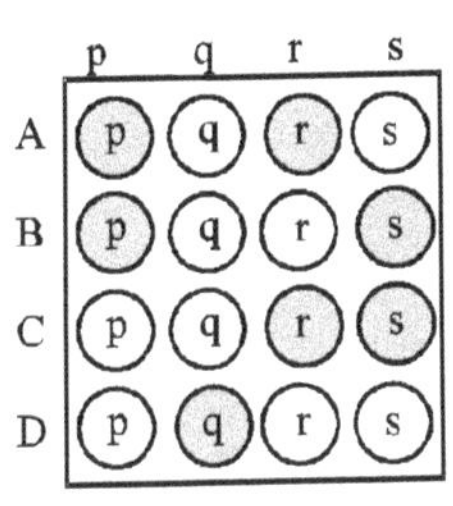

are A-p, A-r, B-p, B-s, C-r, C-s and D-q, then the correctly bubbled matrix will look like the following :

**16.**

| | Column-I | | Column-II |
|---|---|---|---|
| (A) | The area bounded by $y = 3x$ and $y = x^2$ is | p. | $\dfrac{2}{3}$ |
| (B) | The area bounded by $x = 4 - y^2$ and the $y$-axis is | q. | $\dfrac{17}{12}$ |
| (C) | The area in square units of the region bounded by the curve $x^2 = 4y$, the line $x = 2$ and the $x$-axis is | r. | $\dfrac{32}{3}$ |
| (D) | The area bounded by $y = x^3$, $y = x^2$ and $x = 1$, $x = 2$ is | s. | $\dfrac{32}{9}$ |
| | | t. | $\dfrac{9}{2}$ |

**17.**

| | Column-I | | Column-II |
|---|---|---|---|
| (A) | Area enclosed by the curve $(y - \sin^{-1}x)^2 = x - x^2$ is equal to | p. | 0 |
| (B) | The area of the region represented by the expression $\sqrt{2} \le \lvert x + y \rvert + \lvert x - y \rvert \le 2\sqrt{2}$ is equal to | q. | 1 |
| (C) | If the area bounded by $y = x^2 - 3$ and the line $y = ax + 2$ attains its minimum value then the parameter $a$ is equal to | r. | $\pi$ |
| (D) | If k is a positive number and the area of the region bounded by the curves $y = x - kx^2$ and $ky = x^2$ attains its maximum value then k is equal to | s. | 6 |
| | | t. | $\pi/4$ |

## Section - V - Reasoning Type

This section contains 2 reasoning type questions. Each question has 4 choices (a), (b), (c) and (d) out of which **ONLY ONE** is correct.

**DIRECTIONS for (Qs. 18 & 19) : Each of these questions contains two statements: Statement-1 (Assertion) and Statement-2 (Reason). Each of these questions has four alternative choices, only one of which is the correct answer. You have to select the correct choice.**

(a) Statement-1 is True, Statement-2 is True; Statement-2 is a correct explanation for Statement-1.

(b) Statement-1 is True, Statement-2 is True; Statement-2 is NOT a correct explanation for Statement-1.

(c) Statement -1 is True, Statement-2 is False.

(d) Statement -1 is False, Statement-2 is True.

---

**RESPONSE GRID**

14. (a)(b)(c)(d)    15. (a)(b)(c)(d)

16. A - (p)(q)(r)(s)(t); B - (p)(q)(r)(s)(t); C - (p)(q)(r)(s)(t); D - (p)(q)(r)(s)(t)

17. A - (p)(q)(r)(s)(t); B - (p)(q)(r)(s)(t); C - (p)(q)(r)(s)(t); D - (p)(q)(r)(s)(t)

*Space for Rough Work*

18. **Statement -1 :** Let f be a real valued function satisfying

$$f\left(\frac{x}{y}\right) = f(x) - f(y) \text{ and } \lim_{x \to 0} \frac{f(1+x)}{x} = 3.$$

Then the area bounded by the curve y = f (x), the y-axis and the line y = 3 is 3 sq unit.

**Statement -2 :** The function f (x) is concave down.

19. **Statement -1 :** The area of the function $y = \sin^2 x$ from 0 to $\pi$ will be more than that of curve y = sin x from 0 to $\pi$.

**Statement -2 :** $t^2 < t$, if $0 < t < 1$.

## Section - VI - Integer Type

This section contains 5 questions. The answer to each of the questions is a single digit integer ranging from 0 to 9.

20. If A be the area bounded by the curves y = | x − 1 | and

$$y + \frac{3}{|x+1|} = 2,$$ then find the value of (2A + 3 ln 3).

21. Find the value of 'a' (a>0) for which the area bounded by

the curves $y = \frac{x}{6} + \frac{1}{x^2}$ , y = 0, x = a and x = 2a has the least value.

22. Let y = g (x) be the inverse of a bijective mapping $f: R \to R \, f(x) = 3x^3 + 2x$. The area bounded by the graph of g (x), the x-axis and the ordinate at x = 5 is $\frac{A}{B}$. Find A − B.

23. If $a = p^{1/n}$, then the value of the parameter 'a' (a > 0) for each of which the area of the figure bounded by the straight line

$$y = \frac{a^2 - ax}{1 + a^4} \text{ & the parabola } y = \frac{x^2 + 2ax + 3a^2}{1 + a^4} \text{ is the}$$

greatest. Find the value of P + n.

24. Let f be a differentiable function satisfying the condition

$$f\left(\frac{x}{y}\right) = \frac{f(x)}{f(y)} \ (y \neq 0, f(y) \neq 0) \ \forall \ x, y \in R \text{ and } f'(1) = 2. \text{ If the}$$

area enclosed by $y = f(x), x^2 + y^2 = 2$ and x − axis is $\left(\frac{\pi}{P} - \frac{Q}{R}\right)$

sq units, then find the value of P + Q + R.

| | | |
|---|---|---|
| **RESPONSE GRID** | 18. ⓐⓑⓒⓓ  19. ⓐⓑⓒⓓ | 20. ⓪①②③④⑤⑥⑦⑧⑨ |
| | 21. ⓪①②③④⑤⑥⑦⑧⑨ | 22. ⓪①②③④⑤⑥⑦⑧⑨ |
| | 23. ⓪①②③④⑤⑥⑦⑧⑨ | 24. ⓪①②③④⑤⑥⑦⑧⑨ |

## DAILY PRACTICE PROBLEM DPP 63 - MATHS

| Total Questions | 24 | Total Marks | 74 |
|---|---|---|---|
| Attempted | | Correct | |
| Incorrect | | Net Score | |
| Cut-off Score | 15 | Qualifying Score | 49 |
| Success Gap = Net Score – Qualifying Score | | | |

$$\text{Net Score} = \sum_{i=I}^{VI} \left[ (\text{correct}_i \times MM_i) - (In_i - NM_i) \right]$$

*Space for Rough Work*

**Name :**

**Date :**

**Start Time :**

**End Time :**

## MATHEMATICS  M64

**SYLLABUS : Differential Equations-1 :** Order and degree of differential equations, Formation of differential equations

# Max. Marks : 66

# Time : 60 min.

### GENERAL INSTRUCTIONS

- The Daily Practice Problem Sheet contains **22** Questions divided into 6 sections.
  Section I has **8** MCQ's with ONLY 1 correct option. 2 marks for correct answer and No negative marks.
  Section II has **4** MCQ's with 1 or MORE THAN 1 correct option. 4 marks for correct answer(s) and (–1) for wrong answer.
  Section III has **1** PASSAGE with **3** MCQ's with ONLY 1 correct option. 3 marks for correct and (–1) mark for wrong answer.
  Section IV has **2** MCQ's with multiple matchings. 1 mark for the correct matching of each row & No negative marks.
  Section V has **3** Assertion-Reason MCQ's with ONLY 1 correct option. 3 marks for correct and (–1) mark for wrong answer.
  Section VI has **2** single digit integer answer questions. 4 marks for correct answer and (–1) for wrong answer.
- No mark will be given/ deducted if no bubble is filled. Keep a timer in front and stop immediately at the end of 60 min.
- You have to evaluate your Response Grids yourself with the help of Solution Booklet.
- The sheet follows a particular syllabus. Do not attempt the sheet before you have completed your preparation for that syllabus. Refer syllabus sheet in the starting of the book for the syllabus of all the DPP sheets.
- After completing the sheet check your answers with the solution booklet and complete the Result Grid. Finally spend time to analyse your performance and revise the areas which emerge out as weak in your evaluation.

## Section - I - Straight Objective Type

This section contains 8 multiple choice questions. Each question has 4 choices (a), (b), (c) and (d), out of which **ONLY ONE** is correct.

**1.** The differential equation whose general solution is given by, $y = (c_1 \cos(x+c_2)) - (c_3 e^{(-x+c_4)}) + (c_5 \sin x)$, where $c_1, c_2, c_3, c_4, c_5$ are arbitrary constants, is

(a) $\dfrac{d^4 y}{dx^4} - \dfrac{d^2 y}{dx^2} + y = 0$

(b) $\dfrac{d^3 y}{dx^3} + \dfrac{d^2 y}{dx^2} + \dfrac{dy}{dx} + y = 0$

(c) $\dfrac{d^5 y}{dx^5} + y = 0$

(d) $\dfrac{d^3 y}{dx^3} - \dfrac{d^2 y}{dx^2} + \dfrac{dy}{dx} - y = 0$

**2.** The differential equation of all parabolas each of which has a latus rectum '4a' & whose axes are parallel to x-axis is:

(a) of order 1 & degree 2    (b) of order 2 & degree 3
(c) of order 2 and degree 1 (d) of order 2 and degree 2

**3.** Spherical rain drop evaporates at a rate proportional to its surface area. The differential equation corresponding to the rate of change of the radius of the rain drop if the constant of proportionality is $K > 0$, is

(a) $\dfrac{dr}{dt} + K = 0$

(b) $\dfrac{dr}{dt} - K = 0$

(c) $\dfrac{dr}{dt} = Kr$

(d) None of these

**4.** The differential equation of the system of circles touching the x-axis at origin is –

(a) $(x^2 - y^2)\dfrac{dy}{dx} + 2xy = 0$

(b) $(x^2 - y^2)\dfrac{dy}{dx} - 2xy = 0$

(c) $(x^2 + y^2)\dfrac{dy}{dx} + 2xy = 0$

(d) a second order differential equation

**5.** The degree of the differential equation

$$\left(\dfrac{d^3 y}{dx^3}\right)^{2/3} + 4 - 3\dfrac{d^2 y}{dx^2} + 5\dfrac{dy}{dx} = 0 \text{ is}$$

(a) 1     (b) 2     (c) 3     (d) None of these

| RESPONSE GRID | 1. ⓐⓑⓒⓓ | 2. ⓐⓑⓒⓓ | 3. ⓐⓑⓒⓓ | 4. ⓐⓑⓒⓓ | 5. ⓐⓑⓒⓓ |
|---|---|---|---|---|---|

**6.** The order and degree of the differential equation

$$\frac{d^2y}{dx^2}+\left(\frac{dy}{dx}\right)^{1/3}+x^{1/4}=0 \text{ are respectively}$$

(a) 2, 3    (b) 3, 3    (c) 2, 6    (d) 2, 4

**7.** A normal is drawn at a point P (x, y) of a curve. It meets the x-axis at Q. If PQ is of constant length k, then the differential equation describing such a curve is

(a) $y\dfrac{dy}{dx}=\pm\sqrt{k^2-y^2}$    (b) $x\dfrac{dy}{dx}=\pm\sqrt{k^2-x^2}$

(c) $y\dfrac{dy}{dx}=\pm\sqrt{y^2-k^2}$    (d) $x\dfrac{dy}{dx}=\pm\sqrt{x^2-k^2}$

**8.** The differential equation of the family of circles whose centres lie on the y–axis is

(a) $yy''+x(1+y'^2)=0$    (b) $xy''-y'(1+y'^2)=0$

(c) $y'y''-y(1+y'^2)=0$    (d) $y'y''+x(1+y'^2)=0$

## Section - II - Multiple Correct Answer Type

This section contains 4 multiple correct answer(s) type questions. Each question has 4 choices (a), (b), (c) and (d), out of which **ONE OR MORE** is/are correct.

**9.** The differential equation of the curve for which the initial ordinate of any tangent is equal to the corresponding subnormal

(a) is linear

(b) is homogeneous of first degree

(c) has degree 2    (d) is second order

**10.** Which of the following statements are correct ?

(a) The order of the differential equation associated with the primitive $y=c_1+c_2e^x+c_3e^{-2x+c_4}$, where $c_1$, $c_2$, $c_3$, $c_4$ are arbitrary constants, is 3

(b) The order of the differential equation of a family of ellipses with fixed directrix and fixed eccentricity is 2

(c) The differential equation representing the family of hyperbolas $a^2x^2-b^2y^2=c^2$ is $\dfrac{y''}{y'}+\dfrac{y'}{y}=\dfrac{1}{x^2}$

(d) The differential equation of the family of curves represented by $c(y+c)^2=x^3$ is $12y\left(\dfrac{dy}{dx}\right)^2=8x\left(\dfrac{dy}{dx}\right)^3-27x$

**11.** Identify the correct statement from the followings

(a) The differential equation of all parabolas having their axes of symmerty coinciding with the axis of X is $y\dfrac{d^2y}{dx^2}+\left(\dfrac{dy}{dx}\right)^2=0$.

(b) Differential equation of all conics of the form $ax^2+by=1$, a and b being parameters is $xy\dfrac{d^2y}{dx^2}+x\left(\dfrac{dy}{dx}\right)^2-y\dfrac{dy}{dx}=0$.

(c) Differential equation of all conics of the form $ax^2+by=1$, a and b being parameters is $xy\dfrac{d^2y}{dx^2}-x\left(\dfrac{dy}{dx}\right)^2+y\dfrac{dy}{dx}=0$.

(d) The differential equation of all parabolas having their axes of symmerty coinciding with the axis of X is $x\dfrac{d^2x}{dy^2}+\left(\dfrac{dx}{dy}\right)^2=0$.

**12.** The differential equation representing the family of curves $y^2=2c\left(x+\sqrt{c}\right)$, where c is a positive parameter, is of

(a) order 1    (b) order 2    (c) degree 3    (d) degree 4

## Section - III - Linked Comprehension Type

This section contains one paragraph. Based upon the paragraph, 3 multiple choice questions have to be answered. Each question has 4 choices (a), (b), (c) and (d), out of which **ONLY ONE** is correct.

The ORDER of a differential equation is defined as the order of the highest order derivative occuring in the equation. For example, the order of equation $\dfrac{d^2y}{dx^2}+y=0$ is 2, as it contains second order derivative as the highest order derivative. For a given family of curves the order of its differential equation will be equal to the number of arbitrary constants in its equation. For example, the family of curves given by $y=A\cos x+B\sin x$; has two arbitrary constants, so its differential equation will be second order.

| | | | | | |
|---|---|---|---|---|---|
| **RESPONSE GRID** | 6. ⓐⓑⓒⓓ | 7. ⓐⓑⓒⓓ | 8. ⓐⓑⓒⓓ | 9. ⓐⓑⓒⓓ | 10. ⓐⓑⓒⓓ |
| | 11. ⓐⓑⓒⓓ | 12. ⓐⓑⓒⓓ | | | |

*Space for Rough Work*

The DEGREE of a differential equation is the exponent of the highest order derivative in the equation after the equation is expressed as a polynomial in various order derivatives. For example, the equation $\dfrac{d^2y}{dx^2} + y = 0$ is in polynomial form so its degree is the exponent of $\dfrac{d^2y}{dx^2}$, which is 1.

**13.** The order and degree of the differential equation whose solution is $y = cx + c^2 - 3c^{3/2} + 2$, where $c$ is a parameter, are respectively

    (a) 1 and 4   (b) 1 and 3   (c) 2 and 2   (d) 1 and 2

**14.** The order and degree of the differential equation

$$\dfrac{d^2y}{dx^2} = \sin\left(\dfrac{dy}{dx}\right) + xy$$ are respectively

    (a) 2, 1                  (b) 2, infinite

    (c) 2, 0                  (d) 2, not defined

**15.** The order of the differential equation whose general solution is given by $y = (c_1 + c_2)\cos(x + c_3) - c_4 e^{x + c_5}$, where $c_1, c_2, c_3, c_4, c_5$ are arbitrary constants, is

    (a) 5       (b) 4       (c) 3       (d) 2

---

## Section - IV - Matrix-Match Type

This section contains 2 questions. It contains statements given in two columns, which have to be matched. Statements in Column I are labelled as A, B, C and D whereas statements in Column II are labelled as p, q, r and s. The answers to these questions have to be appropriately bubbled as illustrated in the following example. If the correct matches are A-p, A-r, B-p, B-s, C-r, C-s and D-q, then the correctly bubbled matrix will look like the following :

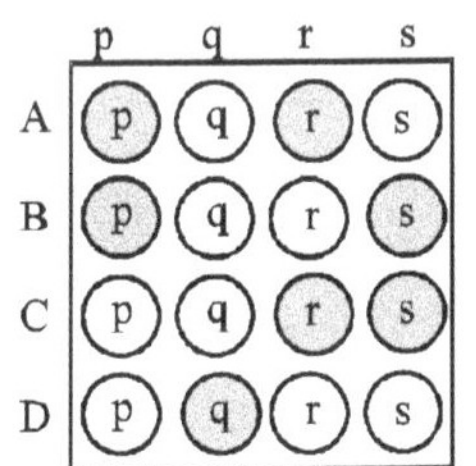

**16.**

| | Column-I | Column-II |
|---|---|---|
| (A) | The order of the differential equation of all conics whose centre lie at the origin is equal to | p. 1 |
| (B) | The order of the differential equation of all circles of radius a is equal to | q. 2 |
| (C) | The order of the differential equation of all parabolas whose axis of symmetry is parallel to x-axis is equal to | r. 3 |
| (D) | The order of the differential equation of all conics whose axes coincide with the axes of coordinates is equal to | s. 4 |

**17.**

| | Column-I | Column-II |
|---|---|---|
| (A) | The differential equation formed by differentiating and eliminating the constants from $y = a\sin^2 x + b\cos^2 x + c\sin 2x + d\cos 2x$, where $a, b, c, d$ are arbitrary constants. If order and degree of the differential equation represented by $O$ and $D$, then | p. $O + 2D = 5$ |
| (B) | The order and degree of the differential equation, whose general solution is given by $y = (c_1 + c_2)\sin(x + c_3) - c_4 e^{x + c_5 + c_6}$, where $c_1, c_2, c_3, c_4, c_5, c_6$ are arbitraty constants, are $O$ and $D$, then | q. $2O + 3D = 5$ |
| (C) | The order and degree of the differential equation satisfying $\sqrt{(1+x^2)} + \sqrt{(1+y^2)} = A(x\sqrt{(1+y^2)} + y\sqrt{(1+x^2)})$ are $O$ and $D$, then | r. $O = D$ |
| | | s. $O^D + D^O = 4$ |
| | | t. $2^O + 3^D = 11$ |

---

## Section - V - Reasoning Type

This section contains 3 reasoning type questions. Each question has 4 choices (a), (b), (c) and (d) out of which **ONLY ONE** is correct.

---



*Space for Rough Work*

**DIRECTIONS for (Qs 18-20) :** Each of these questions contains two statements: Statement-1 (Assertion) and Statement-2 (Reason). Each of these questions has four alternative choices, only one of which is the correct answer. You have to select the correct choice.

(a)  Statement-1 is True, Statement-2 is True; Statement-2 is a correct explanation for Statement-1.

(b)  Statement-1 is True, Statement-2 is True; Statement-2 is NOT a correct explanation for Statement-1.

(c)  Statement -1 is True, Statement-2 is False.

(d)  Statement -1 is False, Statement-2 is True.

18.  **Statement 1 :** The differential equation of family of hyperbola whose asymptote lines are $x + y - 1 = 0$ and

$x - y - 1 = 0$ is $x - 1 = y\dfrac{dy}{dx}$.

**Statement 2 :** Eccentricity of rectangular hyperbola is $\sqrt{2}$.

19.  **Statement-1:** Degree of the differential equation

$y = x \times \dfrac{dy}{dx} + \sqrt{1 + \left(\dfrac{dy}{dx}\right)^2}$ is 2.

**Statement-2:** In the given equation the power of highest order derivative when expressed as a polynomials in derivatives is 2.

20.  **Statement-1:** Degree of differential equation of parabolas having their axis along x–axis and vertex at $(2, 0)$ is 2.

**Statement-2:** Degree of differential equation of parabola having their axis along x–axis and vertex at $(1, 0)$ is 1.

## Section - VI - Integer Type

This section contains 2 questions . The answer to each of the questions is a single digit integer ranging from 0 to 9.

21.  If the function $y = e^{4x} + 2e^{-x}$ is a solution of the differential equation $\dfrac{\dfrac{d^3 y}{dx^3} - 13\dfrac{dy}{dx}}{y} = K$ then find the value of $\dfrac{K}{2}$

22.  The differential equation of all parabolas having their axis of symmetry coinciding with the axis of x has its order "O" and degree "D" . Find the value of O + D.

| | | |
|---|---|---|
| **RESPONSE GRID** | **18.** ⓐⓑⓒⓓ  **19.** ⓐⓑⓒⓓ  **20.** ⓐⓑⓒⓓ | |
| | **21.** ⓪①②③④⑤⑥⑦⑧⑨ | |
| | **22.** ⓪①②③④⑤⑥⑦⑧⑨ | |

## DAILY PRACTICE PROBLEM DPP 64 - MATHS

| Total Questions | 22 | Total Marks | 66 |
|---|---|---|---|
| Attempted | | Correct | |
| Incorrect | | Net Score | |
| Cut-off Score | 13 | Qualifying Score | 42 |
| Success Gap = Net Score – Qualifying Score | | | |

$$\text{Net Score} = \sum_{i=I}^{VI}\left[(\textbf{correct}_i \times MM_i) - (In_i - NM_i)\right]$$

*Space for Rough Work*

# DPP - Daily Practice Problems

**Name :**                                        **Date :**

**Start Time :**                                  **End Time :**

## MATHEMATICS     M65

SYLLABUS : Differential Equations-2 : Variable separable type differential equations

## Max. Marks : 57                                              Time : 60 min.



## Section - I - Straight Objective Type

This section contains 7 multiple choice questions. Each question has 4 choices (a), (b), (c) and (d), out of which **ONLY ONE** is correct.

**1.** Solution of the differential equation

$$\left(e^{x^2} + e^{y^2}\right) y \frac{dy}{dx} + e^{x^2}(xy^2 - x) = 0, \text{ is}$$

(a) $e^{x^2}(y^2 - 1) + e^{y^2} = C$

(b) $e^{y^2}(x^2 - 1) + e^{x^2} = C$

(c) $e^{y^2}(y^2 - 1) + e^{x^2} = C$

(d) $e^{x^2}(y - 1) + e^{y^2} = C$

**2.** The solution of the differential equation,

$$2 x^2 y \frac{dy}{dx} = \tan(x^2 y^2) - 2xy^2 \text{ given } y(1) = \sqrt{\frac{\pi}{2}} \text{ is}$$

(a) $\sin x^2 y^2 = e^{x-1}$      (b) $\sin(x^2 y^2) = x$

(c) $\cos x^2 y^2 + x = 0$        (d) $\sin(x^2 y^2) = e.e^x$

**3.** The general solution of the differential equation, $y' + y\phi'(x) - \phi(x) \cdot \phi'(x) = 0$ where $\phi(x)$ is a known function is :

(a) $y = ce^{-\phi(x)} + \phi(x) - 1$

(b) $y = ce^{+\phi(x)} + \phi(x) - 1$

(c) $y = ce^{-\phi(x)} - \phi(x) + 1$

(d) $y = ce^{-\phi(x)} + \phi(x) + 1$

where $c$ is an arbitrary constant .

**4.** Solution of differential equation

$$x^2 = 1 + \left(\frac{x}{y}\right)^{-1} \frac{dy}{dx} + \frac{\left(\frac{x}{y}\right)^{-2}\left(\frac{dy}{dx}\right)^2}{2!} + \frac{\left(\frac{x}{y}\right)^{-3}\left(\frac{dy}{dx}\right)^3}{3!} + .... \text{ is}$$

(a) $y^2 = x^2(\ln x^2 - 1) + c$      (b) $y = x^2(\ln x - 1) + c$

(c) $y^2 = x(\ln x - 1) + c$          (d) $y = x^2 e^{x^2} + c$

**5.** The general solution of the differential equation $(1 + y^2)dx + (1 + x^2)dy = 0$ is

(a) $mx - y = C(1 - xy)$      (b) $x - y = C(1 + xy)$

(c) $(x + y) = C(1 - xy)$      (d) $x + y = C(1 + xy)$

---

**RESPONSE GRID**  1. ⓐⓑⓒⓓ  2. ⓐⓑⓒⓓ  3. ⓐⓑⓒⓓ  4. ⓐⓑⓒⓓ  5. ⓐⓑⓒⓓ

**6.** The particular solution of the differential equation

$$\sin^{-1}\left(\frac{d^2y}{dx^2}-1\right)=x,\ \text{where}\ y=\frac{dy}{dx}=0\ \text{when}\ x=0,\ \text{is}$$

(a) $\ y=x^2+x-\sin x$

(b) $\ y=\dfrac{x^2}{2}+x-\sin x$

(c) $\ y=\dfrac{x^2}{2}+\dfrac{x}{2}-\sin x$

(d) $\ 2y=x^2+x-\sin x$

**7.** The general solution of $x(1+y^2)^{1/2}\,dx+y(1+x^2)^{1/2}\,dy=0$ is

(a) $\ \cos^{-1}x+\cos^{-1}y=C$

(b) $\ x^2+y^2=(1+x^2)^{1/2}+(1+y^2)^{1/2}+C$

(c) $\ (1+x^2)^{1/2}+(1+y^2)^{1/2}=C$

(d) $\ \tan^{-1}x-\tan^{-1}y=C$

## Section - II - Multiple Correct Answer Type

This section contains 3 multiple correct answer(s) type questions. Each question has 4 choices (a), (b), (c) and (d), out of which **ONE OR MORE** is/are correct.

**8.** The solution of $\left(\dfrac{dy}{dx}\right)^2+2y\cot x\,\dfrac{dy}{dx}=y^2$ is

(a) $\ y-\dfrac{c}{1+\cos x}=0$

(b) $\ y=\dfrac{c}{1-\cos x}$

(c) $\ x=2\sin^{-1}\sqrt{\dfrac{c}{2y}}$

(d) $\ x=2\cos^{-1}\sqrt{\dfrac{c}{2y}}$

**9.** The solution of $\dfrac{dy}{dx}+x=xe^{(n-1)y}$ is

(a) $\ \dfrac{1}{n-1}\log\left(\dfrac{e^{(n-1)y}-1}{e^{(n-1)y}}\right)=\dfrac{x^2}{2}+c$

(b) $\ e^{(n-1)y}=Ce^{(n-1)y+(n-1)x^2/2}+1$

(c) $\ \log\left(\dfrac{e^{(n-1)y}-1}{(n-1)e^{(n-1)y}}\right)=x^2+C$

(d) $\ e^{(n-1)y}=Ce^{(n-1)x^2/2+x}+1$

**10.** The solution of $\dfrac{dy}{dx}=\dfrac{ax+h}{by+k}$ represents a parabola if

(a) $\ a=-2,b=0$

(b) $a=-2,b=2$

(c) $\ a=0,b=2$

(d) $\ a=0,b=0$

## Section - III - Linked Comprehension Type

This section contains one paragraph. Based upon the paragraph, 3 multiple choice questions have to be answered. Each question has 4 choices (a), (b), (c) and (d), out of which **ONLY ONE** is correct.

Let us represent the derivative $\dfrac{dy}{dx}$ by $p$. An equation of the form
$$y=px+f(p) \qquad\qquad \dots(1)$$
is known as Clairut's equation where $f(p)$ is a function of $p$.

To solve equation (1), we differentiate the equation with respect to $x$, we get
$$p=p+x\frac{dp}{dx}+f\,'(p)\frac{dp}{dx}\ \Rightarrow[x+f\,'(p)]\frac{dp}{dx}=0\Rightarrow\frac{dp}{dx}=0\ \dots(2)$$
or, $\ x+f'(p)=0 \qquad\qquad \dots(3)$

Now, (2) gives $p=$ constant $=c$, say.

Then eliminating $p$ from (1) we get $y=cx+f(c) \qquad \dots(4)$

Which is a solution of equation (1).

If we eliminate $p$ between (1) and (3) we will obtain another solution not contained in the general solution (4). This solution is known as the singular solution.

**11.** The general equation of the differential equation $y=px+\log p$ which does not contain the singular solution, is

(a) $\ y=cx+\log c$

(b) $\ y=cx+\dfrac{1}{c}$

(c) $\ y=\log x+c$

(d) $\ y=-\log x+c$

**12.** Singular solution of the differential equation
$$x\frac{dy}{dx}=y-\left(\frac{dy}{dx}\right)^2\ \text{is}$$

(a) $\ y=\dfrac{x}{4}$

(b) $\ y=\dfrac{x^2}{4}$

(c) $\ y=-\dfrac{x^2}{4}$

(d) $\ y=x$

---

**RESPONSE GRID**

6. ⓐ ⓑ ⓒ ⓓ   7. ⓐ ⓑ ⓒ ⓓ   8. ⓐ ⓑ ⓒ ⓓ   9. ⓐ ⓑ ⓒ ⓓ   10. ⓐ ⓑ ⓒ ⓓ

11. ⓐ ⓑ ⓒ ⓓ   12. ⓐ ⓑ ⓒ ⓓ

**13.** Solution of the differential equation

$$x^2\left(y - x\frac{dy}{dx}\right) = y\left(\frac{dy}{dx}\right)^2$$

which does not contain singular solution is

(a) $x^2(y - xc) = yc^2$      (b) $y = cx + c^2$

(c) $y^2 = cx^2 + c^2$      (d) $xy = cx^2 + c$

## Section - IV - Matrix-Match Type

This section contains 2 questions. It contains statements given in two columns, which have to be matched. Statements in Column I are labelled as A, B, C and D whereas statements in Column II are labelled as p, q, r and s. The answers to these questions have to be appropriately bubbled as illustrated in the following example. If the correct matches are

A-p, A-r, B-p, B-s, C-r, C-s and D-q, then the correctly bubbled matrix will look like the following :

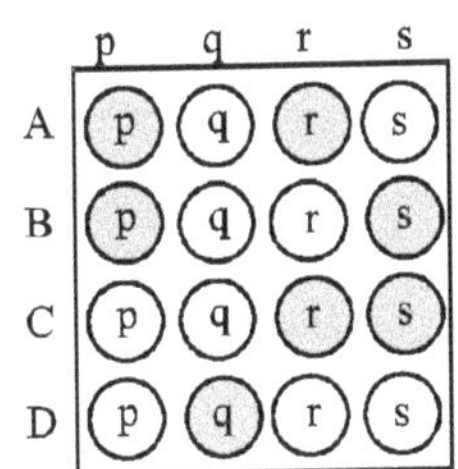

**14.**    **Column - I**        **Column - II**

(A) Solutions of the differential equation

$$\left(\frac{dy}{dx}\right)^2 - \frac{dy}{dx}(e^x + e^{-x}) + 1 = 0$$

are given by

     p. $x + y + 2 = ce^y$, (where c is an arbitrary constant)

(B) Solutions of the differential equation $(x + y + 1)\,dy = dx$ are given by

     q. $\ln(x + y + 2) = c + y$, (where c is an arbitrary constant)

(C) Solutions of the differential equation $(x + y + 2)\,dx + (2x + 2y - 1)\,dy = 0$ are given by

     r. $y + e^{-x} = c$, (where c is an arbitrary constant)

     s. $2(x + y + 2) + 5\ln(x + y - 3) = x + c$, (where c is

     an arbitrary constant)

t. $y - e^x = c$ (where c is an arbitrary constant)

## Section - V - Reasoning Type

This section contains 1 reasoning type question. The question has 4 choices (a), (b), (c) and (d) out of which **ONLY ONE** is correct.

**DIRECTIONS (Qs. 15) : This question contains two statements: Statement-1 (Assertion) and Statement-2 (Reason) and has four alternative choices, only one of which is the correct answer. You have to select the correct choice.**

(a) Statement-1 is True, Statement-2 is True; Statement-2 is a correct explanation for Statement-1.

(b) Statement-1 is True, Statement-2 is True; Statement-2 is NOT a correct explanation for Statement-1.

(c) Statement -1 is True, Statement-2 is False.

(d) Statement -1 is False, Statement-2 is True.

**15.** **Statement-1:** The elimination of four arbitrary constants in

$$y = (c_1 + c_2 + c_3 e^{c_4})\, x$$ results into a differential equation of

the first order $x\dfrac{dy}{dx} = y$.

**Statement-2 :** Elimination of n arbitrary constants requires, in general, a differential equation of the $n^{th}$ order.

## Section - VI - Integer Type

This section contains 4 questions. The answer to each of the questions is a single digit integer ranging from 0 to 9.

**16.** Let C be the curve passing through the point (1, 1) has the property that the perpendicular distance of the origin from the normal at any point P of the curve is equal to the distance of P from the x-axis. If the area bounded by the curve C and x-axis in the first squadrant is $k\pi/2$ square units, then find the value of k.

| | |
|---|---|
| **RESPONSE GRID** | 13. (a)(b)(c)(d)    14. A - (p)(q)(r)(s)(t); B - (p)(q)(r)(s)(t); C - (p)(q)(r)(s)(t) |
| | 15. (a)(b)(c)(d)    16. (0)(1)(2)(3)(4)(5)(6)(7)(8)(9) |

*Space for Rough Work*

**17.** $A$ and $B$ are two separate reservoirs of water, Capacity of reservoir $A$ is double the capacity of reservoir $B$. Both the reservoirs are filled completely with water, their inlets are closed and then the water is released simultaneously from both the reservoirs. The rate of flow of water out of each reservoir at any instant of time is proportional to the quantity of water in the reservoir at the time. One hour after the water is released, the quantity of water in reservoir $A$ is $1\dfrac{1}{2}$ times the quantity of water in reservoir $B$. If both the reservoirs have the same quantity of water after $T$ hours, where $T = \dfrac{\log P}{\log\left(\dfrac{Q}{R}\right)}$, then find the value of $P + Q + R$.

**18.** Let $f(x)$ be a differentiable function such that $f'(x) + f(x) = 4xe^{-x}\cdot\sin 2x$ and $f(0) = 0$. If the value of $\displaystyle Lim_{n\to\infty} \sum_{k=1}^{n} f(k\pi) = \left(\dfrac{-A\pi e^{\pi}}{(e^{\pi}-1)^{B}}\right)$. Find the value of $A + B$.

**19.** If the solution of the differential equation $\dfrac{x\,dx - y\,dy}{x\,dy - y\,dx} = \sqrt{\left(\dfrac{1+x^2-y^2}{x^2-y^2}\right)}$ be $\sqrt{f(x,y)} + \sqrt{1+f(x,y)} = c\left(\dfrac{x+y}{\sqrt{f(x,y)}}\right)$ where $c$ is an arbitrary constant then find the value of $f(3,2)$.

<table>
<tr><td rowspan="2">RESPONSE GRID</td><td>17. ⓪①②③④⑤⑥⑦⑧⑨</td><td>18. ⓪①②③④⑤⑥⑦⑧⑨</td></tr>
<tr><td>19. ⓪①②③④⑤⑥⑦⑧⑨</td><td></td></tr>
</table>

## DAILY PRACTICE PROBLEM DPP 65 - MATHS

| Total Questions | 19 | Total Marks | 57 |
|---|---|---|---|
| Attempted | | Correct | |
| Incorrect | | Net Score | |
| Cut-off Score | 11 | Qualifying Score | 37 |
| Success Gap = Net Score – Qualifying Score | | | |

$$\text{Net Score} = \sum_{i=1}^{VI}\left[(\text{correct}_i \times MM_i) - (In_i - NM_i)\right]$$

# DPP - Daily Practice Problems

**Name :**

**Date :**

**Start Time :**

**End Time :**

## MATHEMATICS    M66

**SYLLABUS : Differential Equation-3 :** Homogeneous differential equations, Linear differential equations, Application of differential equations, Miscellaneous differential equations

## Max. Marks : 75      Time : 60 min.



## Section - I - Straight Objective Type

This section contains 8 multiple choice questions. Each question has 4 choices (a), (b), (c) and (d), out of which **ONLY ONE** is correct.

**1.** Solution of the differential equation

$$x = 1 + xy\frac{dy}{dx} + \frac{x^2 y^2}{2!}\left(\frac{dy}{dx}\right)^2 + \frac{x^3 y^3}{3!}\left(\frac{dy}{dx}\right)^3 + \ldots\ldots \text{ is}$$

(a) $y = \ln(x) + c$      (b) $y = (\ln x)^2 + c$

(c) $y = \pm \ln(x) + c$      (d) $xy = x^y + c$

**2.** A curve $f(x)$ passes through the point $P(1, 1)$. The normal to the curve at point $P$ is $a(y - 1) + (x - 1) = 0$. If the slope of the tangent at any point on the curve is proportional to the ordinate at that point, then the equation of the curve is

(a) $y = e^{ax} - 1$      (b) $y - 1 = e^{ax}$

(c) $y = e^{a(x-1)}$      (d) $y - a = e^{ax}$

**3.** A tangent and a normal to a curve at any point $P$ meet the $x$ and $y$ axes at $A$, $B$ and $C$, $D$ respectively. If the centre of circle through $O$, $C$, $P$ and $B$ lies on the line $y = x$ ($O$ is the origin) then the differential equation of all such curves is :

(a) $\dfrac{dy}{dx} = \dfrac{y - x}{y + x}$      (b) $\dfrac{dy}{dx} = \dfrac{y^2 - x^2}{y^2 + x^2}$

(c) $\dfrac{dy}{dx} = \dfrac{x - y}{xy}$      (d) none of these

**4.** The integrating factor of the differential equation

$$\frac{dy}{dx}(x \ln x) + y = 2\ln x \text{ is given by}$$

(a) $\ln(\ln x)$      (b) $e^x$

(c) $\ln x$      (d) $x$

**5.** The solution of the equation $\dfrac{dy}{dx} + 2y \tan x = \sin x$, is

(a) $y \sec^2 x = \sec x + c$      (b) $y \sec x = \tan x + c$

(c) $y = \sec^3 x + c \sec^2 x$      (d) None of these

---

**RESPONSE GRID**    **1.** ⓐⓑⓒⓓ    **2.** ⓐⓑⓒⓓ    **3.** ⓐⓑⓒⓓ    **4.** ⓐⓑⓒⓓ    **5.** ⓐⓑⓒⓓ

**6.** The value of y (0.2) from the differential equation $\dfrac{dy}{dx} = 2y + 3e^x$ and y (0) = 0 is

(a) 0.40    (b) 8.11    (c) 0.811    (d) 40

**7.** The solution of the boundary value problem $(x^2 - y^2)\,dx + 2xy\,dy = 0$, y (1) = 0, is

(a) $x^2 - y^2 + x = 0$

(b) $x^2 + y^2 - x = 0$

(c) $x^2 + y^2 + x = 0$

(d) None of these

**8.** Solution of the equation $\dfrac{dy}{dx} = \dfrac{ax + by - a}{bx + ay - b}$ is :

(a) $(y - x + 1)^{a-b}\,(y + x - 1)^{a+b} = C$

(b) $(y - x - 1)^{a-b}\,(y + x + 1)^{a+b} = C$

(c) $(y - x + 1)^{a+b}\,(y + x - 1)^{a-b} = C$

(d) $(y - x - 1)^{a-b}\,(y - x + 1)^{a+b} = C$

## Section - II - Multiple Correct Answer Type

This section contains 5 multiple correct answer(s) type questions. Each question has 4 choices (a), (b), (c) and (d), out of which **ONE OR MORE** is/are correct.

**9.** The solution of $xy' + \dfrac{y^2}{x} + y = 0$ is

(a) $x^2 y = k(2x + y)$

(b) $y(kx^2 - 1) = 2x$

(c) $x^2 = ky(2x + y)$

(d) $y = kx^2(2x + y)$

k being an arbitrary constant.

**10.** The differential equation $xy' + \dfrac{y^5}{x^4} + y = 0$

(a) cannot be solved by any method known at this stage

(b) can be solved by the method of variables separable

(c) can be solved by the method for homogeneous equations

(d) can be solved as it is of Bernoulli's type which can be transformed to a linear differential equation

**11.** The differential equation of the curve for which the initial ordinate of any tangent is equal to the corresponding subnormal

(a) is linear

(b) is homogeneous of first degree

(c) has separable variables

(d) is second order

**12.** The curve y = f(x) is such that the area of the trapezium formed by the coordinate axes, ordinate of an arbitrary point and the tangent at this point equals half the square of its abscissa. The equation of the curve can be

(a) $y = cx^2 \pm x$

(b) $y = cx^2 \pm x^3$

(c) $y = cx \pm x^2$

(d) $y = cx^2 \pm x \pm 1$

**13.** Given a function 'g' which has a derivative g'(x) for every real x and satisfies g'(0) = 2 and $g(x + y) = e^y g(x) + e^x g(y)$ for all x and y then

(a) g (x) is increasing for all $x \in [-1, \infty)$

(b) Range of g (x) is $\left[ -\dfrac{2}{e},\ \infty \right)$

(c) $g''(x) > 0\ \forall x$

(d) $\displaystyle \lim_{x \to 0} \dfrac{g(x)}{x} = 1$

## Section - III - Linked Comprehension Type

This section contains one paragraph. Based upon the paragraph, 3 multiple choice questions have to be answered. Each question has 4 choices (a), (b), (c) and (d), out of which **ONLY ONE** is correct.

Newton's law of cooling states that the rate at which a substance cools in moving air is proportional to the difference between the temperatures of the substance and that of the air. If the temperature of the air is 290K.

We can write it as $\dfrac{dT}{dt} = -k(T - 290), k > 0$ constants, where $T$ is temperature of substance.

**14.** The substance cools from $370\,K$ to $330\,K$ in 10 min, then

(a) $T = 290 + 160e^{-kt}$

(b) $T = 290 + 80e^{-kt}$

(c) $T = 290 + 40e^{-kt}$

(d) $T = 290 + 20e^{-kt}$

**15.** The value of $k$ must be

(a) $\ln 2$

(b) $\dfrac{\ln 2}{40}$

(c) $\dfrac{\ln 2}{20}$

(d) $\dfrac{\ln 2}{10}$

| RESPONSE GRID | 6. ⓐⓑⓒⓓ | 7. ⓐⓑⓒⓓ | 8. ⓐⓑⓒⓓ | 9. ⓐⓑⓒⓓ | 10. ⓐⓑⓒⓓ |
|---|---|---|---|---|---|
| | 11. ⓐⓑⓒⓓ | 12. ⓐⓑⓒⓓ | 13. ⓐⓑⓒⓓ | 14. ⓐⓑⓒⓓ | 15. ⓐⓑⓒⓓ |

*Space for Rough Work*

**16.** If $T = f(t)$, then the number of solutions of $|T| = |f(|t|)|$ and $T^2 + t^2 = 1600$ is

(a)  2  (b)  4
(c)  6  (d)  8

## Section - IV - Matrix-Match Type

This section contains 1 question. It contains statements given in two columns, which have to be matched. Statements in Column I are labelled as A, B, C and D whereas statements in Column II are labelled as p, q, r and s. The answers to these questions have to be appropriately bubbled as illustrated in the following example. If the correct matches are A-p, A-r, B-p, B-s, C-r, C-s and D-q, then the correctly bubbled matrix will look like the following :

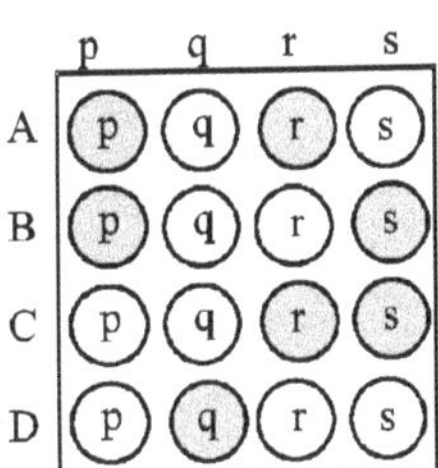

**17.** Let y(x) be the solution of differential equation

$$\frac{dy}{dx} = -2x(y-1) \text{ with } y(0) = 1$$

$g(x) = \min\{|x|, x^2, y(x)\}$ and $h(x) = e^x$, $p(x) = 3 \ln x$

| **Column I** | **Column II** |
|---|---|
| (A) y(x) equals | p.  4 |
| (B) If area bounded by p(x) = 3 ln x, y(x) and the y–axis is $\alpha e^{1/3}$, then $\alpha$ equals | q.  3 |
| (C) If area bounded by the curves y(x); g(x), x = 0, x = 2 and x-axis is $\beta/3$, then $\beta$ equals | r.  1 |
| (D) If h(x) = y(x), then x equals | s.  0 |

## Section - V - Reasoning Type

This section contains 2 reasoning type questions. Each question has 4 choices (a), (b), (c) and (d) out of which **ONLY ONE** is correct.

**DIRECTIONS for Qs (18-19) :** Each of these questions contains two statements: Statement-1 (Assertion) and Statement-2 (Reason). Each of these questions has four alternative choices, only one of which is the correct answer. You have to select the correct choice.

(a)  Statement-1 is True, Statement-2 is True; Statement-2 is a correct explanation for Statement-1.
(b)  Statement-1 is True, Statement-2 is True; Statement-2 is NOT a correct explanation for Statement-1.
(c)  Statement -1 is True, Statement-2 is False.
(d)  Statement -1 is False, Statement-2 is True.

**18.  Statement-1:** The differential equation $\dfrac{dy}{dx} = \dfrac{2xy}{x^2 + y^2}$ can be solved by putting y = vx .

**Statement-2:** Since the given differentiable equation is homogenous.

**19.  Statement-1:** Integrating factor of $\dfrac{dy}{dx} + y = x^2$ is $e^x$.

**Statement-2:** Integrating factor of $\dfrac{dy}{dx} + P(x)y = Q(x)$ is $e^{\int P(x)dx}$

## Section - VI - Integer Type

This section contains 5 questions. The answer to each of the questions is a single digit integer ranging from 0 to 9.



*Space for Rough Work*

**20.** If $y(t)$ is a solution of $(1+t)\dfrac{dy}{dt} - ty = 1$ and $y(0) = -1$, then $y(1) = \dfrac{-1}{P}$. Find the value of P.

**21.** The solution of primitive integral equation $(x^2 + y^2)\, dy = xy\, dx$ is $y = y(x)$. If $y(1) = 1$ and $y(x_0) = e$, then $x_0 = e\sqrt{M}$. Find the value of M.

**22.** The real value of m for which the substitution, $y = u^m$ will transform the differential equation, $2x^4 y\dfrac{dy}{dx} + y^4 = 4x^6$ into a homogeneous equation is $\dfrac{A}{B}$. Find the value of A − B.

**23.** The solution of the boundary value problem $\dfrac{dy}{dx} + y\cot x = 2\cos x$, $y\left(\dfrac{\pi}{6}\right) = \dfrac{3}{2}$ is $Ay\sin x + \cos 2x = B$. Find the value of A + B.

**24.** The solution of the equation $(x^2 - xy)\, dy = (xy + y^2)\, dx$ is $Rxy = ke^{-Px/Qy}$. Find the value of P + Q + R.

<table>
<tr><td rowspan="3">RESPONSE GRID</td><td>20. ⓪①②③④⑤⑥⑦⑧⑨</td><td>21. ⓪①②③④⑤⑥⑦⑧⑨</td></tr>
<tr><td>22. ⓪①②③④⑤⑥⑦⑧⑨</td><td>23. ⓪①②③④⑤⑥⑦⑧⑨</td></tr>
<tr><td>24. ⓪①②③④⑤⑥⑦⑧⑨</td><td></td></tr>
</table>

## DAILY PRACTICE PROBLEM DPP 66 – MATHS

| Total Questions | 24 | Total Marks | 75 |
|---|---|---|---|
| Attempted | | Correct | |
| Incorrect | | Net Score | |
| Cut-off Score | 15 | Qualifying Score | 49 |
| Success Gap = Net Score – Qualifying Score | | | |

$$\textbf{Net Score} = \sum_{i=1}^{\textbf{VI}}\Big[(\textbf{correct}_i \times MM_i) - (In_i - NM_i)\Big]$$

# DPP - Daily Practice Problems

**Name :**                    **Date :**

**Start Time :**              **End Time :**

## MATHEMATICS    M67

**SYLLABUS : Probability - 4 :** Conditional probability, Baye's theorem, Binomial distribution

## Max. Marks : 75                    Time : 60 min.

### GENERAL INSTRUCTIONS

- The Daily Practice Problem Sheet contains **24** Questions divided into 6 sections.
  Section I has **8** MCQ's with ONLY 1 correct option. 2 marks for correct answer and No negative marks.
  Section II has **4** MCQ's with 1 or MORE THAN 1 correct option. 4 marks for correct answer(s) and (–1) for wrong answer.
  Section III has **1** PASSAGE with **3** MCQ's with ONLY 1 correct option. 3 marks for correct and (–1) mark for wrong answer.
  Section IV has **2** MCQ's with multiple matchings. 1 mark for the correct matching of each row & No negative marks.
  Section V has **2** Assertion-Reason MCQ's with ONLY 1 correct option. 3 marks for correct and (–1) mark for wrong answer.
  Section VI has **5** single digit integer answer questions. 4 marks for correct answer and (–1) for wrong answer.
- No mark will be given/ deducted if no bubble is filled. Keep a timer in front and stop immediately at the end of 60 min.
- You have to evaluate your Response Grids yourself with the help of Solution Booklet.
- The sheet follows a particular syllabus. Do not attempt the sheet before you have completed your preparation for that syllabus. Refer syllabus sheet in the starting of the book for the syllabus of all the DPP sheets.
- After completing the sheet check your answers with the solution booklet and complete the Result Grid. Finally spend time to analyse your performance and revise the areas which emerge out as weak in your evaluation.

## Section - I - Straight Objective Type

This section contains 8 multiple choice questions. Each question has 4 choices (a), (b), (c) and (d), out of which **ONLY ONE** is correct.

1. A player 'A' plays a game against a machine. At each round he deposits one rupee in a slot and then flips a coin which has a probability p of showing a head. If a head shows, he gets back the rupee he deposited and one more rupee from the machine. If a tail shows, he loses his rupee. Let A starts with 10 rupees and q = 1 – p. The probability that he is left with no money by the $14^{th}$ round or earlier is

   (a) $q^{10}(1+10pq+45p^2q^2)$    (b) $q^{14}(p^2q+36pq+7)$

   (c) $q^{12}+3pq^{13}+3p^{13}q+p^{12}$    (d) $1 - {}^{10}C_1\, pq^{11} - {}^{10}C_2\, p^2q^{12}$

2. If two events A and B are such that $P\left(A'\right) = 0.3$, P(B) = 0.4 and $P\left(A \cap B'\right) = 0.5$, then $P\left(\dfrac{B}{A \cup B'}\right) =$

   (a) 1/4        (b) 1/5        (c) 3/5        (d) 2/5

3. Two players A and B toss 4 coins and 3 coins respectively. The probability that both of them get the same number of heads is

   (a) $\dfrac{35}{256}$    (b) $\dfrac{35}{128}$

   (c) $\dfrac{1}{16}$    (d) $\dfrac{15}{128}$

4. The probability of the simultaneous occurrence of two events A and B is p. If the probability that exactly one of the events occurs is q, then which of the following is not correct?

   (a) $P(A')+P(B') = 2+2q-p$    (b) $P(A')+P(B') = 2-2p-q$

   (c) $P(A \cap B \,|\, A \cup B) = \dfrac{p}{p+q}$    (d) $P(A' \cap B') = 1-p-q.$

5. A man is known to speak the truth 3 out of 4 times. He throws a die and reports that it is a six. The probability that it is actually a six is

   (a) 3/8        (b) 1/5

   (c) 3/4        (d) none

| RESPONSE GRID | 1. ⓐⓑⓒⓓ | 2. ⓐⓑⓒⓓ | 3. ⓐⓑⓒⓓ | 4. ⓐⓑⓒⓓ | 5. ⓐⓑⓒⓓ |

**6.** Suppose X is a random variable which takes values $0, 1, 2, 3, ...$ and $P(X = r) = pq^r$, where $0 < p < 1$, $q = 1 - p$ and $r = 0, 1, 2, ..$ then :

(a)   $P(X \geq a) = q^a$

(b)   $P(X \geq a + b \mid X \geq a) = P(X \geq b)$

(c)   $P(X = a + b \mid X \geq a) = P(X = b)$

(d)   All of the above

**7.** A pack of playing cards was found to contain only 51 cards. If the first 13 cards which are examined, are all red. The probability that the missing card is black, is

(a)   $\dfrac{2}{3}$     (b) $\dfrac{1}{3}$     (c) $\dfrac{4}{3}$     (d) None of these

**8.** In a bolt factory, machines A, B and C manufacture 60%, 25% and 15% respectively. Of the total of their output 1%, 2%, 1% are defective bolts. A bolt is drawn at random from the total production and found to be defective. From which machine, the defective bolt is most expected to have been manufactured

(a)  A          (b)  B          (c)  C          (d) Cannot be decided

## Section - II - Multiple Correct Answer Type

This section contains 4 multiple correct answer(s) type questions. Each question has 4 choices (a), (b), (c) and (d), out of which **ONE OR MORE** is/are correct.

**9.** Contents of the two urns is as given in this table. A fair die is tossed. If the face 1, 2, 4 or 5 comes, a marble is drawn from the urn A otherwise a marble is chosen from the urn B.

| Urn | Red Marbles | White Marbles | Blue Marbles |
|-----|-------------|---------------|--------------|
| A   | 5           | 3             | 8            |
| B   | 3           | 5             | 0            |

Let $E_1$ : Denote the event a red marble is chosen.

$E_2$ : Denote the event a white marble is chosen.

$E_3$ : Denote the event that a blue marble is chosen. then –

(a)   The event $E_1$, $E_2$ and $E_3$ are equiprobable.

(b)   $P(E_1), P(E_2), P(E_3)$ are in A.P.

(c)   If the marble drawn is red, the probability that it came from the urn A is 1/2

(d)   If the marble drawn is white, the probability that the face 5 appeared on the die is 3/32.

**10.** For any two events A and B defined on a sample space

(a) $P\left(\dfrac{A}{B}\right) \geq \dfrac{P(A) + P(B) - 1}{P(B)}$, $P(B) \neq 0$ is always true

(b) $P(A \cup \bar{B}) = P(A) - P(A \cap B)$

(c) $P(A \cup B) = 1 - P(A^c) \cdot P(B^c)$, if A and B are independent

(d) $P(A \cup B) = 1 - P(A^c) \cdot P(B^c)$, if A and B are disjoint

**11.** If E and F is independent events such that $0 < P(E) < 1$ and $0 < P(F) < 1$, then

(a)   E and F are mutually exclusive

(b)   E and $F^c$ (the complement of the event F) are independent

(c)   $E^c$ and $F^c$ are independent

(d)   $P(E \mid F) + P(E^c \mid F) = 1$.

**12.** The letters of the word PROBABILITY are written down at random in a row. Let $E_1$ denotes the event that two I's are together and $E_2$ denotes the event that two B's are together, then

(a)   $P(E_1) = P(E_2) = \dfrac{3}{11}$     (b)   $P(E_1 \cap E_2) = \dfrac{2}{55}$

(c)   $P(E_1 \cup E_2) = \dfrac{18}{55}$     (d)   $P(E_1 / E_2) = \dfrac{1}{5}$

## Section - III - Linked Comprehension Type

This section contains one paragraph. Based upon the paragraph, 3 multiple choice questions have to be answered. Each question has 4 choices (a), (b), (c) and (d), out of which **ONLY ONE** is correct.

There are n urns, each of these contain $n + 1$ balls. The ith urn contains i white balls and $(n + 1 - i)$ red balls. Let $u_i$ be the event of selecting ith urn, $i = 1, 2, 3 .........., n$ and w the event of getting a white ball.

**13.** If $P(u_i) \propto i$, where $i = 1, 2, 3, ......., n$, then $\displaystyle\lim_{n \to \infty} P(w) = $

(a)   1          (b) 2/3          (c)   3/4          (d) 1/4

**14.** If $P(u_i) = c$, (a constant) then $P(u_n / w) = $

(a)   $\dfrac{2}{n+1}$     (b) $\dfrac{1}{n+1}$     (c)   $\dfrac{n}{n+1}$     (d) $\dfrac{1}{2}$

| RESPONSE GRID | | | | | |
|---|---|---|---|---|---|
| | 6. ⓐⓑⓒⓓ | 7. ⓐⓑⓒⓓ | 8. ⓐⓑⓒⓓ | 9. ⓐⓑⓒⓓ | 10. ⓐⓑⓒⓓ |
| | 11. ⓐⓑⓒⓓ | 12. ⓐⓑⓒⓓ | 13. ⓐⓑⓒⓓ | 14. ⓐⓑⓒⓓ | |

**15.** Let $P(u_i) = \dfrac{1}{n}$, if n is even and E denotes the event of choosing even numbered urn, then the value of $P(w/E)$ is

(a) $\dfrac{n+2}{2n+1}$    (b) $\dfrac{n+2}{2(n+1)}$    (c) $\dfrac{n}{n+1}$    (d) $\dfrac{1}{n+1}$

## Section - IV - Matrix-Match Type

This section contains 2 questions. It contains statements given in two columns, which have to be matched. Statements in Column I are labelled as A, B, C and D whereas statements in Column II are labelled as p, q, r and s. The answers to these questions have to be appropriately bubbled as illustrated in the following example. If the correct matches are A-p, A-r, B-p, B-s, C-r, C-s and D-q, then the correctly bubbled matrix will look like the following :

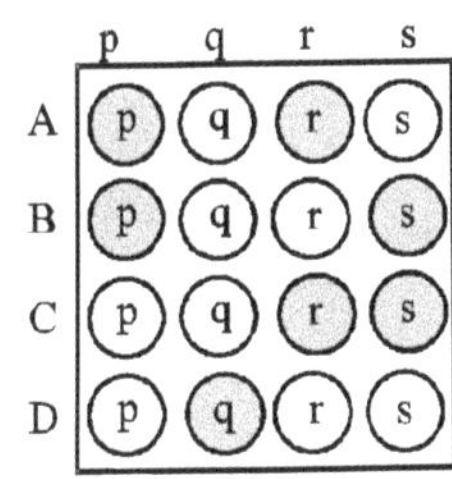

**16.** A bag contains some white and some black balls, all combinations being equally likely. The total number of balls in the bag is 12. Four balls are drawn at random from the bag without replacement. Now match the entries given in the following two columns :

| Column - I | Column-II |
|---|---|
| (A) Probability that all the four balls are black is equal to | p. $\dfrac{14}{33}$ |
| (B) If the bag contains 10 black and 2 white balls then the probability that all four balls are black is equal to | q. $\dfrac{1}{5}$ |
| (C) If all the four balls are black then the probability that the bag contains 10 black balls is equal to | r. $\dfrac{70}{429}$ |
| (D) Probability that two balls are black and two are white is equal to | s. $\dfrac{13}{165}$ |

**17.** Let A and B are two independent events such that $P(A) = \dfrac{1}{3}$ and $P(B) = \dfrac{1}{4}$. Now match the entries from the following two columns :

| Column – I | Column – II |
|---|---|
| (A) $P(A \cup B)$ is equal to | p. $\dfrac{1}{12}$ |
| (B) $P(A/A \cup B)$ is equal to | q. $\dfrac{1}{2}$ |
| (C) $P(B/A' \cap B')$ is equal to | r. $\dfrac{2}{3}$ |
| (D) $P(A'/B)$ is equal to | s. $0$ |

## Section - V - Reasoning Type

This section contains 2 reasoning type questions. Each question has 4 choices (a), (b), (c) and (d) out of which **ONLY ONE** is correct.

**DIRECTIONS for Qs (18-19) :** Each of these questions contains two statements: Statement-1 (Assertion) and Statement-2 (Reason). Each of these questions has four alternative choices, only one of which is the correct answer. You have to select the correct choice.

(a) Statement-1 is True, Statement-2 is True; Statement-2 is a correct explanation for Statement-1.

(b) Statement-1 is True, Statement-2 is True; Statement-2 is NOT a correct explanation for Statement-1.

(c) Statement -1 is True, Statement-2 is False.

(d) Statement -1 is False, Statement-2 is True.

**18.** Let A and B be two independent events of a random experiment.
**Statement–1 :** $P(A \cap B) = P(A) . P(B)$
**Statement–2 :** Probability of occurrence of A is independent of occurrence or non–occurrence of B.

**19.** Let $H_1, H_2, \ldots, H_n$ be mutually exclusive and exhaustive events with $P(H_i) > 0$, $i = 1, 2, \ldots, n$. Let E be any other event with $0 < P(E) < 1$.
**Statement–1 :** $P(H_i | E) > P(E | H_i) . P(H_i)$ for $i = 1, 2, \ldots, n$
**Statement–2 :** $\displaystyle\sum_{i=1}^{n} P(H_i) = 1$.

**RESPONSE GRID**

15. (a)(b)(c)(d)    16. A - (p)(q)(r)(s); B - (p)(q)(r)(s); C - (p)(q)(r)(s); D - (p)(q)(r)(s)

17. A - (p)(q)(r)(s); B - (p)(q)(r)(s); C - (p)(q)(r)(s); D - (p)(q)(r)(s)

18. (a)(b)(c)(d)    19. (a)(b)(c)(d)

*Space for Rough Work*

## Section - VI - Integer Type

This section contains 5 questions. The answer to each of the questions is a single digit integer ranging from 0 to 9.

**20.** All the face cards from a pack of 52 playing cards are removed. From the remaining pack half of the cards are randomly removed without looking at them and then randomly drawn two cards simultaneously from the remaining. If the probability that two cards drawn are both aces is $\dfrac{p(^{38}C_{20})}{^{40}C_{20} \cdot {}^{20}C_2}$, find the value of p.

**21.** Urn-I contains 3 red balls and 9 black balls. Urn-II contains 8 red balls and 4 black balls. Urn-III contains 10 red balls and 2 black balls. A card is drawn from a well shuffled back of 52 playing cards. If a face card is drawn, a ball is selected from Urn-I. If an ace is drawn, a ball is selected from Urn-II. If any other card is drawn, a ball is selected from Urn-III. If the conditional probability that Urn-I was one from which a ball was selected, given that the ball selected was red is $\dfrac{M}{N}$. Find the value of M.

**22.** A number is chosen randomly from one of the two sets, $A = \{1801, 1802, \ldots, 1899, 1900\}$ & $B = \{1901, 1902, \ldots, 1999, 2000\}$. If the number chosen represents a calender year, then the probability that it has 53 sundays is $\dfrac{83X}{14Y}$. Find the value of Y $-X$.

**23.** A company has two plants to manufacture televisions. Plant I manufacture 70% of televisions and plant II manufacture 30%. At plant I, 80% of the televisions are rated as of standard quality and at plant II, 90% of the televisions are rated as of standard quality. A television is chosen at random and is found to be of standard quality. The probability that it has come from plant II is $\dfrac{A^3}{B}$. Find the value of A.

**24.** The probability that a man hits a target is 3/4. He tries 5 times. The probability that he will hit the target at least three times is $\dfrac{X}{Y^9}$. Find the value of Y.

| RESPONSE GRID | | |
|---|---|---|
| | 20. ⓪①②③④⑤⑥⑦⑧⑨ | 21. ⓪①②③④⑤⑥⑦⑧⑨ |
| | 22. ⓪①②③④⑤⑥⑦⑧⑨ | 23. ⓪①②③④⑤⑥⑦⑧⑨ |
| | 24. ⓪①②③④⑤⑥⑦⑧⑨ | |

## DAILY PRACTICE PROBLEM DPP 67 - MATHS

| Total Questions | 24 | Total Marks | 75 |
|---|---|---|---|
| Attempted | | Correct | |
| Incorrect | | Net Score | |
| Cut-off Score | 15 | Qualifying Score | 49 |
| Success Gap = Net Score – Qualifying Score | | | |

$$\text{Net Score} = \sum_{i=1}^{VI} \left[ (\text{correct}_i \times MM_i) - (In_i - NM_i) \right]$$

*Space for Rough Work*

**Name :**

**Date :**

**Start Time :**

**End Time :**

## MATHEMATICS    M68

**SYLLABUS : Vector Algebra-1 :** Modulus of a vector, Direction cosines and Direction ratios of a vector. Algebra of vectors

**Max. Marks : 55**          **Time : 60 min.**

### GENERAL INSTRUCTIONS

- The Daily Practice Problem Sheet contains **18** Questions divided into 5 sections.

  Section I has **6** MCQ's with ONLY 1 correct option. 2 marks for correct answer and No negative marks.

  Section II has **3** MCQ's with 1 or MORE THAN 1 correct option. 4 marks for correct answer(s) and (–1) for wrong answer.

  Section III has **1** PASSAGE with **3** MCQ's with ONLY 1 correct option. 3 marks for correct and (–1) mark for wrong answer.

  Section IV has **2** Assertion-Reason MCQ's with ONLY 1 correct option. 3 marks for correct and (–1) mark for wrong answer.

  Section V has **4** single digit integer answer questions. 4 marks for correct answer and (–1) for wrong answer.

- No mark will be given/ deducted if no bubble is filled. Keep a timer in front and stop immediately at the end of 60 min.

- You have to evaluate your Response Grids yourself with the help of Solution Booklet.

- The sheet follows a particular syllabus. Do not attempt the sheet before you have completed your preparation for that syllabus. Refer syllabus sheet in the starting of the book for the syllabus of all the DPP sheets.

- After completing the sheet check your answers with the solution booklet and complete the Result Grid. Finally spend time to analyse your performance and revise the areas which emerge out as weak in your evaluation.

---

### Section - I - Straight Objective Type

This section contains 6 multiple choice questions. Each question has 4 choices (a), (b), (c) and (d), out of which **ONLY ONE** is correct.

**1.** The position vectors of the vertices A, B, C of a triangle are $\hat{i}-\hat{j}-3\hat{k}$, $2\hat{i}+\hat{j}-2\hat{k}$ and $-5\hat{i}+2\hat{j}-6\hat{k}$ respectively. The length of the bisector AD of the angle BAC where D is on the line segment BC, is

(a) 15/2    (b) 1/4    (c) 11/2    (d) none

**2.** P is a point on the line through the point A whose position vector is $\vec{a}$ and the line is parallel to the vector $\vec{b}$. If PA = 6, the position vector of P is

(a) $\vec{a}+6\vec{b}$

(b) $\vec{a}+\dfrac{6\vec{b}}{|\vec{b}|}$

(c) $\vec{a}-6\vec{b}$

(d) $\vec{b}+\dfrac{6\vec{a}}{|\vec{a}|}$

**3.** If $|\vec{a}+\vec{b}\,|=|\,\vec{a}-\vec{b}\,|$ then the vectors $\vec{a}$ and $\vec{b}$ are adjacent sides of

(a) a rectangle    (b) a square

(c) a rhombus    (d) None of these

**4.** The points having position vectors

$$\vec{a}-2\vec{b}+3\vec{c},\ -2\vec{a}+3\vec{b}+2\vec{c},\ -8\vec{a}+13\vec{b}\ \text{ are}$$

(a) vertices of an equilateral triangle

(b) vertices of an isosceles triangle

(c) vertices of a right-angled triangle

(d) None of these

**5.** If a line makes $\alpha,\beta,\gamma$ angles with the positive directions to the axes, then $\sin^2\alpha+\sin^2\beta+\sin^2\gamma$ is equal to

(a) 1            (b) 2

(c) 0            (d) none

---

**RESPONSE GRID**    **1.** ⓐⓑⓒⓓ    **2.** ⓐⓑⓒⓓ    **3.** ⓐⓑⓒⓓ    **4.** ⓐⓑⓒⓓ    **5.** ⓐⓑⓒⓓ

**6.** A vector has components 2p and 1 with respect to a plane rectangular cartesian system. The axes are rotated through an angle $\theta$ about the origin in the anticlockwise sense. If the vector has components $p + 1$ and 1 with respect to the new system then

(a) $p = 1, -\dfrac{1}{3}$    (b) $p = 0$

(c) $p = -1, \dfrac{1}{3}$    (d) $p = 1, -1$

## Section - II - Multiple Correct Answer Type

This section contains 3 multiple correct answer(s) type questions. Each question has 4 choices (a), (b), (c) and (d), out of which **ONE OR MORE** is/are correct.

**7.** In a parallelogram OABC, vectors $\vec{a}, \vec{b}, \vec{c}$ are respectively by the position vectors of vertices A, B, C with reference to O as origin. A point E is taken on the side BC which divides it in the ratio of 2 : 1. Also, the line segment AE intersects the line bisecting the angle O internally in point P. If CP, when extended meets AB in point F. Then –

(a) The position vector of point P is

$$\frac{3|\vec{a}||\vec{c}|}{3|\vec{c}|+2|\vec{a}|}\left\{\frac{\vec{a}}{|\vec{a}|}+\frac{\vec{c}}{|\vec{c}|}\right\}.$$

(b) The position vector of point F is $\vec{a}+\dfrac{1}{3}\dfrac{|\vec{a}|}{|\vec{c}|}\vec{c}$.

(c) The vector $\overrightarrow{AF}$ is given by $\dfrac{1}{3}\dfrac{|\vec{a}|}{|\vec{c}|}\vec{c}$

(d) The position vector of point P is

$$\frac{2|\vec{c}||\vec{a}|}{3|\vec{c}|+2|\vec{a}|}\left\{\frac{\vec{c}}{|\vec{c}|}+\frac{\vec{a}}{|\vec{a}|}\right\}.$$

**8.** If $\overrightarrow{DA} = \vec{a}, \overrightarrow{AB} = \vec{b}$ and $\overrightarrow{CB} = k\vec{a}$, where k > 0 and X, Y are the mid points of DB and AC respectively such that $|\vec{a}| = 17$ and $|\overrightarrow{XY}| = 4$, then k is equal to

(a) 8/17    (b) 9/17    (c) 25/17    (d) 4/17

**9.** The direction cosines of a line equally inclined to the axes are

(a) $\dfrac{1}{3}, \dfrac{1}{3}, \dfrac{1}{3}$    (b) $\dfrac{-1}{3}, \dfrac{-1}{3}, \dfrac{-1}{3}$

(c) $\dfrac{1}{\sqrt{3}}, \dfrac{1}{\sqrt{3}}, \dfrac{1}{\sqrt{3}}$    (d) $\dfrac{-1}{\sqrt{3}}, \dfrac{-1}{\sqrt{3}}, \dfrac{-1}{\sqrt{3}}$

## Section - III - Linked Comprehension Type

This section contains one paragraph. Based upon the paragraph, 3 multiple choice questions have to be answered. Each question has 4 choices (a), (b), (c) and (d), out of which **ONLY ONE** is correct.

Let the lines $B'B$ and $C'C$ intersect at $A$. Let $\vec{a}$ be the P.V. of $A$ with respect to origin $O$.

Now, let equations of $B'B$ and $C'C$ be respectively

$\vec{r} = \vec{a} + t\vec{b}$ and $\vec{r} = \vec{a} + s\vec{c}$ where $t$ and $s$ are scalars.

and AB is parallal to $\vec{b}$ and AC is parallal to $\vec{c}$.

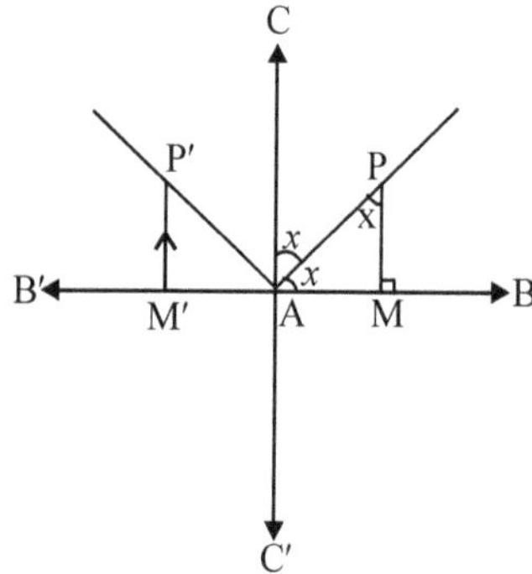


Let P be any point on the bisector of CAB.

Draw PM $\perp$ to AB and let $\overrightarrow{OP} = \vec{r}$

$\therefore \angle CAP = \angle PAM = \angle APM$

$\Rightarrow AM = MP = \lambda$ (say)

$\therefore \overrightarrow{AM} = AM\,\vec{b} = \dfrac{\lambda\vec{b}}{|\vec{b}|}$ and $\overrightarrow{MP} = MP\,\hat{c} = \dfrac{\lambda\vec{c}}{|\vec{c}|}$

| RESPONSE GRID | 6. ⓐⓑⓒⓓ | 7. ⓐⓑⓒⓓ | 8. ⓐⓑⓒⓓ | 9. ⓐⓑⓒⓓ |

—————————*Space for Rough Work*—————————

$$\overrightarrow{AP} = \overrightarrow{AM} + \overrightarrow{MP} = \lambda\left(\frac{\vec{b}}{|\vec{b}|} + \frac{\vec{c}}{|\vec{c}|}\right)$$

But $\overrightarrow{OP} = \overrightarrow{OA} + \overrightarrow{AP} \Rightarrow \vec{r} = \vec{a} + \lambda\left(\frac{\vec{b}}{|\vec{b}|} + \frac{\vec{c}}{|\vec{c}|}\right)$

which is the equation of internal bisector of $\angle CAB$. The bisector $AP'$ of the external $\angle B'$ AC is the bisector of the angle between straight lines whose directions are $-\vec{b}$ and $\vec{c}$. Therefore its equation is

$$\vec{r} = \vec{a} + \mu\left(\frac{\vec{b}}{|\vec{b}|} - \frac{\vec{c}}{|\vec{c}|}\right), \text{ or } \vec{r} = \vec{a} + \mu\left(\frac{\vec{c}}{|\vec{c}|} - \frac{\vec{b}}{|\vec{b}|}\right), \text{ where } \lambda$$

is some scalar.

**10.** A vector $\vec{d}$, directed along the internal bisector of the angle between the vectors $\vec{b} = 7\hat{i} - 4\hat{j} - 4\hat{k}$ and $\vec{c} = -2\hat{i} - \hat{j} + 2\hat{k}$ and $|\vec{d}| = 5\sqrt{6}$ is

(a) $\dfrac{5}{3}(\hat{i} + 7\hat{j} + 2\hat{k})$  (b) $\dfrac{5}{3}(5\hat{i} + 5\hat{j} - 2\hat{k})$

(c) $\dfrac{5}{3}(\hat{i} - 7\hat{j} + 2\hat{k})$  (d) $\dfrac{5}{3}(-5\hat{i} + 5\hat{j} + 2\hat{k})$

**11.** If $ABC$ be a triangle of sides of length $a$, $b$, $c$ with position vectors of $A$, $B$, $C$ as $\vec{a}$, $\vec{b}$ and $\vec{c}$ respectively, then the position vector of its incentre is

(a) $\left(\dfrac{\vec{a} + \vec{b} + \vec{c}}{3}\right)$  (b) $\left(\dfrac{a\vec{a} + b\vec{b} + c\vec{c}}{a + b + c}\right)$

(c) $\left(\dfrac{a\vec{a} + b\vec{b} + c\vec{c}}{3}\right)$  (d) $\left(\dfrac{\vec{a} \times \vec{b} + \vec{b} \times \vec{c} + \vec{c} \times \vec{a}}{a^2 + b^2 + c^2}\right)$

**12.** If the interior and exterior bisectors of the angle $A$ of a triangle $ABC$ meet the base $BC$ at $D$ and $E$, then

(a) $\dfrac{2}{BC} = \dfrac{1}{BD} + \dfrac{1}{BE}$  (b) $2BC = BD + BE$

(c) $(BC)^2 = BD \times BE$  (d) $2BD = BC + BE$

## Section - IV - Reasoning Type

This section contains 2 reasoning type questions. Each question has 4 choices (a), (b), (c) and (d) out of which **ONLY ONE** is correct.

**DIRECTIONS for (Qs. 13 & 14) : Each of these questions contains two statements: Statement-1 (Assertion) and Statement-2 (Reason). Each of these questions has four alternative choices, only one of which is the correct answer. You have to select the correct choice.**

(a) Statement-1 is True, Statement-2 is True; Statement-2 is a correct explanation for Statement-1.

(b) Statement-1 is True, Statement-2 is True; Statement-2 is NOT a correct explanation for Statement-1.

(c) Statement -1 is True, Statement-2 is False.

(d) Statement -1 is False, Statement-2 is True.

**13.** **Statement 1 :** $\vec{a} = \hat{i} + p\hat{j} + 2\hat{k}$ and $\vec{b} = 2\hat{i} + 3\hat{j} + q\hat{k}$ are parallel vectors if $p = \dfrac{3}{2}$, $q = 4$

**Statement 2 :** $\vec{a} = a_1\hat{i} + a_2\hat{j} + a_3\hat{k}$ and $\vec{b} = b_1\hat{i} + b_2\hat{j} + b_3\hat{k}$ are parallel if $\dfrac{a_1}{b_1} = \dfrac{a_2}{b_2} = \dfrac{a_3}{b_3}$

**14.** **Statement 1 :** If I is the incentre of $\Delta ABC$ then $|\overrightarrow{BC}|\,\overrightarrow{IA} + |\overrightarrow{CA}|\,\overrightarrow{IB} + |\overrightarrow{AB}|\,\overrightarrow{IC} = \vec{0}$

**Statement 2 :** The position vector of centroid of $\Delta ABC$ is $\dfrac{\overrightarrow{OA} + \overrightarrow{OB} + \overrightarrow{OC}}{3}$

| RESPONSE GRID | 10. ⓐⓑⓒⓓ | 11. ⓐⓑⓒⓓ | 12. ⓐⓑⓒⓓ | 13. ⓐⓑⓒⓓ | 14. ⓐⓑⓒⓓ |

———————————— *Space for Rough Work* ————————————

## Section - V - Integer Type

This section contains 4 questions. The answer to each of the questions is a single digit integer ranging from 0 to 9.

15. If $\vec{a}, \vec{b}, \vec{c}$ are three non-zero vectors, no two of which are collinear, $\vec{a} + 2\vec{b}$ is collinear with $\vec{c}$ and $\vec{b} + 3\vec{c}$ is collinear with $\vec{a}$, then what is the value of $|\vec{a} + 2\vec{b} + 6\vec{c}|$.

16. If $\vec{a}, \vec{b}, \vec{c}$ are unit vectors such that $|\vec{a} + 2\vec{b} + 3\vec{c}| = \sqrt{3 + 2\sqrt{2}}$. Angle between $\vec{a}$ and $\vec{b}$ is $\alpha$, between $\vec{a}$ and $\vec{c}$ is $\beta$ and angle between $\vec{b}$ and $\vec{c}$ varies in $\left[\dfrac{\pi}{2}, \dfrac{2\pi}{3}\right]$,

then the greatest value of $4\cos\alpha + 6\cos\beta$ is $A\sqrt{A} - 5$. Find the value of A.

17. If A, B, C are the vertices of $\triangle ABC$ having position vectors as the points $(2, 1, 3), (4, 1, 3)$ and $(0, 2, 1)$ respectively, then the magnitude of $\angle BAC$ is $\cos^{-1}\left(\dfrac{A}{B}\right)$. Find the value of B.

18. The projection of the line segment joining the points $(-1, 0, 3)$ and $(2, 5, 1)$ on the line whose direction ratios are $(6, 2, 3)$ is $\dfrac{22}{A}$. Find the value of A.

| RESPONSE GRID | |
|---|---|
| 15. ⓪①②③④⑤⑥⑦⑧⑨ | 16. ⓪①②③④⑤⑥⑦⑧⑨ |
| 17. ⓪①②③④⑤⑥⑦⑧⑨ | 18. ⓪①②③④⑤⑥⑦⑧⑨ |

## DAILY PRACTICE PROBLEM DPP 68 - MATHS

| Total Questions | 18 | Total Marks | 55 |
|---|---|---|---|
| Attempted | | Correct | |
| Incorrect | | Net Score | |
| Cut-off Score | 11 | Qualifying Score | 36 |
| Success Gap = Net Score – Qualifying Score | | | |

$$\text{Net Score} = \sum_{i=1}^{VI}\left[(\text{correct}_i \times MM_i) - (In_i - NM_i)\right]$$

**Name :**

**Date :**

**Start Time :**

**End Time :**

# MATHEMATICS  M69

**SYLLABUS : Vector Algebra-2 :** Scalar or Dot product of two vectors and its applications

**Max. Marks : 58**

**Time : 60 min.**

### GENERAL INSTRUCTIONS

- The Daily Practice Problem Sheet contains **19** Questions divided into 6 sections.
  Section I has **6** MCQ's with ONLY 1 correct option. 2 marks for correct answer and No negative marks.
  Section II has **3** MCQ's with 1 or MORE THAN 1 correct option. 4 marks for correct answer(s) and (–1) for wrong answer.
  Section III has **1** PASSAGE with **3** MCQ's with ONLY 1 correct option. 3 marks for correct and (–1) mark for wrong answer.
  Section IV has **2** MCQ's with multiple matchings. 1 mark for the correct matching of each row & No negative marks.
  Section V has **2** Assertion-Reason MCQ's with ONLY 1 correct option. 3 marks for correct and (–1) mark for wrong answer.
  Section VI has **3** single digit integer answer questions. 4 marks for correct answer and (–1) for wrong answer.
- No mark will be given/ deducted if no bubble is filled. Keep a timer in front and stop immediately at the end of 60 min.
- You have to evaluate your Response Grids yourself with the help of Solution Booklet.
- The sheet follows a particular syllabus. Do not attempt the sheet before you have completed your preparation for that syllabus. Refer syllabus sheet in the starting of the book for the syllabus of all the DPP sheets.
- After completing the sheet check your answers with the solution booklet and complete the Result Grid. Finally spend time to analyse your performance and revise the areas which emerge out as weak in your evaluation.

## Section - I - Straight Objective Type

This section contains 6 multiple choice questions. Each question has 4 choices (a), (b), (c) and (d), out of which **ONLY ONE** is correct.

**1.** In a parallelogram ABCD, the interior bisectors of the consecutive angles B and C intersect at P. Use vector methods to find $\angle BPC$.

(a) $90°$      (b) $60°$

(c) $45°$      (d) $30°$

**2.** If $\vec{a}$ and $\vec{b}$ are unit vectors and $\alpha$ is the angle between them then $\cos \alpha/2$ is equal to

(a) $(1/2)|\vec{a}+\vec{b}|$      (b) $(1/2)|\vec{a}-\vec{b}|$

(c) $|\vec{a}+\vec{b}|$      (d) none

**3.** Determine the value of c so that for all real x, the vector $cx\hat{i} - 6\hat{j} - 3\hat{k}$ and $x\hat{i} + 2\hat{j} - 2cx\hat{k}$ make an obtuse angle with one another.

(a) $-4/3 < c < 0$      (b) $-1/3 < c < 0$

(c) $-2/3 < c < 0$      (d) $-2 < c < 0$

**4.** The resultant moment of three forces $\hat{i} + 2\hat{j} - 3\hat{k}$, $2\hat{i} + 3\hat{j} + 4\hat{k}$ and $-\hat{i} - \hat{j} + \hat{k}$ acting on a particle at a point P $(0, 1, 2)$ about the point A $(1, -2, 0)$ is

(a) $6\sqrt{2}$      (b) $\sqrt{140}$

(c) $\sqrt{21}$      (d) None

**5.** The set of values of 'a' for which the vector $\vec{r} = (a^2 - 4)\hat{i} + 2\hat{j} - (a^2 - 9)\hat{k}$ makes acute angles with the coordinate axes is

(a) $(-3, 3)$      (b) $(-\infty, -2) \cup (2, \infty)$

(c) $(-3, -2) \cup (2, 3)$      (d) $(-\infty, \infty)$

| RESPONSE GRID | 1. ⓐⓑⓒⓓ | 2. ⓐⓑⓒⓓ | 3. ⓐⓑⓒⓓ | 4. ⓐⓑⓒⓓ | 5. ⓐⓑⓒⓓ |
|---|---|---|---|---|---|

---

**6.** If $\vec{u} + \vec{v} + \vec{w} = 0$ and $|\vec{u}| = 3, |\vec{v}| = 4, |\vec{w}| = 5$, then the value of $\vec{u}.\vec{v} + \vec{v}.\vec{w} + \vec{w}.\vec{u}$ is

(a) 25  (b) $-25$  (c) 0  (d) 47

---

## Section - II - Multiple Correct Answer Type

This section contains 3 multiple correct answer(s) type questions. Each question has 4 choices (a), (b), (c) and (d), out of which **ONE OR MORE** is/are correct.

---

**7.** $\vec{a}$ and $\vec{c}$ are unit vectors and $|\vec{b}| = 4$ with $\vec{a} \times \vec{b} = 2\vec{a} \times \vec{c}$. Then angle between $\vec{a}$ and $\vec{c}$ is $\cos^{-1}(1/4)$. Then $\vec{b} - 2\vec{c} = \lambda \vec{a}$, if $\lambda$ is

(a) 3  (b) 1/4  (c) $-4$  (d) $-1/4$

**8.** Let $\vec{a} = 2\hat{i} - \hat{j} + \hat{k}$, $\vec{b} = \hat{i} + 2\hat{j} - \hat{k}$ and $\vec{c} = \hat{i} + \hat{j} - 2\hat{k}$ be three vectors. A vector in the plane of $\vec{b}$ and $\vec{c}$ whose projection on $\vec{a}$ is of magnitude $\sqrt{2/3}$ is

(a) $2\hat{i} + 3\hat{j} - 3\hat{k}$  (b) $2\hat{i} + 3\hat{j} + 3\hat{k}$

(c) $-2\hat{i} - \hat{j} + 5\hat{k}$  (d) $2\hat{i} + \hat{j} + 5\hat{k}$

**9.** If $2\vec{a}, -3\vec{b}, 2(\vec{a} \times \vec{b})$ are position vectors of the vertices $A$, $B$, $C$ of $\Delta ABC$ and $|\vec{a}| = 1, |\vec{b}| = 1, \overrightarrow{OA} \cdot \overrightarrow{OB} = -3$ (where $O$ is the origin), then

(a) triangle $ABC$ is right angled triangle

(b) angle $B$ is $90°$

(c) $A = \cos^{-1}\left(\sqrt{\dfrac{7}{19}}\right)$

(d) The position vector of orthocentre is $2(\vec{a} \times \vec{b})$.

---

## Section - III - Linked Comprehension Type

This section contains one paragraph. Based upon the paragraph, 3 multiple choice questions have to be answered. Each question has 4 choices (a), (b), (c) and (d), out of which **ONLY ONE** is correct.

---

Dot product of two vectors $\vec{A} = (a_1, a_2, a_3)$ and $\vec{B} = (b_1, b_2, b_3)$ is defined as $\vec{A}.\vec{B} = a_1b_1 + a_2b_2 + a_3b_3$. Also, $\vec{A}.\vec{B} = a_1b_1 + a_2b_2$ for $\vec{A} = (a_1, a_2)$ & $\vec{B} = (b_1, b_2)$. Using this definition of dot product of vectors it can be easily proved that following equations/inequations holds true.

I. $\vec{A}.\vec{B} = \vec{B}.\vec{A}$

II. $\vec{A}.(\vec{B} + \vec{C}) = \vec{A}.\vec{B} + \vec{A}.\vec{C}$

III. $C(\vec{A}.\vec{B}) = \vec{A}.(C\vec{B})$, where $C \in R$

IV. $\vec{A}.\vec{A} > 0$ if $\vec{A} \neq 0$ i.e. at least one of $a_i$ not zero for $i = 1, 2, 3$

**10.** If the dot product of two vectors $\vec{A} = (a_1, a_2)$ and $\vec{B} = (b_1, b_2)$ is defined as $\vec{A}.\vec{B} = 2a_1b_1 + a_2b_2 + a_1b_2 + a_2b_1$. All other algebraic operations on vectors remains as usual then –

(a) II is true

(b) II and III are not true

(c) IV is not true

(d) All of I, II, III, IV are not true

**11.** If however dot product of two vectors $\vec{A} = (a_1, a_2, a_3)$ and $\vec{B} = (b_1, b_2, b_3)$ is defined as $\vec{A}.\vec{B} = \left|\sum_{i=1}^{3} a_i b_i\right|$, while all other algebraic operations remains as usual. Then –

(a) I is not true  (b) II is not true

(c) all I, II, III, IV are true  (d) II and III are true

**12.** If the dot product of two vectors $\vec{A} = (a_1, a_2)$ and $\vec{B} = (b_1, b_2)$ is defined as

$$\vec{A}.\vec{B} = \sqrt{a_1b_1} + \sqrt{a_2b_2} + 2\sqrt{a_2b_1} + 2\sqrt{a_1b_2} \text{ and}$$

$|\vec{A}| = a_1 + a_2$, then which of the following always true for $a_i, b_i > 0, \forall i = 1, 2$?

(a) $|\vec{A}.\vec{B}| = |\vec{A}||\vec{B}|$  (b) $|\vec{A}.\vec{B}| > \dfrac{3}{2}(|\vec{A}| + |\vec{B}|)$

(c) $|\vec{A}.\vec{B}| \leq \dfrac{3}{2}(|\vec{A}| + |\vec{B}|)$  (d) $|\vec{A}.\vec{B}| = \dfrac{3}{2}|\vec{A}|$

---

<table>
<tr><td rowspan="2">**RESPONSE GRID**</td><td>6. ⓐⓑⓒⓓ</td><td>7. ⓐⓑⓒⓓ</td><td>8. ⓐⓑⓒⓓ</td><td>9. ⓐⓑⓒⓓ</td><td>10. ⓐⓑⓒⓓ</td></tr>
<tr><td>11. ⓐⓑⓒⓓ</td><td>12. ⓐⓑⓒⓓ</td><td></td><td></td><td></td></tr>
</table>

---

*Space for Rough Work*

## Section - IV - Matrix-Match Type

This section contains 2 questions. It contains statements given in two columns, which have to be matched. Statements in Column I are labelled as A, B, C and D whereas statements in Column II are labelled as p, q, r and s. The answers to these questions have to be appropriately bubbled as illustrated in the following example. If the correct matches are A-p, A-r, B-p, B-s, C-r, C-s and D-q, then the correctly bubbled matrix will look like the following :

|   | p | q | r | s |
|---|---|---|---|---|
| A | ● | q | ● | s |
| B | ● | q | r | ● |
| C | p | q | ● | ● |
| D | p | ● | r | s |

**13.** Let $\vec{a} = 2\hat{i} - 3\hat{j} + 6\hat{k}$, $\vec{b} = -2\hat{i} + 2\hat{j} - \hat{k}$, if $\vec{a} = \lambda\vec{b} + \mu\vec{c}$ where $\vec{c}$ is perpendicular to $\vec{b}$, then

| Column I | | Column II |
|---|---|---|
| (A) | Magnitude of projection of $\vec{a}$ on $\vec{b}$ is | (p) 16/7 |
| (B) | Magnitude of projection of $\vec{b}$ on $\vec{a}$ is | (q) 16/3 |
| (C) | Value of $|\lambda|$ is | (r) $\sqrt{185}/3$ |
| (D) | Value of $|\mu|$ is | (s) 16/9 |

**14.**

| Column I | | Column II |
|---|---|---|

(A) Let $W_1$ be the workdone if two forces $\vec{F}_1 = 3\hat{i} - 2\hat{j} + \hat{k}$ and $\vec{F}_2 = \hat{i} + 3\hat{j} - 5\hat{k}$ act on a particle whose P.V. is $-2\hat{i} + 5\hat{k}$ and displace it to another point whose P.V. is $3\hat{i} - 7\hat{j} + 2\hat{k}$ and $W_2$ be the workdone if three forces $\vec{P} = 2\hat{i} - 2\hat{j} + 6\hat{k}$, $\vec{Q} = -\hat{i} + 2\hat{j} - \hat{k}$ and $\vec{R} = 2\hat{i} + 7\hat{j}$ act on another particle whose P.V. is $4\hat{i} - 3\hat{j} - 2\hat{k}$ and displace it to another point whose P.V. is $6\hat{i} + \hat{j} - 3\hat{k}$, then    **(p)** $W_1 - W_2 = 3$

(B) Let $W_1$ be the workdone if a particle is displaced from the point whose P.V. is $(-2, 5, 7)$ to the point whose P.V. is $(3, 7, 2)$ under the action of constant forces $(2, -3, 1)$ and $(1, 5, -3)$ and $W_2$ be the workdone if other particle displaced from the point whose P.V. is $(4, -3, -2)$ to the point whose P.V. is $(6, 1, -3)$ under the action of constantc forces $(1, -1, 1), (-1, 2, -1)$ and $(1, 0, -1)$, then    **(q)** $W_1 - 3W_2 = 8$

(C) Let $W_1$ be the workdone if constant forces acting on a particle having magnitudes 5, 3, 1 units and act in the directions of the vectors $6\hat{i} + 2\hat{j} + 3\hat{k}$, $3\hat{i} - 2\hat{j} + 6\hat{k}$ and $2\hat{i} - 3\hat{j} - 6\hat{k}$ respectively. Displaced the particle from the point $(2, -1, -3)$ to $(5, -1, 1)$ and $W_2$ be the workdone if constant forces on another particle having magnitudes 1, 2, 3 units and act in the directions of the vectors $\hat{i} + 2\hat{j} + 2\hat{k}$, $2\hat{i} - 2\hat{j} + 2\hat{k}$ and $2\hat{i} - \hat{j} - 2\hat{k}$ respectively. Displaced the particle from the point $(-2, -1, 5)$ to $(3, -4, -5)$, then    **(r)** $2W_2 - W_1 = 9$    **(s)** $3W_2 - 2W_1 = 1$    **(t)** $W_1 - 4W_2 = 1$

## Section - V - Reasoning Type

This section contains 2 reasoning type questions. Each question has 4 choices (a), (b), (c) and (d) out of which **ONLY ONE** is correct.

**RESPONSE GRID**

**13.** A - (p)(q)(r)(s); B - (p)(q)(r)(s); C - (p)(q)(r)(s); D - (p)(q)(r)(s)

**14.** A - (p)(q)(r)(s)(t); B - (p)(q)(r)(s)(t); C - (p)(q)(r)(s)(t)

*Space for Rough Work*

DIRECTIONS for (Qs. 15 & 16) : Each of these questions contains two statements: Statement-1 (Assertion) and Statement-2 (Reason). Each of these questions has four alternative choices, only one of which is the correct answer. You have to select the correct choice.

(a) Statement-1 is True, Statement-2 is True; Statement-2 is a correct explanation for Statement-1.

(b) Statement-1 is True, Statement-2 is True; Statement-2 is NOT a correct explanation for Statement-1.

(c) Statement-1 is True, Statement-2 is False.

(d) Statement-1 is False, Statement-2 is True.

15. **Statement-1 :** If $\left|\vec{a} + \vec{b}\right| = \left|\vec{a} - \vec{b}\right|$ then $\vec{a}$ is parallel to $\vec{b}$.

   **Statement-2 :** If $\left|\vec{a} + \vec{b}\right| = \left|\vec{a} - \vec{b}\right|$ then $\vec{a}.\vec{b} = 0$.

16. **Statement-1 :** If $\vec{a} = \hat{i} + \hat{j}$ and $\vec{b} = \hat{j} - \hat{k}$ then $(\vec{a} + \vec{b}, \vec{a} - \vec{b}) = 90°$

   **Statement-2 :** Projection of $\vec{a} + \vec{b}$ on $\vec{a} - \vec{b}$ is zero.

## Section - VI - Integer Type

This section contains 3 questions. The answer to each of the questions is a single digit intege ranging from 0 to 9.

17. If $\vec{a}, \vec{b}$ and $\vec{c}$ are unit vectors, then

   $\left|\vec{a} - \vec{b}\right|^2 + \left|\vec{b} - \vec{c}\right|^2 + \left|\vec{c} - \vec{a}\right|^2$ does not exceed P then find the value of P.

18. Let $\vec{a}, \vec{b}, \vec{c}$ be unit vectors such that $\vec{a} . \vec{b} = \vec{a} . \vec{c} = 0$ and the angle between $\vec{b}$ and $\vec{c}$ is $\dfrac{\pi}{6}$. If $\vec{a} \times \vec{b} = n(\vec{b} \times \vec{c})$, then the value of n is $\pm R$. Find the value of R.

19. Two forces whose magnitudes are 2 gm wt, and 3 gm wt act on a particle in the directions of the vectors $2\hat{i} + 4\hat{j} + 4\hat{k}$ and $4\hat{i} + 4\hat{j} + 2\hat{k}$ resepectively. If the particle is displaced from the origin to the point (1, 2, 2), then find the work done in gm-cm (the unit of length being 1 cm).

| RESPONSE GRID | 15. ⓐⓑⓒⓓ | 16. ⓐⓑⓒⓓ |
|---|---|---|
| | 17. ⓪①②③④⑤⑥⑦⑧⑨ | 18. ⓪①②③④⑤⑥⑦⑧⑨ |
| | 19. ⓪①②③④⑤⑥⑦⑧⑨ | |

## DAILY PRACTICE PROBLEM DPP 69 - MATHS

| Total Questions | 19 | Total Marks | 58 |
|---|---|---|---|
| Attempted | | Correct | |
| Incorrect | | Net Score | |
| Cut-off Score | 12 | Qualifying Score | 38 |
| Success Gap = Net Score – Qualifying Score | | | |

$$\text{Net Score} = \sum_{i=1}^{VI}\left[(correct_i \times MM_i) - (In_i - NM_i)\right]$$

*Space for Rough Work*

# DPP - Daily Practice Problems

**Name :**  

**Date :**  

**Start Time :**  

**End Time :**  

## MATHEMATICS     M70

**SYLLABUS : Vector Algebra-3 :** Vector or Cross product of two vectors and its applications

**Max. Marks : 72**                     **Time : 60 min.**

### GENERAL INSTRUCTIONS

- The Daily Practice Problem Sheet contains **24** Questions divided into 4 sections.

  Section I has **10** MCQ's with ONLY 1 correct option. 2 marks for correct answer and No negative marks.

  Section II has **5** MCQ's with 1 or MORE THAN 1 correct option. 4 marks for correct answer(s) and (–1) for wrong answer.
  Section III has **4** Assertion-Reason MCQ's with ONLY 1 correct option. 3 marks for correct and (–1) mark for wrong answer.
  Section IV has **5** single digit integer answer questions. 4 marks for correct answer and (–1) for wrong answer.
- No mark will be given/ deducted if no bubble is filled. Keep a timer in front and stop immediately at the end of 60 min.
- You have to evaluate your Response Grids yourself with the help of Solution Booklet.
- The sheet follows a particular syllabus. Do not attempt the sheet before you have completed your preparation for that syllabus. Refer syllabus sheet in the starting of the book for the syllabus of all the DPP sheets.
- After completing the sheet check your answers with the solution booklet and complete the Result Grid. Finally spend time to analyse your performance and revise the areas which emerge out as weak in your evaluation.

---

### Section - I - Straight Objective Type

This section contains 10 multiple choice questions. Each question has 4 choices (a), (b), (c) and (d), out of which **ONLY ONE** is correct.

**1.** Let $\vec{a}, \vec{b}, \vec{c}$ be unit vectors such that $\vec{a} + \vec{b} + \vec{c} = \vec{0}$. Which one of the following is correct ?

(a) $\vec{a} \times \vec{b} = b \times \vec{c} = \vec{c} \times \vec{a} = \vec{0}$

(b) $\vec{a} \times \vec{b} = b \times \vec{c} = \vec{c} \times \vec{a} \neq \vec{0}$

(c) $\vec{a} \times \vec{b} = b \times \vec{c} = \vec{a} \times \vec{c} \neq \vec{0}$

(d) $\vec{a} \times \vec{b},\ b \times \vec{c},\ \vec{c} \times \vec{a}$ are mutually perpendicular

**2.** Given that $\vec{a} = (1, 1, 1)$, $\vec{c} = (0, 1, -1)$,

$\vec{a}.\vec{b} = 3$ and $\vec{a} \times \vec{b} = \vec{c}$, then $\vec{b} =$

(a) $\left(\dfrac{1}{2}, \dfrac{1}{2}, \dfrac{1}{3}\right)$

(b) $\left(\dfrac{2}{2}, \dfrac{1}{2}, \dfrac{1}{4}\right)$

(c) $\left(\dfrac{1}{2}, \dfrac{2}{3}, \dfrac{1}{4}\right)$

(d) $\left(\dfrac{5}{3}, \dfrac{2}{3}, \dfrac{2}{3}\right)$

**3.** The position vectors of two points A and C are $9\hat{i} - \hat{j} + 7\hat{k}$ and $7\hat{i} - 2\hat{j} + 7\hat{k}$ respectively. The point of intersection of vectors $\overrightarrow{AB} = 4\hat{i} - \hat{j} + 3\hat{k}$ and $\overrightarrow{CD} = 2\hat{i} - \hat{j} + 2\hat{k}$ is P. If vector $\overrightarrow{PQ}$ is perpendicular to $\overrightarrow{AB}$ and $\overrightarrow{CD}$ and PQ = 15 units, find the position vector of Q.

(a) $2(\hat{i} + 3\hat{j} - 3\hat{k})$

(b) $(\hat{i} - 3\hat{j} - 3\hat{k})$

(c) $5(2\hat{i} - 3\hat{j} + 3\hat{k})$

(d) $3(\hat{i} - 3\hat{j} - 3\hat{k})$

**4.** $(\vec{a} \times \hat{i})^2 + (\vec{a} \times \hat{j})^2 + (\vec{a} \times \hat{k})^2$ is equal to

(a) $(\vec{a})^2$

(b) $3(\vec{a})^2$

(c) $2(\vec{a})^2$

(d) None of these

---

**RESPONSE GRID**   **1.** ⓐⓑⓒⓓ   **2.** ⓐⓑⓒⓓ   **3.** ⓐⓑⓒⓓ   **4.** ⓐⓑⓒⓓ

**5.** Let $\overrightarrow{OA} = \vec{a}, \overrightarrow{OB} = 10\vec{a} + 2\vec{b}$ and $\overrightarrow{OC} = \vec{b}$, where O, A and C are non-collinear points. Let p denote the area of the quadrilateral OABC, and q denote the area of the parallelogram with OA and OC as adjacent sides. Then p/q is equal to

(a)  4                      (b)  6

(c)  $\dfrac{1}{2}\dfrac{|\vec{a} - \vec{b}|}{|\vec{a}|}$        (d)  None of these

**6.** The perpendicular distance of A$(1, 4, -2)$ from BC, where coordinates of B and C are respectively $(2, 1, -2)$ and $(0, -5, 1)$ is

(a)  $\dfrac{3}{7}$    (b)  $\dfrac{\sqrt{26}}{7}$    (c)  $\dfrac{3\sqrt{26}}{7}$    (d)  $\sqrt{26}$

**7.** Let $\vec{r} \times \vec{a} = \vec{b} \times \vec{a}$ and $\vec{r} \cdot \vec{c} = 0$, where $\vec{a} \cdot \vec{b} \neq 0$, then $\vec{r}$ is equal to

(a)  $\vec{b} + t\vec{a}$ where t is a scalar

(b)  $\vec{a} + \vec{c}$

(c)  $\vec{a} - \vec{c}$

(d)  None of these

**8.** The distance of the point $(1, 1, 1)$ from the plane passing through the points $(2, 1, 1), (1, 2, 1)$ and $(1, 1, 2)$ is

(a)  $1/\sqrt{3}$                (b)  1

(c)  $\sqrt{3}$                (d)  None of these

**9.** Let the vectors $\vec{a}, \vec{b}, \vec{c}$ and $\vec{d}$ be such that

$$\left(\vec{a} \times \vec{b}\right) \times \left(\vec{c} \times \vec{d}\right) = 0$$. Let $P_1$ and $P_2$ be planes determined by the pairs of vectors $\vec{a}, \vec{b}$ and $\vec{c}, \vec{d}$ respectively. Then the angle between $P_1$ and $P_2$ is

(a)  0    (b)  $\dfrac{\pi}{4}$    (c)  $\dfrac{\pi}{3}$    (d)  $\dfrac{\pi}{2}$

**10.** A vector perpendicular to the plane containing the vectors $\hat{i} - 2\hat{j} - \hat{k}$ and $3\hat{i} - 2\hat{j} - \hat{k}$ is inclined to the vector $\hat{i} + \hat{j} + \hat{k}$ at an angle

(a)  $\tan^{-1}\sqrt{14}$        (b)  $\sec^{-1}\sqrt{14}$

(c)  $\tan^{-1}\sqrt{15}$        (d)  $\sec^{-1}\sqrt{15}$

## Section - II - Multiple Correct Answer Type

This section contains 5 multiple correct answer(s) type questions. Each question has 4 choices (a), (b), (c) and (d), out of which **ONE OR MORE** is/are correct.

**11.** Let $\vec{A}$ be vector parallel to line of intersection of planes $P_1$ and $P_2$. Plane $P_1$ is parallel to the vectors $2\hat{j} + 3\hat{k}$ and $4\hat{j} - 3\hat{k}$ and that $P_2$ is parallel to $\hat{j} - \hat{k}$ and $3\hat{i} + 3\hat{j}$, then the angle between vector $\vec{A}$ and a given vector $2\hat{i} + \hat{j} - 2\hat{k}$ is

(a)  $\dfrac{\pi}{2}$    (b)  $\dfrac{\pi}{4}$    (c)  $\dfrac{\pi}{6}$    (d)  $\dfrac{3\pi}{4}$

**12.** Let $\vec{a}$ and $\vec{b}$ be two non-collinear unit vectors. If $\vec{u} = \vec{a} - (\vec{a}.\vec{b})\vec{b}$ and $\vec{v} = \vec{a} \times \vec{b}$, then $|\vec{v}|$ is

(a)  $|\vec{u}|$             (b)  $|\vec{u}| + |\vec{u}.\vec{a}|$

(c)  $|\vec{u}| + |\vec{u}.\vec{b}|$      (d)  $|\vec{u}| + \vec{u}.(\vec{a} + \vec{b})$

**13.** A vector of magnitude 5 perpendicular to the vectors $2\hat{i} + \hat{j} - 3\hat{k}$ and $\hat{i} - 2\hat{j} + \hat{k}$ is

(a)  $\dfrac{5\sqrt{3}}{3}(\hat{i} + \hat{j} + \hat{k})$        (b)  $\dfrac{5\sqrt{3}}{3}(\hat{i} - \hat{j} + \hat{k})$

(c)  $\dfrac{5\sqrt{3}}{3}(\hat{i} + \hat{j} - \hat{k})$        (d)  $-\dfrac{5\sqrt{3}}{3}(\hat{i} + \hat{j} + \hat{k})$

| RESPONSE GRID | | | | | |
|---|---|---|---|---|---|
| **5.** ⓐⓑⓒⓓ | **6.** ⓐⓑⓒⓓ | **7.** ⓐⓑⓒⓓ | **8.** ⓐⓑⓒⓓ | **9.** ⓐⓑⓒⓓ | |
| **10.** ⓐⓑⓒⓓ | **11.** ⓐⓑⓒⓓ | **12.** ⓐⓑⓒⓓ | **13.** ⓐⓑⓒⓓ | | |

14. If a vector $\vec{r}$ satisfies the equation

    $\vec{r} \times (\hat{i} + 2\hat{j} + \hat{k}) = \hat{i} - \hat{k}$, then $\vec{r}$ is equal to

    (a) $\hat{i} + 3\hat{j} + \hat{k}$

    (b) $3\hat{i} + 7\hat{j} + 3\hat{k}$

    (c) $\hat{j} + t(\hat{i} + 2\hat{j} + \hat{k})$ where $t$ is any scalar

    (d) $\hat{i} + (t+3)\hat{j} + \hat{k}$ where $t$ is any scalar

15. Let $\vec{A} = 2\hat{i} + \hat{k}$, $\vec{B} = \hat{i} + \hat{j} + \hat{k}$ and $\vec{C} = 4\hat{i} - 3\hat{j} + 7\hat{k}$. The

    vector $\vec{R}$ which satisfies the equations

    $\vec{R} \times \vec{B} = \vec{C} \times \vec{B}$ and $\vec{R} \cdot \vec{A} = 0$ is given by

    (a) $-2\hat{i} + \hat{k}$

    (b) $-\hat{i} - 8\hat{j} + 2\hat{k}$

    (c) $\dfrac{1}{\sqrt{6}}(\hat{i} - \hat{j} + 2\hat{k})$

    (d) None of these

## Section - III - Reasoning Type

This section contains 4 reasoning type questions. Each question has 4 choices (a), (b), (c) and (d) out of which **ONLY ONE** is correct.

**DIRECTIONS for (Qs 16-19) : Each of these questions contains two statements: Statement-1 (Assertion) and Statement-2 (Reason). Each of these questions has four alternative choices, only one of which is the correct answer. You have to select the correct choice.**

(a) Statement-1 is True, Statement-2 is True; Statement-2 is a correct explanation for Statement-1.

(b) Statement-1 is True, Statement-2 is True; Statement-2 is NOT a correct explanation for Statement-1.

(c) Statement -1 is True, Statement-2 is False.

(d) Statement -1 is False, Statement-2 is True.

16. **Statement 1 :** If $\vec{a}, \vec{b}, \vec{c}, \vec{d}$ are four vectors such that

    $(\vec{a} \times \vec{b}) \times (\vec{c} \times \vec{d}) = \vec{0}$ where $\vec{a}$ and $\vec{b}$ are parallel to plane P

    and $\vec{c}$ and $\vec{d}$ are parallel to plane Q than angle between P

    and Q is $\dfrac{\pi}{2}$.

    **Statement 2 :** Angle between two planes is the angle between their normals.

17. Let the vectors $\overrightarrow{PQ}, \overrightarrow{QR}, \overrightarrow{RS}, \overrightarrow{ST}, \overrightarrow{TU}$ and $\overrightarrow{UP}$ represent the sides of a regular hexagon.

    **Statement–1 :** $\overrightarrow{PQ} \times \left(\overrightarrow{RS} + \overrightarrow{ST}\right) \neq \vec{0}$

    **Statement–2 :** $\overrightarrow{PQ} \times \overrightarrow{RS} = \vec{0}$ and $\overrightarrow{PQ} \times \overrightarrow{ST} \neq \vec{0}$.

18. **Statement–1 :** Let $\vec{a}$ and $\vec{b}$ be two non collinear unit vectors. If $\vec{u} = \vec{a} - (\vec{a} \cdot \vec{b})\vec{b}$ and $\vec{v} = \vec{a} \times \vec{b}$ then $|\vec{v}| = |\vec{u}|$.

    **Statement–2 :** The vector $\dfrac{1}{3}(2\hat{i} - 2\hat{j} + \hat{k})$ makes an angle of $\pi/3$ with the vector $(5\hat{i} - 4\hat{j} + 3\hat{k})$.

19. **Statement-1 :** Three points with position vectors $\vec{a}, \vec{b}, \vec{c}$ are collinear if $\vec{a} \times \vec{b} + \vec{b} \times \vec{c} + \vec{c} \times \vec{a} = 0$

    **Statement-2 :** Three points A, B, C are collinear iff $\overrightarrow{AB} = t \, \overrightarrow{BC}$, where $t$ is scalar.

## Section - IV - Integer Type

This section contains 5 questions. The answer to each of the questions is a single digit integer ranging from 0 to 9.

20. If $\vec{a}$ is a unit vector perpendicular to the plane of $2\hat{i} - \hat{j} + \hat{k}$

    and $3\hat{i} + 4\hat{j} - \hat{k}$, then $\dfrac{1}{\sqrt{155}} |\vec{a}| =$



*Space for Rough Work*

**21.** Find the number of unit vectors perpendicular to the vectors $\vec{a} = (1, 1, 0)$ and $\vec{b} = (0, 1, 1)$

**22.** If three vectors $\vec{a}, \vec{b}, \vec{c}$ are such that $\vec{a} \neq 0$, $\vec{a} \times \vec{b} = 2\vec{a} \times \vec{c}, |\vec{a}| = |\vec{c}| = 1, |\vec{b}| = 4$, the angle between $\vec{b}$ and $\vec{c}$ is $\cos^{-1}\dfrac{1}{4}$ and $\vec{b} - 2\vec{c} = \lambda\vec{a}$ then find the positive value of $\lambda$

**23.** If $\theta$ be the acute angle that the vector $2\hat{i} - 2\hat{j} + \hat{k}$ makes with the plane contained by the two vectors $2\hat{i} + 3\hat{j} - \hat{k}$ and $\hat{i} - \hat{j} + 2\hat{k}$, then $\sqrt{3}\sin\theta =$

**24.** A tetrahedron has vertices at O $(0, 0, 0)$, A$(1, 2, 1)$, B $(2, 1, 3)$ and C $(-1, 1, 2)$. If the angle between the faces OAB and ABC is $\theta$, then $\dfrac{70}{19}\cos\theta =$

| RESPONSE GRID | | |
|---|---|---|
| **21.** ⓪①②③④⑤⑥⑦⑧⑨ | | **22.** ⓪①②③④⑤⑥⑦⑧⑨ |
| **23.** ⓪①②③④⑤⑥⑦⑧⑨ | | **24.** ⓪①②③④⑤⑥⑦⑧⑨ |

## DAILY PRACTICE PROBLEM DPP 70 - MATHS

| Total Questions | 24 | Total Marks | 72 |
|---|---|---|---|
| Attempted | | Correct | |
| Incorrect | | Net Score | |
| Cut-off Score | 14 | Qualifying Score | 47 |
| Success Gap = Net Score – Qualifying Score | | | |

$$\text{Net Score} = \sum_{i=1}^{VI}\left[(correct_i \times MM_i) - (In_i - NM_i)\right]$$

*Space for Rough Work*

Name : 

Date : 

Start Time : 

End Time : 

# MATHEMATICS    M71

SYLLABUS : **Vector Algebra-4** : Scalar triple product and their applications

**Max. Marks : 63**                    **Time : 60 min.**



## Section - I - Straight Objective Type

This section contains 6 multiple choice questions. Each question has 4 choices (a), (b), (c) and (d), out of which **ONLY ONE** is correct.

**1.** The scalar $\vec{A}.(\vec{B}+\vec{C})\times(\vec{A}+\vec{B}+\vec{C})$ equals :

(a) $0$ 

(b) $[\vec{A}\ \vec{B}\ \vec{C}]+[\vec{B}\ \vec{C}\ \vec{A}]$

(c) $[\vec{A}\ \vec{B}\ \vec{C}]$ 

(d) None of these

**2.** For non-zero vectors $\vec{a}, \vec{b}, \vec{c}$ ; $\left|(\vec{a}\times\vec{b}).\vec{c}\right| = |\vec{a}||\vec{b}||\vec{c}|$ holds if and only if

(a) $\vec{a}.\vec{b}=0,\ \vec{b}.\vec{c}=0$ 

(b) $\vec{b}.\vec{c}=0,\ \vec{c}.\vec{a}=0$

(c) $\vec{c}.\vec{a}=0,\ \vec{a}.\vec{b}=0$ 

(d) $\vec{a}.\vec{b}=\vec{b}.\vec{c}=\vec{c}.\vec{a}=0$

**3.** If $\vec{a},\vec{b},\vec{c}$ are non coplanar vectors and $\lambda$ is a real number then $[\lambda(\vec{a}+\vec{b})\ \lambda^2\vec{b}\ \lambda\vec{c}] = [\vec{a}\ \vec{b}+\vec{c}\ \vec{b}]$ for

(a) exactly one value of $\lambda$ 

(b) no value of $\lambda$

(c) exactly three values of $\lambda$ 

(d) exactly two values of $\lambda$

**4.** Let $\vec{a} = \hat{i}-\hat{k}$ , $\vec{b} = x\hat{i}+\hat{j}+(1-x)\hat{k}$ and $\vec{c} = y\hat{i}+x\hat{j}+(1+x-y)\hat{k}$ , then $[\vec{a},\vec{b},\vec{c}]$ depends on

(a) only y 

(b) only x

(c) both x and y 

(d) neither x nor y

**5.** If $\vec{a},\vec{b},\vec{c}$ are non-coplanar vectors, then $\begin{vmatrix} \vec{a}.\vec{a} & \vec{a}.\vec{b} & \vec{a}.\vec{c} \\ \vec{b}.\vec{a} & \vec{b}.\vec{b} & \vec{b}.\vec{c} \\ \vec{c}.\vec{a} & \vec{c}.\vec{b} & \vec{c}.\vec{c} \end{vmatrix}$ equals

(a) $\left[\vec{a}\ \vec{b}\ \vec{c}\right]^2$ 

(b) $\left[\vec{a}\ \vec{b}\ \vec{c}\right]$

(c) $\left[\vec{a}\ \vec{b}\ \vec{c}\right]^3$ 

(d) None of these

**6.** If $\vec{\alpha} = x(\vec{a} \times \vec{b}) + y(\vec{b} \times \vec{c}) + z(\vec{c} \times \vec{a})$ and

$[\vec{a}\ \vec{b}\ \vec{c}] = \dfrac{1}{8}$, then $x + y + z =$

  (a) $8\vec{\alpha}.(\vec{a} + \vec{b} + \vec{c})$      (b) $\vec{\alpha}.(\vec{a} + \vec{b} + \vec{c})$

  (c) $8(\vec{a} + \vec{b} + \vec{c})$      (d) None of these

---

## Section - II - Multiple Correct Answer Type

This section contains 4 multiple correct answer(s) type questions. Each question has 4 choices (a), (b), (c) and (d), out of which **ONE OR MORE** is/are correct.

**7.** If the volume of parallelopiped whose adjacent edges are $\vec{a} = 2\hat{i} + 3\hat{j} + 4\hat{k},\ \vec{b} = \hat{i} + \alpha\hat{j} + 2\hat{k},\ \vec{c} = \hat{i} + 2\hat{j} + \alpha\hat{k}$ is 15, then $\alpha$ can be equal to

  (a) $1$     (b) $\dfrac{5}{2}$     (c) $\dfrac{9}{2}$     (d) $-1$

**8.** If $\vec{a} = \hat{i} + \hat{j} + \hat{k}$ and $\vec{b} = \hat{i} - \hat{j}$ then the vectors $(\vec{a}.\hat{i})\,\hat{i} + (\vec{a}.\hat{j})\,\hat{j} + (\vec{a}.\hat{k})\,\hat{k},\ (\vec{b}.\hat{i})\,\hat{i} + (\vec{b}.\hat{j})\,\hat{j} + (\vec{b}.\hat{k})\,\hat{k},$ and $\hat{i} + \hat{j} - 2\hat{k}$

  (a) are mutually perpendicular
  (b) are coplanar
  (c) form a parallelopiped of volume 6 cubic units
  (d) form a parallelopiped of volume 3 units

**9.** If a is a non-zero real number, then the vectors $\vec{\alpha} = a\hat{i} + 2a\hat{j} - 3a\hat{k},\ \vec{\beta} = (2a+1)\hat{i} + (2a+3)\hat{j} + (a+1)\hat{k},$ $\vec{\gamma} = (3a+5)\hat{i} + (a+5)\hat{j} + (a+2)\hat{k}$ are

  (a) coplanar, if $a < 0$      (b) coplanar, if $a > 0$
  (c) always coplanar      (d) non-coplanar

**10.** Let a, b, c be three distinct positive real numbers. If $\vec{p}, \vec{q}, \vec{r}$ lie in a plane, where $\vec{p} = a\hat{i} - a\hat{j} + b\hat{k},\ \vec{q} = \hat{i} + \hat{k}$ and $\vec{r} = c\hat{i} + c\hat{j} + b\hat{k}$. then b is

  (a) the AM of a,c      (b) the GM of a, c
  (c) the HM of a, c      (d) equal to 0

---

## Section - III - Linked Comprehension Type

This section contains one paragraph. Based upon the paragraph, 3 multiple choice questions have to be answered. Each question has 4 choices (a), (b), (c) and (d), out of which **ONLY ONE** is correct.

Let $\vec{a}, \vec{b}, \vec{c}$ be three vectors such that $|\vec{a}| = |\vec{b}| = |\vec{c}| = 4$ and angle between $\vec{a}$ and $\vec{b}$ is $\pi/3$, angle between $\vec{b}$ and $\vec{c}$ is $\pi/3$ and angle between $\vec{c}$ and $\vec{a}$ is $\pi/3$

**11.** The height of the parallelopiped whose adjacent edges are represented by the vectors $\vec{a}, \vec{b}$ and $\vec{c}$ is

  (a) $4\sqrt{\dfrac{2}{3}}$        (b) $3\sqrt{\dfrac{2}{3}}$

  (c) $4\sqrt{\dfrac{3}{2}}$        (d) $3\sqrt{\dfrac{3}{2}}$

**12.** The height of the tetrahedron whose adjacent edges are represented by the vectors $\vec{a}, \vec{b}$ and $\vec{c}$ is

  (a) $2\sqrt{\dfrac{2}{3}}$    (b) $4\sqrt{\dfrac{2}{3}}$    (c) $3\sqrt{\dfrac{2}{3}}$    (d) $\sqrt{\dfrac{2}{3}}$

**13.** The volume of the triangular prism whose adjacent edges are represented by the vectors $\vec{a}, \vec{b}$ and $\vec{c}$ is

  (a) $12\sqrt{2}$    (b) $12\sqrt{3}$    (c) $16\sqrt{2}$    (d) $16\sqrt{3}$

---

| **Response Grid** | 6. ⓐⓑⓒⓓ | 7. ⓐⓑⓒⓓ | 8. ⓐⓑⓒⓓ | 9. ⓐⓑⓒⓓ | 10. ⓐⓑⓒⓓ |
|---|---|---|---|---|---|
| | 11. ⓐⓑⓒⓓ | 12. ⓐⓑⓒⓓ | 13. ⓐⓑⓒⓓ | | |

*Space for Rough Work*

## Section - IV - Matrix-Match Type

This section contains 2 questions. It contains statements given in two columns, which have to be matched. Statements in Column I are labelled as A, B, C and D whereas statements in Column II are labelled as p, q, r and s. The answers to these questions have to be appropriately bubbled as illustrated in the following example. If the correct matches are A-p, A-r, B-p, B-s, C-r, C-s and D-q, then the correctly bubbled matrix will look like the following :

14. Let $\vec{a}$ be a vector of magnitude 2 and $\vec{b}, \vec{c}$ are non-zero vectors and none collinear with $\vec{a}$, which satisfy the equations $\vec{a} \times \vec{b} = \vec{c}$ and $\vec{b} \times \vec{c} = \vec{a}$ then match the entries from the following two columns :

| Column-I | Column-II |
|---|---|
| (A) $|\vec{b}|$ is equal to | (p) 4 |
| (B) $|\vec{c}|$ is equal to | (q) 3 |
| (C) $[\vec{a}\ \vec{b}\ \vec{c}]$ is equal to | (r) 2 |
| (D) $|\vec{a} + \vec{b} + \vec{c}|$ is equal to | (s) 1 |
| | (t) 0 |

15.

| Column-I | Column-II |
|---|---|
| (A) If $V_1, V_2, V_3$ are the volumes of parallelopiped, triangular prism and tetrahedron respectively. The three coterminus edges of all three figures are the vectors $\hat{i} - \hat{j} - 6\hat{k},\ \hat{i} - \hat{j} + 4\hat{k}$, and $2\hat{i} - 5\hat{j} + 3\hat{k}$, then | (p) $2V_1 + 3V_3 = 5V_2$ |
| (B) If $V_1, V_2, V_3$ are the volumes of parallelopiped, triangular prism and tetrahedron respectively. The three coterminus edges of all three figures are the vectors $-2\hat{i} + 3\hat{j} - 3\hat{k},\ 4\hat{i} + 5\hat{j} - 3\hat{k}$ and $6\hat{i} + 2\hat{j} - 3\hat{k}$, then | (q) $V_1 + V_2 + V_3 = 60$ |
| (C) If $V_1, V_2, V_3$ are the volumes of parallelopiped, triangular prism and tetrahedron respectively. The three coterminus edges of all three figures are the vectors $-3\hat{i} + \hat{j} + \hat{k},\ 4\hat{i} + 2\hat{j} + 4\hat{k}$, and $2\hat{i} + 2\hat{j}$ then | (r) $V_1 + 3V_3 = 3V_2$ |
| | (s) $V_1 + V_2 + V_3 = 50$ |
| | (t) $V_1 : V_2 : V_3 = 6:3:1$ |

## Section - V - Reasoning Type

This section contain 1 reasoning type question. Each question has 4 choices (a), (b), (c) and (d) out of which **ONLY ONE** is correct.

**DIRECTIONS : Each of these questions contains two statements: Statement-1 (Assertion) and Statement-2 (Reason). Each of these questions has four alternative choices, only one of which is the correct answer. You have to select the correct choice.**

(a) Statement-1 is True, Statement-2 is True; Statement-2 is a correct explanation for Statement-1.

(b) Statement-1 is True, Statement-2 is True; Statement-2 is NOT a correct explanation for Statement-1.

(c) Statement -1 is True, Statement-2 is False.

(d) Statement -1 is False, Statement-2 is True.

16. **Statement-1 :** If $\vec{a}, \vec{b}, \vec{c}$ are coplanar, then $\vec{a} \times \vec{b}, \vec{b} \times \vec{c}$ and $\vec{c} \times \vec{a}$ are also coplanar.

**Statement-2 :** $[\vec{a} \times \vec{b}\ \ \vec{b} \times \vec{c}\ \ \vec{c} \times \vec{a}] = 2[\vec{a}\ \vec{b}\ \vec{c}]^2$

**RESPONSE GRID**

14. A - (p)(q)(r)(s)(t); B - (p)(q)(r)(s)(t); C - (p)(q)(r)(s)(t); D - (p)(q)(r)(s)(t)

15. A - (p)(q)(r)(s)(t); B - (p)(q)(r)(s)(t); C - (p)(q)(r)(s)(t)

16. (a)(b)(c)(d)

*Space for Rough Work*

## Section - VI - Integer Type

This section contains 4 questions. The answer to each of the questions is a single digit integer ranging from 0 to 9.

**17.** The volume of the parallelopiped whose sides are given by

$$\overrightarrow{OA} = 2\hat{i} - 2\hat{j}, \ \overrightarrow{OB} = \hat{i} + \hat{j} - \hat{k}, \ \overrightarrow{OC} = 3\hat{i} - \hat{k}, \ \text{is}$$

**18.** Let $\vec{a}, \vec{b}, \vec{c},$ be three non-coplanar vectors and $\vec{p}, \vec{q}, \vec{r},$ are vectors defined by the relations $\vec{p} = \dfrac{\vec{b} \times \vec{c}}{[\vec{a}\vec{b}\vec{c}]},$

$\vec{q} = \dfrac{\vec{c} \times \vec{a}}{[\vec{a}\vec{b}\vec{c}]}, \ \vec{r} = \dfrac{\vec{a} \times \vec{b}}{[\vec{a}\vec{b}\vec{c}]}$ then find the value of the

expression $(\vec{a} + \vec{b}) \cdot \vec{p} + (\vec{b} + \vec{c}) \cdot \vec{q} + (\vec{c} + \vec{a}) \cdot \vec{r}$

**19.** If $\vec{a}, \vec{b}, \vec{c}$ are vectors such that $[\vec{a} \ \vec{b} \ \vec{c}] = 4$ then find the

value of $\dfrac{1}{2}[\vec{a} \times \vec{b} \ \ \vec{b} \times \vec{c} \ \ \vec{c} \times \vec{a}]$

**20.** If $\begin{vmatrix} a & a^2 & 1+a^3 \\ b & b^2 & 1+b^3 \\ c & c^2 & 1+c^3 \end{vmatrix} = 0$ and vectors $(1, a, a^2),$

$(1, b, b^2)$ and $(1, c, c^2)$ are non-coplanar, then find the value of the product abc.

| RESPONSE GRID | | |
|---|---|---|
| **17.** ⓪①②③④⑤⑥⑦⑧⑨ | | **18.** ⓪①②③④⑤⑥⑦⑧⑨ |
| **19.** ⓪①②③④⑤⑥⑦⑧⑨ | | **20.** ⓪①②③④⑤⑥⑦⑧⑨ |

## DAILY PRACTICE PROBLEM DPP 71 - MATHS

| Total Questions | 20 | Total Marks | 63 |
|---|---|---|---|
| Attempted | | Correct | |
| Incorrect | | Net Score | |
| Cut-off Score | 13 | Qualifying Score | 41 |
| Success Gap = Net Score – Qualifying Score | | | |

$$\text{Net Score} = \sum_{i=I}^{VI} \left[ (\text{correct}_i \times MM_i) - (In_i - NM_i) \right]$$

# DPP - Daily Practice Problems

**Name :**

**Date :**

**Start Time :**

**End Time :**

# MATHEMATICS  M72

**SYLLABUS : Co-ordinate Geometry of Three Dimensions-1 :** System of co-ordinates, Direction cosines and direction ratios, Projection

## Max. Marks : 69                    Time : 60 min.

### GENERAL INSTRUCTIONS

- The Daily Practice Problem Sheet contains **24** Questions divided into 6 sections.
  Section I has **10** MCQ's with ONLY 1 correct option. 2 marks for correct answer and No negative marks.
  Section II has **2** MCQ's with 1 or MORE THAN 1 correct option. 4 marks for correct answer(s) and (–1) for wrong answer.
  Section III has **1** PASSAGE with **3** MCQ's with ONLY 1 correct option. 3 marks for correct and (–1) mark for wrong answer.
  Section IV has **1** MCQ's with multiple matchings. 1 mark for the correct matching of each row & No negative marks.
  Section V has **3** Assertion-Reason MCQ's with ONLY 1 correct option. 3 marks for correct and (–1) mark for wrong answer.
  Section VI has **5** single digit integer answer questions. 4 marks for correct answer and (–1) for wrong answer.
- No mark will be given/ deducted if no bubble is filled. Keep a timer in front and stop immediately at the end of 60 min.
- You have to evaluate your Response Grids yourself with the help of Solution Booklet.
- The sheet follows a particular syllabus. Do not attempt the sheet before you have completed your preparation for that syllabus. Refer syllabus sheet in the starting of the book for the syllabus of all the DPP sheets.
- After completing the sheet check your answers with the solution booklet and complete the Result Grid. Finally spend time to analyse your performance and revise the areas which emerge out as weak in your evaluation.

## Section - I - Straight Objective Type

This section contains 10 multiple choice questions. Each question has 4 choices (a), (b), (c) and (d), out of which **ONLY ONE** is correct.

**1.** The projections of the segment PQ on the co-ordinate axes are –9, 12, –8 respectively. The direction cosines of the line PQ are

(a) $\dfrac{-9}{\sqrt{17}}, \dfrac{12}{\sqrt{17}}, \dfrac{-8}{\sqrt{17}}$    (b) $-9, 12, -8$

(c) $-\dfrac{9}{289}, \dfrac{12}{289}, \dfrac{-8}{289}$    (d) $-\dfrac{9}{17}, \dfrac{12}{17}, \dfrac{-8}{17}$

**2.** Let $A(4, 7, 8), B(2, 3, 4), C(2, 5, 7)$ be the position vectors of the vertices of triangle ABC. The length of internal bisector of $\angle A$ is

(a) $\dfrac{\sqrt{34}}{2}$    (b) $\dfrac{3}{2}\sqrt{34}$    (c) $\dfrac{2}{3}\sqrt{34}$    (d) $\dfrac{\sqrt{34}}{3}$

**3.** A line makes the same angle $\theta$ with each of the x and z axis. If the angle $\beta$, which it makes with y-axis, is such that $\sin^2 \beta = 3\sin^2 \theta,$ then $\cos^2\theta$ equals

(a) $\dfrac{2}{5}$    (b) $\dfrac{1}{5}$

(c) $\dfrac{3}{5}$    (d) $\dfrac{2}{3}$

**4.** If the direction cosines of a line are $\left(\dfrac{1}{c}, \dfrac{1}{c}, \dfrac{1}{c}\right),$ then

(a) $0 < c < 1$    (b) $c < 2$

(c) $c > 0$    (d) $c = \pm\sqrt{3}$

**5.** A straight line which makes an angle of $60°$ with each of Y and Z-axis, inclines with X-axis at an angle.

(a) $30°$    (b) $60°$    (c) $75°$    (d) $45°$

| **RESPONSE GRID** | 1. ⓐⓑⓒⓓ | 2. ⓐⓑⓒⓓ | 3. ⓐⓑⓒⓓ | 4. ⓐⓑⓒⓓ | 5. ⓐⓑⓒⓓ |
|---|---|---|---|---|---|

**6.** The points $(5, -4, 2), (4, -3, 1) (7, -6, 4), (8, -7, 5)$ are vertices of

(a) parallelogram      (b) rectangle

(c) rhombus      (d) none.

**7.** Four points P, Q, R and S have the coordinates $(6, -7, 0), (16, -19, -4), (0, 3, -6)$ and $(2, -5, 10)$ respectively. Then

(a) line segments PQ and RS are non-coplanar

(b) line segments PQ and RS are parallel

(c) line segments PQ and RS are intersecting

(d) P, Q, R and S are collinear points

**8.** The vertices of a triangle ABC are A $(-1, 2, -3)$, B $(5, 0, -6)$ and C $(0, 4, -1)$. The direction cosines of the bisector of the angle BAC are

(a) $\dfrac{1}{\sqrt{3}}, -\dfrac{1}{\sqrt{3}}, \dfrac{1}{\sqrt{3}}$      (b) $\dfrac{5}{\sqrt{42}}, \dfrac{4}{\sqrt{42}}, \dfrac{1}{\sqrt{42}}$

(c) $\dfrac{2}{\sqrt{33}}, \dfrac{5}{\sqrt{33}}, \dfrac{2}{\sqrt{33}}$      (d) $\dfrac{25}{\sqrt{714}}, \dfrac{8}{\sqrt{714}}, \dfrac{5}{\sqrt{714}}$

**9.** The angle between the lines whose direction cosines are given by the equations $3l + m + 5n = 0$, $6nm - 2nl + 5lm = 0$ is

(a) $\cos^{-1}\left(\dfrac{1}{6}\right)$      (b) $\cos^{-1}\left(-\dfrac{1}{6}\right)$

(c) $\cos^{-1}\left(\dfrac{2}{3}\right)$      (d) $\cos^{-1}\left(-\dfrac{5}{6}\right)$

**10.** The length intercepted by a line with direction ratios $2, 7, -5$ between the lines $\dfrac{x-5}{3} = \dfrac{y-7}{-1} = \dfrac{z+2}{1}$ and $\dfrac{x+3}{-3} = \dfrac{y-3}{2} = \dfrac{z-6}{4}$ is

(a) $\sqrt{75}$      (b) $\sqrt{78}$

(c) $\sqrt{83}$      (d) None of these

## Section - II - Multiple Correct Answer Type

This section contains 2 multiple correct answer(s) type questions. Each question has 4 choices (a), (b), (c) and (d), out of which **ONE OR MORE** is/are correct.

**11.** The value(s) of $\lambda$, for which the triangle with vertices $(6, 10, 10), (1, 0, -5)$ and $(6, -10, \lambda)$ will be a right angled triangle is / are :

(a) 1      (b) $\dfrac{70}{3}$      (c) 35      (d) 0

**12.** Two coplanar lines having d.c.'s $l_1, m_1, n_1$ and $l_2, m_2, n_2$ are inclined at an angle $\theta$. The d.c.'s of the lines bisecting the angle between them are

(a) $\dfrac{l_1 + l_2}{2\cos\dfrac{\theta}{2}}, \dfrac{m_1 + m_2}{2\cos\dfrac{\theta}{2}}, \dfrac{n_1 + n_2}{2\cos\dfrac{\theta}{2}}$

(b) $\dfrac{l_1 - l_2}{2\cos\dfrac{\theta}{2}}, \dfrac{m_1 - m_2}{2\cos\dfrac{\theta}{2}}, \dfrac{n_1 - n_2}{2\cos\dfrac{\theta}{2}}$

(c) $\dfrac{l_1 + l_2}{2\sin\dfrac{\theta}{2}}, \dfrac{m_1 + m_2}{2\sin\dfrac{\theta}{2}}, \dfrac{n_1 + n_2}{2\sin\dfrac{\theta}{2}}$

(d) $\dfrac{l_1 - l_2}{2\sin\dfrac{\theta}{2}}, \dfrac{m_1 - m_2}{2\sin\dfrac{\theta}{2}}, \dfrac{n_1 - n_2}{2\sin\dfrac{\theta}{2}}$

## Section - III - Linked Comprehension Type

This section contains one paragraph. Based upon the paragraph, 3 multiple choice questions have to be answered. Each question has 4 choices (a), (b), (c) and (d), out of which **ONLY ONE** is correct.

A tetrahedron is a three dimensional figure bounded by four non coplanar triangular planes. So, a tetrahedron has four non-coplanar points as its vertices.

| **RESPONSE GRID** | 6. ⓐⓑⓒⓓ | 7. ⓐⓑⓒⓓ | 8. ⓐⓑⓒⓓ | 9. ⓐⓑⓒⓓ | 10. ⓐⓑⓒⓓ |
|---|---|---|---|---|---|
| | 11. ⓐⓑⓒⓓ | 12. ⓐⓑⓒⓓ | | | |

Suppose a tetrahedron has points A, B, C, D as its vertices, which have coordinates $(x_1, y_1, z_1)$ $(x_2, y_2, z_2)$, $(x_3, y_3, z_3)$ and $(x_4, y_4, z_4)$ respectively. The coordiantes of its centroid are

$$\left( \frac{x_1 + x_2 + x_3 + x_4}{4}, \frac{y_1 + y_2 + y_3 + y_4}{4}, \frac{z_1 + z_2 + z_3 + z_4}{4} \right).$$ The

circumcentre of the tetrahedron is the centre of a sphere pasing through its vertices. So, this is a point equidistant from each of the vertices of tetrahedron.

Let a tetrahedron has three of its vertices represented by the points $(0, 0, 0)$, $(6, -5, -1)$ and $(-4, 1, 3)$ and its centroid lies at the point $(1, -2, 5)$.

Now answer the following questions.

**13.** The coordinate of the fourth vertex of the tetrahedron is
  (a) $(2, -4, 18)$       (b) $(1, -2, 13)$
  (c) $(-2, 4, -2)$       (d) $(1, -1, 1)$

**14.** The coordinates of the centre of the sphere circumscribing the tetrahedron is

  (a) $\left( \dfrac{8}{7}, \dfrac{47}{7}, 8 \right)$       (b) $\left( \dfrac{8}{7}, -\dfrac{45}{7}, -8 \right)$

  (c) $\left( -\dfrac{8}{7}, \dfrac{45}{7}, 8 \right)$       (d) $\left( \dfrac{8}{7}, -\dfrac{45}{7}, 8 \right)$

**15.** The radius of the sphere circumscribing the tetrahedron is

  (a) $\sqrt{209}$       (b) $\dfrac{5}{7}\sqrt{209}$

  (c) $\dfrac{9}{7}\sqrt{209}$       (d) $7\sqrt{209}$

## Section - IV - Matrix-Match Type

This section contains 1 question. It contains statements given in two columns, which have to be matched. Statements in Column I are labelled as A, B, C and D whereas statements in Column II are labelled as p, q, r and s. The answers to these questions have to be appropriately bubbled as illustrated in the following example. If the cor-

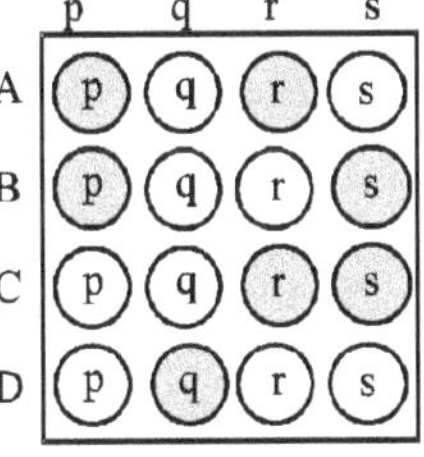

rect matches are A-p, A-r, B-p, B-s, C-r, C-s and D-q, then the correctly bubbled matrix will look like the following :

**16.**

| | Column-I | | Column-II |
|---|---|---|---|
| (A) | Angle between two diagonals of a cube | p. | $\cos^{-1}\left( \dfrac{1}{2} \right)$ |
| (B) | Angle between one diagonal of a cube and a diagonal of one face | q. | $\cos^{-1}\left( \dfrac{2}{6} \right)$ |
| (C) | Angle between the rays with d.r's 4, −3, 5 & 3, 4, 5 | r. | $\cos^{-1}\sqrt{\dfrac{4}{6}}$ |

## Section - V - Reasoning Type

This section contains 3 reasoning type questions. Each question has 4 choices (a), (b), (c) and (d) out of which **ONLY ONE** is correct.

**DIRECTIONS for Qs (17 -19) : Each of these questions contains two statements: Statement-1 (Assertion) and Statement-2 (Reason). Each of these questions has four alternative choices, only one of which is the correct answer. You have to select the correct choice.**

(a) Statement-1 is True, Statement-2 is True; Statement-2 is a correct explanation for Statement-1.
(b) Statement-1 is True, Statement-2 is True; Statement-2 is NOT a correct explanation for Statement-1.
(c) Statement -1 is True, Statement-2 is False.
(d) Statement -1 is False, Statement-2 is True.

**17. Statement-1:** The direction ratio of line joining origin and point (x, y, z) must be x, y, z.
  **Statement-2:** If P is a point (x, y, z) in space and OP = r then directions cosines of OP are $\dfrac{x}{r}, \dfrac{y}{r}, \dfrac{z}{r}$.

<table>
<tr><td rowspan="3">Response Grid</td><td>13. ⓐⓑⓒⓓ    14. ⓐⓑⓒⓓ    15. ⓐⓑⓒⓓ</td></tr>
<tr><td>16. A - ⓟⓠⓡⓢ; B - ⓟⓠⓡⓢ; C - ⓟⓠⓡⓢ</td></tr>
<tr><td>17. ⓐⓑⓒⓓ</td></tr>
</table>

**18.** **Statement -1:** The points $A$ (2, 9, 12), $B$ (1, 8, 8), $C$ (–2,11,8) and $D$ (–1,12,12) are the vertices of a rhombus.

     **Statement -2:** $AB = BC = CD = DA$ and $AC = BD$

**19.** **Statement -1:** If centroid and circumcentre of a triangle are known, its orthocentre can be found.

     **Statement -2:** Centroid, orthocentre and circumcentre of a triangle are collinear.

## Section - VI - Integer Type

This section contains 5 questions. The answer to each of the questions is a single digit integer ranging from 0 to 9.

**20.** If the points $(\lambda, 4, -6)$, $(3, 2, -4)$ and $(9, 8, -10)$ are collinear then find the value of $\lambda$.

**21.** A line passes through the point $(6, -7, -1)$ and $(2, -3, 1)$. If the direction cosines of the line be $l$, m, n and the angle made by it with positive direction of x-axis is acute, then find the value of $-3$ $(l + m + n)$.

**22.** If the angle between the lines whose direction ratios are $2, -1, 2$ and a, 3, 5 is $45°$, then the value of a which is less than 5 is

**23.** P, Q, R, S are the points $(-2, 3, 4)$, $(-4, 4, 6)$, $(4, 3, 5)$ and $(0, 1, 2)$. Then projection of PQ on RS is

**24.** If P (x, y, z) is a point on the line segment joining Q(2, 2, 4) and R (3, 5, 6) such that the projections of $\overrightarrow{OP}$ on the axes are $\dfrac{13}{5}, \dfrac{19}{5}, \dfrac{26}{5}$ respectively, then P divides QR in the ratio $\lambda : 1$. Then find the value of $2\lambda$.

| RESPONSE GRID | | |
|---|---|---|
| **18.** ⓐⓑⓒⓓ   **19.** ⓐⓑⓒⓓ | | **20.** ⓪①②③④⑤⑥⑦⑧⑨ |
| **21.** ⓪①②③④⑤⑥⑦⑧⑨ | | **22.** ⓪①②③④⑤⑥⑦⑧⑨ |
| **23.** ⓪①②③④⑤⑥⑦⑧⑨ | | **24.** ⓪①②③④⑤⑥⑦⑧⑨ |

## DAILY PRACTICE PROBLEM DPP 72 - MATHS

| Total Questions | 24 | Total Marks | 70 |
|---|---|---|---|
| Attempted | | Correct | |
| Incorrect | | Net Score | |
| Cut-off Score | 14 | Qualifying Score | 46 |
| Success Gap = Net Score – Qualifying Score | | | |

$$\textbf{Net Score} = \sum_{i=1}^{VI}\left[(\textbf{correct}_i \times MM_i) - (In_i - NM_i)\right]$$

*Space for Rough Work*

**Name :**

**Date :**

**Start Time :**

**End Time :**

# MATHEMATICS    M73

**SYLLABUS :** Co-ordinate Geometry of Three Dimensions-2 : Line

## Max. Marks : 67

## Time : 60 min.

### GENERAL INSTRUCTIONS

- The Daily Practice Problem Sheet contains **24** Questions divided into 4 sections.

  Section I has **13** MCQ's with ONLY 1 correct option. 2 marks for correct answer and No negative marks.

  Section II has **3** MCQ's with 1 or MORE THAN 1 correct option. 4 marks for correct answer(s) and (–1) for wrong answer.
  Section III has **3** Assertion-Reason MCQ's with ONLY 1 correct option. 3 marks for correct and (–1) mark for wrong answer.
  Section IV has **5** single digit integer answer questions. 4 marks for correct answer and (–1) for wrong answer.

- No mark will be given/ deducted if no bubble is filled. Keep a timer in front and stop immediately at the end of 60 min.
- You have to evaluate your Response Grids yourself with the help of Solution Booklet.
- The sheet follows a particular syllabus. Do not attempt the sheet before you have completed your preparation for that syllabus. Refer syllabus sheet in the starting of the book for the syllabus of all the DPP sheets.
- After completing the sheet check your answers with the solution booklet and complete the Result Grid. Finally spend time to analyse your performance and revise the areas which emerge out as weak in your evaluation.

## Section - I - Straight Objective Type

This section contains 13 multiple choice questions. Each question 4 has choices (a), (b), (c) and (d), out of which **ONLY ONE** is correct.

**1.** The lines whose vector equations are $\vec{r} = \vec{a} + t\vec{b}$, $\vec{r} = \vec{c} + t'\vec{d}$ are coplanar if

(a) $(\vec{a} + \vec{b}).\vec{c} \times \vec{d} = 0$     (b) $(\vec{a} - \vec{c}).\vec{b} \times \vec{d} = 0$

(c) $(\vec{b} - \vec{c}).\vec{a} \times \vec{d} = 0$     (d) $(\vec{b} - \vec{d}).\vec{a} \times \vec{c} = 0$

**2.** The image of the point $(1, 6, 3)$ in the line $\dfrac{x}{1} = \dfrac{y-1}{2} = \dfrac{z-2}{3}$ is :

(a) $(1, 2, 3)$     (b) $(1, 3, 5)$

(c) $(0, 1, 2)$     (d) $(1, 0, 7)$

**3.** The angle between the lines $x = 1, y = 2$ and $y = -1, z = 0$ is

(a) $30°$     (b) $60°$

(c) $90°$     (d) $0°$.

**4.** The equation of the line passing through the point $(1, 2, -4)$ and perpendicular to the two lines $\dfrac{x-8}{3} = \dfrac{y+9}{-16} = \dfrac{z-10}{7}$ and $\dfrac{x-15}{3} = \dfrac{y-2}{8} = \dfrac{z-8}{-5}$ is

(a) $\dfrac{x-1}{2} = \dfrac{y-2}{3} = \dfrac{z+4}{6}$     (b) $\dfrac{x-1}{3} = \dfrac{y-2}{2} = \dfrac{z+4}{6}$

(c) $\dfrac{x-1}{2} = \dfrac{y-2}{6} = \dfrac{z+4}{3}$     (d) $\dfrac{x-1}{3} = \dfrac{y-2}{6} = \dfrac{z+4}{2}$

**5.** The number of the straight lines that are equally inclined to three dimensional co-ordinate axes, is

(a) 2     (b) 4

(c) 6     (d) 8.

| RESPONSE GRID | 1. ⓐⓑⓒⓓ | 2. ⓐⓑⓒⓓ | 3. ⓐⓑⓒⓓ | 4. ⓐⓑⓒⓓ | 5. ⓐⓑⓒⓓ |
|---|---|---|---|---|---|

**6.** The equation of straight line passing through the point $(a, b, c)$ and parallel to z-axis is

(a) $\dfrac{x-a}{1} = \dfrac{y-b}{1} = \dfrac{z-c}{0}$

(b) $\dfrac{x-a}{0} = \dfrac{y-b}{1} = \dfrac{z-c}{1}$

(c) $\dfrac{x-a}{1} = \dfrac{y-b}{0} = \dfrac{z-c}{0}$

(d) $\dfrac{x-a}{0} = \dfrac{y-b}{0} = \dfrac{z-c}{1}$

**7.** The two lines $x = ay + b$, $z = cy + d$; and $x = a'y + b'$, $z = c'y + d'$ are perpendicular to each other if

(a) $aa' + cc' = -1$

(b) $aa' + cc' = 1$

(c) $\dfrac{a}{a'} + \dfrac{c}{c'} = -1$

(d) $\dfrac{a}{a'} + \dfrac{c}{c'} = 1$

**8.** The Cartesian equation of a line is $6x - 2 = 3y + 1 = 2z - 2$. The equation of a line parallel to this line and passing through $(2, -1, -1)$ is

(a) $6x - 12 = 3y + 3 = 2z + 2$

(b) $6x + 2 = 3y + 1 = 2z + 2$

(c) $6x + 2 = 3y + 3 = 2z - 2$

(d) none of these

**9.** The co-ordinates of the foot of the perpendicular drawn from the point $A(1, 0, 3)$ to the join of the points $B(4, 7, 1)$ and $C(3, 5, 3)$ are:

(a) $\left(\dfrac{5}{3}, \dfrac{7}{3}, \dfrac{17}{3}\right)$

(b) $(5, 7, 17)$

(c) $\left(\dfrac{5}{7}, -\dfrac{7}{3}, \dfrac{17}{3}\right)$

(d) $\left(-\dfrac{5}{3}, \dfrac{7}{3}, -\dfrac{17}{3}\right)$

**10.** A line makes angles $\alpha, \beta, \gamma, \delta$ with the four diagonals of a cube, then the value of $\cos^2\alpha + \cos^2\beta + \cos^2\gamma + \cos^2\delta$ is:

(a) 1

(b) 2

(c) $\dfrac{4}{3}$

(d) 4

**11.** The line, $\dfrac{x-2}{3} = \dfrac{y+1}{2} = \dfrac{z-1}{-1}$ intersects the curve $xy = c^2$, $z = 0$ if $c$ is equal to

(a) $\pm 1$

(b) $\pm\dfrac{1}{3}$

(c) $\pm\sqrt{5}$

(d) none of these

**12.** The distance from the point whose position vector is $-\hat{i} + 2\hat{j} + 6\hat{k}$ to the straight line through the point $(2, 3, -4)$ and parallel to the vector $6\hat{i} + 3\hat{j} - 4\hat{k}$ is

(a) 7

(b) 10

(c) 9

(d) none of these

**13.** The perpendicular distance of a corner of a unit cube from a diagonal not passing through it is:

(a) $\dfrac{1}{\sqrt{3}}$

(b) $\dfrac{2}{3}$

(c) $\sqrt{\dfrac{2}{3}}$

(d) $\dfrac{2}{\sqrt{3}}$

---

## Section - II - Multiple Correct Answer Type

This section contains 3 multiple correct answer(s) type questions. Each question has 4 choices (a), (b), (c) and (d), out of which **ONE OR MORE** is/are correct.

---

**14.** The equation of the line $x + y + z - 1 = 0$, $4x + y - 2z + 2 = 0$ written in the symmetrical form is

(a) $\dfrac{x+1}{1} = \dfrac{y-2}{-2} = \dfrac{z-0}{1}$

(b) $\dfrac{x}{1} = \dfrac{y}{-2} = \dfrac{z-1}{1}$

(c) $\dfrac{x+1/2}{1} = \dfrac{y-1}{-2} = \dfrac{z-1/2}{1}$

(d) $\dfrac{x-1}{1} = \dfrac{y+2}{-1} = \dfrac{z-2}{2}$

---

| RESPONSE GRID | 6. ⓐⓑⓒⓓ | 7. ⓐⓑⓒⓓ | 8. ⓐⓑⓒⓓ | 9. ⓐⓑⓒⓓ | 10. ⓐⓑⓒⓓ |
|---|---|---|---|---|---|
| | 11. ⓐⓑⓒⓓ | 12. ⓐⓑⓒⓓ | 13. ⓐⓑⓒⓓ | 14. ⓐⓑⓒⓓ | |

**15.** The direction ratios of the bisector of the angle between the lines whose direction cosines are $l_1, m_1, n_1 ; l_2, m_2, n_2$ are

(a) $l_1 + l_2, m_1 + m_2, n_1 + n_2$

(b) $l_1 - l_2, m_1 - m_2, n_1 - n_2$

(c) $l_1 m_2 - l_2 m_1, m_1 n_2 - m_2 n_1, n_1 l_2 - n_2 l_1$

(d) $l_1 m_2 + l_2 m_1, m_1 n_2 + m_2 n_1, n_1 l_2 + n_2 l_1$

**16.** The lines $\dfrac{x-1}{3} = \dfrac{y-1}{-1} = \dfrac{z+1}{0}$ and $\dfrac{x-4}{2} = \dfrac{y+0}{0} = \dfrac{z+1}{3}$

(a) do not intersect  (b) intersect

(c) intersect at $(4, 0, -1)$  (d) intersect at $(1, 1, -1)$

---

## Section - III - Reasoning Type

This section contains 3 reasoning type questions. Each question has 4 choices (a), (b), (c) and (d) out of which **ONLY ONE** is correct.

---

**DIRECTIONS for Qs (17 - 19) : Each of these questions contains two statements: Statement-1 (Assertion) and Statement-2 (Reason). Each of these questions has four alternative choices, only one of which is the correct answer. You have to select the correct choice.**

(a) Statement-1 is True, Statement-2 is True; Statement-2 is a correct explanation for Statement-1.

(b) Statement-1 is True, Statement-2 is True; Statement-2 is NOT a correct explanation for Statement-1.

(c) Statement -1 is True, Statement-2 is False.

(d) Statement -1 is False, Statement-2 is True.

**17.** The equation of two straight line are $\dfrac{x-1}{2} = \dfrac{y+3}{1} = \dfrac{z-2}{-3}$

and $\dfrac{x-2}{1} = \dfrac{y-1}{-3} = \dfrac{z+3}{2}$

**Statement–1 :** The given lines are coplanar.

**Statement–2 :** The equation $2x_1 - y_1 = 1$, $x_1 + 3y_1 = 4$, $3x_1 + 2y_1 = 5$ are consistent.

**18. Statement–1 :** The shortest distance between the skew lines $\vec{r} = \vec{a} + \alpha \vec{b}$ and $\vec{r} = \vec{c} + \beta \vec{d}$ is $\dfrac{|[\vec{a} - \vec{c} \ \ \vec{b} \ \ \vec{d}]|}{|\vec{b} \times \vec{d}|}$

**Statement–2 :** Two lines are skew lines if there exists no single plane passing through both the lines.

**19.** Given lines $\dfrac{x-4}{2} = \dfrac{y+5}{4} = \dfrac{z-1}{-3}$ and $\dfrac{x-2}{1} = \dfrac{y+1}{3} = \dfrac{z}{2}$

**Statement-1 :** The lines intersect because

**Statement-2 :** They are not parallel.

---

## Section - IV - Integer Type

This section contains 5 questions. The answer to each of the questions is a single digit integer ranging from 0 to 9.

**20.** Find the length of shortest distance between the two lines $\dfrac{x+3}{-4} = \dfrac{y-6}{3} = \dfrac{z}{2}$ and $\dfrac{x+2}{-4} = \dfrac{y}{1} = \dfrac{z-7}{1}$.

**21.** For which value of k, lines $\dfrac{x-2}{1} = \dfrac{y-3}{1} = \dfrac{z-4}{-k}$ and $\dfrac{x-1}{k} = \dfrac{y-4}{2} = \dfrac{z-5}{1}$ are coplanar. (Here k can not be a negative integer)

---

| RESPONSE GRID | | | | | |
|---|---|---|---|---|---|
| | 15. (a)(b)(c)(d) | 16. (a)(b)(c)(d) | 17. (a)(b)(c)(d) | 18. (a)(b)(c)(d) | 19. (a)(b)(c)(d) |
| | 20. (0)(1)(2)(3)(4)(5)(6)(7)(8)(9) | | 21. (0)(1)(2)(3)(4)(5)(6)(7)(8)(9) | | |

---

*Space for Rough Work*

**22.** Let $A(\vec{a})$ and $B(\vec{b})$ be points on the two skew lines $\vec{r} = \vec{a} + \lambda\vec{p}$ and $\vec{r} = \vec{b} + \mu\vec{q}$ and the shortest distance between the skew lines is 1, where $\vec{p}$ and $\vec{q}$ are unit vectors forming adjacent sides of a parallelogram enclosing an area of 1/2 units. If an angle between AB and the line of shortest distance is $60°$, then find the value of AB.

**23.** Foot of perpendicular drawn from the point P $(2, 3, 4)$ to the straight line $\dfrac{x-1}{2} = \dfrac{y-3}{3} = \dfrac{z-3}{6}$ is $\left( \dfrac{A}{D^2}, \dfrac{B}{D^2}, \dfrac{C}{D^2} \right)$. Find the value of D.

**24.** Find the perpendicular distance of P $(1, 2, 3)$ from the line $\dfrac{x-6}{3} = \dfrac{y-7}{2} = \dfrac{z-7}{-2}$.

| RESPONSE GRID | | |
|---|---|---|
| **22.** ⓪①②③④⑤⑥⑦⑧⑨ | | **23.** ⓪①②③④⑤⑥⑦⑧⑨ |
| **24.** ⓪①②③④⑤⑥⑦⑧⑨ | | |

## DAILY PRACTICE PROBLEM DPP 73 - MATHS

| Total Questions | 24 | Total Marks | 67 |
|---|---|---|---|
| Attempted | | Correct | |
| Incorrect | | Net Score | |
| Cut-off Score | 13 | Qualifying Score | 44 |
| Success Gap = Net Score – Qualifying Score | | | |

$$\text{Net Score} = \sum_{i=1}^{VI} \left[ (\text{correct}_i \times MM_i) - (In_i - NM_i) \right]$$

# DPP - Daily Practice Problems

**Name :**                             **Date :**

**Start Time :**                    **End Time :**

# MATHEMATICS   M74

**SYLLABUS : Co-ordinate Geometry of Three Dimensions-3 : Plane**

## Max. Marks : 74          Time : 60 min.

### GENERAL INSTRUCTIONS

- The Daily Practice Problem Sheet contains **24** Questions divided into 6 sections.
  Section I has **8** MCQ's with ONLY 1 correct option. 2 marks for correct answer and No negative marks.
  Section II has **4** MCQ's with 1 or MORE THAN 1 correct option. 4 marks for correct answer(s) and (−1) for wrong answer.
  Section III has **1** PASSAGE with **3** MCQ's with ONLY 1 correct option. 3 marks for correct and (−1) mark for wrong answer.
  Section IV has **1** MCQ's with multiple matchings. 1 mark for the correct matching of each row & No negative marks.
  Section V has **3** Assertion-Reason MCQ's with ONLY 1 correct option. 3 marks for correct and (−1) mark for wrong answer.
  Section VI has **5** single digit integer answer questions. 4 marks for correct answer and (−1) for wrong answer.
- No mark will be given/ deducted if no bubble is filled. Keep a timer in front and stop immediately at the end of 60 min.
- You have to evaluate your Response Grids yourself with the help of Solution Booklet.
- The sheet follows a particular syllabus. Do not attempt the sheet before you have completed your preparation for that syllabus. Refer syllabus sheet in the starting of the book for the syllabus of all the DPP sheets.
- After completing the sheet check your answers with the solution booklet and complete the Result Grid. Finally spend time to analyse your performance and revise the areas which emerge out as weak in your evaluation.

---

## Section - I - Straight Objective Type

This section contains 8 multiple choice questions. Each question has 4 choices (a), (b), (c) and (d), out of which **ONLY ONE** is correct.

---

**1.** If a plane meets the co–ordinate axes in A, B, C such that the centroid of the triangle ABC is the point $(1, r, r^2)$, then equation of the plane is
(a) $x + ry + r^2 z = 3r^2$     (b) $r^2 x + ry + z = 3r^2$
(c) $x + ry + r^2 z = 3$     (d) $r^2 x + ry + z = 3$

**2.** The Cartesian equation of the plane
$$\vec{r} = (1 + \lambda - \mu)\vec{i} + (2 - \lambda)\vec{j} + (3 - 2\lambda + 2\mu)\vec{k} \text{ is}$$
(a) $2x + y = 5$     (b) $2x - y = 5$
(c) $2x + z = 5$     (d) $2x - z = 5$

**3.** The plane $ax + by = 0$ is rotated through an angle $\alpha$ about its line of intersection with the plane $z = 0$. The equation of the plane in new position is

(a) $ax + by \pm z\sqrt{a^2 + b^2}\, \tan\alpha = 0$

(b) $(ax + by)\sqrt{a^2 + b^2} \pm z \tan\alpha = 0$

(c) $\tan\alpha(ax + by) \pm z\sqrt{a^2 + b^2} = 0$

(d) $ax + by \pm \sqrt{a^2 + b^2}\, z = \tan\alpha$

**4.** The image of the point P(1, 3, 4) in the plane $2x - y + z + 3 = 0$ is
(a) $(3, 5, -2)$     (b) $(-3, 5, 2)$
(c) $(3, -5, 2)$     (d) $(3, 5, 2)$

**5.** The three planes $x + y = 0, y + z = 0$ and $x + z = 0$
(a) meet in a unique point
(b) meet in a line
(c) meet taken two at a time in parallel lines
(d) None of these

---

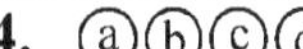

**RESPONSE GRID**    **1.** ⓐⓑⓒⓓ    **2.** ⓐⓑⓒⓓ    **3.** ⓐⓑⓒⓓ    **4.** ⓐⓑⓒⓓ    **5.** ⓐⓑⓒⓓ

**6.** The equation of the plane passing through the line of intersection of the planes $x + 2y + 3z - 5 = 0$ and $3x - 2y - z + 1 = 0$ and cutting off equal intercepts on the OX and OZ axes is

(a) $2x + 5y - 5z - 9 = 0$    (b) $5x - 2y - 5z + 9 = 0$

(c) $5x + 2y + 5z - 9 = 0$    (d) $5x + 5y - 2z + 9 = 0$

**7.** Equation of plane which passes through the point of intersection of lines $\dfrac{x-1}{3} = \dfrac{y-2}{1} = \dfrac{z-3}{2}$ and

$\dfrac{x-3}{1} = \dfrac{y-1}{2} = \dfrac{z-2}{3}$ and at greatest distance from the point $(0, 0, 0)$ is

(a) $4x + 3y + 5z = 25$    (b) $4x + 3y + 5z = 50$

(c) $3x + 4y + 5z = 49$    (d) $x + 7y - 5z = 2$

**8.** The ratio in which the plane $\vec{r} \cdot (\hat{i} - 2\hat{j} + 2\hat{k}) = 17$ divides the line joining the points whose position vectors are $-2\hat{i} + 4\hat{j} + 7\hat{k}$ and $3\hat{i} - 5\hat{j} + 8\hat{k}$ is

(a) $3 : 5$    (b) $1 : 10$    (c) $3 : 10$    (d) $1 : 5$

## Section - II - Multiple Correct Answer Type

This section contains 4 multiple correct answer(s) type questions. Each question has 4 choices (a), (b), (c) and (d), out of which **ONE OR MORE** is/are correct.

**9.** The equation of plane bisecting the angle between the planes $x = 0$ and $z = 0$ and passing through $(1, 2, 3)$ is

(a) $x + y - 4 = 0$    (b) $x + z - 4 = 0$

(c) $x - z + 2 = 0$    (d) $x - y + 2 = 0$

**10.** Consider the planes $3x - 6y + 2z + 5 = 0$ and $4x - 12y + 3z = 3$. The plane $67x - 162y + 47z + 44 = 0$ bisects the angle between the planes

(a) which contains origin    (b) which is acute

(c) which is obtuse    (d) none of these

**11.** If $p_1, p_2, p_3$ denote the distances of the plane $2x - 3y + 4z + 2 = 0$ from the planes $2x - 3y + 4z + 6 = 0$, $4x - 6y + 8z + 3 = 0$ and $2x - 3y + 4z - 6 = 0$ respectively. Then

(a) $p_1 + 8p_2 - p_3 = 0$    (b) $p_3 = 16p_2$

(c) $8p_2 = p_1$    (d) $p_1 + 2p_2 + 3p_3 = \sqrt{29}$

**12.** In three dimensional geometry $ax + by + c = 0$ represents

(a) a straight line on $xy$ plane

(b) a plane parallel to $z$ – axis

(c) a plane perpendicular to $z$ -axis

(d) a plane perpendicular to $xy$ plane

## Section - III - Linked Comprehension Type

This section contains one paragraph. Based upon the paragraph, 3 multiple choice questions have to be answered. Each question has 4 choices (a), (b), (c) and (d), out of which **ONLY ONE** is correct.

Let two planes $P_1 : 2x - y + z = 2$ and $P_2 : x + 2y - z = 3$ are given.

**13.** Equation of the plane which passes through the point $(-1, 3, 2)$ and is perpendicular to each of the planes $P_1$ and $P_2$ is

(a) $x + 3y - 5z + 2 = 0$    (b) $x + 3y + 5z - 18 = 0$

(c) $x - 3y - 5z + 20 = 0$    (d) $x - 3y + 5z = 0$

**14.** The equation of the acute angle bisector of planes $P_1$ and $P_2$ is

(a) $x - 3y + 2z + 1 = 0$    (b) $3x + y - 5 = 0$

(c) $x + 3y - 2z + 1 = 0$    (d) $3x + z + 7 = 0$

| **RESPONSE GRID** | 6. ⓐⓑⓒⓓ | 7. ⓐⓑⓒⓓ | 8. ⓐⓑⓒⓓ | 9. ⓐⓑⓒⓓ | 10. ⓐⓑⓒⓓ |
| | 11. ⓐⓑⓒⓓ | 12. ⓐⓑⓒⓓ | 13. ⓐⓑⓒⓓ | 14. ⓐⓑⓒⓓ | |

**15.** The image of plane $P_1$ in the plane mirror $P_2$ is

(a) $x + 7y - 4z + 5 = 0$   (b) $3x + 4y - 5z + 9 = 0$

(c) $7x - y + 4z - 9 = 0$   (d) $x - 4y + 3z = 0$

## Section - IV - Matrix-Match Type

This section contains 1 question. It contains statements given in two columns, which have to be matched. Statements in Column I are labelled as A, B, C and D whereas statements in Column II are labelled as p, q, r and s. The answers to these questions have to be appropriately bubbled as illustrated in the following example. If the correct matches are A-p, A-r, B-p, B-s, C-r, C-s and D-q, then the correctly bubbled matrix will look like the following :

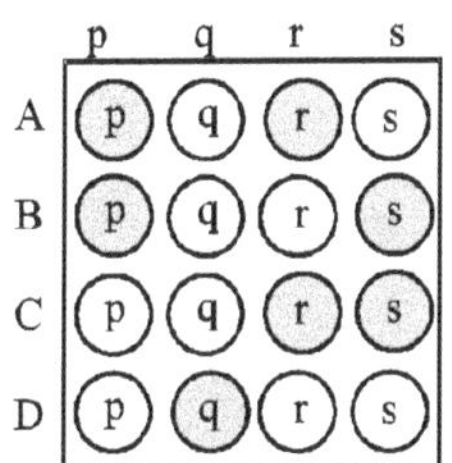

**16.**

| Column I | | Column II |
|---|---|---|
| (A) A plane parallel to the plane $3x - 7y + z = 5$ | (p) | $2x - 2y + 4z = 7$ |
| (B) A plane perpendicular to the plane $3x + 7y + 2z = 5$ | (q) | $3x - 7y + z + 6 = 0$ |
| (C) A plane passing through $(2, 2, 2)$ | (r) | $14x + 6y + 21z = 42$ |
| (D) A plane making intercepts 3, 7, 2 on the coordinate axes | (s) | $3x - 7y + z = 6$ |

## Section - V - Reasoning Type

This section contains 3 reasoning type questions. Each question has 4 choices (a), (b), (c) and (d) out of which **ONLY ONE** is correct.

**DIRECTIONS for Qs (17-19) : Each of these questions contains two statements: Statement-1 (Assertion) and Statement-2 (Reason). Each of these questions has four alternative choices, only one of which is the correct answer. You have to select the correct choice.**

(a) Statement-1 is True, Statement-2 is True; Statement-2 is a correct explanation for Statement-1.

(b) Statement-1 is True, Statement-2 is True; Statement-2 is NOT a correct explanation for Statement-1.

(c) Statement-1 is True, Statement-2 is False.

(d) Statement-1 is False, Statement-2 is True.

**17.** **Statement –1:** The equation $2x^2 - 6y^2 + 4z^2 + 18yz + 2zx + xy = 0$ represents a pair of perpendicular planes.

**Statement –2 :** A pair of planes given by $ax^2 + by^2 + cz^2 + 2fyz + 2gzx + 2hxy = 0$ are perpendicular, if $a + b + c = 0$

**18.** **Statement–1 :** The distance between the planes $4x - 5y + 3z = 5$ and $4x - 5y + 3z + 2 = 0$ is $\dfrac{3}{5\sqrt{2}}$.

**Statement–2 :** The distance between $ax + by + cz + d_1 = 0$ and $ax + by + cz + d_2 = 0$ is $\left| \dfrac{d_1 - d_2}{\sqrt{a^2 + b^2 + c^2}} \right|$.

**19.** **Statement –1 :** The equation of the plane through the intersection of the planes $x + y + z = 6$ and $2x + 3y + 4z + 5 = 0$ and the point $(4,4,4)$ is $29x + 23y + 17z = 276$

**Statement –2 :** Equation of the plane through the line of intersection of the planes $P_1 = 0$ and $P_2 = 0$ is $P_1 + \lambda p_2 = 0$, $\lambda \neq 0$

## Section - VI - Integer Type

This section contains 5 questions. The answer to each of the questions is a single digit integer ranging from 0 to 9.



*Space for Rough Work*

**20.** If the foot of the perpendicular from the origin to a plane is P $(a, b, c)$, then equation of the plane is $ax + by + cz = Pa^2 + Qb^2 + Rc^2$. Find the value of $P + Q + R$

**21.** The distance of the point $(1, 1, 1)$ from the plane passing through the points $(2, 1, 1), (1, 2, 1)$ and $(1, 1, 2)$ is $\dfrac{1}{\sqrt{X}}$. Find the value of X.

**22.** The angle between the two planes $3x - 6y + 2z = 7$ and $2x + 2y - 2z = 5$ is $\cos^{-1} \dfrac{X\sqrt{3}}{21}$. Find the value of X.

**23.** A plane which is perpendicular to two planes $2x - 2y + z = 0$ and $x - y + 2z = 4$, passes through $(1, -2, 1)$. The distance of the plane from the point $(1, 2, 2)$ is $P\sqrt{P}$. Find the value of P.

**24.** The direction ratios of a normal to the plane through $(1, 0, 0), (0, 1, 0)$, which makes an angle of $\dfrac{\pi}{4}$ with the plane $x + y = 3$ are $P : Q : R$. Find the value of $P + Q$.

| RESPONSE GRID | 20. ⓪①②③④⑤⑥⑦⑧⑨ | 21. ⓪①②③④⑤⑥⑦⑧⑨ |
|---|---|---|
| | 22. ⓪①②③④⑤⑥⑦⑧⑨ | 23. ⓪①②③④⑤⑥⑦⑧⑨ |
| | 24. ⓪①②③④⑤⑥⑦⑧⑨ | |

## DAILY PRACTICE PROBLEM DPP 74 - MATHS

| Total Questions | 24 | Total Marks | 74 |
|---|---|---|---|
| Attempted | | Correct | |
| Incorrect | | Net Score | |
| Cut-off Score | 15 | Qualifying Score | 48 |
| Success Gap = Net Score – Qualifying Score | | | |

$$\text{Net Score} = \sum_{i=1}^{VI} \left[ (\text{correct}_i \times MM_i) - (In_i - NM_i) \right]$$

**Name :**  

**Date :**  

**Start Time :**  

**End Time :**  

## MATHEMATICS — M75

**SYLLABUS :** Co-ordinate Geometry of Three Dimensions-4 : Line and Plane

**Max. Marks : 65**                     **Time : 60 min.**

### GENERAL INSTRUCTIONS

- The Daily Practice Problem Sheet contains **24** Questions divided into 4 sections.
  Section I has **15** MCQ's with ONLY 1 correct option. 2 marks for correct answer and No negative marks.
  Section II has **2** MCQ's with 1 or MORE THAN 1 correct option. 4 marks for correct answer(s) and (–1) for wrong answer.
  Section III has **2** MCQ's with multiple matchings. 1 mark for the correct matching of each row & No negative marks.
  Section IV has **5** single digit integer answer questions. 4 marks for correct answer and (–1) for wrong answer.
- No mark will be given/ deducted if no bubble is filled. Keep a timer in front and stop immediately at the end of 60 min.
- You have to evaluate your Response Grids yourself with the help of Solution Booklet.
- The sheet follows a particular syllabus. Do not attempt the sheet before you have completed your preparation for that syllabus. Refer syllabus sheet in the starting of the book for the syllabus of all the DPP sheets.
- After completing the sheet check your answers with the solution booklet and complete the Result Grid. Finally spend time to analyse your performance and revise the areas which emerge out as weak in your evaluation.

### Section - I - Straight Objective Type

This section contains 15 multiple choice questions. Each question has 4 choices (a), (b), (c) and (d), out of which **ONLY ONE** is correct.

**1.** The distance of the point $(1, -2, 3)$ from the plane $x - y + z = 5$ measured parallel to the line $\dfrac{x}{2} = \dfrac{y}{3} = \dfrac{z-1}{-6}$ is

(a) 1    (b) 2    (c) 4    (d) $2\sqrt{3}$

**2.** If $P = (0,1,0), Q = (0,0,1)$, then length of projection of PQ on the plane $x + y + z = 3$ is

(a) $\sqrt{3}$    (b) 3    (c) $\sqrt{2}$    (d) 2

**3.** The line $\dfrac{x-1}{1} = \dfrac{y-2}{-2} = \dfrac{z-1}{3}$ and the plane $x + 2y + z = 6$ meet in

(a) no point        (b) only one point
(c) infinitely many points    (d) none of these

**4.** A square ABCD of diagonal 2a is folded along the diagonal AC so that the planes DAC and BAC are at right angle. The shortest distance between DC and AB is

(a) $\sqrt{2a}$    (b) $2a/\sqrt{3}$    (c) $2a/\sqrt{5}$    (d) $(\sqrt{3}/2)a$

**5.** The distance between the line $\vec{r} = 2\hat{i} - 2\hat{j} + 3\hat{k} + \lambda(\hat{i} - \hat{j} + 4\hat{k})$ and the plane $\vec{r} \cdot (\hat{i} + 5\hat{j} + 4\hat{k}) = 5$ is

(a) $\dfrac{10}{\sqrt{3}}$    (b) $\dfrac{10}{3}$

(c) $\dfrac{10\sqrt{3}}{9}$    (d) none of these

**6.** If $P_1 : \vec{r}.\vec{n}_1 - d_1 = 0$, $P_2 : \vec{r}.\vec{n}_2 - d_2 = 0$ and $P_3 : \vec{r}.\vec{n}_3 - d_3 = 0$ are three planes and $\vec{n}_1, \vec{n}_2$ and $\vec{n}_3$ are three non–coplanar vectors. Three lines $P_1 = P_2 = 0$, $P_2 = P_3 = 0$ and $P_1 = P_3 = 0$ are

(a) parallel lines
(b) coplanar lines
(c) coincident lines
(d) concurrent lines

**7.** Equation of the line passing through $(1, 1, 1)$ and parallel to the plane $2x + 3y + 3z + 5 = 0$ is

(a) $\dfrac{x-1}{1} = \dfrac{y-1}{2} = \dfrac{z-1}{1}$

(b) $\dfrac{x-1}{-1} = \dfrac{y-1}{1} = \dfrac{z-1}{-1}$

(c) $\dfrac{x-1}{3} = \dfrac{y-1}{2} = \dfrac{z-1}{1}$

(d) $\dfrac{x-1}{2} = \dfrac{y-1}{3} = \dfrac{z-1}{1}$

**8.** If line $\dfrac{x - x_1}{\ell} = \dfrac{y - y_1}{m} = \dfrac{z - z_1}{n}$ is parallel to the plane $ax + by + cz + d = 0$, then

(a) $\dfrac{a}{\ell} = \dfrac{b}{m} = \dfrac{c}{n}$

(b) $a\ell + bm + cn = 0$

(c) $\dfrac{a}{\ell} + \dfrac{b}{m} + \dfrac{c}{n} = 0$

(d) none of these

**9.** The equation of the plane containing the two lines $\dfrac{x-1}{2} = \dfrac{y+1}{-1} = \dfrac{z}{3}$ and $\dfrac{x}{2} = \dfrac{y-2}{-1} = \dfrac{z+1}{3}$ is

(a) $8x + y - 5z - 7 = 0$
(b) $8x + y + 5z - 7 = 0$
(c) $8x - y - 5z - 7 = 0$
(d) none of these

**10.** The equation of the PLANE through the line of intersection of planes $ax + by + cz + d = 0$, $a'x + b'y + c'z + d' = 0$ and parallel to the line $y = 0$, $z = 0$ is :

(a) $(ab' - a'b)x + (bc' - b'c)y + (ad' - a'd) = 0$

(b) $(ab' - a'b)x + (bc' - b'c)y + (ad' - a'd)z = 0$

(c) $(ab' - a'b)y + (ac' - a'c)z + (ad' - a'd) = 0$

(d) none of these

**11.** If the straight lines $x = 1 + s, y = -3 - \lambda s, z = 1 + \lambda s$ and $x = \dfrac{t}{2}, y = 1 + t, z = 2 - t$, with parameters $s$ and $t$ respectively, are co-planar, then $\lambda$ equals.

(a) 0
(b) $-1$
(c) $-\dfrac{1}{2}$
(d) $-2$

**12.** If the angle $\theta$ between the line $\dfrac{x+1}{1} = \dfrac{y-1}{2} = \dfrac{z-2}{2}$ and the plane $2x - y + \sqrt{\lambda}\,z + 4 = 0$ is such that $\sin\theta = \dfrac{1}{3}$ then the value of $\lambda$ is

(a) $\dfrac{5}{3}$
(b) $\dfrac{-3}{5}$
(c) $\dfrac{3}{4}$
(d) $\dfrac{-4}{3}$

**13.** The equation of plane containing the line $\dfrac{x+1}{-3} = \dfrac{y-3}{2} = \dfrac{z+2}{1}$ and the point $(0, 7, -7)$ is :

(a) $x + y + z = 1$
(b) $x + y + z = 2$
(c) $x + y + z = 0$
(d) none of these

**14.** The distance of the point $(1, 0, -3)$ from the plane $x - y - z = 9$ measured parallel to the line $\dfrac{x-2}{2} = \dfrac{y+2}{3} = \dfrac{z-6}{-6}$ is

(a) 6
(b) 7
(c) $\dfrac{7}{2}$
(d) $\dfrac{8}{3}$

**15.** If $P$ be any point on the plane $lx + my + nz = p$ and $Q$ be a point on the line $OP$ such that $OP.OQ = p^2$. The locus of the point $Q$ is

(a) $lx + my + nz - p = x^2 + y^2 + z^2$

(b) $lx + my + nz = p(x^2 + y^2 + z^2)$

(c) $p(lx + my + nz) = x^2 + y^2 + z^2$

(d) $x^2 + y^2 + z^2 = p^2$



*Space for Rough Work*

## Section - II - Multiple Correct Answer Type

This section contains 2 multiple correct answer(s) type questions. Each question has 4 choices (a), (b), (c) and (d), out of which **ONE OR MORE** is/are correct.

---

**16.** Let PM be the perpendicular from the point $(1, 2, 3)$ to $x-y$ plane. If OP makes an angle $\theta$ with the positive direction of the z-axis and OM makes an angle $\phi$ with the positive direction of x-axis, where O is the origin then ($\theta$ and $\phi$ are acute angles)

(a)  $\tan\theta = \dfrac{\sqrt{5}}{3}$      (b)  $\sin\theta\sin\phi = \dfrac{2}{\sqrt{14}}$

(c)  $\tan\phi = 2$      (d)  $\cos\theta\cos\phi = \dfrac{1}{\sqrt{14}}$

**17.** The plane $x - 2y + 7z + 21 = 0$

(a)  contains the line $\dfrac{x+1}{-3} = \dfrac{y-3}{2} = \dfrac{z+2}{1}$

(b)  contains the point $(0, 7, -1)$

(c)  is perpendicular to the line $\dfrac{x}{1} = \dfrac{y}{-2} = \dfrac{z}{7}$

(d)  is parallel to the plane $x - 2y + 7z = 0$

## Section - III - Matrix-Match Type

This section contains 2 questions. It contains statements given in two columns, which have to be matched. Statements in Column I are labelled as A, B, C and D whereas statements in Column II are labelled as p, q, r and s. The answers to these questions have to be appropriately bubbled as illustrated in the following example. If the correct matches are A-p, A-r, B-p, B-s, C-r, C-s and D-q, then the correctly bubbled matrix will look like the following :

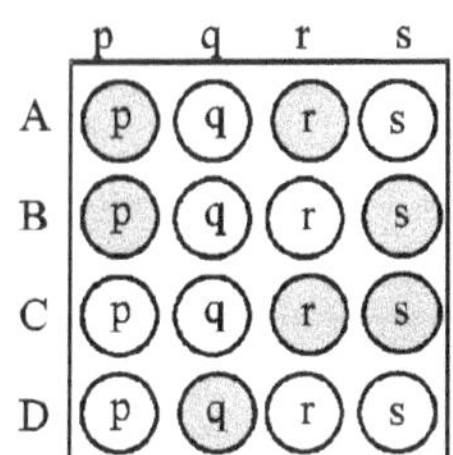

**18.** Consider the following linear equations
$$ax + by + cz = 0$$
$$bx + cy + az = 0$$
$$cx + ay + bz = 0$$

Match the conditions/expressions in Column I with statements in Column II.

| *Column I* | *Column II* |
| --- | --- |
| (A)  $a+b+c \neq 0$ and $a^2+b^2+c^2 = ab+bc+ca$ | (p)  the equations represent planes meeting only at a single point |
| (B)  $a+b+c = 0$ and $a^2+b^2+c^2 \neq ab+bc+ca$ | (q)  the equations represent the line $x = y = z$ |
| (C)  $a+b+c \neq 0$ and $a^2+b^2+c^2 \neq ab+bc+ca$ | (r)  the equations represent identical planes |
| (D)  $a+b+c = 0$ and $a^2+b^2+c^2 = ab+bc+ca$ | (s)  the equations represent the whole of the three dimensional space |

**19.**

| *Column I* | *Column II* |
| --- | --- |
| (A)  If a line makes an angle $\alpha$ with $x$ and $y$-axis, then $\cot\alpha$ can be equal to | (p)  $-3$ |
| (B)  If the straight lines $\dfrac{x-2}{1} = \dfrac{y-3}{1} = \dfrac{4-z}{\lambda}$ and $\dfrac{x-1}{\lambda} = \dfrac{y-4}{2} = \dfrac{z-5}{1}$ intersect, then the value of $\lambda$ is | (q)  $\dfrac{1}{2}$ |
| (C)  If the plane $\lambda x - \mu y + vz = \phi$ contains the line $\dfrac{x-\lambda}{\lambda} = \dfrac{y-2\phi}{\mu} = \dfrac{z-v}{v}$, then the value of $\dfrac{\mu}{\phi}$ is | (r)  $0$ |
|  | (s)  $1$ |
|  | (t)  $2$ |

## Section - IV - Integer Type

This section contains 5 questions. The answer to each of the questions is a single digit integer ranging from 0 to 9.

**20.** If the planes $x - cy - bz = 0$, $cx - y + az = 0$ and $bx + ay - z = 0$ pass through a straight line, then find the value of $a^2 + b^2 + c^2 + 2abc$.

**21.** P is a point on the plane $ax + by + cz = d$. A point Q is taken on the line OP such OP. OQ $= d^2$. If the locus of Q satisfies

$$\frac{d(ax + by + cz)}{x^2 + y^2 + z^2} = k$$ then $k$ is equal to

**22.** If a plane passes through the point $(1, 1, 1)$ and is perpendicular to the line $\frac{x-1}{3} = \frac{y-1}{0} = \frac{z-1}{4}$, then its perpendicular disance from the origin is $\frac{A}{B}$. Find the value of $A - B$.

**23.** If $\frac{x-4}{1} = \frac{y-2}{1} = \frac{z-k}{2}$ lies in the plane $2x - 4y + z = 7$, then find the value of k.

**24.** Let L be the line of intersection of the planes $2x + 3y + z = 1$ and $x + 3y + 2z = 2$. If L makes an angle $\alpha$ with the positive X-axis, then $\cos \alpha = \frac{A}{\sqrt{B}}$ then find the value of $A + B$.

| RESPONSE GRID | | |
|---|---|---|
| 20. ⓪①②③④⑤⑥⑦⑧⑨ | | 21. ⓪①②③④⑤⑥⑦⑧⑨ |
| 22. ⓪①②③④⑤⑥⑦⑧⑨ | | 23. ⓪①②③④⑤⑥⑦⑧⑨ |
| 24. ⓪①②③④⑤⑥⑦⑧⑨ | | |

### DAILY PRACTICE PROBLEM DPP 75 - MATHS

| Total Questions | 24 | Total Marks | 65 |
|---|---|---|---|
| Attempted | | Correct | |
| Incorrect | | Net Score | |
| Cut-off Score | 13 | Qualifying Score | 42 |
| Success Gap = Net Score – Qualifying Score | | | |

$$\text{Net Score} = \sum_{i=1}^{VI} \left[ (\text{correct}_i \times MM_i) - (In_i - NM_i) \right]$$

**1.** **(b)** $(A-B) \cup (B-A) = (A \cup B) - (A \cap B)$

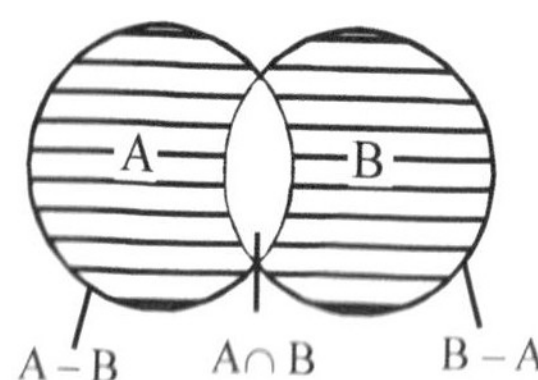


**2.** **(b)** $A = \{x : |x| < 1\} = (-1, 1)$

Since $|x| < 1 \Rightarrow -1 < x < 1$

$B = \{x : |x-1| \geq 1\} = (-\infty, 0] \cup [2, \infty)$

Since $|x-1| \geq 1 \Rightarrow x-1 \leq -1$

or $x - 1 \geq 1 \Rightarrow x \leq 0$ or $x \geq 2$

$\therefore A \cup B = (-\infty, 0] \cup [2, \infty) \cup (-1, 1)$

$= (-\infty, 1) \cup [2, \infty) = R - [1, 2)$

$\therefore D = [1, 2) = \{x : 1 \leq x < 2\}$

**3.** **(c)** The two curves $y = \dfrac{1}{x}$ and $y = -x$

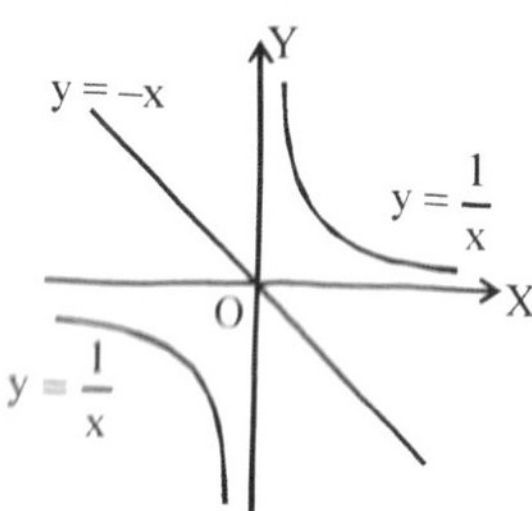


intersect at the point,

where $\dfrac{1}{x} = -x \Rightarrow x^2 = -1$, which has no real solution.

So, the curves do not intersect.

$\therefore A \cap B = \phi$   [see figure also]

**4.** **(c)** $X \cap (X \cup Y)^C = X \cap (X^C \cap Y^C) = (X \cap X^C) \cap Y^C$

$= \phi \cap Y^C = \phi$

**5.** **(d)** $A \cup (A \cap B) = A \;[\because A \cap B \subseteq A]$

**6.** **(c)** Since $y = e^x = 1 + x + \dfrac{x^2}{2!} + \dfrac{x^3}{3!} + \ldots\ldots$

$\therefore e^x > x \; \forall \; x \in R$ so that the two curves given by $y = e^x$ and $y = x$ do not intersect at any point. Hence, there is no common point so that $A \cap B = \phi$.

**7.** **(a)** $R \times (P^C \cup Q^C)^C = R \times [(P^C)^C \cap (Q^C)^C]$

$= R \times (P \cap Q) = (R \times P) \cap (R \times Q)$

**8.** **(a)** Let U be the set of consumers questioned X, the set of consumers who liked the product A and Y, the set of consumers who liked the product B. Then n (U) = 1000, n(X) = 720, n (Y) = 450

$\therefore n (X \cap Y) = 1170 - n (X \cap Y)$

$\therefore n (X \cap Y) = 1170 - n (X \cup Y)$

Clearly $n (X \cap Y)$ is least.

When $n (X \cup Y)$ is maximum.

Now, $X \cup Y \subset U$

$\therefore n(X \cup Y) \leq n (U) = 1000$

$\therefore$ the maximum value of $n (X \cup Y)$ is 1000.

Thus the least value of $n (X \cap Y)$ is 170

**9.** **(b)** $4^n - 3n - 1 = (1+3)^n - 3n - 1$

$= [{}^nC_0 + {}^nC_1.3 + {}^nC_2.3^2 + \ldots\ldots + {}^nC_n 3^n] - 3n - 1$

$= 9\,[{}^nC_2 + {}^nC_3.3 + \ldots + {}^nC_n.3^{n-2}]$

$\therefore 4^n - 3n - 1$ is a multiple of 9 for all n.

$\therefore X = \{x : x \text{ is a multiple of 9}\}$

Also, $Y = \{9(n-1) : n \in \mathbf{N}\} = \{\text{All multiples of 9}\}$

Clearly $X \subset Y$. $\therefore X \cup Y = Y$

**10.** **(a)**

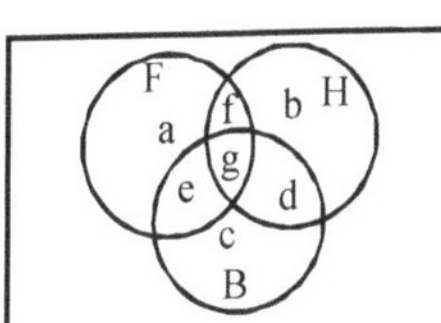


$a + e + f + g = 285, \quad b + d + f + g = 195$

$c + d + e + f = 115, \quad e + g = 45,\; f + g = 70,$

$d + g = 50$

$a + b + c + d + e + f + g = 500 - 50 = 450$

As in previous question, we obtain

$a + f = 240, b + d = 125,\; c + e = 65$

$a + e = 215, b + f = 145, b + c + d = 165$

$a + c + e = 255, a + b + f = 335$

Solving we get

$b = 95, c = 40, a = 190,\; d = 30, e = 25, f = 50$ and $g = 20$

Desired quantity $= a + b + c = 325$

**11.** **(a)** The two sets

$A = \{x : 0 < x < 1\}$ and

$B = \{y : -1 < y < 1\}$ the points $(x, y)$ living inside cartesion plane as shown in the following figure

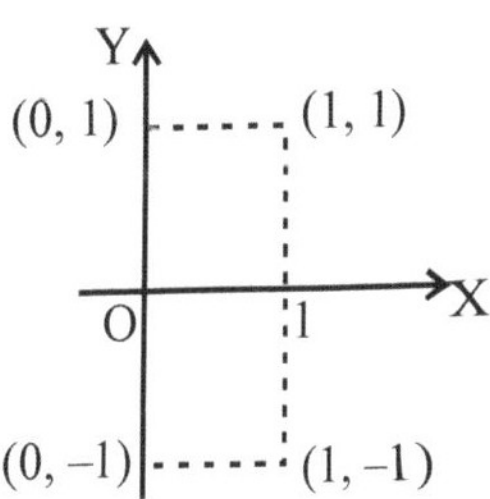


**12.** **(b)** As A has p elements and B has q elements so, $A \times B$ has pq elements.

**13. (d)** We have $3N = \{3x : x \in N\}$
$= \{3, 6, 9, 12, .....\}$ and
$7N = \{7x : x \in N\} = \{7, 14, 21, 28, ....\}$
Hence $3N \cap 7N = \{21, 42, 63, ....\}$
$= \{21x : x \in N\} = 21N$

**14. (a,b,c,)** Let $P$ = set of families buying A,
$Q$ = set of families buying B
and $R$ = set of families buying C.
$\therefore n(P) = 40\%$ of $10,000 = 4,000$, similarly
$n(Q) = 2,000$, $n(R) = 1,000$
$n(P \cap Q) = 500$, $n(Q \cap R) = 300$
$n(P \cap R) = 400$ and $n(P \cap Q \cap R) = 200$
(a) Number of families buying only
$A = n(P \cap Q' \cap R')$
$= n(P \cap (Q \cup R)') = n(P) - n(P \cap (Q \cup R))$
$= n(P) - [n(P \cap Q) + n(P \cap R) - n((P \cap Q) \cap (P \cap R))]$
$= n(P) - n(P \cap Q) - n(P \cap R) + n(P \cap Q \cap R).$
$= 4,000 - 500 - 400 + 200 = 3,300.$
(b) Number of families buying only B
$= n(Q) - n(P \cap Q) - n(Q \cap R) + n(P \cap Q \cap R)$
$= 2,000 - 500 - 300 + 200 = 1,400.$
(c) Number of families buying none of A, B and
$C = n(P' \cap Q' \cap R') = n(P' \cap (Q \cup R)')$
$= n\{(P \cup (Q \cup R))'\} = 10000 - n(P \cup Q \cup R)$
$= 10,000 - [n(P) + n(Q) + n(R) - n(P \cap Q)$
$\qquad - n(Q \cap R) - n(P \cap R) + n(P \cap Q \cap R)]$
$= 10,000 - [4,000 + 2,000 + 1,000$
$\qquad - 500 - 300 - 400 + 200]$
$= 10,000 - 6,000 = 4,000.$
*Note : For sets A, B, we have*
$(A \cap B) \cup (A \cap B') = A \cap (B \cup B')$
$\qquad\qquad\qquad = A \cap U = A$
and $(A \cap B) \cap (A \cap B') = A \cap (B \cap B')$
$\qquad\qquad\qquad = A \cap \phi = \phi$
$\therefore n(A) = n(A \cap B) + n(A \cap B')$
or $n(A \cap B') = n(A) - n(A \cap B)$
Replacing A by P and B by $Q \cup R$, we have
$n(P \cap (Q \cup R)') = n(P) - n(P \cap (Q \cup R))$ *etc.*
*Hence options (a), (b) and (c) are correct.*

**15. (a,c,d,)** We know that the interchange of two adjacent rows
(or columns) changes the value of a determinant only
in sign and not in magnitude. Hence, corresponding to
every element $\Delta$ of B there is an element $\Delta'$ in C obtained
by interchanging two adjacent rows (or columns) in, $\Delta$.
It follows that $n(B) \leq n(C)$.
That is, the number of elements in B is less than or equal
to the number of elements in C.
Similarly $n(C) \leq n(B)$.
Hence $n(B) = n(C)$, that is, B has many elements as C.

**16. (a,b,c)** Since $A \nsubseteq B$, $\exists\ x \in A$ such that $x \notin B$.
Then $x \in B'$
$\therefore A \cup B' \neq \phi$

**17. (a,b,c)**

(a) Let $x \in A - B \Rightarrow x \in A$ and $x \notin B$
$\Rightarrow x \in A$ and $x \in B' \Rightarrow x \in A \cap B'$
$\therefore A - B \leq A \cap B'$ $\qquad$ ...(i)
$x \in A$ and $x \in B'$
$\Rightarrow x \notin A'$ and $x \in B' \Rightarrow x \in B'$ and $x \notin A'$
$\Rightarrow x \in B' - A'$
$\therefore A - B \leq B' - A'$ $\qquad$ ...(ii)
Clearly (a) is not correct. Also from (i) (c) is not correct.
Next let $x \in A - (A - B)$
$\Rightarrow x \in A$ and $x \notin (A - B)$
$\Rightarrow x \in A$ and $[x \notin A$ or $x \in B]$
$\Rightarrow [x \in A$ and $x \notin A]$ or $[x \in A$ and $x \in B]$
$\Rightarrow x \in \phi$ or $x \in A \cap B$
$\Rightarrow x \in \phi \cup (A \cap B)$
$\Rightarrow x \in A \cap B$
$\therefore A - (A - B) \leq A \cap B$
$\therefore$ (b) is also incorrect
The result (d) is correct as can be seen in the following
Venn diagram

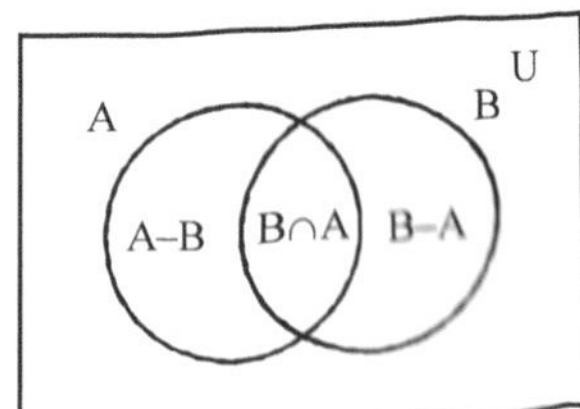


$A \cup B = (A - B) \cup (A \cap B) \cup (B - A)$

**18. (a,b,d)** We have $-1 \leq x \leq 0 \Rightarrow 0 \leq x^2 \leq 1$ ....(i)
and $0 \leq x \leq 1 \Rightarrow 0 \leq x^2 \leq 1$ ...(ii)
$\therefore E = \{x \in \mathbf{R} : -1 \leq x \leq 0\}$
$\Rightarrow f(E) = \{x \in \mathbf{R} : 0 \leq x \leq 1\}$ $\quad$ from(i)
Also $F = \{x \in \mathbf{R} : 0 \leq x \leq 1\}$
$\Rightarrow f(F) = \{x \in \mathbf{R} : 0 \leq x \leq 1\}$ $\quad$ from (ii)
Hence, $f(E) = f(F)$
Again $E \cap F = \{0\} \subset f(E) \cap f(F)$
[Since $f(E) = f(F)$
$\therefore f(E) \cap f(F) = f(E) = f(F)$]
Also $E \cap F = \{0\} \Rightarrow f(E \cap F) = \{0\}$
Next, $E \cup F = \{x \in \mathbf{R} : -1 \leq x \leq 1\}$
and $f(E) \cup f(F) = \{x \in \mathbf{R} : 0 \leq x \leq 1\}$
$\therefore E \cup F \not\subset f(E) \cup f(F)$

**19.** **(d)** $A \times B$ and $B \times A$ have $n^2$ elements common.

**20.** **(5)** Let U denote the set of surveyed students and A denote the set of students taking apple juice and B denote the set of students taking orange juice. Then

$n(U) = 400, n(A) = 100, n(B) = 150$ and

$n(A \cap B) = 75$.

Now $n(A' \cap B') = n(A \cup B)'$

$= n(U) - n(A \cup B)$

$= n(U) - n(A) - n(B) + n(A \cap B)$

$= 400 - 100 - 150 + 75 = 225$

Hence 225 students were taking neither apple juice nor orange juice.

Thus, $9X^2 = 225$

$\Rightarrow \quad X = 5$

**21.** **(3)** We have

$n(A \cup B \cup C) = n(A) + n(B) + n(C)$
$\qquad - n(A \cap B) - n(B \cap C)$
$\qquad - n(C \cap A) + n(A \cap B \cap C)$
$\qquad = 10 + 15 + 20 - 8 - 9$
$\qquad - n(C \cap A) + n(A \cap B \cap C)$
$\qquad = 28 - \{n(C \cap A)$
$\qquad\qquad - n(A \cap B \cap C)\} \ ...(i)$

Since $n(C \cap A) \geq n(A \cap B \cap C)$

We have

$n(C \cap A) - n(A \cap B \cap C) \geq 0 \quad ...(ii)$

From (i) and (ii),

$n(A \cup B \cup C) \leq 28 \qquad\qquad ...(iii)$

Now, $n(A \cup B) = n(A) + n(B) - n(A \cap B)$
$\qquad\qquad = 10 + 15 - 8 = 17$

and $n(B \cup C) = n(B) + n(C) - n(B \cap C)$
$\qquad\qquad = 15 + 20 - 9 = 26$

Since, $n(A \cup B \cup C) \geq n(A \cup C)$ and

$n(A \cup B \cup C) \geq n(B \cup C)$, we have

$n(A \cup B \cup C) \geq 17$ and $n(A \cup B \cup C) \geq 26$

Hence $n(A \cup B \cup C) \geq 26 \quad ...(iv)$

From (iii) and (iv) we obtain

$26 \leq n(A \cup B \cup C) \leq 28$

Also $n(A \cup B \cup C)$ is a positive integer

$\therefore n(A \cup B \cup C) = 26, 27$ or $28$

**22.** **(9)** We have $n(A_i) = 5, 1 \leq i \leq 30$ and

$n(B_j) = 3, 1 \leq j \leq m$.

$\therefore \quad \sum_{i=1}^{30} n(A_i) = 30 \times 5 = 150$

and $\sum_{j=1}^{m} n(B_j) = m \times 3 = 3m$.

Now $\quad S = \bigcup_{i=1}^{30} A_i$ and each element of S belongs to exactly ten of the $A_i$'s.

$\therefore n(S) = \frac{1}{10} \sum_{i=1}^{30} n(A_i) = \frac{1}{10} \times 150 = 15$

Also, $S = \sum_{j=1}^{m} B_j$ and each element of S is in exactly nine of the $B_j$'s.

$\therefore n(S) = \frac{1}{9} \sum_{j=1}^{m} n(B_j) \Rightarrow 15 = \frac{1}{9}(3m) \Rightarrow m = 45.$

Thus, $Y = 9$

**23.** **(5)** See the following Venn diagram

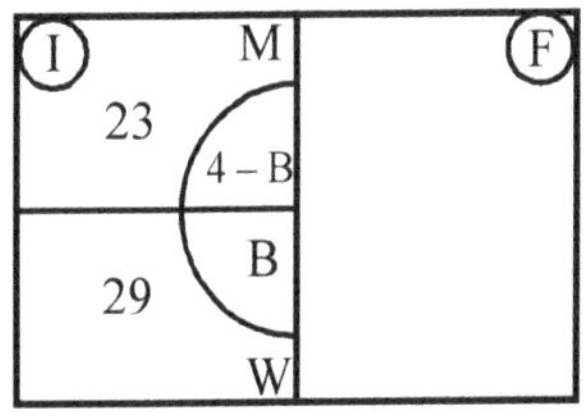


$n(I) = 29 + 23 = 52$

$n(F) = 100 - 52 = 48$

$\therefore 8A = 48 \Rightarrow A = 6$

$n(M \cup D) = n(M) + n(D) - n(M \cap D)$

$24 = 23 + 4 - n(M \cap D)$

$\therefore n(M \cap D) = 3$

$\therefore n(W \cap D) = 4 - 3 = 1$

Thus, $B = 1$

$\therefore A - B = 6 - 1 = 5$

**24.** **(2)** $n(C) = 224, n(H) = 240, n(B) = 336$

$n(H \cap B) = 64, n(B \cap C) = 80$

$n(H \cap C) = 0, n(C \cap H \cap B) = 24$

$n(C^C \cap H^C \cap B^C) = n[(C \cup H \cup B)^C]$
$\qquad\qquad = n(U) - n(C \cup H \cup B) = 160$

Thus, $10 \cdot (X)^4 = 160$

$\Rightarrow (X)^4 = 16$

$\Rightarrow X = 2$

**1.** **(d)** $\left[\dfrac{1}{\ln(x^2+e)}\right] = \begin{cases} 0 & x \neq 0 \\ 1 & x = 0 \end{cases}$

$f(x) = \begin{cases} 2 & x = 0 \\ \dfrac{1}{\sqrt{1+x^2}} & x \neq 0 \end{cases}$

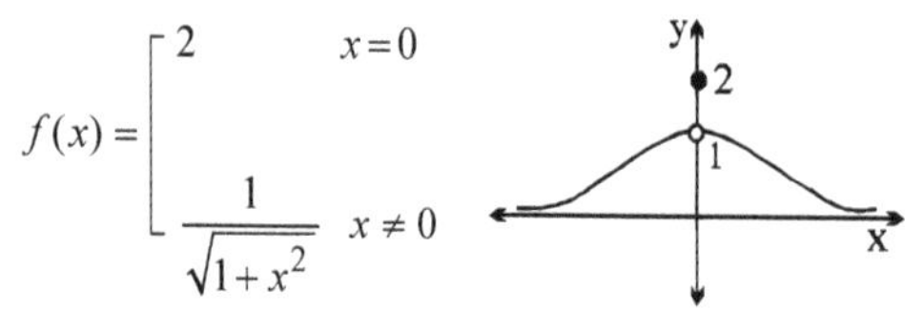

Hence range of $f(x)$ is $(0, 1) \cup \{2\}]$

**2.** **(c)** $y = (x^2 - 1)^2 + 2 \Rightarrow y_{min} = 2$
$\Rightarrow \log_{0.5}(x^4 - 2x^2 + 3) \leq -1$

$\Rightarrow$ range $\left[\dfrac{3\pi}{4}, \pi\right)$

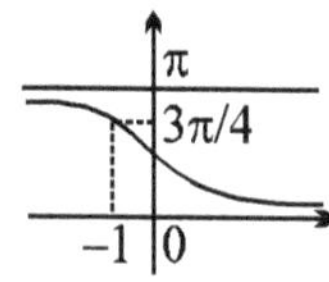

**3.** **(c)** $y = \dfrac{1}{\log_{10}(1-x)} + \sqrt{x+2}$

$y = f(x) + g(x)$
Then domain of given relation is $D_f \cap D_g$

Now, for domain of $f(x) = \dfrac{1}{\log_{10}(1-x)}$

We know it is defined only when $1 - x > 0$ and $1 - x \neq 1$
$\Rightarrow x < 1$ and $x \neq 0$
$\therefore D_f = (-\infty, 1) - \{0\}$

For domain of $g(x) = \sqrt{x+2}$
$x + 2 \geq 0$
$\Rightarrow x \geq -2$
$\therefore D_g = [-2, \infty)$

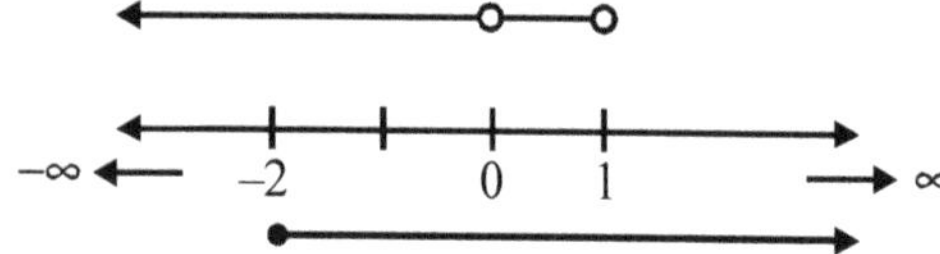

$\therefore$ Common domain is $[-2, 1) - \{0\}$

**4.** **(a)** $f(x)$ is defined on $[0, 1] \Rightarrow 0 \leq x \leq 1$
Now $f(2\sin x)$ shall be defined, if $0 \leq 2\sin x \leq 1$
$\Rightarrow 0 \leq \sin x \leq 1/2$

$\Rightarrow x \in \displaystyle\bigcup_{n \in I}\left\{\left[2n\pi, 2n\pi + \dfrac{\pi}{6}\right] \cup \left[2n\pi + \dfrac{5\pi}{6}, (2n+1)\pi\right]\right\}$

**5.** **(b)** We observe the following properties :
*Reflexivity :* Let $(a, b)$ be an arbitrary element of $\mathbf{N} \times \mathbf{N}$.
Then, $(a, b) \in \mathbf{N} \times \mathbf{N} \Rightarrow a, b \in \mathbf{N}$
$\Rightarrow ab\,(b + a) = ba\,(a + b) \Rightarrow (a, b)\,R\,(a, b)$
Thus, $(a, b)\,R\,(a, b)$ for all $(a, b) \in \mathbf{N} \times \mathbf{N}$.
So, R is reflexive on $\mathbf{N} \times \mathbf{N}$.
*Symmetry :* Let $(a, b), (c, d) \in \mathbf{N} \times \mathbf{N}$ be such that
$(a, b)\,R\,(c, d)$. Then, $(a, b)\,R\,(c, d) \Rightarrow ad\,(b + c)$
$= bc\,(a + d)$
$\Rightarrow cb\,(d + a) = da\,(c + b) \Rightarrow (c, d)\,R\,(a, b)$
Thus, $(a, b)\,R\,(c, d) \Rightarrow (c, d)\,R\,(a, b)$ for all
$(a, b), (c, d) \in \mathbf{N} \times \mathbf{N}$.
So, R is symmetric on $\mathbf{N} \times \mathbf{N}$.
*Transitivity :* Let $(a, b), (c, d), (e, f) \in \mathbf{N} \times \mathbf{N}$ such that $(a, b)$
$R$ (c,d) and $(c, d)\,R\,(e, f)$. Then.
$(a, b)\,R\,(c, d) \Rightarrow ad\,(b + c) = bc\,(a + d)$

$\Rightarrow \dfrac{b+c}{bc} = \dfrac{a+d}{ad} \Rightarrow \dfrac{1}{b} + \dfrac{1}{c} = \dfrac{1}{a} + \dfrac{1}{d}$ ...(i)

and, $(c, d)\,R\,(e, f) \Rightarrow cf(d + e) = de\,(c + f)$

$\Rightarrow \dfrac{d+e}{de} = \dfrac{c+f}{cf} \Rightarrow \dfrac{1}{d} + \dfrac{1}{e} = \dfrac{1}{c} + \dfrac{1}{f}$ ...(ii)

Adding (i) and (ii), we get

$\left(\dfrac{1}{b} + \dfrac{1}{c}\right) + \left(\dfrac{1}{d} + \dfrac{1}{e}\right) = \left(\dfrac{1}{a} + \dfrac{1}{d}\right) + \left(\dfrac{1}{c} + \dfrac{1}{f}\right)$

$\Rightarrow \dfrac{1}{b} + \dfrac{1}{e} = \dfrac{1}{a} + \dfrac{1}{f} \Rightarrow \dfrac{b+e}{be} = \dfrac{a+f}{af}$

$\Rightarrow af(b + e) = be\,(a, + f) \Rightarrow (a, b)\,R\,(e, f)$
Thus, $(a, b)\,R\,(c, d)$ and $(c, d)\,R\,(e, f)$
$\Rightarrow (a, b)\,R\,(e, f)$ for all $(a, b), (c, d), (e, f) \in \mathbf{N} \times \mathbf{N}$.
So, R is transitive on $\mathbf{N} \times \mathbf{N}$.
Hence, R being reflexive, symmetric and transitive, is an
equivalence relation on $\mathbf{N} \times \mathbf{N}$.

**6.** **(c)** $f(x)$ is defined if $3x^2 - 4x + 5 \geq 0$

$\Rightarrow 3\left[x^2 - \dfrac{4}{3}x + \dfrac{5}{3}\right] \geq 0 \Rightarrow 3\left[\left(x - \dfrac{2}{3}\right)^2 + \dfrac{11}{9}\right] \geq 0$

Which is true for all real x
$\therefore$ Domain of $f(x) = (-\infty, \infty)$

Let $y = \sqrt{3x^2 - 4x + 5}$
$\Rightarrow y^2 = 3x^2 - 4x + 5$ i.e. $3x^2 - 4x + (5 - y^2) = 0$

For x to be real , $16 - 12\,(5 - y^2) \geq 0 \Rightarrow y \geq \sqrt{\dfrac{11}{3}}$

$\therefore$ Range of $y = \left[\sqrt{\dfrac{11}{3}}, \infty\right)$

**7.** **(b)** $f(x) = \cos^{-1}\left(\dfrac{2 - |x|}{4}\right) + [\log(3 - x)]^{-1}$

Domain $-1 \leq \dfrac{2 - |x|}{4} \leq 1, \Rightarrow x \in [-6, 6]$

$3 - x > 0, \qquad\qquad \Rightarrow x \in (-\infty, 3)$

$\log(3 - x) \neq 0 \qquad\qquad x \neq 2$

$x \in [-6, 2) \cup (2, 3)$

**8.** **(c)**

**9.** **(c)** For $f(x)$ to be defined, we must have
$x^2 - 10x - 11 \neq 0 \Rightarrow (x - 11)(x + 1) \neq 0$
$\Rightarrow x \neq 1, x \neq -1$
$\therefore$ Domain of $f = (-\infty, \infty) - \{-1, 11\}$

**10.** **(b)** Domain of $\cot^{-1} x$ is R and $\dfrac{x}{\sqrt{x^2 - [x^2]}}$ is defined if

$x^2 > [x^2]$ and $x \neq 0$
$\Rightarrow x$ is a real number but no an integer.
Hence, domain $= R - \{\sqrt{n} : n \geq 0, n \in I\}$

**11.** **(c)** $\because [x]$ is an integer, $\cos(-x) = \cos x$ and

$\cos\left(\dfrac{\pi}{2}\right) = 0, \cos 2\left(\dfrac{\pi}{2}\right) = -1,$

$\cos 0 \left(\dfrac{\pi}{2}\right) = 1,\ \cos 3 \left(\dfrac{\pi}{2}\right) = 0$

Hence range = $\{-1, 0, 1\}$

**12.** **(b)** $\{x\} \neq 0 \Rightarrow 0 < \sin\{x\} < \sin 1 \Rightarrow \left[\dfrac{1}{\sin\{x\}}\right] \in N$

**13.** **(a,b,c)** '$l$' is reflexive since every natural number is a factor of itself, that is n/n for n $\in$ N.
'$l$' is transitive if n is a factor of m and m is a factor of p, then n is surely a factor of P. Thus 'n/m' and 'm/p' $\Rightarrow$ 'n/p'. However '$l$' is not symmetric for ex. 2 is factor of 4 but 4 is not a factor of 2.

**14.** **(c,d)** $f(x) = \left[\dfrac{2\sin x(1+\cos x)}{2\cos x(1+\sin x)}\ \dfrac{1-\cos x}{1-\sin x}\right]^{3/2}$

Hence $x \neq \dfrac{\pi}{2}$ and $x \neq \dfrac{3\pi}{2}$

$\therefore$ Domain is $R - \left\{(4n-1)\dfrac{\pi}{2}, (4n+1)\dfrac{\pi}{2}\right\}$

$\therefore f(x) = \left[\dfrac{\sin x(1-\cos^2 x)}{\cos x(1-\sin^2 x)}\right]^{2/3} = \tan^2 x$

$\Rightarrow$ Range is $[0, \infty)$ ]

**15.** **(b,c,d)** Let A = $\{a, b, c\}$, R = $\{(a, b), (b, c), (a, c)\}$ and S = $\{(b, c), (c, a), (b, a)\}$.
Then, R and S both are transitive.

**16.** **(b)** If $x^4 + y^3 = 1$, then we know $(-x, y)$ is on the graph since $(-x)^4 + y^3 = x^4 + y^3 = 1$. And in general, when the coordinate is raised to an even power every single time in the equation, then symmetry by the other axis occurs. Since y is raised to an odd number, then x-axis and origin symmetry are ruled out. Symmetry about y = x is another story, but since $x^4 + y^3 = x^3 + y^4$ is not necessarily true, it is ruled out. The only symmetry is about the y-axis.

**17.** **(d)** Suppose R is just a rectangle whose 4 vertices are $(1, 2)$, $(1, -2)$, $(-1, 2)$ and $(-1, -2)$. The x-axis and y-axis symmetries in the problem are satisfied, but the point $(2, 1)$ is not contained in R.

**18.** **(b)** Let $y = \dfrac{x-1}{x(x-2)}$

$\Rightarrow x^2 y - 2xy - x + 1 = 0$
$\Rightarrow yx^2 - (2y+1)x + 1 = 0$

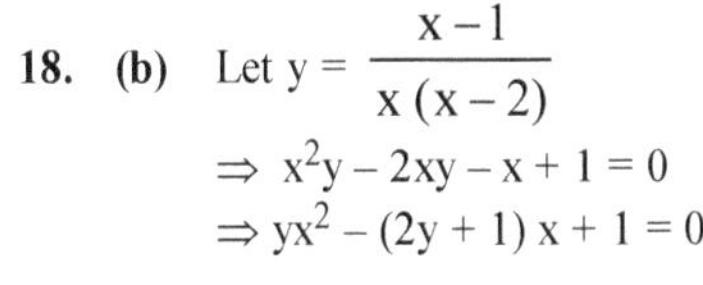

**Case I :** When $y \neq 0$, As $x \in R$ so discreamnent $\geq 0$
$(2y+1)^2 \geq 4y$
$\Rightarrow 4y^2 + 1 \geq 0$, which is true for all non-zero real value of $y$.
**Case II :** When y = 0, we get x = 1
$\therefore$ Option (A) is correct.

**19.** **(b)** For f(x) to be real $\log_2(\sin x) \geq 0$
$\Rightarrow \sin x \geq 2^0 \Rightarrow \sin x = 1$
$\Rightarrow x = (4n+1)\ \dfrac{\pi}{2},\ n \in N.$

**20.** **(1)** $\sqrt{\log_{10}\dfrac{3-x}{x}}$ is defined for $\log_{10}\left(\dfrac{3-x}{x}\right) \geq 0$

$\Rightarrow \dfrac{3-x}{x} \geq 10^0 = 1 \Rightarrow 3 - x \geq x$

$\Rightarrow 2x \leq 3 \Rightarrow x \leq \dfrac{3}{2}$ .........(1)

Also. $\log_{10}\left(\dfrac{3-x}{x}\right)$ is defined for

$\dfrac{3-x}{x} > 0$ or $\dfrac{x(3-x)}{x^2} > 0$
i.e. $x(x-3) < 0$
$\Rightarrow 0 < x < 3$ .........(2)

From (1) and (2), we get domain of $f = \left(0, \dfrac{3}{2}\right]$.

Thus, $A - B = 3 - 2 = 1$

**21.** **(5)** $\log_{2004}(\log_{2003}(\log_{2002}(\log_{2001} x)))$ is defined if $0 < \log_{2003}(\log_{2002}(\log_{2001} x))$,

if $\log_{2002}(\log_{2001} x) > 1$

if $\log_{2001} x > 2002$

if $x > (2001)^{2002}$

Thus $A = 1, B = 2$

$\therefore A + 2B = 1 + 4 = 5$

**22.** **(1)** We have $-1 \leq [2x^2 - 3] \leq 1$
$\Rightarrow -1 \leq 2x^2 - 3 < 2$

$\Rightarrow 1 \leq x^2 < \dfrac{5}{2} \Rightarrow x \in \left(-\sqrt{\dfrac{5}{2}}, -1\right] \cup \left[1, \sqrt{\dfrac{5}{2}}\right)$

$\therefore M = 1$

**23.** **(3)** For f (x) to be defined
$x + 3 > 0$ and $x^2 + 3x + 2 \neq 0$
$\Rightarrow x > -3$ and $(x+1)(x+2) \neq 0$
i.e. $x \neq -1, -2.$
$\therefore$ Domain $= (-3 + \infty) - \{-1, -2\}$
Thus, $P + Q = 1 + 2 = 3$

**24.** **(1)** $f(x) = \dfrac{\sin x}{|\sec x|} - \dfrac{\cos x}{|\cosec x|}$

Range f(x) = sin x . $|\cos x| - \cos x |\sin x|$

$f(x) = \begin{cases} 0 & x \in \left[0, \dfrac{\pi}{2}\right] \\ -\sin 2x & x \in \left(\dfrac{\pi}{2}, \pi\right) \\ 0 & x \in \left(\pi, \dfrac{3\pi}{2}\right) \\ \sin 2x & x \in \left(\dfrac{3\pi}{2}, 2\pi\right) \end{cases}$

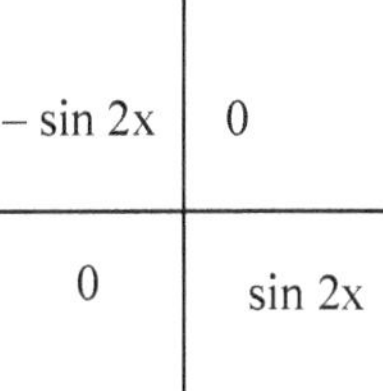

So, range is $[-1, 1]$
Thus, A = 1.

**DAILY PRACTICE PROBLEMS**

# MATHEMATICS SOLUTIONS



**1.** **(b)** $\quad 2 - \dfrac{\log_5 16}{2\log_5 9} = 2 - \log_{81} 16 = 2 - \log_3 2$

$$= \log_3 9 - \log_3 2 = \log_3 \frac{9}{2}$$

$$\left(\frac{1}{\sqrt{27}}\right)^{\log_3 \frac{9}{2}} = \frac{1}{(3)^{\frac{3}{2}\log_3\left(\frac{9}{2}\right)}} = \frac{1}{\left(\frac{9}{2}\right)^{3/2}} = \frac{2\sqrt{2}}{27}$$

**2.** **(d)**

**(a)** The given equation is

$$x^{\log_3 x^2 + (\log_3 x)^2 - 10} = \frac{1}{x^2} = x^{-2}$$

$$\Rightarrow \log_3 x^2 + (\log_3 x)^2 - 10 = -2$$

$$\Rightarrow 2\log_3 x + (\log_3 x)^2 - 8 = 0$$

$$\Rightarrow y^2 + 2y - 8 = 0 \text{, where } y = \log_3 x$$

$$\Rightarrow (y-2)(y+4) = 0 \Rightarrow y = 2 \text{ or } -4$$

$$\Rightarrow \log_3 x = 2 \text{ or } \log_3 x = -4 \Rightarrow x = 3^2 \text{ or } x = 3^{-4}$$

i.e. $x = 9$ or $x = \dfrac{1}{81}$

**(b)** We have, $\dfrac{\log x + \log x^4 + \log x^9 + \dots + \log x^{n^2}}{\log x + \log x^2 + \log x^3 + \dots + \log x^n}$

$$= \frac{(1+4+9+\dots+n^2)\log x}{(1+2+3+\dots+n)\log x} = \frac{\Sigma n^2}{\Sigma n}$$

$$= \frac{\dfrac{n(n+1)(2n+1)}{6}}{\dfrac{n(n+1)}{2}} = \frac{2n+1}{3}$$

**(c)** Let $x = 3^{40}$

$\log x = 40 \log 3 = 40\,(0.477) = 19.08$

$$\Rightarrow x = (10)^{19.08} > 10^{19}$$

Hence the number of digits in $x$ is 20.

**3.** **(b)**

**(a)** $\log_3 x \log_y 3 \log_2 y = 5$

$$\Rightarrow \log_2 y \cdot \log_y 3 \cdot \log_3 x = 5$$

$$\Rightarrow \log_2 x = 5 \Rightarrow x = 2^5 = 32$$

**(b)** Put $\log_2 x = t$

$t\,[t-4] + 4 = 0, \quad \therefore (t-2)^2 = 0$

$$\therefore t = \log_2 x = 2, \Rightarrow \therefore x = 2^2 = 4$$

**(c)** Make the common base 4

$$\log_4 \frac{x^2 + x}{x+1} = \log_4 x = 2 \quad [\because x + 1 \ne 0]$$

$$\Rightarrow x = 2^4 = 16$$

**(d)** From the given relation, we have

$a = y^{1-\log_a x} = z^{1-\log_a y}$

$\therefore \log_a a = (1 - \log_a x)\log_a y = (1 - \log_a y)\log_a z$

$$\Rightarrow \log_a y(1 - \log_a x) = 1 \text{ and } \log_a z(1 - \log_a y) = 1$$

$$\Rightarrow \log_a y = \frac{1}{1 - \log_a x} \text{ and } \log_a z = \frac{1}{1 - \log_a y}$$

Now,

$$\log_a z = \frac{1}{1 - \log_a y} = \frac{1}{1 - \dfrac{1}{1 - \log_a x}} = \frac{1 - \log_a x}{-\log_a x}$$

$$\therefore \frac{1}{1 - \log_a z} = \frac{1}{1 + \dfrac{1 - \log_a x}{\log_a x}} = \log_a x$$

$$\Rightarrow \log_a x = \frac{1}{1 - \log_a z} \Rightarrow x = a^{\frac{1}{1 - \log_a z}}$$

**4.** **(d)** Let $\dfrac{x(y+z-x)}{\log x} = \dfrac{y(z+x-y)}{\log y} = \dfrac{z(x+y-z)}{\log z} = \dfrac{1}{k}$

$$\Rightarrow \log x = kx(y+z-x), \ \log y = ky(z+x-y),$$

$\log z = kz(x+y-z)$

Hence,

$y \log x + x \log y = kxy(y+z-x) + kxy(z+x-y)$

$= 2kxyz$

Similarly $y \log z + z \log y = 2k\,xyz$

and $z \log x + x \log z = 2k\,xyz$

It follows that

$y \log x + x \log y = y \log z + z \log y = z \log x + x \log z$

$$\Rightarrow \log(x^y . y^x) = \log(z^y . y^z) = \log(x^z . z^x)$$

$$\Rightarrow x^y . y^x = z^y . y^z = z^x . x^z$$

**5.** **(c)**

**(a)** $\log(a + 2b) = \dfrac{1}{2}\log(a+2b)^2$

$$= \frac{1}{2}\log(a^2 + 4b^2 + 4ab) = \frac{1}{2}\log(12ab + 4ab)$$

$$= \frac{1}{2}\log(2^4 . ab) = \frac{1}{2}(4\log 2 + \log a + \log b)$$

**(b)** Let $\dfrac{\log x}{b-c} = \dfrac{\log y}{c-a} = \dfrac{\log z}{a-b} = k$

$$\Rightarrow \log x = k(b-c), \ \log y = k(c-a), \ \log z = k(a-b)$$

$$\therefore x^a . y^b . z^c = p^{k[a(b-c)+b(c-a)+c(a-b)]} = p^{k(0)} = 1,$$

where $p$ is any arbitrary base of the log.

**(c)** Given expression $= \log_{xyz} xy + \log_{xyz} yz + \log_{xyz} zx$

$$= \log_{xyz}(xy . yz . zx) = \log_{xyz}(x^2 . y^2 . z^2)$$

$$= 2\log_{xyz}(xyz) = 2 \times 1 = 2$$

**6.** **(b)**

**(a)** We know that $\pi < 3.2$. Also $12 > (3.2)^2$

[Note this carefully]

$$\therefore \frac{1}{\log_3 \pi} + \frac{1}{\log_4 \pi} = \log_\pi 3 + \log_\pi 4$$

$$= \log_\pi 12 > \log_\pi (3.2)^2 = 2\log_\pi (3.2) > 2$$

(b) $\quad 7\log_a \dfrac{16}{15} + 5\log_a \dfrac{25}{24} + 3\log_a \dfrac{81}{80}$

$= 7\log_a\left(\dfrac{2^4}{3\times 5}\right) + 5\log_a\left(\dfrac{5^2}{3\times 2^3}\right) + 3\log_a\left(\dfrac{3^4}{5\times 2^4}\right)$

$= 7[4\log_a 2 - \log_a 3 - \log_a 5]$

$\qquad\qquad + 5[2\log_a 5 - \log_a 3 - 3\log_a 2]$

$\qquad + 3[4\log_a 3 - \log_a 5 - 4\log_a 2] = \log_a 2$

(c) $\quad \sqrt{7\sqrt{7\sqrt{7}}} = \sqrt{7\sqrt{7.7^{1/2}}} = \sqrt{7\sqrt{7^{3/2}}} = \sqrt{7.7^{3/4}} = 7^{7/8}$

$\therefore \log_7 \sqrt{7\sqrt{7\sqrt{7}}} = \dfrac{7}{8}$

$\therefore \log_7 \log_7 \sqrt{7\sqrt{7\sqrt{7}}} = \log_7 \dfrac{7}{8}$

$\qquad = \log_7 7 - \log_7 8 = 1 - 3\log_7 2$

(d) $\quad A = \log_2 \log_2 \log_4 4^4 + 2\log_{2^{1/2}} 2$

$= \log_2 \log_2 4 + \dfrac{2}{1/2}\log_2 2 = \log_2 \log_2 2^2 + 4$

$= \log_2 2 + 4 = 1 + 4 = 5$

**7.** **(d)**

(a) Let r be the common ratio of G.P., then
$b = ar,\ c = ar^2,\ d = ar^3, \ldots\ldots$ etc

$\therefore \log_x b = \log_x(ar) = \log_x a + \log_x r$

$\log_x c = \log_x(ar^2) = \log_x a + 2\log_x r$ and so on

Now $\quad \log_x a,\ \log_x a + \log_x r,\ \log_x a + 2\log_x r, \ldots\ldots$
are in A.P.

$[\because \text{common difference} = \log_x r]$

i.e., $\log_x a,\ \log_x b,\ \log_x c, \ldots\ldots$ are in A.P.

i.e., $\log_a x, \log_b x, \log_c x$ are in H.P.

(b) Let $x^{18} = y^{21} = z^{28} = k$, then

$18\log x = 21\log y = 28\log z = \log k$

Now $3\log_y x = 3\dfrac{\log x}{\log y} = 3.\dfrac{21}{18} = \dfrac{7}{2}$

$3\log_z y = 3.\dfrac{28}{21} = 4, \qquad 7\log_x z = 7.\dfrac{18}{28} = \dfrac{9}{2}$

Hence the numbers are $3,\ 3\dfrac{1}{2},\ 4$ and $4\dfrac{1}{2}$.
which are clearly in A.P.

(c) Since $\log_l x, \log_m x, \log_n x$ are in A.P.

We have $2\log_m x = \log_l x + \log_n x$

$\Rightarrow \dfrac{2}{\log_x m} = \dfrac{1}{\log_x l} + \dfrac{1}{\log_x n} = \dfrac{\log_x l + \log_x n}{\log_x l \times \log_x n}$

$\Rightarrow 2\log_x n = \dfrac{\log_x(\ln).\log_x m}{\log_x l} = \log_x(\ln).\log_l m$

$\Rightarrow \log_x n^2 = \log_x(\ln).\log_l m$

$\Rightarrow n^2 = x^{\log_x(\ln).\log_l m} = x^{(\log_x \ln)^{\log_l m}} = (\ln)^{\log_l m}$

(d) $\quad \log_a n,\ \log_b n,\ \log_c n$ are in H.P.

If $\dfrac{1}{\log_n a},\ \dfrac{1}{\log_n b},\ \dfrac{1}{\log_n c}$ are in H.P.

i.e., if $\log_n a, \log_n b, \log_n c$, are in A.P.

i.e., if $2\log_n b = \log_n a + \log_n c$

i.e., if $\log_n b^2 = \log_n(ac)$

i.e., if $b^2 = ac$ i.e., if a, b, c are in G.P.,
which is given.

**8.** **(b)**

(a) $\log_6 16 = \log_6 2^4 = 4\log_6 2 = \dfrac{4}{\log_2 6}$

$= \dfrac{4}{\log_2 2 + \log_2 3} = \dfrac{4}{1 + \log_2 3} \qquad ....(1)$

and $a = \log_{12} 27 = \log_{12} 3^3 = 3\log_{12} 3$

$= \dfrac{3}{\log_3 12} = \dfrac{3}{\log_3 3 + \log_3 4} = \dfrac{3}{1 + 2\log_3 2}$

$\therefore a + 2a\log_3 2 = 3$ or

$\log_3 2 = \dfrac{3 - a}{2a} \Rightarrow \log_2 3 = \dfrac{2a}{3 - a}$

Now, substituting in (1), we get

$\log_6 16 = \dfrac{4}{1 + \dfrac{2a}{3 - a}} = \dfrac{4(3 - a)}{3 - a + 2a} = 4\left(\dfrac{3 - a}{3 + a}\right)$

(b) Let $\log_a b = \log_b c = \log_c a = \lambda$
Then $b = a^\lambda,\ c = b^\lambda,\ a = c^\lambda$
Now, $a = c^\lambda = (b^\lambda)^\lambda = b^{\lambda^2} = (a^\lambda)^{\lambda^2} = a^{\lambda^3}$

$\therefore \lambda^3 = 1 \Rightarrow \lambda = 1$

$\therefore a = b = c$

(c) Given $\dfrac{1}{\log_a x} + \dfrac{1}{\log_c x} = \dfrac{2}{\log_b x}$

$\Rightarrow \log_x a + \log_x c = 2\log_x b$

$\Rightarrow \log_x ac = \log_x b^2 \Rightarrow ac = b^2$

$\therefore a, b, c$ are in G.P.

(d) Given $\log(3 + 4 + k) = \log 3 + \log 4 + \log k$

$\Rightarrow \log(7 + k) = \log(3.4.k)$

$\Rightarrow 7 + k = 12k \Rightarrow k = \dfrac{7}{11}$

**9.** **(a, c)** $(x + 2y)^2 = 16xy$ or

$2\log_2(x + 2y) = 4 + \log_2 x + \log_2 y$

$\therefore \quad \log_2(x + 2y) = 2 + \dfrac{1}{2}(\log_2 x + \log_2 y)$.

But $1 \le x \le 4, 1 \le y \le 4$.

$\therefore \quad \max \log_2(x + 2y) = 2 + \dfrac{1}{2}(\log_2 4 + \log_2 4) = \mathbf{4}$

$\min \log_2(x + 2y) = 2 + \dfrac{1}{2}(\log_2 1 + \log_2 1) = 2$

Also $\log_2(x+2y)=3 \Rightarrow x+2y=8$
This is satisfied by $x=2, y=3; x=4, y=2; x=6, y=1$

**10.** **(a, b, d)** $\frac{1}{2} \leq \log_{1/10} x \leq 2 \Rightarrow \left(\frac{1}{10}\right)^{1/2} \geq x, \left(\frac{1}{10}\right)^{2} \leq x.$

So, $\frac{1}{100} \leq x \leq \frac{1}{\sqrt{10}}$.

**11.** **(a,b,c)** Taking logarithm, $\left\{\frac{3}{4}(\log_3 x)^2 + \log_3 x - \frac{5}{4}\right\} \log_3 x$

$= \log_3 \sqrt{3}$

or $\quad \frac{3}{4}y^3 + y^2 - \frac{5}{4}y = \frac{1}{2},$ (writing $y$ for $\log_3 x$)

or $\quad 3y^3 + 4y^2 - 5y - 2 = 0$ or $(y-1)(3y^2 + 7y + 2) = 0$

or $\quad (y-1)(3y+1)(y+2) = 0$

$\therefore \quad \log_3 x = 1, -\frac{1}{3}, -2 \Rightarrow x = 3, 3^{-1/3}, 3^{-2}.$

**12.** **(c)** The given equation can be rewriten in the form

$\Rightarrow \frac{1 - 8(\log x)^2}{\log x - 2(\log x)^2} = 1$

Let $\log x = t$

Then $\frac{1 - (8t^2)}{t - 2t^2} - 1 = 0$

$\Rightarrow \frac{1 - t - 6t^2}{t - 2t^2} = 0$

$\Rightarrow \frac{(1+2t)(1-3t)}{t(1-2t)} = 0$

$\Rightarrow \begin{cases} t = -\frac{1}{2} \Rightarrow \log x = -\frac{1}{2} \\ t = \frac{1}{3} \Rightarrow \log x = \frac{1}{3} \end{cases}$

$\Rightarrow \begin{cases} x = (10)^{-1/2} \\ x = (10)^{1/3} \end{cases}$

$\therefore$ Number of solutions is 2.

**13.** **(d)** Put $\log_x 10 = t$ in the given equation,
we get $t^3 - 6t^2 + 11t - 6 = 0$
$(t-1)(t-2)(t-3) = 0$

$\begin{cases} t = 1 \\ t = 2, \text{it follows that} \\ t = 3 \end{cases} \begin{cases} \log_x 10 = 1 \\ \log_x 10 = 2 \\ \log_x 10 = 3 \end{cases} (\because x > 0 \text{ and } x \neq 1)$

$\therefore$ Number of solutions is 3.

**14.** **(c)** Put $\log_5 x = t$ in the given equation, we get

$t^2 + t + 1 = \frac{7}{t-1}$

$\Rightarrow t^2 + t + 1 - \frac{7}{t-1} = 0$

for final solution $\log_5 x = 2$
i.e., only $x = 25$

**15.** **A$\rightarrow$ r,t; B$\rightarrow$p; C$\rightarrow$q,s**

(A) Since, $\log_{100} |x+y| = \frac{1}{2}$

$\Rightarrow |x+y| = (100)^{1/2} = 10$
$\therefore |x+y| = 10 \qquad \qquad ...(i)$
and $\log_{10} y - \log_{10} |x| = \log_{100} 4$

$\Rightarrow \log\left(\frac{y}{|x|}\right) = \log_{10^2} 2^2 = \frac{2}{2}\log_{10} 2$

$\Rightarrow \log_{10}\left(\frac{y}{|x|}\right) = \log_{10} 2$

$\Rightarrow \frac{y}{|x|} = 2 \Rightarrow y = 2|x| \;...(ii)$

From eqs. (i) and (ii),
$|x + 2|x|| = 10$
**Case I :** $x > 0, |3x| = 10$
$\Rightarrow 3|x| = 10$
$\Rightarrow 3x = 10$

$x = \frac{10}{3}$

From Eq. (ii), $y = \frac{20}{3}$

$\left\{\frac{10}{3}, \frac{20}{3}\right\}$ **(t)**

**Case II:** $x < 0, |x - 2x| = 10$
$\Rightarrow |x| = 10 \Rightarrow -x = 10$
$\therefore x = -10$
From eq.(ii), $y = 2|-10| = 20$
$\therefore \{-10, 20\}$ **(r)**

(B) Let $\log_2 x = A$ and $\log_2 y = B$
$\therefore 4A^2 + 1 = 2B \qquad \qquad ...(i)$
and $2A \geq B$
or $4A \geq 2B$
$\Rightarrow 4A \geq 4A^2 + 1 \qquad$ [ from eq. (i)]
$\Rightarrow (2A - 1)^2 \leq 0$

$\Rightarrow 2A - 1 = 0$ or $A = \frac{1}{2}$

From eq. (i), $4\left(\frac{1}{2}\right)^2 + 1 = 2B$

$\therefore B = 1$

$\therefore \log_2 x = \frac{1}{2}$ and $\log_2 y = 1$

$\Rightarrow x = 2^{1/2}$ and $y = 2^1.$

or $x = \sqrt{2}, y = 2$

i.e, $\{\sqrt{2}, 2\}$ **(p)**

(C) $\log_4 x = \log_2 y$

$\Rightarrow \log_{2^2} x = \log_2 y$

$\Rightarrow \frac{1}{2}\log_2 x = \log_2 y$

$\Rightarrow \log_2 x = 2\log_2 y = \log_2 y^2.$
$\Rightarrow x = y^2 \qquad \qquad ...(i)$

And $x^2 - 5y^2 + 4 = 0$
$\Rightarrow x^2 - 5x + 4 = 0 \Rightarrow (x-1)(x-4) = 0$
$x = 1, x = 4$
Then, $y = 1, y = \pm 2$ but $y > 0$
$\therefore$ Solution sets are $\{1, 1\}, \{4, 2\}$ **(q, s)**

**16.** $\quad A \to p, r; B \to q, t; C \to s, t$

(A) $\quad \because 5^2 < 34 < 5^3$.

$\Rightarrow 2 \log_{34} 5 < 1 < 3 \log_{34} 5$

$\therefore \log_{34} 5 < \dfrac{1}{2}$ and $\log_{34} 5 > \dfrac{1}{3}$

$\therefore \log_{34} 5 \in \left(\dfrac{1}{3}, \dfrac{1}{2}\right) \quad \therefore a = \dfrac{1}{3}, b = \dfrac{1}{2}$

$\Rightarrow [10a + 10b] = [3.33 + 5] = [8.33] = 8$**(p)**

Also $[6b - 3a] = [3 - 1] = 2$**(r)**

(B) $\quad \because 4^4 < 300 < 4^5$

$\Rightarrow 4 \log_{300} 4 < 1 < 5 \log_{300} 4$

$\Rightarrow \log_{300} 4 < \dfrac{1}{4}$ and $\log_{300} 4 < \dfrac{1}{5}$

$\therefore \log_{300} 4 \in \left(\dfrac{1}{5}, \dfrac{1}{4}\right)$

$\therefore a = \dfrac{1}{5}, b = \dfrac{1}{4}$

$(10a + 10b) = (2 + 2.5) = 5$ **(q)**

And $(6b - 3a) = (1.5 - 0.6) = (0.9) = 1$**(t)**

(C) $\quad \because 3^5 < 400 < 3^6$

$\Rightarrow 5 \log_{400} 3 < 1 < 6 \log_{400} 3$

$\therefore \log_{400} 3 < \dfrac{1}{5}$ and $\log_{400} 3 > \dfrac{1}{6}$

$\therefore \log_{400} 3 \in \left(\dfrac{1}{6}, \dfrac{1}{5}\right) \quad \therefore a = \dfrac{1}{6}, b = \dfrac{1}{5}$

$(6b - 3a) = \left(\dfrac{6}{5} - \dfrac{3}{6}\right)$

$= (1.2 - 0.5) = (0.7) = 1$ **(t)**

And $[10a + 10b] = \left[\dfrac{10}{6} + \dfrac{10}{5}\right]$

$= [1.67 + 2] = [3.67] = 3$ **(s)**

**17.** **(c)** On solving $\log_{1/5} \dfrac{4x+6}{x} \geq 0, \ 0 < \dfrac{4x+6}{x} \leq 1$

$\dfrac{4x+6}{x} > 0$ and $\dfrac{4x+6}{x} - 1 \leq 0$

$\Rightarrow \ x \in \left(-\infty, -\dfrac{3}{2}\right) \cup (0, \infty)$ and $\dfrac{3x+6}{x} \leq 0$

$\Rightarrow \ x \in \left(-\infty, -\dfrac{3}{2}\right) \cup (0, \infty)$ and $x \in [-2, 0)$

$\Rightarrow \ x \in \left[-2, \dfrac{-3}{2}\right)$

Similarly solving $2^{y-x}(x+y) = 1, \ (x+y)^{x-y} = 2$

We get two pairs of solutions.

$\therefore$ Statement -1 is true and Statement -2 is false.

**18.** **(d)** Statement - 1 is false.

In Statement -2, $\log(2^{100}) = 100 \log 2$

$= 100 \times 0.3010 \ldots = 30.10 \ldots$

$\therefore$ No of digits $= 31$

$\therefore$ Statement -2, is true.

**19.** **(4)** $abc = \dfrac{\log 12}{\log 24} \cdot \dfrac{\log 24}{\log 36} \cdot \dfrac{\log 36}{\log 48} = \dfrac{\log 12}{\log 48}$

$\therefore 1 + abc = \dfrac{\log 48 + \log 12}{\log 48} = \dfrac{\log(48 \cdot 12)}{\log 48}$

$= \dfrac{\log 24^2}{\log 48} = 2 \cdot \dfrac{\log 24}{\log 48} = 2bc$

Thus, $x = 2, p = 0, q = 1, r = 1$

$\therefore \ x + p + q + r = 2 + 0 + 1 + 1 = 4$

**20.** **(9)** $S = 0.1 + 0.01 + 0.001 + \ldots = \dfrac{0.1}{1 - 0.1} = \dfrac{1}{9}$

[Sum of infinite G.P.]

Also, $0.05 = \dfrac{1}{20} = 20^{-1}$

The given expression can be reduce to

$(20^{-1})^{\log_{20^{1/2}}(9^{-1})} = 20^{2 \log_{20} 9} = 20^{\log_{20} 9^2} = 9^2$

$\therefore \ p = 9$

**21.** **(5)** Given $(4)^{\log_9 3} + (9)^{\log_2 4} = (10)^{\log_x 83}$

$\Rightarrow (4)^{\frac{1}{\log_3 9}} + (9)^{\log_2 4} = (10)^{\log_x 83}$

$\Rightarrow 4^{1/2} + (9)^2 = 10^{\log_x 83} \ \Rightarrow 2 + 81 = (10)^{\log_x 83}$

$\Rightarrow 83 = (10)^{\log_x 83} = (83)^{\log_x 10}$

$\Rightarrow 1 = \log_x 10 \ \Rightarrow x = 10$

$\therefore \ p = 5$

**22.** **(9)** $\because \ x + 1 = 2 \log_2(2^x + 3) - 2 \log_{2^2}(1980 - 2^{-x})$

$\Rightarrow \ x + 1 = \log_2(2^x + 3)^2 - \log_2(1980 - 2^{-x})$

$\Rightarrow \ x + 1 = \log_2 \left\{ \dfrac{(2^x + 3)^2}{1980 - 2^{-x}} \right\}$

$\Rightarrow \ 2^x \cdot 2 = \dfrac{2^{2x} + 6 \cdot 2^x + 9}{1980 - 2^{-x}}$

$\Rightarrow \ 2 \times 1980 \times 2^x - 2 = 2^{2x} + 6 \cdot 2^x + 9$

$\Rightarrow \ 2^{2x} - 3954 \cdot 2^x + 11 = 0$

If roots are $\alpha, \beta$, then

$2^\alpha \cdot 2^\beta = \dfrac{11}{1} \ \Rightarrow \ 2^{\alpha + \beta} = 11$

or $\ \alpha + \beta = \log_2 11$

Also,

$\log_{0.5}\left(\dfrac{1}{11}\right) = \log_{1/2}\left(\dfrac{1}{11}\right) = \log_2 11$

$\therefore \ b - a = 11 - 2 = 9$

**23.** **(5)** $\log_5 x = \log_x 5 \Rightarrow (\log_5 x)^2 = 1 \Rightarrow \log_5 x = \pm 1$

$\Rightarrow x = 5, 5^{-1}$

Thus, $a = 5$

1. **(a)** $i^i = \left(e^{i\frac{\pi}{2}}\right) = e^{-\frac{\pi}{2}}$ = a purely real quantity.

2. **(b)** $\sum_{i=1}^{13}(i^n + i^{n+1}) = \sum_{i=1}^{13} i^n(1+i) = (1+i)\sum_{i=1}^{13} i^n$

   This forms a G.P.

   Sum of G.P. $= i\,(1+i)\dfrac{(1-i^{13})}{1-i} = i - 1$ as $i^{13} = i$

3. **(d)** $(1+i)^{n_1} + (1-i)^{n_1} + (1+i)^{n_2} + (1-i)^{n_2}$

   $= \left[{}^{n_1}C_0 - {}^{n_1}C_1 i + {}^{n_1}C_2 i^2 + {}^{n_1}C_3 i^3 + \ldots\ldots\ldots {}^{n_1}C_{n_1}(i)^{n_1}\right]$

   $+ \left[{}^{n_1}C_0 - {}^{n_1}C_1 i + {}^{n_1}C_2 i^2 - {}^{n_1}C_3 i^3 + \ldots + (-1)^{n_1}\,{}^{n_1}C_{n_1}(i)^{n_1}\right]$

   $+ \left[{}^{n_2}C_0 - {}^{n_2}C_1 i + {}^{n_2}C_2 i^2 + {}^{n_2}C_3 i^3 + \ldots + {}^{n_2}C_{n_2}(i)^{n_2}\right]$

   $+ \left[{}^{n_2}C_0 - {}^{n_2}C_2 i + {}^{n_2}C_2 i^2 - {}^{n_2}C_3 i^3 + \ldots + (-1)^{n_2}\,{}^{n_2}C_2(i)^{n_2}\right]$

   $= 2\left[{}^{n_1}C_0 + {}^{n_1}C_2 i^2 + {}^{n_1}C_4 i^4 + \ldots + \left(\dfrac{n_1+1}{2}\right)^{th} \text{or} \left(\dfrac{n_1}{2}\right)^{th}\right]$ term as $n_1$ is odd or even respectively.

   $+ 2\left[{}^{n_2}C_0 + {}^{n_2}C_2 i^2 + {}^{n_2}C_4 i^4 + \ldots + \left(\dfrac{n_2+1}{2}\right)^{th} \text{or} \left(\dfrac{n_2}{2}\right)^{th}\right]$ term as $n_2$ is odd or even respectively.

   $= 2\left[{}^{n_1}C_0 - {}^{n_1}C_2 + {}^{n_1}C_4 + \ldots + \left(\dfrac{n_1+1}{2}\right)^{th} \text{or} \left(\dfrac{n_1}{2}\right)^{th}\right]$ term as $n_1$ is odd or even respectively.

   $+ 2\left[{}^{n_2}C_0 - {}^{n_2}C_2 + {}^{n_2}C_4 - \ldots + \left(\dfrac{n_2+1}{2}\right)^{th} \text{or} \left(\dfrac{n_2}{2}\right)^{th}\right]$ term as $n_2$ is odd or even respectively.

   This is a real number irrespective of the values of $n_1$ and $n_2$.

4. **(c)** $E = 4 + 5(\omega)^{334} + 3(\omega)^{365} = 4 + 5\omega + 3\omega^2$

   $= 1 + 2\omega + 3(1 + \omega + \omega^2) = 1 + (-1 + i\sqrt{3}) = i\sqrt{3}$

5. **(d)** Let $z_1 = \sin x + i\cos 2x$ ; $z_2 = \cos x - i\sin 2x$

   Then ATQ, $\bar{z}_1 = z_2$

   $\Rightarrow \sin x - i\cos 2x = \cos x - i\sin 2x$

   $\Rightarrow \sin x = \cos x$ and $\cos 2x = \sin 2x$

           [Equating real and imaginary parts.]

   $\Rightarrow \tan x = 1$ and $\tan 2x = 1$

   $\Rightarrow x = \dfrac{\pi}{4}$ and $x = \dfrac{\pi}{8}$

   which is not possible at the same time.

   $\therefore$ There is no value of $x$ for which above both are satisfied simultaneously.

   $\therefore$ (d) is correct answer

6. **(c)** Only real numbers can be compared, so imaginary part of both numbers i.e.,
   b and d = 0 and then a > c.

7. **(a)** Let $\alpha$ (purely imaginary) be a root of the given equation then $\alpha = -\bar{\alpha}$. Also $a\alpha^2 + b\alpha + c = 0$   .....(1)

   From (1), $\overline{a\alpha^2 + b\alpha + c} = \bar{0}$

   $\Rightarrow \bar{a}\bar{\alpha}^2 + \bar{b}\bar{\alpha} + \bar{c} = 0 \Rightarrow \bar{a}\alpha^2 - \bar{b}\alpha + \bar{c} = 0$ .....(2)

           $[\because z = -\bar{z}]$

   Solving (1) and (2) simultaneously,

   we get $\dfrac{\alpha^2}{b\bar{c} + c\bar{b}} = \dfrac{\alpha}{c\bar{a} - a\bar{c}} = \dfrac{1}{-a\bar{b} - \bar{a}b}$

   Eliminating $\alpha$, we get $(b\bar{c} + c\bar{b})(a\bar{b} + \bar{a}b) + (c\bar{a} - a\bar{c})^2 = 0$

8. **(b)** $\because \arg\left(\dfrac{z - z_1}{z_2 - z}\right) = \dfrac{\pi}{2} \Rightarrow \operatorname{Re}\left(\dfrac{z - z_1}{z_2 - z}\right) = 0$

   $\Rightarrow \dfrac{z - z_1}{z_2 - z} + \dfrac{\bar{z} - \bar{z}_1}{\bar{z}_2 - \bar{z}} = 0$

   $\Rightarrow (z - z_1)(\bar{z}_2 - \bar{z}) + (z_2 - z)(\bar{z} - \bar{z}_1) = 0$

   $\Rightarrow z(\bar{z}_1 + \bar{z}_2) + \bar{z}(z_1 + z_2) - 2z\bar{z} - (z_1\bar{z}_2 + z_2\bar{z}_1) = 0$

   $\Rightarrow z\bar{z} - (5+i)z - (5-i)\bar{z} + 21 = 0$

   $\Rightarrow |z - (5-i)| = \sqrt{5}$

9. **(a,c,d)** Let $z = c$ be a real root.

   Then $\alpha c^2 + c + \bar{\alpha} = 0$        ...(1)

   Let $\alpha = p + iq$

   Then $(p + iq)c^2 + c + iq = 0$

   $\Rightarrow pc^2 + c + p = 0$ and $qc^2 - q = 0$

   $\Rightarrow c = \pm 1$ $(\because q \neq 0)$

   $\therefore (1) \Rightarrow \alpha \pm 1 + \bar{\alpha} = 0$

   Also $|c| = 1$.

10. **(a,b,c)** The roots of $x^2 + x + 1 = 0$ are $\omega$ and $\omega^2$.

    So, $h(\omega) = 0$ and $h(\omega^2) = 0$

    $\Rightarrow f(1) = g(1) = 0$

    $\therefore h(1) = f(1) + g(1) = 0$

11. **(a,c)** Let $z = x + iy$, then the equation is

    $x^2 + y^2 - 2i(x + iy) + 2c(1 + i) = 0$

    $\Rightarrow (x^2 + y^2 + 2y + 2c) + i(2c - 2x) = 0$

    $\Rightarrow x^2 + y^2 + 2y + 2c = 0$ and $x = c$

    $\Rightarrow c^2 + y^2 + 2y + 2c = 0$

    $\Rightarrow y = -1 \pm \sqrt{1 - 2c - c^2}$

    $\because y \in R \Rightarrow 1 - 2c - c^2 \geq 0$

    $\Rightarrow c^2 + 2c - 1 \leq 0$

    $\Rightarrow -1 - \sqrt{2} \leq c \leq -1 + \sqrt{2}$

    $\therefore$ The equation has a solution,

    If $c \in [-1 - \sqrt{2}, -1 + \sqrt{2}]$ and the solution is given by

    $z = c + i(-1 \pm \sqrt{1 - 2c - c^2})$

    The equation has no solution, if

    $c \in (-\infty, -1 - \sqrt{2}) \cup (-1 + \sqrt{2}, \infty)$

**12.** **(a,b,c)** $|z_1| = |z_2| = 1$

$$\Rightarrow a^2 + b^2 = c^2 + d^2 = 1 \quad ....(1)$$

and $\text{Re}(z_1 \bar{z}_2) = 0 \Rightarrow \text{Re}\{(a + ib)(c - id)\} = 0$

$$\Rightarrow ac + bd = 0 \qquad\qquad ....(2)$$

Now from (1) and (2), $a^2 + b^2 = 1$

$$\Rightarrow a^2 + \frac{a^2 c^2}{d^2} = 1 \Rightarrow a^2 = d^2 \qquad .....(3)$$

Also $c^2 + d^2 = 1$

$$\Rightarrow c^2 + \frac{a^2 c^2}{b^2} = 1 \Rightarrow b^2 = c^2 \qquad ........(4)$$

$|\omega_1| = \sqrt{a^2 + c^2} = \sqrt{a^2 + b^2} = 1$
[From (1) and (4)]

and $|\omega_2| = \sqrt{b^2 + d^2} = \sqrt{c^2 + d^2} = 1$
[From (1) and (4)]

Further $\text{Re}(\omega_1 \bar{\omega}_2) = \text{Re}\{(a + ic)(b - id)\}$

$$= ab + cd = ab + \left(-\frac{ac}{b}\right)c \qquad \text{[From (2)]}$$

$$= \frac{ab^2 - ac^2}{b} = 0 \qquad \text{[From (4)]}.$$

Also, $\text{Im}(\omega_1 \bar{\omega}_2) = bc - ad = bc - a\left(-\frac{ac}{b}\right)$

$$= \frac{(a^2 + b^2)c}{b} = \frac{c}{b} = \pm 1 \neq 0$$

$\therefore |\omega_1| = 1, |\omega_2| = 1$ and $\text{Re}(\omega_1 \bar{\omega}_2) = 0$

**13.** **(c)** $\because \dfrac{A}{B} + \dfrac{B}{C} + \dfrac{C}{A} = 1$

$$\Rightarrow e^{i(\alpha - \beta)} + e^{i(\beta - \gamma)} + e^{i(\gamma - \alpha)} = 1$$

comparing real parts, then

$$\cos(\alpha - \beta) + \cos(\beta - \gamma) + \cos(\gamma - \alpha) = 1$$

$$\sum \cos(\alpha - \beta) = 1$$

**14.** **(c)** $\because \sin^n \alpha + \sin^n \beta + \sin^n \gamma = 3/2$

and $\cos(\alpha + \beta) + \cos(\beta + \gamma) + \cos(\gamma + \alpha) = \lambda$
For $a = b = c = 1$

$$\cos\alpha + \cos\beta + \cos\gamma = 0 = \sin\alpha + \sin\beta + \sin\gamma$$

$$\therefore A + B + C = 0 \text{ and } \frac{1}{A} + \frac{1}{B} + \frac{1}{C} = 0$$

$$\Rightarrow A + B + C = 0 \text{ and } AB + BC + CA = 0$$

$$A^2 + B^2 + C^2 = 0 \text{ and } AB + BC + CA = 0$$

$$\therefore e^{2i\alpha} + e^{2i\beta} + e^{2i\gamma} = 0 \text{ and }$$

$$e^{i(\alpha + \beta)} + e^{i(\beta + \gamma)} + e^{i(\gamma + \alpha)} = 0$$

On comparing real parts on both equations, we get

$$\cos 2\alpha + \cos 2\beta + \cos 2\gamma = 0$$

and $\cos(\alpha + \beta) + \cos(\beta + \gamma) + \cos(\gamma + \alpha) = 0$

$$\Rightarrow 1 - 2\sin^2\alpha + 1 - 2\sin^2\beta + 1 - 2\sin^2\gamma = 0$$

$$\sin^2\alpha + \sin^2\beta + \sin^2\gamma = 3/2$$

Hence, $n = 2$, $\lambda = 0$

$$\therefore (n, \lambda) \equiv (2, 0)$$

**15.** **(c)** Let $\alpha + \beta + \gamma = 0$

$$\therefore \sin(-\beta - \gamma) + 2\sin(-\gamma - \alpha) + 3\sin(-\alpha - \beta) = 0$$

$$\therefore \sin(\beta + \gamma) + 2\sin(\gamma + \alpha) + 3\sin(\alpha + \beta) = 0$$

which is true

$$\therefore \alpha + \beta - \gamma = -\gamma - \gamma = -2\gamma$$

**16.** **(d)** $\displaystyle\sum_{r=1}^{4n+11} i^r = i + i^2 + i^3 + \sum_{r=4}^{4n+11} i^r = i - 1 - i + 0$

$$= -1$$

**17.** **(d)** $3 + ix^2 y$ and $x^2 + y + 4i$ are conjugate.

$$x^2 + y^2 = 3, \ x^2 y = -4, \ x^2 = 4, \ y = -1$$

Statement 1 is false but Statement 2 is true.

**18.** **(9)** If a polynomial has real coefficients then roots occur in complex conjugate

$\therefore$ roots are $2i, -2i, 2 + i, \ 2 - i$

hence $f(x) = (x + 2i)(x - 2i)(x - 2 - i)(x - 2 + i)$

$f(1) = (1 + 2i)(1 - 2i)(1 - 2 - i)(1 - 2 + i)$

$f(1) = 5 \times 2 = 10$

Also $f(1) = 1 + a + b + c + d$

$\therefore 1 + a + b + c + d = 10$

$\Rightarrow a + b + c + d = 9$

**19.** **(4)** We have,

$$\left[i^{19} + \left(\frac{1}{i}\right)^{25}\right]^2 = \left[i^{19} + \left(\frac{1}{i^{25}}\right)\right]^2$$

$$= \left[i^3 + \left(\frac{1}{i}\right)\right]^2 = \left[i + \left(\frac{i^3}{i^4}\right)\right]^2$$

$$= [-i + i^3]^2 = (-i - i)^2 = 4i^2 = -4$$

$$\therefore X = 4$$

**20.** **(1)** $\displaystyle\sum_{k=0}^{100} i^k = x + iy, \Rightarrow 1 + i + i^2 + ........ + i^{100} = x + iy$

Given series is G.P.

$$\Rightarrow \frac{1.(1 - i^{101})}{1 - i} = x + iy \Rightarrow \frac{1 - i}{1 - i} = x + iy$$

$$\Rightarrow 1 + 0i = x + iy$$

Equating real and imaginary parts, we get

$$x = 1, \ y = 0$$

$$\therefore x + y = 1$$

**21.** **(5)** $z^2 = 81 - b^2 + 18bi$

$z^3 = 729 + 243bi - 27b^2 - b^3 i$

Hence, $243b - b^3 = 18b$

and $243 - b^2 = 18$ or $b^2 = 225$

Thus, $\dfrac{b}{3} = \dfrac{15}{3} = 5$

**22.** **(4)** $\dfrac{1 + i}{1 - i} = \dfrac{(1 + i)^2}{(1 - i)(1 + i)} = \dfrac{1 - 1 + 2i}{2} = i$

Now $i^n = 1 \Rightarrow$ the smallest positive integral value of $n$ should be 4.

# MATHEMATICS SOLUTIONS

**1.** **(a)** Let $z_1$, $z_2$ are the two roots with $|z_1| = 1$

$\because z_1 z_2 = \dfrac{c}{a} \Rightarrow |z_2| = \left|\dfrac{c}{a}\right| \dfrac{1}{|z_1|} = 1 \Rightarrow z_1 \overline{z}_1 = z_2 \overline{z}_2 = 1$

$\because z_1 + z_2 = -\dfrac{b}{a}$ and $|b| = |a| \Rightarrow |z_1 + z_2|^2 = 1$

$\Rightarrow (z_1 + z_2)(\overline{z}_1 + \overline{z}_2) = 1$

$\Rightarrow (z_1 + z_2)\left(\dfrac{1}{z_1} + \dfrac{1}{z_2}\right) = 1 \Rightarrow (z_1 + z_2)^2 = z_1 z_2$

$\Rightarrow \left(-\dfrac{b}{a}\right)^2 = \dfrac{c}{a} \Rightarrow b^2 = ac$

**2.** **(c)** $|iz + z_0| = |iz - i^2 + z_0 - 1| = |i(z-i) + 5 + 3i - 1|$

$\qquad = |i(z-i) + (4 + 3i)|$

$\therefore |iz + z_0| \le |i(z-2)| + |(4+3i)| \le 1.2 + 5 \le 7.$

$\therefore$ Maximum value of $|iz + z_0|$ is 7.

**3.** **(a)** Given expression $= \left(\dfrac{z(1+z)}{z+\overline{z}}\right)^4 + \left(\dfrac{z + z\overline{z}}{z(1+z)}\right)^4$

$= \left(\dfrac{z(1+z)}{z + |z|^2}\right)^4 + \left(\dfrac{z + |z|^2}{z(1+z)}\right)^4$

$= \left(\dfrac{z(1+z)}{z+1}\right)^4 + \left(\dfrac{z+1}{z(1+z)}\right)^4$

$= z^4 + \dfrac{1}{z^4} = (\cos\theta + i\sin\theta)^4 + \dfrac{1}{(\cos\theta + i\sin\theta)^4}$

(Since $z = \cos\theta + i\sin\theta$)

$\qquad = \cos 4\theta + i\sin 4\theta + \cos 4\theta - i\sin 4\theta$

$\qquad = 2\cos 4\theta = 2\cos 4(\arg z)$

**4.** **(c)** We have $2 = |z + i\omega| \le |z| + |\omega|$

$\because |z_1 + z_2| \le |z_1| + |z_2|$

$\therefore |z| + |\omega| \ge 2 \qquad\qquad$ ....(1)

But given that $|z| \le 1$ and $|\omega| \le 1$

$\Rightarrow |z| + |\omega| \le 2 \qquad\qquad$ ....(2)

From (1) and (2) $|z| = |\omega| = 1$

Also $|z + i\omega| = |z - i\overline{\omega}|$

$\Rightarrow |z + i\omega|^2 = |z - i\overline{\omega}|^2$

$\Rightarrow (z + i\omega)\overline{(z + i\omega)} = (z - i\overline{\omega})\overline{(z - i\overline{\omega})}$

$\Rightarrow (z + i\omega)(\overline{z} - i\overline{\omega}) = (\overline{z} + i\omega)(z - i\overline{\omega})$

$\Rightarrow z\overline{z} + i\omega\overline{z} - iz\overline{\omega} + \omega\overline{\omega} = \overline{z}z - i\overline{z}\,\overline{\omega} + i\omega z + \omega\overline{\omega}$

$\Rightarrow \omega\overline{z} - z\overline{\omega} + \overline{z}\overline{\omega} - \omega z = 0$

$\Rightarrow (\overline{z} - z)(\omega + \overline{\omega}) = 0$

$\Rightarrow z = \overline{z}$ or $\omega = -\overline{\omega}$

$\Rightarrow \mathrm{Im}(z) = 0$ or $\mathrm{Re}(\omega) = 0$

Also $|z| = 1, |\omega| = 1$

$\Rightarrow z = 1$ or $-1$ and $w = i$ or $-i$.

**Alternative:**

Given that $|z + i\omega| = |z - i\overline{\omega}|$

$\Rightarrow |z - (-i\omega)| = |z - (-i\overline{\omega})|$

$\Rightarrow z$ lies on perpendicular bisector of the line segment joining $(-i\omega)$ and $(-i\overline{\omega})$, which is real axis, $(-i\omega)$ and $(-i\overline{\omega})$ being mirror images of each other.

$\therefore \mathrm{Im}(z) = 0$.

If $z = x$ then $|z| \le 1 \Rightarrow x^2 \le 1 \Rightarrow -1 \le x \le 1$

**5.** **(d)** $\because \dfrac{w - wz}{1 - z}$ is purely real

$\therefore \left(\dfrac{w - \overline{w}z}{1 - z}\right) = \left(\dfrac{w - \overline{w}z}{1 - z}\right) \Rightarrow \dfrac{\overline{w} - w\overline{z}}{1 - \overline{z}} = \dfrac{w - w\overline{z}}{1 - z}$

$\Rightarrow \overline{w} - \overline{w}z - w\overline{z} + wz\overline{z} = w - w\overline{z} - \overline{w}z + \overline{w}z\overline{z}$

$\Rightarrow w - \overline{w} = (w - \overline{w})|z|^2$

$\Rightarrow |z|^2 = 1 \quad (\because w = \alpha + i\beta \text{ and } \beta \ne 0)$

$\Rightarrow |z| = 1$ also given $z \ne 1$

$\therefore$ The required set is $\{z : |z| = 1, z \ne 1\}$

**6.** **(d)** $\because |z| = |\omega|$ and $\arg z = \pi - \arg \omega$

Let $\omega = re^{i\theta}$ then $z = re^{i(\pi - \theta)}$

$\Rightarrow z = re^{i\pi} \cdot e^{i\theta)}$

$\qquad = (re^{-i\theta})(\cos\pi + i\sin\pi) = \overline{\omega}\,(-1) = -\overline{\omega}$

**7.** **(d)** $\left|\dfrac{z_1}{|z_1|} + \dfrac{z_2}{|z_2|}\right| \le \left|\dfrac{z_1}{|z_1|}\right| + \left|\dfrac{z_2}{|z_2|}\right| = \dfrac{|z_1|}{|z_1|} + \dfrac{|z_2|}{|z_2|} = 2$

$\therefore (|z_1| + |z_2|)\left|\dfrac{z_1}{|z_1|} + \dfrac{z_2}{|z_2|}\right| \le 2(|z_1| + |z_2|).$

**8.** **(a)** $\log_{1/2} \dfrac{|z|^2 + 2|z| + 4}{2|z|^2 + 1} < 0$

$\Rightarrow \dfrac{|z|^2 + 2|z| + 4}{2|z|^2 + 1} > 1 \quad$ [Since base < 1]

or, $|z|^2 + 2|z| + 4 > 2|z|^2 + 1$

or, $|z|^2 - 2|z| - 3 < 0$ or, $(|z| + 1)(|z| - 3) < 0$

$\Rightarrow |z| < 3$

**9.** **(b, c, d)** Given $|z - 1| < |z + 3|$

$\Rightarrow |z - 1|^2 < |z + 3|^2$

$\Rightarrow |z|^2 + 1 - 2\mathrm{Re}(z) < |z|^2 + 9 + 2\mathrm{Re}(3z)$

$\Rightarrow 2\mathrm{Re}(4z) > -8$

$\therefore 4z + 4\overline{z} > -8$

or $z + \overline{z} > -2$

and $\omega = 2z + 3 - i \qquad\qquad$ ...(i)

$\therefore \omega + \overline{\omega} = 2z + 3 - i + 2\overline{z} + 3 + i = 2(z + \overline{z}) + 6$ ...(ii)

or $\omega + \overline{\omega} > 2$

(a) $|\omega - 5 - i| < |\omega + 3 + i|$

$\Rightarrow |2z + 3 - i - 5 - i| < |2z + 3 - i + 3 + i|$

$\Rightarrow |2z - 2 - 2i| < |2z + 6|$

$\Rightarrow |z - 1 - i| < |z + 3|$

which is false.

(b) $|\omega - 5| < |\omega + 3|$

$\Rightarrow |2z + 3 - i - 5| < |2z + 3 - i + 3|$

$\Rightarrow |z - 1 - i/2| < |z + 3 - i/2|$

or $|z - 1| < |z + 3|$ which is true.

(c) $\text{Im}(i\omega) > 1$

$\Rightarrow \dfrac{i\omega - i\overline{\omega}}{2i} > 1 \Rightarrow \dfrac{i\omega + i\overline{\omega}}{2i} > 1$

$\Rightarrow \omega + \overline{\omega} > 2$ [which is true from eq. (ii)]

(d) $|\arg(\omega - 1)| < \pi/2$

$|\arg(2z + 2 - i| < \pi/2$

$\left| \tan^{-1}\left( \dfrac{\text{Im}(2z + 2 - i)}{\text{Re}(2z + 2 - i)} \right) \right| < \pi/2$

$\therefore \ \text{Re}(2z + 2 - i) > 0$

$\Rightarrow \dfrac{(2z + 2 - i) + (2\overline{z} + 2 + i)}{2} > 0$

$\Rightarrow z + \overline{z} > -2$ [which is true from eq. (i) ].

**10.** **(a,b)** The locus of $|z + 2| + |z - 2| = 8$ is an ellipse having focii at $(2, 0)$ and $(-2, 0)$ and length of major axis is 8 units.

i.e. $ae = 2$ and $2a = 8$ $\quad \therefore \quad e = \dfrac{1}{2}, a = 4$

Again, the second equation represents a straight line segment such that its locus comprise of all points inside the segement from $(-6, 0)$ to $(6, 0)$ as shown. Hence, it will intersect at two points, i.e., $(-4, 0)$ and $(4, 0)$.

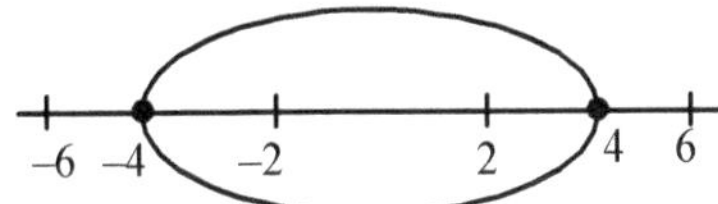

**11.** **(a, d)** Let $z_1 = a + ib$, $a > 0$ and $b \in R$; $z_2 = c + id$, $d < 0, c \in R$

then $|z_1| = |z_2| \Rightarrow a^2 + b^2 = c^2 + d^2$

$\Rightarrow a^2 - c^2 = d^2 - b^2 \qquad ....(1)$

Now, $\dfrac{z_1 + z_2}{z_1 - z_2} = \dfrac{(a + c) + i(b + d)}{(a - c) + i(b - d)}$

$= \dfrac{[(a^2 - c^2) + (b^2 - d^2)] + i[(a - c)(b + d) - (a + c)(b - d)]}{(a - c)^2 + (b - d)^2}$

$= \dfrac{i[(a - c)(b + d) - (a + c)(b - d)]}{(a - c)^2 + (b - d)^2}$ [Using (1)]

$=$ purely imaginary number or zero in case $a + c = b + d = 0$.

$\therefore$ (a) and (d) hold.

**12.** **(a,b,c,d)** $\sqrt{20i - 21} = \pm(2 + 5i)$ and $\sqrt{21 + 20i} = \pm(5 + 2i)$

$\therefore z = 7 + 7i \Rightarrow \arg z = \dfrac{\pi}{4}$ or $z = -3 + 3i \Rightarrow \arg z = \dfrac{3\pi}{4}$

or $z = -7 - 7i \Rightarrow \arg z = -\dfrac{3\pi}{4}$ or $z = 3 - 3i \Rightarrow \arg z = -\dfrac{\pi}{4}$

**13.** **(d)** $\because |z + iw| \le |z| + iw| = |z| + |i||w| \le 2$

$\therefore |z + iw| = 2 \quad \Rightarrow \quad |z| = |w| = 1.$

**14.** **(d)** Let $z = x + iy$ and $w = \alpha + i\beta$

Now $|z + iw| = 2 \Rightarrow (z + iw)(\overline{z} - i\overline{w}) = 4$

$\Rightarrow |z|^2 + |w|^2 + iw\overline{z} - i\overline{w}z = 4 \Rightarrow iw\overline{z} - i\overline{w}z = 2 ...(1)$

and $|z - i\overline{w}| = 2 \Rightarrow (z - i\overline{w})(\overline{z} + iw) = 4$

$\Rightarrow |z|^2 + |w|^2 + iwz - i\overline{w}\,\overline{z} = 4 \Rightarrow iwz - i\overline{w}\,\overline{z} = 2 ..(2)$

Add (1) and (2), $i(w - \overline{w})(z + \overline{z}) = 4 \Rightarrow i(2i\beta)$

$(2x) = 4 \Rightarrow \beta x = -1 \qquad\qquad ....(3)$

Subtract (1) from (2),

$\Rightarrow i(w + \overline{w})(z - \overline{z}) = 0 \Rightarrow \alpha y = 0 \qquad ....(4)$

From (4), either $\alpha = 0$ or $y = 0$.

If $y = 0$, then $x^2 + y^2 = 1 \Rightarrow x = \pm 1 \Rightarrow z = 1 \text{ or } -1$

If $\alpha = 0$, then $\alpha^2 + \beta^2 = 1 \Rightarrow \beta = \pm 1 \Rightarrow w = \pm i$.

So, $I_m(z) = \text{Re}(w) = 0$

**15.** **(b)** As $z = \pm 1$, so two values of $z$ can be obtained.

**16.** $A \to p,t$; $B \to q,r,s$; $C \to s,t$

(A) $|z + 2 + i| \le 1 \to |z - 1 + 3 + i| \le 1$

or $|w + 3 + i| \le 1$ where $w = z - 1$

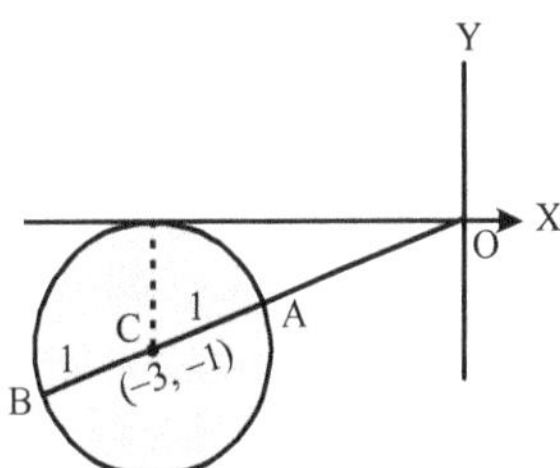

Clearly least value of

$|w| = |z - 1| = OA = OC - CA = \sqrt{10} - 1$

$\therefore L = \sqrt{10} - 1$

and greatest value of

$|w| = |z - 1| = OB = OC + CB = \sqrt{10} + 1$

$\therefore G = \sqrt{10} + 1 \Rightarrow LG = 9, G - L = 2$ **(p, t)**

(B) $1 \le |z - 1| \le 3$

$\Rightarrow 1 \le |(z + 2i) - 2i - 1| \le 3$

$\Rightarrow 1 \le |w - 2i - 1| \le 3$ (where $w = z + 2i$)

$PA = PB = 3$

Greatest value of $|w| = OA = OP + PA$

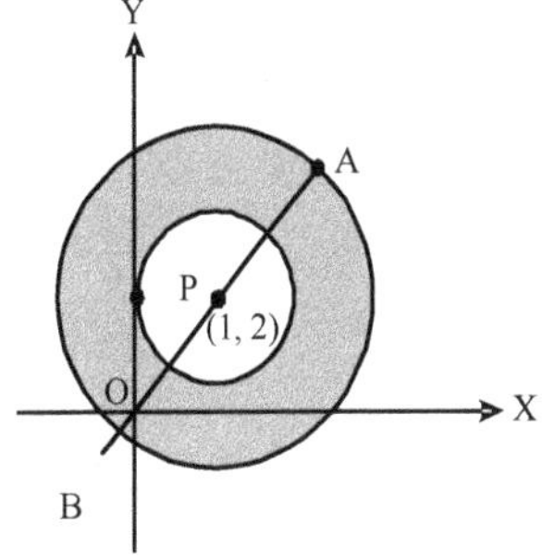

$\therefore \quad G = \sqrt{5} + 3$

and least value of $|w| = OB = BP - OP$

$\therefore \quad L = 3 - \sqrt{5} \quad \Rightarrow \quad L + G = 6, LG = 4$ **(q,s)**

and $\sqrt{2G} = \sqrt{5} + 1$

and $\sqrt{2L} = \sqrt{5} - 1$

$\therefore \sqrt{2G} - \sqrt{2L} = 2$

or $(\sqrt{2G} - \sqrt{2L})^2 = 4$ **(r)**

(C) $|z + i| \le 1 \Rightarrow |(z - 2) + (2 + i)| \le 1$
or $|w + 2 + i| \le 1$ (where $w = z - 2$)
Greatest value of $|w| = OB = OC + CB$

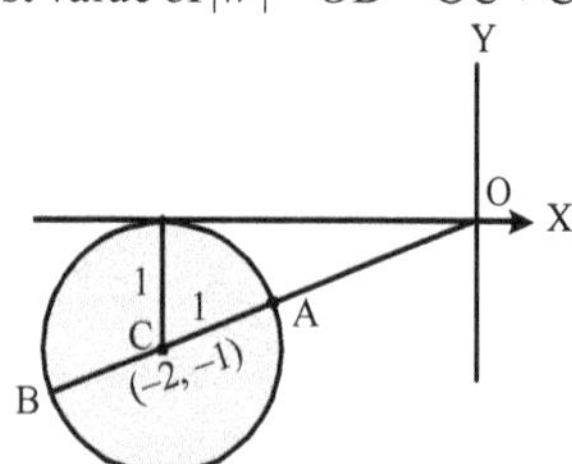

$\therefore G = \sqrt{5} + 1$

and least value of $|w| = OA = OC - CA = \sqrt{5} - 1$

$\therefore \quad L = \sqrt{5} - 1$

Then $LG = 4$, $G - L = 2$ **(s,t)**

**17. A→s; B→q,t; C→s; D→p**

(A) $\angle BOD = \angle COD = A$

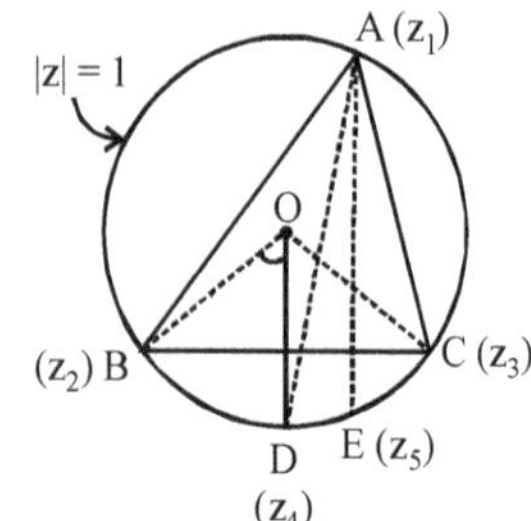

$\therefore \dfrac{z_4 - 0}{z_2 - 0} = e^{iA}$ and $\dfrac{z_3 - 0}{z_4 - 0} = e^{iA}$

$\therefore z_4^2 = z_2 z_3 \Rightarrow \dfrac{z_2 z_3}{z_4^2} = 1$

$\Rightarrow \arg\left(\dfrac{z_2 z_3}{z_4}\right) = 0$ **(s)**

(B) Clearly OD is perpendicular to BC,

$\arg\left(\dfrac{z_4}{z_2 - z_3}\right) = \pm \dfrac{\pi}{2}$ **(q,t)**

(C) $\angle COE = 2\angle CAE = 2\left(\dfrac{\pi}{2} - C\right)$

$\therefore \dfrac{z_3}{z_5} = e^{i(\pi - 2C)} = e^{i2C}$

Also, $\angle AOB = 2C \Rightarrow \dfrac{z_2}{z_1} = e^{i2C}$

$\therefore z_1 z_3 = z_2 z_5 \Rightarrow \dfrac{z_1 z_3}{z_2 z_5} = 1$

$\Rightarrow \arg\left(\dfrac{z_1 z_3}{z_2 z_5}\right) = 0$ **(s)**

(D) $\angle DOE = 2\angle DAE = 2\left\{\dfrac{A}{2} - \left(\dfrac{\pi}{2} - C\right)\right\} = A - \pi + 2C$

$\therefore \dfrac{z_5}{z_4} = e^{i(A - \pi + 2C)} = e^{iA} \cdot e^{-i\pi} \cdot e^{2C} = \dfrac{z_4}{z_2}(-1)\dfrac{z_2}{z_1}$

$\Rightarrow z_1 z_5 = -z_4^2 \Rightarrow \dfrac{z_4^2}{z_1 z_5} = -1 \Rightarrow \arg\left(\dfrac{z_4^2}{z_1 z_5}\right) = \pi$ **(p)**

**18. (a)** $|iz + z_0| = |i(z - i) - 1 + 5 + 3i| = |i(z - i) + 4 + 3i| \le |i|$
$|z - i| + |4 + 3i| = 7$

**19. (a)** Suppose by contradiction

$|z + 1| < \dfrac{1}{\sqrt{2}}$ or $|1 + z^2| < 1$.

Let $z = a + ib$, $z^2 = a^2 - b^2 + 2iab$

$|z + 1| < \dfrac{1}{\sqrt{2}} \Rightarrow (1 + a)^2 + b^2 < \dfrac{1}{2}$

$\Rightarrow 2(a^2 + b^2) + 4a + 1 < 0$ .........(i)

$|z^2 + 1| < 1 \Rightarrow (1 + a^2 - b^2)^2 + 4a^2 b^2 < 1$

$\Rightarrow (a^2 + b^2)^2 + 2(a^2 - b^2) < 0$ .........(ii)

Adding (i) and (ii) gives
$(a^2 + b^2)^2 + (2a + 1)^2 < 0$, which is impossible for $a, b \in R$

**20. (1)**

$|z_1| = |z_2| = z_3|$ (given)

Now, $|z_1| = 1 \Rightarrow |z_1|^2 = 1 \Rightarrow z_1 \bar{z}_1 = 1$

Similarly $z_2 \bar{z}_2 = 1$, $z_3 \bar{z}_3 = 1$

Now, $\left|\dfrac{1}{z_1} + \dfrac{1}{z_2} + \dfrac{1}{z_3}\right| = 1 \Rightarrow |\bar{z}_1 + \bar{z}_2 + \bar{z}_3| = 1$

$\Rightarrow |\overline{z_1 + z_2 + z_3}| = 1$

$\Rightarrow |z_1 + z_2 + z_3| = 1$

**21. (5)** $\sin\dfrac{\pi}{5} + i\left(1 - \cos\dfrac{\pi}{5}\right) = 2\sin\dfrac{\pi}{10}\cos\dfrac{\pi}{10} + i \cdot 2\sin^2\dfrac{\pi}{10}$

$= 2\sin\dfrac{\pi}{10}\left(\cos\dfrac{\pi}{10} + i\sin\dfrac{\pi}{10}\right)$

For amplitude, $\tan\theta = \dfrac{\sin\dfrac{\pi}{10}}{\cos\dfrac{\pi}{10}} = \tan\dfrac{\pi}{10} \Rightarrow \theta = \dfrac{\pi}{10}$

Thus, $p = 5$.

**22. (1)**

We have, $|z_1 + z_2| \le |z_1| + |z_2| \Rightarrow |z_1| + |z_2| \ge |z_1 + z_2|$
$\Rightarrow |z| + |z - 1| = |z| + |1 - z| \ge |z + (1 - z)| = 1$
$[\because |z - 1| = |1 - z|]$
$\therefore |z| + |z - 1| \ge 1$
$\Rightarrow$ Minimum value of $|z| + |z - 1|$ is $1$.

**23. (9)**
$|iz + (3 - 4i)| \le |iz| + |3 - 4i| = |z| + 5 < 4 + 5 = 9$

**24. (8)**

$|z_1| \le 13$

$|z_2 - (-3 + 4i)| \le 5$

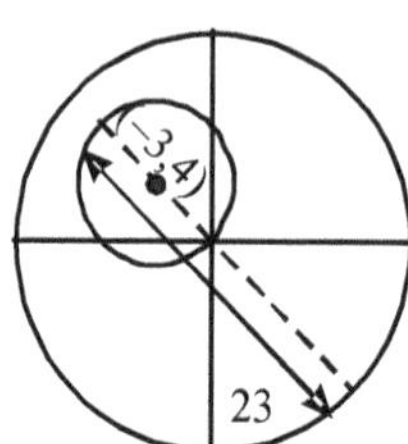

From diagram maximum value of $|z_1 - z_2| = 23$
Thus, $p = 8$.

**1.** **(c)** According to given condition on $z$. $|z| = \dfrac{1}{2}$ ...(1)

Let $\omega = -1 + 4z \Rightarrow z = \dfrac{\omega + 1}{4}$

From (1), $\left|\dfrac{\omega + 1}{4}\right| = \dfrac{1}{2} \Rightarrow |\omega + 1| = 2.$

$\therefore$ $\omega$ lies on a circle of radius 2.

**2.** **(c)** $AP = \dfrac{d}{r} AO. e^{i\pi/2}$

$z' - z_1 = \dfrac{d}{r}(-z_1 i)$ ..........(1)

$BP = \dfrac{d}{r} BO. e^{-i\pi/2}$

$z' - z_2 = \dfrac{d}{r} z_2 i$ .........(2)

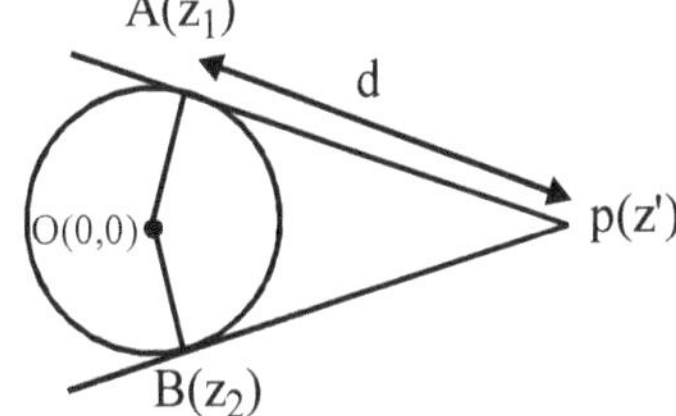


Now from eq. (1) and (2), we get

$\dfrac{z' - z_1}{z' - z_2} = -\dfrac{z_1}{z_2} \Rightarrow z' = \dfrac{2z_1 z_2}{z_1 + z_2}$

**3.** **(b).** Point on $C_1 : |z - 3 - 4i| = 5$
where $|z|$ is maximum is $P \equiv 6 + 8i$

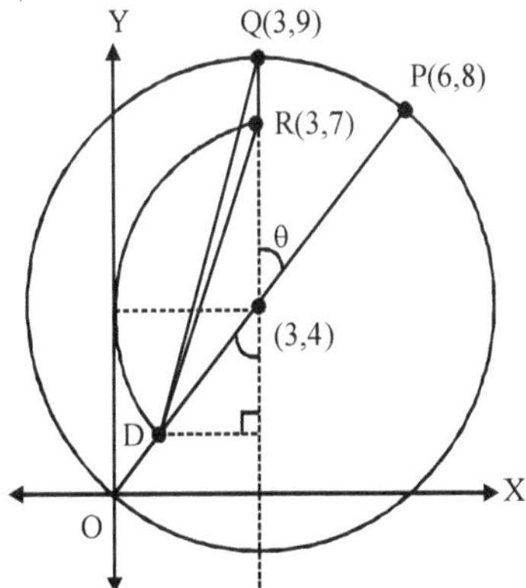


Let complex number coresponding to point Q be $z_2$
Taking rotation of $6 + 8i$ about $3 + 4i$, we get

$\dfrac{z_2 - (3 + 4i)}{6 + 8i - (3 + 4i)} = e^{i \tan^{-1}\left(\frac{3}{4}\right)}$

$z_2 = (3 + 4i) + (3 + 4i)\left(\cos\left(\tan^{-1}\dfrac{3}{4}\right)\right) + i\sin\left(\tan^{-1}\dfrac{3}{4}\right)$

$= 3 + 4i + (3 + 4i)\left(\dfrac{4}{5} + i\dfrac{3}{5}\right)$

$= 3 + 4i + \dfrac{1}{5}(3 + 4i)(4 + 3i) = 3 + 9i$

$\therefore$ Complex number corresponding to R, $z_3 = 3 + 7i$.

**4.** **(c)** $\dfrac{z_1 - z_3}{z_2 - z_3} = \dfrac{1 - i\sqrt{3}}{2}$

$\Rightarrow \arg\left(\dfrac{z_1 - z_3}{z_2 - z_3}\right) = \arg\left(\dfrac{1 - i\sqrt{3}}{2}\right)$

$= \arg(\cos(-\pi/3) + i\sin(-\pi/3)$

$\Rightarrow$ Angle between $z_1 - z_3$ and $z_2 - z_3$ is 60°.

and $\left|\dfrac{z_1 - z_3}{z_2 - z_3}\right| = \left|\dfrac{1 - i\sqrt{3}}{2}\right|$

$\Rightarrow \left|\dfrac{z_1 - z_3}{z_2 - z_3}\right| = 1 \Rightarrow z_1 - z_3 = z_2 - z_3$

$\Rightarrow$ The $\Delta$ with vertices $z_1$, $z_2$ and $z_3$ is isosceles with vertical angle 60°. Hence rest of the two angles should also be 60° each.

$\Rightarrow$ Req. $\Delta$ is an equilateral $\Delta$.

**5.** **(a)** Here we observe that.
$AB = AC = AD = 2$

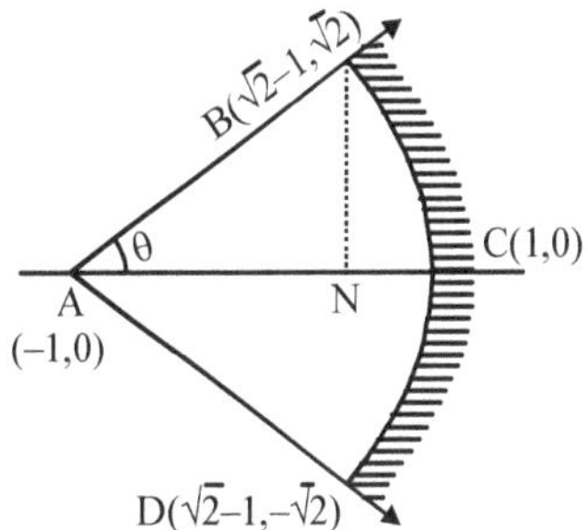


$\therefore$ BCD is an arc of a circle with centre at A and radius 2. Shaded region is outer (exterior) part of this sector ABCDA.

$\therefore$ For any point z on arc BCD, we should have
$$|z - (-1)| = 2$$
and for shaded region, $|z + 1| > 2$ ....(i)

Also $\tan\theta = \dfrac{BN}{AN} = \dfrac{\sqrt{2}}{(\sqrt{2} - 1) - (-1)} = \dfrac{\sqrt{2}}{\sqrt{2}} = 1$

$\Rightarrow$ $\theta = \pi/4$ and by symmetry, $\arg(z + 1)$ varies from $-\pi/4$ to $\pi/4$ as it moves from D to B on arc DCB.
For shaded region we also have
$$-\pi/4 < \arg(z + 1) < \pi/4$$
or $\arg(z + 1), < \pi/4$ ....(ii)
Adding (i) and (ii), (a) is the correct option.

**6.** **(c)** $\log_{0.3}|z - 1| > \log_{0.3}|z - i| \Rightarrow |z - 1| < |z - i|$
$[\because \text{base} < 1]$

$\Rightarrow |z - 1|^2 < |z - i|^2$

$\Rightarrow (z - 1)(\bar{z} - 1) < (z - i)(\bar{z} + i)$

$\Rightarrow z\bar{z} - z - \bar{z} + 1 < z\bar{z} + iz - i\bar{z} + 1$

$\Rightarrow (1 + i)z + (1 - i)\bar{z} > 0$

$\Rightarrow (z + \bar{z}) + i(z - \bar{z}) > 0 \Rightarrow \left(\dfrac{z + \bar{z}}{2}\right) - \left(\dfrac{z - \bar{z}}{2i}\right) > 0$

$\Rightarrow x - y > 0$

**7.** **(c)** Let $z = x + iy$, then $z^2 + \overline{z}^2 = 2 \Rightarrow x^2 - y^2 = 1$, which represents a hyperbola.

**8.** **(d)** Since each of $z_0^2, \overline{z}_0^2, |z_0|^2$ and $a^2$ is a real number the given equation represents is a straight line.

**9.** **(b, d)**

Since $\dfrac{PA}{PB} = 3$, P lies on a circle on CD as diameter where C and D are points which divide AB internally and externally in the ratio $3 : 1$.

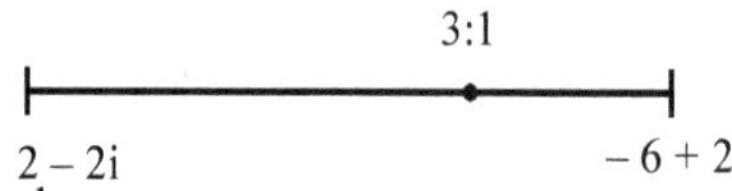


Complex number

C is $\dfrac{3(-6+2i) + 1(2-2i)}{4} = -4 + i$

D is $\dfrac{3(-6+2i) + 1(2-2i)}{2} = -10 + 4i$

C is $(-4, 1)$, D is $(-10, 4)$

Centre $= \left(-7, \dfrac{5}{2}\right)$, Radius $= \dfrac{3}{2}\sqrt{5}$

**10.** **(a, b, c, d)** Let the four points represented by $z_1, z_2, z_3$ and $z_4$ be $A, B, C$ and $D$ respectively. Since $ABCD$ is a square, mid point of $AC$ = mid point of $BD$

$\Rightarrow \dfrac{1}{2}(z_1 + z_3) = \dfrac{1}{2}(z_2 + z_4)$ or $z_1 + z_3 = z_2 + z_4$

Also $AB = BC = CD = DA$

$\Rightarrow |z_1 - z_2| = |z_2 - z_3| = |z_3 - z_4| = |z_4 - z_1|$

Since diagonals of the square $ABCD$ are equal

$\therefore AC = BD$

or $|z_1 - z_3| = |z_2 - z_4|$

Also, since $AC \perp BD$,

$(z_1 - z_3)/z_2 - z_4)$ is purely imaginary.

**11.** **(a, d)** $z_1 + z_2 + z_3 + z_4 = 0 \Rightarrow \dfrac{z_1 + z_2}{2} = -\dfrac{z_3 + z_4}{2}$ ....(1)

$\dfrac{z_1 + z_2}{2}$ represents mid point E of AB

and $\dfrac{z_3 + z_4}{2}$ represents mid point F of DC.

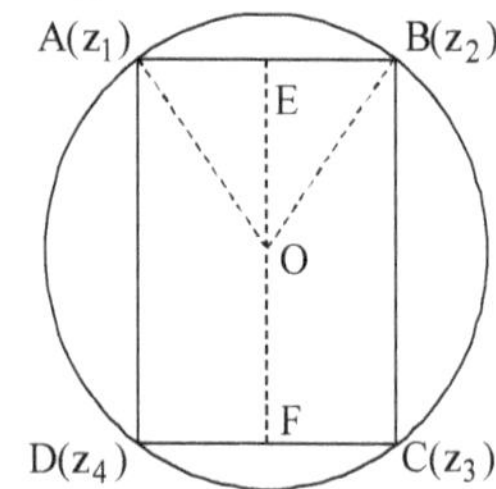


$\therefore$ From (1), OE and OF are in opposite direction and OE = OF

$\therefore$ $\triangle$ OAB is isosceles, since OA = OB = 1 [A, B lie on $|z| = 1$]

Hence OE is perpendicular to AB. Also OF perpendicular to CD.

Hence AB is parallel to CD. Similarly DA is paralled to BC.

$\therefore$ ABCD is a parallelogram inscribed in a circle and hence a rectangle.

**12.** **(b, c, d)** $\operatorname{Re}\left(\dfrac{z+1}{z+i}\right) = 0 \Rightarrow \dfrac{\dfrac{z+1}{z+i} + \dfrac{\overline{z}+1}{z+\overline{i}}}{2} = 0$

$\Rightarrow \dfrac{z+1}{z+i} + \dfrac{\overline{z}+1}{\overline{z}-1} = 0$

$(z+1)(\overline{z} - i) + (\overline{z} + 1)(z + i) = 0$

$\Rightarrow 2z\overline{z} + (1-i)z + (1+i)\overline{z} = 0$

$z\overline{z} + \left(\dfrac{1-i}{2}\right)z + \left(\dfrac{1+i}{2}\right)\overline{z} = 0$, which is a circle whose

radius $= \sqrt{\left(\dfrac{1+i}{2}\right)^2} = \sqrt{\dfrac{i}{2}}$ and passing through $z = 0$

($\because$ no constant term).

**13.** **(c),** **14. (c),** **15. (b).**

$\because f(\alpha) = \dfrac{1}{\alpha - i} \times \dfrac{\alpha + i}{\alpha + i} = \dfrac{\alpha}{\alpha^2 + 1} + i\dfrac{1}{\alpha^2 + 1}$

$\Rightarrow$ Real part x $= \dfrac{\alpha}{\alpha^2 + 1}$, y $= \dfrac{1}{\alpha^2 + 1}$

$\Rightarrow \dfrac{x}{y} = \alpha$, then $x = \dfrac{(x/y)}{(x/y)^2 + 1} \Rightarrow x^2 + y^2 = y$

$\Rightarrow (x-0)^2 + \left(y - \dfrac{1}{2}\right)^2 = \left(\dfrac{1}{2}\right)^2$

$\Rightarrow f(\alpha)$ lies on the circle.

$\therefore \max |f(\alpha) - f(\beta)| = $ diameter of the circle $= 2 \cdot \dfrac{1}{2} = 1$

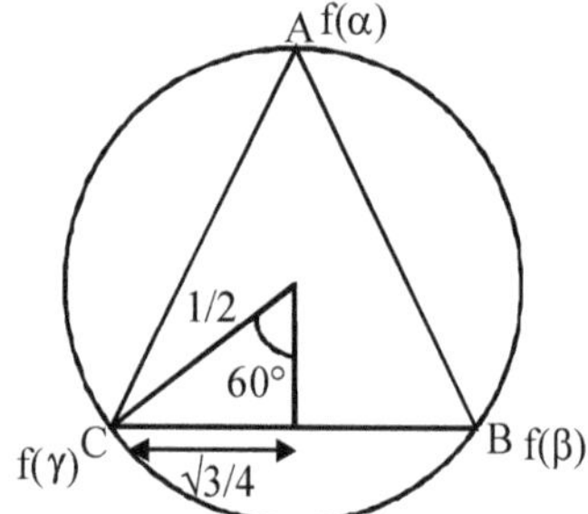


If $f(\alpha), f(\beta), f(\gamma)$, lies on circle, then $\triangle$ ABC for maximum area will be an equilateral triangle

$\Rightarrow R = \dfrac{abc}{4\Delta} \Rightarrow \dfrac{1}{2} = \dfrac{(\sqrt{3}/2)^3}{4\Delta} \Rightarrow \Delta = \dfrac{3\sqrt{3}}{16}$ (units)$^2$

If $f(\alpha), f(\beta), f(\gamma), f(\delta)$ forms a square then its area

$= \dfrac{1}{2}$ (diagonal)$^2$

$= \dfrac{1}{2}(1)^2 = \dfrac{1}{2}$ (units)$^2$ and side $= \dfrac{1}{\sqrt{2}}$ unit

**16.** **A→q, s; B→p, t; C→r**

(A) Since triangle is equilateral then

$z_0 = $ Nine point centre = centroid $= \dfrac{z_1 + z_2 + z_3}{3}$

$\therefore z_1 + z_2 + z_3 = 3z_0$

$AB = BC = CA = a$ (say)

$\angle B = \pi/3$, then by rotation theorem

$\therefore \dfrac{z_1 - z_2}{z_3 - z_2} = \dfrac{a}{a}e^{i\pi/3}$ ...(i)

$\angle A = \pi/3,$ then by rotation theorem

$\therefore \dfrac{z_3 - z_1}{z_2 - z_1} = \dfrac{a}{a} e^{i\pi/3}$ ...(ii)

From eq. (i) and eq. (ii),

$\dfrac{z_1 - z_2}{z_3 - z_2} = \dfrac{z_3 - z_1}{z_2 - z_1}$

$\Rightarrow z_1^2 + z_2^2 + z_3^2 = z_1 z_2 + z_2 z_3 + z_3 z_1$ **(s)** ...(iii)

and $(z_1 + z_2 + z_3)^2 = (3z_0)^2$

$\Rightarrow z_1^2 + z_2^2 + z_3^2 + 2(z_1 z_2 + z_2 z_3 + z_3 z_1) = 9z_0^2$

$\Rightarrow z_1^2 + z_2^2 + z_3^2 + 2(z_1^2 + z_2^2 + z_3^2) = 9z_0^2$ [from eq. (iii)]

or $3(z_1^2 + z_2^2 + z_3^2) = 9z_0^2$

or $z_1^2 + z_2^2 + z_3^2 = 3z_0^2$ **(q)**

(B) $\because \angle C = \pi/2,$ then by rotation theorem

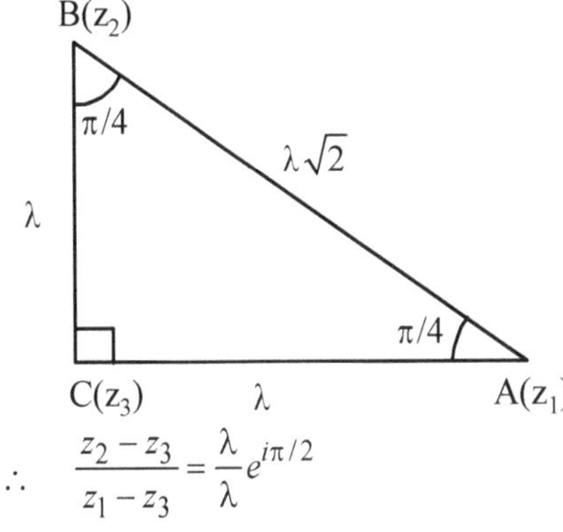


$\therefore \dfrac{z_2 - z_3}{z_1 - z_3} = \dfrac{\lambda}{\lambda} e^{i\pi/2}$

or $\dfrac{z_2 - z_3}{z_1 - z_3} = e^{i\pi/2}$ **(t)**

Also, $\because \angle B = \pi/4$ then by rotation theorem

$\dfrac{z_1 - z_2}{z_3 - z_2} = \dfrac{\lambda\sqrt{2}}{\lambda} e^{i\pi/4}$

or $\dfrac{z_1 - z_2}{z_3 - z_2} = \sqrt{2}\, e^{i\pi/4}$ ...(i)

and $\angle A = \pi/4,$ then by rotation theorem

$\dfrac{z_3 - z_1}{z_2 - z_1} = \dfrac{\lambda}{\lambda\sqrt{2}} e^{i\pi/4}$

or $\dfrac{z_3 - z_1}{z_2 - z_1} = \dfrac{1}{\sqrt{2}} . e^{i\pi/4}$ ...(ii)

Dividing eq. (i) by eq. (ii), we get

$(z_1 - z_2)^2 = 2(z_1 - z_3)(z_3 - z_2)$ **(p)**

(C) Applying sine rule in $\Delta\, ABC,$ then

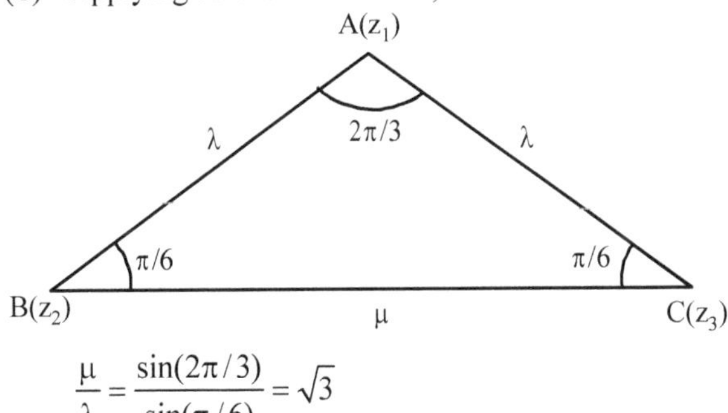


$\dfrac{\mu}{\lambda} = \dfrac{\sin(2\pi/3)}{\sin(\pi/6)} = \sqrt{3}$

$\therefore \quad \mu = \lambda\sqrt{3}$

$\because \quad \angle B = \pi/6,$ applying rotation theorem

$\dfrac{z_1 - z_2}{z_3 - z_2} = \dfrac{\lambda}{\lambda\sqrt{3}} e^{i\pi/6}$ ...(i)

and $\angle C = \pi/6,$ applying rotation theorem

$\dfrac{z_2 - z_3}{z_1 - z_3} = \dfrac{\lambda\sqrt{3}}{\lambda} e^{i\pi/6}$ ...(ii)

Dividing eq. (ii) by eq. (i) then

$\dfrac{(z_2 - z_3)^2}{(z_1 - z_2)(z_3 - z_1)} = 3$

or $(z_2 - z_3)^2 = 3(z_1 - z_2)(z_3 - z_1)$ **(r)**

**17.** **A→q, B→p, C→r,**

(A) $|z - \alpha|^2 = 4\,|z - \overline{\alpha}|^2$

$\Rightarrow z\overline{z} - \alpha\overline{z} - z\overline{\alpha} + \alpha\overline{\alpha} = 4(z\overline{z} - \alpha z - \overline{\alpha}\overline{z} + \alpha\overline{\alpha})$

$\Rightarrow 3z\overline{z} + (\alpha - 4\overline{\alpha})\overline{z} + (\overline{\alpha} - 4\alpha)z + 3\alpha\overline{\alpha} = 0,$

or $z\overline{z} + \dfrac{\alpha - 4\overline{\alpha}}{3}\overline{z} + \dfrac{\overline{\alpha} - 4\alpha}{3} z + \alpha\overline{\alpha} = 0$

which is a circle of radius

$= \sqrt{\left|\dfrac{\alpha - 4\overline{\alpha}}{3}\right|^2 - \alpha\overline{\alpha}} = \sqrt{-\dfrac{4}{9}(\alpha - \overline{\alpha})^2} = \dfrac{2}{3}|\alpha - \overline{\alpha}|$ **(q)**

(B) z lies on a circle of radius 1 and centre at $(1, 0)$

$\angle OPA = \pm\dfrac{\pi}{2} \Rightarrow \dfrac{2 - z}{0 - z} = \dfrac{|2 - z|}{|z|} e^{\pm i\frac{\pi}{2}}$

$\Rightarrow \dfrac{z - 2}{z} = \dfrac{AP}{OP}(\pm i) = \pm i \tan\alpha$

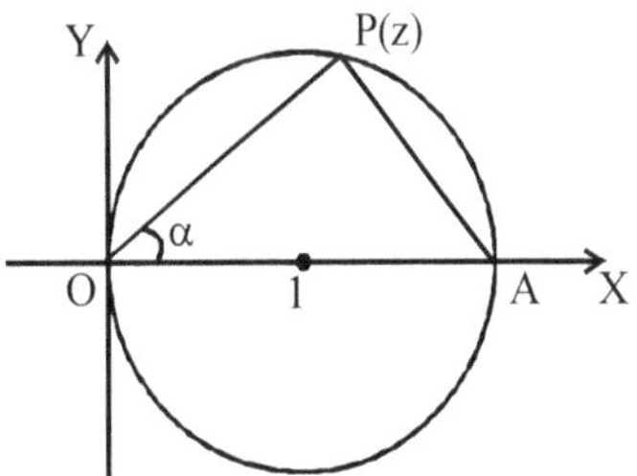


$\therefore \left|\dfrac{z - 2}{z}\right| = |\tan\alpha|$ **(p)**

(C) $z_1 + z_2 = -p$ and $z_1 z_2 = q$

Also, $\dfrac{z_2}{z_1} = \cos\alpha \pm i\sin\alpha \Rightarrow \dfrac{z_2 - z_1\cos\alpha}{z_1} = \pm i\sin\alpha$

or $z_2^2 - 2z_2 z_1 \cos\alpha + z_1^2 \cos^2\alpha = -z_1^2 \sin^2\alpha$

$\Rightarrow z_1^2 + z_2^2 = 2z_1 z_2 \cos\alpha$

or $(z_1 + z_2)^2 = 2z_1 z_2(1 + \cos\alpha) \Rightarrow \dfrac{p^2}{q} = 4\cos^2\dfrac{\alpha}{2}$ **(r)**

**18.** **(d)** $|z_1 - z_2|^2 = |z_1 + z_2|^2$

$\Rightarrow z_1 \bar{z}_2 + \bar{z}_1 z_2 \Rightarrow |z_1 - z_2|^2 = |z_1|^2 + |z_2|^2$

$\Rightarrow \Delta AOB$ is right angled at O.

$\Rightarrow$ orthocentre is the origin.

**19.** **(d)** $|z - 3| \le |z - 1|$

$\Rightarrow |z - 3|^2 \le |z - 1|^2$

$\Rightarrow (z - 3)(\bar{z} - 3) \le (z - 1)(\bar{z} - 1)$

$\Rightarrow 2z + 2\bar{z} \ge 8$

$\Rightarrow x + \bar{z} \ge 4$

$\Rightarrow 2x \ge 4 \qquad \begin{pmatrix} \because z = x + iy \\ \therefore z + \bar{z} = 2x \end{pmatrix}$

$\therefore \quad x \ge 2$

Similarly, $|z - 3| \le |z - 5|$

$\Rightarrow z + \bar{z} \le 8$

$\Rightarrow x \le 4$

$|z - i| \le |z + i|$

$\Rightarrow i(z - \bar{z}) \le 0$

$\Rightarrow y \ge 0 \qquad (\because z - \bar{z} = 2iy)$

and $|z - i| \le |z - 5i|$

$\Rightarrow i(z - \bar{z}) \ge -6 \Rightarrow y \le 3$

Now, combining all cases, we get

$2 \le x \le 4, 0 \le y \le 3$

The region is a rectangle of area

$= 2 \times 3 = 6$ sq. unit

**20.** **(5)** $x^2 + y^2 + (4 - 3i)(x + iy) + (4 + 3i)(x - iy) + 5 = 0$

or, $\quad x^2 + y^2 + 8x + 6y + 5 = 0$

$\therefore$ Radius $= \sqrt{4^2 + 3^2 - 5} = \sqrt{20} = 2\sqrt{5}$ unit

$\therefore P = 5$

**21.** **(0)** $z_1, z_2, 0$ are vertices of an equilateral triangle, so we have

$z_1^2 + z_2^2 + 0^2 = z_1 z_2 + z_2 . 0 + 0 . z_1$

$\Rightarrow z_1^2 + z_2^2 = z_1 z_2 \Rightarrow z_1^2 + z_2^2 - z_1 z_2 = 0$

**22.** **(4)** Let $\sqrt{-8 - 6i} = \pm(a + ib)$

$\Rightarrow -8 - 6i = a^2 - b^2 + 2iab$

$\Rightarrow a^2 - b^2 = -8 \qquad .....(1)$

$\quad 2ab = -6 \Rightarrow ab = -3 \qquad .....(2)$

$\quad (a^2 + b^2)^2 = (a^2 - b^2)^2 + 4a^2 b^2$

$= \quad (-8)^2 + (-6)^2 = 64 + 36 = 100$

$\Rightarrow a^2 + b^2 = 10 \qquad .....(3)$

From equation (2) and (3)

$a = 1, b = -3$

So, $\sqrt{-8 - 6i} = \pm(1 - 3i)$

$\therefore \quad a + b = 1 + 3 = 4$

**23.** **(2)** Let $\quad A = z = x + iy, \qquad B = iz = -y + ix,$

$C = z + iz = (x - y) + i(x + y)$

Now, area of $\Delta ABC = \dfrac{1}{2} \begin{vmatrix} x & y & 1 \\ -y & x & 1 \\ x - y & x + y & 1 \end{vmatrix}$

Operating $R_2 - R_1, R_3 - R_1,$ we get

$\Delta = \dfrac{1}{2} \begin{vmatrix} x & y & 1 \\ -y - x & x - y & 0 \\ -y & x & 0 \end{vmatrix}$

$= \dfrac{1}{2} |x(-y - x) + y(x - y)|$

$= \dfrac{1}{2} |-xy - x^2 + xy - y^2|$

$= \dfrac{1}{2} |-x^2 - y^2|$

$= \dfrac{1}{2} |x^2 + y^2| = \dfrac{1}{2} |z|^2$ Hence Proved.

Thus, P = 2.

**24.** **(2)** $\because BC = AC$ and $\angle C = \pi/2$, we have by rotation about $C$ in anti clockwise sense

$CB = CA \, e^{i \pi/2}$

$\Rightarrow z_2 - z_3 = (z_1 - z_3)^{i \pi/2}$

$\Rightarrow z_2 - z_3 = i(z_1 - z_3)$

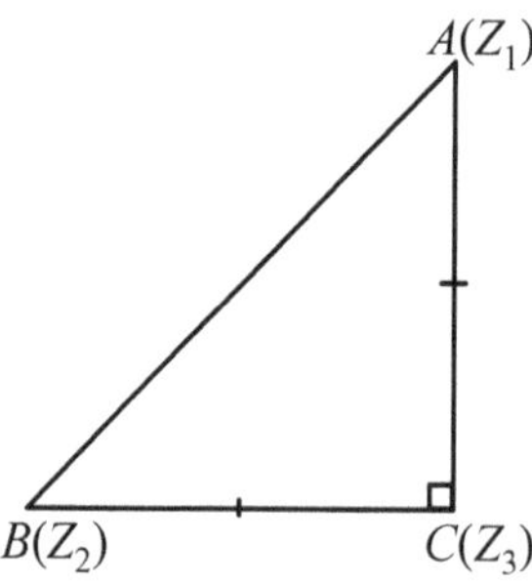


Squaring both sides, we get

$(z_2 - z_3)^2 = -(z_1 - z_3)^2$

$\Rightarrow z_2^2 + z_3^2 - 2z_2 z_3 = -z_1^2 - z_3^2 + 2z_1 z_3$

$\Rightarrow z_1^2 + z_2^2 - 2z_1 z_2 = 2z_1 z_3 + 2z_2 z_3 - 2z_3^2 - 2z_1 z_2$

$\Rightarrow (z_1 - z_2)^2 = 2[(z_1 z_3 - z_3^2) - (z_1 z_2 - z_2 z_3)]$

$\Rightarrow (z_1 - z_2)^2 = 2(z_1 - z_3)(z_3 - z_2)$

Thus, N = 2.

**1.** **(d)** Let $z = (1)^{1/n} = (\cos 2k\pi + i \sin 2k\pi)^{1/n}$

$z = \cos \dfrac{2k\pi}{n} + i \sin \dfrac{2k\pi}{n}, k = 0, 1, 2, ....., n-1.$

Let $z_1 = \cos\left(\dfrac{2k_1\pi}{n}\right) + i\sin\left(\dfrac{2k_1\pi}{n}\right)$

and $z_2 = \cos\left(\dfrac{2k_2\pi}{n}\right) + i\sin\dfrac{2k_2\pi}{n}$

be the two values of z. s.t. they subtend angle of $90°$ at origin.

$\dfrac{2k_1\pi}{n} - \dfrac{2k_2\pi}{n} = \dfrac{\pi}{2} \Rightarrow 4(k_1 - k_2) = \pm n$

As $k_1$ and $k_2$ are integers and $k_1 = k_2$.

$\therefore n = 4k, k \in I$

**2.** **(b)** Key Concept : (D' Moivre's thm)

$(\cos\theta + i\sin\theta)^n = \cos n\theta + i\sin n\theta$, n is any rational no.

$z = \left(\dfrac{\sqrt{3}}{2} + \dfrac{i}{2}\right)^5 + \left(\dfrac{\sqrt{3}}{2} - \dfrac{i}{2}\right)^5$

We have $\dfrac{\sqrt{3}}{2} + \dfrac{i}{2} = \cos \pi/6 + i\sin \pi/6$

and $\dfrac{\sqrt{3}}{2} - \dfrac{i}{2} = \cos \pi/6 - i\sin \pi/6$

$\therefore z = (\cos \pi/6 + i\sin \pi/6)^5 + (\cos \pi/6 - i\sin \pi/6)^5$

$= \cos 5\pi/6 + i\sin 5\pi/6 + \cos 5\pi/6 - i\sin 5\pi/6)$

$= 2\cos 5\pi/6 = -\sqrt{3}$

$\therefore \text{Re}(z) < 0$ and $\text{Im}(z) = 0$

**3.** **(c)** $E = 4 + 5(\omega)^{334} + 3(\omega)^{365} = 4 + 5\omega + 3\omega^2$

$= 1 + 2\omega + 3(1 + \omega + \omega^2) = 1 + (-1 + i\sqrt{3}) = i\sqrt{3}$

**4.** **(b)** $|a\omega^2 + b + c\omega|^2 = \dfrac{1}{2}\left((a-b)^2 + (b-c)^2 + (c-a)^2\right)$

For minimum $b - c = -2, a - b = 2$ and $c - a = 4$

$\Rightarrow |a\omega^2 + b + c\omega| = 2\sqrt{3}$

**5.** **(c)** We have , $1 + \omega + \omega^2 + ... + \omega^{n-1} = \dfrac{1-\omega^n}{1-\omega}$

But $\omega^n = \cos\left(\dfrac{n\pi}{n}\right) + i\sin\left(\dfrac{n\pi}{n}\right) = \cos\pi + i\sin\pi = -1$

and $1 - \omega = 2\sin^2\dfrac{\pi}{2n} - 2i\sin\dfrac{\pi}{2n}\cos\dfrac{\pi}{2n}$

$= -2i\sin\left(\dfrac{\pi}{2n}\right)\left[\cos\dfrac{\pi}{2n} + i\sin\dfrac{\pi}{2n}\right]$

Thus, $1 + \omega + \omega^2 + ... + \omega^{n-1}$

$= \dfrac{2[\cos(\pi/2n) - i\sin(\pi/2n)]}{-2i\sin(\pi/2n)} = 1 + i\cot(\pi/2n)$

**6.** **(b)** We have,

$abcd = \cos(2\alpha + 2\beta + 2\gamma + 2\delta) + i\sin(2\alpha + 2\beta + 2\gamma + 2\delta)$

$\therefore \sqrt{abcd} = [\cos(2\alpha + 2\beta + 2\gamma + 2\delta)$
$\qquad\qquad + i\sin(2\alpha + 2\beta + 2\gamma + 2\delta)]^{1/2}$

or $\sqrt{abcd} = \cos(\alpha + \beta + \gamma + \delta) + i\sin(\alpha + \beta + \gamma + \delta) ... (1)$

[De Moivre's Theorem]

$\therefore \dfrac{1}{\sqrt{abcd}} = \cos(\alpha + \beta + \gamma + \delta) - i\sin(\alpha + \beta + \gamma + \delta) .. (2)$

Adding (1) and (2), we obtain

$\sqrt{abcd} + \dfrac{1}{\sqrt{abcd}} = 2\cos(\alpha + \beta + \gamma + \delta)$

**7.** **(a)** We have, $x = \omega - \omega^2 - 2$ or $x + 2 = \omega - \omega^2$

Squaring, $x^2 + 4x + 4 = \omega^2 + \omega^4 - 2\omega^3$

$= \omega^2 + \omega^3\omega. -2\omega^3 = \omega^2 + \omega - 2 \quad [\omega^3 = 1]$

$= -1 - 2 = -3 \Rightarrow x^2 + 4x + 7 = 0$

Dividing $x^4 + 3x^3 + 2x^2 - 11x - 6$ by $x^2 + 4x + 7$, we get

$x^4 + 3x^3 + 2x^2 - 11x - 6 = (x^2 + 4x + 7)(x^2 - x - 1) + 1$
$\qquad\qquad = (0)(x^2 - x - 1) + 1 = 0 + 1 = 1$

**8.** **(d)** For $x \neq 1$, we have $1 + x + x^2 + ..... + x^n = \dfrac{x^{n+1} - 1}{x - 1}$

Differentiating w.r.t. x, we get

$0 + 1 + 2x + .... + nx^{n-1} = \dfrac{(x-1)(n+1)x^n - (x^{n+1} - 1).1}{(x-1)^2}$

$\Rightarrow 1 + 2x + .... + nx^{n-1} = \dfrac{(n+1)x^n}{x-1} - \dfrac{x^{n+1} - x}{(x-1)^2}$

Multiplying both sides by x, we get

$\Rightarrow x + 2x^2 + .... + nx^n = \dfrac{(n+1)x^{n+1}}{x-1} - \dfrac{x^{n+2} - x}{(x-1)^2}$

Differentiating w.r.t. x, we get

$1 + 4x + ...... + n^2x^{n-1} = \left(\dfrac{(n+1)^2 x^n}{x-1} - \dfrac{(n+1)x^{n+1}}{(x-1)^2}\right)$

$\qquad\qquad - \left(\dfrac{(n+2)x^{n+1} - 1}{(x-1)^2} - \dfrac{2(x^{n+2} - x)}{(x-1)^3}\right)$

$\therefore 1 + 4x + ...... + n^2x^{n-1}$

$= \dfrac{(n+1)^2 x^n}{x-1} - \dfrac{(2n+3)x^{n+1} - 1}{(x-1)^2} + \dfrac{2(x^{x+2} - x)}{(x-1)^3}$

Putting $x = \omega$, we get

$1 + 4\omega + \dots + n^2 \omega^{n-1}$

$= \dfrac{(n+1)^2}{\omega - 1} - \dfrac{(2n+3)\omega - 1}{(\omega - 1)^2} + \dfrac{2(\omega^2 - \omega)}{(\omega - 1)^3}$   $(\because \omega^n = 1)$

$= \dfrac{(n+1)^2(\omega - 1) - (2n+3)\omega + 1 + 2\omega}{(\omega - 1)^2}$

$= \dfrac{(n^2 + 2n + 1 - 2n - 3 + 2)\omega - n^2 - 2n - 1 + 1}{(\omega - 1)^2}$

$= \dfrac{n^2\omega - n^2 - 2n}{(\omega - 1)^2}$

**9.**   **(a, b)** $(n-1)(n-\omega)(n-\omega^2)$

$= (n-1)\{n^2 - (\omega + \omega^2)n + \omega^3\}$

$= (n-1)(n^2 + n + 1) = n^3 - 1$, etc.

$\therefore \text{Sum} = \displaystyle\sum_{n=1}^{n-1}(n^3 - 1) = \{1^3 + 2^3 + 3^3 + \dots + (n-1)^3\} - (n-1).$

**10.**   **(b,c)** $z^3 + (1+i)z^2 + (1+i)z + i = 0$

$\Rightarrow z^2(z+i) + z(z+i) + (z+i) = 0$

$\Rightarrow (z+i)(z^2 + z + 1) = 0$

$\Rightarrow (z+i)(z-\omega)(z-\omega^2) = 0$

$\therefore z = -i, \omega, \omega^2$

Now in $z^{1993} + z^{1994} + 1 = 0$, put $z = -i, \omega, \omega^2$

then $(-i)^{1993} + (-i)^{1994} + 1 = -i - 1 + 1 = -i \neq 0$,

$(\omega)^{1993} + \omega^{1994} + 1 = \omega + \omega^2 + 1 = 0$

and $(\omega^2)^{1993} + (\omega^2)^{1994} + 1 = \omega^2 + \omega + 1 = 0$

Hence $\omega$ and $\omega^2$ are common roots.

**11.**   **(a, b, c, d)** Let $a = \cos\alpha + i\sin\alpha$, $b = \cos\beta + i\sin\beta$ and

$c = \cos\gamma + i\sin\gamma$

We have

$a + b + c = (\cos\alpha + \cos\beta + \cos\gamma)$

$\qquad\qquad + i(\sin\alpha + \sin\beta + \sin\gamma) = 0 + i0 = 0$

Also $\dfrac{1}{a} + \dfrac{1}{b} + \dfrac{1}{c} = a^{-1} + b^{-1} + c^{-1}$

$= (\cos\alpha + \cos\beta + \cos\gamma) - i(\sin\alpha + \sin\beta + \sin\gamma)$

[Using De Moivre's theorem)

$= 0 - i.\,0 = 0$

$\Rightarrow bc + ca + ab = 0$

$\Rightarrow [\cos(\beta+\gamma) + i\sin(\beta+\gamma) + \cos(\gamma+\alpha) + i\sin(\gamma+\alpha)]$

$\qquad\qquad + [\cos(\alpha+\beta) + i\sin(\alpha+\beta)] = 0$

$\Rightarrow \cos(\beta+\gamma) + \cos(\gamma+\alpha) + \cos(\alpha+\beta) = 0$

and $\sin(\beta+\gamma) + \sin(\gamma+\alpha) + \sin(\alpha+\beta) = 0$

Also $a + b + c = 0$

$\Rightarrow (a + b + c)^2 = 0$

$\Rightarrow a^2 + b^2 + c^2 + 2(ab + bc + ca) = 0$

$\Rightarrow a^2 + b^2 + c^2 = 0$   $(\because ab + bc + ca = 0)$

$\Rightarrow [\cos(2\alpha) + i\sin(2\alpha)] + [\cos(2\beta) + i\sin(2\beta)]$

$\qquad + [\cos(2\gamma) + i\sin(2\alpha)] = 0$

$\qquad\qquad\qquad$ [Using De Moivre's theorem]

$\Rightarrow \cos(2\alpha) + \cos(2\beta) + \cos(2\gamma) = 0$

and $\sin(2\alpha) + \sin(2\beta) + \sin(2\gamma) = 0$

**12.**   **(a, b,c)** We have

$\alpha = \cos\dfrac{2\pi}{5} + i\sin\dfrac{2\pi}{5}$ and $1 + \alpha + \alpha^2 + \alpha^3 + \alpha^4 = 0$

$\therefore \left|1 + \alpha + \alpha^2 + \alpha^3\right| = \left|-\alpha^4\right| = |\alpha|^4 = 1$.

Also $\left|1 + \alpha + \alpha^2\right| = \left|-\alpha^3(1+\alpha)\right| = \left|1 + \alpha\right|$ ..... (i)

$= \left|1 + \cos\dfrac{2\pi}{5} + i\sin\dfrac{2\pi}{5}\right|$

$= \left|2\cos\dfrac{\pi}{5}\left(\cos\dfrac{\pi}{5} + i\sin\dfrac{\pi}{5}\right)\right| = 2\cos\dfrac{\pi}{5}$

Again from (i), $\left|1 + \alpha\right| = \left|1 + \alpha + \alpha^2\right| = 2\cos\dfrac{\pi}{5}$

**13.**   **A→r; B→q; C→s**

(A)   $1, \omega, \omega^2, \dots, \omega^{n-1}$ are the $n^{\text{th}}$ roots of unity.

$\Rightarrow 1 + \omega + \omega^2 + \dots + \omega^{n-1} = 0$

$\Rightarrow \omega + \omega^2 + \dots + \omega^{2n-1} + \omega^n = 0$   **(r)**

$(\because \omega^n = 1$, sum of $n^{\text{th}}$ roots of units is zero)

(B)   Let $s = 1 + 2\omega + 3\omega^2 + \dots + n\omega^{n-1}$

$\omega s = \omega + 2\omega^2 + \dots + (n-1)\omega^{n-1} + n\omega^n$

$(1-\omega)s = 1 + \omega + \omega^2 + \dots + \omega^{n-1} - n\omega^n = -n$

$\Rightarrow s = \dfrac{n}{\omega - 1}$   **(q)**

(C)   $x^{n-1} = (x-1)(x-\omega)(x-\omega^2)\dots(n-\omega^{n-1})$

$\Rightarrow (x-\omega)(x-\omega^2)\dots(x-\omega^{n-1}) = \dfrac{x^n - 1}{x - 1}$

$\Rightarrow (1-\omega)(1-\omega^2)\dots(1-\omega^{n-1}) = \displaystyle\lim_{x\to 1}\dfrac{x^n - 1}{x - 1} = n$ **(s)**

**14.**   **A→q; B→r; C→t**

(A)   $\omega_1^4 + \omega_2^4 + \omega_1 + \omega_2 = \omega + \omega^2 = -1 = \dfrac{-1}{\omega^3} = \dfrac{-1}{\omega_1\omega_2}$ **(q)**

(B)   $|x_i - (y+1)| + |x + yi - i| = 2$

$\Rightarrow \sqrt{x^2 + (y+1)^2} + \sqrt{x^2 + (y-1)^2} = 2$

$\Rightarrow x^2 + (y+1)^2 = 4 + x^2 + (y-1)^2 - 4\sqrt{x^2 + (y-1)^2}$

$\Rightarrow 4y - 4 = -4\sqrt{x^2 + (y-1)^2}$

$\Rightarrow y - 1 = -\sqrt{x^2 + (y-1)^2}$

Squaring both the sides,

$y^2 + 1 - 2y = x^2 + y^2 + 1 - 2y \Rightarrow x^2 = 0 \Rightarrow x = 0$,

which represent a straight line **(r)**.

(C)   $z_1 = (e)^{\frac{12r\pi}{n}}$ and $z_2 = (e)^{\frac{12s\pi}{n}}$ where r,s $\in$ z

and $0 \le r,\ s \le n$

$\therefore \arg\left(\dfrac{z_1}{z_2}\right) = \dfrac{2r\pi}{n} - \dfrac{2s\pi}{n} = 2(r-s)\dfrac{\pi}{n}$, which is a

multiple of $\dfrac{2\pi}{n}$ **(t)**.

**15.   (d)**   Statement - 2 is true (a known fact).
Hence if $z_1, z_2, \ldots, z_n$ are roots of $z^n - 1 = 0$, then

$z_1 . z_2 \ldots z_n = (-1)^n . \dfrac{(-1)}{1} = (-1)^{n+1}$,

which is never equal to $(-1)^n$

**16.   (b)**   $\alpha$ is $7^{th}$ roots of unity

$\Rightarrow 1 + \alpha + \ldots\ldots + \alpha^6 = 0$, $p + q = -1$

$pq = \alpha^4 + \alpha^6 + \alpha^7 + \alpha^5 + \alpha^7 + \alpha^8 + \alpha^7 + \alpha^9 + \alpha^{10}$

$= 3 + \alpha + \alpha^2 + \alpha^3 + \alpha^4 + \alpha^5 + \alpha^6 = 3 + (-1) = 2$

$x^2 + x + 2 = 0$

Both Statement-1 and Statement-2 are true and Statement 2 is correct explanation for Statement-1.

**17.   (6)**

$\left[2\left(\cos\dfrac{\pi}{3} + i\sin\dfrac{\pi}{3}\right)\right]^{n/2}$ is real

$2^{n/2}\left[\cos\dfrac{n\pi}{6} + i\sin\dfrac{n\pi}{6}\right]$ is real

hence $\sin\dfrac{n\pi}{6} = 0$,   $\therefore \dfrac{n\pi}{6} = k\pi$, $\therefore n = 6k$

Hence, smallest positive $n$ is 6.

**18.   (4)**
Let x be the $(2009)^{th}$ root of unity $\ne 1$, then
$x^{2009} - 1 = (x-1)(x-w) \ldots\ldots (x - w^{2008})$
Taking ln on both sides, we get
$\ln(x^{2009} - 1) = \ln(x-1) + \ln(x-w) + \ln(x-w^2) \ldots + \ln(x - w^{2008})$
$\therefore$ On differentiate both the side w.r.t. x, we get

$\dfrac{(2009)x^{2008}}{x^{2009} - 1} = \dfrac{1}{x-1} + \sum_{r=1}^{2008} \dfrac{1}{x - w^r}$        ........ (1)

Putting x = 2 in eq. (2), we get

$\Rightarrow 1 + \sum_{r=1}^{2008} \dfrac{1}{2 - w^r} = \dfrac{2009\,(2^{2008})}{2^{2009} - 1}$

Multiplying both sides of above equation by $(2^{2009} - 1)$, we get

$\therefore (2^{2009} - 1) \sum_{r=1}^{2008} \dfrac{1}{2 - w^r} = 2009 . 2^{2008} - 2^{2009} + 1$

$= 2^{2008}(2009 - 2) + 1 = 2^{2008} . 2007 + 1 = [(a)(2^b) + c]$

$\therefore a = 2007, b = 2008, c = 1$

Hence, $a + b + c = 4016$

$\therefore Y = 4$

**19.   (1)**   Given that a, b, c are integers not all equal $\omega$ is cube root of unity $\ne 1$, then

$|a + b\omega + c\omega^2|$

$= \left|a + b\left(\dfrac{-1 + i\sqrt{3}}{2}\right) + c\left(\dfrac{-1 - i\sqrt{3}}{2}\right)\right|$

$= \left|\left(\dfrac{2a - b - c}{2}\right) + i\left(\dfrac{b\sqrt{3} - c\sqrt{3}}{2}\right)\right|$

$= \dfrac{1}{2}\sqrt{(2a - b - c)^2 + 3(b - c)^2}$

$= \dfrac{1}{2}\sqrt{4a^2 + b^2 + c^2 - 4ab + 2bc - 4ac + 3b^2 - 3c^2 - 6bc}$

$= \sqrt{a^2 + b^2 + c^2 - ab + bc - ca}$

$= \sqrt{\dfrac{1}{2}[(a-b)^2 + (b-c)^2 + (c-a)^2]}$

R.H.S. will be min. when a = b = c, but we cannot take a = b = c as per question.
$\therefore$ The min value is obtained when any two are zero and third is a minimum magnitude integer i.e. 1.
Thus b = c = 0, a = 1 gives us the minimum value 1.

**20.   (0)**   Given $\alpha = \omega, \beta = \omega^2$
$\therefore \alpha^4 + \beta^{28} + 1/\alpha\,\beta = \omega^4 + \omega^{56} + 1/\omega^3$
$= \omega + \omega^2 + 1\ (\because \omega^3 = 1) = 0$

**21.   (1)**   $\dfrac{1}{a + \omega} + \dfrac{1}{b + \omega} + \dfrac{1}{c + \omega} + \dfrac{1}{d + \omega} = \dfrac{1}{\omega}$   ........(i)

Taking conjugate we get,

$\dfrac{1}{a + \omega^2} + \dfrac{1}{b + \omega^2} + \dfrac{1}{c + \omega^2} + \dfrac{1}{d + \omega^2} = \dfrac{1}{\omega^2}$ ......(ii)

$\sum\left(\dfrac{1}{a + \omega} - \dfrac{1}{a + \omega^2}\right) = \dfrac{1}{\omega} - \dfrac{1}{\omega^2}$

$\Rightarrow (\omega^2 - \omega)\sum \dfrac{1}{(a + \omega)(a + \omega^2)} = \omega^2 - \omega$

$\Rightarrow \sum \dfrac{1}{a^2 - a + 1} = 1$

**1. (c)** Here $a = 2.6$, $l = 2(6.8) = 96$ ;

$$S = \frac{n}{2}(a + l) = \frac{8}{2}(12 + 96) = 432 \text{ metres}$$

**2. (c)** Given : $a_3 + a_5 + a_8 = 11$

$a + 2d + a + 4d + a + 7d = 11$

$3a + 13d = 11 \qquad \qquad ....(1)$

Given : $\quad a_4 + a_2 = -2$

$a + 3d + a + d = -2$

$a = -1 - 2d \qquad \qquad ....(2)$

Put (2) in (1)

$3(-1-2d) + 13d = 11 \Rightarrow 7d = 14 \Rightarrow d = 2$ and $a = -5$

Now $a_1 + a_6 + a_7$

$\Rightarrow a + a + 5d + a + 6d$

$\Rightarrow 3a + 11d \Rightarrow 3(-5) + 11(2)$

$= -15 + 22 = 7$

**3. (d)** Let the $1^{st}$ 5 terms of the A.P. are

$a - 2d, a - d, a, a + d, a + 2d$

now, $a_1 + a_3 + a_5 = -12$

$\therefore 3a = -12 \Rightarrow a = -4$

also $a_1 . a_2 . a_3 = 8$

$(a - 2d)(a - d)a = 8$

$-4(-4-2d)(-4-d) = 8 \Rightarrow d = -3$

Hence the A.P. is $2, -1, -4, -7, 10, -13 , ......$

Hence $a_2 + a_4 + a_6 = -21$

**4. (a)**

$$\frac{S_{Kx}}{S_x} = \frac{\dfrac{Kx}{2}[2a + (Kx - 1)]}{\dfrac{K}{2}[2a + (x-1)d]} = K\left[\frac{2a - d + Kxd}{2a - d + xd}\right]$$

If $2a - d = 0$ then $\dfrac{S_{Kx}}{S_K} = K\left[\dfrac{Kxd}{xd}\right] = K^2$ which is

possible when $a = d/2$

**5. (b)** $a_1 + a_3 + a_5 = -12$

$a + a + 2d + a + 4d = -12 \quad (d > 0)$

$a + 2d = -4 \qquad ....(1)$

$a_1 a_3 a_5 = 80$

$a(a + 2d)(a + 4d) = 80$

or $a(4)(-4 - 2d + 4d) = 20$ from (1)

or $(-4 - 2d)(-4 + 2d) = 20 \Rightarrow d = \pm 3$

$\therefore$ A.P. is increasing $d = +3$ ; $a = -10$

$a_1 = -10$ ; $a_2 = -7$

$a_3 = a + 2d = -10 + 6 = -4$

$a_5 = a + 4d = -10 + 12 = 2$ $\quad \Big\} \Rightarrow b$

**6. (a)** The general term can be given by

$$t_{r+1} = \frac{a_{2n+1-r} - a_{r+1}}{a_{2n+1-r} + a_{r+1}}, r = 0, 1, 2, ................ n-1$$

$$= \frac{a_1 + (2n - r)d - \{a_1 + rd\}}{a_1 + (2n - r)d + \{a_1 + rd\}} = \frac{(n - r)d}{a_1 + nd}$$

$\therefore$ The required sum,

$$S_n = \sum_{r=0}^{n-1} t_{r+1} = \sum_{r=0}^{n-1} \frac{(n-r)d}{a_1 + nd}$$

$$= \left[\frac{n + (n-1) + (n-2) + .... + 1}{a_1 + nd}\right]d = \frac{n(n+1)d}{2a_{n+1}}$$

$$= \frac{n(n+1)}{2} \cdot \frac{a_2 - a_1}{a_{n+1}} \qquad [\because d = a_2 - a_1]$$

**7. (a)** We know that in an A.P.

$a_1 + a_n = a_2 + a_{n-1} = a_3 + a_{n-2} = ........(i)$

[Using the properties of A.P.]

$$\therefore \frac{1}{a_1 a_n} + \frac{1}{a_2 a_{n-1}} + \frac{1}{a_3 a_{n-2}} + ... + \frac{1}{a_n a_1}$$

$$= \frac{1}{a_1 + a_n}\left[\frac{a_1 + a_n}{a_1 a_n} + \frac{a_1 + a_n}{a_2 a_{n-2}} + \frac{a_1 + a_n}{a_3 a_{n-2}} + .... + \frac{a_1 + a_n}{a_n a_1}\right]$$

$$= \frac{1}{a_1 + a_n}\left[\frac{a_1 + a_n}{a_1 a_n} + \frac{a_2 + a_{n-1}}{a_2 a_{n-2}} + \frac{a_3 + a_{n-2}}{a_3 a_{n-2}}\right.$$

$$\left. + .......... + \frac{a_n + a_1}{a_n a_1}\right] \qquad \text{[Using (i)]}$$

$$= \frac{1}{a_1 + a_n}\left[\left(\frac{1}{a_1} + \frac{1}{a_n}\right) + \left(\frac{1}{a_2} + \frac{1}{a_{n-1}}\right) + \left(\frac{1}{a_3} + \frac{1}{a_{n-2}}\right) + \right.$$

$$\left. .........+ \left(\frac{1}{a_1} + \frac{1}{a_n}\right)\right]$$

$$= \frac{2}{a_1 + a_n}\left[\frac{1}{a_1} + \frac{1}{a_2} + \frac{1}{a_3} + ...... + \frac{1}{a_n}\right]$$

(Each term occurs twice).

**8. (a)** a, b, c, d are in A.P.

$b - a = c - b = d - c = D$

$a - d = -3D$

$b - d = -2D$

$c - a = 2D$

$\Rightarrow -2D + xD^2 + (2D)^3 = -6D + 4D^2 - D^3$

$\Rightarrow 9D^2 + (x - 4)D + 4 = 0$

$\Rightarrow (x - 4)2 - 4 . 4 . 9 \geq 0 \quad \{ \therefore D \text{ is real} \}$

$\Rightarrow x \geq 16$ or $\quad x \leq -8$

**9. (b)** We have $\dfrac{x+y}{2y-x} = \dfrac{x+y}{x+z-x} = \dfrac{x+y}{z}$

$(\because x, y, z \text{ are in A.P.})$

Similarly, $\dfrac{y+z}{2y-z} = \dfrac{y+z}{x}$

Now, $\dfrac{\dfrac{x+y}{2y-x}+\dfrac{y+z}{2y-z}}{2} \geq \sqrt{\dfrac{x+y}{z}\cdot\dfrac{y+z}{x}}$

$= \sqrt{1+\dfrac{y(x+y+z)}{xz}} = \sqrt{1+\dfrac{3y^2}{xz}} \quad ............(i)$

Also, $y$ = A.M. of $x$ and $z$ $\Rightarrow y \geq \sqrt{xz}$ or $\dfrac{y^2}{xz} \geq 1$

$\therefore$ From (i), $\dfrac{x+y}{2y-x}+\dfrac{y+z}{2y-z} \geq 2(\sqrt{1+3\times1}) = 4$

**10.  (b)**  The numbers between 100 and 500, divisible by 7 are 105, 112, 119,.........483, 490, 497 which is an A.P. with common difference 7.
If such numbers be $n$, then
$497 = x_n = 105+(n-1)\times7 \Rightarrow n=57$
The numbers between 100 and 500, divisible by 21 are 105, 126, 147,........483, which is an A.P. with common difference 21.
If such numbers be $m$, then
$483 = x_m = 105+(m-1)\times21 \Rightarrow m = 19$
Hence, the required number $= 57 - 19 = 38$.

**11.  (b)**  If possible let the $m^{th}$ term of the first A.P. be identical with $n^{th}$ term of the second A.P.
That is $2+(m-1)\times3 = 3+(n-1)\times2$
$\Rightarrow 3m-1 = 2n+1 \Rightarrow 3m-6 = 2n-4$
[Subtracting 5 from each side]

$\Rightarrow 3(m-2) = 2(n-2) \Rightarrow \dfrac{m-2}{2} = \dfrac{n-2}{3} = k$  (say)

$\therefore m = 2k+2$  and  $n = 3k+2$

But $1 \leq m \leq 60$ and $1 \leq n \leq 50$

$\therefore 1 \leq 2k+2 \leq 60$ and $1 \leq 3k+2 \leq 50$

$\Rightarrow -\dfrac{1}{2} \leq k \leq 29$ and $-\dfrac{1}{3} \leq k \leq 16$

Hence, $k = 0, 1, 2, 3,........., 16$. Corresponding to each value of $k$ we get one idenlical term. Hence there are 17 identical terms.

**12.  (d)**  Let $\sqrt{2} = a+(p-1)d$, $\sqrt{3} = a+(q-1)d$,

$\sqrt{5} = a+(r-1)d$, $\Rightarrow \sqrt{2}-\sqrt{3} = (p-q)d$

and $\sqrt{3}-\sqrt{5} = (q-r)d$, on dividing we get

$\dfrac{\sqrt{2}-\sqrt{3}}{\sqrt{3}-\sqrt{5}} = \dfrac{p-q}{q-r}$

Clearly LHS is an irrational number but RHS is a rational number, which is a contradiction.

Hence, $\sqrt{2}, \sqrt{3}, \sqrt{5}$ are not terms of an A.P.

**13.  (a)**  Let $2n$ arithmetic means $A_1, A_2, .......,A_{2n}$ be inserted between the numbers $a$ and $b$. Then

$A_1+A_2+.........+A_{2n} = \left(\dfrac{a+b}{2}\right)\times2n = \dfrac{13}{6}\times n$  ...(i)

$\left[\text{Given } a+b = 2\dfrac{1}{6} = \dfrac{13}{6}\right]$

Also, $A_1+A_2+.......+A_{2n} = 2n+1$

$\therefore 2n+1 = \dfrac{13n}{6} \Rightarrow n = 6$

$\therefore$ The number of means $= 2\times6 = 12$

**14.  (b)**  $a_1+a_{2n} = a_2+a_{2n-1} = ...... = a_n+a_{n+1} = k$
Expression

$k = \left\{\dfrac{\sqrt{a_1}+\sqrt{a_2}}{a_1-a_2}+.....+\dfrac{\sqrt{a_n}-\sqrt{a_{n+1}}}{a_n-a_{n+1}}\right\}$

$= \dfrac{k}{-d}(\sqrt{a_1}-\sqrt{a_{n+1}})$, where $d$ = common difference

$= \dfrac{k}{-d}\dfrac{a_1-a_{n+1}}{\sqrt{a_1}+\sqrt{a_{n+1}}} = (a_1+a_{2n})\left(\dfrac{-nd}{-d(\sqrt{a_2}+\sqrt{a_{n+1}})}\right)$

$= \dfrac{n(a_1+a_{2n})}{(\sqrt{a_1}+\sqrt{a_{n+1}})}$

**15.  (a,c)**  $B = 60°$, $b = 9$, $c = 10$
By cosine rule, $\quad 81 = a^2+100-2a$
$\Rightarrow a = 5\pm\sqrt{6}$

**16.  (b,d)**  We have $1072 < 10(2a+19d) < 1162$ and $a+5d = 32$
$\therefore 1072 < 20(a+5d)+90d < 1162$
$\Rightarrow 1072 < 640+90d < 1162$

$\therefore \dfrac{432}{90} < d < \dfrac{522}{90}$ and $d$ is natural number,

So, $d = 5 \Rightarrow a = 7$

**17.  $A \to p, q, s; B \to r, t; C \to q, s$**
(A)  For an AP, sum of $n$ terms is a purely quadratic expression in $n$.
$\therefore a = 0$, then $S_n = bn+cn^2$
$\therefore T_n = S_n-S_{n-1}$
$= (bn+cn^2)-\{b(n-1)+c(n-1)^2\}$
$= b+c(2n-1)$ **(q)**
or $T_n = a+b+c(2n-1)$ **(p)**
$(\because a = 0)$
and $D = T_n-T_{n-1} = \{b+c(2n-1)\}-\{b+c(2n-3)\}$
$= 2c$ **(s)**
(B)  According to reason in (A).
$a-1 = 0 \Rightarrow a = 1$
$\therefore S_n = (b-2)n^2+(c-3)n$
$\Rightarrow T_n = S_n-S_{n-1}$
$= (b-2)\{n-(n-1)^2\}+(c-3)\{n-(n-1)\}$
$= (b-2)(2n-1)+(c-3)$ $\qquad$ ...(i)

$= b(2n-1) - 4n + 2 + c - 3$

$= c - 1 - 4n + b(2n-1)$

$= c - a - 4n + b(2n-a)$ **(r)**  $\qquad (\because a = 1)$

and $D = T_n - T_{n-1}$

$= (b-2)(2) + 0$

$= 2b - 4$ **(t)**

(C) $\quad \because S_n = bn + cn^2$

$\therefore T_n = S_n - S_{n-1}$

$= (bn + cn^2) - \{b(n-1) + c(n-1)^2\}$

$= b + c(2n-1)$  **(q)**

and $D = T_n - T_{n-1}$

$= 2c$ **(s)**

**18.** **(d)** **Case I :** $x < 1$

Then $1 - x, 3, 3 - x$ are in AP.

$6 = 4 - 2x \Rightarrow x = -1$

$\therefore$ terms are 2, 3, 4

$\therefore$ sixth term = 7.

**Case II :** $1 < x < 3$

Then $x - 1, 3, 3 - x$ are in AP.

$\therefore 6 = 2$ (impossible)

**Case III:** $x > 3$

Then $x - 1, 3, x - 3$ are in AP.

$\therefore 6 = 2x - 4 \Rightarrow x = 5$

Then terms are 4, 3, 2

$\therefore$ Sixth term is $-1$

**19.** **(d)** $\quad \because \dfrac{S_n}{S'_n} = \dfrac{(7n+1)}{(4n+17)} = \dfrac{n(7n+1)}{n(4n+17)}$

$\therefore S_n = (7n^2 + n)\lambda,\ S'_n = (4n^2 + 17n)\lambda$

Then $\dfrac{T_n}{T'_n} = \dfrac{S_n - S_{n-1}}{S_n - S'_{n-1}}$

$= \dfrac{7(2n-1)+1}{4(2n-1)+17} = \dfrac{14n-6}{8n+13}$

$\Rightarrow T_n : T'_n = (14n-6) : (8n+13)$

**20.** **(8)**

Let there be $2n + 1$ stones i.e. n stones on each side of the middle stone. The man will run 20 m, to pick up the first stone and return 40 m for the second stone and so on. So he runs $(n/2)(2 \times 20 + (n-1)20) = 10n(n+1)$ meters to pick up the stones on one side, and hence $20\,n(n+1)$ m , to pick up all the stones.

$\therefore 20n(n+1) = 4800$, or $n = 15$.

$\therefore$ there are $2n + 1 = 31$ stones

$\therefore x = 8$

**21.** **(5)**

$$\pi\left[\left(r_2^2 - r_1^2\right) + \left(r_4^2 - r_3^2\right) + \dots + \left(r_{100}^2 - r_{99}^2\right)\right]$$

$\therefore r_2 - r_1 = r_4 - r_3 = \dots = r_{100} - r_{99} = 1$

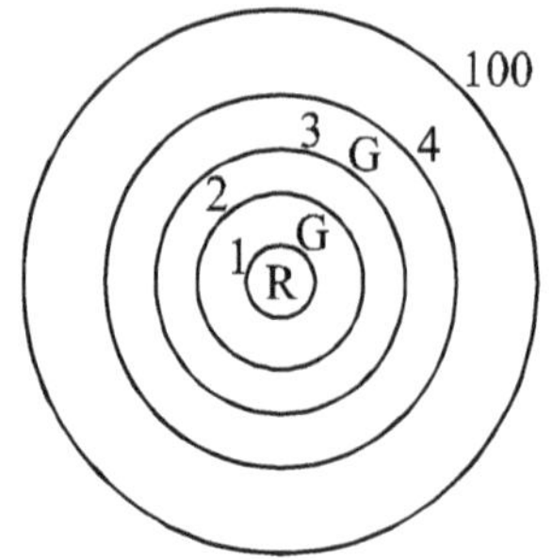


$= \pi\left[r_1 + r_2 + r_3 + r_4 + \dots + r_{100}\right]$

$= \pi\left[1 + 2 + 3 + \dots + 100\right]$

$= 5050\pi$ sq. cm.

$\therefore P = 5$

**22.** **(5)**

Let the 3 consecutive terms are

$\qquad a - d,\ a,\ a + d;\qquad$ where $d > 0$

hence $a^2 - 2ad + d^2 = 36 + K \qquad ....(1)$

$\qquad\qquad a^2 = 300 + K \qquad ....(2)$

$\qquad a^2 + 2ad + d^2 = 596 + K \qquad ....(3)$

now $(2) - (1)$ gives

$= d(2a - d) = 264 \qquad ....(4)$

$(3) - (2)$ gives

$d(2a + d) = 296 \qquad ....(5)$

$(5) - (4)$ gives

$2d^2 = 32 \Rightarrow d^2 = 16 \Rightarrow d = 4$ $(d = -4$ rejected$)$

Hence from (4),

$4(2a - 4) = 264 \Rightarrow 2a - 4 = 66 \Rightarrow 2a = 70 \Rightarrow a = 35$

$\therefore K = 35^2 - 300 = 1225 - 300 = 925$

Thus $P = 5$

**23.** **(2)** Let $S_n$ denote the sum to n terms of the AP. According to the given condition

$\Rightarrow \dfrac{S_n}{S_{2n} - S_n} = k\ \forall\ n \geq 1$

$\Rightarrow \dfrac{S_1}{S_2 - S_n} = \dfrac{S_n}{S_4 - S_2} \Rightarrow S_1 S_4 = S_2^2$

$\Rightarrow a\left[\dfrac{4}{2}(2a + (4-1)d)\right] = (a + a + d)^2$

$\Rightarrow a(4a + 6d) = (2a + d)^2 \Rightarrow 2ad = d^2 \Rightarrow 2a = d$

As $a = 1$, we get $d = 2$

**24.** **(2)** Let the common difference of the given A. P. be t. Then

$d = a^2 + b^2 + c^2 \Rightarrow a + 3t = a^2 + (a+t)^2 + (a+2t)^2$

$\Rightarrow 5t^2 + 3(2a - 1)t + 3a^2 - a = 0 \dots(1)$

$\because$ t is real $\Rightarrow D \geq 0 \Rightarrow 9(2a-1)^2 - 4(5)(3a^2 - a) \geq 0$

$\Rightarrow 24a^2 + 16a - 9 \leq 0 \Rightarrow -\dfrac{1}{3} - \dfrac{\sqrt{70}}{12} < a < -\dfrac{1}{3} + \dfrac{\sqrt{70}}{12}$

$\Rightarrow a = -1, 0 \qquad [\because$ a is integer$]$

When $a = 0$, from $(1): t = 0, \dfrac{3}{5}$

(Since t must be non-zero integer, we rejecting both these values)

When $a = -1$, from $(1); t = 1, \dfrac{4}{5} \Rightarrow t = 1$

$\therefore a + b + c + d = -1 + 0 + 1 + 2 = 2$

**1.** **(b).** $\dfrac{a}{1-r_1} = r_1$ and $\dfrac{a}{1-r_2} = r_2$

hence $r_1$ and $r_2$ are the roots of $\dfrac{a}{1-r} = r \Rightarrow r^2 - r + a = 0$

$\Rightarrow r_1 + r_2 = 1$

**2.** **(c).** $T_n = \dfrac{2^n \cdot 2^2}{4^n \cdot 4^{-2}} = \left(\dfrac{1}{2}\right)^n \cdot 16 \cdot 4$

$\therefore S = 320 \displaystyle\sum_{n=1}^{\infty} \left(\dfrac{1}{2}\right)^n = 320$

**3.** **(a).** Let $\dfrac{\alpha}{\delta}, \alpha, \alpha\delta$ are the roots of the given cubic equation.

$\therefore \alpha^3 = r$ ; $\alpha\left[\dfrac{1}{\delta} + 1 + \delta\right] = p$

$\dfrac{\alpha^2}{\delta} + \alpha^2\delta + \alpha^2 = q$

Hence $\alpha^2\left(\dfrac{1}{\delta} + \delta + 1\right) = q$ $\therefore \alpha = \dfrac{q}{p}$, also $\alpha^3 = r$

$\therefore \dfrac{q^3}{p^3} = r \Rightarrow q^3 = p^3 r$

**4.** **(c).** G.P. : $\dfrac{a}{r}, a, ar, \dots\dots$

$a = 3$ and $r = \dfrac{1}{3}$ or $3$ (rejected)

G.P. is $9, 3, 1, \dfrac{1}{3}, \dots\dots$

$\Rightarrow$ c is not correct.

**5.** **(a).** Let $\quad x_1 = t - a; \qquad y_1 = 3(t - a)^2$
$\qquad\qquad x_2 = t; \qquad\qquad y_2 = 3t^2$
$\qquad\qquad x_3 = t + a; \qquad y_3 = 3(t + a)^2$
since $y_1, y_2$ and $y_3$ are in G.P.
however $\quad 9t^4 = 9(t - a)^2(t + a)^2$
$t^2 = (t - a)(t + a)$ or $-(t - a)(t + a)$
$t^2 = t^2 - a^2$ rejected as $a \neq 0$
$\therefore t^2 = a^2 - t^2$

$2t^2 = a^2 \Rightarrow a = \sqrt{2}\,t$ or $-\sqrt{2}\,t$

$r = \dfrac{t^2}{(t - a)^2} = \dfrac{t^2}{(t - \sqrt{2}\,t)^2} = \dfrac{1}{(\sqrt{2} - 1)^2}$

$= \dfrac{1}{3 - 2\sqrt{2}} = 3 + 2\sqrt{2}$

If $a = -\sqrt{2}\,t$ then $r = 3 - 2\sqrt{2}$

**6.** **(c).** Let $S = \dfrac{1}{2} + \dfrac{3}{4} + \dfrac{7}{8} + \dfrac{15}{16} + \dots.n^{th}$ term

$= \left(1 - \dfrac{1}{2}\right) + \left(1 - \dfrac{1}{4}\right) + \left(1 - \dfrac{1}{8}\right) + \left(1 - \dfrac{1}{16}\right)\dots.n^{th}$ term

$= (1 + 1 + 1 + \dots.n^{th}\text{ term})$

$\left(\dfrac{1}{2} + \dfrac{1}{2^2} + \dfrac{1}{2^3} + \dfrac{1}{2^4} + \dots. + \dfrac{1}{2^n}\right)$

$= n - \left[\dfrac{\dfrac{1}{2}\left(1 - \dfrac{1}{2^n}\right)}{1 - \dfrac{1}{2}}\right] = n - 1 + 2^{-n}$

**7.** **(a)** $a, b$ are the roots of $x^2 - x + p = 0$
$\therefore \alpha + \beta = 1$ ....(1)
$\alpha\beta = p$ ...(2)
$\gamma, \delta$ are the roots of $x^2 - 4x + q = 0$
$\therefore \gamma + \delta = 4$ ....(3)
$\gamma\delta = q$ ....(4)
$\alpha, \beta, \gamma, \delta$ are in G.P. $\therefore$ Let $\alpha = a$; $\beta = ar$,
$\gamma = ar^2$, $\delta = ar^3$.
Substituting these values in equations (1), (2), (3) and (4), we get
$a + ar = 1$ ....(5)
$a^2 r = p$ ....(6)
$ar^2 + ar^3 = 4$ ....(7)
$a^2 r^5 = q$ ....(8)
Dividing (7) by (5), we get

$\dfrac{ar^2(1 + r)}{a(1 + r)} = \dfrac{4}{1} \Rightarrow r^2 = 4 \Rightarrow r = 2, -2$

From equ. (5),

$a = \dfrac{1}{1 + r} = \dfrac{1}{1 + 2}$ or $\dfrac{1}{1 - 2} = \dfrac{1}{3}$ or $-1$

As $p$ is an integer (given), $r$ is also an integer ($2$ or $-2$).

From equ. (6) $\Rightarrow a \neq \dfrac{1}{3}$. Hence $a = -1$ and $r = -2$.

$\therefore \quad p = (-1)^2 \times (-2) = -2$
$\qquad q = (-1)^2 \times (-2)^5 = -32$

**8.** **(b)** $\dfrac{x}{1 - r} = 5 \Rightarrow r = 1 - \dfrac{x}{5}$

Since G.P. contains infinite terms
$\therefore -1 < r < 1$

$\Rightarrow -1 < 1 - \dfrac{x}{5} < 1 \Rightarrow 0 < -\dfrac{x}{5} < 2$

$\Rightarrow \quad -10 < x < 0.$

**9.** **(c)** In the quadratic equation $ax^2 + bx + c = 0$

$$\Delta = b^2 - 4ac \text{ and } \alpha + \beta = -\frac{b}{a}, \alpha\beta = \frac{c}{a}$$

$$\alpha^2 + \beta^2 = (\alpha + \beta)^2 - 2\alpha\beta$$

$$= \frac{b^2}{a^2} - \frac{2c}{a} = \frac{b^2 - 2ac}{a^2}$$

and $= \dfrac{b^3}{a^3} - \dfrac{3c}{a}\left(-\dfrac{b}{a}\right)$

$$= -\left(\frac{b^3 - 3abc}{a^3}\right)$$

ATQ $\alpha + \beta$, $\alpha^2 + \beta^2$, $\alpha^3 + \beta^3$ are in G.P.

$\Rightarrow \quad -\dfrac{b}{a}, -\dfrac{b^2 - 2ac}{a^2}, -\dfrac{(b^3 - 3abc)}{a^3}$ are in G.P.

$$\Rightarrow \quad \left(\frac{b^2 - 2ac}{a^2}\right)^2 = \frac{b}{a}\left(\frac{b^3 - 3abc}{a^3}\right)$$

$$\Rightarrow \quad b^4 + 4a^2c^2 - 4ab^2c = b^4 - 3ab^2c$$

$$\Rightarrow \quad 4a^2c^2 - ab^2c = 0$$

$$\Rightarrow \quad ac\,\Delta = 0$$

$$\Rightarrow \quad c\,\Delta = 0 \qquad (\because \text{ In quadratic } a \neq 0)$$

**10.** **(d)** $T_n = 1 + 2 + 2^2 + \dots\dots + 2^{n-1}$

$$\text{(G.P. with } a = 1 \text{ and } r = 2)$$

$$= (2^n - 1)$$

Hence, sum $= \displaystyle\sum_{n=1}^{n}(2^n - 1) = [(2 + 2^2 + 2^3 + \dots + 2^n) - n]$

$$= 2\,(2^n - 1) - n = 2^{n+1} - 2 - n$$

$$= 2^{n+1} + (0)\,n^2 + (-1)\,n + (-2)$$

Hence $R = 1$, $S = 0$, $T = -1$, $U = -2$

$$R + S + T + U = -2$$

**11.** **(c)** Let the GP be $a$, $ar$, $ar^3$, ... $(0 < r < 1)$

From the equation, $\dfrac{a}{1-r} = 3^3 + 3.3 - 9$

$\{\because f'(x) = 3x^2 + 3 > 0; f(x)$ is monotonically increasing; therefore $f(3)$ is the greatest value in $[-2, 3]\}$

Also, $f'(0) = 3$, So, $a - ar = 3$

Solving $a = 27\,(1 - r)$ and $a\,(1 - r) = 3$

We get $r = \dfrac{2}{3}, \dfrac{4}{3}$ But $r < 1$, $\therefore$ $r = \dfrac{2}{3}$

**12.** **(d)** Let $a = b - d$ and $c = b + d$, then $a + b + c = \dfrac{3}{2}$

$$\Rightarrow b = \frac{1}{2}$$

$\therefore$ The numbers are $\dfrac{1}{2} - d$, $\dfrac{1}{2}$, $\dfrac{1}{2} + d$

$$[d > 0 \text{ as } a < b < c]$$

Now $a^2$, $b^2$, $c^2$ are in G.P. $\Rightarrow (b^2)^2 = a^2c^2$

$$\Rightarrow \left(\frac{1}{2}\right)^4 = \left(\frac{1}{2} - d\right)^2\left(\frac{1}{2} + d\right)^2$$

$$\Rightarrow \frac{1}{16} = \left(\frac{1}{4} - d^2\right)^2 \Rightarrow \frac{1}{4} - d^2 = \pm\frac{1}{4}$$

$$\Rightarrow d = \pm\frac{1}{\sqrt{2}} \Rightarrow d = \frac{1}{\sqrt{2}} \qquad (\because d > 0)$$

**13.** **(c)** $y = 2\sqrt{x}$, being in the first quadrant. The sequence of $x$-coordinate is $1, 2, 4, 8, \dots\dots\dots$

$\therefore$ the sequence of $y$-coordinate is $2$, $2\sqrt{2}$, $2\sqrt{4}$, $2\sqrt{8}$, $\dots\dots\dots$; where the common ratio is $\sqrt{2}$.

$$y_n = 2(\sqrt{2})^{n-1} = (\sqrt{2})^{n+1}$$

**14.** **(b)** $a, b, c, d$ are in G.P. Let they are $a$, $ar$, $ar^2$, $ar^3$

$\therefore (a^2 + b^2 + c^2)(b^2 + c^2 + d^2)$

$= a^2 \times a^2\,[1 + r^2 + r^4]\,[r^2 + r^4 + r^6]$

$= a^4r^2\,[1 + r^2 + r^4]^2 = [a^2r\,(1 + r^2 + r^4)]^2$

$= (ab + bc + cd)^2$

**15.** **(a,b,c,d)** We have

$b_3 > 4b_2 - 3b_1 \Rightarrow b_1 r^2 > 4b_1 r - 3b_1$

$\Rightarrow r^2 > 4r - 3 \qquad\qquad [\because b_1 > 0]$

$\Rightarrow r^2 - 4r + 3 > 0 \Rightarrow (r - 3)(r - 1) > 0 \Rightarrow r > 3$ or $r < 1$

Since $r = 3.5$ and $r = 5.2$ are both greater than 3, so (c) and (d) are true.

**16.** **(a,c,d)** $\dfrac{6\,(r^n - 1)}{r - 1} = \dfrac{45}{4}$ $\quad\dots\dots(1)$

and $\dfrac{1}{6}\left(\dfrac{1 - \dfrac{1}{r^n}}{1 - \dfrac{1}{r}}\right) = \dfrac{5}{2}$ $\quad\dots\dots(2)$

and from (2), $\dfrac{r^n - 1}{r - 1}\cdot\dfrac{1}{r^{n-1}} = 15$, $\dfrac{r^n - 1}{r - 1} = 15r^{n-1}$ $\dots\dots(3)$

Substituting the result of (3) in (1), we get

$6.15.r^{n-1} = \dfrac{45}{4}$ $\Rightarrow r^{n-1} = \dfrac{1}{8}$

$\therefore \qquad r^n = \dfrac{r}{8}$ $\qquad\qquad\dots\dots\dots(4)$

From (1) and (4), we get

$$\frac{6\left(\dfrac{r}{8} - 1\right)}{r - 1} = \frac{45}{4}$$

$$\Rightarrow r = \frac{1}{2}$$

Hence $\quad n = 4$

G.P. is $6 + 3 + \dfrac{3}{2} + \dfrac{3}{4} + \dots\dots\dots\infty \Rightarrow$ **(a)**

$S_\infty = \dfrac{6}{1 - (1/2)} = 12 \Rightarrow$ **(d)**

$t_1 + t_2 = 9 \Rightarrow$ **(c)**

**17.** **(a,b)** Since $\log_x$, $a$, $a^{x/2}$, $\log_b x$ are in GP.

$\therefore a^x = \log_x a.\log_b x = \log_b a$

$\therefore x = \log_a(\log_b a) = \log_a\left(\dfrac{\log_e a}{\log_e b}\right)$

$= \log_a(\log_e a) - \log_a(\log_e b)$.

**18.** **(b,c)** Let the three numbers in G. P. be $a$, $ar$ and $ar^2$, then

$a + ar + ar^2 = \alpha S$ $\qquad\dots\dots\dots(1)$

and $\quad a^2 + a^2r^2 + a^2r^4 = S^2$ $\qquad\dots\dots(2)$

Solving (1) and (2), we have $\dfrac{(1+r+r^2)^2}{1+r^2+r^4} = \alpha^2$

$\Rightarrow \dfrac{(1+r+r^2)^2}{(1+r^2-r)(1+r^2+r)} = \alpha^2$

$\Rightarrow \dfrac{1+r+r^2}{1-r+r^2} = \alpha^2$

$\Rightarrow (\alpha^2-1)r^2 - (\alpha^2+1)r + (\alpha^2-1) = 0$

$\because r \in R \Rightarrow (\alpha^2+1)^2 - 4(\alpha^2-1)^2 \geq 0$

and $\alpha^2 \neq 1$ [If $\alpha^2 = 1 \Rightarrow r = 0$, which is not possible]

$\Rightarrow (3\alpha^2-1)(\alpha^2-3) \leq 0$

and $\alpha^2 \neq 1 \Rightarrow \alpha^2 \in \left(\dfrac{1}{3}, 3\right)$ and $\alpha^2 \neq 1$.

$\therefore \alpha^2 \in \left(\dfrac{1}{3}, 1\right) \cup (1, 3)$

**19.** **(a)** Let $T_{k+1} = ar^k$ and $T'_{k+1} = br^k$.
Since $T''_{k+1} = ar^k + br^k = (a+b)r^k$,
$\therefore T''_{k+1}$ is general term of an another G.P. whose common ratio is r.

**20.** Let $f(x) = x^4 + ax^3 + bx^2 + cx + 1$
As $a$, $b$ and $c$ are non-negative, no root of the equation $f(x) = 0$ can be positive, Futher, as $f(0) \neq 0$, all the roots of the equation, say $x_1, x_2, x_3$ and $x_4$ are negative. We have,
$\Sigma x_1 = -a$, $\Sigma x_1 x_2 = b$, $x_1 x_2 x_3 = -c$ and $x_1 x_2 x_3 x_4 = 1$
Using AM $\geq$ GM for positive numbers $-x_1, -x_2, -x_3$ and $-x_4$, we get

$\dfrac{a}{4} \geq 1 \quad \Rightarrow \quad a \geq 4$

Using AM $\geq$ GM for positive numbers $x_1 x_2, x_1 x_3, x_1 x_4, x_2 x_3, x_2 x_4$ and $x_3 x_4$, we get

$\dfrac{6}{6} \geq 1 \quad \Rightarrow \quad b \geq 6$

Finally, using Am $\geq$ GM for positive numbers $-x_1 x_2 x_3, -x_1 x_2 x_4, -x_1 x_3 x_4$ and $-x_2 x_3 x_4$, we get

$\dfrac{c}{4} \geq 1 \quad \Rightarrow \quad c \geq 4$

$\therefore$ HCF of $\{a, b, c\}$ = HCF $\{4, 6, 4\}$ = 2

**21.** **(5)**

$\tan^2 \dfrac{\pi}{12} = \tan\left(\dfrac{\pi}{12} - x\right) \tan\left(\dfrac{\pi}{12} + x\right)$

$\tan^2 \dfrac{\pi}{12} = \dfrac{\tan\dfrac{\pi}{12} - \tan x}{1 + \tan\dfrac{\pi}{12}\tan x} \cdot \dfrac{\tan\dfrac{\pi}{12} + \tan x}{1 - \tan\dfrac{\pi}{12}\tan x}$

$= \dfrac{\tan^2\dfrac{\pi}{12} - \tan^2 x}{1 - \tan^2\dfrac{\pi}{12}\tan^2 x}$

$\tan^2\dfrac{\pi}{12} - \tan^4\dfrac{\pi}{12}\tan^2 x = \tan^2\dfrac{\pi}{12} - \tan^2 x$

$\Rightarrow \tan^2 x\left(\tan^4\dfrac{\pi}{12} - 1\right) = 0$ ; $\tan x = 0 \Rightarrow x = k\pi$

$\therefore \cos 2x = 1 \Rightarrow x = n\pi$
Sum of solutions is $\pi(1 + 2 + 3 + \dots + 99) = 4950\pi$
$\Rightarrow 990\,A = 4950$
$\Rightarrow A = 5$

**22.** **(2)**

$\displaystyle\sum_{r=0}^{10} \cos^3 \dfrac{\pi r}{3}$

$= \dfrac{1}{4}\left[\displaystyle\sum_{r=0}^{10} \cos \pi r + 3\displaystyle\sum_{r=0}^{10} \cos\dfrac{\pi r}{3}\right]$

$= \dfrac{1}{4}\left[\,(1-1+1-1+\dots+(1-1)+1) + 3\left\{\left(1+\dfrac{1}{2}-\dfrac{1}{2}-1\right)\right.\right.$

$\left.\left. + \left(-\dfrac{1}{2}+\dfrac{1}{2}+1+\dfrac{1}{2}\right) + \left(-\dfrac{1}{2}-1-\dfrac{1}{2}\right)\right\}\,\right]$

$= \dfrac{1}{4}\left[1 - \dfrac{3}{2}\right]$

$= -\dfrac{1}{8}$

Hence value of the expression $= \dfrac{17}{8} - \dfrac{1}{8} = 2$

**23.** **(2)** $1 - \dfrac{1}{2} + \dfrac{1}{4} - \dfrac{1}{8} + \dots\infty = \dfrac{1}{1-\left(-\dfrac{1}{2}\right)} = \dfrac{2}{3}$

Similarly, the other series $= 4/5$

$\therefore \left(3 \times \dfrac{2}{3}\right)^{\log_{10} x} = \left(20 \times \dfrac{4}{5}\right)^{\log_x 10}$

$2^y = \left(2^4\right)^{\frac{1}{y}}$, where $y = \log_{10} x$

$\Rightarrow y = \dfrac{4}{y} \Rightarrow y^2 = 4 \Rightarrow y = \pm 2 \Rightarrow x = 10^2$ or $10^{-2}$

Thus, $A = 2$

**24.** **(2)**
Let $a$, $r$ be the first term and common ratio respectively, then
$t_3 = ar^2 = 64$.
$\therefore t_1 t_2 t_3 t_4 t_5 = a.ar.ar^2.ar^3.ar^4 = a^5 r^{10} = (ar^2)^5$
$\qquad\qquad = 64^5 = 4^{15} = 2^{30}$
Thus, $13A + 4 = 30$
$\Rightarrow A = 2$

**1.** **(b)** a,b,c are in A.P. $\Rightarrow 2b = a + c$     ....(1)

b,c,d are in G.P. $\Rightarrow c^2 = bd$     ....(2)

c,d,e are in H.P. $\Rightarrow d = 2ce/c+e$     ....(3)

put (2) in (3),

$c^2/b = 2ce/c+e = c/b = 2e/c+e$

$\Rightarrow 2c/(a+c) = 2e/c+e \Rightarrow c^2 + ec = ae + ec$

$\Rightarrow c^2 = ae \Rightarrow a$ , c, e are in G.P.

**2.** **(c)** a,b,c are in H.P. $\Rightarrow b = 2ac/a+c$

$\therefore a - b = a - [\, 2ac/(a+c)\,]$

Now, a, a – c, $[a(a-c)]/a+c$ are obviously neither an AP nor GP

If it is H.P., then $\dfrac{1}{a}, \dfrac{1}{a-c}, \dfrac{a+c}{a(a-c)}$ must be an AP, which is True.

**3.** **(a)** b = 2ac/a+c

$e^{\ell n\left((a+c)[(a+c)-2b]\right)} = (a+c)\left[a+c-\dfrac{4ac}{a+c}\right]$

$= (a+c)^2 - 4ac = (a-c)^2$

**4.** **(a)** a, b, c are in G.P. $\Rightarrow b^2 = ac$

Discriminant of $ax^2 + 2bx + c = 0$ is

$4b^2 - 4ac = 4ac - 4ac = 0$

$\Rightarrow$ roots are coincident hence their sum $= -\dfrac{2b}{2a} = -\dfrac{b}{a}$

This must be the common root. Hence $x = -\dfrac{b}{a}$ must satisfy $dx^2 + 2ex + f = 0$

i.e; $d \cdot \dfrac{b^2}{a^2} - 2e \cdot \dfrac{b}{a} + f = 0$

$\Rightarrow 2\dfrac{e}{b} = \dfrac{f}{c} + \dfrac{d}{a}$

Hence, $\dfrac{d}{a}, \dfrac{e}{b}$ and $\dfrac{f}{c}$ are in A.P.

**5.** **(c)** Let the roots of the equation are $ax^2 + bx + c = 0 \ \alpha, \beta$

$\alpha + \beta = \dfrac{1}{\alpha^2} + \dfrac{1}{\beta^2} = \dfrac{(\alpha+\beta)^2 - 2\alpha\beta}{\alpha^2\beta^2}$

$(\alpha+\beta)(\alpha\beta)^2 = (\alpha+\beta)^2 - 2\alpha\beta$

$\left(-\dfrac{b}{a}\right)\left(\dfrac{c^2}{a^2}\right) = \dfrac{b^2}{a^2} - \dfrac{2c}{a}$

$-bc^2 = ab^2 - 2a^2c$

$\dfrac{ab^2 + bc^2 = 2a^2c}{abc}$

$\Rightarrow$ ( Dividing by abc)

$\dfrac{b}{c} + \dfrac{c}{a} = \dfrac{2a}{b}$ or $\dfrac{a}{b} = \dfrac{\dfrac{b}{c} + \dfrac{c}{a}}{2} \Rightarrow \dfrac{b}{c}, \dfrac{a}{b}, \dfrac{c}{a}$ are in A.P.

$\Rightarrow$ result

**6.** **(b)** $a_1 = b_1 = 1$ ; $a_9 = 1 + 8d = b_n = 1 . r^8$

Now $\displaystyle\sum_{r=1}^{9} a_r = \dfrac{9}{2}(1+a_9) = \dfrac{9}{2}(1+r^8) = 369 \Rightarrow r = \sqrt{3}$

$\therefore b_7 = b . r^6 = 1\left(\sqrt{3}\right)^6 = 27$

**7.** **(d)** $D = q^2 - 4pr = \left(\dfrac{2pr}{p+r}\right)^2 - 4pr$

$= -4pr\left[1 - \dfrac{pr}{(p+r)^2}\right] \Rightarrow -4pr\left[\dfrac{p^2 + r^2 + pr}{(p+r)^2}\right]$

$\therefore D < 0$, roots are imaginary

**8.** **(a, b, c)** $\dfrac{a+b+c}{3} > b$ (H.M) $\Rightarrow a + c > 2b$

Also, $\dfrac{a^2 + c^2}{2} > \sqrt{a^2 c^2}$

$\Rightarrow a^2 + c^2 > 2ac > 2b^2$ (G.M. > H.M.)

$\Rightarrow a^2 + c^2 > 2b^2$

**9.** **(b,c,d)**

Let the four numbers $A_1, A_2, A_3, A_4$ be in A.P.

$A_2 - A_1 = A_3 - A_2 = A_4 - A_3 = d$

$A_1 + 5, A_2 + 6, A_3 + 9, A_4 + 15 \Rightarrow$ G.P.

$\dfrac{A_2 + 6}{A_1 + 5} = \dfrac{A_3 + 9}{A_2 + 6} = \dfrac{A_4 + 15}{A_3 + 9} = r$ ;

hence $\dfrac{3 + A_3 - A_2}{1 + A_2 - A_1} = \dfrac{6 + A_4 - A_3}{3 + A_3 - A_2}$ or $\dfrac{d+3}{d+1} = \dfrac{d+6}{d+3}$

On solving we get d = 3

r = 9/6 = 3/2

**10.** **(a,b,d)**

Let x be the first term and y be the (2n–1)th terms of AP, GP and HP whose nth terms are a, b, c respectively.

For AP, y = x + (2n – 2) d

$\Rightarrow d = \dfrac{y-x}{3(n-1)}$

$\therefore a = x + (n-1)d = x + \dfrac{1}{2}(y-x) = \dfrac{1}{2}(x+y)$   ....(1)

For G.P., $y = x\, r^{2n-2} \Rightarrow r = \left(\dfrac{y}{x}\right)^{\frac{1}{2n-2}}$

$\therefore b = x\, r^{n-1} = x.\left(\dfrac{y}{x}\right)^{1/2} = \sqrt{xy}$   ....(2)

For H.P. $\dfrac{1}{y} = \dfrac{1}{x} + (2n-2)d_1$

$\Rightarrow d_1 = \dfrac{x-y}{2xy\,(n-1)}$

$\therefore \dfrac{1}{c} = \dfrac{1}{x} + (n-1)d_1 = \dfrac{1}{x} + \dfrac{x-y}{2xy}$

$\dfrac{1}{c} = \dfrac{x+y}{2xy} \Rightarrow c = \dfrac{2xy}{x+y}$   ....(3)

Thus from (1), (2) and (3), a, b, c are A.M., G.M. and H.M. respectively of x and y.

We know that $AM \geq GM \geq HM$

$\therefore a \geq b \geq c$

Also $(G.M.)^2 = (A.M.)(H.M.)$

$\Rightarrow b^2 = ac$

**11. (a, d)**

Given $(a + nd)^2 = (a + md)(a + rd)$

$\Rightarrow \left(\dfrac{a}{d} + n\right)^2 = \left(\dfrac{a}{d} + m\right)\left(\dfrac{a}{d} + r\right)$  ...........(i)

Also $n = \dfrac{2mr}{m + r} \Rightarrow mr = \dfrac{(m + r)n}{2}$  ...........(ii)

Now from (i),

$\left(\dfrac{a}{d}\right)^2 + 2\left(\dfrac{an}{d}\right) + n^2 = \left(\dfrac{a}{d}\right)^2 + (m + r)\dfrac{a}{d} + mr$

$\Rightarrow \dfrac{a}{d} = \dfrac{n^2 - mr}{m + r - 2n} = \dfrac{n^2 - \dfrac{(m + r)n}{2}}{m + r - 2n}$   (from (ii))

$\therefore \dfrac{a}{d} = -\dfrac{n}{2} = -\dfrac{mr}{m + r}$

**12. (a)** $\sqrt{ab} = 16$

$\Rightarrow ab = 16^2$

$\Rightarrow ab = 256$ and $\dfrac{2ab}{a + b} = 12\dfrac{4}{5}$

$\Rightarrow \dfrac{2 \times 256}{a + b} = \dfrac{64}{5}$

$\Rightarrow a + b = 40 = 8 + 32$

$\therefore \dfrac{a}{b} = \dfrac{8}{32} = \dfrac{1}{4}$

$\therefore a : b = 1 : 4$

**13. (c)** If $a > b$

Then $\dfrac{a + b}{2} + \sqrt{ab} = a - b \Rightarrow 2\sqrt{ab} = a - 3b$

On squaring,

$4ab = a^2 - 6ab + 9b^2$

$\Rightarrow a^2 - 10ab + 9b^2 = 0$

$\therefore a : b = 9 : 1$   $(\because a \neq b)$

**14. A $\rightarrow$ p, r; B $\rightarrow$ q; C $\rightarrow$ s, t**

(A) $\because A = G + \dfrac{3}{2}$   ...(i)

and $G = H + \dfrac{6}{5}$   ...(ii)   $\because G^2 = AH$

$\Rightarrow G^2 = \left(G + \dfrac{3}{2}\right)\left(G - \dfrac{6}{5}\right)$   [from Eqs. (i) and (ii)]

$\therefore G = 6,\ A = \dfrac{15}{2}$   [from Eq. (i)]

a, b are the roots of $x^2 - 15x + 36x = 0$

we get a = 12, b = 3 or a = 3, b = 12

$\therefore \alpha = 15, \beta = 9$

$\Rightarrow \alpha + \beta^2 = 15 + 81 = 96$ **(p)**

and $\alpha^2 + \beta = 225 + 9 = 234$ **(r)**

(B) $\because A = G + 2$   ...(i)

and $H = \dfrac{1}{5}b$   (If b > a)

$\because G^2 = AH = \dfrac{bA}{5}$

$\Rightarrow 5ab = bA \Rightarrow A = 5a$

$\Rightarrow \dfrac{a + b}{2} = 5a \Rightarrow b = 9a$

From Eq. (i) $5a = \sqrt{ab} + 2$

$\Rightarrow 5a = 3a + 2$

$\therefore a = 1$, then b = 9

$\Rightarrow \alpha = a + b = 10$

and $\beta = |a - b| = 8$

$\therefore \alpha + \beta^2 = 10 + 64 = 74$ **(q)**

(C) $H = \dfrac{2ab}{a + b} \Rightarrow 4 = \dfrac{2ab}{a + b} \Rightarrow a + b = \dfrac{ab}{2}$   ...(i)

$2A + G^2 = 27$

$2 \cdot \dfrac{a + b}{2} + ab = 27 \Rightarrow 3(a + b) = 27$

$\Rightarrow a + b = 9$   (From (i))

$\Rightarrow \alpha = 9$

Also $ab = 18$

$|a - b|^2 = (a + b)^2 - 4ab = 81 - 72 = 9 \Rightarrow |a - b| = 3$

$\Rightarrow \beta = 3$

$\alpha^2 + \beta = 81 + 3 = 84$ **(s)**

$1 + \dfrac{\alpha}{\beta} + \left(\dfrac{\alpha}{\beta}\right)^2 + ..... + \left(\dfrac{\alpha}{\beta}\right)^5$

$= \dfrac{\left(\dfrac{\alpha}{\beta}\right)^6 - 1}{\dfrac{\alpha}{\beta} - 1} = \dfrac{3^6 - 1}{2} = 364$ **(t)**

**15. A $\rightarrow$ q; B $\rightarrow$ p; C $\rightarrow$ r; D $\rightarrow$ s**

(A) $A.M \geq H.M \Rightarrow \dfrac{a + b + c}{3} \geq \dfrac{3}{\dfrac{1}{a} + \dfrac{1}{b} + \dfrac{1}{c}}$

$\Rightarrow (a + b + c)\left(\dfrac{1}{a} + \dfrac{1}{b} + \dfrac{1}{c}\right) \geq 9$ **(q)**

(B) $h = \dfrac{2ab}{a + b},\ g = \sqrt{ab} \Rightarrow \dfrac{h}{g} = \dfrac{2ab}{(a + b)\sqrt{ab}}$

$\Rightarrow \dfrac{4}{5} = \dfrac{2\sqrt{ab}}{a + b}$

$\Rightarrow \dfrac{9}{1} = \dfrac{(\sqrt{a} + \sqrt{b})^2}{(\sqrt{a} - \sqrt{b})^2} \Rightarrow \left|\dfrac{\sqrt{a} + \sqrt{b}}{\sqrt{a} - \sqrt{b}}\right| = 3$ or $\dfrac{\sqrt{a} + \sqrt{b}}{\sqrt{a} - \sqrt{b}} = \pm 3$

or $a : b = 1 : 4$ or $4 : 1$ **(p)**

(C) $S = \dfrac{1}{1 - \dfrac{1}{2}} = 2$ and $S_{n+1} = \dfrac{1 - \dfrac{1}{2^{n+1}}}{1 - \dfrac{1}{2}} = 2 - \dfrac{1}{2^n}$

$\therefore S - S_{n+1} = \dfrac{1}{2^n} < \dfrac{1}{1000} \Rightarrow 2^n > 1000$.

But $2^9 < 1000 < 2^{10}$

$\therefore n \geq 10$ **(r)**

(D) $(1+x)(1+x^2)(1+x^4)(1+x^8)..........(1+x^{128})$

$$= \frac{(1-x)(1+x)(1+x^2)(1+x^4)(1+x^8)....(1+x^{128})}{1-x}$$

$$= \frac{(1-x^2)(1+x^2)(1+x^4)(1+x^8)....(1+x^{128})}{1-x}$$

$$= \frac{1-x^{256}}{1-x} = \sum_{r=0}^{255} x^r \Rightarrow n = 255 \quad \text{(s)}$$

**16.** **(d)** Statement-1 is wrong since $S_\infty = \dfrac{a}{1-r}$ is valid for $|r| < 1$

Statement-2 is true

$\because \quad \dfrac{G}{A} = \dfrac{H}{G}$

$\therefore$ Statement-1 is false but statement-2 is true.

**17.** **(c)** For two positive numbers $a$ and $b$, $(AM)(HM) = (GM)^2$. This result will be true for $n$ positive numbers if they are in GP.

**18.** **(b)** $b = $ H.M. of $a$ and $c < $ A.M. of $a$ and $c = \dfrac{a+c}{2}$

Similarly $c < \dfrac{b+d}{2}$.

Adding we get $b + c < a + d$. Hence statement-1 is true.

Further $a, b, c, d$ are in H.P.

$\Rightarrow \dfrac{1}{a}, \dfrac{1}{b}, \dfrac{1}{c}, \dfrac{1}{d}$ in A.P. $\Rightarrow \dfrac{1}{a} + \dfrac{1}{d} = \dfrac{1}{b} + \dfrac{1}{c}$

Hence statement-2 is also true.

Obviously statement-2 is not the correct reasoning of statement-1.

**19.** **(6)**

Let the numbers be

$$\overbrace{A-D, \ A, \ A+D, \ \underbrace{\dfrac{(A+D)^2}{A}}}^{G.P.}$$

$$\underbrace{(a) \quad (b) \quad (c)}_{A.P.} \qquad (d)$$

Given $d - a = 30$

$\Rightarrow \dfrac{(A+D)^2}{A} - (A-D) = 30$

$\Rightarrow (A+D)^2 - A(A-D) = 30A$

$\Rightarrow D^2 + 3AD = 30A$

$D^2 = 3A(10-D)$

$\therefore A = \dfrac{D^2}{3(10-D)} \qquad ....(1)$

since 'A' is a +ve integer

$\therefore 0 < D < 10 \qquad ....(2)$

Also since '3' is prime and A is an integer.

$\therefore D^2$ must be divisible 3

$\Rightarrow D$ must be of the form of $3K$

$\therefore$ possible values of D are 3, 6, 9

$D = 3 \Rightarrow A = \dfrac{3}{7} \qquad$ (rejected)

$D = 6 \Rightarrow A = 3 \qquad$ (rejected)

$D = 9 \Rightarrow A = 27$

$\therefore$ Numbers are 18, 27, 36, 48

As largest number is 48

So, P = 6

**20.** **(8)**

Let the numbers be $a - d, \ a, \ a + d$

$(a - d + 1), \ a, \ (a + d)$ are in G.P.

and $(a - d), \ a, \ (a + d + 2)$ also in G.P.

$(a - d + 1)(a + d) = a^2$

hence $(a^2 - d^2) + (a + d) = a^2 \quad ....(1)$

and $(a - d)(a + d + 2) = a^2$

$(a^2 - d^2) + 2(a - d) = a^2 \qquad ....(2)$

$(2) - (1), \ 2a - 2d - a - d = 0$

$a = 3d \Rightarrow 2^{nd}$ term of A.P. = 3 times its common difference

$\therefore$ from (1), $d^2 - d^2 - 3d = 0 \Rightarrow d = 4$

$d = 4, a = 12$

A.P. is 8, 12, 16

Thus, X = 8

**21.** **(6)**

$a_1 = h_1 = 2, \ a_{10} = h_{10} = 3$

$3 = a_{10} = 2 + 9d \quad \Rightarrow \quad d = 1/9$

$\therefore a_4 = 2 + 3d = 7/3$

$3 = h_{10} \Rightarrow \dfrac{1}{3} = \dfrac{1}{h_{10}} = \dfrac{1}{2} + 9D$

$\therefore D = -\dfrac{1}{54}$

$\dfrac{1}{h_7} = \dfrac{1}{2} + 6D = \dfrac{1}{2} - \dfrac{1}{9} = \dfrac{7}{18}$

$\therefore a_4 h_7 = \dfrac{7}{3} \times \dfrac{18}{7} = 6.$

**22.** **(5)**

Given condition

$\log_{\sqrt{5}} 14, \ \log_{\sqrt{5}} (3^x - 11), \ \log_{\sqrt{5}} \left(3^x - \dfrac{61}{7}\right)$ are in A.P.

$\Rightarrow (3^x - 11)^2 = 14\left(3^x - \dfrac{61}{7}\right)$

$\Rightarrow (3^x)^2 - 36(3^x) + 243 = 0$

$\Rightarrow (3^x - 9)(3^x - 27) = 0 \Rightarrow x = 2$ or $3$

Thus, required sum = 5.

**23.** **(2)**

(i) Let r is the common ratio of G.P.

$\log y = \log rx = \log r + \log x$

$\log z = \log r^2 x = 2 \log r + \log x$

Hence, $\dfrac{1}{1 + \log x}, \dfrac{1}{1 + \log r + \log x}, \dfrac{1}{1 + 2\log r + \log x}$

are in H.P.

(ii) Digits at unit place in $(13)^{1225}$ and $(23)^{1225}$ are equal and get cancelled and digit at unit place in $(11)^{1915}$ is 1. Hence finally the digit at unit's place is equal to 1.

(iii) $\log_2 (x - 1) = 2 \log_2 (x - 3)$

$\Rightarrow \log_2 (x - 1) = \log_2 (x - 3)^2$

$\Rightarrow x - 1 = (x - 3)^2$

$\Rightarrow x^2 - 7x + 10 = 0 \Rightarrow x = 2, 5$

Since x = 2 does not satisfy the original equation thus there is only one solution i.e., x = 5.

**1.** **(c).** $\because \dfrac{1}{\sqrt{n+\sqrt{n^2-1}}} = \dfrac{1}{\sqrt{\left(\sqrt{\dfrac{n+1}{2}}+\sqrt{\dfrac{n-1}{2}}\right)^2}}$

$= \dfrac{1}{\sqrt{\dfrac{n+1}{2}}+\sqrt{\dfrac{n-1}{2}}} = \dfrac{\sqrt{\dfrac{n+1}{2}}-\sqrt{\dfrac{n-1}{2}}}{\dfrac{n+1}{2}-\dfrac{n-1}{2}}$

$= \sqrt{\dfrac{n+1}{2}}-\sqrt{\dfrac{n-1}{2}}$

Hence, $a+b\sqrt{2} = \displaystyle\sum_{n=1}^{49}\left(\sqrt{\dfrac{n+1}{2}}-\sqrt{\dfrac{n-1}{2}}\right)$

$\Rightarrow a+b\sqrt{2} = \left(\sqrt{\dfrac{2}{2}}-0\right)+\left(\sqrt{\dfrac{3}{2}}-\sqrt{\dfrac{1}{2}}\right)$

$+\left(\sqrt{\dfrac{4}{2}}-\sqrt{\dfrac{2}{2}}\right)+\left(\sqrt{\dfrac{5}{2}}-\sqrt{\dfrac{3}{2}}\right)+\ldots+\left(\sqrt{\dfrac{49+1}{2}}-\sqrt{\dfrac{49-1}{2}}\right)$

$= \sqrt{\dfrac{49+1}{2}}+\sqrt{\dfrac{48+1}{2}}-\dfrac{1}{\sqrt{2}}-0 = 5+3\sqrt{2}$

$\Rightarrow a=5, b=3$ and $a+b=8$

**2.** **(b).** $S = \displaystyle\sum_{r=2}^{\infty}\dfrac{1}{r^2-1} = \sum_{r=2}^{\infty}\dfrac{1}{(r-1)(r+1)}$

$T_r = \dfrac{1}{(r-1)(r+1)} = \dfrac{1}{2}\left[\dfrac{1}{r-1}-\dfrac{1}{r+1}\right]$

$\Rightarrow S_\infty = \dfrac{3}{4}$

**3.** **(d)** $\displaystyle\sum_{k=1}^{n}\left(\sum_{m=1}^{k}m^2\right) = \sum_{k=1}^{n}(1^2+2^2+3^2+\ldots+k^2)$

$\displaystyle\sum_{k=1}^{n}\dfrac{k(k+1)(2k+1)}{6} = \dfrac{1}{6}\sum_{k=1}^{n}(2k^3+3k^2+k)$

$= \dfrac{1}{3}\left\{\dfrac{n(n+1)}{2}\right\}^2 + \dfrac{1}{2}\left\{\dfrac{n(n+1)(2n+1)}{6}\right\}$

$+ \dfrac{1}{6}\left\{\dfrac{n(n+1)}{2}\right\} = \dfrac{1}{12}\{n^4+4n^3+5n^2+2n\}$

$\therefore \quad a=\dfrac{1}{12}, b=\dfrac{1}{3}, c=\dfrac{5}{12}, d=\dfrac{1}{6}$ and $e=0$.

So, $a+b+c+d+e=1$

**4.** **(d).** $T_k = \dfrac{(k+2)\sqrt{k}-k\sqrt{k+2}}{k(k+2)^2-k^2(k+2)}$

$= \dfrac{(k+2)\sqrt{k}-k\sqrt{k+2}}{2k(k+2)} = \dfrac{1}{2}\left[\dfrac{1}{\sqrt{k}}-\dfrac{1}{\sqrt{k+2}}\right]$

$T_1 = \dfrac{1}{2}\left[\dfrac{1}{\sqrt{1}}-\dfrac{1}{\sqrt{3}}\right]; \ T_2 = \dfrac{1}{2}\left[\dfrac{1}{\sqrt{2}}-\dfrac{1}{\sqrt{4}}\right]$

$T_3 = \dfrac{1}{2}\left[\dfrac{1}{\sqrt{3}}-\dfrac{1}{\sqrt{5}}\right]$ and so on

$\therefore$ as $k\to\infty$, sum $= \dfrac{1}{2}\left[1+\dfrac{1}{\sqrt{2}}\right] = \dfrac{1+\sqrt{2}}{2\sqrt{2}} = \dfrac{\sqrt{1}+\sqrt{2}}{\sqrt{8}}$

$\Rightarrow a+b+c=11$

**5.** **(a)** We have

$T_n = n(n+1)(n+2) = n^3+3n^2+2n$

$S_n = \Sigma n^3 + 3\Sigma n^2 + 2\Sigma n$

$= \dfrac{1}{4}n^2(n+1)^2 + \dfrac{3}{6}n(n+1)(2n+1) + \dfrac{2}{2}n(n+1)$

$= \dfrac{1}{4}n(n+1)(n^2+5n+6) = \dfrac{1}{4}n(n+1)(n+2)(n+3)$

**6.** **(b)** $A L_1^2 + L_1M_1^2 = (a^2+1)^2 + \{(a-1)^2+1^2\}$

$A L_2^2 + L_2M_2^2 = a^2 + 2^2 + \{(a-2)^2-2^2\}$

$\rule{6cm}{0.4pt}$

$AL_{a-1}^2 + L_{a-1}M_{a-1}^2 = a^2+(a-1)^2+\{1^2+(a-1)^2\}$

$\therefore$ The required sum

$= (a-1)a^2 + \{1^2+2^2+\ldots$

$\qquad\qquad +(a-1)^2\}+2\{1^2+2^2+\ldots+(a-1)^2\}$

$= (a-1)a^2 + a.\dfrac{(a-1)a(2a-1)}{6}$

$= a(a-1)\left\{a+\dfrac{4a-1}{2}\right\} = \dfrac{1}{2}a(a-1)(4a-1)$

**7.** **(c)**

$\dfrac{AL_1}{AB} = \dfrac{L_1M_1}{BC}$

$$\therefore \ \frac{1}{n+1} = \frac{L_1M_1}{a}; \quad \therefore \ L_1M_1 = \frac{a}{n+1}$$

$$\frac{AL_2}{AB} = \frac{L_2M_2}{BC} \quad \therefore \ \frac{2}{n+1} = \frac{L_2M_2}{a}$$

$$\therefore \ L_2M_2 = \frac{2a}{n+1}, \text{ etc}$$

$\therefore$ The required sum

$$= \frac{a}{n+1} + \frac{2a}{n+1} + \frac{3a}{n+1} + \ldots + \frac{na}{n+1}$$

$$= \frac{a}{n+1}(1+2+3+\ldots+n) = \frac{a}{n+1}\cdot\frac{n(n+1)}{2} = \frac{an}{2}$$

**8. (a)** We have $(1^2 - a_1)(2^2 - a_2) + \ldots + (n^2 - a_n)$

$$= \frac{1}{3}(n)(n^2 - 1)$$

$$\Rightarrow \ \sum_{k=1}^{n} k^2 - \sum_{k=1}^{n} a_k = \frac{1}{3}n(n^2 - 1)$$

$$\Rightarrow \ \frac{1}{6}n(n+1)(2n+1) - \frac{1}{3}n(n^2 - 1) = \sum_{k=1}^{n} a_k$$

$$\Rightarrow \ \sum_{k=1}^{n} a_k = \frac{1}{6}n(n+1)\{(2n+1) - 2(n-1)\}$$

$$= \frac{1}{2}n(n+1)$$

Also, $a_n = \displaystyle\sum_{k=1}^{n} a_k - \sum_{k=1}^{n-1} a_k$

$$= \frac{1}{2}n(n+1) - \frac{1}{2}(n-1)n = n$$

**9. (a, c, d)**

$$S_n = \lim_{n\to\infty}\left(\frac{1}{n^6} + \frac{32}{n^6} + \frac{243}{n^6} + \ldots + \frac{1}{n}\right)$$

$$T_n = \lim_{n\to\infty}\left(\frac{1}{n^6} + \frac{32}{n^6} + \frac{243}{n^6} + \ldots + \frac{(n-1)^5}{n^6}\right)$$

$$S_n = \lim_{n\to\infty}\sum_{r=1}^{r^5}\frac{r^5}{n^6} = \int_0^1 x^5\,dx = \left.\frac{x^6}{6}\right|_0^1 = \frac{1}{6}$$

$$\Rightarrow S_n = \left(\frac{1}{6}\right)^+ ; T_n = \left(\frac{1}{6}\right)^-$$

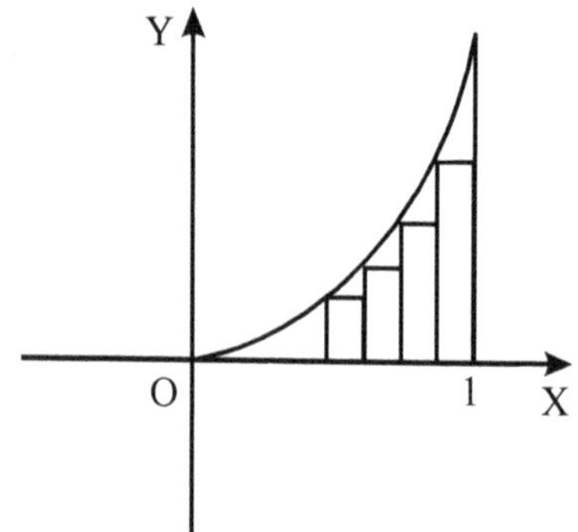

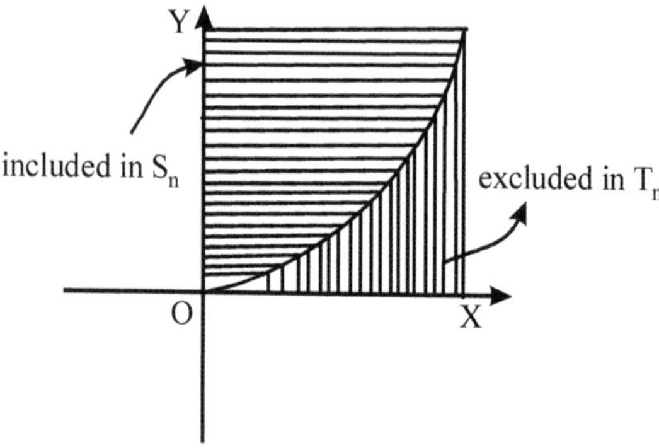


But since $x^5$ is concave upward the area included in $S_n$ for any two consecutive values of r is more than area excluded in $T_n$ for same values of r.

$$\Rightarrow \ S_n - \frac{1}{6} > \frac{1}{6} - T_n \ \Rightarrow \ S_n + T_n > \frac{1}{3}$$

**10. (a,d)** Sum of n terms of series is
$$S = 2 + 6 + 12 + \ldots\ldots + n(n+1)$$

$$= \sum(n^2 + n) = \frac{n(n+1)(2n+1)}{6} + \frac{n(n+1)}{2}$$

$$= \frac{n(n+1)(n+2)}{3}$$

Putting $n = 50$, we get $S = 44200$

also $\dfrac{n(n+1)(n+2)}{3} = 30n$

i.e., $(n+1)(n+2) = 90 = 9 \times 10, \ \therefore \ n = 8$

**11. (a, b,c,d)** $\displaystyle\sum_{r=1}^{n}(2r^3 + 5r^2 + 3r) = an^4 + bn^3 + cn^2 + dn + e$

$$\Rightarrow 2\left\{\frac{n(n+1)}{2}\right\}^2 + 5\left\{\frac{n(n+1)(2n+1)}{6}\right\} + 3\left\{\frac{n(n+1)}{2}\right\}$$

$$= an^4 + bn^3 + cn^2 + dn + e$$

Comparing similar powers of $n$ terms, we get

$$a = \frac{1}{2}, b = \frac{16}{6} = \frac{8}{3}, c = \frac{9}{2}, d = \frac{7}{3} \text{ and } e = 0$$

**12.** **(a, d)** We have $S_n = \dfrac{n}{1 - \dfrac{1}{n+1}} = \dfrac{n(n+1)}{n+1-1} = n+1$

$\Rightarrow S_n^2 = (n+1)^2$

So, $S_1^2 + S_2^2 + ... + S_{2n-1}^2 = 2^2 + 3^2 + ... + (2n)^2$

$= \dfrac{1}{6}(2n)(2n+1)(4n+1) - 1$

$= \dfrac{1}{3}[n(2n+1)(4n+1) - 3]$

**13.** **(b)** Given $S_n = an^2 + bn$

$\therefore \quad S_{n-1} = a(n-1)^2 + b(n-1)$

$\therefore \quad t_n = S_n - S_{n-1} = an^2 + bn - 4(n-1)^2 - b(n-1)$
$\qquad\qquad\qquad = 2an - a + b$

$\therefore \quad t_4 = 8a - a + b = 7a + b$

**14.** **(a)** Given $S_n = \dfrac{1}{4}n(n+1)(n+2)(n+3)$

$\therefore \ t_n = S_n - S_{n-1}$

$= \dfrac{1}{4}n(n+1)(n+2)(n+3) - \dfrac{1}{4}(n-1)n(n+1)(n+2)$

$= \dfrac{1}{4}n(n+1)(n+2)\{n+3-n+1\} = n(n+1)(n+2)$

**15.** **(c)** Given $S_n = \dfrac{n(n+1)(n+2)}{6}$

$\therefore \ n^{th}$ term is given by

$t_n = \dfrac{n(n+1)(n+2)}{6} - \dfrac{(n-1)n(n+1)}{6}$

$= \dfrac{n(n+1)}{6}(n+2-n+1)$

$= \dfrac{n(n+1)}{2} = \Sigma n$

**16.** $\mathbf{A \to r; B \to p; C \to s; D \to q}$

(A) We have $t_r = 1^2 + 3^2 + 5^2 + .... + (2r-1)^2$

$= \sum_{k=1}^{n}(2k-1)^2 = 4\sum_{k=1}^{n}k^2 - 4\sum_{k=1}^{n}k + r$

$= 4 \cdot \dfrac{1}{6}r(r+1)(2r+1) - 4\dfrac{1}{2}r(r+1) + r$

$= \dfrac{1}{3}(4r^3 - r)$

Thus, sum to n terms of the given series is

$\dfrac{4}{3}\sum_{r=1}^{n}r^3 - \dfrac{1}{3}\sum_{r=1}^{n}r = \dfrac{1}{6}n(n+1)(2n^2+2n-1)$

(B) We have $t_r = \dfrac{1}{1+2+3+.....+r} = \dfrac{2}{r(r+1)}$

$= 2\left[\dfrac{1}{r} - \dfrac{1}{r+1}\right]$

Thus, $t_1 + t_2 + ..... t_n$

$= 2\left[\left(1 - \dfrac{1}{2}\right) + \left(\dfrac{1}{2} - \dfrac{1}{3}\right) + .... + \left(\dfrac{1}{n} - \dfrac{1}{n+1}\right)\right] = \dfrac{2n}{n+1}$

(C) We have $S_n = 1^3 + 3.2^3 + 3^3 + 3.4^3 + 5^3 + ............$

Let $n = 2m$

Then $S_{2m} = (1^3 + 3^3 + 5^3 + ...... \text{ to m terms}) +$

$\qquad\qquad\qquad 3(2^3 + 4^3 + 6^3 + ... \text{to m terms})$

$= \{1^3 + 2^3 + 3^3 + 4^3 + ..... + (2m-1)^3 + (2m)^3\} - \{2^3 + 4^3$
$\qquad + ....+(2m)^3\} + 3\{2^3 + 4^3 + 6^3 + ..... + (2m)^3\}$

$= \left[\dfrac{2m(2m+1)}{2}\right]^2 + 8 \times 2\{1^3 + 2^3 + 3^3 + ......... + m^3\}$

$= m^2(2m+1)^2 + 16 \cdot \dfrac{m^2(m+1)^2}{4} = \dfrac{n^2(n^2+3n+1)}{2}$

$\qquad\qquad\qquad\qquad\qquad\qquad \left[\text{Putting } m = \dfrac{n}{2}\right]$

(D) Here, $x_n = \dfrac{1^3 + 2^3 + 3^3 + ......n^3}{1+3+5+.....\text{to n terms}}$

$= \dfrac{\dfrac{n^2(n+1)^2}{4}}{\dfrac{n}{2}\{2+(n-1)\times 2\}} = \dfrac{n^2(n+1)^2}{4n^2} = \dfrac{n^2+2n+1}{4}$

$\therefore S_n = \Sigma x_n = \dfrac{1}{4}\Sigma n^2 + \dfrac{1}{2}\Sigma n + \dfrac{1}{4}\Sigma 1$

$= \dfrac{1}{4} \cdot \dfrac{n(n+1)(2n+1)}{6} + \dfrac{1}{2} \cdot \dfrac{n(n+1)}{2} + \dfrac{1}{4} \cdot n$

$\therefore S_{16} = \dfrac{1}{4} \cdot \dfrac{16.17.33}{6} + \dfrac{1}{2} \cdot \dfrac{16.17}{2} + \dfrac{1}{4} \cdot 16 = 446$

**17.** $\mathbf{A \to r; B \to p; C \to s; D \to q}$

(A) $F(n+1) = \dfrac{2F(n)+1}{2} = F(n) + \dfrac{1}{2}$

$F(1), F(2), F(3).......... $ is an AP with common difference 1/2 **(r)**

$a = F(1) = 2$

$d = \tfrac{1}{2}$

$F = (101) = a + 100\,d$

$\quad = 2 + 100 \times \tfrac{1}{2} = 52$

(B)

$a_1 + 2d + a_1 + 4d + a_1 + 10d + a_1 + 16d + a_1 + 18d = 5a_1 + 50d = 10$

$(a_1 + 10d) = 10$ i.e., $a_1 + 10d = 2$

Now, $\sum_{i=1}^{21} a_i = \dfrac{21}{2}[2a_1 + 20d] = 21(a_1 + 10d) = 42$ **(p)**

(C) $S = 1 + 5 + 13 + 29 + ............. + t_{10}$

$S = \quad 1 + 5 + 13 + ..............t_9 + t_{10}.$

Subtracting,

$t_{10} = 1 + 4 + 8 + 16 + ......... \text{up to 10 terms}$

$\quad = 1 + (4 + 8 + 16 + ........ \text{up to 9 terms}) = 2045$ **(s)**

(D)   Sum of all two digit numbers

$$= \frac{90}{2}(10+99) = (45)(109)$$

Sum of all two digit numbers divisible by 2

$$= \frac{45}{2}(10+98) = (45)(54)$$

Sum of all two digit numbers divisible by 3

$$= \frac{30}{2}(12+99) = 15(111)$$

Sum of all two digit numbers divisible by 6

$$= \frac{15}{2}(12+96) = 15(54)$$

The required sum is $45(109) + 15(54) - (45)(54)$
$- 15(111) = 1620\,\mathbf{(q)}$.

**18.   (a)**   $1 \times 2 + [2 \times 3 + 2 \times 4 + 2 \times 5 + ...] + [3 \times 4 + 3 \times 5 + 3 \times 6$
$+ ... + ... + (n-1).n]$

$$= \frac{1}{2}\left[(1+2+....+n)^2 - (1^2+2^2+...+n^2)\right]$$

$$= \frac{1}{2}\left[\frac{n^2(n+1)^2}{4} - \frac{n(n+1)(2n+1)}{6}\right]$$

$$= \frac{1}{24}(n-1)n(n+1)(3n+2)$$

**19.   (d)**   $T_r = \left[n-(r-1)\right]\left[n+r-1\right] = n^2 - (r-1)^2$

$$\therefore\; S_n = \sum_{r=1}^{n} T_r = \sum_{r=1}^{n}\left[n^2 - (r-1)^2\right]$$

$$= n.\,n^2 - \sum_{r=1}^{n}(r-1)^2 = n^3 - \frac{1}{6}(n-1)n(2n-1)$$

$$= \frac{1}{6}n(n+1)(4n-1)$$

**20.   (5)**

$$S = (1+4+7+...+73) + \sum_{n=1}^{25}(3n-1)(3n)$$

$$= \frac{25}{2}(1+73+) + \sum_{n=1}^{25}(9n^2 - 3n)$$

$$= 25 \times 37 + \frac{9}{6}(25)(26)(51) - \frac{3}{2}(25)(26)$$

$$= 25\,[37 - 39 + 39 \times 51]$$

$$= 25 \times 1987$$

$$\therefore\; \frac{S}{9935} = \frac{25 \times 1987}{5 \times 1987} = 5$$

**21.   (9)**

Given series is an A.G.P. because each term of series is a product of corresponding term of an A.P. 3,5,7.... and a G.P.

$$1, \frac{1}{4}, \frac{1}{4^2} ....$$

Let   $S = 3 + 5.\dfrac{1}{4} + 7.\dfrac{1}{4^2} + ....$   ;   $\dfrac{1}{4}S = 3.\dfrac{1}{4} + 5.\dfrac{1}{4^2} + ....$

After subtraction we get,   $\dfrac{3}{4}S = 3 + 2\left[\dfrac{1}{4} + \dfrac{1}{4^2} + \dfrac{1}{4^3} + ....\right]$

$$= 3 + 2.\frac{1/4}{1-1/4} = \frac{11}{3} \quad \text{i.e.}\quad S = \frac{11}{3} \times \frac{4}{3} = \frac{44}{9}$$

Thus $B = 9$.

**1. (b)** Discriminant $D = (2m-1)^2 - 4(m-2)m = 4m+1$ must be perfect square

$\Rightarrow 4m+1 = k^2$, say for some $k \in \mathbf{I}$

$\Rightarrow m = \dfrac{(k-1)(k+1)}{4}$, clearly $k$ must be odd.

Let $k = 2n+1$.

$\therefore\ m = \dfrac{2n(2n+2)}{4} = n(n+1), n \in I$

**2. (a)**

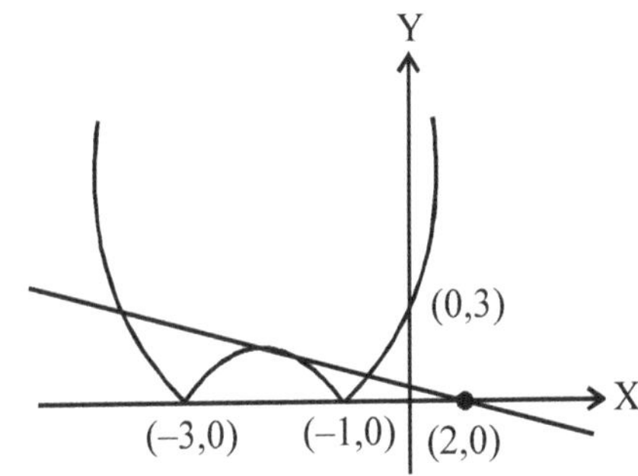


If $|x^2 + 4x + 3| = mx - 2m$ has exactly three solution,

then the curves $y = |x^2 + 4x + 3|$ and $y = m(x-2)$

intersect at exactly three points $\Rightarrow y = m(x-2)$ is

tangent to $y = -x^2 - 4x - 3$

$\Rightarrow\ m(x-2) = -x^2 - 4x - 3$ has equal roots

$\Rightarrow\ (m+4)^2 - 4(3 - 2m) = 0$

$\Rightarrow\ m = -8 \pm 2\sqrt{15}$

$\therefore\ m = -8 + 2\sqrt{15}\ \left(m \neq -8 - 2\sqrt{15}\right)$

**3. (c)** For the equation $px^2 + qx + 1 = 0$ to have real roots

$$D \geq 0 \quad \Rightarrow q^2 \geq 4p$$

If $p = 1$ then $q^2 \geq 4 \Rightarrow q = 2, 3, 4$

If $p = 2$ then $q^2 \geq 8 \Rightarrow q = 3, 4$

If $p = 3$ then $q^2 \geq 12 \Rightarrow q = 4$

If $p = 4$ then $q^2 \geq 16 \Rightarrow q = 4$

$\therefore$ No. of req. equations $= 7$.

**4. (a)** $\because$ a, b, c are sides of a triangle and $a \neq b \neq c$

$\therefore\ |a - b| < |c| \Rightarrow a^2 + b^2 - 2ab < c^2$

Similarly, we have

$b^2 + c^2 - 2bc < a^2$ ; $c^2 + a^2 - 2ca < b^2$

On adding, we get

$a^2 + b^2 + c^2 < 2(ab + bc + ca)$

$\Rightarrow\ \dfrac{a^2 + b^2 + c^2}{ab + bc + ca} \geq 3\lambda - 2$ ....(1)

$\because$ Roots of the given equation are real

$\therefore\ (a+b+c)^2 - 3\lambda(ab+bc+ca) \geq 0$

$\Rightarrow\ \dfrac{a^2 + b^2 + c^2}{ab + bc + ca} \geq 3\lambda - 2$ ....(2)

From (1) and (2), we get $3\lambda - 2 < 2 \Rightarrow \lambda < \dfrac{4}{3}$.

**5. (a)** Key concept : If both roots of a quadratic equation $ax^2 + bx + c = 0$ are less than k then $af(k) > 0$, $D > 0$, $\alpha + \beta < 2\,k$.

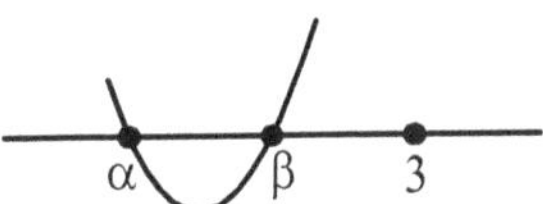


$f(x) = x^2 - 2ax + a^2 + a - 3 = 0$,

$f(3) > 0, \alpha + \beta < 6, \Delta \geq 0$.

$\Rightarrow a^2 - 5a + 6 > 0, a < 3, -4a + 12 > 0$

$\Rightarrow a < 2$ or $a > 3$, $a < 3$, $a < 3 \Rightarrow a < 2$.

**6. (b)** $\dfrac{1}{x+p} + \dfrac{1}{x+q} = \dfrac{1}{r} \Rightarrow \dfrac{2x+p+q}{x^2+(p+q)x+pq} = \dfrac{1}{r}$

$x^2 + (p+q-2r)x + (p+q)r = 0$

Sum of roots $= 0 \Rightarrow p + q = 2r$

**7. (c)** Let $f(x) = x^2 + 2(k+1)x + 9k - 5$. Let $\alpha, \beta$ be the roots of $f(x) = 0$. The equation $f(x) = 0$ will have both negative roots, if –

(i) Disc. $\geq 0$   (ii) $\alpha < 0, \beta < 0$, i.e. $(\alpha + \beta) < 0$ and

(iii) $f(0) > 0$

Now, Discriminant $\geq 0 \Rightarrow 4(k+1)^2 - 36k + 20 \geq 0$

$\Rightarrow\ k^2 - 7k + 6 \geq 0$

$\Rightarrow\ (k-1)(k-6) \geq 0$

$\Rightarrow\ k \leq 1$ or $k \geq 6$          ......(i)

$(\alpha + \beta) < 0 \Rightarrow -2(k+1) < 0$

$\Rightarrow\ k+1 > 0 \Rightarrow k > -1$          ......(ii)

and, $f(0) > 0 \Rightarrow 9k - 5 > 0 \Rightarrow k < 5/9$          ......(iii)

From (i), (ii), (iii), we get $k \geq 6$.

**8. (a,b,c).**

Add all 3 equations, $(a+b+c)x^2 + (a+b+c)x + m(a+b+c) = 0$

or $x^2 + x + m = 0$

Hence if none of the 3 equations have real roots then
$D < 0$

$1 - 4m < 0 \Rightarrow 1 < 4m \Rightarrow$ i.e. $4m > 1$

Hence for atleast one equation to have real roots $4m \leq 1$ or $m \leq 1/4$

**Alternatively:** If atleast one of the equations has real roots then $D_1 + D_2 + D_3 \geq 0$

$(b^2 - 4acm) + (c^2 - 4bam) + a^2 - 4cbm \geq 0$

$a^2 + b^2 + c^2 \geq 4\,(ab + bc + ca)\,m$

$$4m \leq \frac{a^2 + b^2 + c^2}{ab + bc + ca} \qquad \ldots\ldots\ldots\ldots (1) \ \forall \ a, b, c \in R^+$$

but $a^2 + b^2 \geq 2ab$ etc.

$a^2 + b^2 + c^2 \geq ab + bc + ca$

$$\frac{a^2 + b^2 + c^2}{ab + bc + ca} \geq 1$$

$$\therefore \ \left. \frac{a^2 + b^2 + c^2}{ab + bc + ca} \right|_{min} = 1$$

Hence 4m must be less than or equal to the minimum value.

$$\therefore \ 4m \leq \frac{a^2 + b^2 + c^2}{ab + bc + ca}$$

$$\therefore \ 4m \leq 1 \ \Rightarrow \ m \leq \frac{1}{4}$$

$$m \in \left( 0, \frac{1}{4} \right]$$

**9.** **(b,c)** If $x \geq a$, then $|x - a| = x - a$, and the equation

becomes $x^2 - 2ax - a^2 = 0 \Rightarrow x = a(1 \pm \sqrt{2})$

$\because \ a < 0; \quad \therefore \ a(1 + \sqrt{2}) < a,$

hence $x = a(1 + \sqrt{2})$ cannot be the solution.

$\therefore \ x = a(1 - \sqrt{2}) > a$ is the solution, which is positive.

Again if $x < a$, then $|x - a| = -(x - a)$

and the equation becomes

$x^2 + 2ax - 5a^2 = 0 \Rightarrow x = (-1 \pm \sqrt{6})a$

Again as $a < 0; \ \therefore \ a(-1 - \sqrt{6}) > 0 > a$, hence

$x = a(-1 - \sqrt{6})$ cannot be the solution.

$\therefore \ x = a(-1 + \sqrt{6}) < a$ is the solution, which is negative.

**10.** **(a, b, c)** $\because$ Roots are real

$\therefore \quad B^2 - 4AC > 0$

$\Rightarrow \quad a^4 > 4b^2,$

If $f(x) = x^2 + a^2 x + b^2$ ( $\because$ c lies outside the roots)

$\therefore \quad f(c) > 0$, then $c^2 + a^2 c + b^2 > 0$

Also (x − coordinate of vertex) > c

$$\Rightarrow \ -\frac{a^2}{2} > c$$

**11.** **(a,d)** Let $A = a + 2b - 3c, \ B = b + 2c - 3a, \ C = c + 2a - 3b$

$\therefore \quad A + B + C = 0$

Hence, roots are 1 and $\dfrac{C}{A}$.

**12.** **(a)** $f\left( \dfrac{a^2 - 3}{a} + x \right) = f\left( \dfrac{a^2 - 3}{a} - x \right)$

$\Rightarrow f(x)$ is symmetrical about $x = \dfrac{a^2 - 3}{a}$

So, the vertex of the parabola is $\left( \dfrac{a^2 - 3}{a}, \ -\dfrac{\left( a^2 + 3 \right)^2}{a} \right)$

Clearly, discriminant of quadratic $= \left( a^2 + 3 \right)^2 > 0$

Equation of the parabola is

$$\left[ y + \frac{\left( a^2 + 3 \right)^2}{a} \right] = a\left[ x - \left( \frac{a^2 - 3}{a} \right) \right]^2$$

**13.** **(d)** We have $f(0) = -12a$

$$f(1) = (1 - 2a)(a + 6)$$

$$f(0)\,f(1) < 0 \Rightarrow a \in (-\infty, -6) \cup \left( 0, \frac{1}{2} \right)$$

**14.** **(c)** $f(a\lambda) < 0 \Rightarrow a(\lambda - 2)\left( a^2 \lambda + 6 \right) < 0$

$$\Rightarrow -\frac{6}{a^2} < \lambda < 2 \ \ (\because a > 0)$$

**15.** **(A) − s, (B) − q, (C) − r, (D) − p.**

$D > 0 \Rightarrow (k - 3)^2 - 4k > 0$

Sum of roots $> 0 \Rightarrow k - 3 > 0$

Product of roots $> 0 \Rightarrow k > 0$

(B) $D > 0 \Rightarrow (k - 3)^2 - 4k > 0$

Sum of roots $< 0 \Rightarrow k - 3 < 0$

Products of roots $> 0 \Rightarrow k > 0$

(C) $D = 0$

(D) $f(x) = x^2 - (k - 3)x + k$

Now $D \geq 0 \Rightarrow k \in (-\infty, 1] \cup [9, \infty)$ ......... (i)

and because $f(1) = 4$ is positive, it means $f(-1)$ is also positive.

$\Rightarrow k \geq 1$ ......... (ii)

From (i) and (ii) $\Rightarrow k \in \{1\} \cup [9, \infty)$

**16.** $A \to r,t; B \to p,r; C \to s; D \to r,t$

(A)  $\because$ b is AM of a and c. $\Rightarrow b > \sqrt{ac} \Rightarrow b^2 - ac > 0$
$\Rightarrow$ The equation has real and distinct roots. Also a,b, c are positive so the roots are negative. **(r, t)**

(B)  $f(0) = -a^2 - 4 < 0 \Rightarrow f(x) = x^2 - (a+1)x - a^2 - 4 = 0$ has roots of opposite sign. **(p, r,)**

(C)  $\because$ b is HM of a and c $\Rightarrow b < \sqrt{ac} \Rightarrow b^2 - ac < 0$
$\Rightarrow$ The equation has imaginary roots. **(s)**

(D)  Discriminant of the equation is
$$D = (b^2 + a^2 - c^2)^2 - 4a^2b^2$$
$$= \{(a+b)^2 - c^2\}\{(a-b)^2 - c^2\} > 0$$
$$(\because |a \pm b| < c)$$
$\therefore$ roots of equation are real and distinct. Also the product of roots $> 0 \Rightarrow$ roots have same sign. **(r,t)**

**17.** (a)  $f(x) = x^2 + x + 1$, $D = 1 - 4 = -3 < 0$
$\Rightarrow f(x)$ is positive for all $x \in R$ (since $a > 0$)

If $D < 0$, then $ax^2 + bx + c$ and a will have same sign for all $x \in R$.
Both are true and statement -2 is correct reason for statement -1

**18.** (d)  $a^3 + b^3 + c^3 = 3abc$
$$\Rightarrow (a+b+c)(a^2 + b^2 + c^2 - ab - bc - ca) = 0$$
$$\Rightarrow (a+b+c).\frac{1}{2}\{(a-b)^2 + (b-c)^2 + (c-a)^2\} = 0$$
$$\therefore a+b+c = 0$$
$$\left[ \because (a-b)^2 + (b-c)^2 + (c-a)^2 > 0, \text{as } a > b > c \right]$$

But equation is $ax^2 + bx + c = 0$

$\therefore x = 1$ is a root.     $(\because a + b + c = 0)$

If other root is $\alpha$, then $\alpha.1 = \dfrac{c}{a}$

$\Rightarrow \alpha = \dfrac{c}{a} < 1$, which is either +ve or negative

Hence, both roots are real and distinct.

**19.** (9)  $x^2 + x - n = 0$,
Discrminent $= 1 + 4n = $ odd number $= D$ (say)
Now given equation would have an integral solution if $D$ is a perfect square.

Let $D = (2\lambda + 1)^2$

$\Rightarrow n = \lambda + \lambda^2 = \lambda(\lambda + 1) = $ even number
$\Rightarrow$  $n$ can be 2, 6, 12, 20, 30, 42, 56, 72, 90.

**20.** (2)  Given equation : $ax^2 + 2b|x| - c = 0$
**Case I :** when $x > 0$

The equation becomes $ax^2 + 2bx - c = 0$

$\therefore D = 4b^2 + 4ac > 0 \ (\because a,b,c > 0)$
**Case II :** when $x < 0$

The equation becomes $ax^2 - 2bx - c = 0$

$\therefore D = 4b^2 + 4ac > 0 \ (\because a,b,c > 0)$
In both the cases discriminant is positive, so both the roots of the equation must be real.

**1.** **(b)** Cross multiplication and rearranging gives the cubic.

$$x^3 - ax^2 + 23x - b = 0 \begin{cases} \alpha \\ \alpha \\ \beta \end{cases}$$

$2\alpha + \beta = a$ ....(1)

$\alpha^2 + 2\alpha\beta = 23$ ....(2)

and $\alpha^2\beta = \beta$ ....(3)

Also given $\alpha + \beta = 12$ ....(4)

From (2) and (4),

$\alpha^2 + 2\alpha(12 - \alpha) = 23$

$\alpha^2 + 24\alpha - 2\alpha^2 = 23$

$\alpha^2 - 24\alpha + 23 = 0$

$\alpha = 1$ (rejected)    since $x \neq \pm 1$

$\therefore \alpha = 23$      $\therefore \beta = -11$

$\therefore a = 35$ from (4)

and $b = \alpha^2\beta = 529 \times (-11)$

$\Rightarrow b = -5819 \Rightarrow a - b = 35 - (-5819) = 5854$

**2.** **(b)** Since $r_1 r_2 = 2$,

$$\therefore x^2 + px + 2 = 0 \begin{cases} r_1 \\ r_2 \end{cases} \text{ and } r_1 r_2 r_3 r_4 = -8 \Rightarrow r_3 r_4 = -4$$

$\Rightarrow x^4 - x^3 + ax^2 - 8x - 8 = (x^2 + px + 2)(x^2 + qx - 4)$

Compare coefficient of $x^3$ and $x$

$p + q = -1$ .....(1)

and $2q - 4p = -8 \Rightarrow q - 2p = -4$ ....(2)

$\Rightarrow p = 1$ and $q = -2$

On comparing coefficient of $x^2$; $a = -4$

$p = 1 \Rightarrow x^2 + x + 2 = 0$

$\therefore r_{1,2} = \dfrac{-1 \pm i\sqrt{7}}{2}$

**3.** **(a)** $x^2 + ax + b \equiv (x + 1)(x + b) \Rightarrow b + 1 = a$ ....(1)

Also $x^2 + bx + c \equiv (x + 1)(x + c)$

$\Rightarrow c + 1 = b$ or $b + 1 = c + 2$ ....(2)

Hence $b + 1 = a = c + 2$

Also $(x + 1)(x + b)(x + c) \equiv x^3 - 4x^2 + x + 6$

$x^3 + (1 + b + c)x^2 + (b + bc + c)x + bc \equiv x^3 - 4x^2 + x + 6$

$1 + b + c = -4$

$2c + 2 = -4 \Rightarrow c = -3; b = -2$ and $a = -1$

$\Rightarrow a + b + c = -6$

**4.** **(b)** We have $\alpha + \beta = p$ and $\alpha\beta = -(p + q)$.

Also, $(\alpha + 1)(\beta + 1) = (\alpha + \beta) + \alpha\beta + 1 = 1 - q$

Now, $\dfrac{\alpha^2 + 2\alpha + 1}{\alpha^2 + 2\alpha + q} + \dfrac{\beta^2 + 2\beta + 1}{\beta^2 + 2\beta + q}$

$= \dfrac{(\alpha + 1)^2}{(\alpha + 1)^2 + (q - 1)} + \dfrac{(\beta + 1)^2}{(\beta + 1)^2 + (q - 1)}$

$= \dfrac{2(\alpha + 1)^2(\beta + 1)^2 + (q - 1)\{(\alpha + 1)^2 + (\beta + 1)^2\}}{(\alpha + 1)^2(\beta + 1)^2 + (q - 1)^2 + (q - 1)\{(\alpha + 1)^2 + (\beta + 1)^2\}}$

$= \dfrac{2(1 - q)^2 + (q - 1)\{(\alpha + 1)^2 + (\beta + 1)^2\}}{(1 - q)^2 + (q - 1)^2 + (q - 1)\{(\alpha + 1)^2 + (\beta + 1)^2\}} = 1$

**5.** **(a)** $x^2 + px + q = 0$

Roots are $\alpha$ and $\alpha^2$

$\Rightarrow \alpha + \alpha^2 = -p, \alpha\alpha^2 = q \Rightarrow \alpha = q^{1/3}$

$\therefore (q)^{1/3} + (q^{1/3})^2 = -p$

Taking cube of both sides

$q + q^2 + 3q(q^{1/3} + q^{2/3}) = -p^3$

$\Rightarrow q + q^2 - 3pq = -p^3$

$\Rightarrow p^3 + q^2 - q(3p - 1) = 0$

**6.** **(d)** If $f(\alpha)$ and $f(\beta)$ are of opposite sign then there must lie a value $\gamma$ between $\alpha$ and $\beta$ such that $f(\gamma) = 0$.

a, b, c are real numbers and $a \neq 0$.

As $\alpha$ is a root of $a^2x^2 + bx + c = 0$

$\therefore a^2\alpha^2 + b\alpha + c = 0$ ....(1)

Also $\beta$ is a root of $a^2x^2 - bx - c = 0$ $\therefore$

$a^2\beta^2 - b\beta - c = 0$ .... (2)

Now, let $f(x) = a^2x^2 + 2bx + 2c$

Then $f(\alpha) = a^2\alpha^2 + 2b\alpha + 2c$

$= a^2\alpha^2 + 2(b\alpha + c)$

$= a^2a^2 + 2(ba + c)$

$= a^2a^2 + 2(-a^2a^2)$ [Using eq. (1)]

$= -a^2a^2$.

and $f(\beta) = a^2\beta^2 + 2b\beta + 2c$

$= a^2\beta^2 + 2(b\beta + c)$

$= a^2\beta^2 + 2(a^2\beta^2)$ [Using eq. (2)]

$= 3a^2\beta^2 > 0$.

Since $f(\alpha)$ and $f(\beta)$ are of opposite signs and $\gamma$ is a root of equation $f(x) = 0$

$\therefore$ $\gamma$ must lie between $\alpha$ and $\beta$

Thus $\alpha < \gamma < \beta$.

**7.** **(d)** Here $\alpha + \beta = \dfrac{\lambda - 1}{\lambda}$ , $\alpha\beta = \dfrac{5}{\lambda}$

Given $\dfrac{\alpha}{\beta} + \dfrac{\beta}{\alpha} = \dfrac{4}{5} \Rightarrow 5[\alpha^2 + \beta^2] = 4\alpha\beta$

$\Rightarrow \lambda^2 - 16\lambda + 1 = 0$

Now $\lambda_1 + \lambda_2 = 16, \lambda_1\lambda_2 = 1$

$\therefore \dfrac{\lambda_1}{\lambda_2} + \dfrac{\lambda_2}{\lambda_1} = \dfrac{\lambda_1^2 + \lambda_2^2}{\lambda_1\lambda_2} = \dfrac{(-16)^2 - 2}{1} = 254$

**8.** **(d)** Here $\alpha$ and $\beta$ are roots

$\therefore a\alpha^2 + b\alpha + c = 0$ ......(1)

$a\beta^2 + b\beta + c = 0$ .......(2)

Now let us consider (keeping results (1), (2) in mind)

$a S_{n+1} + b S_n + c S_{n-1}$

$= a[\alpha^{n+1} + \beta^{n+1}] + b[\alpha^n + \beta^n] + c[\alpha^{n-1} + \beta^{n-1}]$

$= [a\alpha^{n+1} + b\alpha^n + c\alpha^{n-1}] + [a\beta^{n+1} + b\beta^n + c\beta^{n-1}]$

$= \alpha^{n-1}[a\alpha^2 + b\alpha + c] | \beta^{n-1}[a\beta^2 + b\beta + c] = 0 + 0 = 0$

Hence $aS_{n+1} + cS_{n-1} = -bS_n$

**9.** **(c)** Let the roots of the equation be $\alpha$ and $2\alpha$, then

$$\alpha + 2\alpha = \frac{l}{m-l} \text{ and } \alpha \cdot 2\alpha = \frac{1}{l-m}$$

$$\Rightarrow \alpha = \frac{l}{3(m-l)} \text{ and } \alpha^2 = \frac{1}{2(l-m)}. \text{ Eliminating } \alpha,$$
we get

$$\frac{l^2}{9(m-l)^2} = \frac{1}{2(l-m)} \Rightarrow 2l^2 - 9l + 9m = 0$$

Since $l$ is real, so $(-9)^2 - 4 . 2 . 9m \geq 0 \Rightarrow m \leq \frac{9}{8}$

**10.** **(a)** We are given that $\alpha_1, \alpha_2$ are the roots of

$$ax^2 + bx + c = 0$$

$$\therefore \ \alpha_1 + \alpha_2 = -\frac{b}{a}; \alpha_1 \alpha_2 = \frac{c}{a} \quad ....(1)$$

and $\beta_1, \beta_2$ are the roots of $px^2 + qx + r = 0$

$$\therefore \ \beta_1 + \beta_2 = -\frac{q}{p}; \beta_1 \beta_2 = \frac{r}{p} \quad ....(2)$$

The system of equations, $\quad \alpha_1 y + \alpha_2 z = 0$
and $\beta_1 y + \beta_2 z = 0$ has a non trivial solution.

$$\therefore \text{ We must have } \begin{vmatrix} \alpha_1 & \beta_1 \\ \alpha_2 & \beta_2 \end{vmatrix} = 0$$

$$\Rightarrow \alpha_1 \beta_2 - \alpha_2 \beta_1 = 0$$

$$\Rightarrow \frac{\alpha_1}{\alpha_2} = \frac{\beta_1}{\beta_2}$$

By componendo and dividendo, we get

$$\frac{\alpha_1 + \alpha_2}{\alpha_1 - \alpha_2} = \frac{\beta_1 + \beta_2}{\beta_1 - \beta_2}$$

$$\Rightarrow (\alpha_1 + \alpha_2)(\beta_1 - \beta_2) = (\alpha_1 - \alpha_2)(\beta_1 + \beta_2)$$

$$\Rightarrow (\alpha_1 + \alpha_2)^2 [(\beta_1 + \beta_2)^2 - 4\beta_1 \beta_2]$$

$$= [(\alpha_1 + \alpha_2)^2 - 4\alpha_1 \alpha_2](\beta_1 + \beta_2)^2$$

Using equations (1) and (2), we get

$$\frac{b^2}{a^2}\left[\frac{q2}{p^2} - \frac{4r}{p}\right] = \frac{q^2}{p^2}\left[\frac{b^2}{a^2} - \frac{4c}{a}\right]$$

$$\Rightarrow \frac{b^2 q2}{a^2 p^2} - \frac{4b^2 r}{a^2 p} = \frac{q^2}{p^2}\frac{b^2}{a^2} - \frac{4cq^2}{ap^2}$$

$$\Rightarrow \frac{-4b^2 r}{a^2 p} = \frac{-4cq^2}{ap^2}$$

$$\Rightarrow \frac{b^2 r}{a} = \frac{sq^2}{p} \quad \Rightarrow \frac{b^2}{q^2} = \frac{ac}{pr}.$$

**11.** **(c)** We know that,

$$(\alpha - \beta)^2 = [(\alpha + \delta) - (\beta + \delta)]^2$$

$$\Rightarrow (\alpha + \beta)^2 - 4\alpha\beta = (\alpha + \delta + \beta + \delta)^2 - 4(\alpha + \delta)(\beta + \delta)$$

$$\Rightarrow \frac{b^2}{a^2} - \frac{4c}{a} = \frac{B^2}{A^2} - \frac{4C}{A}$$

$$\frac{4AC - B^2}{}$$

**12.** **(b,d)** The roots are non-real complex, $\Rightarrow$ discriminant,

$$b^2 - 4ac < 0$$

Hence $f(x) = ax^2 + bx + c$ must have the same sign for all real x. Now $f(-1) = a - b + c < 0$ (given condition)

Thus $f(x) < 0$ for all $x \in \mathbf{R}$. In particular $f(-2) < 0$.

That is, $4a - 2b + c < 0 \Rightarrow 4a + c < 2b$
Also, $f(1/2) < 0 \Rightarrow a - 2b + 4c < 0$

**13.** **(a,b)** We can write the given equation as

$$\frac{p}{2x} = \frac{(a+b)x + c(b-a)}{x^2 - c^2}$$

or $\quad p(x^2 - c^2) = 2(a+b)x^2 - 2c(a-b)x$

or $\quad (2a + 2b - p)x^2 - 2c(a-b)x + pc^2 = 0$

For this equation to have equal roots

$$c^2(a-b)^2 - pc^2(2a + 2b - p) = 0$$

$$\Rightarrow (a-b)^2 - 2p(a+b) + p^2 = 0 \quad [\because c^2 \neq 0]$$

$$\Rightarrow [p - (a+b)]^2 = (a+b)^2 - (a-b)^2 = 4ab$$

$$\Rightarrow p - (a+b) = \pm 2\sqrt{ab}$$

$$\Rightarrow p = a + b \pm 2\sqrt{ab} = (\sqrt{a} \pm \sqrt{b})^2$$

**14.** **(d)** $f(0) . f(2) > 0, D > 0$

$$\therefore (a^2 - 2a + 2)(a^2 - 10a + 18) < 0$$

$$\Rightarrow a^2 - 10a + 18 < 0 \quad (\because a^2 - 2a + 2 > 0 \ \forall \ a \in R)$$

$$5 - \sqrt{7} < a < 5 + \sqrt{7} \quad ....(1)$$

Also $(-4a)^2 - 4.4(a^2 - 2a + 2) > 0$

$$\Rightarrow a > 1 \Rightarrow a \in (1, \infty) \quad ....(2)$$

Taking (1) & (2) simultaneously, we obtain

$$5 - \sqrt{7} < a < 5 + \sqrt{7}$$

**15.** **(a)** $4f(0) > 0, 4f(2) > 0, \quad 0 < \dfrac{4a}{2.4} < 2, \ D \geq 0$

$4(a^2 - 2a + 2) > 0,$
And $(4a^2 - 10a + 18) > 0$

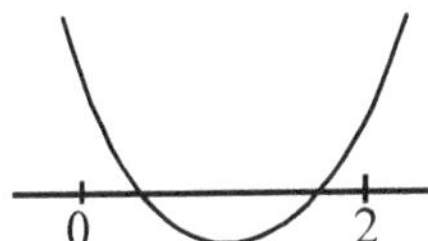

$$\Rightarrow a \in (-\infty, 5 - \sqrt{7}) \cup (5 + \sqrt{7}, \infty)$$

And $a \in (0, 4)$ and $16a^2 - 4.4(a^2 - 2a + 2) \geq 0$

$$a - 1 \geq 0 \Rightarrow a \in [1, 5 - \sqrt{7})$$

**16.** **(a)** We can take D > 0 and $4f(1) < 0$

$$\Rightarrow (4a)^2 - 4.4(a^2 - 2a + 2) > 0 \text{ and } 4(4 - 4a + a^2 - 2a + 2) < 0$$

$$\Rightarrow a > 1 \text{ and } (a-3)^2 < 3$$

$$\Rightarrow a \in (1, \infty) \text{ and } a \in (3 - \sqrt{3}, 3 + \sqrt{3})$$

$$\Rightarrow a \in (3 - \sqrt{3}, 3 + \sqrt{3})$$

**17. (a)** Let $A = b + c - a$, $B = c + a - b$, $C = a + b - c$

$\therefore A + B + C = a + b + c = 0$ $\quad (\because a + b + c = 0)$

Then the given equation can be written as
$Ax^2 + Bx + C = 0$

$\therefore$ Discriminant $= B^2 - 4AC$

$= (-A - C)^2 - 4AC$

$= (A + C)^2 - 4AC$

$= (A - C)^2$

$= [(b + c - a) - (a + b - c)]^2$

$= 4(c - a)^2$, which is a perfect square

Hence, roots of
$(b + c - a)x^2 + (c + a - b)x + (a + b - c) = 0$ are rationals.

**18. (d)** The given equation can be written as

$(a + b + c)x^2 - 2(ab + bc + ca)x + 3abc = 0$

$\therefore$ Discriminant

$= 4(ab + bc + ca)^2 - 12abc(a + b + c) > 0$

$(\because abc < 0, a + b + c > 0)$

Also, product of roots $= \dfrac{3abc}{a + b + c} < 0$

Thus, both roots are of opposite nature.

**19. (6)** $N = \alpha\,(111111)$ is divisible by $7 \times 11 \times 3$
Hence for N to be a divisible by 924, $\alpha = 4$ or $8$
and $\alpha$ and $\beta$ are roots of $x^2 - 11x + \lambda = 0$.

$\Rightarrow \alpha + \beta = 11$

$\Rightarrow (\alpha, \beta) \equiv (4, 7), (8, 3)$

$\Rightarrow$ Possible value of $\lambda = 28, 24$

$\Rightarrow$ Product of values of $\lambda = 672$

$\therefore M = 6$

**20. (2)** Let $2^{111x} = y$, so that

$\log_2 y = 111\,x \Rightarrow x = \dfrac{\log_2 y}{111}$

Equation becomes $\quad \dfrac{y^3}{4} + 2y = 4y^2 + 1$

$y^3 - 16y^2 + 8y - 4 = 0$

Sum of the roots of the given equation is

$x_1 + x_2 + x_3 = \dfrac{\log_2 y_1 + \log_2 y_2 + \log_2 y_3}{111}$

$= \dfrac{\log_2(y_1 y_2 y_3)}{111} = \dfrac{\log_2 4}{111} = \dfrac{2}{111}$

$\Rightarrow S_1 + S_2 = 113$

**21. (2)** Here p, q are roots of $x^2 - 2x + A = 0$

$\therefore\ p + q = 2$ .....(1)

Also r, s are roots of $x^2 - 18x + B = 0$

$\therefore\ r + s = 18$ .....(2)

Now since p, q, r, s are in A.P. say with common difference d.

$\therefore\ q = p + d, r = p + 2d, s = p + 3d$

From (1) and (2),

$\left.\begin{array}{l} 2p + d = 2 \\ 2p + 5d = 18 \end{array}\right\} \Rightarrow 4d = 16 \Rightarrow d = 4$

$\therefore\ 2p + 4 = 2 \Rightarrow p = -1$

Hence $p = -1$, $q = -1 + 4 = 3$

$r = -1 + 8 = 7$, $s = -1 + 12 = 11$

$A = pq = -3$, $B = rs = 77$

$\therefore\ \dfrac{A + B}{37} = \dfrac{74}{37} = 2$

**22. (1)** Since both the roots are less than 2, we have

(i) $D \geq 0 \Rightarrow 15p - 66 \leq 0 \Rightarrow p \leq \dfrac{22}{5}$

(ii) $4f(2) > 0 \Rightarrow 4(25p^2 - 25p - 50) > 0$
$\Rightarrow p^2 - p - 2 > 0 \Rightarrow p < -1$ or $p > 2$

(iii) $-\dfrac{-20p}{2.4} < 2 \Rightarrow p < \dfrac{4}{5}$

Taking the intersection of above three solutions, we get $p < -1$ or $p \in (-\infty, -1)$

$\therefore B = 1$

**23. (3)** The given equation is $m^2 x^2 + (2m - m^2)x + 3 = 0$

$\therefore \alpha + \beta = -\dfrac{2m - m^2}{m^2} = \dfrac{m - 2}{m}$ and $\alpha\beta = \dfrac{3}{m^2}$

Now $\dfrac{\alpha}{\beta} + \dfrac{\beta}{\alpha} = \dfrac{4}{3} \Rightarrow \dfrac{\alpha^2 + \beta^2}{\alpha\beta} = \dfrac{4}{3} \Rightarrow \dfrac{(\alpha + \beta)^2 - 2\alpha\beta}{\alpha\beta} = \dfrac{4}{3}$

Substituting the values, we get

$$\dfrac{\left(\dfrac{m - 2}{m}\right)^2 - 2 \cdot \dfrac{3}{m^2}}{\dfrac{3}{m^2}} = \dfrac{4}{3}$$

$\Rightarrow \dfrac{m^2 - 4m + 4 - 6}{3} = \dfrac{4}{3} \Rightarrow m^2 - 4m - 6 = 0$

$m_1$ and $m_2$ are roots of this equation, therefore $m_1 + m_2 = 4$ and $m_1 m_2 = -6$

The given expression is,

$\dfrac{m_1^2}{m_2} + \dfrac{m_2^2}{m_1} = \dfrac{m_1^3 + m_2^3}{m_1 m_2}$

$= \dfrac{(m_1 + m_2)^3 - 3m_1 m_2(m_1 + m_2)}{m_1 m_2} = \dfrac{(4)^3 - 3.(-6).(4)}{-6} = -\dfrac{68}{3}$

Thus, $P = 3$

**1.** **(c)** $3^{2x^2} - 2.3^{x^2+x+6} + 3^{2(x+6)} = 0$

$(3^{x^2})^2 - 2\,(3^{x^2}).3^{x+6} + (3^{x+6})^2 = 0$

$(3^{x^2} - 3^{x+6})^2 = 0 \Rightarrow 3^{x^2} = 3^{x+6} \Rightarrow x^2 - x - 6 = 0$

$\Rightarrow (x-3)(x+2) = 0 \Rightarrow x = -2, 3$

**2.** **(b)** $x^2 + px + qr = 0$ ......... (i)

$x^2 + qx + rp = 0$ ......... (ii)

$x^2 + rx + pq = 0$ ......... (iii)

Every pair has a common root.

Let the roots are $\alpha, \beta$ for (i), $\beta, \gamma$ for (ii); $\gamma, \alpha$ for (iii).

$\alpha + \beta = -p$ ......... (iv)

$\alpha\beta = qr$ ......... (v)

$\beta + \gamma = -q$ ......... (vi)

$\beta\gamma = rp$ ......... (vii)

Common roots are $\alpha, \beta, \gamma$

By (i) and (ii),

$\beta^2 + p\beta + qr = 0$, $\beta^2 + q\beta + rp = 0$

Subtracting, $(p-q)\beta + r(q-p) = 0$, or $\beta = r$

Put this in (vii),

$r\gamma = rp$ or $\gamma = p$.

Put $\beta = r$ in (v), $\alpha = p$.

$\therefore \ \alpha + \beta + \gamma = q + r + p$ ....... (a)

But $\alpha + \beta = -p$ ; $\beta + \gamma = -q$, $\gamma + \alpha = -r$

$\Rightarrow \alpha + \beta + \gamma = -\dfrac{1}{2}(p + q + r)$ ....... (b)

By (a) and (b),

$\Rightarrow p + q + r = 0 \Rightarrow \alpha + \beta + \gamma = 0$

**3.** **(a)** Let $a^{\cos x} = t \Rightarrow t + \dfrac{1}{t} = 6 \Rightarrow t^2 - 6t + 1 = 0$

$\Rightarrow \ t = \dfrac{6 \pm \sqrt{36-4}}{2} = 3 \pm 2\sqrt{2} \Rightarrow a^{\cos x} = 3 \pm 2\sqrt{2}$

$\Rightarrow \ \cos x = \log_a(3 \pm 2\sqrt{2})$

Since $a > 1$, for all the roots to be real,

We must have $\log_a(3 + 2\sqrt{2}) \le 1$ and

$\log_a(3 - 2\sqrt{2}) \ge -1$,

Both are true for $a \ge 3 + 2\sqrt{2}$.

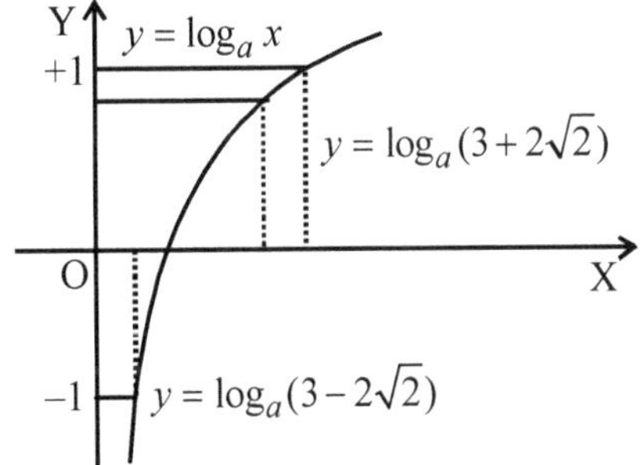


**4.** **(b)** The problem contains one absolute value term $|x - 3|$. Thus, we consider two cases

**CASE : (I)**

Let $x < 3$, then $|x-3| = -(x-3)$, the equation becomes

$x^2 . 2^{x+1} + 2^{-x+5} = x^2 . 2^{-x+7} + 2^{x-1}$

$\Rightarrow x^2 (2^{x+1} - 2^{-x+7}) = 2^{x-1} - 2^{-x+5}$

$\Rightarrow x^2 . 2^{-x+7} (2^{2x-6} - 1) = 2^{-x+5}(2^{2x-6} - 1)$

$\Rightarrow (2^{2x-6} - 1)(x^2 . 2^{-x+7} - 2^{-x+5}) = 0$

$\therefore \ 2^{2x-6} - 1 = 0 \Rightarrow 2x - 6 = 0$

$\Rightarrow x = 3$, rejected $\quad (\because x < 3)$

or $x^2 . 2^{-x+7} - 2^{-x+5} = 0$

$\Rightarrow 2^{-x+5}(2^2 . x^2 - 1) = 0 \Rightarrow x = \pm\dfrac{1}{2}$

$\Rightarrow x \in \left\{ -\dfrac{1}{2}, \dfrac{1}{2} \right\}$

**CASE : (II)**

Let $x \ge 3$, then $|x-3| = x - 3$, the equation becomes

$x^2 . 2^{x+1} + 2^{x-1} = x^2 . 2^{x+1} + 2^{x-1}$ , which is identity.

$\therefore$ All x, such that $x \ge 3$ is the solution of the equation.

The solution set is $\left\{ -\dfrac{1}{2}, \dfrac{1}{2} \right\} \cup [3, \infty)$

**5.** **(b)** $4^{\sin 2x + 2\cos^2 x} + 4^{3 - \left(\sin 2x + 2\cos^2 x\right)} = 65$

Put $y = 4^{\sin 2x + 2\cos^2 x} \Rightarrow y + \dfrac{64}{y} - 65 = 0$

$\therefore y^2 - 65y + 64 = 0 \Rightarrow y = 1$ or $y = 64$

$\Rightarrow \sin 2x + 2\cos^2 x = 0 \Rightarrow \cos^2 x + \sin x \cos x = 0$

$\Rightarrow \cos x (\cos x + \sin x) = 0 \Rightarrow x = \dfrac{\pi}{2}$

Also, $\sin 2x + 2\cos^2 x = 3 \Rightarrow \sin 2x + \cos 2x = 2$ is not possible as maximum of $\sin 2x + \cos 2x = \sqrt{2}$

**6.** **(d)** Given expression $x^{12} - x^9 + x^4 - x + 1 = f(x)$

For $x < 0$ put $x = -y$, where $y > 0$

then we get $f(x) y^{12} + y^9 + y^2 + y + 1 > 0$ for $y > 0$

For $0 < x < 1$, $x^9 < x^4 \Rightarrow -x^9 + x^4 > 0$

Also $1 - x < 0$ and $x^{12} > 0$

$\Rightarrow x^{12} - x^9 + x^4 + 1 - x > 0 \Rightarrow f(x) > 0$

For $x > 1$

$f(x) = x(x^3 - 1)(x^8 + 1) + 1 > 0$

So $f(x) > 0$ for $-\infty < x < \infty$.

**7.** **(b)** Let $3^x = y$, then the inequality is

$$|y^2 - 3y - 15| < 2y^2 - y \qquad ...(1)$$

The inequality holds if $2y^2 - y > 0 \Rightarrow y < 0$ or $y > \dfrac{1}{2}$.

$\because\ y = 3^x \not\le 0 \Rightarrow y > \dfrac{1}{2}$

Now the inequality on solving,

$$-(2y^2 - y) < y^2 - 3y - 15 < 2y^2 - y$$

$$\Rightarrow\ 3y^2 - 4y - 15 > 0 \text{ and } y^2 + 2y + 15 > 0$$

Solution of first inequality

$3y^2 - 4y - 15 > 0$ is $y < -\dfrac{5}{3}$ or $y > 3$.

Solution of second inequality $y^2 + 2y + 15 > 0$ is $y \in \mathbf{R}$

The common solution is $y > 3 \Rightarrow 3^x > 3 \Rightarrow x > 1$
$\Rightarrow x \in (1, \infty)$

**8.** **(b)** **Key concept :** $f(x) = ax^2 + bx + c$ has same sign as that of $a$ if $D < 0$.

$x^2 + 2ax + 10 - 3a > 0 - x$

$\Rightarrow\ D < 0 \Rightarrow 4a^2 - 4(10 - 3a) < 0$

$\Rightarrow\ a^2 + 3a - 10 < 0$

$\Rightarrow\ (a + 5)(a - 2) < 0 \Rightarrow a \in (-5, 2)$

**9.** **(d)** Let $D_1, D_2$ be discriminants of
$2a^2x^2 - 2abx + b^2 = 0$ and $ax^2 + bx - c^2 = 0$ respectively
$D_1 = -4ab < 0$ and $D_2 = b^2 + 4ac^2$
$D_2 > 0$ if $a > 0$ hence no common root if $a > 0$

**10.** **(b)** We have $x^2 - 9 \ne 0$ and $x + 2 \ne 0$ and

$$\dfrac{2x}{x^2 - 9} - \dfrac{1}{x + 2} \le 0 \Rightarrow \dfrac{2x^2 + 4x - x^2 + 9}{(x+2)(x^2 - 9)} \le 0$$

$$\Rightarrow\ \dfrac{x^2 + 4x + 9}{(x+2)(x^2 - 9)} \le 0 \Rightarrow (x+2)(x+3)(x-3) < 0$$

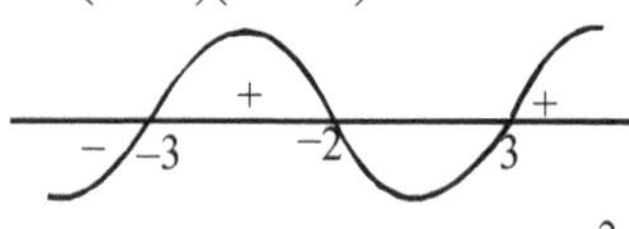

$$(\because\ x^2 + 4x + 9 > 0\ \forall x \in R)$$

From the wavy curve shown,
we have $x \in (-\infty, -3) \cup (-2, 3)$

**11.** **(b,c)**
(a) If for some value of x say $x = x_1$, the equation $E = 0$ has one root infinite and other root a non zero finite, so $u = 0$ and $v \ne 0$
$\therefore\ u = 0$ and $v = 0$ do not have a common root. $\Rightarrow$ (a) is false
(b) If for some value of x say $x = x_2$, the equation $E = 0$ has both infinite roots, so $u = 0$ and $v = 0$
$\therefore\ u = 0$ and $v = 0$ will have a common root. $\Rightarrow$ (b) is true
(c) If for some value of x say $x = x_3$, the equation $E = 0$ becomes an identity in y, so $u = 0$, $v = 0$ and $w = 0$
$\therefore\ u = 0$, $v = 0$ and $w = 0$ must have a root, common to all of them. $\Rightarrow$ (c) is true

(d) If for some value of x say $x = x_4$, the equation $E = 0$ has both roots real and distinct then $v = 0$ and $w = 0$ must have a common root is not necessary $\Rightarrow$ (d) is false.

**12.** **(a, c, d)** $2x^3 + x^2 + 2x - 5 = 0$

$$\Rightarrow\ (x - 1)(2x^2 + 3x + 5) = 0$$

So, one root is 1 and other roots are imaginary.

Also, $ax^3 + (a + b)x^2 + (b + c)x + c = 0$

$$\Rightarrow (x + 1)(ax^2 + bx + c) = 0$$

Clearly the two equations have either 1 as common root or both roots must be common. So,

$a + b + c = 0$ or $\dfrac{a}{2} = \dfrac{b}{3} = \dfrac{c}{5} \Rightarrow a + b + c = 0$

or $a + b + c = 2c$ or $5a$

**13.** **(a,b)** The equation is reciprocal so, $f(x) = 0$ and $f\left(\dfrac{1}{x}\right) = 0$
represent same equation

$\therefore\ x^3 + x^2 + ax + b = 0$ and $\dfrac{1}{x^3} + \dfrac{1}{x^2} + \dfrac{a}{x} + b = 0$

or $bx^3 + ax^2 + x + 1 = 0$ are indentical

$\therefore\ \dfrac{1}{b} = \dfrac{1}{a} = \dfrac{a}{1} = \dfrac{b}{1} \Rightarrow a^2 = 1$ and $a = b$

$\Rightarrow a = b = \pm 1$

**14.** **(b)** Put $x^2 + x + 1 = y$, the equation reduces to

$$(y + 1)^2 - (a - 3)(y + 1)y + (a - 4)y^2 = 0$$

$$\Rightarrow (a - 5)y - 1 = 0 \Rightarrow y = \dfrac{1}{a - 5}$$

$$\therefore\ x^2 + x + 1 = \dfrac{1}{a - 5}.$$

Now $x^2 + x + 1 = \left(x + \dfrac{1}{2}\right)^2 + \dfrac{3}{4} \ge \dfrac{3}{4}$

$$\therefore\ \dfrac{1}{a - 5} \ge \dfrac{3}{4} \Rightarrow \dfrac{4 - 3a + 15}{4(a - 5)} \ge 0$$

$$\Rightarrow\ \dfrac{3a - 19}{a - 5} \le 0 \Rightarrow (a - 5)(3a - 19) \le 0, a \ne 5$$

$$\Rightarrow\ 5 < a \le \dfrac{19}{3} \qquad \because\ 6 < \dfrac{19}{3} < 7$$

$\therefore\ $ Only integral value of $a$, such that

$a \in \left(5, \dfrac{19}{3}\right]$ is $a = 6$.

**15.** **(b)** $f(x) = x^3 - 12x - p$

$f'(x) = 3x^2 - 12 = 3(x^2 - 4) > 0$

$\Rightarrow\ f(x)$ is strictly increasing for $x > 2$ and $x < -2$

$f(3) = -9 - p < 0$

$f(4) = 16 - p > 0 \Rightarrow$ 　 one root lies in $(3, 4)$.

**16. (b)** $f(x) = 2\sin^2\theta x^2 - 3\sin\theta.x + 1$

$f(1) = 2\sin^2\theta - 3\sin\theta + 1 = (2\sin\theta - 1)(\sin\theta - 1) < 0$

$f(2) = 8\sin^2\theta - 6\sin\theta + 1$

$= (4\sin\theta - 1)(2\sin\theta - 1) > 0$

$f(1)f(2) < 0 \Rightarrow$ one real root in the interval (1,2).

**17. (b)** $f(x) = ax^2 + bx + c$, $\qquad f(0) = c < 0$

$f\left(-\dfrac{1}{2}\right) = \dfrac{a - 2b + 4c}{4} > 0$

$\Rightarrow$ one root lies in the interval $\left(-\dfrac{1}{2}, 0\right)$.

**18. (b)** $\because (3)^2 - 4.2.4 = -23 < 0$

$\therefore$ Roots of $2x^2 + 3x + 4 = 0$ are imaginary

Now $\because 2, 3, 4 \in R$

$\therefore$ Roots are conjugate to each other

$\because$ One root is common in $ax^2 + bx + c = 0$

and $2x^2 + 3x + 4 = 0$ (given)

If one root is common then other root is also common

$\because$ Roots are conjugate $(a, b, c \in R)$

Hence, both equations are identical

$\therefore a : b : c = 2 : 3 : 4$

**19. (c)** If $1 \le a \le 2 \Rightarrow 0 \le a - 1 \le 1$

$\Rightarrow \sqrt{a + 2\sqrt{a-1}} + \sqrt{a - 2\sqrt{a-1}}$

$= \sqrt{1} + \sqrt{a-1} + \sqrt{1} - \sqrt{a-1} = 2$

Statement-1 is true but Statement-2 is false.

Hence (c) is correct choice.

**20. (0)** $e^{\sin x} - e^{-\sin x} - 4 = 0$

Let $e^{\sin x} = y$ then $e^{-\sin x} = 1/y$

$\therefore$ Equation becomes, $y - \dfrac{1}{y} - 4 = 0$

$\Rightarrow y^2 - 4y - 1 = 0$

$\Rightarrow y = 2 + \sqrt{5}, 2 - \sqrt{5}$

But y is real +ve number,

$\therefore y \ne 2 - \sqrt{5}$

$\Rightarrow y = 2 + \sqrt{5}$

$\Rightarrow e^{\sin x} = 2 + \sqrt{5}$

$\Rightarrow \sin x = \log_e(2 + \sqrt{5})$

But $2 + \sqrt{5} > e$

$\Rightarrow \log_e(2 + \sqrt{5}) > \log_e e$

$\Rightarrow \log_e(2 + \sqrt{5}) > 1 \qquad$ Hence, $\sin x > 1$

Which is not possible.

$\therefore$ Given equation has no real solution.

**21. (2)** The given equation is

$(5 + 2\sqrt{6})^{x^2-3} + (5 - 2\sqrt{6})^{x^2-3} = 10 \qquad ....(1)$

Let $(5 + 2\sqrt{6})^{x^2-3} = ys \qquad ....(2)$

then $(5 - 2\sqrt{6})^{x^2-3} = \left(\dfrac{(5 - 2\sqrt{6})(5 + 2\sqrt{6})}{5 + 2\sqrt{6}}\right)^{x^2-3}$

$= \left(\dfrac{25 - 24}{5 + 2\sqrt{6}}\right)^{x^2-3} = \left(\dfrac{1}{5 + 2\sqrt{6}}\right)^{x^2-3} = \dfrac{1}{y}$ (Using (2))

$\therefore$ The given equation (1) becomes $y + \dfrac{1}{y} = 10$

$\Rightarrow y^2 - 10y + 1 = 0$

$\Rightarrow y = \dfrac{10 \pm \sqrt{100 - 4}}{2} = \dfrac{10 \pm 4\sqrt{6}}{2}$

$\Rightarrow y = 5 + 2\sqrt{6}$ or $5 - 2\sqrt{6}$

Consider, $y = 5 + 2\sqrt{6}$

$\Rightarrow (5 + 2\sqrt{6})x^2-3 = (5 + 2\sqrt{6})$

$\Rightarrow x^2 - 3 = 1$

$\Rightarrow x^2 = 4 \Rightarrow x = \pm 2$

Again consider

$y = 5 - 2\sqrt{6} = \dfrac{1}{5 + 2\sqrt{6}} = (5 + 2\sqrt{6})^{-1}$

$\Rightarrow (5 + 2\sqrt{6})x^2-3 = (5 + 2\sqrt{6})^{-1}$

$\Rightarrow x^2 - 3 = -1$

$\Rightarrow x^2 = 2$

$\Rightarrow x = \pm\sqrt{2}$

Hence the solutions are $2, -2, \sqrt{2}, -\sqrt{2}$.

**22. (1)** $2 + |e^x - 1| = e^{2x} - 2e^x + 1 = |e^x - 1|^2$

i.e., $|e^x - 1|^2 - |e^x - 1| - 2 = 0$

$\Rightarrow |e^x - 1| = 2$ or $-1 \Rightarrow |e^x - 1| = 2$
$\qquad\qquad$ (negative value not admissible)

$\Rightarrow e^x - 1 = \pm 2 \Rightarrow e^x = 3$ or $-1 \Rightarrow e^x = 3$
$\qquad\qquad$ (negative value not admissible)

$\Rightarrow x = \log_e 3 \Rightarrow$ only one solution.

**23. (4)** $\sqrt{e^{|x|\log 4}} = e^{\frac{|x|2\log 2}{2}} = e^{|x|\log 2} = (e^{\log 2})^{|x|} = 2^{|x|}$

$\therefore$ Given equation is $2^{|x^2-12|} = 2^{|x|}$

$\Rightarrow |x^2 - 12| = |x|$

$\Rightarrow x^4 - 25x^2 + 144 = 0$

$\Rightarrow x^2 = 16, 9$

$\Rightarrow x = \pm 3, \pm 4$

**24. (0)** Let $\alpha$ be the common root of the given equations. Then

$a\alpha^2 + 2c\alpha + b = 0$ and $a\alpha^2 + 2b\alpha + c = 0$

$\Rightarrow 2\alpha(c - b) + (b - c) = 0 \Rightarrow \alpha = \dfrac{1}{2} \qquad [\because b \ne c]$

Puting $\alpha = 1/2$ in $a\alpha^2 + 2c\alpha + b = 0$,

we get $a + 4b + 4c = 0$

**1. (a)** The digit in the units place of n (n + 1) is 0, 2 or 6, therefore digit in the units place of number n (n + 1) + 1 is 1, 3, 7.

5 doesn't divide $n^2 + n + 1$

2005 is not divisor of n (n + 1) + 1

**2. (a)** Total number of words that can be formed using 5 letters out of 10 given different letters

$= 10 \times 10 \times 10 \times 10 \times 10$ (as letters can repeat)

$= 1,00,000$

Number of words that can be formed using 5 different letters out of 10 different letters

$= {}^{10}P_5$ (none can repeat)

$= \dfrac{10!}{5!} = 30,240$

∴ Number of words in which at least one letter is repeated

= total words–words with none of the letter repeated

$= 1,00,000 - 30,240 = 69760$

**3. (a)** $\times \mid \times \mid \times \mid$

The odd place shown by crosses can be filled in

${}^3P_3 - {}^2P_2$ ways.

     (∵ 0 cannot go in the first place from the left).

The remaning place can be filled in 3 ! ways.

∴ The required number of numbers

$= ({}^3P_3 - {}^2P_2) \times 3!$

***ALTERNATIVELY:***

Let the six digit number be $x_1 x_2 x_3 x_4 x_5 x_6$. Then

$x_1$ can take values 2 or 4 that is 2 values.

$x_2$ can take values 1, 3 or 5 that is 3 values.

Now, $x_3$ can take two values as 0 can occur but digit of $x_1$ can not occur.

Similarly $x_4$ can take two values, $x_5$ and $x_6$ each can take 1 value.

∴ Total number of possibilites

$= 2 \times 3 \times 2 \times 2 \times 1 \times 1 = 24$

**4. (d)** We may consider the problem as filling the digits in boxes of the figure :

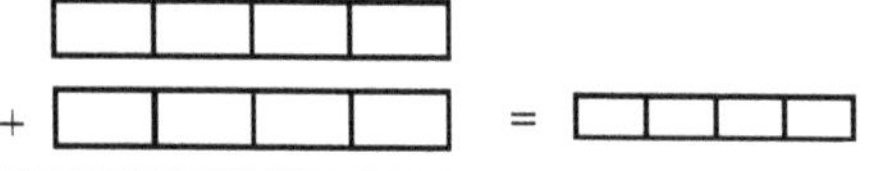

If 0 is placed in the units place of the upper number then the units place of the lower number can be filled in 9 ways (filling by any one of 0, 1, 2, .............., 9).

If 1 is placed in the units place of the upper number then the units place of the lower number can be filled in 9 ways (filling by any one of 0, 1, 2, ......., 8), etc.

∴ The units column can be filled in $10 + 9 + 8 + \ldots\ldots\ldots\ldots$

+ 1, i.e., 55 ways. Similarly for the second and the third columns. The number of ways for the fourth column

$= 8 + 7 + \ldots\ldots\ldots\ldots + 1 = 36$.

∴ The required number of ways $= 55 \times 55 \times 55 \times 36$.

**5. (a)** We know that a number is divisible by 3 if the sum of its digits is divisibly by 3.

Now out of 0, 1, 2, 3, 4, 5 if we take 1, 2, 3, 4, 5 or 0, 1, 2, 4, 5 then the 5 digit numbers will be divisible by 3.

**Case I :** Number of 5 digit numbers formed using the digits 1, 2, 3, 4, 5 = 5! = 120

**Case II :** Taking 0, 1, 2, 4, 5 if we make 5 digit number then

I place can be filled in 4 ways (0 can not come at I place)

II place can be filled in 4 ways

III place can be filled in 3 ways

IV place can be filled in 2 ways

V place can be filled in 1 ways

∴ Total numbers $= 4 \times 4! = 96$

Thus total numbers divisible by 3 are $= 120 + 96 = 216$

**6. (c)** According to questions LCM (p, q) $= r^2 t^4 s^2$. For LCM, (p, q) to contain $r^2$ following are the possible powers of r in p and q. (0, 2); (1, 2) ; (2, 2). Out of these all except (2, 2) can be interchanged for p and q.

∴ Total ways for p, q to contain different powers of r $= 2 \times 3 - 1 = 5$

Similarly, different powers of t that can be given to p and q are (0, 4) (1, 4), (2, 4), (3, 4), (4,4) our of which except (4, 4 ) all others can be interchanged for p and q.

∴ Total ways for p, q to contain different powers of t are $= 2 \times 5 - 1 = 9$

Similarly total ways for p, q to contain different powers of S are $= 2 \times 3 - 1 = 5$

∴ Total ordered pair of p, q can be $= 5 \times 9 \times 5 = 225$

**7. (c)** The letter of word COCHIN in alphabetic order are C, C, H, I, N, O.

Fixing first letter C and keeping C at second place, rest 4 can be arranged in 4! ways.

Similarly the words starting with CH, CI, CN are 4! in each case.

Then fixing first two letters as CO next four places when filled in alphabetic order give the word COCHIN.

∴ Numbers of words coming before COCHIN are $4 \times 4!$

$= 4 \times 24 = 96$

**8. (a)** Number of girls = 3, number of boys = 7. Since there is no restriction on boys, therefore first of all arrange the 7 boys in ${}^7P_7 = 7!$ ways.

$\times$ B $\times$ B $\times$ B $\times$ B $\times$ B $\times$ B $\times$ B $\times$

If the girls are arranged at the places (including the two ends) indicated by crosses, no two of three girls will be consecutive.

Now there are 8 places for 3 girls

∴ 3 girls can be arranged in ${}^8P_3$ ways

∴ Required number $= {}^8P_3 \times 7! = \dfrac{8!}{5!} \times 7! = 4281$.

**9.** **(b,c)** $p = E_2(10!) = \left[\dfrac{10}{2}\right] + \left[\dfrac{10}{2^2}\right] + \left[\dfrac{10}{2^3}\right] = 5 + 2 + 1 = 8$

$q = E_3(10!) = \left[\dfrac{10}{3}\right] + \left[\dfrac{10}{3^2}\right] = 3 + 1 = 4$

$r = E_5(10!) = \left[\dfrac{10}{5}\right] = 2$

$s = E_7(10!) = \left[\dfrac{10}{7}\right] = 1$

**10.** **(a,b,c,d)**

(a) $12 = 2^2 \times 3$

∴ Exponent of 12 in 50 ! $= \min \{ E_2(50!),$

$E_3(50!) \} = E_3(50!) = 22$

(b) We have, $E_2(24!) = 12 + 6 + 3 + 1 = 22$, $E_3(24!) = 8 +$

$2 = 10$, $E_5(24!) = 4$, $E_7(24!) = 3$,

$E_{11}(24!) = 2$, $E_{13}(24!) = 1$, $E_{17}(24!) = 1$, $E_{19}(24!) = 1$,

$E_{23}(24!) = 1$

∴ $24! = 2^{22} \cdot 3^{10} \cdot 5^4 \cdot 7^3 \cdot 11^2 \cdot 13 \cdot 17 \cdot 19 \cdot 23$ Clearly

$24^6 = 2^{18} \cdot 3^6$ divides above.

(c) Number of zero's at the end of 60 ! = exponent of 10 in

60 ! $= \min \{ E_2(60!), E_5(60!) \} = E_5(60!) = 14$.

(d) We have, $\dfrac{^nP_r}{^nP_{r-1}} = \dfrac{\dfrac{n!}{(n-r)!}}{\dfrac{n!}{(n-r+1)!}} = n - r + 1$

∴ $\dfrac{b}{a} = \dfrac{^nP_r}{^nP_{r-1}} = n - r + 1$ ...(1)

and $\dfrac{c}{b} = \dfrac{^nP_{r+1}}{^nP_r} = n - r$ (Put $r = r + 1$ in (1))

∴ $\dfrac{b^2}{a(b+c)} = \dfrac{b}{a\left(1 + \dfrac{c}{b}\right)} = \dfrac{n-r+1}{1+n-r} = 1$

**11.** **(a,c)** $^{n+5}P_{n+1} = \dfrac{11(n-1)}{2} \times {}^{n+3}P_n$

$\Rightarrow {}^{n+5}P_{n+1} = \dfrac{(n+5)!}{4!} = \dfrac{11(n-1)}{2} \dfrac{(n+3)!}{3!}$

$\Rightarrow (n+5)(n+4) = 22(n-1)$

After solving, we get $n = 6$ or $n = 7$.

The number of points of intersection of lines is $^6C_2$ or

$^7C_2 = 15$ or $21$.

**12.** **(a,b,c)** INTERMEDIATE has 3 $E$'s, 2 $I$'s and 2 $T$'s and $A, D,$ $M, N, R$ one each, thus total of 12 letters.

If words start with $I$ and end with $E$ i. e. $I \times \times \times \times \times \times \times$ $\times \times \times E$; the ten places (shown by cross) has to be filled with 2 $E$'s and 2 $T$'s and 6 distinct letters.

∴ Number of words $= \dfrac{10!}{2! \, 2!} = 907200$

If vowels and consonants occupy their original places, then

6 vowels $(E, E, E, I, I, A)$ can be arranged in $\dfrac{6!}{3!2!}$ ways at their original places.

6 consonant $(N, T, T, M, D, R)$ can be arranged in $\dfrac{6!}{2!}$ ways at their original place.

∴ Number of words $= \dfrac{6!}{3! \, 2!} \times \dfrac{6!}{2!} = 21600$

If vowels and consonants occur alternatively, then 6 vowels can be arranged in 6 places in $\dfrac{6!}{3! \, 2!}$ ways.

6 consonants can be arranged in 5 places shown by crosses and one place either extreme left or extreme right in $\dfrac{6!}{2!} \times 2!$.

∴ Number of words $= \dfrac{6!}{3! \, 2!} \times \dfrac{6!}{3!} \times 2! = 43200$

If all the vowels occur together, then group of 6 vowels taken together will be considered one and 6 consonants can be arranged in $\dfrac{7!}{2!}$ ways.

[There are two $T$'s]. But 6 vowels can be arranged in $\dfrac{6!}{3!2!}$ ways.

∴ Number of words $= \dfrac{7!}{2!} \times \dfrac{6!}{3!2!} = 151200 \Rightarrow$ (d) is wrong.

**13. (d), 14. (b), 15. (d)**

(i) Only choice (d) doesn't violate any of the conditions.

(ii) Since Reena cannot select another biography, we eliminate choice (d), also since if B is elected, G must be too, eliminate choice (a). Therefore, the other selections must be three of the four novels A, C, D, and E. If she did not select C, she could not select E either (C ↔ E), and then she would have only two novels. So C must be selected.

∴ (b) holds.

If E is not selected, then neither is C (C ↔ E), so the three novels selected are A, B and D. Since A → F and B → G, F and G must be the selected biographies, H can't be selected.

∴ (d) holds.

**16.** A→p,q, s; B→ p,q,r,s,t; C→p,q,s

(A)  BG B G BG BG BG B

Requird number of ways = 6!5! **( p,q,s)**

(B)  Since here restriction is on girls.

Let us seat the boys first in the form

$\times B \times B \times B \times B \times B \times B \times$

which can be done in 6! ways.

For five girls there are 7 places shows by '×' which can be done in $^7P_5$ ways.

Required number of ways = $^7P_5 \times 6!$

$= \dfrac{7!}{2!} = 6\,! = \dfrac{7 \times 6 \times 5! \times 6!}{2!} = 21 \times 5!6!$ **(p, q, s)**

or $3 \times 5! \times 7!$ **(p,r,t)**

(C)  Total ways without restriction = (11 − 1) = 10!

Number of ways in which all the girls can be seated together = (7 −1)! × 5! = 6!5!

∴ Required number = 10 ! − 6!5! = 41 × 5!6! **(p,q,s)**

**17.** A→p, q; B→q, t; C→p, q,r,s;

(A)  When numbers are of three digits:

| 5 or 6 only | | |

First place can be filled in 2 ways, second place can be filled in 4 ways, and third place can be filled in 3 ways

∴  Number of ways = 2 × 4 × 3 = 24

When numbers are of four digits :

| 2 or 3 only | | | |

First place can be filled in 2 ways, second place can be filled in 4 ways and third place can be filled in 3 ways and fourth place can be filled in 2 ways.

∴  Number of ways = 2 × 4 × 3 × 2 = 48

∴  Total number of ways = 2 4 + 48 = 72

∴ n = 72 = 2 × 2 × 2 × 3 × 3 **(p, q)**

(B)  **Case (I)** : When numbers are of three digits:

(a)  The three digit number with '0' at unit place, first place can be filled in 3 ways  and second place can be filled in 3 ways

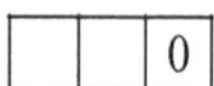


Number of ways = 3 × 3  = 9

(b) The three digit number with 2 or 4 at unit place, first place can be filled in 2 ways and second place can be filled in 3 ways

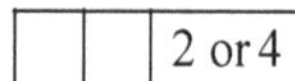


∴ Number of ways = 2 × 3 × 2 = 12

**Case (II)**: When numbers are of four digits:

(a) The four digit numbers with '0' at unit place:

| | | | 0 |

First place can be filled in 2 ways (1 or 2), second place can be filled in 3 ways and third place can be filled in 2 ways.

∴ Number of ways = 2 × 3 × 2 = 12

(b)  The four digits numbers with '2' at unit place:

| | | | 2 |

First place can be filled in  1 way, second place can be filled in 3 ways and third place can be filled in 2 ways.

∴  Number of ways = 1 × 3 × 2 = 6

(c)  The four digits numbers with '4' at unit place:

| | | | 4 |

First place can be filled in 2 ways (1 or 2), second place can be filled in 3 ways and third place can be filled in 2 ways.

∴  Number of ways = 2 × 3 × 2 = 12

∴  Total number of ways = 9 + 12 + 12 + 6 + 12 = 51

n = 51 = 3 × 17 **( q,t)**

(C)  ROORKEE

Number of ways = $\dfrac{7!}{2!2!2!} = 630$

Number of words begin with $R = \dfrac{6!}{2!2!} = 180$

Number of words end with $E = \dfrac{6!}{2!2!} = 180$

and number of words begin with

R and end with $E = \dfrac{5!}{2!} = 60$

∴ Requird number of words

$= 630 − 180 − 180 + 60 = 330$

∴  n = 330 = 2 × 3 × 5 × 11 **(p, q, r, s)**

**18.**  **(c)**  In the given word there are 4 I's, so required number of permutations is $\dfrac{12!}{4!} = 19958392$

**19.**  **(b)**  Since, $1400 = 2^3.5^2.7^1$

⇒ Total no. of factors = $(3 + 1)(2 + 1)(1 + 1) = 24$

⇒ No. of ways of expressing 1400 as a product of two numbers $= \dfrac{1}{2} \times 24 = 12$.

But this does not follow from statement-II, which is obviously true.

**20.**  **(2)**

**Case-I:** All six digits alike × × × × × ×

say 111111, 222222, ...... etc = 5 ways

**Case-II:** 2 alike + 2 other alike + 2 other alike.

$^5C_3$ say 1, 2, 3 and take 11, 22, 33

∴ Number of ways = $\dfrac{6!}{2!2!2!}$ ( in each selection)

⇒ Total = $10 \left( \dfrac{720}{8} \right) = 900$

**Case-III:** 2 alike + 4 other alike e.g. 11 2222 or 221111 etc.

Number of ways selecting 2 digits = $(\,^5C_2\,)(2)$ (in each selection)

$\therefore$ Number of ways $= \dfrac{6!}{2!\,4!}$

$\Rightarrow$ Total $= (^5C_2)\,(2)\,\dfrac{6!}{2!\,4!} = (20)(15) = 300$

**Case-IV:** 3 alike $+$ 3 other alike.
Select $^5C_2$ e.g. 111, 222 etc.

Total ways $^5C_2\ \dfrac{6!}{3!\,3!} = 200$

Total $= 5 + 900 + 300 + 200 = 1405$

$\therefore P = 2$

**21. (5)**

A A A A A | B B B B B B

Middle digit must be A (think !)

$$\overset{\displaystyle M}{\underset{\displaystyle \times\ \times\ \times\ \times\ \times\ \downarrow\ \times\ \times\ \times\ \times\ \times}{}}$$

so that even number of A's and B's are available
Take AABBB on one side of M (6th place) and then their image about M in a unique way

$\therefore$ Number of ways $= \dfrac{5!}{2!\,.3!} = 10$

$\therefore X = 5$

**22. (5)**

**Case-I :** When the two identical digits are both unity as shown.

    $\boxed{1}\ \boxed{x}\ \boxed{y}\ \boxed{1}$ any one place out of 3 block for unity can be taken in 3 ways and the remaining two blocks can be filled in $9 \times 8$ ways.

    Total ways in this case $= 3 \times 9 \times 8 = 216$

**Case-II :** When the two identical digit are other than unity.

    $\boxed{1}\ \boxed{x}\ \boxed{x}\ \boxed{y}$ ; $\boxed{1}\ \boxed{x}\ \boxed{y}\ \boxed{x}$ ; $\boxed{1}\ \boxed{y}\ \boxed{x}\ \boxed{x}$

    two x's can be taken in 9 ways and filled in three ways and y can be taken in 8 ways.

    Total ways in this case $= 9 \times 3 \times 8 = 216$

    Total of both cases $= 432$

$\therefore\quad (A)^3\,(B)^4 = 432$

$= (27)\,(16)$

$= (3)^3 .\,(2)^4$

$\therefore\quad A = 3,\, B = 2.$ Thus $A + B = 3 + 2 = 5$

**23. (3)** $x + 2y = 10$

where x is the number of times he takes single steps and y is the number of times he takes two steps

| Cases | Total number of ways |
|---|---|
| I: $x = 0$ and $y = 5$ | $\dfrac{5!}{5!} = 1$ (2 2 2 2 2) |
| II: $x = 2$ and $y = 4$ | $\dfrac{6!}{2!\cdot 4!} = 15$ (1 1 2 2 2 2) |
| III: $x = 4$ and $y = 3$ | $\dfrac{7!}{4!\cdot 3!} = 35$ (1 1 1 1 2 2 2) |
| IV: $x = 6$ and $y = 2$ | $\dfrac{8!}{2!\cdot 6!} = 28$ (1 1 1 1 1 1 2 2) |
| V: $x = 8$ and $y = 1$ | $^9C_1 = 9$ (1 1 1 1 1 1 1 1 2) |
| VI: $x = 10$ and $y = 0$ | $1$ (1 1 1 1 1 1 1 1 1 1) |

Hence total number of ways $= 1 + 15 + 35 + 28 + 9 + 1 = 89$

$\therefore 10n^2 - 1 = 89$

$\Rightarrow n = 3$

**24. (6)**

$X - X - X - X - X$. The four digits 3, 3, 5, 5 can be

arranged at $(-)$ places in $\dfrac{4!}{2!\,2!} = 6$ ways.

The five digits 2, 2, 8, 8, 8 can be arranged at

(X) places in $\dfrac{5!}{2!\,3!} = 10$ ways.

Total no. of arrangements $= 6 \times 10 = 60$ ways.

$\therefore P = 6.$

**1.** **(a)** $\text{Area} = \dfrac{1}{2}\begin{vmatrix} 0 & 0 & 1 \\ x_1 & 99 - x_1 & 1 \\ x_2 & 99 - x_2 & 1 \end{vmatrix}$

$= \dfrac{1}{2}[x_1(99 - x_2) - x_2(99 - x_1)]$

$\text{Area} = \dfrac{1}{2}\,|\,[(x_1 - x_2)\,99]\,|$

Area is an integer then both $x_1$ and $x_2$ are simultaneously either even or both odd.

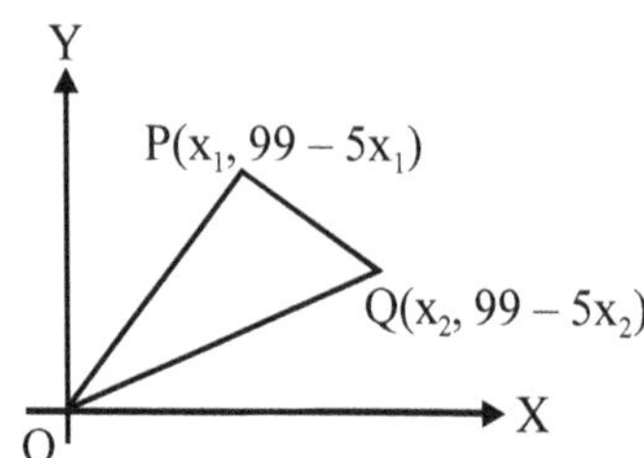


Now $x_1$ varies from 0 to 19 $\Big\langle$ 10 even / 10 odd

hence $^{10}C_2 + {}^{10}C_2 = 2 \cdot {}^{10}C_2 = 90$

**2.** **(c)** $10 \begin{cases} 3m \\ 7w \end{cases}$ ; 3 women can be selected in $^7C_3$ ways and can be paired with 3 men in 3! ways. Remaining 4 women

can be grouped into two pairs in $\dfrac{4!}{2!\,2!\,2!} = 3$ ways

∴  Required number of ways $= {}^7C_3 \cdot 3! \cdot 3 = 630$

**3.** **(a)** There are $^4C_2 = 6$ ways a block can differ from the given block in exactly two ways
(1) material and size, (2) material and colour, (3) material and shape, (4) size and colour, (5) size and shape, and (6) colour and shape. Since there is only 1 choice for different material, 2 choices for different size, 3 choices for a different colour, and 3 choices for a different shape, it follows that the number of blocks in each of the above categories is
$(1 \times 2)$, $(1 \times 3)$, $(1 \times 3)$, $(2 \times 3)$, $(2 \times 3)$ and $(3 \times 3)$, respectively. The answer is the sum of these six numbers
$= 29$

**4.** **(c)** Along horizontal side,
one unit can be taken in $(2m - 1)$ ways
3 units can be taken in $(2m - 3)$ ways
5 units can be taken in $(2m - 5)$ ways
and so on

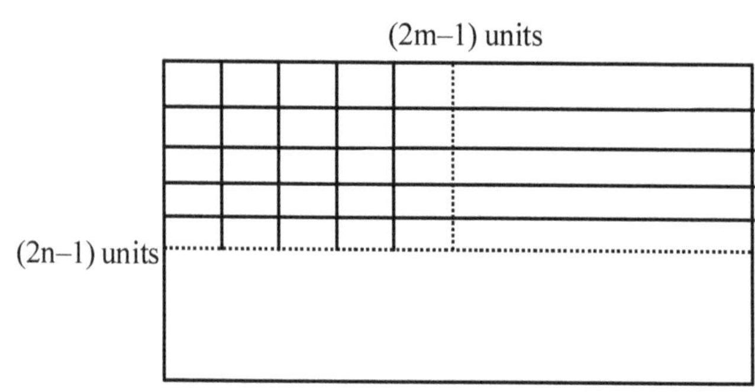


∴  The number of ways of selecting a side horizontally
is $(2m - 1) + (2m - 3) + (2m - 5) + ... + 3 + 1 = m^2$
Similarly the number of ways of selecting a side
vertically is $(2n - 1) + (2n - 3) + (2n - 5) + ... + 3 + 1 = n^2$
∴  Total number of rectangles $= m^2 \times n^2 = m^2 n^2$.

**5.** **(d)** The number of triangles with vertices on sides AB, BC, CD $= {}^3C_1 \times {}^4C_1 \times {}^5C_1$
Similarly for other cases the total number of triangles
$= {}^3C_1 \times {}^4C_1 \times {}^5C_1 + {}^3C_1 \times {}^4C_1 \times {}^6C_1 + {}^3C_1 \times {}^5C_1 \times {}^6C_1$
$\qquad\qquad\qquad\qquad\qquad + {}^4C_1 \times {}^5C_1 \times {}^6C_1$

$= 342$

**6.** **(d)** Given $\dfrac{{}^{n+1}C_{r+1}}{{}^{n}C_r} = \dfrac{11}{6} \Rightarrow \dfrac{\dfrac{n+1}{r+1} \times {}^{n}C_r}{{}^{n}C_r} = \dfrac{11}{6}$

$\Rightarrow 6n + 6 = 11r + 11 \Rightarrow 6n - 11r = 5 \qquad ...(1)$
Also,

$\dfrac{{}^{n}C_r}{{}^{n-1}C_{r-1}} \Rightarrow \dfrac{\dfrac{n}{r} \times {}^{n-1}C_{r-1}}{{}^{n-1}C_{r-1}} = \dfrac{6}{3}$

$\Rightarrow n = 2r \qquad ...(2)$
From (1) & (2);
$r = 5$ & $n = 10 \Rightarrow nr = 50$

**7.** **(c)** Let $A = \{\, a_1, a_2, a_3, .........., a_n \,\}$. For any $a_i \in A$, we may have following situations.

(i) $a_i \in P,\ a_i \in Q$

(ii) $a_i \in P,\ a_i \notin Q$

(iii) $a_i \notin P,\ a_i \in Q$

(iv) $a_i \notin P,\ a_i \notin Q$

∵  $P \cap Q$ contains exactly two elements. Taking 2 elements belonging to case (i) and $(n - 2)$ elements belong to case (ii), (iii) or (iv)
∴  Number of ways $= {}^nC_2 \times 3^{n-2}$

**8.** **(c)** For a particular class total number of different tickets from first intermediate station = 5

Similarly number of different tickets from second intermediate station = 4

So total number of different tickets = $5+4+3+2+1=15$

And same number of tickets for another class

$\Rightarrow$ total number of different tickets = 30 and number of selection = $^{30}C_{10}$

**9.** **(b,c,d)** $\quad 10 \geq x-1 \Rightarrow x \leq 11$ and $10 \geq x \Rightarrow x \leq 10$

$\therefore \quad x \leq 10$

$\because \; ^{10}C_{x-1} > 2.\,^{10}C_x \Rightarrow 1 > 2.\dfrac{^{10}C_x}{^{10}C_{x-1}}$

$\Rightarrow 1 > 2.\dfrac{10-x+1}{x}$

$\Rightarrow x > 22-2x; \Rightarrow x > \dfrac{22}{3} \Rightarrow x > 7\dfrac{1}{3}$

$\therefore \; x = 8, 9, 10$

**10.** **(a,b,c).** No. of ways if both are not present = $^9C_5$

No. of ways if one is present other is not = $^9C_4$

Total = $^9C_5 + 2\,^9C_4 = 3\,^9C_4$

Further, number of ways of selecting 5 of them = $^{11}C_5$

Number of ways in which both must be present = $^9C_3$

Required number of ways = $^{11}C_5 - ^9C_3$.

**11.** **(a,d)** Number of ways = coefficient of $x^{20}$ in

$(x^2+x^3+x^4+x^5)^4 = x^8(1+x+x^2+x^3)^4$

$= \text{coefficient of } x^{12} \text{ in } \left(\dfrac{1-x^4}{1-x}\right)^4 = (1-x^4)^4(1-x)^{-4}$

$= ^{15}C_{12} - 4.\,^{11}C_8 + 6 \times \,^7C_4 - 4 = 1$

**12.** **(a,d)** All AAAAA, BBB, CCC, D, EE and F can be arranged

in $\dfrac{12!}{5!3!2!}$ ways

Between the gaps C, can be arranged in $^{13}C_3$ ways

Total ways = $^{13}C_3 \times \dfrac{12!}{5! \times 3! \times 2!}$

Required number of ways = No. of ways without concidering separation of C − No. of ways in which all C's are together − No. of ways in which exactly two C's are together

$= \dfrac{15!}{5!\,(3!)^2\,2!} - \dfrac{13!}{5!\,3!2!} - \dfrac{12!}{5!\,3!}\,^{13}C_2$

**13.** **(a)** Since one or more boxes remain empty, so the required number of ways = $3^4$

**14.** **(c)** Since each child received at least one ball. It is equivalent to distribution without blank groups. Required number of ways = $3^6 - ^3C_1.\,2^6 + ^3C_2 = 540$

**15.** **(b)** The element not an image can be chosen in $^4C_1$ ways then 6 elements of A have to be distributed over 3 elements of B such that no elements of B remains unassociated. Thus the required number of functions $= ^4C_1\,[\,3^6 - ^3C_1.\,2^6 + ^3C_2\,] = 4 \times 540 = 2160$

**16.** **A→s; B→p; C→t; D→r**

(A) Total number of three digit numbers = $9 \times 10 \times 10$

Half of which will have sum of digits even. **(s)**

(B) $xyz = 140 = 2^2 . 5 . 7$

Therefore number of positive integral solutions $= 3 \times 3 \times {}^4C_2 = 54.$ **(p)**

(C) $x+y+z+t = 10$, where $1 \leq x,\, y,\, z \leq 8,\; 0 \leq t \leq 7$

Therefore desired number of solutions

$= \text{coeff. of } x^{10} \text{ in } (x+x^2+ ..... +x^8)^3 \times (1+x+x^2+ ..... +x^7)$

$= ^{10}C_7 = ^{10}C_3 = 120.$ **(t)**

(D) We must have $i^3 + ai^2 + bi + c = 0$ and

$(-i)^3 + a(-i)^2 + b(-i) + c = 0$

$\Rightarrow b = 1$ and $a = c$

Therefore number of numbers of type abc or cba is $^9C_1$ $= 9$

Number of numbers of type bac or bca is $^{10}C_1 = 10$

But 111 is included in both the counting. **(r)**

**17.** **A→r; B→p; C→t; D→q**

(A) Maximum number of points at which 5-straight lines intersects = $^5C_2$ **(r)**

(B) Number of distinct +ve divisors = $(4+1)(5+1)(3+1) = 120$ **(p)**

(C) Number of triangles = $^5C_3$ **(t)**

(D) $\displaystyle\sum_{r=1}^{n} {}^nC_r = {}^nC_1 + {}^nC_2 + .... + {}^nC_n = 2^n - 1$ **(q)**

**18.** **(d)** Statement-II is true, known as the rule of product. Statement-I is not true, as the two parts of the work are not independent. Three girls can be chosen out of six girls in $^6C_3$ ways, but after this choosing 3 students out of remaining nine students depends on the first part.

**19.** **(c)** $x_1 x_2 x_3 x_4 = 1050 = 2 \times 3 \times 5^2 \times 7$

Thus $5^2$ can assign in $^5C_1 + ^5C_2 = 15$ ways

We can assign 2, 3, or 7 to any of 5 variables.

Hence req. number of solutions = $5 \times 5 \times 5 \times 15 = 1875$

**20.** **3** Number of m = into mappings from A to B

**Case-I:** If exactly one element of set B is not the image of any of the elements of set A then total number of into functions

$= ^3C_1 \times (2^6 - 2) = 3 \times 62 = 186$

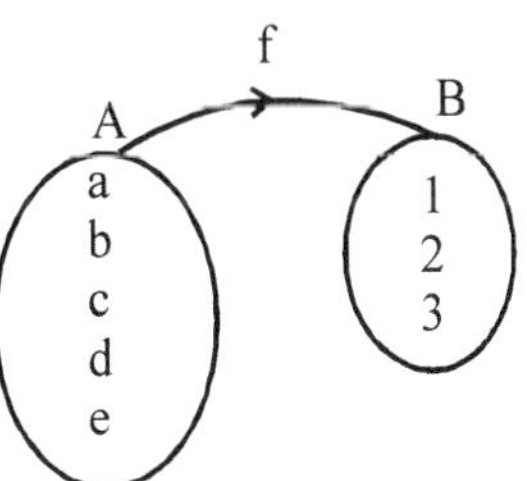

**Case-II:** If exactly two elements of set B is not the image of any of the elements of set A then total number of into functions are $^3C_2 \times 1 = 3$

and hence m $= 186 + 3 = 189$

n = number of injective mapping from B to A.

Injective mapping $= {}^6C_3 \times 3! = 20 \times 6 = 120 = n$

$\therefore$ m $+$ n $= 189 + 120 = 309$

**21.  2**   Total number of ways in which P and Q can be chosen simultaneously

$= (2^5 - 1)(2^5 - 1) = 4^5 - 2^6 + 1$

Number of ways when P and Q have no common element

$= {}^5C_1(2^4 - 1) + {}^5C_2(2^3 - 1) + {}^5C_3(2^2 - 1)$
$$+ {}^5C_4(2^1 - 1) + {}^5C_5(2^0 - 1)$$

$= {}^5C_1 \cdot 2^4 + {}^5C_2 \cdot 2^3 + {}^5C_3 \cdot 2^2 + {}^5C_4 \cdot 2$
$$+ {}^5C_5 - ({}^5C_1 + {}^5C_2 + {}^5C_3 + {}^5C_4 + {}^5C_5)$$

$= ({}^5C_0 \cdot 2^5 + {}^5C_1 \cdot 2^4 + {}^5C_2 \cdot 2^3 + {}^5C_3 \cdot 2^2 + {}^5C_4 \cdot 2$
$$+ {}^5C_5 - 2^5) - (2^5 - 1)$$

$= 3^5 - 2^6 + 1$

Hence P and Q have atleast one common element

$= (4^5 - 2^6 + 1) - (3^5 - 2^6 + 1) = 4^5 - 3^5$

Thus A $+$ B $-$ n $= 4 + 3 - 5 = 2$

**22.  4**

The various possibilities to put 5 different balls in 3 different size boxes, when no box remains empty : The balls can be 1, 1 and 3 in different boxes or 2, 2, 1.

**Case I :** To put 1, 1 and 3 balls in different boxes. Selection of 1, 1 and 3 balls out of 5 balls can be done in ${}^5C_1 \times {}^4C_1 \times {}^3C_3$ ways and then 1, 1, 3 can permute (as defferent size boxes) in 3 ! ways.

$\therefore$   No. of ways

$= {}^5C_1 \times {}^4C_1 \times {}^3C_3 \times 3! = 5 \times 4 \times 1 \times 6 = 120$

**Case II :** To put 2, 2 and 1 ball in different boxes. Selection of 2, 2 and 1 balls out of 5 balls can be done in ${}^5C_2 \times {}^3C_2 \times {}^1C_1$ ways

and then 2, 2, 1 can permute (different boxes) in 3 ! ways

$\therefore$ No. of ways

$= {}^5C_2 \times {}^3C_2 \times {}^1C_1 \times 3! = 10 \times 3 \times 1 \times 6 = 180$

Combining case I and II, total number of required ways

$= 120 + 180 = 300.$

Thus, $75 X = 300, \therefore X = 4$

**23.  3**

Number of ways in which a student can select at least one and atmost n books out of $(2n+1)$ books is equal to

$= {}^{2n+1}C_1 + {}^{2n+1}C_2 + {}^{2n+1}C_3 + \dots + {}^{2n+1}C_n$

$= \dfrac{1}{2}[2 \cdot {}^{2n+1}C_1 + 2 \cdot {}^{2n+1}C_2 + 2 \cdot {}^{2n+1}C_3 + \dots + 2 \cdot {}^{2n+1}C_n]$

$= \dfrac{1}{2}[({}^{2n+1}C_1 + {}^{2n+1}C_{2n}) + ({}^{2n+1}C_2 + {}^{2n+1}C_{2n-1})$
$$+ ({}^{2n+1}C_3 + {}^{2n+1}C_{2n-2}) + \dots + ({}^{2n+1}C_n + {}^{2n+1}C_{n+1})]$$
$$[\text{Using }{}^nC_r = {}^nC_{n-r}]$$

$= \dfrac{1}{2}[{}^{2n+1}C_1 + {}^{2n+1}C_2 + {}^{2n+1}C_3 + \dots + {}^{2n+1}C_n$
$$+ {}^{2n+1}C_{n+1} + {}^{2n+1}C_{n+2} + \dots + {}^{2n+1}C_{2n}]$$

$= \dfrac{1}{2}[{}^{2n+1}C_0 + {}^{2n+1}C_1 + {}^{2n+1}C_2 + \dots + {}^{2n+1}C_{2n+1} - 1 - 1]$

$= \dfrac{1}{2}[2^{2n+1} - 2] = 2^{2n} - 1$

ATQ, $2^{2n} - 1 = 63 \Rightarrow 2^{2n} = 64 = 2^6$

$\Rightarrow 2n = 6 \Rightarrow n = 3$

**24.  7**

Given that

runs scored in $k$th match $= k.2^{n+1-k}, \ 1 \le k \le n$

and runs scored in n matches

$= \dfrac{n+1}{4}(2^{n+1} - n - 2)$

$\therefore \displaystyle\sum_{k=1}^{n} k.2^{n+1-k} = \dfrac{n+1}{4}(2^{n+1} - n - 2)$

$\Rightarrow 2^{n+1}\left[\displaystyle\sum_{k=1}^{n} \dfrac{k}{2^k}\right] = \dfrac{n+1}{4}(2^{n+1} - n - 2)$

$\Rightarrow 2^{n+1}\left[\dfrac{1}{2} + \dfrac{2}{2^2} + \dfrac{3}{2^3} + \dots + \dfrac{n}{2^n}\right]$

$= \dfrac{n+1}{4}(2^{n+1} - n - 2)$    ....(i)

Let $S = \dfrac{1}{2} + \dfrac{2}{2^2} + \dfrac{3}{2^3} + \dots + \dfrac{n}{2^n}$

$\dfrac{1}{2}S = \dfrac{1}{2^2} + \dfrac{2}{2^3} + \dots + \dfrac{n-1}{2^n} + \dfrac{n}{2^{n+1}}$

Subtracting the above two, we get

$\dfrac{1}{2}S = \dfrac{1}{2} + \dfrac{1}{2^2} + \dfrac{1}{2^3} + \dots + \dfrac{1}{2^n} - \dfrac{n}{2^{n+1}}$

$\Rightarrow \dfrac{1}{2}S = \dfrac{\dfrac{1}{2}\left(1 - \dfrac{1}{2^n}\right)}{1 - \dfrac{1}{2}} - \dfrac{n}{2^{n+1}} \Rightarrow S = 2\left[1 - \dfrac{1}{2^n} - \dfrac{n}{2^{n+1}}\right]$

$\therefore$   Equation (i) becomes

$2.2^{n+1}\left[1 - \dfrac{1}{2^n} - \dfrac{n}{2^{n+1}}\right] = \dfrac{n+1}{4}\left[2^{n+1} - n - 2\right]$

$\Rightarrow 2.[2^{n+1} - 2 - n] = \dfrac{n+1}{4}[2^{n+1} - 2 - n]$

$\Rightarrow \dfrac{n+1}{4} = 2 \Rightarrow n = 7$

$A = \dfrac{9!}{2!3!4!}$ is the coefficient of $x^2 y^3 z^4$

$\Rightarrow \quad A = 1260$

Again, coefficient of $x^4 y^4 z$ is $\dfrac{9!}{4!4!1!} = 630 = \dfrac{A}{2}$.

**19.** **(c)** Given expression

$= x \cdot x^2 \cdot x^3 \ldots x^{20}\left(1 - \dfrac{1}{x}\right)\left(1 - \dfrac{2}{x^2}\right)\ldots\left(1 - \dfrac{20}{x^{20}}\right) = x^{210} \cdot P$

where, $P = \left(1 - \dfrac{1}{x}\right)\left(1 - \dfrac{2}{x^2}\right)\left(1 - \dfrac{3}{x^3}\right)\ldots\left(1 - \dfrac{20}{x^{20}}\right)$

Now, coefficient of $x^{203}$ in original expression = coefficient of $x^{-7}$ in P. But,

$P = 1 - \left(\dfrac{1}{x} + \dfrac{2}{x^2} + \dfrac{3}{x^3} + \ldots\right)$

$\quad + \left(\dfrac{1}{x} \cdot \dfrac{6}{x^6} + \dfrac{2}{x^2} \cdot \dfrac{5}{x^3} + \dfrac{3}{x^3} \cdot \dfrac{4}{x^4} + \ldots\right) - \left(\dfrac{1}{x} \cdot \dfrac{2}{x^2} \cdot \dfrac{4}{x^4} + \ldots\right);$

Coefficient of $x^{-7} = -7 + 6 + 10 + 12 - 8 = 13$.

The expression $(2 + x)^2 (3 + x)^3 (4 + x)^4 = x^9 + (2 + 2 + 3 + 3 + 3 + 3 + 4 + 4 + 4 + 4) x^8 + \ldots$

$\Rightarrow$ coefficient of $x^8 = 32$.

**20.** **Ans : 0**

Here, $t_{r+1} = {}^nC_r (a - r)(b - r)(c - r)(-1)^r$

Now, $\displaystyle\sum_{r=0}^{n} t_{r+1} = \sum_{r=0}^{n} {}^nC_r (-1)^r (a - r)(b - r)(c - r)$

$\Rightarrow \quad S = \displaystyle\sum_{r=0}^{n} {}^nC_r (-1)^r \{abc + (a + b + c)r^2 - (ab + bc + ca)r - r^3\}$

$\Rightarrow \quad S = abc\left\{\displaystyle\sum_{r=0}^{n}(-1)^r \, {}^nC_r\right\}$

$\quad + (a + b + c)\left\{\displaystyle\sum_{r=0}^{n}(-1)^r \, r^2 \, {}^nC_r\right\}$

$\quad - (ab + bc + ca)\left\{\displaystyle\sum_{r=0}^{n}(-1)^r \, r \, {}^nC_r\right\} - \displaystyle\sum_{r=0}^{n}(-1)^r \, r^3 \, {}^nC_r$

Since, $\displaystyle\sum_{r=0}^{n}(-1)^r \, {}^nC_r = 0$

Also, $\displaystyle\sum_{r=0}^{n}(-1)^r \, r \, {}^nC_r = \dfrac{d}{dx}(1 - x)^n \Big|_{x=1} = 0$

Similarly,

$\displaystyle\sum_{r=0}^{n}(-1)^r \, r^2 \, {}^nC_r =$ value of $\dfrac{d}{dx}(nx(1 - x)^{n-1}) \Big|_{x=1} = 0$

Hence, $S = abc\,(0) + (a + b + c)\,(0) - (ab + bc + ca)\,(0) - 0$

$\therefore \quad S = 0$.

**21.** **(6)**

$(1 - 2x + 5x^2 + 10x^3)\,[C_0 + C_1 x + C_2 x^2 + \ldots] = 1 + a_1 x + a_2 x^2 + \ldots$

$a_1 = n - 2$ and $a_2 = \dfrac{n(n-1)}{2} - 2n + 5$

put $a_1^2 = 2a_2$

$(n - 2)^2 = n(n - 1) - 4n + 10$

$n^2 - 4n + 4 = n^2 - 5n + 10$

$n = 6$

**22.** **(7)** $\left(x \sin\theta + \dfrac{\cos\theta}{x}\right)^{10}$

$T_{r+1} = {}^{10}C_r (x \sin\theta)^{10-r} \cdot \left(\dfrac{\cos x}{x}\right)^r$

$= {}^{10}C_r (\sin\theta)^{10-r} \cdot x^{10-2r} (\cos\theta)^r$

hence for independent of x, $r = 5$

$T_6 = {}^{10}C_5 (\sin\theta)^5 \cdot (\cos\theta)^5 = \dfrac{{}^{10}C_5 (\sin 2\theta)^5}{2^5}$

For greatest value, $\sin 2\theta = 1$

Thus $T_6 = \dfrac{{}^{10}C_5}{2^5}$

$\therefore \quad A + B = 2 + 5 = 7$

**23.** **(2)**

$(1 + t^2)^{12} (1 + t^{12})(1 + t^{24}) = (1 + t^{12} + t^{24} + t^{36})(1 + t^2)^{12}$

$\therefore$ Coefficient of $t^{24}$ = Coefficient of $t^{24}$ in $(1 + t^2)^{12}$ + Coefficient of $t^{12}$ in $(1 + t^2)^{12}$ + constant term in $(1 + t^2)^{12}$

$= {}^{12}C_{12} + {}^{12}C_6 + {}^{12}C_0 = 1 + {}^{12}C_6 + 1 = {}^{12}C_6 + 2$

Thus $M = 2$

**24.** **(2)** $T_3 = {}^5C_2 \, x^3 \cdot x^{2t} = 10^6$

$x^{3+2t} = 10^5$

$(3 + 2t) \log_{10} x = 5$

$\therefore (3 + 2t)t = 5$ i.e., $2t^2 + 3t - 5 = 0$ i.e., $t = 1, -\dfrac{5}{2}$

$x = 10^t = 10, 10^{-5/2}$

**1. (d).** We have

$${}^{n}C_0 \cdot {}^{2n}C_n - {}^{n}C_1 \cdot {}^{2n-2}C_n + {}^{n}C_2 \cdot {}^{2n-4}C_n - \ldots$$
$$\ldots + (-1)^n \; {}^{n}C_n \; {}^{2n-2n}C_n$$

$$= \text{Coefficient of } x^n \text{ in } [{}^{n}C_0(1+x)^{2n} - {}^{n}C_1(1+x)^{2n-2}$$
$$+ {}^{n}C_2(1+x)^{2n-4} - \ldots + (-1)^n \; {}^{n}C_n(1+x)^{2n-2n}]$$

$$= \text{Coefficient of } x^n \text{ in } [(1+x)^2 - 1]^n$$

$$= \text{Coefficient of } x^n \text{ in } (2x + x^2)^n$$

$$= \text{Coefficient of } x^0 \text{ in } (2+x)^n$$

$$= 2^n$$

Hence, (c) is the correct answer.

**2. (a).** Putting $x = 1$ and $-1$ and adding

$$a_0 + a_2 + \ldots + a_{50} = \frac{3^{25} + 1}{2} = \frac{(1+2)^{25} + 1}{2} \; \left(\frac{\text{odd} + 1}{2} = \frac{\text{even}}{2}\right)$$

$$= \frac{{}^{25}C_0 + {}^{25}C_1 . 2 + {}^{25}C_2 . 2^2 + {}^{25}C_{25} . 2^{25} + 1}{2}$$

$$= \frac{2\left[1 + {}^{25}C_1 + {}^{25}C_2 . 2 + \ldots + {}^{25}C_{25} . 2^{24}\right]}{2}$$

$$= 2\,[13 + {}^{25}C_2 + \ldots + {}^{25}C_{25} . 2^{23}],$$

which is an even.

**3. (a)** To find

$${}^{30}C_0{}^{30}C_{10} - {}^{30}C_1{}^{30}C_{11} + {}^{30}C_2{}^{30}C_{12} - \ldots + {}^{30}C_{20}{}^{30}C_{30}$$

We know that

$$(1+x)^{30} = {}^{30}C_0 + {}^{30}C_1 x + {}^{30}C_2 x^2$$
$$+ \ldots + {}^{30}C_{20}x^{20} + \ldots {}^{30}C_{30}x^{30} \qquad \ldots(1)$$

$$(x-1)^{30} = {}^{30}C_0 x^{30} - {}^{30}C_1 x^{29} + \ldots + {}^{30}C_{10}x^{20}$$
$$- {}^{30}C_{11}x^{19} + {}^{30}C_{12}x^{18} + \ldots {}^{30}C_{30}x^0 \qquad \ldots(2)$$

Multiplying eqn (1) and (2), we get

$$(x^2 - 1)^{30} = (\quad) \times (\quad)$$

Equating the coefficients of $x^{20}$ on both sides, we get

$${}^{30}C_{10} = {}^{30}C_0 {}^{30}C_{10} - {}^{30}C_1{}^{30}C_{11} + {}^{30}C_2{}^{30}C_{12} - \ldots + {}^{30}C_{20}{}^{30}C_{30}$$

$$\therefore \text{Req. value is } {}^{30}C_{10}$$

**4. (d)** We have

$$S = C_0 + (C_0 + C_1) + (C_0 + C_1 + C_2) +$$

$$\ldots + (C_0 + C_1 + \ldots + C_n)$$

$$= (C_0 + C_0 + \ldots (n+1) \text{ times})$$

$$+ (C_1 + C_1 + \ldots n \text{ times})$$

$$(C_2 + C_2 + \ldots (n-1) \text{ times}) + \ldots + (C_{n-1} + C_{n-1}) + C_n$$

$$= (n+1)C_0 + nC_1 + (n-1)C_2 + \ldots + 2C_{n-1} + C_n$$

$$= C_0 + 2C_1 + 3C_2 + \ldots + (n+1)C_n \; [\because C_r = C_{n-r}]$$

General Term, $T_{r+1} = (r+1)C_r$

$$T_{r+1} = r\,{}^{n}C_r + {}^{n}C_r = n.\,{}^{n-1}C_{r-1} + {}^{n}C_r$$

$$\therefore S = \sum_{r=0}^{n} T_{r+1} = n\,[{}^{n-1}C_0 + {}^{n-1}C_1 + \ldots + {}^{n-1}C_{n-1}]$$

$$+ [\,{}^{n}C_0 + {}^{n}C_1 + \ldots + {}^{n}C_n\,]$$

$$= n.\,2^{n-1} + 2^n = (n+2)\,2^{n-1}$$

**5. (b)**

$$\frac{\pi(n)}{\pi(n+1)} = \frac{{}^{n}C_0 . {}^{n}C_1 . {}^{n}C_2 \ldots {}^{n}C_n}{{}^{n+1}C_0 . {}^{n+1}C_1 . {}^{n+1}C_2 \ldots {}^{n+1}C_{n+1}}$$

$$= \frac{1}{{}^{n+1}C_0} \left(\frac{{}^{n}C_0}{{}^{n+1}C_1}\right) \left(\frac{{}^{n}C_1}{{}^{n+1}C_2}\right) \ldots \left(\frac{{}^{n}C_n}{{}^{n+1}C_{n+1}}\right)$$

$$= \frac{1}{1}\left(\frac{1}{n+1}\right)\left(\frac{2}{n+1}\right) \ldots \left(\frac{n+1}{n-1}\right)$$

$$\left[\because \frac{{}^{n}C_r}{{}^{n+1}C_{r+1}} = \frac{r+1}{n+1}\right]$$

$$= \frac{(n+1)!}{(n+1)^{n+1}} = \frac{n!}{(n+1)^n}, \; \therefore \; \frac{\pi(2002)}{\pi(2001)} = \frac{(2002)^{2001}}{(2001)!}$$

**6. (b)** $(1+x)^n = C_0 + C_1 x + C_2 x^2 + \ldots + C_n x^n$

Also, $(x+1)^n = C_n + C_{n-1}x + C_{n-2}x^2 + \ldots + C_0 x^n$

$$[\because C_r = C_{n-r}]$$

Multiplying both sides we get

$$(1+x)^{2n} = (C_0 + C_1 x + C_2 x^2 + \ldots + C_n x^n)$$

$$(C_n + C_{n-1}x + C_{n-2}x^2 + \ldots + C_0 x^n)$$

Comparing coeff. of $x^{n-r}$ on both sides, we get

$$C_0 C_r + C_1 C_{r+1} + C_{n-r}C_n = {}^{2n}C_{n-r} = \frac{2n!}{(n-r)!(n+r)!}$$

**7. (c)** $\because (1+x+2x^2)^{20} = a_0 + a_1 x + a_2 x^2 + \ldots + a_{39}x^{39} + a_{40}x^{40}$

Putting $x = 1 \; \& -1$ we get

$$4^{20} = a_0 + a_1 + a_2 + a_3 + a_4 + a_5 + \ldots$$
$$+ a_{37} + a_{38} + a_{39} + a_{40} \qquad \ldots(1)$$

$$2^{20} = a_0 - a_1 + a_2 - a_3 + a_4 - a_5 + \ldots$$
$$\text{and} \qquad\qquad -a_{37} + a_{38} - a_{39} + a_{40} \qquad \ldots(2)$$

Subtracting (2) from (1) we get,

$$4^{20} - 2^{20} = 2(a_1 + a_3 + a_5 + ..... + a_{37} + a_{39})$$

$$\Rightarrow a_1 + a_3 + a_5 + ..... + a_{39} = \frac{20^{20}(2^{20} - 1)}{2}$$

$$= 2^{19}(2^{20} - 1)$$

[*Note :* In order to find the sum of coefficients of odd terms or sum of coefficients of even terms, we substitute $x = 1$ and $x = -1$ in the expansion and subtract or add].

**8. (c)** Put

$$x = 1 \Rightarrow a_0 + a_1 + a_2 + ..... + a_{30} = 2^{30} \qquad ...(i)$$

$$x = -1 \Rightarrow a_0 - a_1 + a_2 - ..... + a_{30} = 0 \qquad ...(ii)$$

on adding (i) and (ii), we get

$$2(a_0 + a_2 + .... + a_{30}) = 2^{30}$$

$$\Rightarrow a_0 + a_2 + ...... + a_{30} = 2^{29}$$

Also, put $x = \omega$

$$\Rightarrow a_0 + a_1\omega + a_2\omega^2 + a_3 + ..... + a_{30} = (1 + \omega)^{30} = (-\omega^2)^{30}$$

$$\Rightarrow a_0 + a_1\omega + a_2\omega^2 + a_3 + ..... + a_{30} = 1 \quad ...(iii)$$

Put $x = \omega^2$

$$\Rightarrow a_0 + a_1\omega^2 + a_2\omega + a_3 + ..... + a_{30} = (1 + \omega^2)^{30} = (-\omega)^{30}$$

$$\Rightarrow a_0 + a_1\omega^2 + a_2\omega + a_3 + ..... + a_{30} = 1 \quad ...(iv)$$

On adding eqn (i), (iii) and (iv), we get

$$\therefore 3(a_0 + a_3 + a_6 + ..... + a_{30}) = 2^{30} + 1 + 1$$

$$\Rightarrow a_0 + a_3 + a_6 + ..... + a_{30} = \frac{2}{3}(2^{29} + 1)$$

**9. (c,d)** $^{69}C_{3r-1} + {}^{69}C_{3r} = {}^{69}C_{r^2-1} + {}^{69}C_{r^2}$

$$\Rightarrow \qquad {}^{70}C_{3r} = {}^{70}C_{r^2}$$

$\Rightarrow$ either $3r = r^2$ or $r^2 + 3r = 70$

i.e, either $r = 0, 3$ or $r = 7, -10$

But the given equation is not defined for $r = 0, -10$

Hence, $r = 3$ or $7$

**10. (a,b,d)**

$\because n$ is even, let $n = 2m$ then

$$\text{LHS} = S = \frac{2.m!m!}{(2m)!}[C_0^2 - 2C_1^2 + 3C_2^2 .....$$

$$+ (-1)^{2m}(2m+1)C_{2m}^2] \quad ....(1)$$

$$= \frac{2.m!.m!}{(2m)!}\Big[C_{2m}^2 - 2C_{2m-1}^2 + 3C_{2m-2}^2 - .....$$

$$+ (-1)^{2m}(2m+1)C_0^2\Big] \qquad [\text{Using } C_r = C_{n-r}]$$

$$\Rightarrow S = \frac{2.m!m!}{(2m)!}[(2m+1)\,C_0^2 - 2mC_1^2$$

$$+ (2m-1)\,C_2^2 ...... - 2C_{2m-1}^2 + C_{2m}^2] \quad ....(2)$$

Adding (1) and (2):

$$2S = 2\frac{m!m!}{(2m)!}[2m+2]\,[C_0^2 - C_1^2 + C_2^2 + ..... + C_{2m}^2]$$

Now keeping in mind that

$$C_0^2 - C_1^2 + C_2^2 - ...... + C_n^2 = (-1)^{n/2}\,{}^nC_{n/2}$$

If $n$ is even, we get

$$S = \frac{m!m!}{(2m)!}(2m+2)\,[(-1)^m\,{}^{2m}C_m] = \left(2\frac{n}{2} + 2\right)(-1)^{n/2}$$

$$= (-1)^{n/2}(n+2)$$

**11. (a, d)** $(1+x)^n \times (x+1)^n$

$$= (C_0 + C_1x + C_2x^2 + ... + C_{n-2}x^{n-2} + C_{n-1}x^{n-1} + C_nx^n)$$

$$\times (C_0x^n + C_1x^{n-1} + C_2x^{n-2} + C_3x^{n-3} + C_4x^{n-4} + ... + C_n)$$

Coefficient of $x^{n-2}$ in RHS

$$= C_0C_2 + C_1C_3 + C_2C_4 + .... + C_{n-2}C_n \qquad ...(i)$$

Coefficient of $x^{n-2}$ in LHS

$$= {}^{2n}C_{n-2} = \frac{2n!}{(n-2)!(n+2)!} \qquad ...(ii)$$

From eqs. (i) and (ii), we get

$$C_0C_2 + C_1C_3 + C_2C_4 + ... + C_{n-2}C_n = {}^{2n}C_{n-2}$$

$$= \frac{2n!}{(n-2)!(n+2)!}$$

**12. (c, d)** $C_0^2 + 3C_1^2 + 5C_2^2 + ... + (2n+1)C_n^2$

$$\Rightarrow (C_0^2 + C_1^2 + C_2^2 + ... + C_n^2) + 2(C_1^2 + 2C_2^2 + ... + nC_n^2)$$

$$= {}^{2n}C_n + 2(C_1^2 + 2C_2^2 + ... + nC_n^2) \quad ...(i)$$

$\because (1+x)^n = C_0 + C_1x + C_2x^2 + C_3x^3 + ... + C_nx^n$

Differentiating both sides wr.t. x, we get

$$n(1+x)^{n-1} = C_1 + 2C_2x + 3C_3x^2 + ... + nC_nx^{n-1} \quad ..(ii)$$

and $(x+1)^n = C_0x^n + C_1x^{n-1} + C_2x^{n-2} + .... + C_n$

$$...(iii)$$

Multiplying eqs. (ii) and (iii), we get

$$n(1+x)^{2n-1} = (C_1 + 2C_2x + 3C_3x^2 + ... + nC_nx^{n-1}) \times (C_0x^n + C_1x^{n-1} + C_2x^{n-2} + ... + C_n)$$

Comparing the coefficients of $x^{n-1}$ on both sides, we get

$$C_1^2 + 2C_2^2 + 3C_3^2 + ... + nC_n^2 = n\,{}^{2n-1}C_{n-1} \qquad ...(iv)$$

From eqs. (i) and (iv), we get

$$C_0^2 + 3C_1^2 + 5C_2^2 + ... + (2n+1)C_n^2$$

$$= {}^{2n}C_n + 2n.{}^{2n-1}C_{n-1}$$

$$= \frac{2n}{n}.^{2n-1}C_{n-1} + 2n.^{2n-1}C_{n-1}$$

$$= 2(n+1).^{2n-1}C_{n-1} = 2(n+1)^{2n-1}C_n$$

$$= {}^{2n-1}C_{n-1} + (2n+1)^{2n-1}C_{n-1}$$

$$= {}^{2n-1}C_n + (2n+1).^{2n-1}C_{n-1}$$

13. **A-s, B-p, C-r, D-q**

(A) Put $x = 1$, we get $A_0 + A_1 + A_2 + ...... + A_n = (n+1)!$  **(s)**

(B) Multiply by x and differentiate
$(x+1)(x+2)......(x+n) + x(x+2)......(x+n) + ......$
$+ x(x+1)(x+2)......(x+n-1) = A_0 + 2A_1x + 3A_2x^2 +$
$......+(n+1)A_n x^n$
Put $x = 1$, $A_0 + 2A_1 + 3A_2 + ...... + (n+1)A_n = (n+1)! +$

$$\frac{(n+1)!}{2} + - - - - - - + \frac{(n+1)!}{n+1}$$

$$= (n+1)!\left[1 + \frac{1}{2} + \frac{1}{3} + .......... + \frac{1}{n+1}\right] \quad \textbf{(p)}$$

(C) Replace x by $\frac{1}{x}$, then

$(1+x)(1+2x)(1+3x).........(1+nx) = A_0 x^n + A_1 x^{n-1}$
$+..........+A_n$
Differentiate
$(1+2x)(1+3x).........(1+nx)+(1+x).2(1+3x).........$
$(1+nx)+(1+x)(1+2x).3(1+4x).........(1+nx)+.........$
$+(1+x)(1+2x).........\{1+(n-1)x\}.n$
$= n.A_0 x^{n-1} + (n-1)A_1 x^{n-2} +..........+A_{n-1}$
Put $x = 1$, then
$nA_0 + (n-1)A_1 + (n-2)A_2 + ------- + A_{n-1}$

$$= \frac{(n+1)!}{2} + \frac{2(n+1)!}{3} + \frac{3(n+1)!}{4} + - - - - - - \frac{n(n+1)!}{n+1}$$

$$= (n+1)!\left[\frac{1}{2} + \frac{2}{3} + \frac{3}{4} + - - - - - + \frac{n}{n+1}\right] \quad \textbf{(r)}$$

(D) Diff both the sides with respect to x,
$(x+2)(x+3)......(x+n)+(x+1)(x+3)......(x+n)+......+$
$(x+1)(x+2)......(x+n-1) = A_1 + 2A_2x + ...... + nA_n x^{n-1}$
Put $x=1$, $A_1 + 2A_2 + ...... + nA_n$

$$= \frac{(n+1)!}{2} + \frac{(n+1)!}{3} + - - - - - - - + \frac{(n+1)!}{n+1}$$

$$= (n+1)!\left(\frac{1}{2} + \frac{1}{3} + ........... + \frac{1}{n+1}\right) \quad \textbf{(q)}$$

14. **A-r, B-p, C-q**

(A) $\displaystyle\sum\sum_{0\le i<j\le n} {}^nC_i = \sum_{i=0}^{n-1} {}^nC_i(n-i) = \sum_{i=0}^{n}(n-i)^nC_i$

$$= \sum_{i=0}^{n}\{n-(n-i)\}^nC_{n-i} = \sum_{i=0}^{n}i^nC_i = n.2^{n-1} \quad \textbf{(r)}$$

(B) $\displaystyle\sum\sum_{0\le i<j\le n} ({}^nC_i + {}^nC_j) = \sum\sum_{0\le i<j\le n} {}^nC_i + \sum\sum_{0\le i<j\le n} {}^nC_j$

$$= n.2^{n-1} + \sum_{j=1}^{n} j.\,{}^nC_j = n.2^{n-1} + n.2^{n-1} = n.2^n \quad \textbf{(p)}$$

(C) $\displaystyle\sum\sum_{0\le i<j\le n} i^nC_j = \sum_{j=1}^{n} {}^nC_j(0+1+2+.....+j-1)$

$$= \sum_{j=1}^{n} {}^nC_j \frac{j(j-1)}{2} = \frac{1}{2}\sum_{j=1}^{n} j^2\,{}^nC_j - \frac{1}{2}\sum_{j=1}^{n} j\,{}^nC_j$$

$$= \frac{1}{2}(n+1)n.2^{n-2} - \frac{1}{2}n.2^{n-1} = n(n-1).2^{n-3} \quad \textbf{(q)}$$

15. **(d)** $\displaystyle\binom{r}{r} + \binom{r+1}{r} + \binom{r+2}{r} + ...... + \binom{n}{r}$

$$= \left\{\binom{r+1}{r+1} + \binom{r+1}{r}\right\} + \binom{r+2}{r} + ... + \binom{n}{r}$$

$$= \left\{\binom{r+2}{r+1} + \binom{r+2}{r}\right\} + ...... + \binom{n}{r}$$

$$= \binom{r+3}{r+1} + ... + \binom{n}{r} = \binom{n}{r+1} + \binom{n}{r} = \binom{n+1}{r+1}$$

16. **(c).** Statement-1 is true but statement-2 is false.
$2^{2000} = (2^4)^{500} = (16)^{500} = (15+1)^{500} = 15.m+1$,
$m \in I^+$.
$\therefore 2^{2003} = 2^3.(15m+1) = 15.8m + 8$
$\therefore$ Remainder $= 8$

17. **(d).** The given sum $= {}^{10}C_1(2) + {}^{10}C_2(2^2) + {}^{10}C_3(2^3) + ....$
$+ {}^{10}C_{10}(2^{10}) = 3^{10} - 1$

18. **(b).** $\displaystyle\sum_{r=1}^{15} \frac{r.2^r}{(r+2)!}$

$$= \sum_{r=1}^{15} \frac{(r+2)2^r}{(r+2)!} - \sum_{r=1}^{15} \frac{2.2^r}{(r+2)!} = \sum_{r=1}^{15} \frac{2^r}{(r+1)!} - \sum_{r=1}^{15} \frac{2^{r+1}}{(r+2)!}$$

19. **(a)** $2^{21} = {}^{21}C_0 + {}^{21}C_1 + ... + {}^{21}C_{10} + {}^{21}C_{11} + ... + {}^{21}C_{21}$

$$= 2\left({}^{21}C_0 + ... + {}^{21}C_{10}\right)$$

$$\therefore {}^{21}C_0 + {}^{21}C_1 + ... + {}^{21}C_{10} = \frac{2^{21}}{2} = 2^{20}.$$

20. **(2)**
Let $x = C_0 - C_2 + C_4 - C_6 + .....$
and $y = C_1 - C_3 + C_5 - C_7 + .......$
$(1+i)^n = C_0 + C_1 i + C_2 i^2 + C_3 i^3 + C_4 i^4 + ........$
Equating the real and imaginary part
$x_n + i\,y_n = (1+i)^n$
$\therefore |x_n + iy_n| = |1+i|^n = 2^{n/2}$

$$\therefore \ \sqrt{x_n^2 + y_n^2} = 2^{n/2}$$

Hence $x_n^2 + y_n^2 = 2^n$

Thus $p = 2$

**21.** **(2)**

We have $s_n = \dfrac{1 - q^{n+1}}{1 - q}$ ....(1)

and $S_n = \dfrac{1 - \left(\dfrac{q+1}{2}\right)^{n+1}}{1 - \left(\dfrac{q+1}{2}\right)} = \dfrac{2^{n+1} - (q+1)^{n+1}}{2^n(1-q)}$ ....(2)

Now, $^{n+1}C_1 + {}^{n+1}C_2 s_1 + {}^{n+1}C_3 s_2 + .... + {}^{n+1}C_{n+1} s_n$

$= \dfrac{1}{1-q}[{}^{n+1}C_1(1-q) + {}^{n+1}C_2(1-q^2) + {}^{n+1}C_3(1-q^3) + ....$

$\qquad\qquad .... + {}^{n+1}C_n(1-q^{n+1})]$ Using (1)

$= \dfrac{1}{1-q}\left[\left({}^{n+1}C_1 + {}^{n+1}C_2 + .... + {}^{n+1}C_{n+1}\right)\right.$

$\qquad \left. - \left({}^{n+1}C_1 q + {}^{n+1}C_2 q^2 + .... + {}^{n+1}C_{n+1} q^{n+1}\right)\right]$

$= \dfrac{1}{1-q}\left[(2^{n+1}-1) - \left\{(1+q)^{n+1}-1\right\}\right]$

$= \dfrac{2^{n+1} - (1+q)^{n+1}}{(1-q)} = 2^n S_n$ [Using eq. (2)]

Thus, $P = 2$

**22.** **(6)**

$S = \displaystyle\sum\sum C_i C_j$

$0 \le i < j \le n$

$\Rightarrow \ S = C_0(C_1 + C_2 + C_3 + .... + C_n) + C_1(C_2 + C_3 + .... + C_n)$
$\qquad + C_2(C_3 + C_4 + C_5 + .... + C_n) + .... + C_{n-1}(C_n)$

$\Rightarrow \ S = C_0(2^n - C_0) + C_1(2^n - C_0 - C_1)$
$\qquad\qquad\qquad + C_2(2^n - C_0 - C_1 - C_2)$
$\qquad + .... + C_{n-1}(2^n - C_0 - C_1 .... C_{n-1})$
$\qquad + C_n(2^n - C_0 - C_1 .... C_n)$

$\Rightarrow \ S = 2^n(C_0 + C_1 + C_2 + .... + C_{n-1} + C_n)$
$\qquad\qquad\qquad - (C_0^2 + C_1^2 + C_2^2 + .... + C_n^2) - S$

$\Rightarrow \ 2S = 2^n \cdot 2^n - \dfrac{2n!}{(n!)^2} = 2^{2n} - \dfrac{2n!}{(n!)^2}$

$\Rightarrow \ S = 2^{2n-1} - \dfrac{2n!}{2(n!)^2}$

Thus $P = 2$, $Q = 2$, $R = 2$.

$\Rightarrow P + Q + R = 2 + 2 + 2 = 6$.

**23.** **(0)**

We know that

$(1-x)^n = C_0 - C_1 x + C_2 x^2 - C_3 x^3 + .... + (-1)^n C_n x^n$

Multiplying both sides by $x$, we get

$x(1-x)^n = C_0 x - C_1 x^2 + C_2 x^3 - C_3 x^4 + .... + (-1)^n C_n x^{n+1}$

Differentiating both sides w.r. to $x$, we get

$(1-x)^n - nx(1-x)^{n-1}$
$= C_0 - 2C_1 x + 3C_2 x^2 - 4C_3 x^3 + .... + (-1)^n(n+1)C_n x^n$

Again multiplying both sides by $x$, we get

$x(1-x)^n - nx^2(1-x)^{n-1}$
$= C_0 x - 2C_1 x^2 + 3C_2 x^3 - 4C_3 x^4 + .... + (-1)^n(n+1)C_n x^{n+1}$

Differentiating above with respect to $x$, we get

$(1-x)^n - nx(1-x)^{n-1} - 2nx(1-x)^{n-1} + nx^2(n-1)(1-x)^{n-2}$
$= C_0 - 2^2 C_1 x + 3^2 C_2 x^2 - 4^2 C_3 x^3 + .... + (-1)^n(n+1)^2 C_n x^n$

Substituting $x = 1$, in above, we get

$0 = C_0 - 2^2 C_1 + 3^2 C_2 - 4^2 C_3 + .... + (-1)^n(n+1)^2 C_n$

Hence, $P = 0$

**24.** **(0)**

Here, $t_{r+1} = {}^nC_r(a-r)(b-r)(c-r)(-1)^r$

Now, $\displaystyle\sum_{r=0}^{n} t_{r+1} = \sum_{r=0}^{n} {}^nC_r(-1)^r(a-r)(b-r)(c-r)$

$\Rightarrow \ S = \displaystyle\sum_{r=0}^{n} {}^nC_r(-1)^r\{abc + (a+b+c)r^2 - (ab+bc+ca)r - r^3\}$

$\Rightarrow \ S = abc\left\{\displaystyle\sum_{r=0}^{n}(-1)^r {}^nC_r\right\}$

$\qquad\qquad\qquad + (a+b+c)\left\{\displaystyle\sum_{r=0}^{n}(-1)^r r^2 {}^nC_r\right\}$

$\qquad - (ab+bc+ca)\left\{\displaystyle\sum_{r=0}^{n}(-1)^r r {}^nC_r\right\} - \displaystyle\sum_{r=0}^{n}(-1)^r r^3 {}^nC_r$

Since, $\displaystyle\sum_{r=0}^{n}(-1)^r {}^nC_r = 0$

Also, $\displaystyle\sum_{r=0}^{n}(-1)^r r {}^nC_r = \dfrac{d}{dx}(1-x)^n \big|_{x=1} = 0$

Similarly,

$\displaystyle\sum_{r=0}^{n}(-1)^r r^2 {}^nC_r = $ value of $\dfrac{d}{dx}(nx(1-x)^{n-1}) \big|_{x=1} = 0$

Hence, $S = abc(0) + (a+b+c)(0) - (ab+bc+ca)(0) - 0$

$\therefore \ \ S = 0$.

**1.** **(a)** $n = 9$, then median term $= \left(\dfrac{9+1}{2}\right)^{th} = 5^{th}$ term. Last four observations are increased by 2. The median is 5th observation which remains unchanged.

∴ There will be no change in median.

**2.** **(a)** Marks obtained from 3 subjects out of $300 = 75 + 80 + 85 = 240$

If the marks of another subject is added, then the marks will be $\geq 240$ out of 400.

∴ Minimum average marks $= \dfrac{240}{4} = 60\%$

[When marks in the fourth subject = 0].

**3.** **(b)** $M = \dfrac{x_1 + x_2 + x_3 + ..... + x_n}{n}$

$nM = x_1 + x_2 + x_3 + .... + x_{n-1} + x_n$

i.e., $nM - x_n = x_1 + x_2 + x_3 + .... + x_{n-1}$

$\dfrac{nM - x_n + x'}{n} = \dfrac{x_1 + x_2 + x_3 + .... + x_{n-1} + x'}{n}$

∴ New average $= \dfrac{nM - x_n + x'}{n}$

**4.** **(c)** $\dfrac{\Sigma x_i f_i}{\Sigma f_i} = 46.5$

$\Rightarrow \dfrac{15 \times 10 + 30 \times 40 + M \times 30 + 75 \times 10 + 90 \times 10}{10 + 40 + 30 + 10 + 10} = 46.5$

∴ $M = 55$. so the class intervals can be $10 - 20, 20 - 40, 40 - 70, 70 - 80, 80 - 100$

**5.** **(b)** Let the number of workers in two groups be n and 10 n then the mean income

$= \dfrac{n\overline{X} + 10n\overline{Y}}{n + 10n} = \dfrac{\overline{X} + 10\overline{Y}}{11}$

**6.** **(d)** Let $n_1$ and $n_2$ be the number of observations in two groups having means $\overline{x}_1$ and $\overline{x}_2$ respectively. Then,

$\overline{x} = \dfrac{n_1\overline{x}_1 + n_2\overline{x}_2}{n_1 + n_2}$

Now, $\overline{x} - \overline{x}_1 = \dfrac{n_1\overline{x}_1 + n_2\overline{x}_2}{n_1 + n_2} - \overline{x}_1$

$= \dfrac{n_2(\overline{x}_2 - \overline{x}_1)}{n_1 + n_2} > 0 \quad [\because \overline{x}_2 > \overline{x}_1]$

$\Rightarrow \overline{x} > \overline{x}_1 \qquad ..... (i)$

and $\overline{x} - \overline{x}_2 = \dfrac{n(\overline{x}_1 - \overline{x}_2)}{n_1 + n_2} < 0 \quad [\because \overline{x}_2 > \overline{x}_1]$

$\Rightarrow \overline{x} < \overline{x}_2 \qquad ..... (ii)$

From (i) and (ii), $\overline{x}_1 < \overline{x} < \overline{x}_2$.

**7.** **(d)** Since, root mean square $\geq$ arithmetic mean

∴ $\sqrt{\dfrac{\sum\limits_{i=1}^{n} x_i^2}{n}} \geq \dfrac{\sum\limits_{i=1}^{n} x_i}{n} \Rightarrow \sqrt{\dfrac{400}{n}} \geq \dfrac{80}{n} \Rightarrow n \geq 16$

Hence, possible value of $n = 18$

**8.** **(d)** The required mean is

$\overline{x} = \dfrac{0.1 + 1.{}^nC_1 + 2.{}^nC_2 + 3.{}^nC_3 + ..... + n.{}^nC_n}{1 + {}^nC_1 + {}^nC_2 + ..... + {}^nC_n}$

$= \dfrac{\sum\limits_{r=0}^{n} r.{}^nC_r}{\sum\limits_{r=0}^{n} {}^nC_r} = \dfrac{\sum\limits_{r=1}^{n} \dfrac{n}{r}.{}^{n-1}C_{r-1}}{\sum\limits_{r=0}^{n} {}^nC_r}$

$= \dfrac{n\sum\limits_{r=0}^{n} {}^{n-1}C_{r-1}}{\sum\limits_{r=0}^{n} {}^nC_r} = \dfrac{n.2^{n-1}}{2^n} = \dfrac{n}{2}.$

**9.** **(d)** Mean $= \dfrac{1.1 + \dfrac{1}{2}.2 + \dfrac{1}{3}.3 + \dfrac{1}{4}.4 + \dfrac{1}{5}.5 + ..... + \dfrac{1}{n}.n}{1 + 2 + 3 + ..... + n}$

$= \dfrac{1 + 1 + 1 + 1 + ..... + 1}{\dfrac{n(n+1)}{2}} = \dfrac{n}{\dfrac{n(n+1)}{2}} = \dfrac{2}{n+1}$

**10.** **(b)** We know that $\overline{x} = \dfrac{\sum\limits_{i=1}^{n} x_i}{n}$ i.e., $\sum\limits_{i=1}^{n} x_i = n\overline{x}$

∴ $\dfrac{\sum\limits_{i=1}^{n} (x_i + 2i)}{n} = \dfrac{\sum\limits_{i=1}^{n} x_i + 2\sum\limits_{i=1}^{n} i}{n} = \dfrac{n\overline{x} + 2(1 + 2 + ... n)}{n}$

$= \dfrac{n\overline{x} + 2\dfrac{n(n+1)}{2}}{n} = \overline{x} + n + 1.$

**11.** **(c)** Let $x_1, x_2, ....., x_n$ be $n$ items. Then, $\overline{x} = \dfrac{1}{n}\Sigma x_i$

Let $y_1 = x_1 + 1, y_2 = x_2 + 2, y_3 = x_3 + 3, ..., y_n = x_n + n$
Then the mean of the new series is

$\dfrac{1}{n}\Sigma y_i = \dfrac{1}{n}\sum\limits_{i=1}^{n} (x_i + i)$

$= \dfrac{1}{n}\left[ \sum\limits_{i=1}^{n} x_i + \dfrac{1}{n}(1 + 2 + 3 + .... + n) \right]$

$= \overline{x} + \dfrac{1}{n}.\dfrac{n(n+1)}{2} = \overline{x} + \dfrac{n+1}{2}$

**12.** **(a)** A.M. $= \dfrac{1}{n}(1 + 2 + 3 + .... + n)$

$= \dfrac{1}{n}.\dfrac{n(n+1)}{2} = \dfrac{n+1}{2}$

**13.** **(c)** Weighted A.M.

$= \dfrac{1 \times 1 + 2 \times 2 + 3 \times 3 + ... + n \times n}{1 + 2 + 3 + ... + n}$

$= \dfrac{(1^2 + 2^2 + 3^2 + ... + n^2)}{\dfrac{1}{2}n(n+1)} = \dfrac{2n+1}{3}$

**14.** **(c)** Required mean $= \dfrac{1}{n}\sum_{i=1}^{n} x_i = \dfrac{1}{n}\sum_{i=1}^{n}(i+1)i$

$= \dfrac{1}{n}\sum_{i=1}^{n}(i^2+i) = \dfrac{1}{n}\left(\sum_{i=1}^{n}i^2 + \sum_{i=1}^{n}i\right)$

$= \dfrac{1}{n}\left\{\dfrac{n(n+1)(2n+1)}{6} + \dfrac{n(n+1)}{2}\right\}$

$= \dfrac{(n+1)}{2}\left\{\dfrac{2n+1}{3} + 1\right\}$

$= \dfrac{(n+1)(2n+4)}{6} = \dfrac{(n+1)(n+2)}{3}$

**15.** **(a)** We construct the following table [Note that the given discontinuous intervals are converted into continuous interval]

| Class limits | 1 - 10 | 11 - 20 | 21 - 30 | 31 - 40 | 41 - 50 |
|---|---|---|---|---|---|
| Modified class limits | 0.5 - 10.5 | 10.5 - 20.5 | 20.5 - 30.5 | 30.5 - 40.5 | 40.5 - 50.5 |
| Frequency | 8 | 15 | 28 | 16 | 8 |

Clearly, modal class is 20.5 - 30.5, as the maximum frequency occurs in this class. Using the formula for mode

$M_0 = \ell + \dfrac{f_0 - f_{-1}}{2f_0 - f_{-1} - f_1}\times i,$

$\ell = 20.5, \quad f_0 = 28, \quad f_{-1} = 15, \quad f_1 = 16, \ i = 10$

$= 20.5 + \dfrac{28-15}{2\times 28 - 15 - 16}\times 10 = 25.7$

**16.** **(a)** Arranging the data in ascending order, we have

$\alpha - \dfrac{7}{2}, \ \alpha - \dfrac{5}{2}, \ \alpha - \dfrac{3}{2}, \ \alpha - 1, \ \alpha - \dfrac{1}{2}, \ \alpha + \dfrac{1}{2}, \ \alpha + 4, \ \alpha + 5,$

median is

$\dfrac{1}{2}$ (4th observation + 5th observation)   $[\because \ n = 8, \text{ even}]$

$= \dfrac{1}{2}\left(\alpha - 1 + \alpha - \dfrac{1}{2}\right) = \alpha - \dfrac{3}{4}$

**17.** **(c)** The observation in ascending order are $-3, -3, -1, 0, 2,$ $2, 2, 5, 5, 5, 5, 6, 6, 6.$

Number of observation is 14, which is even.

$\therefore$ Median $= \dfrac{1}{2}[7^{\text{th}} \text{ observation} + 8^{\text{th}} \text{ observation}]$

$= \dfrac{1}{2}(2+5) = 3.5$

**18.** **(d)** The median of a given frequency distribution, can be found with the help of an ogive.

**19.** **(c)** If $n_1$ and $n_2$ are the numbers of items in the two distribution, then $\overline{X} = \dfrac{n_1\overline{X}_1 + n_2\overline{X}_2}{n_1 + n_2}$

**20.** **(2)** Let the number of boys be $n_1$ and that of girls be $n_2$

then $60 = \dfrac{80n_1 + 50n_2}{n_1 + n_2}$

$\Rightarrow 60n_1 + 60n_2 = 80n_1 + 50n_2$

$\Rightarrow 10n_2 = 20n_1 \Rightarrow n_1 : n_2 :: 1 : 2$

Thus $X = \dfrac{1}{2} \Rightarrow 4X = 2$

**21.** **(8)** Here for each $x_i = i$, weight $w_i = i^2 + i$
Hence, the required mean

$= \dfrac{\sum w_i x_i}{\sum w_i} = \dfrac{\displaystyle\sum_{i=1}^{n} i(i^2+i)}{\displaystyle\sum_{i=1}^{n}(i^2+i)} = \dfrac{\displaystyle\sum_{i=1}^{n} i^3 + \sum_{i=1}^{n} i^2}{\displaystyle\sum_{i=1}^{n} i^2 + \sum_{i=1}^{n} i}$

$= \dfrac{\dfrac{n^2(n+1)^2}{4} + \dfrac{n(n+1)(2n+1)}{6}}{\dfrac{n(n+1)(2n+1)}{6} + \dfrac{n(n+1)}{2}}$

$= \dfrac{\dfrac{n(n+1)}{2}\left\{\dfrac{n(n+1)}{2} + \dfrac{2n+1}{3}\right\}}{\dfrac{n(n+1)}{2}\left\{\dfrac{2n+1}{3} + 1\right\}}$

$= \dfrac{3n^2 + 7n + 2}{2(2n+4)} = \dfrac{(3n+1)(n+2)}{4(n+2)} = \dfrac{3n+1}{4}$

Thus $A = 3, B = 1, C = 4$

$\Rightarrow \ A + B + C = 3 + 1 + 4 = 8$

**22.** **(5)** Arranging the data in ascending order of magnitude, we obtain

| Height (in cm) | 150 | 152 | 154 | 155 | 156 | 160 | 161 |
|---|---|---|---|---|---|---|---|
| Number of students | 8 | 4 | 3 | 7 | 3 | 12 | 4 |
| Cumulative frequency | 8 | 12 | 15 | 22 | 25 | 37 | 41 |

Here, total number of items is 41 i.e., an odd number.

Hence, the median is $\dfrac{41+1}{2}th$ i.e., $21^{\text{th}}$ item.

From cumulative frequency table, we find that median i.e., $21^{\text{st}}$ item is 155.
(Each items from 16 to $22^{\text{nd}}$ are equal i.e. 155.)
Thus, $X = 155$

$\Rightarrow \dfrac{X}{31} = \dfrac{155}{31} = 5$

**23.** **(4)** Combined mean $= \dfrac{10\times 28 + 35\times n}{10 + n}$

$\Rightarrow \ 30 = \dfrac{280 + 35n}{10 + n}$

$\Rightarrow \ 300 + 30n = 280 + 35n$

$\Rightarrow \ 5n = 20 \Rightarrow n = 4$

**24.** **(9)** Sum of 5 observation $= 5x + 20$

$\therefore \dfrac{5x+20}{5} = 11 \ \Rightarrow \ x = 7$

$\therefore$ Mean of first three

$= \dfrac{x + x + 2 + x + 4}{3} = \dfrac{3x+6}{3} = 9$

**1.** **(b)** Let $y = \dfrac{ax+b}{c}$ i.e., $y = \dfrac{a}{c}x + \dfrac{b}{c}$

i.e., $y = Ax + B$, where $A = \dfrac{a}{c}, B = \dfrac{b}{c}$

$\therefore \ \bar{y} = A\bar{x} + B$

$\therefore \ y - \bar{y} = A(x - \bar{x})$

$\Rightarrow (y - \bar{y})^2 = A^2(x - \bar{x})^2$

$\Rightarrow \Sigma(y - \bar{y})^2 = A^2 \Sigma(x - \bar{x})^2$

$\Rightarrow n\sigma_y^2 = A^2 n\sigma_x^2 \Rightarrow \sigma_y^2 = A^2 \sigma_x^2$

$\Rightarrow \sigma_y = |A|\sigma_x \Rightarrow \sigma_y = \left|\dfrac{a}{c}\right|\sigma_x$

Thus, new S.D. $= \left|\dfrac{a}{c}\right|\sigma$

**2.** **(b)** Let the two unknown items be x and y.
Then, mean = 4.4

$\Rightarrow \dfrac{1+2+6+x+y}{5} = 8.4$

$\Rightarrow x + y = 13 \quad \ldots (i)$

and variance = 8.24

$\Rightarrow \dfrac{1^2 + 2^2 + 6^2 + x^2 + y^2}{5} - (\text{mean}^2) = 8.24$

$\Rightarrow 41 + x^2 + y^2 = 5\{(4.4)^2 + 8.24\}$

$\Rightarrow x^2 + y^2 = 97 \quad \ldots (ii)$

Solving (i) and (ii) for x and y, we get
$x = 9, y = 4$ or $x = 4, y = 9$

**3.** **(d)** Let $x_i/f_i; i = 1, 2 \ldots n$ be a frequency distribution.

Then, S.D. $= \sqrt{\dfrac{1}{N}\sum_{i=1}^{n} f_i (x_i - \bar{x})^2}$

and M.D. $= \dfrac{1}{N}\sum_{i=1}^{n} f_i |x_i - \bar{x}|$

Let, $|x_i - \bar{x}| = z_i \, ; i = 1, 2, \ldots n$

Then, $(\text{S.D.})^2 - (\text{M.D.})^2$

$= \dfrac{1}{N}\sum_{i=1}^{n} f_i z_i^2 - \left(\dfrac{1}{N}\sum_{i=1}^{n} f_i z_i\right)^2 = \sigma_z^2 \geq 0$

$\Rightarrow$ S.D. $\geq$ M.D.

**4.** **(d)** The mean of the given items,

$\bar{x} = \dfrac{3+7+10+18+22}{5} = 12$

Hence, variance $= \dfrac{1}{n}\sum(x_i - \bar{x})^2$

$= \dfrac{1}{5}\{(3-12)^2 + (7-12)^2 + (10-12)^2$

$\qquad\qquad + (18-12)^2 + (22-12)^2\}$

$= \dfrac{1}{5}\{81 + 25 + 4 + 36 + 100\} = \dfrac{246}{5} = 49.2$

**5.** **(b)** $\Sigma x = 170, \Sigma x^2 = 2830$, increase in $\Sigma x = 10$, then

$\Sigma x' = 170 + 10 = 180$

Increase in $\Sigma x^2 = 900 - 400 = 500$ then

$\Sigma x'^2 = 2830 + 500 = 3330$

Variance $= \dfrac{1}{n}\Sigma x'^2 - \left(\dfrac{1}{n}\Sigma x'\right)^2$

$= \dfrac{1}{15} \times 3330 - \left(\dfrac{1}{15} \times 180\right)^2 = 222 - 144 = 78.$

**6.** **(d)** Mode + 2Mean = 3 Median
$\Rightarrow$ Mode $= 3 \times 22 - 2 \times 21 = 66 - 42 = 24.$

**7.** **(c)** We have $n = 200, \ \bar{X} = 40, \sigma = 15$.

$\therefore \bar{X} = \dfrac{1}{N}\sum x_i$

$\Rightarrow \sum x_i = n\bar{X} = 200 \times 40 = 8000$

Corrected $\sum x_i$ = incorrect $\sum x_i$ − (sum of incorrect values) + (sum of correct values)
$= 8000 - 34 + 43 = 8009$

$\therefore$ Corrected mean $= \dfrac{\text{corrected} \sum x_i}{n} = \dfrac{8009}{200}$

$\qquad\qquad\qquad\qquad\qquad = 40.045$

Now, $\sigma = 15$

So, $15^2 = \dfrac{1}{200}\left(\sum x_i^2\right) - \left(\dfrac{1}{200}\sum x_i\right)^2$

$\Rightarrow 225 = \dfrac{1}{200}\left(\sum x_i^2\right) - \left(\dfrac{8000}{200}\right)^2$

$\Rightarrow 225 = \dfrac{1}{200}\left(\sum x_i^2\right) - 1600$

## Left column

$$\Rightarrow \sum x_i^2 = 200 \times 1825 = 365000$$

$$\Rightarrow \text{Incorrect } \sum x_i^2 = 365000$$

Corrected $\sum x_i^2 = (\text{incorrect } \sum x_i^2) - (\text{sum of squares of incorrect values}) + (\text{sum of squares of correct values})$
$= 365000 - (34)^2 + (43)^2 = 365693$

So, corrected

$$\sigma = \sqrt{\frac{1}{n}\sum x_i^2 - \left(\frac{1}{n}\sum x_i\right)^2} = \sqrt{\frac{365693}{200} - \left(\frac{8009}{200}\right)^2}$$

$$= \sqrt{1828.465 - 1603.602} = 14.995$$

**8. (b)** Given $\dfrac{\sum x_i}{18} = 7$ $(\because \text{mean} = 7 \text{ and } n = 18)$

$$\Rightarrow \sum x_i = 18 \times 7 = 126$$

Since, an observation 12 was miscopied as 21, therefore,

correct $\sum x_i = 126 - 21 + 12 = 117$

Hence, true mean $= \dfrac{\text{correct } \sum x_i}{18}$

$$= \frac{117}{18} = 6.5$$

Also variance is given to be $4^2 = 16$,

therefore, $\dfrac{\sum x_i^{\,2}}{18} - (\text{mean})^2 = 16$

$$\Rightarrow \frac{\sum x_i^2}{18} = 4^2 + (\text{mean})^2 = 16 + 7^2$$

$$\Rightarrow \sum x_i^2 = 18(16 + 49) = 1170$$

But, in the summation on R. H.S., one observation 12 was miscopied as 21, therefore, correct

$$\sum x_i^2 = 1170 - 21^2 + 12^2$$

$$= 1160 - 441 + 144 = 873.$$

Hence true variance

$$= \frac{\text{correct} \sum x_i^2}{18} - (\text{true mean})^2$$

$$= \frac{873}{18} - (6.5)^2 = 48.5 - 42.25 = 6.25$$

$\therefore$ True S.D. $= \sqrt{\text{true variance}} = \sqrt{6.25} = 2.5$

$\therefore$ Correct mean $= 6.5$ and correct S.D. $= 2.5$

## Right column

**9. (c)** Let us assume an arbitrary mean $a = 25$.
Class interval, $c = 10$
Construct the following table :

| Class | Freq. | $x_i$ | $u_i = \dfrac{x_i - a}{c}$ | $f_i u_i$ | $f_i u_i^2$ |
|---|---|---|---|---|---|
| $0-10$ | 1 | 5 | $-2$ | $-2$ | 1 |
| $10-20$ | 3 | 15 | $-1$ | $-3$ | 6 |
| $20-30$ | 4 | 25 | 0 | 0 | 0 |
| $30-40$ | 2 | 35 | 1 | 2 | 2 |
| Total | 10 | | | $-3$ | 9 |

$$\sigma^2 = c^2 \left\{ \frac{\sum f_i u_i^2}{\sum f_i} - \left(\frac{\sum f_i u_i}{\sum f_i}\right)^2 \right\}$$

$$= 10^2 \left( \frac{9}{10} - \left(\frac{-3}{10}\right)^2 \right)$$

$$= 90 - 9 = 81 \text{ or } \sigma = \sqrt{81} = 9$$

**10. (d)** Construct the following table taking assumed mean $a = 25$.

| Class | $x_i$ | $f_i$ | $u_i = \dfrac{x_i - a}{10}$ | $f_i u_i$ | $\lvert x_i - 27 \rvert$ | $f_i \lvert x_i - 27 \rvert$ |
|---|---|---|---|---|---|---|
| $0-10$ | 5 | 5 | $-2$ | $-10$ | 22 | 110 |
| $10-20$ | 15 | 8 | $-1$ | $-8$ | 12 | 96 |
| $20-30$ | 25 | 15 | 0 | 0 | 2 | 30 |
| $30-40$ | 35 | 16 | 1 | 16 | 8 | 128 |
| $40-50$ | 45 | 6 | 2 | 12 | 18 | 108 |
| Total | | 50 | | 10 | | 472 |

$$\text{Mean} = a + \frac{\sum f_i u_i}{\sum f_i} \times c = 25 + \frac{10}{50} \times 10 = 27,$$

and mean deviation (about mean)

$$= \frac{\sum f_i \lvert x_i - 27 \rvert}{\sum f_i} = \frac{472}{50} = 9.44 .$$

**11. (d)** There are 11 observations, on arranging these observations in ascending order of magnitude, we get $3, 3, 5, 9, 10, 12, 12, 12, 18, 21, 21$.

The number of observations n $(= 11)$ is an odd number, therfore, median

$$M = \frac{11+1}{2} \text{ the observation}$$

$$= 6\text{th observation} = 12$$

For the mean deviation (about median), construct the following table :

| $x_i$ | 3 | 3 | 5 | 9 | 10 | 12 | 12 | 12 | 18 | 21 | 21 | Total |
|---|---|---|---|---|---|---|---|---|---|---|---|---|
| $x_i-12$ | −9 | −9 | −7 | −3 | −2 | 0 | 0 | 0 | 6 | 9 | 9 | −6 |
| $|x_i-12|$ | 9 | 9 | 7 | 3 | 2 | 0 | 0 | 0 | 6 | 9 | 9 | 54 |

$\therefore$ Mean deviation (about median)

$$= \frac{\sum |x_i - M|}{n} = \frac{\sum |x_i - 12|}{n} = \frac{54}{11} = 4.909$$

**12. (a)** Mean $\overline{x} = \dfrac{1+2+3+4+5+6}{6} = \dfrac{21}{6} = \dfrac{7}{2}$

$$\text{S.D.} = \sigma = \sqrt{\frac{1}{n}\Sigma x_i^2 - (\overline{x})^2}$$

$$= \sqrt{\frac{1}{6}(1+4+9+16+25+36) - \frac{49}{4}}$$

$$= \sqrt{\frac{91}{6} - \frac{49}{4}} = \sqrt{\frac{182-147}{12}} = \sqrt{\frac{35}{12}}$$

**13. (b)** Corrected $\Sigma x = 40 \times 200 - 50 + 40 = 7990$

$$\therefore \text{Corrected } \overline{x} = \frac{7990}{200} = 39.95$$

Incorrect $\Sigma x^2 = n[\sigma^2 + \overline{x}^2] = 200[15^2 + 40^2]$
$$= 365000$$

Correct $\Sigma x^2 = 365000 - 2500 + 1600 = 364100$

$$\therefore \text{Corrected } \sigma = \sqrt{\frac{364100}{200} - (39.95)^2}$$

$$= \sqrt{(1820.5 - 1596)} = \sqrt{224.5} = 14.98$$

**14. (a)** We have $r = \max |x_i - x_j|$

and $S^2 = \dfrac{1}{n-1}\displaystyle\sum_{i=1}^{n}(x_i - \overline{x})^2$

Now, $(x_i - \overline{x})^2 = \left(x_i - \dfrac{x_1 + x_2 + ..... + x_n}{n}\right)^2$

$$= \frac{1}{n^2}[(x_i - x_1) + (x_i - x_2) + .....$$

$$+(x_i - x_{i-1}) + (x_i - x_{i+1}) + .....$$

$$+(x_i - x_n)]^2 \le \frac{1}{n^2}[(n-1)r]^2 \qquad [\because |x_i - x_j| \le r]$$

$$\Rightarrow (x_i - \overline{x})^2 \le r^2 \Rightarrow \sum_{i=1}^{n}(x_i - \overline{x})^2 \le nr^2$$

$$\Rightarrow \frac{1}{n-1}\sum_{i=1}^{n}(x_i - \overline{x})^2 \le \frac{nr^2}{(n-1)}$$

$$\Rightarrow S^2 \le \frac{nr^2}{(n-1)} \Rightarrow S \le r\sqrt{\frac{n}{n-1}}$$

**15. (b)** Let us assume an arbitary mean a = 155. Following table is constructed

| $X_i$ | $f_i$ | $u_i = \dfrac{X_i - 155}{5}$ | $u_i^2$ | $f_i u_i$ | $f_i u_i^2$ |
|---|---|---|---|---|---|
| 140 | 4 | −3 | 9 | −12 | 36 |
| 145 | 6 | −2 | 4 | −12 | 24 |
| 150 | 15 | −1 | 1 | −15 | 15 |
| 155 | 30 | 0 | 0 | 0 | 0 |
| 160 | 36 | 1 | 1 | 36 | 36 |
| 165 | 24 | 2 | 4 | 48 | 96 |
| 170 | 8 | 3 | 9 | 24 | 72 |
| 175 | 2 | 4 | 16 | 8 | 32 |
| Total | 125 | | | 77 | 311 |

$$\therefore \text{Variance} = \sigma^2 = c^2\left(\frac{\sum f_i u_i^2}{n} - \left(\frac{\sum f_i u_i}{n}\right)^2\right)$$

$$= 25 \times \left(\frac{311}{125} - \left(\frac{77}{125}\right)^2\right)$$

$$= 25 \times \frac{311}{125} - \frac{25 \times 77 \times 77}{125 \times 125}$$

$$= 62.2 - 9.4864 = 52.7136$$

$$\Rightarrow \text{S.D.} = \sqrt{52.7136} = 7.26 \text{ nearly}$$

**16. (c)** In this case each value of the variable is increased by the same number 10, therefore, the standard deviation remains unchanged.

**17. (d)** $\displaystyle\sum_{i=1}^{20}(x_i - 30) = 20 \Rightarrow \sum_{i=1}^{20} x_i - 20 \times 30 = 20$

$$\Rightarrow \sum_{i=1}^{20} x_i = 620, \ \text{Mean} = \frac{\displaystyle\sum_{i=1}^{20} x_i}{20} = \frac{620}{20} = 31.$$

**18. (b)** Mean deviation is minimum when it is considered about the item, equidistant from the beginning and the end i.e. the median. In this case median is $\dfrac{101+1}{2}$ th i.e., $51^{st}$ item i.e., $x_{51}$.

**19. (d)** In a positively skewed distribution
$$\text{Mode} < \text{Median} < \text{Mean}$$

**20.  2**

Clearly mean $A = 0$

Standard deviation $\sigma = \sqrt{\dfrac{\sum (x-A)^2}{2n}}$

$2 = \sqrt{\dfrac{(a-0)^2 + (a-0)^2 + \ldots + (2n)^{th}\ \text{term}}{2n}}$

$= \sqrt{\dfrac{a^2 \cdot 2n}{2n}} = |a|$

**21.  1**

$\sigma_x^2 = \dfrac{\sum d_i^2}{n}$ (Here deviations are taken from the mean). Since A and B both have 100 consecutive integers, therefore both have same standard deviation and hence the variance.

$\therefore \dfrac{V_A}{V_B} = 1 \left(\text{As } \sum d_i^2 \text{ is same in both the cases}\right)$

**22.  5**

We construct the following table :

| $x_i$ | $f(x_i)$ | $x_i^2$ | $f(x_i).x_i$ | $f(x_i).x_i^2$ |
|---|---|---|---|---|
| 2 | $\dfrac{1}{3}$ | 4 | $\dfrac{2}{3}$ | $\dfrac{4}{3}$ |
| 3 | $\dfrac{1}{2}$ | 9 | $\dfrac{3}{2}$ | $\dfrac{9}{2}$ |
| 11 | $\dfrac{1}{6}$ | 121 | $\dfrac{11}{6}$ | $\dfrac{121}{6}$ |
| Total | 1 | | 4 | 26 |

$\therefore \ \sigma^2 = \dfrac{\sum f(x_i)x_i^2}{\sum f(x_i)} - \left(\dfrac{\sum f(x_i)x_i}{\sum f(x_i)}\right)^2$

$= \dfrac{26}{1} - \left(\dfrac{4}{1}\right)^2 = 26 - 16 = 10$

Thus, 2M = 10
$\Rightarrow M = 5$

**23.  2**

The relation between Mean, Median and Mode is
$A - M_o = 3(A - M)$ i.e. $2A = 3M - M_o$
$\therefore 2 \times 24 = 3M - 18, \qquad \therefore M = 22$
Thus, P = 2

**24.  1**

$S.D.(\sigma) = \sqrt{\dfrac{250}{10}} = \sqrt{25} = 5$

Hence coefficient of variation

$= \dfrac{\sigma}{\text{mean}} \times 100 = \dfrac{5}{50} \times 100 = 10$

Thus, $\dfrac{X}{10} = 1$.

**1. (c)** If $A + B = 45°$
$\tan(A + B) = 1$
$\tan A + \tan B = 1 - \tan A \tan B$
$(1 + \tan A)(1 + \tan B) = 2$

**2. (c)** Given $\cos x + \sin x = \dfrac{1}{2} \Rightarrow 1 + \sin 2x = \dfrac{1}{4}$

$\sin 2x = -\dfrac{3}{4} \Rightarrow 2x \in (\pi, 2\pi)$

$\Rightarrow x \in (\pi/2, \pi) \Rightarrow \tan x < 0$

$\dfrac{2t}{1+t^2} = -\dfrac{3}{4} \Rightarrow 8t = -3 - 3t^2 \Rightarrow 3t^2 + 8t + 3 = 0$

where $t = \tan x$

$t = \dfrac{-8 \pm \sqrt{64-36}}{2\times 3}$ ; $t = \dfrac{-8 \pm \sqrt{28}}{2\times 3}$ ; $t = \dfrac{-(4+\sqrt 7)}{3}$

or $\dfrac{-4+\sqrt 7}{3}$ (rejected)

**3. (d)** On adding and subtracting

$x = \dfrac{3 - \cos 4\theta + 4\sin 2\theta}{2}$

$y = \dfrac{3 - \cos 4\theta - 4\sin 2\theta}{2}$

$x = \dfrac{4(1 + \sin 2\theta) - (1 + \cos 4\theta)}{2}$ ;

$y = \dfrac{4(1 - \sin 2\theta) - (1 + \cos 4\theta)}{2}$

$x = 2(1 + \sin 2\theta) - \cos^2 2\theta$ ; $y = 2(1 - \sin 2\theta) - \cos^2 2\theta$
$x = 1 + 2\sin 2\theta + \sin^2 2\theta$ ; $y = 1 - 2\sin 2\theta + \sin^2 2\theta$
$x = (1 + \sin 2\theta)^2$ ; $y = (1 - \sin 2\theta)^2$

$\Rightarrow \sqrt x + \sqrt y = 2$

**4. (a)** $\tan(A + B) = \dfrac{\tan A + \tan B}{1 - \tan A \tan B}$

$= \dfrac{\tan A + \dfrac{n\sin A\cos A}{1 - n\cos^2 A}}{1 - \tan A \cdot \dfrac{n\sin A\cos A}{1 - n\cos^2 A}}$

$= \dfrac{\sin A(1 - n\cos^2 A) + n\sin A\cos^2 A}{\cos A(1 - n\cos^2 A) - n\sin^2 A\cos A}$

$= \dfrac{\sin A - 0}{\cos A(1 - n\cos^2 A - n\sin^2 A)}$

$= \dfrac{\sin A}{(1-n)\cos A}$

**5. (b)** $4\cos^2\theta - 2\sqrt 2 \cos\theta - 1 = 0$

$\cos\theta = \dfrac{2\sqrt 2 \pm \sqrt{8+16}}{8}$

$= \dfrac{\sqrt 2 \pm \sqrt 6}{4}$

$\cos\theta = \dfrac{\sqrt 6 + \sqrt 2}{4} \Rightarrow \theta = \dfrac{\pi}{12} ; 2\pi - \dfrac{\pi}{12} = \dfrac{23\pi}{12}$

$\cos\theta = -\dfrac{\sqrt 6 - \sqrt 2}{4}$

$\cos\theta = \cos(\pi - 5\pi/12)$ ; $\cos(\pi + 5\pi/12)$
$\theta = 7\pi/12 ; 17\pi/12$

**6. (d)** $\cot x + \dfrac{\cos(60+x)}{\sin(60+x)} + \dfrac{\cos(x-60)}{\sin(x-60)}$

$= \dfrac{\cos x}{\sin x} + \dfrac{\sin(2x)}{\sin(x+60)\sin(x-60)}$

$= \dfrac{\cos x}{\sin x} + \dfrac{8\sin x\cos x}{4\sin^2 x - 3}$

$= \dfrac{4\sin^2 x\cos x - 3\cos x + 8\sin^2 x\cos x}{4\sin^3 x - 3\sin x}$

$= \dfrac{3[3\cos x - 4\cos^3 x]}{\sin^3 x} = 3\cot 3x$

$\Rightarrow \dfrac{3[1 - 3\tan^2 x]}{3\tan x - \tan^3 x}$

**7. (b)** $(\alpha - \beta) = (\theta - \beta) - (\theta - \alpha)$
$\cos(\alpha - \beta) = \cos(\theta - \beta)\cos(\theta - \alpha) + \sin(\theta - \beta)\sin(\theta - \alpha)$

$\cos(\alpha - \beta) = \dfrac{y}{b}\cdot\dfrac{x}{a} + \sqrt{1 - \dfrac{x^2}{a^2}} \cdot \sqrt{1 - \dfrac{y^2}{b^2}}$

$\Rightarrow \left[\dfrac{xy}{ab} - \cos(\alpha - \beta)\right]^2 = \left(1 - \dfrac{x^2}{a^2}\right)\left(1 - \dfrac{y^2}{b^2}\right)$

$\Rightarrow \dfrac{x^2 y^2}{a^2 b^2} + \cos^2(\alpha - \beta) - \dfrac{2xy}{ab}\cos(\alpha - \beta)$

$= 1 - \dfrac{y^2}{b^2} - \dfrac{x^2}{a^2} + \dfrac{x^2 y^2}{a^2 b^2}$

$\Rightarrow \dfrac{x^2}{a^2} + \dfrac{y^2}{b^2} - \dfrac{2xy}{ab}\cos(\alpha - \beta) = \sin^2(\alpha - \beta)$

**8.** **(a)** $E = \dfrac{3}{2}(1+\cos 20^0)(1+\cos 100^0)(1+\cos 140^0)$

$= \dfrac{3}{2}\, 2\cos^2 10^0 \cdot 2\cos^2 50^0 \cdot 2\cos^2 70^0$

$= 12(\cos 10^0 \cos 50^0 \cos 70^0)^2 = 12 \times \dfrac{3}{64} = \dfrac{9}{16}$

**9.** **(a)** $x = \dfrac{1-\sin\phi}{\cos\phi} = \dfrac{1-\cos(\pi/2-\phi)}{\sin(\pi/2-\phi)}$

$\qquad = \tan(\pi/4 - \phi/2)$

$y = \dfrac{1+\cos\phi}{\sin\phi} = \dfrac{2\cos^2\phi/2}{2\sin(\phi/2)\cos(\phi/2)} = \cot\phi/2$

$x = \dfrac{1-\tan\phi/2}{1+\tan\phi/2} = \dfrac{\cot\phi/2 - 1}{\cot\phi/2 + 1} = \dfrac{y-1}{y+1}$

**10.** **(b)** The expression

$= \left(1+\cos\dfrac{\pi}{10}\right)\left(1+\cos\dfrac{3\pi}{10}\right)\left(1-\cos\dfrac{3\pi}{10}\right)\left(1-\cos\dfrac{\pi}{10}\right)$

$\left[\because \cos\dfrac{7\pi}{10} = \cos\left(\pi - \dfrac{3\pi}{10}\right) = -\cos\dfrac{3\pi}{10}\right.$

$\left.\text{and } \cos\dfrac{9\pi}{10} = \cos\left(\pi - \dfrac{\pi}{10}\right) = -\cos\dfrac{\pi}{10}\right]$

$= \left(1-\cos^2\dfrac{\pi}{10}\right)\left(1-\cos^2\dfrac{3\pi}{10}\right) = \sin^2\dfrac{\pi}{10}\cdot\sin^2\dfrac{3\pi}{10}$

$= \sin^2 18°\cdot\sin^2 54° = \left(\dfrac{\sqrt5-1}{4}\cdot\dfrac{\sqrt5+1}{4}\right)^2 = \dfrac{1}{16}$

**11.** **(a,b,c)** Given $\log\left(\dfrac{a+c}{a}\right) + \log\left(\dfrac{a}{b}\right) = \log 2$

$\Rightarrow \log\left(\dfrac{a+c}{b}\right) = \log 2$

$\Rightarrow a+c = 2b \qquad\qquad .....(1)$
also $a - ax^2 + 2bx + c + cx^2 = 0$
$= (c-a)x^2 + 2bx + (c+a) = 0$ has equal roots
$\therefore D = 0$
$\qquad 4b^2 - 4(c^2 - a^2) = 0$
$\therefore b^2 = c^2 - a^2 \qquad\qquad ....(2)$
From (1) and (2), $b^2 = (c-a)(c+a)$
$\qquad\qquad b^2 = (c-a)\,2b$
$\qquad\qquad \Rightarrow 2(c-a) = b \qquad ....(3)$
From (2) $c^2 = a^2 + b^2 \Rightarrow$ triangle is a right at C.
$\qquad \angle C = 90°$
$\qquad A + B = 90°$
From (3) using sine law,
$\qquad 2(\sin C - \sin A) = \sin B$
$\qquad C = 90° \quad \Rightarrow \sin C = 1$
$\qquad A + B = 90° \Rightarrow B = 90° - A$
$\qquad 2(1 - \sin A) = \sin(90 - A) = \cos A$

Squaring both sides,
$\Rightarrow 4(1-\sin A)^2 = \cos^2 A = (1 - \sin^2 A)$
$\qquad 4(1-\sin A) = (1+\sin A)$
$\qquad 3 = 5\sin A$
$\qquad \sin A = 3/5$
$\qquad B = 90 - A$
$\qquad \sin B = \cos A = 4/5 \ \text{ and } \sin C = 1$

$\Rightarrow \sin A + \sin B + \sin C = \dfrac{3}{5} + \dfrac{4}{5} + 1 = \dfrac{12}{5}$

**12.** **(a,b,c,d)**

$\quad$ **(a)** $A = \sin 82\dfrac{1}{2}^0 \cdot \cos 37\dfrac{1}{2}^0 = \sin\dfrac{165^0}{2}\cdot\cos\dfrac{75^0}{2}$

$\qquad = \dfrac{1}{2}\left[\sin 120^0 + \sin 45^0\right] = \dfrac{\sqrt6+1}{4\sqrt2}$

$\qquad B = \sin 127\dfrac{1}{2}^0 \cdot \sin 97\dfrac{1}{2}^0$

$\qquad = \dfrac{1}{2}\left[\cos 30^0 - \cos 225^0\right] = \dfrac{1}{2}\left[\dfrac{\sqrt3}{2} + \dfrac{1}{\sqrt2}\right] = \dfrac{\sqrt6+2}{4\sqrt2}$

$\qquad \Rightarrow A \neq B$

$\quad$ **(b)** $\tan(A{-}B) = \dfrac{\tan A - \tan B}{1+\tan A\tan B}$

$\qquad = \dfrac{\dfrac{\sqrt3}{4-\sqrt3} - \dfrac{\sqrt3}{4+\sqrt3}}{1 + \dfrac{\sqrt3\cdot\sqrt3}{(4-\sqrt3)(4+\sqrt3)}} = \dfrac{\sqrt3\left[4+\sqrt3 - 4 + \sqrt3\right]}{16-3+3}$

$\qquad = 3/8 \Rightarrow$ rational

$\quad$ **(c)** $\sin 2$ is $+$ve ; $\sin 3$ is $+$ve and $\sin 5$ $-$ve
$\qquad \therefore \ \ 5m2 \cdot 5m3 \cdot \sin 5 : s-ve$

$\quad$ **(d)** $\sin^2\theta = \dfrac{1\pm\sqrt5}{2}$

$\qquad \Rightarrow \sin^2\theta = \dfrac{1-\sqrt5}{2}$ (not possible)

$\qquad \sin^2\theta = \dfrac{1+\sqrt5}{2} > 1$

$\qquad \Rightarrow$ not possible ]

**13.** **(b,d)**

$\tan\left(\dfrac{2\pi}{3} - x\right) = \dfrac{2\cos\left(\dfrac{\pi}{3}+x\right)\sin\left(\dfrac{\pi}{3}-\dfrac{x}{2}\right)}{2\sin\left(\dfrac{\pi}{3}+x\right)\sin\left(\dfrac{\pi}{3}-\dfrac{x}{2}\right)}$

$= -\cot\left(\dfrac{\pi}{3}+x\right) = \tan\left(\dfrac{\pi}{2}+\dfrac{\pi}{3}+x\right) = \tan\left(\dfrac{5\pi}{6}+x\right)$

$\dfrac{5\pi}{6} + x = n\pi + \dfrac{2\pi}{3} - x \Rightarrow 2x = n\pi + \dfrac{\pi}{6}$

$x = \dfrac{n\pi}{2} - \dfrac{\pi}{12} \Rightarrow n = \dfrac{5\pi}{12}$ or $\dfrac{11\pi}{12}$

**14.** **(b,c)** $\cos A + \cos B = 1$

$$\Rightarrow 2\cos\left(\frac{A+B}{2}\right)\cos\left(\frac{A-B}{2}\right) = 1$$

$$\Rightarrow \cos\left(\frac{A-B}{2}\right) = \frac{1}{\sqrt{3}} \Rightarrow 2\cos^2\left(\frac{A-B}{2}\right) - 1 = -\frac{1}{3}$$

$$\Rightarrow \cos(A-B) = -\frac{1}{3} \ (\text{using } \cos 2\theta = 2\cos^2\theta - 1)$$

$$|\cos A - \cos B| = 2\sin\left(\frac{A+B}{2}\right)\sin\left(\frac{B-A}{2}\right)$$

$$= 2 \times \frac{1}{2}\sqrt{\left(1 - \frac{1}{3}\right)} = \sqrt{\frac{2}{3}}$$

**15.** **(b)** Given $P_1 = m \Rightarrow P_1^2 = m^2$

$$\Rightarrow \sin^2\theta + \cos^2\theta + 2\sin\theta\cos\theta$$
$$= m^2 \quad (\text{By defn. of } P_n)$$

$$\Rightarrow \sin\theta\cos\theta = \frac{(m^2-1)}{2}$$

Now, $P_6 = 1 - 3\sin^2\theta\cos^2\theta$

$$\Rightarrow (1 - P_6) = 3(\sin\theta\cos\theta)^2 = \frac{3(m^2-1)^2}{4}$$

$$\qquad\qquad (\text{By putting value of } \sin\theta\cos\theta)$$

Hence, $4(1 - P_6) = 3(m^2 - 1)^2$

**16.** **(c)** Consider $2P_6 - 3P_4 + 10$

$$= 2(1 - 3\sin^2\theta\cos^2\theta) - 3(1 - 2\sin^2\theta\cos^2\theta) + 10$$

$$(\because P_4 = 1 - 2\sin^2\theta\cos^2\theta \text{ and } P_6 = 1 - 3\sin^2\theta\cos^2\theta)$$

$$= 2 - 3 + 10 = 9$$

**17.** **(c)** We have,

$$\frac{P_n - P_{n-2}}{P_{n-4}} = -\sin^2\theta\cos^2\theta$$

Put $n = 7$, then $\dfrac{P_7 - P_5}{P_3} = -\sin^2\theta\cos^2\theta$ ....(1)

Now, put $n = 5$, then $\dfrac{P_5 - P_3}{P_1} = -\sin^2\theta\cos^2\theta$ ....(2)

From Eqs. (1) and (2), we get

$$\frac{P_7 - P_5}{P_3} = \frac{P_5 - P_3}{P_1} \Rightarrow \frac{P_7 - P_5}{P_5 - P_3} = \frac{P_3}{P_1}$$

**18.** $\mathbf{A \to p \,;\, B \to s \,;\, C \to r \,;\, D \to q}$

(A) If M is mid point of PQ, then

$$M = \left(\frac{\theta + \phi}{2}, \frac{\sin\theta + \sin\phi}{2}\right)$$

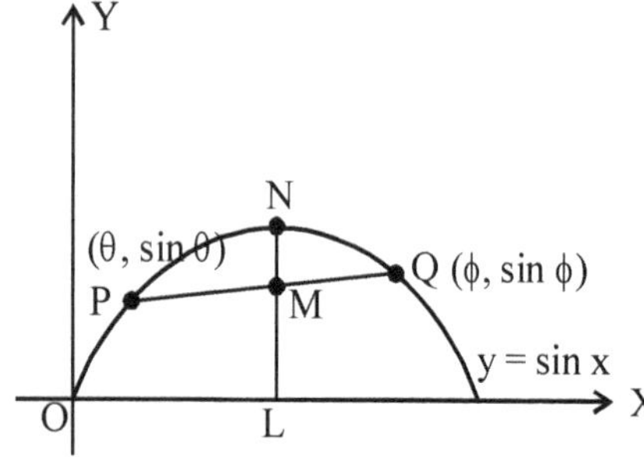


Also, $N \equiv \left(\dfrac{\theta + \phi}{2}, \sin\left(\dfrac{\theta + \phi}{2}\right)\right)$

It is clear from the figure.

$ML \le NL$

$$\Rightarrow \frac{\sin\theta + \sin\phi}{2} \le \sin\left(\frac{\theta+\phi}{2}\right)$$

$$\Rightarrow \sin\theta + \sin\phi \le 2\sin\left(\frac{\theta+\phi}{2}\right)$$

$$\Rightarrow \sin\theta + \sin\phi \le 2\sin\left(\frac{\pi}{4}\right) \quad \left(\because \theta + \phi = \frac{\pi}{2}\right)$$

$\therefore \ \sin\theta + \sin\phi \le \sqrt{2}$ and $(\sin\theta + \sin\phi)\sin\dfrac{\pi}{4} \le 1$ **(p)**

(B) Since, $a^2 + b^2 = (\sin\theta - \sin\phi)^2 + (\cos\theta + \cos\phi)^2$

$$= \sin^2\theta + \cos^2\theta + \sin^2\phi + \cos^2\phi$$
$$-2\sin\theta\sin\phi + 2\cos\theta\cos\phi$$

$$= 2 + 2\cos(\theta + \phi)$$

$$= 4\cos^2\left(\frac{\theta+\phi}{2}\right) \le 4 \ \ \textbf{(s)}$$

$(\text{using } \cos 2\theta = 2\cos^2\theta - 1)$

(C) Since $3\sin\theta + 5\cos\theta = 5$

$\Rightarrow 3\sin\theta = 5(1 - \cos\theta)$

Squaring both sides,

$9\sin^2\theta = 25(1 - \cos\theta)^2$

$\Rightarrow 9(1 - \cos\theta)(1 + \cos\theta) = 25(1 - \cos\theta)^2$

$\qquad (\because \sin^2\theta = 1 - \cos^2\theta)$

$\Rightarrow 9(1 + \cos\theta) = 25(1 - \cos\theta) \ (\because \ 1 - \cos\theta \ne 0)$

$\Rightarrow 34\cos\theta = 16$

$$\cos\theta = \frac{8}{17}, \text{ also } \sin\theta = \frac{15}{17}$$

$$\therefore \ 5\sin\theta - 3\cos\theta = \frac{75}{17} - \frac{24}{17} = 3 \ \textbf{((r)}$$

(D) Let $A = 7\cos x + 6\sin x = 6(2\cos x + \sin x) - 5\cos x$

$= 6 - 5\cos x$

Now, $2\cos x + \sin x = 1 \Rightarrow \sin x = 1 - 2\cos x$

$\Rightarrow \sin^2 x = 1 - \cos^2 x = 1 - 4\cos x + 4\cos^2 x$

$$\therefore \ \cos x = 0 \text{ or } \frac{4}{5}.$$

But $\cos x \ne \dfrac{4}{5} \Rightarrow \cos x = 0 \quad \therefore A = 6$ **(q)**

**19.** **(b)**

$P = 2\sin 2° + 4\sin 4° + 6\sin 6° + \ldots + 178\sin 178°$

$P = 178\sin 2° + 176\sin 4° + \ldots + 2\sin 178°$

$2P = 180[\sin 2° + \sin 4° + \sin 6° + \ldots + \sin 178°]$

$$P = 90\left[\frac{\sin 89°}{\sin 1°}\sin 90°\right] = 90\cot 1° \Rightarrow \frac{P}{90} = \cot 1°$$

S-1 : $\dfrac{\sqrt{1+\cot^2 1°}}{90\cot 1°} = \dfrac{\csc 1°}{90\cot 1°} = \dfrac{\sec 1°}{90}$ which is irrational.

S-2 is not the correct reason as tan 60° is irrational but sec 60° is rational.

**20. (5)**

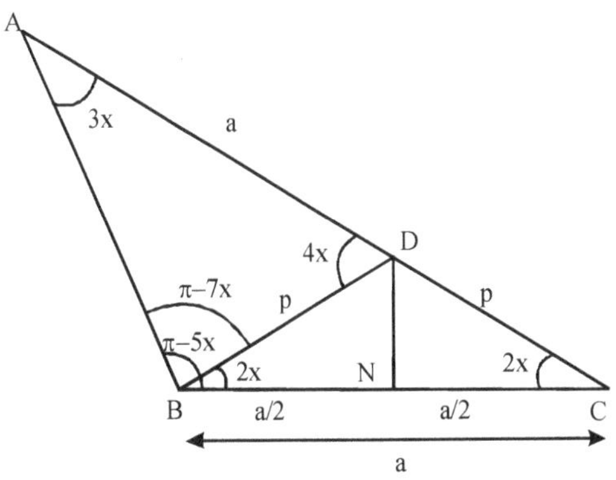

In $\Delta$ ABC, $\dfrac{AC}{\sin 5x} = \dfrac{BC}{\sin 3x}$ ;

$\dfrac{a+p}{\sin 5x} = \dfrac{a}{\sin 3x}$ ..........(1)

In $\Delta$ BDN, (note that $\Delta$ BDC is isosceles)

$\cos 2x = \dfrac{a}{2p}$ ; $a = 2p\cos 2x$

From (1), $\dfrac{2p\cos 2x + p}{\sin 5x} = \dfrac{2p\cos 2x}{\sin 3x}$

$2\sin 3x\cos 2x + \sin 3x = 2\sin 5x\cos 2x$

$\sin 5x + \sin x + \sin 3x = \sin 7x + \sin 3x$

$\sin 7x - \sin 5x = \sin x$

$2\cos 6x \sin x = \sin x$

$\cos 6x = \dfrac{1}{2} \Rightarrow x = 10°, \therefore \dfrac{x}{2} = 5°$

**21. (9)** $k = \dfrac{2\tan x}{1+\tan^2 x} = \sin 2x \Rightarrow \sin 2C = \sin 2B$

But $\angle C > \angle B$

$2C = \pi - 2B \Rightarrow B + C = \pi/2$

$\therefore \angle A = \pi/2$

$= 90°, \therefore \dfrac{A}{10} = 9°$

**22. (5)** Let $y = \cos A \cdot \sin^2\left(\dfrac{A}{2}\right) + \cos B \cdot \sin^2\left(\dfrac{B}{2}\right)$

$\qquad\qquad + \cos C \cdot \sin^2\left(\dfrac{C}{2}\right)$

$= \dfrac{1}{2}[\cos A (1-\cos A) + \cos B (1-\cos B)$

$\qquad\qquad\qquad + \cos C (1-\cos C)]$

$= \dfrac{1}{2}[(\cos A - \cos^2 A) + (\cos B - \cos^2 B) + (\cos C - \cos^2 C)]$

$= \dfrac{1}{2}\left[-\left\{\left(\cos A - \dfrac{1}{2}\right)^2 - \dfrac{1}{4}\right\} - \left\{\left(\cos B - \dfrac{1}{2}\right)^2 - \dfrac{1}{4}\right\} - \left\{\left(\cos C - \dfrac{1}{2}\right)^2 - \dfrac{1}{4}\right\}\right]$

$y = \dfrac{1}{2}\left[\dfrac{3}{4} - \left(\cos A - \dfrac{1}{2}\right)^2 - \left(\cos B - \dfrac{1}{2}\right)^2 - \left(\cos C - \dfrac{1}{2}\right)^2\right]$

Now $y$ will be maximum if $\cos A = \cos B = \cos C = \dfrac{1}{2}$

hence $y_{max} = 3/8$

Thus, $P = 3, Q = 8$

$\Rightarrow Q - P = 5$

**23. (2)** $x = \dfrac{1}{1+x} \Rightarrow x^2 + x - 1 = 0$

$x = \dfrac{-1+\sqrt{5}}{2}$ or $\dfrac{-1-\sqrt{5}}{2}$ (rejected, think!)

hence $x = \left(\dfrac{\sqrt{5}-1}{4}\right)\cdot 2 = 2\sin 18°, \therefore \dfrac{x}{\sin 18°} = 2$

**24. (1)** $\dfrac{3\sin 76°.\sin 16° + \cos 76°\cos 16°}{(\cos 76°\sin 16° + \sin 76°\cos 16°)\cot 44°}$

$= \dfrac{2\sin 76°\sin 16° + [\sin 76°\sin 16° + \cos 76°\cos 16°]}{\sin 92°.\cot 44°}$

$= \dfrac{\cos 60° - \cos 92° + \cos 60°}{\sin 92°.\cot 44°}$

$= \dfrac{1-\cos 92°}{\sin 92°.\cot 44°} = \dfrac{2\sin^2 46°}{2\sin 46°\cos 46°.\cot 44°}$

$= \dfrac{\tan 46°}{\cot 44°} = \dfrac{\cot 44°}{\cot 44°} = 1$

**1.** (d) $S = \dfrac{\sin(n\theta/2)}{\sin(\theta/2)}\cos\dfrac{(n+1)\theta}{2}$, $n = 17$, $\theta = \dfrac{\pi}{9}$

$= \dfrac{\sin(17\pi/18)}{\sin(\pi/18)}.\cos\pi = -1$

**2.** (c) $y = (7\cos\theta + 24\sin\theta) \times (7\sin\theta - 24\cos\theta)$

$r\cos\phi = 7$ ; $r\sin\phi = 24$

$r^2 = 625$ ; $\tan\phi = \dfrac{24}{7}$

$y = r\cos(\theta-\phi).r\sin(\theta-\phi)$

$= \dfrac{r^2}{2}.2\sin(\theta-\phi)\cos(\theta-\phi) = \dfrac{r^2}{2}.(\sin2(\theta-\phi))$

$y_{max} = \dfrac{25^2}{2} = \dfrac{625}{2}$

**3.** (c) For $\alpha = -\pi/2$, $\beta = -\pi/2$ and $\gamma = 2\pi$

$\sin\alpha + \sin\beta + \sin\gamma = -2 \Rightarrow$ min value of the expression is negative.

**4.** (b) Given that $A + B = \dfrac{\pi}{4}$

$\Rightarrow \cos A\cos B = \cos A\cos\left(\dfrac{\pi}{4} - A\right)$

$= \cos A\left[\cos\dfrac{\pi}{4}\cos A + \sin\dfrac{\pi}{4}\sin A\right]$

$= \dfrac{\cos A}{\sqrt{2}}(\cos A + \sin A)$

$= \dfrac{\cos^2 A}{\sqrt{2}} + \dfrac{\sin A\cos A}{\sqrt{2}}$

$= \dfrac{1+\cos 2A}{2\sqrt{2}} + \dfrac{\sin 2A}{2\sqrt{2}}$

$= \dfrac{1}{2\sqrt{2}} + \dfrac{\cos 2A + \sin 2A}{2\sqrt{2}}$

$= \dfrac{1}{2\sqrt{2}} + \dfrac{1}{2}\sin\left(\dfrac{\pi}{4} + 2A\right).$

$\Rightarrow$ maximum value of $\cos A\cos B$ is

$\dfrac{1}{2\sqrt{2}} + \dfrac{1}{2} = \dfrac{1+\sqrt{2}}{2\sqrt{2}}$

**5.** (c) $f(\theta) = \sin\theta(\sin\theta + \sin 3\theta)$

$= (\sin\theta + 3\sin\theta - 4\sin^3\theta).\sin\theta$

$= (4\sin\theta - 4\sin^3\theta)\sin\theta = \sin^2\theta(4 - 4\sin^2\theta)$

$= 4\sin^2\theta(1 - \sin^2\theta)$

$= 4\sin^2\theta\cos^2\theta = (2\sin\theta\cos\theta)^2 = (\sin 2\theta)^2 \geq 0$

which is true for all $\theta$.

**6.** (a) We have

$\left(a\tan\beta - \sqrt{a^2-1}\tan\alpha\right)^2 + \left(\sqrt{a^2+1}\tan\beta - \sqrt{a^2-1}\tan\gamma\right)^2$

$+ \left(a\tan\gamma - \sqrt{a^2+1}\tan\alpha\right)^2 \geq 0$

$\Rightarrow \{a^2 + a^2 - 1 + a^2 + 1\}(\tan^2\alpha + \tan^2\beta + \tan^2\gamma)$

$-\left\{a\tan\alpha + \sqrt{a^2-1}\tan\beta + \sqrt{a^2+1}\tan\gamma\right\}^2 \geq 0$

$\Rightarrow \tan^2\alpha + \tan^2\beta + \tan^2\gamma \geq \dfrac{4a^2}{3a^2} \Rightarrow 3\sum\tan^2\alpha \geq 4$

**7.** (a) Numerator of given expression

$= (\sin 8x + \sin 6x) + 6(\sin 6x + \sin 4x) + 12(\sin 4x + \sin 2x)$

$= 2\sin 7x\cos x + 12\sin 5x\cos x + 24\sin 3x\cos x$

$= 2\cos x(\sin 7x + 6\sin 5x + 12\sin 3x)$

Hence, given expression

$= \dfrac{2\cos x(\sin 7x + 6\sin 5x + 12\sin 3x)}{\sin 7x + 6\sin 5x + 12\sin 3x} = 2\cos x$

**8.** (b) Since $\cos\theta \leq 1$ for all real $\theta$,

$\therefore$ the given expression $\leq 1$ for all x.

Hence, the greatest value $= 1$.

**9.** (b) $\tan\theta = n\tan\phi$

$\tan(\theta-\phi) = \dfrac{\tan\theta - \tan\phi}{1 + \tan\theta\tan\phi} = \dfrac{(n-1)\tan\phi}{1 + n\tan^2\phi} = \dfrac{n-1}{\cot\phi + n\tan\phi}$

$\Rightarrow \tan^2(\theta-\phi) = \dfrac{(n-1)^2}{\cot^2\phi + n^2\tan^2\phi + 2n}$

Since, denominator $= (n\tan\phi - \cot\phi)^2 + 4n$

$\therefore$ Denominator is minimum at $\tan^2\phi = \dfrac{1}{n}$

So, maximum value of $\tan^2(\theta-\phi) = \dfrac{(n-1)^2}{0+4n} = \dfrac{(n-1)^2}{4n}$

**10.** (a,b,d)

We have, $u = \sin^6 x + \cos^6 x = (\sin^2 x)^3 + (\cos^2 x)^3$

$= (\sin^2 x + \cos^2 x)^3 - 3\sin^2 x\cos^2 x(\sin^2 x + \cos^2 x)$

$= 1 - 3\sin^2 x\cos^2 x = 1 - \dfrac{3}{4}(2\sin x\cos x)^2$

$= 1 - \dfrac{3}{4}\sin^2 2x = 1 - \dfrac{3}{8}(1 - \cos 4x) = \dfrac{5}{8} + \dfrac{3}{8}\cos 4x$

Since the maximum value of $\cos 4x$ is 1 and its minimum value is $-1$;

$\therefore$ Maximum value of $u = \dfrac{5}{8} + \dfrac{3}{8}.1 = 1$

Minimum value of $u = \dfrac{5}{8} + \dfrac{3}{8}\times -1 = \dfrac{1}{4}$.

**11.** **(a, b, c)** Let $\dfrac{\tan x}{1} = \dfrac{\tan y}{2} = \dfrac{\tan z}{3} = \lambda$ (say)

$\therefore\quad \tan x = \lambda,\ \tan y = 2\lambda,\ \tan z = 3\lambda$

$\because\quad x + y + z = \pi$

$\therefore\quad \tan x + \tan y + \tan z = \tan x \tan y \tan z$

$\Rightarrow\quad 6\lambda = 6\lambda^3$

$\therefore\quad 6\lambda(\lambda^2 - 1) = 0$

$\qquad \lambda = \pm 1 \quad (\lambda \neq 0)$

$\therefore\quad \tan x = \pm 1,\ \tan y = \pm 2,\ \tan z = \pm 3,$

$\qquad \tan x + \tan y + \tan z = \pm 6$

Maximum and minimum values of $\tan x + \tan y + \tan z$ are 6 and $-6$ respectively.

**12.** **(d)** $\cos\dfrac{2\pi}{7}\cos\dfrac{4\pi}{7}\cos\dfrac{6\pi}{7}$

$= \cos\dfrac{2\pi}{7}\cos\dfrac{4\pi}{7}\cos\left(2\pi - \dfrac{8\pi}{7}\right)$

$= \cos\dfrac{2\pi}{7}\cos\dfrac{4\pi}{7}\cos\dfrac{8\pi}{7}$

$= \dfrac{\sin\left(2^3 \cdot \dfrac{2\pi}{7}\right)}{2^3 \sin\left(\dfrac{2\pi}{7}\right)} = \dfrac{\sin\left(2\pi + \dfrac{2\pi}{7}\right)}{8\sin\left(\dfrac{2\pi}{7}\right)} = \dfrac{\sin\left(\dfrac{2\pi}{7}\right)}{8\sin\left(\dfrac{2\pi}{7}\right)} = \dfrac{1}{8}$

**13.** **(b)** Since, $\sin\left(\dfrac{\pi}{18}\right)\sin\left(\dfrac{5\pi}{18}\right)\sin\left(\dfrac{7\pi}{18}\right)$

$= \cos\left(\dfrac{\pi}{2} - \dfrac{\pi}{18}\right)\cos\left(\dfrac{\pi}{2} - \dfrac{5\pi}{18}\right)\cos\left(\dfrac{\pi}{2} - \dfrac{7\pi}{18}\right)$

$= \cos\left(\dfrac{8\pi}{18}\right)\cos\left(\dfrac{4\pi}{18}\right)\cos\left(\dfrac{2\pi}{18}\right)$

$= \cos\left(\dfrac{\pi}{9}\right)\cos\left(\dfrac{2\pi}{9}\right)\cos\left(\dfrac{4\pi}{9}\right)$

$= \dfrac{1}{2^3}\left(\text{here } \alpha = \dfrac{\pi}{2^3 + 1}\right) = \dfrac{1}{8}$

**14.** **(b)** $\because 64\sqrt{3}\,\sin\left(\dfrac{\pi}{48}\right)\cos\left(\dfrac{\pi}{48}\right)\cos\left(\dfrac{\pi}{24}\right)\cos\left(\dfrac{\pi}{12}\right)\cos\left(\dfrac{\pi}{6}\right)$

$= 32\sqrt{3}\left(2\sin\left(\dfrac{\pi}{48}\right)\cos\left(\dfrac{\pi}{48}\right)\right)\cos\left(\dfrac{\pi}{24}\right)\cos\left(\dfrac{\pi}{12}\right)\cos\left(\dfrac{\pi}{6}\right)$

$= 32\sqrt{3}\left(\sin\dfrac{\pi}{24}\right)\cos\left(\dfrac{\pi}{24}\right)\cos\left(\dfrac{\pi}{12}\right)\cos\left(\dfrac{\pi}{6}\right)$

$= 16\sqrt{3}\left(2\sin\left(\dfrac{\pi}{24}\right)\cos\left(\dfrac{\pi}{24}\right)\right)\cos\left(\dfrac{\pi}{12}\right)\cos\left(\dfrac{\pi}{6}\right)$

$= 16\sqrt{3}\,\sin\left(\dfrac{\pi}{12}\right)\cos\left(\dfrac{\pi}{12}\right)\cos\left(\dfrac{\pi}{6}\right)$

$= 8\sqrt{3}\left(2\sin\left(\dfrac{\pi}{12}\right)\cos\left(\dfrac{\pi}{12}\right)\right)\cos\left(\dfrac{\pi}{6}\right)$

$= 8\sqrt{3}\,\sin\left(\dfrac{\pi}{6}\right)\cos\left(\dfrac{\pi}{6}\right) = 8\sqrt{3}\cdot\dfrac{1}{2}\cdot\dfrac{\sqrt{3}}{2} = 6$

**15.** **A $\to$ r, s ; B $\to$ r, t ; C $\to$ p, q**

(A) Let $y = \dfrac{7 + 6\tan\theta - \tan^2\theta}{(1 + \tan^2\theta)}$

$= 7\cos^2\theta + 6\sin\theta\cos\theta - \sin^2\theta$

$= 7\left(\dfrac{1 + \cos 2\theta}{2}\right) + 3\sin 2\theta - \left(\dfrac{1 - \cos 2\theta}{2}\right)$

$= -3\sin 2\theta + 4\cos 2\theta + 3$

Now, $-\sqrt{(3^2 + 4^2)} + 3 \le 3\sin 2\theta + 4\cos 2\theta + 3$

$\le \sqrt{(3^2 + 4^2)} + 3$

$\therefore\ -2 \le y \le 8$

$\Rightarrow\ \lambda = 8,\ \mu = -2$

$\Rightarrow\ \lambda + \mu = 6\ \textbf{(r)},\ \lambda - \mu = 10\ \textbf{(s)}$

(B) Let $y = 5\cos\theta + 3\cos(\theta + \pi/3) + 3$

$= 5\cos\theta + 3\left(\dfrac{1}{2}\cos\theta - \dfrac{\sqrt{3}}{2}\sin\theta\right) + 3$

$= \dfrac{13}{2}\cos\theta - \dfrac{3\sqrt{3}}{2}\sin\theta + 3$

$\therefore\ 3 - \sqrt{\left(\dfrac{13}{2}\right)^2 + \left(\dfrac{-3\sqrt{3}}{2}\right)^2} \le \dfrac{13}{2}\cos\theta - \dfrac{3\sqrt{3}}{2}\sin\theta + 3$

$\le 3 + \sqrt{\left(\dfrac{13}{2}\right)^2 + \left(\dfrac{-3\sqrt{3}}{2}\right)^2}$

$\Rightarrow\ 3 - 7 \le y \le 3 + 7$

$\Rightarrow\ -4 \le y \le 10$

$\therefore\ \lambda = 10,\ \mu = -4$

$\Rightarrow\ \lambda + \mu = 6\ \textbf{(r)},\ \lambda - \mu = 14\ \textbf{(t)}$

(C) Let $y = 1 + \sin\left(\dfrac{\pi}{4} + \theta\right) + 2\cos\left(\dfrac{\pi}{4} - \theta\right)$

$= 1 + \cos\left(\dfrac{\pi}{2} - \left(\dfrac{\pi}{4} + \theta\right)\right) + 2\cos\left(\dfrac{\pi}{4} - \theta\right)$

$= 1 + \cos\left(\dfrac{\pi}{4} - \theta\right) + 2\cos\left(\dfrac{\pi}{4} - \theta\right)$

$= 1 + 3\cos\left(\dfrac{\pi}{4} - \theta\right)$

Since, $-1 \le \cos\left(\dfrac{\pi}{4} - \theta\right) \le 1$

$\Rightarrow\ -3 \le 3\cos\left(\dfrac{\pi}{4} - \theta\right) \le 3$

$\Rightarrow\ 1 - 3 \le 1 + 3\cos\left(\dfrac{\pi}{4} - \theta\right) \le 1 + 3$

$\therefore\ -2 \le y \le 4$

$\Rightarrow\ \lambda = 4,\ \mu = -2$

$\therefore\ \lambda + \mu = 2\ \textbf{(p)},\ \lambda - \mu = 6\ \textbf{(q)}$

**16.** A - p,q,r,s; B - r,s; C - q,r,s; D - q, s

(A) $f(\theta) = (\sin\theta + \mathrm{cosec}\,\theta)^2 + (\cos\theta + \sec\theta)^2$

$$= \sin^2\theta + \cos^2\theta + \sec^2\theta + \mathrm{cosec}^2\theta + 4$$

$$= 5 + 1 + \cot^2\theta + 1 + \tan^2\theta = 9 + (\tan\theta - \cot\theta)^2 \geq 9$$

(B) $\sin\alpha - \sin\beta = a, \quad \cos\alpha + \cos\beta = b$

$$\Rightarrow a^2 + b^2 = 2 + 2\cos(\alpha + \beta) = 4\cos^2\frac{\alpha+\beta}{2} \leq 4$$

(C) $\dfrac{\sin A + \sin B}{2} \leq \sin\left(\dfrac{A+B}{2}\right)$

$$\therefore \sin A + \sin B \leq 2\sin\frac{\pi}{4}$$

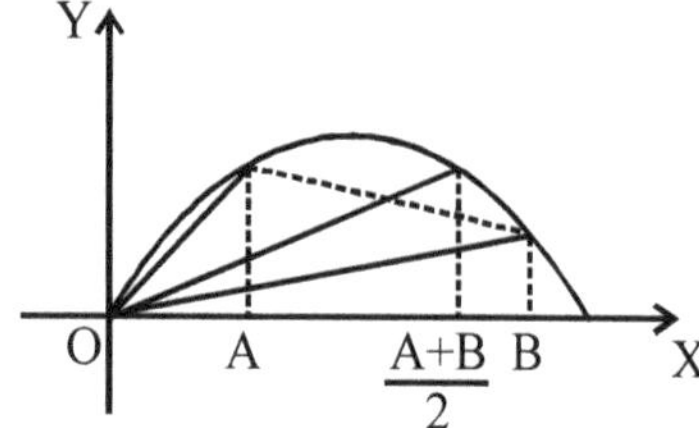

or $\dfrac{1}{\sqrt{2}}(\sin A + \sin B) \leq 1$

(D) Let $A = 7\cos x + 6\sin x = 6(2\cos x + \sin x) - 5\cos x$

$$= 6 - 5\cos x$$

Now, $2\cos x + \sin x = 1 \Rightarrow \sin x = 1 - 2\cos x$

$$\Rightarrow \sin^2 x = 1 - \cos^2 x = 1 - 4\cos x + 4\cos^2 x$$

$$\therefore \cos x = 0 \text{ or } \frac{4}{5}. \text{ So, } A = 6 \text{ or } 2$$

**17. (a)** $\cos\dfrac{\pi}{7}\cos\dfrac{2\pi}{7}\cos\dfrac{4\pi}{7} = \dfrac{\sin\left(\dfrac{8\pi}{7}\right)}{8\sin\left(\dfrac{\pi}{7}\right)} = \dfrac{-\sin\dfrac{\pi}{7}}{8\sin\dfrac{\pi}{7}} = -\dfrac{1}{8}$

$$\cos\theta\cos 2\theta\cos 2^2\theta \dots \cos(2^{n-1}\theta) = -\frac{1}{2^n},$$

if $\theta = \dfrac{\pi}{2^n - 1}$

**18. (a)** Let $g(x) = 6\sin x - 8\cos x + 5$

Max. value of $g(x) = \sqrt{6^2 + 8^2} + 5 = 5 + 10 = 15$

Min. value of $g(x) = -\sqrt{6^2 + 8^2} + 5 = 5 - 10 = -5$

$\therefore$ The range of $f(x) = \dfrac{1}{g(x)}$ is $R - \left(-\dfrac{1}{5}, \dfrac{1}{15}\right)$

$\Rightarrow$ It is an unbounded function.

$\Rightarrow$ f(x) has no maximum and no minimum values.

**19. (8)**

$$\pi/10 = \theta$$

$$E = -\frac{2\sin 2\theta(\cos 2\theta.\cos 4\theta.\cos 8\theta.\cos 16\theta)}{2\sin 2\theta}$$

$$= -\frac{\sin 32\theta}{16\sin 2\theta} = -\frac{\sin(30\theta + 2\theta)}{16.\sin 2\theta} = \frac{1}{16}$$

Thus $\dfrac{1}{2X} = \dfrac{1}{16}$.

$\therefore \quad X = 8.$

**20. (9)**

Note that $(\tan C - \sin A)^2 + (\cot C - \cos B)^2$ denotes the square of the distance PQ

now $\quad d^2_{PQ} = (Q - OP)^2$

$$d^2_{PQ} = \left[\sqrt{(\tan^2 C + \cot^2 C)} - 1\right]^2$$

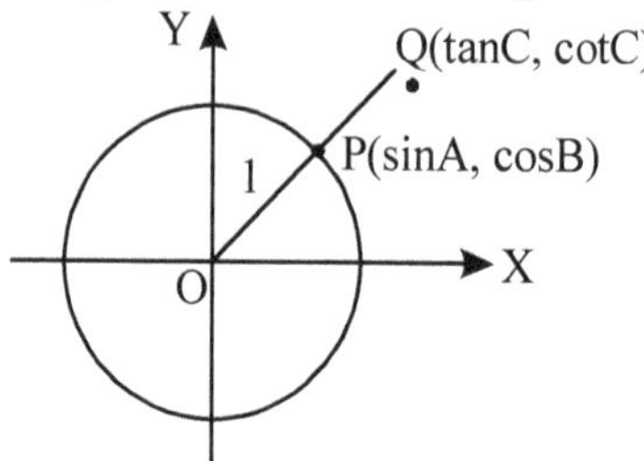


$$\therefore \ d^2_{PQ} = \left[\sqrt{(\tan C - \cot C)^2 + 2} - 1\right]^2$$

$$\therefore \ d^2_{min} = \left(\sqrt{2} - 1\right)^2 = 3 - 2\sqrt{2}$$

$$\Rightarrow a = 3; \ b = 2 \Rightarrow a^3 + b^3 = 27 - 8 = 19$$

$$\therefore \ a^3 + b^3 - 10 = 9.$$

**21. (4)**

Let $x = r\cos\theta$ and $y = r\sin\theta$

$$\Rightarrow r^2 = x^2 + y^2; \quad \tan\theta = \frac{y}{x} \qquad \theta \in (0, \pi/2)$$

$$N = \frac{r^2}{r^2[\cos^2\theta + \sin\theta\cos\theta + 4\sin^2\theta]}$$

$$= \frac{r^2}{(1 + \cos 2\theta) + \sin 2\theta + 4(1 - \cos 2\theta)}$$

$$= \frac{2}{5 + \sin 2\theta + 3\cos 2\theta}$$

$$N_{max} = \frac{2}{5 - \sqrt{10}} = \frac{2}{15}\left(5 + \sqrt{10}\right) = M$$

$$N_{min} = \frac{2}{5 + \sqrt{10}} = \frac{2}{15}\left(5 - \sqrt{10}\right) = m$$

$$A = \frac{M + m}{2} = \frac{2 \cdot 10}{15 \cdot 2} = \frac{2}{3};$$

$$\therefore \ 6A = 4.$$

**22. (4)**

Maximum value of $4\sin^2 x + 3\cos^2 x$ i.e., $\sin^2 x + 3$ is 4 and that of $\sin\dfrac{x}{2} + \cos\dfrac{x}{2}$ is $\dfrac{1}{\sqrt{2}} + \dfrac{1}{\sqrt{2}} = \sqrt{2}$, both attained at

$$x = \pi/2.$$

Hence the given function has maximum value 4.

**23. (4)**

Given : $\sin x + \sin^2 x + \sin^3 x = 1$

$\sin x + \sin^2 x = 1 - \sin^2 x$

$\sin x [1 + \sin^2 x] = \cos^2 x$

$\sin x [2 - \cos^2 x] = +\cos^2 x$

Squaring we have,

$(1 - \cos^2 x)(2 - \cos^2 x)^2 = \cos^4 x$

or $4 + \cos^4 x - 4\cos^2 x - 4\cos^2 x - \cos^6 x + 4\cos^4 x = \cos^4 x$

or $\cos^6 x - 4\cos^4 x + 8\cos^2 x = 4.$

**1.** **(b)** $(a+1)^2 + \csc^2\left(\dfrac{\pi a}{2} + \dfrac{\pi x}{2}\right) - 1 = 0$

or $(a+1)^2 + \cot^2\left(\dfrac{\pi a}{2} + \dfrac{\pi x}{2}\right) = 0$

from option [b]  If $a = -1 \Rightarrow \tan^2 \pi x/2 = 0 \Rightarrow x/2 \in I$

**2.** **(b)** $4\cos^2\theta - 2\sqrt{2}\,\cos\theta - 1 = 0$

$\cos\theta = \dfrac{2\sqrt{2} \pm \sqrt{8+16}}{8} = \dfrac{\sqrt{2} \pm \sqrt{6}}{4}$

$\cos\theta = \dfrac{\sqrt{6} + \sqrt{2}}{4} \Rightarrow \theta = \dfrac{\pi}{12}; 2\pi - \dfrac{\pi}{12} = \dfrac{23\pi}{12}$

$\cos\theta = -\dfrac{\sqrt{6} - \sqrt{2}}{4}$

$\cos\theta = \cos(\pi - 5\pi/12) \; ; \cos(\pi + 5\pi/12)$

$\theta = 7\pi/12 \,; 17\pi/12$

**3.** **(a)** $\tan(5\pi\cos\theta) = \cot(5\pi\sin\theta)$

$\tan(5\pi\cos\theta) = \tan\left(\dfrac{\pi}{2} - 5\pi\sin\theta\right)$

$5\pi\cos\theta = n\pi + \pi/2 - 5\pi\sin\theta$

$(\cos\theta + \sin\theta) = \left(\dfrac{2n+1}{10}\right)$

$\Rightarrow -1 < \dfrac{2n+1}{10\sqrt{2}} < 1$

$\Rightarrow -\dfrac{10\sqrt{2} - 1}{2} < n < \dfrac{10\sqrt{2} - 1}{2}$

$n = 14$ for each 'n' there are two values of $\theta$

$\therefore$   no. of solutions = 28

**4.** **(b)** $\cos 2x + a\sin x = 2a - 7$

i.e. $2\sin^2 x - a\sin x + 2a - 8 = 0$

$\sin x = \dfrac{a \pm \sqrt{a^2 - 8(2a-8)}}{4} = \dfrac{a \pm (a-8)}{4}$

$\sin x = \dfrac{a-4}{2}$ or 2

Hence $-1 \le (a-4)/2 \le 1$

$\Rightarrow a \in [2, 6]$

**5.** **(b)** $\left|\dfrac{x}{2} - \dfrac{\pi}{2}\right| \le \dfrac{3\pi}{4}$

$\Rightarrow -\dfrac{3\pi}{4} \le \dfrac{x}{2} - \dfrac{\pi}{2} \le \dfrac{3\pi}{4} \Rightarrow -\dfrac{\pi}{4} \le \dfrac{x}{2} \le \dfrac{5\pi}{4}$

$\Rightarrow -\dfrac{\pi}{2} \le x \le \dfrac{5\pi}{4}$

Also, $x = \dfrac{n\pi}{2}$

$\therefore \; x = -\dfrac{\pi}{2}, 0, \dfrac{\pi}{2}, \pi, \dfrac{3\pi}{2}, 2\pi, \dfrac{5\pi}{2} \quad \ldots(i)$

Now, $\sin\dfrac{x}{2} - \cos\dfrac{x}{2} = \left(\sin\dfrac{x}{2} - \cos\dfrac{x}{2}\right)^2$

$\Rightarrow \sin\dfrac{x}{2} - \cos\dfrac{x}{2} = 0 \quad \Rightarrow \qquad \ldots(ii)$

or $\sin\dfrac{x}{2} - \cos\dfrac{x}{2} = 1 \qquad \ldots(iii)$

Out of the values of $x$ in equation (i), only $\dfrac{\pi}{2}$, $\pi$, $2\pi$

and $\dfrac{\pi}{2}$, satisfy either equations (ii) or (iii).

Hence $n = 1, 2, 4, 5$

$\text{Tan } 3x = \text{Tan}(2x + x)$

$\Rightarrow \text{Tan } 3x = \dfrac{\tan 2x + \tan x}{1 - \tan 2x \tan x}$

$\Rightarrow \text{Tan } 3x + \text{Tan } 2x \cdot \text{Tan } x = \text{Tan } 3x - \text{Tan } 2x - \text{Tan } x$

only circled angle satisfy one of the above equation when n = 1, 2, 4, 5

**6.** **(d)** $\tan x + \tan 2x + \tan 3x = \tan 3x - \tan 2x - \tan x$

$\Rightarrow \tan x + \tan 2x = 0$

$\therefore \tan 2x = \tan(-x)$

$2x = n\pi - x$

$x = \dfrac{n\pi}{3}, \; n \in I$

**7.** **(c)** $(1 - \tan q)(1 + \tan q)\sec^2 q + 2^{\tan^2\theta} = 0$

$\Rightarrow (1 - \tan^2\theta)(1 + \tan^2\theta) + 2^{\tan^2\theta} = 0$

$\Rightarrow 1 + 2\tan^2\theta = \tan^4\theta$. By observation, we have $\tan^2\theta = 3$

$\Rightarrow \theta = n\pi \pm \left(\dfrac{\pi}{3}\right)$

Moreover there will be values of $\theta$, satisfying, $3 < \tan^2\theta < 4$ and satisfying the given equation as if $f(x) = x^2 - 2^x - 1$, then $f(3^+)\,f(4^-) < 0$.

So, number of values of $\theta$ is 4.

Hence, (c) is the correct answer.

**8.    (c)** We have, $\dfrac{-\pi}{2} \le \theta \le \dfrac{\pi}{2}$.

$\Rightarrow \quad -1 \le \sin\theta \le 1$

$\therefore\ -1 \le \sin\theta \le 1$, here $0 < \sin\theta < 1$

Now, $\log_{\sin\theta} \cos 2\theta = 2$

$\Rightarrow\ \cos 2\theta = \sin^2\theta \Rightarrow 1 - 2\sin^2\theta = \sin^2\theta$

$\Rightarrow\ 3\sin^2\theta = 1 \Rightarrow \sin\theta = \pm 1/\sqrt{3}$

Now, $\pm\dfrac{1}{\sqrt{3}} \in [-1, 1]$

Hence, there are two solutions.

**9.    (b)** $|\tan x + \sec x| = |\tan x| + |\sec x|$ iff $\sec x$ and $\tan x$ both have same sign.

$\Rightarrow\ \sec x.\tan x \ge 0 \Rightarrow \dfrac{\sin x}{\cos^2 x} \ge 0$

$\Rightarrow\ \sin x \ge 0$, but $\cos x \ne 0 \Rightarrow x \in \left[0, \dfrac{\pi}{2}\right) \cup \left(\dfrac{\pi}{2}, \pi\right]$

**10.    (ab,d)**

$\sin\theta = \sin\alpha$

$\theta = n\pi + (-1)^n\alpha$

$n = 0 \ \Rightarrow\ \theta = \alpha \ \Rightarrow\ \sin\theta/3 = \sin\alpha/3 \ \Rightarrow\ $ (A)

$n = 1 \ \Rightarrow\ \theta = \pi - \alpha \ \Rightarrow\ \sin\theta/3 = \sin(\pi/3 - \alpha/3) \Rightarrow$ (B)

$n = -1 \Rightarrow\ \theta = -\pi - \alpha$

$\Rightarrow \sin\theta/3 = \sin(-\pi/3 - \alpha/3) = -\sin(\pi/3 + \alpha/3) \Rightarrow$ (D)

**11.    (b,c)**

We have,

$3^{\sin 2x + 1 + \cos 2x} + 3^{1 - \sin 2x + 1 - \cos 2x} = 28$

$\Rightarrow\ 3^1 . 3^y + 3^2 . 3^{-y} = 28$

where $y = \sin 2x + \cos 2x$

$\Rightarrow\ 3t + \dfrac{9}{t} = 28 \Rightarrow t = 1/3, 9$

$\therefore\ \cos 2x + \sin 2x = -1$

$\Rightarrow\ \cos x = 0$ or $\tan x = -1$

$\therefore\ x = (2n+1)\dfrac{\pi}{2}\ $ or $\ x = n\pi - (\pi/4)$

**12.    (a,b,c)** The given equation can be written as

$\sqrt{\cos^2 x - \sin^2 x} + \sqrt{(\cos x + \sin x)^2} = 2\sqrt{\cos x + \sin x}$

$\Rightarrow\ \sqrt{\cos x + \sin x}\,[\sqrt{\cos x - \sin x} + \sqrt{\cos x + \sin x}]$

$= 2\sqrt{\cos x + \sin x}$

$\Rightarrow$ Either $\cos x + \sin x = 0$

$\Rightarrow \tan x = -1 \Rightarrow x = n\pi - \dfrac{\pi}{4}\ (n \in I)$

$\Rightarrow$ (a) and (c) are correct

---

or $\sqrt{\cos x - \sin x} + \sqrt{\cos x + \sin x} = 2$

$\Rightarrow\ 2\cos x + 2\sqrt{\cos^2 x - \sin^2 x} = 4$

$\Rightarrow\ \cos^2 x - \sin^2 x = (2 - \cos x)^2$

$\Rightarrow\ \cos^2 x + 4\cos x - 5 = 0$

$\Rightarrow\ \cos x = \dfrac{-4 \pm \sqrt{16 + 20}}{2} = -5$ or $1$

But $\cos x \ne -5$ so $\cos x = 1 \Rightarrow x = 2n\pi$ and thus (b) is correct.

**13.    (b,c)** $\cos(x - y) - 2\sin x + 2\sin y = 3$

$\Rightarrow 1 - 2\sin^2\dfrac{x-y}{2} - 4\sin\dfrac{x-y}{2}\cos\dfrac{x+y}{2} - 3 = 0$

$\Rightarrow \sin^2\dfrac{x-y}{2} + 2\sin\dfrac{x-y}{2}\cos\dfrac{x+y}{2} + 1 = 0$

$\Rightarrow \sin\dfrac{x-y}{2} = \dfrac{-2 \pm \sqrt{4\cos^2\dfrac{x+y}{2} - 4}}{2}$

For real values of $\sin\dfrac{x-y}{2}$, we have $\cos^2\dfrac{x+y}{2} = 1$

$\Rightarrow \sin^2\dfrac{x+y}{2} = 0$ or $\sin\dfrac{x+y}{2} = 0 \Rightarrow x + y = 2n\pi$ and

then $\quad \sin\dfrac{x-y}{2} = -1, \Rightarrow x - y = (4k+1)\,\pi$.

Hence = (b) is correct.

If $\sin x = \sin y$ then the given equation becomes $\cos(x - y) = 3$ which is not correct; (a) is not correct.

Next if $x = 2k\pi - \dfrac{\pi}{2}$ and $y = 2n\pi + \dfrac{\pi}{2}$.

Then, $\cos(x-y) - 2\sin x + 2\sin y = -1 + 2 + 2 = 3$ so (c) is correct finally if $\cos(x-y) = -1$, the given equation becomes $\sin x - \sin y = -2$ which is not true for all values of $x$ and $y$ so (d) is not correct.

**14.    (a)** Let $\cos x - \sin x = t$

$\therefore\ 1 - 2\sin x \cos x = t^2$

Then, the given equation can be written as $t^2 = t$

$\Rightarrow\ t(t - 1) = 0$

$\therefore\ t = 0, t = 1$

$\Rightarrow\ \cos x - \sin x = 0,\ \cos x - \sin x = 1$

$\therefore\ \tan x = 1,\ \dfrac{1}{\sqrt{2}}\cos x - \dfrac{1}{\sqrt{2}}\sin x = \dfrac{1}{\sqrt{2}}$

$\Rightarrow\ \tan x = 1,\ \cos\left(x + \dfrac{\pi}{4}\right) = \cos\dfrac{\pi}{4}$

$\therefore\ x = n\pi + \dfrac{\pi}{4}, x + \dfrac{\pi}{4} = 2n\pi \pm \dfrac{\pi}{4}$

Hence, $x = 2n\pi, 2n\pi - \dfrac{\pi}{2}, n\pi + \dfrac{\pi}{4}, n \in I$

**15. (b)** $\because 1 + \sin^3 x + \cos^3 x = \dfrac{3}{2}\sin 2x$

$\Rightarrow 1 + (\sin x + \cos x)^3 - 3\sin x \cos x(\sin x + \cos x)$

$= \dfrac{3}{2}\sin 2x \qquad\qquad ....(i)$

Let $\sin x + \cos x = t$

$\therefore \sin x \cos x = \dfrac{t^2 - 1}{2}$

Then, from eq. (i),

$1 + t^3 - \dfrac{3(t^2 - 1)}{2}t = \dfrac{3}{2}(t^2 - 1)$

$\Rightarrow 2 + 2t^3 - 3t^3 + 3t = 3t^2 - 3$

$\Rightarrow t^3 + 3t^2 - 3t - 5 = 0$

$\Rightarrow (t + 1)(t^2 + 2t - 5) = 0$

$\Rightarrow t = -1, -1 \pm \sqrt 6$

$\Rightarrow \sin x + \cos x = -1, \ \sin x + \cos x \neq -1 \pm \sqrt 6$

$(\because -\sqrt 2 \le \sin x + \cos x \le \sqrt 2)$

$\therefore \ \sin x + \cos x = -1$

$\Rightarrow \dfrac{1}{\sqrt 2}\cos x + \dfrac{1}{\sqrt 2}\sin x = -\dfrac{1}{\sqrt 2}$

$\Rightarrow \cos\left(x - \dfrac{\pi}{4}\right) = \cos\dfrac{3\pi}{4}$

$\therefore \ x - \dfrac{\pi}{4} = 2n\pi \pm \dfrac{3\pi}{4} \qquad \text{or} \quad x = 2n\pi \pm \dfrac{3\pi}{4} + \dfrac{\pi}{4}$

$\therefore \ x = (2n+1)\pi, (4n-1)\pi/2,\ n \in I$

**16. (a)** $\because (\sin x + \cos x) - 2\sqrt 2 \sin x \cos x = 0 \qquad ....(i)$

Let $\sin x + \cos x = t$

$\therefore \ 1 + \sin 2x = t^2 \qquad\qquad ...(ii)$

From eq. (i), $t - \sqrt 2\,(t^2 - 1) = 0$

or $\sqrt 2\,t^2 - t - \sqrt 2 = 0$

$\Rightarrow \sqrt 2\,t^2 - 2t + t - \sqrt 2 = 0$

$\therefore \ t = \sqrt 2, -\dfrac{1}{\sqrt 2}$

From eq. (ii), $1 + \sin 2x = 2,\ \dfrac{1}{2} \qquad \therefore \sin 2x = 1, -\dfrac{1}{2}$

or $2x = 2n\pi + \dfrac{\pi}{2}$ and $2x = n\pi + (-1)^n\left(\dfrac{-\pi}{6}\right)$

or $x = n\pi + \dfrac{\pi}{4},\ x = \dfrac{n\pi}{2} - \dfrac{(-1)^n \pi}{12},\ n \in I$

Hence, $x = 2n\pi + \dfrac{\pi}{4},\ n \in I$

**17.** $A \to q, s;\ B \to p, t;\ C \to s, t, r$

**(A)** $\because \sin x = -\dfrac{1}{2} = -\sin\dfrac{\pi}{6}$

$= \sin\left(\pi + \dfrac{\pi}{6}\right), \sin\left(2\pi - \dfrac{\pi}{6}\right)$

$\therefore \ x = \dfrac{7\pi}{6}, \dfrac{11\pi}{6} \qquad\qquad ....(i)$

and $\cos x = -\dfrac{\sqrt 3}{2} = -\cos\dfrac{\pi}{6}$

$= \cos\left(\pi - \dfrac{\pi}{6}\right), \cos\left(\pi + \dfrac{\pi}{6}\right)$

$\therefore \qquad x = \dfrac{5\pi}{6}, \dfrac{7\pi}{6} \qquad\qquad .... (ii)$

From equations (i) and (ii), it is clear that

$\alpha = \dfrac{7\pi}{6},\ \beta = \dfrac{11\pi}{6},\ \gamma = \dfrac{5\pi}{6}$

$\Rightarrow \alpha + \beta = 3\pi\ \textbf{(s)},\ \beta - \gamma = \pi\ \textbf{(q)}$

**(B)** $\because \cot x = -\sqrt 3 = -\cot\dfrac{\pi}{6}$

$= \cot\left(\pi - \dfrac{\pi}{6}\right), \cot\left(2\pi - \dfrac{\pi}{6}\right)$

$\therefore \ x = \dfrac{5\pi}{6}, \dfrac{11\pi}{6} \qquad\qquad ....(i)$

and $\operatorname{cosec} x = -2 = -\operatorname{cosec}\dfrac{\pi}{6}$

$= \operatorname{cosec}\left(\pi + \dfrac{\pi}{6}\right), \operatorname{cosec}\left(2\pi - \dfrac{\pi}{6}\right)$

$\therefore \ x = \dfrac{7\pi}{6}, \dfrac{11\pi}{6} \qquad\qquad ....(ii)$

From Eqs. (i) and (ii), it is clear that

$\alpha = \dfrac{11\pi}{6},\ \beta = \dfrac{5\pi}{6},\ \gamma = \dfrac{7\pi}{6}$

$\Rightarrow \beta + \gamma = 2\pi\ \textbf{(t)},\ \alpha - \beta = \pi\ \textbf{(p)}$

**(C)** $\because \sin x = -\dfrac{1}{2} = -\sin\dfrac{\pi}{6}$

$= \sin\left(\pi + \dfrac{\pi}{6}\right), \sin\left(2\pi - \dfrac{\pi}{6}\right)$

$\therefore \ x = \dfrac{7\pi}{6}, \dfrac{11\pi}{6} \qquad\qquad ....(i)$

and $\tan x = \dfrac{1}{\sqrt 3}$

$= \tan\dfrac{\pi}{6}, \tan\left(\pi + \dfrac{\pi}{6}\right)$

$\therefore \quad x = \dfrac{\pi}{6}, \dfrac{7\pi}{6}$ ....(ii)

From Eqs. (i) and (ii), it is clear that

$\alpha = \dfrac{7\pi}{6}, \beta = \dfrac{11\pi}{6}, \gamma = \dfrac{\pi}{6}$

$\Rightarrow \alpha + \beta = 3\pi$ **(s)**, $\beta + \gamma = 2\pi$ **(t)**, $\alpha - \gamma = \pi$ **(r)**

**18. (b)** $\because \sin(\cos x) = \cos(\sin x)$

$\Rightarrow \cos(\sin x) = \cos\left(\dfrac{\pi}{2} - \cos x\right)$

$\Rightarrow \sin x = 2n\pi \pm \left(\dfrac{\pi}{2} - \cos x\right), n \in I$

$\Rightarrow \sin x \pm \cos x = \left(2n \pm \dfrac{1}{2}\right)\pi$

Squaring both sides, we get

$1 \pm \sin 2x = \left(2n \pm \dfrac{1}{2}\right)^2 \pi^2$

$\Rightarrow |\sin 2x| = \left(2n \pm \dfrac{1}{2}\right)^2 \pi^2 - 1$

But $\left(2n \pm \dfrac{1}{2}\right)^2 \pi^2 > 2$ for all $n \in I$

$\therefore \quad |\sin 2x| > 1$ which is inadmissive.

Hence, the given equation does not possess real roots.

and $\because \sin x > 0$ ($x$ lies in I and II quadrant)

$\therefore 2n\pi < x < (2n+1)\pi, n \in I$

**19. (b)** $|\sin x| + |\cos x| = \sqrt{1 + |\sin 2x|}$

$\because 0 \le |\sin 2x| \le 1 \Rightarrow 1 \le |\sin x| + |\cos x| \le \sqrt{2}$,

hence the equation

$|\sin x| + |\cos x| = \dfrac{\sqrt{3}}{2}$ has no real solution

**20. (7)** $\tan x + \cot x + 1 = \cos\left(x + \dfrac{\pi}{4}\right)$

$\underbrace{\tan x + \cot x}_{\ge 2 \text{ or } \le -2} = \underbrace{\cos\left(x + \dfrac{\pi}{4}\right) - 1}_{-2 \le x \le 0}$

$\Rightarrow$ Equality holds when both sides are $-2$

$\therefore \cos\left(x + \dfrac{\pi}{4}\right) = -1$

$\Rightarrow x + \dfrac{\pi}{4} = (2m+1)\pi \Rightarrow x = \dfrac{3\pi}{4}$ or $\dfrac{11\pi}{4}$

$\Rightarrow$ Sum of the solutions is $\dfrac{3\pi}{4} + \dfrac{11\pi}{4} = \dfrac{7\pi}{2} = k\pi$

$\Rightarrow k = 3.5 \quad \therefore 2k = 7$

**21. (8)** Given equation can be written as
$3 \sin\theta - 4\sin^3\theta = 4\sin\theta \sin 2\theta \sin 4\theta$
Hence either $\sin\theta = 0 \Rightarrow \theta = n\pi$
or $3 - 4\sin^2\theta = 4 \sin 2\theta \sin 4\theta$
$3 - 2(1 - \cos 2\theta) = 2(\cos 2\theta - \cos 6\theta)$
or $1 = -2\cos 6\theta$

$\cos 6\theta = -\dfrac{1}{2} = \cos \dfrac{2\pi}{3}$

$6\theta = 2n\pi \pm \dfrac{2\pi}{3}$

If $0 \le \theta \le \pi$ then total solution are

$0, \dfrac{\pi}{9}, \dfrac{2\pi}{9}, \dfrac{4\pi}{9}, \dfrac{5\pi}{9}, \dfrac{7\pi}{9}, \dfrac{8\pi}{9}, \pi$ is 8 real solutions.

**22. (3)** $\sin x + \sin 5x = \sin 2x + \sin 4x$
$2 \sin 3x \cos 2x = 2 \sin 3x \cos x$
$2\sin 3x [\cos 2x - \cos x] = 0$

On solving we get $x = n\pi/3$, $\therefore \dfrac{9x}{n\pi} = 3$

**23. (4)** $1 - \sin^2 x + \dfrac{\sqrt{3}+1}{2}\sin x - \dfrac{\sqrt{3}}{4} - 1 = 0$

$\sin^2 x - \dfrac{\sqrt{3}+1}{2}\sin x + \dfrac{\sqrt{3}}{4} = 0$

$4\sin^2 x - 2\sqrt{3}\sin x - 2\sin x + \sqrt{3} = 0$

On solving we get

$\sin x = 1/2 \; ; \; \dfrac{\sqrt{3}}{2}$

$\therefore x = \pi/6, 5\pi/6 ; \pi/3, 2\pi/3$

Hence there are 4 roots.

**24. (2)** The given eq is $\tan x + \sec x = 2 \cos x$

$\Rightarrow \dfrac{\sin x}{\cos x} + \dfrac{1}{\cos x} = 2 \cos x$

$\Rightarrow \sin x + 1 = 2\cos^2 x$

$\Rightarrow \sin x + 1 = 2 - 2\sin^2 x$

$\Rightarrow 2\sin^2 x + \sin x - 1 = 0$

$\Rightarrow (2\sin x - 1)(\sin x + 1) = 0$

$\Rightarrow \sin x = \dfrac{1}{2}, -1$

$\Rightarrow x = \dfrac{\pi}{6}, \dfrac{5\pi}{6}, \dfrac{3\pi}{2} \in [0, 2\pi]$

But for $x = \dfrac{3\pi}{2}$ given eq. is not satisfied, as $\infty - \infty = 0$ indeterminate form

$\therefore$ only 2 solutions.

**1. (a)** Area $= \dfrac{1}{2}ab$ ; also $a^2 + b^2 = 3600$

$AD : y = x + 3$

$\left. \begin{array}{l} BE : y = 2x + 4 \end{array} \right\}$ solve to get $G = (-1, 2)$

acute angle $\alpha$ between the medians is given by

$\tan\alpha = \left| \dfrac{m_1 - m_2}{1 + m_1 m_2} \right| = \dfrac{2-1}{1+2} = \dfrac{1}{3} \Rightarrow \tan\alpha = \dfrac{1}{3}$

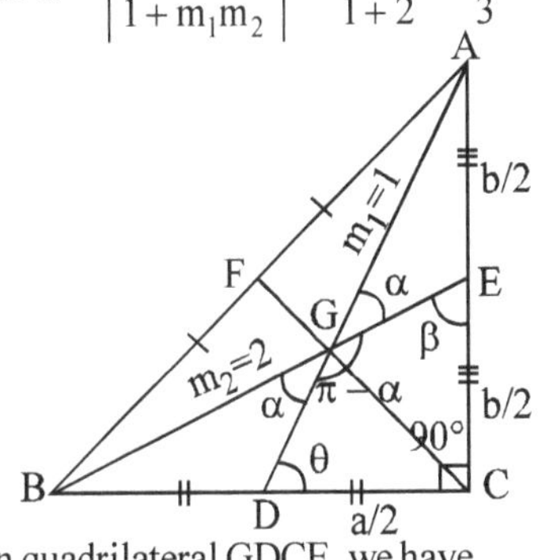

In quadrilateral GDCE, we have

$(180 - \alpha) + 90° + \theta + \beta = 360°$

$\Rightarrow \alpha = \theta + \beta - 90°$

$\cot\alpha = -\tan(\theta + \beta)$

$-3 = \dfrac{\tan\theta + \tan\beta}{1 - \tan\theta\tan\beta}$ or $-3 = \dfrac{\dfrac{2b}{a} + \dfrac{2a}{b}}{1 - \dfrac{2b}{a}\cdot\dfrac{2a}{b}}$

$\Rightarrow 9 = \dfrac{2(a^2 + b^2)}{ab}$

$9ab = 2 \times 3600 \Rightarrow \dfrac{1}{2}ab = 400$

$\therefore$ Area $= 400$ sq. units

**2. (b)** $x = r\, \mathrm{cosec}\,\dfrac{A}{2}$ ; $a = r\left(\cot\dfrac{B}{2} + \cot\dfrac{C}{2}\right)$

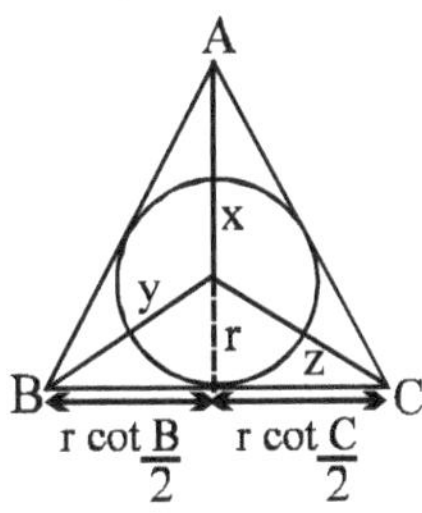

$\dfrac{a}{x} = \left(\cot\dfrac{B}{2} + \cot\dfrac{C}{2}\right).\sin\dfrac{A}{2} = \dfrac{\sin\dfrac{A}{2}.\cos\dfrac{A}{2}}{\sin\dfrac{B}{2}.\sin\dfrac{C}{2}}$

$\therefore \dfrac{abc}{xyz} = \dfrac{\cos\dfrac{A}{2}.\cos\dfrac{B}{2}.\cos\dfrac{C}{2}}{\sin\dfrac{A}{2}\sin\dfrac{B}{2}.\sin\dfrac{C}{2}} = \cot\dfrac{A}{2}.\cot\dfrac{B}{2}.\cot\dfrac{C}{2}$

In a triangle, $\prod \cot\dfrac{A}{2} = \sum \cot\dfrac{A}{2}$

**3. (c)** Using $R = \dfrac{abc}{4\Delta} \Rightarrow \dfrac{a}{R} = \dfrac{4\Delta}{bc}$

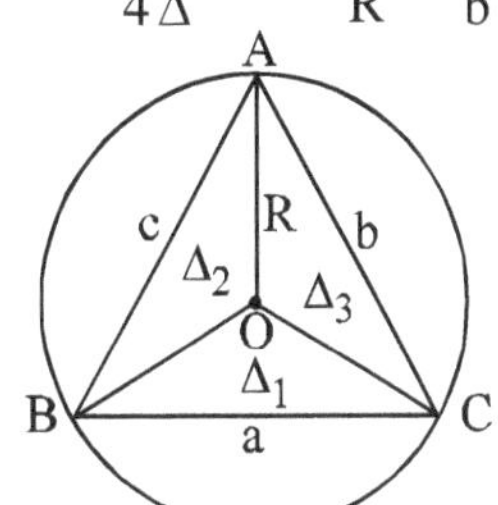

$\dfrac{a}{R_1} + \dfrac{b}{R_2} + \dfrac{c}{R_3} = \dfrac{4}{R^2}(\Delta_1 + \Delta_2 + \Delta_3) = \dfrac{4\Delta}{R^2}$

**4. (d)** put $p = 1$, we get $a_2 = 4 \Rightarrow b = 4$

put $p = 2$, we get $a_3 = 4 \Rightarrow c = 4$

Hence the $\Delta ABC$ is isosceles

Now $\Delta = \sqrt{15}$

$\therefore \quad r_1 = \dfrac{\Delta}{s-a} = \dfrac{\sqrt{15}}{3}$

and $r_2 = \dfrac{\Delta}{s-b} = \dfrac{\sqrt{15}}{1} = r_3$

hence $r_2 = r_3 = 3r$

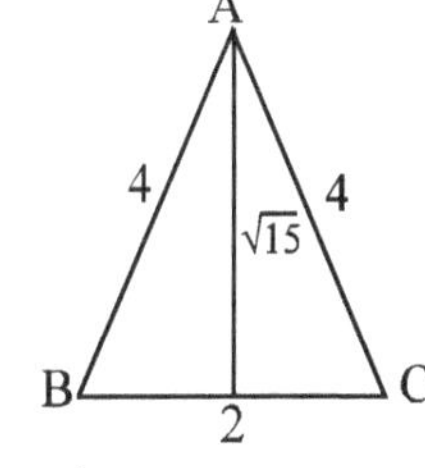

**5. (a)** We have $\tan\dfrac{C}{2} = \tan\left(90° - \dfrac{A+B}{2}\right)$

$\cot\dfrac{A+B}{2} = \dfrac{\cot(A/2)\cot(B/2) - 1}{\cot(A/2) + \cot(B/2)}$

$= \dfrac{\dfrac{6}{5}\cdot\dfrac{37}{20} - 1}{\dfrac{6}{5} + \dfrac{37}{20}} = \dfrac{222 - 100}{120 + 185} = \dfrac{122}{305} = \dfrac{2}{5}$

Also $\tan\dfrac{A}{2}\tan\dfrac{C}{2}$

$= \sqrt{\dfrac{(s-b)(s-c)}{s(s-a)}}\sqrt{\dfrac{(s-a)(s-b)}{s(s-c)}}$

$\Rightarrow \dfrac{5}{6}\cdot\dfrac{2}{5} = \dfrac{s-b}{s} \Rightarrow 3(s-b) = s \Rightarrow 2s = 3b$

$\Rightarrow a + b + c = 3b \Rightarrow a + c = 2b$

which shows that a, b and c are in A.P.

**6. (b)** Let $\theta$ be the angle opposite to side c of $\Delta ABC$

$\Rightarrow c^2 = a^2 + b^2 - 2ab\cos\theta$

$= (a - b)^2 + 2ab(1 - \cos\theta)$

Also $\Delta = \dfrac{1}{2}ab\sin\theta \Rightarrow 2ab = \dfrac{4\Delta}{\sin\theta}$

$\Rightarrow c^2 = (a-b)^2 + 4\Delta\dfrac{1 - \cos\theta}{\sin\theta} = (a-b)^2 + 4\Delta\tan\dfrac{\theta}{2}$

For minimum of c, $a = b$

$\Rightarrow 2ab = 2a^2 = \dfrac{4\Delta}{\sin\theta} \Rightarrow a = \sqrt{\dfrac{2\Delta}{\sin\theta}} = b$

**7. (c)** We have from $\triangle OAC$,

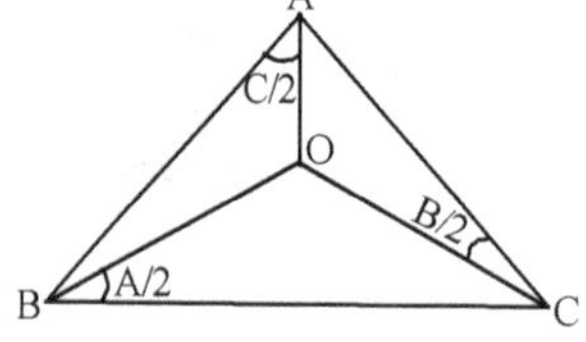

$$\frac{\sin\left(A - \frac{C}{2}\right)}{\sin\left(\frac{B}{2}\right)} = \frac{OC}{OA}$$

Similarly, $\dfrac{\sin\left(B - \frac{A}{2}\right)}{\sin\left(\frac{C}{2}\right)} = \dfrac{OA}{OB}$

and $\dfrac{\sin\left(C - \frac{B}{2}\right)}{\sin\left(\frac{A}{2}\right)} = \dfrac{OB}{OC}$

So, the given expression is equal to 1.

**8. (d)** A, B, C be in A. P. Then $2B = A + C$ and $A + B + C = 180°$
$\Rightarrow B = 60°$ and $A + C = 120°$
Let $A = 2C \Rightarrow A = 80°, C = 40°$

Let AD be the median of length $2\sqrt{3}$ cm

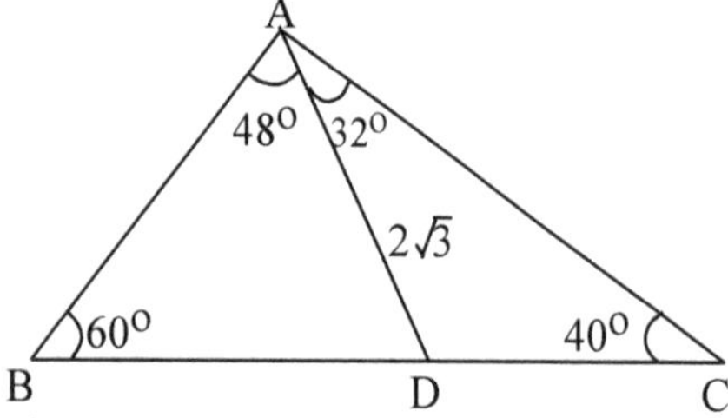

Then $\angle BAD + \angle DAC = 80°$
Since $\angle BAD : \angle DAC = 3 : 2$
$\therefore \angle BAD = 48°, \angle DAC = 32°$
From $\triangle BAD$, $\dfrac{BD}{\sin 48°} = \dfrac{AD}{\sin 60°}$
$\Rightarrow BD = \dfrac{2\sqrt{3}\sin 48°}{\frac{\sqrt{3}}{2}} = 4\sin 48°$
$\therefore BC = 8\sin 48° = 8\cos 42°$

**9. (a,b,c,d)**

**(a)** $r_1 = 2r_2 = 2r_3$
$\dfrac{\Delta}{s-a} = \dfrac{2\Delta}{s-b} = \dfrac{2\Delta}{s-c}$, now $\dfrac{\Delta}{s-a} = \dfrac{2\Delta}{s-b}$
$\Rightarrow \quad s - b = 2s - 2a = b + c - a$
$\dfrac{a+c-b}{2} = b + c - a \Rightarrow a + c - b = 2b + 2c - 2a$
$3a = 3b + c \qquad\qquad ....(1)$
Now $\dfrac{2\Delta}{s-b} = \dfrac{2\Delta}{s-c}$
$s - b = s - c \Rightarrow b = c \qquad ....(2)$
From (1) & (2), $3a = 4b$

**(b)** $\dfrac{\sin A}{\sin C} = \dfrac{\sin(A - B)}{\sin(B - C)}$

$\dfrac{\sin(B + C)}{\sin(A + B)} = \dfrac{\sin(A - B)}{\sin(B - C)}$
$\sin^2 B - \sin^2 C = \sin^2 A - \sin^2 B$
$\therefore 2b^2 = a^2 + c^2 \Rightarrow a^2, b^2, c^2$ are in A.P.

**(c)** $\cos A + \cos B = 2(1 - \cos C) = 4\sin^2\dfrac{C}{2}$

or, $2\cos\dfrac{A+B}{2}\cos\dfrac{A-B}{2} = 4\sin^2\dfrac{C}{2}$

or, $\cos\dfrac{A-B}{2} = 2\sin\dfrac{C}{2}$

or, $2\cos\dfrac{C}{2}\cos\dfrac{A-B}{2} = 4\sin\dfrac{C}{2}\cos\dfrac{C}{2} = 2\sin C$

or, $2\sin\dfrac{A+B}{2}\cos\dfrac{A-B}{2} = 2\sin C$

or, $\sin A + \sin B = 2\sin C$
$\Rightarrow$ a, c, b are in A.P.

**(d)** $\dfrac{1}{2}ra + \dfrac{1}{2}rb = \dfrac{1}{2}ab\sin C$
$r(a + b) = 2\Delta$

$$r = \frac{2\Delta}{a + b}$$

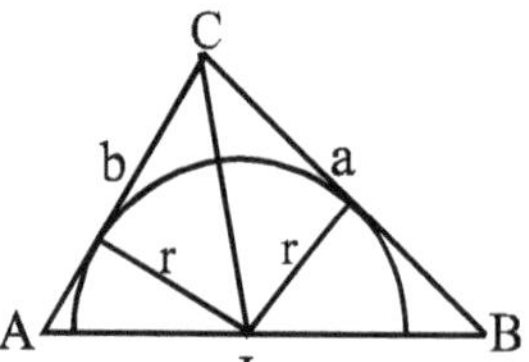

**10. (a, b)**

**(a)** Produce the median AM to D such that
GM = MD. Join D to B and C. Now GBDC
is a parallelogram. Note that the sides of the
$\triangle$ GDC are 6, 8, 10 $\Rightarrow \angle GDC = 90°$

$$Area\ of\ \triangle ADC = \frac{12 \times 8}{2} = 48$$
$$Area\ of\ \triangle MDC = \frac{3 \times 8}{2} = 12$$

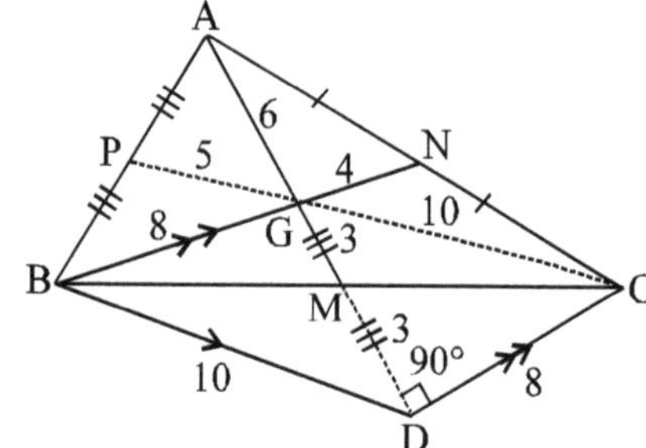

$\Rightarrow$ Area of $\triangle$ AMC = 36
$\Rightarrow$ Area of $\triangle$ ABC = 72 cm$^2$ ]

**(b)** OAMB is a cyclic quadrilateral
using sine law in $\triangle$ OBM and $\triangle$ OAM
$$\frac{d}{\sin 90°} = \frac{x}{\sin(60° - \theta)} \qquad .....(1)$$
and $\dfrac{d}{\sin 90°} = \dfrac{y}{\sin\theta} \qquad ....(2)$

(1) and (2) $\Rightarrow \dfrac{x}{\sin(60° - \theta)} = \dfrac{y}{\sin\theta}$

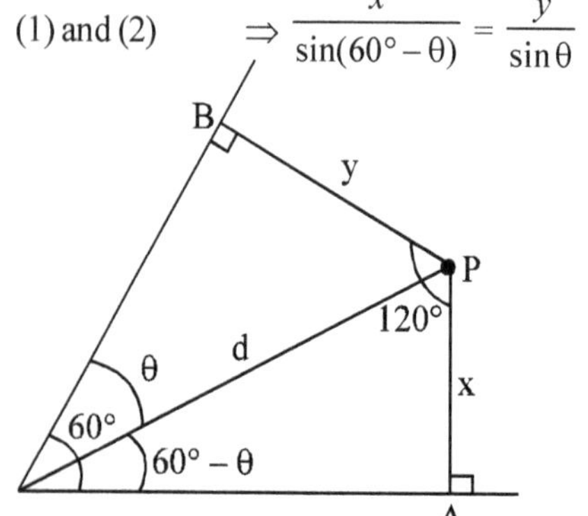

$$\therefore \ \frac{x}{y} = \frac{\sin(60° - \theta)}{\sin\theta} = \frac{\sqrt{3}}{2}\cot\theta - \frac{1}{2}$$

$$\Rightarrow \frac{2x}{y} + 1 = \sqrt{3}\cot\theta \Rightarrow \frac{2x+y}{\sqrt{3}y} = \cot\theta$$

from (2), $d = y\,\mathrm{cosec}\,\theta$

$$d^2 = y^2(1 + \cot^2\theta) \Rightarrow d^2 = y^2\left(1 + \frac{(2x+y)^2}{3y^2}\right)$$

$$\Rightarrow d^2 = y^2 + \frac{(2x+y)^2}{3}$$

$$d^2 = \frac{3y^2 + 4x^2 + y^2 + 4xy}{3}$$

$$\Rightarrow d^2 = \frac{4x^2 + 4y^2 + 4xy}{3}$$

$$\Rightarrow d = \frac{2}{\sqrt{3}}\sqrt{x^2 + y^2 + xy}$$

**11. (a,b,c,d)**

By simple geometry in $\Delta AFE$, $AF = AE$

$\therefore \Delta AFE$ is an isosceles $\Delta$. **(d)**

Now ar $(\Delta ABC) = $ ar $(\Delta ABD) + $ ar $(\Delta ADC)$

$$\Rightarrow \frac{1}{2}bc\sin A = \frac{1}{2}c(AD)\sin\frac{A}{2} + \frac{1}{2}b(AD)\sin\frac{A}{2}$$

$$\Rightarrow \quad AD = \frac{2bc\cos\dfrac{A}{2}}{b+c} \quad \textbf{(b)}$$

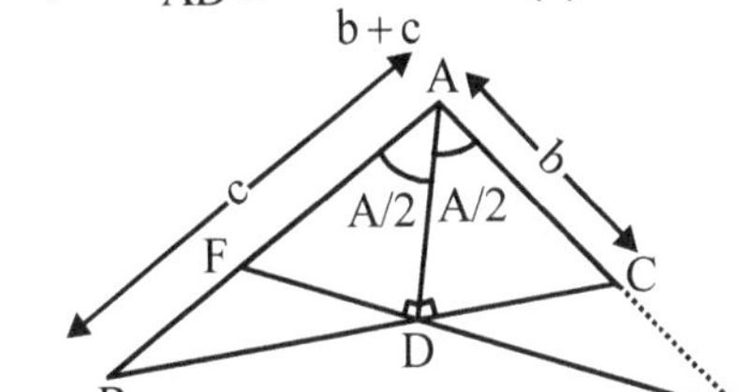

Also $AD = AE\cos\dfrac{A}{2}$

$$\Rightarrow \quad AE = \frac{2bc}{b+c} = \text{HM of } b \text{ and } c. \quad \textbf{(a)}$$

Again $EF = 2DE = 2.\,AD\tan\dfrac{A}{2} = \dfrac{4bc\sin\dfrac{A}{2}}{b+c}$ **(c)**

**12. (a,b,d)** Draw BE perpendicular to CA produced.

Then, $BD = DC = \dfrac{a}{2}$ and $EA = AC = b$

From $\Delta$ ADC, $\cos C = \dfrac{b}{a} = \dfrac{2b}{a}$

From $\Delta$ ABC, $\cos(\pi - A) = \dfrac{b}{c}$

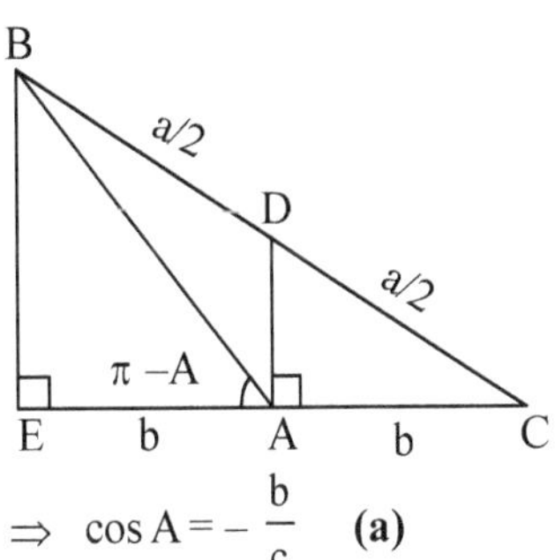

$$\Rightarrow \ \cos A = -\frac{b}{c} \quad \textbf{(a)}$$

So that $\cos A \cos C = -\dfrac{2b^2}{ac}$ **(b)**

Also $\cos A = -\dfrac{b}{c}$

$$\Rightarrow \quad \frac{b^2 + c^2 - a^2}{2bc} = -\frac{b}{c}$$

$$\Rightarrow \quad a^2 - 3b^2 - c^2 = 0 \quad \textbf{(d)}$$

and $\cos B = \dfrac{c^2 + a^2 - b^2}{2ca}$

$$= \frac{c^2 + 3b^2 + c^2 - b^2}{2ca} = \frac{b^2 + c^2}{ca}$$

**13. (c)** $\dfrac{bx}{c} + \dfrac{cy}{a} + \dfrac{az}{b} = b\sin B + c\sin C + a\sin A$

$$= \frac{b^2 + c^2 + a^2}{2R} \qquad \therefore \ k = 2R$$

**14. (c)** $\dfrac{1}{x^2} + \dfrac{1}{y^2} + \dfrac{1}{z^2} = \dfrac{a^2}{4\Delta^2} + \dfrac{b^2}{4\Delta^2} + \dfrac{c^2}{4\Delta^2} = \dfrac{a^2 + b^2 + c^2}{4\Delta^2}$

$\cos A + \cos B + \cot C = \dfrac{R}{abc}(b^2 + c^2 - a^2 + c^2 + a^2$
$- b^2 + a^2 + b^2 - c^2)$

$$\frac{R}{abc}(b^2 + c^2 + a^2) = \frac{R}{abc}\left(\frac{4\Delta^2}{x^2} + \frac{4\Delta^2}{y^2} + \frac{4\Delta^2}{z^2}\right)$$

$$= \frac{4\Delta^2 R}{abc}\left(\frac{1}{x^2} + \frac{1}{y^2} + \frac{1}{z^2}\right)$$

$$= \frac{4\Delta R}{abc}.\Delta\left(\frac{1}{x^2} + \frac{1}{y^2} + \frac{1}{z^2}\right) = \Delta\left(\frac{1}{x^2} + \frac{1}{y^2} + \frac{1}{z^2}\right)$$

$$\therefore \quad k = \Delta$$

**15. (d)** $\sum \dfrac{c\sin B + b\sin C}{x}, = \sum \dfrac{x + x}{x} = 6$

**16.** $A \to r, B \to s, C \to p, D \to q$

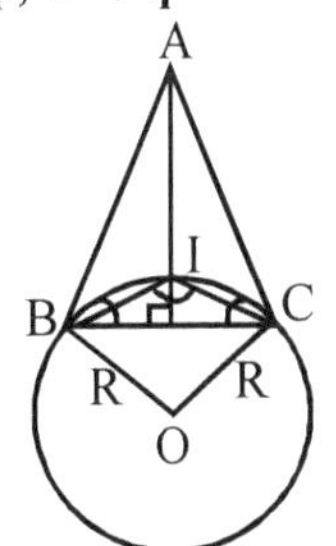

$\angle BOC = 2\pi - (\pi + A) = \pi - A$

$$\left[\because \angle BIC = \pi - \left(\frac{B}{2} + \frac{C}{2}\right) = \frac{\pi}{2} + \frac{A}{2}\right]$$

From $\Delta$ BOC, $\cos\angle BOC = \dfrac{R^2 + R^2 - a^2}{2a^2}$

$$\Rightarrow -\cos A = \frac{2R^2 - a^2}{2R^2}$$

$$\Rightarrow a^2 = 2R^2 + 2R^2\cos A = 2R^2[1 + \cos A]$$

$$= 2R^2 . 2\cos^2\frac{A}{2}$$

$$\Rightarrow a = 2R\cos\frac{A}{2} \Rightarrow R = \frac{a}{2}\sec\frac{A}{2} \quad \textbf{(r)}$$

**(B)** $r_1 = 2r_2 = 3r_3$

$\Rightarrow \dfrac{\Delta}{s-a} = \dfrac{2\Delta}{s-b} = \dfrac{3\Delta}{s-c} = \dfrac{\Delta}{k}$

$\therefore s-a = k, \; s-b = 2k, \; s-c = 3k$

$\therefore 3s - (a+b+c) = 6k \Rightarrow s = 6k$

$\therefore 6k - a = k \Rightarrow a = 5k$

Similar, $b = 4k, \; c = 3k$

$\therefore a^2 = b^2 + c^2$

$\therefore \Delta ABC$ is a right angled triangle with $A = 90°$ ($\because$ D is the mid point of BC)

AD = DC (radius of the circumcircle)

$\therefore \angle DAC = C$

$\Rightarrow \angle ADC = 180° - 2C$

$\Rightarrow \cos \angle ADC = \cos(180° - 2C) = -\cos 2C$

$\qquad = -(2\cos^2 C - 1) = 1 - 2\cos^2 C$

$\qquad = 1 - 2 \times \dfrac{16}{25} = -\dfrac{7}{25}$ **(s)**

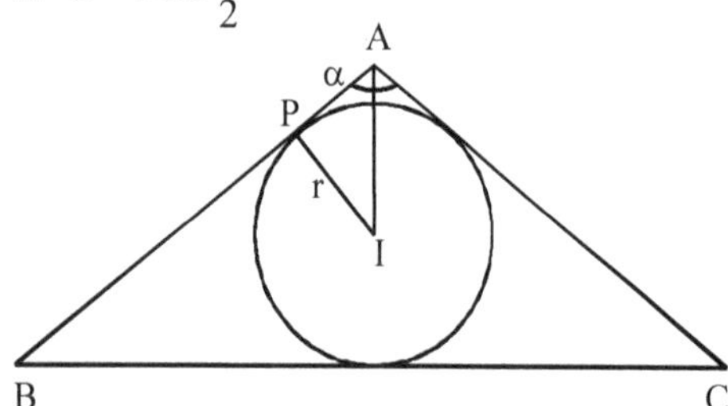

**(C)** H.M. of $r_1, r_2, r_3 = \dfrac{3}{\dfrac{1}{r_1} + \dfrac{1}{r_2} + \dfrac{1}{r_3}} = \dfrac{3}{\dfrac{s-a}{\Delta} + \dfrac{s-b}{\Delta} + \dfrac{s-c}{\Delta}}$

$\qquad = \dfrac{3\Delta}{3s - 2s} = \dfrac{3\Delta}{s} = 3r$ **(p)**

**(D)** From right angle $\Delta$ API, $\dfrac{r}{\alpha} = \tan \dfrac{A}{2}$

$\therefore \alpha = r \cot \dfrac{A}{2}$

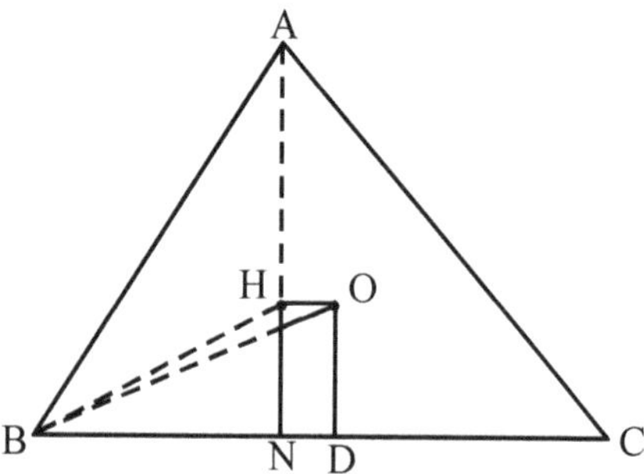

Similarly, $\beta = r \cot \dfrac{B}{2}, \; \gamma = r \cot \dfrac{C}{2}$

$\therefore \dfrac{\alpha}{r} + \dfrac{\beta}{r} + \dfrac{\gamma}{r} = \cot \dfrac{A}{2} + \cot \dfrac{B}{2} + \cot \dfrac{C}{2}$

$\Rightarrow \dfrac{\alpha + \beta + \gamma}{r} = \cot \dfrac{A}{2} \cot \dfrac{B}{2} \cot \dfrac{C}{2}$

$\qquad = \dfrac{\alpha}{r} \cdot \dfrac{\beta}{r} \cdot \dfrac{\gamma}{r} = \dfrac{\alpha\beta\gamma}{r^3} \Rightarrow \dfrac{\alpha\beta\gamma}{\alpha+\beta+\gamma} = r^2$ **(Q)**

**17.** $A \to s, \; B \to q, \; C \to p, \; D \to r.$

**(A)** $\dfrac{\tan^4 A + \tan^4 B + \tan^4 C}{3} \geq \left(\dfrac{\tan A + \tan B + \tan C}{3}\right)^4$ ... (i)

Also, $\tan A + \tan B + \tan C \geq 3\sqrt{3}$ ... (ii)

Now from (i) and (ii), we get

$\tan^4 A + \tan^4 B + \tan^4 C \geq 27$ **(S)**

**(B)** $\dfrac{A}{2} + \dfrac{B}{2} + \dfrac{C}{2} = \dfrac{\pi}{2}$

So, $\cot \dfrac{A}{2} + \cot \dfrac{B}{2} + \cot \dfrac{C}{2} = \cot \dfrac{A}{2} \cot \dfrac{B}{2} \cot \dfrac{C}{2}$

Also $\dfrac{\cot \dfrac{A}{2} + \cot \dfrac{B}{2} + \cot \dfrac{C}{2}}{3} \geq \left(\cot \dfrac{A}{2} \cot \dfrac{B}{2} \cot \dfrac{C}{2}\right)^{1/3}$

$\Rightarrow \left(\cot \dfrac{A}{2} \cot \dfrac{B}{2} \cot \dfrac{C}{2}\right)^{2/3} \geq 3$

$\Rightarrow \left(\cot \dfrac{A}{2} \cot \dfrac{B}{2} \cot \dfrac{C}{2}\right) \geq 3\sqrt{3}$ **(Q)**

**(C)** $\tan A + \tan B + \tan C = \tan A \tan B \tan C$

$\Rightarrow \tan A + \tan B + \tan C = 2 \tan B$

$\Rightarrow \tan A + \tan C = \tan B$

Multiply both sides by $\tan C$

$\tan A \tan C + \tan^2 C = \tan B \tan C = 18$

$\Rightarrow 2 + \tan^2 C = 18$

$\Rightarrow \tan^2 C = 16$ **(P)**

**(D)** $1 + \sin\left(\dfrac{\pi}{4} + \theta\right) + 2\cos\left(\dfrac{\pi}{4} - \theta\right)$

$= 1 + \dfrac{1}{\sqrt{2}}(\cos\theta + \sin\theta) + \dfrac{2}{\sqrt{2}}(\cos\theta + \sin\theta)$

$= 1 + \dfrac{3}{\sqrt{2}}(\cos\theta + \sin\theta)$

maximum value of $\cos\theta + \sin\theta = \sqrt{2}$

Hence maximum value $1 + \sin\left(\dfrac{\pi}{4} + \theta\right) + 2\cos\left(\dfrac{\pi}{4} - \theta\right)$

$\qquad = 1 + \dfrac{3}{\sqrt{2}} \times \sqrt{2} = 4$

**18. (a)** a, b, c are in A.P. as well as in G.P.

$\Rightarrow a = b = c$

So the triangle is equilateral.

So, $r = 4R \sin \dfrac{A}{2} \sin \dfrac{B}{2} \sin \dfrac{C}{2} = \dfrac{R}{2}$

**19. (d)** If $\tan A, \tan B, \tan C$ are in A.P. then

$2 \tan A = \tan A + \tan C \Rightarrow 3 \tan B = \tan A \tan B \tan C$

$\because \tan B \neq 0 \Rightarrow \tan A \tan C = 3$

Now in $\Delta ABC$

OH is parallel to BC, so

$OD = HN \Rightarrow R \cos A = 2R \cos B \cos C$

$\Rightarrow -\cos(B+C) = 2\cos B \cos C$

$\Rightarrow \sin B \sin C = 3 \cos B \cos C$

$\Rightarrow \tan B \tan C = 3 \Rightarrow \tan A + \tan B + \tan C = 3 \tan A$

$\Rightarrow \tan B + \tan C = 2 \tan A$

$\Rightarrow \tan B, \tan A, \tan C$ and in A.P.

**20. (5)** Let G be the centroid : $AD = x$ ; $BE = y$

$\therefore AG = \dfrac{2x}{3}$ ; $GD = \dfrac{x}{3}$ ; $BG = \dfrac{2y}{3}$ ; $GE = \dfrac{y}{3}$

In $\Delta AGE: \dfrac{4x^2}{9} + \dfrac{y^2}{9} = \dfrac{9}{4}$ or $16x^2 + 4y^2 = 81$ .....(1)

In $\triangle BGD$ : $\dfrac{x^2}{9} + \dfrac{4y^2}{9} = 4$

or $\quad x^2 + 4y^2 = 36$ .....(ii)

(i) − (ii) , $15x^2 = 45$

$\Rightarrow \quad x = \sqrt{3}$

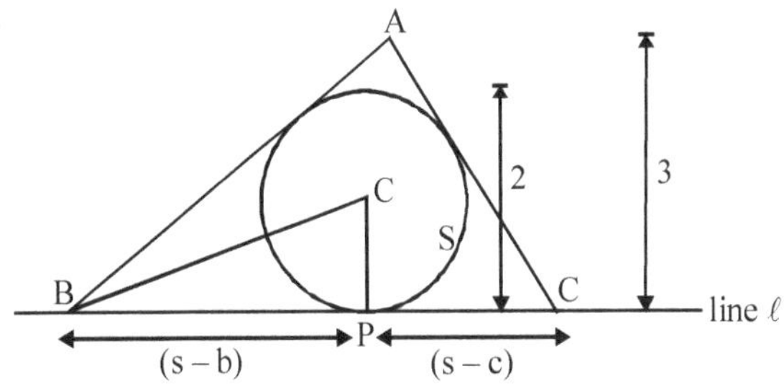

In $\triangle ADC$, $\cos C = \dfrac{9 + 4 - 3}{2(2)(3)} = \dfrac{5}{6} = \dfrac{9 + 16 - c^2}{2(4)(3)}$

$\Rightarrow 20 = 25 - c^2$ or $\quad c = \sqrt{5} \; \therefore \; c^2 = 5$

**21.** **(6)** From the identity

$$r = 4R \cdot \sin\frac{A}{2} \cdot \sin\frac{B}{2} \cdot \sin\frac{C}{2}$$

or, $r = 4\left(\sqrt{3} + 1\right) r \cdot \sin\dfrac{A}{2} \cdot \sin\dfrac{B}{2} \cdot \sin\dfrac{C}{2}$

or, $\dfrac{1}{2\left(\sqrt{3} + 1\right)} = 2\left(\sin\dfrac{A}{2} \cdot \sin\dfrac{C}{2}\right) \cdot \sin\dfrac{B}{2}$

let $\angle A \ge \angle B$, $\quad \therefore \quad \angle A - \angle C = 30°$

then $\dfrac{\sqrt{3} - 1}{4} = \left(\cos\dfrac{A-C}{2} - \cos\dfrac{A+C}{2}\right)\sin\dfrac{B}{2}$

$\dfrac{\sqrt{3} - 1}{4} = \left(\dfrac{\sqrt{6} + \sqrt{2}}{4} - \sin\dfrac{B}{2}\right)\sin\dfrac{B}{2}$

Let $\sin\dfrac{B}{2} = x$ yields $x^2 - \dfrac{\sqrt{6} + \sqrt{2}}{4}x + \dfrac{\sqrt{3} - 1}{4} = 0$,

whose solutions are $x = \dfrac{\sqrt{6} - \sqrt{2}}{4}$ and $x = \dfrac{\sqrt{2}}{2}$.

It follows that $\dfrac{B}{2} = 15°$ or $\dfrac{B}{2} = 45°$. The second solution is not acceptable, because $A \ge B$.

Hence $B = 30°$, $A = 90°$ and $C = 60°$, $\therefore \; \dfrac{1}{10}C = 6°$

**22.** **(1)** Area $A = \dfrac{1}{2}b^2 \sin 2\theta = b^2 \sin\theta\cos\theta$ ....(1)

Now $\sin\theta = \dfrac{x}{24} = \dfrac{65 - x}{36}$

$60x = 24 \times 65$

$x = 26$

$\therefore \; \sin\theta = \dfrac{12}{13}$ and $\cos\theta = \dfrac{5}{13}$

Again, $\dfrac{b}{\sin\theta} = \dfrac{65}{\sin 2\theta}$

$\Rightarrow b = \dfrac{65}{2\sin\theta} = \dfrac{65 \cdot 13}{2 \cdot 5} = \dfrac{13^2}{2}$

From (1), Area $= \dfrac{13^4}{4} \cdot \dfrac{12}{13} \cdot \dfrac{5}{13} = 2535$

$\therefore \; \dfrac{1}{2535} \times$ Area $= 1$

**23.** **(3)**

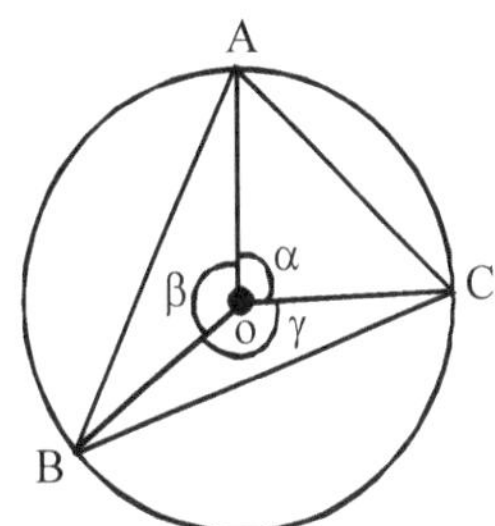

$(PB)(PC) = (s - b)(s - c) = \dfrac{s(s-a)(s-b)(s-c)}{s(s-a)}$

$= \dfrac{\Delta \cdot \Delta}{s(s-a)} = r \cdot s \dfrac{\Delta}{s(s-a)}$

$= \dfrac{\Delta}{s - a}(\because r = 1) = \dfrac{\Delta}{\Delta - a} \quad \left(r = \dfrac{\Delta}{s} = 1 \Rightarrow s = \Delta\right)$

$= \dfrac{3a}{2\left(\dfrac{3a}{2} - a\right)} = \dfrac{3}{3 - 2} = 3$

**24.** **(9)** Given, arc $AC = 3$, arc $AB = 4$ and arc $BC = 5$. Let $r$ be the radius of the circle,

Then $AC = r\alpha$, $BC = r\gamma$, $AB = r\beta$

$\Rightarrow \alpha = \dfrac{3}{r}$, $\beta = \dfrac{4}{r}$, $\gamma = \dfrac{5}{r}$

Now, $3 + 4 + 5 = 2\pi r \Rightarrow r = \dfrac{6}{\pi} \Rightarrow \dfrac{1}{r} = \dfrac{\pi}{6}$

$\triangle ABC = \triangle OAC + \triangle OAB + \triangle OBC$

$= \dfrac{1}{2}r^2\left[\sin\left(\dfrac{3}{r}\right) + \sin\left(\dfrac{4}{r}\right) + \sin\left(\dfrac{5}{r}\right)\right]$

$= \dfrac{1}{2}\dfrac{36}{\pi^2}\left(\sin\dfrac{\pi}{2} + \sin\dfrac{2\pi}{3} + \sin\dfrac{5\pi}{6}\right)$

$= \dfrac{18}{\pi^2}\left(1 + \dfrac{\sqrt{3}}{2} + \dfrac{1}{2}\right) = \dfrac{9\sqrt{3}(1 + \sqrt{3})}{\pi^2}$

$\Rightarrow x = \dfrac{9\sqrt{3}(1 + \sqrt{3})}{\pi^2}$,

$\therefore \; \dfrac{\pi^2}{\sqrt{3}(1 + \sqrt{3})}x = 9$

**1. (b)** $f(x) = \dfrac{[x]}{x} = \begin{bmatrix} 0/x & x < 1 \\ 1/x & x > 1 \end{bmatrix}$

$\ell = \lim\limits_{x \to 1} \dfrac{[x]}{x} \begin{cases} \text{R.H.L.}=1 \\ \text{L.H.L.}=0 \end{cases} \Rightarrow \ell$ does not exist

$m = \lim\limits_{x \to 1^+} \dfrac{x}{[x]} = 1 \Rightarrow m$ exists

$g(x) = \dfrac{x}{[x]} = \begin{bmatrix} x & x > 1 \\ \text{N.D. for } 0 \le x < 1 \end{bmatrix}$

Note: $1^-$ not in domain

**2. (c)** $\lim\limits_{x \to 0} \dfrac{(\cos x)^{1/m} - (\cos x)^{1/n}}{x^2}$

$= \lim\limits_{x \to 0} \dfrac{(1 - 2\sin^2 x/2)^{1/m} - (1 - 2\sin^2 x/2)^{1/n}}{x^2}$

$\left(1 - \dfrac{1}{m}(2\sin^2 x/2) + \dfrac{1/m \, (1/m - 1)}{2!}(2\sin^2 x/2)^2 .....\right)$

$= \lim\limits_{x \to 0} \dfrac{-\left(1 - \dfrac{1}{n}(2\sin^2 x/2) + \dfrac{1/n \,(1/n - 1)}{2!}(2\sin^2 x/2)^2 .....\right)}{x^2}$

$= \lim\limits_{x \to 0} \dfrac{2\sin^2 x/2 \left(\dfrac{1}{n} - \dfrac{1}{m}\right)}{x^2}$

$= \dfrac{1}{2}\left(\dfrac{1}{n} - \dfrac{1}{m}\right) = \dfrac{m - n}{2mn}$

**3 (a)** $\lim\limits_{x \to 0} \dfrac{\sin 3x}{x^3} + \dfrac{a}{x^2} + b$

$= \lim\limits_{x \to 0} \dfrac{\sin 3x + ax + bx^3}{x^3}$

$= \lim\limits_{x \to 0} \dfrac{3\dfrac{\sin 3x}{3x} + a + bx^2}{x^2}$

for existence of limit $3 + a = 0 \Rightarrow a = -3$

$\therefore \quad l = \lim\limits_{x \to 0} \dfrac{\sin 3x - 3x + bx^3}{x^3}$

$= 27 . \dfrac{\sin t - t}{t^3} + b = 0 \quad (3x = t)$

$= -\dfrac{27}{6} + b = 0 \Rightarrow b = \dfrac{9}{2}$

[ OR use L' Hospital's rule ]

**4. (c)** $l = e^{\displaystyle\lim_{n \to \infty} n\left(\left(\frac{n}{n+1}\right)^\alpha + \sin\frac{1}{n} - 1\right)}$

$= e^{\displaystyle\lim_{n \to \infty} n \sin\frac{1}{n} + \lim_{n \to \infty} n\left(\left(\frac{n}{n+1}\right)^\alpha - 1\right)}$

Consider $= \lim\limits_{n \to \infty} n\left(\left(\dfrac{n}{n+1}\right)^\alpha - 1\right)$

$= \lim\limits_{n \to \infty} n\left(\left(\dfrac{1}{1 + 1/n}\right)^\alpha - 1\right);$ put $n = \dfrac{1}{y}$

$= \lim\limits_{y \to 0} \dfrac{1}{y}\left(\left(\dfrac{1}{1+y}\right)^\alpha - 1\right)$

$= \lim\limits_{y \to 0} \dfrac{1 - (1+y)^\alpha}{y(1+y)} = -\alpha \qquad \text{(using binomial)}$

$\therefore \ l = e^{1-\alpha}$

**5. (c)** Given that $f ; R \to R$ such that

$f(1) = 3$ and $f'(1) = 6$

Then $\lim\limits_{x \to 0}\left[\dfrac{f(1+x)}{f(1)}\right]^{1/x}$

$= e^{\displaystyle\lim_{x \to 0} \frac{1}{x}[\log f(1+x) - \log f(1)]}$

$= e^{\displaystyle\lim_{x \to 0} \frac{\frac{1}{f(1+x)} f'(1+x)}{1}}$ [Using L' Hospital rule]

$= \dfrac{f'(1)}{e f(1)} = e^{6/3} = e^2$

**6. (d)** $l = \lim\limits_{h \to 0} \dfrac{f(2h + 2 + h^2) - f(2)}{f(h - h^2 + 1) - f(1)} = \left[\dfrac{0}{0} \text{form}\right]$

$\therefore$ Applying L' Hospital's rule, we get

$l = \lim\limits_{h \to 0} \dfrac{f'(2h + 2 + h^2).(2 + 2h)}{f'(h - h^2 + 1).(1 - 2h)} = \dfrac{f'(2).2}{f'(1).1} = \dfrac{6 \times 2}{4 \times 1} = 3$

**7. (c)** $\lim\limits_{x \to \infty}\left(\dfrac{x^2 + 5x + 3}{x^2 + x + 2}\right)^x = \lim\limits_{x \to \infty}\left(1 + \dfrac{4x + 1}{x^2 + x + 2}\right)^x$

$= \lim\limits_{x \to \infty}\left\{\left(1 + \dfrac{4x + 1}{x^2 + x + 2}\right)^{\frac{x^2 + x + 2}{4x + 1}}\right\}^{\frac{(4x+1)}{x^2 + x + 2} \cdot x}$

$$= \lim_{x \to \infty} \left\{ \left(1 + \frac{1}{n}\right) \right\}^{\lim\limits_{x \to \infty} \left\{ \frac{4 + \frac{1}{x}}{1 + \frac{1}{x} + \frac{2}{x^2}} \right\}},$$

where $n = \dfrac{x^2 + x + 2}{4x + 1} = e^4.$

**8.** **(b,c)** $\lim\limits_{x \to 0} \left(1 + ax + bx^2\right)^{\frac{2-x}{x}} = e^3$

$$\Rightarrow \quad e^{\lim\limits_{x \to \infty} \frac{2}{x}\left(ax + bx^2\right)}$$

Since, limit value $e^{2a}$ does not involve $b$.

$\therefore$ $b$ can have any value.

Thus, $\quad a = \dfrac{3}{2}, \ b \in R$

**9.** **(a,c)** If $m < 0$, then for values of $x$ sufficiently close to 0

$$1 + \frac{1}{m} < \frac{\sin x}{x} < 1$$

$$\therefore \quad m + 1 > m\frac{\sin x}{x} > m$$

$$\therefore \quad \left[ m\frac{\sin x}{x} \right] = m$$

$$\therefore \quad \lim_{x \to 0}\left[ m\frac{\sin x}{x} \right] = m$$

If $m > 0$, then for values of $x$ sufficiently close to 0, we can have

$$1 - \frac{1}{m} < \frac{\sin x}{x} < 1$$

$$\therefore \quad m - 1 < m\frac{\sin x}{x} < m$$

$$\therefore \quad \lim_{x \to 0}\left[ m\frac{\sin x}{x} \right] = m - 1$$

**10.** **(b,c)** We have

$$\lim_{x \to 0^+} f(x) = \lim_{x \to 0^+} \frac{\tan^2\{x\}}{(x^2 - [x]^2)} = \lim_{x \to 0^+} \frac{\tan^2 x}{x^2} = 1 \quad ....(1)$$

$[\text{As } x \to 0^+; [x] = 0 \Rightarrow \{x\} = x ]$

Also $\lim\limits_{x \to 0^-} f(x) = \lim\limits_{x \to 0^-} \sqrt{\{x\}\cot\{x\}} = \sqrt{\cot 1} \quad ....(2)$

$[\text{As } x \to 0^-; [x] = -1 \Rightarrow \{x\} = x + 1 \Rightarrow \{x\} \to 1]$

Also $\cot^{-1}\left( \lim\limits_{x \to 0^-} f(x) \right)^2 = \cot^{-1}(\cot 1) = 1$

**11.** **(a)** $\lim\limits_{x \to \infty} \left(1 + \dfrac{2}{x}\right)^x = e^{\lim\limits_{x \to \infty} \frac{2x}{x}} = e^2$

**12.** **(b)** $\lim\limits_{x \to 0} (1 + \sin x)^{2\cot x} \Rightarrow e^{\lim\limits_{x \to 0} \sin x . 2\cot x}$

$$\Rightarrow e^{\lim\limits_{x \to 0} 2\cos x} = e^2$$

**13.** **(c)** $\lim\limits_{x \to 1} (\log_3 3x)^{\log_x 3} \Rightarrow \lim\limits_{x \to 1} (\log_3 3 + \log_3 x)^{\log_x 3}$

$$\Rightarrow e^{\lim\limits_{x \to 1} \log_3 x . \frac{1}{\log_3 x}} = e$$

**14.** **A - q; B - p; C - t; D - r, s**

**(A)** $\lim\limits_{x \to a} \dfrac{g(x)f(a) - g(a)f(x)}{x - a}$

$$= \lim_{h \to 0} \frac{g(a+h)f(a) - g(a)f(a+h)}{h}$$

$$= \lim_{h \to 0} \frac{g(a+h)f(a) - g(a)f(a) + g(a)f(a) - g(a)f(a+h)}{h}$$

$$= \lim_{h \to 0} f(a)\left[ \frac{g(a+h) - g(a)}{h} \right]^h - g(a)\left[ \frac{f(a+h) - f(a)}{h} \right]$$

$$= f(a)g'(a) - g(a)f'(a) = 2 \times 2 - (-1) \times 1 = 5 \ \textbf{(q)}$$

**(B)** At $\underset{x=k}{LD} = \lim\limits_{h \to 0} \dfrac{f(k) - f(k-h)}{h}$

$(k = \text{integer})$

$$= \lim_{h \to 0} \frac{[k]\sin k\pi - [k-h]\sin(k-h)\pi}{h}$$

$$= \lim_{h \to 0} \frac{-(k-1)\sin(k-h)\pi}{h} \qquad [\because \sin k\pi = 0]$$

$$= \lim_{h \to 0} \frac{-(k-1)\sin(k\pi - h\pi)}{h} \, [\sin(kx - \theta) = (-1)^{k-1}\theta]$$

$$= \lim_{h \to 0} \frac{-(k-1)(-1)^k \sin h\pi}{h\pi} \times \pi = \pi(k-1)(-1)^{k-1} \ \textbf{(P)}$$

**(C)** We know that

$$\cos A \cos 2A \cos 4A .... \cos 2^{n-1}A = \frac{\sin 2^n A}{2^n \sin A}$$

Taking $A = \dfrac{x}{2^n}$, we get

$$\cos\left(\frac{x}{2^n}\right)\cos\left(\frac{x}{2^{n-1}}\right)....\cos\left(\frac{x}{4}\right)\cos\left(\frac{x}{2}\right)$$

$$= \frac{\sin x}{2^n \sin\left(\dfrac{x}{2^n}\right)}$$

$$\therefore \lim_{n \to \infty} \cos\left(\frac{x}{2}\right)\cos\left(\frac{x}{4}\right)....\cos\left(\frac{x}{2^{n-1}}\right)\cos\left(\frac{x}{2^n}\right)$$

$$= \lim_{n \to \infty} \frac{\sin x}{2^n \sin\left(\dfrac{x}{2^n}\right)} = \lim_{n \to \infty} \frac{\sin x}{x} \frac{(x/2^n)}{\sin(x/2^n)} = \frac{\sin x}{x} \ \textbf{(t)}$$

**(D)** Case I : If n is even, say n = 2k. Then limit is

$$\lim_{k \to \infty} \frac{-6k + (-1)^{2k}}{8k - (-1)^{2k}} = \lim_{k \to \infty} \frac{-6k + 1}{8k - 1}$$

$$= \lim_{k \to \infty} \frac{-6 + \dfrac{1}{k}}{8 - \dfrac{1}{k}} = \frac{-6}{8} = \frac{-3}{4}$$

$\left(\text{as } \dfrac{1}{k} \to 0 \text{ where } k \to \infty\right)$

Case II : If n is odd, say $n = 2k + 1$. Then limit is

$$\lim_{k \to \infty} \frac{-3(2k+1) - (-1)^{2k+1}}{4(2k+1) - (-1)^{2k+1}} = \lim_{k \to \infty} \frac{-6k - 3 + 1}{8k + 4 + 1}$$

$$= \lim_{k \to \infty} \frac{-6 - \dfrac{2}{k}}{8 + \dfrac{5}{k}} = \frac{-3}{4}$$

$$\therefore \lim_{n \to \infty} \frac{-3n + (-1)^n}{4n - (-1)^n} = \frac{-3}{4} \text{, n even or odd} \quad \textbf{(r, s)}$$

**15. A-p; B-s; C-t; D-r**

**(A)** $\displaystyle \lim_{x \to \infty} \frac{1}{2} \frac{\sin\left(\dfrac{\pi}{4}\right) \cdot \dfrac{1}{x}}{\left(\dfrac{1}{x}\right)} = \frac{\pi}{8}$ **(p)**

**(B)** $\therefore \pi^2 = 9.8$

$\Rightarrow \displaystyle \lim_{x \to 0} \frac{\tan^2(-10x^2) + 10x^2}{x^2} = \frac{-10x^2 + 10x^2}{x^2} = 0$ **(s)**

**(C)** $\displaystyle \lim_{x \to \infty} \sqrt{\frac{2 - \dfrac{1}{x} \cdot \sin x + \dfrac{1}{x} \cdot \cos x}{1 + \dfrac{1}{x}}} = \sqrt{\frac{2 - 0 + 0}{1 + 0}} = \sqrt{2}$ **(t)**

**(D)** Put $x - 1 = h$, as $x \to 1$, $h \to 0$

$$\lim_{h \to 0} \left(1 + \frac{(n-1)}{2} h\right)^{1/h} = \lim_{h \to 0} \left(\frac{1 + nh + \dfrac{n(n+1)}{2!} h^2 \dots - 1}{nh}\right)^{1/h}$$

$$= \lim_{h \to 0} \left(1 + \frac{(n-1)}{2} h\right)^{1/n} = e^{n - 1/2} \quad \textbf{(r)}$$

**16. (a)** Clearly $\cos^2 x < 1$ in the neighbourhood of the point $x = 0 \Rightarrow \mathrm{cosec}^{-1}(\cos^2 x)$ is well defined at $x = 0$ but not in the neighbourhood of the point $x = 0 \Rightarrow$ limit does not exist.

**17. (a)** $\displaystyle \lim_{x \to 0} \frac{\sqrt{2}\,|\sin x|}{x}$

Now, $\displaystyle \lim_{x \to 0^+} \frac{\sqrt{2} \sin x}{x} = \sqrt{2}$, $\displaystyle \lim_{x \to 0^-} \frac{-\sqrt{2} \sin x}{x} = -\sqrt{2}$

Limit does not exists. Both A and R are true and R is correct reason of A.

**18. 3**

We have $\left(1 + \dfrac{1}{n}\right)^{n + x_n} = e$ $\qquad \dots \dots (1)$

Taking log on both sides of eq. (1), we get

$\Rightarrow (n + x_n) \ln\left(1 + \dfrac{1}{n}\right) = 1$

$\Rightarrow n + x_n = \dfrac{1}{\ln\left(1 + \dfrac{1}{n}\right)}$

$\Rightarrow x_n = \dfrac{1}{\ln\left(1 + \dfrac{1}{n}\right)} - n$ $\qquad \dots \dots (2)$

Let $\dfrac{n+1}{n} = u \Rightarrow nu = n + 1 \Rightarrow n = \dfrac{1}{u - 1}$

$\therefore \displaystyle \lim_{n \to \infty} x_n = \lim_{u \to 1} \left(\frac{1}{\ln u} - \frac{1}{u - 1}\right)$

$= \displaystyle \lim_{u \to 1} \frac{(u - 1) - \ln u}{(u - 1) \ln u} \quad \left(\frac{0}{0}\right) \text{ form}$

$= \displaystyle \lim_{u \to 1} \frac{1 - \dfrac{1}{u}}{\dfrac{u - 1}{u} + \ln u} = \lim_{u \to 1} \frac{\dfrac{1}{u^2}}{\dfrac{1}{u^2} + \dfrac{1}{u}} = \frac{1}{2}$

Thus, $A + B = 1 + 2 = 3$

**19. 5**

Let given limit $= L$, then

$$L = \lim_{n \to \infty} \left(\frac{1}{2n+1} + \frac{1}{2n+2} + \frac{1}{2n+3} + \dots + \frac{1}{4n}\right)$$

$$- \lim_{n \to \infty} \left(\frac{1}{2n+2} + \frac{1}{2n+4} + \frac{1}{2n+6} + \dots + \frac{1}{4n}\right)$$

$$= \lim_{n \to \infty} \left[\frac{1}{n} \sum_{r=1}^{2n} \frac{n}{2n+r} - \frac{1}{n} \sum_{r=1}^{2n} \frac{n}{2n+2r}\right]$$

$$= \lim_{n \to \infty} \left[\frac{1}{n} \sum_{r=1}^{2n} \frac{1}{2 + \dfrac{r}{n}} - \frac{1}{n} \sum_{r=1}^{n} \frac{1}{2 + 2(r/n)}\right]$$

$$= \int_0^2 \frac{1}{2+x}\,dx - \int_0^1 \frac{1}{2+2x}\,dx$$

$$= \big[\ln(2+x)\big]_0^2 - \frac{1}{2}\big[\ln(1+x)\big]_0^1$$

$$= \ln 4 - \ln 2 - \frac{1}{2}\ln 2 = \left(2 - \frac{3}{2}\right)\ln 2 = \frac{1}{2}\ln 2 = \frac{A}{B}\ln C$$

Hence least value of $A + B + C = 1 + 2 + 2 = 5$

**20.  3**

For limit to exist and equal to 1
coefficient of $x^4$ in denominator $= 0$
(as degree of x in $D^r > N^r$)
Now degree of x in $D^r$ is 2 and degree of x in $N^r$ is 3
$\therefore$  coefficient of $x^3$ in $N^r = 0$ otherwise $L \neq 1$ and will be
   infinity

and  $\dfrac{\text{coefficient of } x^2 \text{ in } N^r}{\text{coefficient of } x^2 \text{ in } D^r} = 1$

now  coefficient of $x^4$ in $D^r = 5a - b + 4c = 0$ ....(1)
coefficient of $x^3$ in $N^r = 2a + b - 3c = 0$              ....(2)

$\dfrac{\text{coefficientl of } x^2 \text{ in } N^r}{\text{coefficientl of } x^2 \text{ in } D^r} = 1 \Rightarrow \dfrac{-a + 5b - c}{2} = 1$

$\therefore$  $a - 5b + c + 2 = 0$                          ....(3)
Solving (1), (2) and (3) we get

$$a = \frac{-2}{109}, \ b = \frac{46}{109} \text{ and } c = \frac{14}{109}$$

$$\Rightarrow a + b + c = \frac{58}{109} = \frac{p}{q}$$

$$\Rightarrow \frac{q - p}{17} = \frac{109 - 58}{17} = 3.$$

**21.  1**

$$\underset{x \to \infty}{\text{Lim it}} \ \frac{\cot^{-1}\left(\dfrac{\log_a x}{x^a}\right)}{\sec^{-1}\left(\dfrac{a^x}{\log_a x}\right)} \ ; \quad \underset{x \to \infty}{as} \left(\frac{\log_a x}{x^a}\right) \to 0 \ \text{ and}$$

$$\left(\frac{a^x}{\log_a x}\right) \to \infty \ \text{(using L'Hospital rule)}$$

$$\therefore \ l = \frac{\pi/2}{\pi/2} = 1$$

**22.  6**

$$\lim_{x \to 0} \frac{x(1 + a\cos x) - b\sin x}{\{f(x)\}^3} = 1$$

$$\Rightarrow \lim_{x \to 0} \frac{x + ax\left\{1 - \dfrac{x^2}{2!} + \dfrac{x^4}{4!} - \ldots\right\} - b\left\{x - \dfrac{x^3}{3!} + \dfrac{x^5}{5!} - \ldots\right\}}{\{f(x)\}^3} = 1$$

$$\Rightarrow \lim_{x \to 0} \frac{\dfrac{1 + a - b}{x^2} + \left(-\dfrac{a}{2!} + \dfrac{b}{3!}\right) + x^2\left(\dfrac{a}{4!} - \dfrac{b}{5!}\right) + \ldots}{\left\{\dfrac{f(x)}{x}\right\}^3} = 1$$

$$\Rightarrow 1 + a - b = 0 \ \text{ and } \ -\frac{a}{2!} + \frac{b}{3!} = 1$$

$$\Rightarrow a = -\frac{5}{2} \ \text{ and } \ b = -\frac{3}{2}. \text{ Thus } b - 3a = 6$$

**1.** **(a)** $(H-h)\cot 15° = (H+h)\cot 45°$

or $H = \dfrac{h\,(\cot 15° + 1)}{(\cot 15° - 1)}$

Since, h = 2500 and

$\cot 15° = 2+\sqrt{3}$ , $H = 2500\sqrt{3}$

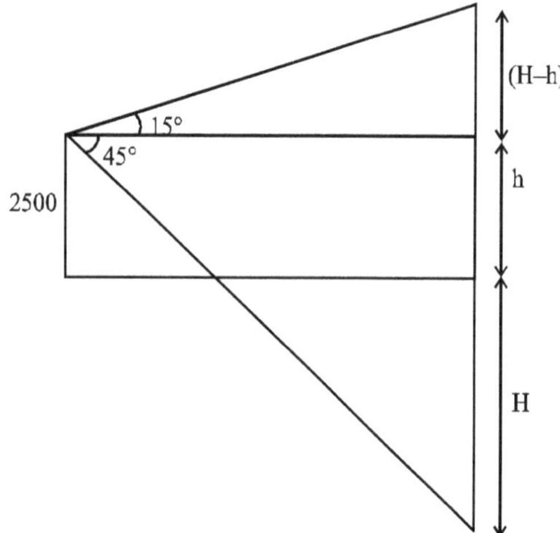


**2.** **(b)** Figure shows the tower OP standing at O, the midpoint of BC.
We are given $\angle PAO = 45° = \angle PBO = \angle PCO$.
Let the height of the tower be h meter.

Clearly, $\Delta\,PAO \cong \Delta\,PBO \cong \Delta\,PCO$ (AAS direction)

In $\Delta\,PAO$,

$\dfrac{OP}{OA} = \tan 45° \Rightarrow OA = h\cot 45° = h$ ........ (1)

In $\Delta\,BOP$,

$\dfrac{OP}{OB} = \tan 45° \Rightarrow OB = OP \Rightarrow OB = h$ ....... (2)

In $\Delta\,AOB$, $AO^2 + OB^2 = AB^2$

$\Rightarrow h^2 + h^2 = 100^2$   [From (1) and (2)]

$\Rightarrow h = 50\sqrt{2}$ m

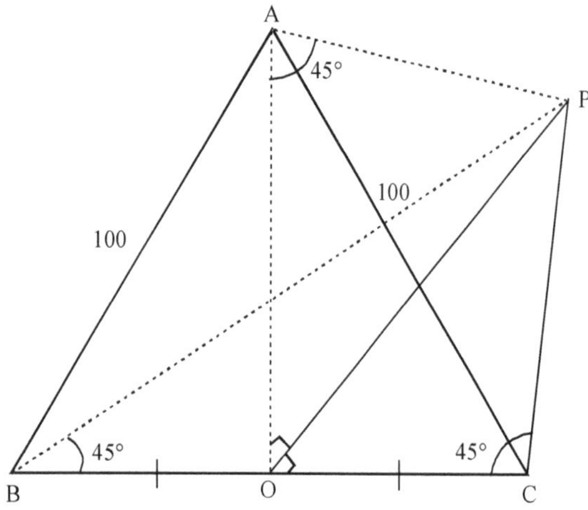


**3.** **(b)** $\dfrac{PQ}{x} = \tan\alpha,$   $\therefore PQ = x\tan\alpha$

Also $\dfrac{QR}{x} = \tan[90° - \beta - (90° - \alpha)] = \tan(\alpha - \beta)$

$\therefore QR = x\tan(\alpha - \beta)$
$h = PQ - QR = x\,[\tan\alpha - \tan(\alpha - \beta)]$

$\therefore x = \dfrac{h}{\tan\alpha - \tan(\alpha - \beta)}$

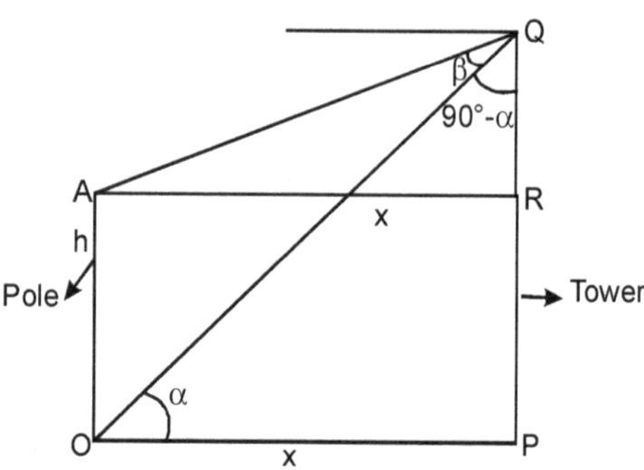


$\therefore PQ = \dfrac{h\tan\alpha}{\tan\alpha - \tan(\alpha - \beta)} = \dfrac{h.\dfrac{\sin\alpha}{\cos\alpha}}{\dfrac{\sin\alpha}{\cos\alpha} - \dfrac{\sin(\alpha - \beta)}{\cos(\alpha - \beta)}}$

$= h.\dfrac{\sin\alpha}{\sin\alpha}\dfrac{\cos\alpha.\cos(\alpha - \beta)}{\sin\alpha\cos(\alpha - \beta) - \cos\alpha\sin(\alpha - \beta)}$

$= \dfrac{h\cos(\alpha - \beta)\sin\alpha}{\sin(\alpha - (\alpha - \beta))} = \dfrac{h\sin\alpha\cos(\alpha - \beta)}{\sin\beta}$

**4.** **(a)** Let $\angle APC = \alpha, AC = CB = x$.

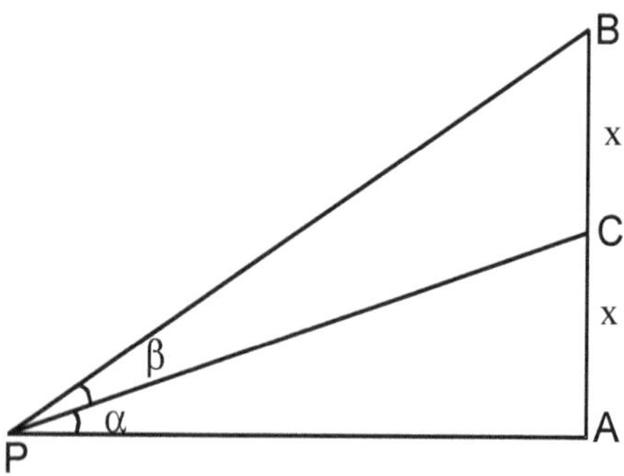


It is given that $AP = nAB$ or $AP = 2nx$

$\Rightarrow$ In $\Delta\,APC$, we have $\tan\alpha = \dfrac{AC}{AP}$

$\Rightarrow \tan\alpha = \dfrac{x}{2nx} = \dfrac{1}{2n}$   ...(1)

From $\Delta$ APB, we have

$$\tan(\alpha+\beta) = \frac{AB}{AP} \Rightarrow \tan(\alpha+\beta) = \frac{2x}{2nx}$$

$$\Rightarrow \tan(\alpha+\beta) = \frac{1}{n} \qquad \text{...(2)}$$

Now $\tan\beta = \tan[(\alpha+\beta) - \alpha]$

$$= \frac{\tan(\alpha+\beta) - \tan\alpha}{1 + \tan(\alpha+\beta)\tan\alpha}$$

$$\Rightarrow \tan\beta = \frac{1/n - 1/2n}{1 + 1/n.(1/2n)} = \frac{n}{2n^2 + 1}$$

$$[\text{By (1) and (2)}]$$

**5.** **(c)**

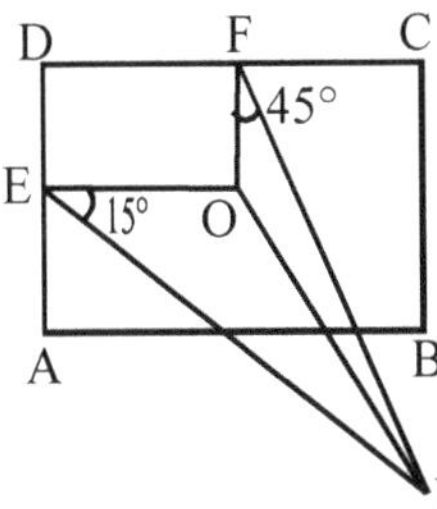

Let OP be the flagstaff of height 'h' standing at the centre O of the rectangular field ABCD subtending angles 15° and 45° at E the F, the mid points of the sides AD and DC of the field (see fig.), then

$OE = h \cot 15° = h(2 + \sqrt{3})$

and $OF = h \cot 45° = h$.

$$\Rightarrow EF = h\sqrt{1^2 + (2+\sqrt{3})^2} = 2h\sqrt{2+\sqrt{3}}$$

$$\Rightarrow 1200 = AC = 2EF = 4h\sqrt{(2+\sqrt{3})}$$

$$\Rightarrow h = \frac{300}{\sqrt{2+\sqrt{3}}} = 300\sqrt{2-\sqrt{3}}$$

**6.** **(b)**

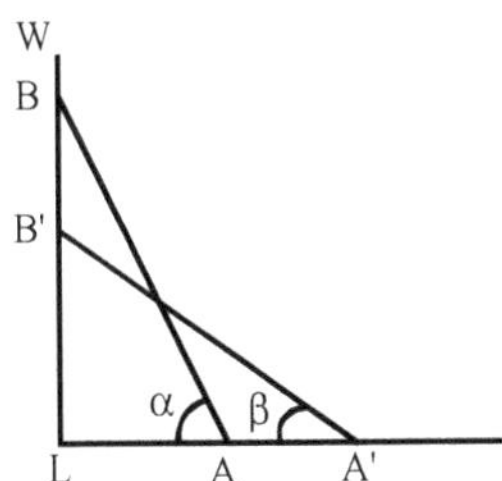

Let AB be the original position of the ladder. After sliding it takes the position A'B'. Let the length of the ladder be $\ell$.

Then AA'=a, BB'=b, AB = A'B'=$\ell$

In $\Delta$ABL, $\cos\alpha = \dfrac{AL}{\ell}$

In $\Delta$A'B'L, $\cos\beta = \dfrac{A'L}{\ell}$

$$\therefore \cos\beta - \cos\alpha = \frac{A'L - AL}{\ell} = \frac{a}{\ell} \qquad \text{...(1)}$$

Similarly,

$$\sin\alpha - \sin\beta = \frac{BL - B'L}{\ell} = \frac{b}{\ell} \qquad \text{...(2)}$$

$\therefore$ From (1) and (2),

$$\frac{\cos\beta - \cos\alpha}{\sin\alpha - \sin\beta} = \frac{a}{b} \Rightarrow a = b\tan\frac{\alpha+\beta}{2}$$

**7.** **(a)** Let C be the centre of the top of the circular tower. Draw QQ', PP', CC' and RR' perpendicular to the horizontal plane.

Since A is the point on the horizontal plane nearest to Q, hence A will be on the line Q'A, where Q'A $\perp$ QQ'.

$\angle$ QAQ' = 60° and $\angle$ PAP' = 45°

From right angled triangle QQ'A

$$\tan 60° = \frac{h}{AQ'} , \qquad \therefore \quad AQ' = \frac{h}{\sqrt{3}}$$

From right angle triangle,

$$PP'A \quad \tan 45° = \frac{h}{AP'} , \therefore AP' = h$$

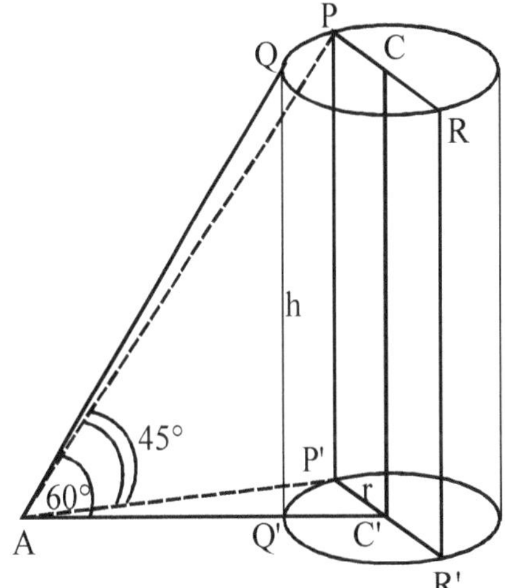

Now, $AC' = AQ' + Q'C' = \dfrac{h}{\sqrt{3}} + r$

C'P' = r and $\angle$AC'P' = 90°

From right angled triangle AC'P,

$AP'^2 = AC'^2 + C'P'^2$

$$\text{or,} \quad h^2 = \left(\frac{h}{\sqrt{3}} + r\right)^2 + r^2$$

$$\text{or,} \quad 2h^2 - 2\sqrt{3}hr - 6r^2 = 0$$

$$\text{or,} \quad h^2 - \sqrt{3}rh - 3r^2 = 0$$

$$\therefore \quad h = \frac{\sqrt{3}r \pm \sqrt{3r^2 - 4\times 1(-3r^2)}}{2}$$

$$\text{or,} \quad h = \frac{\sqrt{3}r[1\pm\sqrt{5}]}{2}, \quad \therefore \quad \frac{h}{r} = \frac{\sqrt{3}[1+\sqrt{5}]}{2}$$

**8.** **(a)** Let O be the centre of the square, OP the pole. Shadow of the pole OP is OQ. From question, BQ = y and CO = x. Then, BC = x + y.

Let OR ⊥ BC

$$\therefore OR = \frac{x+y}{2} \text{ and}$$

$$BR = \frac{x+y}{2}, \ RQ = \frac{x+y}{2} - y = \frac{x-y}{2}$$

Let h be the height of the pole.
From right angled triangle POQ,

$$\tan \alpha = \frac{h}{OQ}, \qquad \therefore \ OQ = h \cot \alpha$$

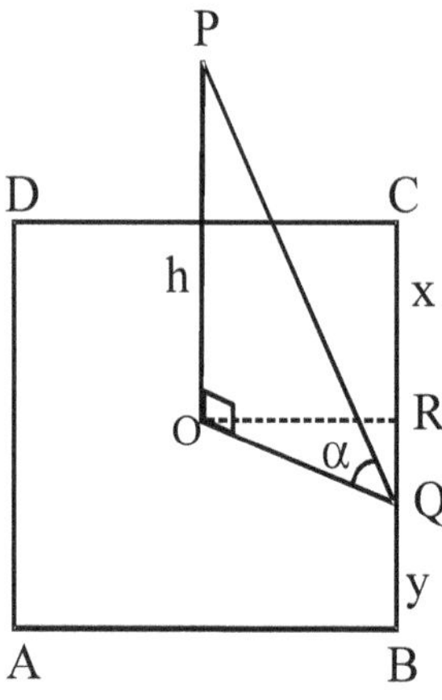

Now, from right angled triangle ORQ,
$$OQ^2 = OR^2 + RQ^2$$

or $h^2 \cot^2 \alpha = \left(\frac{x+y}{2}\right)^2 + \left(\frac{x-y}{2}\right)^2$

or $h^2 \cot^2 \alpha = \dfrac{2(x^2+y^2)}{4}$

$$\therefore \ h = \sqrt{\frac{x^2+y^2}{2}}.\tan \alpha$$

**9.** **(b)** Let ABC be an equilateral triangle with each side =a, AP be the pillar of height h. making an angle of 45° at C then

AC = h tan 45° = h ⟹ a = h.

If the elevation of the pillar at D is θ.
(see figure)

Then $\tan \theta = \dfrac{h}{AD} = \dfrac{h}{\sqrt{3}\,a/2} = \dfrac{2h}{\sqrt{3}\,a} = \dfrac{2}{\sqrt{3}}$

$$\Rightarrow \theta = \tan^{-1}\left(\frac{2}{\sqrt{3}}\right)$$

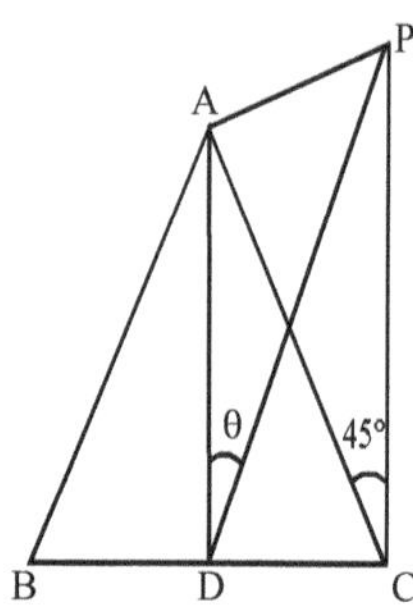

**10.** **(c)** Suppose the man is initially at O and observes the balloon at position A, and the final position of the man is C, when balloon is at B just above C.

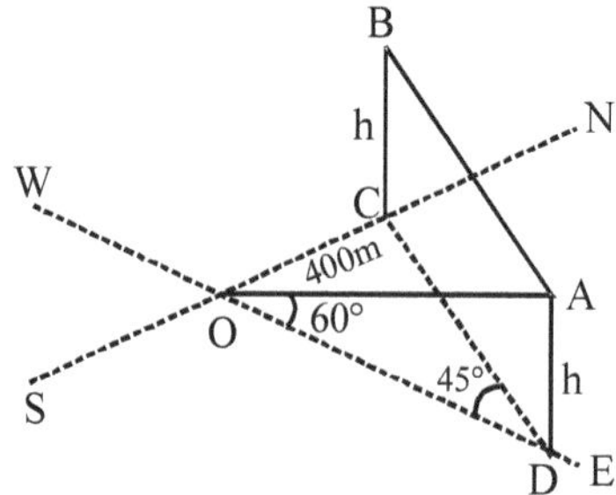

The balloon remains in the same horizontal plane. So the vertical height AD = the vertical height BC = h

∠OCD = ∠ODC = 45°     [∵ ∠EON = 90°]

OD = OC = 400 m

$$\tan 60° = \frac{AD}{OD} = \frac{h}{400} \Rightarrow h = 400\sqrt{3}$$

**11.** **(a)** In the △AOB, ∠AOB = 60°, and ∠OBA = ∠OAB (since OA = OB = AB radius of same circle). ∴ △AOB is an equilateral triangle. Let the height of tower is h m.

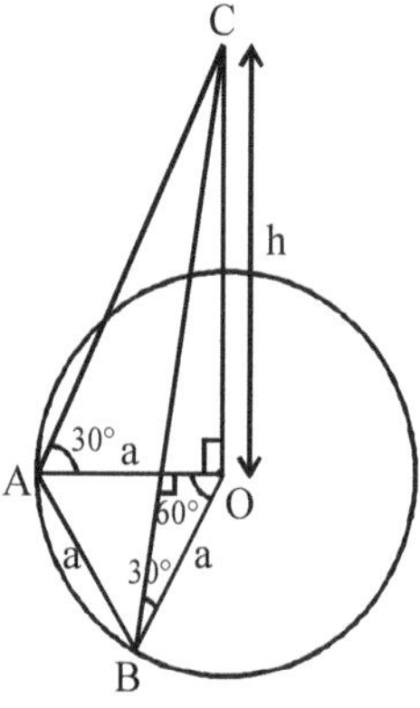

Given distance between two points A & B lie on boundary of circular park, subtends an angle of 60° at the foot of the tower AB i.e. AB = a. A tower OC stands at the centre of a circular park. Angle of elevation of the top of the tower from A and B is 30°. In △ OAX

$$\tan 30° = \frac{h}{a}$$

∴ ∠OBA = ∠AOB = ∠OAB = 60°

$$\Rightarrow \ \frac{1}{\sqrt{3}} = \frac{h}{a} \ \Rightarrow \ h = \frac{a}{\sqrt{3}}$$

**12. (a)**

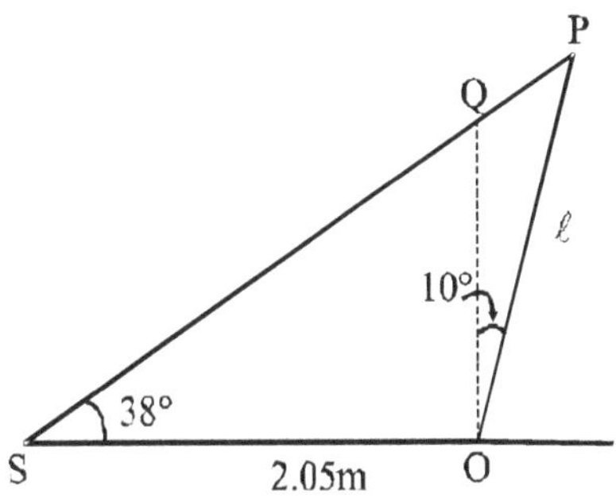


$$\frac{\sin 38°}{\ell} = \frac{\sin (SPO)}{2.05}$$

$$= \frac{\sin (180° - 38° - 90° - 10°)}{2.05}, \ \therefore \ \ell = \frac{2.05 \sin 38°}{\sin 42°}$$

**13. (c)** Let P be the vertex of the pyramid with a square base ABCD. At P the flag staff is PQ. Let the foot of the perpendicular from P to the ABCD is O. Also suppose L is a point on DC at which the shadow of the Flag staff touches the side DC.

Clearly,

PQ = 6 m, OP = 34 m

LC = 8m and DL = 56m

$$OC = \frac{AC}{2} = \frac{64}{2}\sqrt{2} = 32\sqrt{2}\,m \ \text{ and } \ \angle OCL = 45°$$

$$\therefore \ \cos OCL = \cos 45° = \frac{8^2 + (32\sqrt{2})^2 - OL^2}{2.8.32\sqrt{2}}$$

or, $64 + 32^2.2 - 16.32 = OL^2$

or, $OL^2 = 64\,(1 + 32 - 8) = 64.25$

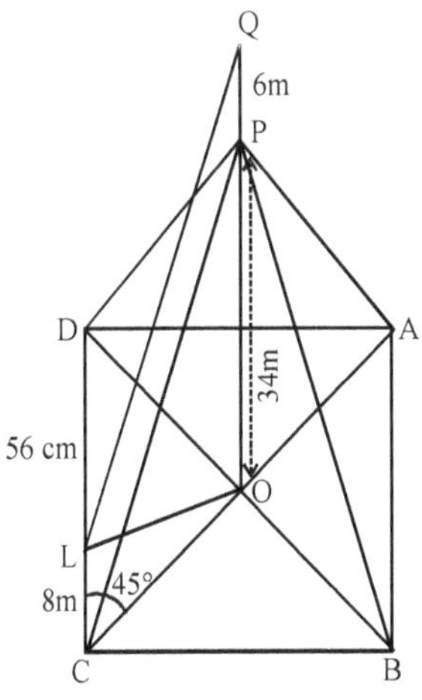


$\therefore \ OL = 40m$

Hence $\ \tan QLO = \dfrac{QO}{OL} = \dfrac{40}{40} = 1$

$\therefore \ \angle QLO = $ Sun's altitude $= 45°$

**14. (d)**

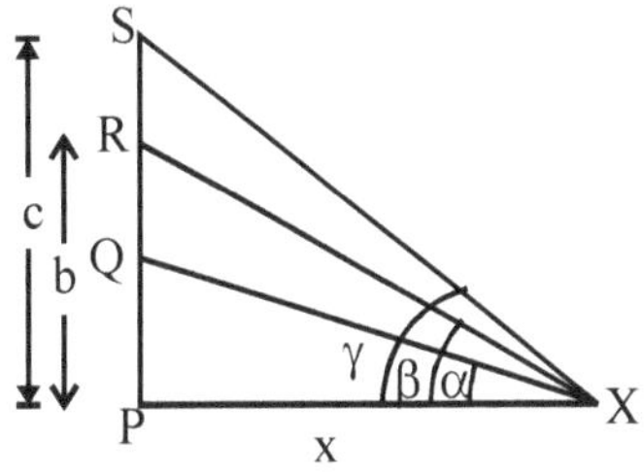


We have $\ \tan\alpha = \dfrac{a}{x}, \ \tan\beta = \dfrac{b}{x} \ \text{ and } \ \tan\gamma = \dfrac{c}{x}$

$\therefore \quad \alpha + \beta + \gamma = 180°$, so

$$\tan\alpha + \tan\beta + \tan\gamma = \tan\alpha \tan\beta \tan\gamma$$

or $\dfrac{a}{x} + \dfrac{b}{x} + \dfrac{c}{x} = \dfrac{a}{x}\cdot\dfrac{b}{x}\cdot\dfrac{c}{x}$

$\therefore \ x^2 = \dfrac{abc}{a+b+c}$

**15. (d)**

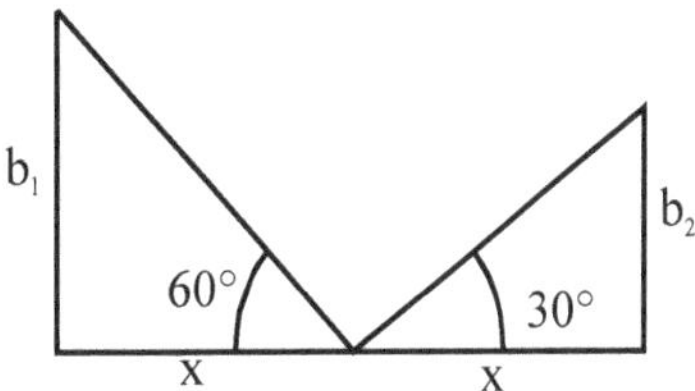


$$\tan 60° = \frac{b_1}{x} \ \text{ and } \ \tan 30° = \frac{b_2}{x}$$

$\therefore \quad \dfrac{b_1}{b_2} = \dfrac{\tan 60°}{\tan 30°} = \dfrac{3}{1}$

**16. (c)** We have

$$\angle CAD = 45°, \ \angle BAD = 30°, \ \angle CBH = 60° \ \text{(see figure)}$$

$$\Rightarrow \angle ACD = 45°, \ \angle BCH = 30°,$$

so that $\ \angle ACB = 15°$ and

$$\angle CAB = 45° - 30° = 15° \Rightarrow \angle ABC = 150°$$

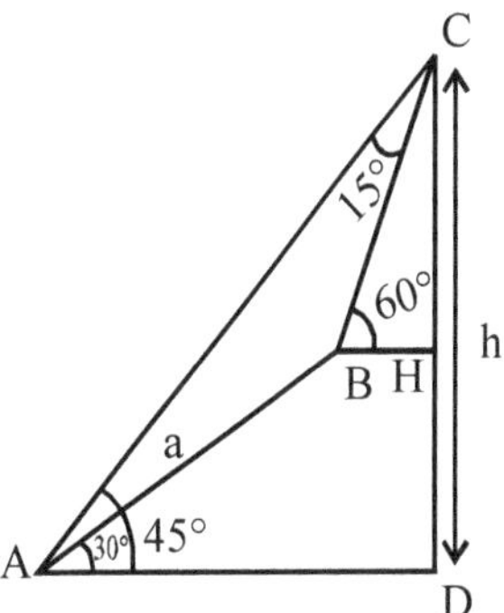


From $\triangle ADC$, $AC^2 = h^2 + h^2 = 2h^2 \quad [\because AD=CD=h]$

and from $\triangle ABC$,

$$\frac{AB}{\sin 15°} = \frac{AC}{\sin 150°} \Rightarrow \frac{a}{\sin 15°} = \frac{\sqrt{2}h}{\sin 150°}$$

$$\therefore a = \left(\frac{\sqrt{2}\sin 15°}{\sin 30°}\right)h, \quad [\because \sin 150° = \sin 30°]$$

$$= \frac{\sqrt{2}\left(\frac{\sqrt{3}-1}{2\sqrt{2}}\right)}{\frac{1}{2}}h = h\left(\sqrt{3}-1\right)$$

**17. (a)** Let OP be the tower of height h and PQ be the flag staff of height $l$.

$\angle PRO = 30°, \angle QRO = 60°$

Let OR = x

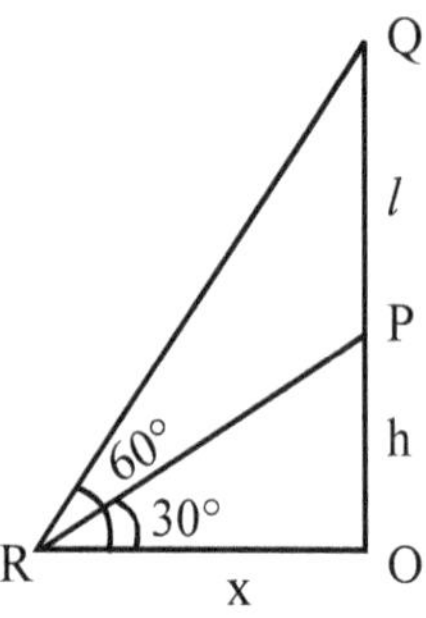


In $\Delta PRO$, $\dfrac{h}{x} = \tan 30° \Rightarrow \sqrt{3}h = x$ ...(1)

In $\Delta QRO$, $\dfrac{h+l}{x} = \tan 60° \Rightarrow \dfrac{h+l}{\sqrt{3}} = x$ ...(2)

From eqs. (i) and (ii), we have

$$\sqrt{3}h = \frac{h+l}{\sqrt{3}} \Rightarrow 3h = h+l \Rightarrow 2h = l$$

**18. (a)** Let P be the position of man's eye and O be the centre of the spherical ball and let PL and PM be the tangents to the spherical ball.

$\therefore \quad \angle MPL = \alpha \quad$ and $\quad \angle OPL = \dfrac{\alpha}{2}$

Draw OQ perpendicular to the horizontal line through P. Let OQ = h

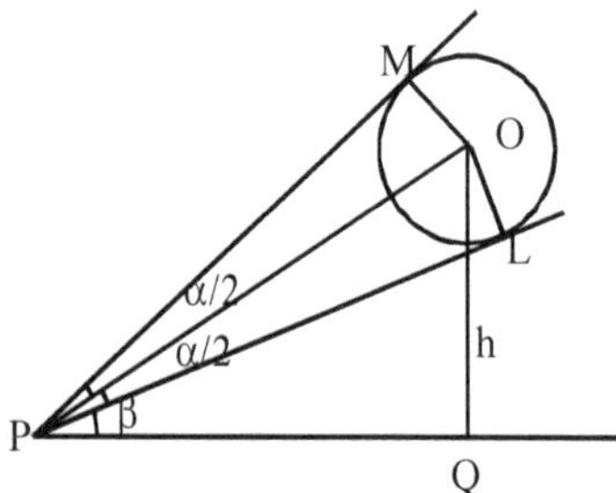


Since the diameter of the spherical ball is d

$\therefore \quad$ Its radius OL = $\dfrac{d}{2}$

In the rt. angled triangle OPL

$$\frac{OP}{OL} = \text{cosec}\,\frac{\alpha}{2}, \qquad \therefore OP = OL\,\text{cosec}\,\frac{\alpha}{2}$$

i.e., $OP = \dfrac{d}{2}\text{cosec}\,\dfrac{\alpha}{2}$

Now in rt. angled triangle PQO,

$$h = \frac{d}{2}\text{cosec}\,\frac{\alpha}{2}\sin\beta$$

**19. (a)** Let AB is the ladder, the man is at D, initially and the object is O. $\theta$ is the inclination of the ladder.

$$\sin\theta = \frac{DM}{\frac{1}{3}l} \Rightarrow DM = \frac{1}{3}l\sin\theta.$$

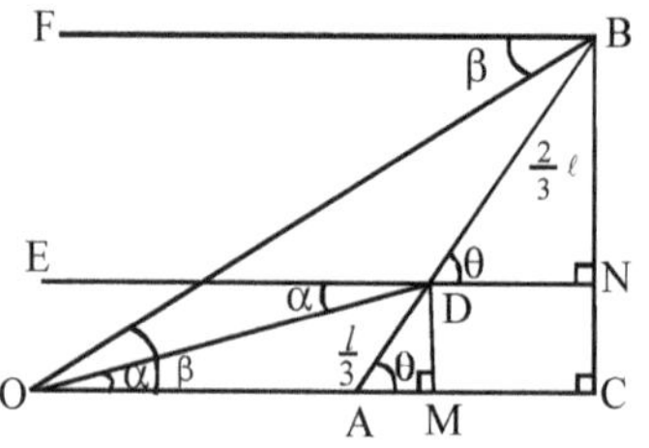


Again, $\sin\theta = \dfrac{BC}{l} \Rightarrow BC = l\sin\theta.$

$$\cot\alpha = \frac{OM}{DM} \Rightarrow OM = \frac{1}{3}l\sin\theta\cot\alpha.$$

Again $\cot\beta = \dfrac{OC}{BC} \Rightarrow OC = l\sin\theta\cot\beta$

$$MC = OC - OM = l\sin\theta\cot\beta - \frac{1}{3}l\sin\theta\cot\alpha$$

But $MC = DN = \dfrac{2}{3}l\cos\theta$

$$\therefore l\sin\theta\cot\beta - \frac{1}{3}l\sin\theta\cot\alpha = \frac{2}{3}l\cos\theta$$

$$\Rightarrow (3\cot\beta - \cot\alpha)\sin\theta = 2\cos\theta$$

$$\Rightarrow \cot\theta = \frac{3\cot\beta - \cot\alpha}{2}$$

**20. (0)**

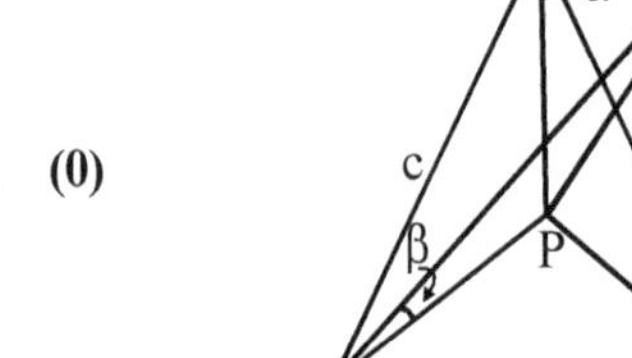


We have $\angle APB = \angle BPC = \angle CPA = 120°$. If h is the height of the tower at P subtending angles $\alpha$, $\beta$, $\gamma$ at A, B, C respectively (see fig.) then PA = h cot $\alpha$, PB = h cot $\beta$, PC = h cot $\gamma$,

From $\Delta PBC$, $\cos 120° = \dfrac{PB^2 + PC^2 - BC^2}{2PB.PC}$

$\Rightarrow -\dfrac{1}{2} = \dfrac{h^2 \cot^2 \beta + h^2 \cot^2 \gamma - a^2}{2h^2 \cot \beta \cot \gamma}$

$\Rightarrow a^2 = h^2 [\cot^2 \beta + \cot^2 \gamma + \cot \beta \cot \gamma]$

$\Rightarrow a^2 (\cot \beta - \cot \gamma) = h^2 [\cot^3 \beta - \cot^3 \gamma]$

Similarly $b^2 (\cot \gamma - \cot \alpha) = h^2 [\cot^3 \gamma - \cot^3 \alpha]$ and

$c^2 (\cot \alpha - \cot \beta) = h^2 (\cot^3 \alpha - \cot^3 \beta)$

On adding, we find the given expression is equal to zero.

**21. (1)** Let OP be the tower of height h. A be a point due south of it such that $\angle OAP = \alpha$ and B, a point due east of it such that $\angle OBP = \beta$. (see figure)

It is given that $\tan \alpha = 0.6 = \dfrac{3}{5}$ and $\tan \beta = 0.75 = \dfrac{3}{4}$

Now, $OA = h \cot \alpha = \dfrac{5h}{3}$ and $OB = h \cot \beta = \dfrac{4h}{3}$.

So that from right angled triangle AOB,

$(AB)^2 = (OA)^2 + (OB)^2 = \dfrac{41}{9} h^2$

$\Rightarrow AB = \lambda h$, where $\lambda^2 = 41/9$

$\therefore \dfrac{9}{41} \lambda^2 = 1$

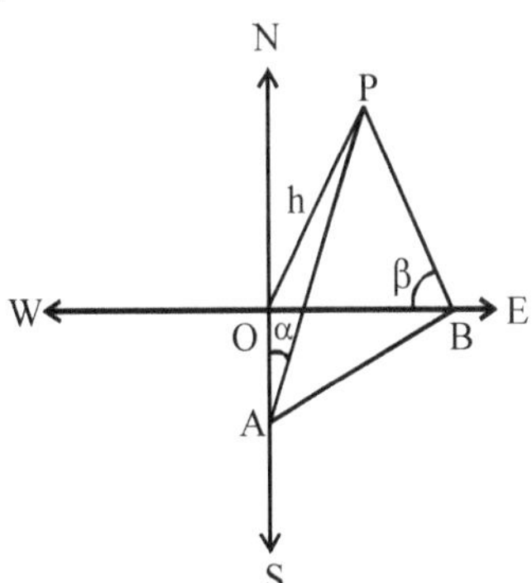

**22. (0)** Let h be the height of the tower PQ (fig) then
$h = AQ \tan \alpha = BQ$

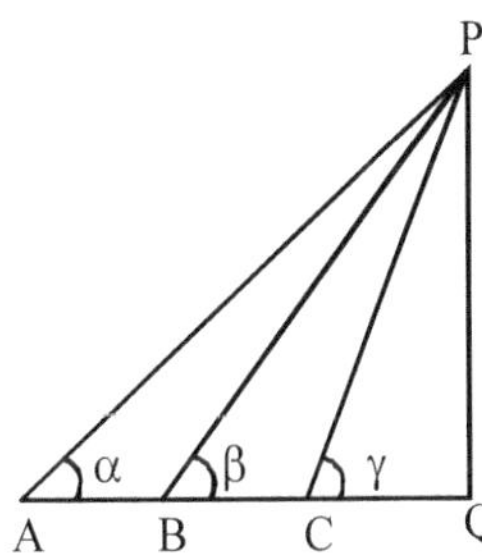

$\tan \beta = CQ \tan \gamma$

$\Rightarrow BC = BQ - CQ = h[\cot \beta - \cot \gamma]$,

$CA = h [\cot \alpha - \cot \gamma]$
and $AB = h (\cot \alpha - \cot \beta)$
So that BC $\cot \alpha$ – CA $\cot \beta$ + AB $\cot \gamma$

$= h[\cot \alpha(\cot \beta - \cot \gamma)$

$\quad - \cot \beta(\cot \alpha - \cot \gamma) + \cot \gamma(\cot \alpha - \cot \beta)] = 0$

**23. (9)** Clearly, one side AB of the rectangle $= 9 \cot 45° = 9$ m

Diagonal AC $= 9 \cot 30° = 9\sqrt{3}$ m

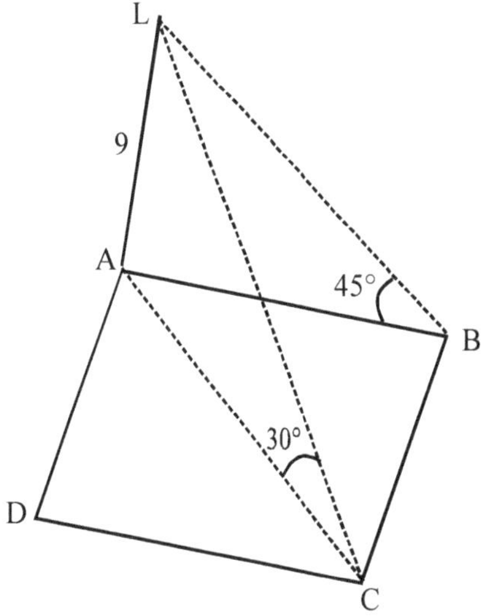

$\therefore$ the other side $= \sqrt{(9\sqrt{3})^2 - 9^2} = 9\sqrt{2}$ m .

So, area $= 9 \times 9\sqrt{2}$ m$^2 = 81\sqrt{2}$ m$^2$, $\therefore \dfrac{x}{9\sqrt{2}} = 9$ m$^2$

**24. (8)**

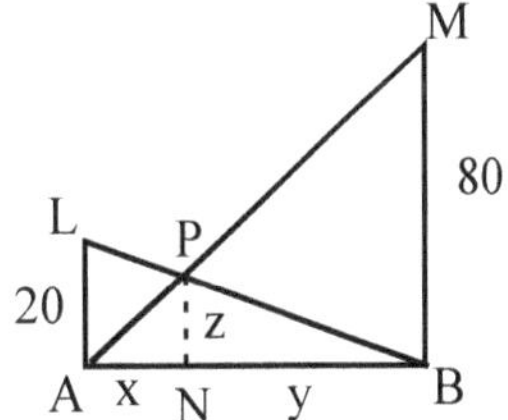

$\dfrac{20}{x+y} = \dfrac{z}{y} \Rightarrow y = \dfrac{z(x+y)}{20}$

$\dfrac{80}{x+y} = \dfrac{z}{x} \Rightarrow x = \dfrac{z(x+y)}{80}$

$\therefore x + y = (x+y)\left(\dfrac{z}{20} + \dfrac{z}{80}\right) \Rightarrow z = 16$

$\therefore \dfrac{Z}{2} = 8$

**1.** **(b)** Let P (n) be the statement given by :

$$P(n): \left(1+\frac{3}{1}\right)\left(1+\frac{5}{4}\right)\left(1+\frac{7}{9}\right)...\left(1+\frac{(2n+1)}{n^2}\right)$$

$$= (n+1)^2$$

**Step 1 :** For n = 1, we have

$$P(1): \left(1+\frac{2\times 1+1}{1^2}\right) = (1+1)^2$$

$$P(1): \left(1+\frac{3}{1}\right) = 2^2$$

P(1) : 4 = 4

Thus, P (1) is true.

**Step 2 :** Let us assume that P (k) is true. Then,

$$P(k): \left(1+\frac{3}{1}\right)\left(1+\frac{5}{4}\right)\left(1+\frac{7}{9}\right)....\left(1+\frac{2k+1}{k^2}\right) =$$

$$(k+1)^2 \quad ..... (1)$$

**Step 3 :** For n = k + 1, we have
P(k+1) :

$$\left(1+\frac{3}{1}\right)\left(1+\frac{5}{4}\right)\left(1+\frac{7}{9}\right)....\left(1+\frac{2k+1}{k^2}\right)\left(1+\frac{2(k+1)+1}{(k+1)^2}\right)$$

$$= (k+1+1)^2$$

$$P(k+1): (k+1)^2\left[1+\frac{2k+3}{(k+1)^2}\right] = (k+2)^2$$

$$P(k+1): (k+1)^2\left[\frac{(k+1)^2+2k+3}{(k+1)^2}\right]$$

$$P(k+1): (k^2+2k+1+2k+3) = (k+2)^2$$
$$P(k+1): (k+2)^2 = (k+2)^2$$
Therefore, P (k + 1) is true.
Thus P (k) is true $\Rightarrow$ P (k + 1) is true
Hence, by the principle of mathematical induction P (n)
is true for all n $\in$ N

**2.** **(a)** Let P(n) be the statement given by

$$P(n): 1+3+3^2+.....+3^{n-1} = \frac{(3^n-1)}{2}$$

**Step 1 :** For n = 1, we have

$$P(1): 3^{1-1} = \frac{3^1-1}{2}$$

P (1) : 1 = 1
Thus, P (1) is true.
**Step 2 :** For n = k, assume that P (k) is true.

Then $1+3+3^2+.....+3^{k-1} = \frac{3^k-1}{2}$

**Step 3 :** For n = k + 1, we have to show that

$$1+3+3^2+.....+3^{k-1}+3^{k+1-1} = \frac{3^{k+1}-1}{2}$$

Now, L.H.S. $= 1+3+3^2+.....+3^{k-1}+3^{k+1-1}$

$$= \frac{3^k-1}{2}+3^{k+1-1}$$

$$= \frac{3^k-1}{2}+3^k = \frac{3^k-1+2.3^k}{2} = \frac{3^k(1+2)-1}{2}$$

$$= \frac{3.3^k-1}{2} = \frac{3^{k+1}-1}{2}$$

Therefore, P (k + 1) is true.
Thus, P (k) is true $\Rightarrow$ P (k + 1) is true for all n $\in$ N.

**3.** **(d)** Unless we prove P(1) is true, nothing can be said.

**4.** **(b)** Let $P(n): \left(\frac{n+1}{2}\right)^n \geq n!$

$P(1): 1^1 \geq 1!$ TRUE

$P(2): \left(\frac{3}{2}\right)^2 \geq 2!$ TRUE

$P(3): 2^3 \geq 3!$ TRUE

$P(4): \left(\frac{5}{2}\right)^4 \geq 4!$ TRUE

$\therefore$ The given statement is true $\forall n \geq 1$

**5.** **(a)** Let

$$U_n = \frac{1}{n}+\frac{1}{n+1}+\frac{1}{n+2}+....+\frac{1}{2n-1}$$

$$V_n = 1-\frac{1}{2}+\frac{1}{3}-\frac{1}{4}+.....+\frac{1}{2n-1}$$

Let T(n) be the statement $U_n = V_n$
Then T(1) is true. For $U_1 = 1$ and $V_1 = 1$, so that $U_1 = V_1$
Let T(k) be true for some positive integer K. Now,

$$U_{k+1} - U_k = \left[\frac{1}{k+1}+\frac{1}{k+2}+....+\frac{1}{2k+1}\right] -$$

$$\left[\frac{1}{k}+\frac{1}{k+1}+....+\frac{1}{2k-1}\right] = \frac{1}{2k}+\frac{1}{2k+1}-\frac{1}{k} =$$

$$-\frac{1}{2k}+\frac{1}{2k+1} \qquad ...(i)$$

Also,

$$V_{k+1} - V_k = \left[1 - \frac{1}{2} + \frac{1}{3} - \ldots\ldots + \frac{1}{2k+1}\right]$$

$$-\left[1 - \frac{1}{2} + \frac{1}{3} - \ldots.. + \frac{1}{2k-1}\right] = -\frac{1}{2k} + \frac{1}{2k+1} \quad \ldots(ii)$$

From (i) and (ii), we find that

$U_{k+1} - U_k = V_{k+1} - V_k$

Since, $U_k = V_k$, therefore, it follows that $U_{k+1} = V_{k+1}$

$\therefore$ T(n) is true for all $n \in \mathbf{N}$.

**6. (b)** When k = 1, LHS = 1 but RHS = 1 + 10 = 11

$\therefore$ T(1) is not true

Let T(k) is true.

That is $1 + 3 + 5 + \ldots.. + (2k-1) = k^2 + 10$

Now, $1 + 3 + 5 + \ldots.. + (2k-1) + (2k+1)$

$= k^2 + 10 + 2k + 1 = (k+1)^2 + 10$

$\therefore$ T(k+1) is true.

That is T(k) is true $\Rightarrow$ T(k+1) is true.

But T(n) is not true for all $n \in \mathbf{N}$, as T(1) is not true.

**7. (b)** $S(k) = 1 + 3 + 5 + \ldots + (2k-1) = 3 + k^2$

$S(1) = 1 = 3 + 1$, which is not true

$\because$ S(1) is not true.

$\therefore$ P.M.I cannot be applied

Let S(k) is true, i.e. $1 + 3 + 5 \ldots. + (2k-1) = 3 + k^2$

$\Rightarrow 1 + 3 + 5 \ldots. + (2k-1) + 2k + 1$

$= 3 + k^2 + 2k + 1 = 3 + (k+1)^2$,

$\therefore S(k) \Rightarrow S(k+1)$

**8. (d)** $P(n) = n^2 + n$. It is always odd (statement) but square of any odd number is always odd and also, sum of two odd number is always even. So for no any 'n' for which this statement is true.

**9. (c)** Putting n = 1 in $11^{n+2} + 12^{2n+1}$

we get, $11^{1+2} + 12^{2 \times 1+1} = 11^3 + 12^3 = 3059$, which is divisible by 133.

**10. (b)** $n! > 2^{n-1}$ is not true for n = 1 and n = 2

$(\because 1! = 2^0$ and $2! = 2^{2-1})$

For $n = 3, n! = 3! = 6$

and $2^{n-1} = 2^{3-1} = 4$

$\therefore$ inequality is true for n = 3

Also, if it is true for n = m > 2

i.e., $m! > 2^{m-1}$,

then $(m+1)! = (m+1)m! > (m+1)2^{m-1} > 2.2^{m-1}$

$\Rightarrow (m+1)! > 2^{m+1-1} \quad (\because m > 2, \therefore m+1 > 3)$

$\therefore$ Result is true by principle of induction for all $n \geq 3$ i.e., for all n > 2.

**11. (b)** P(3) is true

Assume P(k) is true $\Rightarrow$ P(k + 1) is true means if P(3) is true $\Rightarrow$ P(4) is true $\Rightarrow$ P(5) is true and so on. So statement is true for all $n \geq 3$.

**12. (a)** Given $u_1 = 1, u_2 = 1, u_{n+2} = u_{n+1} + u_n, n \geq 1$

$$u_n = \frac{1}{\sqrt{5}}\left[\left(\frac{1+\sqrt{5}}{2}\right)^n - \left(\frac{1-\sqrt{5}}{2}\right)^n\right]$$

$$\therefore \quad u_2 = \frac{1}{\sqrt{5}}\left[\left(\frac{1+\sqrt{5}}{2}\right)^2 - \left(\frac{1-\sqrt{5}}{2}\right)^2\right]$$

$$= \frac{1}{\sqrt{5}}\left(\frac{1+\sqrt{5}}{2} + \frac{1-\sqrt{5}}{2}\right)\left(\frac{1+\sqrt{5}}{2} - \frac{1-\sqrt{5}}{2}\right)$$

$$= \frac{1}{\sqrt{5}}[1.\sqrt{5}] = 1$$

$\therefore$ $u_n$ is true for $n = 2$ (as given $u_2 = 1$).

Let it be true for $n \geq k > 2$ then

$$u_k = \frac{1}{\sqrt{5}}\left[\left(\frac{1+\sqrt{5}}{2}\right)^k - \left(\frac{1-\sqrt{5}}{2}\right)^k\right]$$

.... (Induction Hypothesis)

Consider $U_{k+1} = u_k + u_{k-1}$ [Using $u_{n+2} = u_{n+1} + u_n$]

$$\therefore \quad u_{k+1} = \frac{1}{\sqrt{5}}\left[\left(\frac{1+\sqrt{5}}{2}\right)^k - \left(\frac{1-\sqrt{5}}{2}\right)^k\right]$$

$$+ \frac{1}{\sqrt{5}}\left[\left(\frac{1+\sqrt{5}}{2}\right)^{k-1} - \left(\frac{1-\sqrt{5}}{2}\right)^{k-1}\right]$$

$$= \frac{1}{\sqrt{5}}\left[\left(\frac{1+\sqrt{5}}{2}\right)^k + \left(\frac{1+\sqrt{5}}{2}\right)^{k-1}\right]$$

$$- \frac{1}{\sqrt{5}}\left[\left(\frac{1-\sqrt{5}}{2}\right)^k + \left(\frac{1-\sqrt{5}}{2}\right)^{k-1}\right]$$

$$= \frac{1}{\sqrt{5}}\left[\left(\frac{1+\sqrt{5}}{2}\right)^{k-1}\left(\frac{1+\sqrt{5}}{2} + 1\right)\right.$$

$$\left. - \left(\frac{1-\sqrt{5}}{2}\right)^{k-1}\left\{\frac{1-\sqrt{5}}{2} + 1\right\}\right]$$

$$= \frac{1}{\sqrt{5}}\left[\left(\frac{1+\sqrt{5}}{2}\right)^{k-1}\left\{\frac{6+2\sqrt{5}}{4}\right\}\right.$$

$$\left. - \left(\frac{1-\sqrt{5}}{2}\right)^{k-1}\left\{\frac{6-2\sqrt{5}}{4}\right\}\right]$$

$$= \frac{1}{\sqrt{5}}\left[\left(\frac{1+\sqrt{5}}{2}\right)^{k-1}\left\{\frac{(\sqrt{5})^2 + 1^2 + 2\sqrt{5}}{4}\right\}\right.$$

$$\left. - \left(\frac{1-\sqrt{5}}{2}\right)^{k-1}\left\{\frac{1^2 + (\sqrt{5})^2 - 2\sqrt{5}}{4}\right\}\right]$$

$$= \frac{1}{\sqrt{5}}\left[\left(\frac{1+\sqrt{5}}{2}\right)^{k+1} - \left(\frac{1-\sqrt{5}}{2}\right)^{k+1}\right]$$

$\therefore$ $u_{k+1}$ is also true.

Hence by principle of mathematical induction $u_n$ is true $\forall\ n \geq 1$

**13.** **(a)** It can be proved with the help of mathematical induction that $\dfrac{n}{2} < a(n) \le n$.

$\therefore \dfrac{200}{2} < a(200) \Rightarrow a(200) > 100$ and $a(100) \le 100$.

**14.** **(d)** No conclusion can be drawn on the basis of principle of mathematical induction as P(1) is not given to be true.

**15.** **(a,b)** Since $\alpha, \beta$ are the roots of $x^2 - (p+1)x + 1 = 0$

$\therefore \quad \alpha + \beta = p+1; \ \alpha\beta = 1$

Here $p \ge 3$ and $p \in Z$

(a) To prove that $\alpha^n + \beta^n$ is an integer.

Let us consider the statement, "$\alpha^n + \beta^n$ is an integer."

Then for $n = 1, \alpha + \beta = p+1$ which is an integer, $p$ being an integer.

$\therefore$ Statement is true for $n = 1$

Let the statement be true for $n \le k$, i.e., $\alpha^k + \beta^k$ is an integer

Then ,

$\alpha^{k+1} + \beta^{k+1} = \alpha^k . \alpha + \beta^k . \beta$

$= \ \alpha(\alpha^k + \beta^k) + \beta(\alpha^k + \beta^k) - \alpha\beta^k - \alpha^k\beta$

$= \ (\alpha + \beta)(\alpha^k + \beta^k) - \alpha\beta(\alpha^{k-1} + \beta^{k-1}$

$= \ (\alpha + \beta)(\alpha^k + \beta^k) - (\alpha^{k-1} + \beta^{k-1})$ .....(1)

$\qquad\qquad\qquad\qquad$ [as $\alpha\beta = 1$]

$= \ $ difference of two integers

$= \ $ some integral value

$\Rightarrow \ $ Statement is true for $n = k+1$.

$\therefore$ By the principle of mathematical induction the given statement is true $\forall \, n \in N$.

(b) Let $R_n$ be the remainder of $\alpha^n + \beta^n$ when divided by $p$ where $0 \le R_n \le p-1$

Since $\alpha + \beta = p+1 \quad \therefore \quad R_1 = 1$

Also $\alpha^2 + \beta^2 = (\alpha + \beta)^2 - 2\alpha\beta = (p+1)^2 - 2$

$\qquad\qquad\qquad = p^2 + 2p - 1 = p(p+1) + p - 1$

$\therefore \quad R_2 = p - 1$

Also from equation (1) of previous part (i), we have

$\alpha^{n+1} + \beta^{n+1} = (p+1)(\alpha^n + \beta^n) - (\alpha^{n-1} + \beta^{n-1})$

$= p(\alpha^n + \beta^n) + (\alpha^n + \beta^n) - (\alpha^{n-1} + \beta^{n-1})$

$\Rightarrow \ R_{n+1}$ is the remainder of $R_n - R_{n-1}$ when divided by $p$

$\therefore \ $ We observe that $R_2 - R_1 = p - 1 - 1$

$\therefore \ R_3 = p - 2$

Similarly, $R_4$ is the remainder when $R_3 - R_2$ is divided by $p$ where

$R_3 - R_2 = p - 2 - p + 1 = -1 = -p + (p-1) \therefore \quad R_4 = p-1$

$R_4 - R_3 = p - 1 - p + 1 = 1 \qquad\qquad \therefore \quad R_5 = 1$

$R_5 - R_4 = 1 - p + 1 = -p + 2 \qquad\quad \therefore \quad R_6 = p - 2$

It is evident for above that the remainder is either 1 or $p-1$ or $p-2$.

Since $p \ge 3$, so none is divisible by $p$.

**16.** **(a, b)** Let $P(n) : \dfrac{(2n)!}{2^{2n}(n!)^2} \le \dfrac{1}{(3n+1)^{1/2}}$

For $n = 1, \ P(1) : \dfrac{2!}{2^2 (1!)^2} \le \dfrac{1}{(3+1)^{1/2}}$

$\Rightarrow \quad \dfrac{1}{4} \le \dfrac{1}{2}$

$\Rightarrow \quad \dfrac{1}{2} \le \dfrac{1}{2}$ which is true for $n = 1$

Assume that P(k) is true, then

$P(k) : \dfrac{(2k)!}{2^{2k}(k!)^2} \le \dfrac{1}{(3k+1)^{1/2}}$ ....(1)

For $n = k+1$,

$\dfrac{[2(k+1)]!}{2^{2(k+1)}[(k+1)!]^2} = \dfrac{(2k+2)!}{2^{2k+2}[(k+1)!]^2}$

$= \ \dfrac{(2k+2)(2k+1)(2k)!}{4.2^{2k}(k+1)^2(k!)^2}$

$\le \ \dfrac{(2k+2)\,(2k+1)}{4(k+1)^2} . \dfrac{1}{(3k+1)^{1/2}}$

[Using Induction hypothesis (1)]

$= \ \dfrac{(2k+1)}{2.(k+1)\,(3k+1)^{1/2}}$

Thus, $\dfrac{[2(k+1)]!}{2^{2(k+1)}\,[(k+1)!]^2} \le \dfrac{(2k+1)}{2\,(k+1)\,(3k+1)^{1/2}}$ ....(2)

In order to prove $P(k+1)$, it is sufficient to prove that

$\dfrac{(2k+1)}{2\,(k+1)\,(3k+1)^{1/2}} \le \dfrac{1}{(3k+4)^{1/2}}$ ....(3)

Squaring eq. (3), we get

$\dfrac{(2k+1)^2}{4(k+1)^2(3k+1)} \le \dfrac{1}{3k+4}$

$\Rightarrow \ (2k+1)^2(3k+4) - 4(k+1)^2(3k+1) \le 0$

$\Rightarrow \ (4k^2 + 4k + 1)(3k+4) - 4(k^2 + 2k + 1)(3k+1) \le 0$

$\Rightarrow (12k^3 + 28k^2 + 19k + 4) - (12k^3 + 28k^2 + 20k + 4) \le 0$

$\Rightarrow \ -k \ \le 0$

which is true.

Hence from (2) and (3), we get

$\dfrac{(2k+2)!}{2^{2k+2}\,[(k+1)!]^2} \le \dfrac{1}{(3k+4)^{1/2}}$

Hence the above inequation is true for $n = k+1$ and by the principle of induction it is true for all $n \in N$.

**17.** **(a,b,c,)** $P(n) : 2 + 4 + 6 + \ldots\ldots + 2n = n(n+1) + 2$

$P(3) : 2 + 4 + 6 = 3(3+1) + 2$, which is not true.

Hence P(n) is not true for $n \ge 1, \ n \ge 2$ or $n \ge 3$

**18.** **(a,c)** $P(1) : 1 \times 1! = (1+1)! - 1$

$\Rightarrow P(1) : 1 = 1$, which is true

Let $P(k) : 1 \times 1! + 2 \times 2! + 3 \times 3! + ... + k \times k! = (k+1)! - 1$

Now $P(k+1) : (k+1)! - 1 + (k+1)(k+1)! = (k+2)! - 1$

$\Rightarrow P(k+1) : (k+1)!(1+k+1) - 1 = (k+2)! - 1$

$\Rightarrow P(k+1) : (k+2)(k+1)! - 1 = (k+2)! - 1$

$\Rightarrow P(k+1) : (k+2)! - 1 = (k+2)! - 1$, which is true

Hence, the given statement is true for all $n \in N$.

**19.** **(A) – p; B – p; (C) – s; (D) – r.**

(A)   Let $2^{n+1} - 1 = k$

$N = 2^n k$

Factors of N are $1, 2, 2^2 ......... 2^n, k, 2k, 2^2 k ........ 2^n k$

Sum of all factors $= (1+k)(1+2+2^2 ....... 2^n)$

$= (1+k)(2^{n+1} - 1)$

$= 2^{n+1}(2^{n+1} - 1) = 2 . 2^n (2^{n+1} - 1) = 2N$

(B)   $\text{sum} = \left(1 + \frac{1}{2} + \frac{1}{2^2} + ... \frac{1}{2^n}\right) + \left(\frac{1}{k} + \frac{2}{2k} + \frac{1}{2^2 k} + ... + \frac{1}{2^n k}\right)$

$= \left(1 + \frac{1}{k}\right) \frac{\left(2^{n+1} - 1\right)}{2^{n+1}} \times 2$

(C)   $x^3 - 8x^2 + 20x - 13 = (x-1)(x^2 - 7x + 13)$

Three positive integral value of x is possible i.e., $x = 2, 3, 4$

(D) Let $x_1, x_2$ are two positive integral solutions

$x_1 + x_2 = -k$

$x_1 x_2 = p$

p is prime so either $x_1 = 1$ for $x_2 = 1$ i.e. roots of equations are 1 and p.

$\Rightarrow 1 + p = -k \Rightarrow k + p = -1$

**20.** **(2)** $N = 2^{10} \cdot 6^{20}$

$= 1024 [(7-1)^{20}] = 1024 [(1-7)^{20}]$

$= 1024 [^{20}C_0 - {}^{20}C_1 \cdot 7 + {}^{20}C_2 \, 7^2 + .......]$

$= 1024 - 7 \, I$ where I is an integer $\Rightarrow$ remainder is 2

**21.** **(5)** Putting $n = 1$ in $7^{2n} + 2^{3n-3} . 3^{n-1}$

then, $7^{2 \times 1} + 2^{3 \times 1 - 3} . 3^{1-1}$

$= 7^2 + 2^0 . 3^0 = 49 + 1 = 50$      ...(i)

Also, $n = 2$

$7^{2 \times 2} + 2^{3 \times 2 - 3} . 3^{2-1} = 2401 + 24 = 2425$      ... (ii)

From (i) and (ii), $(7^{2n} + 2^{3n-3} . 3^{n-1})$ is always divisible by 25.

Hence $\frac{1}{5}(7^{2n} + 2^{3n-3} . 3^{n-1})$ is always divisible by 5.

**22.** **(9)** $10^n + 3(4^{n+2}) + 5$

Taking $n = 2$, $10^n + 3(4^{n+2}) + 5 = 10^2 + 3 \times 4^4 + 5$

$= 100 + 768 + 5 = 873$

Therefore, this is divisible by 9.

**23.** **(2)** Let $P(n) = 2 . 4^{2n+1} + 3^{3n+1}$

Then $P(1) = 2 . 4^3 + 3^4 = 209$, which is divisible by 11 but not divisible by 2, 7 or 27.

Further, let $P(k) = 2 . 4^{2k+1} + 3^{3k+1}$ is divisible by 11, that is,

$2 . 4^{2k+1} + 3^{3k+1} = 11q$ for some integer q. Now

$P(k+1) = 2 . 4^{2k+3} + 3^{3k+4}$

$= 2 . 4^{2k+1} . 4^2 + 3^{3k+1} . 3^3$

$= 16 . 2 . 4^{2k+1} + 27 . 3^{3k+1}$

$= 16 . 2 . 4^{2k+1} + (16 + 11) . 3^{3k+1}$

$= 16 [2 . 4^{2k+1} + 3^{3k+1}] + 11 . 3^{3k+1}$

$= 16 . 11q + 11 . 3^{3k+1} = 11(16q + 3^{3k+1}) = 11m$

where $m = 16q + 3^{3k+1}$ is another integer.

$\therefore P(k+1)$ is divisible by 11.

$\therefore P(n) = 2 . 4^{2n+1} + 3^{3n+1}$ is divisible by 11 for all $n \in \mathbf{N}$.

Hence $\frac{2}{11}(2.4^{2n+1} + 3^{n+1})$ is divisible by 2 for all $n \in N$

**24.** **(2)** $P(1)$ is not true. For $n = 2$, $P(2)$ is $2! < \left(\frac{3}{2}\right)^2$

i.e. $2 < \frac{9}{4}$ which is true.

Hence the smallest integer for which $n! < \left(\frac{n+1}{2}\right)^n$ is true for $n = 2$.

Let $P(k)$ be true for some, $k \geq 2$,

i.e., $k! < \left(\frac{k+1}{2}\right)^k$      .....(1)

Now $(k+1)! = (k+1)k! < (k+1)\left(\frac{k+1}{2}\right)^k$

$= \frac{(k+1)^{k+1}}{2^k}$      ....(2) [From (1)]

Now, $\left(\frac{k+2}{2}\right)^{k+1} - \frac{(k+1)^{k+1}}{2^k} = \frac{(k+1)^{k+1}}{2^k}\left[\frac{1}{2}\left(\frac{k+2}{k+1}\right)^{k+1} - 1\right]$

$= \frac{(k+1)^{k+1}}{2^k}\left[\frac{1}{2}\left\{1 + \frac{1}{k+1}\right\}^{k+1} - 1\right]$

$= \frac{(k+1)^{k+1}}{2^k}\left[\frac{1}{2}\left\{1 + (k+1)\frac{1}{k+1} + \frac{(k+1)k}{2!}\frac{1}{(k+1)^2} + ...\right\} - 1\right]$

(using binomial theorem)

$= \frac{(k+1)^{k+1}}{2^{k+1}}\left[\frac{(k+1)k}{2!}\frac{1}{(k+1)^2} + .......\right] > 0$

$\therefore \frac{(k+1)^{k+1}}{2^k} < \left(\frac{k+2}{2}\right)^{k+1}$      Substituting in (2),

we get $(k+1)! < \left[\frac{k+2}{2}\right]^{k+1} = \left[\frac{(k+1)+1}{2}\right]^{k+1}$

$\therefore P(k+1)$ is true.      $\therefore P(n)$ is true for all $n \geq 2$.

**1.** **(c).** Minimum distance of $(2, 3)$ from the line $3x + 4y = 5$ is

$$\frac{|6+12-5|}{\sqrt{3^2+4^2}} = 2.6$$

**2.** **(b)** The point is $((1-t)x_1 + tx_2, (1-t)y_1 + ty_2)$

$\because\ 1 - t + t = 1$, so above point dividing join of $(x_1, y_1)$

and $(x_2, y_2)$ internally, if $(1-t)t > 0 \Rightarrow 0 < t < 1$

**3.** **(d)** Distance $= \sqrt{a^2(\cos\alpha - \cos\beta)^2 + a^2(\sin\alpha - \sin\beta)^2}$

$$= a\sqrt{\begin{array}{c} \sin^2\alpha + \cos^2\alpha + \cos^2\beta + \sin^2\beta \\ -2\cos\alpha\cos\beta - 2\sin\alpha\sin\beta \end{array}}$$

$$= a\sqrt{2\{1 - \cos(\alpha - \beta)\}} = 2a\sin\left(\frac{\alpha-\beta}{2}\right)$$

**Trick:** Put $a = 1$, $\alpha = \dfrac{\pi}{2}$, $\beta = \dfrac{\pi}{6}$, then the points will be

$(0, 1)$ and $\left(\dfrac{\sqrt{3}}{2}, \dfrac{1}{2}\right)$.

Obviously, the distance between these two points is 1 which is given by (d).

$$\left\{\because\ 2a\sin\frac{\alpha-\beta}{2} = 2\times 1\times\sin\frac{(\pi/2)-(\pi/6)}{2} = 2\times\frac{1}{2} = 1\right\}$$

**4.** **(b)** We can see that all these points are of the type

$\left(am, \dfrac{a}{m}\right)$.

Let these points be at a distance 'r' from a fixed point $(\alpha, \beta)$.

Then, we have $(am - \alpha)^2 + \left[\dfrac{a}{m} - \beta\right]^2 = r^2$

i.e. $a^2 m^4 - (2a\alpha)m^3 + (\alpha^2 + \beta^2 - r^2)m^2 - (2a\beta)$

$m + a^2 = 0$ ...............(1)

Which is a biquadratic equation whose product of the roots is equal to 1.

This shows that there will be four points of the type

$\left(am, \dfrac{a}{m}\right)$ which satisfy equation (1) provided the

product of their m's is equal to one.

Since the four given points do satisfy this condition.

**5.** **(a)** Let A be taken as the origin, AB as the x-axis and AD as the y-axis.

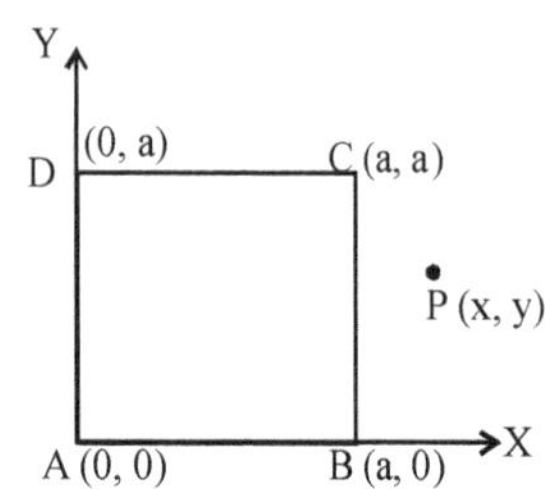


If each side of the square $= a$

then $A = (0, 0)$, $B = (a, 0)$, $C = (a, a)$, $D = (0, a)$

Let $P = (x, y)$

Now, by distance formula we get

$PA^2 = (x-0)^2 + (y-0)^2 = x^2 + y^2$

$PB^2 = (x-a)^2 + (y-0)^2 = x^2 - 2ax + a^2 + y^2$

$PC^2 = (x-a)^2 + (y-a)^2 = x^2 - 2ax + a^2 + y^2 - 2ay + a^2$

$PD^2 = (x-0)^2 + (y-a)^2 = x^2 + y^2 - 2ay + a^2$

$PA^2 + PC^2 = x^2 + y^2 + x^2 - 2ax + a^2 + y^2 - 2ay + a^2$

$\qquad = 2x^2 + 2y^2 - 2ax - 2ay + 2a^2$

$PB^2 + PD^2 = x^2 - 2ax + a^2 + y^2 + x^2 + y^2 - 2ay + a^2$

$\qquad = 2x^2 + 2y^2 - 2ax - 2ay + 2a^2$

$\therefore\ PA^2 + PC^2 = PB^2 + PD^2$.

**6.** **(b)** The point L $\left(\dfrac{5a+3b}{8}, \dfrac{5x+3y}{8}\right)$ divides PT in the ratio

$3 : 5$ and hence in the middle point of QR.

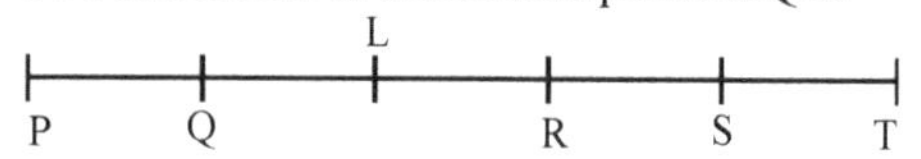


**7.** **(d)** We have $(x + 1 + x)/2 = 3/2 \Rightarrow x = 1$ and

$(y + 1 + y + 2)/2 = 5/2 \Rightarrow y = 1$.

Now co-ordinates of the required mid-point are

$\left(\dfrac{x-1+x+1}{2}, \dfrac{y+1+y-1}{2}\right) = (x, y) = (1, 1)$

**8.** **(c)** From triangle $OQ_1Q_2$, by applying cosine formula.

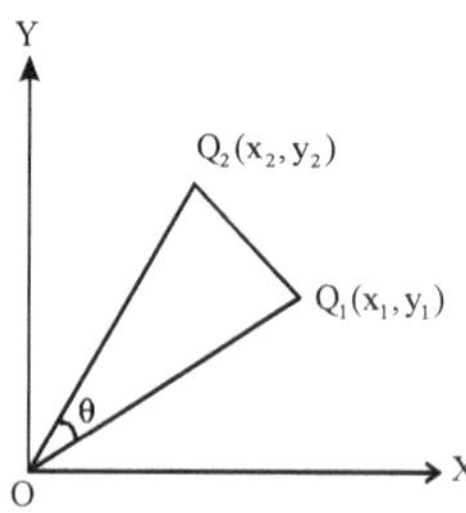


$Q_1Q_2^2 = OQ_1^2 + OQ_2^2 - 2OQ_1.OQ_2\cos Q_1OQ_2$

or $(x_1 - x_2)^2 + (y_1 - y_2)^2$

$= x_1^2 + y_1^2 + x_2^2 + y_2^2 - 2OQ_1.OQ_2\cos\theta$

or $\ x_1 x_2 + y_1 y_2 = OQ_1.OQ_2\cos Q_1OQ_2$

**9.** **(c)** Since $\angle RPQ = \dfrac{\pi}{2}$, therefore

Slope of RP × slope of PQ $= -1$

$\Rightarrow \dfrac{y-1}{x-3} \times \dfrac{5-1}{6-3} = -1 \Rightarrow 3x + 4y = 13$ ...(i)

Also, area of $\triangle RPQ = 7$ $\Rightarrow \begin{vmatrix} x & y & 1 \\ 3 & 1 & 1 \\ 6 & 5 & 1 \end{vmatrix} = \pm 7$

$\Rightarrow 3y - 4x = 5$ or $3y - 4x = -23$ ...(ii)

Solving (i) and (ii), we get two points.

**10. (b)** Area of a triangle

$$= \frac{1}{2}[(x_1 y_2 - x_2 y_1) + (x_2 y_3 - x_3 y_2) + (x_3 y_1 - x_1 y_3)]$$

$$= \frac{\text{an integer}}{2} = \text{a rational number}$$

whereas area of an equilateral triangle of side a is equal

to $\frac{\sqrt{3}}{4}a^2$, which is an irrational number.

Hence, a traingle whose vertices have integral coordinates cannot be equilateral.

[Note that $a^2 = (x_2 - x_1)^2 + (y_2 - y_1)^2 = $ integer

$\therefore \frac{\sqrt{3}}{4}a^2$ is always irrational ]

**11. (b)** Since the diagonals of a rhombus bisect each other at right angles.

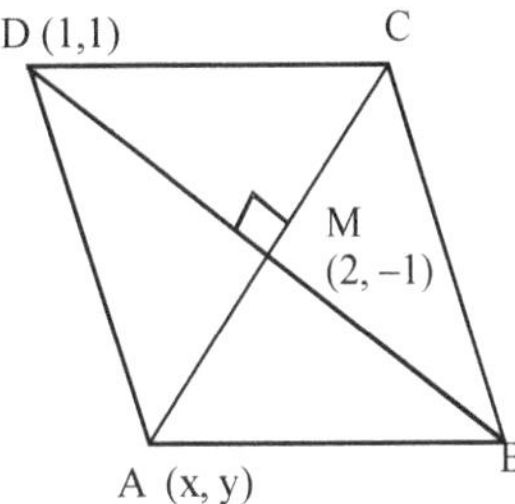

AM is perpendicular to DM and $AM = \frac{1}{2}$ MD.

(given)

Let the coordinates of A be (x, y) then

$$\frac{y+1}{x-2} \times \frac{1+1}{1-2} = -1$$

$$\Rightarrow 2(y+1) = x-2 \Rightarrow \quad x - 2y - 4 = 0 \quad \text{.......(i)}$$

(only the coordinates in (b), $\left(1, -\frac{3}{2}\right)$ satisfy the equation and hence is the correct answer).

Next, $(AD)^2 = (AM)^2 + (MD)^2$

$$\Rightarrow (x-1)^2 + (y-1)^2$$

$$= \left[1 + \frac{1}{4}\right][(2-1)^2 + (-1-1)^2] = \frac{25}{4}$$

$$\Rightarrow (2y+3)^2 + (y-1)^2 = \frac{25}{4}$$

$$\Rightarrow 5y^2 + 10y + 10 = \frac{25}{4}$$

$$\Rightarrow 4y^2 + 8y + 3 = 0 \Rightarrow y = -\frac{3}{2} \text{ or } -\frac{1}{2}$$

$y = -\frac{3}{2} \Rightarrow x = 1; \quad y = -\frac{1}{2} \Rightarrow x = 3$

Hence (b) gives the correct answer.

**12. (b)** Let $A(0, 0)$, $B(a, 0)$ and $C\left(\frac{a}{2}, \frac{a\sqrt{3}}{2}\right)$

Hence $AB = \sqrt{a^2 + 0} = a$, $BC = \sqrt{\left(\frac{a}{2}\right)^2 + \left(\frac{a\sqrt{3}}{2}\right)^2} = a$

and $AC = \sqrt{\left(\frac{a}{2}\right)^2 + \left(\frac{a\sqrt{3}}{2}\right)^2} = a$

Hence the triangle is equilateral.

**13. (d)** Let a point on x-axis is $(x_1, 0)$, then its distacne from the

point $(2, 3) = \sqrt{(x_1 - 2)^2 + 9} = c$

or $(x_1 - 2)^2 = c^2 - 9$

$\therefore x_1 - 2 = \sqrt{c^2 - 9}$

But $c < 3 \Rightarrow c^2 - 9 < 0$

$\therefore x_1$ will be imaginary

**14. (a)**

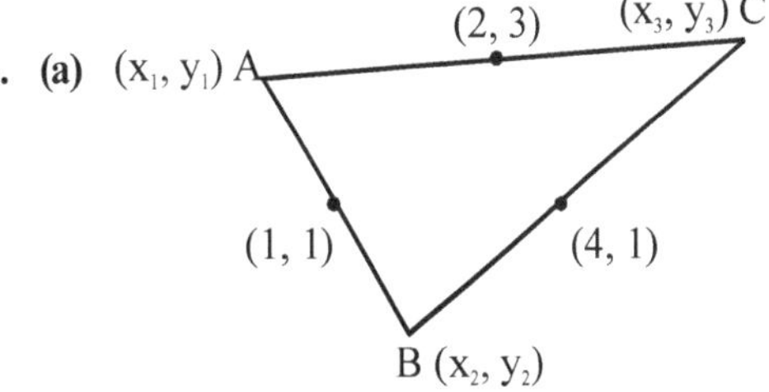

Let the coordinates of the vertices be $A(x_1, y_1)$, $B(x_2, y_2)$ and $C(x_3, y_3)$.

Then, we have

$x_1 + x_2 = 2$, $x_2 + x_3 = 8$, $x_3 + x_1 = 4$

and, $y_1 + y_2 = 2$, $y_2 + y_3 = 2$, $y_3 + y_1 = 6$

From the above equations, we have

$x_1 + x_2 + x_3 = 7$ and $y_1 + y_2 + y_3 = 5$

Solving together, we have $x_1 = -1$, $x_2 = 3$, $x_3 = 5$

and $y_1 = 3$, $y_2 = -1$, $y_3 = 3$

Therefore the coordinates of the vertices are $(-1, 3)$, $(3, -1)$ and $(5, 3)$.

Hence, the centroid is $\left(\frac{-1+3+5}{3}, \frac{3-1+3}{3}\right)$ i.e. $\left(\frac{7}{3}, \frac{5}{3}\right)$.

**15. (d)**

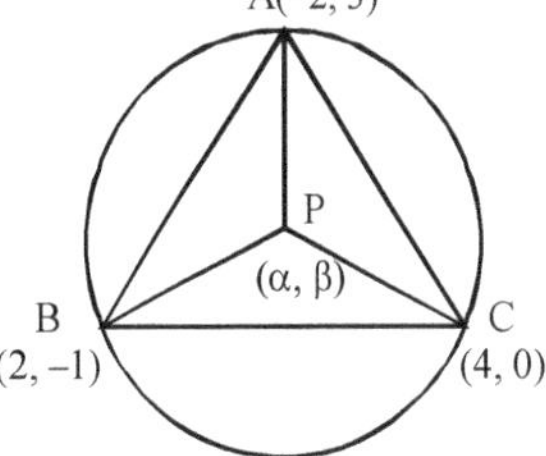

Let $A = (-2, 3)$, $B = (2, -1)$, $C = (4, 0)$

Let the centre of the circumcircle of the $\triangle ABC$ be $P = (\alpha, \beta)$

Then $PA = PB = PC$ i.e. $PA^2 = PB^2 = PC^2 \text{...(i)}$

$(\alpha + 2)^2 + (\beta - 3)^2 = (\alpha - 2)^2 + (\beta + 1)^2 = (\alpha - 4)^2 + (\beta - 0)^2$

or, $\alpha^2 + \beta^2 + 4\alpha - 6\beta + 13 = \alpha^2 + \beta^2 - 4\alpha + 2\beta + 5$

$$= \alpha^2 + \beta^2 - 8\alpha + 16$$

Subtracting $\alpha^2 + \beta^2$ from each,

$4\alpha - 6\beta + 13 = -4\alpha + 2\beta + 5 = -8\alpha + 16$

From the first two, $8\alpha - 8\beta + 8 = 0 \Rightarrow \alpha - \beta + 1 = 0$ ....(ii)

From the last two, $4\alpha + 2\beta - 11 = 0$ ....(iii)

Solving (ii) and (iii) we get $\alpha = \dfrac{3}{2}$ and $\beta = \dfrac{5}{2}$

$\therefore (\alpha, \beta) = \left(\dfrac{3}{2}, \dfrac{5}{2}\right) = $ circumcentre.

Now radius = PC = $\sqrt{\left(\dfrac{3}{2} - 4\right)^2 + \left(\dfrac{5}{2} - 0\right)^2}$

$= \sqrt{\left(\dfrac{-5}{2}\right)^2 + \left(\dfrac{5}{2}\right)^2} = \sqrt{\left(\dfrac{25}{4}\right) + \left(\dfrac{25}{4}\right)} = \sqrt{\dfrac{50}{4}} = \dfrac{5\sqrt{2}}{2}$

**16. (c)** The coordinates of the centroid are

$$\left(\dfrac{ab + bc + ca}{3}, \dfrac{\dfrac{1}{ab} + \dfrac{1}{bc} + \dfrac{1}{ca}}{3}\right)$$

i.e. $\left(\dfrac{ab + bc + ca}{3}, \dfrac{a + b + c}{3abc}\right)$

From the given cubic equation $x^3 - 3x^2 + 6x + 1 = 0$, we have

$\left.\begin{array}{l} a + b + c = 3 \\ ab + bc + ca = 6 \\ \text{and } abc = -1 \end{array}\right\}$ Relations between roots and coefficients of an equation

Hence, using the above results, we have the coordinates of the centroid as $\left(\dfrac{6}{3}, \dfrac{3}{-3}\right)$ i.e. $(2, -1)$

**17. (a,c)** O and the point lie to the opposite sides w.r.to
$2x + 3y - 1 = 0$

$2x + 3y - 1 = -1 < 0 \Rightarrow 2\alpha + 3\alpha^2 - 1 > 0$ ......(1)
O and the point $(\alpha, \alpha^2)$ lie to the same side w.r.to
$x + 2y - 3 = 0$

$x + 2y - 3 = -3 < 0 \Rightarrow \alpha + 2\alpha^2 - 3 < 0$ ......(2)

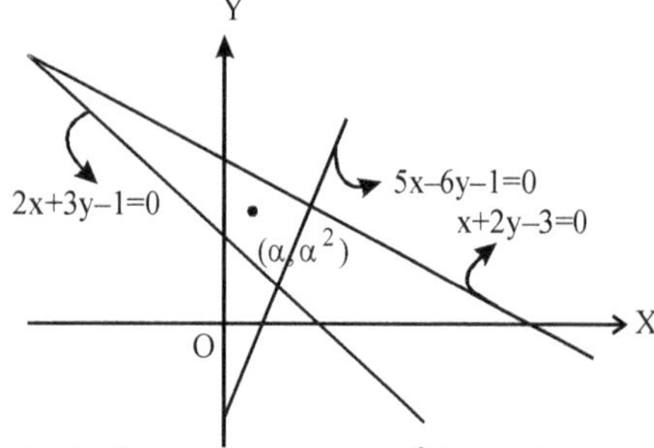


Again O and the point $(\alpha, \alpha^2)$ lie to the same side w.r.to
$5x - 6y - 1 = -1 < 0$

$\Rightarrow 5\alpha - 6\alpha^2 - 1 < 0 \Rightarrow 6\alpha^2 - 5\alpha + 1 > 0$

**18. (c)** Point of intersection of $L_1$ and $L_2$ is A $(0, 0)$.
Also P $(-2, -2)$, Q $(1, -2)$

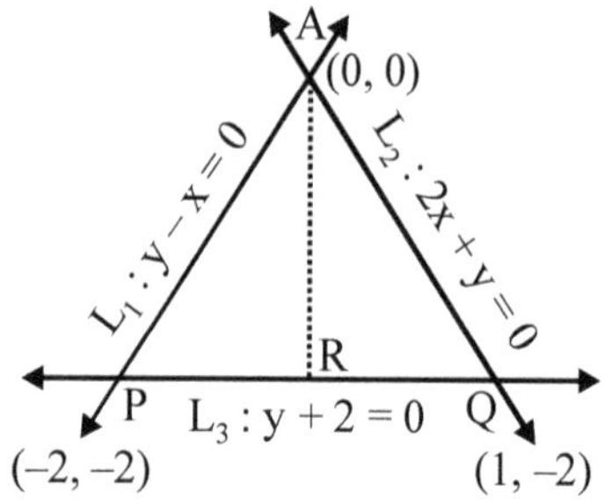


$\because$ AR is the bisector of $\angle$PAQ, therefore R divides PQ in the same ratio as AP : AQ.

Thus PR : RQ = AP : AQ = $2\sqrt{2} : \sqrt{5}$

$\therefore$ Statement-1 is true.
Statement-2 is clearly false.

**19. (6)** Since, C $(2, -1)$ is the mid-point of P $(4, -x)$ and Q$(-2, 4)$.

$\therefore \dfrac{4 - x}{2} = -1 , x = -6$

**20. (3)** Let y-axis divide the join of points $(-3, -4)$ and $(1, -2)$ in the ratio $\lambda : 1$ then $(\lambda - 3)/(\lambda + 1) = 0 \Rightarrow \lambda = 3$

**21. (8)** The mid point of PQ is the mid-point of AB and hence its co-ordinates are

$\left(\dfrac{25 + 55}{2}, \dfrac{37 - 21}{2}\right)$ or $(40, 8)$.

Hence Y-coordinate of the mid-point = 8

**22. (0)** Let $(x, y)$ be the co-ordinates of the fourth vertex. Since the diagonals of a parallelogram bisect each other; the mid points of the two diagonals coincide. So that

$\dfrac{y + 1}{2} = \dfrac{-4 + 5}{2} \Rightarrow y = 0$

**23. (2)** Diagonals cut each other at middle points.

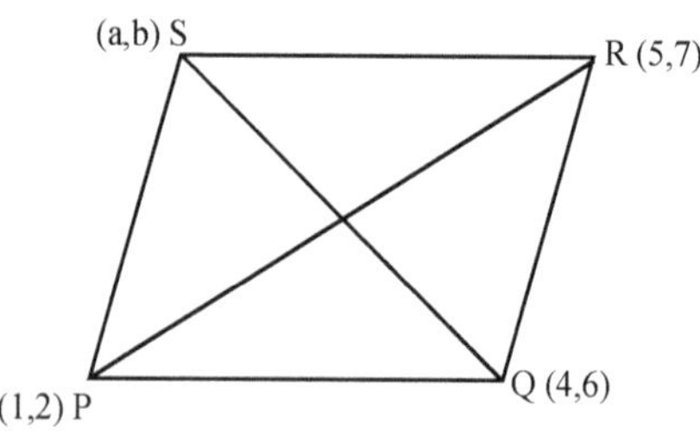


Hence $\dfrac{a + 4}{2} = \dfrac{1 + 5}{2} \Rightarrow a = 2$

$\dfrac{b + 6}{2} = \dfrac{2 + 7}{2} \Rightarrow b = 3$

$\therefore \dfrac{3a}{b} = \dfrac{3 \times 2}{3} = 2$

**1.** **(a).** Distance of all vertices from origin is 2. So, circum-centre is origin.

$$\text{Centroid} = \left( \frac{1 + 2\cos\theta + 2\sin\theta}{3}, \frac{\sqrt{3} + 2\sin\theta - 2\cos\theta}{3} \right)$$

Let orthocentre is (h, k)

$h = 1 + 2(\cos\theta + \sin\theta) \, ; \, k = \sqrt{3} + 2(\sin\theta - \cos\theta)$

$$\left( \frac{h-1}{2} \right)^2 + \left( \frac{k-\sqrt{3}}{2} \right)^2 = 2 \text{ locus is}$$

$(x-1)^2 + (y - \sqrt{3})^2 = 8$

**2.** **(b).** $(x+y)^2 - 3(x+y) + 2$

$\Rightarrow t^2 - 3t + 2 \Rightarrow (t-2)(t-1) \Rightarrow (x+y-2)(x+y-1)$

$\Rightarrow$ two parallel lines which are non coincident.

**3.** **(c)** The coordinates of the centroid are

$$\left( \frac{ab + bc + ca}{3}, \frac{\dfrac{1}{ab} + \dfrac{1}{bc} + \dfrac{1}{ca}}{3} \right)$$

*i.e.* $\left( \dfrac{ab + bc + ca}{3}, \dfrac{a+b+c}{3abc} \right)$

From the given cubic equation $x^3 - 3x^2 + 6x + 1 = 0$, we have

$\left. \begin{array}{l} a + b + c = 3 \\ ab + bc + ca = 6 \\ \text{and } abc = -1 \end{array} \right\}$ Relations between roots and coefficients of an equation

Hence, using the above results, we have the coordinates of the centroid as $\left( \dfrac{6}{3}, \dfrac{3}{-3} \right)$ i.e. (2, –1)

**4.** **(d)**

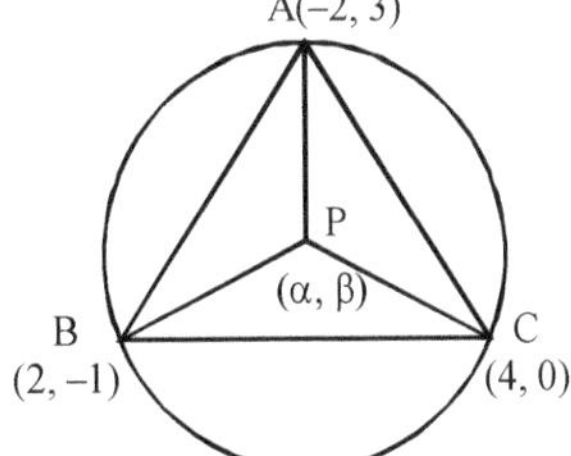


Let A = (–2, 3), B = (2, –1), C = (4, 0)

Let the centre of the circumcircle of the $\triangle ABC$ be P = (α, β)

Then PA = PB = PC i.e. $PA^2 = PB^2 = PC^2$ ...(i)

$(\alpha + 2)^2 + (\beta - 3)^2 = (\alpha - 2)^2 + (\beta + 1)^2 = (\alpha - 4)^2 + (\beta - 0)^2$

or, $\alpha^2 + \beta^2 + 4\alpha - 6\beta + 13 = \alpha^2 + \beta^2 - 4\alpha + 2\beta + 5$

$= \alpha^2 + \beta^2 - 8\alpha + 16$

Subtracting $\alpha^2 + \beta^2$ from each,

$4\alpha - 6\beta + 13 = -4\alpha + 2\beta + 5 = -8\alpha + 16$

From the first two, $8\alpha - 8\beta + 8 = 0 \Rightarrow \alpha - \beta + 1 = 0$ ....(ii)

From the last two, $4\alpha + 2\beta - 11 = 0$ ....(iii)

Solving (ii) and (iii) we get $\alpha = \dfrac{3}{2}$ and $\beta = \dfrac{5}{2}$

$\therefore (\alpha, \beta) = \left( \dfrac{3}{2}, \dfrac{5}{2} \right) = \text{circumcentre.}$

---

Now, radius $= PC = \sqrt{\left( \dfrac{3}{2} - 4 \right)^2 + \left( \dfrac{5}{2} - 0 \right)^2}$

$= \sqrt{\left( \dfrac{-5}{2} \right)^2 + \left( \dfrac{5}{2} \right)^2} = \sqrt{\dfrac{25}{4} + \dfrac{25}{4}} = \sqrt{\dfrac{50}{4}} = \dfrac{5\sqrt{2}}{2}$

**5.** **(d)** Circurmcentre of the triangle is (0, 0)

Centroid is $\left( \dfrac{3 + 5\cos\theta + 5\sin\theta}{3}, \dfrac{4 + 5\sin\theta - 5\cos\theta}{3} \right)$

[$\because$ Centroid divides the join of orthocentre and circumcentre in 2 : 1 ratio]

$\therefore$ $h = 3 + 5\cos\theta + 5\sin\theta$

$k = 4 + 5\sin\theta - 5\cos\theta$, where (h, k) represents orthocentre

$\Rightarrow \sin\theta = \dfrac{h + k - 7}{10} ; \cos\theta = \dfrac{h - k + 1}{10}$

$\Rightarrow (h + k - 7)^2 + (h - k + 1)^2 = 100$

$\therefore$ Locus of orthocentre is $(x + y - 7)^2 + (x - y + 1)^2 = 100$.

**6.** **(b)** Coordinates of a triangle are

($a\cos t$, $a\sin t$), ($b\sin t$, $-b\cos t$) and (1, 0)

x - cordinate of Centroid, $x = \dfrac{a\cos t + b\sin t + 1}{3}$

$\Rightarrow 3x - 1 = a\cos t + b\sin t$ ....(i)

y - cordinate of centroid, $y = \dfrac{a\sin t - b\cos t + 0}{3}$

$\Rightarrow 3y = a\sin t - b\cos t$ ....(ii)

Squiring and adding Eqs. (i) and (ii), we get

$(3x - 1)^2 + (3y)^2 = (a\cos t + b\sin t)^2 + (a\sin t - b\cos t)^2$

or $(3x - 1)^2 + (3y)^2 = a^2 + b^2$

**7.** **(c)** Let O is the orthocentre of the triangle formed by A, B, C. Then each point is the orthocentre of the triangle formed by the remaing three points.

$\Rightarrow$ Orthocentre of $\triangle OAC$ is B = (– 2, 3).

**8.** **(d)** Let $R$ be the radius of the circumcircle and $O$ be the origin, then $AO = \sqrt{x_1^2 + x_2^2 \tan^2 \alpha}$

$\Rightarrow R = x_1 \sec\alpha \Rightarrow x_1 = R\cos\alpha$.

Similarly, $x_2 = R\cos\beta$ and $x_3 = R\cos\gamma$

So, the coordinates of vertices are $A(R\cos\alpha, R\sin\alpha)$, $B(R\cos\beta, R\sin\beta)$, $C(R\cos\gamma, R\sin\gamma)$. Hence, the coordinates of centroid $G$ are

$$\left( \dfrac{\sum R\cos\alpha}{3}, \dfrac{\sum R\sin\alpha}{3} \right).$$

Since the orthocentre $H(a, b)$, Circumcentre $O(0, 0)$ and the centroid $G$ are collinear, therefore Slope of $OH = $ Slope of $OG$

$\Rightarrow \dfrac{b}{a} = \dfrac{R(\sin\alpha + \sin\beta + \sin\gamma)}{R(\cos\alpha + \cos\beta + \cos\gamma)}$

**9.** **(a,b,c)**

(a) Slope of $AH$, is $\dfrac{4-1}{2-1} = 3$

$\Rightarrow \left(-\dfrac{a}{b}\right)3 = -1$

$\Rightarrow 3a = b$

$b - 3a = 0$

Also, $a + c = 2b$

$\Rightarrow a - 2b + c = 0$

$a(1) + b(-2) + c = 0$

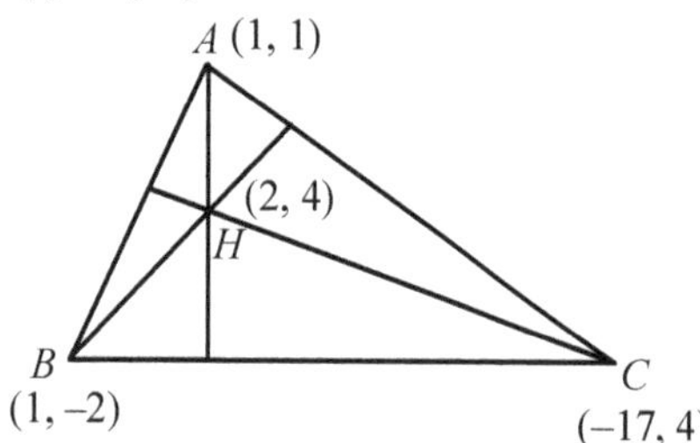


$\Rightarrow$ Lines are concurrent

at $(1, -2)$. So, $B$ is $(1, -2)$

(b) If $C$ be $(\alpha, \beta)$ then

$AH \perp^r BC \Rightarrow \dfrac{\beta+2}{\alpha-1} \times 3 = -1 \Rightarrow \alpha + 3\beta + 5 = 0$

$BH \perp^r CA \Rightarrow \dfrac{\beta-1}{\alpha-1} \times 6 = -1 \Rightarrow \alpha + 6\beta - 7 = 0$

Solving we get $\alpha = -17$ and $\beta = 4$

So, $C$ is $(-17, 4)$

(c) Slope of $AC(m_1) = \dfrac{1-4}{1+17} = -\dfrac{3}{18} = -\dfrac{1}{6}$

Slope of $BC(m_2) = \dfrac{-2-4}{1+17} = -\dfrac{6}{18} = -\dfrac{1}{3}$

$\therefore \tan C = \dfrac{m_2 - m_1}{1 + m_1 m_2} = \dfrac{-\dfrac{1}{3} + \dfrac{1}{6}}{1 + \left(-\dfrac{1}{6}\right)\left(-\dfrac{1}{3}\right)} < 0$

$\Rightarrow \angle BCA$ is obtuse.

**10.** **(a,b,c,d)** The given point are collinear if

$$0 = \begin{vmatrix} a & x & 1 \\ b & y & 1 \\ c & z & 1 \end{vmatrix} = \begin{vmatrix} a & x & 1 \\ b-a & y-x & 0 \\ c-b & z-y & 0 \end{vmatrix},$$

$$\begin{bmatrix} R_2 \rightarrow R_2 - R_1 \\ R_3 \rightarrow R_3 - R_2 \end{bmatrix}$$

or if $(b-a)(z-y) - (c-b)(y-x) = 0$

or if $z - y = y - x$ [a, b, c being in A.P]

or if $2y = x + z$    or    if $x = z = y$.

[x, y, z being in G.P.]

**11.** **(a,c,d)** Since a is an integer, $\sqrt{2}$ a is irrational. Now incentre will be

$$\left(\dfrac{ax_1 + ax_2 + \sqrt{2}ax_3}{2a + a\sqrt{2}}, \dfrac{ay_1 + ay_2 + \sqrt{2}ay_3}{2a + a\sqrt{2}}\right)$$

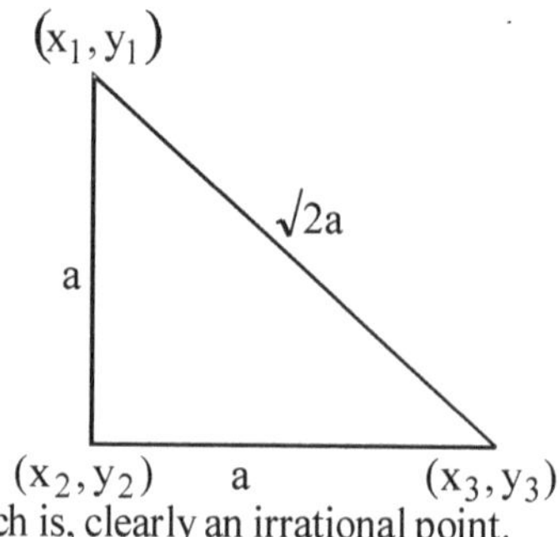


which is, clearly an irrational point.

**12.** **(a, b, c)** Vertices of the given triangle are $(0, 0)$, $\left(\dfrac{a}{m_1}, a\right)$

and $\left(\dfrac{a}{m_2}, a\right)$

so that the area of the triangle is equal to

$$\dfrac{a^2(m_2 - m_1)}{2 m_1 m_2}$$

Since $m_1$, $m_2$ are the roots of $x^2 - ax - a - 1 = 0$

so $m_1 + m_2 = a$, $m_1 m_2 = -(a+1)$

$\Rightarrow (m_1 - m_2)^2 = a^2 + 4(a+1) = (a+2)^2$

$\Rightarrow m_1 - m_2 = \pm(a+2)$

So the required area is $\Delta = \pm \dfrac{a^2(a+2)}{-2(a+1)}$

$= \pm \dfrac{a^2(a+2)}{2(a+1)}$

Since the area $\Delta$ is a positive quantity.

$\Delta = \dfrac{a^2(a+2)}{2(a+1)}$ if $a > -1$   or   $a < -2$

and $\Delta = -\dfrac{a^2(a+2)}{2(a+1)}$ if $-2 < a < -1$.

**13.** **(d).**

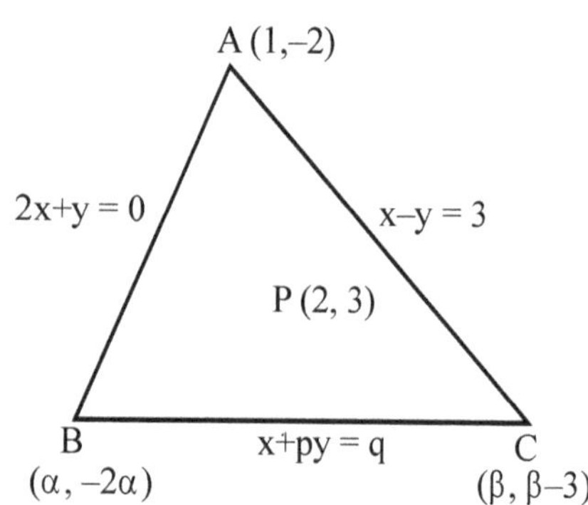


$A(1, -2)$, $B(\alpha, -2\alpha)$, $C(\beta, \beta-3)$

$1 + \alpha + \beta = 6$, $-2 - 2\alpha + \beta - 3 = 9$

$\Rightarrow \alpha = -3, \beta = 8$

$B = (-3, 6)$, $C = (8, 5)$

Equation of BC is $x + 11y = 63$

$\therefore p + q = 63 + 11 = 74$

**14.** **(b).** Slope of BP $= -1 \Rightarrow \dfrac{3+2\alpha}{2-\alpha} = -1 \Rightarrow \alpha = -5$

Slope of CP $= \dfrac{1}{2} \Rightarrow \dfrac{\beta-6}{\beta-2} = \dfrac{1}{2} \Rightarrow \beta = 10$

B $(-5, 10)$, C $(10, 7)$

Equation of BC : $x + 5y = 45$

$\therefore$ $p + q = 50$

**15.** **(a).** $PA^2 = 26 = PB^2 = PC^2$

$\Rightarrow$ $(\alpha-2)^2 + (3+2\alpha)^2 = (\beta-2)^2 + (\beta-6)^2 = 26$

$\Rightarrow$ $\alpha = \dfrac{-13}{5}$ or $1$ (rejected because vertices A and B coincide )

Similarly other equation gives $\beta = 7$ or $1$ (rejected because vertices A and C coincide)

Hence $\alpha = \dfrac{-13}{5}$ and $\beta = 7$

$B = \left(\dfrac{-13}{5}, \dfrac{26}{5}\right), C = (7, 4)$

The equation of BC is $x + 8y = 39 \Rightarrow (p+q) = 47$

Alternatively for (iii): Slope of line EP $= \dfrac{1}{2}$

$\dfrac{1}{2} = \dfrac{3+\alpha+1}{2-\dfrac{\alpha+1}{2}}; \quad \dfrac{1}{2} = 2\left(\dfrac{4+\alpha}{3-\alpha}\right)$

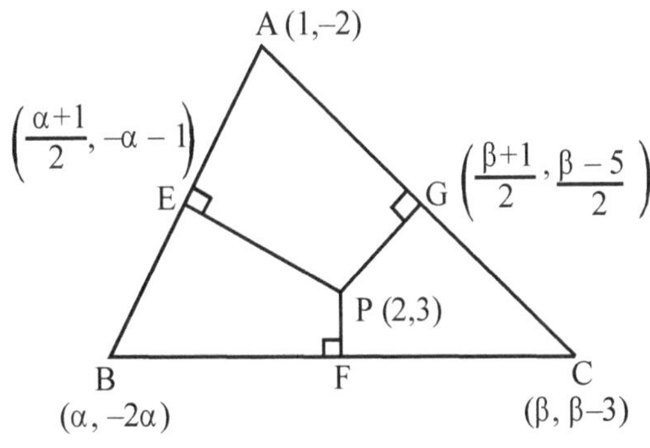

$3 - \alpha = 16 + 4\alpha \Rightarrow 5\alpha = -13 \Rightarrow \alpha = -13/5$

Slope of line PG $= -1$

$-1 = \dfrac{\dfrac{\beta-5}{2} - 3}{\dfrac{\beta+1}{2} - 2} = \dfrac{\beta-11}{\beta-3}$ ;

$-\beta + 3 = \beta - 11$ ; $2\beta = 14$ ; $\beta = 7$

$B = \left(\dfrac{-13}{5}, \dfrac{26}{5}\right), C = (7, 4)$

The equation of BC is $x + 8y = 39 \Rightarrow (p+q) = 47$

**16.** A→s; B→t; C→q; D→p

(A) $x = ct, y = \dfrac{c}{t} \Rightarrow xy = c^2$

(B) $x = \dfrac{a}{2}\left(t + \dfrac{1}{t}\right), y = \dfrac{a}{2}\left(t - \dfrac{1}{t}\right)$

$\Rightarrow \dfrac{4x^2}{a^2} - \dfrac{4y^2}{a^2} = 4 \Rightarrow x^2 - y^2 = a^2$

(C) $x = \cos^2 t, y = 2\sin t \Rightarrow y^2 = 4[1 - \cos^2 t] = 4[1-x]$
$\Rightarrow y^2 + 4x = 4$

(D) $x = a\cosh\theta, y = b\sinh\theta; \quad \left(\dfrac{x}{a}\right)^2 - \left(\dfrac{y}{b}\right)^2 = 1$

**17.** **(a).** Let A $(\alpha, f(\alpha))$, B $(\beta, f(\beta))$, C $(\gamma, f(\gamma))$

P is centroid

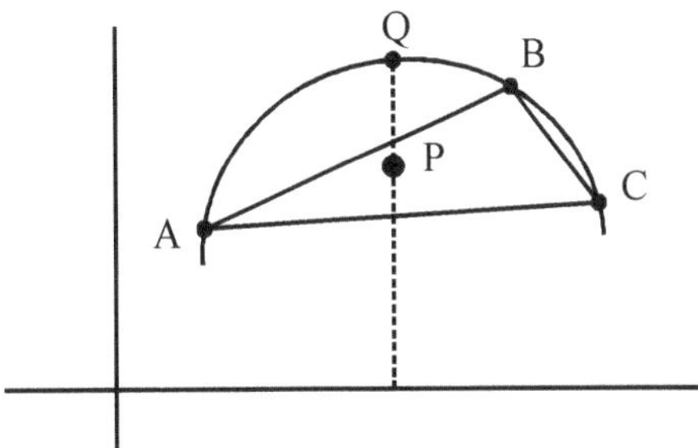

$P \equiv \left(\dfrac{\alpha+\beta+\gamma}{3}, \dfrac{f(\alpha)+f(\beta)+f(\gamma)}{3}\right),$

$Q \equiv \left(\dfrac{\alpha+\beta+\gamma}{3}, f\left(\dfrac{\alpha+\beta+\gamma}{3}\right)\right)$

Centroid lies inside, so

$f\left(\dfrac{\alpha+\beta+\gamma}{3}\right) > \dfrac{f(\alpha)+f(\beta)+f(\gamma)}{3}$

**18.** **(a)** Area of triangle is unaltered by shifting origin to any point. If origin is shifted to $(2000, 2002)$
A, B, C become P $(0, 0)$, Q $(1, 2)$, R $(2, 1)$. Both are true.

**19.** **(c)** We know that incentre is equidistant from the three sides of the triangle.
$(0, 0)$ is equidistance from three given lines. Therefore incentre $= (0, 0)$.

**20.** **(3)** A line passing through $P(h, k)$ and parallel to $x$-axis is
$y = k.$ ...(1)
The other two lines given are
$y = x$ ...(2)
and $x + y = 2$ ...(3)
Let $ABC$ be the $\Delta$ formed by the points of intersection of the lines (1), (2) and (3), as shown in the figure.

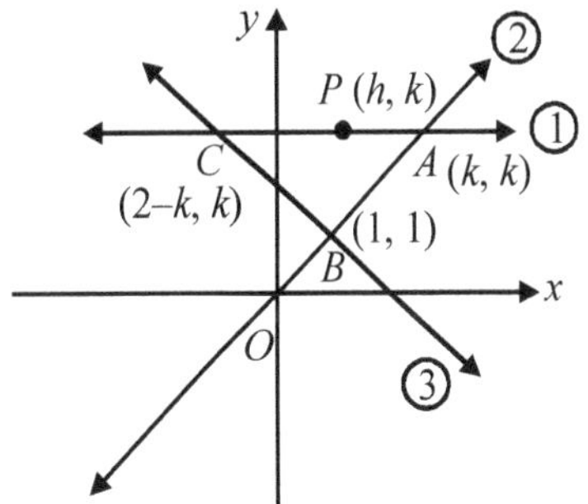

Then $A(k, k), B(1, 1), C(2-k, k)$

$\therefore$ Area of $\Delta ABC = \dfrac{1}{2}\begin{vmatrix} k & k & 1 \\ 1 & 1 & 1 \\ 2-k & k & 1 \end{vmatrix} = 4h^2$

Operating $C_1 - C_2$ we get

$$\frac{1}{2}\begin{vmatrix} 0 & k & 1 \\ 0 & 1 & 1 \\ 2-2k & k & 1 \end{vmatrix} = 4h^2$$

$\Rightarrow \quad \dfrac{1}{2}\,|\,(2-2k)(k-1)\,| = 4h^2$

$\Rightarrow \quad (k-1)^2 = 4h^2$

$\Rightarrow \quad k-1 = 2h \qquad$ or $\qquad k-1 = -2h$

$\Rightarrow \quad k = 2h+1 \qquad$ or $\qquad k = -2h+1$

$\therefore \quad$ Locus of $(h, k)$ is, $y = 2x + 1$ or $y = -2x + 1$.

Thus, P = 2, Q = 1

$\Rightarrow$ P + Q = 3.

**21.** **(8)** The area of the triangle formed by the first set of verticles is

$$\Delta = \frac{1}{2}\begin{vmatrix} b & c & 1 \\ c & a & 1 \\ a & b & 1 \end{vmatrix} = \frac{1}{2}\begin{vmatrix} b-a & c-b & 0 \\ c-a & a-b & 0 \\ a & b & 1 \end{vmatrix}$$

$$= \frac{1}{2}\left[-(a-b)^2 - (c-b)(c-a)\right]$$

$$= \frac{1}{2}\left(bc + ca + ab - a^2 - b^2 - c^2\right).$$

For the second set of vertices, the required area is given by

$$\Delta' = \frac{1}{2}\begin{vmatrix} ac-b^2 & ab-c^2 & 1 \\ ba-c^2 & bc-a^2 & 1 \\ cb-a^2 & ca-b^2 & 1 \end{vmatrix}$$

$$= \frac{1}{2}\begin{vmatrix} ac-b^2-cb+a^2 & ab-c^2-ca+b^2 & 0 \\ ba-c^2-cb+a^2 & bc-a^2-ca+b^2 & 0 \\ cb-a^2 & ca-b^2 & 1 \end{vmatrix}$$

$$= \frac{1}{2}\begin{vmatrix} (a+b+c)(a-b) & (a+b+c)(b-c) & 0 \\ (a+b+c)(a-c) & (a+b+c)(b-a) & 0 \\ cb-a^2 & ca-b^2 & 1 \end{vmatrix}$$

$$= \frac{1}{2}(a+b+c)^2\begin{vmatrix} a-b & b-c \\ a-c & b-a \end{vmatrix}$$

$$= \frac{1}{2}(a+b+c)^2\left[-(a-b)^2 - (b-c)(a-c)\right]$$

$$= \frac{1}{2}(a+b+c)^2\left(bc + ca + ab - a^2 - b^2 - c^2\right).$$

Hence $\Delta' = (a+b+c)^2\,\Delta = (16)^2\,\Delta$

$\therefore \dfrac{\Delta'}{32\Delta} = 8$

**22.** **(0)** As $C$ lies on the line $y = x + 3$, let the co-ordinates of $C$ be $(\lambda, \lambda + 3)$. Also $A(2, 1)$, $B(3, -2)$. Then area of $\triangle ABC$ is given by

$$\frac{1}{2}\begin{vmatrix} 2 & 1 & 1 \\ 3 & -2 & 1 \\ \lambda & \lambda+3 & 1 \end{vmatrix} = \pm 5$$

$\Rightarrow \quad |2(-2-\lambda-3) - 1(3-\lambda)(3\lambda+9+2\lambda)| = 10$

$\Rightarrow \quad |-2\lambda - 10 - 3 + \lambda + 5\lambda + 9| = 10$

$\Rightarrow \quad |4\lambda - 4| = 10$

$\Rightarrow \quad 4\lambda - 4 = 10 \qquad$ or $\qquad 4\lambda - 4 = -10$

$\Rightarrow \quad \lambda = 7/2$ or $\qquad \lambda = -3/2$

$\therefore \quad$ Coordinates of $C$ are $\left(\dfrac{P}{2}, \dfrac{Q}{2}\right)$ or $\left(\dfrac{-R}{2}, \dfrac{S}{2}\right)$

Hence, value of
$P - Q - R + S = 7 - 13 - (-3) + 3 = 7 - 13 + 3 + 3 = 13 - 13 = 0$.

**23.** **(4)** We know orthocentre of $\Delta$ is meeting point of altitudes.

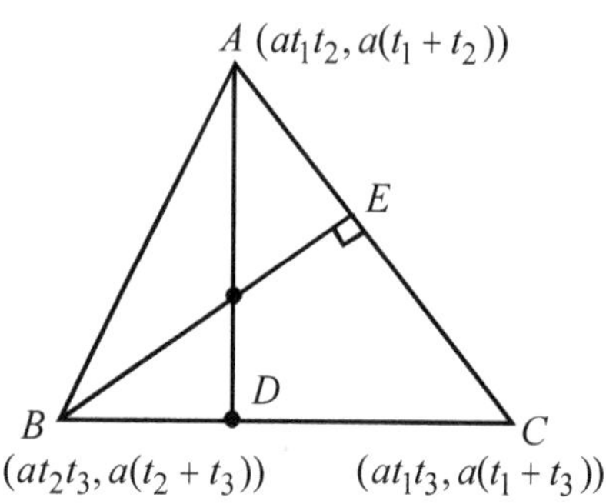


Slope of $BC = \dfrac{a(t_1+t_3) - a(t_2+t_3)}{at_1t_3 - at_2t_3}$

$$= \frac{a(t_1+t_3-t_2-t_3)}{at_3(t_1-t_2)} = \frac{1}{t_3}$$

$\therefore \quad$ Slope of $AD = -t_3$

$\therefore \quad$ Eq. of $AD$,

$\quad y - a(t_1+t_2) = -t_3(x - at_1t_2)$

or $\quad x t_3 + y = a t_1t_2t_3 + a(t_1+t_2) \qquad$ ....... (1)

Similarly, by symm. equation of $BE$ is

$\Rightarrow \quad xt_1 + y = at_1t_2t_3 + a(t_2+t_3) \qquad$ ....... (2)

Solving (1) and (2), we get

$\quad x = -a$

$\quad y = a(t_1+t_2+t_3) + at_1t_2t_3)$

$\therefore \quad$ Orthocentre $H(-a,\ a(t_1+t_2+t_3) + at_1t_2t_3)$

If $a = 1$, $t_1 + t_2 + t_3 = 2$, $t_1t_2t_3 = 3$

then orthocentre is

$H(-1, 2+3) = H(-1, 5)$

$\Rightarrow s = -1, t = 5$

Hence, $s + t = -1 + 5 = 4$.

**1.** **(d).** $\tan\theta = 7$; $OA = OB = r$ $\qquad \sin\theta = \dfrac{7}{5\sqrt{2}}$, $\cos\theta = \dfrac{1}{5\sqrt{2}}$

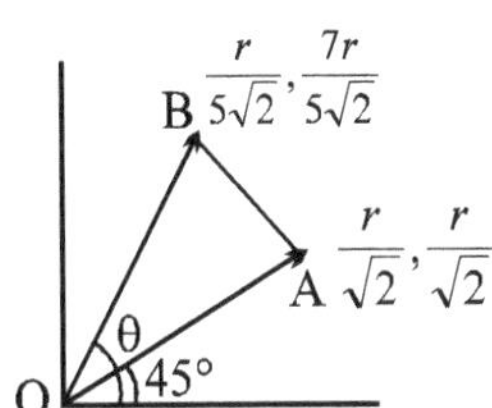


now $m_{AB} = \dfrac{-1}{2}$

**2.** **(b)** Any line passing through the intersection of the given lines is

$x + 3y + 4 + \lambda(3x + y + 4) = 0$ ....(i)

or, $(1 + 3\lambda)x + (3 + \lambda)y + 4(1 + \lambda) = 0$

The slope of the line $m = -\dfrac{1 + 3\lambda}{3 + \lambda}$

As the line is equally inclined with the axes,

$m = \tan 45°$ or $\tan 135° = \pm 1$

$\therefore -\dfrac{1 + 3\lambda}{3 + \lambda} = \pm 1, \Rightarrow \lambda = \pm 1$

$\therefore$ The required lines are (putting $\lambda = -1$, 1 in (i))

$x + 3y + 4 \pm (3x + y + 4) = 0$

or, $x + y + 2 = 0$ and $x - y = 0$

**3.** **(c)** $\tan\theta = \sqrt{3} \Rightarrow \theta = 60° \Rightarrow \angle PQR = 120°$

$\Rightarrow$ Bisector will have slope $\tan 120°$

$\Rightarrow$ Equation of bisector is $\sqrt{3}x + y = 0$

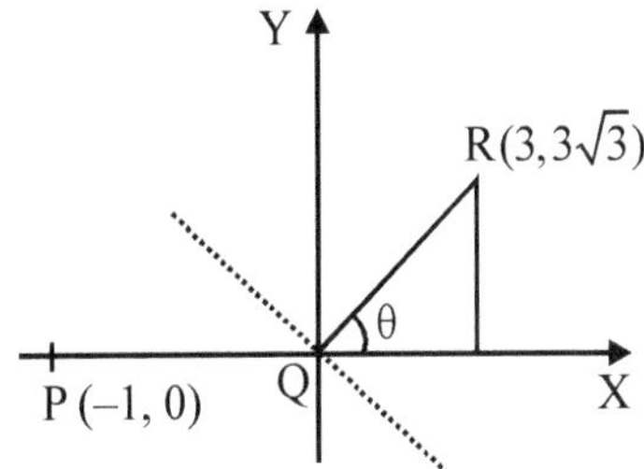


**Alternative:**

Equation of PQ is $y = 0$

Equation of QR is $y = \dfrac{3\sqrt{3}x}{3}$

$\therefore$ Angle bisector of $\angle PQR$ is given by

$y = \pm\left(\dfrac{y - \sqrt{3}x}{\sqrt{1^2 + \left(\sqrt{3}\right)^2}}\right) = \pm\left(\dfrac{y - \sqrt{3}x}{2}\right)$

$\Rightarrow y + \sqrt{3}x = 0$ or $\sqrt{3}y - x = 0$

But from figure, $\angle PQR$ is obtuse angle.

$\therefore$ Its bisector is the one obtained taking positive sign

i.e. $\sqrt{3}x + y = 0$

**4.** **(d)** We have $y = \cos x \cos(x + 2) - \cos^2(x + 1)$

$y = \dfrac{1}{2}\{2\cos x \cos(x + 2) - 2\cos^2(x + 1)\}$

$= \dfrac{1}{2}\{\cos(2x + 2) + \cos 2 - 1 - \cos(2x + 2)\}$

$= \dfrac{1}{2}(\cos 2 - 1) = \dfrac{1}{2}(1 - 2\sin^2 1 - 1) = -\sin^2 1$

Which is a straight line passing through $\left(\dfrac{\pi}{2}, -\sin^2 1\right)$

and parallel to the x-axis.

**5.** **(a)** Let $L_1(x, y) = x + y + 1$ and $L_2(x, y) = 2x - 3y - 5$

$\therefore L_1(10, -20) = 10 - 20 + 1 = -9$, which is −ve

and $L_2(10, -20) = 20 + 60 - 5 = 75$, which is +ve

$\therefore$ Equation of the bisector will be

$\dfrac{x + y + 1}{\sqrt{2}} = -\left(\dfrac{2x - 3y - 5}{\sqrt{13}}\right)$

$\Rightarrow x(\sqrt{13} + 2\sqrt{2}) + y(\sqrt{13} - 3\sqrt{2}) + (\sqrt{13} - 5\sqrt{2}) = 0$

**6.** **(a)** Clearly the point $(3, 0)$ does not lie on the diagonal $x = 2y$.

Let m be the slope of a side passing through $(3, 0)$. Then its equation is

$y - 0 = m(x - 3)$ ....(i)

Since the angle between a diagonal and a side of a square is $\dfrac{\pi}{4}$. Therefore angle between

$x = 2y$ & $y - 0 = m(x - 3)$ is also $\dfrac{\pi}{4}$

Consequently, $\tan\dfrac{\pi}{4} = \pm\dfrac{m - \dfrac{1}{2}}{1 + \dfrac{m}{2}} \Rightarrow m = 3, -\dfrac{1}{3}$

$\therefore$ From (i), we get the required equations

$y = 3(x - 3) \Rightarrow y - 3x + 9 = 0$ or

$y = -\dfrac{1}{3}(x - 3) \Rightarrow 3y + x - 3 = 0$

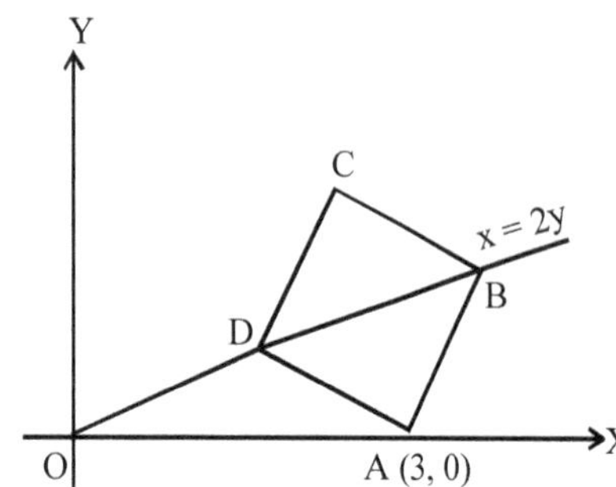



**7.** **(a)** Perpendicular bisector of AB is parallel to $x - y - 4 = 0$, $m = 1$

Passing through circumcentre $= \left(\dfrac{3}{2}, \dfrac{5}{2}\right)$

Equation of perpendicular bisector of side AB,
$2x - 2y + 2 = 0 \Rightarrow x - y + 1 = 0$

**8.** **(b)** Given equation is $(x^2 + y^2)\sin^2\alpha = (x\cos\beta - y\sin\beta)^2$
$\Rightarrow x^2(\sin^2\alpha - \cos^2\beta) + 2xy\sin\beta\cos\beta$
$\qquad + y^2(\sin^2\alpha - \sin^2\beta) = 0 \quad …(1)$
Let the angle between the lines representing by (1) is $\theta$

$\therefore \tan\theta = 2\left|\dfrac{\sqrt{h^2 - ab}}{a + b}\right|$

$= 2\dfrac{\sqrt{\sin^2\beta\cos^2\beta - (\sin^2\alpha - \cos^2\beta)(\sin^2\alpha - \sin^2\beta)}}{|\sin^2\alpha - \cos^2\beta + \sin^2\alpha - \sin^2\beta|}$

$= 2\dfrac{\sqrt{\begin{array}{c}\{\sin^2\beta\cos^2\beta - \sin^4\alpha + \sin^2\alpha\sin^2\beta \\ + \sin^2\alpha\cos^2\beta - \sin^2\beta\cos^2\beta\}\end{array}}}{|(2\sin^2\alpha - 1)|}$

$= 2\dfrac{\sqrt{\sin\alpha(1 - \sin^2\alpha)}}{|-\cos 2\alpha|} = \dfrac{2\sin\alpha\cos\alpha}{|-\cos 2\alpha|} = \tan 2\alpha$

$\Rightarrow \theta = 2\alpha$

**9.** **(a,b)** $(a + b)x + (a - b)y - 2ab = 0$
and $(a - b)x + (a + b)y - 2ab = 0$
Equation of the angle bisectors are
$(a + b)x + (a - b)y - 2ab = \pm((a - b)x + (a + b)y - 2ab)$
$2bx - 2by = 0$ i.e., $x = y$
and $2ax + 2ay - 4ab = 0$ i.e., $x + y = 2b$
$\therefore$ Equation of third side is given by
(i) $x - y = k$ satisfying the point $(b - a, a - b)$
$\therefore k = 2b - 2a$
$\therefore$ The line is $x - y = 2(b - a)$
(ii) $x + y - 2b = k$ passing through the point $(b - a, a - b)$
$\therefore k = -2b$
$\therefore$ The line is $x + y = 0$

**10.** **(a,b,c,d)** Let the slope of $u = 0$ be m then the slope of $v = 0$ is $9m/2$

$\therefore \dfrac{7}{9} = \left|\dfrac{m - \dfrac{9m}{2}}{1 + m.\dfrac{9m}{2}}\right| = \left|\dfrac{-7m}{2 + 9m^2}\right|$

i.e., $\dfrac{7m}{2 + 9m^2} = \pm\dfrac{7}{9}$ i.e., $2 + 9m^2 = \pm 9m$

i.e., $9m^2 - 9m + 2 = 0$ or $9m^2 + 9m + 2 = 0$

$m = \dfrac{9 \pm \sqrt{81 - 72}}{18} = \dfrac{9 \pm 3}{18} = \dfrac{2}{3}, \dfrac{1}{3}$

or $m = \dfrac{-9 \pm 3}{18} = -\dfrac{2}{3}, -\dfrac{1}{3}$

$\therefore$ Equations of the lines are
(i) $3y = x$ and $2y = 3x$
(ii) $3y = 2x$ and $y = 3x$
(iii) $x + 3y = 0$ and $3x + 2y = 0$
(iv) $2x + 3y = 0$ and $3x + y = 0$

**11.** **(a,b,c,d)** The two lines will be identical if their exists some real number $k$ such that
$b^3 - c^3 = k(b - c)$, $c^3 - a^3 = k(c - a)$
and $a^3 - b^3 = k(a - b)$
$\Rightarrow b - c = 0$ or $b^2 + c^2 + bc = k$
$\quad c - a = 0$ or $c^2 + a^2 + ca = k$
and $a - b = 0$ or $a^2 + b^2 + ab = k$
$\Rightarrow a = b$ or $b = c$ or $c = a$
or $b^2 + c^2 + bc = c^2 + a^2 + ca$
$\Rightarrow b = c$ or $c = a$
or $a = b$ or $a + b + c = 0$

**12.** **(b,d)** Equation of any line through the point of intersection of the given lines is $(3x + y - 5) + \lambda(x - y + 1) = 0$. since this line is perpendicular to one of the given lines

$\dfrac{3 + \lambda}{\lambda - 1} = -1$ or $\dfrac{1}{3}$

$\Rightarrow \lambda = -1$ or $-5$, therefore the required straight line is $x + y - 3 = 0$ or $x - 3y + 5 = 0$

**13.** **(a)** If the line passes through the pole then obviously for any point $p(r, \theta)$ on it $\theta = \alpha$

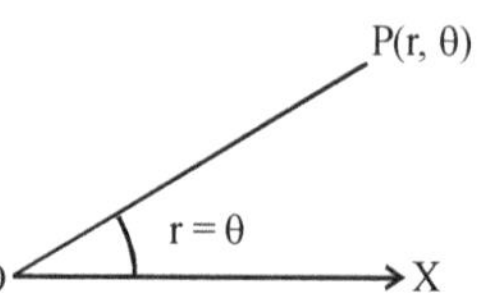



**14.** **(c)** $a\cos\theta + b\sin\theta = \dfrac{l}{r}$ has cartesian form $ax + by = l$

Any line parallel to it is $ax + by = l'$

$\Rightarrow a\cos\theta + b\sin\theta = \dfrac{l'}{r}$

**15.** **(b)** As solved in question (2), the cartesian form of the desired line is $bx - ay = 0 \Rightarrow b\cos\theta = a\sin\theta$

$$\Rightarrow \theta = \tan^{-1}\left(\frac{b}{a}\right)$$

**16.** **A - t, r; B - s, p; C -q**

Given two lines are

$\because 4x + 3y - 6 = 0$ and $5x + 12y + 9 = 0$

$\Rightarrow -4x - 3y + 6 = 0$ and $5x + 12y + 9 = 0$

$\because (-4)(5) + (-3)(12) = -56 < 0$

$\therefore$ Bisectors are $\left(\dfrac{-4x - 3y + 6}{5}\right) = \pm\left(\dfrac{5x + 12y + 9}{13}\right)$

$\Rightarrow (-52x - 39y + 78) = \pm(25x + 60y + 45)$

O : $(-52x - 39y + 78) = -(25x + 60y + 45)$

or $27x - 21y - 123 = 0$

or $9x - 7y - 41 = 0$

$\therefore$ O : $9x - 7y - 41 = 0$ **(t)**

and A : $(-52x - 39y + 78) = (25x + 60y + 45)$

or $77x + 99y - 33 = 0$

or $7x + 9y - 3 = 0$

$\therefore$ A : $7x + 9y - 3 = 0$ **(r)**

**(B)** Given two lines $4x - 3y - 6 = 0$ and $5x - 12y + 9 = 0$

$\Rightarrow -4x + 3y + 6 = 0$

$\because (-4)(5) + 3(-12) = -56 < 0$

$\therefore$ Bisectors are $\left(\dfrac{-4x + 3y + 6}{5}\right) = \pm\left(\dfrac{5x - 12y + 9}{13}\right)$

$\Rightarrow (-52x + 39y + 78) = \pm(25x - 60y + 45)$

O : $(-52x + 39y + 78) = -(25x - 60y + 45)$

or $27x + 21y - 123 = 0$

or $9x + 7y - 41 = 0$

$\therefore$ O : $9x + 7y - 41 = 0$ **(s)**

and A : $(-52x + 39y + 78) = (25x - 60y + 45)$

or $77x - 99y - 33 = 0$

or $7x - 9y - 3 = 0$

$\therefore$ A : $7x - 9y - 3 = 0$ **(p)**

**(C)** $\because 4x - 3y + 6 = 0$ and $5x - 12y - 9 = 0$

or $4x - 3y + 6 = 0$ and $-5x + 12y + 9 = 0$

$\because (4)(-5) + (-3)(12) = -56 < 0$

$\therefore$ Bisectors are $\left(\dfrac{4x - 3y + 6}{5}\right) = \pm\left(\dfrac{-5x + 12y + 9}{13}\right)$

$\Rightarrow (52x - 39y + 78) = \pm(-25x + 60y + 45)$

O : $(52x - 39y + 78) = -(-25x + 60y + 45)$

or $27x + 21y + 123 = 0$

or $9x + 7y + 41 = 0$

$\therefore$ O : $9x + 7y + 41 = 0$

and A : $(52x - 39y + 78) = (-25x + 60y + 45)$

or $77x - 99y + 33 = 0$

or $7x - 9y + 3 = 0$

$\therefore$ A : $7x - 9y + 3 = 0$ **(q)**

**17.** **(b)** Any line through the intersection of $x + y + 4 = 0$ & $3x - y - 8 = 0$ is $(x + y + 4) + \lambda(3x - y - 8) = 0$. Since it passes through $(2, -3)$ so $\lambda = -3$. Hence required equation is $2x - y - 7 = 0$.

**18.** **(d)** Equation of $AB$ is $y - 1 = \dfrac{0 - 1}{2 - 0}(x - 0)$

or $x + 2y - 2 = 0$

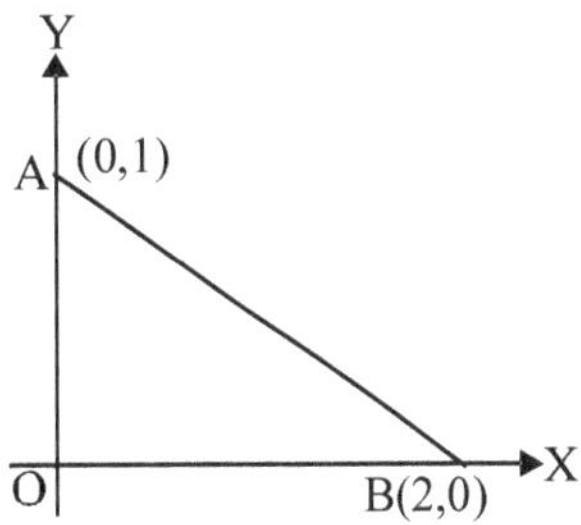

$|PA - PB| \le |AB|$ thus $|PA - PB|$ to be maximum then $A$, $B$ and $P$ must be collinear.

Hence, solving $x + 2y - 2 = 0$ and $4x + 3y + 9 = 0$

we get, $P\left(-\dfrac{24}{5}, \dfrac{17}{5}\right)$.

**19.** **(a)** The pair of bisectors of $2x^2 + 6xy + y^2 = 0$

and $4x^2 + 18xy + y^2 = 0$ coincides

$\Rightarrow$ angle between $\ell_1, m_2$ is same as angle between $\ell_2, m_1$.

Both are true and it is correct reason.

Hence (a) is correct choice.

**20.** **(3)** Equation of the bisectors of the angles between the lines $a^2x^2 + 2axy + y^2 = 0$ is $\dfrac{x^2 - y^2}{a^2 - 1} = \dfrac{xy}{a}$ which is

satisfied by $y = 3x$ if $\dfrac{1 - 9}{a^2 - 1} = \dfrac{3}{a}$

i.e., if $3a^2 + 8a - 3 = 0$ or if $a = -3, \dfrac{1}{3}$.

Thus X = 3.

**21.** **(6)** Let $m$ and $m^2$ be the slopes of the lines represented by $ax^2 + 2hxy + by = 0$

Then, $m + m^2 = -\dfrac{2h}{b}$    ...(1)

$m.m^2 = \dfrac{a}{b}$ or $m^3 = \dfrac{a}{b}$    ...(2)

from (1) $(m + m^2)^3 = \left(-\dfrac{2h}{b}\right)^3$

$\Rightarrow m^3 + m^6 + 3.\,m.m^2(m + m^2) = -\dfrac{8h^3}{b^3}$

$\Rightarrow \dfrac{a}{h} + \dfrac{a^2}{b^2} + \dfrac{3a}{b}\left(-\dfrac{2h}{b}\right) = -\dfrac{8h^3}{b^3}$ {from (1) and (2)}

$\Rightarrow \dfrac{a}{b^2}(a + b)\dfrac{8h^3}{b^3} = \dfrac{6ah}{b^2}$ or $\dfrac{(a + b)}{h} + \dfrac{8h^2}{ab} = 6$

**22. (4)**

Pair of bisectors of

$a(x-1)^2 + 2h(x-1)(y-2) + b(y-2)^2 = 0$ is

$$\frac{(x-1)^2 - (y-2)^2}{a-b} = \frac{(x-1)(y-2)}{h}$$

$\Rightarrow\quad h\{x^2 - y^2 - 2x + 4y - 3\} = (a-b)(xy - 2x - y + 2)$

$\Rightarrow\quad hx^2 - hy^2 - (a-b)xy + 2x(a-b-h) + y(a-b+4h) - 2(a-b) - 3h = 0$

Given one bisector is $x + 2y - 5 = 0$

then let other bisector is $2x - y + \lambda = 0$

$\therefore$ pair of bisector is $(x + 2y - 5)(2x - y + \lambda) = 0 \Rightarrow 2x^2 - 2y^2 + 3xy - 10x + \lambda x + 2\lambda y + 5y - 5\lambda = 0$

Comparing (1) and (2) we get

$h = 2, a - b = -3, 2a - 2b - 2h = -10 + \lambda$

$\therefore\quad 2(-3) - 4 = -10 + \lambda \Rightarrow \lambda = 0$

$\therefore$ The other bisector is $2x - y = 0$

So, $2\alpha - (\alpha - 4) = 0 \Rightarrow \alpha = 4$

**23. (5)** The given equation can be written as

$(x^2 + y^2)(\cos^2\theta \sin^2\alpha + \sin^2\theta) = x^2 \tan^2\alpha - 2xy \tan\alpha \sin\theta + y^2\sin^2\theta$

or $(\cos^2\theta \sin^2\alpha + \sin^2\theta - \tan^2\alpha)x^2 + 2(\tan\alpha \sin\theta)xy + \cos^2\theta \sin^2\alpha \, y^2 = 0$

Since the slope of these lines are given as $\tan\theta_1$ and $\tan\theta_2$

Sum of the slopes $= \dfrac{-2\tan\alpha \sin\theta}{\cos^2\theta \sin^2\alpha}$ $\quad \left(\because \theta = \dfrac{\pi}{6}\right)$

$\Rightarrow \tan\theta_1 + \tan\theta_2 = \dfrac{-2\tan\theta \times \dfrac{1}{2}}{\dfrac{3}{4} \times \sin^2\alpha} = -\dfrac{8}{3}\operatorname{cosec}2\alpha$

Thus, $A - B = 8 - 3 = 5$.

**24. (2)**

Intersection of $3x + 4y = 9$ and $y = mx + 1$.

For x co-ordinate

$3x + 4(mx + 1) = 9 \Rightarrow (3 + 4m)x = 5$

$\Rightarrow x = \dfrac{5}{3 + 4m}$

For x to be an integer $3 + 4m$ should be a divisor of 5 i.e., $1, -1, 5$ or $-5$.

$3 + 4m = 1 \quad \Rightarrow m = -1/2$ (not integer)

$3 + 4m = -1 \Rightarrow m = -1$ (integer)

$3 + 4m = 5 \quad \Rightarrow m = 1/2$ (not an integer)

$3 + 4m = -5 \Rightarrow m = -2$ (integer)

$\therefore$ There are 2 integral values of m.

**1. (a)** Mid point of QS = Mid point of PS

$0 = h + x_1$

$\Rightarrow x_1 = -h$

$PQ \equiv y = mx + c$

passes through $(-h, 0)$

$c = mh$

$\therefore \quad y = mx - mh$

since Q lies on it

$\Rightarrow y_1 = ma - mh$

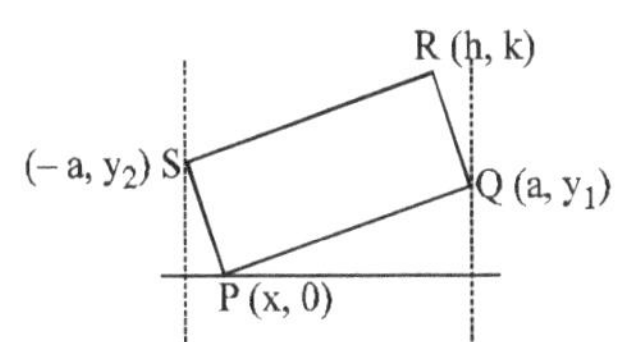


now $m_{QR} = -\dfrac{1}{m} = \dfrac{y_1 - K}{a - h}$

$-\dfrac{1}{m} = \dfrac{m(a - h) - K}{a - h}$

simplifying $h + mk = a + (a - h)m^2 \Rightarrow$ a st. line

**2. (d)** Let the coordinates of C be $(1, c)$

$m_2 = \dfrac{c - y}{1 - x}$ ;

$m_2 = \dfrac{c - m_1 x}{1 - x}$

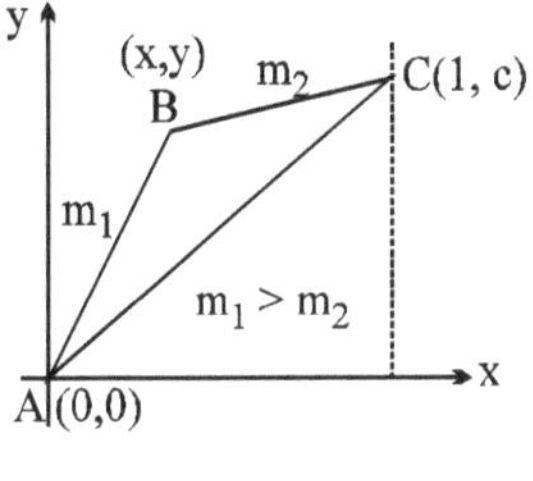


$m_2 - m_2 x = c - m_1 x$

$(m_1 - m_2)x = c - m_2$

$c = (m_1 - m_2)x + m_2 \;....(1)$

now area of $\Delta ABC = \dfrac{1}{2}\begin{vmatrix} 0 & 0 & 1 \\ x & m_1 x & 1 \\ 1 & c & 1 \end{vmatrix}$

$= \dfrac{1}{2}[cx - m_1 x] = \dfrac{1}{2}\left| [((m_1 - m_2)x + m_2)x - m_1 x] \right|$

$= \dfrac{1}{2}\left| [(m_1 - m_2)x^2 + m_2 x - m_1 x] \right|$

$= \dfrac{1}{2}(m_1 - m_2)(x - x^2) \quad (x > x^2 \text{ in } (0, 1))$

Hence, $f(x) = \dfrac{1}{2}(x - x^2); f(x)]_{max} = \dfrac{1}{8}$ when $x = \dfrac{1}{2}$

**3. (a)**

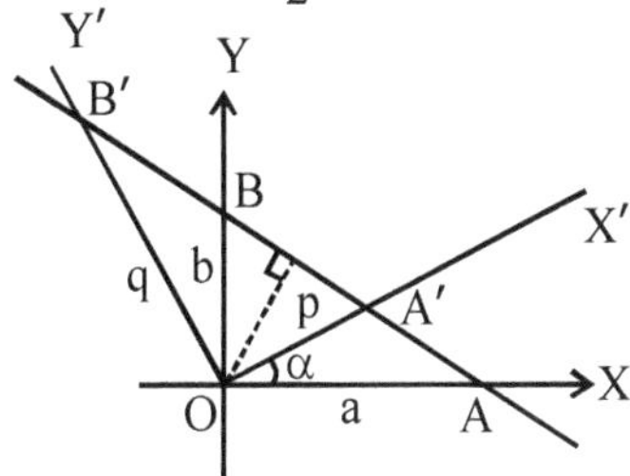


The length of the perpendicular from the origin to the line in both the cases is the same. So,

$\dfrac{\dfrac{0}{a} + \dfrac{0}{b} - 1}{\sqrt{\dfrac{1}{a^2} + \dfrac{1}{b^2}}} = \dfrac{\dfrac{0}{p} + \dfrac{0}{q} - 1}{\sqrt{\dfrac{1}{p^2} + \dfrac{1}{q^2}}} \Rightarrow \dfrac{1}{a^2} + \dfrac{1}{b^2} = \dfrac{1}{p^2} + \dfrac{1}{q^2}$

$\therefore \dfrac{1}{p^2} + \dfrac{1}{q^2} = \dfrac{1}{a^2} + \dfrac{1}{b^2}$

**4. (b)** The axes are rotated by angle $\theta$, where $\tan \theta = 2$.

Thus, $\sin \theta = \dfrac{2}{\sqrt{5}}$ and $\cos \theta = \dfrac{1}{\sqrt{5}}$

Now replacing x by $X \cos\theta - Y \sin\theta$ and y by $X \sin\theta + Y \cos\theta$,

$14\left(\dfrac{x}{\sqrt{5}} - \dfrac{2y}{\sqrt{5}}\right)^2 - 4\left(\dfrac{x}{\sqrt{5}} - \dfrac{2y}{\sqrt{5}}\right)\left(\dfrac{2x}{\sqrt{5}} + \dfrac{y}{\sqrt{5}}\right)$

$+11\left(\dfrac{2x}{\sqrt{5}} - \dfrac{y}{\sqrt{5}}\right)^2 = 60$

$\Rightarrow 10x^2 + 15y^2 = 60 \Rightarrow \dfrac{x^2}{6} + \dfrac{y^2}{4} = 1$

**5. (c)** $\dfrac{s_1}{s} = \dfrac{p^2}{a^2} \Rightarrow \sqrt{\dfrac{s_1}{s}} = \dfrac{p}{a}$

Similarly $\sqrt{\dfrac{s_2}{s}} = \dfrac{q}{a}$ and $\sqrt{\dfrac{s_3}{s}} = \dfrac{r}{a}$

$\Rightarrow \dfrac{\sqrt{s_1} + \sqrt{s_2} + \sqrt{s_3}}{\sqrt{s}} = \dfrac{p + q + r}{a} = 1$

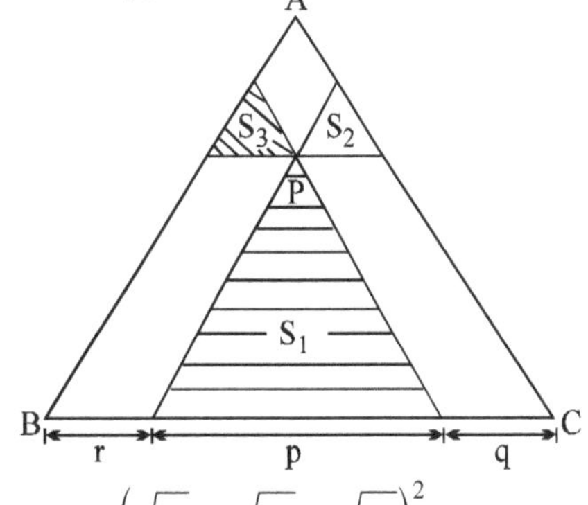


$\Rightarrow s = \left(\sqrt{s_1} + \sqrt{s_2} + \sqrt{s_3}\right)^2$

**6. (d)** Clearly $OP = OQ = 1$ and $\angle QOP = \alpha - \theta - \theta = \alpha - 2\theta$.

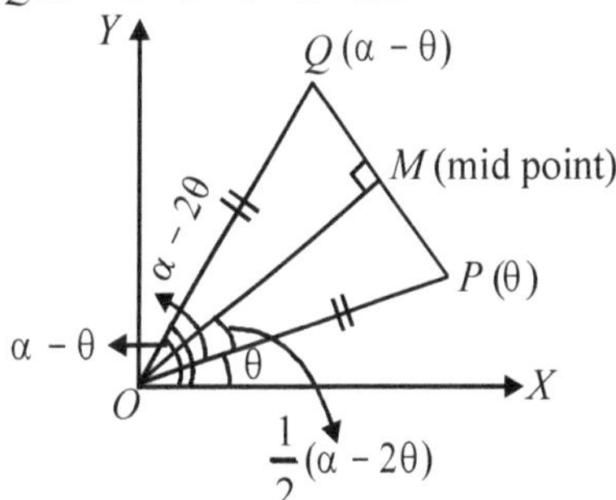


The bisector of $\angle QOP$ will be a perpendicular to $PQ$ and also bisect it. Hence $Q$ is reflection of $P$ in the line $OM$ which makes an angle $\angle MOP + \angle POX$ with $x$-axis, i.e.,

$\dfrac{1}{2}(\alpha - 2\theta) + \theta = \alpha / 2.$

So that slope of $OM$ is $\tan \alpha/2$.

**7. (b)** Lines $x \cos\alpha + y \sin\alpha = p$ and $x \sin\alpha - y \cos\alpha = 0$ are mutually perpendicular. Thus $ax + by + p = 0$ will be equally inclined to these line and would be the angle bisector of these lines. Now equations of angle bisectors is,

$x \sin\alpha - y \cos\alpha = \pm (x \cos\alpha + y \sin\alpha - p)$

$\Rightarrow x(\cos\alpha - \sin\alpha) + y(\sin\alpha + \cos\alpha) = p$

or $x(\sin\alpha + \cos\alpha) - y(\cos\alpha - \sin\alpha) = p$

Comparing these lines with $ax + by + p = 0$, we get

$$\frac{a}{\cos\alpha - \sin\alpha} = \frac{b}{\sin\alpha + \cos\alpha} = 1 \Rightarrow a^2 + b^2 = 2$$

or $$\frac{a}{\sin\alpha + \cos\alpha} = \frac{b}{\sin\alpha - \cos\alpha} = 1 \Rightarrow a^2 + b^2 = 2$$

**8. (c)** Reflection about the line $y = x$, changes the point $(4, 1)$ to $(1, 4)$.

On translation of $(1, 4)$ through a distance of 2 units along +ve direction of x-axis the point becomes $(1 + 2, 4)$, i.e., $(3, 4)$.

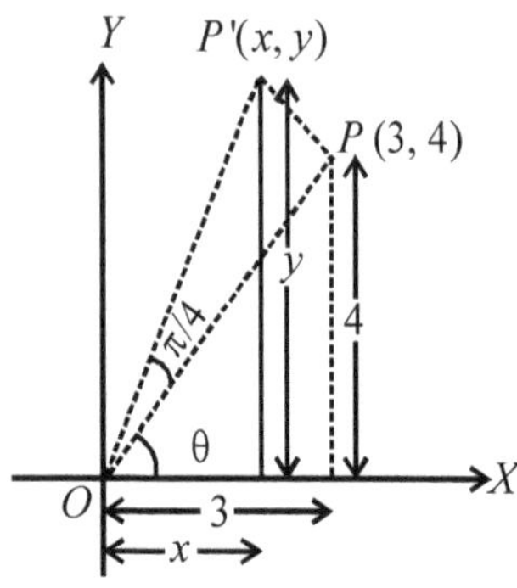

On rotation about origin through an angle $\pi/4$ the point $P$ takes the position $P'$ such that
$$OP = OP'$$

Also $OP = 5 = OP'$ and $\cos\theta = \dfrac{3}{5}$, $\sin\theta = \dfrac{4}{5}$

Now, $x = OP' \cos\left(\dfrac{\pi}{4} + \theta\right)$

$= 5\left(\cos\dfrac{\pi}{4}\cos\theta - \sin\dfrac{\pi}{4}\sin\theta\right)$

$= 5\left(\dfrac{3}{5\sqrt{2}} - \dfrac{4}{5\sqrt{2}}\right) = -\dfrac{1}{\sqrt{2}}$

$y = OP' \sin\left(\dfrac{\pi}{4} + \theta\right)$

$= 5\left(\sin\dfrac{\pi}{4}\cos\theta + \cos\dfrac{\pi}{4}\sin\theta\right)$

$= 5\left(\dfrac{3}{5\sqrt{2}} + \dfrac{4}{5\sqrt{2}}\right) = \dfrac{7}{\sqrt{2}}$

$\therefore \quad P' = \left(-\dfrac{1}{\sqrt{2}}, \dfrac{7}{\sqrt{2}}\right)$

**9. (c,d)** Equation of given line is $2x + y = 2$ ... (i)

When axes are rotated by an angle of $45°$ in anticlockwise direction then equation of the line with respect to new axes will be

$2(x \cos 45° - y \sin 45°) + (x \sin 45° + y \cos 45°) = 2$

or $\quad 3x - y = 2\sqrt{2}$ . ... (ii)

Length of intercepts made by this line on new axes are

$\dfrac{2\sqrt{2}}{3}$ and $2\sqrt{2}$

When the axes are rotated by an angle of $45°$ in clockwise direction, then equation of line (i) with respect to new axes will be

$2(x \cos 45° + y \sin 45°) + (-x \sin 45° + y \cos 45°) = 2$

or $\quad x + 3y = 2\sqrt{2}$ ... (iii)

Length of intercept of line (iii) on new axes are $2\sqrt{2}$

and $\dfrac{2\sqrt{2}}{3}$ .

**10. (b, d)** If $B$ lies on $y$ - axis, then coordinates of $B$ are $(0, a)$ or $(0, -a)$

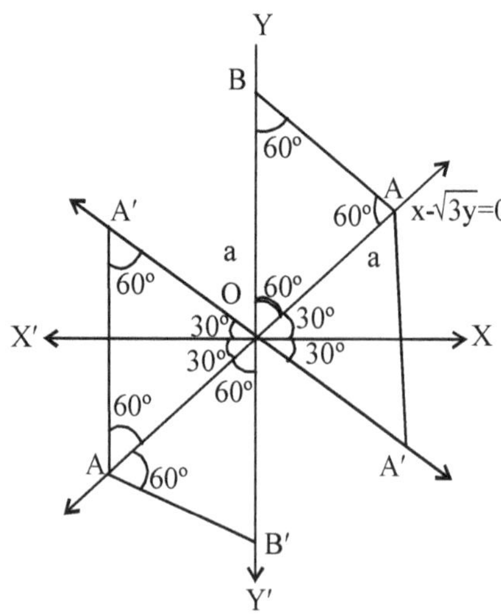


If third vertex in IV quadrant or in II quadrant, then its coordinates are $(a \cos 30°, -a \sin 30°)$
or $(-a \cos 30°, a \sin 30°)$

i.e, $\left(\dfrac{a\sqrt{3}}{2}, -\dfrac{a}{2}\right)$ or $\left(-\dfrac{a\sqrt{3}}{2}, \dfrac{a}{2}\right)$

**11. (a, c)** $\dfrac{x - \dfrac{a}{2}}{\dfrac{b}{\sqrt{a^2 + b^2}}} = \dfrac{y - \dfrac{b}{2}}{\dfrac{a}{\sqrt{a^2 + b^2}}} = \pm\dfrac{\sqrt{a^2 + b^2}}{2}$

$x = \dfrac{a}{2} + \dfrac{b}{2}, \; y = \dfrac{b}{2} + \dfrac{a}{2}$

and $x = \dfrac{a}{2} - \dfrac{b}{2}, \; y = \dfrac{b}{2} - \dfrac{a}{2}$

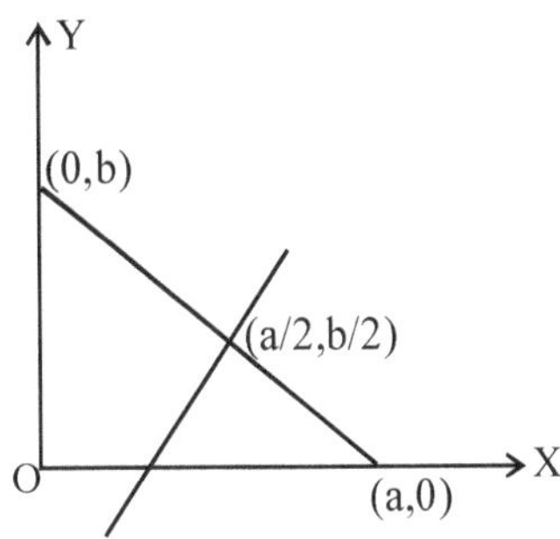

$\therefore$ The required points are

$\left(\dfrac{a+b}{2}, \dfrac{a+b}{2}\right)$ and $\left(\dfrac{a-b}{2}, \dfrac{b-a}{2}\right)$

**12. (c)** Any point on the line $3x - y = 2$ is $(t, 3t - 2)$, $t$ being parameter.

If $(x, y)$ be image of the point $(t, 3t - 2)$ in the line $y = x - 1$ or $x - y - 1 = 0$, then

$$\frac{x-t}{1} = \frac{y-(3t-2)}{-1} = -\frac{2(t-3t+2-1)}{1+1}$$

$$\Rightarrow \quad \frac{x-t}{1} = \frac{y-3t+2}{-1} = 2t-1$$

or $\quad x - t = 2t - 1$

$\Rightarrow \quad x + 1 = 3t \qquad\qquad ....(i)$

and $\quad y - 3t + 2 = -2t + 1$

$\Rightarrow y + 1 = t \qquad\qquad ... (ii)$

From Eqs. (i) and (ii), we get

$x + 1 = 3(y + 1)$

$\Rightarrow \quad x - 3y = 2$

**13. (d)** Any point on the circle $x^2 + y^2 = 4$ is $(2\cos\theta, 2\sin\theta)$, $\theta$ being parameter.

If $(x, y)$ be image of the point $(2\cos\theta, 2\sin\theta)$ in the line $x + y = 2$, then

$$\frac{x-2\cos\theta}{1} = \frac{y-2\sin\theta}{1} = \frac{-2(2\cos\theta+2\sin\theta-2)}{1+1}$$

or $x - 2\cos\theta = y - 2\sin\theta = -2\cos\theta - 2\sin\theta + 2$ ....(i)

or $\quad x - 2\cos\theta = -2\cos\theta - 2\sin\theta + 2$

$\Rightarrow \quad x - 2 = -2\sin\theta$

and $y - 2\sin\theta = -2\cos\theta - 2\sin\theta + 2$

$\Rightarrow y - 2 = -2\cos\theta \qquad ....(ii)$

From Eqs. (i) and (ii),

$(x - 2)^2 + (y - 2)^2 = 4$

$\Rightarrow \quad x^2 + y^2 - 4x - 4y + 4 = 0$

**14. (b)** Any point on the parabola $x^2 = 4y$ is $(2t, t^2)$, $t$ being parameter.

If $(x, y)$ be image of the point $(2t, t^2)$ in the line $x + y = a$, then

$$\frac{x-2t}{1} = \frac{y-t^2}{1} = \frac{-2(2t+t^2-a)}{1+1} = -2t - t^2 + a$$

$\therefore \quad x - 2t = -2t - t^2 + a$

$\Rightarrow \quad x - a = -t^2 \qquad ...(i)$

and $y - t^2 = -2t - t^2 + a$

$\Rightarrow \quad y - a = -2t \qquad ... (ii)$

From Eqs. (i) and (ii)

$(y - a)^2 = 4t^2 = -4(x - a)$

or $\quad (y - a)^2 = 4(a - x)$

**15.** **A - s; B - p; C - q; D - r**

If image of $(2, -3)$ with respect to $y$-axis be $(x, -3)$ then

$x + 2 = 0 \Rightarrow x = -2$

If image of $(-3, 4)$ with respect to point $(1, 2)$ be $(x, y)$ then

$\dfrac{x-3}{2} = -1$ and $\dfrac{y+4}{2} = 2 \Rightarrow x = 5, y = 0$

If image of $(2, 1)$ with respect to $x + 1 = 0$ be $(x, 1)$ then

$\dfrac{x+2}{2} = -1 \Rightarrow x = -4$

If image of $(4, 3)$ with respect to $2x + y - 1 = 0$ be $(x, y)$ then

$\dfrac{x-4}{2} = \dfrac{y-3}{1} = -\dfrac{2(8+3-1)}{5} = -4$

$\Rightarrow x = -4, y = -1$

**16.** **A→t; B→p; C→r; D→q**

(A) Let the desired line be $x + 2y - 1 + \lambda(x - y + 2) = 0$,

which is perpendicular to $3x + y + 5 = 0$. So, $\lambda = -\dfrac{5}{2}$.

Thus the line is $x - 3y + 4 = 0$.

(B) Any point on the line $x - 2y = 1$ is $(1 + 2t, t)$. The image of the point in $x + y = 0$ is given by $x = -t$, $y = -1 - 2t$.

Eliminating $t$ we get $y = -1 + 2x \Rightarrow 2x - y = 1$

(C) In right angled triangles ACB and OCN,

$\angle CBA = \angle CON$

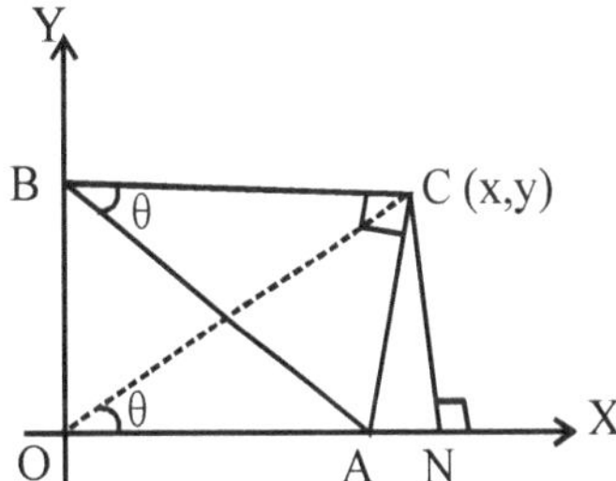

$\therefore$ The triangles are similar

$$\Rightarrow \frac{CN}{ON} = \frac{AC}{BC} \Rightarrow \frac{y}{x} = \frac{3}{4}$$

(D) The third vertex C is $(h, k)$ then centroid

$$x = \frac{1-1+h}{3} \Rightarrow h = 3x$$

and $y = \dfrac{2+5+k}{3} \Rightarrow k = 3y - 7$.

Now $2h + k = 2 \Rightarrow 6x + 3y - 7 = 2 \Rightarrow 2x + y = 3$.

**17. (d)** The statement-1 is false since

$(x - 2) + (2x - 3) + (5 - 3x) = 0$ but the lines $x - 2 = 0$, $2x - 3 = 0$ and $5 - 3x = 0$ are parallel. The Statement-2 is a standard true result whose more general form is.

If $L_1 = 0$ and $L_2 = 0$, $L_3 = 0$ be three lines. If we could find $\lambda, \mu, \nu$ (not all zero) such that $\lambda L_1 + \mu L_2 + \nu L_3 = 0$ then the three lines $L_1 = 0$, $L_2 = 0$, $L_3 = 0$ are either concurrent or are parallel.

**18.** **(c)** The image of $P(a, b)$ on
$y = -x$ is $Q(-b, -a)$
(interchange $x, y$ and change signs)

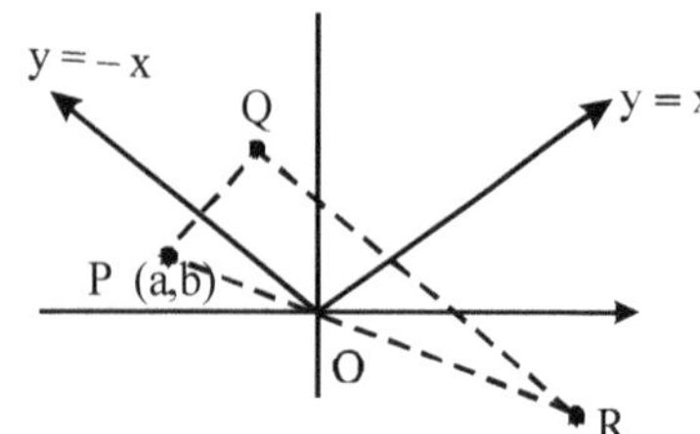

and the image of $Q(-b, -a)$ on $y = x$ is $R(-a, -b)$ (merely interchange).
$\therefore$ The mid point of $PR$ is $(0, 0)$.

**19.** **(1)**
Lines are $x + y + 1 = 0$; $4x + 3y + 4 = 0$ and
$x + \alpha y + \beta = 0$, where $\alpha^2 + \beta^2 = 2$

$$\begin{vmatrix} 1 & 1 & 1 \\ 4 & 3 & 4 \\ 1 & \alpha & \beta \end{vmatrix} = 0$$

$1(3\beta - 4\alpha) - 1(4\beta - 4) + 1(4\alpha - 3)$
$= 3\beta - 4\alpha - 4\beta + 4 + 4\alpha - 3$
$= -\beta + 1 = 0 \Rightarrow \beta = 1$
$\therefore \alpha = \pm 1$

**20.** **(2)**

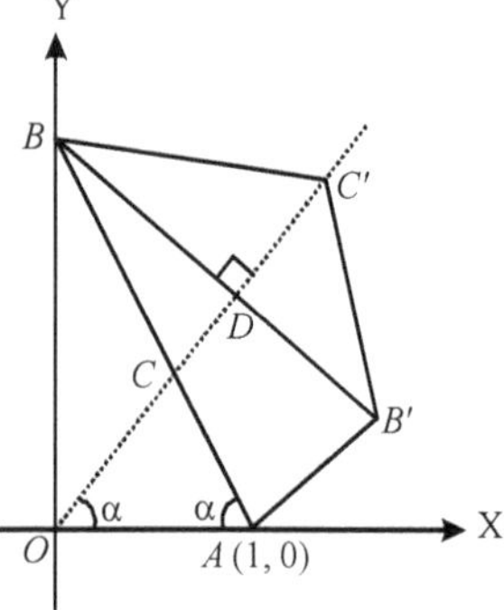

From figure $OB = \tan\alpha$ and $\angle COA = \alpha$
So, equation of line $OC$ is $y = x \tan\alpha$
and $AB = \sec\alpha$
So,
In $\triangle BDC$
angle $BCD = (180° - 2\alpha)\left(\because \angle COA = \alpha\right)$
$\Rightarrow BD = BC\sin(180 - 2\alpha)$

$$= BC \times \sin 2\alpha = \frac{1}{2} \times \sec\alpha \times 2\sin\alpha \times \cos\alpha = \sin\alpha$$

$\Rightarrow BD = B'D' = \sin\alpha$
Clearly $\triangle BDC$ and $\triangle BDC'$ are congruent

$$BC' = BC = \frac{1}{2}\sec\alpha \text{ and } \angle ABB' = \angle B'BC' \qquad ...(2)$$

Now, $\dfrac{\text{area of } \triangle ABB'}{\text{area of } \triangle BB'C'} = \dfrac{AB \times BB' \times \sin\angle ABB'}{BB' \times BC' \times \sin\angle B'BC'}$

$$= \frac{AB}{BC'} = \frac{\sec\alpha}{\frac{1}{2}\sec\alpha} = 2 \text{ (Since } \angle ABB' = \angle B'BC')$$

**21.** **(3)**
Equation of any line through $(2, 3)$ is $y - 3 = m(x - 2)$
$y = mx - 2m + 3$
with the help of the fig. area of $\triangle OAB = \pm 12$

ie. $\dfrac{1}{2}\left(\dfrac{2m - 3}{m}\right)(3 - 2m) = \pm 12$

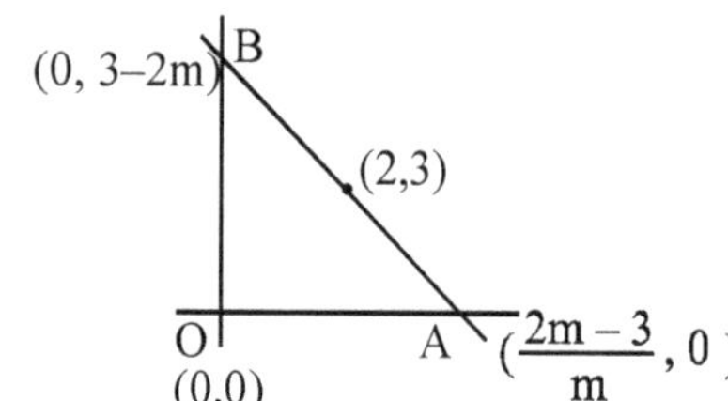

taking $+$ sign me get $(2m + 3)^2 = 0$
this gives one value of $m = -3/2$
taking negative sign we get
$4m^2 - 36m + 9 = 0 \qquad (D > 0)$
quadratic in m gives 2 values of m
$\Rightarrow$ 3 st. lines are possible.

**22.** **(2)**
The slope of the line $x - y + 1 = 0$ is 1. So it makes an angle of $45°$ with x axis.
The equation of a line passing through $(2, 3)$ and making an angle of $45°$ is

$$\frac{x - 2}{\cos 45°} = \frac{y - 3}{\sin 45°} = r$$

Coordinates of any point on this line are

$$(2 + r\cos 45°, 3 + r\sin 45°) \text{ or } \left(2 + \frac{r}{\sqrt{2}}, 3 + \frac{r}{\sqrt{2}}\right)$$

If this point lies on this line $2x - 3y + 9 = 0$, then

$$4 + r\sqrt{2} - 9 - \frac{3r}{\sqrt{2}} + 9 = 0 \Rightarrow r = 4\sqrt{2}$$

So the required distance $= 4\sqrt{2}$ units
Thus, $A = 2$.

**23.** **(5)**
$x + 2y - 1 = 0$, $ax + y + 3 = 0$, $bx - y + 2 = 0$ are concurrent.

$$\therefore \begin{vmatrix} 1 & 2 & -1 \\ a & 1 & 3 \\ b & -1 & 2 \end{vmatrix} = 0 \Rightarrow 5 - 2(2a - 3b) + a + b = 0$$

$\Rightarrow 7b - 3a + 5 = 0$
$\therefore$ Locus of $(a, b)$ is $3x - 7y = 5$
$\therefore$ Least distance from $(0, 0) = $ length of perpendicular from

$$(0, 0) = \frac{5}{\sqrt{58}}.$$

Thus $A = 5$ and $B = 58$.

**1.** **(a)** Centre is $x = t^2 - 3t + 1$ ....(1)

$y = t^2 + 2t$ ....(2)

eliminating t, we get

$x = t^2 + 2t - 5t + 1 = y - 5t + 1$

$t = \dfrac{y - x + 1}{5}$

Substituting the value of t in (2)

$y = \left(\dfrac{y - x + 1}{5}\right)^2 + 2\left(\dfrac{y - x + 1}{5}\right)$

$25y = (y - x + 1)^2 + 10(y - x + 1)$

$25y = y^2 + x^2 + 1 - 2xy - 2x + 2y + 10y - 10x + 10$

$x^2 + y^2 - 2xy - 12x - 13y + 11 = 0$

which is a parabola

as $\Delta \neq 0$ and $h^2 = ab$

**2.** **(a)** Given $r = 3k$ and P is centroid

$g^2 + f^2 = (3k)^2$ ....(1)   because $c = 0$

$\therefore 3h_1 = a$ and $3k_1 = b$

also $2\sqrt{g} = a \Rightarrow 2g = a$ and $2f = b$

$\Rightarrow 2g = \dfrac{3h_1}{2}$ and $2f = \dfrac{3k_1}{2}$ substitute in (1)

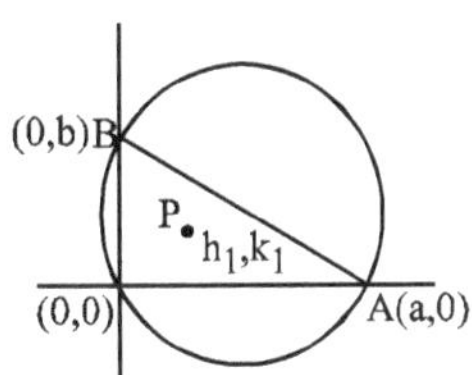

$\dfrac{9h_1^2}{4} + \dfrac{9k_1^2}{4} = 9k^2 \Rightarrow x^2 + y^2 = (2k)^2$

**3.** **(d)** Equation of circle is $x^2 + y^2 + 2gx + 2fy + c = 0$

$(1, t) \Rightarrow 1 + t^2 + 2g + 2ft + c = 0$

$(t, t) \Rightarrow t^2 + t^2 + 2gt + 2ft + c = 0$

$(t, 1) \Rightarrow 1 + t^2 + 2gt + 2f + c = 0$

subtract        $1 + 2g - t^2 - 2gt = 0$

$\Rightarrow 1 - t^2 + 2g(1 - t) = 0$

$\Rightarrow (1 - t)(1 + t + 2g) = 0$

$\Rightarrow t = 1$

$\therefore$ one point $(t, t)$

$\therefore$ passes through $(1, 1)$

**4.** **(c)** Equation of line PQ is

$y - k = -\dfrac{h}{k}(x - h) \Rightarrow hx + ky = h^2 + k^2$

Also $2a = \sqrt{x_1^2 + y_1^2} \Rightarrow x_1^2 + y_1^2 = 4a^2$

$\therefore$ points $Q\left(\dfrac{h^2 + k^2}{h}, 0\right)$ and $P\left(0, \dfrac{h^2 + k^2}{k}\right)$

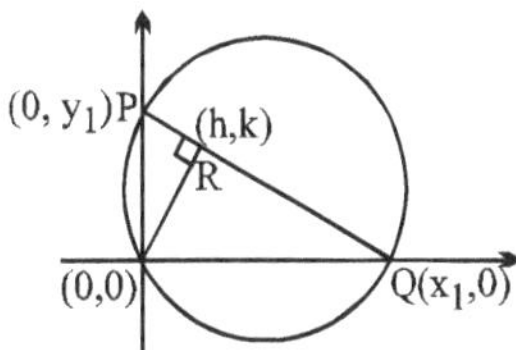

$(x^2 + y^2)^2\left(\dfrac{1}{x^2} + \dfrac{1}{y^2}\right) = 4a^2\,]$

**5.** **(c)** $r = \sqrt{\dfrac{a^2}{4} + \dfrac{b^2}{4}} = \dfrac{\sqrt{a^2 + b^2}}{2}$

$\sin 45° = \dfrac{\sqrt{\left(h - \dfrac{a}{2}\right)^2 + \left(k - \dfrac{b}{2}\right)^2}}{\dfrac{\sqrt{a^2 + b^2}}{2}}$

$\Rightarrow \dfrac{1}{2} = 4\left[\dfrac{\dfrac{(2h - a)^2}{4} + \dfrac{(2k - b)^2}{4}}{a^2 + b^2}\right]$

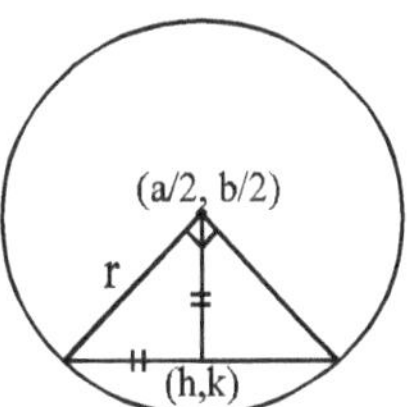

simplify to get locus $x^2 + y^2 - ax - by - \dfrac{a^2 + b^2}{8} = 0$

**6.** **(b)**

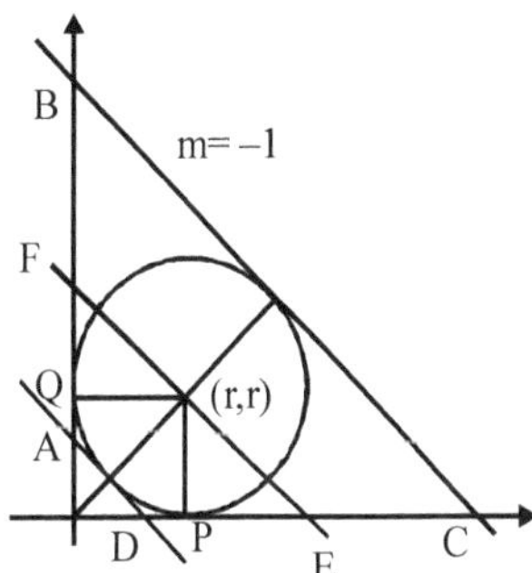

$\Delta = $ Area of ABCD $= \dfrac{1}{2}(a + b)\,h$

{as ABCD is a trapezium}

where $\dfrac{a+b}{2} = EF$ (median) and $h = 2r$

Hence $\Delta = 2r\,(EF)$

Equation of EF is $y = -x + c$ passes through $(r, r)$

$\Rightarrow c = 2r$

Hence EF is $y = -x + 2r$

$\Rightarrow E = (2r, 0)$ and $F \equiv (0, 2r) \Rightarrow EF = 2\sqrt{2}r$

$\Delta = (2r)(2\sqrt{2}r) = 4\sqrt{2}r^2 = 900\sqrt{2} \Rightarrow r = 15$

**7.** **(c)** As $2x - 3y - 5 = 0$ and $3x - 4y - 7 = 0$ are diameters of the circle.

∴ Centre of the circle is solution of these two equations i.e.

$$\dfrac{x}{21-20} = \dfrac{y}{-15+14} = \dfrac{1}{-8+9}$$

$\Rightarrow \quad x = 1,\, y = -1$

∴ $\quad C(1, -1)$

Also area of circle, $\pi r^2 = 154$

$\Rightarrow \quad r^2 = \dfrac{154}{22} \times 7 = 49 \Rightarrow r = 7$

∴ $\quad$ Equation of required circle is

$(x-1)^2 + (y+1)^2 = 7^2$

$\Rightarrow \quad x^2 + y^2 - 2x + 2y = 47$

**8.** **(d)** Let $(h, k)$ be the centre of the circle which touches the circle

$x^2 + y^2 - 6x - 6y + 14 = 0$ and y-axis.

Now, $x^2 + y^2 + 2(-3)x + 2(-3)y + 14 = 0$, the centre

of this circle is $(3, 3)$ and radius is $\sqrt{3^2 + 3^2 - 14} = 2$.

Since, the circle touches y-axis, the distance from its centre to y - axis must be equal to its radius, therefore its radius is h. Again the circles touch externally, therefore the distance between two centres = sum of the radii of the two circles.

Hence, $(h-3)^2 + (k-3)^2 = (2+h)^2$

$\Rightarrow k^2 - 10h - 6k + 14 = 0$

Thus, the locus of $(h, k)$ is $y^2 - 10x - 6y + 14 = 0$

**9.** **(c,d)**

$2h = \alpha + r\cos\theta$

$2k = \beta + r\sin\theta \Rightarrow (2h - \alpha)^2 + (2k - \beta)^2 = r^2$

$$\left(h - \dfrac{\alpha}{2}\right)^2 + \left(k - \dfrac{\beta}{2}\right)^2 = \left(\dfrac{r}{2}\right)^2$$

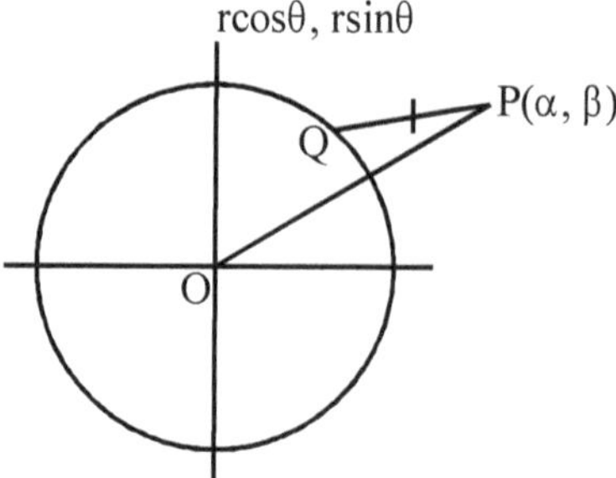


locus is $\left(x - \dfrac{\alpha}{2}\right)^2 + \left(y - \dfrac{\beta}{2}\right)^2 = \left(\dfrac{r}{2}\right)^2$

which is a circle with centre as midpoint of OP and radius r/2.

**10.** **(a,d)** $x^2 + y^2 + 8x - 10y - 40 = 0$

Centre of the circle is $(-4, 5)$

radius $= 9$

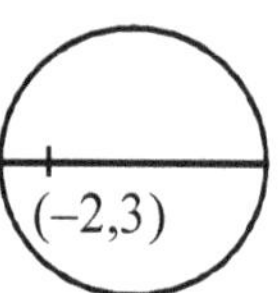


Distance of the centre $(-4, 5)$

from the point $(-2, 3)$ is $\sqrt{4+4} = 2\sqrt{2}$

∴ $a = 2\sqrt{2} + 9$ and $b = -2\sqrt{2} + 9$

∴ $a + b = 18$, $a - b = 4\sqrt{2}$, $a.b = 81 - 8 = 73$

**11.** **(a,b,c,d)** Since $(a, 0)$ is a point on the diameter of the circle $x^2 + y^2 = 4$,

So maximum value of $a^2$ is 4

Let $f(x) = x^2 - 4x - a^2$

clearly $f(-1) = 5 - a^2 > 0$

$f(2) = -(a^2 + 4) < 0$

$f(0) = -a^2 < 0$ and $f(5) = 5 - a^2 > 0$

so graph of $f(x)$ will be as shown

**12.** **(c,d)** Distance between $(4, 3)$ and $(0, 0)$ is 5.

Radius of the circle $x^2 + y^2 = 1$ is 1

∴ $\quad$ radii of the required circles are 4, 6

∴ $\quad$ Equation of the circles are

$(x-4)^2 + (y-3)^2 = 16, 36$

i.e., $x^2 + y^2 - 8x - 6y + 9 = 0$

or $\quad x^2 + y^2 - 8x - 6y - 11 = 0$

**13.** **(c)** The equation of the coaxal system is

$x^2 + y^2 + 4x + 2y + 5 + \lambda(x^2 + y^2 + 2x + 4y + 7) = 0$

or $x^2 + y^2 + \dfrac{2(2+\lambda)}{1+\lambda}x + \dfrac{2(1+2\lambda)}{1+\lambda}y + \dfrac{5+7\lambda}{1+\lambda} = 0$

Equating radius to zero, we get

$$\frac{(2+\lambda)^2+(1+2\lambda)^2-(5+7\lambda)(1+\lambda)}{(1+\lambda)^2}=0$$

$$\Rightarrow 2\lambda^2+4\lambda=0 \Rightarrow \lambda=0 \ or\ -2$$

The centre of above system is $\left(-\dfrac{2+\lambda}{1+\lambda},\ -\dfrac{1+2\lambda}{1+\lambda}\right)$

Substituting the values of $\lambda$, we get the coordinates of limiting points $(-2,-1)$ and $(0,-3)$.

**14. (d)** The point circles represented by the limiting points are $(x-1)^2+(y+1)^2=0$ and $(x-2)^2+y^2=0$

So, the equation of coaxal system is,

$$(x-1)^2+(y+1)^2+\lambda\{(x-2)^2+y^2\}=0 \quad ....(1)$$

It passes through $(0,0)$, so, $\lambda=-\dfrac{1}{2}$ putting into (1)

we get the equation to the desired circle as
$x^2+y^2+4y=0$

**15. (b)** The equation of the given coaxal system is

$$x^2+y^2-2\alpha x-2\beta y+c+\lambda(x^2+y^2)=0$$

or $x^2+y^2-\dfrac{2\alpha}{1+\lambda}x-\dfrac{2\beta}{1+\lambda}y+\dfrac{c}{1+\lambda}=0$

Its centre is $\left(\dfrac{\alpha}{1+\lambda},\dfrac{\beta}{1+\lambda}\right)$ and radius is

$$\frac{\sqrt{\alpha^2+\beta^2-c(1+\lambda)}}{|1+\lambda|}$$

The radius vanishes if $1+\lambda=\dfrac{\alpha^2+\beta^2}{c}$

So, the other limiting point is $\left(\dfrac{c\alpha}{\alpha^2+\beta^2},\dfrac{c\beta}{\alpha^2+\beta^2}\right)$.

**16. A → q,s; B → r,t; C → p, s**

(A) Since $P=(10,7)$

and $S=x^2+y^2-4x-2y-20$

$\therefore S_1=100+49-40-14-20>0$

$\therefore P$ outside the circle

Radius $r=\sqrt{4+1+20}=5$

Centre $C=(2,1)$

$\therefore$ Shortest distance, $L=CP-r$

$$=\sqrt{(10-2)^2+(7-1)^2}-5$$

$$=\sqrt{(64+36)}-5$$

$= 10-5=5$

And largest distance, $M=CP+r$

$\qquad = 10+5$

$\qquad = 15$

$M+L=20,$ (q) $M-L=10$ (s)

(B) $\because P\equiv(3,-6)$

and $S\equiv x^2+y^2-16x-12y-125$

$\therefore \quad S_1=9+36-48+72-125<0$

$\therefore \quad P$ inside the circle

Radius $r=\sqrt{64+36+125}=15$

Centre $C\equiv(8,6)$

$\therefore \quad$ Shortest distance, $L=r-CP$

$$=15-\sqrt{(8-3)^2+(6-6)^2}$$

$$=15-13=2$$

And largest distance, $M=r+CP$

$\qquad = 15+13$

$\qquad = 28$

$M+L=30$ (r),

$M-L=26$ (t)

(C) $P\equiv(6,-6)$

and $S\equiv x^2+y^2-4x+6y-12$

$\therefore \quad S_1=(6)^2+(-6)^2-24-36-12=0$

$P$ on the circle

$\therefore \quad$ Radius $r=\sqrt{(4+9+12)}=5$

$\therefore \quad$ Shortest distance, $L=0$

And largest distance, $M=2r=10$ $M+L=10$ (p),

$M-L=10$ (s)

**17. A → p; B→s; C→ q**

(A) Greatest distance is $AD=C_1C_2+AC_1+DC_2$

$\qquad =5+1+3=9$

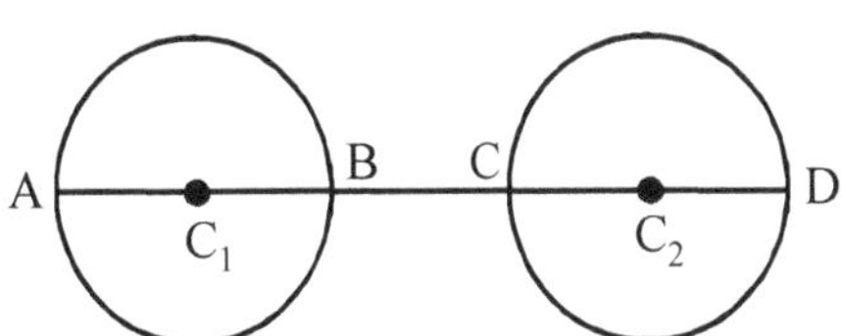


$9=3\lambda \Rightarrow \lambda=3$

(B) $x^2=200$ ; $2x^2=4r^2$ ; $2r^2=200 \Rightarrow r=10$

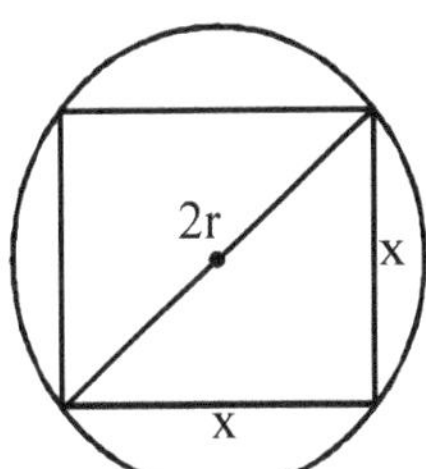


(C) Distance between $\left(\dfrac{1}{3},\dfrac{1}{3}\right)$ and $\left(\dfrac{8}{3},\dfrac{8}{3}\right)$ is $\dfrac{7}{3}\sqrt{2}$

$\therefore \quad \dfrac{\ell}{\sqrt{2}}=7$

**18. (a)** Let the equation of circle be

$x^2 + y^2 + 2gx + 2fy + c = 0$

Since its passes through $(1, 0)$ and $(0, 1)$, then

$1 + 0 + 2g + 0 + c = 0$

$\Rightarrow g = -\dfrac{(1+c)}{2}$

and $\quad 0 + 1 + 0 + 2f + c = 0$

$\Rightarrow f = -\dfrac{(1+c)}{2}$

$\therefore$ Radius $= \sqrt{(g^2 + f^2 - c)}$

$$= \sqrt{\left( \dfrac{(1+c)^2}{4} + \dfrac{(1+c)^2}{4} - c \right)}$$

$$= \sqrt{\dfrac{2(1+c^2)}{4}}$$

For minimum radius, c must be equal to zero.

$\therefore$ Radius $= \sqrt{\dfrac{1}{2}} = \dfrac{1}{\sqrt{2}}$,

then $g = -\dfrac{1}{2}, f = -\dfrac{1}{2}, c = 0$

$\therefore$ Circle is $x^2 + y^2 - x - y = 0$

Which pass through origin.

**19. (a)** Two circles touch each other $C_1 C_2 = r_1 \pm r_2$

$\sqrt{a^2 + b^2} = \sqrt{a^2 - c} \pm \sqrt{b^2 - c}$

$\Rightarrow a^2 + b^2 = a^2 - c + b^2 - c \pm 2\sqrt{(a^2 - c)(b^2 - c)}$

$c^2 = (a^2 - c)(b^2 - c) \Rightarrow a^2 b^2 = \left( a^2 + b^2 \right)$

$\Rightarrow \dfrac{1}{c} = \dfrac{1}{a^2} + \dfrac{1}{b^2}$

**20. (8)** $2x - y + 1 = 0$ is tangent slope of line $OA = -\dfrac{1}{2}$

equation of OA, $(y - 5) = -\dfrac{1}{2}(x - 2)$

$2y - 10 = -x + 2$

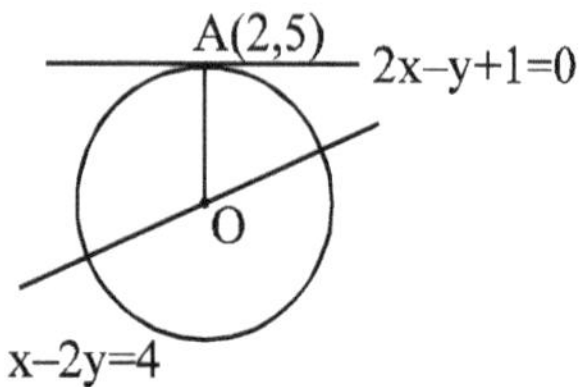


$x + 2y = 12$

$\therefore$ intersection with $x - 2y = 4$ will give coordinates of centre

Solving we get $(8, 2)$

distance OA $= \sqrt{(8-2)^2 + (2-5)^2}$

$\qquad\qquad = \sqrt{36 + 9} = \sqrt{45} = 3\sqrt{5}$

Thus $A = 3$, $B = 5$.

$\therefore A + B = 8$.

**21. (5)**

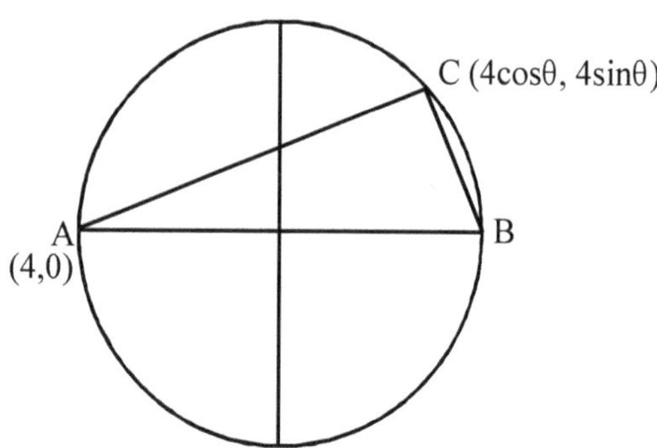


$A = \dfrac{1}{2} \times 8 \times 4\sin\theta = |16\sin\theta|$

Now $\sin\theta$ can be $\dfrac{1}{16}, \dfrac{2}{16}, \dots \dfrac{15}{16}$

i.e. 15 points in each quadrant

$\Rightarrow 60 + 2$ more with $\sin\theta = 1$

$\Rightarrow$ total $= 62$

On comparing, we get,

$11P + 7 = 62$

$\Rightarrow P = 5$.

**22. (1)** Equation of line : $y - 1 = m(x - 7)$

$mx - y + 1 - 7m = 0$

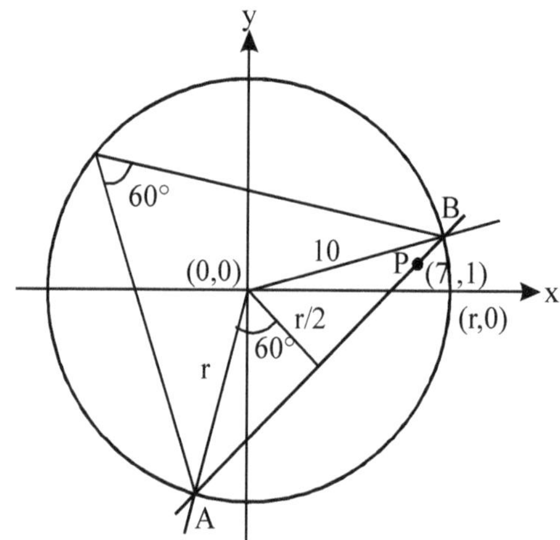


Perpendicular distance from $(0, 0) = \dfrac{r}{2}$

$\Rightarrow \dfrac{|7m - 1|}{\sqrt{1 + m^2}} = \dfrac{r}{2} = 5$

$(7m-1)^2 = 25(1+m^2)$

$49m^2 - 14m + 1 = 25 + 25m^2$

$24m^2 - 14m - 24 = 0$

$\Rightarrow m_1 m_2 = -1$

$\therefore P = 1.$

**23. (1)** The given circle

$$S(x,y) \equiv x^2 + y^2 - x - y - 6 = 0 \qquad ........(i)$$

has centre at $C \equiv \left(\dfrac{1}{2}, \dfrac{1}{2}\right)$

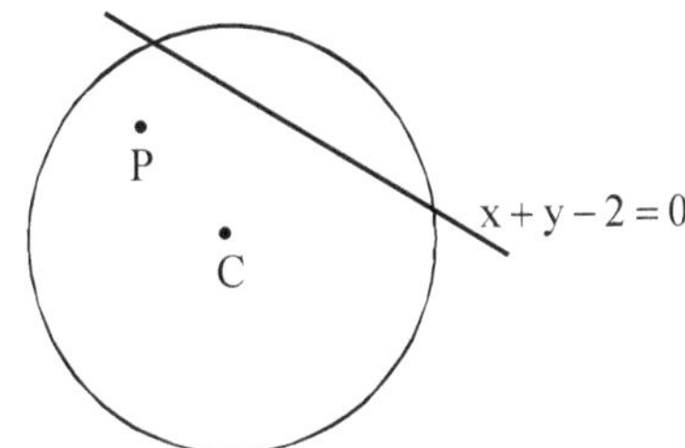


According to the required conditions, the given point $P(\alpha - 1, \alpha + 1)$ must lie inside the given circle

i.e. $S(\alpha - 1, \alpha + 1) < 0$ i.e. $(\alpha - 1)^2 + (\alpha + 1)^2 - (\alpha - 1) - (\alpha + 1) - 6 < 0$

i.e. $\alpha^2 - \alpha - 2 < 0$ i.e. $(\alpha - 2)(\alpha + 1) < 0$

i.e. $-1 < \alpha < 2$ ........(ii)

and also $P$ and $C$ must lie on the same side of the line (see fig.).

$$L(x,y) \equiv x + y - 2 = 0 \qquad .........(iii)$$

i.e. $L\left(\dfrac{1}{2}, \dfrac{1}{2}\right)$ and $L(\alpha - 1, \alpha + 1)$ must have the same sign.

Now, since $L\left(\dfrac{1}{2}, \dfrac{1}{2}\right) = \dfrac{1}{2} + \dfrac{1}{2} - 2 < 0$

therefore, we have $L(\alpha - 1, \alpha + 1) = (\alpha - 1) + (\alpha + 1) - 2 < 0$ i.e. $\alpha < 1$ ........(iv)

Inequalities (ii) and (iv) together give the permissible values of $\alpha$ as $-1 < \alpha < 1$

**24. (3)** Equation of a curve passing through the intersection points of the given curves

$$a\,x^2 + 2hxy + b\,y^2 - 2gx - 2fy + c = 0 \qquad .......(i)$$

and

$$a'\,x^2 - 2hxy + (a' + a - b)\,y^2 - 2g'x - 2f'y + c = 0 ..(ii)$$

can be written as

$$\{a'\,x^2 - 2hxy + (a' + a - b)\,y^2 - 2g'x - 2f'y + c\} +$$

$$\lambda\,\{a\,x^2 + 2hxy + b\,y^2 - 2gx - 2fy + c\} = 0$$

i.e. $(a' + \lambda a)\,x^2 + 2h(\lambda - 1)xy + (a' + a - b + \lambda b)\,y^2$

$$-2(g' + \lambda g)x - 2(f' + \lambda f)y + (1 + \lambda)c = 0 \qquad ......(iii)$$

According to the given condition equation (iii) must represent a circle, therefore we have

coeff. of $x^2$ = coeff. of $y^2$ i.e. $a' + \lambda a = a' + a - b + \lambda b$

i.e. $\lambda(a - b) = a - b$ gives $\lambda = 1$

and coeff. of $xy = 0$ i.e. $\lambda - 1 = 0$ gives $\lambda = 1$

The identical values prove that the curve is a circle.

Putting the above value of $\lambda$ in equation (iii) gives the equation of the circle passing through the intersection points of the curves represented by equations (i) and (ii) as

$$(a' + a)\,(x^2 + y^2) - 2(g' + g)\,x - 2(f' + f)y + 2c = 0$$

which has its centre at the point $\left(\dfrac{g'+g}{a'+a}, \dfrac{f'+f}{a'+a}\right)$

We can see that the co-ordinates of the given point P is the same as the centre of the circle passing through the points A, B, C and D. Therefore, we have

$$PA^2 = PB^2 = PC^2 = PD^2 = \text{radius of the circle.}$$

So, $PA^2 + PB^2 + PC^2 = 3\,PD^2$

**1.** **(d).** $C_1C_2 = r_1 + r_2$

$C_1 = (0, 0)$ ; $C_2 = (3\sqrt{3}, 3)$ & $r_1 = 2, r_2 = 4$

$\Rightarrow$ circle touch each other externally

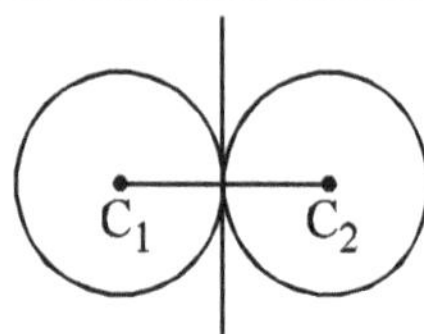

equation of common tangent is,

$\sqrt{3}\, x + y - 4 = 0$ ....(1)

comparing it with $x\cos\theta + y\sin\theta = 2$

$\theta = \dfrac{\pi}{6}$

**2.** **(c).** $(x_1, y_1)$ lies on $2x + y = 4$

$\Rightarrow 2x_1 + y_1 = 4$ ....(1)

chord of contact w.r.t. $(x_1, y_1)$

$xx_1 + yy_1 = 1$

also equation of chord whose mid point is (h, k)

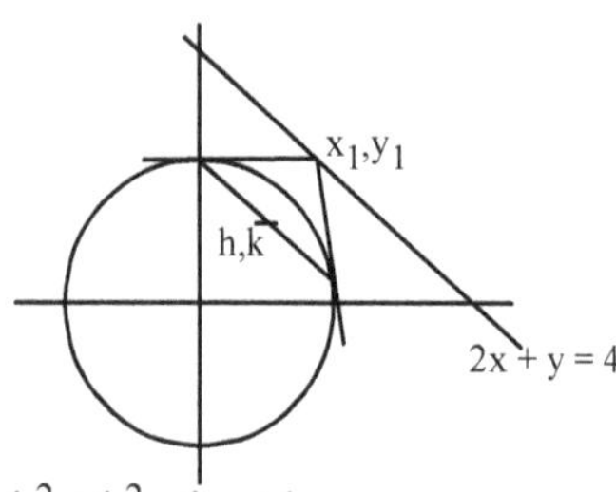

$h^2 + k^2 = hx + ky$

$\therefore \dfrac{x_1}{h} = \dfrac{y_1}{k} = \dfrac{1}{h^2 + k^2}$

$\Rightarrow x_1 = \dfrac{h}{h^2 + k^2}$ ; $y_1 = \dfrac{k}{h^2 + k^2}$

substitute in (1)

$2 \cdot \dfrac{h}{h^2 + k^2} + \dfrac{k}{h^2 + k^2} = 4$

locus $= 4(x^2 + y^2) = 2x + y$ ]

**3.** **(a).** Locus of point of intersection of tangents

chord of contact of $(x_1, y_1)$ w.r.t. $x^2 + y^2 = 1$ is

$xx_1 + yy_1 = 1$ (AB) .....(1)

AB is also common chord between two circles

$\therefore -1 + (\lambda + 6)x - (8 - 2\lambda)y + 3 = 0$

$\Rightarrow (\lambda + 6)x - (8 - 2\lambda)y + 2 = 0$ .....(2)

comparing (1) and (2) we get

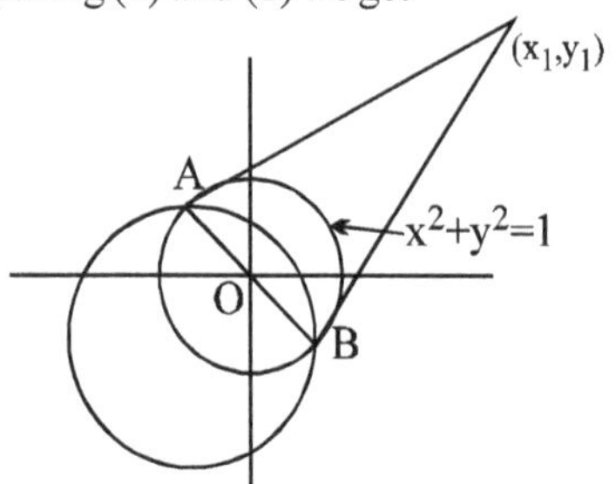

$\dfrac{x_1}{\lambda + 6} = \dfrac{y}{2\lambda - 8} = \dfrac{-1}{2}$

eliminate $\lambda \Rightarrow 2x - y + 10 = 0$

**4.** **(a)** Let $\angle RPS = \theta$

$\angle XPQ = 90 - \theta$

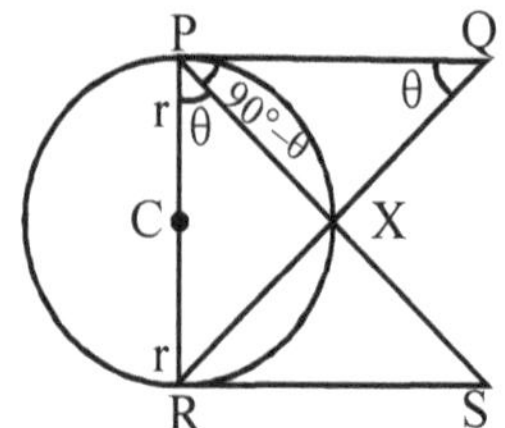

$\therefore \quad \angle PQX = \theta$ $(\because \angle PXQ = 90°)$

$\therefore \quad \Delta PRS \sim \Delta QPR$ (AA similarity)

$\therefore \quad \dfrac{PR}{QP} = \dfrac{RS}{PR}$

$\Rightarrow \quad PR^2 = PQ \cdot RS$

$\Rightarrow \quad PR = \sqrt{PQ.RS}$

**5.** **(b)** Equation of the given circle is

$$x^2 + y^2 + 2gx + 2fy + c = 0 \quad ......(i)$$

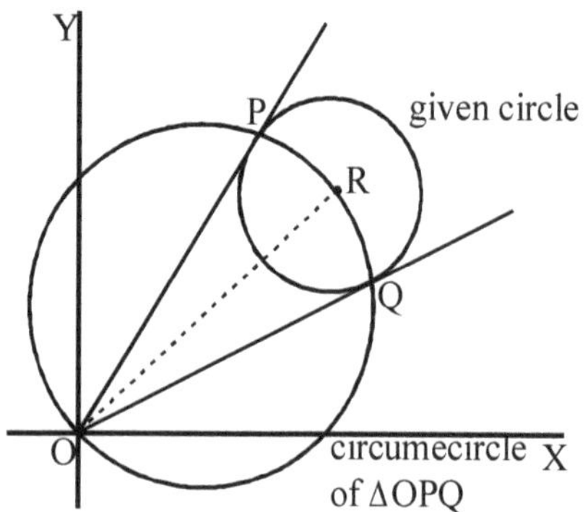

Equation of the chord of contact $PQ$, drawn from the origin $(0, 0)$ to the given circle will be

$gx + fy + c = 0$ .....(ii)

Eq. of any circle passing through the intersection points of the given circle and the chord $PQ$ can be written as

$(x^2 + y^2 + 2gx + 2fy + c) + \lambda(gx + fy + c) = 0$ .....(iii)

If this circle passes through the origin, then we have,

$c + \lambda c = 0$ gives $\lambda = -1$

Putting the above value of $\lambda$ in equation (iii) gives the equation of the required circle as

$$x^2 + y^2 + gx + fy = 0$$

**6.** **(a)** The circles are given as $x^2 + y^2 = 12$ ......(i)

and $x^2 + y^2 - 5x + 3y - 2 = 0$. ......(ii)

If $A$ and $B$ are the points of intersection of (i) and (ii), clearly $AB$ will be the common chord whose equation will be

$$(x^2 + y^2 - 12) - (x^2 + y^2 - 5x + 3y - 2) = 0$$

or $5x - 3y - 10 = 0$ ....(iii)

If $P$ be the point where the tangents at $A$ and $B$ with respect to (i), meet each other, $AB$ will be the chord of contact of $P$. Let the coordinates of $P$ be $(\alpha, \beta)$.

Equation of the chord of contact of $(\alpha, \beta)$ with respect to (i) is $x\alpha + y\beta - 12 = 0$ ....(iv)

As (iii) and (iv) represent the same equation, comparing the coefficients, we get

$\dfrac{\alpha}{5} = \dfrac{\beta}{-3} = \dfrac{-12}{-10}$, which, we get $\alpha = 6$ and

$\beta = -\dfrac{18}{5}$. Hence the required point is $\left(6, -\dfrac{18}{5}\right)$

**7.** **(b)**

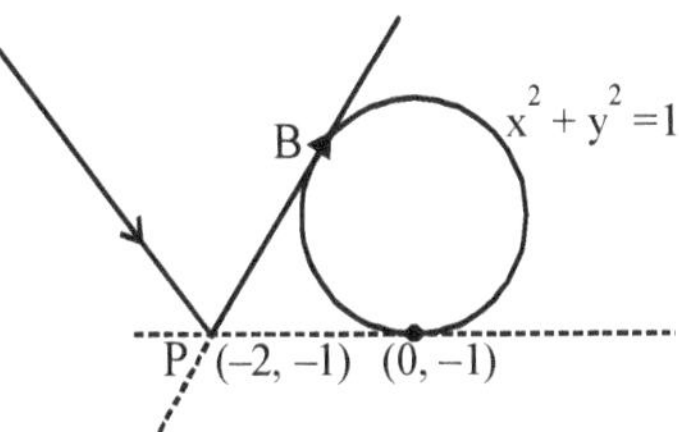


Any line through $(-2, -1)$ is $y + 1 = m(x + 2)$

It touches the circle if $\left|\dfrac{2m - 1}{\sqrt{1 + m^2}}\right| = 1 \Rightarrow m = 0, \dfrac{4}{3}$

$\therefore$ Equation of PB is $y + 1 = \dfrac{4}{3}(x + 2)$

$\Rightarrow 4x - 3y + 5 = 0$

A point on PB is $(-5, -5)$, (we can choose some other point as well)

Its image by the line $y = -1$ is $P'(-5, 3)$.

Hence equation of incident ray PP' is

$$y - 3 = \dfrac{3 + 1}{-5 + 2}(x + 5) \Rightarrow \qquad 4x + 3y + 11 = 0$$

**8.** **(a)** We have $\dfrac{\pi}{3} < \theta < \pi$

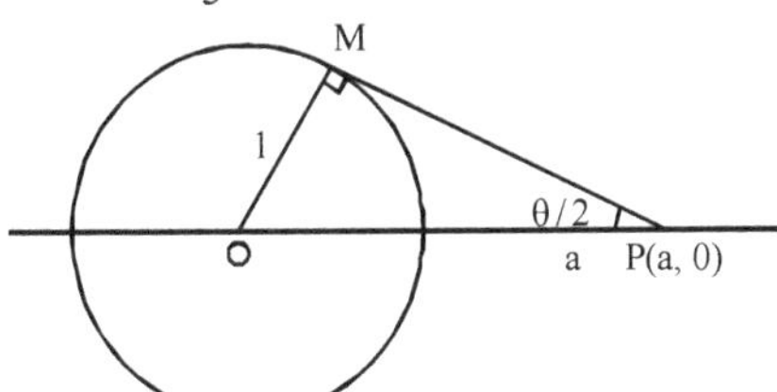


i.e. $\dfrac{\pi}{6} < \dfrac{\theta}{2} < \dfrac{\pi}{2}$ i.e. $\dfrac{1}{2} < \sin\left(\dfrac{\theta}{2}\right) < 1$

i.e. $\dfrac{1}{2} < \dfrac{1}{a} < 1$ $\left[\because \sin\left(\dfrac{\theta}{2}\right) = \dfrac{1}{a} (see\ fig.)\right]$

i.e. $1 < a < 2$

There can be symmetrical points on the $-ve$ x-axis too.

Hence, we have $a \in (-2, -1) \cup (1, 2)$.

**9.** **(a, b)**

(a) Equation of tangent from point $(3, -3)$ to the given circle

is $y + 3 = m(x - 3)$

$mx - 3m - y - 3 = 0$

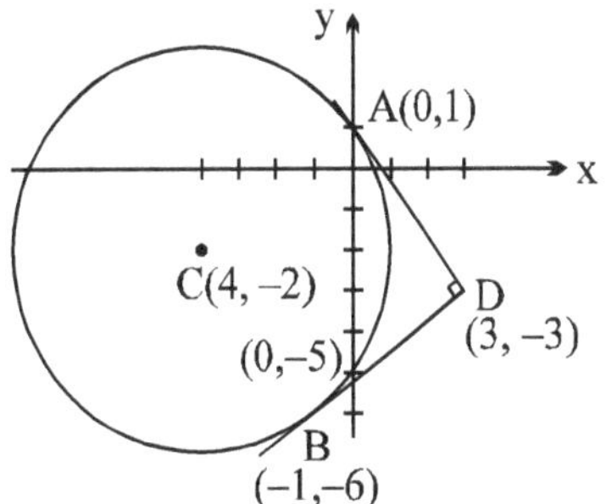


and also $\left|\dfrac{-4m - 3m + 2 - 3}{\sqrt{1 + m^2}}\right| = 5$

$(1 + 7m)^2 = 25(1 + m^2) \Rightarrow 1 + 49m^2 + 14m = 25 + 25m^2$

$\Rightarrow 12m^2 + 7m - 12 = 0$

$\Rightarrow (4m - 3)(3m + 4) = 0$

$\therefore m = 3/4$ or $m = -4/3$

$\therefore$ equation of tangent at point A and B are

$y + 3 = -\dfrac{4}{3}(x - 3)$ and $y + 3 = \dfrac{3}{4}(x - 3)$

$3y + 9 = -4x + 12$ $\qquad$ $4y + 12 = 3x - 9$

$4x + 3y = 3$ $\qquad\qquad$ $3x - 4y = 21$

(b) Equation of normals to these 2 tangents are

$y + 2 = \dfrac{3}{4}(x + 4)$ and $y + 2 = -\dfrac{4}{3}(x + 4)$

$4y + 8 = 3x + 12$ $\qquad$ $3y + 6 = -4x - 16$

$3(3x - 4y + 4 = 0)$ $\qquad$ $4(4x + 3y = -22)$

$9x - 12y = -12$ $\qquad$ $16x + 12y = -88$

$\underline{16x + 12y = 12}$ $\qquad$ $\underline{9x - 12y = 63}$

$\Rightarrow \quad 25x = 0;$ $\qquad\qquad$ $25x = -25$

$\Rightarrow \quad x = 0;$ $\therefore y = 1$ $\qquad$ $\Rightarrow x = -1;$ $\therefore y = -6$

$\therefore$ points A and B are $(0, 1)$ and $(-1, -6)$

**10.** **(a, c)** The given circle is $x^2 + y^2 - 2rx - hy + h^2 = 0$ with centre $(r, h)$ and radius $= r$.

Clearly circle touches y-axis so one of its tangent is $x = 0$.

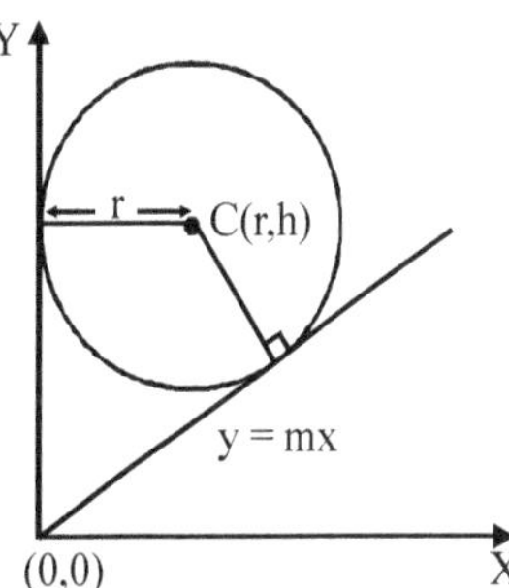


Let $y = mx$ be the other tangent through origin.

Then length of perpendicular from C (r, h) to $y - mx$ should be equal to r.

$\therefore \qquad \left|\dfrac{mr - h}{\sqrt{m^2 + 1}}\right| = r$

$$\Rightarrow \quad m^2r^2 - 2mrh + h^2 = m^2r^2 + r^2$$

$$\Rightarrow \quad m = \frac{h^2 - r^2}{2rh}$$

$\therefore$ Other tangent is $y = \dfrac{h^2 - r^2}{2rh}x$

or $\quad (h^2 - r^2)x - 2rhy = 0$

**11.** **(a,b,d)** The combined equation of the tangents drawn from $(0, 0)$ to
$x^2 + y^2 - 2rx - 2hy + h^2 = 0$ is
$(x^2 + y^2 - 2rx - 2hy + h^2)h^2 = (-rx - hy + h^2)^2$
This equation represents a pair of perpendicular straight lines if coeff. of $x^2$ + coeff. of $y^2 = 0$  i.e. $2h^2 - r^2 - h^2 = 0$
$$\Rightarrow \quad r^2 = h^2 \text{ or } r = \pm h.$$

**12.** **(a, c)**

$$OP = 5\sqrt{2}\sec\theta, \qquad OP_1 = 5\sqrt{2}\operatorname{cosec}\theta$$

$$\Delta PP_1P_2 = \frac{100}{\sin 2\theta}, \qquad (\Delta PP_1P_2)_{min} = 100$$

$$\Rightarrow \quad \theta = \pi/4 \Rightarrow OP = 10$$
$$\Rightarrow \quad P = (10, 0), (-10, 0).$$

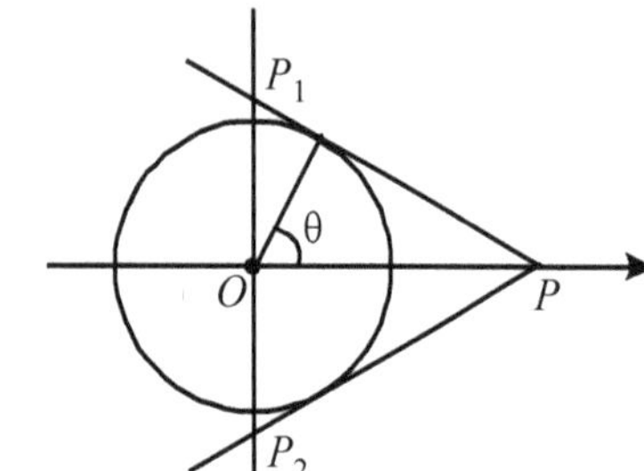

**13.** **(b)** $14 \cdot x \cdot (-3) + 14 \cdot y \cdot 6 + 108(x-3) - \dfrac{69}{2}(y+6) + 432 = 0$

$$\Rightarrow \quad x(108 - 42) + y\left(84 - \frac{69}{2}\right) + (432 - 531) = 0$$

$$\Rightarrow \quad 4x + 3y - 6 = 0$$

**14.** **(c)** $g = \dfrac{216}{28}, \; f = -\dfrac{69}{28}, \; c = \dfrac{432}{14}$

$$\text{Radius} = \sqrt{g^2 + f^2 - c} = \frac{165}{28}$$

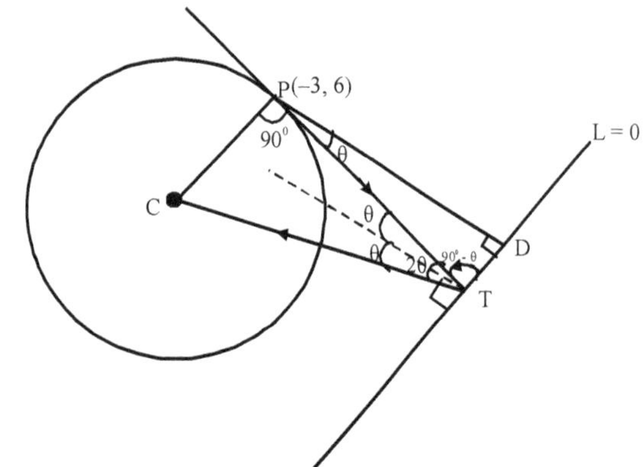

**15.** **(b)** $\angle DPT = \theta$ , Slope of $PT = -4/3$

Let $PT = \ell$, $\tan 2\theta = \dfrac{165}{28\,\ell}$ ...........(i)

$$\cos\theta = \frac{11\sqrt{130}}{13\,\ell} \qquad ...........\text{(ii)}$$

Dividing (i) by (ii) $\quad \dfrac{\tan 2\theta}{\cos\theta} = \dfrac{15.13}{28 \cdot \sqrt{13} \cdot \sqrt{10}}$

$$\sin\theta = \frac{-56\sqrt{10} \pm 74\sqrt{10}}{60\sqrt{13}}$$ (only positive value is possible )

$$\Rightarrow \quad \tan\theta = \frac{3}{11}$$

**16.** $A \to p, q, r, s;\; B \to p, q, r, s, t;\; C \to r, s$

(A) Distance from centre $(0, 10)$ to the line $(y - mx = 0)$

$$= \quad \frac{10}{\sqrt{(1 + m^2)}} \geq \text{radius}$$

$$\Rightarrow \quad \frac{10}{\sqrt{(1 + m^2)}} \geq \sqrt{10}$$

$$\Rightarrow \quad \sqrt{10} \geq \sqrt{1 + m^2}$$

$$\Rightarrow \quad m^2 \leq 9$$

$$\therefore \quad -3 \leq m \leq 3$$

Then $0 \leq |m| \leq 3$

$\therefore \quad |m| = 0\,1, 2, 3$ . (p, q, r, s)

(B) Distance from the centre $(2, 4)$ to the line $(3x - 4y - 5k = 0)$

$$= \frac{|6 - 16 - 5k|}{5} \leq \text{radius}$$

$$\Rightarrow \quad \frac{|10 + 5k|}{5} \leq 5$$

$$\Rightarrow \quad |10 + 5k| \leq 25 \Rightarrow 0 \leq |2 + k| \leq 5$$

$$\therefore \quad |2 + k| = 0, 1, 2, 3, 4, 5 \text{ (p, q, r, s, t)}$$

(C) The given circles will cut orthogonally, if

$$2\left(\frac{1}{2}\right)(-5) + 2\left(\frac{p}{2}\right)(p) = -7 + 1$$

$$\Rightarrow \quad -5p + p^2 = -6$$
$$\Rightarrow \quad p^2 - 5p + 6 = 0$$
$$\Rightarrow \quad (p-2)(p-3) = 0$$
$$\therefore \quad p = 2, 3 \text{ (r, s)}$$

**17.** $A \to s;\; B \to t;\; C \to p,q$

(A) $CD = \sqrt{5}$ and $AC = 2$

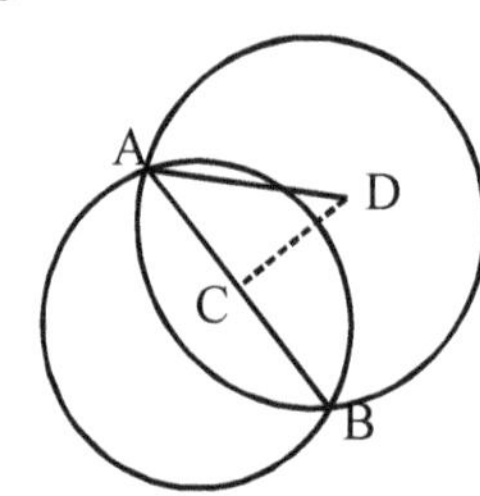

$$\therefore AD = \sqrt{5 + 4} = 3$$

(B) $OD = 4 \Rightarrow \sin\theta = \dfrac{4}{5}$ so, $AC = OA\cot\theta = 5\times\dfrac{3}{4} = \dfrac{15}{4}$

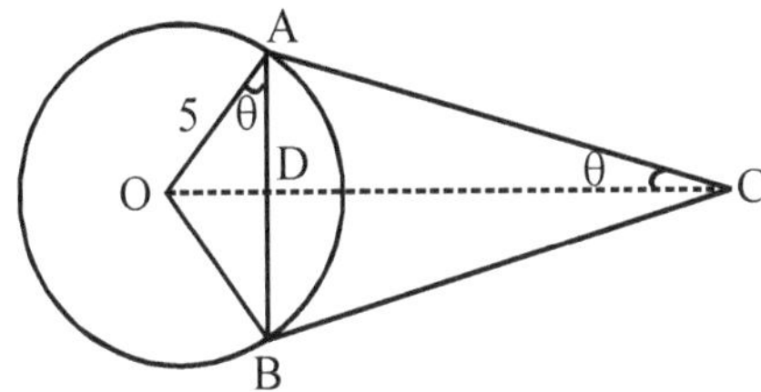

$\therefore$ Area of quadrilateral $OACB = OA \times AC = \dfrac{75}{4}$

(C) The circle $C$ is $x^2 + y^2 - 2x - 2y + 1 = 0$ and $C_1$ is

$x^2 + y^2 - 2rx - 2ry + r^2 = 0$.

They intersect orthogonally if $2(r + r) = 1 + r^2 \Rightarrow r^2 - 4r + 1 = 0$

so, $r = 2 \pm \sqrt{3}$ **(p, q)**

**18. (a)** $\because$ Now, replacing $x$ by $x - 3$, $y$ by $y - 3$ and $a$ by 1, then $x\cos\theta + y\sin\theta = a$ reduce in $(x - 3)\cos\theta + (y - 3)\sin\theta = 1$, and $x^2 + y^2 = a^2$ reduce in $(x - 3)^2 + (y - 3)^2 = 1$

**19. (b)** For $x^2 + y^2 + 2x = 0$, $C_1(-1, 0)$, $r_1 = 1$, for $x^2 + y^2 - 6x = 0$, $C_2(3, 0)$, $r_2 = 3$.

$\Rightarrow$ Point of contact of circle $E = \left(\dfrac{3+3}{1-3}, 0\right) = (-3, 0)$,

Angle between the tangents from $(-3, 0)$ to the circle

$x^2 + y^2 + 2x = 0$ is $\theta = 2\tan^{-1}\left(\dfrac{1}{\sqrt{9 + 0 - 6}}\right) = \dfrac{\pi}{3}$

and $C_1C_2 = r_1 + r_2$.

Therefore the common tangents form an equilateral triangle and they touch each other externally.

The statement-1 is correct and statement-2 is also correct, but statement-2 is not the correct explanation of statement-1.

**20. (1)** $\sin\dfrac{\theta}{2} = \dfrac{3}{5}$ ; $\cos\dfrac{\theta}{2} = \dfrac{4}{5}$

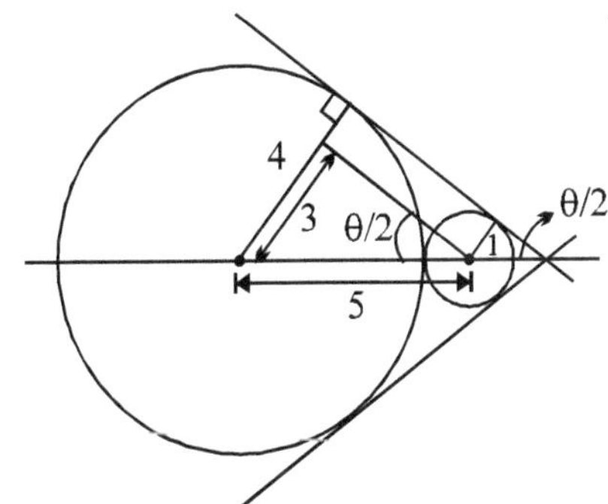

$\therefore \sin\theta = 2\cdot\dfrac{3}{5}\cdot\dfrac{4}{5} = \dfrac{24}{25}$

Thus $B - A = 25 - 24 = 1$

**21. (5)**

The equation of given circle is

$S(x, y) = x^2 + y^2 - 6x - 2py + 17 = 0$

$\Rightarrow (x - 3)^2 + (y - p)^2 = (p^2 - 8)$

$S(0, 0) = 17 > 0$.

$\therefore$ $(0, 0)$ lies outside the circle.

Equation of director circle of $S = 0$ will be

$(x - 3)^2 + (y - p)^2 = 2(p^2 - 8)$.

$\therefore$ Tangents drawn from $(0, 0)$ to $S = 0$ are perpendicular to each other

$\therefore$ $(0, 0)$ must lie on director circle.

$\Rightarrow$ $(0 - 3)^2 + (0 - p)^2 = 2(p^2 - 8)$

$\Rightarrow$ $p^2 = 25 \Rightarrow p = \pm 5$

Hence $\dfrac{(p_1^2 + p_2^2)}{10} = \dfrac{(5)^2 + (-5)^2}{10} = \dfrac{25 + 25}{10} = \dfrac{50}{10} = 5$

**22. (5)**

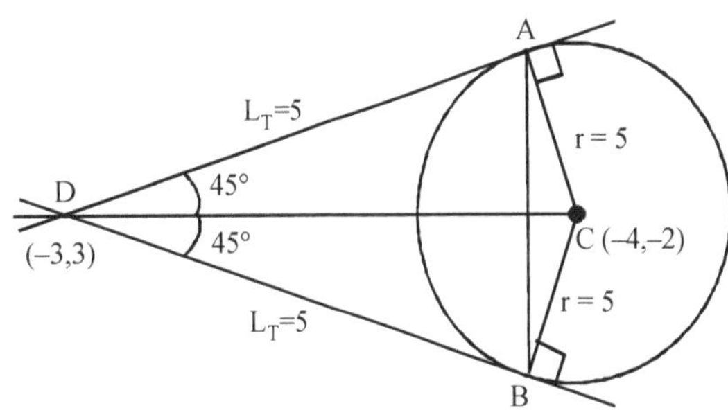

$L = \sqrt{S_1} = 5$

Area of quadrilateral $ABCD = 2$ Area of $\triangle ACD$

$= 2\left(\dfrac{1}{2}\times 5\times 5\right) = 25$ sq. units

Thus, $M^2 = 25$

$\Rightarrow M = 5$

**23. (5)**

Line $5x - 2y + 6 = 0$ is intersected by tangent at P to circle $x^2 + y^2 + 6x + 6y - 2 = 0$ on y-axis at $Q(0, 3)$.

In other words tangent passes through $(0, 3)$

$\therefore$ $PQ = $ length of tangent to circle from $(0, 3)$

$= \sqrt{0 + 9 + 0 + 18 - 2}$

$= \sqrt{25} = 5$

**1.** **(a).** $AB = \sqrt{a^2 + b^2}$

hence $D = \sqrt{b^2 + a^2}$ ....(1)

Now $\dfrac{d}{2} = \dfrac{\Delta}{s} = \dfrac{ab}{2s}$

$\therefore \quad \dfrac{d}{2} = \dfrac{ab}{a + b + \sqrt{a^2 + b^2}}$

or $d = \dfrac{2ab}{a + b + \sqrt{a^2 + b^2}}$ ....(2)

from (1) and (2)

$d + D = \dfrac{\sqrt{a^2 + b^2}\left[(a+b) + \sqrt{a^2 + b^2}\right] + 2ab}{a + b + \sqrt{a^2 + b^2}}$

$= \dfrac{(a+b)^2 + (a+b)\sqrt{a^2 + b^2}}{a + b + \sqrt{a^2 + b^2}}$

**2.** **(c).** Radius of circle are $r_1, r_2$ and 1

line $y = x + 1$

perpendicular from $(0, 0)$ on line $y = x + 1 = \dfrac{1}{\sqrt{2}}$

now $r_1 > \dfrac{1}{\sqrt{2}} \Rightarrow r_1 = 1 - 2d \Rightarrow \dfrac{1 - r_1}{2} = d$

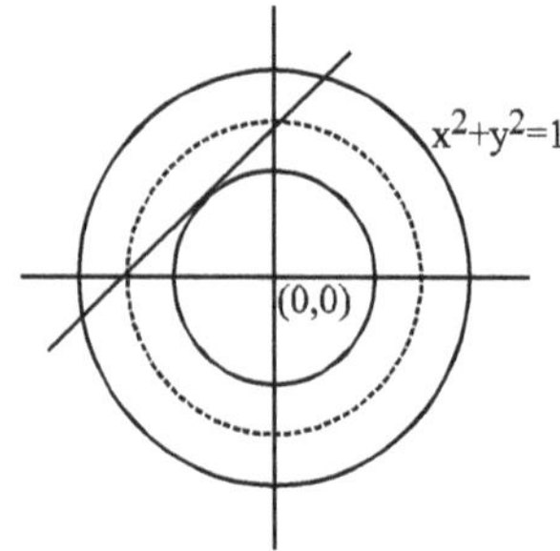


$\therefore d = \dfrac{\sqrt{2} - 1}{2\sqrt{2}}$

**Aliter :** Equation of circle are

$x^2 + y^2 = 1$

$x^2 + y^2 = (1 - d)^2$

$x^2 + y^2 = (1 - 2d)^2$

$\Rightarrow$ solve any of circle with line $y = x + 1$

e.g. $x^2 + y^2 = (1 - d)^2 \Rightarrow 2x^2 + 2x + 2d - d^2 = 0$ cuts the circle in real and distinct point hence $\Delta > 0$

$\Rightarrow 2d^2 - 4d + 1 > 0 \Rightarrow d = \dfrac{2 \pm \sqrt{2}}{4}$

**3.** **(c).** Equation of the two circles be $(x - r)^2 + (y - r)^2 = r^2$

i.e. $x^2 + y^2 - 2rx - 2ry + r^2 = 0$ where $r = r_1 \& r_2$.

Condition of orthogonality gives

$2 r_1 r_2 + 2 r_1 r_2 = r_1^2 + r_2^2 \Rightarrow 4 r_1 r_2 = r_1^2 + r_2^2$. Circle passes through $(a, b)$

$\Rightarrow a^2 + b^2 - 2ra - 2rb + r^2 = 0$

i.e. $r^2 - 2r(a + b) + a^2 + b^2 = 0$

$r_1 + r_2 = 2(a + b)$ and $r_1 r_2 = a^2 + b^2$

**4.** **(b).** $\cos\theta = \dfrac{10 + 5 - 5}{2 \cdot \sqrt{10} \cdot \sqrt{5}} = \dfrac{1}{\sqrt{2}}$

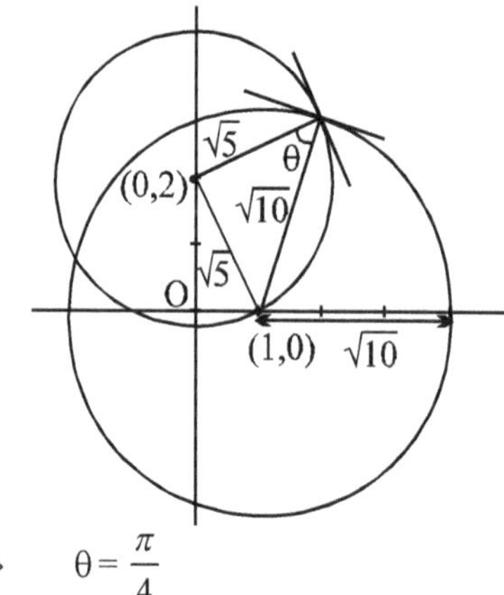


$\Rightarrow \quad \theta = \dfrac{\pi}{4}$

**5.** **(c).** Locus of the centre of the $\odot$ cutting $S_1 = 0$ and $S_2 = 0$ orthogonally is the radical axis between $S_1 = 0$ and $S_2 = 0$ ]

Let out circle be $x^2 + y^2 + 2gx + 2fy + c = 0$

conditions $2(-g)(-2) + 2(-f)(3) = c + 9$

and $2(-g)(5/2) + 2(-f)(-2) = c - 2$

$\therefore \quad ag - 10 f = 11$

$\therefore \quad$ locus of centre $9x - 10y + 11 = 0$

**6.** **(a)** Let $P$ be $(1 + \sqrt{2} \cos\theta, \sqrt{2} \sin\theta)$ and C is $(1, 0)$.

Circum centre of triangle ABC lies on midpoint of PC

$\Rightarrow \quad 2h = 1 + \sqrt{2} \cos\theta + 1$ and $2k \sqrt{2} \sin\theta$

$\Rightarrow \quad [2(h - 1)]^2 + (2k)^2 = 2$

$\Rightarrow \quad [2(h - 1)]^2 + k^2 - 1 = 0$

$\Rightarrow \quad 2x^2 + 2y^2 - 4x + 1 = 0$

**7.** **(c)** Let $P \equiv (x_1, y_1)$ and $Q \equiv (x_2, y_2)$

Let the equation of given circle be $x^2 + y^2 = a^2$

The equation of chord of contact of tangent drawn from the point $P(x_1, y_1)$ to the given circle is

$xx_1 + yy_1 = a^2$

Since it passes through $Q(x_2, y_2)$

$\therefore xx_1 + yy_1 = a^2$ ...(1)

Now, $l_1 = \sqrt{x_1^2 + y_1^2 - a^2}$, $l_2 = \sqrt{x_2^2 + y_2^2 - a^2}$

and $PQ = \sqrt{(x_2 - x_1)^2 + (y_2 - y_1)^2}$

$= \sqrt{\left(x_1^2 + y_1^2\right) + \left(x_2^2 + y_2^2\right) - 2(x_1 x_2 + y_1 y_2)}$

$= \sqrt{\left(x_1^2 + y_1^2\right) + \left(x_2^2 + y_2^2\right) - 2a^2}$ [Using (1)]

$= \sqrt{\left(x_1^2 + y_1^2 - a^2\right) + \left(x_2^2 + y_2^2 - a^2\right)} = \sqrt{l_1^2 + l_2^2}$

**8. (a)** Given circles are $S_1 \equiv x^2 + y^2 + 2x = 0$ ... (1)

and $S_2 \equiv x^2 + y^2 + 2y = 0$ ...(2)

Equation of chord say AB of circles (1) and (2) is

$S_1 - S_2 = 0 \Rightarrow 2x - 2y = 0$ ... (3)

Equation of any circle having AB as a chord is

$x^2 + y^2 + 2x + \lambda(2x - 2y) = 0$

or $x^2 + y^2 + (2 + 2\lambda)x - 2\lambda y = 0$ ...(4)

Its centre is $C(-(1 + \lambda), \lambda)$.

If line AB is the diameter of circle (4), then $C(-(1 + \lambda), \lambda)$ will lie on line (3)

$\therefore \; -2(1 + \lambda) - 2\lambda = 0$ or $\lambda = -\dfrac{1}{2}$

Putting the value of $\lambda$ in (4), we get the equation of the required circle as $x^2 + y^2 + 2x - \dfrac{1}{2}(2x - 2y) = 0$

or $x^2 + y^2 + x + y = 0$

**9. (b, c)** The given circles are $x^2 + y^2 - 4x = 0$, $x > 0$

i.e. $(x - 2)^2 + y^2 = 2^2$, $x > 0$

and $x^2 + y^2 + 4x = 0$, $x < 0$

i.e. $(x + 2)^2 + y^2 = 2^2$, $x < 0$

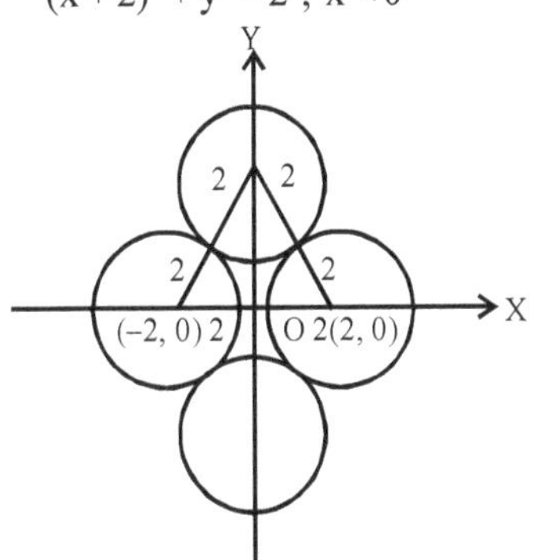


Clearly, from the figure, the centres of the required circles are at $(0, \sqrt{12})$ and $(0, -\sqrt{12})$.

$\therefore$ Equations of the required circles are

$(x - 0)^2 + (y \mp \sqrt{12})^2 = 2^2$

i.e., $x^2 + y^2 + 2\sqrt{12}y + 8 = 0$

and $x^2 + y^2 - 2\sqrt{12}y + 8 = 0$

**10. (b)** Clearly, from the figure, the radius of the smallest circle touching the given circles is

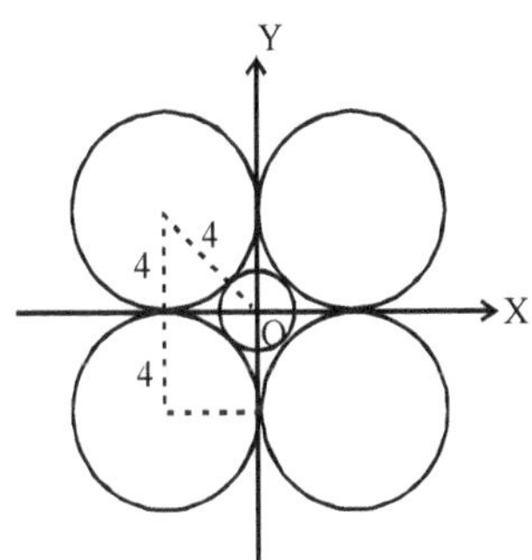


$= \sqrt{4^2 + 4^2} - 4$ i.e. $4\sqrt{2} - 4$

**11. (a, c)** Radius of inner circle $= OR - a$

$= \sqrt{a^2 + a^2} - a$

$= a(\sqrt{2} - 1)$

Radius of outer circle $= OR + RQ$

$= a\sqrt{2} + a = a(\sqrt{2} + 1)$

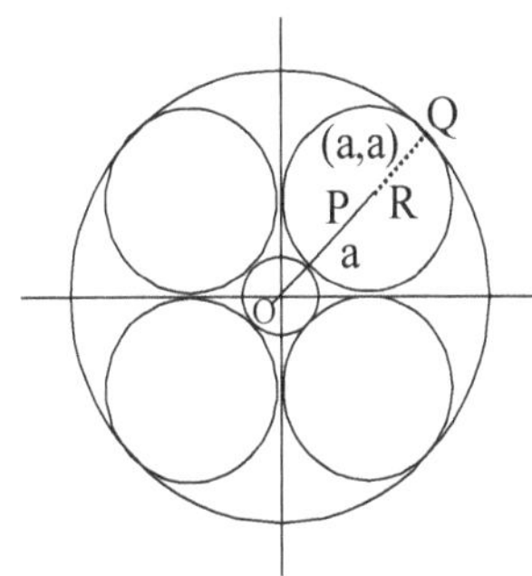


**12. (b,c).** $x^2 + y^2 - 8x - 16y + 60 = 0$

Equation of chord of contact from $(-2, 0)$ is

$-2x - 4(x - 2) - 8y + 60 = 0$

$-6x - 8y + 68 = 0$

$3x + 4y - 34 = 0$

$x^2 + \left(\dfrac{34 - 3x}{4}\right)^2 - 8x - 16\left(\dfrac{34 - 3x}{4}\right) + 60 = 0$

$16x^2 + 1156 - 204x + 9x^2 - 128x - 2176 + 192x + 960 = 0$

$25x^2 - 140x - 60 = 0$

$5x^2 - 28x - 12 = 0$

$x = \dfrac{28 \pm \sqrt{784 + 240}}{10} = \dfrac{28 \pm \sqrt{1024}}{10} = \dfrac{28 \pm 32}{10} = 6, -\dfrac{2}{5}$

$(6, 4)$ and $\left(-\dfrac{2}{5}, \dfrac{44}{5}\right)$

**13. (b)**      **14. (c)**      **15. (c).**

Equation of a member of the family S with AB as diameter is

$S : (x - 3)(x - 6) + (y - 7)(y - 5) + \lambda(2x + 3y - 27) = 0$

or $\; S : x^2 + y^2 + (2\lambda - 9)x + (3\lambda - 12)y + 53 - 27\lambda = 0$

....... (1)

Equation of the common chord of (i) and C is $S_1 - S_2 = 0$

$(2\lambda - 9 + 4)x + (3\lambda - 12 + 6)y + 53 - 27\lambda + 3 = 0$

or $(5x + 6y - 56) - \lambda(2x + 3y - 27) = 0$ ....... (2)

which passes through $\left(2, \dfrac{23}{3}\right)$, the point of intersection of

$5x + 6y - 56 = 0$ and $2x + 3y - 27 = 0$ for all values of $\lambda$.

(1) bisects the circumference of C if the centre $(2, 3)$ of C lies on the common chord (2)

$\Rightarrow \; -28 + 14\lambda = 0 \; \Rightarrow \lambda = 2$ and from (1), the equation is $x^2 + y^2 - 5x - 6y - 1 = 0$

Difference of the squares of the lengths of tangents from A and B to the circle C is

$|(9 + 49 - 12 - 42 - 3) - (36 + 25 - 24 - 30 - 3)| = 3$

$(AB)^2 = 13$, $(OP)^2 = 13$, $(AP)^2 = 17$, $(BP)^2 = 20$

**16.** (A) – s, (B) – r, (C) – q, (D) – p

Equation of circle touching the coordinates axes and centre $(r, r)$ in the first quadrant is

$$x^2 + y^2 - 2xr - 2yr + r^2 = 0$$

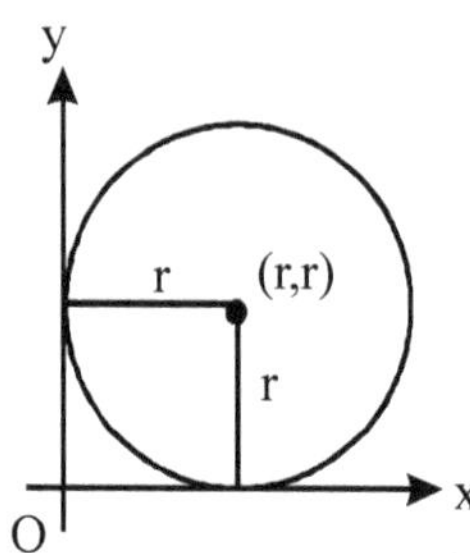


For $r = a$ or $b$

Hence $C_1 : x^2 + y^2 - 2ax - 2ay + a^2$ ....(1)

Centre $(a, a)$, radius $= a$, $a > 0$

$C_2 : x^2 + y^2 - 2bx - 2by + b^2$ ....(2)

Centre $(b, b)$, radius $b$, $b > 0$

$C_1$ and $C_2$ touch each other radical axis between (1) and (2) is

$(1) - (2) = 0$

$2(b - a)x + 2(b - a)y - (b^2 - a^2) = 0$

$2x + 2y - (b + a) = 0$ ....(3)

If it touches both $C_1$ and $C_2$ then perpendicular from $(a, a) = $ radius 'a'

$$\left| \frac{2a + 2a - (b + a)}{\sqrt{8}} \right| = a \qquad ....(4)$$

$$|3a - b| = 2\sqrt{2}\,a \qquad ....(5)$$

now origin and $(a, a)$ must lie on the same side of (3) but $(0, 0)$ gives – ve sign with (3).

hence $(a, a)$ should also give the same sign i.e. $4a - b - a < 0 \Rightarrow 3a - b < 0$

Hence (5) becomes

$$b - 3a = 2\sqrt{2}a \Rightarrow \frac{b}{a} = 3 + 2\sqrt{2}$$

**Alternativly:**

(A) As $C_1$ and $C_2$ touch each other externally so, distance between their centre = sum of their radius

$$\Rightarrow \sqrt{(a-b)^2 + (a-b)^2} = (a + b)$$

$$\Rightarrow 2(a-b)^2 = (a+b)^2 \Rightarrow a^2 + b^2 - 6ab = 0$$

$$\therefore \frac{b}{a} = \frac{6 \pm \sqrt{36 - 4}}{2} = \frac{6 \pm 4\sqrt{2}}{2} = 3 \pm 2\sqrt{2}$$

but $\frac{b}{a} = 3 - 2\sqrt{2}$ (rejected as $\frac{b}{a} > 1$. Hence $\frac{b}{a} = 3 + 2\sqrt{2}$

(B) If (1) and (2) are orthogonal then

$$2g_1 g_2 + 2f_1 f_2 = C_1 + C_2$$

i.e. $2(-a)(-b) + 2(-a)(-b) = a^2 + b^2$

$4ab = a^2 + b^2$

$$\left( \frac{b}{a} \right)^2 - 4 \left( \frac{b}{a} \right) + 1 = 0$$

If $\frac{b}{a} = t$, $t^2 - 4t + 1 = 0$

$$\Rightarrow (t - 2)^2 = 3 \Rightarrow t - 2 = +\sqrt{3} \text{ or } -\sqrt{3}$$

$$t = 2 + \sqrt{3}$$

as $t > 1 \Rightarrow 2 - \sqrt{3}$ is not possible

$$\therefore \frac{b}{a} = 2 + \sqrt{3} \Rightarrow r$$

(C) If common chord is longest then (3) must pass through the centre $(a, a)$ of $C_1$.

i.e. $4a - b - a = 0$

$$3a = b \Rightarrow \frac{b}{a} = 3 \Rightarrow q$$

(D) If $C_2$ passes through the centre of $C_1$ then $(a, a)$ must satisfy (2)

i.e. $a^2 + a^2 - 2b(2a) + b^2 = 0$

$$\Rightarrow 2a^2 - 4ab + b^2 = 0$$

$$\left( \frac{b}{a} \right)^2 - 4 \left( \frac{b}{a} \right) + 2 = 0$$

Put $\frac{b}{a} = t$

$$t^2 - 4t + 2 = 0$$

$$\Rightarrow (t - 2)^2 = 4 - 2 = 2$$

$$\Rightarrow t - 2 = \sqrt{2} \text{ or } -\sqrt{2}$$

$$t = 2 + \sqrt{2},\ t \neq 2 - \sqrt{2} \ (\text{as } t > 1) \Rightarrow p$$

**17.** **(b)** no. of radical axes = no. of radical centres

$nc_2 = nc_3 \Rightarrow n = 5$ both are true

**18.** **(7)**

Note that triangles BCM and OCN are similar

now let $ON = p$. N will be mid point of chord PQ

$$\therefore \frac{p}{1} = \frac{1}{2} \Rightarrow p = \frac{1}{2}$$

now $R = 2\sqrt{r^2 - p^2}$ for large circle

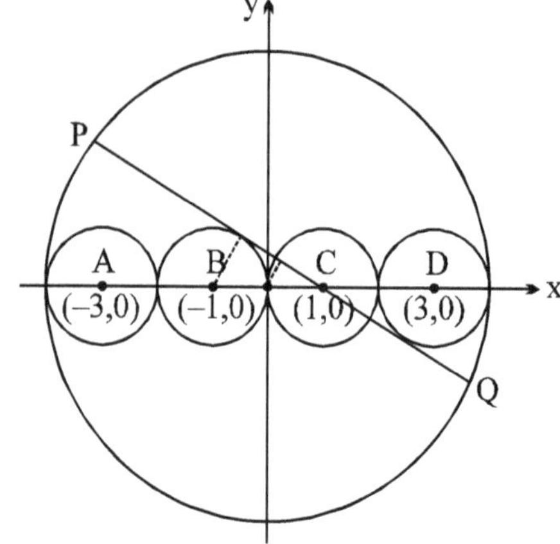


$$= 2\sqrt{16 - (1/4)} = \sqrt{63}$$

Thus $3\sqrt{x} = \sqrt{63}$

$$\Rightarrow x = 7$$

**19. (3)**

Let r be the radius of circle A
and R be the radius of circle B

$\therefore$  $r + R = 12$ and $r = 3R$

$\therefore$  $4R = 12$; $\therefore R = 3$ and $r = 9$

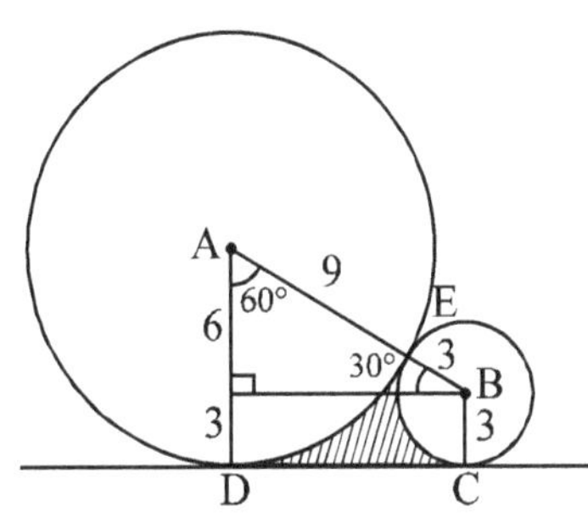

Area of trapezium ABCD $= \dfrac{1}{2}(3+9)\sqrt{(12)^2 - 6^2}$

$$= 6\sqrt{108} = 36\sqrt{3}$$

Area of arc ADC $= \dfrac{1}{2} \times 81 \times \dfrac{\pi}{3} = \dfrac{27\pi}{2}$

Area of arc BCE $= \dfrac{1}{2} \times 9 \times \dfrac{2\pi}{3} = 3\pi$

$\therefore$  required area $= 36\sqrt{3} - \left(\dfrac{27\pi}{2} + 3\pi\right)$

$$= 36\sqrt{3} - \dfrac{33\pi}{2}$$

$\therefore a = 36, \quad b = 33$

$\therefore a - b = 3$

**20. (2)**

Radius of the first circle $= \dfrac{\Delta}{S} = \dfrac{6}{6} = 1$

$\sin \dfrac{C}{2} = \dfrac{1-r}{1+r}$ $\qquad ....(1) \qquad (r < 1)$

also, $\sin C = \dfrac{4}{5}$

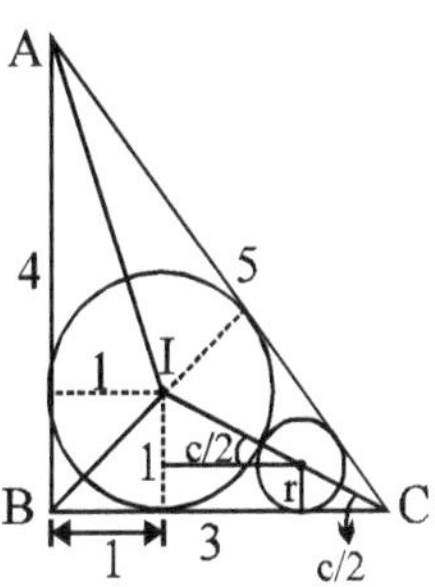

now $\quad 2\sin^2 \dfrac{C}{2} = 1 - \cos C = 1 - \dfrac{3}{5} = \dfrac{2}{5}$

$\sin^2 \dfrac{C}{2} = \dfrac{1}{5}$

$\left(\dfrac{1-r}{1+r}\right)^2 = \dfrac{1}{5} \quad \Rightarrow 5(1-r)^2 = (1+r)^2$

$\Rightarrow \sqrt{5}(1-r) = 1 + r \Rightarrow \sqrt{5} - 1 = (\sqrt{5}+1)r$

$\Rightarrow r = \dfrac{\sqrt{5}-1}{\sqrt{5}+1} = \dfrac{\sin 18°}{\cos 36°}$

$\Rightarrow \dfrac{w}{k} = 2$

**21. (3)**

$W_1: C_1 = (-5, 12) \qquad W_2: C_2 = (5, 12)$

$r_1 = 16 \qquad\qquad r_2 = 4$

now, $\quad CC_2 = r + 4$

$CC_1 = 16 - r$

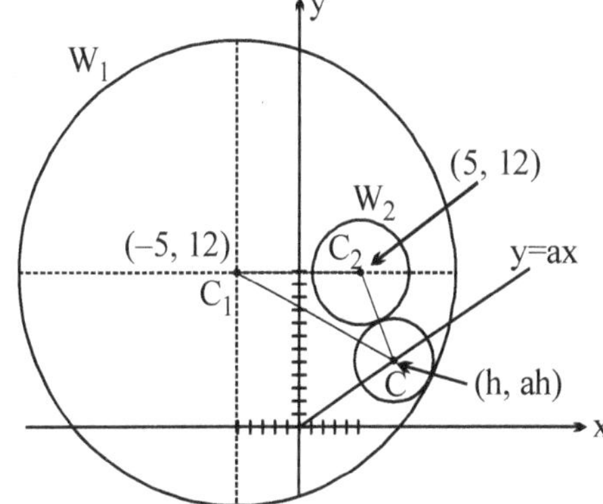

let $C(h, k) = c(h, ah)$

$CC_1^2 = (16 - r)^2$

$\Rightarrow \quad (h+5)^2 + (12 - ah)^2 = (16 - r)^2$

$\quad CC_2^2 = (4 + r)^2$

$\Rightarrow (h-5)^2 + (12 - ah)^2 = (4 + r)^2$

By subtraction

$20h = 240 - 40r$

$\Rightarrow h = 12 - 2r \Rightarrow 12r = 72 - 6h \;...(1)$

By addition

$2[h^2 + 25 + a^2h^2 - 24ah + 144] = 272 - 24r + 2r^2$

$h^2(1+a^2) - 24ah + 169 = 136 - 12r + r^2 = 136 + (6h - 72)$

$\qquad + \left(\dfrac{12-h}{2}\right)^2 \quad [\text{using (1)}]$

$\Rightarrow 4[h^2(1+a^2) - 24ah + 169] = 4[64 + 6h] + (12-h)^2$

$\qquad\qquad\qquad = 256 + 144 + h^2$

$\Rightarrow h^2(3 + 4a^2) - 96ah + 105 \cdot 4 - 36 \cdot 4 = 0$

$\Rightarrow h^2(3 + 4a^2) - 96ah + 69 \cdot 4 = 0$; for 'h' to be real $D \geq 0$

$\Rightarrow (96a)^2 - 4 \cdot 4 \cdot 69(3 + 4a^2) \geq 0$

$\Rightarrow 576a^2 - 69.3 - 276a^2 \geq 0$

$300a^2 \geq 207 \Rightarrow a^2 \geq \dfrac{69}{100}$; hence m (smallest) $= \dfrac{13}{10}$

So, $\therefore p - q = 13 - 10 = 3$

**22. (2)**

Circles are orthogonal

$\Rightarrow \dfrac{\lambda}{2}(2) - \left(\dfrac{1+\lambda^2}{2}\right)(3) = -\dfrac{10}{2} + 3 \Rightarrow 3\lambda^2 - 2\lambda - 1 = 0$

$\Rightarrow (3\lambda + 1)(\lambda - 1) = 0$

$\Rightarrow \lambda = -\dfrac{1}{3}, 1 \Rightarrow \lambda$ has two values.

**1.** **(a)**

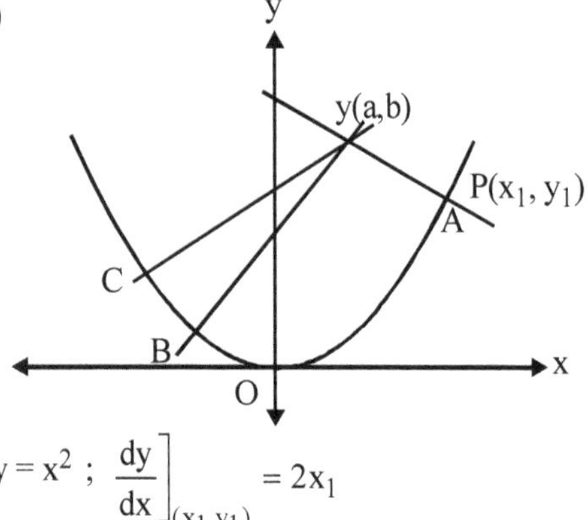

$$y = x^2 \; ; \; \left.\frac{dy}{dx}\right]_{(x_1,y_1)} = 2x_1$$

$$\therefore \; m \text{ (slope of normal)} = \frac{-1}{2x_1}$$

Equation of normal at $(x, x_1{}^2)$ is

$$y - x_1^2 = \frac{-1}{2x_1}(x - x_1) \qquad \dots\dots(1)$$

As eq. (1) passes through $(a, b)$, so

$$b - x_1^2 = \frac{-1}{2x_1}(a - x_1)$$

$$\Rightarrow 2x_1(b - x_1^2) = x_1 - a$$

$$\Rightarrow 2x_1^3 + x_1(1 - 2b) - a = 0 \qquad \dots\dots(2)$$

$\therefore$ Sum of all the x-coordinates = 0 (As there is no coefficient of $x_1{}^2$ in eq. (2))

**2.** **(c).** $SP_1 = a(1 + t_1^2)$ ; $SP_2 = a(1 + t_2^2)$

$$\Rightarrow t_1 t_2 = -1$$

$$\frac{1}{SP_1} = \frac{1}{a(1 + t^2)} \; ; \; \frac{1}{SP_2} = \frac{t^2}{a(1 + t^2)}$$

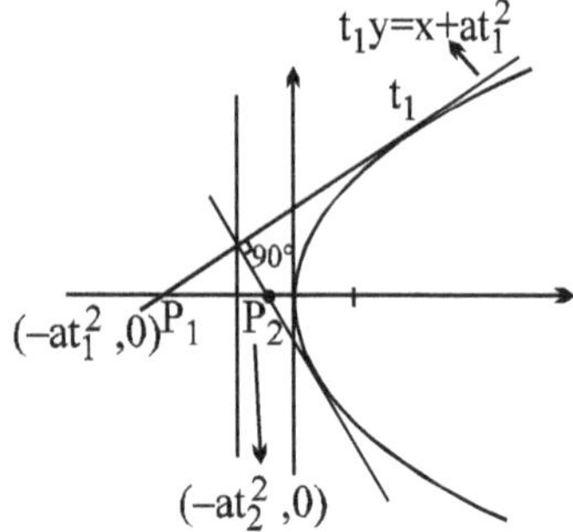

$$\therefore \; \frac{1}{SP_1} + \frac{1}{SP_2} = \frac{1}{a}$$

**3.** **(c).** Slope of tangent $= \frac{1}{t}$ $(m_1)$ at P on parabola

$$\text{slope of PS} = \frac{2at}{a(t^2 - 1)} = \frac{2t}{t^2 - 1}$$

$\therefore$ Slope of tangent at P on circle $= \frac{1 - t^2}{2t}$ $(m_2)$

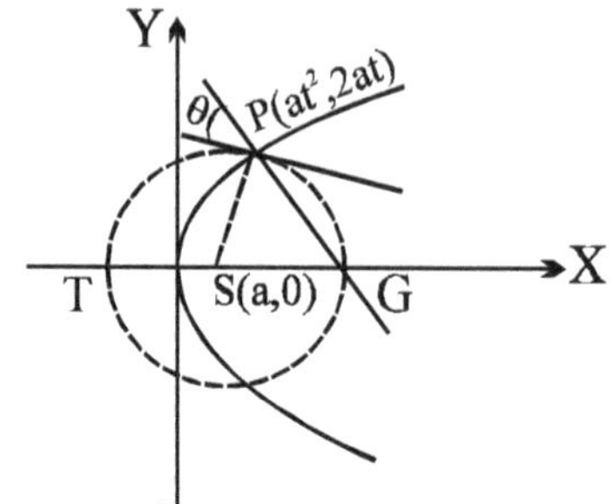

$$\therefore \; \tan\theta = \frac{\dfrac{1}{t} - \dfrac{1 - t^2}{2t}}{1 + \dfrac{1 - t^2}{2t^2}} = \frac{\left(2 - 1 + t^2\right)2t^2}{2t(1 + t^2)} = t$$

$$\therefore \; \theta = \tan^{-1} t$$

**4.** **(c).** $\vec{V} = (T^2 - 1)\hat{i} + 2T\hat{j}$

$$\vec{n} = \hat{j} - \hat{i}$$

direction of $\vec{V}$ on $\vec{n}$

$$y = \frac{\vec{V} \cdot \vec{n}}{|\vec{n}|} = \frac{(1 - T^2) + 2T}{\sqrt{2}}$$

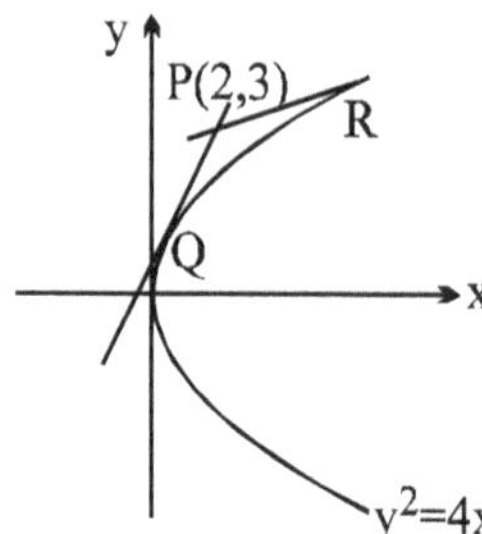

$$\sqrt{2}\,y - 1 - T^2 + 2T \; ; \; \sqrt{2}\frac{dy}{dx} = -2T\frac{dT}{dt} + 2\frac{dT}{dt}$$

Given $\dfrac{dx}{dt} = u$; but $x = T^2$; $\dfrac{dx}{dt} = 2T\dfrac{dT}{dt}$

when $P(4, 4)$ then $T = 2 \Rightarrow u = 2 \cdot 2\dfrac{dT}{dt}$; $\dfrac{dT}{dt} = 1$

$$\therefore \; \sqrt{2}\frac{dy}{dt} = -4 + 2 = -2 \qquad \Rightarrow \frac{dy}{dt} = -\sqrt{2}$$

**5.** **(b).**

$$\left.\begin{array}{l} t_1 t_2 = 2 \\[4pt] t_1 + t_2 = 3 \end{array}\right\} \Rightarrow t_1 = 1 \text{ and } t_2 = 2$$

Hence point $\left(t_1^2, 2t_1\right)$ and $\left(t_2^2, 2t_2\right)$

i.e. $(1, 2)$ and $(4, 4)$

**6.** (c). $y = mx + \dfrac{1}{m}$

or $m^2 h - mk + 1 = 0$

$m_1 + m_2 = \dfrac{k}{h}$ ; $m_1 m_2 = \dfrac{1}{h}$

given $\theta_1 + \theta_2 = \dfrac{\pi}{4} \Rightarrow \dfrac{m_1 + m_2}{1 - m_1 m_2}$

$\Rightarrow \dfrac{k}{h} = 1 - \dfrac{1}{h} \qquad \Rightarrow y = x - 1$

**7.** (c). $t_2 = -t_1 - \dfrac{2}{t_1} \Rightarrow t_1 t_2 + t_1{}^2 = -2$

Equation of the line through P parallel to AQ

$y - 2at_1 = \dfrac{2}{t_2}(x - at_1{}^2)$

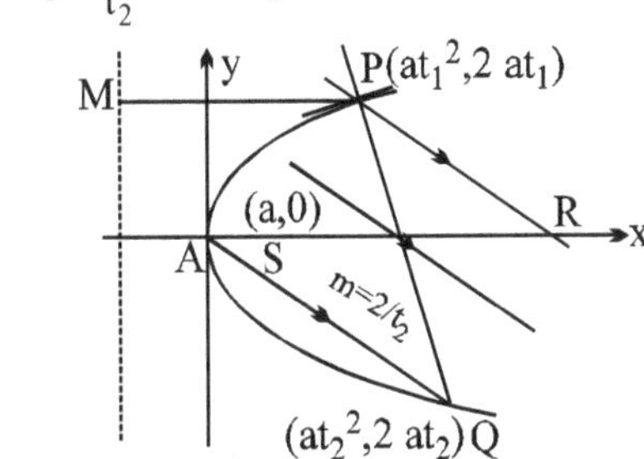


put $y = 0 \Rightarrow x = at_1{}^2 - at_1 t_2$

$= at_1^2 - a(-2 - t_1^2) = 2a + 2at_1^2 = 2(a + at_1^2)$

= twice the focal distance of P

**8.** (b) Let P $(at^2, 2at)$ be any point on the parabola $y^2 = 4ax$.
The equation of the tangent at P is $ty = x + at^2$
Since the tangent meets the axis of parabola in T and tangent at the vertex A in Y,

∴ coordinates of T and Y are $(-at^2, 0)$ and $(0, at)$ respectively.

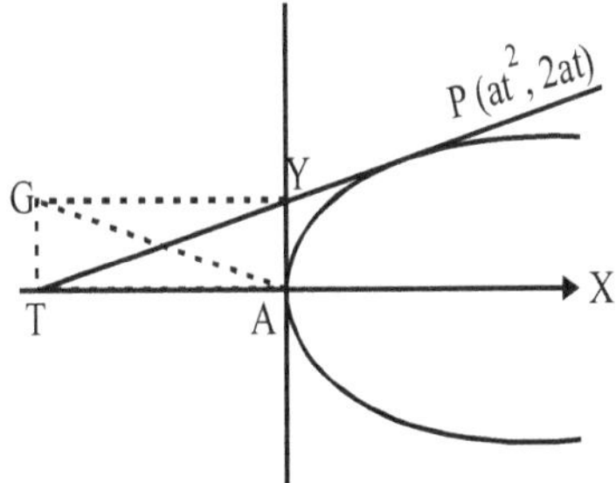


Let the coordinate of G be $(x_1, y_1)$
Since TAYG is a rectangle. So, $x_1 = -at^2$ and $y_1 = at$
Eliminating t, we get

$x_1 = -a\left(\dfrac{y_1}{a}\right)^2 \Rightarrow y_1^2 + ax_1 = 0$

∴ The locus of G $(x_1, y_1)$ is $y^2 + ax = 0$

**9.** **(a, b, c, d)**
$y = ax^2 + bx + c$, where $c = 3$ and $a = 1$ hence curve lies completely above the x-axis.
$f(x) = y = x^2 + bx + c$. Line of symmetry being 1 hence minima occurs at $x = 1$
∴ $f'(1) = 0 \Rightarrow 2x + b = 0$ at $x = 1$
$\qquad\qquad b = -2$
Hence, $f(x) = x^2 - 2x + 3$ ...(1)
Vertex is (1,2)

if $y_2 = 11$, then $11 = x^2 - 2x + 3$
$x^2 - 2x - 8 = 0$
$(x - 4)(x + 2) = 0$ ; $x = 4$ or $-2$
Now, $\overrightarrow{OA} = \hat{i} + 2\hat{j}$ and $\overrightarrow{OB} = 4\hat{i} + 11\hat{j}$

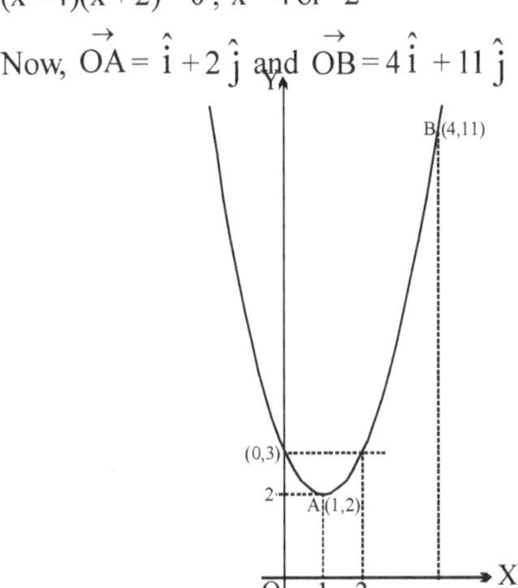


$\overrightarrow{OA} \cdot \overrightarrow{OB} = 4 + 22 = 26$
if $y = 3$, then $x^2 - 2x = 0 \Rightarrow x = 0$ or 2
Hence, area bounded

$= \displaystyle\int_0^2 3 - (x^2 - 2x + 3)dx = \int_0^2 (2x - x^2)dx$

$= x^2 - \dfrac{x^3}{3}\Big|_0^2 = 4 - \dfrac{8}{3} = \dfrac{4}{3}$ Ans.

$y = x^2 - 2x + 3 = (x - 1)^2 + 2$
$(x - 1)^2 = y - 2$
$X^2 = Y$ where $x - 1 = X$ ; $y - 2 = Y$
focus $(0, 1/4)$
if $X = 0$; $x = 1$
$Y = 1/4$; $y = 9/4$
Hence focus is $(1, 9/4)$

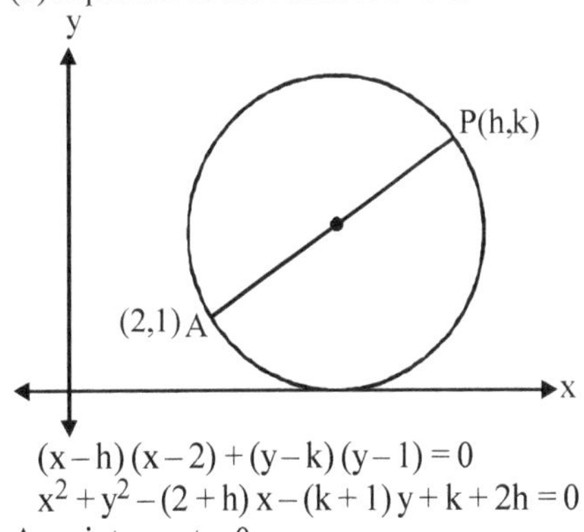


**10.** **(a, b, c)**
(a) Equation of the variable circles



$(x - h)(x - 2) + (y - k)(y - 1) = 0$
$x^2 + y^2 - (2 + h)x - (k + 1)y + k + 2h = 0$
As x-intercept $= 0$
$\Rightarrow g^2 = C$

∴ $\dfrac{(h + 2)^2}{4} = k + 2h$

$\Rightarrow (h + 2)^2 = 4k + 8h$
$\Rightarrow (h - 2)^2 = 4k$
∴ Locus is $(x - 2)^2 = 4y$
$\Rightarrow$ L.R. $= 4$

(b) $N \equiv (2, -1)$
(c) Figure is a square

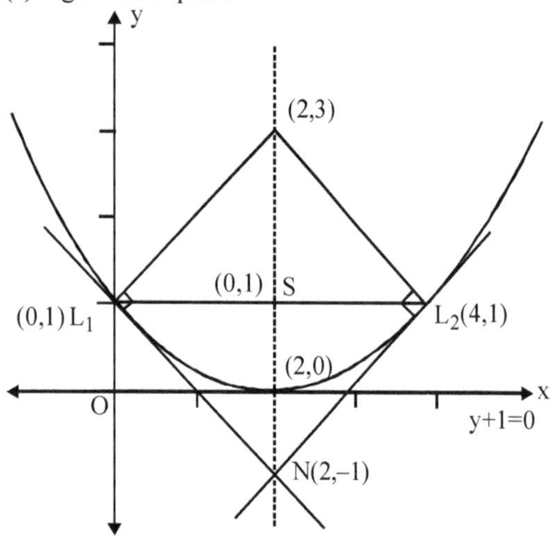


$\therefore$ Area $= \dfrac{(4)(4)}{2} = 8$ sq. unit.

**11.** **(c,d).** We have $x = y^2 + ay + b$ .......... (1)
and $x^2 = y$ .......... (2)
As (1) passing through $(1, 1)$
$\Rightarrow 1 = 1 + a + b \Rightarrow a + b = 0$

Now, $1 = 2y \dfrac{dy}{dx} + a \dfrac{dy}{dx}$

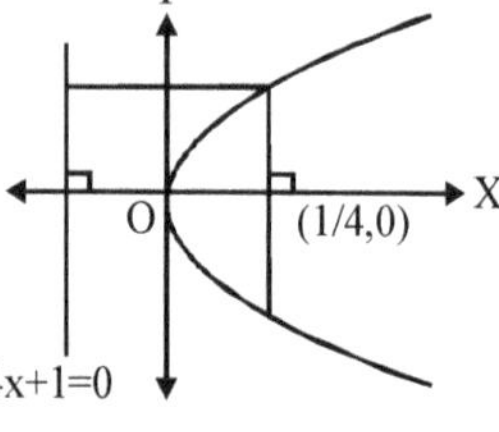


$\dfrac{dy}{dx}\Big]_{(x_1, y_1)} = \dfrac{1}{2 + a}$ and for

$y = x^2$, $\dfrac{dy}{dx} = 2x \Rightarrow \dfrac{dy}{dx}\Big]_{(1,1)} = 2$ $\therefore \dfrac{2}{2 + a} = -1$

$\Rightarrow -2 = 2 + a \Rightarrow a = -4$ and $b = 4$
Hence parabola is $y^2 - 4y + 4 = x \Rightarrow (y - 2)^2 = x$
Let $y - 2 = Y$
$\therefore Y^2 = X$
Hence required area

$= 2 \int\limits_0^{1/4} \sqrt{x}\, dx = (2)\left(\dfrac{2}{3}\right)\left(x^{3/2}\right)_0^{1/4} = \dfrac{1}{6}$ sq. units.

Equation of directirx is $x = \dfrac{-1}{4} \Rightarrow 4x + 1 = 0$

**12.** **(a,b,c).** Equation of AB
$y = 2x - 1$
solving it $y^2 = 4x$
$y^2 = 2(y + 1) \quad \Rightarrow \quad y^2 - 2y - 2 = 0$



but $y_1 + y_2 + y_3 = 0$ but $y_1 + y_2 = 2$ $\therefore y_3 = -2$
putting in $y^2 = 4x$ ; $x_3 = 1$
hence coordinates of c are $(1, -2)$

$\therefore$ sum of the x and y coordinates of C are $-1$
$\Rightarrow$ (a) is correct.
obviously normal at C passes through the lower end of the latus rectum $\Rightarrow$ (b) is correct

again centroid of $\triangle ABC = \dfrac{x_1 + x_2 + x_3}{3}$

now solving $y = 2x - 1$ with $y^2 = 4x$
$(2x - 1)^2 = 4x$
$4x^2 - 8x + 1 = 0 \Rightarrow x_1 + x_2 = 2$; also $x_3 = 1$

$\therefore$ centroid of the $\triangle ABC = \dfrac{2 + 1}{3} = (1, 0)$

again equation of the normal at C
$y + 2 = -(-2/2)(x - 1)$
$y + 2 = x - 1 \Rightarrow x - y - 3 = 0$
hence gradient of chord at C is $1 \Rightarrow$ (d) is incorrect

**13.** **(b)** The equation can be written as $(x - 4)^2 = -16(y - 1)$ ...(1)
We know that focal distance of any point $(x, y)$ on $y^2 = 4ax$ is $|x + a|$.
So, the focal distance of point $(x, y)$ on the parabola (1) is $|y - 1 - 4| = |y - 5|$

**14.** **(c)** The parabola is $(x - 4)^2 = 16(y + 1)$
The equation of normal to
$y^2 = 4ax$ is $y = mx - 2am - am^3$
So, the equation of normal to
$(x - 4)^2 = 16(y + 1)$ is $x - 4 = m(y + 1) - 8m - 4m^3$
It passes through $(7, 14)$, so, $3 = 15m - 8m - 4m^3$
$\Rightarrow 4m^3 - 7m + 3 = 0 \Rightarrow (m - 1)(2m - 1)(2m + 3) = 0$
$\therefore m = 1, \dfrac{1}{2}, -\dfrac{3}{2}$

So, the slope of normals is $\dfrac{1}{m} = 1, 2, -\dfrac{2}{3}$
(**NOTE :** here slope $\neq$ m)

**15.** **(c)** The foot of normals $y = mx - 2am - am^3$ on $y^2 = 4ax$ is $(am^2, -2am)$. So, the feet of normal on $(x - h)^2 = 4a(y - k)$ is $(h - 2am, k + am^2)$.
So, the desired feet of normals are $(4 - 8 \times 1, -1 + 4 \times 1)$,

$\left(4 - 8 \times \dfrac{1}{2}, -1 + 4 \times \dfrac{1}{4}\right)$ and

$\left(4 - 8 \times -\dfrac{3}{2}, -1 + 4 \times \dfrac{9}{4}\right)$, i.e. $(-4, 3)$, $(0, 0)$ and $(16, 8)$.

**16.** $A \to r$; $B \to p, s$; $C \to q, t$
(A) $\because 25(x^2 + y^2) = (4x + 3y - 12)^2$
or $25x^2 + 25y^2 = 16x^2 + 9y^2 + 24xy - 96x - 72y + 144$
$\Rightarrow 9x^2 + 16y^2 - 24xy = -96x - 72y + 144$
$\Rightarrow (3x - 4y)^2 = -24(4x + 3y - 6)$

$\Rightarrow 25 \times \left(\dfrac{3x - 4y}{5}\right)^2 = -24\left(\dfrac{4x + 3y - 6}{5}\right) \times 5$

$\Rightarrow \left(\dfrac{3x - 4y}{5}\right)^2 = -\dfrac{24}{5}\left(\dfrac{4x + 3y - 6}{5}\right)$

Let $\dfrac{3x - 4y}{5} = Y$ and $\dfrac{4x + 3y - 6}{5} = X$

$\therefore Y^2 = -\dfrac{24}{5}X$

On comparing with $Y^2 = 4pX$, we get

$4p = \dfrac{24}{5} \Rightarrow p = \dfrac{6}{5}$

$\therefore$ Equation of directrix is $X - p = 0$

i.e., $\dfrac{4x + 3y - 6}{5} - \dfrac{6}{5} = 0$

or $4x + 3y = 12$

Axis of the parabola is $Y = 0$

ie, $\dfrac{3x - 4y}{5} = 0$

or $3x - 4y = 0$

(B) $\because 25(x^2 + y^2) = (4x - 3y + 12)^2$

or $25x^2 + 25y^2 = 16x^2 + 9y^2 - 24xy + 96x - 72y + 144$

$\Rightarrow 9x^2 + 16y^2 + 24xy = 96x - 72y + 144$

$\Rightarrow (3x + 4y)^2 = 24(4x - 3y + 6)$

or $25 \times \left(\dfrac{3x + 4y}{5}\right)^2 = 24\left(\dfrac{4x - 3y + 6}{5}\right) \times 5$

$\Rightarrow \left(\dfrac{3x + 4y}{5}\right)^2 = \dfrac{24}{5}\left(\dfrac{4x - 3y + 6}{5}\right)$

Let $\dfrac{3x + 4y}{5} = Y$ and $\dfrac{4x - 3y + 6}{5} = X$

$\therefore Y^2 = \dfrac{24}{5} X$

On comparing with $Y^2 = 4pX$, we get

$\therefore 4p = \dfrac{24}{5} \Rightarrow p = \dfrac{6}{5}$

Equation of directrix is $X + p = 0$

ie, $\dfrac{4x - 3y + 6}{5} + \dfrac{6}{5} = 0$

$\Rightarrow 4x - 3y + 12 = 0$   (p)

and axis of the parabola is $Y = 0$

ie, $\dfrac{3x + 4y}{5} = 0$

or $3x + 4y = 0$ (s)

(C) $\because 25(x^2 + y^2) = (3x - 4y + 12)^2$

or $25x^2 + 25y^2 = 9x^2 + 16y^2 - 24xy + 72x - 96y + 144$

$\Rightarrow 16x^2 + 9y^2 + 24xy = 72x - 96y + 144$

$\Rightarrow (4x + 3y)^2 = 24(3x - 4y + 6)$

or $25 \times \left(\dfrac{4x + 3y}{5}\right)^2 = 24\left(\dfrac{3x - 4y + 6}{5}\right) \times 5$

$\Rightarrow \left(\dfrac{4x + 3y}{5}\right)^2 = \dfrac{24}{5}\left(\dfrac{3x - 4y + 6}{5}\right)$

Let $\dfrac{4x + 3y}{5} = Y$ and $\dfrac{3x - 4y + 6}{5} = X$

$\therefore Y^2 = \dfrac{24}{5} X$

On comparing with $Y^2 = 4pX$, we get

$4p = \dfrac{24}{5} \Rightarrow p = \dfrac{6}{5}$

$\therefore$ Equation of directrix is $X + p = 0$

$\dfrac{3x - 4y + 6}{5} + \dfrac{6}{5} = 0$

or $\quad 3x - 4y + 12 = 0$   (t)

and axis of the parabola is $Y = 0$

ie, $4x + 3y = 0$ (q)

17. **A→s; B→r; C→p; D→q**

(A) T : $ty = x + at^2$        ....(1)

line perpendicular to (1) through (a,0)

$tx + y = ta$        ....(2)

equation of OP : $y - \dfrac{2}{t}x = 0$  ....(3)

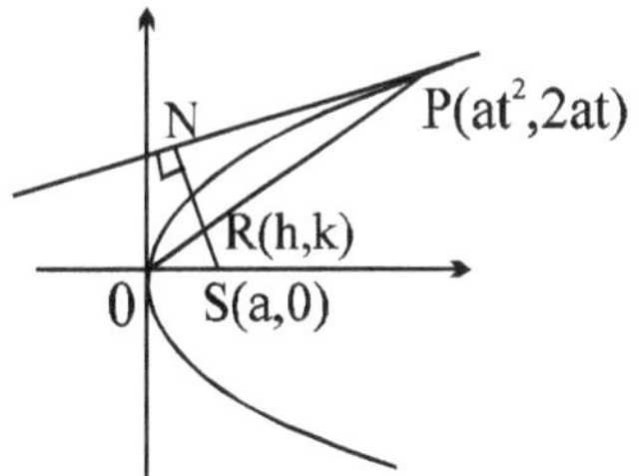


from (2) & (3) eliminating t we get locus

$2x^2 + y^2 - 2ax = 0$

(B) put $x^2 = \dfrac{y}{a}$ in circle, $x^2 + (y - 1)^2 = 1$, we get

(Note that for a < 0 they cannot intersect other than origin)

$\dfrac{y}{a} + y^2 - 2y = 0$ ; hence we get $y = 0$ or $y = 2 - \dfrac{1}{a}$

substituting $y = 2 - \dfrac{1}{a}$ in $y = ax^2$, we get

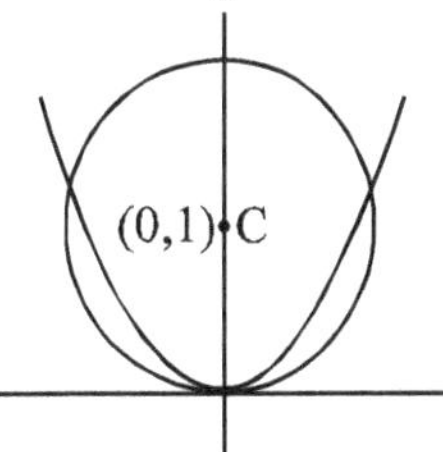


$ax^2 = 2 - \dfrac{1}{a}$ ; $x^2 = \dfrac{2a - 1}{a^2} > 0 \Rightarrow a > \dfrac{1}{2}$ ]

(C) Chord of contact of (h, k)

$ky = 2a(x + h)$. It passes through $(-a, b)$

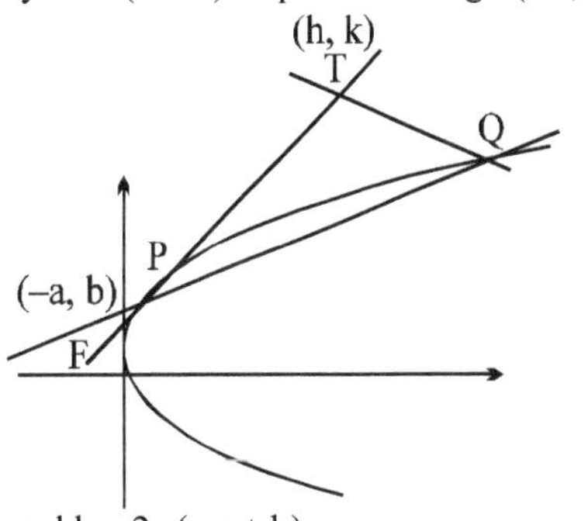


$\Rightarrow bk = 2a(-a + h)$

$\Rightarrow$ Locus is $by = 2a(x - a)$

(D) Slope of tangant at P is $\dfrac{1}{t_1}$ and at Q $= \dfrac{1}{t_2}$

$\Rightarrow \cot\theta_1 = t_1$ and $\cot\theta_2 = t_2$

Slope of PQ $= \dfrac{2}{t_1 + t_2}$

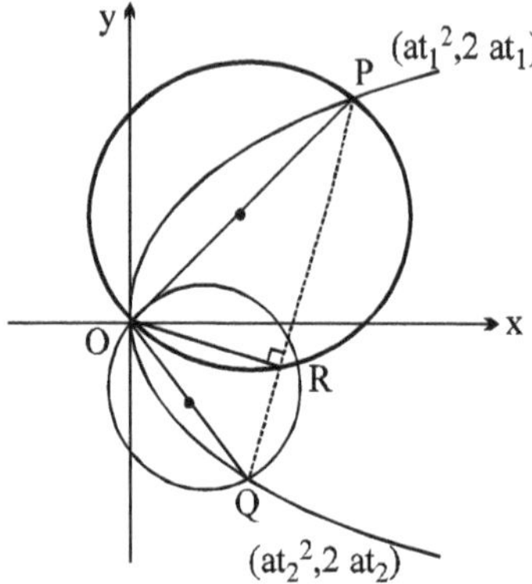


$\Rightarrow$ Slope of OR is $-\dfrac{t_1 + t_2}{2} = \tan\phi$

(Note angle in a semicircle is 90°)

$\Rightarrow \tan\phi = -\dfrac{1}{2}(\cot\theta_1 + \cot\theta_2)$

$\Rightarrow \cot\theta_1 + \cot\theta_2 = -2\tan\phi$

**18.** **(a)** The given curve is $y = -\dfrac{x^2}{2} + x + 1$

or $(x-1)^2 = -2(y - 3/2)$

which is a parabola, so it should be symmetric with respect to its axis $x - 1 = 0$

$\therefore$ Both the statements are true and statement 2 is a correct explanation for statement 1.

**19.** **(a)** Any point on $x + 2 = 0$ is $(-2, k)$

If it lies on the tangent $ty = x + 2t^2$

then $tk = -2 + 2t^2$ i.e. $2t^2 - kt - 2 = 0$

$\therefore t_1 t_2 = -1$

$\therefore \dfrac{1}{t_1} \cdot \dfrac{1}{t_2} = -1$

$\therefore$ The two tangents are perpendicular

$\therefore$ Statement-2 is true.

Further the point $(-2, 5)$ lies on $x = -2$

$\therefore$ The tangents drawn through $(-2, 5)$ are perpendicular to each other.

$\therefore$ Statement-1 is true.

Statement 2 is correct explanation of statement-1.

**20.** **(7)**

$y = x^2$

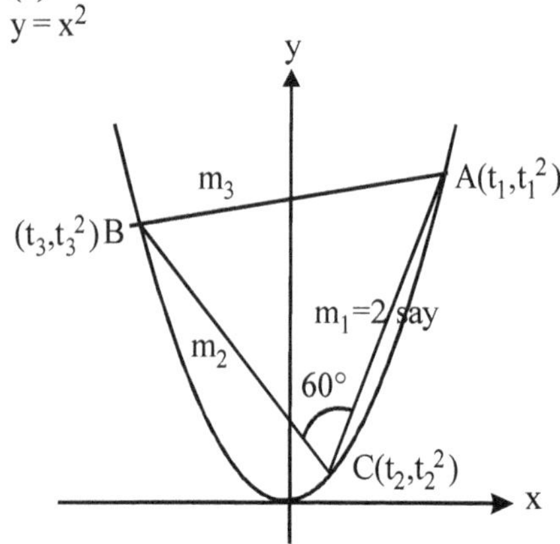


To find : $t_1 + t_2 + t_3 = ?$

$m_1 = \dfrac{t_2^2 - t_1^2}{t_2 - t_1} = t_2 + t_1$

Similarly, $m_2 = t_2 + t_3$ and $m_3 = t_3 + t_1$

Hence, $\Sigma\, t_i = \dfrac{m_1 + m_2 + m_3}{2}$

Now, $\tan 60° = \left|\dfrac{m - 2}{1 + 2m}\right|$

$\Rightarrow \pm\sqrt{3}\,(1 + 2m) = m - 2$

Taking +ve sign, we get

$\sqrt{3}\,(1 + 2m) = m - 2$

$\Rightarrow m\,(2\sqrt{3} - 1) = -(2 + \sqrt{3})$

$\Rightarrow m = \dfrac{-(2 + \sqrt{3})}{2\sqrt{3} - 1}$

Takin −ve sign, we get

$m - 2 = -2\sqrt{3}m - \sqrt{3}$

$\Rightarrow m\,(2\sqrt{3} + 1) = 2 - \sqrt{3} \Rightarrow m = \dfrac{2 - \sqrt{3}}{2\sqrt{3} + 1}$

$\therefore m_1 = \dfrac{-(2 + \sqrt{3})}{2\sqrt{3} - 1},\ m_2 = \dfrac{2 - \sqrt{3}}{2\sqrt{3} + 1}$ and $m_3 = 2$

$\therefore \displaystyle\sum_{i=1}^{3} t_i = \dfrac{m_1 + m_2 + m_3}{2}$

$= \dfrac{\dfrac{-(2 + \sqrt{3})}{2\sqrt{3} - 1} + \dfrac{2 - \sqrt{3}}{2\sqrt{3} + 1} + 2}{2}$

$= \dfrac{\dfrac{-4\sqrt{3} - 2 - 6 - \sqrt{3} + 4\sqrt{3} - 6 - 2 + \sqrt{3} + 22}{11}}{2}$

$= \dfrac{6}{22} = \dfrac{3}{11} = \dfrac{p}{q} \Rightarrow \dfrac{(p + q)}{2} = \dfrac{14}{2} = 7$

**21.** **(4)**

$T : ty = x + t^2,\ \tan\theta = \dfrac{1}{t}$

$A = \dfrac{1}{2}\,(AN)(PN) = \dfrac{1}{2}\,(2t^2)(2t)$

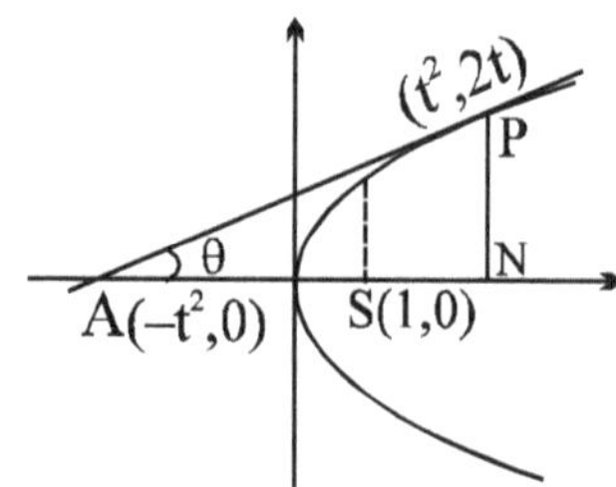


$A = 2t^3 = 2(t^2)^{3/2}$

i.e. $t^2 \in [1, 4]$ & $A_{max}$ occurs when $t^2 = 4 \Rightarrow A_{max} = 16$

Thus $4X = 16$

$\Rightarrow X = 4$

**22.** **(2)**

$\tan \alpha = -t_1$ and $\tan \beta = -t_2$

also $t_2 = -t_1 - \dfrac{2}{t_1}$

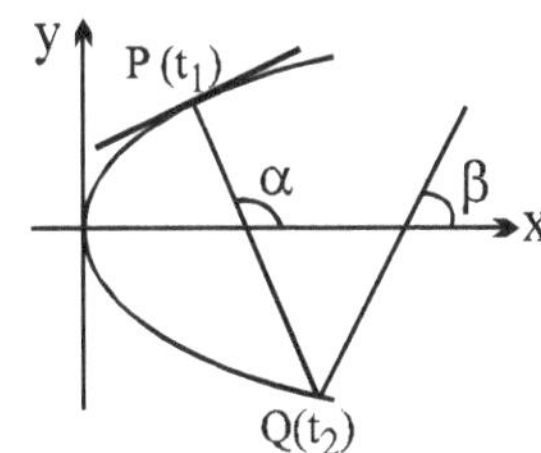

$t_1 t_2 + t_1^2 = -2$

$\tan \alpha \tan \beta + \tan^2 \alpha = -2$

Thus $N = 2$

**23.** **(8)**

$SS_1 = T^2$

$(y^2 - 4x)(y_1^2 - 4x_1) = (yy_1 - 2(x + x_1))^2$

$(y^2 - 4x)(4 + 4) = [2y - 2(x - 1)]^2 = 4(y - x + 1)^2$

$2(y^2 - 4x) = (y - x + 1)^2 \quad ;$

solving with the line $x = 2$ we get,

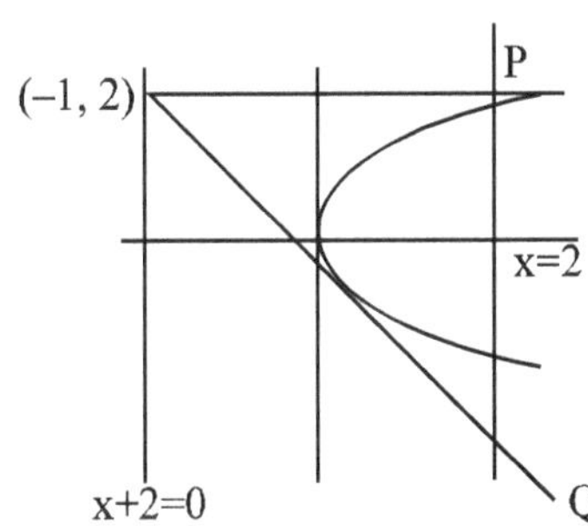

$2(y^2 - 8) = (y - 1)^2 \quad$ or $2(y^2 - 8) = y^2 - 2y + 1$

or $y^2 + 2y - 17 = 0$

where $y_1 + y_2 = -2$ and $y_1 y_2 = -17$

Now $|y_1 - y_2|^2 = (y_1 + y_2)^2 - 4 y_1 y_2$

or $|y_1 - y_2|^2 = 4 - 4(-17) = 72$

$\therefore (y_1 - y_2) = \sqrt{72} = 6\sqrt{2}$

Thus, $A = 6$

$B = 2$

$\Rightarrow A + B = 6 + 2 = 8$

**24.** **(4)**

$y = ax^2$

$\left. \dfrac{dy}{dt} \right|_T = 2ax_0 = m$

hence line is $y = (2ax_0)x - b \qquad .....(1)$

$\therefore (x_0, a x_0^2)$ lies on parabola and the line (1)

$a x_0^2 = 2a x_0^2 - b$

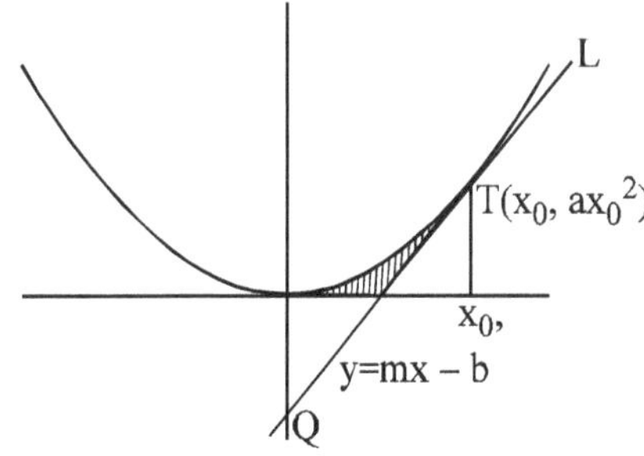

$b = a x_0^2$. Hence $Q = (0, -b) = (0, -a x_0^2)$

now using $(TQ)^2 = 1$

$x_0^2 + 4a^2 x_0^4 = 1$

$a^2 = \dfrac{(1 - x_0^2)}{4x_0^4} \qquad .....(2)$

now $A = \displaystyle\int_0^{x_0} (ax^2 - mx + b)\,dx$

$= \left. \dfrac{ax^3}{3} - \dfrac{mx^2}{2} + bx \right|_0^{x_0} = \dfrac{ax_0^3}{3} - \dfrac{mx_0^2}{2} + bx_0$

$= \dfrac{ax_0^3}{3} - ax_0^3 + ax_0^3 = \dfrac{ax_0^3}{3}$

$\therefore A^2 = \dfrac{a^2 x_0^6}{9} = \dfrac{x_0^6}{9}\left(\dfrac{1 - x_0^2}{4x_0^4}\right) = \dfrac{x_0^2(1 - x_0^2)}{36}$

let $A^2 = f(x_0) = \dfrac{x_0^2(1 - x_0^2)}{36}$

This is maximum when $x_0^2 = \dfrac{1}{2}$

$A^2 \Big]_{max} = \dfrac{1}{2} \cdot \dfrac{1}{2} \cdot \dfrac{1}{36} = \dfrac{1}{144} \, ;$

$\therefore A_{max} = \dfrac{1}{12} \Rightarrow \dfrac{1}{3A} = 4$

**1.** **(b).**
$$9(x-3)^2 + 9(y-4)^2 = y^2$$
$$9(x-3)^2 + 8y^2 - 72y + 14y = 0$$
$$9(x-3)^2 + 8(y^2 - 9y) + 144 = 0$$
$$9(x-3)^2 + 8\left[\left(y-\frac{9}{2}\right)^2 - \frac{81}{4}\right] + 144 = 0$$
$$\Rightarrow\quad 9(x-3)^2 + 8\left(y-\frac{9}{2}\right)^2 = 162 - 144 = 18$$
$$\frac{9(x-3)^2}{18} + \frac{8\left(y-\frac{9}{2}\right)}{18} = 1$$
$$\Rightarrow\quad \frac{(x-3)^2}{2} + \frac{\left(y-\frac{9}{2}\right)}{9/4} = 1$$
$$e^2 = 1 - \frac{2\cdot 4}{9} = \frac{1}{9}\quad ;\quad \therefore\ e = \frac{1}{3}$$

**2.** **(a).** $\quad T: \dfrac{x\cos\theta}{a} + \dfrac{y\sin\theta}{b} = 1$

$$p_1 = \left|\frac{ab}{\sqrt{b^2\cos^2\theta + a^2\sin^2\theta}}\right| \qquad ....(1)$$

$$N_1: \frac{ax}{\cos\theta} - \frac{by}{\sin\theta} = a^2 - b^2$$

$$p_2 = \left|\frac{(a^2-b^2)\sin\theta\cos\theta}{\sqrt{a^2\sin^2\theta + b^2\cos^2\theta}}\right| \qquad ....(2)$$

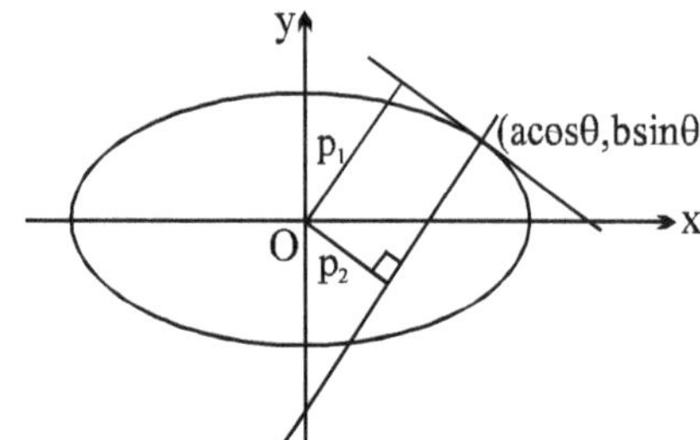


$$p_1 p_2 = \frac{ab(a^2 - b^2)}{2\left(\dfrac{a^2}{2} + \dfrac{b^2}{2}\right)} \qquad \text{when } \theta = \pi/4;$$

$$p_1 p_2 = \frac{ab(a^2 - b^2)}{a^2 + b^2}$$

**3.** **(a)** Proceeding, we get

$$m_1 + m_2 = \frac{2x_1 y_1}{x_1^2 - a^2} \quad \text{and} \quad m_1 m_2 = \frac{y_1^2 - b^2}{x_1^2 - a^2}$$

Given $\theta_1 + \theta_2 = \text{constant} = \alpha$ (say)

$\therefore\ \tan(\theta_1 + \theta_2) = \tan\alpha$

$$\Rightarrow\quad \frac{\tan\theta_1 + \tan\theta_2}{1 - \tan\theta_1 . \tan\theta_2} = \tan\alpha$$

or $\quad \dfrac{m_1 + m_2}{1 - m_1 m_2} = \tan\alpha$

$$\Rightarrow\quad \frac{2x_1 y_1 /(x_1^2 - a^2)}{1 - (y_1^2 - b^2)/(x_1^2 - a^2)} = \tan\alpha$$

$$\Rightarrow\quad 2x_1 y_1 \cot\alpha = x_1^2 - y_1^2 + b^2 - a^2$$

**4.** **(b)** Let $P \equiv (a\cos\alpha,\ b\sin\alpha)$

and $Q \equiv (a\cos\beta,\ b\sin\beta)$

The Equation of the chord PQ is

$$\frac{x}{a}\cos\left(\frac{\alpha+\beta}{2}\right) + \frac{y}{b}\sin\left(\frac{\alpha+\beta}{2}\right) = \cos\left(\frac{\alpha-\beta}{2}\right)$$

Since it cuts the major axis of the ellipse at a distance d from the centre.

It must pass through the point (d, 0)

i.e. $\quad \dfrac{d}{a}\cos\left(\dfrac{\alpha+\beta}{2}\right) = \cos\left(\dfrac{\alpha-\beta}{2}\right)$

$$\Rightarrow\quad \frac{d-a}{d+a} = \frac{\cos\left(\dfrac{\alpha-\beta}{2}\right) - \cos\left(\dfrac{\alpha+\beta}{2}\right)}{\cos\left(\dfrac{\alpha-\beta}{2}\right) + \cos\left(\dfrac{\alpha+\beta}{2}\right)}$$

[By componendo and dividendo]

$$= \frac{2\sin\alpha/2 \sin\beta/2}{2\cos\alpha/2 \cos\beta/2} = \tan\alpha/2 . \tan\beta/2$$

$$\therefore\quad \tan\alpha/2 . \tan\beta/2 = \frac{d-a}{d+a}$$

**5.** **(a)** Let the Equation of the ellipse be $\dfrac{x^2}{a^2} + \dfrac{y^2}{b^2} = 1$

It is given that it passes through $(7, 0)$ and $(0, -5)$

$\therefore\ a^2 = 49$ and $b^2 = 25$

Since $b^2 = a^2(1 - e^2)$

$\therefore\ 25 = 49(1 - e^2)$

$$\Rightarrow\ 1 - e^2 = \frac{25}{49} \Rightarrow e^2 = \frac{24}{49}$$

$e = 2\sqrt{6}/7$

**6.** **(d)** The given ellipse is $\dfrac{x^2}{9} + \dfrac{y^2}{5} = 1$

Then $a^2 = 9,\ b^2 = 5$

$$\Rightarrow\ e = \sqrt{1 - \frac{5}{9}} = \frac{2}{3}$$

$\therefore$ End point of latus rectum in first quadrant is
$\quad L(2, 5/3)$

Equation of tangent at L is $\dfrac{2x}{9} + \dfrac{y}{3} = 1$

It meets x-axis at A $(9/2, 0)$ and B at $(0, 3)$

$$\therefore \quad \text{Area of } \Delta OAB = \frac{1}{2} \times \frac{9}{2} \times 3 = \frac{27}{4}$$

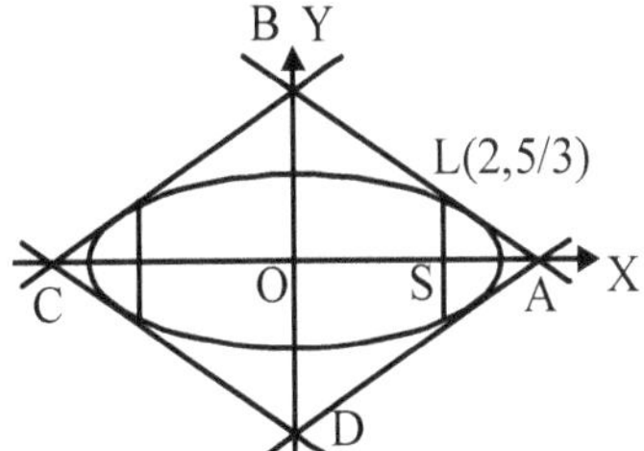


By symmetry area of quadrilateral

$= 4 \times (\text{Area } \Delta OAB)$

$= 4 \times \dfrac{27}{4} = 27$ sq. units.

**7.**   **(a)**   Equation of the tangent at $\dfrac{\pi}{4}$ is

$$\frac{x\left(\frac{1}{\sqrt{2}}\right)}{a} + \frac{y\left(\frac{1}{\sqrt{2}}\right)}{b} = 1$$

i.e., $\dfrac{x}{a} + \dfrac{y}{b} - \sqrt{2} = 0$  ..........(i)

Equation of the normal at $\dfrac{\pi}{4}$ is

$$\frac{x}{b} - \frac{y}{a} = \frac{a}{b\sqrt{2}} - \frac{b}{a\sqrt{2}} \quad ..........(ii)$$

$p_1$ = length of the perpendicular from the centre to the

$$\text{tangent} = \left| \frac{-\sqrt{2}}{\sqrt{\frac{1}{a^2} + \frac{1}{b^2}}} \right| = \frac{\sqrt{2}ab}{\sqrt{a^2 + b^2}}$$

$p_2$ = length of the perpendicular from the centre to the

$$\text{normal} = \left| \frac{\frac{a}{b\sqrt{2}} - \frac{b}{a\sqrt{2}}}{\sqrt{\frac{1}{a^2} + \frac{1}{b^2}}} \right| = \frac{a^2 - b^2}{\sqrt{2}\sqrt{a^2 + b^2}}.$$

Area of the rectangle $= p_1 \, p_2 = \dfrac{ab(a^2 - b^2)}{a^2 + b^2}$

**8.**   **(b)**   Let the points of intersection of the line and the ellipse

be $(a\cos\theta, \, b\sin\theta)$ and $\left(a\cos\left(\frac{\pi}{2}+\theta\right), b\sin\left(\frac{\pi}{2}+\theta\right)\right)$.

Since they lie on the given line $lx + my + n = 0$,

$\qquad la\cos\theta + mb\sin\theta + n = 0$

$\Rightarrow la\cos\theta + mb\sin\theta = -n$

and $-la\sin\theta + mb\cos\theta + n = 0$

$\Rightarrow la\sin\theta - mb\cos\theta = n.$

Squaring and adding, we get $a^2l^2 + b^2m^2 = 2n^2$

$\Rightarrow \dfrac{a^2l^2 + b^2m^2}{n^2} = 2.$

**9**   **(a, b, c)**

Let PN is normal to ellipse at point P.

$F_1 \equiv (4, 3), F_2 \equiv (10, \beta)$

Slope PN = 1,

Slope $PF_1 = 1/3$

Let slope $PF_2 = m$

$$\frac{m-1}{1+m} = \frac{1 - \frac{1}{3}}{1 + \frac{1}{3}} \Rightarrow m = 3 \Rightarrow \beta = 29$$

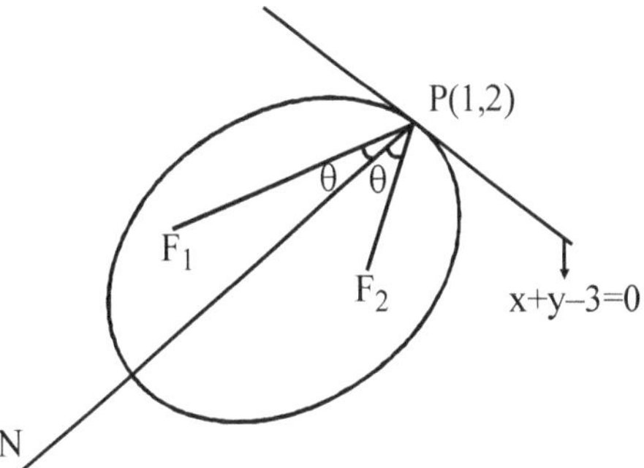


Also, $PF_1 + PF_2 = 2a \Rightarrow a = 5\sqrt{10}$

Also $b^2 = 72 \Rightarrow b = 6\sqrt{2} \Rightarrow 2b = 12\sqrt{2}$

$$e^2 = 1 - \frac{b^2}{a^2} = \frac{89}{125}$$

**10.**   **(a,b).** $h = \pm ae \,; k = \pm \dfrac{b^2}{a}$

$$k = \pm a(1 - e^2) = \pm a\left(1 - \frac{h^2}{a^2}\right) = \pm \left(a - \frac{h^2}{a}\right)$$

$+$ ve sign, $k = a - \dfrac{h^2}{a} \Rightarrow \dfrac{h^2}{a} = a - k$

$\Rightarrow h^2 = a(a-k) \Rightarrow$(a)

$-$ ve sign, $k = -a + \dfrac{h^2}{a} \Rightarrow h^2 = a(a+k)$

**11.**   **(b,d)** Let $(x_1, y_1)$ be the point at which tangent to ellipse $4x^2 + 9y^2 = 1$ are parallel to $8x = 9y$ then slope of tangent at

$(x_1, y_1) = \dfrac{8}{9}$

$\Rightarrow \left(\dfrac{dy}{dx}\right)_{(x_1, y_1)} = \dfrac{8}{9}$    ...(1)

Differentiating equation of ellipse w.r.t. to x we get

$8x + 18y\dfrac{dy}{dx} = 0$

$\Rightarrow \left(\dfrac{dy}{dx}\right)_{(x_1, y_1)} = \dfrac{-8x_1}{18y_1} = \dfrac{-4x_1}{9y_1}$

Substituting in equation (1) we get

$\dfrac{-4x_1}{9y_1} = \dfrac{8}{9} \Rightarrow -x_1 = 2y_1$ ...(2)

Also $(x_1, y_1)$ being pt of contact must be on curve

$\therefore \quad 4x_1^2 + 9y_1^2 = 1$

$\Rightarrow 4.4y_1^2 + 9y_1^2 = 1 \qquad$ (Using (2))

$\Rightarrow y_1^2 = \dfrac{1}{25} \qquad \Rightarrow \qquad y_1 = \pm\dfrac{1}{5}$

$\Rightarrow x_1 = \mp\dfrac{2}{5}$

Thus the req. pts are $\left(\dfrac{-2}{5}, \dfrac{1}{5}\right)$ and $\left(\dfrac{2}{5}, \dfrac{-1}{5}\right)$

**12. (a,c,d)** Coordinates of $V \equiv \left(-a, \dfrac{b(1+\cos\theta)}{\sin\theta}\right)$

$V' \equiv \left(a, \dfrac{b(1-\cos\theta)}{\sin\theta}\right)$

$\ell(AV) = \dfrac{b(1+\cos\theta)}{\sin\theta}, \quad \ell(A'V') = \dfrac{b(1-\cos\theta)}{\sin\theta}$

$\Rightarrow \ell(AV).\ell(A'V') = b^2$

Slope of V'S $= \dfrac{b(1-\cos\theta)}{a\sin\theta(1+e)}$

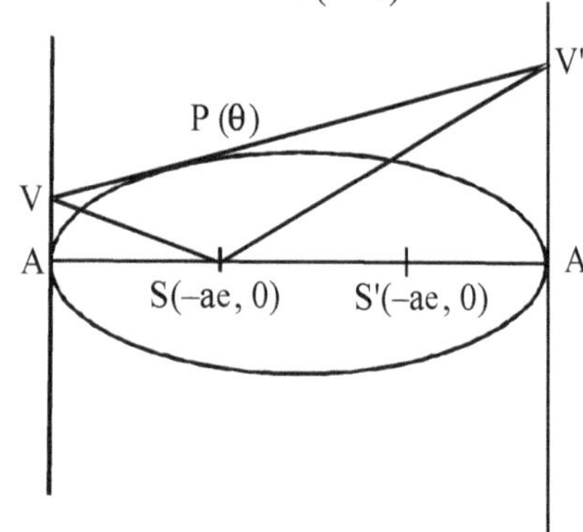

Slope of VS $= \dfrac{b(1+\cos\theta)}{a\sin\theta(e-1)}$

Product of slope of V'S and VS $= \dfrac{b^2\sin^2\theta}{a^2\sin^2\theta(e^2-1)} = -1$

$\Rightarrow \angle V'SV = 90°$. Also $\angle VS'V' = 90°$

Hence V'S' VS is a cyclic quadrilateral.

**13. (b)** If $C$ is the centre of the ellipse then slope of $CP$, where $C(0, 0)$ and $P(a\cos\phi_1, b\sin\phi_1)$ is

$m_1 = \dfrac{b\sin\phi_1}{a\cos\phi_1} = \dfrac{b}{a}\tan\phi_1.$

Similarly slope of $CQ$ is $\dfrac{b}{a}\tan\phi_2.$

Since $CP$ and $CQ$ are conjugate,

$\dfrac{b^2}{a^2}\tan\phi_1\tan\phi_2 = -\dfrac{b^2}{a^2} \quad \Rightarrow \quad \tan\phi_1\tan\phi_2 = -1$

$\Rightarrow \sin\phi_1\sin\phi_2 + \cos\phi_1\cos\phi_2 = 0$

$\Rightarrow \cos(\phi_1 \sim \phi_2) = 0 \qquad \Rightarrow \qquad \phi_1 \sim \phi_2 = \pm 90°.$

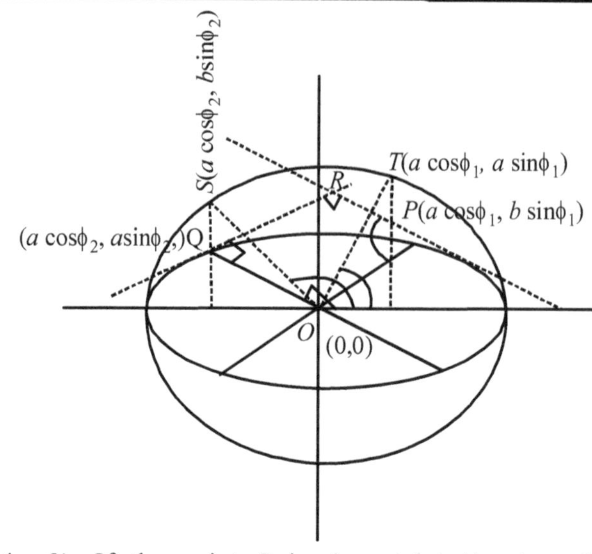


**14. (b)** If the point $P$ is $(a\cos\phi, b\sin\phi)$, then $Q$ is $(-a\sin\phi, b\cos\phi)$, and hence

$CP^2 + CQ^2 = a^2\cos^2\phi + b^2\sin\phi$
$\qquad\qquad\qquad + a^2\sin^2\phi + b^2\cos^2\phi$
$= a^2 + b^2.$

**15. (c)** By definition the tangent at $P$ is parallel to $CQ$ and tangent at $Q$ is parallel to $CP$

$\Rightarrow CPRQ$ is a parallelogram. Also

$P$ and $Q$ are respectively $P(a\cos\phi, b\sin\phi)$, and $Q(-a\sin\phi, b\cos\phi)$. Equation of the tangent at P is $\dfrac{x\cos\phi}{a} + \dfrac{y\sin\phi}{b} = 1.$ The length of the perpendicular from $C$ to this tangent

i.e. $PR = \dfrac{ab}{\sqrt{b^2\cos^2\phi + a^2\sin\phi}} = \dfrac{ab}{CQ}$

$\Rightarrow$ area of parallelogram $CPRQ = ab.$

**16. (A) – s, (B) – r, (C) – p, (D) – q.**

(A) Locus will be director circle $x^2 + y^2 = a^2 + b^2$

(B) Locus of foot of perpendicular upon any tangent from focus is auxiliary circle $x^2 + y^2 = a^2.$

(C) Equation of tangent $\dfrac{x}{a}\cos\theta + \dfrac{y}{b}\sin\theta = 1 \qquad$ ....... (i)

Perpendicular on tangent passing through centre is

$y = \dfrac{a}{b}x\tan\theta \qquad$ ......... (ii)

$\tan\theta = \dfrac{by}{ax}$ ; $\sin\theta = \dfrac{by}{\sqrt{a^2x^2 + b^2y^2}}$ ;

$\cos\theta = \dfrac{ax}{\sqrt{a^2x^2 + b^2y^2}}$

Put value in (i) $(x^2 + y^2)^2 = a^2x^2 + b^2y^2.$

(D) Replace x by 2x and y by 2y in $(x^2 + y^2)^2 = (a^2x^2 + b^2y^2)$

**17. (a)** Equation of PQ (i.e., chord of contact) to the ellipse $x^2 + 2y^2 = 6$ is

$$\frac{hx}{6} + \frac{ky}{3} = 1 \qquad \ldots(1)$$

Any tangent to the ellipse $x^2 + 4y^2 = 4$ is

$$x/2\cos\theta + y\sin\theta = 1 \qquad \ldots(2)$$

$\Rightarrow$ (1) & (2) represent the same line $h = 3\cos\theta, k = 3\sin\theta$

Locus of $(h, k)$ is $x^2 + y^2 = 9$

**18. (a)** $S_1O + S_2O = 2a \Rightarrow 13 + 20 = 2a$   ($\because$ O lies on ellipse)

Also $S_1S_2 = 2ae$

$$\Rightarrow 2ae = \sqrt{65}$$

$$\therefore e = \frac{\sqrt{65}}{33}$$

**19. (4)**

$a = 3 ; b = 2$

$$T : \frac{x\cos\theta}{3} + \frac{y\sin\theta}{2} = 1$$

$x = 0 ; y = 2\,\text{cosec}\theta$

chord A'P,  $\quad y = \dfrac{2\sin\theta}{3(\cos\theta + 1)}(x + 3)$

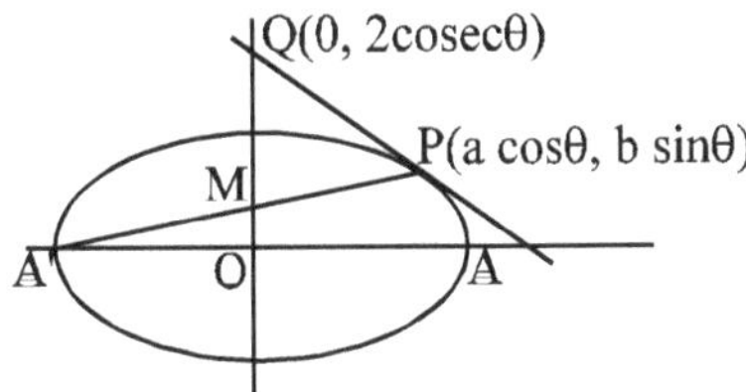


put $x = 0$  $y = \dfrac{2\sin\theta}{1 + \cos\theta} = OM$

Now $OQ^2 - MQ^2 = OQ^2 - (OQ - OM)^2 = 2(OQ)(OM) - OM^2$

$$= OM\{2(OQ) - (OM)\}$$

$$= \frac{2\sin\theta}{1 + \cos\theta}\left[\frac{y}{\sin\theta} - \frac{2\sin\theta}{1 + \cos\theta}\right] = 4$$

**20. (3)**

$x + y = 17 ; xy = 60$, To find $\sqrt{x^2 + y^2}$ ]

now, $x^2 + y^2 = (x + y)^2 - 2xy = 289 - 120 = 169$

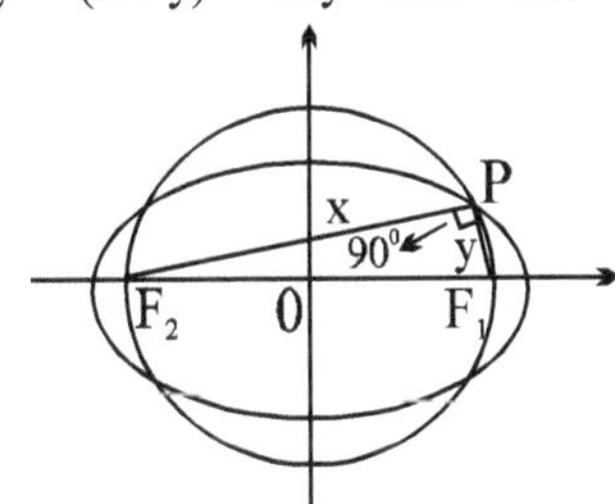


$$\Rightarrow \sqrt{x^2 + y^2} = 13$$

Thus $3P + 4 = 13 \Rightarrow P = 3$

**21. (5)**

$a^2 e^2 = 36 \Rightarrow a^2 - b^2 = 36$ — (1)

Using  $r = (s - a)\tan\dfrac{A}{2}$  in $\triangle$ OCF

$1 = (s - a)\tan 45°$ when $a = CF$

$2 = 2(s - a)$

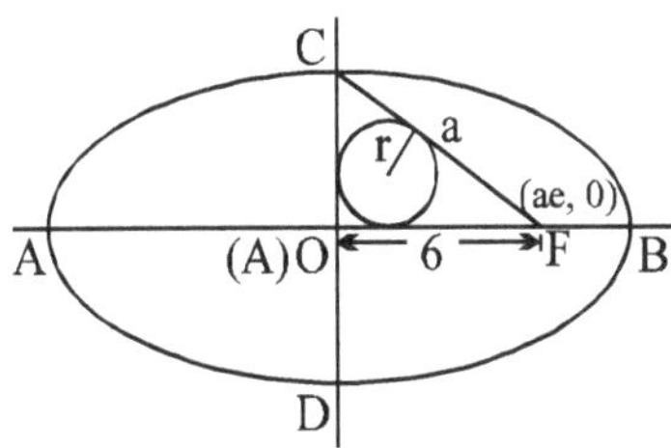


$$= 2s - 2a = 2s - AB$$

$$= (OF + FC + CO) - AB$$

$$2 = 6 + \frac{AB}{2} + \frac{CD}{2} - AB$$

$$\frac{AB - CD}{2} = 4 \Rightarrow 2(a - b) = 8 \Rightarrow a - b = 4 \text{ — (2)}$$

From (1) & (2) $a + b = 9 \Rightarrow 2a = 13 ; 2b = 5$

$\Rightarrow (AB)(CD) = 65$

$\Rightarrow X = 5$

**22. (3)**

Equation of normal,

$$Y - y = -\frac{1}{m}(X - x)$$

$Y = 0$ gives  $X = x + my$  and

$X = 0$ gives  $Y = \dfrac{x + my}{m}$   Hence $\dfrac{x + x + my}{2} = 0$

$$\Rightarrow 2x + y\frac{dy}{dx} = 0$$

$$x^2 + \frac{y^2}{2} = C \; ; \text{ passes through } (1, 4)$$

$$\Rightarrow C = 9$$

$$\Rightarrow \text{conic is } \frac{x^2}{9} + \frac{y^2}{18} = 1 \text{ with } e = \frac{1}{\sqrt{2}}$$

$\Rightarrow$ focii are $(0, 3) \& (0, -3)$

Thus, $A = 3$

1.  (a). $e_1^2 = 1 + \dfrac{b^2}{a^2} = 1 + \dfrac{12}{4} = 4 \Rightarrow e_1 = 2$

   now $\dfrac{1}{e_1^2} + \dfrac{1}{e_2^2} = 1$

   $\dfrac{1}{e_2^2} = 1 - \dfrac{1}{4} = \dfrac{3}{4} \Rightarrow e_2^2 = \dfrac{4}{3} \Rightarrow e_2 = \dfrac{2}{\sqrt{3}}$

2.  (a). $A = ab = a^2 \tan \lambda \Rightarrow b/a = \tan \lambda$, hence $e^2 = 1 + (b^2/a^2)$
   $\Rightarrow e^2 = 1 + \tan^2 \lambda \Rightarrow e = \sec \lambda$

3.  (d). $\dfrac{y^2}{1/16} - \dfrac{x^2}{1/9} = 1$

   Locus will be the auxilary circle
   $x^2 + y^2 = 1/16$

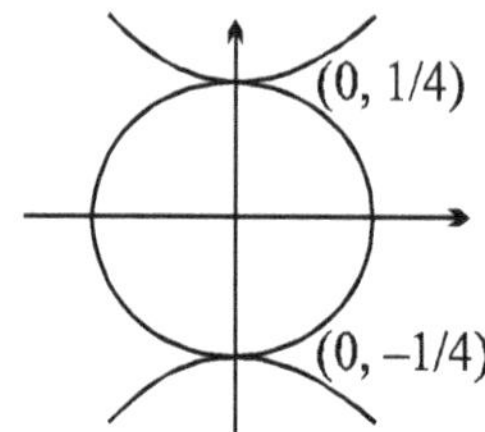


4.  (d)  Normal at $\theta, \phi$ are $\begin{cases} ax \cos\theta + by \cot\theta = a^2 + b^2 \\ ax \cos\theta + by \cot\phi = a^2 + b^2 \end{cases}$

   where $\phi = \dfrac{\pi}{2} - \theta$ and these pass through (h, k)

   $\therefore \quad ah \cos\theta + bk \cot\theta = a^2 + b^2$
   $ah \sin\theta + bk \tan\theta = a^2 + b^2$
   Eliminate h, $bk (\cot\theta \ \sin\theta - \tan\cos\theta)$
   $= (a^2 + b^2)(\sin\theta - \cos\theta)$ or $k = -(a^2 + b^2)/b$

5.  (b)  Chord $x = 9$ meets $x^2 - y^2 = 9$ at $(9, 6\sqrt{2})$ and $(9, -6\sqrt{2})$
   at which tangents are
   $$9x - 6\sqrt{2}y = 9 \ \text{ and } \ 9x + 6\sqrt{2}y = 9$$
   or $\quad 3x - 2\sqrt{2}y - 3 = 0$ and $3x + 2\sqrt{2}y - 3 = 0$
   $\therefore \quad$ Combined equation of tangents is
   $$(3x - 2\sqrt{2}y - 3)(3x + 2\sqrt{2}y - 3) = 0$$
   or, $\quad 9x^2 - 8y^2 - 18x + 9 = 0$

6.  (b)  The given eq$^n$ of hyperbola is
   $$\dfrac{x^2}{\cos^2 \alpha} - \dfrac{y^2}{\sin^2 \alpha} = 1$$

$\Rightarrow \quad a = \cos\alpha, b = \sin\alpha$

$\Rightarrow \quad e = \sqrt{1 + \dfrac{b^2}{a^2}} = \sqrt{1 + \tan^2\alpha} = \sec\alpha$

$\Rightarrow \quad ae = 1$

$\therefore \quad$ foci $\equiv (\pm 1, 0)$

$\therefore \quad$ focii remain constant with respect to $\alpha$.

7.  (c)  Let P be the point $(a \sec\theta, b \tan\theta)$.
   Equation of tangent at P is
   $$\dfrac{x}{a} \sec\theta - \dfrac{y}{b} \tan\theta = 1 \qquad \dotsc\dotsc(1)$$

   It meets the line $\dfrac{x}{a} - \dfrac{y}{b} = 0 \qquad \dotsc\dotsc(2)$

   in Q. From (2) $\dfrac{x}{a} = \dfrac{y}{b}$. From (1)

   $\dfrac{y}{b}(\sec\theta - \tan\theta) = 1$

   $\Rightarrow \ y = \dfrac{b}{\sec\theta - \tan\theta} ; \quad x = \dfrac{a}{b} y = \dfrac{a}{\sec\theta - \tan\theta}$

   $\therefore$ Co-ordinates of Q are
   $$\left( \dfrac{a}{\sec\theta - \tan\theta}, \dfrac{b}{\sec\theta - \tan\theta} \right).$$
   The tangent at P i.e. (1), meets
   $$\dfrac{x}{a} + \dfrac{y}{b} = 1 \qquad \dotsc\dotsc(3)$$
   in R.

   From (3), $\dfrac{x}{a} = -\dfrac{y}{b}$,

   From (1), $\dfrac{-y}{b}(\sec\theta - \tan\theta) = 1$

   $\Rightarrow \ y = \dfrac{-b}{\sec\theta + \tan\theta} ;$

   $x = \dfrac{-a}{b} y = \dfrac{a}{\sec\theta + \tan\theta}$

   Co-ordinates of R are
   $$\left( \dfrac{a}{\sec\theta + \tan\theta}, \dfrac{-b}{\sec\theta + \tan\theta} \right).$$

Mid point of QR is

$$\left( \dfrac{\dfrac{a}{\sec\theta - \tan\theta} + \dfrac{a}{\sec\theta + \tan\theta}}{2},\ \dfrac{\dfrac{b}{\sec\theta - \tan\theta} + \dfrac{b}{\sec\theta + \tan\theta}}{2} \right)$$

i.e. $(a\sec\theta, b\tan\theta)$. These are the co-ordinates of P.
Hence P is the mid point of QR.

**8.  (a)**  Equation of hyperbola is $\dfrac{x^2}{a^2} - \dfrac{y^2}{a^2} = 1$    ....(1)

Equation of any normal to it is

$$\dfrac{ax}{\sec\theta} + \dfrac{ay}{\tan\theta} = a^2 + a^2$$

i.e. $\dfrac{x}{\sec\theta} + \dfrac{y}{\tan\theta} = 2a$    ....(2)

Let $(x_1, y_1)$ be its mid point.
Eq. of chord with $(x_1, y_1)$ as mid-point is

$$\dfrac{xx_1}{a^2} - \dfrac{yy_1}{a^2} = \dfrac{x_1^2}{a^2} - \dfrac{y_1^2}{a^2}$$

$$\Rightarrow xx_1 - yy_1 = x_1^2 - y_1^2 \qquad ....(3)$$

Comparing coefficient (2) and (3),

$$\dfrac{x_1}{1/\sec\theta} = \dfrac{-y_1}{1/\tan\theta} = \dfrac{x_1^2 - y_1^2}{2a}$$

$$\Rightarrow \sec\theta = \dfrac{x_1^2 - y_1^2}{2ax_1},\ \tan\theta = \dfrac{x_1^2 - y_1^2}{-2ay_1}$$

Also, $\sec^2\theta - \tan^2\theta = 1$

$$\dfrac{(x_1^2 - y_1^2)^2}{4a^2 x_1^2} - \dfrac{(x_1^2 - y_1^2)^2}{4a^2 y_1^2} = 1$$

$$\Rightarrow (y_1^2 - x_1^2)^3 = 4a^2 x_1^2 y_1^2$$

The locus of $(x_1, y_1)$ is

$$(y^2 - x^2)^3 = 4a^2 x^2 y^2.$$

**9.  (b,d).** $p_1 p_2 = \dfrac{a^2 b^2}{a^2 + b^2}$ ; $e = \sec\theta$

$e^2 = 1 + \dfrac{9}{3} = 4 \Rightarrow e = 2 = \sec\theta$  (b is correct)

$\Rightarrow \theta = 60^0$
angle between the two asymptotes is $120^0$
$\Rightarrow$ acute angle is $60^0 \Rightarrow$ (a) is correct

$C : LLR = \dfrac{2b^2}{a} = 2.\dfrac{3}{3} = 2 \Rightarrow$ (c) is correct

$$p_1 p_2 = \dfrac{ab(\sec\theta + \tan\theta)}{\sqrt{a^2 + b^2}} \dfrac{ab(\sec\theta - \tan\theta)}{\sqrt{a^2 + b^2}}$$

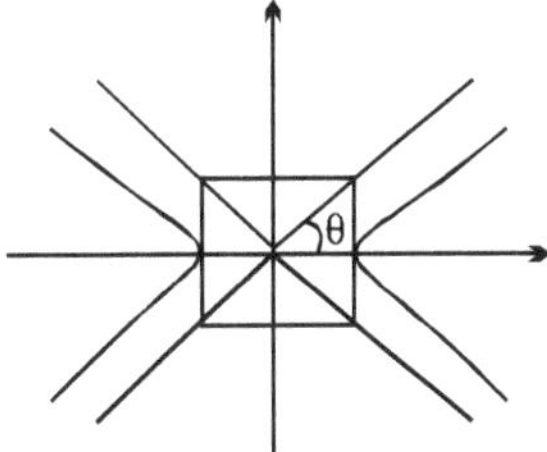


$$= \dfrac{a^2 b^2}{a^2 + b^2}(\sec^2\theta - \tan^2\theta) = \dfrac{9.3}{12} = \dfrac{9}{4}$$

$\Rightarrow$ (d) is incorrect

**10.  (a,b,c,d).**

$$\dfrac{x^2}{a^2} - \dfrac{y^2}{b^2} = 1 \quad ....(1) \qquad\qquad \text{and}$$

$$\dfrac{y^2}{a^2} - \dfrac{x^2}{b^2} = 1 \quad ....(2)$$

Tangent to (1) $y = mx \pm \sqrt{a^2 m^2 - b^2}$

If this is also tangent to $\dfrac{x^2}{(-b^2)} - \dfrac{y^2}{(-a^2)} = 1$

then $a^2 m^2 + b^2 = (-b^2)\, m^2 - (-a^2) = a^2 - b^2 m^2$

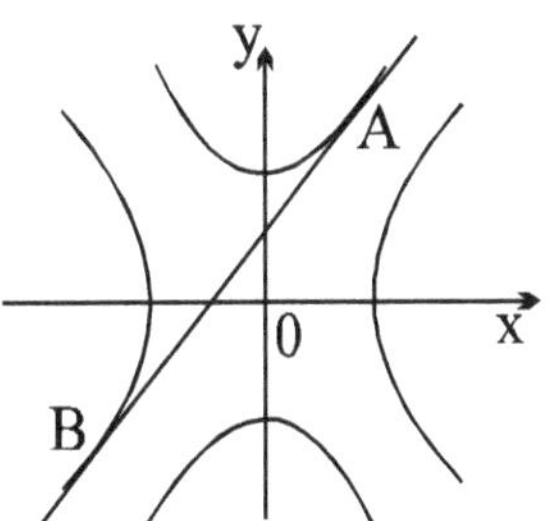


$(a^2 - b^2)\, m^2 = a^2 - b^2$

$m = \pm 1$

Hence 4 common tangents are   $y = \pm x \pm \sqrt{a^2 - b^2}$

**11.  (b,d).** Let the line is normal to the hyperbola at $P(x_1, y_1)$ hence
$2x_1 + 4y_1 + k = 0$ ....(1)

differentiate the curve $\dfrac{dy}{dx}\bigg|_P = \dfrac{3x_1}{y_1}$

$\therefore$ slope of normal $= -\dfrac{y_1}{3x_1}$ ; slope of line $= -\dfrac{2}{9}$

$\therefore \ -\dfrac{y_1}{3x_1} = -\dfrac{2}{9} \quad \Rightarrow 2x_1 = 3y_1$

line $(x_1, y_1)$ lies on the hyperbola

$$3x_1^2 - y_1^2 = 23 \ \Rightarrow \ 3x_1^2 - \dfrac{4x_1^2}{9} = 23$$

$$\Rightarrow 23\,x_1^2 = 23 \cdot 9 \Rightarrow \ x_1 = 3 \quad \text{or} \ -3$$

hence P is $(3, 2)$ or $(-3, -2)$

$\therefore k = 24$ or $-24 \Rightarrow$ b.d

**12.** **(b,c,d).** $16(x^2 - 2x + 1) - 3(y^2 - 4y + 4) = 48$

$$\Rightarrow \dfrac{(x-1)^2}{3} - \dfrac{(y-2)^2}{16} = 1$$

So length of transverse axis is $\sqrt{3}$, length of conjugate axis is 4.

Centre $(1, 2)$ and $e = \sqrt{\dfrac{19}{3}}$

**13.** **(d)** Let the asymptotes be $2x + 3y + \lambda = 0$ and $3x + 2y + \mu = 0$.

Since, asymptotes passes through $(1, 2)$, therefore

$\lambda = -8$ and $\mu = -7$

Let the equation of hyperbola be

$(2x + 3y - 8)(3x + 2y - 7) + \gamma = 0 \qquad \text{....(i)}$

$\because$ It passes through $(5, 3)$, then

$(10 + 9 - 8)(15 + 6 - 7) + \gamma = 0$

$\Rightarrow \ 11 \times 14 + \gamma = 0$

$\therefore \gamma = -154$

Putting the value of $\gamma$ in Eq. (i), then

$(2x + 3y - 8)(3x + 2y - 7) = 154$

**14.** **(b)** $2\tan^{-1}\left(\dfrac{b}{a}\right) = \dfrac{\pi}{3} \Rightarrow \tan^{-1}\left(\dfrac{b}{a}\right) = \dfrac{\pi}{6}$

$$\Rightarrow \quad \dfrac{b}{a} = \dfrac{1}{\sqrt{3}} \ \text{or} \ a = b\sqrt{3}$$

Let $e$ be an eccentricity of conjugate hyperbola, then
$a^2 = b^2(e^2 - 1) \Rightarrow 3b^2 = b^2(e^2 - 1)$

$\Rightarrow \quad e^2 = 4 \Rightarrow e = 2$

**15.** **(c)** The transverse axis is the bisector of the angle between asymptotes containing the origin and the conjugate axis is the other bisector. The bisectors of the angle between asymptotes are

$$\dfrac{(3x - 4y - 1)}{5} = \pm \dfrac{(4x - 3y - 6)}{5}$$

$\Rightarrow \quad (3x - 4y - 1) = \pm \ (4x - 3y - 6)$

$\Rightarrow \quad x + y - 5 = 0 \ \text{and} \ x - y - 1 = 0$

Hence, transverse axis and conjugate axis are $x + y - 5 = 0$ and $x - y - 1 = 0$.

**16.** **(A)** $\to$**r, s; B**$\to$**p,s; C**$\to$**q,t**

(A)   Let    $f(x, y) = x^2 - 4y^2 - 2x + 24y - 37$

$\therefore \quad f(3, 4) = 9 - 64 - 6 + 96 - 37 = -2$

$\therefore \quad f(3, 4) < 0$

$\Rightarrow$   Point $(3, 4)$ lies outside the hyperbola **(r)**

   and $f(5, 2) = 25 - 16 - 10 + 48 - 37 = 10$

$\therefore \quad f(5, 2) > 0$

$\Rightarrow$ Point $(5, 2)$ lies inside the hyperbola **(s)**

(B)   Let    $f(x, y) = xy + 2x + 3y - 12$

$\therefore \quad f(3, 4) = 12 + 6 + 12 - 12 = 18$

$\therefore \quad f(3, 4) > 0$

$\Rightarrow$   Point $(3, 4)$ lies inside the hyperbola **(p)**

   and $f(5, 2) = 10 + 10 + 6 - 12 = 14 > 0$

$\Rightarrow$   Point $(5, 2)$ lies inside the hyperbola **(s)**

(C)   Let    $f(x, y) = xy - 12$

$\therefore \quad f(3, 4) = 12 - 12 = 0$

$\Rightarrow$   Point $(3, 4)$ lies on the hyperbola **(t)**

   and $f(5, 2) = 5 \times 2 - 12 = -2$

$\therefore \quad f(5, 2) < 0$

$\Rightarrow$   Point $(5, 2)$ lies outside the hyperbola **(q)**

**17.** **(a).** Circle is $x^2 + y^2 = a^2$      ..... (i)

Hyperbola is $xy = c^2$      ...... (ii)

Take $P\left(ct, \dfrac{c}{t}\right)$ any point on (ii)

To find intersection of (i) and (ii), we put P in (i), $(ct)^2 +$

$$\left(\dfrac{c}{t}\right)^2 = a^2$$

$\Rightarrow c^2t^4 - a^2t^2 + c^2 = 0$

$\Rightarrow c^2t^4 - 0t^3 - a^2t^2 + c^2 = 0$

$$\Rightarrow t^4 - 0t^3 - \dfrac{a^2}{c^2}t^2 + 1 = 0$$

$\Rightarrow t_1 + t_2 + t_3 + t_4 = 0, \ t_1 t_2 t_3 t_4 = 1$

**18.** **(a)** $\dfrac{x_1 + x_2 + x_3 + x_4}{4} = 0, \ \dfrac{y_1 + y_2 + y_3 + y_4}{4} = 0$

So $(0, 0)$ is average point which is also the mid point of line joining the centres of circle & rectangular hyperbola.

**19.** **(d)** The locus of point of intersection of two mutually perpendicular tangents drawn on to hyperbola

$\dfrac{x^2}{a^2} - \dfrac{y^2}{b^2} = 1$ is its director circle whose equation is $x^2 +$

$y^2 = a^2 - b^2$. For $\dfrac{x^2}{9} - \dfrac{y^2}{16} = 1$, $x^2 + y^2 = 9 - 16$

So director circle does not exist.

**20.** **(3)**

$x = ct \Rightarrow \dfrac{dx}{dt} = c$

$y = \dfrac{c}{t} \Rightarrow \dfrac{dy}{dt} = -\dfrac{c}{t^2}$

$$\frac{dy}{dx} = -\frac{1}{t^2}$$

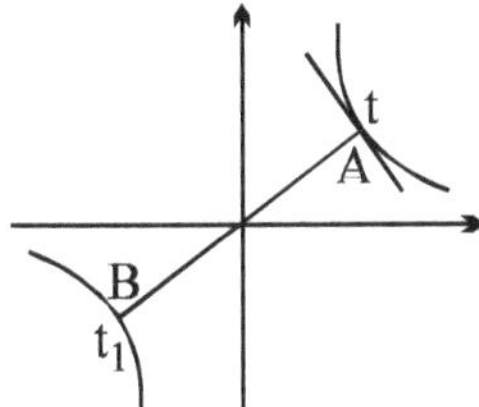

$$\therefore \ m_N = t^2 \ \therefore \ t^2 = m_{AB} = -\frac{1}{t_1 \, t} \ \therefore \ t^3 t_1 = -1$$

$$\Rightarrow \ -3t^3 t_1 = 3$$

**21. (2)**

$$e^2 = 1 + \frac{16}{9} = \frac{25}{9} \ \Rightarrow \ e = \frac{5}{3}$$

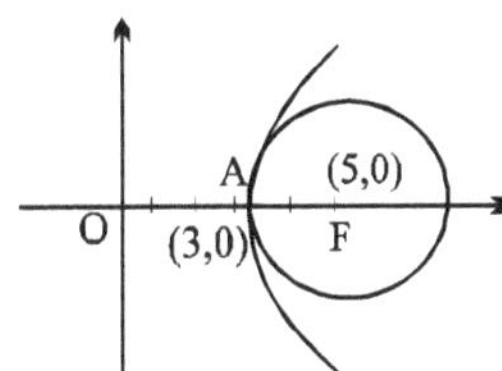

$$\therefore \quad \text{focus} = (5, 0)$$

Use reflection property to prove that circle cannot touch at two points. It can only be tangent at the vertex

$$r = 5 - 3 = 2$$

**22. (2)**

Equation to the hyperbola where $S = (0, 0)$ ;

directrix is $x + y + 1 = 0$ and $e = \sqrt{2}$ is

$$\sqrt{x^2 + y^2} = \sqrt{2}\left(\frac{x + y + 1}{\sqrt{2}}\right)$$

$$\therefore \quad x^2 + y^2 = (x + y + 1)^2$$

$$2xy + 2x + 2y + 1 = 0$$

Let the combined equation of the asymptotes is

$$2xy + 2x + 2y + c = 0$$

put $D = 0$ to get $c = 2$

hence combined equation of the asymptotes are

$$xy + x + y + 1 = 0$$

$$(x + 1)(y + 1) = 0$$

$$\Rightarrow \ x + 1 = 0 \ \text{ and } \ y + 1 = 0$$

Thus $M = 1, N = 1$

$$\Rightarrow \quad M + N = 1 + 1 = 2$$

**23. (9)**

Equation $(2 + \lambda) x^2 - 2\lambda xy + (\lambda - 1) y^2 - 4x - 2 = 0$

represents a hyperbola if $\Delta \neq 0, \ h^2 > ab$

$$\Rightarrow \lambda \neq \frac{4}{3} \ \& \ \lambda < 2 \ \Rightarrow \ \lambda \in \left(-\infty, \frac{4}{3}\right) \cup \left(\frac{4}{3}, 2\right)$$

Thus $A + B + C = 4 + 3 + 2 = 9$

**24. (7)**

Equation of hyperbola is

$$\frac{x^2}{a^2} - \frac{y^2}{b^2} = 1 \qquad\qquad ......(1)$$

Equation of the two lines are

$$2x + 3y + 4 = 0 \qquad\qquad .....(2)$$

and $3x - 2y + 5 = 0 \qquad\qquad .....(3)$

Let $(x_1, y_1)$ be the pole of (2) w.r.t. (1)

Polar of $(x_1, y_1)$ w.r.t (1) is

$$\frac{xx_1}{a^2} - \frac{yy_1}{b^2} = 1 \qquad\qquad .....(4)$$

Since (2) and (4) both represents the polar of $(x_1, y_1)$ w.r.t. (1) Comparing coefficients,

$$\frac{x_1 / a^2}{2} = \frac{-y_1 / b^2}{3} = \frac{1}{-4}$$

$$\Rightarrow \ x_1 = \frac{-a^2}{2}, y_1 = \frac{3b^2}{4}$$

Pole of (2) w.r.t. (1) is $\left(\frac{-a^2}{2}, \frac{3b^2}{4}\right)$.

The lines (2) and (3) will be conjugate if the pole of (2) lies on (3) i.e. if

$$3\left(\frac{-a^2}{2}\right) - 2\left(\frac{3b^2}{4}\right) + 5 = 0$$

$$\Rightarrow \ 3(a^2 + b^2) = 10 \Rightarrow a^2 + b^2 = \frac{10}{3}$$

Thus $P - Q = 10 - 3 = 7$.

**1. (d)** Given that $\dfrac{x^2}{1-r} - \dfrac{y^2}{1+r} = 1,\ r > 1$

As $r > 1$

$\therefore\quad 1 - r < 0$ and $1 + r > 0$

$\therefore\quad$ Let $1 - r = -a^2,\ 1 + r = b^2$

Then we get

$$\dfrac{x^2}{-a^2} - \dfrac{y^2}{b^2} = 1 \qquad \Rightarrow \dfrac{x^2}{a^2} + \dfrac{y^2}{b^2} = -1$$

Which is not possible for any values of x and y.

**2. (c)** (a) $x^2 + 2y^2 \leq 1$ represents exterior region of an ellipse where on taking any two pts the mid pt of that segment will also lie inside that ellipse

(b) Max $\{|x|, |y|\} \leq 1$

$\Rightarrow\ |x| \leq 1, |y| \leq 1 \Rightarrow -1 \leq x \leq 1$ and $-1 \leq y \leq 1$

Which represents the interior region of a square with its sides $x = \pm 1$ and $y = \pm 1$ in which for any two points, their mid point also lies inside the region.

(c) $x^2 - y^2 \geq 1$ represents interior regions on both the sides (left and right) of hyperbola in which if we take two points $(2, 0)$ and $(-2, 0)$ then their mid point $(0, 0)$ lies in the same region (as show in the figure.)

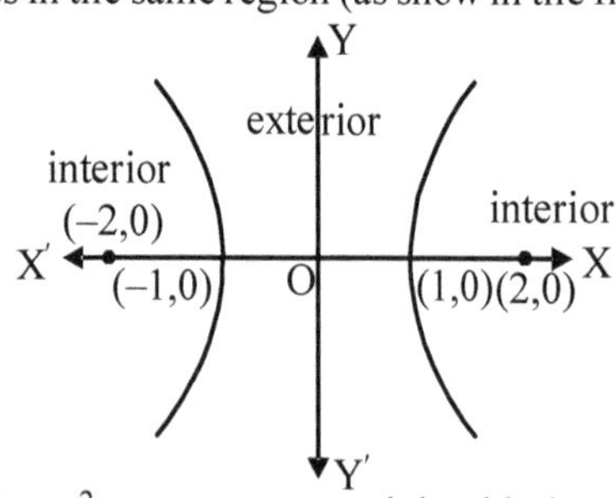


(d) $y^2 \leq x$ represents right side interior region of parabola in which for any two pts, their mid point also lies inside the region.

**3. (c)** $\dfrac{x+y}{2} = t^2 + 1,\ \dfrac{x-y}{2} = t$

Eliminating t, $2(x+y) = (x-y)^2 + 4$

Since 2nd degree terms form a perfect square, it represents a parabola.

**4. (c)** We have $2x^2 + 3y^2 - 8x - 18y + 35 = k$

$\Rightarrow\ 2(x^2 - 4x) + 3(y^2 - 6y) + 35 = k$

$\Rightarrow\ 2(x-2)^2 + 3(y-3)^2 = k$

For $k = 0$, we get $2(x-2)^2 + 3(y-3)^2 = 0$ wich represents the point $(2, 3)$.

**5. (a)** The length of transverse axis $= 2\sin\theta = 2a$

$\Rightarrow\ a = \sin\theta$

Also for ellipse $3x^2 + 4y^2 = 12$

or $\dfrac{x^2}{4} + \dfrac{y^2}{3} = 1,\ a^2 = 4, b^2 = 3$

$$e = \sqrt{1 - \dfrac{b^2}{a^2}} = \sqrt{1 - \dfrac{3}{4}} = \dfrac{1}{2}$$

$\therefore$ Focus of ellipse $= \left(2 \times \dfrac{1}{2}, 0\right) \Rightarrow (1, 0)$

As hyperbola is confocal with ellipse, focus of hyperbola $= (1, 0)$

$\Rightarrow\quad ae = 1 \Rightarrow \sin\theta \times e = 1$

$\Rightarrow\quad e = \operatorname{cosec}\theta$

$\therefore\quad b^2 = a^2(e^2 - 1) = \sin^2\theta\,(\operatorname{cosec}^2\theta - 1) = \cos^2\theta$

$\therefore\quad$ Equation of hyperbola is

$$\dfrac{x^2}{\sin^2\theta} - \dfrac{y^2}{\cos^2\theta} = 1$$

or, $x^2 \operatorname{cosec}^2\theta - y^2 \sec^2\theta = 1$

**6. (b)** $y = \dfrac{-2p}{\sqrt{1-p^2}}\, x + \dfrac{1}{\sqrt{1-p^2}};\ m = \dfrac{-2p}{\sqrt{1-p^2}}$

$\Rightarrow\ m^2 = \dfrac{4p^2}{1-p^2} \Rightarrow m^2 = (4 + m^2)p^2$

$\Rightarrow\ p^2 = \dfrac{m^2}{4 + m^2}$

$$y = mx + \dfrac{1}{\sqrt{1 - \dfrac{m^2}{4 + m^2}}} \Rightarrow y = mx + \sqrt{\dfrac{4 + m^2}{4}}$$

$$\Rightarrow y = mx + \sqrt{1 + \dfrac{1}{4}m^2}$$

Which touches the ellipse $\dfrac{x^2}{1/4} + \dfrac{y^2}{1} = 1$ whose

eccentricity $e = \sqrt{1 - \dfrac{1}{4}} = \dfrac{\sqrt{3}}{2}$.

**7. (c)** Let $P(h, k)$ be a point on the hyperbola $x^2 - y^2 = a^2 - b^2$.

Then $h^2 - k^2 = a^2 - b^2$ ........(i)

The equation of a tangent to the ellipse $\dfrac{x^2}{a^2} + \dfrac{y^2}{b^2} = 1$

is $y = mx + \sqrt{a^2 m^2 + b^2}$

If it passes through $(h, k)$, then $k = mh + \sqrt{a^2 m^2 + b^2}$

$\Rightarrow (k - mh)^2 = a^2 m^2 + b^2$

$\Rightarrow m^2(h^2 - a^2) - 2mhk + k^2 - b^2 = 0$

Let $m_1$ and $m_2$ be the roots of this equation. Then,

$m_1 m_2 = \dfrac{k^2 - b^2}{h^2 - a^2} = 1 \Rightarrow \tan\alpha \tan\beta = 1$

**8.** **(c)** Angle bisector of focal distances is tangent at that point and whose slope is always greater than the slope of asymptote hence $\alpha \in (0, a]$

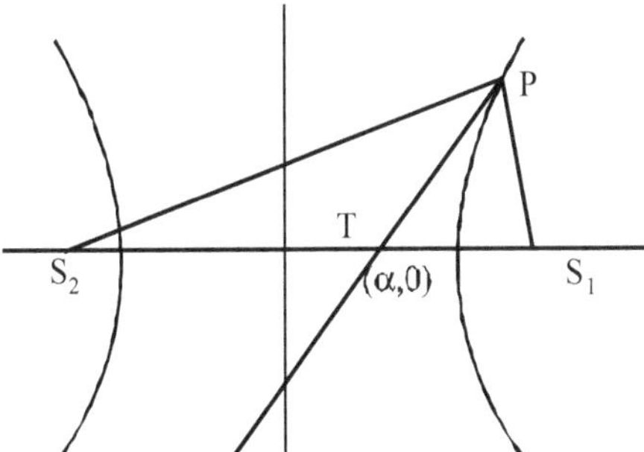


**9.** **(d)** Equation of any tangent to $x^2 - y^2 = a^2$

i.e $\dfrac{x^2}{a^2} - \dfrac{y^2}{a^2} = 1$ is $\dfrac{x}{a}\sec\theta - \dfrac{y}{a}\tan\theta = 1$

or $\quad x\sec\theta - y\tan\theta = a \qquad\qquad$ ...(1)

Equation of other two sides of the triangle are

$\quad x - y = 0$ ...(2) and $x + y = 0$ ...(3)

[The two asymptotes of the hyperbola $x^2 - y^2 = a^2$ are

$\quad x - y = 0$ and $x + y = 0$]

Solving (1) (2) and (3) in pairs, the coordinates of the vertices of the triangle are (0, 0);

$\left( \dfrac{a}{\sec\theta + \tan\theta},\ -\dfrac{a}{\sec\theta + \tan\theta} \right)$

and $\left( \dfrac{a}{\sec\theta - \tan\theta},\ \dfrac{a}{\sec\theta - \tan\theta} \right)$

$\therefore$ Area of triangle $= \dfrac{1}{2}\left[ \dfrac{a^2}{\sec^2\theta - \tan^2\theta} + \dfrac{a^2}{\sec^2\theta - \tan^2\theta} \right]$

$= \dfrac{1}{2}(a^2 + a^2) \qquad\qquad [\because \sec^2\theta - \tan^2\theta = 1]$

$= a^2$

**10.** **(a,b,c)**

**(a)** Equation of hyperbola can be written as

$(x - 1)(y + 1) = 8$

Let $X = x - 1, Y = y + 1 \Rightarrow XY = 8$

Equation of transverse axis is

$\quad Y = X$

$\quad x - 1 = y + 1,\ x - y = 2$

$\quad P(4, 2)$

Let equation of parabola be $y = ax^2 + bx + c$

$\quad\quad 2 = 16a + 4b + \Rightarrow c \qquad$ ...(1)

also $\left.\dfrac{dy}{dx}\right|_{4,2} = 0 \Rightarrow 8a + b = 0 \qquad$ ...(2)

Parabola passes through $(1, 3) \Rightarrow 3 = a + b + c$ ...(3)

Solving (1), (2), (3) we get $a = \dfrac{1}{9}, b = -\dfrac{8}{9}, c = \dfrac{34}{9}$

So parabola is $9y = x^2 - 8x + 34$

**(b)** Now tangent at $P$ is $y = 2$

$P'$ is $\left(\dfrac{11}{3}, 2\right)$; C is $(1, -1)$

$A = \dfrac{1}{2}\begin{vmatrix} 1 & -1 & 1 \\ 4 & 2 & 1 \\ 11/3 & 2 & 1 \end{vmatrix}$

$= \dfrac{1}{2}\left[ 1(2 - 2) + 1\left(4 - \dfrac{11}{3}\right) + \left(8 - \dfrac{22}{3}\right) \right]$

$= 1/2$ sq. units.

**(c)** Let latus rectum be $y + x + \lambda = 0$

Now length of $\perp$ from centre $= 4\sqrt{2} = ae$

$\dfrac{|\lambda|}{\sqrt{2}} = 4\sqrt{2} \Rightarrow \lambda = \pm 8$

So equation of latus rectum is $y + x - 8 = 0$

**11.** **(b,c,d)** $(x - \alpha)^2 + (y - \beta)^2 = k\,(\ell x + my + n)^2$

$= k\,(\ell^2 + m^2)\left( \dfrac{\ell x + my + n}{\sqrt{\ell^2 + m^2}} \right)^2$

$\Rightarrow \quad \dfrac{PS^2}{PM^2} = k\,(\ell^2 + m^2) = e^2,\ e$ being eccentricity

If $\quad k\,(\ell^2 + m^2) = 1$, P lies on parabola

If $\quad k\,(\ell^2 + m^2) < 1$, P lies on ellipse

If $\quad k\,(\ell^2 + m^2) > 1$, P lies on hyperbola

If $\quad k = 0$, P lies on a point circle.

**12.** **(a,b,c)** $\quad y = x + 5$

Comparing with $y = mx + c$

$\therefore \quad m = 1, c = 5$

(a) Condition of tangency

$\quad c = \dfrac{a}{m} \Rightarrow 5 = \dfrac{5}{1},\quad$ which is true.

(b) $\quad 9x^2 + 16y^2 = 144$

$\Rightarrow \quad \dfrac{x^2}{16} + \dfrac{y^2}{9} = 1$

$\therefore \quad$ Condition of tangency

$\quad\quad c^2 = a^2m^2 + b^2$

$\Rightarrow \quad 25 = 16 \times 1 + 9 = 25$, which is true.

(c): $\quad \dfrac{x^2}{29} - \dfrac{y^2}{4} = 1$

$\because \quad$ Condition of tangency

$\quad\quad c^2 = a^2m^2 - b^2$

$\quad\quad 25 = 29 \times 1 - 4 = 25$, which is true.

(d) Now length of perpendicular from centre $(0, 0)$

to the line $y = x + 5$ is $\dfrac{|5|}{\sqrt{2}}$

ie, $\quad \dfrac{5}{\sqrt{2}} \neq$ radius (5).

**13.** **(a, b, c, d)** Equation of tangent in terms of slope of $y^2 = 32x$ is

$\quad\quad y = mx + \dfrac{8}{m} \qquad\qquad$ ....(i)

Which is also tangent of $9x^2 - 9y^2 = 8$

i.e., $\quad x^2 - y^2 = \dfrac{8}{9}$

then $\left(\dfrac{8}{m}\right)^2 = \dfrac{8}{9}m^2 - \dfrac{8}{9}$ $\Rightarrow$ $\dfrac{8}{m^2} = \dfrac{m^2}{9} - \dfrac{1}{9}$

$\Rightarrow \quad 72 = m^4 - m^2$

$\Rightarrow \quad m^4 - m^2 - 72 = 0$

$\Rightarrow \quad (m^2 - 9)\,(m^2 + 8) = 0$

$\therefore \quad m^2 = 9,\ m^2 + 8 \neq 0$

$\therefore \quad m = \pm 3.$

From eq. (i), $y = \pm 3x \pm \dfrac{8}{3}$

$\Rightarrow \quad 3y = \pm 9x \pm 8$

or $\quad \pm 9x - 3y \pm 8 = 0$

i.e., $\quad 9x - 3y + 8 = 0,\ 9x - 3y - 8 = 0$

$\qquad - 9x - 3y + 8 = 0,\ - 9x - 3y - 8 = 0$

or $\quad 9x - 3y + 8 = 0,\ 9x - 3y - 8 = 0$

$\qquad 9x + 3y - 8 = 0$

and $\ 9x + 3y + 8 = 0$

**14. (b), 15. (a), 16. (d).**

Equation of a normal $y = mx - 2m - m^3$ passes through (h, k)

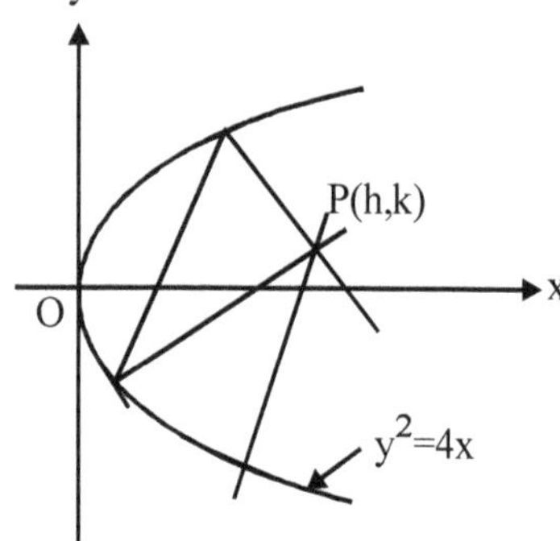

$m^3 + (2 - h)\,m + k = 0 \quad \dots\dots (i)$

$m_1 m_2 m_3 = -k$

but $m_1 m_2 = 2 \Rightarrow m_3 = -k/2$

this must satisfy equation (i) ; $\dfrac{k^3}{8} - (2 - h)\dfrac{k}{2} + k = 0$

$\Rightarrow k^3 - 4k\,(2 - h) + 8k = 0 \ \ (k \neq 0)$

$\Rightarrow k^2 - 8 - 4h + 8 = 0$

Locus of P is $y^2 = 4x$ which is a parabola.

Now chord passing through $(1, 0)$ is the focal chord.

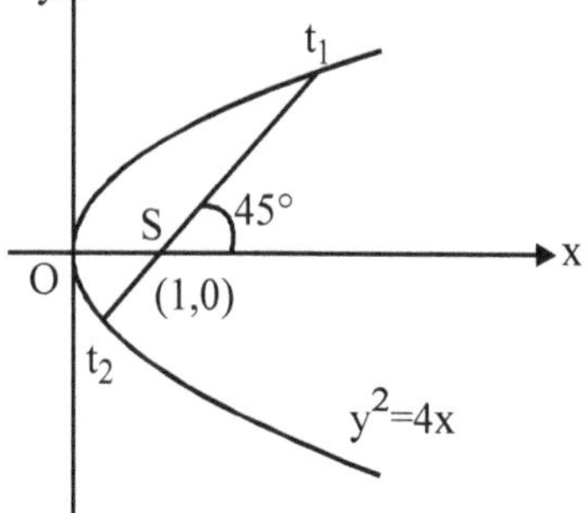

Given that gradient of focal chord is 1.

$\Rightarrow \dfrac{2}{t_1 + t_2} = 1 \Rightarrow t_1 + t_2 = 2.$ Also $t_1 t_2 = -1$

Equation of circle described on $t_1 t_2$ as diameter is

$(x - t_1^2)\,(x - t_2^2) + (y - 2t_1)\,(y - 2t_2) = 0$

$\Rightarrow x^2 + y^2 - x\,(t_1^2 + t_2^2) + t_1^2 t_2^2 - 2y\,(t_1 + t_2) + 4t_1 t_2 = 0$

$\Rightarrow x^2 + y^2 - x\,(4 + 2) + 1 - 2y\,(2) - 4 = 0$

$\Rightarrow x^2 + y^2 - 6x - 4y - 3 = 0$

Centre $a = 3$ and $b = 2,\ r = 4$

Now the hyperbola is $\dfrac{x^2}{9} - \dfrac{y^2}{4} = 1$

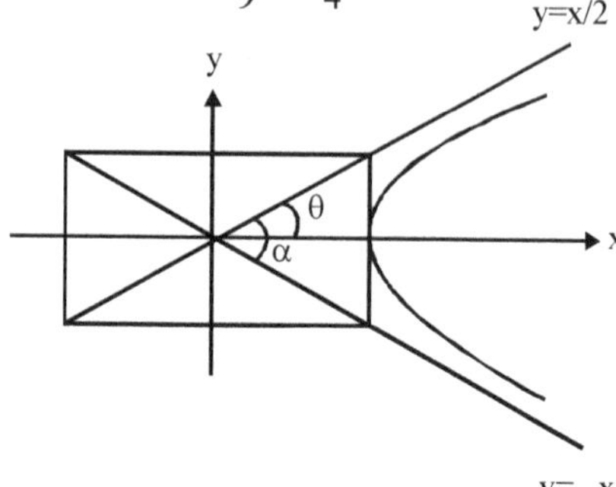

Asymptotes are $y = \dfrac{2x}{3}$ and $y = -\dfrac{2x}{3}$

Now $\tan\theta = 2/3,\ \therefore\ \alpha = 2\theta$

$\tan\alpha = \dfrac{2.(2/3)}{1 - (4/9)}$ ; $\tan\alpha = \dfrac{12}{5}$ ; $\alpha = \tan^{-1}\left(\dfrac{12}{5}\right)$

Hence $\alpha \in (60°, 75°)$

**17.** $(A) - r, (B) - p, (C) - q, (D) - p, q$

(A) Points of intersection is $(0, 0)$ and $(1, 1)$

$\therefore$ Length of common chord $= \sqrt{2}$

(B) $a = 4,\ b = 3,\ b^2 = a^2\,(1 - e^2)$

$\Rightarrow 9 = 16\,(1 - e^2) \Rightarrow e = \dfrac{\sqrt{7}}{4}$

$\Rightarrow ae = \sqrt{7}$

$\Rightarrow$ Focci are $(\pm\sqrt{7}, 0)$

$\Rightarrow$ Radius of circle $= \sqrt{7 + 9} = 4$

(c) $r_1 = \sqrt{r_2^2 + 5} = \sqrt{2^2 + 5} = 3$

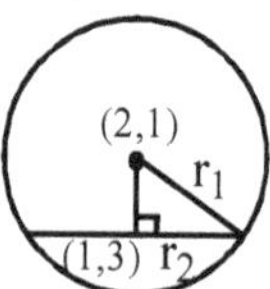

(d) K must be greater than $\sqrt{2}$

**18.** $A \to p;\ B \to s, t;\ C \to r;\ D \to q, s$

(p) As the line $hx + ky = 1$, touches the circle $x^2 + y^2 = 4$

$\therefore$ Length of perpendicular from centre $(0, 0)$ of circle to line = radius of the circle

$\Rightarrow \dfrac{1}{\sqrt{h^2 + k^2}} = 2 \Rightarrow h^2 + k^2 = \dfrac{1}{4}$

$\therefore$ Locus of $(h, k)$ is $x^2 + y^2 = \dfrac{1}{4}$, which is a circle.

(q) We know that if $|z - z_1| - |z - z_2| = k$

where $|k| < |z_1 - z_2|$

then $z$ traces a hyperbola.

Here $|z + 2| - |z - 2| = \pm 3$

$\therefore$ Locus of $z$ is a hyperbola.

(r)   We have $x = \sqrt{3}\left(\dfrac{1-t^2}{1+t^2}\right)$, $y = \dfrac{2t}{1+t^2}$

$$\Rightarrow \quad \frac{x}{\sqrt{3}} = \frac{1-t^2}{1+t^2} \quad \text{and} \quad y = \frac{2t}{1+t^2}$$

On squaring and adding, we get

$$\frac{x^2}{3} + y^2 = \frac{(1-t^2)^2 + 4t^2}{(1+t^2)^2} = 1$$

or $\dfrac{x^2}{3} + \dfrac{y^2}{1} = 1$

which is the equation of an ellipse.

(s)   We know eccentricity  for a parabola $= 1$

for an ellipse $< 1$

for a hyperbola $> 1$

$\therefore$ The conics whose eccentricity lies in $1 \le x < \infty$ are parabola and hyperbola.

(t)   Let $z = x + iy$ then

$$\text{Re}\,[(x+1)+iy]^2 = x^2 + y^2 + 1$$

$$\Rightarrow \quad (x+1)^2 - y^2 = x^2 + y^2 + 1$$

$$\Rightarrow \quad y^2 = x, \text{ which is a parabola.}$$

**19.  (5)**

$$\frac{x^2}{5} - \frac{y^2}{5\cos^2\alpha} = 1$$

$$\Rightarrow \quad e_1^2 = 1 + \frac{b^2}{a^2} = 1 + \frac{5\cos^2\alpha}{5} = 1 + \cos^2\alpha \quad ;$$

and $\dfrac{x^2}{25\cos^2\alpha} + \dfrac{y^2}{25} = 1$ is

$$\Rightarrow \quad e_2^2 = 1 - \frac{25\cos^2\alpha}{25} = \sin^2\alpha \quad ;$$

put $e_1 = \sqrt{3}\,e_2 \Rightarrow e_1^2 = 3\,e_2^2$

$\Rightarrow 1 + \cos^2\alpha = 3\sin^2\alpha \Rightarrow 2 = 4\sin^2\alpha$

$\Rightarrow \sin\alpha = \dfrac{1}{\sqrt{2}}$

$\Rightarrow \alpha = \dfrac{\pi}{4}$

Thus $A = 1$, $B = 4$

$\Rightarrow A + B = 5$

**20.  (8)**   Equation of the normal of the parabola is

$$y = mx - 2am - am^3$$

It touches the rectangular hyperbola

$x^2 - y^2 = a^2$ if $(-2am - am^3)^2 = a^2 m^2 - a^2$

$\left[\because y = mx + c \text{ touches } \dfrac{x^2}{a^2} - \dfrac{y^2}{b^2} = 1 \text{ if } c^2 = a^2 m^2 - b^2\right]$

$\Rightarrow \quad a^2 m^2 (2 + m^2)^2 = a^2 (m^2 - 1)$

$\Rightarrow \quad m^2 (m^4 + 4m^2 + 4) = m^2 - 1$

$\Rightarrow \quad m^6 + 4m^4 + 3m^2 + 1 = 0$

$\Rightarrow \quad A = 6, B = 2$

Hence, $A + B = 6 + 2 = 8$

**21.  (4)**   Equation of hyperbola is $3x^2 - y^2 = 3$

or $\dfrac{x^2}{1} - \dfrac{y^2}{3} = 1$ .........(1)

Here $a^2 = 1$ and $b^2 = 3$

Equation of any tangent to (1) is

$$y = mx + \sqrt{m^2 - 3} \qquad \text{.........(2)}$$

(2) touches the parabola $y^2 = 8x$

$$\sqrt{m^2 - 3} = \frac{2}{m} \quad \left[c = \frac{a}{m}; \text{Here } c = \sqrt{m^2 - 3}, a = 2\right]$$

$\Rightarrow m^2(m^2 - 3) = 4 \quad \Rightarrow \quad m^4 - 3m^2 - 4 = 0$

$m^2 = 4, -1.$

But $m^2 \ne -1$

$\because m^2 = 4 \Rightarrow m = \pm 2.$

Hence the equations of common tangents are

$$y = \pm\,2x + \sqrt{4 - 3}$$

i.e. $2x - y + 1 = 0$  and  $2x + y - 1 = 0$

on comparing we get

$A = 2, B = 2,$ So, $A + B = 2 + 2 = 4$

**22.  (0)**   Let $A\,(5, 12)$ and $B\,(24, 7)$ be two fixed points,

so $|OA - OB| = 12$; $|OA + OB| = 38$ if conic is ellipse

$$e = \frac{\sqrt{386}}{38} \quad \text{and if conic is hyperbola } e = \frac{\sqrt{386}}{3}$$

$\Rightarrow A = 386$ and $B = 386$

So, $A - B = 0$

**1.** **(b)** The total number of squares is
$$1^2 + 2^2 + 3^2 + 4^2 + \ldots + 14^2 + [1 \times 13^2 + 2 \times 12^2 + 3 \times 11^2 \ldots\ldots 13 \times 1^2] = 4200$$
The total number of squares with length of side as integer is
$$(1^2 + 2^2 + 3^2 + \ldots + 14^2) + (2 \times 8 \times 8) + (2 \times 1 \times 1) = 1145$$
Hence probability $= \dfrac{1145}{4200} = \dfrac{229}{840}$

**2.** **(a)** We have $P(A) = P(7) = \dfrac{6}{36}$, $P(B) = P(4) = \dfrac{3}{36}$

Since equal throws are disregarded,
Hence in each throw A is twice as likely to win as B.
Let $P(B) = p$, $P(A) = 2p$
$\therefore 3p = 1 \Rightarrow p = 1/3$

**3.** **(b)** $n(S) = 4 \times 4 \times 4 = 64$
$n(A) = 211$ or $312$ or $413$ or $431$ or $422$

$$\therefore P(E) = \frac{6}{64} = \frac{3}{32} = \frac{3}{3+29}$$

odds in favour $3 : 29$ Ans

**4.** **(a)** Probability of getting head $= 1/2$ and probability of throwing 5 or 6 with a dice $= 2/6 = 1/3$.
He starts with a coin and alternatively tosses the coin and throws the dice and he will win if he gets a head before he gets 5 or 6. Hence probability

$$= \frac{1}{2} + \left(\frac{1}{2} \cdot \frac{2}{3}\right)\frac{1}{2} + \left(\frac{1}{2} \cdot \frac{2}{3}\right)\cdot\left(\frac{1}{2} \times \frac{2}{3}\right) \times \frac{1}{2} + \ldots$$

$$= \frac{1}{2}\left[1 + \frac{1}{3} + \left(\frac{1}{3}\right)^2 + \ldots\right]$$

$$= \frac{1}{2} \cdot \frac{1}{1 - \dfrac{1}{3}} = \frac{1}{2} \times \frac{3}{2} = \frac{3}{4}.$$

**5.** **(a)** In a single throw the favourable points are 2, 3, 4 and 5 whose number is 4.
$\therefore$ All possible outcomes are 6.
$\therefore$ P = Probability that in a single throw the minimum face value is not less then 2 and the maximum face value is not greater than $5 = 4/6 = 2/3$.
Since the dice is rolled 4 times and all the four throw's are independent events therefore the required probability

$$= \left(\frac{2}{3}\right)^4 = \frac{16}{81}.$$

**6.** **(b)** The word 'SOCIETY' contains seven distinct letters and they can be arranged at random in a row in $^7P_7$ ways, i.e. in $7! = 5040$ ways.
Let us now consider those arrangements in which all the three vowels come together. So in this case we have to arrange four letters. S,C,T,Y and a pack of three vowels in a row which can be done in $^5P_5$ i.e. $5! = 120$ ways.
Also, the three vowels in their pack can be arranged in $^3P_3$ i.e. $3! = 6$ ways.
Hence, the number of arrangements in which the three vowels come together is $120 \times 6 = 720$
$\therefore$ The probability that the vowels come together
$$= \frac{720}{5040} = \frac{1}{7}$$

**7.** **(c)** Total number of possibilities $= 2 \times 2 \times 2 \times 2 = 16$
Determinannts whose value is positive are
$$\begin{vmatrix} 1 & 0 \\ 0 & 1 \end{vmatrix}, \begin{vmatrix} 1 & 1 \\ 0 & 1 \end{vmatrix} \text{ and } \begin{vmatrix} 1 & 0 \\ 1 & 1 \end{vmatrix}$$

So, the desired probability $= \dfrac{3}{16}$

**8.** **(b, c)** According to the problem,
$$m + p + c - mp - mc - pc + mpc = 3/4 \quad \ldots(1)$$
$$mp(1-c) + mc(1-p) + pc(1-m) = 2/5$$
$$\text{or } mp + mc + pc - 3mpc = 2/5 \quad \ldots(2)$$
$$\text{Also } mp + pc + mc - 2mpc = 1/2 \quad \ldots(3)$$

From (2) and (3) $\Rightarrow mpc = \dfrac{1}{2} - \dfrac{2}{5} = \dfrac{1}{10}$

$\therefore mp + mc + pc = \dfrac{2}{5} + \dfrac{3}{10} = \dfrac{7}{10}$

$\therefore m + p + c = \dfrac{3}{4} + \dfrac{7}{10} - \dfrac{1}{10}$

$$= \frac{15 + 14 - 2}{20} = \frac{27}{20}$$

**9.** **(a,d)** Let $\alpha$ and $\beta$ be the number of heads and tails thrown by A respectively,
then $\alpha + \beta = n + 1 \quad \ldots(1)$
Let $\gamma$ and $\delta$ be the number of heads and tails thrown by B respectively,
then $\gamma + \delta = n \quad \ldots(2)$
Required probability is $P(\alpha > \gamma) = p$ (say)
Due to symmetry P (A will have more heads than B) = P (A will have more tails than B) $\quad \ldots(3)$

Now $P(\alpha \leq \gamma) = 1 - p$

[$\because$ $\alpha \leq \gamma$ is the complementary event of $\alpha > \gamma$]

Also $\alpha \leq \gamma \Rightarrow n + 1 - \beta \leq n - \delta$

$\Rightarrow 1 + \delta \leq \beta \Rightarrow \delta < \beta$ [From (1) and (2)]

$\therefore P(\alpha \leq \gamma) = P(\delta < \beta)$

$\Rightarrow 1 - p = P(A \text{ will throw more tails than } B) = p$

[From (3)]

$\therefore p = \dfrac{1}{2}$

**10. (a,b,c)** Let S denote the set of points inside a square with corners $(x, y)$, $(x, y + 1)$, $(x + 1, y)$, $(x + 1, y + 1)$, x and y are integers. Clearly each of the four points belong to the set X.

Let P denote the set of points in S with distance less than $\dfrac{1}{4}$ from any corner point. P consists of four quarter circles each of radius $\dfrac{1}{4}$.

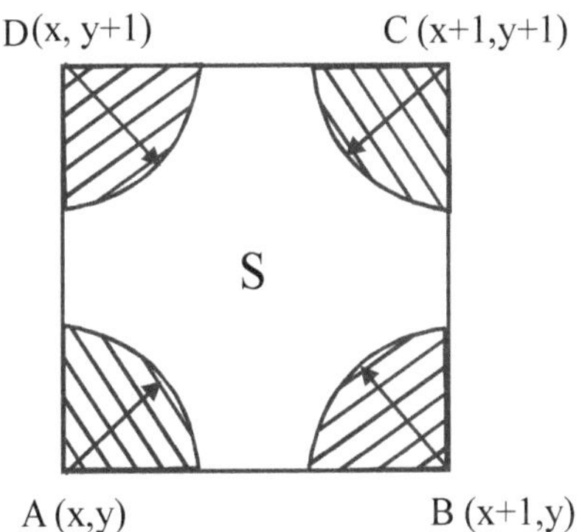


A coin, whose centre falls in S, will cover a point of X if and only if its centre falls in P.

Hence, the required probability,

$$p = \frac{\text{area of P}}{\text{area of S}} = \frac{\pi(\frac{1}{4})^2}{1 \times 1} = \frac{\pi}{16}$$

**11. (c)** $P(\overline{A} \cap \overline{B} \cap \overline{C}) = P(\overline{A \cup B \cup C}) = 1 - P(A \cup B \cup C) = b$

**12. (b)** $x = P(\overline{A} \cap \overline{B} \cap \overline{C}) = P\{(\overline{A \cup B}) \cap C\} = P(C) - P\{(A \cup B) \cap C\}$

$= P(C) - P(A \cap C \cup A \cap B)$

$= P(C) - P(A \cap C) - P(B \cap C) + P(A \cap B \cap C)$

$= P(C) - P(A)P(C) - P(B)P(C) + P(A)P(B)P(C)$

$= P(C)\{1 - P(A)\}\{1 - P(B)\}$

$\therefore x = (1 - a)P(C)\{1 - P(B)\}$

$\Rightarrow P(C) - P(C)P(B) = \dfrac{x}{1 - a}$ .....(1)

Also, $1 - c = P(A \cap B \cap C) = P(A) \cap P(B) \cap P(C)$

$\Rightarrow P(B)P(C) = \dfrac{1 - c}{a}$ ....(2)

And

$P(\overline{A} \cap \overline{B} \cap \overline{C}) = b \Rightarrow \{1 - P(A)\}\{1 - P(B)\}\{1 - P(C)\} = b$

$\Rightarrow \{1 - P(B)\}\{1 - P(C)\} = \dfrac{b}{1 - a}$ ....(3)

From (1) and (3), $\dfrac{P(C)}{1 - P(C)} = \dfrac{x}{b} \Rightarrow P(C) = \dfrac{x}{x + b}$ and

from (2), $P(B) = \dfrac{(1 - c)(x + b)}{ax}$

**13. (a)** As obtained earlier $P(C) = \dfrac{x}{x + b}$

**14. A→ q, s; B→ p, t; C → r, t**

(A) $\lambda = 1 -$ Problem will not be solved

$= 1 - P(\overline{A} \cap \overline{B} \cap \overline{C}) = 1 - P(\overline{A})P(\overline{B})P(\overline{C})$

$= 1 - \left(1 - \dfrac{1}{2}\right)\left(1 - \dfrac{1}{3}\right)\left(1 - \dfrac{1}{4}\right)$

$= 1 - \dfrac{1}{2} \times \dfrac{2}{3} \times \dfrac{3}{4}$

$= 1 - \dfrac{1}{4} = \dfrac{3}{4}$

and $\mu = P(A \cap \overline{B} \cap \overline{C}) + P(\overline{A} \cap B \cap \overline{C}) + P(\overline{A} \cap \overline{B} \cap C)$

$= P(A)P(\overline{B})P(\overline{C}) + P(\overline{A})P(B)P(\overline{C}) + P(\overline{A})P(\overline{B})P(C)$

$= \dfrac{1}{2}\cdot\left(1 - \dfrac{1}{3}\right)\cdot\left(1 - \dfrac{1}{4}\right) + \left(1 - \dfrac{1}{2}\right)\cdot\dfrac{1}{3}\cdot\left(1 - \dfrac{1}{4}\right)$

$\qquad\qquad + \left(1 - \dfrac{1}{2}\right)\left(1 - \dfrac{1}{3}\right)\cdot\dfrac{1}{4}$

$= \dfrac{6}{24} + \dfrac{3}{24} + \dfrac{2}{24} = \dfrac{11}{24}$

$\therefore \lambda + \mu = \dfrac{3}{4} + \dfrac{11}{24} = \dfrac{29}{24}$ (q) and $\lambda - \mu = \dfrac{7}{24}$ (s)

(B) Here, $P(A) = \dfrac{1}{2}$, $P(B) = \dfrac{1}{3}$, $P(C) = \dfrac{1}{4}$

$\therefore \lambda = P(A \cap B \cap \overline{C}) + P(\overline{A} \cap B \cap C) + P(A \cap \overline{B} \cap C)$

$= P(A)P(B)P(\overline{C}) + P(\overline{A})P(B)P(C) + P(A)P(\overline{B})P(C)$

$$= \frac{1}{2}\cdot\frac{1}{3}\cdot\frac{3}{4} + \frac{1}{2}\cdot\frac{1}{3}\cdot\frac{1}{4} + \frac{1}{2}\cdot\frac{2}{3}\cdot\frac{1}{4}$$

$$= \frac{6}{24}$$

and $\mu = \lambda + P(A)\cdot P(B)\cdot P(C)$

$$= \lambda + \frac{1}{24} = \frac{7}{24}$$

and $\mu - \lambda = \dfrac{1}{24}$ (t) and $\lambda + \mu = \dfrac{13}{24}$ (p)

(C) $\quad \lambda = \dfrac{2}{6}\times\dfrac{5}{8} = \dfrac{5}{24}$ and $\mu = \dfrac{4}{6}\times\dfrac{3}{8} = \dfrac{6}{24}$

$$\therefore \mu - \lambda = \frac{1}{24}\ (t)\ \text{ and }\ \mu + \lambda = \frac{11}{24}\ (r)$$

**15.** $A \to p, q, t; B \to r; C \to p, s$

(A) The chance of getting a head with a coin is $\dfrac{1}{2}$. A can win in 1st, 4th or 7th...... throws

$\therefore p =$ The chance of A's winning

$$= \frac{1}{2} + \left(\frac{1}{2}\right)^3 \times \frac{1}{2} + \left(\frac{1}{2}\right)^6 \times \frac{1}{2} + ...$$

$$= \frac{\dfrac{1}{2}}{1 - \left(\dfrac{1}{2}\right)^3} = \frac{4}{7}$$

$B$ can win in 2nd, 5th or 8th .....throws

$\therefore q =$ The chance of B's winning

$$= \left(\frac{1}{2}\right)^1 \times \frac{1}{2} + \left(\frac{1}{2}\right)^4 \times \frac{1}{2} + \left(\frac{1}{2}\right)^7 \times \frac{1}{2} + ...$$

$$= \frac{\dfrac{1}{2}\times\dfrac{1}{2}}{1 - \left(\dfrac{1}{2}\right)^3} = \frac{2}{7}$$

and $r =$ The chance of C's winning

$$= 1 - (p + q)$$

$$= 1 - \left(\frac{4}{7} + \frac{2}{7}\right)$$

$$= \frac{1}{7}$$

$p : q = 2 : 1$ (t)

$$p - r = \frac{3}{7}\ (q),\quad q - r = \frac{1}{7}\ (p)$$

(B) The chance of getting a 'six' when a dice is thrown $= \dfrac{1}{6}$

$\therefore$ The chance of not getting a 'six', when a dice is not thrown $= 1 - \dfrac{1}{6} = \dfrac{5}{6}$

$\therefore \quad p =$ The probability of A's winning

$$= \frac{1}{6} + \left(\frac{5}{6}\right)^3 \times \frac{1}{6} + \left(\frac{5}{6}\right)^6 \times \frac{1}{6} + ....$$

$$= \frac{\dfrac{1}{6}}{1 - \left(\dfrac{5}{6}\right)^3}$$

$$= \frac{36}{91}$$

$q =$ The probability of B's winning

$$= \frac{5}{6} \times \frac{1}{6} + \left(\frac{5}{6}\right)^4 \times \frac{1}{6} + \left(\frac{5}{6}\right)^7 \times \frac{1}{6} + ...$$

$$= \frac{\dfrac{5}{6}\times\dfrac{1}{6}}{1 - \left(\dfrac{5}{6}\right)^3} = \frac{30}{91}$$

and $r = 1 - (p + q)$

$$= 1 - \left(\frac{36 + 30}{91}\right)$$

$$= 1 - \frac{66}{91}$$

$$= \frac{25}{91}$$

$p : q = 6 : 5$ (r)

(C) $p =$ The probability of A's winning

$$= \frac{2}{3} + \left(\frac{1}{3}\times\frac{1}{2}\times\frac{3}{4}\right) \times \frac{2}{3} + \left(\frac{1}{3}\times\frac{1}{2}\times\frac{3}{4}\right)^2 \times \frac{2}{3} + ...$$

$$= \frac{\dfrac{2}{3}}{1 - \left(\dfrac{1}{3}\times\dfrac{1}{2}\times\dfrac{3}{4}\right)}$$

$$= \frac{\dfrac{2}{3}}{\dfrac{7}{8}} = \frac{16}{21}$$

$q$ = The probability of B's winning

$$= \frac{1}{3} \cdot \frac{1}{2} + \left(\frac{1}{3} \cdot \frac{1}{2} \cdot \frac{3}{4}\right) \frac{1}{3} \cdot \frac{1}{2} + \left(\frac{1}{3} \cdot \frac{1}{2} \cdot \frac{3}{4}\right)^2 \frac{1}{3} \cdot \frac{1}{2} + \ldots$$

$$= \frac{\dfrac{1}{3} \cdot \dfrac{1}{2}}{1 - \left(\dfrac{1}{3} \cdot \dfrac{1}{2} \cdot \dfrac{3}{4}\right)}$$

$$= \frac{\dfrac{1}{6}}{\dfrac{7}{8}} = \frac{4}{21}$$

$$\therefore r = 1 - (p + q)$$

$$= 1 - \left(\frac{16}{21} + \frac{4}{21}\right)$$

$$= \frac{1}{21}$$

$$\therefore q - r = \frac{3}{21} = \frac{1}{7} \text{ (p)}$$

$$p - r = \frac{15}{21} = \frac{5}{7} \text{ (s)}$$

**16. (c)** Statement – I is true as there are six equally likely possibilities of which only two are favourable (4 and 6). Hence P(obtained number is composite) =

$$\frac{2}{6} = \frac{1}{3}.$$

Statement – II is not true, as the three possibilities are not equally likely.

Hence (c) is the correct answer.

**17. (d)** Given $P(E_1 \cap E_2) \le 0.3$

$$\Rightarrow P(E_1) . P(E_2) \le 0.3$$

$$\Rightarrow (0.5) P(E_2) \le (0.3)$$

$$\therefore \quad P(E_2) \le \frac{(0.3)}{(0.5)}$$

$$\Rightarrow P(E_2) \le 0.6$$

$$\therefore \quad P(E_2) \ne 0.9$$

**18. 2**

Let $P(A) = a$ and $P(B) = b$ Then $P(A \cap B) = \frac{1}{6}$

$$\Rightarrow P(A) P(B) = \frac{1}{6},$$

because A and B are independent .

$$\therefore a\,b = \frac{1}{6} \qquad \ldots\text{(i)}$$

Also $P(\overline{A} \cap \overline{B}) = [1 - P(A)][1 - P(B)];$ .

$$\therefore [1 - a][1 - b] = \frac{1}{3} \Rightarrow 1 - a - b + a\,b = \frac{1}{3} \qquad \ldots\text{(ii)}$$

From (i) and (ii), we have $a + b = \frac{5}{6}$ $\qquad \ldots\text{(iii)}$

Solving (i) and (iii), we get, $a = \frac{1}{2}$, $b = \frac{1}{3}$, $\therefore P(A) = \frac{1}{2}$.

Thus, $X = 2$

**19. 5**

Consider the probability that, for example, an ace and a king are together. There are 4 aces and 4 kings in a deck.

Hence an ace can be chosen in 4 ways, and when that is done a king can be chosen in 4 ways.

Thus an ace and then a king can be selected in $4 \times 4 = 16$ ways. Similarly, a king and then an ace can be selected in 16 ways.

Then an ace and a king can be together in $2 \times 16 = 32$ ways.

For every one way the combination (ace, king) occurs, the remaining 50 cards and the (ace, king) combination can be permuted in $51 \times 50 \times 49 \times 48 \ldots\ldots$ ways. The number of favourable arrangements is thus

$32 (51 \times 50 \times 49 \times 48 \ldots\ldots \times 1)$

$$\therefore \quad \text{The required probability is } \frac{32}{52} = \frac{8}{13}.$$

Thus, $Q - P = 13 - 8 = 5$

**20. 5**

| odd | even | odd | even | odd |
|-----|------|-----|------|-----|

Odd digits = 1, 3, 5, 7, 9
Even digits = 0, 2, 4, 6, 8
Since odd digits at odd place and even digit at even place
Places of odd digit = 3 and places of even digits = 2
$\therefore$ Favourable ways = = 1200
Total five digit numbers = $9 \times 10 \times 10 \times 10 \times 10$

$$\therefore \text{ Required probability} = \frac{1200}{9 \times 10 \times 10 \times 10 \times 10} = \frac{1}{75}.$$

Thus, $P = 5$

**1. (d)** Total number of cases obtained by taking multiplication of any two numbers out of $100 = {}^{100}C_2$. Out of hundred $(1, 2 \ldots 100)$ given numbers, there are the numbers 3, 6, 12, .... 99, which are 33 in numbers such that when any one of these is multiplied with any one of the remaining 67 numbers or any two of these 33 are multiplied then the resulting product is divisible by 3.

Thus the number of numbers which are the products of two of the given numbers and are divisible by 3

$$= {}^{33}C_1 \times {}^{67}C_1 + {}^{33}C_2$$

Hence the required probability

$$= \frac{{}^{33}C_1 \times {}^{67}C_1 + {}^{33}C_2}{{}^{100}C_2} = \frac{2739}{4950} = 0.55 .$$

**2. (c)** Required probability = probability of drawing 3 W and 3 B balls in 6 draws and drawing a white ball in

$7^{th}$ draw

$$= {}^6C_3 \left(\frac{12}{24}\right)^3 \left(\frac{12}{24}\right)^3 \left(\frac{12}{24}\right) = \frac{5}{32}$$

**3. (c)** The probabilities of obtaining 0, 2, 3 in a single throw are respectively

$$\frac{4}{6}, \frac{1}{6}, \frac{1}{6} \text{ or } \frac{2}{3}, \frac{1}{6}, \frac{1}{6}$$

In 5 throws, the number 12 can be obtained as follows:
(1) 3 in 4 throws and 0 in 1 throw.
(2)  3 in 2 throws and 2 in 3 throws.
Hence, the required probability

$$= {}^5C_4 \left(\frac{1}{6}\right)^4 \left(\frac{2}{3}\right) + {}^5C_2 \left(\frac{1}{6}\right)^2 \left(\frac{1}{6}\right)^3 = \frac{30}{6^5} = \frac{5}{1296}$$

**4. (a)** Let $A = \{a_1, a_2, a_3, \ldots\ldots\ldots a_n\}$. For any $a_i \in A$, $1 \le i \le n$, we have following choices

(1) $a_i \in P$ and $a_i \in Q$ (2) $a_i \in P$ and $a_i \notin Q$

(3) $a_i \notin P$ and $a_i \in Q$ (4) $a_i \notin P$ and $a_i \notin Q$

So, for each $a_i \in A$, there are four possibilities.

$\therefore$ Total no. of cases $= 4 \times 4 \times \ldots\ldots\ldots \times 4$ (n times)
$= 4^n$

Further out of above four possibilities, first three satisfy

$a_i \in P \cup Q$

So, the number of cases, when exactly r element of A

belong to $P \cup Q = {}^nC_r (3)^r$

$\therefore$ Required probability $= \dfrac{{}^nC_r (3)^r}{4^n}$

**5. (d)** Since there are r cars in N places. Total number of selection of places out of $N - 1$ places for $r - 1$ cars (excepting the owner's car)

$$= {}^{N-1}C_{r-1} = \frac{(N-1)!}{(r-1)!(N-r)!}$$

If neighbouring places are empty, then $r - 1$ cars must be parked in $N - 3$ places.

So, the favourable cases $= {}^{N-3}C_{r-1}$

$$= \frac{(N-3)!}{(r-1)!(N-r-2)!}$$

$\therefore$ Required probability

$$= \frac{(N-3)!}{(r-1)!(N-r-2)!} \times \frac{(r-1)!(N-r)!}{(N-1)!}$$

$$= \frac{(N-r)(N-r-1)}{(N-1)(N-2)} = \frac{{}^{N-r}C_2}{{}^{N-1}C_2}$$

**6. (b)** The no. of ways of placing 3 black ball is ${}^{10}C_3$. The no. of ways in which two black balls are not together is equal to the number of ways of choosing 3 places marked with X out of eight places.
X W X W X W X W X W X W X W X
This can be done in ${}^8C_3$ ways.

$$\text{Pro.} = \frac{{}^8C_3}{{}^{10}C_3} = \frac{7}{15}$$

**7. (c)** A number is divisible by 9, if the sum of its digits is divisible by 9. Here $1 + 2 + 3 + 4 + 5 + 6 + 7 + 8 + 9 = 45$ is divisible by 9.
$\therefore$ The two numbers should be removed such that their sum is 9.
$\therefore$ They can be any one of the following pairs $(1, 8), (2, 7), (3, 6), (4, 5)$.
Hence the number of favourable cases = 4
Total number of cases of removing two numbers $= {}^9C_2$

$\therefore$ The required probability $= \dfrac{4}{{}^9C_2} = \dfrac{4}{36} = \dfrac{1}{9} .$

**8. (d)** Let $p_1, p_2, p_3, \ldots\ldots, p_9$ denote, the probability of drawing black, black, white, white white, white, red, red and red respectively in this order without replacement. Then

$P =$ required probability $= p_1 p_2 p_3 \ldots\ldots p_9$.

$p_1 = \dfrac{{}^2C_1}{{}^9C_1} = \dfrac{2}{9}$ [Since one black ball can be drawn out of 2 in

${}^2C_1$ ways and total number of way ${}^9C_1$]

$p_2 = \dfrac{^1C_1}{^8C_1} = \dfrac{1}{8}$. Since one black remaining after first draw.

$p_3 = \dfrac{^4C_1}{^7C_1} = \dfrac{4}{7}$. Since in the remaining 7 balls 4 are white.

Similarly, $p_4 = \dfrac{^3C_1}{^6C_1} = \dfrac{3}{6}$, $p_5 = \dfrac{^2C_1}{^5C_1} = \dfrac{2}{5}$, $p_6 = \dfrac{1}{4}$

Now the remaining three balls are red so that $p_7 = p_8 = p_9 = 1$

Hence $p = \dfrac{2}{9} \cdot \dfrac{1}{8} \cdot \dfrac{4}{7} \cdot \dfrac{1}{2} \cdot \dfrac{2}{5} \cdot \dfrac{1}{4} = \dfrac{1}{1260}$.

**9.**   **(c)**   Two squares out of 64 can be selected in

$^{64}C_2 = \dfrac{64 \times 63}{2} = 32 \times 63$ ways

The number of ways of selecting those pairs which have a

side in common $= \left(\dfrac{1}{2}\right)(4 \times 2 + 24 \times 3 + 36 \times 4) = 112$

[Since each of the corner squares has two neighbours each of 24 squares in border other than corner ones has three neighbours and each of the remaining 36 squares have four neighbours and in this computation, each pair of squares has been counted twice].

Hence required probability $= \dfrac{112}{32 \times 63} = \dfrac{1}{18}$.

**10.**   **(b)**   $p_1 = \dfrac{^{15}C_2}{^{42}C_4} = \dfrac{15 \times 14 \times 4!}{2! \times 42 \times 41 \times 40 \times 39} = \dfrac{1}{41 \times 26}$ and

$p_2 = \dfrac{^{30}C_4}{^{84}C_8} = \dfrac{15 \times 14 \times 13 \times 12 \times 8!}{4! \times 84 \times 83 \times 82 \times ..... \times 77}$

$= \dfrac{15 \times 14 \times 13 \times 12 \times 8 \times 7 \times 6 \times 5}{84 \times 83 \times 82 \times 81 \times 79 \times 78 \times 77} < p_1 \Rightarrow p_1 > p_2$.

**11.**   **(b)**   Since each ball can be put into any one of the three boxes. So, the total number of ways in which 12 balls can be put into three boxes is $3^{12}$.
Out of 12 balls, 3 balls can be chosen in $^{12}C_3$ ways. Now, remaining 9 balls can be put in the remaining 2 boxes in $2^9$ ways. So, the total number of ways in which 3 balls are put in the first box and the remaining in other two boxes is $^{12}C_3 \times 2^9$.

Hence, required probability $= \dfrac{^{12}C_3 . 2^9}{3^{12}}$

**12.**   **(a)**   The number of possible outcomes of 2n tosses is $2^{2n}$. There are $^nC_r$ ways of getting r heads, with $0 \le r \le n$, in n tosses. Therefore, the number of ways of getting r heads in both the first n and last n tosses is $(^nC_r)^2$. Summing over all values of r, the number of favourable ways is

$(^nC_0)^2 + (^nC_1)^2 + (^nC_2)^2 + .... + (^nC_n)^2 = \,^{2n}C_n$,

[Refer to properties of binomial coefficients for above result].

So that the required probability is $\dfrac{^{2n}C_n}{2^{2n}}$.

**13. (a, b, c, d)**

**(a)**   If a no. is to be divisible by both 2 and 3. It should be divisible by their L.C.M.
$\therefore$   L.C.M. of (2 and 3) = 6
$\therefore$   Numbers are 6, 12, 18 ... 96.
Total numbers = 16

$\therefore$   Probability $= \dfrac{^{16}C_3}{^{100}C_3} = \dfrac{4}{1155}$

**(b)**   Total number of ways of selecting 3 integers from 20 natural numbers $= \,^{20}C_3 = 1140$
Their product is a multiple of 3 means, at least one number is divisible by 3.
The numbers which are divisible by 3 are 3, 6, 9, 12, 15, 18 and the number of ways of selecting atleast one of them is

$^6C_1 \times \,^{14}C_2 + \,^6C_2 \times \,^{14}C_1 + \,^6C_3 = 776$

Probability $= \dfrac{776}{1140} = \dfrac{194}{285}$

**(c)**   Total number of balls = 12.

Required probability $= \dfrac{^5C_2 \, ^7C_2}{^{12}C_4} = \dfrac{14}{33}$.

**(d)**   The given word is made up of the letters of the word BRILLIANT Possibilities of arrangements :

(i)   two alike + two alike + one different $1 \times 5 \times \dfrac{5!}{(2!)^2}$

$\quad = 150$

(ii)   two alike + three different $\quad 2 \times \,^6C_3 \times \dfrac{5!}{2!} = 2400$

(iii)   all are different $\quad ^7C_5 \times 5! = 2520$
Total number of different arrangements = 5070.

The required probability $= \dfrac{2520}{5070} = \dfrac{252}{507}$.

**14.**   **(a,d)**   $\because \, P(X=4), P(X=5)$ and $P(X=6)$ are in $AP$,
$\therefore \quad 2P(X=5) = P(X=4) + P(X=6)$

$\Rightarrow \quad 2 = \dfrac{P(X=4)}{P(X=5)} + \dfrac{P(X=6)}{P(X=5)}$

$2 = \dfrac{^nC_4}{^nC_5} + \dfrac{^nC_6}{^nC_5}$

$\Rightarrow \quad n^2 - 21n + 98 = 0$
$\therefore \quad n = 7, 14$

**15. (a, c)**   $X = \{a_1, a_2, a_3, ... a_n\}$
$\therefore$   Number of subsets $= 2^n$
The number of ways of choosing $A$ and $B$ is
$= 2^n \times 2^n = 2^{2n}$.
The number of ways of choosing $A$ and $B$ so that

they have the same number of elements is
$${}^{n}C_{0} \cdot {}^{n}C_{0} + {}^{n}C_{1} \cdot {}^{n}C_{1} + {}^{n}C_{2} \cdot {}^{n}C_{2} + ... + {}^{n}C_{n} \cdot {}^{n}C_{n}$$
$$= {}^{2n}C_{n} = \frac{2^{n} \cdot (1.3.5 .... 2n - 1)}{n!}$$

$\therefore$ Probability $= \dfrac{{}^{2n}C_{n}}{2^{2n}} = \dfrac{1.3.5 .... (2n-1)}{2^{n} \cdot n!}$

**16. (a, c)** The total number of cases $= 6 \times 6 \times 6 = 216$
The number of favourable ways

$=$ coefficient of $x^{k}$ in $(x + x^{2} + .... + x^{6})^{3}$

$=$ coefficient of $x^{k-3}$ in $(1-x^{6})^{3}(1-x)^{-3}$

$=$ coefficient of $x^{k-3}$ in $(1-x)^{-3} [0 \le k-3 \le 5]$

$= {}^{k-3+2}C_{2} = {}^{k-1}C_{2} = \dfrac{(k-1)(k-2)}{2}$

$\therefore$ Required probability $= \dfrac{(k-1)(k-2)}{2 \times 216}$

$= \dfrac{(k-1)(k-2)}{432}$

**17. (a,b,c)** The number of ways in which $m$ boys and $m$ girls can take their seats around a circle
$$= ((m+m)-1)! = (2m-1)!$$

**(a)** : No two boys sit together
We make the girls sit first around the table. This can be done in (m-1)! ways.  After this boys can take their seats in m! ways

$\therefore$ The probability no two boys sit together

$= \dfrac{m!(m-1)!}{(2m-1)!} = \dfrac{1}{{}^{2m-1}C_{m}}$

$= ({}^{2m-1}C_{m})^{-1}$

**(b) :** No two girls sit together
We make the boys sit first around the table. This can be done in $(m-1)!$ ways. After this girls can take their seats in (m)!

$\therefore$ The probability no two girls sit together

$= \dfrac{m!(m-1)!}{(2m-1)!} = \dfrac{1}{{}^{2m-1}C_{m}}$

$= ({}^{2m-1}C_{m})^{-1}$

**(c)** : Boys and girls sit alternatively ie, no two boys (girls) sit together

$\therefore$ Required probability $= ({}^{2m-1}C_{m})^{-1}$

**(d) :** All the boys sit together
$\because$ All the boys sit together. Let treat them as a single boy.
Here, (m + 1) objects (m girls + 1 boy)
$\therefore$ We can put (m + 1) objects around a circle in m! ways.
But boys can be tied in m! boys.
So boys will sit together in m! m! ways

$\therefore$ Required probability $= \dfrac{m!m!}{(2m-1)!} \ne ({}^{2m-1}C_{m})^{-1}$

**18.** **(d)** $2n+1 = 5 \Rightarrow n = 2$

$P(E) = \dfrac{3n}{4n^{2}-1} = \dfrac{6}{15} = \dfrac{2}{5}$

For a, b, c are in A.P. $a + c = 2b \Rightarrow a + c$ is even
$\therefore$ a and c are both even or both odd.
So, number of ways of choosing a and c is ${}^{n}C_{2} + {}^{n+1}C_{2}$
$= n^{2}$

$\therefore n^{2} P(E) = \dfrac{n^{2}}{{}^{2n+1}C_{3}} = \dfrac{3n}{4n^{2}-1}$

**19.** **(b)** For statement 1, $n(S) = {}^{6}C_{3} = 20$

Only two triangle formed are equilateral, they are $\Delta A_{1}A_{3}A_{5}$ and $\Delta A_{2}A_{4}A_{6}$. $\therefore n(E) = 2$

$\Rightarrow P(E) = \dfrac{n(E)}{n(S)} = \dfrac{2}{20} = \dfrac{1}{10}$

For statement $-2$, $n(S) = 216$

No. of favourable ways $= \displaystyle\sum_{i=1}^{6}(i-1)(6-i) = 20$

$\therefore$ Required probability $= \dfrac{20}{216} = \dfrac{5}{54}$.

**20.** 7
Total number of ways of selecting x and y $= 11 \times 11 = 121$
Favourable ways are as follows.

| x | y |
|---|---|
| 0 | 0 to 5 |
| 1 | 0 to 6 |
| 2 | 0 to 7 |
| 3 | 0 to 8 |
| 4 | 0 to 9 |
| 5 | 0 to 10 |
| 6 | 1 to 10 |
| 7 | 2 to 10 |
| 8 | 3 to 10 |
| 9 | 4 to 10 |
| 10 | 5 to 10 |

So, number of ways $= 2(6 + 7 + 8 + 9 + 10) + 11$
$= 2 \times 40 + 11 = 91$

Thus $P = \dfrac{91}{121} \Rightarrow \dfrac{121}{13} P = 7$

**21.** 3
E : all the 5 persons leave at different floors
$n(S) = 8^{5}$
$n(A) = {}^{8}C_{5} \cdot 5!$

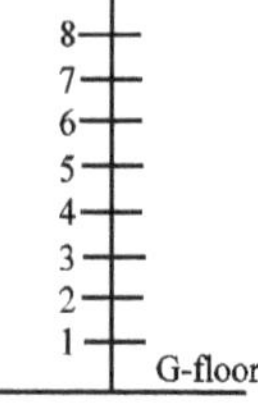

$$\therefore P(E) = \frac{^8C_5 \cdot 5!}{8^5}$$

Thus $P = 8, Q = 5$

$\Rightarrow P - Q = 8 - 5 = 3$

**22.** **9**

$1, 2, 3, 4, 5, 6, 7, 8, 9$

$x + y = 45$ ; $x - y = 11$ $\qquad \Rightarrow x = 28$ ; $y = 17$

Now to realise a sum 17 using 4 digits we can have different cases ,

$$\left.\begin{matrix} 9 & 4 & 3 & 1 \\ 9 & 5 & 2 & 1 \end{matrix}\right] ; \quad \left.\begin{matrix} 8 & 6 & 2 & 1 \\ 8 & 5 & 3 & 1 \\ 8 & 4 & 3 & 2 \end{matrix}\right| ; \left.\begin{matrix} 7 & 6 & 3 & 1 \\ 7 & 5 & 4 & 1 \\ 7 & 5 & 3 & 2 \end{matrix}\right| ;$$

$$\left.\begin{matrix} 6 & 5 & 4 & 2 \end{matrix}\right] \qquad (\,9 \text{ cases}\,)$$

If we use five digits then $\quad 7, 1, 2, 3, 4$

$\quad (\,2 \text{ cases}\,)$

$\qquad\qquad\qquad\qquad\qquad 6, 5, 3, 2, 1$

Hence $p = \dfrac{4! \times 5! \times 9 + 5! \times 4! \times 2}{9!}$

$$= \frac{11 \times 5! \times 4!}{9!} \quad = \frac{11}{126}$$

[ odd in favour $11 : 115$ ]

Thus $X + 2 = 11 \Rightarrow X = 9$

**23.** **5**

Required probability = P (I in 1st draw) $\times$ P (I in 2nd draw) $\times$ P (T in 3rd draw)

$$= \frac{^{10}C_1}{^{20}C_1} \times \frac{^9C_1}{^{19}C_1} \times \frac{^{10}C_1}{^{18}C_1} = \frac{10}{20} \times \frac{9}{19} \times \frac{10}{18} = 5/38.$$

Thus $A = 5$

**24.** **6**

Required probability = P (yellow in 1st toss) $\times$ P (Red in 2nd toss) $\times$ P(Blue in 3rd toss) $= \dfrac{^3C_1}{^6C_1} \times \dfrac{^2C_1}{^6C_1} \times \dfrac{^1C_1}{^6C_1}$

$$= \frac{3}{6} \times \frac{2}{6} \times \frac{1}{6} = \frac{1}{2} \times \frac{1}{3} \times \frac{1}{6} = 1/36$$

Thus $P = 6$

**1.** **(c)** $P(A' \cap B') = (P \cup B)' = 1 - P(A \cup B)$
$= 1 - [P(A) + P(B) - P(A \cap B)]$
$= P(B') - P(A) + P(A \cap B)$
$\Rightarrow P(A \cap B) = 0$

**2.** **(a)**
We have $P(E) = P(TTTTH + TTTTT)$
$= \dfrac{1}{32} + \dfrac{1}{32} = \dfrac{1}{16} = \dfrac{p}{q} \Rightarrow p + q = 17$

**3.** **(d)** $P(A) = \dfrac{1}{6}$, $P(B) = \dfrac{1}{2}$, A and B are independent events,

that means $P(AB) = P(A)\,P(B) = \dfrac{1}{6}\cdot\dfrac{1}{2} = \dfrac{1}{12}$

and $P(A^c B^c) = 1 - P(A \cup B)$
$= 1 - P(A) - P(B) + P(AB)$
$= 1 - \dfrac{1}{6} - \dfrac{1}{2} + \dfrac{1}{12} = \dfrac{12 - 2 - 6 + 1}{12} = \dfrac{5}{12}$

**4.** **(d)** Let $A \equiv$ event of selecting first purse
$B \equiv$ event of selecting second purse
$C \equiv$ event of drawing a copper coin from first purse
$D \equiv$ event of drawing a copper coin from second purse
Then given event has two disjoint cases : AC and BD
$\therefore$ Reqd. prob. $= P(AC + BD) = P(AC) + P(BD)$
$= P(A)\,P(C) + P(B)\,P(D) = \dfrac{1}{2}\cdot\dfrac{4}{7} + \dfrac{1}{2}\cdot\dfrac{6}{8} = \dfrac{37}{56}$

**5.** **(a)** $P(A \cup B) = P(A) + P(B) - P(A \cap B)$
$= 0.25 + 0.50 - 0.14 = 0.61$
$\therefore P(A' \cap B') = P((A \cup B)') = 1 - P(A \cup B)$
$= 1 - 0.61 = 0.39$

**6.** **(a)** We know that P (exactly one of A or B occurs)
$= P(A) + P(B) - 2P(A \cap B)$
$= P(A) + P(B) - 2P(A \cap B) = p \qquad \dots(1)$
Similarly, $P(B) + P(C) - 2P(B \cap C) = p \qquad \dots(2)$
and $P(C) + P(A) - 2P(C \cap A) = p \dots(3)$
Adding (1), (2) and (3) we get
$2\,[P(A) + P(B) + P(C) - P(A \cap B)$
$- P(B \cap C) - P(C \cap A)] = 3p$
$\Rightarrow \quad P(A) + P(B) + P(C) - P(A \cap B)$
$- P(B \cap C) - P(C \cap A)] = \dfrac{3}{2}p \qquad \dots(4)$
We are also given that,
$P(A \cap B \cap C) = p^2 \qquad \dots(5)$
Now, P (at least one of A, B and C)
$= P(A) + P(B) + P(C) - P(A \cap B) - P(B \cap C)$
$- P(C \cap A) + P(A \cap B \cap C)$
$= \dfrac{3p}{2} + p^2 \qquad$ [using (4) and (5)]
$= \dfrac{3p + 2p^2}{2}$

**7.** **(b)** We have $P(B') = 1/2$
$\Rightarrow \quad P(B) = 1/2$
Now, $P(A \cup B) = 5/6$
$\Rightarrow \quad P(A) + P(B) - P(A \cap B) = 5/6$
$\Rightarrow \quad P(A) = 2/3$
Since $P(A)\,P(B) = (2/3)(1/2) = 1/3 = P(A \cap B)$
A and B are independent events.

**8.** **(a)** $P(A \cap B) = P(A) + P(B) - P(A \cup B)$
$= 0.6 + 0.4 - 0.8 = 0.2.$
$P(A \cup B \cup C) = P(A) + P(B) + P(C) - P(A \cap C) + P(A \cap B \cap C) - P(A \cap B) - P(B \cap C)$
$\Rightarrow \quad P(B \cap C) = 1.2 - P(A \cup B \cup C) \dots(1)$
$\because \quad 0.85 \le P(A \cup B \cup C) \le 1$
$\therefore \quad (1) \Rightarrow P(B \cap C) \le 1.2 - 0.85$
and $\quad P(B \cap C) \ge 1.2 - 1$
$\Rightarrow \quad 0.2 \le P(B \cap C) \le 0.35$

**9.** **(c)** $P(\overline{A \cup B}) = \dfrac{1}{6}; P(A \cap B) = \dfrac{1}{4}$ and $P(\overline{A}) = \dfrac{1}{4}$
$\Rightarrow P(A \cup B) = \dfrac{5}{6} ; \quad P(A) = \dfrac{3}{4}$
Also $P(A \cup B) = P(A) + P(B) - P(A \cap B)$
$\Rightarrow P(B) = \dfrac{5}{6} - \dfrac{3}{4} + \dfrac{1}{4} = \dfrac{1}{3}$
$\Rightarrow P(A)\,P(B) = \dfrac{3}{4}\cdot\dfrac{1}{3} = \dfrac{1}{4} = P(A \cap B)$
Hence A and B are independent but not equally likely.

**10.** **(d)** P (exactly one of A and B occurs)
$= P[A \cap B') \cup (A' \cap B)] = P(A \cap B') + P(A' \cap B) \dots(1)$
$= P(A) - P(A \cap B) + P(B) - P(A \cap B)$
$= P(A) + P(B) - 2P(A \cap B) \qquad \dots(2)$
$= P(A \cup B) - P(A \cap B) \qquad \dots(3)$
$= [1 - P(A \cup B)'] - [1 - P(A \cap B)']$
$= P(A' \cup B') - P(A' \cap B')$
[De morgans Law]
$= P(A') + P(B') - 2P(A' \cap B') \qquad \dots(4)$
Clearly (d) is not correct

**11.** **(a)** The probability of 4 being the minimum number $= \dfrac{^6C_2}{^{10}C_3}$
(because, after selecting 4 any two can be selected from 5, 6, 7, 8, 9, 10).

The probability of 8 being the maximum number $= \dfrac{^7C_2}{^{10}C_3}$
The probability of 4 being the minimum number and 8 being the maximum number $= \dfrac{3}{^{10}C_3}$
$\therefore$ The required probability
$= P(A \cup B) = P(A) + P(B) - P(A \cap B)$
$= \dfrac{^6C_2}{^{10}C_3} + \dfrac{^7C_2}{^{10}C_3} - \dfrac{3}{^{10}C_3} = \dfrac{11}{40}$

**12.** **(a)** Given
$P(A \cap B) = P(A).P(B), P(B \cap C) = P(B).P(C),$
$P(C \cap A) = P(C) \cdot P(A)$ and
$P(A \cap B \cap C) = P(A) \cdot P(B) \cdot P(C)$
we have $P\{A \cap (B \cup C)\} = P\{(A \cap B) \cup (A \cap C)\}$
$= P(A \cap B) + P(A \cap C) - P(A \cap B \cap C)$

$$= P(A)\,P(B) + P(A)\,P(C) - P(A)\,P(B)\,P(C)$$
$$= P(A)\cdot\{P(B) + P(C) - P(B)P(C)\}$$
$$= P(A)\cdot\{P(B) + P(C) - P(B\cap C)\}$$
$$= P(A)\cdot P(B\cup C)$$

$\therefore$ A and $B\cup C$ are independent ie, $S_1$ is true

Also, $P\{A\cap(B\cap C)\} = P(A\cap B\cap C)$
$$= P(A)\cdot P(B)\cdot P(C)$$
$$= P(A)\cdot P(B\cap C)$$

$\Rightarrow$ A and $B\cap C$ are independent
ie, $S_2$ is true
Hence, $S_1$ and $S_2$ are true.

**13.** **(a,c,d)** P(exactly two of A, B, C occur)

$= \quad P(A\cap B) + P(B\cap C) + P(C\cap A) - 3P(A\cap B\cap C)$

$\leq P(A\cap B) + P(B\cap C) + P(C\cap A) \qquad ....(1)$

Thus (a) is wrong.
Also,
$P(A\cup B\cup C) \leq P(A\cup B) + P(C) \leq P(A) + P(B) + P(C)$
$$....(2)$$

Again P (exactly one of A, B, C occurs)
$= P(A) + P(B) + P(C) - 2P(A\cap B) - 2P(B\cap C)$
$$\qquad - 2P(C\cap A) + 3P(A\cap B\cap C)$$
$= P(A) + P(B) + P(C) - P(A\cap B) - P(B\cap C) - P(C\cap A)$
$$- [P(A\cap B) + P(B\cap C) + P(C\cap A) - 3P(A\cap B\cap C)]$$
$= P(A) + P(B) + P(C) - P(A\cap B) - P(B\cap C) - P(C\cap A)$
$- P$ (exactly two of A, B, C occour) [see (1)]

$\leq P(A) + P(B) + P(C) - P(A\cap B) - P(B\cap C) - P(C\cap A) ...(3)$
$$[\because \text{ Probability of any event } \geq 0]$$

Further, P (A and at least one of B, C occur)
$= P[A\cap(B\cup C)] = P[(A\cap B)\cup(A\cap C)]$
$= P(A\cap B) + P(A\cap C) - P[(A\cap B)\cap(A\cap C)]$
$= P(A\cap B) + P(A\cap C) - P[(A\cap B\cap C) \leq P(A\cap B) + P(A\cap C)$
$$....(4)$$

From (2), only (b) is correct.

**14.** **(a, c, d)** Given that M and N are any two events. To check the probability that exactly one of them occurs. We check all the options one by one.

(a) $P(M) + P(N) - 2\,P(M\cap N)$
$= [P(M) + P(N) - P(M\cap N)] - P(M\cap N)$
$= P(M\cup N) - P(M\cap N)$
$=$ Prob. that exactly one of M and N occurs.

(b) $P(M) + P(N) - P(M\cap N) = P(M\cup N) =$ Prob. that at least one of M and N occurs.

(c) $P(M^c) + P(N^c) - 2P(M^c\cap N^c)$
$= 1 - P(M) + 1 - P(N) - 2P(M\cup N)^c$
$= 2 - P(M) - P(N) - 2[1 - P(M\cup N)]$
$= 2 - P(M) - P(N) - 2 + 2P(M\cup N)$
$= P(M\cup N) + P(M\cup N) - P(M) - P(N)$
$= P(M\cup N) - P(M\cap N)$
$=$ Prob. that exactly one of M and N occurs.

(d) $P(M\cap N^c) + P(M^c\cap N)$
$=$ Prob that M occurs but not N or prob that M does not occur but N occurs.
$=$ Prob. that exactly one of M and N occurs.
Thus we can conclude that (a), (c) and (d) are the correct options.

**15.** **(a, b, c)** We know that,
$$P(A\cap B) = P(A) + P(B) - P(A\cup B) \qquad ...(1)$$
Also $P(A\cup B) \leq 1$
$$\Rightarrow -P(A\cup B) \geq -1 \qquad ...(2)$$
$\therefore \quad P(A\cap B) \geq P(A) + P(B) - 1$ [Using (1) and (2)]
$\therefore \quad$ (a) is true.
Again $P(A\cup B) \geq 0$
$$\Rightarrow \quad -P(A\cup B) \leq 0 \qquad ...(3)$$
$$\Rightarrow \quad P(A\cap B) \leq P(A) + P(B) \qquad \text{[Using (1) and (3)]}$$
$\therefore \quad$ (b) is also correct.
From (1) (c) is true. and (d) is not correct.

**16.** **(a, d)** Let $P(E) = x$ and $P(F) = y$

According to the ques $P(E\cap F) = \dfrac{1}{12}$

As E and F are independent events
$\therefore \quad P(E\cap F) = P(E)\,P(F)$

$$\Rightarrow \quad \frac{1}{12} = xy$$

$$\Rightarrow \quad xy = \frac{1}{12} \qquad ...(1)$$

Also $P(\overline{E}\cap\overline{F}) = P(\overline{E\cup F}) = 1 - P(E\cup F)$

$$\Rightarrow \quad \frac{1}{2} = 1 - [P(E) + P(F) - P(E)P(F)]$$

$$\Rightarrow \quad x + y - xy = \frac{1}{2}$$

$$\Rightarrow \quad x + y = \frac{7}{12} \qquad ...(2)$$

Solving (1) and (2) we get

either $x = \dfrac{1}{3}$ and $y = \dfrac{1}{4}$

or $\qquad x = \dfrac{1}{4}$ and $\qquad y = \dfrac{1}{3}$

$\therefore \quad$ (a) and (b) are the correct options.

**17.(a, b)** Let A = {minimum of the chosen number is 3)
and B = {maximum of the chosen number is 7}
$\therefore$ P(A) = probability of choosing 3 and two other numbers from 4 to 10.

$$= \frac{{}^{7}C_2}{{}^{10}C_3} = \frac{\dfrac{7.6}{1.2}}{\dfrac{10.9.8}{1.2.3}} = \frac{7}{40}$$

P(B) = probability of choosing 7 and two other numbers from 1 to 6

$$= \frac{{}^{6}C_2}{{}^{10}C_3} = \frac{\dfrac{6.5}{1.2}}{\dfrac{10.9.8}{1.2.3}} = \frac{1}{8}$$

Now, $P(A\cap B) =$ Probability of choosing 3 and 7 and one other number from 4 to 6.

$$= \frac{3}{{}^{10}C_3} = \frac{3}{\dfrac{10.9.8}{1.2.3}} = \frac{1}{40}$$

$\therefore \quad P(A\cup B) = P(A) + P(B) - P(A\cap B)$

$$= \frac{7}{40} + \frac{1}{8} - \frac{1}{40} = \frac{11}{40} < \frac{11}{30}$$

but $\dfrac{11}{40} > \dfrac{11}{50}$ and $\dfrac{11}{40} > \dfrac{11}{60}$

**18.** **(a)** $\because P(A \cup B \cup C) = P(A) + P(B) + P(C)$
$$-P(A \cap B) - P(B \cap C)$$
$$-P(A \cap C) + P(A \cap B \cap C)$$
Using all the given values we get that $P(B \cap C) \in (0.23, 0.48)$.

**19.** **(c)** We have
$$P(A \cup B) \geq \max \{P(A), P(B)\} = \frac{2}{3}$$
or $\quad P(A \cup B) \geq \frac{2}{3}$
$$P(A \cap B) = P(A) + P(B) - P(A \cup B) \geq P(A) + P(B) - 1$$
$$= \quad \frac{1}{2} + \frac{2}{3} - 1$$
$$= \quad \frac{1}{6}$$
or $\quad P(A \cap B) \geq \frac{1}{6} \qquad ....(i)$
and $\quad P(A \cap B) \leq \min\{P(A), P(B)\} = \frac{1}{2}$
$\therefore \quad P(A \cap B) \leq \frac{1}{2}$
From Eqs. (i) and (ii), we get
$$\frac{1}{6} \leq P(A \cap B) \leq \frac{1}{2}$$

**20.** **1** If $A$, $B$, $C$ represent events that the student is sucessful in tests I, II, III respectively. Then
$P$(The student is successful )
$$= P\left[(A \cap B \cap \bar{C}) \cup (A \cap \bar{B} \cap C) \cup (A \cap B \cap C)\right]$$
$$= P(A \cap B \cap \bar{C}) + P(A \cap \bar{B} \cap C) + P(A \cap B \cap C)$$
$$= P(A)P(B)\,P(\bar{C}) + P(A)\,P(\bar{B})\,P(C) + P(A)\,P(B)\,P(C)$$
$$[\because A, B, C, \text{ are independent events}]$$
$$= pq\left(1 - \frac{1}{2}\right) + p(1-q)\frac{1}{2} + pq\frac{1}{2} = pq + \frac{1}{2}p - \frac{1}{2}pq$$
$$= \frac{1}{2}(pq + p)$$
$$\therefore \quad \frac{1}{2}p(1+q) = \frac{1}{2} \Rightarrow p(1+q) = 1$$

**21.** **1**
Here, $P(A \cup B) = \frac{3}{5}$ and $P(A \cap B) = \frac{1}{5}$
So from the addition theorem,
$$\frac{3}{5} = P(A) + P(B) - \frac{1}{5}$$

or $\quad \frac{4}{5} = 1 - P(A') + 1 - P(B')$
$$\therefore \quad P(A') + P(B') = 2 - \frac{4}{5} = \frac{6}{5}$$
Thus, $M = 6$, $N = 5$
$\Rightarrow \quad M - N = 1$

**22.** **2**
Probability that exactly one event out of A and B occur is $P(A) + P(B) - 2P(A \cap B)$
$\therefore P(A) + P(B) - 2P(A \cap B) = 1 - a \qquad ...(1)$
Similarly, $\quad P(B) + P(C) - 2P(B \cap C) = 1 - 2a \quad ...(2)$
and $\quad P(C) + P(A) - 2P(C \cap A) = 1 - a \qquad ......(3)$
Now, Probability that at least one out of A, B, C will occur is
$$P(A \cup B \cup C) = P(A) + P(B) + P(C) - P(A \cap B)$$
$$- P(B \cap C) - P(C \cap A) + P(A \cap B \cap C)$$
$$= \frac{1}{2}\Big[\{P(A) + P(B) - 2P(A \cap B)\} + \{P(B) + P(C) - 2P(B \cap C)\}$$
$$+ \{P(C) + P(A) - 2P(C \cap A)\}\Big] + P(A \cap B \cap C)$$
$$= \frac{1}{2}\Big[(1-a) + (1-2a) + (1-a)\Big] + a^2$$
$$= a^2 - 2a + \frac{3}{2} = a^2 - 2a + 1 + \frac{1}{2} = (a-1)^2 + \frac{1}{2} > \frac{1}{2}$$
$$[\because a \neq 1]$$
Thus $x = 2$

**23.** **7**
$$P(A \cup B) = P(A) + P(B) - P(A \cap B);$$
$$\Rightarrow \frac{3}{4} = 1 - P(\bar{A}) + P(B) - \frac{1}{4}$$
$$\Rightarrow 1 = 1 - \frac{2}{3} + P(B) \Rightarrow P(B) = \frac{2}{3};$$
Now, $P(\bar{A} \cap B) = P(B) - P(A \cap B) = \frac{2}{3} - \frac{1}{4} = \frac{5}{12}.$
Thus $W = 5$, $Z = 12$
$\Rightarrow Z - W = 7$

**24.** **4**
Since the events are mutually exclusive (if a card is King it cannot be Queen and vice versa) $\therefore$ the probability of drawing a King is 4/52 and similarly of drawing a Queen is 4/52 (as there are 4 Kings and 4 Queens in the pack) The probability that the card is either a King or a Queen is
$$P(A \text{ or } B) = P(A) + P(B) = \frac{4}{52} + \frac{4}{52} = \frac{2}{13}.$$
Thus $26X = 26\left(\frac{2}{13}\right) = 4$

1.  (a)  $\sim p \vee q$ means $F \vee F = F$,

$\sim r$ means $F(\sim p \vee q) \wedge \sim r$ means F.

$\because [(\sim p \vee q) \wedge \sim r] \Rightarrow p$ means T

$[\because$ in $p \Rightarrow q$ we have FTT]

2.  (a)  $p \Rightarrow q$ is false only when p is true and q is false.

$\therefore p \Rightarrow q$ is false when p is true and $q \vee r$ is false, and $q \vee r$ is false when both q and r are false.

Hence, truth values of p, q and r are respectively T, F, F.

3.  (d)  $p \Rightarrow (\sim p \vee q)$ is false means p is true and $\sim p \vee q$ is false.

$\Rightarrow$ p is true and both $\sim p$ and q are false.

$\Rightarrow$ p is true and q is false.

4.  (b)  p : A number is a prime

q : It is odd

We have $p \Rightarrow q$

The inverse of $p \Rightarrow q$ is $\sim p \Rightarrow \sim q$

i.e., If a number is not a prime then it is not odd.

5.  (c)  p : we control population. q : we prosper.

$\therefore$ we have $p \Rightarrow q$

Its negation is $\sim (p \Rightarrow q)$ i.e., $p \wedge \sim q$

i.e., we control population but we do not prosper.

6.  (c)  $p \Rightarrow q$ is false, when p is true and q is false.

Since q, r are false, $\therefore q \vee r$ is false.

Since r is false, $\therefore \sim r$ is true

Since $p \wedge \sim r$ is true, $\therefore$ p is true.

7.  (c)  Let $p : 2 + 3 = 5, q : 8 < 10$

Given proposition is : $p \wedge q$

Its negation is $\sim (p \wedge q) = \sim p \vee \sim q$

$\therefore$ we have $2 + 3 \neq 5$ or $8 \not< 10$

8.  (a)

| p | q | $\sim p$ | $\sim q$ | $p \wedge \sim q$ | $\sim p \vee q$ | $(p \wedge \sim q) \wedge (\sim p \vee q)$ |
|---|---|---|---|---|---|---|
| T | T | F | F | F | T | F |
| T | F | F | T | T | F | F |
| F | T | T | F | F | T | F |
| F | F | F | T | F | T | F |

Clearly, $(p \wedge \sim q) \wedge (p \vee \sim q)$ is a contradiction.

9.  (c)

| p | $\sim p$ | $p \Rightarrow \sim p$ | $\sim p \Rightarrow p$ | $(p \Rightarrow \sim p) \wedge (\sim p \Rightarrow p)$ |
|---|---|---|---|---|
| T | F | F | T | F |
| F | T | T | F | F |

Clearly, $(p \Rightarrow \sim p) \wedge (\sim p \Rightarrow q)$ is a contradiction.

10. (a)  $\sim [p \vee (\sim p \vee q)] \equiv \sim p \wedge \sim (\sim p \vee q)$

$\equiv \sim p \wedge (\sim (\sim p) \wedge \sim q) \equiv \sim p \wedge (p \wedge \sim q)$

11. (c)  $\sim [(p \wedge q) \to (\sim p \vee r)]$

$\equiv (p \wedge q) \vee [\sim (\sim p \vee r)] \equiv (p \wedge q) \wedge (p \wedge \sim r)$

12. (b)  Let p : Paris is in France, q : London is in England

$\therefore$ we have $p \wedge q$

Its negation is $\sim (p \wedge q) = \sim p \vee \sim q$

i.e Paris is not in France or London is not in England.

13. (a)  $\sim ((\sim p) \wedge q) \equiv \sim (\sim p) \vee \sim q \equiv p \vee (\sim q)$

14. (c)  Contrapositive of $p \Rightarrow q$ is $\sim q \Rightarrow \sim p$

$\therefore$ contrapositive of $(p \vee q) \Rightarrow r$ is

$\sim r \Rightarrow \sim (p \vee q)$ i.e. $\sim r \Rightarrow (\sim p \wedge \sim q)$

15. (b)  $p \wedge q$ : It is a cold day and temperature is $5^{\circ}C$.

So, $\sim (p \wedge q)$ : It is not true that it is a cold day and temperature is $5^{\circ}C$.

16. (b)  Here, $\sim q$ : It is not raining;

$r \wedge p$ : It is cold and today is Tuesday.

So, $\sim q \Rightarrow (r \wedge p)$ follows

(b) as $\Rightarrow$ stands for then.

17. (b)  $p \wedge (-q)$ stands for Anil and Ram are both rich .

So, $\sim [p \wedge (-q)]$ is the required symbolic form.

18. (a,b,d)  Mathematics is interesting is not a logical sentence. It may be interesting for some persons and may not be interesting for others.

$\therefore$ This is not a proposition.

19. (a,b,d)  $\sim (p \Rightarrow q) \equiv p \wedge \sim q$

$\therefore \sim (\sim p \Rightarrow \sim q) \equiv \sim p \wedge \sim (\sim q) \equiv \sim p \wedge q$

Thus $\sim (\sim p \Rightarrow \sim q) \equiv \sim p \wedge q$

20. (b,c,d)

| p | q | $p \wedge q$ | $p \vee q$ | $\sim (p \vee q)$ | $(p \wedge q) \wedge \sim (p \vee q)$ |
|---|---|---|---|---|---|
| T | T | T | T | F | F |
| T | F | F | T | F | F |
| F | T | F | T | F | F |
| F | F | F | F | T | F |

$\therefore (p \wedge q) \wedge (\sim (p \vee q))$ is a contradiction.

21. (a,c,d)  $p \Rightarrow q$ is logically equivalent to $\sim q \Rightarrow \sim p$

$\therefore (p \Rightarrow q) \Leftrightarrow (\sim q \Rightarrow \sim p)$ is a tautology but not a contradiction.

22. (d)  The statement contains "and" but not as a connective.

23. (a)  Define the statements

p = It is cloudy tonight

q = It will rain tomorrow

r = I shall be on leave tomorrow

The assumptions are $p \Rightarrow q, q \Rightarrow r$ and the conclusion is $p \Rightarrow r$, validity can be checked using truth table.

24. (a)  Truth table has been given below :

| p | q | $\sim p$ | $p \vee q$ | $(p \vee q) \wedge \sim p$ | $\sim p \wedge q$ |
|---|---|---|---|---|---|
| T | T | F | T | F | F |
| T | F | F | T | F | F |
| F | T | T | T | T | T |
| F | F | T | F | F | F |

**1.** **(d)** Putting $y = 1$ in the given relation.

$$2f(x) = f(x) + [f(1)]^x \Rightarrow f(x) = (f(1))^x = a^x$$

Now, $\sum_{i=l}^{n} f(i) = a + a^2 + a^3 + \dots + a^n = \dfrac{a(a^n - 1)}{a - 1}$

$$\therefore (a-1)\sum_{i-l}^{n} f(i) = a^{n+1} - a$$

**2.** **(d)** Since codomain $= \left[0, \dfrac{\pi}{2}\right)$

$\therefore$ for $f$ to be onto, range $= \left[0, \dfrac{\pi}{2}\right)$

This is possible only when $x^2 + x + a \geq 0$

$\therefore 1^2 - 4a \leq 0 \Rightarrow a \geq \dfrac{1}{4}$ $\because$ for $a > \dfrac{1}{4}$, range will not

be entire $\left[0, \dfrac{\pi}{2}\right)$; So $a = \dfrac{1}{4}$

**3.** **(d)** $f(x) = x^2$ is many one as $f(1) = f(-1) = 1$
Also f is into as $-$ ve real number have no preimage.
$\therefore$ F is neither injective nor surjective.

**4.** **(c)** Let $h(x) = |x|$ then
$g(x) = |f(x)| = |h(f(x)|$
Since composition of two continuous function is continues, g is continuous if f is continuous.

**5.** **(a)** Given that
$f(x) = 2x + \sin x$, $x \in R$
$\Rightarrow f'(x) = 2 \cos x$
but $-1 \leq \cos x \leq 1$
$\Rightarrow 1 \leq 2 + \cos x \leq 3$
$\Rightarrow 1 \leq 2 + \cos x \leq 3$
$\therefore f'(x) > 0$, $\forall x \in R$
$\Rightarrow f(x)$ is strictly increasing and hence one one
Also as $x \to \infty$, $f(x) \to \infty$ and $x \to -\infty$, $f(x) - \infty$
$\therefore$ Range of $f(x) = R =$ domain of $f(x) \Rightarrow f(x)$ is onto.
Thus, $f(x)$ is one one and onto.

**6.** **(d)** We have $f \circ g(x) = f(g(x)) = \sin(\ln |x|)$
$\therefore R_1 = \{u : -1 \leq u \leq 1\}$
$(\because -1 \leq \sin \theta \leq 1, \forall \theta)$
Also $g \circ f(x) = g(f(x)) = \ln |\sin x|$
$\therefore 0 < |\sin x| \leq 1$
$\Rightarrow -\infty < \ln |\sin x| \leq 0$
$\therefore R_2 = \{v : -\infty < v \leq 0\}$

**7.** **(d)**
**(a)** $f(x) = x^4 + 2x^3 - x^2 + 1 \to$ A polynomial of degree even will always be into
say $f(x) = a_0 x^{2n} + a_1 x^{2n-1} + a_2 x^{2n-2} + \dots + a_{2n}$

$\underset{x \to \pm\infty}{\text{Limit}} f(x) = \underset{x \to \pm\infty}{\text{Limit}}$

$$\left[x^{2n}\left(a_0 + \dfrac{a_1}{x} + \dfrac{a_2}{x^2} + \dots + \dfrac{a_{2n}}{x^{2n}}\right)\right] = \begin{bmatrix} \infty & \text{if } a_0 > 0 \\ -\infty & \text{if } a_0 < 0 \end{bmatrix}$$

Hence it will never approach $\infty / -\infty$

**(b)** $f(x) = x^3 + x + 1$
$\Rightarrow f'(x) = 3x^2 + 1 -$ injective as well as surjective

**(c)** $f(x) = \sqrt{1 + x^2}$ $-$ neither injective nor surjective
(minimum value $= 1$)
$f(x) = x^3 + 2x^2 - x + 1$
$\Rightarrow f'(x) = 3x^2 + 4x - 1 \Rightarrow D > 0$
Hence $f(x)$ is surjective but not injective.

**8.** **(b,c,d)**
**Option (a)** $\because \sin(\sin^{-1} x) = x$

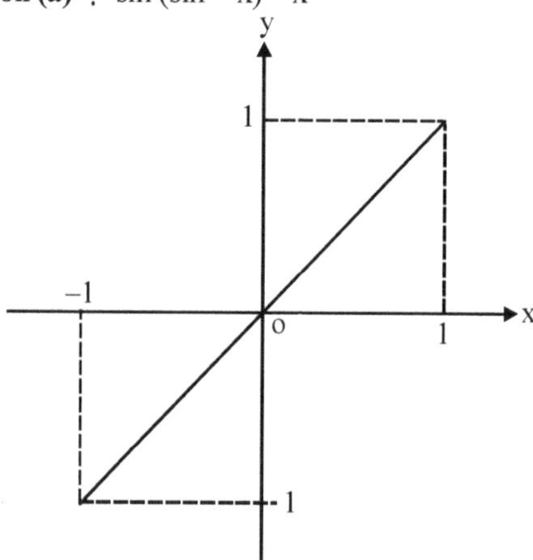

Which is bijective
**Option (b)** $\because x \in [-1, 1]$

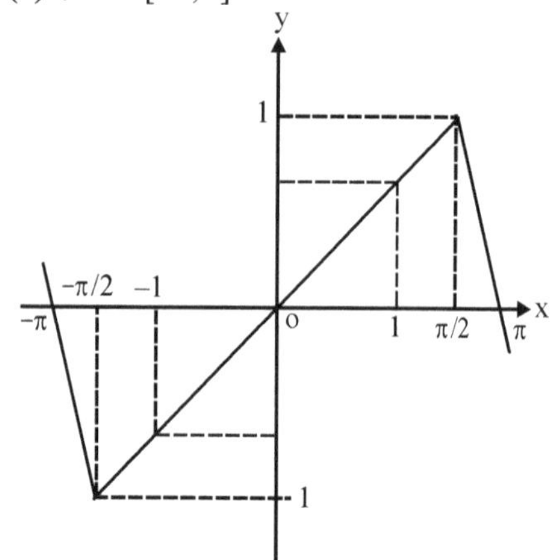

Here, range $<$ codomain
ie, not bijective.

**Option (c) :**

$$\frac{\text{Sgn}(x)}{\ln e^x} = \frac{\text{Sgn}(x)}{x} = \begin{cases} \dfrac{1}{x}, & x > 0 \\ -\dfrac{1}{x}, & x < 0 \end{cases}$$

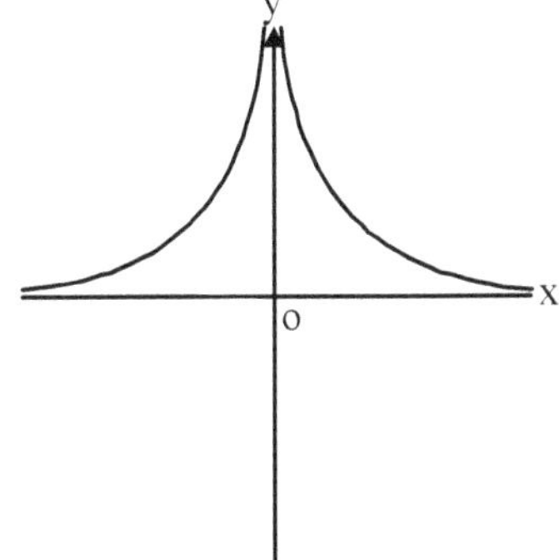

Which is many one into
ie, not bijective

**Option (d) :**

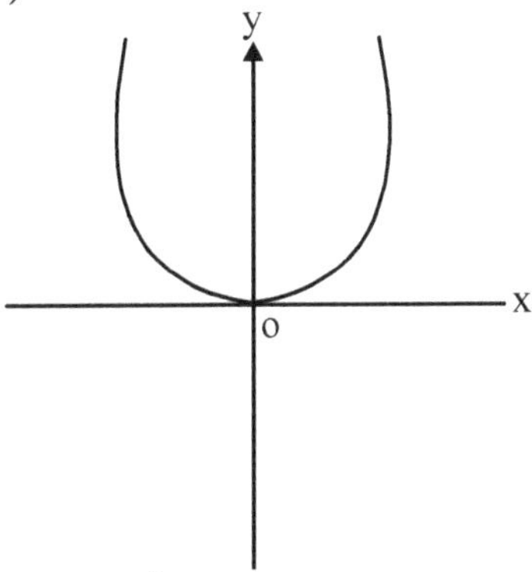

$$x^3 \,\text{Sgn}(x) = \begin{cases} x^3, & x > 0 \\ -x^3, & x < 0 \\ 0, & x = 0 \end{cases}$$

Which is many one into
ie, not bijective.

**9.  (a,b)**

$$f(x) = [x]^2 + [x+1] - 3$$
$$= [x]^2 + 1 + [x] - 3$$
$$= ([x]+2)([x]-1)$$

$f(x) = 0$, then $[x] = -2$

$\Rightarrow \quad -2 \le x < -1$

and $[x] = 1 \Rightarrow 1 \le x < 2$

many one and into

**10.  (a,b,c)**

$\because \quad f(x) = [x]$, $[.]$ denotes the greatest integer function.
and $g(x) = |x|$

Now, $(fog)\,x = f(g(x)) = f(|x|) = [|x|]$
and $(gof)\,x = g(f(x)) = g([x]) = |[x]|$

**Option (a) :**

$$(gof - fog)\left(-\frac{5}{3}\right) = (gof)\left(-\frac{5}{3}\right) - (fog)\left(-\frac{5}{3}\right)$$

$$= \left|\left[-\frac{5}{3}\right]\right| - \left[\left|-\frac{5}{3}\right|\right]$$

$$= |-2| - \left[\frac{5}{3}\right] = 2 - 1 = 1$$

**Option (b) :** $(f + 2g)(-1) = f(-1) + 2g(-1)$
$= [-1] + 2|-1| = -1 + 2 = 1$

**Option (c) :** $(gof - fog)\left(\dfrac{5}{3}\right) = (gof)\left(\dfrac{5}{3}\right) - (fog)\left(\dfrac{5}{3}\right)$

$$= \left|\left[\frac{5}{3}\right]\right| - \left[\left|\frac{5}{3}\right|\right]$$

$$= |1| - \left[\frac{5}{3}\right] = 1 - 1 = 0$$

**Option (d) :**
$(f + 2g)(1) = f(1) + 2g(1) = [1] + 2|1| = 1 + 2 = 3$

**11.  (d)**  Let $y = 1 - 2^{-x} \Rightarrow 2^{-x} = 1 - y \Rightarrow -x = \log_2(1-y)$
Therefore $f^{-1}(x) = -\log_2(1-x)$

**12.  (b)**  As $f(x) = 1 - 2^{-x}$ and $g(x) = -\log_2(1-x)$

Therefore $f(x) = g(x) \Rightarrow 1 - 2^{-x} = x = -\log(1-x)$

Now graph of $y = 1 - 2^{-x}$ and $y = x$ can intersect only
once at $x = 0$

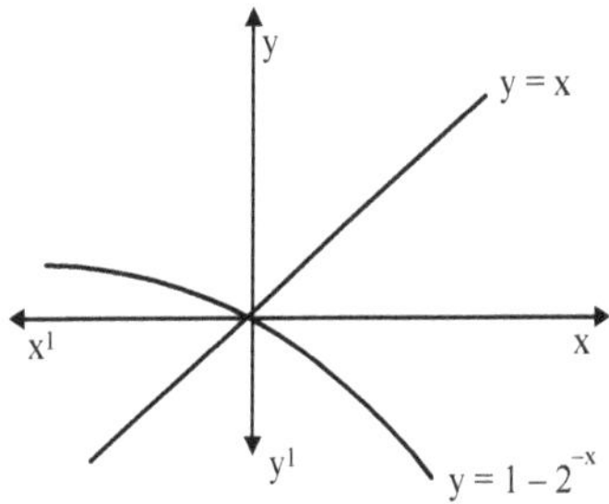


Therefore $x = 0$ is the only solution of

$$1 - 2^{-x} = -\log(1-x) \Rightarrow 1 + \log(1-x) = 2^{-x}$$

**13.  (b)**  Let $y = x^2 + 2ax + \dfrac{1}{16} = (x+a)^2 + \dfrac{1}{16} - a^2$

$$\Rightarrow x + a = \pm\sqrt{a^2 + y - \frac{1}{16}} \Rightarrow x = -a \pm \sqrt{a^2 + y - \frac{1}{16}}$$

Therefore $f^{-1}(x) = -a + \sqrt{a^2 + x - \dfrac{1}{16}} \quad (\because x > -a)$

**14.  A-p, r, s; B-r,s; C-t; D-q,t**

(A)  Put $x = y = 0$, then $2f(0) = 2\{f(0)\}^2 \Rightarrow f(0) = 1$.
Now put $x = 0$, then $f(y) + f(-y) = 2f(0)f(y)$
$\therefore f(y) = f(-y) \Rightarrow f(x)$ is even $\Rightarrow f(x)$ is many one
Again $f(0) = 1 \Rightarrow f(x)$ cannot be onto

(B)  If $x \le 0$, then $f(x) = 0 \Rightarrow f(x)$ is many one and neither
even nor odd. Clearly $f(x)$ is not onto, for example
$f(x) \ne -1$ for any $x$.

(C)  $f(x)$ is either $-x^n + 1$ or $x^n + 1$. But $f(3) = 28$.
$\therefore f(x) = x^3 + 1$, which is neither even nor odd but
one-one and onto both.

(D)  Obviously $f(x)$ is odd and $f'(x) = 2 + \cos x > 0$, so $f(x)$
is one-one.
Also,
$f(x) \to \infty$ if $x \to \infty$ and $f(x) \to -\infty$ as $x \to -\infty$,
so $f(x)$ is onto.

**15.** **(c)** $f(x) = \tan^{-1} x$, $f'(x) > 0$
for all x in the domain of f but $\tan^{-1} x$ is not one-one, it is many one.

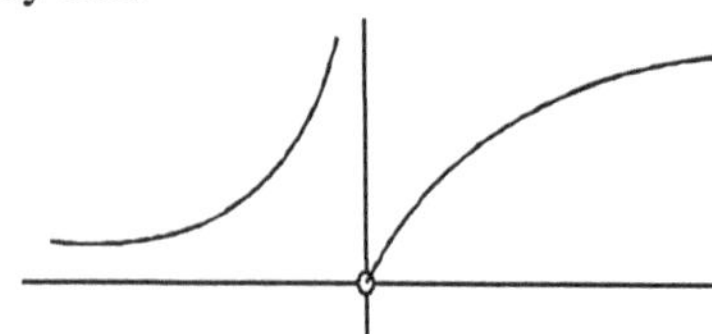

**16.** **(c)** f is injective since $x \neq y$ $(x, y \in R)$

$$\Rightarrow \log_a \left\{ x + \sqrt{x^2 + 1} \right\} \neq \log_a \left\{ y + \sqrt{y^2 + 1} \right\}$$

$f(x) \neq f(y)$
f is onto because

$$\log_a \left( x + \sqrt{x^2 + 1} \right) = y$$

$$\Rightarrow x = \frac{a^y - a^{-y}}{2}$$

**17.** **(c)** For one to one function if $x_1 \neq x_2$
$\Rightarrow f(x_1) \neq f(x_2)$ for all $x_1, x_2 \in D_f$
$\sqrt{3} > 1 \Rightarrow f(\sqrt{3}) < f(1)$ and $5 > 1 \Rightarrow f(5) > f(1)$.
$f(x)$ is one-to-one but non-monotonic

**18.** **(6)**

$(f(x)) = f(x)$ ; $f(x) = y \Rightarrow f(y) = y$
**Case-1:** range contains exactly one element it can be done in $^4C_1$ ways say 1 remaining 3 elements i.e. 2, 3, 4 can be mapped only in one ways $\Rightarrow$ total $= {}^4C_1 = 4$

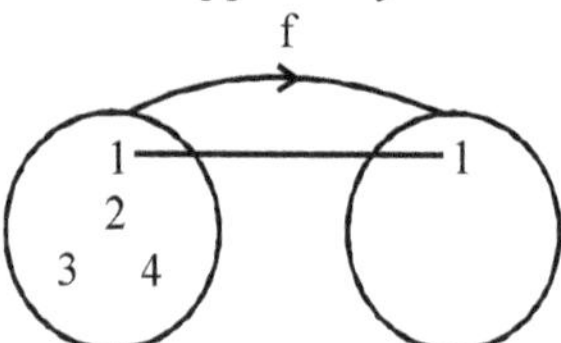

**Case-2:** range contains two elements this can this can be done in $^4C_2$ ways say 1, 2
$\therefore f(1) = 1; f(2) = 2$
remaining 2 elements i.e. 3 and 4 each can be mapped in 2 ways
Total $= {}^4C_2 \cdot 2^2 = 24$

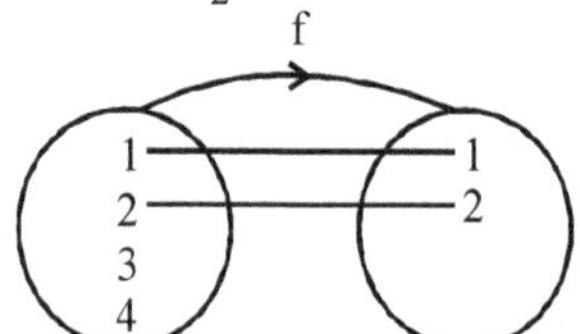

**Case-3:** range contains 3 elements which can be done in $^4C_3$ ways say 1, 2, 3
$\Rightarrow f(1) = 1; f(2) = 2$ and $f(3) = 3$
now remaining 4 can be mapped only in 3 ways.

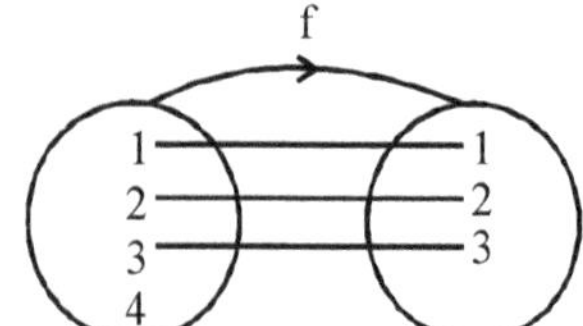

Total $= {}^4C_3 \cdot 3 = 12$ ways
**Case 4 :** range contains all 4 elements
$f(1) = 4, f(2) = 2, f(3) = 3, f(4) = 4$
only 1 way
Total $4 + 24 + 12 + 1 = 41$
Thus $P = 6$.

**19.** **(1)**

$$f(x) = \frac{\alpha x}{x + 1}, x \neq -1$$
$$ff(x)) = x$$

$$\Rightarrow \frac{\alpha \left( \dfrac{\alpha x}{x + 1} \right)}{\dfrac{\alpha x}{x + 1} + 1} = x$$

$$\Rightarrow \frac{\alpha^2 x}{(\alpha + 1)x + 1} = x$$

$\Rightarrow (\alpha + 1)x^2 + (1 - \alpha^2)x = 0 \qquad \ldots(1)$
$\Rightarrow \alpha + 1 = 0$ and $1 - \alpha^2 = 0$

$$\left[ \begin{array}{l} \text{As true} \forall x \neq -1 \\ \therefore \text{Eq.(1) is an identity} \end{array} \right]$$

$\Rightarrow \alpha = -1$
Thus, $M = 1$.

**20.** **(7)**

Let us put $y = \dfrac{\alpha x^2 + 6x - 8}{\alpha + 6x - 8x^2}$

$\Rightarrow \quad (\alpha + 6x - 8x^2)y = \alpha x^2 + 6x - 8$
$\Rightarrow \quad (\alpha + 8y)x^2 + 6(1 - y)x - (8 + \alpha y) = 0$
Since $x$ is real, $D \geq 0$
$\Rightarrow \quad 36(1 - y)^2 + 4(\alpha + 8y)(8 + \alpha y) \geq 0$
$\Rightarrow \quad 9(1 - 2y + y^2) + [8\alpha + (64 + \alpha^2)y + 8\alpha y^2] \geq 0$
$\Rightarrow \quad y^2(9 + 8\alpha) + y(46 + \alpha^2) + (9 + 8\alpha) \geq 0 \ldots(1)$
For $(1)$ to hold for each $y \in R$, $9 + 8\alpha > 0$
and $(46 + \alpha^2)^2 - 4(9 + 8\alpha)^2 \leq 0$
$\Rightarrow \quad \alpha > -9/8$
and $[46 + \alpha^2 - 2(9 + 8\alpha)][46 + \alpha^2 + 2(9 + 8\alpha)] \leq 0$
$\Rightarrow \alpha > -9/8$
and $(\alpha^2 - 16\alpha + 28)(\alpha^2 + 16\alpha + 64) \leq 0$
$\Rightarrow \alpha > -9/8$
and $(\alpha - 2)(\alpha - 14)(\alpha + 8)^2 \leq 0$
$\Rightarrow \alpha > -8/9$

and $(\alpha - 2)(\alpha - 14) \leq 0 \qquad [\because (\alpha + 8)^2 \geq 0]$
$\Rightarrow \alpha > -8/9$ and $2 \leq \alpha \leq 14$
$\Rightarrow 2 \leq \alpha \leq 14$

Thus, $f(x) = \dfrac{\alpha x^2 + 6x - 8}{\alpha + 6x - 8x^2}$ will be onto if $2 \leq \alpha \leq 14$.
Thus $P = 2$, $Q = 14$

$$\Rightarrow \frac{Q}{P} = 7.$$

**21.** **(4)**
The problem is equivalent to deragement. The required number of functions

$$= 5! \left[ 1 - \frac{1}{1!} + \frac{1}{2!} - \frac{1}{3!} + \frac{1}{4!} - \frac{1}{5!} \right] = 44.$$

Thus, $P = 4$

**22.** **(3)**
$4x^2 + 4x + 4 + \sin(\pi x) = (2x + 1)^2 + \sin(\pi x) + 3 \geq 2$.
Now as $1 < 2 < e$, the required value of $n$ is 3.

**1.** **(d)** $\tan\left(-\sin^{-1}\left(\dfrac{4}{5}\right)-\pi+\cos^{-1}\left(\dfrac{5}{13}\right)\right)$

$=-\tan\left(\pi+\sin^{-1}\dfrac{4}{5}-\cos^{-1}\dfrac{5}{13}\right)$

$=-\tan(\alpha-\beta)$ where $\sin\alpha=\dfrac{4}{5}$ and $\cos\beta=\dfrac{5}{13}$

$=-\left(\dfrac{\tan\alpha-\tan\beta}{1+\tan\alpha\tan\beta}\right)=\dfrac{\dfrac{4}{3}-\dfrac{12}{5}}{1+\dfrac{4}{3}\cdot\dfrac{12}{5}}=-\left(\dfrac{20-36}{63}\right)$

$=\dfrac{16}{63}$

**2.** **(b)** $T_n=\cot^{-1}\left(n^2+\dfrac{3}{4}\right)=\tan^{-1}\left(\dfrac{1}{n^2+(3/4)}\right)$

$=\tan^{-1}\left(\dfrac{1}{1+n^2-(1/4)}\right)$

$=\tan^{-1}\dfrac{1}{1+\left(n-\dfrac{1}{2}\right)\left(n+\dfrac{1}{2}\right)}$

$=\tan^{-1}\left(\dfrac{\left(n+\dfrac{1}{2}\right)-\left(n-\dfrac{1}{2}\right)}{1+\left(n+\dfrac{1}{2}\right)\left(n-\dfrac{1}{2}\right)}\right)$

**3.** **(a)** $\tan^{-1}\left(\dfrac{1}{2}\tan 2A\right)+\tan^{-1}(\cot A)+\tan^{-1}(\cot^3 A)$

$=\tan^{-1}\left(\dfrac{1}{2}\tan 2A\right)+\tan^{-1}\left(\dfrac{\cot A+\cot^3 A}{1-\cot^4 A}\right)+\pi$

$\qquad\qquad\left(0<A<\dfrac{\pi}{4}\Rightarrow\cot A>1\right)$

$=\tan^{-1}\left(\dfrac{\tan A}{1-\tan^2 A}\right)+\pi$

$\qquad+\tan^{-1}\dfrac{\cot A(1+\cot^2 A)}{(1-\cot^2 A)(1+\cot^2 A)}$

$=\pi+\tan^{-1}\left(\dfrac{\tan A}{1-\tan^2 A}\right)+\tan^{-1}\left(\dfrac{\cot A}{1-\cot^2 A}\right)$

$=\pi\quad\Rightarrow\quad 4\tan^{-1}(1)$

**4.** **(d)** $x=\cos^{-1}(\cos 4)$

$y=\sin^{-1}(\sin 3)=\sin^{-1}\sin(\pi-3)=\pi-3$

or $x=\cos^{-1}(\cos(2\pi-4))$

$\therefore x=2\pi-4$

$x+y=3\pi-7$

$\tan(x+y)=-\tan 7$

**5.** **(a)** $\sin^{-1}x+\cos^{-1}x=\dfrac{\pi}{2}$

and $\sin^{-1}x-\cos^{-1}x=\sin^{-1}(3x-2)$

$\qquad -\qquad\quad+\qquad\quad -$

———————————————————

$2\cos^{-1}x=\cos^{-1}(3x-2)$

Also $x\in[-1,1]$

$\cos^{-1}(2x^2-1)=\cos^{-1}(3x-2)$

and $(3x-2)\in[-1,1]$ i.e. $-1\le 3x-2\le 1$

$2x^2-1=3x-2\quad$ hence $\quad x\in\left[\dfrac{1}{3},1\right]$

$2x^2-3x+1=0\Rightarrow x=1$ or $\dfrac{1}{2}\Rightarrow$ A

**6.** **(a)** $y=\operatorname{cosec}^{-1}(\operatorname{cosec}x)\ ;\quad x\in R-\{n\pi,n\in I\}\ ;$

$y\in[-\pi/2,0)\cup(0,\pi/2]$

and $y=\operatorname{cosec}(\operatorname{cosec}^{-1}x)\ ;\ |x|\ge 1\ ;\ |y|\ge 1$

$\therefore$ range of value of $x\quad y\in\left[-\dfrac{\pi}{2},-1\right]\cup\left[1,\dfrac{\pi}{2}\right]$

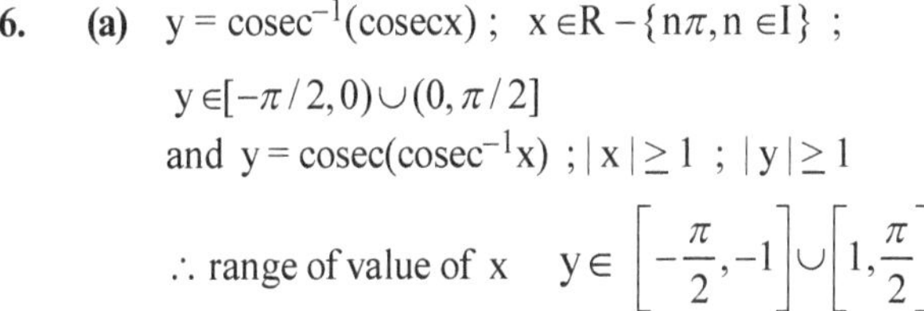
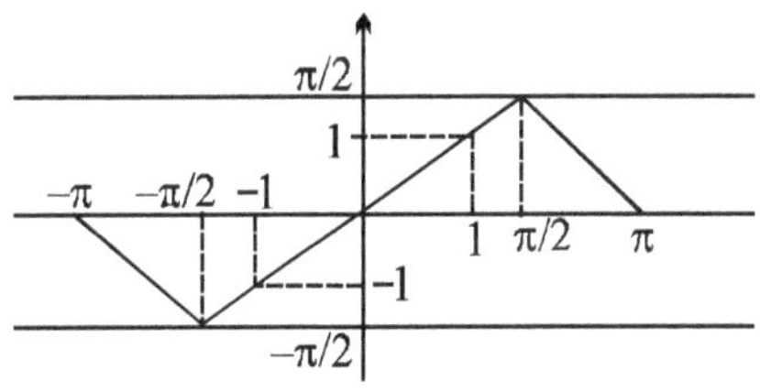


**7.** **(d)** $2\cos^{-1}\{\cot(2\tan^{-1}x)=n\pi.$

$\Rightarrow\ \cos^{-1}[\cot(2\tan^{-1}x)]=n\pi/2\ (n\in I)$

$n$ can take only three values $0, 1, 2.$

$\Rightarrow\ \cot(2\tan^{-1}x)=\cos\dfrac{n\pi}{2}=\begin{cases}0, & \text{if } n=1\\ \pm 1, & \text{if } n=0,2\end{cases}$

From $\cot(2\tan^{-1}x)=0,$

we get $\ 2\tan^{-1}x=k\pi+\dfrac{\pi}{2},$ where $k=-1$ or $0$

$\Rightarrow\ \tan^{-1}x=\dfrac{\pi}{4}\ $ or $\ -\dfrac{\pi}{4}$

$\Rightarrow x=\pm 1$

and $\cot(2\tan^{-1}x)=\pm 1\Rightarrow\tan(2\tan^{-1}x)=\pm 1$

$$\Rightarrow \frac{2x}{1-x^2} = \pm 1 \Rightarrow 1-x^2 = \pm\, 2x$$

$$\Rightarrow x^2 \pm 2x - 1 = 0 \Rightarrow (x \pm 1)^2 = 2$$

$$\Rightarrow x = \pm\,\sqrt{2} \pm 1$$

Thus, $x = \pm 1,\ \pm\sqrt{2} \pm 1$

**8. (d)** The solution of $y = \sqrt{y}$ is $y = 0$ or $y = 1$

If $\sin^{-1}|\sin x| = 1$

$\Rightarrow x = 1$ or $\pi - 1$ (in the interval $(0,\,\pi)$)

But $y = \sin^{-1}|\sin x|$ is periodic with period $\pi$, so

$x = n\pi + 1$ or $n\pi - 1$

Again if $\sin^{-1}|\sin x| = 0 \Rightarrow x = n\pi$

**9. (b,c)**

$$2x = \tan(2\tan^{-1}a) + 2\tan(\tan^{-1}a + \tan^{-1}a^3)$$

$$2x = \frac{2a}{1-a^2} + \frac{2(a + a^3)}{1-a^4}$$

$$\therefore a \neq \pm 1 \Rightarrow D \quad \left(\text{Using } \tan 2\theta = \frac{2\tan\theta}{1-\tan^2\theta}\right)$$

$$x = \frac{a}{1-a^2} + \frac{a}{1-a^2} = \frac{2a}{1-a^2}$$

$$\Rightarrow x(1-a^2) = 2a$$

$$\Rightarrow a^2 x + 2a = x \Rightarrow A$$

Hence (b) & (c) are invalid

**10. (a,b,c,d)**

(a) T domain $[-1, 0) \cup (0, 1]$ (b) T (c) T

(d) T , $\dfrac{1}{\sqrt{1+x^2}}$

(a) $y = \tan(\cos^{-1}x)$
note that $0 < \cos^{-1}x < \pi$
but $\tan(\pi/2)$ is not defined
hence $\cos^{-1}x \neq \pi/2 \Rightarrow x \neq 0$
hence domain is $[-1,1] - \{0\}$
and range is R.
The graph is as shown.

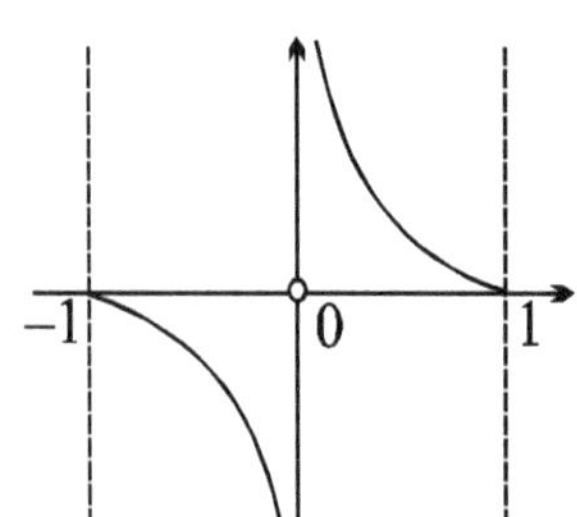

(b) $y = \tan(\cot^{-1}x)$
note that $0 < \cot^{-1}x < \pi$
$\Rightarrow \tan(\pi/2)$ is not defined
hence $\cos^{-1}x \neq \pi/2 \Rightarrow x \neq 0$
hence domain $= R - \{0\}$
since $\cot^{-1}x \neq 0,\,\pi \Rightarrow y \neq 0$

hence range is $R - \{0\}$
The graph is as shown.

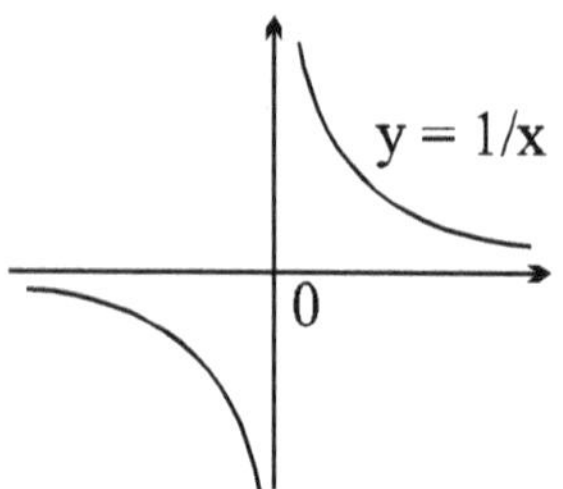


(c) $y = \sin(\tan^{-1}x)$

$$-\frac{\pi}{2} < \tan^{-1}x < \frac{\pi}{2} \ \Rightarrow y \in (-1, 1)$$

since $\tan^{-1}x$ is defined for all $x \in R$
and sin is also defined for all $x \in R$
$\Rightarrow$ domain is R

$$y = \frac{x}{\sqrt{1+x^2}}$$

The graph is as shown.

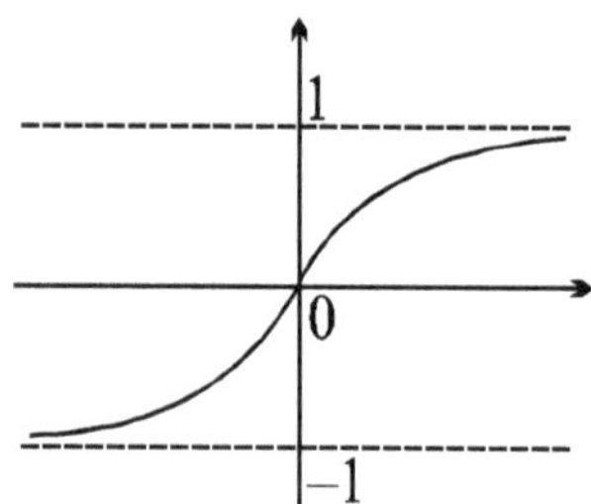


(d) $y = \cos(\tan^{-1}x)$

$$\tan^{-1} \in \left(-\frac{\pi}{2}, \frac{\pi}{2}\right) \ \Rightarrow y \in (0, 1]$$

Domain is R

$$y = \frac{1}{\sqrt{1+x^2}}$$

Note that $\sin^{-1}(\cot^{-1}x)$ also has the same graph

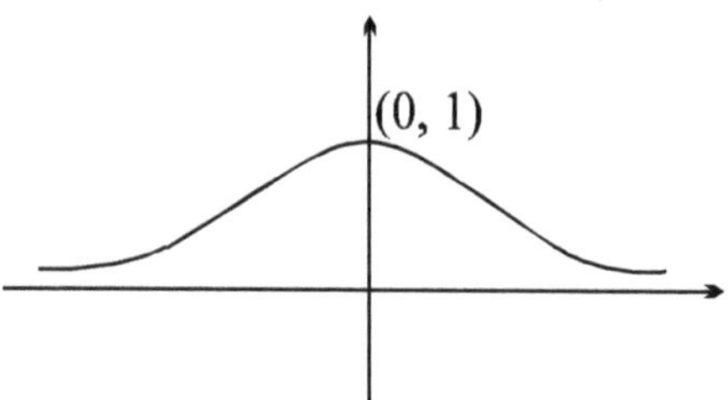


The graph is as shown.

**11. (a,b)** $\cos^{-1}x + \cos^{-1}y + \cos^{-1}z = \pi$

$$\Rightarrow \sin^{-1}x + \sin^{-1}y + \sin^{-1}z = \frac{\pi}{2}$$

$$\cos^{-1}x + \cos^{-1}y = \cos^{-1}(-z)$$

$$\Rightarrow xy - \sqrt{1-x^2}\ \sqrt{1-y^2} = -z$$

$$\Rightarrow x^2 + y^2 + z^2 + 2xyz = 1$$

**12. (a, b, d)**

$$|\tan^{-1}x| = \begin{cases} \tan^{-1}x, & \text{if } 0 \le \tan^{-1}x < \pi/2 \\ -\tan^{-1}x, & \text{if } -\pi/2 < \tan^{-1}x < 0 \end{cases}$$

$$= \begin{cases} \tan^{-1}x & \text{if } x \ge 0 \\ -\tan^{-1}x & \text{if } x < 0 \end{cases}$$

$\Rightarrow |\tan^{-1}x| = \tan^{-1}|x|, \quad \forall x \in R$

$\Rightarrow \tan|\tan^{-1}x| = \tan(\tan^{-1}|x|) = |x|, \forall\, x \in R$

Likewise, $\sin|\sin^{-1}x| = \sin(\sin^{-1}|x|)$

$$= |x| \quad \forall |x| \le 1$$

As $0 < |\cot^{-1}x| < \pi \; \forall x \in R$

$\therefore \quad \cot|\cot^{-1}x| = \cot\cot^{-1}x = x$

since $|\tan x|$ is not necessarily always equal to $\tan|x|$

**13. (d)** $\because \cos\left(\dfrac{4\pi}{3}\right) = \cos\left(\pi + \dfrac{\pi}{3}\right) = -\cos\dfrac{\pi}{3} = -\dfrac{1}{2} < 0$

$\therefore \quad \dfrac{\pi}{2} < \cos^{-1}\left(\cos\dfrac{4\pi}{3}\right) \le \pi$

$\Rightarrow \quad \cos^{-1}\left(\cos\dfrac{4\pi}{3}\right) = \cos^{-1}\left\{\cos\left(2\pi - \dfrac{2\pi}{3}\right)\right\}$

$$= \cos^{-1}\left(\cos\dfrac{2\pi}{3}\right) = \dfrac{2\pi}{3}$$

and $\sin\dfrac{4\pi}{3} = \sin\left(\pi + \dfrac{\pi}{3}\right) = -\sin\dfrac{\pi}{3} = \dfrac{-\sqrt{3}}{2} < 0$

$\therefore \quad -\dfrac{\pi}{2} \le \sin^{-1}\left(\sin\dfrac{4\pi}{3}\right) < 0$

$\therefore \quad \sin^{-1}\left(\sin\dfrac{4\pi}{3}\right) = \sin^{-1}\left\{\sin\left(\pi + \dfrac{\pi}{3}\right)\right\} = -\dfrac{\pi}{3}$

Hence, $\sin^{-1}\left(\sin\dfrac{4\pi}{3}\right) + \cos^{-1}\left(\cos\dfrac{4\pi}{3}\right)$

$$= -\dfrac{\pi}{3} + \dfrac{2\pi}{3} = \dfrac{\pi}{3}$$

**14. (a)** $\because \tan^{-1}\tan\left(-\dfrac{3\pi}{4}\right)$

$$= \tan^{-1}\left(\tan\left(-\dfrac{3\pi}{4} + \pi\right)\right) = -\dfrac{3\pi}{4} + \pi = \dfrac{\pi}{4}$$

and $\cot^{-1}\cot\left(-\dfrac{3\pi}{4}\right)$

$$= \cot^{-1}\cot\left(-\dfrac{3\pi}{4} + \pi\right) = -\dfrac{3\pi}{4} + \pi = \dfrac{\pi}{4}$$

$\therefore \tan^{-1}\tan\left(-\dfrac{3\pi}{4}\right) + \cot^{-1}\left\{\cot\left(-\dfrac{3\pi}{4}\right)\right\}$

$$= \dfrac{\pi}{4} + \dfrac{\pi}{4} = \dfrac{\pi}{2}$$

**15. (d)** $\because \sin^{-1}[\cos\{\cos^{-1}(\cos x) + \sin^{-1}(\sin x)\}]$

$$= \sin^{-1}\{\cos(x + \pi - x)\} \text{ as } x \in \left(\dfrac{\pi}{2}, \pi\right)$$

$$= \sin^{-1}(\cos\pi) = \sin^{-1}(-1) = -\dfrac{\pi}{2}$$

**16. $A \to q, t \,; B \to p, s \,; C \to q, r$**

(A) $\lambda = -\dfrac{\pi}{6} + \dfrac{\pi}{3} = \dfrac{\pi}{6}$ and $\mu = \dfrac{2\pi}{3}$

$\therefore \quad \lambda + \mu = \dfrac{\pi}{6} + \dfrac{2\pi}{3} = \dfrac{5\pi}{6}$ **(t)**

and $\mu - \lambda = \dfrac{2\pi}{3} - \dfrac{\pi}{6} = \dfrac{\pi}{2}$ **(q)**

(B) $\lambda = \pi - \dfrac{7\pi}{6} = -\dfrac{\pi}{6}$

and $\mu = \cos^{-1}\left(-\sin\dfrac{5\pi}{6}\right) = \cos^{-1}\left(-\dfrac{1}{2}\right)$

$$= \cos^{-1}\left(\cos\dfrac{2\pi}{3}\right) = \dfrac{2\pi}{3}$$

$\therefore \quad \lambda + \mu = -\dfrac{\pi}{6} + \dfrac{2\pi}{3} = \dfrac{\pi}{2}$ **(p)**

and $\mu - \lambda = \dfrac{2\pi}{3} + \dfrac{\pi}{6} = \dfrac{5\pi}{6}$ **(s)**

(C) $\lambda = \sin^{-1}\left(-\dfrac{\sqrt{3}}{2}\right) = \sin^{-1}\left(\sin\left(-\dfrac{\pi}{3}\right)\right) = -\dfrac{\pi}{3}$

$\mu = \sin^{-1}\left(\cos\left(\sin^{-1}\dfrac{\sqrt{3}}{2}\right)\right) = \sin^{-1}\left(\cos\dfrac{\pi}{3}\right)$

$$= \sin^{-1}\left(\dfrac{1}{2}\right) = \dfrac{\pi}{6}$$

$\therefore \quad \lambda + \mu = -\dfrac{\pi}{6}$ **(r)** and $\mu - \lambda = \dfrac{\pi}{2}$ **(q)**

**17. $A \to q, r \,; B \to s, t \,; C \to p, s, t$**

(A) $\because \tan^{-1}x + \tan^{-1}y + \tan^{-1}z = \pi$

$\Rightarrow \quad \tan^{-1}\left(\dfrac{x + y + z - xyz}{1 - xy - yz - zx}\right) = \pi$

$\Rightarrow \quad \dfrac{x + y + z - xyz}{1 - xy - yz - zx} = 0$

$\therefore \quad x + y + z - xyz = 0$

or $\quad x + y + z = xyz$ **(r)**

Also, $\quad AM \geq GM$

$\Rightarrow \quad \dfrac{x + y + z}{3} \geq (xyz)^{1/3}$

$\Rightarrow \quad (xyz)^{2/3} \geq 3 \quad$ or $\quad xyz \geq 3\sqrt{3}$ **(q)**

(B) $\quad \because \tan^{-1} x + \tan^{-1} y + \tan^{-1} z = \dfrac{\pi}{2}$

$\Rightarrow \quad \tan^{-1}\left(\dfrac{x + y + z - xyz}{1 - xy - yz - zx}\right) = \dfrac{\pi}{2}$

$\Rightarrow \quad \dfrac{x + y + z - xyz}{1 - xy - yz - zx} = \infty$ or $1 - xy - yz - zx = 0$

$\therefore \quad xy + yz + zx = 1$ **(t)**

Also, $\quad AM \geq GM$

$\Rightarrow \quad \dfrac{xy + yz + zx}{3} \geq (xy.yz.zx)^{1/3}$

$\Rightarrow \quad \dfrac{1}{3} \geq (x^2 y^2 z^2)^{1/3} \quad (\because xy + yz + zx = 1)$

$\Rightarrow \quad \left(\dfrac{1}{3}\right)^{3/2} \geq xyz \quad$ or $\quad xyz \leq \dfrac{1}{3\sqrt{3}}$ **(s)**

(C) $\quad \because \tan^{-1} x + \tan^{-1} y + \tan^{-1} z = \dfrac{\pi}{2}$

Then, $x y + y z + z x = 1$ (t) (from above)

and $x + y + z = \sqrt{3}$

$\because \quad (x + y + z)^2 = x^2 + y^2 + z^2 + 2(xy + yz + zx)$

$\Rightarrow \quad 3 = x^2 + y^2 + z^2 + 2$

$\therefore \quad x^2 + y^2 + z^2 = 1$

Hence, $(x - y)^2 + (y - z)^2 + (z - x)^2$

$= 2(x^2 + y^2 + z^2 - xy - yz - zx)$

$= 2(1 - 1) = 0$

$\therefore \quad x - y = 0, y - z = 0$ and $z - x = 0$

$\therefore \quad x = y = z$ **(p)**

$\because \quad AM \geq GM \Rightarrow \dfrac{x + y + z}{3} \geq (xyz)^{1/3}$

$\Rightarrow \quad \dfrac{\sqrt{3}}{3} \geq (xyz)^{1/3}$

$\therefore \quad xyz \leq \dfrac{1}{3\sqrt{3}}$ **(s)**

**18. (d)** If $x < 0$, $\tan^{-1}\left(\dfrac{1}{x}\right) = -\pi + \cot^{-1} x$

$\tan^{-1} x + \tan^{-1}\dfrac{1}{x} = \tan^{-1} x - \pi + \cot^{-1} x$

$= -\pi + \dfrac{\pi}{2} = -\dfrac{\pi}{2}$

Statement 1 is false. Statement 2 is true.

**19. (b)** In statement 1 put $x = \cos\theta$ then $0 \leq \pi \leq \pi/3$

$\text{L.H.S.} = \cos^{-1}(\cos\theta) + \cos^{-1}\left[\dfrac{1}{2}\cos\theta + \dfrac{\sqrt{3}}{2}\sin\theta\right]$

$= \theta + \cos^{-1}(\cos(\pi/3 - \theta)) = \theta + \pi/3 - \theta = \dfrac{\pi}{3}$

So statement 1 is true.

In statement 2, put $x = \sin\theta$ then $-\pi/4 \leq \theta \leq \pi/4$

So, $\sin^{-1}\left(2x\sqrt{1 - x^2}\right) = \sin^{-1}(2\sin\theta\cos\theta)$

$= \sin^{-1}(\sin 2\theta) = 2\theta = 2\sin^{-1} x$

**20. (2)**

$\tan\left\{\underbrace{\arctan(2)}_{A} + \underbrace{\arctan(20k)}_{B}\right\} = k;$

$\dfrac{\tan A + \tan B}{1 - \tan A \tan B} = k \; ; \; \dfrac{2 + 20k}{1 - (2)(20k)} = k$

or $40k^2 + 19k + 2 = 0$

$\therefore$ sum of solutions, $k_1 + k_2 = -19/40$,

$\therefore \quad -\dfrac{80}{19}(k_1 + k_2) = -\dfrac{80}{19}\left(-\dfrac{19}{40}\right) = 2$

**21. (3)**

$\tan^{-1}\left(\dfrac{x}{3}\right) + \tan^{-1}\left(\dfrac{x}{2}\right) = \tan^{-1} x$

or $\tan^{-1}\left(\dfrac{x/3 + x/2}{1 - x^2/6}\right) = \tan^{-1}x$

where $x > 0$ & $x^2/6 < 1 \Rightarrow x^2 < 6 \Rightarrow -\sqrt{6} < x < \sqrt{6}$

now, $\left(\dfrac{5x}{6 - x^2}\right) = x \Rightarrow x\left[\dfrac{5}{6 - x^2} - 1\right] = 0$

$\Rightarrow x = 0$ or $x^2 - 1 = 0 \qquad \Rightarrow \qquad x = \pm 1$

$\therefore x = \{-1, 0, 1\} \qquad \Rightarrow \qquad 3$ solution

**22. (2)**

$\tan\left[\cos^{-1}\left(\dfrac{4}{5}\right) + \tan^{-1}\left(\dfrac{2}{3}\right)\right]$

$= \tan\left[\tan^{-1}\dfrac{3}{4} + \tan^{-1}\dfrac{2}{3}\right]$

$= \tan\left[\tan^{-1}\left(\dfrac{3/4 + 2/3}{1 - 3/4 \times 2/3}\right)\right] = \dfrac{17}{12} \times \dfrac{12}{6} = \dfrac{17}{6}$

$\therefore \quad \dfrac{12}{17} x = \dfrac{12}{17} \times \dfrac{17}{6} = 2$

**23. (2)**

$\sin\left[\cot^{-1}(1 + x)\right] = \cos(\tan^{-1} x)$

$\Rightarrow \quad \sin\left[\sin^{-1}\left(\dfrac{1}{\sqrt{1 + (1 + x)^2}}\right)\right] = \cos\left[\cos^{-1}\left(\dfrac{1}{\sqrt{1 + x^2}}\right)\right]$

$$\Rightarrow \quad \frac{1}{\sqrt{1+(1+x)^2}} = \frac{1}{\sqrt{1+x^2}}$$

$$\Rightarrow \quad 1+1+2x+x^2 = 1+x^2$$

$$\Rightarrow \quad 2x+1 = 0$$

$$\Rightarrow \quad x = -\frac{1}{2}; \therefore \; -4x = -4 \times \left(-\frac{1}{2}\right) = 2$$

**Alternative**

$$\sin[\cot^{-1}(1+x)] = \cos(\tan^{-1}x)$$

$$\Rightarrow \quad \sin[\cot^{-1}(1+x)] = \sin\left(\frac{\pi}{2} \pm \tan^{-1}x\right)$$

$$\left[\therefore \; \sin\left(\frac{\pi}{2}-\theta\right) = \cos\theta \atop \sin\left(\frac{\pi}{2}+\theta\right) = \cos\theta\right]$$

$$\Rightarrow \quad \cot^{-1}(1+x) = \frac{\pi}{2} \pm \tan^{-1}x$$

$$\Rightarrow \quad \cot^{-1}(1+x) = \frac{\pi}{2} - \tan^{-1}(\mp x)$$

$$(\because \; \tan^{-1}(-x) = -\tan^{-1}x)$$

$$\Rightarrow \quad \cot^{-1}(1+x) = \cot^{-1}(\pm x)$$

$$\Rightarrow \quad 1+x = \pm x$$

$$\Rightarrow \quad 1+2x = 0 \; [1+x = x \text{ not possible}]$$

$$\Rightarrow \quad x = -1/2, \therefore -4x = 2$$

**24. (3)**

$$(\sin^{-1}x)^3 + (\cos^{-1}x)^3 = (\sin^{-1}x + \cos^{-1}x)^3 - 3\sin^{-1}x\cos^{-1}x(\sin^{-1}x + \cos^{-1}x)$$

$$= \left(\frac{\pi}{2}\right)^3 - \left(3\sin^{-1}x\cos^{-1}x\right)\left(\frac{\pi}{2}\right)$$

$$= \frac{\pi^3}{8} - \frac{3\pi}{2}\sin^{-1}x\left(\frac{\pi}{2} - \sin^{-1}x\right)$$

$$= \frac{\pi^3}{8} + \frac{3\pi}{2}\left[(\sin^{-1}x)^2 - \frac{\pi}{2}\sin^{-1}x\right]$$

$$= \frac{\pi^3}{8} + \frac{3\pi}{2}\left[\left(\sin^{-1}x - \frac{\pi}{4}\right)^2\right] - \frac{3\pi^3}{32}$$

$$= \frac{\pi^3}{32} + \frac{3\pi}{2}\left(\sin^{-1}x - \frac{\pi}{4}\right)^2$$

$$\Rightarrow \text{the least value is } \frac{\pi^3}{32}, \therefore \; \frac{96}{\pi^3}\theta = \frac{96}{\pi^3} \times \frac{\pi^3}{32} = 3$$

**1.** **(d).** Write 1 as $\sin^2\alpha + \cos^2\alpha$ etc. to get

$$\begin{vmatrix} \sin^2\alpha + \cos^2\alpha & \cos\beta\cos\alpha + \sin\beta\sin\alpha \\ \cos\alpha\cos\beta + \sin\alpha\sin\beta & \cos^2\beta + \sin^2\beta \\ \cos\alpha\cos\gamma + \sin\alpha\sin\gamma & \cos\beta\cos\gamma + \sin\beta\sin\gamma \end{vmatrix}$$

$$\begin{matrix} \cos\gamma\cos\alpha + \sin\gamma\sin\alpha \\ \cos\gamma\cos\beta + \sin\gamma\sin\beta \\ \sin^2\gamma + \cos^2\gamma \end{matrix}$$

can be factorized into 2 determinant

$$\begin{vmatrix} \cos\alpha & \sin\alpha & x \\ \cos\beta & \sin\beta & x \\ \cos\gamma & \sin\gamma & x \end{vmatrix} \begin{vmatrix} \cos\alpha & \cos\beta & \cos\gamma \\ \sin\alpha & \sin\beta & \sin\gamma \\ x & x & x \end{vmatrix} = 0$$

**2.** **(a).** Using $\to C_3 \to C_3 - (C_1 + C_2)$, $D_1 = \begin{vmatrix} a & b & a+b \\ c & d & c+d \\ a & b & a-b \end{vmatrix}$ and

$$D_2 = \begin{vmatrix} a & c & a+c \\ b & d & b+d \\ a & c & a+b+c \end{vmatrix}$$

$$\therefore \frac{D_1}{D_2} = \frac{-2b(ad-bc)}{b(ad-bc)} = -2$$

**3.** **(d).** $\dfrac{1}{abc}\begin{vmatrix} a^2+b^2 & c^2 & c^2 \\ a^2 & b^2+c^2 & a^2 \\ b^2 & b^2 & c^2+a^2 \end{vmatrix}$

use $R_1 \to R_1 - (R_2 + R_3)$

$$\frac{1}{abc}\begin{vmatrix} 0 & -2b^2 & -2a^2 \\ a^2 & b^2+c^2 & a^2 \\ b^2 & b^2 & c^2+a^2 \end{vmatrix}$$

$R_2 \to R_2 + 1/2R_1$ and $R_3 \to R_3 + 1/2\,R_1$

$$\frac{1}{abc}\begin{vmatrix} 0 & -2b^2 & -2a^2 \\ a^2 & c^2 & 0 \\ b^2 & 0 & c^2 \end{vmatrix}$$

$$\frac{1}{abc}\,[\,2b^2\,(a^2\,c^2) - 2a^2\,(-b^2\,c^2)\,]$$

$$= \frac{4a^2\,b^2\,c^2}{abc} = 4abc$$

**4.** **(d).** Multiply $R_1$ by a, $R_2$ by b & $R_3$ by c & divide the determinant by abc. Now take a, b & c common from $c_1, c_2$ & $c_3$. Now use $C_1 \to C_1 + C_2 + C_3$ to get

$$(a^2+b^2+c^2+1)\begin{vmatrix} 1 & 1 & 1 \\ b^2 & b^2+1 & b^2 \\ c^2 & c^2 & c^2+1 \end{vmatrix} = 1.$$

Now use $c_1 \to c_1 - c_2$ & $c_2 \to c_2 - c_3$
we get $1 + a^2 + b^2 + c^2 = 1 \Rightarrow a = b = c = 0$

**5.** **(b).** $\begin{vmatrix} x^4+x & x^3y & x^3z \\ xy^3 & y^4+y & y^3z \\ xz^3 & yz^3 & z^4+z \end{vmatrix} = 11$

$$\frac{1}{xyz}\begin{vmatrix} x^3+1 & x^3 & x^3 \\ y^3 & y^3+1 & y^3 \\ z^3 & z^3 & z^3+1 \end{vmatrix} = 11$$

use $R_1 \to R_1 + R_2 + R_3$

$$D = (x^3+y^3+z^3+1)\begin{vmatrix} 1 & 1 & 1 \\ y^3 & y^3+1 & y^3 \\ z^3 & z^3 & z^3+1 \end{vmatrix} = 11$$

hence $x^3 + y^3 + z^3 = 10$
$(2,1,1),(1,2,1),(1,1,2)$

**6.** **(b)** Given $\begin{vmatrix} xp+y & x & y \\ yp+z & y & z \\ 0 & xp+y & yp+z \end{vmatrix} = 0$

Operating $C_1 - p\,C_2 - C_3$

$$\begin{vmatrix} 0 & x & y \\ 0 & y & z \\ -(xp^2+2py+z) & xp+y & yp+z \end{vmatrix} = 0$$

$\Rightarrow (xz - y^2)(xp^2 + 2py + z) = 0$
$\Rightarrow xz - y^2 = 0$
[also for this D = 0 for other quad. factor in P which shows second factor is a perfect square]
$\Rightarrow y^2 = xz$
$\Rightarrow x, y, z$ are in G.P.

**7.**   **(b)**   Let

$$\Delta = \begin{vmatrix} 1+a^2 & a & a^2 \\ \cos(p-d)x & \cos px & \cos(p+d)x \\ \sin(p-d)x & \sin px & \sin(p+d)x \end{vmatrix}$$

Applying $c_1 \to c_1 + c_3$

$$\Delta = \begin{vmatrix} 1+a^2 & a & a^2 \\ \cos(p-d)x+\cos(p+d)x & \cos px & \cos(p+d)x \\ \sin(p-d)x+\sin(p+d)x & \sin px & \sin(p+d)x \end{vmatrix}$$

$$\Rightarrow \Delta = \begin{vmatrix} 1+a^2 & a & a^2 \\ 2\cos px \cos dx & \cos px & \cos(p+d)x \\ 2\sin px \cos dx & \sin px & \sin(p+d)x \end{vmatrix}$$

$c_1 \to c_1 - (2\cos dx)c_2$

$$\Rightarrow \Delta = \begin{vmatrix} 1+a^2-2a\cos dx & a & a^2 \\ 0 & \cos px & \cos(p+d)x \\ 0 & \sin px & \sin(p+d)x \end{vmatrix}$$

Expanding along $c_1$, we get
$\Rightarrow \Delta = (1+a^2-2a\cos dx)\,[\sin(p+d)\,x\cos px - \sin px$
$\cos(p+d)x]$
$\Delta \Delta = (1+a^2-2a\cos dx)\,[\sin\{(p+d)x - px\}]$
$\Delta \Delta = (1+a^2-2a\cos dx)\,[\sin dx]$
which is independent of p.

**8.**   **(a)**   $\Delta_a = \begin{vmatrix} a-1 & n & 6 \\ (a-1)^2 & 2n^2 & 4n-2 \\ (a-1)^3 & 3n^3 & 3n^2-3n \end{vmatrix}$

$$\sum_{a=1}^{n} \Delta_a = \Delta_1 + \Delta_2 + \Delta_3 + \ldots + \Delta_n$$

$$= \begin{vmatrix} 0+1+2+\ldots+(n-1) & n & 6 \\ 0+1^2+2^2+\ldots+(n-1)^2 & 2n^2 & 4n-2 \\ 0+1^3+2^3+\ldots+(n-1)^3 & 3n^3 & 3n^2-3n \end{vmatrix}$$

[∵ 2nd and 3rd column remain unchanged in each of

    $\Delta_1, \Delta_2, \ldots, \Delta_n$]

$$= \begin{vmatrix} \dfrac{n(n-1)}{2} & n & 6 \\ \dfrac{(n-1)n(2n-1)}{6} & 2n^2 & 4n-2 \\ \left[\dfrac{n(n-1)}{2}\right]^2 & 3n^3 & 3n^2-3n \end{vmatrix}$$

$$= \frac{n(n-1)}{12} \begin{vmatrix} 6 & n & 6 \\ 4n-2 & 2n^2 & 4n-2 \\ 3n^2-3n & 3n^3 & 3n^2-3n \end{vmatrix} = 0$$

[∵ 1st and 3rd column are identical]

**9.**   **(a,b).** Directly open by $R_1$ to get
   $\cos^2(\theta+\phi) + \sin^2(\theta+\phi) + \cos 2\phi$
   $= 1 + \cos 2\phi$.
   Which is independent of $\theta$

   At $\phi = \dfrac{\pi}{4}$, given determinant becomes $1 + \cos 2\left(\dfrac{\pi}{4}\right)$

    $= 1 + 0 = 1$

**10.**   **(a, b)** ATQ $\begin{vmatrix} a & b & a\alpha+b \\ b & c & b\alpha+c \\ a\alpha+b & b\alpha+c & 0 \end{vmatrix} = 0$

Operating $C_3 - C_1 a - C_2$, we get

$$\begin{vmatrix} a & b & 0 \\ b & c & 0 \\ a\alpha+b & b\alpha+c & -(a\alpha^2+b\alpha+b\alpha+c) \end{vmatrix} = 0$$

$$\Rightarrow (a\alpha^2+2b\alpha+c)\begin{vmatrix} a & b & 0 \\ b & c & 0 \\ a\alpha+b & b\alpha+c & 1 \end{vmatrix} = 0$$

$\Rightarrow (ac-b^2)(a\alpha^2+2b\alpha+c) = 0$
For non-trival solution of the equations
$\Rightarrow$ either $ac-b^2 = 0$ or $a\alpha^2+2b\alpha+c = 0$
$\Rightarrow$ either a, b, c are in G.P. or $(x-\alpha)$ is a factor of
                      $ax^2+2bx+c$

$\Rightarrow$ (a) and (b) are the correct answers.

**11.**   **(a,c).**

$$0 = \begin{vmatrix} 1+\sin^2\theta & \cos^2\theta & 4\sin 4\theta \\ \sin^2\theta & 1+\cos^2\theta & 4\sin 4\theta \\ \sin^2\theta & \cos^2\theta & 1+4\sin 4\theta \end{vmatrix}$$

$$= \begin{vmatrix} 2 & \cos^2\theta & 4\sin 4\theta \\ 2 & 1+\cos^2\theta & 4\sin 4\theta \\ 1 & \cos^2\theta & 1+4\sin 4\theta \end{vmatrix}$$

$$= \begin{vmatrix} 2 & \cos^2\theta & 4\sin 4\theta \\ 0 & 1 & 0 \\ -1 & 0 & 1 \end{vmatrix} = 2 + 4\sin 4\theta = 0$$

$\therefore \sin 4\theta = -\dfrac{1}{2} \quad \therefore 4\theta = \dfrac{7\pi}{6}, \dfrac{11\pi}{6}$ i.e. $\dfrac{7\pi}{24}, \dfrac{11\pi}{24}$

**12.** **(b,c).** As $1 + \omega + \omega^2 = 0$, the given determinant can be written as

$$\begin{vmatrix} -\dfrac{x}{\omega^2} & -y & -\dfrac{z}{\omega} \\[2mm] -y & -\dfrac{z}{\omega} & -\dfrac{x}{\omega^2} \\[2mm] -\dfrac{z}{\omega} & -\dfrac{x}{\omega^2} & -y \end{vmatrix} = x^3 + y^3 + z^3 - 3xyz$$

$$= \frac{1}{2}(x + y + z)\{(x-y)^2 + (y-z)^2 + (z-x)^2\}$$

$$= (x + y\omega + z\omega^2)(x^2 + y^2\omega^2 + z^2\omega - xy\omega - yz - zx\omega^2)$$

The determinant vanishes if either

$x = y = z$ or $x + y\omega + z\omega^2 = 0$

**13.** **(c)** $\Delta'(x) = \begin{vmatrix} 6x^2 - 6x & 5x + 7 & 2 \\ 12x^2 - 7 & 3x + 2 & 1 \\ 21x^2 - 16x & x - 1 & 3 \end{vmatrix} + \begin{vmatrix} 2x^3 - 3x^2 & 5 & 2 \\ 4x^3 - 7x & 3 & 1 \\ 7x^3 - 8x^2 & 1 & 3 \end{vmatrix}$

$\qquad a_1 = \Delta(0) = 161$

**14.** **(b)** Put $1/x = t$ in $\Delta(x)/x^4$ and write

$$\Delta_1(t) = \begin{vmatrix} 2 - 3t & 5 + 7t & 2 \\ 4 - 7t^2 & 3 + 2t & 1 \\ 7 - 8t & 1 - t & 3 \end{vmatrix}$$

$$\Delta_1'(t) = \begin{vmatrix} -3 & 5 + 7t & 2 \\ -14t & 3 + 2t & 1 \\ -8 & 1 - t & 3 \end{vmatrix} + \begin{vmatrix} 2 - 3t & 7 & 2 \\ 4 - 7t^2 & 2 & 1 \\ 7 - 8t & -1 & 3 \end{vmatrix}$$

$a_3 = \Delta_1'(0) = -73$

**15.** **(b)** $\dfrac{\Delta(x)}{x^4} = \begin{vmatrix} 2 - 3/x & 5 + 7/x & 2 \\ 4 - 7/x^2 & 3 + 2/x & 1 \\ 7 - 8/x & 1 - 1/x & 3 \end{vmatrix}$

Taking limit as $x \to \infty$, we get

$$a_4 = \begin{vmatrix} 2 & 5 & 2 \\ 4 & 3 & 1 \\ 7 & 1 & 3 \end{vmatrix} = -43$$

**16.** **(A)** $\to$ q, r ; **(B)** $\to$ r, s ; **(C)** $\to$ p, q ; **(D)** $\to$ p, q

$$\Delta = \begin{vmatrix} 2 & p & 6 \\ 1 & 2 & q \\ 1 & 1 & 3 \end{vmatrix} = 2(6 - q) - p(3 - q) + 6(1 - 2)$$

$$= 12 - 2q - 3p + pq - 6 = pq - 2q - 3p + 6 = (p - 2)(q - 3)$$

$$\Delta_1 = \begin{vmatrix} 8 & p & 6 \\ 5 & 2 & q \\ 4 & 1 & 3 \end{vmatrix} = 8(6 - q) - p(15 - 4q) + 6(5 - 8)$$

$$= 48 - 8q - 15p + 4pq - 18 = 4pq - 8q - 15p + 30$$
$$= 4q(p - 2) - 15(p - 2)$$

$$= (4q - 15)(p - 2)$$

$$\Delta_2 = \begin{vmatrix} 2 & 8 & 6 \\ 1 & 5 & q \\ 1 & 4 & 3 \end{vmatrix} = 2(15 - 4q) - 8(3 - q) + 6(4 - 5) = 0$$

$$\Delta_3 = \begin{vmatrix} 2 & p & 8 \\ 1 & 2 & 5 \\ 1 & 1 & 4 \end{vmatrix} = 2(8 - 5) - p(4 - 5) + 8(1 - 2)$$

$$= p - 2$$

(A) : When $q = 3$, $p \neq 2$, $\Delta = 0$, $\Delta_1 \neq 0$. Given equation has no solution.

(B) : When $\Delta \neq 0$ i.e., $p \neq 2$, $q \neq 3$, given system of equation has unique solution.

(C) : When $\Delta = 0 \Rightarrow p = 2$ or $q = 3$
When $p = 2$, $\Delta = 0$, $\Delta_1 = 0$, $\Delta_2 = 0$, $\Delta_3 = 0$
$\therefore$ Given system of equation has infinitely many solutions.

(D) When $\Delta = 0 \Rightarrow p = 2$, $q = 3$.

**17.** **A-q; B-s; C-r; D-q**

(A) Put $x = 0 \Rightarrow \begin{vmatrix} 1 & 0 & 0 \\ 0 & 1 & 0 \\ 0 & 0 & 1 \end{vmatrix} = f \Rightarrow f = 1$

(B) Differentiate both the sides and put $x = 0$

$$\Rightarrow \begin{vmatrix} 1 & 1 & 0 \\ 0 & 1 & 0 \\ 0 & 0 & 0 \end{vmatrix} + \begin{vmatrix} 1 & 0 & 0 \\ 1 & 1 & 0 \\ 0 & 0 & 1 \end{vmatrix} + \begin{vmatrix} 1 & 0 & 0 \\ 0 & 1 & 0 \\ 0 & 1 & 1 \end{vmatrix} = e \Rightarrow e = 3$$

(C) Put $x = 1$, then $\begin{vmatrix} 2 & 1 & 1 \\ 1 & 2 & 1 \\ 1 & 1 & 2 \end{vmatrix} = -a + b - c + d - e + f$

$\Rightarrow 4 = a + b + c + d + 3 + 1 \Rightarrow a + b + c + d = 0 ...(1)$
Put $x = -1$, then

$\begin{vmatrix} 0 & -1 & 1 \\ -1 & 0 & 1 \\ 1 & -1 & 0 \end{vmatrix} = -a + b - c + d - e + f \Rightarrow 0 = -a + b - c + d$

$-3 + 1 \Rightarrow -a + b - c + d = 2$

Solving (1) and (2), $b + d = 1$ and $a + c = -1$ ...(2)

**18.** **(a)** If the G.P. be $a$, $ar$, $ar^2$, .... then $a_n = ar^{n-1}$

$$D = \begin{vmatrix} \log a + (n-1)\log r & \log a + n\log r & \log a + (n+1)\log r \\ \log a + n\log r & \log a + (n+1)\log r & \log a + (n+2)\log r \\ \log a + (n+1)\log r & \log a + (n+2)\log r & \log a + (n+3)\log r \end{vmatrix}$$

$R_3 : R_3 - R_2$ and $R_2 : R_2 - R_1$ gives,

$$= \begin{vmatrix} \log a + (n-1)\log r & \log a + n\log r & \log a + (n+1)\log r \\ \log r & \log r & \log r \\ \log r & \log r & \log r \end{vmatrix}$$

$= 0$, since $R_2 = R_3$

**19. (c)** Statement (2) is false. We have

$$A'(x) = \begin{vmatrix} 1 & a_{12}+x & a_{13}+x \\ 1 & a_{22}+x & a_{23}+x \\ 1 & a_{32}+x & a_{33}+x \end{vmatrix}$$

$$+ \begin{vmatrix} a_{11}+x & 1 & a_{13}+x \\ a_{21}+x & 1 & a_{23}+x \\ a_{31}+x & 1 & a_{33}+x \end{vmatrix} + \begin{vmatrix} a_{11}+x & a_{12}+x & 1 \\ a_{21}+x & a_{22}+x & 1 \\ a_{31}+x & a_{32}+x & 1 \end{vmatrix}$$

Using $C_2 \to C_2 - x\,C_1$, $C_3 \to C_3 - xC_1$ in the first determinant etc. and then evaluating the determinant we obtain

$$A'(x) = \sum_{k=0}^{3} \sum_{\ell=0}^{3} A_{\ell k}$$

Integrating we get $A(x) = c + x \sum_{k=0}^{3} \sum_{\ell=0}^{3} A_{\ell k}$ where c is a constant. Putting $x = 0$, we obtain $c = A(0)$.

**20. (5)**

$$\Delta = \alpha\,\beta\,\gamma \begin{vmatrix} \dfrac{1}{1-\alpha} & \dfrac{1}{1-\beta} & \dfrac{1}{1-\gamma} \\ 1 & 1 & 1 \\ \alpha & \beta & \gamma \end{vmatrix}$$

$$= \alpha\,\beta\,\gamma \begin{vmatrix} \dfrac{1}{1-\alpha} & \dfrac{1}{1-\beta}-\dfrac{1}{1-\alpha} & \dfrac{1}{1-\gamma}-\dfrac{1}{1-\alpha} \\ 1 & 0 & 0 \\ \alpha & \beta-\alpha & \gamma-\alpha \end{vmatrix}$$

$$= \frac{\alpha\beta\gamma\,(-1)\,(\beta-\alpha)\,(\gamma-\alpha)}{(1-\alpha)\,(1-\beta)\,(1-\gamma)} \begin{bmatrix} 1-\gamma & 1-\beta \\ 1 & 1 \end{bmatrix}$$

$$= \frac{\alpha\beta\gamma\,(\alpha-\beta)\,(\beta-\gamma)\,(\gamma-\alpha)}{(1-\alpha)\,(1-\beta)\,(1-\gamma)}$$

Since, $\alpha, \beta, \gamma$ are the roots of $ax^3 + bx^2 + cx + d = 0$

$\therefore ax^3 + bx^2 + cx + d = a\,(x-\alpha)\,(x-\beta)\,(x-\gamma)$ and $\alpha\,\beta\,\gamma$

$$= -\frac{d}{a}$$

$$\therefore \Delta = \frac{\left(-\dfrac{d}{a}\right)\left(\dfrac{25}{2}\right)}{\dfrac{(a+b+c+d)}{a}} = -\frac{25d}{2\,(a+b+c+d))}$$

$\therefore$ Required value $= 25$

Thus $X^2 = 25$

$X = 5$

**21. (2)**

$$C_1 \to C_1 + C_2 + C_3$$

$$\begin{vmatrix} 1+2x+x(a^2+b^2+c^2) & (1+b^2)x & (1+c^2)x \\ 1+2x+x(a^2+b^2+c^2) & 1+b^2x & (1+c^2)x \\ 1+2x+x(a^2+b^2+c^2) & (1+b^2)x & 1+c^2x \end{vmatrix}$$

$$\begin{vmatrix} 1 & (1+b^2)x & (1+c^2)x \\ 1 & 1+b^2x & (1+c^2)x \\ 1 & (1+b^2)x & 1+c^2x \end{vmatrix}$$

$$R_2 \to R_2 - R_1 \quad \& \quad R_3 \to R_3 - R_1$$

$$\begin{vmatrix} 1 & (1+b^2)x & (1+c^2)x \\ 0 & 1-x & 0 \\ 0 & 0 & 1-x \end{vmatrix}$$

$$f(x) = (1-x)^2 = 1 - 2x + x^2$$

**22. (0)**

Given,     $au + bv + cw = 0$     ....(1)

          $au' + bv' + cw' = 0$     ....(2)

and   $au'' + bv'' + cw'' = 0$     ....(3)

For non trivial solution (non zero) solution of a, b and c.

We must have $\begin{vmatrix} u & v & w \\ u' & v' & w' \\ u'' & v'' & w'' \end{vmatrix} = 0$

**23. (2)**

$$\begin{vmatrix} x & y & a \\ a & x & x \\ x & a & y \end{vmatrix} \begin{vmatrix} x & a & x \\ y & x & a \\ a & x & y \end{vmatrix} = \begin{vmatrix} x & a & x \\ y & x & a \\ a & x & y \end{vmatrix}^2$$

$= [x\,(xy-ax) - a(y^2-a^2) + x\,(xy-ax)\,]^2$

$= [2x^2\,(y-a) - a\,(y-a)\,(y+a)\,]^2$

$= (y-a)^2\,[2x^2 - a(y+a)]^2$

Hence $D = (y^2 + a^2 - 2ay)\,(2x^2 - ay - a^2)^2$

On comparing, we get $p = 1$, $q = 1$

Thus, $p + q = 1 + 1 = 2$.

**24. (0)**

Apply $C_3 \to C_3 - C_1$

$$\Rightarrow \begin{vmatrix} \sin^2\left(x+\dfrac{3\pi}{2}\right) & \sin^2\left(x+\dfrac{5\pi}{2}\right) & \sin(2x+5\pi)\sin(2\pi) \\ \sin\left(x+\dfrac{3\pi}{2}\right) & \sin\left(x+\dfrac{5\pi}{2}\right) & 2\cos\left(x+\dfrac{5\pi}{2}\right)\sin(\pi) \\ \sin\left(x-\dfrac{3\pi}{2}\right) & \sin\left(x-\dfrac{5\pi}{2}\right) & 2\cos\left(x-\dfrac{5\pi}{2}\right)\sin(-\pi) \end{vmatrix} = 0$$

$\because$ All elements of $C_3$ are zero.

1. **(b).** Let $D = \begin{bmatrix} d_1 & 0 & 0 \\ 0 & d_2 & 0 \\ 0 & 0 & d_3 \end{bmatrix}$. Clearly $D' = D \Rightarrow A$ is correct

Also, $AD = \begin{bmatrix} a_{11} & a_{12} & a_{13} \\ a_{21} & a_{22} & a_{23} \\ a_{31} & a_{32} & a_{33} \end{bmatrix} \begin{bmatrix} d_1 & 0 & 0 \\ 0 & d_2 & 0 \\ 0 & 0 & d_3 \end{bmatrix}$

$= \begin{bmatrix} d_1 a_{11} & d_2 a_{12} & d_3 a_{13} \\ d_1 a_{21} & d_2 a_{22} & d_3 a_{23} \\ d_1 a_{31} & d_2 a_{32} & d_3 a_{33} \end{bmatrix}$

and, $DA = \begin{bmatrix} d_1 & 0 & 0 \\ 0 & d_2 & 0 \\ 0 & 0 & d_3 \end{bmatrix} \begin{bmatrix} a_{11} & a_{12} & a_{13} \\ a_{21} & a_{22} & a_{23} \\ a_{31} & a_{32} & a_{33} \end{bmatrix}$

$= \begin{bmatrix} d_1 a_{11} & d_1 a_{12} & d_1 a_{13} \\ d_2 a_{21} & d_2 a_{22} & d_2 a_{23} \\ d_3 a_{31} & d_3 a_{32} & d_3 a_{33} \end{bmatrix}$

This shows that in general $AD \neq DA$

If $d_1, d_2, d_3 \neq 0$, then $D^{-1} = \begin{bmatrix} d_1^{-1} & 0 & 0 \\ 0 & d_2^{-1} & 0 \\ 0 & 0 & d_3^{-1} \end{bmatrix}$

$\Rightarrow$ (c) is correct

2. **(a).** We have $A^2 = \begin{pmatrix} 1 & a \\ 0 & 1 \end{pmatrix} \begin{pmatrix} 1 & a \\ 0 & 1 \end{pmatrix} = \begin{pmatrix} 1 & 2a \\ 0 & 1 \end{pmatrix}$

$A^3 = A^2 A = \begin{pmatrix} 1 & 2a \\ 0 & 1 \end{pmatrix} \begin{pmatrix} 1 & a \\ 0 & 1 \end{pmatrix} = \begin{pmatrix} 1 & 3a \\ 0 & 1 \end{pmatrix}$

In general by induction, $A^n = \begin{pmatrix} 1 & na \\ 0 & n \end{pmatrix}, \, \forall \, n \in N$

3. **(d).** We have $A^2 = \begin{pmatrix} a & b \\ c & d \end{pmatrix} \begin{pmatrix} a & b \\ c & d \end{pmatrix}$

$= \begin{pmatrix} a^2 + bc & ab + bd \\ ac + cd & bc + d^2 \end{pmatrix}$

$\therefore A^2 - (a+d)A = \begin{pmatrix} bc - ad & 0 \\ 0 & bc - da \end{pmatrix} = (bc - ad)\, I$

As $A^2 - (a+d)A + kI = 0$, we get $(bc - ad)I + kI = 0$

$\Rightarrow k = ad - bc$

4. **(b).** $A \text{ adj } A = |A|\, I$

$(AB)(\text{adj } AB) = |AB|\, I$

Also $(AB)(\text{adj } B \cdot \text{adj } A) = A(B \text{ adj } B)\text{ adj } A$

$= A |B| I_n \text{ AdjA} = |B| A \text{ adj } A$

$= |B| |A| I_n$ or $|AB| I_n$

5. **(b).** $A = 3 \times 4$ ; $A' = 4 \times 3$

As $A'\,B$ is defined $\Rightarrow$ let order of $B = 3 \times n$

now $BA' = (3 \times n) \times (4 \times 3) \Rightarrow n = 4$

$\therefore$ order of $B$ is $3 \times 4$

$\therefore$ order of $B' = 4 \times 3$

order of $B'A = (4 \times 3) \times (3 \times 4) = 4 \times 4$

6. **(b).** $A - \lambda I$

$= \begin{bmatrix} 1 & 3 \\ 2 & 2 \end{bmatrix} - \begin{bmatrix} \lambda & 0 \\ 0 & \lambda \end{bmatrix} = \begin{bmatrix} 1-\lambda & 3 \\ 2 & 2-\lambda \end{bmatrix} = (1-\lambda)(2-\lambda) = \lambda^2$

$-3\lambda + 2 = 0$

i.e. for $A - \lambda I$ to be singular $\lambda^2 - 3\lambda + 2 = 0$

since $A - \lambda I$ is singular $\Rightarrow \det. (A - \lambda I) = 0$

hence $\begin{bmatrix} 1-\lambda & 3 \\ 2 & 2-\lambda \end{bmatrix} = 0$

$\Rightarrow 2 - \lambda - 2\lambda + \lambda^2 - 6 = 0$ or $\lambda^2 - 3\lambda - 4 = 0$

7. **(c).** $|A| = \begin{vmatrix} 1 & \sin\theta & 1 \\ -\sin\theta & 1 & \sin\theta \\ -1 & -\sin\theta & 1 \end{vmatrix}$

$= 1(1 + \sin^2\theta) - \sin\theta\,(-\sin\theta + \sin\theta) + (1 + \sin^2\theta)$

$= 2\,(1 + \sin^2\theta)$

$|\sin\theta| \leq 1 \Rightarrow -1 \leq \sin\theta \leq 1 \Rightarrow 0 \leq \sin^2\theta \leq 1$

$\Rightarrow 1 \leq 1 + \sin^2\theta \leq 2 \Rightarrow 2 \leq 2(1 + \sin^2\theta) \leq 4$

$\Rightarrow |A| \in [2, 4]$

8. **(c)** $A^2 = 2A - I \Rightarrow A^3 = 2A^2 - IA = 2(2A - I) - A$

$A^3 = 3A - 2I$

$A^4 = 3A^2 - 2A = 3(2A - I) - 2A$

$A^4 = 4A - 3I$

$A^5 = 5A - 4I$

$\vdots$

$A^n = nA - (n-1)I$

9. **(a,b,d)** We have $A(A + I) = -2I$

$\Rightarrow |A(A+I)| = |-2I| \Rightarrow |A||A+I| = 2 \neq 0$

Thus, $|A| \neq 0$

Also, $A\left\{-\dfrac{1}{2}(A+I)\right\} = I$

$\Rightarrow A^{-1} = -\dfrac{1}{2}(A+I)$

Clearly $A \neq O$ for otherwise $|A| = 0$

**10.** **(a,b,c).** Let We have

$|A| = \begin{vmatrix} a_1 & a_2 & a_3 \\ a_4 & a_5 & a_6 \\ a_5 & a_6 & a_7 \end{vmatrix} = \begin{vmatrix} a_1 & a_2 & a_3 \\ 3d & 3d & 3d \\ d & d & d \end{vmatrix} = 0$

[ Using $R_3 \to R_3 - R_2$, and $R_2 \to R_2 - R_1$ ]

$\Rightarrow A$ is singular

$\therefore$ The given system of homogeneous equations has infinite number of solutions.

Also $|B| = a_1^2 + a_2^2 \neq 0$. Thus B is non- singular

**11.** **(a,b,d).** $A^2 = \begin{bmatrix} 1 & 2 & 2 \\ 2 & 1 & 2 \\ 2 & 2 & 1 \end{bmatrix}\begin{bmatrix} 1 & 2 & 2 \\ 2 & 1 & 2 \\ 2 & 2 & 1 \end{bmatrix} = \begin{bmatrix} 9 & 8 & 8 \\ 8 & 9 & 8 \\ 8 & 8 & 9 \end{bmatrix}$

We have $A^2 - 4A - 5I_3$

$= \begin{bmatrix} 9 & 8 & 8 \\ 8 & 9 & 8 \\ 8 & 8 & 9 \end{bmatrix} - 4\begin{bmatrix} 1 & 2 & 2 \\ 2 & 1 & 2 \\ 2 & 2 & 1 \end{bmatrix} - 5\begin{bmatrix} 1 & 0 & 0 \\ 0 & 1 & 0 \\ 0 & 0 & 1 \end{bmatrix} = O$

$\Rightarrow 5I_3 = A^2 - 4A = A(A - 4I_3)$

$\Rightarrow I_3 = A\left[\dfrac{1}{5}(A - 4I_3)\right] \Rightarrow A^{-1} = \dfrac{1}{5}(A - 4I_3)$

Note that $|A| = 5$. Since $|A^3| = |A|^3 = 5^3 \neq 0$, $A^3$ is invertible Similarly, $A^2$ is invertible

**12.** **(a, b)** For simiplicity we just consider a fourth order matrix, then

$A = \begin{bmatrix} 0 & -1 & -8 & -15 \\ 1 & 0 & -5 & -12 \\ 8 & 5 & 0 & -7 \\ 15 & 12 & 7 & 0 \end{bmatrix}$

which is a skew-symmetric. Also,

$|A| = (1 \times 5 - 8 \times 12 + 7 \times 15)^2 = $ perfect square.

**13. (a), 14. (a), 15. (b).**

Let $A = \begin{bmatrix} a_{11} & a_{12} & a_{13} \\ a_{21} & a_{22} & a_{23} \\ a_{31} & a_{32} & a_{33} \end{bmatrix}$ and $\vec{x} = x_1\hat{i} + x_2\hat{j} + x_3\hat{k}$

$\therefore A\vec{x} = \begin{bmatrix} a_{11} & a_{12} & a_{13} \\ a_{21} & a_{22} & a_{23} \\ a_{31} & a_{32} & a_{33} \end{bmatrix}\begin{bmatrix} x_1 \\ x_2 \\ x_3 \end{bmatrix} = \begin{bmatrix} a_{11}x_1 + a_{12}x_2 + a_{13}x_3 \\ a_{21}x_1 + a_{22}x_2 + a_{23}x_3 \\ a_{31}x_1 + a_{32}x_2 + a_{33}x_3 \end{bmatrix}$

Since, $A\vec{x}$ is orthogonal to $\vec{x}$ for every $\vec{x}$ in $R^3$,

so $A\vec{x}.\vec{x} = 0$

$\Rightarrow (a_{11}x_1 + a_{12}x_2 + a_{13}x_3)x_1 + (a_{21}x_1 + a_{22}x_2 + a_{23}x_3)x_2$
$\qquad + (a_{31}x_1 + a_{32}x_2 + a_{33}x_3)x_3 = 0$

$\Rightarrow (a_{11}x_1^2 + a_{12}x_2^2 + a_{13}x_3^2) + (a_{12} + a_{21})x_1x_2$
$+ (a_{13} + a_{31})x_1x_3 + (a_{23} + a_{32})x_2x_3 = 0 \qquad \ldots\ldots (1)$

$\because$ Above relation (1) hold good for every $\vec{x}$ in $R^3$

$\qquad\qquad\qquad$ (i.e., $\forall\, x_1, x_2, x_3$)

Hence, $a_{ii} = 0\; \forall i$ and $a_{ij} = -a_{ji}\; \forall\, i \neq j$

$\Rightarrow$ Matrix A must be skew symmetric. Also order of matrix A is 3 and every skew symmetric matrix of odd order is singular.

Hence matrix A is singular also.

(i) Clearly option (a) is the only correct option.

(ii) We have $a_{13} = -2$, $a_{32} = 5$

$\therefore\; a_{31} = 2$, $a_{23} = -5$

Hence option (a) & (d) are correct.

(iii) As matrix A is skew symmetric so sum of all the elements of matrix A is zero, although matrix A cannot be uniquely determined.

We know that maximum number of distinct entries in a skew symmetric matrix of order n is $n^2 - n + 1$

$\therefore$ For n = 3, maximum number of distinct entries
$\qquad\qquad\qquad = 3^2 - 3 + 1 = 7$

As all the diagonal elements of skew symmetric matrix are zero, so trace of matrix A is also zero. Also pair of conjugate elements of skew-symmetric matrix are additive inverse of each other.

Hence option (a), (c), (d) are true.

**16.** **(A) $\to$ q ; (B) $\to$ s ; (C) $\to$ r ; (D) $\to$ p**

(A) $A^2 = -I \quad \therefore\;$ A is of even order

(B) $(I + A)^n = C_0 I^n + C_1 IA + C_2 IA^2 + \ldots\ldots + C_n IA^n$
$\quad = C_0 I + C_1 A + C_2 A + \ldots\ldots + C_n A = I + (2^n - 1)A$
$\quad \therefore\; \lambda = 2^n - 1$

(C) $A^2 = A$ and $B = I - A$
$\quad AB + BA + I - (I + A^2 - 2A)$
$\quad = AB + BA - A + 2A = AB + BA + A$
$\quad = A(I - A) + (I - A)A + A$
$\quad = A - A + A - A + A = A$

(D) $\overline{A} = A,\; \overline{B} = B$

$\quad (\overline{AB - BA}) = \overline{B}\,\overline{A} - \overline{A}\,\overline{B} = BA - AB$

**17.** **A-q; B-s; C-p; D-r**

If A is non-singular matrix then

$A\left(\dfrac{\text{Adj } A}{|A|}\right) = \dfrac{\text{Adj } A}{|A|}.A = I$

(A) $(\text{Adj } A)^{-1} = \dfrac{A}{|A|}$

(B) $\text{Adj}\,(A^{-1}) = \dfrac{\text{adj (adj } A)}{|A|^2}$

(C) $\text{Adj. }(kA) = k^{n-1}.\,\text{Adj } A$

(D) $\text{Adj (Adj } A) = |A|^{n-2}\, A$

**18.** **(a).** $A^2 + B^2 = A \cdot A + B \cdot B$

$= A(BA) + B(AB) = (AB)A + (BA)B = BA + AB = A + B$

**19.** **(b)** $A^{-1} = \dfrac{1}{\det A}\, \text{adj}A = \dfrac{1}{abc}\begin{bmatrix} bc & 0 & 0 \\ 0 & ca & 0 \\ 0 & 0 & ab \end{bmatrix}$

$= \begin{bmatrix} \dfrac{1}{a} & 0 & 0 \\ 0 & \dfrac{1}{b} & 0 \\ 0 & 0 & \dfrac{1}{c} \end{bmatrix}$

**20.** **(5)**

Given $A^2 - 4A - 5I = 0$

$A^3 = A \cdot A^2 = A(4A + 5I) = 4A^2 + 5A = 4(4A + 5I) + 5A$

$\quad = 21A + 20I$

$= \begin{bmatrix} 21 & 42 & 42 \\ 42 & 21 & 42 \\ 42 & 42 & 21 \end{bmatrix} + \begin{bmatrix} 20 & 0 & 0 \\ 0 & 20 & 0 \\ 0 & 0 & 20 \end{bmatrix} = 315 + 60 = 375$

Thus, $3P^3 = 375$

$\Rightarrow P = 5$

**21.** **(2)**

$A$ is involutary $\Rightarrow \ A^2 = I \Rightarrow A = A^{-1}$

Also $(KA)^{-1} = \dfrac{1}{k}(a)^{-1}$ ;

hence $\left(\dfrac{1}{2}A\right)^{-1} = 2(a)^{-1} \Rightarrow 2A$

On comparing we found that $P = 2$

**22** **(0)**

$|A| = 2(a-2) \Rightarrow a \neq 2$

cofactor of $0$ in $|A|$ is $2 - 3a$. According to value of $A^{-1}$,

$\dfrac{2-3a}{|A|} = \dfrac{1}{2} \Rightarrow \dfrac{2-3a}{2(a-2)} = \dfrac{1}{2}$

$\Rightarrow 2 - 3a = a - 2 \Rightarrow a = 1$

Again $c = \dfrac{\text{cofactor of } a \text{ in } |A|}{|A|} = \dfrac{\begin{vmatrix} 0 & 2 \\ 1 & 3 \end{vmatrix}}{2(a-2)}$

$\quad = \dfrac{2}{2(1-2)} = -1$

Thus, $a + c = 0$

**23.** **(6)**

Possible orders

$[(1 \times 12) ; (12 \times 1) ; (2 \times 6) ; (6 \times 2) ; (3 \times 4) ; (4 \times 3)]$

**24.** **(6)**

$BC = \begin{bmatrix} 3 & 4 \\ 2 & 3 \end{bmatrix}\begin{bmatrix} 3 & -4 \\ -2 & 3 \end{bmatrix}$

$\Rightarrow BC = \begin{bmatrix} 1 & 0 \\ 0 & 1 \end{bmatrix} = I$

$t_r(a) + t_r\left(\dfrac{A}{2}\right) + t_r\left(\dfrac{A}{2^2}\right) + \ldots$

$= t_r(a) + \dfrac{1}{2}t_r(a) + \dfrac{1}{2^2}t_r(a) + \ldots$

$= \dfrac{t_r(A)}{1 - (1/2)} = 2\,t_r(a) = 2(2+1) = 6$

**1.** **(d)** We have $y \lim_{x \to 0} f(\cos^3 x - \cos^2 x)$

$= x \lim_{x \to 0} f(\sin^2 x - \sin^3 x)$

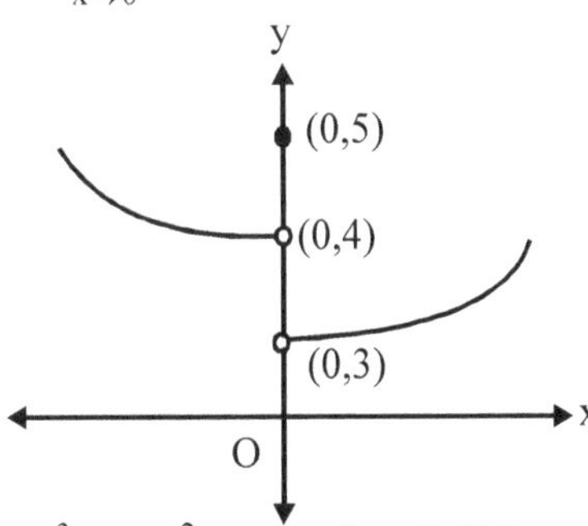

$\cos^3 x - \cos^2 x \to 0$    from L.H.S.

$\therefore \lim_{x \to 0} f(\cos^3 x - \cos^2 x) = 4$

$\sin^2 x - \sin^3 x \to 0$    from R.H.S.

$\therefore \lim_{x \to 0} f(\sin^2 x - \sin^3 x) = 3$

$\therefore$ Equation of the line is $4y = 3x$ ........(1)

Equation of line perpendicular to $y = \dfrac{3}{4}x$ and passing

$(0, 1)$, is $y - 1 = \dfrac{-4}{3}x$     ........(2)

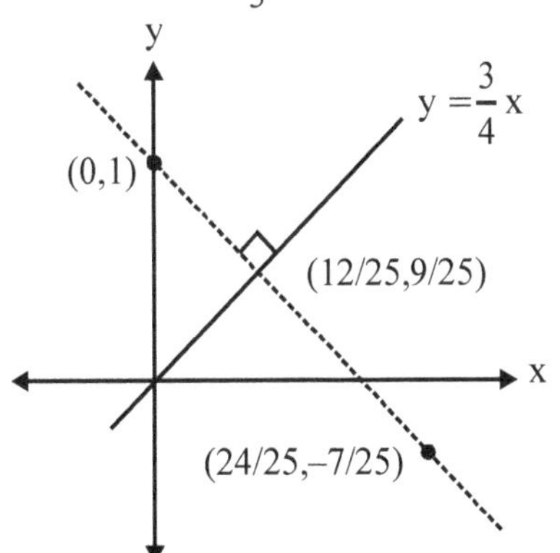

On solving eq. (1) and eq. (2), we get

$x = \dfrac{12}{25}, \ y = \dfrac{9}{25}$

Hence image point is $\left( \dfrac{24}{25}, \dfrac{-7}{25} \right)$

**2.** **(a)** $\lim_{x \to 0^+} g(x) = \lim_{x \to 0^+} f(|x|) + |f(x)|$

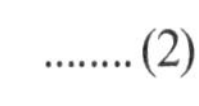

$= \lim_{x \to 0^+} f(x) + |f(x)| = \lim_{x \to 0^+} 2x + 1 + |2x + 1| = 2$

$\lim_{x \to 0^-} g(x) = \lim_{x \to 0^-} f(|x|) + |f(x)|$

$= 1 + |-1| = 2$ g(x) is discontinuous at $x = -2, -1$

**3.** **(b)** $f(0^+) = \lim_{x \to 0^+} |x|^{\sin x} = e^{\lim_{x \to 0^+} \sin x \ln|x|}$

$= e^{\lim_{x \to 0^+} \frac{\ln|x|}{\operatorname{cosec} x}} = e^{\lim_{x \to 0^+} \frac{1/x}{-\operatorname{cosec} x \cot x}}$

$= e^{-\lim_{x \to 0^+} \left( \frac{\sin x}{x} \right) \tan x} = e^{-1 \times 0} = 1$

$\therefore \ f(0^-) = g(0) = 1$

Let $g(x) = ax + b$

$\Rightarrow b = 1 \Rightarrow g(x) = ax + 1$

For $x > 0$, $f'(x) = e^{\sin x \ln(|x|)} \left[ \cos x \ln(|x|) + \dfrac{\sin x}{x} \right]$

$f'(1) = 1(0 + \sin 1) = \sin 1$

$f(-1) = -a + 1 \Rightarrow a = 1 - \sin 1$

$g(x) = (1 - \sin 1)x + 1.$

**4.** **(c)** When x is not an integer, both the functions [x] and $\cos\left( \dfrac{2x - 1}{2} \right) \pi$ are continuous.

$\therefore$ f(x) is continuous on all non integral points.

For $x = n \in 1$

$\lim_{x \to n^-} f(x) = \lim_{x \to n^-} [x] \cos\left( \dfrac{2x - 1}{2} \right) \pi = (n - 1) \cos \left( \dfrac{2x - 1}{2} \right) \pi = 0$

$\lim_{x \to n^+} f(x) = \lim_{x \to n^+} [x] \cos\left( \dfrac{2x - 1}{2} \right) \pi$

$= n \cos\left( \dfrac{2x - 1}{2} \right) \pi = 0$

Also $f(n) = n \cos \dfrac{(2n - 1)\pi}{2} = 0$

$\therefore$ f is continuous at all integral pts as well. The, f is continuous everywhere.

**5.** **(b)** For $|x| < 1$, $\lim_{n \to \infty} x^{2n} = 0$ and hence $f(x) = -1$

For $|x| > 1$, $\lim_{n \to \infty} \dfrac{1}{x^{2n}} = 0$ and hence $\lim_{n \to \infty} \dfrac{x^{2n} - 1}{x^{2n} + 2} =$

$\lim_{n \to \infty} \dfrac{1 - \dfrac{1}{x^{2n}}}{1 + \dfrac{1}{x^{2n}}}$

For $|x| > 1$, $f(x) = 0$

Thus, $f(x) = \begin{cases} 1 \text{ when } |x| > 1 \\ 0 \text{ when } |x| = 1 \\ -1 \text{ when } |x| < 1 \end{cases}$ and hence $f(x)$ is not

continuous at $-1$ and $1$.

**6.** **(b, c)** If $0 \le \sin^2 x < 1$ then $f(x) = \sec^{-1}(-1) = 0$

If $\sin^2 x = 1$ then $f(x) = \sec^{-1}(2) = \dfrac{\pi}{3}$

Thus, $f(x)$ is not continuous if $\sin x = \pm 1$ i.e,

$x =$ Odd multiple of $\dfrac{\pi}{2}$

**7.** **(a,c)**

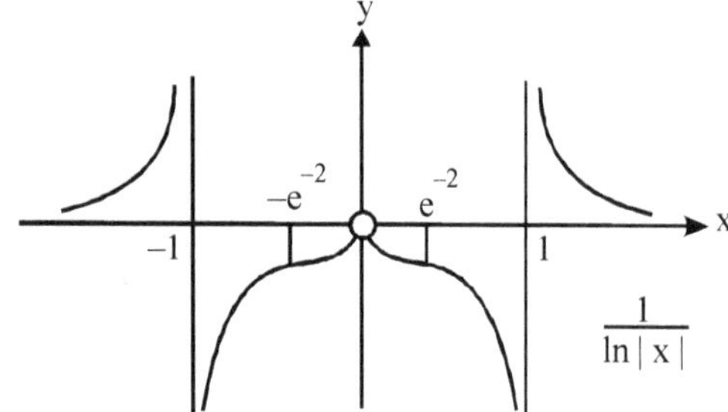

$$f(x) = \frac{1}{\ln |x|} = \begin{cases} \dfrac{1}{\ln x} & \text{if } x > 0 \\[2mm] \dfrac{1}{\ln(-x)} & \text{if } x < 0 \end{cases}$$

**8.** **(a, c)** Continuity at $x = 0$

L.H.L at $x = 0$ $\displaystyle\lim_{x\to 0^-} f(x) = \lim_{x\to 0^-} (1) = 1$

R.H.L at $x = 0$ $\displaystyle\lim_{x\to 0^+} f(x) = \lim_{x\to 0^+} (1+\sin x) = 1$

$f(0) = 1 + \sin 0 = 1$

$= $ L.H.L $=$ R.H.L $= f(0)$

so $f(x)$ is continuous at $x = 0$.

continuity at $x = \pi/2$

L.H.L at $x = \dfrac{\pi}{2} = \displaystyle\lim_{x\to\frac{\pi}{2}^-} f(x) = \lim_{x\to\frac{\pi}{2}^-} (1+\sin x) = 1+1 = 2$

R.H.L at $x = \dfrac{\pi}{2} = \displaystyle\lim_{x\to\frac{\pi}{2}^+} f(x) = 2 + \left(\dfrac{\pi}{2} - \dfrac{\pi}{2}\right)^2 = 2$

$f\left(\dfrac{\pi}{2}\right) = 2 + \left(\dfrac{\pi}{2} - \dfrac{\pi}{2}\right)^2 = 2$

$\therefore$ L.H.L $=$ R.H.L $= f\left(\dfrac{\pi}{2}\right)$

so, $f(x)$ is continuous at $x = \left(\dfrac{\pi}{2}\right)$

Hence, $f(x)$ is continuous over the whole real number.

**9.** **(d)** For any $x \ne 0$, $-1 \le \sin\dfrac{1}{x} \le 1$, but As $x \to 0$, $\sin\dfrac{1}{x}$

does not approach to any particular value but oscillates between $-1$ and $1$.

**10.** **(a)** $\displaystyle\lim_{x\to 1^+} f(x) = \lim_{h\to 0} \dfrac{h}{e^{\frac{1}{h}}+1} = 0 \qquad \left(\because \lim_{h\to 0} e^{\frac{1}{h}} = \infty\right)$

$\displaystyle\lim_{x\to 1^-} f(x) = \lim_{h\to 0} \dfrac{-h}{e^{-\frac{1}{h}}+1} = 0 \qquad \left(\because \lim_{h\to 0} e^{-\frac{1}{h}} = 0\right)$

Therefore $f(x)$ is continuous at $x = 0$.

**11.** **(d)** We have

$\displaystyle\lim_{x\to 0^-} f(x) = \lim_{h\to 0} \sin(\log_e |-h|) = \lim_{h\to 0} \sin(\log_e h)$

which does not exist but lies between $-1$ and $1$. Similarly

$\displaystyle\lim_{x\to 0^+} f(x)$ lies between $-1$ and $1$ but cannot be determined.

**12.** **A-t; B-p,q,r; C-q,s;**

(A) LHL $= \displaystyle\lim_{x\to 0-} f(x) = \lim_{h\to 0} f(0-h)$

$= \displaystyle\lim_{h\to 0} \dfrac{a+3\cos(0-h)}{(0-h)^2} = \lim_{h\to 0} \dfrac{a+3\cos h}{h^2}$

at $h \to 0$, Numerator $= a + 3$ must be 0

$\therefore a = -3$ ($\because f(x)$ is continuous)

$\Rightarrow$ LHL $= \displaystyle\lim_{h\to 0} \dfrac{-3(1-\cos h)}{h^2} = -\dfrac{3}{2}$

V.F. $= f(0) = b\tan\left(\dfrac{\pi}{3}\right) = b\sqrt{3}$

$\because f(x)$ is continuous, $\therefore$ LHL $=$ V.F.

$-\dfrac{3}{2} = b\sqrt{3} \Rightarrow b = -\dfrac{\sqrt{3}}{2}$

Hence, $a = -3, b = -\dfrac{\sqrt{3}}{2}$

$[a - 2b] = [-3 + \sqrt{3}] = -2$

(B) $\because f(x)$ is continuous in $[-\pi, \pi]$

$\therefore$ at $x = -\dfrac{\pi}{2}$

V.F. $=$ RHL

$\Rightarrow \qquad f(-\pi/2) = \displaystyle\lim_{x\to -\frac{\pi}{2}+} f(x)$

$-2\sin\left(-\dfrac{\pi}{2}\right) = \displaystyle\lim_{h\to 0} f\left(-\dfrac{\pi}{2}+h\right)$

$-2(-1) = \displaystyle\lim_{h\to 0}\left(a\sin\left(-\dfrac{\pi}{2}+h\right)+b\right)$

$2 = -a + b \qquad \text{...(i)}$

and at $x = \dfrac{\pi}{2}$

V.F. $=$ LHL

$f\left(\dfrac{\pi}{2}\right) = \displaystyle\lim_{x\to \pi/2-} f(x)$

$\cos\dfrac{\pi}{2} = \displaystyle\lim_{h\to 0} f\left(\dfrac{\pi}{2}-h\right)$

$0 = \displaystyle\lim_{h\to 0} a\sin\left(\dfrac{\pi}{2}-h\right)+b$

$\Rightarrow 0 = a + b \qquad \text{...(ii)}$

From Eqs. (i) and (ii), $b = 1, a = -1$

$a + b = 0, a - b = -2, a + 2b = 1$

$|a+b| = 0, |a-b| = 2, |a+2b| = 1$ (P, Q, R)

(C) $V.F. = f(\pi/2) = b + 3$     (i)

$$LHL = \lim_{x \to \pi/2-} f(x) = \lim_{h \to 0} f\left(\frac{\pi}{2} - h\right)$$

$$= \lim_{h \to 0} \left(\frac{3}{2}\right)^{\cot\left(\frac{3\pi}{2} - 3h\right)/\cot(\pi - 2h)}$$

$$= \lim_{h \to 0}\left(\frac{3}{2}\right)^{-\frac{\tan 3h}{\cot 2h}} = \lim_{h \to 0}\left(\frac{3}{2}\right)^0 = 1 \ \dots(ii)$$

$$RHL = \lim_{x \to \frac{\pi}{2}+} f(x) = \lim_{h \to 0} f\left(\frac{\pi}{2} + h\right)$$

$$= \lim_{h \to 0}\left(1 + \left|\cos\left(\frac{\pi}{2} + h\right)\right|\right)^{\frac{a\left|\tan\left(\frac{\pi}{2}+h\right)\right|}{b}}$$

$$= \lim_{h \to 0}(1 + \sin h)^{\frac{a \cot h}{b}} = e^{\lim_{h \to 0}\frac{a \cos h}{b}} = e^{a/b}$$

$\therefore LHL = RHL = V.F.$

$\Rightarrow 1 = e^{a/b} = b + 3$

$\therefore b = -2, a = 0$

$a - b = 2, \ a + 2b = -4$

$|a - b| = 2, | \ | a + 2b| = 4$

**13. (a)** $\displaystyle \operatorname*{Lt}_{t \to 0} \frac{1 - \cos(1 - \cos t)}{t^4} = \operatorname*{Lt}_{t \to 0} \frac{1 - \cos(1 - \cos t)}{(1 - \cos t)^2} \cdot \frac{(1 - \cos t)^2}{t^4}$

$$= \frac{1}{2} \cdot \frac{1}{4} = \frac{1}{8} \qquad \left(\because \operatorname*{Lt}_{x \to 0} \frac{1 - \cos ax}{x^2} = \frac{a^2}{2}\right)$$

**14. (c)** Since $\displaystyle \lim_{n \to \infty} x^{2n} = \begin{cases} 0 \text{ if } 0 < x < 1 \\ 1 \text{ if } x = 1 \\ \infty \text{ if } x > 1 \end{cases}$

$\therefore \ L.H.L. = f(1 - 0)$

$$= \lim_{n \to 1^-}\left[\lim_{n \to \infty} \frac{\log_e(1 + x) - x^{2n}\sin(2x)}{1 + x^{2n}}\right] = \log_e(2)$$

$R.H.L. = f(1 + 0) =$

$$\lim_{n \to 1^+}\left[\lim_{n \to \infty} \frac{\log_e(1 + x) - x^{2n}\sin(2x)}{1 + x^{2n}}\right]$$

$$= \lim_{n \to 1^+}\left[\lim_{n \to \infty} \frac{x^{-2n}\log_e(1 + x) - \sin 2x}{x^{-2n} + 1}\right] = -\sin 2$

Also $f(1) = \dfrac{\log 2 - \sin 2}{2}$

$\therefore L.H.L. \neq R.H.L. \neq f(1)$

$\therefore f(x)$ is discontinuous at $x = 1$ $\therefore$ Statement-1 is true.

But statement-2 is false $\because L.H.L. \neq R.H.L. \neq f(1)$

**15. 4**

$$f(0) = \lim_{x \to 0} \frac{e^{2x} - (1 + 4x)^{1/2}}{\ln(1 - x^2)} = \lim_{x \to 0} \frac{e^{2x} - (1 + 4x)^{1/2}}{\frac{\ln(1 - x^2)}{-x^2}(-x^2)}$$

$$= \lim_{x \to 0} \frac{(1 + 4x)^{1/2} - e^{2x}}{x^2}$$

$$= \lim_{x \to 0} \frac{\left(1 + \frac{1}{2}4x + \frac{1}{2}\left(\frac{1}{2} - 1\right)\frac{1}{2!}16x^2 + \dots\right) - \left(1 + \frac{2x}{1!} + \frac{4x^2}{2!} + \dots\right)}{x^2}$$

$$= -2 - 2 = -4$$

Thus, $P = 4$.

**16. 0**

$f(x)$ is continuous at $x = 1$

$\Rightarrow \operatorname*{Lim}_{x \to 1} f(x) = \operatorname*{Lim}_{x \to 1^+} f(x) = f(1)$

$\Rightarrow \operatorname*{Lim}_{x \to 1^-} a[x + 1] + b[x - 1] = \operatorname*{Lim}_{x \to 1^+} a[x + 1] + b[x - 1]$

$\Rightarrow a - b = 2a + 0b \Rightarrow a + b = 0$

**17. 0**

Since $|x - 1|$, $|x - 2|$ and $\cos x$ are continuous functions and the sum of continuous functions is also continuous, so the given function is continuous every where, i.e., there is no point of discontinuity.

**18. 7**

As $f(x)$ is continuous at $x = 0$,

$\therefore$ and both $f(0)$ and $\displaystyle \lim_{x \to 0} f(x)$ are finite.

$$\Rightarrow f(0) = \lim_{x \to 0} \frac{\sin 2x + A \sin x + B \cos x}{x^3}$$

As denominator $\to 0$, when $x \to 0$.

Numerator should also $\to 0$, when $x \to 0$

which is possible only if

$\Rightarrow \sin 2(0) + A \sin(0) + B \cos(0) = 0 \Rightarrow B = 0$

$$\therefore f(0) = \lim_{x \to 0} \frac{\sin 2x + A \sin x}{x^3}$$

$$\Rightarrow f(0) = \lim_{x \to 0}\left(\frac{\sin x}{x}\right)\left(\frac{2\cos x + A}{x^2}\right) = \lim_{x \to 0}\left(\frac{2\cos x + A}{x^2}\right)$$

Again we can see that denominator $\to 0$ as $x \to 0$

$\therefore$ Numerator should also approach 0 as $x \to 0$

$\Rightarrow 2 + A = 0 \Rightarrow A = -2$

$$\Rightarrow f(0) = \lim_{x \to 0}\left(\frac{2\cos x - 2}{x^2}\right)$$

$$= \lim_{x \to 0}\left(\frac{-4\sin^2 x/2}{x^2}\right) = \lim_{x \to 0}\left(\frac{-\sin^2 x/2}{x^2/4}\right) = -1$$

So, we get $A = -2, B = 0$ and $f(0) = -1$

Thus, $f(0) - 4A + B = -1 + 8 + 0 = 7$.

**1.** **(c)** $f(x) = (x-1)(x-2) \,|\, (x-1)(x-2)(x-3)\,|$

$$+ \left| \sin\left( x + \frac{\pi}{4} \right) \right|.$$

Clearly $f(x)$ is not differentible at $x = 3, \dfrac{3\pi}{4}, \dfrac{7\pi}{4}$.

**2.** **(c)** $\therefore$ f(x) is differntiable in $(0,\infty)$

hence $\lim\limits_{x\to\infty}$ f(x) must exist and is finite.

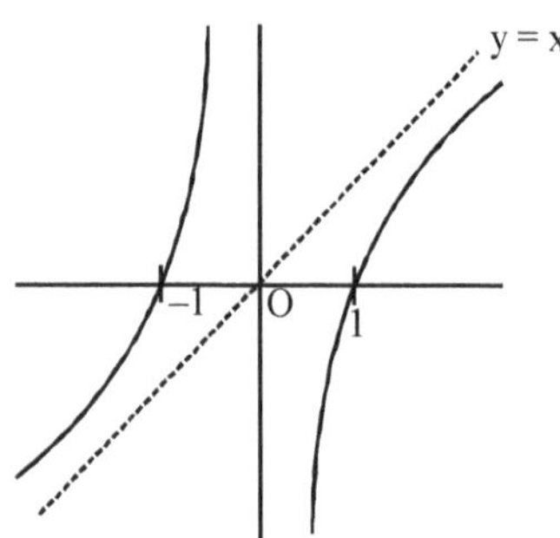


$\therefore$ y = f(x) must have a horizontal asymptote as $x \to \infty$ then only $\lim\limits_{x\to\infty}$ f(x) will exist.

If f(x) has an inclined asymptote as $y = x - \dfrac{1}{x}$

then $\lim\limits_{x\to\infty}$ f(x) $\to \infty$

$\therefore$ f(x) has a horizontal asymptote

hence $\lim\limits_{x\to\infty}$ f'(x) $\to 0$

$\Rightarrow$ (C) (also see figure for f(x) = $\tan^{-1}$ x)

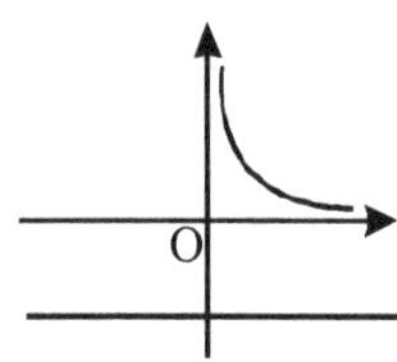

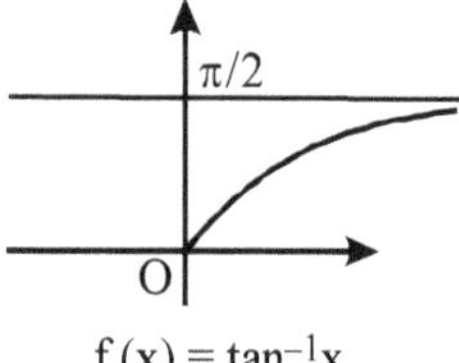


e.g. Take the example given

(i) Let f(x) = $x \sin \dfrac{1}{x}$ which is differentiable in $(0, \infty)$

$$f'(x) = \sin\frac{1}{x} - \frac{1}{x}\cos\frac{1}{x}$$

$$f(x) + f'(x) = \underbrace{\left( x\sin\frac{1}{x} \right)}_{\substack{\lim \to 1 \\ x\to\infty}} + \underbrace{\left( \sin\frac{1}{x} - \frac{1}{x}\cos\frac{1}{x} \right)}_{\substack{\lim \to 0 \\ x\to\infty}}$$

hence $\lim\limits_{x\to\infty}$ f(x) = L and $\lim\limits_{x\to\infty}$ f'(x) = 0

(ii) f(x) = $\tan^{-1}$x in $(0,\infty)$

**3.** **(c)** We have,

$$f_1(x) = 2 \sum_{r=1}^{n} \frac{\sin\left( \left( x + \dfrac{r\pi}{6} \right) - \left( x + (r-1)\dfrac{\pi}{6} \right) \right)}{\cos\left( x + (r-1)\dfrac{\pi}{6} \right) . \cos\left( x + \dfrac{r\pi}{6} \right)}$$

$$= 2 \left[ \left( \tan\left( x + \frac{\pi}{6} \right) - \tan x \right) + \left( \tan\left( x + \frac{2\pi}{6} \right) - \tan\left( x + \frac{\pi}{6} \right) \right) \right.$$
$$+ \left( \tan\left( x + \frac{3\pi}{6} \right) - \tan\left( x + \frac{2\pi}{6} \right) \right)$$
$$\left. + \dots\dots\dots + \left( \tan\left( x + \frac{n\pi}{6} \right) - \tan\left( x + (n-1)\frac{\pi}{6} \right) \right) \right]$$

$$\Rightarrow f_1(x) = 2\left( \tan\left( x + \frac{n\pi}{6} \right) - \tan x \right)$$

for n = 3, $f_1(x) = 2\left( \tan\left( \dfrac{\pi}{2} + x \right) - \tan x \right)$

$$= 2(-\cot x - \tan x) = -2\frac{1}{\sin x \cos x}$$

$$2f_2(x) = f_1(x) - 2\tan\left( x + \frac{n\pi}{6} \right)$$

$$= 2\tan\left( x + \frac{n\pi}{6} \right) - 2\tan x - 2\tan\left( x + \frac{n\pi}{6} \right)$$

$\therefore$ $f_2(x) = -\tan x$
$\quad f_3(x) = -f_2(x)$, so
$\quad f_3(x) = \tan x$

Now, $f_4(x) = \begin{cases} \dfrac{e^{(e^x-1)}-1}{e^{2(e^x-1)}} & ; x < 0 \\ k_1 & ; x = 0 \\ (1+|\tan x|)^{\frac{k_2}{\tan x}} & ; x > 0 \end{cases}$

Clearly, $f(0^-) = e^{\frac{1}{2}\ln e} = \sqrt{e}$

$$f(0^-) = e^{k_2} \ \& \ f(0) = k_1$$

(ii) As $y = f_3(x) = \tan x$
Clearly $f_3(x)$ is continuous as well as derivable every where in $(0, \pi/2)$

**4.**    **(d)**    Given : $g(x)$ is not differentiable at $x = a$

$$\therefore \text{ LHD of } g(x) = \lim_{h \to 0^+} \frac{(a-h-a)\,f(a-h) - 0}{-h}$$

$$= \lim_{h \to 0^+} f(a-h) = L_1$$

Similarly RHD of $g(x) = \lim_{h \to 0^+} f(a+h) = L_2$

Given $L_1 \neq L_2$

$\therefore f(X)$ is discontinuous at $x = a$.

**5.**    **(d)**    $f(x) = \max.\{x, x^3\} = \begin{cases} x & ; x < -1 \\ x^3 & ; -1 \le x \le 0 \\ x & ; 0 \le x \le 1 \\ x^3 & ; x \ge 1 \end{cases}$

$$\therefore f'(x) = \begin{cases} 1 & ; x < -1 \\ 3x^2 & ; -1 \le x \le 0 \\ 1 & ; 0 \le x \le 1 \\ 3x^2 & ; x \ge 1 \end{cases}$$

Clearly $f$ is not differentiable at $-1, 0$ and $1$.

**6.**    **(d)**

(a)    $f(x) = \cos|x| + |x| = \begin{cases} \cos x - x, & x < 0 \\ \cos x + x, & x \ge 0 \end{cases}$

$$f'(x) = \begin{cases} -\sin x - 1, & x < 0 \\ -\sin x + 1, & x \ge 0 \end{cases}$$

At $x = 0$
LD $= -1$
RD $= 1$
$\therefore$ Not differentiable

(b)    $f(x) = \cos|x| - |x| = \begin{cases} \cos x + x, & x < 0 \\ \cos x - x, & x \ge 0 \end{cases}$

$\therefore$ Not differentiable at $x = 0$

(c)    $f(x) = \sin|x| + |x| = \begin{cases} -\sin x - x, & x < 0 \\ +\sin x - x, & x \ge 0 \end{cases}$

$\therefore$ Not differentiable at $x = 0$

(d)    $f(x) = \sin|x| - |x| = \begin{cases} -\sin x + x, & x < 0 \\ \sin x - x, & x \ge 0 \end{cases}$

$$f'(x) = \begin{cases} -\cos x + 1, & x < 0 \\ +\cos x - 1, & x \ge 0 \end{cases}$$

At $x = 0$
LD $= 0$
RD $= 0$
$\therefore f$ is differentiable at $x = 0$.

**7.**    **(b)**    If $f(x)$ is differentiable, $\{f(x)\}^2$. i.e. $|f(x)|^2$ is also differentiable.

Taking $f(x) = x$, we have $|f(x)| = |f(x)| = |x|$, which is not differentiable at $x = 0$.

---

Thus $f$ is differentiable in $R \not\Rightarrow |f|$ is differentiable in R.

Also $(f|f|)(x) = f(x)|f(x)|$

$$= \begin{cases} -\{f(x)\}^2 & \text{if } f(x) < 0 \\ \{f(x)\}^2 & \text{if } f(x) \ge 0 \end{cases}$$

Which is differentiable in R if $f$ is differentiable in R.

**8.**    **(b)**    For the domain of $f(x)$

(i)    $2x - 4 \ge 0 \Rightarrow x \ge 2$

(ii)    $x + 2\sqrt{2x-4} \ge 0 \Rightarrow 2\sqrt{2x-4} \ge -x$

which holds if $x$ is positive.

(iii)    $x - 2\sqrt{2x-4} \ge 0 \Rightarrow 2\sqrt{2x-4} \le x$

$\Rightarrow x \ge 0$ and $4(2x-4) \le x^2$

$\Rightarrow x^2 - 8x + 16 \ge 0 \Rightarrow x \in \mathbf{R}$

$\therefore f(x)$ is defined if $x \ge 2$

Further $f(x)$ is not differentiable if the expressions inside the radical sign vanish, i.e., if $2x - 4 = 0$ or

$x + 2\sqrt{2x-4} = 0$

or $x - 2\sqrt{2x-4} = 0$    or if $x = 2$ or $4$

$\therefore f(x)$ is differentiable in $(2, \infty) - \{4\}$

**9.**    **(a, c)** We have $\begin{bmatrix} 3(x-1), & x > 1 \\ 0, & x = 1 \\ (1-x), & x < 1 \end{bmatrix}$ As $\begin{array}{l}[x] = 1 \\ [-x] = -2 \\ [x] = 0 \\ [-x] = -1 \end{array}$

$$\Rightarrow f'(1^+) = \lim_{h \to 0} \frac{3(h) - 0}{h} = 3,$$

$$f'(1^-) = \lim_{h \to 0} \frac{[1 - (1-h)] - 0}{-h} = \lim_{h \to 0} \frac{h}{-h} = -1$$

**10.**    **(a, c)**

$$f(x) = \begin{bmatrix} x^3 & \text{if } x \le 1 \\ x^2 & \text{if } x > 1 \end{bmatrix}; \quad g(x) = \begin{bmatrix} x+2 & -1 < x < 0 \\ x & 0 \le x < 2 \\ x+2 & 2 \le x < 3 \end{bmatrix}$$

also $g(x)$ be continuous at $x \in I$.

$g(n) = n^2$ ; $g(n^+) = n^2$ ; $g(n^-) = (n-1)^2 + 1$

$\therefore n^2 = (n-1)^2 \Rightarrow n = 1$

$\Rightarrow g(x)$ is continuous only at one integer $x = 1$

**11.**    **(c, d )** For continuity at $x = 0$

$$f(0) = 0 \,;\, f(0^-) = 0;\, f(0^+) = \lim_{h \to 0} h^n \sin\frac{1}{h} = 0 \Rightarrow n > 0$$

For derivability at $x = 0$

$$f'(0^-) = 0;\, f'(0^+) = \lim_{h \to 0} \frac{h^n \sin\dfrac{1}{h}}{h} \text{ for this limit not to}$$

exist $n \le 1$

for this limit not to exist $n \le 1$

hence $0 < n \le 1$

$\Rightarrow n$ can not be $3/2$ or $2$

**12.** **(a, b, c)**

$$f(x) = \begin{cases} x-3 & \text{if } x \geq 3 \\ 3-x & \text{if } 1 \leq x < 3 \\ \dfrac{x^2}{4} - \dfrac{3x}{2} + \dfrac{13}{4} & \text{if } x < 1 \end{cases}$$

$$f'(1^+) = \operatorname*{Limit}_{h \to 0} \frac{f(1+h) - f(1)}{h}$$

$$= \operatorname*{Limit}_{h \to 0} \frac{3-(1+h)-2}{h} = -1$$

$$f'(1^-) = \operatorname*{Limit}_{h \to 0} \frac{\dfrac{(1-h)^2}{4} - \dfrac{3}{2}(1-h) + \dfrac{13}{4} - 2}{-h}$$

$$= \operatorname*{Limit}_{h \to 0} \frac{(1-h)^2 - 6(1-h) + 5}{-4h}$$

$$= \operatorname*{Limit}_{h \to 0} \frac{h^2 - 2h + 6h}{-4h} = -1$$

$\Rightarrow f$ is continuous at $x = 1$

**13-15.**

$$\because \ f'(x) = \lim_{h \to 0} \frac{f(x+h) - f(x)}{h}$$

$$= \lim_{h \to 0} \frac{f\left(\dfrac{3x+3h}{3}\right) - f\left(\dfrac{3x+0}{3}\right)}{h}$$

$$= \lim_{h \to 0} \frac{\dfrac{2+f(3x)+f(3h)}{h} - \dfrac{2+f(3x)+f(0)}{3}}{h}$$

$$= \lim_{h \to 0} \frac{f(3h) - f(0)}{3h - 0} = f'(0)$$

$\Rightarrow f'(2) = f'(0) = 2 \qquad (\because f'(2) = 2)$

$\Rightarrow f'(x) = 2$

$\Rightarrow f(x) = 2x + C \qquad \qquad ...(1)$

Put $x = y = 0$ in $f\left(\dfrac{x+y}{3}\right) = \dfrac{2+f(x)+f(y)}{3}$

$\Rightarrow f(0) = 2$

Now, from eq. (1) $f(0) = 0 + C = 2$

$\qquad \qquad \qquad \qquad C = 2$

From eq. (1), $f(x) = 2x + 2$

$\because f(|x|) = 2|x| + 2 \geq 2$

$\because$ Range is $[2, \infty)$

**13.** **(c)** $\because f(|x|) = 2|x| + 2$

$\therefore f(|x|) - 3 = 2|x| - 1$

and $g(x) = |f(|x|) - 3| = |2|x| - 1|$

Now, graphs of $y = 2x - 1$

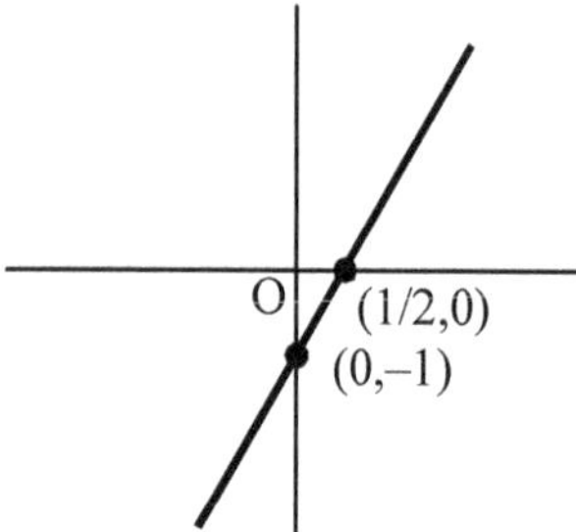


Now, graph of $y = 2|x| - 1$

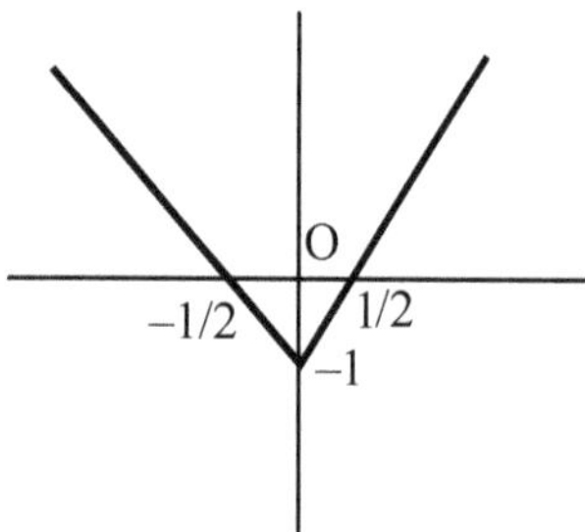


And in last graph of $g(x) = |2|x| - 1|$

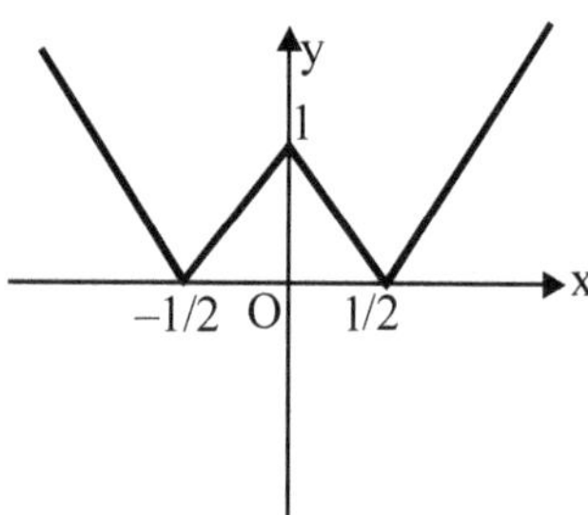


Number of non-differentiable points $= 3$.

**14.** **(c)** $\because f(x) = 2x + 2$

Here, gives $x \in [-2, 3]$

or $\quad -2 \leq x \leq 3$

$\Rightarrow \quad -4 \leq 2x \leq 6$

$\Rightarrow \quad -4 + 2 \leq 2x + 2 \leq 6 + 2$

$\therefore -2 \leq f(x) \leq 8$

Hence, Range of $f(x)$ is $[-2, 8]$.

**15.** **(b)** Let $y = f(|x|) = (2|x| + 2)$ then $x^2 + y^2 = 3^2$

$\therefore$ Number of solutions $= 2$.

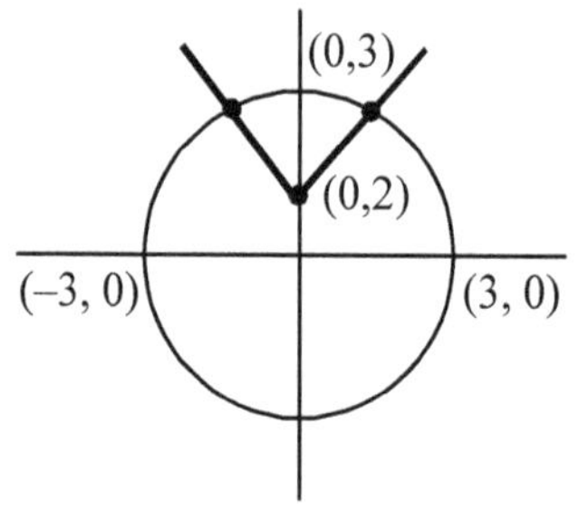

**16.** $(A) \to (s); (B) \to (p); (C) \to (q); (D) \to (t)$

(A)  We have, for $-1 \le x \le 1$

$\Rightarrow \quad 0 \le x \sin \pi x \le 1/2$

$\therefore \quad f(x) = [x \sin \pi x] = 0$

Also $x \sin \pi x$ becomes negative and numerically less than 1 when x is slightly less than 1 and so by definition of $[x]$,

$f(x) = [x \sin \pi x] = -1$ when $1 < x < 1 + h$

Thus $f(x)$ is constant and equal to 0 in the closed interval $[-1, 1]$ and so $f(x)$ is continuous and differentiable in the open interval $(-1, 1)$.

At $x = 1$, $f(x)$ is clearly discontinuous, since $f(1-0) = 0$ and $f(1 + 0) = -1$ and $f(x)$ is non-differentiable at $x = 1$.

Hence (a), (b) and (d) are correct answers.

(B)

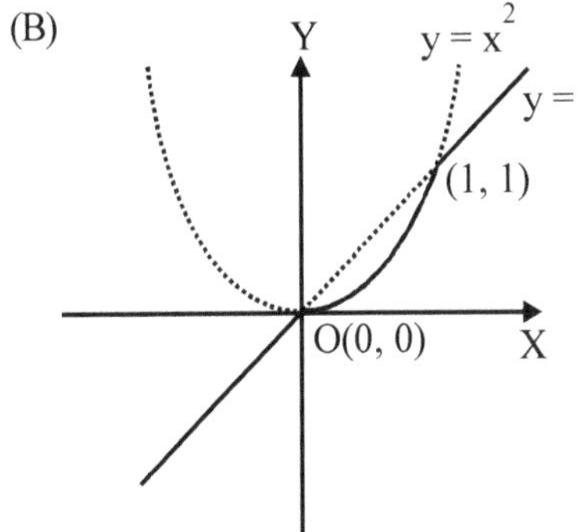

From the graph it is clear that h is continuous for all $x \in R$, $h'(x) = 1$ for all $x > 1$ and h is not differentiable at $x = 0$ and 1.

$\therefore$ (a), (c) and (d) are the correct options.

(C)  We have $g(x) = \begin{cases} x^2 \sin\left(\dfrac{1}{x}\right), & x \ne 0 \\ 0, & x = 0 \end{cases}$

If $x \ne 0$, $g'(x) = x^2 \cos(1/x)\left(-\dfrac{1}{x^2}\right) + 2x \sin\dfrac{1}{x}$

$= -\cos\left(\dfrac{1}{x}\right) + 2x \sin\left(\dfrac{1}{x}\right)$, which exists for $\forall x \ne 0$.

If $x = 0$ then $g'(0)$

$= \lim_{x \to 0} \dfrac{g(x) - g(0)}{x - 0} = \lim_{x \to 0} \dfrac{x^2 \sin(1/x) - 0}{x - 0}$

$= \lim_{x \to 0} x \sin\left(\dfrac{1}{x}\right) = 0$

$\Rightarrow g'(x) = \begin{cases} -\cos\left(\dfrac{1}{x}\right) + 2x \sin\dfrac{1}{x}, & x \ne 0 \\ 0, & x = 0 \end{cases}$

At $x = 0$, $\cos\left(\dfrac{1}{x}\right)$ is not continuous, therefore $g'(x)$ is not continuous at $x = 0$.

At $x = 0$

$Lf' = \lim_{x \to 0} \dfrac{0 - (-x)\sin\left(-\dfrac{1}{x}\right)}{x} = \sin\left(\dfrac{1}{x}\right)$

which does not exist.

$\therefore$ f is not differentiable.

(D)  $y = 1 - x$

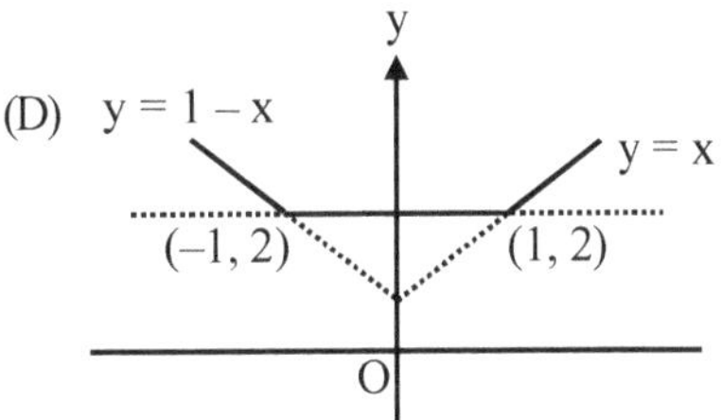

From graph it is clear that $f(x)$ is continuous everywhere and also differentiable everywhere except at $x = 1$ and $-1$.

**17.** $(A) \to (p, q); B \to (s, t); C \to (r)$

(A)  $Rf'(1) = \lim_{h \to 0} \dfrac{f(1 + h) - f(1)}{h}$

$= \lim_{h \to 0} \dfrac{\{b(1 + h) + 2\} - \{1 + 3 + a\}}{h}$

when $h \to 0$, Numerator $= b - a - 2$ must be zero ($\because$ $f(x)$ is differentiable)

Then, $Rf'(1) = \lim_{h \to 0} \dfrac{bh}{h} = b$

$Lf'(1) = \lim_{h \to 0} \dfrac{f(1 - h) - f(1)}{-h}$

$= \lim_{h \to 0} \dfrac{((1 - h)^2 + 3(1 - h) + a) - (4 + a)}{-h}$

$= \lim_{h \to 0} \dfrac{h^2 - 5h}{-h} = 5$

$\therefore Lf'(1) = Rf'(1)$

$\Rightarrow b = 5$

Also, $a = b - 2 = 5 - 2 = 3$

$\therefore a - b = -2$

(B)  $f(x) = \begin{cases} -\dfrac{1}{x}, & x \le -1 \\ \dfrac{1}{x}, & x \ge 1 \\ ax^2 + b, & -1 < x < 1 \end{cases}$

$\because$ $f(x)$ is differentiable, then it is also continuous.

$\therefore f(1) = \lim_{x \to 1-} f(x) = \lim_{h \to 0} f(1 - h)$

$\Rightarrow 1 = \lim_{h \to 0} a(1 - h)^2 + b$

$$\Rightarrow 1 = a + b \text{ and } f'(x) = \begin{cases} \dfrac{1}{x^2}, & x \le -1 \\ -\dfrac{1}{x^2}, & x \ge 1 \\ 2ax, & -1 < x < 1 \end{cases}$$

$$f'(1) = \lim_{x \to 1-} f'(x) = \lim_{h \to 0} f'(1-h)$$

$$\Rightarrow -1 = \lim_{h \to 0} 2a(1-h)$$

$$\Rightarrow -1 = 2a$$

$$\Rightarrow a = -\frac{1}{2}$$

Then, $b = \dfrac{3}{2}$     $\therefore a - b = -2$

(C)   $f(x)$ is also continuous.

$$\therefore f(3) = \lim_{x \to 3-} f(x)$$

$$9b - 3 = \lim_{h \to 0} f(3-h)$$

$$= \lim_{h \to 0} a(3-h)^2 - b(3-h) + 2$$

$$= 9a - 3b + 2$$

or $9a - 12b = -5$       ...(i)

Also, $f'(x) = \begin{cases} 2ax - b, & x < 3 \\ 2bx; & x \ge 3 \end{cases}$

$$\therefore f'(3) = \lim_{x \to 3-} f(x) = \lim_{h \to 0} f(3-h)$$

$$6b = \lim_{h \to 0} 2a(3-h) - b = 6a - b$$

or          $6a = 7b$      ...(ii)

From eqs. (i) and (ii), we get

$$a = \frac{35}{9}, b = \frac{10}{3}$$

**18. (a)**   $f'(0) = \lim\limits_{h \to 0} \dfrac{f(0+h) - f(0)}{h} = \lim\limits_{h \to 0} \dfrac{h^n \sin\left(\dfrac{1}{h}\right) - 0}{h}$

$$= \lim_{h \to 0} h^{n-1} \sin\left(\frac{1}{h}\right) \quad (n \ge 2)$$

$= 0$ finite number $= 0$

**19. (c)**   The Statements-1: is true. If f is differentiable at 'c' then f'(c) exists.

$$\Rightarrow \lim_{h \to 0} \frac{f(c+h) - f(c)}{h} \text{ exists}$$

$$\Rightarrow \lim_{h \to 0} \frac{f(c) + f(h) - f(c)}{h} \text{ exists}$$

$$\Rightarrow \lim_{h \to 0} \frac{f(h)}{h} \text{ exists. Now if p be some other point then}$$

$$f'(p) = \lim_{h \to 0} \frac{f(p+h) - f(p)}{h} = \lim_{h \to 0} \frac{f(h)}{h} \text{ which exists.}$$

Now any function is either differentiable nowhere or differentiable atleast one point, then it is differentiable for all x. Thus statement-1 is true.

The statement-2 is false since any function is either differentiable nowhere is differentiable at one point.

**20. 1**

$$f'(x) = 1 - 2x > 0 \text{ If } x < \frac{1}{2} \text{ and } < 0 \text{ if } x > \frac{1}{2}$$

$$\therefore f(x) \text{ is increasing in } 0 \le x \le \frac{1}{2}$$

$$\Rightarrow \max f(t) = f(x)$$

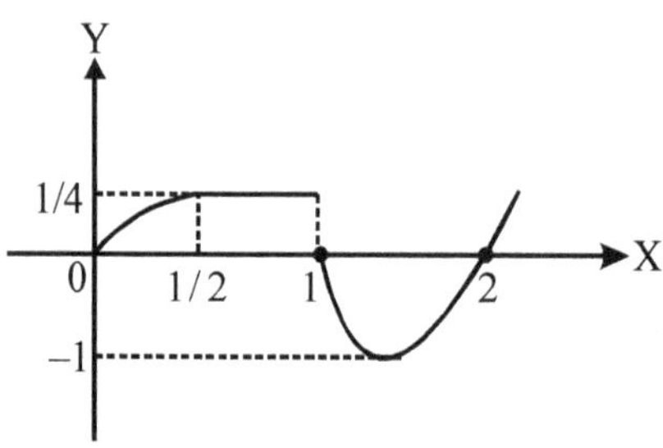

Also maximum of

$$f(x) = f\left(\frac{1}{2}\right) = \frac{1}{4} \qquad (0 \le x \le 1)$$

$$\therefore \text{ Max } f(t) = f\left(\frac{1}{2}\right) = \frac{1}{4} \qquad \text{If } \frac{1}{2} \le x \le 1$$

$$\text{so } g(x) = \begin{cases} x - x^2, & 0 \le x \le \dfrac{1}{2} \\ \dfrac{1}{4}, & \dfrac{1}{2} \le x \le 1 \\ \sin \pi x, & x > 1 \end{cases}$$

It is clear from the graph that $g(x)$ is continuous every where except at $x = 1$, hence not differentiable at $x = 1$

Thus, P = 1

**21. 5**

$$f(x) = \begin{cases} [\cos \pi x], & x \le 1 \\ |2x - 3| [x - 2], & x > 1 \end{cases}$$

$$\text{i.e } f(x) = \begin{cases} [\cos \pi x], & 0 \le x \le 1 \\ -|2x - 3|, & 1 < x < 2 \\ 0, & x = 2 \end{cases}$$

$$\Rightarrow f(x) = \begin{cases} 1, & \text{if } x = 0 \\ 0, & \text{if } 0 < x \le \dfrac{1}{2} \\ -1, & \text{if } \dfrac{1}{2} < x \le 1 \\ 2x-3, & \text{if } 1 \le x < \dfrac{3}{2} \\ 3-2x, & \text{if } \dfrac{3}{2} \le x < 2 \\ 0, & \text{if } x = 2 \end{cases}$$

From graph,

$f(x)$ is discontinuous at $x = 0, \dfrac{1}{2}, 2$

$f(x)$ is non differentiable at $x = 0, \dfrac{1}{2}, 1, \dfrac{3}{2}, 2.$

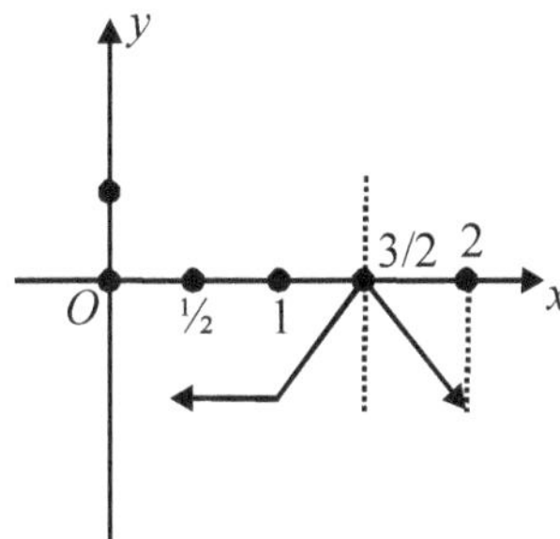

**22. 1**

We have $f(x) = -1$, $-2 \le x \le 0$ $= x-1$, $0 < x \le 2$
and $g(x) = f(|x| + |f(x)|)$
Hence $g(x)$ involves $|x|$ and $|x-1|$ or $|-1| = 1$
Therefore we should divide the given interval $(-2, 2)$
into the following intervals.

| $I_1$ | $I_2$ | $I_3$ |
|---|---|---|
| $[-2, 2] = [-2, 0)$ | $[0, 1)$ | $[1, 2]$ |
| $x = -ve$ | $+ve$ | $+ve$ |
| $|x| = -x$ | $x$ | $x$ |
| $f(x) = -1$ | $x-1$ | $x-1$ |
| $f(|x|) = -1$ | $= x-1$ | $= x-1$ |
| $|f(x)| = |-1|$ | $|x-1|$ | $|x-1|$ |
| $= 1$ | $= -(x-1)$ | $= x-1$ |

$\therefore$ Using above we get
$g(x) = f|x| + |f(x)|$
$\quad = -1 + 1 = 0$ in $I_1$
$\quad = x-1 - (x-1) = 0$ in $I_2$
$\quad = x-1 + x-1 = 2(x-1)$ in $I_3$
Hence g $(x)$ is defined as follows :

$$g(x) = \begin{cases} 0, & -2 \le x < 1 \\ 2(x-1), & 1 \le x \le 2 \end{cases}$$

$Lg'(1) = 0;\ Rg'(1) = 2$ (not equal )
Hence $g(x)$ is not differentiable at $x = 1$.
Thus A = 1

**23. 2**

We have $|x| = \begin{cases} -x & \text{if } x < 0 \\ x & \text{if } x \ge 0 \end{cases}$

$\Rightarrow |x^2 - 3x + 2| = |(x-1)(x-2)|$

$$= \begin{cases} (1-x)(2-x) & \text{if } x \le 1 \\ (x-1)(2-x) & \text{if } 1 \le x \le 2 \\ (x-1)(x-2) & \text{if } x \ge 2 \end{cases}$$

As $\cos(-\theta) = \cos\theta \Rightarrow \cos|x| = \cos x$

$\therefore$ Given function can be written as

$\therefore \quad f(x) = \begin{cases} (x^2-1)(x-1)(x-2) + \cos x & \text{if } x \le 1 \\ -(x^2-1)(x-1)(x-2) + \cos & \text{if } 1 < x \le 2 \\ (x^2-1)(x-1)(x-2) + \cos x & \text{if } x > 2 \end{cases}$

This function is differentiable at all points except possibly at x = 1 and x = 2.

$$Lf'(1) = \left\{ \frac{d}{dx}[(x^2-1)(x-1)(x-2) + \cos x] \right\}_{x=1}$$
$$= -\sin 1$$

$$Rf'(1) = \left\{ \frac{d}{dx}(-(x^2-1)(x-1)(x-2) + \cos x] \right\}_{x=1}$$
$$= -\sin 1$$

$\because \quad Lf'(1) = Rf'(1)$
$\therefore \quad$ f is differentiable at x = 1.

$$Lf'(2) = \left\{ \frac{d}{dx}(-x^2-1)(x-1)(x-2) + \cos x) \right\}_{x=2}$$
$$= -3 - \sin 2$$

$$Rf'(2) = \left\{ \frac{d}{dx}((x^2-1)(x-1)(x-2) + \cos x) \right\}_{x=2}$$
$$= 3 - \sin 2$$

$Lf'(2) \ne Rf'(2)$
$\therefore \quad$ f is not differentiable at x = 2.

**24. 2**

Let $x = y = 0 \Rightarrow f(0) = 0$
Now we have

$$\frac{f(x+2y) - f(x)}{2y} = 2x + \frac{f(2y)}{2y} = 2x + \frac{f(2y) - f(0)}{2y}$$

Taking limit on both sides as $2y \to 0$ , we get

$$f'(x) = 2x + f'(0) \text{ as}$$

$$f(0) = 0 \Rightarrow f'(0) = f'(1) - 2$$

$$\Rightarrow f'(1) - f'(0) = 2$$

**1.** **(a)** $y = f(x) - f(2x)$
$y' = f'(x) - 2f'(2x)$
$y'(1) = f'(1) - 2f'(2) = 5$ ....(1)
and $y'(2) = f'(2) - 2f'(4) = 7$ ....(2)
now let $y = f(x) - f(4x)$
$y' = f'(x) - 4f'(4x)$
$y'(1) = f'(1) - 4f'(4)$ ....(3)
substituting the value of $f'(2) = 7 + 2f'(4)$ in (1)
$f'(1) - 2[7 + 2f'(4)] = 5$
$f'(1) - 4f'(4) = 19$

**2.** **(b)** $y = \dfrac{(x^2+1)^2 - 3x^2}{x^2 + \sqrt{3}x + 1}$

$= \dfrac{(x^2 + 1 + \sqrt{3}x)(x^2 + 1 - \sqrt{3}x)}{x^2 + 1 + \sqrt{3}x}$

$\dfrac{dy}{dx} = 2x - \sqrt{3} \Rightarrow a = 2 \ \& \ b = -\sqrt{3}$

$a + b = 2 - \sqrt{3} = \tan\dfrac{\pi}{12} = \cot\dfrac{5\pi}{12}$

**3.** **(c)** $y = (\sin x)^{\ln x} \csc(e^x(a + bx))$ ; $(a + b) = \dfrac{\pi}{2e}$

$\dfrac{dy}{dx} = (\sin)^{\ln x}(-\csc E \cdot \cot E)\{e^x(b) + (a + bx)e^x\}$

$+ \csc(e^x(a + bx))e^{\ln x \ln(\sin x)} \cdot \left\{\ln x \cot x + \dfrac{\ln \sin x}{x}\right\}$

$\dfrac{dy}{dx}\Big]_{x=1} = (1)(-1).(0)\{be + (a+b)e\} + (1)(1)[\ln \sin 1]$

$= \ln(\sin 1)$

**4.** **(c)** $f(x) = \dfrac{1}{3}\tan^3 x + 3\tan x - 3\cot x - \dfrac{1}{3}\cot^3 x$

$f'(x) = \sec^2 x(\sec^2 x + 2) + \csc^2 x(\csc^2 x + 2)$
$= (\sec^2 x + \csc^2 x)^2$

$= (\sec^2 x \csc^2 x)^2 = \dfrac{16}{\sin^4 x \cos^4 x}$

$= 16\csc^4(2x)$

**5.** **(d)** $f(x) = -\dfrac{x^3}{3} + x^2\sin 6 - x\sin 4.\sin 8 - 5\sin^{-1}((a-4)^2 + 1)$

$f'(x) = -x^2 + 2x\sin 6 - \sin 4 \sin 8$
$f'(\sin 8) = -\sin^2 8 + 2\sin 6 \sin 8 - \sin 4 \sin 8$
$= \sin 8[-\sin 8 + 2\sin 6 - \sin 4]$
$= -\sin 8[\sin 8 + \sin 4 - 2\sin 6]$
$= -\sin 8[2\sin 6 \cos 2 - 2\sin 6]$
$= 2\sin 8 \sin 6[1 - \cos 2]$

**6.** **(b)** $\dfrac{d}{dx}(\cos^{-1}x + \sin^{-1}x) = \dfrac{d}{dx}\left(\dfrac{\pi}{2}\right) = 0$

**7.** **(c)** Around $x = \dfrac{2\pi}{3}$, $|\cos x| = -\cos x$
and $|\sin x| = \sin x$.

$\therefore y = -\cos x + \sin x$ $\qquad \therefore \dfrac{dy}{dx} = \sin x + \cos x$

At $x = \dfrac{2\pi}{3}$, $\dfrac{dy}{dx} = \sin\dfrac{2\pi}{3} + \cos\dfrac{2\pi}{3}$

$= \dfrac{\sqrt{3}}{2} - \dfrac{1}{2} = \dfrac{\sqrt{3} - 1}{2}$

**8.** **(d)** $y = x\tan\dfrac{x}{2}$

$\Rightarrow \dfrac{dy}{dx} = 1.\tan\dfrac{x}{2} + x.\sec^2\dfrac{x}{2}.\dfrac{1}{2}$

$= \tan\dfrac{x}{2} + \dfrac{x}{2}\sec^2\dfrac{x}{2}$

$= \dfrac{\sin\dfrac{x}{2}}{\cos\dfrac{x}{2}} + \dfrac{x}{2\cos^2\dfrac{x}{2}}$

$= \dfrac{2\sin\dfrac{x}{2}\cos\dfrac{x}{2} + x}{2\cos^2\dfrac{x}{2}} = \dfrac{\sin x + x}{1 + \cos x}$

$\Rightarrow (1 + \cos x)\dfrac{dy}{dx} - \sin x = x$

**9.** **(b)** We have, $y = f\left(\dfrac{2x-1}{x^2+1}\right)$

$\Rightarrow \dfrac{dy}{dx} = f'\left(\dfrac{2x-1}{x^2+1}\right) \cdot \left[\dfrac{(x^2+1)2 - (2x-1).2x}{(x^2+1)^2}\right]$

$= \sin\left(\dfrac{2x-1}{x^2+1}\right)^2 \cdot \left[\dfrac{2 + 2x - 2x^2}{(x^2+1)}\right]$

$\left[\because f'(x) = \sin x^2, \ \therefore f'\left(\dfrac{2x-1}{x^2+1}\right) = \sin\left(\dfrac{2x-1}{x^2+1}\right)^2\right]$

**10. (c)** If $f(x) = \dfrac{1 + \tan x}{1 - \tan x}$. Then

$$f'(x) = \dfrac{\dfrac{d(1+\tan x)}{dx}.(1-\tan x) - (1+\tan x).\dfrac{d(1-\tan x)}{dx}}{(1-\tan x)^2}$$

$$= \dfrac{(0+\sec^2 x)(1-\tan x) - (1+\tan x)(0-\sec^2 x)}{(1-\tan x)^2}$$

$$= \dfrac{2\sec^2 x}{1+\tan^2 x - 2\tan x} = \dfrac{2\sec^2 x}{\sec^2 x - 2\tan x} = \dfrac{2}{1-\sin 2x}$$

$\therefore$ When $x = \dfrac{\pi}{6}$, $f'\left(\dfrac{\pi}{6}\right) = \dfrac{2}{1-\sin\dfrac{\pi}{3}} = \dfrac{2}{1-\dfrac{\sqrt{3}}{2}} = \dfrac{4}{2-\sqrt{3}}$

$$= 4\left(2+\sqrt{3}\right)$$

**11. (a)** $y = \dfrac{a + bx^{3/2}}{x^{5/4}}$

$$\Rightarrow y' = \dfrac{\dfrac{3}{2}bx^{7/4} - \dfrac{5}{4}(a+bx^{3/2})x^{1/4}}{x^{5/2}}$$

$\therefore$ $y' = 0$ at $x = 5$

$\therefore$ $\dfrac{3}{2}bx^{7/4} - \dfrac{5}{4}(a+bx^{3/2})x^{1/4} = 0$ at $x = 5$

$\Rightarrow 6bx^{3/2} - 5(a+bx^{3/2}) = 0$ at $x = 5$

$\Rightarrow bx^{3/2} = 5a$ at $x = 5 \Rightarrow b(5)^{3/2} = 5a$

$\Rightarrow \dfrac{a}{b} = \dfrac{5^{3/2}}{5} \Rightarrow a : b = \sqrt{5} : 1$.

**12. (d)** If $y = \sin^{-1}\left(\dfrac{\sin\alpha \sin x}{1 - \cos\alpha \sin x}\right)$

$$\Rightarrow \dfrac{dy}{dx} = \dfrac{1}{\sqrt{1 - \dfrac{\sin^2\alpha \sin^2 x}{(1-\cos\alpha \sin x)^2}}} \cdot \dfrac{d}{dx}\left(\dfrac{\sin\alpha \sin x}{1-\cos\alpha \sin x}\right)$$

$$= \dfrac{1-\cos\alpha \sin x}{\sqrt{(1-\cos\alpha \sin x)^2 - \sin^2\alpha \sin^2 x}} \cdot$$

$$\dfrac{(1-\cos\alpha \sin x).\sin\alpha \cos x + \sin\alpha \cos x(\cos\alpha \cos x)}{(1-\cos\alpha \sin x)^2}$$

$$= \dfrac{1}{\sqrt{1 + (\cos^2\alpha - \sin^2\alpha)\sin^2 x - 2\cos\alpha \sin x}} \cdot$$

$$\dfrac{\sin\alpha \cos x}{(1-\cos\alpha \sin x)}$$

$\therefore$ $\dfrac{dy}{dx}\Bigg]_{x=0} = \dfrac{1}{\sqrt{1+0-0}} \cdot \dfrac{\sin\alpha.1}{1-0} = \sin\alpha$

$\Rightarrow y'(0) = \sin\alpha$

**13. (c)** Given $3f(\cos x) + 2f(\sin x) = 5x$ .....(i)

Replace $x$ by $\dfrac{\pi}{2} - x$ we get

$$3f\left\{\cos\left(\dfrac{\pi}{2} - x\right)\right\} + 2f\left\{\sin\left(\dfrac{\pi}{2} - x\right)\right\} = 5\left(\dfrac{\pi}{2} - x\right)$$

or $3f(\sin x) + 2f(\cos x) = 5\left(\dfrac{\pi}{2} - x\right)$ .....(ii)

Solving (i) and (ii) simultaneously,
we get $f(\cos x) = 5x - \pi$
Differentiating we get

$$(-\sin x)f'(\cos x) = 5 \Rightarrow f'(\cos x) = -\dfrac{5}{\sin x} \cdot$$

**14. (a, b, c)**

**(a)** $f'(x) = \dfrac{\sqrt{x}.1 - (x-4)\dfrac{1}{2\sqrt{x}}}{2x}$

$$= \dfrac{2x - x + 4}{4x\sqrt{x}} = \dfrac{x+4}{4x\sqrt{x}}$$

which is not defined at $x = 0$
i.e. $f'(0)$ does not exist

**(b)** $f'(t) = \dfrac{d}{dt}\left[\dfrac{1-t}{1+t}\right] = \dfrac{(1+t)(-1) - (1-t)\times(1)}{(1+t)^2}$

$$= \dfrac{-1-t-1+t}{(1+t)^2} = \dfrac{-2}{(1+t)^2}$$

$$f'[1/t] = \dfrac{-2}{\left(1+\dfrac{1}{t}\right)^2} = \dfrac{-2t^2}{(t+1)^2}$$

**(c)** $\dfrac{dy}{dx} = \dfrac{d}{dx}\left[\tan^{-1}\dfrac{x}{2}\right] - \dfrac{d}{dx}\left[\cot^{-1}\dfrac{x}{2}\right]$

$$= \dfrac{4}{4+x^2} \cdot \dfrac{1}{2} + \dfrac{4}{1+x^2} \cdot \dfrac{1}{2}$$

$$= \dfrac{2.2}{4+x^2} = \dfrac{4}{1+x^2}$$

**(d)** If $\varphi(x) = \log_5(\log_3 x) = \log_5\left(\dfrac{\log_e x}{\log_e 3}\right)$

$$= \log_5\left(\log_e x\right) - \log_5\left(\log_e 3\right)$$

$$= \dfrac{\log_e(\log_e x)}{\log_e 5} - \log_5(\log_e 3)$$

$\therefore$ $\varphi'(x) = \dfrac{1}{\log_e 5} \cdot \dfrac{1}{\log_e x} \cdot \dfrac{1}{x} - 0$

$\Rightarrow \varphi'(e) = \dfrac{1}{\log_e 5} \cdot \dfrac{1}{\log_e e} \cdot \dfrac{1}{e} = \dfrac{1}{e\log_e 5}$

**15.** **(a,c)** $f'(x) = nx^{n-1}$

$\therefore n(a+b)^{n-1} = na^{n-1} + nb^{n-1}$

$\Rightarrow n(a+b)^{n-1} - a^{n-1}b^{n-1} = 0$

$\therefore n = 0$

$\Rightarrow (a+b)^{n-1} = a^{n-1} + b^{n-1}$ it is true for n = 2.

**16.** **(a,b)** $y = \log_2(\log_2 x)$

$\therefore \dfrac{dy}{dx} = \dfrac{1}{\log_2 x} \times \log_2 e \times \dfrac{1}{x}\log_2 e$

$= \dfrac{1}{x\,\log_2 x . \log_e 2 . \log_e 2}$

$= \dfrac{1}{x\,\log_e x . \log_e 2}$

$= \dfrac{\log_2 e}{x\,\log_e x}$

**17.** $A \to r,t;\ B \to r,t;\ C \to p,q,s$

(A) $\because\ \ y = \sin^{-1}(3x - 4x^3)$

$$= \begin{cases} -\pi - 3\sin^{-1} x\,, & -1 \le x \le -\dfrac{1}{2} \\[2mm] 3\sin^{-1} x\,, & -\dfrac{1}{2} \le x \le \dfrac{1}{2} \\[2mm] \pi - 3\sin^{-1} x\,, & \dfrac{1}{2} \le x \le 1 \end{cases}$$

$$\therefore\ \dfrac{dy}{dx} = \begin{cases} -\dfrac{3}{\sqrt{1-x^2}}\,, & -1 \le x \le -\dfrac{1}{2} \\[3mm] \dfrac{3}{\sqrt{1-x^2}}\,, & -\dfrac{1}{2} \le x \le \dfrac{1}{2}\ \textbf{(r,t)} \\[3mm] -\dfrac{3}{\sqrt{(1-x^2)}}\,, & \dfrac{1}{2} \le x \le 1 \end{cases}$$

(B) $\because\ \ y = \cos^{-1}(4x^3 - 3x)$

$$= \begin{cases} 3\cos^{-1} x - 2\pi\,, & -1 \le x \le -\dfrac{1}{2} \\[2mm] 2\pi - 3\cos^{-1} x\,, & -\dfrac{1}{2} \le x \le \dfrac{1}{2} \\[2mm] 3\cos^{-1} x\,, & \dfrac{1}{2} \le x \le 1 \end{cases}$$

$$\therefore\ \dfrac{dy}{dx} = \begin{cases} \dfrac{-3}{\sqrt{1-x^2}}\,, & -1 \le x \le -\dfrac{1}{2} \\[3mm] \dfrac{3}{\sqrt{1-x^2}}\,, & -\dfrac{1}{2} \le x \le \dfrac{1}{2}\ \textbf{(r,t)} \\[3mm] \dfrac{-3}{\sqrt{(1-x^2)}}\,, & \dfrac{1}{2} \le x \le 1 \end{cases}$$

(C) $\because\ \ y = \tan^{-1}\left(\dfrac{3x - x^3}{1 - 3x^2}\right)$

$$= \begin{cases} 3\tan^{-1} x\,, & -\dfrac{1}{\sqrt{3}} < x < \dfrac{1}{\sqrt{3}} \\[2mm] \pi + 3\tan^{-1} x\,, & x < -\dfrac{1}{\sqrt{3}} \\[2mm] -\pi + 3\tan^{-1} x\,, & x > \dfrac{1}{\sqrt{3}} \end{cases}$$

$$\therefore\ \dfrac{dy}{dx} = \begin{cases} \dfrac{3}{1+x^2}\,, & -\dfrac{1}{\sqrt{3}} < x < \dfrac{1}{\sqrt{3}} \\[3mm] \dfrac{3}{1+x^2}\,, & x < -\dfrac{1}{\sqrt{3}} \\[3mm] \dfrac{3}{1+x^2}\,, & x > \dfrac{1}{\sqrt{3}} \end{cases}$$

**18.** **(d)** $\because\ \dfrac{d}{dx}(\ln|x|) = \dfrac{1}{x}$

Now, $\left(\because \dfrac{d}{dx}\ell n|x| = \dfrac{d}{dx}\ell n(-x) = \dfrac{1}{(-x)}\,(-1) = \dfrac{1}{x}\right)$

**19.** **(a)** $\because f(x) = \sin^2 x + \sin^2\left(x + \dfrac{\pi}{3}\right) + \cos x \cos\left(x + \dfrac{\pi}{3}\right)$

$= \dfrac{1}{2}\left\{2\sin^2 x + 2\sin^2\left(x + \dfrac{\pi}{3}\right) + 2\cos x \cos\left(x + \dfrac{\pi}{3}\right)\right\}$

$= \dfrac{1}{2}\left\{(1 - \cos 2x) + \left(1 - \cos\left(2x + \dfrac{2\pi}{3}\right)\right)\right.$

$\left. + \cos\left(2x + \dfrac{\pi}{3}\right) + \cos\dfrac{\pi}{3}\right\}$

$= \dfrac{1}{2}\left\{\dfrac{5}{2} + \cos\left(2x + \dfrac{\pi}{3}\right) - \cos 2x - \cos\left(2x + \dfrac{2\pi}{3}\right)\right\}$

$= \dfrac{1}{2}\left\{\dfrac{5}{2} + \cos\left(2x + \dfrac{\pi}{3}\right) - 2\cos\left(2x + \dfrac{\pi}{3}\right) . \cos\dfrac{\pi}{3}\right\}$

$= \dfrac{1}{2}\left\{\dfrac{5}{2} + 0\right\} = \dfrac{5}{4}$

$\therefore\ f'(x) = 0$

**20.** **4**

- By definition $f'(1)$ is the limit of the slope of the secant line when $s \to 1$.

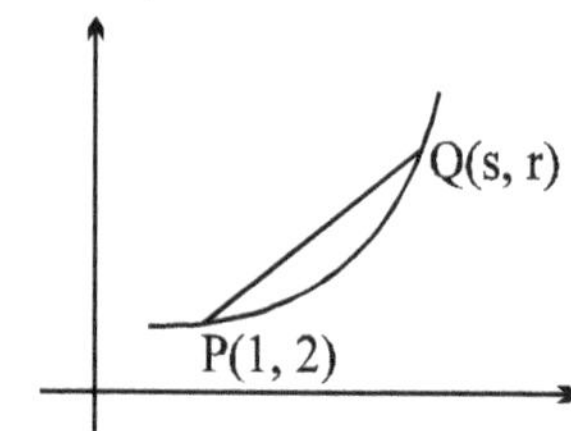

Thus $f'(1) = \underset{s \to 1}{\text{Lim}} \dfrac{s^2 + 2s - 3}{s - 1}$

$= \underset{s \to 1}{\text{Lim}} \dfrac{(s-1)(s+3)}{s-1}$

$= \underset{s \to 1}{\text{Lim}}(s+3) = 4$

- By substituting $x = s$ into the equation of the secant line, and cancelling by $s - 1$ again, we get
  $y = s^2 + 2s - 1$. This is $f(s)$, and its derivative is
  $f'(s) = 2s + 2$, so $f'(1) = 4$

**21.  1**

$y = (1 + x^{1/2})(1 - x^{1/2}) = 1 - x$

$\therefore \quad dy/dx = -1$

Thus, $Q = 1$

**22.  0**

As we know

$1 < \sqrt[3]{\dfrac{\pi}{2}} < 2, \qquad \therefore \text{ If } x = \sqrt[3]{\dfrac{\pi}{2}} \Rightarrow [x] = 1$

So, $f(x) = \cos\left\{\dfrac{\pi}{2} - x^3\right\} = \sin x^3$

$\Rightarrow f'(x) = \cos x^3 . 3x^2$

$\therefore \quad f'\left(\sqrt[3]{\dfrac{\pi}{2}}\right) = 3\left(\dfrac{\pi}{2}\right)^{2/3} . \cos\dfrac{\pi}{2} = 0 \Rightarrow f'\left(\sqrt[3]{\dfrac{\pi}{2}}\right) = 0$

**23.  0**

If $y = 2^{\log_2(x^{2x})} - \left(\tan\dfrac{\pi x}{4}\right)^{\frac{4}{\pi x}} = x^{2x} - \left(\tan\dfrac{\pi x}{4}\right)^{\frac{4}{\pi x}}$

$$[\because a^{\log_a x} = x]$$

$= e^{2x \log x} - e^{\frac{4}{\pi x}\log\left(\tan\frac{\pi x}{4}\right)} \qquad (\text{using } a^x = e^{x \log a})$

$\therefore \dfrac{dy}{dx} = e^{2x \log x}\left[2x.\dfrac{1}{x} + 2.\log x\right]$

$- e^{\frac{4}{\pi x}\log\left(\tan\frac{\pi x}{4}\right)}\left[-\dfrac{4}{\pi x^2}\log\left(\tan\dfrac{\pi x}{4}\right) + \dfrac{4}{\pi x}.\dfrac{\sec^2\dfrac{\pi x}{4}}{\tan\dfrac{\pi x}{4}}.\dfrac{\pi}{4}\right]$

$\therefore \left.\dfrac{dy}{dx}\right|_{x=1} = e^0[2+0] - e^0\left[0 + \dfrac{4}{\pi.1}.\dfrac{\left(\sqrt{2}\right)^2}{1}.\dfrac{\pi}{4}\right] = 2 - 2 = 0$

**24.  0**

If $y = \dfrac{1}{x}, \quad \therefore \dfrac{dy}{dx} = -\dfrac{1}{x^2}.$

Now, $\dfrac{\sqrt{1+y^4}}{\sqrt{1+x^4}} = \dfrac{\sqrt{1+\dfrac{1}{x^4}}}{\sqrt{1+x^4}} = \dfrac{\dfrac{\sqrt{x^4+1}}{x^2}}{\sqrt{x^4+1}} = \dfrac{1}{x^2} = -\dfrac{dy}{dx}.$

Writing in the form of differentials, we have

$\dfrac{dx}{\sqrt{1+x^4}} = -\dfrac{dy}{\sqrt{1+y^4}}; \Rightarrow \dfrac{dx}{\sqrt{1+x^4}} + \dfrac{dy}{\sqrt{1+y^4}} = 0.$

**1.  (d)**  $y = x^{(\ell n\, x)^{\ell n\,(\ell n\, x)}}$

$$\ell n\, y = (\ell n\, x)^{\ell n(\ell n x)} . \ell n\, x \qquad .....(1)$$

$$\ell n\,(\ell n\, y) = \ell n\,(\ell n\, x). \ell n(\ell n x) + \ell n(\ell n x)$$

$$\frac{1}{\ell n\, y}.\frac{1}{y}\frac{dy}{dx} = \frac{2\,\ell n(\ell n x)}{\ell n\, x}.\frac{1}{x} + \frac{1}{x\,\ell n x}$$

$$= \frac{2\,\ell n(\ell n x) + 1}{x\,\ell n x}$$

$$\therefore \;\; \frac{dy}{dx} = \frac{y}{x}.\frac{\ell n\, y}{\ell n x}(2\ell n(\ell n x) + 1) \;\Rightarrow\; D$$

Substituting the value of $\ell n\, y$ from (1)

$$\frac{dy}{dx} = \frac{y}{x}(\ell n x)^{\ell n(\ell n x)}(2\ell n(\ell n x) + 1) \;\Rightarrow\; B$$

**2.  (a)**  $f(x) = f'(x) + f''(x) + f'''(x) + ...... \infty$
$f'(x) = f''(x) + f'''(x) + f''''(x) + ........ \infty$

$$\therefore 2f'(x) = f'(x) + f''(x) + f'''(x) + ......$$

$$\Rightarrow\; 2f'(x) = f(x) \;\Rightarrow\; \frac{f'(x)}{f(x)} = \frac{1}{2}$$

$$\ell n\, f(x) = \frac{1}{2}x + c$$

$$\text{if } x = 0\,;\, f(0) = 1 \;\Rightarrow\; c = 0$$

$$\text{hence } \ell n\, f(x) = \frac{x}{2} \;\Rightarrow\; f(x) = e^{\frac{x}{2}}$$

**3.  (a)**  $y = (\sin x)^{\tan x} \Rightarrow \log y = \tan x . \log \sin x$

Differentiating w.r.t. x,

$$\frac{1}{y}\frac{dy}{dx} = \sec^2 x \log \sin x + \tan x . \frac{1}{\sin x}.\cos x$$

$$\frac{dy}{dx} = (\sin x)^{\tan x}[1 + \sec^2 x \log \sin x]$$

**4.  (b)**  $\dfrac{dy}{dx} = \dfrac{e^t(\sin t + \cos t)}{e^t(\cos t - \sin t)} = \dfrac{\sin t + \cos t}{\cos t - \sin t}$

$$\therefore \;\; \left.\frac{d^2 y}{dx^2}\right]_{t=0}$$

$$= \frac{(\cos 0 - \sin 0)(\cos 0 - \sin 0) - (\sin 0 + \cos 0)(-\sin 0 - \cos 0)}{(\cos 0 - \sin 0)^2 \times \dfrac{1}{e^0(\cos 0 - \sin 0)}}$$

$$= 2$$

**5.  (c)**  $\dfrac{dy}{dx} = \dfrac{(\sec^2 t - \mathrm{cosec}^2 t)}{-2\mathrm{cosec}^2 t}\cot t$

$$= \frac{-1}{2}\frac{(\sin^2 t - \cos^2 t)}{\cos^2 t} \times \frac{\cos t}{\sin t}$$

$$\Rightarrow \;\; \sin 2t\,\frac{dy}{dx} = -[\sin^2 t - \cos^2 t]$$

$$= -(1 - \cos^2 t) + \cos^2 t = -1 + 2\cos^2 t.$$

**6.  (a)**  From given condition we have

$$\cos\!\left(y\sqrt{a^2 - b^2}\right) = \frac{a\cos(x-a) + b}{a + b\cos(x-\alpha)}$$

Differentiating w.r.t. x on both sides we have

$$\sqrt{a^2 - b^2}\,\sin(y\sqrt{a^2 - b^2})\,\frac{dy}{dx} = \frac{(a^2 - b^2)\sin(x-\alpha)}{\theta^2}$$

$$\text{or } \sin(y\sqrt{a^2 - b^2})\,\frac{dy}{dx} = \frac{\sqrt{a^2 - b^2}.\sin(x-\alpha)}{\theta^2}$$

$$\text{Now, } \sin(y\sqrt{a^2 - b^2}) = \frac{\sqrt{a^2 - b^2}.\sin(x-\alpha)}{\theta}$$

$$\therefore \;\; \frac{dy}{dx} = \frac{1}{\theta}$$

**7.  (c)**  $\dfrac{dx}{dt} = -f(t)\sin t + f'(t)\cos t - f'(t)\cos t - f''(t)\sin t$

$$= -[f(t) + f''(t)]\sin t$$

$$\text{and } \frac{dy}{dt} = f(t)\cos t + f'(t)\sin t - f'(t)\sin t + f''(t)\cos t$$

$$= [f(t) + f''(t)]\cos t$$

$$\therefore \;\; \left(\frac{dx}{dt}\right)^2 + \left(\frac{dy}{dt}\right)^2 = [f(t) + f''(t)]^2$$

**8.  (a)**  Taking logarithm of both sides, we get

$$\log y = x\left[\log\left(1 + \frac{1}{x}\right)\right]$$

$$\Rightarrow \frac{1}{y}y_1(x) = \frac{x^2}{x+1}\left(-\frac{1}{x^2}\right) + \log\left(1 + \frac{1}{x}\right)$$

$$= -\frac{1}{x+1} + \log\left(1 + \frac{1}{x}\right) \qquad ........(1)$$

Since $y(2) = (1 + 1/2)^2 = 9/4$

$$\text{so } y_1(2) = (9/4)\left(-\frac{1}{3} + \log\frac{3}{2}\right)$$

Multiplying (1) by y and then differentiating, we get

$$y_2(x) = y_1(x)\left(-\frac{1}{x+1} + \log\left(1+\frac{1}{x}\right)\right)$$

$$+y(x)\times\left(\frac{1}{(x+1)^2} + \frac{x}{x+1}\left(-\frac{1}{x^2}\right)\right)$$

So, $y_2(2) = y_1(2)\left(-\frac{1}{3} + \log\frac{3}{2}\right) + y(2)\left(\frac{1}{9} - \frac{1}{6}\right)$

$$= \left(\frac{9}{4}\right)\left(-\frac{1}{3} + \log\frac{3}{2}\right)^2 - \frac{1}{8}$$

**9.** **(a, b, c)**

**(a)** $y = \tan^{-1}\left[\dfrac{2^x(2-1)}{1+2^x.2^{x+1}}\right] = \tan^{-1}\left[\dfrac{2^{x+1}-2^x}{1+2^x.2^{x+1}}\right]$

$= \tan^{-1}(2^{x+1}) - \tan^{-1}(2^x) \Rightarrow \dfrac{dy}{dx} = \dfrac{2^{x+1}\log 2}{1+2^{2(x+1)}} - \dfrac{2^x\log 2}{1+2^{2x}}$

$\therefore \left(\dfrac{dy}{dx}\right)_{x=0} = (\log 2)\left(\dfrac{2}{5}-1\right) = \log 2\left(-\dfrac{3}{5}\right)$

**(b)** If $y = \sqrt{\sin x + \sqrt{\sin x + \sqrt{\sin x + \dots\dots\infty}}}$

Squaring both sides, we get

$$y^2 = \sin x + \sqrt{\sin x + \sqrt{\sin x + \sqrt{\sin x + \dots\dots\text{to }\infty}}};$$

$\therefore y^2 = \sin x + y.$

Differentiating both sides with respect to x, we get

$$\frac{d(y^2)}{dy} \times \frac{dy}{dx} = \frac{d(\sin x)}{dx} + \frac{dy}{dx} \text{ or } 2y\frac{dy}{dx} = \cos x + \frac{dy}{dx}$$

or $(2y-1)\dfrac{dy}{dx} = \cos x;$ or $\dfrac{dy}{dx} = \dfrac{\cos x}{2y-1}.$

**(c)** $y = \tan^{-1}\left[\dfrac{2^x(2-1)}{1+2^x.2^{x+1}}\right] = \tan^{-1}\left[\dfrac{2^{x+1}-2^x}{1+2^x.2^{x+1}}\right]$

$= \tan^{-1}(2^{x+1}) - \tan^{-1}(2^x) \Rightarrow \dfrac{dy}{dx} = \dfrac{2^{x+1}\log 2}{1+2^{2(x+1)}} - \dfrac{2^x\log 2}{1+2^{2x}}$

$\therefore \left(\dfrac{dy}{dx}\right)_{x=0} = (\log 2)\left(\dfrac{2}{5}-1\right) = \log 2\left(-\dfrac{3}{5}\right)$

**(d)** If $y = \sqrt{\sin x + \sqrt{\sin x + \sqrt{\sin x + \dots\dots\infty}}}$

Squaring both sides, we get

$$y^2 = \sin x + \sqrt{\sin x + \sqrt{\sin x + \sqrt{\sin x + \dots\dots\text{to }\infty}}};$$

$\therefore y^2 = \sin x + y.$

Differentiating both sides with respect to x, we get

$$\frac{d(y^2)}{dy} \times \frac{dy}{dx} = \frac{d(\sin x)}{dx} + \frac{dy}{dx} \text{ or } 2y\frac{dy}{dx} = \cos x + \frac{dy}{dx}$$

or $(2y-1)\dfrac{dy}{dx} = \cos x;$ or $\dfrac{dy}{dx} = \dfrac{\cos x}{2y-1}.$

**10.** **(c, d)** We have, $e^{xy} + y\cos x = 2$ ....(1)

Put $x = 0$, we get

$1 + y = 2$

$\therefore y = 1$

$\Rightarrow (0, 1)$ lies on the given curve.

On differentiating (1) w.r.t. x, we get

$$e^{xy}\left[x\frac{dy}{dx} + y\right] + y(-\sin x) + \cos x\frac{dy}{dx} = 0 \quad ....(2)$$

As $(0, 1)$ satisfying it, we get

$$0 + 1 + \frac{dy}{dx} = 0 \Rightarrow y'(0) = -1 \Rightarrow (C)$$

Again differentiating (2), we get

$$e^{xy}\left[x\frac{d^2y}{dx^2} + \frac{dy}{dx} + \frac{dy}{dx}\right] + e^{xy}\left[x\frac{dy}{dx} + y\right]^2$$

$$-\left[y\cos x + \sin x\frac{dy}{dx}\right] + \cos x\frac{d^2y}{dx^2} - \sin x\frac{dy}{dx} = 0$$

As $(0, 1)$ satisfy it we get $-2 + 1 - 1 + y''(0) = 0$

$\therefore y''(0) = 2$

**11.** **(a, b, c)**

$$f'(x) = \begin{vmatrix} -\sin(x+\alpha) & -\sin(x+\beta) & -\sin(x+\gamma) \\ \sin(x+\alpha) & \sin(x+\beta) & \sin(x+\gamma) \\ \sin(\beta-\gamma) & \sin(\gamma-\alpha) & \sin(\alpha-\beta) \end{vmatrix} +$$

$$\begin{vmatrix} \cos(x+\alpha) & \cos(x+\beta) & \cos(x+\gamma) \\ \cos(x+\alpha) & \cos(x+\beta) & \cos(x+\gamma) \\ \sin(\beta-\gamma) & \sin(\gamma-\alpha) & \sin(\alpha-\beta) \end{vmatrix}$$

$= 0 + 0 \Rightarrow f(x)$ is a constant function.

Thus $f(\alpha) = f(\beta) = f(\gamma)$

**12.** **(a,c)** $u = \sin^{-1} x$

$$v = \sin^{-1}(3x - 4x^3) = \begin{cases} -\pi - 3\sin^{-1} x, & -1 \le x \le -\dfrac{1}{2} \\ 3\sin^{-1} x, & -\dfrac{1}{2} \le x \le \dfrac{1}{2} \\ \pi - 3\sin^{-1} x, & \dfrac{1}{2} \le x \le 1 \end{cases}$$

$$\therefore \frac{du}{dv} = \begin{cases} -\dfrac{1}{3}, & -1 \le x \le -\dfrac{1}{2} \\ \dfrac{1}{3}, & -\dfrac{1}{2} \le x \le \dfrac{1}{2} \\ -\dfrac{1}{3}, & \dfrac{1}{2} \le x \le 1 \end{cases}$$

**13. (a)** We have

$$(1+x)(1+x^2)(1+x^4)\ldots\ldots(1+x^{2^{n-1}})$$

$$=\frac{1}{1-x}(1-x^2)(1+x^2)(1+x^4)\ldots\ldots(1+x^{2^{n-1}})$$

$$=\frac{1}{1-x}(1-x^4)(1+x^4)\ldots\ldots(1+x^{2^{n-1}})=\ldots\ldots$$

$$=\frac{(1-x^{2^{n-1}})(1+x^{2^{n-1}})}{1-x}=\frac{1-x^{2^n}}{1-x}$$

**14. (a)** Taking log of product obtained in (1), we get

$$\log(1+x)+\log(1+x^2)+\log(1+x^4)+\ldots\ldots+\log(1+x^{2^{n-1}})$$

$$=\log(1-x^{2^n})-\log(1-x)$$

Differentiating both the sides, we get

$$\frac{1}{1+x}+\frac{2x}{1+x^2}+\frac{4x^3}{1+x^4}+\ldots\ldots+\frac{2^{n-1}.x^{2^{n-1}-1}}{1+x^{2^{n-1}}}$$

$$=\frac{1}{1-x}-\frac{2^n x^{2^n-1}}{1-x^{2^n}}$$

**15. (c)** $\cos\dfrac{x}{2}\cos\dfrac{x}{2^2}\cos\dfrac{x}{2^3}\ldots\ldots\cos\dfrac{x}{2^n}$

$$=\frac{1}{2\sin\dfrac{x}{2^n}}\left(2\sin\dfrac{x}{2^n}\cos\dfrac{x}{2^n}\right)\cos\dfrac{x}{2^{n-1}}\ldots\ldots\cos\dfrac{x}{2}$$

$$=\frac{1}{2\sin\dfrac{x}{2^n}}\sin\dfrac{x}{2^{n-1}}\cos\dfrac{x}{2^{n-1}}\ldots\ldots\cos\dfrac{x}{2}$$

$$=\frac{1}{2^2\sin\dfrac{x}{2^n}}\sin\dfrac{x}{2^{n-2}}\ldots\ldots\cos\dfrac{x}{2}$$

$$=\frac{1}{2^{n-1}\sin\dfrac{x}{2^n}}\sin\dfrac{x}{2}\cos\dfrac{x}{2}=\frac{\sin x}{2^n\sin\dfrac{x}{2^n}}$$

**16.** $A\to r; B\to p; C\to s; D\to q$

**(A)** On differentiating, $2^x\log2+2^y\log2.\dfrac{dy}{dx}$

$$=2^x.2^y\frac{dy}{dx}.\log2+2^y.2^x\log2$$

$$\Rightarrow 2^x+2^y\frac{dy}{dx}=2^{x+y}\frac{dy}{dx}+2^{x+y}$$

$$\Rightarrow \frac{dy}{dx}=\frac{2^{x+y}-2^x}{2^y-2^{x+y}}$$

$$\Rightarrow \frac{dy}{dx}=\frac{2^x+2^y-2^x}{2^y-2^x-2^y}=-2^{y-x}$$

**(B)** We have $x^y+y^x=1$

Let $u=x^y$ and $v=y^x$ then $u+v=1$

$$\therefore \frac{du}{dx}+\frac{dv}{dx}=0.\qquad\ldots\ldots(1)$$

Taking logarithm with base e of $u=x^y$, we get

$\log u=y\log x$;

$$\therefore \frac{1}{u}\frac{du}{dx}=\frac{dy}{dx}\log x+y.\frac{1}{x}\ \text{ or }\ \frac{du}{dx}=u\left(\frac{dy}{dx}\log x+\frac{y}{x}\right)$$

$$=x^y.\left(\frac{dy}{dx}\log x+\frac{y}{x}\right).$$

Again taking logarithm with base e of $v=y^x$, we get

$\log v=x\log y$

$$\therefore \frac{1}{v}.\frac{dv}{dx}=\log y+x.\frac{1}{y}.\frac{dy}{dx}$$

$$\text{or }\frac{dv}{dx}=v\left(\log y+\frac{x}{y}.\frac{dy}{dx}\right)=y^x\left(\log y+\frac{x}{y}.\frac{dy}{dx}\right)$$

Substituting these values in (1), we get

$$x^y\left(\frac{dy}{dx}\log x+\frac{y}{x}\right)+y^x\left(\log y+\frac{x}{y}.\frac{dy}{dx}\right)=0$$

$$\text{or }\frac{dy}{dx}[x^y\log x+y^{x-1}.x]=-(y^x\log y+x^{y-1}.y)$$

$$\Rightarrow \frac{dy}{dx}=-\frac{y(x^{y-1}+y^{x-1}\log y)}{x(y^{x-1}+x^{y-1}\log x)}.$$

**(C)** If $x=a(\cos\theta+\theta\sin\theta)$ and $y=a(\sin\theta-\theta\cos\theta)$

Then $\dfrac{dx}{d\theta}=a(-\sin\theta+\sin\theta+\theta\cos\theta)=a\theta\cos\theta$

and $\dfrac{dy}{d\theta}=a(\cos\theta-\cos\theta+\theta\sin\theta)=a\theta\sin\theta$

$$\therefore \frac{dy}{dx}=\frac{a\theta\sin\theta}{a\theta\cos\theta}=\tan\theta$$

Now, $\dfrac{d^2y}{dx^2}=\dfrac{d}{dx}\left(\dfrac{dy}{dx}\right)=\dfrac{d}{dx}(\tan\theta)=\dfrac{d}{d\theta}\tan\theta.\dfrac{d\theta}{dx}$

$$=\sec^2\theta.\frac{1}{a\theta\cos\theta}=\frac{\sec^3\theta}{a\theta}$$

**(D)** Differentiating w.r.t. to x,

$$3x^2+3y^2\frac{dy}{dx}=3y+3x\frac{dy}{dx}$$

$$\Rightarrow 3(x^2-y)=3\frac{dy}{dx}(x-y^2)$$

$$\Rightarrow \frac{dy}{dx}=\frac{x^2-y}{x-y^2}$$

**17.** A→r; B→q; C→t; D→p

(A) Take log on both sides

$\Rightarrow y \log x = \log_e e^{x-y} = x - y$

$\Rightarrow y = \dfrac{x}{1 + \log x}, \therefore \dfrac{dy}{dx} = \dfrac{\log x}{(1 + \log x)^2}$

(B) $(a-b)^2 = (a+b)^2 - 4ab$

$\Rightarrow x^2 = y^2 - 4, \therefore 2x = 2y\dfrac{dy}{dx} \Rightarrow \dfrac{dy}{dx} = \dfrac{x}{y}$

(C) Put $x = 3\cos t$

$\Rightarrow \cos^{-1}\left(\dfrac{4x^3}{27} - x\right) = \cos^{-1}(4\cos^3 t - 3\cos t)$

$\Rightarrow \cos^{-1}(\cos 3t) = 3t = 3\cos^{-1}\left(\dfrac{x}{3}\right)$

$\dfrac{dx}{dt} = 3 \cdot \dfrac{-1}{\sqrt{1 - \dfrac{x^2}{9}}} \cdot \dfrac{1}{3} = \dfrac{-3}{\sqrt{9 - x^2}}$

(D) Take log on both sides, $\log x + \log y = n\log(x+y)$

Diff. w.r. to 'x' we get $\dfrac{1}{x} + \dfrac{1}{y}\dfrac{dy}{dx} = n\left(\dfrac{1}{x+y}\right)\left(1 + \dfrac{dy}{dx}\right)$

$\Rightarrow \dfrac{1}{x} + \dfrac{1}{y} \cdot \dfrac{y}{x} = n\left(\dfrac{1}{x+y}\right)\left(1 + \dfrac{y}{x}\right)$

$\Rightarrow \dfrac{2}{x} = n\left(\dfrac{1}{x+y}\right)\left(\dfrac{x+y}{x}\right) \Rightarrow n = 2$

**18.** (c) $\because \quad \sin^{-1}\left(\dfrac{2x}{1+x^2}\right)$

$= \begin{cases} \pi - 2\tan^{-1}x & , \ x > 1 \\ 2\tan^{-1}x & , \ -1 \le x \le 1 \\ -\pi - 2\tan^{-1}x & , \ x < -1 \end{cases}$

and $\cos^{-1}\left(\dfrac{1-x^2}{1+x^2}\right) = \begin{cases} 2\tan^{-1}x, & x \ge 0 \\ -2\tan^{-1}x, & x < 0 \end{cases}$

For $\qquad 0 < x < 1$

$\sin^{-1}\left(\dfrac{2x}{1+x^2}\right) = \cos^{-1}\left(\dfrac{1-x^2}{1+x^2}\right)$

Let $u = \sin^{-1}\left(\dfrac{2x}{1+x^2}\right)$ and $v = \cos^{-1}\left(\dfrac{1-x^2}{1+x^2}\right)$

$\therefore \quad \dfrac{du}{dv} = 1 \qquad (\because u = v)$

**19.** (d) $\because \dfrac{d}{dx}(x^{x^x}) = \dfrac{d}{dx}(x)^{x^x} = \dfrac{d}{dx}e^{\ln(x)^{x^x}}$

$= \dfrac{d}{dx}e^{x^x \ln x}$

$= e^{x^x \cdot \ln x}\{x^x \cdot \dfrac{1}{x} + \ln x \cdot x^x (1 + \ln x)\}$

$= x^{x^x} \cdot x^{x-1}\{1 + x\ln x(1 + \ln x)\}$

**20.** 3

$y^2\left(e^{xy}\left(x\dfrac{dy}{dx} + y\right)\right) + e^{xy} \cdot 2y\dfrac{dy}{dx} = 9e^{-3} \cdot 2x$

put $x = -1$ and $y = 3$

$9\left(e^{-3}\left(-1\dfrac{dy}{dx} + 3\right)\right) + e^{-3} \cdot 6\dfrac{dy}{dx} = -9e^{-3} \cdot 2$

$-9\left(\dfrac{dy}{dx} - 3\right) + 6\dfrac{dy}{dx} = -18$

$3\dfrac{dy}{dx} = 45 \quad \Rightarrow \qquad \dfrac{dy}{dx} = 15$

Thus M = 3

**21.** 9

Given $y^3 - y = 2x$

Differentiate both sides with respect to x, we get

$$(3y^2 - 1)\dfrac{dy}{dx} = 2 \Rightarrow \dfrac{dy}{dx} = \dfrac{2}{(3y^2 - 1)} \ \dots\dots(1)$$

Again differentiating both sides with respect to x, we get

$\dfrac{d^2y}{dx^2} = \dfrac{-2.6y\dfrac{dy}{dx}}{(3y^2 - 1)^2} \qquad$ Using (1) we get

$\dfrac{d^2y}{dx^2} = \dfrac{-24y}{(3y^2 - 1)^3} \qquad \dots\dots(2)$

Now, $\left(x^2 - \dfrac{1}{27}\right)\dfrac{d^2y}{dx^2} + x\dfrac{dy}{dx}$

$= \left(x^2 - \dfrac{1}{27}\right)\left(\dfrac{-24y}{(3y^2 - 1)^3}\right) + \dfrac{2x}{(3y^2 - 1)}$ [From (1) and (2)]

$= \left(\dfrac{y^2(y^2 - 1)^2}{4} - \dfrac{1}{27}\right)\left(\dfrac{-24y}{(3y^2 - 1)^3}\right) + \dfrac{y(y^2 - 1)}{(3y^2 - 1)}$

$(\because y^3 - y = 2x)$

$= \dfrac{\{27y^2(y^2 - 1)^2 - 4\}}{108}\dfrac{(-24y)}{(3y^2 - 1)^3} + \dfrac{y(y^2 - 1)}{(3y^2 - 1)}$

$= \dfrac{y}{9}\left\{\dfrac{-54y^2(y^2 - 1)^2 + 8}{(3y^2 - 1)^3} + \dfrac{9(y^2 - 1)}{(3y^2 - 1)}\right\}$

$= \dfrac{y}{9}\left\{\dfrac{-2(1+\alpha)(\alpha - 2)^2 + 8}{\alpha^3} + \dfrac{3(\alpha - 2)}{\alpha}\right\} = \dfrac{y}{9} \ (\alpha = 3y^2 - 1)$

**22.   1**

$\log(x+y) = 2xy$ when $x = 0 \Rightarrow y = 1$

Differentiating w.r.t. x

$\Rightarrow \quad \dfrac{1}{x+y}\left[1+\dfrac{dy}{dx}\right] = 2y + \dfrac{2xdy}{dx}$

$\Rightarrow \quad \dfrac{dy}{dx} = \dfrac{1/x + 1 - 2y}{2x - 1/x + y}$

$\Rightarrow \quad y'(0) = \dfrac{1-2}{0-1} = 1$

**23.   3**

Equation can be written as

$(y^2 + 2)\left(y - \dfrac{\cos x}{1+\sin x}\right) = 0$. As $y^2 + 2 \neq 0$.

$y = \dfrac{\cos x}{1+\sin x}$ with $t = \tan\dfrac{x}{2}$, $y(t) = \dfrac{1-t^2}{1+t^2+2t} = \dfrac{1-t}{1+t} = \dfrac{2}{1+t} - 1$

$y'(t) = \dfrac{-2}{(1+t)^2}$

At $x = \dfrac{\pi}{2}$, $t = 1$ and $y'(1) = -\dfrac{1}{2}$

Thus, $A + B = 1 + 2 = 3$

**24.   0**

$y\sqrt{x^2+1} = \log\left\{\sqrt{x^2+1} - x\right\}$

Differentiating both sides w.r.t.x we get

$\dfrac{dy}{dx}\sqrt{x^2+1} + y.\dfrac{1}{2\sqrt{x^2+1}}.2x$

$= \dfrac{1}{\sqrt{x^2+1} - x} \times \left\{\dfrac{1}{2}\dfrac{2x}{\sqrt{x^2+1}} - 1\right\}$

$\Rightarrow (x^2+1)\dfrac{dy}{dx} + xy = \sqrt{x^2+1}.\dfrac{-1}{\sqrt{x^2+1}}$

$\Rightarrow (x^2+1)\dfrac{dy}{dx} + xy + 1 = 0$.

**1. (c)** We have $y^2 = P(x)$, where $P(x)$ is a polynomial of degree 3 and hence thrice differentiable.

Then $\qquad y^2 = P(x) \qquad\qquad ........(1)$

Differentiating (1) w.r. to x, we get

$$2y\frac{dy}{dx} = p'(x) \qquad\qquad .........(2)$$

Again differentiating with respect to x, we get

$$2\left(\frac{dy}{dx}\right)^2 + 2y\frac{d^2y}{dx^2} = p''(x)$$

$$\Rightarrow \quad \frac{[P'(x)]^2}{2y^2} + 2y\frac{d^2y}{dx^2} = p''(x) \quad [\text{Using}\,(2)]$$

$$\Rightarrow \quad 4y^3\frac{d^2y}{dx^2} = 2y^2 p''(x) - [P'(x)]^2$$

$$\Rightarrow \quad 4y^3\frac{d^2y}{dx^2} = 2P(x)P''(x) - [P'(x)]^2 \quad [\text{Using}\,(1)]$$

$$\Rightarrow \quad 2y^3\frac{d^2y}{dx^2} = P(x)P''(x) - \frac{1}{2}[P'(x)]^2$$

Again differentiating w.r. to x, we get

$$2\frac{d}{dx}\left(y^3\frac{d^2y}{dx^2}\right)$$

$$= P'''(x)P(x) + P''(x)P'(x) - P'(x)P''(x)$$

$$= P'''(x)P(x)$$

**2. (b)** Let $f(x) = ax^2 + bx + c$

As given that $f(x) > 0,\ \forall\ x \in R$

$\therefore\quad a > 0$ and $D < 0$

$\Rightarrow\quad a > 0$ and $b^2 - 4ac < 0 \qquad .....(1)$

Now, $g(x) = f(x) + f'(x) + f''(x)$

$\qquad\quad = ax^2 + bx + c + 2ax + b + 2a$

$\qquad\quad = ax^2 + (2a + b)x + (2a + b + c)$

Here, $D = (2a + b)^2 - 4a(2a + b + c)$

$\qquad\quad = 4a^2 + b^2 + 4ab - 8a^2 - 4ab - 4ac$

$\qquad\quad = b^2 - 8a^2 - 4ac = -8a^2 + b^2 - 4ac$

$\qquad\quad = (-ve) + (-ve) = -ve \qquad [\text{Using eq. (1)}]$

Also $a > 0$ from (1), $g(x) > 0,\ \forall\ x \in R$

**3. (d)** We are given,

$$f(x) = \begin{vmatrix} x^3 & \sin x & \cos x \\ 6 & -1 & 0 \\ p & p^2 & p^3 \end{vmatrix}\quad \text{where p is constant.}$$

Now keeping in mind that

$$\frac{d}{dx}\begin{vmatrix} f_1(x) & f_2(x) & f_3(x) \\ g_1(x) & g_2(x) & g_3(x) \\ h_1(x) & h_2(x) & h_3(x) \end{vmatrix}$$

$$= \begin{vmatrix} f_1'(x) & f_2'(x) & f_3'(x) \\ g_1(x) & g_2(x) & g_3(x) \\ h_1(x) & h_2(x) & h_3(x) \end{vmatrix}$$

$$+ \begin{vmatrix} f_1(x) & f_2(x) & f_3(x) \\ g_1'(x) & g_2'(x) & g_3'(x) \\ h_1(x) & h_2(x) & h_3(x) \end{vmatrix}$$

$$+ \begin{vmatrix} f_1(x) & f_2(x) & f_3(x) \\ g_1(x) & g_2(x) & g_3(x) \\ h_1'(x) & h_2'(x) & h_3'(x) \end{vmatrix}$$

We get, $f'(x) = \begin{vmatrix} 3x^2 & \cos x & \sin x \\ 6 & -1 & 0 \\ p & p^2 & p^3 \end{vmatrix}$

$$\Rightarrow\quad f''(x) = \begin{vmatrix} 6x & -\sin x & -\cos x \\ 6 & -1 & 0 \\ p & p^2 & p^3 \end{vmatrix}$$

$$\Rightarrow\quad f'''(x) = \begin{vmatrix} 6 & -\cos x & \sin x \\ 6 & -1 & 0 \\ p & p^2 & p^3 \end{vmatrix}$$

$$\therefore\quad f'''(0) = \begin{vmatrix} 6 & -1 & 0 \\ 6 & -1 & 0 \\ p & p^2 & p^3 \end{vmatrix} = 0 \qquad (\because R_1 \equiv R_2)$$

$\qquad = $ independent of p.

**4. (b)** $x^2 + y^2 \Rightarrow 2x + 2yy' = 0 \Rightarrow x + yy' = 0$

$$\Rightarrow\quad 1 + yy'' + (y')^2 = 0 \Rightarrow yy'' + (y')^2 + 1 = 0$$

**5. (c)** $f'(x) = \underset{h \to 0}{\text{Lim}}\ \frac{f(x+h) - f(x)}{h} = \underset{h \to 0}{\text{Lim}}\ \frac{f(x)\{f(h)-1\}}{h}$

$$= \underset{h \to 0}{\text{Lim}}\ \frac{f(x)(1 + hg(h) - 1)}{h}$$

$$= \underset{h \to 0}{\text{Lim}}\ f(x)g(h) = (\log a)\ f(x)$$

Hence $f''(x) = (\log a)(f'(x)) = (\log a)^2 f(x)$

Thus $f^n(x) = (\log a)^n f(x)$ so $K = (\log a)^n$

**6.  (a)**  $x = e^{y+x} \Rightarrow \log x = x + y \Rightarrow \dfrac{1}{x} = 1 + \dfrac{dy}{dx}$

$\therefore \quad \dfrac{dy}{dx} = \dfrac{1-x}{x}$

**7.  (a)**  Given that $g^{-1}(x) = f(x)$

$\Rightarrow \quad x = g(f(x))$ or $g'(f(x))f'(x) = 1$

$\Rightarrow \quad g'(f(x)) = \dfrac{1}{f'(x)}$

$\Rightarrow \quad g''(f(x)).f'(x) = -\dfrac{f''(x)}{[f'(x)]^2}$

$\Rightarrow \quad g''(f(x)) = -\dfrac{f''(x)}{[f'(x)]^3}$

**8.  (c)**  Given $y^3 - y = 2x$
Differentiating both sides w.r.t. x, we get

$(3y^2 - 1)\dfrac{dy}{dx} = 2 \Rightarrow \dfrac{dy}{dx} = \dfrac{2}{(3y^2 - 1)}$ .....(1)

Again differentiating both sides w.r.t. x, we get

$\dfrac{d^2y}{dx^2} = \dfrac{-2.6y\dfrac{dy}{dx}}{(3y^2-1)^2}$

Using (1), we get $\dfrac{d^2y}{dx^2} = \dfrac{-24y}{(3y^2-1)^3}$ .....(2)

Now, L.H.S. $= \left(x^2 - \dfrac{1}{27}\right)\dfrac{dy^2}{dx^2} + x\dfrac{dy}{dx}$

$= \left(x^2 - \dfrac{1}{27}\right)\left(\dfrac{-24y}{(3y^2-1)^3}\right) + \dfrac{2x}{(3y^2-1)}$

[From (1) and (2)]

$= \left(\dfrac{y^2(y^2-1)^2}{4} - \dfrac{1}{27}\right)\left(\dfrac{-24y}{(3y^2-1)^3}\right) + \dfrac{y(y^2-1)}{(3y^2-1)}$

$(\because\ y^3 - y = 2x)$

$= \dfrac{\{27y^2(y^2-1)^2 - 4\}}{108}\dfrac{(-24y)}{(3y^2-1)^3} + \dfrac{y(y^2-1)}{(3y^2-1)}$

$= \dfrac{y}{9}\left\{\dfrac{-54y^2(y^2-1)^2 + 8}{(3y^2-1)^3} + \dfrac{9(y^2-1)}{(3y^2-1)}\right\}$

$= \dfrac{y}{9}\left\{\dfrac{-2(1+\alpha)(\alpha-2)^2 + 8}{\alpha^3}\right\} + \dfrac{3(\alpha-2)}{\alpha} = \dfrac{y}{9}$

$(\alpha = 3y^2 - 1)$

**9.  (a)**  If $y = e^{ax}\sin(bx+c)$  ....(i)

Then, $\dfrac{dy}{dx} = ae^{ax}\sin(bx+c) + b\cos(bx+c)e^{ax}$

$= ay + be^{ax}\cos(bx+c)$  ....(ii)

Again $\dfrac{d^2y}{dx^2} = a\dfrac{dy}{dx} + b.ae^{ax}\cos(bx+c) - b^2e^{ax}\sin(bx+c)$

$= a\dfrac{dy}{dx} + a\left(\dfrac{dy}{dx} - ay\right) - b^2y$  [from (i) & (ii)]

$\dfrac{dy}{dx} = 2a\dfrac{dy}{dx} - (a^2+b^2)y \Rightarrow \dfrac{d^2y}{dx^2} - 2a\dfrac{dy}{dx} + (a^2+b^2)y = 0$

**10.  (a)**  $y_1 = m(x+\sqrt{x^2+1})^{m-1}\left\{1 + \dfrac{2x}{2\sqrt{x^2+1}}\right\}$

$= \dfrac{my}{\sqrt{x^2+1}}$

$\Rightarrow\ y_1^2(x^2+1) = m^2y^2$

Diff. $2y_1y_2(x^2+1) + y_1^2(2x) = m^2(2yy_1)$

$\Rightarrow\ 2y_1[y_2(x^2+1) + xy_1 - m^2y] = 0$

**11.  (d)**  $y = e^{\sqrt{x}} + e^{-\sqrt{x}}$

$\Rightarrow\ y_1 = (e^{\sqrt{x}} - e^{-\sqrt{x}})\dfrac{1}{2\sqrt{x}}$

$\Rightarrow\ 2y_1\sqrt{x} = e^{\sqrt{x}} - e^{-\sqrt{x}}$

$\Rightarrow\ 2y_2\sqrt{x} + 2y_1.\dfrac{1}{2\sqrt{x}}$

$= (e^{\sqrt{x}} + e^{-\sqrt{x}})\dfrac{1}{2\sqrt{x}}$

$\Rightarrow\ 4y_2 x + 2y_1 = y$

**12.  (b,c)**  $y = 1 - 2\sin^2 x\cos^2 x = 1 - \dfrac{1}{2}\sin^2 2x$

$= 1 - \dfrac{1}{4}(1 - \cos 4x)$

$\therefore\quad y_n = \dfrac{1}{4}.4^n\cos(4x + n\pi/2)$

$= 4^{n-1}\sin\left(\dfrac{\pi}{2} - 4x - \dfrac{n\pi}{2}\right)$

$= 4^{n-1}\sin\left(\dfrac{\pi}{2}(n-1) - 4x\right)$

**13. (a,b,c)** Given

$$f(x) = x^3 + x^2 f'(1) + x f''(2) + f'''(3)$$
$$\Rightarrow f'(x) = 3x^2 + 2x f'(1) + f''(2)$$
$$\Rightarrow f'(1) = 3 + 2f'(1) + f''(2)$$
$$\Rightarrow f'(1) + f''(2) = -3 \qquad ....(i)$$
$$\Rightarrow \text{and } f''(x) = 6x + 2f'(1)$$
$$\therefore f''(2) = 12 + 2f'(1)$$
$$\therefore -2f'(1) + f''(2) = 12 \qquad ....(ii)$$

Solving Eqs. (i) and (ii) we get

$$f'(1) = -5 \text{ and } f''(2) = 2$$

And $f'''(x) = 6$

$$\therefore \quad f'''(3) = 6 \qquad ....(iii)$$

**Substituting the values of** $f'(1), f''(2)$ and $f'''(3)$
from Eq. (i), (ii) and (iii) in $f(x)$

$$\therefore f(x) = x^3 - 5x^2 + 2x + 6$$
$$\Rightarrow f(0) = 6, f(1) = 4, f(2) = -2, f(3) = -6$$

Hence, $f(0) + f(2) = f(1)$

$$f(0) + f(3) = 0$$

and $f(1) + f(3) = f(2)$

**14. (a,b,c)** $f(x) = x^2 + xg'(1) + g''(2)$

and $g(x) = x^2 + xf'(2) + f''(3)$
$$f'(x) = 2x + g'(1), f''(x) = (2)$$
$$g'(x) = 2x + f'(2), g''(x) = 2$$
At $x = 1$, $f'(1) = 2 + g'(1)$ and $g'(1) = 2 + f'(2)$
$$\Rightarrow f'(1) = 4 + f'(2)$$
Putting $x = 2$, $f'(2) = 4 + g'(1)$, $g'(2) = 4 + f'(2)$
$$\therefore g'(2) = 4 + 4 + g'(1) = 8 + g'(1)$$
and $g''(2) + f''(3) = 2 + 2 = 4$

**15. (a,b,c)** Given $F(x) = f(x) \cdot g(x)$ $\qquad ....(1)$

Differentiating both sides w.r.t., x we get

$$F'(x) = f'(x).g(x) + g'(x).f(x)$$

$$\Rightarrow F'(x) = f'(x)g'(x)\left[\frac{f(x)}{f'(x)} + \frac{g(x)}{g'(x)}\right]$$

$$\Rightarrow F' = c\left[\frac{f}{f'} + \frac{g}{g'}\right]$$

Again differentiating both sides w.r.t., x we get

$$F''(x) = f''(x).g(x) + g''(x).f(x) + 2f'(x).g'(x)$$

$$\Rightarrow F''(x) = f''(x).g(x) + g''(x).f(x) + 2c \qquad .....(2)$$

Dividing both sides by $F(x) = f(x) \cdot g(x)$

$$\{\because f'(x).g'(x) = c\}$$

then $\dfrac{F''(x)}{F(x)} = \dfrac{f''(x)}{f(x)} + \dfrac{g''(x)}{g(x)} + \dfrac{2c}{f(x)g(x)}$

or $\dfrac{F''}{F} = \dfrac{f''}{f} + \dfrac{g''}{g} + \dfrac{2c}{fg}$

Again given $f'(x)g'(x) = c$

Differentiating both sides w.r.t., x we get

$$f'(x)g''(x) + g'(x) - f''(x) = 0$$

From (2), $F''(x) = f''(x) \cdot g(x) + g''(x) \cdot f(x) + 2c$

Differentiating both sides w.r.t., x we get

$$F'''(x) = f''(x).g'(x) + f'''(x).g(x) + g''(x).f'(x) + f(x).g'''(x)$$
$$+ 0 = f'''(x).g(x) + g'''(x).f(x) + 0 \quad \text{[from (3)]}$$

Now dividing both sides by $F(x) = f(x) g(x)$

Then $\dfrac{F'''(x)}{F(x)} = \dfrac{f'''(x)}{f(x)} + \dfrac{g'''(x)}{g(x)}$

or $\dfrac{F'''}{F} = \dfrac{f'''}{f} + \dfrac{g'''}{g}$

**16. (d)** $y = \dfrac{x^2 + 1}{(x-1)(x-2)(x-3)}$

Breaking into partial fractions,

$$\frac{x^2 + 1}{(x-1)(x-2)(x-3)} = \frac{A}{x-1} + \frac{B}{x-2} + \frac{C}{x-3}$$

Then, $A = \dfrac{1^2 + 1}{(1-2)(1-3)} = 1$

$$B = \frac{2^2 + 1}{(2-1)(2-3)} = -5$$

$$C = \frac{3^2 + 1}{(3-1)(3-2)} = 5$$

[Also, see partial fractions]

Thus, $y = \dfrac{x^2 + 1}{(x-1)(x-2)(x-3)}$

$$= \frac{1}{x-1} - \frac{5}{x-2} + \frac{5}{x-3}$$

$$\therefore \quad y_n = (-1)^n n! \frac{1}{(x-1)^{n+1}}$$

$$-5(-1)^n n! \frac{1}{(x-2)^{n+1}} + 5(-1)^n n! \frac{1}{(x-3)^{n+1}} = (-1)^n n!$$

$$\left[\frac{1}{(x-1)^{n+1}} - \frac{5}{(x-2)^{n+1}} + \frac{5}{(x-3)^{n+1}}\right]$$

**17. (c)** We have,

$$D^n(x^2 y_2) = x^2 y_{n+2} + n.(2x)y_{n+1} + \frac{n(n-1)}{2!}.2y_n$$

$$D^n(xy_1) = xy_{n+1} + n.y_n$$

$$D^n(y) = y_n$$

Adding, we get

$0 = x^2 y_{n+2} + (2n+1)\, xy_{n+1} + (n^2+1)\, y_n$

$\therefore\ x^2 y_{n+2} + (2n+1)xy_{n+1} + n^2 y_n = -y_n$

**18. (c)** If $y = x^{2n}$, then

$$y_n = \frac{(2n)!}{(2n-n)!}\, x^{2n-n} = \frac{(2n)!}{n!}\, x^n \qquad \dots\text{(i)}$$

Again regard $x^{2n}$ as $x^n . x^n$.

$\therefore\ D^n\,(x^{2n}) = D^n(x^n.x^n)$

$= D^n(x^n).x^n + {}^nC_1 D^{n-1}(x^n).Dx^n +$

${}^nC_2 D^{n-2}(x^n).D^2 x^n + \dots\dots\dots x^n . D^n\,(x^n)$

$= n!\,x^n + n.\dfrac{n!}{1!}x.nx^{n-1} + \dfrac{n(n-1)}{2!}\dfrac{n!}{2!}x^2 \times n\,(n-$

$1)\,x^{n-2} + \dots\dots\dots x^n .n!$

$= x^n .n!\left[1 + \dfrac{n^2}{1^2} + \dfrac{n^2(n-1)^2}{2!.2!} + \dots\dots\dots\right]$

$= \dfrac{(2n)!}{n!}\, x^n \qquad \text{[by (i)]}$

$\therefore\ 1 + \dfrac{n^2}{1^2} + \dfrac{n^2(n-1)^2}{1^2.2^2} + \dots\dots\dots = \dfrac{(2n)!}{(n!)^2}$

**19.**  **A→r; B→p; C→q; D→t**

(A)  Put $x = \cos 2\theta$

$$\Rightarrow \frac{d}{dx}(\sin^2 .\cot^{-1}(\cot\theta)) = \frac{d}{dx}\left(\frac{1-\cos 2\theta}{2}\right)$$

$$= \frac{d}{dx}\left(\frac{1-x}{2}\right) = \frac{-1}{2}\ \textbf{(r)}$$

(B)  $\log(h(x)) = e^x \Rightarrow \dfrac{1}{h(x)}h^1(x) = e^x = \log(h(x))$ **(p)**

(C)  $f'(x) = \sqrt{a}.\dfrac{1}{2\sqrt{x}} + a\sqrt{a}.\left(\dfrac{-1}{2}\right)(x)^{\frac{-3}{2}}$ ;

$f'(a) = \dfrac{1}{2} - \dfrac{1}{2}a\sqrt{a}.\dfrac{1}{a\sqrt{a}} = 0$ **(q)**

(D)  $\tan y = e^{2\cos 2x}.\sin^2 x$

$\sec^2 y\dfrac{dy}{dx} = \sin 2x\ e^{2\cos 2x} - 4e^{2\cos 2x}.\sin^2 x.\sin 2x$

$\sec^2 y\dfrac{dy}{dx} = \sin 2x.e^{2\cos 2x} - 4\sin^2 x.\tan y$

$\Rightarrow \dfrac{dy}{dx} = \sin 2y[\cot x - 2\sin 2x]$ **(t)**

**20.  0**

$f(2x^2 - 1) = 2x\, f(x) \qquad \dots\text{(1)}$

Replace $x$ by $-x$ then

$f(2x^2 - 1) = -2x\, f(-x) \quad \dots\text{(2)}$

From (1) and (2)

$2x\big[f(x) + f(-x)\big] = 0 \Rightarrow f(x) + f(-x) = 0$

$\therefore\ f(x)$ is an odd function.

$\Rightarrow\ f^{iv}(x)$ is also odd $\Rightarrow f^{iv}(0) = 0$

**21.  3**

Let $x = a\cos^2\theta + b\sin^2\theta$

$\therefore\ a - x = a - a\cos^2\theta - b\sin^2\theta = (a-b)\sin^2\theta$

and $x - b = a\cos^2\theta + b\sin^2\theta - b = (a-b)\cos^2\theta$

$\therefore\ y = (a-b)\sin\theta\cos\theta - (a-b)\tan^{-1}\tan\theta$

$= \dfrac{a-b}{2}\sin 2\theta - (a-b)\theta$

$\therefore\ \dfrac{dy}{dx} = \dfrac{dy/d\theta}{dx/d\theta} = \dfrac{(a-b)\cos 2\theta - (a-b)}{(b-a)\sin 2\theta}$

$= \dfrac{1-\cos 2\theta}{\sin 2\theta} = \tan\theta = \sqrt{\dfrac{a-x}{x-b}}$

Thus, $P = 1, Q = 2$

$\Rightarrow P + Q = 3$

**22.  3**

With $\theta = \cos^{-1}x,\ \tan^{-1}\sqrt{\dfrac{1-x}{1+x}}$

$= \tan^{-1}\sqrt{\dfrac{2\sin^2\frac{\theta}{2}}{2\cos^2\frac{\theta}{2}}} = \dfrac{\theta}{2} = \dfrac{1}{2}\left(\dfrac{\pi}{2} - \sin^{-1}x\right)$

as $\cos^{-1}x + \sin^{-1}x = \dfrac{\pi}{2}$.

Required derivative $= -1/2$

$\therefore A + B = 1 + 2 = 3$.

**23.  3**

$z = (\cos x)^5,\ y = \sin x$

$\dfrac{dz}{dx} = -5\cos^4 x.\sin x\ ,\ \dfrac{dy}{dx} = \cos x$

$\therefore\ \dfrac{dz}{dy} = -5\cos^3 x.\sin x$

now $\dfrac{d^2z}{dy^2} = \dfrac{d}{dx}\left(\dfrac{dz}{dy}\right).\dfrac{dx}{dy}$

$= -5\dfrac{d}{dx}[\cos^3 x.\sin x]\dfrac{1}{\cos x}$

$= -5\,[\cos^4 x - 3\sin^2 x.\cos^2 x]\dfrac{1}{\cos x}$

$= -5(\cos^3 x - 3\sin^2 x.\cos x)$

$= -5(\cos^3 x - 3\cos x(1 - \cos^2 x))$

$= -5(4\cos^3 x - 3\cos x) = -5\cos 3x$

$\therefore \dfrac{d^2z}{dy^2}\bigg|_{x=\frac{2\pi}{9}} = -5\cos 120° = \dfrac{5}{2}$

Thus, $P - Q = 5 - 2 = 3$

**24.  0**

If $y = ke^{a\sin^{-1}x}$

$\therefore \dfrac{dy}{dx} = k.e^{a\sin^{-1}x}\dfrac{a}{\sqrt{1-x^2}} = \dfrac{ay}{\sqrt{1-x^2}}$

$\Rightarrow \sqrt{1-x^2}\dfrac{dy}{dx} = ay \Rightarrow (1-x^2)\left(\dfrac{dy}{dx}\right)^2 = a^2y^2$

Differentiating again, we get

$\left(1-x^2\right).2\dfrac{dy}{dx}.\dfrac{d^2y}{dx^2} + \left(\dfrac{dy}{dx}\right)^2(-2x) = a^2.2y\dfrac{dy}{dx}$

$\therefore \ 2\dfrac{dy}{dx}\left[(1-x^2)\dfrac{d^2y}{dx^2} - x\dfrac{dy}{dx} - a^2y\right] = 0$

$\Rightarrow (1-x^2)\dfrac{d^2y}{dx^2} - x\dfrac{dy}{dx} - a^2y = 0$

**1.** **(d).** Given, $V = \pi r^2 h$

Differentiating both sides

$$\frac{dV}{dt} = \pi\left(r^2\frac{dh}{dt} + 2r\frac{dr}{dt}h\right) = \pi r\left(r\frac{dh}{dt} + 2h\frac{dr}{dt}\right)$$

$$\frac{dr}{dt} = \frac{1}{10} \quad \text{and} \quad \frac{dh}{dt} = -\frac{2}{10}$$

$$\frac{dV}{dt} = \pi r\left(r\left(-\frac{2}{10}\right) + 2h\left(\frac{1}{10}\right)\right) = \frac{\pi r}{5}(-r + h)$$

Thus, when $r = 2$ and $h = 3$,

$$\frac{dV}{dt} = \frac{\pi(2)}{5}(-2+3) = \frac{2\pi}{5}$$

**2.** **(d).** For cylindrical pot $V = \pi r^2 h$

$$\frac{dV}{dt} = \pi\left[r^2\frac{dh}{dt} + h\cdot 2r\frac{dr}{dt}\right] \quad (r = \text{constant}, \ \frac{dr}{dt} = 0)$$

hence, $\quad 100 = \pi r^2\dfrac{dh}{dt}$

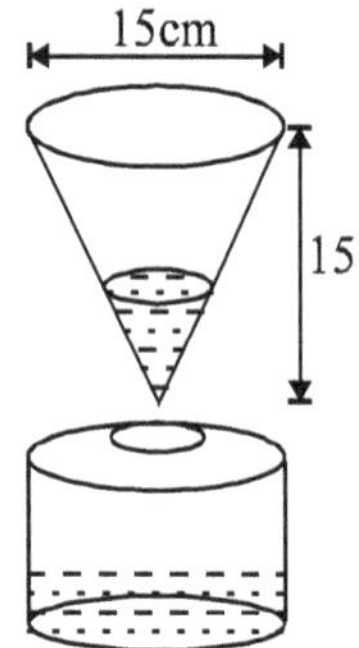

$$100 = \pi \cdot \frac{225}{4} \cdot \frac{dh}{dt} \qquad (r = \frac{15}{2} \text{ cm})$$

$$\frac{dh}{dt} = \frac{400}{225\pi} = \frac{16}{9\pi} \text{ cm/min}$$

**3.** **(d).** $\dfrac{dr}{dt} = c$ and $\quad h = ar + b$

Also $\quad \dfrac{dh}{dt} = 3\dfrac{dr}{dt}$ (given)

$$\therefore \ a\frac{dr}{dt} = 3\frac{dr}{dt} \Rightarrow \ a = 3$$

hence $\quad h = 3r + b$

when $r = 1$ ; $h = 6 \Rightarrow 6 = 3 + b \Rightarrow b = 3$

$\therefore h = 3(r+1)$

$V = \pi r^2 h = 3\pi r^2(r+1) = 3\pi(r^3 + r^2)$

$$\frac{dV}{dt} = 3\pi(3r^2 + 2r)\frac{dr}{dt}$$

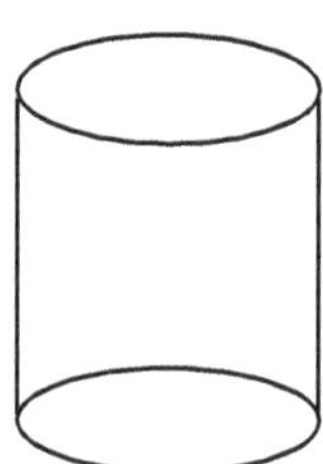

where $\ r = 6$ ; $\dfrac{dV}{dt} = 1$ cc/sec

$$\therefore \ 1 = 3\pi(108+12)\frac{dr}{dt} \Rightarrow \ 360\pi\frac{dr}{dt} = 1$$

again when $r = 36$, $\dfrac{dV}{dt} = n$

$$n = 3\pi((3.36)^2 + 2.36)\frac{dr}{dt}$$

$$n = 3\pi \cdot 36(110) \cdot \frac{1}{360\pi}$$

$$n = 33$$

**4.** **(b).** $V = \dfrac{4}{3}\pi(r^3 - 10^3)$, $r$ being the distance of outer coat

of ice from the centre

$$\therefore \ \frac{dV}{dt} = 4\pi r^2\frac{dr}{dt} \Rightarrow 4\pi r^2\frac{dr}{dt} = 50$$

$$\Rightarrow \frac{dr}{dt} = \frac{50}{4\pi r^2} = \frac{1}{18\pi} \text{ cm/min}$$

$$(\because r = 10 + 5)$$

**5.** **(c).** $A_2 = (x - x^2)^2$, $A_1 = x^2$

$$\frac{dA_2}{dx} = 2(x - x^2)(1 - 2x)$$

$$\Rightarrow \frac{dA_1}{dx} = 2x$$

Req. ratio $= 1 + 2x^2 - 3x$

**6.** **(d)** $V = 5x - \dfrac{x^2}{6} \Rightarrow \dfrac{dV}{dt} = 5\dfrac{dx}{dt} - \dfrac{x}{3} \cdot \dfrac{dx}{dt}$

$\Rightarrow \dfrac{dx}{dt} = \dfrac{\dfrac{dV}{dt}}{\left(5 - \dfrac{x}{3}\right)}$

$\Rightarrow \left(\dfrac{dx}{dt}\right)_{x=2} = \dfrac{5}{5 - \dfrac{2}{3}} = \dfrac{15}{13} \, \text{cm/sec}.$

**7.** **(d)** Let at any instant, the radius of the base and height of the cone formed by the water in the filter be x and y respectively

∴ Volume of water in the filter at that time is

$V = \dfrac{1}{3}\pi x^2 y \quad \text{But} \quad \dfrac{x}{y} = \dfrac{10}{20} = \dfrac{1}{2} \quad \therefore x = \dfrac{1}{2}y$

$\therefore V = \dfrac{1}{3}\pi \dfrac{1}{4}y^2 \cdot y = \dfrac{\pi y^3}{12}$

$\therefore \dfrac{dV}{dt} = \dfrac{\pi}{12} 3y^2 \dfrac{dy}{dt} = \dfrac{\pi y^2}{4}\dfrac{dy}{dt}$

Given $\dfrac{dV}{dt} = 5$

We have to find $\dfrac{dy}{dt}$, when y = 15

$\therefore 5 = \pi \dfrac{(15)^2}{4}\dfrac{dy}{dt}$

$\therefore \dfrac{dy}{dt} = \dfrac{5 \times 4}{15 \times 15} \cdot \dfrac{1}{\pi} = \dfrac{4}{45\pi} \, \text{cm/sec}.$

**8.** **(b)** Let velocity v = 5cm/sec

$\dfrac{da}{dt} = 5 \qquad\qquad \ldots\text{(i)}$

Where a is distance and t is time.
But if a is edge of a cube. then $V = a^3$.
Differentiating w.r.t. time t. so

$\dfrac{dV}{dt} = 3a^2\dfrac{da}{dt} = 3a^2 .5 = 15a^2 = 15 \times (12)^2$

$= 2160 \, \text{cm}^3/\text{sec} \qquad (\because \text{edge } a = 12\text{cm}).$

**9.** **(a)** Given that rate of metal increasing

$= 4\text{cm/sec} = v = \dfrac{da}{dt}$

We know that area of square sheet (a) = $a^2$, (where a is side).

$\therefore \dfrac{dA}{dt} = 2a\dfrac{da}{dt} = 2 \times 2 \times 4 = 16\,\text{cm}^2/\text{sec}$

**10.** **(a)** Given the rate of increasing the radius

$= \dfrac{dr}{dt} = 3.5 \, \text{cm/sec} \text{ and } r = 10 \, \text{cm}$

Area of circle = A = $\pi r^2$.

$\Rightarrow \dfrac{dA}{dt} = 2\pi r.\dfrac{dr}{dt} \Rightarrow \dfrac{dA}{dt} = 2\pi \times 10 \times 3.5$

$\Rightarrow \dfrac{dA}{dt} = 220\,\text{cm}^2/\text{sec}.$

**11.** **(c)** $V = \dfrac{4}{3}\pi r^3$

Differentiate with respect to t,

$\dfrac{dV}{dt} = \dfrac{4}{3}\pi 3r^2.\dfrac{dr}{dt} \Rightarrow \dfrac{dr}{dt} = \dfrac{1}{4\pi r^2}.\dfrac{dV}{dt}$

$\dfrac{dr}{dt} = \dfrac{1}{4\pi \times 15 \times 15} \times 900 \Rightarrow \dfrac{dr}{dt} = \dfrac{1}{\pi} = \dfrac{7}{22}$

**12.** **(d)** Given curve is $y^2 = 18x$

$\therefore 2y\dfrac{dy}{dt} = 18\dfrac{dx}{dt} \Rightarrow 2y.2 = 18\left[\because \dfrac{dy}{dt} = 2\dfrac{dx}{dt}\right]$

$\Rightarrow y = \dfrac{9}{2} \qquad\qquad \therefore x = \dfrac{y^2}{18} = \dfrac{81}{4 \times 18} = \dfrac{9}{8}$

$\therefore$ Required point is $\left(\dfrac{9}{8}, \dfrac{9}{2}\right)$.

**13.** **(a)** Let h be the height and r be the radius of the 'water cylinder' formed at a time t.
The volume V of the 'water cylinder' is given

$V = \pi r^2 h$, but r = 3 ft. Thus we have

$V = 9\pi h \Rightarrow \dfrac{dv}{dt} = 9\pi.\dfrac{dh}{dt} \Rightarrow 12 = 9\pi\dfrac{dh}{dt}$

$\Rightarrow \dfrac{dh}{dt} = \dfrac{4}{3\pi} \, \text{ft/min.} \qquad \left(\because \dfrac{dV}{dt} = 12\right)$

**14.** **(b)** Let r and h be the radius and height of the sand – cone at time t respectively.

$h = \dfrac{r}{6} \qquad \ldots\text{(i)}$

Let V be the volume of the cone

$V = \dfrac{1}{3}\pi r^2 h = \dfrac{1}{3}\pi (6h)^2 \cdot h = \dfrac{1}{3}\pi \times 36\,h^2 . h = 12\,\pi h^3$

$\dfrac{dV}{dt} = 12\,\pi (3\,h^2).\dfrac{dh}{dt} \Rightarrow \dfrac{dV}{dt} = 36\,\pi h^2\dfrac{dh}{dt}$

It is given that sand is pouring at the rate of 12 $\text{cm}^3/\text{sec}.$

$\therefore \dfrac{dV}{dt} = 12. \therefore 12 = 36\,\pi h^2\dfrac{dh}{dt} \Rightarrow \dfrac{dh}{dt} = \dfrac{12}{36\,\pi h^2} = \dfrac{1}{3\pi h^2}$

Hence the rate of increase of height of sand – cone w.r.t. – t.

When $h = 4$ is $\left(\dfrac{dh}{dt}\right)_{h=4} = \dfrac{1}{3\pi\,(4)^2} = \dfrac{1}{48\pi}$ cm / sec.

**15. (b)** We have $6y = x^3 + 2$  ...(i)

Differentiating w.r.t. t of equ. (i)

$$6\frac{dy}{dt} = 3x^2\frac{dx}{dt} \quad \Rightarrow \quad 2\frac{dy}{dt} = x^2\frac{dx}{dt} \qquad ...(ii)$$

Now, y coordinate changes 8 times as fast as x coordinate i.e.,

$$\frac{dy}{dt} = 8\frac{dx}{dt}$$

Putting this value of $\dfrac{dy}{dt}$ in (ii), we have

$$2\left(8\frac{dx}{dt}\right) = x^2\left(\frac{dx}{dt}\right) \;\Rightarrow\; x^2 = 16 \Rightarrow x = \pm 4$$

When $x = 4$, then from (i)

$$y = \frac{1}{6}\,(4^3 + 2) = \frac{1}{6}\,(64 + 2) = \frac{66}{6} = 11$$

When $x = -4$, then from (i)

$$y = \frac{1}{6}\,(-64 + 2) = \frac{-62}{6} = -\frac{31}{3}$$

Hence, the required points are $(4, 11), \left(-4, \dfrac{-31}{3}\right)$

**16. (d)** Diameter of the sphere $= \dfrac{3}{2}\,(2x + 1)$

$\therefore$ Radius of the sphere $= \dfrac{3}{4}\,(2x + 1)$

Volume of the sphere

$$V = \frac{4}{3}\,\pi \cdot \frac{27}{64}\,(2x + 1)^3 \;, \qquad V = \frac{9\pi}{16}\,(2x + 1)^3$$

$\therefore$ Rate of change of volume with respect to x

$$\frac{dV}{dx} = \frac{9\pi}{16}\cdot 3\,(2x + 1)^2\cdot 2 \qquad \frac{dv}{dx} = \frac{27\pi}{8}\,(2x + 1)^2$$

**17. (b, c)** Let at time t the area of the circle $= A$, the radius $= r$.

$\therefore A = \pi r^2$.

Differentiating with respect to t, we get

$$\frac{dA}{dt} = \pi 2r\frac{dr}{dt} \qquad .......(1).$$

By question, the rate of increase of area of the circle =

$$\frac{dA}{dt} = K \quad \text{(a constant quantity)}$$

$\therefore$ from (1), $K = \pi.2r\dfrac{dr}{dt};\; \therefore \dfrac{dr}{dt} = \dfrac{K}{2\pi r}.$

Now, the circumference $= P = 2\pi r$. Differentiating with respect to t,

we get $\dfrac{dP}{dt} = 2\pi\dfrac{dr}{dt};\; \therefore \dfrac{dP}{dt} = 2\pi.\dfrac{K}{2\pi r} = \dfrac{K}{r},\; \therefore \dfrac{dP}{dt} \propto \dfrac{1}{r}.$

**18. (a, b)**

**(a)** The given function between number of words and time (t) is

$$N(t) = \frac{70t^2}{30 + t^2} \text{ words per minute (wpm)}$$

$$N'(t) = \frac{\left(30 + t^2\right)\left(70 \times 2t\right) - 70t^2\,(2t)}{\left(30 + t^2\right)^2}$$

$$= \frac{4200t + 140t^3 - 140t^3}{\left(30 + t^2\right)^2}$$

$$= \frac{4200t}{\left(30 + t^2\right)^2}$$

**(b)** When $t = 5$ hours,

$$N'(5) = \frac{4200(5)}{\left(30 + 5^2\right)^2} = \frac{21000}{55^2} = 7 \text{ wpm (approx)}$$

After 5 hours the student is improving (positive sign) at 7 wpm.

**19. A→r; B→t; C→q; D→p**

**(A)** Let r, s and v be the radius, surface area and volume of a sphere at time t. We have to find $\left(\dfrac{dv}{ds}\right)_{r=2}$

Now, $v = \dfrac{4}{3}\pi r^3$ and $S = 4\pi r^2$

$\therefore \dfrac{dv}{dr} = 4\pi r^2$ and $\dfrac{ds}{dr} = 8\pi r$

$\therefore \dfrac{dv}{ds} = \dfrac{dv/dr}{ds/dr} = \dfrac{4\pi r^2}{8\pi r} = \dfrac{r}{2}$

$\therefore \left(\dfrac{dv}{ds}\right)_{r=2} = \dfrac{1}{2}(2) = 1 \text{ cm}^3/\text{cm}^2.$

**(B)** Let r be the radius of the air bubble. If V is the volume

of at time t, then $V = \dfrac{4}{3}\pi r^3$

The rate of increase of radius w.r.t time t i.e.

$$\frac{dr}{dt} = \frac{1}{2} \text{ cm / sec.}$$

The rate of increase of volume V w.r.t. time t

i.e. $\dfrac{dv}{dt} = \dfrac{d}{dt}\left(\dfrac{4}{3}\pi r^3\right) = \dfrac{4}{3}\pi \cdot 3r^2 \cdot \dfrac{dr}{dt}$

$$= 4\pi r^2 \cdot \dfrac{1}{2} = 2\pi r^2$$

Hence, the rate of increase of volume when radius is 1 cm $= 2\pi \times 1^2 = 2\pi\ cm^3/sec$.

**(C)** Let R and S be the positions of men P and Q at any time t. Since velocities are same

$\therefore$ OR = OS = x (say) ....(i)

$\dfrac{dx}{dt} = v$ and let SR = y

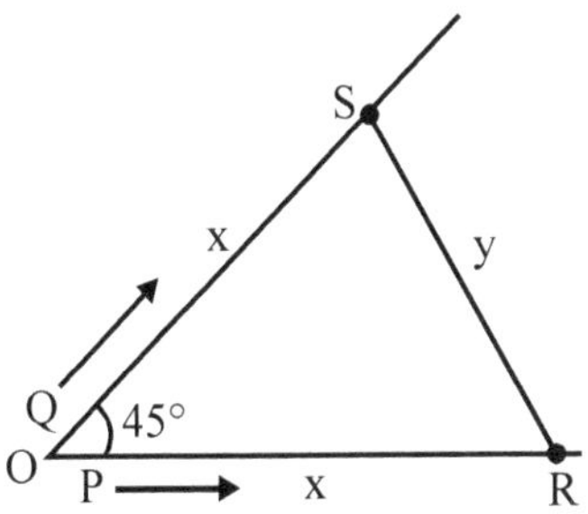

Now in triangle ORS, applying cosine rule, we get
$$y^2 = x^2 + x^2 - 2x \cdot x \cos 45°$$

$= 2x^2 - x^2\sqrt{2}$

$\therefore\ y = x\sqrt{(2-\sqrt{2})}$

$\therefore\ \dfrac{dy}{dt} = \{\sqrt{(2-\sqrt{2})}\}\dfrac{dx}{dt} = v\sqrt{(2-\sqrt{2})}$

Hence the required rate at which they are being separated is $v\sqrt{2-\sqrt{2}}$.

**(D)** Let CD be the position of man at any time t.
Let BD = x, then EC = x. Let $\angle ACE = \theta$

Given, AB = 41.6 m, CD = 1.6 m and $\dfrac{dx}{dt} = 2\,m/sec$.

AE = AB − EB = AB − CD = 41.6 − 1.6 = 40 m

We have to find $\dfrac{d\theta}{dt}$ when x = 30 m.

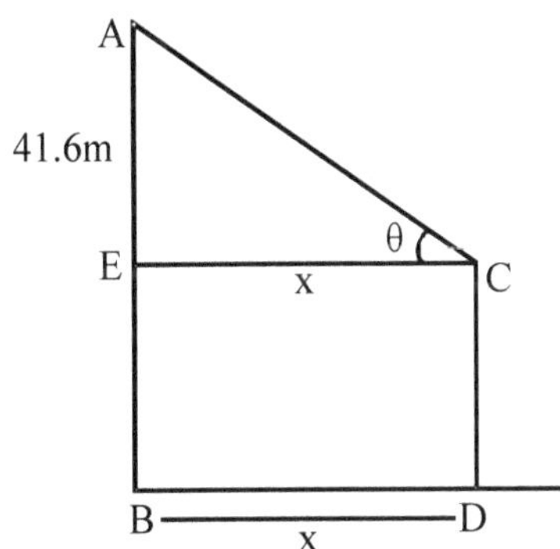

From $\triangle AEC$, $\tan\theta = \dfrac{AE}{EC} = \dfrac{40}{x}$ .....(1)

Differentiating w.r. to t, we get [From (1)]

$\sec^2\theta\,\dfrac{d\theta}{dt} = -\dfrac{40}{x^2}\dfrac{dx}{dt}$ or $\sec^2\theta\,\dfrac{d\theta}{dt} = -\dfrac{40}{x^2}.2$

$\therefore\ \dfrac{d\theta}{dt} = \dfrac{-80}{x^2}\cos^2\theta = -\dfrac{80}{x^2}\cdot\dfrac{x^2}{x^2+40^2}$

$$\left[\because \cos\theta = \dfrac{x}{\sqrt{x^2+40^2}}\right]$$

or $\dfrac{d\theta}{dt} = -\dfrac{80}{x^2+40^2}$ when x = 30 m

$\dfrac{d\theta}{dt} = -\dfrac{80}{30^2+40^2} = -\dfrac{4}{125}$ radian/sec

**20.  6**

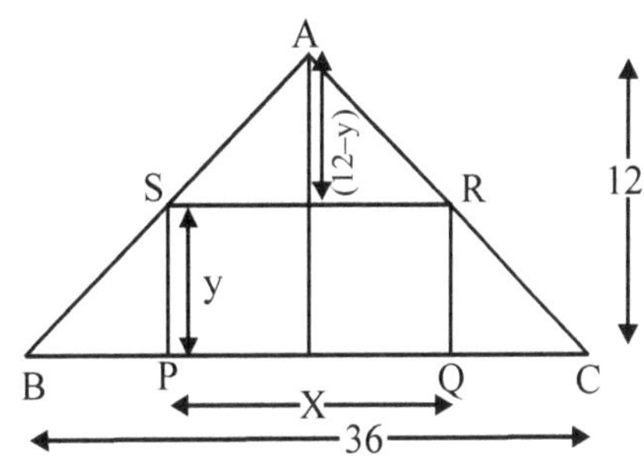

Area of rectangle = A = xy ..........(1)

Also, $\dfrac{36}{x} = \dfrac{12}{12-y} \Rightarrow 3y = (36-x)$ ..........(2)

$\therefore\ A = \dfrac{x}{3}(36-x) = \dfrac{1}{3}(36x-x^2)$

Now, $A'(x) = 0 \Rightarrow 36 - 2x = 0 \Rightarrow x = 18$

$A''(x) = \dfrac{1}{3}(-2) < 0$

Also, $y = \dfrac{36-x}{3} = \dfrac{36-18}{3} = 6$

$\therefore\ A_{max} = 18 \times 6 = 108$ sq. feet
Thus, X = 6

**21.  4**
Given $S = x^2 + 4xh = 1200$ and $V = x^2 h$

$V(x) = \dfrac{x^2(1200-x^2)}{4x}$ ; $V(x) = \dfrac{1}{4}(1200x - x^3)$

Put $V'(x) = 0$ gives x = 20
If x = 20, h = 10
Hence, $V_{max.} = x^2 h = (400)(10) = 4000$ cubic cm.
Thus, M = 4

**22.  6**

$5x + 3x > 8 \Rightarrow x > 1$

$5x + 8 > 3x \Rightarrow x > -4$

and $3x + 8 > 5x \Rightarrow x < 4$

Hence, $x \in (1, 4)$. Now perimeter of the triangle = 8 $(x + 1)$

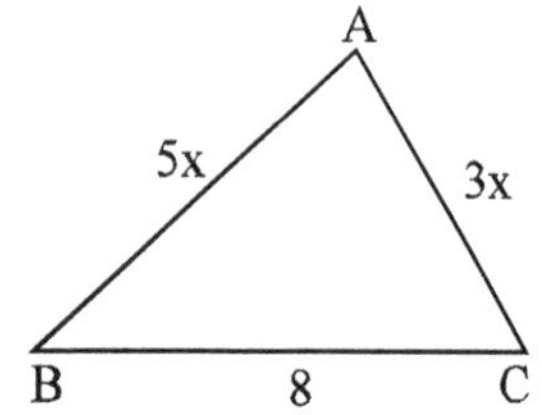


$s = 4x + 4$

$A^2(x) = (4(x+4)(4-x)(4x-4)(x+4))$

$\qquad = -16(x^2 - 1)(x^2 - 16)$

$A^2(t) = -16(t-1)(t-16)$, where $x^2 = t$, $t \in (1, 16)$

$A^2(t) = -16[t^2 - 17t + 16] = f(t)$

$f'(t) = 0 \qquad\qquad \Rightarrow t = 17/2$

$$A^2(t)\Big|_{max} = -16\left(\frac{17}{2} - 1\right)\left(\frac{17}{2} - 16\right)$$

$$= 16 \times \frac{15}{2} \times \frac{15}{2} = (2 \times 15)^2$$

$(\text{Area})_{max} = 30$ sq. units

Thus, $N = 6$

**23.  6**

At time t, let OA = x and OB = y.

Then $\dfrac{dx}{dt} = 2\dfrac{1}{2}$ ft./sec.

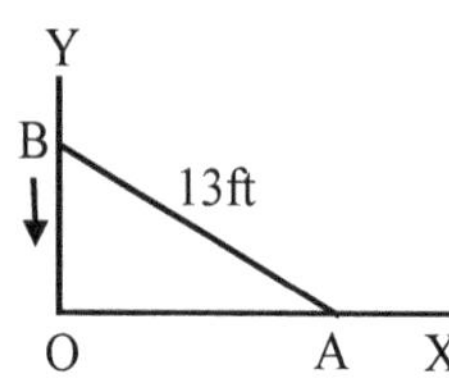


and we have to find $\dfrac{dy}{dt}$.

From right angled $\triangle AOB$, we have $AB^2 = OA^2 + OB^2$

$\Rightarrow 13^2 = x^2 + y^2$ \qquad\qquad ....(1)

Differentiating with respect to t, we get

$\therefore\ x\dfrac{dx}{dt} + y\dfrac{dy}{dt} = 0$ \qquad\qquad ....(2)

When OA = 12, i.e. x = 12 then from (1),

$13^2 = 12^2 + y^2$

or $\ y = \sqrt{13^2 - 12^2} = 5.$

Putting the values of y and $\dfrac{dx}{dt}$ in (2), we get

$$12 \times \frac{5}{2} + 5 \times \frac{dy}{dt} = 0$$

or $30 + 5\dfrac{dy}{dt} = 0;\ \ \therefore\ \dfrac{dy}{dt} = -6\,\text{ft} / \sec.$

Hence the end B is moving at the rate of 6ft/sec. The negative sign shows the downward tendency of B i.e.y decreases when t increases.

**24.  2**

The length x of a rectangle is decreaing at the rate of 5 cm/min.

$\Rightarrow \dfrac{dx}{dt} = -5\,\text{cm/min}$ \qquad\qquad ...(i)

The width in increasing at the rate of 4 cm/min.

$\Rightarrow \dfrac{dy}{dt} = -4\,\text{cm/ min.}$ \qquad\qquad ...(ii)

The perimeter p of the rectangle is p = 2 (x + y)

$$\frac{dp}{dt} = 2\left(\frac{dx}{dt} + \frac{dy}{dt}\right)$$

From (i) & (ii) $\dfrac{dp}{dt} = 2(-5 + 4) = -2$ cm/min.

This shows the perimeter decreases at the rate of 2 cm/min.

**1.** **(c).** $x^2 y = c^3$

$$x^2 \frac{dy}{dx} + 2xy = 0 \Rightarrow \frac{dy}{dx} = -\frac{2y}{x}$$

equation of tangent at $(x, y)$

$$Y - y = -\frac{2y}{x}(X - x)$$

$Y = 0$, gives, $X = \dfrac{3x}{2} = a$

and $X = 0$, gives, $Y = 3y = b$

Now $a^2 b = \dfrac{9x^2}{4} \cdot 3y = \dfrac{27}{4} x^2 y = \dfrac{27}{4} c^3 \Rightarrow (C)$

**2.** **(d).** $f'(a) = \sqrt{3}$ and $f'(b) = 1$ ; now put $f'(x) = t$ or I.B.P.

Now $I = \left[ \dfrac{f'(x)}{2} \right]_a^b = \dfrac{(f'(b))^2 - (f'(a))^2}{2}$

$$= \frac{1 - 3}{2} = -1 \,]$$

**3.** **(d).** Eliminating t gives $y^2(x - 1) = 1$.
Equation of tangent at $P(2, 1)$ is $x + 2y = 4$.

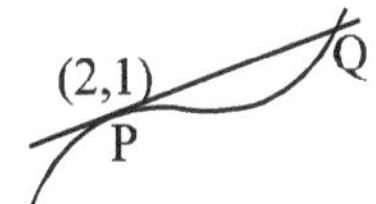


Solving with curve $x = 5$ & $y = -1/2$

$$\Rightarrow Q(5, 1/2) \Rightarrow PQ = \frac{3\sqrt{5}}{2} \,]$$

**4.** **(c).** $\dfrac{a}{x^2} + \dfrac{b}{y^2} = 1 \Rightarrow ay^2 + bx^2 = x^2 y^2$ .....(1)

$$-\frac{2a}{x^3} - \frac{2b}{y^3} \frac{dy}{dx} = 0 \Rightarrow \frac{dy}{dx} = -\frac{ay^3}{bx^3}$$

equation of tangent

$$Y - y = -\frac{ay^3}{bx^3}(X - x)$$

for x-intercept, put $Y = 0$

$$\therefore X = \frac{bx^3}{ay^2} + x$$

$$X = x \left[ \frac{bx^2 + ay^2}{ay^2} \right] = x \left[ \frac{x^2 y^2}{ay^2} \right] = \frac{x^3}{a}$$

$\Rightarrow$ x-intercept is proportional to cube of abscissa

**5.** **(a)** Slope of the normal at $(1, 1)$ is $-1/a$
$\Rightarrow$ Slope of the tangent at $(1, 1)$ is a

i.e., $\left. \dfrac{dy}{dx} \right]_{(1, 1)} = a$ ......(1)

We are given that $\dfrac{dy}{dx} \propto y$; $\dfrac{dy}{dx} = ky$,

where k is some constant $\dfrac{dy}{y} = k\, dx$

$\log |y| = kx + c$, where c is a constant
$|y| = e^{kx + c}$
$\quad y = \pm e^c \, e^{kx} = Ae^{kx}$, where A is a constant.
Since the curve passes through $(1, 1)$, therefore
$\quad 1 = Ae^k \Rightarrow A = e^{-k}$
Therefore, $y = e^{-k} \cdot e^{kx} = e^{k(x - 1)}$

$$\Rightarrow \frac{dy}{dx} = ke^{k(x - 1)}$$

$$\Rightarrow \left. \frac{dy}{dx} \right]_{(1, 1)} = k \Rightarrow a = k \qquad [\text{Using (1)}]$$

Thus, the required curve is $y = e^{a(x - 1)}$.

**6.** **(b)** $\dfrac{dy}{dx} = \dfrac{dy/dt}{dx/dt} = \dfrac{3a \sin^2 t \cos t}{-3a \cos^2 t \sin t} = -\tan t$

$\therefore$ Equation of the tangent at 't' is
$y - a \sin^3 t = -\tan t \, (x - a \cos^3 t)$
$\Rightarrow x \tan t + y - a (\sin^3 t + \sin t \cdot \cos^2 t) = 0$
$\Rightarrow x \tan t + y - a \sin t = 0$
$\therefore$ Distance from the origin of this tangent

$$= \frac{|-a \sin t|}{\sqrt{\tan^2 t + 1}} = \frac{a \sin t}{\sec t} = \frac{a}{2} \sin 2t$$

**7.** **(a)** $\dfrac{dy}{d\theta} = a\sqrt{\cos 2\theta} \cdot \cos\theta + a \cdot \dfrac{1}{2\sqrt{\cos 2\theta}}(-2\sin 2\theta)\sin\theta$

$$= \frac{a}{\sqrt{\cos 2\theta}} \cdot \cos 3\theta \ .$$

$$\left. \frac{dy}{d\theta} \right]_{\theta = \pi/6} = 0 \quad \Rightarrow \quad \left. \frac{dy}{dx} \right]_{\theta = \pi/6} = 0$$

$$\left( \because \left. \frac{dx}{d\theta} \right]_{\theta = \pi/6} \neq 0 \right)$$

**8.** **(a, b, c)**
**(a)** By replacing 't' by $-t$
$x = 1 - 3t^2,\ y = t - 3t^3 \Rightarrow x = 1 - 3t^2,\ y = -t + 3t^3$
as $(x, y)$ as well as $(x, -y)$ lies on the curve, curve is
symmetrical about x–axis $\Rightarrow y = 0$

**(b)** $\dfrac{dy}{dx} = \dfrac{1-9t^2}{-6t} = \tan\theta$

$\Rightarrow 9t^2 - 6\tan\theta.t - 1 = 0$

$\Rightarrow 3t = \tan\theta \pm \sec\theta \Rightarrow \tan\theta + \sec\theta = 3t$

**(c)** $P(-2, 2) \Rightarrow t = -1 \Rightarrow \dfrac{dy}{dx}\Big|_{t=-1} = -\dfrac{4}{3}$

Equation of tangent, $Y - 2 = -\dfrac{4}{3}(x + 2)$

$\Rightarrow t - 3t^3 - 2 = -\dfrac{4}{3}(1 - 3t^2 + 2)$

$\Rightarrow 9t^3 + 12t^2 - 3t - 6 = 0 \Rightarrow t_1 + t_2 + t_3 = -12/9$

$\Rightarrow (-1) + (-1) + t_3 = -4/3$

$\Rightarrow t_3 = \dfrac{2}{3} \Rightarrow Q \equiv \left(-\dfrac{1}{3}, -\dfrac{2}{9}\right)$

Thus, statements (a) (b) and (c) are true.

**9.** **(b, c)** Let the line $ax + by + c = 0$ be normal to the curve

$xy = 1$ at the point $(x', y')$, then

$x'y' = 1 \ldots (1)$ [pt$(x', y')$ lies on the curve]

Also differentiating the curve $xy = 1$ with respect to x, we get

$$y + x\dfrac{dy}{dx} = 0 \Rightarrow \dfrac{dy}{dx} = -\dfrac{y}{x}$$

$$\Rightarrow \dfrac{dy}{dx}\bigg)_{(x',y')} = \dfrac{-y'}{x'}$$

$\therefore$ Slope of normal $= \dfrac{x'}{y'}$

Also equation of normal suggests, slope of normal

$$= \dfrac{-a}{b}$$

$\therefore$ We must have,

$$\dfrac{x'}{y'} = -\dfrac{a}{b} \qquad \ldots (2)$$

Now from eq. (1), $x'y' > 0 \Rightarrow x', y'$ are of same sign

$$\Rightarrow \dfrac{x'}{y'} = +\text{ve} \Rightarrow -\dfrac{a}{b} = +\text{ve} \Rightarrow \dfrac{a}{b} = -\text{ve}$$

$\Rightarrow$ a and b are of opposite sign.

$\Rightarrow$ either $a < 0$ and $b > 0$ or $a > 0$ and $b < 0$.

**10.** **(a,b,c,d)** We have, $y = c\,e^{x/a}$

$$\Rightarrow \dfrac{dy}{dx} = \dfrac{c}{a}e^{x/a} \Rightarrow \dfrac{dy}{dx} = \dfrac{1}{a}y$$

$$\Rightarrow \dfrac{y}{dy/dx} = a = \text{const.}$$

$\Rightarrow$ subtangent = const.

Length of the subnormal $= y\dfrac{dy}{dx}$

$$= y.\dfrac{y}{a} = \dfrac{y^2}{a} \propto \text{(square of the ordinate)}$$

Equation of the tangent at $(x_1, y_1)$ is

$$y - y_1 = \dfrac{-y_1}{a}(x - x_1)$$

This meets x-axis at a point given by

$$-y = \dfrac{y_1}{a}(x - x_1) \Rightarrow x = x_1 - a$$

The curve meets y-axis at $(0, c)$

$$\therefore \left(\dfrac{dy}{dx}\right)_{(0,c)} = \dfrac{c}{a}$$

So, equation of the normal at $(0, c)$ is

$$y - c = -\dfrac{1}{c/a}(x - 0) \Rightarrow ax + cy = c^2$$

**11.** **(a,b,c)** $y = x^3 - ax^2 + x + 1$

$$\Rightarrow \dfrac{dy}{dx} = 3x^2 - 2ax + 1 > 0 \text{ for all x}$$

$$\Rightarrow 4a^2 - 12 \Rightarrow a \in (-\sqrt{3}, \sqrt{3})$$

**12. (a), 13. (b), 14. (d).**

Tangent to the curves are $Y - f(x) = f'(x)(X - x)$

$Y - g(x) = g'(x)(X - x)$

The two tangents intersect on y-axis

$f(x) - xf'(x) = g(x) - xg'(x)$

$f(x) - g(x) = x\{f'(x) - g'(x)\}$

$$\Rightarrow \dfrac{f'(x) - g'(x)}{f(x) - g(x)} = \dfrac{1}{x}$$

$\Rightarrow \log(f(x) - g(x)) = \log x + \log C$

$\Rightarrow f(x) - g(x) = Cx \qquad \ldots\ldots(i)$

Normal to the two curves are $Y - f(x) = \dfrac{-1}{f'(x)}(X - x)$

$$Y - g(x) = \dfrac{-1}{g'(x)}(X - x)$$

The two normal intersect on x-axis

$x + f(x)f'(x) = x + g(x)g'(x)$

$f(x)f'(x) = g(x)g'(x)$

Integrating both sides $f(x)^2 - g(x)^2 = C_1$

$(f(x) + g(x))(f(x) - g(x)) = C_1$

$$f(x) + g(x) = \dfrac{C_1}{Cx} \qquad \ldots\ldots(ii)$$

Solving eq. (i) and (ii)

$$f(x) = \dfrac{1}{2}\left(Cx + \dfrac{C_1}{Cx}\right) \qquad \ldots\ldots(iii)$$

$$g(x) = \dfrac{1}{2}\left(\dfrac{C_1}{Cx} - Cx\right)$$

Satisfy (iii) by $(1, 1)$ and (iv) by $(2, 3)$

$C = -2$ and $C_1 = -8$

$$f(x) = -x + \frac{2}{x} \text{ and } g(x) = \frac{2}{x} + x$$

**15.  A→q; B→r; C→p**

(A)  Point of intersection is $(0, b)$. $\dfrac{dy}{dx} = be^{-\frac{x}{a}}\left(-\dfrac{1}{a}\right)$;

$$m = \left(\frac{dy}{dx}\right)_{(0,\,b)} = -\frac{b}{a}$$

∴ Equation of tangent is $y - b = -\dfrac{b}{a}(x - 0)$ **(q)**

(B)  $\dfrac{dy}{dx} = -\dfrac{y}{x}$,

$$\text{Subnormal} = \left|y\frac{dy}{dx}\right| = \left|y \cdot \left(\frac{-y}{x}\right)\right| = \frac{y^2}{x} = \frac{y^2}{\dfrac{e^2}{y}} = \frac{y^3}{e^2} \text{ (r)}$$

(C)  $m = \dfrac{dy}{dx} = \dfrac{xb^2}{ya^2}$ (take $x = a\cos\theta$, $y = b\sin\theta$);

Length of subtangent $\quad =$

$$\left|\frac{y}{\dfrac{dy}{dx}}\right| = \left|\frac{b\sin\theta}{-\dfrac{b}{a}\cdot\dfrac{\cos\theta}{\sin\theta}}\right| = a\sin^2\theta\,|\sec\theta| \text{ (p)}$$

**16.  A→q; B→s; C→s; D→q**

(A)  $\dfrac{d}{dx}(1 - \cos x) = \dfrac{d}{dx}\left(\dfrac{\sqrt{3}}{2}x + a\right)$ assuming $x \geq 0$

$$\Rightarrow \sin x = \frac{\sqrt{3}}{2} \Rightarrow x = \frac{\pi}{3} \text{ and } \frac{2\pi}{3}$$

Due to symmetry $x = -\dfrac{\pi}{3}$ and $-\dfrac{2\pi}{3}$ can also be the

points and so the points $\left(\pm\dfrac{\pi}{3}, \dfrac{1}{2}\right)$ and $\left(\pm\dfrac{2\pi}{3}, \dfrac{3}{2}\right)$

satisfy $y = \dfrac{\sqrt{3}}{2}|x| + a$

giving $a = \dfrac{1}{2} - \dfrac{\pi}{2\sqrt{3}}$ or $\dfrac{3}{2} - \dfrac{\pi}{\sqrt{3}}$ **(q)**

(B)  Slope of the curves at the point of contact are

$\dfrac{2a}{y}$ and $\dfrac{x}{2a}$ Thus $\dfrac{2a}{y} = \dfrac{x}{2a} \Rightarrow xy = 4a^2$ **(s)**

(C)  The least distance will occur along the common nornal. Normal to parabola at $(t^2, 2t)$ is $y = -tx + 2t + t^3$ which is normal to circle if $12 = 2t + t^3 \Rightarrow t = 2$. Hence the point is $(4,4)$ **(s)**

(D)  Differentiating we get

$$3y^2\frac{dy}{dx} + 6x = 12\frac{dy}{dx} \Rightarrow \frac{dy}{dx} = -\frac{2x}{y^2 - 4}$$

$$\Rightarrow y^2 - 4 = 0 \quad or \quad y = \pm 2$$

If $y = 2$, then $x = \pm\dfrac{4}{\sqrt{3}}$ if $y = -2$, then $x \notin R$.

So the points are $\left(\pm\dfrac{4}{\sqrt{3}}, 2\right)$ **(q)**

**17.  (a).** $y\sqrt{1 + \left(\dfrac{dx}{dy}\right)^2} = y\sqrt{1 + \left(\dfrac{dy}{dx}\right)^2}$

$$\Rightarrow \frac{\sqrt{1 + \left(\dfrac{dy}{dx}\right)^2}}{\dfrac{dy}{dx}} = \sqrt{1 + \left(\dfrac{dy}{dx}\right)^2} \Rightarrow \frac{dy}{dx} = 1$$

Equation of tangent $y - 2 = 1(x - 1) \Rightarrow x - y + 1 = 0$

**18.  (a)**  Given $f'(x) = f(x)$

$\Rightarrow 2x = x^2 \Rightarrow x = 0, 2$

at $x = 0, y = 0$ and at $x = 2, y = 4$

So we have to find equation of tangents at $(0,0)$ and $(2, 4)$

At $(0, 0)$, $f'(0) = 0$ and at $(2, 4)$, $f'(2) = 4$

∴ Tangents are $y - 0 = 0(x - 0)$ and $y - 4 = 4(x - 2)$

i.e., $y = 0$ and $4x - y - 4 = 0$

**19.  2**

$y = x^n$

$\dfrac{dy}{dx} = n\,x^{n-1} = na^{n-1}$

Slope of normal $= -\dfrac{1}{na^{n-1}}$

equation of normal $y - a^n = -\dfrac{1}{na^{n-1}}(x - a)$

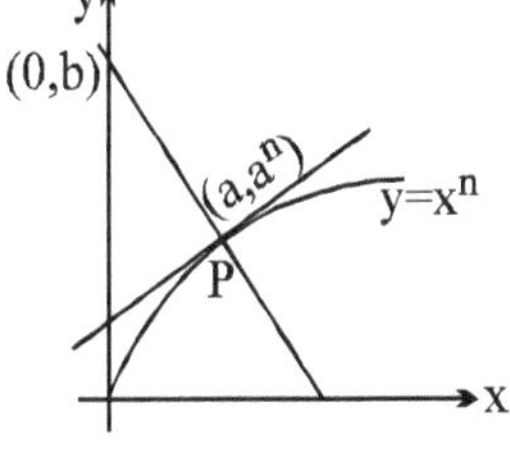


put $x = 0$ to get y-intercept

$y = a^n + \dfrac{1}{na^{n-2}}$ ; Hence $b = a^n + \dfrac{1}{na^{n-2}}$

$$\lim_{a\to 0} b = \begin{cases} 0 & \text{if } n < 2 \\ \dfrac{1}{2} & \text{if } n = 2 \\ \infty & \text{if } n > 2 \end{cases}$$

**20.  3.**

$$\frac{dx}{dt} = 3t^2 - 8t - 3; \quad \frac{dy}{dt} = 4t + 3$$

$\therefore \dfrac{dy}{dx} = \dfrac{4t+3}{3t^2 - 8t - 3}$

Hence H means $4t + 3 = 0 \Rightarrow t = -3/4 \Rightarrow H = 1$
 V means $3t^2 - 8t - 3 = 0 \Rightarrow t = 3$ & $t = -1/3$
$\Rightarrow V = 2$
Thus, $H + V = 1 + 2 = 3$

**21.  9**

Given, $9y^2 = x^3$
Let the point on the curve be $x = t^2$ and $y = t^3/3$

$\dfrac{dx}{dt} = 2t$ ; $\dfrac{dy}{dt} = t^2$

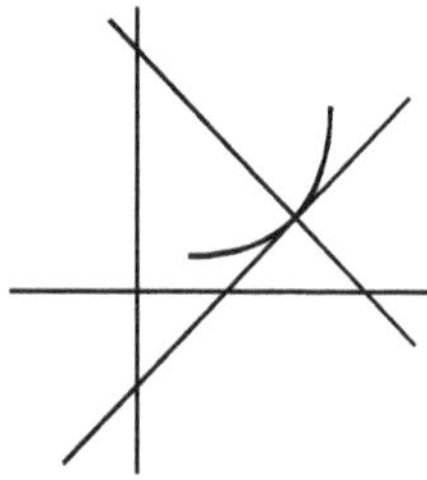

$\dfrac{dy}{dx} = \dfrac{dy}{dt} \times \dfrac{dt}{dx} = \dfrac{t^2}{2t} = \dfrac{t}{2}$

$\Rightarrow$ slope of the normal $= -\dfrac{2}{t}$

$\therefore$ normal makes equal intercept

hence $-\dfrac{2}{t} = -1 \Rightarrow t = 2$

Hence $P = (4, 8/3) \Rightarrow \dfrac{a}{4} + 3b = \dfrac{4}{4} + 3 \cdot \dfrac{8}{3} = 1 + 8 = 9$

**22.  2**

Slope of the normal $m = \dfrac{1}{2x_1 - 1}$

$\Rightarrow x_1 = \dfrac{m-1}{2m} \Rightarrow y_1 = \dfrac{3m^2 + 1}{4m^2}$ ;

equation of the normal in terms of slope of the normal is

$y = mx + \dfrac{5m^2 - 2m^3 + 1}{4m^2}.$

It passes through $(7/2, 9/2) \Rightarrow 12m^3 - 13m^2 + 1 = 0$
Also $(m-1)(3m-1)(4m+1) = 0$
$\Rightarrow m_1 = 1$ ; $m_2 = 1/3$ ; $m_3 = -1/4$
$\Rightarrow$ sum $= 13/12$.

Thus, $\dfrac{13X}{24} = \dfrac{13}{12} \Rightarrow X = 2$

**23.  7**

$4x^3 + 4y^3 (dy/dx) = 0 \Rightarrow dy/dx = -x^3/y^3$
Equation of tangent, $Y - y = -x^3/y^3 (X-x)$
$\Rightarrow y^3 Y + x^3 X = x^4 + y^4 = a^4$

$\Rightarrow \dfrac{X}{a^4/x^3} + \dfrac{Y}{a^4/y^3} = 1$

Here, $p = a^4/x^3$, $q = a^4/y^3$

$\Rightarrow p^{-4/3} + q^{-4/3} = \dfrac{a^{-16/3}}{x^{-4}} + \dfrac{a^{-16/3}}{y^{-4}}$

$= a^{-16/3}\left(x^4 + y^4\right)$

$= a^{-16/3}(a^4) = a^{-4/3}$

Thus, $P = 4$, $Q = 3$
Hence, $P + Q = 7$

**1.** **(b).** In $-1 \le x < 0$, $f'(x) = 3x^2 + 2x - 10$
$$= 2x^2 + (x+1)^2 - 11 < 0$$
$\therefore$ $f(x)$ is monotonically decreasing in the interval
$-1 \le x < 0$

In $0 < x < \dfrac{\pi}{2}$, $f'(x) = -\sin x < 0$, $\therefore$ $f(x)$ is m.d.

In $\dfrac{\pi}{2} < x \le \pi$, $f'(x) = \cos x < 0$, $\therefore$ $f(x)$ is m.d.

Displaying the trend of values of the function in different intervals, we get the adjoining graph.

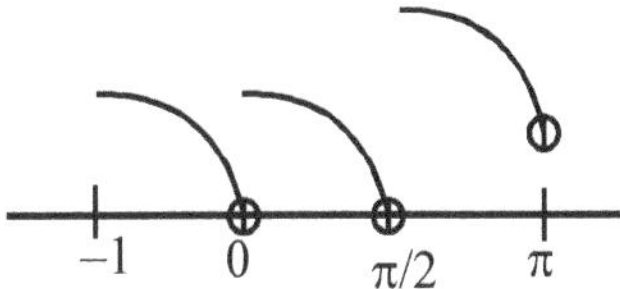

$\therefore$ $f\left(\dfrac{\pi}{2} - h\right) < \left(2 = f\left(\dfrac{\pi}{2}\right)\right)$, $f\left(\dfrac{\pi}{2} + h\right) < f\left(\dfrac{\pi}{2}\right)$

$\therefore$ $f(x)$ has a local maximum at $x = \dfrac{\pi}{2}$

**2.** **(b).** $f'(x) = 6(x^2 - 3ax + 2a^2) = 6(x - 2a)(x - a) = 0$
$\Rightarrow$ $x = 2a$ or $a$
$f''(x) = 6(2x - 3a)$

$\left.\begin{array}{l} f''(2a) = a \\ f''(a) = -a \end{array}\right] \Rightarrow$
If $a > 0$ then $x_1 = a$
$x_2 = 2a$
If $a < 0$ then $x_1 = 2a$
$x_2 = a$

Now $x_1^2 = x_2$ $\Rightarrow$ $a^2 = 2a$ $\Rightarrow$ $a = 2$
other option not valid ]

**3.** **(b).** $2A = xy \sin\theta$ ; $4A^2 = x^2 y^2 \sin^2\theta$ ;

$f(x) = \dfrac{x^4}{2x - 1}$ ; $f'(x) = 0$ $\Rightarrow$ $x = \dfrac{2}{3}$ ]

**4.** **(c).** $f'(x) = 0 \Rightarrow (\sin x + \cos x)(\text{non zero quantity}) = 0$
$\Rightarrow \tan x = -1$ $\Rightarrow x = 3\pi/4$ or $7\pi/4$.
Global Min $= x = 2n\pi + (3\pi/4)$ ;
global max $= x = 2n\pi + (7\pi/4)$

$M = \dfrac{4}{8 - \sqrt{2}}$ ; $m = \dfrac{4}{8 + \sqrt{2}}$

**5.** **(c)** We have $f(x) = \begin{cases} (-1)^{m+n} x^m (x-1)^n & \text{if } x < 0 \\ (-1)^n x^m (x-1)^n & \text{if } 0 \le x < 1 \\ x^m (x-1)^n & \text{if } x \ge 1 \end{cases}$

Let $g(x) = x^m (x-1)^n$ then

$g'(x) = mx^{m-1}(x-1)^n + nx^m(x-1)^{n-1}$

Put $x^{m-1}(x-1)^{n-1}\{mx - m + nx\} = 0$

Now $f'(x) = 0 \Rightarrow g'(x) = 0 \Rightarrow x = 0, 1$ or $\dfrac{m}{m+n}$

$f(0) = 0$, $f(1) = 0$ and

$f\left(\dfrac{m}{m+n}\right) = (-1)^n \dfrac{m^m n^n (-1)^n}{(m+n)^{m+n}}$ $\left[\because 0 < \dfrac{m}{m+n} < 1\right]$

$= \dfrac{m^m n^n}{(m+n)^{m+n}} > 0$

$\therefore$ The maximum value $= \dfrac{m^m n^n}{(m+n)^{m+n}}$

**6.** **(b)** $\because 0 < x < \dfrac{\pi}{2}$, $\therefore \tan x > 0$, $\cot x > 0$

Now $f(x) = \dfrac{ab(a^2 - b^2)\sin x \cos x}{a^2 \sin^2 x + b^2 \cos^2 x}$

$= \dfrac{ab(a^2 - b^2)}{a^2 \tan x + b^2 \cot x} = \dfrac{ab(a^2 - b^2)}{(a\sqrt{\tan x} - b\sqrt{\cot x})^2 + 2ab}$

$f(x)$ will be max. when $(a\sqrt{\tan x} - b\sqrt{\cot x})^2$ is minimum. But its minimum value is zero.

$\therefore$ max value of $f(x) = \dfrac{ab(a^2 - b^2)}{2ab} = \dfrac{a^2 - b^2}{2}$

**7.** **(c)** Maximum value at $x = a$ is $b$
$\therefore$ $f(x) = b - (x - a)^{2n+2}$. $(\because f^{(2n+2)}(a) = -\text{ve})$

**8.** **(c)** The given polynomial is

$p(x) = a_0 + a_1 x^2 + a_2 x^4 + \ldots + a_n x^{2n}, x \in R$

and $0 < a_0 < a_1 < a_2 < \ldots < a_n$

Here we observe that all coefficients of different powers of x, i.e., $a_0, a_1, a_2, \ldots, a_n$ are positive.

Also only even powers of x are involved.
$\therefore$     $P(x)$ can not have any max. value.
Moreover $P(x)$ is minimum, when $x = 0$, i.e., $a_0$.
$\therefore$     $P(x)$ has only one minimum.

**9.** **(a,c).**

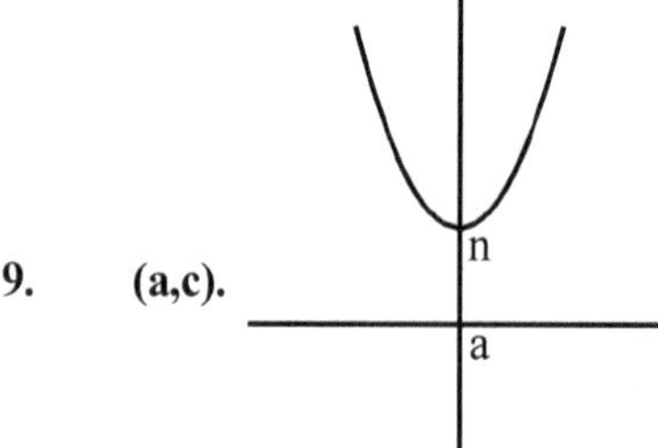

Clearly $\lim_{x \to a} [f(x)]$ is an integer and LHL and RHL should

be same for existence of $\lim_{x \to a} f(x)$

Let $\lim_{x \to a} [f(x)] = n \ (n \in I)$

Clearly LHL and RHL both should be just greater than n as $f(x)$ is cont. at $x = a$

$\therefore$ $f(x)$ has local minimum at $x = a$.

**10.** **(a,b,c).** $f(x) = \dfrac{\sin(x+a)}{\sin(x+b)}$

$f'(x) = \dfrac{\sin(x+b) \times \cos(x+a) - \sin(x+a)\cos(x+b)}{\sin^2(x+b)}$

$\qquad = \dfrac{\sin(b-a)}{\sin^2(x+b)}$

If $\sin(b-a) = 0$ then $f'(x) = 0 \Rightarrow f(x)$ will be constant i.e. $b - a = n\pi$ or $n\pi$ or $b - a = (2n+1)\pi$ or $b - a = 2n\pi$ then $f(x)$ has no minima

**11.** **(a,b)** $\dfrac{dy}{dx} = (x-1)(x-2) = 0$ when $x = 1$ & $x = 2$.

$\dfrac{d^2y}{dx^2} = 2x - 3$ ; $\left.\dfrac{d^2y}{dx^2}\right]_{x=1} < 0$

$\Rightarrow$ $y$ is maximum at $x = 1$ and

$\left.\dfrac{d^2y}{dx^2}\right]_{x=2} < 0$ $\Rightarrow$ $y$ is minimum at $x = 2$

Hence extreme values are

$y_{max} = \displaystyle\int_0^1 (t^2 - 3t + 2)\, dt$ &

$y_{min} = \displaystyle\int_0^2 (t^2 - 3t + 2)\, dt$ ]

**12.** **(a, b)** $\because$ $g(x) = \displaystyle\int_0^x f(t)\, dt$

$\Rightarrow$ $g'(x) = f(x) = \begin{cases} e^x, & 0 \le x \le 1 \\ 2 - e^{x-1}, & 1 < x \le 2 \\ x - e, & 2 < x \le 3 \end{cases}$

$\therefore$ $g'(x) = 0 \Rightarrow e^{x-1} = 2$

or $\quad x - e = 0 \Rightarrow x - 1 = \ln 2$

$\Rightarrow \quad x = 1 + \ln 2$ or $e$

$g''(x) = \begin{cases} e^x, & 0 \le x \le 1 \\ -e^{x-1}, & 1 < x \le 2 \\ 1, & 2 < x \le 3 \end{cases}$

$\therefore$ $g''(1 + \ln 2) = -2$ and $g''(e) = 1 \Rightarrow g(x)$ has local max. at $x = 1 + \ln 2$ and local min. at $x = e$.

**13.** **(a)** For exactly one point of local maxima and local minima of $f(x)$, quadratic equation $f'(x)$ has two distinct and real roots

So $D > 0 \Rightarrow (a-3)^2 - 4a > 0$

$\qquad a^2 + 9 - 10a > 0$

$(a-1)(a-9) > 0 \Rightarrow a \in (-\infty, 1) \cup (9, \infty)$

**14.** **(c)** For local minima at some negative real x, quadratic equation $f'(x)$ has both roots negative So

$D > 0 \Rightarrow a \in (-\infty, 1) \cup (9, \infty)$

$-\dfrac{B}{A} < 0 \Rightarrow a - 3 < 0 \Rightarrow a \in (-\infty, 3)$

$\dfrac{C}{A} > 0 \Rightarrow a > 0 \Rightarrow a \in (0, \infty) \Rightarrow a \in (0, 1)$

**15.** **(d)** For local maxima at some negative real x and local minima at some positive real x of f(x), quadratic equation f' (x) has one root positive and other root negative

So $f'(0) < 0 \Rightarrow a \in (-\infty, 0)$

**16.** $A \to r; B \to t; C \to q; D \to p$

**(A)** Note the graph of $f(x)$. Least value coincides with local minima

$y = (x^2 + 3x)(x^2 + 3x + 2) = z(z+2)$

$\quad = (z+1)^2 - 1 = (x^2 + 3x + 1)^2 - 1$

$y_{least} = -1$ ; this occurs where $z = -1$

i.e. $x^2 + 3x + 1 = 0$

or $\dfrac{dy}{dx} = 2(2x+3)(x^2 + 3x + 1) = 0$

$\Rightarrow x = \dfrac{-3 + \sqrt{5}}{2}, \ -\dfrac{3}{2}$ or $\dfrac{-3 - \sqrt{5}}{2}$

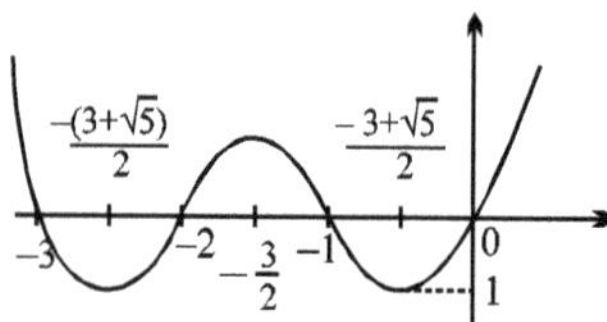

Here $x = \dfrac{-3+\sqrt{5}}{2}$ & $x = \dfrac{-3-\sqrt{5}}{2}$ are the points of local minima and $x = -3/2$ is the point of local maxima . Local maximum value $= 9/16$

**(B)** $f(x)$ has a period equal to $\pi$ & can take values $(-\infty, \infty)$
$\Rightarrow$ 3 is the local minimum value.

$$y = \frac{2\sin\left(x+\frac{\pi}{6}\right)\cos x}{2\sin x \cos\left(x+\frac{\pi}{6}\right)} = \frac{\sin\left(2x+\frac{\pi}{6}\right)+\sin\frac{\pi}{6}}{\sin\left(2x+\frac{\pi}{6}\right)-\sin\frac{\pi}{6}}$$

$$= 1 + \frac{1}{\sin\left(2x+\frac{\pi}{6}\right)-\sin\frac{\pi}{6}}$$

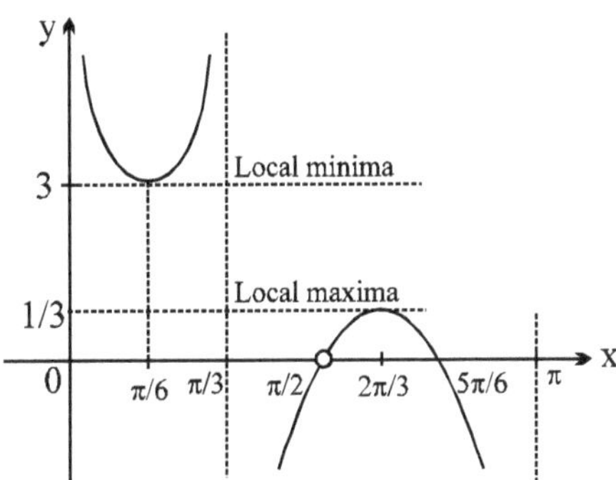

$y$ is minimum if $2x + \dfrac{\pi}{6} = \dfrac{\pi}{2}$

$$\Rightarrow \ x = \frac{\pi}{6} \ \Rightarrow \ y_{min} = 1+2 = 3 \ ]$$

**(C)** $f(x) = e^x \cos x$

$f'(x) = e^x(\cos x - \sin x)$

$f''(x) = e^x(\cos x - \sin x - \sin x - \cos x) = -2e^x \sin x$

$f''(x) = 0 \Rightarrow x = 0$

So, $f'(x)$ is maximum at $x = 0$

**(D)** $y = x(\ln x - 2)$

$$y' = x\left(\frac{1}{x}\right) + (\ln x - 2) = \ln x - 1$$

$$\frac{dy}{dx} = \ln x - 1 = 0 \qquad \Rightarrow x = e$$

now $f(1) = -2$
$f(e) = -e$ (least)
$f(e^2) = 0$   (greatest)
$\therefore$ difference $= 0 - (-e) = e$ Ans.

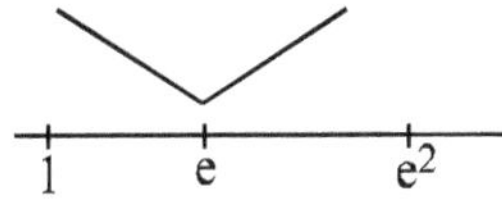

**17.** $\mathbf{A \to q,s; \ B \to q; \ C \to t}$

$g(x)$ can be defined as $g(x) = \begin{cases} f(x), & -2 \le x < -1 \\ -1, & -1 \le x < 0 \\ 0, & 0 \le x < 2 \\ f(x), & 2 \le x \le 3 \end{cases}$

or $g(x) = \begin{cases} x^2 + 2x, & -2 \le x < -1 \\ -1, & -1 \le x < 0 \\ 0, & 0 \le x < 2 \\ x^2 - 2x, & 2 \le x \le 3 \end{cases}$

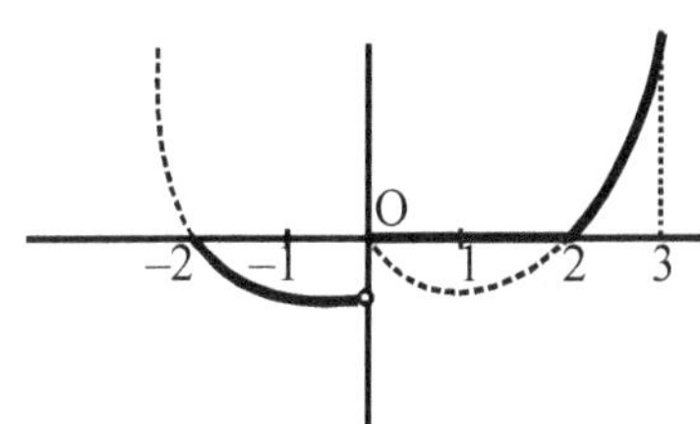

(A) $g(x)$ is not differentiable at $x = 0, 2$ **(q, s)**
(B) $g(x)$ has no extremum **(q)**
(C) Absolute maximum value $= f(3) = 3$ **(t)**

**18.** **(d)** Consider the function $f(x) = x^3$.
Its derivative $f'(x) = 3x^2$, vanishes at $x = 0$.
However, as the graph shows that $x = 0$ is not a local extremum of $f(x) = x^3$.

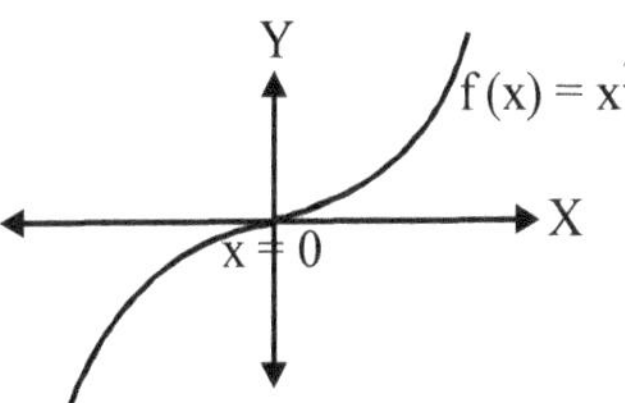

**19.** **(a)** $f'(x) = x^x(1 + \log_e x)$ it is clear that $f'(x) < 0$ for $x < 1/e$ and $f'(x) > 0$ for $x > 1/e$.

**20.** **8**

$f(x) = 7e^{\sin^2 x} - e^{\cos^2 x} + 2$

Let $e^{\sin^2 x} = t \Rightarrow t \in [1, e]$

$g(t) = 7t - \dfrac{e}{t} + 2$

$g'(t) = 7 + \dfrac{e}{t^2} = 0 \Rightarrow$ no critical point

$g(1) = 9 - e = $ minimum value
$g(e) = 7e + 1 = $ maximum value

$\sqrt{7f_{min} + f_{max}} = 8$

**21.**  **6**

We have $F(x) = \dfrac{x^3}{3} + (a-3)x^2 + x - 13$ .

$\therefore$ For F (x) to have negative point of local minimum, the equation F '(x) = 0 must have two distinct negative roots.

Now, $F'(x) = x^2 + 2(a-3)x + 1$

$\therefore$ Following condition(s) must be satisfied simultaneously.

(i) Discriminant > 0; (ii) Sum of roots < 0 ; (iii) Product of roots > 0

Now, D > 0

$\Rightarrow 4(a-3)^2 > 4 \Rightarrow (a-3)^2 - 1 > 0 \Rightarrow (a-2)(a-4) > 0$

$\therefore$ $a \in (-\infty, 2) \cup (4, \infty)$ .........(i)

Also, $-2(a-3) < 0 \Rightarrow a - 3 > 0 \Rightarrow a > 3$ .........(ii)

And product of root(s) = 1 > 0 $\forall$ a $\in$ R

$\therefore$ (i) $\cap$ (ii) $\cap$ (iii) $\Rightarrow$ a $\in (4, \infty)$ .........(iii)

Hence sum of value(s) of a = 5 + 6 + 7 + ..... + 100 = 5040

Thus, $14M^2 = 5040$

M = 6

**22.**  **2**

Let the number of passengers be x ( x $\geq$ 200)

Fair changed per person $= 10 - (x-100)\dfrac{2}{100}$

Total revenue $= x . \left[10 - (x-200)\dfrac{2}{100}\right]$

$= 10x - \dfrac{2x}{100}(x-200) = 10x - \dfrac{2x^2}{100} + 4x$

$f(x) = 14x - \dfrac{2x^2}{100}$

$f'(x) = 14 - \dfrac{4x}{100} = 0 \Rightarrow x = 350$

$f''(x) < 0 \Rightarrow x = 350$ gives maxima

Thus 10PQ = 350

$\Rightarrow$ P = 5, Q = 7 or Q = 5, P = 7

$\therefore$ Difference = 2

**23.**  **9**

$x^4 - 10x^2 + 9 \leq 0$

$(x^2 - 9)(x^2 - 1) \leq 0$

hence $\quad -3 \leq x \leq -1$ or $\quad 1 \leq x \leq 3$

now $\quad f(x) = x^3 - 3x$

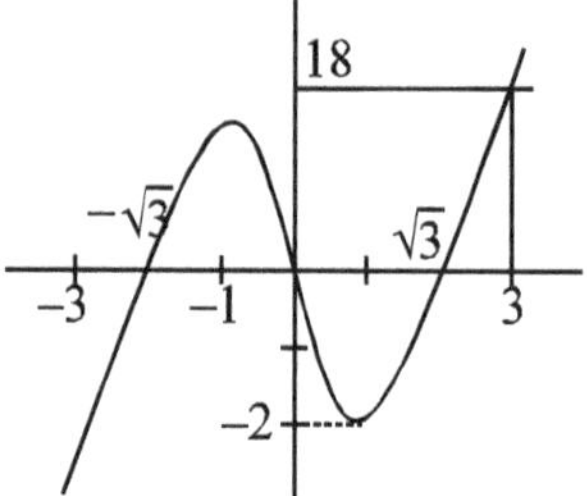

$f'(x) = 3x^2 - 3 = 0$

$x = \pm 1$

maximum occurs when x = 3

$f(3) = 18$

Thus, N = 9

**24.**  **4**

Let $y = x^{25}(1-x)^{75}$

$\Rightarrow \dfrac{dy}{dx} = 25x^{24}(1-x)^{75} - 75x^{25}(1-x)^{74}$

$= 25x^{24}(1-x)^{74}(1-x-3x)$

$= 25x^{24}(1-x)^{74}(1-4x)$

For maximum value of y, $\dfrac{dy}{dx} = 0$

$\Rightarrow$ x = 0, 1, 1/4

$x = 1/4 \in [0,1]$

Also at x = 0, y = 0, at x = 1, y = 0, and at x = 1/4, y > 0

$\therefore$ Max. value of y occurs at x = 1/4.

Thus, B = 4

**1.** **(a)**

$$f'(x) = 2x \log 27 - 6 \log 27 (6x - 18) \log(x^2 - 6x + 8)$$

$$+ \frac{(3x^2 - 18x + 24)(2x - 6)}{x^2 - 6x + 8}$$

$$= 6(x-3)\left[\log 3 + \log\left(x^2 - 6x + 8\right) + 1\right]$$

$$= 6(x-3) \log 3e\left(x^2 - 6x + 8\right)$$

For $f(x)$ to be defined $x^2 - 6x + 8 > 0$
$\Rightarrow x < 2$ or $x > 4$

If $x > 4$ then $f'(x) < 0$ if $\log 3(x^2 - 6x + 8)e < 0$

i.e. $3(x^2 - 6x + 8)e < 1$ i.e. $x^2 - 6x + (8 - 1/3e) < 0$

i.e. $(x - (3 + \sqrt{1 + 1/3e}))(x - (3 - \sqrt{1 + 1/3e}) < 0$

$\Leftrightarrow 3 - \sqrt{1 + 1/3e} < x < (3 + \sqrt{1 + 1/3e})$

Hence $x \in (4, 3 + \sqrt{1 + 1/3e})$

Similiarly if $x < 2$, then $f'(x) < 0$,
If $\log 3(x^2 - 6x + 8) e > 0$

i.e., $x < 3 - \sqrt{1 + 1/3e}$ or $x > 3 + \sqrt{1 + 1/3e}$

Hence $x \in (3 - \sqrt{1 + 1/3e}, 2)$

**2.** **(b).** $\dfrac{dx}{dt} = -\dfrac{2t}{(1+t)^2}$

$$\frac{dy}{dt} = -\frac{1 + 3t^2}{t^2 (1+t^2)^2}$$

$$\frac{dy}{dx} = \frac{1 + 3t^2}{2t^3} > 0 \text{ for } t > 0$$

$\therefore$ y is increasing for every $x \in (0,1)$

**3.** **(c)** We have $f(x) = \dfrac{x}{\sin x}, 0 < x \le 1$

$$\Rightarrow \quad f'(x) = \frac{\sin x - x \cos x}{\sin^2 x}$$

where $\sin^2 x$ is always +ve when $0 < x \le 1$. To check
Nr., let
$\qquad h(x) = \sin x - x \cos x$
$\Rightarrow \quad h'(x) = x \sin x > 0$ for $0 < x \le 1$
$\Rightarrow \quad h(x)$ is increasing
$\Rightarrow \quad h(0) < h(x)$ when $0 < x$
$\Rightarrow \quad 0 < \sin x - x \cos x$

$\Rightarrow \quad \sin x - x \cos x > 0$

$\Rightarrow \quad f'(x) > 0, x \in (0,1]$

$\Rightarrow \quad f(x)$ is increasing on $(0, 1]$

Again $g(x) = \dfrac{x}{\tan x}$

$$\Rightarrow \quad g'(x) = \frac{\tan x - x \sec^2 x}{\tan^2 x}$$

Here $\tan^2 x > 0$ but to check Nr. we consider
$p(x) = \tan x - x \sec^2 x$

$$p'(x) = \sec^2 x - \sec^2 x - x.2 \sec x. \sec x \tan x$$

$\Rightarrow \quad p'(x) = -2x \sec^2 x \tan x < 0$ for $0 < x \le 1$

$\Rightarrow \quad p(x)$ is decreasing, when $0 < x \le 1$
$\Rightarrow \quad p(0) > p(x)$
$\Rightarrow \quad 0 > \tan x - x \sec^2 x$
$\therefore \quad g'(x) < 0$

Hence g (x) is decreasing when $0 < x \le 1$.

**4.** **(a)** $f(x) = x e^{x(1-x)}$
$\Rightarrow \quad f'(x) = e^{x(1-x)} + (1 - 2x) x e^{x(1-x)}$
$\qquad = e^{x(1-x)}(2x^2 - x - 1)$
$\qquad = -e^{x(1-x)}(2x + 1)(x - 1)$

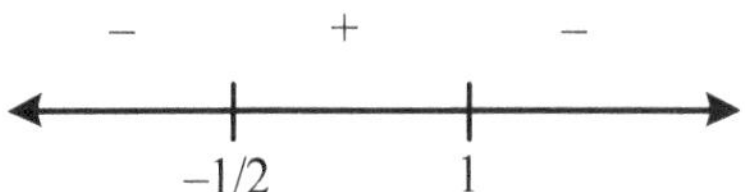

$\therefore \quad f(x)$ is increasing on $[-1/2, 1]$

**5.** **(d)** $f'(x) = -(x + 2)e^{-x} = -(x + 1)e^{-x} = 0$

$\Rightarrow \quad x = -1$

For $x \in (-\infty, -1), f'(x) > 0$ and for

$x \in (-1, \infty), f'(x) < 0$

$\therefore \quad f(x)$ is increasing on $(-\infty, -1)$ and decreasing on

$(-1, \infty)$

**6.** **(c)** $f(x) = \begin{vmatrix} x + a^2 & ab & ac \\ ab & x + b^2 & bc \\ ac & bc & x + c^2 \end{vmatrix}$

$f'(x) = 3x^2 + 2kx$, where $k = a^2 + b^2 + c^2$

$f(x)$ is an increasing function if $f'(x) > 0$.

$\Rightarrow \quad x < -\dfrac{2k}{3}, \quad$ or $\quad x > 0$

Thus, $f(x)$ is increasing for

$\left(-\infty, \dfrac{-2k}{3}\right) \cup (0, \infty)$

Also f(x) is decreasing function if $f'(x) < 0$

$\Rightarrow \dfrac{-2k}{3} < x < 0$

Therefore, f(x) is decreasing for $\left(\dfrac{-2k}{3}, 0\right)$.

**7. (c)** $f(x) = \begin{cases} xe^{ax} & ; \ x \le 0 \\ x + ax^2 - x^3; & x > 0 \end{cases}$

[f(x) is continuous at x = 0]

$\Rightarrow f'(x) = \begin{cases} axe^{ax} + e^{ax} & ; \ x \le 0 \\ 1 + 2ax - 3x^2; & x > 0 \end{cases}$

[f'(x) is continuous at x = 0]

and $f''(x) = \begin{cases} 2ae^{ax} + a^2 xe^{ax}; & x \le 0 \\ 2a - 6x & ; \ x > 0 \end{cases}$

[f''(x) is continuous at x = 0]

Now $f''(x) > 0 \Rightarrow 2a - 6x > 0$ if $x > 0$

**8. (a)** Since f(x) decreases for all x, therefore

$f'(x) \le 0 \ \forall \ x$

$\Rightarrow \cos x + \sin x - a \le 0 \ \forall \ x$

$\Rightarrow \sin x + \cos x \le a \ \forall \ x$

$\Rightarrow \sin x\left(x + \dfrac{\pi}{4}\right) \le \dfrac{a}{\sqrt{2}} \ \forall \ x$

$\Rightarrow \dfrac{a}{\sqrt{2}} \ge 1 \qquad \left[\because \sin\left(x + \dfrac{\pi}{4}\right) \le 1\right]$

$\Rightarrow a \ge \sqrt{2}$

**9. (d)** $g'(x) = f' (\cot^2 x + 2\cot x + 2)$

$\qquad \{-2\cot x \cosec^2 x - 2\cosec^2 x\} < 0$

$\Rightarrow f'\{(\cot x + 1)^2 + 1\}.(\cot x + 1) > 0 .....(1)$

Now given $f''(x) > 0$, so $f'(x)$ is increasing.

$\Rightarrow f'\{(\cot x + 1)^2 + 1\} > f'(1) = 0 \, \forall \, x \in (0, \pi) - \left\{\dfrac{3\pi}{4}\right\}$

$\therefore$ From (1), $g'(x) < 0$ if $\cot x + 1 > 0 \Rightarrow x \in \left(0, \dfrac{3\pi}{4}\right)$

**10. (a)** Since g is decreasing in $[0, \infty)$

$\therefore$ For $x \ge y \ge 0, \quad g(x) \le g(y) \qquad ........(1)$

Also g(x), g(y) $\in [0, \infty)$ and f is increasing in $[0, \infty)$.

$\therefore$ For $g(x), g(y) \in [0, \infty)$

such that $g(x) \le g(y)$

$\Rightarrow f(g(x)) \le f(g(y))$, where $x \ge y$

$\Rightarrow h(x) \le h(y)$

$\Rightarrow$ h is decreasing function in $[0, \infty)$

$\therefore \quad h(x) \le h(0), \ \forall \ x \ge 0$

But, h (0) = 0 (given)

$\therefore \quad h(x) \le 0 \, \forall \ x \ge 0 \qquad ...(2)$

Also, $h(x) \ge 0 \, \forall \ x \ge 0 \qquad ...(3)$

as h (x) $\in [0, \infty)$

From (2) and (3), we get h (x) = 0, $\forall \, x \ge 0$

Hence, h (x) − h (1) = 0 − 0 $\forall \, x \ge 0$

**11. (a, c)** We have

$h'(x) = f'(x)[1 - 2f(x) + 3(f(x))^2]$

$\qquad = 3f'(x)\left[(f(x))^2 - \dfrac{2}{3}f(x) + \dfrac{1}{3}\right]$

$\qquad = 3f'(x)[\{f(x) - 1/3\}^2 + 2/9]$

Note that $h'(x) < 0$ whenever $f'(x) < 0$ and $h'(x) > 0$

whenever $f'(x) > 0$. Thus, h (x) increases (decreases)

whenever f (x) increases (decreases).

**12. (b, d)** We have : $f(x) = x - e^x + \tan\left(\dfrac{2\pi}{7}\right)$

$\Rightarrow f'(x) = 1 - e^x$

For f (x) to be increasing, we must have

$f'(x) > 0 \Rightarrow 1 - e^x > 0 \Rightarrow e^x < 1$

$\Rightarrow x < 0 \Rightarrow x \in (-\infty, 0)$

**13. (a, d)** We have, $y = 2x + \cot^{-1} x + \log\left[\sqrt{1 + x^2} - x\right]$

$\Rightarrow \dfrac{dy}{dx} = 2 - \dfrac{1}{1+x^2} + \dfrac{1}{\sqrt{1+x^2} - x} \times \left[\dfrac{x}{\sqrt{1+x^2}} - 1\right]$

$\qquad = \dfrac{2x^2 + 1}{1 + x^2} - \dfrac{1}{\sqrt{1+x^2}} = \dfrac{(2x^2 + 1) - \sqrt{1+x^2}}{1 + x^2}$

Now, $\dfrac{dy}{dx} \ge 0$

$\Rightarrow (2x^2 + 1) - \sqrt{1 + x^2} \ge 0$

$\Rightarrow (2x^2 + 1)^2 \ge 1 + x^2$

$\Rightarrow 4x^4 + 3x^2 \ge 0,$

which is true for all real values of x.

∴ y increases for all real values of x.

**14. (b, c)** $f(x) = 2\log(x-2) - x^2 + 4x + 1$

$$\Rightarrow f'(x) = \frac{2}{x-2} - 2x + 4$$

$$\Rightarrow f'(x) = 2\left[\frac{1-(x-2)^2}{x-2}\right] = -2\frac{(x-1)(x-3)}{x-2}$$

$$\Rightarrow f'(x) = \frac{2(x-1)(x-3)(x-2)}{(x-2)^2}$$

∴ $f'(x) > 0 \Rightarrow -2(x-1)(x-3)(x-2) > 0$

$\Rightarrow (x-1)(x-2)(x-3) < 0$

$\Rightarrow x \in (-\infty, 1) \cup (2, 3)$

Thus, f(x) is increasing on $(-\infty, 1) \cup (2, 3)$.

**15. (b,d)** We have $g(x) = f(\sin x) + f(\cos x)$

$$\Rightarrow g'(x) = f'(\sin x)\cos x + f'(\cos x)(-\sin x)$$

$$\Rightarrow g''(x) = -f'(\sin x).\sin x + f''(\sin x)\cos^2 x$$

$$-f'(\cos x)\cos x + f''(\cos x).\sin^2 x$$

As $f'(\sin x) < 0, f''(\sin x) > 0$,

$$\sin x > 0, \cos x > 0 \,\forall\, x \in \left(0, \frac{\pi}{2}\right)$$

$$\therefore g''(x) > 0 \,\forall\, x \in \left(0, \frac{\pi}{2}\right)$$

Note that $f'(\sin x) < 0 \Rightarrow f'(\cos x) = f'\left(\sin\left(\frac{\pi}{2} - x\right)\right) < 0$

and $f''(\sin x) > 0$

$$\Rightarrow f''(\cos x) = f''\left(\sin\left(\frac{\pi}{2} - x\right)\right) > 0$$

∴ $g'(x)$ is increasing function for $x \in \left(0, \frac{\pi}{2}\right)$

We have $g'(x) = 0$

$$\Rightarrow f'(\sin x)\cos x - f'(\cos x).\sin x = 0 \text{ if } x = \frac{\pi}{4}$$

∴ $g'(x) > 0$ if $\sin x > \cos x \Rightarrow x \in \left(\frac{\pi}{4}, \frac{\pi}{2}\right)$

and $g'(x) < 0$, $\cos x > \sin x \Rightarrow x \in \left(0, \frac{\pi}{4}\right)$

$[\because f'(\sin x) < 0]$

**16. A → s,t; B → p,t; C → p,q,s,t; D → r,s,t**

(A) $f'(x) > 0 \,\forall\, x \in R \Rightarrow f'(x)$ is an increasing function.

Now $g'(x) = -f'(4-x) + f'(2+x)$

If $g'(x) > 0 \Rightarrow f'(2+x) > f'(4-x)$

$\Rightarrow 2 + x > 4 - x$ or $x > 1$

(B) $f'(x) = 3(x-1)(x+1) \Rightarrow f'(x) = 0$ has roots $x = -1, 1$

∴ $f(x) = 0$ will have exactly one real root if

$f(-1)f(1) > 0$

$\Rightarrow (a+2)(a-2) > 0 \Rightarrow a < -2$ or $a > 2$.

(C) $f'(x) = -\sin x + a^2 \geq 0 \,\forall\, x \in R$

$\Rightarrow a^2 \geq \sin x \,\forall\, x \in R$

∴ $a^2 \geq 1 \Rightarrow a \leq -1$ or $a \geq 1$.

(D) $f'(x) = 2e^x + ae^{-x} + 2a + 1 = 2e^{-x}(e^x + a)\left(e^x + \frac{1}{2}\right)$

f(x) increases for all x if $f'(x) \geq 0 \,\forall\, x \in R$

∴ $e^x + a \geq 0 \,\forall\, x \in R \Rightarrow a \geq 0$

**17. A → p, s; B → p, q, r,s, t; C → p, q**

(A) ∵ $f(x) = \frac{x}{(1+x^2)}$

∴ $f'(x) = \frac{(1-x^2)}{(1+x^2)^2}$

∵ $f'(x) < 0 \Rightarrow \frac{1-x^2}{(1+x^2)^2} < 0$

$\Rightarrow (1-x^2) < 0 \Rightarrow x^2 - 1 > 0$

∴ $x \in (-\infty, -1) \cup (1, \infty)$ **(p, s)**

(B) ∵ $f(x) = \tan^{-1} x - x$

∴ $f'(x) = \frac{1}{1+x^2} - 1 = -\frac{x^2}{1+x^2} < 0$

$f'(x) < 0 \,\forall\, x \in R$ **(p,q,r,s,t)**

(C) ∵ $f(x) = x - e^x + \tan\left(\frac{2\pi}{7}\right)$

∴ $f'(x) = 1 - e^x > 0$

or $e^x < 1$

or $f^x < e^0$

∴ $x < 0$

$x \in (-\infty, 0)$ **(p,q)**

**18. (a)** $f'(x) = \ln(x + \sqrt{1+x^2}) = -\ln(\sqrt{1+x^2} - x)$

$\Rightarrow f'(x) > 0$

$\Rightarrow f(x)$ is decreasing when $x < 0$

$\Rightarrow f(x)$ is increasing when $x > 0$.

$\Rightarrow f(x) > f(0) \Rightarrow f(x) > 0$.

Again f(x) is decreasing in $(-\infty, 0)$

$\Rightarrow f(x) > f(0) \Rightarrow f(x) > 0$.

**19. (c)** Every increasing or decreasing function is one-one

$f'(x) = 3x^2 + 2x + 3 + \cos x$

$$= 3\left(x + \frac{1}{3}\right)^2 + \frac{8}{3} + \cos x > 0$$

$$\left[\because\ |\cos x| < 1 \text{ and } 3\left(x + \frac{1}{3}\right)^2 + \frac{8}{3} \geq \frac{8}{2}\right]$$

$\therefore$   f(x) is strictly increasing.

**20.**   **3**

We have, $F(x) = \begin{cases} -2x + \log_{1/2}(k^2 - 6k + 8), & -2 \leq x < -1 \\ x^3 + 3x^2 + 4x + 1, & -1 \leq x \leq 3 \end{cases}$

Also F(x) is increasing on [–1, 3] because

   F'(x) > 0 $\forall$ x $\in$ [–1, 3]

And F'(x) = –2 $\forall$ x $\in$ [–2, –1), so F(x) is decreasing on [–2, –1).

$\therefore$ If F(x) has smallest value at x = –1, then we must have

$$\lim_{h \to 0} F(-1-h) \geq F(-1)$$

$\Rightarrow 2 + \log_{1/2}(k^2 - 6k + 8) \geq -1$

$\Rightarrow \log_{1/2}(k^2 - 6k + 8) \geq -3$

$\Rightarrow k^2 - 6k + 8 \leq 8$

$\Rightarrow k^2 - 6k \leq 0$

$\Rightarrow k \in [0, 6]$        ........ (1)

But in order to define $\log_{1/2}(k^2 - 6k + 8)$

We must have $k^2 - 6k + 8 > 0$

$\Rightarrow (k-2)(k-4) > 0$

$\Rightarrow k < 2$ or $k > 4$        ........ (2)

$\therefore$ From (1) and (2), we get k $\in$ [0, 2) $\cup$ (4, 6]

$\Rightarrow$ Possible integer(s) in the range of k are 0, 1, 5, 6

Hence the sum of all possible positive integer(s) in the range of k = 1 + 5 + 6 = 12

Thus, M = 3

**21.**   **4**

If $f(x)$ is decreasing then $f'(x) < 0$

$\Rightarrow \log_{1/3}(\log_3(\sin x + a)) < 0$

$\Rightarrow \log_3(\sin x + a) > 1$

$\sin x + a > 3$

$a > 3 - \sin x$

$a > 4$

$\Rightarrow a \in (4, \infty)$

Thus P = 4

**22.**   **8**

Here $f'(x) > 0 \forall x \in R$

$\Rightarrow 2\cos 2x - 8(a+1)\cos x - (4a^2 + 8a - 14) > 0 \forall x \in R$

$\Rightarrow 4\cos^2 x - 8(a+1)\cos x - (4a^2 + 8a - 12) > 0$

$\Rightarrow \cos^2 x - 2(a+1)\cos x - (a^2 + 2a - 3) > 0$

$\Rightarrow (\cos x - \alpha)(\cos x - \beta) > 0$

where $\alpha = (a+1) + \sqrt{2a^2 + 4a - 2}$ and

$\beta = (a+1) - \sqrt{2a^2 + 4a - 2}$

$\Rightarrow \cos x - \beta < 0$ since $\cos x - \alpha < 0 \ \forall a > 0$

$\Rightarrow (a+1) - \sqrt{2a^2 + 4a - 2} > \cos x \ \forall x \in R$

$\Rightarrow (a+1) - \sqrt{2a^2 + 4a - 2} > 1$

$\Rightarrow \sqrt{2a^2 + 4a - 2} < a$

$\Rightarrow a^2 + 4a - 2 < 0$

$\Rightarrow a \in (-2 - \sqrt{6}, \sqrt{6} - 2)$

Hence $a \in (0, \sqrt{6} - 2)$ since $a > 0$.

Thus, P + Q + R = 0 + 6 + 2 = 8

**23.**   **1**

$f(x) = xe^{x(1-x)}$

$\Rightarrow f'(x) = e^{x(1-x)} + (1-2x)x\,e^{x(1-x)}$

$= -e^{x(1-x)}(2x^2 - x - 1)$

$= -e^{x(1-x)}(2x+1)(x-1)$

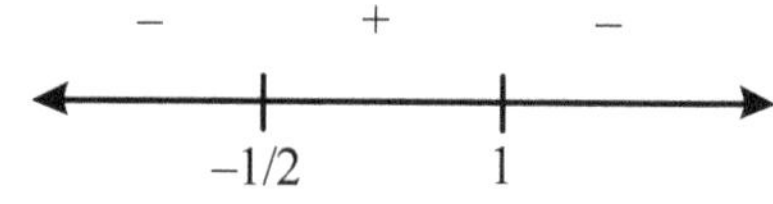


$\therefore$   $f(x)$ is increasing on [–1/2, 1]

Thus, $\dfrac{P + Q + R}{4} = \dfrac{1 + 2 + 1}{4} = 1$

**24.**   **3**    $3\sin x - 4\sin^3 x = \sin 3x$ which increases for

$$3x \in \left(-\frac{\pi}{2}, \frac{\pi}{2}\right) \Rightarrow x \in \left(-\frac{\pi}{6}, \frac{\pi}{6}\right) \text{ whose length is } \frac{\pi}{3}.$$

Thus Y = 3

**1.** **(b)** We have $ax^3 + bx^2 + cx + d = 0$

Let $f(x) = \dfrac{ax^4}{4} + \dfrac{bx^3}{3} + \dfrac{cx^2}{2} + dx + e$   $\therefore$  $f(0) = e$

$f(2) = 4a + \dfrac{8b}{3} + 2c + 2d + e$

$\quad = \dfrac{(12a + 8b + 6c + 6d)}{3} + e$

$\quad = \dfrac{2}{3}(6a + 4b + 3c + 3d) + e = 0 + e$

$f(2) = e$

$\therefore$  By Rolle's theorem, there exist atleast one value of $x \in (0, 2)$ such that $f'(x) = 0$
The equation $ax^3 + bx^2 + cx + d = 0$ has atleast one real root in $[0, 2]$.

**2.** **(d)** Consider $h(x) = g(x) - 4f(x)$, in $[2, 4]$

Also $h(2) = g(2) - 4f(2) = -32$; $h(4) = -32$
$\Rightarrow h'(x) = 0$ for atleast one $x \in (2, 4)$ using Rolle's theorem

**3.** **(d)** Consider $\phi(x) = f(x) - g(x) \Rightarrow \phi'(x) = f'(x) - g'(x)$
$\phi(x)$ is also continuous and derivable in $[x_0, x]$
Using LMVT for $Q(x)$ in $[x_0, x]$

$\phi'(x) = \dfrac{\phi(x) - \phi(x_0)}{x - x_0}$.

since $\phi'(x) = f'(x) - g'(x)$ are $f'(x) - g'(x) > 0$
$\therefore \qquad \phi'(x) > 0$
hence  $\phi(x) - \phi(x_0) > 0$
$\qquad \phi(x) > \phi(x_0)$
$\qquad f(x) - g(x) > 0$
are $\quad f(x_0) = f(x_0) - f(x_0) = 0$

**4.** **(a)** By Rolle's theorem $f(1) = f(3)$ gives
$a + b + 11 - 6 = 27a + 9b + 33 - 6$
$\Rightarrow 26a + 8b + 22 = 0$
$\Rightarrow 13a + 4b + 11 = 0$ $\qquad$ ...(1)
Again $f'(x) = 3ax^2 + 2bx + 11$

Since $f'\left(2 + \dfrac{1}{\sqrt{3}}\right) = 0$

$\therefore 3a\left(2 + \dfrac{1}{\sqrt{3}}\right)^2 + 2b\left(2 + \dfrac{1}{\sqrt{3}}\right) + 11 = 0$

Simplify it, we get $b + 6a = 0$ $\qquad$ .....(2)
From eqn (1) and (2)
$a = 1, b = -6$

**5.** **(c)** From mean value theorem $f'(c) = \dfrac{f(b) - f(a)}{b - a}$

$a = 0, f(a) = 0 \Rightarrow b = \dfrac{1}{2}, f(b) = \dfrac{3}{8}$

$f'(x) = (x - 1)(x - 2) + x(x - 2) + x(x - 1)$
$f'(c) = (c - 1)(c - 2) + c(c - 2) + c(c - 1)$
$\quad = c^2 - 3c + 2 + c^2 - 2c + c^2 - c$
$f'(c) = 3c^2 - 6c + 2$

According to mean value theorem, $f'(c) = \dfrac{f(b) - f(a)}{b - a}$

$\Rightarrow 3c^2 - 6c + 2 = \dfrac{(3/8) - 0}{(1/2) - 0} = \dfrac{3}{4}$

$\Rightarrow 3c^2 - 6c + \dfrac{5}{4} = 0$

$c = \dfrac{6 \pm \sqrt{36 - 15}}{2 \times 3} = \dfrac{6 \pm \sqrt{21}}{6} = 1 \pm \dfrac{\sqrt{21}}{6}$.

**6.** **(a)** $f'(x_1) = \dfrac{-1}{x_1^2}$

$\therefore \dfrac{-1}{x_1^2} = \dfrac{\dfrac{1}{b} - \dfrac{1}{a}}{b - a} = -\dfrac{1}{ab} \Rightarrow x_1 = \sqrt{ab}$

**7.** **(a,b,c,d).**
(a) $f(x) = x - \cos x$ ; $f(0) < 0, f(\pi/2) > 0$
(b) $f(x) = x + \sin x - 1$

$\qquad f(0) = -1 < 0 ; f(\pi/6) = \dfrac{\pi}{6} + \dfrac{1}{2} - 1 > 0$

(c) $f(x) = a(x - 3) + b(x - 1)$ in $[1, 3]$
$\qquad f(1) = -2a < 0 ; f(3) = 2b > 0 \Rightarrow f(x) = 0$ in $(1, 3)$
(d) $h(x) = f(x) - g(x)$
$\qquad h(a) = f(a) - g(a) > 0$
$\qquad h(b) = f(b) - g(b) < 0$
$\qquad$ hence using IVT all the four have at least one root in indicated interval.

**8.** **(a,b,c,d).** As Rolle's theorem is applicable, the function should be continuous and differentiable in $[-3, 3]$.
So, at $x = 1$, $a + b = 1 = c$ (continuity) and

$2a = \lim_{h \to 0} \dfrac{\dfrac{c}{1+h} - 1}{h}$ (differentiability)

$\Rightarrow 2a = \lim_{h \to 0} \dfrac{1 - (1 + h)}{h(1 + h)}$ $\;(c = 1)$

$\Rightarrow a = \dfrac{-1}{2}, \; b = \dfrac{3}{2}$ and $c = 1$

**9.** **(a,b,d).** $f(x) = x - 1, 1 \le x \le 2$

$g(x) = x - 1 + b \sin \dfrac{\pi}{2} x, \ 1 \le x \le 2$

$f(1) = 0$ ; $f(2) = 1 \Rightarrow$ Rolle's theorem is not applicable to ' f ' but LMVT is applicable to f.

($\because$ $x - 1$ is continuous and differentiable in $[1, 2]$ and $(1, 2)$ respectively)

Now, $g(1) = b$ ; $g(2) = 1$ and

Function $x - 1$, $\sin \dfrac{\pi}{2} x$ are both continuous in $[1, 2]$ and $(1, 2)$

$\therefore$ For Rolle's theorem to be applicable to g.

We must have $b = 1$

**10.** **(a,b,d).**

(a) This statement is true, every continuous function is bounded on a closed interval.

(b) True again, by Intermediate Value Theorem

(c) Not true, because maximum and/or minimum values could also occur at a or b, without the derivatives being 0.

(d) True. By the Mean Value Theorem there exist a point between a and b where the derivative is exactly

$\dfrac{f(b) - f(a)}{b - a}$, a clearly positive value.

Thus the true statements are (a), (b) and (d).

**11.** **(c)** Given $e^{\alpha} \cos \alpha = 1$ ....(1)

and $e^{\beta} \cos \beta = 1$ .....(2)

Let $f(x) = e^{-x} - \cos x$, then $f(x)$ is continuous and differentiable.

Also, $f(\alpha) = f(\beta) = 0$  (from (1) and (2))

Therefore by Rolle's MVT, $f'(x) = 0$ has at least one root in $(\alpha, \beta)$.

$\Rightarrow -e^{-x} + \sin x = 0$  for at least one $x \in (\alpha, \beta)$

$\Rightarrow e^{x} \sin x = 1$ has at least one root in $(\alpha, \beta)$.

**12.** **(d)** Let $f(x) = \tan^{-1} x$, then using Lagrange's MVT, for some

$\alpha \in (x, y); \ f'(\alpha) = \dfrac{f(x) - f(y)}{x - y}$

$\Rightarrow \left| \dfrac{1}{1 + \alpha^2} \right| = \left| \dfrac{\tan^{-1} x - \tan^{-1} y}{x - y} \right|$

$\because 1 + \alpha^2 \ge 1 \Rightarrow \dfrac{1}{1 + \alpha^2} \le 1 \Rightarrow$ So, $\left| \dfrac{\tan^{-1} x - \tan^{-1} y}{x - y} \right| \le 1$

Again if $f(x) = \sin x$, then as above

$\left| \dfrac{\sin x - \sin y}{x - y} \right| = |\cos \alpha| \le 1$

**13.** **(b)** Let $h(x) = \{f(x) - f(a)\} \{g(b) - g(x)\}$

Then $h(x)$ is continuous and differentiable and $h(a) = h(b) = 0$

Therefore $h(x)$ satisfies the conditions of Rolle's MVT.

Therefore for some $c \in (a, b)$, $f'(c) = 0$

$\Rightarrow f'(c)\{g(b) - g(c)\} - g'(c)\{f(c) - f(a)\} = 0$

$\Rightarrow \dfrac{f(c) - f(a)}{g(b) - g(c)} = \dfrac{f'(c)}{g'(c)}$

**14.** **A $\to$ q, s; B $\to$ p, r; C $\to$ p, r**

**(A)** $f(x) = |x|$

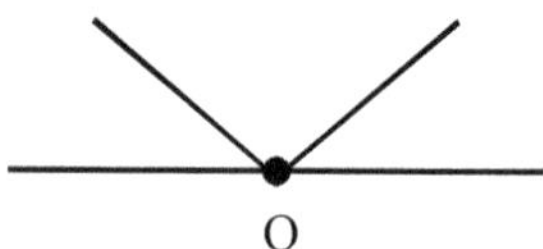

is not differentiable at $x = 0$

$f(x) = \ln |x|$

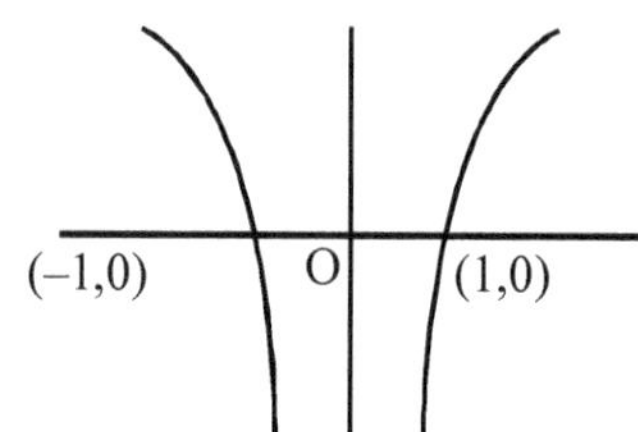


is discontinuous at $x = 0$,

$f(x) = x^2 + x + 1$

$f(-1) \ne f(1)$

**(B)** $f(x) = \begin{cases} \left( \dfrac{1}{2} - x \right)^2, & x > \dfrac{1}{2} \\[3mm] \left( \dfrac{1}{2} - x \right), & x \le \dfrac{1}{2} \end{cases}$

$\therefore f'(x) = \begin{cases} -2\left( \dfrac{1}{2} - x \right), & x > \dfrac{1}{2} \\[3mm] -1 & x \le \dfrac{1}{2} \end{cases}$

$f'\left( \dfrac{1^{+}}{2} \right) \ne f'\left( \dfrac{1^{-}}{2} \right)$

$\Rightarrow f(x)$ is not differentiable at $x = \dfrac{1}{2}$

and $f(x) = \begin{cases} 1, & 0 \le x < \dfrac{1}{2} \\[3mm] 2, & \dfrac{1}{2} \le x \le 1 \end{cases}$

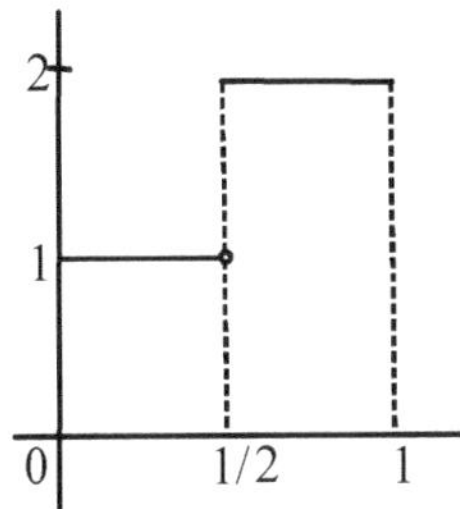

$f(x)$ is discontinuous at $x = 1/2$

**(C)** From (B)

**15. (b)** For Rolle's theorem and LMVT, $f(x)$ must be continuous in [a, b] and differentiable in (a, b).

∴ If Rolle's theorem be applied in $f(x)$, then LMVT is also applied in $f(x)$

∵ $f(x) = |\sin|x||$ in $\left[-\dfrac{\pi}{4}, \dfrac{\pi}{4}\right]$ is non differentiable at $x = 0$

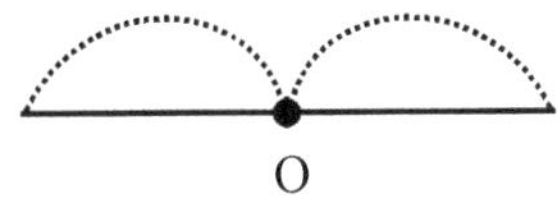

∴ Rolle's theorem and LMVT cannot be applicable for

$f(x) = |\sin|x|| \; \forall \; x \in \left[-\dfrac{\pi}{4}, \dfrac{\pi}{4}\right]$.

**16. (b)** ∵ $x(x+3)$ and $e^{-x/2}$ are continuous and differentiable everywhere

∴ $x(x+3)\,e^{-x/2}$ is continuous and differentiable and $f(-3) = f(0) = 0$

$f'(x) = (x^2 + 3x)\,e^{-x/2}\left(-\dfrac{1}{2}\right) + e^{-x/2}(2x+3)$

$= -\dfrac{1}{2}e^{-x/2}(x^2 + 3x - 4x - 6)$

$= -\dfrac{1}{2}e^{-x/2}(x^2 - x - 6)$

$= -\dfrac{1}{2}e^{-x/2}(x-3)(x+2)$

Put $f'(x) = 0 \Rightarrow x = 3, -2$

$3 \notin [-3, 0]$

∴ $x = -2 \in [-3, 0]$

∴ Rolle's theorem applies in $[-3, 0]$

LMVT is also applied.

∵ $f'(c) = \dfrac{f(b) - f(a)}{b - a} = 0$

$\Rightarrow f(a) = f(b)$

But it is not possible for all integral [a, b].

**17. 7**

Using LMVT in [0, 2]

$\dfrac{f(2) - f(0)}{2 - 0} = f'(c)$ where $c \in (0, 2)$

$\dfrac{f(2) + 3}{2} \leq 5$

$f(2) \leq 7$

**18. 4**

Using LMVT for $f$ in [1, 2]

$\forall \; c \in (1, 2) \; \dfrac{f(2) - f(1)}{2 - 1} = f'(c) \leq 2$

$f(2) - f(1) \leq 2 \Rightarrow \qquad f(2) \leq 4 \quad ....(1)$

again using LMVT in [2, 4]

$\forall \; d \in (2, 4)$

$\dfrac{f(4) - f(2)}{4 - 2} = f'(d) \leq 2$

∴ $f(4) - f(2) \leq 4$

$8 - f(2) \leq 4$

$4 \leq f(2) \qquad \Rightarrow f(2) \geq 4 \qquad ....(2)$

from (1) and (2)

$f(2) = 4$

**19. 1**

$\dfrac{f(2) - f(0)}{2 - 0} = f'(x) \Rightarrow \dfrac{f(2) - 0}{2} = f'(x)$

$\Rightarrow \dfrac{df(x)}{dx} = \dfrac{f(2)}{2}, \Rightarrow f(x) = \dfrac{f(2)}{2}x + c$

∴ $f(0) = 0 \Rightarrow c = 0$;

∴ $f(x) = \dfrac{f(2)}{2}x \qquad ...(i)$

Given $|f'(x)| \leq \dfrac{1}{2} \Rightarrow \left|\dfrac{f(2)}{2}\right| \leq \dfrac{1}{2} \quad ...(ii)$

$(i) \Rightarrow |f(x)| = \left|\dfrac{f(2)}{2}x\right| = \left|\dfrac{f(2)}{2}\right| |x| \leq \dfrac{1}{2}|x|$

$\qquad\qquad\qquad\qquad\qquad\qquad$ [from (ii)]

In [0, 2], for maximum $x \, (x = 2)$

$|f(x)| \leq \dfrac{1}{2} \cdot 2 \Rightarrow |f(x)| \leq 1$.

Thus, $P = 1$.

**20. 5**

Given that equation of curve $y = x^3 = f(x)$

So $f(2) = 8$ and $f(-2) = -8$

$f'(x) = 3x^2$

Now $f'(x) = \dfrac{f(2) - f(-2)}{2 - (-2)}$

$\Rightarrow \dfrac{8 - (-8)}{4} = 3x^2; \therefore x = \pm\dfrac{2}{\sqrt{3}}$.

Thus, $A = 2, B = 3$

$\Rightarrow A + B = 2 + 3 = 5$

**21. 2**

To determine 'c' in Rolle's theorem, $f'(c) = 0$

Here $f'(x) = (x^2 + 3x)e^{-(1/2)x}\left(-\dfrac{1}{2}\right) + (2x + 3)e^{-(1/2)x}$

$= e^{-(1/2)x}\left\{-\dfrac{1}{2}(x^2 + 3x) + 2x + 3\right\}$

$= -\dfrac{1}{2}e^{-(x/2)}\{x^2 - x - 6\}$

∴ $f'(c) = 0 \Rightarrow c^2 - c - 6 = 0 \Rightarrow c = 3, -2$

But $c = 3 \notin [-3, 0]$, Thus $c = -2 \Rightarrow -c = 2$

**1. (c)** $\int\left(3x^2\tan\dfrac{1}{x}-x\sec^2\dfrac{1}{x}\right)dx$

$=\int 3x^2\tan\dfrac{1}{x}dx-\int x\sec^2\dfrac{1}{x}dx$

$=\tan\dfrac{1}{x}x^3-\int\left(\sec^2\dfrac{1}{x}\right)\left(-\dfrac{1}{x^2}\right).x^3dx-\int x\sec^2\dfrac{1}{x}dx$

$=x^3.\tan\dfrac{1}{x}+c$

**2. (d)** $f(x)=(-1)^3\begin{vmatrix} 0 & \sin x-x^2 & 2-\cos x \\ x^2-\sin x & 0 & 2x-1 \\ \cos x-2 & 1-2x & 0 \end{vmatrix}$

$=-f(x)$

Since the value of a determinant does not change if rows are changed into columns. Thus $f(x)=0$ for all x and

$\int f(x)\,dx=$ a constant.

**3. (b)** $\int\left(1+x+\dfrac{x^2}{2!}+\dfrac{x^3}{3!}+........\right)dx=\int e^x dx=e^x+C$.

**4. (b)** $\int(1+2x+3x^2+4x^3+....)dx$

$=\int(1-x)^{-2}dx=(1-x)^{-1}+C$

**5. (a)** $\int\dfrac{\cos 2x-\cos 2\alpha}{\cos x-\cos\alpha}dx$

$=\int\dfrac{2(\cos^2 x-\cos^2\alpha)}{\cos x-\cos\alpha}dx$

$=2\int(\cos x+\cos\alpha)dx=2(\sin x+x\cos\alpha)$

**6. (c)** $\int\left\{1+2\tan^2 x+2\tan x\sec x\right\}^{1/2}dx$

$=\int(\sec^2 x+\tan^2 x+2\tan x\sec x)^{1/2}dx$

$=\int(\sec x+\tan x)dx$

$=\log\sec x(\sec x+\tan x)+C$

**7. (d)** $\int\log 10^x\,dx=\int\dfrac{\log x}{\log 10}dx$

$=\int\dfrac{1}{\log 10}[x\log x-x]$

$=x[\log_{10}x-\log_{10}e]+C$

**8. (a)** $I=\int\tan^{-1}\left(\dfrac{\cos 2x}{1+\sin 2x}\right)dx$

$I=\int\tan^{-1}\left(\dfrac{2\sin\left(\dfrac{\pi}{4}-x\right)\cos\left(\dfrac{\pi}{4}-x\right)}{2\cos^2\left(\dfrac{\pi}{4}-x\right)}\right)$

$I=\int\tan^{-1}\tan\left(\dfrac{\pi}{4}-x\right)dx=\int\left(\dfrac{\pi}{4}-x\right)dx$

$=\dfrac{\pi}{4}x-\dfrac{x^2}{2}+C$

**9. (a)** $f'(x)=\int\tan^2 x\,dx=\int(\sec^2 x-1)\,dx$

$=\tan x-x+K$

$\therefore\qquad f'(0)=K=0$

$\therefore\qquad f'(x)=\tan x-x$

$f(x)=\int(\tan x-x)\,dx$

$=\log\sec x-\dfrac{x^2}{2}+C$

$\therefore\ f(0)=C=0$

**10. (a)** $\int\dfrac{\sin^8 x-\cos^8 x}{1-2\sin^2 x\cos^2 x}dx$

$=-\int\dfrac{\cos 2x.(1-2\sin^2 x\cos^2 x)}{(1-2\sin^2 x\cos^2 x)}dx$

$=-\int\cos 2x\,dx=-\dfrac{1}{2}\sin 2x+B$

$A=-\dfrac{1}{2}$.

**11. (d)** $I=\int\dfrac{\cos 5x+\cos 4x}{1-2\cos 3x}dx$

(multiply by. 2sin3x in $N^r$ and $D^r$)

$=\int\left(\dfrac{2\cos 5x\sin 3x+2\cos 4x\sin 3x}{2\sin 3x-2\sin 6x}\right)dx$

$=\int\dfrac{\sin 8x-\sin 2x+\sin 7x-\sin x}{2(\sin 3x-\sin 6x)}dx$

$=\int\dfrac{(\sin 8x-\sin x)+(\sin 7x-\sin 2x)}{2(\sin 3x-\sin 6x)}dx$

$=\int\dfrac{2\cos\dfrac{9x}{2}.\sin\dfrac{7x}{2}+2\cos\dfrac{9x}{2}.\sin\dfrac{5x}{2}}{-2.2\cos\dfrac{9x}{2}.\sin\dfrac{3x}{2}}dx$

$=-\dfrac{1}{2}\int\left(\dfrac{\sin\dfrac{7x}{2}+\sin\dfrac{5x}{2}}{\sin\dfrac{3x}{2}}\right)dx$

$=-\int\dfrac{2\sin\dfrac{3x}{2}\cos\dfrac{3x}{2}.\cos\dfrac{x}{2}}{\sin\dfrac{3x}{2}}dx$

$=-\int 2\cos\dfrac{3x}{2}.\cos\dfrac{x}{2}.dx$

$=-\int(\cos x+\cos 2x)dx$

$$= -\left(\sin x + \frac{\sin 2x}{2}\right) + C$$

**12. (b)** $\tan 3x = \tan(2x + x) = \dfrac{\tan 2x + \tan x}{1 - \tan 2x \tan x}$

$$\Rightarrow \quad \tan 3x \tan 2x \tan x = \tan 3x - \tan 2x - \tan x$$

$$\therefore \ I = \int \tan x \cdot \tan 2x \tan 3x\, dx$$

$$= \int (\tan 3x - \tan 2x - \tan x)dx$$

$$= \frac{1}{3}\log|\sec 3x| - \frac{1}{2}\log|\sec 2x| - \log|\sec x| + C$$

**13. (c)** $I = \int \sqrt{1 + 2\tan^2 x + 2\tan x \sec x}\ dx$

$$= \int \sqrt{\sec^2 x + \tan^2 x + 2\tan x \sec x}\ dx$$

$$= \int (\sec x + \tan x)\, dx = \ln(\sec x + \tan x) + \ln \sec x + C$$

**14. (b)**

$$\int \frac{\sin^8 x - \cos^8 x}{1 - 2\sin^2 x \cos^2 x}dx = \int \frac{(\sin^4 x + \cos^4 x)(\sin^2 x - \cos^2 x)}{1 - 2\sin^2 x \cos^2 x}dx$$

$$= \int \frac{(1 - 2\sin^2 x \cos^2 x)(\sin^2 x - \cos^2 x)}{(1 - 2\sin^2 x \cos^2 x)}dx$$

$$= -\int \cos 2x\, dx = -\frac{1}{2}\sin 2x + C$$

**15. (a)** $\int \sqrt{(1 + \sin 2x)}\ dx$

$$= \int \sqrt{(\sin^2 x + \cos^2 x + 2\sin x \cos x)}\ dx$$

$$= \int \sqrt{(\sin x + \cos x)^2}\ dx = \int (\sin x + \cos x)\ dx$$

$$= \int \sin x\, dx + \int \cos x\, dx = -\cos x + \sin x + C$$

**16. (c)** $\int \dfrac{1.dx}{\sin^2 x \cos^2 x} = \int \dfrac{(\sin^2 x + \cos^2 x)}{\sin^2 x \cos^2 x}dx$

[Putting $(\sin^2 x + \cos^2 x)$ in place of 1 in the numberator]

$$= \int \left(\frac{\sin^2 x}{\sin^2 x \cos^2 x} + \frac{\cos^2 x}{\sin^2 x \cos^2 x}\right)dx$$

$$= \int \left(\frac{1}{\cos^2 x} + \frac{1}{\sin^2 x}\right)dx$$

$$= \int \sec^2 x\, dx + \int \cos ec^2 x\, dx = \tan x - \cot x + C$$

**17. (b)** $\int e^{x\log a} + e^{a\log x} + e^{a\log a}\ dx$

$$= \int e^{\log a^x} + e^{\log x^a} + e^{\log a^a}\ dx\ [\because e^{\log \lambda} = \lambda\,]$$

$$= \int (a^x + x^a + a^a)\ dx = \int a^x dx + \int x^a dx + \int a^a dx$$

$$= \frac{a^x}{\log a} + \frac{x^{a+1}}{a+1} + a^a \cdot x + C$$

**18. (a,b)** $\int \sqrt{\dfrac{1-x}{1+x}}\ dx$

$$= \int \left(\frac{1}{\sqrt{1-x^2}} - \frac{x}{\sqrt{1-x^2}}\right)dx$$

$$= \sin^{-1}x + \sqrt{1-x^2} + C$$

$$= -\cos^{-1}x + \sqrt{1-x^2} + C$$

**19. (c,d)** $\int \dfrac{\sin x}{\sin(x-\alpha)}dx = \int \dfrac{\sin\{x-\alpha\}+\alpha\}}{\sin(x-\alpha)}dx$

$$= \int \frac{\sin(x-\alpha)\cos\alpha + \cos(x-\alpha)\sin\alpha}{\sin(x-\alpha)}dx$$

$$= \int \cos\alpha\, dx + \sin\alpha \int \cot(x-\alpha)dx$$

$$= x\cos\alpha + \sin\alpha \ln \sin(x-\alpha) + C$$

**20. (1)**

Since $\int [f(x)]^n\ f'(x)\, dx = \dfrac{[f(x)]^{n+1}}{n+1} + C$

$$\therefore \int f(x)\cos x\, dx = \frac{f^2(x)}{2} + C$$

$$\Rightarrow f'(x) = \cos x \Rightarrow f(x) = \sin x$$

Thus, $P = 1$

**21. (3)** $\int x^{51}(\tan^{-1} x + \cot^{-1} x)\, dx$

$$= \int x^{51} \cdot \frac{\pi}{2}dx \quad \left\{\because \tan^{-1}x + \cot^{-1}x = \frac{\pi}{2}\right\}$$

$$= \frac{\pi x^{52}}{104} + C = \frac{x^{52}}{52}(\tan^{-1}x + \cot^{-1}x) + C.$$

Thus $M = 52,\ N = 52,$
$\quad P = 1,\ Q = 1$

$$\Rightarrow \frac{M}{N} + P + Q = 1 + 1 + 1 = 3$$

**22. (1)** $\int \dfrac{\cos 4x + 1}{\cot x - \tan x}dx$

$$= \int \frac{2\cos^2 2x}{\cos^2 x - \sin^2 x} \cdot \sin x \cos x\, dx$$

$$= \int \cos 2x \sin 2x\, dx = \frac{1}{2}\int \sin 4x\, dx = -\frac{1}{8}\cos 4x + C$$

Hence $K = -1/8$.
Thus, $-8K = 1$

**23. (2)** Here $I = \int \sin^{-1}(\cos x)dx$

$$\Rightarrow \int \sin^{-1}\sin\left(\frac{\pi}{2} - x\right)dx$$

$$\Rightarrow \int \left(\frac{\pi}{2} - x\right)dx = \frac{\left(\frac{\pi}{2} - x\right)^2}{-2} + C$$

Thus $K = 2$

**24. (7)** $\int \left(\dfrac{4 + 3\sin x}{\cos^2 x}\right)dx = \int \left(\dfrac{4}{\cos^2 x} + \dfrac{3\sin x}{\cos^2 x}\right)dx$

$$= 4\int \sec^2 dx + 3\int \sec x \tan x\, dx = 4\tan x + 3\sec x + C$$

Thus $P + Q = 4 + 3 = 7$

**1. (c)** Put $\sec\theta + \tan\theta = t$
or IBP twice taking
$\sec\theta \cdot (\sec\theta + \tan\theta)$ as the first function and remaining as the $2^{nd}$ function

$$\sec\theta + \tan\theta = y \qquad ....(1)$$
$$\sec\theta\,(\tan\theta + \sec\theta)\,d\theta = dy$$

now, $\sec\theta \cdot \tan\theta = \dfrac{1}{y} \qquad ....(2)$

from (1) and (2), $2\sec\theta = y + \dfrac{1}{y}$

$$\therefore I = \frac{1}{2}\int y\left(y + \frac{1}{y}\right)dy = \frac{1}{2}\left[\frac{y^3}{3} + y\right] + C$$

$$\frac{1}{2}\left[\frac{(\sec\theta + \tan\theta)^3}{3} + (\sec\theta + \tan\theta)\right]$$

$$= \frac{(\sec\theta + \tan\theta)}{6}[(\sec\theta + \tan\theta)^2 + 2]$$

**2. (d)** $I = \int\left(\dfrac{f(x)}{x^2}\right)^{\frac{1}{2}}dx = \int\left(\dfrac{x+2}{2x+3}\right)^{\frac{1}{2}}\dfrac{dx}{x}$

Put $\dfrac{x+2}{2x+3} = y^2 \Rightarrow x = \dfrac{3y^2 - 2}{1 - 2y^2}$

and $dx = \dfrac{-2y\,dy}{(1-2y^2)^2}$

$$\therefore\ I = -\int y \cdot \frac{2y}{(1-2y^2)^2} \cdot \frac{1-2y^2}{3y^2-2}\,dy$$

$$= 2\int \frac{y^2 dy}{(2y^2-1)(3y^2-2)}$$

$$= 2\int\left(\frac{2}{3y^2-2} - \frac{1}{2y^2-1}\right)dy$$

$$= \frac{4}{3}\int\frac{dy}{y^2 - \dfrac{2}{3}} - \int\frac{dy}{y^2 - \dfrac{1}{2}}$$

**3. (c)** Let $I =$

$$\int\frac{\cos^3 x + \cos^5 x}{\sin^2 x + \sin^4 x}dx = \int\frac{(\cos^2 x + \cos^4 x)\cos x}{\sin^2 x(1+\sin^2 x)}dx$$

$$= \int\frac{(2 - 3\sin^2 x + \sin^4 x)\cos x}{\sin^2 x(1+\sin^2 x)}dx$$

$$= \int\frac{[1 - \sin^2 x + (1-\sin^2 x)^2]\cos x}{\sin^2 x(1+\sin^2 x)}dx$$

Put $\sin x = t \Rightarrow \cos x\,dx = dt$

$$I = \int\frac{2 - 3t^2 + t^4}{t^4 + t^2}dt = \int\left(1 + \frac{2}{t^2} - \frac{6}{t^2+1}\right)dt$$

$$= t - \frac{2}{t} - 6\tan^{-1}(t) + C$$

$$= \sin x - 2(\sin x)^{-1} - 6\tan^{-1}(\sin x) + C$$

**4. (b)** $I = \displaystyle\int\frac{x^2\left(1 - \dfrac{1}{x^2}\right)dx}{x^2\left(x + \dfrac{1}{x}\right)\left(x^2 + \dfrac{1}{x^2}\right)^{1/2}}$

Let $x + \dfrac{1}{x} = p \Rightarrow \left(1 - \dfrac{1}{x^2}\right)dx = dp$

$$I = \int\frac{dp}{p\sqrt{p^2 - 2}} = \frac{1}{\sqrt{2}}\sec^{-1}\frac{p}{\sqrt{2}}$$

$$= \frac{1}{\sqrt{2}}\sec^{-1}\left(\frac{x^2+1}{\sqrt{2}x}\right) + C$$

**5. (a)** $I = \displaystyle\int\frac{dx}{a^2\cos^2 x + b^2\sin^2 x}$

Dividing numerator and denominator by $\cos^2 x$

$$I = \int\frac{\sec^2 x\,dx}{a^2 + b^2\tan^2 x}$$

Let $b\tan x = t, \qquad \therefore\ \sec^2 x\,dx = \dfrac{dt}{b}$

$$\Rightarrow I = \frac{1}{b}\int\frac{dt}{a^2 + t^2} = \frac{1}{ab} + \tan^{-1}\frac{t}{a}$$

$$\Rightarrow \frac{1}{ab}\tan^{-1}\left(\frac{b}{a}\tan x\right) + C$$

**6. (a)** $I = \displaystyle\int\frac{a^x}{\sqrt{1 - a^{2x}}}dx = \int\frac{a^x}{\sqrt{1^2 - (a^x)^2}}dx$

Let $a^x = t$. Then, $d(a^x) = dt$

$\Rightarrow a^x \log_e a\, dx = dt \Rightarrow dx = \dfrac{dt}{a^x \log_e a}$

$\therefore I = \int \dfrac{a^x}{\sqrt{1^2 - t^2}} \dfrac{dt}{a^x \log a} = \dfrac{1}{\log a}\int \dfrac{dt}{\sqrt{1^2 - t^2}}$

$= \dfrac{1}{\log a}\sin^{-1} t + C = \dfrac{1}{\log a}\sin^{-1}(a^x) + C$

**7.** **(a, c)** Put $\tan x = t$,

$I = \int (1 + t^2)\dfrac{(1 + t^2)}{t^4}\dfrac{dt}{1 + t^2}$

$I = \int \dfrac{1 + t^4 + 2t^2}{t^4}dt = \int \dfrac{dt}{t^4} + \int dt + \int \dfrac{2}{t^2}dt$

$= -\dfrac{1}{4}(\tan x)^{-3} + \tan x - 2(\tan x)^{-1} + C$

$= -\dfrac{1}{4}\cot^3 x + \tan x - 2\cot x + C$

Therefore, $K = -1/4,\ L = 1,\ M = -2$

**8.** **(b, d)** $\int \dfrac{\sin x}{\sin(x - \pi/4)}dx$

$= \int \dfrac{\sin(u + \pi/4)}{\sin u}du \quad (u = x - \pi/4)$

$= \int \dfrac{\sin u \cos(\pi/4) + \cos u \sin(\pi/4)}{\sin u}du$

$= \dfrac{1}{\sqrt{2}}\int du + \dfrac{1}{\sqrt{2}}\int \cot u\, du$

$= \dfrac{1}{\sqrt{2}}u + \dfrac{1}{\sqrt{2}}\log|\sin u| + \text{const.}$

$= \dfrac{1}{\sqrt{2}}(x - \pi/4) + \log|\sin(x - \pi/4)| + \text{const.}$

$= \dfrac{1}{\sqrt{2}}\left(x + \log|\sin x - \cos x| + \log\dfrac{1}{\sqrt{2}}\right) + \text{const.}$

$= \dfrac{1}{\sqrt{2}}(x + \log|\sin x - \cos x|) + \text{const.}$

Thus $A = 1/\sqrt{2}$ and $f(x) = x$

**9.** **(b, c, d)**

Numerator $= \ell\,(\text{Denominator}) + m\dfrac{d}{dx}(\text{Denominator})$

$\Rightarrow 4e^x + 6e^{-x} = \ell(9e^x - 4e^{-x}) + m(9e^x + 4e^{-x})$

On comparing coefficient of $e^x$ and $e^{-x}$, then

$4 = 9\ell + 9m$ and $6 = -4\ell + 4m$

Then, we get $\ell = -\dfrac{19}{36},\ m = \dfrac{35}{36}$

$\therefore \int \left(\dfrac{4e^x + 6e^{-x}}{9e^x - 4e^{-x}}\right)dx$

$= \int \dfrac{\ell(9e^x - 4e^{-x}) + m(9e^x + 4e^{-x})}{(9e^x - 4e^{-x})}dx$

$= \ell x + m\,\ell n\,(9e^x - 4e^{-x}) + n$

$= \ell x + m\ln\left(\dfrac{9e^{2x} - 4}{e^x}\right) + n$

$= (\ell - m)x + m\,\ell n\,(9e^{2x} - 4) + n$

$= -\dfrac{3}{2}x + \dfrac{35}{36}\ln(9e^{2x} - 4) + n$

On comparing, we get

$A = -\dfrac{3}{2},\ B = \dfrac{35}{36},\ C = n = \text{(indefinite)}$

and $A + B = -\dfrac{19}{36}$

**10.** **(a)** $\int \dfrac{x^2 + 1}{x^4 + 1}dx = \int \dfrac{1 + \dfrac{1}{x^2}}{x^2 + \dfrac{1}{x^2}}dx = \int \dfrac{1 + \dfrac{1}{x^2}}{\left(x - \dfrac{1}{x}\right)^2 + 2}$

Put $x - \dfrac{1}{x} = t \Rightarrow \left(1 + \dfrac{1}{x^2}\right)dx = dt$

$\therefore I = \int \dfrac{dt}{t^2 + 2} = \dfrac{1}{\sqrt{2}}\tan^{-1}\dfrac{t}{\sqrt{2}} + C = \dfrac{1}{\sqrt{2}}\tan^{-1}\dfrac{x^2 - 1}{\sqrt{2}x} + C$

**11.** **(c)** $I = \int \dfrac{x^2 - 1}{(x^4 + 3x^2 + 1)\tan^{-1}\left(x + \dfrac{1}{x}\right)}dx$

$= \int \dfrac{1 - \dfrac{1}{x^2}}{\left(x^2 + \dfrac{1}{x^2} + 3\right)\tan^{-1}\left(x + \dfrac{1}{x}\right)}dx$

Put $x + \dfrac{1}{x} = t \Rightarrow \left(1 - \dfrac{1}{x^2}\right)dx = dt$

and $x^2 + \dfrac{1}{x^2} + 2 = t^2$

$\therefore I = \int \dfrac{dt}{(t^2 + 1)\tan^{-1} t} = \ln|\tan^{-1} t| + C$

$= \ln\left|\tan^{-1}\left(x + \dfrac{1}{x}\right)\right| + C$

**12.** **(b)** $I = \int \dfrac{x^4 - 2}{x^2\sqrt{x^4 + x^2 + 2}}dx = \int \dfrac{x^4 - 2}{x^3\sqrt{x^2 + 1 + \dfrac{2}{x^2}}}dx$

$$= \int \frac{x - \dfrac{2}{x^3}}{\sqrt{x^2 + 1 + \dfrac{2}{x^2}}}\, dx$$

Put $x^2 + \dfrac{2}{x^2} + 1 = t \Rightarrow \left(x - \dfrac{2}{x^3}\right)dx = \dfrac{dt}{2},$ we get

$$I = \int \frac{dt}{2\sqrt{t}} = \sqrt{t} + C = \sqrt{x^2 + 1 + \frac{2}{x^2}} + C$$

**13.  A-r; B-p; C-q**

**(A)** $\displaystyle\int (x^a + a^x)dx = \frac{x^{a+1}}{a+1} + \frac{a^x}{(\log a)} + C$

**(B)** $\displaystyle\int \frac{1 + \dfrac{1}{x^2}}{x^2 + \dfrac{1}{x^2}}\, dx$  put $x - \dfrac{1}{x} = t, \left(x^2 + \dfrac{1}{x^2}\right)dx = dt$

$$\Rightarrow \int \frac{dt}{t^2 + (\sqrt{2})^2} = \frac{1}{\sqrt{2}} \tan^{-1}\left(\frac{x^2 - 1}{\sqrt{2}x}\right) + C$$

**(C)** $\dfrac{1}{4}\displaystyle\int \frac{\sec^2 x\, dx}{\tan^2 x + \tan x + \dfrac{5}{4}} = \dfrac{1}{4}\int \frac{\sec^2 x\, dy}{\left(\tan x + \dfrac{1}{2}\right)^2 + 1}$

$$= \frac{1}{4}\tan^{-1}\left(\tan x + \frac{1}{2}\right) + C$$

**14.  A-q, s; B-t; C-p,**

**(A)** $\displaystyle\int \frac{dx}{x(x^n + 1)} = \int \frac{dx}{x^{n+1}\left(1 + \dfrac{1}{x^n}\right)}$

Put $1 + \dfrac{1}{x^n} = t$

$\therefore \dfrac{-n}{x^{n+1}}dx = dt$

Then $\displaystyle\frac{dx}{x(x^n + 1)} = -\frac{1}{n}\int \frac{dt}{t} = -\frac{1}{n}\ln|t|$

$$= -\frac{1}{n}\ln\left|1 + \frac{1}{x^n}\right| + C$$

$$= -\frac{1}{n}\{\ln|1 + x^n| - n\ln|x|\} + C$$

$$= \ln|x| - \frac{1}{n}\ln|1 + x^n| + C$$

**(B)** $\displaystyle\int \frac{dx}{x^2(x^n + 1)^{(n-1)/n}} = \int \frac{dx}{x^2 . x^{n-1}.\left(1 + \dfrac{1}{x^n}\right)^{(n-1)/n}}$

$$= \int \frac{dx}{x^{n+1}\left(1 + \dfrac{1}{x^n}\right)^{(n-1)/n}}$$

Put $1 + \dfrac{1}{x^n} = t$

$$\Rightarrow \frac{-n}{x^{n+1}}dx = dt$$

Then, $\displaystyle\int \frac{dx}{x^2(x^n + 1)^{(n-1)/n}} = -\frac{1}{n}\int \frac{dt}{t^{(n-1)/n}}$

$$= -\frac{1}{n}\int t^{-(n-1)/n}dt$$

$$= \frac{-1}{n} . \frac{t^{\frac{-(n-1)}{n} + 1}}{\frac{-(n-1)}{n} + 1} + C$$

$$= -\left(1 + \frac{1}{x^n}\right)^{1/n} + C$$

$$= -(1 + x^{-n})^{1/n} + C$$

**(C)** $\displaystyle\int \frac{dx}{x^n(1 + x^n)^{1/n}} = \int \frac{dx}{x^{n+1}\left(\dfrac{1}{x^n} + 1\right)^{1/n}}$

Put $\dfrac{1}{x^n} + 1 = t$

$\therefore \quad -\dfrac{n}{x^{n+1}}dx = dt$

Then, $\displaystyle\int \frac{dx}{x^n(1 + x^n)^{1/n}} = -\frac{1}{n}\int \frac{dt}{t^{1/n}}$

$$= -\frac{1}{n}\int t^{-1/n}dt$$

$$= -\frac{1}{n} . \frac{t^{-\frac{1}{n} + 1}}{\left(-\dfrac{1}{n} + 1\right)} + C$$

$$= \frac{1}{(1-n)}t^{1-1/n} + C$$

$$= \frac{1}{(1-n)}(x^{-n} + 1)^{1-1/n} + C$$

$$= \frac{1}{(1-n)}\left(\frac{(1+x^n)^{1-1/n}}{x^{n-1}}\right) + C$$

$$= \frac{x^{1-n}}{(1-n)}(1+x^n)^{1-1/n} + C$$

**15. (a)** $\displaystyle\int \frac{(x^2-2)}{(x^4+5x^2+4)\tan^{-1}\left(\dfrac{x^2+2}{x}\right)}\,dx$

Put $x + 2/x = z,\ \therefore (1-2/x^2)\,dx = dz$

$$\int \frac{dz}{(z^2+1)\tan^{-1}z} = \log|\tan^{-1}(x+2/x)| + C$$

**16. (a)** $\because 5x = 3x + 2x$

$$\therefore \tan 5x = \frac{\tan 3x + \tan 2x}{1 - \tan 3x \tan 2x}$$

$$\therefore \tan 5x - \tan 3x - \tan 2x = \tan 5x \tan 3x \tan 2x$$

**17. (3)**

$$I = \int \frac{\sin^3\dfrac{\theta}{2}}{\cos\dfrac{\theta}{2}\sqrt{\cos^3\theta + \cos^2\theta + \cos\theta}}\,d\theta$$

$$= \int \frac{\left(2\sin\dfrac{\theta}{2}.\cos\dfrac{\theta}{2}\right).\sin^2\dfrac{\theta}{2}}{2\cos^2\dfrac{\theta}{2}\sqrt{\cos^3\theta + \cos^2\theta + \cos\theta}}\,d\theta$$

$$= \int \frac{2\sin^2\dfrac{\theta}{2}\sin\theta\,d\theta}{2\cos^2\dfrac{\theta}{2}\sqrt{\cos^3\theta + \cos^2\theta + \cos\theta}}$$

Put $\cos\theta = t \Rightarrow -\sin\theta\,d\theta = dt$

Also $\cos\theta = 2\cos^2\dfrac{\theta}{2} - 1 = 1 - 2\sin^2\dfrac{\theta}{2} = t$

$$\therefore \ I = \int \frac{\dfrac{1-t}{2}(-dt)}{(1+t)\sqrt{t^3+t^2+t}} = \frac{1}{2}\int \frac{(t^2-1)dt}{(t+1)^2\sqrt{t^3+t^2+t}}$$

$$= \frac{1}{2}\int \frac{\left(1-\dfrac{1}{t^2}\right)(dt)}{\left(t+\dfrac{1}{t}+2\right)\sqrt{t+\dfrac{1}{t}+1}}$$

Put $t + \dfrac{1}{t} + 1 = u^2 \Rightarrow \left(1 - \dfrac{1}{t^2}\right)dt = 2u\,du$

$$I = \frac{1}{2}\int \frac{2u\,du}{\left(1+u^2\right)u} = \tan^{-1}u = \tan^{-1}\sqrt{1+\dfrac{1}{t}+1} + c$$

$$= \tan^{-1}(\cos\theta + \sec\theta + 1)^{1/2} + c$$

So, $f(\theta) = \cos\theta + \sec\theta + 1 \geq 2 + 1 = 3$

**18. (2)**

$$I = \int \sin 4x\, e^{\tan^2 x}\,dx = \int 2\sin 2x \cos 2x\, e^{\tan^2 x}\,dx$$

$$= 4\int \sin x \cos x \left(\frac{1-\tan^2 x}{1+\tan^2 x}\right)e^{\tan^2 x}\,dx$$

$$= 4\int \tan x.\sec^2 x.\cos^6 x(1-\tan^2 x)e^{\tan^2 x}\,dx$$

Put $\tan^2 x = t \Rightarrow 2\tan x \sec^2 x\,dx = dt$

$$\therefore\ I = 2\int \frac{(1-t)e^t}{(1+t)^3}\,dt = -2\int \left[\frac{t+1-2}{(t+1)^3}\right]e^t\,dt$$

$$= -2\int \left[\frac{1}{(t+1)^2} + \frac{-2}{(t+1)^3}\right]e^t\,dt$$

$$= -2\frac{e^t}{(t+1)^2} + c = -2\cos^4 x.e^{\tan^2 x} + c$$

**19. (2)**

$$I = \sqrt{2}\int \frac{(\cos x - \sin x)}{\sqrt{\sin 2x}(4+3\sin 2x)}\,dx$$

Put $\cos x + \sin x = z$
$(\cos x - \sin x)\,dx = dz$

$$\therefore\ I = \sqrt{2}\int \frac{dz}{\sqrt{(z^2-1)(4+3)(z^2-1))}}$$

Put $z = \sec\theta \qquad dz = \sec\theta\tan\theta\,d\theta$

$$I = \sqrt{2}\int \frac{\sec\theta\tan\theta\,d\theta}{\tan\theta(3\sec^2\theta + 1)}$$

$$\therefore\ I = \sqrt{2}\int \frac{\dfrac{\sin\theta}{\cos^2\theta}}{\dfrac{\sin\theta}{\cos\theta}\left(\dfrac{3+\cos^2\theta}{\cos^2\theta}\right)}\,d\theta$$

$$= \sqrt{2}\int \frac{\cos\theta}{4-\sin^2\theta}\,d\theta$$

Let $\sin\theta = t \Rightarrow \cos\theta\,d\theta = dt$

$$\therefore I = \sqrt{2}\int \frac{dt}{4-t^2} \Rightarrow \frac{1}{2\sqrt{2}}\ell n\left|\frac{t+2}{t-2}\right| + c$$

$$= \frac{1}{2\sqrt{2}}\ell n\left|\frac{\sin\theta+2}{\sin\theta-2}\right| + c,$$

where $\sin\theta = \dfrac{\sqrt{z^2-1}}{z} = \dfrac{\sqrt{\sin 2x}}{\sqrt{1+\sin 2x}}$

**1. (d)** Let $I = \int \dfrac{e^x(2-x^2)}{(1-x)\sqrt{(1-x^2)}}dx$

$I = \int \dfrac{e^x(1+1-x^2)}{(1-x)\sqrt{(1-x^2)}}dx$

$= \int e^x \left\{ \dfrac{1}{(1-x)\sqrt{(1-x^2)}} + \sqrt{\left(\dfrac{1+x}{1-x}\right)} \right\} dx$

Let $f(x) = \sqrt{\left(\dfrac{1+x}{1-x}\right)}$ ; $f'(x) = \dfrac{1}{(x-1)\sqrt{(1-x^2)}}$

$\because \int e^x(f(x)+f'(x))dx = e^x f(x) + c$

$\therefore I = e^x\sqrt{\left(\dfrac{1+x}{1-x}\right)} + c = \dfrac{e^x(1+x)}{\sqrt{1-x^2}} + C$

**2. (a)** Let, $I = \int \dfrac{x^2 dx}{(x\sin x + \cos x)^2}$

$\because \dfrac{d}{dx}(x\sin x + \cos x) = x\cos x$ , we write

$I = \int \left(\dfrac{x}{\cos x}\right) \cdot \left(\dfrac{x\cos x}{(x\sin x + \cos x)^2}\right) dx$

Integrating by part taking $\dfrac{x\cos x}{(x\sin x + \cos x)^2}$

as second function, we get

$I = \left(\dfrac{x}{\cos x}\right)\left(-\dfrac{1}{x\sin x + \cos x}\right)$

$\qquad + \int \dfrac{(x\sin x + \cos x)}{\cos^2 x} \cdot \dfrac{1}{(x\sin x + \cos x)} dx$

$= -\dfrac{x}{\cos x(x\sin x + \cos x)} + \int \sec^2 x\, dx$

$= -\dfrac{x}{\cos x(x\sin x + \cos x)} + \tan x + c$

$= -\dfrac{x}{\cos x(x\sin x + \cos x)} + \dfrac{\sin x}{\cos x} + c$

$= \dfrac{-x + \sin x(x\sin x + \cos x)}{\cos x(x\sin x + \cos x)} + c$

$= \dfrac{(\sin x - x\cos x)}{(x\sin x + \cos x)} + c$

**3. (c)** $\int \dfrac{e^x(1+nx^{n-1}-x^{2n})}{(1-x^n)\sqrt{1-x^{2n}}}dx$

$= \int e^x \left( \sqrt{\dfrac{1+x^n}{1-x^n}} + \dfrac{nx^{n-1}}{(1-x^n)\sqrt{1-x^{2n}}} \right) dx$

$= \dfrac{e^x\sqrt{1-x^{2n}}}{1-x^n} + C$

**4. (a)** $\int x\tan^{-1} x\, dx$

$= \tan^{-1}x \cdot \dfrac{x^2}{2} - \int \left(\dfrac{1}{1+x^2}\dfrac{x^2}{2}\right) dx$

$= \dfrac{x^2}{2}\tan^{-1} x - \dfrac{1}{2}\int \dfrac{x^2}{1+x^2}dx$

$= \dfrac{x^2}{2}\tan^{-1} x - \dfrac{1}{2}\int \left[1 - \dfrac{1}{1+x^2}\right]dx$

$= \dfrac{1}{2}(x^2+1)\tan^{-1} x - \dfrac{1}{2}x + C$

**5. (a)** $I = e^x\left[\dfrac{2+\sin 2x}{1+\cos 2x}\right]dx$

$\Rightarrow I = \int e^x \left[\dfrac{2}{1+\cos 2x} + \dfrac{\sin 2x}{1+\cos 2x}\right]dx$

$\Rightarrow I = e^x\left[\dfrac{2}{2\cos^2 x} + \dfrac{2\sin x\cos x}{2\cos^2 x}\right]dx$

$= \int e^x[\sec^2 x + \tan x]dx$

$\Rightarrow I = \int e^x[\tan x + \sec^2 x]dx = e^x\tan x + C$

**6. (c)** $I = \int 2\sin x.\cos x.\log\cos x\, dx$

Put $\log\cos x = z$

$\therefore -\dfrac{\sin x}{\cos x}dx = dz$

$\therefore I = \int 2\sin x.\cos x.z.\dfrac{\cos x}{-\sin x}dz$

$= -2\int \cos^2 x.z.dz = -2\int ze^{2z}dz$

$= -2\left[z.\dfrac{e^{2z}}{2} - \int \dfrac{e^{2z}}{2}dz\right]$

$= -z.e^{2z} + \dfrac{1}{2}e^{2z} + K = e^{2z}\left(\dfrac{1}{2} - z\right) + K$

$= \cos^2 x\left(\dfrac{1}{2} - \log\cos x\right) + K$

**7. (a)** We integrate by parts, taking $\tan^{-1} x$ as the first

function and $\dfrac{x}{\sqrt{1+x^2}}$ as the second.

$\displaystyle\int \dfrac{x}{\sqrt{1+x^2}}dx = \dfrac{1}{2}\int\dfrac{dt}{\sqrt{t}} = \dfrac{1}{2}\dfrac{\sqrt{t}}{1/2}$

$= \sqrt{t} = \sqrt{1+x^2}$     [where $x^2 + 1 = t$]

$\Rightarrow \displaystyle\int \dfrac{x\tan^{-1}x}{\sqrt{1+x^2}}dx = \tan^{-1}x\sqrt{1+x^2}$

$\qquad\qquad\qquad -\displaystyle\int \dfrac{1}{1+x^2}\sqrt{1+x^2}\,dx$

$= \sqrt{1+x^2}\,\tan^{-1}x - \displaystyle\int \dfrac{dx}{\sqrt{1+x^2}}$

$= \sqrt{1+x^2}\,\tan^{-1}x - \log(x+\sqrt{x^2+1}) + C$

Thus, $f(x) = \tan^{-1}x$, $K = -1$.

**8. (d)** The given integral equals

$\displaystyle\int x\log\left(\dfrac{x+1}{x}\right)dx$

$= \displaystyle\int x\log(x+1)dx - \int x\log x\,dx$

$= \dfrac{x^2}{2}\log(x+1) - \dfrac{1}{2}\int\dfrac{x^2}{x+1}dx - \dfrac{x^2}{2}\log x + \dfrac{1}{2}\int\dfrac{x^2}{x}dx$

$= \dfrac{x^2}{2}\log(x+1) - \dfrac{x^2}{2}\log x - \dfrac{1}{2}\int\left(x-1+\dfrac{1}{x+1}\right)dx +$

$\qquad\qquad\qquad\qquad \dfrac{1}{2}\int x\,dx$

$= \dfrac{x^2}{2}\log(x+1) - \dfrac{x^2}{2}\log x + \dfrac{x}{2} - \dfrac{1}{2}\log(x+1) + C$

$\Rightarrow f(x) = \dfrac{x^2}{2} - \dfrac{1}{2}$, $g(x) = -\dfrac{1}{2}\log x$ and

$\qquad\qquad L = 1/2.$

**9. (b,c)** $I = \displaystyle\int e^x\left\{\dfrac{2\tan x}{1+\tan x} + \cot^2\left(x+\dfrac{\pi}{4}\right)\right\}dx$

$= \displaystyle\int e^x\left\{\dfrac{2}{1+\cot x} - 1 + \cos ec^2\left(x+\dfrac{\pi}{4}\right)\right\}dx$

$= \displaystyle\int e^x\left\{-\cot\left(x+\dfrac{\pi}{4}\right) + \cos ec^2\left(x+\dfrac{\pi}{4}\right)\right\}dx$

$= -e^x\cot\left(x+\dfrac{\pi}{4}\right) + C = e^x\cot\left(\dfrac{3\pi}{4} - x\right) + C$

Again,

$I = e^x\cot\left(\dfrac{3\pi}{4} - x\right) + C = e^x\cot\left(\dfrac{\pi}{2} + \dfrac{\pi}{4} - x\right) + C$

$= e^x\tan\left(x - \dfrac{\pi}{4}\right) + C$

**10. (b, d)** Let $I = \displaystyle\int \dfrac{xe^x}{\sqrt{(1+e^x)}}dx$

$= \displaystyle\int x.\dfrac{e^x}{\sqrt{(1+e^x)}}dx$

$= x.2\sqrt{(1+e^x)} - \displaystyle\int 1.2\sqrt{(1+e^x)}\,dx$

$= 2x\sqrt{(1+e^x)} - 2\displaystyle\int\sqrt{(1+e^x)}\,dx$

In second integral
Put $\qquad\qquad\qquad 1+e^x = t^2$

$\therefore\ dx = \dfrac{2t\,dt}{t^2-1}$

Then, $I = 2x\sqrt{(1+e^x)} - 4\displaystyle\int\dfrac{t^2-1+1}{(t^2-1)}\,dt$

$= 2x\sqrt{(1+e^x)} - 4\displaystyle\int\left(1+\dfrac{1}{t^2-1}\right)dt$

$= 2x\sqrt{(1+e^x)} - 4\left\{t + \dfrac{1}{2}\ln\left(\dfrac{t-1}{t+1}\right)\right\} + C$

$= 2x\sqrt{(1+e^x)} - 4\sqrt{(1+e^x)} - 2\ln\left(\dfrac{\sqrt{(1+e^x)}-1}{\sqrt{(1+e^x)}+1}\right) + C$

$= (2x-4)\sqrt{(1+e^x)} - 2\ln\left(\dfrac{\sqrt{(1+e^x)}-1}{\sqrt{(1+e^x)}+1}\right) + C$

On comparing

$f(x) = 2x-4,\ g(x) = \dfrac{\sqrt{(1+e^x)}-1}{\sqrt{(1+e^x)}+1} + C$

**11. (a, b, c, d)** Let $I = \displaystyle\int \sin(\ln x)\,dx$

Put $\ln x = t$
$\therefore\quad x = e^t$
$\Rightarrow\quad dx = e^t\,dt$

Then, $I = \displaystyle\int e^t\sin t\,dt$

$= \dfrac{e^t}{2}(\sin t - \cos t) + C$

$$= \frac{x}{2}\{\sin(\ln x) - \cos(\ln x)\} + C$$

On comparing, we get

$$f(x) = \frac{x}{2}, g(x) = \ln x, h(x) = \ln x$$

$$\lim_{x \to 2} f(x) = \lim_{x \to 2} \frac{x}{2} = \frac{2}{2} = 1$$

$$\lim_{x \to 1} \frac{g(x)}{f(x)} = \lim_{x \to 1} \frac{\ln x}{\ln x} = 1$$

$$g(e^3) = \ln e^3 = 3 \ln e = 3$$

$$h(e^5) = \ln e^5 = 5 \ln e = 5$$

**12.** **(b,d)** $\cos^{-1}\sqrt{1-x^2} = -\sin^{-1} x, \ x < 0$

$$\therefore \int \left( \cos^{-1} x + \cos^{-1}\sqrt{1-x^2} \right) dx$$

$$= \int \left( \cos^{-1} x - \sin^{-1} x \right) dx$$

$$= \int \left( \frac{\pi}{2} - 2\sin^{-1} x \right) dx = \frac{\pi}{2} x - 2x \sin^{-1} x + \int \frac{2x}{\sqrt{1-x^2}} dx$$

$$= \frac{\pi}{2} x - 2x \sin^{-1} x - 2\sqrt{1-x^2} + C$$

**13.** **(d)** $I = \int \frac{xe^x}{(x+1)^2} dx = \int \frac{(x+1-1)e^x}{(x+1)^2} dx$

$$= \int e^x \left\{ \frac{1}{x+1} + \frac{-1}{(x+1)^2} \right\} dx$$

$$= \frac{e^x}{x+1} + C \qquad \left[ \because \frac{d}{dx}\left(\frac{1}{x+1}\right) = -\frac{1}{(x+1)^2} \right]$$

**14.** **(a)** $I = \int e^{\sin x}.x \cos x \ dx - \int e^{\sin x} \sec x \tan x \ dx$

$$= \left\{ xe^{\sin x} - \int e^{\sin x} \ dx \right\} - \left\{ e^{\sin x}.\sec x - \int e^{\sin x} \ dx \right\}$$

$$= xe^{\sin x} - e^{\sin x} \sec x + C$$

**15.** **(b)** $I = \int \left[ \log(\log x) + \frac{1}{(\log x)^2} \right] dx = \int \left( \log t + \frac{1}{t^2} \right) e^t \ dt$

$$[\text{Putting } \log x = t]$$

$$= \int e^t \left\{ \left( \log t + \frac{1}{t} \right) - \left( \frac{1}{t} - \frac{1}{t^2} \right) \right\} dt$$

$$= e^t \left( \log t - \frac{1}{r} \right) = x \log(\log x) - \frac{x}{\log x}$$

**16.** **A-s; B-t; C-r; D-q**

(A) Since $\int \frac{f'(x)}{a^2 + (f(x))^2} dx = \frac{1}{a} \tan^{-1}(f(x)) + C$

$$\Rightarrow 2\int \frac{1}{3^2 + (\sqrt{x})^2} \left( \frac{1}{2\sqrt{x}} \right) dx$$

$$= \frac{2}{3} \tan^{-1}\sqrt{x} + C$$

(B) $\because \int e^x(f(x) + f'(x))dx = e^x f(x) + C$

$$\Rightarrow \int e^x(\cos ec^2 x + (-\cot x))dx = e^x(-\cot x) + C$$

(C) $\int (\tan x \sec x + \cot x \cos ecx)dx = \sec x - \cos ecx + C$

(D) $\int \dfrac{dx}{2\sin^2\left(\dfrac{x}{2}\right) - 2\sin^2\left(\dfrac{x}{2}\right)\cos\left(\dfrac{x}{2}\right)}$

$$= \int \frac{\cos^2\left(\dfrac{x}{2}\right)\dfrac{1}{2}}{1-\cot\left(\dfrac{x}{2}\right)} dx = \int \frac{f'(x)}{f(x)} dx = \log\left|1-\cot\left(\frac{x}{2}\right)\right| + C$$

**17.** **A→r; B→s; C→p; D→q**

(A) $\int e^x \left[ \dfrac{1}{x+2} + \log(x+2) \right] dx = e^x \log(x+2) + C$

(B) $\int \sin^2 x(1 - \sin^2 x)\cos x dx$

$$= \int \sin^2 x \cos x dx - \int \sin^4 x.\cos x \ dx$$

$$= \frac{\sin^3 x}{3} - \frac{\sin^5 x}{5} + C$$

(C) $\int \dfrac{dx}{\sqrt{\left(\dfrac{\sqrt{17}}{2}\right)^2 - \left(x + \dfrac{3}{2}\right)^2}} = \sin^{-1}\left(\dfrac{2x+3}{\sqrt{17}}\right) + C$

(D) Put $x = \tan\theta, \ \therefore \dfrac{dx}{d\theta} = \sec^2\theta$

$$\Rightarrow dx = \sec^2\theta. \ d\theta$$

$$\int \frac{x^5}{x^2 + 1} dx = \int \frac{\tan^5\theta}{\tan^2\theta + 1}.\sec^2\theta d\theta$$

$$= \int \tan^5\theta d\theta = \int \tan^3\theta.(\sec^2\theta - 1) d\theta$$

$$= \int \tan^3\theta.\sec^2\theta.d\theta - \int \tan^3\theta \ d\theta$$

$$= \frac{\tan^4\theta}{4} - \int \tan\theta(\sec^2\theta - 1)d\theta$$

$$= \frac{\tan^4\theta}{4} - \frac{\tan^2\theta}{2} + \int \tan\theta d\theta$$

$$= \frac{\tan^4\theta}{4} - \frac{\tan^2\theta}{2} + \log|\sec\theta| + C$$

$$= \frac{x^4}{4} - \frac{x^2}{2} + \frac{1}{2}\log(x^2+1) + C$$

**18. (d)** $I = \int e^{ax} \sin bx \, dx$

$$= \sin bx \, \frac{e^{ax}}{a} - \int b\cos bx \, \frac{e^{ax}}{a} \, dx$$

$$I = \frac{e^{ax}}{a^2+b^2}(a\sin bx - b\cos by) + 2$$

Here $A = a^2 + b^2$

$$\int e^x(\sec^2 x + \tan x)\,dx = e^x + ax + C$$

**19. (b)** $\int g(x)\,(f(x)+f'(x))\,dx$

$$= \int g(x)\,f(x)\,dx + \int g(x)\,f'(x)\,dx$$

$$= f(x)\int g(x)\,dx - \int(f'(x)\int g(x)\,dx)\,dx$$

$$+ \int g(x)\,f'(x)\,dx$$

$$= f(x)g(x) - \int f'(x)g(x)\,dx + \int g(x)f'(x)\,dx$$

$$(\because \int g(x)\,dx = g(x))$$

$$= f(x)\,g(x) + C$$

Now, $\int g(x)\,(f(x)-f''(x))\,dx$

$$= \int g(x)\{(f(x)+f'(x))-(f'(x)+f''(x))\}\,dx$$

$$= g(x)\,f(x) - g(x)\,f'(x) + C$$

**20. 1**

Let $P = \int e^{ax}\cos bx\,dx$, $Q = \int e^{ax}\sin bx\,dx$

$$P + iQ = \int e^{ax}(\cos bx + i\sin bx)\,dx$$

[We may apply integration by parts twice also]

$$\therefore \quad \int e^{ax}\cdot e^{ibx}\,dx = \int e^{(a+ib)x}\,dx$$

$$= \frac{e^{(a+ib)x}}{(a+ib)} + c \;=\; \frac{e^{ax}(\cos bx + i\sin bx)(a-ib)}{a^2+b^2} + c$$

$$= \frac{e^{ax}\{(a\cos bx + b\sin bx)\} + ie^{ax}\{(a\sin bx - b\cos bx)\}}{(a^2+b^2)}$$

$$= \frac{e^{ax}(a\cos bx + b\sin bx)}{(a^2+b^2)} + i\frac{e^{ax}(a\sin bx - b\cos bx)}{a^2+b^2}$$

Equating real and imaginary parts on both sides, we get

$$P = \int e^{ax}\cos bx\,dx = \frac{e^{ax}(a\cos bx + b\sin bx)}{(a^2+b^2)} + c$$

$$= \frac{1}{r}e^{ax}\cos(bx-\phi) + c \quad\text{and}$$

$$Q = \int e^{ax}\sin bx\,dx = \frac{e^{ax}(a\sin bx - b\cos bx)}{(a^2+b^2)} + c$$

$$= \frac{1}{r}e^{ax}\sin(bx+\phi) + c$$

where $r = \sqrt{a^2+b^2}$ and $\phi = \tan^{-1}\left(\frac{b}{a}\right)$

$$\therefore \; (P^2+Q^2)r^2 = e^{2ax}$$

(neglecting constant of integration)

$$\therefore \; (P^2+Q^2)(a^2+b^2) = e^{2ax}$$

**21. 4** $f(x) = I = \int\left\{\frac{1+\cos(2\ln x)}{2}\right\}dx$

$$= \frac{x}{2} + \frac{1}{2}\int\cos(2\ln x)\,dx = \frac{x}{2} + \frac{1}{2}I_1$$

$$I_1 = \int\cos(2\ln x)\,dx = \int\cos(2\ln x)\cdot 1\,dx$$

Integrating by parts using 1 as second function

$$= x\cos(2\ln x) + \int x\sin(2\ln x)\frac{2}{x}\,dx$$

$$= x\cos(2\ln x) + 2\int\sin(2\ln x)\,dx$$

$$= x\cos(2\ln x) + 2\{x\sin(2\ln x)\} - 4\int\cos(2\ln x)\,dx$$

$$\Rightarrow 5I_1 = x\cos(2\ln x) + 2x\sin(2\ln x)$$

$$\Rightarrow I_1 = \frac{x}{5}[\cos(2\ln x) + 2\sin(2\ln x)]$$

$$I = f(x) = \frac{x}{2} + \frac{x\cos(2\ln x) + 2x\sin(2\ln x)}{10} + C$$

Thus, $P = 2$, $Q = 2$

$$\Rightarrow P + Q = 4$$

**22. 7** Integrating by parts, we have

$$I_{4,3} = -\frac{\cos 3x \cos^4 x}{3} - \frac{4}{3}\int\cos^3 x\sin x\cos 3x\,dx$$

But $\sin x\cos 3x = -\sin 2x + \sin 3x\cos x$ so.

$$I_{4,3} = -\frac{\cos 3x\cos^4}{4} + \frac{4}{3}$$

$$\int\cos^3 x\sin 2x - \frac{4}{3}\int\cos^4 x\sin 3x\,dx + C$$

$$= -\frac{\cos 3x\cos^4 x}{3} + \frac{4}{3}I_{3,2} - \frac{4}{3}I_{4,3} + C$$

Therefore, $\dfrac{7}{3}I_{4,3} - \dfrac{4}{3}I_{3,2} = -\dfrac{\cos 3x\cos^4 x}{3} + C$ or

$7I_{4,3} - 4I_{3,2} = -\cos 3x \cos^4 x + \text{const.}$

Thus, $A + B = 4 + 3 = 7$

**23.** **5** Integrating by parts, the given integral is equal to

$= (3x - 1)\sin x - 3\int \sin x\, dx - (1 - 2x)\cos x - 2\int \cos x\, dx$

$= (3x - 1)\sin x + 3\cos x - (1 - 2x)\cos x - 2\sin x$

$= (3x - 3)\sin x + (2 + 2x)\cos x$

Hence $Q = 3(x - 1)$ and $P = 2(1 + x)$

$\Rightarrow \dfrac{P}{1+x} + \dfrac{Q}{x-1} = 2 + 3 = 5$

**24.** **3** $I = \displaystyle\int \log_e\left(\sqrt{1-x} + \sqrt{1+x}\right).1\, dx$

Integrating by parts taking 1 as the second function.

$I = \log\left(\sqrt{1-x} + \sqrt{1+x}\right)x - \displaystyle\int \dfrac{1}{\sqrt{1-x} + \sqrt{1+x}}$

$\left[-\dfrac{1}{2\sqrt{1-x}} + \dfrac{1}{2\sqrt{1+x}}\right](x)\, dx$

$= x\log\left(\sqrt{1-x} + \sqrt{1+x}\right)$

$\quad -\dfrac{1}{2}\displaystyle\int \dfrac{\sqrt{1-x} - \sqrt{1+x}}{\sqrt{1-x} + \sqrt{1+x}} \cdot \dfrac{1}{\sqrt{1-x^2}} \cdot x\, dx$

$= x\log\left(\sqrt{1-x} + \sqrt{1+x}\right)$

$\quad -\dfrac{1}{2}\displaystyle\int \dfrac{(1-x) + (1+x) - 2\sqrt{1-x^2}}{(1-x) - (1+x)} \cdot \dfrac{1}{\sqrt{1-x^2}} \cdot x\, dx$

$= x\log\left(\sqrt{1-x} + \sqrt{1+x}\right) - \dfrac{1}{2}\displaystyle\int \dfrac{\sqrt{1-x^2} - 1}{\sqrt{1-x^2}}\, dx$

$= x\log\left(\sqrt{1-x} + \sqrt{1+x}\right) - \dfrac{1}{2}\left[\displaystyle\int 1\, dx - \int \dfrac{1}{\sqrt{1-x^2}}\, dx\right]$

$= x\log\left(\sqrt{1-x} + \sqrt{1+x}\right) + \dfrac{1}{2}\left[\sin^{-1} x - x\right] + C$

Thus, $A = 1, B = 2$

$\Rightarrow A + B = 1 + 2 = 3$

**1.** **(a)** $I_n = \int \cot^n x \, dx = \int \cot^{n-2} x \cot^2 x \, dx$

$= \int \cot^{n-2} x (\cosec^2 x - 1) dx$

$= \int \cot^{n-2} x \cosec^2 x \, dx - I_{n-2}$

Thus $I_n + I_{n-2} = \dfrac{\cot^{n-1} x}{n-1}$ ......(i)

$I_0 + I_1 + 2(I_2 + ...... + I_8) + I_9 + I_{10}$

$= (I_2 + I_0) + (I_3 + I_1) + (I_4 + I_2) + (I_5 + I_3)$

$\qquad + (I_6 + I_4) + (I_7 + I_5). + (I_8 + I_6) + (I_9 + I_7)$

$\qquad\qquad\qquad\qquad\qquad + (I_{10} + I_8)$

$= -\left( \dfrac{\cot x}{1} + \dfrac{\cot^2 x}{2} + ....... + \dfrac{\cot^9 x}{9} \right)$ [using (i)]

$= -\sum_{k=1}^{9} \dfrac{\cot^k x}{k}$

**2.** **(b)** $\dfrac{2x}{(x-1)(x-4)} = \dfrac{P}{x-1} + \dfrac{Q}{x-4}$

$2x = P(x-4) + Q(x-1)$

$\therefore P = -2/3, \; Q = 8/3$

$\therefore \int \dfrac{e^{x-1}}{(x-1)(x-4)} 2x \, dx = \int e^{x-1} \left( \dfrac{-2/3}{x-1} + \dfrac{8/3}{x-4} \right) dx$

$= -\dfrac{2}{3} F(x-1) + \dfrac{8}{3} e^3 F(x-4) + C$

$\therefore A = -2/3, \; B = 8/3 \; e^3$

**3.** **(a)** Let $f(x) = \dfrac{x-1}{(2x+1)(x-2)(x-3)}$

$= \dfrac{P}{2x+1} + \dfrac{Q}{x-2} + \dfrac{R}{x-3}$

$-P = \dfrac{x-1}{(x-2)(x-3)} \Bigg]_{x=-\frac{1}{2}} = -\dfrac{6}{35}$

$Q = \dfrac{x-1}{(2x+1)(x-3)} \Bigg]_{x=2} = -\dfrac{1}{5}$

$R = \dfrac{x-1}{(2x+1)(x-2)} \Bigg]_{x=3} = \dfrac{2}{7}$

$\int f(x) dx = \dfrac{-6}{35} \int \dfrac{dx}{2x+1} - \dfrac{1}{5} \int \dfrac{dx}{x-2} + \dfrac{2}{7} \int \dfrac{dx}{x-3}$

$= \dfrac{3}{35} \ln|2x+1| - \dfrac{1}{5} \ln|x-2| + \dfrac{2}{7} \ln|x-3| + C$

**4.** **(a)** $\int \dfrac{1}{9x^2 - 4} dx = \dfrac{1}{9} \int \dfrac{1}{x^2 - (2/3)^2} dx$

$= \dfrac{1}{9} \cdot \dfrac{1}{2 \times \frac{2}{3}} \log \left| \dfrac{x - \frac{2}{3}}{x + \frac{2}{3}} \right| + C = \dfrac{1}{12} \log \left| \dfrac{3x-2}{3x+2} \right| + C$

**5.** **(a)** $I = \int \dfrac{x^2 + 1}{x^4 + 1} dx = \int \dfrac{1 + \frac{1}{x^2}}{x^2 + \frac{1}{x^2}} dx$

[Dividing the num. and denom. by $x^2$]

$= \int \dfrac{1 + \frac{1}{x^2}}{\left( x - \frac{1}{x} \right)^2 + 2} dx$

Let $x - \dfrac{1}{x} = t \Rightarrow d\left( x - \dfrac{1}{x} \right) = dt$

$\Rightarrow \left( 1 + \dfrac{1}{x^2} \right) dx = dt$

$\therefore I = \int \dfrac{dt}{t^2 + (\sqrt{2})^2} = \dfrac{1}{\sqrt{2}} \tan^{-1} \left( \dfrac{t}{\sqrt{2}} \right) + C$

$= \dfrac{1}{\sqrt{2}} \tan^{-1} \left( \dfrac{x - 1/x}{\sqrt{2}} \right) + C$

$= \dfrac{1}{\sqrt{2}} \tan^{-1} \left( \dfrac{x^2 - 1}{\sqrt{2} \, x} \right) + C$

**6.** **(c)** Let

$I = \int \dfrac{\cos^3 x + \cos^5 x}{\sin^2 x + \sin^4 x} dx = \int \dfrac{(\cos^2 x + \cos^4 x) \cos x}{\sin^2 x (1 + \sin^2 x)} dx$

$= \int \dfrac{[1 - \sin^2 x + (1 - \sin^2 x)^2] \cos x}{\sin^2 x (1 + \sin^2 x)} dx$

$= \int \dfrac{((2 - 3\sin^2 x + \sin^4 x) \cos x}{\sin^2 x (1 + \sin^2 x)} dx$

Put $\sin x = t \Rightarrow \cos dx = dt$

$I = \int \dfrac{2 - 3t^2 + t^4}{t^4 + t^2} dt$

$I = \int \left(1 + \dfrac{2}{t^2} - \dfrac{6}{t^2+1}\right) dt = t - \dfrac{2}{t} - 6\tan^{-1}(t) + C$

$= \sin x - 2(\sin x)^{-1} - 6\tan^{-1}(\sin x) + C$

**7.** **(d)** Let $g_n(x) = 1 + x^2 + x^4 + \dots + x^{2n} = \dfrac{x^{2n+2}-1}{x^2-1}$

So, $2x + 4x^3 + \dots + 2nx^{2n-1} =$

$h_n(x) = g'_n(x) = \dfrac{2x(nx^{2n+2} - (n+1)x^{2n} + 1)}{(x^2-1)^2}$

Now $f(x) = \lim_{n\to\infty} h_n(x) = \dfrac{2x}{(x^2-1)^2}$ as $0 < x < 1$

Thus $\int f(x)dx = \int \dfrac{2x}{(x^2-1)^2} dx$

$= -\dfrac{1}{x^2-1} = \dfrac{1}{1-x^2} + c$

**8.** **(d)** $\int \dfrac{dx}{3\sin x + \sin^3 x} = \int \dfrac{\sin x \, dx}{(3 + \sin^2 x)\sin^2 x}$

$= \int \dfrac{\sin x \, dx}{(4 - \cos^2 x)(1 - \cos^2 x)}$

$= -\int \dfrac{dt}{(4 - t^2)(1 - t^2)}$

$= \dfrac{-1}{3} \int \left(\dfrac{1}{t^2-4} - \dfrac{1}{t^2-1}\right) \quad (t = \cos x)$

$= \dfrac{1}{3}\cdot\dfrac{1}{4}\log\dfrac{2+t}{2-t} + \dfrac{1}{3}\cdot\dfrac{1}{2}\log\dfrac{t-1}{t+1} + C$

$= \dfrac{1}{6}\log\dfrac{t-1}{t+1} + \dfrac{1}{12}\log\dfrac{2+t}{2-t} + C$

**9.** **(a)** Put $1 + x^4 = x^4 z^4$

$x^4 = \dfrac{1}{z^4-1} \Rightarrow dx = \dfrac{-z^3}{x^3(z^4-1)^2} dz$

$\therefore \quad \int \dfrac{dx}{\sqrt[4]{1+x^4}} = \int \dfrac{1}{xz}\left(\dfrac{-z^3}{x^3(z^4-1)^2}\right) dz$

$= -\int \dfrac{z^2}{z^4-1} dz = \dfrac{1}{2}\int \left(\dfrac{1}{1-z^2} - \dfrac{1}{1+z^2}\right) dz$

$= \dfrac{1}{2}\left(\dfrac{1}{2}\log\dfrac{1+z}{1-z} - \tan^{-1} z\right) + C$

where $z = \dfrac{\sqrt[4]{1+x^4}}{x}$.

**10.** **(a,b,d)** $\int \dfrac{1}{(e^x-1)^2} dx = \int \dfrac{e^x dx}{e^x(e^x-1)^2}$

$= \int \dfrac{dt}{t(t-1)^2} \quad (t = e^x)$

$= \int \left[\dfrac{1}{(t-1)^2} - \dfrac{1}{(t-1)} + \dfrac{1}{t}\right] dt$

$= \dfrac{1}{1-t} - \log(t-1) + \log t + c$

$= (1 - e^x)^{-1} - \log(1 - e^{-x}) + c$

Hence, $f(x) = (1 - e^x)^{-1}$ and
$g(x) = 1 - e^{-x}$

The domain of $f = R \sim \{0\}$

**11.** **(a,d)** Let $I = \int \dfrac{x^3+x}{x^4-9} dx$

$= \int \dfrac{x^3}{x^4-9} dx + \int \dfrac{x}{x^4-9} dx = I_1 + I_2 + C \text{ (say)}$

where $I_1 = \int \dfrac{x^3}{x^4-9} dx$ and $I_2 = \int \dfrac{x}{x^4-9} dx$

Put $x^4 - 9 = t$, so that $4x^3 dx = dt$

$\therefore \quad I_1 = \dfrac{1}{4}\int \dfrac{1}{t} dt = \dfrac{1}{4}\log_e |t| = \dfrac{1}{4}\log_e |x^4-9|$

$I_2 = \int \dfrac{x}{x^4-9} dx = \int \dfrac{x}{(x^2)^2 - 3^2} dx$

Put $x^2 = t$ so that $2x \, dx = dt$

$I_2 = \dfrac{1}{2}\int \dfrac{dt}{t^2-3^2} = \dfrac{1}{2}\cdot\dfrac{1}{2\times 3}\log_e\left|\dfrac{t-3}{t+3}\right|$

Hence, $I = \dfrac{1}{4}\log_e |x^4-9| + \dfrac{1}{12}\log_e\left|\dfrac{x^2-3}{x^2+3}\right| + C$

**12.** **(c,d)** $\lim_{n\to\infty} \tan(1/n)\ln(1/n)$

$= \lim_{n\to\infty} \dfrac{\tan(1/n)}{(1/n)}\cdot\dfrac{\ln(1/n)}{n}$

$= -\lim_{n\to\infty} \dfrac{\tan(1/n)}{(1/n)}\cdot\dfrac{\ln(n)}{(n)}$

$= -1\cdot\lim_{n\to\infty} \dfrac{1/n}{1}$

$= 0$

Then, $f(x) = e^0 = 1$

$\therefore \int \dfrac{f(x)}{\sqrt[3]{(\sin^{11} x \cos x)}} dx = \int \dfrac{1}{\sin^{11/3} x \cos^{1/3} x} dx$

$$= \int \sin^{-11/3} x \cos^{-1/3} x \, dx$$

$$= \int (\tan x)^{-11/3} \cos^{-4} x \, dx = \int (\tan x)^{-11/3} \cdot \sec^4 x \, dx$$

$$= \int (\tan x)^{-11/3} \cdot (1 + \tan^2 x) \cdot \sec^2 x \, dx$$

$$= \frac{(\tan x)^{-\frac{11}{3}+1}}{\left(-\frac{11}{3}+1\right)} + \frac{(\tan x)^{-2/3}}{(-2/3)} + C$$

$$= -\frac{3}{8}(\tan x)^{-8/3} - \frac{3}{2}(\tan x)^{-2/3} + C$$

$$\therefore \ g(x) = -\frac{3}{8}(\tan x)^{-8/3} - \frac{3}{2}(\tan x)^{-2/3}$$

$$\therefore \ g(\pi/4) = -\frac{3}{8} - \frac{3}{2} = -\frac{15}{8}$$

and $g(x)$ is non differentiable at $\tan x = 0$

or $x = n\pi, \ n \in I$

**13. (a, b)** Let $I = \displaystyle\int_0^x \frac{(t - |t|)^2}{(1 + t^2)} \, dt$

***Case I* :** $x > 0$, then $0 < t < x, |t| = t$

$$\therefore \qquad = \int_0^x \frac{(t - t)^2}{1 + t^2} \, dt = 0$$

***Case II* :** $x < 0$, then $x < t < 0 \Rightarrow |t| = -t$

$$\therefore \quad I = \int_0^x \frac{4t^2}{1 + t^2} dt = 4 \int_0^x \left(1 - \frac{1}{1 + t^2}\right) dt$$

$$= 4(x - \tan^{-1} x) + C$$

**14. (c)** Let $P = \sin^{m-1} x \cdot \cos^{n+1} x$

$$\therefore \ \frac{dP}{dx} = \sin^{m-1} x(n+1)\cos^n x(-\sin x)$$

$$+ \cos^{n+1} x \cdot (m-1)\sin^{m-2} x \cdot \cos x$$

$$= -(n+1)\sin^m x \cos^n x + (m-1)\sin^{m-2} x \cos^{n+2} x$$

On integrating both sides, we get

$$(n+1)I_{m,n} = -\sin^{m-1} x \cos^{n+1} x + (m-1)I_{m-2, n+2}$$

or $\ I_{m,n} = -\dfrac{\sin^{m-1} x \cos^{n+1} x}{(n+1)} + \dfrac{(m-1)}{(n+1)} I_{m-2, n+2}$

Here, $f(m,n) = \dfrac{m-1}{n+1}$

$$\therefore \ f(2,3) = \frac{1}{4}$$

**15. (a)** $I_n = \int (x \sin^{n-1} x) \sin x \, dx$

$$= x \sin^{n-1} x(-\cos x) - \int \{x(n-1)\sin^{n-2} x \cdot \cos x$$

$$+ \sin^{n-1} x \cdot 1\}(-\cos x) dx$$

$$= -x \sin^{n-1} x \cos x$$

$$+ (n-1)\int x \sin^{n-2} x(1 - \sin^2 x) dx + \frac{\sin^n x}{n}$$

$$nI_n = -x \sin^{n-1} x \cos x + \frac{\sin^n x}{n^2} + (n-1)I_{n-2}$$

or $\ I_n = -\dfrac{x \sin^{n-1} x \cos x}{n} + \dfrac{\sin^n x}{n^2} + \dfrac{(n-1)}{n} I_{n-2}$

$$\therefore \ f(n) = \frac{n-1}{n}$$

**16. (b)** $I_n = \int \sin^{n-1} x \cdot (e^{ax} \sin x) dx$

$$= \sin^{n-1} x \cdot \left(\frac{e^{ax}}{(1+a^2)}(a\sin x - \cos x)\right)$$

$$- \frac{1}{(1+a^2)} \int (n-1)\sin^{n-2} x \cos x[e^{ax}(a\sin x - \cos x)] dx$$

$$= \frac{e^{ax} \sin^{n-1} x(a\sin x - \cos x)}{(1+a^2)}$$

$$- \frac{(n-1)}{(1+a^2)} \int (a\sin^{n-1} x \cos x - \sin^{n-2} x(1 - \sin^2 x)) dx$$

$$= \frac{e^{ax} \sin^{n-1} x(a\sin x - \cos x)}{(1+a^2)} - \frac{(n-1)a}{(1+a^2)} \cdot \frac{\sin^n x}{n}$$

$$+ \frac{(n-1)}{(1+a^2)} I_{n-2} - \frac{(n-1)}{(1+a^2)} I_n$$

or $\ I_n = \dfrac{e^{ax} \sin^{n-1} x(a\sin x - \cos x)}{(n+a^2)}$

$$- \frac{(n-1)a\sin^n x}{n(n+a^2)} + \frac{(n-1)}{(n+a^2)} I_{n-2}$$

Here, $A = \dfrac{(n-1)a}{n(n+a^2)}, \ B - \dfrac{(n-1)}{(n+a^2)}$

$$\therefore \quad A + B = \frac{(n-1)a + n(n-1)a}{n(n+a^2)} = \frac{a(n^2-1)}{n(n+a^2)}$$

**17.** $A \to r,t; \ B \to p,s; \ C \to q$

(A) $I = \int \dfrac{dx}{e^{2x}+1} = \int \dfrac{e^{-2x}}{1+e^{-2x}}dx = -\dfrac{1}{2}\ln(1+e^{-2x})+C$ **(r)**

$= -\dfrac{1}{2}\ln\left(\dfrac{1+e^{2x}}{e^{2x}}\right)+C$

$= -\dfrac{1}{2}\{\ln(1+e^{2x})-2x\}+C$

$= x - \dfrac{1}{2}\ln(1+e^{2x})+C$ **(t)**

(B) $I = \dfrac{e^x dx}{\sqrt{(e^{2x}+1)}}$

Put $e^x = t$

$\Rightarrow \ e^x dx = dt$

Then, $I = \int \dfrac{dt}{\sqrt{(t^2+1)}} = \ln\{t+\sqrt{t^2+1}\}+C$

$= \ln\{e^x+\sqrt{(e^{2x}+1)}\}+C$ **(p)**

$= \ln\{e^x(1+\sqrt{(1+e^{-2x})})\}+C$

$= x + \ln(1+\sqrt{(1+e^{-2x})})+C$ **(s)**

(C) $I = \int \dfrac{dx}{\left(e^{2x}+1\right)^2} = \int \dfrac{e^x\, dx}{e^x(e^{2x}+1)^2}$

Put $e^x = \tan\theta$

$\therefore \ e^x dx = \sec^2\theta\, d\theta$

Then, $I = \int \dfrac{\sec^2\theta\, d\theta}{\tan\theta.\sec^4\theta} = \int \dfrac{d\theta}{\tan\theta.\sec^2\theta}$

$= \int \dfrac{\cos^3\theta\, d\theta}{\sin\theta} = \int \dfrac{(1-\sin^2\theta)\cos\theta\, d\theta}{\sin\theta}$

Put $\sin\theta = t$

$\Rightarrow \ \cos\theta\, d\theta = dt$

Then, $I = \int \dfrac{(1-t^2)dt}{t}$

$= \ln t - \dfrac{t^2}{2}+C$

$= \ln\sin\theta - \dfrac{\sin^2\theta}{2}+C$

$= \ln\left(\dfrac{e^x}{\sqrt{e^{2x}+1}}\right) - \dfrac{1}{2}\cdot\dfrac{e^{2x}}{(e^{2x}+1)}+C$

$= x - \dfrac{1}{2}\ln(1+e^{2x})+\dfrac{1}{2}\left(\dfrac{1}{e^{2x}+1}\right)+C$ **(q)**

**18.** **(a)** Put $x^{11/2}=t \Rightarrow \dfrac{11}{2}x^{\frac{11}{2}-1}dx = dt$

$\Rightarrow x^{9/2}\,dx = \dfrac{2}{11}dt$

$\therefore$ Given integral

$= \dfrac{2}{11}\int \dfrac{dt}{\sqrt{1+t^2}} = \dfrac{2}{11}\ln|\,t+\sqrt{1+t^2}\,|+C$

$= \dfrac{2}{11}\ln|\,x^{11/2}+\sqrt{1+x^{11}}\,|+C$

**19.** **(d)** $I_n = \int \tan^n x\, dx$

$= \int (\tan^{n-2}x\sec^2 x - \tan^{n-2}x)\,dx$

$= \dfrac{\tan^{n-1}}{n-1} - I_{n-2}$

Put $n=6,\ \ 5(I_6+I_4) = \tan^5 x$

Statement 1 is true. Statement 2 is false.

**20.** **1** $\displaystyle\int \dfrac{ax^2-b}{x\sqrt{c^2x^2-\left(ax^2+b\right)^2}}dx = \int \dfrac{a-b/x^2}{\sqrt{c^2-\left(ax+\dfrac{b}{x}\right)^2}}$

Now put $ax + \dfrac{b}{x}=t;\ \left(a-\dfrac{b}{x^2}\right)dx = dt$,

the integral becomes

$\displaystyle\int \dfrac{dt}{\sqrt{c^2-t^2}} = \sin^{-1}\dfrac{t}{c} = \sin^{-1}\left(\dfrac{ax+b/x}{c}\right)+K$

Thus $P = 1$

**21.** **5** $I = \displaystyle\int \sqrt{\dfrac{x}{4-x^3}}\,dx = \int \dfrac{\sqrt{x}\,dx}{\sqrt{4-x^3}}$

Here integral of $\sqrt{x} = \dfrac{2}{3}x^{3/2}$ and

$4-x^3 = 4-(x^{3/2})^2$

Put $x^{3/2}=t \Rightarrow \sqrt{x}\,dx = \dfrac{2}{3}dt$

So $I = \dfrac{2}{3}\displaystyle\int \dfrac{dt}{\sqrt{4-t^2}} = \dfrac{2}{3}\sin^{-1}\left(\dfrac{x^{3/2}}{2}\right)+C$

Thus $A = 2,\ B = 3$

$\Rightarrow A+B = 2+3 = 5$

**22.** **1** $\displaystyle\int \frac{dx}{2+\cos x}$

$$= \int \frac{dx}{2\sin^2\left(\frac{x}{2}\right) + 2\cos^2\left(\frac{x}{2}\right) + \cos^2\left(\frac{x}{2}\right) - \sin^2\left(\frac{x}{2}\right)}$$

$$= \int \frac{dx}{\sin^2\left(\frac{x}{2}\right) + 3\cos^2\left(\frac{x}{2}\right)} = \int \frac{\sec^2\left(\frac{x}{2}\right)}{\tan^2\left(\frac{x}{2}\right) + 3}\, dx$$

Put $\tan\left(\frac{x}{2}\right) = t \Rightarrow \sec^2\left(\frac{x}{2}\right) dx = 2dt$, then it reduces

to

$$2\int \frac{dt}{t^2 + 3} = \frac{2}{\sqrt{3}} \tan^{-1}\left(\frac{t}{\sqrt{3}}\right) + C$$

$$= \frac{2}{\sqrt{3}} \tan^{-1}\left(\frac{\tan\left(\frac{x}{2}\right)}{\sqrt{3}}\right) + C.$$

Thus, $(P + Q + R) - (A + B) = (1 + 3 + 2) - (2 + 3) = 1$

**23.** **4** Putting $5x^2 - 3 = t^2$, so $5x\,dx = t\,dt$

$$\int \frac{dx}{x\sqrt{5x^2 - 3}} = \int \frac{x\,dx}{x^2\sqrt{5x^2 - 3}}$$

$$= \frac{1}{5} \int \frac{5t\,dt}{(t^2 + 3)t}$$

$$= \int \frac{dt}{t^2 + 3} = \frac{1}{\sqrt{3}} \tan^{-1}\frac{t}{\sqrt{3}} + C$$

$$= \frac{1}{\sqrt{3}} \tan^{-1}\sqrt{\frac{5x^2 - 3}{3}} + C$$

Thus $M = 1$, $K = 3$

$\Rightarrow M + K = 4$

**24.** **3**

Let $I = \displaystyle\int \frac{(\cos^2 x + \sin 2x)}{(2\cos x - \sin^2 x)}\, dx$

$$= \int \frac{(\cos x + 2\sin x)\cos x}{(2\cos x - \sin x)^2}\, dx$$

Integrating by part, taking $\cos x$ as the first and

$\dfrac{(\cos x + 2\sin x)}{(2\cos x - \sin x)^2}$ as the second function, we have

$$= \cos x\left\{\frac{1}{2\cos x - \sin x}\right\} - \int \frac{-\sin x\,dx}{(2\cos x - \sin x)}$$

$$= \cos x\left\{\frac{1}{2\cos x - \sin x}\right\} + \int \frac{-\sin x\ dx}{(2\cos x - \sin x)}$$

$$= \frac{\cos x}{(2\cos x - \sin x)} +$$

$$\int \frac{-\frac{1}{5}(2\cos x - \sin x) - \frac{2}{5}(-2\sin - \cos x)}{(2\cos x - \sin x)}\, dx$$

$$\left[ N^\gamma = \lambda D^\gamma + \mu \frac{d}{dx} D^\gamma \right]$$

$$= \frac{\cos x}{(2\cos x - \sin x)} - \frac{1}{5}\int dx - \frac{2}{5}\int \frac{(-2\sin x - \cos x)}{2\cos x - \sin x}\, dx$$

$$= \frac{\cos x}{(2\cos x - \sin x)} - \frac{1}{5}x - \frac{2}{5}\ln|2\cos x - \sin x| + C$$

Thus $5a - 10b = 5\left(\frac{-1}{5}\right) - 10\left(\frac{-2}{5}\right)$

$$= -1 + 4$$

$$= 3$$

**1. (a)** $I = \displaystyle\int_1^\infty \frac{dx}{(e \cdot e^x + e^3 \cdot e^{-x})} = \int_1^\infty \frac{e^x\, dx}{e(e^{2x} + e^2)}$

(multiply $N^r$ and $D^r$ by $e^x$)

put $e^x = t$

$\Rightarrow \quad e^x\, dx = dt$

$I = \dfrac{1}{e} \displaystyle\int_e^\infty \frac{dt}{t^2 + e^2}$

$= \dfrac{1}{e^2} \tan^{-1} \dfrac{t}{e} \Big|_e^\infty = \dfrac{1}{e^2}\left[\dfrac{\pi}{2} - \dfrac{\pi}{4}\right] = \dfrac{\pi}{4e^2}$

**2. (d)** $f'(x) = f(x) \Rightarrow f(x) = C\, e^x$ and since $f(0) = 1$

$\therefore\ 1 = f(0) = C \quad \therefore\ f(x) = e^x$ and hence $g(x) = x^2 - e^x$

Thus, $\displaystyle\int_0^1 f(x)g(x)\,dx = \int_0^1 (x^2 e^x - e^{2x})\,dx$

$= x^2 e^x \Big|_0^1 - 2\displaystyle\int_0^1 x e^x\, dx - \left[\dfrac{e^{2x}}{2}\right]_0^1$

$= (e - 0) - 2\,[\, x e^x \big|_0^1 - e^x \big|_0^1 \,] - \dfrac{1}{2}(e^2 - 1)$

$= (e - 0) - 2\,[(e - 0) - (e - 1)] - \dfrac{1}{2}(e^2 - 1)$

$= e - \dfrac{1}{2} e^2 - \dfrac{3}{2}$

**3. (c)** $I = \displaystyle\int_0^\infty (x^2)^n \cdot x\, e^{-x^2}\, dx$

put $x^2 = t \Rightarrow x\, dx = -dt/2 = \dfrac{1}{2}\displaystyle\int_0^\infty t^n\, e^{-t}\, dt$

$= \dfrac{1}{2}\left[\ t^n\, e^{-t} \Big|_0^\infty + n\displaystyle\int_0^\infty t^{n-1}\, e^{-t}\, dt\ \right]$

$= \dfrac{1}{2}\left[\ 0 + n\displaystyle\int_0^\infty t^{n-1}\, e^{-t}\, dt\ \right]$

Hence $I = \dfrac{n!}{2}$

**4. (a)** $\beta + \displaystyle\int_0^1 \underbrace{x}_{I}\, \underbrace{2x e^{-x^2}}_{II}\, dx = \int_0^1 e^{-x^2}\, dx$

$\beta + \left[\, -x e^{-x^2}\, \right]_0^1 - \displaystyle\int_0^1 -e^{-x^2}$

$dx = \displaystyle\int_0^1 e^{-x^2}\, dx \qquad \beta = \dfrac{1}{e}\ ]$

**5. (a)** $I = \displaystyle\int_0^{\pi/2} \frac{\sin x \cos x}{x\left(\dfrac{\pi}{2} - x\right)}\,dx = \int_0^{\pi/2} \frac{\sin 2x}{x(\pi - 2x)}\,dx$

put $2x = t$

$I = \displaystyle\int_0^\pi \frac{\sin t}{t(\pi - t)}\,dt = \dfrac{1}{\pi}\int_0^\pi \left(\frac{\sin t}{t} + \frac{\sin t}{(\pi - t)}\right)dt$

$= \dfrac{1}{\pi}\displaystyle\int_0^\pi \frac{\sin t}{t}\,dt + \dfrac{1}{\pi}\int_0^\pi \frac{\sin t}{\pi - t}\,dt$

$= \dfrac{1}{\pi}\displaystyle\int_0^\pi \frac{\sin t}{t}\,dt + \dfrac{1}{\pi}\int_0^\pi \frac{\sin t}{t}\,dt = \dfrac{2}{\pi}\int_0^\pi \frac{\sin t}{t}\,dt$

**6. (c)** In first integral putting $t = \sin^2 y$ and in second putting $t = \cos^2 z$, we have

$I = \displaystyle\int_0^x y \sin 2y\, dy - \int_{\pi/2}^x z \sin 2z\, dz$

$= \displaystyle\int_0^x y \sin 2y\, dy + \int_x^{\pi/2} z \sin 2z\, dz$

$= \displaystyle\int_0^{\pi/2} \theta \sin 2\theta\, d\theta$

$= \left[\theta\left(-\dfrac{\cos 2\theta}{2}\right) + \dfrac{\sin 2\theta}{4}\right]_0^{\pi/2} = \pi/4$

**7. (a)** The integral

$= \dfrac{1}{2}\displaystyle\int_{\log \pi/2}^{\log x} e^x \cosec^2\left(\dfrac{1}{3}e^x\right)dx$

$= \dfrac{-3}{2}\left[\cot\left(\dfrac{1}{3}e^{\log \pi}\right) - \cot\left(\dfrac{1}{3}e^{\log\frac{\pi}{2}}\right)\right]$

$= \dfrac{-3}{2}\left[\cot\left(\dfrac{\pi}{3}\right) - \cot\left(\dfrac{\pi}{6}\right)\right] = \sqrt{3}\,.$

**8.** **(c)** $\displaystyle\int_0^\pi \frac{dx}{1+2^{\cos x}} = \int_0^\pi \frac{dx}{1+2^{\cos(\pi-x)}} = \int_0^\pi \frac{dx}{1+2^{-\cos x}}$

$\displaystyle = \int_0^\pi \frac{dx}{2^{\cos x}+1}\,dx = \frac{1}{2}\int_0^\pi \frac{1+2^{\cos x}}{2^{\cos x}+1}\,dx = \frac{\pi}{2}$

**9.** **(a, b)** We have $\cot^{-1}\dfrac{1}{x} = \begin{bmatrix} \pi + \tan^{-1}x, & x < 0 \\ \tan^{-1}x, & x > 0 \end{bmatrix}$

and $\tan^{-1}x + \cot^{-1}x = \dfrac{\pi}{2} \; \forall\, x \in R$

Now, let $J = \displaystyle\int_{-1}^{2}\left(\cot^{-1}\frac{1}{x} + \cot^{-1}x\right)dx$

$\displaystyle = \int_{-1}^{0}\left(\cot^{-1}\frac{1}{x} + \cot^{-1}x\right)dx + \int_{0}^{2}\left(\cot^{-1}\frac{1}{x} + \cot^{-1}x\right)dx$

$\displaystyle = \frac{3\pi}{2} + \pi = \frac{5\pi}{2}$

And $K = \displaystyle\int_{-2\pi}^{7\pi}\frac{\sin x}{|\sin x|}dx = \int_{6\pi}^{7\pi} 1.dx = \pi$

**10.** **(a,b,d)** Given $U_n = \displaystyle\int_0^1 x^n.(2-x)^n\,dx$

$V_n = \displaystyle\int_0^1 x^n.(1-x)^n\,dx$

in $U_n$ put $x = 2t \Rightarrow dx = 2dt$

$\therefore \;\; U_n = 2\displaystyle\int_0^{1/2} 2^n.t^n\, 2^n (1-t)^n\; dt \;\;....(1)$

Now, $V_n = 2\displaystyle\int_0^{1/2} x^n (1-x)^n \; dx \;\;....(2)$

From (1) and (2)

$U_n = 2^{2n}.V_n$

**11.** **(a,b)** $P(x) \equiv 4a_0 x^3 + 3a_1 x^2 + 2a_2 x + a_3$ is a polynomial and hence is continuous for all x. $P(x) = 0$ has a root in $(-1, 0)$ iff it takes both positive and negative values in $(-1, 0)$ as continuity implies that $P(x) = 0$ at one point at least. This will happen if either $P(-1).\,P(0) < 0$ or the area enclosed by the graph of $P(x)$, the x-axis and the ordinates at $x = -1$ and $x = 0$ is zero.
As $P(0) = a_3 > 0$,
$P(-1) = -4a_0 + 3a_1 - 2a_2 + a_3 < 0$
or $4a_0 + 2a_2 > 3a_1 + a_3$.

$\displaystyle\int_{-1}^{0} P(x)\,dx = 0$ gives $a_0 + a_2 = a_1 + a_3$.

**12.** **(a,b)** $I_n = \displaystyle\int_0^1 \frac{dx}{(1+x^2)^n} = \int_0^1 (1+x^2)^{-n}\,dx$

$\displaystyle = \frac{x}{(1+x^2)^n}\Big|_0^1 - \int_0^1 (-n)(1+x^2)^{-n-1}.2x.x\,dx$

$\displaystyle = \frac{1}{2^n} + 2n\int_0^1 (-n)(1+x^2)^{-n-1}.2x.x\,dx$

$\displaystyle = \frac{1}{2^n} + 2n\int_0^1 \frac{x^2}{(1+x^2)^{n+1}} = \frac{1}{2^n} + 2n\int_0^1 \frac{1+x^2-1}{(1+x^2)^{n+1}}\,dx$

$\displaystyle = \frac{1}{2^n} + 2nI_n - 2nI_{n+1}$

$\therefore \; 2n\,I_{n+1} = 2^{-n} + (2n-1)\,I_n$

$\therefore \; 2I_2 = \dfrac{1}{2} + I_1 = \dfrac{1}{2} + \tan^{-1}x\,\big|_0^1$

$\therefore \; I_2 = \dfrac{1}{4} + \dfrac{\pi}{8}$

**13.** **(c)** Let $I(\alpha) = \displaystyle\int_0^1\left(\frac{x^{\cos\alpha}-1}{\ell nx}\right)dx \;\;......(1)$

$\therefore \; I'(\alpha) = \displaystyle\int_0^1 \frac{x^{\cos\alpha}\,\ell nx(-\sin\alpha)}{\ell nx}\,dx$

$\displaystyle = (-\sin\alpha)\int_0^1 x^{\cos\alpha}\,dx = (-\sin\alpha)\left\{\frac{x^{\cos\alpha+1}}{\cos\alpha+1}\right\}_0^1$

$\displaystyle = \frac{(-\sin\alpha)}{(1+\cos\alpha)}$

Integrating both sides w.r.t. $\alpha$ then
$I(\alpha) = \ell n(1+\cos\alpha) + c$

$I(\pi/2) = \ell n1 + c \Rightarrow \displaystyle\int_0^1 \frac{x^0-1}{\ell nx}\,dx = \ell n1 + c$ [form (1)]

So, $0 = 0 + c \Rightarrow c = 0$. Hence $I(\alpha) = \ell n(1+\cos x)$

**14.** **(d)** Let $I(\alpha) = \displaystyle\int_0^1 \frac{x^{2\alpha}-1}{\log x}\,dx$

$\Rightarrow I'(\alpha) = 2\displaystyle\int_0^1 \frac{x^{2\alpha}\log x}{\log x}\,dx = 2\frac{x^{2\alpha+1}}{2\alpha+1}\Big|_0^1 = \frac{2}{2\alpha+1}$

$I(\alpha) = 2\displaystyle\int \frac{d\alpha}{2\alpha+1} + C = \log(2\alpha+1) + C$

If $\alpha = 0$, then $I(\alpha) = 0$. So, $C = 0$.

Hence $I(\alpha) = \log(2\alpha+1) = \log 2n = \log 2 + \log n$

**15.** **(b)** Let $F(a) = \int_0^\infty \dfrac{e^{-ax} - e^{-x}}{x}\,dx, \ a > 0$  ...(1)

then $F'(a) = \int_0^\infty \dfrac{(-x)e^{-ax}}{x}\,dx = \int_0^\infty (-e^{-ax})\,dx$

$$= \left[\dfrac{e^{-ax}}{a}\right]_0^\infty = -\dfrac{1}{a} \qquad (\because \lim_{x\to\infty} e^{-ax} = 0)$$

$\therefore \qquad F(a) = -\ln a + c$

Let $a = 1$ then $F(1) = c$

Also, from (1), $F(1) = 0 \ \Rightarrow c = 0$

$$\therefore \ F(a) = \int_0^\infty \dfrac{e^{-ax} - e^{-x}}{x}\,dx = -\ln a$$

Thus

$$\int_0^\infty \dfrac{e^{-ax} - e^{-bx}}{x}\,dx = \int_0^\infty \left[\dfrac{e^{-ax} - e^{-x}}{x} - \dfrac{e^{-bx} - e^{-x}}{x}\right]dx$$

$$= -\ln a + \ln b = \ln\left(\dfrac{b}{a}\right)$$

**16.** **A-p; B-r; C-p; D-q, r**

**(A)** $f'(x) = \dfrac{16 - 2x^3}{(x^3 + 16)^2} > 0 \ \ \forall \ x \in [0, 1]$

$\therefore$ Least value of $f(x) = f(0) = 0$ and greatest value of $f(x)$

$$= f(1) = \dfrac{1}{17}$$

$$\therefore 0(1-0) \le \int_0^1 f(x)\,dx \le \dfrac{1}{17}(1-0) \Rightarrow 0 \le I \le \dfrac{1}{17} \Rightarrow [I] = 0$$

**(B)** $\displaystyle\int_0^\pi f(x)\sin\,dx + \int_0^\pi f''(x)\sin x\,dx = 2 \Rightarrow [f(x)(-\cos x)]_0^\pi$

$$-\int_0^\pi f'(x)(-\cos x)\,dx + \int_0^\pi f''(x)\sin x\,dx = 2$$

$$\Rightarrow f(\pi) + f(0) + [f'(x)\sin x]_0^\pi - \int_0^\pi f''(x)\sin x\,dx$$

$$+\int_0^\pi f''(x)\sin x\,dx = 0$$

$$\Rightarrow f(\pi) + f(0) = 2 \Rightarrow f(0) = 2 - f(\pi) = 2 - 5 = -3$$

**(C)** $I = \displaystyle\int_0^{\pi/2} \log\left(\dfrac{4 + 3\sin x}{4 + 3\cos x}\right)dx = \int_0^{\pi/2} \log\left(\dfrac{4 + 3\sin\left(\dfrac{\pi}{2} - x\right)}{4 + 3\cos\left(\dfrac{\pi}{2} - x\right)}\right)dx$

$$= \int_0^{\pi/2} \log\left(\dfrac{4 + 3\cos x}{4 + 3\sin x}\right)dx = -I$$

$\therefore I = 0$

**(D)** $x = \displaystyle\int_0^y \dfrac{dt}{\sqrt{1 + 9t^2}} \Rightarrow \dfrac{dx}{dy} = \dfrac{1}{\sqrt{1 + 9y^2}} \Rightarrow \dfrac{dy}{dx} = \sqrt{1 + 9y^2}$

$$\Rightarrow \dfrac{d^2y}{dx^2} = \dfrac{18y}{2\sqrt{1 + 9y^2}} \times \dfrac{dy}{dx} = 9y \Rightarrow a^2 = 9 \ \text{ or } a = \pm 3$$

**17.** **A-r, t; B-p, r; C-q, s**

**(A)** Since, $0 < \dfrac{x^7}{\sqrt[3]{\left(1 + x^8\right)}} < x^7 \ \forall \ 0 < x < 1$

Then, $\displaystyle\int_0^1 0\,dx < \int_0^1 \dfrac{x^7}{\sqrt[3]{\left(1 + x^8\right)}}\,dx < \int_0^1 x^7\,dx$

Hence, $0 < \displaystyle\int_0^1 \dfrac{x^7\,dx}{\sqrt[3]{\left(1 + x^8\right)}} < \dfrac{1}{8}$

$\therefore \ \lambda = \dfrac{1}{8}, \mu = 0$

$[\lambda + \mu] = 0, [\lambda - \mu] = 0$

**(B)** Since $\sqrt{(1 - x^2)} < \sqrt{(1 + x^6)} < \sqrt{(1 + x^2)} \ \forall \ x \in (0, 1)$

$$\Rightarrow \dfrac{1}{\sqrt{(1 - x^2)}} > \dfrac{1}{\sqrt{(1 + x^6)}} > \dfrac{1}{\sqrt{(1 + x^2)}} \ \forall \ x \in (0, 1)$$

$$\Rightarrow \int_0^1 \dfrac{dx}{\sqrt{(1 + x^2)}} < \int_0^1 \dfrac{dx}{\sqrt{(1 + x^6)}} < \int_0^1 \dfrac{dx}{\sqrt{(1 - x^2)}}$$

$$\Rightarrow \text{In } \{x + \sqrt{(1 + x^2)}\}_0^1 < \int_0^1 \dfrac{dx}{\sqrt{(1 + x^6)}} < \{\sin^{-1} x\}_0^1$$

$$\Rightarrow \text{In } 2 < \int_0^1 \dfrac{dx}{\sqrt{(1 + x^6)}} < \dfrac{\pi}{2}$$

$$\therefore \ \lambda = \dfrac{\pi}{2} \approx 1.57, \mu = \text{In } 2 \approx 0.693$$

$$[\lambda + \mu] = 2, [\lambda - \mu] = 0$$

**(C)** Since, $4 - x^2 > 4 - x^2 - x^3 > 4 - 2x^2 \ \forall \ x \in (0, 1)$

$$\Rightarrow \sqrt{(4 - x^2)} > \sqrt{(4 - x^2 - x^3)} > \sqrt{(4 - 2x^2)} \forall x \in (0, 1)$$

$\Rightarrow \quad \dfrac{1}{\sqrt{(4-x^2)}} < \dfrac{1}{\sqrt{(4-x^2-x^3)}} < \dfrac{1}{\sqrt{(4-2x^2)}} \ \forall \, x \in (0,1)$

$\therefore \quad \displaystyle\int_0^1 \dfrac{dx}{\sqrt{(4-x^2)}} < \int_0^1 \dfrac{dx}{\sqrt{(4-x^2-x^3)}} < \int_0^1 \dfrac{dx}{\sqrt{(4-2x^2)}}$

$\Rightarrow \quad \left[\sin^{-1}\left(\dfrac{x}{2}\right)\right]_0^1 < \displaystyle\int_0^1 \dfrac{dx}{\sqrt{(4-x^2-x^3)}} < \dfrac{1}{\sqrt{2}}\left[\sin^{-1}\dfrac{x}{\sqrt{2}}\right]_0^1$

$\Rightarrow \quad \dfrac{\pi}{6} < \displaystyle\int_0^1 \dfrac{dx}{\sqrt{(4-x^2-x^3)}} < \dfrac{\pi}{4\sqrt{2}}$

$\therefore \quad \lambda = \dfrac{\pi}{4\sqrt{2}} \approx 4.43 \ \text{and} \ \mu = \dfrac{\pi}{6} \approx 0.52$

$[\lambda + \mu] = 4, [\lambda - \mu] = 3$

**18. (d)** $\because \ m(b-a) \le \displaystyle\int_a^b f(x)\,dx \le M(b-a)$

$16 < \displaystyle\int_4^6 2x\,dx < 24$.

**19. (b)** For $x > 0$

$\sin x < x$

$\Rightarrow \quad \dfrac{\sin x}{x} < 1$

$\Rightarrow \quad \displaystyle\int_0^{\pi/2} \dfrac{\sin x}{x}\,dx < \int_0^{\pi/2} 1.dx$

$\Rightarrow \quad \displaystyle\int_0^{\pi/2} \dfrac{\sin x}{x}\,dx < \dfrac{\pi}{2} \ \text{and} \ \lim_{x\to 0} \dfrac{\sin x}{x} = 1$

**20. 2**

Note that in $\left(-\dfrac{1}{2}, \dfrac{1}{2}\right)$,

$\sin^{-1}(3x - 4x^3) = 3\sin^{-1}x$

and $\cos^{-1}(4x^3 - 3x) = 2\pi - 3\cos^{-1}x$

Hence, $f(x) = 3\sin^{-1}x - 2\pi + 3\cos^{-1}x = -\dfrac{\pi}{2}$

$\therefore \quad I = -\dfrac{\pi}{2} \displaystyle\int_{-1/2}^{1/2} dx = -\dfrac{\pi}{2}$

Thus $A = 2$

**21. 9** $\left.\dfrac{t^3}{3}\right|_0^{f(x)} = x \cos \pi x \Rightarrow [f(x)]^3 = 3x \cos \pi x \ ....(1)$

$[f(9)]^3 = -27 \Rightarrow f(9) = -3$

Also differentiating $\displaystyle\int_0^{f(x)} t^2\,dt = x \cos \pi x$

$[f(x)]^2 \cdot f'(x) = \cos \pi x - x \pi \sin \pi x$

$\therefore [f(9)]^2 \cdot f'(9) = -1$

$\Rightarrow f'(9) = -\dfrac{1}{\left(f(9)\right)^2} = -\dfrac{1}{9}$

$f'(9) = -\dfrac{1}{9}$

Thus $P = 9$

**22. 5**

$I = \displaystyle\int_0^1 (acx^{b+1} + a^3 b x^{3b+5})\,dx \,;$

$ac\cdot \left.\dfrac{x^{b+2}}{b+2} + \dfrac{a^3 b x^{3b+6}}{3b+6}\right]_0^1 = \dfrac{ac}{b+2} + \dfrac{a^3 b}{3(b+2)}$

$I(b) = \dfrac{1}{3(b+2)}[3ac + a^3 b] \quad \Rightarrow \dfrac{a^3\left(b + \dfrac{3c}{a^2}\right)}{3(b+2)}$

If this is independent of b, then $\dfrac{3c}{a^2} = 2$

Thus $P + Q = 3 + 2 = 5$

**23. 4**

$u = \displaystyle\int_0^1 \dfrac{\ln(x+1)}{x^2+1}\,dx \qquad \text{put } x = \tan\theta$

$= \displaystyle\int_0^{\pi/4} \ln(1+\tan\theta)\,d\theta = \int_0^{\pi/4} \ln\left(1 + \dfrac{1-\tan\theta}{1+\tan\theta}\right)d\theta$

$= \displaystyle\int_0^{\pi/4} \ln\dfrac{2}{1+\tan\theta}\,d\theta = \dfrac{\pi}{4}\ln 2 - u$

$\therefore u = \dfrac{\pi}{8}\ln 2 \Rightarrow 4u = \dfrac{\pi}{2}\ln 2 \qquad ....(1)$

Again $v = \displaystyle\int_0^{\pi/2} \ln(\sin 2x)\,dx \ \ (\text{put } 2x = t)$

$v = \dfrac{1}{2}\displaystyle\int_0^\pi \ln(\sin t)\,dt = \int_0^{\pi/2} \ln(\sin x)\,dx$

$v = -\dfrac{\pi}{2}\ln 2 \qquad ....(2)$

$(1) + (2) \qquad \Rightarrow 4u + v = 0$

$\Rightarrow \dfrac{-v}{u} = 4$

**24.** **7** Using $\sin 2x = \dfrac{2\tan x}{1+\tan^2 x}$

$$I = \int_0^{\pi/2} \frac{1 - \dfrac{2\tan x}{1+\tan^2 x}}{1 + \dfrac{2\tan x}{1+\tan^2 x}}\,dx$$

$$= \int_0^{\pi/2} \frac{(1-\tan x)^2}{(1+\tan x)^4}\cdot(1+\tan^2 x)\,dx$$

$$= \int_0^{\pi/2} \frac{(1-\tan x)^2}{(1+\tan x)^4}\cdot\sec^2 x\,dx$$

put $y = \tan x \Rightarrow dy = \sec^2 x\,dx$

$$\therefore\ I = \int_0^{\infty} \frac{(1-y)^2}{(1+y)^4}\,dy$$

now put $1+y = z \Rightarrow dy = dz$

$$\therefore\ I = \int_1^{\infty} \frac{(2-z)^2}{z^4}\,dz = -\left.\frac{3z^2-6z+4}{3z^3}\right|_1^{\infty} = \frac{1}{3}$$

Thus $a = 1,\ b = 3$

$\Rightarrow a + b + ab = 1 + 3 + 1 \times 3 = 7$

**1.** **(d)** $I = \int_{-\pi}^{\pi} (\cos px - \sin qx)^2 \, dx$

$I = \int_{-\pi}^{\pi} (\cos px + \sin qx)^2 \, dx$

$2I = 2\int_{-\pi}^{\pi} (\cos^2 px + \sin^2 qx) \, dx$

$I = \int_{0}^{\pi} (2\cos^2 px + 2\sin^2 qx) \, dx$

$= \int_{0}^{\pi} (1 + \cos 2px) + (1 - \cos 2qx) \, dx$

$= 2\pi$ (Both the integrals vanish)

**2.** **(c)** $T_r = \dfrac{1}{\sqrt{\dfrac{r}{n}} \cdot n \left( 3\sqrt{\dfrac{r}{n}} + 4 \right)^2}$

$S = \dfrac{1}{n} \sum_{1}^{4n} \dfrac{1}{\left( 3\sqrt{\dfrac{r}{n}} + 4 \right)^2 \cdot \sqrt{\dfrac{r}{n}}}$

$= \int_{0}^{4} \dfrac{dx}{\sqrt{x}\,(3\sqrt{x} + 4)^2}$

Put $3\sqrt{x} + 4 = t \Rightarrow \dfrac{3}{2}\dfrac{1}{\sqrt{x}}dx = dt$

$= \dfrac{2}{3} \int_{4}^{10} \dfrac{dt}{t^2} = \dfrac{2}{3}\left[\dfrac{1}{t}\right]_{10}^{4} = \dfrac{2}{3}\left[\dfrac{1}{4} - \dfrac{1}{10}\right]$

$= \dfrac{2}{3} \cdot \dfrac{6}{40} = \dfrac{1}{10}$

**3.** **(d)** We have,

$I = \int_{-\pi/2}^{\pi/2} \{f(x) + f(-x)\}\{g(x) - g(-x)\}dx$

Let $F(x) = (f(x) + f(-x))(g(x) - g(-x))$

then $F(-x) = (f(-x) + f(x))(g(-x) - g(x))$

$\qquad = -[f(x) + f(-x)][g(x) - g(-x)]$

$\qquad = -F(x)$

$\therefore \quad F(x)$ is an odd function.

$\therefore \quad$ Using the properly $\int_{-a}^{a} f(x)dx = 0$

If $f(-x) = -f(x)$ we get $I = 0$

If $f(-x) = -f(x)$

we get $I = 0$

**4.** **(c)** Given that for $f$ to be a positive function

$I_1 = \int_{1-k}^{k} xf(x(1-x))dx;$

$I_2 = \int_{1-k}^{k} f[x(1-x)]dx$

Here $I_1 = \int_{1-k}^{k} xf[x(1-x)]dx \qquad \ldots(1)$

$= \int_{1-k}^{k} (1-x)\,f[(1-x)x]dx \qquad \ldots(2)$

$$\left[ \text{Using the prop. } \int_{a}^{b} f(x)\,dx = \int_{a}^{b} f(a+b-x)dx \right]$$

Adding (1) and (2) we get,

$2I_1 = \int_{1-k}^{k} f[x(1-x)]dx = I_2$

$\Rightarrow \quad \dfrac{I_1}{I_2} = \dfrac{1}{2}$

**5.** **(a)** We have

$I = \int_{\pi/4}^{3\pi/4} \dfrac{dx}{1 + \cos x} \qquad \ldots(1)$

$= \int_{\pi/4}^{3\pi/4} \dfrac{dx}{1 + \cos(\pi - x)}$

$$\left[ \text{Using the prop. } \int_{a}^{b} f(x)dx = \int_{a}^{b} (f(a+b-x)\,dx \right]$$

$= \int_{\pi/4}^{3\pi/4} \dfrac{dx}{1 - \cos x} \qquad \ldots(2)$

Adding (1) and (2), we get

$2I = \int_{\pi/4}^{3\pi/4} \left( \dfrac{1}{1 + \cos x} + \dfrac{1}{1 - \cos x} \right) dx$

$$= \int_{\pi/4}^{3\pi/4} 2\csc^2 x\, dx = 2(-\cot x)_{\pi/4}^{3\pi/4}$$

$$= -2[\cot 3\pi/4 - \cot \pi/4] = -2(-1-1) = 4$$

$$\Rightarrow \quad I = 2$$

**6.** **(d)** Consider

$$0 \le \int_0^1 \left( f'(x-1) \right)^2 dx$$

$$= \int_0^1 \left( f'(x) \right)^2 dx - 2\int_0^1 f'(x)dx + \int_0^1 dx$$

$$= \int_0^1 \left( f'(x) \right)^2 dx - 2\left[ f'(x) \right]_0^1 + 1$$

$$= \int_0^1 \left( f'(x) \right)^2 dx - 2(1-0) + 1$$

$$\therefore \int_0^1 (f'(x))^2 dx \ge 1$$

and the value 1 will be minimum.

**7.** **(b)** Applying the method of summation for a definite integral

$$\lim_{n \to \infty} \frac{1}{n} \sum_{r=0}^{20} \left( \frac{n+r}{n} \right)^5$$

$$= \int_0^1 (1+x)^5 \, dx = \frac{2^6 - 1}{6} = \frac{21}{2}$$

**8.** **(b)** $I = \displaystyle\int_\alpha^{\frac{\pi}{2}-\alpha} \frac{d\theta}{1+\cot^n \theta} = \int_\alpha^{\frac{\pi}{2}-\alpha} \frac{d\theta}{1+\cot^n\left( \alpha + \frac{\pi}{2} - \alpha - \theta \right)}$

$$I = \frac{\frac{\pi}{2} - \alpha - \alpha}{2} \Rightarrow \frac{\pi}{4} - \alpha$$

**9.** **(a,b,d)**

**(a)** $L = \displaystyle\lim_{n \to \infty} n \int_0^{\pi/2} (1 - \sqrt[n]{\sin x})\, dx$ ; put $n = 1/t$

$$= \lim_{n \to 0^+} \int_0^{\pi/2} \left( \frac{1 - (\sin x)^t}{t} \right) dx$$

$$L = \lim_{t \to 0} \int_0^{\pi/2} \left( \frac{1 - e^{t\ln(\sin x)}}{t \ln(\sin x)} \cdot \ln(\sin x) \right) dx$$

but $\displaystyle\lim_{t \to 0} \frac{1 - e^{t\ln(\sin x)}}{t\ln(\sin x)} = -1$

$$\therefore \quad L = -\int_0^{\pi/2} \ln(\sin x)\, dx = \frac{\pi}{2} \ln 2$$

**(b)** Put $e^{-z} = \sin \theta$

**(c)** $I = \displaystyle\int_0^\pi \frac{x\,|\sin x|}{1 + |\cos x|} dx \qquad \ldots\ldots(1)$

or $\quad I = \displaystyle\int_0^\pi \frac{(\pi - x)\,|\sin x|}{1 + |\cos x|} dx \qquad \ldots\ldots(2)$

**10.** **(b, c)** $\displaystyle\lim_{n \to \infty} \frac{1}{n} \sum_{r=1}^n f\left( \frac{r}{n} \right) = \int_1^2 f(x)\, dx$

$$\lim_{n \to \infty} \frac{1}{n} \sum_{r=1}^n f\left( \frac{r+n}{n} \right) = \int_0^1 f(1+x)\, dx$$

$$= \int_1^2 f(t)\, dt = \int_1^2 f(x)\, dx$$

$$\lim_{n \to \infty} \frac{1}{n} \sum_{r=1}^n f\left( \frac{r}{n} \right) = \int_0^1 f(x)\, dx$$

$$\lim_{n \to \infty} \frac{1}{n} \sum_{r=1}^{2n} f\left( \frac{r}{n} \right) = \int_0^2 f(x)\, dx$$

**11.** **(a, b, c)** **Case I :** $0 < a < b$

$$\therefore \qquad |x| = x$$

then $\quad \displaystyle\int_a^b \frac{|x|}{x}\, dx = b - a$

**Case II :** $a < 0 < b$

Then $\displaystyle\int_a^b \frac{|x|}{x}\, dx = \int_a^0 \frac{|x|}{x}\, dx + \int_0^b \frac{|x|}{x}\, dx$

$$= \int_a^0 (-1)\, dx + \int_0^b (1)\, dx = a + b$$

**Case III :** $a < b < 0$

$$\int_a^b \frac{|x|}{x}\, dx = \int_a^b (-1)\, dx = -(b-a) = a - b$$

**12.** **(a, c, d)** Let $I = \displaystyle\int_0^\pi x\, f(\sin x)\, dx \qquad \ldots(i)$

$$= \int_0^\pi (\pi - x)\, f(\sin x)\, dx \qquad \ldots(ii)$$

(by property)

Adding Eqs. (i) and (ii), we get

$$2I = \pi \int_0^\pi f(\sin x)\, dx$$

$$\therefore \quad I = \frac{\pi}{2} \int_0^\pi f(\sin x)\, dx$$

$$= \frac{\pi}{2} \cdot 2 \int_0^{\pi/2} f(\sin x)\, dx$$

$$= \pi \int_0^{\pi/2} f(\sin x)\, dx \quad \text{(by property)}$$

$$= \pi \int_0^{\pi/2} f(\cos x)\, dx \quad \text{(by property)}$$

**13. (a)** $g(-x) = \int_0^{-x} f(t)\, dt = -\int_0^{x} f(-y)\, dy \quad (\text{where } t = -y)$

$$= -\int_0^{x} f(y)\, dy = -g(x)$$

so $g(x)$ is in odd function.

**14. (b)** $g(x+2) - g(2) = \int_0^{x+2} f(t)\, dt - \int_0^{2} f(t)\, dt$

$$= \int_0^{x} f(y+2)\, dy \quad (\text{where } t = y+2)$$

$$= \int_0^{x} f(y)\, dy = g(x)$$

$\Rightarrow g(x+2) - g(x) = g(2)$ for all x.

**15. (c)** If $g(x)$ is periodic function with period 2, then $g(x+2)$
$= g(x)$ for all x
$g(x+2) - g(x) = g(2) = 2\alpha$
$\Rightarrow 2\alpha = 0 \qquad \Rightarrow \alpha = 0$
Hence $g(x)$ is periodic with period 2 if $\alpha = 0$

**16. A-p; B-r; C-q; D-s**

**(A)** $\int_{-4}^{-5} e^{(x+5)^2} dx + 3 \int_{1/3}^{2/3} e^{9\left(x-\frac{2}{3}\right)^2} dx$

$\underset{\text{Put } t = x+5}{\text{I}} \qquad \underset{\text{Put } -t=3x-2}{\text{II}}$

$$\Rightarrow \int_1^0 e^{t^2} dt + \int_1^0 e^{t^2}(-dt) = 0$$

**(B)** $\int_{-n}^{n} [x]\, dx = -n$

**(C)** $\int_{-1}^{0} \frac{\pi}{2} dx + \int_{0}^{3} \frac{\pi}{2}\, dx = \frac{\pi}{2}(0+1)\frac{\pi}{2}(3) = 2\pi$

**(D)** $\because \sin x < x \text{ for } x \in \left(0, \frac{\pi}{2}\right) \Rightarrow \frac{\sin x}{x} < 1$

$$\therefore \int_0^{\pi/2} \frac{\sin x}{x} dx < \int_0^{\pi/2} 1\, dx < \frac{\pi}{2}$$

**17. A-q,s,t; B-p, q; C-r,t**

**(A)** $\int_1^4 |x-3|\, dx = \int_1^3 (3-x)\, dx + \int_3^4 (x-3)\, dx$

$$= \left\{ 3x - \frac{x^2}{2} \right\}_1^3 + \left\{ \frac{x^2}{2} - 3x \right\}_3^4$$

$$= \left\{ \left(9 - \frac{9}{2}\right) - \left(3 - \frac{1}{2}\right) \right\} + \left\{ (8-12) - \left(\frac{9}{2} - 9\right) \right\}$$

$$= 5/2$$

$\therefore 2a + b = 5/2$

$\therefore a = 1, b = \dfrac{1}{2} ; a = 2, b = -3/2 : a = \dfrac{1}{2}, b = \dfrac{3}{2}$

**(B)** $\int_{-1}^{1} \frac{|x|}{x} dx = \int_{1}^{0} (-1)\, dx + \int_{0}^{1} 1 dx$

$$= -(0+1) + 1(1-0) = 0$$

$\therefore a - 2b = 0 \quad \text{or} \quad a = 2b$

$\therefore \qquad a = 3, b = \dfrac{3}{2}; \quad a = 1, \quad b = \dfrac{1}{2}$

**(C)** $\int_0^{2\pi} |\sin x|\, dx = \int_0^{\pi} \sin x\, dx - \int_{\pi}^{2\pi} \sin x\, dx$

$$= -[\cos x]_0^{\pi} + [\cos x]_{\pi}^{2\pi}$$

$$= -(-1-1) + (1-(-1)) = 4$$

$\therefore \qquad 5a + b = 4$

$\therefore \qquad a = 1, b = -1 \ a = \dfrac{1}{2}, b = \dfrac{3}{2}$

**18. (a)** $\int_0^{10} x - [x]\, dx = 10 \int_0^{1} x - [x]\, dx = 5$

$$\int_0^{na} f(x)\, dx = n \int_0^{a} f(x)\, dx$$

If 'a' is period of f. Both A and R true and R is the correct explantion of A.

**19. (a)** $\int_{-2}^{2} \log\left(\frac{1+x}{1-x}\right) dx = 0 \Rightarrow f(x) = \log\left(\frac{1+x}{1-x}\right)$

$$f(-x) = \log f(x) = \log\left(\frac{1+x}{1-x}\right) = -\log\left(\frac{1+x}{1-x}\right)$$

$= -f(x) \text{ f is an odd function} \Rightarrow \int_{-a}^{a} f(x)\, dx = 0$

**20.  2**

$$I_1 = \int_{-\pi/4}^{\pi/4} \ln(\sin x + \cos x)\, dx$$

$$= \int_{-\pi/4}^{\pi/4} \ln(\cos x - \sin x)\, dx \qquad \text{(using king)}$$

$$\Rightarrow 2I_1 = \int_{-\pi/4}^{\pi/4} \ln\cos 2x\, dx = 2\int_{0}^{\pi/4} \ln(\cos 2x)$$

$$= \int_{0}^{\pi/2} \ln(\cos t)\, dt \quad \text{where } 2x = t$$

$$\int_{0}^{\pi/2} \ln(\sin t)\, dt = I \Rightarrow I_1 = I/2$$

Thus, $P = 2$

**21.  8**   Let $\theta = \dfrac{\pi}{4} + x \Rightarrow \qquad d\theta = dx$

or $4\theta = \pi + 4x \Rightarrow \pi - 4\theta = -4x$

$$= \int_{-\pi/2}^{0} \frac{(-4x)\tan\left(\dfrac{\pi}{4}+x\right)}{1-\tan\left(\dfrac{\pi}{4}+x\right)}\,dx = -4\int_{-\pi/2}^{0} \frac{x\dfrac{(1+\tan x)}{1-\tan x}}{1-\dfrac{1+\tan x}{1-\tan x}}\,dx$$

$$= -4 \int_{-\pi/2}^{0} \frac{x(1+\tan x)}{1-\tan x}\cdot\frac{(1-\tan x)}{(-2)\tan x}\,dx$$

$$= 2 \int_{-\pi/2}^{0} \frac{x(1+\tan x)}{\tan x}\,dx = 2\int_{-\pi/2}^{0}\left(\frac{x}{\tan x}+x\right)dx$$

$$I = x^2\Big]_{-\pi/2}^{0} + \int_{-\pi/2}^{0} \frac{x}{\tan x}\,dx$$

$$I = -\frac{\pi^2}{4} + 2\int_{0}^{\pi/2} \frac{t}{\tan t}\,dt \qquad x = -t$$

$$\text{now } I_1 = \int_{0}^{\pi/2} \underset{I}{\underbrace{t}}\ \underset{II}{\underbrace{\cot t}}\,dt = t\ln\sin t\Big]_{0}^{\pi/2} - \int_{0}^{\pi/2} \ln\sin t\, dt$$

$$I_1 = 0 + \frac{\pi}{2}\,\ln 2$$

Hence, $2\cdot\dfrac{\pi}{2}\,\ln 2 - \dfrac{\pi^2}{4} = \pi\ln 2 - \dfrac{\pi^2}{4}$

$\Rightarrow k = 2,\ w = 4 \Rightarrow \quad kw = 8$

**22.  6**

We know that in integration as a limit sum

$$\int_{0}^{1} f(x)\,dx = \lim_{n\to\infty} \frac{1}{n}\sum_{r=1}^{n} f(r/n)$$

Similarly the given series can be written as

$$\lim_{n\to\infty}\left(\frac{1}{n+1}+\frac{1}{n+2}+...+\frac{1}{6n}\right) = \lim_{n\to\infty}\sum_{r=1}^{5n}\frac{1}{n+r}$$

$$= \lim_{n\to\infty}\frac{1}{n}\sum_{r=1}^{5n}\frac{1}{1+\dfrac{r}{n}}$$

$$= \int_{0}^{5} \frac{1}{1+x}\,dx = [\log|1+x|]_{0}^{5} = \log 6 - \log 1 = \log 6$$

**23.  7**

Let $I = \displaystyle\int_{0}^{1} \frac{\log(1+x)}{1+x^2}\,dx = \int_{0}^{\pi/4} \frac{\log(1+\tan\theta)}{(1+\tan^2\theta)}\sec^2\theta\, d\theta$

[Putting $x = \tan\theta \Rightarrow dx = \sec^2\theta\, d\theta$]

$$= \int_{0}^{\pi/4} \log(1+\tan\theta)\, d\theta$$

$$= \int_{0}^{\pi/4} \log\left[1+\tan\left(\frac{\pi}{4}-\theta\right)\right] d\theta$$

$$= \int_{0}^{\pi/4}\left(1+\frac{1-\tan\theta}{1+\tan\theta}\right)d\theta = \int_{0}^{\pi/4}\log\left(\frac{2}{1+\tan\theta}\right)d\theta$$

$$= \log 2\int_{0}^{\pi/4} 1\, d\theta - I \Rightarrow 2I = \frac{\pi}{4}\,\log 2$$

$$\therefore \qquad I = \frac{\pi}{8}\,\log 2$$

Thus, $A = 1,\ B = 8$ and $C = 2$

$\Rightarrow A + B - C = 1 + 8 - 2 = 7$

**24.  2**

Using property $\displaystyle\int_{a}^{b} f(x)\,dx = \int_{a}^{b} f(a+b-x)\,dx$

$$I = \int_{2}^{3} \frac{\sqrt{2+3-x}}{\sqrt{5-(2+3-x)}+\sqrt{5-x}}\,dx$$

$$= \int_{2}^{3} \frac{\sqrt{5-x}}{\sqrt{x}+\sqrt{5-x}}\,dx \qquad\qquad ...(i)$$

$$I = \int_{2}^{3} \frac{\sqrt{x}}{\sqrt{5-x}+\sqrt{x}}\,dx \qquad\qquad ...(ii)$$

Adding equation (i) and (ii)

$$2I = \int_{2}^{3}\left(\frac{\sqrt{5-x}}{(\sqrt{x}+\sqrt{5-x})} + \frac{\sqrt{x}}{\sqrt{5-x}+\sqrt{x}}\right)dx$$

$$= \int_{2}^{3} 1.dx = 3 - 2 = 1$$

$$I = 1/2$$

Thus $4x = 4\left(\dfrac{1}{2}\right) = 2$

**1.** **(a)** $\left(x-\dfrac{\pi}{2}\right)^2+y^2=\left(\dfrac{\pi}{2}\right)^2$

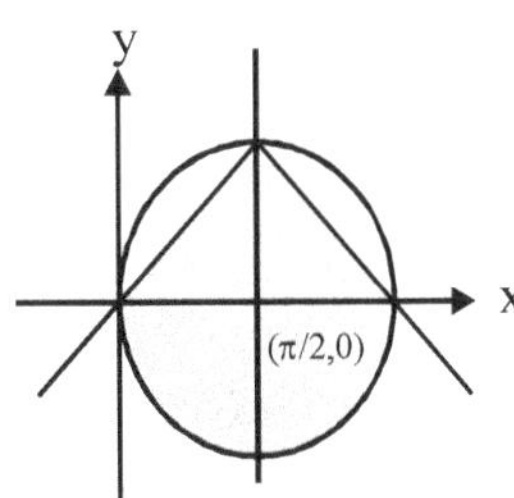


Required area $=\dfrac{1}{2}\pi\left(\dfrac{\pi}{2}\right)^2+\dfrac{1}{2}\pi\dfrac{\pi}{2}$

$=\dfrac{\pi^3}{8}+\dfrac{\pi^2}{4}=\dfrac{\pi^2}{4}\left(\dfrac{\pi}{2}+1\right)$ (units)$^2$

**2.** **(b)** $\cos ax = 0$ if $ax = \dfrac{\pi}{2}$ or $\dfrac{3\pi}{2}$

$x = \dfrac{\pi}{2a}$ or $\dfrac{3\pi}{2a}$

$A_1 = \displaystyle\int_{\frac{\pi}{6a}}^{\frac{\pi}{2a}} \cos ax\, dx$

$=\dfrac{1}{a}\displaystyle\int_{\pi/6}^{\pi/2}\cos t\, dt = \dfrac{1}{a}[\sin t]_{\pi/6}^{\pi/2} = \dfrac{1}{2a}$

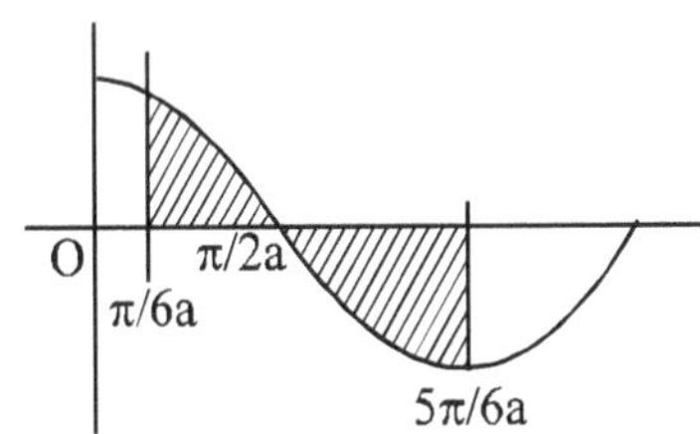


Similarly $A_2 = \left|\displaystyle\int_{\frac{\pi}{2a}}^{\frac{\pi}{6a}}\cos ax\, dx\right| = \left|-\dfrac{1}{2a}\right| = \dfrac{1}{2a}$

$\therefore$ Total area $=\dfrac{1}{a}>3$ $\therefore$ $0<a<\dfrac{1}{3}$

**3.** **(a)** (a, 0) lies on the given curve

$\therefore 0 = \sin 2a - \sqrt{3}\,\sin a \Rightarrow \sin a = 0$ or $\cos a = \sqrt{3}/2$

$\Rightarrow a = \dfrac{\pi}{6}$ (as $a>0$ and the first point of intersection with positive X-axis)

and $A = \displaystyle\int_0^{\pi/6}(\sin 2x - \sqrt{3}\sin x)\,dx$

$=\left(-\dfrac{\cos 2x}{2}+\sqrt{3}\cos x\right)_0^{\pi/6}$

$=\left(-\dfrac{1}{4}+\dfrac{3}{2}\right)-\left(-\dfrac{1}{2}+\sqrt{3}\right)=\dfrac{7}{4}-\sqrt{3}$

$\Rightarrow 4A + 8\cos a = 7$

**4.** **(c)** Let the drawn tangents be PA and PB. AB is clearly the chord of contact of point P.

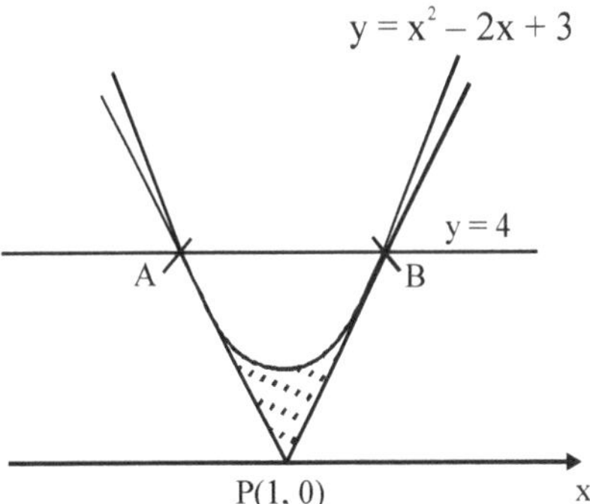


Thus equation of AB is

$\dfrac{1}{2}\cdot(y+0) = x.1 - (2+1)+3$ i.e., $y = 4$

x coordinates of points A and B will be given by,
$x^2 - 2x + 3 = 4$ i.e., $x^2 - 2x - 1 = 0$

$\Rightarrow x = 1 \pm \sqrt{2}$

Thus $AB = 2\sqrt{2}$ units.

Hence $\Delta_{PAB} = \dfrac{1}{2}(2\sqrt{2}).4 = 4\sqrt{2}$ sq. units

Now area bounded by line AB and parabola is equal to

$\displaystyle\int_{1-\sqrt{2}}^{1+\sqrt{2}}(4\sqrt{2}-(x^2-2x+3))\,dx = \dfrac{4\sqrt{2}}{3}$ sq. units.

Thus required area $= 4\sqrt{2}-\dfrac{4\sqrt{2}}{3}=\dfrac{8\sqrt{2}}{3}$ sq. units.

**5.** **(a)**

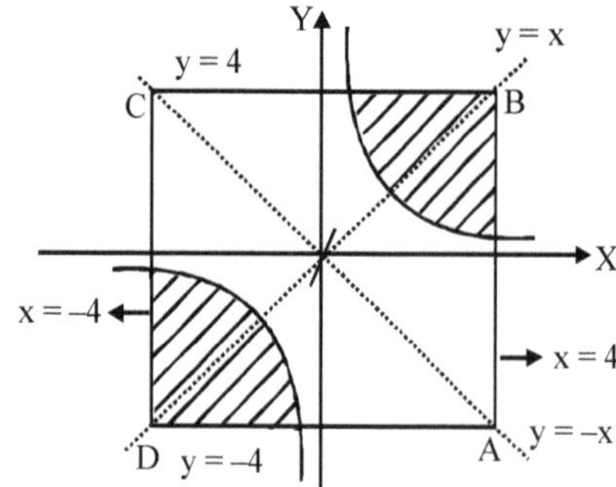

The expression $|x-y|+|x+y| \le 8$,

$x=\pm 4$, $y=\pm 4$ and $xy \ge 2$ represents the

interior region of the square formed by the lines represents the region lying inside the hyperbola $xy = 2$. Required area,

$$\Delta = 2\int_{1/2}^{4}\left(4-\frac{2}{x}\right)dx = \left[2(4x-2\ell n\, x)\right]_{1/2}^{4}$$

$$= 4(7-3\,\ell n\, 2) \text{ sq. units}$$

**6.** **(b)** $y = \sin^4 \pi x$ intersects the x-axis at $x=0$, $x=1$.

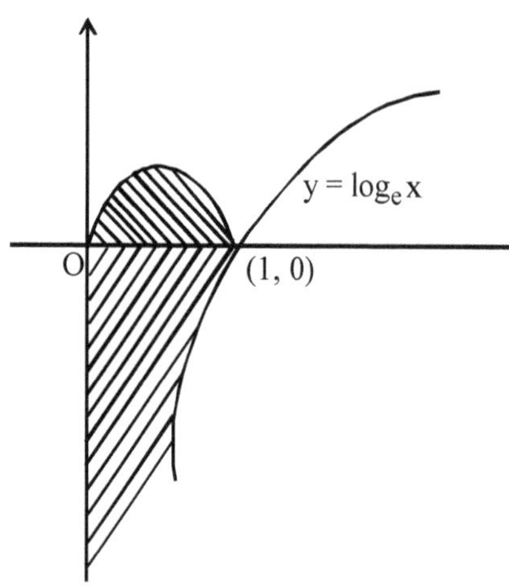

The curve, $y = \log x$ also passes through $(1, 0)$

$$\text{Required area} = \left|\int_0^1 \sin^4 \pi x \, dx\right| + \left|\int_0^1 \log_e x \, dx\right|$$

$$= \left|\int_0^{\pi} \sin^4 \theta \frac{d\theta}{\pi}\right| + \left|\left[x\log_e x - x\right]_0^1\right|$$

$$= \frac{2}{\pi}\int_0^{\pi/2} \sin^4 \theta \, d\theta + 1 = \frac{2}{\pi} \times \frac{3}{4} \times \frac{1}{2} \times \frac{\pi}{2} + 1 = \frac{11}{8}.$$

**7.** **(d)** If $[\,|x|\,]=1$ and $[\,|y|\,]=0$

then $1 \le |x| < 2$, $0 \le |y| < 1$

$\Rightarrow x \in (-2, -1] \cup [1, 2)$, $y \in (-1,1)$

if $[\,|x|\,]=0, [\,|y|\,]=1$

Then, $x \in (-1, 1)$, $y \in (-2, -1] \cup [1, 2]$

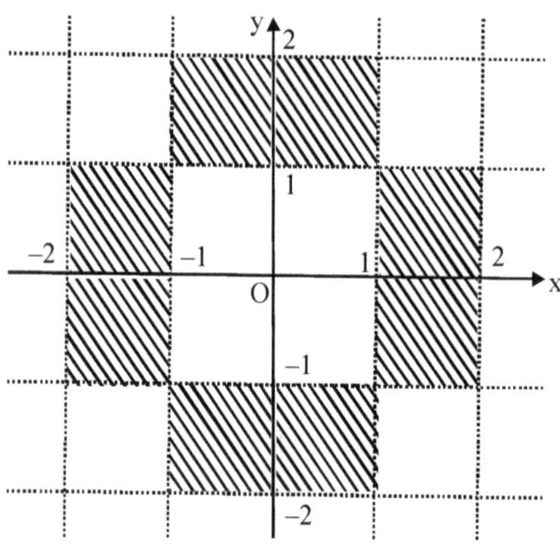

Area of required region

$$= 4(2-1)(1-(-1)) = 8 \text{ sq. units.}$$

**8.** **(a)** Case (I):

$$x+y \ge 0$$
$$2xy \le x+y \le x^2+y^2$$

This gives,

(i) $\left(x-\dfrac{1}{2}\right)\left(y-\dfrac{1}{2}\right) \le \dfrac{1}{4}$, which is one side of a

rectangular hyperbola, and

(ii) $x^2+y^2 \ge x+y$  $\left(x-\dfrac{1}{2}\right)^2 \left(y-\dfrac{1}{2}\right)^2 \ge \dfrac{1}{2}$ which

represents the region outside a circle.

The hyperbola, $x+y = 2xy$ meets $y = 2$ at $x = \dfrac{2}{3}$

The area of the unshaded portion on right top corner at A

$$= \int_{2/3}^{2}\left(2-\frac{x}{2x-1}\right)dx, \text{ since the equation of the}$$

hyperbola is $y = \dfrac{x}{2x-1}$

$$= \left[2x-\frac{1}{2}x-\frac{1}{4}\log(2x-1)\right]_{2/3}^{2} = 2-\frac{1}{2}\log 3$$

The area bounded by the circle $= \pi\left(\dfrac{1}{\sqrt{2}}\right)^2 = \dfrac{\pi}{2}.$

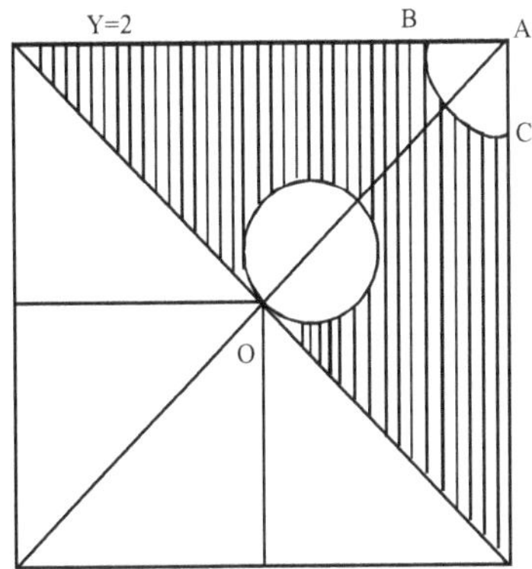

Hence, the area of the shaded portion

$$= \frac{1}{2} \times 4 \times 4 - \frac{\pi}{2} - \left(2 - \frac{1}{2}\log 3\right) = 6 - \frac{\pi}{2} + \frac{1}{2}\log 3$$

**Case (II) :**

$$x + y < 0$$

This refers to the region below the line $x + y = 0$ and equation of the hyperbola is

$$\left(x + \frac{1}{2}\right)\left(y + \frac{1}{2}\right) = \frac{1}{4}.$$

The equation of the corresponding circle is

$$\left(x + \frac{1}{2}\right)^2 + \left(y + \frac{1}{2}\right)^2 = \frac{1}{2}.$$

The area required is also $6 - \frac{\pi}{2} + \frac{1}{2}\log 3$ by symmetry.

$$\therefore \quad \text{Total area} = 12 - \pi + \log 3.$$

**9.** **(a).** $\sin x \dfrac{dy}{dx} + y\cos x = 1$

$$\frac{dy}{dx} + y\cot x = \operatorname{cosec} x$$

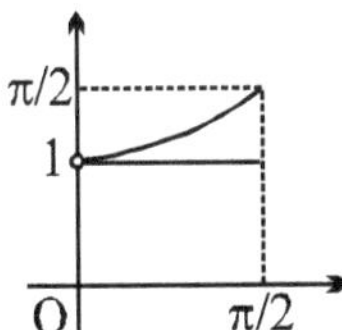

$$\text{I.F.} = e^{\int \cot x\, dx} = e^{ln(\sin x)} = \sin x$$

$$y\sin x = \int \operatorname{cosec} x \cdot \sin x\, dx$$

$$y\sin x = x + C$$

if $x = 0$, $y$ is finite

$$\therefore \quad C = 0$$

$$y = x\,(\operatorname{cosec} x) = \frac{x}{\sin x}$$

Now $I < \dfrac{\pi^2}{4}$ and $I > \dfrac{\pi}{2}$

Hence $\dfrac{\pi}{2} < I < \dfrac{\pi^2}{4}$

**10.** **(a,b,c,d)**

(a) Bold lines represents the graph of $y = \max\{\sin x, \cos x\}$.

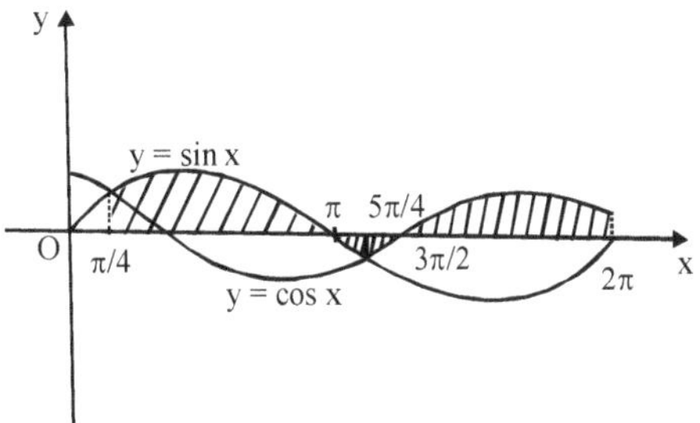


Required area,

$$\Delta = \int_{\pi/4}^{\pi} \sin x\, dx - \int_{\pi}^{5\pi/4} \sin x\, dx \int_{5\pi/4}^{3\pi/2} \cos x\, dx + \int_{3\pi/2}^{2\pi} \cos x\, dx$$

$$= \frac{(4\sqrt{2} - 1)}{\sqrt{2}} \text{ sq.units}$$

(b) The curves given are

$$y = \sqrt{x} \qquad \qquad ...(1)$$

and $\qquad 2y + 3 = x \qquad \qquad ...(2)$

and $x$-axis $\qquad y = 0 \qquad \qquad ...(3)$

$Eq^n$ (1) $[y^2 = x]$ represents right handed parabola but with +ve values of $y$ i.e., part of curve lying above $x$-axis.

Solving (1) and (2) we get,

$$2y + 3 = y^2$$

$$\Rightarrow \quad y^2 - 2y - 3 = 0$$

$$\Rightarrow \quad (y - 3)(y + 1) = 0$$

$$\Rightarrow \quad y = 3 \qquad \qquad (\text{as } y \neq -ve)$$

$$\Rightarrow \quad x = 9$$

Also (2) meets x-axis at $(3, 0)$

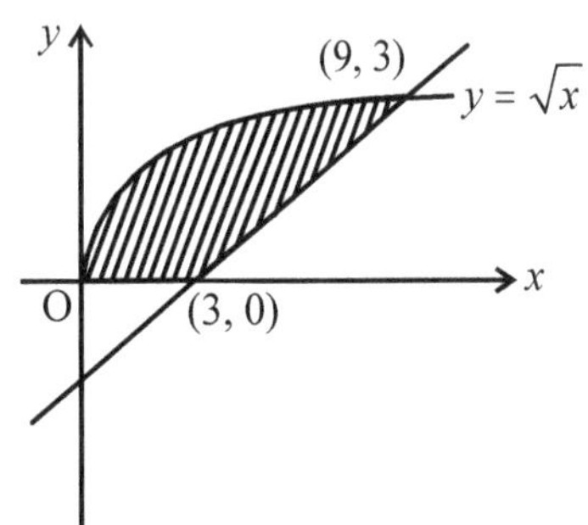


Shaded area is the required area given by

$$A = \int_0^9 \sqrt{x}\, dx - \int_3^9 \frac{x - 3}{2}\, dx$$

$$= \left[\frac{2x^{3/2}}{3}\right]_0^9 - \frac{1}{2}\left[\frac{x^2}{2} - 3x\right]_3^9$$

$$= \frac{2 \times 27}{3} - \frac{1}{2}\left[\frac{81}{2} - 27 - \frac{9}{2} + 9\right]$$

$$= \frac{54}{3} - \frac{1}{2}[18]$$

$$= 18 - 9 = 9 \text{ sq. units}$$

(c) The given region is represented by the equations
$$y = 1 - x,\ x \le 1 \text{ and } y = x - 1,\ x \ge 1$$
and $y = 1$; $C = (2, 1)$ and $B = (0, 1)$

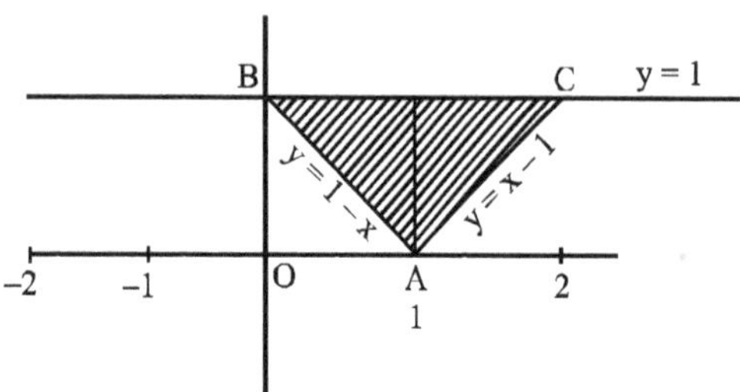


∴ The shaded area in the figure
$$= \frac{1}{2}\, BC \cdot AC = \frac{1}{2}\, 2 \cdot 1 = 1.$$

(d) The required area

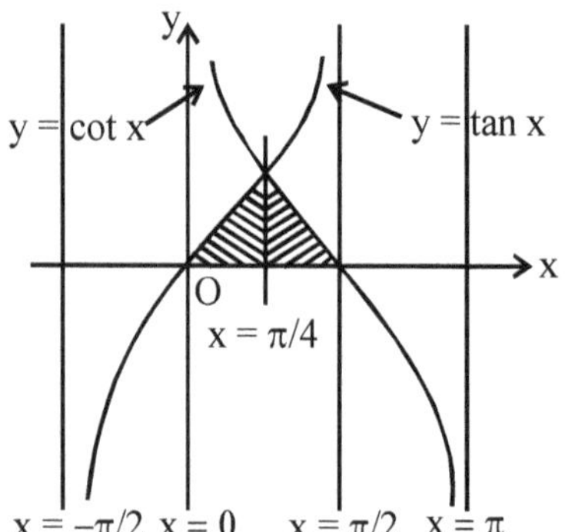


$$= \int_{0}^{\pi/4} \tan x\, dx + \int_{\pi/4}^{\pi/2} \cot x\, dx$$

$$= [\log \sec x]_{0}^{\pi/4} + [\log \sec x]_{\pi/4}^{\pi/2}$$

$$= [\log \sqrt{2} - \log 1] + [\log 1 - \log 1/\sqrt{2}]$$

$$= \log \sqrt{2} - \log 1 + \log \sqrt{2}$$

$$= 2 \log \sqrt{2} = \log (\sqrt{2})^2 = \log 2.$$

**11.** **(b, d)** The two curves meet at $mx = x - x^2$ or $x^2 = x(1 - m)$
$$\therefore \qquad\qquad x = 0,\ 1 - m$$

$$\int_{0}^{1-m} (y_1 - y_2)\, dx = \int_{0}^{1-m} (x - x^2 - mx)\, dx$$

$$= \left[(1 - m)\frac{x^2}{2} - \frac{x^3}{3}\right]_{0}^{1-m} = \frac{9}{2} \text{ (given)}$$

If $m < 1$

or $(1 - m)^3 \left[\frac{1}{2} - \frac{1}{3}\right] = \frac{9}{2}$

or $(1 - m)^3 = 27$
$$\therefore\ m = -2$$
Now, if $m > 1$, (c)n $1 - m$ is −ve, then

$$\left[(1 - m)\frac{x^2}{2} - \frac{x^3}{3}\right]_{1-m}^{0} = \frac{9}{2}$$

$$-(1 - m)^3 \left(\frac{1}{2} - \frac{1}{3}\right) = \frac{9}{2}$$

$$\therefore\quad -(1 - m)^3 = -27$$
or $\quad 1 - m = -3$
$$\Rightarrow\quad m = 4$$

**12.** **(a,b,c)** ∵ Curves $x^2 = y$ and $y^2 = x$ intersect at $(0, 0)$ and $(1, 1)$
.

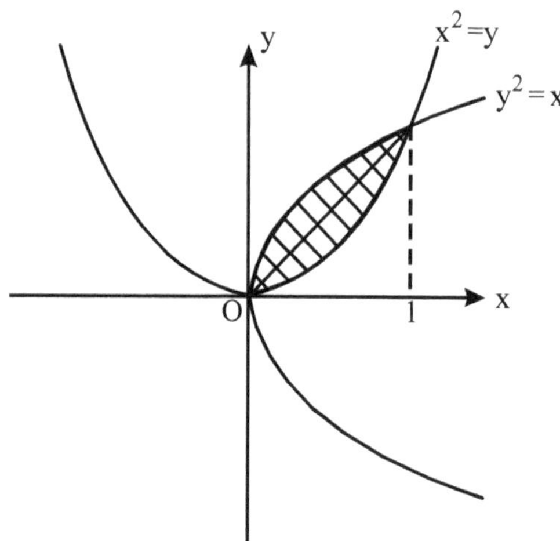


∴ Required area $= \int_{0}^{1} (\sqrt{x} - x^2)\, dx$

$$= \frac{2}{3} - \frac{1}{3} = \frac{1}{3} \text{ sq unit.}$$

Also, both curves $x^2 = y$ and $y^2 = x$ are symmetric about $y = x$.

∴ Required area $= 2 \int_{0}^{1} (x - x^2)\, dx$

**Option (c):** $x^2 \le y \le |x|$

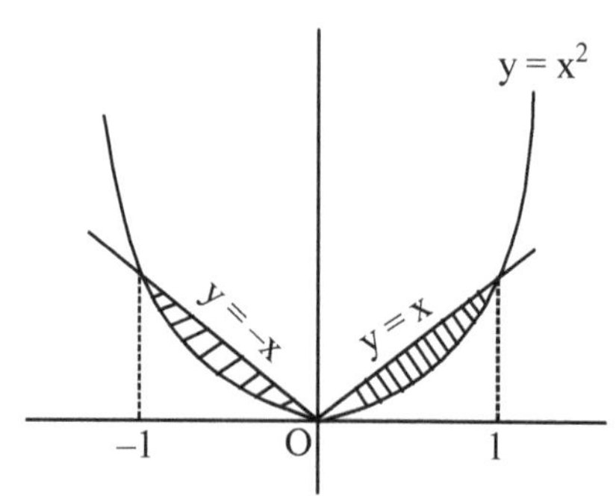

$y = x^2, y = |x|$ points of intersection are $(0, 0)$ and $(1, 1)$.

$\therefore$ Required area $= 2\int_0^1 (x - x^2)\,dx$

$$= 2\left(\frac{1}{2} - \frac{1}{3}\right) = 1 - \frac{2}{3} = \frac{1}{3} \text{ sq unit.}$$

**13. (c)** $A = \int_{-\infty}^{0} e^y\,dy$

**14. (c)** $A = \left|\int_0^{\pi/4} \tan y\,dy\right| + \left|\int_{\pi/4}^{\pi/2} \cot y\,dy\right|$

$$= 2\ln\sqrt{2} = \ln 2$$

**15. (b)**

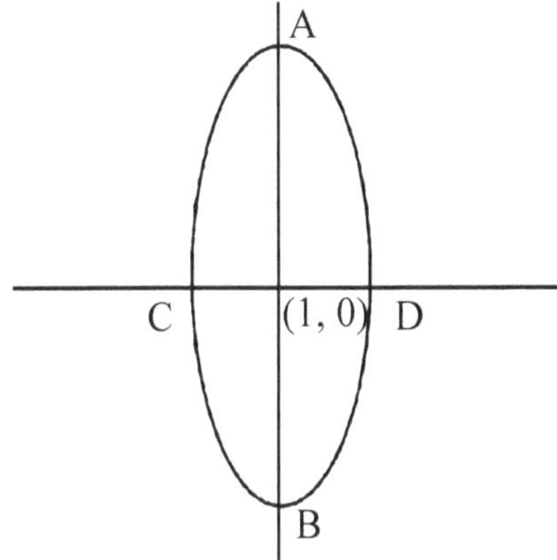

Area of the region is given by

$$A = \int_{-1}^{3}\left[(y+1) - \left(\frac{y^2 - 1}{2}\right)\right]dy = \frac{16}{3}$$

**16. A→t; B→r; C→p; D→q**

**(A):** $\int_0^3 (3x - x^2)\,dx = 4.5$ **(t)**

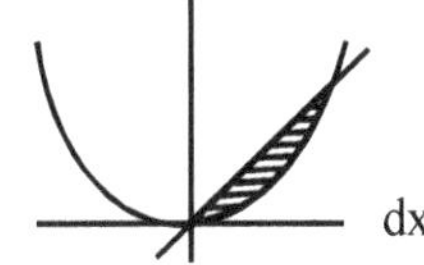


**(B):** $2\int_0^2 (4 - y^2)\,dy = \frac{32}{3}$ **(r)**

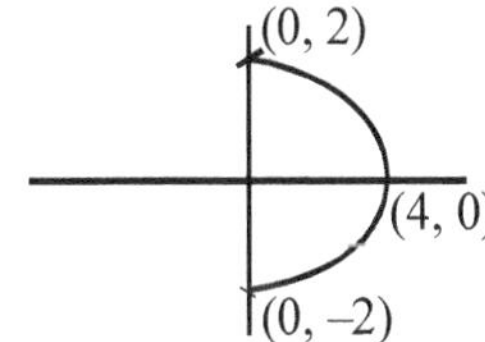


**(C):** $\int_0^2 \frac{x^2}{4}\,dx = \frac{2}{3}$ **(p)**

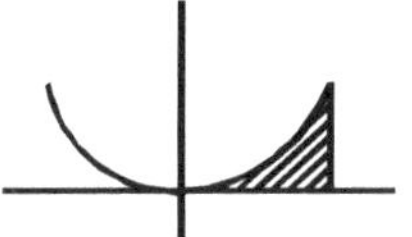

**(D):** $\int_1^2 (x^3 - x^2)\,dx = \frac{17}{12}$ **(q)**

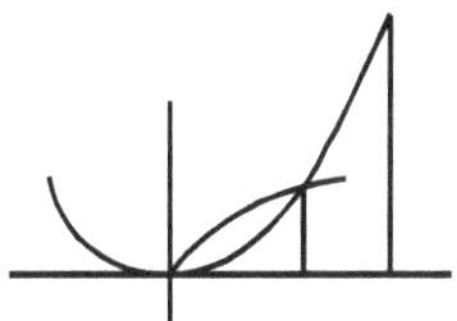

**17. A→t; B→s; C→p; D→q**

**(A)** We have $-1 \le x \le 1$ and $x - x^2 \ge 0 \Rightarrow 0 \le x \le 1$, curve has two branches

$y = \sin^{-1} x \pm \sqrt{x - x^2}$ and lies between $x = 0$ and $x = 1$

$\therefore$ Desired area $= \int_0^1 |y_1 - y_2|\,dx = 2\int_0^1 \sqrt{x - x^2}\,dx$

$$= 2\left[\frac{2x - 1}{4}\sqrt{x - x^2}\right]_0^1 + \frac{2}{8}\sin^{-1}(2x - 1)\ \bigg|_0^1 = \frac{\pi}{4} \textbf{ (t)}$$

**(B)** If $x + y \ge 0$ and $x - y \ge 0$, then $\dfrac{1}{\sqrt{2}} \le x \le \sqrt{2}$

If $x + y \ge 0$ and $x - y < 0$, then $\dfrac{1}{\sqrt{2}} \le y \le \sqrt{2}$

If $x + y < 0$ and $x - y \ge 0$ then $-\sqrt{2} \le y \le -\dfrac{1}{\sqrt{2}}$

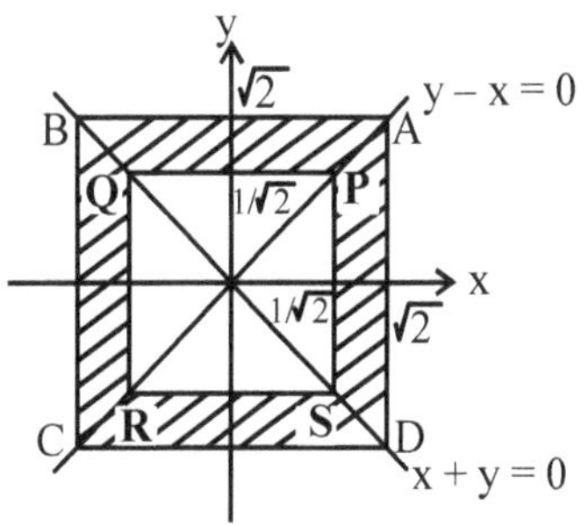


If $x + y < 0$ and $x - y < 0$ then $-\sqrt{2} \le x \le -\dfrac{1}{\sqrt{2}}$

Desired area $= (2\sqrt{2})^2 - (\sqrt{2})^2 = 6$ **(s)**

**(C)** Area, $A = \int_\alpha^\beta [(ax + 2) - (x^2 - 3)]\,dx$

$$= \left[\frac{ax^2}{2} + 5x - \frac{x^3}{3}\right]_\alpha^\beta$$

**Left column:**

$$= (\beta - \alpha)\left[\frac{a}{2}(\beta + \alpha) - \frac{1}{3}(\beta^2 + \alpha^2 + \beta\alpha) + 5\right]$$

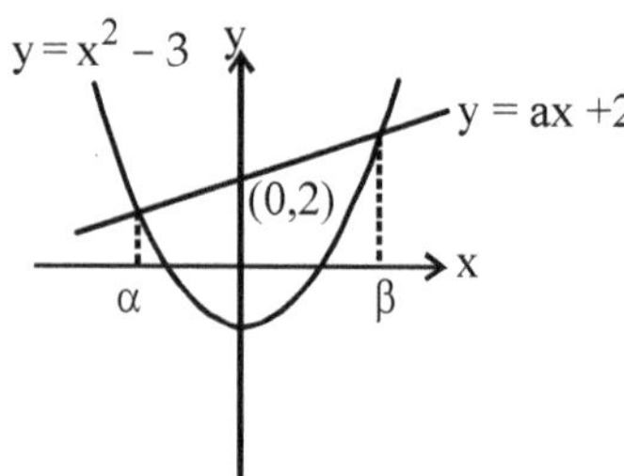


$\alpha, \beta$ are roots of $x^2 - ax - 5 = 0 \Rightarrow \alpha + \beta = a,\ \alpha\beta = -5$

$$\therefore A = \sqrt{a^2 + 20}\left[\frac{a^2}{6} + \frac{10}{3}\right],\ \text{which is minimum if } a = 0\ \textbf{(p)}$$

(D) On solving two equations, we get

$$x = 0,\ x = \frac{k}{1 + k^2} = \alpha\ (\text{say})$$

$$\text{So, the area } A = \int_0^{\alpha}\left(x - kx^2 - \frac{x^2}{k}\right)dx$$

$$\Rightarrow A = \frac{\alpha^2}{2} - \frac{k\alpha^3}{3} - \frac{\alpha^3}{3k} \Rightarrow \frac{\alpha^2}{6}\left(3 - 2k\alpha - \frac{2\alpha}{k}\right)$$

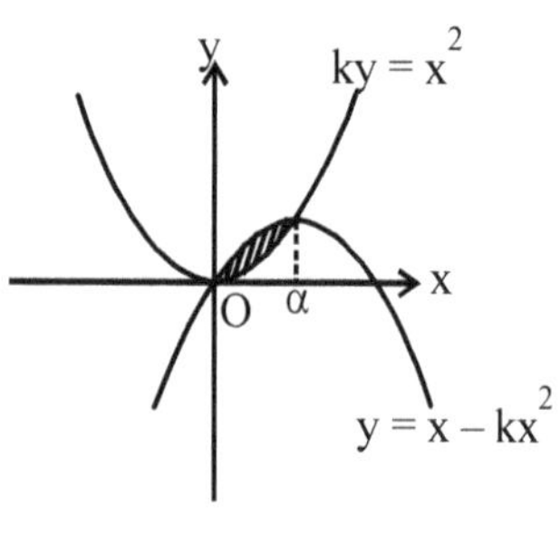


$$= \frac{\alpha^2}{6}\left[3 - \frac{2k^2}{1 + k^2} - \frac{2}{1 + k^2}\right] = \frac{k^2}{6(1 + k^2)^2}$$

Clearly it attains its maximum when $k = 1$. **(q)**

**18. (b)** Given, $f\left(\dfrac{x}{y}\right) = f(x) - f(y)$ ....(i)

Puting $x = y$, then $\Rightarrow f(1) = 0$

$$\therefore\quad f'(x) = \lim_{h \to 0}\frac{f(x + h) - f(x)}{h}$$

$$= \lim_{h \to 0}\frac{f\left(1 + \dfrac{h}{x}\right)}{h}\qquad [\text{from Eq. (i)}]$$

$$= \lim_{h \to 0}\frac{f\left(1 + \dfrac{h}{x}\right)}{x\,\dfrac{h}{x}}$$

**Right column:**

$$= \frac{3}{x}\left\{\because\ \lim_{x \to 0}\frac{f(1 + x)}{x} = 3\right\}$$

$\therefore\quad f(x) = 3\ln x + c$

Putting $x = 1$, then

$f(1) = 0 + c = 0$

$\Rightarrow\quad f(x) = 3\ln x = y\ (\text{say})$

$\therefore\quad x = e^{y/3}$

$\therefore\quad$ Required area $= \displaystyle\int_{-\infty}^{3} x\,dy$

$$= \int_{-\infty}^{3} e^{y/3}\,dy$$

$$= 3\ \{e^{y/3}\}_{-\infty}^{3} = 3(e - 0) = 3e\ \text{sq. unit.}$$

$\because\quad f''(x) = -\dfrac{3}{x^2} < 0$

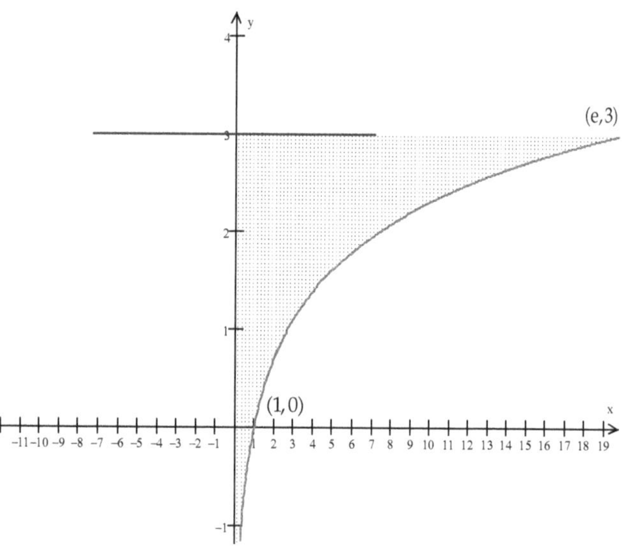


$\Rightarrow\quad f(x)$ is concave down.

**19. (d)** For $0 < t < 1$

$t^2 < t$

$\therefore\quad \sin^2 x < \sin x$

$$\Rightarrow\quad \int_0^{\pi} \sin^2 x\,dx < \int_0^{\pi} \sin x\,dx$$

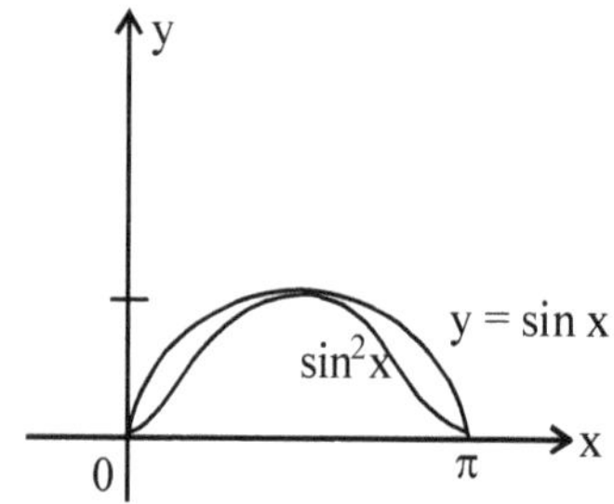

**20.** **(4)**

Solving the two functions we get $x = 2,\ \sqrt{3}-1$

So, required area $= \displaystyle\int_{\sqrt{3}-1}^{2}\left[2-\dfrac{3}{(x+1)}-|x-1|\right]dx$

$= \displaystyle\int_{\sqrt{3}-1}^{1}\left[2-\dfrac{3}{(x+1)}+(x-1)\right]dx$

$+ \displaystyle\int_{1}^{2}\left[2-\dfrac{3}{(x+1)}+(1-x)\right]dx$

$A = \left(2-\dfrac{3}{2}\ln 3\right)$ sq. units

$2A = 4 - 3\ln 3$
$2A + 3\ln 3 = 4$

**21.** **(1)**

$A = \displaystyle\int_{a}^{2a}\left(\dfrac{x}{6}+\dfrac{1}{x^2}\right)dx = \left.\dfrac{x^2}{12}-\dfrac{1}{x}\right]_{a}^{2a}$

$= \left(\dfrac{a^2}{3}-\dfrac{1}{2a}\right)-\left(\dfrac{a^2}{12}-\dfrac{1}{a}\right)$

$f(a) = \dfrac{a^2}{4}+\dfrac{1}{2a}$

Now, $f'(a) = \dfrac{a}{2}-\dfrac{1}{2a^2} = 0 \ \Rightarrow\ a^3 = 1 \ \Rightarrow\ a = 1$

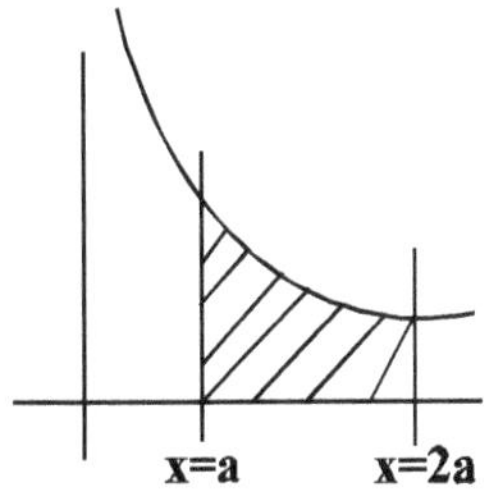


**22.** **(9)**

Note for inverse function y axis will be the x axis and x axis will be the y axis

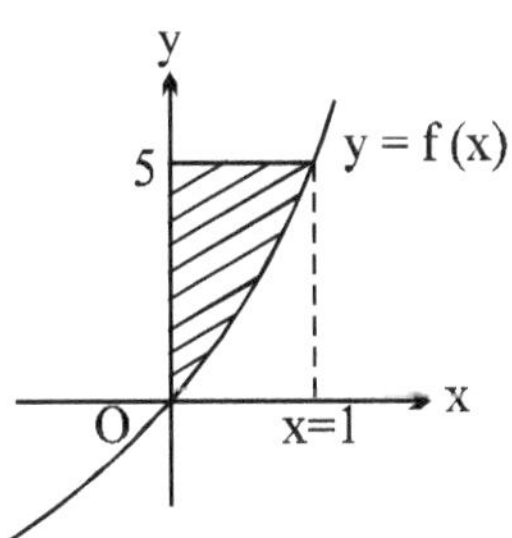


Required area $=$ Area of rectangle $-\displaystyle\int_{0}^{1}f(x)\,dx$

$= 5 - \displaystyle\int_{0}^{1}(3x^3 + 2x)\,dx$

$= 5-\left(\dfrac{3}{4}+1\right) = 3\dfrac{1}{4} = \dfrac{13}{4}$

Thus, $A - B = 13 - 4 = 9$

**23.** **(7)**

$A = \displaystyle\int_{x_1}^{x_2}\dfrac{\left(a^2 - a\,x\right)-\left(x^2 + 2a\,x + 3a^2\right)}{1+a^4}\,dx$

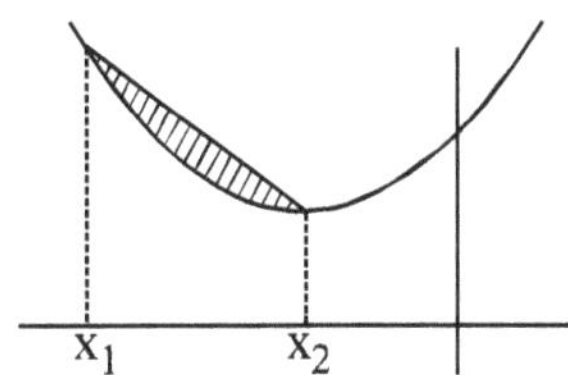


where $x_1$ & $x_2$ are the roots of,
$x^2 + 2a\,x + 3a^2 = a^2 - a\,x$
$x = -a$ or $x = -2a$

$A = \dfrac{a^3}{6(1+a^4)} \ \Rightarrow\ \dfrac{dA}{da} = 0$ gives $a = 3^{1/4}$

Thus, $P = 3,\ n = 4$
$\Rightarrow P + n = 7$

**24.** **6**

$f'(x) = \underset{h\to 0}{\text{Limit}}\ \dfrac{f(x+h)-f(x)}{h}$

$= \underset{h\to 0}{\text{Limit}}\dfrac{f(x)\cdot\left[\dfrac{f(x+h)}{f(x)}-1\right]}{h}$

$= f(x)\cdot\underset{h\to 0}{\text{Limit}}\dfrac{f\left(\dfrac{x+h}{x}\right)-1}{h}$

$= f(x)\cdot\underset{h\to 0}{\text{Limit}}\dfrac{f\left(1+\dfrac{h}{x}\right)-1}{x\cdot\dfrac{h}{x}}$

$= \dfrac{f(x)}{x}\underset{t\to 0}{\text{Limit}}\dfrac{f(1+t)-1}{t}$

Now putting $x = 1,\ y = 1$ in functional rule

$f(1) = \dfrac{f(1)}{f(1)} = 1$

$\therefore f'(x) = \dfrac{f(x)}{x} \cdot f'(1) \qquad = \dfrac{2f(x)}{x}$

$\dfrac{f'(x)}{f(x)} = \dfrac{2}{x}$

$ln\,(f(x)) = 2lnx + C$

$x = 1;\ f(1) = 0 \Rightarrow C = 0 \qquad \therefore f(x) = x^2$

Now solving $y = x^2$ and $x^2 + y^2 = 2$

$y^2 + y - 2 = 0$

$(y + 2)(y - 1) = 0$

$y = 1$

$A = 2 \displaystyle\int_0^1 \left( \sqrt{2 - y^2} - \sqrt{y} \right) dy$

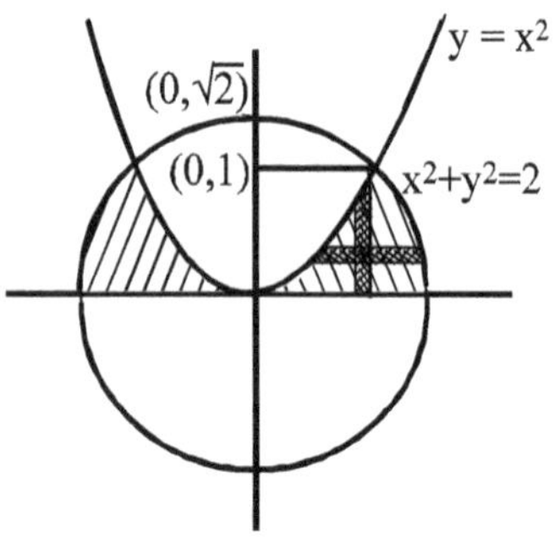


$= 2\left[ \displaystyle\int_0^1 \sqrt{2 - y^2}\,dy - \int_0^1 \sqrt{y}\ dy \right]$

$= \displaystyle\int_0^1 \sqrt{y}\ dy = \dfrac{2}{3} y^{\frac{1}{2}+1} \Big|_0^1 = \dfrac{2}{3}$

and $\displaystyle\int_0^1 \sqrt{2 - y^2}\ dy$

$y = \sqrt{2}\sin\theta$

$\displaystyle\int_0^{\pi/4} \sqrt{2}\cos\theta \sqrt{2}\cos\theta\, d\theta$

$\Rightarrow \displaystyle\int_0^{\pi/4} 2\cos^2\theta\ d\theta = \int_0^{\pi/4} (1 + \cos 2\theta)\ d\theta$

$= \left. \theta + \dfrac{1}{2}\sin 2\theta \right]_0^{\pi/4} \Rightarrow \dfrac{\pi}{4} + \dfrac{1}{2}$

Hence $A = 2\left[ \dfrac{\pi}{4} + \dfrac{1}{2} - \dfrac{2}{3} \right] \quad ; A = \left( \dfrac{\pi}{2} - \dfrac{1}{3} \right)$ sq. units

Thus, $P = 2,\ Q = 1$ and $R = 3$

$\Rightarrow P + Q + R = 6$

**1.** **(b).** $y = c_1 \cos(x + c_2) - (c_3 e^{-x + c_4}) + (c_5 \sin x)$

$\therefore\ y = c_1(\cos x\ \cos c_2 - \sin x\ \sin c_2)$

$\qquad - (c_3 e^{c_4} e^{-x}) + (c_5 \sin x)$

$\therefore\ y = (c_1 \cos c_2)\cos x - (c_1 \sin c_2 - c_5)\sin x - (c_3 e^{c_4})e^{-x}$

$\therefore\ y = l\cos x + m\sin x - n\,e^{-x}$ ....(i)

where $l, m, n$ are arbitrary constant

$\therefore\ \dfrac{dy}{dx} = -l\sin x + m\cos x + n\,e^{-x}$ ....(ii)

$\therefore\ \dfrac{d^2 y}{dx^2} = -l\cos x - m\sin x - n\,e^{-x}$ ....(iii)

$\therefore\ \dfrac{d^3 y}{dx^3} = l\sin x - m\cos x + n\,e^{-x}$ ....(iv)

(i) + (iii) gives $\dfrac{d^2 y}{dx^2} + y = -2n\,e^{-x}$ ....(v)

(ii) + (iv) gives $\dfrac{d^3 y}{dx^3} + \dfrac{dy}{dx} = 2n\,e^{-x}$ ....(vi)

From (v) and (vi) we get $\dfrac{d^3 y}{dx^3} + \dfrac{dy}{dx} = -\left(\dfrac{d^2 y}{dx^2} + y\right)$

or $\dfrac{d^3 y}{dx^3} + \dfrac{d^2 y}{dx^2} + \dfrac{dy}{dx} + y = 0$

is the required differential equation

**2.** **(c).** Equation to the family of parabolas is

$(y - k)^2 = 4a(x - h)$

$2(y - k)\dfrac{dy}{dx} = 4a \ \Rightarrow (y - k)\dfrac{dy}{dx} = 2a)$

$(y - k)\dfrac{d^2 y}{dx^2} + \left(\dfrac{dy}{dx}\right)^2 = 0$

$2a\dfrac{d^2 y}{dx^2} + \left(\dfrac{dy}{dx}\right)^3 = 0.$

Hence order is 2 and degree is 1.

**3.** **(a).** $\dfrac{dV}{dt} = -k4\pi r^2$ ....(1)

but $V = \dfrac{4}{3}\pi r^3 \ \Rightarrow\ \dfrac{dV}{dt} = 4\pi r^2\dfrac{dr}{dt}$ ....(2)

hence $\dfrac{dr}{dt} = -K$

**4.** **(b).** $x^2 + (y - r)^2 = r^2$ ......... (1)

$\therefore\ x + (y - r)\dfrac{dy}{dx} = 0 \ \therefore\ (r - y)\dfrac{dy}{dx} = x$

$\therefore\ r = y + \dfrac{x}{(dy/dx)}$

Put it in (i) we get $(x^2 - y^2)\dfrac{dy}{dx} - 2xy = 0$

**5.** **(b)** $\left(\dfrac{d^3 y}{dx^3}\right)^{2/3} + 4 - 3\dfrac{d^2 y}{dx^2} + 5\dfrac{dy}{dx} = 0$

$\Rightarrow\ \left(\dfrac{d^3 y}{dx^3}\right)^2 = \left[3\dfrac{d^2 y}{dx^2} - 5\dfrac{dy}{dx} - 4\right]^3$

It is a differential equation of degree 2.

**6.** **(a)** Clearly order of the differential eq. is 2.

Again $\dfrac{d^2 y}{dx^2} + x^{1/4} = -\left(\dfrac{dy}{dx}\right)^{1/3}$

$\Rightarrow \left(\dfrac{d^2 y}{dx^2} + x^{1/4}\right)^3 = -\dfrac{dy}{dx}$

Which shows that degree of the differential equation is 3.

**7.** **(a)** We have, k = PQ = length of normal

$\Rightarrow k = y\sqrt{1 + \left(\dfrac{dy}{dx}\right)^2} \ \Rightarrow \dfrac{k^2}{y^2} = 1 + \left(\dfrac{dy}{dx}\right)^2$

$\therefore\ y\dfrac{dy}{dx} = \pm\sqrt{k^2 - y^2}$

Which is the required differential equation.

**8.** **(b)** The equation of the family is $x^2 + (y - b)^2 = a^2$

[where the centre is (0,b) and radius = a]

Differentiating, $2x + 2(y - b)y' = 0$

Differentiating again $1 + (y - b)y'' + y'^2 = 0.$

Eliminating b, we get $xy'' = y'(1 + y'^2)$

**9.** **(a,b)** If $y = f(x)$ is the curve, $Y - y = f'(x)(X - x)$ is the equation of the tangent at $(x, y)$, with $f'(x) = \dfrac{dy}{dx}$.

Putting $X = 0$, the initial ordinate of the tangent is therefore $y - x f'(x)$. The subnormal at this point is given by $y\dfrac{dy}{dx}$, so we have

$y\dfrac{dy}{dx} = y - x\dfrac{dy}{dx} \Rightarrow \dfrac{dy}{dx} = \dfrac{y}{x + y}$

This is a homogeneous equation and, by rewriting it as

$$\frac{dx}{dy} = \frac{x+y}{y} = \frac{x}{y}+1 \Rightarrow \frac{dx}{dy} - \frac{x}{y} = 1$$

we see that it is also a linear equation.

**10.** **(a,b,d)**

**(a)** $y = C_1 + C_2 e^x + C_3 e^{-2x+c_4}$

$$= C_1 + C_2 e^x + C_3 e^{c_4} . e^{-2x}$$

So, Differential equation will be of order 3.

**(b)** Let the directrix be $x = 0$ (y-axis) and fixed eccentricity is e. If the focus S be (h, k) then the equation of such an

$$\text{ellipse is } \frac{\text{Distance from focus}}{\text{Distance from directrix}} = \text{eccentricity}$$

$$\Rightarrow \frac{\sqrt{(x-h)^2 + (y-k)^2}}{|x|} = e \Rightarrow (x-h)^2 + (y-k)^2 = e^2 x^2$$

Clearly it contains two arbitrary constants h and k. Therefore the order of the equation is 2.

**(c)** Differentiating the equation twice with respect to x, we have
$2a^2 x - 2b^2 yy' = 0$, $a^2 - b^2(y'^2 + yy'') = 0$.
Eliminating $a^2$ and $b^2$, we have the differential equation

$$\frac{y''}{y'} + \frac{y'}{y} = \frac{1}{x}$$

**(d)** The equation $c(y+c)^2 = x^3$ ...(i)

has one arbitrary constant, so the equation must be of the first order. Differentiating (i) we get

$$2c(y+c)\frac{dy}{dx} = 3x^2 \qquad \text{...(ii)}$$

$$\Rightarrow \qquad 4c^2(y+c)^2 \left(\frac{dy}{dx}\right)^2 = 9x^4 \qquad \text{...(iii)}$$

Divide (iii) by (i), we get $4c\left(\frac{dy}{dx}\right)^2 = 9x$

$$\Rightarrow \quad c = \frac{9}{4}\frac{x}{\left(\frac{dy}{dx}\right)^2}$$

Put the value of c in (ii), we get

$$2 \cdot \frac{9}{4}\frac{x}{\left(\frac{dy}{dx}\right)^2}\left[y + \frac{9}{4}\frac{x}{\left(\frac{dy}{dx}\right)^2}\right]\left(\frac{dy}{dx}\right) = 3x^2$$

$$\Rightarrow 9x\left[y + \frac{9}{4}\frac{x}{\left(\frac{dy}{dx}\right)^2}\right] = 6x^2\left(\frac{dy}{dx}\right)$$

$$\Rightarrow 3y\left(\frac{dy}{dx}\right)^2 + \frac{27}{4}x = 2x\left(\frac{dy}{dx}\right)^3$$

$$\Rightarrow 12y\left(\frac{dy}{dx}\right)^2 = 8x\left(\frac{dy}{dx}\right)^3 - 27x$$

**11.** **(a, b)**

**(a)** The given equation is $ax^2 + by^2 = 1$.

Differentiating we get, $2ax + 2by\frac{dy}{dx} = 0$

$$\Rightarrow ax + by\frac{dy}{dx} = 0 \qquad \text{....(1)}$$

Differentiating again, $a + b\left(y\frac{d^2y}{dx^2} + \left(\frac{dy}{dx}\right)^2\right) = 0$, ...(2)

From eqs. (1) and (2), we get

$$a = -\frac{by}{x}\frac{dy}{dx} = -b\left(y\frac{d^2y}{dx^2} + \left(\frac{dy}{dx}\right)^2\right)$$

$$\Rightarrow xy\frac{d^2y}{dx^2} + x\left(\frac{dy}{dx}\right)^2 - y\frac{dy}{dx} = 0$$

**(b)** The equation of such a parabola is

$$y^2 = l(x+h) \qquad \text{...(i)}$$

where $l$ and h are arbitrary constants. Differentiating (i) we get

$$2y\frac{dy}{dx} = l \qquad \text{…(ii)}$$

Differentiating again,

$$2y\frac{d^2y}{dx^2} + 2\left(\frac{dy}{dx}\right)^2 = 0 \Rightarrow y\frac{d^2y}{dx^2} + \left(\frac{dy}{dx}\right)^2 = 0$$

**12.** **(a, c)** $2yy_1 = 2c \Rightarrow c = yy_1$

Elimanating, c we get,

$$y^2 = 2yy_1(x + \sqrt{yy_1}) \text{ or } (y - 2xy_1)^2 = 4yy_1^3$$

It involves only Ist order derivative, its order is 1 but its degree is 3 as $y_1^3$ is there.

**13.** **(a)** Differentiating the equation, we get $\frac{dy}{dx} = c$.

So, eliminating $c$ we get

$$y = x\frac{dy}{dx} + \left(\frac{dy}{dx}\right)^2 - 3\left(\frac{dy}{dx}\right)^{3/2} + 2.$$

Clearly its order is 1 and removing the fractional power, it will result into 4th degree.

**14.** **(d)** Order is 2 but degree can not be determine because the equation is not expressible as polynomial.

**15.** **(c)** The equation can be written as $y = a\cos(x+b) + ce^x$

**16.** **A→r; B→q; C→r; D→q**

**(A)** The general equation of all such conic is $ax^2 + 2hxy + by^2 = 1$, which has three arbitrary constants. **(r)**

(B) The general equation of all such circles is
$(x - h)^2 + (y - k)^2 = a^2$, which has two arbitrary
constants. **(q)**

(C) The general equation of all such parabolas is
$x = ay^2 + by + c$, which has three arbitrary constants. **(r)**

(D) The general equation of all such conics is
$ax^2 + by^2 = 1$, which has two arbitrary constants. **(q)**

**17.** $A \to p,s,t;\ B \to r,s,t;\ C \to q,r$

(A) $\because\ y = a\left(\dfrac{1-\cos 2x}{2}\right) + b\left(\dfrac{1+\cos 2x}{2}\right)$

$$+ c\sin 2x + d\cos 2x$$

$$= A + B\sin 2x + C\cos 2x$$

$$\therefore\ \frac{dy}{dx} = 2B\cos 2x - 2C\sin 2x \qquad ...(i)$$

$$\Rightarrow\ \frac{d^2 y}{dx^2} = -4B\sin 2x - 4C\cos 2x$$

$$\Rightarrow\ \frac{d^3 y}{dx^3} = -8B\cos 2x + 8C\sin 2x$$

$$= -4\frac{dy}{dx} \qquad \text{[From eq. (i)]}$$

$$\Rightarrow\ \frac{d^3 y}{dx^3} + 4\frac{dy}{dx} = 0$$

$$\therefore\ O = 3,\ D = 1$$
$$O + 2D = 5,\ O^D + D^O = 4,\ 2^O + 3^D = 8 + 3 = 11\ \textbf{(p,s,t)}$$

(B) $\because\ y = (c_1 + c_2)\sin(x + c_3) - c_4 e^{c_5 + c_6 . e^x}$

or $\quad y = A\sin(x + B) + Ce^6 \qquad ...(i)$

$$\therefore\ \frac{dy}{dx} = A\cos(x + B) + Ce^x \qquad ...(ii)$$

Subtracting eq. (i) from eq. (ii), then

$$\frac{dy}{dx} - y = A\cos(x + B) - A\sin(x + B) \qquad ...(iii)$$

$$\frac{d^2 y}{dx^2} - \frac{dy}{dx} = -A\sin(x + B) - A\cos(x + B)$$

$$= -\left(\frac{dy}{dx} - y\right) \qquad \text{[from eq. (iii)]}$$

$$\frac{d^3 y}{dx^3} - \frac{d^2 y}{dx^2} + \frac{dy}{dx} - y = 0$$

$$O = 3,\ D = 1$$

$$O + 2D = 5,\ O^D + D^O = 4,\ 2^O + 3^D = 11\ \textbf{(r, s, t)}$$

(C) Put $x = \tan\theta,\ y = \tan\phi$

Then, $(\sec\theta + \sec\phi) = A(\tan\theta\sec\phi + \tan\phi\sec\theta)$

$$\Rightarrow\ \left(\frac{\cos\theta + \cos\phi}{\cos\theta\cos\phi}\right) = A\left(\frac{\sin\theta + \sin\phi}{\cos\theta\cos\phi}\right)$$

$$\Rightarrow\ 2\cos\left(\frac{\theta+\phi}{2}\right)\cos\left(\frac{\theta-\phi}{2}\right) = A.2\sin\left(\frac{\theta+\phi}{2}\right)\cos\left(\frac{\theta-\phi}{2}\right)$$

$$\Rightarrow\ \cot\left(\frac{\theta+\phi}{2}\right) = A$$

$$\Rightarrow\ \frac{\theta+\phi}{2} = \cot^{-1} A$$

$$\Rightarrow\ \theta + \phi = 2\cot^{-1} A$$

$$\Rightarrow\ \tan^{-1} x + \tan^{-1} y = 2\cot^{-1} A$$

or $\quad \dfrac{1}{(1+x^2)} + \dfrac{1}{(1+y^2)}\dfrac{dy}{dx} = 0$

$$\therefore\ O = 1,\ D = 1$$
Then $O = D$ and $2O + 3D = 5$ **(q, r)**

**18. (b)** Centre of hyperbola is $(1, 0)$.

Equation of hyperbola is $\dfrac{(x-1)^2}{a^2} - \dfrac{y^2}{a^2} = 1$

**19. (a)** $y = x\dfrac{dy}{dx} + \sqrt{1 + \left(\dfrac{dy}{dx}\right)^2}$ becomes

$$(x^2 - 1)\left(\frac{dy}{dx}\right)^2 - 2xy\frac{dy}{dx} + (y^2 - 1) = 0,$$

when expressed as a polynomial in derivatives.

**20. (d)** Equation of parabola will be $y^2 = a(x - 1)$

$$\Rightarrow 2y\frac{dy}{dx} = a \ \Rightarrow \text{D.E. is } y = 2\frac{dy}{dx}(x - 1)$$

$$\Rightarrow \text{Degree of this D.E. is } 1.$$

**21.** 6

$y = e^{4x} + 2e^{-x}\ ;\ y_1 = 4e^{4x} - 2e^{-x}$
$y_2 = 16e^{4x} + 2e^{-x}\ ;\ y_3 = 64e^{4x} - 2e^{-x}$
Now, $y_3 - 13y_1 = (64e^{4x} - 2e^{-x}) - 13(4e^{4x} - 2e^{-x})$
$$= 12e^{4x} + 24e^{-x}$$
$$= 12(e^{4x} + 2e^{-x}) = 12y$$

$$\therefore\ \frac{y_3 - 13y_1}{y} = 12$$

Thus, $\dfrac{K}{2} = 6$

**22.** 3

Equation $(x - a)^2 + y^2 = (x - b)^2$
$[S = (a, 0)\ ;\ D : x = b\,]$
$y^2 = (b^2 - a^2) + 2x(a - b)$

differentiate twice to get $y\dfrac{d^2 y}{dx^2} + \left[\dfrac{dy}{dx}\right]^2 = 0\ ;$

$$y\frac{d^2 y}{dx^x} + \left(\frac{dy}{dx}\right)^2 = 0$$

Thus $O = 2,\ D = 1$

**1.** **(a).** $y^2 = t$ ; $2y\dfrac{dy}{dx} = \dfrac{dt}{dx}$ ; Hence the differential equation

becomes $\left(e^{x^2} + e^t\right)\dfrac{dt}{dx} + 2\,e^{x^2}(x\,t - x) = 0$

$e^{x^2} + e^t + 2\,e^{x^2}\cdot x(t-1)\dfrac{dx}{dt} = 0$

put $e^{x^2} = z$ ; $e^{x^2}\cdot 2x\dfrac{dx}{dt} = \dfrac{dz}{dt}$

$z + e^t + \dfrac{dz}{dt}(t-1) = 0$

$\dfrac{dz}{dt} + \dfrac{z}{(t-1)} = -\dfrac{e^t}{(t-1)}$ ;

I.F. $= e^{\int \frac{dt}{t-1}} = e^{\ln(t-1)} = t-1$

$z(t-1) = -\int (e^t)\,dt$

$z(t-1) = -e^t + C$

$e^{x^2}(y^2-1) = -e^{y^2} + C$

$e^{x^2}(y^2-1) + e^{y^2} = C$ .

**2.** **(a).** Put $x^2 y^2 = z$

Given $x^2.2y\dfrac{dy}{dx} + y^2.2x = \tan(x^2 y^2)$

$\dfrac{d}{dx}(x^2 y^2) = \tan(x^2 y^2)$ put $x^2 y^2 = z$

Now given expression transforms to $\dfrac{dz}{dx} = \tan z$

$\therefore \int dx = \int \cot z\,dz$

$x = \ln(\sin z) + C$

when $x = 1$ , $y = \sqrt{\dfrac{\pi}{2}} \Rightarrow z = \dfrac{\pi}{2} \Rightarrow C = 1$

$\therefore x = \ln \sin(x^2 y^2) + 1$

$\therefore \ln \sin(x^2 y^2) = x - 1$

$\sin(x^2 y^2) = e^{x-1}$

**3.** **(a).** $\dfrac{dy}{dx} + y\,\phi'(x) = \phi(x).\phi'(x)$

I.F. $= e^{\int \phi'(x)\,dx} = e^{\phi(x)}$

hence $y.e^{\phi(x)} = \int e^{\phi(x)}.\phi(x).\phi'(x)\,dx = \int e^t.t\,dt$

where $\phi(x) = t$
$= te^t - e^t + C = \phi(x).e^{\phi(x)} - e^{\phi(x)} + C$
$\therefore y = ce^{-\phi(x)} + \phi(x) - 1$

**4.** **(a)** $x^2 = e^{\left(\frac{x}{y}\right)^{-1}\left(\frac{dy}{dx}\right)}$

$x^2 = e^{\left(\frac{y}{x}\right)\left(\frac{dy}{dx}\right)}$ or $\ln x^2 = \dfrac{y}{x}\dfrac{dy}{dx}$

or $\int x \ln x^2\,dx = \int y\,dy$
$x^2 = t \Rightarrow 2x\,dx = dt$

$\dfrac{1}{2}\int \ln t\,dt = \dfrac{y^2}{2}$

$c + t \ln t - t = y^2$ or $y^2 = x^2(\ln x^2 - 1) + c$

**5.** **(c)** $(1+y^2)\,dx + (1+x^2)\,dy = 0$

$\Rightarrow \dfrac{dx}{1+x^2} + \dfrac{dy}{1+y^2} = 0$

On integration, we get
$\tan^{-1}x + \tan^{-1}y = \tan^{-1}C$

$\Rightarrow \dfrac{x+y}{1-xy} = C \Rightarrow x+y = C(1-xy)$

**6.** **(b)** The differential equation is

$$\dfrac{d^2 y}{dx^2} = 1 + \sin x \qquad\qquad ....(i)$$

Integrating we get $\dfrac{dy}{dx} = x - \cos x + c \qquad ....(ii)$

When $x = 0$, $\dfrac{dy}{dx} = 0 \Rightarrow c = 1$

$\therefore$ Equation (ii) is $\dfrac{dy}{dx} = x - \cos x + 1$

Integrating again, we get $y = \dfrac{x^2}{2} - \sin x + x + d$ ...(iii)

When $x = 0$, $y = 0 \Rightarrow d = 0$

$\therefore$ The particular solution is $y = \dfrac{x^2}{2} + x - \sin x$

**7.** **(c)** $x(1+y^2)^{1/2}\,dx + y(1+x^2)^{1/2}\,dy = 0$

$\Rightarrow \dfrac{xdx}{(1+x^2)^{1/2}} + \dfrac{ydy}{(1+y^2)^{1/2}} = 0$

Integrating we get

$2\sqrt{1+x^2} + 2\sqrt{1+y^2} = 2C$

or $(1+x^2)^{1/2} + (1+y^2)^{1/2} = C$

**8.** **(a,b,c,d)** Solving for $\dfrac{dy}{dx}$, we obtain

$\dfrac{dy}{dx} = \dfrac{-2y\cot x \pm \sqrt{4y^2\cot^2 x + 4y^2}}{2}$

$= y(-\cot x \pm \operatorname{cosec} x)$

Thus, we have $\dfrac{dy}{y} = (-\cot x + \operatorname{cosec} x)dx$

$\Rightarrow \ln y = -\ln \sin x + \ln \tan\dfrac{x}{2} + \ln c$

$\Rightarrow y = \dfrac{c\tan\dfrac{x}{2}}{\sin x} = \dfrac{c}{2\cos^2\dfrac{x}{2}} = \dfrac{c}{1+\cos x}$

Also, solving $\dfrac{dy}{y} = -(\cot x + \operatorname{cosec} x)\,dx$, we get

$y = \dfrac{c}{1-\cos x} \Rightarrow x = 2\sin^{-1}\sqrt{\dfrac{c}{2y}}$

**9.** **(a,b)** Rewriting the given equation, we get

$\dfrac{dy}{dx} = x(e^{(n-1)y} - 1)$

$\Rightarrow \dfrac{dy}{e^{(n-1)y} - 1} = x\,dx$

$\Rightarrow \dfrac{1}{n-1}\int \dfrac{(n-1)e^{(n-1)y}}{(e^{(n-1)y}-1)e^{(n-1)y}}dy = \dfrac{x^2}{2} + c$

$\Rightarrow \dfrac{1}{n-1}\int \dfrac{du}{u(u-1)} = \dfrac{x^2}{2} + c$ (Where $u = e^{(n-1)y}$)

$\Rightarrow \dfrac{1}{n-1}\log\dfrac{u-1}{u} = \dfrac{x^2}{2} + c$

$\Rightarrow \dfrac{1}{n-1}\log\left(\dfrac{e^{(n-1)y}-1}{e^{(n-1)y}}\right) = \dfrac{x^2}{2} + c$

$\Rightarrow e^{(n-1)y} = Ce^{(n-1)y+(n-1)x^2/2} + 1$

**10.** **(a,c)** We have

$\int (by+k)\,dy = \int (ax+h)\,dx$

or $\dfrac{by^2}{2} + ky = \dfrac{ax^2}{2} + hx + c$

Clearly for $\qquad a = -2,\, b = 0$

and for $\qquad a = 0,\, b = 2$

It represents a parabola ($\because y = ax^2 + bx + c$ and $x = ay^2 + by + c$ represent their respective parabolas.)

**11.** **(a)** The general solution will be obtained by replacing $p$ by $c$, where $c$ is an arbitrary constant. So, the solution is $y = cx + \log c$.

**12.** **(c)** Putting $\dfrac{dy}{dx} = p$ the equation becomes $y = xp + p^2$, which is the Clairut's equation. So the solution is obtained by replacing $p$ by $c$, so $y = cx + c^2$, where $c$ is the arbitrary constant.

Singular form is $x + f'(p) = 0 \Rightarrow x + 2p = 0$

Therefore $p = -\dfrac{x}{2}$ putting in the given equation,

We get $y = x\left(-\dfrac{x}{2}\right) + \dfrac{x^2}{4} \Rightarrow y = -\dfrac{x^2}{4}$

**13.** **(c)** Put $x^2 = u$ and $y^2 = v$, then $\dfrac{dy}{dx} = \dfrac{x}{y}\left(\dfrac{dv}{du}\right)$

The equation then becomes,

$x^2\left(y - \dfrac{x^2}{y}\dfrac{dv}{du}\right) = y\cdot\dfrac{x^2}{y^2}\left(\dfrac{dv}{du}\right)^2 \Rightarrow y^2 - x^2\dfrac{dv}{du} = \left(\dfrac{dv}{du}\right)^2$

or $v = u\dfrac{dv}{du} + \left(\dfrac{dv}{du}\right)^2$

which is Clairut's equation in variables u and v, so the solution is $v = uc + c^2 \Rightarrow y^2 = cx^2 + c^2$.

**14.** **A→ r, t; B→ p, q; C→ s**

(A) The given equation can be written as

$\left(\dfrac{dy}{dx} - e^{-x}\right)\left(\dfrac{dy}{dx} - e^{x}\right) = 0$

$\Rightarrow \dfrac{dy}{dx} - e^{-x} = 0$ or $\dfrac{dy}{dx} - e^{x} = 0$

$\Rightarrow dy - e^{-x}\,dx = 0$ or $dy - e^{x}\,dx = 0$

$\Rightarrow y + e^{-x} = c$ **(r)** or $y - e^{x} = c$ **(t)**

(B) $(x+y+1)\,dy = dx$

Put $\qquad x + y + 1 = v$

Then, $dx + dy = dv$

and the given equation reduces to

$\qquad v(dv - dx) = dx$

$\Rightarrow dx = \dfrac{vdv}{v+1} = \left(1 - \dfrac{1}{v+1}\right)dv$

$\Rightarrow\ x + C = v - \ln(v+1)$

$\Rightarrow\ \ln(v+1) = v - x - C$

or $\ln(x+y+2) = y + 1 - C = y + c$ **(q)**

Also, $x + y + 2 = e^{y+C} = e^y \cdot e^C = ce^y$ **(p)**

(C)　$\dfrac{dy}{dx} + \dfrac{(x+y+2)}{(2x+2y-1)} = 0$

Put $x + y = v$

$\therefore\quad 1 + \dfrac{dy}{dx} = \dfrac{dv}{dx}$, then

$\dfrac{dv}{dx} - 1 + \dfrac{v+2}{2v-1} = 0$

$\Rightarrow\quad \dfrac{dv}{dx} - \dfrac{(v-3)}{(2v-1)} = 0$

or　$\dfrac{(2v-1)}{(v-3)} dv = dx$

$\Rightarrow\quad \left(2 + \dfrac{5}{v-3)}\right) dv = dx$

$\Rightarrow 2v + 5\ln(v-3) = x + c$

or $2(x+y) + 5\ln(x+y-3) = x + c$

or $2(x+y+2) + 5\ln(x+y-3) = x + c_1$

$\hspace{5cm} = x + c$ **(s)**

**15.　(a)**　Let $c_1 + c_2 + c_3 e^{c_4} = A$ (constant)

Then, $y = Ax \Rightarrow \dfrac{dy}{dx} = A$

or $y = x\dfrac{dy}{dx}$

or $x\dfrac{dy}{dx} = y$

**16.　1**

Equation of normal is

$Y - y = -\dfrac{1}{m}(X - x)$

$X + mY - (x + my) = 0 \hspace{2cm} \ldots\ldots(1)$

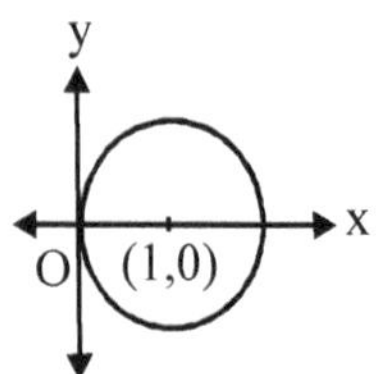

Perpendicular distance from $(0, 0)$ to eq. (1) is

$\left|\dfrac{x+my}{\sqrt{1+m^2}}\right| = |y|$

$\Rightarrow (x+my)^2 = y^2(1+m^2)$

$\Rightarrow x^2 + 2mxy = y^2$

$\Rightarrow m = \dfrac{y^2 - x^2}{2x} \Rightarrow 2xy\dfrac{dy}{dx} = y^2 - x^2 \ldots\ldots\ldots(2)$

Put $y^2 = t \Rightarrow 2y\dfrac{dy}{dx} = \dfrac{dt}{dx}$

$\therefore$ Equation (2) becomes

$x\dfrac{dt}{dx} = t - x^2 \Rightarrow \dfrac{dt}{dx} - \dfrac{1}{x}t = -x$

$\therefore$ I.F. $= e^{-\int \frac{1}{x}dx} = e^{-\ln x} = \dfrac{1}{x}$

Now general solution is given by

$t\left(\dfrac{1}{x}\right) = -x + C \Rightarrow y^2\left(\dfrac{1}{x}\right) = -x + C$

As $(1, 1)$ satisfy it, so $C = 2$

$\Rightarrow y^2 = -x^2 + 2x$

$\Rightarrow x^2 + y^2 - 2x = 0$

Hence, required area $= \dfrac{k\pi}{2}$

$\therefore k = 1$

**17.　9**

Let at any instant $t$, $x$ be the vol. of water in the reservoir $A$ and $y$ of that in $B$.

Then $\dfrac{dx}{dt} \propto x \Rightarrow \dfrac{dx}{dt} = k_1 x$

and $\dfrac{dy}{dt} \propto y \Rightarrow \dfrac{dy}{dt} = k_2 y$

$\Rightarrow \dfrac{dx}{x} = k_1 dt \Rightarrow \log x = k_1 t + C_1$

and $\dfrac{dy}{y} = k_2 dt \Rightarrow \log y = k_2 t + C_2$

$\Rightarrow x = e^{k_1 t} \cdot e^{C_1} \hspace{3cm} \ldots(1)$

and $y = e^{k_2 t} \cdot e^{C_2} \hspace{3cm} \ldots(2)$

Now at $t = 0$, $x = 2y$ i.e., $\dfrac{x}{y} = 2$

$\therefore$　From (1) and (2) we get

$\dfrac{e^{C_1}}{e^{C_2}} = 2 \hspace{3cm} \ldots(3)$

Also at $t = 1$, $x = \dfrac{3}{2}y$, i.e., $\dfrac{x}{y} = \dfrac{3}{2}$

$\Rightarrow \dfrac{e^{k_1}}{e^{k_2}}\dfrac{e^{C_1}}{e^{C_2}} = \dfrac{3}{2} \Rightarrow e^{k_1 - k_2} = \dfrac{3}{4}$

Let at $t = T$, $x = y$, i.e. $\dfrac{x}{y} = 1$

then $\dfrac{e^{k_1 T}}{e^{k_2 T}} \dfrac{e^{C_1}}{e^{C_2}} = 1 \Rightarrow e^{(k_1 - k_2)T} . 2 = 1$

$\Rightarrow \left(\dfrac{3}{4}\right)^T = \dfrac{1}{2}$

Taking log on both sides, we get

$$T \log\left(\dfrac{3}{4}\right) = \log\left(\dfrac{1}{2}\right)$$

$\Rightarrow T = \dfrac{-\log 2}{-\log \dfrac{4}{3}} \Rightarrow T = \left(\dfrac{\log 2}{\log \dfrac{4}{3}}\right)$

Thus, $P = 2, Q = 4, R = 3$
$\Rightarrow P + Q + R = 2 + 4 + 3 = 9.$

**18.**    **4**

Let $f(x) = y$

$\therefore \dfrac{dy}{dx} + y = 4xe^{-x} \cdot \sin 2x$    (linear differenial equation)

I.F. $e^x$

$ye^x = 4 \int \underset{I}{x} \; \underset{II}{\sin 2x} \; dx$

$ye^x = 4\left[x\left(-\dfrac{\cos 2x}{2}\right) + \dfrac{1}{2}\int \cos 2x \, dx\right]$

$ye^x = 4\left[-\dfrac{x\cos 2x}{2} + \dfrac{\sin 2x}{4}\right] + C$

$ye^x = (\sin 2x - 2x\cos 2x) + C$

$f(0) = 0 \Rightarrow C = 0$

$\therefore y = e^{-x}(\sin 2x - 2x\cos 2x)$

**now** $f(k\pi) = e^{-k\pi}(\sin 2k\pi - 2k\pi \cdot \cos 2k\pi)$

$\qquad = e^{-k\pi}(0 - 2k\pi)$

$f(k\pi) = -2\pi(k \cdot e^{-k\pi})$

$\sum f(k\pi) = -2\pi \underbrace{\sum_{k=1}^{\infty} k e^{-k\pi}}_{S}$

$S \quad = 1 \cdot e^{-\pi} + 2e^{-2\pi} + 3e^{-3\pi} + \dots\dots + \infty$

$S \, e^{-\pi} = \qquad\quad + e^{-2\pi} + 2e^{-3\pi} + \dots\dots + \infty$

---

$S(1 - e^{-\pi}) = e^{-\pi} + e^{-2\pi} + e^{-3\pi} + \dots\dots \infty$

$S(1 - e^{-\pi}) = \dfrac{e^{-\pi}}{1 - e^{-\pi}} = \dfrac{1}{e^{\pi} - 1}$

$S = \dfrac{1}{(e^{\pi} - 1)(1 - e^{-\pi})} = \dfrac{e^{\pi}}{(e^{\pi} - 1)^2}$

$\displaystyle \lim_{x \to \infty} \sum_{n=1} f(k\pi) = \dfrac{-2\pi e^{\pi}}{(e^{\pi} - 1)^2}$

Thus $A + B = 2 + 2 = 4$

**19.**    **5**

Put $x = r\sec\theta$ and $y = r\tan\theta$ So, $x^2 - y^2 = r^2$ ........(1)

and $\sin\theta = \dfrac{y}{x}$         ........(2)

then differentiating (1) we get, $2\,xdx - 2ydy = 2rdr$

or $xdx - ydy = rdr$       ...... (3)

and differentiaing (2) we get, $\dfrac{xdy - ydx}{x^2} = \cos\theta d\theta$

or $xdy - ydx = x^2 \cos\theta d\theta$

$= r^2 \sec^2\theta \cos\theta d\theta = r^2 \sec\theta d\theta$   ........(4)

Substituting values from (3) and (4) in the given differetial equation, we get

$$\dfrac{rdr}{r^2 \sec^2\theta d\theta} = \sqrt{\left(\dfrac{1 + r^2}{r^2}\right)} = \dfrac{\sqrt{1 + r^2}}{r}$$

or $\dfrac{dr}{\sqrt{(1 + r^2)}} = \sec\theta d\theta$

Intergrating both sides,

$\ell n(r + \sqrt{(1 + r^2)}) = \ell n(\sec\theta + \tan\theta) + \ell n\, c$

Where $c$ is an arbitrary constant.

or $(r + \sqrt{(1 + r^2)}) = c(\sec\theta + \tan\theta)$

or $(\sqrt{(x^2 - y^2)} + \sqrt{(1 + x^2 - y^2)}) = c\left(\dfrac{x + y}{\sqrt{(x^2 - y^2)}}\right)$

Thus $f(x, y) = x^2 - y^2$

$\Rightarrow f(3, 2) = 3^2 - 2^2 = 9 - 4 = 5.$

**1.** **(c)** The given equation is reduced to

$$x = e^{xy(dy/dx)}$$

$$\Rightarrow\ \ln x = xy\frac{dy}{dx} \Rightarrow \int y\,dy = \int \frac{1}{x}\ln x\,dx$$

$$\Rightarrow\ \frac{y^2}{2} = \frac{(\ln x)^2}{2} + C$$

$$\Rightarrow\ y = \pm\sqrt{(\ln x)^2} + C = \pm\ell n\,x + c$$

**2.** **(c)** Given, equation of normal at $P(1,1)$ is $ay + x = a + 1$

$$\therefore \text{ Slope of tangent at } P = a \Rightarrow \left(\frac{dy}{dx}\right)_{(1,1)} = a \text{ Given}$$

$$\frac{dy}{dx} \propto y \Rightarrow \frac{dy}{dx} = ky \Rightarrow \left(\frac{dy}{dx}\right)_{(1,1)} = k = a$$

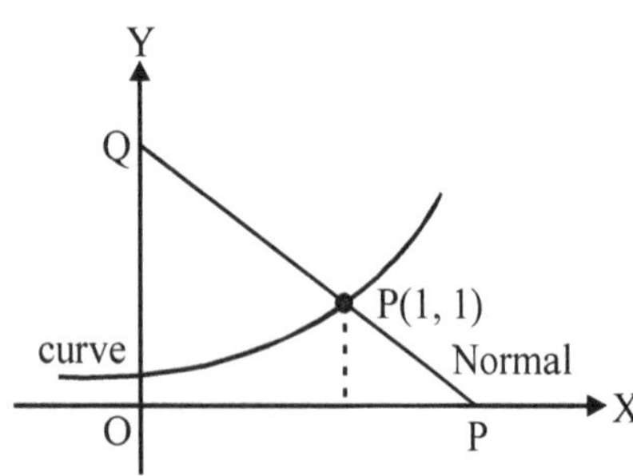


$$\frac{dy}{dx} = ay \Rightarrow \frac{dy}{y} = a\,dx \text{ (variable being separated)}$$

$$\Rightarrow \ln y = ax + c$$

It is passing through (1, 1) then $c = -a \Rightarrow$ equation of the curve is $y = e^{a(x-1)}$

**3.** **(a)** Let $P$ be $(x, y)$. $C$ is $\left(x + y\frac{dy}{dx}, 0\right)$ and $B$ is

$\left(0, y - x\frac{dy}{dx}\right)$. Centre of the circle through $O, C, P$ and $B$ has its centre at the mid-point of $BC$. Let it be $(\alpha, \beta)$ then

$$2\alpha = x + y\frac{dy}{dx} \text{ and } 2\beta = y - x\frac{dy}{dx}$$

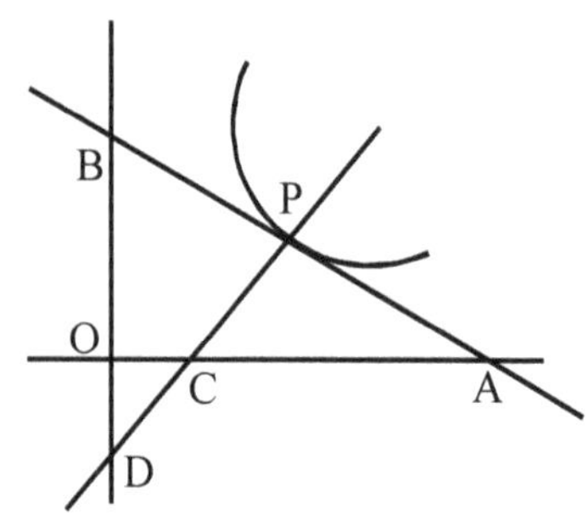


Now, $(\alpha, \beta)$ lies on $y = x$

so, $y - x\dfrac{dy}{dx} = x + y\dfrac{dy}{dx} \Rightarrow \dfrac{dy}{dx} = \dfrac{y-x}{x+y}$

**4.** **(c)** Given differential equation can be written as

$$\frac{dy}{dx} + \frac{1}{x\ln x}y = \frac{2}{x}, \text{ which is linear in y}$$

$$\text{Integrating factor } = e^{\int \frac{1}{x\ln x}dx} = e^{\ln(\ln x)} = \ln x$$

**5.** **(a)** Given equation is linear.

$$\text{I.F.} = e^{\int 2\tan x\,dx} = e^{2\log\sec x} = \sec^2 x$$

$\therefore$ Its solution is

$$y \times \sec^2 x = \int \sec^2 x \sin x\,dx$$

$$\Rightarrow y\sec^2 x = \int \sec x \tan x\,dx$$

$$\Rightarrow y\sec^2 x = \sec x + c$$

**6.** **(c)** Given equation is $\dfrac{dy}{dx} - 2y = 3e^x$,

which is linear.

$$\text{I.F} = e^{\int -2dx} = e^{-2x}$$

$\therefore$ Its solution is $y \times e^{-2x} = \int 3e^x \times e^{-2x}dx$

$$\Rightarrow y \times e^{-2x} = 3\int e^{-x}dx$$

$$\Rightarrow y\,e^{-2x} = -3\,e^{-x} + c \qquad\qquad ........(i)$$

Putting $x = 0$ and $y = 0$ in (i), we get

$$c = 3$$

$$\therefore\quad y\,e^{-2x} = -3\,e^{-x} + 3$$

$$\Rightarrow y = 3\,(e^{2x} - e^x)$$

$$\Rightarrow y(0.2) = 3\,(e^{0.4} - e^{0.2})$$

$$= 3\,(1.4918 - 1.2214) = 3\,(0.2704) = 0.8112$$

**7. (b)** Given equation is $\dfrac{dy}{dx} = \dfrac{y^2 - x^2}{2xy}$

This is homogeneous.

Putting $y = vx$ and $\dfrac{dy}{dx} = v + x\dfrac{dv}{dx}$, we get,

$$v + x\dfrac{dv}{dx} = \dfrac{v^2 - 1}{2v}$$

$$\Rightarrow \quad x\dfrac{dv}{dx} = \dfrac{-1 - v^2}{2v}$$

$$\therefore \quad \int \dfrac{2v}{1 + v^2}\,dv = -\int \dfrac{1}{x}\,dx$$

$$\Rightarrow \quad \log(1 + v^2) = -\log x + \log c$$

$$\Rightarrow \quad x\left(1 + \dfrac{y^2}{x^2}\right) = c$$

$$\Rightarrow \quad x^2 + y^2 = cx \qquad \ldots\ldots\ldots\ldots(i)$$

Putting $x = 1$ and $y = 0$, we get, $c = 1$

$\therefore \quad x^2 + y^2 = x$ i.e. $x^2 + y^2 - x = 0$.

**8. (c)** We have, $\dfrac{dy}{dx} = \dfrac{ax + by - a}{bx + ay - b}$

Put $x = X + h$ and $y = Y + k$

So that $\dfrac{dY}{dX} = \dfrac{dy}{dx}$

$$\therefore \quad \dfrac{dY}{dX} = \dfrac{aX + bY + ah + bk - a}{bX + aY + bh + ak - b}$$

Choosing h and k such that

$$ah + bk - a = 0$$
and $$bh + ak - b = 0$$

Solving, $\dfrac{h}{a^2 - b^2} = \dfrac{k}{0} = \dfrac{1}{a^2 - b^2}$

i.e. $h = 1, k = 0$

The reduced equation is

$$\dfrac{dY}{dX} = \dfrac{aX + bY}{bX + aY}$$

Which is homogenous,

Put $Y = VX$

So that $\dfrac{dY}{dX} = V + X\dfrac{dV}{dX}$

Hence $V + X\dfrac{dV}{dx} = \dfrac{a + bV}{b + aV}$

$$\Rightarrow X\dfrac{dV}{dX} = \dfrac{a + bV}{b + aV} - V = \dfrac{a(1 - V^2)}{b + aV}$$

$$\Rightarrow \dfrac{dX}{X} = \dfrac{b + aV}{a(1 - V^2)}\,dV$$

$$\Rightarrow \dfrac{dX}{X} + \dfrac{b + aV}{a(V^2 - 1)}\,dV = 0$$

$$\Rightarrow \dfrac{dX}{X} + \dfrac{b}{a}\cdot\dfrac{1}{V^2 - 1}\,dV + \dfrac{1}{2}\cdot\dfrac{2V}{V^2 - 1}\,dV = 0$$

Integrating,

$$\log X + \dfrac{b}{2a}\,\log\left|\dfrac{V - 1}{V + 1}\right| + \dfrac{1}{2}\log|V^2 - 1| = \dfrac{1}{2}\log C'$$

$$\Rightarrow X^2(V - 1)^{\frac{a+b}{a}}\cdot(V + 1)^{\frac{a-b}{a}} = C'$$

$$\Rightarrow X^2\left(\dfrac{Y}{X} - 1\right)^{\frac{a+b}{a}}\cdot\left(\dfrac{Y}{X} + 1\right)^{\frac{a-b}{a}} = C'$$

$$\Rightarrow (Y - X)^{\frac{a+b}{a}}\cdot(Y + X)^{\frac{a-b}{a}} = C'$$

$$\Rightarrow (Y - X)^{a+b}(Y + X)^{a-b} = (C')^a = C \text{ (say)}$$

$$\Rightarrow (y - x + 1)^{a+b}\cdot(y + x - 1)^{a-b} = C$$

**9. (a,b)** $y' = -\dfrac{y(y + x)}{x^2}$ is a homogeneous differential equation.

With $y = vx$ it reduces to $\dfrac{v'}{v(v + 2)} = \dfrac{-1}{x}$ which on

integration gives $\dfrac{v}{v + 2}x^2 = k$. Substituting $v = \dfrac{y}{x}$ we

get the solution as $x^2y = k(y + 2x)$ or $y(kx^2 - 1) = 2x$, in

case $\dfrac{1}{k}$ is taken instead of k.

**10. (c,d)** If we write the equation in the form

$$y' = -\dfrac{y^5 + yx^4}{x^5}$$ is a homogeneous equation. Instead,

written in the form $\dfrac{1}{y^5}\cdot\dfrac{dy}{dx} + \dfrac{1}{xy^4} = -\dfrac{1}{x^5}$ it is of

Bernoulli's type and can be transformed to a linear differential equation by the substitution

$$z = \dfrac{1}{y^4}$$

**11. (a,b)** If $y = f(x)$ is the curve, $Y - y = f'(x)(X - x)$ is the

equation of the tangent at $(x, y)$, with $f'(x) = \dfrac{dy}{dx}$.

Putting $X = 0$, the initial ordinate of the tangent is therefore $y - xf'(x)$. The subnormal at this point is given

by $y\dfrac{dy}{dx}$, so we have

$$y\frac{dy}{dx} = y - x\frac{dy}{dx} \Rightarrow \frac{dy}{dx} = \frac{y}{x+y}$$

This is a homogeneous equation and, by rewriting it as

$$\frac{dx}{dy} = \frac{x+y}{y} = \frac{x}{y}+1 \Rightarrow \frac{dx}{dy} - \frac{x}{y} = 1$$

we see that it is also a linear equation.

**12. (a)** Let P $(x, y)$ be any point on the curve. Length of intercept on y-axis by any tangent at

$$P(x,y) = OT = y - x\frac{dy}{dx}$$

$\therefore$ Area of trapezium OLPTO $= \dfrac{1}{2}(PL + OT)OL$

$$= \frac{1}{2}\left(y + y - x\frac{dy}{dx}\right)x = \frac{1}{2}\left(2y - x\frac{dy}{dx}\right)x$$

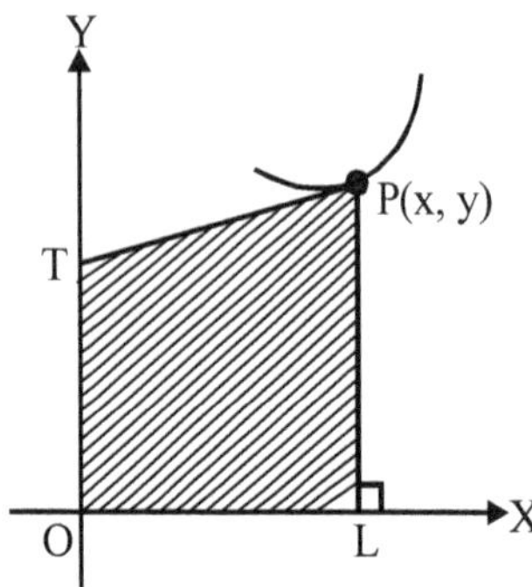

According to question, area of trapezium

$$OLPTO = \frac{1}{2}x^2$$

i.e., $\dfrac{1}{2}\left(2y - x\dfrac{dy}{dx}\right)x = \pm\dfrac{1}{2}x^2$

$$\Rightarrow 2y - x\frac{dy}{dx} = \pm x \quad \text{or} \quad \frac{dy}{dx} - \frac{2y}{x} = \pm 1$$

Which is linear differential equation and

$$\text{I.F.} = e^{-2\ln x} = \frac{1}{x^2}$$

$\therefore$ The solution is $\dfrac{y}{x^2} = \int \pm\dfrac{1}{x^2}\,dx + c = \pm\dfrac{1}{x} + c$

$$\therefore \qquad y = cx^2 \pm x$$

Where c is an arbitrary constant.

**13. (a, b)** Put $x = y = 0$ we get g $(0) = 0$. Differentiating the given equation with respect to x, we get

$$g'(x+y)\left[1+\frac{dy}{dx}\right]$$

$$= e^y g'(x) + e^y g(x)\frac{dy}{dx} + e^x g(y) + e^x g'(y)\frac{dy}{dx}$$

$\because$ x and y are independent so $\dfrac{dy}{dx} = 0$ and we have

$$g'(x+y) = e^y g'(x) + e^x g(y)$$

Putting, $x = 0$, $g'(y) = 2e^y + g(y)$

or $g'(y) - g(y) = 2e^y$

which is a linear differential equation, I.F. $= e^{-y}$

$\therefore$ Solution is $g(y)e^{-y} = \int 2\,dy + C \Rightarrow g(y)e^{-y} = 2y + C$

$\because g(0) = 0 + C \Rightarrow C = 0$

$\therefore g(y) = 2ye^y$ or $g(x) = 2xe^x$

Now, $g'(x) = 2(x+1)e^x > 0 \,\forall\, x > -1$. Also, g(x) attains

absolute minimum at $x = -1$ and $f(-1) = \dfrac{-2}{e}$

$\therefore$ Range $= \left[-\dfrac{2}{e}, \infty\right)$.

Further $g''(x) = 2(x+2)e^x > 0\ \forall x$ and $\lim\limits_{x\to 0}\dfrac{g(x)}{x} = 2$

**14. (b)** $\because \dfrac{dT}{dt} = -k(T - 290)$

$$\Rightarrow \frac{dT}{(T-290)} = -k\,dt$$

$\Rightarrow \ln(T - 290) = -kt + c$ \hfill ...(i)

Initially, T = 370 K and t = 0, then

$\qquad \ln(80) = c$

From eq. (i), $\ln(T - 290) = -kt + \ln 80$

$$\ln\left(\frac{T-290}{80}\right) = -kt$$

$$\Rightarrow \frac{T-290}{80} = e^{-kt}$$

or $\qquad T = 290 + 80e^{-kt}$

**15. (d)** For t = 10 min, T = 330 K

Then, $330 - 290 = 80e^{-10k}$

$$\Rightarrow \frac{1}{2} = e^{-10k}$$

$$\Rightarrow e^{10k} = 2$$

$$\Rightarrow 10k = \ln 2$$

Or $\qquad k = \dfrac{\ln 2}{10}$

**16. (a)**

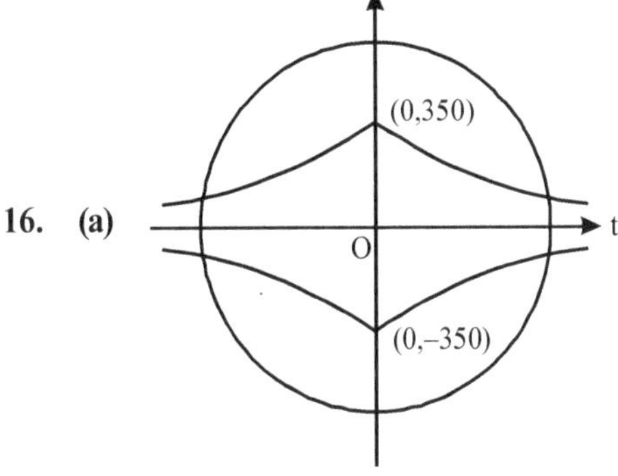



∴ Time can never be negative.
Number of solutions = 2.

**17.** $A \to r; B \to q; C \to p; D \to s$

**(A)** $\dfrac{dy}{dx} = -2x(y-1) \Rightarrow \dfrac{dy}{dx} + 2xy = 2x$

I.F $= e^{x^2}$

∴ solution $y \cdot e^{x^2} = \int 2x \cdot e^{x^2} dx$

$\Rightarrow y \cdot e^{x^2} = e^{x^2} = c$

Given $y(0) = 1 \Rightarrow c = 0$

∴ $y \cdot e^{x^2} = e^{x^2} \Rightarrow y = 1 \Rightarrow y(x) = 1$ **(r)**

**(B)** Required area $= \displaystyle\int_{-\infty}^{1} e^{y/3} dy$

$= \left[ 3e^{y/3} \right]_{-\infty}^{1} = 3e^{1/3}$ **(q)**

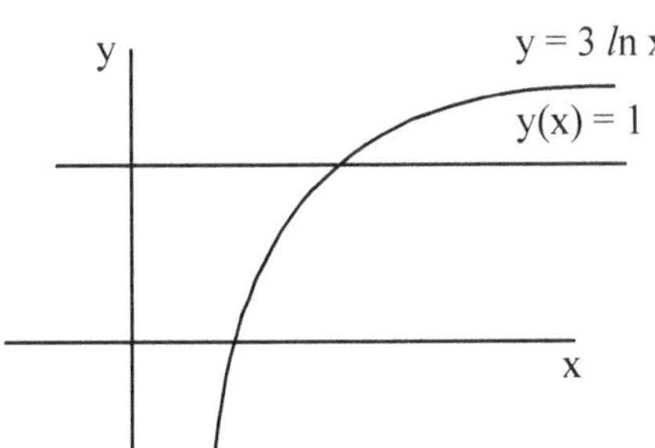



**(C)** Required area $= \displaystyle\int_{-\infty}^{1} x^2 dx + 1 = \dfrac{1}{3} + 1 = \dfrac{4}{3}$ **(p)**

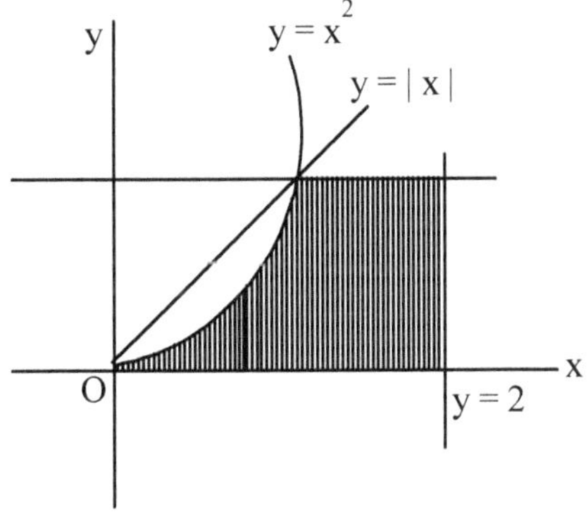



**(D)** $h(x) = y(x)$

$\Rightarrow e^x = 1 \Rightarrow x = 0$ is the only solution. **(s)**

**18. (a)** $\dfrac{dy}{dx} = \dfrac{2xy}{x^2 + y^2}$ ...(1)

This is homogenous differential equation
Put $\quad y = vx$

From (1) $\dfrac{dy}{dx} = v + x \dfrac{dv}{dx}$

$\Rightarrow v + \dfrac{xdv}{dx} = \dfrac{2x^2 v}{x^2(1 + v^2)}$

$x \dfrac{dv}{dx} = \dfrac{2v}{1 + v^2} - v = \dfrac{2v - v - v^3}{1 + v^2} = \dfrac{v(1 - v^2)}{1 + v^2}$

$\displaystyle\int \dfrac{(1 + v^2)}{v(1 - v^2)} dv = \int \dfrac{dx}{x}$

**19. (a)** I.F. $= e^{\int 1.dx} = e^x$

**20. 2**

The given differential equation is

$\dfrac{dy}{dt} - \dfrac{t}{1+t} y = \dfrac{1}{1+t}$

I.F. $= e^{-\int \frac{t}{1+t} dt} = e^{-\int \left(1 - \frac{1}{1+t}\right) dt} = e^{-(t - \log(1+t))}$

$= e^{-t} \cdot e^{\log(1+t)} = (1+t)e^{-t}$

∴ Solution is

$y.e^{-t}(1+t) = \displaystyle\int \dfrac{1}{(1+t)} e^{-t}(1+t)\, dt + C$

$\Rightarrow y.e^{-t}(1+t) = -e^{-t} + C$

$\Rightarrow y = -\dfrac{1}{1+t} + \dfrac{Ce^t}{1+t}$

Given that $y(0) = -1$

$\Rightarrow -1 = -1 + C \Rightarrow C = 0$

∴ $y = -\dfrac{1}{1+t}$

∴ $y(1) = -\dfrac{1}{1+1} = -\dfrac{1}{2}$

Thus, P = 2

**21. 3**

The given D.E. is $(x^2 + y^2)dy = xy\, dx$ s.t. $y(1) = 1$
and $y(x_0) = e$
The given eq$^n$ can be written as

$\dfrac{dy}{dx} = \dfrac{xy}{x^2 + y^2}$

Put $y = vx$ to get $v + x\dfrac{dv}{dx} = \dfrac{v}{1+v^2}$

$\Rightarrow \quad x\dfrac{dv}{dx} = \dfrac{-v^3}{1+v^2}$

$\Rightarrow \quad \displaystyle\int \dfrac{1+v^2}{v^3}dv + \int \dfrac{dx}{x} = 0$

$\Rightarrow \quad -\dfrac{1}{2v^2} + \log|v| + \log|x| = C$

$\Rightarrow \quad \log y = C + \dfrac{x^2}{2y^2} \quad (\text{using } v = y/x)$

Also, $y(1) = 1$

$\Rightarrow \quad \log 1 = C + \dfrac{1}{2} \Rightarrow C = -\dfrac{1}{2}$

$\therefore \quad \log y = \dfrac{x^2 - y^2}{2y^2}$

But given $y(x_0) = e$

$\Rightarrow \quad \log e = \dfrac{x_0^2 - e^2}{2e^2} \Rightarrow x_0^2 = 3e^2 \Rightarrow x_0 = e\sqrt{3}$

**22. 1**

$y = u^m \Rightarrow \dfrac{dy}{du} = m\, u^{m-1}$

Hence $2\,x^4 . u^m . m\, u^{m-1} . \dfrac{du}{dx} + u^{4m} = 4\,x^6$.

$\dfrac{du}{dx} = \dfrac{4\,x^6 - u^{4m}}{2m\ x^4\ u^{2m-1}}$

$\Rightarrow 4m = 6 \text{ and } 2m - 1 = 2 \Rightarrow m = 3/2$

Thus, $A - B = 3 - 2 = 1$

**23. 4**

Given equation is linear

I.F. $= e^{\int \cot x\, dx} = e^{\log \sin x} = \sin x$

$\therefore$ Its solution is $y \sin x = \displaystyle\int 2\sin x \cos x \ dx$

$\Rightarrow \quad y \sin x = -\dfrac{\cos 2x}{2} + c$

$\Rightarrow \quad 2y \sin x + \cos 2x = 2c \qquad \text{.........(i)}$

Putting $x = \dfrac{\pi}{6}$ and $y = \dfrac{3}{2}$, we get $c = 1$

$\therefore \quad 2y \sin x + \cos 2x = 2.$
Thus, $A + B = 2 + 2 = 4$

**24. 3**

Given equation is $\dfrac{dy}{dx} = \dfrac{xy + y^2}{x^2 - xy}$

This is homogeneous.

Putting $y = vx$ and $\dfrac{dy}{dx} = v + x\dfrac{dv}{dx}$, we get,

$v + x\dfrac{dv}{dx} = \dfrac{v + v^2}{1 - v}$

$\Rightarrow \quad x\dfrac{dv}{dx} = \dfrac{2v}{1-v}$

$\therefore \quad \displaystyle\int \dfrac{(1-v)}{v^2}dv = \int \dfrac{2}{x}dx$

$\Rightarrow \quad \displaystyle\int \left(\dfrac{1}{v^2} - \dfrac{1}{v}\right)dv = \int \dfrac{2}{x}dx$

$\Rightarrow -\dfrac{1}{v} - \log v = 2 \log x + \log c$

$\Rightarrow -\dfrac{x}{y} = \log(cxy)$

$\Rightarrow cxy = e^{-x/y}$

$\Rightarrow xy = \dfrac{1}{c} e^{-x/y} = k e^{-x/y}.$

Thus $P = 1, Q = 1, R = 1$
$\Rightarrow P + Q + R = 1 + 1 + 1 = 3$

**1.** **(a)** Again he cannot be drained at the 13th round if A gets at least 2 heads in the first 10 rounds. To finish at the 14th round, A must get exactly 2 heads in the first 10 rounds and a tail on all the rounds from 11th to 14th.

This has a probability $^{10}C_2 \, p^2 \, q^{12}$.

Therefore required probability

$= q^{10} + {}^{10}C_1 \, pq^{11} + {}^{10}C_2 \, p^2 q^{12} = q^{10} (1 + 10 \, pq + 45 p^2 q^2)$

**2.** **(a)** $P\left(B / A \cup B'\right) = \dfrac{P\left(B \cap (A \cup B')\right)}{P(A \cup B')}$

$= \dfrac{P(A \cap B)}{P(A) + P(B') - P(A \cap B')} = \dfrac{P(A) - P(A \cap B')}{0.7 + 0.6 - 0.5}$

$= \dfrac{0.7 - 0.5}{0.8} = \dfrac{1}{4}$

**3.** **(b)** The number of heads that they can get is either 0 or 1 or 2 or 3.

∴ the required probability

$= \ ^4C_0 \left(\dfrac{1}{2}\right)^0 \left(\dfrac{1}{2}\right)^4 \cdot {}^3C_0 \left(\dfrac{1}{2}\right)^0 \left(\dfrac{1}{2}\right)^3$

$+ {}^4C_1 \left(\dfrac{1}{2}\right) \left(\dfrac{1}{2}\right)^3 \cdot {}^3C_1 \left(\dfrac{1}{2}\right) \left(\dfrac{1}{2}\right)^2$

$+ {}^4C_2 \left(\dfrac{1}{2}\right)^2 \left(\dfrac{1}{2}\right)^2 \cdot {}^3C_2 \left(\dfrac{1}{2}\right)^2 \left(\dfrac{1}{2}\right)$

$+ {}^4C_3 \left(\dfrac{1}{2}\right)^3 \left(\dfrac{1}{2}\right) \cdot {}^3C_3 \left(\dfrac{1}{2}\right)^3 \left(\dfrac{1}{2}\right)^0$

$= \dfrac{1}{2^7} (1 + 12 + 18 + 4) = \dfrac{35}{128}.$

**4.** **(a)** It is given that

$P(A \cap B) = p$ and $P(A' \cap B) + P(A \cap B') = q$.

Therefore, since

$P(A' \cap B) = P(B) - P(A \cap B)$, we get

$q = P(B) - P(A \cap B) + P(A) - P(A \cap B)$

$\Rightarrow P(A) + P(B) = q + 2p$

$\Rightarrow P(A') + P(B') = 1 - P(A) + 1 - P(B)$

$\qquad\qquad\qquad = 2 - q - 2p,$

showing that (b) is correct. The answer (c) is also correct because

$P(A \cap B \mid A \cup B) = \dfrac{P[(A \cap B) \cap (A \cup B)]}{P(A \cup B)}$

$= \dfrac{P(A \cap B)}{P(A \cup B)} = \dfrac{P(A \cap B)}{P(A) + P(B) - P(A \cap B)}$

$= \dfrac{p}{q + 2p - p} = \dfrac{p}{p + q}$

Finally, (d) is correct because

$P(A' \cap B') = 1 - P(A \cup B)$

$= 1 - [P(A) + P(B) - P(A \cap B)]$

$= 1 - (q + 2p - p) = 1 - p - q$

**5.** **(a)** $P(E) = 1/6$, $P(E') = 5/6$, $P(A/E) = 3/4$ and $P(A/E') = 1/4$.

By Bayes' Theorem

$P(E/A) = \dfrac{(1/6)(3/4)}{(1/6)(3/4) + (5/6)(1/4)} = \dfrac{3}{8}$

**6.** **(d)** We have, $P(X \ge a) = \displaystyle\sum_{x=a}^{\infty} pq^x = \dfrac{pq^a}{1-q} = q^a$

Next, $P(X \ge a + b \mid X \ge a)$

$= \dfrac{P[(X \ge a + b) \cap (X \ge a)]}{P(X \ge a)}$

$= \dfrac{P(X \ge a + b)}{P(X \ge a)} = \dfrac{q^{a+b}}{q^a} = q^b = P(X \ge b)$

Also,

$P[X = a + b / X \ge a] = \dfrac{P(X = a + b) \cap P(X \ge a)}{P(X \ge a)}$

$= \dfrac{P(X = a + b)}{P(X \ge a)} = \dfrac{pq^{a+b}}{q^a} = pq^b = P(X = b)$

**7.** **(a)** $A_1$ be the event that black card is lost, $A_2$ be the event that red card is lost and let A denote occurrence of first 13 cards which are examined are found to be all red. Then we have to find $P(A_1/A)$

$P(A_1) = P(A_2) = 1/2$

Also $P\left(\dfrac{A}{A_1}\right) = \dfrac{^{26}C_{13}}{^{51}C_{13}}$

and $P\left(\dfrac{A}{A_2}\right) = \dfrac{^{25}C_{13}}{^{51}C_{13}}$

Then by Baye's rule, $P\left(\dfrac{A_1}{A}\right)$

$$= \dfrac{P(A_1).P\left(\dfrac{A}{A_1}\right)}{P(A_1).P\left(\dfrac{A}{A_1}\right) + P(A_2).P\left(\dfrac{A}{A_2}\right)}$$

$$= \dfrac{\dfrac{1}{2}.\dfrac{{}^{26}C_{13}}{{}^{51}C_{13}}}{\dfrac{1}{2}.\dfrac{{}^{26}C_{13}}{{}^{51}C_{13}} + \dfrac{1}{2}.\dfrac{{}^{25}C_{13}}{{}^{51}C_{13}}}$$

$$= \dfrac{{}^{26}C_{13}}{{}^{26}C_{13} + {}^{25}C_{13}} = \dfrac{2}{2+1} = \dfrac{2}{3}.$$

**8.** **(a)** Let $E_1$, $E_2$, $E_3$ be the events of drawing a bolt produced by machine A, B and C respectively. Let D be the event of drawing a defective bolt. We have

$$P(E_1) = \dfrac{60}{100}, \;\; P(E_2) = \dfrac{25}{100}, \;\; P(E_3) = \dfrac{15}{100}$$

$$P(D/E_1) = \dfrac{1}{100}, \;\; P(D/E_2) = \dfrac{2}{100}, \;\; P(D/E_3) = \dfrac{1}{100}$$

The events $E_1$, $E_2$ and $E_3$ are mutually exclusive and exhaustive.

P (defective bolt is produced by A)

$$= P(E_1/D) = \dfrac{P(E_1)P(D/E_1)}{P(E_1)P(D/E_1) + P(E_2)P(D/E_2) + P(E_3)P(D/E_3)}$$

$$= \dfrac{\dfrac{60}{100} \times \dfrac{1}{100}}{\dfrac{60}{100} \times \dfrac{1}{100} + \dfrac{25}{100} \times \dfrac{2}{100} + \dfrac{15}{100} \times \dfrac{1}{100}}$$

$$= \dfrac{60}{125} = \dfrac{12}{25} \;\; \text{[Using Baye's Theorem]}$$

Similarly, P (defective bolt is produced by B)

$$= P(E_2/D) = \dfrac{P(E_2)P(D/E_2)}{P(E_1)P(D/E_1) + P(E_2)P(D/E_2) + P(E_3)P(D/E_3)}$$

$$= \dfrac{\dfrac{25}{100} \times \dfrac{2}{100}}{\dfrac{60}{100} \times \dfrac{1}{100} + \dfrac{25}{100} \times \dfrac{2}{100} + \dfrac{15}{100} \times \dfrac{1}{100}} = \dfrac{50}{125} = \dfrac{10}{25}$$

P(defective bolt is produced by C)

$$= P(E_3/D) = \dfrac{P(E_3)P(D/E_3)}{P(E_1)P(D/E_1) + P(E_2)P(D/E_2) + P(E_3)P(D/E_3)}$$

$$= \dfrac{\dfrac{15}{100} \times \dfrac{1}{100}}{\dfrac{60}{100} \times \dfrac{1}{100} + \dfrac{25}{100} \times \dfrac{2}{100} + \dfrac{15}{100} \times \dfrac{1}{100}} = \dfrac{15}{125} = \dfrac{3}{25}$$

Form the above three probabilities it is clear that the machine A has the highest probability of producing a defective bolt.

**9.** **(a,b,d)**

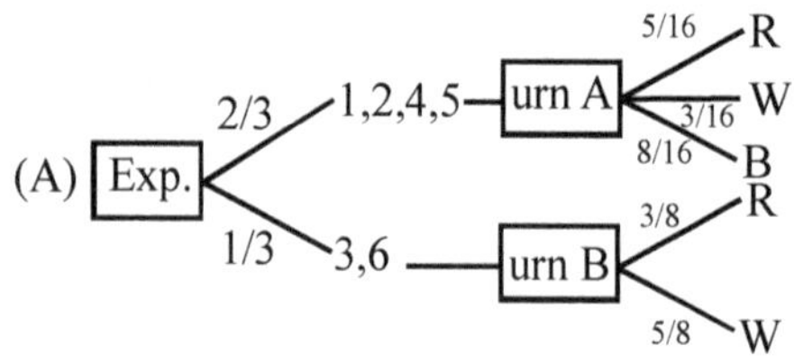


| Urn | Red Marbles | Red Marbles | Red Marbles |
|---|---|---|---|
| A | 5 | 3 | 8 |
| B | 3 | 5 | 0 |

$$P(E_1) = P(R) = \left(\dfrac{2}{3}\right)\left(\dfrac{5}{16}\right) + \left(\dfrac{1}{3}\right)\left(\dfrac{3}{8}\right) = \dfrac{10}{48} + \dfrac{6}{48} = \dfrac{1}{3}$$

$$P(E_2) = P(W) = \left(\dfrac{2}{3}\right)\left(\dfrac{3}{16}\right) + \left(\dfrac{1}{3}\right)\left(\dfrac{5}{8}\right) = \dfrac{6}{48} + \dfrac{10}{48} = \dfrac{1}{3}$$

$$P(E_3) = P(B) = \left(\dfrac{2}{3}\right)\left(\dfrac{8}{16}\right) = \dfrac{1}{3}$$

$\Rightarrow E_1$, $E_2$, $E_3$ can equiprobable $\Rightarrow$ (a)

(c) Let A : event that urn A is chosen

$$P(A/R) = \dfrac{P(A \cap R)}{P(R)} = \dfrac{\left(\dfrac{2}{3}\right)\left(\dfrac{5}{16}\right)}{\dfrac{1}{3}} = \left(\dfrac{10}{48}\right)(3) = \dfrac{5}{8}$$

$\Rightarrow$ (c) is incorrect

(d) $P(A/W) = \dfrac{P(A \cap W)}{P(W)} = \dfrac{\left(\dfrac{2}{3}\right)\left(\dfrac{3}{16}\right)}{\dfrac{1}{3}} = \left(\dfrac{6}{48}\right)(3) = \dfrac{3}{8}$

$$P \,(\text{face five/W}) = \left(\dfrac{3}{8}\right)\left(\dfrac{1}{4}\right) = \dfrac{3}{32}$$

$\Rightarrow$ (d) is correct

**10.** **(a, c)**

(a) $P(A/B) = \dfrac{P(A \cap B)}{P(B)} = \dfrac{P(A) + P(B) - P(A \cup B) - 1}{P(B)}$

$$\geq \dfrac{P(A) + P(B) - 1}{P(B)}, \;\; P(B) \neq 0$$

(c) $P(A \cup B) = 1 - P((A \cup B)^c) = 1 - P(A^c \cap B^c)$

$$= 1 - P(A^c).P(B^c)$$

if A and B are independent.

**11.** **(b,c, d)** Since E and F are independent

$\therefore \quad P(E \cap F) = P(E).P(F) \qquad ...(1)$

Now, $P(E \cap F^c) = P(E) - P(E \cap F)$

$= P(E) - P(E)\,P(F)$       [Using (1)]

$= P(E)\,[1 - P(F)]$

$= P(E)\,P(F^c)$

$\therefore$ E and $F^c$ are independent.

Again $P(E^c \cap F^c) = P(E \cup F)^c = 1 - P(E \cup F)$

$= 1 - P(E) - P(F) + P(E \cap F)$

$= 1 - P(E) - P(F) + P(E)\,P(F)$

$= (1 - P(E))\,(1 - P(F)) = P(E^c)\,P(F^c)$

$\therefore$ $E^c$ and $F^c$ are independent.

Also $P(E/F) + P(E^c/F)$

$$= \frac{P(E \cap F)}{P(F)} + \frac{P(E^c \cap F)}{P(F)}$$

$$= \frac{P(E)\,P(F) + P(E^c)\,P(F)}{P(F)}$$

$$= \frac{P(F)[P(E) + P(E^c)]}{P(F)} = 1$$

**12.** **(b,c,d)** $P(E_1) = P(E_2) = \dfrac{\dfrac{10!}{2!}}{\dfrac{11!}{2!2!}} = \dfrac{2}{11}$

$\Rightarrow$ (a) is not correct

$P(E_1 \cap E_2) =$ Probability that two I's are together and

two B's are together $= \dfrac{\dfrac{9!}{}}{\dfrac{11!}{2!2!}} = \dfrac{2}{55}$

$\Rightarrow$ (b) is correct.

$P(E_1 \cup E_2) = P(E_1) + P(E_2) - P(E_2 \cap E_2)$

$= \dfrac{2}{11} + \dfrac{2}{11} - \dfrac{2}{55} = \dfrac{18}{55} \Rightarrow$ (c) is correct.

$P(E_1/E_2) = \dfrac{P(E_1 \cap E_2)}{P(E_2)} = \dfrac{\dfrac{2}{55}}{\dfrac{2}{11}} = \dfrac{1}{5}$

$\Rightarrow$ (d) is correct.

**13.** **(b)** $P(u_i) \propto i \Rightarrow P(u_i) = ki,$ But $\sum P(u_i) = 1$

$\Rightarrow \quad \sum ki = 1 \Rightarrow k \sum i = 1 \Rightarrow k = \dfrac{2}{n\,(n+1)}$

$\Rightarrow \quad P(u_i) = \dfrac{2i}{n(n+1)}$

By total prob. theorem $P(w) = \displaystyle\sum_{i=1}^{n} P(u_i)\,P(w/u_i)$

$$= \sum_{i=1}^{n} \frac{2i}{n(n+1)} \times \frac{i}{n+1}$$

$$= \frac{2}{n(n+1)^2} \cdot \frac{n(n+1)(2n+1)}{6} = \frac{2n+1}{3n+3}$$

$\therefore \quad \displaystyle\lim_{n\to\infty} P(w) = \lim_{n\to\infty} \frac{2n+1}{3n+3} = \lim_{n\to\infty} \frac{2+1/n}{3+3/n} = \frac{2}{3}$

**14.** **(a)** $P(u_i) = c$

Using Baye's thm.

$$P(u_n/w) = \frac{P(w/u_n)\,P(u_n)}{\displaystyle\sum_{i=1}^{n} P(w/u_i)\,P(u_i)}$$

$$= \frac{c \times \dfrac{n}{n+1}}{c\left[\dfrac{1}{n+1} + \dfrac{2}{n+1} + \ldots + \dfrac{n}{n+1}\right]}$$

$$= \frac{n}{n+1} \times \frac{n+1}{\dfrac{n(n+1)}{2}} = \frac{2}{n+1}$$

**15.** **(b)** $P(w/E) = \dfrac{P(w \cap E)}{P(E)}$

$$= \frac{\dfrac{1}{n}\times\dfrac{2}{n+1} + \dfrac{1}{n}\times\dfrac{4}{n+1} + \dfrac{1}{n}\times\dfrac{6}{n+1} + \ldots + \dfrac{1}{n}\times\dfrac{n}{n+1}}{\dfrac{1}{n} + \dfrac{1}{n} + \ldots + \dfrac{1}{n}\left(\dfrac{n}{2}\ \text{times}\right)}$$

$$= \frac{\dfrac{1}{n}\times\dfrac{2}{n+1}\left[1+2+3\ldots+\dfrac{n}{2}\right]}{\dfrac{1}{n}\times\dfrac{n}{2}}\ \text{(n being even)}$$

$$= \frac{2}{n(n+1)}\left[\frac{n}{2}\left(\frac{n}{2}+1\right)\right]$$

$$= \frac{n+2}{2(n+1)}$$

**16.** **A$\to$q; B$\to$p; C$\to$r; D$\to$q**

Let $E_i$ denotes the event that the bag contains i black and $(12 - i)$ white balls $(i = 0, 1, 2, \ldots\ldots\ldots, 12)$ and A denotes the event that the four balls drawn are all black. Then

$$P(E_i) = \frac{1}{13}\ (i - 0, 1, 2, \ldots\ldots, 12)$$

$$P\!\left(\frac{A}{E_i}\right) = 0\ \text{ for } i = 0, 1, 2, 3$$

$$P\left(\frac{A}{E_i}\right) = \frac{{}^iC_4}{{}^{12}C_4} \quad \text{for } i \geq 4$$

(A) $\quad P(A) = \sum_{i=0}^{12} P(E_i)\, P\left(\frac{A}{E_i}\right)$

$$= \frac{1}{13} \times \frac{1}{{}^{12}C_4}\left[{}^4C_4 + {}^5C_4 + \ldots + {}^{12}C_4\right]$$

$$= \frac{{}^{13}C_5}{13 \times {}^{12}C_4} = \frac{1}{5}$$

(B) $\quad$ Clearly, $P\left(\frac{A}{E_{10}}\right) = \frac{{}^{10}C_4}{{}^{12}C_4} = \frac{14}{33}$

(C) $\quad$ By Baye's theorem,

$$P\left(\frac{E_{10}}{A}\right) = \frac{P(E_{10})\, P\left(\dfrac{A}{E_{10}}\right)}{P(A)} = \frac{\dfrac{1}{13} \times \dfrac{14}{33}}{\dfrac{1}{5}} = \frac{70}{429}$$

(D) $\quad$ Let B denotes the probability of drawing 2 white and 2 black balls then

$$P\left(\frac{B}{E_i}\right) = 0 \quad \text{if } i = 0, 1 \text{ or } 11, 12$$

$$P\left(\frac{B}{E_i}\right) = \frac{{}^iC_2 \times {}^{12-i}C_2}{{}^{12}C_4} \quad \text{for } i = 2, 3, \ldots, 10$$

$$\therefore\ P(B) = \sum_{i=0}^{12} P(E_i)\, P\left(\frac{B}{E_i}\right)$$

$$= \frac{1}{13} \times \frac{1}{{}^{12}C_4}\left[{}^2C_2 \times {}^{10}C_2 + {}^3C_2 \times {}^9C_2 + \ldots + {}^{10}C_2 \times {}^2C_2\right]$$

$$= \frac{1}{13} \times \frac{1}{{}^{12}C_4}\left[2\left\{{}^2C_2 \times {}^{10}C_2 + {}^3C_2 \times {}^9C_2\right.\right.$$

$$\left.\left. + \ldots + {}^5C_2 \times {}^7C_2\right\} + {}^6C_2 \times {}^6C_2\right]$$

$$= \frac{1}{13} \times \frac{1}{495}(1287) = \frac{1}{5}$$

**17.** $\quad$ **A→q; B→r; C→s; D→r**

We have, $P(A \cap B) = P(A)\,.\,P(B) = \dfrac{1}{12}$

(A) $\quad P(A \cup B) = P(A) + P(B) - P(A \cap B) = \dfrac{1}{3} + \dfrac{1}{4} - \dfrac{1}{12} = \dfrac{1}{2}$

(B) $\quad P\left(\dfrac{A}{A \cup B}\right) = \dfrac{P(A \cap (A \cup B))}{P(A \cup B)} = \dfrac{P(A)}{P(A \cup B)} = \dfrac{2}{3}$

(C) $\quad P\left(\dfrac{B}{A' \cap B'}\right) = \dfrac{P(B \cap (A' \cap B'))}{P(A' \cap B')} = \dfrac{P(\phi)}{P(A' \cap B')} = 0$

(D) $\quad P\left(\dfrac{A'}{B}\right) = \dfrac{P(A' \cap B)}{P(B)} = \dfrac{P(A')\,P(B)}{P(B)} = P(A') = \dfrac{2}{3}$

**18.** $\quad$ **(a)** $\quad$ Statement $-2$ is true as this is the definition of the independent events.

Statement $-1$ is also true, as if events are independent, then $P(A/B) = P(A)$

$$\Rightarrow \frac{P(A \cap B)}{P(B)} = P(A) \Rightarrow P(A \cap B) = P(A)\,.\,P(B)$$

Obviously Statement $-2$ is a correct reasoning of Statement $-1$

**19.** $\quad$ **(d)** $\quad$ We know $P(H_i/E) = \dfrac{P(H_i \cap E)}{P(E)}$

$$= \frac{P(E/H_i)P(H_i)}{P(E)}$$

$$\Rightarrow P(H_i/E)\, P(E) = P(E/H_i)\, P(H_i)$$

$$\Rightarrow P(E) = \frac{P(E/H_i)P(H_i)}{P(H_i/E)}$$

Now given that $0 < P(E) < 1$

$$\Rightarrow\ 0 < \frac{P(E/H_i)P(H_i)}{P(H_i/E)} < 1$$

$\Rightarrow P(E/H_i)\, P(H_i) < P(H_i/E)$

But if $P(H_i \cap E) = 0$ then

$P(H_i/E) = P(E/H_i) = 0$

Then $P(E/H_i)\, P(H_i) < P(H_i/E)$ is not true.

$\therefore\quad$ Statement -1 is not always true.

Also as $H_1, H_2, \ldots H_n$ are mutually exclusive and exhaustive events, therefore $\displaystyle\sum_{i=1}^{n} P(H_i) = 1$.

$\therefore\quad$ Statement -2 is true.

**20.** $\quad$ **6**

$52 \xrightarrow{\text{face card removed}} 40 \xrightarrow{\text{20 drawn randomly}}$

Let

$E_0$ : 20 cards randomly removed has no aces.

$E_1$ : 20 cards randomly removed has exactly one ace.

$E_2$ : 20 cards randomly removed has exactly 2 aces.

$E$ : event that 2 drawn from the remaining 20 cards has both the aces.

$$P(E) = P(E \cap E_0) + P(E \cap E_1) + P(E \cap E_2)$$
$$= P(E_0) \cdot P(E/E_0) + P(E_1) \cdot P(E/E_1) + P(E_2) \cdot P(E/E_2)$$

$$= 40 \begin{cases} 4 \text{ aces} \\ \\ 36 \text{ other} \end{cases}$$

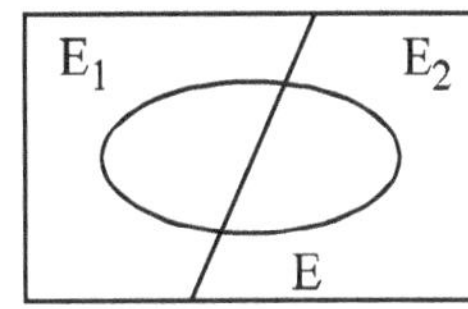

$$= \frac{{}^4C_0 \cdot {}^{36}C_{20}}{{}^{40}C_{20}} \cdot \frac{{}^4C_2}{{}^{20}C_2} + \frac{{}^4C_1 \cdot {}^{36}C_{19}}{{}^{40}C_{20}} \cdot \frac{{}^3C_2}{{}^{20}C_2}$$

$$+ \frac{{}^4C_2 \cdot {}^{36}C_{18}}{{}^{40}C_{20}} \cdot \frac{{}^2C_2}{{}^{20}C_2}$$

$$= \frac{{}^{36}C_{20} \cdot {}^4C_2 + {}^4C_1 \cdot {}^{36}C_{19} \cdot {}^3C_2 + {}^4C_2 \cdot {}^{36}C_{18} \cdot {}^2C_2}{{}^{40}C_{20} \cdot {}^{20}C_2}$$

$$= \frac{6 \cdot {}^{36}C_{20} + 12 \cdot {}^{36}C_{19} + 6 \cdot {}^{36}C_{18}}{{}^{40}C_{20} \cdot {}^{20}C_2}$$

$$= \frac{6[{}^{36}C_{20} + {}^{36}C_{19} + {}^{36}C_{19} + {}^{36}C_{18}]}{{}^{40}C_{20} \cdot {}^{20}C_2}$$

$$= \frac{6({}^{37}C_{20} + {}^{37}C_{19})}{{}^{40}C_{20} \cdot {}^{20}C_2} = \frac{6({}^{38}C_{20})}{{}^{40}C_{20} \cdot {}^{20}C_2} \Rightarrow p = 6$$

**21.   9**

A : red ball is selected
$B_1$ : Face card is drawn
$B_2$ : ace card is drawn
$B_3$ : neither face nor ace is drawn

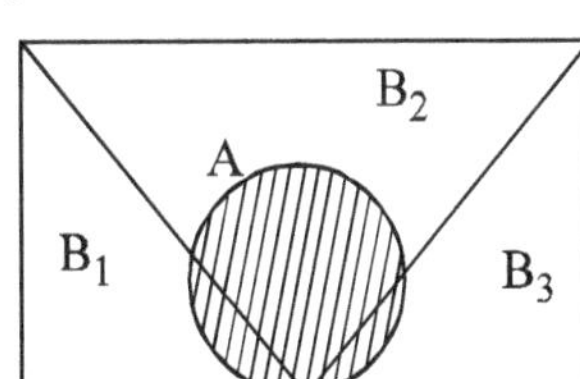

$$P(A) = \frac{12}{52} \cdot \frac{3}{12} + \frac{4}{52} \cdot \frac{8}{12} + \frac{36}{52} \cdot \frac{10}{12} = \frac{107}{156}$$

$$P(B_1/A) = \left(\frac{12}{52} \cdot \frac{3}{12}\right) \cdot \frac{156}{107} = \frac{9}{107}$$

**22.   7**

A = {1801, 1802,....,1899, 1900}
B = {1901, 1902,....,1999, 2000}

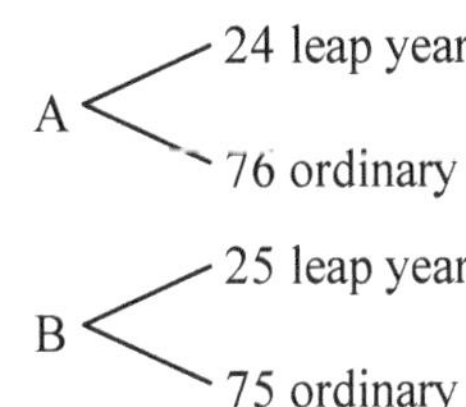


E : randomly chosen year has 53 sundays
$$P(E) = P(E \cap L) + P(E \cap O)$$
$$= P(L) \cdot P(E/L) + P(O) \cdot P(E/O)$$

$$= \frac{1}{2}\left[\frac{24}{100} \cdot \frac{2}{7} + \frac{76}{100} \cdot \frac{1}{7}\right] + \frac{1}{2}\left[\frac{25}{100} \cdot \frac{2}{7} + \frac{75}{100} \cdot \frac{1}{7}\right]$$

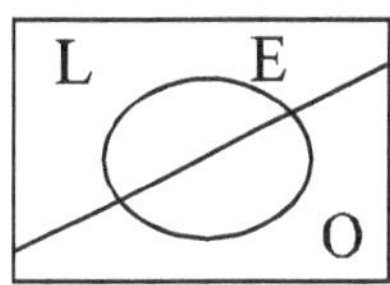

$$= \frac{249}{1400}$$

On comparing the result with given expression, we get
Y = 10 and X = 3
Thus, Y – X = 10 – 3 = 7

**23.   3**

Let E be the event that a television chosen randomly is of standard quality. We have to find

$$P(II/E) = \frac{P(E/II) \cdot P(II)}{P(E/I) \cdot P(I) + P(E/II) \cdot P(II)}$$

$$= \frac{(9/10)(3/10)}{(4/5)(7/10) + (9/10)(3/10)} = \frac{27}{83}$$

Thus $\dfrac{A^3}{B} = \dfrac{27}{83}$

$$\Rightarrow A = 3$$

**24.   2**

Probability that he hits the target
$= 3/4 = P$
Probability that he doesn't hit the target
$= 1 - 3/4 = 1/4 = q$
Required probability = he hits the target 3 times + he hits the target 4 times + he hits the target 5 times

$$= {}^5C_3\left(\frac{3}{4}\right)^3\left(\frac{1}{4}\right)^{5-3} + {}^5C_4\left(\frac{3}{4}\right)^4\left(\frac{1}{4}\right)^{5-4} +$$

$$\qquad\qquad {}^5C_5\left(\frac{3}{4}\right)^5\left(\frac{1}{4}\right)^{5-5}$$

$$= \frac{5 \times 4}{2} \cdot \frac{(3)^3}{(4)^3}\left(\frac{1}{4}\right)^2 + 5 \times \frac{3^4}{4^4} \times \frac{1}{4} + 1 \times \frac{3^5}{4^5} \times 1$$

$$= \frac{918}{4 \times 256} = \frac{459}{512}.$$

$$\Rightarrow \text{Thus } \frac{X}{Y^9} = \frac{459}{2^9}$$

$$\Rightarrow Y = 2$$

**1.** **(a)** $\overrightarrow{AB} = \overrightarrow{OB} - \overrightarrow{OA} = (2\hat{i} + \hat{j} - 2\hat{k})$

$$-(\hat{i} - \hat{j} - 3\hat{k}) = \hat{i} + 2\hat{j} + \hat{k}$$

$$\overrightarrow{AC} = \overrightarrow{OC} - \overrightarrow{OA} = (-5\hat{i} + 2\hat{j} - 6\hat{k})$$

$$-(\hat{i} - \hat{j} - 3\hat{k}) = -6\hat{i} + 3\hat{j} - 3\hat{k}$$

A vector along the bisector of the angle BAC

$$= \frac{\overrightarrow{AB}}{|\overrightarrow{AB}|} + \frac{\overrightarrow{AC}}{|\overrightarrow{AC}|} = \frac{\hat{i} + 2\hat{j} + \hat{k}}{\sqrt{1^2 + 2^2 + 1^2}} + \frac{-6\hat{i} + 3\hat{j} - 3\hat{k}}{\sqrt{(-6)^2 + 3^2 + (-3)^2}}$$

$$= \frac{1}{\sqrt{6}}(\hat{i} + 2\hat{j} + \hat{k}) + \frac{1}{3\sqrt{6}}(-6\hat{i} + 3\hat{j} - 3\hat{k})$$

$$= \frac{1}{3\sqrt{6}}(-3\hat{i} + 9\hat{j}) = \frac{-\hat{i} + 3\hat{j}}{\sqrt{6}}$$

$\therefore$ The unit vector along $AD = \dfrac{-\hat{i} + 3\hat{j}}{\sqrt{10}}$

$\therefore \quad \overrightarrow{AD} = \dfrac{-\hat{i} + 3\hat{j}}{10} AD$

As D is on BC, $\overrightarrow{BD} = t\,\overrightarrow{BC}$

$\therefore \quad \overrightarrow{BA} + \overrightarrow{AD} = t(\overrightarrow{BA} + \overrightarrow{AC})$

or $\quad -\hat{i} - 2\hat{j} - \hat{k} + \dfrac{-\hat{i} + 3\hat{j}}{10} AD$

$$= t\{-\hat{i} - 2\hat{j} - \hat{k} - 6\hat{i} + 3\hat{j} - 3\hat{k}\}$$

$$= t(-7\hat{i} + \hat{j} - 4\hat{k})$$

$$\Rightarrow \quad -1 - \frac{AD}{10} = -7t, \, -2 + \frac{3}{10}AD = t,$$

$$-1 = -4t$$

$\therefore \quad t = 1/4.$

$\therefore \quad -1 - \dfrac{AD}{10} = -\dfrac{7}{4}$ or $\dfrac{AD}{10} = \dfrac{3}{4}$

$\therefore \quad AD = \dfrac{15}{2}.$

**2.** **(b)**

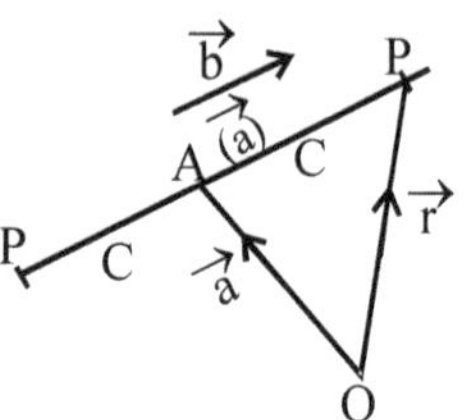


Clearly, $\vec{r} = \vec{a} + \overrightarrow{AP} = \vec{a} \pm 6\dfrac{\vec{b}}{|\vec{b}|}$

**3.** **(a)**

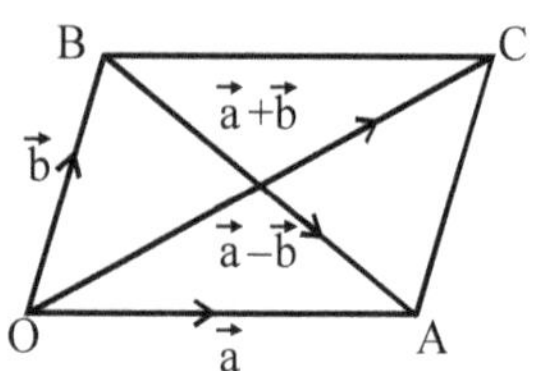


Let $\overrightarrow{OA} = \vec{a}$ and $\overrightarrow{OB} = \vec{b}$.

Complete the parallelogram OACB.

$$\vec{a} + \vec{b} = \overrightarrow{OA} + \overrightarrow{OB} = \overrightarrow{OC} \Rightarrow |\vec{a} + \vec{b}| = OC$$

Again $\vec{a} - \vec{b} = \overrightarrow{OA} - \overrightarrow{OB} = \overrightarrow{BA} \Rightarrow |\vec{a} - \vec{b}| = BA$

Given $|\vec{a} + \vec{b}| = |\vec{a} - \vec{b}| \Rightarrow OC = BA$

$\therefore$ Diagonals of the parallelogram OACB are equal.

$\therefore$ OACB is a rectangle.

$\therefore \quad \vec{a}$ and $\vec{b}$ are adjacent sides of a rectangle.

**4.** **(d)** Let the given position vectors represent points P, Q and R respectively. Then

$$\overrightarrow{PQ} = \text{P.V. of } Q - \text{P.V. of } P$$

$$= (-2\vec{a} + 3\vec{b} + 2\vec{c}) - (\vec{a} - 2\vec{b} + 3\vec{c})$$

$$= -3\vec{a} + 5\vec{b} - \vec{c}$$

$$\overrightarrow{QR} = \text{P.V. of } R - \text{P.V. of } Q$$

$$= (-8\vec{a} + 13\vec{b}) - (-2\vec{a} + 3\vec{b} + 2\vec{c}) = -6\vec{a} + 10\vec{b} - 2\vec{c}$$

$$= 2(-3\vec{a} + 5\vec{b} - \vec{c}) = 2\overrightarrow{PQ}$$

$\therefore \overrightarrow{QR}$ and $\overrightarrow{PQ}$ are collinear vectors.

$\therefore$ P, Q and R are collinear points.

**5. (b)** We know that $\ell^2 + m^2 + n^2 = 1$

$\therefore \cos^2\alpha + \cos^2\beta + \cos^2\gamma = 1$.

Changing cosines into sines, we get

$(1 - \sin^2\alpha) + (1 - \sin^2\beta) + (1 - \sin^2\gamma) = 1$.

$\Rightarrow \sin^2\alpha + \sin^2\beta + \sin^2\gamma = 3 - 1 = 2$

**6. (a)** Here, $\vec{a} = 2p\hat{i} + \hat{j}$. After rotation, let the vectors be

$\vec{b}$ and let the unit vectors along the new axes be $\hat{\alpha}, \hat{\beta}$.

Then $\vec{b} = (p+1)\hat{\alpha} + \hat{\beta}$. But the magnitude of a vector does not change with rotation of axes.

$\therefore |\vec{a}| = |\vec{b}| \Rightarrow \sqrt{(2p)^2 + 1^2} = \sqrt{(p+1)^2 + 1^2}$

$\Rightarrow 4p^2 + 1 = p^2 + 2p + 2$ or $3p^2 - 2p - 1 = 0$

$\therefore p = 1, -\dfrac{1}{3}$

**7. (a,b,c)**

Since E divides BC in the ratio of $2 : 1$

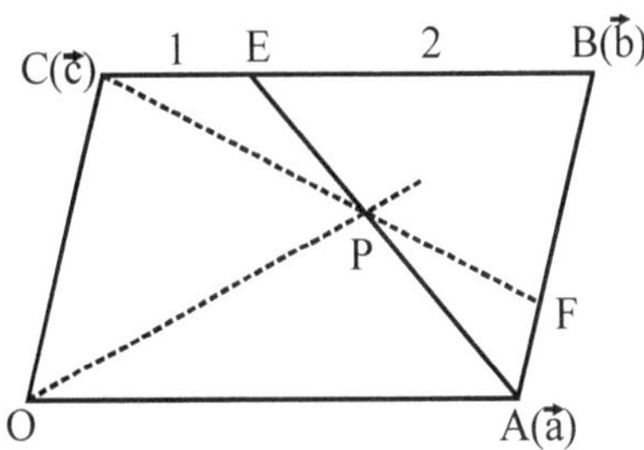


Therefore, position vector of

$E = \dfrac{\vec{b} + 2\vec{c}}{3}$ ........ (i)

But, $\overrightarrow{OA} + \overrightarrow{AB} = \overrightarrow{OB}$

$\Rightarrow \vec{a} + \vec{c} = \vec{b}$ ........ (ii)

$\therefore$ Position vector of $E = \dfrac{\vec{a} + 3\vec{c}}{3}$, by (i) and (ii)

The vector equation of the bisector of $\angle$ AOC is

$\vec{r} = \lambda \left\{ \dfrac{\vec{a}}{|\vec{a}|} + \dfrac{\vec{c}}{|\vec{c}|} \right\}$ ........ (iii)

The vector equation of AE is

$\vec{r} = \vec{a} + \mu \left\{ \dfrac{\vec{a} + 3\vec{c}}{3} - \vec{a} \right\}$

or $\vec{r} = \vec{a} + \mu \left\{ \dfrac{3\vec{c} - 2\vec{a}}{3} \right\}$ ........ (iv)

Lines (iii) and (iv) intersect at P.

$\therefore$ For point P, we must have

$\lambda \left\{ \dfrac{\vec{a}}{|\vec{a}|} + \dfrac{\vec{c}}{|\vec{c}|} \right\} = \vec{a} + \mu \left\{ \dfrac{3\vec{c} - 2\vec{a}}{3} \right\}$

$\Rightarrow \left\{ \dfrac{\lambda}{|\vec{a}|} - 1 + \dfrac{2\mu}{3} \right\} \vec{a} + \left\{ \dfrac{\lambda}{|\vec{c}|} - \mu \right\} \vec{c} = \vec{0}$

$\Rightarrow \dfrac{\lambda}{|\vec{a}|} - 1 + \dfrac{2\mu}{3} = 0$ and $\dfrac{\lambda}{|\vec{c}|} - \mu = 0$

$[\because \ \vec{a}$ and $\vec{c}$ are non-collinear$]$

$\Rightarrow \lambda = \dfrac{3|\vec{a}||\vec{c}|}{3|\vec{c}| + 2|\vec{a}|}$ and $\mu = \dfrac{3|\vec{a}|}{3|\vec{c}| + 2|\vec{a}|}$

Putting the value of $\lambda$ in (iii) or that of $\mu$ in (iv), we obtain the position vector of P as

$\vec{r_1} = \dfrac{3|\vec{a}||\vec{c}|}{3|\vec{c}| + 2|\vec{a}|} \left\{ \dfrac{\vec{a}}{|\vec{a}|} + \dfrac{\vec{c}}{|\vec{c}|} \right\}$

Now vector equation of line CP is

$\vec{r_1} = \vec{c} + \lambda_1 \left\{ \dfrac{3|\vec{a}||\vec{c}|}{3|\vec{c}| + 2|\vec{a}|} \left\{ \dfrac{\vec{a}}{|\vec{a}|} + \dfrac{\vec{c}}{|\vec{c}|} \right\} - \vec{c} \right\}$ ........ (v)

Vector equation of line AB is $\vec{r} = \vec{a} + \lambda_2 \vec{c}$ ........ (vi)

These two lines intersect at F, we must have for F,

$\vec{c} + \lambda_1 \left[ \dfrac{3|\vec{a}||\vec{c}|}{2|\vec{a}| + 3|\vec{c}|} \left\{ \dfrac{\vec{a}}{|\vec{a}|} + \dfrac{\vec{c}}{|\vec{c}|} \right\} - \vec{c} \right] = \vec{a} + \lambda_2 \vec{c}$

$\Rightarrow \left[ \dfrac{3|\vec{a}||\vec{c}|\lambda_1}{3|\vec{c}| + 2|\vec{a}|} \dfrac{1}{|\vec{a}|} - 1 \right] \vec{a}$

$\qquad + \left[ 1 + \dfrac{3\lambda_1|\vec{a}|}{3|\vec{c}| + 2|\vec{a}|} - \lambda_1 - \lambda_2 \right] \vec{c} = 0$

$\Rightarrow \dfrac{3|\vec{c}|\lambda_1}{3|\vec{c}| + 2|\vec{a}|} - 1 = 0$ and

$\qquad 1 + \dfrac{3\lambda_1|\vec{a}|}{3|\vec{c}| + 2|\vec{a}|} - \lambda_1 - \lambda_2 = 0$

$[\because \ \vec{a}$ and $\vec{c}$ are non-collinear$]$

$\Rightarrow \lambda_1 = \dfrac{3|\vec{c}| + 2|\vec{a}|}{3|\vec{c}|}$ and $\lambda_2 = \dfrac{1}{3} \dfrac{|\vec{a}|}{|\vec{c}|}$

Putting values of $\lambda_2$ in (vi), we get $\vec{r_4} = \vec{a} + \dfrac{1}{3} \dfrac{|a|}{|c|} \vec{c}$

$\overrightarrow{AF} = \vec{r_4} - \vec{a} = \dfrac{1}{3} \dfrac{|a|}{|c|} \vec{c}$

**8.** **(b, c)** We have $\overrightarrow{DA} = \vec{a}, \overrightarrow{AB} = \vec{b}$ and $\overrightarrow{CB} = k\vec{a}$,

Given X & Y are the mid points of $DB$ and $AC$

Then $\overrightarrow{OX} = \dfrac{\overrightarrow{OB}+\overrightarrow{OD}}{2}, \overrightarrow{OY} = \dfrac{\overrightarrow{OA}+\overrightarrow{OC}}{2}$

$\therefore \overrightarrow{XY} = \overrightarrow{OY} - \overrightarrow{OX}$

$= \dfrac{\overrightarrow{OA}+\overrightarrow{OC}-\overrightarrow{OB}-\overrightarrow{OD}}{2} = \dfrac{\overrightarrow{DA}+\overrightarrow{BC}}{2} = \dfrac{\vec{a}-k\vec{a}}{2}$

$\overrightarrow{XY} = \dfrac{(1-k)\vec{a}}{2}$

$\therefore |\overrightarrow{XY}| = \left(\dfrac{1-k}{2}\right)a = 4$     (given)

$\Rightarrow \left(\dfrac{1-k}{2}\right)17 = 4$  (taking + ve sign)

$\Rightarrow 1 - k = \dfrac{8}{17} \Rightarrow k = \dfrac{9}{17}$

And $-\left(\dfrac{1-k}{2}\right)a = 4$   (taking –ve sign)

$\Rightarrow (k-1)\,17 = 8 \Rightarrow k = \dfrac{25}{17}$

**9.** **(c, d)** If a line makes angles $\alpha,\beta,\gamma$ with the axes, we have

$\alpha = \beta = \gamma$

$\therefore \quad \cos\alpha = \cos\beta = \cos\gamma \Rightarrow \ell = m = n$

$\because \quad \ell^2 + m^2 + n^2 = 1,$

$\ell^2 + \ell^2 + \ell^2 = 1 \Rightarrow 3\ell^2 = 1,$

$\therefore \quad \ell^2 = \dfrac{1}{3}$ or $\ell = \pm\dfrac{1}{\sqrt{3}}$

$\therefore$   The d.c's of the line are $\left(\pm\dfrac{1}{\sqrt{3}}, \pm\dfrac{1}{\sqrt{3}}, \pm\dfrac{1}{\sqrt{3}}\right)$.

**10.** **(c)** The vector along the bisector of the given angle is

$\vec{d} = \lambda\left(\dfrac{\vec{b}}{|\vec{b}|} + \dfrac{\vec{c}}{|\vec{c}|}\right)$

$= \lambda\left(\dfrac{7\hat{i} - 4\hat{j} - 4\hat{k}}{\sqrt{81}} + \dfrac{-2\hat{i} - \hat{j} + 2\hat{k}}{\sqrt{9}}\right)$

$= \lambda\left(\dfrac{\hat{i} - 7\hat{j} + 2\hat{k}}{9}\right)$    ...(i)

$\therefore |\vec{d}| = \lambda\sqrt{\left(\dfrac{54}{81}\right)}$

$\Rightarrow 5\sqrt{6} = \lambda\cdot\dfrac{3\sqrt{6}}{9} \Rightarrow \lambda = 15$

Then, from eq. (i),

$\vec{d} = \dfrac{5}{3}(\hat{i} - 7\hat{j} + 2\hat{k})$

**11.** **(b)** Incentre is the point of intersection of the internal bisectors of angles $A$, $B$ and $C$. Equations of the bisectors of angles $A$ and $B$ are

$\vec{r} = \vec{a} + \lambda\left(\dfrac{\vec{c}-\vec{a}}{b} + \dfrac{\vec{b}-\vec{a}}{c}\right)$    ...(i)

and $\vec{r} = \vec{b} + \mu\left(\dfrac{\vec{a}-\vec{b}}{c} + \dfrac{\vec{c}-\vec{b}}{a}\right)$    ...(ii)

Now, equating the coefficients of $\vec{a}, \vec{b}$ and $\vec{c}$, then

$1 - \dfrac{\lambda}{b} - \dfrac{\lambda}{c} = \dfrac{\mu}{c}$    ...(iii)

$\dfrac{\lambda}{c} = \dfrac{\mu}{c} - \dfrac{\mu}{a}$    ...(iv)

and $\dfrac{\lambda}{b} = \dfrac{\mu}{a}$    ...(v)

From eqs. (iii) and (v), we get

$\therefore \quad 1 - \dfrac{\lambda}{b} - \dfrac{\lambda}{c} = \dfrac{1}{c}\left(\dfrac{a\lambda}{b}\right)$

$\Rightarrow 1 = \lambda\left(\dfrac{1}{b} + \dfrac{1}{c} + \dfrac{a}{bc}\right)$

$\therefore \quad \lambda = \left(\dfrac{bc}{c+b+a}\right)$

Now, from eq. (i), we get

$\vec{r} = \left(\dfrac{a\vec{a} + b\vec{b} + c\vec{c}}{a+b+c}\right)$

**12.** **(a)** Let $A$ be the initial point and the PV of B and C be $\vec{b}$ and $\vec{c}$ respectively. Hence, let $AB = c$ and $AC = b$. The

internal bisector is $\vec{r} = t\left(\dfrac{\vec{b}}{c} + \dfrac{\vec{c}}{b}\right)$ and the equation of

the line BC is $\vec{r} = \vec{b} + \lambda(\vec{c} - \vec{b})$ and hence the position

vector of $D$ is $\left(\dfrac{b\vec{b} + c\vec{c}}{b+c}\right)$

$\Rightarrow \overrightarrow{BD} = \left(\dfrac{b\vec{b} + c\vec{c}}{b+c}\right) - \vec{b} = \dfrac{c(\vec{c} - \vec{b})}{(b+c)}$

$\Rightarrow BD = |\overrightarrow{BD}| = \dfrac{c}{(b+c)}|\vec{c} - \vec{b}| = \dfrac{ca}{(b+c)}$

$$BE = |\overrightarrow{BE}| = \frac{c}{(c-b)}|\vec{c}-\vec{b}| = \frac{ca}{(c-b)}$$

$$\therefore \quad \frac{1}{BE} + \frac{1}{BD} = \frac{c-b}{ca} + \frac{b+c}{ca}$$

$$= \frac{2c}{ca} = \frac{2}{a} = \frac{2}{BC}$$

$$\Rightarrow \quad \frac{2}{BC} = \frac{1}{BE} + \frac{1}{BD}$$

**13. (a)** $\vec{a} = a_1\hat{i} + a_2\hat{j} + a_3\hat{k}, \vec{b} = b_1\hat{i} + b_2\hat{j} + b_3\hat{k}$ are parallel

$$\Rightarrow \quad \frac{a_1}{b_1} = \frac{a_2}{b_2} = \frac{a_3}{b_3}$$

$\vec{a} = \hat{i} + p\hat{j} + 2\hat{k}$, $\vec{b} = 2\hat{i} + 3\hat{j} + 9\hat{k}$ are parallel

$$\Rightarrow \quad \frac{1}{2} = \frac{p}{3} = \frac{2}{q}, \ p = \frac{3}{2}, \ q = 4$$

**14. (b)** I is incentre

$$\Rightarrow \quad \overline{OI} = \frac{|\overline{BC}|\overline{OA}| + |\overline{CA}|\overline{OB} + |\overline{AB}|\overline{OC}}{|\overline{AB}| + |\overline{BC}| + |\overline{CA}|}$$

$$\Rightarrow \quad |\overline{BC}|\overline{IA} + |\overline{CA}|\overline{IB} + |\overline{AB}|\overline{IC} = 0$$

Position vector of centroid, $\overline{OG} = \dfrac{\overline{OA} + \overline{OB} + \overline{OC}}{3}$

**15. (0)** $\vec{a} + 2\vec{b} = \lambda\vec{c}$ and $\vec{b} + 3\vec{c} = \mu\vec{a}$. where $\vec{a}$, $\vec{b}$ and $\vec{c}$ are non-collinear vectors

$$\Rightarrow \quad \vec{a} - 6\vec{c} = \lambda\vec{c} - 2\mu\vec{a}$$

$$\Rightarrow \quad \vec{a}(1 + 2\mu) = (\lambda + 6)\vec{c}$$

$$\Rightarrow \quad \mu = -\frac{1}{2} \text{ and } \lambda = -6 \text{ as } \vec{a} \text{ and } \vec{c} \text{ are non-collinear.}$$

$$\therefore \quad |\vec{a} + 2\vec{b} + 6\vec{c}| = |-6\vec{c} + 6\vec{c}| = |\vec{0}| = 0$$

**16. (2)** Let angle between $\vec{b}$ and $\vec{c}$ be $\gamma$.

Now $|\vec{a} + 2\vec{b} + 3\vec{c}|^2 = 3 + 2\sqrt{2}$

$$\Rightarrow \quad 1 + 4 + 9 + 4\cos\alpha + 6\cos\beta + 12\cos\gamma \Rightarrow 3 + 2\sqrt{2}$$

$$\Rightarrow \quad 4\cos\alpha + 6\cos\beta = -11 + 2\sqrt{2} - 12\cos\gamma$$

$$\because \quad \cos\gamma \in \left[-\frac{1}{2}, 0\right] \Rightarrow -12\cos\gamma \in [0, 6]$$

$$\therefore \quad 4\cos\alpha + 6\cos\beta \in [-11 + 2\sqrt{2}, -5 + 2\sqrt{2}]$$

on comparing we get greatest value is

$$2\sqrt{2} - 5 \Rightarrow A = 2$$

**17. (3)** P.V. of A $= 2\hat{i} + \hat{j} + 3\hat{k}$ ; P.V. of B $= 4\hat{i} + \hat{j} + 3\hat{k}$ ;

P.V. of C $= 2\hat{j} + \hat{k}$ .

$$\therefore \quad \overrightarrow{BA} = \text{P.V. of } A - \text{P.V. of } B = -2\hat{i}$$

Similarly, $\overrightarrow{AC} = -2\hat{i} + \hat{j} - 2\hat{k}$

$$\therefore \quad \cos(\angle BAC) = \frac{\overrightarrow{BA} \cdot \overrightarrow{AC}}{|\overrightarrow{BA}| \cdot |\overrightarrow{AC}|} = \frac{4}{\sqrt{4}\sqrt{9}} = \frac{4}{2 \cdot 3} = \frac{2}{3}$$

$$\Rightarrow \quad \angle BAC = \cos^{-1}\left(\frac{2}{3}\right).$$

$$\Rightarrow \quad A = 2, B = 3$$

**18. (7)** Direction cosines of the line are

$$\frac{6}{\sqrt{\{(6)^2 + (2)^2 + (3)^2\}}}, \frac{2}{\sqrt{\{(6)^2 + (2)^2 + (3)^2\}}},$$

$$\frac{3}{\sqrt{\{(6)^2 + (2)^2 + (3)^2\}}} \text{ i.e., } \frac{6}{7}, \frac{2}{7}, \frac{3}{7}$$

$\therefore$ Projection of the line segment joining the points on the

given line $= \dfrac{6}{7}(2+1) + \dfrac{2}{7}(5-0) + \dfrac{3}{7}(1-3) = \dfrac{22}{7}$.

$$\Rightarrow \quad B = 7$$

**1. (a)** Take B as the origin and let $\vec{a}$ and $\vec{b}$ be unit vectors along BA and BC. Then from the equation of the bisector of the angle.

$$\overrightarrow{BP} = \ell(\vec{a} + \vec{b}) \text{ and } \overrightarrow{CP} = m(\vec{a} - \vec{b})$$

for some scalars $\ell$ and m.

Then

$$\overrightarrow{BP}.\overrightarrow{CP} = \ell m (\vec{a} + \vec{b}).(\vec{a} - \vec{b}) = \ell m (|\vec{a}|^2 - |\vec{b}|^2) = 0,$$

since $|\vec{a}| = |\vec{b}| = 1$.

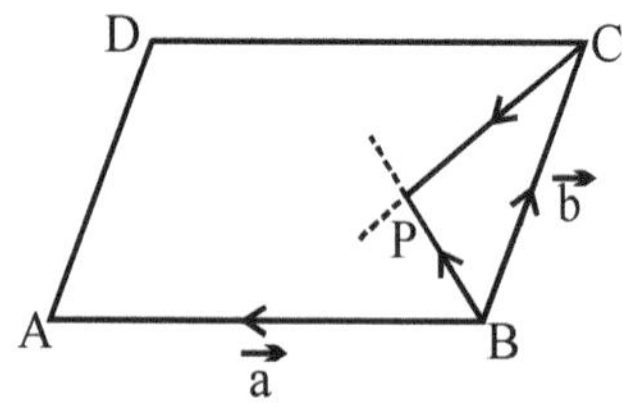

$$\therefore \ \overrightarrow{BP} \perp \overrightarrow{CP}$$

That is, the angle between $\overrightarrow{BP}$ and $\overrightarrow{CP}$ is 90°.

Hence $\angle BPC = 90°$.

**2. (a)** Here $\cos\alpha = \vec{a}.\vec{b}$

or $2\cos^2\dfrac{\alpha}{2} - 1 = \vec{a}.\vec{b}$

or $4\cos^2\dfrac{\alpha}{2} = 2 + 2\vec{a}.\vec{b}$

$$\therefore \left(2\cos\dfrac{\alpha}{2}\right)^2 = \vec{a}^2 + \vec{b}^2 + 2\vec{a}.\vec{b}$$

$$= (\vec{a} + \vec{b})^2 = |\vec{a} + \vec{b}|^2$$

or $2\cos\dfrac{\alpha}{2} = |\vec{a} + \vec{b}|$

$$\therefore \cos\dfrac{\alpha}{2} = \dfrac{1}{2}|\vec{a} + \vec{b}|$$

**3. (a)** We know that $\vec{a}.\vec{b} = |\vec{a}||\vec{b}|\cos\theta$.

If the vectors make obtuse angle with each other, then $\cos\theta < 0$.

Let $\vec{a} = cx\hat{i} - 6\hat{j} - 3\hat{k}$ and $\vec{b} = x\hat{i} + 2\hat{j} - 2cx\hat{k}$

Then $\vec{a}.\vec{b} = cx^2 - 12 + 6cx$

Since the vectors $\vec{a}$ and $\vec{b}$ make an obtuse angle with each other, therefore

$cx^2 + 6cx - 12 < 0 \Rightarrow -cx^2 - 6cx + 12 > 0$

This is possible if $(-c) > 0$ i.e. $c < 0$ and

$$(6c)^2 - 4 \times (-c)(12) < 0$$

$$\Rightarrow 36c^2 + 48c < 0 \Rightarrow 12c(3c + 4) < 0 \Rightarrow -\dfrac{4}{3} < c < 0.$$

**4. (b)** If $\vec{F}$ be the resultant of the three given forces then

$$\vec{F} = (\hat{i} + 2\hat{j} - 3\hat{k}) + (2\hat{i} + 3\hat{j} + 4\hat{k}) + (-\hat{i} - \hat{j} + \hat{k}) = 2\hat{i} + 4\hat{j} + 2\hat{k}$$

If O be the origin, then $\overrightarrow{OP} = $ p.v. of P $= \hat{j} + 2\hat{k}$

$$\overrightarrow{OA} = \text{p.v. of A} = \hat{i} - 2\hat{j}$$

$$\therefore \overrightarrow{AP} = \overrightarrow{OP} - \overrightarrow{OA} = (\hat{j} + 2\hat{k}) - (\hat{i} - 2\hat{j}) = -\hat{i} + 3\hat{j} + 2\hat{k}$$

$\therefore$ Vector moment of the given forces about

A = vector moment of $\vec{F}$ about A $= \overrightarrow{AP} \times \vec{F}$

$$= (-\hat{i} + 3\hat{j} + 2\hat{k}) \times (2\hat{i} + 4\hat{j} + 2\hat{k}) = -2\hat{i} + 6\hat{j} - 10\hat{k}$$

The magnitude of the moment $= \sqrt{4 + 36 + 100} = \sqrt{140}$

**5. (c)**

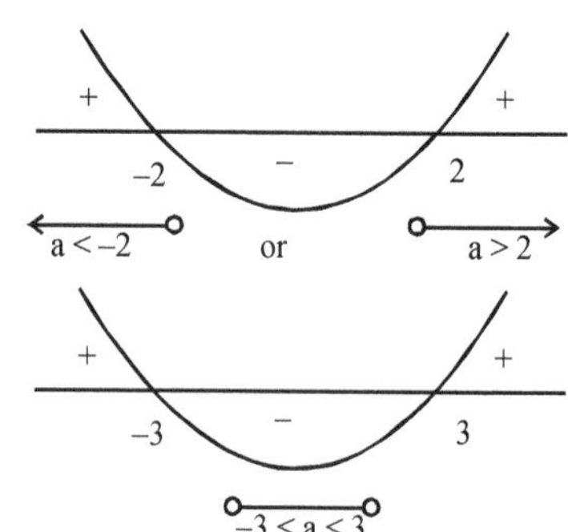

For $\theta$ to be acute, $\cos\theta = \dfrac{\vec{a}.\vec{b}}{|\vec{a}||\vec{b}|}$ is +ve,

i.e., $\cos\theta > 0 \Rightarrow \vec{a}.\vec{b} > 0$.

$\therefore$ For vector $\vec{r}$ to be inclined at acute angles with the coordinate axes, we must have

$\vec{r}.\hat{i} > 0$, $\vec{r}.\hat{j} > 0$ and $\vec{r}.\hat{k} > 0$ since $\vec{r}.\hat{j} = 2 > 0$

$\Rightarrow \vec{r}.\hat{i} > 0$, and $\vec{r}.\hat{k} > 0$

Now, $\vec{r}.\hat{i} = [(a^2 - 4)\hat{i} + 2\hat{j} - (a^2 - 9)\hat{k}].\hat{i} = a^2 - 4$

$\vec{r}.\hat{k} = [(a^2 - 4)\hat{i} + 2\hat{j} - (a^2 - 9)\hat{k}].\hat{k} = -(a^2 - 9)$

$\therefore$ From (i), $(a^2 - 4) > 0$ and $-(a^2 - 9) > 0$ i.e., $a^2 - 9 < 0$

$\Rightarrow (a - 2)(a + 2) > 0$ and $(a + 3)(a - 3) < 0$

$\Rightarrow a < -2$ or $a > 2$ and $-3 < a < 3$ $\Rightarrow a \in (-3, -2) \cup (2, 3)$.

**6. (b)** Taking the dot product of $\vec{u} + \vec{v} + \vec{w}$ with $\vec{u}$, $\vec{v}$, $\vec{w}$ respectively, we get

$$\vec{u}.\vec{u} + \vec{u}.\vec{v} + \vec{u}.\vec{w} = 0$$

$$\Rightarrow 9 + \vec{u}.\vec{v} + \vec{u}.\vec{w} = 0$$

$$\therefore \ \vec{u}.\vec{v} + \vec{u}.\vec{w} = -9 \qquad \qquad ..........(1)$$

Again, $\vec{v}.\vec{u} + \vec{v}.\vec{v} + \vec{v}.\vec{w} = 0$

$$\Rightarrow \vec{u}.\vec{v} + 16 + \vec{v}.\vec{w} = 0$$

$$\therefore \ \vec{u}.\vec{v} + \vec{v}.\vec{w} = -16 \qquad \qquad ..........(2)$$

Again, $\vec{w}.\vec{u} + \vec{w}.\vec{v} + \vec{w}.\vec{w} = 0$

$$\Rightarrow \vec{w}.\vec{u} + \vec{v}.\vec{w} + 25 = 0$$

$$\therefore \ \vec{w}.\vec{u} + \vec{v}.\vec{w} = -25 \qquad \qquad ..........(3)$$

Adding (1), (2) and (3), we get

$$2(\vec{u}.\vec{v} + \vec{v}.\vec{w} + \vec{w}.\vec{u}) = -50$$

$$\therefore \ \vec{u}.\vec{v} + \vec{v}.\vec{w} + \vec{w}.\vec{u} = -25$$

**7. (a,c)** We have, $\vec{a}.\vec{c} = |\vec{a}||\vec{c}|\cos\theta$, if $\theta$ is the angle between

the vectors $\vec{a}$ and $\vec{c}$

$$= 1.1 \cdot \cos\{\cos^{-1}(1/4)\}; \text{ (given)}$$
$$= 1/4. \qquad \qquad .....(1)$$

Also, given $\vec{b} - 2\vec{c} = \lambda\vec{a}$

Taking scalar product by $\vec{a}$, we get

$$\vec{a}.\vec{b} - 2\vec{a}.\vec{c} = \lambda\vec{a}.\vec{a}$$

$$\Rightarrow \ \vec{a}.\vec{b} - 2.\frac{1}{4} = \lambda; \qquad \text{from (1) and also } |\vec{a}| = 1$$

$$\Rightarrow \ \vec{a}.\vec{b} = \lambda + \frac{1}{2} \qquad \qquad .....(2)$$

Again, taking scalar product of (1), by $\vec{b}$, we get

$$\vec{b}.\vec{b} - 2\vec{b}.\vec{c} = \lambda\vec{a}.\vec{b}$$

$$\Rightarrow \ 16 - 2\vec{b}.\vec{c} = \lambda\left(\lambda + \frac{1}{2}\right); \qquad \text{from (2)}$$

$$\Rightarrow \ 2\vec{b}.\vec{c} = 16 - \lambda^2 - \frac{\lambda}{2}$$

$$\Rightarrow \ \vec{b}.\vec{c} = 8 - \frac{\lambda^2}{2} - \frac{\lambda}{4} \qquad \qquad ....(3)$$

Again, taking scalar product of (1) by $\vec{c}$, we get

$$\vec{b}.\vec{c} - 2\vec{c}.\vec{c} = \lambda\vec{c}.\vec{a}$$

$$\Rightarrow \left(8 - \frac{\lambda^2}{2} - \frac{\lambda}{4}\right) - 2 = \lambda\left(\frac{1}{4}\right); \qquad \text{(from (1) and (3))}$$

$$\Rightarrow 32 - 2\lambda^2 - \lambda - 8 = \lambda$$

$$\Rightarrow 2\lambda^2 + 2\lambda - 24 = 0$$

$$\Rightarrow \lambda^2 + \lambda - 12 = 0$$

$$\Rightarrow (\lambda - 3)(\lambda + 4) = 0$$

$$\therefore \ \lambda = 3 \text{ or } \lambda = -4.$$

**8. (a,c)** Any vector $\vec{r}$ in the plane of $\vec{b}$ and $\vec{c}$ is

$$\vec{r} = \vec{b} + t\,\vec{c} \qquad \qquad ..........(1)$$

$$= \left(\hat{i} + 2\hat{j} - \hat{k}\right) + t\left(\hat{i} + \hat{j} - 2\hat{k}\right)$$

$$= (1+t)\hat{i} + (2+t)\hat{j} - (1+2t)\hat{k} \qquad \qquad ..........(2)$$

Then the projection of $\vec{r}$ on $\vec{a}$ is

$$\frac{\vec{r}.\vec{a}}{|\vec{a}|} = \frac{2(1+t) - (2+t) - (1+2t)}{\sqrt{2^2 + 1 + 1}}$$

$$= \frac{2 + 2t - 2 - t - 1 - 2t}{\sqrt{6}} = \frac{-1-t}{\sqrt{6}} = \frac{-(1+t)}{\sqrt{6}}$$

Given the projection of $\vec{r}$ on $\vec{a}$ is $\pm\sqrt{2/3}$.

$$\therefore -\frac{(1+t)}{\sqrt{6}} = \pm\frac{\sqrt{2}}{\sqrt{3}} \Rightarrow -(1+t) = \pm 2$$

$$\therefore \ t = -3 \text{ or } 1.$$

Putting the value of t in (1), we get

$$\vec{r} = -2\hat{i} - \hat{j} + 5\hat{k} \text{ or } \vec{r} = 2\hat{i} + 3\hat{j} - 3\hat{k}$$

**9. (a, c, d)** $\overrightarrow{OA}.\overrightarrow{OB} = -3$

$$2.3\cos\theta = -3$$

$$\cos\theta = -\frac{1}{2} \Rightarrow \theta = \frac{2\pi}{3}$$

$$(2(\vec{a} \times \vec{b}) - 2\vec{a}).(2(\vec{a} \times \vec{b}) - 3\vec{b})$$

$$= 4|\vec{a}|^2|\vec{b}|^2 \sin^2\theta + 6\vec{a}.\vec{b} = 4.\frac{3}{4} - 6.\frac{1}{2} = 0.$$

Angle $C$ is $90°$.

**10. (a), 11. (b), 12. (c).**

$$\vec{A}.\vec{B} = 2a_1b_1 + a_2b_2 + a_1b_2 + a_2b_1$$

$\vec{A}.\vec{B} = \vec{B}.\vec{A}$ as expression on RHS remains unchanged if $a_1$ and $b_1$ are interchanged and $a_2$ and $b_2$ are interchanged. Hence I holds.

$$\vec{A}.(\vec{B} + \vec{C}) = (a_1, a_2).(b_1 + c_1, b_2 + c_2)$$

$$= 2a_1(b_1 + c_1) + a_2(b_2 + c_2) + a_1(b_2 + c_2) + a_2(b_1 + c_1)$$

$$= (2a_1b_1 + a_2b_2 + a_1b_2 + a_2b_1) + 2a_1c_1 + a_2c_2 + a_1c_2 + a_2c_1$$

$$= \vec{A}.\vec{B} + \vec{A}.\vec{C}. \text{ Hence II holds true.}$$

$$(c\vec{A}).\vec{B} = (ca_1, ca_2).(b_1, b_2) = 2ca_1b_1 + ca_2b_2 + ca_1b_2 + ca_2b_1$$

$$= 2a_1.(cb_1) + a_2.(cb_2) + a_1.(cb_2) + a_2.(cb_1) = \vec{A}.(c\,\vec{B}).$$

Hence III holds true.

$$\vec{A}.\vec{A} = (a_1, a_2).(a_1, a_2) = 2a_1^2 + a_2^2 + a_1a_2 + a_2a_1$$

$$= a_1^2 + a_1^2 + a_2^2 + 2a_1a_2$$

$$= a_1^2 + (a_1 + a_2)^2 > 0 \ \text{if } a_1 \text{ or } a_2 \text{ is not zero.}$$

Hence IV holds.

(ii) $\vec{A}.\vec{B} = \left| \sum\limits_{i=1}^{3} a_i b_i \right| = |a_1b_1 + a_2b_2 + a_3b_3| = \vec{B}.\vec{A}$.

Hence I holds true.

$$\vec{A}.(\vec{B}+\vec{C}) = |(a_1, a_2, a_3).(b_1 + c_1, b_2 + c_2, b_3 + c_3)|$$

$$= |(a_1(b_1 + c_1) + a_2(b_2 + c_2) + a_3(b_3 + c_3)|$$
$$= |(a_1b_1 + a_2b_2 + a_3b_3) + (a_1c_1 + a_2c_2 + a_3c_3)|$$
$$\neq |a_1b_1 + a_2b_2 + a_3b_3| + |a_1c_1 + a_2c_2 + a_3c_3| \ \text{in general.}$$
$$\Rightarrow \text{II don't hold true.}$$

Similarly III and IV can be checked.

(iii) $\vec{A}.\vec{B} = \sqrt{a_1b_1} + \sqrt{a_2b_2} + 2\sqrt{a_2b_1} + 2\sqrt{a_1b_2}$

$$\Rightarrow \vec{A}.\vec{B} \leq \left( \frac{a_1 + b_1}{2} \right) + \left( \frac{a_2 + b_2}{2} \right) + (a_2 + b_1) + (a_1 + b_2)$$

$$\Rightarrow \vec{A}.\vec{B} \leq \frac{3}{2}(a_1 + a_2 + b_1 + b_2) = \frac{3}{2}(|\vec{A}| + |\vec{B}|)$$

**13.** $\mathbf{(A) \to q; (B) \to p; (C) \to s; (D) \to r}$

(A) Magnitude of projection of $\vec{a}$ on $\vec{b}$

$$= \left| \frac{(2\hat{i} - 3\hat{j} + 6\hat{k}).(-2\hat{i} + 2\hat{j} - \hat{k})}{3} \right| = \frac{16}{3} \ \textbf{(q)}$$

(B) Magnitude of projection of $\vec{b}$ on $\vec{a}$

$$= \left| \frac{(-2\hat{i} + 2\hat{j} - \hat{k}).(2\hat{i} - 3\hat{j} + 6\hat{k})}{7} \right| = \frac{16}{7} \ \textbf{(p)}$$

(C) $\lambda\vec{b} = \left( \dfrac{(2\hat{i} - 3\hat{j} + 6\hat{k}).(-2\hat{i} + 2\hat{j} - \hat{k})}{9} \right)\vec{b}$

$$\therefore |\lambda| = \frac{16}{9} \ \textbf{(s)}$$

(D) $\mu\vec{c} = \vec{a} - \lambda\vec{b} = \dfrac{-14\hat{i} + 5\hat{j} + 38\hat{k}}{9}$

$$\therefore |\mu| = \frac{\sqrt{185}}{3} \ \textbf{(r)}$$

**14.** $\mathbf{A \to r, s; \ B \to q, t; \ C \to p}$

(A) $\vec{F} = \vec{F_1} + \vec{F_2} = (3\hat{i} - 2\hat{j} + \hat{k}) + (\hat{i} + 3\hat{j} - 5\hat{k})$

$$\therefore \vec{F} = 4\hat{i} + \hat{j} - 4\hat{k}$$

and let $\overrightarrow{OA} = -2\hat{i} + 5\hat{k}$,

$$\overrightarrow{OB} = 3\hat{i} - 7\hat{j} + 2\hat{k}$$

$\therefore \overrightarrow{AB} = \overrightarrow{OB} - \overrightarrow{OA} = 5\hat{i} - 7\hat{j} - 3\hat{k}$

Then $W_1 = \vec{F}.\overrightarrow{AB} = 20 - 7 + 12 = 25$ unit

And also $\vec{F'} = \vec{P} + \vec{Q} + \vec{R}$

$$= (2\hat{i} - 5\hat{j} + 6\hat{k}) + (-\hat{i} + 2\hat{j} - \hat{k}) + (2\hat{i} + 7\hat{j})$$

$$= 3\hat{i} + 4\hat{j} + 5\hat{k}$$

and $\overrightarrow{OM} = 4\hat{i} - 3\hat{j} - 2\hat{k}$

$$\overrightarrow{ON} = 6\hat{i} + \hat{j} - 3\hat{k}$$

$\therefore \overrightarrow{MN} = \overrightarrow{ON} - \overrightarrow{OM} = 2\hat{i} + 4\hat{j} - \hat{k}$

Then, $W_2 = \vec{F'}.\overrightarrow{MN} = 6 + 16 - 5 = 17$ unit

$\because W_1 = 25, W_2 = 17$

$\therefore 3W_2 - 2W_1 = 1$ **(s)** and $2W_2 - W_1 = 9$ **(r)**

(B) Let $\overrightarrow{OA} = -2\hat{i} + 5\hat{j} + 7\hat{k}$ and

$$\overrightarrow{OB} = 3\hat{i} + 7\hat{j} + 2\hat{k}$$

$\therefore \overrightarrow{AB} = \overrightarrow{OB} - \overrightarrow{OA} = 5\hat{i} + 2\hat{j} - 5\hat{k}$

and let $\vec{F_1} = 2\hat{i} - 3\hat{j} + \hat{k}, \vec{F_2} = \hat{i} + 5\hat{j} - 3\hat{k}$

$\therefore \vec{F} = \vec{F_1} + \vec{F_2} = 3\hat{i} + 2\hat{j} - 2\hat{k}$

Then, $W_1 = \vec{F}.\overrightarrow{AB} = 15 + 4 + 10 = 29$ unit

and also let $\overrightarrow{OM} = 4\hat{i} - 3\hat{j} - 2\hat{k}$

and $\overrightarrow{ON} = 6\hat{i} + \hat{j} - 2\hat{k}$

$\therefore \overrightarrow{MN} = \overrightarrow{ON} - \overrightarrow{OM} = 2\hat{i} + 4\hat{j} - \hat{k}$

and also let $\vec{P} = \hat{i} - \hat{j} + \hat{k},$

$\vec{Q} = -\hat{i} + 2\hat{j} - \hat{k}$ and $\vec{R} = \hat{i} + 0\hat{j} - \hat{k}$

$\therefore \vec{F} = \vec{P} + \vec{Q} + \vec{R} = \hat{i} + \hat{j} - \hat{k}$

Then, $W_2 = \vec{F'}.\overrightarrow{MN} = 2 + 4 + 1 = 7$ unit

$\because W_1 = 29, W_2 = 7$

$W_1 - 3W_2 = 8$ **(q)**

and $W_1 - 4W_2 = 1$ **(t)**

(C) Let $F_1 = 5$ unit $F_2 = 3$ unit, $F_3 = 1$ unit

and let $\vec{a} = 6\hat{i} + 2\hat{j} + 3\hat{k},$

$\vec{b} = 3\hat{i} - 2\hat{j} + 6\hat{k}$ and $\vec{c} = 2\hat{i} - 3\hat{j} - 6\hat{k}$

$\therefore \hat{a} = \dfrac{(6\hat{i} + 2\hat{j} + 3\hat{k})}{7},$

$\hat{b} = \dfrac{(3\hat{i} - 2\hat{j} + 6\hat{k})}{7}$

and $\hat{c} = \dfrac{(2\hat{i} - 3\hat{j} - 6\hat{k})}{7}$

$\therefore \vec{F_1} = F_1\,\hat{a} = \dfrac{5}{7}(6\hat{j} + 2\hat{j} + 3\hat{k})$

$\vec{F_2} = F_2\,\hat{b} = \dfrac{3}{7}(3\hat{i} - 2\hat{j} + 6\hat{k})$

and $\vec{F_3} = F_3\,\hat{c} = \dfrac{1}{7}(2\hat{i} - 3\hat{j} - 6\hat{k})$

$\therefore \vec{F} = \vec{F_1} + \vec{F_2} + \vec{F_3} = \dfrac{1}{7}(41\,\hat{i} + \hat{j} + 27\hat{k})$

and $\overrightarrow{OA} = 2\hat{i} - \hat{j} - 3\hat{k},\ \overrightarrow{OB} = 5\hat{i} - \hat{j} + \hat{k}$

$\therefore \overrightarrow{AB} = \overrightarrow{OB} - \overrightarrow{OA} = 3\hat{i} + 4\hat{k}$

Then, $W_1 = \vec{F}.\overrightarrow{AB}$

$= \dfrac{1}{7}(123 + 0 + 108)$

$= \dfrac{1}{7}(231) = 33\ \text{unit}$

And also let

$P = 1$ unit, $Q = 2$ unit, $R = 3$ unit

and let $\vec{P} = \hat{i} + 2\hat{j} + 2\hat{k},\ \vec{q} = 2\hat{i} - 2\hat{j} + \hat{k},\ \vec{r} = 2\hat{i} - \hat{j} - 2\hat{k}$

$\therefore \hat{p} = \dfrac{1}{3}(\hat{i} + 2\hat{j} + 2\hat{k})$

$\hat{q} = \dfrac{1}{3}(2\hat{i} - 2\hat{j} + \hat{k})$

And $\hat{r} = \dfrac{1}{3}(2\hat{i} - \hat{j} + 2\hat{k})$

$\therefore \vec{P} = P\hat{p} = \dfrac{1}{3}(\hat{i} + 2\hat{j} + 2\hat{k})$

$\vec{Q} = Q\hat{q} = \dfrac{2}{3}(2\hat{i} - 2\hat{j} + \hat{k})$

and $\vec{R} = R\hat{r} = \dfrac{3}{3}(2\hat{i} - \hat{j} - 2\hat{k})$

$\therefore \vec{F} = \vec{P} + \vec{Q} + \vec{R} = \dfrac{1}{3}(11\hat{i} - 5\hat{j} - 2\hat{k})$

and $\overrightarrow{OM} = -2\hat{i} - \hat{j} + 5\hat{k},$

$\overrightarrow{ON} = 3\hat{i} - 4\hat{j} - 5\hat{k}$

$\therefore \overrightarrow{MN} = \overrightarrow{ON} - \overrightarrow{OM} = 5\hat{i} - 3\hat{j} - 10\hat{k}$

Then, $W_2 = \vec{F}.\overrightarrow{MN} = \dfrac{1}{3}(55 + 15 + 20)$

$= 30\ \text{unit}$

$\because W_1 = 33,\ W_2 = 30$

$\therefore W_1 - W_2 = 3$ **(p)**

**15. (d)** $\ \left|\vec{a} + \vec{b}\right| = \left|\vec{a} - \vec{b}\right|$

$\Rightarrow \vec{a}.\vec{b} = 0 \Rightarrow \vec{a}$ is perpendicular to $\vec{b}$.

**16. (a)** Statement-1 :

$\cos(\vec{a} + \vec{b},\ \vec{a} - \vec{b}) = \dfrac{(\hat{i} + 2\hat{j} - \hat{k}).(\hat{i} + \hat{k})}{\sqrt{6}\sqrt{2}} = \dfrac{1 + 0 - 1}{\sqrt{12}} = 0\ ;$

$(\vec{a} + \vec{b},\ \vec{a} - \vec{b}) = 90°$

Statement-2 : $\dfrac{(\vec{a} + \vec{b}).(\vec{a} - \vec{b})}{|\vec{a} - \vec{b}|} = \dfrac{0}{\sqrt{2}} = 0$

**17. (9)** $\hat{a}, \hat{b}, \hat{c}$ are units vectors.

$\therefore \hat{a}.\hat{a} = \hat{b}.\hat{b} = \hat{c}.\hat{c} = 1$

Now, $x = |\hat{a} - \hat{b}|^2 + |\hat{b} - \hat{c}|^2 + |\hat{c} - \hat{a}|^2$

$= \hat{a}.\hat{a} + \hat{b}.\hat{b} - 2\hat{a}.\hat{b} + \hat{b}.\hat{b} + \hat{c}.\hat{c} - 2\hat{b}.\hat{c} + \hat{c}.\hat{c} + \hat{a}.\hat{a} - 2\hat{c}.\hat{a}$

$\Rightarrow x = 6 - 2(\hat{a}.\hat{b} + \hat{b}.\hat{c} + \hat{c}.\hat{a})$ ...(1)

Also

$\Rightarrow |\hat{a} + \hat{b} + \hat{c}| \geq 0$

$\Rightarrow |\hat{a} + \hat{b} + \hat{c}|^2 \geq 0$

$\Rightarrow \hat{a}.\hat{a} + \hat{b}.\hat{b} + \hat{c}.\hat{c} + 2(\hat{a}.\hat{b} + \hat{b}.\hat{c} + \hat{c}.\hat{a}) \geq 0$

$\Rightarrow 3 + 2(\hat{a}.\hat{b} + \hat{b}.\hat{c} + \hat{c}.\hat{a}) \geq 0$

$\Rightarrow 2(\hat{a}.\hat{b} + \hat{b}.\hat{c} + \hat{c}.\hat{a}) \geq -3$

$\Rightarrow 6 - 2(\hat{a}.\hat{b} + \hat{b}.\hat{c} + \hat{c}.\hat{a}) \leq 9$ ...(2)

From (1) and (2), $x \leq 9$

$\therefore x$ does not exceed 9

Thus P = 9

**18. (2)**

Given $\vec{a}.\vec{b} = 0 \Rightarrow \vec{a}$ is perpendicular to $\vec{b}$.

$\vec{a}.\vec{c} = 0 \Rightarrow \vec{a}$ is perpendicular to $\vec{c}$.

$\therefore \vec{a}$ is perpendicular to the plane of $\vec{b}$ and $\vec{c}$.

Also $\vec{a}$ is a unit vector. Therefore, $\vec{a} = \pm \dfrac{\vec{b} \times \vec{c}}{|\vec{b} \times \vec{c}|}$ ...(1)

But $|\vec{b} \times \vec{c}| = |\vec{b}||\vec{c}| \sin \dfrac{\pi}{6} = 1 \cdot 1 \cdot \dfrac{1}{2} = \dfrac{1}{2}$. $\therefore$ From (1) we

have $\vec{a} = \pm 2(\vec{b} \times \vec{c})$. $\qquad \therefore n = \pm 2$.

Thus, $R = 2$.

**19. (6)**

The unit vectors in the given direction being

$\dfrac{1}{6}(2\hat{i} + 4\hat{j} + 4\hat{k})$ and $\dfrac{1}{6}(4\hat{i} + 4\hat{j} + 2\hat{k})$, the vectors

representing the forces are $\dfrac{1}{3}(2\hat{i} + 4\hat{j} + 4\hat{k})$ and

$\dfrac{1}{2}(4\hat{i} - 4\hat{j} + 2\hat{k})$ respectively, of which the resultant is

$\left(\dfrac{2}{3} + 2\right)\hat{i} + \left(\dfrac{4}{3} - 2\right)\hat{j} + \left(\dfrac{4}{3} + 1\right)\hat{k}$ i.e., $\dfrac{1}{3}(8\hat{i} - 2\hat{j} + 7\hat{k})$.

The displacement is represented by the vector $\hat{i} + 2\hat{j} + 2\hat{k}$.

Hence the work done

$= \dfrac{1}{3}(8\hat{i} - 2\hat{j} + 7\hat{k}) \cdot (\hat{i} + 2\hat{j} + 2\hat{k}) = \dfrac{1}{3}(8 - 4 + 14) = 6 \text{ gm cm}$.

**1.** **(b)** $\vec{a} + \vec{b} + \vec{c} = 0$ and $\vec{a}, \vec{b}, \vec{c}$ are unit vectors, therfore

$\vec{a}, \vec{b}, \vec{c}$ form an equilateral triangle.

$\Rightarrow \vec{a} \times (\vec{a} + \vec{b} + \vec{c}) = \vec{0}$

$\Rightarrow \vec{a} \times \vec{a} + \vec{a} \times \vec{b} + \vec{a} \times \vec{c} = \vec{0}$

$\Rightarrow \vec{a} \times \vec{b} = \vec{c} \times \vec{a}$

Similarly $\vec{b} \times \vec{c} = \vec{c} \times \vec{a}$

$\therefore \vec{a} \times \vec{b} = \vec{b} \times \vec{c} = \vec{c} \times \vec{a}$

Also since $\vec{a}, \vec{b}, \vec{c}$ are non parallel (these form an equilateral $\Delta$).

$\therefore \vec{a} \times \vec{b} = \vec{b} \times \vec{c} = \vec{c} \times \vec{a} \neq \vec{0}$

**2.** **(d)** We have $\vec{a} = \hat{i} + \hat{j} + \hat{k}$, $\hat{c} = \hat{j} - \hat{k}$

Let $\vec{b} = b_1 \hat{i} + b_2 \hat{j} + b_3 \hat{k}$

Then $\vec{a}.\vec{b} = 3 \Rightarrow b_1 + b_2 + b_3 = 3$ .... (1)

Also, given $\vec{a} \times \vec{b} = \vec{c}$

Therefore $\begin{vmatrix} \hat{i} & \hat{j} & \hat{k} \\ 1 & 1 & 1 \\ b_1 & b_2 & b_3 \end{vmatrix} = \hat{j} - \hat{k}$

$\Rightarrow \hat{i}(b_3 - b_2) - \hat{j}(b_3 - b_1) + \hat{k}(b_2 - b_1) = \hat{j} - \hat{k}$.

On comparing the coefficients of $\vec{i}, \vec{j}, \vec{k}$ on both sides, we get $b_3 - b_2 = 0$, $b_1 - b_3 = 1$ and $b_1 - b_2 = 1$
$\Rightarrow b_3 = b_2$ and $b_1 = 1 + b_2$.
But from (1), $b_1 + b_2 + b_3 = 3 \Rightarrow b_1 + 2b_2 = 3$
$\Rightarrow (1 + b_2) + 2b_2 = 3 \Rightarrow 3b_2 = 2$ $\therefore b_2 = 2/3$.
Hence, $b_3 = b_2 = 2/3$

and $b_1 = 1 + b_2 = 1 + \dfrac{2}{3} = \dfrac{5}{3}$

$\therefore \vec{b} = (b_1, b_2, b_3) = \left( \dfrac{5}{3}, \dfrac{2}{3}, \dfrac{2}{3} \right)$.

**3.** **(d)** The vector normal to the plane of $\overrightarrow{AB}$ and $\overrightarrow{CD}$ is

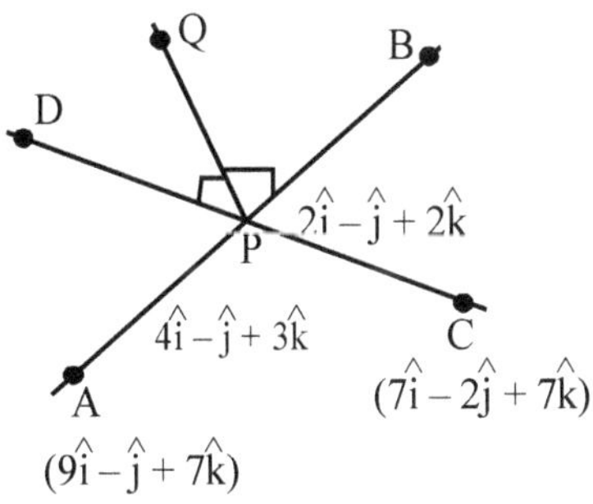


$\overrightarrow{AB} \times \overrightarrow{CD} = \begin{vmatrix} \hat{i} & \hat{j} & \hat{k} \\ 4 & -1 & 3 \\ 2 & -1 & 2 \end{vmatrix}$

$= \hat{i}(-2 + 3) - \hat{j}(8 - 6) + \hat{k}(-4 + 2) = \hat{i} - 2\hat{j} - 2\hat{k}$

$\therefore$ The magnitude of this vector is $\sqrt{1 + 4 + 4} = 3$.

Hence the vector normal to the plane of $(\overrightarrow{AB}, \overrightarrow{CD})$

having magnitude 15 units will be $5(\hat{i} - 2\hat{j} - 2\hat{k})$.
Now to find out the position vector of P, we need to find the equations of AB and CD.

Now, the equation of $\overrightarrow{AB}$ is (by using $\vec{r} = \vec{a} + t\vec{b}$)

$\vec{r} = 9\hat{i} - \hat{j} + 7\hat{k} + t(4\hat{i} - \hat{j} + 3\hat{k})$

$= \hat{i}(9 + 4t) + \hat{j}(-t - 1) + \hat{k}(3t + 7)$ .... (1)

Similarly the equation of $\overrightarrow{CD}$ is

$\vec{r} = 7\hat{i} - 2\hat{j} + 7\hat{k} + s(2\hat{i} - \hat{j} + 2\hat{k})$

$= \vec{i}(7 + 2s) + \hat{j}(-s - 2) + \hat{k}(2s + 7)$ ............ (2)

Therefore for the point of intersection P, we shall have
$9 + 4t = 7 + 2s$, $t + 1 = s + 2$ and $3t + 7 = 2s + 7$.
Now solving them, we get $t = -2$, $s = -3$.
Hence putting $t = -2$ in (1) or putting $s = -3$ in (2), we

find that the position vector of P is $\hat{i} + \hat{j} + \hat{k}$.
Let O be the origin of reference.

Now, the position vector of Q i.e. $\overrightarrow{OQ}$ is

$\overrightarrow{OP} + \overrightarrow{OQ} = \hat{i} + \hat{j} + \hat{k} + 5(\hat{i} - 2\hat{j} - 2\hat{k})$
$= 6\hat{i} - 9\hat{j} - 9\hat{k} = 3(\hat{i} - 3\hat{j} - 3\hat{k})$

**4.** **(c)** Let $\vec{a} = a_1\hat{i} + b_1\hat{j} + c_1\hat{k}$

$\therefore \vec{a} \times \hat{i} = (a_1\hat{i} + b_1\hat{j} + c_1\hat{k}) \times \hat{i} = -b_1\hat{k} + c_1\hat{j}$

$(\vec{a} \times \hat{i})^2 = [(\vec{a} \times \hat{i}).(\vec{a} \times \hat{i})]$

$= (c_1\hat{j} - b_1\hat{k}).(c_1\hat{j} - b_1\hat{k}) = c_1^2 + b_1^2$

Similarly, $(\vec{a} \times \hat{j})^2 = a_1^2 + c_1^2 \Rightarrow (\vec{a} \times \hat{k})^2 = a_1^2 + b_1^2$

Hence, $(\vec{a} \times \hat{i})^2 + (\vec{a} \times \hat{j})^2 + (\vec{a} \times \hat{k})^2$

$$= c_1^2 + b_1^2 + a_1^2 + c_1^2 + a_1^2 + b_1^2 = 2(a_1^2 + b_1^2 + c_1^2)$$

$$= 2|\vec{a}|^2 = 2(\vec{a})^2$$

**5. (b)** Here, $|\vec{a} \times \vec{b}| = q$ and

$$\frac{1}{2}|\vec{b} \times (10\vec{a} + 2\vec{b})| + \frac{1}{2}|\vec{a} \times (10\vec{a} + 2\vec{b})| = p$$

$$\therefore \quad 5|\vec{b} \times \vec{a}| + |\vec{a} \times \vec{b}| = p$$

$$\Rightarrow \quad 6q = p \Rightarrow \frac{p}{q} = 6.$$

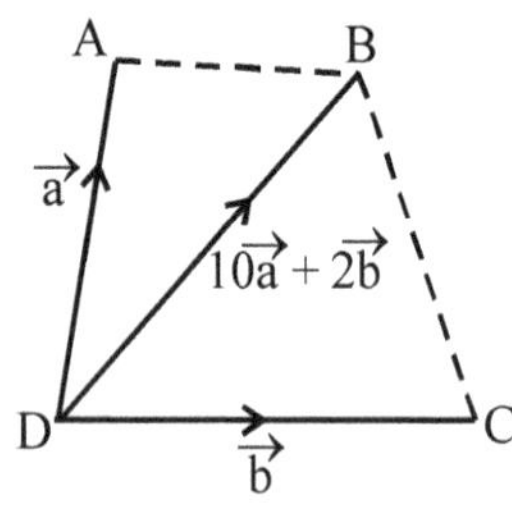

**6. (c)**

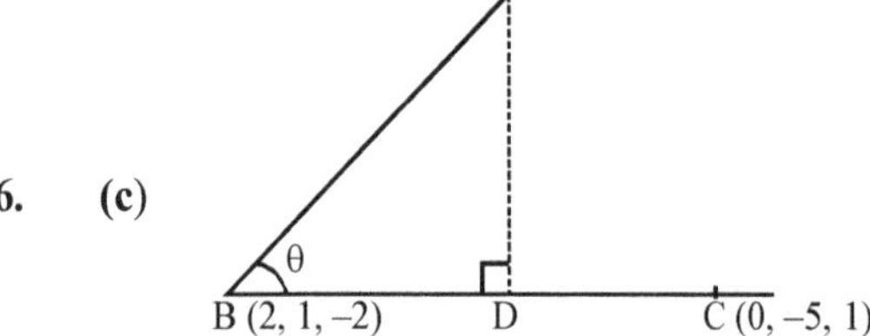

$$AD = AB \sin\theta = AB \cdot \frac{|\overrightarrow{BC} \times \overrightarrow{BA}|}{|\overrightarrow{BC}| \cdot |\overrightarrow{BA}|} = \frac{|\overrightarrow{BC} \times \overrightarrow{BA}|}{|\overrightarrow{BC}|}$$

$$[\because |\overrightarrow{BA}| = BA = AB]$$

Now $\overrightarrow{BC} = -2\hat{i} - 6\hat{j} + 3\hat{k}$ and $\overrightarrow{BA} = -\hat{i} + 3\hat{j}$

$$\therefore \overrightarrow{BC} \times \overrightarrow{BA} = \begin{vmatrix} \hat{i} & \hat{j} & \hat{k} \\ -2 & -6 & 3 \\ -1 & 3 & 0 \end{vmatrix} = -9\hat{i} - 3\hat{j} - 12\hat{k}$$

$$|\overrightarrow{BC} \times \overrightarrow{BA}| = \sqrt{9^2 + 3^2 + (12)^2} = 3\sqrt{26}$$

and $|\overrightarrow{BC}| = \sqrt{4 + 36 + 9} = 7$

$$\therefore AD = \frac{3\sqrt{26}}{7}$$

**7. (d)** Here, $(\vec{r} - \vec{b}) \times \vec{a} = 0$, so $(\vec{r} - \vec{b}) \parallel \vec{a}$

$$\therefore \qquad \vec{r} - \vec{b} = t\vec{a} \quad \text{or} \quad \vec{r} = \vec{b} + t\vec{a}$$

But $\qquad \vec{r} \cdot \vec{c} = 0$.

$$\therefore \qquad 0 = \vec{b} \cdot \vec{c} + t\,\vec{a} \cdot \vec{c}$$

$$\therefore \qquad t = -\frac{\vec{b} \cdot \vec{c}}{\vec{a} \cdot \vec{c}}$$

$$\therefore \qquad \vec{r} = \vec{b} - \frac{\vec{b} \cdot \vec{c}}{\vec{a} \cdot \vec{c}}\,\vec{a}$$

**8. (a)**

$$\overrightarrow{AP} = \overrightarrow{OP} - \overrightarrow{OA}$$

$$= (\hat{i} + \hat{j} + \hat{k}) - (2\hat{i} + \hat{j} + \hat{k}) = -\hat{i}$$

$$\overrightarrow{AB} = \overrightarrow{OB} - \overrightarrow{OA}$$

$$= (\hat{i} + 2\hat{j} + \hat{k}) - (2\hat{i} + \hat{j} + \hat{k}) = -\hat{i} + \hat{j}$$

$$\overrightarrow{AC} = \overrightarrow{OC} - \overrightarrow{OA}$$

$$= (\hat{i} + \hat{j} + 2\hat{k}) - (2\hat{i} - \hat{j} + \hat{k}) = -\hat{i} + \hat{k}$$

$$\overrightarrow{AC} \times \overrightarrow{AB} = (-\hat{i} + \hat{k}) \times (\hat{i} + \hat{j}) = -\hat{k} - \hat{j} - \hat{i}$$

$\therefore$ The unit vector perpendicular to the plane ABC

$$= \frac{-\hat{k} - \hat{j} - \hat{i}}{\sqrt{3}}$$

The required distance $= \overrightarrow{AP} \cdot \dfrac{-\hat{k} - \hat{j} - \hat{i}}{\sqrt{3}}$

$$= (-\vec{i}) \cdot \frac{-\hat{k} - \hat{j} - \hat{i}}{\sqrt{3}} = \frac{1}{\sqrt{3}}$$

**9. (a)** $\left.\begin{array}{l} N_1 = \vec{a} \times \vec{b}, \\ N_2 = \vec{c} \times \vec{d}, \end{array}\right\} N_1 \times N_2 = 0$

If $\theta$ is the angle between $P_1$ and $P_2$,

then $|N_1| \times |N_2| \sin\theta = 0$   or   $\sin\theta = 0 \Rightarrow \theta = 0$

**10. (a)** A vector $\perp$ to the plane is $(\hat{i} - 2\hat{j} - \hat{k}) \times (3\hat{i} - 2\hat{j} - \hat{k})$

$$= \begin{vmatrix} \hat{i} & \hat{j} & \hat{k} \\ 1 & -2 & -1 \\ 3 & -2 & -1 \end{vmatrix} = -2\hat{j} + 4\hat{k}$$

$$\Rightarrow \text{unit vector } \hat{a} = \frac{-2\hat{j} + 4\hat{k}}{\sqrt{4 + 16}} = \frac{-2\hat{j} + 4\hat{k}}{2\sqrt{5}}$$

Angle between the unit vector and $\vec{r} = \hat{i} + \hat{j} + \hat{k}$

$$= \cos^{-1} \frac{\vec{r} \cdot \hat{a}}{|\vec{r}| \cdot |\hat{a}|}$$

$$= \cos^{-1} \frac{1}{\sqrt{15}} = \sec^{-1} \sqrt{15} = \tan^{-1} \sqrt{14}$$

**11. (b, d)** Normal to plane $P_1$ is

$$\vec{n_1} = (2\hat{i} + 3\hat{k}) \times (4\hat{j} - 3\hat{k}) = -18\hat{i}$$

Normal to plane $P_2$ is

$$\vec{n_2} = (\hat{j} - \hat{k}) \times (3\hat{i} + 3\hat{j}) = 3\hat{i} - 3\hat{j} - 3\hat{k}$$

$\therefore \vec{A}$ is parallel to $\pm(\hat{n_1} \times \hat{n_2}) = \pm(-54\hat{j} + 54\hat{k})$

Now, angle between $\vec{A}$ and $2\hat{i} + \hat{j} - 2\hat{k}$ is given by

$$\cos\theta = \pm \frac{(-54\hat{j}) + 54\hat{k}).(2\hat{i} + \hat{j} - 2\hat{k})}{54\sqrt{2}.3} = \pm \frac{1}{\sqrt{2}}$$

$$\theta = \frac{\pi}{4} \text{ or } \frac{3\pi}{4}$$

**12. (a, c)** Here $|\vec{a}| = 1 = |\vec{b}|$.

Let $\theta$ be the angle between $\vec{a}$ and $\vec{b}$.

Then $|\vec{v}| = |\vec{a} \times \vec{b}| = |\vec{a}||\vec{b}| \sin\theta$

$$= 1.1 \sin\theta = \sin\theta \qquad \ldots\ldots\ldots(1)$$

Now, $\vec{u} = \vec{a} - (\vec{a}.\vec{b})\vec{b}$

$$= \vec{a} - (|\vec{a}||\vec{b}|\cos\theta)\vec{b} = \vec{a} - \cos\theta\vec{b}$$

$$\Rightarrow u^2 = |\vec{u}|^2 = (\vec{a} - \cos\theta\,\vec{b})^2$$

$$= a^2 + \cos^2\theta \cdot b^2 - 2\cos\theta \cdot \vec{a} \cdot \vec{b}$$

$$= 1 + \cos^2\theta \cdot 1 - 2\cos\theta\,(\cos\theta)$$

$$= 1 + \cos^2\theta - 2\cos^2\theta = 1 - \cos^2\theta = \sin^2\theta.$$

$\therefore |\vec{u}| = \sin\theta$.

Hence from (1), $|\vec{v}| = |\vec{u}|$.

Again, $\vec{u}.\vec{b} = \{\vec{a} - (\vec{a}.\vec{b})\vec{b}\}.\vec{b} = \cos\theta - \cos\theta = 0$.

$\therefore |\vec{u}| + |\vec{u}.\vec{b}| = |\vec{u}| + 0 = |\vec{u}|$

**13. (a,d)** Let $\vec{a} = 2\hat{i} + \hat{j} - 3\hat{k}$ and $\hat{b} = \hat{i} - 2\hat{j} + \hat{k}$

Then $\quad \vec{a} \times \vec{b} = \begin{vmatrix} \hat{i} & \hat{j} & \hat{k} \\ 2 & 1 & -3 \\ 1 & -2 & 1 \end{vmatrix}$

$$= \hat{i}(1 - 6) - \hat{j}(2 + 3) + \hat{k}(-4 - 1) = -5\hat{i} - 5\hat{j} - 5\hat{k}.$$

Therefore the unit vector perpendicular to $\vec{a}$ and $\vec{b}$ is

$$\pm \frac{\vec{a} \times \vec{b}}{|\vec{a} \times \vec{b}|} = \pm \frac{5\hat{i} + 5\hat{j} + 5\hat{k}}{\sqrt{5^2 + 5^2 + 5^2}}$$

$$= \pm \frac{5(\hat{i} + \hat{j} + \hat{k})}{5\sqrt{3}} = \pm \frac{1}{\sqrt{3}}(\hat{i} + \hat{j} + \hat{k})$$

Hence the required vector of magnitude 5 is

$$\pm \frac{5}{\sqrt{3}}(\hat{i} + \hat{j} + \hat{k}).$$

**14. (a,b,c)** $\vec{r} \times (\hat{i} + 2\hat{j} + \hat{k}) = \hat{i} - \hat{k}$

Let $\vec{r} = x\hat{i} + y\hat{j} + z\hat{k}$

$\therefore (x\hat{i} + y\hat{j} + z\hat{k}) \times (\hat{i} + 2\hat{j} + \hat{k}) = \hat{i} - \hat{k}$

$$\Rightarrow \begin{vmatrix} \hat{i} & \hat{j} & \hat{k} \\ x & y & z \\ 1 & 2 & 1 \end{vmatrix} = \hat{i} - \hat{k}$$

$$\Rightarrow \hat{i}(y - 2z) - \hat{j}(x - z) + \hat{k}(2x - y) = \hat{i} - \hat{k}$$

On comparing

$y - 2z = 1, x - z = 0$ and $2x - y = -1$

$\therefore z = x, y = 2x + 1$

$\therefore \vec{r} = x\hat{i} + (2x + 1)\hat{j} + x\hat{k} \qquad \ldots.(i)$

For $x = 1$ and $x = 3$

$$\vec{r} = \hat{i} + 3\hat{j} + \hat{k}$$

and $\vec{r} = 3\hat{i} + 7\hat{j} + 3\hat{k}$

(alternate (b) is correct)

Now, from eq. (i)

$$\vec{r} = \hat{j} + x(\hat{i} + 2\hat{j} + \hat{k})$$

or $\quad \vec{r} = \hat{j} + t(\hat{i} + 2\hat{j} + \hat{k})$

where $t$ is scalar.

**15. (b)** Let $\vec{R} = x\hat{i} + y\hat{j} + z\hat{k}$. Then

$$\vec{R} \times \vec{B} = \vec{C} \times \vec{B} \Rightarrow (\vec{R} - \vec{C}) \times \vec{B} = \vec{0}$$

$$\Rightarrow \begin{vmatrix} \hat{i} & \hat{j} & \hat{k} \\ x - 4 & y + 3 & z - 7 \\ 1 & 1 & 1 \end{vmatrix} = \vec{0}$$

$$\Rightarrow (y - z + 10)\hat{i} + (z - x - 3)\hat{j} + (x - y - 7)\hat{k} = \vec{0}$$

$$\Rightarrow y - z = -10, z - x = 3, x - y = 7$$

Also $\vec{R} \cdot \vec{A} = 0 \Rightarrow 2x + 0 \cdot y + z = 0 \Rightarrow z = -2x \cdot$

Solving, we obtain

$x = -1, y = -8, z = 2$. Hence $\vec{R} = -\hat{i} - 8\hat{j} + 2\hat{k}$.

**16.**   **(d)** $\vec{a} \times \vec{b}$ is normal to plane P

$\vec{c} \times \vec{d}$ is normal to plane Q

$(\vec{a} \times \vec{b}) \times (\vec{c} \times \vec{b}) = 0 \Rightarrow \vec{a} \times \vec{b} \parallel \vec{c} \times \vec{d}$

Normals are parallel so planes are also parallel.

**17.**   **(c)**   $\overrightarrow{PQ} \times (\overrightarrow{RS} + \overrightarrow{ST}) = \overrightarrow{PQ} \times \overrightarrow{RT}$

$|\overrightarrow{PQ}| \times |\overrightarrow{RT}| \sin 120° \hat{n} \neq 0$

Statement-1 is true.

Also, $|\overrightarrow{PQ}| \times |\overrightarrow{RS}| = |\overrightarrow{PQ}| \times |\overrightarrow{RS}| \sin 120° \times \hat{n}_1 \neq 0$

And $|\overrightarrow{PQ}| \times |\overrightarrow{ST}| = |\overrightarrow{PQ}| \times |\overrightarrow{ST}| \sin 180° \times \hat{n}_2 = 0$

$\therefore$ Statement-2 is false.

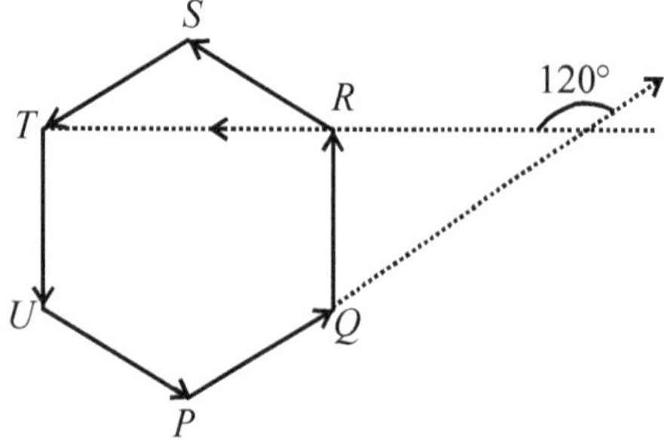


**18.**   **(c)**   $|\vec{v}| = |\vec{a} \times \vec{b}| = |\vec{a}||\vec{b}| \sin\theta = \sin\theta$

$\vec{u} = \vec{a} - (\vec{a} \cdot \vec{b})\vec{b} = \vec{a} - \vec{b}\cos\theta$

$\Rightarrow |\vec{u}| = |\vec{a}|^2 + |\vec{b}|^2 \cos^2\theta - 2\vec{a} \cdot \vec{b}\cos\theta$

$= 1 + \cos^2\theta - 2\cos^2\theta = \sin^2\theta \Rightarrow |\vec{u}| = |\vec{v}|$

If $\theta$ is the angle between the vectors

$\dfrac{1}{3}(2\hat{i} - 2\hat{j} + \hat{k})$ and $(2i - 4j + 3k)$, then

$\cos\theta = \dfrac{\dfrac{1}{3}(4 + 8 + 3)}{\sqrt{29}} = \dfrac{15}{3\sqrt{29}} \Rightarrow \theta = \cos^{-1}\left(\dfrac{5}{\sqrt{29}}\right)$

**19.**   **(a)**   $\because \overrightarrow{OA} = \vec{a}, \overrightarrow{OB} = \vec{b}, \overrightarrow{OC} = \vec{c}$

$\therefore \overrightarrow{AB} = \overrightarrow{OB} - \overrightarrow{OA} = \vec{b} - \vec{a}$

and $\overrightarrow{BC} = \overrightarrow{OC} - \overrightarrow{OB} = \vec{c} - \vec{b}$

$\overrightarrow{AB}$ is parallel to $\overrightarrow{BC}$

$\therefore \overrightarrow{AB} \times \overrightarrow{BC} = \vec{0} \Rightarrow (\vec{b} - \vec{a}) \times (\vec{c} - \vec{b}) = 0$

$\Rightarrow \vec{b} \times \vec{c} - \vec{b} \times \vec{b} - \vec{a} \times \vec{c} + \vec{a} \times \vec{b} = 0$

$\Rightarrow \vec{b} \times \vec{c} - 0 + \vec{c} \times \vec{a} + \vec{a} \times \vec{b} = 0$

Hence, $\vec{a} \times \vec{b} + \vec{b} \times \vec{c} + \vec{c} \times \vec{a} = 0$

**20.**   **(1)**

Vector perpendicular to the plane of given vectors is

$\vec{a} = (2\hat{i} - \hat{j} + \hat{k}) \times (3\hat{i} + 4\hat{j} - \hat{k})$

$= \begin{vmatrix} \hat{i} & \hat{j} & \hat{k} \\ 2 & -1 & 1 \\ 3 & 4 & -1 \end{vmatrix} = -3\hat{i} + 5\hat{j} + 11\hat{k}$.

$|\vec{a}| = \sqrt{3^2 + 5^2 + 11^2} = \sqrt{155}$

$\therefore \dfrac{1}{\sqrt{155}} |\vec{a}| = 1$.

**21.**   **(2)**

The vector perpendicular to $\vec{a}$ and $\vec{b}$ is

$\vec{a} \times \vec{b} = \begin{vmatrix} \hat{i} & \hat{j} & \hat{k} \\ 1 & 1 & 0 \\ 0 & 1 & 1 \end{vmatrix} = \hat{i}(1-0) - \hat{j}(1-0) + \hat{k}(1-0)$

$= \hat{i} - \hat{j} + \hat{k}$

$\therefore |\vec{a} \times \vec{b}| = \sqrt{1 + 1 + 1} = \sqrt{3}$.

Hence the unit vector perpendicular to $\vec{a}$ and $\vec{b}$ is

$\pm \dfrac{\vec{a} \times \vec{b}}{|\vec{a} \times \vec{b}|} = \pm \dfrac{1}{\sqrt{3}}(\hat{i} - \hat{j} + \hat{k})$.

Hence the number of such vectors is 2.

**22.**   **(4)**

Given, $\vec{a} \times \vec{b} = 2\vec{a} \times \vec{c} \Rightarrow \vec{a} \times (\vec{b} - 2\vec{c}) = 0$

Since the vectors are non zero.

$\therefore \vec{b} - 2\vec{c}$ is parallel to $\vec{a}$. Let $\vec{b} - 2\vec{c} = \lambda \vec{a}$

Now $|\vec{b} - 2\vec{c}|^2 = b^2 + 4c^2 - 4\vec{b} \cdot \vec{c}$

$= 16 + 4 - 4 \times 4 \times 1 \times \dfrac{1}{4} = 16$

i.e., $\lambda^2 a^2 = 16 \Rightarrow \lambda^2 = 16 \Rightarrow \lambda = \pm 4$

$\therefore$ Positive value of $\lambda = 4$.

**23.**   **(1)**   Let $\vec{a} = 2\hat{i} + 3\hat{j} - \hat{k}$ and $\vec{b} = \hat{i} - \hat{j} + 2\hat{k}$, then

$\vec{a} \times \vec{b} = \begin{vmatrix} \hat{i} & \hat{j} & \hat{k} \\ 2 & 3 & -1 \\ 1 & -1 & 2 \end{vmatrix} = 5\hat{i} - 5\hat{j} - 5\hat{k}$

Unit vector perpendicular to the plane of $\vec{a}$ and $\vec{b}$ is

$\dfrac{1}{\sqrt{3}}(\hat{i} - \hat{j} - \hat{k})$.

$$\cos\left(\frac{\pi}{2}-\theta\right) = \frac{2\hat{i}-2\hat{j}+\hat{k}}{3} \cdot \frac{1}{\sqrt{3}}(\hat{i}-\hat{j}-\hat{k}) = \frac{1}{\sqrt{3}}$$

$$\Rightarrow \sqrt{3}\sin\theta = 1$$

**24. (2)**

Angle between the faces OAB and ABC is the same as the angle between their normals.

Now $\overrightarrow{n_1}$ = the vector normal to face OAB

$$= \overrightarrow{OA} \times \overrightarrow{OB} = \begin{vmatrix} \hat{i} & \hat{j} & \hat{k} \\ 1 & 2 & 1 \\ 2 & 1 & 3 \end{vmatrix} = 5\hat{i} - \hat{j} - 3\hat{k}$$

$\overrightarrow{n_2}$ = the vector normal to face ABC

$$= \overrightarrow{AB} \times \overrightarrow{AC} = \begin{vmatrix} \hat{i} & \hat{j} & \hat{k} \\ 1 & -1 & 2 \\ -2 & -1 & 1 \end{vmatrix} = \hat{i} - 5\hat{j} - 3\hat{k}$$

The angle between the faces,

$$\cos\theta = \frac{\overrightarrow{n_1}.\overrightarrow{n_2}}{|\overrightarrow{n_1}||\overrightarrow{n_2}|} = \frac{5+5+9}{\sqrt{35}\sqrt{35}} = \frac{19}{35}$$

$$\therefore \frac{35}{19}\cos\theta = 1$$

$$\Rightarrow \frac{70}{19}\cos\theta = 2.$$

**1. (a)** $\vec{A}.\big((\vec{B}+\vec{C})\times(\vec{A}+\vec{B}+\vec{C})\big)$

It is scalar triple product of three vectors namely

$\vec{A}, \vec{B}+\vec{C}, \vec{A}+\vec{B}+\vec{C}$

Clearly first cross product will take place and then dot product

Hence the given product

$= \vec{A}.[\vec{B}\times\vec{A}+\vec{B}\times\vec{B}+\vec{B}\times\vec{C}+\vec{C}\times\vec{A}+\vec{C}\times\vec{B}+\vec{C}\times\vec{C}]$

$= \vec{A}.\vec{B}\times\vec{A}+\vec{A}.\vec{B}\times\vec{C}+\vec{A}.\vec{C}\times\vec{A}+\vec{A}.\vec{C}\times\vec{B}$

$\hfill (\text{Using } \vec{a}\times\vec{a}=0)$

$= 0+[\vec{A}\,\vec{B}\,\vec{C}]+0+[\vec{A}\,\vec{C}\,\vec{B}]$

(as $\big[\vec{a}\,\vec{b}\,\vec{c}\big]=0$ if any two vector are equal out of $\vec{a},\vec{b},\vec{c}$ )

$= \big[\vec{A}\,\vec{B}\,\vec{C}\big]-\big[\vec{A}\,\vec{B}\,\vec{C}\big]$   [Using $[\vec{a}\,\vec{b}\,\vec{c}]=-[\vec{a}\,\vec{c}\,\vec{b}]$]

$= 0$

**2. (d)** $|(\vec{a}\times\vec{b}).\vec{c}|=|\vec{a}||\vec{b}||\vec{c}|$

$\Rightarrow ||\vec{a}||\vec{b}|\sin\theta\ \hat{n}.\vec{c}|=|\vec{a}||\vec{b}||\vec{c}|$

$\Rightarrow |\vec{a}||\vec{b}||\vec{c}|\sin\theta\cos\alpha=|\vec{a}||\vec{b}||\vec{c}|$

$\Rightarrow |\sin\theta||\cos\alpha|=1$

$\Rightarrow \theta=\pi/2$ and $\alpha=0$

$\Rightarrow \vec{a}\perp\vec{b}$ and $\vec{c}\parallel\hat{n}$

i.e., $\vec{c}$ is perpendicular to both $\vec{a}$ and $\vec{b}$

$\Rightarrow \vec{a}.\vec{b}=\vec{b}.\vec{c}=\vec{c}.\vec{a}=0$

**3. (b)** $[\lambda(\vec{a}+\vec{b})\quad \lambda^2\vec{b}\quad \lambda\vec{c}]=[\vec{a}\quad \vec{b}+\vec{c}\quad \vec{b}]$

$\begin{vmatrix}\lambda & \lambda & 0\\ 0 & \lambda^2 & 0\\ 0 & 0 & \lambda\end{vmatrix}=\begin{vmatrix}1 & 0 & 0\\ 0 & 1 & 1\\ 0 & 1 & 0\end{vmatrix} \Rightarrow \lambda^4=-1$

Hence no real value of $\lambda$.

**4. (d)** $\vec{a}=\hat{i}-\hat{k},\ \vec{b}=x\hat{i}+\hat{j}+(1-x)\hat{k}$

and $\vec{c}=y\hat{i}+x\hat{j}+(1+x-y)\hat{k}$

$[\vec{a}\,\vec{b}\,\vec{c}]=\vec{a}.(\vec{b}\times\vec{c})$

$\vec{b}\times\vec{c}=\begin{vmatrix}\hat{i} & \hat{j} & \hat{k}\\ x & 1 & 1-x\\ y & x & 1+x-y\end{vmatrix}$

$= \hat{i}(1+x-y-x+x^2)$

$\qquad -\hat{j}(x+x^2-xy-y+xy)+\hat{k}(x^2-y)$

$\vec{a}.(\vec{b}\times\vec{c})=1$, which does not depend on x and y.

**5. (a)** $\begin{vmatrix}\vec{a}\cdot\vec{a} & \vec{a}\cdot\vec{b} & \vec{a}\cdot\vec{c}\\ \vec{b}\cdot\vec{a} & \vec{b}\cdot\vec{b} & \vec{b}\cdot\vec{c}\\ \vec{c}\cdot\vec{a} & \vec{c}\cdot\vec{b} & \vec{c}\cdot\vec{c}\end{vmatrix}$

$= \begin{vmatrix}a_1^2+a_2^2+a_3^2 & a_1b_1+a_2b_2+a_3b_3 & a_1c_1+a_2c_2+a_3c_3\\ a_1b_1+a_2b_2+a_3b_3 & b_1^2+b_2^2+b_3^2 & b_1c_1+b_2c_2+b_3c_3\\ a_1c_1+a_2c_2+a_3c_3 & b_1c_1+b_2c_2+b_3c_3 & c_1^2+c_2^2+c_3^2\end{vmatrix}$

$= \begin{vmatrix}a_1 & a_2 & a_3\\ b_1 & b_2 & b_3\\ c_1 & c_2 & c_3\end{vmatrix}\begin{vmatrix}a_1 & a_2 & a_3\\ b_1 & b_2 & b_3\\ c_1 & c_1 & c_3\end{vmatrix} = [\vec{a}\,\vec{b}\,\vec{c}]^2$

**6. (a)** We have $\vec{\alpha}=x(\vec{a}\times\vec{b})+y(\vec{b}\times\vec{c})+z(\vec{c}\times\vec{a})$

Taking dot products with $\vec{a},\ \vec{b},\ \vec{c}$, we get

$\vec{\alpha}.\vec{a}=y[\vec{a}\,\vec{b}\,\vec{c}]\Rightarrow y=8(\vec{\alpha}.\vec{a})$

$\vec{\alpha}.\vec{b}=z[\vec{a}\,\vec{b}\,\vec{c}]\Rightarrow z=8(\vec{\alpha}.\vec{b})$

$\vec{\alpha}.\vec{c}=x[\vec{a}\,\vec{b}\,\vec{c}]\Rightarrow x=8(\vec{\alpha}.\vec{c})$

$\therefore x+y+z=8\vec{\alpha}.(\vec{a}+\vec{b}+\vec{c})$

**7. (c,d)** $\begin{vmatrix}2 & 3 & 4\\ 1 & \alpha & 2\\ 1 & 2 & \alpha\end{vmatrix}=15\Rightarrow 2(\alpha^2-4)+3(2-\alpha)+4(2-\alpha)=15$

$\Rightarrow 2\alpha^2-7\alpha-9=0\ \Rightarrow\alpha=-1,\dfrac{9}{2}$

**8. (a,c)** Let $\vec{A}=(\vec{a}.\hat{i})\,\hat{i}+(\vec{a}.\hat{j})\,\hat{j}+(\vec{a}.\hat{k})\,\hat{k}$

$\qquad = \hat{i}+\hat{j}+\hat{k}$

and $\vec{B}=(\vec{b}.\hat{i})\,\hat{i}+(\vec{b}.\hat{j})\,\hat{j}+(\vec{c}.\hat{k})\,\hat{k}$

$\qquad = \hat{i}-\hat{j}+0$

$\vec{C}=\hat{i}+\hat{j}-2\hat{k}$

$\vec{A}.\vec{B}=0,\ \vec{B}.\vec{C}=0,\ \vec{C}.\vec{A}=0$

$[\vec{A}\,\vec{B}\,\vec{C}]=\begin{vmatrix}1 & 1 & 1\\ 1 & -1 & 1\\ 1 & 1 & -2\end{vmatrix}$

$= 1(2-1)-1(-2-1)+1(1+1)=6$

$\therefore \vec{A},\vec{B},\vec{C}$ are mutually perpendicular and form a parallelopiped of volume 6 cube unit.

**9. (d)** We have $[\vec{\alpha}\ \vec{\beta}\ \vec{\gamma}]=\begin{vmatrix}a & 2a & -3a\\ 2a+1 & 2a+3 & a+1\\ 3a+5 & a+5 & a+2\end{vmatrix}$

$$= a\{(2a+3)(a+2)-(a+5)(a+1)\}$$
$$\quad -2a\{(2a+1)(a+2)-(3a+5)(a+1)\}$$
$$\quad -3a\{(2a+1)(a+5)-(3a+5)(2a+3)\}$$

$$= a(15a^2+31a+37), \text{ on simplification}$$

$$= 15a\left\{\left(a+\frac{31}{30}\right)^2+\frac{1259}{900}\right\} \neq 0 \quad \text{[for all non-zero a]}$$

Hence, the given vectors are non-coplanar, for all $a \neq 0$.

**For Qs. (10-12)**

$$\because \; [\vec{a}\,\vec{b}\,\vec{c}][\vec{u}\,\vec{v}\,\vec{w}] = \begin{vmatrix} \vec{a}.\vec{u} & \vec{b}.\vec{u} & \vec{c}.\vec{u} \\ \vec{a}.\vec{v} & \vec{b}.\vec{v} & \vec{c}.\vec{v} \\ \vec{a}.\vec{w} & \vec{b}.\vec{w} & \vec{c}.\vec{w} \end{vmatrix}$$

$$\therefore \; [\vec{a}\,\vec{b}\,\vec{c}]^2 = [\vec{a}\,\vec{b}\,\vec{c}][\vec{a}\,\vec{b}\,\vec{c}]$$

$$= \begin{vmatrix} \vec{a}.\vec{a} & \vec{b}.\vec{a} & \vec{c}.\vec{a} \\ \vec{a}.\vec{b} & \vec{b}.\vec{b} & \vec{c}.\vec{b} \\ \vec{a}.\vec{c} & \vec{b}.\vec{c} & \vec{c}.\vec{c} \end{vmatrix}$$

Now, $\vec{a}.\vec{a} = a^2 = |\vec{a}|^2 = 16$

$$\vec{a}.\vec{b} = \vec{b}.\vec{a} = |\vec{a}||\vec{b}|\cos \pi/3 = 4.4.\frac{1}{2} = 8$$

$$\vec{a}.\vec{c} = \vec{c}.\vec{a} = |\vec{a}||\vec{c}|\cos \pi/3 = 4.4.\frac{1}{2} = 8$$

$$\vec{b}.\vec{b} = b^2 = |\vec{b}|^2 = 16$$

$$\vec{b}.\vec{c} = \vec{c}.\vec{b} = |\vec{b}||\vec{c}|\cos \pi/3 = 4.4.\frac{1}{2} = 8$$

$$\vec{c}.\vec{c} = |\vec{c}|^2 = 4^2 = 16$$

From Eq. (i),

$$[\vec{a}\,\vec{b}\,\vec{c}]^2 = \begin{vmatrix} 16 & 8 & 8 \\ 8 & 16 & 8 \\ 8 & 8 & 16 \end{vmatrix}$$

$$= 8^3 \begin{vmatrix} 1 & 1 & 1 \\ 1 & 2 & 1 \\ 1 & 1 & 2 \end{vmatrix}$$

$$= 8^3.4 = 64 \times 32$$

$$\therefore \; \left|[\vec{a}\,\vec{b}\,\vec{c}]\right| = 32\sqrt{2}$$

**10. (c)** Here $[\vec{p}\,\vec{q}\,\vec{r}] = 0$

So, $\begin{vmatrix} a & -a & b \\ 1 & 0 & 1 \\ c & c & b \end{vmatrix} = 0$

or $a(0-c)+a(b-c)+b(c-0) = 0$

$\Rightarrow ab + bc = 2ac \Rightarrow b = \dfrac{2ac}{a+c}$

So, b is the HM of a, c.

**11. (a)** Volume of the parallelopiped = (base area) × (height)

$$32\sqrt{2} = \left(4 \times 4 \times \sin \pi/3\right) h$$
$$= 8\sqrt{3} \times h$$
$$\therefore \; h = 4\sqrt{\frac{2}{3}}$$

**12. (b)** Volume of the tetrahedron

$$= \frac{1}{3}(\text{base area})(\text{height})$$

$$\frac{16\sqrt{2}}{3} = \frac{1}{3}\left(\frac{\sqrt{3}}{4}(4)^2\right) \times h$$

$$\therefore \; h = \frac{\dfrac{16\sqrt{2}}{3}}{\dfrac{4\sqrt{3}}{3}}$$

$$= \frac{4\sqrt{2}}{\sqrt{3}} = 4\sqrt{\frac{2}{3}}$$

**13. (c)** Volume of the triangular prism $= \dfrac{1}{2}[\vec{a}\,\vec{b}\,\vec{c}]$

$$= \frac{1}{2} \times (32\sqrt{2}) = 16\sqrt{2}$$

**14. A→s; B→r; C→p; D→q**

(A) We have $\vec{b} \times (\vec{a} \times \vec{b}) = \vec{b} \times \vec{c} = \vec{a}$

$\Rightarrow |\vec{b}|^2 \vec{a} - (\vec{a}.\vec{b})\vec{b} = \vec{a} \Rightarrow |\vec{b}|^2 = 1 \textbf{(s)}$

and $\vec{a}.\vec{b} = 0$

(B) $|\vec{a} \times \vec{b}| = |\vec{c}| \Rightarrow |\vec{a}||\vec{b}|.\sin\dfrac{\pi}{2} = |\vec{c}| \Rightarrow |\vec{a}| = |\vec{c}|$ **(r)**

(C) $[\vec{a}\,\vec{b}\,\vec{c}] = (\vec{a} \times \vec{b}).\vec{c} = \vec{c}.\vec{c} = 4$ **(p)**

(D) Clearly $\vec{a}, \vec{b}, \vec{c}$ are mutually perpendicular so

$$|\vec{a}+\vec{b}+\vec{c}| = \sqrt{|\vec{a}|^2+|\vec{b}|^2+|\vec{c}|^2} = 3 \textbf{ (q)}$$

**15. A → r, s, t; B→p,r,t; C→p,q,r,t**

If $\vec{a}, \vec{b}$ and $\vec{c}$ are three conterminus edges of parallelopiped, triangular prism and tetrahedron, then

$$V_1 = [\vec{a}\,\vec{b}\,\vec{c}], V_2 = \frac{1}{2}[\vec{a}\,\vec{b}\,\vec{c}] \text{ and } V_3 = \frac{1}{6}[\vec{a}\,\vec{b}\,\vec{c}]$$

$$\therefore \; V_1:V_2:V_3 = 1:\frac{1}{2}:\frac{1}{6} = 6:3:1$$

(A) Here, $\vec{a} = \hat{i}-\hat{j}-6\hat{k}, \vec{b} = \hat{i}-\hat{j}+4\hat{k}$

and $\vec{c} = 2\hat{i}-5\hat{j}+3\hat{k}$

$$\therefore \; V_1 = \begin{vmatrix} 1 & -1 & -6 \\ 1 & -1 & 4 \\ 2 & -5 & 3 \end{vmatrix}$$

$$= 1(-3+20)+1(3-8)-6(-5+2)$$
$$= 17-5+18 = 30$$

$\therefore V_2 = 15$ and $V_3 = 5$

$V_1 + V_2 + V_3 = 50$ **(s)**

$V_1 + 3V_3 = 30 + 15 = 45 = 3V_2$ **(r)**

and $V_1 : V_2 : V_3 = 6 : 3 : 1$ **(t)**

(B)  Here, $\vec{a} = -2\hat{i} + 3\hat{j} - 3\hat{k}$

$\vec{b} = 4\hat{i} + 5\hat{j} - 3\hat{k}$

and  $\vec{c} = 6\hat{i} + 2\hat{j} - 3\hat{k}$

$$\therefore \quad V_1 = \begin{vmatrix} -2 & 3 & -3 \\ 4 & 5 & -3 \\ 6 & 2 & -3 \end{vmatrix}$$

$= -2(-15 + 6) - 3(-12 + 18) - 3(8 - 30)$

$= 18 - 18 + 66 = 66$

$\therefore \qquad V_2 = 33$ and $V_3 = 11$

$\because \qquad 2V_1 + 3V_3 = 132 + 33 = 165 = 5V_2$ **(p)**

$V_1 + V_2 + V_3 = 110$

$V_1 + 3V_3 = 66 + 33 = 3V_2$ **(r)**

and $\qquad V_1 : V_2 : V_3 = 6 : 3 : 1$ **(t)**

(C)  Here, $\vec{a} = -3\hat{i} + \hat{j} + \hat{k}$, $\vec{b} = 4\hat{i} + 2\hat{j} + 4\hat{k}$

and  $\vec{c} = 2\hat{i} + 2\hat{j}$

$$\therefore \quad V_1 = \begin{vmatrix} -3 & 1 & 1 \\ 4 & 2 & 4 \\ 2 & 2 & 0 \end{vmatrix}$$

$= -3(0 - 8) - 1(0 - 8) + 1(8 - 4)$

$= 24 + 8 + 4$

$= 36$

$\therefore V_2 = 18$ and $V_3 = 6$

$2V_1 + 3V_3 = 72 + 18 = 90 = 5V_2$ **(p)**,

$V_1 + V_2 + V_3 = 60$ **(q)**

$V_1 + 3V_3 = 36 + 18 = 54 = 3V_2$ **(r)**

$V_1 : V_2 : V_3 = 6 : 3 : 1$ **(t)**

**16. (c)**  $\because [\vec{a} \times \vec{b} \;\; \vec{b} \times \vec{c} \;\; \vec{c} \times \vec{a}] = (\vec{a} \times \vec{b}) . \{(\vec{b} \times \vec{c}) \times (\vec{c} \times \vec{a})\}$

$= (\vec{a} \times \vec{b}) . \{(\vec{b} . (\vec{c} \times \vec{a})) \vec{c} - (\vec{c} . (\vec{c} \times \vec{a})) \vec{b}\}$

$= (\vec{a} \times \vec{b}) . \{[\vec{b} \;\; \vec{c} \;\; \vec{a}] \vec{c} - 0\}$

$= (\vec{a} \times \vec{b} . \vec{c}) [\vec{b} \;\; \vec{c} \;\; \vec{a}] = [\vec{a} \;\; \vec{b} \;\; \vec{c}]^2$

$\because \vec{a}, \vec{b}, \vec{c}$ are coplanar.

$\therefore [\vec{a} \;\; \vec{b} \;\; \vec{c}] = 0$

And then $[\vec{a} \times \vec{b} \;\; \vec{b} \times \vec{c} \;\; \vec{c} \times \vec{a}] = 0$

Hence, $\vec{a} \times \vec{b}$, $\vec{b} \times \vec{c}$ and $\vec{c} \times \vec{a}$ are also coplanar.

**17. 2**

Vol. of parallelopiped $= [\vec{a} \;\; \vec{b} \;\; \vec{c}]$

$$= \begin{vmatrix} 2 & -2 & 0 \\ 1 & 1 & -1 \\ 3 & 0 & -1 \end{vmatrix} = 2(-1) + 2(-1 + 3) = 2$$

**18. 3**

Given that $\vec{a}, \vec{b}, \vec{c}$ are non coplanar

$\therefore |\vec{a}, \vec{b}, \vec{c}| \neq 0$

Also $\vec{p} = \dfrac{\vec{b} \times \vec{c}}{[\vec{a} \; \vec{b} \; \vec{c}]}$, $\vec{q} = \dfrac{\vec{c} \times \vec{a}}{[\vec{a} \; \vec{b} \; \vec{c}]}$, $\vec{r} = \dfrac{\vec{a} \times \vec{b}}{[\vec{a} \; \vec{b} \; \vec{c}]}$   ..(1)

Now, $(\vec{a} + \vec{b}) . \vec{p} + (\vec{b} + \vec{c}) . \vec{q} + (\vec{c} + \vec{a}) . \vec{r}$

$= (\vec{a} + \vec{b}) . \dfrac{\vec{b} \times \vec{c}}{[\vec{a} \vec{b} \vec{c}]} + (\vec{b} + \vec{c}) . \dfrac{\vec{c} \times \vec{a}}{[\vec{a} \vec{b} \vec{c}]} + (\vec{c} + \vec{a}) . \dfrac{\vec{a} \times \vec{b}}{[\vec{a} \vec{b} \vec{c}]}$

$= \dfrac{\vec{a} . \vec{b} \times \vec{c}}{[\vec{a} \; \vec{b} \; \vec{c}]} + \dfrac{\vec{b} . \vec{c} \times \vec{a}}{[\vec{a} \; \vec{b} \; \vec{c}]} + \dfrac{\vec{c} . \vec{a} \times \vec{b}}{[\vec{a} \; \vec{b} \; \vec{c}]}$

$[\text{Using } \vec{b} . \vec{b} \times \vec{c} = \vec{c} . \vec{c} \times \vec{a} = \vec{a} . \vec{a} \times \vec{b} = 0]$

$= \dfrac{[\vec{a} \; \vec{b} \; \vec{c}]}{[\vec{a} \; \vec{b} \; \vec{c}]} + \dfrac{[\vec{a} \; \vec{b} \; \vec{c}]}{[\vec{a} \; \vec{b} \; \vec{c}]} + \dfrac{[\vec{a} \; \vec{b} \; \vec{c}]}{[\vec{a} \; \vec{b} \; \vec{c}]} = 1 + 1 + 1 = 3$

**19. 8**

We have,

$\dfrac{1}{2} [\vec{a} \times \vec{b} \;\; \vec{b} \times \vec{c} \;\; \vec{c} \times \vec{a}]$

$= \dfrac{1}{2} (\vec{a} \times \vec{b}) . \left\{ (\vec{b} \times \vec{c}) \times (\vec{c} \times \vec{a}) \right\}$

$= \dfrac{1}{2} (\vec{a} \times \vec{b}) . \left\{ (\vec{m} . \vec{a}) \vec{c} - (\vec{m} . \vec{c}) \vec{a} \right\}$

$\qquad\qquad\qquad\qquad$ (where $\vec{m} = \vec{b} \times \vec{c}$ )

$= \dfrac{1}{2} \left\{ (\vec{a} \times \vec{b}) . \vec{c} \right\} . \left\{ \vec{a} . (\vec{b} \times \vec{c}) \right\}$

$= \dfrac{1}{2} [\vec{a} \; \vec{b} \; \vec{c}]^2 = \dfrac{4^2}{2} = 8.$

**20. 1**

$$\begin{vmatrix} a & a^2 & 1 + a^3 \\ b & b^2 & 1 + b^3 \\ c & c^2 & 1 + c^3 \end{vmatrix} = 0 \Rightarrow \begin{vmatrix} a & a^2 & 1 \\ b & b^2 & 1 \\ c & c^2 & 1 \end{vmatrix} + \begin{vmatrix} a & a^2 & a^3 \\ b & b^2 & b^3 \\ c & c^2 & c^3 \end{vmatrix} = 0$$

$$\Rightarrow (1 + abc) \begin{vmatrix} 1 & a & a^2 \\ 1 & b & b^2 \\ 1 & c & c^2 \end{vmatrix} = 0$$

As $\begin{vmatrix} 1 & a & a^2 \\ 1 & b & b^2 \\ 1 & c & c^2 \end{vmatrix} \neq 0$ (given condition ) $\therefore abc = -1$

$\therefore |abc| = 1.$

**1. (d)** The projection of the segment on the coordinates axes are –9, 12, –8. Thus the direction ratios of the segment PQ are –9, 12, –8. Hence the direction cosines are

$$-\frac{9}{17}, \frac{12}{17}, \frac{-8}{17}.$$

**2. (c)** $AB = 6$, $BC = \sqrt{13}$, $CA = 3$

$\therefore \ AB : AC = 2 : 1$

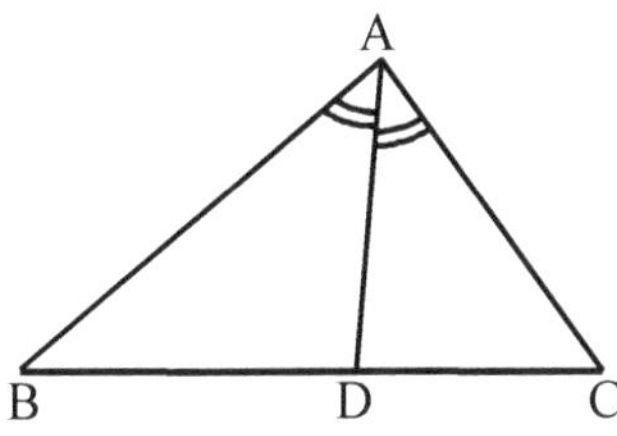

Internal bisector of an angle divides the opposite side in the ratio of adjacent sides

$$\therefore \frac{BD}{CD} = \frac{AB}{AC} = \frac{2}{1}$$

$\therefore$ Coordinate of D are $\left(2, \dfrac{13}{3}, 6\right)$

$\therefore$ Length $AD = \dfrac{2}{3}\sqrt{34}$

**3. (c)** The direction cosines of the line are $\cos\theta$, $\cos\beta$, $\cos\theta$

$$\therefore \cos^2\theta + \cos^2\beta + \cos^2\theta = 1$$

$$\Rightarrow 2\cos^2\theta = \sin^2\beta = 3\sin^2\theta \text{ (given)}$$

$$\Rightarrow 2\cos^2\theta = 3 - 3\cos^2\theta \quad \therefore \cos^2\theta = \frac{3}{5}$$

**4. (d)** Since d.c. of line are $\dfrac{1}{c}, \dfrac{1}{c}, \dfrac{1}{c}$

$$\therefore \ \frac{1}{c^2} + \frac{1}{c^2} + \frac{1}{c^2} = 1 \Rightarrow c^2 = 3$$

$$\Rightarrow \ c = \pm\sqrt{3}$$

**5. (d)** Clearly $\cos^2 60° + \cos^2 60° + \cos^2\alpha = 1$

where $\alpha$ is the angle which the st. line makes with x-axis.

$$\therefore \quad \cos^2\alpha = 1 - \frac{1}{4} - \frac{1}{4} = \frac{1}{2}$$

$$\Rightarrow \quad \cos\alpha = \frac{1}{\sqrt{2}} \Rightarrow \alpha = 45°$$

**6. (a)** Let A $(5, -4, 2)$, B $(4, -3, 1)$, C $(7, -6, 4)$, D$(8, -7, 5)$ be the given points.

Mid point of AC $= \left(\dfrac{5+7}{2}, \dfrac{-4-6}{2}, \dfrac{2+4}{2}\right)$

i.e. $(6, -5, 3)$.

Mid point of BD is $\left(\dfrac{4+8}{2}, \dfrac{-3-7}{2}, \dfrac{1+5}{2}\right)$

i.e. $(6, -5, 3)$.

Since mid point of AC and BD coincide

$\therefore \qquad$ ABCD is a parallelogram.

**7. (c)** Let the lines PQ and RS intersect at A $(x, y, z)$ then the point A lies on both the lines PQ and RS and so, it divide PQ and RS in some ratio. Let the point A divides PQ in the ratio $\lambda : 1$ and RS in the ratio $\mu : 1$ where $\lambda \neq -1$ and $\mu \neq -1$. Then

$$x = \frac{16\lambda + 6}{\lambda + 1} = \frac{2\mu}{\mu + 1} \qquad \qquad ...(1)$$

$$y = \frac{-19\lambda - 7}{\lambda + 1} = \frac{-5\mu + 3}{\mu + 1} \ . \qquad \qquad ..(2)$$

$$z = \frac{-4\lambda}{\lambda + 1} = \frac{10\mu - 6}{\mu + 1} \qquad \qquad ...(3)$$

From (1) and (2), we get

$$7\lambda\mu + 8\lambda + 2\mu + 3 = 0 \qquad \qquad ...(4)$$

and $\quad 7\lambda\mu + 11\lambda + \mu + 5 = 0 \qquad \qquad ...(5)$

Subtracting (5) from (4), we get, $-3\lambda + \mu - 2 = 0$

or $\mu = 3\lambda + 2$.

Putting this value of $\mu$ in (4), we get,

$$7\lambda(3\lambda + 2) + 8\lambda + 2(3\lambda + 2) + 3 = 0$$

$$\Rightarrow (\lambda + 1)(3\lambda + 1) = 0 \text{ or } \lambda = -1 \text{ or } \lambda = -\frac{1}{3}.$$

But $\lambda \neq -1$ so $\lambda = -\dfrac{1}{3}$.

$$\therefore \mu = -\frac{3}{3} + 2 = 1$$

Putting these values of $\lambda$ and $\mu$ in (3), we get

$$\frac{-4\lambda}{\lambda + 1} = \frac{4/3}{1 - \left(\dfrac{1}{3}\right)} = 2, \ \frac{10\mu - 6}{\mu + 1} = \frac{4}{2} = 2$$

$\therefore \lambda = -\dfrac{1}{3}$, $\mu = 1$ satisfy all the three equations (1), (2) and (3) and so lines PQ and RS intersect at A. Putting $\lambda = -\dfrac{1}{3}$ or $\mu = 1$ in (1), (2) and (3), coordinates of the point of intersection A are $(1, -1, 2)$.

**8.** **(d)** $AB = \sqrt{(5+1)^2 + (0-2)^2 + (-6+3)^2} = \sqrt{49} = 7$

$AC = \sqrt{(0+1)^2 + (4-2)^2 + (-1+3)^2} = \sqrt{9} = 3$.

By geometry, the bisector of $\angle BAC$ will divide the side BC in the ratio AB : AC i.e., in the ratio 7 : 3 internally. Let the bisector of $\angle BAC$ meets the side BC at point D. Therefore, D divides BC in the ratio 7 : 3.

$\therefore$ Coordinates of D are

$$\left( \frac{7 \times 0 + 3 \times 5}{7+3}, \frac{7 \times 4 + 3 \times 0}{7+3}, \frac{7 \times (-1) + 3 \times (-6)}{7+3} \right)$$

i.e., $\left( \dfrac{3}{2}, \dfrac{14}{5}, -\dfrac{5}{2} \right)$.

Therefore, direction ratios of the bisector AD are

$\dfrac{3}{2} - (-1), \dfrac{14}{5} - 2, \dfrac{-5}{2} + 3$ i.e., $\dfrac{5}{2}, \dfrac{4}{5}, \dfrac{1}{2}$.

Hence, direction cosines of the bisector AD are

$$\frac{\frac{5}{2}}{\sqrt{\left(\frac{5}{2}\right)^2 + \left(\frac{4}{5}\right)^2 + \left(\frac{1}{2}\right)^2}}, \frac{\frac{4}{5}}{\sqrt{\left(\frac{5}{2}\right)^2 + \left(\frac{4}{5}\right)^2 + \left(\frac{1}{2}\right)^2}},$$

$$\frac{\frac{1}{2}}{\sqrt{\left(\frac{5}{2}\right)^2 + \left(\frac{4}{5}\right)^2 + \left(\frac{1}{2}\right)^2}} \text{ i.e., } \frac{25}{\sqrt{714}}, \frac{8}{\sqrt{714}}, \frac{5}{\sqrt{714}}$$

**9.** **(b)** The given equations are $3l + m + 5n = 0$ ....(i)

and $6mn - 2nl + 5lm = 0$ ...(ii)

From (i), we have $m = -3l - 5n$. Putting $m = -3l - 5n$ in (ii), we get $6(-3l - 5n)n - 2nl + 5l(-3l - 5n) = 0$

$\Rightarrow 2n^2 + 3ln + l^2 = 0 \Rightarrow (n+l)(2n+l) = 0$

$\Rightarrow$ either $l = -n$ or $l = -2n$.

If $l = -n$, then putting $l = -n$ in (i), we obtain $m = -2n$. If $l = -2n$, then putting $l = -2n$ in (i), we obtain $m = n$.

Thus, the direction ratios of two lines are $-n, -2n, n$ and $-2n, n, n$ i.e., $1, 2, -1$ and $-2, 1, 1$.

Hence, the direction cosines are

$\dfrac{1}{\sqrt{6}}, \dfrac{2}{\sqrt{6}}, \dfrac{-1}{\sqrt{6}}$ or $\dfrac{-2}{\sqrt{6}}, \dfrac{1}{\sqrt{6}}, \dfrac{1}{\sqrt{6}}$.

The angle $\theta$ between the lines is given by

$\cos \theta = \dfrac{1}{\sqrt{6}} \times \dfrac{-2}{\sqrt{6}} + \dfrac{2}{\sqrt{6}} \times \dfrac{1}{\sqrt{6}} + \dfrac{-1}{\sqrt{6}} \times \dfrac{1}{\sqrt{6}} = \dfrac{-1}{6}$

$\Rightarrow \theta = \cos^{-1}\left( \dfrac{-1}{6} \right)$.

**10.** **(b)** The general points on the given lines are respectively $P(5 + 3t, 7 - t, -2 + t)$ and $Q(-3 - 3s, 3 + 2s, 6 + 4s)$. Direction numbers of PQ are

$< -3 - 3s - 5 - 3t, 3 + 2s - 7 + t, 6 + 4s + 2 - t >$

i.e., $< -8 - 3s - 3t, -4 + 2s + t, 8 + 4s - t >$

If PQ is the desired line then direction numbers of PQ should be proportional to $<2, 7, -5>$, therefore,

$$\frac{-8 - 3s - 3t}{2} = \frac{-4 + 2s + t}{7} = \frac{8 + 4s - t}{-5}$$

Taking first and second numbers, we get

$-56 - 21s - 21t = -8 + 4s + 2t$

$\Rightarrow 25s + 23t = -48$ ....(i)

Taking second and third members, we get

$20 - 10s - 5t = 56 + 28s - 7t$

$\Rightarrow 38s - 2t = -36$ ....(ii)

Solving (i) and (ii) for t and s, we get $s = -1$ and $t = -1$. The coordinates of P and Q are respectively

$(5 + 3(-1), 7 - (-1), -2 - 1) = (2, 8, -3)$

and $(-3 - 3(-1), 3 + 2(-1), 6 + 4(-1)) = (0, 1, 2)$

$\therefore$ The said line intersects the given lines in the points $(2, 8, -3)$ and $(0, 1, 2)$ respectively.

Length of the line intercepted between the given lines

$= |PQ| = \sqrt{(0-2)^2 + (1-8)^2 + (2+3)^2} = \sqrt{78}$.

**11.** **(b,d)** Let the given points be A, B and C respectively. Then

$AB^2 = 350, AC^2 = 500 - 20\lambda + \lambda^2, BC^2$

$= 150 + 10\lambda + \lambda^2$

Now $AB^2 + AC^2 = BC^2$

$\Rightarrow 350 + 500 - 20\lambda + \lambda^2$

$= 150 + 10\lambda + \lambda^2 \Rightarrow \lambda = \dfrac{70}{3}$

Next, $AB^2 + BC^2 = AC^2$

$\Rightarrow 250 + 150 + 10\lambda + \lambda^2 = 500 - 20\lambda + \lambda^2 \Rightarrow \lambda = 0$

Further, $BC^2 + AC^2 = AB^2$

$\Rightarrow 150 + 10\lambda + \lambda^2 + 500 - 20\lambda + \lambda^2 = 350$

$\Rightarrow \lambda^2 - 5\lambda + 150 = 0$, which have no real solution

$\therefore$ The triangle is right angles for $\lambda = 0, \dfrac{70}{3}$

**12.** **(a,c)** Unit vectors along the lines are

$$\vec{a} = l_1\vec{i} + m_1\vec{j} + n_1\vec{k} \text{ and } \vec{b} = l_2\vec{i} + m_2\vec{j} + n_2\vec{k}.$$

The unit vectors along the angular bisectors are

$$\frac{\vec{a} + \vec{b}}{|\vec{a} \pm \vec{b}|}. \text{ Now } |\vec{a} + \vec{b}|^2 = 2 + 2\cos\theta = 4\cos^2\frac{\theta}{2} \text{ and}$$

$$|\vec{a} - \vec{b}|^2 = 2 - 2\cos\theta = 4\sin^2\frac{\theta}{2}.$$

So, D.C. are $\dfrac{l_1 + l_2}{2\cos\dfrac{\theta}{2}}, \dfrac{m_1 + m_2}{2\cos\dfrac{\theta}{2}}, \dfrac{n_1 + n_2}{2\cos\dfrac{\theta}{2}}$ and

$$\frac{l_1 + l_2}{2\sin\dfrac{\theta}{2}}, \frac{m_1 + m_2}{2\sin\dfrac{\theta}{2}}, \frac{n_1 + n_2}{2\sin\dfrac{\theta}{2}}$$

**13.** **(a)** Here, the three vertices of tetrahedron are O $(0, 0, 0)$; A $(6, -5, -1)$; B $(-4, 1, 3)$ and centroid G $(1, -2, 5)$. Let the fourth vertex be $(x_1, y_1, z_1)$

$\therefore$ Centroid $\equiv$

$$\left(\frac{x_1 + 0 + 6 + (-4)}{4}, \frac{y_1 + 0 + (-5) + 1}{4}, \frac{z_1 + 0 - 1 + 3}{4}\right)$$

$$\Rightarrow \quad \left(\frac{x_2 + 2}{2}, \frac{y_1 - 4}{4}, \frac{z_1 + 2}{4}\right) = (1, -2, 5)$$

$$\Rightarrow \quad x_1 = 2, y_1 = -4, z_1 = 18$$

$\therefore$ Fourth vertex $(2, -4, 18)$

**14.** **(d)** Now, to find the radious of sphere circumscribing the tetrahedron (let radius be r, and centre be P $(\alpha, \beta, \gamma)$)

$$\therefore r^2 = (\alpha - 0)^2 + (\beta - 0)^2 + (\gamma - 0)^2$$
$$= (\alpha - 2)^2 + (\beta + 4)^2 + (\gamma - 18)^2$$
$$= (\alpha - 6)^2 + (\beta + 5)^2 + (\gamma + 1)^2$$

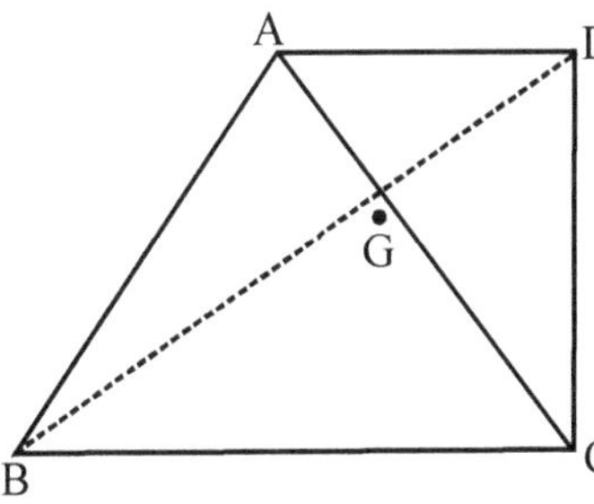


$$= (\alpha + 4)^2 + (\beta - 1)^2 + (\gamma - 3)^2$$

Using $r^2 = PA^2 = PB^2 = PC^2$ (P being centre)

$$\Rightarrow -6\alpha + 5\beta + 6\gamma + 26 = 0 \qquad ...(i)$$
$$8\alpha - 2\beta - 6\gamma + 26 = 0 \qquad ...(ii)$$
and $-\alpha + 2\beta - 9\gamma + 86 = 0 \qquad ...(iii)$

Solving (i), (ii) and (iii), we get

$$\alpha = \frac{8}{7}, \beta = -\frac{45}{7}, \gamma = 8$$

**15.** **(b)** $r^2 = \alpha^2 + \beta^2 + \gamma^2 = \left(\dfrac{8}{7}\right)^2 + \left(-\dfrac{45}{7}\right)^2 + (8)^2$

$$= \frac{64 + 2050 + 2025}{49}$$

$$\Rightarrow r = \frac{5}{7}\sqrt{209}$$

**16.** **A→q; B→r; C→p**

(A) Angle between two diagonals of a

cube $= \cos^{-1}\left(\dfrac{1}{3}\right)$ **(q)**

(B) Angle between the diagonal of a cube and a diagonal

of one face $= \cos^{-1}\sqrt{\dfrac{2}{3}}$ **(r)**

(C) $\cos\theta = \dfrac{a_1 a_2 + b_1 b_2 + c_1 c_2}{\sqrt{a_1^2 + b_1^2 + c_1^2} \cdot \sqrt{a_2^2 + b_2^2 + c_2^2}}$

$$= \frac{12 - 12 + 25}{\sqrt{16 + 9 + 25} \cdot \sqrt{9 + 16 + 25}} = \frac{1}{2}$$

$$\theta = \cos^{-1}\left(\frac{1}{2}\right) \text{ (p)}$$

**17.** **(b)** DR's of line joining $(0,0,0)$ and $(x, y, z)$ is $x - 0, y - 0, z - 0$, i.e., $x, y, z$

DC's are $\dfrac{x}{OP}, \dfrac{y}{OP}, \dfrac{z}{OP}$ i.e., $\dfrac{x}{r}, \dfrac{y}{r}, \dfrac{z}{r}$

**18.** **(d)** $AB = \sqrt{(2-1)^2 + (9-8)^2 + (12-8)^2} = \sqrt{18} = 3\sqrt{2}$

$BC = \sqrt{\{(1+2)^2 + (8-11)^2 + (8-8)^2\}} = \sqrt{18} = 3\sqrt{2}$

$CD = \sqrt{\{(-2+1)^2 + (11-12)^2 + (8-12)^2\}} = \sqrt{18} = 3\sqrt{2}$

$DA = \sqrt{\{(-1-2)^2 + (12-9)^2 + (12-12)^2\}} = \sqrt{18} = 3\sqrt{2}$

$AC = \sqrt{\{(2+2)^2 + (9-11)^2 + (12-8)^2\}} = \sqrt{36} = 6$

and $BD = \sqrt{\{(1+1)^2 + (8-12)^2 + (8-12)^2\}} = \sqrt{36} = 6$

Hence, $AB = BC = CD = DA$ and $AC = BD$.

$\therefore$ it is a square not a rhombus

**19.** **(b)** $\therefore$ Orthocentre, centroid and circumcentre are collinear and cenroid divides orthocentre and circumcentre in the ratio 2 : 1 (internally).

$$\therefore \quad \alpha = \frac{x + 2\gamma}{2 + 1}$$
$$\Rightarrow \quad x = 3\alpha - 2\gamma$$
and $\beta = \dfrac{y + 2\delta}{2 + 1}$

$$\Rightarrow \quad y = 3\beta - 2\delta$$

$\therefore$ Orthocentre is $(3\alpha - 2\gamma, 3\beta - 2\delta)$

**20. 5**

If the given points $(\lambda, 4, -6)$, $(3, 2, -4)$ and $(9, 8, -10)$ are collinear then

$$\frac{\lambda - 3}{9 - 3} = \frac{4 - 2}{8 - 2} = \frac{-6 + 4}{-10 + 4} \Rightarrow \lambda = 5$$

**21. 1**

Let $l$, m, n be the DCs of the given line. Then as it makes an acute angle with x-axis, therefore $l > 0$. The line passes through $(6, -7, -1)$ and $(2, -3, 1)$, therefore its DRs are $6 - 2, -7 + 3, -1 - 1$ or $4, -4, -2$

Hence DCs of the given line are $\dfrac{2}{3}$, $-\dfrac{2}{3}$, $-\dfrac{1}{3}$

$$\therefore -3\,(l + m + n) = -3\left(\frac{2}{3} - \frac{2}{3} - \frac{1}{3}\right) = 1.$$

**22. 4**

The direction cosines of the lines are $\dfrac{2}{3}, \dfrac{-1}{3}, \dfrac{2}{3}$ and

$\dfrac{a}{\sqrt{a^2 + 34}}, \dfrac{3}{\sqrt{a^2 + 34}}, \dfrac{5}{\sqrt{a^2 + 34}}$. Since the angle between the lines is 45°, we have

$$\cos 45° = \left(\frac{2}{3}\right)\left(\frac{a}{\sqrt{a^2 + 34}}\right) + \left(\frac{-1}{3}\right)\left(\frac{3}{\sqrt{a^2 + 34}}\right)$$

$$+ \left(\frac{2}{3}\right)\left(\frac{5}{\sqrt{a^2 + 34}}\right)$$

$$\Rightarrow \frac{1}{\sqrt{2}} = \frac{2a - 3 + 10}{3\sqrt{a^2 + 34}}$$

$$\Rightarrow 3\sqrt{a^2 + 34} = \sqrt{2}\,(2a + 7)$$

$$\Rightarrow 9\,(a^2 + 34) = 2\,(4a^2 + 28a + 49)$$

$$\Rightarrow (a - 4)\,(a - 52) = 0 \Rightarrow a = 4, 52.$$

$$\because \quad a < 5 \qquad\qquad \therefore a = 4.$$

**23. 0**

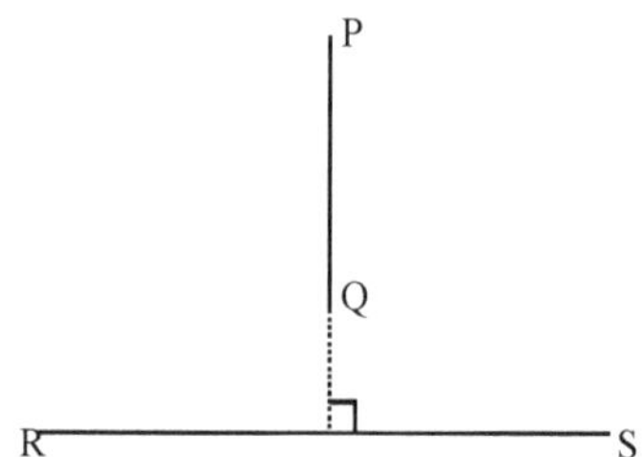


The four points are P $(-2, 3, 4)$, Q $(-4, 4, 6)$, R $(4, 3, 5)$, S $(0, 1, 2)$.

$\therefore$ direction ratios of RS are $0 - 4, 1 - 3, 2 - 5$, i.e., $4, 2, 3$.

Dividing each by $\sqrt{(4)^2 + (2)^2 + (3)^2}$, i.e., $\sqrt{29}$, the actual direction cosines' of RS are $\dfrac{4}{\sqrt{29}}, \dfrac{2}{\sqrt{29}}, \dfrac{3}{\sqrt{29}}$.

$\therefore$ Projection of PQ on RS

$$= \frac{4}{\sqrt{29}}(-4 + 2) + \frac{2}{\sqrt{29}}(4 - 3) + \frac{3}{\sqrt{29}}(6 - 4)$$

$$= \frac{1}{\sqrt{29}}(-8 + 2 + 6) = 0$$

**24. 3**

Since $\overrightarrow{OP}$ has projections $\dfrac{13}{5}$, $\dfrac{19}{5}$ and $\dfrac{26}{5}$ on the co-ordinate axes, therefore $\overrightarrow{OP} = \dfrac{13}{5}\hat{i} + \dfrac{19}{5}\hat{j} + \dfrac{26}{5}\hat{k}$

Now, P divides the join of Q $(2, 2, 4)$ and R $(3, 5, 6)$ in the ration $\lambda : 1$. Then the position vector of P is

$$\left(\frac{3\lambda + 2}{\lambda + 1}\right)\hat{i} + \left(\frac{5\lambda + 2}{\lambda + 1}\right)\hat{j} + \left(\frac{6\lambda + 4}{\lambda + 1}\right)\hat{k}$$

$$\therefore \frac{13}{5}\hat{i} + \frac{19}{5}\hat{j} + \frac{26}{5}\hat{k}$$

$$= \left(\frac{3\lambda + 2}{\lambda + 1}\right)\hat{i} + \left(\frac{5\lambda + 2}{\lambda + 1}\right)\hat{j} + \left(\frac{6\lambda + 4}{\lambda + 1}\right)\hat{k}$$

$$\Rightarrow \frac{3\lambda + 2}{\lambda + 1} = \frac{13}{5}, \frac{5\lambda + 2}{\lambda + 1} = \frac{19}{5}, \frac{6\lambda + 4}{\lambda + 1} = \frac{26}{5}$$

$$\Rightarrow \lambda = \frac{3}{2} \quad \therefore 2\lambda = 3.$$

**1. (b)** Lines are co-planar if $\vec{a}-\vec{c}$, $\vec{b},\vec{d}$ are co-planar

then $(\vec{a}-\vec{c}).\vec{b}\times\vec{d}=0$

**2. (d)** Any point on the given line is $(\lambda,1+2\lambda,2+3\lambda)$. Let it represents the co-ordinates of foot N of perpendicular from P(1, 6, 3) then direction ratios of PN are $\lambda-1$, $2\lambda-5$, $3\lambda-1$. Now PN is perpendicular to the given line

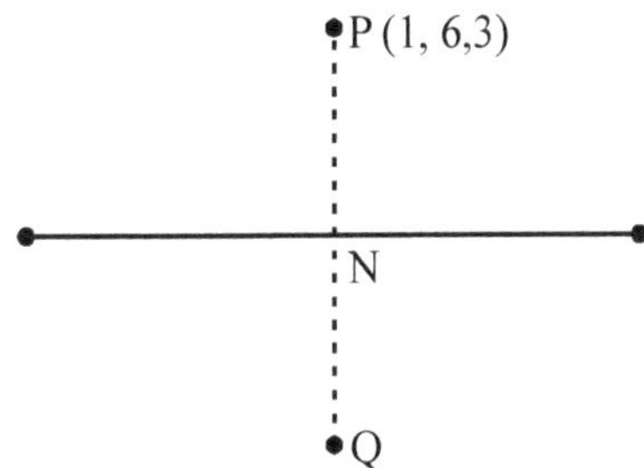

So, $1(\lambda-1)+2(2\lambda-5)+3(3\lambda-1)=0$

$\Rightarrow \lambda=1$. So coordinates of N are $(1,3,5)$

If $Q(x_1,y_1,z_1)$ be the image of P, then N is mid point of PQ

$\therefore 1=\dfrac{x_1+1}{2}, 3=\dfrac{y_1+6}{2}, 5=\dfrac{z_1+3}{2}$

$\Rightarrow x_1=1, y_1=0, z_1=7$

**3. (c)** Lines are $\dfrac{x-1}{0}=\dfrac{y-2}{0}=\dfrac{z}{1}$ and $\dfrac{x}{1}=\dfrac{y+1}{0}=\dfrac{z}{0}$

$\therefore \cos\theta=0.1+0.0+1.0=0\Rightarrow\theta=90°$.

**4. (a)** Equations of the given lines are

$\dfrac{x-8}{3}=\dfrac{y+9}{-16}=\dfrac{z-10}{7}$ ....(1)

and $\dfrac{x-15}{3}=\dfrac{y-2}{8}=\dfrac{z-8}{-5}$ ....(2)

Let the equations of the line through the point

$(1,2,-4)$ be $\dfrac{x-1}{a}=\dfrac{y-2}{b}=\dfrac{z+4}{c}$ .....(3)

where a, b, c are its direction ratios.

Since (3) is perpendicular to (1) and (2), we have

$3a-16b+7c=0$ ....(4)

and $3a+8b-5c=0$ .....(5)

Solving (4) and (5) for a, b, c by the method of cross multiplication, we get

$\dfrac{a}{80-56}=\dfrac{b}{21+15}=\dfrac{c}{24+48}\Rightarrow\dfrac{a}{24}=\dfrac{b}{36}=\dfrac{c}{72}$

or $\dfrac{a}{2}=\dfrac{b}{3}=\dfrac{c}{6}$ .....(6)

From (3) and (6), we obtain the required line as

$\dfrac{x-1}{2}=\dfrac{y-2}{3}=\dfrac{z+4}{6}$.

**5. (b)** If $\alpha,\beta,\gamma$ are the angles made by the line with x, y and z-axes respectively, then

$\cos^2\alpha+\cos^2\beta+\cos^2\gamma=1$.

Given $\alpha=\beta=\gamma$,

$\therefore\quad 3\cos^2\alpha=1\Rightarrow\cos\alpha=\pm1/\sqrt{3}$

Possible direction cosines are

$\left(\pm\dfrac{1}{\sqrt{3}},\pm\dfrac{1}{\sqrt{3}},\pm\dfrac{1}{\sqrt{3}}\right)$.

Different sets of DC's are

$\left(\dfrac{1}{\sqrt{3}},\dfrac{1}{\sqrt{3}},\dfrac{1}{\sqrt{3}}\right)$,

$\left(\dfrac{1}{\sqrt{3}},\dfrac{1}{\sqrt{3}},-\dfrac{1}{\sqrt{3}}\right)$, $\left(\dfrac{1}{\sqrt{3}},\dfrac{-1}{\sqrt{3}},\dfrac{1}{\sqrt{3}}\right)$ and

$\left(\dfrac{-1}{\sqrt{3}},\dfrac{1}{\sqrt{3}},+\dfrac{1}{\sqrt{3}}\right)$.

Thus four lines are equally inclined to axes.

**6. (d)** Direction cosines of a line parallel to z-axis are $(\cos 90°,\cos 90°,\cos 0)=(0,0,1)$

Hence the line through $(a, b, c)$ having direction cosines 0, 0, 1 is

$\dfrac{x-a}{0}=\dfrac{y-b}{0}=\dfrac{z-c}{1}$.

**7. (a)** Equation of lines $\dfrac{x-b}{a}=y=\dfrac{z-d}{c}$

$\dfrac{x-b'}{a'}=y=\dfrac{z-d'}{c'}$

Line are perpendicular $\Rightarrow$ $aa'+1+cc'=0$

**8. (a)** The given line is $6\left(x-\dfrac{1}{3}\right)=3\left(y+\dfrac{1}{3}\right)=2(z-1)$

Divide by 6, we get the equation in standard form

$\dfrac{x-\dfrac{1}{3}}{1}=\dfrac{y+\dfrac{1}{3}}{2}=\dfrac{z-1}{3}$

$\therefore$ direction ratios are 1, 2, 3. Therefore directions

cosines are $+\dfrac{1}{\sqrt{14}},\pm\dfrac{2}{\sqrt{14}},\pm\dfrac{3}{\sqrt{14}}$

Hence, the direction cosines of the line parallel to this

line are $\pm\dfrac{1}{\sqrt{14}},\pm\dfrac{2}{\sqrt{14}},\pm\dfrac{3}{\sqrt{14}}$. That is direction ratios are 1, 2, 3.

$\therefore$ The equation of the required line is

$$\frac{x-2}{1} = \frac{y+1}{2} = \frac{z+1}{3} \Rightarrow 6x-12 = 3y+3 = 2z+2$$

**9.** **(a)** Let D be the foot of perpendicular and let it divides BC in the ratio $\lambda : 1$. Then the co-ordinates of

D are $\dfrac{3\lambda+4}{\lambda+1}, \dfrac{5\lambda+7}{\lambda+1}, \dfrac{3\lambda+1}{\lambda+1}$. Now

$$\overrightarrow{AD} \perp \overrightarrow{BC} = \overrightarrow{AD}.\overrightarrow{BC} = 0$$

$$\Rightarrow -(2\lambda+3)-2(5\lambda+7)-4 = 0 \Rightarrow \lambda = -\frac{7}{4}$$

$\therefore$ Co-ordinates of D $\left(\dfrac{5}{3}, \dfrac{7}{3}, \dfrac{17}{3}\right)$.

**10.** **(c)** Let the cube be shown in the figure. Where, four diagonals are OP, AL, BM and CN such that.
and A (a, 0, 0), B (0, a, 0), C(0, 0, a), L(0, a, a), M (a, 0, a), N (a, a, 0) and P (a, a, a) hence, direction cosines of OP are

$$\frac{a}{\sqrt{a^2+a^2+a^2}}, \frac{a}{\sqrt{a^2+a^2+a^2}}, \frac{a}{\sqrt{a^2+a^2+a^2}}$$

$$= \left(\frac{1}{\sqrt{3}}, \frac{1}{\sqrt{3}}, \frac{1}{\sqrt{3}}\right)$$

Similarly,

The direction cosines of AL are $-\dfrac{1}{\sqrt{3}}, \dfrac{1}{\sqrt{3}}, \dfrac{1}{\sqrt{3}}$

The direction cosines of BM are $\dfrac{1}{\sqrt{3}}, -\dfrac{1}{\sqrt{3}}, \dfrac{1}{\sqrt{3}}$

The direction cosines of CN are $\dfrac{1}{\sqrt{3}}, \dfrac{1}{\sqrt{3}}, -\dfrac{1}{\sqrt{3}}$

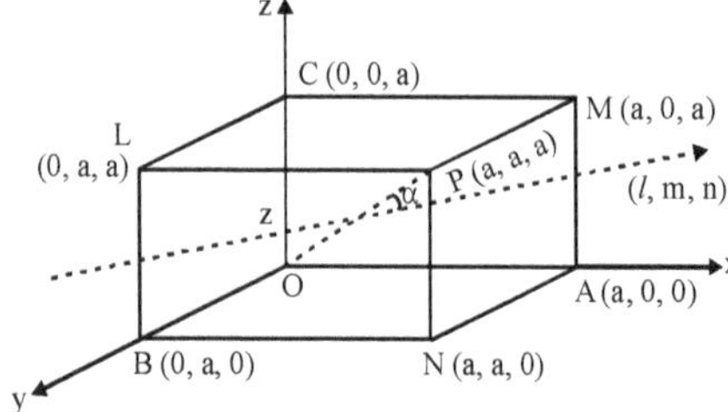


If the direction cosines of the line be $l$, m, n then

$$\cos\alpha = \frac{l+m+n}{\sqrt{3}}, \quad \cos\beta = \frac{-l+m+n}{\sqrt{3}},$$

$$\cos\gamma = \frac{l-m+n}{\sqrt{3}}, \quad \cos\delta = \frac{l+m-n}{\sqrt{3}}$$

$\therefore \cos^2\alpha + \cos^2\beta + \cos^2\gamma + \cos^2\delta$

$$= \frac{1}{3}\{(l+m+n)^2 + (-l+m+n)^2$$

$$+ (l-m+n)^2 + (l+m-n)^2\}$$

$$= \frac{1}{3}[4(l^2+m^2+n^2)] = \frac{4}{3}$$

**11.** **(c)** We have $z = 0$ for the point where the line intersects the curve

Therefore, $\dfrac{x-2}{3} = \dfrac{y+1}{2} = \dfrac{0-1}{-1} \Rightarrow \dfrac{x-2}{3} = 1$ and

$$\frac{y+1}{2} = 1 \Rightarrow x = 5 \text{ and } y = 1$$

Put these value in $xy = c^2$, we get

$$5 = c^2 \Rightarrow c = \pm\sqrt{5}$$

**12.** **(a)** We have $\overrightarrow{AP} = -3\hat{i} - \hat{j} + 10\hat{k}$

$$\therefore \quad |\overrightarrow{AP}| = \sqrt{9+1+100} = \sqrt{110}$$

$\overrightarrow{AN}$ = Projection of $\overrightarrow{AP}$ on $6\hat{i}+3\hat{j}-4\hat{k}$

$$= \left|\frac{\overrightarrow{AP}.(6\hat{i}+3\hat{j}-4\hat{k})}{|6\hat{i}+3\hat{j}-4\hat{k}|}\right| = \left|\frac{-8-3-40}{\sqrt{61}}\right| = \sqrt{61}$$

$\therefore PN = \sqrt{AP^2 - AN^2} = \sqrt{110-61} = 7$

**13.** **(c)** Let the edges OA, OB, OC of the unit cube along OX, OY, OZ respectively.
Since OA = OB = OC = 1 unit

$$\therefore \quad \overrightarrow{OA} = \hat{i}, \ \overrightarrow{OB} = \hat{j}, \ \overrightarrow{OC} = \hat{k}$$

Let CM be perpendicular from the corner C on the diagonal OP. The vector equation of OP is;

$$\vec{r} = \lambda(\hat{i}+\hat{j}+\hat{k})$$

$\therefore$ OM = projection of $\overrightarrow{OC}$ on $\overrightarrow{OP}$ = $\overrightarrow{OC}$ . $\overrightarrow{OP}$

$$= \hat{k} = \frac{(\hat{i}+\hat{j}+\hat{k})}{\sqrt{3}} = \frac{1}{\sqrt{3}}$$



Now $OC^2 = OM^2 + CM^2$

$$\Rightarrow CM^2 = |OC^2| - OM^2 = 1 - \frac{1}{3} = \frac{2}{3}$$

$$\Rightarrow CM = \sqrt{\frac{2}{3}}$$

**14.** **(a,b,c)** Given : $x+y+z-1 = 0, 4x+y-2z+2 = 0$
$\therefore$ Direction ratios of the line are $(-3, 6, -3)$
i.e., $(1, -2, 1)$
Let $z = k$, then $x = k-1, y = 2-2k$
i.e., $(k-1, 2-2k, k)$ is any point on the line

$\therefore (-1, 2, 0), (0, 0, 1)$ and $\left(-\dfrac{1}{2}, 1, \dfrac{1}{2}\right)$ are points on the line.

**15.** **(a, b)** Let $OP = OQ = r$

$M$ is the mid point of $PQ$, then coordinates of

$$M\left(\frac{l_1+l_2}{2}\right)r, \left(\frac{m_1+m_2}{2}\right)r, \left(\frac{n_1+n_2}{2}\right)r$$

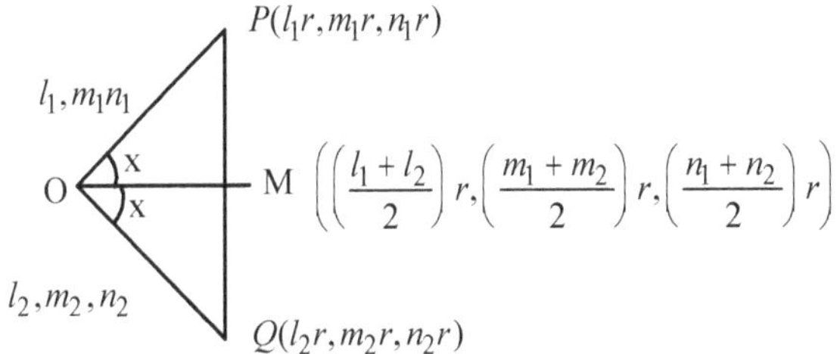

$\therefore$ DR's of the bisector are $l_1+l_2, m_1+m_2, n_1+n_2$

DR's of other bisector are $l_1-l_2, m_1-m_2, n_1-n_2$

**16.** **(b, c)** For the given lines

$$\begin{vmatrix} 4-1 & 0-1 & -1-(-1) \\ 3 & -1 & 0 \\ 2 & 0 & 3 \end{vmatrix} = \begin{vmatrix} 3 & -1 & 0 \\ 3 & -1 & 0 \\ 2 & 0 & 3 \end{vmatrix} = 0$$

So, the given lines intersect.

Any point on the first line is $(3r_1+1, -r_1+1, -1)$ and

any point on the second line is $(2r_2+4, 0, 3r_2-1)$

Since, the lines intersect, at a point

$$3r_1+1 = 2r_2+4, -r_1+1 = 0, -1 = 3r_2-1$$

$$\Rightarrow \quad r_1 = 1, r_2 = 0$$

Hence, the point of intersection is $(4, 0, -1)$

**17.** **(a)** Any point on the first line is $(2x_1+1, x_1-3, -3x_1+2)$

Any point on the second line is $(y_1+2, -3y_1+1, 2y_1-3)$

If two lines are coplanar then

$2x_1 - y_1 = 1, x_1 + 3y_1 = 4, 3x_1 + 2y_1 = 5$ are consistent.

**18.** **(b)** Statement-1 : Definition, Statement-2 : Definition

**19.** **(d)** $L_1$ and $L_2$ are obviously non-parallel

Consider the determinant

$$D = \begin{vmatrix} 2 & -4 & 1 \\ 2 & 4 & -3 \\ 1 & 3 & 2 \end{vmatrix} = 2(8+9) + 4(4+3) + 1(6-4)$$

$$= 34 + 28 + 2 \Rightarrow D \neq 0 \Rightarrow \text{skew}$$

Hence Statement-1 is false.

**20.** **9**

Let $l, m, n$ be the direction cosines of the line $MN$ which is perpendicular to each of the given lines

$\therefore \ -4l + 3m + 2n = 0$ and $-4l + m + n = 0$

Solving $\dfrac{l}{3-2} = \dfrac{m}{-8+4} = \dfrac{n}{-4+12}$

$$\Rightarrow \frac{l}{1} = \frac{m}{-4} = \frac{n}{8} = \frac{\sqrt{l^2+m^2+n^2}}{\sqrt{1+16+64}} = \frac{1}{9}$$

$$\Rightarrow l = \frac{1}{9}, m = -\frac{4}{9}, n = \frac{8}{9}$$

It is obvious that the points $P(-3, 6, 0)$ and $Q(-2, 0, 7)$ are situated on the given line

$\therefore$ Length of shortest distance

$=$ Projection of $PQ$ on the common perpendicular $MN$

$$\frac{1}{9}\{(-2)-(-3)\} + \left(-\frac{4}{9}\right)[0-6] + \frac{8}{9}[7-0] = 9$$

**21.** **0**

The given lines are coplanar if

$$0 = \begin{vmatrix} 2-1 & 3-4 & 4-5 \\ 1 & 1 & -k \\ k & 2 & 1 \end{vmatrix} = \begin{vmatrix} 1 & -1 & -1 \\ 1 & 1 & -k \\ k & 2 & 1 \end{vmatrix}$$

$$= \begin{vmatrix} 1 & 0 & 0 \\ 1 & 2 & 1-k \\ k & k+2 & 1+k \end{vmatrix}$$

or $\quad 2(1+k) - (k+2)(1-k) = 0$ or $k^2 + 3k = 0$

or $\quad$ if $k = 0, -3$.

Thus $k = 0$.

**22.** **2**

$$1 = \left|(\vec{b}-\vec{a}).\frac{(\vec{p}\times\vec{q})}{|\vec{p}\times\vec{q}|}\right| \Rightarrow |\vec{b}-\vec{a}|.|\vec{p}\times\vec{q}|.\cos 60° = \frac{1}{2}$$

$$\Rightarrow AB.\frac{1}{2}.\frac{1}{2} = \frac{1}{2} \Rightarrow AB = 2$$

**23.** **7**

Let the foot of perpendicular be $Q(1+2r, 2+3r, 3+6r)$

Direction ratios of PQ are $< 2r-1, 3r-1, 6r-1 >$

Since PQ is perpendicular to the line,

$\therefore \ 2(2r-1) + 3(3r-1) + 6(6r-1) = 0$

i.e., $49r - 11 = 0$ i.e., $r = \dfrac{11}{49}$

$\therefore$ Coordinates of the foot are $\left(\dfrac{71}{49}, \dfrac{131}{49}, \dfrac{213}{49}\right)$

Thus $D = 7$.

**24.** **7**

The point $A(6, 7, 7)$ is on the line. Let the perpendicular from P meet the line in L. Then

$AP^2 = (6-1)^2 + (7-2)^2 + (7-3)^2 = 66$.

Also $AL = $ Projection of AP on line

$$\left(\text{actual d.c's } \frac{3}{\sqrt{17}}, \frac{2}{\sqrt{17}}, \frac{-2}{\sqrt{17}}\right).$$

$$= (6-1)\frac{3}{\sqrt{17}} + (7-2)\frac{2}{\sqrt{17}} + (7-3)\frac{-2}{\sqrt{17}} = \sqrt{17}.$$

$\therefore$ Perpendicular distance d of P from the line is given by

$$d^2 = AP^2 - AL^2 = 66 - 17 = 49, \ d = 7.$$

**1.** **(b)** Let an equation of the required plane be

$$\frac{x}{a}+\frac{y}{b}+\frac{z}{c}=1$$

This meets the coordinates axes in
A(a, 0, 0), B(0, b, 0) and C(0, 0, c).
So that the coordinates of the centroid of the triangle

ABC are $\left(\dfrac{a}{3},\dfrac{b}{3},\dfrac{c}{3}\right)=(1,r,r^2)$ (given)

$\Rightarrow a=3, b=3r, c=3r^2$

Hence the required equation of the plane is

$$\frac{x}{3}+\frac{y}{3r}=1 \text{ or } r^2x+ry+z=3r^2$$

**2.** **(c)** We have,

$$\vec{r}=(1+\lambda-\mu)\hat{i}+(2-\lambda)\hat{j}+(3-2\lambda+2\mu)\hat{k}$$

$$\Rightarrow \vec{r}=(\hat{i}+2\hat{j}+3\hat{k})+\lambda(\hat{i}-\hat{j}-2\hat{k})+\mu(-\hat{i}+2\hat{k})$$

which is a plane passing through $\vec{a}=\hat{i}+2\hat{j}+3\hat{k}$ and

parallel to the vectors $\vec{b}=\hat{i}-\hat{j}-2\hat{k}$ and $\vec{c}=-\hat{i}+2\hat{k}$

Therefore, it is $\perp$ to the vector $\vec{n}=\vec{b}\times\vec{c}=2\hat{i}-\hat{k}$

Hence, its vector equation is $(\vec{r}-\vec{a}).\vec{n}=0$

$$\Rightarrow \vec{r}.\vec{n}=\vec{a}.\vec{n} \Rightarrow \vec{r}(-2\hat{i}-\hat{k})=-2-3 \Rightarrow \vec{r}(2\hat{i}+\hat{k})=5$$

So, the cartesion equation is $(x\hat{i}+y\hat{j}+z\hat{k}).(2\hat{i}+\hat{k})=5$

or $2x+z=5$

**3.** **(a)** Given planes are $ax+by=0$ ........(i)

and $z=0$ .......(ii)

$\therefore$ Equation of any plane passing through the line of intersection of planes (i) and (ii) may be taken as

$$ax+by+\lambda z=0 \quad ......(iii)$$

The direction cosines of a normal to the plane (iii) are :

$$\frac{a}{\sqrt{a^2+b^2+\lambda^2}},\frac{b}{\sqrt{a^2+b^2+\lambda^2}},\frac{\lambda}{\sqrt{a^2+b^2+\lambda^2}}$$

The direction cosines of a normal to the plane (i) are :

$$\frac{a}{\sqrt{a^2+b^2}},\frac{b}{\sqrt{a^2+b^2}},0$$

Since the angle between the plane (i) and (iii) is $\alpha$,

$$\cos\alpha=\frac{a.a+b.b+\lambda.0}{\sqrt{a^2+b^2+\lambda^2}\sqrt{a^2+b^2}}=\sqrt{\frac{a^2+b^2}{a^2+b^2+\lambda^2}}$$

$$\Rightarrow \lambda^2\cos^2\alpha=a^2(1-\cos^2\alpha)+b^2(1-\cos^2\alpha)$$

$$\Rightarrow \lambda^2=\frac{(a^2+b^2)\sin^2\alpha}{\cos^2\alpha}$$

$$\Rightarrow \lambda=\pm\sqrt{a^2+b^2}\tan\alpha=0$$

Putting in (iii) we get, eq. of plane as

$$ax+by\pm z\sqrt{a^2+b^2}\tan\alpha=0$$

**4.** **(b)** Let image of the point P(1, 3, 4) in the given plane be the point Q. The equation of the line through P and normal to the given plane is

$$\frac{x-1}{2}=\frac{y-3}{-1}=\frac{z-4}{1}$$

Since this line passes through Q, so let the coordinates of Q be $(2r+1,-r+3,r+4)$.
The coordinates of the mid-point of PQ are

$$\left(r+1,-\frac{r}{2}+3,\frac{r}{2}+4\right).$$

This point lies on the given plane. Therefore, $r=-2$.
Hence (b) is the correct answer because the coordinates of Q are $(-3,5,2)$.

**5.** **(a)** The planes $x+y=0$ i.e. $x=-y$ and $y+z=0$ i.e. $z=-y$

meet in the line $\dfrac{x}{1}=\dfrac{y}{-1}=\dfrac{z}{1}$. Any point on this line is

$(t,-t,t)$. This point lies in the plane $x+z=0$ if $t+t=0$
$\Rightarrow t=0$. So the three planes meet in a unique point
$(0,0,0)$.

**6.** **(c)** Any plane passing through the line of intersection of the given planes is

$$(x+2y+3z-5)+\lambda(3x-2y-z+1)=0$$

$$\Rightarrow (1+3\lambda)x+(2-2\lambda)y+(3-\lambda)z+(-5+\lambda)=0 \ ...(1)$$

Intercept on X-axis is $\dfrac{5-\lambda}{1+3\lambda}$      [Put $y=z=0$]

Intercept on Z-axis is $\dfrac{5-\lambda}{3-\lambda}$.

Given $\dfrac{5-\lambda}{1+3\lambda}=\dfrac{5-\lambda}{3-\lambda}\Rightarrow\lambda=\dfrac{1}{2}$

[$\lambda=5$ is not admissible as in that case each intercept is zero].

Put $\lambda=\dfrac{1}{2}$ in (1), we get the equation of the required plane as $5x + 2y + 5z - 9 = 0$.

**7.** **(b)** Let a point $(3\lambda + 1, \lambda + 2, 2\lambda + 3)$ of the first line also lies on the second line.

Then, $\dfrac{3\lambda + 1 - 3}{1} = \dfrac{\lambda + 2 - 1}{2} = \dfrac{2\lambda + 3 - 2}{3} \Rightarrow \lambda = 1$

Hence, the point of intersection P of the two lines is $(4, 3, 5)$

Equation of plane perpendicular to OP where O is $(0, 0, 0)$ and passing through P is $4x + 3y + 5z = 50$

**8.** **(c)** Let the plane $\vec{r}.(\hat{i} - 2\hat{j} + 3\hat{k}) = 17$ divide the line joining the points $-2\hat{i} + 4\hat{j} + 7\hat{k}$ and $3\hat{i} - 5\hat{j} + 8\hat{k}$ in the ratio t : 1 at the point P.

$\therefore$ P is $\dfrac{3t - 2}{t + 1}\hat{i} + \dfrac{-5t + 4}{t + 1}\hat{j} + \dfrac{8t + 7}{t + 1}\hat{k}$

This lies on the given plane,

$\therefore$ $20t = 17 - 21 + 10 = 6$

$$t = \dfrac{6}{20} = \dfrac{3}{10}$$

Reqd. ratio is 3 : 10.

**9.** **(b, c)** The equation of the angle bisector of the given planes is $\quad x = \pm z$

i.e. $x + z = 0$ or $x - z = 0$ ....(1)

Equation of plane parallel to (1) is

$x + z + d = 0$ or $x - z + d_1 = 0$.

It passes through $(1, 2, 3)$

therefore, $d = -4$ or $d_1 = 2$

so, $(x + z - 4)$ and $(x - z + 2) = 0$

**10** **(a,b)** $3x - 6y + 2z + 5 = 0$ ........(1)

$4x - 12y + 3z = 3$ ........(2)

$\dfrac{3x - 6y + 2z + 5}{\sqrt{9 + 36 + 4}} = \dfrac{-4x + 12y - 3z + 3}{\sqrt{16 + 144 + 9}}$

bisects the angle between the planes that contains the origin.

$13(3x - 6y + 2z + 5) = 7(-4x + 12y - 3z + 3)$

$39x - 78y + 26z + 65 = -28x + 84y - 21z + 21$

$67x - 162y + 47z + 44 = 0$ ........(3)

Further, $3 \times 4 + (-6)(-12) + 2 \times 3 > 0$

$\therefore$ origin lies in acute angle.

**11.** **(a,b,c,d)** Since, the planes are all parallel planes.

$$p_1 = \dfrac{|2 - 6|}{\sqrt{2^2 + 3^2 + 4^2}}$$

$$= \dfrac{4}{\sqrt{4 + 9 + 16}} = \dfrac{4}{\sqrt{29}}$$

Equation of the plane $4x - 6y + 8z + 3 = 0$ can be written

as $2x - 3y + 4z + \dfrac{3}{2} = 0$

So, $p_2 = \dfrac{\left|2 - \dfrac{3}{2}\right|}{\sqrt{2^2 + 3^2 + 4^2}} = \dfrac{1}{2\sqrt{29}}$

and $p_3 = \dfrac{|2 + 6|}{\sqrt{2^2 + 3^2 + 4^2}} = \dfrac{8}{\sqrt{29}}$

We find $p_3 = 16p_2 = 2p_1$

$p_1 + 2p_2 + 3p_3 = \dfrac{4}{\sqrt{29}} + \dfrac{1}{\sqrt{29}} + \dfrac{24}{\sqrt{29}} = \dfrac{29}{\sqrt{29}}$

$\qquad = \sqrt{29}$

and $p_1 + 8p_2 - p_3 = \dfrac{4}{\sqrt{29}} + \dfrac{4}{\sqrt{29}} - \dfrac{8}{\sqrt{29}} = 0$

**12.** **(b,d)** It is clear that plane is parallel to $z$ - axis *i.e.* perpendicular to $xy$ plane.

**13.** **(c)** The equation of any plane through $(-1, 3, 2)$ is $a(x + 1) + b(y - 3) + c(z - 2) = 0$ ....(i)

If this plane (i) is perpendicular to $P_1$,

then $2a - b + c = 0$ ....(ii)

and if the plane (ii) is perpendicualr to $P_2$

then $a + 2b - c = 0$ ....(iii)

From eqs. (ii) and (iii), we get $\dfrac{a}{-1} = \dfrac{b}{3} = \dfrac{c}{5}$

Substituting these proportionate values of $a$, $b$, $c$ in eq (i), we get the required equation as

$-(x + 1) + 3(y - 3) + 5(z - 2) = 0$

or $\quad x - 3y - 5z + 20 = 0$

**14.** **(a)** The given planes can be written as

$-2x + y - z + 2 - 0$ and $-x - 2y + z + 3 = 0$

Here, $(-2)(-1) + (1)(-2) + (-1)(1) = -1 < 0$

Equation of bisectors

$$\dfrac{(-2x + y - z + 2)}{\sqrt{(4 + 1 + 1)}} = \pm \dfrac{(-x - 2y + z + 3)}{\sqrt{1 + 4 + 1}}$$

$\therefore$ Acute angle bisector is

$(-2x + y - z + 2) = (-x - 2y + z + 3)$

$\Rightarrow \quad x - 3y + 2z + 1 = 0$

**15.** **(c)** The image of plane $P_1$ in the plane mirror $P_2$, is

$2(2.1 + (-1).2 + 1.(-1))(x + 2y - z - 3)$

$= (1 + 4 + 1)(2x - y + z - 2)$

$\Rightarrow -(x + 2y - z - 3) = 3(2x - y + z - 2)$

$\Rightarrow 7x - y + 4z - 9 = 0$.

**16.** **(A)** $\rightarrow$ s; **(B)** $\rightarrow$ p; **(C)** $\rightarrow$ q; **(D)** $\rightarrow$ r

(A) Two planes $A_1x + B_1y + C_1z = D_1$ and

$A_2x + B_2y + C_2z = D_2$ are parallel

If $\dfrac{A_1}{A_2} = \dfrac{B_1}{B_2} = \dfrac{C_1}{C_2} \neq \dfrac{D_1}{D_2}$,

Hence (A)→ **(s)**

(B) Two planes $A_1x + B_1y + C_1z = D_1$ and $A_2x + B_2y + C_2z = D_2$ are perpendicular

If $A_1A_2 + B_1B_2 + C_1C_2 = 0$

For planes $3x + 7y + 2z = 5$

and $2x - 2y + 4z = 7$

$A_1A_2 + B_1B_2 + C_1C_2 = 3 \times 2 + 7 \times (-2) + 2 \times 4 = 0$

Hence (B)→ **(p)**

(C) Putting the co-ordinates of the point $(2,2,2)$ in the plane $3x - 7y + z + 6 = 0$,

we get

$3 \times 2 - 7 \times 2 + 2 + 6 = 0$

$\Rightarrow 0 = 0$

Hence, equation of the plane passing through the point $(2, 2, 2)$ is $3x - 7y + z + 6 = 0$

Hence (C)→ **(q)**

(D) For the plane $14x + 6y + 21z = 42$,

$\dfrac{x}{3} + \dfrac{y}{7} + \dfrac{z}{2} = 1$

Hence, equation of the plane making intercepts 3, 7, 2 on the coordinate axes is $14x + 6y + 21z = 42$

Hence (D) → **(r)**

**17. (d)** Here, $a = 2, b = -6, c = 4, f = 9, g = 1, h = \dfrac{1}{2}$

$\therefore \quad abc + 2fgh - af^2 - bg^2 - ch^2$

$= (2)(-6)(4) + 2(9)(1)\left(\dfrac{1}{2}\right) - (2)(81) + 6(1)^2 - 4\left(\dfrac{1}{2}\right)^2$

$= -48 + 9 - 162 + 6 - 1$

$= -196 \neq 0$

$\therefore$ given equation cannot represent a pair of planes.

**18. (d)** Distance $= \left|\dfrac{5+2}{\sqrt{50}}\right| = \dfrac{7}{5\sqrt{2}}$.

**19. (a)** $\because$ Equation of the plane through the line of intersection of the planes $x + y + z = 6$ and $2x + 3y + 4z + 5 = 0$ is

$(x + y + z - 6) + \lambda(2x + 3y + 4z + 5) = 0$ ...(i)

Since, it passes through $(4, 4, 4)$, then

$(4 + 4 + 4 - 6) + \lambda(8 + 12 + 16 + 5) = 0$

$\Rightarrow 6 + 41\lambda = 0$

$\therefore \quad \lambda = -\dfrac{6}{41}$

Then from Eq. (i),

$41(x + y + z - 6) - 6(2x + 3y + 4z + 5) = 0$

$\Rightarrow 29x + 23y + 17z = 276$

**20. 3**

Direction ratios of OP are $(a, b, c)$

$\therefore$ equation of the plane is

$a(x - a) + b(y - b) + c(z - c) = 0$

$ax + by + cz = a^2 + b^2 + c^2$

Thus, $P = 1, Q = 1, R = 1$

$\Rightarrow P + Q + R = 3$.

**21. 3**

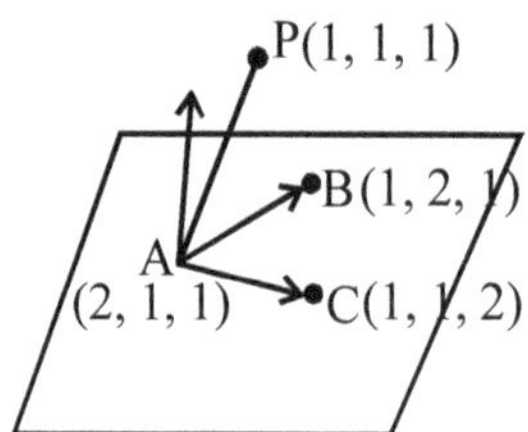


$\overrightarrow{AP} = \overrightarrow{OP} - \overrightarrow{OA} = (\hat{i} + \hat{j} + \hat{k}) - (2\hat{i} + \hat{j} + \hat{k}) = -\hat{i}$

$\overrightarrow{AB} = \overrightarrow{OB} - \overrightarrow{OA} = (\hat{i} + 2\hat{j} + \hat{k}) - (2\hat{i} + \hat{j} + \hat{k}) = -\hat{i} + \hat{j}$

$\overrightarrow{AC} = \overrightarrow{OC} - \overrightarrow{OA} = (\hat{i} + \hat{j} + 2\hat{k}) - (2\hat{i} - \hat{j} + \hat{k}) = -\hat{i} + \hat{k}$

$\overrightarrow{AC} \times \overrightarrow{AB} = (-\hat{i} + \hat{k}) \times (\hat{i} + \hat{j}) = -\hat{k} - \hat{j} - \hat{i}$

$\therefore$ The unit vector perpendicular to the plane ABC

$= \dfrac{-\hat{k} - \hat{j} - \hat{i}}{\sqrt{3}}$

The required distance $= \overrightarrow{AP} \cdot \dfrac{-\hat{k} - \hat{j} - \hat{i}}{\sqrt{3}}$

$= (-\vec{i}) \cdot \dfrac{-\hat{k} - \hat{j} - \hat{i}}{\sqrt{3}} = \dfrac{1}{\sqrt{3}}$

Thus, $X = 3$.

**22. 5**

Comparing the given equations of the planes with the equations $A_1x + B_1y + C_1z + D_1 = 0$ and $A_2x + B_2y + C_2z + D_2 = 0$

We get $A_1 = 3, B_1 = -6, C_1 = 2$

$A_2 = 2, B_2 = 2, C_2 = -2$

$\cos\theta = \left|\dfrac{3 \times 2 + (-6)(2) + (2)(-2)}{\sqrt{(3^2 + (-6)^2 + (-2)^2)}\sqrt{(2^2 + 2^2 + (-2)^2)}}\right|$

$= \left|\dfrac{-10}{7 \times 2\sqrt{3}}\right| = \dfrac{5}{7\sqrt{3}} = \dfrac{5\sqrt{3}}{21}$

Therefore, $\theta = \cos^{-1}\left(\dfrac{5\sqrt{3}}{21}\right)$

Thus $X = 5$.

**23.** **2**

The equation of plane through the point $(1, -2, 1)$ and perpendicular to the planes $2x - 2y + z = 0$ and $x - y + 2z = 4$ is given by

$$\begin{vmatrix} x-1 & y+2 & z-1 \\ 2 & -2 & 1 \\ 1 & -1 & 2 \end{vmatrix} = 0$$

$$\Rightarrow \quad x + y + 1 = 0$$

It's distance from the point $(1, 2, 2)$ is $\left| \dfrac{1+2+1}{\sqrt{2}} \right| = 2\sqrt{2}$.

Thus, $P = 2$.

**24.** **2**

Any plane through $(1, 0, 0)$ is

$$A(x-1) + B(y-0) + C(z-0) = 0 \qquad \text{...(1)}$$

It contains $(0, 1, 0)$ if $-A + B = 0$ $\qquad$ ...(2)

Also, (1) makes an angle of $\dfrac{\pi}{4}$ with the plane $x + y = 3$,

therefore, $\cos \dfrac{\pi}{4} = \dfrac{|A + B|}{\sqrt{A^2 + B^2 + C^2}\,\sqrt{1^2 + 1^2}}$

$$\Rightarrow (A + B)^2 = A^2 + B^2 + C^2 \quad \Rightarrow 2AB = C^2 \quad \text{...(3)}$$

From (2) and (3), $C^2 = 2A^2 \Rightarrow C = \pm\sqrt{2}A$

Hence $A : B : C :: A : A : \pm\sqrt{2}A$ .

$\therefore$ Direction ratios are $1 : 1 : \pm\sqrt{2}$

Thus, $P + Q = 2$.

**1. (a)** Equation of the line passing through $(1, -2, 3)$ parallel to the line $\dfrac{x}{2} = \dfrac{y}{3} = \dfrac{z-1}{-6}$ is

$$\frac{x-1}{2} = \frac{y+2}{3} = \frac{z-3}{-6} = r \ (\text{say}) \qquad ...(1)$$

Then any point on (1) is $(2r + 1, 3r - 2, -6r + 3)$

If this point lies on the plane $x - y + z = 5$ then

$$(2r+1) - (3r-2) + (-6r+3) = 5 \Rightarrow r = \frac{1}{7}$$

Hence, the point is $\left(\dfrac{9}{7}, -\dfrac{11}{7}, \dfrac{15}{7}\right)$

Distance between $(1, -2, 3)$ and $\left(\dfrac{9}{7}, -\dfrac{11}{7}, \dfrac{15}{7}\right)$

$$= \sqrt{\left(\frac{4}{49} + \frac{9}{49} + \frac{36}{49}\right)} = \sqrt{\left(\frac{49}{49}\right)} = 1$$

**2. (c)** Given plane is $x + y + z - 3 = 0$.

From point P and Q, draw PM and QN perpendiculars on the given plane.

$$|MP| = \frac{0+1+0-3}{\sqrt{1^2+1^2+1^2}} = \frac{2}{\sqrt{3}}, |NQ| = \frac{2}{\sqrt{3}}$$

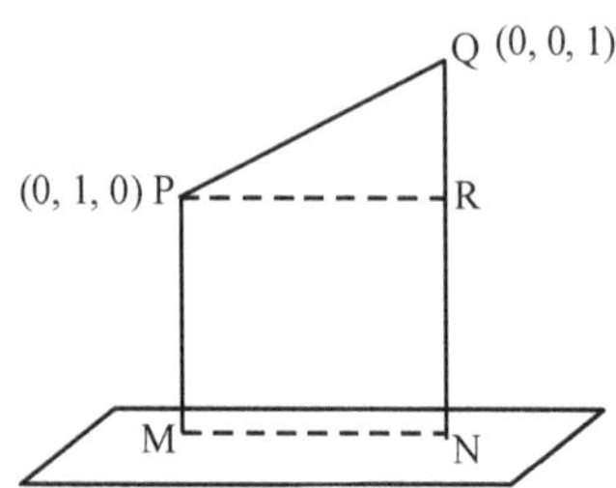

$$|PQ| = \sqrt{(0-0)^2 + (0-1)^2 + (1-0)^2} = \sqrt{2}$$

$$\because |MP| = |NQ|$$

$$\therefore QR = 0, \qquad \therefore MN = PQ = \sqrt{2}$$

**3. (c)** Direction ratios of given line are $1, -2, 3$ and the d.r. of normal to the given plane are $1, 2, 1$.

Since $1 \times 1 + (-2) \times 2 + 3 \times 1 = 0$, therefore, the line is parallel to the plane, Also, the base point of the line $(1, 2, 1)$ lies in the given plane.

$(1 + 2 \times 2 + 1 = 6 \text{ is true})$

Hence, the given line lies in the given plane.

**4. (b)** When folded co-ordinates will be D $(0, 0, a)$; C$(a, 0, 0)$; A$(-a, 0, 0)$; B $(0, -a, 0)$

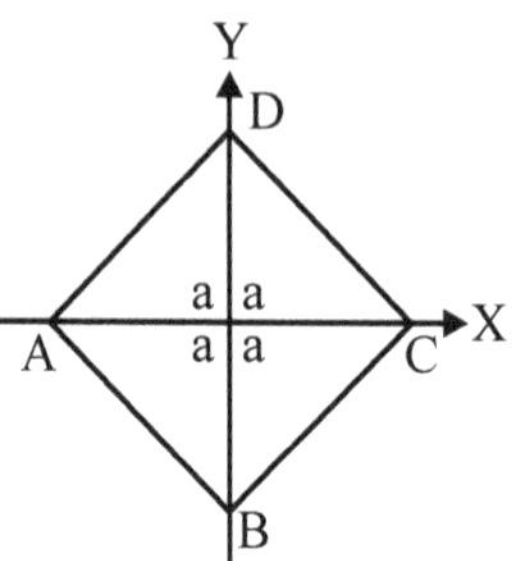

Equation of DC is, $\dfrac{x}{a} = \dfrac{y}{0} = \dfrac{z-a}{-a}$

Equation of AB is, $\dfrac{x+a}{a} = \dfrac{y}{-a} = \dfrac{z}{0}$

Shortest distance between DC and AB is given by

$$S.D = \frac{\begin{vmatrix} -a & 0 & -a \\ a & 0 & -a \\ a & -a & 0 \end{vmatrix}}{\sqrt{(0-a^2) + (-a^2-0)^2 + (-a^2-0)^2}}$$

Using the formula

$$S.D = \pm \frac{\begin{vmatrix} x_2 - x_1 & y_2 - y_1 & z_2 - z_1 \\ \ell_1 & m_1 & n_1 \\ \ell_2 & m_2 & n_2 \end{vmatrix}}{\sqrt{(m_1 n_2 - m_2 n_1)^2 + (n_1 \ell_2 - n_2 \ell_1)^2 + (\ell_1 m_2 - \ell_2 m_1)^2}}$$

$$= \frac{2a^3}{\sqrt{3a^4}} = \frac{2a}{\sqrt{3}}$$

**5. (c)** The given line is $\hat{r} = 2\hat{i} - 2\hat{j} + 3\hat{k} + \lambda(\hat{i} - \hat{j} + 4\hat{k})$ or $\vec{r} = \vec{a} + \lambda\vec{b}$ where $\vec{a} = 2\hat{i} - 2\hat{j} + 3\hat{k}$, $\vec{b} = \hat{i} - \hat{j} + 4\hat{k}$. The given plane is $\vec{r} = (\hat{i} + 5\hat{j} + \hat{k}) = 5$ or $\vec{r}\vec{n} = d$. where $\vec{n} = (\hat{i} + 5\hat{j} + \hat{k})$.

Since $\vec{b}\vec{n} = (\hat{i} - \hat{j} + 4\hat{k}).(\hat{i} + 5\hat{j} + \hat{k}) = 1 - 5 + 4 = 0$.

Therefore, the line is parallel to the plane. Thus, the distance between the line and the plane is equal to the length of the $\perp$ from a point $\vec{a} = 2\hat{i} - 2\hat{j} + 3\hat{k}$ on the line to the given plane.

Hence, the required distance

$$= \left| \frac{(2\hat{i} - 2\hat{j} + 3\hat{k}).(\hat{i} - 5\hat{j} + \hat{k}) - 5}{\sqrt{1 + 25 + 1}} \right|$$

$$= \left| \frac{2 - 10 + 3 - 5}{\sqrt{27}} \right| = \frac{10}{3\sqrt{3}}$$

**6.** **(d)** $P_1 = P_2 = 0$, $P_2 = P_3 = 0$ and $P_3 = P_1 = 0$ are lines of intersection of the three planes $P_1$, $P_2$ and $P_3$.

As $\vec{n}_1, \vec{n}_2$ and $\vec{n}_3$ are non-coplanar, planes $P_1$, $P_2$ and $P_3$ will intersect at unique point. So the given lines will pass through a fixed point.

**7.** **(b)** If the direction ratios of the line are $l$, m, n then it is perpendicular to the normal to the plane.

$\therefore \qquad 2l + 3m + n = 0$

And the only values of $l$, m, n that satisfy this equation are $-1$, 1, $-1$.

**8.** **(b)** Angle between line

$$\frac{x - x_1}{l} = \frac{y - y_1}{m} = \frac{z - z_1}{n} \text{ and plane}$$

$ax + by + cz + d = 0$ is

$$\sin\theta = \frac{al + bm + cn}{\sqrt{a^2 + b^2 + c^2}\sqrt{l^2 + m^2 + n^2}}$$

If line is parallel to plane then $\theta = 0°$

$$\therefore \sin\theta = \frac{al + bm + cn}{\sqrt{a^2 + b^2 + c^2}\sqrt{l^2 + m^2 + n^2}} = 0$$

or $al + bm + cn = 0$

**9.** **(a)** Equation of any plane through the first line is

$a(x - 1) + b(y + 1) + cz = 0 \qquad .....(1)$

where $2a - b + 3c = 0 \qquad .....(2)$

It will pass through the second line if $(0, 2, -1)$, a point on the second line lies on it i.e. if

$-a + 3b - c = 0 \qquad .....(3)$

By (2) and (3), we get

$$\frac{a}{-8} = \frac{b}{-1} = \frac{c}{5} \text{ or } \frac{a}{8} = \frac{b}{1} = \frac{c}{-5}$$

Hence equation of required plane is

$8(x - 1) + (y + 1) - 5z = 0$.

$\Rightarrow \qquad 8x + y - 5z - 7 = 0$.

**10.** **(c)** Equation of a plane through the line of intersection of given planes is

$$ax + by + cz + d + \lambda(a'x + b'y + c'z + d') = 0$$

$$(a + \lambda a')x + (b + \lambda b')y + (c + \lambda c')z + (d + \lambda d') = 0$$

It is a parallel to $y = 0$, $z = 0$

i.e. x-axis whose direction ratios are 1, 0, 0.

$\therefore \ 1(a + \lambda a') + 0(b + \lambda b') + 0(c + \lambda c') = 0$

$$\Rightarrow \lambda = -\frac{a}{a'}$$

Hence the required plane is

$$y(a'b - ab') + z(a'c - ac') + (a'd - ad') = 0$$

**11.** **(d)** The given lines are

$$x - 1 = \frac{y + 3}{-\lambda} = \frac{z - 1}{\lambda} = s \text{ -------(1)}$$

and $2x = y - 1 = \dfrac{z - 2}{-1} = t \text{ .........(2)}$

The lines are coplanar, if

$$\begin{vmatrix} 0 - 1 & 1 - (-3) & 2 - (1) \\ 1 & -\lambda & \lambda \\ \frac{1}{2} & 1 & -1 \end{vmatrix} = 0$$

$$\begin{vmatrix} 1 & -5 & -1 \\ 1 & 0 & \lambda \\ \frac{1}{2} & 0 & -1 \end{vmatrix} = 0; \quad C_2 \to C_2 + C_3$$

$$\Rightarrow 5\left(-1 - \frac{\lambda}{2}\right) = 0 \Rightarrow \lambda = -2$$

**12.** **(a)** Angle between line and normal to plane is

$$\cos\left(\frac{\pi}{2} - \theta\right) = \frac{2 - 2 + 2\sqrt{\lambda}}{3 \times \sqrt{5} + \lambda};$$

where $\theta$ is angle between line and plane

$$\Rightarrow \sin\theta = \frac{2\sqrt{\lambda}}{3\sqrt{5} + \lambda} = \frac{1}{3} \Rightarrow \lambda = \frac{5}{3}.$$

**13.** **(c)** The equation of the plane containing the line

$$\frac{x + 1}{-3.} = \frac{y - 3}{2} = \frac{z + 2}{1} \text{ is}$$

$a(x + 1) + b(y - 3) + c(z + 2) = 0 \quad ......(1)$

where $-3a + 2b + c = 0 \quad ......(2)$

This passes through $(0, 7, -7)$ $\qquad \therefore$

$a + 4b - 5c = 0 \qquad ......(3)$

From (2) and (3) $\dfrac{a}{-14} = \dfrac{b}{-14} = \dfrac{c}{-14}$ or $\dfrac{a}{1} = \dfrac{b}{1} = \dfrac{c}{1}$.

So the required plane is $x + y + z = 0$

**14.** **(b)** Given plane is $x - y - z = 9 \quad ......(1)$

Given line AB is $\dfrac{x - 2}{2} = \dfrac{y + 2}{3} = \dfrac{z - 6}{-6} \quad ......(2)$

Eq. of line passing through $(1, 0, -3)$ and parallel to

$\dfrac{x - 2}{2} = \dfrac{y + 2}{3} = \dfrac{z - 6}{-6}$ is :

$$\frac{x-1}{2} = \frac{y-0}{3} = \frac{z+3}{-6} = r \quad ........(3)$$

Co-ordinates of any point on (3) may be given as

$P(2r+1, \ 3r, \ -6r-3)$

If $P$ is intersection of (1) and (3) then it must lie on (1);

$$(2r+1)-(3r)-(-6r-3)=9$$

$$2r+1-3r+6r+3=9 \ \Rightarrow r=1$$

$\therefore$    Co-ordinate of $P$ are $(3,3,-9)$

$\therefore$    Required distance = distance between $(1,0,-3)$ and $(3,3,-9) = 7$

**15.**   **(c)**   Let $P$ be the point $(x_1, y_1, z_1)$ on the given plane, then

$$lx_1 + m\,y_1 + n\,z_1 = p \quad .....(i)$$

Let $Q$ be $(\alpha, \beta, \gamma)$   $O, P, Q$ are collinear so

$$\frac{x_1}{\alpha} = \frac{y_1}{\beta} = \frac{z_1}{\gamma} = k \ \text{(say)} .........(ii)$$

Now $OP.OQ = p^2$

$$\Rightarrow \sqrt{x_1^2 + y_1^2 + z_1^2}\ \sqrt{\alpha^2 + \beta^2 + \gamma^2} = p^2$$

$$\Rightarrow k(\alpha^2 + \beta^2 + \gamma^2) = p^2 \quad ......(iii)$$

Also from (i) and (ii), $k(l\alpha + m\beta + n\gamma) = p$ ; From (iii)

and (iv), $p(l\alpha + m\beta + n\gamma) = (\alpha^2 + \beta^2 + \gamma^2)$

$\therefore$   Locus of $Q = (\alpha, \beta, \gamma)$ is

$$p(lx + my + nz) = x^2 + y^2 + z^2$$

**16.**   **(a,b,c)** Here, P be (x, y, z)

Then, $x = r\sin\theta.\cos\phi, \ y = r\sin\theta\sin\phi, \ z = r\cos\theta$

$\Rightarrow 1 = r\sin\theta.\cos\phi, \ 2 = r\sin\theta\sin\phi, \ 3 = r\cos\theta \quad ...(i)$

$\Rightarrow 1^2 + 2^2 + 3^2$

$\qquad = r^2\sin^2\theta\cos^2\phi + r^2\sin^2\theta\sin^2\phi + r^2\cos^2\theta$

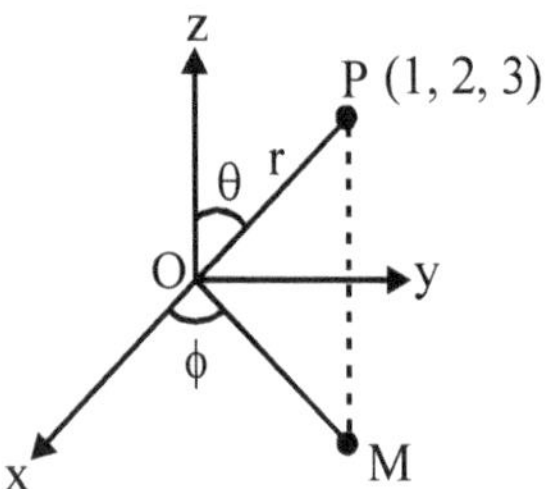


$\qquad = r^2\sin^2\theta(\cos^2\phi + \sin^2\phi) + r^2\cos^2\theta$

$\qquad = r^2\sin^2\theta + r^2\cos^2\theta = r^2$

$\Rightarrow r = \pm\sqrt{14}$

$\therefore$ From (i), we have

$$\sin\theta\cos\phi = \pm\frac{1}{\sqrt{14}}, \ \sin\theta + \cos\phi = \frac{2}{\sqrt{14}},$$

$$\cos\theta = \frac{3}{\sqrt{14}}$$

    (neglecting –ve sign assuming acute angles)

$\therefore \ \dfrac{\sin\theta\sin\phi}{\sin\theta\cos\phi} = \dfrac{2}{1}$ and $\tan\theta = \dfrac{\sin\theta}{\cos\theta} = \dfrac{\sqrt{5}}{3}$

$\Rightarrow \ \tan\phi = 2$ and $\tan\theta = \dfrac{\sqrt{5}}{3}$

**17.**   **(a,b,c,d)**

(a)   We know that the plane $ax + by + cz + d = 0$ contains

the line $\dfrac{x-\alpha}{l} = \dfrac{y-\beta}{m} = \dfrac{z-\gamma}{n}$

if $a\alpha + b\beta + c\gamma + d = 0$ and $al + bm + cn = 0$.

Now, since $(-1)-2(3)+7(-2)+21=0$

and $(-3)(1)+2(-2)+1(7)=0$

The line given in (a) lies on the given plane

(b)   Since, $0-2(7)+7(-1)+21=0$

The point $(0,7,-1)$ lies on the plane.

(c)   Direction ratios of the normal to the given plane are $(1, -2, 7)$ which are same as those of the given in (c). So, the plane is perpendicular to the lines.

(d)   The direction ratios of the normal to the planes given in (d) are same as those of the given plane. SO, the plane in (d) is parallel to the given plane.

**18.**   **A→r; B→q; C→p; D→s**

Here we have, the determinent of the coefficient matrix of given equation, as

$$\Delta = \begin{vmatrix} a & b & c \\ b & c & a \\ c & a & b \end{vmatrix}$$

$$= -(a+b+c)(a^2 + b^2 + c^2 - ab - bc - ca)$$

$$= -\frac{1}{2}(a+b+c)[(a-b)^2 + (b-c)^2 + (c-a)^2]$$

(A) $a+b+c \neq 0$ and $a^2 + b^2 + c^2 - ab - bc - ca = 0$

$\Rightarrow \quad (a-b)^2 + (b-c)^2 + (c-a)^2 = 0$

$\Rightarrow \quad a = b = c \,(\text{but} \neq 0 \text{ as } a+b+c \neq 0)$

$\therefore$    This equation represent identical planes.

(B) $a+b+c = 0$ and $a^2 + b^2 + c^2 - ab - bc - ca \neq 0$

$\Rightarrow \quad \Delta = 0$ and $a, b, c$ are not all equal.

$\therefore$ all equations are not identical but have infinite many solutions.

$\therefore \quad ax + by = (a+b)z$ (using $a+b+c=0$)

and $bx + cy = (b+c)z$

$\Rightarrow \quad (b^2 - ac)y = (b^2 - ac)z$

$\Rightarrow y=z$

$\Rightarrow \quad ax + by + cy = 0 \quad \Rightarrow \quad ax = ay$

$\Rightarrow \quad x = y = z$

$\therefore \quad$ the equations represent the line $x = y = z$

(C) $a + b + c \neq 0$ and $a^2 + b^2 + c^2 - ab - bc - ca \neq 0$

$\Rightarrow \quad \Delta \neq 0 \Rightarrow$ Equations have only trivial solution

i.e., $x = y = z = 0$

$\therefore$ The equations represents the three planes meeting at a single point namely origin.

(D) $a + b + c = 0$ and $a^2 + b^2 + c^2 - ab - bc - ca = 0$

$\Rightarrow \quad a = b = c$ and $\Delta = 0$

$\Rightarrow \quad a = b = c = 0$

$\Rightarrow \quad$ All equations are satisfied by all $x$, $y$, and $z$.

$\Rightarrow \quad$ The equations represent the whole of the three dimensional space (all points in 3–D)

**19.** $\mathbf{A \to q, r, s,; B \to p, r; C \to t}$

(A) Let the line makes an angle $\theta$ with $z$-axis

Then, $\cos^2 \alpha + \cos^2 \alpha + \cos^2 \theta = 1$

$\Rightarrow \quad \cos^2 \theta = -\cos 2\alpha$

$\therefore \quad 0 \leq \cos^2 \theta \leq 1$

$\Rightarrow \quad 0 \leq -\cos 2\alpha \leq 1$

$\Rightarrow \quad -1 \leq \cos 2\alpha \leq 0$

$\Rightarrow \quad \cos^{-1}(0) \leq 2\alpha \leq \cos^{-1}(-1)$

$\Rightarrow \quad \dfrac{\pi}{2} \leq 2\alpha \leq \pi$

or $\quad \dfrac{\pi}{4} \leq \alpha \leq \dfrac{\pi}{2}$

Then, $0 \leq \cot \alpha \leq 1$

(B) Let $\dfrac{x-2}{1} = \dfrac{y-3}{1} = \dfrac{4-z}{\lambda} = r_1$ (say)

then general point on Ist line is $(2 + r_1, 3 + r_1, 4 - \lambda r_1)$

and Let $\dfrac{x-1}{\lambda} = \dfrac{y-4}{2} = \dfrac{z-5}{1} = r_2$ (say)

Then, general point on IInd line is

$\quad (1 + \lambda r_2, 4 + 2r_2, 5 + r_2)$

$\because \quad$ lines intersect, then

$2 + r_1 = 1 + \lambda r_2, \ 3 + r_1 = 4 + 2r_2, \ 4 - \lambda r_1 = 5 + r_2$

Eliminating $r_1$ and $r_2$, we get, $\lambda^2 + 3\lambda = 0$

$\therefore \quad \lambda = 0, -3$

(C) $\because$ Line is perpendicular to normal of the plane

$\therefore \quad \lambda . \lambda + (-\mu) . \mu + v . v = 0$

$\Rightarrow \quad \lambda^2 - \mu^2 + v^2 = 0 \qquad ....(i)$

and point $(\lambda, 2\phi, v)$ lies on the plane

then, $\lambda^2 - 2\mu\phi + v^2 = 0 \qquad ....(ii)$

From eqs. (i) and (ii), we get

$2\mu\phi = \mu^2$

or $\quad 2\phi = \mu$

$\therefore \quad \dfrac{\mu}{\phi} = 2$

**20.** **1**

Given planes are : $x - cy - bz = 0$ ..... (1)

$\qquad\qquad cx - y + az = 0$ ...... (2)

$\qquad\qquad bx + ay - z = 0$ ..... (3)

Equation of plane passing through the line of intersection of plane (1) and (2) may be taken as;

$\qquad (x - cy - bz) + \lambda(cx - y + az) = 0$

or $\quad x(1 + \lambda c) - y(c + \lambda) - z(-b + a\lambda) = 0$ ...... (4)

If plane (3) and (4) are same ; then equation (3) and (4) will be identical

$\therefore \quad \dfrac{1 + c\lambda}{b} = \dfrac{-(c + \lambda)}{a} = \dfrac{-b + a\lambda}{-1}$

or $\lambda = -\dfrac{(a + bc)}{(ac + b)}$ and $\lambda = -\dfrac{(a + bc)}{(1 - a^2)}$

$\therefore \qquad \dfrac{-(a + bc)}{(ac + b)} = -\dfrac{(ab + c)}{(1 - a^2)}$

$\Rightarrow \quad a - a^3 + bc - a^2 bc = a^2 bc + ac^2 + ab^2 + bc$

$\Rightarrow \quad 2a^2 bc + ac^2 + a^3 - a = 0$

$\Rightarrow \quad a(2abc + c^2 + b^2 + a^2 - 1) = 0$

$\Rightarrow \quad a^2 + b^2 + c^2 + 2abc = 1$

**21.** **1**

Let P $(x_1, y_1, z_1)$ be a point on $ax + by + cz = d$. Then $ax_1 + by_1 + cz_1 = d$

Let $OP = r$. Then direction cosines of $OP$ are $\dfrac{x_1}{r}, \dfrac{y_1}{r}, \dfrac{z_1}{r}$

Equation of line $OP$ is $\dfrac{x - 0}{\dfrac{x_1}{r}} = \dfrac{y - 0}{\dfrac{y_1}{r}} = \dfrac{z - 0}{\dfrac{z_1}{r}}$,

Let $Q \ (\alpha, \beta, \gamma)$ be a point on $OP$ such that $OQ = \lambda$. Then coordinates of $Q\left(\dfrac{x_1 \lambda}{r}, \dfrac{y_1 \lambda}{r}, \dfrac{z_1 \lambda}{r}\right)$. Thus

$x_1 = \dfrac{\alpha r}{\lambda}, y_1 = \dfrac{\beta r}{\lambda}, z_1 = \dfrac{\gamma r}{\lambda}$

Now $ax_1 + by_1 + cz_1 = d$

$\Rightarrow \dfrac{r}{\lambda}(a\alpha + b\beta + c\gamma) = d$

Now $OP . OQ = d^2$

$\Rightarrow r\lambda = d^2$

$\Rightarrow r\lambda = d . \dfrac{r}{\lambda}(a\alpha + b\beta + c\gamma)$

$$\Rightarrow (a\alpha + b\beta + c\gamma)d = \lambda^2$$

$$\Rightarrow (a\alpha + b\beta + c\gamma)d = \alpha^2 + \beta + \gamma^2$$

So, locus of $(\alpha, \beta, \gamma)$ is $(ax + by + cz)\,d = x^2 + y^2 + z^2$

or $\dfrac{(ax + by + cz)\,d}{x^2 + y^2 + z^2} = 1$

**22.  2**

Equation of plane through $(1, 1, 1)$ and perpendicular to line

$$\frac{x-1}{3} = \frac{y-1}{0} = \frac{z-1}{4} \text{ is}$$

$$3(x-1) + 0(y-1) + 4.(z-1) = 0$$

or $3x + 4z - 7 = 0$

Distance of plane from the origin $= \left| \dfrac{0+0-7}{\sqrt{9+16}} \right| = \dfrac{7}{5}$

$\therefore$ A $-$ B $= 7 - 5 = 2.$

**23.  7**

As the line $\dfrac{x-4}{1} = \dfrac{y-1}{1} = \dfrac{z-k}{2}$ lies in the plane

$2x - 4y + z = 7$, the point $(4, 2, k)$ through which line passes must also lie on the given plane and hence

$2 \times 4 - 4 \times 2 + k = 7$

$k = 7$

**24.  4**

Let the direction cosines of line L be $l$, m, n, then

$2l + 3m + n = 0$ ....(i)

and $l + 3m + 2n = 0$ ....(ii)

On solving equation (i) and (ii), we get

$$\frac{l}{6-3} = \frac{m}{1-4} = \frac{n}{6-3} \quad \Rightarrow \quad \frac{l}{3} = \frac{m}{-3} = \frac{n}{3}$$

Now $\dfrac{l}{3} = \dfrac{m}{-3} = \dfrac{n}{3} = \dfrac{\sqrt{l^2 + m^2 + n^2}}{\sqrt{3^2 + (-3)^2 + 3^2}}$

$\because \ l^2 + m^2 + n^2 = 1$

$\therefore \ \dfrac{l}{3} = \dfrac{m}{-3} = \dfrac{n}{3} = \dfrac{1}{\sqrt{27}}$

$\Rightarrow \ l = \dfrac{3}{\sqrt{27}} = \dfrac{1}{\sqrt{3}}, m = -\dfrac{1}{\sqrt{3}}, n = \dfrac{1}{\sqrt{3}}$

Line L, makes an angle $\alpha$ with +ve x-axis

$\therefore \ l = \cos\alpha \ \Rightarrow \ \cos\alpha = \dfrac{1}{\sqrt{3}}$

Thus A $= 1$, B $= 3$

$\Rightarrow$ A $+$ B $= 1 + 3 = 4.$

# CHAPTER-WISE
# DPP SHEETS
# WITH SOLUTIONS

Date :       Start Time :       End Time :

# MATHEMATICS $\boxed{\text{CM01}}$

**SYLLABUS : Sets**

**Max. Marks : 67**            **Time : 60 min.**

## GENERAL INSTRUCTIONS

- The Daily Practice Problem Sheet contains 20 Questions divided into 5 sections.
  **Section I** has **6** MCQs with ONLY 1 Correct Option, **3** marks for each correct answer and **−1** for each incorrect answer.
  **Section II** has **4** MCQs with ONE or MORE THAN ONE Correct options.
  For each question, marks will be awarded in one of the following categories:
  Full marks: **+4** If only the bubble(s) corresponding to all the correct option(s) is (are) darkened.
  Partial marks: **+1** For darkening a bubble corresponding to each correct option provided NO INCORRECT option is darkened.
  Zero marks:  If none of the bubbles is darkened.
  Negative marks: **−2** In all other cases.
  **Section III** has **5** Single Digit Integer Answer Type Questions, **3** marks for each Correct Answer and **0** mark in all other cases.
  **Section IV** has Comprehension Type Questions having **4** MCQs with ONLY ONE corect option, **3** marks for each Correct Answer and **0** mark in all other cases.
  **Section V** has **1** Matching Type Question, **2** marks for the correct matching of each row and **0** mark in all other cases.
- You have to evaluate your Response Grids yourself with the help of Solutions.

## Section I - Straight Objective Type

This section contains 6 multiple choice questions. Each question has 4 choices (a), (b), (c) and (d), out of which **ONLY ONE** is correct.

**1.** Consider the following relations:
1.  $A - B = A - (A \cap B)$
2.  $A = (A \cap B) \cup (A - B)$
3.  $A - (B \cup C) = (A - B) \cup (A - C)$
Which of these is/are correct?

(a) (1) and (3)      (b) (2) only
(c) (2) and (3)      (d) (1) and (2)

**2.** The value of $(A \cup B \cup C) \cap (A \cap B^c \cap C^c)^c \cap C^c$, is
(a) $B \cap C^c$      (b) $B^c \cap C^c$
(c) $B \cap C$      (d) $A \cap B \cap C$

**3.** A survey shows that 63% of the Americans like cheese whereas 76% like apples. If $x\%$ of the Americans like both cheese and apples, then
(a) $x = 39$      (b) $x = 63$
(c) $39 \le x \le 63$      (d) None of these

---

**RESPONSE GRID**    **1.** ⓐⓑⓒⓓ    **2.** ⓐⓑⓒⓓ    **3.** ⓐⓑⓒⓓ

*Space for Rough Work*

**4.** Let $X$ and $Y$ be two non-empty sets such that $X \cap A = Y \cap A = \phi$ and $X \cup A = Y \cup A$ for some non-empty set $A$. Then
(a) $X$ is a proper subset of $Y$
(b) $Y$ is a proper subset of $X$
(c) $X = Y$
(d) $X$ and $Y$ are disjoint sets

**5.** If $n(A) = 1000$, $n(B) = 500$ and if $n(A \cap B) \geq 1$ and $n(A \cup B) = p$, then
(a) $500 \leq p \leq 1000$   (b) $1001 \leq p \leq 1498$
(c) $1000 \leq p \leq 1498$   (d) $1000 \leq p \leq 1499$

**6.** In a battle 70% of the combatants lost one eye, 80% an ear, 75% an arm, 85% a leg, $x$ % lost all the four limbs. The minimum value of $x$ is
(a) 10   (b) 12
(c) 15   (d) None of these

## Section II - Multiple Correct Answer Type

This section contains 4 multiple correct answer(s) type questions. Each question has 4 choices (a), (b), (c) and (d), out of which **ONE OR MORE** is/are correct.

**7.** In a certain town 25% families own a phone and 15% own a car 65% own neither a phone nor a car. 2000 families own both a car and a phone.
(a) 10% families own both a car and a phone
(b) 35% families own either a car or a phone.
(c) 40,000 families live in the town.
(d) All above are correct

**8.** At a certain conference of 100 people, there are 29 Indian women and 23 Indian men. Of these Indian people 4 are doctors and 24 are either men or doctors. There are no foreign doctors. If the no. of foreigners and women doctors who are attending the conference are $n_1$ and $n_2$.
(a) $n_1^2 + n_2^2 = 2305$   (b) $n_1 + n_2 - n_1 n_2 = 1$
(c) $n_1^2 - n_2^2 = 2303$   (d) $n_1 + n_2 + n_1 n_2 = 98$

**9.** Let A, B, C be finite sets. Suppose that n (A) = 10, n (B) = 15, n (C) = 20, n (A∩B) = 8 and n (B∩C) = 9. Then the possible value of n (A∪B∪C) is
(a) 26
(b) 27
(c) 28
(d) 29

**10.** In a class of 60 students, 23 play Hockey 15 Play Basket-ball and 20 play cricket. 7 play Hockey and Basket-ball, 5 play cricket and Basket-ball, 4 play Hockey and Cricket and 15 students do not play any of these games. Then
(a) 4 play Hockey, Basket-ball and Cricket
(b) 19 play Hockey but not Cricket
(c) 1 plays Hockey and Cricket but not Basket-ball
(d) All above are correct

## Section III - Integer Type

This section contains 5 questions. The answer to each of the questions is a single digit integer ranging from 0 to 9.

**11.** A survey shows that 61%, 46% and 29% of the people watched "3 idiots", "Rajneeti" and "Avatar" respectively. 25% people watched exactly two of the three movies and 3% watched none. What percentage of people watched all the three movies?



*Space for Rough Work*

**12.** Two finite sets have $m$ and $n$ elements. The number of subsets of the first set is 112 more than that of the second set. The values of $m - n$ is

**13.** There are 20 students in a chemistry class and 30 students in a physics class. If ten students are to be enrolled in both the courses. Let k be the number of students which are either in physics class or chemistry class if two classes meet at different hours, then find $\dfrac{k}{8}$.

**14.** If A is the set of the divisors of the number 15, B is the set of prime numbers smaller than 10 and C is the set of even numbers smaller than 9, then the number of elements in $(A \cup C) \cap B$ is

**15.** The number of elements in the set

$\{\dfrac{a}{b} \in I^+ : 2a^2 + 3b^2 = 35, a, b \in Z\}$, where Z is the set of all integers, is

## Section IV - Comprehension Type

Based upon the given paragraphs, 4 multiple choice questions have to be answered. Each question has 4 choices (a), (b), (c) and (d), out of which **ONLY ONE** is correct.

### PARAGRAPH-1

In a society 60 family read Times Of India (TOI), 70 read Hindustan Times (HT), and 40 read Telegraph (Tel). 10 family read both HT and Tel but not TOI, 18 family read HT & TOI, number of family who read only TOI & Tel but not HT is 10 less than the number of family who read all the three newspaper.

**16.** What could be the total number of family in the society assuming that each family read at least one news paper?

(a) 114  (b) 126

(c) 129  (d) None of these

**17.** If number of family who read both TOI and HT but not Tel is more than the number of family who read both TOI and Tel but not HT then what could be the number of family who read only Tel?

(a) 15  (b) 10

(c) 16  (d) None of these

### PARAGRAPH-2

In a college student can opt for any one or more available sports, these are Foot Ball (FB), Carom (Cr), Chess (Ch), and Volley Ball (VB), number of students who play FB and any one more game is 10, (I.e FB and Ch is 10, FB and Cr is 10 and so on), similarly number of students who play Cr and any one more game (Except FB as it is already defined as 10) is 8 and number of students who play FB and any two more games is 12. Total count for each of four Game is 100.

**18.** How many student play Cricket and exactly one more game?

(a) 26  (b) 28

(c) 32  (d) None of these

**19.** If number of students who play Ch and Exactly one more game is maximum possible then what is the number of students who play only Cr.

(a) 25  (b) 50

(c) 46  (d) None of these

<table>
<tr><td rowspan="3">**RESPONSE GRID**</td><td>12. ⓪①②③④⑤⑥⑦⑧⑨</td><td>13. ⓪①②③④⑤⑥⑦⑧⑨</td></tr>
<tr><td>14. ⓪①②③④⑤⑥⑦⑧⑨</td><td>15. ⓪①②③④⑤⑥⑦⑧⑨</td></tr>
<tr><td>16. ⓐⓑⓒⓓ  17. ⓐⓑⓒⓓ</td><td>18. ⓐⓑⓒⓓ  19. ⓐⓑⓒⓓ</td></tr>
</table>

──────────────── *Space for Rough Work* ────────────────

## Section V - Matrix-Match Type

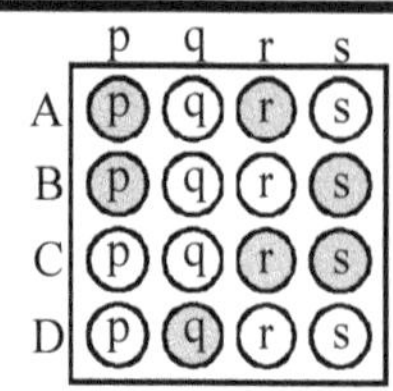

This section contains 1 question. It contains statements given in two columns, which have to be matched. Statements in column I are labelled as A, B, C and D whereas statements in column II are labelled as p, q, r and s. The answers to these questions have to be appropriately bubbled as illustrated in the following example. If the correct matches are A-p, A-r, B-p, B-s, C-r, C-s and D-q, then the correctly bubbled matrix will look like the following:

20. The proportion of male students and the proportion of vegetarian students in a school are given below. The school has a total of 800 students, 80% of whom are in the secondary section and rest equally divided between class 11 & 12.

|  | Male (M) | Vegetarian (V) |
|---|---|---|
| Class 12 | 0.60 |  |
| Class 11 | 0.55 | 0.55 |
| Secondary Section |  | 0.55 |
| Total | 0.475 | 0.53 |

Now, Match the columns.

| **Column-I** | | **Column-II** |
|---|---|---|
| (A) | What is the percentage of vegetarian students in class-12 | (p) 45 |
| (B) | In class 12, 25% of vegetarians are male. What is the difference between the number of female vegetarians and male non-vegetarians. | (q) 40 |
| (C) | What is the percentage of Male students in the secondary section | (r) 38 |
|  |  | (s) 16 |

| **RESPONSE GRID** | 20. A - (p)(q)(r)(s); B - (p)(q)(r)(s); C - (p)(q)(r)(s) |
|---|---|

## DAILY PRACTICE PROBLEM DPP CM01 - MATHEMATICS

| Total Questions | 20 | Total Marks | 67 |
|---|---|---|---|
| Attempted |  | Correct |  |
| Incorrect |  | Net Score |  |
| Cut-off Score | 27 | Qualifying Score | 38 |

$$\text{Net Score} = \sum_{i=I}^{V}\left[\left(\text{correct}_i \times MM_i\right) - \left(In_i - NM_i\right)\right]$$

*Space for Rough Work*

Date :                Start Time :               End Time :

# MATHEMATICS CM02

**SYLLABUS : Relations and Functions**

**Max. Marks : 74**                  **Time : 60 min.**

## GENERAL INSTRUCTIONS

- The Daily Practice Problem Sheet contains 20 Questions divided into 5 sections.

**Section I** has **5** MCQs with ONLY 1 Correct Option, **3** marks for each correct answer and **−1** for each incorrect answer.

**Section II** has **4** MCQs with ONE or MORE THAN ONE Correct options.

For each question, marks will be awarded in one of the following categories:

Full marks: **+4** If only the bubble(s) corresponding to all the correct option(s) is (are) darkened.

Partial marks: **+1** For darkening a bubble corresponding to each correct option provided NO INCORRECT option is darkened.

Zero marks: If none of the bubbles is darkened.

Negative marks: **−2** In all other cases.

**Section III** has **4** Single Digit Integer Answer Type Questions, **3** marks for each Correct Answer and **0** mark in all other cases.

**Section IV** has Comprehension/Matching Cum-Comprehension Type Questions having **5** MCQs with ONLY ONE correct option, **3** marks for each Correct Answer and **0** mark in all other cases.

**Section V** has **2** Matching Type Questions, **2** marks for the correct matching of each row and **0** mark in all other cases.

- You have to evaluate your Response Grids yourself with the help of Solutions.

## Section I - Straight Objective Type

This section contains 5 multiple choice questions. Each question has 4 choices (a), (b), (c) and (d), out of which **ONLY ONE** is correct.

**1.** Let $f: R \to R$ be a periodic function such that

$$f(T+x) = 1 + [1 - 3f(x) + 3(f(x))^2 - (f(x))^3]^{1/3}$$

where $T$ is a fixed positive number, then period of $f(x)$ is

(a) $T$            (b) $2T$

(c) $3T$          (d) None of these

**2.** If $f(x) . f(y) = f(x) + f(y) + f(xy) - 2 \ \forall \ x, y \in R$ and if $f(x)$ is not a constant function, then the value of $f(a)$ is –

(a) 1            (b) 2

(c) 0            (d) −1

**3.** If $f(x)$ is a polynomial function that $f(x) . f(-x) = f(2x)$, then–

(a) No such function exists

(b) $f(x)$ is linear

(c) Number of such functions are exactly one

(d) Number of such functions are exactly two

---

| RESPONSE GRID | 1. ⓐⓑⓒⓓ | 2. ⓐⓑⓒⓓ | 3. ⓐⓑⓒⓓ |
|---|---|---|---|

*———— Space for Rough Work ————*

**4.** Let $f(x) = \dfrac{x}{1-x}$ and '$a$' be a real number.

If $x_0 = a$, $x_1 = f(x_0)$, $x_2 = f(x_1)$, $x_3 = f(x_2)$.......

and $x_{2009} = 1$, then the value of a is

(a) 0

(b) $\dfrac{2009}{2010}$

(c) $\dfrac{1}{2009}$

(d) $\dfrac{1}{2010}$

**5.** If $\{\ \}$ denotes the fractional part of $x$, the range of the function

$f(x) = \sqrt{\{x\}^2 - 2\{x\}}$ is

(a) $\phi$

(b) $[0, 1/2]$

(c) $\{0, 1/2\}$

(d) $\{0\}$

## Section II - Multiple Correct Answer Type

This section contains 4 multiple correct answer(s) type questions. Each question has 4 choices (a), (b), (c) and (d), out of which **ONE OR MORE** is/are correct.

**6.** If A, B and C are three sets, consider

(i) $A \times (B \cap C) = (A \times B) \cap (A \times C)$

(ii) $A \times (B' \cup C')' = (A \times B) \cap (A \times C)$ then :

(a) (i) is correct

(b) (i) and (ii) are both correct

(c) (ii) is correct

(d) None of these

**7.** The relation R defined on the set A = {1, 2, 3, 4, 5} by R = {(x, y) : |x² – y²| < 16} is not given by

(a) {(1, 1), (2, 1), (3, 1), (4, 1), (2, 3)}

(b) {(2, 2), (3, 2), (4, 2), (2, 4)}

(c) {(3, 3), (4, 3), (5, 4), (3, 4)}

(d) None of these

**8.** Which of the following function is periodic

(a) $Sgn\ (e^{-x})$

(b) $\sin x + |\sin x|$

(c) $\min (\sin x, |x|)$

(d) $\left[x + \dfrac{1}{2}\right] + \left[x - \dfrac{1}{2}\right] + 2[-x]$

**9.** $f(x) = \sqrt{|x|^2 - 5|x| + 6} + \sqrt{8 + 2|x| - |x|^2}$

is real for all x in

(a) $[-4, -3]$

(b) $[-3, -2]$

(c) $[-2, 2]$

(d) $[3, 4]$

## Section III - Integer Type

This section contains 4 questions. The answer to each of the questions is a single digit integer ranging from 0 to 9.

**10.** The number of elements in the domain of relation R = {(x, y) : x² + y² = 16, x, y $\in$ Z} is

**11.** If $2f(xy) = \left(f(x)\right)^y + \left(f(y)\right)^x$, for all $x, y \in$ R and

$f(1) = 2$, then $f(3) =$

**12.** Consider $f(x) = \dfrac{4^x}{4^x + 2}$, if $f\left(\dfrac{1}{1997}\right) +$

$f\left(\dfrac{2}{1997}\right) + .... + f\left(\dfrac{1196}{1997}\right) = 499q$, then $q$ is equal to

**13.** If $a$, $b$ be two fixed positive integers such that $f(a + x) = b + [b^3 + 1 - 3b^2 f(x) + 3b \{f(x)\}^2 - \{f(x)\}^3]^{1/3}$ for all real $x$, if period of $f(x)$ is $ka$, then $k =$

## Section IV - Comprehension/Matching Cum-Comprehension Type

**Directions (Qs. 14 and 15) :** Based upon the given paragraph, 2 multiple choice questions have to be answered. Each question has 4 choices (a), (b), (c) and (d), out of which **ONLY ONE** is correct.

### PARAGRAPH

If $(f(x))^2 \times f\left(\dfrac{1-x}{1+x}\right) = 64x, x \neq 0,1$, then

**14.** $f(x)$ is equal to

(a) $4x^{2/3}\left(\dfrac{1+x}{1-x}\right)^{1/3}$
(b) $x^{1/3}\left(\dfrac{1-x}{1+x}\right)^{1/3}$
(c) $x^{2/3}\left(\dfrac{1-x}{1+x}\right)^{1/3}$
(d) $x\left(\dfrac{1+x}{1-x}\right)^{1/3}$

**15.** The value of $f(9/7)$ is
(a) $8\,(7/9)^{2/3}$
(b) $4\,(9/7)^{1/3}$
(c) $-8\,(9/7)^{2/3}$
(d) None of these

**Directions (Qs. 16-18) :** This passage contains a table having 3 columns and 4 rows. Based on the table, there are three questions. Each question has four options (a), (b), (c) and (d) **ONLY ONE** of these four options is correct.

Column 1, 2 and 3 contain informations about functions, domain of the functions and codomain of the functions respectively.

| Column 1 | Column 2 | Column 3 |
|---|---|---|
| (I) $f(x)=\dfrac{1}{\log_a x},\ a>0,\ a\neq 1$ | (i) $R-\{0\}$ | (P) $(1,\infty)$ |
| (II) $f(x)=\dfrac{1}{[x]}$ | (ii) $R-I$ | (Q) $R-\{0\}$ |
| (III) $f(x)=\dfrac{1}{\{x\}}$ | (iii) $R^+ - \{1\}$ | (R) $R^+$ |
| (IV) $f(x)=\dfrac{1}{|x|}$ | (iv) $R-[0,1)$ | (S) $\left\{\dfrac{1}{n}, n \in I - \{0\}\right\}$ |

**16.** Which of the following options is the only correct combination?
(a) (II)(i)(P)   (b) (I)(iv)(R)   (c) (III)(ii)(P)   (d) (IV)(iii)(Q)

**17.** Which of the following options is the only in incorrect combination?
(a) (II)(i)(Q)   (b) (IV)(iii)(P)   (c) (I)(iv)(R)   (d) (IV)(ii)(S)

**18.** Which of the following options is the only incorrect combination?
(a) (III)(iii)(P)   (b) (IV)(ii)(S)   (c) (II)(i)(S)   (d) (I)(iv)(R)

| RESPONSE GRID | | | | | |
|---|---|---|---|---|---|
| | 14. ⓐⓑⓒⓓ | 15. ⓐⓑⓒⓓ | 16. ⓐⓑⓒⓓ | 17. ⓐⓑⓒⓓ | 18. ⓐⓑⓒⓓ |

*Space for Rough Work*

## Section V - Matrix-Match Type

This section contains 2 questions. It contains statements given in two columns, which have to be matched. Statements in column I are labelled as A, B, C and D whereas statements in column II are labelled as p, q, r and s. The answers to these questions have to be appropriately bubbled as illustrated in the following example. If the correct matches are A-p, A-r, B-p, B-s, C-r, C-s and D-q, then the correctly bubbled matrix will look like the following:

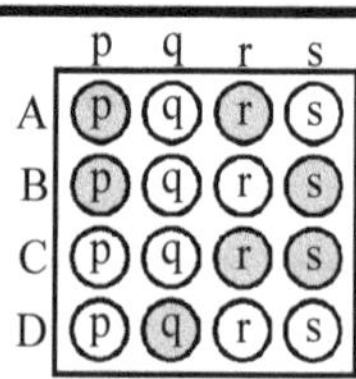

**19.**  **Column-I: Function**          **Column-II: Type of function**

(A) $f(x) = \{(\text{sgn } x)^{\text{sgn } x}\}^n$; $x \neq 0$, $n$ is an odd integer     (p)  odd function

(B) $f(x) = \dfrac{x}{e^x - 1} + \dfrac{x}{2} + 1$     (q)  even function

(C) $f(x) = \begin{cases} 0, & \text{If } x \text{ is rational} \\ 1, & \text{If } x \text{ is irrational} \end{cases}$     (r)  neither odd nor even function

(D) $f(x) = \max \{\tan x, \cot x\}$     (s)  periodic

**20.**  **Column-I**         **Column-II**

(A) Domain of $f(x) = (x^2 - 1)^{-1/2}$ is     (p) $\left(1, \dfrac{7}{3}\right]$

(B) Range of the function $f(x) = \dfrac{x^2 + x + 2}{x^2 + x + 1}$, $x \in \mathbb{R}$ is     (q) $(-\infty, -1) \cup (1, \infty)$

(C) The range of $f(x) = \sec\left(\dfrac{\pi}{4} \cos^2 x\right)$, $-\infty < x < \infty$ i is     (r) $(-\infty, 5] \cup [9, \infty)$

(D) Range of $f(x) = \dfrac{x^2 + 34x - 71}{x^2 + 2x - 7}$ is     (s) $[1, \sqrt{2}]$

| RESPONSE GRID | |
|---|---|
| 19. A - (p)(q)(r)(s); B - (p)(q)(r)(s); C - (p)(q)(r)(s); D - (p)(q)(r)(s) | |
| 20. A - (p)(q)(r)(s); B - (p)(q)(r)(s); C - (p)(q)(r)(s); D - (p)(q)(r)(s) | |

## DAILY PRACTICE PROBLEM DPP CM02 - MATHEMATICS

| Total Questions | 20 | Total Marks | 74 |
|---|---|---|---|
| Attempted | | Correct | |
| Incorrect | | Net Score | |
| Cut-off Score | 26 | Qualifying Score | 38 |

$$\text{Net Score} = \sum_{i=1}^{V} \left[ (correct_i \times MM_i) - (In_i - NM_i) \right]$$

---

*Space for Rough Work*

Date :            Start Time :        End Time :

# MATHEMATICS $\boxed{\text{CM03}}$

**SYLLABUS :** Trigonometric Functions

**Max. Marks : 74**                                          **Time : 60 min.**

### GENERAL INSTRUCTIONS

- The Daily Practice Problem Sheet contains 20 Questions divided into 5 sections.
  **Section I** has **6** MCQs with ONLY 1 Correct Option, **3** marks for each correct answer and **–1** for each incorrect answer.
  **Section II** has **4** MCQs with ONE or MORE THAN ONE Correct options.
  For each question, marks will be awarded in one of the following categories:
  Full marks: **+4** If only the bubble(s) corresponding to all the correct option(s) is (are) darkened.
  Partial marks: **+1** For darkening a bubble corresponding to each correct option provided NO INCORRECT option is darkened.
  Zero marks:  If none of the bubbles is darkened.
  Negative marks: **–2** In all other cases.
  **Section III** has **4** Single Digit Integer Answer Type Questions, **3** marks for each Correct Answer and **0** mark in all other cases.
  **Section IV** has Comprehension Type Questions having **4** MCQs with ONLY ONE corect option, **3** marks for each Correct Answer and **0** mark in all other cases.
  **Section V** has **2** Matching Type Questions, **2** marks for the correct matching of each row and **0** mark in all other cases.
- You have to evaluate your Response Grids yourself with the help of Solutions.

## Section I - Straight Objective Type

This section contains 6 multiple choice questions. Each question has 4 choices (a), (b), (c) and (d), out of which **ONLY ONE** is correct.

**1.** If $x\sin a + y\sin 2a + z\sin 3a = \sin 4a$
$x\sin b + y\sin 2b + z\sin 3b = \sin 4b$
$x\sin c + y\sin 2c + z\sin 3c = \sin 4c$

Then, the roots of the equation

$$t^3 - \frac{z}{2}t^2 - \frac{y+2}{4}t + \frac{z-x}{8} = 0 , a, b, c \neq n\pi, \text{ are}$$

(a) $\sin a, \sin b, \sin c$  
(b) $\cos a, \cos b, \cos c$  
(c) $\sin 2a, \sin 2b, \sin 2c$  
(d) $\cos 2a, \cos 2b, \cos 2c$

**2.** If $u = \sqrt{a^2\cos^2\theta + b^2\sin^2\theta} + \sqrt{a^2\sin^2\theta + b^2\cos^2\theta}$, then the difference between the maximum and minimum values of $u^2$ is given by

(a) $(a-b)^2$  
(b) $2\sqrt{a^2+b^2}$  
(c) $(a+b)^2$  
(d) $2(a^2+b^2)$

| RESPONSE GRID | 1. ⓐⓑ©ⓓ | 2. ⓐⓑ©ⓓ |
| --- | --- | --- |

*Space for Rough Work*

**3.** For $0 < \theta < \dfrac{\pi}{2}$, the solution (s) of $\sum\limits_{m=1}^{6} \operatorname{cosec}\left(\theta + \dfrac{(m-1)\pi}{4}\right)\operatorname{cosec}\left(\theta + \dfrac{m\pi}{4}\right) = 4\sqrt{2}$ is (are)

(a) $\dfrac{\pi}{4}$

(b) $\dfrac{\pi}{6}$

(c) $\dfrac{\pi}{12}$

(d) $\dfrac{7\pi}{12}$

**4.** Let $S = \left\{ x \in (-\pi, \pi) : x \neq 0, \pm\dfrac{\pi}{2} \right\}$. The sum of all distinct solutions of the equation $\sqrt{3}\sec x + \operatorname{cosec} x + 2(\tan x - \cot x) = 0$ in the set S is equal to

(a) $-\dfrac{7\pi}{9}$

(b) $-\dfrac{2\pi}{9}$

(c) $0$

(d) $\dfrac{5\pi}{9}$

**5.** The maximum value of $(\cos \alpha_1).(\cos \alpha_2)...(\cos \alpha_n)$, under the restrictions $0 \leq \alpha_1, \alpha_2, ..., \alpha_n \leq \dfrac{\pi}{2}$ and $(\cot \alpha_1).(\cot \alpha_2) ... (\cot \alpha_n) = 1$ is

(a) $1/2^{n/2}$

(b) $1/2^n$

(c) $1/2n$

(d) $1$

**6.** If $\alpha, \beta, \gamma, \delta$ are the smallest positive angles in ascending order of magnitude which have their sines equal to the positive quantity $k$, then the value of

$$4\sin\dfrac{\alpha}{2} + 3\sin\dfrac{\beta}{2} + 2\sin\dfrac{\gamma}{2} + \sin\dfrac{\delta}{2}$$ is equal to

(a) $2\sqrt{1-k}$

(b) $2\sqrt{1+k}$

(c) $2\sqrt{k}$

(d) None of these

## Section II - Multiple Correct Answer Type

This section contains 4 multiple correct answer(s) type questions. Each question has 4 choices (a), (b), (c) and (d), out of which **ONE OR MORE** is/are correct.

**7.** Let, $f_n(\theta) = \tan\dfrac{\theta}{2}(1+\sec\theta)(1+\sec2\theta)(1+\sec4\theta)$ $......(1 + \sec 2^n\theta)$ then

(a) $f_2\left(\dfrac{\pi}{16}\right) = 1$

(b) $f_3\left(\dfrac{\pi}{32}\right) = 1$

(c) $f_4\left(\dfrac{\pi}{64}\right) = 1$

(d) $f_5\left(\dfrac{\pi}{128}\right) = 1$

**8.** Given that $\sin\beta = \dfrac{12}{13}, 0 < \beta < \pi$, then $\{5\sin(\alpha + \beta) - 12\cos(\alpha + \beta)\}\operatorname{cosec}\alpha$ is equal to :

(a) $13\sin\alpha$ if $\tan\beta > 0$

(b) $13\sin\alpha$ if $\tan\beta < 0$

(c) $\dfrac{119 + 120\cot\alpha}{13}$ if $\tan\beta < 0$

(d) $\dfrac{119 + 120\cot\alpha}{13}$ if $\tan\beta > 0$

**9.** If $(a-b)\sin(\theta + \phi) = (a+b)\sin(\theta - \phi)$ and $a\tan\dfrac{\theta}{2} - b\tan\dfrac{\phi}{2} = c$, then

(a) $b\tan\phi = a\tan\theta$

(b) $a\tan\phi = b\tan\theta$

(c) $\sin\phi = \dfrac{2bc}{a^2 - b^2 - c^2}$

(d) $\sin\theta = \dfrac{2ac}{a^2 - b^2 + c^2}$

| RESPONSE | 3. ⓐⓑⓒⓓ | 4. ⓐⓑⓒⓓ | 5. ⓐⓑⓒⓓ | 6. ⓐⓑⓒⓓ | 7. ⓐⓑⓒⓓ |
| GRID | 8. ⓐⓑⓒⓓ | 9. ⓐⓑⓒⓓ | | | |

*Space for Rough Work*

10. If $\dfrac{\tan 3A}{\tan A} = k,\ (k \neq 1)$, then

(a) $\dfrac{\cos A}{\cos 3A} = \dfrac{k^2 - 1}{2k}$

(b) $\dfrac{\sin 3A}{\sin A} = \dfrac{2k}{k-1}$

(c) $k < \dfrac{1}{3}$

(d) $k > 3$

## Section III - Integer Type

This section contains 4 questions. The answer to each of the questions is a single digit integer ranging from 0 to 9.

11. If a $\tan\alpha + \sqrt{a^2 - 1}\,\tan\beta + \sqrt{a^2 + 1}\,\tan\gamma = 2a$, where a is constant and $\alpha,\ \beta,\ \gamma$ are variable angles. Then the least value of 3 $(\tan^2\alpha + \tan^2\beta + \tan^2\gamma)$ is equal to

12. If $\cos\alpha = \dfrac{2\cos\beta - 1}{2 - \cos\beta}$ $(0 < \alpha < \beta < \pi)$, then find the value of

$$\sqrt{3}\left(\dfrac{\tan\dfrac{\alpha}{2}}{\tan\dfrac{\beta}{2}}\right)$$

13. If $x\cos\theta = y\cos\left(\theta + \dfrac{2\pi}{3}\right) = z\cos\left(\theta + \dfrac{4\pi}{3}\right)$ then find the value of $xy + yz + zx$.

14. Suppose that $\sin^3 x \sin 3x = \displaystyle\sum_{m=0}^{n} c_m \cos mx$ is an identity in x, where $c_0, c_1, c_2, \ldots, c_n$ are constants and $c_n \neq 0$, find the value of n.

## Section IV - Comprehension Type

Based upon the given paragraphs, 4 multiple choice questions have to be answered. Each question has 4 choices (a), (b), (c) and (d), out of which **ONLY ONE** is correct.

### PARAGRAPH-1

If $P_n = \sin^n\theta + \cos^n\theta$ where $n \in W$ (whole number) and $\theta \in R$ (real number)

15. If $P_1 = m$, then the value of $4(1 - P_6)$ is

(a) $3\,(m-1)^2$

(b) $3\,(m^2 - 1)^2$

(c) $3\,(m+1)^2$

(d) $3\,(m^2 + 1)^2$

16. The value of $6P_{10} - 15P_8 + 10P_6 + 7$ is

(a) 8

(b) 6

(c) 4

(d) 2

### PARAGRAPH-2

Consider the equations

$5\sin^2 x + 3\sin x \cos x - 3\cos^2 x = 2$     (1)

$\sin^2 x - \cos 2x = 2 - \sin 2x$     (2)

17. If $\alpha$ is a root of (1) and $\beta$ is a root of (2) then $\tan\alpha + \tan\beta$ can be equal to

(a) $1 + \sqrt{69}/4$

(b) $1 - \sqrt{69}/6$

(c) $\dfrac{-3 + \sqrt{69}}{6}$

(d) $\dfrac{-3 - \sqrt{69}}{3}$

18. If $\tan\alpha,\ \tan\beta$ satisfy (1) and $\cos\gamma,\ \cos\delta$ satisfy (2) then $\tan\alpha \tan\beta + \cos\gamma + \cos\delta$ can be equal to

(a) $-1$

(b) $-\dfrac{5}{3} + \dfrac{3}{\sqrt{13}}$

(c) $\dfrac{5}{3} - \dfrac{2}{\sqrt{13}}$

(d) $-\dfrac{5}{3} - \dfrac{2}{\sqrt{13}}$

---

**RESPONSE GRID**

10. (a)(b)(c)(d)    11. (0)(1)(2)(3)(4)(5)(6)(7)(8)(9)    12. (0)(1)(2)(3)(4)(5)(6)(7)(8)(9)

13. (0)(1)(2)(3)(4)(5)(6)(7)(8)(9)    14. (0)(1)(2)(3)(4)(5)(6)(7)(8)(9)

15. (a)(b)(c)(d)    16. (a)(b)(c)(d)    17. (a)(b)(c)(d)    18. (a)(b)(c)(d)

*Space for Rough Work*

## Section V - Matrix-Match Type

This section contains 2 questions. It contains statements given in two columns, which have to be matched. Statements in column I are labelled as A, B, C and D whereas statements in column II are labelled as p, q, r and s. The answers to these questions have to be appropriately bubbled as illustrated in the following example. If the correct matches are A-p, A-r, B-p, B-s, C-r, C-s and D-q, then the correctly bubbled matrix will look like the following:

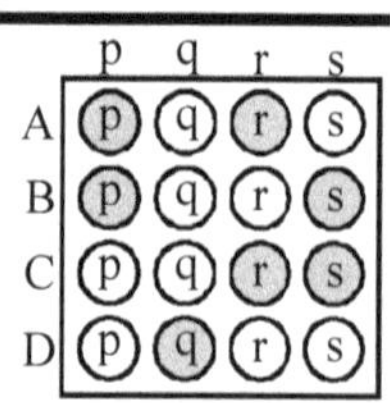

**19.**  **Column-I**                                                                                          **Column-II**

(A)  If $f(\theta) = (\sin\theta + \mathrm{cosec}\theta)^2 + (\cos\theta + \sec\theta)^2$, then $f(\theta)$ cannot be less than      p.  1

(B)  If $\sin\alpha - \sin\beta = a$ and $\cos\alpha + \cos\beta = b$ then $a^2 + b^2$ cannot exceed      q.  2

(C)  If $A + B = \dfrac{\pi}{2}$, where $A$ and $B$ are positive then $(\sin A + \sin B)\cos\dfrac{\pi}{4}$      r.  4

   is always less than

(D)  If $2\cos x + \sin x = 1$, then the value of $7\cos x + 6\sin x$ is equal to      s.  6

**20.**  **Column-I**                                                                                          **Column-II**

(A)  The values of $\cos^2\theta + \sin^4\theta$ for all $\theta$      p.  belong to $(0, 1]$

(B)  In a $\triangle ABC$ if $\tan A < 0$ then values of $\tan B \tan C$      q.  belong to $\left[\dfrac{3}{4}, 1\right]$

(C)  For any real $\theta \neq n\pi,\ n \in I$ then values of $\dfrac{\cos^2\theta - 1}{\cos^2\theta + \cos\theta}$      r.  are less than 0 or greater than 2

(D)  If $A > 0, B > 0$ and $A + B = \dfrac{\pi}{3}$ then the values of $3\tan A \tan B$      s.  belong to $(0, 1)$

---

**RESPONSE GRID**

19. A - p q r s ; B - p q r s ; C - p q r s ; D - p q r s
20. A - p q r s ; B - p q r s ; C - p q r s ; D - p q r s

## DAILY PRACTICE PROBLEM DPP CM03 - MATHEMATICS

| Total Questions | 20 | Total Marks | 74 |
|---|---|---|---|
| Attempted |  | Correct |  |
| Incorrect |  | Net Score |  |
| Cut-off Score | 26 | Qualifying Score | 38 |

$$\text{Net Score} = \sum_{i=1}^{V}\left[\left(\text{correct}_i \times MM_i\right) - \left(In_i - NM_i\right)\right]$$

*Space for Rough Work*

## Chapter-wise Sheets

**Date :** [blank]    **Start Time :** [blank]    **End Time :** [blank]

# MATHEMATICS $\boxed{\text{CM04}}$

**SYLLABUS :** Complex Numbers and Quadratic Equations

**Max. Marks : 69**                                                                     **Time : 60 min.**

### GENERAL INSTRUCTIONS

- The Daily Practice Problem Sheet contains 20 Questions divided into 5 sections.
  **Section I** has **6** MCQs with ONLY 1 Correct Option, **3** marks for each correct answer and **−1** for each incorrect answer.
  **Section II** has **4** MCQs with ONE or MORE THAN ONE Correct options.
  For each question, marks will be awarded in one of the following categories:
  Full marks: **+4** If only the bubble(s) corresponding to all the correct option(s) is (are) darkened.
  Partial marks: **+1** For darkening a bubble corresponding to each correct option provided NO INCORRECT option is darkened.
  Zero marks:  If none of the bubbles is darkened.
  Negative marks: **−2** In all other cases.
  **Section III** has **5** Single Digit Integer Answer Type Questions, **3** marks for each Correct Answer and **0** mark in all other cases.
  **Section IV** has Comprehension Type Questions having **4** MCQs with ONLY ONE corect option, **3** marks for each Correct Answer and **0** mark in all other cases.
  **Section V** has **1** Matching Type Question, **2** marks for the correct matching of each row and **0** mark in all other cases.
- You have to evaluate your Response Grids yourself with the help of Solutions.

## Section I - Straight Objective Type

This section contains 6 multiple choice questions. Each question has 4 choices (a), (b), (c) and (d), out of which **ONLY ONE** is correct.

**1.** A complex number $z$ satisfies the equation $|z|^2 - 2iz + 2c\,(1 + i) = 0$, where $c$ is real. The values of $c$ for which the above equation has no solution can be given by

(a)  $c \in (-\infty, -1-\sqrt{2})$

(b)  $c \in [-1-\sqrt{2}, -1+\sqrt{2}]$

(c)  $c \in (-1-\sqrt{2}, \infty)$

(d)  $c \in \mathbf{R}$

**2.** If $z_1 = a + ib$ and $z_2 = c + id$ are complex numbers such that $|z_1| = |z_2| = 1$ and $\mathrm{Re}\,(z_1\bar{z}_2) = 0$, then the pair of complex numbers $\omega_1 = a + ic$ and $\omega_2 = b + id$ do not satisfy

(a)  $|\omega_1| = 1$

(b)  $|\omega_2| = 1$

(c)  $\mathrm{Re}(\omega_1\bar{\omega}_2) = 0$

(d)  $\mathrm{In}\,(\omega_1\bar{\omega}_2) = 0$

| RESPONSE GRID | 1. ⓐⓑⓒⓓ | 2. ⓐⓑⓒⓓ |
|---|---|---|

*Space for Rough Work*

 

**3.** If $A$, $G$ and $H$ are the Arithmetic mean, Geometric mean and Harmonic mean between two unequal positive integers. Then the equation $Ax^2 - |G|x - H = 0$ does not have
(a) both roots fractions
(b) one negative fraction root
(c) exactly one positive root
(d) no root greater than 2

**4.** If $a$, $b$, $c$ are positive rational numbers such that $a > b > c$ and the quadratic equation
$(a + b - 2c)x^2 + (b + c - 2a)x + (c + a - 2b) = 0$ has a root in the interval $(-1, 0)$, then
(a) $c + a > 2b$
(b) Both roots of the given equation are irrational
(c) The equation $ax^2 + 2bx + c = 0$ has both negative real roots
(d) The equation $cx^2 + 2ax + b = 0$ has both positive real roots

**5.** Let $[a]$ denote the greatest integer less than or equal to $a$. Given that the quadratic equation
$x^2 + [a^2 - 5a + b + 4]x + b = 0$ has roots $-5$ and $1$. Then the set of values of $a$ is

(a) $\left(-1, \dfrac{5 - 3\sqrt{5}}{2}\right] \cup \left[\dfrac{5 + 3\sqrt{5}}{2}, 6\right)$

(b) $\left(\dfrac{5 - 3\sqrt{5}}{2}, \dfrac{5 + 3\sqrt{5}}{2}\right)$

(c) $(-\infty, -1] \cup [6, \infty)$

(d) $(-\infty, \infty)$

**6.** The point of intersection of the curves $\arg(z - 3i) = \dfrac{3\pi}{4}$

and $\arg(2z + 1 - 2i) = \dfrac{\pi}{4}$ is

(a) $\dfrac{1}{4}(3 + 9i)$
(b) $\dfrac{1}{4}(3 - 9i)$

(c) $\dfrac{1}{2}(3 + 2i)$
(d) None of these

## Section II - Multiple Correct Answer Type

This section contains 4 multiple correct answer(s) type questions. Each question has 4 choices (a), (b), (c) and (d), out of which **ONE OR MORE** is/are correct.

**7.** Let $z_1$, $z_2$, $z_3$ be complex number such that $|z_1| = |z_2| = |z_3| = 1$ and $\dfrac{z_1^2}{z_2 z_3} + \dfrac{z_2^2}{z_3 z_1} + \dfrac{z_3^2}{z_1 z_2} = -1$, then value of $|z_1 + z_2 + z_3|$ can be

(a) 2
(b) 3
(c) 4
(d) 1

**8.** Consider the quadratic equation $x^2 - 2px + p^2 - 1 = 0$ where $p$ is parameter, then
(a) Both the roots of the equation are less than 4 if $p \in (-\infty, 3)$
(b) Both the roots of the equation are greater than $-2$ if $p \in (-\infty, -1)$
(c) Exactly one root of the equation lies in the interval $(-2, 4)$ if $p \in (-1, 3)$
(d) 1 lies between the roots of the equation if $p \in (0, 2)$

**9.** Equation $\dfrac{\pi^e}{x - e} + \dfrac{e^\pi}{x - \pi} + \dfrac{\pi^\pi + e^e}{x - \pi - e} = 0$ has

(a) one real root in $(e, \pi)$ and other in $(\pi - e, e)$
(b) one real root in $(e, \pi)$ and other in $(\pi, \pi + e)$
(c) Two real roots in $(\pi - e, \pi + e)$
(d) No real root

**10.** If $S = \sum\limits_{k=1}^{10} \left( \sin \dfrac{2\pi k}{11} - i \cos \dfrac{2\pi k}{11} \right)$ then

(a) $S + \bar{S} = 0$
(b) $S\bar{S} = 1$
(c) $\sqrt{S} = \pm \dfrac{1}{\sqrt{2}}(1 + i)$
(d) $S - \bar{S} = 0$



*Space for Rough Work*

## Section III - Integer Type

This section contains 5 questions. The answer to each of the questions is a single digit integer ranging from 0 to 9.

11. If $z^2 - z + 1 = 0$, and the value of

$$\left(z + \frac{1}{z}\right)^2 + \left(z^2 + \frac{1}{z^2}\right)^2 + \left(z^3 + \frac{1}{z^3}\right)^2 + \dots + \left(z^{24} + \frac{1}{z^{24}}\right)$$

    is 8k, then k =

12. Let $a$ and $b$ be the roots of the equation $x^2 - 10cx - 11d = 0$ and those of $x^2 - 10ax - 11b = 0$ are $c, d$ then find the value

    of $\dfrac{a+b+c+d}{605}$, when $a \neq b \neq c \neq d \neq 0$

13. If the roots of equation $ax^2 + bx + c = 0$ $(a \neq 0)$ are $\alpha$ and $\beta$, and the roots of the equation $a^5 x^2 + ba^2 c^2 x + c^5 = 0$ are 4 and 8 then the numerical value of $\alpha\beta$ is __________ .

14. If $\omega$ and $\omega^2$ be the non-real cube roots of unity and

    $$\frac{1}{a+\omega} + \frac{1}{b+\omega} + \frac{1}{c+\omega} = 2\omega^2 \text{ and}$$

    $$\frac{1}{a+\omega^2} + \frac{1}{b+\omega^2} + \frac{1}{c+\omega^2} = 2\omega, \text{ where } a, b, c \text{ are real}$$

    then the value of $\dfrac{1}{a+1} + \dfrac{1}{b+1} + \dfrac{1}{c+1}$ is equal to :

15. If $z = \dfrac{1}{2}\left(\sqrt{3} - i\right)$, and the smallest value of positive integer $n$ for which $(z^{89} + i^{97})^{94} = z^n$ is 2k, then k =

## Section IV - Comprehension Type

Based upon the given paragraphs, 4 multiple choice questions have to be answered. Each question has 4 choices (a), (b), (c) and (d), out of which **ONLY ONE** is correct.

### PARAGRAPH-1

Suppose $z$ and $w$ be two complex numbers such that $|z| \leq 1$, $|w| \leq 1$ and $|z + iw| = |z - iw| = 2$. Use the results $|z|^2 = z\bar{z}$ and $|z + w| \leq |z| + |w|$, answer the following questions

16. Which of the following is true about $|z|$ and $|\omega|$

    (a) $|z| = |w| = \dfrac{1}{2}$     (b) $|z| = \dfrac{1}{2}, |w| = \dfrac{3}{4}$

    (c) $|z| = |w| = \dfrac{3}{4}$     (d) $|z| = |w| = 1$

17. Which of the following is true for $z$ and $\omega$

    (a) $\text{Re}(z) = \text{Re}(w)$     (b) $I_m(z) = I_m(w)$

    (c) $\text{Re}(z) = I_m(w)$     (d) $I_m(z) = \text{Re}(w)$

### PARAGRAPH-2

Suppose $z_1, z_2$ and $z_3$ represent the vertices $A$, $B$ and $C$ of an equilateral triangle $ABC$ on the Argand plane.

Then $AB = BC = CA$

$\Rightarrow |z_2 - z_1| = |z_3 - z_2| = |z_1 - z_3|$

Also $\angle CAB = \dfrac{\pi}{3}$

$\Rightarrow \arg \dfrac{z_3 - z_1}{z_2 - z_1} = \pm \dfrac{\pi}{3}$

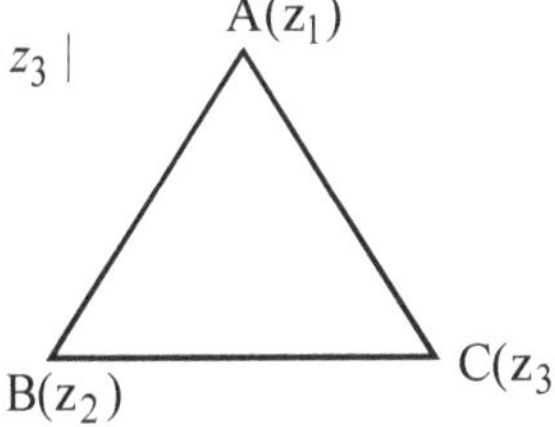


**Now solve the following questions :**

18. If $a$ and $b$ are two real numbers lying between 0 and 1 such that $z_1 = a + i$, $z_2 = 1 + bi$ and $z_3 = 0$ form an equilateral triangle then

    (a) $a = 2 + \sqrt{3}$     (b) $b = 4 - \sqrt{3}$

    (c) $a = b = 2 - \sqrt{3}$     (d) $a = 2, \ b = \sqrt{3}$

<table>
<tr><td rowspan="3">RESPONSE<br>GRID</td><td>11. ⓪①②③④⑤⑥⑦⑧⑨</td><td>12. ⓪①②③④⑤⑥⑦⑧⑨</td></tr>
<tr><td>13. ⓪①②③④⑤⑥⑦⑧⑨</td><td>14. ⓪①②③④⑤⑥⑦⑧⑨</td></tr>
<tr><td>15. ⓪①②③④⑤⑥⑦⑧⑨</td><td>16. ⓐⓑⓒⓓ   17. ⓐⓑⓒⓓ   18. ⓐⓑⓒⓓ</td></tr>
</table>

———————————— *Space for Rough Work* ————————————

**19.** Let the complex numbers $z_1$, $z_2$ and $z_3$ be the vertices of an equilateral triangle. Let $z_0$ be the circumcentre of the triangle, then

$$z_1^2 + z_2^2 + z_3^2 =$$

(a) $z_0^2$  (b) $3z_0^2$

(c) $9z_0^2$  (d) $0$

---

## Section V - Matrix-Match Type

This section contains 1 question. It contains statements given in two columns, which have to be matched. Statements in column I are labelled as A, B, C and D whereas statements in column II are labelled as p, q, r and s. The answers to these questions have to be appropriately bubbled as illustrated in the following example. If the correct matches are A-p, A-r, B-p, B-s, C-r, C-s and D-q, then the correctly bubbled matrix will look like the following:

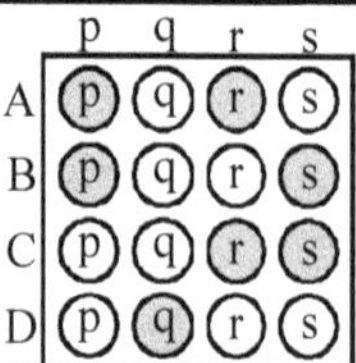

**20.** 

| Column-I | Column-II |
|---|---|

(A) The roots of cubic equation $(z + \alpha\beta)^3 = \alpha^3$ $(\alpha \neq 0, \alpha \in R)$ represent the vertices of a triangle of area equal to

    p.  $|\tan \alpha|$

(B) If $\alpha$ is a complex number then the radius of the circle $\left|\dfrac{z-\alpha}{z-\overline{\alpha}}\right| = 2$ is equal to

    q.  $\dfrac{3\sqrt{3}}{4}|\alpha|^2$

(C) If $\arg z = \alpha$ and $|z-1| = 1$ then $\left|\dfrac{z-2}{z}\right|$ is equal to

    r.  $\dfrac{2}{3}|\alpha - \overline{\alpha}|$

(D) Let A and B represent complex numbers $z_1$ and $z_2$, which are roots of the equation $z^2 + pz + q = 0$. If $\angle AOB = \alpha \neq 0$ and $OA = OB$, where $O$ is the origin then $\dfrac{p^2}{q}$ is equal to

    s.  $4\cos^2 \dfrac{\alpha}{2}$

| RESPONSE GRID | 19. ⓐⓑⓒⓓ   20. A - ⓟⓠⓡⓢ; B - ⓟⓠⓡⓢ; C - ⓟⓠⓡⓢ; D - ⓟⓠⓡⓢ |
|---|---|

## DAILY PRACTICE PROBLEM DPP CM04 - MATHEMATICS

| Total Questions | 20 | Total Marks | | 69 |
|---|---|---|---|---|
| Attempted | | Correct | | |
| Incorrect | | Net Score | | |
| Cut-off Score | 22 | Qualifying Score | | 33 |

$$\text{Net Score} = \sum_{i=1}^{V}\left[\left(\text{correct}_i \times MM_i\right) - \left(In_i - NM_i\right)\right]$$

---

*Space for Rough Work*

Date :          Start Time :          End Time :

# MATHEMATICS $\boxed{\text{CM05}}$

**SYLLABUS :** Permutations and Combinations

**Max. Marks : 74**　　　　　　　　　　　　　　　　　　　**Time : 60 min.**

**GENERAL INSTRUCTIONS**

- The Daily Practice Problem Sheet contains 20 Questions divided into 5 sections.
  **Section I** has **5** MCQs with ONLY 1 Correct Option, **3** marks for each correct answer and **−1** for each incorrect answer.
  **Section II** has **4** MCQs with ONE or MORE THAN ONE Correct options.
  For each question, marks will be awarded in one of the following categories:
  Full marks: **+4** If only the bubble(s) corresponding to all the correct option(s) is (are) darkened.
  Partial marks: **+1** For darkening a bubble corresponding to each correct option provided NO INCORRECT option is darkened.
  Zero marks:  If none of the bubbles is darkened.
  Negative marks: **−2** In all other cases.
  **Section III** has **4** Single Digit Integer Answer Type Questions, **3** marks for each Correct Answer and **0** mark in all other cases.
  **Section IV** has Comprehension/Matching Cum-Comprehension Type Questions having **5** MCQs with ONLY ONE correct option, **3** marks for each Correct Answer and **0** mark in all other cases.
  **Section V** has **2** Matching Type Questions, **2** marks for the correct matching of each row and **0** mark in all other cases.
- You have to evaluate your Response Grids yourself with the help of Solutions.

---

## Section I - Straight Objective Type

This section contains 5 multiple choice questions. Each question has 4 choices (a), (b), (c) and (d), out of which **ONLY ONE** is correct.

1. The largest integer '$n$' such that $33\,!$ is divisible by $2^{n}$ is
   (a)　33
   (b)　32
   (c)　31
   (d)　None of these

2. If $a, b, c, d$ are odd natural numbers such that
   $a + b + c + d = 20$ then the number of values of $a, b, c, d$ is
   (a)　165
   (b)　455
   (c)　310
   (d)　255

3. The total number of 5-digit numbers of different digits in which the digit in the middle is the largest is
   (a)　$\sum\limits_{n=4}^{9}{}^{n}P_4$
   (b)　4563
   (c)　2688
   (d)　5292

---

<table>
<tr><td>**RESPONSE GRID**</td><td>**1.** (a)(b)(c)(d)</td><td>**2.** (a)(b)(c)(d)</td><td>**3.** (a)(b)(c)(d)</td></tr>
</table>

*Space for Rough Work*

**4.** Two 4-digits numbers are to be formed such that the sum of the number is also a 4-digit number and in no place the addition is with carrying. The number of ways of forming the numbers under above conditions is

(a) $55^4$ 

(b) 220

(c) $45^4$ 

(d) $36 \times 55^3$

**5.** Given that $n$ is odd, the number of ways in which three numbers in A. P. can be selected from $1, 2, 3 ....., n$ is

(a) $\dfrac{(n-1)^2}{2}$ 

(b) $\dfrac{(n+1)^2}{2}$

(c) $\dfrac{n^2-1}{4}$ 

(d) $\dfrac{(n-1)^2}{4}$

## Section II - Multiple Correct Answer Type

This section contains 4 multiple correct answer(s) type questions. Each question has 4 choices (a), (b), (c) and (d), out of which **ONE OR MORE** is/are correct.

**6.** The number of ways of choosing triplet $(x, y, z)$ such that $z \geq \max\{x, y\}$ and $x, y, z \in \{1, 2, ..., n, n+1\}$ is

(a) $^{n+1}C_3 + {}^{n+2}C_3$ 

(b) $^{n+1}C_2 + 2(^{n+1}C_3)$

(c) $1^2 + 2^2 + ... + n^2$ 

(d) $2(^{n+2}C_3) - {}^{n+1}C_2$

**7.** Number of triangles which can be formed by joining vertices of a regular polygon of $n \ (> 5)$ sides such that no side is common with the side of polygon is equal to

(a) $\dfrac{n}{n-3} {}^{n-3}C_3$ 

(b) $^{n}C_3 - n - n(n-4)$

(c) $^{n-4}C_2 + {}^{n-3}C_3$ 

(d) $^{n+2}C_3$

**8.** For n > 1, let

$E = (2n+1)(2n+3)(2n+5)...(4n-3)(4n-1)$

Then

(a) $2^n$ E is divisible by $^{4n}C_{2n}$ 

(b) $2^n$ E is divisible by n!

(c) $\dfrac{2^n E}{n!}$ is a positive integer 

(d) $\dfrac{2^n E}{(4n)!}$ is not an integer

**9.** Let A = { 1, 2, 3} and B = { 1, 2, 3, 4, 6, 7}. Among all the functions from A to B, the number of functions $f$ such that

(a) f (i) < f (j) whenever i < j, is 35

(b) f (i) $\leq$ f (j) whenever i < j, is 84

(c) f(i) > f(j) whenever i < j is 35

(d) none of these

## Section III - Integer Type

This section contains 4 questions. The answer to each of the questions is a single digit integer ranging from 0 to 9.

**10.** If the number of ordered pairs $(m, n)$; $m, n \in \{1, 2, 3, ........., 20\}$ such that $3^m + 7^n$ is a multiple of 10, is equal to 20k, then k =

**11.** A person has 6 friends and during a certain vacation he met them during several dinners. He found that he dinned with all the 6 exactly on one day, with every 5 of them on 2 days, with every 4 of them on 3 days, with every 3 on 4 days; with every 2 on 5 days. Furthers every friend was present at 7 dinners and every friend was absent at 7 dinners. The number of dinner(s) he had alone is equal to

**12.** If the number of ordered triplets $(a, b, c)$ such that L.C.M. $(a,b) = 1000$, L.C.M. $(b,c) = 2000$ and L.C.M. $(c,a) = 2000$ is 10q, then q =

**13.** If all the permutations of the letters of the word TACKLE are written in order as in a dictionary, also if the rank of the word TACKLE is equal to 100 a + b, then a − b =

| | | | | | |
|---|---|---|---|---|---|
| **RESPONSE GRID** | 4. (a)(b)(c)(d) | 5. (a)(b)(c)(d) | 6. (a)(b)(c)(d) | 7. (a)(b)(c)(d) | 8. (a)(b)(c)(d) |
| | 9. (a)(b)(c)(d) | 10. (0)(1)(2)(3)(4)(5)(6)(7)(8)(9) | | 11. (0)(1)(2)(3)(4)(5)(6)(7)(8)(9) | |
| | 12. (0)(1)(2)(3)(4)(5)(6)(7)(8)(9) | 13. (0)(1)(2)(3)(4)(5)(6)(7)(8)(9) | | | |

*Space for Rough Work*

## Section IV - Comprehension/Matching Cum-Comprehension Type

**Directions (Qs. 14 and 15) :** Based upon the given paragraph, 2 multiple choice questions have to be answered. Each question has 4 choices (a), (b), (c) and (d), out of which ONLY ONE is correct.

### PARAGRAPH

If $p$ is a prime, then exponent of $p$ in $n!$ equals

$$E_p(n) = \left[\frac{n}{p}\right] + \left[\frac{n}{p^2}\right] + \left[\frac{n}{p^3}\right] + \dots$$

14. The largest two digit prime that divides $^{200}C_{100}$ is
    (a) 59            (b) 53            (c) 47            (d) none of these
15. The number of natural numbers n for n! ends in 26 zeros, is
    (a) 4            (b) 5            (c) 6            (d) 7

**Directions (Qs. 16-18) :** This passage contains a table having 3 columns and 4 rows. Based on the table, there are three questions. Each question has four options (a), (b), (c) and (d) **ONLY ONE** of these four options is correct.

Column-1 contains information about the numbers to be formed.

Column-2 contains digits with condition to be used to form the numbers mentioned in the column-1.

Column-3 contains number of numbers formed mentioned in the column-1 using the digits mentioned in the column-2.

| | Column 1 | | Column 2 | | Column 3 |
|---|---|---|---|---|---|
| (I) | Four digit odd-numbers | (i) | 0, 1, 2, 3, 4, 5 (without repetition) | (P) | 216 |
| (II) | Numbers greater than 1000 but less than 4000 | (ii) | 0, 1, 2, 3, 5, 7 (with repetition) | (Q) | 72 |
| (III) | Five digit numbers divisible by 3 | (iii) | 1, 2, 3 (with repetition) | (R) | 77 |
| (IV) | Seven digit integers with sum of the digits equal to 10 | (iv) | 0, 1, 2, 3, 4 (without repetition) | (S) | 720 |

16. Which of the following options is the only correct combination?
    (a) (I)(ii)(R)      (b) (III)(i)(P)      (c) (II)(iv)(S)      (d) (IV)(ii)(Q)
17. Which of the following options is the only correct combination?
    (a) (IV)(iii)(R)      (b) (III)(ii)(Q)      (c) (II)(iv)(P)      (d) (I)(i)(S)
18. Which of the following options is the only incorrect combination?
    (a) (I)(ii)(S)      (b) (III)(i)(P)      (c) (II)(iv)(R)      (d) (IV)(iii)(R)



*Space for Rough Work*

## Section V - Matrix-Match Type

This section contains 2 questions. It contains statements given in two columns, which have to be matched. Statements in column I are labelled as A, B, C and D whereas statements in column II are labelled as p, q, r and s. The answers to these questions have to be appropriately bubbled as illustrated in the following example. If the correct matches are A-p, A-r, B-p, B-s, C-r, C-s and D-q, then the correctly bubbled matrix will look like the following:

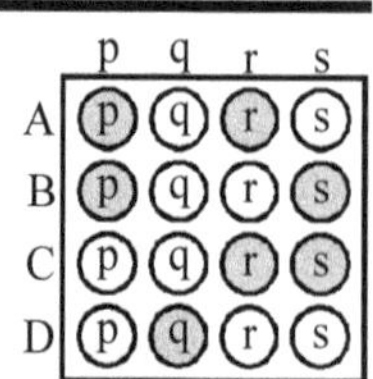

19. **Match the columns :**

| Column-I | | Column-II |
|---|---|---|
| (A) The number of 6 digit natural numbers, where each digit appears at least twice is | p. | 1800 |
| (B) In how many ways can five different books be tied up in 3 bundles? | q. | 677 |
| (C) In how many ways 5 different subjects can be distributed in 6 periods in a timetable if each subject must occur. | r. | 11754 |
| (D) How many students do you need in a school to guarantee that there are atleast 2 students, who have the same $1^{st}$ two initials in their $1^{st}$ names? | s. | 25 |

20. **Match the columns :**

| Column-I | | Column-II |
|---|---|---|
| (A) The total number of three digit numbers, the sum of whose digits is even is equal to | p. | 18 |
| (B) Total number of positive intergal solutions of the equation $xyz = 140$ is equal to | q. | 54 |
| (C) Total number of positive intergal solutions of $x + y + z \leq 10$ is equal to | r. | 120 |
| (D) If the cubic $x^3 + ax^2 + bx + c$ is divisible by $x^2 + 1$, then the number of three digit numbers of the form abc or bca or cab which can be formed is equal to | s. | 450 |

| **RESPONSE GRID** | 19. A - ⓟⓠⓡⓢ; B - ⓟⓠⓡⓢ; C - ⓟⓠⓡⓢ; D - ⓟⓠⓡⓢ |
|---|---|
| | 20. A - ⓟⓠⓡⓢ; B - ⓟⓠⓡⓢ; C - ⓟⓠⓡⓢ; D - ⓟⓠⓡⓢ |

## DAILY PRACTICE PROBLEM DPP CM05 - MATHEMATICS

| Total Questions | 20 | Total Marks | 74 |
|---|---|---|---|
| Attempted | | Correct | |
| Incorrect | | Net Score | |
| Cut-off Score | 25 | Qualifying Score | 38 |

$$\text{Net Score} = \sum_{i=1}^{V} \left[ \left( \text{correct}_i \times MM_i \right) - \left( In_i - NM_i \right) \right]$$

Date : Start Time : End Time :

# MATHEMATICS $\boxed{\text{CM06}}$

**SYLLABUS :** Binomial Theorem

**Max. Marks : 74**  **Time : 60 min.**

## GENERAL INSTRUCTIONS

- The Daily Practice Problem Sheet contains 20 Questions divided into 5 sections.
  **Section I** has **6** MCQs with ONLY 1 Correct Option, **3** marks for each correct answer and **−1** for each incorrect answer.
  **Section II** has **4** MCQs with ONE or MORE THAN ONE Correct options.
  For each question, marks will be awarded in one of the following categories:
  Full marks: **+4** If only the bubble(s) corresponding to all the correct option(s) is (are) darkened.
  Partial marks: **+1** For darkening a bubble corresponding to each correct option provided NO INCORRECT option is darkened.
  Zero marks:  If none of the bubbles is darkened.
  Negative marks: **−2** In all other cases.
  **Section III** has **4** Single Digit Integer Answer Type Questions, **3** marks for each Correct Answer and **0** mark in all other cases.
  **Section IV** has Comprehension Type Questions having **4** MCQs with ONLY ONE corect option, **3** marks for each Correct Answer and **0** mark in all other cases.
  **Section V** has **2** Matching Type Questions, **2** marks for the correct matching of each row and **0** mark in all other cases.
- You have to evaluate your Response Grids yourself with the help of Solutions.

## Section I - Straight Objective Type

This section contains 6 multiple choice questions. Each question has 4 choices (a), (b), (c) and (d), out of which **ONLY ONE** is correct.

**1.** If $(1 + x - 2x^2)^6 = 1 + a_1x + a_2x^2 + a_3x^3 + ....$ and $k = a_2 + a_4 + a_6 + ... + a_{12}$ then which one of the following is true about k?
(a) k is a perfect square
(b) k is a prime number
(c) k is a perfect cube
(d) k is more than 64

**2.** Consider a function $f(x) = \left(1 - \dfrac{1}{x}\right)$. Then term independent of $x$ in the expansion of $\left(f(x)\right)^n \cdot \left(f\left(-\dfrac{1}{x}\right)\right)^n$ is
(a) $0$, if $n$ is odd
(b) $(-1)^{\frac{n-1}{2}} \cdot {}^nC_{\frac{n-1}{2}}$, if $n$ is odd
(c) $(-1)^{n/2} \cdot {}^nC_{\frac{n}{2}-1}$, if $n$ is even
(d) None of the above

| **RESPONSE GRID** | 1. ⓐⓑⓒⓓ | 2. ⓐⓑⓒⓓ |
| --- | --- | --- |

*Space for Rough Work*

**3.** If $(1+x)^n = C_0 + C_1 x + C_2 x^2 + \dots + C_n x^n$, then

$\displaystyle \sum_{0 \le i \le j} \sum_{j \le n} \left(C_i + C_j\right)^2$ is equal to

(a) $(n-1)\ ^{2n}C_n + 2^{2n}$

(b) $n\ ^{2n}C_n + 2^{2n}$

(c) $(n+1)\ ^{2n}C_n + 2^{2n}$

(d) None of these

**4.** The number of integral solutions of the equation
$x + y + z + w = 20$, if $x \ge 1,\ y \ge 2,\ z \ge 3,\ w \ge 4$, is

(a) 286            (b) 78

(c) 715            (d) 1001

**5.** If $I$ is integral part of $(2+\sqrt{3})^n$ and $f$ is its fractional part.
Then $(I+f)(1-f)$ is

(a) $I+1$          (b) 1

(c) $n$             (d) $2^n$

**6.** If coefficient of $x^n$ in $(1+x)^{101}(1-x+x^2)^{100}$ is non-zero, then $n$ cannot be of the form

(a) $3r+1$         (b) $3r$

(c) $3r+2$         (d) $4r+1$

**8.** Which all statements are correct?

(a) The number of integral terms in the expansion of $(\sqrt{3} + \sqrt[8]{5}\ )^{256}$ is k then $k > 30$

(b) The number of integral terms in the expansion of $(\sqrt{3} + \sqrt[8]{5}\ )^{256}$ is k then $k < 40$

(c) Number of distinct terms in the expansion of $(x+y-z)^{16}$ is k then $k > 140$

(d) Number of distinct terms in the expansion of $(x+y-z)^{16}$ is k then $k < 150$

**9.** If $f(n) = \displaystyle\sum_{r=1}^{n} [r\left(n^{n-1}C_{r-1} - r\ ^nC_{r-1}\right) + (2r+1)\ ^nC_r]$,

then

(a) $f(10) = 120$      (b) $f(20) = 440$

(c) $\displaystyle\sum_{n=1}^{10} f(n) = 495$     (d) $\displaystyle\sum_{n=1}^{10} f(n) = 374$

**10.** The integer just greater than $\left(\sqrt{3}+1\right)^{2m}$ is

(a) divisible by $2^{m+1}$     (b) divisible by $3^{m+1}$

(c) divisible by $2^m$       (d) divisible by $3^m$

## Section II - Multiple Correct Answer Type

This section contains 4 multiple correct answer(s) type questions. Each question has 4 choices (a), (b), (c) and (d), out of which **ONE OR MORE** is/are correct.

**7.** Suppose $x_1, x_2, \dots, x_n\,(n>2)$ are real numbers such that $x_i = -x_{n-i+1}$ for $1 \le i \le n$. Consider the sum $S_n = \displaystyle\sum \sum \sum x_i x_j x_k$

$(1 < i, j, k \le n)\,(i,j,k\ distinct)$ then which of the following is true?

(a) $S_{10} = 121$      (b) $S_{10} = S_{20}$

(c) $S_{14} = 0$        (d) $S_{30} > S_{31}$

## Section III - Integer Type

This section contains 4 questions. The answer to each of the questions is a single digit integer ranging from 0 to 9.

**11.** If $\displaystyle\sum_{r=0}^{n} \left(\frac{r+2}{r+1}\right) C_r = \frac{2^8 - 1}{6}$, then $n$ is equal to



*Space for Rough Work*

12. Given $\left(1 - 2x + 5x^2 - 10x^3\right)\left(1 + x\right)^n = 1 + a_1 x + a_2 x^2 + ...$ and that $a_1^{\,2} = 2a_2$, then the value of $n$ is

13. If the expansion of $(1 + x + x^2)^n$ be written as $a_0 + a^1 x + a_2 x^2 + ..... + a_{2n} x^{2n}$, then the value of
$$\frac{a_0 + a_1 + a_3 + a_4 + a_6 + a_7 + ...}{a_2 + a_5 + a_8 + ...}$$ if $n$ is a multiple of 3.

14. If $(1 + ax)^n = 1 + 8x + 24x^2 + ........$; then $9\left(\dfrac{n-a}{a+n}\right)$ is equal to

 (n being a positive Integer)

---

## Section IV - Comprehension Type

Based upon the given paragraphs, 4 multiple choice questions have to be answered. Each question has 4 choices (a), (b), (c) and (d), out of which **ONLY ONE** is correct.

---

### PARAGRAPH-1

If $^nC_0, ^nC_1, ^nC_2,..., ^nC_n$ denote the binomial coefficients in the expansion of $(1 + x)^n$ and $a + b = 1$, then

15. Find the value of $\displaystyle\sum_{r=0}^{n} r \; ^nC_r a^r b^{n-r}$ is

 (a) $na^2$
 (b) $nab$
 (c) $na$
 (d) None of these

16. If $^nC_0, ^nC_1, ^nC_2,...., ^nC_n$ denote the binomial coefficients in the expansion of $(1 + x)^n$ and $p + q = 1$, then $\displaystyle\sum_{r=0}^{n} r^2 \; ^nC_r p^r q^{n-r}$ is

 (a) $np$
 (b) $npq$
 (c) $n^2 p^2 + npq$
 (d) None of these

### PARAGRAPH-2

The binomial expansion is defined as
$$\left(x + y\right)^n = \sum_{r=0}^{n} C_r \; x^{n-r} y^r \text{, where } C_r = \; ^nC_r.$$

17. The value of $\displaystyle\sum_{0 \le i < j \le n} \sum i \cdot \; ^nC_j$ is equal to

 (a) $n(n+1)2^{n-3}$
 (b) $n^2 2^{n-3}$
 (c) $n(n-1)2^{n-3}$
 (d) None of these

18. The value of $\displaystyle\sum_{0 \le i < j \le n} \sum j \cdot \; ^nC_i$ is equal to

 (a) $n^2 2^{n-3}$
 (b) $n(n+3)2^{n-3}$
 (c) $(n+3)2^{n-3}$
 (d) None of these

<table>
<tr><td rowspan="3">RESPONSE GRID</td><td>12. ⓪①②③④⑤⑥⑦⑧⑨</td><td>13. ⓪①②③④⑤⑥⑦⑧⑨</td><td></td><td></td></tr>
<tr><td>14. ⓪①②③④⑤⑥⑦⑧⑨</td><td>15. ⓐⓑⓒⓓ</td><td>16. ⓐⓑⓒⓓ</td><td>17. ⓐⓑⓒⓓ</td></tr>
<tr><td>18. ⓐⓑⓒⓓ</td><td></td><td></td><td></td></tr>
</table>

*Space for Rough Work*

## Section V - Matrix-Match Type

This section contains 2 questions. It contains statements given in two columns, which have to be matched. Statements in column I are labelled as A, B, C and D whereas statements in column II are labelled as p, q, r and s. The answers to these questions have to be appropriately bubbled as illustrated in the following example. If the correct matches are A-p, A-r, B-p, B-s, C-r, C-s and D-q, then the correctly bubbled matrix will look like the following:

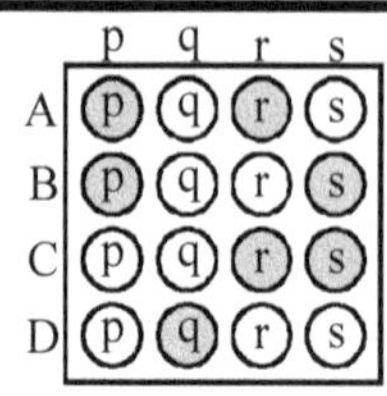

**19. Match the statement of Column I with values of Column II.**

**Column I**

(A) If $(r+1)$th term is the first negative term in the expansion of $(1+x)^{7/2}$, then the value of $r$ where $|x| < 1$ is ($x$ is + ve).

(B) The coefficient of y in the expansion of $(y^2 + 1/y)^5$ is

(C) If the second term in the expansion $\left( a^{\frac{1}{13}} + \dfrac{a}{\sqrt{a^{-1}}} \right)^n$ is $14a^{5/2}$, then the value of $n$ is

(D) The sum of coefficient of $x^2, x^4, x^6, x^8$ in the expression $(1 + 2x + 3x^2 + 4x^3 + \dots \text{ up to } \infty)^{1/2}$ is (where $|x| < 1$) is

**Column II**

(p) Divisible by 7

(q) A perfect square

(r) Divisible by 10

(s) A prime number

**20. Match the following.**

**Column I**

(A) Let n be an odd natural number greater than 1. Then the number of zeroes at the end of the sum $99^n + 1$ is

(B) Let $f(n) = 10^n + 3 \cdot 4^{n+2} + 5$, $n \in N$. The greatest value of the integer which divides $f(n)$ for all n is

(C) If $x + \dfrac{1}{x} = 1$ and $p = x^{1000} + \dfrac{1}{x^{1000}}$ and q be the digit at unit place in the number $2^{4n} + 1$, $n \in N$ and $n > 1$, then $p + q =$

(D) For integer $n > 1$, the digit at unit place in the number $\displaystyle\sum_{r=0}^{100} r! + 2^{2n}$ is

**Column II**

(p) 6

(q) 0

(r) 2

(s) 9

| RESPONSE GRID | |
|---|---|
| **19.** A - (p)(q)(r)(s); B - (p)(q)(r)(s); C - (p)(q)(r)(s); D - (p)(q)(r)(s) | |
| **20.** A - (p)(q)(r)(s); B - (p)(q)(r)(s); C - (p)(q)(r)(s); D - (p)(q)(r)(s) | |

## DAILY PRACTICE PROBLEM DPP CM06 - MATHEMATICS

| Total Questions | 20 | Total Marks | 74 |
|---|---|---|---|
| Attempted | | Correct | |
| Incorrect | | Net Score | |
| Cut-off Score | 25 | Qualifying Score | 36 |

$$\text{Net Score} = \sum_{i=1}^{V} \left[ (\text{correct}_i \times MM_i) - (In_i - NM_i) \right]$$

*Space for Rough Work*

Date : ____    Start Time : ____    End Time : ____

# MATHEMATICS CM07

**SYLLABUS :** Sequences and Series

**Max. Marks : 74**                    **Time : 60 min.**

## GENERAL INSTRUCTIONS

- The Daily Practice Problem Sheet contains 20 Questions divided into 5 sections.
  **Section I** has **6** MCQs with ONLY 1 Correct Option, **3** marks for each correct answer and **−1** for each incorrect answer.
  **Section II** has **4** MCQs with ONE or MORE THAN ONE Correct options.
  For each question, marks will be awarded in one of the following categories:
  Full marks: **+4** If only the bubble(s) corresponding to all the correct option(s) is (are) darkened.
  Partial marks: **+1** For darkening a bubble corresponding to each correct option provided NO INCORRECT option is darkened.
  Zero marks:   If none of the bubbles is darkened.
  Negative marks: **−2** In all other cases.
  **Section III** has **4** Single Digit Integer Answer Type Questions, **3** marks for each Correct Answer and 0 marks in all other cases.
  **Section IV** has Comprehension Type Questions having **4** MCQs with ONLY ONE corect option, 3 marks for each Correct Answer and **0** marks in all other cases.
  **Section V** has **2** Matching Type Questions, **2** mark for the correct matching of each row and 0 marks in all other cases.
- You have to evaluate your Response Grids yourself with the help of Solutions.

## Section I - Straight Objective Type

This section contains 6 multiple choice questions. Each question has 4 choices (a), (b), (c) and (d), out of which **ONLY ONE** is correct.

1. If $a_1, a_2, a_3, \ldots$ are in H.P. and $f(k) = \left(\displaystyle\sum_{r=1}^{n} a_r\right) - a_k$, then

   $\dfrac{a_1}{f(1)}, \dfrac{a_2}{f(2)}, \dfrac{a_3}{f(3)} \ldots \dfrac{a_n}{f(n)}$ are in

   (a)  A.P.                     (b)  G.P.
   (c)  H.P.                     (d)  None of these

2. If $a, b, c, d$ are non−zero real numbers such that

   $\left(a^2 + b^2 + c^2\right)\left(b^2 + c^2 + d^2\right) \le \left(ab + bc + cd\right)^2$, then $a, b, c, d$ are in

   (a)  AP                       (b)  GP
   (c)  HP                       (d)  None of these

**RESPONSE GRID**    1. ⓐⓑⓒⓓ    2. ⓐⓑⓒⓓ

*Space for Rough Work*

**3.** If $a > 0$, $b > 0$, $c > 0$ and the minimum value of $a\left(b^2 + c^2\right) + b\left(c^2 + a^2\right) + c\left(a^2 + b^2\right)$ is $\lambda abc$, then find the value of $\lambda$

(a)  2  
(b)  1  
(c)  6  
(d)  3

**4.** If $S_r$ denotes the sum of the first $r$ terms of an AP, and the value of $\dfrac{S_r}{S_{kr}}$ = pr + q then find the value of $p + q$

(a)  −1  
(b)  1  
(c)  3  
(d)  None of these

**5.** If $H_1, H_2, ....H_n$ are $n$ harmonic means between $a$ and $b(\neq a)$, then find the value of $\dfrac{H_1 + a}{H_1 - a} + \dfrac{H_n + b}{H_n - b}$

(a)  $n + 1$  
(b)  $n - 1$  
(c)  $2n$  
(d)  $2n + 3$

**6.** If $a_1, a_2, ........, a_n$ are in H.P., then the expression $a_1 a_2 + a_2 a_3 + ..........+ a_{n-1} a_n$ is equal to

(a)  $n(a_1 - a_n)$  
(b)  $(n-1)(a_1 - a_n)$  
(c)  $na_1 a_n$  
(d)  $(n-1)a_1 a_n$

---

### Section II - Multiple Correct Answer Type

This section contains 4 multiple correct answer(s) type questions. Each question has 4 choices (a), (b), (c) and (d), out of which **ONE OR MORE** is/are correct.

---

**7.** If $a, b, c$ are in AP and $a^2, b^2, c^2$ are in HP, then

(a)  $a = b = c$  
(b)  $a, b, -\dfrac{1}{2}c$ are in GP  
(c)  $a, b, c$ are in GP  
(d)  $-\dfrac{1}{2}a, b, c$ are in GP

**8.** Sum to $n$ terms of the series $S_n = \dfrac{1}{(1+x)(1+2x)}$
$+ \dfrac{1}{(1+2x)(1+3x)} + \dfrac{1}{(1+3x)(1+4x)} + ...$ is

(a)  $S_{10} = \dfrac{10}{(1+x)(1+11x)}$

(b)  $S_{10} = \dfrac{10}{(1+2x)(1+11x)}$

(c)  $S_{16} = \dfrac{16}{(1+x)(1+17x)}$

(d)  $S_{18} = \dfrac{18}{(1+x)(1+17x)}$

**9.** For $0 < \phi < \pi / 2$, if

$$x = \sum_{n=0}^{\infty} \cos^{2n}\phi \ , \ y = \sum_{n=0}^{\infty} \sin^{2n}\phi, \ z = \sum_{n=0}^{\infty} \cos^{2n}\phi \sin^{2n}\phi \text{ then:}$$

(a)  $xyz = xz + y$  
(b)  $xyz = xy + z$  
(c)  $xyz = x + y + z$  
(d)  $xyz = yz + x$

**10.** Given that $\alpha, \gamma$ are roots of the equation $Ax^2 - 4x + 1 = 0$ and $\beta, \delta$ the roots of the equation $Bx^2 - 6x + 1 = 0$, and $\alpha, \beta, \alpha, \gamma$ and $\delta$ are in HP, then

(a)  $A = 3, B = 8$  
(b)  $A = 8, B = 3$  
(c)  $A = 3, B = -8$  
(d)  $A + B = 11$

---

<table>
<tr><td rowspan="2">RESPONSE<br>GRID</td><td>3. ⓐⓑⓒⓓ</td><td>4. ⓐⓑⓒⓓ</td><td>5. ⓐⓑⓒⓓ</td><td>6. ⓐⓑⓒⓓ</td><td>7. ⓐⓑⓒⓓ</td></tr>
<tr><td>8. ⓐⓑⓒⓓ</td><td>9. ⓐⓑⓒⓓ</td><td>10. ⓐⓑⓒⓓ</td><td></td><td></td></tr>
</table>

*Space for Rough Work*

## Section III - Integer Type

This section contains 4 questions. The answer to each of the questions is a single digit integer ranging from 0 to 9.

**11.** Let $a_1$, $a_2$, ..., $a_{10}$ be in AP and $h_1$, $h_2$,...,$h_{10}$ be in HP. If $a_1 = h_1 = 2$ and $a_{10} = h_{10} = 3$, then find the value of $a_4 h_7$

**12.** If $a$, $b$, $c$ are in $G.P.$, $x$ and $y$ be the $A.M.$s between $a$, $b$ and $b$, $c$ respectively, then $\left(\dfrac{a}{x} + \dfrac{c}{y}\right)\left(\dfrac{b}{x} + \dfrac{b}{y}\right)$ is equal to.

**13.** If $\left(1+x\right)\left(1+x^2\right)\left(1+x^4\right)...\left(1+x^{128}\right) = \sum\limits_{r=0}^{n} x^r$ , then unit digit of $n$ is

**14.** Sum to $n$ terms of the series $\dfrac{1}{5!} + \dfrac{1!}{6!} + \dfrac{2!}{7!} + \dfrac{3!}{8!} +$

$... = \dfrac{1}{a}\left[\dfrac{1}{b!} - \dfrac{(n+c)!}{(n+d)!}\right]$ then $(a + b - c - d)$ is

## Section IV - Comprehension Type

Based upon the given paragraphs, 4 multiple choice questions have to be answered. Each question has 4 choices (a), (b), (c) and (d), out of which **ONLY ONE** is correct.

### PARAGRAPH-1

If $a_1$, $a_2$, ..., $a_n$ are in A.P., then $\dfrac{1}{a_1}$, $\dfrac{1}{a_2}$, ..., $\dfrac{1}{a_n}$ are in H.P. and vice–versa.

If $a_1$, $a_2$, ..., $a_n$ are in A. P. with common difference d, then for any b ($> 0$), the number $b^{a_1}, b^{a_2}, b^{a_3} ..., b^{a_n}$ are in G.P. with common ratio $b^d$.

If $a_1$, $a_2$, ... $a_n$ are positive and in G.P. with common ratio $r$, then for any base b ($b > 0$), $\log_b a_1$, $\log_b a_2$, ... $\log_b a_n$ are in A.P. with common difference $\log_b r$.

**15.** If a, b, c are in H.P., then $e^{(-a)^{-1}}, e^{(-b)^{-1}}, e^{(-c)^{-1}}$ are in
(a) A.P.        (b) GP
(c) H.P.        (d) None of these.

**16.** If $x$, $y$, $z$ are respectively the p[th,] q[th] and the r[th] terms of an A.P., as well as of a G.P., then the value of $(x^{y-z})$, $(y^{z-x})$, $(z^{x-y})$ is
(a) 1        (b) −1
(c) 0        (d) 2

### PARAGRAPH-2

Let $V_r$ denote the sum of first $r$ terms of an arithmetic progression (A.P.) whose first term is $r$ and the common difference is $(2r - 1)$. Let $T_r = V_{r+1} - V_r - 2$ and $Q_r = T_{r+1} - T_r$ for $r = 1, 2, ...$

**17.** The sum $V_1 + V_2 + ... + V_n$ is
(a) $\dfrac{1}{12} n(n+1)(3n^2 - n + 1)$

(b) $\dfrac{1}{12} n(n+1)(3n^2 + n + 2)$

(c) $\dfrac{1}{2} n(2n^2 - n + 1)$

(d) $\dfrac{1}{3}(2n^3 - 2n + 3)$

**18.** $T_r$ is always
(a) an odd number    (b) an even number
(c) a prime number    (d) a composite number

| | |
|---|---|
| **RESPONSE GRID** | 11. ⓪①②③④⑤⑥⑦⑧⑨  12. ⓪①②③④⑤⑥⑦⑧⑨ <br> 13. ⓪①②③④⑤⑥⑦⑧⑨  14. ⓪①②③④⑤⑥⑦⑧⑨ <br> 15. ⓐⓑⓒⓓ  16. ⓐⓑⓒⓓ  17. ⓐⓑⓒⓓ  18. ⓐⓑⓒⓓ |

*Space for Rough Work*

## Section V - Matrix-Match Type

This section contains 2 questions. It contains statements given in two columns, which have to be matched. Statements in column I are labelled as A, B, C and D whereas statements in column II are labelled as p, q, r and s. The answers to these questions have to be appropriately bubbled as illustrated in the following example. If the correct matches are A-p, A-r, B-p, B-s, C-r, C-s and D-q, then the correctly bubbled matrix will look like the following:

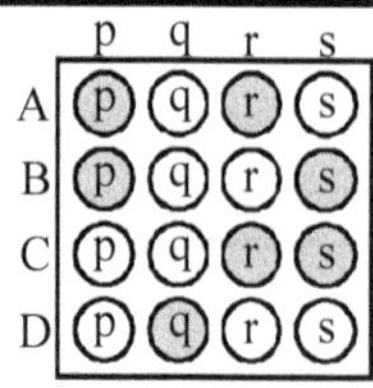

**19.** Match the columns

| **Column I** | | **Column II** | |
|---|---|---|---|
| (A) | The sum of the first $n$ natural number is one – fifth of the sum of their squares, then $n$ is | ($p$) | 4 |
| (B) | The harmonic mean of the roots of the equation $(5 + \sqrt{2})x^2 - (4 + \sqrt{3})x + 8 + 2\sqrt{3} = 0$ is | ($q$) | 2 |
| (C) | If $x, y, z$ are in HP, $(z > y > x)$. The value of $\dfrac{\left(\log(x+z) + \log(x - 2y + z)\right)}{\log(z-x)}$ is | ($r$) | 1 |
| (D) | The nth term of GP is 128 and the sum to its $n$ terms is 255. If its common ratio is 2, the its first term is | ($s$) | 7 |

**20.** Match the columns

| **Column I** | | **Column II** | |
|---|---|---|---|
| (A) | The arithmetic mean of two positive numbers is 6 and their geometric mean G and harmonic mean H satisfy $G^2 + 3H = 48$ then $G^2$ is equal to | ($p$) | 308 |
| (B) | $S_n = n^3 - (n-1)^3 + (n-2)^3 - \dots + (-1)^{n-1} \cdot 1^3$ Then find $\dfrac{S_{39}}{100}$ | ($q$) | 32 |
| (C) | If the first two terms of a harmonic progression be ½ and 1/3, then the harmonic mean of the first four terms is | ($r$) | $\dfrac{240}{77}$ |
| (D) | Find the number of numbers lying between 100 and 500 that are divisible by 7 but not by 21. | ($s$) | 38 |

| **RESPONSE** | 19. A - ⓟⓠⓡⓢ; B - ⓟⓠⓡⓢ; C - ⓟⓠⓡⓢ; D - ⓟⓠⓡⓢ |
|---|---|
| **GRID** | 20. A - ⓟⓠⓡⓢ; B - ⓟⓠⓡⓢ; C - ⓟⓠⓡⓢ; D - ⓟⓠⓡⓢ |

## DAILY PRACTICE PROBLEM DPP CM07 - MATHEMATICS

| | | | |
|---|---|---|---|
| Total Questions | 20 | Total Marks | 74 |
| Attempted | | Correct | |
| Incorrect | | Net Score | |
| Cut-off Score | 26 | Qualifying Score | 37 |

$$\text{Net Score} = \sum_{i=1}^{V} \left[ (\text{correct}_i \times MM_i) - (In_i - NM_i) \right]$$

*Space for Rough Work*

Date : | Start Time : | End Time :

# MATHEMATICS $\boxed{\text{CM08}}$

**SYLLABUS :** Straight Lines and Pair of Straight Lines

**Max. Marks : 67**                                                                                   **Time : 60 min.**

## GENERAL INSTRUCTIONS

- The Daily Practice Problem Sheet contains 20 Questions divided into 5 sections.

  **Section I** has **6** MCQs with ONLY 1 Correct Option, **3** marks for each correct answer and **−1** for each incorrect answer.

  **Section II** has **4** MCQs with ONE or MORE THAN ONE Correct options.

  For each question, marks will be awarded in one of the following categories:

  Full marks: **+4** If only the bubble(s) corresponding to all the correct option(s) is (are) darkened.

  Partial marks: **+1** For darkening a bubble corresponding to each correct option provided NO INCORRECT option is darkened.

  Zero marks:  If none of the bubbles is darkened.

  Negative marks: **−2** In all other cases.

  **Section III** has **5** Single Digit Integer Answer Type Questions, **3** marks for each Correct Answer and **0** mark in all other cases.

  **Section IV** has Comprehension Type Questions having **4** MCQs with ONLY ONE corect option, **3** marks for each Correct Answer and **0** mark in all other cases.

  **Section V** has **1** Matching Type Question, **2** marks for the correct matching of each row and **0** mark in all other cases.

- You have to evaluate your Response Grids yourself with the help of Solutions.

## Section I - Straight Objective Type

This section contains 6 multiple choice questions. Each question has 4 choices (a), (b), (c) and (d), out of which **ONLY ONE** is correct.

**1.** If $a$ and $b$ are positive numbers ($a < b$), then the range of values of $K$ for which a real $\lambda$ can be found such that the equation $ax^2 + 2\lambda xy + by^2 + 2K(x + y + 1) = 0$ represents a pair of straight lines is :

(a)  $a < K^2 < b$

(b)  $a \le K^2 \le b$

(c)  $K^2 \le a$ or $K^2 \ge b$

(d)  $K \le 2a$ or $K \ge 2b$

**2.** Let $ax + by + c = 0$ be a variable straight line, where $a$, $b$ and $c$ are 1st, 3rd and 7th terms of an increasing A.P. Then the variable straight line always passes through a fixed point which lies on

(a)  $x^2 + y^2 = 13$

(b)  $x^2 + y^2 = 5$

(c)  $y^2 = 4x$

(d)  $3x + 4y = 9.$

**3.** If $5a + 5b + 20c = t$, then the value of $t$ for which the line $ax + by + c - 1 = 0$ always passes through a fixed point is

(a)  0

(b)  20

(c)  30

(d)  None on these

**RESPONSE GRID**     **1.** ⓐⓑⓒⓓ     **2.** ⓐⓑⓒⓓ     **3.** ⓐⓑⓒⓓ

*Space for Rough Work*

**4.** The range of values of $\beta$ such that $(0, \beta)$ lie on or inside the triangle formed by the lines $y + 3x + 2 = 0$, $3y - 2x - 5 = 0$, $4y + x - 14 = 0$ is

(a) $5 < \beta \leq 7$

(b) $\dfrac{1}{2} \leq \beta \leq 1$

(c) $\dfrac{5}{3} \leq \beta \leq \dfrac{7}{2}$

(d) None of these

**5.** If $a^2 + b^2 - c^2 - 2ab = 0$, then the point of concurrency of family of straight lines $ax + by + c = 0$ lies on the line

(a) $y = x$

(b) $y = x + 1$

(c) $y = -x$

(d) $x + y = 1$

**6.** If the area of the rhombus enclosed by the lines $lx \pm my \pm n = 0$ be 2 square units, then

(a) $l, m, n$ are in G.P.

(b) $l, n, m$ are in G.P.

(c) $lm = n$

(d) $ln = m$

---

### Section II - Multiple Correct Answer Type

This section contains 4 multiple correct answer(s) type questions. Each question has 4 choices (a), (b), (c) and (d), out of which **ONE OR MORE** is/are correct.

---

**7.** The equation of straight line(s) passing through ordered pairs $(a,\ b)$ satisfying equation

$$\sec^2(a+2)b + a^2 - 1 = 0, -\pi < b < \pi$$

and haveing slope $\dfrac{1}{2}$ is

(a) $x - 2y = 0$

(b) $x - 2y = 1$

(c) $x - 2y = \pi$

(d) $x - 2y + \pi = 0$

**8.** Let $0 < p < q$ and $a \neq 0$ such that the equation
$$px^2 + 4\lambda xy + qy^2 + 4a(x + y + 1) = 0$$
represents a pair of straight lines, then $a$ can lie in the interval

(a) $(-\infty, \infty)$

(b) $(-\infty, p]$

(c) $[p, q]$

(d) $[q, \infty)$

**9.** If the points $\left(\dfrac{a^3}{a-1}, \dfrac{a^2-3}{a-1}\right)$, $\left(\dfrac{b^3}{b-1}, \dfrac{b^2-3}{b-1}\right)$ and

$\left(\dfrac{c^3}{c-1}, \dfrac{c^2-3}{c-1}\right)$, where $a, b, c$ are different from $1$, lie on the line $lx + my + n = 0$, then

(a) $a + b + c = -\dfrac{m}{l}$

(b) $ab + bc + ca = \dfrac{n}{l}$

(c) $abc = \dfrac{m+n}{l}$

(d) $abc - (bc + ca + ab) + 3(a + b + c) = 0$

**10.** If $m_1$ and $m_2$ are the roots of the equation $x^2 - ax - a - 1 = 0$, then the area of the triangle formed by the three straight lines $y = m_1 x, y = m_2 x$ and $y = a\,(a \neq -1)$ is

(a) $\dfrac{a^2\,(a+2)}{2(a+1)}$ if $a > -1$

(b) $\dfrac{-a^2\,(a+2)}{2\,(a+1)}$ if $-2 < a < -1$

(c) $\dfrac{a^2\,(a+2)}{2\,(a+1)}$ if $a < -2$

(d) $0$ for all $a$

---

| RESPONSE | 4. (a)(b)(c)(d) | 5. (a)(b)(c)(d) | 6. (a)(b)(c)(d) | 7. (a)(b)(c)(d) | 8. (a)(b)(c)(d) |
| --- | --- | --- | --- | --- | --- |
| GRID | 9. (a)(b)(c)(d) | 10. (a)(b)(c)(d) | | | |

*Space for Rough Work*

## Section III - Integer Type

This section contains 5 questions. The answer to each of the questions is a single digit integer ranging from 0 to 9.

11. If $ax^2 + 2hxy + by^2 + 2gx + 2fy + 10 = 0$ represents a pair of straight lines, equidistant from the origin, if $\dfrac{f^4 - g^4}{bf^2 - ag^2}$ is equal to 2s, then s =

12. Number or integral values of '$b$' for which the origin and the point $(1, 1)$ lie on the same side of the straight line $a^2x + aby + 1 = 0$, for all $a \in \mathbf{R} - \{0\}$ is

13. A straight line $L$ with negative slope passes through the points $(8, 2)$ and cuts the positive coordinate axes at points $P$ and $Q$. As $L$ varies the absolute minimum value of $OP + OQ$ is ($O$ is origin) 9t, then t =

14. If $(\sin\theta, \cos\theta)$, $\theta \in [0, 2\pi]$ and $(1, 4)$ lie on the same side or on the line $\sqrt{3}x - y + 1 = 0$, then the maximum value of $\sin\theta$ will be

15. If the lines $x = a + m$, $y = -2$ and $y = mx$ are concurrent, if the least value of $|a|$ is $\ell\sqrt{k}$, then $\ell k =$

## Section IV - Comprehension Type

Based upon the given paragraphs, 4 multiple choice questions have to be answered. Each question has 4 choices (a), (b), (c) and (d), out of which **ONLY ONE** is correct.

### PARAGRAPH-1

A triangle $ABC$ is given where vertex $A$ is $(1, 1)$ and the orthocentre is $(2, 4)$. Also sides $AB$ and $BC$ are members of the family of lines $ax + by + c = 0$ where $a, b, c$ are in $A.P$

16. The vertex $B$ is
    (a) $(2, 1)$      (b) $(1, -2)$
    (c) $(-1, 2)$      (d) $(1, 2)$

17. Triangle $ABC$ is a/an
    (a) obtuse angled triangle   (b) right angled triangle
    (c) acute angled triangle    (d) equilateral triangle

### PARAGRAPH-2

Let $ABCD$ be a parallelogram the equation of whose diagonals are $AC : x + 2y = 3; BD : 2x + y = 3$. If length of diagonal $AC = 4$ units and area of $ABCD = 8$ sq. units.

18. The length of other diagonal $BD$ is
    (a) $\dfrac{10}{3}$      (b) $2$
    (c) $\dfrac{20}{3}$      (d) $5$

19. The length of side $AB$ is equal to
    (a) $\dfrac{2\sqrt{58}}{3}$      (b) $\dfrac{2\sqrt{58}}{9}$
    (c) $\dfrac{3\sqrt{58}}{9}$      (d) $\dfrac{4\sqrt{58}}{9}$

<table>
<tr><td rowspan="4">RESPONSE GRID</td><td>11. ⓪①②③④⑤⑥⑦⑧⑨</td><td>12. ⓪①②③④⑤⑥⑦⑧⑨</td></tr>
<tr><td>13. ⓪①②③④⑤⑥⑦⑧⑨</td><td>14. ⓪①②③④⑤⑥⑦⑧⑨</td></tr>
<tr><td>15. ⓪①②③④⑤⑥⑦⑧⑨</td><td>16. ⓐⓑⓒⓓ   17. ⓐⓑⓒⓓ   18. ⓐⓑⓒⓓ</td></tr>
<tr><td>19. ⓐⓑⓒⓓ</td><td></td></tr>
</table>

*Space for Rough Work*

## Section V - Matrix-Match Type

This section contains 1 question. It contains statements given in two columns, which have to be matched. Statements in column I are labelled as A, B, C and D whereas statements in column II are labelled as p, q, r and s. The answers to these questions have to be appropriately bubbled as illustrated in the following example. If the correct matches are A-p, A-r, B-p, B-s, C-r, C-s and D-q, then the correctly bubbled matrix will look like the following:

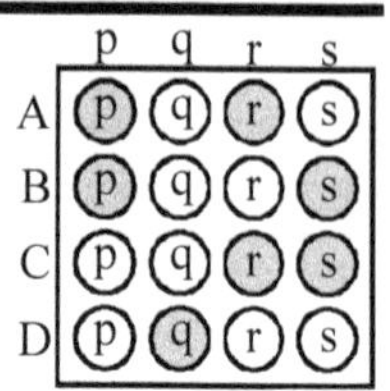

**20.** **Match the following column :**

| Column-I | Column-II |
|---|---|
| (A) If the equation $12x^2 - 10xy + 2y^2 + 11x - 5y + c = 0$ represents a pair of straight lines and $\theta$ be the angle between them, then $7|\tan\theta|$ is equal to | p. $-2$ |
| (B) If the lines $x^2 + 4xy - 2y^2 + 4x + 2fy + c^2 = 0$ intersect on the $x$-axis then $f$ is equal to | q. $2$ |
| (C) In the equation given in (C) the value of $c$ is equal to | r. $4$ |
|  | s. $1$ |

| RESPONSE GRID | 20. A - ⓟⓠⓡⓢ; B - ⓟⓠⓡⓢ; C - ⓟⓠⓡⓢ |
|---|---|

## DAILY PRACTICE PROBLEM DPP CM08 - MATHEMATICS

| Total Questions | 20 | Total Marks | 67 |
|---|---|---|---|
| Attempted |  | Correct |  |
| Incorrect |  | Net Score |  |
| Cut-off Score | 23 | Qualifying Score | 33 |

$$\text{Net Score} = \sum_{i=1}^{V} \left[ (\text{correct}_i \times MM_i) - (In_i - NM_i) \right]$$

*Space for Rough Work*

Date :        Start Time :        End Time :

# MATHEMATICS $\boxed{CM09}$

**SYLLABUS :** Conic Sections

**Max. Marks : 69**                            **Time : 60 min.**

### GENERAL INSTRUCTIONS

- The Daily Practice Problem Sheet contains 20 Questions divided into 5 sections.
  **Section I** has **6** MCQs with ONLY 1 Correct Option, **3** marks for each correct answer and **−1** for each incorrect answer.
  **Section II** has **4** MCQs with ONE or MORE THAN ONE Correct options.
  For each question, marks will be awarded in one of the following categories:
  Full marks: **+4** If only the bubble(s) corresponding to all the correct option(s) is (are) darkened.
  Partial marks: **+1** For darkening a bubble corresponding to each correct option provided NO INCORRECT option is darkened.
  Zero marks: If none of the bubbles is darkened.
  Negative marks: **−2** In all other cases.
  **Section III** has **5** Single Digit Integer Answer Type Questions, **3** marks for each Correct Answer and **0** mark in all other cases.
  **Section IV** has Comprehension Type Questions having **4** MCQs with ONLY ONE corect option, **3** marks for each Correct Answer and **0** mark in all other cases.
  **Section V** has **1** Matching Type Question, **2** marks for the correct matching of each row and **0** mark in all other cases.
- You have to evaluate your Response Grids yourself with the help of Solutions.

## Section I - Straight Objective Type

This section contains 6 multiple choice questions. Each question has 4 choices (a), (b), (c) and (d), out of which **ONLY ONE** is correct.

**1.** The value of $\alpha$ for which the points $(\alpha, \alpha + 2)$ is an interior point of the smaller segment of the circle $x^2 + y^2 - 4 = 0$ made by the chord whose equation is $3x + 4y + 12 = 0$ is

(a) $\left(-\infty, \dfrac{-20}{7}\right)$      (b) $(-2, 0)$

(c) $\left(-\infty, \dfrac{-20}{7}\right) \cup (-2, 0)$      (d) None of these

**2.** If one of two circle $x^2 + y^2 + \lambda_1(x - y) + c = 0$, and $x^2 + y^2 + \lambda_2(x - y) + c = 0$, where $\lambda_1, \lambda_2 \in R$, $\lambda_1 \neq \lambda_2$ lies within the other then

(a) $c < 0$    (b) $c = 0$    (c) $c > 0$    (d) $c \geq 0$

**3.** The condition that the parabolas $y^2 = 4ax$ and $y^2 = 4c(x - b)$ have a common normal other than $x$-axis ($a$, $b$, $c$ being distinct positive real numbers) is

(a) $\dfrac{b}{a - c} < 2$      (b) $\dfrac{b}{a - c} > 2$

(c) $\dfrac{b}{a - c} < 1$      (d) $\dfrac{b}{a - c} > 1$

**RESPONSE GRID**    **1.** ⓐⓑⓒⓓ    **2.** ⓐⓑⓒⓓ    **3.** ⓐⓑⓒⓓ

*Space for Rough Work*

**4.** If the circle $(x+c)^2 + y^2 = a^2$ and ellipse $\dfrac{(x-h)^2}{b^2} + \dfrac{y^2}{a^2} = 1$ ($a, b, c, h$ are positive) have common tangent parallel to x-axis only then

(a) $c > b + a - h$        (b) $c < b + a - h$

(c) $c > b + a$             (d) None of these

**5.** If a rectangular hyperbola $(x-1)(y-2) = 4$ cuts a circle $x^2 + y^2 + 2gx + 2fy + c = 0$ at points $(3, 4), (5, 3), (2, 6)$ and $(-1, 0)$, then the value of $(g + f)$ is equal to

(a) $-8$    (b) $-9$    (c) $8$    (d) $9$

**6.** A normal to the hyperbola $\dfrac{x^2}{4} - \dfrac{y^2}{1} = 1$, has equal intercepts on the positive $x$ and $y$ axes. If this normal touches the ellipse $\dfrac{x^2}{a^2} + \dfrac{y^2}{b^2} = 1$, then $a^2 + b^2$ is equal to

(a) $5$    (b) $25$    (c) $16$    (d) $\dfrac{25}{3}$

## Section II - Multiple Correct Answer Type

This section contains 4 multiple correct answer(s) type questions. Each question has 4 choices (a), (b), (c) and (d), out of which **ONE OR MORE** is/are correct.

**7.** The value of $\alpha$ in $[0, 2\pi]$ so that $x^2 + y^2 + 2\sqrt{\sin\alpha}\,x + (\cos\alpha - 1) = 0$ having intercept on x-axis always greater than 2 is/are

(a) $\left(\dfrac{\pi}{4}, \dfrac{\pi}{2}\right]$          (b) $\left(\dfrac{\pi}{4}, \pi\right]$

(c) $\left(\dfrac{\pi}{4}, \dfrac{5\pi}{4}\right)$        (d) $[0, \pi]$

**8.** The equation $\left|\sqrt{x^2 + (y-1)^2} - \sqrt{x^2 + (y+1)^2}\right| = K$ will represent a hyperbola for

(a) $K \in (0, 2)$        (b) $K \in (0, 1)$

(c) $K \in (1, \infty)$       (d) $K \in (0, \infty)$

**9.** If the circle $x^2 + y^2 = 1$ cuts the rectangular hyperbola $xy = 1$ in four points $(x_i, y_i)$ $i = 1, 2, 3, 4$ then.

(a) $x_1 x_2 x_3 x_4 = -1$     (b) $y_1 y_2 y_3 y_4 = 1$

(c) $x_1 + x_2 + x_3 + x_4 = 0$    (d) $y_1 + y_2 + y_3 + y_4 = 0$

**10.** If the straight line $3x + 4y = 24$ intersects the axes at $A$ and $B$ and the straight line $4x + 3y = 24$ at $C$ and $D$, then points $A, B, C, D$ lies on

(a) circle            (b) parabola

(c) ellipse           (d) hyperbola

## Section III - Integer Type

This section contains 5 questions. The answer to each of the questions is a single digit integer ranging from 0 to 9.

**11.** If the circle passing through the distinct points $(1, t), (t, 1)$ and $(t, t)$ for all values of $t \in R$ also passes through fixed point $(a, b)$ then $a^2 + b^2$ is equal to

**12.** $C$ is the centre of the hyperbola $\dfrac{x^2}{4} - \dfrac{y^2}{1} = 1$, and $'A'$ is any point on it. The tangent at A to the hyperbola meets the line $x - 2y = 0$ and $x + 2y = 0$ at $Q$ and $R$ respectively. The value of $CQ . CR$ is equal to



*Space for Rough Work*

**13.** A chord is drawn from a point $P(1, t)$ to the parabola $y^2 = 4x$ which cuts the parabola at $A$ and $B$. If $PA.PB = 3|t|$, then the maximum value of $t$ is equal to

**14.** Maximum number of common normal of $y^2 = 4ax$ and $x^2 = 4by$ may be equal to

**15.** If the sum of the squares of the lengths of the chords intercepted by the line $x + y = n$, $n \in \mathbf{N}$ on the circle $x^2 + y^2 = 4$ is 11k, then k =

## Section IV - Comprehension Type

Based upon the given paragraphs, 4 multiple choice questions have to be answered. Each question has 4 choices (a), (b), (c) and (d), out of which **ONLY ONE** is correct.

### PARAGRAPH-1

The line $x + 2y + a = 0$ intersects the circle $x^2 + y^2 - 4 = 0$ at two distinct points $A$ and $B$. Another line $12x - 6y - 41 = 0$ intersects the circle $x^2 + y^2 - 4x - 2y + 1 = 0$ at two distinct points $C$ and $D$.

**16.** The value for '$a$' so that the line $x + 2y + a = 0$ intersect the circle $x^2 + y^2 - 4 = 0$ at two distinct points $A$ and $B$ is

(a) $-2\sqrt{5} < a < 2\sqrt{5}$     (b) $0 < a < 2\sqrt{5}$

(c) $-\sqrt{5} < a < \sqrt{5}$     (d) $0 < a < 2\sqrt{5}$

**17.** The equation of circle passing through the points $A, B, C$ and $D$ is

(a) $5x^2 + 5y^2 + 8x + 16y - 36 = 0$

(b) $5x^2 + 5y^2 + 8x - 16y - 36 = 0$

(c) $5x^2 + 5y^2 - 8x - 16y - 36 = 0$

(d) $5x^2 + 5y^2 + 8x - 16y + 36 = 0$

### PARAGRAPH-2

An ellipse whose major axis is parallel to x-axis such that the segments of a focal chord are 1 and 3 units. The lines $ax + by + c = 0$ are the chords of the ellipse such that $a$, $b$, $c$, are in $AP$ and bisected by the point at which they intersent. The equation of its auxiliary circle is

$$x^2 + y^2 + 2\alpha x + 2\beta y - 2\alpha - 1 = 0 \text{ then.}$$

**18.** Equation of the director circle is

(a) $x^2 + y^2 - 2x + 4y + 1 = 0$

(b) $x^2 + y^2 + 2x + 2y - 3 = 0$

(c) $x^2 + y^2 + 2x + 4y + 1 = 0$

(d) $x^2 + y^2 - 2x + 4y - 2 = 0$

**19.** Eccentricity of ellipse is

(a) $\dfrac{\sqrt{13}}{4}$     (b) $\dfrac{1}{2}$     (c) $\dfrac{\sqrt{3}}{2}$     (d) $\dfrac{1}{\sqrt{2}}$

<table>
<tr><td rowspan="3">**RESPONSE GRID**</td><td>13. ⓪①②③④⑤⑥⑦⑧⑨</td><td>14. ⓪①②③④⑤⑥⑦⑧⑨</td><td></td></tr>
<tr><td>15. ⓪①②③④⑤⑥⑦⑧⑨</td><td>16. ⓐⓑⓒⓓ     17. ⓐⓑⓒⓓ</td><td>18. ⓐⓑⓒⓓ</td></tr>
<tr><td>19. ⓐⓑⓒⓓ</td><td></td><td></td></tr>
</table>

——————————————————— *Space for Rough Work* ———————————————————

## Section V - Matrix-Match Type

This section contains 1 question. It contains statements given in two columns, which have to be matched. Statements in column I are labelled as A, B, C and D whereas statements in column II are labelled as p, q, r and s. The answers to these questions have to be appropriately bubbled as illustrated in the following example. If the correct matches are A-p, A-r, B-p, B-s, C-r, C-s and D-q, then the correctly bubbled matrix will look like the following:

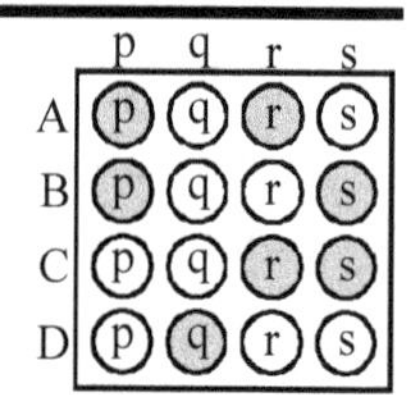

**20.** Normal to parabola $y^2 = 4x$ at points $P$ and $Q$ of parabola meet at $R\,(x_2, 0)$ and tangents at $P$ and $Q$ meets at T $(x_1, 0)$. Let $x_2 = 3$

Match the entries of two columns.

| Column – I | Column – II |
|---|---|
| (A) The area of quadrilateral $PTQR$ is | p. 3 |
| (B) If the quadrilateral PTQR can be inscribed in a circle then the value of $\dfrac{\text{circumferecnce}}{4\pi}$ is | q. 4 |
| (C) The number of nomals that can be drawn to the parabola from $R$ is | r. 1 |
| (D) The square of the length $PT$ is | s. 8 |

| RESPONSE GRID | 20. A - ⓟⓠⓡⓢ; B - ⓟⓠⓡⓢ; C - ⓟⓠⓡⓢ; D - ⓟⓠⓡⓢ |
|---|---|

## DAILY PRACTICE PROBLEM DPP CM09 - MATHEMATICS

| Total Ques! ons | 20 | Total Marks | 69 |
|---|---|---|---|
| Attempted | | Correct | |
| Incorrect | | Net Score | |
| Cut-off Score | 23 | Qualifying Score | 32 |

$$\text{Net Score} = \sum_{i=1}^{V} \left[ (\text{correct}_i \times MM_i) - (In_i - NM_i) \right]$$

*Space for Rough Work*

Date : [        ]   Start Time : [        ]   End Time : [        ]

# MATHEMATICS $\boxed{\text{CM10}}$

**SYLLABUS** : Limits and Derivatives

**Max. Marks : 72**                                              **Time : 60 min.**

### GENERAL INSTRUCTIONS

- The Daily Practice Problem Sheet contains 20 Questions divided into 5 sections.

**Section I** has **6** MCQs with ONLY 1 Correct Option, **3** marks for each correct answer and **−1** for each incorrect answer.

**Section II** has **4** MCQs with ONE or MORE THAN ONE Correct options.

For each question, marks will be awarded in one of the following categories:

Full marks: **+4** If only the bubble(s) corresponding to all the correct option(s) is (are) darkened.

Partial marks: **+1** For darkening a bubble corresponding to each correct option provided NO INCORRECT option is darkened.

Zero marks: If none of the bubbles is darkened.

Negative marks: **−2** In all other cases.

**Section III** has **4** Single Digit Integer Answer Type Questions, **3** marks for each Correct Answer and **0** mark in all other cases.

**Section IV** has Comprehension Type Questions having **4** MCQs with ONLY ONE corect option, **3** marks for each Correct Answer and **0** mark in all other cases.

**Section V** has **2** Matching Type Questions, **2** marks for the correct matching of each row and **0** mark in all other cases.

- You have to evaluate your Response Grids yourself with the help of Solutions.

## Section I - Straight Objective Type

This section contains 6 multiple choice questions. Each question has 4 choices (a), (b), (c) and (d), out of which **ONLY ONE** is correct.

**1.** For $m,\ n \in I^{+}$, $\lim\limits_{x \to 0} \dfrac{\sin x^{n}}{(\sin x)^{m}}$ is equal to

(a)  1, if $n < m$              (b)  0, if $n > m$

(c)  $n/m$                     (d)  0, if $n = m$

**2.** Let $f(x)$ be a polynomial function of second degree. If $f(a) = f(-1)$ and $a, b, c$ are in AP, then $f'(a), f'(b)$ and $f'(c)$ are in –

(a)  A P      (b)  GP      (c)  HP      (d)  AGP

**3.** If $S_n = \sum\limits_{k=1}^{n} a_k$ and $\lim\limits_{n \to \infty} a_n = a$, then

$\lim\limits_{n \to \infty} \dfrac{S_{n+1} - S_n}{\sqrt{\sum\limits_{k=1}^{n} k}}$ is equal to

(a)  0      (b)  $a$      (c)  $\sqrt{2}a$      (d)  $2a$

**4.** If A.M. of the products of all distinct pair of positive integers whose sum is $n$, is denoted by $S_n$, then the value of

$\lim\limits_{n \to \infty} \left( \dfrac{S_n}{n^2} \right)$ is equal to

(a)  1/6                          (b)  1/4

(c)   1/12                    (d)   None of these

**5.** If $\phi(x)$ be a polynomial function of the second degree. If $\phi(1) = \phi(-1)$ and $a_1, a_2, a_3$ are in AP, then $\phi'(a_1), \phi'(a_2), \phi'(a_3)$ are in

(a)   AP                  (b)   GP

(c)   HP                  (d)   None of these

**6.** Let $a = \min\{x^2 + 2x + 3, x \in R\}$ and

$$b = \lim_{\theta \to 0} \frac{1 - \cos\theta}{\theta^2}.$$ The value of $\sum_{r=0}^{n} a^r \cdot b^{n-r}$ is

(a)   $\dfrac{2^{n+1} - 1}{3 \cdot 2^n}$         (b)   $\dfrac{2^{n+1} + 1}{3 \cdot 2^n}$

(c)   $\dfrac{4^{n+1} - 1}{3 \cdot 2^n}$         (d)   None of these

## Section II - Multiple Correct Answer Type

This section contains 4 multiple correct answer(s) type questions. Each question has 4 choices (a), (b), (c) and (d), out of which **ONE OR MORE** is/are correct.

**7.** $f(x) = |x^2 - 3|x| + 2|$, then which of the following is/are true

(a)   $f'(x) = 2x - 3$ for $x \in (0, 1) \cup (2, \infty)$

(b)   $f'(x) = 2x + 3$ for $x \in (-\infty, -2) \cup (-1, 0)$

(c)   $f'(x) = -2x - 3$ for $x \in (-2, -1)$

(d)   None of these

**8.** $f(x) = \lim_{n \to \infty} \dfrac{x}{x^{2n} + 1}$, then

(a)   $f(1^+) + f(1^-) = 0$

(b)   $f(1^+) + f(1^-) + f(1) = 3/2$

(c)   $f(-1^+) + f(-1^{-1}) = -1$

(d)   $f(1^+) + f(-1^{-1}) = 0$

**9.** If $\lim_{x \to 1}(2 - x + a[x - 1] + b[1 + x])$ exists, then $a$ and $b$ can take the values (where [.] denotes the greatest integer function)

(a)   $a = 1/3, b = 1$       (b)   $a = 1, b = -1$

(c)   $a = 9, b = -9$       (d)   $a = 2, b = 2/3$

**10.** Let $f(x) = \lim_{n \to \infty} \dfrac{x^{2n} - 1}{x^{2n} + 1}$, then

(a)   $f(x) = 1$ for $|x| > 1$

(b)   $f(x) = -1$ for $|x| < 1$

(c)   $f(x)$ is not defined for any value of $x$

(d)   $f(x) = 1$ for $|x| = 1$

## Section III - Integer Type

This section contains 4 questions. The answer to each of the questions is a single digit integer ranging from 0 to 9.

**11.** Find the sum of all the values of n for which $f'(x + y) + 1 = f'(x) + f'(y)$ holds where $f(x) = x^n + x$ ($n$ : whole number)

**12.** Find the value of $\lim_{x \to 0} \left[ \dfrac{\sin(\mathrm{sgn}(x))}{(\mathrm{sgn}(x))} \right]$, where [.] denotes the greatest integer function.

**13.** Find the value of $\lim_{x \to \infty} \dfrac{-\ln x^n + [x]}{[x]}$, where $n \in N$ and [ . ] denotes the greatest integer function.

**14.** If $y = (1 + x)(1 + x^2)(1 + x^4)\dots\dots(1 + x^{2^n})$, then find the value of $\dfrac{dy}{dx}$ at $x = 0$.

<table>
<tr><td rowspan="3">RESPONSE<br>GRID</td><td>5. ⓐⓑⓒⓓ</td><td>6. ⓐⓑⓒⓓ</td><td>7. ⓐⓑⓒⓓ</td><td>8. ⓐⓑⓒⓓ</td><td>9. ⓐⓑⓒⓓ</td></tr>
<tr><td>10. ⓐⓑⓒⓓ</td><td colspan="2">11. ⓪①②③④⑤⑥⑦⑧⑨</td><td colspan="2">12. ⓪①②③④⑤⑥⑦⑧⑨</td></tr>
<tr><td colspan="2">13. ⓪①②③④⑤⑥⑦⑧⑨</td><td colspan="3">14. ⓪①②③④⑤⑥⑦⑧⑨</td></tr>
</table>

*Space for Rough Work*

## Section IV - Comprehension Type

Based upon the given paragraphs, 4 multiple choice questions have to be answered. Each question has 4 choices (a), (b), (c) and (d), out of which **ONLY ONE** is correct.

### PARAGRAPH-1

If $L = \lim\limits_{x \to 0} \dfrac{\sin x + ae^{x} + be^{-x} + c\ln(1+x)}{x^{3}} \neq \infty$

**15.** The value of $L$ is

(a)  1/2  
(b)  $-1/3$  
(c)  $-1/6$  
(d)  3

**16.** The solution set of $\| x + c| - 2a| < 4b$ is

(a)  $[-2, 2]$  
(b)  $[0, 2]$  
(c)  $[-1, 1]$  
(d)  $[-2, 1]$

### PARAGRAPH-2

$AP$ is a diameter of a unit circle with centre at $O$. Let $AC$ be an arc of this circle, which subtends angle $\theta$ radian at centre $O$. A tangent line is drawn to the circle at the point $A$ and a segment $AB$ on this tangent is laid off whose length is equal to that of the arc $AC$. A straight line $BC$ is drawn to intersect the extension of the diameter $AP$ at $Q$. $CD$ is the perpendicular let fall from the point $C$ upon the diameter $AP$.

**17.** The area of the trapezoid $ABCD$ is

(a)  $\dfrac{1 - \cos\theta}{\theta - \sin\theta}$  
(b)  $(\theta + \sin\theta)\sin^{2}\dfrac{\theta}{2}$  

(c)  $2\cos^{2}\dfrac{\theta}{2}(\theta - \sin\theta)$  
(d)  $\theta(\theta + \sin\theta)$

**18.** The value of the limit $\lim\limits_{\theta \to 0^{+}} (AQ)$ is

(a)  0  
(b)  1  
(c)  2  
(d)  3

## Section V - Matrix-Match Type

This section contains 2 questions. It contains statements given in two columns, which have to be matched. Statements in column I are labelled as A, B, C and D whereas statements in column II are labelled as p, q, r and s. The answers to these questions have to be appropriately bubbled as illustrated in the following example. If the correct matches are A-p, A-r, B-p, B-s, C-r, C-s and D-q, then the correctly bubbled matrix will look like the following:

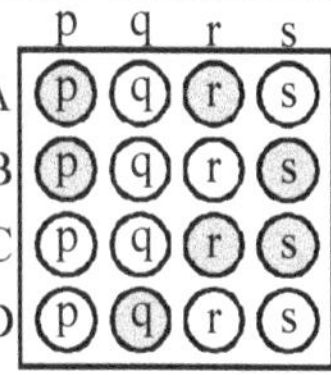

**19.**

| Column-I | Column-II |
|---|---|
| (A) If $\lim\limits_{x \to \infty} (\sqrt{(x^{2} - x - 1)} - ax - b) = 0$, where $a > 0$, then there exists at least one a and b for which point $(a, 2b)$ lies on the line. | (p)  $y = -3$ |
| (B) If $\lim\limits_{x \to \infty} \dfrac{(1 + a^{3}) + 8e^{1/x}}{1 + (1 - b^{3})e^{1/x}} = 2$, then there exists at least one $a$ and $b$ for which point $(a, b^{3})$ lies on the line | (q)  $3x - 2y - 5 = 0$ |



*Space for Rough Work*

(C)   If $\lim_{x\to\infty}(\sqrt{(x^4-x^2+1)}-ax^2-b)=0$, then      (r)   $15x-2y-11=0$

     there exists at least one $a$ and $b$ for which point $(a,-2b)$ lies on the line

(D)   If $\lim_{x\to-a}\dfrac{x^7+a^7}{x+a}=7$, where $a<0$, then      (s)   $y=2$

     there exists at least one $a$ for which point $(a,2)$ lies on the line

**20.**     **Column-I**                                         **Column-II**

(A)   If $f(x)=\left(\dfrac{|x|}{|x|+2}\right)^{-x}$, then      (p)   $\lim_{x\to\infty}f(x)=e^2$

(B)   If $f(x)=\dfrac{(1+x)^{1/x}-e}{x}$, then      (q)   $\lim_{x\to 0}f(x)=e^2$

(C)   If $f(x)=\left(\dfrac{1+5x^2}{1+3x^2}\right)^{1/x^2}$, then      (r)   $\lim_{x\to-\infty}f(x)=e^{-2}$

                                            (s)   $\lim_{x\to 0}f(x)=-e/2$,

                                            (t)   $\lim_{x\to 0}f(x)<-1$

| RESPONSE GRID | 20. A - ⓟⓠⓡⓢ; B - ⓟⓠⓡⓢ; C - ⓟⓠⓡⓢ; D - ⓟⓠⓡⓢ |
| --- | --- |

## DAILY PRACTICE PROBLEM DPP CM10 - MATHEMATICS

| Total Questions | 20 | Total Marks | 72 |
| --- | --- | --- | --- |
| Attempted | | Correct | |
| Incorrect | | Net Score | |
| Cut-off Score | 25 | Qualifying Score | 36 |

$$\text{Net Score} = \sum_{i=1}^{V}\left[(\text{correct}_i \times MM_i)-(In_i-NM_i)\right]$$

*Space for Rough Work*

Date : 　　　　　　　　Start Time : 　　　　　　　　End Time :

# MATHEMATICS $\boxed{\text{CM11}}$

**SYLLABUS :** Mathematical Reasoning

**Max. Marks : 76**　　　　　　　　　　　　　　　　　　**Time : 60 min.**

### GENERAL INSTRUCTIONS

- The Daily Practice Problem Sheet contains 20 Questions divided into 3 sections.
  **Section I** has **8** MCQs with ONLY 1 Correct Option, **3** marks for each correct answer and **−1** for each incorrect answer.
  **Section II** has **11** MCQs with ONE or MORE THAN ONE Correct options.
  For each question, marks will be awarded in one of the following categories:
  Full marks: **+4** If only the bubble(s) corresponding to all the correct option(s) is (are) darkened.
  Partial marks: **+1** For darkening a bubble corresponding to each correct option provided NO INCORRECT option is darkened.
  Zero marks:　If none of the bubbles is darkened.
  Negative marks: **−2** In all other cases.
  **Section III** has **1** Matching Type Question, **2** marks for the correct matching of each row and **0** mark in all other cases.
- You have to evaluate your Response Grids yourself with the help of Solutions.

## Section I - Straight Objective Type

This section contains 8 multiple choice questions. Each question has 4 choices (a), (b), (c) and (d), out of which **ONLY ONE** is correct.

1. $\sim(p \Rightarrow q) \Leftrightarrow \sim p \vee \sim q$ is

   (a)　A tautology

   (b)　A contradiction

   (c)　Neither a tautology nor a contradiction

   (d)　Cannot come to any conclusion

2. The inverse of the statement $(p \wedge \sim q) \to r$ is

   (a)　$\sim(p \vee \sim q) \to \sim r$　　　(b)　$(\sim p \wedge q) \to \sim r$

   (c)　$(\sim p \vee q) \to \sim r$　　　(d)　None of these

3. Let f be a function from a set X to a set Y. Consider the following statements:

   P :　For each $x \in X$, there exists unique $y \in Y$ such that $f(x) = y$

   Q :　For each $y \in Y$, there exists $x \in X$ such that $f(x) = y$.

   R :　There exist $x_1, x_2 \in X$ such that $x_1 \neq x_2$ and $f(x_1) = f(x_2)$.

   The negation of the statement "f is one-to-one and onto" is

   (a)　P or not R　　　　　(b)　R or not P

   (c)　R or not Q　　　　　(d)　P and not R

4. The contrapositive of $p \to (\sim q \to \sim r)$ is –

   (a)　$(\sim q \wedge r) \to \sim p$　　　(b)　$(q \to r) \to \sim p$

   (c)　$(q \vee \sim r) \to \sim p$　　　(d)　None of these

---

**RESPONSE GRID**　　1. ⓐⓑⓒⓓ　　2. ⓐⓑⓒⓓ　　3. ⓐⓑⓒⓓ　　4. ⓐⓑⓒⓓ

**5.** If $S^*(p, q, r)$ is the dual of the compound statement $S(p,q,r)$ and $S(p,q,r) = \sim p \wedge [\sim (q \vee r)]$ then $S^*(\sim p, \sim q, \sim r)$ is equivalent to –

   (a)   $S(p, q, r)$             (b)   $\sim S(\sim p, \sim q, \sim r)$

   (c)   $\sim S(p, q, r)$           (d)   $S^*(p, q, r)$

**6.** $\sim(p \to q) \to [(\sim p) \vee (\sim q)]$ is

   (a)   a tautology

   (b)   a contradiction

   (c)   neither a tautology nor contradicion

   (d)   cannot come any conclusion.

**7.** The statement $p \to (q \to p)$ is equivalent to

   (a)   $p \to (p \to q)$       (b)   $p \to (p \vee q)$

   (c)   $p \to (p \wedge q)$       (d)   $p \to (p \leftrightarrow q)$

**8.** In the truth table for the statement $(p \to q) \leftrightarrow (\sim P \vee q)$, the last column has the truth value in the following order is

   (a)   TTFF              (b)   FFFF

   (c)   TTTT              (d)   FTFT

## Section II - Multiple Correct Answer Type

This section contains 11 multiple correct answer(s) type questions. Each question has 4 choices (a), (b), (c) and (d), out of which **ONE OR MORE** is/are correct.

**9.** Let p, q and r be any three logical statements. Which of the following are not correct?

   (a)   $\sim [p \wedge (\sim q)] \equiv (\sim p) \wedge q$

   (b)   $\sim [(p \vee q) \wedge (\sim r)] \equiv (\sim p) \vee (\sim q) \vee (\sim r)$

   (c)   $\sim [p \vee (\sim q)] \equiv (\sim p) \wedge q$

   (d)   $\sim [p \vee (\sim q)] \equiv (\sim p) \wedge \sim q$

**10.** If $p$ and $q$ are two statement then $(p \leftrightarrow \sim q)$ is true when –

   (a)   $p$ and $q$ both are true

   (b)   $p$ and $q$ both are false

   (c)   $p$ is false and $q$ is true

   (d)   $p$ is true and $q$ is flase

**11.** Identify the correct statements

   (a)   $\sim [p \vee (\sim q)] \equiv (\sim p) \vee q$

   (b)   $[p \vee q] \vee (\sim p)$ is a tautology

   (c)   $[p \wedge q) \wedge (\sim p)$ is a contradiction

   (d)   $\sim [p \vee q] \equiv (\sim p) \vee (\sim q)$

**12.** Which of the following statements are tautology?

   (a)   $(\sim p \vee \sim q) \vee (p \vee \sim q)$   (b)   $(p \to q) \vee (p \wedge \sim q)$

   (c)   $(\sim p \wedge q) \wedge (\sim q)$      (d)   $(\sim p \wedge q) \vee (\sim q)$



*Space for Rough Work*

13. Which of the following are correct?

    (a)  $p \vee \sim p$ is a tautology

    (b)  $\sim(\sim p) \leftrightarrow p$ is a tautology

    (c)  $p \wedge \sim p$ is a contradiction

    (d)  $((p \wedge q) \to q) \to p$ is a tautology

14. If p is any statement, t is tautology and c is a contradiction, then which of the following are correct?

    (a)  $p \vee (\sim p) = c$      (b)  $p \vee t = t$

    (c)  $p \wedge t = p$      (d)  $p \wedge c = c.$

15. Dual of following statement are given which are correct?

    (a)  $(p \vee q) \wedge (r \vee s), (p \wedge q) \vee (r \wedge s)$

    (b)  $[p \vee (\sim q) \wedge (\sim p), [p \wedge (\sim q)] \vee (\sim p)$

    (c)  $(p \wedge q) \vee r, (p \vee q) \wedge r$

    (d)  $(p \vee q) \vee s, \wedge (p \wedge q) \vee s.$

16. Which of the following are incorrect?

    (a)  $(\sim p \Rightarrow q) = \sim q \Rightarrow \sim p$

    (b)  $(\sim p \vee q) \equiv \vee p \vee \sim q$

    (c)  $\sim(p \Rightarrow q) \equiv p \wedge \sim q$

    (d)  $\sim(p \vee q) \equiv \sim p \wedge \sim q$

17. Which of the following is not true for the statements p and q ?

    (a)  $p \wedge q$ is true when at least one of $p$ and $q$ is true

    (b)  $p \to q$ is true when $p$ is true and $q$ is false

    (c)  $p \leftrightarrow q$ is true only when both $p$ and $q$ are true

    (d)  $\sim(p \vee q)$ is true only when both $p$ and $q$ are false

18. Which of the following are correct?

    (a)  $p \to q$ is logically equivalent to $\sim p \vee q$

    (b)  If the truth values of $p, q, r$ are T, F, T respectively, then the truth value of $(p \vee q) \wedge (q \vee r)$ is T

    (c)  $\sim(p \vee q \vee r) \cong \sim p \wedge \sim q \wedge \sim r$

    (d)  The truth value of $p \wedge \sim (p \vee q)$ is always T.

19. Which of the following are not true?

    (a)  $(\sim p \vee \sim q) \equiv (p \wedge q)$

    (b)  $(p \to q) \equiv (\sim q \to \sim p)$

    (c)  $\sim(p \to \sim q) \equiv (p \wedge \sim q)$

    (d)  $\sim(p \leftrightarrow q) \equiv (p \to q) \to (q \to p)$



*Space for Rough Work*

## Section III - Matrix-Match Type

This section contains 1 question. It contains statements given in two columns, which have to be matched. Statements in column I are labelled as A, B, C and D whereas statements in column II are labelled as p, q, r and s. The answers to these questions have to be appropriately bubbled as illustrated in the following example. If the correct matches are A-p, A-r, B-p, B-s, C-r, C-s and D-q, then the correctly bubbled matrix will look like the following:

**20.** **Match the followings:**

| Column-I | | Column-II |
|---|---|---|
| (A) Dual of statement $[(p \vee q) \wedge (\sim q)] \vee (\sim p)$ | p. | $[p \wedge \sim q] \vee (\sim p)$ |
| (B) Logically equivalent of $[(p \vee q) \wedge (\sim q)] \vee (\sim p)$ | q. | $[(\sim p \wedge \sim q) \vee q] \wedge p$ |
| (C) Negation of $[(p \vee q) \wedge (\sim q)] \vee (\sim p)$ | r. | $[(\sim p \wedge \sim q) \vee q] \vee (\sim p)$ |
| (D) Contrapositive of $[(p \vee q) \wedge (\sim q)] \to (\sim p)$ | s. | $[(p \wedge q) \vee \sim q] \wedge (\sim p)$ |

**RESPONSE GRID**    20. A - ⓅⓆⓇⓈ; B - ⓅⓆⓇⓈ; C - ⓅⓆⓇⓈ; D - ⓅⓆⓇⓈ

## DAILY PRACTICE PROBLEM DPP CM11 - MATHEMATICS

| Total Questions | 20 | Total Marks | 76 |
|---|---|---|---|
| Attempted | | Correct | |
| Incorrect | | Net Score | |
| Cut-off Score | 27 | Qualifying Score | 38 |

$$\text{Net Score} = \sum_{i=1}^{V} \left[ \left(\text{correct}_i \times MM_i\right) - \left(In_i - NM_i\right) \right]$$

*Space for Rough Work*

Date :      Start Time :      End Time :

# MATHEMATICS CM12

SYLLABUS : Statistics

**Max. Marks : 69**      **Time : 60 min.**

## GENERAL INSTRUCTIONS

- The Daily Practice Problem Sheet contains 20 Questions divided into 5 sections.
  **Section I** has **7** MCQs with ONLY 1 Correct Option, **3** marks for each correct answer and **−1** for each incorrect answer.
  **Section II** has **4** MCQs with ONE or MORE THAN ONE Correct options.
  For each question, marks will be awarded in one of the following categories:
  Full marks: **+4** If only the bubble(s) corresponding to all the correct option(s) is (are) darkened.
  Partial marks: **+1** For darkening a bubble corresponding to each correct option provided NO INCORRECT option is darkened.
  Zero marks: If none of the bubbles is darkened.
  Negative marks: **−2** In all other cases.
  **Section III** has **6** Single Digit Integer Answer Type Questions, **3** marks for each Correct Answer and **0** mark in all other cases.
  **Section IV** has Comprehension Type Questions having **2** MCQs with ONLY ONE corect option, **3** marks for each Correct Answer and **0** marks in all other cases.
  **Section V** has **1** Matching Type Question, **2** marks for the correct matching of each row and **0** mark in all other cases.
- You have to evaluate your Response Grids yourself with the help of Solutions.

## Section I - Straight Objective Type

This section contains 7 multiple choice questions. Each question has 4 choices (a), (b), (c) and (d), out of which **ONLY ONE** is correct.

**1.** In a series of $2n$ observations, half of them equals '$a$' and remaining equals '$-a$'. If S.D. is 2, then $|a|$ equals

(a) $\dfrac{1}{n}$      (b) $\sqrt{2}$

(c) $2$      (d) $\dfrac{\sqrt{2}}{n}$

**2.** For $(2n+1)$ observations $x_1, -x_1, x_2, -x_2, \ldots\ldots x_n, -x_n$ and $0$ where $x$'s are all distinct. Let S.D. and M.D. denote the standard deviation and median respectively. Then which of the following is always true?

(a) S.D $<$ M.D.

(b) S.D $>$ M.D.

(c) S.D $=$ M.D.

(d) Nothing can be said in general about the relationship of S.D. and M.D.



*Space for Rough Work*

**3.** The standard deviation of 25 numbers is 40. If each of the number is increased by 5, then the new standard deviation is

(a) 40

(b) 45

(c) $40 + \dfrac{21}{25}$

(d) $40 - \dfrac{21}{25}$

**4.** If $\sum_{i=1}^{9}(x_i - 5) = 9$ and $\sum_{i=1}^{9}(x_i - 5)^2 = 45$, then the standard deviation of the 9 items $x_1, x_2, ...., x_9$ is

(a) 9

(b) 4

(c) 3

(d) 2

**5.** Two variables X and U are related by the relationship $X = 5 + 2U$. The mean and the coefficient of variation of X are 10 and 2.6 respectively. The coefficient of variation of the variable U is

(a) 5.2

(b) 2.6

(c) 1.3

(d) 52

**6.** The mean deviation from the mean of the A.P.

$a, a+d, a+2d, ........ a, a+2nd$ is

(a) $n(n+1)d$

(b) $\dfrac{n(n+1)d}{2n+1}$

(c) $\dfrac{n(n+1)d}{2n}$

(d) $\dfrac{n(n-1)d}{2n+1}$

**7.** The variance of first $n$ natural numbers is

(a) $\dfrac{n^2+1}{12}$

(b) $\dfrac{n^2-1}{12}$

(c) $\dfrac{(n+1)(2n+1)}{6}$

(d) $\left[\dfrac{n(n+1)}{2}\right]^2$

## Section II - Multiple Correct Answer Type

This section contains 4 multiple correct answer(s) type questions. Each question has 4 choices (a), (b), (c) and (d), out of which **ONE OR MORE** is/are correct.

**8.** The mean of the numbers $a, b, 8, 5, 10$ is 6 and the variance is 6.80. Then which one of the following gives possible values of $a$ and $b$ ?

(a) $a = 0, b = 7$

(b) $a = 4, b = 3$

(c) $a = 1, b = 6$

(d) $a = 3, b = 4$

**9.** The mean of five observations is 4 and their variance is 5.2. If three of these observations are 2, 4 and 6, then the other two observations are

(a) 3 and 5

(b) 2 and 6

(c) 5 and 5

(d) 1 and 7

**10.** Let $x_1, x_2, .......... x_n$ be n observations such that $\sum x_i^2 = 400$ and $\sum x_i = 80$. Then the possible value of $n$ among the following is

(a) 15

(b) 18

(c) 20

(d) 12



*Space for Rough Work*

11. If the standard deviation of the numbers 2, 3, a and 11 is 3.5, then which of the following is true?

    (a) Sum of possible values of a is less than 11.

    (b) Difference of possible values of a is greater than 1.

    (c) Product of possible values of a is 28.

    (d) Each possible value of a is less than or equal to 6.

## Section III - Integer Type

This section contains 6 questions. The answer to each of the questions is a single digit integer ranging from 0 to 9.

12. The standard deviation of 9, 16, 23, 30, 37, 44, 51 is $k + 10$ where $k =$

13. If the variance of 1, 2, 3, 4, 5, ..., 10 is $\dfrac{99}{12}$, then the standard deviation of 3, 6, 9, 12, ..., 30 is $\dfrac{3}{2}\sqrt{30 + m}$ where $m =$

14. Let a, b, c, d and e be the observations with mean m and standard deviation s. The standard deviation of the observations $a + k$, $b + k$, $c + k$, $d + k$ and $e + k$ is $s + k\,\alpha$ where $\alpha =$

15. If M. D. is 12, the value of S.D. will be $20 - p$ where, $p =$

16. Consider the following frequency distribution

| x | A | 2A | 3A | 4A | 5A | 6A |
|---|---|----|----|----|----|----|
| f | 2 | 1  | 1  | 1  | 1  | 1  |

    where, A is a positive integer and has variance 160. Then the value of A is

17. Consider the following data.
    36, 72, 46, 42, 60, 45, 53, 46, 51, 49
    Then the mean deviation about the median for the data is

## Section IV - Comprehension Type

Based upon the given paragraph, 2 multiple choice questions have to be answered. Each question has 4 choices (a), (b), (c) and (d), out of which **ONLY ONE** is correct.

### PARAGRAPH

Let $\bar{x}$ and $\sigma^2$ be respectively the mean and variance of n observations $x_1, x_2, ..., x_n$ and $d_i = -x_i; -a$, $i = 1, 2, ....n$, where a is any numbers.

18. Variance of $d_1, d_2, .... d_n$ is :

    (a) $\sigma^2 - a$       (b) $\sigma^2$

    (c) $\sigma^2 + a$       (d) $2\sigma^2$

19. variance of first n even natural numbers is :

    (a) $n^2$       (b) $n^2 - 1$

    (c) $\dfrac{n^2 - 1}{3}$       (d) $\dfrac{n^2 - 1}{4}$



──────────── *Space for Rough Work* ────────────

## Section V - Matrix-Match Type

This section contains 1 question. It contains statements given in two columns, which have to be matched. Statements in column I are labelled as A, B, C and D whereas statements in column II are labelled as p, q, r and s. The answers to these questions have to be appropriately bubbled as illustrated in the following example. If the correct matches are A-p, A-r, B-p, B-s, C-r, C-s and D-q, then the correctly bubbled matrix will look like the following:

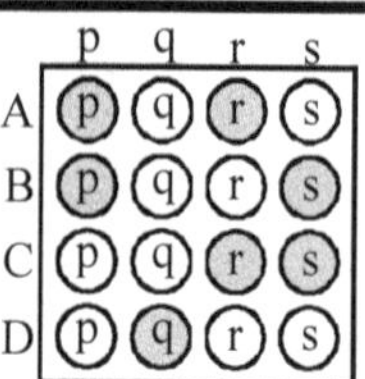

**20.**

**Column - I**

(A) Mean deviation about the median for the data 3, 9, 5, 3, 12, 10, 18, 4, 7, 19, 21, is

(B) Mean deviation about the median for the data 13, 17, 16, 14, 11, 13, 10, 16, 11, 18, 12, 17, is

(C) The standard deviation of n observations $x_1, x_2, \ldots, x_n$ is given by

(D) The coefficient of variation (CV) is defined as

**Column - II**

p. $\dfrac{\sigma}{\bar{x}} \times 100$

q. $\sqrt{\dfrac{1}{n}\sum_{i=1}^{n}\left(x_i - \bar{x}\right)^2}$

r. 2.33

s. 5.27

---

**RESPONSE GRID**

20. A - (p)(q)(r)(s); B - (p)(q)(r)(s); C - (p)(q)(r)(s); D - (p)(q)(r)(s)

---

## DAILY PRACTICE PROBLEM DPP CM12 - MATHEMATICS

| Total Questions | 20 | Total Marks | 67 |
|---|---|---|---|
| Attempted | | Correct | |
| Incorrect | | Net Score | |
| Cut-off Score | 27 | Qualifying Score | 38 |

$$\text{Net Score} = \sum_{i=1}^{V}\left[\left(correct_i \times MM_i\right) - \left(In_i - NM_i\right)\right]$$

*Space for Rough Work*

Date :       Start Time :       End Time :

# MATHEMATICS $\boxed{\text{CM13}}$

**SYLLABUS : Probability**

**Max. Marks : 69**           **Time : 60 min.**

## GENERAL INSTRUCTIONS

- The Daily Practice Problem Sheet contains 20 Questions divided into 5 sections.
  **Section I** has **6** MCQs with ONLY 1 Correct Option, **3** marks for each correct answer and **−1** for each incorrect answer.
  **Section II** has **4** MCQs with ONE or MORE THAN ONE Correct options.
  For each question, marks will be awarded in one of the following categories:
  Full marks: **+4** If only the bubble(s) corresponding to all the correct option(s) is (are) darkened.
  Partial marks: **+1** For darkening a bubble corresponding to each correct option provided NO INCORRECT option is darkened.
  Zero marks:  If none of the bubbles is darkened.
  Negative marks: **−2** In all other cases.
  **Section III** has **5** Single Digit Integer Answer Type Questions, **3** marks for each Correct Answer and **0** marks in all other cases.
  **Section IV** has Comprehension Type Questions having **4** MCQs with ONLY ONE corect option, **3** marks for each Correct Answer and **0** mark in all other cases.
  **Section V** has **1** Matching Type Question, **2** marks for the correct matching of each row and **0** mark in all other cases.
- You have to evaluate your Response Grids yourself with the help of Solutions.

## Section I - Straight Objective Type

This section contains 6 multiple choice questions. Each question has 4 choices (a), (b), (c) and (d), out of which **ONLY ONE** is correct.

**1.** A die is rolled three times, the probability of getting a larger number than the previous number is :

(a) $\dfrac{5}{216}$    (b) $\dfrac{5}{54}$    (c) $\dfrac{1}{6}$    (d) $\dfrac{5}{36}$

**2.** A natural number $x$ is chosen at random from the first 100 natural numbers. The probability that $\dfrac{x^2 - 60x + 800}{x - 30} < 0$ is

(a) $\dfrac{3}{25}$    (b) $\dfrac{1}{50}$    (c) $\dfrac{7}{25}$    (d) $\dfrac{3}{50}$

**3.** If $p$ is chosen at random in the closed interval $[0, 5]$, then the pobability that the equation $x^2 + px + \dfrac{1}{4}(p+2) = 0$ has real roots is

(a) $\dfrac{1}{2}$    (b) $\dfrac{1}{4}$    (c) $\dfrac{3}{5}$    (d) $\dfrac{2}{5}$

**4.** Out of $3n$ consecutive integers, three are selected at random. The chance that their sum is divisible by 3 is

(a) $\dfrac{3n^2 - 3n + 2}{(3n-1)(3n-2)}$      (b) $\dfrac{3n^2 - 3n + 2}{n(3n-1)(3n-2)}$

(c) $\dfrac{n^3}{(3n-1)(n-2)(n-3)}$      (d) None of these

| RESPONSE GRID | 1. ⓐⓑⓒⓓ | 2. ⓐⓑⓒⓓ | 3. ⓐⓑⓒⓓ | 4. ⓐⓑⓒⓓ |

*Space for Rough Work*

**5.** The probablilty that the length of a randomly chosen chord of a circle lies between $\dfrac{2}{3}$ and $\dfrac{5}{6}$ of its diameter is

(a) $\dfrac{5}{16}$  (b) $\dfrac{1}{16}$

(c) $\dfrac{1}{4}$  (d) $\dfrac{5}{12}$

**6.** 10 persons sit around a circular table with 10 numbered chairs. The probability that the two particular persons $A$ and $B$ are always together is

(a) $\dfrac{2}{9}$  (b) $\dfrac{1}{5}$

(c) $\dfrac{1}{9}$  (d) $\dfrac{2}{5}$

---

## Section II - Multiple Correct Answer Type

This section contains 4 multiple correct answer(s) type questions. Each question has 4 choices (a), (b), (c) and (d), out of which **ONE OR MORE** is/are correct.

---

**7.** A square in inscribed in a circle. If $p_1$ is the probability that a randomly chosen point of the circle lies within the square and $p_2$ is the probability that the point lies outside the square, then

(a) $p_1 = p_2$  (b) $p_1 > p_2$

(c) $p_1 < p_2$  (d) $p_1^2 - p_2^2 < \dfrac{1}{3}$

**8.** If $\dfrac{1+4p}{4}, \dfrac{1-p}{4}, \dfrac{1-2p}{4}$ are probabilities of three mutually exclusive and exhaustive events, then the possible values of $p$ belong to the set

(a) $\left(0, \dfrac{2}{3}\right)$  (b) $\left[0, \dfrac{1}{2}\right]$

(c) $\left[-\dfrac{1}{4}, \dfrac{1}{2}\right]$  (d) $\left[-\dfrac{2}{3}, \dfrac{2}{3}\right]$

**9.** The probabilities of three events $A$, $B$ and $C$ are $P(A) = 0.6$, $P(B) = 0.4$ and $P(C) = 0.5$. If $P(A \cup B) = 0.8$, $P(A \cap C) = 0.3$, $P(A \cap B \cap C) = 0.2$ and $P(A \cup B \cup C) \geq 0.85$. Then

(a) $P(A \cap B) < 0.35$  (b) $P(B \cap C) \geq 0.2$

(c) $P(B \cap C) \leq 0.35$  (d) $P(A \cap B) > 0.25$

**10.** There is a key-ring which has 'n' keys of which only one is the right key of the lock. A person tries to open the lock at random. If he discards the key already tried, and the probability that he opens the lock at $k^{\text{th}}$ trial is P then which all statements are correct?

(a) P is less than k/n  (b) P is independent of k

(c) $1/n \leq P \leq k/n$  (d) P = k/2n

---



*Space for Rough Work*

## Section III - Integer Type

This section contains 5 questions. The answer to each of the questions is a single digit integer ranging from 0 to 9.

11. Two friends Ankur and Rahul have equal number of sons. There are only 3 mangoes which are to be distributed among the sons. The probability that 2 mangoes go to the sons of the one friend and one mango to the son of the other is 6/7. Find how many sons each of the two friends have

12. A bag contains four tickets with numbers 00, 01, 10, 11. A ticket is drawn and replaced. In this way five tickets are drawn. If the probability that the sum of the number on the ticket drawn is 23 is P. then find $[\dfrac{1}{10p}]$ here [.] is greatest integer function.

13. Arti and Bharti are two candidates seeking admission in I.I.T. The probability that Arti is selected is 0.5 and the probability that both Arti and Bharti are selected is at most 0.3. If probability of Bharti getting selected P then find the maximum possible value of 10P.

14. 5 girls and 10 boys sit at random in a row having 15 chairs numbered as 1 to 15. If the probability that the end seats are occupied by the girls and between any two girls odd number of boys take seat is $\dfrac{20}{n}$, then $\dfrac{n}{1001}$ is equal to

15. A fair coin is tossed 15 times. If the probability of getting head as many times in the first ten throw as in the last five is $k$, then $\dfrac{32768k}{1001}$ is equal to.

## Section IV - Comprehension Type

Based upon the given paragraphs, 4 multiple choice questions have to be answered. Each question has 4 choices (a), (b), (c) and (d), out of which **ONLY ONE** is correct.

### PARAGRAPH-1

There are two dice $A$ and $B$ both having six faces. Die $A$ has 3 faces marked with 1, 2 faces marked with 2 and 1 face marked with 3. Die $B$ has 1 face marked with 1, 2 faces marked with 2 and 3 faces marked with 3. Both dice are thrown randomly once. If $E$ be the event of getting sum of the numbers appearing on top faces equal to $x$ and let $P(E)$ be the probability of event $E$, then

16. $P(E)$ is maximum when $x$ equals to

    (a)  5               (b)  3
    (c)  4               (d)  6

17. $P(E)$ is minimun when $x$ equals to

    (a)  3               (b)  4
    (c)  5               (d)  6

### PARAGRAPH-2

If the squares of a $8 \times 8$ chess board are painted either red or black at random.

18. The probability that not all squares is any column are alternating in colour is

    (a)  $\left(1-\dfrac{1}{2^7}\right)^8$        (b)  $\dfrac{1}{2^{56}}$

    (c)  $1-\dfrac{1}{2^7}$              (d)  none of these



*Space for Rough Work*

**19.** The probability that the chess board contains equal number of red and black squares is

(a) $\dfrac{^{64}C_{32}}{2^{64}}$ 　　(b) $\dfrac{\lfloor 64}{2^{64}\lfloor 32}$ 　　(c) $\dfrac{2^{32}-1}{2^{64}}$ 　　(d) None of these

---

## Section V - Matrix-Match Type

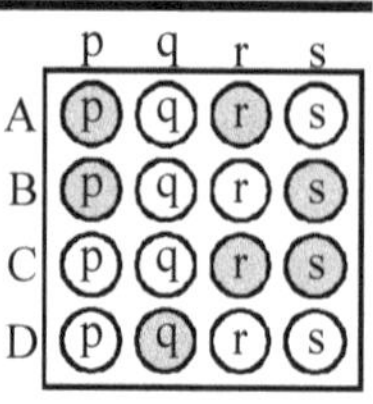

This section contains 1 question. It contains statements given in two columns, which have to be matched. Statements in column I are labelled as A, B, C and D whereas statements in column II are labelled as p, q, r and s. The answers to these questions have to be appropriately bubbled as illustrated in the following example. If the correct matches are A-p, A-r, B-p, B-s, C-r, C-s and D-q, then the correctly bubbled matrix will look like the following:

**20.**

| Column 1 | | Column 2 |
|---|---|---|
| **(A)** A bag contains 4 red, & 6 white. Two balls are drawn at random. What is the probability that one of them is red and other is white | **(p)** | 31/32 |
| **(B)** A bag contains 6 apples, 4 bananas and 8 mangoes. If three fruits are drawn at random, then what is the probability that all the three are apples | **(q)** | 8/15 |
| **(C)** Five coins are tossed together. What is the probability that at least one tail will appear? | **(r)** | 75/198 |
| **(D)** Team of 5 is to be constituted out of 6 girls and 6 boys then what is probability that team has 3 girls 2 boys | **(s)** | 5/204 |

---

| **RESPONSE GRID** | 19. (a)(b)(c)(d)　　20. A - (p)(q)(r)(s); B - (p)(q)(r)(s); C - (p)(q)(r)(s); D - (p)(q)(r)(s) |
|---|---|

## DAILY PRACTICE PROBLEM DPP CM13 - MATHEMATICS

| Total Questions | 20 | Total Marks | 69 |
|---|---|---|---|
| Attempted | | Correct | |
| Incorrect | | Net Score | |
| Cut-off Score | 22 | Qualifying Score | 33 |

$$\text{Net Score} = \sum_{i=1}^{V}\left[\left(\text{correct}_i \times MM_i\right) - \left(In_i - NM_i\right)\right]$$

---

*Space for Rough Work*

Date : Start Time : End Time :

# MATHEMATICS CM14

**SYLLABUS :** Relation and Functions

**Max. Marks : 72**                                                              **Time : 60 min.**

### GENERAL INSTRUCTIONS

- The Daily Practice Problem Sheet contains 20 Questions divided into 5 sections.

**Section I** has **5** MCQs with ONLY 1 Correct Option, **3** marks for each correct answer and **−1** for each incorrect answer.

**Section II** has **4** MCQs with ONE or MORE THAN ONE Correct options.

For each question, marks will be awarded in one of the following categories:

Full marks: **+4** If only the bubble(s) corresponding to all the correct option(s) is (are) darkened.

Partial marks: **+1** For darkening a bubble corresponding to each correct option provided NO INCORRECT option is darkened.

Zero marks:  If none of the bubbles is darkened.

Negative marks: **−2** In all other cases.

**Section III** has **4** Single Digit Integer Answer Type Questions, **3** marks for each Correct Answer and **0** mark in all other cases.

**Section IV** has Comprehension/Matching Cum-Comprehension Type Questions having **5** MCQs with ONLY ONE corect option, **3** marks for each Correct Answer and **0** mark in all other cases.

**Section V** has **2** Matching Type Questions, **2** mark for the correct matching of each row and **0** mark in all other cases.

- You have to evaluate your Response Grids yourself with the help of Solutions.

---

### Section I - Straight Objective Type

This section contains 5 multiple choice questions. Each question has 4 choices (a), (b), (c) and (d), out of which **ONLY ONE** is correct.

1.  Let $f(x) = \dfrac{2}{x+1}$, $g(x) = \cos x$ and

    $h(x) = \sqrt{x+3}$ then the range of the composite function

    fogoh, is

    (a)  $R^+$                     (b)  $R - \{0\}$

    (c)  $[1, \infty)$               (d)  $R^+ - \{1\}$

2.  Let R be the relation on the set R of all real numbers defined by $aRb$ iff $|a - b| \leq 1$. Then R is

    (a)  reflexive and symmetric

    (b)  symmetric and transitive

    (c)  transitive and reflexive

    (d)  Equivalence Relation

3.  Let $g : R \to R$ be given by $g(x) = 3 + 4x$.

    If $g^n(x) = gogo....... og(x)$, then $g^{-n}(x) = $ (where $g^{-n}(x)$

    denotes inverse of $g^n(x)$ )

    (a)  $(4^n - 1) + 4^n x$        (b)  $(x+1)4^{-n} - 1$

    (c)  $(x+1)4^n - 1$             (d)  $(4^{-n} - 1)x + 4^n$

---

**RESPONSE GRID**     **1.** ⓐⓑⓒⓓ     **2.** ⓐⓑⓒⓓ     **3.** ⓐⓑⓒⓓ

*Space for Rough Work*

**4.** $x^2 = xy$ is a relation which is
- (a) symmetric and reflexive
- (b) reflexive only
- (c) transitive and reflexive
- (d) Equivalence Relation

**5.** Let $f : R \to R$ be a function defined by

$$f(x) = \frac{e^{|x|} - e^{-x}}{e^x + e^{-x}} \cdot \text{Then}$$

- (a) $f$ is both one-one and onto
- (b) $f$ is one-one but not onto
- (c) $f$ is onto but not one-one
- (d) $f$ is neither one-one nor onto.

## Section II - Multiple Correct Answer Type

This section contains 4 multiple correct answer(s) type questions. Each question has 4 choices (a), (b), (c) and (d), out of which **ONE OR MORE** is/are correct.

**6.** Let $f : A \to B$ and $g : B \to C$ be functions and $gof : A \to C$. Which of the following statement is true
- (a) If gof is one-one then f and g both are one-one
- (b) If gof is one-one then f is one-one
- (c) If gof is bijection then f is one-one and g is onto
- (d) If f and g are both one-one then gof is one-one.

**7.** Let $f : D \circledR R$ be defined by $f(x) = ln\ (ln\ (ln\ (ln\,x)))$ then
- (a) $f(x)$ is into
- (b) $f(x)$ is one-one
- (c) $f(x)$ is onto
- (d) $D = (e^e, \infty)$

**8.** $f : R \to [-1, \infty)$ and $f(x) = \ln\ ( [\ |\sin 2x| + |\cos 2x|\ ])$ (where $[.]$ is the greatest integer function).
- (a) Z
- (b) $f(x)$ is periodic with fundamental period $\pi/4$
- (c) $f(x)$ is invertible in $\left[ 0, \dfrac{\pi}{4} \right]$
- (d) $f(x)$ is into function

**9.** Let $f(x) = \max \{1 + \sin x, 1, 1 - \cos x\}$, $x \in [0, 2\pi]$ and $g(x) = \max \{1, |x - 1|\}$ $x \in R$, then
- (a) $g(f(0)) = 1$
- (b) $g(f(0)) = 1$
- (c) $f(g(1)) = 1$
- (d) $f(g(0)) = 1 + \sin 1$

## Section III - Integer Type

This section contains 4 questions. The answer to each of the questions is a single digit integer ranging from 0 to 9.

**10.** If the function $f(x) = \dfrac{x-1}{c - x^2 + 1}$ does not take any value in the internal $\left[ -1, -\dfrac{1}{3} \right]$, then the largest integral value that $c$ can attain is equal to

**11.** Let $f$ be a function such that $f(x + f(y)) = f(x) + y$, $\forall\ x, y \in R$, if $f(1000)$ is equal to 200k, then k =

**12.** Let $f : [0, 1] \to [0, 1]$ defined by $f(x) = \dfrac{1-x}{1+x}$, for $0 \le x \le 1$ and let $g : [0, 1] \to [0, 1]$ defined by $g(x) = 4x\,(1-x)$, $0 \le x \le 1$. If range of $fog\,(x)$ is $[\alpha, \beta]$, then $\alpha + \beta =$

**13.** If $f : R - \{2\} \to R$ satisfying

$$2f(x) + 3f\left( \frac{2x + 29}{x - 2} \right) = 100x + 80,$$ then unit digit of $f(3)$ is



*Space for Rough Work*

## Section IV - Comprehension/Matching Cum-Comprehension Type

**Directions (Qs. 14 and 15) :** Based upon the given paragraph, 2 multiple choice questions have to be answered. Each question has 4 choices (a), (b), (c) and (d), out of which **ONLY ONE** is correct.

**PARAGRAPH**

Consider to functions

$$f(x) = \begin{cases} [x], & -2 \le x \le -1 \\ |x|+1, & -1 < x \le 2 \end{cases} \text{ and}$$

$$g(x) = \begin{cases} [x], & -\pi \le x < 0 \\ |x|+1, & 0 \le x \le \pi \end{cases},$$

where [.] denotes the greatest integer function.

**14.** The exhaustive domain of $g(f(x))$ is
- (a) $[0, 2]$  (b) $[-2, 0]$
- (c) $[-2, 2]$  (d) $[-1, 2]$

**15.** The range of $g(f(x))$ is
- (a) $[\sin 3, \sin 1]$
- (b) $[\sin 3, 1] \cup \{-2, -1, 0\}$
- (c) $[\sin 3, 1] \cup \{-2, -1\}$
- (d) $[\sin 1, 1]$

**Directions (Qs. 16-18) :** This passage contains a table having 3 columns and 4 rows. Based on the table, there are 3 questions. Each question has four options (a), (b), (c) and (d) **ONLY ONE** of these four options is correct.

By appropriately matching the information given in the three columns of the following table, give the answer of the questions that follows.

| Column 1 | Column 2 | Column 3 |
|---|---|---|
| (I) $x^2 = 2y + 1$ is | (i) Not injective but surjective for | (P) $R \to [0, \infty)$ |
| (II) $y = |x| + 2$ is | (ii) Neither injective nor surjective for | (Q) $R \to \left[-\dfrac{1}{2}, \infty\right)$ |
| (III) $y = x + \dfrac{1}{x}$ is | (iii) Injective and surjective for | (R) $R \to R$ |
| (IV) $y^2 = 2x - 4$ is | (iv) Injective but not surjective for | (S) $R - \{0\} \to R \sim (-2, 2)$ |

**16.** Which of the following options is the only correct combination?
- (a) (I)(ii)(P)  (b) (II)(iii)(S)
- (c) (III)(i)(S)  (d) (IV)(iv)(Q)

**17.** Which of the following options is the only correct combination?
- (a) (I)(iii)(S)  (b) (II)(ii)(R)
- (c) (III)(iv)(P)  (d) (IV)(i)(Q)

**18.** Which of the following options is the only incorrect combination?
- (a) (I)(i)(Q)  (b) (II)(ii)(R)
- (c) (III)(i)(S)  (d) (IV)(i)(P)

| RESPONSE GRID | | | |
|---|---|---|---|
| 14. ⓐⓑ©ⓓ | 15. ⓐⓑ©ⓓ | 16. ⓐⓑ©ⓓ | 17. ⓐⓑ©ⓓ |
| 18. ⓐⓑ©ⓓ | | | |

*Space for Rough Work*

## Section V - Matrix-Match Type

This section contains 2 questions. It contains statements given in two columns, which have to be matched. Statements in column I are labelled as A, B, C and D whereas statements in column II are labelled as p, q, r and s. The answers to these questions have to be appropriately bubbled as illustrated in the following example. If the correct matches are A-p, A-r, B-p, B-s, C-r, C-s and D-q, then the correctly bubbled matrix will look like the following:

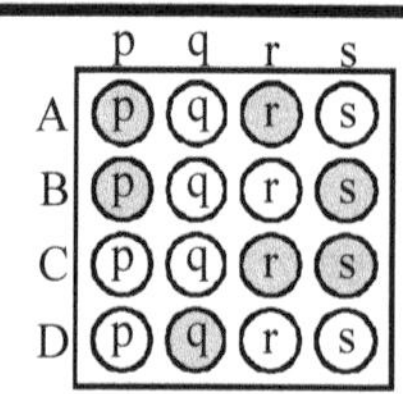

**19.** Let $f : R \to R$ and $g : R \to R$ be functions such that $f(g(x))$ is a one-one function.

| **Column-I** | | **Column-II** |
|---|---|---|
| (A) Then $g(x)$ | | (p) must be one-one |
| (B) Then $f(x)$ | | (q) may not be one-one |
| (C) If $g(x)$ is onto then $f(x)$ | | (r) may be many-one |
| (D) If $g(x)$ is into then $f(x)$ | | (s) must be many-one |

**20.**

**Column-I**       **Column-II**

(A) Let $f(x) = \max\{1 + \sin x, 1, 1 - \cos x\}, x \in [0, 2\pi]$ and $g(x) = \max\{1, |x - 1|\}, x \in R$, then

(p) $g(f(a)) = 1$

(q) $f(g(0)) = 0$

(B) Let $f(x) = \ell n\left(\dfrac{1+x}{1-x}\right) \cdot \forall x \in (-1, 1)$ and $g(x) = \left(\dfrac{3x + x^3}{1 + 3x^2}\right)$, then

(r) $f(g(0)) = 1$

(C) Let $f(x) = 1 + x^2$ and $g(x) = x - x^2$, then

(s) $g(f(0)) = 1$

(t) $g\left(f\left(\dfrac{e-1}{e+1}\right)\right) = 1$

---

| **RESPONSE GRID** | |
|---|---|
| **19.** A - p q r s; B - p q r s; C - p q r s; D - p q r s | |
| **20.** A - p q r s; B - p q r s; C - p q r s; D - p q r s | |

## DAILY PRACTICE PROBLEM DPP CM14 - MATHEMATICS

| Total Questions | 20 | Total Marks | 72 |
|---|---|---|---|
| Attempted | | Correct | |
| Incorrect | | Net Score | |
| Cut-off Score | 24 | Qualifying Score | 35 |

$$\text{Net Score} = \sum_{i=1}^{V} \left[ \left(\text{correct}_i \times MM_i\right) - \left(In_i - NM_i\right) \right]$$

*Space for Rough Work*

Date :        Start Time :        End Time :

# MATHEMATICS (CM15)

**SYLLABUS :** Inverse Trigonometric Functions

**Max. Marks : 69**         **Time : 60 min.**

## GENERAL INSTRUCTIONS

- The Daily Practice Problem Sheet contains 20 Questions divided into 5 sections.

**Section I** has **5** MCQs with ONLY 1 Correct Option, **3** marks for each correct answer and **−1** for each incorrect answer.

**Section II** has **4** MCQs with ONE or MORE THAN ONE Correct options.

For each question, marks will be awarded in one of the following categories:

Full marks: **+4** If only the bubble(s) corresponding to all the correct option(s) is (are) darkened.

Partial marks: **+1** For darkening a bubble corresponding to each correct option provided NO INCORRECT option is darkened.

Zero marks:  If none of the bubbles is darkened.

Negative marks: **−2** In all other cases.

**Section III** has **5** Single Digit Integer Answer Type Questions, **3** marks for each Correct Answer and **0** mark in all other cases.

**Section IV** has Comprehension/Matching cum-comprehension Type Questions having **5** MCQs with ONLY ONE corect option, **3** marks for each Correct Answer and **0** mark in all other cases.

**Section V** has **1** Matching Type Question, **2** marks for the correct matching of each row and **0** mark in all other cases.

- You have to evaluate your Response Grids yourself with the help of Solutions.

## Section I - Straight Objective Type

This section contains 5 multiple choice questions. Each question has 4 choices (a), (b), (c) and (d), out of which **ONLY ONE** is correct.

**1.** The set of values of $x$ for which the identity
$$\cos^{-1} x + \cos^{-1}\left(\frac{x}{2} + \frac{1}{2}\sqrt{3 - 3x^2}\right) = \frac{\pi}{3} \text{ holds good, is}$$

(a) $[0, 1]$        (b) $\left[0, \frac{1}{2}\right]$

(c) $\left[\frac{1}{2}, 1\right]$        (d) $\{-1, 0, 1\}$

**2.** $\sin^{-1}\left(a - \frac{a^2}{3} + \frac{a^3}{9} + .....\right) + \cos^{-1}(1 + b + b^2 + ...) = \frac{\pi}{2}$

when

(a) $a = -3 \ \& \ b = 1$        (b) $a = 1 \ \& \ b = -\dfrac{1}{3}$

(c) $a = \dfrac{1}{6} \ \& \ b = \dfrac{1}{2}$        (d) none of these

**3.** The number of all possible 5-tuples $(a_1, a_2, a_3, a_4, a_5)$ such that $a_1 + a_2 \sin x + a_3 \cos x + a_4 \sin 2x + a_5 \cos 2x = 0$ holds for all $x$ is

(a) zero        (b) 1

(c) 2        (d) infinite

| RESPONSE GRID | 1. ⓐⓑⓒⓓ | 2. ⓐⓑⓒⓓ | 3. ⓐⓑⓒⓓ |
|---|---|---|---|

**4.** $x = n\pi - \tan^{-1} 3$ is a solution of the equation

$$12\tan 2x + \frac{\sqrt{10}}{\cos x} + 1 = 0 \text{ for}$$

(a) no value of $n$  
(b) all integral values of $n$  
(c) even values of $n$  
(d) odd values of $n$

**5.** If $S_n$ denotes the sum to $n$ terms of the series

$$\cot^{-1}\frac{7}{4} + \cot^{-1}\frac{19}{4} + \cot^{-1}\frac{39}{4} + \dots \text{ then}$$

(a) $S_n = \tan^{-1}\dfrac{n}{2n+5}$  
(b) $S_n = \cot^{-1}\dfrac{n+5}{2n}$  

(c) $S_n = \cot^{-1}\dfrac{4n}{2n+5}$  
(d) $S_\infty = \cot^{-1}\dfrac{1}{2}$

## Section II - Multiple Correct Answer Type

This section contains 4 multiple correct answer(s) type questions. Each question has 4 choices (a), (b), (c) and (d), out of which **ONE OR MORE** is/are correct.

**6.** If $\tan^{-1}y = 4\tan^{-1}x$, then $y$ is not finite if

(a) $x^2 = 3 + 2\sqrt{2}$  
(b) $x^2 = 3 - 2\sqrt{2}$  

(c) $x^4 = 6x^2 - 1$  
(d) $x^4 = 6x^2 + 1$

**7.** If the equation $\sin^{-1}(x^2 + x + 1) + \cos^{-1}(ax + 1) = \dfrac{\pi}{2}$ has exactly two solutions then $a$ can not have the integral value

(a) –1  (b) 0  (c) 1  (d) 2

**8.** If $\tan^{-1}(\sin^2\theta + 2\sin\theta + 2) + \cot^{-1}(4^{\sec^2\phi} + 1) = \dfrac{\pi}{2}$ has solution for some $\theta$ and $\phi$ then

(a) $\sin\theta = -1$  
(b) $\sin\theta = 1$

(c) $\cos\phi = 1$  
(d) $\cos\phi = -1$

**9.** If $\alpha, \beta, \gamma$ are the roots of $\tan^{-1}(x-1) + \tan^{-1}x + \tan^{-1}(x+1) = \tan^{-1} 3x$, then

(a) $\alpha + \beta + \gamma = 0$  
(b) $\alpha\beta + \beta\gamma + \gamma\alpha = -1/4$  

(c) $\alpha\beta\gamma = 1$  
(d) $|\alpha - \beta|_{\max} = 1$

## Section III - Integer Type

This section contains 5 questions. The answer to each of the questions is a single digit integer ranging from 0 to 9.

**10.** The sum of the solutions of the equation

$$2\sin^{-1}\sqrt{x^2 + x + 1} + \cos^{-1}\sqrt{x^2 + x} = \frac{3\pi}{2} \text{ is } -p. \text{ The value}$$

of p is –

**11.** Find the value of $-\cos\left[\cos^{-1}\left(-\dfrac{\sqrt{3}}{2}\right) + \dfrac{\pi}{6}\right]$.

**12.** If $\sin^{-1}\left(x - \dfrac{x^2}{2} + \dfrac{x^3}{4} - \dots\right) +$

$$\cos^{-1}\left(x^2 - \frac{x^4}{2} + \frac{x^6}{4} - \dots\right) = \frac{\pi}{2} \text{ for } 0 < |x| < \sqrt{2}, \text{ then find}$$

the value of x.

**13.** If $\sin^{-1}\left(\dfrac{x}{5}\right) + \text{cosec}^{-1}\left(\dfrac{5}{4}\right) = \dfrac{\pi}{2}$, then find the value of x.

**14.** If $\cos^{-1}x - \cos^{-1}\dfrac{y}{2} = a$ then $4x^2 - 4xy\cos\alpha + y^2$ is equal to $k\sin^2\alpha$. The value of k is –

## Section IV - Comprehension/Matching Cum-Comprehension Type

**Directions (Qs. 15 and 16) :** Based upon the given paragraph, 2 multiple choice questions have to be answered. Each question has 4 choices (a), (b), (c) and (d), out of which **ONLY ONE** is correct.

### PARAGRAPH

The function $\sin^{-1}x$, $\cos^{-1}x$, $\tan^{-1}x$, $\cot^{-1}x$, $\csc^{-1}x$ and $\sec^{-1}x$ are called inverse circular functions. Each of the inverse circular function is multivalued. To make each inverse circular function single valued let us define the principal values as follow.

$$\sin^{-1}x \in \left[\frac{3\pi}{2}, \frac{5\pi}{2}\right], \cos^{-1}x \in [2\pi, 3\pi]$$

(in both cases $x \in [-1, -1]$ )and $\tan^{-1}x \in \left(\frac{3\pi}{2}, \frac{5\pi}{2}\right), x\,(-\infty, \infty)$.

**15.** Number of possible solutions for the equation

$$\sin^{-1}x + \cos^{-1}y = \frac{11\pi}{2} \text{ is /are}$$

(a)  0        (b)  1

(c)  2        (d)  infinite

**16.** Range of values of $x$ for which $2\sin^{-1}x = \sin^{-1}\left(2x\sqrt{1-x^2}\right)$ holds, is

(a)  $\left[-\dfrac{1}{2}, \dfrac{1}{2}\right]$        (b)  $\left[-\dfrac{1}{\sqrt{2}}, \dfrac{1}{\sqrt{2}}\right]$

(c)  $[-1, 1]$        (d)  $\left[-\infty, -\dfrac{1}{\sqrt{2}}\right]$

---

**Directions (Qs. 16-17) :** This passage contains a table having 3 columns and 4 rows. Based on the table, there are three questions. Each question has four options (a), (b), (c) and (d) **ONLY ONE** of these four options is correct.

Column 1 contains information about inverse trigonometric equations.

Column 2 contains information about constraints on $x$.

Column 3 contains information about the value of $x$.

| Column 1 | Column 2 | Column 3 |
|---|---|---|
| (I)   $\tan^{-1}\sqrt{x(x+1)} + \sin^{-1}\sqrt{x^2+x+1} = \dfrac{\pi}{2}$ | (i)   $0 < |x| < \sqrt{2}$ | (P)   1 |
| (II)   $\sin[\cot^{-1}(1+x)] = \cos(\tan^{-1}x)$ | (ii)   $-\infty < x < \infty$ | (Q)   $-1$ |
| (III)   $\sin^{-1}\left(x - \dfrac{x^2}{2} + \dfrac{x^3}{3} \cdots\right) + \cos^{-1}\left(x^2 - \dfrac{x^4}{2} + \dfrac{x^6}{4} \cdots\right) = \dfrac{\pi}{2}$ | (iii)   $-\infty < x < 0$ | (R)   $\dfrac{25}{23}$ |
| (IV)   $\displaystyle\sum_{n=1}^{23}\left[\cot^{-1}\left(1 + \sum_{k=1}^{n} 2k\right)\right] = x$ | (iv)   $1 < x < 2$ | (S)   $\dfrac{-1}{2}$ |

**RESPONSE GRID**

**15.** (a)(b)(c)(d)      **16.** (a)(b)(c)(d)

---

*Space for Rough Work*

**17.** Which of the following is the only correct option?

(a) (III)(i)(P)     (b) (II)(iv)(S)

(c) (IV)(iii)(R)    (d) (I)(ii)(Q)

**18.** Which of the following is the only correct combination?

(a) (I)(iii)(P)     (b) (IV)(i)(Q)

(c) (II)(ii)(S)     (d) (III)(iv)(R)

**19.** Which of the following is the only incorrect option?

(a) (I)(iii)(Q)     (b) (II)(ii)(S)

(c) (III)(i)(P)     (d) (IV)(iv)(S)

## Section V - Matrix-Match Type

This section contains 1 question. It contains statements given in two columns, which have to be matched. Statements in column I are labelled as A, B, C and D whereas statements in column II are labelled as p, q, r and s. The answers to these questions have to be appropriately bubbled as illustrated in the following example. If the correct matches are A-p, A-r, B-p, B-s, C-r, C-s and D-q, then the correctly bubbled matrix will look like the following:

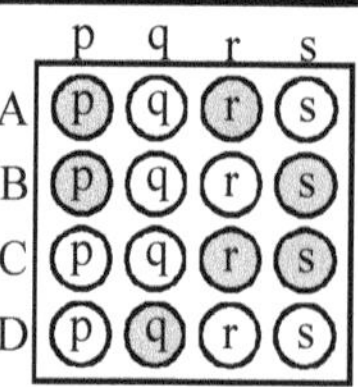

**20.**

| Column-I | Column-II |
|---|---|
| (A) $(\sin^{-1} x)^2 + (\sin^{-1} y)^2 = \dfrac{\pi^2}{2} \Rightarrow x^3 + y^3 =$ | p.   1 |
| (B) $(\cos^{-1} x)^2 + (\cos^{-1} y)^2 = 2\pi^2 \Rightarrow x^5 + y^5 =$ | q.   –2 |
| (C) $(\sin^{-1} x)^2 (\cos^{-1} y)^2 = \dfrac{\pi^4}{4} \Rightarrow |x-y| =$ | r.   0 |
| (D) $|\sin^{-1} x - \sin^{-1} y| = \pi \Rightarrow x^y =$ | s.   2 |

**RESPONSE GRID**

17. (a)(b)(c)(d)     18. (a)(b)(c)(d)     19. (a)(b)(c)(d)

20. A - (p)(q)(r)(s); B - (p)(q)(r)(s); C - (p)(q)(r)(s); D - (p)(q)(r)(s)

## DAILY PRACTICE PROBLEM DPP CM15 - MATHEMATICS

| Total Questions | 20 | Total Marks | 69 |
|---|---|---|---|
| Attempted |  | Correct |  |
| Incorrect |  | Net Score |  |
| Cut-off Score | 22 | Qualifying Score | 31 |

$$\text{Net Score} = \sum_{i=I}^{V} \left[ \left(\text{correct}_i \times MM_i\right) - \left(In_i - NM_i\right) \right]$$

---

*Space for Rough Work*

Date :     Start Time :     End Time :

# MATHEMATICS (CM16)

**SYLLABUS : Matrices**

**Max. Marks : 69**         **Time : 60 min.**

## GENERAL INSTRUCTIONS

- The Daily Practice Problem Sheet contains 20 Questions divided into 5 sections.
  **Section I** has **6** MCQs with ONLY 1 Correct Option, **3** marks for each correct answer and **−1** for each incorrect answer.
  **Section II** has **4** MCQs with ONE or MORE THAN ONE Correct options.
  For each question, marks will be awarded in one of the following categories:
  Full marks: **+4** If only the bubble(s) corresponding to all the correct option(s) is (are) darkened.
  Partial marks: **+1** For darkening a bubble corresponding to each correct option provided NO INCORRECT option is darkened.
  Zero marks: If none of the bubbles is darkened.
  Negative marks: **−2** In all other cases.
  **Section III** has **5** Single Digit Integer Answer Type Questions, **3** marks for each Correct Answer and **0** mark in all other cases.
  **Section IV** has Comprehension Type Questions having **4** MCQs with ONLY ONE corect option, **3** marks for each Correct Answer and **0** mark in all other cases.
  **Section V** has **1** Matching Type Question, **2** marks for the correct matching of each row and **0** mark in all other cases.
- You have to evaluate your Response Grids yourself with the help of Solutions.

---

### Section I - Straight Objective Type

This section contains 6 multiple choice questions. Each question has 4 choices (a), (b), (c) and (d), out of which **ONLY ONE** is correct.

**1.** If $A_1, A_3, ..., A_{2n-1}$ are n skew – symmetric matrices of same order, then

$$X = \sum_{r=1}^{n} (2r-1)\,(A_{2r-1})^{2r-1} \text{ will be}$$

(a) symmetric

(b) skew – symmetric

(c) neither symmetric nor skew symmetric

(d) depends on 'n' is even or odd

**2.** If B, C are square matrices of order n and if
$A = B + C,\ BC = CB,\ C^2 = 0$, then for any positive integer N,
$A^{N+1} = B^K[B + (N+1)\,C]$, then K/N is

(a) 1        (b) $\dfrac{1}{2}$

(c) 2        (d) None of these

---



*Space for Rough Work*

3. Consider $A = \begin{bmatrix} a & b & c \\ c & a & b \\ b & c & a \end{bmatrix}$ and $AA' = I$ if and only if a, b, c are

the roots of the equation

(a) $x^3 + abc = 0$

(b) $x^3 + x^2 - abc = 0$

(c) $x^3 - 2x^2 + abc = 0$

(d) $x^3 \pm x^2 + abc = 0$

4. If A and B are symmetric matrices and A B = BA, then $A^{-1}B$ is a

(a) symmetric matrix

(b) skew–symmetric matrix

(c) unit matrix

(d) None of these

5. If A and B are two matrices such that $AB = B$ and $BA = A$, then $A^2 + B^2$ is equal to

(a) 2AB

(b) 2BA

(c) A + B

(d) AB

6. If $A = \begin{bmatrix} \alpha & 0 \\ 1 & 1 \end{bmatrix}$ and $B = \begin{bmatrix} 9 & a \\ b & c \end{bmatrix}$ and $A^2 = B$, then the value of

a + b + c is

(a) 1 or –1

(b) 5 or –1

(c) 5 or 1

(d) No real values

## Section II - Multiple Correct Answer Type

This section contains 4 multiple correct answer(s) type questions. Each question has 4 choices (a), (b), (c) and (d), out of which **ONE OR MORE** is/are correct.

7. Let $A = \begin{bmatrix} 2 & 3 \\ -1 & 2 \end{bmatrix}$ and $f(x) = x^2 - 4x + 7$. Then

(a) $f(A) = 0$

(b) $f(A) = \begin{bmatrix} 1 & 2 \\ -1 & 3 \end{bmatrix}$

(c) $A^5 = \begin{bmatrix} 118 & -93 \\ 31 & -118 \end{bmatrix}$

(d) $A^5 = \begin{bmatrix} -118 & -93 \\ 31 & -118 \end{bmatrix}$

8. For $k = \dfrac{1}{\sqrt{50}}$ and $PP' = I$, where $P = \begin{bmatrix} 2/3 & 3k & a \\ -1/3 & -4k & b \\ 2/3 & -5k & c \end{bmatrix}$,

then

(a) $a = \dfrac{\pm 13}{2\sqrt{5}}$

(b) $b = \dfrac{\pm 16}{5\sqrt{2}}$

(c) $a = \dfrac{\pm 13}{5\sqrt{2}}$

(d) $c = \dfrac{\pm 1}{2\sqrt{3}}$

9. If $A = \begin{bmatrix} i & 0 \\ 0 & i \end{bmatrix}$, $n \in N$, then $A^{75}$ is not equal to

(a) $\begin{bmatrix} 0 & i \\ i & 0 \end{bmatrix}$

(b) $\begin{bmatrix} 1 & i \\ i & 1 \end{bmatrix}$

(c) $\begin{bmatrix} 1 & 0 \\ 0 & 1 \end{bmatrix}$

(d) None of these

10. If the matrix $\begin{bmatrix} 0 & 2\beta & \gamma \\ \alpha & \beta & -\gamma \\ \alpha & -\beta & \gamma \end{bmatrix}$ is orthogonal, then

(a) $\alpha = \pm \dfrac{1}{\sqrt{2}}$

(b) $\beta = \pm \dfrac{1}{\sqrt{3}}$

(c) $\gamma = \pm \dfrac{1}{\sqrt{2}}$

(d) $\beta = \pm \dfrac{1}{\sqrt{6}}$



*Space for Rough Work*

## Section III - Integer Type

This section contains 5 questions. The answer to each of the questions is a single digit integer ranging from 0 to 9.

**11.** Let $A = \begin{bmatrix} 0 & \alpha \\ 0 & 0 \end{bmatrix}$ and $(A + I)^{50} - 50A = \begin{bmatrix} a & b \\ c & d \end{bmatrix}$, find $abc + abd + bcd + acd$

**12.** If matrix $A = \begin{bmatrix} -5 & -8 & 0 \\ 3 & 5 & 0 \\ 1 & 2 & -1 \end{bmatrix}$ then find sum of digits of $\text{tr}(A) + \text{tr}(A^2) + \text{tr}(A^3) + \ldots + \text{tr}(A^{100})$

**13.** If matrix $A = \begin{bmatrix} a & b & c \\ b & c & a \\ c & a & b \end{bmatrix}$ where a, b c are real positive numbers, $abc = 1$ and $A^T A = I$. Then the value of $a^3 + b^3 + c^3$ is

**14.** Consider a matrix $A = \begin{bmatrix} a_{11} & a_{12} \\ a_{21} & a_{22} \end{bmatrix}$ and another matrix $B = \begin{bmatrix} 1 & 1 \\ 2 & 1 \end{bmatrix}$ such that $AB = BA$ then find the value of $\left(\dfrac{a_{11}}{a_{12}}\right)^2$

**15.** Consider a $2 \times 2$ matrix $A = \begin{bmatrix} 1 & 1 \\ -1 & 1 \end{bmatrix}$ and then find the value of matrix

$B = A^{10} - A^9 + 2A^8 - A^7 + 4A^6 - 2A^5$
$+4A^4 + A^3 - A^2 + A + I = \begin{bmatrix} a & b \\ c & d \end{bmatrix}$

find $(a + b + c + d)$

## Section IV - Comprehension Type

Based upon the given paragraphs, 4 multiple choice questions have to be answered. Each question has 4 choices (a), (b), (c) and (d), out of which **ONLY ONE** is correct.

### PARAGRAPH-1

If $(x + a)^n = \sum_{k=0}^{n} \left(C_r^n\right) x^k a^{n-k}$

Let $a_k = k(^{10}C_k)$, $b_k = (10 - k)(^{10}C_k)$ and

$$A_k = \begin{bmatrix} a_k & 0 \\ 0 & b_k \end{bmatrix}$$

If $A = \sum_{k=1}^{9} A_k = \begin{bmatrix} a & 0 \\ 0 & b \end{bmatrix}$.

**16.** Find the sum of digits of trace of the matrix A
(a) 5       (b) 14
(c) 8       (d) None of these

**17.** Which of the following is correct about 'ab'
(a) 'ab' has 4 prime factors
(b) Largest prime factor of 'ab' is a three digit prime number
(c) 'ab' is a 5 digit number
(d) None of these

### PARAGRAPH-2

Let $a_k = {}^nC_k$ for $0 \le k \le n$ and $A_k = \begin{bmatrix} a_{k-1} & 0 \\ 0 & a_k \end{bmatrix}$ for $0 \le k \le n$ and

$$\sum_{k=1}^{n-1} A_k \cdot A_{k+1} = \begin{bmatrix} a & 0 \\ 0 & b \end{bmatrix},$$



*Space for Rough Work*

**18.** Find 'a'

  (a) $^{2n}C_{n+1}$         (b) $^{2n}C_{n}$

  (c) $^{2n-1}C_{n}$        (d) None of these

**19.** Find 'b'

  (a) $^{2n}C_{n+1}$         (b) $^{2n}C_{n}$

  (c) $^{2n-1}C_{n}$        (d) None of these

## Section V - Matrix-Match Type

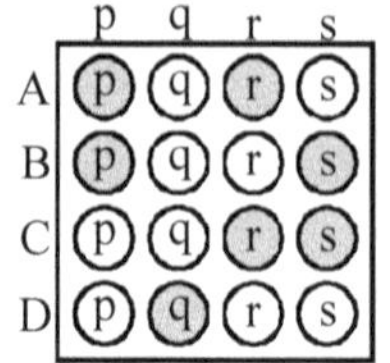

This section contains 1 question. It contains statements given in two columns, which have to be matched. Statements in column I are labelled as A, B, C and D whereas statements in column II are labelled as p, q, r and s. The answers to these questions have to be appropriately bubbled as illustrated in the following example. If the correct matches are A-p, A-r, B-p, B-s, C-r, C-s and D-q, then the correctly bubbled matrix will look like the following:

**20.**

|  | Column - I | | Column - II |
|---|---|---|---|
| (A) | Find the trace of the matrix X for which $\begin{bmatrix} 1 & -4 \\ 3 & -2 \end{bmatrix} X = \begin{bmatrix} -16 & -6 \\ 7 & 2 \end{bmatrix}$ | | (p)  2 |
| (B) | If $\begin{bmatrix} 2 & -1 \\ 1 & 0 \\ -3 & 4 \end{bmatrix} \begin{bmatrix} 1 & m & n \\ x & y & z \end{bmatrix} = \begin{bmatrix} -1 & -8 & -10 \\ 1 & -2 & -5 \\ 9 & 22 & 15 \end{bmatrix}$, then the value of $l + m + n + x + y + z$ is? | | (q)  0 |
| (C) | Find the number of rational values of X which satisfy $[|x|]\begin{bmatrix} 1 & 3 & 2 \\ 0 & 5 & 1 \\ 0 & 3 & 2 \end{bmatrix} \begin{bmatrix} 1 \\ 1 \\ x \end{bmatrix} = 0$ | | (r)  1 |
| (D) | If $\begin{bmatrix} 1/25 & 0 \\ x & 1/25 \end{bmatrix} = \begin{bmatrix} 5 & 0 \\ -a & 5 \end{bmatrix}^{-2}$, then the value of $\dfrac{125x}{a}$ is | | (s)  8 |

| RESPONSE GRID | 18. ⓐⓑⓒⓓ   19. ⓐⓑⓒⓓ |
|---|---|
| | 20. A - ⓟⓠⓡⓢ; B - ⓟⓠⓡⓢ; C - ⓟⓠⓡⓢ; D - ⓟⓠⓡⓢ |

## DAILY PRACTICE PROBLEM DPP CM16 - MATHEMATICS

| Total Questions | 20 | Total Marks | 69 |
|---|---|---|---|
| Attempted | | Correct | |
| Incorrect | | Net Score | |
| Cut-off Score | 21 | Qualifying Score | 32 |

$$\text{Net Score} = \sum_{i=1}^{V} \left[ \left(\text{correct}_i \times MM_i\right) - \left(In_i - NM_i\right) \right]$$

*Space for Rough Work*

Date : [ ]  Start Time : [ ]  End Time : [ ]

# MATHEMATICS (CM17)

**SYLLABUS : Determinants**

**Max. Marks : 69**  **Time : 60 min.**

## GENERAL INSTRUCTIONS

- The Daily Practice Problem Sheet contains 20 Questions divided into 5 sections.
  **Section I** has **6** MCQs with ONLY 1 Correct Option, **3** marks for each correct answer and **−1** for each incorrect answer.
  **Section II** has **4** MCQs with ONE or MORE THAN ONE Correct options.
  For each question, marks will be awarded in one of the following categories:
  Full marks: **+4** If only the bubble(s) corresponding to all the correct option(s) is (are) darkened.
  Partial marks: **+1** For darkening a bubble corresponding to each correct option provided NO INCORRECT option is darkened.
  Zero marks: If none of the bubbles is darkened.
  Negative marks: **−2** In all other cases.
  **Section III** has **5** Single Digit Integer Answer Type Questions, **3** marks for each Correct Answer and **0** mark in all other cases.
  **Section IV** has Comprehension Type Questions having **4** MCQs with ONLY ONE corect option, **3** marks for each Correct Answer and **0** mark in all other cases.
  **Section V** has **1** Matching Type Question, **2** marks for the correct matching of each row and **0** mark in all other cases.
- You have to evaluate your Response Grids yourself with the help of Solutions.

## Section I - Straight Objective Type

This section contains 6 multiple choice questions. Each question has 4 choices (a), (b), (c) and (d), out of which **ONLY ONE** is correct.

**1.** If $x \neq 0$, $y \neq 0$, $z \neq 0$ and $\begin{vmatrix} 1+x & 1 & 1 \\ 1+y & 1+2y & 1 \\ 1+z & 1+z & 1+3z \end{vmatrix}$

$= pxyz\left(q + \dfrac{1}{x} + \dfrac{1}{y} + \dfrac{1}{z}\right)$, then, $(p+q)$ is equal to

(a) 7  (b) 5
(c) 9  (d) None of these

**2.** The system of equations $(a\alpha + b)x + ay + bz = 0$
$(b\alpha + c)x + by + cz = 0$
$(a\alpha + b)y + (b\alpha + c)z = 0$

has a non-trivial solution, if

(a) a, b, c are in A.P
(b) a, b, c are in G.P
(c) a, b, c are in H.P
(d) $\alpha$ is a root of $ax^2 - 2bx + c = 0$

<table><tr><td>**RESPONSE GRID**</td><td>**1.** ⓐⓑⓒⓓ</td><td>**2.** ⓐⓑⓒⓓ</td></tr></table>

*Space for Rough Work*

**3.** If $a, b, c, d > 0$ and $(a^2 + b^2 + c^2)^2 x^2 - 2(ab + bc + cd)x + b^2 + c^2 + d^2 \leq 0$.

Then, $\begin{vmatrix} p & x & \log a \\ q & y & \log b \\ r & z & \log c \end{vmatrix}$ is equal to, here $p, q, r, x, y,$ and $z$ are in AP

(a)  1      (b)  $-1$      (c)  2      (d)  0

**4.** If $U_n = \begin{vmatrix} 1 & k & k \\ 2n & k^2 + k + 1 & k^2 + k \\ 2n - 1 & k^2 & k^2 + k + 1 \end{vmatrix}$ and $\sum_{n=1}^{k} U_n = 110$, then $k$ is equal to

(a) 10           (b)  9

(c) 6            (d)  None of these

**5.** Let $f(n) = \begin{vmatrix} n & n+1 & n+2 \\ {}^nP_n & {}^{n+1}P_{n+1} & {}^{n+2}P_{n+2} \\ {}^nC_n & {}^{n+1}C_{n+1} & {}^{n+2}C_{n+2} \end{vmatrix}$ where the symbols have their usual meanings. Then $f(n)$

(a)  $f(5) = 3720$      (b)  $f(5) = 2040$

(c)  $f(4) = 5040$      (d)  None of these

**6.** The value of the determinant of nth order $\begin{vmatrix} x & 1 & 1 & \ldots \\ 1 & x & 1 & \ldots \\ 1 & 1 & x & \ldots \\ \ldots & \ldots & \ldots & \ldots \end{vmatrix}$, is

(a)  $(x-1)^{n-1}(x+n-1)$      (b)  $(x-1)^n(x+n-1)$

(c)  $(1-x)^{n-1}(x+n-1)$      (d)  None of these.

## Section II - Multiple Correct Answer Type

This section contains 4 multiple correct answer(s) type questions. Each question has 4 choices (a), (b), (c) and (d), out of which ONE OR MORE is/are correct.

**7.** If $f(x)$ satisfies the equation

$$\begin{vmatrix} f(x-3) & f(x+5) & f\left[(x+1)(x-2)-(x-1)^2\right] \\ 5 & 4 & -5 \\ 5 & 6 & 15 \end{vmatrix} = 0$$

for all real $x$, then:

(a)  $f(13) = f(53)$      (b)  $f(7) = f(127)$

(c)  $f(9) = f(25)$      (d)  $f(-4) = f = (4)$

**8.** If $f(x) = \begin{vmatrix} x & a & a & a \\ a & x & a & a \\ a & a & x & a \\ a & a & a & x \end{vmatrix}$ then

(a)  $f(2a) = 5a^4$      (b)  $f(3a) = 48a^4$

(c)  $f(4a) = 64a^4$      (d)  $f(-a) = -16a^4$

**9.** If $\Delta = \begin{vmatrix} my + nz & mq + nr & mb + nc \\ kz - mx & kr - mp & kb - ma \\ -nx - ky & -np - kq & -na - kb \end{vmatrix}$

(a)  $\Delta$ is independent of $a, b, c$

(b)  $\Delta$ is independent of $x, y, z$

(c)  $\Delta$ is independent of $p, q, r$.

(d)  $\Delta$ is independent of $x, y, z$ but dependent on $a, b, c$

**10.** If a point $(x, y)$ moves on a curve and satisfies the equation $\begin{vmatrix} a & b & ax + by \\ b & c & bx + cy \\ ax + by & bx + ay & 0 \end{vmatrix} = 0$. Then,

(a)  $a, b, c$ form a GP

(b)  $a, b, c$ form an HP

(c)  the point $(x, y)$ lies on a curve that passes through the origin

(d)  the point $(x, y)$ lies on a curve that does not pass through the origin



*Space for Rough Work*

### Section III - Integer Type

This section contains 5 questions. The answer to each of the questions is a single digit integer ranging from 0 to 9.

11. For a non–zero, real a, b and c
$$\begin{vmatrix} \dfrac{a^2+b^2}{c} & c & c \\ a & \dfrac{b^2+c^2}{a} & a \\ b & b & \dfrac{c^2+a^2}{b} \end{vmatrix} = (\alpha abc)$$
then the values of $[\alpha]+3$ is, where $[x]$ is greatest integer less than or equal to $x$.

12. If A and B are two matrices of order $3 \times 3$ where $|A| = -2$, $|B| = 2$ then $|(A^{-1}\text{adj}(B^{-1})\text{adj}(2A^{-1})|$ is equal to

13. If $a_1, a_2, \ldots\ldots a_{12}$ are in AP, and $A=\begin{vmatrix} a_1a_5 & a_1 & a_2 \\ a_2a_6 & a_2 & a_3 \\ a_3a_7 & a_3 & a_4 \end{vmatrix}$, $B=\begin{vmatrix} a_2a_{10} & a_2 & a_3 \\ a_3a_{11} & a_3 & a_4 \\ a_4a_{12} & a_4 & a_5 \end{vmatrix}$

    Find the sum of the digits AB if common difference of AP is 2

14. If $a^2 + b^2 + c^2 = -2$ and then the equation
$$\begin{vmatrix} 1+a^2x & (1+b^2)x & (1+c^2)x \\ (1+a^2)x & 1+b^2x & (1+c^2)x \\ (1+a^2)x & (1+b^2)x & 1+c^2x \end{vmatrix} = 0$$
has how many distinct roots?

15. a and b are real and
    $ax + (\sin b)y + (\cos b)z = 0$; $x + (\cos b)y + (\sin b)z = 0$
    $-x + (\sin b)y - (\cos b)z = 0$
    Find the number of integral values of 'a' for which the system of linear equations has a non-trivial solution

### Section IV - Comprehension Type

Based upon the given paragraphs, 4 multiple choice questions have to be answered. Each question has 4 choices (a), (b), (c) and (d), out of which **ONLY ONE** is correct.

#### PARAGRAPH-1

**Read the paragraph carefully and answer the following questions:**
A determinant is called cyclic if it follows the arrangement symmetrically with $a$, $b$, $c$ for example $\begin{vmatrix} 1 & 1 & 1 \\ a & b & c \\ a^2 & b^2 & c^2 \end{vmatrix}$ is a cyclic determinant

Now, if we increase the degree of any row in this determinant symmetrically its value will be multiplied by expression which is also cyclic and increases the degree of the value of determinant,

16. The value of $\begin{vmatrix} 1 & 1 & 1 \\ a^2 & b^2 & c^2 \\ bc & ca & ab \end{vmatrix}$ is equal to

    (a) $(a-b)(b-c)(c-a)$
    (b) $(a-b)(b-c)(c-a)(a+b+c)$
    (c) $(a-b)(b-c)(c-a)(ab+bc+ca)$
    (d) $(a-b)(b-c)(c-a)\,abc$

17. The value of $\begin{vmatrix} a & b & c \\ a^2 & b^2 & c^2 \\ bc & ca & ab \end{vmatrix}$ is equal to

    (a) $(a-b)(b-c)(c-a)(a+b+c)^2$
    (b) $(a-b)(b-c)(c-a)(a+b+c)$
    (c) $(a-b)(b-c)(c-a)(ab+bc+ca)$
    (d) $(a-b)(b-c)(c-a)\left(a^2+b^2+c^2+ab+bc+ca\right)$

| | |
|---|---|
| **RESPONSE GRID** | **11.** ⓪①②③④⑤⑥⑦⑧⑨  **12.** ⓪①②③④⑤⑥⑦⑧⑨ <br> **13.** ⓪①②③④⑤⑥⑦⑧⑨  **14.** ⓪①②③④⑤⑥⑦⑧⑨ <br> **15.** ⓪①②③④⑤⑥⑦⑧⑨  **16.** ⓐⓑⓒⓓ  **17.** ⓐⓑⓒⓓ |

*Space for Rough Work*

### PARAGRAPH-2

The system of equations $a_1x + b_1y + c_1z = d_1$,

$a_2x + b_2y + c_2z = d_2$, $a_3x + b_3y + c_3z = d_3$ can be written as

$$AX = B \text{ where } A = \begin{bmatrix} a_1 & b_1 & c_1 \\ a_2 & b_2 & c_2 \\ a_3 & b_3 & c_3 \end{bmatrix}, X = \begin{bmatrix} x \\ y \\ z \end{bmatrix} \text{ and } B = \begin{bmatrix} d_1 \\ d_2 \\ d_3 \end{bmatrix} \text{ the}$$

system is

(i)  consistent with unique solution iff $|A| \neq 0$

(ii)  either inconsistent or consistent with infinite solutions if $|A| = 0$ and (adj. $A$) $B = 0$

(iii)  Inconsistent iff $|A| = 0$ and (adj $A$) $B \neq 0$

18.  The system of equations $x + y + z = 3$, $2x + y + 2z = 5$, $x - y + 3z = 3$ has
(a)  only solution $x = 1, y = 1, z = 1$
(b)  Infinite solutions
(c)  no solution
(d)  None of these

19.  The system of equations $x + y + z = 3$, $2x + 2y + 2z = 7$, $x - y + 3z = 3$ has
(a)  only solution $x = 1, y = 1, z = 1$
(b)  Infinite solution
(c)  no solution
(d)  None of these

---

## Section V - Matrix-Match Type

This section contains 1 question. It contains statements given in two columns, which have to be matched. Statements in column I are labelled as A, B, C and D whereas statements in column II are labelled as p, q, r and s. The answers to these questions have to be appropriately bubbled as illustrated in the following example. If the correct matches are A-p, A-r, B-p, B-s, C-r, C-s and D-q, then the correctly bubbled matrix will look like the following:

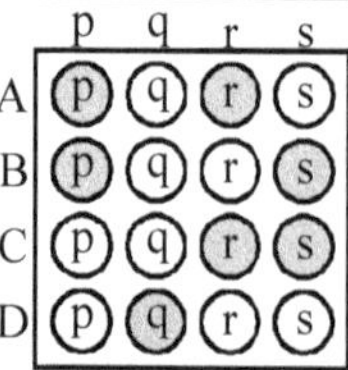

20.  **Column - I**  **Column - II**

(A)  Simplify $\begin{vmatrix} 1 + \sin^2\theta & \cos^2\theta & \sin 2\theta \\ \sin^2\theta & 1 + \cos^2\theta & \sin 2\theta \\ \sin^2\theta & \cos^2\theta & 1 + \sin 2\theta \end{vmatrix}$  (p)  $(3\cos\theta - \sin\theta)2$

(B)  If $\begin{bmatrix} 1 & -\tan\theta \\ \tan\theta & 1 \end{bmatrix} \begin{bmatrix} 1 & \tan\theta \\ -\tan\theta & 1 \end{bmatrix}^{-1} = \begin{bmatrix} a & -b \\ b & a \end{bmatrix}$ then a =  (q)  $2 + \sin 2\theta$

(C)  If $\begin{bmatrix} 1 & -\tan\theta \\ \tan\theta & 1 \end{bmatrix} \begin{bmatrix} 1 & \tan\theta \\ -\tan\theta & 1 \end{bmatrix}^{-1} = \begin{bmatrix} a & -b \\ b & a \end{bmatrix}$ then b =  (r)  $\cos 2\theta$

(D)  $\begin{vmatrix} 1 & 3\cos\theta & 1 \\ \sin\theta & 1 & 3\cos\theta \\ 1 & \sin\theta & 1 \end{vmatrix}$ equals  (s)  $\sin 2\theta$

---



## DAILY PRACTICE PROBLEM DPP CM17 - MATHEMATICS

| Total Questions | 20 | Total Marks | 69 |
|---|---|---|---|
| Attempted |  | Correct |  |
| Incorrect |  | Net Score |  |
| Cut-off Score | 23 | Qualifying Score | 34 |

$$\text{Net Score} = \sum_{i=1}^{V} \left[ (\text{correct}_i \times MM_i) - (In_i - NM_i) \right]$$

---

*Space for Rough Work*

Date : [ ]  Start Time : [ ]  End Time : [ ]

# MATHEMATICS CM18

**SYLLABUS :** Continuity and Differentiability

**Max. Marks : 74**  **Time : 60 min.**

### GENERAL INSTRUCTIONS

- The Daily Practice Problem Sheet contains 20 Questions divided into 5 sections.
  **Section I** has **5** MCQs with ONLY 1 Correct Option, **3** marks for each correct answer and **−1** for each incorrect answer.
  **Section II** has **4** MCQs with ONE or MORE THAN ONE Correct options.
  For each question, marks will be awarded in one of the following categories:
  Full marks: **+4** If only the bubble(s) corresponding to all the correct option(s) is (are) darkened.
  Partial marks: **+1** For darkening a bubble corresponding to each correct option provided NO INCORRECT option is darkened.
  Zero marks: If none of the bubbles is darkened.
  Negative marks: **−2** In all other cases.
  **Section III** has **4** Single Digit Integer Answer Type Questions, **3** marks for each Correct Answer and **0** mark in all other cases.
  **Section IV** has Comprehension/Matching Cum-Comprehension Type Questions having **5** MCQs with ONLY ONE correct option, **3** marks for each Correct Answer and **0** mark in all other cases.
  **Section V** has **2** Matching Type Questions, **2** marks for the correct matching of each row and **0** mark in all other cases.
- You have to evaluate your Response Grids yourself with the help of Solutions.

## Section I - Straight Objective Type

This section contains 5 multiple choice questions. Each question has 4 choices (a), (b), (c) and (d), out of which **ONLY ONE** is correct.

**1.** If $f(x)=\begin{cases}\dfrac{e^{[x]+|x|}-2}{[x]+|x|}, & x\neq 0\\ -1, & x=0\end{cases}$ ([.]denotes the greatest integer function) then

(a) $f(x)$ is continuous at $x=0$

(b) $\lim\limits_{x\to 0^{+}} f(x)=-1$

(c) $\lim\limits_{x\to 0^{-}} f(x)=1$

(d) None of these

**2.** If $f''(x)=-f(x)$ and $g(x)=f'(x)$ and

$F(x)=\left(f\left(\dfrac{x}{2}\right)\right)^{2}+\left(g\left(\dfrac{x}{2}\right)\right)^{2}$ and given that

$F(5)=5$, then $F(10)$ is equal to

(a) 5  (b) 10
(c) 0  (d) 15

| RESPONSE GRID | 1. ⓐⓑⓒⓓ | 2. ⓐⓑⓒⓓ |
| --- | --- | --- |

*Space for Rough Work*

**3.** Given $f : [-2a, 2a] \rightarrow R$ is an odd function such that the left hand derivative at $x = a$ is zero and $f(x) = f(2a - x) \; \forall \; x \in (a, 2a)$, then its left had derivative at $x = -a$ is

(a) 0
(b) $a$
(c) $-a$
(d) does not exist

**4.** If $f(x) = \cos x \cos 2x \cos 2^2 x \cos 2^3 x \ldots \cos 2^{n-1} x$ and $n > 1$, then $f'\left(\dfrac{\pi}{2}\right)$ is

(a) 1
(b) 0
(c) $-1$
(d) None of these

**5.** Let $f$ be $a$ differentiable function satisfying $[f(x)]^n = f(nx)$ for all $x \in R$.
Then, $f'(x) f(nx) =$

(a) $f(x)$
(b) 0
(c) $f(x) f'(nx)$
(d) None of these

## Section II - Multiple Correct Answer Type

This section contains 4 multiple correct answer(s) type questions. Each question has 4 choices (a), (b), (c) and (d), out of which **ONE OR MORE** is/are correct.

**6.** If $f(x) = \begin{vmatrix} x^n & \sin x & \cos x \\ n! & \sin(n\pi/2) & \cos(n\pi/2) \\ a & a^2 & a^3 \end{vmatrix}$, then the value of

$\dfrac{d^n}{dx^n}(f(x))$ at $x = 0$ for $n = 2m + 1$, is

(a) $-1$
(b) 0
(c) $a$
(d) independent of $a$

**7.** If $f(x) = x + |x| + \cos([\pi^2]x)$ and $g(x) = \sin x$, where $[.]$ denotes the greatest integer function, then
(a) $f(x) + g(x)$ is continuous everywhere
(b) $f(x) + g(x)$ is differentiable everywhere
(c) $f(x) \times g(x)$ is differentiable everywhere
(d) $f(x) \times g(x)$ is continuous but not differentiable at $x = 0$

**8.** Let $f(x) = x^3 + 3x^2 - 33x - 33$ for $x > 0$ and '$g$' be its inverse, then the value of '$k$' such that $kg'(2) = 1$, is equal to

(a) $-36$
(b) 51
(c) 72
(d) 42

**9.** If $f(x) = \begin{cases} (\sin^{-1} x)^2 \cos(1/x), & x \neq 0 \\ 0, & x = 0 \end{cases}$ then

(a) $f(x)$ is continuous everywhere in $x \in (-1, 1)$
(b) $f(x)$ is discontinuous in $x \in [-1, 1]$
(c) $f(x)$ is differentiable everywhere in $x \in (-1, 1)$
(d) $f(x)$ is non-differentiable anywhere in $x \in [-1, 1]$

## Section III - Integer Type

This section contains 4 questions. The answer to each of the questions is a single digit integer ranging from 0 to 9.

**10.** If the number of points of non-differentiability of $f(x) = \max\{\sin x, \cos x, 0\}$ in $(0, 2n\pi)$ is $pn$, then find the value of $p$.

**11.** If $\dfrac{d^2 x}{dy^2}\left(\dfrac{dy}{dx}\right)^3 + \dfrac{d^2 y}{dx^2} = k$, then find the value of $k$.

**12.** Let $f(x) = \begin{cases} \dfrac{1 - \cos 4x}{x^2}, & x < 0 \\ a, & x = 0 \\ \dfrac{\sqrt{x}}{\sqrt{16 + \sqrt{x}} - 4}, & x > 0 \end{cases}$

Determine the value of '$a$' if possible, so that the function is continuous at $x = 0$.

**13.** Let $f(x)$ and $g(x)$ be differentiable for $0 \leq x \leq 1$, such that $f(0) = 0, g(0) = 0, f(1) = 6$. Let there exist $a$ real number $c$ in $(0, 1)$ such that $f'(c) = 2 g'(c)$, then find the value of $g(1)$

## Section IV - Comprehension/Matching Cum-Comprehension Type

**Directions (Qs. 14 and 15) :** Based upon the given paragraph, 2 multiple choice questions have to be answered. Each question has 4 choices (a), (b), (c) and (d), out of which **ONLY ONE** is correct.

### PARAGRAPH

If $y = f(x)$ be a differentiable function of $x$ such that whose second, third, ..., nth derivatives exist. *i.e.*, nth derivative of $y$ is denoted by

$$y_n, \frac{d^n y}{dx^n}, D^n y, y^n, f^n(x)$$

$$\Rightarrow \quad \frac{d^n y}{dx^n} = \lim_{h \to 0} \frac{f^{n-1}(x+h) - f^{n-1}(x)}{h}$$

On the basis of above information, answer the following questions :

14. If $y = e^{3x+7}$, then the value of $y_n(0)$ is

   (a)   1
   (b)   $3^n$
   (c)   $3^n . e^7$
   (d)   $3^n . e^7 . 7!$

15. If $y = \dfrac{\ln x}{2 - 3x}$, then the value of $y_n(1)$ is

   (a)   0
   (b)   $(-1)^n . 3^n$
   (c)   $(-1)^n . 3^n . n!$
   (d)   None of these

---

**Directions (Qs. 16-18) :** This passage contains a table having 3 columns and 4 rows. Based on the table, there are three questions. Each question has four options (a), (b), (c) and (d) **ONLY ONE** of these four options is correct.

Column 1 contains information about the functions.

Column 2 contains information about continuity and differentiability of functions given in column I.

Column 3 contains information about points/intervals where given function is either continuous or differentiable.

| Column I | Column II | Column III |
|---|---|---|
| (I) $f(x) = \begin{cases} x^p \sin \dfrac{1}{x} & x \neq 0 \\ 0 & x = 0 \end{cases}$ | (i) Neither continuous nor derivable | (P) $\{2\}$ |
| (II) $f(x) = \begin{cases} 4x^2 + [2x]\,x, & -\dfrac{1}{2} \leq x < 0 \\ ax^2 - bx, & 0 \leq x < \dfrac{1}{2} \end{cases}$ | (ii) Continuous but not differentiable | (Q) $(-1, 0)$ |
| (III) $f(x) = [x^2] + [-x]^2$ | (iii) Continuous and differentiable | (R) $\{0\}$ |
| (IV) $f(x) = \cos \pi\,(|x| + [x])$ | (iv) Differentiable but not continuous | (S) $\left(\dfrac{-1}{2}, \dfrac{1}{2}\right)$ |

<table>
<tr><td rowspan="2">RESPONSE<br>GRID</td><td>14. ⓐⓑⓒⓓ</td><td>15. ⓐⓑⓒⓓ</td></tr>
</table>

———————————————— *Space for Rough Work* ————————————————

16. Which of the following options is the only correct combination?

(a) (II)(i)(S)
(b) (III)(i)(P)
(c) (I)(ii)(Q)
(d) (IV)(iv)(R)

17. For $0 < p \le 1$, check the continuity and differentiability at $x = 0$ of the function $f(x) = \begin{cases} x^p \sin \dfrac{1}{x} & x \ne 0 \\ 0 & x = 0 \end{cases}$

(a) Continuous but not differentiable
(b) Continuous and differentiable
(c) Differentiable but not continuous
(d) Neither continuous nor derivable

18. Which of the following options is the only incorrect combination?

(a) (I)(ii)(R)
(b) (II)(iii)(S)
(c) (III)(i)(P)
(d) (IV)(ii)(Q)

---

## Section V - Matrix-Match Type

This section contains 2 questions. It contains statements given in two columns, which have to be matched. Statements in column I are labelled as A, B, C and D whereas statements in column II are labelled as p, q, r and s. The answers to these questions have to be appropriately bubbled as illustrated in the following example. If the correct matches are A-p, A-r, B-p, B-s, C-r, C-s and D-q, then the correctly bubbled matrix will look like the following:

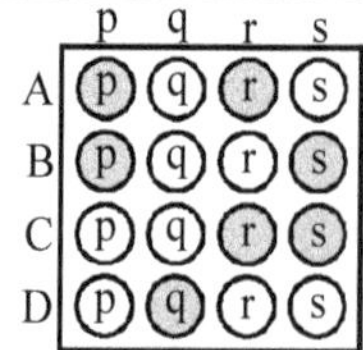

19. Let $f(x) = \begin{cases} \dfrac{5e^{1/x} + 2}{3 - e^{1/x}}, & x \ne 0 \\ 0, & x = 0 \end{cases}$

| Column I | Column II |
|---|---|
| (A) $y = f(x)$ is | (p) continuous at $x = 0$ |
| (B) $y = xf(x)$ is | (q) discontinuous at $x = 0$ |
| (C) $y = x^2 f(x)$ is | (r) differentiable at $x = 0$ |
| (D) $y = x^{-1} f(x)$ is | (s) non-differentiable at $x = 0$ |

20.

| Column I | Column II |
|---|---|
| (A) $f(x) = |x^3|$ is | (p) continuous in $(-1, 1)$ |
| (B) $f(x) = \sqrt{|x|}$ is | (q) differentiable in $(-1, 1)$ |
| (C) $f(x) = |\sin^{-1}x|$ is | (r) differentiable in $(0, 1)$ |
| (D) $f(x) = \cos^{-1}|x|$ | (s) not differentiable at least one point in $(-1, 1)$ |

---



## DAILY PRACTICE PROBLEM DPP CM18 - MATHEMATICS

| Total Questions | 20 | Total Marks | 74 |
|---|---|---|---|
| Attempted | | Correct | |
| Incorrect | | Net Score | |
| Cut-off Score | 23 | Qualifying Score | 34 |

$$\text{Net Score} = \sum_{i=1}^{V} \left[ \left( \text{correct}_i \times MM_i \right) - \left( In_i - NM_i \right) \right]$$

*Space for Rough Work*

**Date :**        **Start Time :**        **End Time :**

# MATHEMATICS $\boxed{\text{CM19}}$

**SYLLABUS :** Application of Derivatives

**Max. Marks : 74**                                 **Time : 60 min.**

**GENERAL INSTRUCTIONS**

- The Daily Practice Problem Sheet contains 20 Questions divided into 5 sections.

**Section I** has **6** MCQs with ONLY 1 Correct Option, **3** marks for each correct answer and **−1** for each incorrect answer.

**Section II** has **4** MCQs with ONE or MORE THAN ONE Correct options.

For each question, marks will be awarded in one of the following categories:

Full marks: **+4** If only the bubble(s) corresponding to all the correct option(s) is (are) darkened.

Partial marks: **+1** For darkening a bubble corresponding to each correct option provided NO INCORRECT option is darkened.

Zero marks: If none of the bubbles is darkened.

Negative marks: **−2** In all other cases.

**Section III** has **4** Single Digit Integer Answer Type Questions, **3** marks for each Correct Answer and **0** mark in all other cases.

**Section IV** has Comprehension Type Questions having **4** MCQs with ONLY ONE corect option, **3** marks for each Correct Answer and **0** mark in all other cases.

**Section V** has **2** Matching Type Questions, **2** marks for the correct matching of each row and **0** mark in all other cases.

- You have to evaluate your Response Grids yourself with the help of Solutions.

---

### Section I - Straight Objective Type

This section contains 6 multiple choice questions. Each question has 4 choices (a), (b), (c) and (d), out of which **ONLY ONE** is correct.

1. The value of $\theta$, $\theta \in [0, \pi/2]$ for which the sum of intercepts on co-ordinate axes by tangent at point $(3\sqrt{3}\cos\theta, \sin\theta)$ of ellipse $\dfrac{x^2}{27} + y^2 = 1$ is minimum, is :

  (a) $\dfrac{\pi}{6}$   (b) $\dfrac{\pi}{4}$   (c) $\dfrac{\pi}{3}$   (d) $\dfrac{\pi}{2}$

2. Function $f(x) = \tan^{-1}(\sin x + \cos x)$ is monotonic increasing when

  (a) $x < 0$       (b) $x > 0$

  (c) $0 < x < \pi/2$   (d) $0 < x < \pi/4$

3. The equation of one of the tangents to the curve $y = \cos(x + y)$, $-2\pi \le x \le 2\pi$ that is parallel to the line $x + 2y = 0$ is

  (a) $x + 2y = 1$   (b) $x + 2y = \pi/2$

  (c) $x + 2y = \pi/4$   (d) None of these

---

**RESPONSE GRID**    **1.** ⓐⓑⓒⓓ    **2.** ⓐⓑⓒⓓ    **3.** ⓐⓑⓒⓓ

*Space for Rough Work*

**4.** The ratio of the altitude of the cone of greatest volume which can be inscribed in a given sphere to the diameter of the sphere is

(a)   2/3

(b)   3/4

(c)   1/3

(d)   1/4

**5.** Let $y = f(x)$ be the equation of a parabola which is touched by the line $y = x$ at the point where $x = 1$. Then,

(a)   $f'(0) = f'(1)$

(b)   $f'(1) = -1$

(c)   $f(0) + f'(0) + f'(0) = 1$

(d)   $2f(0) = 1 - f'(0)$

**6.** In a $\triangle ABC$, $B = 90°$ and $a + b = 4$. The area of the triangle is maximum when $C$ is

(a)   $\dfrac{\pi}{4}$

(b)   $\dfrac{\pi}{6}$

(c)   $\dfrac{\pi}{3}$

(d)   None of these

---

### Section II - Multiple Correct Answer Type

This section contains 4 multiple correct answer(s) type questions. Each question has 4 choices (a), (b), (c) and (d), out of which **ONE OR MORE** is/are correct.

**7.** The point on the curve $9y^2 = x^3$, where the normal to the curve makes equal intercepts with the axes is

(a)   $\left(4, \dfrac{8}{3}\right)$

(b)   $\left(-4, \dfrac{8}{3}\right)$

(c)   $\left(4, -\dfrac{8}{3}\right)$

(d)   None of these

**8.** If $f(x)$ is defined in $[-3, 3]$ by

$$f(x) = \max. \left\{\sqrt{9-x^2}, \sqrt{1+x^2}\right\}, -3 \le x \le 0$$

$$= \min. \left\{\sqrt{9-x^2}, \sqrt{1+x^2}\right\}, 0 \le x \le 3, \text{ then } f(x) \text{ has}$$

(a)   a point of discontinuity at $x = 0$

(b)   a point of maximum at $x = -2$ and a point of minimum at $x = 2$

(c)   a point of minimum at $x = -2$ and a point of maximum at $x = 2$

(d)   no turning point

**9.** Let the function $f(x) = \sin x + \cos x$, be defined in $[0, 2\pi]$, then $f(x)$

(a)   increases in $\left(\dfrac{\pi}{4}, \dfrac{\pi}{2}\right)$

(b)   decreases in $\left(\dfrac{\pi}{4}, \dfrac{5\pi}{4}\right)$

(c)   increases in $\left[0, \dfrac{\pi}{4}\right) \cup \left(\dfrac{5\pi}{4}, \dfrac{7\pi}{4}\right]$

(d)   decreases in $\left[0, \dfrac{\pi}{4}\right) \cup \left(\dfrac{\pi}{2}, 2\pi\right]$

**10.** The normal to the curve represented parametrically by $x = a(\cos\theta + \theta\sin\theta)$ and $y = a(\sin\theta - \theta\cos\theta)$ at any point $\theta$, is such that it

(a)   makes a constant angle with the $x$-axis

(b)   is at a constant distance from the origin

(c)   touches a fixed circle

(d)   passes through the origin



---

*Space for Rough Work*

## Section III - Integer Type

This section contains 4 questions. The answer to each of the questions is a single digit integer ranging from 0 to 9.

**11.** Find the point of inflexion of $(x-5)^{55}(x-6)^{66}$.

**12.** If $\theta$ be the angle of intersection of curves $y = [|\sin x| + |\cos x|]$ and $x^2 + y^2 = 5$, where [.] denotes the greatest integer function, then find the value of $\tan^2\theta$.

**13.** Find the greatest value of $f(x) = (x+1)^{1/3} - (x-1)^{1/3}$ on $[0, 1]$.

**14.** The altitude of a cone is 20 cm and its semi-vertical angle is $30°$. If the semi-vertical angle is increasing at the rate of $2°$ per second, if the radius of the base is increasing at the rate of $\dfrac{160}{b}$, then b =

## Section IV - Comprehension Type

Based upon the given paragraphs, 4 multiple choice questions have to be answered. Each question has 4 choices (a), (b), (c) and (d), out of which **ONLY ONE** is correct.

### PARAGRAPH-1

A conical vessel is to be prepared out of a circular sheet of copper of unit radius as shown in the figure where $\alpha$ be the angle of the sector removed (i.e. $\angle$ AOB), then

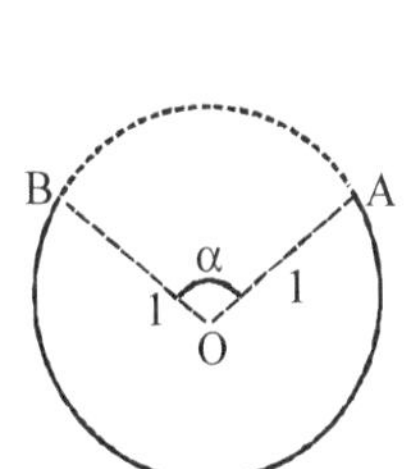 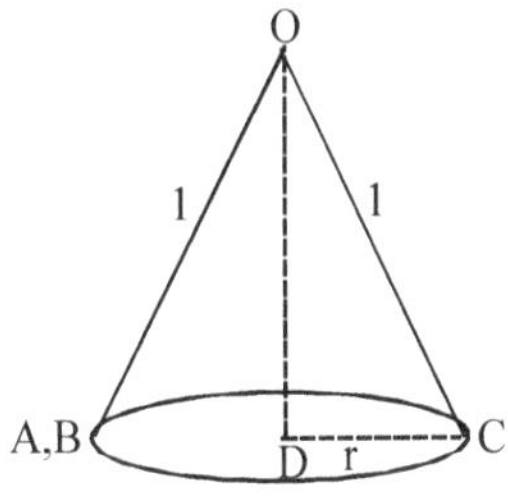

Then, $\alpha = \dfrac{AB}{1}$

$\Rightarrow AB = \alpha \Rightarrow ABC = 2\pi - \alpha$

Circumference of the base of the cone $= 2\pi - \alpha$

Let $r$ be the radius of the base of the cone then

$$2\pi r = 2\pi - \alpha \Rightarrow r = 1 - \dfrac{\alpha}{2\pi}$$

**15.** The volume of the vessel. ( If $\alpha = \pi$ )

(a) $\dfrac{\pi}{24}$      (b) $\dfrac{\sqrt{3}\,\pi^2}{6}$

(c) $\dfrac{\sqrt{3}\,\pi}{24}$      (d) None of these

**16.** The value of '$r$' for which volume is maximum (when $\alpha$ is variable)

(a) $\sqrt{2}/3$      (b) $2/\sqrt{3}$

(c) $\sqrt{2/3}$      (d) None of these

### PARAGRAPH-2

Analyse the following graph of derivative of a function $f(x)$, i.e. $y = g(x)$, where $g(x) = f'(x)$ and answer the following questions : ($a \le x \le b$). Given $f(c) = 0$.

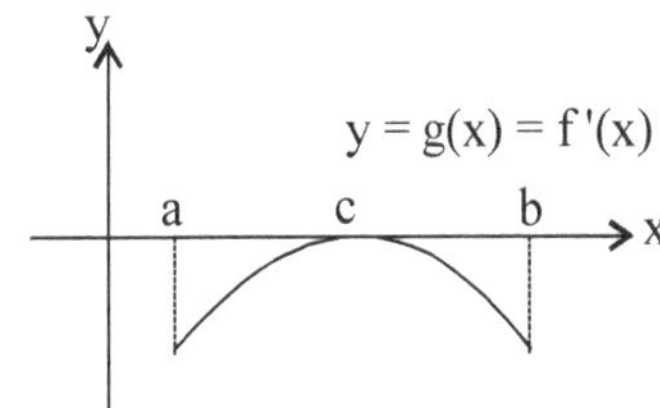


**17.** The graph of $y = f(x)$ will intersect $x$-axis

(a) never      (b) once

(c) twice      (d) cannot be determined

**18.** The equation $f(x) = 0$, $a \le x \le b$ has

(a) no real roots

(b) two distinct real roots

(c) two repeated roots

(d) at least three repeated roots

<table>
<tr><td>RESPONSE GRID</td><td>11. ⓪①②③④⑤⑥⑦⑧⑨   12. ⓪①②③④⑤⑥⑦⑧⑨<br>13. ⓪①②③④⑤⑥⑦⑧⑨   14. ⓪①②③④⑤⑥⑦⑧⑨<br>15. ⓐⓑⓒⓓ   16. ⓐⓑⓒⓓ   17. ⓐⓑⓒⓓ   18. ⓐⓑⓒⓓ</td></tr>
</table>

*Space for Rough Work*

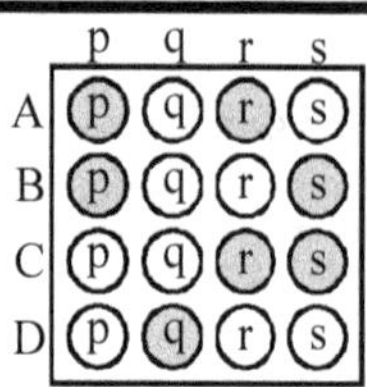

## Section V - Matrix-Match Type

This section contains 2 questions. It contains statements given in two columns, which have to be matched. Statements in column I are labelled as A, B, C and D whereas statements in column II are labelled as p, q, r and s. The answers to these questions have to be appropriately bubbled as illustrated in the following example. If the correct matches are A-p, A-r, B-p, B-s, C-r, C-s and D-q, then the correctly bubbled matrix will look like the following:

**19.**

**Column-I**

(A) The normal line to $y = be^{-x/a}$ where it crosses $y$-axis, has slope equal to    (p)   $\dfrac{a^2}{b^2}$

(B) Subnormal length to $xy = a^2 b^2$ at any point $(x, y)$ is $p$ then $\dfrac{1}{p}\left|y^3\right|$ is equal to    (q)   $\dfrac{a}{b}$

(C) The length of subtangent at any point $(x, y)$ on the ellipse $\dfrac{x^2}{a^2} + \dfrac{y^2}{b^2} = 1$ is $p$ then    (r)   $a^2 b^2$

     $\dfrac{p\,|x|}{y^2}$ is equal to

(D) If $m$ be slope of tangent at any point $(x, y)$ on the curve $\dfrac{x^2}{a^2} - \dfrac{y^2}{b^2} = 1$ then $\dfrac{my}{x}$ is equal to    (s)   $\dfrac{b^2}{a^2}$

**20.**

**Column-I**      **Column-II**

(A) A circular plate is expanded by heat from radius 6 cm to 6.06 cm. Approximate increase in the area is    (p)   5

(B) If an edge of a cube increases by 2%, then percentage increase in the volume is    (q)   $0.72\,\pi$

(C) If the rate of decrease of $\dfrac{x^2}{2} - 2x + 5$ is thrice the rate of decrease of $x$, then $x$ is equal to    (r)   6

     (rate of decrease is non zero)

(D) The rate of increase in the area of an equailateral triangle of side 30 cm, when each side increases at the rate of 0.1 cm/s is    (s)   $\dfrac{3\sqrt{3}}{2}$

| RESPONSE GRID | |
|---|---|
| **19.** A - (p)(q)(r)(s); B - (p)(q)(r)(s); C - (p)(q)(r)(s); D - (p)(q)(r)(s) | |
| **20.** A - (p)(q)(r)(s); B - (p)(q)(r)(s); C - (p)(q)(r)(s); D - (p)(q)(r)(s) | |

## DAILY PRACTICE PROBLEM DPP CM19 - MATHEMATICS

| Total Questions | 20 | Total Marks | 74 |
|---|---|---|---|
| Attempted | | Correct | |
| Incorrect | | Net Score | |
| Cut-off Score | 23 | Qualifying Score | 34 |

$$\text{Net Score} = \sum_{i=1}^{V}\left[\left(\text{correct}_i \times MM_i\right) - \left(In_i - NM_i\right)\right]$$

Date : ___________   Start Time : ___________   End Time : ___________

# MATHEMATICS CM20

**SYLLABUS :** Integrals

**Max. Marks : 74**                                      **Time : 60 min.**

## GENERAL INSTRUCTIONS

- The Daily Practice Problem Sheet contains 20 Questions divided into 5 sections.
  **Section I** has **6** MCQs with ONLY 1 Correct Option, **3** marks for each correct answer and **−1** for each incorrect answer.
  **Section II** has **4** MCQs with ONE or MORE THAN ONE Correct options.
  For each question, marks will be awarded in one of the following categories:
  Full marks: **+4** If only the bubble(s) corresponding to all the correct option(s) is (are) darkened.
  Partial marks: **+1** For darkening a bubble corresponding to each correct option provided NO INCORRECT option is darkened.
  Zero marks:  If none of the bubbles is darkened.
  Negative marks: **−2** In all other cases.
  **Section III** has **4** Single Digit Integer Answer Type Questions, **3** marks for each Correct Answer and **0** mark in all other cases.
  **Section IV** has Comprehension Type Questions having **4** MCQs with ONLY ONE corect option, **3** marks for each Correct Answer and **0** mark in all other cases.
  **Section V** has **2** Matching Type Questions, **2** marks for the correct matching of each row and **0** mark in all other cases.
- You have to evaluate your Response Grids yourself with the help of Solutions.

### Section I - Straight Objective Type

This section contains 6 multiple choice questions. Each question has 4 choices (a), (b), (c) and (d), out of which **ONLY ONE** is correct.

**1.** $\displaystyle\int \frac{dx}{3\sin^2 x + 4\cos^2 x} =$

(a)  $\dfrac{1}{2\sqrt{3}}\tan^{-1}\left(\dfrac{1}{2}\tan x\right)+c$

(b)  $\dfrac{1}{2}\tan^{-1}\left(\dfrac{\sqrt{3}}{2}\tan x\right)+c$

(c)  $\dfrac{1}{2\sqrt{3}}\tan^{-1}\left(\dfrac{\sqrt{3}}{2}\tan x\right)+c$

(d)  None of these

**2.** $\displaystyle\int |x|\ln|x|\,dx$ equals $(x \neq 0)$

(a)  $\dfrac{x^2}{2}\ln|x| - \dfrac{x^2}{4} + c$

(b)  $\dfrac{1}{2}x|x|\ln x + \dfrac{1}{4}x|x| + c$

(c)  $-\dfrac{x^2}{2}\ln|x| + \dfrac{x^2}{4} + c$

(d)  $\dfrac{1}{2}x|x|\ln|x| - \dfrac{1}{4}x|x| + c$

| **RESPONSE GRID** | **1.** ⓐⓑⓒⓓ | **2.** ⓐⓑⓒⓓ |
| --- | --- | --- |

*Space for Rough Work*

**3.** If $\displaystyle\int \frac{(\sqrt{x})^5}{(\sqrt{x})^7 + x^6}\,dx = \lambda\,\ln\left(\frac{x^a}{x^a+1}\right) + c$, then

$a+\lambda$ is

(a)  $=2$  (b)  $>2$
(c)  $<2$  (d)  $=1$

**4.** A student evaluate $\displaystyle\int_0^\infty \frac{\tan^{-1}x}{\sqrt{x}(1+x)}\,dx$ by substituting $x = 1/t$

and obtains the correct answer equal $\dfrac{502\pi^2}{k}$. Using the same substitution or otherwise, find the value of $k$.

(a)  2008  (b)  1008
(c)  880  (d)  750

**5.** $\displaystyle\lim_{n\to\infty}\left(\tan\frac{\pi}{2n}\cdot\tan\frac{2\pi}{2n}\cdot\tan\frac{3\pi}{2n}\ldots\tan\frac{n\pi}{2n}\right)^{\frac{1}{n}} =$

(a)  0  (b)  1
(c)  $e$  (d)  $1/e$

**6.** If $p, q, r, s$ are in arithmetic progression and

$$f(x) = \begin{vmatrix} p+\sin x & q+\sin x & p-r+\sin x \\ q+\sin x & r+\sin x & -1+\sin x \\ r+\sin x & s+\sin x & s-q+\sin x \end{vmatrix}$$ such that

$\displaystyle\int_0^2 f(x)\,dx = -4$, then the common difference of the progession is

(a)  $\pm 1$  (b)  $\dfrac{1}{2}$
(c)  $\pm 2$  (d)  None of these

**Section II - Multiple Correct Answer Type**

This section contains 4 multiple correct answer(s) type questions. Each question has 4 choices (a), (b), (c) and (d), out of which **ONE OR MORE** is/are correct.

**7.** If $\displaystyle I = \int \frac{\sin^3(\theta/2)}{\cos(\theta/2)\sqrt{\cos^3\theta + \cos^2\theta + \cos\theta}}\,d\theta$

then $I$ equals

(a)  $\cot^{-1}(\tan\theta + \sec\theta) + c$
(b)  $\cot^{-1}(\cos\theta + \sec\theta + 1) + c$
(c)  $\tan^{-1}\left(\tan\dfrac{\theta}{2} + \sec\dfrac{\theta}{2} + 1\right) + c$
(d)  $\tan^{-1}(\cos\theta + \sec\theta + 1) + c$

**8.** If $\displaystyle I = \int \frac{(x^2+n)(n-1)x^{2n-1}}{(x\sin x + n\cos x)^2}\,dx$

$$= f(x) + g(x) + c,\ \text{then}$$

(a)  $f(x) = \dfrac{x^n}{x^n\sin x + n\cos x}$

(b)  $f(x) = -\dfrac{x^n\sec x}{x^n\sin x + nx^{n-1}\cos x}$

(c)  $g(x) = \tan x$

(d)  $g(x) = \sec x$

**9.** If $\displaystyle\int \sin^{-1}x\cos^{-1}x\,dx = f^{-1}(x)$

$$\left[Ax - x\,f^{-1}(x) - 2\sqrt{1-x^2}\right] + 2x + c,\ \text{then}$$

(a)  $f(x) = \sin x$  (b)  $f(x) = \cos x$

(c)  $A = \dfrac{\pi}{4}$  (d)  $A = \dfrac{\pi}{2}$

**10.** Let $e$ be the eccentricity of a hyperbola and $f(e)$ be the eccentricity of its conjugate hyperbola then

$\displaystyle\int_1^3 \underbrace{fff\ldots f}_{n\ \text{times}}(e)de$ is equal to

(a)  4, if $n$ is even  (b)  4, if $n$ is odd

(c)  2, if $n$ is even  (d)  $2\sqrt{2}$, if $n$ is odd

| RESPONSE GRID | | | | | |
|---|---|---|---|---|---|
| **3.** ⓐⓑⓒⓓ | **4.** ⓐⓑⓒⓓ | **5.** ⓐⓑⓒⓓ | **6.** ⓐⓑⓒⓓ | **7.** ⓐⓑⓒⓓ |
| **8.** ⓐⓑⓒⓓ | **9.** ⓐⓑⓒⓓ | **10.** ⓐⓑⓒⓓ | | |

### Section III - Integer Type

This section contains 4 questions. The answer to each of the questions is a single digit integer ranging from 0 to 9.

11.  If the value of $\displaystyle\int_{0}^{100\pi} ([\cot^{-1} x]+[\tan^{-1} x])\,dx$ is $100\pi + p\cot p,$ then the value of $p$ is (where $[.]$ denotes greatest integer function).

12.  Let $f:(0,\infty) \to R$ be a differentiable function such that

$$x\int_{0}^{x}(1-t)f(t)dt = \int_{0}^{x} t\,f(t)dt \ \forall x \in (0,\infty) \text{ and } f(1)=1. \text{ The}$$

value of $\displaystyle\lim_{x\to\infty} f(x)$ is equal to

13.  If $\displaystyle I(n) = \int_{0}^{\pi/2} \theta\sin^{n}\theta\,d\theta,\ n\in N,\ n>3,$ and $[2010\,I(2010) - 2009\,I(2008)]^{-1}$ is equal to $1005\,a$ then $a=$

14.  If $\displaystyle\int \cos ec^2 x\, ln\left(\cos x + \sqrt{\cos 2x}\right)dx$

$$= f(x)\, ln\left(\cos x + \sqrt{\cos 2x}\right)+ g(x) + f(x) - x + c,$$

then $f^2(x) - g^2(x)$ is equal to $\left(0 < x \le \dfrac{\pi}{2}\right).$

---

## Section IV - Comprehension Type

Based upon the given paragraphs, 4 multiple choice questions have to be answered. Each question has 4 choices (a), (b), (c) and (d), out of which **ONLY ONE** is correct.

---

### PARAGRAPH-1

Let $f(x)$ and $\phi(x)$ are two continuous functions on $R$ satisfying $\displaystyle\phi(x) = \int_{a}^{x} f(t)\,dt,\ a \ne 0$ and another continuous function $g(x)$ satisfying $g(x + \alpha) + g(x) = 0\ \forall\, x \in R, \alpha > 0$ and $\displaystyle\int_{b}^{2k} g(t)\,dt$ is independent of $b.$

15.  If $f(x)$ is an even function, then
 (a)  $\phi(x)$ is also an even function
 (b)  $\phi(x)$ is an odd function
 (c)  If $f(a-x) = -f(x),$ then $\phi(x)$ is an even function
 (d)  If $f(a-x) = -f(x),$ then $\phi(x)$ is an odd function

16.  Least positive value of $c$ if $c, k, b$ are in A.P., is
 (a)  0  (b)  1
 (c)  $\alpha$  (d)  $2\alpha$

### PARAGRAPH-2

If $A$ is square matrix and $e^A$ is defined as

$$e^A = I + A + \frac{A^2}{2!} + \frac{A^3}{3!} + ... = \frac{1}{2}\begin{bmatrix} f(x) & g(x) \\ g(x) & f(x) \end{bmatrix}, \text{ where } A = \begin{bmatrix} x & x \\ x & x \end{bmatrix}$$

and $0 < x < 1,$ $I$ is an identity matrix.

17.  $\displaystyle\int \frac{g(x)}{f(x)}\,dx$ is equal to
 (a)  $\log(e^x + e^{-x}) + c$  (b)  $\log(e^x - e^{-x}) + c$
 (c)  $\log(e^{2x} - 1) + c$  (d)  none of these

18.  $\displaystyle\int (g(x)+1)\,\sin x\,dx$ is equal to
 (a)  $\dfrac{e^x}{2}(\sin x - \cos x)$  (b)  $\dfrac{e^{2x}}{5}(2\sin x - \cos x)$
 (c)  $\dfrac{e^x}{5}(\sin 2x - \cos 2x)$  (d)  none of these

---

<table>
<tr><td rowspan="3">**RESPONSE GRID**</td><td>11. ⓪①②③④⑤⑥⑦⑧⑨</td><td>12. ⓪①②③④⑤⑥⑦⑧⑨</td></tr>
<tr><td>13. ⓪①②③④⑤⑥⑦⑧⑨</td><td>14. ⓪①②③④⑤⑥⑦⑧⑨</td></tr>
<tr><td>15. ⓐⓑⓒⓓ    16. ⓐⓑⓒⓓ</td><td>17. ⓐⓑⓒⓓ    18. ⓐⓑⓒⓓ</td></tr>
</table>

*Space for Rough Work*

## Section V - Matrix-Match Type

This section contains 2 questions. It contains statements given in two columns, which have to be matched. Statements in column I are labelled as A, B, C and D whereas statements in column II are labelled as p, q, r and s. The answers to these questions have to be appropriately bubbled as illustrated in the following example. If the correct matches are A-p, A-r, B-p, B-s, C-r, C-s and D-q, then the correctly bubbled matrix will look like the following:

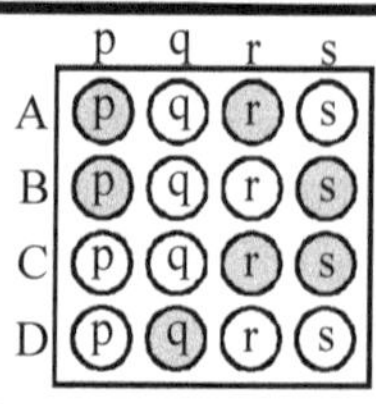

**19.** If $\displaystyle\int \frac{\log_e(x+\sqrt{1+x^2})}{\sqrt{1+x^2}}\,dx = fog(x) + c$, Now match the entries from the following two columns:

| Column-I | Column-II |
|---|---|
| (A) $f(2)$ is equal to | (p) 0 |
| (B) $g(0)$ is equal to | (q) 1 |
| (C) If $\displaystyle\int f(x)g(x)dx = ax^3 g(x) + b(1+x^2)^{3/2} + c(1+x^2)^{1/2} + d$, then $a+c$ is equal to | (r) 2 |
| (D) If $\displaystyle\int e^{g(x)}dx = ax(x+\sqrt{1+x^2}+ag(x)+c)$ then $a$ is equal to | (s) $\dfrac{1}{2}$ |
| | (t) $\dfrac{1}{3}$ |

**20.**

| Column-I | Column-II |
|---|---|
| (A) $\displaystyle\sqrt{2}\int_0^\infty \left[\frac{3}{x^2+1}\right]dx$ is equal to | (p) 1 |
| (B) $\displaystyle\ln 3\int_{-10}^{10} \frac{3^x}{3^{[x]}}dx$ is equal to | (q) 2 |
| (C) $\displaystyle\int_{-1}^{1} [x[1+\sin\pi x]+1]\,dx$ is equal to | (r) 3 |
| (D) If $\displaystyle\int_0^{\pi/3}\left\{a^2\left(\frac{\cos 3x}{4}+\frac{3}{4}\cos x\right)a\sin x - 20\cos x\,dx \le -\frac{a^2}{3}\right\}$, then $a$ can be equal to | (s) 4 |
| (In all of the above, [.] represents the greatest integer function) | (t) 40 |

| | |
|---|---|
| **RESPONSE** | **19.** A - ⓟⓠⓡⓢ; B - ⓟⓠⓡⓢ; C - ⓟⓠⓡⓢ; D - ⓟⓠⓡⓢ |
| **GRID** | **20.** A - ⓟⓠⓡⓢ; B - ⓟⓠⓡⓢ; C - ⓟⓠⓡⓢ; D - ⓟⓠⓡⓢ |

## DAILY PRACTICE PROBLEM DPP CM20 - MATHEMATICS

| Total Questions | 20 | Total Marks | 74 |
|---|---|---|---|
| Attempted | | Correct | |
| Incorrect | | Net Score | |
| Cut-off Score | 24 | Qualifying Score | 35 |

$$\text{Net Score} = \sum_{i=1}^{V}\left[(\text{correct}_i \times MM_i) - (In_i - NM_i)\right]$$

*Space for Rough Work*

**Date :**  **Start Time :**  **End Time :**

# MATHEMATICS CM21

**SYLLABUS :** Application of Integrals

**Max. Marks : 69**  **Time : 60 min.**

## GENERAL INSTRUCTIONS

- The Daily Practice Problem Sheet contains 20 Questions divided into 5 sections.
  **Section I** has **5** MCQs with ONLY 1 Correct Option, **3** marks for each correct answer and **−1** for each incorrect answer.
  **Section II** has **4** MCQs with ONE or MORE THAN ONE Correct options.
  For each question, marks will be awarded in one of the following categories:
  Full marks: **+4** If only the bubble(s) corresponding to all the correct option(s) is (are) darkened.
  Partial marks: **+1** For darkening a bubble corresponding to each correct option provided NO INCORRECT option is darkened.
  Zero marks:  If none of the bubbles is darkened.
  Negative marks: **−2** In all other cases.
  **Section III** has **5** Single Digit Integer Answer Type Questions, **3** marks for each Correct Answer and **0** mark in all other cases.
  **Section IV** has Comprehension/Matching Cum-Comprehension Type Questions having **5** MCQs with ONLY ONE corect option, **3** marks for each Correct Answer and **0** mark in all other cases.
  **Section V** has **1** Matching Type Questions, **2** marks for the correct matching of each row and **0** mark in all other cases.
- You have to evaluate your Response Grids yourself with the help of Solutions.

---

### Section I - Straight Objective Type

This section contains 5 multiple choice questions. Each question has 4 choices (a), (b), (c) and (d), out of which **ONLY ONE** is correct.

**1.** The area bounded by $y = \sec^{-1} x$,

$y = \operatorname{cosec}^{-1} x$ and line $x - 1 = 0$ is

(a) $\left( \log(3 + 2\sqrt{2}) - \dfrac{\pi}{2} \right)$ sq.units

(b) $\left( \dfrac{\pi}{2} - \log(3 + 2\sqrt{2}) \right)$ sq.units

(c) $(\pi - \log_e 3)$ sq. units

(d) None of these

**2.** The area of the loop of the curve, $ay^2 = x^2(a - x)$ is

(a) $4a^2$ sq. units

(b) $\dfrac{8a^2}{15}$ sq.units

(c) $\dfrac{16a^2}{9}$ sq.units

(d) None of these

---

| RESPONSE GRID | **1.** ⓐⓑⓒⓓ  **2.** ⓐⓑⓒⓓ |
| --- | --- |

*Space for Rough Work*

**3.** The area enclosed by the curves, $xy^2 = a^2(a-x)$ and $(a-x)y^2 = a^2 x$ is

(a) $(\pi - 2)a^2$ sq. units    (b) $(4 - \pi)a^2$ sq. units

(c) $\pi a^2 / 3$ sq. units    (d) None of these

**4.** If $f(x) = \begin{cases} \sqrt{\{x\}}, & x \notin z \\ 1, & x \in z \end{cases}$ and $g(x) = \{x\}^2$, (where $\{.\}$ denotes fractional part of x), then area bounded by $f(x)$ and $g(x)$ for $x \in [0,10]$ is

(a) 5/3        (b) 5

(c) 10/3       (d) None of these

**5.** The area bounded by $y = 2 - |2 - x|$, $y = \dfrac{3}{|x|}$ is

(a) $\left(\dfrac{5 - 4 \ln 2}{3}\right)$ sq. units

(b) $\left(\dfrac{2 - \ln 3}{2}\right)$ sq. units

(c) $\left(\dfrac{4 - 3 \ln 3}{2}\right)$ sq. units

(d) None of these

### Section II - Multiple Correct Answer Type

This section contains 4 multiple correct answer(s) type questions. Each question has 4 choices (a), (b), (c) and (d), out of which **ONE OR MORE** is/are correct.

**6.** $y = f(x)$ and $y = g(x)$ are two continuous positive functions intersecting only at three points (0, 1), (3, 4) and (5, 6). A function $h(x) = $ max. $(f(x),$ $g(x))$ is defined as $h(x) = \begin{cases} f(x), 0 \le x < 3 \\ g(x), 3 \le x \le 5 \end{cases}$.

If $\displaystyle\int_0^5 f(x)\, dx = a$,

$\displaystyle\int_0^5 g(x)\, dx = b, \int_3^5 f(x)\, dx = c, \int_0^3 g(x)\, dx = d$,

then area of region bounded between $f(x)$ and $g(x)$ from $x = 0$ to $x = 5$ is

(a) $a - 2c + b - d$

(b) $a + b - 2c - 2d$

(c) $\displaystyle\int_0^3 f(x)\, dx + \int_5^3 f(x)\, dx + \int_3^0 g(x)\, dx + \int_3^5 g(x)\, dx$

(d) $\displaystyle\int_0^3 (g(x) - f(x))\, dx + \int_3^5 (f(x) - g(x))\, dx$

**7.** Which of the following have the same bounded area ?

(a) $f(x) = \sin x, g(x) = \sin^2 x$, where $0 \le x \le 10\pi$

(b) $f(x) = \sin x, g(x) = |\sin x|$, where $0 \le x \le 20\pi$

(c) $f(x) = |\sin x|, g(x) = \sin^3 x$, where $0 \le x \le 10\pi$

(d) $f(x) = \sin x, g(x) = \sin^4 x$, where $0 \le x \le 10\pi$

**8.** Let $f$ and $g$ be continuous function on $a \le x \le b$ and $p(x) = $ max $\{f(x), g(x)\}$ and $q(x) = $ min $\{f(x), g(x)\}$. The area bounded by the curves $y = p(x)$, $y = q(x)$ and the ordinates $x = a$ and $x = b$ is given by

(a) $\displaystyle\int_a^b (f(x) - g(x))\, dx$    (b) $\displaystyle\int_a^b (p(x) - q(x))\, dx$

(c) $\displaystyle\int_a^b |p(x) - q(x)|\, dx$    (d) $\displaystyle\int_a^b |f(x) - g(x)|\, dx$

**9.** Let S be the area of the region enclosed by $y = e^{-x^2}$, $y = 0, x = 0$ and $x = 1$; then

(a) $S \ge \dfrac{1}{e}$

(b) $S \ge 1 - \dfrac{1}{e}$

(c) $S \le \dfrac{1}{4}\left(1 + \dfrac{1}{\sqrt{e}}\right)$

(d) $S \le \dfrac{1}{\sqrt{2}} + \dfrac{1}{\sqrt{e}}\left(1 - \dfrac{1}{\sqrt{2}}\right)$

---

**RESPONSE GRID**

3. (a)(b)(c)(d)   4. (a)(b)(c)(d)   5. (a)(b)(c)(d)   6. (a)(b)(c)(d)   7. (a)(b)(c)(d)
8. (a)(b)(c)(d)   9. (a)(b)(c)(d)

---

*Space for Rough Work*

## Section III - Integer Type

This section contains 5 questions. The answer to each of the questions is a single digit integer ranging from 0 to 9.

**10.** The area of the region bounded between the curves $|y| - |\sin x| \geq 0$ and $x^2 + y^2 - \pi^2 \leq 0$ is $\pi^3 - A$. Find the value of $A$.

**11.** Area of the region bounded by the curve $y = \{x^2\}$, where $\{.\}$ denotes fractional part function $\forall\ x \in [-2,\ 2]$ is $p\left(\sqrt{q} + \sqrt{r} - \dfrac{7}{3}\right)$. Find the value of $p + q + r$.

**12.** If the area of the region bounded by the curves $|y + x| \leq 1$, $|y - x| \leq 1$ and $3x^2 + 3y^2 = 1$ is $\left(p - \dfrac{\pi}{p+1}\right)$ square unit then $p$ is equal to

**13.** If $14 + 1nk$ be the area bounded by the curves $|y| = e^{-|x|} - \dfrac{1}{2}$ and $\dfrac{|x| + |y|}{2} + \left|\dfrac{|x| - |y|}{2}\right| \leq 2$ then $k$ is equal to

**14.** If the total area between the curves $f(x) = \cos^{-1}(\sin x)$ and $g(x) = \sin^{-1}(\cos x)$ on the interval $[0, 98\pi]$ is $A$, then find the last digit of $A$ (Given $\pi = 22/7$).

## Section IV - Comprehension/Matching Cum-Comprehension Type

**Directions (Qs. 15 and 16) :** Based upon the given paragraph, 2 multiple choice questions have to be answered. Each question has 4 choices (a), (b), (c) and (d), out of which **ONLY ONE** is correct.

**PARAGRAPH**

Consider the areas $S_0, S_1, S_2, \ldots\ldots$ bounded by the $x$-axis and half-waves of the curve $y = e^{-x}\sin x$, where $x \geq 0$.

**15.** The value of $S_0$ is

(a) $\dfrac{1}{2}(1 + e^{\pi})$ sq. units

(b) $\dfrac{1}{2}(1 + e^{-\pi})$ sq. units

(c) $\dfrac{1}{2}(1 - e^{-\pi})$ sq. units

(d) $\dfrac{1}{2}(e^{\pi} - 1)$ sq. units

**16.** The sequence $S_0, S_1, S_2, \ldots\ldots$ forms a G.P. with common ratio

(a) $\dfrac{e^{\pi}}{2}$ 　　　　(b) $e^{-\pi}$

(c) $e^{\pi}$ 　　　　(d) $\dfrac{e^{-\pi}}{2}$

**Directions (Qs. 17-19) :** This passage contains a table having 3 columns and 4 rows. Based on the table, there are three questions. Each question has four options (a), (b), (c) and (d) **ONLY ONE** of these four options is correct.

Column 1 contains information about equations in two variables $x$ and $y$ where $p$, $q$ and $k$ are arbitrary constants.

Column 2 contains information about shape of the graphs of given equations in column-1.

Column 3 contains information about the area of the regions bounded by the graphs in column-2.

**RESPONSE GRID**

10. ⓪①②③④⑤⑥⑦⑧⑨　11. ⓪①②③④⑤⑥⑦⑧⑨
12. ⓪①②③④⑤⑥⑦⑧⑨　13. ⓪①②③④⑤⑥⑦⑧⑨
14. ⓪①②③④⑤⑥⑦⑧⑨　15. ⓐⓑⓒⓓ　　16. ⓐⓑⓒⓓ

*Space for Rough Work*

| Column 1 | Column 2 | Column 3 |
|---|---|---|
| (I) $\ |x-p|+|y-q|=k$ | (i) Rectangle | (P) $\dfrac{2k^2}{pq}$ |
| (II) $|x-p|-|y-q|=k$ | (ii) Rhombus | (Q) $2k^2$ |
| (III) $p\,|x|+q\,|y|=k$ | (iii) Square | (R) Undetermined |
| (IV) $|x+y|=p$ and $|x-y|=q$ | (iv) Non-quadrilateral | (S) $2pq$ |

**17.** Which of the following options is the only correct combination?

    (a) (II)(i)(S)       (b) (III)(ii)(P)       (c) (I)(iii)(S)       (d) (IV)(ii)(P)

**18.** For $\left|x-\dfrac{1}{p}\right|+\left|y-\dfrac{1}{q}\right|=k,$ the area bounded by region is similar to

    (a) (I)(iii)(Q)       (b) (II)(iv)(R)       (c) (III)(ii)(P)       (d) (IV)(i)(S)

**19.** Which of the following options is the only incorrect combination?

    (a) (I)(iii)(Q)       (b) (III)(ii)(P)       (c) (II)(iv)(R)       (d) (IV)(i)(Q)

### Section V - Matrix-Match Type

This section contains 1 questions. It contains statements given in two columns, which have to be matched. Statements in column I are labelled as A, B, C and D whereas statements in column II are labelled as p, q, r and s. The answers to these questions have to be appropriately bubbled as illustrated in the following example. If the correct matches are A-p, A-r, B-p, B-s, C-r, C-s and D-q, then the correctly bubbled matrix will look like the following:

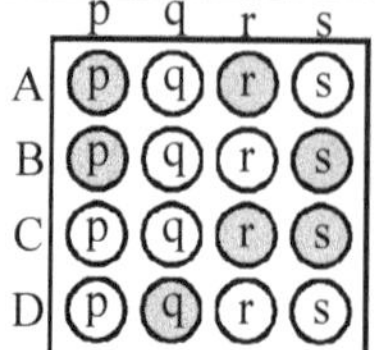

**20.**

| Column - I | Column - II |
|---|---|
| (A) Area enclosed by $y=[\,x\,]$ and $y=\{x\}$, where [.] and {.} represent greatest integer and fractional part functions, is | (p) 16/5 sq. units |
| (B) The area bounded by the curves $y^2=x^3$ and $|y|=2x$, is | (q) 1 sq. units |
| (C) The smaller area included between the curves $\sqrt{x}+\sqrt{|y|}=1$ and $|x|+|y|=1$, is | (r) 4 sq. units |
| (D) Area bounded by the curves $y=\left[\dfrac{x^2}{64}+2\right]$ (where [.] denotes the greatest integer function), $y=x-1$ and $x=0$ above the $x$-axis, is | (s) 2/3 sq. units |



## DAILY PRACTICE PROBLEM DPP CM21 - MATHEMATICS

| Total Questions | 20 | Total Marks | 69 |
|---|---|---|---|
| Attempted | | Correct | |
| Incorrect | | Net Score | |
| Cut-off Score | 22 | Qualifying Score | 33 |

$$\text{Net Score} = \sum_{i=1}^{V}\left[\left(\text{correct}_i \times MM_i\right)-\left(In_i - NM_i\right)\right]$$

Date : [ ]　　　　Start Time : [ ]　　　　End Time : [ ]

# MATHEMATICS CM22

**SYLLABUS :** Differential Equations

**Max. Marks : 74**　　　　　　　　　　　　　**Time : 60 min.**

### GENERAL INSTRUCTIONS

- The Daily Practice Problem Sheet contains 20 Questions divided into 5 sections.
  **Section I** has **5** MCQs with ONLY 1 Correct Option, **3** marks for each correct answer and **−1** for each incorrect answer.
  **Section II** has **4** MCQs with ONE or MORE THAN ONE Correct options.
  For each question, marks will be awarded in one of the following categories:
  Full marks: **+4** If only the bubble(s) corresponding to all the correct option(s) is (are) darkened.
  Partial marks: **+1** For darkening a bubble corresponding to each correct option provided NO INCORRECT option is darkened.
  Zero marks:　If none of the bubbles is darkened.
  Negative marks: **−2** In all other cases.
  **Section III** has **4** Single Digit Integer Answer Type Questions, **3** marks for each Correct Answer and **0** mark in all other cases.
  **Section IV** has Comprehension/Matching Cum–Comprehension Type Questions having **5** MCQs with ONLY ONE corect option, **3** marks for each Correct Answer and **0** mark in all other cases.
  **Section V** has **2** Matching Type Questions, **2** marks for the correct matching of each row and **0** mark in all other cases.
- You have to evaluate your Response Grids yourself with the help of Solutions.

---

### Section I - Straight Objective Type

This section contains 5 multiple choice questions. Each question has 4 choices (a), (b), (c) and (d), out of which **ONLY ONE** is correct.

**1.** The gradient of the curve passing through the point $(4, 0)$ is given by $\dfrac{dy}{dx} - \dfrac{y}{x} + \dfrac{5x}{(x+2)(x-3)} = 0$. If the point $(5, a)$ lies on the curve, then the value of '$a$', is

(a) $5\ln\dfrac{7}{12}$

(b) $\dfrac{67}{12}$

(c) $5\sin\dfrac{7}{12}$

(d) None of these

**2.** If for the differential equation $y' = \dfrac{y}{x} + \phi\left(\dfrac{x}{y}\right)$, the general solution is $y = \dfrac{x}{\log|Cx|}$, then $\phi\,(x/y)$ is given by

(a) $-x^2/y^2$

(b) $y^2/x^2$

(c) $x^2/y^2$

(d) $-y^2/x^2$

---

| **RESPONSE GRID** | **1.** ⓐⓑⓒⓓ　**2.** ⓐⓑⓒⓓ |
|---|---|

---

*Space for Rough Work*

**3.** If $\phi(x)$ is a differentiable function, then the solution of the differential equation $dy + \{y\,\phi'(x) - \phi(x)\,\phi'(x)\}\,dx = 0$ is

(a) $y = \{\phi(x) - 1\} + ce^{-\phi(x)}$

(b) $y\phi(x) = \{\phi(x)\}^2 + c$

(c) $ye^{\phi(x)} = \phi(x)\,e^{\phi(x)} + c$

(d) $y - \phi(x) = \phi(x)\,e^{-\phi(x)}$

**4.** Choose the incorrect statements

(a) The order of differential equation $\sqrt{1 + \dfrac{d^2 y}{dx^2}} = x$ is 1.

(b) The solution of differential equation

$x\,dy - y\,dx = \sqrt{x^2 + y^2}\,dx$ is

$y + \sqrt{x^2 + y^2} = cx^2 \cdot$

(c) $\dfrac{d^2 y}{dx^2} = 2\left(\dfrac{dy}{dx} - y\right)$ is differential equation of family

curves $y = e^x(A\cos x + B\sin x)$.

(d) The solution of differential equation

$(1 + y^2) + (x - 2e^{\tan^{-1} y})\dfrac{dy}{dx} = 0$ is

$x\,e^{\tan^{-1} y} = e^{2\tan^{-1} y} + k$

**5.** The solution of $\dfrac{xdx + ydy}{xdy - ydx} = \sqrt{\dfrac{a^2 - x^2 - y^2}{x^2 + y^2}}$ is

(a) $\sqrt{x^2 + y^2} = a\left\{\sin\left(\tan^{-1}\dfrac{y}{x} + c\right)\right\}$

(b) $\sqrt{x^2 + y^2} = a\cos\left\{\left(\tan^{-1}\dfrac{y}{x} + c\right)\right\}$

(c) $\sqrt{x^2 + y^2} = a\left\{\tan\left(\sin^{-1}\dfrac{y}{x} + c\right)\right\}$

(d) None of these

**6.** The differential equation $\dfrac{d^2 x}{dy^2} + y + \cot^2 x = 0$ must be satisfied by

(a) $2 + c_1 \cos x + \sqrt{c_2}\,\sin x$

(b) $\cos x.\ln\left(\tan\dfrac{x}{2}\right) + 2$

(c) $2 + c_1 \cos x + c_2 \sin x + \cos x\,\log\left(\tan\dfrac{x}{2}\right)$

(d) all the above

**7.** The curve for which the area of the triangle formed by the $x$-axis, the tangent line and radius vector of the point of tangency is equal to $a^2$ is

(a) $x = cy + \dfrac{a^2}{y}$      (b) $y = x - cx^2$

(c) $y = cx + \dfrac{a^2}{x}$      (d) $x = cy - \dfrac{a^2}{y}$

(where $c$ is arbitrary constant)

**8.** Which one of the following functions is / are homogeneous ?

(a) $f(x, y) = \dfrac{x - y}{x^2 + y^2}$

(b) $f(x, y) = x^{\frac{1}{3}} y^{-\frac{2}{3}} \tan^{-1}\dfrac{x}{y}$

(c) $f(x, y) = x\,(\ln\sqrt{x^2 + y^2} - \ln y) + y\,e^{x/y}$

(d) $f(x, y) = x\left[\ln\dfrac{2x^2 + y^2}{x} - \ln(x + y)\right] + y^2 \tan\dfrac{x + 2y}{3x - y}$

**9.** The orthogonal trajectories of the family of coaxial circle $x^2 + y^2 + 2gx + c = 0$, where $g$ is a parameter are

(a) family of circles with center on $y$-axis

(b) system of coaxial parabolas

(c) $x^2 + y^2 - c'x - cy = 0$, where $c'$ is an arbitrary constant

(d) system of coaxial circles with radical axis along $x$-axis

## Section III - Integer Type

This section contains 4 questions. The answer to each of the questions is a single digit integer ranging from 0 to 9.

**10.** If the equation of a curve $y = y(x)$ satisfies the differential equation

$$x\int_0^x y(t)\,dt = (x + 1)\int_0^x ty(t)\,dt, \; x > 0, \text{ and } y(1) = e, \text{ then } y\left(\dfrac{1}{2}\right)$$

is equal to

## Section II - Multiple Correct Answer Type

This section contains 4 multiple correct answer(s) type questions. Each question has 4 choices (a), (b), (c) and (d), out of which **ONE OR MORE** is/are correct.

<table>
<tr><td rowspan="2">**RESPONSE GRID**</td><td>3. ⓐⓑⓒⓓ</td><td>4. ⓐⓑⓒⓓ</td><td>5. ⓐⓑⓒⓓ</td><td>6. ⓐⓑⓒⓓ</td><td>7. ⓐⓑⓒⓓ</td></tr>
<tr><td>8. ⓐⓑⓒⓓ</td><td>9. ⓐⓑⓒⓓ</td><td colspan="3">10. ⓪①②③④⑤⑥⑦⑧⑨</td></tr>
</table>

11. The population of a country increases at a rate proportional to the number of inhabitants. If the population doubles in 30 years then the number of years in the nearest integer when the population will triple is equal to 6 m, where m equals,

12. If the differential equation corresponding to $y = \sum\limits_{i=1}^{3} C_i e^{m_i x}$

where $C_i$'s are arbitrary constants and $m_1, m_2, m_3$ are roots of $m^3 - 7m + 6 = 0$ is $\dfrac{d^3 y}{dx^3} - 7\dfrac{dy}{dx} + ky = 0$ then $k$ is equal to

13. Find the degree of the following differential equations:

$$\left(\frac{dy}{dx}\right)^4 - 2x\left(\frac{d^3 y}{dx^3}\right)^2 = x^2 y \frac{d^2 y}{dx^2} - \frac{d^3 y}{dx^3}$$

---

## Section IV - Comprehension/Matching Cum-Comprehension Type

**Directions (Qs. 14 and 15) :** Based upon the given paragraph, 2 multiple choice questions have to be answered. Each question has 4 choices (a), (b), (c) and (d), out of which **ONLY ONE** is correct.

### PARAGRAPH

For certain curves $y = f(x)$ satisfying $\dfrac{d^2 y}{dx^2} = 6x - 4$, $f(x)$ has local minimum value 5 when $x = 1$.

14. Number of critical point for $y = f(x)$ for $x \in [0, 2]$ is
    (a) 0        (b) 1
    (c) 2        (d) 3

15. Global minimum value of $y = f(x)$ for $x \in [0, 2]$ is
    (a) 5        (b) 7
    (c) 8        (d) 9

---

**Directions (Qs. 16-18) :** This passage contains a table having 3 columns and 4 rows. Based on the table, there are two questions. Each question has four options (a), (b), (c) and (d) **ONLY ONE** of these four options is correct.

### PARAGRAPH

Appropriately match the information given in the three columns of the given table.

| | Column 1 [Differential Equations] | | Column 2 [Integrating factors (I.F.)] | | Column 3 [Solutions of Differential equations] |
|---|---|---|---|---|---|
| (I) | $(1+x^2)\dfrac{dy}{dx} + 2xy - 4x^2 = 0$ | (i) | $e^{x/\sqrt{1-x^2}}$ | (P) | $x = y^3 + cy$ |
| (II) | $(x + 2y^3)\dfrac{dy}{dx} = y$ | (ii) | $e^{-x}(1+x)$ | (Q) | $y(1+x^2) = \dfrac{4}{3}x^3 + c$ |
| (III) | $(1+x)\dfrac{dy}{dx} - xy = 1 - x$ | (iii) | $2y^2$ | (R) | $y = \dfrac{x}{\sqrt{1-x^2}} + ce^{-x/\sqrt{1-x^2}}$ |
| (IV) | $\dfrac{dy}{dx} + \dfrac{y}{(1-x^2)^{3/2}} = \dfrac{x + \sqrt{1-x^2}}{(1-x^2)^2}$ | (iv) | $1 + x^2$ | (S) | $y(1+x) = x + ce^x$ |

16. Which of the following options is the only correct combination?
    (a) (I)(i)(R)      (b) (II)(ii)(S)
    (c) (III)(iv)(P)      (d) (IV)(i)(R)

17. Which of the following options is the only correct combination?
    (a) (IV)(iii)(R)      (b) (II)(iv)(P)
    (c) (III)(ii)(S)      (d) (I)(i)(S)

18. Which of the following options is the only incorrect combination?
    (a) (II)(iv)(R)      (b) (III)(ii)(S)
    (c) (I)(iv)(Q)      (d) (IV)(i)(R)



*Space for Rough Work*

## Section V - Matrix-Match Type

This section contains 2 questions. It contains statements given in two columns, which have to be matched. Statements in column I are labelled as A, B, C and D whereas statements in column II are labelled as p, q, r and s. The answers to these questions have to be appropriately bubbled as illustrated in the following example. If the correct matches are A-p, A-r, B-p, B-s, C-r, C-s and D-q, then the correctly bubbled matrix will look like the following:

**19.** Let a function $y = f(x)$ satisfies the following conditions

1. $\dfrac{dy}{dx} = y + \int\limits_0^1 y\,dx$  2. $f(0) = 1$

**Column-I**

A. $f''(0)$ is equal to

B. $f(1)$ is equal to

C. $\lim\limits_{x \to 0} \dfrac{f(x) - 1}{x}$ is equal to

D. $\dfrac{1}{2} f'(\ln(3\text{-e}))$ is equal to

**Column-II**

(p) $f(0)$

(q) $\dfrac{2}{3-e}$

(r) $\dfrac{e+1}{3-e}$

(s) $f'(0)$

(t) 1

**20.**

**Column-I**

(A) Let $f(x)$ is a derivable function satisfying $f(x) = \int\limits_0^x e^t \sin(x - t)\,dt$ and $g(x) = f''(x) - f(x)$ then the possible integers in the range of $g(x)$ is

(B) If the substitution $x = \tan^{-1}(t)$ transforms the differential equation $\dfrac{d^2y}{dx^2} + xy\dfrac{dy}{dx} + \sec^2 x = 0$ into a differential equation $(1+t^2)\dfrac{d^2y}{dt^2} + (2t + y\tan^{-1}(t))\dfrac{dy}{dt} = k$ then $k$ is equal to

(C) If $a^2 + b^2 = 1$ then $(a^3b - ab^3)$ can be equal to

(D) If the system of equations $\left.\begin{array}{r} x - \lambda y - z = 0 \\ \lambda x - y - z = 0 \\ x + y - z = 0 \end{array}\right\}$ has a unique solution, then the value of $\lambda$ can be

**Column-II**

(p) $-1$

(q) 0

(r) 1

(s) 2



## DAILY PRACTICE PROBLEM DPP CM22 - MATHEMATICS

| Total Questions | 20 | Total Marks | 74 |
|---|---|---|---|
| Attempted | | Correct | |
| Incorrect | | Net Score | |
| Cut-off Score | 22 | Qualifying Score | 32 |

$$\text{Net Score} = \sum_{i=1}^{V} \left[ (\text{correct}_i \times MM_i) - (In_i - NM_i) \right]$$

*Space for Rough Work*

Date :        Start Time :        End Time :       

# MATHEMATICS CM23

**SYLLABUS :** Vector Algebra

**Max. Marks : 69**                  **Time : 60 min.**

## GENERAL INSTRUCTIONS

- The Daily Practice Problem Sheet contains 20 Questions divided into 5 sections.
  **Section I** has **6** MCQs with ONLY 1 Correct Option, **3** marks for each correct answer and **−1** for each incorrect answer.
  **Section II** has **4** MCQs with ONE or MORE THAN ONE Correct options.
  For each question, marks will be awarded in one of the following categories:
  Full marks: **+4** If only the bubble(s) corresponding to all the correct option(s) is (are) darkened.
  Partial marks: **+1** For darkening a bubble corresponding to each correct option provided NO INCORRECT option is darkened.
  Zero marks:  If none of the bubbles is darkened.
  Negative marks: **−2** In all other cases.
  **Section III** has **5** Single Digit Integer Answer Type Questions, **3** marks for each Correct Answer and **0** mark in all other cases.
  **Section IV** has Comprehension Type Questions having **4** MCQs with ONLY ONE corect option, **3** marks for each Correct Answer and **0** mark in all other cases.
  **Section V** has **1** Matching Type Question, **2** marks for the correct matching of each row and **0** mark in all other cases.
- You have to evaluate your Response Grids yourself with the help of Solutions.

## Section I - Straight Objective Type

This section contains 6 multiple choice questions. Each question has 4 choices (a), (b), (c) and (d), out of which **ONLY ONE** is correct.

1. Let $\vec{a} = 2\hat{i} + \hat{j} - 2\hat{k}, \vec{b} = \hat{i} + \hat{j}$. If $\vec{c}$ is a vector such that $\vec{a} \bullet \vec{c} = |\vec{c}|, |\vec{c} - \vec{a}| = 2\sqrt{2}$ and the angle between $\vec{a} \times \vec{b}$ and $\vec{c}$ is $30°$, then $|(\vec{a} \times \vec{b}) \times \vec{c}|$ equals:

   (a) $\dfrac{1}{2}$        (b) $\dfrac{3\sqrt{3}}{2}$

   (c) $3$        (d) $\dfrac{3}{2}$

2. If $\hat{x}, \hat{y}$ and $\hat{z}$ are three unit vectors in three-dimensional space, then the minimum value of $|\hat{x} + \hat{y}|^2 + |\hat{y} + \hat{z}|^2 + |\hat{z} + \hat{x}|^2$

   (a) $\dfrac{3}{2}$        (b) $3$

   (c) $3\sqrt{3}$        (d) $6$

3. $ABCD$ is parallelogram. The position vectors of $A$ and $C$ are respectively, $3\hat{i} + 3\hat{j} + 5\hat{k}$ and $\hat{i} - 5\hat{j} - 5\hat{k}$. If $M$ is the midpoint of the diagonal $DB$, then the magnitude of the projection of $\overrightarrow{OM}$ on $\overrightarrow{OC}$, where $O$ is the origin, is

   (a) $7\sqrt{51}$        (b) $\dfrac{7}{\sqrt{50}}$

   (c) $7\sqrt{50}$        (d) $\dfrac{7}{\sqrt{51}}$

---

**RESPONSE GRID**    **1.** ⓐⓑⓒⓓ    **2.** ⓐⓑⓒⓓ    **3.** ⓐⓑⓒⓓ

*Space for Rough Work*

**4.** Let $\vec{p} = a\hat{i} + b\hat{j} + c\hat{k}$ and $\vec{q} = b\hat{i} + c\hat{j} + a\hat{k}$, where a, b, $c \in R$. If '$\theta$' be the angle between $\vec{p}$ and $\vec{q}$ then,

(a) $\theta \in (0, \pi/2)$      (b) $\theta \in [0, 2\pi/3]$

(c) $\theta \in (2\pi/3, \pi]$      (d) $\theta \in [\pi/2, \pi]$

**5.** If $\cos\alpha \neq 1$, $\cos\beta \neq 1$ and $\cos\gamma \neq 1$, then the vector

$\vec{a} = \hat{i}\cos\alpha + \hat{j} + \hat{k}$, $\vec{b} = \hat{i} + \hat{j}\cos\beta + \hat{k}$,

$\vec{c} = \hat{i} + \hat{j} + \hat{k}\cos\gamma$ are

(a) Coplanar vectors

(b) Coplanar vectors if $\cos\alpha = \cos\beta = \cos\gamma \neq 1$

(c) Coplanar vectors if $\cos\alpha \neq \cos\beta \neq \cos\gamma$

(d) Never coplanar

**6.** If the vector $\vec{b} = (\tan\alpha, -1, 2\sqrt{\sin\alpha/2})$ and

$\vec{c} = \left(\tan\alpha, \tan\alpha, -\dfrac{3}{\sqrt{\sin\alpha/2}}\right)$ are orthogonal and a

vector $\vec{a} = (1, 3, \sin 2\alpha)$ makes an obtuse angle with the z-axis then the value of $\alpha$ is

(a) $\alpha = (4n+1)\pi - \tan^{-1}2$

(b) $\alpha = (4n+2)\pi - \tan^{-1}2$

(c) $\alpha = (4n+1)\pi + \tan^{-1}2$

(d) $\alpha = (4n+2)\pi + \tan^{-1}2$

## Section II - Multiple Correct Answer Type

This section contains 4 multiple correct answer(s) type questions. Each question has 4 choices (a), (b), (c) and (d), out of which **ONE OR MORE** is/are correct.

**7.** If $\vec{b}$ is vector whose initial point divides the join of $5\hat{i}$ and $5\hat{j}$ in the ratio $k : 1$ and terminal point is origin and $|\vec{b}| \leq \sqrt{37}$, then $k$ belongs to

(a) $\left[-6, -\dfrac{1}{6}\right]$      (b) $(-\infty, -6) \cup \left[-\dfrac{1}{6}, \infty\right)$

(c) $[0, 6]$      (d) $\left[-\dfrac{1}{6}, \infty\right)$

**8.** Let $\vec{a} = \alpha\hat{i} + 2\hat{j} - 3\hat{k}$, $\vec{b} = \hat{i} + 2\alpha\hat{j} - 2\hat{k}$, $\vec{c} = 2\hat{i} - \alpha\hat{j} + \hat{k}$ and $(\vec{a} \times \vec{b}) \times (\vec{b} \times \vec{c})\} \times (\vec{c} \times \vec{a}) = \vec{0}$, then

(a) $\alpha = \dfrac{2}{3}$

(b) if $\alpha = 0$, then given vectors product is $-60(2\hat{i} + \hat{k})$

(c) $(\vec{a}.\vec{b})\vec{c} - (\vec{b}.\vec{c})\vec{a} = 0$ will give no real value of $\alpha$

(d) none of these

**9.** Let $\Delta PQR$ be a triangle. Let $\vec{a} = \overrightarrow{QR}$, $\vec{b} = \overrightarrow{RP}$ and $\vec{c} = \overrightarrow{PQ}$. If $|\vec{a}| = 12$, $|\vec{b}| = 4\sqrt{3}$, $\vec{b}.\vec{c} = 24$, then which of the following is (are) true?

(a) $\dfrac{|\vec{c}|^2}{2} - |\vec{a}| = 12$      (b) $\dfrac{|\vec{c}|^2}{2} + |\vec{a}| = 30$

(c) $|\vec{a} \times \vec{b} + \vec{c} \times \vec{a}| = 48\sqrt{3}$      (d) $\vec{a}.\vec{b} = -72$

**10.** Let $\vec{x}$, $\vec{y}$ and $\vec{z}$ be three vectors each of magnitude $\sqrt{2}$ and the angle between each pair of them is $\dfrac{\pi}{3}$. If $\vec{a}$ is a non-zero vector perpendicular to $\vec{x}$ and $\vec{y} \times \vec{z}$ and $\vec{b}$ is a non-zero vector perpendicular to $\vec{y}$ and $\vec{z} \times \vec{x}$, then

(a) $\vec{b} = \left(\vec{b}.\vec{z}\right)\left(\vec{z} - \vec{x}\right)$

(b) $\vec{a} = \left(\vec{a}.\vec{y}\right)\left(\vec{y} - \vec{z}\right)$

(c) $\vec{a}.\vec{b} = -\left(\vec{a}.\vec{y}\right)\left(\vec{b}.\vec{z}\right)$

(d) $\vec{a} = -\left(\vec{a}.\vec{y}\right)\left(\vec{z} - \vec{y}\right)$

## Section III - Integer Type

This section contains 5 questions. The answer to each of the questions is a single digit integer ranging from 0 to 9.

11. $ABCD$ is a regular tetrahedron; $A$ is the origin; $AB$ is the $x$-axis; $ABC$ lies in the $xy$-plane; $AB = d$. Under these conditions the number of possible tetrahedra is

12. Let $\vec{u}$ and $\vec{v}$ be two unit vectors. If $\vec{w}$ be any vector such that $\vec{w} + (\vec{w} \times \vec{u}) = \vec{v}$, then the least value of $|(\vec{u} \times \vec{v}).\vec{w}|^{-1}$ is equal to

13. Let $\vec{a} = \hat{i} + \hat{j} + \hat{k}, \vec{b} = x_1\hat{i} + x_2\hat{j} + x_3\hat{k}$,

    where $x_1, x_2, x_3 \in \{-3, -2, -1, 0, 1, 2\}$.

    Number of possible vectors $\vec{b}$ such that $\vec{a}$ and $\vec{b}$ are mutually perpendicular is 5k, where k equals.

14. Two points $P$ and $Q$ are given in the rectangular cartesian co-ordinates on the curve $y = 2^{x+2}$, such that $\overrightarrow{OP}.\hat{i} = -1$ and $\overrightarrow{OQ}.\hat{i} = 2$, where $\hat{i}$ is a unit vector along the $x$-axis. The magnitude of the vector $\overrightarrow{OQ} - 4\overrightarrow{OP}$, is 2k, where k equal.

15. Let $\vec{a}$, $\vec{b}$ and $\vec{c}$ be three non-coplanar unit vectors such that the angle between every pair of them is $\dfrac{\pi}{3}$. If $\vec{a} \times \vec{b} + \vec{b} \times \vec{c} = p\vec{a} + q\vec{b} + r\vec{c}$, where $p, q$ and $r$ are scalars, then the value of $\dfrac{p^2 + 2q^2 + r^2}{q^2}$ is

## Section IV - Comprehension Type

Based upon the given paragraphs, 4 multiple choice questions have to be answered. Each question has 4 choices (a), (b), (c) and (d), out of which **ONLY ONE** is correct.

### PARAGRAPH-1

The vertices of a $\triangle ABC$ are $A\,(2, 0, 2)$, $B\,(-1, 1, 1)$ and $C\,(1, -2, 4)$. The points $D$ and $E$ divide the sides $AB$ and $AC$ in the ratio 1 : 2 respectively. Another point $F$ is taken in space such that perpendicular drawn from $F$ on $\triangle ABC$ meet the $\Delta$ at the point of intersection of line segment $CD$ and $BE$ at $P$. If distance of $F$ from plane of $\triangle ABC$ is $\sqrt{2}$ units, then

16. The position vector of $P$ is
    - (a) $\hat{i} - \hat{j} + 3\hat{k}$
    - (b) $\hat{i} - \hat{j}$
    - (c) $2\hat{i} - \hat{j} - 3\hat{k}$
    - (d) $\hat{i} + \hat{j} + 3\hat{k}$

17. The volume of tetrahedron $ABCF$ is
    - (a) $\dfrac{7}{3}$ cubic units
    - (b) $\dfrac{7}{5}$ cubic units
    - (c) $\dfrac{3}{5}$ cubic units
    - (d) 7 cubic units

### PARAGRAPH-2

Let $\vec{a}_1$ be projection of $\vec{a}$ on $\vec{b}$ and $\vec{a}_2$ be the projection of $\vec{a}_1$ on $\vec{c}$, then

18. $\vec{a}_2 =$
    - (a) $\dfrac{943}{49}(2\hat{i} - 3\hat{j} - 6\hat{k})$
    - (b) $\dfrac{943}{49^2}(2\hat{i} - 3\hat{j} - 6\hat{k})$
    - (c) $\dfrac{943}{49}(-2\hat{i} + 3\hat{j} + 6\hat{k})$
    - (d) $\dfrac{943}{49^2}(-2\hat{i} + 3\hat{j} + 6\hat{k})$

19. $\vec{a}_1.\vec{b} =$
    - (a) $-41$
    - (b) $-\dfrac{41}{7}$
    - (c) $41$
    - (d) $287$

## Section V - Matrix-Match Type

This section contains 1 question. It contains statements given in two columns, which have to be matched. Statements in column I are labelled as A, B, C and D whereas statements in column II are labelled as p, q, r and s. The answers to these questions have to be appropriately bubbled as illustrated in the following example. If the correct matches are A-p, A-r, B-p, B-s, C-r, C-s and D-q, then the correctly bubbled matrix will look like the following:

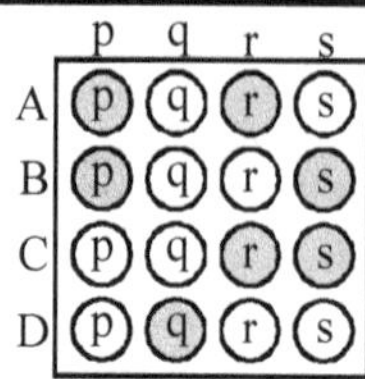

**20.** 

**Column-I**

(A) If $\vec{a}+\vec{b}+\vec{c} = \alpha\vec{d}, \vec{b}+\vec{c}+\vec{d} = \beta\vec{a}$ and $\vec{a},\vec{b},\vec{c}$ are non-coplanar then the $|\vec{a}+\vec{b}+\vec{c}+\vec{d}|$ is

(B) If $\vec{a}$ and $\vec{b}$ are unit vectors inclined at an angle $\theta$ to each other and $|\vec{a}+\vec{b}| < 1$, then $\theta$ can be equal to

(C) If $\vec{a}$ is unit vector perpendicular to another unit vector $\vec{b}$ then $|\vec{a}\times[\vec{a}\times\{\vec{a}\times(\vec{a}\times\vec{b})\}]|$ is equal to

(D) Let $\vec{a},\vec{b},\vec{c}$ be three unit vectors such that $\vec{a}+\vec{b}+\vec{c} = \vec{0}$, then the angle between $\vec{a}$ and $\vec{b}$ is equal to

**Column-II**

p. $\dfrac{2\pi}{3}$

q. $\dfrac{3\pi}{4}$

r. $\dfrac{5\pi}{6}$

s. $0$

t. $1$

**RESPONSE GRID**

20. A - (p)(q)(r)(s); B - (p)(q)(r)(s); C - (p)(q)(r)(s); D - (p)(q)(r)(s)

## DAILY PRACTICE PROBLEM DPP CM23 - MATHEMATICS

| Total Questions | 20 | Total Marks | 69 |
|---|---|---|---|
| Attempted | | Correct | |
| Incorrect | | Net Score | |
| Cut-off Score | 21 | Qualifying Score | 32 |

$$\text{Net Score} = \sum_{i=1}^{V}\left[\left(\text{correct}_i \times MM_i\right) - \left(In_i - NM_i\right)\right]$$

Date : [ ]   Start Time : [ ]   End Time : [ ]

# MATHEMATICS CM24

**SYLLABUS :** Three Dimensional Geometry

**Max. Marks : 74**                                **Time : 60 min.**

### GENERAL INSTRUCTIONS

- The Daily Practice Problem Sheet contains 20 Questions divided into 5 sections.
  **Section I** has **5** MCQs with ONLY 1 Correct Option, **3** marks for each correct answer and **−1** for each incorrect answer.
  **Section II** has **4** MCQs with ONE or MORE THAN ONE Correct options.
  For each question, marks will be awarded in one of the following categories:
  Full marks: **+4** If only the bubble(s) corresponding to all the correct option(s) is (are) darkened.
  Partial marks: **+1** For darkening a bubble corresponding to each correct option provided NO INCORRECT option is darkened.
  Zero marks:  If none of the bubbles is darkened.
  Negative marks: **−2** In all other cases.
  **Section III** has **4** Single Digit Integer Answer Type Questions, **3** marks for each Correct Answer and **0** mark in all other cases.
  **Section IV** has Comprehension/Matching Cum-Comprehension Type Questions having **5** MCQs with ONLY ONE corect option, **3** marks for each Correct Answer and **0** mark in all other cases.
  **Section V** has **2** Matching Type Questions, **2** marks for the correct matching of each row and **0** mark in all other cases.
- You have to evaluate your Response Grids yourself with the help of Solutions.

## Section I - Straight Objective Type

This section contains 5 multiple choice questions. Each question has 4 choices (a), (b), (c) and (d), out of which **ONLY ONE** is correct.

**1.** A rectangle $ABCD$ of dimension $r$ and $2r$ is folded along diagonal $BD$ such that planes $ABD$ and $CBD$ are perpendicular to each other, then the distance $AC'$(in new position is)

(a) $\sqrt{3}\,r$   (b) $\sqrt{85}\,r$   (c) $\dfrac{\sqrt{85}}{5}r$   (d) $\sqrt{\dfrac{17}{5}}\,r$

**2.** Let Q be the foot of perpendicular from the origin to the plane $4x - 3y + z + 13 = 0$ and $R$ be a point $(-1, -6)$ on the plane. Then length QR is :

(a) $\sqrt{14}$   (b) $\sqrt{\dfrac{19}{2}}$

(c) $3\sqrt{\dfrac{7}{2}}$   (d) $\dfrac{3}{\sqrt{2}}$

**3.** Equation of the line of the shortest distance between the lines $\dfrac{x}{1} = \dfrac{y}{-1} = \dfrac{z}{1}$ and $\dfrac{x-1}{0} = \dfrac{y+1}{-2} = \dfrac{z}{1}$ is:

(a) $\dfrac{x}{1} = \dfrac{y}{-1} = \dfrac{z}{-2}$   (b) $\dfrac{x-1}{1} = \dfrac{y+1}{-1} = \dfrac{z}{-2}$

(c) $\dfrac{x-1}{1} = \dfrac{y+1}{-1} = \dfrac{z}{1}$   (d) $\dfrac{x}{-2} = \dfrac{y}{1} = \dfrac{z}{2}$

---

**RESPONSE GRID**   **1.** ⓐⓑⓒⓓ   **2.** ⓐⓑⓒⓓ   **3.** ⓐⓑⓒⓓ

*Space for Rough Work*

**4.** Consider the triangle AOB in the x-y plane where A $\equiv$ (1, 0, 0); B $\equiv$ ( 0,2, 0) ; and O $\equiv$ ( 0, 0, 0). The new position of O, when triangle is rotated about side AB by $90°$ can be

(a) $\left(\dfrac{4}{5},\dfrac{3}{5},\dfrac{2}{\sqrt{5}}\right)$
(b) $\left(\dfrac{-3}{5},\dfrac{\sqrt{2}}{5},\dfrac{2}{\sqrt{5}}\right)$

(c) $\left(\dfrac{4}{5},\dfrac{2}{5},\dfrac{2}{\sqrt{5}}\right)$
(d) $\left(\dfrac{4}{5},\dfrac{2}{5},\dfrac{1}{\sqrt{5}}\right)$

**5.** The median AD of the triangle ABC is bisected at E, BE meets AC in F, then AF: AC =
(a) $3:4$  (b) $1:3$  (c) $1:2$  (d) $1:4$

## Section II - Multiple Correct Answer Type

This section contains 4 multiple correct answer(s) type questions. Each question has 4 choices (a), (b), (c) and (d), out of which **ONE OR MORE** is/are correct.

**6.** If $OABC$ is a tetrahedron such that $OA^2 + BC^2 = OB^2 + CA^2 = OC^2 + AB^2$ then
(a) $OA$ is perpendicular to $BC$
(b) $OB$ is perpendicular to $CA$
(c) $OC$ is perpendicular to $AB$
(d) $AB$ is perpendicular to $BC$

**7.** The x-y plane in rotated about its line of intersection with the y-z plane by $45°$, then the equation of the new plane is/are
(a) $z + x = 0$  (b) $z - y = 0$
(c) $x + y + z = 0$  (d) $z - x = 0$

**8.** The equation of the plane which is equally inclined to the lines $\dfrac{x-1}{2} = \dfrac{y}{-2} = \dfrac{z+2}{1}$ and $\dfrac{x+3}{8} = \dfrac{y-4}{1} = \dfrac{z}{-4}$
(a) $14x - 5y - 7z = 0$  (b) $2x + 7y - z = 0$
(c) $3x - 4y - z = 0$  (d) $x + 2y - 5z = 0$

**9.** A rod of length 2 units whose one end is $(1, 0 -1)$ and other end touches the plane $x - 2y + 2z + 4 = 0$, then
(a) The rod sweeps the figure whose volume is $3\pi$ cubic units.
(b) The area of the region which the rod traces on the plane is $2\pi$.
(c) The length of the projection of the rod on the plane is $\sqrt{3}$ units.
(d) The centre of the region which the rod traces on the plane is $(4/3, -2/3, 1/3)$.

## Section III - Integer Type

This section contains 4 questions. The answer to each of the questions is a single digit integer ranging from 0 to 9.

**10.** $P$ is a point and $PM$, $PN$ are perpendiculars from $P$ to the ZX and $XY$ planes respectively. If $OP$ makes angles $\theta$, $\alpha$, $\beta$, $\gamma$ with the plane $OMN$ and the $XY$, $YZ$, $ZX$ plane respectively then $\sin^2\theta\,(\operatorname{cosec}^2\alpha + \operatorname{cosec}^2\beta + \operatorname{cosec}^2\gamma)$ is equal to

**11.** A plane passing through (1 1, 1) cuts positive direction of co-ordinate axes at A, B and C the volume of tetrahedron OABC satisfies $V \geq \dfrac{k}{l}$, then $(k - l)$ equals.

**12.** If the ratio in which the plane $\vec{r}.(\vec{i} - 2\vec{j} + 3\vec{k}) = 17$ divides the line joining the points $-2\vec{i} + 4\vec{j} + 7\vec{k}$ and $3\vec{i} - 5\vec{j} + 8\vec{k}$ is $\dfrac{a}{b}$, then $|a - b| =$

**13.** $L_1$ and $L_2$ are two lines whose vector equations are
$L_1 : \vec{r} = \lambda\left(\left(\cos\theta + \sqrt{3}\right)\hat{i} + \left(\sqrt{2}\sin\theta\right)\hat{j} + \left(\cos\theta - \sqrt{3}\right)\hat{k}\right)$
$L_2 : \vec{r} = \mu\left(a\hat{i} + b\hat{j} + c\hat{k}\right)$, where $\lambda$ and $\mu$ are scalars and $\alpha$ is the acute angle between $L_1$ and $L_2$. If the angle '$\alpha$' (independent of $\theta$) is equal to $\dfrac{\pi}{k}$, then $k =$

## Section IV - Comprehension/Matching Cum-Comprehension Type

**Directions (Qs. 14 and 15) :** Based upon the given paragraph, 2 multiple choice questions have to be answered. Each question has 4 choices (a), (b), (c) and (d), out of which **ONLY ONE** is correct.

### PARAGRAPH

If the projections of three points A, B, C on a given plane are A', B', C', then $\Delta A'B'C' = \cos\theta(\Delta ABC)$, where $\theta$ is the angle between the planes ABC and A'B'C' (i.e., the angle that the positive direction of a normal to one makes with the positive direction of a normal to the other). In general, if $A_0$ is the area of any plane curve and A is the area of its projection on any given plane, then $A = \cos\theta\,A_0$.

**14.** Suppose $AB$ is a diameter of a circle and $P$ is a plane through $AB$ making an angle $\theta$ with the plane of the circle. If diameter of the circle be $2a$, then the eccentricity of the curve of projection of the circle on P is
(a) $\sin\theta$
(b) $\dfrac{2a\sin\theta}{1+a}$
(c) $\dfrac{a\cos\theta}{1+a}$
(d) $1 + \sin^2\theta$

**15.** A plane makes intercepts $OA$, $OB$, $OC$ whose measures are $a$, $b$, $c$ on the axes $OX$, $OY$, $OZ$. The area of the triangle $ABC$ is

(a) $\sqrt{a^4 + b^4 + c^4 - a^2b^2 - b^2c^2 - c^2a^2}$

(b) $\dfrac{1}{2}\sqrt{a^2b^2 + b^2c^2 + c^2a^2}$

(c) $a^2 + b^2 + c^2 - bc - ca - ab$

(d) $\dfrac{1}{4}\sqrt{(a+b+c)(b+c-a)(c+a-b)(a+b-c)}$

---

**Directions (Qs. 16-18) :** This passage contains a table having 3 columns and 4 rows. Based on the table, there are three questions. Each question has four options (a), (b), (c) and (d) **ONLY ONE** of these four options is correct.

---

Consider the lines $L_1$, $L_2$ and the planes $P_1$, $P_2$. Let $ax + by + cz = d$ be the equation of the plane passing through the point of intersection of lines $L_1$ and $L_2$, and perpendicular to planes $P_1$ and $P_2$.

Column 1, 2 and 3 contains equation of lines, equation of planes and values of $a$, $b$, $c$ & $d$ respectively.

| Column 1 | Column 2 | Column 3 |
|---|---|---|
| (I)  $L_1 : \dfrac{x-1}{2} = \dfrac{y}{-1} = \dfrac{z+3}{1}$, | (i)  $P_1 : 7x + y + 2z = 3$ | (P)  $a = 5; b = 4$ |
| $L_2 : \dfrac{x-4}{1} = \dfrac{y+3}{1} = \dfrac{z+3}{2}$ | $P_2 : 3x + 5y - 6z = 4$ | $c = -7; d = 1$ |
| (II)  $L_1 : \dfrac{x-2}{3} = \dfrac{y-3}{4} = \dfrac{z-1}{5}$, | (ii)  $P_1 : 2x + 5y + 3z = 4$ | (Q)  $a = 1; b = -2$ |
| $L_2 : \dfrac{x-4}{1} = \dfrac{y-2}{3} = \dfrac{z-1}{2}$ | $P_2 : 5x + 3y + 7z = 3$ | $c = 1; d = 0$ |
| (III)  $L_1 : \dfrac{x-1}{1} = \dfrac{y-0}{0} = \dfrac{z-0}{0}$ | (iii)  $P_1 : x + 2y + 3z = 2$ | (R)  $a = 1; b = -3$ |
| $L_2 : \dfrac{x-0}{0} = \dfrac{y-1}{1} = \dfrac{z-0}{0}$ | $P_2 : 2x + 3y + 4z = 4$ | $c = -2; d = 13$ |
| (IV)  $L_1 : \dfrac{x-2}{5} = \dfrac{y-3}{4} = \dfrac{z-1}{3}$ | (iv)  $P_1 : 5x + 4y + z = 2$ | (S)  $a = 2; b = 3$ |
| $L_2 : \dfrac{x-3}{3} = \dfrac{y-4}{2} = \dfrac{z-2}{5}$ | $P_2 : 3x + 2y + 5z = 4$ | $c = 3; d = -4$ |

**16.** Which of the following options is the only correct combination?
(a) (I)(i)(R)     (b) (II)(ii)(Q)     (c) (III)(iii)(P)     (d) (IV)(iv)(S)

**17.** Which of the following options is the only correct combination?
(a) (II)(iii)(S)     (b) (IV)(i)(Q)     (c) (III)(iv)(P)     (d) None of these

**18.** Which of the following options is the only correct combination?
(a) (I)(iv)(R)     (b) (II)(i)(S)     (c) (III)(iii)(Q)     (d) (IV)(ii)(P)



*Space for Rough Work*

## Section V - Matrix-Match Type

This section contains 2 questions. It contains statements given in two columns, which have to be matched. Statements in column I are labelled as A, B, C and D whereas statements in column II are labelled as p, q, r and s. The answers to these questions have to be appropriately bubbled as illustrated in the following example. If the correct matches are A-p, A-r, B-p, B-s, C-r, C-s and D-q, then the correctly bubbled matrix will look like the following:

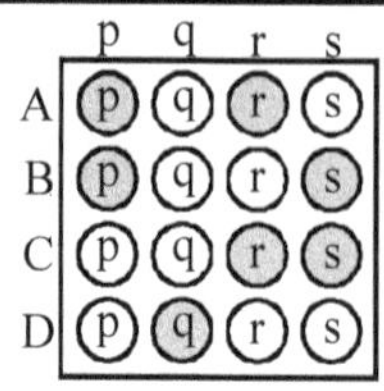

**19.**

**Column I**

(A) If the coordinates of the mid-points of the sides $BC, CA, AB$ of $\triangle ABC$ are $(a, 0, 0), (0, b, 0), (0, 0, c)$ respectively then $\dfrac{AB^2 + BC^2 + CA^2}{a^2 + b^2 + c^2}$ is equal to

(B) The distance of the image of the point $(1, -2, 3)$ in the plane $x - y + z = 5$ from the origin is equal to

(C) If $\theta$ be the angle between a diagonal of a cube and an edge of the cube intersecting the diagonal then $\tan\theta$ is equal to

(D) If the equation $px^2 + y^2 + qz^2 + 2yz + zx + 3xy = 0$ represents a pair of mutually perpendicular planes then q is equal to

**Column II**

p.   3/4

q.   $-3$

r.   8

s.   $\sqrt{2}$

t.   $5\sqrt{2}$

**20.**

**Column I**

(A) If the plane $ax - by + cz = d$ contains the line $\dfrac{x-a}{a} = \dfrac{y-2d}{b} = \dfrac{z-c}{c}$, then $\dfrac{b}{d}$ is equal to

(B) The distance of the point $(1, -2, 3)$ from the plane $x - y + z - 5 = 0$ measured parallel to $\dfrac{x}{2} = \dfrac{y}{3} = \dfrac{z-1}{-6}$ is equal to

(C) If the straight lines $\dfrac{x-2}{1} = \dfrac{y-3}{1} = \dfrac{4-z}{k}$ and $\dfrac{x-1}{k} = \dfrac{y-4}{2} = \dfrac{z-5}{1}$ intersect then k is equal to

(D) If a line makes an angle $\theta$ with $x$ and $y$-axis then $\cot\theta$ can be equal to

**Column II**

p.   0

q.   1

r.   2

s.   $\dfrac{1}{3}$

t.   $-3$

| RESPONSE GRID | |
|---|---|
| **19.** A - Ⓟ Ⓠ Ⓡ Ⓢ; B - Ⓟ Ⓠ Ⓡ Ⓢ; C - Ⓟ Ⓠ Ⓡ Ⓢ; D - Ⓟ Ⓠ Ⓡ Ⓢ | |
| **20.** A - Ⓟ Ⓠ Ⓡ Ⓢ; B - Ⓟ Ⓠ Ⓡ Ⓢ; C - Ⓟ Ⓠ Ⓡ Ⓢ; D - Ⓟ Ⓠ Ⓡ Ⓢ | |

## DAILY PRACTICE PROBLEM DPP CM24 - MATHEMATICS

| | | | |
|---|---|---|---|
| Total Questions | 20 | Total Marks | 74 |
| Attempted | | Correct | |
| Incorrect | | Net Score | |
| Cut-off Score | 26 | Qualifying Score | 36 |

$$\text{Net Score} = \sum_{i=1}^{V} \left[ \left(\text{correct}_i \times MM_i\right) - \left(In_i - NM_i\right) \right]$$

Date :  Start Time :  End Time :

# MATHEMATICS CM25

**SYLLABUS :** Probability

**Max. Marks : 74**                                                   **Time : 60 min.**

## GENERAL INSTRUCTIONS

- The Daily Practice Problem Sheet contains 20 Questions divided into 5 sections.
  **Section I** has **5** MCQs with ONLY 1 Correct Option, **3** marks for each correct answer and **−1** for each incorrect answer.
  **Section II** has **4** MCQs with ONE or MORE THAN ONE Correct options.
  For each question, marks will be awarded in one of the following categories:
  Full marks: **+4** If only the bubble(s) corresponding to all the correct option(s) is (are) darkened.
  Partial marks: **+1** For darkening a bubble corresponding to each correct option provided NO INCORRECT option is darkened.
  Zero marks:  If none of the bubbles is darkened.
  Negative marks: **−2** In all other cases.
  **Section III** has **4** Single Digit Integer Answer Type Questions, **3** marks for each Correct Answer and **0** mark in all other cases.
  **Section IV** has Comprehension/Matching Cum-Comprehension Type Questions having **5** MCQs with ONLY ONE correct option, **3** marks for each Correct Answer and **0** mark in all other cases.
  **Section V** has **2** Matching Type Questions, **2** marks for the correct matching of each row and **0** mark in all other cases.
- You have to evaluate your Response Grids yourself with the help of Solutions.

## Section I - Straight Objective Type

This section contains 5 multiple choice questions. Each question has 4 choices (a), (b), (c) and (d), out of which **ONLY ONE** is correct.

**1.** The probabilities that a student passes in Mathematics, physics and chemistry are m, p and c, respectively. Of these subjects, the student has a 75% chance of passing in at least one, a 50% chance of passing in exactly two. Which of the following relations are true?

(a)  $p + m + c = 19/20$       (b)  $p + m + c = 27/20$
(c)  $pmc = 1/10$              (d)  $pmc = 1/4$

**2.** Raj and Sanchita are playing game in which they throw two dice alternately till one of them gets 9. Which one of the following could be the probability that Sanchita win the game?

(a)  7/15 or 8/15             (b)  6/11 or 5/11
(c)  8/17 or 9/17            (d)  None of these

---

**RESPONSE GRID**   **1.** ⓐⓑⓒⓓ   **2.** ⓐⓑⓒⓓ

---

*Space for Rough Work*

**3.** Suppose $A$ and $B$ shoot independently until each hits his target. They have probabilities $\dfrac{3}{5}$ and $\dfrac{5}{7}$ of hitting the targets at each shot. The probability that $B$ will require more shots than $A$ is

(a) $\dfrac{6}{31}$    (b) $\dfrac{7}{31}$    (c) $\dfrac{8}{31}$    (d) $\dfrac{1}{2}$

**4.** Two persons $A$ and $B$ agree to meet at a place between 5 to 6 p.m. The first one to arrive waits for 20 minutes and then leaves. If the time of their arrival be independent and at random, then the probability that $A$ and $B$ meet is

(a) $\dfrac{1}{3}$    (b) $\dfrac{4}{9}$    (c) $\dfrac{5}{9}$    (d) $\dfrac{2}{3}$

**5.** If X has a binomial distribution, B(n, p) with parameters n and p such that $P(X = 2) = P(X = 3)$, then E(X), the mean of variable X, is

(a) $2 - p$             (b) $3 - p$

(c) $\dfrac{p}{2}$              (d) $\dfrac{p}{3}$

## Section II - Multiple Correct Answer Type

This section contains 4 multiple correct answer(s) type questions. Each question has 4 choices (a), (b), (c) and (d), out of which **ONE OR MORE** is/are correct.

**6.** Let $P(X = r) = pq^r$ and $P(Y = r) = pq^r$, where $r = 1, 2, \ldots\ldots\ldots\ldots$, $0 < p < 1$, $q = 1 - p$. Suppose $X$ and $Y$ are independent. Let $Z = \max(X, Y)$. Then

(a) $P(Z \le m) = (1 - q^m)^2$

(b) $P(Z = m) = 2 pq^{m-1} - p(1 + q) q^{2m-2}$

(c) $\displaystyle\sum_{m \ge 1} P(Z = m) = \dfrac{1}{p}$

(d) $P(X \le m) = 1 - q^m$

**7.** $n$ letters to each of which corresponds an addressed envelope are placed in the envelopes at random. What is the probability that no letter is placed in the right envelope?

(a) first $n - 2$ terms in the expansion of $e^{-1}$.

(b) first n-1 terms in the expansion of $e^{-1}$.

(c) $= \dfrac{1}{2!} - \dfrac{1}{3!} + \dfrac{1}{4!} - \ldots + (-1)^n \cdot \dfrac{1}{n!}$

(d) first n-3 terms in the expansion of $e^{-1}$.

**8.** There is 30% chance that it rains on any particular day. Then in a period of 7 days

(a) The probability that there is at least one rainy day within a period of 7 days is $1 - \left(\dfrac{7}{10}\right)^6$

(b) The probability that there is at least one rainy day within a period of 7 days is $1 - \left(\dfrac{7}{10}\right)^7$

(c) Given that there is at least one rainy day, what is the probability that there are at least two rainy days is

$$\dfrac{1 - \left(\dfrac{7}{10}\right)^7 - 7\left(\dfrac{3}{10}\right)\left(\dfrac{7}{10}\right)^7}{1 - \left(\dfrac{7}{10}\right)^7}$$

(d) Given that there is at least one rainy day, what is the probability that there are at least two rainy days is

$$\dfrac{1 - \left(\dfrac{7}{10}\right)^7 - 7\left(\dfrac{3}{10}\right)\left(\dfrac{7}{10}\right)^6}{1 - \left(\dfrac{7}{10}\right)^7}$$

**9.** An urn contains four tickets with numbers 112, 121, 211, 222 and one ticket is drawn. Let $A_i$ ($i = 1, 2, 3$) be the event that the ith digit of the number of tickets drawn is 1. Then

(a) $P(A_1) = P(A_2) = P(A_3)$

(b) $A_1, A_2, A_3$ are pairwise independent.

(c) $A_1, A_2, A_3$ are the not mutually independent although they are pairwise independent.

(d) $P(A_1) = 1/2$

## Section III - Integer Type

This section contains 4 questions. The answer to each of the questions is a single digit integer ranging from 0 to 9.

**10.** Rahul has to write a project, Probability that he will get a project copy is 'p', probability that he will get a blue pen is 'q' and probability that he will get a black pen is ½. If he can complete the project either with blue or with black pen or with both and probability that he completed the project is ½ then find p(1 + q).

11. An urn contains five balls. Two balls are drawn and are found to be white. If P is the probability that all the balls are white and P = a/b in simplest form then find a + b.

12. A fair coin is tossed n times. Let X denote the number of heads appeared. If $P(X = 4)$, $P(X = 5)$ and $P(X = 6)$ are in AP, then the smallest values of $n$ is ___________.

13. An artillery target may be either at point I with probability $\frac{8}{9}$ or at the point (II) with probability $\frac{1}{9}$. There are 21 shells each of which can be fired either at point I or II. Each shell may hit the target independently of the other shell with probability $\frac{1}{2}$. Minimum number of shells that must be fired at point I to hit the target with maximum probability is equal to 2k. Then value of k is.

## Section IV - Comprehension/Matching Cum-Comprehension Type

**Directions (Qs. 14 and 15) :** Based upon the given paragraph, 2 multiple choice questions have to be answered. Each question has 4 choices (a), (b), (c) and (d), out of which **ONLY ONE** is correct.

### PARAGRAPH

Suppose there are three urns 1st containing 2 white and 3 black balls 2nd contain 3 white and 2 black balls, and 3rd contain 4 white and one black ball respectively. There is equal probability of each urn being chosen.

14. One ball is drawn from an urn chosen at random. What is the probability that a white ball is drawn?
    (a) 2/5          (b) 3/5
    (c) 2/9          (d) None of these

15. If it is known that a white ball has been drawn, find the probability that it was drawn from the first urn.
    (a) 2/5          (b) 3/5
    (c) 2/9          (d) None of these

**Directions (Qs. 16-18) :** This passage contains a table having 3 columns and 4 rows. Based on the table, there are three questions. Each question has four options (a), (b), (c) and (d) **ONLY ONE** of these four options is correct.

| Column 1 | Column 2 | Column 3 |
|---|---|---|
| (I) $P(A^C) = 0.3$, $P(b) = 0.4$ $P(A \cap B^C) = 0.5$ | (i) $P(A \cap B \cap C^C) + P(A \cap B^C \cap C)$ $+ P(A^C \cap B \cap C) + P(A \cap B \cap C)$ | (P) $\frac{26}{31}$ |
| (II) $P(A) = \frac{1}{5}$, $P(B) = \frac{4}{5}$, $P(C) = \frac{7}{100}$ | (ii) $P[B/(A \cap B^C)]$ | (Q) $\frac{3}{4}$ |
| (III) $P(A) = \frac{1}{2}$; $P(B) = \frac{1}{4} = P(C)$ | (iii) $P(B/\bar{C})$ | (R) $\frac{1}{4}$ |
| (IV) If A, B, C are pairwise independent events and $P(A) = \frac{1}{2}$, $P(B) = \frac{1}{3}$, $P(C) = \frac{1}{4}$ | (iv) $P(A \cup B \cup C)$ | (S) $\frac{5}{31}$ |

16. Which of the following options is the only correct combination?
    (a) (I)(ii)(R)          (b) (II)(iii)(P)
    (c) (III)(iv)(S)          (d) (IV)(i)(Q)



*Space for Rough Work*

**17.** Which of the following options is the only correct combination?

(a) (I)(iii)(R)
(b) (II)(ii)(Q)
(c) (III)(i)(S)
(d) (II)(iii)(P)

**18.** Which of the following options is the only incorrect combination?

(a) (I)(ii)(R)
(b) (III)(i)(S)
(c) (II)(iii)(P)
(d) (IV)(iv)(Q)

---

## Section V - Matrix-Match Type

This section contains 2 questions. It contains statements given in two columns, which have to be matched. Statements in column I are labelled as A, B, C and D whereas statements in column II are labelled as p, q, r and s. The answers to these questions have to be appropriately bubbled as illustrated in the following example. If the correct matches are A-p, A-r, B-p, B-s, C-r, C-s and D-q, then the correctly bubbled matrix will look like the following:

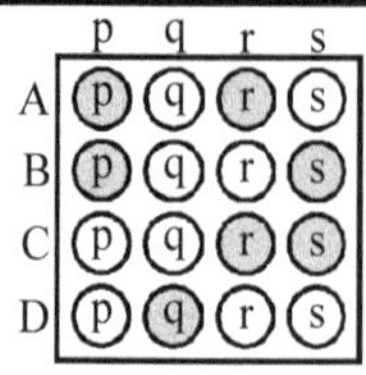

**19.** Match the columns.

**Column-I**

(A) Aman and Binay are playing dart game and it is known that Aman can hit the target 4 out of 5 shots while Binay can hit the target 3 out of 4 shots, what is the probability that target will be hit if both of them try

(B) Kushal and Karina are playing with a dice wherein they throw a dice alternately. Kushal wins if he throws a prime number and Karina wins if she throws a composite number. Kushal starts the game and game continues till one of them win. What is the probability that Kushal will win the game

(C) In the above question (B) what is the probability that Karina wins the game

(D) Raj and Sanchita are playing game in which they throw a die alternately till one of them gets a six. Which one of the following could be the probability that Sanchita win the game

**Column-II**

(p) 5/11
(q) 1/4
(r) 19/20
(s) 3/4

**20.** In a tournament there are twelve players $S_1, S_2, ..., S_{12}$ and divided into six pairs at random. From each game a winner is decided on the basis of a game played between the two players of the pair. Assuming all the pairs are of equal strength, then match the following :

**Column-I**

(A) Probability that $S_2$ is among the losers is

(B) Probability that exactly one of $S_3$ and $S_4$ is among the losers, is

(C) Probability that both $S_2$ and $S_4$ are among the winners is

(D) Probability of $S_4$ and $S_5$ not playing against each other is

**Column-II**

p. $\dfrac{5}{22}$

q. $\dfrac{10}{11}$

r. $\dfrac{1}{2}$

s. $\dfrac{6}{11}$

| **RESPONSE GRID** | **17.** ⓐⓑⓒⓓ **18.** ⓐⓑⓒⓓ |
|---|---|
| | **19.** A - ⓟⓠⓡⓢ; B - ⓟⓠⓡⓢ; C - ⓟⓠⓡⓢ; D - ⓟⓠⓡⓢ |
| | **20.** A - ⓟⓠⓡⓢ; B - ⓟⓠⓡⓢ; C - ⓟⓠⓡⓢ; D - ⓟⓠⓡⓢ |

## DAILY PRACTICE PROBLEM DPP CM25 - MATHEMATICS

| Total Questions | 20 | Total Marks | 74 |
|---|---|---|---|
| Attempted | | Correct | |
| Incorrect | | Net Score | |
| Cut-off Score | 26 | Qualifying Score | 36 |

$$\text{Net Score} = \sum_{i=1}^{V} \left[ (\text{correct}_i \times MM_i) - (In_i - NM_i) \right]$$

---

*Space for Rough Work*

Date :     Start Time :     End Time :

# MATHEMATICS CM26

**SYLLABUS :** Properties of Triangles

**Max. Marks : 74**　　　　　　　　　　　　　　**Time : 60 min.**

### GENERAL INSTRUCTIONS

- The Daily Practice Problem Sheet contains 20 Questions divided into 5 sections.
  **Section I** has **6** MCQs with ONLY 1 Correct Option, **3** marks for each correct answer and **−1** for each incorrect answer.
  **Section II** has **4** MCQs with ONE or MORE THAN ONE Correct options.
  For each question, marks will be awarded in one of the following categories:
  Full marks: **+4** If only the bubble(s) corresponding to all the correct option(s) is (are) darkened.
  Partial marks: **+1** For darkening a bubble corresponding to each correct option provided NO INCORRECT option is darkened.
  Zero marks: If none of the bubbles is darkened.
  Negative marks: **−2** In all other cases.
  **Section III** has **4** Single Digit Integer Answer Type Questions, **3** marks for each Correct Answer and **0** mark in all other cases.
  **Section IV** has Comprehension Type Questions having **4** MCQs with ONLY ONE corect option, **3** marks for each Correct Answer and **0** mark in all other cases.
  **Section V** has **2** Matching Type Questions, **2** marks for the correct matching of each row and **0** mark in all other cases.
- You have to evaluate your Response Grids yourself with the help of Solutions.

## Section I - Straight Objective Type

This section contains 6 multiple choice questions. Each question has 4 choices (a), (b), (c) and (d), out of which **ONLY ONE** is correct.

**1.** In $\Delta ABC$, if $\cot \theta = \cot A + \cot B + \cot C$, then
$\sin(A-\theta) \cdot \sin(B-\theta) \cdot \sin(C-\theta) =$
(a) $\sin^3 \theta$      (b) $\sin A \sin B \sin C$
(c) $3\sin\theta$      (d) $1$

**2.** If $A+B+C = \pi$, then the greatest value of $\cos A + \cos B + \cos C$ is
(a) $2$      (b) $3$
(c) $\dfrac{3}{2}$      (d) $1$

**3.** If $a$, $b$, $c$ be the sides of a triangle and
$P = \dfrac{(a+b+c)^2}{ab+bc+ca}$, then
(a) $P \in [1, 2]$      (b) $P \in [3, 4)$
(c) $P \in (2, 4]$      (d) None of these

| **RESPONSE GRID** | 1. ⓐⓑⓒⓓ | 2. ⓐⓑⓒⓓ | 3. ⓐⓑⓒⓓ |
| --- | --- | --- | --- |

*Space for Rough Work*

**4.** In a triangle $ABC$, if $\dfrac{a^2+b^2}{a^2-b^2}\sin(A-B)=1$, and $C$ is not a right angle, then $\cos(A-B)=$

(a) $\tan\left(\dfrac{C}{2}+\dfrac{\pi}{4}\right)$     (b) $\tan\left(\dfrac{C}{2}-\dfrac{\pi}{4}\right)$

(c) $\cos\left(\dfrac{C}{2}+\dfrac{\pi}{4}\right)$     (d) $\sin\left(\dfrac{C}{2}-\dfrac{\pi}{4}\right)$

**5.** The angle of elevation of the top of a tower from a point A due south of it is $\tan^{-1}0.6$, and that from B due east of it is $\tan^{-1}0.75$. If h is the height of the tower, and $AB=\lambda h$, then $\lambda^2=$

(a) $\dfrac{41}{9}$     (b) $\dfrac{40}{9}$

(c) $\dfrac{41}{2}$     (d) None

**6.** The angle of elevation of the top C of a vertical tower CD of height h from a point A in the horizontal plane is $45°$ and from a point B at a distance a from A on the line making an angle $30°$ with AD in the vertical plane, it is $60°$, then

(a) $a=h(\sqrt{3}+1)$     (b) $h=a(\sqrt{3}+1)$

(c) $a=h(\sqrt{3}-1)$     (d) $h=a(\sqrt{3}-1)$

## Section II - Multiple Correct Answer Type

This section contains 4 multiple correct answer(s) type questions. Each question has 4 choices (a), (b), (c) and (d), out of which **ONE OR MORE** is/are correct.

**7.** If in a triangle $ABC$, $b\cos^2\dfrac{A}{2}+a\cos^2\dfrac{B}{2}=\dfrac{3c}{2}$, then

(a) $c^2\geq ab$     (b) $2c>\sqrt{ab}$

(c) $\dfrac{a+c}{2c-a}+\dfrac{b+c}{2c-b}\leq 4$     (d) $\dfrac{a}{c}+\dfrac{c}{b}+\dfrac{b}{a}\geq 3$

**8.** If the sides $a$, $b$, $c$ of a triangle $ABC$ form successive terms of $G.P.$ with common ratio $r\,(>1)$, then which of the following is / are correct

(a) $r<\dfrac{\sqrt{5}+1}{2}$     (b) $A<B<\dfrac{\pi}{3}$

(c) $B>\dfrac{\pi}{3}$     (d) $C>\dfrac{\pi}{3}$

**9.** In a $\triangle ABC$, the incircle touches the sides $BC$, $CA$, and $AB$ at $P$, $Q$ and $R$ respectively and its radius is 4 units. If the lengths $BP$, $CQ$ and $AR$ are consecutive integers then

(a) sides are also consecutive integers
(b) Sides are in $A.P.$
(c) Perimeter of the triangle is 42 unit
(d) diameter of the circumcircle is 65 unit

**10.** In a triangle $ABC$, if $\sec A$, $\sec B$, $\sec C$ are in H.P. then

(a) $a$, $b$, $c$ are in H.P.

(b) $\cot\dfrac{A}{2}$, $\cot\dfrac{B}{2}$, $\cot\dfrac{C}{2}$ are in H.P.

(c) $r_1, r_2, r_3$ are in A.P.

(d) $\cot\dfrac{A}{2}$, $\cot\dfrac{B}{2}$, $\cot\dfrac{C}{2}$ are in A.P.

## Section III - Integer Type

This section contains 4 questions. The answer to each of the questions is a single digit integer ranging from 0 to 9.

**11.** For a triangle $ABC$, with altitudes $h_1$, $h_2$, $h_3$ and in radius $r$, the minimum value of $\dfrac{h_1+r}{h_1-r}+\dfrac{h_2+r}{h_2-r}+\dfrac{h_3+r}{h_3-r}$ is



*Space for Rough Work*

**12.** If in the triangle $ABC$, $\tan\dfrac{A}{2}$, $\tan\dfrac{B}{2}$ and $\tan\dfrac{C}{2}$ are in harmonic progression then the least value of $\cot^2\dfrac{B}{2}$ is equal to

**13.** Let $ABC$ be a triangle of area $\Delta$ and $A'B'C'$ be the triangle formed by the altitudes of $\Delta ABC$ as its sides with area $\Delta'$ and $A''B''C''$ be the triangle formed by the altitudes of $\Delta A'B'C'$ as its sides with area $\Delta''$. If $\Delta' = 30$ and $\Delta'' = 20$ then the value of $\dfrac{\Delta}{9}$ is

**14.** If $p_1$, $p_2$, $p_3$ are the altitudes of a triangle which circumscribes a circle of diameter $\dfrac{4}{3}$ units, then the least value of $p_1 + p_2 + p_3$ is equal to

---

## Section IV - Comprehension Type

Based upon the given paragraphs, 4 multiple choice questions have to be answered. Each question has 4 choices (a), (b), (c) and (d), out of which **ONLY ONE** is correct.

### PARAGRAPH–1

Let $r$ and $R$ represent the inradius and circum radius of a triangle $ABC$ of which $r_1$, $r_2$, $r_3$ are respectively the radii of excircles opposite to vertices $A$, $B$ and $C$. Perimeter of triangle is $2s$.

**15.** The cubic equation with $r_1, r_2, r_3$ as three roots is given by
(a) $x^3 - x^2(R+r) + sx - rs^2 = 0$
(b) $x^3 - x^2(R-2r) + s^2 x - rs^2 = 0$
(c) $x^3 - x^2(4R+r) + s^2 x - rs^2 = 0$
(d) $x^3 - 4x^2(R+r) + s^2 x - rs^2 = 0$

**16.** The expression $(s+r_1)(s+r_2)(s+r_3)$ equals to
(a) $2s^2(s+r+2R)$ (b) $2s^2(s+2R)$
(c) $R(s^2+r^2)$ (d) None of these

### PARAGRAPH–2

When any two sides and the angle opposite to one of them are given then either no triangle, or one triangle or two triangles are possible. Let the sides $a$, $b$ and the angle $A$ be given

Then, $\cos A = \dfrac{b^2 + c^2 - a^2}{2bc}$

$\Rightarrow c^2 - (2b\cos A)c + b^2 - a^2 = 0$

This is a quadratic equation in $c$. So, two values of $c$ will be obtained real, coincident or imaginary. Values of $c$ from the above equation are given by $c_1 = b\cos A \pm \sqrt{a^2 - b^2 \sin^2 A}$, say $c_1$ and $c_2$
The discriminant of the above equation is

$D = 4b^2 \cos^2 A - 4(b^2 - a^2) = 4(a^2 - b^2 \sin^2 A)$

**We can have following cases :**
(i) If $D < 0$, i.e. $a < b\sin A$, then no triangle is possible
(ii) If $D = 0$, i..e., $a = b\sin A$, then only one triangle is possible provided $A$ is acute. In case $A$ is obtuse then no triangle is possible as then $c_1$ and $c_2$ will be negative.
(iii) If $D > 0$, i.e., $a > b\sin A$, then two triangles are possible provided $c_1$ and $c_2$ are both positive.

**17.** If $A$ is acute then two different triangles are possible if and only if
(a) $a < b\sin A$ (b) $a > b\sin A$ and $a < b$
(c) $a > b\sin A$ and $a > b$ (d) $a > b\sin A$ and $a = b$

**18.** If $a > b\sin A$ and $a = b$ then
(a) No triangle is possible
(b) Only one triangle is possible
(c) Two distinct triangles are possible
(d) Any of the (a), (b), (c) may be true



———————————————— *Space for Rough Work* ————————————————

## Section V - Matrix-Match Type

This section contains 2 questions. It contains statements given in two columns, which have to be matched. Statements in column I are labelled as A, B, C and D whereas statements in column II are labelled as p, q, r and s. The answers to these questions have to be appropriately bubbled as illustrated in the following example. If the correct matches are A-p, A-r, B-p, B-s, C-r, C-s and D-q, then the correctly bubbled matrix will look like the following:

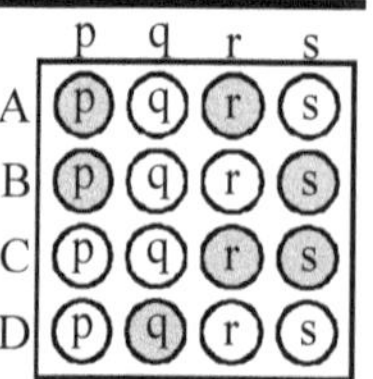

**19.**

**Column-I**

(A) If in a triangle $ABC$, $\dfrac{r}{r_1} = \dfrac{1}{4}$, then the value of $\tan\dfrac{A}{2}\left(\tan\dfrac{B}{2} + \tan\dfrac{C}{2}\right)$ is equal to

(B) In a triangle the least value of $\dfrac{r_1 r_2 r_3}{r^3}$ is

(C) If the sides $a$, $b$, $c$ of a triangle $ABC$ are in A.P. then the ratio $\dfrac{b}{c}$ can be equal to

(D) Let $P$ be an interior point of the triangle $ABC$ and the lines $AP$, $BP$ and $CP$ when produced meet the opposite sides in $D$, $E$ and $F$ respectively then $\dfrac{PD}{AD} + \dfrac{PE}{BE} + \dfrac{PE}{CF}$ is equal to

**Column-II**

p. $\dfrac{3}{4}$

q. 1

r. 3

s. 27

**20.**

**Column-I**

(A) If $\alpha$, $\beta$, $\gamma$ be the lengths of medians of triangle $ABC$ then $\dfrac{\alpha^2 + \beta^2 + \gamma^2}{a^2 + b^2 + c^2}$ is equal to

(B) Let the point $P$ lies interior of an equilateral triangle $ABC$ of side length 2 and its distances from the sides $BC$, $CA$ and $AB$ are respectively $x$, $y$ and $z$, then $x + y + z$ is equal to

(C) In a triangle $ABC$. $A$, $B$, $C$ are in A.P. and $a$, $b$, $c$ are in G.P. then $\dfrac{a^2 b + b^2 c + c^2 a}{a^3 + b^3 + c^3}$ is equal to

(D) In triangle $ABC$, the least value of $\sqrt{\dfrac{abc(a+b+c)}{\Delta}}$ is

**Column-II**

p. 1

q. $\sqrt{3}$

r. $\dfrac{3}{4}$

s. 4

| RESPONSE GRID | |
|---|---|
| 19. A - ⓟⓠⓡⓢ; B - ⓟⓠⓡⓢ; C - ⓟⓠⓡⓢ | |
| 20. A - ⓟⓠⓡⓢ; B - ⓟⓠⓡⓢ; C - ⓟⓠⓡⓢ | |

## DAILY PRACTICE PROBLEM DPP CM26 - MATHEMATICS

| Total Questions | 20 | Total Marks | 74 |
|---|---|---|---|
| Attempted | | Correct | |
| Incorrect | | Net Score | |
| Cut-off Score | 28 | Qualifying Score | 39 |

$$\text{Net Score} = \sum_{i=1}^{V}\left[\left(\text{correct}_i \times MM_i\right) - \left(In_i - NM_i\right)\right]$$

*Space for Rough Work*

**1.** **(d)** Statement (1) and (2) are correct. Hence, option (d) is correct.

**2.** **(b)**

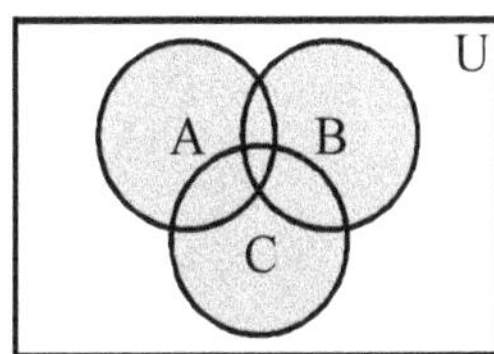

(i) $A \cup B \cup C$

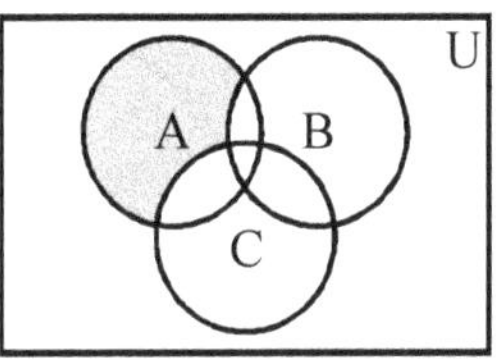

(ii) $(A \cap B^c \cap C^c)$

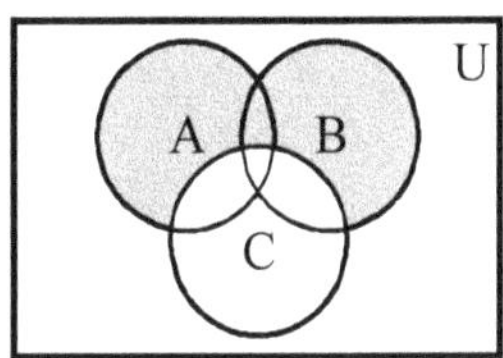

(iii) $C^c$

From Fig. (i), (ii) and (iii), we get

$(A \cup B \cup C) \cap (A \cap B^c \cap C^c)^c \cap C^c = (B^c \cap C^c)$

**3.** **(c)** Let C represents the set of Americans like cheese and A represents the set of Americans like apples.

$C \cap A$ represents the set of Americans like both cheese and apples.

$\therefore n(C) = 63$, $n(A) = 76$, and $n(C \cap A) = x$

We know that,

$n(C \cup A) = n(C) + n(A) - n(C \cap A)$

$100 = 63 + 76 - x$

$\Rightarrow x = 139 - 100 = 39$ and $n(C \cap A) \le n(C)$

$\Rightarrow x \le 63$

$\therefore 39 \le x \le 63.$

**4.** **(c)** Suppose $a \in X$ and $a \in A$

$\Rightarrow a \in X \cup A \Rightarrow a \in Y \cup A$

$\Rightarrow a \in Y$ and $a \in A \cap (\because X \cup A = Y \cup A)$

$\Rightarrow a \in Y \cap A \Rightarrow Y \cap A$ is non-empty

This contradicts that $Y \cap A = \phi$

So, $X = Y$

**5.** **(d)** $n(A) = 1000$, $n(B) = 500$, $n(A \cap B) \ge 1$,

$n(A \cup B) = p$

$n(A \cup B) = n(A) + n(B) - n(A \cap B)$

$p = 1000 + 500 - n(A \cap B)$

$1 \le n(A \cap B) \le 500$

Hence $p \le 1499$ and $p \ge 1000$

$1000 \le p \le 1499$

**6.** **(a)** Minimum value of $x = 100 - (30 + 20 + 25 + 15)$

$= 100 - 90 = 10$

**7.** **(b, c)** Let there are x families

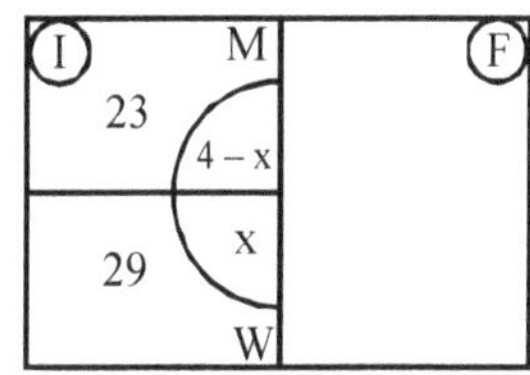

$a + b + c + d = x$

$a + c = 2.5 x$, $b + c = 0.15 x$

$d = 0.65x$, $c = 2000$

$\therefore a + b + 2c + d = 1.05x$

$x + c = 1.05x$

$\therefore 0.05x = c = 2000 \Rightarrow x = 40,000$

So $a = 8000$, $b = 4000$ $d = 26000$

$c = 2000 \Rightarrow 5\%$ families own both a car and a phone

$a + b + c = 14000$

$\Rightarrow 35\%$ families own either a car or a phone

**8.** **(a, b, c)** See the following Venn diagram

$n(I) = 29 + 23 = 52$

$n(F) = 100 - 52 = 48 = n_1$

$n(m \cup D) = n(m) + n(D) - n(m \cap D)$

$24 = 23 + 4 - n(m \cap D)$

$\therefore n(m \cap D) = 3$

$\therefore n(W \cap D) = 4 - 3 = 1 = n_2$

**9.** **(a, b, c)** We have

$n(A \cup B \cup C) = n(A) + n(B) + n(C) -$

$n(A \cap B) - n(B \cap C) - n(C \cap A) + n(A \cap B \cap C)$

$= 10 + 15 + 20 - 8 - 9 - n(C \cap A) + n(A \cap B \cap C)$

$= 28 - \{n(C \cap A) - n(A \cap B \cap C)\}$ ...(i)

Since $n(C \cap A) \ge n(A \cap B \cap C)$

We have $n(C \cap A) - n(A \cap B \cap C) \ge 0$ ...(ii)

From (i) and (ii)

$n(A \cup B \cup C) \le 28$ ...(iii)

Now, $n(A \cup B) = n(A) + n(B) - n(A \cap B)$

$= 10 + 15 - 8 = 17$

and $n(B \cup C) = n(B) + n(C) - n(B \cap C)$

$= 15 + 20 - 9 = 26$

Since, $n(A \cup B \cup C) \ge n(A \cup C)$ and

$n(A \cup B \cup C) \ge n(B \cup C)$, we have

$n(A \cup B \cup C) \ge 17$ and $n(A \cup B \cup C) \ge 26$

Hence $n(A \cup B \cup C) \ge 26$ ...(iv)

From (iii) and (iv) we obtain

$26 \le n(A \cup B \cup C) \le 28$

Also $n(A \cup B \cup C)$ is a positive integer

$\therefore n(A \cup B \cup C) = 26$ or $27$ or $28$

**10.** **(b, c)** $a + e + f + g = 23$
$b + d + f + g = 15$
$c + d + e + g = 20$
$f + g = 7; \quad d + g = 5$
$e + g = 4$

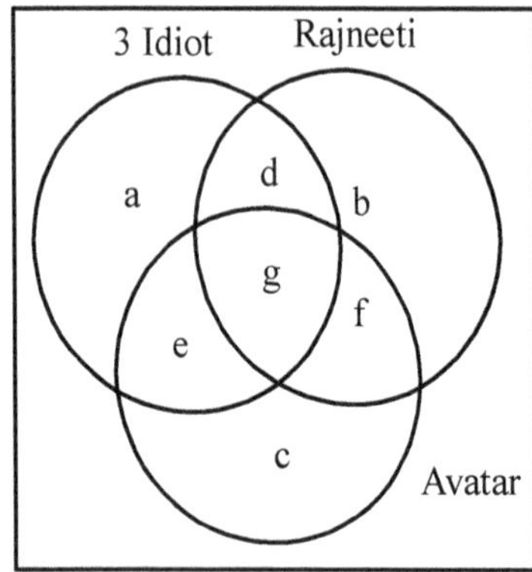

$a + b + c + d + e + f + g = 60 - 15 = 45$
By substitutions,
$a + e = 16, \ b + d = 8, \ b + f = 10, \ c + e = 15, \ c + d = 16$
Also, $b + c + d = 22$
$a + c + e = 30, \ a + b + f = 25$
From these, we get
$b = 6, a = 15, c = 14 \ e = 1, d = 2, f = 4 \ $ and $g = 3$
Clearly (a) is not correct
for (b) $a + f = 19 \Rightarrow$ (b) is correct
for (c) $e = 1 \Rightarrow$ (c) is correct

**11.** **(7)** The given condition is as follows-



We know that $\{(a + d + e + g) + (b + d + f + g) +$
$(c + e + f + g)\} - (d + e + f) - 2g$
$= a + b + c + d + e + f + g$
or $61x + 46x + 29x - 25x - 2g = 97x$
or $2g = 14x$ or $g = 7x$

**12.** **(3)** $2^m - 2^n = 112 \Rightarrow 2^n(2^{m-n} - 1) = 16.7$

$\therefore \ 2^n(2^{m-n} - 1) = 2^4(2^3 - 1)$
Comparing we get $n = 4$ and $m - n = 3$
$\Rightarrow n = 4$ and $m = 7 \Rightarrow m - n = 3$

**13.** **(5)** Let C be the set of students in chemistry class and P
be the set of students in physics class.
Given $n(C) = 20, n(P) = 30$ and $n(C \cap P) = 10$. We have
to find $n(C \cup P)$
If two classes meet at different hours, then
$n(C \cap P) = 10$ (given)
So, $n(C \cup P) = n(C) + \cap(P) - (C \cap P) = 40$

**14.** **(3)** $A = \{1, 3, 5, 15\}, B = \{2, 3, 5, 7\} \ C = \{2, 4, 6, 8\}$

$\therefore A \cup C = \{1, 2, 3, 4, 5, 6, 7, 8, 15\}$

$(A \cup C) \cap B = \{2, 3, 5\}$

**15.** **(2)** Given set is $\{\dfrac{a}{b} \in I^+ : 2a^2 + 3b^2 = 35, a, b \in Z\}$

We can see that, $2(\pm 2)^2 + 3(\pm 3)^2 = 35$

and $2(\pm 4)^2 + 3(\pm 1)^2 = 35$

$\therefore (2, 3), (2, -3), (-2, -3), (-2, 3), (4, 1), (4, -1),$
$(-4, -1), (-4, 1)$

**For 16-17**

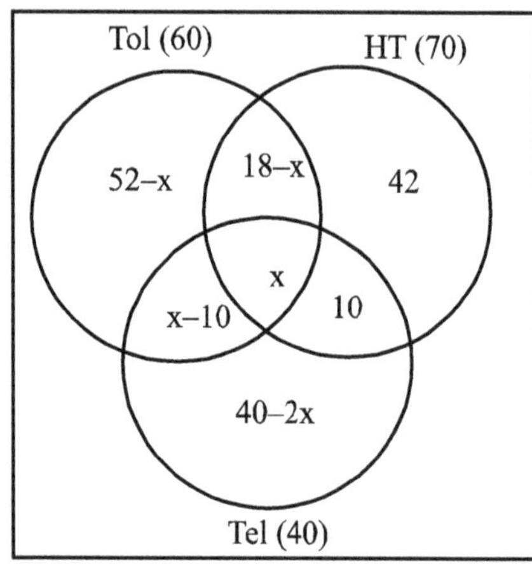


Let us assume that the number of family who read all
the news paper is x, then remaining is as given the
venn diagram.

**16.** **(b)** Total number of family is $152 - 2x$
From venn diagram $10 \leq x \leq 18$
So minimum total number of family
$= 152 - 2 \times 18 = 152 - 36 = 116$
And maximum number of family
$= 152 - 2 \times 10 = 152 - 20 = 132$
So total number of family must be between 132 and 116
and an even number hence 126 is a possible option.

**17.** **(c)** From the given condition $18 - x > x - 10$
or $28 > 2x$ or $x < 14$
But we have seen that $x \geq 10$ hence range of x is $10 \leq x < 14$
Number of family who read only Tel is
$40 - 2x$ whose minimum value is 12 and maximum value
is 20 with even number.

**For 18-19**

From the given condition number of students who play FB
and any one more game is 10 we can conclude $e = g = i = 10$,

From the given condition number of students who play Cr
and any one more game is 8 we can conclude, $h = j = 8$.

From the given condition number of students who play FB
and any two more games is 12 we can conclude $k = n = l = 12$

Hence the Venn diagram will be as follows -

Since total number of students who play FB is 100 hence
$a + e + g + k + l + o + i + n = 100$
or $a + o = 34$
Similarly $o + m + b = 50$
$o + m + c + f = 58$

$o + m + d + f = 58$

Or $c + f = 8 + b$

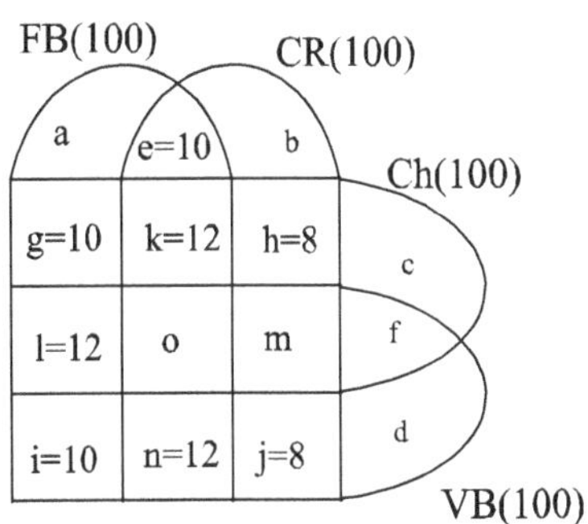


18. **(a)** From the Venn Diagram we have to find the value of Cr + FB, Cr + Ch , and Cr + VB or we have to find the value of e+ h + j = 10+8+8= 26

19. **(b)** Since number of students who play Chess and exactly 1 more game is g + h + f = 18 + f is maximum when f is maximum and since c+f = 8 + b hence for f is maximum b has to be maximum and maximum value of b is 50 when o = m = 0.

20. **(A) → (q); (B) → (s); (C) → (p)**

**(A)** Total no. of male students = 0.475 × 800 =380,

Total no. of veg. students = 0.53 × 800 = 424

Total number of students in secondary section = 0.80 × 800 = 640, out of these 0.55 × 640

= 352 are vegetarian, so we can re-write and complete the table as follows

|  | Male (M) | Vegetarian (V) |
|---|---|---|
| Class12 | 48 | 32 |
| Class 11 | 44 | 40 |
| Secondary Section | 288 | 352 |
| Total | 380 | 424 |

Hence % of vegetarian students in class 12

= 32/80 ×100 = 40%

**(B)** The number of vegetarian male in class 12 = 0.25 × 32 =8, since total number of males in class 12 is 48, hence the number of non-vegetarian males in this class = 48 – 8 = 40.

The number of vegetarian female = 32 – 8 = 24

Hence required difference = 40 – 24 = 16

**(C)** Total number of male students in secondary section = 288, and total number of students in this section is 640, hence required %

= 288/640 × 100 = 45%

**1. (b)** Given :

$$f(T+x) = 1 + \left[ \left\{ 1 - f(x) \right\}^3 \right]^{1/3}$$

$$= 1 + (1 - f(x))$$

$$\Rightarrow f(T+x) + f(x) = 2 \qquad \qquad .....(1)$$

$$\Rightarrow f(2T+x) + f(T+x) = 2 \qquad \qquad .....(2)$$

$$(2) - (1) \Rightarrow f(2T + x) - f(x) = 0$$

$$\Rightarrow f(2T + x) = f(x)$$

Also $T$ is positive and least therefore period of $f(x) = 2T$

**2. (b)** Put $x = y = 1$, $(f(1))^2 = 3f(1) - 2$

$\Rightarrow f(1) = 1$ or $2$

Let $f(1) = 1$, then put $y - 1$

$f(x) \cdot f(1) = f(x) + f(1) + f(x) - 2$

$\Rightarrow f(x) = 1$ constant function

$\therefore f(1) \neq 1$, hence $f(1) = 2$

**3. (d)** Let degree of $f(x)$ is n

Equating the degree of LHS and RHS, we get

$n + n = n \Rightarrow n = 0$

$\Rightarrow f(x) = c \Rightarrow c^2 = c$

$\Rightarrow c = 0, 1 \Rightarrow f(x) = 0, 1$

**4. (d)** $x_0 = a$, $x_1 = f(x) = \dfrac{x_0}{1 - x_0} = \dfrac{a}{1 - a}$ ;

$$x_2 = f(x_1) = \frac{x_1}{1 - x_1} = \frac{\dfrac{a}{1-a}}{1 - \dfrac{a}{1-a}} = \frac{a}{1 - 2a}$$

$$\therefore x_{2009} = \frac{a}{1 - 2009\,a} = 1 \Rightarrow 1 - 2009\,a = a$$

$$\Rightarrow a = \frac{1}{2010}$$

**5. (d)** $\{x^2\} - 2\{x\} \geq 0$

$\Rightarrow \{x\}(\{x\} - 2) \geq 0$

$\Rightarrow \{x\} \leq 0$ or $\{x\} \geq 2$

Second case is not possible. Hence $\{x\} = 0$, as $\{x\} \leq [0, 1)$ Hence range of $f(x)$ contains only one element 0.

**6. (a, b, c)** Let $(a, b) \in A \times (B \cap C)$

$\Rightarrow \quad a \in A$ and $b \in (B \cap C)$

$\Rightarrow \quad a \in A$ and $(b \in B$ and $b \in C)$

$\Rightarrow \quad (a \in A$ and $b \in B)$ and $(a \in A$ and $b \in C)$

$\Rightarrow \quad (a, b) \in A \times B$ and $(a, b) \in (A \times C)$

$\quad (a, b) \in (A \times B) \cap (A \times C)$

$\Rightarrow \quad A \times (B \cap C) \subset (A \times B) \cap (A \times C) \quad ... (i)$

Again, let $(x, y) \in (A \times B) \cap (A \times C)$

$(x, y) \in A \times B$ and $(x, y) \in A \times C$

$\Rightarrow \quad (x \in A$ and $y \in B)$ and $(x \in A$ and $y \in C)$

$\Rightarrow \quad x \in A$ and $(y \in B$ and $y \in C)$

$\Rightarrow \quad x \in A$ and $y \in (B \cap C)$

$\Rightarrow \quad (x, y) \in A \times (B \cap C)$

$\Rightarrow \quad (A \times B) \cap (A \times C) \subset A \times (B \cap C) \quad ... (ii)$

From equations (i) and (ii), we get

$A \times (B \cap C) = (A \times B) \cap (A \times C) \quad ... (iii)$

Now, $A \times (B' \cup C')' = A \times \left[ (B')' \cap (C')' \right]$

[by De-Morgan's law]

$$= A \times (B \cap C) \qquad \left[ \because (A')' = A \right]$$

$$= (A \times B) \cap (A \times C) \qquad \text{[by equation (iii)]}$$

**7. (a, b, c)** We have $R = \{(x, y) : |x^2 - y^2| < 16\}$

Let $x = 1$,

$|x^2 - y^2| < 16 \Rightarrow |1 - y^2| < 16$

$\Rightarrow \quad |y^2 - 1| < 16 \Rightarrow y = 1, 2, 3, 4$

Let $x = 2$,

$\quad |x^2 - y^2| < 16 \Rightarrow |4 - y^2| < 16$

$\Rightarrow \quad |y^2 - 4| < 16 \Rightarrow y = 1, 2, 3, 4$

Let $x = 3$,

$\quad |x^2 - y^2| < 16 \Rightarrow |9 - y^2| < 16$

$\Rightarrow \quad |y^2 - 9| < 16 \Rightarrow y = 1, 2, 3, 4$

Let $x = 4$,

$\quad |x^2 - y^2| < 16 \Rightarrow |16 - y^2| < 16$

$\Rightarrow \quad |y^2 - 16| < 16 \Rightarrow y = 1, 2, 3, 4, 5$

Let $x = 5$,

$\quad |x^2 - y^2| < 16 \Rightarrow |25 - y^2| < 16$

$\Rightarrow \quad |y^2 - 25| < 16 \Rightarrow y = 4, 5$

$\therefore \quad R = \{(1, 1), (1, 2), (1, 3), (1, 4), (2, 1), (2, 2), (2, 3), (2, 4), (3, 1), (3, 2), (3, 3), (3, 4), (4, 1), (4, 2), (4, 3), (4, 4), (4, 5), (5, 4), (5, 5)\}.$

**8. (a, b, c, d)**

**Option (a) :** $Sgn\,(x) = \begin{cases} 1, & x > 0 \\ 0, & x = 0 \\ -1, & x < 0 \end{cases}$

$\therefore \quad Sgn\,(e^{-x}) = 1 \qquad (\because e^{-x} > 0)$

$Sgn\,(e^{-x})$ is constant function. Hence, it is periodic.

**Option (b) :** $\because$ Period of $\sin x$ is $2\pi$

and period of $|\sin x|$ is $\pi$

$\therefore$ Period of $\sin x + |\sin x|$ is LCM $\{2\pi, \pi\}$

**Option (c) :** Let $f(x) = \min\,\{\sin x, |x|\} = \sin x$

$[\because \sin x < |x|]$

$\sin x$ is periodic with period $2\pi$.

**Option (d) :**

$$f(x) = \left[x + \frac{1}{2}\right] + \left[x - \frac{1}{2}\right] + 2\left[-x\right]$$

$$= \left(x + \frac{1}{2}\right) - \left\{x + \frac{1}{2}\right\} + \left(x - \frac{1}{2}\right) - \left\{x - \frac{1}{2}\right\}$$

$$+ 2\left(-x - \{-x\}\right)$$

$$= -\left\{x + \frac{1}{2}\right\} - \left\{x - \frac{1}{2}\right\} - 2\{-x\}$$

Hence, $f(x)$ is periodic.

**9.  (a, c, d)** $\sqrt{|x^2| - 5|x| + 6} = \sqrt{(|x| - 2)(|x| - 3)}$

is real for $0 \le |x| \le 4$

$\therefore f(x)$ is real for all $0 \le |x| \le 2$ or $3 \le |x| \le 4$.

**10.  (3)**  We have, $(x, y) \in R$, if $x^2 + y^2 = 16$

i.e.,  $y = \pm\sqrt{16 - x^2}$

For, $x = 0$, $y = \pm 4$

For, $x = \pm 4$, $y = 0$

We observe that no other values of x, $y \in Z$, which satisfy $x^2 + y^2 = 16$

$R = \{(0, 4), (0, -4), (4, 0), (-4, 0)\}$

$\therefore$  Domain of $R = \{0, 4, -4\}$.

**11.  (8)**  Given $2f(xy) = \left(f(x)\right)^y + \left(f(y)\right)^x$  ...(1)

Putting $y = 1$, we get $2f(x) = f(x) + \left(f(1)\right)^x$

$\Rightarrow$  $f(x) = \left(f(1)\right)^x = 2^x$  $\left[\because f(1) = 2\right]$

$\Rightarrow$  $f(3) = 2^3 = 8$

**12.  (2)**  Given, $f(x) = \dfrac{4^x}{4^x + 2}$  ...(1)

We observe that $f\left(\dfrac{1}{1997}\right)$ and $f\left(\dfrac{1996}{1997}\right)$ are such that

$$\frac{1}{1997} + \frac{1996}{1997} = 1$$

$\therefore$  If $x = \dfrac{1}{1997}, \dfrac{1996}{1997} = 1 - x$

Also, $f\left(\dfrac{2}{1997}\right)$ and $f\left(\dfrac{1995}{1997}\right)$ are such that

$\dfrac{2}{1997} + \dfrac{1995}{1997} = 1$ $\therefore$

If $x = \dfrac{2}{1997}$, then $\dfrac{1995}{1997} = 1 - x$

Now, $f(x) + f(1-x) = \dfrac{4^x}{4^x + 2} + \dfrac{4^{1-x}}{4^{1-x} + 2}$

$$= \frac{4^x}{4^x + 2} + \frac{4}{4 + 2.4^x} = \frac{4^x}{4^x + 2}$$

$$+ \frac{2}{2 + 4^x} = \frac{4^x + 2}{4^x + 2} = 1$$

Thus, $f(x) + f(1-x) = 1$

Now, $f\left(\dfrac{1}{1997}\right) + f\left(\dfrac{2}{1997}\right) + f\left(\dfrac{3}{1997}\right)$

$$+ .... + f\left(\frac{1995}{1997}\right) + f\left(\frac{1996}{1997}\right)$$

$$= \left[f\left(\frac{1}{1997}\right) + f\left(\frac{1996}{1997}\right)\right] +$$

$$\left[f\left(\frac{2}{1997}\right) + f\left(\frac{1995}{1997}\right)\right] + ... \text{ to } 998 \text{ terms}$$

$= 1 + 1 + 1 + ...$ to 998 terms $= 998$

**13.  (2)**  $f(a + x) = b + [1 + b^3 - 3b^2 f(x) + 3b\{f(x)\}^2$
$$- \{f(x)\}^3]^{1/3}$$

$$= b + [1 + \{b - f(x)\}^3]^{1/3}$$

$\Rightarrow$  $f(a+x) - b = [1 - \{f(x) - b\}^3]^{1/3}$

$\Rightarrow$  $\phi(a+x) = [1 - \{\phi(x)\}^3]^{1/3}$  ...(1)

where $\phi(x) = f(x) - b$

$\Rightarrow$  $\phi(2a+x) = [1 - \{\phi(x+a)\}^3]^{1/3} = \phi(x)$ form (1)

$\Rightarrow$  $f(x + 2a) - b = f(x) - b$

$\Rightarrow$  $f(x + 2a) = f(x)$

$\therefore$  $f(x)$ is periodic with period $2a$.

**14. (a),  15. (c)**

$$(f(x))^2 f\left(\frac{1-x}{1+x}\right) = 64x$$

$\Rightarrow$  $(f(x))^4 \left\{f\left(\dfrac{1-x}{1+x}\right)\right\}^2$  ....(1)

Putting $\dfrac{1-x}{1+x} = y$, and $x = \dfrac{1-y}{1+y}$, we get

$$\left\{f\left(\frac{1-y}{1+y}\right)\right\}^2 . f(y) = 64\left(\frac{1-y}{1+y}\right)$$

$\Rightarrow$  $f(x).\left\{f\left(\dfrac{1-x}{1+x}\right)\right\}^2 = 64\left(\dfrac{1-x}{1+x}\right)$ ...(2)

Equation (1) by (2), we get

$$\frac{\{f(x)\}^4 \left\{f\left(\frac{1-x}{1+x}\right)\right\}^2}{f(x)\left\{f\left(\frac{1-x}{1+x}\right)\right\}^2} = \frac{(64x)^2}{64\left(\frac{1-x}{1+x}\right)}$$

$$\Rightarrow \quad \{f(x)\}^3 = 64x^2 \left(\frac{1+x}{1-x}\right)$$

$$\Rightarrow \quad f(x) = 4x^{2/3}\left(\frac{1+x}{1-x}\right)^{1/3}$$

$$f(9/7) = -8(9/7)^{2/3}$$

**16.** **(b)**

**17.** **(b)**

**18.** **(c)**

**Sol.** (I) $f(x) = \dfrac{1}{\log_a x}, a > 0, \ a \neq 1$

Domain $= R - [0, 1)$

Co-domain $= R^+$

(II) $f(x) = \dfrac{1}{[x]}$

Domain $= R - \{0\}$

Co-domain $= R - \{0\}$

(III) $f(x) = \dfrac{1}{\{x\}}$

Domain $= R^+ - \{1\}$

Co-domain $= (1, \infty)$

(IV) $f(x) = \dfrac{1}{|x|}$

Domain $= R - I$

Co-domain $= \left\{ \dfrac{1}{n}, n \in I - \{0\} \right\}$

**19.** (A)–(p); (B)–(q); (C)–(q, s);

(A) $f(x) = \{(\operatorname{sgn} x)^{\operatorname{sgn} x}\}^n = \begin{cases} [(x)^1]^n, x > 0 \\ [(-1)^{-1}]^n, x < 0 \end{cases}$

$$= \begin{cases} 1, x > 0 \\ -1, x < 0 \end{cases}$$

Hence, $f(x)$ is an odd function.

(B) $f(x) = \dfrac{x}{e^x - 1} + \dfrac{x}{2} + 1$

$$\Rightarrow \quad f(-x) = \frac{-x}{e^{-x} - 1} - \frac{x}{2} + 1 = \frac{xe^x}{e^x - 1} - \frac{x}{2} + 1$$

$$= \frac{xe^x - x + x}{e^x - 1} - \frac{x}{2} + 1$$

$$= x + \frac{x}{e^x - 1} - \frac{x}{2} + 1 = \frac{x}{e^x - 1} + \frac{x}{2} + 1$$

$$= f(x)$$

(C) $f(x) = \begin{cases} 0, & \text{if } x \text{ is rational} \\ 1, & \text{if } x \text{ is irrational} \end{cases}$

$$f(-x) = \begin{cases} 0, & \text{if } -x \text{ is rational} \\ 1, & \text{if } -x \text{ is irrational} \end{cases}$$

**20.** (A) $\to$ (q); (B) $\to$ (p); (C) $\to$ (s); (D) $\to$ (r)

**1.** **(b)** The first equation can be written as

$$x \sin a + y \times 2 \sin a \cos a + z \sin a (3 - 4\sin^2 a)$$

$$= 2 \times 2 \sin a \cos a \cos 2a$$

$$\Rightarrow x + 2y \cos a + z(3 + 4\cos^2 a - 4)$$

$$= 4 \cos a (2\cos^2 a - 1) \ as \sin a \neq 0$$

$$\Rightarrow 8\cos^3 a - 4z\cos^2 a - (2y+4)\cos a + (z-x) = 0$$

$$\Rightarrow \cos^3 a - \frac{z}{2}\cos^2 a - \frac{y+2}{4}\cos a + \frac{z-x}{8} = 0$$

which shows that cos a is root of the equation

$$t^3 - \frac{z}{2}t^2 - \frac{y+2}{4}t + \frac{z-x}{8} = 0$$

Similarly from second and third equations we can varify that cos $b$ and cos $c$ are the roots of the above equation

**2.** **(a)** $$u^2 = a^2 + b^2 + 2\sqrt{\frac{(a^4+b^4)\cos^2\theta\sin^2\theta}{+\ a^2b^2(\cos^4\theta+\sin^4\theta)}} \quad \ldots(i)$$

Now $(a^4+b^4)\cos^2\theta\sin^2\theta + a^2b^2(\cos^4\theta+\sin^4\theta)$

$$= (a^4+b^4)\cos^2\theta\sin^2\theta + a^2b^2(1-2\cos^2\theta\sin^2\theta)$$

$$= (a^4+b^4-2a^2b^2)\cos^2\theta\sin^2\theta + a^2b^2$$

$$= (a^2-b^2)^2 \cdot \frac{\sin^2 2\theta}{4} + a^2b^2 \quad \ldots(ii)$$

$\because 0 \le \sin^2 2\theta \le 1$

$$\Rightarrow 0 \le (a^2-b^2)^2 \frac{\sin^2 2\theta}{4} \le \frac{(a^2-b^2)^2}{4}$$

$$\Rightarrow a^2b^2 \le (a^2-b^2)^2 \frac{\sin^2 2\theta}{4} + a^2b^2$$

$$\le (a^2-b^2)^2 \cdot \frac{1}{4} + a^2b^2 \quad \ldots(iii)$$

$\therefore$ from (i), (ii) and (iii)

Minimum value of $u^2 = a^2 + b^2 + 2\sqrt{a^2b^2} = (a+b)^2$

Maximum value of $u^2$

$$= a^2 + b^2 + 2\sqrt{\left(a^2-b^2\right)^2 \cdot \frac{1}{4} + a^2b^2}$$

$$= a^2 + b^2 + \frac{2}{2}\sqrt{(a^2+b^2)^2} \ = 2(a^2+b^2)$$

$\therefore$ Max value – Min value

$$= 2(a^2+b^2) - (a+b)^2 = (a-b)^2$$

**3.** **(c)** We have

$$\sum_{m=1}^{6} \operatorname{cosec}\left[\theta + \frac{(m-1)\pi}{4}\right] \operatorname{cosec}\left[\theta + \frac{m\pi}{4}\right] = 4\sqrt{2}$$

$$\Rightarrow \sum_{m=1}^{6} \frac{\sin\dfrac{\pi}{4}}{\sin\left[\theta + \dfrac{(m-1)\pi}{4}\right]\sin\left[\theta + \dfrac{m\pi}{4}\right]} = 4$$

$$\Rightarrow \sum_{m=1}^{6} \frac{\sin\left[\left(\theta + \dfrac{m\pi}{4}\right) - \left(\theta + \dfrac{(m-1)\pi}{4}\right)\right]}{\sin\left(\theta + \dfrac{(m-1)\pi}{4}\right)\sin\left(\theta + \dfrac{m\pi}{4}\right)} = 4$$

$$\Rightarrow \sum_{m=1}^{6} \frac{\left[\begin{array}{l}\sin\left(\theta+\dfrac{m\pi}{4}\right)\cos\left(\theta+\dfrac{(m-1)\pi}{4}\right)\\ -\cos\left(\theta+\dfrac{m\pi}{4}\right)\sin\left(\theta+\dfrac{(m-1)\pi}{4}\right)\end{array}\right]}{\sin\left(\theta+\dfrac{(m-1)\pi}{4}\right)\sin\left(\theta+\dfrac{m\pi}{4}\right)} = 4$$

$$\Rightarrow \sum_{m=1}^{6}\left[\cot\left(\theta+\frac{(m-1)\pi}{4}\right) - \cot\left(\theta+\frac{m\pi}{4}\right)\right] = 4$$

$$\Rightarrow \left[\cot\theta - \cot\left(\theta+\frac{\pi}{4}\right)\right] + \left[\cot\left(\theta+\frac{\pi}{4}\right) - \cot\left(\theta+\frac{2\pi}{4}\right)\right]$$

$$+ \ldots + \left[\cot\left(\theta+\frac{5\pi}{4}\right) - \cot\left(\theta+\frac{6\pi}{4}\right)\right] = 4$$

$$\Rightarrow \cot\theta - \cot\left(\theta+\frac{3\pi}{2}\right) = 4 \Rightarrow \cot\theta + \tan\theta = 4$$

$$\Rightarrow \cos^2\theta + \sin^2\theta = 4\sin\theta\cos\theta$$

$$\Rightarrow \sin 2\theta = \frac{1}{2} \Rightarrow 2\theta = \frac{\pi}{6} \text{ or } \frac{5\pi}{6} \Rightarrow \theta = \frac{\pi}{12} \text{ or } \frac{5\pi}{12}$$

**4.** **(c)** $\sqrt{3}\ \sec x + \operatorname{cosec} x + 2(\tan x - \cot x) = 0$

$$\Rightarrow \frac{\sqrt{3}}{2}\sin x + \frac{1}{2}\cos x \ = \cos^2 x \ \sin^2 x$$

$$\Rightarrow \cos\left(x - \frac{\pi}{3}\right) = \cos 2x$$

$$\Rightarrow x - \frac{\pi}{3} = 2n\pi \pm 2x$$

$$\Rightarrow x = \frac{2n\pi}{3} + \frac{\pi}{9} \text{ or } x = -2n\pi - \frac{\pi}{3}$$

For $x \in S$, $n = 0 \Rightarrow x = \dfrac{\pi}{9}, -\dfrac{\pi}{3}$

$n = 1 \Rightarrow x = \dfrac{7\pi}{9}$

$n = -1 \Rightarrow x = \dfrac{-5\pi}{9}$

$\therefore$ Sum of all values of $x = \dfrac{\pi}{9} - \dfrac{\pi}{3} + \dfrac{7\pi}{9} - \dfrac{5\pi}{9} = 0$

**5.** **(a)** We are given that

$(\cot \alpha_1).(\cot \alpha_2) \, .... \, (\cot \alpha_n) = 1$

$\Rightarrow (\cos \alpha_1)(\cos \alpha_2) \, .... \, (\cos \alpha_n)$

$= (\sin \alpha_1)(\sin \alpha_2) \, ....(\sin \alpha_n)$ \qquad ....(i)

Let $y = (\cos \alpha_1)(\cos \alpha_2) \, .... \, (\cos \alpha_n)$ (to be max.)

Squaring both sides, we get

$y^2 = (\cos^2 \alpha_1)(\cos^2 \alpha_2) \, .... \, (\cos^2 \alpha_n)$

$= \cos \alpha_1 \sin \alpha_1 \cos \alpha_2 \sin \alpha_2 \, .... \, \cos \alpha_n \sin \alpha_n$

(Using (i))

$= \dfrac{1}{2^n}[\sin 2\alpha_1 \sin 2\alpha_2 \, .... \, \sin 2\alpha_n]$

As $0 \le \alpha_1, \alpha_2, ..... \alpha_n \le \pi/2$

$\therefore \; 0 \le 2\alpha_1, 2\alpha_2, ..... 2\alpha_n \le \pi$

$\Rightarrow \; 0 \le \sin 2\alpha_1, \sin 2\alpha_2, ..... \sin 2\alpha_n \le 1$

$\therefore \; y^2 \le \dfrac{1}{2^n}.1 \Rightarrow y \le \dfrac{1}{2^{n/2}}$

$\therefore$ Max. value of $y$ is $1/2^{n/2}$.

**6.** **(b)** $\alpha < \beta < \gamma < \delta$ and $\sin\alpha = \sin\beta = \sin\gamma = \sin\delta = k$

$\Rightarrow \beta = \pi - \alpha, \; \gamma = 2\pi + \alpha, \; \delta = 3\pi - \alpha$

So that the given expression is equal to

$4\sin\dfrac{\alpha}{2} + 3\sin\left(\dfrac{\pi - \alpha}{2}\right) + 2\sin\dfrac{2\pi + \alpha}{2} + \sin\dfrac{3\pi - \alpha}{2}$

$= 4\sin\dfrac{\alpha}{2} + 3\cos\dfrac{\alpha}{2} - 2\sin\dfrac{\alpha}{2} - \cos\dfrac{\alpha}{2}$

$= 2\left(\sin\dfrac{\alpha}{2} + \cos\dfrac{\alpha}{2}\right) = 2\sqrt{1 + 2\sin\dfrac{\alpha}{2}\cos\dfrac{\alpha}{2}} = 2\sqrt{1 + k}$

**7.** **(a,b,c,d)** We have, $1 + \sec\theta = \dfrac{1 + \cos\theta}{\cos\theta} = \dfrac{2\cos^2\dfrac{\theta}{2}}{\cos\theta}$,

similarly for others.

$f_n(\theta) = \tan\dfrac{\theta}{2} \cdot \dfrac{2\cos^2\dfrac{\theta}{2}}{\cos\theta} \cdot \dfrac{2\cos^2\theta}{\cos 2\theta} ..... \dfrac{2\cos^2 2^{n-1}\theta}{\cos 2^n\theta}$

$= \tan\dfrac{\theta}{2} . 2^{n+1} \dfrac{[\cos\theta.\cos 2\theta.......\cos 2^{n-1}\theta]\cos^2\dfrac{\theta}{2}}{\cos 2^n\theta}$

$= \dfrac{\sin\theta}{\cos 2^n\theta} . 2^n . \dfrac{\sin 2^n\theta}{2^n \sin\theta} = \tan 2^n\theta$

$\therefore \; f_2\left(\dfrac{\pi}{16}\right) = \tan\left(4.\dfrac{\pi}{16}\right) = 1,.$

$f_3\left(\dfrac{\pi}{32}\right) = \tan\left(8.\dfrac{\pi}{32}\right) = 1$

Similarly others are also true.

**8.** **(a,c)** $\sin\beta = \dfrac{12}{13} \Rightarrow \cos\beta = \pm\dfrac{5}{13}$

according as $\tan\beta > 0$ or $< 0$

$\therefore \; 5\sin(\alpha + \beta) - 12\cos(\alpha + \beta)$

$= 5[\sin\alpha\cos\beta + \cos\alpha\sin\beta]$

$\qquad - 12[\cos\alpha\cos\beta - \sin\alpha\sin\beta]$

$= (5\cos\beta + 12\sin\beta)\sin\alpha$

$\qquad\qquad + (5\sin\beta - 12\cos\beta)\cos\alpha$

$= \left(\dfrac{25}{13} + \dfrac{144}{13}\right)\sin\alpha + \left(\dfrac{60}{13} - \dfrac{60}{13}\right)\cos\alpha$

$= 13\sin\alpha \;$ if $\; \tan\beta > 0$

$\Rightarrow \{(5\sin(\alpha + \beta) - 12\cos(\alpha + \beta)\}\cos ec\alpha = 13$

If $\; \tan\beta < 0 \;$ then $\; 5\sin(\alpha + \beta) - 12\cos(\alpha + \beta)$

$= \dfrac{119}{13}\sin\alpha + \dfrac{120}{13}\cos\alpha$

$\Rightarrow [5\sin(\alpha + \beta) - 12\cos(\alpha + \beta)]\cos ec\alpha$

$= \dfrac{119}{13} + \dfrac{120}{13}\cot\alpha$

**9.** **(b, c, d)** From the first relation we have

$a[\sin(\theta + \phi) - \sin(\theta - \phi)] = b[\sin(\theta - \phi) + \sin(\theta + \phi)]$

$\Rightarrow 2a\sin\phi\cos\theta = 2b\sin\theta\cos\phi$

$\Rightarrow a\tan\phi = b\tan\theta \Rightarrow$ (b) is correct

$$\Rightarrow \frac{2a\tan\frac{\phi}{2}}{1-\tan^2\frac{\phi}{2}} = \frac{2b\tan\frac{\theta}{2}}{1-\tan^2\frac{\theta}{2}}$$

From the second relation replacing

$$\tan\frac{\theta}{2} = \frac{1}{a}[b\tan\frac{\phi}{2}+c] \text{ we have}$$

$$\frac{a\tan\frac{\phi}{2}}{1-\tan^2\frac{\phi}{2}} = \frac{\left(b(b\tan\frac{\phi}{2}+c)\right)}{a\left[1-\left\{\frac{1}{a}(b\tan\frac{\phi}{2}+c)\right\}^2\right]}$$

$$\Rightarrow \tan\frac{\phi}{2}\left[a^2-(b\tan\frac{\phi}{2}+c)^2\right]$$

$$= b\left(b\tan\frac{\phi}{2}+c\right)\left(1-\tan^2\frac{\phi}{2}\right)$$

$$\Rightarrow \tan\frac{\phi}{2}(a^2-b^2-c^2) = bc\left(1+\tan^2\frac{\phi}{2}\right)$$

$$\Rightarrow \frac{2\tan\frac{\phi}{2}}{1+\tan^2\frac{\phi}{2}} = \frac{2bc}{a^2-b^2-c^2}$$

$$\Rightarrow \sin\phi = \frac{2bc}{a^2-b^2-c^2}$$

Similarly we get $\sin\theta = \dfrac{2ac}{a^2-b^2+c^2}$

**10. (b, c, d)** Given : $\dfrac{\tan 3A}{\tan A} = k$       ...(1)

$$\Rightarrow \frac{\tan 3A-\tan A}{\tan A} = k-1 \Rightarrow \frac{\sin 2A}{\cos 3A\sin A} = k-1$$

$$\Rightarrow \frac{2\cos A}{\cos 3A} = k-1 \Rightarrow \frac{\cos A}{\cos 3A} = \frac{k-1}{2}$$

$\Rightarrow$ (a) is incorrect

Again $\dfrac{\tan 3A}{\tan A} = k \Rightarrow \dfrac{\sin 3A}{\cos 3A}\cdot\dfrac{\cos A}{\sin A} = k$

$$\Rightarrow \frac{\sin 3A}{\sin A} = k.\frac{2}{k-1} = \frac{2k}{k-1}$$

$$\Rightarrow \frac{3\sin A-4\sin^3 A}{\sin A} = \frac{2k}{k-1}$$

$$\Rightarrow 3-4\sin^2 A = \frac{2k}{k-1} \text{ or } 4\sin^2 A = \frac{k-3}{k-1}$$

$$\Rightarrow 0 < \frac{k-3}{k-1} < 4 \ [\sin A \neq 0 \text{ or } 1]$$

Now, $\dfrac{k-3}{k-1} > 0$   is $k<1$ or $k>3$    ...(ii)

and $\dfrac{k-3}{k-1} < 4$

$$\Rightarrow \frac{3k-1}{k-1} > 0 \Rightarrow k < \frac{1}{3} \text{ or } k > 1 \quad ...(iii)$$

(ii) and (iii) simultaneously hold if $k < \dfrac{1}{3}$ or $k > 3$

**11. (4)**

We have

$$\left(a\tan\beta - \sqrt{a^2-1}\tan\alpha\right)^2 + \left(\sqrt{a^2+1}\tan\beta - \sqrt{a^2-1}\tan\gamma\right)^2$$

$$+\left(a\tan\gamma - \sqrt{a^2+1}\tan\alpha\right)^2 \geq 0$$

$$\Rightarrow \{a^2+a^2-1+a^2+1\}(\tan^2\alpha+\tan^2\beta+\tan^2\gamma)$$

$$-\left\{a\tan\alpha+\sqrt{a^2-1}\tan\beta+\sqrt{a^2+1}\tan\gamma\right\}^2 \geq 0$$

$$\Rightarrow \tan^2\alpha+\tan^2\beta+\tan^2\gamma \geq \frac{4a^2}{3a^2} \Rightarrow 3\sum\tan^2\alpha \geq 4$$

**12. (3)**

$$1+\cos\alpha = 1+\frac{2\cos\beta-1}{2-\cos\beta}$$

$$= \frac{2-\cos\beta+2\cos\beta-1}{2-\cos\beta} = \frac{1+\cos\beta}{2-\cos\beta}$$

$$\Rightarrow 2\cos^2\frac{\alpha}{2} = \frac{2\cos^2(\beta/2)}{1+2\sin^2(\beta/2)}$$

$\Rightarrow \cos^2\dfrac{\alpha}{2} = \dfrac{\cos^2(\beta/2)}{1+2\sin^2(\beta/2)}$ ...(1)

$\Rightarrow 1-\cos^2\dfrac{\alpha}{2} = 1-\dfrac{\cos^2(\beta/2)}{1+2\sin^2(\beta/2)}$

$= \dfrac{1+2\sin^2(\beta/2)-\cos^2(\beta/2)}{1+2\sin^2(\beta/2)} = \dfrac{3\sin^2\dfrac{\beta}{2}}{1+2\sin^2\dfrac{\beta}{2}}$

$\Rightarrow \sin^2\dfrac{\alpha}{2} = \dfrac{3\sin^2(\beta/2)}{1+2\sin^2(\beta/2)}$ ...(2)

Divide eqs. (2) by (1), we get

$\tan^2\dfrac{\alpha}{2} = 3\tan^2\dfrac{\beta}{2} \Rightarrow \dfrac{\tan(\alpha/2)}{\tan(\beta/2)} = \sqrt{3}$

$\Rightarrow \sqrt{3}\,\dfrac{\tan(\alpha/2)}{\tan(\beta/2)} = 3$

**13. (0)**

We have $xy+yz+zx = xyz\left(\dfrac{1}{x}+\dfrac{1}{y}+\dfrac{1}{z}\right)$

Now, $x\cos\theta = y\cos\left(\theta+\dfrac{2\pi}{3}\right) = z\cos\left(\theta+\dfrac{4\pi}{3}\right) = k$ (say)

then $x = \dfrac{k}{\cos\theta}, y = \dfrac{k}{\cos\left(\theta+\dfrac{2\pi}{3}\right)}$ and $z = \dfrac{k}{\cos\left(\theta+\dfrac{4\pi}{3}\right)}$

$\Rightarrow \dfrac{1}{x}+\dfrac{1}{y}+\dfrac{1}{z} = \dfrac{1}{k}\left[\cos\theta+\cos\left(\theta+\dfrac{2\pi}{3}\right)+\cos\left(\theta+\dfrac{4\pi}{3}\right)\right]$

$= \dfrac{1}{k}\left[\cos\theta+\cos\theta\left(\dfrac{-1}{2}\right)-\sin\theta\left(\dfrac{\sqrt{3}}{2}\right)+\cos\theta\left(-\dfrac{1}{2}\right)-\sin\theta\left(-\dfrac{\sqrt{3}}{2}\right)\right]$

$= \dfrac{1}{k}\left[\cos\theta-\cos\theta-\dfrac{\sqrt{3}}{2}\sin\theta-\dfrac{\sqrt{3}}{2}\sin\theta\right] = 0$

$\therefore xy+yz+zx = 0$

**14. (6)**

Given that $\sin^3 x\sin 3x = \displaystyle\sum_{m=0}^{n} c_m\cos mx$

or $\left(\dfrac{3\sin x-\sin 3x}{4}\right)\cdot\sin x = \displaystyle\sum_{m=0}^{n} c_m\cos mx$

or $\dfrac{3}{8}\cdot(2\sin 3x\sin x)-\dfrac{1}{8}\cdot 2\sin^2 3x = \displaystyle\sum_{m=0}^{n} c_m\cos mx$

or $\dfrac{3}{8}\cdot[\cos 2x-\cos 4x]-\dfrac{1}{8}[1-\cos 6x] = \displaystyle\sum_{m=0}^{n} c_m\cos mx$

or $-\dfrac{1}{8}+\dfrac{3}{8}\cos 2x-\dfrac{3}{8}\cos 4x+\dfrac{1}{8}\cos 6x = \displaystyle\sum_{m=0}^{n} c_m\cos mx$ .

Comparing, we get $n=6$.

**15. (b)** $\because$ $P_1 = m$

$P_1{}^2 = m^2$

$\sin^2\theta+\cos^2\theta+2\sin\theta\cos\theta = m^2$

$\Rightarrow \sin\theta\cos\theta = \dfrac{(m^2-1)}{2}$

Now, from eq. (iii), we get
$P_6 = 1-3\sin^2\theta\cos^2\theta$

$\Rightarrow (1-P_6) = 3(\sin\theta\cos\theta)^2 = \dfrac{3(m^2-1)^2}{4}$

$\Rightarrow 4(1-P_6) = 3(m^2-1)^2$

**16. (a)** Let $\sin^2\theta\cos^2\theta = k$, then from eq. (i), we get
$P_n - P_{n-2} = -kP_{n-4}$.
From eq. (ii), $P_4 = 1-2k$
and from eq. (iii), $P_6 = 1-3k$
Put $n=10$,
then $P_{10}-P_8 = -kP_6 = -k(1-3k)$
$\therefore P_{10}-P_8 = 3k^2-k$ ...(iv)
and put $n=8$, then $P_8-P_6-kP_4 = -k(1-2k)$
$P_8 = P_6+2k^2-k$
$= 1-3k+2k^2-k$
$\Rightarrow P_8 = 2k^2-4k+1$
From eq. (iv), $P_{10} = 5k^2-5k+1$
$\therefore 6P_{10}-15P_8+10P_6+7$
$= 6(5k^2-5k+1)-15(2k^2-4k+1)+10(1-3k)+7$
$= 8$

**17. (b)** $5\sin^2 x+3\sin x\cos x-3\cos^2 x = 2(\sin^2 x+\cos^2 x)$
$\Rightarrow 3\tan^2 x+3\tan x-5 = 0$

$\Rightarrow \tan x = \dfrac{-3\pm\sqrt{69}}{6}$

and $\sin^2 x-\cos 2x = 2-\sin 2x$
$3\sin^2 x+2\sin x\cos x = 3(\sin^2 x+\cos^2 x)$
$\Rightarrow \cos x(2\sin x-3\cos x) = 0$

Either $\cos x = 0$ or $\tan x = \dfrac{3}{2} \Rightarrow \cos x = \pm\dfrac{2}{\sqrt{13}}$

Taking $= \alpha = \dfrac{-3\pm\sqrt{69}}{6}$, $\tan\beta = \dfrac{3}{2}$

we get $\tan\alpha+\tan\beta = 1\pm\sqrt{69}/6$

**18. (d)** Taking $\tan\alpha = \dfrac{-3+\sqrt{69}}{6}$, $\tan\beta = \dfrac{-3-\sqrt{69}}{6}$

$\cos\gamma = 0, \cos\delta = \pm\dfrac{2}{\sqrt{13}}$

we get $\tan\alpha\tan\beta+\cos\gamma+\cos\delta = -\dfrac{5}{3}\pm\dfrac{2}{\sqrt{13}}$

**19.**   **A - p,q,r,s; B - r,s; C - q,r,s; D - q, s**

**(A)**   $f(\theta) = (\sin\theta + \mathrm{cosec}\,\theta)^2 + (\cos\theta + \sec\theta)^2$

$$= \sin^2\theta + \cos^2\theta + \sec^2\theta + \mathrm{cosec}^2\theta + 4$$

$$= 5 + 1 + \cot^2\theta + 1 + \tan^2\theta = 9 + (\tan\theta - \cot\theta)^2 \geq 9$$

**(B)**   $\sin\alpha - \sin\beta = a,\ \cos\alpha + \cos\beta = b$

$$\Rightarrow a^2 + b^2 = 2 + 2\cos(\alpha+\beta) = 4\cos^2\frac{\alpha+\beta}{2} \leq 4$$

**(C)**   $\dfrac{\sin A + \sin B}{2} \leq \sin\left(\dfrac{A+B}{2}\right)$

$$\therefore \sin A + \sin B \leq 2\sin\frac{\pi}{4}$$

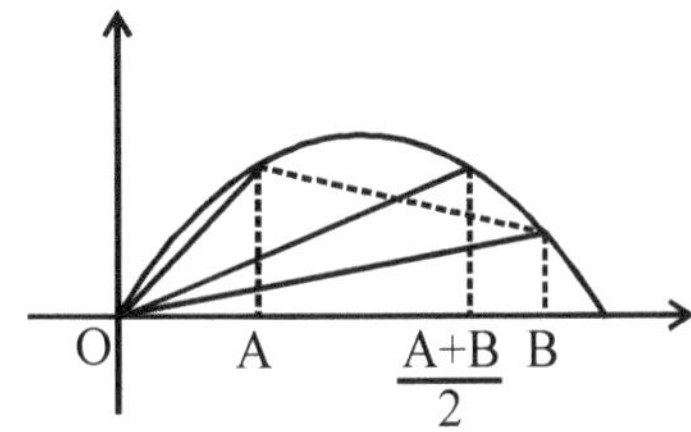

or $\dfrac{1}{\sqrt{2}}(\sin A + \sin B) \leq 1$

**(D)**   Let $A = 7\cos x + 6\sin x = 6\,(2\cos x + \sin x) - 5\cos x$
$$= 6 - 5\cos x$$
Now, $2\cos x + \sin x = 1 \Rightarrow \sin x = 1 - 2\cos x$
$\Rightarrow \sin^2 x = 1 - \cos^2 x = 1 - 4\cos x + 4\cos^2 x$

$$\therefore \cos x = 0 \text{ or } \frac{4}{5}. \text{ So, } A = 6 \text{ or } 2$$

**20.**   **A - q; B - p, s; C - r; D - p**

**(A)**   $y = \cos^2\theta + \sin^4\theta = \cos^2\theta + \sin^2\theta(1 - \cos^2\theta)$

$$= 1 - \frac{1}{4}\sin^2 2\theta \ \Rightarrow\ \frac{3}{4} \leq A \leq 1$$

**(B)**   $\tan A < 0 \ \Rightarrow\ A > \dfrac{\pi}{2} \ \Rightarrow\ 0 < B + C < \dfrac{\pi}{2}$

$$\Rightarrow\ \tan(B+C) > 0 \ \Rightarrow\ \frac{\tan B + \tan C}{1 - \tan B \tan C} > 0$$

$$\Rightarrow\ 0 < \tan B \tan C < 1$$

**(C)**   Let $y = \dfrac{\cos^2\theta - 1}{\cos^2 + \cos\theta}$

$$\Rightarrow\ (y-1)\cos^2\theta + y\cos\theta + 1 = 0$$

$$\Rightarrow\ \cos\theta = -1 \text{ or } \cos\theta = \frac{1}{1-y}$$

$$-1 < \frac{1}{1-y} < 1$$

$$\Rightarrow\ y < 0 \text{ or } y > 2$$

**(D)**   $y = \tan A \tan B = \tan A \tan\left(\dfrac{\pi}{3} - A\right)$

$$= x\left(\frac{\sqrt{3} - x}{1 + \sqrt{3}x}\right), \text{ where } x = \tan A$$

$$\Rightarrow\ x^2 + \sqrt{3}x(y-1) + y = 0$$

$$\because\ x \in R \ \Rightarrow\ 3(y-1)^2 - 4y \geq 0 \ \Rightarrow\ y \leq \frac{1}{3} \text{ or } y \geq 3$$

Also, $0 < A, B < \dfrac{\pi}{3} \ \Rightarrow\ 0 < \tan A, \tan B < \sqrt{3}$

$$\Rightarrow\ 0 < \tan A \tan B < 3$$

$$\therefore\ 0 < y \leq \frac{1}{3}$$

**1.** **(a)** Let $z = x + iy$, then the equation is

$$x^2 + y^2 - 2i(x+iy) + 2c(1+i) = 0$$

$$\Rightarrow (x^2 + y^2 + 2y + 2c) + i(2c - 2x) = 0$$

$$\Rightarrow x^2 + y^2 + 2y + 2c = 0 \text{ and } x = c$$

$$\Rightarrow c^2 + y^2 + 2y + 2c = 0$$

$$\Rightarrow y = -1 \pm \sqrt{1 - 2c - c^2}$$

$$\because y \in \mathbf{R} \Rightarrow 1 - 2c - c^2 \geq 0$$

$$\Rightarrow c^2 + 2c - 1 \leq 0 \Rightarrow -1 - \sqrt{2} \leq c \leq -1 + \sqrt{2}$$

$\therefore$ The equation has a solution, if

$c \in [-1 - \sqrt{2}, -1 + \sqrt{2}]$ and the solution is given by

$$z = c + i(-1 \pm \sqrt{1 - 2c - c^2})$$

The equation has no solution, if

$$c \in (-\infty, -1 - \sqrt{2}) \cup (-1 + \sqrt{2}, \infty)$$

**2.** **(d)** $|z_1| = |z_2| = 1 \Rightarrow a^2 + b^2 = c^2 + d^2 = 1$ ...(1)

and Re $(z_1 \bar{z}_2) = 0 \Rightarrow \text{Re}\{(a + ib)(c - id)\} = 0$

$$\Rightarrow ac + bd = 0 \qquad \qquad ...(2)$$

Now from (1) and (2), $a^2 + b^2 = 1$

$$\Rightarrow a^2 + \frac{a^2 c^2}{d^2} = 1 \Rightarrow a^2 = d^2 \qquad ...(3)$$

Also $c^2 + d^2 = 1 \Rightarrow c^2 + \frac{a^2 c^2}{b^2} = 1$

$$\Rightarrow b^2 = c^2 \qquad \qquad ...(4)$$

$$|\omega_1| = \sqrt{a^2 + c^2} = \sqrt{a^2 + b^2} = 1$$

$$[\text{From (1) and (4)}]$$

and $|\omega_2| = \sqrt{b^2 + d^2} = \sqrt{c^2 + d^2} = 1$

$$[\text{from (1) and (4)}]$$

Further Re $(\omega_1 \bar{\omega}_2) = \text{Re}\{(a + ic)(b - id)\}$

$$= ab + cd = ab + \left(-\frac{ac}{b}\right) c \quad [\text{From (2)}]$$

$$= \frac{ab^2 - ac^2}{b} = 0 \ [\text{from (4)}].$$

Also, $\text{Im}(\omega_1 \bar{\omega}_2) = bc - ad = bc - a\left(-\frac{ac}{b}\right)$

$$= \frac{(a^2 + b^2)c}{b} = \frac{c}{b} = \pm 1 \neq 0$$

$\therefore |\omega_1| = 1, |\omega_2| = 1$ and Re$(\omega_1 \bar{\omega}_2) = 0$

**3.** **(a)** If $f(x) = Ax^2 - |G| x - H$, then $f(0) = -H < 0$ and $f(-1) = A + |G| - H > 0$. So, $f(x) = 0$ has one root in $(-1, 0)$ hence the equation has a negative fraction root. Also,
$f(2) = 4A - 2|G| - H = 2(A - |G|) + (A - H) + A > 0$.
So, $f(x) = 0$ has one root in $(0, 2)$, hence the equation has a positive root, which cannot exceed 2.

**4.** **(c)** $a > b > c$ ...(1)
and given equation is

$$(a + b - 2c)x^2 + (b + c - 2a)x + (c + a - 2b) = 0 \ ...(2)$$

$\because$ Equation (2) has a root in the interval $(-1, 0)$

$$\therefore \ f(-1) f(0) < 0$$

$$\Rightarrow (2a - b - c)(c + a - 2b) < 0 \qquad ...(3)$$

From (1), $a > b \Rightarrow a - b > 0$ and

$$a > c \Rightarrow a - c > 0 \ \therefore \ 2a - b - c > 0 \qquad ...(4)$$

From (3) and (4), $c + a - 2b < 0$ or $c + a < 2b$. Option (a) is wrong. Again, the sum of coefficients of the equation

$= 0$, that is one root is 1 and the other root is $\dfrac{c + a - 2b}{a + b - 2c}$,

which is a rational number as $a, b, c$ are rational. Hence, both the roots of the equation are rational.
$\Rightarrow$ (b) is wrong. Further, the discriminate of equation

$ax^2 + 2bx + c = 0$ is $D = 4b^2 - 4ac$.

As deduced earlier, $c + a < 2b$

$$\Rightarrow 4b^2 > (c + a)^2$$

$$\Rightarrow 4b^2 > c^2 + a^2 + 2ac$$

$$\Rightarrow 4b^2 - 4ac > c^2 + a^2 - 2ac$$

$$= (c - a)^2 \Rightarrow 4b^2 - 4ac > 0 \Rightarrow D > 0. \text{ Also, each of}$$

$a, b, c$ are positive.

$\therefore$ The equation $ax^2 + 2bx + c = 0$ has real and negative roots. So (c) is correct.

**5.** **(a)** Since $-5$ and 1 are the roots. Product of roots

$$= -5 \times 1 = b \Rightarrow b = -5 \text{ and}$$

Sum of roots $= -5 + 1 = -[a^2 - 5a + b + 4]$

$\Rightarrow [a^2 - 5a - 1] = 4 \Rightarrow 4 \le a^2 - 5a - 1 < 5$

$$[\because [x] = n \Rightarrow n \le x < n+1]$$

$\Rightarrow a^2 - 5a - 5 \ge 0$ and $\qquad a^2 - 5a - 6 < 0$

$\Rightarrow a \le \dfrac{5 - \sqrt{45}}{2}$ or $a \ge \dfrac{5 + \sqrt{45}}{2}$ and $-1 < a < 6$

$\Rightarrow -1 < a \le \dfrac{5 - 3\sqrt{5}}{2}$ or $\dfrac{5 + 3\sqrt{5}}{2} \le a < 6$

$\Rightarrow a \in \left( -1, \dfrac{5 - 3\sqrt{5}}{2} \right] \cup \left[ \dfrac{5 + 3\sqrt{5}}{2}, 6 \right)$

**6.** **(d)** Let $z = x + iy$, then $\arg(z - 3i) = \arg(x + iy - 3i) = \dfrac{3\pi}{4}$

$\Rightarrow x < 0, y - 3 > 0 \quad (\because \dfrac{3\pi}{4}$ is in II quadrant$)$

and $\dfrac{y - 3}{x} = \tan \dfrac{3\pi}{4} = -1$

$\Rightarrow y = -x + 3 \ \forall \ x < 0$ and $y > 3$ ...(1)

and $\arg(2z + 1 - 2i) = \arg[(2x + 1) + i(2y - 2)] = \dfrac{\pi}{4}$

$\Rightarrow 2x + 1 > 0, 2y - 2 > 0 \quad (\because \dfrac{\pi}{4}$ is in I quadrant$)$

and $\dfrac{2y - 2}{2x + 1} = \tan \dfrac{\pi}{4} = 1 \Rightarrow 2y - 2 = 2x + 1$

$\Rightarrow y = x + \dfrac{3}{2} \ \forall \ x > -\dfrac{1}{2}, y > 1$ .....(2)

From equations (1) and (2), we get graph

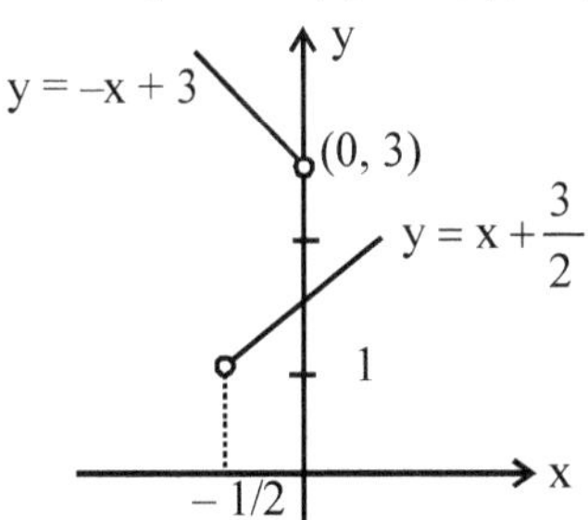


It is clear from the graph that two lines do not intersect.
∴ No point of intersection.
***Caution :*** *It is most likely that the students after getting two straight lines, solve them to get the point of intersection* $\left( \dfrac{3}{4}, \dfrac{9}{4} \right)$. *Clearly the principal values of arguments must be considered.*

**7.** **(a, d)**
We have $z_1^3 + z_2^3 + z_3^3 = -z_1 z_2 z_3$.

$\Rightarrow -4z_1 z_2 z_3 = z_1^3 + z_2^3 + z_3^3 - 3z_1 z_2 z_3$

$= (z_1 + z_2 + z_3)(z_1^2 + z_2^2 + z_3^2 - z_2 z_3 - z_3 z_1 - z_1 z_2)$

$= (z_1 + z_2 + z_3)[(z_1 + z_2 + z_3)^2 - 3(z_2 z_3 + z_3 z_1 + z_1 z_2)]$

$\Rightarrow z^3 - 3z(z_2 z_3 + z_3 z_1 + z_1 z_2) + 4z_1 z_2 z_3 = 0$

where $z = z_1 + z_2 + z_3$

$\Rightarrow z^3 = z_1 z_2 z_3 \left[ 3z \left( \dfrac{1}{z_1} + \dfrac{1}{z_2} + \dfrac{1}{z_3} \right) - 4 \right]$

$= z_1 z_2 z_3 \left[ 3z \left( \bar{z}_1 + \bar{z}_2 + \bar{z}_3 \right) - 4 \right] \quad \left[ \because |z_1| = |z_2| = |z_3| = 1 \right]$

$= z_1 z_2 z_3 \left[ 3z \bar{z} - 4 \right]$

$\Rightarrow |z|^3 = |z_1| \, |z_2| \, |z_3| \, |3|z|^2 - 4|$

$\Rightarrow |z|^3 - |3|z|^2 - 4| = 0$

If $|z| \ge 2/\sqrt{3}$, we get

$\quad |z|^3 - |3|z|^2 + 4| = 0$

$\Rightarrow (|z| - 2)(|z|^2 - |z| - 2) = 0$

$\Rightarrow (|z| - 2)^2 (|z| + 1) = 0$

$\Rightarrow |z| - 2 = 0$ or $|z| = 2$

If $|z| < 2/3$, we get

$\quad |z|^3 + 3|z|^2 - 4 = 0$

$\Rightarrow (|z| - 1)(|z|^2 + 4|z| + 4) = 0$

$\Rightarrow |z| - 1 = 0 \Rightarrow |z| = 1$

**8.** **(a,d)** Discriminant $D = 4p^2 - 4(p^2 - 1) = 4 > 0$

∵ Roots of the equation are real and distinct
Now both the roots are less than 4 if

$D \ge 0, \ f(4) > 0$ and $4 > -\dfrac{2p}{2}$

$\Rightarrow 16 - 8p + p^2 - 1 > 0$ and

$4 > p \Rightarrow (p - 3)(p - 5) > 0$ and $p < 4$

$\Rightarrow p < 3$ or $p > 5$ and $p < 4 \Rightarrow p \in (-\infty, 3)$

Again both the roots are greater than

$-2$ if $D \ge 0, f(-2) > 0$ and $-2 < -\dfrac{2p}{2}$

$\Rightarrow (4 + 4p + p^2 + 1) > 0$ and

$3 < p \Rightarrow (p + 3)(p + 1) > 0$ and $p > -3$

$\Rightarrow p < -3$ or $p > -1$ and $p > -3 \Rightarrow p \in (-1, \infty)$

Further exactly one root lies in the interval $(-2, 4)$ if

$D > 0$ and $f(-2) f(4) < 0$

$\Rightarrow (p + 3)(p + 1)(p - 3)(p - 5) < 0$

$\Rightarrow p \in (-3, -1) \cup (3, 5)$

Finally, 1 lies between the roots if $D > 0$ and $f(1) < 0$

$\Rightarrow 1 - 2p + p^2 - 1 < 0 \Rightarrow p(p-2) < 0$

$\Rightarrow 0 < p < 2 \Rightarrow p \in (0, 2)$

***Alternatively :***

$x^2 - 2px + p^2 - 1 = 0 \Rightarrow (x-p)^2 = 1$

$\therefore x = p \pm 1$

Both the roots are less than 4 if $p + 1 < 4$ and $p - 1 < 4 \Rightarrow p < 3$

Both the roots are greater than $-2$ if $p + 1 > -2$ and $p - 1 > -2 \Rightarrow p > -1$

Exactly one root lies in $(-2, 4)$ if $-2 < p + 1 < 4$ or $-2 < p - 1 < 4$ but not both

$\Rightarrow p \in (-3, -1) \cup (3, 5)$

One root is less than 1 and other greater than 1 if $p + 1 < 1 < p - 1$ or $p - 1 < 1 < p + 1 \Rightarrow 0 < p < 2$

***NOTE : The alternate method is easier than the general method, so if the roots of quadratic in terms of parameter come out to be free of radical the alternative method is better.***

**9.** **(b,c)** The given equation is,

$$\pi^e (x - \pi)(x - \pi - e) + e^\pi (x - e)(x - \pi - e)$$
$$+ (\pi^\pi + e^e)(x - e)(x - \pi) = 0$$

Let $f(x) = \pi^e (x - \pi)(x - \pi - e) + e^\pi (x - e)(x - \pi - e)$
$$+ (\pi^\pi + e^e)(x - e)(x - \pi)$$

Then $f(e) = \pi^e (e - \pi)(-\pi) > 0 \;[\because e < \pi]$

and $f(\pi) = e^\pi (\pi - e)(-e) < 0$

$\therefore$ Equation $f(x) = 0$ has a real root in $(e, \pi)$.

Again $f(\pi + e) = (\pi^\pi + e^e)(\pi)(e) > 0$.

$\therefore$ Equation $f(x) = 0$ has a real root in $(\pi, e + \pi)$.

$\therefore\; f(x) = 0$ has a real roots in $(e, \pi)$

and other in $(\pi, \pi + e)$

Also, $\pi - e < e$

$\therefore$ Equation $f(x) = 0$ has two real roots in

$(\pi - e, \pi + e)$.

**10.** **(a,b,c)**

Put $\omega = \cos\dfrac{2\pi}{11} + i\sin\dfrac{2\pi}{11}$,

so that for $1 \le k \le 10$

$$\sin\dfrac{2\pi}{11} - i\cos\dfrac{2\pi k}{11}$$

$$= -i\left(\cos\dfrac{2\pi k}{11} + i\sin\dfrac{2\pi k}{11}\right)$$

$= -i\omega^k$ \qquad [De Moivre's theorem]

Thus,

$$S = -i\sum_{k=1}^{10} \omega^k = -\dfrac{i\omega(1 - \omega^{10})}{1 - \omega} = \dfrac{i\omega(1 - \omega^{11})}{1 - \omega}$$

But $\omega^{11} = \cos 2\pi + i\sin 2\pi = 1 + i0 = 1$

$\therefore\quad S = i$

$\Rightarrow\quad S + \overline{S} = 0,\; S\overline{S} = 1$

and $\sqrt{S} = \pm\dfrac{1}{\sqrt{2}}(1 + i)$

**11.** **(6)**

Solving $z^2 - z + 1 = 0 \Rightarrow z = \dfrac{1 \pm i\sqrt{3}}{2}$

Taking $z = \dfrac{1 + i\sqrt{3}}{2} = \cos\dfrac{\pi}{3} + i\sin\dfrac{\pi}{3}$

$\Rightarrow z^n = \cos\dfrac{n\pi}{3} + i\sin\dfrac{n\pi}{3}, n = 1, 2, \dots\dots\dots, 24$

$\therefore\quad z^n + \dfrac{1}{z^n} = 2\cos\dfrac{n\pi}{3}$

$\therefore\quad \left(z + \dfrac{1}{z}\right)^2 + \left(z^2 + \dfrac{1}{z^2}\right)^2 + \left(z^3 + \dfrac{1}{z^3}\right)^2 +$

$$\dots\dots\dots\dots\dots + \left(z^{24} + \dfrac{1}{z^{24}}\right)^2$$

$= 2^2 \cos^2\dfrac{\pi}{3} + 2^2\cos^2\dfrac{2\pi}{3} + 2^2\cos^2\dfrac{3\pi}{3} + 2^2\cos^2\dfrac{24\pi}{3}$

$= 2\left[\left(1 + \cos\dfrac{2\pi}{3}\right) + \left(1 + \cos\dfrac{4\pi}{3}\right) + \left(1 + \cos\dfrac{6\pi}{3}\right) + \right.$

$$\left. \dots\dots\dots\dots + \left(1 + \cos\dfrac{48\pi}{3}\right)\right]$$

$$= 2\left[24 + \dfrac{\cos\left\{\dfrac{2\pi}{3} + \dfrac{23\pi}{3}\right\}\sin\dfrac{24\pi}{3}}{\sin\dfrac{\pi}{3}}\right] = 2(24+0) = 48$$

Using the formula,

$$\cos\alpha + \cos(\alpha+\beta) + \cos(\alpha+2\beta) + \ldots\ldots +$$

$$\cos\{\alpha + (n-1)\beta\} = \dfrac{\cos\left\{\alpha + \dfrac{(n-1)\beta}{2}\right\}\sin\dfrac{n\beta}{2}}{\sin\dfrac{\beta}{2}}$$

**12. (2)** Roots of $x^2 - 10cx - 11d = 0$ are $a$ and $b \Rightarrow a+b = 10c$
and $ab = -11d$
Similarly $c$ and $d$ are the roots of
$x^2 - 10ax - 11b = 0 \Rightarrow c+d = 10a$ and $cd = -11b$
$\Rightarrow a+b+c+d = 10(a+c)$ and $abcd = 121bd$
$\Rightarrow b+d = 9(a+c)$ and $ac = 121$
Also we have $a^2 - 10ac - 11d = 0$ & $c^2 - 10ac - 11b = 0$
$\Rightarrow a^2 + c^2 - 20ac - 11(b+d) = 0$
$\Rightarrow (a+c)^2 - 22 \times 121 - 99(a+c) = 0 \Rightarrow a+c = 121$ or $-22$
For $a+c = -22$ we get $a = c$
$\therefore$ rejecting this value we have $a+c = 121$
$\therefore a+b+c+d = 10(a+c) = 1210$

**13. (2)** $ax^2 + bx + c = 0$ has roots $\alpha$ and $\beta$

$$\Rightarrow \alpha + \beta = -\dfrac{b}{a},\ \alpha\beta = \dfrac{c}{a}.$$

If the roots of equation $a^5 x^2 + ba^2 c^2 x + c^5 = 0$ are
$\gamma$ and $\delta$, then

$$\gamma + \delta = -\dfrac{b}{a}\left(\dfrac{c}{a}\right)^2 = (\alpha+\beta)\alpha^2\beta^2 = \alpha^3\beta^2 + \alpha^2\beta^3$$

Clearly roots are $\alpha^3\beta^2$ and $\alpha^2\beta^3$

$$\Rightarrow \alpha^5\beta^5 = 32 \Rightarrow \alpha\beta = 2$$

**14. (2)** The given relation can be rewritten as

$$\dfrac{1}{a+\omega} + \dfrac{1}{b+\omega} + \dfrac{1}{c+\omega} = \dfrac{2}{\omega}$$

$$\text{and}\ \dfrac{1}{a+\omega^2} + \dfrac{1}{b+\omega^2} + \dfrac{1}{c+\omega^2} = \dfrac{2}{\omega^2}$$

$$\Rightarrow \omega\ \text{and}\ \omega^2\ \text{are roots of}\ \dfrac{1}{a+x} + \dfrac{1}{b+x} + \dfrac{1}{c+x} = \dfrac{2}{x}$$

$$\Rightarrow \dfrac{3x^2 + 2(a+b+c)x + bc + ca + ab}{(a+x)(b+x)(c+x)} = \dfrac{2}{x}$$

$$\Rightarrow x^3 - (bc + ca + ab)x - 2abc = 0 \qquad \ldots(1)$$

Two roots of the equation (1) are $\omega$ and $\omega^2$. Let the
third root be $\alpha$, then

$$\alpha + \omega + \omega^2 = 0 \Rightarrow \alpha = -\omega - \omega^2 = 1.$$

$\therefore\ \ \alpha = 1$ will satisfy equation (1)

$$\Rightarrow \dfrac{1}{a+1} + \dfrac{1}{b+1} + \dfrac{1}{c+1} = 2$$

**15. (5)** We have $z = \dfrac{1}{2}\left(\sqrt{3} - i\right)$

$$= -\dfrac{1}{2}i\left(1 + i\sqrt{3}\right) = i\,\omega^2$$

where $\omega \neq 1$ is a cube of unity.

$\therefore\ \ z^{89} = (i\omega^2)^{89} = i^{89}\,\omega^{178} = i\omega$

Also, $i^{97} = i^{96}\,i = i$

Thus, $(z^{89} + i^{97})^{94} = (i\omega + i)^{94} = [i(-\omega^2)]^{94} = -\omega^2$

Also, $z^n = i^n\,\omega^{2n}$

$\therefore$ The given equation becomes

$$-\omega^2 = i^n\,\omega^{2n} \Rightarrow i^n\,\omega^{2n-2} = -1$$

This is possible if n is of the type $4k + 2$ and $2n - 2$ is a
multiple of 3.

That is $2(4k+2) - 2 = 8k + 2$ is multiple of 3.

The least value of k for which this is possible is 2.
Therefore, $n = 10$.

**16. (d)** $\because\ |z + i\omega| \leq |z| + |i\omega| = |z| + |i||\omega| \leq 2$
$\therefore\ |z + i\omega| = 2 \Leftrightarrow |z| = |\omega| = 1.$

**17. (d)** Let $z = x + iy$ and $\omega = \alpha + i\beta$

Now $|z + i\omega| = 2 \Rightarrow (z + i\omega)(\overline{z} - i\overline{\omega}) = 4$

$\Rightarrow |z|^2 + |\omega|^2 + i\omega\,\overline{z} - i\overline{\omega}\,z = 4$

$\Rightarrow i\omega\,\overline{z} - i\overline{\omega}\,z = 2 \qquad \ldots(1)$

and $|z - i\overline{\omega}| = 2 \Rightarrow (z - i\overline{\omega})(\overline{z} + i\omega) = 4$

$\Rightarrow |z|^2 + |\omega|^2 + i\omega\,z - i\overline{\omega}\,\overline{z} = 4$

$\Rightarrow i\omega z - i\overline{\omega}\,\overline{z} = 2 \qquad \ldots(2)$

Add (1) and (2), $\Rightarrow i(\omega - \overline{\omega})(z + \overline{z}) = 4$

$\Rightarrow i(2i\beta)(2x) = 4 \Rightarrow \beta x = -1 \qquad \ldots(3)$

Subtract (1) from (2),

$\Rightarrow i(\omega + \overline{\omega})(z - \overline{z}) = 0 \Rightarrow \alpha y = 0 \qquad \ldots(4)$

From (4), either $\alpha = 0$ or $y = 0$.

If $y = 0$, then $x^2 + y^2 = 1 \Rightarrow x = \pm 1 \Rightarrow z = 1$ or $-1$

If $\alpha = 0$, then $\alpha^2 + \beta^2 = 1 \Rightarrow \beta = \pm 1 \Rightarrow w = \pm i.$

So, $I_m(z) = \mathrm{Re}(w) = 0$

**18. (c)** Using the result

$$z_1^2 + z_2^2 + z_3^2 - z_1 z_2 - z_2 z_3 - z_3 z_1 = 0 \text{, we get}$$

$$a^2 - 1 + 2ai + 1 - b^2 + 2bi + 0 - a + b - i - abi = 0$$

$$\therefore \ a^2 - b^2 - a + b = 0 \text{ and } 2a + 2b - ab - 1 = 0$$

$$\Rightarrow \ a = b \text{ and } 2a + 2b - ab - 1 = 0$$

$(\because \ a + b = 1 \text{ does not give real solution})$

$$\therefore \ a = b \text{ and } a^2 - 4a + 1 = 0$$

$$a = b = 2 - \sqrt{3} \qquad\qquad (\because \ a < 1, b < 1)$$

**19. (b)** $\quad z_0 = \dfrac{z_1 + z_2 + z_3}{3}$

$$\Rightarrow \ z_1^2 + z_2^2 + z_3^2 - 2z_1 z_2 - 2z_2 z_3 - 2z_3 z_1 = 9z_0^2$$

$$\Rightarrow \ 3(z_1^2 + z_2^2 + z_3^2) = 9z_0^2 \ \Rightarrow \ z_1^2 + z_2^2 + z_3^2 = 3z_0^2$$

$$(\because \ z_1^2 + z_2^2 + z_3^2 = z_1 z_2 + z_2 z_3 + z_3 z_1)$$

**20. A - q; B - r; C - p; D - s**

**(A)** $\ (z + \alpha\beta)^3 = \alpha^3 \Rightarrow z + \alpha\beta = \alpha, \omega\alpha, \omega^2\alpha$

$$\Rightarrow z = \alpha - \alpha\beta, \ \omega\alpha - \alpha\beta, \ \omega^2\alpha - \alpha\beta \text{, say } z_1, z_2, z_3$$
respectively

Now, $|z_1 - z_2| = |z_2 - z_3| = |z_3 - z_1| = \sqrt{3}\,|\alpha|$

So, the triangle is equilateral and has area

$$= \frac{\sqrt{3}}{4} |z_1 - z_2|^2$$

**(B)** $\ |z - \alpha|^2 = 4 |z - \bar{\alpha}|^2$

$$\Rightarrow z\bar{z} - \alpha\bar{z} - \bar{\alpha}z + \alpha\bar{\alpha} = 4(z\bar{z} - \alpha z - \bar{\alpha}\bar{z} + \alpha\bar{\alpha})$$

$$\Rightarrow 3z\bar{z} + (\alpha - 4\bar{\alpha})\bar{z} + (\bar{\alpha} - 4\alpha)z + 3\alpha\bar{\alpha} = 0$$

or $\ z\bar{z} + \dfrac{\alpha - 4\bar{\alpha}}{3}\bar{z} + \dfrac{\bar{\alpha} - 4\alpha}{3}z + \alpha\bar{\alpha} = 0$

which is a circle of radius

$$= \sqrt{\left|\frac{\alpha - 4\bar{\alpha}}{3}\right|^2 - \alpha\bar{\alpha}} = \sqrt{-\frac{4}{9}(\alpha - \bar{\alpha})^2} = \frac{2}{3}|\alpha - \bar{\alpha}|$$

**(C)** z lies on a circle of radius 1 and centre at $(1, 0)$

$$\angle OPA = \pm\frac{\pi}{2} \Rightarrow \frac{2 - z}{0 - z} = \frac{|2 - z|}{|z|}e^{\pm i\frac{\pi}{2}}$$

$$\Rightarrow \frac{z - 2}{z} = \frac{AP}{OP}(\pm i) = \pm i\tan\alpha$$

$$\therefore \ \left|\frac{z - 2}{z}\right| = |\tan\alpha|$$

**(D)** $\ z_1 + z_2 = -p$ and $z_1 z_2 = q$
Also,

$$\frac{z_2}{z_1} = \cos\alpha \pm i\sin\alpha$$

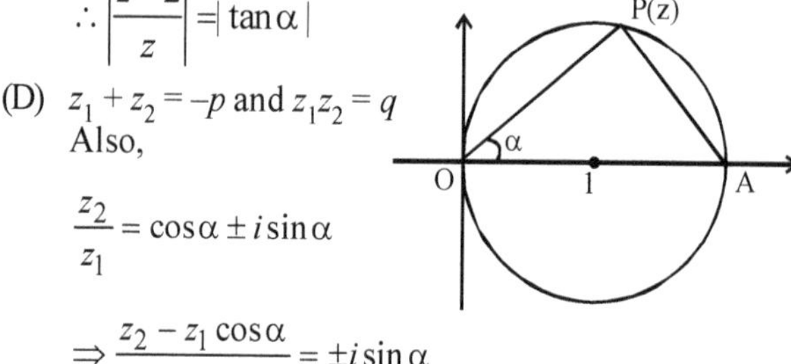


$$\Rightarrow \frac{z_2 - z_1\cos\alpha}{z_1} = \pm i\sin\alpha$$

or $\ z_2^2 - 2z_2 z_1 \cos\alpha + z_1^2 \cos^2\alpha = -z_1^2 \sin^2\alpha$

$$\Rightarrow z_1^2 + z_2^2 = 2z_1 z_2 \cos\alpha$$

or $\ (z_1 + z_2)^2 = 2z_1 z_2(1 + \cos\alpha) \Rightarrow \dfrac{p^2}{q} = 4\cos^2\dfrac{\alpha}{2}$

**1. (c)**

$33! = 1.2.3.5 \ldots\ldots\ldots\ldots 33$

$= (2.4.6 \ldots\ldots\ldots\ldots 32)(1.3.5 \ldots\ldots\ldots\ldots 33)$

$= 2^{16}(1.2.3.4 \ldots\ldots\ldots 16)(1.3.5 \ldots\ldots\ldots 33)$

$= 2^{16}(2.4.6 \ldots\ldots\ldots 16)(1.3.5 \ldots\ldots\ldots 15)$
$\qquad\qquad\qquad\qquad (1.3.5 \ldots\ldots\ldots 33)$

$= 2^{16}.2^8(1.2.3 \ldots\ldots\ldots 8)(1.3.5 \ldots\ldots\ldots 15)$
$\qquad\qquad\qquad\qquad (1.3.5 \ldots\ldots\ldots 33)$

$= 2^{24}(2.4.6.8)(1.3.5.7)(1.3.5 \ldots\ldots\ldots 15)$
$\qquad\qquad\qquad\qquad (1.3.5 \ldots\ldots\ldots 33)$

$= 2^{24}.2^4(1.2.3.4)(1.3.5.7)(1.3.5 \ldots\ldots\ldots 15)$
$\qquad\qquad\qquad\qquad (1.3.5 \ldots\ldots\ldots 33)$

$= 2^{28}(2.4)(1.3)(1.3.5.7)(1.3.5 \ldots\ldots\ldots 15)$
$\qquad\qquad\qquad\qquad (1.3.5 \ldots\ldots\ldots 33)$

$= 2^{28}.2^2(1.2)(1.3)(1.3.5.7)(1.3.5 \ldots\ldots 15)$
$\qquad\qquad\qquad\qquad (1.3.5 \ldots\ldots\ldots 33)$

$= 2^{31}(1.3)(1.3.5.7)(1.3.5 \ldots\ldots 15)$
$\qquad\qquad\qquad\qquad (1.3.5 \ldots\ldots\ldots 33)$

Thus the maximum value of '$n$' for which $33!$ is divisible by $2^n$ is 31.

***ALTERNATIVELY,*** the exponent of 2 in $33!$ is given by

$$E_2(33!) = \left[\frac{33}{2}\right] + \left[\frac{33}{2^2}\right] + \left[\frac{33}{2^3}\right] + \left[\frac{33}{2^4}\right] + \left[\frac{33}{2^5}\right]$$

$$= 16 + 8 + 4 + 2 + 1 = 31.$$

**NOTE :** If $p$ is a prime number then largest-power $k$ of $p$ such that $p^k$ divides $n!$ is given by

$$\left[\frac{n}{p}\right] + \left[\frac{n}{p^2}\right] + \left[\frac{n}{p^3}\right] + \ldots\ldots\ldots$$

It is also called exponent of $p$ in $n!$ and we write $E_p(n!)$

Where $[x]$ represents integral part of $x$

**2. (a)** Let $a = 2p + 1$, $b = 2q + 1$, $c = 2r + 1$, $d = 2s + 1$ where $p, q, r$ and $s$ are non-negative integers.

$\therefore \ 2p + 1 + 2q + 1 + 2r + 1 + 2s + 1 = 20$ or

$p + q + r + s = 8$

The required number of solutions = The number of non-negative integral solutions of $(p + q + r + s = 8)$.

$= {}^{8+4-1}C_{4-1} = {}^{11}C_3$

$= 165.$

**3. (d)** The smallest number, which can occur in the middle is 4.

The number of numbers with 4 in the middle

$= {}^4P_4 - {}^3P_3$

($\because$ The other four places are to be filled by 0, 1, 2 and 3, and a number cannot begin with 0)

Similarly, the number of numbers with 5 in the middle

$= {}^5P_4 - {}^4P_3$ , etc.

$\therefore$ The required number of numbers

$= ({}^4P_4 - {}^3P_3) + ({}^5P_4 - {}^4P_3) + ({}^6P_4 - {}^5P_3) +$

$\ldots\ldots\ldots\ldots + ({}^9P_4 - {}^8P_3) = \displaystyle\sum_{n=4}^{9} ({}^nP_4 - {}^{n-1}P_3)$

**4. (d)** We may consider the problem as filling the digits in boxes of the figure :

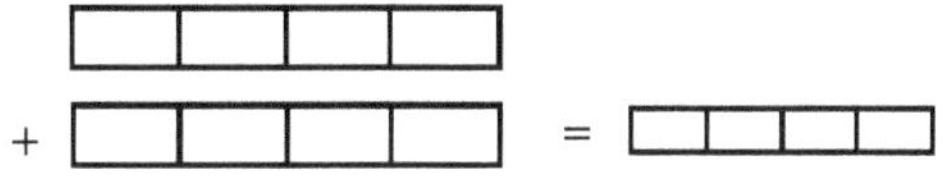

If 0 is placed in the units place of the upper number then the units place of the lower number can be filled in 9 ways (filling by any one of 0, 1, 2 \ldots\ldots\ldots, 9).

If 1 is placed in the units place of the upper number then the units place of the lower number can be filled in 9 ways (filling by any one of 0, 1, 2, \ldots\ldots, 8), etc.

$\therefore$ The units column can be filled in $10 + 9 + 8 + \ldots\ldots\ldots + 1$, i.e., 55 ways. Similarly for the second and the third columns. The number of ways for the fourth column $= 8 + 7 + \ldots\ldots\ldots + 1 = 36$.

$\therefore$ The required number of ways $= 55 \times 55 \times 55 \times 36$.

**5. (d)** Let $n = 2m + 1$

For the three numbers in A. P., we have the following pattern, Common Numbers Ways difference

| Common difference | Numbers | Ways |
|---|---|---|
| 1 | $(1, 2, 3), (2, 3, 4), \ldots\ldots (n-2, n-1, n)$ | $(n-2)$ |
| 2 | $(1, 3, 5), (2, 4, 6), \ldots\ldots (n-4, n-2, n)$ | $(n-4)$ |
| 3 | $(1, 4, 7), (2, 5, 8), \ldots\ldots(n-6, n-3, n)$ | $(n-6)$ |
| 4 | \ldots\ldots\ldots\ldots\ldots\ldots\ldots\ldots\ldots\ldots | |
| 5 | \ldots\ldots\ldots\ldots\ldots\ldots\ldots\ldots\ldots\ldots | |
| . | \ldots\ldots\ldots\ldots\ldots\ldots\ldots\ldots\ldots\ldots | |
| . | \ldots\ldots\ldots\ldots\ldots\ldots\ldots\ldots\ldots\ldots | |
| . | \ldots\ldots\ldots\ldots\ldots\ldots\ldots\ldots\ldots\ldots | |
| $m$ | $(1, m+1, 2m+1)$ | 1 |

$\therefore$ Favourable number of ways

$= (n-2) + (n-4) + (n-6) + \ldots\ldots\ldots + 3 + 1$

$m$ terms $= \dfrac{m}{2}(n - 2 + 1) = \dfrac{n-1}{2} \cdot \dfrac{n-1}{2} = \dfrac{(n-1)^2}{4}$

**Alternatively,** if $a, b, c$ are in A. P., then $a + c = 2b$

$\therefore$    Sum of terminal digits is even.

$\therefore$    Terminal digits must be either both even or both odd.

$\therefore$    Required number of selections $=$ number of ways of selecting 2 odd numbers from $\dfrac{n+1}{2}$ odd numbers $+$ number of ways of selecting 2 even numbers from $\dfrac{n-1}{2}$ even number    [$\because$ $n$ is odd]

$$= {}^{\frac{n+1}{2}}C_2 + {}^{\frac{n-1}{2}}C_2 = \frac{\frac{n+1}{2} \times \frac{n-1}{2}}{2} + \frac{\frac{n-1}{2} \times \frac{n-3}{2}}{2}$$

$$= \frac{(n-1)^2}{4}.$$

**6.    (b, c, d)**    When $z = n+1$ we can choose $x, y$ from $\{1, 2, ..., n\}$

$\therefore$ when $z = n+1, x, y$ can be chosen in $n^2$ ways

and if $z = n, x, y$ can be chosen in $(n-1)^2$ ways and so on

$$\therefore n^2 + (n-1)^2 + ... + 1^2 = \frac{1}{6}n(n+1)(2n+1)$$

ways of choosing triplets
*ALTERNATIVELY* triplets with
$x = y < z, x < y < z, y < z < x$

can be chosen in ${}^{n+1}C_2, {}^{n+1}C_3, {}^{n+1}C_3$ ways.

There are ${}^{n+1}C_2 + 2({}^{n+1}C_3) = {}^{n+2}C_2 + {}^{n+1}C_3$

$$= 2({}^{n+2}C_3) - {}^{n+1}C_2.$$

**7.    (a, b, c)**    Number of all possible triangles $= {}^{n}C_3$

Out of these $n$ triangles have two sides common with polygon and $n(n-4)$ triangles have exactly one side common with polygon.
So, desired number of triangles

$$= {}^{n}C_3 - n - n(n-4)$$

$$= \frac{n(n-1)(n-2)}{6} - n - n(n-4)$$

$$= \frac{n}{6}(n-4)(n-5) = \frac{n}{n-3}{}^{n-3}C_3$$

***ALTERNATIVELY:***
If we consider a particular vertex, say $A_i$. If $A_i$ is not included in the selection then we have to select 3 vertices from remaining $(n-1)$ vertices on a circle such that no two are consecutive, which can be done in ${}^{(n-1)-3+1}C_3$ ways $= {}^{n-3}C_3$ ways.

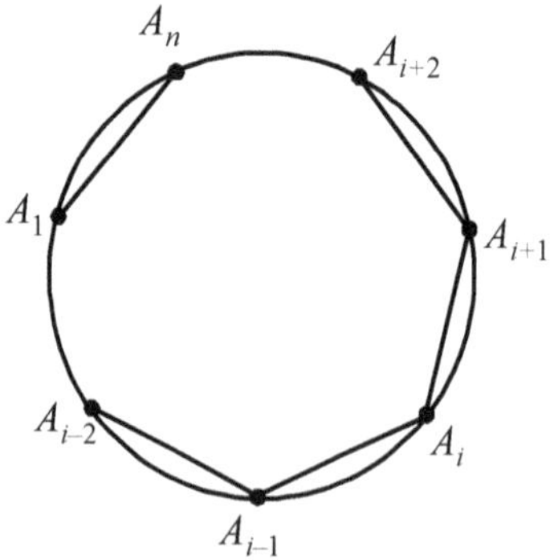


If $A_i$ is included, then $A_{i-1}$ and $A_{i+1}$ can not be included, so we can choose 2 points from remaining $n - 3$ points such that they are not adjacent in ${}^{n-3-2+1}C_2 = {}^{n-4}C_2$ ways. So, desired number of triangles $= {}^{n-3}C_3 + {}^{n-4}C_2$

**8.    (a, b, c, d)**
We have
$$E = (2n + 1)(2n + 3)(2n + 5) ... (4n - 3)(4n - 1)$$

$$= \frac{(2n)!(2n+1)(2n+2)(2n+3)(2n+4)...(4n-1)(4n)}{(2n)!(2n+2)(2n+4)...(4n)}$$

$$= \frac{(4n)!\,n!}{(2n)!\,2^n\,n!(n+1)(n+2)...(2n)} = \frac{1}{2^n}\cdot\frac{(4n)!\,n!}{(2n)!(2n)!}$$

$\Rightarrow 2^n\,E = ({}^{4n}C_{2n})(n!)$
This shows that $2^n\,E$ is divisible by ${}^{4n}C_{2n}$ and also by n!

$$\Rightarrow \frac{2^n\,E}{n!} = {}^{4n}C_{2n}, \text{ a positive integer.}$$

Also, note that

$$\frac{2^n\,E}{(4n)!} = \frac{n!}{(2n)!(2n)!} \text{ is not an integer as } n > 1.$$

**9.    (a, b, c)**    For $f(i) < f(j)$ whenever $i < j$, is equivalent to choose 3 numbers out of $\{1, 2, 3, 4, 5, 6, 7\}$ in ${}^{7}C_3$. For $f(i) \le f(j)$ whenever $i < j$, the number of ways is ${}^{7}C_3 + 2\,({}^{7}C_2) + {}^{7}C_1 = 84$
For (c), see (a).

**10.    (5)**    The terminal digit in the different powers of 3 and 7 are as follows :

$$\begin{cases} 3^1 = 3 & 3^2 = 9 & 3^3 = ........7 & 3^4 = ........1 \\ 3^5 = .....3 & 3^6 = .......9 & 3^7 = ......... & 3^8 = ........1 \\ 3^9 = .....3 \end{cases}$$

$$\begin{cases} 7^1 = 7 & 7^2 = 9 & 7^3 = ........3 \\ 7^5 = .....7 & 7^6 = .......9 & 7^7 = ........3 \\ 7^9 = .....7 \end{cases}$$

$$7^4 = ..........1$$
$$7^8 = ..........1$$

$$\begin{cases} m = 1; \ n = 1, 5, 9, 13, 17, \} \ 5 \text{ pairs} \\ m = 2; \ n = 4, 8, 12, 16, 20, \} \ 5 \text{ pairs} \\ m = 3; \ n = 3, 7, 11, 15, 19, \} \ 5 \text{ pairs} \\ m = 4; \ n = 2, 6, 10, 14, 18, \} \ 5 \text{ pairs} \\ \qquad \cdots\cdots\cdots\cdots\cdots\cdots \\ m = 20; \ n = 2, 6, 10, 14, 18, \} \ 5 \text{ pairs} \end{cases}$$

$\therefore$ required $(m, n)$ pairs $= 20 \times 5 = 100$ pairs

***ALTERNATIVELY :***

End digits in power of 3 and 7 repeat in cycle of 4

$$3^m \to 3^{4k} = 1 \quad 3^{4k+1} = 3 \qquad 3^{4k+2} = 9 \quad 3^{4k+3} = 7$$

$$7^n \to 7^{4k} = 1 \quad 7^{4k+1} = 7 \qquad 7^{4k+2} = 9 \quad 7^{4k+3} = 3$$

So the numbers $\{1, 2, 3, \ldots, 20\}$ can be divided into 4 sets

| | |
|---|---|
| $4k$ type | $\{4, 8, 12, 16, 20\} = A$ |
| $4k + 1$ type | $\{1, 5, 9, 13, 17\} = B$ |
| $4k + 2$ type | $\{2, 6, 10, 14, 18\} = C$ |
| $4k + 3$ type | $\{3, 7, 11, 15, 19\} = D$ |

Now $3^m + 7^n$ is divisible by 10, if end digit of the number is 0.

Thus if $m \in A$ then $n \in C$, if $m \in B$ then $n \in B$

if $m \in C$ then $n \in A$, if $m \in D$ then $n \in D$

So, desired number of ordered pairs $(m, n)$
$= 5 \times 5 + 5 \times 5 + 5 \times 5 + 5 \times 5 = 100$

**11. (1)** Let $A_t$, $t = 1, 2, \ldots\ldots 6$ be the set of days on which the friend is present at dinner and $B_t$ be the set of days on which the friend is absent at dinner. Then $|A_t| = |B_t| = 7$

Also $|A_i \cap A_j| = 7$, $|A_i \cap A_j \cap A_k| = 4$

$|A_i \cap A_j \cap A_k \cap A_l| = 3$, $|A_i \cap A_j \cap A_k \cap A_l \cap A_m| = 2$

and

$|A_1 \cap A_2 \cap A_3 \cap A_4 \cap A_5 \cap A_6| = 1$

Where $i, j, k, l, m$, vary from 1 to 6 and are distinct. Now the number of dinners at which at least one friend was present

$= |A_1 \cup A_2 \cup \ldots\ldots\ldots \cup A_6| = \sum |A_i| - \sum |A_i \cap A_j| + \sum$

$$|A_i \cap A_j \cap A_k|$$

$$- \sum |A_i \cap A_j \cap A_k \cap A_l| + \sum |A_i \cap A_j \cap A_k$$

$$\cap A_l \cap A_m| - |A_1 \cap A_2 \cap \ldots\ldots \cap A_6|$$

$$= {}^6C_1 \times 7 - {}^6C_2 \times 5 + {}^6C_3 \times 4 - {}^6C_4$$

$$\times 3 + {}^6C_5 \times 2 - {}^6C_6 \times 1 = 13$$

Total number of dinners is $|A_t| + |B_t| = 7 + 7 = 14$

$\therefore$ Number of dinners the person had alone $= 14 - 13 = 1$

**12. (7)**

$$1000 = 2^3.5^3, \ 2000 = 2^4.5^3$$

So, $a = 2^A.5^R, b = 2^B.5^S, c = 2^C.5^T,$

$\max(A, B) = 3, \max(A, C) = \max(B, C) = 4$

$\max(R, S) = \max(R, T) = \max(S, T) = 3.$

We can choose $R, S, T$ in following ways

(1) $R = S = T = 3$ in 1 ways
(2) Two of $R, S$ and $T$ are 3 and one is 2 in 3 ways
(3) Two of $R, S$ and $T$ are 3 and one is 1 in 3 ways
(4) Two of $R, S$ and $T$ are 3 and one is 0 in 3 ways

So, $R, S$ and $T$ can be selected in 10 ways

Now, we can choose $A, B, C$ in following ways

(1) $C$ is necessarily 4
(2) One of $A$ and $B$ is 3 and other 2 in two ways
(3) One of $A$ and $B$ is 3 and other 1 in two ways
(4) One of $A$ and $B$ is 3 and other 0 in two ways
(5) $A = B = 3$ in one way

So, $A, B,$ and $C$ can be selected in 7 ways

So, the required number $= 10 \times 7 = 70.$

**13. (2)**

Dictionary will have first the words starting with the letter $A$, then by $C, E, K, L$ and finally the words starting with $T$.

Number of words starting with $A = 5! = 120$      [Since there are 5 letters other than $A$, and position of $A$ is fixed]

Number of words starting with $C = 5! = 120$

Number of words starting with $E = 5! = 120$

Number of words starting with $K = 5! = 120$

Number of words starting with $L = 5! = 120$

Now, we consider the words starting with $T$. Before the word TACKLE occurs, there will be the words TACEKL, TACELK, TACKEL then TACKLE.

$\therefore$ Rank of TACKLE $= 120 + 120 + 120 + 120 + 120 + 4 = 604.$

**14. (d)** $$\,{}^{200}C_{100} = \frac{(200)(199)\ldots\ldots(101)}{(1)\,(2)\ldots(100)}$$

All the two digit numbers occur in the denominator.

Thus, the exponent of the largest two digit prime must at least 3 in $(200)!$. Since $[200/3] = 66$, we find the required largest two digit prime is 61.

**15. (b)** $$E_5(n) = \sum_{k=1}^{\infty} \left[\frac{n}{5^k}\right] < \sum_{k=1}^{\infty} \left(\frac{n}{5^k}\right) = \frac{n}{4}$$

$$\Rightarrow n > 4 E_5(n) = 104$$

But for $n \leq 109$, $E_5(n) < 26$

$\therefore n \geq 110$

The desired numbers are 110, 111, 112, 113, 114.

**Solution For 16 - 18**

- Number of four digit odd-number which are formed by using $0, 1, 2, 3, 5, 7$ (with repetition)
  $= 5 \times 6 \times 6 \times 4 = 36 \times 20 = 720$

- Number of numbers greater than 1000 but less than 4000 which are formed by using the digits $0, 1, 2, 3, 4, 5$ (without repetition)
  $= 3 \times 4 \times 3 \times 2 = 72$

- We know that a number is divisible by 3 only when the sum of the digits is divisible by 3.
  Now the possible number of combinations of 5 digits out of 6 different digits $0, 1, 2, 3, 4, 5$ (without repetition) are ${}^6C_5 = 6$, which are as follows–

$1 + 2 + 3 + 4 + 5 = 15 = 3 \times 5$ (divisible by 3)
$0 + 2 + 3 + 4 + 5 = 14$ (not divisible by 3)
$0 + 1 + 3 + 4 + 5 = 13$ (not divisible by 3)
$0 + 1 + 2 + 4 + 5 = 12 = 3 \times 4$ (divisible by 3)
$0 + 1 + 2 + 3 + 5 = 11$ (not divisible by 3)
$0 + 1 + 2 + 3 + 4 = 10$ (not divisible by 3)

Thus the number should certain the digits 1, 2, 3, 4, 5 or the digits 0, 1, 2, 4, 5.

Taking 1, 2, 3, 4, 5, the 5 digit numbers are $= \lfloor 5 = 120$

Taking 0, 1, 2, 4, 5, the 5 digit numbers are $= \lfloor 5 - \lfloor 4$
$= 96$

∴    Total number of numbers $= 120 + 96 = 216$

• Now the 7 digit numbers using the digits 1, 2 and 3 only such that the sum of digits in a number is 10

This can be done by taking 2, 2, 2, 1, 1, 1, 1 or by taking 2, 3, 1, 1, 1, 1, 1.

∴    Number of ways $= \dfrac{\lfloor 7}{\lfloor 3 \ \lfloor 4} + \dfrac{\lfloor 7}{\lfloor 5} = 77$

**16.** **(b)**

**17.** **(a)**

**18.** **(c)**

**19.** **A - r; B - s; C - p; D - q**

(A) Number of 6 digit numbers which can be formed using only 1 digit $= 9$

Number of 6 digit numbers can be formed using 2 digits
**Case 1 :** When zero is included

$$= {}^9C_6 \left[ \frac{\lfloor 5}{\lfloor 3.\lfloor 2} + \frac{\lfloor 5}{\lfloor 3.\lfloor 2} + \frac{\lfloor 5}{\lfloor 4} \right] = 225$$

**Case 2 :** When zero is not included

$$= {}^9C_2 \left[ \frac{\lfloor 6}{\lfloor 2.\lfloor 4} + \frac{\lfloor 6}{\lfloor 3.\lfloor 3} + \frac{\lfloor 6}{\lfloor 2.\lfloor 4} \right] = 1800$$

Number of such numbers using 3 digits
**Case 1 :** When zero is included

$$= {}^9C_2 \left[ \frac{\lfloor 5}{\lfloor 2.\lfloor 2} + \frac{\lfloor 5}{\lfloor 2.\lfloor 2} \right] = 2160$$

**Case 2 :** When zero is excluded

$$= {}^9C_3 \left[ \frac{\lfloor 6}{\lfloor 2.\lfloor 2.\lfloor 2} \right] = 7560$$

Total number $= 9 + 225 + 1800 + 2160 + 7560 = 11754$.

(B) Since books are to be tied up in a bundle so that books are to be kept in a group or set and hence required number of ways

$$= \frac{1}{\lfloor 3}[3^5 - {}^3C_1 2^5 + {}^3C_2] = 25.$$

(C) One subject must be repeated in two periods. So the required number of ways $= 5 \times \dfrac{6!}{2!} = 1800$

(D) There are $26 \times 26 = 676$ different possible set of two initials possible. So there are to be minimum $676 + 1 = 677$ students to guarantee.

**20.** **A - s; B - q; C - r; D - p**

(A) Total number of three digit numbers $= 9 \times 10 \times 10$
Half of which will have sum of digits even.

(B) $xyz = 140 = 2^2 . 5 . 7$
Therefore number of positive integral solutions
$= 3 \times 3 \times {}^4C_2 = 54.$

(C) $x + y + z + t = 10$, where $1 \le x,\ y,\ z \le 8,\ 0 \le t \le 7$
Therefore desired number of solutions $=$ coeff. of $x^{10}$ in
$(x + x^2 + \ ..... + x^8)^3 \times (1 + x + x^2 + ..... + x^7)$
$\qquad\qquad\qquad = {}^{10}C_7 = {}^{10}C_3 = 120.$

(D) We must have $i^3 + ai^2 + bi + c = 0$ and
$(-i)^3 + a(-i)^2 + b(-i) + c = 0$

$\Rightarrow b = 1$ and $a = c$

Therefore number of numbers of type $abc$ or $cba$ is ${}^9C_1 = 9$

Number of numbers of type bac or $bca$ is ${}^{10}C_1 = 10$
But 111 is included in both the counting.

**1.** **(b)** Given, $(1 + x - 2x^2)^6 = 1 + a_1 x + a_2 x^2 + \ldots$

Putting x = 1, we get $0 = 1 + a_1 + a_2 + a_3 + \ldots a_{12}$ ...(i)

Putting x = –1, we get 64

$= 1 - a_1 + a_2 - a_3 + \ldots + a_{12}$ ... (ii)

On adding Eqs. (i) and (ii), we get

$64 = 2 + 2a_2 + 2a_4 + 2a_6 + \ldots + 2a_{12}$

$\Rightarrow \quad a_2 + a_4 + a_6 + \ldots + a_{12} = 31.$

**2.** **(a)** The given question is same as to find the term independent of $x$ in the expansion of

$$(1 + x)^n \cdot \left(1 - \frac{1}{x}\right)^n$$

The given expression can be written as

$$= (-1)^n \cdot \frac{(1 - x^2)^n}{x^n}$$

$\therefore$ The term independent of $x$ in the above expansion is same as the coefficient of $x^n$ in $(-1)^n \cdot (1 - x^2)^n$ which in turn is equal to the coefficient of $x^n$ in

$$(-1)^n \left\{ {}^nC_0 + {}^nC_1 (-x)^2 + {}^nC_2 \left(-x^2\right)^2 + \right.$$

$$\left. \ldots + {}^nC_n \left(-x^2\right)^n \right\},$$

and the expansion contains only even powers of $x$.
So, if $n$ is odd

$\Rightarrow$ Coefficient is zero.

**3.** **(a)** Given expression is $\displaystyle\sum_{0 \le i \le j\, j \le n} \sum \left(C_i + C_j\right)^2$

$$= n\left(C_0^2 + C_1^2 + \ldots + C_n^2\right) + 2 \sum_{0 \le i \le j\, j \le n} \sum C_i C_j$$

$$= n \cdot {}^{2n}C_n + [(C_0 + C_1 + \ldots + C_n)^2$$

$$-(C_0^2 + C_1^2 + \ldots + C_n^2)]$$

$$= n \cdot {}^{2n}C_n + \left(2^n\right)^2 - {}^{2n}C_n = (n-1) \cdot {}^{2n}C_n + 2^{2n}$$

**4.** **(a)** Required number of positive integral solutions

= coefficient of $\alpha^{20}$ in $(\alpha + \alpha^2 + \ldots)(\alpha^2 + \alpha^3$

$+ \ldots)(\alpha^3 + \alpha^4 + \ldots)(\alpha^4 + \alpha^5 + \ldots)$

= coefficient of $\alpha^{20}$ in $\alpha^4 \cdot \alpha^3 \cdot \alpha^2 \cdot \alpha$

$(1 + \alpha + \alpha^2 + \ldots)$

= coefficient of $\alpha^{10}$ in $(1 - \alpha)^{-4} = {}^{10 + 4 - 1}C_{10}$

$= {}^{13}C_{10} = 286$

**5.** **(b)** Given $(2 + \sqrt{3})^n = I + f$, where $I$ is integer and

$0 \le f < 1$. We note that $(2 + \sqrt{3})(2 - \sqrt{3}) = 1$. So let us assume that

$F = (2 - \sqrt{3})^n$. Clearly $0 < F < 1$. Now,

$I + f + F = (2 + \sqrt{3})^n + (2 - \sqrt{3})^n$

$= 2[{}^nC_0 2^n + {}^nC_2 2^{n-2} \cdot 3 + {}^nC_4 \cdot 2^{n-4} \cdot 3^2 + \ldots]$

$= 2 \times$ Integer = Integer

$\because$ $I + f + F$ is integer $\Rightarrow f + F$ must be integer.

$\therefore$ $0 \le f < 1$ and $0 < F < 1 \Rightarrow 0 < f + F < 2$

$\Rightarrow f + F = 1 \Rightarrow F = 1 - f$

$\therefore (I + f)(1 - f) = (I + f)F = (2 + \sqrt{3})^n (2 - \sqrt{3})^n = 1$

**6.** **(c)** The expression is $(1 + x)^{101}(1 - x + x^2)^{100}$

$= (1 + x)\left((1 + x)(1 - x + x^2)\right)^{100}$

$= (1 + x)(1 + x^3)^{100}$

$= (1 + x)\{C_0 + C_1 x^3 + C_2 x^6 + \ldots + C_{100} x^{300}\}$

$$= (1 + x)\sum_{r=0}^{100} {}^nC_r x^{3r} = \sum_{r=0}^{100} {}^nC_r x^{3r} + \sum_{r=0}^{100} {}^nC_r x^{3r+1}$$

Hence there will be no term containing $3r + 2$.

**7.** **(b, c)** Since i, j, k are distinct, $n - i + 1, n - j + 1, n - k + 1$ are also distinct and they all lie from 1 to $n$. Now,

$$S = \sum \sum \sum \left(-x_{n-i+1}\right)\left(-x_{n-j+1}\right)\left(-x_{n-k+1}\right)$$

$$= -\sum \sum \sum x_i x_j x_k = -S$$

$\Rightarrow S = 0$ for all $n$

**8.** **(a, b, c)** Consider option (a) and (b) we get

$$T_{r+1} = {}^{256}C_r (3)^{\frac{256-r}{2}} \cdot 5^{r/8}$$

for $r = 0, 8, 16, 24 \ldots, 256$ are rational, thus 33 terms are rational

So option (a) and (b) are correct.

Consider option (c) and (d) we get

Number of distinct terms is ${}^{(16+3-1)}C_{3-1} = {}^{18}C_2$

$= \dfrac{18 \times 17}{2} = 9 \times 17 = 153$

Option (c) is correct but (d) is wrong.

**9.** **(a, b, c)** $f(n) = \sum_{r=1}^{n}\left((r+1)^2\ {}^nC_r - r^2\ {}^nC_{r-1}\right)$

$$= (n+1)^2 - 1$$

Now,

$$\sum_{n=1}^{n} f(n) = \left(2^2 - 1\right) + \left(3^2 - 1\right) + \left(4^2 - 1\right) + \left(5^2 - 1\right)$$

$$+ \left(6^2 - 1\right) + \left(7^2 - 1\right) + \left(8^2 - 1\right) + \left(9^2 - 1\right)$$

$$+ \left(10^2 - 1\right)$$

So $f(10) = 11^2 - 1 = 120$

$$f(20) = 21^2 - 1 = 440$$

**10.** **(a, c)** Let $\left(\sqrt{3}+1\right)^{2m} = I + F$, where $I \in N$ and $0 < F < 1$

Let $G = \left(\sqrt{3}-1\right)^{2m}$ then,

$$I + F + G = \left(\sqrt{3}+1\right)^{2m} + \left(\sqrt{3}-1\right)^{2m}$$

$$= 2^m\left(2+\sqrt{3}\right)^m + 2^m\left(2-\sqrt{3}\right)^m = 2^{m+1} \times$$

$$\text{an integer .... (i)}$$

$\Rightarrow$  $I + F + G = $ an even integer

$\Rightarrow$  $F + G = $ an even integer $- I$

$\Rightarrow$  $F + G = $ an integer

$\Rightarrow$  $F + G = 1$ [since $0 < F < 1, 0 < G < 1$]

Putting $F + G = 1$ in Eq.(i), we get

$I + 1 = 2^{m+1} \times$ an integer

$\Rightarrow$  $2^{m+1}$ is a factor of the integer just greater than $\left(\sqrt{3}+1\right)^{2m}$

**11.** **(5)** Now, $\sum_{r=0}^{n}\left(\dfrac{r+1+1}{r+1}\right){}^nC_r$

$$= \sum_{r=0}^{n}{}^nC_r + \frac{1}{(n+1)}\sum_{r=0}^{n}{}^{n+1}C_{r+1}$$

$$= 2^n + \frac{1}{(n+1)}\left(2^{n+1} - 1\right)$$

Since, $\sum_{r=0}^{n}\left(\dfrac{r+2}{r+1}\right){}^nC_r = \dfrac{2^8 - 1}{6}$ (given)

$\therefore\ 2^n + \dfrac{2^{n+1} - 1}{n+1} = \dfrac{2^8 - 1}{6}$ therefore, n = 5

**12.** **(6)** $(1 - 2x + 5x^2 - 10x^3)[C_0 + C_1x + C_2x^2 + ...]$

$$= 1 + a_1x + a_2x^2 + ...$$

$$a_1 = n-2 \text{ and } a_2 = \frac{n(n-1)}{2} - 2n + 5$$

Put $a_1^2 = 2a_2$

$$(n-2)^2 = n(n-1) - 4n + 10$$

$$n^2 - 4n + 4 = n^2 - 5n + 10 \quad n = 6$$

**13.** **(2)** Since, $\left(1 + x + x^2\right)^n = a_0 + a_1x + a_2x^2 + ... + a_{2n}x^{2n}$

$$....(i)$$

Substituting $x = \omega, \omega^2$ and 1 and then, adding them together $a_0 + a_3 + a_6 + ... = 3^{n-1}$

Multiplying Eq. (i) by $x^2$ and then repeating the same process again $a_1 + a_4 + a_7 + ... = 3^{n-1}$

$\Rightarrow a_0 + a_3 + a_6 + ... = a_1 + a_4 + a_7 + ...$

$$= a_2 + a_5 + a_8 + ...$$

Since the required ratio is $\dfrac{2 \cdot 3^{n-1}}{3^{n-1}} = 2$

**14.** **(3)** We know that

$$(1 + ax)^n = {}^nC_0 + {}^nC_1(ax)^1 + {}^nC_2(ax)^2 + ........=$$

$$1 + 8x + 24x^2 + .... \quad ....(i)$$

Now comparing coefficients of $x^0, x^1, x^2$ we get

$${}^nC_0 = 1 \Rightarrow 1 = 1$$

$${}^nC_1 = 8 \Rightarrow na = 8$$

and ${}^nC_2 \cdot a^2 = 24 \Rightarrow \dfrac{n(n-1)}{2}a^2 = 24$

Put $n = \dfrac{8}{a}$ we get

$$\Rightarrow \left[\left(\frac{8}{a}\right)^2 - \frac{8}{a}\right]a^2 = 48$$

$$\Rightarrow 64 - 8a = 48 \Rightarrow a = 2$$

$$\therefore\ n = 4$$

$$\therefore\ \frac{n-a}{a+n} = \frac{4-2}{2+4} = \frac{1}{3}$$

$$9\left(\frac{n-a}{a+n}\right) = 3$$

**15.** **(c)** We have,

$$\sum_{r=0}^{n} r\,{}^nC_r a^r b^{n-r}$$

$$= \sum_{r=0}^{n} r \cdot \frac{n}{r}\,{}^{n-1}C_{r-1} a \cdot a^{r-1} b^{(n-1)-(r-1)}$$

$$= na \left\{ \sum_{r=0}^{n} {}^{n-1}C_{r-1} a^{r-1} \, b^{(n-1)-(r-1)} \right\}$$

$$= na(a+b)^{n-1}$$

**16. (c)** We have, $\displaystyle\sum_{r=0}^{n} r^2 \, {}^nC_r p^r q^{n-r}$

$$= \sum_{r=0}^{n} \left[ r(r-1) + r \right] {}^nC_r p^r q^{n-r}$$

$$= \sum_{r=0}^{n} r(r-1) {}^nC_r p^r q^{n-r} + \sum_{r=0}^{n} r \cdot {}^nC_r p^r q^{n-r}$$

$$= \sum_{r=0}^{n} r(r-1) \frac{n}{r} \cdot \frac{n-1}{r-1} \, {}^{n-2}C_{r-2} p^r q^{n-r}$$

$$+ \sum_{r=0}^{n} r \cdot \frac{n}{r} \, {}^{n-1}C_{r-1} p^r q^{n-r}$$

$$= n(n-1) p^2 (p+q)^{n-2} + np(p+q)^{n-1}$$

$$= n(n-1) p^2 + np \left[\text{since } p+q=1\right]$$

$$= n^2 p^2 - np^2 + np$$

$$= n^2 p^2 + npq \left[\text{since } p+q=1\right]$$

**17. (c)** $\displaystyle\sum_{0 \le i < j \le n} \sum i \cdot {}^nC_j = \sum_{r=1}^{n} {}^nC_r (0+1+2+\ldots r-1)$

$$= \frac{1}{2} \left\{ n(n-1) \cdot 2^{n-2} + n \cdot 2^{n-1} - n \cdot 2^{n-1} \right\}$$

$$= n(n-1) \cdot 2^{n-3}$$

**18. (b)** $\displaystyle\sum_{0 \le i < j \le n} \sum j \cdot {}^nC_i$

$$= \sum_{r=0}^{n-1} {}^nC_r \left[ (r+1) + (r+2) + \ldots (n) \right]$$

$$= \sum_{r=0}^{n-1} {}^nC_r \left( \frac{n-r}{2}(r+1+n) \right)$$

$$= \sum_{r=0}^{n-1} {}^nC_r \left( \frac{n+1}{2}(n-r) + \frac{r(n-r)}{2} \right)$$

$$= \frac{n+1}{2} \cdot \sum_{r=0}^{n} (n-r) \cdot {}^nC_r + \frac{n}{2} \sum_{r=0}^{n} r \cdot {}^nC_r$$

$$- \frac{1}{2} \sum_{r=0}^{n} r^2 \cdot {}^nC_r$$

$$= \frac{n+1}{2} \sum_{r=0}^{n} r \cdot {}^nC_r - \frac{n}{2} \sum_{r=0}^{n} r \cdot {}^nC_r + \frac{1}{2} \sum_{r=0}^{n} r^2 \cdot {}^nC_r$$

$$= \frac{1}{2} \left( \sum_{r=0}^{n} r \cdot {}^nC_r + \sum_{r=0}^{n} r^2 \cdot {}^nC_r \right)$$

$$= n(n+3) \cdot 2^{n-3}$$

**19. (A) → (s); (B) → (r); (C) → (p); (D) → (q)**

**(A)** $\displaystyle T_{r+1} = \frac{\frac{7}{2}\left(\frac{7}{2}-1\right)\left(\frac{7}{2}-2\right)\ldots\left(\frac{7}{2}-r+1\right) x^r}{r!}$

First negative term, if $\frac{7}{2} - r + 1 < 0$ *i.e.*, $r > \frac{9}{2}$.

Hence, $r = 5$

**(B)** $\displaystyle T_{r+1} = {}^5C_r \left(y^2\right)^{5-r} \left(\frac{1}{y}\right)^r = {}^5C_r y^{10-3r}$

$$\therefore 10 = 3r + 1 \implies r = 3.$$

So, coefficient of $y = {}^5C_3 = 10$

**(C)** $T_2 = 14a^{5/2}$

$$\implies {}^nC_1 \left( a^{\frac{1}{13}} \right)^{n-1} (a^{3/2})^1 = 14a^{5/2}$$

$$\implies na^{\frac{n-1}{13}} = 14a$$

$$\implies n = 14$$

**(D)** $\left( 1 + 2x + 3x^2 + 4x^3 + \ldots \right)^{1/2}$

$$= \left[ (1-x)^{-2} \right]^{1/2}$$

$$= (1-x)^{-1} = 1 + x + x^2 + \ldots + x^n + \ldots$$

Required sum is $1+1+1+1 = 4$

**20. (A) → (r); (B) → (s); (C) → (p); (D) → (q)**

**(A)** $1 + 99^n = 1 + (100-1)^n = 1 + \{ {}^nC_0 \, 100^n - {}^nC_1 \, 100^{n-1} + \ldots - {}^nC_n \}$

Since n is odd

$= 100 \{ C_0 \, 100^{n-1} - {}^nC_1 \, 100^{n-2} + \ldots - {}^nC_{n-2} \, 100 + {}^nC_{n-1} \}$

$= 100 \times$ integer whose unit place is different from 0 there are two zeroes at the end of the sum $99^n + 1$.

**(B)** $f(n) = 10^n + 3.4^{n+2} + 5$

$$= 10^n - 1 + 3.4^{n+2} + 6 = (10^n - 1) + 6\left(2^{2n+3} + 1\right)$$

$= (10-1)\{10^{n-1} + 10^{n-2} + \ldots + 10 + 1\} + 6(2+1)\{2^{2n+2} - 2^{2n+1} + \ldots - 2 + 1\}$

Which is divisible by 9

**(C)** $x + \dfrac{1}{x} = 1 \Rightarrow x^2 - x + 1 = 0 \Rightarrow x = \dfrac{1 \pm \sqrt{3}i}{2}$

$$\Rightarrow x = -\omega, -\omega^2$$

$\Rightarrow$ Now , $p = \omega^{1000} + \dfrac{1}{\omega^{1000}} = = (\omega^3)^{333}.\ \omega +$

$\dfrac{1}{\left(\omega^3\right)^{333}.\omega} = \omega + \dfrac{1}{\omega} + = \omega + \omega^2 = -1$

Similarly, for $x = -\omega^2$, also $p = -1$

For $n > 1, 2^n = 4k,\ k \in N$

$\therefore\ q = (\text{the digit at unit place in } 2^n) + 1 = 6 + 1 = 7$

$\therefore\ p + q = 7 + (-1) = 6$

**(D)** We know that the digit at unit place in each of
$5!, 6!, .........., 100!$ is $0$ and

$0! + 1! + 2! + 3! + 4! = 34$

$\therefore$ Digit at unit place in $\sum_{r=0}^{100} r!$ is 4. Now

$2^{2n} = 2^{4k}$

$(k \in N, = 2^n \text{ is multiple of } 4\, n > 1)$,

$\therefore$ The digit at unit place in $2^{2n} = 2^{4k} = \left(16\right)^k$ is 6.

$\therefore$ The digit at unit place in $\sum_{r=0}^{100} r! + 2^{2n} = 0$

**1.** **(c)** We have

$$f(k) = \left(\sum_{r=1}^{n} a_r\right) - a_k = S_n - a_k$$

$$\Rightarrow \frac{f(k)}{a_k} = \frac{S_n}{a_k} - 1 \, \forall k = 1, 2, \ldots, n$$

Given $a_1, a_2, \ldots, a_n$ are in H.P.

$$\Rightarrow \frac{1}{a_1}, \frac{1}{a_2}, \ldots\ldots\ldots, \frac{1}{a_n} \text{ are in A.P.}$$

$$\Rightarrow \frac{S_n}{a_1} - 1, \frac{S_n}{a_2} - 1 \ldots\ldots\ldots, \frac{S_n}{a_n} - 1 \text{ are in A.P.}$$

$$\Rightarrow \frac{f(1)}{a_1}, \frac{f(2)}{a_2}, \ldots\ldots\ldots, \frac{f(n)}{a_n} \text{ are in A.P.}$$

**2.** **(b)** On simplification,

$$\left(b^2 - ac\right)^2 + \left(c^2 - bd\right)^2 + \left(ad - bc\right)^2 \le 0,$$

which is possible iff; each of

$$\left(b^2 - ac\right) = \left(c^2 - bd\right) = \left(ad - bc\right) = 0$$

$$\Rightarrow b^2 = ac, c^2 = bd, ad = bc \Rightarrow \frac{b}{a} = \frac{c}{b} = \frac{d}{c}$$

**3.** **(c)** We know that $AM \ge GM$

$$\frac{ab^2 + ac^2 + bc^2 + ba^2 + ca^2 + cb^2}{6} \ge \left(a^6 b^6 c^6\right)^{1/6}$$

$$\Rightarrow a\left(b^2 + c^2\right) + b\left(c^2 + a^2\right) + c\left(a^2 + b^2\right) \ge 6abc$$

**4.** **(c)** $\dfrac{S_{3r} - S_{r-1}}{S_{2r} - S_{2r-1}}$

$$= \frac{\frac{3r}{2}\left[2a + (3r-1)d\right] - \frac{(r-1)}{2}\left[2a + (r-2)d\right]}{\frac{2r}{2}\left[2a + (2r-1)d\right] - \frac{(2r-1)}{2}\left[2a + (2r-2)d\right]}$$

$$\Rightarrow \frac{2a(2r+1) + d\left(8r^2 - 2\right)}{2a + d(4r-2)}$$

$$= \frac{(2r+1)\left[2a + 2(2r-1)d\right]}{\left[2a + 2(2r-1)d\right]}$$

$= (2x + 1) = (pr + q)$

so $p = 2$ and $q = 1$

$\qquad p + q = 2 + 1 = 3$

**5.** **(c)** As $a, H_1, H_2, \ldots, H_n, b$ are in HP.

$$\frac{1}{a}, \frac{1}{H_1}, \frac{1}{H_2}, \ldots, \frac{1}{H_n}, \frac{1}{b} \text{ are in AP}$$

Let $d$ be the common difference of the AP, then

$$\frac{1}{b} = \frac{1}{a} + (n+1)d \Rightarrow d = \frac{1}{n+1}\frac{a-b}{ab}$$

Thus, $\dfrac{1}{H_1} = \dfrac{1}{a} + d$ and $\dfrac{1}{H_n} = \dfrac{1}{b} - d$

$$\Rightarrow \frac{a}{H_1} = 1 + ad \text{ and } \frac{b}{H_n} = 1 - bd$$

Now, $\dfrac{H_1 + a}{H_1 - a} + \dfrac{H_n + b}{H_n - b} = \dfrac{1 + \dfrac{a}{H_1}}{1 - \dfrac{a}{H_1}} + \dfrac{1 + \dfrac{b}{H_n}}{1 - \dfrac{b}{H_n}}$

$$= \frac{1 + 1 + ad}{1 - 1 - ad} + \frac{1 + 1 - ba}{1 - 1 + bd}$$

$$= \frac{2 + ad}{-ad} + \frac{2 - bd}{bd} = \frac{2a - abd - 2b - abd}{abd}$$

$$= \frac{2\left[(a - b) - abd\right]}{abd}$$

$$= \frac{2\left[(n+1)dab - abd\right]}{abd} = 2n$$

**6.** **(d)** $\dfrac{1}{a_2} - \dfrac{1}{a_1} = \dfrac{1}{a_3} - \dfrac{1}{a_2} = \ldots\ldots\ldots = \dfrac{1}{a_n} - \dfrac{1}{a_{n-1}} = d$ (say)

Then $a_1 a_2 = \dfrac{a_1 - a_2}{d}$, $a_2 a_3 = \dfrac{a_2 - a_3}{d}$,

$$\ldots\ldots\ldots, a_{n-1}a_n = \frac{a_{n-1} - a_n}{d}$$

$\therefore \quad a_1 a_2 + a_2 a_3 + \ldots\ldots\ldots + a_{n-1} a_n$

$$= \frac{a_1 - a_2}{d} + \frac{a_2 - a_3}{d} + \ldots + \frac{a_{n-1} - a_n}{d}$$

$$= \frac{1}{d}[a_1 - a_2 + a_2 - a_3 + \ldots + a_{n-1} - a_n]$$

$$= \frac{a_1 - a_n}{d}$$

Also, $\dfrac{1}{a_n} = \dfrac{1}{a_1} + (n-1)d$

$$\Rightarrow \frac{a_1 - a_n}{a_1 a_n} = (n-1)d \Rightarrow \frac{a_1 - a_n}{d} = (n-1)a_1 a_n$$

Which is the required result.

**7.** **(a, b, d)** Since three numbers in AP so $2b = a + c$ and

$$b^2 = \frac{2a^2c^2}{a^2 + c^2}$$

Eliminating $b$, we get $\left(\frac{a+c}{2}\right)^2 = \frac{2a^2c^2}{a^2 + c^2}$

$\Rightarrow \quad \left(a^2 + c^2\right)^2 + 2ac\left(a^2 + c^2\right) - 8a^2c^2 = 0$

$\Rightarrow \quad \left(a^2 + c^2 + 4ac\right)\left(a^2 + c^2 - 2ac\right) = 0$

$\Rightarrow \quad \left[(a+c)^2 + 2ac\right](a-c)^2 = 0$

$\Rightarrow \quad 4\left(b^2 + \frac{1}{2}ac\right)(a-c)^2 = 0$

$\Rightarrow \quad a - c = 0 \quad or \quad b^2 = -\frac{1}{2}ac$

If $a = c$, we get $a = b = c$

If $b^2 = -\frac{1}{2}ac$, then either $a, b, -\frac{1}{2}c$ are in GP

or $-\frac{1}{2}a, b, c$ are in GP

**8.** **(a, c)** If $t_r$ denotes the rth term of the series, then

$$xt_r = \frac{x}{(1+rx)\left(1+(r+1)x\right)}$$

$$= \frac{1}{1+rx} - \frac{1}{1+(r+1)x}$$

$\Rightarrow \quad x\sum_{r=1}^{n} t_r = \sum_{r=1}^{n}\left[\frac{1}{1+rx} - \frac{1}{1+(r+1)x}\right]$

$$= \frac{1}{1+x} - \frac{1}{1+(n+1)x} = \frac{nx}{(1+x)\left(1+(n+1)x\right)}$$

$\Rightarrow \quad S_n = \sum_{r=1}^{n} t_r = \frac{n}{(1+x)\left[1+(n+1)x\right]}$

**9.** **(b, c)** We have for $0 < \phi < \frac{\pi}{2}$

$$x = \sum_{n=0}^{\infty} \cos^{2n}\phi = 1 + \cos^2\phi + \cos^4\phi + ....\infty$$

$$\frac{1}{1 - \cos^2\phi} = \frac{1}{\sin^2\phi} \qquad ....(1)$$

[Using sum of infinite G.P. $\cos^2\alpha$ being $< 1$]

$$y = \sum_{n=0}^{\infty} \sin^{2n}\phi = 1 + \sin^2\phi + \sin^4\phi + ....\infty$$

$$= \frac{1}{1 - \sin^2\phi} = \frac{1}{\cos^2\phi} \qquad ....(2)$$

$$z = \sum_{n=0}^{\infty} \cos^{2n}\phi \sin^{2n}\phi$$

$$= 1 + \cos^2\phi\sin^2\phi + \cos^4\phi\sin^4\phi + ... \infty$$

$$= \frac{1}{1 - \cos^2\phi\sin^2\phi} \qquad ....(3)$$

Substituting the values of $\cos^2\phi$ and $\sin^2\phi$ in (3), from (1) and (2), we get

$$z = \frac{1}{1 - \frac{1}{x}\cdot\frac{1}{y}} \Rightarrow z = \frac{xy}{xy - 1}$$

$\Rightarrow xyz - z = xy \Rightarrow xyz = xy + z.$

Also, $\quad x + y + z = \frac{1}{\cos^2\phi} + \frac{1}{\sin^2\phi} + \frac{1}{1 - \cos^2\phi\sin^2\phi}$

$$= \frac{[\sin^2\phi(1 - \cos^2\phi\sin^2\phi) + \cos^2\phi(1 - \cos^2\phi\sin^2\phi) + \cos^2\phi\sin^2\phi]}{\cos^2\phi\sin^2\phi\,(1 - \cos^2\phi\sin^2\phi)}$$

$$= \frac{(\sin^2\phi + \cos^2\phi)\,(1 - \cos^2\phi\sin^2\phi) + \cos^2\phi\sin^2\phi}{\cos^2\phi\sin^2\phi\,(1 - \cos^2\phi\sin^2\phi)}$$

$$= \frac{1}{\cos^2\phi\sin^2\phi\,(1 - \cos^2\phi\sin^2\phi)} = xyz$$

Thus $(b)$ and $(c)$ both are correct.

**10.** **(a, d)** $\alpha, \beta, \gamma$ and $\delta$ are in HP

$\Rightarrow \quad \frac{1}{\alpha}, \frac{1}{\beta}, \frac{1}{\gamma}, \frac{1}{\delta}$ are in AP

Let d be the common difference of this AP.

Now, a, $\gamma$ are roots of $Ax^2 - 4x + 1 = 0$

$$\therefore \quad \frac{\alpha + \gamma}{\alpha\gamma} = \frac{\frac{4}{A}}{\frac{1}{A}} = 4$$

or $\quad \frac{1}{\alpha} + \frac{1}{\gamma} = 4 ie, \frac{1}{\alpha} + \frac{1}{\alpha} + 2d = 4$

or $\quad \frac{1}{\alpha} + d = 2 \qquad ...(i)$

$\beta, \delta$ are roots of $Bx^2 - 6x + 1 = 0$

$$\therefore \quad \frac{\beta + \delta}{\beta\delta} = \frac{1}{\beta} + \frac{1}{\delta} = \frac{6/B}{1/B} = 6$$

or $\quad \frac{1}{\alpha} + d + \frac{1}{\alpha} + 3d = 6$

or $\quad \frac{1}{\alpha} + 2d = 3 \qquad ...(ii)$

From Eqs. (i) and (ii), on solving, we get

$\dfrac{1}{\alpha} = 1,\ d = 1\ \therefore\ \dfrac{1}{\alpha} = 1,\ \dfrac{1}{\beta} = 2,\ \dfrac{1}{\gamma} = 3,\ \dfrac{1}{\delta} = 4$

Since, $\dfrac{1}{\alpha\gamma} = A \Rightarrow A = 3$

Also, $\dfrac{1}{\beta\delta} = B, \Rightarrow B = 8$

Hence, A = 3 and B = 8.

**11.** **(6)** Given that $a_{10} = 3 \Rightarrow a_1 + 9d = 3$

$\Rightarrow\ 2 + 9d = 3\ [a_1 = 2]$

$\Rightarrow\ d = \dfrac{1}{9}$

$\therefore\ a_4 = a_1 + 3d = 2 + \dfrac{3}{9} = \dfrac{7}{3}$

$h_{10} = 3$

$\Rightarrow\ \dfrac{1}{h_{10}} = \dfrac{1}{3}$

$\Rightarrow\ $ Common difference of corresponding AP is $D = -\dfrac{1}{54}$

$\therefore\ \dfrac{1}{h_7} = \dfrac{1}{h_1} + 6D = \dfrac{1}{2} - \dfrac{1}{9} = \dfrac{7}{18}$

$\Rightarrow\ h_7 = \dfrac{18}{7}$

so, $a_4 h_7 = \dfrac{7}{3} \times \dfrac{18}{7} = 6$

**12.** **(4)** Given $b^2 = ac,\ x = \dfrac{a+b}{2},\ y = \dfrac{b+c}{2}$

Now, $\dfrac{a}{x} + \dfrac{c}{y} = \dfrac{2a}{a+b} + \dfrac{2c}{b+c}$

$= \dfrac{2(ab + ac + ac + bc)}{ab + ac + b^2 + bc} = 2 \qquad \left[\because b^2 = ac\right]$

Again $\dfrac{b}{x} + \dfrac{b}{y} = 2b\left[\dfrac{1}{a+b} + \dfrac{1}{b+c}\right]$

$= \dfrac{2b(b + c + a + b)}{ab + ac + b^2 + bc} = 2$

$\therefore\ \left(\dfrac{a}{x} + \dfrac{c}{y}\right)\left(\dfrac{b}{x} + \dfrac{b}{y}\right) = 4.$

**13.** **(5)** $(1+x)(1+x^2)(1+x^4)\ldots(1+x^{128})$

$= 1 + x + x^2 + \ldots + x^n$

$\Rightarrow\ (1-x)\left\{(1+x)(1+x^2)(1+x^4)\ldots(1+x^{128})\right\}$

$= 1 - x^{n+1}$

$\Rightarrow\ (1-x^2)\left\{(1+x^2)\ldots(1+x^{128})\right\} = 1 - x^{n+1}$

$\Rightarrow\ (1-x^4)(1+x^4)\ldots(1+x^{128}) = 1 - x^{n+1}$

$\Rightarrow\ 1 - x^{256} = 1 - x^{n+1}$

$\therefore\ n+1 = 256\ \text{ or }\ n = 255$

**14.** **(4)** We have $t_r = \dfrac{(r-1)!}{(r+4)!}$

And $t_{r+1} = \dfrac{r!}{(r+5)!}$

Now, $rt_r - (r+5)t_{r+1} = \dfrac{r!}{(r+4)!} - \dfrac{r!}{(r+4)!} = 0$

$\Rightarrow\ rt_r - (r+1)t_{r+1} = 4t_{r+1}$

$\Rightarrow\ 4\displaystyle\sum_{r=1}^{n-1} t_{r+1} = \sum_{r=1}^{n-1}\left[rt_r - (r+1)t_{r+1}\right]$

$\Rightarrow\ 4(t_2 + t_3 + \ldots + t_n) = 1t_1 - nt_n$

$\Rightarrow\ 4(t_1 + t_2 + \ldots + t_n) = 5t_1 - nt_n$

$= 5\left(\dfrac{0!}{5!}\right) - \dfrac{n(n-1)!}{(n+4)!} = \dfrac{1}{4!} - \dfrac{n!}{(n+4)!}$

$\Rightarrow\ t_1 + t_2 + \ldots + t_n = \dfrac{1}{4}\left[\dfrac{1}{4!} - \dfrac{n!}{(n+4)!}\right]$

So a = 4, b = 4, c = 0 and d = 4 and a + b–c–d = 4

**15.** **(b)** Here a, b, c, are in H.P.

$\Rightarrow\ a^{-1}, b^{-1}, c^{-1}$ are in A.P.

$\Rightarrow\ e^{(-a)^{-1}}, e^{(-b)^{-1}}, e^{(-c)^{-1}}$ are in G.P.

**16.** **(a)** Since $x, y, z$ are respectively the $p^{th},\ q^{th}$ and the $r^{th}$ terms of a G.P so $\ln x,\ \ln y,\ \ln z$ are in A.P. with common difference $\ln t$. Here $t$ is the common ratio
Also, $x, y, z$ are in A.P.(say with common difference d.)
Hence, $x - y = (p-q)d$ etc.
and $\ln x - \ln y = (p - q)\ln t.$
Let $S = (x^{y-z}), (y^{z-x}), (z^{x-y})$
so that $\ln S = (y - z)\ln x + (z - x)\ln y$
$\hspace{5cm} + (x - y)\ln z$
$= (q - r)d\ln x + (r - p)d\ln y + (p - q)d\ln z$
$= d[p(\ln z - \ln y) + q(\ln x - \ln z)$
$\hspace{4cm} + r(\ln y - \ln x)]$
$= d\ln t\ [p(r-q) + q(p-r) + r(q-p)] = 0$

$\Rightarrow\ S = 1$

**17.** **(b)** $V_1 + V_2 + \ldots\ldots + V_n = \displaystyle\sum_{r=1}^{n} V_r = \sum_{r=1}^{n}\left(r^3 - \dfrac{r^2}{2} + \dfrac{r}{2}\right)$

$= \displaystyle\sum n^3 - \dfrac{\sum n^2}{2} + \dfrac{\sum n}{2}$

$$= \frac{n^2(n+1)^2}{4} - \frac{n(n+1)(2n+1)}{12} + \frac{n(n+1)}{4}$$

$$= \frac{n(n+1)}{4}\left[n(n+1) - \frac{2n+1}{3} + 1\right]$$

$$= \frac{n(n+1)(3n^2+n+2)}{12}$$

**18. (d)** $T_r = V_{r+1} - V_r - 2$

$$= \left[(r+1)^3 - \frac{(r+1)^2}{2} + \frac{r+1}{2}\right] - \left[r^3 - \frac{r^2}{2} + \frac{r}{2}\right] - 2$$

$$= 3r^2 + 2r + 1$$

$T_r = (r+1)(3r-1)$

For each r, $T_r$ has two different factors other than 1 and itself.

∴ T is always a composite number.

**19.** $(A) \to (s), (B) \to (p), (C) \to (q), (D) \to (r)$

(A) Given, $\Sigma n = \frac{1}{5}\left(\Sigma n^2\right)$

or $\quad \frac{n(n+1)}{2} = \frac{1}{5}\frac{n(n+1)(2n+1)}{6}$

$\Rightarrow \quad 2n+1 = 15$

$\Rightarrow \quad 2n = 14$

$\Rightarrow \quad n = 7$

(B) Let $\alpha$ and $\beta$ be the roots of the given equation,

$$\alpha + \beta = \frac{4+\sqrt{3}}{5+\sqrt{2}} \text{ and } \alpha\beta = \frac{8+2\sqrt{3}}{5+\sqrt{2}}$$

Hence, required harmonic mean

$$= \frac{2\alpha\beta}{\alpha+\beta} = \frac{2\left(\dfrac{8+2\sqrt{3}}{5+\sqrt{2}}\right)}{\dfrac{4+\sqrt{3}}{5+\sqrt{2}}} = 4$$

(C) $x, y, z$ are in HP.

$$y = \frac{2xz}{x+z}$$

$\Rightarrow \quad x - 2y + z = x + z - \dfrac{4xz}{x+z}$

$$= \frac{(x+z)^2 - 4xz}{x+z} = \frac{(z-x)^2}{x+z}$$

$\Rightarrow \quad (x+z)(x-2y+z) = (z-x)^2$

$\Rightarrow \quad \log(x+z) + \log(x-2y+z) = 2\log(z-x)$

**(D)** $\dfrac{128r - a}{r-1} = 255$

$\Rightarrow \quad \dfrac{256 - a}{2-1} = 255$ $\qquad$ [since $r = 2$]

$\Rightarrow \quad 256 - a = 225$

$\Rightarrow \quad a = 1$

**20.** $(A) \to (q); (B) \to (p); (C) \to (r); (D) \to (s)$

(A) $a + b = 12$

$$ab + \frac{6ab}{a+b} = 48$$

$$ab + \frac{ab}{2} = 48$$

∴ $ab = 32$

(B) As $n = 39$ is odd, the value of the given expression

$$= 1^3 - 2^3 + 3^3 - \ldots + n^3$$

$$= \left(1^3 + 2^3 + 3^3 + \ldots + n^3\right) - 2\left\{2^3 + 4^3 + \ldots + (n-1)^3\right\}$$

$$= \left\{\frac{n(n+1)}{2}\right\}^2 - 16\left\{1^3 + 2^3 + \ldots + \left(\frac{n-1}{2}\right)^3\right\}$$

$$= \frac{n^2(n+1)^2}{4} - 16 \cdot \left\{\frac{\frac{n-1}{2}\cdot\frac{n+1}{2}}{2}\right\}^2$$

$$= \frac{(n+1)^2 \cdot (2n-1)}{4}$$

On putting the value we get $\dfrac{S_{39}}{100} = \dfrac{30800}{100} = 308$

(C) HM of $\dfrac{1}{2}, \dfrac{1}{3}, \dfrac{1}{4}, \dfrac{1}{5}$ is

$$\frac{4}{\dfrac{1}{2} + \dfrac{1}{3} + \dfrac{1}{4} + \dfrac{1}{5}} = \frac{240}{77}$$

(D) The numbers between 100 and 500 that are divisible by 7 are 105, 112, 119, 126, 133, 140, 147, … …, 483, 490, 497.

Let such numbers be $n$.

Then, $497 = 105 + (n-1) \times 7$ or $n = 57$

So there are 57 number of numbers lying between 100 and 500 that are divisible by 7

The number between 100 and 500 that are divisible by 21 are 105, 126, 147, …, 483.

Let such number be m.

Then, $483 = 105 + (m-1) \times 21$ or $n = 19$

So there are 19 number of numbers lying between 100 and 500 that are divisible by 21

Hence, the required number $= n - m = 57 - 19 = 38$

**1. (d)** We have $ax^2 + 2\lambda xy + by^2 + 2Kx + 2Ky + 2K = 0$

$h = \lambda,\ g = K,\ c = 2K,\ f = K$

$= abc + 2fgh - af^2 - bg^2 - ch^2 = 0$

$ab.(2K) + 2\lambda K^2 + aK^2 - bK^2 - 2\lambda^2 K = 0$

$2K\lambda^2 - 2K^2\lambda + (a+b)K^2 - 2abK = 0$

For real $\lambda$, $B^2 - 4AC \geq 0$

$4K^4 - 4\,2K[(a+b)\,K^2 - 2aK\,] \geq 0$

$K^2 - 2(a+b)\,K + 4ab \geq 0,\ (K - 2a)\,(K - 2b) \geq 0$

$K \leq 2a$ or $K \geq 2b$.

**2. (a)** Let $d$ be common difference of A.P, then $b = a + 2d$ and $c = a + 6d$. Clearly $(b - a) \times 3 = c - a$

$\Rightarrow 2a - 3b + c = 0.$

So, the straight line $ax + by + c = 0$, passes through $(2, -3)$, which also satisfies $x^2 + y^2 = 13$.

**3. (b)** Equation of line $\dfrac{ax}{c-1} + \dfrac{by}{c-1} + 1 = 0$ has two independent parameters. It can pass through a fixed point if it contains only one independent parameter.

So, there must be one relation between $\dfrac{a}{c-1}$ and $\dfrac{b}{c-1}$

indepentent of $a$, $b$ and $c$ so that $\dfrac{a}{c-1}$ can be expressed

in terms of $\dfrac{b}{c-1}$ and straight line contains only one independent parameter. The given relation can be

expressed as $\dfrac{5a}{c-1} + \dfrac{4b}{c-1} = \dfrac{t - 20c}{c-1}$. Now $RHS$ be independent of $c$ if $t = 20$.

**4. (c)**

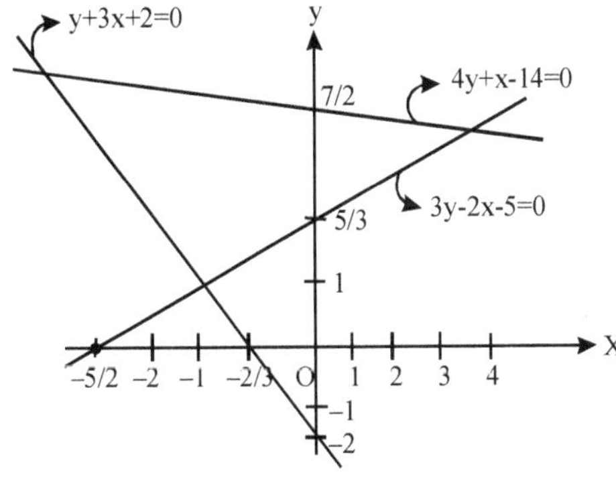


From diagram it is clear that $\dfrac{5}{3} \leq \beta \leq \dfrac{7}{2}$.

**5. (c)** We have, $(a - b)^2 - c^2 = 0$

$\Rightarrow (a - b + c)(a - b - c) = 0.$

$\Rightarrow$ Line $ax + by + c = 0$ passes through either of two points $(1, -1)$ and $(-1, 1)$.

**6. (b)** By solving the sides of the rhombus, its vertices are

$$\left(0, -\frac{n}{m}\right),\ \left(-\frac{n}{\ell}, 0\right),\ \left(0, \frac{n}{m}\right) \text{and} \left(\frac{n}{\ell}, 0\right)$$

$\therefore$ area $= \dfrac{1}{2} \times \dfrac{2n}{m} \times \dfrac{2n}{1} = 2$

$\Rightarrow n^2 = lm$ or $l, n, m$ are in G.P.

**7. (a,c,d)** The given equation is

$\sec^2(a+2)b + a^2 - 1 = 0$

$\Rightarrow \tan^2(a+2)b + a^2 = 0,$ which holds if and only if

$a = 0, \tan^2(a+2)b = 0$

$\Rightarrow \tan^2 2b = 0$

$\Rightarrow b = 0, \dfrac{\pi}{2}, -\dfrac{\pi}{2}$

$(a, b) = (0, 0), \left(0, \dfrac{\pi}{2}\right), \left(0, -\dfrac{\pi}{2}\right)$

$y - 0 = \dfrac{1}{2}(x - 0),\ y - \dfrac{\pi}{2} = \dfrac{1}{2}(x - 0)$

and $y + \dfrac{\pi}{2} = \dfrac{1}{2}(x - 0)$

$2y = x,\ 2y - \pi = x,\ 2y + \pi = x.$

**8. (b,d)** $p.q.4a + 2.2a.2a.2\lambda - p.4a^2 - q.4a^2 - 4a.4\lambda^2 = 0$

$\Rightarrow 4\lambda^2 - 4a\lambda + \{(p+q)\,a - pq\} = 0 \quad (\because a \neq 0)$

$\because \lambda \in R,\ 16a^2 - 4.4\{(p+q)a - pq\} \geq 0$

$or\ (a - p(a - q) \geq 0$

$\therefore a \leq p$ or $a \geq q$

**9. (a,b,d)** Since the given points lie on the line $lx + my + n = 0$, $a$, $b$, $c$ are the roots of the equation

$$l\left(\frac{t^3}{t-1}\right) + m\left(\frac{t^2 - 3}{t-1}\right) + n = 0$$

Or $\ l\,t^3 + mt^2 + nt - (3m + n) = 0 \qquad \ldots(i)$

$$\Rightarrow \quad a+b+c=-\frac{m}{l}\;;\quad ab+bc+ca=\frac{n}{l}\quad ...(ii)$$

and $\quad abc=\dfrac{3m+n}{l}\qquad\qquad ...(iii)$

So, that from (i), (ii) and (iii) we get
$abc-(bc+ca+ab)+3(a+b+c)=0.$

**10. (a,b,c)** Verticles of the given triangle are $(0,0)$, $\left(\dfrac{a}{m_1},a\right)$

and $\left(\dfrac{a}{m_2},a\right)$ so that the area of the triangle is

equal to $=\dfrac{a^2(m_2-m_1)}{2\,m_1\,m_2}$

Since $m_1$, $m_2$ are the roots of $x^2-ax-a-1=0$
so $m_1+m_2=a,\ m_1m_2=-(a+1)$

$\Rightarrow (m_1-m_2)^2=a^2+4(a+1)=(a+2)^2$

$\Rightarrow m_1-m_2=\pm(a+2)$

So the required area is

$\Delta=\pm\dfrac{a^2(a+2)}{-2(a+1)}=\pm\dfrac{a^2(a+2)}{2(a+1)}$

Since the area $\Delta$ is a positive quantity.

$\Delta=\dfrac{a^2(a+2)}{2(a+1)}$ if $a>-1$.

or $a<-2$ and $\Delta=-\dfrac{a^2(a+2)}{2(a+1)}$ if $-2<a<-1$.

**11. (5)** We have $ax^2+2hxy+by^2+2gx+2fy+c=0$, where $c=10$
Let $ax^2+2hxy+by^2+2gx+2fy+c\equiv(l_1x+m_1y+n_1)(l_2x+m_2y+n_2)$
Comparing the coefficient of similar terms, we get
$l_1l_2=a,\ m_1m_2=b,\ n_1n_2=c$
$l_1m_2+l_2m_1=2h,\ l_1n_2+l_2n_1=2g,\ m_1n_2+m_2n_1=2f$
Now, the two lines are equidistant from origin

$\therefore\ \dfrac{0.l_1+0m_1+n_1}{\sqrt{l_1^2+m_1^2}}=\dfrac{0.l_2+0.m_2+n_2}{\sqrt{l_1^2+m_2^2}}$

$\Rightarrow n_1^2(l_2^2-m_2^2)=n_2^2(l_1^2-m_1^2)$

$\Rightarrow n_1^2l_2^2-n_2^2l_1^2=n_2^2m_1^2-n_1^2m_2^2$. On squaring, we get

$\left(n_1l_2+n_2l_1\right)^2[(n_1l_2+n_2l_1)^2-4n_1n_2l_1l_2]$

$=(m_1n_2+m_2n_1)^2.[(m_1n_2+m_2n_1)^2-4m_1m_2n_1n_2]$

$\therefore\quad 4g^2[4g^2-4ac]=4f^2[4f^2-4bc]$

$\Rightarrow f^4-g^4=c(bf^2-ag^2)\Rightarrow\dfrac{f^4-g^4}{bf^2-ag^2}=c=10$

**12. (3)** Since $(0,0)$ and $(1,1)$ lie on the same side, so

$a^2+ab+1>0$

$\because a\in R\Rightarrow D<0\Rightarrow b^2-4<0$

$\Rightarrow -2<b<2\Rightarrow b=-1,0,1$

**13. (2)** Let the equation of the line $L$ be $y-2=m(x-8),\,m<0$

Coordinates of $P$ and $Q$ are $P\left(8-\dfrac{2}{m},0\right)$ and

$Q(0,2-8m)$

So, $OP+OQ=8-\dfrac{2}{m}+2-8m=10+\dfrac{2}{-m}+8(-m)$

$\geq 10+2\sqrt{\dfrac{2}{-m}\times 8(-m)}\geq 18$

So, absolute minimum value of $OP+OQ=18$

**14. (0)** Since $\sqrt{3}.1-4+1<0$, so $\sqrt{3}\sin\theta-\cos\theta+1\leq 0$

$\Rightarrow \dfrac{\sqrt{3}}{2}\sin\theta-\dfrac{1}{2}\cos\theta\leq-\dfrac{1}{2}$

$\Rightarrow \sin\left(\theta-\dfrac{\pi}{6}\right)\leq-\dfrac{1}{2}$

$\Rightarrow \dfrac{7\pi}{6}\leq\theta-\dfrac{\pi}{6}\leq\dfrac{11\pi}{6}\Rightarrow\dfrac{4\pi}{3}\leq\theta\leq 2\pi$

$\Rightarrow$ maximum value of $\sin\theta$ is 0.

**15. (4)** Eliminating $x$ and $y$ from three equations, we get

$-2=m(a+m)\Rightarrow m^2+am+2=0$.

Since $m\in R\Rightarrow$ discriminant $\geq 0$

$\therefore a^2-8\geq 0\Rightarrow|a|\geq 2\sqrt{2}$.

**16. (b)** Slope of $AH$, is $\dfrac{4-1}{2-1}=3$

$\Rightarrow \left(-\dfrac{a}{b}\right)3=-1$

$\Rightarrow 3a=b$

$b-3a=0$

Also, $a+c=2b$

$\Rightarrow a-2b+c=0$

$a(1)+b(-2)+c=0$

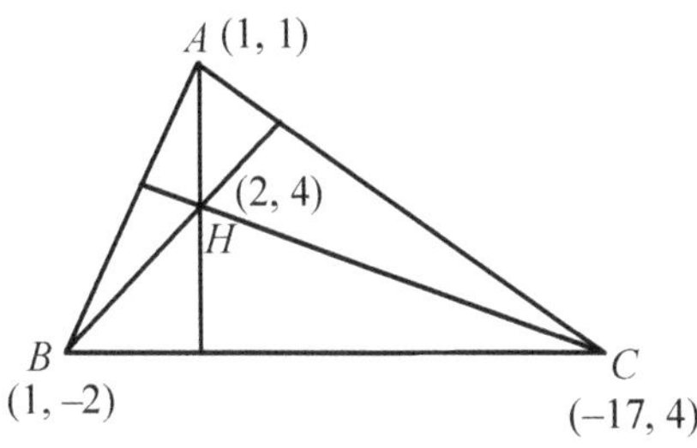

$\Rightarrow$ Lines are concurrent

at $(1, -2)$. So, $B$ is $(1, -2)$

**17.** **(a)** Slope of $AC(m_1) = \dfrac{1-4}{1+17} = -\dfrac{3}{18} = -\dfrac{1}{6}$

Slope of $BC(m_2) = \dfrac{-2-4}{1+17} = -\dfrac{6}{18} = -\dfrac{1}{3}$

$\therefore \tan C = \dfrac{m_2 - m_1}{1 + m_1 m_2} = \dfrac{-\dfrac{1}{3} + \dfrac{1}{6}}{1 + \left(-\dfrac{1}{6}\right)\left(-\dfrac{1}{3}\right)} < 0$

$\Rightarrow \angle BCA$ is obtuse.

**18.** **(c)** $\tan\theta = \left|\dfrac{-\dfrac{1}{2} + 2}{1 + 1}\right| = \dfrac{3}{4}$

$\Rightarrow \sin\theta = \dfrac{3}{5}$

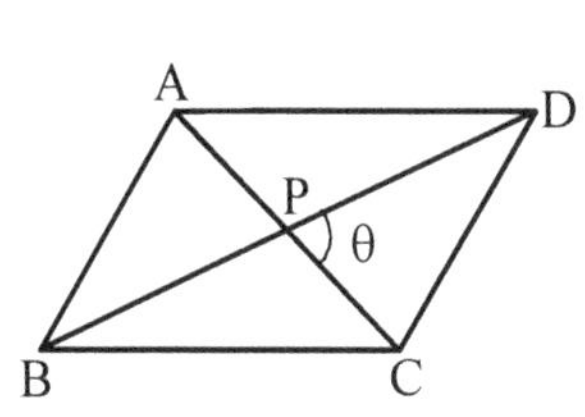

$\therefore$ area of $\triangle CPD = \dfrac{1}{2} \times PC \times PD \sin\theta = 2$

$\Rightarrow \dfrac{1}{2} \times 2 \times PD \times \dfrac{3}{5} = 2$

$\Rightarrow PD = \dfrac{10}{3} \Rightarrow BD = \dfrac{20}{3}$

**19.** **(a)** $\cos(\pi - \theta) = \dfrac{PB^2 + PC^2 - BC^2}{2PB.PC}$

$\Rightarrow -\dfrac{4}{5} = \dfrac{4 + \dfrac{100}{9} - BC^2}{2 \times 2 \times \dfrac{10}{3}} \Rightarrow BC = \dfrac{2\sqrt{58}}{3}.$

**20.** $(A) \to (s);\ (B) \to (r);\ (C) \to (p, q)$

(A) $|\tan\theta| = \dfrac{2\sqrt{25-24}}{12+2} = \dfrac{1}{7}$

(B) Put $y = 0$, we get $x^2 + 4x + c^2 = 0$, which gives equal roots if $c^2 = 4$, then equation becomes

$x^2 + 4xy - 2y^2 + 4x + 2fy + 4 = 0$ which pepresents a pair of st. lines if $f = 4$

(C) As obtained in (C) $c^2 = 4$

**1. (d)** Since point $(\alpha, \alpha+2)$ lies inside the circle

$$\Rightarrow \quad \alpha^2 + (\alpha+2)^2 - 4 < 0$$

$$\Rightarrow \quad -2 < \alpha < 0 \quad ....(1)$$

and also point $(\alpha, \alpha+2)$ lies in the smaller segment made by the line so that

$$\Rightarrow \quad 3\alpha + 4(\alpha+2) + 12 < 0$$

$$\Rightarrow \quad \alpha < -\frac{20}{7} \quad ...(2)$$

(since centre of circle $(0,0)$ and point $(\alpha, \alpha+2)$ lies in the opposite sides of the given line)

From (1) and (2), $\alpha \in \phi$.

**2. (c)** $x^2 + y^2 + \lambda_1(x-y) + c = 0$ ...(1)

$$x^2 + y^2 + \lambda_2(x-y) + c = 0$$

Radical axes $(\lambda_1 - \lambda_2)(x-y) = 0 \Rightarrow x = y$.

Putting in (1) $\qquad 2x^2 + c = 0$

$\Rightarrow \quad c > 0$ for non real $x$.

**3. (b)** For $y^2 + 4ax$, Normal : $y = mx - 2am - am^3$ ... (i)

For $y^2 = 4c(x-b)$, normal : $y = m(x-b) - 2cm - cm^3$ ... (ii)

If two parabolas have common normal :
Then (i) & (ii) must be identical
After comparing the coeffecients we get

$$m = \pm \sqrt{\frac{2(a-c)-b}{(c-a)}}$$

which is real of $-2 - \dfrac{b}{c-a} > 0 \Rightarrow \dfrac{b}{a-c} > 2$.

**4. (b)** The given circle and ellipse have common tangent parallel to x-axis only.

$\Rightarrow$ the circle and the ellipse intersect at 2 distinct points.

$\Rightarrow \quad h + c < a + b$

$\Rightarrow \quad c < a + b - h$.

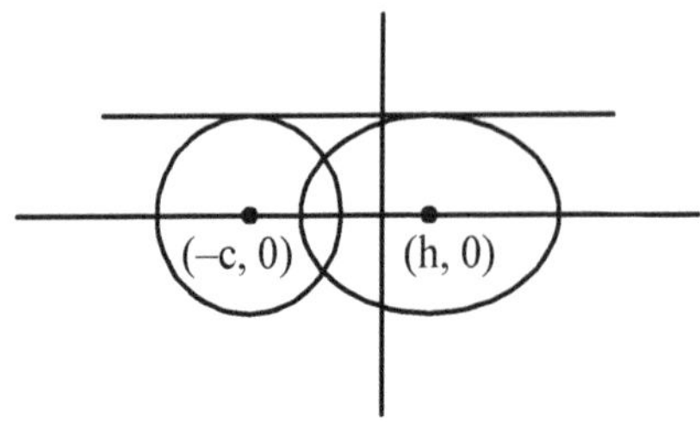

**5. (a)** We know that if a circle cuts a rectangular hyperbola then arithmetic mean of points of intersection is the mid-point of centre of hyperbola and circle.

So, $\dfrac{3+5+2+(-1)}{4} = \dfrac{-g+1}{2}, \dfrac{4+3+6+0}{4} = \dfrac{-f+2}{2}$

$$\Rightarrow \quad g + f = \left(-\frac{7}{2}\right) + \left(-\frac{9}{2}\right) = -8.$$

**6. (d)** The equation of the normal to the hyperbola $\dfrac{x^2}{4} - \dfrac{y^2}{1} = 1$ at $(2\sec\theta, \tan\theta)$ is

$$2x\cos\theta + y\cot\theta = 5 \qquad ...(1)$$

Slope of the normal $= -2\sin\theta = -1 \Rightarrow \sin\theta = \dfrac{1}{2}$

$$\Rightarrow \quad \theta = \frac{\pi}{6}.$$

$Y$–intercept of the normal $= \dfrac{5}{\cot\theta} = \dfrac{5}{\sqrt{3}}$

Since it touches the ellipse $\dfrac{x^2}{a^2} + \dfrac{y^2}{b^2} = 1$

$$\therefore \quad \left(\frac{5}{\sqrt{3}}\right)^2 = a^2(-1)^2 + b^2 \Rightarrow a^2 + b^2 = \frac{25}{3}$$

**7. (a,b)** Here circle equation is

$$x^2 + y^2 + 2\sqrt{\sin\alpha}\,x + (\cos\alpha - 1) = 0$$

so $\sqrt{\sin\alpha}$ will be defined for $\sin\alpha \geq 0$

$$\Rightarrow \quad \alpha \in [0, \pi] \qquad ...(1)$$

also, Length of intercept on x-axis

$$= 2\sqrt{g^2 - c} = 2\sqrt{\sin\alpha - \cos\alpha + 1} > 2$$

$$\Rightarrow \quad \sin\alpha - \cos\alpha > 0$$

$$\frac{\pi}{4} < \alpha < \frac{5\pi}{4} \qquad ...(2)$$

from (1) and (2)

$$\alpha \in \left(\frac{\pi}{4}, \pi\right]$$

**8. (a,b)** We have $\left|\sqrt{x^2 + (y-1)^2} - \sqrt{x^2 + (y+1)^2}\right| = K$

Which is equivalent to $|S_1P - S_2P| = $ Const.

Where $S_1 \equiv (0, 1)$, $S_2 \equiv (0, -1)$ and $P \equiv (x, y)$.

Using properties of a hyperbola, the above equation represents a hyperbola, then we have.

$$2a = K$$

[where 2a is the transverse axis and $e$ is the eccentricity]

and $\quad 2ae = S_1 S_2 = 2$

Dividing, we have $\quad e = \dfrac{2}{K}$

Since, $e > 1$ for a hyperbola, therefore $K < 2$.

Also, $K$ must be a positive quantity. Hence, we have, $K \in (0, 2)$.

**9.** **(b,c,d)** Let $(x_i, y_i) = \left( t_i, \dfrac{1}{t_i} \right) \quad i = 1, 2, 3, 4.$

Any point on the rectangular hyperbola $xy = 1$ is $\left( t, \dfrac{1}{t} \right)$ which lies on the circle

$$x^2 + y^2 = 1 \text{ if } t^2 + \frac{1}{t^2} = 1 \Rightarrow t^4 - t^2 + 1 = 0$$

The roots of this equation are $t_1, t_2, t_3, t_4$ where

$$t_1 + t_2 + t_3 + t_4 = 0 \Rightarrow x_1 + x_2 + x_3 + x_4 = 0$$

$$\sum t_1 t_2 = -1, \sum t_1 t_2 t_3 = 0$$

$$t_1 t_2 t_3 t_4 = 1 \Rightarrow x_1 x_2 x_3 x_4 = y_1 y_2 y_3 y_4 = 1$$

and $\quad y_1 + y_2 + y_3 + y_4 = \dfrac{1}{t_1} + \dfrac{1}{t_2} + \dfrac{1}{t_3} + \dfrac{1}{t_4}$

$$= \frac{\sum t_1 t_2 t_3}{t_1 t_2 t_3 t_4} = 0.$$

**10.** **(a, b, c, d)**

Equation of the curve passing through all four points A, B, C, D can be written as

$$(3x + 4y - 24)(4x + 3y - 24) + \lambda xy = 0.$$

$$\Rightarrow 12x^2 + 12y^2 + (25 + \lambda) xy - 168x - 168y + 576 = 0$$

Clearly for $\lambda = -25$, it represents a circle for different values of $\lambda$, it can represent other curves

**11.** **(2)**

Let circle $x^2 + y^2 + 2gx + 2fy + c = 0 \ldots(A)$

it is passing through $(1, t), (t, 1)$ and $(t, t)$

then $\quad 1 + t^2 + 2g + 2ft + c = 0 \qquad \ldots(i)$

$\quad t^2 + 1 + 2gt + 2f + c = 0 \qquad \ldots(ii)$

$\quad 2t^2 + 2gt + 2ft + c = 0 \qquad \ldots(iii)$

(ii) − (i) and (iii) − (ii),

Then $2g (t - 1) + 2f (1 - t) = 0 \quad$ or $\quad g - f = 0$ and

$t^2 - 1 + 2f(t - 1) = 0$

$$\therefore \quad f = -\frac{(t+1)}{2} = g$$

From (iii), $2t^2 - t(t+1) - t(t+1) + c = 0 \Rightarrow c = 2t$

From (A), $x^2 + y^2 - (t+1)x - (t+1)y + 2t = 0 \Rightarrow (x^2 + y^2 - x - y) - t(x + y - 2) = 0,$

Which is of the form $S + \lambda L = 0$. Hence always pass through points of intersection of

$x^2 + y^2 - x - y = 0$ and $x + y - 2 = 0$. On solving we get $x = 1$ and $y = 1$. So, $a = 1, b = 1$

**12.** **(5)**

The tangent at any point $A(2\sec\theta, \tan\theta)$ is given by

$$\frac{x\sec\theta}{2} - \frac{y\tan\theta}{1} = 1.$$

It meets the line $x - 2y = 0$

$$\Rightarrow \frac{x\sec\theta}{2} - \frac{x\tan\theta}{2} = 1 \Rightarrow x = \frac{2}{\sec\theta - \tan\theta}$$

$$\Rightarrow Q \equiv \left( \frac{2}{\sec\theta - \tan\theta}, \frac{1}{\sec\theta - \tan\theta} \right) \qquad \ldots(1)$$

Also, the tangent meets the line $x + 2y = 0$ at $R$, so

$$\Rightarrow \frac{x}{2}\sec\theta + \frac{x}{2}\tan\theta = 1 \Rightarrow x = \frac{2}{\sec\theta + \tan\theta}$$

$$\Rightarrow R \equiv \left( \frac{2}{\sec\theta + \tan\theta}, \frac{-1}{\sec\theta + \tan\theta} \right) \qquad \ldots(2)$$

Now, $CQ.CR = \sqrt{\dfrac{2^2 + 1^2}{(\sec\theta - \tan\theta)^2}} \sqrt{\dfrac{2^2 + 1^2}{(\sec\theta + \tan\theta)^2}}$

$$= 2^2 + 1^2$$

$$\Rightarrow CQ.CR = 5$$

**13.** **(4)**

Let equation of line passing through $P(1, t)$ be

$$\frac{x-1}{\cos\theta} = \frac{y-t}{\sin\theta} = r$$

$$\Rightarrow x = r\cos\theta + 1 \text{ and } y = r\sin\theta + t.$$

Line meets the parabola at $A$ and $B$

$$\Rightarrow (r\sin\theta + t)^2 = 4(r\cos\theta + 1)$$

$$\Rightarrow r^2 \sin^2\theta + 2r(t\sin\theta - 2\cos\theta) + t^2 - 4 = 0$$

$$\therefore \quad PA.PB = \left| \frac{t^2 - 4}{\sin^2\theta} \right| = 3|t|$$

$$\Rightarrow \frac{|t^2 - 4|}{3|t|} = \sin^2\theta \le 1$$

$\Rightarrow \quad t^2 - 3|t| - 4 \le 0$

$\Rightarrow \quad (|t| + 1)(|t| - 4) \le 0$

$\Rightarrow \quad |t| \le 4$

Hence the maximum value of $t$ is 4.

**14. (5)** Equation of normal to $y^2 = 4ax$ and $x^2 = 4by$ in terms of $m$ are given by

$$y = mx - 2am - a m^3 \text{ and } y = mx + 2b + \frac{b}{m^2}$$

For common normal $2b + \dfrac{b}{m^2} + 2am + am^3 = 0$

$\Rightarrow a m^5 + 2a m^3 + 2b m^2 + b = 0.$

So, a maximum of 5 normals are possible.

**15. (2)** $AB^2 = 4A\,M^2$　　　　(See figure)

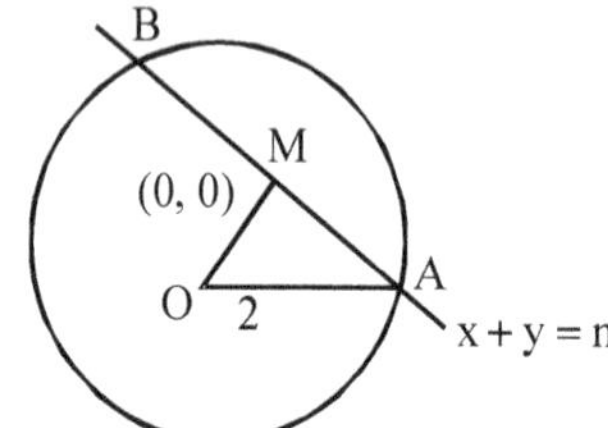


$$4\left(4 - \frac{n^2}{2}\right) = 2(8 - n^2),\, n \in \mathbf{N} \Rightarrow n = 1 \text{ or } 2$$

Hence required sum $= 2(8 - 1^2 + 8 - 2^2) = 2 \times 11$

**16. (a)** Line $x + 2y + a = 0$ intersects the circle

$x^2 + y^2 - 4 = 0$ if $\left|\dfrac{0 + 0 + a}{\sqrt{1 + 4}}\right| < 2$

$\Rightarrow -2\sqrt{5} < a < 2\sqrt{5}.$

**17. (c)** Equation of circle passing through point of intersection of circle $x^2 + y^2 - 4 = 0$ and $x + 2y + 2 = 0$ is given by

$x^2 + y^2 - 4 + \lambda(x + 2y + 2) = 0$　　　　...(1)

again common chord of circle represented by equation

(1) and circle $x^2 + y^2 - 4x - 2y + 1 = 0$ is

$(\lambda + 4)x + 2(\lambda + 1)y + 2\lambda - 5 = 0$　　　...(2)

since equation (2) and $12x - 6y - 41 = 0$ represent the same line

$\therefore \dfrac{\lambda + 4}{14} = \dfrac{2(\lambda + 1)}{-6} = \dfrac{2\lambda - 5}{-41} \Rightarrow \lambda = -\dfrac{8}{5}.$

Hence equation of required circle is

$5x^2 + 5y^2 - 8x - 16y - 36 = 0.$

**For (18-19)** $a - 2b + c = 0$

$\Rightarrow ax + by + c = 0$

passes through $(1, -2)$

So, the centre of the ellipse is $(1, -2)$, which is also the centre of the auxiliary circle, so, $-\alpha = 1, -\beta = -2$

$\Rightarrow \alpha = -1,\ \beta = 2.$

Radius of auxiliary circle $= \sqrt{1 + 4 - 1} = 2$

$\therefore$ Major axis of ellipse $= 4$. Also if segments of focal

chord are $l_1$ and $l_2$ then $\dfrac{1}{l_1} + \dfrac{1}{l_2} = \dfrac{2}{(b^2 / a)}$

$\therefore \dfrac{1}{1} + \dfrac{1}{3} = \dfrac{4}{b^2} \Rightarrow b^2 = 3$

$\therefore$ Equation of director circle is

$(x - 1)^2 + (y + 2)^2 = 4 + 3$

Eccentricity $= \sqrt{1 - \dfrac{3}{4}} = \dfrac{1}{2}$

**18. (d)**

**19. (b)**

**20.** $(A) \to (s);\ (B) \to (r);\ (C) \to (p),\ (D) \to (s)$

(A)　　　$y^2 = 4x$　　　　　　　　.....(1)

Clearly, if $P(at^2, 2at)$ then by symmetry,

$$Q(at^2, -2at)$$

Equation of tangent is $ty = x + at^2$

For $T,\ y = 0,\ x_1 = -at^2$

and equation of normal is

$$y = -tx + 2at + at^3$$

For $R,\ y = 0,\ x_2 = (2at + at^2)$　　　.....(2)

Here, $a = 1 \Rightarrow x_1 = -t^2$ and $x_2 = (2 + t^2)$

$x_2 = 3 = 2 + t^2 \Rightarrow t^2 = 1 \Rightarrow t = \pm 1$

Take $t = 1$, then $x_1 = -1$,

$\therefore \quad PM = 2at = 2 \times 1 \times 1 = 2$

$RT = x_1 + x_2 = (1 + 3) = 4$

$\therefore \quad$ Area of quadrilateral $PTQR$

$$= 2 \times \left(\frac{1}{2} \times 4 \times 2\right) = 8 \text{ sq. units}$$

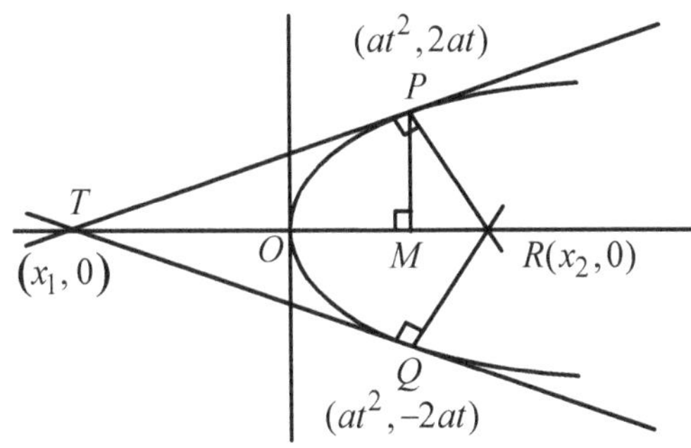


(B)  Clearly, $RT$ will be the diameter of circle
∴ Circumference $= (\pi \times \text{diameter})$

$$= \pi \times RT = \frac{\pi \times 4}{4\pi} = 1.$$

(C)  Since in the part (1), we have found $x_2\left(2a + at^2\right) > 2a$,

$$\left(\text{ if } t \neq 0\right)$$

∴   For three real normals, $x_2 > 2a = 2 \times 1 = 2$
i.e. $x_2 > 2$.

(D)  Equation of $PT$ is $y = x + a \Rightarrow \angle\, PTM = \dfrac{\pi}{4}$

$$\Rightarrow \sin\frac{\pi}{4} = \frac{PM}{PT} = \frac{2}{PT}$$

$$\therefore PT = 2\sqrt{2}$$

**1. (b)** Writing the given expression in the form

$$\left(\frac{\sin x^n}{x^n}\right)\left(\frac{x^n}{x^m}\right)\left(\frac{x}{\sin x}\right)^m \quad \text{and noting that the}$$

$$\lim_{\theta \to 0}\frac{\sin\theta}{\theta}=1 \text{, we see that the required limit equals to 1}$$

if $n = m$, and 0 if $n > m$.

**2. (a)** Let $f(x) = ax^2 + bx + c$

Then, $f(1) = a + b + c$

and $f(-1) = a - b + c$

Since $f(1) = f(-1)$

$\Rightarrow \quad a + b + c = a - b + c$

$\Rightarrow \quad 2b = 0 \ \text{ or } \ b = 0$

i.e., $f(x) = ax^2 + c$

$\therefore \quad f'(x) = 2ax$

$f'(a) = 2a^2, f'(b) = 2ab, f'(c) = 2ac$

Now, $2f'(b) = f'(a) + f'(c)$

If $2.2ab = 2a^2 + 2ac$

If $2b = a + c$

If $a, b, c$ are in AP, which is given.

$\therefore \quad f'(a), f'(b), f'(c)$ are in AP.

**3. (a)** $\displaystyle\lim_{n\to\infty}\frac{S_{n+1} - S_n}{\sqrt{\displaystyle\sum_{k=1}^{n} k}} = \lim_{n\to\infty}\frac{a_{n+1}}{\sqrt{\dfrac{n(n+1)}{2}}} = 0$

$$(\because a_{n+1} = a)$$

**4. (a)** It can be easily shown that,

$$S_n = \begin{cases} \dfrac{n}{6}\left(n + \dfrac{1}{2}\right), & \text{when } n \text{ is even} \\[2mm] \dfrac{n}{6}\,(n + 1), & \text{when } n \text{ is odd} \end{cases}$$

Thus $\dfrac{S_n}{n^2} = \begin{cases} \dfrac{1}{6}\left(1 + \dfrac{1}{2n}\right), & \text{when } n \text{ is even} \\[2mm] \dfrac{1}{6}\left(1 + \dfrac{1}{n}\right), & \text{when } n \text{ is odd} \end{cases}$

$\Rightarrow \quad \displaystyle\lim_{n\to\infty}\frac{S_n}{n^2} = \frac{1}{6}$

**5. (a)** $\phi(x) = ax^2 + bx + c$

$\because \quad \phi(1) = \phi(-1) \Rightarrow a + b + c = a - b + c$

$\Rightarrow b = 0$

$\therefore \quad \phi(x) = ax^2 + c$

$\Rightarrow \quad \phi'(x) = 2ax$

$\therefore \quad \phi'(a_1) = 2aa_1, \phi'(a_2) = 2aa_2, \phi'(a_3) = 2aa_3$

$\because \quad a_1, a_2, a_3$ are in AP

$\therefore \quad \phi'(a_1), \phi'(a_2), \phi'(a_3)$ are also in AP.

**6. (c)** $a = \min\{x^2 + 2x + 3, x \in R\}$

$\quad = \min\{(x+1)^2 + 2, x \in R\}$

$\quad = 2$

and $b = \displaystyle\lim_{\theta \to 0}\frac{1 - \cos\theta}{\theta^2}$

$\quad = \displaystyle\lim_{\theta \to 0}\frac{(1 - \cos\theta)(1 + \cos\theta)}{\theta^2(1 + \cos\theta)} = \frac{1}{2}$

$\therefore \quad \displaystyle\sum_{r=0}^{n} a^r \cdot b^{n-r} = b^n \sum_{r=0}^{n}\left(\frac{a}{b}\right)^r$

$\quad = \left(\dfrac{1}{2}\right)^n \displaystyle\sum_{r=0}^{n}(4)^r$

$\quad = \dfrac{1}{2^n}(1 + 4 + 4^2 + \ldots + 4^n)$

$\quad = \dfrac{1}{2n}\cdot 1\cdot\left(\dfrac{4^{n+1} - 1}{4 - 1}\right)$

$\quad = \dfrac{4^{n+1} - 1}{3\cdot 2^n}$

**7. (a, b, c)**

$f(x) = |x^2 - 3|x| + 2|$

$\quad = \begin{cases} |x^2 - 3x + 2|, & x \geq 0 \\ |x^2 + 3x + 2|, & x < 0 \end{cases}$

$\quad = \begin{cases} x^2 - 3x + 2, & x^2 - 3x + 2 \geq 0, \ x \geq 0 \\ -x^2 + 3x - 2, & x^2 - 3x + 2 < 0, \ x \geq 0 \\ x^2 + 3x + 2, & x^2 + 3x + 2 \geq 0, \ x < 0 \\ -x^2 - 3x - 2, & x^2 + 3x + 2 < 0, \ x < 0 \end{cases}$

$\quad = \begin{cases} x^2 - 3x + 2, & x \in [0,1] \cup [2, \infty) \\ -x^2 + 3x - 2, & x \in (1, 2) \\ x^2 + 3x + 2, & x \in (-\infty, -2] \cup [-1, 0) \\ -x^2 - 3x + 2, & x \in (-2, -1) \end{cases}$

$\Rightarrow \quad f'(x) = \begin{cases} 2x - 3, & x \in (0,1) \cup (2, \infty) \\ -2x + 3, & x \in ((1, 2) \\ 2x + 3, & x \in (-\infty, -2) \cup (-1, 0) \\ -2x - 3, & x \in (-2, -1) \end{cases}$

**8.** **(b,c,d)** $f(x) = \lim\limits_{x \to \infty} \dfrac{x}{x^{2n}+1}$

$$= \begin{cases} x, & x^2 < 1 \\ 0, & x^2 > 1 \\ 1/2, & x = 1 \\ -1/2, & x = -1 \end{cases}$$

$\Rightarrow \quad f(1^+) = f(-1^-) = 0$

$f(1^-) = 1, \; f(-1^+) = -1$

$f(1) = 1/2$

**9.** **(b, c)** Since the greatest integer function is discontinuous (sensitive) at integral values of $x$, then for a given limit to exist both left- and right-hand limit must be equal.

$$\text{L.H.L.} = \lim\limits_{x \to 1^-} (2 - x + a[x-1] + b[1+x])$$
$$= 2 - 1 + a(-1) + b(1) = 1 - a + b$$
$$\text{R.H.L.} = \lim\limits_{x \to 1^+} (2 - x + a[x-1] + b[1+x])$$
$$= 2 - 1 + a(0) + b(2) = 1 + 2b$$

On comparing, we have $-a = b$

**10.** **(a, b, c)**

$$f(x) = \lim\limits_{n \to \infty} \frac{x^{2n}-1}{x^{2n}+1}$$

Option (a) : $|x| > 1$

Then $f(x) = \lim\limits_{n \to \infty} \dfrac{1 - \dfrac{1}{x^{2n}}}{1 + \dfrac{1}{x^{2n}}} = \dfrac{1-0}{1+0} = 1$

Option (b) : $|x| < 1$

Then $f(x) = \lim\limits_{n \to \infty} \dfrac{x^{2n}-1}{x^{2n}+1} = \dfrac{0-1}{0+1} = -1$

Option (c) : From alternate (a) and (b),
$f(x) = 1$, for $|x| > 1$
$f(x) = -1$, for $|x| < 1$
But $1 \ne -1$
$\therefore f(x)$ is not defined for any value of $x$.
Option (d) : $|x| = 1$
Then $f(x) = 0$

**11.** **(2)** $f'(x) = nx^{n-1} + 1 \; ; \; f'(y) = ny^{n-1} + 1 \,;$

$f'(x+y) = n(x+y)^{n-1} + 1$

by given equation we get,

$n(x+y)^{n-1} + 2 = n(x)^{n-1} + n(y)^{n-1} + 2$

$\Rightarrow \quad (x+y)^{n-1} = x^{n-1} + y^{n-1} \qquad ....(1)$

For $n - 1 \le 1, \; \therefore \; n = 0, 2$ ; since for $n = 1$ equation (1) does not holds.

**12.** **(0)** $\lim\limits_{x \to 0^+} \left[ \dfrac{\sin(\operatorname{sgn} x)}{\operatorname{sgn}(x)} \right]$

$= \lim\limits_{x \to 0^+} \left[ \dfrac{\sin 1}{1} \right]$

$= 0$

And $\lim\limits_{x \to 0^-} \left[ \dfrac{\sin(\operatorname{sgn} x)}{\operatorname{sgn}(x)} \right]$

$= \lim\limits_{x \to 0^-} \left[ \dfrac{\sin(-1)}{-1} \right]$

$= \lim\limits_{x \to 0^-} [\sin 1]$

$= 0$

**13.** **(1)** $\lim\limits_{x \to \infty} \dfrac{-\ln x^n + [x]}{[x]} = \lim\limits_{x \to \infty} \dfrac{-n \ln x + [x]}{[x]}$

$= 1 - n \lim\limits_{x \to \infty} \dfrac{\ln x}{[x]} \qquad ........(1)$

$0 < x - 1 < [x] \le x$

$\Rightarrow \dfrac{1}{x} \le \dfrac{1}{[x]} < \dfrac{1}{x-1} \Rightarrow \dfrac{\ln x}{x} \le \dfrac{\ln x}{[x]} < \dfrac{\ln x}{x-1}$

$\Rightarrow \lim\limits_{x \to \infty} \dfrac{\ln x}{x} \le \lim\limits_{x \to \infty} \dfrac{\ln x}{[x]} < \lim\limits_{x \to \infty} \dfrac{\ln x}{x-1}$

$\Rightarrow 0 \le \lim\limits_{x \to \infty} \dfrac{\ln x}{[x]}$

$\therefore \lim\limits_{x \to \infty} \dfrac{\ln x}{[x]} = 0 \qquad ........(2)$

From (1) and (2) we get, $\lim\limits_{x \to \infty} \dfrac{-\ln x^n + [x]}{[x]} = 1$

**14.** **(1)** Here,

$y = (1+x)(1+x^2)(1+x^4)........(1+x^{2^n})$

$= \dfrac{1}{1-x} \{(1-x)(1+x)(1+x^2)(1+x^4)$

$\qquad\qquad\qquad\qquad\qquad ......(1+x^{2^n})\}$

$= \dfrac{1}{1-x} \{(1-x^2)(1+x^2)(1+x^4)........(1+x^{2^n})\}$

$= \dfrac{1}{1-x} \{(1-x^4)(1+x^4)..........(1+x^{2^n})\}$

$$\therefore \quad y = \frac{(1 - x^{2^{n+1}})}{(1 - x)}$$

$$\therefore \quad \frac{dy}{dx} = \frac{-2^{n+1}.(x^{2^{n+1}-1})\ (1-x) - (1 - x^{2^{n+1}}).(-1)}{(1-x)^2}$$

Now, $\dfrac{dy}{dx}$ at $x = 0$ ;

$$\left(\frac{dy}{dx}\right)_{x=0} = \frac{-2^{n+1}.(0).(1) + (1 - 0)}{(1 - 0)^2} = 1.$$

**For 15–16.**

$$L = \lim_{x \to 0} \frac{\sin x + ae^x + be^{-x} + c\ln(1+x)}{x^3}$$

$$= \lim_{x \to 0} \left[ \frac{\left(x - \dfrac{x^3}{3!}\right) + a\left(1 + \dfrac{x}{1!} + \dfrac{x^2}{2!} + \dfrac{x^3}{3!}\right)}{x^3} \right.$$

$$\left. + \frac{b\left(1 - \dfrac{x}{1!} + \dfrac{x^2}{2!} - \dfrac{x^3}{3!}\right) + c\left(x - \dfrac{x^2}{2} + \dfrac{x^3}{3}\right)}{x^3} \right]$$

$$= \lim_{x \to 0} \left[ \frac{(a+b) + (1 + a - b + c)x + \left(\dfrac{a}{2} + \dfrac{b}{2} - \dfrac{c}{a}\right)x^2}{x^3} \right.$$

$$\left. + \frac{\left(-\dfrac{1}{3!} + \dfrac{a}{3!} - \dfrac{b}{3!} + \dfrac{c}{3}\right)x^3}{x^3} \right]$$

$$\Rightarrow a + b = 0, 1 + a - b + c = 0, \frac{a}{2} + \frac{b}{2} - \frac{c}{2} = 0$$

and $L = -\dfrac{1}{3!} + \dfrac{a}{3!} - \dfrac{b}{3!} + \dfrac{c}{3}$

Solving first three equations,
we get $c = 0$, $a = -1/2$, $b = 1/2$.
Then, L $= -1/3$

Equation $ax^2 + bx + c = 0$ reduces to

$x^2 - x = 0 \Rightarrow x = 0, 1$

$||\,x + c\,| -2a\,| < 4b$

reduces to $||\,x\,| + 1\,| < 2$

$$\Rightarrow -2 < |\,x\,| + 1 < 2$$

$$\Rightarrow 0 \le |\,x\,| < 1$$

$$\Rightarrow x \in [-1, 1]$$

**15.** **(b)**   **16. (c)**

**17.** **(b)**   $\overset{\frown}{AC} = \theta = AB$
$CD = \sin\theta$ and $OD = \cos\theta$

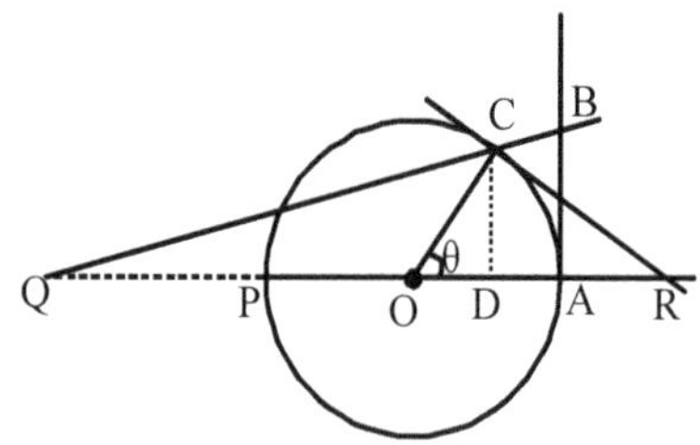

Therefore $AD = 1 - \cos\theta$
Therefore area of trapezoid,

$$ABCD = \frac{1}{2}(AB + CD) \times AD$$

$$= \frac{(\theta + \sin\theta)(1 - \cos\theta)}{2} = (\theta + \sin\theta)\sin^2\frac{\theta}{2}$$

**18.** **(d)**   $\triangle ABQ$ and $DCQ$ are similar, so

$$\frac{AB}{CD} = \frac{AQ}{DQ} = \frac{AQ}{AQ - AD}$$

$$\Rightarrow \frac{\theta}{\sin\theta} = \frac{AQ}{AQ - (1 - \cos\theta)}$$

or, $AQ = \dfrac{\theta(1 - \cos\theta)}{\theta - \sin\theta}$

$$\therefore \lim_{\theta \to 0^+} AQ = \lim_{\theta \to 0^+} \frac{\theta(1 - \cos\theta)}{\theta - \sin\theta}$$

$$= \lim_{\theta \to 0^+} \frac{1 - \cos\theta + \theta\sin\theta}{1 - \cos\theta}$$

$$= \lim_{\theta \to 0^+} \frac{2\sin\theta + \theta\cos\theta}{\sin\theta} = 3$$

**19.**   **(A) → (q); (B) → (p, q, r); (C) → (r, s); D → (s)**
(A)  Here, a > 0, if a $\le$ 0, then limit $= \infty$

$$\therefore \lim_{x \to \infty} \frac{(\sqrt{x^2 - x + 1} - ax - b)(\sqrt{x^2 - x + 1} + ax + b)}{(\sqrt{x^2 - x + 1}) + ax + b}$$

$$= \lim_{x \to \infty} \frac{(x^2 - x + 1) - (ax + b)^2}{\sqrt{(x^2 - x + 1)} + ax + b}$$

$$= \lim_{x \to \infty} \frac{(1-a^2)x^2 - (1+2ab)x + (1-b^2)}{\sqrt{(x^2-x+1)}+ax+b}$$

This is possible only when $1-a^2 = 0$ and $1+2ab = 0$

$$\therefore \quad a = \pm 1$$
$$\Rightarrow a = 1 \qquad (\because a > 0)$$
$$\Rightarrow b = -1/2$$
$$\Rightarrow (a, 2b) = (1, -1)$$

(B)  Divide numerator and denominator by $e^{1/x}$, then

$$\lim_{x \to \infty} \frac{(1+a^3)e^{\frac{1}{x}}+8}{e^{\frac{1}{x}}+(1-b^3)} = 2$$

$$\Rightarrow \frac{0+8}{0+1-b^3} = 2$$

$$\Rightarrow 1-b^3 = 4$$

$$\therefore \quad b^3 = -3 \Rightarrow b = -3^{1/3}$$

Then, $a \in R$

$$\Rightarrow (a, b^3) = (a, -3)$$

(C)  $\displaystyle \lim_{x \to \infty} \left(\sqrt{(x^4-x^2+1)} - ax^2 - b\right) = 0$

Put $x = \dfrac{1}{t}$

$$\therefore \quad \lim_{t \to 0}\left( \sqrt{\left(\frac{1}{t^4} - \frac{1}{t^2}+1\right)} - \frac{a}{t^2} - b \right) = 0$$

$$\Rightarrow \lim_{t \to 0} \frac{\sqrt{(1-t^2+t^4)}-a-bt^2}{t^2} = 0 \quad ...(1)$$

Since R.H.S. is finite, numerator must be equal to 0 at t $\to 0$.

$$\therefore \quad 1-a = 0, \therefore a = 1$$

From equation (1),

$$\lim_{t \to 0} \frac{\sqrt{(1-t^2+t^4)}-1-bt^2}{t^2} = 0$$

$$\lim_{t \to 0}(-1+t^2)\left( \frac{(1-t^2+t^4)^{1/2} - (1)^{1/2}}{(1-t^2+t^4)-1} \right) = b$$

$$\Rightarrow (-1)\left(\frac{1}{2}\right) = b \Rightarrow a = 1, b = -\frac{1}{2}$$

$$\Rightarrow (a, -2b) = (1, 2)$$

(D)  $\displaystyle \lim_{x \to -a} \frac{a^7 - (-x)^7}{a-(-x)} = 7$

$$\Rightarrow \quad 7a^6 = 7 \Rightarrow a^6 = 1 \Rightarrow a = -1$$

**20.**  **A→(p, r) ; B→(s, t) ; C→(q)**

(A)  For $x \to \infty, |x| = x$

$$\therefore \; f(x) = \left(\frac{x}{x+2}\right)^{-x} = \left(\frac{x+2}{x}\right)^x = \left(1+\frac{2}{x}\right)^x$$

$$\Rightarrow \lim_{x \to \infty} f(x) = \lim_{x \to \infty}\left(1+\frac{2}{x}\right)^x = e^2$$

and for $x \to -\infty, |x| = -x$

$$\therefore \; f(x) = \left(\frac{-x}{-x+2}\right)^{-x} = \left(\frac{-x+2}{-x}\right)^x = \left(1-\frac{2}{x}\right)^x$$

$$\Rightarrow \lim_{x \to -\infty} f(x) = \lim_{x \to -\infty}\left(1-\frac{2}{x}\right)^x = e^{-2}$$

(B)  $\because \; f(x) = \dfrac{(1+x)^{1/x} - e}{x}$

$$= \frac{e\left\{1-\dfrac{x}{2}+\dfrac{11}{24}x^2 +...\right\}-e}{x}$$

$$= \frac{e\left(-\dfrac{x}{2}+\dfrac{11}{24}x^2 +...\right)}{x}$$

$$= e\left(-\frac{1}{2}+\frac{11}{24}x+...\right)$$

$$\Rightarrow \lim_{x \to 0} f(x) = -\frac{e}{2} < -1$$

(C)  $f(x) = \left(\dfrac{1+5x^2}{1+3x^2}\right)^{1/x^2}$

$$\therefore \; \lim_{x \to 0} f(x) = \lim_{x \to 0}\left(\frac{1+5x^2}{1+3x^2}\right)^{1/x^2}$$

$$= e^{\displaystyle \lim_{x\to 0}\left(\frac{1+5x^2}{1+3x^2}-1\right)\frac{1}{x^2}}$$

$$= e^{\displaystyle \lim_{x\to 0}\left(\frac{2}{1+3x^2}\right)} = e^2$$

**1.** **(c)**

| $p$ | $q$ | $p \Rightarrow q$ | $\sim (p \Rightarrow q)$ | $\sim p$ | $\sim q$ | $\sim p \vee \sim q$ | $\sim (p \Rightarrow q) \Leftrightarrow \sim p \vee \sim q$ |
|---|---|---|---|---|---|---|---|
| $T$ | $T$ | $T$ | $F$ | $F$ | $F$ | $F$ | $T$ |
| $T$ | $F$ | $F$ | $T$ | $F$ | $T$ | $T$ | $T$ |
| $F$ | $T$ | $T$ | $F$ | $T$ | $F$ | $T$ | $F$ |
| $F$ | $F$ | $T$ | $F$ | $T$ | $T$ | $T$ | $F$ |

Last column shows that result is neither a tautology nor a contradiction.

**2.** **(c)** The inverse of the proposition $(p \wedge \sim q) \to r$ is

$\sim (p \wedge \sim q) \to \sim r$

$\equiv \sim p \vee \sim (\sim q) \to \sim r$

$\equiv \sim p \vee q \to \sim r$

**3.** **(c)** Negation of 'f is one to one and onto' is R or not Q.

**4.** **(a)** We know that the contropositive of $p \to q$ is

$\sim q \to \sim p$. So contra positive of $p \to (\sim q \to \sim r)$ is

$\sim (\sim q \to \sim r) \to \sim p$

$\equiv \sim q \wedge [\sim (\sim r)] \sim p$

$\because \sim (p \to q) \equiv p \wedge \sim q$

$\equiv \sim q \wedge r \to \sim p$

**5.** **(c)** $S(p, q, r) = \sim p \wedge [\sim (q \vee r)]$

So, $S(\sim p, \sim q, \sim r) \equiv \sim (\sim p) \wedge [\sim (\sim q \vee \sim r)] \equiv p \wedge (q \vee r)$

$S^*(p, q, r) \equiv \sim p \vee [\sim (q \wedge r)]$

$S^* (\sim p, \sim q, \sim r) \equiv p \vee (q \vee r)$

Clearly, $S^* (\sim p, \sim q, \sim r) \equiv \sim S(p, q, r)$

**6.** **(a)**

**7.** **(b)** Let us make the truth table for the given statements, as follows :

| $p$ | $q$ | $p \vee q$ | $q \to p$ | $p \to (q \to p)$ | $p \to (p \vee q)$ |
|---|---|---|---|---|---|
| T | T | T | T | T | T |
| T | F | T | T | T | T |
| F | T | T | F | T | T |
| F | F | F | T | T | T |

From table we observe

$p \to (q \to p)$ is equivalent to $p \to (p \vee q)$

**8.** **(c)**

| p | q | p→q | ~p | ~p∨ q | (p→ q)↔ ~ (p∨ q) |
|---|---|---|---|---|---|
| T | T | T | F | T | T |
| T | F | F | F | F | T |
| F | T | T | T | T | T |
| F | F | T | T | T | T |

**9.** **(a, b, d)** Statement given in option (c) is only correct.

$\sim [p \vee (\sim q)] = (\sim p) \wedge \sim (\sim q)$

$= (\sim p) \wedge q$

**10.** **(c, d)** We know that $p \leftrightarrow q$ is true if $p$ and $q$ both are true or false.

so $p \leftrightarrow \sim q$ is true when if $p$ and $\sim q$ is true.

i.e., $p$ is true and $q$ is false.

or $p$ and $\sim q$ is false, i.e. $p$ is false and $q$ is true.

Hence, options (c) and (d) are correct

**11.** **(a, b , c)** Since $\sim (p \vee q) \equiv \sim p \wedge \sim q$

(By De-Morgans' law)

$\therefore \sim (p \vee q) \neq \sim p \vee \sim q$

$\therefore$ (d) is the false statement

**12.** **(a, b, d)** We consider following truth table.

| $p$ | $q$ | $\sim p$ | $\sim q$ | $p \wedge q$ | $p \vee q$ | $(\sim (p \vee q))$ | $(p \wedge q) \wedge (\sim (p \vee q))$ |
|---|---|---|---|---|---|---|---|
| T | T | F | F | T | T | F | F |
| T | F | F | T | F | T | F | F |
| F | T | T | F | F | T | F | F |
| F | F | T | T | F | F | T | F |

Clearly last column of the above truth table contains only F. Hence $(p \wedge q) \wedge (\sim (p \vee q))$ is a contradiction

**13.** **(a, b , c)** The truth value of $\sim (\sim p) \leftrightarrow p$ as follow

| $p$ | $\sim p$ | $\sim (\sim p)$ | $\sim (\sim p) \to p$ | $p \to \sim (\sim p)$ | $\sim (\sim p) \leftrightarrow p$ |
|---|---|---|---|---|---|
| T | F | T | T | T | T |
| F | T | F | T | T | T |

Since last column of above truth table contains only T.

Hence $\sim (\sim p) \to p$ is a tautology.

**14.** **(b , c, d)**

**15.** **(a, b , c)**

**16.** **(a, b , d)** $p \Rightarrow q \equiv \sim p \vee q \therefore \sim (p \Rightarrow q) \equiv p \wedge \sim q$.

**17.** **(a, b , c)** We know that $p \wedge q$ is true when both $p$ and $q$ are true.

So, option (a) is not true.

We know that $p \to q$ is false when $p$ is true and $q$ is false.

So, option (b) is not true.

We know that $p \leftrightarrow q$ is true when either both $p$ and $q$ are true or both are false. So, option (c) is not true.

If $p$ and $q$ both are false, then

$p \vee q$ is false $\Rightarrow \sim (p \vee q)$ is true.

Hence, option (d) is true.

**18.** **(a, b , c)** The truth tables of $p \to q$ and $\sim p \vee q$ are given below:

| $p$ | $q$ | $\sim p$ | $p \to q$ | $\sim (p \vee q)$ |
|---|---|---|---|---|
| $T$ | $T$ | $F$ | $T$ | $T$ |
| $T$ | $F$ | $F$ | $F$ | $F$ |
| $F$ | $T$ | $T$ | $T$ | $T$ |
| $F$ | $F$ | $T$ | $T$ | $T$ |

Clearly, truth tables of $p \to q$ and $\sim p \vee q$ are same.

So, $p \to q$ is logically equivalent to $\sim p \vee q$.

Hence, option (a) is correct.

If the truth value of $p, q, r$ are T, F, T respectively, then the truth values of $p \vee q$ and $q \vee r$ are each equal to T. Therefore, the truth value of $(p \vee q) \wedge (q \vee r)$ is T. Hence, option (b) is correct.

We have, $\sim (p \vee q \vee r) \cong (\sim p \wedge \sim q \wedge \sim r)$

So, option, (c) is correct.

If $p$ is true and $q$ is false, then $p \vee q$ is true. Consequently,

$\sim (p \vee q)$ is false and hence $p \wedge \sim (p \vee q)$ is false.

Hence, option (d) is wrong.

**19.** **(a, c , d)** Since $\sim (p \vee q) \equiv (\sim p \wedge \sim q)$ and $\sim (p \wedge q) \equiv (\sim p \vee q)$

So option (b) and (d) are not true.

$(p \to q) \equiv p \wedge \sim q)$, so option (c) is not true.

Now $p \to q \sim p \vee q$

$\sim q \to \sim p \equiv [\sim (\sim q) \vee \sim p] \equiv q \vee \sim p \equiv \sim p \vee q$

$p \to q \equiv \sim q \to \sim p$

**20.** **(A) $\to$ (s); (B) $\to$ (p); (C) $\to$ (q); (D) $\to$ (r)**

(A) Dual of statement $[(p \vee q) \wedge (\sim q)] \vee (\sim p)$ is

$[(p \wedge q) \vee (\sim q)] \wedge (\sim p)$

(B) Logically equivalent of $[(p \vee q) \wedge (\sim q)] \vee \sim p$ is

$[(p \wedge \sim q) \vee (q \wedge \sim q)] \vee \sim p$ or $[p \wedge \sim q] \vee \sim p$

(C) Negation of $[(p \vee q) \wedge (\sim q)] \vee (\sim p)$ is

$\sim [(p \vee q) \wedge (\sim q)] \wedge \sim (\sim p)$ or $[(\sim p \wedge \sim q) \vee q)] \wedge p$

(D) Contrapositive of $[(p \vee q) \wedge (\sim q)] \to (\sim p)$ is $\sim (\sim p) \to$

$\sim [(p \vee q) \wedge (\sim q)]$ or $p \to [\sim (p \vee q) \vee q]$

or $(\sim p) \vee [(\sim p \wedge \sim q) \vee q]$

**1.** **(c)** $\because \ \sigma = \sqrt{\dfrac{\Sigma xi^2}{N} - \left(\dfrac{\Sigma x_i}{N}\right)^2}$

$\therefore \ 2 = \sqrt{\dfrac{(a^2 + a^2 \dots \,'2n'\ \text{times})}{2n} - 0}$

$\Rightarrow \ 4 = \dfrac{2na^2}{2n} \Rightarrow a^2 = 4 \Rightarrow |a| = 2$

**2.** **(b)** On arranging the given observations in ascending order, we get

$$\text{All negative terms} \underbrace{\phantom{xx}}_{(n+1)^{th}\ \text{term}}^{0} \text{All positive terms}$$

The median of given observations $= (n+1)^{th}$term $= 0$

$\therefore$ S.D.>M.D.

**3.** **(a)** If each item of a data is increased or decreased by the same constant, then the standard deviation of the data remains unchanged.

**4.** **(d)** Let $\displaystyle\sum_{i=1}^{9}(x_i - 5) = 9$

$\Rightarrow \displaystyle\sum_{i=1}^{9} x_i - \sum_{i=1}^{9} 5 = 9$

$\Rightarrow \displaystyle\sum_{i=1}^{9} x_i - (9 \times 5) = 9$

$\displaystyle\sum x_i - 45 = \Rightarrow \sum x_i = 54$

Similarly,

$\displaystyle\sum x_i^2 - 10 \times 54 + 25 \times 9 = 45$

$\Rightarrow \displaystyle\sum x_i^2 = 360$

$\Rightarrow \sigma = \sqrt{\dfrac{360}{9} - \left(\dfrac{54}{9}\right)^2} = \sqrt{\dfrac{324}{81}} = 2$

**5.** **(c)** Two distributions are linerarly related

**6.** **(b)** The mean of the series

$\bar{X} = \dfrac{1}{2n+1}\{a + (a+d) + (a+2d) + \dots + (a+2nd)\}$

$= \dfrac{1}{2n+1}\left\{\dfrac{2n+1}{2}(2a + 2nd)\right\} = a + nd$

Therefore, mean deviation from mean

$\dfrac{1}{2n+1}\displaystyle\sum_{r=0}^{2n}\left|\,(a+rd) - (a+nd)\,\right| = \dfrac{1}{2n+1}\sum_{r=0}^{2n}|r-n|\,d$

$= \dfrac{[2(1+2+\dots+n)+0]\,d}{2n+1} = \dfrac{n(n+1)d}{2n+1}$

**7.** **(b)** We know that variance $(\sigma^2) = \dfrac{\Sigma x_i^2}{n} - \left(\dfrac{\Sigma x_i}{n}\right)^2$

First $n$ natural numbers are:

| $x_i$ | $x_i^2$ |
|---|---|
| 1 | $1^2$ |
| 2 | $2^2$ |
| 3 | $3^2$ |
| 4 | $4^2$ |
| 5 | $5^2$ |
| $\vdots$ | $\vdots$ |
| $n$ | $n^2$ |

$\therefore \ \displaystyle\sum x_i^2 = \dfrac{n(n+1)(2n+1)}{6} \ $ and $\ \sum x_i = \dfrac{n(n+1)}{2}$

$\therefore \ \sigma^2 = \dfrac{\Sigma x_i^2}{n} - \left(\dfrac{\Sigma x_i}{n}\right)^2$

$= \dfrac{n(n+1)(2n+1)}{6n} - \left[\dfrac{n(n+1)}{2n}\right]^2$

$= \dfrac{(2n^2 + 3n + 1)}{6} - \left(\dfrac{n+1}{2}\right)^2$

$= \dfrac{2[2n^2 + 3n + 1] - 3(n^2 + 1 + 2n)}{12}$

$= \dfrac{4n^2 + 6n + 2 - 3n^2 - 3 - 6n}{12} = \dfrac{n^2 - 1}{12}.$

**8.** **(b,d)** Mean of $a, b, 8, 5, 10$ is 6

$\Rightarrow \dfrac{a + b + 8 + 5 + 10}{5} = 6 \Rightarrow a + b = 7 \qquad \dots(i)$

Variance of $a, b, 8, 5, 10$ is 6.80

$\Rightarrow \dfrac{(a-6)^2 + (b-6)^2 + (8-6)^2 + (5-6)^2 + (10-6)^2}{5} = 6.80$

$\Rightarrow a^2 - 12a + 36 + (1-a)^2 + 21 = 34 \quad$ [using eq. (i)]

$\Rightarrow 2a^2 - 14a + 24 = 0 \Rightarrow a^2 - 7a + 12 = 0$

$\Rightarrow \quad a = 3 \text{ or } 4$

$\Rightarrow \quad b = 4 \text{ or } 3$

$\therefore \quad$ The possible values of $a$ and $b$ are $a = 3$ and $b = 4$

or, $\quad a = 4$ and $b = 3$

**9. (c, d)** Let the other two observations be '$a$' and '$b$'

$\therefore$ mean $= \dfrac{2+4+6+a+b}{5}$

$\Rightarrow 4 = \dfrac{12+a+b}{5} \Rightarrow a+b = 8$

Variance $= \dfrac{1}{n}\sum x^2 - \bar{x}^2 = 5.2$

$\Rightarrow \dfrac{1}{5}\left(4+16+36+a^2+b^2\right) - 16 = 5.2$

$\Rightarrow a^2 + b^2 = 50$

**10. (b, c)** We know that for positive real numbers $x_1, x_2, ...., x_n$, we have

$\dfrac{\sum x_i^2}{n} \geq \left(\dfrac{\sum x_i}{n}\right)^2 \Rightarrow \dfrac{400}{n} \geq \left(\dfrac{80}{n}\right)^2$

$\Rightarrow n \geq 16$ . So only possible value for $n = 18, 20$

**11. (a, b, c, d)** $\bar{x} = \dfrac{2+3+a+11}{4} = \dfrac{a}{4} + 4$

$\sigma = \sqrt{\sum \dfrac{x_i^2}{n} - \left(\bar{x}\right)^2}$

$\Rightarrow 3.5 = \sqrt{\dfrac{4+9+a^2+121}{4} - \left(\dfrac{a}{4}+4\right)^2}$

$\Rightarrow \dfrac{49}{4} = \dfrac{4(134+a^2) - (a^2+256+32a)}{16}$

$\Rightarrow 3a^2 - 32a + 84 = 0$

**12. (4)** Standard deviation $= \sigma = d\sqrt{\dfrac{n^2-1}{12}}$

$d$ = size between each observation = 7

$n$ = total number of observation = 7

$\therefore \quad \sigma = 7\sqrt{\dfrac{(7)^2-1}{12}} = 7\sqrt{\dfrac{49-1}{12}}$

$= 7\sqrt{\dfrac{48}{12}} = 7 \times 2 = 14$

**13. (3)** Variance of $1, 2, 3, 4, 5, ... 10$ is $\dfrac{99}{12}$

$\therefore$ variance of $3, 6, 9, 12, ... 30$ is $9 \times \dfrac{99}{12}$

$\therefore$ S.D. of $3, 6, 9, 12, ... 30 = \sqrt{9 \times \dfrac{99}{12}} = \dfrac{3}{2}\sqrt{33}$

**14. (0)** We know that, if any constant is added in each observation, then standard deviation remains same.

$\therefore$ The standard deviation of the observations $a+k, b+k, c+k, d+k, e+k$ is s.

**15. (5)** We know that $Q.D = \dfrac{5}{6} \times M.D. = \dfrac{5}{6} \times 12 = 10$

$\therefore S.D = \dfrac{3}{2} \times Q.D. = \dfrac{3}{2} \times 10 \Rightarrow S.D. = 15.$

**16. (7)**

| $x_i$ | $f_i$ | $f_i x_i$ | $f_i x_i^2$ |
|---|---|---|---|
| A | 2 | 2A | $2A^2$ |
| 2A | 1 | 2A | $4A^2$ |
| 3A | 1 | 3A | $9A^2$ |
| 4A | 1 | 4A | $16A^2$ |
| 5A | 1 | 5A | $25A^2$ |
| 6A | 1 | 6A | $36A^2$ |
| **Total** | **7** | **22A** | **$92A^2$** |

$\because \quad \sigma^2 = \dfrac{\sum f_i x_i^2}{\sum f_i} - \left(\dfrac{\sum f_i x_i}{\sum f_i}\right)^2$

$\Rightarrow 160 = \dfrac{92A^2}{7} - \left(\dfrac{22A}{7}\right)^2$

$\Rightarrow 160 = \dfrac{92A^2}{7} - \dfrac{484A^2}{49} \Rightarrow 160 = \dfrac{92 \times 7A^2 - 484A^2}{49}$

$\Rightarrow 160 \times 49 = 644A^2 - 484A^2 \Rightarrow 160A^2 = 7840$

$\Rightarrow A^2 = \dfrac{7840}{160} \Rightarrow A^2 = 49 \Rightarrow A = \pm 7$

A = 7 as A is a positive integer.

**17. (7)** The given data is 36, 72, 46, 42, 60, 45, 53, 46, 51, 49

Arranging the data in ascending order,

36, 42, 45, 46, 46, 49, 51, 53, 60, 72

Number of observation = 10 (even)

Median (M)

$= \dfrac{\left(\dfrac{N}{2}\right)^{th} \text{observation} + \left(\dfrac{N}{2}+1\right)^{th} \text{observation}}{2}$

$= \dfrac{\left(\dfrac{10}{2}\right)^{th} \text{observation} + \left(\dfrac{10}{2}+1\right)^{th} \text{observation}}{2}$

$= \dfrac{5^{th} \text{observation} + 6^{th} \text{observation}}{2} = \dfrac{46+49}{2} = 47.5$

| $x_i$ | $|x_i - M|$ |
|---|---|
| 36 | $|36 - 47.5| = 11.5$ |
| 42 | $|42 - 47.5| = 5.5$ |
| 45 | $|45 - 47.5| = 2.5$ |
| 46 | $|46 - 47.5| = 1.5$ |
| 46 | $|46 - 47.5| = 1.5$ |
| 49 | $|49 - 47.5| = 1.5$ |
| 51 | $|51 - 47.5| = 3.5$ |
| 53 | $|53 - 47.5| = 5.5$ |
| 60 | $|60 - 47.5| = 12.5$ |
| 72 | $|72 - 47.5| = 24.5$ |
| | $\Sigma|x_i - M| = 70$ |

$\therefore$ Mean deviation about median

$$= \frac{\sum |x_i - M|}{n} = \frac{70}{10} = 7$$

**18. (b)** $\quad \overline{x} = \dfrac{x_1 + x_2 + x_3 + ... + x_n}{n}$

$$\sigma^2 = \frac{1}{n}\sum_{i=1}^{n}(x_i - \overline{x})^2$$

Mean of $d_1, d_2, d_3, ...., d_n$

$$= \frac{d_1 + d_2 + d_3 + .... + d_n}{n}$$

$$= \frac{(-x_1 - a) + (-x_2 - a) + (-x_3 - a) + .... + (-x_n - a)}{n}$$

$$= -\left[\frac{x_1 + x_2 + x_3 + .... + x_n}{n}\right] - \frac{na}{n}$$

$$= -\overline{x} - a$$

Since, $d_i = -x_i - a$ and we multiply or subtract each observation by any number the mode remains the same. Hence mode of $-x_i - a$ i.e. $d_i$ and $x_i$ are same. Now variance of $d_1, d_2, ...., d_n$

$$= \frac{1}{n}\sum_{i=1}^{n}[d_i - (-\overline{x} - a)]^2$$

$$= \frac{1}{n}\sum_{i=1}^{n}[-x_i - a + \overline{x} + a]^2$$

$$= \frac{1}{n}\sum_{i=1}^{n}(-x_i + \overline{x})^2$$

$$= \frac{1}{n}\sum_{i=1}^{n}(\overline{x} - x_i)^2 = \sigma^2$$

**19. (c)** For the numbers $2, 4, 6, 8, ......., 2n$

$$\overline{x} = \frac{2[n(n+1)]}{2n} = (n+1)$$

And $Var = \dfrac{\Sigma(x - \overline{x})^2}{2n} = \dfrac{\Sigma x^2}{n} - (\overline{x})^2$

$$= \frac{4\Sigma n^2}{n} - (n+1)^2$$

$$= \frac{4n(n+1)(2n+1)}{6n} - (n+1)^2$$

$$= \frac{2(2n+1)(n+1)}{3} - (n+1)^2$$

$$= (n+1)\left[\frac{4n+2-3n-3}{3}\right]$$

$$= \frac{(n+1)(n-1)}{3} = \frac{n^2-1}{3}$$

$\therefore$ Statement-1 is false. Clearly, statement - 2 is true.

**20.** $\quad$ **(A) $\rightarrow$ s; (B) $\rightarrow$ r; (C) $\rightarrow$ q; (D) $\rightarrow$ p**

(A) Given data is

$3, 3, 4, 5, 7, 9, 10, 12, 18, 19, 21.$

Median $(M) = 6^{\text{th}}$ obs $= 9$

$|x_i - M|$ are $6, 6, 5, 4, 2, 0, 1, 3, 9, 10, 12$

$$\therefore \sum_{i=1}^{11}|x_i - M| = 58$$

$$\text{M.D}(M) = \frac{1}{11} \times 58 = 5.27$$

(B) Data in ascending order is

$10, 11, 11, 12, 13, 13, 14, 16, 16, 17, 17, 18$

$$\text{Median} = \frac{6^{\text{th}} \text{ obs} + 7^{\text{th}} \text{ obs}}{2} = \frac{13+14}{2} = \frac{27}{2}$$

$$= 13.5$$

Now, $\sum |x_i - M| = 28$

$$\therefore \quad \text{M.D}(M) = \frac{28}{12} = 2.33$$

**1. (b)** Total number of cases $= 6 \times 6 \times 6 = 216$

Let the second number is $i$ (clearly $1 < i < 6$), then first number can be chosen in $i - 1$, ways and third number can be chosen in $6 - i$ ways.

Hence number of ways $= (i - 1)(6 - i)$.

$\therefore$ $i$ can take values 2 to 5.

$\therefore$ Favourable no. of cases

$$= \sum_{i=2}^{5} (i-1)(6-i) = 1 \times 4 + 2 \times 3 + 3 \times 2 + 4 \times 1 = 20$$

$\therefore$ Required probability $= \dfrac{20}{216} = \dfrac{5}{54}$

**2. (c)** $\dfrac{x^2 - 60x + 800}{x - 30} < 0 \Rightarrow \dfrac{(x-20)(x-40)}{x-30} < 0$

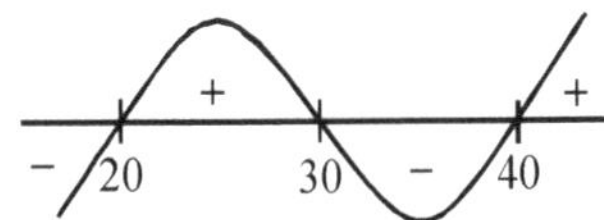

$\therefore$ $x \in \{1, 2, ........, 19\} \cup \{31, 32, ............, 39\}$

$[\because x \in N]$

$\therefore$ Number of favourable cases $= 19 + 9 = 28$. Total no. of cases $= 100$

$\therefore$ Required probability $= \dfrac{28}{100} = \dfrac{7}{25}$

**3. (c)** Here, $n(S) = $ length of the interval $[0, 5] = 5$

$n(E) = $ length of the interval $\subseteq [0, 5]$ in which $p$ belongs such that the given equation has real roots.

Now, $x^2 + px + \dfrac{1}{4}(p+2) = 0$ will have real roots if

$p^2 - 4.1.\dfrac{1}{4}(p+2) \geq 0 \qquad \Rightarrow p^2 - p - 2 \geq 0$

$\Rightarrow (p+1)(p-2) \geq 0$

$\Rightarrow p \leq -1$ or $p \geq 2$

But $p \in [0, 5]$. So, $E = [2, 5]$

$\therefore$ $n(E) = $ length of the interval $[2, 5] = 3$

$\therefore$ Required probability $= \dfrac{3}{5}$

**4. (a)** Let $3n$ consecutive integers be

$N+1, N+2, N+3, ................., N+3n$ (starting with the integer $N$)

We write these $3n$ numbers in 3 rows as following;

$N+1, N+4, N+7, ................, N+3n-2$

$N+2, N+5, N+8, ................, N+3n-1$

$N+3, N+6, N+9, ................, N+3n$

The sum of three selected number will be divisible by 3 it either all three belong to the same row or all three belong to different rows. So, the favourable no. of cases

$= 3(^nC_3) + (^nC_1)(^nC_1)(^nC_1)$

$= \dfrac{3n(n-1)(n-2)}{3!} + n^3 = \dfrac{3n^3 - 3n^2 + 2n}{2}$

Also, the total no of cases

$= {}^{3n}C_3 = \dfrac{3n(3n-1)(3n-2)}{3!} = \dfrac{n(3n-1)(3n-2)}{2!}$

$\therefore$ Required probability

$= \dfrac{\dfrac{3n^3 - 3n^2 + 2n}{2}}{\dfrac{n(3n-1)(3n-2)}{2}} = \dfrac{3n^2 - 3n + 2}{(3n-1)(3n-2)}$

**5. (c)** Let $l$ be the length of the chord $AB$ of the given circle of radius $a$ and $r$ be the distance of the mid point $D$ of the chord from the centre $C$, then $r = a\cos\theta$ and $l = 2a\sin\theta$. According to given condition :

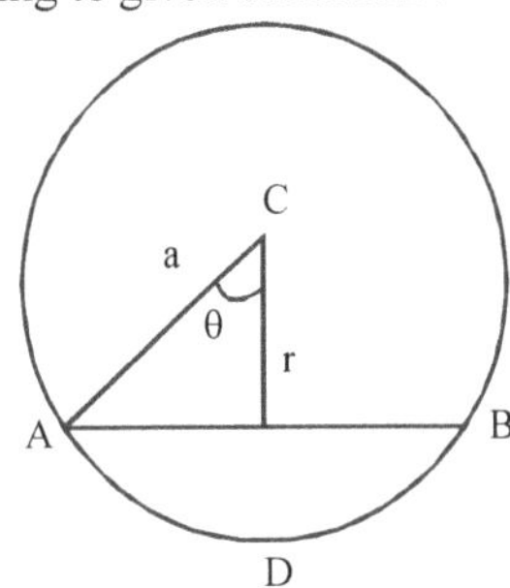

$\dfrac{2}{3}(2a) < 2a\sin\theta < \dfrac{5}{6}(2a) \Rightarrow \dfrac{2}{3} < \sin\theta < \dfrac{5}{6}$

$\Rightarrow \dfrac{\sqrt{11}}{6} < \cos\theta < \dfrac{\sqrt{5}}{3} \Rightarrow \dfrac{\sqrt{11}}{6}a < r < \dfrac{\sqrt{5}}{3}a$

$\therefore$ The given condition is satisfied if the mid point of the chord lies within the region

between the concentric circles of radii $\dfrac{\sqrt{11}}{6}a$ and

$\dfrac{\sqrt{5}}{3}a$.

Hence, the required probability

$$= \dfrac{\pi\left(\dfrac{\sqrt{5}}{3}a\right)^2 - \pi\left(\dfrac{\sqrt{11}}{6}a\right)^2}{\pi a^2} = \dfrac{1}{4}$$

**6. (a)** Since the chairs are numbered, so for counting of total number of cases it is equivalent to linear permutation. Hence, total number of cases $= 10!$

If two particular persons A and B sit together then the total number of linear arrangements $= 2! \, 9!$. Consider one of such arrangements in which the arrangement started at chair 1 $(C_1)$ and ends at chair 10 $(C_{10})$.

$C_1 - C_2 - C_3 - ......... - C_9 - C_{10}$

If two persons sit at $C_1$ and $C_{10}$ then it will lead to $2!\,8!$ new arrangements. So the favourable number of cases $= 2!\,9! + 2!\,8! = 2!8!\,(10)$

$\therefore$ Probability $= \dfrac{2!\,8!\,(10)}{10!} = \dfrac{2}{9}$

**7.** **(b, d)** If $a$ be the radius of the circle, the area of the inscribed sqrare $= 2a^2$

$\therefore\ p_1 = \dfrac{2a^2}{\pi a^2} = \dfrac{2}{\pi}$ and $p_2 = 1 - p, = \dfrac{\pi - 2}{\pi}$

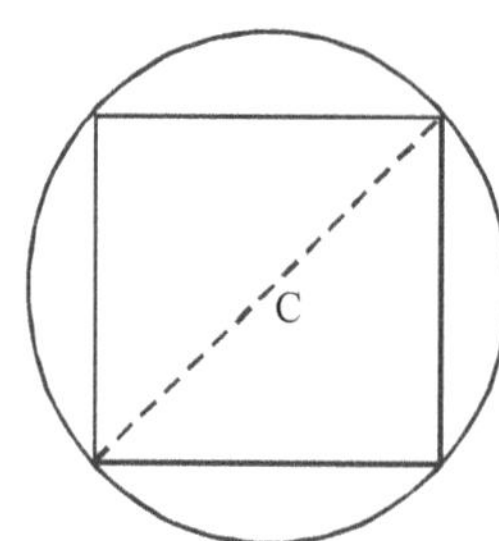

$\because\ \pi - 2 < 2 \Rightarrow \dfrac{\pi - 2}{\pi} < \dfrac{2}{\pi} \Rightarrow p_2 < p_1$

Again, $p_1^2 - p_2^2 = (p_1 + p_2)(p_1 - p_2) = \dfrac{4 - \pi}{\pi} < \dfrac{1}{3}$

$[\because 3 < \pi < 4]$

**8.** **(b, c)** We must have, $0 \le \dfrac{1 + 4p}{4} \le 1,\ \ 0 \le \dfrac{1 - p}{4} \le 1$ and

$0 \le \dfrac{1 - 2p}{4} \le 1,$

$\Rightarrow\ -\dfrac{1}{4} \le p \le \dfrac{3}{4},\ -3 \le p \le 1,\ -\dfrac{3}{2} \le p \le \dfrac{1}{2}$

Again the events are mutually exclusive and

exhaustive, so $0 \le \dfrac{1 + 4p}{4} + \dfrac{1 - p}{4} + \dfrac{1 - 2p}{4} \le 1$

$\Rightarrow\ -3 \le p \le 1$

Taking intersection of all four intervals of $p$, we get

$-\dfrac{1}{4} \le p \le \dfrac{1}{2}$

**9.** **(a, b, c)** $P(A \cup B) = P(A) + P(B) - P(A \cap B)$

$0.8 = 0.6 + 0.4 - P(A \cap B)$

$\therefore\ \ P(A \cap B) = 0.2$

$P(A \cup B \cup C) = (0.6 + 0.4 + 0.5)$

$-(0.2 + P(B \cap C) + 0.3) + 0.2$

$= 1.5 - 0.3 - P(B \cap C)$

We know $0.85 \le P(A \cup B \cup X) \le 1$

or $\ \ 0.85 \le 1.2 - P(B \cap X) \le 1$

$\therefore\ \ 0.2 \le P(B \cap X) \le 0.35.$

**10.** **(a, b, c)** We have to find the probability that the person unlocks the lock at $k^{\text{th}}$ trial. It means that he fails in first $(k - 1)$

trials.

$= P(\text{he fails in } k - 1 \text{ trials}) \times P(\text{he succeeds in } k^{\text{th}} \text{ trial})$

$= \left[\dfrac{n-1}{n} \cdot \dfrac{n-2}{n-1} \cdot \dfrac{n-3}{n-2} \cdots \dfrac{n-(k-1)}{n-(k-2)}\right]$

$\times \left[\dfrac{1}{n-(k-1)}\right] = \dfrac{1}{n}$

**11.** **(4)** Let each of them have n sons. Hence we have to distribute 3 mangoes amongst the sons of Ankur and Rahul, in such a manner that one mango goes to the sons of one and two mango to the sons of other.

1 to Ankur's sons and 2 to Rahul's son + 2 to Ankur's son and 1 to Rahul's son

$=$ Total number of ways of distributing

$= {}^nC_1 \cdot {}^nC_2 + {}^nC_2\,{}^nC_1 = 2 \cdot {}^nC_1\,{}^nC_2 = m$

And total number of ways is ${}^{2n}C_3 = n.$

$\therefore\ \ 2 \cdot \dfrac{{}^nC_1\,{}^nC_2}{{}^{2n}C_3} = \dfrac{6}{7}$

$7 \cdot \dfrac{n(n-1)}{2} \cdot n = 3 \cdot \dfrac{2n(2n-1)(2n-2)}{6}$

$\Rightarrow$ n $= 4.$

**12.** **(1)** Consider one combination $01, 01, 01, 10, 10$.

In each case numbers can come in different orders. Hence the required probability

$= \dfrac{5!}{2!\,2!1!}\left(\dfrac{1}{4}\right)^5 + \dfrac{5!}{2!1!1!1!}\left(\dfrac{1}{4}\right)^5 + \dfrac{5!}{3!2!}\left(\dfrac{1}{4}\right)^5$

$= 5!\left(\dfrac{1}{4}\right)^5\left[\dfrac{1}{4} + \dfrac{1}{2} + \dfrac{1}{12}\right]\ \ = \dfrac{1}{4^5} \cdot 120\left[\dfrac{10}{12}\right] = \dfrac{100}{4^5}$

$= \left[\dfrac{1}{10p}\right] = \left[\dfrac{1024}{1000}\right] = 1$

**13.** **(8)** Let A denote the event that he candidate A is selected and B the event that B is selected. It is given that

$P(A) = .5$

$P(A \cap B) \le .3$

Now $P(A) + P(B) - P(A \cap B) = (A \cup B) \le 1$

or $\ \ 0.5 + P(B) - P(A \cap B) \le 1$, by (1)

or $\ \ P(B) \le .5 + P(A \cap B) \le 0.5 + .3,$

by (2) or $P(B) \le .8$

So maximum possible value of 10P is 8.

**14.** **(3)** Total no. of arrangements $= 15!$

Extreme chairs are occupied by girls, thus there are

four gaps among 5 girls where boys can be seated. Let the number of boys in these four gaps be $2x+1, 2y+1, 2z+1$ and $2t+1$, then

$$2x+1+2y+1+2z+1+2t+1 = 10 \Rightarrow x+y+z+t = 3$$

Where $x, y, z, t$ are integers and

$$0 \le x \le 3,\ 0 \le y \le 3,\ 0 \le z \le 3,\ 0 \le t \le 3$$

∴ The number of ways of selecting positions for boys
$=$ coefficient of $x^3$ in $(1 + x + x^2 + x^3)^4$

$= $ coefficient of $x^3$ in $\left( \dfrac{1-x^4}{1-x} \right)^4$

$=$ coefficent of $x^3$ in $(1 - x^4)^4 (1-x)^{-4} = {}^6C_3 = 20$

∴ Number of arrangements of boys and girls with given condition $= 20 \times 10\,! \times 5\,!$

∴ Required probability $= \dfrac{20 \times 10! \times 5!}{15!} = \dfrac{20}{3003}$

$\Rightarrow \dfrac{n}{1001} = \dfrac{3003}{1001} = 3$

**15. (3)** In the last five throws there can be 0, 1, 2, 3, 4 or 5 heads and the same should be the case in the first ten throws.

$n\,(E) =$ number of favourable cases

$= {}^5C_0 {}^{10}C_0 + {}^5C_1 {}^{10}C_1 + {}^5C_2 {}^{10}C_2 + {}^5C_3 {}^{10}C_3 + {}^5C_4 {}^{10}C_4$

$+ {}^5C_5 {}^{10}C_5 = 3003$

and $n\,(S) =$ total number of ways $= 2^{15} = 32768$

$k = \dfrac{n(E)}{n(S)} = \dfrac{3003}{32768} \Rightarrow \dfrac{32768k}{1001} = 3$

**16. (c)** $x$ can be 2, 3, 4, 5, 6.
The number of ways in which sum 2, 3, 4, 5, 6 can occur are the coefficients of $x^2, x^3, x^4, x^5, x^6$, in

$$\left(3x + 2x^2 + x^3\right)\left(x + 2x^2 + 3x^3\right)$$

$$= 3x^2 + 8x^3 + 14x^4 + 8x^5 + 3x^6.$$

The greatest coefficient of 14 occurs with $x^4$, so $P(E)$ is maximum when $x = 4$

This shows that sum that occurs most often is 4.

**17. (d)** Sum that occurs minimum times is 2 or 6.

**18. (a)** Total number of ways of painting first column when colours are not alternating is $2^8 - 2$.

$\Rightarrow$ The probability when no column has alternating colours is $\left( \dfrac{2^8 - 2}{2^8} \right)^8 = \left( 1 - \dfrac{1}{2^7} \right)^8$.

**19. (a)** The number of ways the square has equal number of red and black squares is ${}^{64}C_{32}$

$\Rightarrow$ probability $= \dfrac{{}^{64}C_{32}}{2^{64}}$

**20. (A) → (q); (B) → (s); (C) → (p); (D) →(r)**

(A) Here sample space is selecting 2 out of 10 i.e ${}^{10}C_2$ and 2 balls can be selected in ${}^4C_1 \times {}^6C_1$ ways such that one of them is red and the other is white hence required probability is

$\dfrac{4 \times 6 \times 2}{10 \times 9} = \dfrac{8}{15}$

(B) Total number of fruits is $6 + 4 + 8 = 18$, so three fruits can be selected in ${}^{18}C_3$ ways and that represents the sample space.

3 apples can be selected out of 6 in ${}^6C_3$ ways so required probability is $= \dfrac{{}^6C_3}{{}^{18}C_3} = \dfrac{6 \times 5 \times 4}{18 \times 17 \times 16} = \dfrac{5}{204}$

**Alternately:** Probability that $1^{st}$ one is apple is 6/18, $2^{nd}$ one apple is 5/17 and $3^{rd}$ one apple is 4/16 so required probability is $\dfrac{6 \times 5 \times 4}{18 \times 17 \times 16} = \dfrac{5}{204}$

(C) Probability that none of them will appear tail is $(1/2)^5 = 1/32$

So required probability that at least one tail will appear is $1 - 1/32 = 31/32$

(D) Out of 12 students 5 can be selected in ${}^{12}C_5 = (12 \times 11 \times 10 \times 9 \times 8)/120 = 792$ ways and the number of ways of selecting 3 girls and 2 boys is ${}^6C_3 \times {}^6C_2 = 20 \times 15 = 300$.

So required probability is $300/792 = 75/198$

**1.** **(c)** $f$ image of goh image

Let $fogoh = F(x) = f[goh(x)]$

$$= f[g(\sqrt{x+3})] = f(\cos\sqrt{x+3})$$

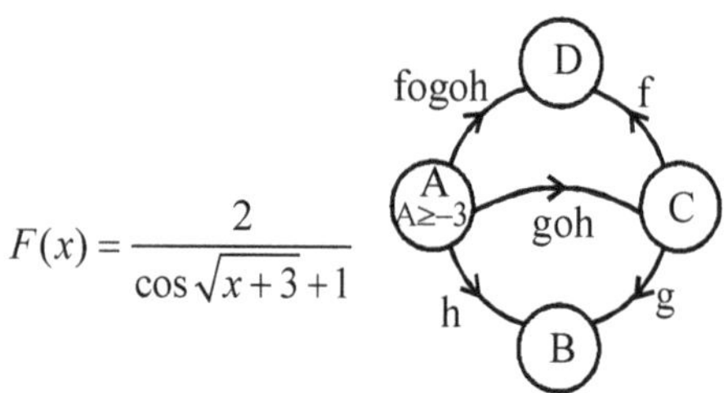


$$F(x) = \frac{2}{\cos\sqrt{x+3}+1}$$

Domain : $x+3 \geq 0$

now $-1 < \cos\sqrt{x+3} \leq 1$

$\sqrt{x+3} \neq (2n-1)\pi, n \in N$

**2.** **(a)** $a\,R\,b \implies |a-b| \leq 1$

$\therefore$ $a\,R\,b$ as $|a-a| = 0 \leq 1$

$\implies$ R is reflexive.

Let $a = 2$, $b = 2.5$, $c = 3.4$, then $|a-b| = 0.5 < 1$ and $|b-c| = 0.9 < 1$

But $|a-c| = |2-3.4| = 1.4 \nleq 1$

$\implies$ $(a, c) \notin R$

$\implies$ R is not transitive.

Clearly $|a-b| \leq 1$

$\implies$ $|b-a| \leq 1$

$\implies$ R is symmetric.

**3.** **(b)** Here

$$g^2(x) = gog(x) = g\{g(x)\} = g(3+4x)$$

$$= 15 + 4^2 x = (4^2 - 1) + 4^2 x$$

$$g^3(x) = gogog(x)$$

$$= g(15 + 4^2 x) = 3 + 4(15 + 4^2 x)$$

$$= 63 + 4^3 x = (4^3 - 1) + 4^3 x$$

Generalizing, we get

$$g^n(x) = (4^n - 1) + 4^n x = y \text{ (say)}$$

then $x = (y+1-4^n)4^{-n}$

$\implies$ $g^{-n}(y) = (y+1)4^{-n} - 1$

$\therefore$ $g^{-n}(x) = (x+1)4^{-n} - 1$

**4.** **(b)** $\because x^2 = xy \implies x(x-y) = 0$

$\implies$ $x = 0$ or $x = y$

$\because$ $x = x \,\forall\, x \in A \implies$ R is reflexive

Also $x\,R\,y \implies x = 0$ or $x = y$

When $x = 0$, then $x^2 = xy$; $y \neq 0$, then $y^2 \neq yx$ as L.H.S $\neq 0$, R.H.S $= 0$

$\implies$ R is not symmetric.

Let $x\,R\,y$ and $y\,R\,z$

$\implies$ Either $x = 0$ or $x = y$ and $y = 0$ or $y = z$

Case (i) : $x = 0$, $y = 0$ and $z \neq 0$, then $x^2 = xz$

$\implies$ $x\,R\,z$

Case (ii) : $x = 0$, $y = z \neq = 0$, then $x^2 = xz$

$\implies$ $x = z \implies x\,R\,z$

Case (iii) : $x = y \neq 0$; $y = z$

$\implies$ R is transitive.

**5.** **(d)** $f$ is not one-one as $f(0) = 0$ and $f(-1) = 0$.

$f$ is also not onto a for $y = 1$ there is no $x \in R$ such that $f(x) = 1$. If there is such an $x \in R$, then

$$e^{|x|} - e^{-x} = e^x + e^{-x}.$$

Clearly $x \neq 0$. For $x > 0$, this equation gives

$e^{-x} = 0$ which is not possible and for $x < 0$, $\dfrac{e^{2x} + 1}{e^x} = 0$,

which is also not possible.

**6.** **(b,c,d)** As shown gof is one-one but g is many-one

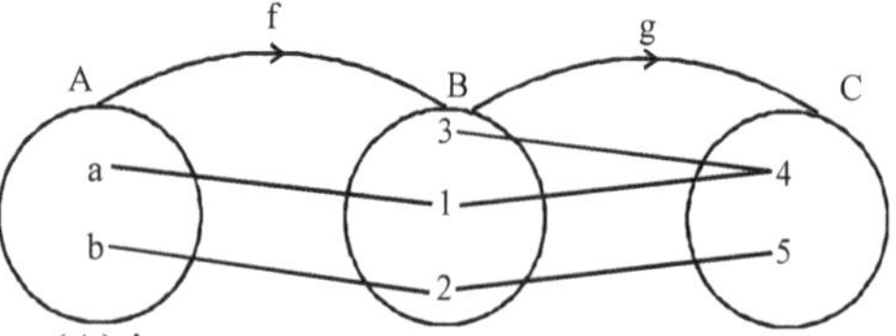


$\implies$ (A) is not correct.

(b) If gof is one-one then f is also one-one,

If f is many-one then gof can not be one-one

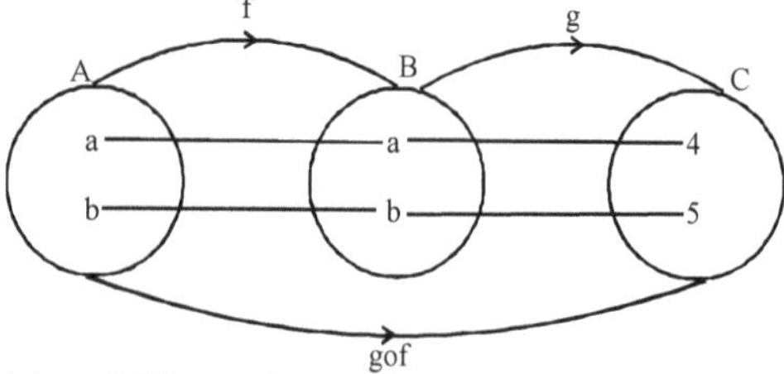


(c) and (d) are obviously true.

**7.** **(b, c, d)**

For $f(x)$ to be real

$x > 0$, $\ln x > 0$, $\ln(\ln x) > 0$ and

$$\ln(\ln(\ln x)) > 0$$

$\implies$ $x > 0$, $x > 1$, $x > e$ and $x > e^e$

$\implies$ $D = (e^e, \infty)$

Clearly range of $f(x) = R \implies f(x)$ is onto

Also, $f'(x) = \dfrac{1}{x \ln(x) \ln(\ln x)} > 0$ if $x > e^e$

$\therefore$ $f(x)$ is one-one in its domain.

**8.** **(b, d)**

The period of $f(x) = |\sin 2x| + |\cos 2x|$ is $\pi/4$

$\Rightarrow$ $[f(x)]$ is also periodic with period $\pi/4$.

Also $1 \le f(x) \le \sqrt{2}$

$\Rightarrow$ $[f(x)] = 1 f(x)$ is a many-one and into function.

**9.** **(a, b, d)**

$$f(x) = \max\{1 + \sin x,\ 1,\ 1 - \cos x\} = \begin{cases} 1 + \sin x, & 0 \le x \le \dfrac{3\pi}{4} \\ 1 - \cos x, & \dfrac{3\pi}{4} \le x \le \dfrac{3\pi}{2} \\ 1, & \dfrac{3\pi}{2} \le x \le 2\pi \end{cases}$$

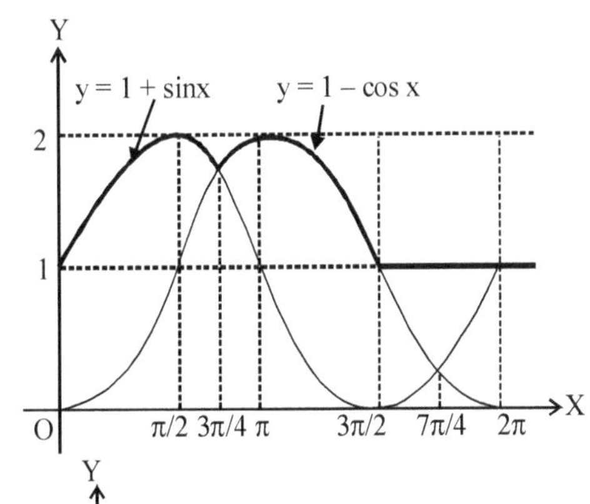


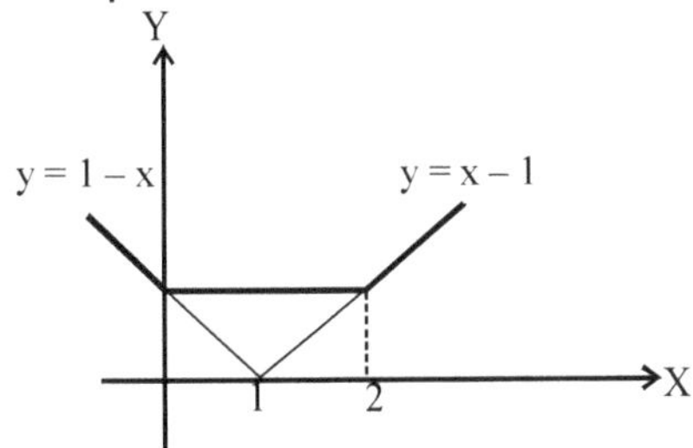


$$g(x) = \max\{1,\ |x-1|\} = \begin{cases} 1 - x, & x \le 0 \\ 1, & 0 \le x \le 2 \\ x - 1, & x \ge 2 \end{cases}$$

$\therefore f(0) = 1 \Rightarrow g(f(0)) = 1$ and $f(1) = 1 + \sin 1$

$\left( \because 0 < 1 < \dfrac{3\pi}{4} \right)$

$\Rightarrow g(f(1)) = 1$  $\qquad (\because 1 < 1 + \sin 1 < 2)$

Again $g(1) = 1 \Rightarrow f(g(1)) = 1 + \sin 1$ and

$g(0) = 1 \Rightarrow f(g(0)) = 1 + \sin 1$

**10.** **(0)**

Let $y = f(x) = \dfrac{x-1}{c - x^2 + 1}$

Take $y = -t$, where $t \in \left[ \dfrac{1}{3}, 1 \right]$,

$\therefore \quad -t = \dfrac{x-1}{c - x^2 + 1}$

$\Rightarrow \quad x^2 - c - 1 = \dfrac{x-1}{t} \Rightarrow x^2 - \dfrac{1}{t}x + \dfrac{1}{t} - c - 1 = 0$

As $-t \in \left[ -1, -\dfrac{1}{3} \right]$, hence the above must not possess real solution

$\therefore \quad \left( \dfrac{1}{t} \right)^2 - 4\left( \dfrac{1}{t} - c - 1 \right) < 0 \Rightarrow \dfrac{1}{t^2} - \dfrac{4}{t} + 4 < -4c$

$\Rightarrow c < -\dfrac{1}{4}\left( \dfrac{1}{t} - 2 \right)^2$

Now, $\dfrac{1}{3} \le t \le l \Rightarrow 1 \le \dfrac{1}{t} - 2 \le 1 \Rightarrow -\dfrac{1}{4} \le \dfrac{1}{4}\left( \dfrac{1}{t} - 2 \right)^2 \le 0$

Hence, $c \in \left( -\infty, -\dfrac{1}{4} \right]$

**11.** **(5)**

Given $f\big(x + f(y)\big) = f(x) + y, \ \forall\ x, y \in R$

Putting $y = x$, we get $f\big(x + f(x)\big) = f(x) + x$

$\Rightarrow \quad f\big(x + f(x)\big) = x + f(x)$

$\Rightarrow f(t) = t$  $\quad \big[$ Putting $t$ in place of $x + f(x)\big]$

$\Rightarrow f(x) = x \ \forall\ x \in R$

$\Rightarrow f(1000) = 1000$

**12.** **(1)**

$fog\,(x) = f(g(x)) = f(4x(1-x))$

$\Rightarrow \dfrac{1 - 4x(1-x)}{1 + 4x(1-x)}$ when $0 \le 4x(1-x) \le 1$ and $0 \le x \le 1$

But $4x - 4x^2 \ge 0 \Rightarrow 0 \le x \le 1$

$4x - 4x^2 \le 1 \Rightarrow (2x - 1)^2 \ge 0 \Rightarrow x \in R$

Hence $fog\,(x) = \dfrac{1 - 4x + 4x^2}{1 + 4x - 4x^2},\ 0 \le x \le 1$

Let $y = \dfrac{4x^2 - 4x + 1}{-(4x^2 - 4x) + 1}, \qquad 0 \le x \le 1$

Put $4x^2 - 4x = t \qquad\qquad t \in [-1, 0]$

$y = \dfrac{1 + t}{1 - t}, \dfrac{dy}{dt} = \dfrac{1 - t + 1 + t}{(1 - t)^2} > 0$

Range of $fog\,(x) = [0, 1]$

$\Rightarrow \alpha + \beta = 1$

**13.** **(6)**

Given, $2f(x) + 3f\left( \dfrac{2x + 29}{x - 2} \right) = 100x + 80$

Putting $\dfrac{2x + 29}{x - 2}$ in place of $x$, we get

$2f\left( \dfrac{2x + 29}{x - 2} \right) + 3f\left( \dfrac{\dfrac{2(2x + 29)}{x - 2} + 29}{\dfrac{2x + 29}{x - 2} - 2} \right) = 100\left( \dfrac{2x + 29}{x - 2} \right) + 80$

or $\quad 2f\left(\dfrac{2x+29}{x-2}\right)+3f(x)=100\dfrac{(2x+29)}{x-2}+80$

$2.(1)-3.(2)\Rightarrow -5f(x)$

$= 200x+160-300\dfrac{(2x+29)}{x-2}-240$

$= -300\dfrac{(2x+29)}{x-2}+200x-80$

$\therefore\ f(x)=60\left(\dfrac{2x+29}{x-2}\right)-40x+16$

$\therefore\ f(3)=60\times 35-120+16=1996$

**For Qs. 14 & 15**

$$g(f(x))=\begin{cases}[f(x)] & -\pi\le f(x)<0\\ \sin f(x), & 0\le f(x)\le \pi\end{cases}$$

$$=\begin{cases}[[x]], & -\pi\le [x]<0,\ -2\le x\le -1\\ [|x|+1], & -\pi\le |x|+1<0,\ -1<x\le 2\\ \sin[x], & 0\le [x]\le \pi,\ -2\le x\le -1\\ \sin(|x|+1), & 0\le |x|+1\le \pi,\ -1<x\le 2\end{cases}$$

$$=\begin{cases}[x], & -2\le x\le -1\\ \sin(|x|+1), & -1<x\le 2\end{cases}$$

Hence, the domain is $[-2,2]$.
Also for $-2\le x\le -1$, $[x]=-2,-1$
and for $-1<x\le 2$, $|x|+1\in[1,3]$
$\Rightarrow\ \sin(|x|+1)\in[\sin 3,1]$
Hence, the range is $\{-2,-1\}\cup[\sin 3,1]$

Also for $y\in[\sin 3,1],[y]=0.1$

Hence, the number of integral points in the range is 4.

**14.**  **(c)**    **15. (c)**

**16.**  **(c)**    Since $y=x+\dfrac{1}{x}$

Clearly the given relation is many one and therefore not an injective relation with domain $R\sim\{0\}$ and range $R\sim(-2,2)$

**17.**  **(b)**    Since, $y=|x|+2$
Clearly, this relation is many-one and so not injective. Here, domain of this solution is $(-\infty,\infty)$ and range is $(2,\infty)$. Hence, this solution is not surjective from R to R whereas it is surjective from R to $[2,\infty)$.

**18.**  **(d)**    Since $y^2=2x-4=2(x-2)$
Clearly there are infinitely many pairs of points having same abscissa in $(2,\infty)$
So, the given relation is one-many relation.
Here, domain of $y^2=2x-4$ is $[2,\infty)$ and range is $(-\infty,\infty)$.
Hence, this relation is surjective from $R\to R$ and also in $R\to[0,\infty)$

**19.**  **(A)–(p); (B)–(q, r); (C)–( p); (D)–(q, r)**
Since $f(g(x))$ is a one-one function.

$f(g(x_1))\ne f(g(x_2))$ whenever $g(x_1)=g(x_2)$
$\Rightarrow\ f(g(x_1))\ne (g(x_2))$ whenever $x_1\ne x_2$
$\Rightarrow\ (g(x_1))\ne (g(x_2))$ whenever $x_1\ne x_2$
$\Rightarrow\ g(x)$ is one-one.
If $f(x)$ is not one-one, then $f(x)=y$ is satisfied by $x=x_1$, $x_2$
$\Rightarrow\ f(x_1)=f(x_2)=y$ also if $g(x)$ is onto, then
let $g(x_1)=x_1$ and $g(x_2)=x_2$
$\Rightarrow\ f(g(x_1))=f(g(x_2))$
$\Rightarrow\ f(g(x))$ cannot be one-one.

**20.**  **A–(s, p); (B)–(q, t); (C)–(r)**
(A)   $\because\ f(x)=\max\{1+\sin x,\ 1,\ 1-\cos x\}$

$$=\begin{cases}1+\sin x, & 0\le x\le \dfrac{3\pi}{4}\\[2mm] 1-\cos x, & \dfrac{3\pi}{4}\le x\le \dfrac{3\pi}{2}\\[2mm] 1, & \dfrac{3\pi}{2}\le x\le 2\pi\end{cases}$$

$$g(x)=\max\{1,|x-1|\}=\begin{cases}1-x, & x\le 0\\ 1, & 0\le x\le 2\\ x-1, & x\ge 2\end{cases}$$

$\therefore\ f(0)=1\Rightarrow g(f(0)=g(1)=1$
$\therefore\ g(f(0))=1$ (S)

and $f(1)=1+\sin 1\qquad\left(\because 0<1<\dfrac{3\pi}{4}\right)$

$\therefore\ g(f(1))=g(1+\sin 1)=1$

$\hspace{4cm}(\because 1<1+\sin 1<2)$

$\therefore\ g(f(1))=1$ (p)

(B)   $\because\ f(g(x))=\ell n\left(\dfrac{1+g(x)}{1-g(x)}\right)$

$\therefore\ f(g(0))=\ell n\left(\dfrac{1+g(0)}{1-g(0)}\right)$

$\hspace{2cm}=\ell n\left(\dfrac{1+0}{1-0}\right)=\ell n\ 1=0$ (q)

and $g\left(f\left(\dfrac{e-1}{e+1}\right)\right)=g\left(\ell n\dfrac{1+\dfrac{e-1}{e+1}}{1-\dfrac{e-1}{e+1}}\right)$

$\hspace{2cm}=g(\ell n\ (e))=g(1)$

$\hspace{2cm}=\dfrac{3+1}{1+3}=\dfrac{4}{4}=1$ (t)

(C)   $f(g(0))=f(0)=1+0^2=1$ (r)
$\hspace{1cm}gf(0)=g(1)=1-1^2=0$
$\hspace{1cm}gf((1))=g(2)=2-2^2=-2$

**1.** **(c)** **Case 1 :** If $0 \le x \le \dfrac{1}{2}$, then

$$\cos^{-1}\left(\dfrac{x}{2}+\dfrac{1}{2}\sqrt{3-3x^2}\right) = \cos^{-1}\left(x.\dfrac{1}{2}+\sqrt{1-x^2}.\dfrac{\sqrt{3}}{2}\right)$$

$$= \cos^{-1} x - \cos^{-1}\dfrac{1}{2}$$

$\therefore$ Equation is

$$\cos^{-1} x + \cos^{-1} x - \cos^{-1}\dfrac{1}{2} = \dfrac{\pi}{3} \Rightarrow x = \dfrac{1}{2}$$

**Case 2 :** If $\dfrac{1}{2} \le x \le 1$, then

$$\cos^{-1}\left(\dfrac{x}{2}+\dfrac{1}{2}\sqrt{3-3x^2}\right) = \cos^{-1}\dfrac{1}{2} - \cos^{-1} x$$

$\therefore$ Equation is $\cos^{-1} x + \cos^{-1}\dfrac{1}{2} - \cos^{-1} x = \dfrac{\pi}{3}$,

which is identity

Hence the identity holds good for $x \in \left[\dfrac{1}{2},1\right]$.

**2.** **(b)** The given relation is possible when

$$a - \dfrac{a^2}{3} + \dfrac{a^3}{9} + ... = 1 + b + b^2 + ...$$

Also

$$-1 \le a - \dfrac{a^2}{3} + \dfrac{a^3}{9} + ... \le 1 \ \& \ -1 \le 1+b+b^2+... \le 1$$

$$\Rightarrow |b| < 1 \Rightarrow |a| < 3 \text{ and } \dfrac{a}{1+\dfrac{a}{3}} = \dfrac{1}{1-b}$$

$$\Rightarrow \dfrac{3a}{a+3} = \dfrac{1}{1-b}, \text{ there are infinitely many solution.}$$

But in given options it is satisfied only when $a = 1$

and $b = -\dfrac{1}{3}$.

**3.** **(b)** Since the equation

$$a_1 + a_2 \sin x + a_3 \cos x + a_4 \sin 2x + a_5 \cos 2x = 0$$

holds for all values of $x$,

$$a_1 + a_3 + a_5 = 0 \qquad \text{(on putting } x = 0)$$
$$a_1 - a_3 + a_5 = 0 \qquad \text{(on putting } x = \pi)$$
$$\Rightarrow a_3 = 0 \text{ and } a_1 + a_5 = 0 \qquad ...(1)$$

Putting $x = \dfrac{\pi}{2}$ and $\dfrac{3\pi}{2}$, we get

$$a_1 + a_2 - a_5 = 0 \text{ and } \quad a_1 - a_2 - a_5 = 0 \qquad ...(2)$$
$$\Rightarrow a_2 = 0 \text{ and } a_1 - a_5 = 0 \quad (1) \text{ and } (2) \text{ give}$$
$$a_1 = a_2 = a_3 = a_5 = 0$$

The given equation reduces to $a_4 \sin 2x = 0$. This is true for all values of $x$, therefore $a_4 = 0$

Hence, $a_1 = a_2 = a_3 = a_4 = a_5 = 0$

Thus the number of 5-tuples is one.

**4.** **(d)** $x = n\pi - \tan^{-1} 3 \Rightarrow \tan^{-1} 3 = n\pi - x$

$$\Rightarrow \tan(n\pi - x) = 3 \Rightarrow -\tan x = 3$$

$$\Rightarrow \tan 2x = \dfrac{2\tan x}{1-\tan^2 x} = \dfrac{3}{4} \text{ and}$$

$$\cos x = \pm\dfrac{1}{\sqrt{1+\tan^2 x}} = \pm\dfrac{1}{\sqrt{10}}$$

on substituting these value in the given equation we

find only $\cos x = -\dfrac{1}{\sqrt{10}}$ satisfies the equation, so

that the given equation holds for values of $x$ for

which $\tan x = -3$ and $\cos x = -\dfrac{1}{\sqrt{10}}$ which is

possible if $x$ lies in the second quadrant only and so $n$ must be an odd integer.

**5.** **(d)** $T_r = \cot^{-1}\left(\dfrac{4r^2+3}{4}\right) = \tan^{-1}\dfrac{1}{1+r^2-\dfrac{1}{4}}$

$$= \tan^{-1}\dfrac{\left(r+\dfrac{1}{2}\right)-\left(r-\dfrac{1}{2}\right)}{1+\left(r+\dfrac{1}{2}\right)\left(r-\dfrac{1}{2}\right)}$$

$$= \tan^{-1}\left(r+\dfrac{1}{2}\right) - \tan^{-1}\left(r-\dfrac{1}{2}\right)$$

$$S_n = \sum T_r = \tan^{-1}\left(n+\dfrac{1}{2}\right) - \tan^{-1}\dfrac{1}{2} = \tan^{-1}\left(\dfrac{4n}{2n+5}\right)$$

$$S_\infty = \lim_{n\to\infty} S_n = \tan^{-1} 2 = \cot^{-1}\dfrac{1}{2}.$$

**6.** **(a,b,c)** If we put $x = \tan\theta$, the given equality becomes

$$\tan^{-1} y = 4\theta$$

$$\Rightarrow y = \tan 4\theta = \dfrac{2\tan 2\theta}{1-\tan^2 2\theta} = \dfrac{2\left[\dfrac{2\tan\theta}{1-\tan^2\theta}\right]}{1-\left(\dfrac{2\tan\theta}{1-\tan^2\theta}\right)^2}$$

$$= \frac{2 \times 2x(1-x^2)}{(1-x^2)^2 - 4x^2} = \frac{4x(1-x^2)}{1-6x^2+x^4}$$

so that $y$ is finite if $x^4 - 6x^2 + 1 \neq 0$

$$\Rightarrow x^2 \neq \frac{6 \pm \sqrt{36-4}}{2} \neq 3 \pm 2\sqrt{2}$$

**7.** **(a, c, d)** The given equation holds if $x^2 + x + 1 = ax + 1$ and

$-1 \leq x^2 + x + 1 \leq 1$

$\Rightarrow x(x+1+a) = 0$ and $-1 \leq x \leq 0$

$\Rightarrow x = 0$ or $a - 1$ and $-1 \leq x \leq 0$

$\therefore x = 0$ is one solution and for another different

solution $-1 \leq a - 1 < 0$

$\Rightarrow 0 \leq a < 1$. So only integral value a can have

is 0.

**8.** **(a,c,d)** The equation holds if

$$\sin^2 \theta + 2\sin \theta + 2 = 4^{\sec^2 \phi} + 1$$

Now LHS $= (\sin \theta + 1)^2 + 1 \leq 5$ and RHS $\geq 5$

$(\because \sec^2 \phi \geq 1)$

So, LHS = RHS $\Rightarrow \sin \theta = -1$ and $\sec^2 \phi = 1$

**9.** **(a, b, d)**

$\tan^{-1}(x-1) + \tan^{-1}(x) + \tan^{-1}(x+1) = \tan^{-1} 3x$

$\Rightarrow \tan^{-1}(x-1) + \tan^{-1}(x) = \tan^{-1} 3x - \tan^{-1}(x+1)$

$$\Rightarrow \tan^{-1}\left[\frac{(x-1)+x}{1-(x-1)(x)}\right] = \tan^{-1}\left[\frac{3x-(x+1)}{1+3x(x+1)}\right]$$

$$\Rightarrow \frac{2x-1}{1-x^2+x} = \frac{2x-1}{1+3x^2+3x}$$

$$\Rightarrow (1-x^2+x)(2x-1) = (1+3x^2+3x)(2x-1)$$

$$\Rightarrow x = 0, \pm\frac{1}{2}$$

**10.** **(1)** $0 \leq x^2 + x + 1 \leq 1$ and $0 \leq x^2 + x \leq 1$

$\therefore x = -1, 0$

for $x = -1$

L.H.S $= 2\sin^{-1} 1 + \cos^{-1} 1 + 0 = \frac{3\pi}{2}$

$\therefore x = -1$ is a solution.

For $x = 0$, L.H.S. $= 2\sin^{-1} 1 + \cos^{-1} 0 = \frac{3\pi}{2}$

$\therefore x = 0$ is a solution.

$\therefore$ sum of the solutions $= -1$.

**11.** **(1)**

$$-\cos\left[\cos^{-1}\left(-\frac{\sqrt{3}}{2}\right) + \frac{\pi}{6}\right] = -\cos\left[\pi - \cos^{-1}\left(\frac{\sqrt{3}}{2}\right) + \frac{\pi}{6}\right]$$

$$[\because \cos^{-1}(-x) = \pi - \cos^{-1} x]$$

$$= -\cos\left(\pi - \frac{\pi}{6} + \frac{\pi}{6}\right) = -1\cos \pi = -(-1) = 1$$

**12.** **(1)** We know that, $\sin^{-1} y + \cos^{-1} y = \frac{\pi}{2}, |y| \leq 1$

$\therefore$ According to question

$$x - \frac{x^2}{2} + \frac{x^3}{3} - \ldots = x^2 - \frac{x^4}{2} + \frac{x^6}{4} \ldots$$

$$\Rightarrow \frac{x}{1+\frac{x}{2}} = \frac{x}{1+\frac{x^2}{2}}, \quad (\because 0 < |x| < \sqrt{2}) \Rightarrow \frac{x}{2+x} = \frac{x^2}{2+x^2}$$

$\Rightarrow 2x + x^3 = 2x^2 + x^3 \Rightarrow x = x^2$

But $x \neq 0$, hence $x = 1$

**13.** **(3)** $\sin^{-1}\left(\frac{x}{5}\right) + \mathrm{cosec}^{-1}\left(\frac{5}{4}\right) = \frac{\pi}{2}$ ... (i)

Let $\theta = \mathrm{cosec}^{-1}\left(\frac{5}{4}\right); \quad \mathrm{cosec}\,\theta = \frac{5}{4}$

$\therefore \sin \theta = \frac{1}{\mathrm{cosec}\,\theta} = \frac{4}{5} \Rightarrow \theta = \sin^{-1}\left(\frac{4}{5}\right)$ ... (ii)

We know that $\sin\frac{\pi}{2} = 1 \quad \therefore \frac{\pi}{2} = \sin^{-1}(1)$ ... (iii)

From eq. (i), $\sin^{-1}\left(\frac{x}{5}\right) = \frac{\pi}{2} - \mathrm{cosec}^{-1}\left(\frac{5}{4}\right) = \frac{\pi}{2} - \theta$

Using eq. (ii) and eq. (iii)

$$\sin^{-1}\left(\frac{x}{5}\right) = \sin^{-1}(1) - \sin^{-1}\left(\frac{4}{5}\right) = \sin^{-1}\left(\sqrt{1-\frac{16}{25}} - \frac{4}{5}\sqrt{1-1}\right)$$

(Using Formula of $\sin^{-1} A - \sin^{-1} B$)

$$\Rightarrow \sin^{-1}\frac{x}{5} = \sin^{-1}\left(\frac{3}{5} - 0\right)$$

$$\Rightarrow \sin^{-1}\frac{x}{5} = \sin^{-1}\frac{3}{5} \Rightarrow x = 3$$

**14.** **(4)** We have $\cos^{-1} x - \cos^{-1}\frac{y}{2} = \alpha$

$$\Rightarrow x = \cos\left(\cos^{-1}\frac{y}{2} + \alpha\right)$$

$$= \cos\left(\cos^{-1}\frac{y}{2}\right)\cos \alpha - \sin\left(\cos^{-1}\frac{y}{2}\right)\sin \alpha$$

$$\Rightarrow 2x = y\cos \alpha - \sin \alpha\sqrt{4-y^2}$$

$$\Rightarrow 2x - y\cos \alpha = -\sin \alpha\sqrt{4-y^2}$$

Squaring, we get

$4x^2 + y^2\cos^2 \alpha - 4xy\cos \alpha = 4\sin^2 \alpha - y^2\sin^2 \alpha$

$\Rightarrow 4x^2 - 4xy\cos \alpha + y^2 = 4\sin^2 \alpha$

**15.** **(b)** Extreme value of $\sin^{-1} x = \frac{5\pi}{2}$ and $\cos^{-1} y = 3\pi$

$$\Rightarrow \sin^{-1} x + \cos^{-1} y \leq \frac{11\pi}{2}$$

$\therefore$ Only 1 possible ordered pairs $(1, -1)$.

**16. (b)** We have $2\theta = \sin^{-1}(\sin 2\theta)$ [let $\sin^{-1} x = \theta$].

$$\Rightarrow \frac{3\pi}{2} \le 2\theta \le \frac{5\pi}{2} \Rightarrow \frac{3\pi}{4} \le \theta \le \frac{5\pi}{4}$$

$$\Rightarrow -\frac{1}{\sqrt{2}} \le x \le \frac{1}{\sqrt{2}}.$$

**17. (a)** $\sin^{-1}\left(x - \frac{x^2}{2} + \frac{x^3}{3}\ldots\right) + \cos^{-1}\left(x^2 - \frac{x^4}{2} + \frac{x^6}{4}\ldots\right)$

$$= \frac{\pi}{2}$$

$$\Rightarrow \cos^{-1}\left(x^2 - \frac{x^4}{2} + \frac{x^6}{4}\ldots\right)$$

$$= \frac{\pi}{2} - \sin^{-1}\left(x - \frac{x^2}{2} + \frac{x^3}{4}\ldots\right)$$

$$\Rightarrow \cos^{-1}\left(x^2 - \frac{x^4}{2} + \frac{x^6}{4}\ldots\right)$$

$$= \cos^{-1}\left(x - \frac{x^2}{2} + \frac{x^3}{4}\ldots\right)$$

$$\Rightarrow x^2 - \frac{x^4}{2} + \frac{x^6}{4}\ldots = x - \frac{x^2}{2} + \frac{x^3}{4}\ldots$$

On both sides we have G.P. of infinite terms

$$\therefore \quad \frac{x^2}{1 - \left(\dfrac{-x^2}{2}\right)} = \frac{x}{1 - \left(\dfrac{-x}{2}\right)} \Rightarrow \frac{2x^2}{2 + x^2} = \frac{2x}{2 + x}$$

$$\Rightarrow 2x + x^3 = 2x^2 + x^3 \Rightarrow x(x - 1) = 0$$

$$\Rightarrow x = 0, 1 \text{ but } 0 < |x| < \sqrt{2} \Rightarrow x = 1$$

**18. (c)** $\sin[\cot^{-1}(1 + x)] = \cos(\tan^{-1} x)$

$$\Rightarrow \sin\left[\sin^{-1}\left(\frac{1}{\sqrt{1 + (1 + x)^2}}\right)\right]$$

$$= \cos\left[\cos^{-1}\left(\frac{1}{\sqrt{1 + x^2}}\right)\right]$$

$$\Rightarrow \frac{1}{\sqrt{1 + (1 + x)^2}} = \frac{1}{\sqrt{1 + x^2}}$$

$$\Rightarrow 1 + 1 + 2x + x^2 = 1 + x^2$$

$$\Rightarrow 2x + 1 = 0$$

$$\Rightarrow x = \frac{-1}{2}$$

**19. (d)** $\cot^{-1}\left(1 + \displaystyle\sum_{k=1}^{n} 2k\right) = \cot^{-1}[1 + n(n + 1)]$

$$= \tan^{-1}\left[\frac{(n + 1) - n}{1 + (n + 1)n}\right] = \tan^{-1}(n + 1) - \tan^{-1} n$$

$$\therefore \quad \sum_{n=1}^{23}[\tan^{-1}(n + 1) - \tan^{-1} n]$$

$$= \tan^{-1} 24 - \tan^{-1} 1$$

$$= \tan^{-1}\frac{23}{25}$$

$$\therefore \quad \cot\left[\sum_{n=1}^{23}\cot^{-1}\left(1 + \sum_{k=1}^{n} 2k\right)\right]$$

$$= \cot\left[\tan^{-1}\frac{23}{25}\right] = \frac{25}{23} > 1$$

**20.** $A \to (q, r, s); (B) \to (q); (C) \to (r, s); (D) \to (p)$

(A) $(\sin^{-1} x)^2 + (\sin^{-1} y)^2 = \dfrac{\pi^2}{2}$

$$\Rightarrow (\sin^{-1} x)^2 = (\sin^{-1} y)^2 = \frac{\pi}{4}$$

$$\Rightarrow \sin^{-1} x = \pm\frac{\pi}{2}, \sin^{-1} y = \pm\frac{\pi}{2}$$

$$\Rightarrow x = \pm 1 \text{ and } y = \pm 1$$

$$\Rightarrow x^3 + y^3 = -2, 0, 2$$

(B) $(\cos^{-1} x)^2 + (\cos^{-1} y)^2 = 2\pi^2$

$$\Rightarrow (\cos^{-1} x)^2 = (\cos^{-1} y)^2 = \pi$$

$$\Rightarrow x = y = -1$$

$$\Rightarrow x^5 + y^5 = -2$$

(C) $(\sin^{-1} x)^2 (\cos^{-1} y)^2 = \dfrac{\pi^4}{4}$

$$\Rightarrow (\sin^{-1} x)^2 = \frac{\pi^2}{4} \text{ and } (\cos^{-1} y)^2 = \pi^2$$

$$\Rightarrow (\sin^{-1} x) = \pm\frac{\pi}{2} \text{ and } (\cos^{-1} y) = \pi$$

$$\Rightarrow x = \pm 1 \text{ and } y = -1$$

$$\Rightarrow |x - y| = 0, 2$$

(D) $|\sin^{-1} x - \sin^{-1} y| = \pi$

$$\Rightarrow \sin^{-1} x = -\frac{\pi}{2} \text{ and } \sin^{-1} y = \frac{\pi}{2}$$

or $\sin^{-1} x = \dfrac{\pi}{2}$ and $\sin^{-1} y = -\dfrac{\pi}{2}$

$$\Rightarrow x^y = 1^{(-1)} \text{ or } (-1)^1 = 1 \text{ or } -1$$

**1.** **(b)** Given that $X = A_1 + 3$

$$A_3^2 + \dots (2n-1)\left(A_{2n-1}\right)^{2n-1}$$

We know that if A is a skew-symmetric matrix then $A^T = -A$

$$X^T = -\left[A_1 + 3A_3^3 + \dots (2n-1)\left(A_{2n-1}\right)^{2r-1}\right]$$

$= -X$, so skew-symmetric

**2.** **(a)** We have, $BC = CB$, and

$A^{N+1} = (B+C)^{N+1}$

$= {}^{N+1}C_0 B^{N+1} + {}^{N+1}C_1 B^N C + {}^{N+1}C_2 B^{N-1}C^2 +$

$\qquad\qquad \dots + {}^{N+1}C_r B^{N+1-r}C^r + \dots$

But given that $C^2 = 0 \Rightarrow C^3 = C^4 = \dots = C^r = 0$

Hence, $A^{N+1} = {}^{N+1}C_N B^{N+1} + {}^{N+1}C_1 B^N C$

$= B^{N+1} + (N+1)B^N C$

$= B^N[B + (N+1)C]$

Thus $K = N$

**3.** **(d)** Consider $AA' = \begin{bmatrix} a & b & c \\ c & a & b \\ b & c & a \end{bmatrix}\begin{bmatrix} a & c & b \\ b & a & c \\ c & b & a \end{bmatrix}$

$$= \begin{bmatrix} a^2 + b^2 + c^2 & ac + ab + bc & ab + bc + ca \\ ca + ab + bc & a^2 + b^2 + c^2 & cb + ba + ac \\ ab + cb + ac & bc + ca + ab & a^2 + b^2 + c^2 \end{bmatrix} = I$$

$\therefore \quad a^2 + b^2 + c^2 = 1$ and $ab + bc + ca = 0$.

$\Rightarrow \quad a + b + c = \pm 1$

So a, b, c are the roots of the equation

$x^2 \pm x^2 + abc = 0$

**4.** **(a)** We have,

$AB = BA \Rightarrow B'A' = (AB)' \Rightarrow AB$ is symmetric

Also, $ABA^{-1} = BAA^{-1} = B$

$\Rightarrow A^{-1}ABA^{-1} = A^{-1}B \Rightarrow BA^{-1} = A^{-1}B$

$\Rightarrow (A^{-1}B)' = (BA^{-1})' \Rightarrow (A^{-1})'B' = A^{-1}B$

(Since, $A^{-1}$ is symmetric)

So $A^{-1}B$ is a symmetric matrix.

**5.** **(c)** We have,

$A^2 + B^2 = AA + BB = A(BA) + B(AB)$

$(\therefore \ AB = B$ and $BA + A)$

$= (AB)A + (BA)B$

$= BA + AB = A + B \ (\therefore \ AB = B$ and $BA = A)$

**6.** **(b)** We have

$$A^2 = \begin{bmatrix} \alpha & 0 \\ 1 & 1 \end{bmatrix}\begin{bmatrix} \alpha & 0 \\ 1 & 1 \end{bmatrix} = \begin{bmatrix} \alpha^2 & 0 \\ \alpha+1 & 1 \end{bmatrix} = \begin{bmatrix} 9 & a \\ b & c \end{bmatrix}$$

$\Rightarrow$ we get $\alpha^2 = 9$

$\Rightarrow$ $\alpha = \pm 3$ and $a = 0$, $c = 1$, $b = a + 1 = 3 + 1 = 4$

or $b = -3 + 1 = -2$

So $a + b + c = (0 + 4 + 1) = 5$ or $(0 - 2 + 1) = -1$

**7.** **(a, d)** $A = \begin{bmatrix} 2 & 3 \\ -1 & 2 \end{bmatrix}$, $f(x) = x^2 - 4x + 7$

$f(A) = A^2 - 4A + 7I_2$

$$= \begin{bmatrix} 2 & 3 \\ -1 & 2 \end{bmatrix}\begin{bmatrix} 2 & 3 \\ -1 & 2 \end{bmatrix} - 4\begin{bmatrix} 2 & 3 \\ -1 & 2 \end{bmatrix} + 7\begin{bmatrix} 1 & 0 \\ 0 & 1 \end{bmatrix}$$

$$= \begin{bmatrix} (4-3) & (6+6) \\ (-2-2) & (-3+4) \end{bmatrix} + \begin{bmatrix} -8 & -12 \\ 4 & -8 \end{bmatrix} + \begin{bmatrix} 7 & 0 \\ 0 & 7 \end{bmatrix}$$

$$= \begin{bmatrix} 0 & 0 \\ 0 & 0 \end{bmatrix} = 0$$

Thus, $A^2 - 4A + 7I_2 = 0$

$\Rightarrow A^2 = 4A - 7I_2$

$A^3 = A(4A - 7I_2) = 4A^2 - 7A = 4(4A - 7I_2) - 7A$

$\qquad = 16A - 28I_2 - 7A = 9A - 28I_2$

$A^4 = A(9A - 28I_2) = 9A^2 - 28A$

$= 9(4A - 7I_2) - 28A = 8A - 63I_2$

$A^5 = A(8A - 63I_2) = 8A^2 - 63A = 8(4A - 7I_2) - 63A$

$= -31A - 56I_2$

Put, $A = \begin{bmatrix} 2 & 3 \\ -1 & 2 \end{bmatrix}$, $I_2 = \begin{bmatrix} 1 & 0 \\ 0 & 1 \end{bmatrix}$

$$A^5 = -31\begin{bmatrix} 2 & 3 \\ -1 & 2 \end{bmatrix} - 56\begin{bmatrix} 1 & 0 \\ 0 & 1 \end{bmatrix}$$

$$= \begin{bmatrix} -62 & -93 \\ 31 & -62 \end{bmatrix} + \begin{bmatrix} -56 & 0 \\ 0 & -56 \end{bmatrix}$$

$$= \begin{bmatrix} -118 & -93 \\ 31 & -118 \end{bmatrix}$$

**8.** **(b, c)** For $PP' = I$

$$\begin{bmatrix} 2/3 & 3k & a \\ -1/3 & -4k & b \\ 2/3 & -5k & c \end{bmatrix}\begin{bmatrix} 2/3 & -1/3 & 2/3 \\ 3k & -4k & -5k \\ a & b & c \end{bmatrix}$$

$$= \begin{bmatrix} \dfrac{4}{9}+9k^2+a^2 & -\dfrac{2}{9}-12k^2+ab & \dfrac{4}{9}-15k^2+ac \\[2mm] -\dfrac{2}{9}-12k^2+ab & \dfrac{1}{9}+16k^2+b^2 & -\dfrac{2}{9}+20k^2+bc \\[2mm] \dfrac{4}{9}-15k^2+ac & -\dfrac{2}{9}+20k^2+bc & \dfrac{4}{9}+25k^2+c^2 \end{bmatrix}$$

$$= \begin{bmatrix} 1 & 0 & 0 \\ 0 & 1 & 0 \\ 0 & 0 & 1 \end{bmatrix}$$

$$\frac{4}{9}+9k^2+a^2=1$$

$$-\frac{2}{9}-12k^2+ab=0$$

$$\frac{4}{9}-15k^2+ac=0$$

$$\frac{1}{9}+16k^2+b^2=1$$

$$-\frac{2}{9}+20k^2+bc=0$$

$$\frac{4}{9}+25k^2+c^2=1$$

On solving these equations we get

$$ab=\frac{208}{450},\ bc=-\frac{80}{450},\ ac=\frac{-65}{450}$$

and $a^2=\dfrac{169}{450},\ b^2=\dfrac{256}{450},\ c^2=\dfrac{25}{450}$

Hence, $a=\pm\dfrac{13}{5\sqrt{2}},\ b=\pm\dfrac{16}{5\sqrt{2}},\ c=\pm\dfrac{1}{3\sqrt{2}}$

**9.** **(a, b, c)** We have,

$$A^2=\begin{bmatrix} i & 0 \\ 0 & i \end{bmatrix}\begin{bmatrix} i & 0 \\ 0 & i \end{bmatrix}=\begin{bmatrix} i^2 & 0 \\ 0 & i^2 \end{bmatrix}=\begin{bmatrix} -1 & 0 \\ 0 & -1 \end{bmatrix}$$

$$A^3=\begin{bmatrix} -1 & 0 \\ 0 & -1 \end{bmatrix}\begin{bmatrix} i & 0 \\ 0 & i \end{bmatrix}=\begin{bmatrix} -i & 0 \\ 0 & -i \end{bmatrix}$$

$$A^4=\begin{bmatrix} -1 & 0 \\ 0 & -1 \end{bmatrix}\begin{bmatrix} -i & 0 \\ 0 & -i \end{bmatrix}=\begin{bmatrix} 1 & 0 \\ 0 & 1 \end{bmatrix}$$

$$A^{75}=A^3=\begin{bmatrix} -i & 0 \\ 0 & -i \end{bmatrix}$$

**10.** **(a, d)** Let $A=\begin{bmatrix} 0 & 2\beta & \gamma \\ \alpha & \beta & -\gamma \\ \alpha & -\beta & \gamma \end{bmatrix}$

Then $A'=\begin{bmatrix} 0 & \alpha & \alpha \\ 2\beta & \beta & -\beta \\ \gamma & -\gamma & \gamma \end{bmatrix}$

Given that, A is orthogonal. $\quad \therefore AA'=I$

$$\Rightarrow \begin{bmatrix} 0 & 2\beta & \gamma \\ \alpha & \beta & -\gamma \\ \alpha & -\beta & \gamma \end{bmatrix}\begin{bmatrix} 0 & \alpha & \alpha \\ 2\beta & \beta & -\beta \\ \gamma & -\gamma & \gamma \end{bmatrix}=\begin{bmatrix} 1 & 0 & 0 \\ 0 & 1 & 0 \\ 0 & 0 & 1 \end{bmatrix}$$

$$\Rightarrow \begin{bmatrix} 4\beta^2+\gamma^2 & 2\beta^2-\gamma^2 & -2\beta^2+\gamma^2 \\ 2\beta^2-\gamma^2 & \alpha^2+\beta^2+\gamma^2 & \alpha^2-\beta^2-\gamma^2 \\ -2\beta^2+\gamma^2 & \alpha^2-\beta^2-\gamma^2 & \alpha^2+\beta^2+\gamma^2 \end{bmatrix}$$

$$= \begin{bmatrix} 1 & 0 & 0 \\ 0 & 1 & 0 \\ 0 & 0 & 1 \end{bmatrix}$$

Equating the corresponding elements, we have

$$\left.\begin{array}{l} 4\beta^2+\gamma^2=1 \\ 2\beta^2-\gamma^2=0 \end{array}\right\} \Rightarrow \beta=\pm\frac{1}{\sqrt{6}},\ \gamma=\pm\frac{1}{\sqrt{3}}$$

$$\alpha^2+\beta^2+\gamma^2=1 \ \Rightarrow \alpha^2+\frac{1}{6}+\frac{1}{3}=1$$

$$\Rightarrow \alpha=\pm\frac{1}{\sqrt{2}}$$

**11.** **(0)** As $A^2=0, A^k=0\ \forall\ k\geq 2$.

Thus, $(A+I)^{50}=I+50A$

$\Rightarrow (A+I)^{50}-50A=I$

$\therefore a=1, b=0, c=0, d=1$

abc + abd + bcd + acd = 0

**12.** **(2)** Consider $A^2 = \begin{bmatrix} -5 & -8 & 0 \\ 3 & 5 & 0 \\ 1 & 2 & -1 \end{bmatrix}\begin{bmatrix} -5 & -8 & 0 \\ 3 & 5 & 0 \\ 1 & 2 & -1 \end{bmatrix}$

$$= \begin{bmatrix} 25-24+0 & 40-40+0 & 0+0+0 \\ -15+15+0 & -24+25+0 & 0+0+0 \\ -5+6-1 & -8+10-2 & 0+0+1 \end{bmatrix}$$

$$= \begin{bmatrix} 1 & 0 & 0 \\ 0 & 1 & 0 \\ 0 & 0 & 1 \end{bmatrix} = I$$

So $A^3 = \begin{bmatrix} -5 & -8 & 0 \\ 3 & 5 & 0 \\ 1 & 2 & -1 \end{bmatrix}$ and so on

$tr(A) + tr(A^2)\, tr(A^3) +...+tr(A^{100})$
$= (-1)+(3)+(-1)+(3)+...+(-1)+(3) = 200$

**13.** **(4)** Given that $A^T A = I$ so

$$\begin{bmatrix} a & b & c \\ b & c & a \\ c & a & b \end{bmatrix}\begin{bmatrix} a & b & c \\ b & c & a \\ c & a & b \end{bmatrix} = \begin{bmatrix} 1 & 0 & 0 \\ 0 & 1 & 0 \\ 0 & 0 & 1 \end{bmatrix}$$

$$\Rightarrow \begin{bmatrix} a^2+b^2+c^2 & ab+bc+ca & ab+bc+ca \\ ab+bc+ca & a^2+b^2+c^2 & ab+bc+ca \\ ab+bc+ca & ab+bc+ca & a^2+b^2+c^2 \end{bmatrix}$$

$$= \begin{bmatrix} 1 & 0 & 0 \\ 0 & 1 & 0 \\ 0 & 0 & 1 \end{bmatrix}$$

$\Rightarrow \quad a^2 + b^2 + c^2 = 1 \qquad\qquad ... (i)$
And $ab + bc + ca = 0 \qquad\qquad ..(ii)$
We know
$a^3 + b^3 + c^3 = (a + b + c)$
$(a^2 + b^2 + c^2 - ab - bc - ca) + 3abc$
$= (a + b + c) + 3 \qquad\qquad ...(iii)$
Now, $(a + b + c)^2 = a^2 + b^2 + c^2 + 2(ab + bc + ca)$
$= 1 + 2.0 = 1$
$\Rightarrow \quad a + b + c = 1$ (Since, a, b, c are real positive number)
Now, From Eq. (iii), $a^3 + b^3 + c^3 = 4$

**14.** **(2)** Given that AB = BA

So $\begin{bmatrix} a_{11} & a_{12} \\ a_{21} & a_{22} \end{bmatrix}\begin{bmatrix} 1 & 1 \\ 2 & 1 \end{bmatrix} = \begin{bmatrix} 1 & 1 \\ 2 & 1 \end{bmatrix}\begin{bmatrix} a_{11} & a_{12} \\ a_{21} & a_{22} \end{bmatrix}$

So $a_{11} + 2a_{12} = a_{11} + a_{21} \qquad ...(i)$
$a_{11} + a_{12} = a_{12} + a_{22} \qquad ...(ii)$
$a_{21} + 2a_{22} = 2a_{11} + a_{21} \qquad ...(iii)$
$a_{21} + a_{22} = 2a_{12} + a_{22} \qquad ...(iv)$
On solving these we get

$$\frac{a_{11}}{a_{12}} = \frac{\sqrt{2}}{1}$$

$$\left(\frac{a_{11}}{a_{12}}\right)^2 = 2$$

**15.** **(0)** Since $A = \begin{bmatrix} 1 & 1 \\ -1 & 1 \end{bmatrix}$ so $A^2 - 2A + 2I = 0$

$B = A^{10} - A^9 + 2A^8 - A^7 + 4A^6 - 2A^5 + 4A^4$
$\qquad + A^3 - A^2 + A + I = (A^2 - 2A + 2I)\, f(A) + (A - I)$
so $B = A - 1$

$$= \begin{bmatrix} 1 & 1 \\ -1 & 1 \end{bmatrix} - \begin{bmatrix} 1 & 0 \\ 0 & 1 \end{bmatrix} = \begin{bmatrix} 0 & 1 \\ -1 & 0 \end{bmatrix} = \begin{bmatrix} a & b \\ c & d \end{bmatrix}$$

So $a + b + c + d = 0$

**16.** **(a)** Trace of the matrix A is $a + b$

$$= \sum_{k=1}^{9}\left(a_k + b_k\right) = 10 \sum_{k=1}^{9} C_k^{10} = 10(2^{10} - 2)$$

$= 10220$
Sum of digits is 5

**17.** **(b)** $a = \sum_{k=1}^{9} k\,(^{10}C_k) = \sum_{k=1}^{10} k\,(^{10}C_k)$

$\qquad\qquad\qquad - 10(^{10}C_{10}) = 10(2^9) - 10 = 10(2^9 - 1)$
Similarly, $b = 10(2^9 - 1)$
Thus, $ab = 100(2^9 - 1)^2$
Largest prime factor is 511

**For Questions 18 & 19**
Consider

$$A_1.A_2 = \begin{bmatrix} a_0 & 0 \\ 0 & a_1 \end{bmatrix}\begin{bmatrix} a_1 & 0 \\ 0 & a_2 \end{bmatrix} = \begin{bmatrix} a_0 a_1 & 0 \\ 0 & a_1 a_2 \end{bmatrix}$$

And so on.

Given that $\sum_{k=1}^{n-1} A_k \cdot A_{k+1} = \begin{bmatrix} a & 0 \\ 0 & b \end{bmatrix}$

$a = a_0 a_1 + a_1 a_2 + ... + a_{n-2} a_{n-1} = a_n a_1 + a_{n-1} a_2 + ... + a_2 a_{n-1}$
= number of ways of selecting $(n + 1)$ persons out of $n$ men and $n$
women = $^{2n}C_{n+1}$
Similarly $b = {}^{2n}C_{n+1}$

**18. (a)          19. (a)**

**20.    (A) $\to$ (s); (B) $\to$ (r); (C) $\to$ (q); (D) $\to$ (p)**

(A)  Let $X = \begin{bmatrix} a & b \\ c & d \end{bmatrix}$ then

$\begin{bmatrix} 1 & -4 \\ 3 & -2 \end{bmatrix} \begin{bmatrix} a & b \\ c & d \end{bmatrix} = \begin{bmatrix} -16 & -6 \\ 7 & 2 \end{bmatrix}$

Or  $\begin{bmatrix} a-4c & b-4d \\ 3a-2c & 3b-2d \end{bmatrix} = \begin{bmatrix} -16 & -6 \\ 7 & 2 \end{bmatrix}$

On equating we get $a = 6$, $b = 2$, $c = 11/2$ and $d = 2$
So trace of the matrix = $6 + 2 = 8$

(B)  Given

$\begin{bmatrix} 2 & -1 \\ 1 & 0 \\ -3 & 4 \end{bmatrix} \begin{bmatrix} l & m & n \\ x & y & z \end{bmatrix} = \begin{bmatrix} -1 & -8 & -10 \\ 1 & -2 & -5 \\ 9 & 22 & 15 \end{bmatrix}$

$\begin{bmatrix} 2l-x & 2m-y & 2n-z \\ l & m & n \\ -3l+4x & -3m+4y & -3n+4z \end{bmatrix}$

$= \begin{bmatrix} -1 & -8 & -10 \\ 1 & -2 & -5 \\ 9 & 22 & 15 \end{bmatrix}$

$\Rightarrow$  $2l-x=-1, 2m-y=-8, 2n-z=-10, l=1, m=-2, n=-5$
$\Rightarrow$  $x=3, y=4, z=0, l=1, m=-2, n=-5$

$\Rightarrow \begin{bmatrix} l & m & n \\ x & y & z \end{bmatrix} = \begin{bmatrix} 1 & -2 & -5 \\ 3 & 4 & 0 \end{bmatrix}$

So $l + m + n + x + y + z = 1 - 2 - 5 + 3 + 4 + 0 = 1$

(C)  We have $\begin{bmatrix} 1 & x & 1 \end{bmatrix} \begin{bmatrix} 1 & 3 & 2 \\ 0 & 5 & 1 \\ 0 & 3 & 2 \end{bmatrix} \begin{bmatrix} 1 \\ 1 \\ x \end{bmatrix} = 0$

$\Rightarrow \begin{bmatrix} 1 & 5x+6 & x+4 \end{bmatrix} \begin{bmatrix} 1 \\ 1 \\ x \end{bmatrix} = 0$

$\Rightarrow \begin{bmatrix} 1 + 5x + 6 + x^2 + 4x \end{bmatrix} = 0$

$\Rightarrow x^2 + 9x + 7 = 0$

$\Rightarrow x = \dfrac{-9 \pm \sqrt{53}}{2}$

(D)  We multiply both sides by $\begin{bmatrix} 5 & 0 \\ -a & 5 \end{bmatrix}$ then

$\begin{bmatrix} 1/5 & 0 \\ -a/25+5x & 1/5 \end{bmatrix} = \begin{bmatrix} 5 & 0 \\ -a & 5 \end{bmatrix}^{-1}$

Again multiply both sides by $\begin{bmatrix} 5 & 0 \\ -a & 5 \end{bmatrix}$,

$\begin{bmatrix} 1/5 & 0 \\ -a/25+5x & 1/5 \end{bmatrix} \begin{bmatrix} 5 & 0 \\ -a & 5 \end{bmatrix} = \begin{bmatrix} 1 & 0 \\ 0 & 1 \end{bmatrix}$

Or  $\dfrac{-2a}{5} + 25x = 0$

Or  $\dfrac{125x}{a} = 2$

**1.** **(b)** Given $\begin{vmatrix} 1+x & 1 & 1 \\ 1+y & 1+2y & 1 \\ 1+z & 1+z & 1+3z \end{vmatrix}$

$= xyz \begin{vmatrix} 1+\dfrac{1}{x} & \dfrac{1}{x} & \dfrac{1}{x} \\ 1+\dfrac{1}{y} & 2+\dfrac{1}{y} & \dfrac{1}{y} \\ 1+\dfrac{1}{z} & 1+\dfrac{1}{z} & 3+\dfrac{1}{z} \end{vmatrix}$

$= xyz\left(3+\dfrac{1}{x}+\dfrac{1}{y}+\dfrac{1}{z}\right) \begin{vmatrix} 1+\dfrac{1}{x} & \dfrac{1}{x} & \dfrac{1}{x} \\ 1+\dfrac{1}{y} & 2+\dfrac{1}{y} & \dfrac{1}{y} \\ 1+\dfrac{1}{z} & 1+\dfrac{1}{z} & 3+\dfrac{1}{z} \end{vmatrix}$

$$(R_1 \to R_1 + R_2 + R_3)$$

$= xyz\left(3+\dfrac{1}{x}+\dfrac{1}{y}+\dfrac{1}{z}\right) \begin{vmatrix} 1 & 0 & 0 \\ 1+\dfrac{1}{y} & 1 & -1 \\ 1+\dfrac{1}{z} & 0 & 2 \end{vmatrix}$

$= 2xyz\left(3+\dfrac{1}{x}+\dfrac{1}{y}+\dfrac{1}{z}\right)$

$(p+q)=5$

**2.** **(b)** The given system of equations will have a non-trivial solution if

$\Delta = \begin{vmatrix} a\alpha+b & a & b \\ b\alpha+c & b & c \\ 0 & a\alpha+b & b\alpha+c \end{vmatrix} = 0$

Applying $R_3 \to R_3 - \alpha R_1 - R_2$, we get

$\Delta = \begin{vmatrix} a\alpha+b & a & b \\ b\alpha+c & b & c \\ -\left(a\alpha^2+2b\alpha+c\right) & 0 & 0 \end{vmatrix} = 0$

$\Rightarrow \quad -(a\alpha^2+2b\alpha+c)\,(ac-b^2)=0$

$\Rightarrow \quad a\alpha^2+2b\alpha+c=0$ or $(ac-b^2)=0$

$\Rightarrow \quad \alpha$ is a root of $ax^2+2bx+c=0$ or $a$, $b$, $c$ are in G.P.

**3.** **(d)** Given

$(a^2+b^2+c^2)^2\,x^2-2\,(ab+bc+cd)x+b^2+c^2+d^2\le 0$

$\Rightarrow \quad (ax-b)^2+(bx-c)^2+(cx-d)^2\le 0$

$\Rightarrow \quad (ax-b)^2+(bx-c)^2+(cx-d)^2=0$

$\Rightarrow \quad \dfrac{b}{a}=\dfrac{c}{b}=\dfrac{d}{c}=x \Rightarrow$ or $2\log b = \log a + \log c$

Now, $\Delta = \begin{vmatrix} p & x & \log a \\ q & y & \log b \\ r & z & \log c \end{vmatrix}$

In each row, terms are in AP so $\Delta = 0$

**4.** **(a)** We have,

$\displaystyle\sum_{n=1}^{k} U_n = \begin{vmatrix} \displaystyle\sum_{n=1}^{k} 1 & k & k \\ 2\displaystyle\sum_{n=1}^{k} n & k^2+k+1 & k^2+k \\ 2\displaystyle\sum_{n=1}^{k} n - \displaystyle\sum_{n=1}^{k} 1 & k^2 & k^2+k+1 \end{vmatrix}$

$= \begin{vmatrix} k & k & k \\ k(k+1) & k^2+k+1 & k^2+k \\ k^2 & k^2 & k^2+k+1 \end{vmatrix}$

$= \begin{vmatrix} k & 0 & k \\ k^2+k & 1 & k^2+k \\ k^2 & 0 & k^2+k+1 \end{vmatrix}$

$$[\text{Applying } C_2 \to C_2 - C_1]$$

$= k\,(k^2+k+1)-k^3 = k\,(k+1) = 110$

$\Rightarrow \quad k=10$

**5.** **(a)** $f(n) = \begin{vmatrix} n & n+1 & n+2 \\ n! & (n+1)! & (n+2)! \\ 1 & 1 & 1 \end{vmatrix}$

$= \begin{vmatrix} n & 1 & 1 \\ n! & nn! & (n+1)(n+1)! \\ 1 & 0 & 0 \end{vmatrix}$

$=$ Using $C_3 \to C_3 - C_2,\ C_2 \to C_2 - C_1$

$= (n+1)(n+1)! - nn! = n![(n+1)^2 - n]$

$= n!(n^2+n+1)$

$f(5) = 3720$

**6.** **(a)** We have,
$$\begin{vmatrix} x & 1 & 1 & \cdots \\ 1 & x & 1 & \cdots \\ 1 & 1 & x & \cdots \\ \cdots & \cdots & \cdots & \cdots \end{vmatrix}$$

$$= \begin{vmatrix} x & 1 & 1 & \cdots \\ (1-x) & (x-1) & 0 & \cdots \\ (1-x) & 0 & (x-1) & \cdots \\ \cdots & \cdots & \cdots & \cdots \end{vmatrix}$$

[Applying $R_2 \to R_2 - R_1$, $R_3 \to R_3 - R_1$
$$\vdots \; R_n \to R_n - R_1]$$

$$x(x-1)^{n-1} + \underbrace{(x-1)^{n-1} + (x-1)^{n-1} + \cdots + (x-1)^{n-1}}_{(n-1)\text{ times}}$$

[Expanding along $R_1$]
$$= x(x-1)^{n-1} + (x-1)^{n-1}[1 + 1 + \cdots + (n-1)\text{ times}]$$
$$= (x-1)^{n-1}(x+n-1).$$

**7.** **(a, b, c, d)** The determinant of L.H.S on expansion $= 0$
$$= 90 f(x-3) - 100 f(x+5) + 10 f(x-3) = 0$$

$$100 f(x-3) = 100 f(x+5)$$

So, $f(x)$ satisfies the equation $f(x+5) = f(x-3)$.
Hence $f(x)$ is periodic with period 8.

**8.** **(a, b, d)** We have,

$$f(x)\begin{vmatrix} x & a & a & a \\ a & x & a & a \\ a & a & x & a \\ a & a & a & x \end{vmatrix} = (x+3a)\begin{vmatrix} 1 & a & a & a \\ 1 & x & a & a \\ 1 & a & x & a \\ 1 & a & a & x \end{vmatrix}$$

[Applying $C_1 \to C_1 + C_2 + C_3 + C_4$ and taking $(x+3a)$ common from $C_1$]

$$= (x+3a)\begin{vmatrix} 1 & a & a & a \\ 0 & x-a & 0 & 0 \\ 0 & 0 & x-a & 0 \\ 0 & 0 & 0 & x-a \end{vmatrix}$$

[Applying $R_2 \to R_2 - R_1$, $R_3 \to R_3 - R_1$ and $R_4 \to R_4 - R_1$] $f(x) = (x+3a)(x-a)^3$
[Expanding along $C_1$]

**9.** **(a, b, c)** $\Delta = \begin{vmatrix} x & y & z \\ p & q & r \\ a & b & c \end{vmatrix}\begin{vmatrix} 0 & m & n \\ -m & 0 & k \\ -n & -k & 0 \end{vmatrix}$.

where $\begin{vmatrix} 0 & m & n \\ -m & 0 & k \\ -n & -k & 0 \end{vmatrix}$ is skew-symmetric

$$\therefore \; \Delta = 0$$

**10.** **(a, c)** Apply $C_3 \to C_3 - x\,C_1 - y\,C_2$

$$\Delta = \begin{vmatrix} a & b & 0 \\ b & c & 0 \\ ax + by & bx + ay & -\left(ax^2 + ay^2 + 2bxy\right) \end{vmatrix} = 0$$

$$\Rightarrow \left(b^2 - ac\right)\left(ax^2 + 2bxy + ay^2\right) = 0$$

$\Rightarrow$ Either $b^2 = ac$ or $ax^2 + 2bxy + ay^2 = 0$
Thus, the point $(x, y)$ lies on a curve through the origin.

**11.** **(7)** $R_1 \to c\,R_1$, $R_2 \to a\,R_2$, $R_3 \to b\,R_3$

$$\Rightarrow \frac{1}{abc}\begin{vmatrix} a^2 + b^2 & c^2 & c^2 \\ a^2 & b^2 + c^2 & a^2 \\ b^2 & b^2 & c^2 + a^2 \end{vmatrix}$$

Use $R_1 \to R_1 - (R_2 + R_3)$

$$\Rightarrow \frac{1}{abc}\begin{vmatrix} 0 & -2b^2 & -2a^2 \\ a^2 & b^2 + c^2 & a^2 \\ b^2 & b^2 & c^2 + a^2 \end{vmatrix}$$

$$R_2 \to R_2 + 1/2\,R_1 \text{ and } R_3 \to R_3 + 1/2\,R_1$$

$$\Rightarrow \frac{1}{abc}\begin{vmatrix} 0 & -2b^2 & -2a^2 \\ a^2 & c^2 & 0 \\ b^2 & 0 & c^2 \end{vmatrix}$$

$$\Rightarrow \frac{1}{abc} \Rightarrow [2\,b^2\,(a^2\,c^2) - 2\,a^2\,(-b^2 c^2)]$$

$$= \frac{4a^2 b^2 c^2}{abc} = 4\,a\,b\,c$$

So $[\alpha] + 3 = 7$

**12.** **(2)** We know that $\left|A^{-1}\right| = \dfrac{1}{|A|}$ and $|\text{adj } B| = |B|^{n-1}$ here 'n' is the order of matrix
Now consider

$$\left\||\left(A^{-1} adj\left(B^{-1}\right)\right) adj\left(2A^{-1}\right)\right\| = \left|\frac{1}{|A|}\frac{1}{|B|^2}\frac{64}{|A|^2}\right|$$

$$= \left|\frac{64}{(-2)(4)(4)}\right| = |-2| = 2$$

**13.** **(7)** Consider

$$A = \begin{vmatrix} a_1 a_5 & a_1 & a_2 \\ a_2 a_6 & a_2 & a_3 \\ a_3 a_7 & a_3 & a_4 \end{vmatrix}$$

$$= \begin{vmatrix} a_1 a_5 - a_3 a_7 & a_1 - a_3 & a_2 - a_4 \\ a_2 a_6 - a_3 a_7 & a_2 - a_3 & a_3 - a_4 \\ a_3 a_7 & a_3 & a_4 \end{vmatrix}$$

$= d(a_1 - a_2)(a_2 - a_3)(a_3 - a_1) = -2d^4$

Similarly $B = -2d^4$

So $AB = 4d^8 = 1024$

**14.** **(1)** $C_1 \to C_1 + C_2 + C_3$

$$\begin{vmatrix} 1 + 2x + x(a^2 + b^2 + c^2) & (1 + b^2)x & (1 + c^2)x \\ 1 + 2x + x(a^2 + b^2 + c^2) & 1 + b^2 x & (1 + c^2)x \\ 1 + 2x + x(a^2 + b^2 + c^2) & (1 + b^2)x & 1 + c^2 x \end{vmatrix} = 0$$

Since $a^2 + b^2 + c^2 = -2$

$$\begin{vmatrix} 1 & (1 + b^2)x & (1 + c^2)x \\ 1 & 1 + b^2 x & (1 + c^2)x \\ 1 & (1 + b^2)x & 1 + c^2 x \end{vmatrix} = 0$$

$$R_2 \to R_2 - R_1 \text{ and } R_3 \to R_3 - R_1$$

$$\begin{vmatrix} 1 & (1 + b^2)x & (1 + c^2)x \\ 0 & 1 - x & 0 \\ 0 & 0 & 1 - x \end{vmatrix} = 0$$

On expanding we get $(1 - x)^2 = 1 - 2x + x^2 = 0$

It has only one root.

**15.** **(3)** For non-trivial solution,

$$\Delta = \begin{vmatrix} a & \sin b & \cos b \\ 1 & \cos b & \sin b \\ -1 & \sin b & -\cos b \end{vmatrix} = 0$$

$\Rightarrow$ $a[-\cos^2 b - \sin^2 b] - \sin b \,[-\cos b + \sin b]$
$$+ \cos b[\sin b + \cos b] = 0$$

$\Rightarrow$ $-a + \sin 2b + \cos 2b = 0$

$\Rightarrow$ $a = \cos 2b + \sin 2b = \sqrt{2} \cos\left(2b - \dfrac{\pi}{4}\right),$

since, $-1 \le \cos\left(2b - \dfrac{\pi}{4}\right) \le 1$

$\Rightarrow$ $-\sqrt{2} \le \sqrt{2} \cos\left(2b - \dfrac{\pi}{4}\right) \le \sqrt{2}$

$\Rightarrow$ $-\sqrt{2} \le a \le \sqrt{2}$

$\Rightarrow$ $a \in [-\sqrt{2}, \sqrt{2}\,]$

Possible integral values are $-1$, $0$ and $1$

**(For Q. 16 – Q.17)**

Let $\Delta = \begin{vmatrix} 1 & 1 & 1 \\ a & b & c \\ a^2 & b^2 & c^2 \end{vmatrix}$

$$= \begin{vmatrix} 1 & 0 & 0 \\ a & b - a & c - a \\ a^2 & b^2 - a^2 & c^2 - a^2 \end{vmatrix}$$

$(C_2 \to C_2 - C_1, C_3 \to C_3 - C_1)$

$$= (b - a)(c - a) \begin{vmatrix} 1 & 0 & 0 \\ a & 1 & 1 \\ a^2 & b + a & c + a \end{vmatrix}$$

$= (b - a)(c - a)(c - b) = (a - b)(b - c)(c - a)$

**16.** **(b)** $\Delta_1 = \begin{vmatrix} 1 & 1 & 1 \\ a^2 & b^2 & c^2 \\ bc & ca & ab \end{vmatrix} = \dfrac{1}{abc} \begin{vmatrix} a & b & c \\ a^3 & b^3 & c^3 \\ abc & abc & abc \end{vmatrix}$

$$= \begin{vmatrix} a & b & c \\ a^3 & b^3 & c^3 \\ 1 & 1 & 1 \end{vmatrix} = \begin{vmatrix} 1 & 1 & 1 \\ a & b & c \\ a^3 & b^3 & c^3 \end{vmatrix}$$

$\because$ $\Delta_1$ is cyclic and obtained by increasing the degree of third row of $\Delta$ by unity (1), so the value of $\Delta$ will be multiplied by a linear cyclic expression, i.e. $(a + b + c)$, so, $\Delta_1 = \Delta\,(a + b + c)$

**17.** **(c)** $\Delta_2 = \begin{vmatrix} a & b & c \\ a^2 & b^2 & c^2 \\ bc & ca & ca \end{vmatrix} = \begin{vmatrix} 1 & 1 & 1 \\ a^2 & b^2 & c^2 \\ a^3 & b^3 & c^3 \end{vmatrix}$

Now $\Delta_2$ is obtained by increasing the degree of second row and third row by unity each, so the value of $\Delta$ will be multiplied by a quadratic cyclic expression, say, $\{k_1\,(a^2 + b^2 + c^2) + k_2\,(bc + ca + ab)\}$
So, $\Delta_2 = \Delta\,[k_1\,(a^2 + b^2 + c^2) + k_2\,(bc + ca + ab)]$
The values of $k_1$ and $k_2$ can be obtained by substituting suitable unequal values of $k_1$ and $k_2$. For example.
Put $a = 0$, $b = 1$, $c = -1$ then we get $2k_1 - k_2 = -1$
Put $a = 0$, $b = 1$, $c = 2$ then we get $5k_1 + 2k_2 = 2$
Thus $k_1 = 0$ and $k_2 = 1$
Thus $\Delta_2 = \Delta\,(bc + ca + ab)$

**18.** **(a)** $\Delta = \begin{vmatrix} 1 & 1 & 1 \\ 2 & 1 & 2 \\ 1 & -1 & 3 \end{vmatrix} = \begin{vmatrix} 1 & 2 & 0 \\ 2 & 3 & 0 \\ 1 & 0 & 2 \end{vmatrix} = -2$

$\therefore$ System of equation has unique solution

Now $A = \begin{vmatrix} 1 & 1 & 1 \\ 2 & 1 & 2 \\ 1 & -1 & 3 \end{vmatrix} \Rightarrow \text{adj } A = \begin{bmatrix} 5 & -4 & 1 \\ -4 & 2 & 0 \\ -3 & 2 & -1 \end{bmatrix}$

$$B = \begin{bmatrix} 3 \\ 5 \\ 3 \end{bmatrix} \Rightarrow (\text{adj } A)\, B = \begin{bmatrix} -2 \\ -2 \\ -2 \end{bmatrix}$$

$$\therefore \quad A^{-1} B = \frac{1}{\Delta}(\text{adj } A)\, B = -\frac{1}{2}\begin{bmatrix} -2 \\ -2 \\ -2 \end{bmatrix} = \begin{bmatrix} 1 \\ 1 \\ 1 \end{bmatrix}$$

$$\therefore \quad X = \begin{bmatrix} x \\ y \\ z \end{bmatrix} = \begin{bmatrix} 1 \\ 1 \\ 1 \end{bmatrix} \Rightarrow x = y = z = 1$$

***ALTERNATIVELY :***

After finding $\Delta \neq 0$, we can check the option (a) which satisfies the given equation. [If it do not satisfy the system of equations. (d) will be the answer]

**19. (c)** $A = \begin{bmatrix} 1 & 1 & 1 \\ 2 & 2 & 2 \\ 1 & -1 & 3 \end{bmatrix} \Rightarrow |A| = 0 \ \text{adj } A = \begin{bmatrix} 8 & -4 & 0 \\ -4 & 2 & 0 \\ -4 & 2 & 0 \end{bmatrix}$

$$\therefore (\text{adj } A)\, B = \begin{bmatrix} 8 & -4 & 0 \\ -4 & 2 & 0 \\ -4 & 2 & 0 \end{bmatrix}\begin{bmatrix} 3 \\ 7 \\ 3 \end{bmatrix} = \begin{bmatrix} -4 \\ 2 \\ 2 \end{bmatrix} \neq 0$$

$\therefore$ The system has no solution.

**20. (A) $\rightarrow$ (q); (B) $\rightarrow$ (r); (C) $\rightarrow$ (s); (D) $\rightarrow$ (p)**

(A) Applying $C_1 \rightarrow C_1 + C_2$, we get

$$\begin{vmatrix} 2 & \cos^2\theta & \sin 2\theta \\ 2 & 1+\cos^2\theta & \sin 2\theta \\ 1 & \cos^2\theta & 1+\sin 2\theta \end{vmatrix}$$

Applying $R_2 \rightarrow R_2 - R_1$ and $R_3 \rightarrow R_3 - R_1$,

we get $\begin{vmatrix} 2 & \cos^2\theta & \sin 2\theta \\ 0 & 1 & 0 \\ -1 & 0 & 1 \end{vmatrix} = 2 + \sin^2 2\theta$

(B) $\begin{bmatrix} 1 & -\tan\theta \\ \tan\theta & 1 \end{bmatrix}\begin{bmatrix} 1 & \tan\theta \\ -\tan\theta & 1 \end{bmatrix}^{-1}$

$= \begin{bmatrix} 1 & -\tan\theta \\ \tan\theta & 1 \end{bmatrix}\left( \dfrac{1}{1+\tan^2\theta} \right) \begin{bmatrix} 1 & -\tan\theta \\ \tan\theta & 1 \end{bmatrix}$

$= \dfrac{1}{1+\tan^2\theta}\begin{bmatrix} 1-\tan^2\theta & -2\tan\theta \\ 2\tan\theta & 1-\tan^2\theta \end{bmatrix}$

$= \begin{bmatrix} \cos 2\theta & -\sin 2\theta \\ \sin 2\theta & \cos 2\theta \end{bmatrix} \quad \therefore a = \cos 2\theta,\ b = \sin 2\theta$

$$\therefore a = \cos 2\theta,\ b = \sin 2\theta$$

(D) we have,

$$= \begin{vmatrix} 1 & 3\cos\theta & 1 \\ \sin\theta & 1 & 3\cos\theta \\ 0 & \sin\theta - 3\cos\theta & 0 \end{vmatrix}$$

$$[\text{Applying } R_3 \rightarrow R_3 - R_1]$$

$$= \begin{vmatrix} 1 & 3\cos\theta & 1 \\ \sin\theta & 1 & 3\cos\theta \\ 0 & \sin\theta - 3\cos\theta & 0 \end{vmatrix}$$

$= -(\sin\theta - 3\cos\theta)(3\cos - \sin\theta)$

$= (3\cos\theta - \sin\theta)^2$

**1. (d)** $f(x) = \begin{cases} \dfrac{e^{[x]+|x|}-2}{[x]+|x|}, & x \neq 0 \\ -1, & x = 0 \end{cases}$

$\underset{x\to 0^-}{\text{Lt}}\, f(x) = \underset{x\to 0^-}{\text{Lt}}\, \dfrac{e^{[x]+|x|}}{[x]+|x|} = \dfrac{e^{-1}-2}{-1}$

$\underset{x\to 0^+}{\text{Lt}}\, f(x) = \underset{x\to 0^+}{\text{Lt}}\, \dfrac{e^{[x]+|x|}-2}{[x]+|x|}$

$= \underset{x\to 0^+}{\text{Lt}}\, \dfrac{e^x-2}{x} \to -\infty$

Clearly none of (a), (b), (c) is correct.

**2. (a)** $F'(x) = \left[ f\left(\dfrac{x}{2}\right).f'\left(\dfrac{x}{2}\right) + g\left(\dfrac{x}{2}\right)g'\left(\dfrac{x}{2}\right)\right]$

Here, $g(x) = f'(x)$
and $g'(x) = f''(x) = -f(x)$

So, $F'(x) = f\left(\dfrac{x}{2}\right)g\left(\dfrac{x}{2}\right) - f\left(\dfrac{x}{2}\right)g\left(\dfrac{x}{2}\right) = 0$

$\Rightarrow F(x)$ is constant function
So, $F(10) = 5$

**3. (a)** Given

$f'(a) = \lim_{h\to 0} \dfrac{f(a-h)-f(a)}{-h} = 0 \quad \dots (1)$

Now $f'(-a^-) = \lim_{h\to 0} \dfrac{f(-a-h)-f(-a)}{-h}$

$= \lim_{h\to 0} \dfrac{-f(a+h)+f(a)}{-h}$

$[\because f(x) \text{ is odd function}]$

$= \lim_{h\to 0} \dfrac{-f(a-h)+f(a)}{-h}$

$[\because f(2a-x) = f(x) \Rightarrow f(a+x) = f(a-x)]$

$= \lim_{h\to 0} \dfrac{f(a-h)-f(a)}{h} = 0 \quad [\text{From (1)}]$

**4. (a)** We have,
$f(x) = \cos x \cos 2x \cos 2^2 x \cos 2^3 x \,..... \cos 2^{\,n-1}x$

$\Rightarrow f(x) = \dfrac{\sin 2^n x}{2^n \sin x}$

$\Rightarrow f'(x) = \dfrac{2^n \cos 2^n x \sin x - \sin 2^n x \cos x}{2^n \sin^2 x}$

$\Rightarrow f'\left(\dfrac{\pi}{2}\right) = \dfrac{2^n \cos 2^{n-1}\pi}{2^n} = \cos 2^{n-1}\pi = (-1)2^{n-1} = 1$

**5. (c)** We have,
$[f(x)]^n = f(nx)$ for all $x$
$\Rightarrow n[f(x)]^{n-1} f'(x) = nf'(nx)$
$\Rightarrow n[f(x)]^n f'(x) = nf(x)f'(nx)$
[Multiplying both sides by $f(x)$]
$\Rightarrow f(nx)f'(x) = f(x)f'(nx)$
$[\because [f(x)]^n = f(nx)]$
$\Rightarrow f(nx)f'(x) = f(x)f'(nx)$

**6. (b, d)** $\dfrac{d^n}{dx^n}[f(x)] =$

$\begin{vmatrix} \dfrac{d^n}{dx^n}x^n & \dfrac{d^n}{dx^n}\sin x & -\dfrac{d^n}{dx^n}\cos x \\ n! & \sin(n\pi/2) & \cos(n\pi/2) \\ a & a^2 & a^3 \end{vmatrix}$

$= \begin{vmatrix} n! & \sin\left(\dfrac{n\pi}{2}+x\right) & \cos\left(\dfrac{n\pi}{2}+x\right) \\ n! & \sin n\pi/2 & \cos n\pi/2 \\ a & a^2 & a^3 \end{vmatrix}$

$\therefore$ At $x = 0$, $R_1 = R_2$

$\therefore \dfrac{d^n}{dx^n}\left[f(x)\right] = 0$

**7. (a, c)** $f(x) = x + |x| + \cos 9x, \, g(x) = \sin x$

Since both $f(x)$ and $g(x)$ are continuous everywhere,
$f(x) + g(x)$ is also continuous everywhere
$f(x)$ is non-differentiable and $x = 0$

Hence $f(x) + g(x)$ is non-differentiable at $x = 0$

Now $h(x) = f(x) \times g(x)$

$= \begin{cases} (\cos 9x)(\sin x), & x < 0 \\ (2x + \cos 9x)(\sin x), & x \geq 0 \end{cases}$

Clearly, $h(x)$ is continuous at $x = 0$
Also

$h'(x) = \begin{cases} \cos x \cos 9x - 9\sin x \sin 9x, & x < 0 \\ (2 - 9\sin 9x)\sin x + \cos x(2x + \cos 9x), & x > 0 \end{cases}$

$h'(0^-) = 1, h'(0^+) = 1$

$\Rightarrow f(x) \times g(x)$ is differentiable everywhere.

**8. (a, b, c)**

$g(f(x)) = x \Rightarrow g'(f(x)) f'(x) = 1$

$\Rightarrow \quad g'(f(x)) = \dfrac{1}{f'(x)}$

Now, $f(x) = 2$

$\Rightarrow x^3 + 3x^2 - 33x - 33 = 2$

$\Rightarrow x^3 + 3x^2 - 33x - 35 = 0$

$\Rightarrow x^3 - 5x^2 + 8x^2 - 40x + 7x - 35 = 0$

$\Rightarrow (x - 5)(x^2 + 8x + 7) = 0$

$\Rightarrow (x - 5)(x + 1)(x + 7) = 0$

$\therefore \quad x = -7, -1, 5$

Thus, we have

$k = f'(-1) = 3(-1)^2 + 6(-1) - 33$

$= 3 - 6 - 33 = -36$

$k = f'(-7) = 3(-7)^2 + 6(-7) - 33$

$= 147 - 63 - 33 = 51$

$k = f'(5) = 3.5^2 + 6.5 - 33$

$= 75 + 30 - 33 = 72$

**9. (a, c)** $f(x) = \begin{cases} (\sin^{-1} x)^2 \cos\left(\dfrac{1}{x}\right), & x \neq 0 \\ \\ 0, & x = 0 \end{cases}$

$\lim_{x \to 0} f(x) = \lim_{x \to 0} (\sin^{-1} x)^2 \cos\left(\dfrac{1}{x}\right)$

$= 0 \times (\text{any value between} - 1 \text{ to } 1) = 0$

Hence $f(x)$ is continuous at $x = 0$

$f'(0^+) = \lim_{h \to 0} \dfrac{(\sin^{-1} h)^2 \cos\left(\dfrac{1}{h}\right) - 0}{h}$

$= \left( \lim_{h \to 0} \dfrac{\sin^{-1} h}{h} \right)\left( \lim_{h \to 0} \sin^{-1} h \right)\left( \lim_{h \to 0} \cos\left(\dfrac{1}{h}\right) \right)$

$= 1 \times (0) \times (\text{any value between} - 1 \text{ to } 1) = 0$

Similarly, $f'(0^-) = 0$

Hence, $f(x)$ is continuous and differentiable in $[-1, 1]$ and $(-1, 1)$, respectively.

**10. (3)** Here, we know $\sin x$ and $\cos x$ are periodic with period $2\pi$. Thus we could sketch the curve(In the interval 0 to $2\pi$) as

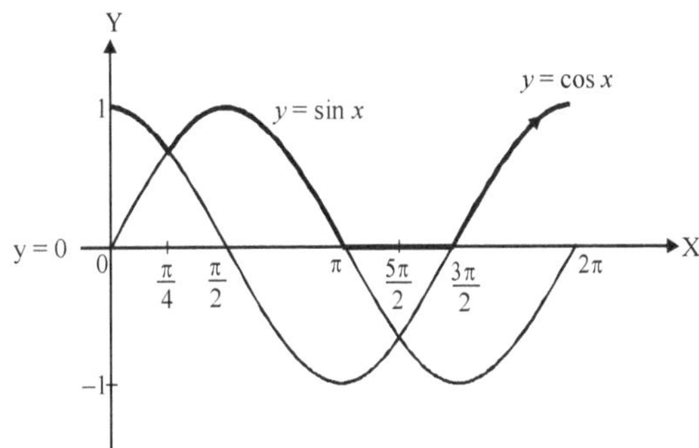


Which shows,

$y = \max \{\sin x, \cos x, 0\}$

$= \begin{cases} \cos x, & 0 < x < \dfrac{x}{4} \text{ or } \dfrac{3\pi}{2} < x < 2\pi \\ \\ 0, & \pi < x < \dfrac{3\pi}{2} \\ \\ \sin x, & \dfrac{\pi}{4} < x < \pi \end{cases}$

Clearly, $y = \max\{\sin x, \cos x, 0\}$ is not differentiable at 3 points when $x = (0, 2\pi)$.

Thus, $y = \max \{\sin x, \cos x, 0 \}$ is not differentiable at 3n points. Hence, $p = 3$.

**11. (0)** $\dfrac{dy}{dx} = \left(\dfrac{dx}{dy}\right)^{-1} \Rightarrow \dfrac{d^2 y}{dx^2} = -\left(\dfrac{dx}{dy}\right)^{-2}\left\{\dfrac{d}{dx}\left(\dfrac{dx}{dy}\right)\right\}$

$\Rightarrow \dfrac{d^2 y}{dx^2} = -\left(\dfrac{dx}{dy}\right)^{-2}\left\{\dfrac{d}{dy}\left(\dfrac{dx}{dy}\right)\dfrac{dy}{dx}\right\}$

$= -\left(\dfrac{dy}{dx}\right)^2 \left\{\dfrac{d^2 x}{dy^2} \cdot \dfrac{dy}{dx}\right\} = -\left(\dfrac{dy}{dx}\right)^3 \dfrac{d^2 x}{dy^2}$

$\Rightarrow \dfrac{d^2 y}{dx^2} + \left(\dfrac{dy}{dx}\right)^3 \dfrac{d^2 x}{dy^2} = 0$

**12. (8)** As, $f(x)$ is continuous at $x = 0$.

$\therefore$ We must have

RHL (at $x = 0$) = LHL (at $x = 0$) = $f(0)$

RHL (at $x = 0$) = $\lim_{x \to 0^+} f(x)$

$= \lim_{x \to 0^+} \dfrac{\sqrt{x}}{\sqrt{16 + \sqrt{x}} - 4}$

Put $x = 0 + h$

$= \lim_{h \to 0} \dfrac{\sqrt{0 + h}}{\sqrt{16 + \sqrt{0 + h}} - 4} \times \dfrac{\sqrt{16 + \sqrt{h}} + 4}{\sqrt{16 + \sqrt{h}} + 4}$

$= \lim_{h \to 0} \dfrac{\sqrt{h}\left\{\sqrt{16 + \sqrt{h}} + 4\right\}}{16 + \sqrt{h} - 16}$

$$= \lim_{h \to 0}\left\{\sqrt{16+\sqrt{h}}+4\right\} = 8$$

Also LHL (at $x = 0$) $= \lim_{x \to 0^-} f(x)$

$$= \lim_{x \to 0^-}\frac{1-\cos 4x}{x^2}$$

$$= \lim_{h \to 0}\frac{1-\cos 4(0-h)}{(0-h)^2}\left[\text{put}\quad x = 0-h\right]$$

$$= \lim_{h \to 0}\frac{1-\cos 4}{h^2} = \lim_{h \to 0}\frac{2\sin^2 2h}{h^2}$$

$$= \lim_{h \to 0}8\left(\frac{\sin 2h}{2h}\right)^2 = 8$$

and $f(x) = a$.

Since $f(x)$ is continuous at $x = 0$

$\Rightarrow$    $f(0) = \text{RHL} = \text{LHL}$

or    $f(0) = 8$.

or    $a = 8$

**13.**  **(3)**   Apply Rolle's theorem to $F(x) = f(x) - 2g(x)$

$F(0) = 0$, $F(1) = f(1) - 2g(1)$

$\Rightarrow$   $0 = 6 - 2g(1) \Rightarrow g(1) = 3$.

**14.**  **(c)**

$\because$   $y = e^{3x+7}$

$\therefore$   $y_1 = 3e^{3x+7}, y_2 = 3^2 e^{3x+7}\ ...$

$\therefore$   $y_n(x) = 3^n.\, e^{3x+7}$

     Then $y_n(0) = 3^n.\, e^7$

**15.**  **(d)**

$\because$   $y = (2-3x)^{-1}$

$\therefore$   $y_1 = (-1)(2-3x)^{-2}(-3)$

     $y_2 = (-1)(-2)(2-3x)^{-3}(-3)^2$

     $y_3 = (-1)(-2)(-3)(2-3x)^{-4}.(-3)^3$

     .................................................

     $y_n = (-1)^n.\, n!\, (2-3x)^{-n-1}(-3)^n$

$\therefore$   $y_n(1) = (-1)^n.\, n!\, (-1)^{-n-1}(-3)^n$

     $= (-1)^{n+1}.\, 3^n.n!$

**16.**  **(b)**   Here $-\dfrac{1}{2} \le x < 0$ gives $-1 \le 2x < 0$

So that $[2x] = -1$ in $\dfrac{-1}{2} \le x < 0$

Thus $f(x) = 4x^2 - x,\ \dfrac{-1}{2} \le x < 0$

$f(x) = ax^2 - bx,\ 0 \le x < \dfrac{1}{2}$

The function is differentiable in $\dfrac{-1}{2} \le x < 0$ and also in

$0 < x < \dfrac{1}{2}$ as it is a polynomial of degree 2 in each of the

subinterval.

Since $f(0^-) = f(0) = f(0^+) = 0$. $f(x)$ is continuous at $x = 0$ for all a, $b$

Now, $f'(0^-) = -1$ and $f'(0^+) = -b$.

It follows that $f'(0)$ exists, if $b = 1$, independent of $a$.

**17.**  **(a)**   Here $f(0) = 0$

So, $f(x)$ will be continuous, if $\lim_{x \to 0} x^p \sin\dfrac{1}{x} = 0$

This is possible only when $p > 0$         ... (i)

$$f'(0) = \lim_{h \to 0}\frac{f(0+h)-f(0)}{h}$$

$$= \lim_{h \to 0}\frac{h^p \sin\dfrac{1}{h}-0}{h} = \lim_{h \to 0} h^{p-1}\sin\frac{1}{h}$$

$f'(0)$ will exist only when $p > 1$

$\therefore$   $f(x)$ will not be differentiable if $p \le 1$     ... (ii)

From (i) and (ii), for $f(x)$ to be not differentiable but continuous at $x = 0$, possible values of $p$ are given by $0 < p \le 1$

**18.**  **(d)**   $f(x) = \cos \pi\,(|x|+[x])$

$$= \begin{cases} \cos \pi\,(-x+(-1)), & -1 \le x < 0 \\ \cos \pi\,(x+0), & 0 \le x < 1 \end{cases}$$

$$= \begin{cases} -\cos \pi x & -1 \le x < 0 \\ \cos \pi x & 0 \le x < 1 \end{cases}$$

Obviously $f(x)$ is discontinuous at $x = 0$ otherwise $f(x)$ is continuous and differentiable in $(-1, 0)$ and $(0, 1)$.

**19.**  $(A) \to (q, s); (B) \to (p, s); (C) \to (p, r); (D) \to (q, s)$

(A)   $f(x) = \begin{cases} \dfrac{5e^{1/x}+2}{3-e^{1/x}}, & x \ne 0 \\ 0, & x = 0 \end{cases}$

$$f(0^+) = \lim_{h \to 0}\frac{5e^{1/h}+2}{3-e^{1/h}} = \lim_{h \to 0}\frac{5+2e^{-1/h}}{3e^{-1/h}-1} = -5$$

Hence, $f(x)$ is discontinuous and non-differentiable at $x = 0$

(B)   $g(x) = x\, f(x) = \begin{cases} x\dfrac{5e^{1/x}+2}{3-e^{1/x}}, & x \ne 0 \\ 0, & x = 0 \end{cases}$

$$f(0^+) = \lim_{h \to 0} h\frac{5e^{1/h}+2}{3-e^{1/h}} = \lim_{h \to 0} h\frac{5+2e^{-1/h}}{3e^{-1/h}-1}$$

$$= 0 \times (-5) = 0$$

$$f(0^-) = \lim_{h \to 0} h\frac{5e^{-1/h}+2}{3-e^{-1/h}} = 0 \times (2/3) = 0$$

Hence, $f(x)$ is continuous at $x = 0$

$$Lg'(0) = \lim_{h \to 0}\frac{g(0-h)-g(0)}{-h}$$

$$= \lim_{h\to 0} \frac{-hf(-h)-0}{-h} = \lim_{h\to 0} f(-h)$$

$$= \lim_{h\to 0} \frac{5e^{-1/h}+2}{3-e^{-1/h}} = \frac{0+2}{3-0} = \frac{2}{3}$$

$$Rg'(0) = \lim_{h\to 0} \frac{g(0+h)-g(0)}{h}$$

$$= \lim_{h\to 0} \frac{g(h)-0}{h}$$

$$= \lim_{h\to 0} f(h) = \lim_{h\to 0} \frac{5e^{1/h}+2}{3-e^{1/h}}$$

$$= \lim_{h\to 0} \frac{5+2e^{-1/h}}{3e^{-1/h}-1}$$

$$= \frac{5+0}{0-1} = -5$$

$\because LF'(0) = RF'(0)$ hence, $F(x)$ is not differentiable, but continuous at $x = 0$.

(C) For $x^2 f(x)$,

Let $F(x) = x^2 f(x)$

$$\therefore \ LF'(0) = \lim_{h\to 0} \frac{F(0-h)-F(0)}{-h}$$

$$= \lim_{h\to 0} \frac{h^2 f(-h)-0}{-h} = 0$$

$$RF'(0) = \lim_{h\to 0} \frac{F(0+h)-F(0)}{h}$$

$$= \lim_{h\to 0} \frac{h^2 f(h)-0}{h} = 0$$

$$\therefore LF'(0) = RF'(0)$$

Hence, $F(x)$ is differentiable at $x = 0$, then it is always continuous at $x = 0$.

**20.** **(A) → (p, q, r); (B) → (p, r, s); (C) → (p, r, s); (D) → (p, r, s)**

(A) $f(x) = |x^3| = x(x|x|)$ is continuous and differentiable.

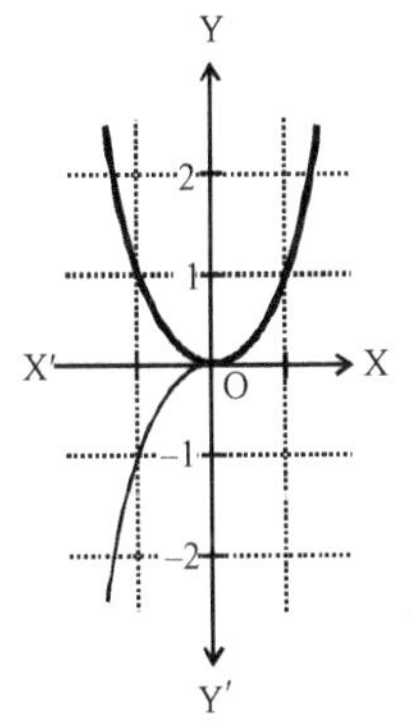

(B) $f(x) = \sqrt{|x|}$ is continuous

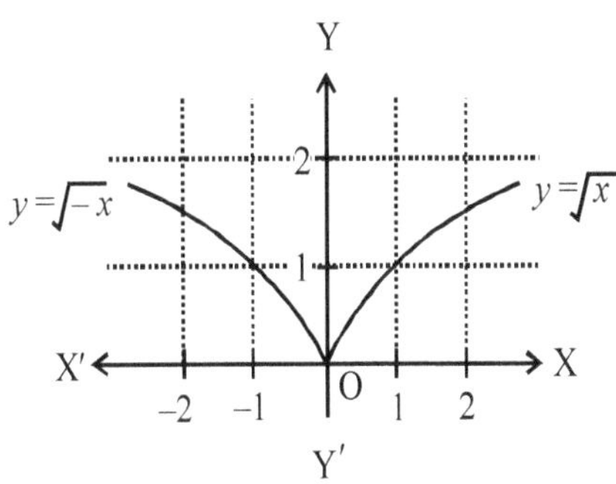

Clearly from the graph, $f(x)$ is non-differentiable at $x = 0$

(C) $f(x) = \left|\sin^{-1} x\right|$ is continuous.

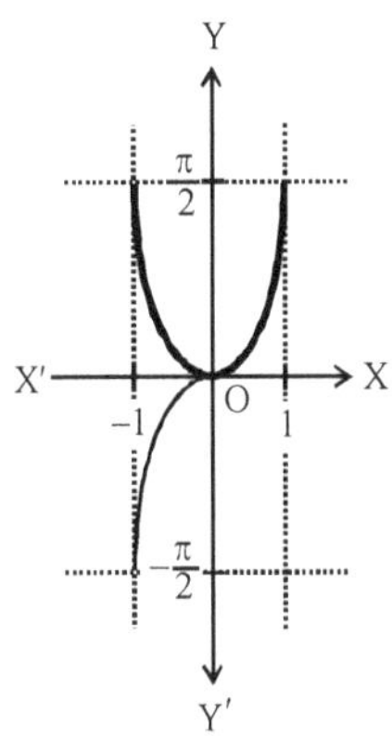

Clearly from the graph, $f(x)$ is non-differentiable at $x = 0$

(D) $f(x) = \cos^{-1}|x|$ is continuous

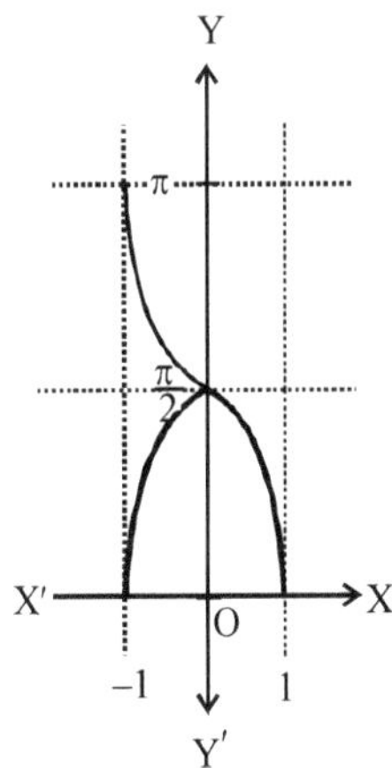

Clearly from the graph, $f(x)$ is non-differentiable at $x = 0$.

**1. (a)** Here $a^2 = 27$, $b^2 = 1$,

$a = 3\sqrt{3}$ , $b = 1$

The point $(a \cos\theta, b \sin\theta)$ is

$(3\sqrt{3} \cos\theta, \sin\theta)$.

Tangent at the above point is

$$\frac{x^3\sqrt{3}\cos\theta}{9} + \frac{y\sin\theta}{1} = 1$$

$\therefore$ Sum of intercepts $= \dfrac{9}{\sqrt{3}\cos\theta} + \dfrac{1}{\sin\theta}$

or $s = 3\sqrt{3}\ \sec\theta + \csc\theta$

$\Rightarrow \dfrac{ds}{d\theta} = 3\sqrt{3}\ \sec\theta\tan\theta - \csc\theta\cot\theta = 0$

$\Rightarrow \tan^3\theta = \dfrac{1}{3\sqrt{3}}\ \therefore \tan\theta = \dfrac{1}{\sqrt{3}} \Rightarrow \theta = \dfrac{\pi}{6}$

$\dfrac{d^2 s}{d\theta^2}$ is positive at $\theta = \dfrac{\pi}{6}$.

Therefore, sum is minimum at $\theta = \pi/6$.

**2. (d)** $f'(x) = \dfrac{\cos x - \sin x}{1 + (\sin x + \cos x)^2}$

$f(x)$ is monotonic increasing when $f'(x) > 0$

$\Rightarrow \dfrac{\cos x - \sin x}{1 + (\sin x + \cos x)^2} > 0$

$\Rightarrow \cos x - \sin x > 0$

$\Rightarrow \sqrt{2}\cos(x + \pi/4) > 0$

$\Rightarrow -\pi/2 < x + \pi/4 < \pi/2$

($\because \cos\theta$ is positive when $-\pi/2 < \theta < \pi/2$)

$\therefore -3\pi/4 < x < \pi/4$

**3. (b)** $\dfrac{dy}{dx} = -\sin(x + y).\,[1 + dy/dx]$ ...(1)

Since the tangent is parallel to $x + 2y = 0$

therefore, $\dfrac{dy}{dx} = $ slope $= -\dfrac{1}{2}$

Putting in (1), $\sin(x + y) = 1 = \sin(\pi/2)$

$\therefore \cos(x + y) = 0$

$\therefore y = \cos(x + y) = 0$

$\therefore \sin(x + y) = 1 \Rightarrow \sin x = 1,\ \because y = 0$

$\therefore x = \dfrac{\pi}{2}, -\dfrac{3\pi}{2}$ as $-2\pi < x < 2\pi$

Hence the points are $[(-3\pi)/2,\ 0]$ and $[\pi/2,\ 0]$ , where the tangents are parallel to the line $x + 2y = 0$

$\therefore$ The equation of tangents are

$$y - 0 = -\frac{1}{2}(x + 3\pi/2) \text{ and } y - 0$$

$$= -\frac{1}{2}(x - \pi/2)$$

or $x + 2y + 3\pi/2 = 0$ and $x + 2y - \pi/2 = 0$

**4. (a)** Let $h$ be the height of the cone and $r$ be its radius.

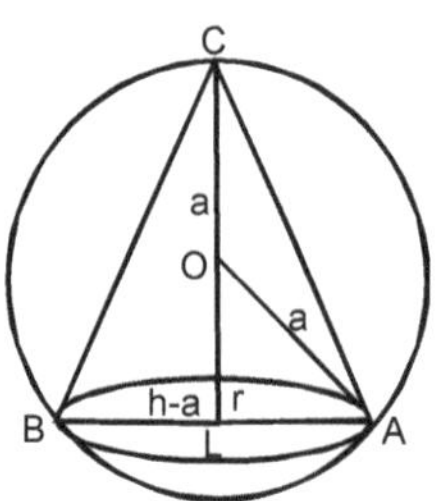

$\therefore\quad h = CL = CO + OL = a + OL$
$\therefore\quad OL = h - a$

$r = LA = \sqrt{(OA^2 - OL^2)}$

or $r = \sqrt{\{a^2 - (h-a)^2\}}$

$\quad = (2ah - h^2)$

$V = \dfrac{1}{3}\pi r^2 h = \dfrac{1}{3}\pi(2ah - h^2)h$

$\quad = \dfrac{1}{3}\pi(2ah^2 - h^3)$

$\dfrac{dy}{dh} = (\pi/3)(4ah - 3h^2) = 0$

$\therefore\quad h = 0$ or $4a/3$

$h = 0$ is rejected, $\therefore h = 4a/3 = (2/3)(2a)$

$h = \dfrac{2}{3}$ (diameter)

**5. (d)** Let $y = ax^2 + bx + c$ be the given parabola. Then,
$f(x) = ax^2 + bx + c$

Clearly, $\dfrac{dy}{dx} = 2ax + b$

It is given that $y = x$ touches the parabola at $x = 1$.

$\therefore \left(\dfrac{dy}{dx}\right)_{x=1} = $ (Slope of the line $y = x$)

$\Rightarrow 2a + b = 1$ ...............(i)

Putting $x = 1$ in $y = x,$ we get $y = 1.$
So, the line $y = x$ touches the parabola
$y = ax^2 + bx + c$ at $(1, 1).$
$a + b + c = 1$ ................ (ii)
Now,
$f(x) = ax^2 + bx + c \Rightarrow f'(x) = 2ax + b$ and
$f''(x) = 2a$
$\therefore \quad f(0) = c, f'(0) = b, f''(0) = 2a$ and
$f'(1) = 2a + b.$
From (ii), we have
$a + b + c = 1$
$\Rightarrow \quad 2a + 2b + 2c = 2$
$\Rightarrow \quad 2a + b + (b + 2c) = 2$
$\Rightarrow \quad 1 + (b + 2c) = 2 \quad [\because\ 2a + b = 1 \text{ from (i)}]$
$\Rightarrow \quad b + 2c = 1$
$\Rightarrow \quad 2c = 1 - b \Rightarrow 2f(0) = 1 - f'(0)$
Also, $f'(1) = 2a + b = 1 \quad [\text{using (i)}]$

**6. (c)** Let $\angle C = \theta.$ Then,
$a = b \cos \theta$
$\therefore \quad a + b = 4$

$\Rightarrow \quad a + b \cos \theta = 4 \Rightarrow b = \dfrac{4}{1 + \cos \theta}$

$\therefore \quad a = b \cos \theta \Rightarrow a = \dfrac{4 \cos \theta}{1 + \cos \theta}$

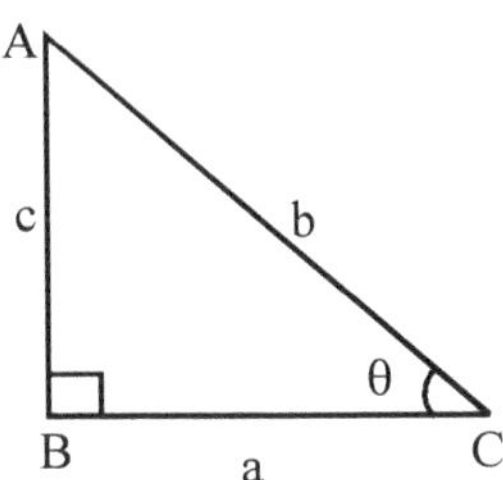


Let $\Delta$ be the area of $\Delta\, ABC.$ Then,

$\Delta = \dfrac{1}{2}\, ab \sin \theta$

$\Rightarrow \quad \Delta = \dfrac{1}{2} \times \dfrac{4 \cos \theta}{1 + \cos \theta} \times \dfrac{4}{1 + \cos \theta} \times \sin \theta$

$\Rightarrow \quad \Delta = \dfrac{8 \sin \theta \cos \theta}{(1 + \cos \theta)^2} = \dfrac{4 \sin 2\theta}{(1 + \cos \theta)^2}$

$\dfrac{d(\Delta)}{d\theta} = \dfrac{(1 + \cos 2\theta)^2 \times 8 \cos 2\theta + 8 \sin 2\theta (1 + \cos \theta) \sin \theta}{(1 + \cos \theta)^4}$

$\Rightarrow \dfrac{d(\Delta)}{d(\theta)} = \dfrac{8 \cos 2\theta + (1 + \cos\theta) 8 \sin 2\theta \sin \theta}{(1 + \cos \theta)^3}$

$\Rightarrow \quad \dfrac{d(\Delta)}{d\theta} = \dfrac{8 \cos \theta + 8 \cos 2\theta}{(1 + \cos \theta)^2}$

$\Rightarrow \quad \dfrac{d(\Delta)}{d\theta} = \dfrac{8(2\cos^2 \theta + \cos \theta - 1)}{(1 + \cos \theta)^2} = 8\left(\dfrac{2 \cos \theta - 1}{1 + \cos \theta}\right)$

For $\Delta$ to be maximum, we must have

$\dfrac{d(\Delta)}{d\theta} = 0 \Rightarrow 2 \cos \theta - 1 = 0 \Rightarrow \cos\theta$

$= \dfrac{1}{2} \Rightarrow \theta = \dfrac{\pi}{3}$

Now,

$\dfrac{d^2(\Delta)}{d\theta^2} = 8\left\{\dfrac{-2(1 + \cos\theta)\sin\theta + (2\cos\theta - 1)\sin\theta}{(1 + \cos\theta)^2}\right\}$

Clearly, $\dfrac{d^2(\Delta)}{d\theta^2} < 0$ for $\theta = \dfrac{\pi}{3}$

Hence, $(\Delta)$ is maximum when $\theta = \dfrac{\pi}{3}$

**7. (a,c)**
We have, $9y^2 = x^3 \quad ........(1)$
Differentiating w.r.t. $x$, we get

$18y \dfrac{dy}{dx} = 3x^2 \Rightarrow \dfrac{dy}{dx} = \dfrac{x^2}{6y}$

Slope of the normal $= -\dfrac{6y^2}{x^2} = \pm 1 \qquad ........(2)$

($\because$ any line making equal intercepts on axes will have its
slope as $1$ or $-1$)
Now from (2), we have

$y = -\dfrac{x^2}{6}$ or $y = \dfrac{x^2}{6}$

Solving these with the equation (1), we get the points

$\left(4, \dfrac{8}{3}\right), \left(4, -\dfrac{8}{3}\right).$

**8. (a,c)**

$y = \sqrt{9 - x^2}$ is the semicircle on the line segment joining $(-3, 0)$ and $(3, 0),$

$y = \sqrt{1 + x^2}$ is the hyperbola with its transverse axis along
the y-axis and one vertex at $(0, 1).$ Points of intersection : $A = (-2, \sqrt{5}), A' = (2, \sqrt{5}).$

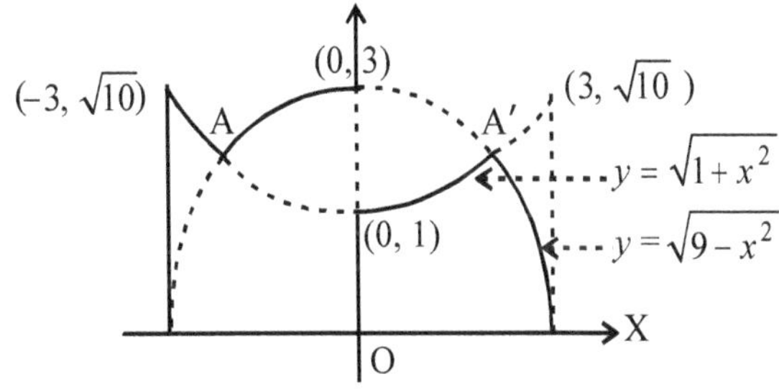

As shown in figure, $f(x)$ consists of the segment of the hyperbola between $(-3, \sqrt{10})$ and $A\,(-2, \sqrt{5})$, the segment of the semicircle between $(-2, \sqrt{5})$ and $(0, 3)$, the segment of the hyperbola between $(0, 1)$ and $A'\,(2, \sqrt{5})$ and the segment of the semicircle between $(2, \sqrt{5})$ and $\left(3, \sqrt{10}\right)$.

$x = 0$ is a point of discontinuity of $f(x)$. $(-2, \sqrt{5})$ is a point of minimum and $(2, \sqrt{5})$ is a point of maximum.

**9.** **(b, c)**

We have, $f(x) = \sin x + \cos x$

$$\Rightarrow f'(x) = \cos x - \sin x = \sqrt{2}\,\cos\left(x + \frac{\pi}{4}\right)$$

$f'(x) > 0$, if $0 \le x + \dfrac{\pi}{4} < \dfrac{\pi}{2}$

or $\dfrac{3\pi}{2} < x + \dfrac{\pi}{4} \le 2\pi$

i.e. $-\dfrac{\pi}{4} \le x < \dfrac{\pi}{4}$ or $\dfrac{5\pi}{4} < x \le \dfrac{7\pi}{4}$

But $f(x)$ is defined in $[0, 2\pi]$.

$$\therefore\ f'(x) > 0 \text{ in } \left[0, \frac{\pi}{4}\right) \cup \left(\frac{5\pi}{4}, \frac{7\pi}{4}\right]$$

$$\Rightarrow f(x) \text{ is increasing in } \left[0, \frac{\pi}{4}\right) \cup \left(\frac{5\pi}{4}, \frac{7\pi}{4}\right]$$

Also, $f'(x) < 0$, if $\dfrac{\pi}{2} < x + \dfrac{\pi}{4} < \dfrac{3\pi}{2}$

i.e., $\dfrac{\pi}{4} < x < \dfrac{5\pi}{4}$.

$$\therefore\ f(x) \text{ is decreasing in } \left(\frac{\pi}{4}, \frac{5\pi}{4}\right).$$

**10.** **(b, c)**

$\therefore\ x = a\,(\cos\theta + \theta\sin\theta)$

and $y = a\,(\sin\theta - \theta\cos\theta)$

$$\therefore\ \frac{dx}{d\theta} = a\,(\theta\cos\theta), \frac{dy}{d\theta} = a\,(\theta\cos\theta)$$

$$\therefore\ \frac{dy}{dx} = \frac{\sin\theta}{\cos\theta}$$

$$\therefore\ \text{Slope of normal} = -\frac{\cos\theta}{\sin\theta}$$

Equation of normal at '$\theta$' is

$$y - a\,(\sin\theta - \theta\cos\theta) = -\frac{\cos\theta}{\sin\theta}\,(x - a)$$

$(\cos\theta + \sin\theta))$

$\Rightarrow\ y\sin\theta - a\,(\sin^2\theta - \theta\sin\theta\cos\theta)$

$-x\cos\theta + a(\cos^2\theta + \theta\sin\theta\cos\theta)$

$\Rightarrow\ x\cos\theta + y\sin\theta = a$ ............(i)

Distance from origin to (i) $= a = $ constant

Hence, $x\cos\theta + y\sin\theta = a$

touches a fixed circle $x^2 + y^2 = a^2$, whose centre $(0, 0)$ and radius a.

**11.** **(5)** Let $f(x) = (x-5)^{55}(x-6)^{66}$

$f'(x) = (x-5)^{55}\,66\,(x-6)^{65} +$
$$\qquad\qquad\qquad\qquad (x-6)^{66}\,55\,(x-5)^{54}$$
$$= (x-5)^{54}\,(x-6)^{65}\,(66\,(x-5) + 55\,(x-6))$$
$f'(x) = 0 \Rightarrow (x-5)^{54}\,(x-6)^{65}$
$$\qquad\qquad\qquad\qquad\qquad (121x - 660) = 0$$

$$\Rightarrow\ x = 5, 6, \frac{660}{121}$$

Now, applying method of intervals

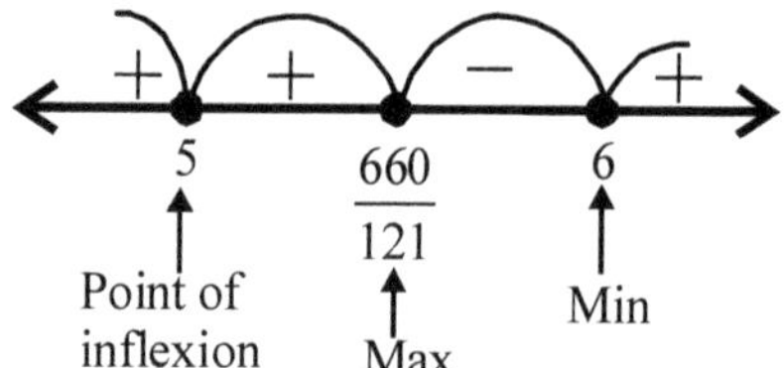


**12.** **(4)**

**(a)** We know that, $1 \le |\sin x| + |\cos x| \le \sqrt{2},$ for all real values of $x$

[Note that $(|\sin x| + |\cos x|)^2 + |\sin 2x| \ge 1$

$\therefore\ y = [|\sin x| + |\cos x|] = 1$

Let $P$ and $Q$ be the points of intersection of given curves

Clearly the given curves meet at points where $y = 1$ so, we get

$x^2 + 1 = 5$, $x = \pm 2$

Now, $P\,(2, 1)$ and $Q\,(-2, 1)$

Now, $x^2 + y^2 = 5$

Differentiating the above equation with respect to $x$ we get

$$2x + 2y\frac{dy}{dx} = 0 \Rightarrow \frac{dy}{dx} = -\frac{x}{y}$$

$$\therefore\ \left(\frac{dy}{dx}\right)_{(2,1)} = -2$$

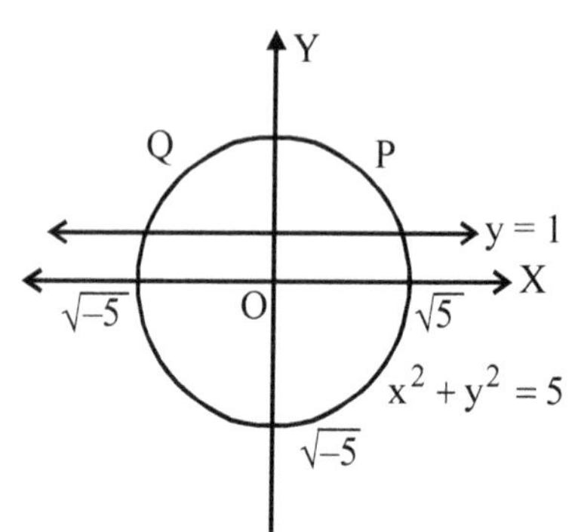

$$\left(\frac{dy}{dx}\right)_{(-2,1)} = 2$$

Clearly the slope of line $y = 1$ is zero and the slope of the tangents at $P$ and $Q$ are $(-2)$ and $(2)$ respectively. Thus, the angle of intersection is $\tan^{-1}(2)$.

**13.** **(2)** We have, $f(x) = (x+1)^{1/3} - (x-1)^{1/3}$

$$\therefore \quad f'(x) = \frac{1}{3}\left[\frac{1}{(x+1)^{1/3}} - \frac{1}{(x-1)^{1/3}}\right]$$

$$= \frac{(x-1)^{2/3} - (x+1)^{2/3}}{3(x^2-1)^{2/3}}$$

Clearly, $f'(x)$ does not exist at $x = \pm 1$

Now, $f'(x) = 0 \Rightarrow (x-1)^{2/3} = (x+1)^{2/3} \Rightarrow x = 0$

Clearly $f'(x) \neq 0$ for any other value of $x \in [0, 1]$ The value of $f(x)$ at $x = 0$ is 2.

Hence, the greatest value of $f(x)$ is 2

**14.** **(3)** Let $\theta$ be the semi-vertical angle and $r$ be the radius of the cone at time $t$. Then,

$$r = 20 \tan \theta$$

$$\Rightarrow \quad \frac{dr}{dt} = 20 \sec^2 \theta \frac{d\theta}{dt}$$

$$\Rightarrow \quad \frac{dr}{dt} = 20 \sec^2 30° \times 2$$

$$\left[\because \theta = 30° \text{ and } \frac{d\theta}{dt} = 2 \text{ (given)}\right]$$

$$\Rightarrow \quad \frac{dr}{dt} = 20 \times \frac{4}{3} \times 2 \, \text{cm/sec} = \frac{160}{3} \text{cm/sec}$$

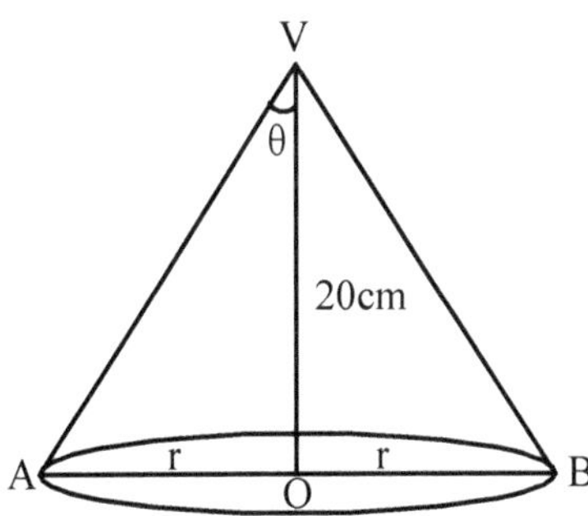


**15.** **(c)** $\alpha = 2\pi r = \pi \Rightarrow r = 1/2,$

Also, $h = \sqrt{1 - r^2} = \frac{\sqrt{3}}{2}$

$$\Rightarrow \quad v = \frac{1}{3}\pi r^2 h \Rightarrow \frac{\sqrt{3}\pi}{24}$$

**16.** **(c)** $$\frac{dV}{d\alpha} = \frac{\pi}{3}\left[2r\frac{dr}{d\alpha}.\sqrt{1-r^2} - \frac{r^3}{\sqrt{1-r^2}}.\frac{dr}{d\alpha}\right]$$

$$\Rightarrow \quad \frac{dV}{d\alpha} = \frac{1}{6}\left[\frac{2r - 3r^3}{\sqrt{1-r^2}}\right]\left\{\because \frac{dr}{d\alpha} = -\frac{1}{2\pi}\right\}$$

For maximum or minimum values of V, we must have

$$\frac{dV}{d\alpha} = 0 \Rightarrow r = \sqrt{\frac{2}{3}}$$

$$\frac{d^2V}{d\alpha^2} = -\frac{1}{6}\left\{\frac{\sqrt{1-r^2}(2-9r^2)\frac{dr}{d\alpha} + (2r-3r^3)\frac{r}{\sqrt{1-r^2}}.\frac{dr}{d\alpha}}{1-r^2}\right\}$$

Putting $r = \sqrt{\frac{2}{3}}$ and $\frac{dr}{d\alpha} = \frac{1}{2\pi}$, we get

$$\frac{d^2V}{d\alpha^2} = -\frac{1}{6}\times\frac{1}{\left(1-\frac{2}{3}\right)}(2-6).\frac{-1}{2\pi} < 0$$

Hence V is maximum, when $r = \sqrt{2/3}$

**17.** **(b)** $f'(x) \leq 0 \ \forall x \in [0, b]$, so $f(x)$ is decreasing function and $f(c) = 0 \Rightarrow f(x)$ cuts $x$ – axis once when $x = c$

**18.** **(d)** We note that $f(c) = 0, f'(c) = 0$. Also tangent to $f'(x)$ at $x = c$ is $y = 0$. So $f'(c) = 0$

$\therefore x = c$ is repeated root of third order. That is the equation

$f(x) = 0$ has at least three repeated roots.

**19.** **(A)** $\rightarrow$ **(q); (B)** $\rightarrow$ **(r); (C)** $\rightarrow$ **(p); (D)** $\rightarrow$ **(s)**

(A) Point of intersection

$$(0, b), \frac{dy}{dx} = be^{-\frac{x}{a}}\left(-\frac{1}{a}\right);$$

$$m = \left(\frac{dy}{dx}\right)_{(0, b)} = -\frac{b}{a}$$

$$\Rightarrow \text{Slope of normal} = \frac{a}{b}$$

(B) $\dfrac{dy}{dx} = -\dfrac{y}{x}$, Subnormal $= \left|y\dfrac{dy}{dx}\right|$

$$= \left| y \cdot \left( \frac{-y}{x} \right) \right| = \left| \frac{y^2}{x} \right| = \left| \frac{y^2}{\dfrac{a^2 b^2}{y}} \right| = \frac{|y^3|}{a^2 b^2}$$

(C)  $m = \dfrac{dy}{dx} = \dfrac{xb^2}{ya^2}$ ;

Length of subtangent

$$= \left| \frac{y}{\dfrac{dy}{dx}} \right| = \left| \frac{y}{\dfrac{xb^2}{ya^2}} \right| = \frac{y^2}{|x|} \frac{a^2}{b^2}$$

(D)  $\dfrac{x^2}{a^2} - \dfrac{y^2}{b^2} = 1 \;\Rightarrow\; \dfrac{2x}{a^2} - \dfrac{2y}{b^2} \dfrac{dy}{dx} = 0$

$$\Rightarrow \dfrac{dy}{dx} = \dfrac{b^2 x}{a^2 y}$$

**20.**  (A) → (q); (B) → (r); (C) → (p); (D) → (s)

(A).  r = 6 cm  δ r = 0.06

$A = \pi r^2 \,\delta A = 2\pi r \delta r = 2\pi(6)(0.06) = 0.72\pi$

(B).  $v = x^3, \delta v = 3x^2 \delta x$

$$\frac{\delta v}{v} \times 100 = 3 \frac{\delta x}{x} \times 100 = 3 \times 2 = 6$$

(C)  $(x - 2) \dfrac{dx}{dt} = 3 \dfrac{dx}{dt}$

$\Rightarrow x = 5$

(D)  $A = \dfrac{\sqrt{3}}{4} x^2 \;\Rightarrow\; \dfrac{dA}{dt} = \dfrac{\sqrt{3}}{2} \left( x \dfrac{dx}{dt} \right)$

$$= \frac{\sqrt{3}}{2} \times 30 \times \frac{1}{10} = \frac{3\sqrt{3}}{2}$$

**1.** **(c)** $\displaystyle\int \frac{dx}{3\sin^2 x + 4\cos^2 x} = \int \frac{\sec^2 x}{3\tan^2 x + 4}\,dx$

$\displaystyle = \int \frac{dt}{3t^2 + 4},$ where $t = \tan x$

$\displaystyle = \frac{1}{3}\int \frac{dt}{t^2 + \left(2/\sqrt{3}\right)^2} = \frac{1}{2\sqrt{3}}\tan^{-1}\left(\frac{t}{2/\sqrt{3}}\right) + c$

$\displaystyle = \frac{1}{2\sqrt{3}}\tan^{-1}\left(\frac{\sqrt{3}}{2}\tan x\right) + c$

**2.** **(d)** **Case -I :** If $x > 0$, then $|x| = x$

$\displaystyle \therefore \int |x|\ln|x|\,dx$

$\displaystyle = \int x\ln x\,dx = \ln x.\frac{x^2}{2} - \int \frac{1}{x}.\frac{x^2}{2}\,dx$

$\displaystyle = \frac{x^2}{2}.\ln x - \frac{x^2}{4} + c$

$\displaystyle = \frac{x^2}{2}.\ln|x| - \frac{x^2}{4} + c$

**Case- II :** If $x < 0$, then $|x| = -x$

$\displaystyle \int |x|\ln|x|\,dx = -\int x\ln(-x)\,dx$

$\displaystyle = -\left\{\ln(-x).\frac{x^2}{2} - \frac{x^2}{4}\right\} + c$

$\displaystyle = -\frac{x^2}{2}\ln|x| + \frac{x^2}{4} + c$

Combining both cases, then we get

$\displaystyle \frac{1}{2}x|x|\ln|x| - \frac{1}{4}x|x| + c$

**3.** **(b)** Let $\displaystyle I = \int \frac{(\sqrt{x})^5}{(\sqrt{x})^7 + x^6}\,dx$

$\displaystyle = \int \frac{dx}{(\sqrt{x})^2 + (\sqrt{x})^7}$

$\displaystyle = \int \frac{dx}{(\sqrt{x})^7\left(\dfrac{1}{(\sqrt{x})^5} + 1\right)}$

Put $\displaystyle \frac{1}{(\sqrt{x})^5} + 1 = t$

$\displaystyle \therefore dt = -5/2\,(x)^{-7/2}\,dx = -\frac{5}{2}.\frac{1}{(\sqrt{x})^7}\,dx$

or $\displaystyle \frac{dx}{(\sqrt{x})^7} = -\frac{2}{5}\,dt$

$\displaystyle \therefore I = -\frac{2}{5}\int \frac{dt}{t} = -\frac{2}{5}\ln|t| + c$

$\displaystyle = -\frac{2}{5}\ln\left|\frac{1}{(\sqrt{x})^5} + 1\right| + c$

$\displaystyle = \frac{2}{5}\ln\left(\frac{(\sqrt{x})^5}{(\sqrt{x})^5 + 1}\right) + c$

$\displaystyle = \frac{2}{5}\ln\left(\frac{x^{5/2}}{x^{5/2} + 1}\right) + c$

On comparing, we get

$\displaystyle \lambda = \frac{2}{5} \text{ and } a = \frac{5}{2}$

$\because$ AM $>$ GM

$\displaystyle \therefore \frac{\lambda + a}{2} > \sqrt{\lambda a} = 1$

$\therefore \lambda + a > 2$

**4.** **(a)** Let $\displaystyle I = \int_0^\infty \frac{\tan^{-1} x}{\sqrt{x}\,(1+x)}\,dx$ ...(i)

put $\displaystyle x = \frac{1}{t} \implies dx = -\frac{1}{t^2}\,dt$

$\displaystyle \therefore \int_\infty^0 \frac{\tan^{-1}\left(\dfrac{1}{t}\right)}{\dfrac{1}{\sqrt{t}}\left(1 + \dfrac{1}{t}\right)}\frac{1}{t^2}\,dt\ ;$

$\displaystyle \int_0^\infty \frac{\tan^{-1}\left(\dfrac{1}{t}\right)}{\sqrt{t}\,(1+t)}\,dt = \int_0^\infty \frac{\tan^{-1}\left(\dfrac{1}{x}\right)}{\sqrt{x}\,(1+x)}\,dx$ ...(ii)

Adding (i) and (ii),

$\displaystyle 2I = \frac{\pi}{2}\int_0^\infty - \frac{dx}{\sqrt{x}\,(x+1)}$

(put $x = y^2$, $dx = 2y\,dy$)

$$2I = \frac{\pi}{2} \int_0^\infty \frac{2y \, dy}{y(1+y^2)}$$

$$\Rightarrow \; 2I = \left[\pi \cdot \tan^{-1} y\right]_0^\infty = \frac{\pi^2}{2} \; \Rightarrow \; I = \frac{\pi^2}{4}$$

Hence, $\dfrac{502\pi^2}{k} = \dfrac{\pi^2}{4} \Rightarrow k = 2008$

**5. (b)** Let

$$l = \lim_{n \to \infty} \left( \tan\frac{\pi}{2n} \cdot \tan\frac{2\pi}{2n} \dots \dots \tan\frac{n\pi}{2n} \right)^{\frac{1}{n}}$$

$$\therefore \quad \log l = \lim_{n \to \infty} \frac{1}{n} \sum_{r=1}^{n} \log\left( \tan\frac{r\pi}{2n} \right)$$

$$\log l = \int_0^1 \log\left( \tan\frac{\pi}{2}x \right) dx \qquad \dots(i)$$

$$\Rightarrow \; I = \int_0^1 \log\left( \tan\frac{\pi}{2}(1-x)\, dx \right)$$

$$\Rightarrow \; I = \int_0^1 \log\left( \cot\frac{\pi}{2}x \right) dx \qquad \dots(ii)$$

Adding equations (i) and (ii), we get

$$2\log l = \int_0^1 \left\{ \log\tan\frac{\pi}{2}x + \log\cot\frac{\pi}{2}x \right\} dx$$

$$= \int_0^1 \log\left( \tan\frac{\pi}{2}x \cdot \cot\frac{\pi}{2}x \right) dx$$

$$= \int_0^1 0 \cdot dx = 0, \; \therefore \qquad l = e^0 = 1.$$

**6. (a)** Let $q = p+d, r = p+2d, s = p+3d$

$$\therefore f(x) = \begin{vmatrix} p+\sin x & p+d+\sin x & -2d+\sin x \\ p+d+\sin x & p+2d+\sin x & -1+\sin x \\ p+2d+\sin x & p+3d+\sin x & 2d+\sin x \end{vmatrix}$$

Applying $R \to R_1 + R_3 - 2R_2$, we get

$$f(x) = \begin{vmatrix} 0 & 0 & 2 \\ p+d+\sin x & p+2d+\sin x & -1+\sin x \\ p+2d+\sin x & p+3d+\sin x & 2d+\sin x \end{vmatrix}$$

$$= 2[(p+d+\sin x)(p+3d+\sin x)$$
$$\qquad\qquad\qquad - (p+2d+\sin x)^2]$$
$$= -2d^2$$

Given $\displaystyle\int_0^2 f(x)\,dx = -4$

$$\Rightarrow \int_0^2 (-2d^2)\,dx = -4$$

$$d^2 = 1 \; \Rightarrow \; d = \pm 1$$

**7. (b,d)** $\displaystyle I = \int \frac{\sin(\theta/2)\sin^2(\theta/2)\sin^2(\theta/2)}{(\cos^2\theta/2)\sqrt{\cos^3\theta + \cos^2\theta + \cos\theta}}\,d\theta$

$$= \frac{1}{2}\int \frac{\sin\theta\,(1-\cos\theta)}{(1+\cos\theta\,\sqrt{\cos^3\theta + \cos^2\theta + \cos\theta}}\,d\theta$$

Put $\cos\theta = x$, so that

$$I = -\frac{1}{2}\int \frac{(1-x)}{(1+x)\sqrt{x^3+x^2+x}}\,dx$$

$$= \frac{1}{2}\int \frac{x^2-1}{(x+1)^2\, x\sqrt{x+\dfrac{1}{x}+1}}\,dx$$

$$= \frac{1}{2}\int \frac{x^2-1}{x^2\left(x+\dfrac{1}{x}+2\right)\sqrt{x+\dfrac{1}{x}+1}}\,dx$$

Put $x + \dfrac{1}{x} + 1 = t^2$

$$\Rightarrow \; \left(1 - \frac{1}{x^2}\right) dx = 2 + dt$$

$$\therefore \; I = \frac{1}{2}\int \frac{2t\,dt}{(t^2+1)\,t} = \tan^{-1} t + c$$

$$= \tan^{-1}(\cos\theta + \sec\theta + 1) + c$$

**8. (b, c)** $\displaystyle I = \int \frac{x^2 + n(n-1)}{(x\sin x + n\cos x)^2}\,dx$

Multiplying and dividing by $x^{2n-2}$

$$I = \int \frac{(x^2 + n(n-1)).x^{2n-2}}{(x\sin x + n\cos x)^2 .x^{2n-2}}\,dx$$

$$I = \int \frac{(x^2 + n(n-1))x^{2n-2}}{(x^n \sin x + nx^{n-1}\cos x)^2}\,dx$$

Let $x^n \sin x + nx^{n-1}\cos x = t$

$$\Rightarrow \quad (nx^{n-1}\sin x + x^n\cos x + n(n-1))x^{n-2}$$
$$\cos x - nx^{n-1}\sin x)dx = dt$$
$$\Rightarrow \quad x^{n-2}\cos x \cdot (x^2 + n(n-1))dx = dt$$

$$I = \int \frac{(x^2 + n(n-1)) \cdot x^{n-2} \cos x}{(x^n \sin x + nx^{n-1} \cos x)^2} \cdot x^n \cdot \sec x \, dx$$

Integrating by parts; we get

$$I = x^n \sec x \cdot \left( -\frac{1}{x^n \sin x + nx^{n-1} \cos x} \right)$$

$$+ \int \frac{x^n \sec x \tan x + nx^{n-1} \sec x}{(x^n \sin x + nx^{n-1} \cos x)} \, dx$$

$$= -\frac{x^n \sec x}{x^n \sin x + nx^{n-1} \cos x} + \tan x + c$$

**9.**   **(a,d)**   $\int \sin^{-1} x \cos^{-1} x \, dx$

$$= \int \left[ \frac{\pi}{2} \sin^{-1} x - (\sin^{-1} x)^2 \right] dx$$

$$= \frac{\pi}{2} \left( x \sin^{-1} x + \sqrt{1-x^2} \right)$$

$$- \left( x(\sin^{-1} x)^2 + \sin^{-1} x \sqrt{1-x^2} - x \right) + c$$

(integrating by parts)

$$= \sin^{-1} x \left[ \frac{\pi}{2} x - x \sin^{-1} x - 2\sqrt{1-x^2} \right]$$

$$+ \frac{\pi}{2}\sqrt{1-x^2} + 2x + c$$

$$\therefore f^{-1}(x) = \sin^{-1} x, f(x) = \sin x$$

**10.**   **(a,d)** The eccentricities of a hyperbola and its conjugate $e_1$ and $e_2$ are related by

$$\frac{1}{e_1^2} + \frac{1}{e_2^2} = 1 \Rightarrow e_2 = \frac{e_1}{\sqrt{e_1^2 - 1}}$$

$$\therefore f(e) = \frac{e}{\sqrt{e^2 - 1}} \Rightarrow ff(e) = e$$

$$\therefore \underbrace{fff \,\ldots\, f}_{n \text{ times}} (e)$$

$$= \begin{cases} \dfrac{e}{\sqrt{e^2 - 1}}, & \text{if } n \text{ is odd} \\[2mm] e, & \text{if } n \text{ is even} \end{cases}$$

$$\therefore \int_1^3 fff \ldots f(e) \, de = \begin{cases} 2\sqrt{2}, & \text{if } n \text{ is odd} \\ 4, & \text{if } n \text{ is even} \end{cases}$$

**11.**   **(2)**

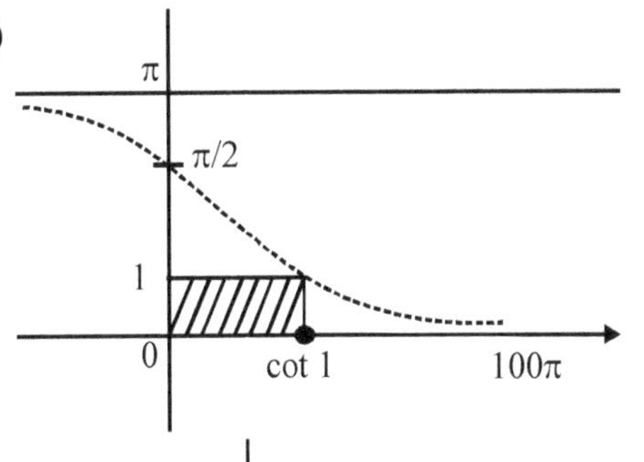


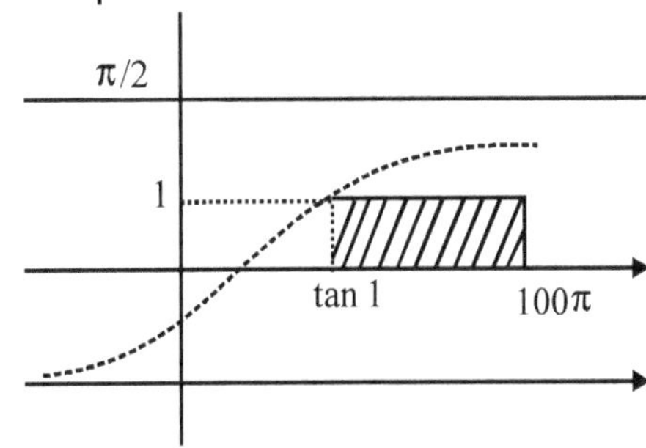


$$\int_0^{100\pi} ([\cot^{-1} x] + [\tan^{-1} x]) \, dx$$
$$= \cot 1 + (100\pi - \tan 1)$$

$$= 100\pi + \frac{1 - \tan^2 1}{\tan 1} = 100\pi + 2\cot 2$$

**12.**   **(0)**   We have $x \int_0^x (1-t)f(t)dt = \int_0^x t f(t)dt$

Differentating both sides with respect to $x$, we get

$$x(1-x)f(x) + \int_0^x (1-t)f(t)dt = x f(x)$$

$$\Rightarrow \quad x^2 f(x) = \int_0^x (1-t)f(t)dt$$

Differentiating again with respect to $x$ on both sides, we get

$$x^2 f'(x) + 2x f(x) = (1-x) f(x)$$

$$\Rightarrow \quad \frac{f'(x)}{f(x)} = \frac{1-3x}{x^2}$$

Integrating both the sides, we get

$$\ln |f(x)| = -\frac{1}{x} + 3 \ln x + \lambda$$

$$\Rightarrow \quad \ln \left[ x^3 |f(x)| \right] + \frac{1}{x} = \lambda \text{ and } f(1) = 1$$

$$\Rightarrow \quad \lambda = 1$$

$$\Rightarrow \quad |f(x)| = \frac{1}{x^3} e^{\left(1 - \frac{1}{x}\right)}.$$

Thus $\lim_{x \to \infty} f(x) = 0$

**13.** **(2)** $I(n) = \int\limits_0^{\pi/2} \theta . \sin^n \theta \, d\theta$

$\Rightarrow \quad I(n) = \int\limits_0^{\pi/2} \theta . \sin^{n-2}\theta (1 - \cos^2 \theta) d\theta$

$= I(n-2) - \int\limits_0^{\pi/2} (\theta . \cos \theta) . \cos \theta . \sin^{n-2} \theta \, d\theta$

$= \left[ I(n-2) - \theta . \cos \theta . \dfrac{\sin^{n-1} \theta}{n-1} \right]_0^{\pi/2}$

$\qquad + \int\limits_0^{\pi/2} [\theta .(-\sin \theta) + \cos \theta] . \dfrac{\sin^{n-1} \theta}{n-1} d\theta$

$= I(n-2) - \dfrac{1}{(n-1)} \int\limits_0^{\pi/2} \theta . \sin^n \theta \, d\theta$

$\qquad + \dfrac{1}{n-1} \int\limits_0^{\pi/2} \cos \theta . \sin^{n-1} \theta \, d\theta$

$= I(n-2) - \dfrac{1}{(n-1)} . I(n)$

$\qquad + \dfrac{1}{(n-1)(n)} . \left[ \sin^n \theta \right]_0^{\pi/2}$

$\Rightarrow \quad \dfrac{n}{n-1} I(n) = I(n-2) + \dfrac{1}{(n-1)(n)}$

$\Rightarrow \quad I(n) - I(n-2) . \dfrac{n-1}{n} = \dfrac{1}{n^2}$

$\Rightarrow \quad n \, I(n) - (n-1) \, I(n-2) = \dfrac{1}{n}$

Put $n = 2010$, then

$2010 \ I(2010) - 2009 \ I(2008) = \dfrac{1}{2010}$

$\Rightarrow \quad [2010 \ I(2010) - 2009 \ I(2008)]^{-1}$

$\qquad = 2010 = 1005 \times 2$

**14.** **(1)**

$I = \int \operatorname{cosec}^2 x \, ln \left( \cos x + \sqrt{\cos 2x} \right) dx$

$= -\cot x . \log_e \left( \cos x + \sqrt{\cos 2x} \right)$

$\qquad - \int (-\cot x), \dfrac{1}{\cos x + \sqrt{\cos 2x}}$

$\qquad \left\{ -\sin x + \dfrac{1}{2} (\cos 2x)^{-\frac{1}{2}} (-\sin 2x) . 2 \right\} dx$

$= -\cot x \, ln \left( \cos x + \sqrt{\cos 2x} \right)$

$\qquad - \int \cot x \dfrac{\sin x \sqrt{\cos 2x} + \sin 2x}{\sqrt{\cos 2x} \left( \cos x + \sqrt{\cos 2x} \right)} dx$

$= -\cot x \, ln \left( \cos x + \sqrt{\cos 2x} \right)$

$\qquad - \int \dfrac{\cos x \sqrt{\cos 2x} - \cos^2 x \cos 2x}{\cos 2x \sin^2 x} dx$

$= -\cot x \, ln \left( \cos x + \sqrt{\cos 2x} \right)$

$\qquad - \int \dfrac{\cos x}{\sqrt{\cos 2x} \sin^2 x} dx + \int \cot^2 x \, dx$

Now, $I_1 = \int \dfrac{\cos x \, dx}{\sqrt{\cos 2x} \sin^2 x}$

$\qquad = \int \dfrac{\cos x \, dx}{\sin^2 x \sqrt{1 - 2\sin^2 x}} = \int \dfrac{dt}{t^2 \sqrt{1 - 2t^2}}$

Put $t = \dfrac{1}{u} \Rightarrow dt = -\dfrac{1}{u^2} du$

$\therefore \ I_1 = -\int \dfrac{u \, du}{\sqrt{u^2 - 2}} = -\sqrt{u^2 - 2} = -\sqrt{\operatorname{cosec}^2 x - 2}$

Thus $I = -\cot x \, ln \left( \cos x + \sqrt{\cos 2x} \right)$

$\qquad + \sqrt{\operatorname{cosec}^2 x - 2} - \cot x - x + c$

$\therefore \ f(x) = -\cot x \ and \ g(x) = \sqrt{\operatorname{cosec}^2 x - 2}$

**15.** **(d)** If $f(x)$ is an even function, then

$\phi(-x) = -\int\limits_{-a}^{x} f(t) \, dt$

$\qquad = -\int\limits_{-a}^{a} f(t) \, dt - \int\limits_{a}^{x} f(t) \, dt$

$$= -2\int_0^a f(t)\,dt - \int_a^x f(t)\,dt$$

( as $f(x)$ is an even function )

Now, $\displaystyle\int_0^a f(t)\,dt = \int_0^a f(a-t)\,dt$

$$= -\int_0^a f(t)\,dt \quad [\text{ using } f(a-x) = -f(x)]$$

$$\Rightarrow \quad \int_0^a f(t)\,dt = 0$$

$$\Rightarrow \quad \phi(-x) = -\int_a^x f(t)\,dt = -\phi(x)$$

$\Rightarrow \quad \phi(x)$ is an odd function.

**16.** **(d)** $g(x+\alpha) + g(x) = 0$

$\Rightarrow g(x) + 2\alpha) + g(x+\alpha) = 0$

$\Rightarrow g(x + 2\alpha) = g(x)$

$\Rightarrow g(x)$ is periodic with period $2\alpha$

$$\Rightarrow \int_b^{2k} g(t)\,dt = \int_b^{b+c} g(x)\,dx$$

( $\because$  $b, k, c$ are in A. P.)

This is independent of $b$ then $c$ has least value $2\,\alpha$.

**For Qs. 17 & 18**

$$A = \begin{bmatrix} x & x \\ x & x \end{bmatrix} \Rightarrow A^2 = \begin{bmatrix} 2x^2 & 2x^2 \\ 2x^2 & 2x^2 \end{bmatrix},$$

$$A^3 = \begin{bmatrix} 2^2 x^2 & 2^2 x^2 \\ 2^2 x^2 & 2^2 x^2 \end{bmatrix} \quad \text{and so on}$$

Then $e^A = I + A + \dfrac{A^2}{2!} + \dfrac{A^3}{3!} + \dots +$

$$= \begin{bmatrix} 1 + x + \dfrac{2x^2}{2!} + \dfrac{2^2 x^3}{3!} + \dots & x + \dfrac{2x^2}{2!} + \dfrac{2^2 x^3}{3!} + \dots \\ x + \dfrac{2x^2}{2!} + \dfrac{2^2 x^3}{3!} + \dots & 1 + x + \dfrac{2x^2}{2!} + \dfrac{2^2 x^3}{3!} + \dots \end{bmatrix}$$

$$= \begin{bmatrix} \dfrac{1}{2}\left(1 + 2x + \dfrac{2^2 x^2}{2!} + \dfrac{2^3 x^3}{3!} + \dots\right) + \dfrac{1}{2} & \dfrac{1}{2}\left(1 + 2x + \dfrac{2^2 x^2}{2!} + \dots\right) - \dfrac{1}{2} \\ \dfrac{1}{2}\left(1 + 2x + \dfrac{2^2 x^2}{2!} + \dfrac{2^3 x^3}{3!} + \dots\right) - \dfrac{1}{2} & \dfrac{1}{2}\left(1 + 2x + \dfrac{2^2 x^2}{2!} + \dots\right) + \dfrac{1}{2} \end{bmatrix}$$

$$= \frac{1}{2}\begin{bmatrix} e^{2x} + 1 & e^{2x} - 1 \\ e^{2x} - 1 & e^{2x} + 1 \end{bmatrix}$$

$\Rightarrow \quad f(x) = e^{2x} + 1$ and $g(x) = e^{2x} - 1$

**17.** **(a)** $\displaystyle\int \frac{e^{2x} - 1}{e^{2x} + 1}\,dx = \int \frac{e^x - e^{-x}}{e^x + e^{-x}}\,dx$

**18.** **(b)** $\displaystyle\int (g(x) + 1)\sin x\,dx$

$$= \int e^{2x}\sin x\,dx = \frac{e^{2x}}{5}(2\sin x - \cos x)$$

**19.** $(A) \rightarrow (r); (B) \rightarrow (p); (C) \rightarrow (t); (D) \rightarrow (s)$

$$\int \frac{\ln(x + \sqrt{1+x^2})}{\sqrt{1+x^2}}\,dx = I$$

Put $\ln(x + \sqrt{1+x^2}) = t \Rightarrow \dfrac{dx}{\sqrt{1+x^2}} = dt$

So, $I = \displaystyle\int t\,dt = \frac{t^2}{2} + c = \frac{1}{2}\left\{\ln\left(x + \sqrt{1+x^2}\right)\right\}^2 + c$.

Thus,

**(A)** $f(x) = \dfrac{x^2}{2}$

**(B)** $g(x) = \ln(x + \sqrt{x^2 + 1})$

**(C)** Now, $\displaystyle\int \frac{x^2}{2}\ln(x + \sqrt{x^2+1})\,dx$

$$= \frac{x^3}{6}\ln(x + \sqrt{x^2+1})$$

$$- \frac{1}{2}\int \frac{x^3}{3} \times \frac{1}{x + \sqrt{x^2+1}}\left\{1 + \frac{2x}{2\sqrt{x^2+1}}\right\}dx$$

$$= \frac{x^3}{6}\ln(x + \sqrt{x^2+1}) - \frac{1}{6}\int \frac{x^3\,dx}{\sqrt{x^2+1}}$$

$$= \frac{x^3}{6}\ln(x + \sqrt{x^2+1}) - \frac{1}{6}\int (t^2 - 1)\,dt$$

Putting $x^2 + 1 = t^2$

$$= \frac{x^3}{6}\ln(x + \sqrt{x^2+1}) - \frac{1}{18}(1+x^2)^{3/2}$$

$$+ \frac{1}{6}(1+x^2)^{1/2} + c$$

**(D)** $\int e^{g(x)} dx = \int (x + \sqrt{1+x^2}) dx$

$$= \frac{x^2}{2} + \frac{x}{2}\sqrt{1+x^2} + \frac{1}{2}\ln(x + \sqrt{1+x^2}) + c$$

$$= \frac{1}{2}x(x + \sqrt{1+x^2}) + \frac{1}{2}g(x) + c$$

**20.** **(A)** $\to$ **(r); (B)** $\to$ **(t); (C)** $\to$ **(q); (D)** $\to$ **(p, q, r, s)**

**(A)** $0 < \dfrac{3}{x^2+1} \leq 3$

$\Rightarrow \dfrac{3}{x^2+1} = 2$

$\Rightarrow x = \dfrac{1}{\sqrt{2}}$ and $\dfrac{3}{x^2+1} = 1$

$\Rightarrow x = \sqrt{2}$

$$I = \int_{0}^{1/\sqrt{2}} 2\,dx + \int_{1/\sqrt{2}}^{\sqrt{2}} 1.dx$$

$$+ \int_{\sqrt{2}}^{\infty} 0\,dx = \sqrt{2} + \sqrt{2} - \frac{1}{\sqrt{2}}$$

$$= 2\sqrt{2} - \frac{1}{\sqrt{2}} = \frac{3}{\sqrt{2}}$$

**(B)** $\displaystyle\int_{-10}^{10} \frac{3}{3^{[x]}}dx = 20\int_{0}^{1} 3^{x-[x]}dx = 20\int_{0}^{1} 3^x\,dx$

$$= 20\left[\frac{3^x}{\ln 3}\right]_{0}^{1} = \frac{40}{\ln 3}$$

**(C)** $\displaystyle\int_{-1}^{1} [x[1 + \sin \pi x] + 1]\,dx$

$$= \int_{-1}^{0} [x[1 + \sin \pi x] + 1]\,dx + \int_{0}^{1} [x[1 + \sin \pi x] + 1]dx$$

Now, $-1 < x < 0 \Rightarrow [1 + \sin \pi x] = 0$

And $0 < x < 1 \Rightarrow [1 + \sin \pi x] = 1$

$\Rightarrow [x[1 + \sin \pi x] + 1] = 1$

So, $\displaystyle\int_{-1}^{1} [x[1 + \sin \pi x] + 1]\,dx = 2$

**(D)** The L.H.S. of given inequality is equal to

$$\left[ a^2\left(\frac{\sin 3x}{12} + \frac{3}{4}\sin x\right) - a\cos x - 20\sin x \right]_{0}^{\pi/2}$$

$$= a^2\left(-\frac{1}{12} + \frac{3}{4}\right) - a(0-1) - 20$$

$$= \frac{2a^2}{3} + a - 20$$

Thus the given inequality is $\dfrac{2a^2}{3} + a - 20 \leq -\dfrac{a^2}{3}$ i.e.,

$a^2 + a - 20 \leq 0$

$\Rightarrow -5 \leq a \leq 4$

Since '$a$' is a positive integer so, $a = 1, 2, 3, 4$.

**1. (a)**

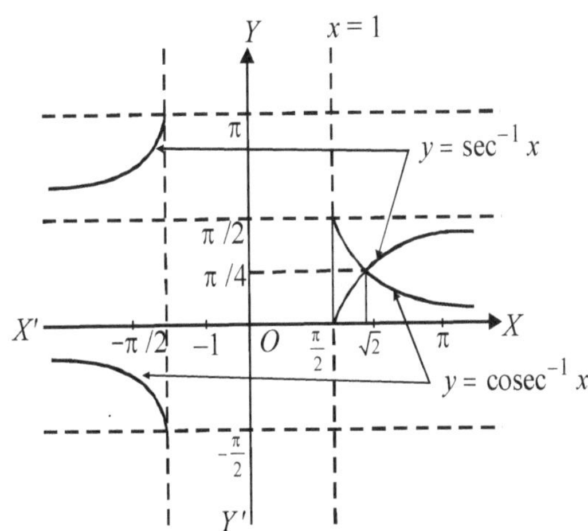

Integrating along $x$-axis, we get

$$A = \int_{1}^{\sqrt{2}} (\text{cosec}^{-1} x - \sec^{-1} x)\, dx$$

Integrating along $y$-axis, we get

$$A = 2 \int_{0}^{\pi/4} (\sec y - 1)\, dy$$

$$= 2[\log|\sec y + \tan y| - y]_{0}^{\pi/4}$$

$$= 2\left[\log|\sqrt{2}+1| - \frac{\pi}{4}\right] = \left(\log(3+2\sqrt{2}) - \frac{\pi}{2}\right) \text{ sq.units}$$

**2. (b)** $ay^2 = x^2(a-x) \Rightarrow y = \pm x\sqrt{\dfrac{a-x}{a}}$

Curve tracing : $y = x\sqrt{\dfrac{a-x}{a}}$

We must have $x \le a$

For $0 < x \le a$, $y > 0$ and for $x < 0$, $y < 0$

Also $y = 0 \Rightarrow x = 0, a$

Curve is symmetrical about $x$-axis.

When $x \to -\infty$, $y \to -\infty$

Also, it can be varified that $y$ has only one point of maxima for $0 < x < a$.

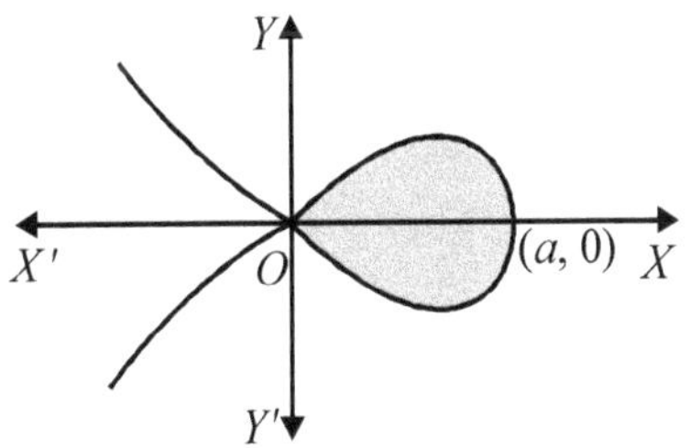

$$\text{Area} = 2\int_{0}^{a} x\sqrt{\frac{a-x}{a}}\, dx$$

$$\sqrt{\frac{a-x}{a}} = t \Rightarrow 1 - \frac{x}{a} = t^2 \Rightarrow x = a(1-t^2)$$

$$\Rightarrow \quad A = 2\int_{1}^{0} a(1-t^2)\, t\,(-2at)\, dt$$

$$= 4a^2 \int_{0}^{1} (t^2 - t^4)\, dt$$

$$= 4a^2\left[\frac{t^3}{3} - \frac{t^5}{5}\right]_{0}^{1}$$

$$= 4a^2\left[\frac{1}{3} - \frac{1}{5}\right] = \frac{8a^2}{15} \text{ sq.units}$$

**3. (a)** The two curves are

$$xy^2 = a^2(a-x) \Rightarrow x = \frac{a^3}{a^2 + y^2} \qquad \text{...(i)}$$

and $(a-x)y^2 = a^2 x$

$$\Rightarrow \quad x = \frac{ay^2}{a^2 + y^2} = \frac{ay^2 + a^3 - a^3}{a^2 + y^2}$$

$$= a - \frac{a^3}{a^2 + y^2} \qquad \text{...(ii)}$$

Curve (i) is symmetrical about $x$-axis and have $y$-axis as the asymptote.

Curve (ii) is symmetrical about $x$-axis, tangent at origin as $y$-axis and the asymptote $x = a$.

The two curve intersect at the point $P(a/2, a)$ and $Q(a/2, -a)$.

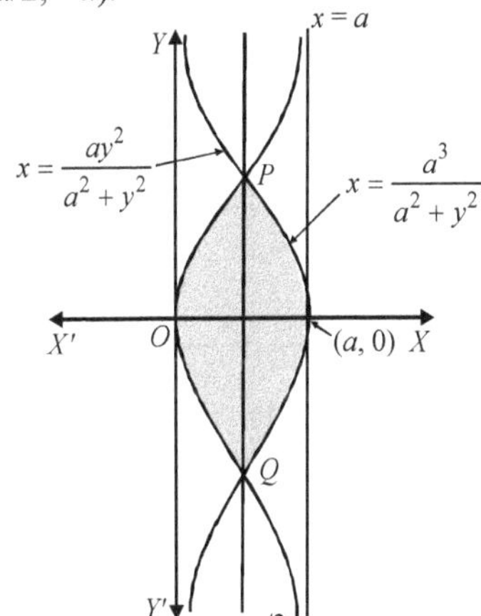

Required area $= 2\int_0^a \left[ a - \dfrac{a^3}{a^2+y^2} - \dfrac{a^3}{a^2+y^2} \right] dy$

(integrating along $y$-axis)

$= 2\left[ ay - 2a^2 \tan^{-1}\dfrac{y}{a} \right]_0^a$

$= 2\left[ a^2 - 2a^2 \dfrac{\pi}{4} \right]$

$= (\pi - 2)\, a^2$ sq. units

**4. (c)** As, $f(x) = \begin{cases} \sqrt{\{x\}}, & x \notin z \\ 1, & x \in z \end{cases}$ and $g(x) = \{x\}^2$, where

both $f(x)$ and $g(x)$ are periodic with period '1' shown as,

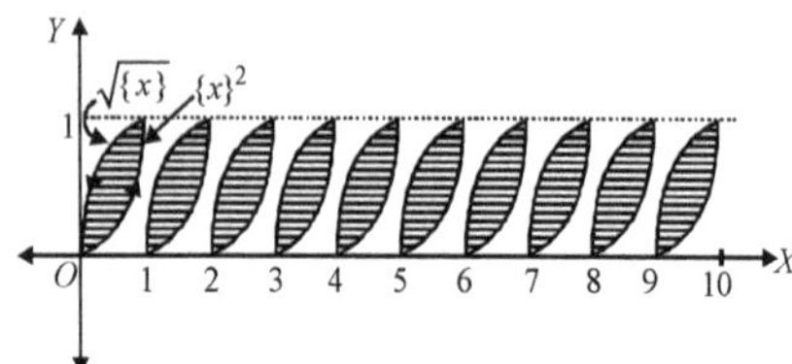


Thus required area $= 10\int_0^1 (\sqrt{\{x\}} - \{x\}^2)\,dx$

$= 10\int_0^1 ((x)^{1/2} - x^2)\,dx = 10\left\{ \dfrac{x^{3/2}}{3/2} - \dfrac{x^3}{3} \right\}_0^1$

$= 10\left\{ \dfrac{2}{3} - \dfrac{1}{3} \right\} = \dfrac{10}{3}$ sq. unit

**5. (c)** $y = 2 - |2 - x|,\ y = \dfrac{3}{|x|}$

$y = \begin{cases} x, & x \le 2 \\ 4 - x, & x \ge 2 \end{cases};\quad y = \begin{cases} \dfrac{3}{x}, & x > 0 \\ -\dfrac{3}{x}, & x < 0 \end{cases}$

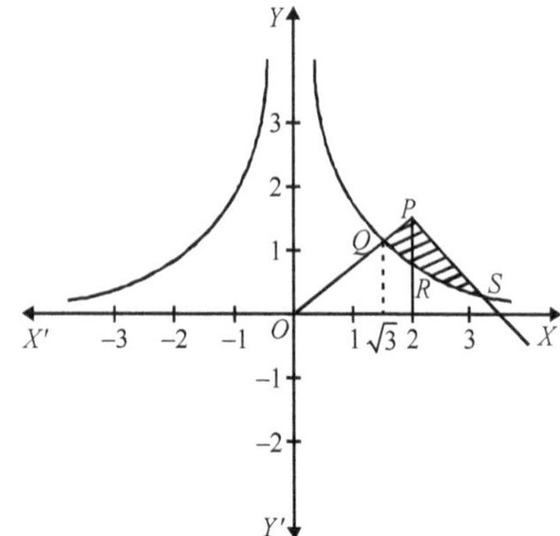


Hence, required area = Area of region $PQRSP$
= area of region $PQRP$ + area of region $PRSP$

$= \left| \int_{\sqrt3}^2 \left( x - \dfrac{3}{x} \right) dx \right| + \left| \int_2^3 \left( (4 - x) - \dfrac{3}{x} \right) dx \right|$

$= \left( \dfrac{4 - 3\ln 3}{2} \right)$ sq. units

**6. (b, c)** $\text{Area} = \int_0^3 (f(x) - g(x))\,dx + \int_3^5 (g(x) - f(x))\,dx$

$= \int_0^3 f(x)\,dx - \int_0^3 g(x)\,dx + \int_3^5 g(x)\,dx - \int_3^5 f(x)\,dx$

$= (a - c) - (d) + (b - d) - c$

$= a + b - 2c - 2d$

**7. (a, c, d)**

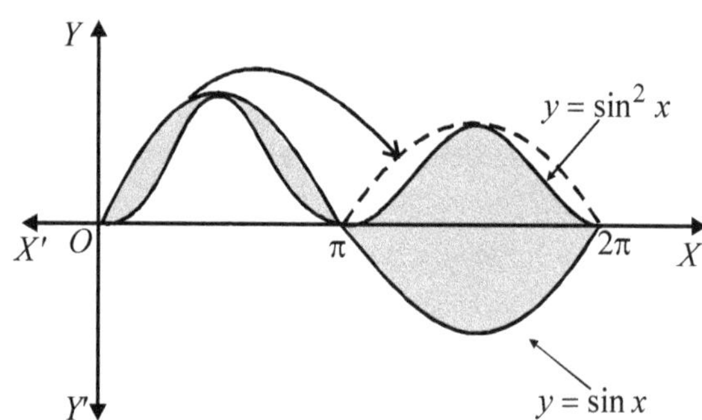


We know that area bounded by $y = \sin x$ and $x$-axis for $x \in [0, \pi]$ is 2 sq. units.

Then area bounded by $y = \sin x$ and $y = \sin^2 x$ is 4 sq. units for $x \in [0, 2\pi]$.

Then for $x \in [0, 10\pi]$, the area bounded is 20 sq. units.

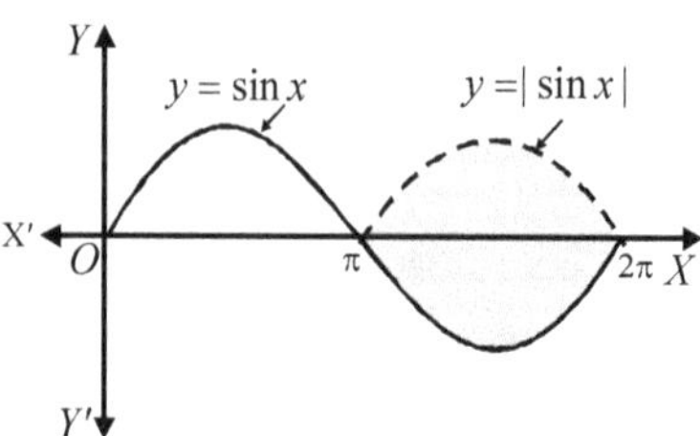


The area bounded by $y = \sin x$ and $y = |\sin x|$ for $x \in [0, 2\pi]$ is 4 sq. units.

Then for $x \in [0, 2\pi]$, the area bounded is 40 sq. units.

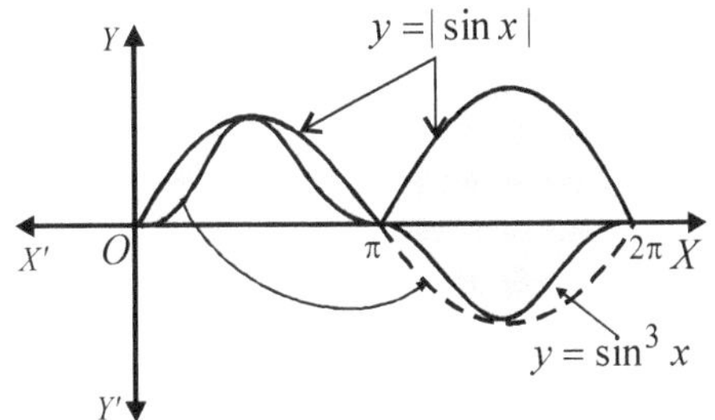


The area bounded by $y = \sin x$ and $y = \sin^3 x$ for $x \in [0, 2\pi]$ is 4 sq. units.

Then for $x \in [0, 10\pi]$, the area bounded is 20 sq. units. Similarly, the area bounded by $y = \sin x$ and $y = \sin^4 x$ for $x \in [0, 10\pi]$ is 20 sq. units.

**8.** **(c, d)** Here, curve $ABCD$ is max $\{f(x),\ g(x)\} = p(x)$ and curve $EBCF$ is min $\{f(x),\ g(x)\} = q(x)$.

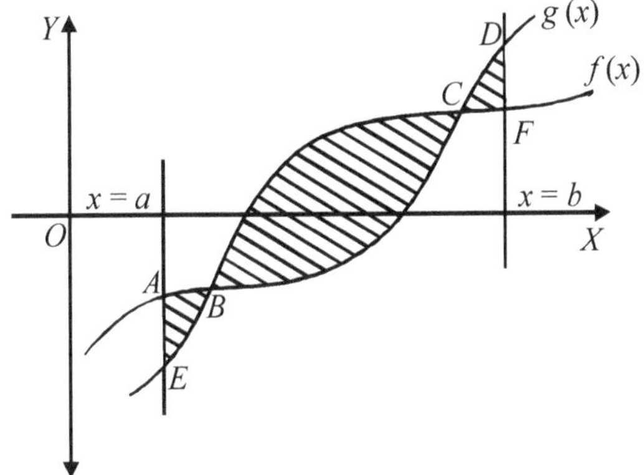


Thus, area can be determine by either (c) or (d).

**9.** **(a, b, d)** First of all let us draw a rough sketch of $y = e^{-x}$.
At $x = 0$, $y = 1$ and at $x = 1$, $y = 1/e$

Also $\dfrac{dy}{dx} = -2xe^{-x^2} < 0 \ \ \forall \ x \in (0,1)$

$\therefore y = e^{-x^2}$ is decreasing on $(0, 1)$
Hence its graph is as shown in figure given below

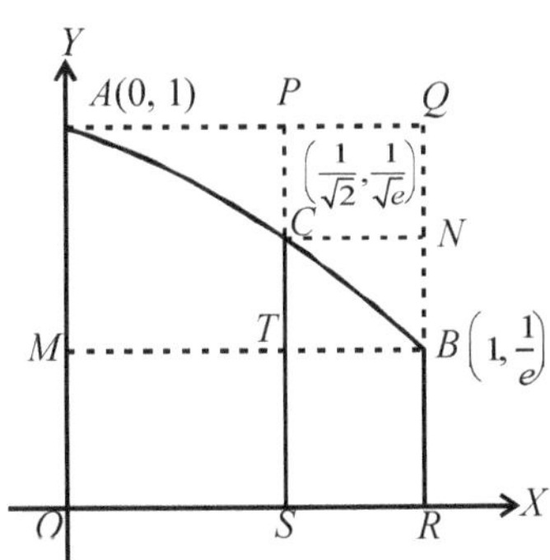


Now, S = area exclosed by curve = ABRO

and area of rectangle ORBM = $\dfrac{1}{e}$

Clearly $S > \dfrac{1}{e}$ $\quad \therefore$ A is true.

Also $x^2 < x \ \ \forall \ x \in [0,1]$

$\Rightarrow \ -x^2 > -x \ \ \Rightarrow \ e^{-x^2} \geq e^{-x} \ \forall \ x \in [0,1]$

$\Rightarrow \displaystyle\int_0^1 e^{-x^2} dx > \int_0^1 e^{-x} dx = 1 - \dfrac{1}{e}$

$\Rightarrow \ S > 1 - \dfrac{1}{e} \qquad \therefore$ (b) is true.

Now S < area of rectangle APSO + area of rectangle CSRN

$\Rightarrow \ S < \dfrac{1}{\sqrt{2}} \times 1 + \left(1 - \dfrac{1}{\sqrt{2}}\right) \dfrac{1}{\sqrt{e}}$

$\therefore \quad S < \dfrac{1}{\sqrt{2}} + \dfrac{1}{\sqrt{e}}\left(1 - \dfrac{1}{\sqrt{2}}\right) \qquad \because$ (d) is true

Also as $\dfrac{1}{4}\left(1 + \dfrac{1}{\sqrt{e}}\right) < 1 - \dfrac{1}{e} \qquad \therefore$ (c) is incorrect.

**10.** **(8)**

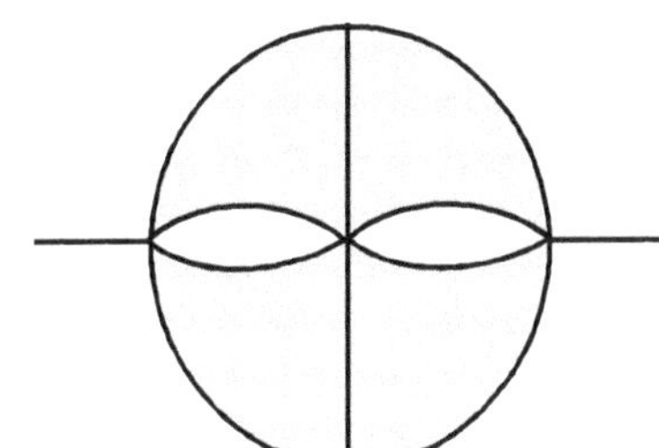

Required area

$= \pi(\pi^2) - 4\displaystyle\int_0^{\pi} \sin x\, dx = \pi^3 - 8$

**11.** **(7)**

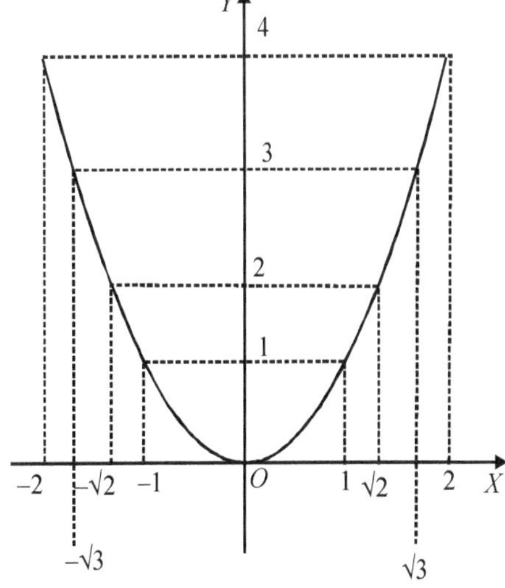


As we know that fractional part of any thing must lie between 0 and 1 thus

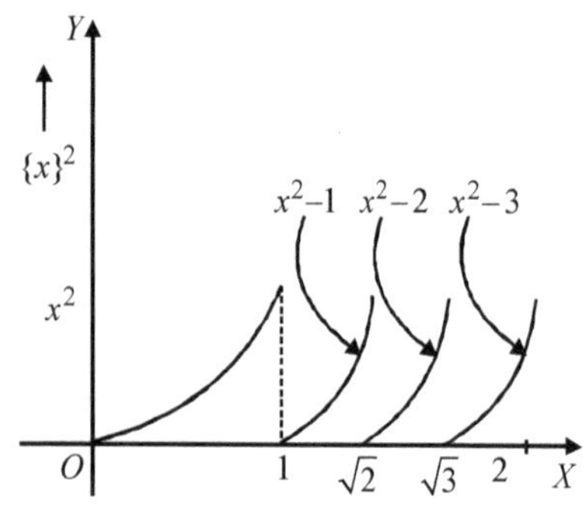

$\therefore$ Area of region bounded by $y = \{x\}^2$ between $x$-axis for the $x \in [0, 2]$ is

$$= \int_0^1 x^2\, dx + \int_1^{\sqrt{2}} (x^2 - 1)\, dx + \int_{\sqrt{2}}^{\sqrt{3}} (x^2 - 2)\, dx$$

$$+ \int_{\sqrt{3}}^{2} (x^2 - 3)\, dx$$

$$A_0 = \sqrt{2} + \sqrt{3} - \frac{7}{3}$$

$\therefore$ Required area $= 2A_0 = 2\left(\sqrt{2} + \sqrt{3} - \frac{7}{3}\right)$

**12. (2)** $|y + x| \le 1 \quad \Rightarrow \quad -1 \le x + y \le 1$

It represents the region between the lines $x + y = 1$ and $x + y = -1$

Similarly, $|y - x| \le 1$

$\Rightarrow \quad -1 \le y - x \le 1$ represents the region between the lines $x - y = 1$ and $-x + y = 1$

$\Rightarrow$ Both together form a square of side $\sqrt{2}$ units

$3x^2 + 12y^2 = 2$ is an ellipse with

$$a = \sqrt{\frac{2}{3}}, \quad b = \frac{1}{\sqrt{6}}$$

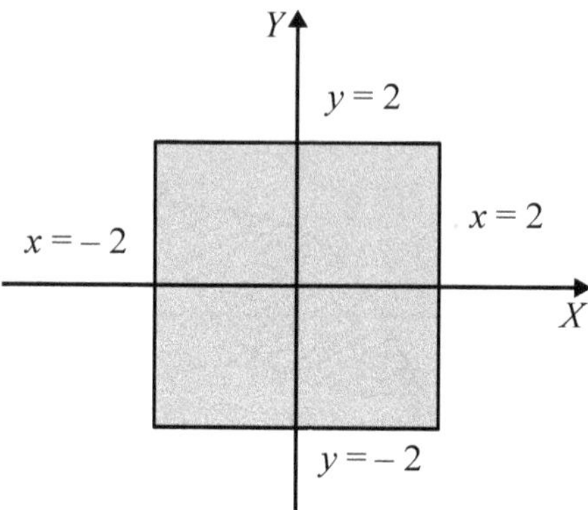

Area of the ellipse $= \pi ab = \dfrac{\pi}{3}$

Area of the square $= 2$ sq. units

Required area $= \left(2 - \dfrac{\pi}{3}\right)$ sq. units.

**13. (4)** $\dfrac{|x| + |y|}{2} + \left|\dfrac{|x| - |y|}{2}\right| \le 2$

$\Rightarrow \quad ||x| - |y|| \le 4 - |x| + |y|)$ ( here $|x| + |y| \le 4$)

$\Rightarrow \quad |x| + |y| - 4 \le |x| - |y| \le 4 - (|x| + |y|)$

$\Rightarrow \quad |x| \le 2$ and $|y| \le 2$

So, that the region satisfying

$$|x| \le 2, |y| \le 2 \text{ and } |x| + |y| \le 4 \text{ is}$$

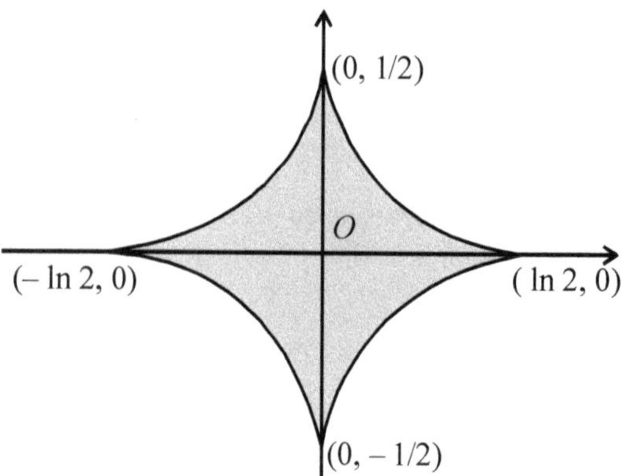

Also curve $|y| = e^{-|x|} - \dfrac{1}{2}$ is symmetric about both $x$ and $y$-axis. So that the curve is

So that the required region is the the shaded region $=$ (area of square $ABCD$) $-$ (area of curve $A'B'C'D'$ )

$$= 16 - 4 \int_0^{\ln 2} \left(e^{-x} - \frac{1}{2}\right) dx$$

$$= 14 + \ln 4 \text{ sq. units}$$

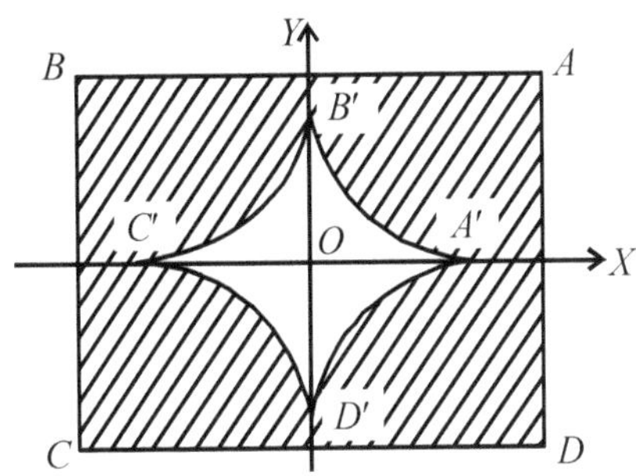

**14.** **(4)** $f(x) = \dfrac{\pi}{2} - \sin^{-1}(\sin x)$ ; $g(x) = \dfrac{\pi}{2} - \cos^{-1}(\cos x)$

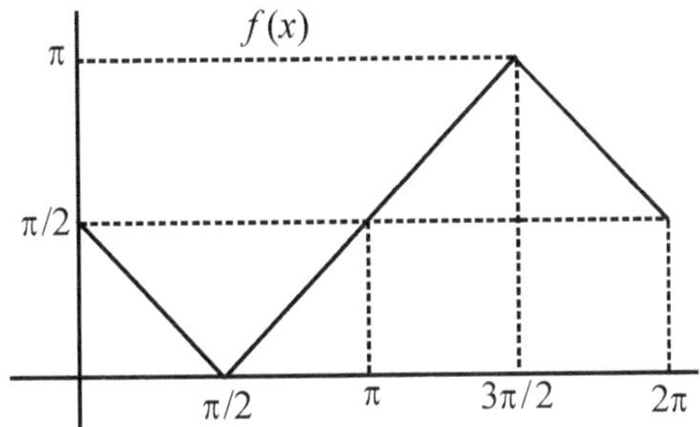

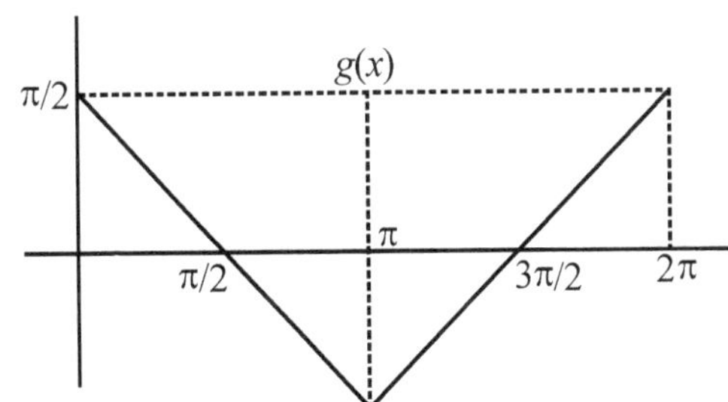

Both $f(x)$ and $g(x)$

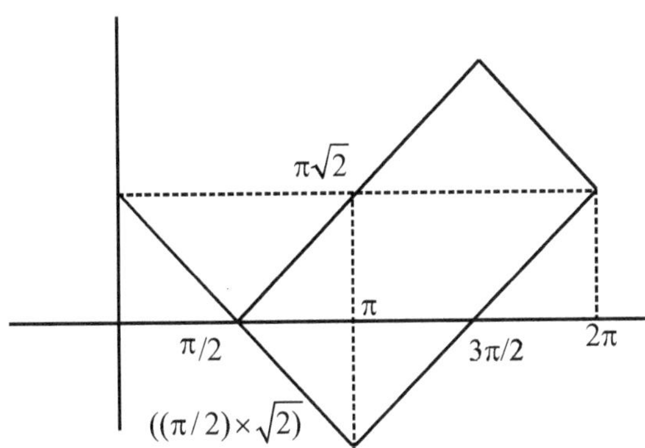

So, area $= \pi\sqrt{2} \times \dfrac{\pi}{2}\sqrt{2} = \pi^2$

From 0 to $98\pi$, there are 49 period

So, $A = 49\pi^2 = 49 \times \dfrac{22}{7} \times \dfrac{22}{7} = (22)^2 = 484$

**For Q. 15—16**

Since $-1 \le \sin x \le 1$, the curve $y = e^{-x}\sin x$ is bounded by the curves $y = e^{-x}$ and $y = e^{-x}$.

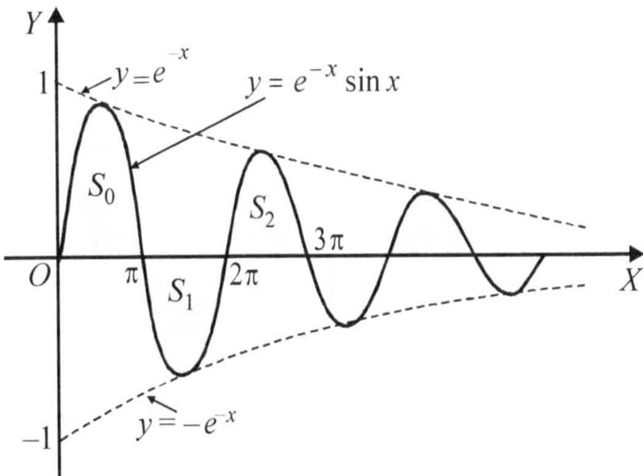

Also, the curve $y = e^{-x}\sin x$ intersects the positive semi-axis $OX$ at the points where $\sin x = 0$, where $x_n = n\pi$, $n \in Z$.

Also $|y_n| = |y$ coordinate in the half-wave $S_n| = (-1)^n e^{-x}$ $\sin x$, and in $S_n$, $n\pi \le x \le (n+1)\pi$

$$\therefore \ S_n = (-1)^n \int_{n\pi}^{(n+1)\pi} e^{-x}\sin x\, dx$$

$$= \frac{(-1)^{n+1}}{2}\left[e^{-x}(-\sin x + \cos x)\right]_{n\pi}^{(n+1)\pi}$$

$$= \frac{(-1)^{n+1}}{2}[e^{-(n+1)\pi}(-1)^{n+1} - e^{n\pi}\beta(-1)^n]$$

$$= \frac{e^{-n\pi}}{2}\left(1 + e^\pi\right)$$

$$\Rightarrow \quad \frac{S_{n+1}}{S_n} = e^{-\pi} \ \text{ and } \ S_0 = \frac{1}{2}(1 + e^\pi)$$

$\therefore$ The sequence $S_0, S_1, S_2, \dots$ forms an infinite G.P. with common ratio $e^{-\pi}$

**15.** **(a)**  **16. (b)**

**For Q. 17 - 19**

- The graph of $|x - p| + |y - q| = k$ is a square. Area of the region bounded by $|x - p| + |y - q| = k$ is given by $2k^2$ (area is independent of $p$ and $q$).

- The resultant figure for $a|x - p| + b|y - q| = k$ is a rhombus. Area of the region bounded by $a|x - p| + b|y - q| = k$ is given by $\dfrac{2k^2}{ab}$ (area is independent of $p$ and $q$)

- The resultant figure for $|x - p| - |y - q| = k$ is not a closed loop so we cannot find the area bounded by the graph.

- The resultant figure which is bounded by $|x+y|=p$ and $|x-y|=q$ is a rectangle and its area will be $(\sqrt{2}p)(\sqrt{2}q)$ i.e., $2pq$.

  Area of the regions bounded by $|x-p|+|y-q|=k$ and $\left|x-\dfrac{1}{p}\right|+\left|y-\dfrac{1}{q}\right|=k$ is same.

**17.** (b)

**18.** (a)

**19.** (d)

**20.** $(A)\to(q)$ ; $(B)\to(p)$; $(C)\to(s)$; $(D)\to(r)$

(A) Area $= 2\left(\dfrac{1}{2}.1.1\right) = 1$ sq. units. $(q)$

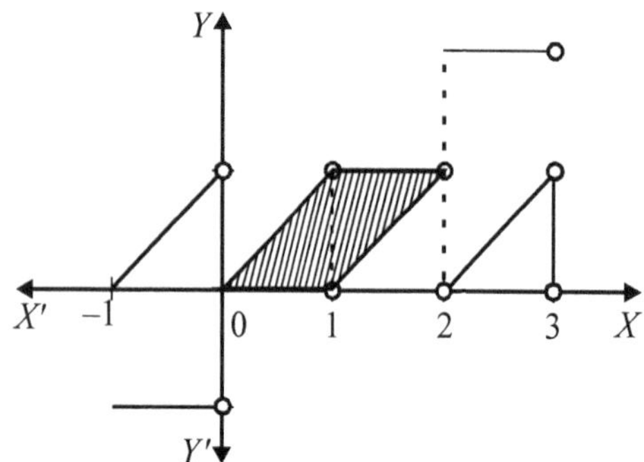

(B) $y^2 = x^3$ and $|y| = 2x$, both the curve are symmetric about $y$-axis

$4x^2 = x^3 \Rightarrow x = 0, 4.$

Required area $= 2\displaystyle\int_0^4 (2x - x^{3/2})dx$

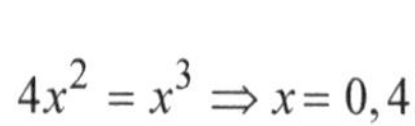

$= \dfrac{16}{5}$ sq. units. **(p)**

(C) $\sqrt{x} + \sqrt{|y|} = 1$

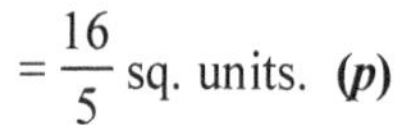

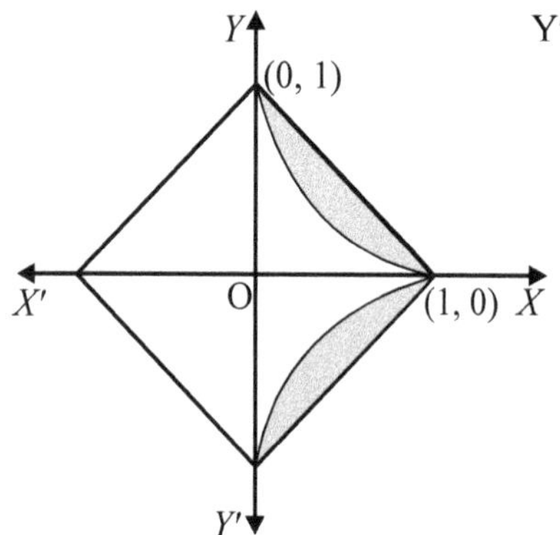


The curve is symmetrical about $x$-axis, because

$\sqrt{|y|} = 1 - \sqrt{x}$ and $\sqrt{x} = 1 - \sqrt{|y|}$

$\Rightarrow$ for $x > 0,\ y > 0,\ \sqrt{y} = 1 - \sqrt{x}$

$\dfrac{1}{2\sqrt{y}}\dfrac{dy}{dx} = -\dfrac{1}{2\sqrt{x}}$

$\dfrac{dy}{dx} = -\sqrt{\dfrac{x}{y}}$

$\dfrac{dy}{dx} < 0,$ function is decreasing. Required area

$= 2\displaystyle\int_0^1 (1-x) - (1 - 2\sqrt{x} + x)dx = 4\displaystyle\int_0^1 (\sqrt{x} - x)dx$

$= 4\left[\dfrac{x^{3/2}}{3/2} - \dfrac{x^2}{2}\right]_0^1 = 4\left[\dfrac{2}{3} - \dfrac{1}{2}\right]$

$= \dfrac{2}{3}$ sq. units  **(s)**

(D) If $-8 < x < 8$, then $y = 2$

If $x \in (-8\sqrt{2}, -8] \cup [8, \sqrt{2})$, then $y = 3$, and so on

Intersection of $y = x - 1$ and $y = 2$. We get $x = 3 \in (-8, 8).$

Intersection of $y = x - 1$ and $y = 3$, we get $x = 4 \notin (-8\sqrt{2}, -8] \cup [8, 8\sqrt{2}).$

Similarly, $y = x - 1$ will not intersect $y = \left[\dfrac{x^2}{64} + 2\right]$ at any other interval, except in the interval $x \in (-8, 8).$

The required area (shaded region)

$= 2 \times 3 - \dfrac{1}{2} \times 2 \times 2 = 4$ sq. units $(r)$

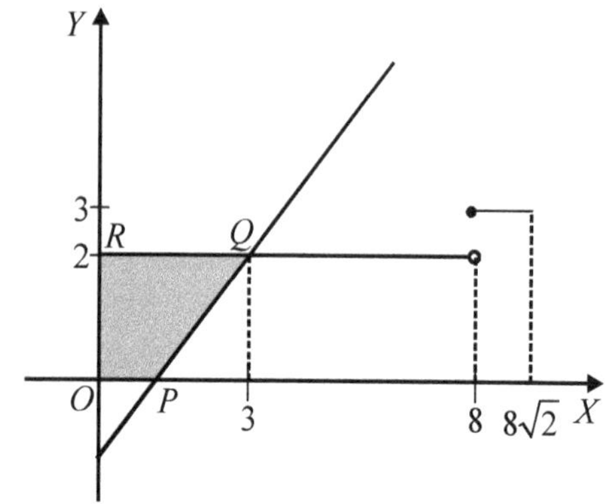

**1.** **(a)** $\dfrac{dy}{dx} - \dfrac{y}{x} = -\dfrac{5x}{(x+2)(x-3)}$,

which is linear in $y$

I.F. $= e^{\int -\frac{1}{x}dx} = e^{-\ln x} = \dfrac{1}{x}$

So the solution is

$y.\dfrac{1}{x} = -\int \dfrac{5}{(x+2)(x+3)} dx + c$

$y.\dfrac{1}{x} = \ln\left(\dfrac{x+2}{x-3}\right) + c$

It passes through $(4, 0)$

$\therefore \quad 0 = \ln 6 + c \Rightarrow c = -\ln 6$

$\therefore \quad \dfrac{y}{x} = \ln \dfrac{x+2}{x-3} - \ln 6$

Then point $(5, a)$ lies on it

$\therefore \quad a = 5 \ln (7/12)$

**2.** **(d)** Putting $v = y/x$ so that $x\dfrac{dv}{dx} + v = \dfrac{dy}{dx}$

We have $x\dfrac{dv}{dx} + v = v + \phi(1/v)$

$\Rightarrow \quad \dfrac{dv}{\phi(1/v)} = \dfrac{dx}{x}$

$\Rightarrow \quad \log|Cx| = \int \dfrac{dv}{\phi(1/v)}$

($C$ being constant of integration)

But $y = \dfrac{x}{\log|Cx|}$ is the general solution,

So $\dfrac{x}{y} = \dfrac{1}{v} = \log|Cx| = \int \dfrac{dv}{\phi(1/v)}$

$\Rightarrow \quad \phi(1/v) = -1/v^2$

(differentiating w.r.t. $v$ both sides)

$\Rightarrow \quad \phi(x/y) = -y^2/x^2$

**3.** **(a)** We have

$dy + \{y\phi'(x) - \phi(x)\phi'(x)\} dx = 0$

$\Rightarrow \quad \dfrac{dy}{dx} + \phi'(x).y = \phi(x)\phi'(x)$

This is a linear differential equation with

I.F. $= e^{\int \phi'(x)dx = e^{\phi(x)}}$.

Multiplying (i) by $\phi(x)$ and integrating we get

$ye^{\phi(x)} = \int \phi(x)\phi'(x)e^{\phi(x)}dx$

$\Rightarrow \quad ye^{\phi(x)} = \int e^{\phi(x)}\phi(x)\phi'(x)\,dx$

$\Rightarrow \quad ye^{\phi(x)} = \int \underset{\text{I}}{\phi(x)}\, \underset{\text{II}}{e^{\phi(x)}\phi'(x)}dx$

$\Rightarrow \quad ye^{\phi(x)} = \phi(x)e^{\phi(x)} - \int \phi'(x)e^{\phi(x)}\,dx$

$\Rightarrow \quad ye^{\phi(x)} = \phi(x)e^{\phi(x)} - e^{\phi(x)} + c$

$\Rightarrow \quad y = (\phi(x) - 1) + ce^{-\phi(x)}$

**4.** **(a)**

(a) Order of the differential equation is 2.

(b) $\dfrac{xdy - ydx}{\sqrt{x^2+y^2}} = dx \Rightarrow \dfrac{\dfrac{xdy - ydx}{x^2}}{\sqrt{1 + \dfrac{y^2}{x^2}}} = \dfrac{dx}{x}$ ...(i)

Put $t = \dfrac{y}{x}$, $\therefore \dfrac{dt}{dx} = \dfrac{x.\dfrac{dy}{dx} - y}{x^2}$

$\Rightarrow \quad \dfrac{dt}{dx} = \dfrac{xdy - ydx}{x^2.dx} \Rightarrow dt = \dfrac{xdy - ydx}{x^2}$

L.H.S. of equation (i) $= \dfrac{1}{\sqrt{1-t^2}}dt$

$\therefore \int \dfrac{1}{\sqrt{1-t^2}}dt = \int \dfrac{1}{x}dx$

$\therefore \int \dfrac{1}{\sqrt{1-t^2}}dt = \int \dfrac{1}{x}dx$

$\Rightarrow \quad \ln\left| \dfrac{y}{x} + \sqrt{1 + \dfrac{y^2}{x^2}} \right| = \ln|cx|,$

$\Rightarrow \quad \dfrac{y}{x} + \dfrac{\sqrt{x^2+y^2}}{x} = cx$

$\Rightarrow \quad y + \sqrt{x^2+y^2} = cx^2$

(c) $y = e^x(A\cos x + B\sin x)$

$\dfrac{dy}{dx} = e^x(A\cos x + B\sin x)$

$\qquad\qquad\qquad + e^x(-A\sin x + B\cos x)$

$$= y + e^x(-A\sin x + B\cos x)$$

$$\therefore \quad \frac{d^2 y}{dx^2} = \frac{dy}{dx} + e^x(-A\sin x + B\cos x)$$

$$+ e^x(-A\cos x - B\sin x)$$

$$\therefore \quad \frac{d^2 y}{dx^2} = \frac{dy}{dx} + e^x(-A\sin x + B\cos x) - y$$

$$= \frac{dy}{dx} + \frac{dy}{dx} - y - y = 2\left(\frac{dy}{dx} - y\right)$$

(d) $\quad \dfrac{dx}{dy} + \dfrac{x}{1+y^2} = \dfrac{2e^{\tan^{-1} y}}{1+y^2}$ ;

$$\text{I.F.} = e^{\int \frac{1}{1+y^2}} = e^{\tan^{-1} y}$$

$$\Rightarrow \quad x.e^{\tan^{-1} y} = 2\int e^{\tan^{-1} y} \cdot \frac{e^{\tan^{-1} y}}{1+y^2} dy$$

$$\Rightarrow \quad x.e^{\tan^{-1} y} = e^{2\tan^{-1} y} + k$$

**5. (a)** Taking $x = r\cos\theta$ and $y = r\sin\theta$, so that

$x^2 + y^2 = r^2$ and $y/x = \tan\theta$, we have

$x\,dx + y\,dx = r\,dr$ and

$x\,dy - y\,dx = x^2 \sec^2\theta\,d\theta = r^2 d\theta$ .

The given equation can be transformed into

$$\frac{r\,dr}{r^2 d\theta} = \sqrt{\frac{a^2 - r^2}{r^2}} \Rightarrow \frac{dr}{d\theta} = \sqrt{a^2 - r^2}$$

$$\Rightarrow \quad c + \sin^{-1} r/a = \theta = \tan^{-1} y/x$$

$$\Rightarrow \quad y = x\tan\left(c + \sin^{-1}\frac{1}{a}\sqrt{x^2 + y^2}\right)$$

or $\quad \sqrt{x^2 + y^2} = a\sin\left(\text{const.} + \tan^{-1}\frac{y}{x}\right)$

**6. (b, c)**

(a): $\quad y = 2 + c_1 \cos x + \sqrt{c_2}\,\sin x$

$$\frac{dy}{dx} = -c_1 \sin x + \sqrt{c_2}\,\cos x$$

$$\frac{d^2 y}{dx^2} = -c_1 \cos x - \sqrt{c_2}\,\sin x = 2 - y$$

$$\frac{d^2 y}{dx^2} + y + 2 = 0$$

(b): $\quad y = \cos x \ln\left(\tan\frac{x}{2}\right)$

$$\frac{dy}{dx} = \cos x \, \frac{\sec^2(x/2)}{2\tan(x/2)} - \sin x \ln\left(\tan\frac{x}{2}\right)$$

$$\frac{dy}{dx} = \cot x - \sin x \ln\left(\tan\frac{x}{2}\right)$$

$$\frac{d^2 y}{dx^2} = -\cot^2 x - 2 - \cos x \ln\left(\tan\frac{x}{2}\right)$$

$$\frac{d^2 y}{dx^2} + y + \cot^2 x = 0$$

(c): $\quad y = 2 + c_1 \cos x + c_2 \sin x + \cos x \ln\tan\frac{x}{2}$

$$\frac{dy}{dx} = -c_1 \sin x + c_2 \cos x$$

$$+ \frac{d}{dx}\left(\cos x \ln\left(\tan\frac{x}{2}\right)\right)$$

$$\frac{d^2 y}{dx^2} = -(c_1 \cos x + c_2 \sin x)$$

$$+ \frac{d^2}{dx^2}\left(\cos x \ln\left(\tan\frac{x}{2}\right)\right)$$

$$\Rightarrow \quad \frac{d^2 y}{dx^2} = -c_1 \cos x - c_2 \sin x - \cot^2 x$$

$$- 2 - \cos x \ln\left(\tan\frac{x}{2}\right)$$

$$\Rightarrow \quad \frac{d^2 y}{dx^2} + y + \cot^2 x = 0$$

**7. (a, d)** Equation of tangent at $(x, y)$,

$$Y - y = \frac{dy}{dx}(X - x)$$

$\therefore \quad$ Coordinate of $A$ is $\left(x - y\dfrac{dx}{dy}, 0\right)$

Radius vector $OP = \sqrt{x^2 + y^2}$

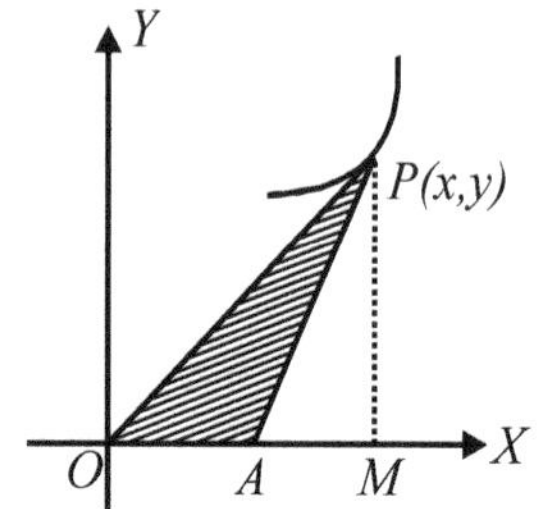

Area of $\triangle OAP = \triangle OPM - \triangle APM$

$$= \frac{1}{2}xy - \frac{1}{2}\left(y\frac{dx}{dy}\right) \quad y = \pm a^2 \text{ (given)}$$

$$\Rightarrow \quad xy - y^2\frac{dx}{dy} = \pm 2a^2$$

$$\Rightarrow \quad y^2\frac{dx}{dy} - xy \pm 2a^2 = 0$$

$$\Rightarrow \quad \frac{dx}{dy} - \frac{x}{y} = \pm\frac{2a^2}{y^2}$$

This is a linear equation and

$$\text{I.F.} = e^{-\ln y} = \frac{1}{y}$$

$\therefore$ Solution is $x\left(\dfrac{1}{y}\right) = \mp\, 2a^2\displaystyle\int\frac{1}{y^3}dy + c$

$$\Rightarrow \quad \frac{x}{y} = \pm\frac{a^2}{y^2} + c \;\Rightarrow\; x = cy \pm\frac{a^2}{y},$$

where $c$ is an arbitrary constant.

**8. (a, b, c)**

(a) $\quad f(\lambda x, \lambda y) = \dfrac{\lambda(x-y)}{\lambda^2(x^2+y^2)} = \lambda^{-1}f(x,y)$

$\Rightarrow$ homogeneous of degree $(-1)$.

(b) $\quad f(\lambda x, \lambda y) = (\lambda x)^{1/3}(\lambda y)^{-2/3}\tan^{-1}\dfrac{x}{y}$

$$= \lambda^{-1/3}x^{1/3}y^{-2/3}\tan^{-1}\frac{x}{y}$$

$$= \lambda^{-\frac{1}{3}}f(x,y)$$

$\Rightarrow$ homogeneous

(c) $\quad f(\lambda x, \lambda y) = \lambda x\big(\ln\sqrt{\lambda^2(x^2+y^2)}$

$$-\ln \lambda y\big) + \lambda\, y e^{x/y}$$

$$= \lambda x\left[\ln\left(\frac{\lambda\sqrt{(x^2+y^2)}}{\lambda y}\right)\right] + \lambda y e^{x/y}$$

$$= \lambda[\,x(\ln\sqrt{x^2+y^2} - \ln y) + y e^{x/y}\,]$$

$$= \lambda f(x,y)$$

$\Rightarrow$ homogeneous

(d) $\quad f(\lambda x, \lambda y) = \lambda x\left[\ln\dfrac{2\lambda^2 x^2 + \lambda^2 y^2}{\lambda x\,\lambda(x+y)}\right.$

$$\left. + \lambda^2 x^2\tan\frac{x+2y}{3x-y}\right.$$

$$= \lambda x\left[\ln\frac{2x^2+y^2}{x(x+y)}\right] + \lambda^2 x^2\tan\frac{x+2y}{3x-y}$$

$\Rightarrow$ non homogeneous

**9. (a, d)** Differentiating the given equation, we have

$$2x + 2y\frac{dy}{dx} + 2g = 0$$

$$\Rightarrow \quad g = -\left(x + y\frac{dy}{dx}\right)$$

Putting this value in

$x^2 + y^2 + 2gx + c = 0$, we have

$$x^2 + y^2 - 2x\left(x + y\frac{dy}{dx}\right) + c = 0$$

Replacing $\dfrac{dy}{dx}$ by $-\dfrac{dx}{dy}$, we have the differential equation of orthogonal trajectories as

$$y^2 - x^2 + 2xy\frac{dy}{dx} + c = 0$$

$$\Rightarrow \quad 2x\frac{dx}{dy} - \frac{1}{y}x^2 = -\frac{c}{y} - y$$

Putting $x^2 = v$, we have $\dfrac{dv}{dy} - \dfrac{1}{y}v = -\dfrac{c}{y} - y$,

which is linear in $v$ and $y$ whose I.F. is $\dfrac{1}{y}$. Hence

$$\frac{v}{y} = \int\left(-\frac{c}{y^2} - 1\right)dy + c' = \frac{c}{y} - y + c'$$

$\Rightarrow \quad x^2 + y^2 - c'y - c = 0,$ which represent system of circles with center on $y$-axis.

**10. (8)** Differentiating both sides of the given equation w.r.t. $x$, we get

$$x.y(x) + \int_0^x y(t)dt.1 = (x+1)x.y(x) + \int_0^x ty(t)dt$$

or $\quad \displaystyle\int_0^x y(t)dt = x^2 y(x) + \int_0^x ty(t)dt$

Again differentiating both sides w.r.t. $x$

$$y(x) = x^2 y'(x) + y(x)2x + xy(x)$$

$$\Rightarrow \quad (1-3x)y(x) = x^2 y'(x)$$

$\Rightarrow \quad \dfrac{y'(x)}{y(x)} = \left( \dfrac{1}{x^2} - \dfrac{3}{x} \right)$

Integrating, we get

$\ln y(x) = -\dfrac{1}{x} - 3\ln x + \ln c$

$\Rightarrow \quad \ln\left( \dfrac{x^3 y(x)}{c} \right) = -\dfrac{1}{x} \quad \text{or} \quad \dfrac{x^3 y(x)}{c} = e^{-1/x}$

$\Rightarrow \quad y(x) = \dfrac{c e^{-1/x}}{x^3}$

So, $\quad y(1) = e \Rightarrow c = e^2$

$\therefore \quad y\left( \dfrac{1}{2} \right) = 8$

**11.**    **(8)**

Let population $= x$, at time t years

Give $\dfrac{dx}{dt} \propto x \Rightarrow \dfrac{dx}{dt} = kx$

Where k is constant of proportionality or $\dfrac{dx}{x} = kdt$

Integrating, we get $\ln x = kt + \ln c \Rightarrow \dfrac{x}{c} = e^{kt}$

or $x = c e^{kt}$

If initially i.e., when time $t = 0, x = x_0$ then $x_0 = c e^0 = c$

$\therefore \quad x = x_0 e^{kt}$

Given $x = 2x_0$ when $t = 30$ then $2x_0 = x_0 e^{30k}$

$\Rightarrow \quad 2 = e^{30k} \hspace{3cm} \text{........ (1)}$

$\therefore \quad \ln 2 = 30k$

To find t, when it tripples, $x = 3x_0$

$\therefore \quad 3x_0 = x_0 e^{kt} \Rightarrow 3 = e^{kt} \hspace{1.5cm} \text{.......(2)}$

$\therefore \quad \ln 3 = kt$

Diving (2) by (1) then $\dfrac{t}{30} = \dfrac{\ln 3}{\ln 2}$

or $t = 30 \times \dfrac{\ln 3}{\ln 2} = 30 \times 1.5849 = 48$ years. (approx.)

$\Rightarrow \quad 6\,\text{m} = 48$

$\Rightarrow \quad \text{m} = 8$

**12.**    **(6)**

Given $y = C_1 e^{m_1 x} + C_2 e^{m_2 x} + C_3 e^{m_3 x} \hspace{1cm} \text{...... (1)}$

so, $y_1 = C_1 m_1 e^{m_1 x} + C_2 m_2 e^{m_2 x} + C_3 m_3 e^{m_3 x}$

$\quad = m_1(y - C_2 e^{m_2 x} - C_3 e^{m_3 x}) + C_2 m_2 e^{m_2 x} + C_3 m_3 e^{m_3 x}$

$\hspace{3cm} \{\text{from}\,(1)\}$

$\quad = m_1 y + C_2(m_2 - m_1) e^{m_2} + C_3(m_3 - m_1) e^{m_3 x} \hspace{0.5cm} \text{...(2)}$

Next $y_2 = m_1 y_1 + C_2 m_2 (m_2 - m_1) e^{m_2 x}$

$\hspace{3cm} + C_3 m_3 (m_3 - m_1) e^{m_3 x}$

$\quad = m_1 y_1 + m_2[y_1 - m_1 y - C_3(m_3 - m_1) e^{m_3 x}]$

$\hspace{3cm} + C_3 m_3 (m_3 - m_1) e^{m_3 x}$

$\hspace{3.5cm} [\text{from } (2)]$

$\quad = (m_1 + m_2)y_1 - m_1 m_2 y$

$\hspace{2cm} + C_3(m_3 - m_1)(m_3 - m_2) e^{m_3 x} \hspace{0.7cm} \text{......(3)}$

Further, $y_3 = (m_1 + m_2)y_2 - m_1 m_2 y_1$

$\hspace{2cm} + C_3 m_3 (m_3 - m_1)(m_3 - m_2) e^{m_2 x}$

$\quad = (m_1 + m_2)y_2 - m_1 m_2 y_1$

$\hspace{1.5cm} + m_3[y_2 - (m_1 + m_2)y_1 + m_1 m_2 y]\,[\text{from }(3)]$

$\quad = (m_1 + m_2 + m_3)y_2 - (m_1 m_2 + m_1 m_3 + m_2 m_3)y_1$

$\hspace{4cm} + m_1 m_2 m_3 y$

$\quad = 0 . y_2 - (-7)y_1 - 6y \Rightarrow y_3 - 7y_1 + 6y = 0$

**13.**    **(2)**   The given differential equation is in the form of a

polynomial in the differential coefficient $\dfrac{dy}{dx}, \dfrac{d^2 y}{dx^2}$ and

$\dfrac{d^3 y}{dx^3}$. The differential coefficient $\dfrac{d^3 y}{dx^3}$ is the highest

order differential coefficient out of $\dfrac{dy}{dx}, \dfrac{d^2 y}{dx^2}$ and $\dfrac{d^3 y}{dx^3}$.

The highest exponent of this highest order differential

coefficient $\dfrac{d^3 y}{dx^3}$ is 2. Hence degree of the given

differential equation is 2.

**For Qs.14 – 15**

Integrating $\dfrac{d^2 y}{dx^2} = 6x - 4$, we get

$\dfrac{dy}{dx} = 3x^2 - 4x + A$

When $x = 1, \dfrac{dy}{dx} = 0$ and hence $A = 1.$

$\therefore \quad \dfrac{dy}{dx} = 3x^2 - 4x + 1 \hspace{1cm} \text{...(i)}$

Integrating, we get $y = x^3 - 2x^2 + x + B.$

When $x = 1, y = 5$, then $B = 5.$

Thus, we have, $y = x^3 - 2x^2 + x + 5$

From equation (i), we get the critical points $x = 1/3$, $x = 1$

At the critical point $x = \dfrac{1}{3}, \dfrac{d^2 y}{dx^2}$ is $-$ve

Therefore, at $x = 1/3$, $y$ has a local maximum.

At $x = 1$, $\dfrac{d^2 y}{dx^2}$ is $+$ve.

Therefore, at $x = 1$, $y$ has a local minimum.

Also $f(1) = 5$, $f\left(\dfrac{1}{3}\right) = \dfrac{157}{27}$, $f(0) = 5$,

$f(2) = 7$

Hence the global maximum value $= 7$ and the global

minimum value $= 5$

**14.** (c)        **15.**    (a)

**For Qs. 16 – 18**

$(1 + x^2)\dfrac{dy}{dx} + 2xy - 4x^2 = 0$

$\text{I.F.} = e^{\int \frac{2x}{1+x^2}\,dx} = 1 + x^2$

So, $y(1 + x^2) = \int \dfrac{4x^2}{1 + x^2}(1 + x^2)dx + c$

$y(1 + x^2) = \dfrac{4}{3}x^3 + c$

Similarly for, $(x + 2y^3)\dfrac{dy}{dx} = y$

$\text{I.F.} = \dfrac{1}{y}$

So, $x = y^3 + cy$

For, $(1 + x)\dfrac{dy}{dx} - xy = 1 - x$

$\text{I.F.} = e^{-x}(1 + x)$

So, $y(1 + x) = x + ce^x$

For, $\dfrac{dy}{dx} + \dfrac{y}{(1 - x^2)^{3/2}} = \dfrac{x + \sqrt{1 - x^2}}{(1 - x^2)^2}$

$\text{I.F.} = e^{\frac{x}{\sqrt{1 - x^2}}}$

$y = \dfrac{x}{\sqrt{1 - x^2}} + ce^{-x/\sqrt{1 - x^2}}$

**16.** (d)

**17.** (c)

**18.** (a)

**19.** (A) $\rightarrow$ (q,s) ; (B) $\rightarrow$ (r) ; (C) $\rightarrow$ (q,s) ; (D) $\rightarrow$ (p,t)

We have

$\dfrac{dy}{dx} = y + \int_0^1 y\, dx \Rightarrow \dfrac{d}{dx}\left(\dfrac{dy}{dx}\right) = \dfrac{dy}{dx} + 0 \Rightarrow \dfrac{d}{dx}p = p$

(where $p = \dfrac{dy}{dx}$)

Integrating we get $\ln p = x + \ln k \Rightarrow p = k\, e^x$.

$\therefore \dfrac{dy}{dx} = k\, e^x$       .....(1)

Integrating again $y = k e^x + c$    .....(2)

Now $f(0) = 1 \Rightarrow 1 = c + k$ or $c = 1 - k$

Also $\dfrac{dy}{dx} = y + \int_0^1 y\, dx \Rightarrow ke^x = ke^x + 1 - k + \int_0^1 (ke^x + 1 - k)\, dx$

$\therefore 0 = 1 - k + ke + 1 - k - k \Rightarrow k = \dfrac{2}{3 - e}$

Clearly $\dfrac{dy}{dx}\bigg|_{x=0} = f'(0) = k = \dfrac{2}{3 - e}$

$\dfrac{d^2 y}{dx^2}\bigg|_{x=0} = f''(0) = k = \dfrac{2}{3 - e}$

Also, $y = f(x) = \dfrac{2e^x + 1 - e}{3 - e} \Rightarrow f(1) = \dfrac{e + 1}{3 - e}$

$\displaystyle \lim_{x \to 0} \dfrac{f(x) - 1}{x} = \lim_{x \to 0} \dfrac{2e^x + 1 - e - 3 + e}{x(3 - e)}$

$= \dfrac{2}{3 - e} \displaystyle\lim_{x \to 0} \dfrac{e^x - 1}{x} = \dfrac{2}{3 - e}$

**20.** (A) $\rightarrow$ (p, q, r); (B) $\rightarrow$ (p); (C) $\rightarrow$ (q); (D) $\rightarrow$ (q, s)

(A)   $f(x) = \displaystyle\int_0^x e^t \sin(x - t)\, dt$

$= \displaystyle\int_0^x e^{x-t} \sin(t)\, dt$

$f(x) = e^x \displaystyle\int_0^x e^{-t} \sin t\, dt$

$f'(x) = e^x . e^{-x} \sin x + \left(\displaystyle\int_0^x e^{-t} \sin t\, dt\right) e^x$

$f'(x) = \sin x + f(x)$       ...(i)

$f''(x) = \cos x + f'(x) = \cos x + \sin x + f(x)$

                        [Using (i)]

$f''(x) - f(x) = \sin x + \cos x$       ...(ii)

$g(x) = \sin x + \cos x \Rightarrow g(x) \in [-\sqrt{2}, \sqrt{2}]$

(B) $x = \tan^{-1} t \Rightarrow \dfrac{dx}{dt} = \dfrac{1}{1+t^2}$

$$\dfrac{dy}{dx} = \dfrac{dy}{dt} \cdot \dfrac{dt}{dx} = \dfrac{dy}{dt}(1+t^2) \qquad \ldots(i)$$

$$\dfrac{d^2 y}{dx^2} = \dfrac{d}{dt}\left[\dfrac{dy}{dt}(1+t^2)\right] \cdot \dfrac{dt}{dx}$$

$$= \left[\dfrac{dy}{dt} 2t + (1+t^2)\dfrac{d^2 y}{dt^2}\right](1+t^2) \qquad \ldots(ii)$$

Hence the given differential equation

$$\dfrac{d^2 y}{dx^2} + xy\dfrac{dy}{dx} + \sec^2 x > 0 \text{, becomes}$$

$$(1+t^2)\left[2t\dfrac{dy}{dt} + (1+t^2)\dfrac{d^2 y}{dt^2}\right]$$

$$+ y\tan^{-1} t\left[\dfrac{dy}{dt}(1+t^2)\right] + (1+t^2) = 0$$

Cancelling $(1+t^2)$ throughout we get

$$(1+t^2)\dfrac{d^2 y}{dt^2} + (2t + y\tan^{-1} t)\dfrac{dy}{dt} = -1$$

$\Rightarrow \quad k = -1$

(C) Let $a = \cos\theta$, $b = \sin\theta$

$\quad \therefore \ E = ab(a^2 - b^2) = \cos\theta \sin\theta (\cos 2\theta)$

$\quad = \dfrac{1}{2}\sin 2\theta \cos 2\theta = \dfrac{1}{4}\sin 2\theta.$

$\Rightarrow \quad -\dfrac{1}{4} \le E \le \dfrac{1}{4}$ ; Possible vlaue $= 0$

(D) Obviously $D_1 = D_2 = D_3 = 0$

$$D = \begin{vmatrix} 1 & -\lambda & -1 \\ \lambda & -1 & -1 \\ 1 & 1 & -1 \end{vmatrix} \ne 0$$

$$= \begin{vmatrix} 0 & -\lambda & -1 \\ \lambda-1 & -1 & -1 \\ 0 & 1 & -1 \end{vmatrix} = (\lambda-1)(\lambda+1) \ne 0$$

$\Rightarrow \quad \lambda \ne 1, -1$

Hence, $\lambda = R - \{-1, 1\}$

**1.** **(d)** $\vec{a} = 2\hat{i} + \hat{j} - 2\hat{k},\ \vec{b} = \hat{i} + \hat{j}$

$\Rightarrow |\vec{a}| = 3$

and $\vec{a} \times \vec{b} = \begin{vmatrix} \hat{i} & \hat{j} & \hat{k} \\ 2 & 1 & -2 \\ 1 & 1 & 0 \end{vmatrix} = 2\hat{i} - 2\hat{j} + \hat{k}$

$|\vec{a} \times \vec{b}| = \sqrt{4+4+1} = 3$

Now, $|\vec{c} - \vec{a}| = 2\sqrt{2} \Rightarrow |\vec{c} - \vec{a}|^2 = 8$

$\Rightarrow |\vec{c} - \vec{a}| . (\vec{c} - \vec{a}) = 8$

$\Rightarrow |\vec{c}|^2 + |\vec{a}|^2 - 2\vec{c}.\vec{a} = 8$

$\Rightarrow |\vec{c}|^2 + 9 - 2|\vec{c}| = 8$

$\Rightarrow (|\vec{c}| - 1)^2 = 0 \Rightarrow |\vec{c}| = 1$

$\therefore |(\vec{a} \times \vec{b}) \times \vec{c}| = |\vec{a} \times \vec{b}||\vec{c}| \sin 30° = 3 \times 1 \times \dfrac{1}{2} = \dfrac{3}{2}$

**2.** **(b)** $(\hat{x} + \hat{y} + \hat{z})^2 \geq 0$

$\Rightarrow 3 + 2\Sigma \hat{x}.\hat{y} \geq 0$

$\Rightarrow 2\Sigma \hat{x}.\hat{y} \geq -3$

Now, $|\hat{x} + \hat{y}|^2 + |\hat{y} + \hat{z}|^2 + |\hat{z} + \hat{x}|^2$

$= 6 + 2\Sigma \hat{x}.\hat{y} \geq 6 + (-3)$

$\Rightarrow |\hat{x} + \hat{y}|^2 + |\hat{y} + \hat{z}|^2 + |\hat{z} + \hat{x}|^2 \geq 3$

**3.** **(d)**

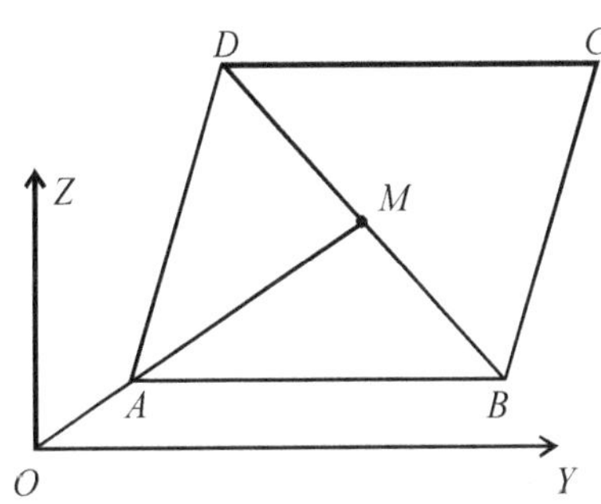

In a parallelogram, diagonals bisect each other. So, mid point of $DB$ is also the mid-point of $AC$.

Mid-point of $M = 2\hat{i} - \hat{j}$

Direction ratio of $OC = (1, -5, -5)$

Direction ratio of $OM = (2, -1, 0)$

Angle $\theta$ between $OM$ and $OC$ is given by

$\cos\theta = \dfrac{(1 \times 2) + (-5)(-1) + (-5)(0)}{\sqrt{2^2 + (-1)^2}\sqrt{(1)^2 + (-5)^2 + (-5)^2}}$

$= \dfrac{2+5}{\sqrt{5}\sqrt{51}} = \dfrac{7}{\sqrt{5}\sqrt{51}}$

Projection of $\overrightarrow{OM}$ on $\overrightarrow{OC}$ is given by

$|OM| . \cos\theta = \sqrt{5} \times \dfrac{7}{\sqrt{5} \times \sqrt{51}} = \dfrac{7}{\sqrt{51}}$

**4.** **(b)** $\vec{p}.\vec{q} = ab + bc + ca$

$= \sqrt{a^2 + b^2 + c^2}\sqrt{b^2 + c^2 + a^2} \cos\theta$

$\Rightarrow \cos\theta = \dfrac{ab + bc + ca}{(a^2 + b^2 + c^2)}$

$\Rightarrow$ Now $(a-b)^2 + (b-c)^2 + (c-a)^2 \geq 0$

$a^2 + b^2 + c^2 \geq ab + bc + ca$

$\Rightarrow \dfrac{ab + bc + ca}{a^2 + b^2 + c^2} \leq 1$

Also

$(a + b + c)^2 = a^2 + b^2 + c^2 + 2(ab + bc + ca) \geq 0$

$\Rightarrow \dfrac{ab + bc + ca}{a^2 + b^2 + c^2} \geq -1/2$

$\Rightarrow -\dfrac{1}{2} \leq \cos\theta \leq 1$

$\Rightarrow \theta \in [0, 2\pi/3].$

**5.** **(d)** Suppose that $\vec{a}, \vec{b}, \vec{c}$ are coplanar.

$\Rightarrow \begin{vmatrix} \cos\alpha & 1 & 1 \\ 1 & \cos\beta & 1 \\ 1 & 1 & \cos\gamma \end{vmatrix} = 0$

applying $R_2 \longrightarrow R_2 - R_1$ and $R_3 \longrightarrow R_1$

or $\begin{vmatrix} \cos\alpha & 1 & 1 \\ 1 - \cos\alpha & \cos\beta - 1 & 1 \\ 1 - \cos\alpha & 0 & \cos\gamma - 1 \end{vmatrix} = 0$

or $\cos\alpha(\cos\beta - 1)(\cos\gamma - 1)$

$-(1 - \cos\alpha)(\cos\gamma - 1) - (1 - \cos\alpha)(\cos\beta - 1) = 0$

Dividing through out by

$(1-\cos\alpha)(1-\cos\beta)(1-\cos\gamma)$ ; we get

$$\frac{\cos\alpha}{1-\cos\alpha}+\frac{1}{1-\cos\beta}+\frac{1}{1-\cos\gamma}=0$$

$$\Rightarrow \frac{-(1-\cos\alpha)+1}{(1-\cos\alpha)}+\frac{1}{(1-\cos\beta)}+\frac{1}{(1-\cos\gamma)}=0$$

$$\Rightarrow -1+\frac{1}{1-\cos\alpha}+\frac{1}{1-\cos\beta}+\frac{1}{1-\cos\gamma}=0$$

$$\Rightarrow \frac{1}{1-\cos\alpha}+\frac{1}{1-\cos\beta}+\frac{1}{1-\cos\gamma}=1$$

$$\Rightarrow \operatorname{cosec}^2\frac{\alpha}{2}+\operatorname{cosec}^2\frac{\beta}{2}+\operatorname{cosec}^2\frac{\gamma}{2}=2 \text{ which is not}$$

possible as $\operatorname{cosec}^2\frac{\alpha}{2}\geq 1$, $\operatorname{cosec}^2\frac{\beta}{2}\geq 1$, $\operatorname{cosec}^2\frac{\gamma}{2}\geq 1$.
So the vectors cannot be coplanar.

**6. (a)** $\vec{a}=(1, 3, \sin 2\alpha)$ makes an obtuse angle with the z-axis.

$$\therefore \quad \sin 2\alpha < 0$$

Since $\vec{b}$ and $\vec{c}$ are orthogonal

$$\Rightarrow \vec{b}.\vec{c}=0. \qquad\qquad .......(1)$$

$$\therefore \tan^2\alpha-\tan\alpha-6=0 \Rightarrow \tan\alpha=3 \text{ or} -2.$$

If $\tan\alpha=3$, then $\sin 2\alpha=\dfrac{2\tan\alpha}{1+\tan^2\alpha}=\dfrac{3}{5}>0$, which

is not possible (from (1))

$$\therefore \quad \tan\alpha=-2.$$

Again $\tan 2\alpha=\dfrac{2\tan\alpha}{1-\tan^2\alpha}=\dfrac{4}{3}>0$. Also $\sin 2\alpha<0$.

$\therefore 2\alpha$ lies in the third quadrant

$$\Rightarrow \frac{\alpha}{2} \text{ lies in the first quadrant}$$

$$\therefore \sqrt{\sin\frac{\alpha}{2}} \text{ is valid and } \alpha=(4n+1)\pi-\tan^{-1}2.$$

**7. (b,d)** The point that divides $5\hat{i}$ and $5\hat{j}$ in the ratio of

$$k:1 \text{ is } \frac{k(5\hat{j})+(5\hat{i}).1}{k+1}$$

$$\therefore \vec{b}=\frac{5\hat{i}+5k\hat{j}}{k+1}$$

also $|\vec{b}|\leq\sqrt{37} \Rightarrow \frac{1}{k+1}\sqrt{25+25k^2}\leq\sqrt{37}$

$$\Rightarrow 5\sqrt{1+k^2}\leq\sqrt{37}(k+1)$$

Squaring both sides

$$25(1+k^2)\leq 37(k^2+2k+1) \text{ or } 6k^2+37k+6\geq 0$$

$$\Rightarrow (6k+1)(k+6)\geq 0$$

$$k\in(-\infty,-6)\cup\left[-\frac{1}{6},\ \infty\right)$$

**8. (a, b, c)** $\{(\vec{a}\times\vec{b})\times(\vec{b}\times\vec{c})\}\times(\vec{c}\times\vec{a})=\vec{0}$

$$\{(\vec{a}\cdot\vec{b})\vec{c}-(\vec{b}\cdot\vec{c})\vec{a}\}\left[\vec{a}\ \vec{b}\ \vec{c}\right]=0$$

$$(\vec{a}\cdot\vec{b})\vec{c}=(\vec{b}\cdot\vec{c})\vec{a}$$

Leads to $2\alpha^3+10\alpha+12=0$, $\alpha^2+6\alpha=0$,

$6\alpha^2-6\alpha-6=0$ which do not have a common solution.

If $\left[\vec{a}\ \vec{b}\ \vec{c}\right]=0 \Rightarrow \alpha=\dfrac{2}{3}$

$$\alpha=0$$

then $\left[\vec{a}\ \vec{b}\ \vec{c}\right]=-10$

$$\vec{a}.\vec{b}=6$$

$$\vec{b}.\vec{c}=0$$

$$\therefore \quad \text{The vector product is } -60(2\hat{i}+\hat{k}).$$

**9. (a, c, d)**

$$\vec{a}+\vec{b}+\vec{c}=\vec{o}$$

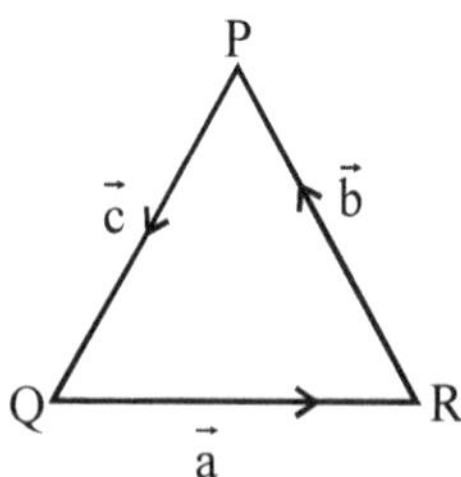


$$\Rightarrow \left|\vec{b}+\vec{c}\right|^2=\left|-\vec{a}\right|^2$$

$$\Rightarrow \left|\vec{b}\right|^2+\left|\vec{c}\right|^2+2\vec{b}.\vec{c}=\left|\vec{a}\right|^2$$

$$\Rightarrow 48+\left|\vec{c}\right|^2+48=144 \Rightarrow \left|\vec{c}\right|^2=48 \Rightarrow \left|\vec{c}\right|=4\sqrt{3}$$

$$\therefore \frac{\left|\vec{c}\right|^2}{2}-\left|\vec{a}\right|=\frac{48}{2}-12=12$$

$$\frac{\left|\vec{c}\right|^2}{2}+\left|\vec{a}\right|=24\neq 30$$

Also $\left|\vec{b}\right| = \left|\vec{c}\right| \Rightarrow \angle Q = \angle R$

and $\cos(180 - P) = \dfrac{\vec{b}.\vec{c}}{\left|\vec{b}\right|\left|\vec{c}\right|} = \dfrac{1}{2}$

$\Rightarrow \quad \angle P = 120° \therefore \angle Q = \angle R = 30°$

Again $\vec{a} + \vec{b} + \vec{c} = 0 \Rightarrow \vec{a} \times (\vec{a} + \vec{b} + \vec{c}) = 0 \Rightarrow \vec{a} \times \vec{b} = \vec{c} \times \vec{a}$

$\therefore \quad \left|\vec{a} \times \vec{b} + \vec{c} \times \vec{a}\right| = 2\left|\vec{a} \times \vec{b}\right| = 2 \times 12 \times 4\sqrt{3} \times \sin 150 = 48\sqrt{3}$

And $\vec{a}.\vec{b} = 12 \times 4\sqrt{3} \times \cos 150 = -72$

**10. (a, b, c)** $\left|\vec{x}\right| = \left|\vec{y}\right| = \left|\vec{z}\right| = \sqrt{2}$

Angle between each pair is $\dfrac{\pi}{3}$

$\vec{a} = \lambda\left[\vec{x} \times \left(\vec{y} \times \vec{z}\right)\right]$

$= \lambda\left[\left(\vec{x} \cdot \vec{z}\right)\vec{y} - \left(\vec{x} \cdot \vec{y}\right)\vec{z}\right]$

$= \lambda\left[\left(\sqrt{2}.\sqrt{2}\cos\dfrac{\pi}{3}\right)\vec{y} - \left(\sqrt{2}.\sqrt{2}\cos\dfrac{\pi}{3}\right)\vec{z}\right]$

$= \lambda\left(\vec{y} - \vec{z}\right)$

$\vec{b} = \mu\left[\vec{y} \times \left(\vec{z} \times \vec{x}\right)\right]$

$= \mu\left[\left(\vec{y} \cdot \vec{x}\right)\vec{z} - \left(\vec{y} \cdot \vec{z}\right)\vec{x}\right]$

$= \mu\left[\left(\sqrt{2}.\sqrt{2}.\cos\dfrac{\pi}{3}\right)\vec{z} - \left(\sqrt{2}.\sqrt{2}.\cos\dfrac{\pi}{3}\right)\vec{x}\right]$

$= \mu\left(\vec{z} - \vec{x}\right)$

Now $\vec{b} . \vec{z} = \mu\left[\vec{z} . \vec{z} - \vec{x} . \vec{z}\right]$

$= \mu(2 - 1) = \mu$

$\therefore \vec{b} = \left(\vec{b} . \vec{z}\right)\left(\vec{z} - \vec{x}\right)$ is correct

Also $\vec{a} . \vec{y} = \lambda\left(\vec{y} . \vec{y} - \vec{z} . \vec{y}\right) = \lambda(2 - 1) = \lambda$

$\therefore \vec{a} = \left(\vec{a} . \vec{y}\right)\left(\vec{y} - \vec{z}\right)$ is also correct

$\vec{a} . \vec{b} = \lambda\mu\left(\vec{y} . \vec{z} - \vec{y} . \vec{x} - \vec{z} . \vec{z} + \vec{z} . \vec{x}\right)$

$= \lambda\mu(1 - 1 - 2 + 1) = -\lambda\mu = -\left(\vec{a} . \vec{y}\right)\left(\vec{b} . \vec{z}\right)$

$\therefore$ (c) is correct.

$-\left(\vec{a} . \vec{y}\right)\left(\vec{z} - \vec{y}\right) = \lambda\left(\vec{z} - \vec{y}\right) = -\vec{a}$

(d) is not correct.

**11. (4)**

We have $\overrightarrow{AB} = d\hat{i}$. Let $\overrightarrow{AC} = x\hat{i} + y\hat{j}$. Then we have

$AC = d \Rightarrow x^2 + y^2 = d^2,$

$\overrightarrow{AB} . \overrightarrow{AC} = AB \times AC \times \cos 60°$

$[\triangle ABC$ in $xy$ plane is equilateral$]$

$d\hat{i}.(x\hat{i} + y\hat{i}) = d.d\dfrac{1}{2}$

$\Rightarrow dx = \dfrac{d^2}{2} \Rightarrow x = \dfrac{d}{2} \quad$ and $\quad y = \pm\dfrac{\sqrt{3}}{2}d$

Now, let $\overrightarrow{AD} = p\hat{i} + q\hat{j} + r\hat{k}$. Then

$AD = d \Rightarrow p^2 + q^2 + r^2 = d^2;$

$\overrightarrow{AD} . \overrightarrow{AB} = \overrightarrow{AD} . \overrightarrow{AC} = \dfrac{d^2}{2}$

$\Rightarrow pd = px + qy = \dfrac{d^2}{2} \Rightarrow p = \dfrac{d}{2}$

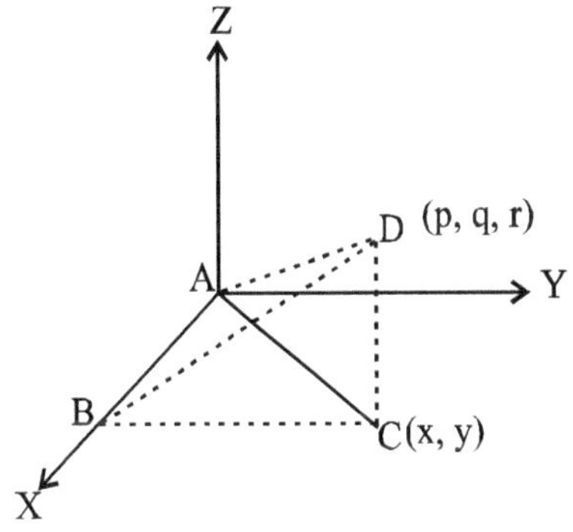


If $\quad y = \dfrac{\sqrt{3}}{2}d$, then $q = \dfrac{pd - px}{q} = \dfrac{d}{2\sqrt{3}}$

and $r^2 = d^2 - p^2 - q^2 = \dfrac{2d^2}{3} \Rightarrow r = \pm\dfrac{\sqrt{2}}{\sqrt{3}}d$

If $\quad y = -\dfrac{\sqrt{3}}{2}d$, then $q = -\dfrac{d}{2\sqrt{3}}$ and $r = \pm\dfrac{\sqrt{2}}{\sqrt{3}}d$.

So, $\overrightarrow{AB}$, $\overrightarrow{AC}$ and $\overrightarrow{AD}$ can be

(i) $\quad d\hat{i}, \dfrac{d}{2}\hat{i} + \dfrac{d\sqrt{3}}{2}\hat{j}, \dfrac{d}{2}\hat{i} + \dfrac{d}{2\sqrt{3}}\hat{j} + \dfrac{d\sqrt{2}}{\sqrt{3}}\hat{k}$

(ii) $\quad d\hat{i}, \dfrac{d}{2}\hat{i} + \dfrac{d\sqrt{3}}{2}\hat{j}, \dfrac{d}{2}\hat{i} + \dfrac{d}{2\sqrt{3}}\hat{j} - \dfrac{d\sqrt{2}}{\sqrt{3}}\hat{k}$

(iii) $\quad d\hat{i}, \dfrac{d}{2}\hat{i} - \dfrac{d\sqrt{3}}{2}\hat{j}, \dfrac{d}{2}\hat{i} - \dfrac{d}{2\sqrt{3}}\hat{j} + \dfrac{d\sqrt{2}}{\sqrt{3}}\hat{k}$

(iv) $\quad d\hat{i}, \dfrac{d}{2}\hat{i} - \dfrac{d\sqrt{3}}{2}\hat{j}, \dfrac{d}{2}\hat{i} - \dfrac{d}{2\sqrt{3}}\hat{j} - \dfrac{d\sqrt{2}}{\sqrt{3}}\hat{k}$

Hence, 4 tetrahedra are possible.

**12.**    **(2)**

$\vec{w} + (\vec{w} \times \vec{u}) = \vec{v} \qquad\qquad ........(i)$

$\Rightarrow \quad \vec{w} \times \vec{u} = \vec{v} - \vec{w}$

$\Rightarrow \quad (\vec{w} \times \vec{u})^2 = \vec{v}^2 + \vec{w}^2 - 2\vec{v}.\vec{w}$

$\Rightarrow \quad 2\vec{v}.\vec{w} = 1 + \vec{w}^2 - (\vec{u} \times \vec{w})^2 \quad ..........(ii)$

Also taking dot product of (i) with $\vec{v}$ we get

$\vec{w}.\vec{v} + (\vec{w} \times \vec{u}).\vec{v} = \vec{v}.\vec{v}$

$\Rightarrow \vec{v}.(\vec{w} \times \vec{u}) = 1 - \vec{w}.\vec{v} \qquad ........(iii) \quad [\vec{v}.\vec{v} = |\vec{v}|^2 = 1]$

Now $\vec{v}.(\vec{w} \times \vec{u}) = 1 - \dfrac{1}{2}(1 + w^2 - (\vec{u} \times \vec{w})^2)$

(Using (ii) and (iii))

$= \dfrac{1}{2} - \dfrac{w^2}{2} + \dfrac{(\vec{u} \times \vec{w})^2}{2} \qquad (\because 0 \le \cos^2\theta \le 1)$

$= \dfrac{1}{2}(1 - w^2 + w^2\sin^2\theta) = \dfrac{1}{2}(1 - w^2\cos^2\theta) \quad ........(iv)$

as we know $0 \le w^2\cos^2\theta \le w^2$

$\therefore \quad \dfrac{1}{2} \ge \dfrac{1 - w^2\cos^2\theta}{2} \ge \dfrac{1 - w^2}{2} \qquad ......... (v)$

$\Rightarrow \quad \dfrac{1 - w^2\cos^2\theta}{2} \le \dfrac{1}{2}$

From (iv) and (v) $|\vec{v}.(\vec{w} \times \vec{u})| \le \dfrac{1}{2}$

$\Rightarrow |\vec{v}.(\vec{w} \times \vec{u})|^{-1} \ge 2 \ or \ |(\vec{u} \times \vec{v}).\vec{w}|^{-1} \ge 2$

**13.**    **(5)**

$\vec{a}.\vec{b} = 0 \Rightarrow x_1 + x_2 + x_3 = 0$

We have to obtain the number of integral solution of this equation $\Rightarrow$ Coefficient of

$x^0$ in $(x^{-3} + x^{-2} + x^{-1} + x^0 + x + x^2)^3$

$= $ Coeff. of $x^0$ in $\left(\dfrac{1 + x + x^2 + x^3 + x^4 + x^5}{x^3}\right)^3$

$= $ Coeff. of $x^9$ in $(1 - x^6)^3(1 - x)^{-3} = {}^{11}C_9 - 3.{}^5C_3 = 25$

**14.**    **(5)**

Let $P(x_1 y_1)$ and $Q(x_2, y_2)$ be the two points on

$y = 2^{x+2}$

$\overrightarrow{OP}.\hat{i} = $ Projection on $\overrightarrow{OP}$ on the x-axis

$\Rightarrow \quad x_1 = -1 \qquad\qquad [\because \overrightarrow{OP}.\hat{i} = -1]$

Also $(x_1, y_1)$ lies on $y = 2^{x+2}$

$\therefore \quad y_1 = 2^{x_1+2} \Rightarrow y_1 = 2$

Also $\overrightarrow{OQ}.\ \hat{i} = $ projection of $\overrightarrow{OQ}$ on x-axis

$\Rightarrow \quad x_2 = 2 \quad [\text{given } \overrightarrow{OQ}.\hat{i} = 2]$

as $(x_2, y_2)$ lies on $y = 2^{x+2}$

$\therefore \quad y_2 = 2^{x_2+2} \Rightarrow y_2 = 16$

Thus, $\overrightarrow{OP} = x_1\hat{i} + y_1\hat{j} = -\hat{i} + 2\hat{j}$

and $\overrightarrow{OQ} = x_2\hat{i} + y_2\hat{j} = 2\hat{i} + 16\hat{j} \Rightarrow \overrightarrow{OQ} - 4\overrightarrow{OP} = 6\hat{i} + 8\hat{j}$

$\Rightarrow |\overrightarrow{OQ} - 4\overrightarrow{OP}| = \sqrt{36 + 64} = 10 = 2k$

**15.**   **(4)**    $\vec{a}.\vec{b} = \vec{b}.\vec{c} = \vec{c}.\vec{a} = \cos\dfrac{\pi}{3} = \dfrac{1}{2}$

Given $p\,\vec{a} + q\,\vec{b} + r\,\vec{c} = \vec{a} \times \vec{b} + \vec{b} \times \vec{c}$

Taking its dot product with $\vec{a}, \vec{b}, \vec{c}$, we get

$$p + \frac{1}{2}q + \frac{1}{2}r = \begin{bmatrix} \vec{a} & \vec{b} & \vec{c} \end{bmatrix} \quad ...(1)$$

$$\frac{1}{2}p + q + \frac{1}{2}r = 0 \quad ...(2)$$

$$\frac{1}{2}p + \frac{1}{2}q + r = \begin{bmatrix} \vec{a} & \vec{b} & \vec{c} \end{bmatrix} \quad ...(3)$$

From (1) and (3), $p = r$ Using (2) $q = -p$

$$\therefore \quad \frac{p^2 + 2q^2 + r^2}{q^2} = \frac{p^2 + 2p^2 + p^2}{p^2} = 4$$

**16. (a)** Vector equation of $CD$ and $BE$ are

$$\vec{r} = \hat{i} - 2\hat{j} + 4\hat{k} + \frac{\lambda}{3}(7\hat{j} - 7\hat{k}) \quad ....(1)$$

and $\quad \vec{r} = -\hat{i} + \hat{j} + \hat{k} + \frac{\mu}{3}(7\hat{i} - 7\hat{j} + 7\hat{k}) \quad ....(2)$

At point of intersection $P$,

$$1 = -1 + \frac{7\mu}{3}, \ -2 + \frac{7\lambda}{3} = 1 - \frac{7\mu}{3}, \ 4 - \frac{7\lambda}{3} = 1 + \frac{7\mu}{3}$$

$$\mu = \frac{6}{7}, \ \lambda = \frac{3}{7}$$

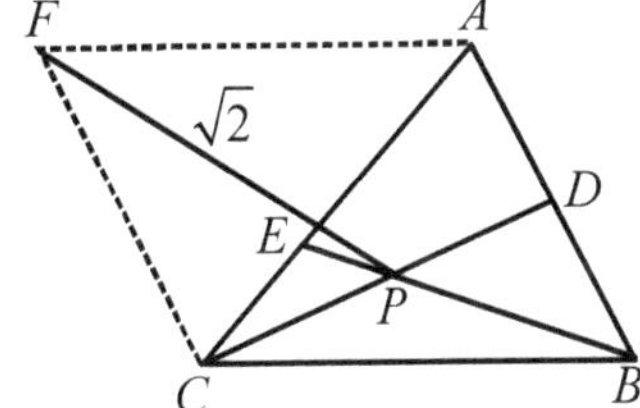

Position vector of $P$ is $\hat{i} - \hat{j} + 3\hat{k}$.

**17. (a)** Area of $\triangle ABC = \frac{1}{2}\left| \overrightarrow{AB} \times \overrightarrow{AC} \right|$

$$= \frac{1}{2}\left| (-3\hat{i} + \hat{j} - \hat{k}) \times (-\hat{i} - 2\hat{j} + 2\hat{k}) \right|$$

$$= \frac{1}{2}\left| 7\hat{j} + 7\hat{k} \right| = \frac{7\sqrt{2}}{2} \text{ sq. units.}$$

Volume of tetrahedron $ABCF$

$$= \frac{1}{3} \times \text{area of base} \times \text{height} = \frac{7}{3} \text{ cubic units.}$$

**18. (b)** $\vec{a}_1 = \left[ (2\hat{i} + 3\hat{j} - 6\hat{k}) . \dfrac{(2\hat{i} - 3\hat{j} + 6\hat{k})}{7} \right] \dfrac{2\hat{i} - 3\hat{j} + 6\hat{k}}{7}$

$$= \frac{-41}{49}(2\hat{i} - 3\hat{j} + 6\hat{k})$$

$$\vec{a}_2 = \frac{-41}{49}\left(2\hat{i} - 3\hat{j} + 6\hat{k}.\right)\left(\frac{(-2\hat{i} + 3\hat{j} + 6\hat{k})}{7}\right)\frac{(-2\hat{i} + 3\hat{j} + 6\hat{k})}{7}$$

$$= \frac{-41}{(49)^2}(-4 - 9 + 36)(-2\hat{i} + 3\hat{j} + 6\hat{k})$$

$$= \frac{943}{49^2}(2\hat{i} - 3\hat{j} - 6\hat{k})$$

**19. (a)** $\vec{a}_1.\vec{b} = \dfrac{-41}{49}(2\hat{i} - 3\hat{j} + 6\hat{k}).(2\hat{i} - 3\hat{j} + 6\hat{k}) = -41$

**20.** **(A) → (s); (B) → (q, r); (C) → (t); (D) → (p)**

(A) $\vec{a} + \vec{b} + \vec{c} + \vec{d} = (\alpha + 1)\vec{d} = (\beta + 1)\vec{a}$

If $\alpha \neq -1$, then $\vec{d} = \left(\dfrac{\beta + 1}{\alpha + 1}\right)\vec{a}$

$$\Rightarrow \vec{a} + \vec{b} + \vec{c} = \alpha\vec{d} = \alpha\left(\frac{\beta + 1}{\alpha + 1}\right)\vec{a}$$

$$\Rightarrow \left\{1 - \alpha\left(\frac{\beta + 1}{\alpha + 1}\right)\right\}\vec{a} + \vec{b} + \vec{c} = 0 \Rightarrow \vec{a}, \vec{b}, \vec{c}$$

are coplanar, which is against the given condition,

so $\alpha = -1$ and hence $\vec{a} + \vec{b} + \vec{c} + \vec{d} = \vec{0}$

(B) $|\vec{a} + \vec{b}| < 1 \Rightarrow |\vec{a}|^2 + |\vec{b}|^2 + 2|\vec{a}||\vec{b}|\cos\theta < 1$

$$\Rightarrow \cos\theta < -\frac{1}{2}$$

So, $\dfrac{2\pi}{3} < \theta < \pi$

(C) $\vec{a} \times (\vec{a} \times \vec{b}) = (\vec{a}.\vec{b})\vec{a} - (\vec{a}.\vec{a})\vec{b} = -\vec{b}$

$$a \times \{\vec{a} \times (\vec{a} \times \vec{b})\} = \vec{a} \times -\vec{b} = -\vec{a} \times \vec{b}$$

$$a \times [\vec{a} \times \{\vec{a} \times (\vec{a} \times \vec{b})\}] = \vec{a} \times (-\vec{a} \times \vec{b})$$

$$= (\vec{a}.\vec{a})\vec{b} - (\vec{a}.\vec{b})\vec{a} = \vec{b}$$

(D) $\vec{a} + \vec{b} = -\vec{c} \Rightarrow |\vec{a} + \vec{b}|^2 = |\vec{c}|^2 = 1$

$$\Rightarrow \vec{a}.\vec{b} = -\frac{1}{2} \Rightarrow \theta = \frac{2\pi}{3}$$

**1. (c)**

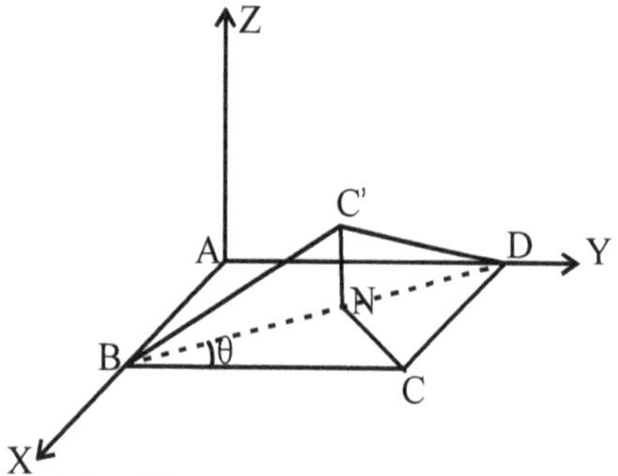

Let $AB = CD = r$ and $BC = AD = 2r$

then $\tan\theta = \dfrac{CD}{BC} = \dfrac{1}{2}$

Also,

$\sin\theta = \dfrac{CN}{BC} \Rightarrow \dfrac{1}{\sqrt{5}} = \dfrac{CN}{2r} \Rightarrow CN = C'N = \dfrac{2}{\sqrt{5}}r$

In $xy$ plane the equation of $BD$ is $\dfrac{x}{r} + \dfrac{y}{2r} = 1$

$\Rightarrow 2x + y - 2r = 0$ and $C$ is $(r, 2r)$

$\therefore$ Coordinates of $N$ are given by

$\dfrac{x-r}{2} = \dfrac{y-2r}{1} = \dfrac{-(2r+2r-2r)}{5}$

$\therefore \quad x = r - \dfrac{4r}{5} = \dfrac{r}{5}$ and $y = 2r - \dfrac{2r}{5} = \dfrac{8r}{5}$

$\therefore$ Coordinate of $C'$ in three dimensions are

$\left( \dfrac{r}{5}, \dfrac{8r}{5}, \dfrac{2}{\sqrt{5}}r \right)$

$\therefore AC' = \sqrt{\dfrac{r^2}{25} + \dfrac{64r^2}{25} + \dfrac{4r^2}{5}} = \dfrac{\sqrt{85}r}{5}$

**2. (c)** Let $P$ be the image of $O$ in the given plane.

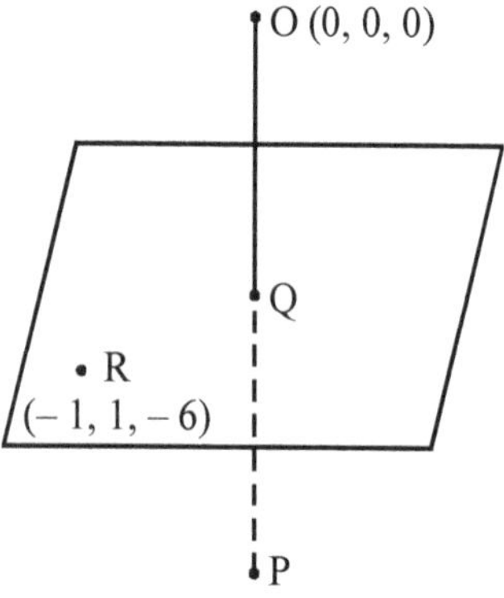


Equation of the plane, $4x - 3y + z + 13 = 0$
$OP$ is normal to the plane, therefore direction ratio of $OP$ are proportional to $4, -3, 1$
Since $OP$ passes through $(0, 0, 0)$ and has direction ratio proportional to $4, -3, 1$. Therefore equation of $OP$ is

$\dfrac{x-0}{4} = \dfrac{y-0}{-3} = \dfrac{z-0}{1} = r$ (let)

$\therefore x = 4r, y = -3r, z = r$

Let the coordinate of $P$ be $(4r, -3r, r)$
Since $Q$ be the mid point of $OP$

$\therefore Q = \left( 2r, -\dfrac{3}{2}r, \dfrac{r}{2} \right)$

Since $Q$ lies in the given plane
$4x - 3y + z + 13 = 0$

$\therefore 8r + \dfrac{9}{2}r + \dfrac{r}{2} + 13 = 0$

$\Rightarrow r = \dfrac{-13}{8 + \dfrac{9}{2} + \dfrac{1}{2}} = \dfrac{-26}{26} = -1$

$\therefore Q = \left( -2, \dfrac{3}{2}, -\dfrac{1}{2} \right)$

$QR = \sqrt{(-1+2)^2 + \left(1 - \dfrac{3}{2}\right)^2 + \left(-6 + \dfrac{1}{2}\right)^2}$

$= \sqrt{1 + \dfrac{1}{4} + \dfrac{121}{4}} = 3\sqrt{\dfrac{7}{2}}$

**3. (b)** Let equation of the required line be

$\dfrac{x - x_1}{a} = \dfrac{y - y_1}{b} = \dfrac{z - z_1}{c}$ ...(i)

Given two lines

$\dfrac{x}{1} = \dfrac{y}{-1} = \dfrac{z}{1}$ ...(ii)

and $\dfrac{x-1}{0} = \dfrac{y+1}{0} = \dfrac{z}{1}$ ...(iii)

Since the line (i) is perpendicular to both the lines (ii) and (iii), therefore
$a - b + c = 0$ ...(iv)
$-2b + c = 0$ ...(v)
From (iv) and (v) $c = 2b$ and $a + b = 0$, which are not satisfy by options (c) and (d). Hence options (c) and (d) are rejected.

Thus point $(x_1, y_1, z_1)$ on the required line will be either $(0, 0, 0)$ or $(1, -1, 0)$.

Now foot of the perpendicular from point $(0, 0, 0)$ to the line (iii)

$= (1, -2r - 1, r)$

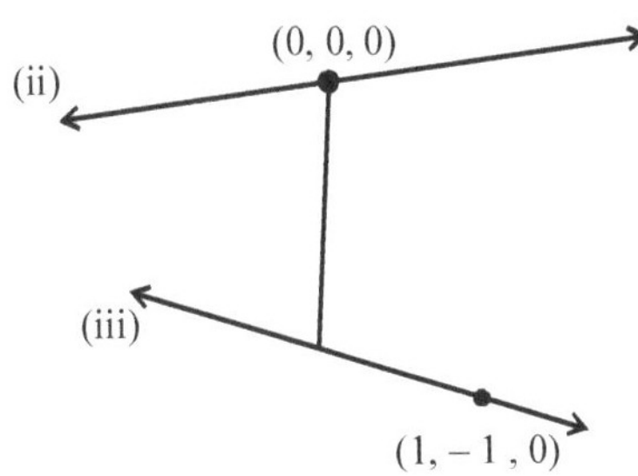

The direction ratios of the line joining the points $(0, 0, 0)$ and $(1, -2r - 1, r)$ are $1, -2r - 1, r$

Since sum of the $x$ and $y$-coordinate of direction ratio of the required line is 0.

$\therefore 1 - 2r - 1 = 0, \Rightarrow r = 0$

Hence direction ratio are $1, -1, 0$

But the z-direction ratio of the required line is twice the $y$-direction ratio of the required line

i.e. $0 = 2(-1)$, which is not true.

Hence the shortest line does not pass through the point $(0, 0, 0)$. Therefore option (a) is also rejected

**4.　(c)**

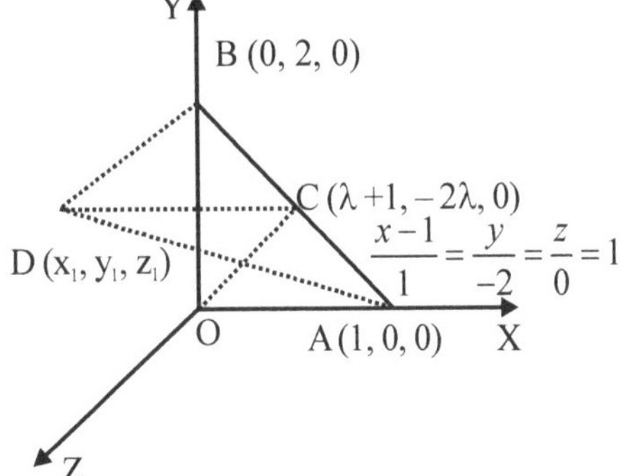

Equation of line AB is $\dfrac{x-1}{1} = \dfrac{y}{-2} = \dfrac{z}{0} = \lambda$

Now $AB \perp OC \Rightarrow 1(\lambda + 1) + (-2\lambda)(-2) = 0 \Rightarrow 5\lambda = -1$

$\Rightarrow \lambda = -\dfrac{1}{5}$

C is $\left(\dfrac{4}{5}, \dfrac{2}{5}, 0\right)$. Now

$x_1^2 + (y_1 - 2)^2 + z_1^2 = 4$

and $(x_1 - 1)^2 + y_1^2 + z_1^2 = 1$

Now $OC \perp CD$

$\Rightarrow \left(x_1 - \dfrac{4}{5}\right)\dfrac{4}{5} + \left(y_1 - \dfrac{2}{5}\right)\dfrac{2}{5} + (z_1 - 0)0 = 0$

Form (i), and (ii), we get

$-4y_1 + 2x_1 = 0 \Rightarrow x_1 = 2y_1$

From (iii), Putting $x_1 = 2y_1 \Rightarrow 2y_1 = \dfrac{4}{5} \Rightarrow y_1 = \dfrac{2}{5}$

$\Rightarrow x_1 = \dfrac{4}{5}.$

Putting this value of $x_1$ and $y_1$ in (i), we get

$= z_1 \pm \dfrac{2}{\sqrt{5}}$

**5.　(b.)**

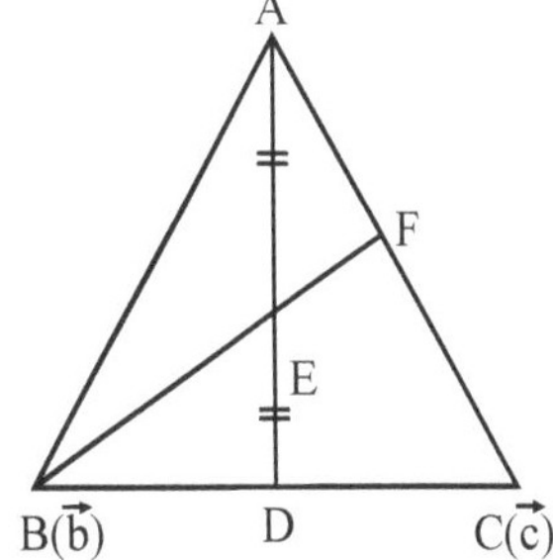

Taking A is the origin, let P.V. of B and C be $\vec{b}$ and $\vec{c}$, respectively.

P.V. of D is $\dfrac{\vec{b} + \vec{c}}{2}$ and P.V. of E is $\dfrac{\vec{b} + \vec{c}}{4}$

Equation of line BF is $\vec{r} = \vec{b} + \lambda\left(\dfrac{\vec{b} + \vec{c}}{4} - \vec{b}\right)$

Equation of line AC is $\vec{r} = 0 + \mu \vec{c}$

For the point of intersection, $\vec{b} + \lambda\left(\dfrac{\vec{b} + \vec{c}}{4} - \vec{b}\right) = \mu \vec{c}$

$\Rightarrow 1 - \dfrac{3\lambda}{4} = 0$ and $\dfrac{\lambda}{4} = \mu\left(\dfrac{\vec{b} + \vec{c}}{2}\right)$

$\Rightarrow \lambda = \dfrac{4}{3}$ and $\mu = \dfrac{1}{3}$. therefore, P.V., of F is

$\vec{r} = \dfrac{1}{3}\vec{c} \Rightarrow \overrightarrow{AF} = \dfrac{1}{3}\overrightarrow{AC} \Rightarrow AF : AC = 1 : 3$

**6.　(a, b, c)** Let $\overrightarrow{OA} = \vec{a}$, $\overrightarrow{OB} = \vec{b}$, $\overrightarrow{OC} = \vec{c}$, then we have

$\vec{a} \cdot \vec{a} + (\vec{b} - \vec{c}) \cdot (\vec{b} - \vec{c}) = \vec{b} \cdot \vec{b} + (\vec{c} - \vec{a}) \cdot (\vec{c} - \vec{a})$

$\Rightarrow -2\vec{b} \cdot \vec{c} = -2\vec{c} \cdot \vec{a} \Rightarrow (\vec{a} - \vec{b}) \cdot \vec{c} = 0$ or $\overrightarrow{BA} \cdot \overrightarrow{OC} = 0$

Hence $AB$ is perpendicular to $OC$. Similarly, $BC$ is perpendicular to $OA$ and $CA$ is perpendicular to $OB$.

**7.** **(a, d)**

The equation of a plane passing through the line of intersection of the x-y and y-z planes is $z + \lambda x = 0$, $\lambda \in R$

This plane makes an angle $45°$ with the x-y plane $(z = 0)$.

$$\Rightarrow \cos 45° = \frac{1}{\sqrt{1}\sqrt{\lambda^2 + 1}}$$

$$\Rightarrow \lambda = \pm 1$$

**8.** **(a, b)** The plane is equally inclined to the lines. Hence, it is perpendicular to the angle bisector of the vectors $2\hat{i} - 2\hat{j} - \hat{k}$ and $8\hat{i} + \hat{j} - 4\hat{k}$.

Vector along the angle bisectors of the vectors are

$$\frac{2\hat{i} - 2\hat{j} - \hat{k}}{3} \pm \frac{8\hat{i} + \hat{j} - 4\hat{k}}{9}, \text{ or}$$

$$\frac{14\hat{i} - 5\hat{j} - 7\hat{k}}{9} \text{ and } \frac{-2\hat{i} - 7\hat{j} + \hat{k}}{9}.$$

Hence, the equation of the planes is $14x - 5y - 7z = 0$ or $2x + 7y - z = 0$

**9.** **(a, c, d)**

The rod sweeps out the figure which is a cone.

The distance of point $A(1, 0, -1)$ from the plane is

$$\frac{|1 - 2 + 4|}{\sqrt{9}} = 1 \text{ unit.}$$

The slant height $l$ of the cone is 2 units.

Then the radius of the base of the cone is

$$\sqrt{l^2 - 1} = \sqrt{4 - 1} = \sqrt{3}.$$

Hence, the volume of the cone is $\pi\left(\sqrt{3}\right)^2 (1) = 3\pi$ cubic units.

Area of the circle on the plane which the rod traces is $3\pi$.

Also, the centre of the circle is $Q(x, y, z)$. Then

$$\frac{x - 1}{1} = \frac{y - 0}{-2} = \frac{z + 1}{2} = \frac{-(1 - 0 - 2 + 4)}{1^2 + (-2)^2 + 2^2}, \text{ or}$$

$$Q(x, y, z) \equiv \left(\frac{4}{3}, \frac{-2}{3}, -\frac{1}{3}\right).$$

**10.** **(1)**

Let $P$ be $(x_1, y_1, z_1)$. Point $M$ is $(x_1, 0, z_1)$ and $N$ is $(x_1, y_1, 0)$

So normal to plane $OMN$ is $\overrightarrow{OM} \times \overrightarrow{ON} = \vec{x}$ (say)

*i.e.* $\begin{vmatrix} \hat{i} & \hat{j} & \hat{k} \\ x_1 & 0 & z_1 \\ x_1 & y_1 & 0 \end{vmatrix} = \hat{i}(-y_1 z_1) - \hat{j}(-x_1 z_1) + \hat{k}(x_1 y_1)$

therefore, $\sin\theta = \dfrac{-x_1 y_1 z_1 + x_1 y_1 z_1 + x_1 y_1 z}{\sqrt{x_1^2 + y_1^2 + z_1^2}\sqrt{\sum x_1^2 y_1^2}}$

or $\left(\because \sin = \dfrac{\vec{n} \times \overrightarrow{OP}}{|n|\,|\overrightarrow{OP}|}\right)$

$$\Rightarrow \cosec^2\theta = \frac{\sum x_1^2 \sum x_1^2 y_1^2}{(x_1 y_1 z_1)^2}$$

$$= \frac{\sum x_1^2}{x_1^2} + \frac{\sum x_1^2}{y_1^2} + \frac{\sum x_1^2}{z_1^2}$$

Now, $\sin\alpha = \dfrac{\overrightarrow{OP}.\hat{k}}{|\overrightarrow{OP}|} = \dfrac{z_1}{\sqrt{\sum x_1^2}}$

$$\sin\beta = \frac{x_1}{\sqrt{\sum x_1^2}} \text{ and } \sin\gamma = \frac{y_1}{\sqrt{\sum x_1^2}}$$

Now, $\cosec^2\alpha + \cosec^2\beta + \cosec^2\gamma$

$$= \frac{x_1^2 + y_1^2 + z_1^2}{x_1^2} + \frac{\sum x_1^2}{y_1^2} + \frac{\sum x_1^2}{z_1^2} = \cosec^2\theta$$

**11** **(7)** Let the equation of the plane be $\dfrac{x}{a} + \dfrac{y}{b} + \dfrac{z}{c} = 1$

$$\Rightarrow \frac{1}{a} + \frac{1}{b} + \frac{1}{c} = 1$$

$$\Rightarrow \text{ volume of tetrahedron } OABC = V = \frac{1}{6}(a\,b\,c)$$

Now $(abc)^{1/3} \geq \dfrac{3}{\dfrac{1}{a} + \dfrac{1}{b} + \dfrac{1}{c}} \geq 3. (G.M. \geq H.M.)$

$$\Rightarrow a\,b\,c \geq 27 \Rightarrow V \geq \frac{9}{2}$$

**12.** **(7)** Let the plane $\vec{r} \cdot (\hat{i} - 2\hat{j} + 3\hat{k}) = 17$ divide the line joining the points

$-2\vec{i}+4\vec{j}+7\vec{k}$ and $3\vec{i}-5\vec{j}+8\vec{k}$ in the ratio t : 1 at the point P.

Therefore, point P is

$$\frac{3t-2}{t+1}\vec{i}+\frac{-5t+4}{t+1}\vec{j}+\frac{8t+7}{t+1}\vec{k}$$

This lies on the given plane

$$\therefore \frac{3t-2}{t+1}.(1)+\frac{-5t+4}{t+1}(-2)+\frac{8t+7}{t+1}(3)=17$$

Solving, we get

$$t=\frac{3}{10}$$

**13.  (6)** Both the lines pass through origin. Line $L_1$ is parallel to the vector

$$\vec{V}_1 = (\cos\theta+\sqrt{3})\hat{i}+\left(\sqrt{2}\sin\theta\right)\hat{j}+(\cos\theta-\sqrt{3})\hat{k}$$

and $L_2$ is parallel to the vector

$$\vec{V}_2 = a\hat{i}+b\hat{j}+c\hat{k}$$

$$\therefore \cos\alpha = \frac{\vec{V}_1 \times \vec{V}_2}{|\vec{V}_1||\vec{V}_2|}$$

$$= \frac{a(\cos\theta+\sqrt{3})+(b\sqrt{2})\sin\theta+c(\cos\theta-\sqrt{3})}{\sqrt{a^2+b^2+c^2}\sqrt{(\cos\theta+\sqrt{3})^2+2\sin^2\theta+(\cos\theta-\sqrt{3})^2}}$$

$$= \frac{(a+c)\cos\theta+b\sqrt{3}\sin\theta+(a-c)\sqrt{3}}{\sqrt{a^2+b^2+c^2}\sqrt{2+6}}$$

In order that cos $\alpha$ is independent of $\theta$, we get $a+c=0$ and $b=0$

$$\therefore \cos\alpha = \frac{2a\sqrt{3}}{a\sqrt{2}\,2\sqrt{2}} = \frac{\sqrt{3}}{2}$$

$$\Rightarrow \alpha = \frac{\pi}{6}$$

**14.  (a)**  The projection will be an ellipse whose major axis is $AB=2a$.

If its minor axis be b, then $\pi ab = (\cos\theta)\pi a^2$

$$\Rightarrow b = a\cos\theta.$$

$$\therefore e = \sqrt{1-\frac{b^2}{a^2}} = \sin\theta.$$

**15.  (b)**  Let the positive direction of the normal to the plane $ABC$ from O has direction cosines cos$\alpha$, cos$\beta$, cos$\gamma$. Since $\triangle OBC$ is the projection of $\triangle ABC$ on the plane $YOZ$, so

$$\cos\alpha.\Delta = \frac{1}{2}bc.$$

Similarly

$$\cos\beta.\Delta = \frac{1}{2}ca, \cos\gamma.\Delta = \frac{1}{2}ab.$$

Using $\cos^2\alpha+\cos^2\beta+\cos^2\gamma = 1$, we get

$$\Delta = \frac{1}{2}\sqrt{a^2b^2+b^2c^2+c^2a^2}.$$

**16.  (a)**

(I)   Any point on $L_1$ is $(2\lambda+1,-\lambda,\lambda-3)$
and that on $L_2$ is $(\mu+4,\mu-3,2\mu-3)$
For point of intersection of $L_1$ and $L_2$
$2\lambda+1=\mu+4, -\lambda=\mu-3, \lambda-3=2\mu-3$
$\Rightarrow \lambda=2, \mu=1$
$\therefore$   Intersection point of $L_1$ and $L_2$ is $(5,-2,-1)$
$\because$   $ax+by+cz=d$ is perpendicular to $P_1$ and $P_2$
$\therefore$   $7a+b+2c=0$ and $3a+5b-6c=0$

$$\Rightarrow \frac{a}{-16}=\frac{b}{48}=\frac{c}{32} \Rightarrow \frac{a}{1}=\frac{b}{-3}=\frac{c}{-2}$$

$\therefore$   Equation of plane is $x-3y-2z=d$
As it passes through $(5,-2,-1)$
$\therefore$   $5+6+2=d=13$
$\therefore$   $a=1, b=-3, c=-2, d=13$
(I) (i) (R) is the correct matching.

**17.  (d)**  All options (a), (b) and (c) are incorrect combinations.

**18.  (c)**  (III)  Any point on $L_1$ is $(\lambda+1,0,0)$
and that on $L_2$ is $(0,\mu+1,0)$
For point of intersection of $L_1$ and $L_2$
$\lambda+1=0, \quad 0=\mu+1, \quad 0=0$
$\Rightarrow \lambda=-1, \mu=-1$
$\therefore$   Intersection point of $L_1$ and $L_2$ is $(0,0,0)$
$\because$   $ax+by+cz=d$ is perpendicular to $x+2y+3z=2$ and $2x+3y+4z=4$
$\therefore$   $a+2b+3c=0$ and $2a+3b+4c=0$

$$\Rightarrow \frac{a}{8-9}=\frac{b}{6-4}=\frac{c}{3-4} \Rightarrow \frac{a}{-1}=\frac{b}{2}=\frac{c}{-1}$$

or   $\dfrac{a}{1}=\dfrac{b}{-2}=\dfrac{c}{1}$

$\therefore$   Equation of plane is $x-2y+z=d$
As it passes through $(0,0,0)$
$\therefore$   $0-0+0=d=0$
$\therefore$   $a=1, b=-2, c=1, d=0$
(III) (iii) (Q) is the correct matching.

**19.  (A)−(r), (B)−(t), (C)−(s), (D)−(p,q)**
(A) Let $D, E, F$ be the mid points then

$$EF^2 = \frac{BC^2}{4} \Rightarrow BC^2 = 4(b^2+c^2)$$

Similarly $AB^2 = 4(a^2+b^2)$ and $AC^2 = 4(a^2+c^2)$

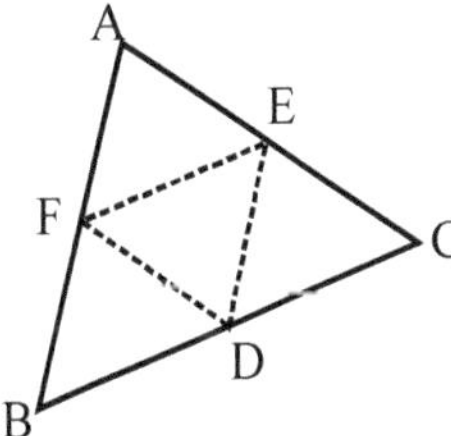

$$\therefore \frac{AB^2 + BC^2 + CA^2}{a^2 + b^2 + c^2} = 8$$

(B)  The image $(x_1, y_1, z_1)$ is given by

$$\frac{x_1 - 1}{1} = \frac{y_1 + 2}{-1} = \frac{z_1 - 3}{1} = -\frac{2}{3}(1 - 2 + 3 - 5)$$

$$\Rightarrow (x_1, y_1, z_1) \equiv (3, -4, 5)$$

$$\therefore \text{ desired distance} = \sqrt{50} = 5\sqrt{2}$$

(C)  *D. R.* of edge *OA* are $1, 0, 0$ and *D. R.* of diagonal *OP* are $1, 1, 1$.

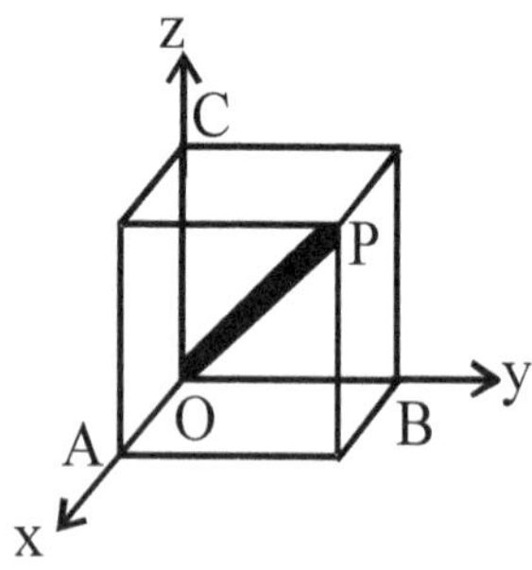


$$\therefore \cos\theta = \frac{1}{\sqrt{3}} \Rightarrow \tan\theta = \sqrt{2}$$

(D)  We have $\begin{vmatrix} p & \dfrac{3}{2} & \dfrac{1}{2} \\[2mm] \dfrac{3}{2} & 1 & 1 \\[2mm] \dfrac{1}{2} & 1 & q \end{vmatrix} = 0$ and $p + 1 + q = 0.$

$$\Rightarrow 4pq - 4p - 5q + 5 = 0 \text{ and } p + 1 + q = 0$$

Eliminating $p$, we get $q = -3, \dfrac{3}{4}.$

**20.**  **(A) - r, (B) - q, (C) - p, t, (D) - p, q, s**

(A)  We have $a^2 - b^2 + c^2 = 0$ and $a^2 - 2bd + c^2 = 0$

$$\Rightarrow b^2 = 2bd. \ As \ b \neq 0 \Rightarrow \frac{b}{d} = 2.$$

(B)  Equation of line through $(1, -2, 3)$ and parallele to given

line is $\dfrac{x - 1}{2} = \dfrac{y + 2}{3} = \dfrac{z - 3}{-6}.$

Any point on it is $(2r + 1, 3r - 2, -6r + 3).$

This point lies on the plane if $r = \dfrac{1}{7}$. So, the point is

$$\left( \frac{9}{7}, -\frac{11}{7}, \frac{15}{7} \right).$$

Desired distance

$$= \sqrt{\left( \frac{9}{7} - 1 \right)^2 + \left( -\frac{11}{2} + 2 \right)^2 + \left( \frac{15}{7} - 3 \right)^2} = 1.$$

(C)  General points on two given lines may be written as $(r_1 + 2, r_1 + 3, -kr_1 + 4)$ and $(kr_2 + 1, 2r_2 + 4, r_2 + 5).$ If two lines intersect then for some $r_1$ and $r_2$

$$r_1 + 2 = kr_2 + 1, r_1 + 3 = 2r_2 + 4 \text{ and } -kr_1 + 4 = r_2 + 5$$

Eliminating $r_1$ and $r_2$, $k^2 + 3k = 0 \Rightarrow k = 0$ or $-3$

(D)  $\cos^2\theta + \cos^2\theta + \cos^2\gamma = 1 \Rightarrow \cos^2\gamma = -\cos 2\theta$

$$\cos 2\theta \leq 0 \Rightarrow \theta \in \left[ \frac{\pi}{4}, \frac{\pi}{2} \right] \Rightarrow 0 \leq \cot\theta \leq 1$$

**1.** **(c)** This question is based on principle of inclusion and exclusion

Let X, Y and Z be the events that the student passes in Maths, Physics and chemistry.

$P(X) = m$, $P(Y) = p$ and $P(Z) = c$ and P (passing in at least one) $= P(X \cup B \cup C) = 0.75$ [given]

Now, $1 - P(X_d^c \cap Y_d^c \cap Z_d^c) = 0.75$, $P(X) = 1 - P(X_d^c)$ and $P(X \cup B \cup C)_d^c = P(X \cap Y \cap Z)$

$\Rightarrow 1 - P(X_d^c)P(Y_d^c)P(Z_d^c) = 0.75$

X, Y and Z are independent event therefore $X_d^c$, $Y_d^c$ and $Z_d^c$ are also independent.

$1 - (1 - m)(1 - p)(1 - c) = 0.75$

$(1 - m)(1 - p)(1 - c) = 0.25$ ...(i)

also P( passing exactly in one subject) = 0.4

$\square$ $P( X \cap Y \cap Z_d^c \cup X \cap Y_d^c \cap Z \cup Z \cap X_d^c$

$\cap Y \cap Z) = 0.4$

$\square$ $P(X Y Z)P(X Y Z)$

$P(X Y Z) = 0.4$

$pm - pmc + pc - pmc + mc - pmc = 0.4$ ...(ii)

Again P(passing at least in two subjects) = 0.5

$P(X Y Z)\ P(X Y Z)\ P(X Y Z)\ P(X Y Z)$

$= 0.5$

$(pm + pc + mc) - pcm = 0.5$ ...(iii)

From (ii) we get

$(pm + pc + mc) - 3pcm = 0.4$ ...(iv)

From (i) we get,

$1 - (m + p + c) + (pm + pc + cm) - pcm$

$= 0.25$ ...(v)

Now from (iii), (iv) and (v) we get,

$p + m + c = 1.35 = 27/20$

and pmc = 1/10

**2.** **(c)** When two dice is thrown then sample space has $6 \times 6$ $= 36$ elements so n(S) = 36

Now consider the event of getting 9 is (3, 6), (4, 5), (5, 4) and (6, 3)

So probability of getting 9 when two dice is thrown is 4/36 = 1/9

If Sanchita starts the game then the probability that she wins is

$\left(\dfrac{1}{9}\right) + \left(\dfrac{8}{9}\right)\left(\dfrac{8}{9}\right)\left(\dfrac{1}{9}\right) + ..... \dfrac{n}{k}$

$= \dfrac{\dfrac{1}{9}}{1 - \dfrac{64}{81}} = \dfrac{1}{9} \times \dfrac{81}{17} = \dfrac{9}{17}$

And if Raj starts the game then probability that Sanchita wins the game is $1 - 9/17 = 8/17$

**3.** **(a)** Let $X$ = Number of times $A$ shoots at the target to hit it for the first time.

$Y$ = Number of times $B$ shoots at the target to hit it for the first time.

Then $P(X = m) = \left(\dfrac{2}{5}\right)^{m-1}\left(\dfrac{3}{5}\right)$ and

$P(Y = n) = \left(\dfrac{2}{7}\right)^{n-1}\left(\dfrac{5}{7}\right)$

We have $P(Y > X) = \displaystyle\sum_{m=1}^{\infty} \sum_{n=m+1}^{\infty} P(X = m)P(Y = n)$

$[\because X \text{ and } Y \text{ are independent}]$

$= \displaystyle\sum_{m=1}^{\infty} \left[\left\{\left(\dfrac{2}{5}\right)^{m-1}\left(\dfrac{3}{5}\right)\right\} \sum_{n=m+1}^{\infty} \left\{\left(\dfrac{2}{7}\right)^{n-1}\left(\dfrac{5}{7}\right)\right\}\right]$

$= \displaystyle\sum_{m=1}^{\infty} \left(\dfrac{2}{5}\right)^{m-1}\left(\dfrac{3}{5}\right)\left\{\dfrac{5}{7} \cdot \dfrac{\left(\dfrac{2}{7}\right)^{m}}{1 - \dfrac{2}{7}}\right\} =$

$\displaystyle\sum_{m=1}^{\infty} \left(\dfrac{2}{5}\right)^{m-1}\left(\dfrac{3}{5}\right)\left(\dfrac{2}{7}\right)^{m}$

$= \dfrac{6}{35} \displaystyle\sum_{m=1}^{\infty} \left(\dfrac{4}{35}\right)^{m-1} = \dfrac{6}{35} \cdot \dfrac{1}{1 - \dfrac{4}{35}} = \dfrac{6}{31}$

**4.** **(c)** Let $A$ and $B$ arrive at the place of their meeting '$a$' minutes and '$b$' minutes after 5 pm. Their meeting is possible only if $|a-b| \le 20$ ...(i)

Clearly, $0 \le a \le 60$ and $0 \le b \le 60$.

$\therefore$ $a$ and $b$ can be selected as an ordered pair $(a, b)$ from the set $[0, 60] \times [0, 60]$.

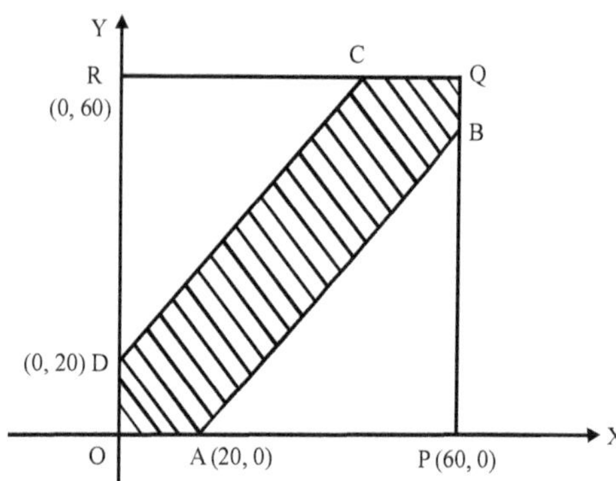

Alternatively, it is equivalent to selecting a point $(a, b)$ from the square $OPQR$, where $P$ is $(60, 0)$ and $R$ is $(0, 60)$ in the cartesian plane.

Now, $|a-b| \le 20 \Rightarrow -20 \le a-b \le 20$

$\therefore$ Points $(a, b)$ satisfy the equation $-20 \le x-y \le 20$

$\therefore$ Favourble condition is equivlent to selecting a point from the region bounded by

$y \le x+20$ and $y \ge x-20$

$\therefore$ Required probability $= \dfrac{\text{Area of } OABQCDO}{\text{Area of square } OPQR}$

$= \dfrac{[Ar(OPQR) - 2Ar(\triangle APB)]}{Ar(OPQR)}$

$= \dfrac{[60 \times 60 - \dfrac{2}{2} \times 40 \times 40]}{60 \times 60} = \dfrac{5}{9}$

**5.** **(b)** Since X has a binomial distribution, B $(n, p)$

$\therefore$ P $(X = 2) = {}^nC_2 \, (p)^2 \, (1 - p)^{n-2}$

and P $(X = 3) = {}^nC_3 \, (p)^3 \, (1 - p)^{n-3}$

Given P $(X = 2) = $ P $(X = 3)$

$\Rightarrow {}^nC_2 \, p^2 \, (1 - p)^{n-2} = {}^nC_3 \, (p)^3 \, (1 - p)^{n-3}$

$\Rightarrow \dfrac{n!}{2!(n-2)!} \cdot \dfrac{p^2(1-p)^n}{(1-p)^2} = \dfrac{n!}{3!(n-3)!} \cdot \dfrac{p^3(1-p)^n}{(1-p)^3}$

$\Rightarrow \dfrac{1}{n-2} = \dfrac{1}{3} \cdot \dfrac{p}{1-p}$

$\Rightarrow 3 \, (1 - p) = p \, (n - 2)$

$\Rightarrow 3 - 3p = np - 2p$

$\Rightarrow np = 3 - p$

$\Rightarrow$ E$(X) = $ mean $= 3 - p$

$(\because$ mean of B $(n, p) = np)$

**6.** **(a, b, d)** Note that $P(Z \le m) = P\{X \le m, Y \le m\}$

$= P\{X \le m\} \, P\{Y \le m\}$

But $P\{Y \le m\} = P\{X \le m\}$

$= P(X = 0) + P(X = 1) + \ldots\ldots\ldots + P(X = m)$

$= p + pq + pq^2 + \ldots\ldots\ldots$

$+ pq^{m-1} = \dfrac{p(1 - q^m)}{1 - q} = 1 - q^m$

$\therefore P(Z \le m) = (1 - q^m)^2$

Now, $P(Z = m) = P(Z \le m) - P(Z \le m-1)$

$= (1 - q^m)^2 - (1 - q^{m-1})^2$

$= 1 - 2q^m + q^{2m} - (1 - 2q^{m-1} + q^{2m-2})$

$= 2 \, pq^{m-1} - p(1 + q) \, q^{2m-2}$ $[\because 1 - q = p]$

Clearly, $\displaystyle\sum_{m \ge 1} P(Z = m)$

$= \displaystyle\sum_{m \ge 1} [2pq^{m-1} - p \, (1 + q) \, q^{2m-2}]$

$= \dfrac{2p}{1-q} - \dfrac{p(1+q)}{1-q^2} = 2 - 1 = 1.$

**7.** **(a, c)** Let $A_i$ denote the event that the $i^{th}$ letter is placed in the right envelope. Then the required probability is

$P(\overline{A_1} \cap \overline{A_2} \cap \ldots\ldots \cap \overline{A_n})$

$= P(\overline{A_1 \cup A_2 \cup \ldots\ldots A_n})$ [By De-Morgan law]

$= 1 - P(A_1 \cup A_2 \cup \ldots \cup A_n)$

$= 1 - [\Sigma P(A_i) - \Sigma P(A_i \cap A_j) + \Sigma P(A_i \cap A_j \cap A_k) - \ldots\ldots$

$+ (-1)^{n-1} P(A_1 \cap A_2 \cap \ldots \cap A_n)]$

$i \ne j \ne k$

Now $P(A_i) = \dfrac{(n-1)!}{n!}$ as having placed $i^{th}$ letter in the

right envelope, the remaining letters can be placed in $(n - 1)!$ ways.

Similarly $P(A_1 \cap A_2 \cap \ldots \cap A_r) = $ Prob. of r particular

letters in right envelopes $= \dfrac{(n-r)!}{n!}$.

$\therefore \Sigma P(A_1 \cap A_2 \cap \ldots \cap A_r)$

$= {}^nC_r \cdot \dfrac{(n-r)!}{n!} = \dfrac{1}{r!}$

Where $r = 1, 2, 3, \ldots\ldots, n.$

$$\therefore \quad \Sigma(\overline{A_i} \cap \overline{A_2} \cap ..... \cap \overline{A_n})$$

$$= 1 - \left\{\frac{1}{1!} - \frac{1}{2!} + \frac{1}{3!} - ... + (-1)^{n-1} \cdot \frac{1}{n!}\right\}$$

$$= \frac{1}{2!} - \frac{1}{3!} + \frac{1}{4!} - ..... + (-1)^n \cdot \frac{1}{n!}$$

which is equal to first $n-2$ terms in the expansion of $e^{-1}$.

**8. (b, d)** $p(r) = \dfrac{3}{10}$ so $p(\overline{r}) = \dfrac{7}{10}$.

The probability of at least one rainy day in 7 days

$$P(A) = 1 - \left(\frac{7}{10}\right)^7$$

Now the probability that at least two rainy days in 7 days.

$$P(B) = 1 - \left(\frac{7}{10}\right)^7 - {}^7C_1\left(\frac{3}{10}\right)\left(\frac{7}{10}\right)^6$$

Hence $P(B/A) = \dfrac{P(B \cap A)}{P(A)}$

$$= \frac{1 - \left(\frac{7}{10}\right)^7 - {}^7C_1\left(\frac{3}{10}\right)\left(\frac{7}{10}\right)^6}{1 - \left(\frac{7}{10}\right)^7}$$

$$= \left\{\frac{1 - \left(\frac{7}{10}\right)^7 - 7\left(\frac{3}{10}\right)\left(\frac{7}{10}\right)^6}{1 - \left(\frac{7}{10}\right)^7}\right\}$$

**9. (a, b, c, d)** We have

$$P(A_1) = \frac{2}{4} = \frac{1}{2} = P(A_2) = P(A_3).$$

[Note that $P(A_1)$ is the probability of the event that the first digit is 1 and since there are two numbers having 1 at the first place out of four, we have $P(A_1) = $

$\dfrac{2}{4} = \dfrac{1}{2}$. Similarly for $P(A_2)$ and $P(A_3)$].

$A_1 \cap A_2$ is the event that the first two digits in the numbers drawn are each equal to 1 and so $P(A_1 \cap A_2)$

$$= \frac{1}{4} = \frac{1}{2} = P(A_1) P(A_2)$$

Similarly $P(A_2 \cap A_3) = P(A_2)(A_3)$
and $P(A_3 \cap A_1) = P(A_3) P(A_1)$.
Thus the events $A_1$, $A_2$ and $A_3$ are equal to 1 and since there is no such number, we have

$$P(A_1 \cap A_2 \cap A_3) = 0.$$
$$\neq P(A_1) P(A_2) P(A_3).$$

Hence the events $A_1$, $A_2$, $A_3$ are the not mutually independent although they are pairwise independent.

**10. (1)** Lets define the events as

Probability of getting project copy (A) = p
Probability of getting blue pen (B) = q
Probability of getting black pen (C) = 1/2

Then $P(AB\overline{C}) + p(AC\overline{B}) + p(ABC) = \dfrac{1}{2}$

$$p \cdot q \cdot \frac{1}{2} + p \cdot \frac{1}{2}(1-q) + p \cdot q \cdot \frac{1}{2} = \frac{1}{2}$$

$$= pq + p - pq + pq = 1 \quad \therefore \quad p(1+q) = 1$$

**11. (3)** Let $A_i (i = 1, 2, 3, 4)$ be the event that the urn contains 2, 3, 4 or 5 white balls and B the event that two white balls are drawn.

We have to find $P(A_4/B)$.

Since the four events $A_1$, $A_2$, $A_3$, $A_4$ are equally likely, we have

$$P(A_1) = P(A_2) = P(A_3) = P(A_4) = \frac{1}{4}.$$

$P(B/A_1)$ is the probability of event that the urn contains 2 white balls and both have been drawn.

Hence $P(B/A_1) = \dfrac{{}^2C_2}{{}^5C_2} = \dfrac{1}{10}.$

Similarly $P(B/A_2) = \dfrac{{}^3C_2}{{}^5C_2} = \dfrac{3}{10}.$

$$P(B/A_3) = \frac{{}^4C_2}{{}^5C_2} = \frac{6}{10} = \frac{3}{5}.$$

and $P(B/A_4) = \dfrac{{}^5C_2}{{}^5C_2} = 1.$

$\therefore$ by Baye's theorem

$$P(A_4/B) = \frac{P(A_4)P(B/A_4)}{\displaystyle\sum_{i+1}^{4} P(A_i)P(B/A_i)}$$

$$= \frac{\frac{1}{4} \cdot 1}{\frac{1}{4}(\frac{1}{10} + \frac{3}{10} + \frac{3}{5} + 1)} = \frac{1}{2}$$

**12. (7)** Since the coin is fair,

$$P(H) = P(T) = \frac{1}{2}$$

By binomial distribution,

$$P(X = K) = {}^nC_k \left(\frac{1}{2}\right)^{n-k} \left(\frac{1}{2}\right)^{k}$$

$$= {}^nC_k \left(\frac{1}{2}\right)^{n}$$

By hypothesis
$$2P(X = 5) = P(X = 4) + P(X = 6)$$

Therefore, $2\left({}^nC_5\right) = {}^nC_4 + {}^nC_6$

$n^2 - 21n + 98 = 0$

$n = 7, 14$

Therefore, $n = 7$ (smaller value).

**13. (6)** Let $x$ shell are fixed at point I. Define the following events

$E_1$ : The target is at point I $\Rightarrow P(E_1) = \dfrac{8}{9}$

$E_2$ : The target is at point II $\Rightarrow P(E_2) = \dfrac{1}{9}$

$A$ : The target is hit

The target will be hit if at least one shell hits the target.

$P(A / E_1) = 1 - $ None of the shells hit when the target

is at point I $= 1 - \left(\dfrac{1}{2}\right)^{x}$ and $P(A / E_2) = 1 - \left(\dfrac{1}{2}\right)^{21-x}$

$$\therefore \quad P(A) = \frac{8}{9}\left[1 - \left(\frac{1}{2}\right)^{x}\right] + \frac{1}{9}\left[1 - \left(\frac{1}{2}\right)^{21-x}\right]$$

$$= 1 - \frac{1}{9}\left[\left(\frac{1}{2}\right)^{x-3} + \left(\frac{1}{2}\right)^{21-x}\right]$$

For maximum probability; $\dfrac{dP(A)}{dx} = 0$

$$\Rightarrow -\frac{1}{9}\left[\left(\frac{1}{2}\right)^{21-x} ln\,2 - \left(\frac{1}{2}\right)^{x-3} ln\,2\right] = 0 \Rightarrow x = 12$$

Also,

$$\frac{d^2 P(A)}{dx^2} = -\frac{1}{9}\left[\left(\frac{1}{2}\right)^{x-3}(ln2)^2 + \left(\frac{1}{2}\right)^{21-x}(ln2)^2\right] < 0$$

$\therefore P(A)$ is maximum when $x = 12$.

$\Rightarrow k = 6$

**14. (b)** Let $A_i (i = 1, 2, 3)$ be the event that ith urn is chosen and B the event that a white ball is drawn.
Since all the urns are equally likely to be selected, we have

$$P(A_1) = P(A_2) = P(A_3) = \frac{1}{3}$$

and $P(B/A_1) = \dfrac{2}{5}$, $P(B/A_2) = \dfrac{3}{5}$

$$P(B/A_3) = \frac{4}{5}.$$

Hence $P(B) = P(A_1)\,P(B/A_2) = \dfrac{3}{5}$, $P(B/A_2) = \dfrac{4}{5}$,

Hence $P(B) = P(A_1)\,P(B/A_1) + P(A_2)\,P(B/A_2) + P(A_3)\,P(B/A_3)$

$$= \frac{1}{3} \cdot \frac{2}{5} + \frac{1}{3} \cdot \frac{3}{5} + \frac{1}{3} \cdot \frac{4}{5} = \frac{9}{15} = \frac{3}{5}.$$

**15. (c)** Here we have to find $P(A_1/B)$

By Baye's theorem required probability

$$= \frac{\frac{1}{3} \cdot \frac{2}{5}}{\frac{3}{5}} = \frac{2}{9}.$$

**16. (a)** $P(A^C) = 0.3$, $P(b) = 0.4$ and $P(A \cap B^C) = 0.5$

$$P[B/(A \cap B^C)] = \frac{P[B \cap (A \cup B^C)]}{P(A \cup B^C)}$$

$$= \frac{P((B \cap A) \cup (B \cap B^C))}{P(A \cup B^C)}$$

$$= \frac{P(A \cap B)}{P(A) + P(B^C) - P(A \cap B^C)}$$

$$= \frac{P(A) - P(A \cap B^C)}{1 - P(A^C) + 1 - P(B) - P(A \cap B^C)}$$

$$= \frac{1 - 0.3 - 0.5}{1 - 0.3 + 1 - 0.4 - 0.5} = \frac{0.2}{0.8} = \frac{1}{4}$$

**17. (d)** $P(A) = \dfrac{1}{5}$, $P(B) = \dfrac{4}{5}$, $P(C) = \dfrac{7}{100}$

$$P\left(\frac{B}{C}\right) = \frac{P\left(\dfrac{\overline{C}}{B}\right) P(B)}{P\left(\dfrac{\overline{C}}{A}\right) P(A) + P\left(\dfrac{\overline{C}}{B}\right) P(B)}$$

$$= \cfrac{\dfrac{80}{100} \times \dfrac{39}{40}}{\dfrac{20}{100} \times \dfrac{30}{40} + \dfrac{80}{100} \times \dfrac{39}{40}}$$

$$\left[ \because \ P\left(\frac{\overline{C}}{A}\right) = \frac{30}{40}, P\left(\frac{\overline{C}}{B}\right) = \frac{39}{40} \right]$$

$$= \frac{156}{186} = \frac{26}{31}$$

**18.  (b)**  $P(A) = \dfrac{1}{2} \cdot P(B) = \dfrac{1}{4} = P(C)$

$P(A \cap B \cap C^C) + P(A \cap B^C \cap C)$
$\qquad\qquad + P(A^C \cap B \cap C) + P(A \cap B \cap C)$

$$= \frac{1}{2} \times \frac{1}{4} \times \frac{3}{4} + \frac{1}{2} \times \frac{3}{4} \times \frac{1}{4} + \frac{1}{2} \times \frac{1}{4} \times \frac{1}{4}$$
$$+ \frac{1}{2} \times \frac{1}{4} \times \frac{1}{4}$$

$$= \frac{1}{4}$$

**19.  $A \to (r); B \to (s); C \to (q); D \to (p)$**

(A)  Probability that Aman will hit the target is $P(A) = 4/5$ and probability that Aman will not hit the target is $P(A') = 1 - 4/5 = 1/5$.

Probability that Binay will hit the target is $P(A) = 3/4$ and probability that Binay will not hit the target is $P(A') = 1 - 3/4 = 1/4$

Probability that none of them will hit the target is $P(A' \cap B')$

$= 1/5 \times \frac{1}{4} = 1/20$

So probability that at least one of them will hit the target is $1 - 1/20 = 19/20$

(B)  Let $P(A)$ probability of getting a prime number $= 3/6 = 1/2$ then $P(A') = 1/2$

And $P(B) =$ probability of getting a composite number $2/6 = 1/3$ then $P(B') = 2/3$

Now consider Kushal wins the game it is possible in following cases-

Case (1) in one throw- if kushal gets a prime
$= P(A) = 1/2$

Case (2) in three throws- If kushal fails to get a prime in $1^{st}$ throw, Karina fails to get composite in $2^{nd}$ throw and Kushal gets a prime in $3^{rd}$ throw, in this case probability is $P(A') \times P(B') \times P(A) = 1/2 \times 2/3 \times 1/2 = 1/6$

Case (3) in 5 throw then similar to above case probability is $(1/2) \times (2/3) \times (1/2) \times (2/3) \times (1/2) = 1/18$

And this process will continue and the required probability is $(1/2) + (1/6) + (1/18) + \ldots \infty$

Or required probability $\cfrac{\dfrac{1}{2}}{1 - \dfrac{1}{3}} = \dfrac{3}{4}$

(C)  Probability that Karina will win the game is $1 - 3/4 = 1/4$

(D)  Probability of getting a six is $1/6$

If Sanchita starts the game then the probability that she wins is

$$\left(\frac{1}{6}\right) + \left(\frac{5}{6}\right)\left(\frac{5}{6}\right)\left(\frac{1}{6}\right) + \ldots \infty = \cfrac{\dfrac{1}{6}}{1 - \dfrac{25}{56}} = \frac{6}{11}$$

And if Raj starts the game then probability that Sanchita wins the game is $1 - 6/11 = 5/11$

**20.  (A) $\to$ r; (B) $\to$ s; (C) $\to$ p; (D) $\to$ q**

(A)  $\dfrac{^{11}C_5}{^{12}C_6} = \dfrac{1}{2}.$

(B)  Let $E_1$ be the event that $S_3$ and $S_4$ are in same group

Let $E_2$ be the event that $S_3$ and $S_4$ are in different group.

$$P(E_1) = \frac{1}{11}$$

$$P(E_2) = \frac{10}{11}$$

Ler E be the event that exactly one of $S_3$ and $S_4$ is among the losers, then

$$P(E) = P(E_1)P(E/E_1) + P(E_2) \ P(E/E_2)$$

$$= \frac{1}{11} \times 1 + \frac{10}{11} \times \left(\frac{1}{2} \cdot \frac{1}{2} + \frac{1}{2} \cdot \frac{1}{2}\right) = \frac{6}{11}.$$

(C)  $S_2$ and $S_4$ should be in different groups for both winner

Required probability $= \dfrac{10}{11}\left(\dfrac{1}{2} \cdot \dfrac{1}{2}\right) = \dfrac{5}{22}$

or  $\dfrac{^{10}C_4}{^{12}C_6} = \dfrac{5}{22}.$

(D)  $S_4$ and $S_5$ will not play against each other if they are paired together whose probability $= \dfrac{10}{11}$

**1.** **(a)** Given $\cot\theta = \cot A + \cot B + \cot C$

$\Rightarrow \cot\theta - \cot A = \cot B + \cot C$

$\Rightarrow \dfrac{\cos\theta\sin A - \sin\theta\cos A}{\sin\theta\sin A} = \dfrac{\cos B\sin C + \sin B\cos C}{\sin B\sin C}$

$\Rightarrow \sin(A-\theta) = \dfrac{\sin A\sin\theta\sin(B+C)}{\sin B\sin C} = \dfrac{\sin^2 A\sin\theta}{\sin B\sin C}$

$[\because A+B+C=\pi]$

Similarly, $\sin(B-\theta) = \dfrac{\sin^2 B\sin\theta}{\sin A\sin C}$ and

$\sin(C-\theta) = \dfrac{\sin^2 C\sin\theta}{\sin A\sin B}$

$\therefore \sin(A-\theta)\sin(B-\theta)\sin(C-\theta) = \sin^3\theta$

**2.** **(c)** $\cos A + \cos B + \cos C$

$= 2\cos\dfrac{A+B}{2}\cos\dfrac{A-B}{2} + 1 - 2\sin^2\dfrac{C}{2}$

$= 2\sin\dfrac{C}{2}\cdot\left(\cos\dfrac{A-B}{2} - \sin\dfrac{C}{2}\right) + 1 \ (\because A+B=\pi-C)$

$\leq 2\sin\dfrac{C}{2}\left(1 - \sin\dfrac{C}{2}\right) + 1$

$\left(\because \text{ the greatest value of } \cos\dfrac{A-B}{2} \text{ is } 1\right)$

and equality holds when $\cos\dfrac{A-B}{2} = 1$ ...(1)

$\therefore \ \cos A + \cos B + \cos C \leq 1 - 2\left(\sin^2\dfrac{C}{2} - \sin\dfrac{C}{2}\right)$

$= 1 - 2\left(\sin^2\dfrac{C}{2} - \sin\dfrac{C}{2} + \dfrac{1}{4}\right) + 2\cdot\dfrac{1}{4}$

$= \dfrac{3}{2} - 2\left(\sin\dfrac{C}{2} - \dfrac{1}{2}\right)^2 \leq \dfrac{3}{2}$

equality holding when $\sin\dfrac{C}{2} = \dfrac{1}{2}$

Thus, $\cos A + \cos B + \cos C \leq \dfrac{3}{2}$

equality holding when (1) and (2) both hold, i.e., when

$A = B = C = \dfrac{\pi}{3}$

**3.** **(b)** $a$, $b$, $c$ are sides of a triangle

$\therefore a+b>c,\ b+c>a,\ c+a>b$

$\therefore a>|b-c|,\ b>|c-a|,\ c>|a-b|$ square and add

$a^2+b^2+c^2 < 2(ab+bc+ca)$

$\Rightarrow a^2+b^2+c^2 + 2(ab+bc+ac) < 4(ab+bc+ca)$

$\Rightarrow \dfrac{(a+b+c)^2}{ab+bc+ca} < 4 \Rightarrow P < 4$

Again $(a-b)^2 + (b-c)^2 + (c-a)^2 \geq 0$

$\Rightarrow \dfrac{(a+b+c)^2}{ab+bc+ca} \geq 3 \Rightarrow P \geq 3$

$\therefore 3 \leq P < 4$ or $P \in [3, 4)$

**4.** **(b)** $\dfrac{a^2+b^2}{a^2-b^2}\sin(A-B) = 1$

$\Rightarrow \dfrac{\sin^2 A + \sin^2 B}{\sin^2 A - \sin^2 B}\cdot\sin(A-B) = 1$

$\Rightarrow \dfrac{\sin^2 A + \sin^2 B}{\sin(A+B)\sin(A-B)}\times\sin(A-B) = 1$

$\Rightarrow \sin^2 A + \sin^2 B = \sin(A+B) = \sin C$

$\Rightarrow 1 - \cos 2A + 1 - \cos 2B = 2\sin C$

$\Rightarrow \cos 2A + \cos 2B = 2(1 - \sin C)$

$\Rightarrow 2\cos(A+B)\cos(A-B) = 2(1 - \sin C)$

$\Rightarrow \cos(A-B) = \dfrac{1-\sin C}{-\cos C} \qquad \left(\text{if } C \neq \dfrac{\pi}{2}\right)$

$\Rightarrow \cos(A-B) = \dfrac{\left(\sin\dfrac{C}{2} - \cos\dfrac{C}{2}\right)^2}{\sin^2\dfrac{C}{2} - \cos^2\dfrac{C}{2}} = \dfrac{\sin\dfrac{C}{2} - \cos\dfrac{C}{2}}{\sin\dfrac{C}{2} + \cos\dfrac{C}{2}}$

$= \dfrac{\tan(C/2) - 1}{\tan(C/2) + 1} = \tan\left(\dfrac{C}{2} - \dfrac{\pi}{4}\right)$

**5.** **(a)** Let OP be the tower of height h, A be a point due south of it such that $\angle OAP = \alpha$ and B, a point due east of it such that $\angle OBP = \beta$. (see figure)

It is given that $\tan\alpha = 0.6 = \dfrac{3}{5}$ and $\tan\beta = 0.75 = \dfrac{3}{4}$

Now, $OA = h\cot\alpha = \dfrac{5h}{3}$ and $OB = h\cot\beta = \dfrac{4h}{3}$. So that from right angled triangle AOB

$$(AB)^2 = (OA)^2 + (OB)^2 = \dfrac{41}{9}h^2$$

$\Rightarrow AB = \lambda h$, where $\lambda^2 = 41/9$

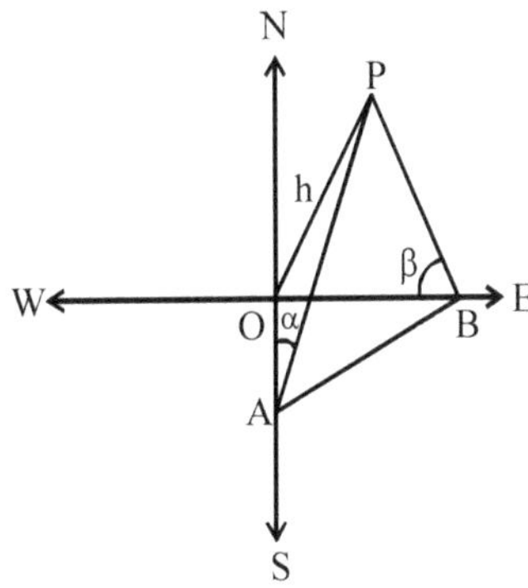


**6.** **(c)** We have
$\angle CAD = 45°, \angle BAD = 30°, \angle CBH = 60°$ (see figure)
$\Rightarrow \angle ACD = 45°, \angle BCH = 30°$,
so that $\angle ACB = 15°$ and
$\angle CAB = 45° - 30° = 15° \Rightarrow \angle ABC = 150°$

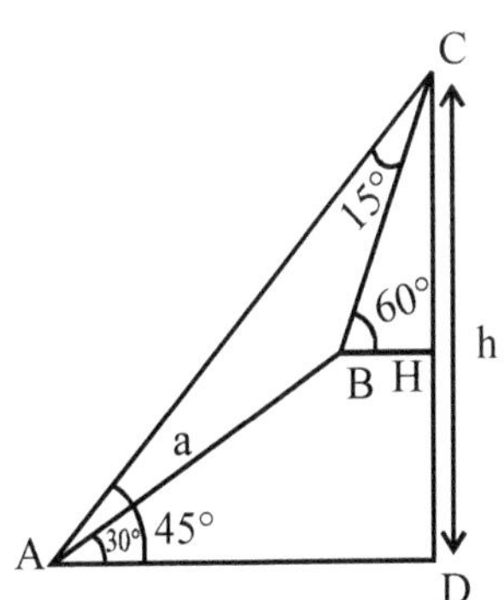


From $\triangle ADC$, $AC^2 = h^2 + h^2 = 2h^2$ $\quad[\because AD = CD = h]$
and from $\triangle ABC$

$$\dfrac{AB}{\sin 15°} = \dfrac{AC}{\sin 150°} \Rightarrow \dfrac{a}{\sin 15°} = \dfrac{\sqrt{2}h}{\sin 150°}$$

$$\therefore a = \left(\dfrac{\sqrt{2}\sin 15°}{\sin 30°}\right)h, \quad [\because \sin 150° = \sin 30°]$$

$$= \dfrac{\sqrt{2}\left(\dfrac{\sqrt{3}-1}{2\sqrt{2}}\right)}{\dfrac{1}{2}}h = h\left(\sqrt{3}-1\right)$$

**7.** **(a,b,d)** $\quad b\cos^2\dfrac{A}{2} + a\cos^2\dfrac{B}{2} = \dfrac{3c}{2}$

$$\Rightarrow \dfrac{b}{2}(1+\cos A) + \dfrac{a}{2}(1+\cos B) = \dfrac{3c}{2}$$

$$\Rightarrow b + a + (b\cos A + a\cos B) = 3c$$

$$\Rightarrow b + a + c = 3c \Rightarrow a + b = 2c$$

Thus, $a + b \geq 2\sqrt{ab}$

$$\Rightarrow 2c \geq 2\sqrt{ab} > \sqrt{ab}$$

Also $2c \geq 2\sqrt{ab} \Rightarrow c^2 \geq ab$

Moreover, $\dfrac{a+c}{2c-a} + \dfrac{b+c}{2c-b} = \dfrac{a+c}{b} + \dfrac{b+c}{a}$

$$= \dfrac{a}{b} + \dfrac{c}{b} + \dfrac{b}{a} + \dfrac{c}{a} \geq 4\left(\dfrac{c^2 ab}{a^2 b^2}\right)^{1/4} \geq 4 \text{ and}$$

$$\dfrac{a}{c} + \dfrac{c}{b} + \dfrac{b}{a} \geq 3\left(\dfrac{acb}{cba}\right)^{1/3} = 3$$

**8.** **(a,b,d)** Let the sides of a triangle be $a, ar, ar^2$
$\because ar^2$ is the greater side $(r > 1)$.

$$\therefore a + ar > ar^2$$

$$\because r^2 - r - 1 < 0 \Rightarrow \dfrac{1-\sqrt{5}}{2} < r < \dfrac{1+\sqrt{5}}{2}$$

$$\Rightarrow 1 < r < \dfrac{1+\sqrt{5}}{2}$$

Therefore (a) is correct.

Also $r^2 < \dfrac{1}{4}(6+2\sqrt{5}) = \dfrac{1}{2}(3+\sqrt{5})$

and $r^4 < \dfrac{1}{4}(14+6\sqrt{5}) = \dfrac{1}{2}(7+3\sqrt{5})$

$$\therefore 1 + r^2 - r^4 < 1 + \dfrac{1}{2}(3+\sqrt{5}) - \dfrac{1}{2}(7+3\sqrt{5})$$

$$= -1 - \sqrt{5} < r$$

$$\cos C = \dfrac{a^2 + a^2 r^2 - a^2 r^4}{2a^2 r} = \dfrac{1 + r^2 - r^4}{2r} < \dfrac{1}{2}$$

$$\therefore \cos C < \cos\dfrac{\pi}{3} \Rightarrow C > \dfrac{\pi}{3}$$

Therefore (d) is correct.

Also, $\cos B = \dfrac{a^2 + a^2 r^4 - a^2 r^2}{2a^2 r^2} = \dfrac{1 + r^4 - r^2}{2r^2}$

$$= \frac{1}{2}\left[ r^2 + \frac{1}{r^2} - 1 \right] = \frac{1}{2}\left[ \left( r - \frac{1}{2} \right)^2 + 1 \right] > \frac{1}{2}$$

$$\therefore \cos B > \cos\frac{\pi}{3} \Rightarrow B < \frac{\pi}{3}$$

Also,

$$a < ar < ar^2 \Rightarrow A < B < C \Rightarrow A < B < \frac{\pi}{3} < C$$

Hence (b) is also correct and (c) is incorrect.

**9.** **(a,b,c)** Let $BP = n, CQ = n+1, AR = n+2$

Then $BP = BR = n$

$CQ = CP = n+1$ and $AR = AQ = n+2$

$$\therefore \ BC = 2n+1,\ CA = 2n+3,\ AB = 2n+2 \ \text{ and }$$

$$S = \frac{1}{2}[2n+1+2n+3+2n+2] = 3n+3$$

$$\Delta = \sqrt{(3n+3)(n+2)(n)(n+1)} \ \text{ and inradius}$$

$$= \frac{\Delta}{s} = 4$$

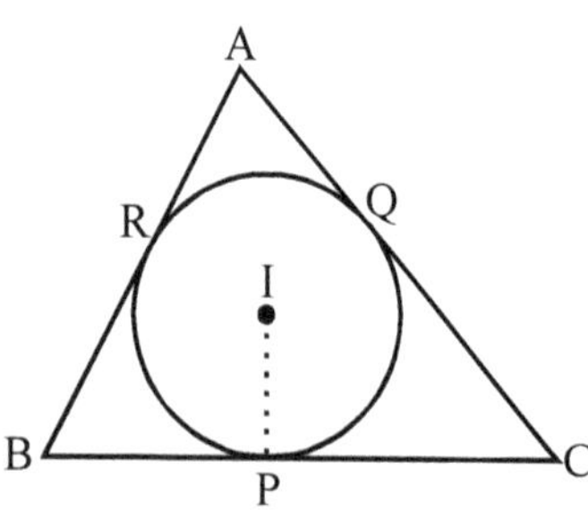

$$\therefore \ \sqrt{\frac{n(n+2)}{3}} = 4 \Rightarrow n^2 + 2n - 48 = 0 \Rightarrow n = 6$$

So, the sides are 13, 14, 15. and perimeter
$= 2s = 42$ unit

$$\Delta = \sqrt{31 \times 8 \times 6 \times 7} = 7 \times 3 \times 4 = 84 \ \text{unit}$$

$\therefore$ radius of circumcircle

$$R = \frac{13 \times 14 \times 15}{4 \times 84} = \frac{65}{8} \ \text{cm}$$

**10.** **(b, c)** Here $\cos A,\ \cos B,\ \cos C$ are in A.P.

$$\Rightarrow 2\cos B = \cos A + \cos C$$

$$= 2 \cos \frac{A+C}{2} \cos \frac{A-C}{2}$$

$$\Rightarrow \left( 1 - 2\sin^2 \frac{B}{2} \right) = \sin \frac{B}{2} \cos \frac{A-C}{2}$$

$$\text{or } \cos^2 \frac{B}{2} = \sin \frac{B}{2}\left[ \sin \frac{B}{2} + \cos \frac{A-C}{2} \right]$$

$$= \sin \frac{B}{2}\left[ \cos \frac{A+C}{2} + \cos \frac{A-C}{2} \right]$$

$$= 2 \sin \frac{B}{2} \cos \frac{A}{2} \cos \frac{C}{2}.$$

$$\Rightarrow \cot \frac{B}{2} = \frac{2 \cos \dfrac{A}{2} \cos \dfrac{C}{2}}{\sin \left( \dfrac{A+C}{2} \right)}$$

$$= \frac{2 \cos \dfrac{A}{2} \cos \dfrac{C}{2}}{\sin \dfrac{A}{2} \cos \dfrac{C}{2} + \cos \dfrac{A}{2} \sin \dfrac{C}{2}}$$

$$\Rightarrow \cot \frac{B}{2} = \frac{2}{\tan \dfrac{A}{2} + \tan \dfrac{C}{2}}$$

$$\Rightarrow \tan \frac{A}{2} + \tan \frac{C}{2} = 2 \tan \frac{B}{2}$$

$$\Rightarrow \tan \frac{A}{2}, \tan \frac{B}{2}, \tan \frac{C}{2} \ \text{are in A.P.}$$

$$\Rightarrow \sqrt{\frac{(s-b)(s-c)}{s(s-a)}} + \sqrt{\frac{(s-a)(s-b)}{s(s-c)}}$$

$$= 2 \sqrt{\frac{(s-a)(s-c)}{s(s-b)}}$$

$$\text{or } \frac{\Delta}{s(s-a)} + \frac{\Delta}{s(s-c)} = 2 \frac{\Delta}{s(s-b)}$$

$$\text{or } r_1 + r_2 = 2r_2 \Rightarrow r_1, r_2, r_3 \ \text{are in A.P.}$$

**11.** **(6)** We have $\dfrac{1}{2} ah_1 = \Delta = rs$

$$\Rightarrow \frac{h_1}{r} = \frac{2s}{a} = \frac{a+b+c}{a}$$

$$\Rightarrow \frac{h_1 + r}{h_1 - r} = \frac{2a+b+c}{b+c} = \frac{2(a+b+c)}{b+c} - 1$$

Hence $\displaystyle\sum \frac{h_1 + r}{h_1 - r} = 2(a+b+c)\left[ \frac{1}{b+c} + \frac{1}{c+a} + \frac{1}{a+b} \right] - 3$

$$\geq 2(a+b+c).3\frac{3}{(b+c)+(c+a)+(a+b)} - 3$$

$$\text{(A.M.} \geq \text{H.M.)}$$

i.e., $\displaystyle\sum \frac{h_1 + r}{h_1 - r} \geq 6$ .

**12.** **(3)** Given $A + B + C = \pi$

$\Rightarrow \cot\dfrac{A}{2}\cot\dfrac{B}{2}\cot\dfrac{C}{2} = \cot\dfrac{A}{2} + \cot\dfrac{B}{2} + \cot\dfrac{C}{2}$ ... (i)

But $\tan\dfrac{A}{2}, \tan\dfrac{B}{2}, \tan\dfrac{C}{2}$ are in H.P.

$\Rightarrow \cot\dfrac{A}{2}, \cot\dfrac{B}{2}, \cot\dfrac{C}{2}$ are in A.P.

$\Rightarrow \cot\dfrac{A}{2} + \cot\dfrac{C}{2} = 2\cot\dfrac{B}{2}$ ... (ii)

From (i) and (ii), we get $\cot\dfrac{A}{2}.\cot\dfrac{B}{2}.\cot\dfrac{C}{2} = 3\cot\dfrac{B}{2}$

$\therefore \cot\dfrac{A}{2}.\cot\dfrac{C}{2} = 3$

Now, $\dfrac{\cot\dfrac{A}{2} + \cot\dfrac{C}{2}}{2} \geq \sqrt{\cot\dfrac{A}{2}\cot\dfrac{C}{2}}$

$\Rightarrow \dfrac{2\cot\dfrac{B}{2}}{2} \geq \sqrt{3}$  [From (ii) an (iii)]

$\therefore \cot\dfrac{B}{2} \geq \sqrt{3}$

**13.** **(5)** Let $h_a, h_b, h_c$ be sides of $\Delta A'B'C'$ and $h_a', h_b', h_c'$ be sides of $A''B''C''$

Then $\dfrac{1}{2}ah_a = \dfrac{1}{2}bh_b = \dfrac{1}{2}ch_c = \Delta$ ....(1)

Also, $\dfrac{1}{2}h_a h'_a = \dfrac{1}{2}h_b h'_b = \dfrac{1}{2}h_c h'_c = \Delta'$ ...(2)

$\therefore h'_a = \dfrac{2\Delta'}{h_a} = \dfrac{2\Delta'}{\dfrac{2\Delta}{a}} = \dfrac{a\Delta'}{\Delta}$  from (1)

Now $\Delta''^2 = \left(\dfrac{h'_a + h'_b + h'_c}{2}\right)\left(\dfrac{h'_a + h'_b - h'_c}{2}\right)$

$\left(\dfrac{h'_a - h'_b + h'_c}{2}\right)\left(\dfrac{-h'_a + h'_b + h'_c}{2}\right)$

$= \dfrac{1}{2^4}\left[\dfrac{a\Delta'}{\Delta} + \dfrac{b\Delta'}{\Delta} + \dfrac{c\Delta'}{\Delta}\right]\left[\dfrac{a\Delta'}{\Delta} + \dfrac{b\Delta'}{\Delta} - \dfrac{c\Delta'}{\Delta}\right]$

$\left[\dfrac{a\Delta'}{\Delta} - \dfrac{b\Delta'}{\Delta} + \dfrac{c\Delta'}{\Delta}\right]\left[-\dfrac{a\Delta'}{\Delta} + \dfrac{b\Delta'}{\Delta} + \dfrac{c\Delta'}{\Delta}\right]$

$= \dfrac{(\Delta')^4}{2^4 \Delta^4}(a+b+c)(a+b-c)(a-b+c)$

$(-a+b+c) = \dfrac{(\Delta')^4 \Delta^2}{\Delta^4}$

$\therefore \Delta^2 = \dfrac{(\Delta')^4}{(\Delta'')^2} = \dfrac{(30)^4}{(20)^2} = \dfrac{3^4 \times 10^2}{2^2}$

$\therefore \Delta = \dfrac{3^2 \times 10}{2} = 45 \Rightarrow \dfrac{\Delta}{9} = 5$

**14.** **(6)** $p_1 = \dfrac{2\Delta}{a}, \; p_2 = \dfrac{2\Delta}{b}, \; p_3 = \dfrac{2\Delta}{c}$

$\therefore p_1 + p_2 + p_3 \geq 3(p_1 p_2 p_3)^{1/3}$

$= 3\left\{\dfrac{(2\Delta)^3}{abc}\right\}^{1/3} = 6\Delta\left(\dfrac{1}{abc}\right)^{1/3}$

$= 6rs\left(\dfrac{1}{abc}\right)^{1/3} = 6r\dfrac{a+b+c}{2}\left(\dfrac{1}{abc}\right)^{1/3}$

$= 9r\left(\dfrac{a+b+c}{3}\right)\left(\dfrac{1}{abc}\right)^{1/3} \geq 9r \; (AM/GM \geq 1)$

(Equality occurs when $p_1 = p_2 = p_3$ and $a = b = c$, i.e. when $\Delta ABC$ is equilateral)

$\therefore p_1 + p_2 + p_3 \geq 9 \times \dfrac{2}{3} = 6$

**15.** **(c)** $r_1 + r_2 + r_3 - r = \Delta\left[\dfrac{1}{s-a} + \dfrac{1}{s-b} + \dfrac{1}{s-c} - \dfrac{1}{s}\right]$

$= \Delta\left[\dfrac{2s-a-b}{(s-a)(s-b)} + \dfrac{s-s+c}{s(s-c)}\right]$

$= \Delta c\left[\dfrac{s(s-c)+(s-a)(s-b)}{s(s-a)(s-b)(s-c)}\right]$

$= \dfrac{\Delta c}{\Delta^2}\left[2s^2 - s(a+b+c) + ab\right] = \dfrac{abc}{\Delta} = 4R$

$\therefore r_1 + r_2 + r_3 = r + 4R$

$r_1 r_2 + r_2 r_3 + r_3 r_1$

$= \Delta^2\left[\dfrac{1}{(s-a)(s-b)} + \dfrac{1}{(s-b)(s-c)} + \dfrac{1}{(s-c)(s-a)}\right]$

$= \dfrac{\Delta^2(s-c+s-a+s-b)}{(s-a)(s-b)(s-c)} = s^2$

$r_1 r_2 r_3 = \dfrac{\Delta^2}{(s-a)(s-b)(s-c)} = \Delta s = rs^2$

$\therefore r_1, r_2, r_3$ are roots of the equations

$x^3 - x^2(r_1 + r_2 + r_3) + x(r_1 r_2 + r_2 r_3 + r_3 r_1) - r_1 r_2 r_3 = 0$

$\Rightarrow x^3 - x^2(4R+r) + x(s^2) - rs^2 = 0$

**16. (a)** We have
$$x^3 - (4R+r)x^2 + s^2x - rs^2 = (x-r_1)(x-r_2)(x-r_3)$$
$$\Rightarrow (-s)^3 - (4R+r)(-s)^2 + s^2(-s) - rs^2$$
$$= (-s-r_1)(-s-r_2)(-s-r_3)$$
$$\therefore (s+r_1)(s+r_2)(s+r_3) = 2s^2(s+r+2R)$$

**17. (b)** For real roots $c_1$ and $c_2$, $D > 0$, i.e., $a > b\sin A$
Consider the smaller root, say
$$c_1 = b\cos A - \sqrt{a^2 - b^2\sin^2 A}$$
$c_1 > 0$ if $b\cos A > \sqrt{a^2 - b^2\sin^2 A}$, i.e., if
$b^2\cos^2 A > a^2 - b^2\sin^2 A$ and $\cos A > 0$
or if $b^2 > a^2$ and $\cos A > 0$.
Hence, two different triangles are possible if
$a > b\sin A$, $b > a$ and $A$ is acute.
***ALTERNATIVELY***
The equation $c^2 - (2b\cos A)c + b^2 - a^2 = 0$ has two
distinct positive roots $c_1$ and $c_2$ if and only if
discriminant $> 0$, $c_1 + c_2 > 0$ and $c_1c_2 > 0$
$\Rightarrow a > b\sin A$, $2b\cos A > 0$ and $b^2 - a^2 > 0$
$\Rightarrow a > b\sin A$ and $b > a$

**18. (b)** If $a = b$, then $a^2 = b^2(\cos^2 A + \sin^2 A)$
$$\Rightarrow a^2 - b^2\sin^2 A = b^2\cos^2 A$$
$$\therefore \sqrt{a^2 - b^2\sin^2 A} = b\cos A \Rightarrow G = 0$$
but $c_2 > 0$. So, only one triangle is possible.

**19.** $(A) \to (p)$; $(B) \to (s)$; $(C) \to (p,q)$; $(D) \to (q)$
**(A)** We have,
$$\frac{r}{r_1} = \frac{4R\sin\dfrac{A}{2}\sin\dfrac{B}{2}\sin\dfrac{C}{2}}{4R\sin\dfrac{A}{2}\cos\dfrac{B}{2}\cos\dfrac{C}{2}} = \tan\frac{B}{2}\tan\frac{C}{2} = \frac{1}{4}$$
$$\therefore \tan\frac{A}{2}\left(\tan\frac{B}{2} + \tan\frac{C}{2}\right)$$
$$= 1 - \tan\frac{B}{2}\tan\frac{C}{2} = 1 - \frac{1}{4} = \frac{3}{4}$$

**(B)** We have, $(r_1r_2r_3)^{1/3} \geq \dfrac{3}{\dfrac{1}{r_1} + \dfrac{1}{r_2} + \dfrac{1}{r_3}} = 3r$
$$\therefore \frac{r_1r_2r_3}{r^3} \geq 27$$

**(C)** $a+b > c \Rightarrow 2b-c+b > c \Rightarrow \dfrac{b}{c} > \dfrac{2}{3}$
Also, $b+c > a \Rightarrow b+c > 2b-c \Rightarrow \dfrac{b}{c} < 2$
Again, $c+a > b \Rightarrow 2b > b$ $\therefore \dfrac{b}{c} \in \left(\dfrac{2}{3}, 2\right)$

**(D)** We have, $\dfrac{PD}{AD} = \dfrac{ar(\triangle BPC)}{ar(\triangle BAC)}$, ........etc.

$$\therefore \frac{PD}{AD} + \frac{PE}{BE} + \frac{PF}{CF}$$
$$= \frac{ar(\triangle BPC) + ar(\triangle CPA) + ar(\triangle APB)}{ar(\triangle ABC)} = 1$$

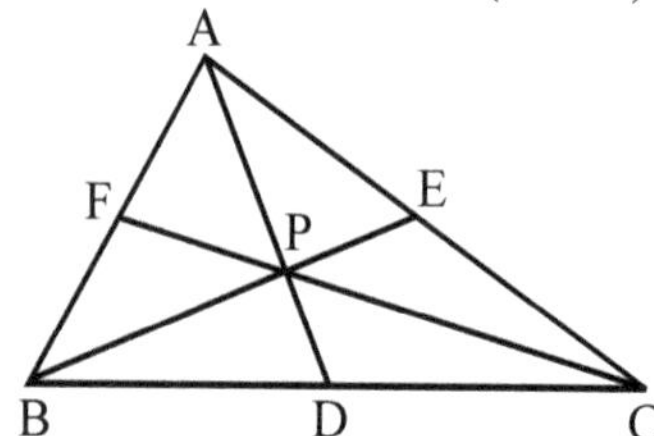

**20.** $(A) \to (r)$; $(B) \to (q)$; $(C) \to (p)$; $(D) \to (s)$

**(A)** $\alpha = \dfrac{1}{2}\sqrt{2b^2 + 2c^2 - a^2}$, $\beta = \dfrac{1}{2}\sqrt{2c^2 + 2a^2 - b^2}$,
$$= \frac{1}{2}\sqrt{2a^2 + 2b^2 - c^2}$$
$$\therefore \alpha^2 + \beta^2 + \gamma^2 = \frac{1}{4}(3a^2 + 3b^2 + 3c^2)$$
$$\Rightarrow \frac{\alpha^2 + \beta^2 + \gamma^2}{a^2 + b^2 + c^2} = \frac{3}{4}$$

**(B)** $ar(\triangle ABC) = ar(\triangle PBC) + ar(\triangle CPA) + ar(\triangle APB)$
$$\frac{\sqrt{3}}{4} \times 4 = \frac{1}{2}[x \times 2 + y \times 2 + z \times 2]$$

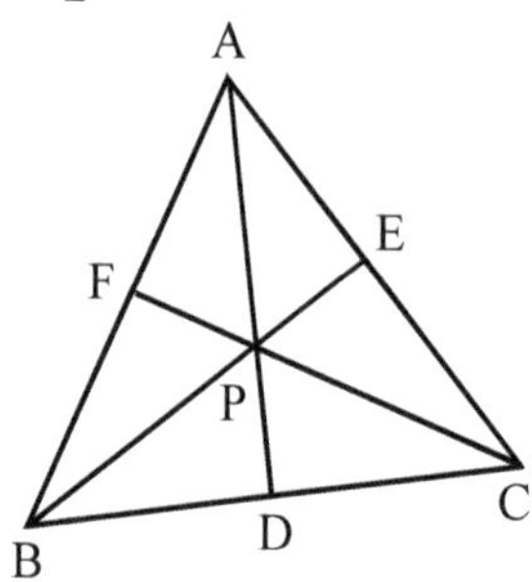

$$\therefore x + y + z = \sqrt{3}$$

**(C)** $2B = A+C \Rightarrow B = \dfrac{\pi}{3}$ and $A+C = \dfrac{2\pi}{3}$
$$b^2 = ac \Rightarrow \sin^2 B = \sin A\sin C \Rightarrow \sin A\sin C = \frac{3}{4}$$
$$\therefore \cos(A-C) - \cos(A+C) = \frac{3}{2} \Rightarrow \cos(A-C) = 1$$
$$\therefore A = C \Rightarrow A = B = C = \frac{\pi}{3}$$
so the triangle is equilateral.

**(D)** $\dfrac{\sqrt{abc(a+b+c)}}{\Delta} = \dfrac{1}{\Delta}\sqrt{4R\Delta \cdot 2s}$
$$= \sqrt{\frac{8Rs}{\Delta}} = \sqrt{\frac{8R}{r}} \geq \sqrt{8 \times 2} = 4$$

CPSIA information can be obtained
at www.ICGtesting.com
Printed in the USA
LVHW061505230623
750475LV00009B/111

# Remembering Childhood

## Workbook Your Way to a Finished Memoir

# LESLIE RUPLEY

DAMELIAM BOOKS

*For Michael and Jon*

# Contents

# Remembering Childhood

# Introduction

I wrote this collection of vignettes to illustrate how my child-hood shaped me hoping that you, too, will think about your childhood and how it molded the person you have become. My goal in sharing these accounts is to encourage a reimagining of your own youth, evoke memories that may be similar to mine, and inspire you to write about the experiences and relationships that have been part of your life.

My stories model how you can write brief scenes that collectively tell your life story. After each vignette I pose questions that are designed to stir your imagination and stimulate your recall of specific events. Additionally, I link you to a series of videos with tips about how to start writing, how to persist, and how to make your stories more engaging. You can scan the codes in the text or type the URL in your browser for access to this information. Think of *Remembering Childhood* as your book as well as mine—a place to collect ideas and impressions that might "jump-start" and help organize your own memoir.

Maybe you have wanted to write about your past but didn't know where to begin. Here is an opportunity. Allow my memories to open the door to your own recollections and retrieve the sights, sounds, smells, tastes, and feelings you have stored there. Write them down on the pages provided or in a separate notebook. Plumb your mental archives for as many details as possible. They are the grist of your story.

For the past eight years I've helped clients write their life stories. All have reported feeling grateful for the opportunity to review their lives in perspective, realizing as they probed their memories how over the course of time they had created a satisfactory life, despite dark episodes or regretted decisions they had long ago buried. Without exception, my clients have conveyed to me a satisfaction about writing and sharing memories of a time and place that no longer exists.

If this book enables you to examine your life with a fresh perspective, put pen to paper and compose your stories, I will have accomplished my goal.

# How to Use This Book

Approach this book by reading it sequentially, or skip to a section that interests you at the moment.

Here are some suggestions for getting started:

1.  Write down the memories that my prompts suggest or choose your own topics.

2.  Draw a picture of a particular scene or create a piece of artwork that ties to your memory.

3.  Make notes about what you want to include in your story.

4.  Reference photos you'd like to dig out.

5.  Reference documents such as birth and marriage certificates.

6.  Write a poem or song lyrics about a particular memory.

7. Write a note to a loved one.

8. Engage your contemporaries in conversation about a particular memory, but remember that your versions will differ. Most important, keep in mind that your own recollection is your reality.

Scan the video codes on your smart phone with a QR app like Bakodo, type in the URL, or see all of the videos on my website at http://leslierupley.com/rememberingchildhood/jump-start-your-memoir.

Find a comfy place to read and write. Let the memories flow!

*You Can Write That Memoir Now*
https://youtu.be/C1dTLn6FAFQ

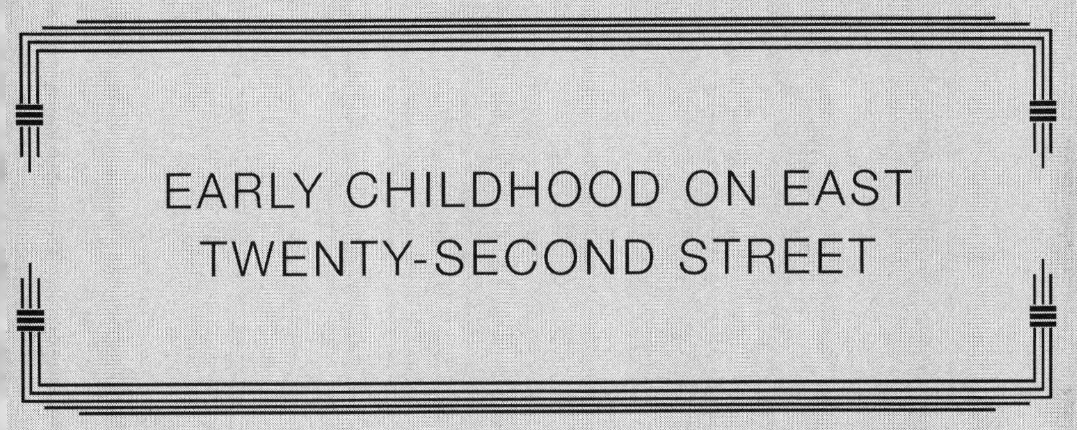
EARLY CHILDHOOD ON EAST
TWENTY-SECOND STREET

# My Imaginary Friend

An only child gets a lot of love, but perhaps a share of loneliness, too. Although I was a beloved first child, adored exclusively until I was four years old, there were times during the day when I needed companionship. Georgie Kaplan came to visit when solitary play lost its allure, when puzzles, dolls, and crayons failed to entertain.

Georgie was *a nice Jewish boy*, as Nana would say, who befriended me when I was three. I would stand in front of a full-length mirror with Georgie at my side, he childlike in stature, heroic in deed. Georgie was my height and had dark hair and brown eyes. He was spotlessly dressed in gray, pleated gabardine slacks with a pressed white shirt and tie. No little-boy clothes for him.

He asked about my day, and I told him my dreams. "I want to go to California," I said, fueled with images of the Golden State where sidewalks are paved à la Oz.

"Who are you talking to?" my mother asked when she overheard me.

"Georgie Kaplan, but he's gone now."

"Oh, the one who's going to take you to California?"

"Uh huh."

She knew all about my friend. Sometimes I hid on the floor behind my dad's seat when he drove.

"Where's Leslie?" Mom asked Dad.

"She went to California with Georgie Kaplan," piped a little voice from the rear.

"Ah, yes. Georgie. What a good friend," my mother replied.

Somewhere within me still resides a Georgie, a strong, clear voice that guides me, ensuring my safety as he did when I was a small child.

*Did you have an imaginary friend? Describe this character, their appearance, and the things you may have done together. If you didn't have an imaginary companion, how did you occupy yourself when you were alone?*

# MY STORY...

# Will It Ever Cool Off?

Even after dark, the damp heat smothered us with its clammy breath. My dad stripped to his jockey shorts and sleeveless undershirt. Mom undid her top buttons, and I still wore my sweaty bathing suit bottoms. It would be another sleepless night.

Dad put on his slacks, and we went down four flights to sit on the back stoop. Our first-floor neighbors brought out chairs and sat on the pavement facing us. It was too hot to talk.

The strong, spicy fragrance of deep-pink roses from our neighbor's yard exuded a nippy sweetness in the heavy air. This lingering childhood memory is haunting and almost out of reach, but like my mother's particular scent, I think it would be evocative should I inhale it today.

Lightning bugs flashed then disappeared, blinking in a different spot. Too hot to chase and catch them.

The air resounded with the music of crickets, the droning

repetition. The feeling of distance, yet closeness. The primordial evocation of jungle swamps, deep wet places.

A feral cat screamed like an infant. A screech owl pierced the heavy air.

Mrs. Rudolph summoned her dog. "Here, Benji. Come in."

Mrs. Gross and my mom held ice cubes wrapped in washcloths to their foreheads. My mother gave me her cloth when the ice melted, and I sucked out the remaining cool water. At times the women fanned themselves with accordion-pleated newspaper, but the puny breeze did little good.

We sat on that wooden stoop under a starless sky praying that clouds would burst. There was no clap of thunder, only the sounds of deep inhalation and long sighs offered up in surrender to the smothering night.

# MY STORY...

*What specifics can you recall about hot summer weather? What did you do to cool off?*

# MY STORY...

# Screaming and Splashing

"Mommy, come quick," I shouted from the porch. "It's open now! Mommy, Donny's opened the hydrant! He did it again."

I was barefoot on the front porch of our third-story flat, bibbed seersucker sunsuit over my naked chest, my blonde curls wet from perspiration that dripped onto my shoulders. The afternoon was more than sultry. It was a steam bath. Nearby, Nana drank water with a pinch of salt.

"Come and put on your bathing suit," Mommy called out to me.

After a quick change into the pink bottoms, I ran down the spiral staircase leading to the front door and then outside to cool jets of water.

My mother followed, holding out a pair of rubber slippers. "Don't go outside without your slippers. The pavement's hot."

*Can't wait.* I ran. Mommy followed.

This great treat, Donny's doing, was an occasion for local children to act with abandon, running through the strong spray as close to the source as we dared, screaming and splashing, laughing and teasing.

By the time I got to the hydrant, all of the kids were running amok, my friends among them. Oh, the screeching, the gentle pushing, and the not-so-gentle shoving from the bigger kids. I hesitated to rush in. *They'll push me.*

Then I squeezed my body tight, bent over, and resolved to not back away. Putting aside fears of pain and big kids, I stood up and ran into the mix.

I squealed and ran close to the spray and out again. I grabbed Marcy's hand and we romped and dared ourselves to run closer to the hydrant. Tiny needles poked at my bare midriff, and I let go of her hand and jumped in a circle to even out the thrusts of spray. Pain and thrill, fear and recklessness were at war within me, but I stayed until I was no longer afraid.

Mothers sat on front stoops wearing similar buttoned housedresses, their hair tied up in a scarf or pinned. Most held towels, but others didn't see the need. They stayed near enough to monitor their children, keeping an eye on them as they gossiped with one other.

Jenny started to cry and run for her mother. "Owie, owie," she yelled.

"What darling? Come to Mommy."

"My toe. I hurt my toe," she cried.

Two minutes later she was back in the frenzy.

I was doing my jumping-up-and-down dance when I felt the kids pushing to get out of the spray. Then I heard it, the disturbing wail of the police car siren, rising and falling, nearer, nearer. The black-and-white Ford with a flashing roof light veered onto East Twenty-Second Street and screeched to a halt across from our hydrant. Officer Scotch in his yellow slicker strode toward us waving his baton.

"Awww. Not yet. Leave it on. Just a little while longer." It was no use. We scrambled.

Mommy called to me and wrapped a towel around my shivering body. In no time I was sweating on the front porch again, my hair dripping wet, awaiting the next respite from the heat.

*How Accurate is Your Memory?*
https://youtu.be/noEJW7Y0hAw

# MY STORY...

*What were popular summer activities in your neighborhood?*
*Tell about a time that you overcame your fear.*

# MY STORY...

# The Runaway

One evening as our newly expanded family was about to sit down to dinner, my father grumbled, "Your dolls are all over the floor in your bedroom, and your mother could trip on her way to Michael's crib. Clean it up before you eat. You're five years old now, big enough to be in charge of that."

"But Daddy, I can do it before bed."

"No, do it now."

"You always worry about that baby of yours," I said.

He didn't relent as I imagined he would, so I pulled the ace from my sleeve.

"I'll run away."

"That's a good idea," he said, winking at my mother over her mild protest.

It was getting dark that October evening, but I was a girl of my word. I went into the walk-in cupboard and packed a few Ritz crackers and some raisins in a paper bag and headed for the door. No one stopped me.

The stairwell was dim, and I inched down the first flight holding the wall and counting the steps until I reached the first landing where my baby brother's navy blue carriage was stowed. Pram-like, it was about my height with a chrome chassis suspended high above thin rubber wheels. The hood cranked down with a handle. On occasion I would bring a doll to the stroller and pretend I was the mother, but I had to climb onto the suspension to peer inside.

I waited there, thinking that if not Dad, my mother would come after me. Not a sound. I took a deep breath, exhaled, and crept down the flight to the second floor where my teenage idol, Angie, lived. Maybe she would hear me and come out to look. I came down hard on the last two steps before her door, but she didn't seem to hear. I listened for a while, but there was nothing. Not even the pungent smell of pasta sauce wafted through the crack under the door.

With two flights to go before the ground floor I hesitated, but I was determined to carry out my plan. I stepped onto each riser with two feet, advancing with baby steps until I reached the bottom. I considered the door to the coal cellar. Too scary.

Instead I went straight out the back door to the stoop. The yard was dark. Even in my playclothes and jacket I was stunned by the cold. I sat on the top step and waited, eyeing the crescent moon.

After a chilly few minutes, I opened my bag and ate the Ritz crackers, knowing that my mother would come to get me before I could eat the raisins. I waited. A cat screeched. I waited. I began to count stars, losing track of my count when I heard Bobby's dog growling in the next yard, claws clutching at the chain-link fence.

I began on the raisins, one by one. I thought I heard my mother call, "Leslie, where are you?" Only the wind, I guessed. I finished the raisins and folded the paper bag. Put it in my pocket.

Where could I go? I stood up and turned to go back inside. I put my hand on the doorknob but reconsidered. *No.* I wouldn't retreat. I faced the yard again and listened for Bobby's dog. My skin prickled at the nighttime sounds. I shivered, raced inside, and scuttled up to the landing where my brother's carriage beckoned.

I grabbed on to the side, stepped on the suspension, and landed within its soft, welcoming shelter. I curled up, closed my eyes, and waited.

My mom and dad's whispering aroused me, but I kept my eyes shut pretending to sleep.

"I'll pick her up. You get her bed ready." Comforting arms lifted me out of the carriage, brought me to bed, and tucked me in. I was safe, and all was forgiven.

*Describe the details of running away or a similar rebellious adventure. What is it about your personality that prompted your behavior?*

*If you had siblings, did you experience rivalry? How did it surface?*

# MY STORY...

# Wet Mittens

I pulled off my mittens, stuffed them in my pockets, and stomped the snow from my rubber galoshes. Before I unzipped my parka in the back hallway, I saw Nana trudging up from the coal cellar with a tiny drop of blood suspended from the tip of her nose. I ran and hugged her around the waist.

"What happened to you? You're bleeding."

"It's nothing. The shovel handle hit...*Ach!* Shoveling the coal is hard. Your mama and papa are busy at their work. I have to make sure the fire don't run out before they come home. We go upstairs now, and I'll make for you hot cocoa."

Nana pulled a wrinkled hankie from her coat pocket, wiped her nose, and squeezed her nostrils hard. She sniffed in, crumpled the bloodstained cloth into a ball, and smiling, pulled out the lace handkerchief I'd given her as a birthday gift.

"See? I wouldn't use your present on a bloody nose."

"I made a snow fort today—"

"Come," she said. "You tell me about it when we go up where it's warm."

I took Nana's hand, and we trudged up to our third-floor flat in silence. *Will Nana's apple strudel be ready?*

I handed her my thick woolen mittens, pulled off my galoshes, and stripped off my leggings, parka, and scarf in the hall outside our flat. Once inside, kitchen warmth chased the cold from my face. Nana put my mittens on the steaming radiator.

She filled the small dented saucepan with milk and turned on the white enamel gas stove. I watched her mix the cocoa powder in my mug and stir in three Charlie McCarthy spoonfuls of sugar (Mom never let me have three spoons). Then she opened the oven door, and the yummy aroma of apples, cinnamon, and raisins flooded the room. Strudel!

I warmed my hands over the radiator's clanking irons. The musty smell of damp woolen mittens reminded me of hugging my dad when he came up from the coal cellar in his sweaty maroon woolen sweater. To this day, the smell of damp wool recalls those winter days when Nana made cocoa, and Dad hugged me tight.

# MY STORY...

*What do you recall of snowy weather activities? What did you feel and do when you came in from the snow and cold?*

# MY STORY...

# Nana's Darling

I was my grandmother's darling throughout my early child-hood years. Nana lived with us and captivated me with her stories and games in the early mornings, allowing my parents the privacy they craved in our crowded flat. Later on when their "privacy" led to the birth of my two younger brothers, she taught me handcrafts and cooking while my mom cared for my brothers.

In winter she dressed me in snowsuits, boots, scarves, and mittens and walked me down three flights to the yard so I could build a snowman. In sweltering summer she took me downstairs in my swimsuit and hosed me off as I squealed with delight on a small grassy patch beyond the cement.

She served home-baked cookies or strudel with milk after school when my mother went back to work. She catered to me, made me sweaters, and taught me how to sew and knit.

Nana also took me on an occasional trip to New York City by bus. This particular day was steamy, well into the nineties, and East Coast muggy. My bare thighs stuck to the woven seat on the bus. I wore my favorite white polished cotton pinafore dress with its delicate black trim around the hem and cuff of the baby-doll sleeves. A self-tie corded bow trimmed the neckline.

My sandy blonde hair hung in baloney curls that Nana fashioned by wrapping strands around a rat-tailed comb as it dried. In the oppressive heat of the bus, perspiration poured down my forehead and drenched the hair that clung to the back of my neck. I squirmed in my seat.

"Too hot?" Nana asked.

I nodded and wiped the sweat from my forehead with my hand.

"No, *Shainela*, my little beauty," said Nana as she fished in her pocketbook. "Use this hankie."

"My neck is all wet, Nana." The hankie was soon saturated.

Nana clicked her tongue and tore the bow from my neckline.

"Nana!"

"*Nisht geferlich*, it's not so terrible," she said, tying my hair up and away from my neck.

"*Nisht geferlich*," I parroted and smiled.

After we arrived at the newly built Port Authority Bus Terminal in Manhattan we took a quick hike north to Times Square where, at Forty-Sixth and Broadway, Horn & Hardart's automat beckoned us. This gleaming restaurant was my first experience with self-service dining. Instead of waiting at a table to be served, we could choose from an assortment of appealing food items that were displayed on shelves inside rotating glass cylinders. Some had sandwiches, others salads, and the best ones held desserts.

Nana inserted a nickel into a slot and a door opened, exuding the aroma of cinnamon and permitting access to a huge slice of apple pie. I indulged with gusto, contrasting it with the tiny servings of sweets that were doled out as rewards for finishing dinner at home.

After my lunch of a cheese sandwich minus the crusts, cold milk, and apple pie, we walked farther uptown to Radio City Music Hall to see the Rockettes perform. We sat toward the front in the world's largest theater, stretching our necks to see. I gazed at the longest legs imaginable, all kicking high in unison, and bodies clad in shimmering, sequined leotards cut as high as 1950s decency allowed. At that moment, I knew I would become a dancer.

Later on my mother fueled this ambition to dance by performing in the chorus line at the annual "Y Parents" fundraisers in Paterson. She stored her costumes, including fishnet stockings, in a cedar chest, and she used their decorative trim to embellish my Halloween outfits.

Unknown to me, Nana had her own agenda for our trip to Radio City Music Hall. With the enticement of the Rockettes, she intended to educate me about the great tenor, Enrico Caruso, whom she adored. For her, the feature attraction was not the dancers who came first. It was a newly released biographical film with Mario Lanza singing Caruso's great arias.

At six, I wasn't prepared to sit still for an eternity listening to his operatic tenor voice. I fidgeted. I shifted to my knees and then into a squat. I poked Nana and pointed to the door, but she had other ideas.

Nana withdrew a volume of *Stuart Little* by E.B. White from her pocketbook. With her finger to her lips, she handed me the book and pointed to the thick red-carpeted step on the aisle where I could sit and read by dimmed light. While Caruso sang *Celeste Aida* in his exquisite tenor voice, I consumed *Stuart Little*.

*Describe a special relationship you had with an adult who pampered you. What characteristics did this person have? Describe him or her.*

# MY STORY...

# Reverie: Aunt Sadie Died

Her head rested on a satin pillow in an open coffin, cheeks rosier than life. Bright lipstick I had never seen. I sniffed hard, but couldn't smell the sweetness of Auntie Sadie. I cried, and Mama pulled me away from the altar. White Shoulders perfume. Whenever I catch a whiff, Aunt Sadie appears, arms wide open, smile broad.

# MY STORY...

*What is your first memory of attending a funeral? What feelings of the person's presence did you experience afterward?*

# MY STORY...

# Reverie: She Adored Me

Mommy cupped my chin in her hand and brought my face close to hers. Eyes crinkled and lips parted in a smile showing only the tips of small teeth. Auburn hair drawn into a bun at the back of her head, she wagged my chin from side to side. "Such a *punem*, only a mother could love." I grinned, mouth wide, showing all of my baby teeth.

# MY STORY...

*What specific moment can you recall when you felt adored by a parent or other family member? Describe the relationship, the emotional characteristics of this person, and his/her physical appearance.*

MY STORY...

# The Daily Drudge

Every chore had its own routine. Dusting came before pulling out the Hoover upright, so particles that settled on the floor could be vacuumed up. Sheets had to have their hospital corners. Even washing the linoleum kitchen floor required its own system. Mom crouched on her hands and knees with a bucket of water, rags, and a scrub brush. She worked from the far corner by the back door toward the opposite hall. First the soapy scrub. Then she spread rags over the wet floor to dry it. Finally, she squeezed the rags into the bucket and sidled back to do the next area. This was a midday chore to prevent my father from stepping on a wet floor when he came home from work.

———————◼︎———————

Twice a week my mother put a scrub board in the kitchen sink to wash clothes. She bent over the sink in her housedress, an apron tied at the waist. A print scarf, knotted above her forehead, held her lavish auburn tresses in place.

On this day my mother hunched over the sink as she squeezed and rubbed the dirty wash against the ridged board with a bar of Fels-Naptha soap. It was quiet in the room except for the rhythmic grating sound on the board and the occasional splat as she slapped the next piece onto it. Steam rose from the hot-water faucet, and when her face got sweaty she would stick out the left side of her lower lip and blow a dangling strand of hair from her cheek.

I watched her wring the clean garment into the sink and toss it into the laundry basket.

"Can I help, Mommy?"

"Could you hand me that shirt off the pile?" she said.

I grinned, stuck out my chest, and reached for one of Dad's pin-striped Sunday shirts. Mom stretched for it, and I saw her knuckles, red and angry. No wedding ring when she did the wash.

I climbed up on a kitchen chair and watched her hands pummel those shirts. When she finished, she lugged the wet load into the tiny bathroom that served all four of us.

"I'll get the mat."

I jumped down from the chair and ran ahead of her. She needed a cushion on the hard, tessellated black-and-white tile floor to rest her knees.

The wringer dominated the claw-foot bathtub, and my mother knelt on the mat and struggled with the revolving handle to squeeze the excess moisture from the clean laundry. I grabbed each shirt or cotton dress as it fell from the wringer and put it in the basket.

She wiped the beads of sweat from her forehead with the back of her wrist.

"They have a Bendix machine that would do all this work. Maybe one day we'll get one," she said.

Each of the identical three flats in our building had a pulley clothesline that extended from the rear bedroom window across the grassy backyard to a telephone pole at the far end of the property. Our third-floor line was above my friend Angie's in the middle flat and the Grosses' on the first floor. After the washing, rinsing and squeezing ordeal, Mom toted the laundry basket to a table near the back-bedroom window.

On occasion, Angie's mom or Mrs. Gross hung clothes at the same time. They might exchange news of the day as they stuck their heads out the window and twisted to see each other amid the flapping clothes. Meanwhile, a fresh breeze infused our clothing with a healthy smell I can still recall, a remembrance from another era.

Mom would let her hair down to enjoy the breeze of the open window. I remember her stretching out the window from her waist, a wooden clothespin held in her mouth while both hands worked to fasten one end of a sheet to the pulley line. She was gorgeous. Her smile made her eyes go crescent moon-shaped, and the memory of it sustains me long after her death.

Her wraparound cotton housedress came a bit below her knees. The muscles of her shapely bare calves tightened as she stood on tiptoe to lean out the window. Sometimes I sat on the nearby bed and talked to her, admired her.

Taking in the laundry was the reverse of hanging it to dry. She put the clothespins in her mouth to free up her hands and handed the dry pieces to me to put in the basket. Then she dropped the pins into a drawstring bag that hung by a nail on the window casement.

I buried my face in the fresh towels and bedding and helped her fold the sheets, each of us holding up an end. She nodded when it was time to walk forward to meet at the corners. Her eyes smiled when we were through, and we stacked everything in the linen closet.

"Good job," she would say.

"Good job," I recall today when my ego needs a little boost.

On clothes-washing day, Mom and I took the dry garments from the clothesline to the kitchen table to dampen them for ironing.

One day Mom got that moon-eyed look on her face, the one that spelled joy. Snatching up the sprinkle bottle she said, "Hot day," and began shaking water at my head and face.

I giggled and grabbed the bottle to sprinkle her back. She laughed.

"OK, fill it up again so we can get started."

With determination and the will to please, I would spread out each garment on the white-speckled Formica kitchen table and dampen it with a shake of the water bottle.

Next, Mom would roll each piece tightly and pile it into a neat pyramid to keep it damp. We didn't have a misting or steam iron in those days. Our iron was black handled and heavy, with a chrome body and a thick brown, ropelike cord.

At six or seven I learned to iron the straight pieces—the handkerchiefs, dishtowels, and napkins. I started from one corner and moved to the next. I learned to hold the hankie or napkin far from the tip of the iron. I scorched one or two napkins in the beginning, but soon became proficient.

By ten I had learned to iron a shirt doing the collar, yoke, cuffs, and sleeves before the front and back, to prevent those larger parts from wrinkling.

Washing, hanging out to dry, sprinkling, ironing…routines of the past. I miss the slow pace when I rush to "put a load in" before starting my busy day.

*A Slice of Life*
https://youtu.be/QGfIClUC4eI

# MY STORY...

*What housekeeping skills, habits, and attitudes did you learn in childhood? Write about your early responsibilities. What is your current attitude toward housekeeping?*

# MY STORY...

# Shoplifting

My mother smoked Camel cigarettes. I imagined she chose the brand because of the alluring package with its gold and brown picture of a desert camel under a cellophane wrap. I can see her sitting in a wicker chair on our third-floor porch, hair in a bun, relaxing with her cigarette. I sensed the sophistication of smoking even then, and one idle day when she gave me twenty-five cents to buy Camels at Charlie's corner store, I was eager to go.

While in the store I noticed a pack of Wrigley's spearmint gum under the rack on the floor. I squatted and reached for it, put the gum in my pocket, and went to the cash register to pay for the Camels. I skipped up the four flights of stairs to our flat, cigarettes in hand. With naiveté, I showed the gum to my mom. "Look what I found!"

"Where did you find it?"

"On the floor under the rack in Charlie's store." *Finders keepers!*

"How do you think it got there?" she asked.

Here was a stumper. It occurred to me for the first time that it must have fallen from the rack and been pushed under by the slip of someone's toe. I reddened and looked up at her from beneath my eyelids.

"You're not going to like this, but—"

"I know, Mom."

I put the gum in my pocket and headed back to Charlie's store.

I was hoping to replace it on the rack without notice, but Charlie greeted me when I came in. *No chance.*

"Uh, Charlie, I found this on the floor," I said, handing over my booty.

Charlie smiled. "Thanks, Leslie. I knew you'd bring it back."

*What childhood transgressions did you commit? What was the outcome, and what lessons did you learn?*

MY STORY...

# A Dream: The Pleasure of Riches

"Step on a crack, break your mother's back. Step on a line, break your father's spine." This was my walking mantra as I took baby steps or long strides as necessary to avoid stepping on any fissures in the cement.

In one recurring dream, a sidewalk with a void on both sides and haze in the distance were the only features. I sighted a gleaming penny on the pavement and picked it up. I continued my chant, but another penny appeared nearby, and I picked that one up, too. Before I could stand up, a third penny surfaced and then a fourth. My fist soon bulged with pennies, and I gathered the corners of my white pinafore with my left hand, leaving the right free to pick up and deposit the coins. Chanting had given way to looking for pennies.

I was still bent over when a nickel materialized, as if a gnome had pushed it up through the pavement. Another penny, another nickel, and then a shiny silver Roosevelt dime. As soon as I dropped a coin into my apron, a new one glistened on the ground.

My apron was becoming too heavy to lift by the corners. I hesitated before picking up another coin and weighed my options, to go home with my riches or risk dropping the lot. I awoke before learning how greedy I might have been.

# MY STORY...

*Do you recall any fantastical childhood dreams? Was money an issue in your childhood? What dreams or actual childhood events involved found money?*

# MY STORY...

# Knit for Your Life

Lace doilies everywhere. Nana crocheted them from fine mercerized white cotton with a tiny Boyd crochet hook. She didn't use a pattern, but churned out a prolific number of antimacassars, lace circles draped over the arms of every upholstered piece of furniture. Before we had television, she crocheted while listening to our cabinet-sized radio. Later she crocheted while watching *As the World Turns*. She didn't even have to look at her work.

Everyone dear to her owned a crocheted afghan, colorful affairs made from leftover yarn with his or her initials chain-stitched into the cotton lining. I wore intricate baby sweaters with tiny pearl buttons, still wrapped for posterity, and sported a new cardigan to celebrate each birthday or special occasion.

Nana learned this art from her mother in the impoverished Jewish ghetto of Lodz, Poland, where she sold initialed doilies in the marketplace to earn money. Her mother, Greta, brought her handcrafting skill to her married life in Lodz from her birthplace in Warsaw where she had been exposed to a more cosmopolitan lifestyle.

Today I knit sweaters and worry about arthritis while recalling Nana. She taught me to knit and much more. My first lessons, even before starting school, were the finger exercises that she intuitively knew would develop my small finger muscles in preparation for handwork.

She had me hold my hands in front of me, palms away and fingers together. The task was to separate each finger from the others simultaneously on both hands. First the index finger came apart and returned. Then I formed a "V" by holding my ring and pinkie fingers apart from my joined index and middle fingers. Apart, together, apart, together. These exercises prepared me to use a crochet hook and a pencil as a preschooler, and I could easily string beads and write my name before I entered kindergarten.

I made chain-stitch cotton ropes until I begged to learn a double crochet. Over the years we moved on to knitting, a more complicated two-handed skill. She knit doll clothes for me, and I knitted would-be scarves in garter stitch on large needles. I learned to purl next, and my facility by age eight was good enough for stockinet and seed-stitch scarves.

Through all of this crocheting and knitting I learned concentration, persistence, attention to detail, and the joy of knitting for others. Nana gave me a skill that I could expand and that has carried me through every stage of my life. I knit for myself, my children, my husband. It's calming, creative, and it's always fun to have a new sweater.

# MY STORY...

*What skills and attitudes did you learn in your childhood that have carried over to the present? How did you learn them? Of what value were they at the time, and are they still of importance today?*

# MY STORY...

# Saturday Calm

Dad was a marksman. He looked forward to a Saturday when he could drive to the shooting range far out in the country and away from his workaday anxieties. He delighted in handling his guns in preparation, and I would watch him clean the rifles at our kitchen table. He covered the Formica top with newspaper and laid out his guns. Then he'd haul his sturdy hinged oak box of cleaning paraphernalia onto the table and sit on a yellow-padded chrome chair.

He'd swab out the barrel of the Winchester .22 caliber rifle using tender care, but he only cradled his custom Mannlicher-Schoenauer .243 hunting rifle. The latter was a rarely used deer rifle whose walnut stock and precision he admired.

"See this here grain, Leslie. Beautiful," he might say. "Ya gotta respect a gun. Remember that."

"Yeah, Dad," I would reply, feeling eight-year-old pride at being his confidante.

"You know when I go into a farmer's field I only hunt the wood-chucks that eat his grain. I don't shoot them for pleasure," he would tell me.

"You don't like to go shooting, Dad?"

It seemed to me he had a good time on the rare occasion he took me with him to a farm and not to the shooting range.

"It's not the killing I like. It's the quiet of the field. Feels good out there in farm country."

I knew what he meant. I'd seen the Saturday calm on his face when he lay on the grass waiting for a chuck to pop its head up. I, too, felt the warmth of the sun as I lay next to him. The breeze that stirred the grasses, the hum of a bee in passing. A pungent inhalation. My dad and me.

━━━━◼━━━━

On this Saturday in May, Mom stayed home to care for my younger brothers when Dad and I went to the shooting range. I think the boys were an excuse. My mother didn't like guns. She was happy to make sandwiches and pack us a good lunch.

Dad had retrieved the car from the rented garage space and parked it in front of the house.

He said, "Come on, Leslie. Help me pack the DeSoto."

I grabbed the wicker basket, the kind with a carrying handle and a wood lid that opens on both sides. I was hoping for a picnic treat inside. Mom got the blankets that Dad used to pad the rifles. I navigated the stairs from the third floor carrying the basket in one hand and the blankets over my other arm. Dad cradled both rifles so he wouldn't have to leave one in the car while he went up for the second.

Trunk packed, we set off for the shooting range. Dad's face relaxed as the DeSoto glided beyond the confines of pavement and houses crammed along dreary alleyways. It seems that this outing liberated him, at least for a little while, from his job in the Kearfott factory. That was the "plant" where he labored until his retirement, wearing the one-piece navy jumpsuit that he would shed as soon as he walked in the door after work.

I sensed the timing might be right to ask, "Dad, will you let me shoot today? Will you teach me? You said I might be able to handle the .22."

"I guess you're big enough to shoot that rifle. Today it is."

We were silent after that, each anticipating our own pleasures.

Once the open-forested road replaced the city grit, we rolled down the windows to inhale the woodsy pine smell. I stuck my arm out the window to feel the rush of wind and looked over to see a broad smile on Dad's face.

"I know a good place to stop for an early lunch before we go to the range," Dad said.

He turned off onto a narrow tree-lined dirt lane where, beyond the road, the occasional dogwood bloomed white. At the end of the lane Dad parked beside a rock-studded brook. We got out of the car and he extended his arms, presenting our private Eden.

"Let's get our picnic stuff," he said.

When relaxed, my dad was charming and gallant. He was tall, reedy, dark-skinned, with a head of thick, combed-back crinkly black hair. He spread a blanket beside the flowing water, brought out the lunch basket, and we sat together near the edge of the pristine brook.

I pulled out the Wonder Bread sandwiches. Mom used cream cheese on everything. We often had cream cheese and sardines, cream cheese and chopped olives, and cream cheese with jelly. To my relief, we didn't have sardines today. There were apples and, lucky us, bottles of Coke with a church-key opener. Best of all, we had a package of day-old Hostess cupcakes, the chocolate kind with the cream filling from the Wonder Bread factory around the corner from our house.

After we ate and cleaned up, Dad said, "Take off your shoes, Les."

He did the same and we moved over to sit on a rock and put our feet in the water. I wiggled my toes in the ripples, sat back, and grinned.

"Hear any birds?" Dad asked. "Shhh. Listen."

I froze so I could concentrate on the sounds of the birds and the brook's passage over the rocks. I watched every insect moving on the surface, long-legged critters and those flitting with translucent wings.

Dad said, "Leslie, you will remember this for your whole life."

*Describe any special memories of time spent outdoors with your father, mother, or other important adult. Describe the surroundings, the emotions you felt, and the impact it had on your life at the time.*

# MY STORY...

# Dinner at Angie's

I was a bee, crammed in a hive with incessant buzzing around me. Nana was the queen, situated in her own quiet bedroom. Mom and Dad slept in the converted living room with baby Jon's cradle pushed up against their bed, leaving little room for their armoire doors to open. I shared a bedroom with three-year-old Michael.

Most of the time we inhabited the hive with a minimum of collisions, but sometimes it was too much for me. That's when I would escape to visit Angie who lived with her parents in the flat below us.

I idolized this kindly and sometimes bored teenager who in my imagination had the figure of Marilyn Monroe. Her dresses were calf length, unlike mine that displayed my often-scraped knees.

After school, spelling sentences written or math facts completed, I would tromp down the two narrow staircases and rap on her door, hoping for an invitation.

One day when Angie answered, the intense aroma of Italian seasoning exploded from the cracked doorway. I peeked inside to see her mama standing over the porcelain Wedgewood stove, apron tied over her prodigious hips. She was stirring a gigantic pot of tomato sauce with meatballs.

"Can you play?" I asked.

"OK. Wanna play Jacks?"

Angie sat me down in a corner of the spacious kitchen to wait while she got the Jacks from her bedroom. I ran my fingers along the seam of the swirly black-and-white linoleum floor trying to be inconspicuous while sniffing the aroma of that scrumptious pot on the stove. *Wish I could stay for dinner.*

I spread the skirt of my new cotton plaid dress over my bent knees. My skinny arms stuck out of the baby-doll sleeves, and I recalled my mother's comment: "Maybe a sweater to cover your elbows."

The dress had cost $2.99, and I knew Mom wouldn't want it soiled. I remember watching her remove the three single dollars from her billfold one by one, leaving me to wonder if she might change her mind.

Angie returned with the Jacks, the "good" kind. They were sturdy and colorful while mine were tinny and gray. She was a master at whisking up a specified number of jacks and never made allowances for my age. I didn't win a game, but I didn't care. I was with Angie in her mama's luscious-smelling kitchen.

"I can play till dinner," she said.

"That's OK," I said.

Angie's mama snapped her head around. "Hey, you stay here for the dinner?"

I grinned and nodded.

"You telephone to you mama."

Now I would be able to play Jacks without thinking about dinner.

Mealtime was quiet compared to our house, and Angie's parents wanted to know everything about her day. She got their attention all the time. No younger brothers. I relaxed and soaked up the peacefulness of this household as if from a ceasefire. Angie told her mom that I came close to winning Jacks today, and I lowered my head to hide my satisfied blush.

Peaceful meal. Praise. Meatballs stuffed into hungry mouths. Chaos at my kitchen table on the floor above. I had escaped for this night.

*Skeletons in the Closet*
https://youtu.be/kSJQYEAlUmk

*Was there a special teenager in your life, and how did you relate to him or her? Describe a situation in which you felt a need to escape and tell what you did about it. Did you have a refuge, either in reality or in your daydreams?*

MY STORY...

# To the Library—Alone

On this Saturday morning, I ate my soft-boiled egg from the orange, fluted glass cup that I had used since my nursery school days. I rushed to the sink to wash out the sticky remains and collected my library books.

"Bye, Mom. I'm going to the library."

"Watch the crossings," she called from the back bedroom.

My mother had taken me to visit the Danforth Public Library at 250 Broadway since I was a toddler, pushing me along in a blue and white metal stroller. By the time I was seven, I walked almost a mile there on my own.

I marched over to Broadway from Fifteenth Avenue and turned left to the library, the head of my own parade. I gloried in my new-found freedom to walk the long distance from home by myself, balancing the "return" books on my forearm against my chest the way I'd seen Angie carry her high school books.

I walked tall, head up, chest out. My blonde curls bounced on my shoulders as I strode down Broadway.

The aroma of baking bread from the Wonder Bread factory distracted me until I glanced across the street at the Catholic Church whose rituals and clerical garments were unfamiliar to my culture. My paced quickened as I recalled two fearsome black-clad nuns who had once glided toward me on the narrow pavement, white-banded wimples tight across their foreheads and broad white-lined veils afloat.

I continued my walk without such an encounter until I reached the library where I stopped to admire the daunting yet wondrous façade with its four imposing Ionic columns and broad stone steps that seemed to stretch across the whole city block.

I ascended the steps to my haven. I set down my books, tugged hard on the heavy door handle, and held the door open with my body as I bent down to retrieve them. Once inside, the dank mustiness and silence of the newspaper reading room stupefied me. I had a gauntlet to cross before I could turn right, then proceed around the corner to the children's room.

Rectangular library tables were arranged horizontal to the street. Old men, some wearing battered fedoras or homburgs, and most others with shabby tweed jackets and flat peaked caps, hunched over spread newspapers. Gray grizzled hair twisted on their necks and fuzzed on their ears. Day-old beards spoke disarray, poverty even.

"*Sha*," a few rattled as they bent over *The Paterson Evening News* or the *Yiddish Forward* newspaper. "Such noise she makes," one whispered aloud to another. "Pull the door shut," another growled. My price of admittance was a tight stomach and the unwelcome sensation that I had invaded their domain.

The bitter heaviness of recently smothered pipe tobacco

cautiously reserved for later, suffused the air. The outer door, ajar for a mere moment, had barely stirred the hazy atmosphere that was the color of decaying newspapers. I tried to tiptoe, but no matter how small and quiet I made myself, the old men grumbled.

"Excuse me," I whispered.

"*Sha*," they replied.

Once I passed through the gauntlet, I made my way to the children's room where the librarian was waiting for me. The room was still, but not foreboding, a peaceful quiet that settled my spirits. I sighed. Miss Arlett and I would be alone in the early hours of the morning with a feast of books.

Miss Arlett, in her twin sweater set and mid-calf skirt, was standing over the oak card catalog when I came in. I saw her brown French twist from behind, expertly pinned up, and wondered how hair could be managed in that fashion. I waited for her to turn around and notice me. When she did, I beamed in reply to her welcoming smile.

"Leslie, did you have a chance to read *The Peanut Man*?" she asked.

"Here it is, and I want to read more about George Washington Carver."

She asked why I liked the book and what I thought about the man who rose up from slavery to become a famous botanist and inventor.

"I liked everything about his life and how he tried to help the poor people by teaching them how to grow peanuts instead of cotton."

I believe this was the beginning of my fascination with the history of slavery. It may have been the onset of my lifelong yearning to hear true stories from the past.

"If you liked *The Peanut Man*, let's go to the biography section and see what else we have."

We each carried a small wooden chair to the Dewey 920s section, and she pulled out a biography of Booker T. Washington that I examined and placed on a table to start my collection for the week.

I liked stories about people who worked their way out of poverty to achieve success. Knowing this, Miss Arlett brought me a volume of Horatio Alger's that I hadn't yet read, *Ben Logan's Triumph*. My great-aunt was a New York City librarian and had introduced me to the series with the gift of *Andy Grant's Pluck*.

After those two picks, I was free to browse the shelves for two more books. I deemed the picture books too babyish to bring home, but I read them with pleasure under Miss Arlett's watchful eye, dreaming that I might become an illustrator or a writer.

I chose *Abraham Lincoln* by Genevieve Foster and *Story of the Negro* by Arna Bontemps for my mother to read to me.

Miss Arlett walked me to the door.

"I'll see you next week," I said.

The trip back through the gauntlet was easier on the way out, but nonetheless elicited a number of grumbles from the old men. With four new books in hand, I scampered down the steps, turned at the bottom to admire the building once more, and then strode back up Broadway.

# MY STORY...

*What experiences marked your increasing independence in child-hood? Describe what they were and how they made you feel. Did you visit your local library often? If so, what made it appealing to you?*

MY STORY...

# Taboos at Camp Te-Ata

## WATCH YOUR REAR

My folks saved all year to send me away to summer camp. Beginning at age seven, I spent two weeks sleeping away at Brownie Camp Te-Ata on Lake Kanawauke in Harriman State Park. The weeks were a mixture of delight and torment.

I sang camp songs that I remember today, songs I've taught my children, but I was also sent outside at night to sit on a log near the reeking cesspool for talking after lights-out. I thrilled at the raising of the flag and was proud when I was chosen to raise it in the morning or fold it at sunset, but I dreaded swimming. I definitely hated "bug juice" punch.

My parents were always the last to arrive on visiting day, and I waited in the parking lot wondering if they were coming at all. It was worse than the mixed feeling of seeing them drive off at the end of the day.

The log cabins at Camp Te-Ata slept eight of us seven-year-old first-timers on cots with tight hospital corners. The top halves of the walls were screened and open to the woodsy perfumes. We could hear the night creatures scratching on the ground near the cabin, and sometimes the piercing screams of raccoons in combat sent me burrowing deeper under my blanket.

Breezes chased the piney air through one screened window and out the other side. Sometimes the scent of mountain laurel danced in on the winds. These fragrances were new to city kids, and I thrived in the nearness of the forest.

That first summer at Te-Ata I learned why bringing food into our sleeping quarters was taboo. If a mom sent a care package with snacks, we were required to turn it over for safekeeping. What kid, given the opportunity to hide food, would turn it over? Not anyone I knew. Marian opened her package of marshmallows, hid the squishy bag under her covers, and kept it close while she slept.

That night we were awakened by a human shriek. Marian jumped from her bed yelling, "My tush, my tush. He bit my tush."

Miss Ann, our counselor, came running in with a flashlight to reveal a stealthy raccoon hopping down from Marian's bed. He slipped into the shadows and scooted out the door. We all rushed to gather round her.

Miss Ann pulled down the bedcovers to reveal a half-eaten bag of marshmallows, its wrapper punctured and torn by long, sharp raccoon nails. She grabbed the bag but didn't berate Marian when she saw the damage to her rear end. Miss Ann wrapped her in a blanket and propelled her off to the infirmary. None of us saw the wound, but speculation kept us awake well into the night.

# A STICKY MESS

Betty got her care package after lunch and brought her prize back to the bunk to open during rest period. It was a shoebox wrapped in stiff brown paper from a grocery bag her mother had taken pains to cut apart and secure with tape and string. We watched as she tore into the wrapping. Inside the shoebox, cushioned by several pairs of white anklets and a tube of toothpaste, were two cans of once frozen lemonade concentrate.

In those days, frozen juice was a rarity. Orange juice concentrate was introduced during World War II, but many of us hadn't seen the cardboard tubes it came in.

Unfamiliar with the product, we didn't understand what "concentrate" meant, and we didn't read the label to learn that the contents required mixing with three cans of water.

Betty turned the can around and around, and seeing no opening or spout from which to drink, she pulled off the tin bottom and squeezed. The thick syrup oozed onto her lap.

"We'd better hurry up and eat it," she said. "It's getting over everything."

"Yeah, it's not juice. It's gooey mush."

Without ceremony, we each scooped out some concentrate with two fingers and unwound the cardboard spiral as we probed deeper into the can. By the time we finished the treat, our hands were sticky, and our clothes were smeared with the evidence of our transgression.

We knew we should have taken it to the office for later, and now we were in a sticky fix. Our solution was to sneak out to the toilets one by one so as not to attract attention, and wash our hands and faces. When one girl came back, she changed her soiled shorts and shirt, and the next girl went to wash.

Still disappointed about the yucky mush Betty's mother had sent, we turned our attention to other rest period activities—making lanyards, writing postcards, and playing with quiet puzzles like Hi-Q. Soon it would be time for afternoon sports, and I began to invent ways to get out of dreaded swim instruction.

*Tell about an experience you may have had at a camp or a retreat and your feelings associated with it. What was your inclination toward participating in organized group activities?*

# MY STORY...

# A Trip to Paradise

In my working-class neighborhood, any family cars were usually models from before World War II. My dad had a 1936 DeSoto Airstream Custom sedan with front and rear doors that opened outward from the center. It was shiny black with a running board, the rear curved almost like today's VW Bug, only larger and far sturdier. The hood ornament was a nude winged goddess with an arched back, a gleaming silver curiosity.

My father pampered this fifteen-year-old DeSoto, hand washed it, and garaged "her" a few blocks from home, since our ancient apartment house was built before autos and driveways were commonplace.

On a Sunday afternoon, especially if it was too hot to stay inside our flat, we would take a ride with the windows open to let the fresh air stream through.

"I'll get the DeSoto," I would hear my father say.

"Can we go to Howard Johnson's?" I'd ask.

In the fifties, a restaurant was a rare treat for us. In the heat of summer, getting an ice cream cone at Howard Johnson's was the closest thing to heaven, but the joy for me was thinking about the twenty-eight flavors during the ride, weighing fudge ripple over burgundy cherry. Brick boxes of Breyer's chocolate, strawberry, and vanilla at the corner store or the A&P were our other options, but my parents didn't buy ice cream except for birthday parties.

With the windows down, we would drive off to an area that is likely a suburban tract today, but in my memory, it was a considerable distance out to the "country." I giggled as the cool breeze blew curls off my sweaty face. From the rear seat I recall my mother's profile looking out the window, relaxed, smiling, as she brushed the hair from her face with the back of her hand.

My father would turn completely around to talk to me in the backseat. "Har," my mother would yell, "Watch the road."

We would park facing a wooden railing and walk across gravel and through the gate to the colonial building with the orange roof. "28 Flavors," the sign said. Twenty-eight flavors were lined up in a long glass case at the entrance. Paradise.

By this time I would have decided between my two favorites. My dad always had chocolate and my mother raspberry. We'd walk outside licking our dripping cones and lean up against the gate to finish. No ice cream allowed in the DeSoto.

All that we said was, "Mmmm." All that we heard were slurps and the smacking of our own lips.

We'd feel content during the ride home with me sitting in the backseat licking my sticky fingers. Soon enough, though, my thoughts would turn to the future. Maybe next time Dad would buy me a double-dip cone. Then I could have fudge ripple *and* burgundy cherry, or I might even try something new.

*Write the details about a favorite weekend destination or "treat spot" your family liked to frequent. What was it you enjoyed most about it?*

# MY STORY...

# To Brownies on the Bus

I wasn't my sit-up-and-fold-your-hands self on this or any other Brownie meeting day. Instead of my usual attentive behavior in school, I had trouble keeping still. My wooden seat was harder on Tuesdays than other days, and confinement behind the attached desk made me squirm.

I worried about the bus. Would it be on time? Would I miss it? I worried about my seven cents fare, and I reached into my sock to feel the nickel and two pennies at every opportunity to move around. When Miss Levi would say, "Take out your math book," I'd probe my sock. If we got up for recess, I'd check my sock yet again.

I wore my cotton Brownie uniform to school, adorned with the badges that Nana taught me to sew on using tiny stitches around the edges. The belted, above-the-knee dress was buttoned from the waist up and had short sleeves. In retrospect it wasn't flattering, but at the time it represented proud membership in a group that defined my identity as distinct from my family. The bus trip downtown to the Van Houten Street YM/YWHA, like my Saturday walks to the library, built confidence.

During the afternoon, the minute hand on the white-faced wall clock moved with interminable clicks, marking time with each loud advance. Miss Levi's voice was a distant drone. My ears were attuned to the street sounds, the truck horns, the whoosh of air when a bus stopped at the corner. Even the pigeons cooing in the play yard received more attention than my teacher did.

The ring of the three o'clock bell, the slamming of desktops, and the final check of assignments would combine to make my scalp tingle in anticipation. I perched on the edge of my seat, legs facing the aisle. I waited to hear, "Good-bye class." Then I scampered up the aisle and out to the hall. Crammed among the throng of second- and third-grade kids, I navigated the stairs down to the first floor and ran out the door.

I was the wind blowing across the cement playground in my navy blue Keds. I'd fly to the bus stop, out of breath and squeezing my schoolbooks near to me. There on the corner of East Twenty-Second and Ellison Streets my breathing would become more regular, but my mind would race.

I'd reach into my sock to check the coins, and rather than wait until the bus appeared, I'd pull out the nickel and two pennies and clench them in my perspiring hand. I'd keep my eye on the yellow gloves of my Mickey Mouse watch as I shifted from right leg to left and back until 3:10 p.m. *Five more minutes.* For the last few minutes I'd periodically venture off the curb to look up the street for the brown and orange #26 bus.

There was rarely another kid at the bus stop. Some girls in the troop came from other schools and several had mothers who drove them. We had one car, the DeSoto, and my father took it to work.

"Mommy," I had asked. "Why can't you get a car and drive like some of the other mothers?"

"I don't know how to drive," she said.

"But, Mommy, you could…"

"We can't afford another car, but I'm proud of you for taking the bus by yourself."

Sometimes I couldn't help pondering my mother's tone of voice as she cut off my questioning, but whooshing brakes would bring the #26 to a halt at the curb to interrupt my musing.

The acrid exhaust invaded my nostrils, overwhelming, yet welcome. I climbed the deep steps to the driver's area, poured my seven cents into the fare box, and wobbled into a seat as the bus took off. With knees together and books held securely on my lap, I'd fix my sight on the passing buildings, each familiar to me.

The grand white funeral home signaled that I was nearing my stop, and I'd get my right leg under me and push up on my knee to reach the overhead pull-cord. It wasn't easy to balance my books during this maneuver, but I had it down pat. *Ringggg.*

When the bus came to a shuddering halt I'd stand, sway, and usually fall against the metal bar that separated the driver's cab from the passenger seats. Ignoring the indignity, I'd straighten up and walk down two steps with as much grace as I could muster. Once on the curb I'd hold my breath against the bus's exhaust as it belched ahead.

The block-long walk to the YM/YWHA was a quick one, and I'd forget my poise as I sped to the three-story brick building, a welcoming haven where I socialized throughout my childhood and teenage years.

# MY STORY...

*How were you able to get to places on your own as a child? Describe a time when you first used public transportation or perhaps a bike to leave your immediate neighborhood on your own. How did this new way of getting around affect your feelings about yourself?*

# MY STORY...

# Catskill Summers

The Catskills' "Borscht Belt" was a summer haven for metropolitan New York's *Ashkenazi* (Eastern European) Jewish community. Most families with a little savings spent a week or more in the mountains, free from the debilitating city mugginess. It was a chance to breathe clean air, for the children to escape the hot pavement, and for families to make and enjoy friendships with other Jews.

Grossinger's and The Nevele were two hotels that catered to families wealthier than mine. The array of food was ostentatious, course after course, abundant, and ethnic. Bagels, lox, kugel, white-fish, brisket...there was no end to the rich food or the number of young college boys who waited and bused the tables.

In the evenings parents enjoyed stand-up comics like Mel Brooks, Jackie Mason, Milton Berle, and Sid Caesar, who made their names by entertaining at the Catskill hotels. Meanwhile, babysitters tended their exhausted children, sound sleepers after a long day of outdoor camp.

Less affluent families stayed in bungalow colonies, rented by the week or month where the whole *mishpocheh* or extended family could stay in cabins and cook their own food. *Bubbies* (grandmas) sat on Adirondack lawn chairs knitting or crocheting. *Zaidehs* (grandpas) sat on the bungalow steps with their whittling. They watched their grandchildren run amok while the middle generation of mothers gossiped nearby.

Some families spent almost the whole summer at a bungalow colony. The dads stayed home and worked during the week, then drove up to join their wives and children on weekends.

Our family chose another option. We stayed at Mootz's, a farm whose owners operated a summer boarding house where guests stayed in small cabins and ate communally in the screened-in porch of the "big house." They didn't have organized programs like the big hotels or day camps like some of the bungalow colonies, but for us, the freedom from summer heat and having to cook and clean was more than enough.

<hr>

J. Fred Mootz and his family operated a boarding house on their farm in Callicoon, New York, where they kept cows and raised rye. In the spring I would overhear my parents talking about summer plans to stay there, because their income tax refunds had arrived by March. They always waited to reserve a cabin at Mootz's until then, since the amount determined the length of time we could stay.

"I think we can squeeze ten days at Mootz's out of this tax

refund," my mother, the budget keeper, might say. From the moment she hung up the phone with Mrs. Mootz, having secured a cabin for a week or ten days, the six of us, Nana included, began to look forward in earnest to our stay at Mootz's.

I began to anticipate the long hot ride from Paterson to the Catskill Mountains in upstate New York. Piled into the DeSoto with overflow packages from the trunk squeezed between us, we would head for Route 17, the only road that led to our destination. What today might take an hour or two was then a grueling, bumper-to-bumper daylong trip along a four-lane highway.

With the three of us kids crammed into the backseat and the three adults in the front, there was no room for comfort. Our sweaty bodies brushed against each other, and our impatience with the heat and long ride caused us to lose sight of the joyous time we would have once we arrived.

In those days we had no videos or computer games to keep us numbed against boredom. My mother encouraged word games like *I Spy* or *Geography*, and she led us in song, but we also did the "When will we get there?" whine. There was nudging, finger-poking, and teasing in the backseat that at its peak would necessitate a stop for a snack from the picnic hamper and maybe a pee in the bushes.

When we arrived at the farm I'd take in the familiar weathered buildings. We would make our way to one of the bare-bones cabins after checking in with Alice Mootz, and as we unpacked I'd anticipate the lazy and familiar rhythm of the coming days. Ladies sitting on the lawn in the Adirondack chairs, perhaps playing cards, maybe knitting. Dipping in the pool, walking to town, and washing my hair in the tiny waterfalls near the pool. Woodchuck hunting with my dad, if I wasn't roaming around by myself exploring the unknown.

I recall in particular the gray wooden barn whose door I feared might come off with a slight tug. I would drop by the barn to find one of the older Mootz children hand-milking their dozen or so cows.

A wet-dog smell emanated through the open door, a sense of closeness inside. I bristled, feeling when I entered as if I, too, were confined to a stall. The animals' bulk, their lowing, and their constant shifting of legs consumed all of the space. I recoiled at each flick of a cow's tail, worried that it might swish me onto the fetid straw-covered floor.

The boy would tolerate my visit, and once he let me try milking. I looked at the udder with apprehension, but grabbed it nonetheless. My inexperienced hands did little other than cause the cow to stomp and complain, so the Mootz boy pushed me out of the way in a hurry.

Another time I recall waking from a nap in my cot against the wall under the window. I opened my eyes, having felt a nudge on my abdomen, and let out a scream that brought my family and the surrounding vacationers to investigate.

A massive black-and-white Holstein had poked her entire cow head into my open window, but was making her way out as the crowd assembled. No one understood my fuss over a cow, but they hadn't had a Bossy nosing around in their beds.

Mom and I often walked "to town" along a dusty country road. Right after breakfast we would stroll hand in hand before the heat of the day set in. Perhaps we would buy film for the Brownie camera whose then ubiquitous black-and-white-photos of us "having fun" lay in boxes in the attic for decades.

We would anticipate each landmark on our way to town. Not far from Mootz's we'd begin holding our noses, and I'd cry, "Yucky, yucky," as we passed the chicken farm set back from the road. The stink kept me from wanting to investigate, though I otherwise might have been curious. I'd squeeze my mother's hand and pull her along to get ahead of the stench.

The village had one row of shops along a wooden boardwalk. It too appeared to have survived a much earlier time, and I'd step onto the walkway by grabbing the hitching post for support. The general store was the only place of interest to me, because I'd get an ice cream cone for the walk back, even though it would "spoil" my lunch.

Mom would stay in the store, lingering over the postcards, buying a stamp, or fingering the *tchotchkes* as she was inclined to do. I'd station myself on the boardwalk, eyeing the passers-by, licking drips from my cone, and wondering what she found interesting about shelves full of junky souvenirs.

Walking home, I would start thinking about lunch, a nap, and a dip in the pool, to which I'd only succumb if held in my mother's arms. Lots of photographs in the attic of me in the pool, squinting into the sun and hanging on for dear life.

The days passed in quiet waves, and the family relaxed into summer mode, Dad's good humor returning for a week or more, and the escape from family tension restoring Mom's face to calm. Even Nana, who spent all of her time among the other old ladies in the Adirondack chairs, wore a summery lilac dress with her arms and neck exposed to the sun, allowing herself the rare pleasure of repose.

The packing for home was in slow motion. We children dawdled over collecting our things and reluctantly deflated our plastic tubes.

Michael emptied his squirt gun, and Jon stuffed a toy car in his pocket for the trip. Mom put away her sun hat. Nana packed her lilac dress, and Dad no doubt became increasingly tense in anticipation of the long ride home.

# MY STORY...

*How did your family spend summer vacations? Did you travel somewhere special every year? What memories do you have of your family's recreation and relaxation time?*

MY STORY...

# My Bicycle Crusade

"When can I have a bicycle?" At almost ten years old, I still didn't own a two-wheeler, but not for lack of begging. I needed that bike. Everyone else in the neighborhood had one, and I was left out of Saturday rides. Why couldn't my parents understand?

I rarely let suppertime pass without a reminder, even though my pleas for a bike were seldom heard above the cacophony. My father, a picky eater, exhausted the family's emotions with his complaints like, "This beef tastes gamey. I want a sandwich."

Nana was forever tsk-tsking, my brothers elbowed each other, and my frantic mom tended to everyone's needs but her own.

I figured that I needed another way to reach my father, who was beginning to show cracks in his emotional foundation. Mom wrote the checks, but he set the priorities, and I couldn't rely on his good humor.

My parents were very close-mouthed about money. It seemed

that we had enough for good food and clothes to start the school year, but a bicycle was an extra, out of the question with the expense of raising three children.

I wondered how I could get their attention and sympathy. We had a wall-sized chalkboard in the kitchen, hung when I was in nursery school so I could learn to write. Now my mother used it for grocery lists. One day I covered the entire six-foot surface with a drawing of a three-speed English racer. I labeled it: "Raleigh 3 speed girl's English racer."

That evening after Nana took the boys away from the dinner table, my parents called me into their bedroom. *Oh, no. Dad's mad at something. The drawing?*

They sat on the side of their bed and beckoned me to sit between them. This was a good sign, so I squished in like a favored baby doll.

"Leslie, you have US bonds that you got when you were born. They might be worth enough to buy you a bicycle," my father said.

"Bonds? Is that money?" I asked.

My father smiled. "It's paper that can be changed into money, but they were gifts to save for your future," he said.

Now I was puzzled but didn't have the savvy to ask about "mixed messages."

"Can I get my bike?"

My father looked at my mother with eyebrows raised. She held out her arms, palms up, and shrugged.

"I guess the future might be now," he said. "On Saturday we'll look at bicycles."

"But Daddy, it has to be an English racer and it has to have three speeds and it has to be black and—"

"Whoa, we'll see what your money can buy on Saturday."

———————◼———————

I awoke early on Saturday morning, and I was not quiet in the kitchen when I poured myself a bowl of Rice Krispies. I plopped down on the yellow vinyl cushion and nursed my bowl of cereal. I kicked my legs up to hit the underside of the Formica table. I squeaked the chair seat.

"Hey, we're still sleeping in here," my father shouted from their front bedroom.

Once my cereal was gone, I clomped back into the bedroom that I shared with my brother. Now with him astir and Jon awakening in my parents' bedroom, they would have to get up.

The hubbub in the kitchen, the family breakfast, the washing up, the dressing seemed to take forever. Clad in pedal pushers and a sleeveless cotton blouse, I sat down for a second breakfast with the family.

"Can't we hurry up a little?"

"The store isn't even open yet," my father said. "Hold your horses."

———————◼———————

The array of children's bikes in the store might have confused some kids, but I made a beeline for the black Raleigh English racer. "Here's my bike, Daddy."

"Mmm. Forty-six ninety-five. I'm not sure we have that much money."

Before disappointment set in, an astute salesman intervened and showed us the twenty-three-inch model, my size and less pricey. Did I want to try it out?

*Did I want to try it out?* I didn't even know how to ride it.

My father and the salesman pulled the bicycle into the passage-way. I stood astride it, then edged onto the seat. The two steadied the bike while I sat on the elongated saddle and tested the distance to the pedals. *Just right.*

I fingered the three-speed lever and squeezed the hand brakes, sitting up straight and proud in the seat. I grasped the handlebars and said, "OK."

"OK what?" my father asked.

"OK, Daddy. This is the bike I want. I need a basket on the back."

"What you need is a bell on the handlebars to warn the world you're coming," he said.

*Tell about something that you yearned for as a child. How persistent were you about getting what you wanted, and did you cherish it once it was yours?*

# MY STORY...

# A Cowgirl

I've always been enthralled with the crispness of a New Jersey autumn. The other seasons couldn't compete with the mingled essence of fall, the clean fragrance of dry October air inhaled to capacity. Not summer mugginess, winter's sting, or even the perfume of spring blossoms. The premonition of a long sleep, maple leaves clinging to life, and the magnificent panoply of fleeting colors evoked the stirrings of my artistic nature as yet unnamed.

During autumn I wore my hand-knit sweaters before the drudgery of donning winter snowsuits and boots suffocated my spirit. I reveled in tromping through the gutters, kicking piled leaves so high they floated, or crushing them underfoot to hear the crackle. I even liked the smell of burning leaves.

In those childhood days, an excursion to the country for pony rides was the most gratifying autumn trip. We'd drive to a farm far away from the city where they sold succulent sweet corn in summer and jugs of apple cider in the fall. We'd gawk at the throng of gobbling turkeys, ignorant of the farmer's imminent Thanksgiving plans.

The toms would strut with red wattles bobbing from their necks as their brown tail feathers opened straight up like a Japanese fan, edges scraping the ground on either side. They could be aggressive, too, nudging other birds while picking through the ground straw for feed.

But turkey watching wasn't my main goal at the farm. Ponies. They were the lure. I would choose my mount, hopefully one with Appaloosa coloration, and my dad would hoist me onto its saddle. A teenager decked out with a red cowboy hat and bandana would lead me around the ring with a guide rope. Maybe two or three rotations, and then my plea for Dad to pay a nickel for another ride.

Dad's nickels and the effortless use of my imagination were the only requirements. I treasured the smell of the hay and manure, and I was a cowgirl. I sat straight and tall, visualizing the imagined dangers of the wide-open range. For a few moments I was courageous and powerful, like Annie Oakley, six-gun at the ready.

# MY STORY...

*What sparked your imagination as a child? How did it come to
life for you?*

# MY STORY...

PUBLIC SCHOOL NUMBER 13

# A Painful Crash

I thought the cement playground at Public School Number 13 was enormous. It felt as if a hundred different groups of kids of all ages had room to play within the chain-link enclosure. Today the yard still fronts Fifteenth Avenue, but a brick addition to the school has diminished the former play space.

We lived across the street from the corner of the yard that's farthest from the main entrance. Some big kids had pulled up the bottom of the fence near that corner to create a shortcut. I could slip under it and jump down the two feet into the playground near the swings without walking around the block to the "real" entrance. After school hours or on weekends when the gate was padlocked, I could still get under the fence to play.

I recall a Saturday when the yard was deserted except for the pigeons. They cooed and bobbled around, picking at peanut shells or bits of discarded bread crusts. A breeze wafted empty potato chip bags, and a Coke bottle rolled to a stop against the wall.

I hopped onto a wooden swing, swayed gently, and imagined licking a fudge-ripple ice cream cone. I never pumped high because it made me dizzy, but I envied the kids who could. At recess I had watched them scream with delight, and some boys even jumped off while the swing was in motion. I once saw a girl pump so high that her swing flipped over the top bar.

This day a strange kid appeared on the lonely yard, and we teetered up and down on the adjustable green-painted seesaw enjoying the equal balance of our weights. Then without warning, the girl got off while I was up in the air, and I crashed to the cement in pain and outrage. My teeth shook in my head it seemed, but I didn't have the courage to pursue her and take revenge.

*Axe Those Tired Verbs*
https://youtu.be/OBxUvHoy6Xw

# MY STORY...

*What childhood injustice do you recall? Were there "bullies" in your life?*

# MY STORY...

# Dick and Jane Aren't Fun

Reading instruction began in the first grade after a semester of kindergarten song, dance, and play. Now we sat crammed in rows with last name "A" in the first seat near the door and "Z" at the far back of the last row. This was to become the enduring pattern for eight years, and "Pay attention!" was the enduring command.

The essential tool for learning to read was a center-stitched, black-and-white mottled composition book with black tape on the spine. Teacher would write new words each day for us to commit to memory that night. While waiting to be called to her desk to recite them, we would rehearse our word lists *sotto voce* to prevent the admonition, "Read to yourselves."

Beginning with "A" last names, Miss McDonough would call each student to her desk. I was "T" and had to sweat out the success or failure of most of the class before my turn.

"Read the words you learned last night, Leslie," she would say as I stood quivering beside her desk.

We read by rote, phonics out of vogue, I guess. At first I confused the *th* words like *this*, *these*, and *that* because it took me a while to learn their configuration. As a visual learner, I didn't intuitively make the aural connection between sound and symbol.

However, with help from my mom, I'd memorize everything, and I soared through *Fun with Dick and Jane*, eventually reading fluently as if by magic. Despite my proficiency, I became sick to my stomach when less fortunate classmates came to Teacher's desk to recite the words they had memorized the prior evening.

Their agony almost brought me to tears. Some kids didn't have patient moms. Others didn't have recall ability. Perspiration would collect on their foreheads. Their legs would shake, and the slight odor of a panicky urine leak might permeate the air.

Miss McDonough would say "Mmmm" to the successful, and then write new words from the next chapter of *Fun with Dick and Jane* on the next page in our composition books.

"Didn't you study these words last night?" she might say to the failures. "Learn them tonight." Some repeated the same list day after dreaded day.

Following each of our turns at mortification and back in our rows, we read aloud from our readers "round robin" style, which was humiliation for some and embarrassment for sympathetic others. A kindly soul might whisper the forgotten word, only to be rebuked by the teacher.

"It's not *your* turn," Teacher would say to a helpful friend.

The classroom became overheated from our anxiety, close, as if the feverish tension had released itself onto the sickly green walls.

"Pay attention!"

*What was the transition to first grade like for you? Tell how you learned to read and about your early attitude toward reading.*

MY STORY...

# Navigating Recess

*Ringggg*! A flurry. We'd sit up straight, fold our quiet hands, and appear more attentive than for our lessons. Recess.

"I see that you are ready for recess," Teacher would say. "Jeffrey, you may get the balls and go outside. Rows one and four are excused."

Every kid would strain to sit straighter than the others. Backs riveted.

"Row three may go."

So it went until the girls got the jump ropes and every row was excused.

Once on the yard, some girls would form little cliques, friendship knots, two or three together to talk about the boys or the other girls. Usually my friend Selina and I wandered the yard from group to group, observing and at times joining in, but on this day Selina nudged me when we came near the double-Dutch game.

"C'mon. Grab the end." Selina admired my mastery of the rhythm and the consistency required to keep the two ropes going for the talented double-Dutch skippers.

She followed the last jumper and ran into the game, her nimble feet hopping from one foot to the next, a skillful ropedancer. I relieved the turner on one end and spun the synchronous ropes. They grazed the cement in time with Selina's rhythmic jumping and with the onlookers' pulsing count.

A boisterous boy holding another boy's hat above his head bumped into me as he ran from his pursuers. Our rhythm interrupted, we had to restart turning the ropes, and then Selina ran back in and began her count. "…five, six, seven…one hundred, a hundred one…"

We muttered, "Boys. Wish they'd stay away." But the muttering was bravado. We took a secret pleasure in their attention and in the break from tedious counting.

Selina and I eventually left the game and wandered around the yard observing other kids. Along the shady side of the school building, groups of boys tossed baseball cards at the wall. The closest toss to the wall won the others' cards. "Dumb," I thought.

Other boys stood in klatches comparing or trading their cards. Some pulled fistfuls of marbles from their pockets. "Oooh. I'll trade ya two cat's eyes for that aggie."

Pairs of girls recited hand jives using complicated patterns of clapping their palms together, all the while singing rhyming songs.

"My boyfriend's name is Matty. He comes from Cincinnati, with five fat toes and a cherry on is nose. This is how my story goes…" or

"One day when I was walking, I heard my boyfriend talking, to a pretty little girl with a strawberry curl, and this is what he said to her. I L-O-V-E love you, to K-I-S-S- kiss you…"

*Ringggg!*

"It!"

"Not It."

Tag came to an end. Jump ropes were coiled. Cards put in pockets. Marbles stashed. Reluctant boys and girls lined up according to height and traipsed back into classrooms.

*What was recess like for you? Were you shy or did you join right in with others? What playground games do you remember?*

MY STORY...

# The Foreboding Basement

P ublic School Number 13 had classes from kindergarten through eighth grade, each of its three floors housing successively older children. There was a separate class on the first floor for what we now call Special Education. Some staircases were "up," and others were "down." I learned the right one early on to avoid an onslaught of "big" kids scrambling pell-mell down the stairs toward me. It happened only once, and I scooted to the wall, shaking with terror to avoid the stampede.

The basement could also be an alarming place if I chanced to be on the "boys'" side while doing an errand for the teacher. I could hear each footfall in this cement-shrouded passageway, the domain of the janitor and the boys' shop classes. Rumor had it that misbehaving boys were sent to the janitor for a whipping, legal at the time, as were gender-specific classes for shop and home economics.

I remember once walking by the janitor's door on a teacher's errand when I heard a tortured scream from a disobedient boy. *It's true. He does whip the boys.* I shuddered and recoiled at the sound.

The basement was also used as a bomb shelter. In those early years after World War II, disaster drills were as routine as fire drills.

"Class, line up," the teacher would say when the alarm blared.

In no time we shoved books into our desks and lined up by gender and height. I was the second shortest girl next to Barbie. We'd march single-file to the basement where we stood, backs against the wall in designated places, mouths shut. I worried that the Russians were coming to bomb us. It was my prevailing nightmare in those post-war days.

# MY STORY...

*Was there something frightening about your elementary school building or environment? Can you describe the details of the building and your emotions at the time?*

# MY STORY...

# A Dream: Horror Unleashed

In 1951 during the Cold War with Russia, the Federal Civil Defense Administration produced a horrific piece of propaganda to show school children. *Duck and Cover* was a nine-minute film that featured Bert the Turtle, who demonstrated how he withdrew into his shell for protection. Likewise, children were shown how to duck under their desks and cover their heads for self-protection against the atomic bomb. The archive is still available at https://archive.org/details/gov.ntis.ava11109vnb1, and the quote below is taken from it:

"We must be ready for a new danger," says the narrator. "The atomic bomb...If you are not ready...it could hurt you....Getting ready means we will all have to take care of ourselves. The bomb might explode when there are no grown-ups near...so duck and cover....It might be a beautiful spring day...but always try to remember what to do if the atom bomb explodes right then. It's a bomb. Duck and cover."

Accordingly, we held regular drills as we did for fire. In the case of a routine fire drill, we'd line up by classroom on the playground. A bomb alert would send us hustling to the basement where we lined up against the wall, standing straight and tall. Teachers patrolled. We stood like soldiers, faces forward, arms at sides, quiet. Each one of us harbored our own fears, but mine haunted me at night.

My atomic bomb dreams were a conflagration of blood, fire, and loss. Loss of family. Loss of home. Loss of friends. Terrifying images of burning alive. Some nights my hair caught fire. Other times a draft of air would force the burning hem of my dress up toward my face. The piercing rise and fall of sirens and shrill whistle blasts provided sound effects to these dreams.

I would wake up screaming in the night, perspiring, shaking. My mother would rush to comfort me, to envelop and console me.

"There, there. It's OK. You're home. Safe. Shhhhh."

I recall the assurance of her touch, the warmth of her hip next to my snuggled body, and the rhythm of her soft breath in the dark as she tucked me in.

# MY STORY...

*How did you respond to the anxiety of the post-WWII Cold War era? Describe the impact the Cold War atmosphere had on your life. If you had a different wartime experience, begin by describing your cognizance of the war and your emotional reactions.*

# MY STORY...

# I Disappointed Nana

Nana had three special pieces of jewelry. Two of them are in my jewelry box today. One is a gnarled necklace made of half-inch knobby coral rods that poke out from the wire strand every which way. A gold-plated screw clasp still holds the necklace together.

The other piece, the one I treasure, was brought from the old country. It's a 14K gold sun pendant with a diamond at the center and radiating curved rays, each embedded with graduated seed pearls, the tiniest lying at the outer points. At my request, Nana would open a small and ancient cardboard box stuffed with cotton and extract the "sun." She'd hold it in her open palm so I could admire it.

"It was my mama's in the old country," she'd say. "Sit, and I'll let you hold it."

With deliberate care she would place the treasure in my hand,

and we'd both look at it for a while. Then, holding it by the edges as she might a vinyl record, she put it back in its original gold-leaf box.

The third piece has disappeared. It was a child-sized gold ring that had a rectangular onyx stone with a small diamond in the center. Nana let me wear the ring in the house, and it fit my middle finger when I was about seven years old.

"Nana, can I wear the ring to the playground for a while? No one is there on Sunday, and I'll stay near the swings," I said.

I had asked this of her many times, but this time she relented. With the ring on the middle finger of my right hand, I went downstairs and crossed Fifteenth Avenue at the corner of East Twenty-Second Street to the playground. I walked with my fingers outstretched, my eyes fixed on the diamond.

After crossing the street, I squeezed under the pulled-up chain-link fence and hopped down to the cement playground. The swing set and a seesaw were deserted, and, as I predicted, no one was in sight.

I pulled myself onto a swing and began to pump, still viewing the diamond ring while clutching the swing's chain with one hand. As I pumped higher I lost interest in the ring and focused on the breeze generated by the swing as it flew higher and higher.

At some point I knew I would become sick from the motion, and I allowed the swing to settle into a comfortable arc without any more pumping. In daydream mode, I was mesmerized by the gentle motion until the swing came to a near stop. *Time to go home.*

Still absorbed by the sensation of movement, I walked home and went upstairs where Nana was waiting for me.

"I'll take the ring back now," she said.

I looked down at the ring on my finger and opened my eyes wide. I couldn't speak.

Nana grabbed my hand and saw that the diamond was missing from the onyx stone.

"The diamond—" she began.

"It's gone," I said. "I don't—"

"You didn't see when it came out? *Oy!* This is what I get for allowing such nonsense. Giving a child a diamond ring."

She grabbed me by the shoulders. "You go back and find that diamond," she said.

I wiped the dribble from my nose with the back of my hand and adopted a brave posture.

"I'll find it, Nana."

I retraced my steps to the schoolyard, eyes on the ground the entire distance to the swing. I got down on my hands and knees and swept my hand over the cement beneath the swings. When the sun shone on the pavement, there was a slight sparkle. Each time I saw a glint I felt momentary hope until I ran my hand over the spot and came up with nothing.

I sat on the ground, tears welling and then dripping down my cheeks. I couldn't find the diamond. The ring isn't in my jewelry box today. In its place is the memory of disappointing Nana.

# MY STORY...

*Describe an instance when you lost something of value, or perhaps lost the trust of someone dear to you. Were you able to regain the object or the trust, and what were the aftereffects of the loss?*

MY STORY...

# Rote Learning, Routine Days

I didn't relish the thought of going to school, nor did I dread it in the extreme. It was tedious for the most part, and routine. Learning was rote except in the rare classroom led by a particularly creative or oddball teacher.

Several of my teachers had also taught my unruly father, and on the first day of third grade my physical education teacher, Miss K, reported aloud what she had heard from his teachers. "I'm glad to learn that you're not like your father. A troublemaker."

Here's the story from circa 1927 that he told me when I related what Miss K had said:

> "I hated PE, especially jumping jacks. The guys were
> all lined up in the gym doing those fool jumping
> jacks, and I guess I didn't have my heart in it. Miss K,
> the redheaded ole battleax, came and stood right in

front of me, almost in my face. She grabbed my hair and tried to pull me up, so I hauled off and punched her in the gut. Got sent to the principal. They called Ma, and she came and gave Miss K what-for. I guess the ole battleax held a grudge after that."

After Miss K's public rebuke of my father, I lowered my eyes on future occasions when the class list was read on the first day of school. I felt both the shame of having a troublemaker for a father and pride in my reputation for being unlike him—a well-behaved, good student.

The following year, my fourth-grade teacher nodded and smiled when she called certain names on the first day. Miss L scowled at others. She wasn't the neutral type, so I was glad she didn't know my father. Even when a new student came to school, she gave a warning.

"You're new. We behave in this school."

We sat in straight alphabetical rows and were instructed how to conduct ourselves, as if we hadn't heard this every year since we were five years old, and in my case, four and a half. Admonishments rolled over us like the tides onto the Atlantic City shore. We nodded and said, "Yes, *Miss Just-Like-All-The-Others.*"

On the first day of school, Miss L announced that each of us would have opportunities to choose and read a daily selection from the Bible during the morning's opening exercise. I always chose the twenty-third psalm. This teacher picked her favorites to lead the Pledge of Allegiance. Then she would blow her pitch pipe, and we'd sing a patriotic song like *America the Beautiful.*

Days followed routine days. I could sleepwalk through them except for lunch and recess. My excellent memory served me well all through elementary school. When I got to high school I realized that I had mistaken a superb memory for intellectual development, and I had considerable growth to accomplish over the next few years.

# MY STORY...

*What kind of student were you? How do you believe that your school's academic environment supported or inhibited your growth? Did a particular teacher leave a mark on you? How?*

MY STORY...

# Unlikely Friends

I n the second and third grades I played with several friends during recess. Selina, a favorite classmate, knew all of the hand jives and could jump double-Dutch far better than anyone else. I invited her to my house after school.

We set up a school in the kitchen using the wall-sized chalkboard and dolls from my bedroom. My dad came home from work and looked in on us without commenting.

After my friend left he said, "Why did you bring that little *pickaninny*, that Negro girl home? Aren't there enough Jewish girls for you to play with?"

I stood up from the floor where I was arranging my dolls, hands on hips and eyes wide. "She's no pickaninny. I like her, Daddy. She plays jump rope good," I said.

"Don't bring her home again. Stick with your own kind."

I knew what he meant, but I wondered why only Jews were my

kind. I hadn't yet realized how age-old anti-Semitism had created clannishness among Jewish communities, nor did I know that not every Jewish parent reacted to persecution with counter prejudice.

In my experience, Selina was a better friend than most girls, Jews included. She was loyal, smart, and fun to play with.

A few years later I developed a friendship with Marylou, the girl with one dress, holes in her outgrown shoes, and no friends to play with after school. Here was a kind soul, grateful perhaps for my friendship, but independent. I knew better than to invite her to my house, so I accepted an invitation to hers. Neither my mom nor my nana asked questions about my whereabouts. They trusted my common sense. It was my father who might have objected.

After school, Marylou led me a block away from my house to Park Avenue where the railroad tracks crossed the intersection at East Twenty-Second Street. We entered a shack that was perched not ten feet from the rails. The wooden structure had unpainted walls, no foundation, and one bare lightbulb hanging inside. Tattered café curtains hung in the window that faced the tracks, and as we entered I inhaled the dankness of poverty.

Marylou's home had one all-purpose room with screened-off areas beyond my line of sight. We were sitting with her mother at the only table in the room to get acquainted and have a glass of milk, when a deep roaring noise from outside startled me. It grew louder and closer until I felt engulfed by it. The thunder made my insides pulsate, and I wanted to run. The shack rocked side to side, the curtains swayed, and the milk glasses slid on the table.

Marylou grabbed our glasses, and as impassive as I was rattled, she drank her milk.

Once the din receded I whispered, "What—"

"Don't worry," said Marylou. "It's only the train on its way through. Sometimes it's longer than that one."

Her mother began to croon a song from their Tennessee home, and my friend joined in harmony.

> There's a church in the valley by the wildwood
> No lovelier place in the dale
> No spot is so dear to my childhood
> As the little brown church in the vale

I chimed in on the chorus. "Oh, come, come, come, come. Come to the church by the wildwood …"

The train had unsettled me, but their song passed over me like a warm breeze. I left for home with regret, not for having visited, but for knowing I wouldn't be able to share with my parents this family's warmth and ability to soothe their own souls.

# MY STORY...

*Describe a childhood experience with someone of another culture or social class. What attracted you to that person and what did you find in common that prolonged your companionship?*

# MY STORY...

# Suffering Cursive

Our oak desk and chair units had hinged tops that slanted downward for correct penmanship position. Ink bottles fit into recessed wells on a level portion of the desks above the hinge.

On Mondays the teacher toted a gallon-size ink container up and down each row to siphon ink into our glass bottles. Her clunky shoes resounded on the oak floor while desks squeaked from our fidgeting and covert monkeyshines.

We endured The Palmer Method of penmanship daily. Half-sized drab blue booklets filled with "push-pull" and "circle" exercises were designed to make the fluent strokes of one's pen become a natural habit.

"Push, pull. No. No. Not that way," Miss B would say. She strode to the blackboard to demonstrate the correct form. I remember the fat of her upper arm jiggling below her short sleeves while her raised arm glided up and down to create admirable push-pull strokes.

Our wooden pens held a delicate steel nib with a small oval hole at its center. The nib fit into a groove in the wood handle for easy exchange. We learned the art of dipping the pen into the inkwell and tapping it on the side to release excess ink. In a way, it was an elegant procedure that inspired a few future calligraphers. Years later I was proud to own a modern fountain pen that I filled with South Sea Blue ink.

During our lesson we held the pen lightly between our index finger and thumb of our right hand, with the other fingers gently lying on the desk and curved inward. "The pen must be held, not gripped, near the nib, but not too close to the nib. It should rest against the first knuckle of the middle finger, which allows it to rise precisely between the second and third knuckle of the index finger," we were told.

A callus on the inside of our middle finger was a sign that the grip was too tight. Lucky for me she chose not to notice my telltale pad, a sure indication of penmanship anxiety.

If all this wasn't enough, the underside of our wrists were to lay flat on the desk, and the formation of each letter required that we move our entire arm up and down, keeping our fingers still.

The teacher monitored our positions as she tromped up and down the aisles with a ruler, stopping to rap the knuckles of each "poor writer." I was repulsed by this cruelty and was never rapped, being a natural "righty," dexterous, and eager to please. Lefties were made to conform, creating miserable converts to right-handedness or claw-shaped southpaws with ink all over their sleeves.

By fifth grade I secretly practiced my unique signature, looking forward to my release from Palmer in the coming year. I covered both sides of composition paper testing a series of assumed identities, and

I adopted my favorites in succession until I settled on the iteration I would use in the future.

# MY STORY...

*Relate your experience of learning cursive and how your signature has evolved over time. What is your attitude toward good penmanship?*

MY STORY...

# Smoldering Books

In the 1950s, students had to put paper covers on their personally assigned textbooks. Some people bought precut book jackets with folding guides. In our house we made book covers from cut-up brown paper bags. I decorated mine with extravagant script and crayon designs.

One morning when I was late for school I scurried around the house to collect my schoolbooks. I had the math and geography books, but I couldn't find the history book.

"Where's my history book?" I screeched. "Mom, Michael took my history book."

"Michael, where is Leslie's book?" she asked.

Innocent blue eyes looked up from his angelic face. "I don't know," he said.

"He has my book, I know it. Maaa, get it from him."

Michael inched his way backward and disappeared into the bathroom, a sure sign of guilt.

By this time I was wailing, looking under furniture, and rifling through linens in the hall closet.

Mom grabbed my arm. "Smell," she said.

Sure enough, I caught a whiff of burning paper. We headed for the steaming radiator. The smell was unmistakable, and Mom reached behind it to extract my scorched history book.

I grabbed it and raced off to school, not even waiting to see if Michael got punished.

*What childhood pranks did you or your siblings play? Were you punished for them?*

# MY STORY...

# Leslie Meets the Mayor

Miss Feeney was my favorite teacher at Public School Number 13. She was the only one who put aside the fragile pages of old textbooks and gave us assignments that related to the world outside. I recall her tall, willowy body, long straight skirt, and well-managed salt-and-pepper pageboy. She showed marked indulgence as she listened patiently to each one of us. This teacher instilled confidence in my ability to reach beyond the familiar.

Edward J. O'Byrne was the mayor of Paterson when I was in fifth grade. One of my assignments that year was to interview him, sit on a class panel as if I were the mayor, and answer questions from the other students about his role in Paterson politics.

My neck reddened when Teacher assigned me the task. I knew I could never call the mayor's office on the phone to make an appointment, much less go there and ask him questions. I went home shaking.

At dinnertime, the six of us sat around the chrome kitchen table. Competition for attention was keen because my younger brothers were boisterous, and my father was often the center of attention with his silly jokes or worse yet, his complaining about the food. Even with the chaos, it wasn't difficult for my mother to perceive my stress.

Usually talkative, I was silent, head down. My neck turned red thinking about the interview. I pushed the lumpy mashed potatoes around with my fork. This was not one of the nights my father said, "I'll give you twenty-five cents if you can shut up for five minutes."

"Miss Feeney wants me to interview Mayor O'Byrne," I murmured when Mom leaned over and asked about my silence.

"What about?"

"I don't know, and I'm not going to do it."

"Wait a minute," she said. "Tell me the whole story."

I described the panel discussion as best I could. It would include other city notables, represented by three other classmates.

"What should I ask him?" I blubbered.

"Let's see," said Mom.

After the dinner was cleared away and the dishes done, Nana took my two little brothers to bed so Mom could spend time with me. My mother was steadfast and patient, the latter a trait I struggle to match.

We took out the *Paterson Evening News* and scoured it for topics of interest in the city, and I wrote them down. Tomorrow we would write some questions, and the next day after school I would call the mayor's office to make an appointment.

It seemed like a reasonable strategy, and I was temporarily mollified, but my dreams were not peaceful that night.

Everything went according to plan, and I had an appointment

to meet the mayor at four o'clock in his office. I went home after school and changed into a clean dress with tiny green flowers and short puffed sleeves. I had a black-and-white composition notebook for the occasion, and I had written a different question on each page so I could take notes.

I was ten years old. Much too young, I thought, for this ordeal. When I was ushered into the mayor's office I stood in the doorway, paralyzed. The room was paneled in dark wood. The floor had a lush Oriental rug, and law books lined one wall.

The mayor sat across the room behind a vast, forbidding mahogany desk, its top clear of all but a blotter, an ink pen set, and a photograph I assume was of his family. There was no sign of an ashtray, but cigar smoke hung in the air. *Did he hide it from visitors?*

Seeing my discomfort, he rose and showed me to a seat across from his desk. My head barely reached above it, and I felt like a shrunken Alice.

Somehow I asked questions and took notes. Afterward, Mayor O'Byrne guided me to the door. I must have said thank you, because I had been properly coached, but my time with him is a blur. I walked home in a daze, clutching my black-and-white notebook.

On the day of the panel discussion I was shaking from anxiety. Miss Feeney had secured a long table for the panel to sit behind, and it stood at the front of the class. Seated thus, facing the class with Miss Feeney at the rear, I reddened and felt a momentary buzz in my head. I looked up at her, and she nodded and smiled.

My classmates directed questions about city affairs to the various panel members. After I answered my first question, the panic left. I breathed easily and sensed that my neck had lost its blush. I had perfect recall of Mayor O'Byrne's positions. I knew what he would have said, and I was able to answer fluently. I *was* Mayor O'Byrne, and to my surprise, I felt smart.

On this day in fifth grade a new Leslie emerged. I regained confidence in my intelligence after the prior year's setback when I struggled to catch up in math after having skipped third grade. I was a self-assured student once more.

That was my gift from Miss Feeney, my favorite teacher.

# MY STORY...

*Describe your favorite teacher and how she or he enabled you to grow as a student. Describe a memorable event when you shone in the classroom.*

# MY STORY...

# THE NEIGHBORHOOD

# Treasures From the Corner Store

The "candy store" was an institution among the ethnic neighborhoods in metropolitan New York City. Charlie and Edith owned our corner store, and they worked seven days a week, morning to night, relieving each other for meals and necessary breaks. With wrinkled brow and probing eyes, they kept vigilance against the theft of a nickel candy bar, Black Jack chewing gum, or a pack of Camel cigarettes.

A friend told me about his childhood as the son of neighborhood candy store proprietors, and I can see in retrospect what life must have been like for Charlie and Edith.

Herb's parents worked without any vacation time. They couldn't close the store, and there was no one to manage it for a weekend or even a family visit on Sunday. Eventually his parents sold the store, took a vital respite, and then bought another candy store. It was the only way they could manage a rest.

Regardless of what I learned as an adult about the wearisome burdens of candy store ownership, Charlie and Edith's store was a wonderland for me and for the neighborhood kids. The irresistible draw was a tall, glass-enclosed, kid-proof case filled with an alluring assortment of penny candies. It opened from the back, to prevent eager fingers from digging through the buckets.

We pondered over our choices—candy necklaces, jawbreakers, sweet wax lips, Bazooka gum, wiggly worms, or wax milk bottles—while fingering the pennies in our pockets.

I liked the yard-long, two-inch-wide strips of white paper with four rows of pink, blue, yellow, and green hard sugar dots. My friend and I differed in our method of attack on candy dots. I was thoughtful about which colors I ate first in order to leave an artistic design before finishing them all. I would fold the paper back under a dot to release the edge, maneuver it into my mouth, and savor the sugar. My friend gobbled her dots and then, eyebrows raised and tongue licking her lips, she looked enviously at my remaining pattern.

*Share?*

*Noooo.*

We imitated our parents by smoking King's fiery red-tipped candy cigarettes in the days before anyone believed smoking was harmful. We bought wax Coke bottles, bit off the necks, and held spitting contests to see who could propel them the farthest. Last, we savored the sweet "Coke" syrup and chewed the wax bottle before spitting it out.

While young kids came for penny candy, the teenage boys piled into the store, pushed us little kids aside, and gathered around the refrigerated drinks case with the bottle opener attached to the side. They were tall enough to open the case from the top and reach in for a thin-waisted bottle of Coke, a cream soda, or better still, a black cherry soda.

Then, with the flick of a wrist, they jerked the serrated metal cap under the opener and let it fall to the floor before tossing money onto the counter and strutting out. Those big guys with leather jackets and DA (duck's ass) haircuts were so cool. We little ones huddled until they left and then ran to grab the cork-lined caps for our wooden cigar-box collections.

At other times we scavenged bottle caps from the gutter. Often in the after-school hours a passerby could see six- to eight-year-old foragers trudging in the gutters, heads down, looking for the rare Dr. Brown's Black Cherry bottle top. Such a prize could be traded for two or three Coca-Cola caps to beef up the numbers of a thin stockpile.

The stashes were our bragging rights, a sign of our ingenuity in tracking down or trading for rare treasures. We guarded our wooden Cuban cigar boxes and squirreled them away under our beds or in the dark corner of a closet.

I recall an episode with Bobby, the *mamzer*, as Nana called him, who lived next door. I thought that *mamzer* meant "naughty" until much later when I discovered the literal Yiddish meaning—bastard. A chain-link fence separated his yard from ours. A thin but flowering privet bush lined the fence, and lily-of-the-valley clumped on our side in a small, rarely tended border.

Bobby called to me from his yard.

"Ya wanna trade bottle caps?"

"What do you have?" I asked.

"I got a Black Cherry."

*Wonder what he'd take for it.*

We went into our respective homes and brought out our collections, each on our own side of the fence. He showed me his Black Cherry, and I had Dr. Brown's Cel-Ray, not as rare as the cherry. But I also had a variety of Coke caps, some NEHI, and a Yoo-Hoo chocolate soda top.

"Trade ya my Black Cherry for your NEHI and a Coke," he said.

I thought about it. The idea of having that Black Cherry in my cigar box won me over.

"OK," I said.

"Aw. OK. Toss those two over the fence," he said.

"You toss yours first," I countered.

"No."

"Then we'll both throw them at the same time."

He nodded.

"I'll count to three, and then we'll both toss."

"OK," he said.

"One. Two. Three." I flung the NEHI and the Coke caps over the fence, and Bobby bent to pick them up.

"Hey, you didn't toss yours!" I called.

"Nope, I didn't."

My face reddened and I blustered, but Bobby was a *mamzer*, and I was no match for him.

*What details can you recall about neighborhood candy stores, how you got spending money, and what you bought with it? What did you collect in your childhood and what became of those collections?*

# MY STORY...

# Picking Moss

A grumpy old blue-haired lady chased kids from her property with a bat, and I tried to avoid meeting up with her when I went exploring in our neighborhood.

This woman had a side yard with a large oak tree, and under the tree was a bed of the softest and velvetiest emerald green moss. I loved to stroke the moss, and once when she was nowhere in sight I tried to dig up a swath of it to bring home. I had no notion about where moss grows and how it survives, and I must have imagined laying it down in my backyard.

She spied me from her window and apron clad, bat in hand, she darted out. As fast as she moved, not a wisp of her curled blue hair came loose. Her jowls wagged as she yelled, "Get away. Stay out of my yard!"

I dropped the tattered moss and started to run, but she hustled closer and yelled, "Stop."

I froze, and then turned to face the old woman.

"Now let me show you how to pat that moss back into place," she said, suddenly a different woman. "You live over there," she added, pointing to my catty-corner yard.

I nodded and wondered what had overcome the troll to be speaking to me so kindly. Did she know my family?

"You see, this moss grows in the shade of the tree. This is its home," she told me, patting the moss firmly back into place. "It won't grow anywhere else."

I leaned over to watch and she said, "Here, you pat it down." I bent down and put a tentative palm on the soft green carpet, now ragged with soil around the edges.

"Will it grow smooth again?" I asked.

Mrs. Peale, that was her name I learned, said yes, it would grow again. We surveyed the repaired sod, and I began to relax. I could feel myself let go and breathe. I looked up at her and saw her differently this time. She wore a rose-print housedress, and her apron was a soft pink with pockets. Her hair didn't seem quite so blue, and her kind eyes smiled at me.

"Would you like to come and sit on my porch and have a lemonade?" she asked.

I nodded, and she served me lemonade and ginger cookies.

The next time I passed her mossy turf I bent down to stroke it, and if she was sitting on her front porch she beckoned me to come and sit with her. I had a new friend.

# MY STORY...

*Were there scary adults in your neighborhood? What was frightening about them, and how did you relate to them? Do you recall how curiosity led to new understandings of people in your childhood?*

# MY STORY...

# Gleaning Coal

Anthracite coal, a source of warmth in winter, was also a delight for neighborhood children. A monthly delivery of lustrous ebony chunks brought out the scavengers among us, because each chunk was a valuable implement that could be used for drawing graffiti or a hopscotch grid, depending on gender in those days.

I would draw a hopscotch outline on the sidewalk in front of my house with coal if I didn't have chalk, hoping for a friend to come by. If no one came, I'd practice anyway. I owned a perfect potsy, the discarded heel of a shoe I had wheedled out of the shoemaker, although a flat stone would do in a pinch.

Our cellar had three adjacent coal bins facing the street, one for each flat. They measured about six feet wide and eight feet deep with a small opening high up at street level, wide enough to fit a metal chute.

When the smoking truck would rumble down our street and stop at our house, two enormous men, muscles bulging, would climb down from the truck and position a chute from it into the coal bin. They wore thick gloves and coal-stained overalls. We kids would gather round, wide-eyed and enthralled as we held our ears against the thunderous roar of coal careening down the chute into the bin.

The moment the last bit of coal left the chute, the kids would rush in to grab errant chunks, but I would wait a moment for the "gleaner" to fill his sack as best he could.

Once I asked my dad about the olive-skinned boy with shabby clothing whose face was always smudged with coal.

"Dad, do you know about the boy who follows the coal truck with his sack? It seems there's always more coal slipping from the chute on his side."

"His family lives in one of those garages in gasoline alley around the corner. They don't have a coal bin like us, and they can't afford to buy coal for heat. I think they use a stove they rigged up."

"But, Dad, what about more coal falling off near him?" I asked.

"Think about it, Leslie. Would the coal always fall that way by itself?"

My eyes lit, and I smiled at my dad. "They do it on purpose, huh?"

My dad smiled too. "It's a *mitzvah*, a good deed."

Anthracite coal, a source of warmth, and two working guys who shared the wealth.

# MY STORY...

*What memories do you have about heating your home? Were you aware of any mitzvahs in your life? What memories do you have about being encouraged to do good deeds?*

# MY STORY...

# The Flasher

A fading three-family gray clapboard house built at the turn of the twentieth century was our Paterson, New Jersey, home until I was ten years old. It stood among a row of similar buildings along East Twenty-Second Street, but ours was next to the corner store that was across from Public School Number 13.

Four cement steps led to a landing with a brown-painted tubular banister. Six more stairs to the right accessed a railed porch. A heavy mahogany door with a brass handle and a small window above my sight guarded the entrance to the foyer. It took a two-handed tug for me to open the massive door.

There was something frightening, too adult-like about the dark paneling and carpeting in that entryway. It smelled of old people to me. The first-floor flat was on the left. On the right, a creaky spiral staircase with a thick carved banister wound up to the second- and third-floor landings. Children rarely used the front entrance.

Instead, we walked the narrow alleyway between the houses to go into the backyard and up the rear staircase.

I was six years old, playing jump rope alone on the street in front of the house one day when a strange man wearing a long brown coat and a black fedora asked, "Is your mother at home?"

"You can ring the bell up on the porch," I said, thinking how commonplace it was to see a door-to-door salesman. I remember a Fuller Brush man, the encyclopedia salesman, the vacuum cleaner man, not to mention the whip-cracking ragman with his horse and wagon, the milkman, and the seltzer man. I didn't think to question why this man didn't have any wares.

He wanted me to go inside with him to show the way. I hesitated for a moment and pointed. "It's right there. See the bells?"

"I'd like you to go with me, so I don't make a mistake."

I didn't want to, but I did what I thought was polite and led him into the foyer. "Go up there and knock on the door," I said, pointing to the staircase.

"Wait," he said. "I have something to show you."

The salesman unbuttoned his long wool coat and quickly unzipped his pants. He pulled out his erect penis.

I was paralyzed for a moment, and then I flushed, feeling a buzzing in my head. I backed up to the door. He reached out to stay me, but I twisted the knob, pushed the door open with the weight of my body and fled. I dashed down the two sets of steps, and then around to the alleyway, nearly tripping on a crack in the narrow passage where I raced for the safety of the back door.

I imagined that he was following me, but I was too frightened to look back. Breathing hard, I ran up the porch steps, into the hallway, and up to the third floor where I burst into the kitchen, a tearful quivering child. Mommy was in the kitchen, her back to me at the sink. She turned when she heard me, and I ran into her arms.

"What—?"

"A man, Mommy, a man opened his pants."

She swooped me up onto her lap, held me tight, and smoothed my hair. "Shh, Baby, you're all right now. Shh. No one will hurt you. Shhhh."

# MY STORY...

*Do you remember witnessing any exhibitionism or other bizarre behavior from an adult? How did it affect you at the time?*

MY STORY...

# A Strange Girl

One day I was hanging upside down by my knees from the brown banister on the cement landing in front of my house when a pair of bare legs, smeared with dirt, appeared before my eyes, close enough that I could see a brown birthmark on tan skin. I thought I was seeing things because of all the blood rushing to my head.

I scuttled off the bar and came face-to-face with a girl, older and taller than my six years. She had shoulder-length, thick tangled brown hair and fiery dark cat-shaped eyes with thick lashes and brows. She wore a tattered dress, too short for her age, I thought. The red polish had worn from the tips of her toenails so I could see the dirt under them.

Without a word she pushed me away from the bar and in an instant was standing on it. She got up so fast I didn't see how she managed. My mouth agape, I watched her grip her long toes around the bar and walk from one end to the other and back. Then she bent down, gripped the bar with one hand, and jumped off as quickly as an alley cat pouncing on a mouse. She stood up straight, looked at me with a "take that" kind of grin, and disappeared around the corner.

My nana said a Syrian family lived in the neighborhood and that she was likely one of their many children. I never saw her in school or on my street again, and I lost interest in my knee-hanging trick after that.

# MY STORY...

*Does this girl remind you of anyone you've known? How so? Describe your experience with an exotic stranger or acquaintance. What did you learn or wish to know about that person or their culture?*

MY STORY...

PHOTOS AND MEMORABILIA

*This infant bracelet with the inverted letter "T" was placed on my wrist at birth in Barnert Memorial Hospital, Paterson, New Jersey.*

*A photo of me in bibbed shorts with tangled, sweat-soaked hair inspired the story "Screaming and Splashing."*

*The stream at Mootz's Farm provided water for the swimming pool and a miniature waterfall where little girls could wash their hair.*

*Mom coaxed me to eat soft-boiled "eggy-in-the-cup" from this orange glass teacup before leaving for nursery school in the morning.*

*Mom at the stove in our East Twenty-Second Street flat inspired "The Daily Drudge."*

*Dad wearing a woolen sweater like the one I remembered when writing "Wet Mittens."*

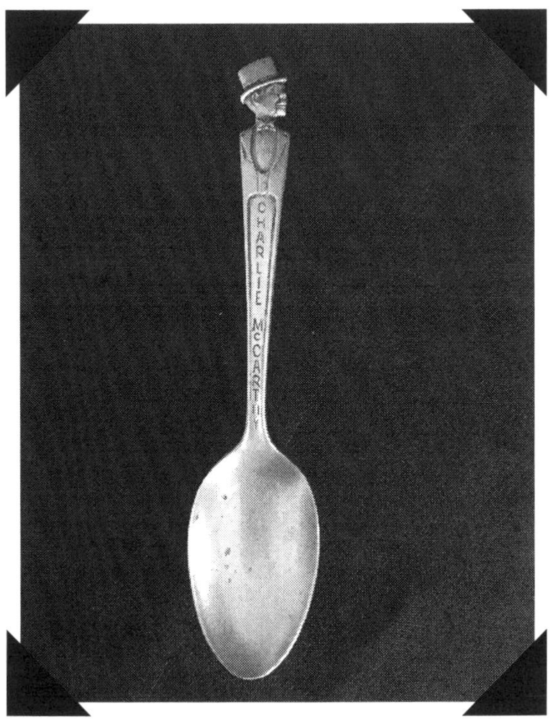

*This Charlie McCarthy spoon was used to stir cocoa in
the "Wet Mittens" story.*

*Taken near the hole in the playground fence of PS #13, this photo
with me on the left evoked the incident "A Painful Crash"
and other memories about school life.*

*My dad, here on East Twenty-Second Street, cared for his clothing and his auto with equal meticulousness.*

*Mom (third from left) kicking high in a "Y" Parents' Group fundraiser, inspired my love of dance and costume as described in "Nana's Darling."*

*A collection of pins and badges from my Brownie uniform and Girl Scout sash inspired the story "To Brownies on the Bus."*

*The elegant Danforth Memorial Library was my destination in "To the Library—Alone."*

Laurie took her bike out of the
garage. She ____ liked that old bike.
Every day that summer she ____ rode
it around and
around the block all by herself.
Each time she passed
past the empty lot where the boys
played baseball. she would slow down a little
Not unless Joe or
Kevin would call out "I'll race
you around the block, Laurie!"
Then she would yell "Beat ya back here!"
And they would take off. Skinny
little Laurie pumping like mad
and just hardly ____ ____
Kevin Joe ____ feeling the wind
against her face and arms. She felt
proud then and she thought that
everyone they passed must be looking
and saying "there goes Laurie. She's
going to beat that boy clear around the
block." And sometimes she did.

And those times when she did
win, the boys might ask her to play
out field, but Laurie would just
take off again on her bike. She'd stand
up and pump real hard and then sit

see p. 9

Top: Long after I had written "My Bicycle Crusade," I found this essay written at age eleven.

Bottom: I described this black, Raleigh 3-speed English racer in "My Bicycle Crusade."

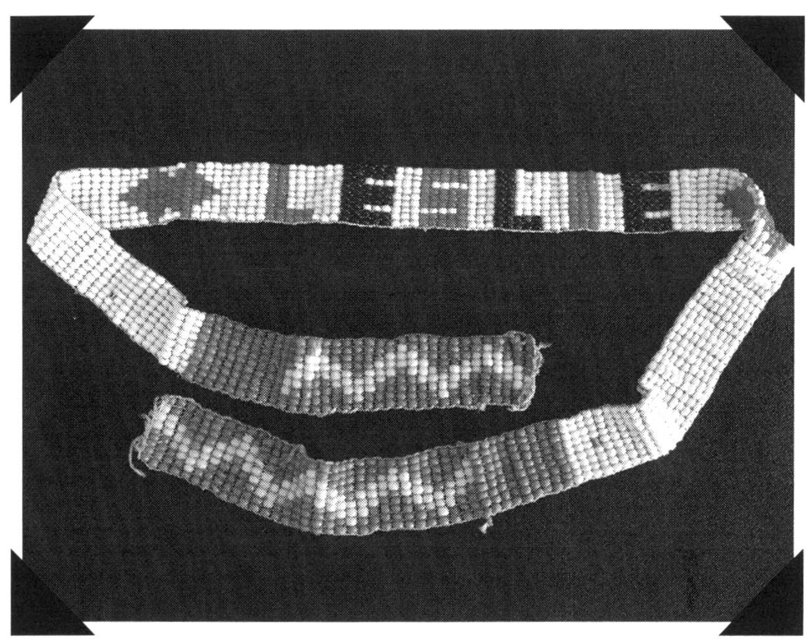

*An Indian beaded belt is one of many arts and crafts projects
I made at summer camp.*

*At age fourteen I met the young man described in
"Love in the Mountains."*

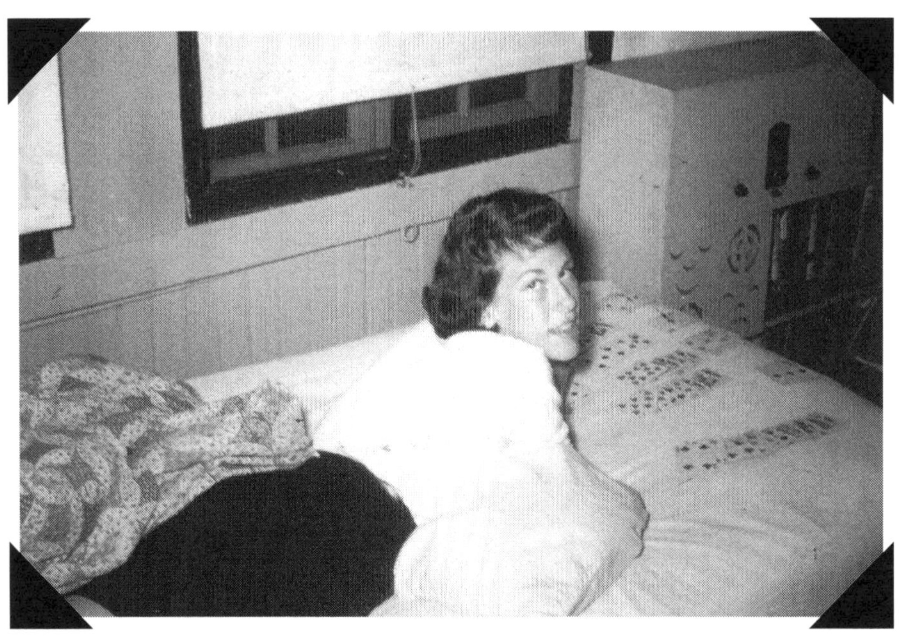

*As described in "Nana and I Share a Room," I spent summers in this screened-in porch.*

*Eighth grade graduates of PS #20 in Paterson, New Jersey, were awarded this pin.*

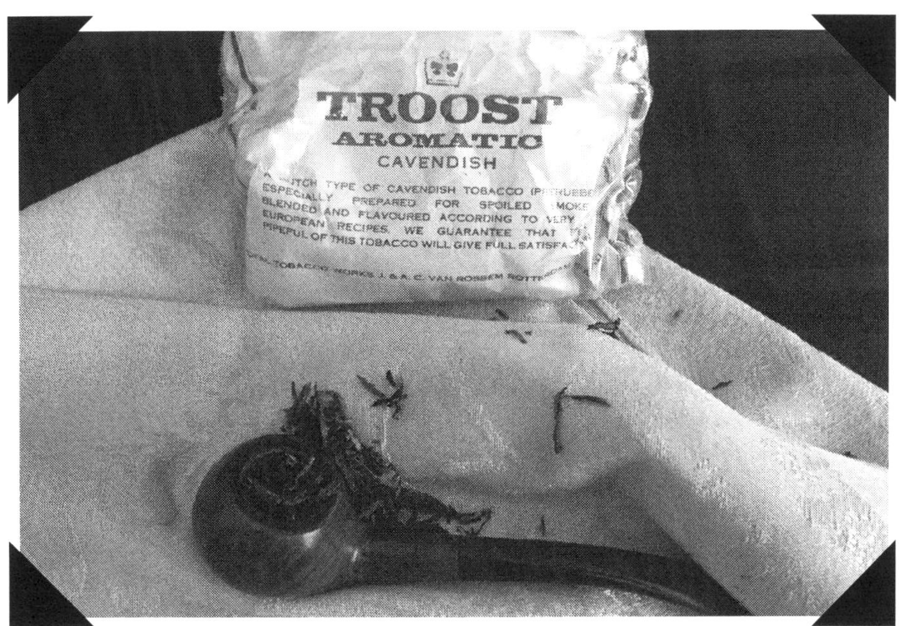


*My pipe and tobacco were a calling card to youthful rebellion as described in "What Was I Thinking?"*

*Rhinestone shoe clips and hair comb added sparkle to my Junior Prom outfit. Long silver gloves completed the ensemble.*

*As a sophomore at Eastside High School I was elected to the International Zonta Club, a junior division of a women's service and advocacy organization.*

*Emma, daughter Lillian, and husband Meyer dressed in finery in 1912.*

*Nana (center row, fourth from left) and daughter Lillian (bottom row, second from left) among the family including her brothers, their wives and children. Photo taken circa 1915.
My great-grandparents, Greta and Louis Kaufman, are seated in the front row. Emma's husband, Meyer, is not present.*

*Lillian and Emma are fashionably arrayed for winter in the 1920s.*

WE MOVE UPTOWN

# Nana's Sorrow

When I asked Nana about her past, she revealed only snippets, and my father filled me in on some of the rest. She was born into a family of weavers in the Jewish ghetto of Lodz in Poland. She was the youngest of seven children and the only girl. Her emotional and physical hardships, which I couldn't have understood in my youth, required courage and perseverance to endure, but I felt the distortion of those traits and the reverberations of her suffering as I grew older.

"What was it like when you lived in Lodz?" I asked when I was a preteen.

"Soldiers came through our city. Czar Nicholas, that '*Bloody Czar,*' hated us Jews. Once I hid when they came through. I looked out of a window."

"Did you get caught?"

"*Na.* I didn't go out on the street."

"Nana, you must have been afraid."

"*Vell*, sure I was afraid, but I saw."

"What? What did you see? Tell me, Nana."

"*Ach*. I don't like to remember. The *goyim*, they followed the soldiers and they carried big sticks. They beat what Jews were on the street with those sticks…fire…burned some houses…stole from Jewish shops."

"Later we came out. We helped the people that was hurt."

"Dad told me that your brothers were against the czar. They hid a press in your house and printed handbills about rebelling against the czar. Right?"

"*Yah*. They tried to make, what you say? Demonstrations against that czar."

I learned much more from subsequent reading than from what Nana told me. In addition to the danger of being discovered, her brothers were subject to conscription into the Russian army, and once conscripted, would never be seen again.

"Your brothers left Poland?"

"*Yah*. They had to go or they would be caught. They got out. One by one they left."

My father told me about her escape. The brothers sent for her when all six got to Paterson, New Jersey. She had to sneak out and bribe her way along the walk north from her home in central Poland to the port city of Gdansk on the Baltic. That was two hundred miles on foot, and she was pregnant with her first child.

"Dad said you had another baby before Lillian, and she died."

"*Ve* stop now," she said.

I couldn't get her to talk about the death of her baby, Jewel. It seemed that her guilt and anguish were too great. My dad said that

Jewel died from tetanus, likely caused by bacteria from a fecal-contaminated diaper pin (so my research indicates). The symptoms, including high fever, convulsions, difficulty swallowing, chills, and extreme pain would have been horrific for both Jewel and Nana.

Later in her married life and a few years prior to my birth, Nana lost her forty-year-old daughter, Lillian, to chronic kidney disease. Soon after that, her husband died, leaving her in a large flat with my father, her remaining child. After he married, he brought my mother to live with them.

My birth was an opportunity for Nana to relive Lillian's infancy and childhood. I was named for Lillian, and in her mind, perhaps I was Lillian. That would explain the doting, her attempt at surrogate parenting until I was about ten years old.

As my independence grew, Nana came to realize that I wasn't the reincarnation of her departed daughter, and she couldn't contain her bitter disappointment. Gradually, the person who once pampered me turned hostile, and we both lost the opportunity to continue a loving relationship, I with my only living grandparent.

# MY STORY...

*What do you know about ordeals that your grandparents may have endured? How did their experiences strengthen or hamper them? Can you see some of your grandparents' traits in yourself?*

# MY STORY...

# Nana and I Share a Room

I was ten years old when we moved from East Twenty-Second Street to East Thirty-First Street in Paterson. We had arrived. Dad had wanted us closer to the wealthier Jewish neighborhood, and this flat on the first floor of a two-family house was on that fringe. "You'll go to a good school now," he said. "More Jews. Even the principal is Jewish."

The main advantage for my dad as I saw it was that oil heat replaced the coal furnace. I would watch him walk up to the thermostat on the dining room wall to admire it. "Look here at this little gadget," my father would say. "I move this lever with one finger and the heat goes on."

Even I could appreciate this. My dad was thirty-eight years old, and he had shoveled coal every winter since he could manage it as a boy.

"No shoveling coal," he'd mutter to himself, and then he would shake his head from side to side as if he couldn't quite understand how this miracle had befallen him. "Tsk, tsk, tsk. Such a wonder."

"Yeah, Dad." *Not worth moving.* Unlike my father, I didn't appreciate our new home. I had farther to walk to school, I had to make new friends in sixth grade, and I still didn't have my own room.

In our old home, I had shared a bedroom with Michael who was four years younger. Jon, three years old when we moved, had slept in my parents' makeshift bedroom, the intended "front room" of the flat. My grandmother was the only one who had her own bedroom.

In the new arrangement, Michael and Jon shared a room, and my parents enjoyed a real bedroom with a door that closed. Both of the intended bedrooms were off the kitchen. Now it was my turn to sleep in a makeshift bedroom, but this time with Nana.

Our new flat must have been luxurious in its day. It had high ceilings, oak floors, and decorative moldings. The walls were clean and painted, not dressed with peeling floral wallpaper. There was a spacious living room and a sunny dining room with glass French doors that opened onto a sitting room. The screened but unheated front porch was almost the width of the house.

Our flat would have been the perfect home for three or four people, but we were six. My parents put shades on the French doors and moved Nana and me into twin beds pushed against opposite walls in the former sitting room. There was a hooked rug between the beds and we shared the dresser at the foot of my bed. Our armoire was on Nana's side. We each had a night table. That was it. Nana and me.

A seventy-seven-year-old woman shared my room. She wore flowered housedresses buttoned down the front with a crumpled handkerchief peeking from a patch pocket on her breast. Seamed hosiery rolled up with garter bands dug into the flesh below her knees, and she stuffed her feet into black lace-up shoes with clunky two-inch heels and decorative holes on the tips. Naturally curly steel-gray hair, parted on the side, hung below her dangly earlobes.

Wire rim glasses completed the picture of a stern, opinionated lady. The doting Nana of my early childhood had evolved into a severe woman. Once adoring and compliant, I had passed my malleable stage, and she grew increasingly strident.

Nana and I retired to our bedroom on the first night in our new home. Her breath smelled of the schnapps-soaked bread she enjoyed every night before sleep. She switched on her bedside light then drew the French doors shut and pulled down the shades, locking us into a windowless prison. I sat on the edge of my bed and waited, not knowing what to expect. She opened and closed her dresser drawers, satisfied that her garments were in place. She went to the armoire and examined her dresses and straightened her two pairs of sturdy shoes on the bottom shelf.

I got up and switched on my light.

She sat on the edge of her bed facing me, quiet.

"Are you going to read, Nana?"

"What? Read? It's time to sleep."

"Nana, I always read in bed. I'm reading *Secret of the Andes*. I used to read to Michael when we shared a room."

I felt as if I would suffocate in this room. The air had begun to take on a musty odor, and I wanted to knock on the wall by my bed and yell to my parents on the other side, "Get me out of here!"

"*Nu?* Time to get ready," she said.

I got my pajamas from the dresser and climbed under the covers to change in private. Once my PJs were on, I slipped out of bed and put my clothes away. I reached for my book on the nightstand.

Nana unbuttoned her lavender print housedress and hung it up in the armoire. She pulled her slip over her head and sat in her brassiere and heavy cotton panties. She pulled on white cotton gloves and began to unroll her hosiery.

"Always I used gloves with my silk stockings, but still I wear them for nylon so I shouldn't make a rip," she said.

I nodded, certain that I wouldn't go to that extreme when I could wear nylons.

Then I gawked at her wrinkled chest, the folds of skin that hung from her arms, and small rolls of sagging flesh around her middle. I flinched, swallowed hard, and turned away from Nana.

"What's the matter? You never saw a naked woman?"

"Mom looks different," I said as I turned back to face her.

All was quiet again and I started to read my book.

"You don't say your prayers?" asked Nana.

"I say them when I close my eyes. To myself."

Nana, now dressed in her nightgown, pulled down her covers and got into bed. She turned off her light and began her prayer.

"Dear God, Keep me busy. Keep me fit. By windows I don't want to sit, watching my neighbors hurry by. Keep me fit until I die."

Every night the same prayer. Every single night.

◼

As the months passed I grew unhappier and overwhelmed by Nana's toilette, her aging body, and her routines. I longed for a space of my own, for a little piece of turf I could arrange to my satisfaction.

Mom had the solution that would save me in the coming spring. The front screened-in porch, a long, narrow room, was unheated and unused in winter. While the storm windows protected it from the elements, it was too cold for daily use. In April, however, Dad would exchange the storm windows for screens, and I'd finally have a space of my own.

Mom and I found used bedroom furniture, a bookcase, and a desk that we painted white. We bought a coverlet, and when spring finally came, I began to move my things. During summer vacation when the light streamed in through the east-facing windows, I was in heaven. I spent hours lying on my bed reading. In later years I had a portable radio. I wrote poetry. I sketched. I daydreamed. I even had a bulletin board.

I tucked away the memory of my retreat all winter. I would go into the porch on occasion to reassure myself of the coming season when my life would be renewed with the changing of the storm windows, and the drab winter porch would once again become my cozy refuge from Nana.

*Did you have grandparents or relations living in your home when you were a child? How did it affect you? If you shared a bedroom with a family member, describe your feelings about it.*

# MY STORY...

# A Tin Mug of Root Beer

"Root beer, please." I daydreamed about an icy tin mug of root beer, a dewy mug with the big-eared handle. Tall. Foaming right up to the top. Stinging in the nostrils. Lasting forever. I'd hop onto the padded revolving stool in the drugstore and plunk down my nickel.

But I didn't have five cents or even a penny. Whatever might have been left from my Friday dime was long gone.

One more hot summer day and I'd been reading *Nancy Drew* mysteries on the screened-in sun porch all morning, lying on my tummy, propped up on my bony preteen elbows. I'd finished *The Secret of the Wooden Lady* and moved on to *The Clue of the Black Keys*, but I couldn't get that mug of root beer out of my mind. My mouth was dry, and I could feel the void in my stomach.

I jumped up and padded to the Frigidaire for a thirst quencher.

Seltzer or milk. No frosty root beer. I spritzed some seltzer from the nozzle into a juice glass, but it wasn't what I wanted.

My parents were both working, and Nana was glued to the living room TV with the shades drawn to keep out the summer heat. She was watching *As the World Turns*, like a million other women who sat mesmerized by the soaps for two hours every weekday.

No one would know if I happened to come upon five pennies somewhere in the house. I listened for Nana's footsteps before entering my parents' bedroom, almost certain she was still rapt, seated two feet from the television set.

The forbidden bedroom was dark and warm like a womb, the double bed neatly made, and the air suffused with Attar of Roses. Two night tables and dressers were crammed in the remaining space. I crept in and faced Mom's dresser, listening for a stirring from Nana. *Safe.*

I lifted the lid of Mom's tiny porcelain box, the one with the hinge and the pink flowers painted on the top. No pennies today. Only a tiny pearled button from Dad's shirt cuff.

I tiptoed to my father's dresser to check the square wooden box with the inlaid top and ran my fingers across the smooth, oiled surface before I took off the lid. No pennies there.

The kitchen junk drawer wasn't any better, so I went to the last place where money might be, the hall closet. It was perilously close to the TV. *Don't turn your head now, Nana.*

Mom's khaki raincoat pocket yielded only a crumpled hankie, but my father's navy blue spring jacket held the ticket: a nickel and two pennies. I left the two pennies for another day and went to the porch for my pink beaded Indian moccasins.

"Nana, I'm going for a walk," I called. No answer.

"Nana, I said I'm going out."

When I tapped her on the shoulder, she startled. "Wait for the commercials," she said.

"I'm going out."

"*Yah*," she said, her eyes still on the screen. How could I have been so thoughtless as to interrupt *As the World Turns*? Anyway, I was glad she didn't look to see my bare legs in soiled white shorts. She would have made me change.

With the nickel in my pocket I headed for Caroline's house one block down the street. She wasn't at summer camp this week either.

Her mother let me in and called to Caroline. "Leslie's here to see you."

I whispered in my friend's ear, "Do you have five cents for a root beer?"

She grinned. "Yep."

We were off to Park Avenue where the drugstore's soda fountain beckoned. Arms linked, we skipped along the sidewalk singing a Yiddish-American chant, the one popularized decades later on TV by Laverne and Shirley: "1, 2, 3, 4, 5, 6, 7, 8 Schlemiel! Schlimazel! Hasenpfeffer Incorporated!"

At the drugstore we hopped onto the padded stools and plunked down our five cents. "Root beer, please."

# MY STORY...

*Tell about your memories of a local drugstore counter or soda fountain you liked to visit when you were young. How did you get pocket money as a child? Do you recall being sneaky to get something you wanted?*

MY STORY...

# Becoming June Cleaver

*Why can't I play with the blocks?* I liked my dolls, but I'd wanted other options from as early as I can remember. In kindergarten, girls played "school," "nurse," or "dolls," while the boys got to play with wooden blocks, fire engines, and toy trucks. I'd peek over the half wall that separated the boys' and girls' play areas to watch intense little guys build towers and noisy guys imitate fire engine sounds, but another girl, or worse yet, the teacher, would coax me back to my *place.*

Beginning in the sixth grade we left our homeroom class several times a week for extended periods of either home economics or wood shop. These gender-specific "classrooms" occupied opposite sides of the cement-walled basement. Choice was not an option, but I yearned to define my person beyond presumptions of what was right for me well before the eyes-wide-open sixties.

My brothers took pride in their bookshelves and birdhouses. I examined their projects to see how they were made, confident that I could do as well. My own take-home project was an apron that I had sewn on a treadle Singer machine. I stuffed it in the bottom of a kitchen drawer.

In eighth grade we girls produced identical, princess style, dotted-swiss graduation dresses with V-necks and short, capped sleeves. No variations were allowed for us, but the boys could choose their own ties.

Mrs. June Cleavers in the making, we learned cooking and housekeeping skills while wearing identical white-bibbed aprons. Miss Beemer, our home economics teacher, wore a 38 EEE brassiere, we were certain. We watched her, intent not on her direction but on the sure possibility that she would fall forward, drawn to the floor by the weight of her bosom. She was a sweet young woman, a competent homemaker, yet little match for preadolescent girls.

One day while stirring cupcake frosting, Terri whispered, "Pssst. Watch me." She held a frosting-laden spoon like a slingshot, ready to fire it off at Miss Beemer, who in a prescient moment, hastened off to the housekeeping rooms. Thwarted, Terri licked her spoon, and we all dug into our bowls for a taste.

The home economics area had six kitchen workspaces and a complete suite of rooms—a model living room, dining room, and bedroom—for instruction. In the austere dining room, a long wooden table awaited our ministrations. The windowless, over-furnished room was cellar dark, and the still air held not a hint of cooking aroma.

"Jean, select the tablecloth, and Terri, help her lay it. Girls, each of you please take silverware from the sideboard and set your place. Stand behind your chair when you're ready," said Miss Beemer. We had learned the correct placement of two forks, two spoons, and a knife. Next week, we would add the fish fork, learn how to arrange the china, and record all of our homemaking wisdom in notebooks for the day we would reign in our own homes.

We moved on to the living room to vacuum and dust, each in its proper order. Vacuum first so what is kicked up can be dusted off. Or was it dust first so what floats down can be vacuumed up? Regardless, I recall the swirling haze in the light of table lamps, and I would sneeze at each swipe of the rag.

In the bedroom we learned to make tightly pulled hospital corners of the flat-bottomed sheet. We paired up to add the top sheet, blanket, and quilted coverlet. Miss Beemer inspected every step, leaving nothing to chance in molding our future course.

We girls graduated to high school, competent to keep house, steered toward an early marriage, and encouraged to be ladylike in every situation. Soon after, the sixties hit, and all bets were off.

*Did you feel thwarted by gender expectations in school? How have your attitudes changed with respect to gender roles since the 1950s?*

# MY STORY...

# Out to Impress

W hen the snowdrifts wore a coating of frost and the front steps needed salt to melt the ice, the pond would be frozen deep enough to skate.

Dad pulled his 1950 black Buick Riviera out of the detached garage that was his bonus with our move uptown in 1955. He had shoveled the snow to either side of the driveway that morning, and I heard his tires crush the residue of ice that crackled as he maneuvered out of the garage.

I came out of the back kitchen door, wearing two heavy sweaters, hand-knit by Nana, with my ice skates tied together and slung over my shoulder like the "real" ice skaters. I kicked away the ice on the back landing with the tip of my boot and tested each step for slipperiness on my way down.

Dad warmed the car while I struggled with my gloved hands to pull the garage door shut, sliding it sideways along its channel.

Then I climbed into the front seat and laid my skates on the floor next to me.

I grinned when Dad patted me on the knee and backed down the driveway. We drove out of the city to a small pond with only a few skaters on it. My father walked onto the ice, tested it with the heel of his boot, and then helped me change into my skates.

I put on a show for him alone. I skated away in an arabesque, my arms stuck straight out in front and behind as he watched from the edge. I sped around the circumference of the pond with newly acquired turning skills. I slowed down and hummed the romantic *Melody of Love*, imagining that Ricky Nelson was holding me around the waist and admiring my grace and skill on ice.

When I returned to my dad, face flushed and fingertips frozen, he sat me on a log and pulled off my skates. He was my hero. A thin, olive-complexioned man with curly black hair combed back from his forehead. In those days he smiled readily and gazed with pride at his stellar daughter. He held out a thermos of hot cocoa. Soon, though, no execution of flashy moves on the ice would elicit my father's admiration again.

*How did you elicit your parents' admiration or pride and how did they show it? Did you have specific skills that they held in high regard or were they proud of you in general?*

# MY STORY...

# An Impending Storm

My childhood ended long before Mother Nature awoke my womanhood. My tenth year was the last peaceful one I can remember at home. For the next two years our family lived with an impending storm, menacing clouds on the horizon.

With my father's growing angst, the clouds burst and returned with increasing vigor over time. After a while there were no warning clouds. Anger erupted from nowhere and put an end to harmony in our family.

Eventually, turmoil squeezed the happiness from my father's soul. Discontent overruled his emotions until he sucked the joy out of the air whenever he was home. My serenity dissolved when I heard him drive up after work, open the creaky garage door, and pull his shiny black Buick forward, the car he seemed to love more than me. Then the kitchen door would fly open. The air screamed silent terror.

Sometimes my dad would eat alone, and on other occasions with us. By the time I was twelve years old, we three kids regularly ate dinner before he came home from work. Mom and Nana cleared our dishes and set Dad's place early in case he arrived before the usual time. It was more relaxing for everyone that way.

On very hot summer days he would take off his work clothes in the bedroom and come out with a towel wrapped around his waist. My mother would have laid a fresh one on their bed. He would go through the kitchen and out to the backyard to hose off before dinner. Although I didn't see this, I know he would have taken off his gold-rimmed glasses and placed them on the pavement before washing. I can visualize him removing his house slippers and then wiping his feet completely dry before putting them back on.

Refreshed, he would return with the towel once more around his waist and change into his dinner outfit—pinstripe boxer shorts, the top snap undone, and the waistband hanging open. He was thin except for the tiny paunch that swelled from beneath the elastic waistband, and bones jutted out everywhere else.

We scooted out of the kitchen at this point. Michael, the elder of my two brothers, did his homework with me at the dining room table while Nana shepherded Jon out of sight. I would imagine the grimace on Dad's face, the look of discontent as my mother waited on him.

He would have sniffed the air. "What's for dinner?"

"Nice roast beef and potatoes. Salad."

"Gimme the salad with some of that French dressing on it."

Sometimes it went OK, but too often we would hear a variation on their dialog. "Do ya think I'm going to eat this meat? It's like shoe leather. Gimme a cream cheese and olive sandwich. Make it two."

"But it's a good piece of meat from the butcher, well done the way you like it…"

"Get it out of my sight, and get me the sandwiches."

The sandwiches pacified him, or perhaps it was my mother's meek response to his bullying. They spoke softly, but I could almost make out their conversation through the closed kitchen door. I knew they must be talking about me. Maybe he was telling her about the schoolbooks I left on the table or my shoes cluttering the living room. I could never predict what he might seize upon next.

I noticed that he began to suffer extreme stomach pain at about the same time. On occasion he retreated to his bedroom and I could hear his faint moans from behind the door. "Moe," he'd call. "Come sit by me."

My dad was no longer pleasant to look at. He often held his protruding belly, a bulge like that of a starving child. The corners of his mouth turned downward, and the commas between his nose and mouth grew deeper. His swarthy complexion turned sallow, and the embers of his good humor flickered and died.

I didn't think to connect his physical discomfort with his outbursts, and I never had evidence of their being linked, but I learned to live with the new man who was my father. Over time my roiling anxiety about his unpredictable mood abated, but my heart hardened like a jewelry box locked tight. Love for my dad was a once-gleaming gem whose brightness slowly dimmed until it finally faded away.

I always had and always would love my mom, but instead of

feeling empathy, I vowed never to be like her. I wouldn't let any man boss and disrespect me as she did.

———————■———————

Dad favored my brothers as they grew old enough to be companions. I tried to recapture his love by excelling in school, but if I got 95 percent he scowled. "Why not 100 percent?"

"It's too bad you're a girl," he would say. "You have brains. If you were a boy, you could go to college and be somebody. You could even be a mathematician."

"I could still go to college, Dad. I want to be a teacher or a librarian."

"Just get married."

*Never. Not if all men are like you.*

It remained difficult to reconcile the adoring father of my early years with the man he had become, and harder yet to retain my own inner peace. I watched out for my brothers, did my chores, and developed an early independence, but things would never be the same. My youngest brother became reclusive to avoid my father's sudden flare-ups. Michael, our lighthearted, charming middle child, drew Dad's fire. He became the target of verbal abuse and my father's "spare the rod, spoil the child" philosophy. Perhaps the experience of watching my innocent brother suffer and realizing that my mother didn't have the power to intervene was harder to bear than my own pain.

The iciness that I felt toward my father melted somewhat when I approached my middle years. I came to understand that despite his bullying, my father was a fragile man with gnawing anxiety and obsessive behaviors, a man who at a relatively young age had lost his vigor, his charm, and worst of all, his thirst for life.

JUMP-START
YOUR MEMOIR

*Paint Unique Characters*
https://youtu.be/qSQUvu5FgEk

*What challenges did you have within your family? How did you cope with difficult times? If there was anyone in your family whose personality or behavior changed dramatically or unpredictably, can you describe its impact?*

# MY STORY...

# ADOLESCENCE

# A Dream: I Learn to Soar

I was eleven or twelve years old when I began to dream about learning to fly, not from an enemy, but for pleasure. These early dreams began on the street in front of our former home, the three-story building on East Twenty-Second Street.

In one of them, neighborhood kids surrounded me. They crowded closer with an edge of confrontation, seeming to say, "What makes you so great?" I felt the need to prove myself, to brag.

"I can fly," I said.

"Aw, your mother's uncle," one boy shouted.

"Go tell it to the pope," said another.

"I can," I said. "Watch me."

The crowd moved to create a path on the sidewalk. I ran with a long stride, faster, faster, until I pushed off and levitated, but not quite high enough. I hovered in stagnant air, afloat merely a few feet above the ground, unable to soar.

I could hear the doubtful taunts below me. The unbelievers were almost close enough to grab my heels.

My nerve endings tingled with determination and I filled my lungs, peering up at endless blue. With one big exhale, I shot up well beyond their reach.

I wafted in a cloudless sky. Below were Manhattan's apartment buildings where clothes dangled on lines strung from windows across narrow alleys. I landed on a rooftop among pigeon coops, crisscrossed wires, and protruding pipes.

Another rooftop caught my attention, one that had a garden profuse with red azaleas and all manner of yellow and gold daisies. I pushed off and soared, coming to a graceful landing near a lounge chair. The allure of weightlessness kept me flying from one building to another until I simply floated and enjoyed the ride.

I reveled in the infinite freedom and independence of these flights. After days of confined classrooms and hectic dinner hours, I might be able to escape to the skies and adventures without limit.

*If you had flying dreams, describe how you felt. Did you have dreams about experiences other than flying that created a sense of exhilaration or an awakening of new powers? Describe those.*

# MY STORY...

# The Social Group

In seventh grade I discovered how far I would go to be in the popular group, and to this day I feel the pain of it. I was still new to a school that included grades kindergarten to eight. My family had moved up in the world, but not far enough. We lived on the poor end of a wealthy neighborhood, not next door to the popular girls.

From the first school recess I had distinguished the elite from the "drips," those unaffiliated but undisturbed loners. The popular girls had their own social group with a formal invitation required for membership. A few pairs and triads of friends were content as long as no one bothered them. Solitary "drips" stood unnoticed on the sidelines of the playground. Cynthia was one of these.

She was a frail blonde with skirts well above her knees, pre-adolescent in body with no breasts or hair in the important places. Cynthia was an average student, but uncoordinated in physical education class and last picked for teams. She cried easily. "Victim!" she emanated.

Not physically mature, but a good student and highly coordinated in PE, I could shinny to the top of a rope suspended from the gymnasium ceiling. I could broad jump, run fast, and swing a bat. I wasn't *cute*, but I didn't have silly pigtails or too-short skirts.

I was just about good enough to be popular, but like my family's fringe status in wealth, I became fringe popular as a result of an unexpected phone call. About a month into the school year my mom called me to the telephone. "Marcy's on the line."

"I called to say that you could join our social group. We're having a get-together on Friday night at Barbara's house at 7:00 p.m. Be there if you want to join," she said.

Having seen some of their nasty ways, I was leery about my true welcome at the get-together, and I wondered if it was a setup where I would be targeted as the "drip." I went to bed in agony, wanting to be accepted yet fearful of rejection.

The next day at school, Jeannette called me aside. "I was the one who said to invite you into our social group. The boys'll be at the get-together on Friday."

One or two others in the group made friendly gestures during recess. "Come talk to us," they said. Playground games were below them, but gossip carried weight.

Friday night arrived, and my father drove me to Barbara's house, a three-story white stucco mansion near Eastside Park. In addition to M&Ms and bottles of Coke, her mother served potato chips, dip, and English muffin pizzas on a tray. There was a record player and a stack of 45-rpm hits. Her parents had rolled a massive rug aside so we could dance on the bare living room floor. *Young Love* and

*Tammy* were my favorite songs, but no one asked me to "slow dance." Actually, no one asked me to dance at all that night.

I became a member of the social group, but I was still an outsider. My mother couldn't afford to serve appealing refreshments on a tray, and our flat in a two-family house wasn't large enough for get-togethers. I was invited to them, but instead of planning or hosting, I was relegated to the telephone tree to inform everyone where to meet on Friday night.

Saturday morning meant meeting at the deli, eating lunch, and walking to Eastside Park where the boys and some of the girls might play tennis. I had my father's old wooden tennis racket for show. I was anxious lest I be left out of something—a Friday night party, a huddle on the playground, or an after-school invitation to play canasta at someone's home.

My life went on in this manner for the remaining years of elementary school. I had a few close friends outside of the social group, but I continued to hover in the group's light, building the self-assuredness I would need to strike out on my own.

# MY STORY...

*Describe a situation in which popularity played a role in your childhood.*

# MY STORY...

# The "Drip"

P E was one of the most vulnerable times of the school day for the "drips." As we all changed into royal blue one-piece bloomers in the locker room, I was sure to imitate the girls who knew the cool way to wear them. I rolled up the short sleeves, then tucked the mid-thigh puffy bloomers securely under hiked-up elasticized cuffs to make them sleeker and shorter.

Cynthia seemed oblivious. She dressed in a corner, hiding her undershirt and panties. No one wore an undershirt. By then I had convinced my mother to buy me a AAA training bra to cover my nonexistent breasts. Cynthia obviously hadn't caught on to that, nor did she arrange her bloomers the right way.

Taunting this girl was locker room entertainment for the social group. "Baby! Baby! Where are your breasts? You don't even have any hair under your arms!"

Too innocent to protect herself, Cynthia crossed her arms over her chest. I shuddered and didn't participate, but I didn't defend her. I was a coward, too afraid to jeopardize my tenuous standing in the social group.

One day on the playground, a few of the girls pulled baby rattles from their pockets. They shook them at Cynthia saying, "Baby want her rattle? Baby want her rattle?"

She shook her head and backed off. They crowded closer to her. I watched. My body was trembling. I wanted to cry out, "Stop it!" but I couldn't. Instead I cringed in silence.

Cynthia ran, and they ran after her, all the while yelling, "Don't you want your rattle?"

I played the scene over in my mind before sleep, weighing different intervention scenarios, but I couldn't muster the courage to speak in the ensuing days. I knew that by allowing my "friends" to taunt her I was guilty too, and it plagued me. A disturbing memory of this unfortunate girl emerges now and again, and it evokes the shame of my youthful impotence.

# MY STORY...

*Were you ever complicit with bullies? How did it affect you at the time and in your later life?*

# MY STORY...

# A Torso in the Window

Self-importance swelled my twelve-year-old ego when I paraded "my" baby girl up and down the residential streets of one- and two-family homes on East Thirty-First Street. This first summer job as a mother's helper fulfilled my nurturing instincts with the joy of caring for an eighteen-month-old blonde toddler.

When I dressed her in the morning I nuzzled close to smell her baby-ness, that fragrance unique to bathed and powdered privilege. I chose a stroller to walk through the neighborhood in the morning before the day's mugginess claimed the outdoors.

Our final destination was Park Avenue, where the local shops lined two blocks. I might have an errand or two for the mom, picking up a prescription from the pharmacy or buying fresh rye bread and meats from the deli. Most of the shopkeepers knew the family, and when they fussed over the baby I felt as proud as if I were her mother.

One warm Saturday morning, wearing cuffed-up shorts and a

baby-doll blouse, I sang "Old MacDonald" as I pushed the stroller and encouraged "my baby" to respond with the appropriate animal sound, as I had learned to do when caring for my brothers.

I stopped to pick a dandelion puffball and blow the seeds into the air. I bent down to smile into baby's face, and then I heard a wolf-whistle from above. "Whip-woo. Whip-woo."

The whistle wouldn't be for me I knew, and I stood at the handle of the stroller ready to move on.

"Whip-woo. Whip-woo."

This time I looked up to see where the sound originated. It was a second-floor window, open wide with a lace curtain swaying at either side. There in the window was a naked male torso, its penis gyrating for attention.

I reached for a blanket to cover my baby's face. She cried, and I hustled down the street before removing the covering from her eyes.

I was stupefied by the starkness of this nude torso, pale as a winter sky. Rather than tell anyone and avoid the scene, my curiosity drew me back to that block on my own. Although I felt furtive and unclean, I couldn't help wondering about that torso and why I chose to revisit the site of that open window.

Two years later I overheard a conversation about the family who lived in the apartment of the dangling penis, and I was able to identify their eldest son. I had seen him in the halls of Eastside High School, tall, blonde, with a pompadour that fell across his right eye. He seemed to ooze sexuality, and I wondered what bizarre notion led him to display his body the way he did.

# MY STORY...

*Did you have a similar unsettling experience of a sexual nature that you were too embarrassed to tell anyone? What did you do, and how do you think about it in retrospect?*

# MY STORY...

# She Couldn't Do It

One day I heard my mom talking on the phone to her sister. "He stopped taking the Miltown. Won't take pills for anxiety."

—"No. Says he can control his temper. He's getting worse."

—"I know that I could get a job with Scott Company as a bookkeeper," she said. "Could we live with you until I find an apartment? His mother would take care of him. It would only be me and the kids."

That night I heard my parents whispering in their bedroom on the other side of the wall. I heard the hushed speech, not the words. Then a long wail. "Noooooo! You can't do that," my father sobbed. It seems like he cried all night.

The next morning when I was getting breakfast before school, I looked into their bedroom and saw him lying in bed with the covers thrown off, curled into a fetal ball. Mom was seated at his side, and she glanced at me with red eyes. She got up and shut the door.

I could still hear him moaning, "Don't leave. My stomach hurts. The pain is killing me. Call the doctor."

"I won't leave you, Shhh. I won't leave you."

"I need the doctor."

And that's how it went. Every time my mother gathered the courage to leave him, my father had a stomach attack, and she promised not to go.

MY STORY...

*Did anyone in your family suffer from a condition that seemed agonizing for you or others? How did it affect your life?*

# MY STORY...

TEENAGE YEARS

# My First Date

I began my Saturday *toilette* in the afternoon hours before Mark's seven o'clock arrival. A few days earlier, my gangly friend with oversized feet, a peach-fuzz mustache, and a voice that often cracked or rose mid word had invited me to a movie.

He had stammered, "Uh. I mean…would you like to go to the movies with me on Saturday night? Um…my father can drive us." His adolescent voice came in bursts and broke on the word *movies*, rising an octave. He blushed and faced me.

I had been eager to accept. "What will I wear?" was my first thought, and even before answering yes I envisioned my new green pleated jumper skirt and matching blouse.

Now I laid out my outfit and strategized how to get enough time in the bathroom that served all six of us. I waited until my five- and eight-year-old brothers were watching cartoons on the television set before I got into the tub, anticipating a long, bubbly soak. Before filling it, I washed and rinsed my hair under the running faucet, but as soon as I closed the drain, I heard a knock on the door.

"Let me in. I gotta go." The door wasn't locked, but we were all trained to knock first.

*Darn.* I could imagine Jon jumping up and down holding on to his crotch, so I pulled the shower curtain around the bathtub and called, "OK, come on, but hurry up."

I knew Michael would follow suit, so I waited to fill the tub since I didn't want to spoil the pleasure of pouring the bubble powder into the running water and watching it foam up.

Finally, I sat back in a tub full of light-infused bubbles, languidly raising each leg in turn like the ballerina I imagined myself to be. I lay back and closed my eyes, dreaming of a Cinderella evening.

Following the bath, I set my hair in curlers and sat under the plastic hood of my portable hair dryer reading *Seventeen* magazine and pondering which makeup would pass muster with my father.

Dressed after dinner and awaiting the doorbell, I paced through the living room and the dining room. All of this primping was too much for my father's brand of humor to resist.

"When will Mmm-arrk get here?" he asked, his voice rising in the middle to mimic the inevitable crack he'd hear.

"Da-aad! Don't you dare embarrass him."

"Why-eee not?" he mocked with a crescendo.

"Oh, you!" I stomped my foot, annoyed by his continual teasing, swerved around, and huffed my way to the kitchen to wait with Mom.

———————■———————

Mark rang the bell, looking special in a jacket and tie. He greeted my dad with, "Hello, Sir," and promised to have me home on time. I unclenched my fists, relieved to be out the door without Dad's ridicule.

Mark and I sat in the backseat, rigid and silent while Mr. Hirsch drove us downtown to the Fabian Theater where Mark bought our tickets for *April Love*. Once inside, we groped our way into seats and blinked in the unfamiliar darkness. The sound of candy wrappers, shuffling feet, and hushed whispers filled the movie house, and the longer we sat, the queasier I felt from the smell of buttered popcorn. We sat side by side, my sensing Mark's awkwardness, and feeling edgy in return.

I tried to concentrate on the opening credits. *Photographed in CinemaScope* and *DeLuxe Color*. I could feel Mark squirming in his seat, unsure of what to do. Other couples were settling in, arms draped over shoulders. We sat erect in unaccustomed silence.

I became absorbed in the movie, thinking how cute Shirley Jones was as a tomboy, and I tingled when Pat Boone sang the title song. Mark and I were still trying to ignore the discomfort between us when Liz (Shirley Jones) bent over and kissed Nick (Pat Boone) on the cheek. Emboldened, Mark reached for my hand. We relaxed after that, but I was afraid to move and disturb the fragile bond we had made.

Mr. Hirsch was at the curb after the movie, and when we climbed into the backseat, Mark reached out to resume our tentative connection. Our clasped hands rested on the seat between us on the way to a dairy barn outside of town. Mark's dad waited in the car while we went in for ice cream and sat opposite each other licking our cones. I sensed that Mark was stalling, pausing between licks to prolong the evening perhaps, but soon enough we were back in the car, our hands once again intertwined.

"What flavor did ya have?" Mr. Hirsch asked.

"Chocolate," Mark said with a heavy stress on the first syllable, a vocal signal for Mr. Hirsch to butt out.

Mark walked me to my front door. I opened it, and he followed me into the lighted hallway. He stepped close, and when he leaned in to kiss me goodnight, I saw the dark fuzz of a forthcoming beard on his face before he pecked at my lips and vanished.

I rested my head against the closed door to review the evening in my mind, but was interrupted when my mother scampered toward me from the kitchen in the back of the flat.

"Did you have a nice time, Hon?"

"Mom, he kissed me goodnight, but it wasn't anything."

"Yeah, I know," she said as she hugged me and walked me toward my bedroom.

"Was that it?" I thought. Where was the glamour? Where were the butterflies I expected to feel in my stomach? I didn't feel anything that Shirley Jones seemed to feel, and I undressed for bed wondering what all the fuss was about.

# MY STORY...

*Relate the details of your first date. How did it originate, what did you do, and how did it meet or not meet your expectations? When and where was your first kiss and how did it feel?*

# MY STORY...

# What's Wrong With Dancing?

Sweat moistened my armpits where new hairs had sprouted, and perspiration soaked my swimsuit. I was dancing along with American Bandstand trying new steps in front of the full-length mirror on the hall closet door, my back to the living room TV. Perhaps my hips gyrated a bit more than they might have in public, but at thirteen I was beginning to feel the stir of puberty.

*"Well I said come over baby we got chicken in the barn oooh... huh...*

*I said shake it baby shake it. Come on over. Whole lot of shakin' goin'*

*on ..."*

*Dang!* The television went dead. I turned to see what had happened, and there was my father watching me, his hand on the TV knob. He wore his familiar scowl, mouth turned downward, neck veins throbbing.

"That's disgusting! Go and put some clothes on, and don't let me see you like that again!"

I ran to my bedroom, the one I shared with Nana, tears mingling with sweat. She had been resting in her bed across from mine, thick stockings rolled down to her ankles, print duster unbuttoned at the collar revealing the translucent skin on her neck and chest. She was waving a straw fan in front of her face.

"Something happened?" she said.

"What's wrong with dancing? I was only watching TV and dancing by the mirror. He turned it off and yelled at me. Why?" I wiped the sweat and tears from my cheeks with my fingertips and knuckled my eyes.

"Ah, your papa is tired. It's easy to make him upset."

"He's always upset. I hate him!" I flung myself on my bed and buried my face in the pillow crying, "I hate him. I wish he would die."

"A *shandeh*, a shame to talk about a father like that. Tsk, tsk, tsk," said Nana.

As I lay crying, blocking out Nana's words, I wondered, "Where's Mom?" I sobbed louder, but still she didn't come to soothe me, and I knew that my father had forbidden her again. *Why do you always have to listen to him?*

I sniffed back my tears and gave up on my mother, but during my silence, Nana droned on.

"Tsk, tsk, tsk. No respect for a father. A *shandeh*."

*Oh, shut up.*

*But what if I am a bad person?* "Disgusting," he had said, and I had wished ill, even death, for my own father. He and Nana planted the seed of self-doubt that day, and it grew to a leafy plant that encroached on my flowering consciousness.

*How did your parent(s) react to your growing maturity? What doubts did you have about your own self-worth? Can you pinpoint their origin?*

# MY STORY...

# Making New Friends

Moping is a good fallback for a young teenager when life doesn't cooperate, and I did *maudlin* well. In midafternoon I reclined on the camelback sofa in my bathrobe, head resting on the arm I had draped over the hump, legs drawn up under me. I sighed. I grieved like a dying swan.

My first year at Eastside High School was about to begin, and I dreaded going back to school. Instead of welcoming the opportunity to meet new people, I feared the inevitability of losing my connection to "the social group," although I'd grown tired of keeping up with them. They would join one of the two popular sororities, but I wanted to be true to myself, not one of their social set.

We had moved to this neighborhood and school before I entered sixth grade, and I had made friends then, but not without angst. Now at age thirteen, I would be facing newness once again.

Mom joined me on the sofa after enduring my *mope* for two days. She pulled me into her embrace, and I nuzzled close to her.

She smoothed my hair, fingered my curls.

"What are you suffering from?" she asked, her voice soft, comforting.

"I don't want to go back to school."

"Is it the new kids from other schools? Change again after you got used to your friends here?"

I nodded.

"Do you remember the ice cream social you had when we moved here?" she asked. "It helped with getting to know the kids."

"Sure, but we can't make ice cream sundaes and play stick ball in the street anymore, Mom. I'm in high school."

She had known that my leave-taking from "the social group" was imminent. Given my growing interest in art and literature as well as my longer periods of quiet thought, she knew of my approaching independence with greater certainty than I did.

"What about a dance party?"

"Oh, sure. Right in our tiny living room in this flat," I snapped.

"No. Let's make a party in the garage," she said.

"But it's old and musty and…"

"And it's big, and kids can't harm the furniture," she said. "You could have it about a month after school starts when you'll know who you want to invite. You'll meet your friends from the old neighborhood…"

"…and some from other schools that I know from the 'Y.'"

Mom and I would transform the nearly empty two-car garage into a party room. It was perfect, because the doors slid sideways on a track and we could leave one side open to the driveway.

I jumped off the sofa and came back from my room, now dressed in shorts and a shirt and holding a pad and pencil. We began our "to do" list:

1.  Get Dad to string up more lights, lots of lights.

2.  Order a keg of birch beer.

3.  Buy cups, plates, napkins, and crepe paper.

4.  Buy balloons.

5.  Make a "Welcome" sign.

6.  Drag a worn rug into the garage.

7.  Borrow a phonograph and my friends' 45-rpm records.

8.  Make and distribute invitations.

---

It didn't take as long as I had feared to reconnect with old friends and develop an interest in new ones. As the time approached I began to create invitations. Using my favorite South Sea Blue ink and perfect penmanship I wrote and distributed individual notes to each guest:

> Please come to a party with music, dancing, and
> snacks at my house on October 4, 1958…

Alone in the garage the night of the party I waited, handling each vinyl record and worrying. I had all the good songs—*All I Have to Do is Dream, The Witch Doctor, Catch a Falling Star, Tequila, The Purple People Eater.* The birch beer keg was in place and the tap worked.

I had sampled it. A mild breeze fluttered orange and black crepe paper streamers that Mom and I had tacked over the open doorway.

I ambled around to sample the snacks—chips, nuts, frosted chocolate cupcakes that we had labored over, and dishes of M&Ms. I consulted my watch. The sun had set about six thirty, but it was still light at seven and I peered down the long, empty driveway. I thought about walking to the curb to look for cars or walkers, but I was concerned my anxiety would be obvious if someone caught me checking for arrivals.

Mom poked her head out from the back door.

"No one's here yet," I said.

"They'll be here. You'll see."

Soon a small group of girls wandered up the driveway, followed by some boys and more girls. They all drifted in, someone set up the phonograph, and the party began.

As the dusk turned to dark, the music played, the birch beer keg was tapped, and we danced in the garage and on the driveway. A warm familiarity developed as girls gossiped in corners of the lighted garage, and guys punched each other in the arm, laughing and heckling. I danced with most of the boys during that perfect evening.

My mother appeared as an occasional apparition to refill candy bowls. She cast an essence of parental order—not enough to embarrass me, but enough to provide assurance and calm.

When the designated time arrived, my mom went out to meet the parents who had come to collect their teens. She knew some from her volunteer work at the "Y," and she introduced herself to others. A gracious woman, she always filled the void left by my father's increasing unsociability.

As the weeks passed I found my place at Eastside High School, resumed contact with old friends, and formed new relationships. I eventually did join a sorority, the *other* one, the one with an eclectic mix of accepting girls who met at the Paterson "Y," my home away from home since early childhood.

# MY STORY...

*If you had to change schools when you were young, how did you adjust? What was it like for you to make new friends? Describe your high school friends, how you chose them, and the activities you enjoyed together.*

# MY STORY...

# A Dreamy Smile and a Thick
# Black Pompadour

One summer day two teenage guys, hair slicked back into DAs and driving a 1957 aqua Chevy Bel Air with white tail fins, pulled up near the curb and crept alongside me while I was walking on Broadway near McLean Boulevard in Paterson. I tried not to look. Kept walking. Upped it to a stride.

I wore "short shorts," not provocative because I was physically immature for my fourteen years, but nevertheless, I was a lone young girl, languid, strolling on a wide but not busy street.

"Hey, get in and we'll go for a spin," said the one leaning out the window. I sucked in my breath when I saw his dreamy smile and thick black pompadour. *Gosh, he looks like Fabian.*

After an adrenaline spurt I began to perspire, but I thought of a way to protect myself. In my whiniest voice I called out, "What do you want with a twelve-year-old?" Lying about my age was the only thing I could think of to deter the boys, and it worked.

The car took off with a screech. The back of that Chevy Bel Air with the wide V on the trunk faded into the distance faster than I could read the license plate. My heart continued to flutter as I looked after the fleeing car, and I felt a surge of pride for my attractiveness and witty deception. *Those guys were interested in ME!*

*Describe a particular teenager who sparked your interest and how you interacted with him or her. Describe any close calls you may have had with an aggressive suitor.*

# MY STORY...

# A Summer Romance

My family's usual summer trip to Mootz's no longer held appeal for me when I became a teenager. My father would spend most of his time with my brothers who got to go woodchuck hunting with him, and I would feel the angst of losing his attention. Besides, there wouldn't be any guys my age or much to do at the farm.

The summer I was fourteen I sat arms-crossed in the backseat of the car, nestled against the door and pouting. *I hate this trip.* After two hours in the car the boys were getting rowdy and bumping up against me with their sweaty bodies.

"Will you stop it already?" I yelled at them. Dad pulled off the road and made me sit between them to break up their horseplay. Now I would have to contend with their sticky arms reaching across me to shove one another.

Our irritable family arrived at the Mootz farm three hours later and unpacked the car as usual. We rested in our cabin until dinner, and then, halfheartedly, I shuffled along to the dining porch.

"Why do I have to be here?" I grumbled. "I'm tired of this place. Why couldn't I stay home with Nana?"

"Oh, hush up," my father said.

I slumped into my dining chair and looked around. Same old people, I thought, until I saw him—a slim young man with a blonde crew cut, maybe a year or two older than me, sitting at the opposite end of the plank table. He looked my way and smiled. I sat up straight and ate my dinner with impeccable manners.

I lingered on the steps after dinner and ambled away from my family toward a remote pair of lawn chairs. Tom took the hint, and we were soon in eager conversation about his home in Virginia and what good fortune it was to have met each other.

As the evening wore on, we strolled the farm's vast lawn, tramped through the grain fields beyond, and dawdled on the path near the creek.

When dusk settled he said, "Ask your parents if you can stay out later."

Dad gave me the usual, "Watch yourself. Don't stay out too late."

A full moon rose that evening, bright, almost orange. We sat on a bench apart from the lingering guests and he took my hand and held it. We listened to the nighttime noises of owls and insects, convinced that each sound was especially for us. Everything about the evening became ours—"our moon," "our crickets," and "our owl." When we heard my father's footsteps approaching we dropped our clasped hands.

"I'll see you at breakfast," he whispered into my ear.

We were inseparable for the remainder of the week, mooning

and hand-holding, kissing with lips closed, walking through fields with a picnic lunch. By the end of our stay my parents had met his family and approved of our writing to each other.

"Promise you'll write," he said when we parted that last day.

"Every day," I answered.

———————■———————

In August I started my job as a counselor-in-training at a local day camp, and my responses to Tom's love letters became less frequent. Toward the end of the summer I received a letter of a different nature. Tom wanted to take the train from Virginia to New Jersey to visit me over Labor Day and, without much enthusiasm, I fell into planning our weekend together.

When I saw him again, I noticed his acne and his too-slim physique as if for the first time. *This is the same boy?*

During his stay, my parents took us for a Sunday ride in the Buick without Nana and my brothers. He nudged closer to me in the backseat. I nudged closer to the window and looked out. He reached for my hand. I withdrew it. We sat in silence. My mother turned around, and seeing us sitting apart, she jerked her head toward him as if to say, "Be sweet and hold his hand."

It wasn't to be. He left the next day, a very disappointed young man, a sad casualty of summer love.

# MY STORY...

*What do you recall about a summer romance or the first time a relationship ended? Describe your feelings when you met, what you did together, and how you felt when you parted.*

MY STORY...

# Love in the Mountains

Cousin Fanny's grandparents lived in a small town in the Catskills, and as children she and I visited them for a week or two during the summers. Grandma and Gramps's house, a source of wonderment, was a gray clapboard Victorian with a wraparound porch. There were endless things to discover about the house, especially in the two-story circular turret with curved windows on each level.

"Let's go up in the turret," I would have said.

The shaded windows were always closed, and both floors were crowded with dust-covered remnants of former lives. It was musty and dark, and the first time we crept in there we had to thread our way through boxes and sheeted furniture.

On subsequent visits Fanny and I became bolder. We uncovered late nineteenth-century chairs with sagging needlework upholstery and a sofa with carved flowers. We rifled through yellowed boxes of old photos.

Other times we explored the cellar where Great-Grandma's green tomatoes and sour pickles floated in brine-filled wooden barrels. Near the brambles, we gathered Highbush blueberries for pies. Gramps took us to the summer carnival and to the local Fourth of July fireworks. We read comic books on the porch swing.

———————◼———————

When our teenage hormones kicked in, our interest in boys replaced the lure of the turret and the pickle barrels, but our physical maturation occurred on different timelines. Cousin Fanny's breasts announced an early start to womanhood, and her height and wavy blonde hair added allure. I was still waiting for my feminine figure, although my interest in boys was keen. We mooned over movie star magazines, and Fanny even sent away for autographed photos of Fabian and Tab Hunter.

One day we lounged on the porch, bored and listless in the summer heat. We talked about the boys we knew at home and about Saturday evenings in Fanny's basement dancing to rock and roll 45-rpm records with our friends. We joked about how girls jitterbugged with each other if the boys wouldn't dance and about playing spin-the-bottle when we wanted to generate some excitement. We laughed thinking about the elected couple who would go into another room where they might share a chaste kiss, or pretend they had.

That sultry day in the mountains we had little interest in the movie magazines. They lay on the nearby table along with sweating glasses of lemonade. The porch swing chains squeaked as the lushly padded two-seater swayed from the overhang. I scratched the mosquito bites on my bare legs.

"I wish there were some boys we could meet here," said Fanny.

For the first summer ever, I wanted to go home to Paterson.

Fanny's Aunt Sarah came out to the porch and sat on the wicker chair beside the swing.

"What are you girls going to do today?" she asked.

"We're bored," said Fanny. I was glad Fanny said it, because as a guest I felt I had to be cheerful.

"No berry picking? Want a ride into town to go shopping?"

"No," said Fanny. "We want to meet some boys."

"Ahh." Aunt Sarah raised her eyebrows and nodded her head. "I see. Well, maybe I can do something about that," she said as she rose to go inside. I watched her walk away and imagined that Fanny would look like her one day. She would be glamorous, and I'd be skinny forever.

⬛

On Saturday we fussed over our appearance all day, because Aunt Sarah had organized dates with two young men, sons of local families whose parents were happy to arrange an outing at her suggestion. I had my hair in rollers. Fanny's did its usual gorgeous thing, flowing to her shoulders in gentle waves with her thick bangs lying perfectly straight. We wore our new wash-and-wear skirts and blouses with rolled sleeves.

Jonathan and Stuart arrived in chinos and button-down, short-sleeve shirts. Their crew cuts stuck straight up. Both were sixteen and had cars, a rural necessity. This evening they carried our sweaters to Stuart's car and opened the doors for us. Aunt Sarah watched from the porch.

Jonathan claimed Fanny, and they sat in the backseat on the way to the movies. I sat in the front next to Stuart. He was sweet-natured, attentive, and polite. He worked in his father's store, and planned to expand it when his father grew old.

The four of us were together for as much time as they could spare from their summer work. We went to the carnival and Stuart held me tight while I squeezed my eyes shut on the roller coaster. We went to the movies, and we drank lemonade on Grandma's wraparound porch. Stuart put his arm around me when he drove, while Fanny and Jerry necked in the backseat. Stuart and I kissed in the back when Jerry drove.

Fanny and I were enchanted, and we left for Paterson at the end of our visit knowing our memories would sustain us for the school year. Perhaps the feeling of having arrived as real teenagers was as important to us as the actual relationships we'd had. When school opened we had stories to tell, and that was a thrill in itself.

Thoughts of the summer dimmed with the beginning of high school activities. I didn't think about what my relationship with Stuart might have meant to him, a boy from a rural town, and I was surprised that he called me regularly that year. We didn't talk of love, but rather about day-to-day goings-on. Stuart had become a good friend.

<hr>

I didn't go back to visit Fanny's family again, because I began working summers as a day camp counselor. Stuart and I continued to talk on the phone and he came to visit once or twice. Once we spent the day in Manhattan, going to a Broadway play and afterward to Lindy's for their famous cheesecake. But our relationship had changed, and Stuart didn't even try to kiss me. Things appeared to be what we girls called "platonic."

Even during the four-year period between ages sixteen and twenty when I had a serious boyfriend, Stuart continued to call. He was a backstage presence in my life. Our conversations were casual, and on occasion he asked about my boyfriend. He didn't mention having a girlfriend, and he continued to work in his father's business while I was in college.

"How are your classes going?" he might ask, or "Have you been to the City lately?"

One time he said, "Jonathan's marrying his high school girlfriend."

I wondered about Stuart's social life and finally ventured to ask, "Are you dating anyone?"

"No."

Stuart talked about the store and how he was preparing to take over when his father retired. Once a year he made a casual visit to New Jersey, but I was shocked by the nature of his June visit the year I graduated from college.

I assumed he was coming to congratulate me, but he had a different agenda. That evening while at a restaurant, he got quiet and then flushed. He fumbled in his pocket and withdrew a small gold box which he held open, revealing a solitaire diamond ring.

"May I put this on your finger?" he asked.

Now it was my turn to flush. My head buzzed, and I was speechless.

"Are you blushing? Does it mean that you'll marry me?"

Stuart had been my friend. We hadn't been romantic since my first visit with Fanny. We hadn't kissed since. Then it occurred to me that he had been waiting. Waiting for seven years.

He sat across from me waiting still, this time for an answer. He scrutinized my reaction, and when I searched his face I found the same boy with the blonde crew cut and the button-down shirt I had met seven summers ago. He was taller and beefier, but I knew that this small-town young man would be the same in middle age and even old age as he was then.

It terrified me to imagine a small-town existence without the excitement of city life.

Stuart saw it in my face. He knew the answer before I could speak. His eyes deadened and he replaced the ring in its nest and put it in his pocket. Head down, he peered at me from under his brow. His silent resignation was unbearable.

I began to chatter. "You knew I was going to graduate school. I'm going to Michigan in September. I'm not ready to marry, I—"

"You don't have to talk anymore. My parents came with me, and they're at the motel waiting. Will you meet us for breakfast in the morning?"

I nodded and hung my head. He paid the bill and drove me home in silence. After our dismal breakfast with his parents the next morning, I neither saw nor heard from Stuart again.

*What can you remember about a blind date or an early romance? Do you recall any misinterpreted relationships with people you dated? How did they work out?*

MY STORY...

# A Nightmare Resolved

In 1958 when I was thirteen years old, I read *The Wall* by John Hersey, followed by Anne Frank's *Diary of a Young Girl,* and *Exodus* by Leon Uris. *The Wall* is narrated as a first-person diary of one of the 40 escapees from the dehumanizing Warsaw Ghetto where more than 400,000 Jews were confined to a part of the city that encompassed little more than a square mile. Escapees were shot on sight.

WWII newsreels with parades of goose-stepping soldiers and heartrending images of concentration camp victims lingered in my imagination, and these visuals fueled my nightmares.

In one version I was alone on a playground that stretched to infinity. The wind came up. My dress blew around my knees, and lightning streaked the sky. Through the rush of the wind and cracks of lightning I perceived Nazi soldiers, rows of them marching behind me and then breaking ranks to chase me.

The scene changed to our former flat on the third floor where the chase continued. I ran toward the front stairs that spiraled down three floors and burst through the door to the stairwell. The Nazis were gaining on me. I leaped onto the first stair, and then I took them three at a time. I looked back to see the soldiers still behind. My toes barely touched each step as I sprinted forward, skipping three, four steps at a time. In a splinter of time I was safe.

I awoke gasping, but I had learned to comfort myself. I would sit up in the dark and listen to my grandmother snoring lightly in her bed across the room, reminding myself I was safe at home. I took slow, deep breaths. I became alert to house noises, and hearing nothing amiss, I would snuggle down and close my eyes, calm and ready to sleep again.

*Do you recall learning about the Holocaust or other horrific world event when you were a child? What effect did it have on you? If you were ever in the midst of a terrifying experience or nightmare, how did you respond?*

# MY STORY...

# Dinnertime Feuds

Anti-Semitism was rampant in post-war days, and my father had experienced it before World War II and throughout his working life. Someone might have *accidentally* shoved him in the corridors at work. "*Kike*" resounded in his ears as if it had been bellowed and not murmured. The aftereffects of his trauma visited our dinner table when he mocked his non-Jewish coworkers and disparaged other ethnic groups.

He seized on opportunities to extol the hard work and good sense of the Jewish community as opposed to the *goyim*. "We Jews make something of ourselves," he'd say. "We're hard workers, smart, and you'll never hear of a Jew getting drunk and beating his wife."

Dinnertime grew more uncomfortable when I was old enough to challenge my father's distorted aggression. I confronted him on his use of stereotypes, and the dinner hour became a battlefield. The more he vented, the angrier I became.

During these stormy dinners, my brothers would shrink into their chairs. My mom might have said, "Har, that's enough," but she was meek, and he washed away her plea the way an incoming tide obliterates castles in the sand.

Nana would begin to clear the table, and Mom would follow her into the kitchen. Michael and Jon would drift away into their own worlds, and I carried on a righteous battle until my father slammed his fist on the table and shouted, "You don't know what you're talking about."

His solution to my logic was a win by *force majeure*. He was older, louder, and resorted to intimidation to end our debates. I would leave the table in face-saving indignation, beginning a pattern that persisted for years.

*Were you or a family member ever a target of prejudice? What were the effects on your family life?*

*What was dinnertime like at your house? Did your family eat meals together or have particular rituals?*

# MY STORY...

# My Jewish Community

A tight-knit community nourished me from early childhood through my young adult years. Elementary school was largely Jewish. In the wider high school population, I enjoyed casual friendships with classmates from other ethnic and religious groups, but my advanced academic classes were heavily Jewish. Even though I was curious and wished for more than brief glimpses of other schoolmates' lives, I was content within my own sphere.

Religious school occupied me on Sunday mornings between ages five and thirteen. While many boys attended more intensive Hebrew School after the regular school day and learned Torah in preparation for their Bar Mitzvahs and lives as Jewish men, few girls had the option in those days. Sunday was the only day of religious instruction for most girls and some younger boys.

I remember religious school at the "Y" in detail, because Israel became a state in 1948, soon after my birth. Our community gave generous support to the new nation, and we had pride in our identity at a time when Jews were building a new homeland after the Holocaust. We stood together in our Sunday morning assembly singing the Jewish national anthem *Hatikvah* in Hebrew, our souls filled with reverence. I didn't learn the English lyrics that expressed hopes for a Jewish homeland until I reached adulthood.

My Brownie and Girl Scout troops met at the "Y" as well, and I took the bus downtown once a week for meetings. We marched in the Labor Day parade as a troop, attended regional jamborees in the armory, and went to Scout camp together. Between public school, Sunday school, Scouts, and family time, there was little room for life outside the Jewish community.

In high school my sorority and social activities took precedence. There were three exclusively Jewish sororities, mostly distinguished by levels of wealth and popularity. At thirteen, I had finally become comfortable with my family's income level and no longer aspired to fit in with the wealthier set. I joined the sorority that was focused more on camaraderie than social status.

We met in members' homes and paired with a boys' group called the Spartans for social occasions at the "Y." Our remarkable youth leader, Moe Liss, sponsored dances and other events for us. My young life had a coherency that nourished my friends and me during our crucial adolescent and teen years. It gave me the confidence to participate with courage and curiosity in the outside world.

# MY STORY...

*Did you ever feel isolated in your own ethnic neighborhood or community? To what extent? What did you feel was the value or disadvantage of self-selected clannishness?*

# MY STORY...

# MY STORY...

# LIFE IN SUBURBIA

# No Jews Wanted

We went hunting for our family's first home when I was fifteen years old. One Sunday afternoon in 1960 my parents and I cruised the nearby suburbs in search of the perfect dwelling, a place of our own with no neighbors upstairs or down, our own garden, even freedom to bang down a wall if Dad had an itch to remodel.

Back then the asking price was printed on the "For Sale" sign, and I read them off as we coasted by: $12,500… $15,000… $17,000.

As Dad drove, Mom would comment. "Looks small." "Too far from shopping." "Too expensive."

Once in a while she yelled, "Stop here, Har." He'd slam on the brakes mid road. Hopes up, I would wait for Mom to write down an address and phone number to telephone the agent, but I hadn't seen the inside of a house yet.

"Why don't we look in Packanack Lake? I heard they have nice houses there," I said.

"Swell. You want to live among the *goyim* who skirt the law to keep you out of their town?" my father asked. "Is that what you want?"

"Jews can't live there?"

"Not unless you want to fight city hall. And I suppose you want to join one of those 'No Jews Wanted' country clubs," he said.

*Ahh. That's why there were two Jewish-only country clubs.*

I had been insulated by my community in school, at play, and at social events. With a preponderance of Jews in our neighborhood, the schools even closed for two days on the Jewish High Holidays.

I fell mute. I pulled my feet up onto the seat and hugged my knees, head bent, tears at the ready. I squeezed myself into a compact ball of misery, and for the first time I identified with the hurt and rejection that overwhelmed my father in the workplace. I didn't say anything more and neither did my folks. The air had been poisoned, the outing ruined.

*Were you aware of de facto segregation of any ethnic or religious groups in your city or town and if so, how did it affect you personally?*

# MY STORY...

# This Is It

A red door and red azaleas under the front windows. A small patch of grass on either side of the walkway. Dad pulled into the single-car driveway of our 1941 brick Cape Cod-style house. It didn't strike my fancy. It was almost the same as all the other houses on the street, too tiny for six people and to my dismay, it had only one bathroom.

"Twelve hundred eighty-three square feet and a huge basement," Dad said when we kids piled out of the car to see it for the first time. He fished out his house key, already on an IOOF (Independent Order of the Odd Fellows) brass key fob, and he flung the front door open to welcome us into our empty house.

I pinched my nose. *Musty.* Achoo! Undaunted, he ran to open the windows.

"Listen to this," he said as he pounded the living room wall with his fist. "That's solid plaster. Built like a brick shithouse."

*Who wants to live in a shithouse?*

Dad spread his arms wide as he beheld the room, and he grinned like the proud Jolly Green Giant on the "Corn Niblets" can.

Mom hovered on the side. She'd seen it and didn't seem any more thrilled than I.

My brothers sprinted through the house to explore its secrets. Mom wandered into the kitchen.

Done with showing off the thick plaster walls, Dad pulled me outside to see the yard.

"Oak trees! Will ya look at that? And over here, yellow forsythia."

"Nice, Dad."

"Wait till you see your room," he said.

Well, that caught my interest. The attic dormer had bright yellow walls, a yellow linoleum floor, and an odd mishmash of slanted walls with an acoustic-tiled ceiling. A door led to a roomy closet in an unfinished attic with extra storage space over the garage.

There was even a window fan in the wall facing the side yard and a space heater along the floor under the front window. Despite my bad humor, I began to imagine how I would furnish this room, the private space I had craved. For the first time, I had a door to shut out the world. I would have a cozy hideaway.

When Dad and I came downstairs, Mom was in the tiny kitchen with all the drawers open, a scissors and rolls of white liner paper on the counter. I saw her rounded shoulders and sagging posture before she noticed us, and I heard her heavy sigh that escaped my dad. I wondered if she had settled for this affordable Cape Cod to live in Fair Lawn with its large Jewish population and quality schools.

Michael and Jon, now twelve and nine years old, broke my musing when they came hurling into the kitchen.

"Hey, you should see our room. The ceilings are slanted all over the place, and there's a huge closet. It's so big we could all walk in it," said Michael.

"Yeah," said Jon. "Coo-ool. We can each have a bed under a crooked ceiling. They're all crooked!"

"Dad has a workbench in the basement," said Mom.

"And you have your own laundry room down there, Moe. We'll get you a washing machine and I know a guy who wants to sell an automatic ironing machine."

"Someday maybe we can finish the basement and have a real rumpus room," said Mom.

"Well," said Dad, "starting tomorrow we'll bring our tools and peel off the living room wallpaper."

It was the only family project I recall. The six of us combined forces to steam off the ugly dark floral wallpaper. We had tin buckets of boiling water for soaking rags. Nana refilled the cooled-off buckets, Michael toted them into the front room, and Jon squeezed out the steaming rags for Mom and me to saturate the wallpaper. As soon as the moisture loosened it, Dad scraped it off. There were four layers of wallpaper, one uglier than the last.

I grudgingly admitted satisfaction and pride of ownership after the big cleanup and our move in. My yellow bedroom walls heard all the teenage confidences my best friend Roberta and I shared. It was there that I studied, wrote poetry, mused in my diary, and talked on my own telephone extension. Short lived though it was, my yellow room became the haven I had always sought.

*Did your family move to a new home while you were growing up, either to a different apartment or into a single-family dwelling? What memories do you have of it and your transition? Which of its attributes mattered most to you?*

# MY STORY...

# A Valuable Find

On the day before we moved furniture into our new home, I explored every nook of my bedroom. I stretched above my line of sight to the closet shelf and ran my fingertips over it. Expecting dust, I was startled to feel a wad of folded paper.

Money! I opened it and counted, feeling stealthy and uncertain about what to do.

I imagined what I could buy if I stashed these four ten dollar bills (worth over three hundred dollars in 2016). New clothes, a record player, toys for my brothers. I put the money in my pocket to enjoy the feel of it. I took it out, unfolded it, and peered at Alexander Hamilton in anticipation of my secret purchases.

I was about to stuff the money back into my pocket when my conscience caught up with me. The money belonged to the old grandpa who had lived in the room before me. Anyway, how could I hide a closetful of new clothes and a record player?

Money in hand, I ambled down a few steps and turned back. *I'll keep it.* Then I started down again, halted, and finally jogged down the remaining narrow wooden steps to turn over the loot.

"Dad, Mom. I found this." With a slow and dramatic reveal of the fisted money, I offered it up.

Dad wasn't hesitant. "That's forty dollars! Moe, we could buy a lawn mower and tools for the garden," he said, taking the money from my open palm.

"Har, I know we can't afford them yet, but…"

"It belongs to the grandpa who lived here," I said.

Dad was quick to answer. "We can't get hold of him now. They moved far away weeks ago. I don't know where."

My father bought a new lawn mower and pushed it back and forth across the narrow swaths of grass, front yard and back, every Saturday. He planted tomatoes and berries behind the back hedges. He clipped and he mowed. He dug and he planted with the well-earned pride of tending to his own home.

# MY STORY...

*Consider the ethics of found money or valuables. What experience have you had finding something of value?*

# MY STORY...

# The Vacuum Cleaner Roars

"There's dirt on the carpet," my father might say at any time of day or evening, even if he had just come home from work or was sitting in his favorite wing chair. It wasn't enough that we all had chores or that we might have dusted and vacuumed the day before. We never left a bit of personal clutter to mar the pristine living room—not a book, not a pencil case, and certainly not one of Jon's die-cast toy cars.

At the sight of a speck of anything, out came the Kirby upright vacuum cleaner, its dust bag inflated, and my father attacking the carpet to rid the house of dirt.

We kids knew to get out of the way when this happened. None of us wanted to be accused of dropping a shred of paper or a particle of lint from a sweater. We'd scuttle to the safety of our attic rooms until the Kirby's buzzing vibrations faded. We waited for a few extra minutes to ensure that Dad had calmed down and put the monster away before we trotted down "the wooden hill," as he called the steps.

There was something else. Late at night I would hear my father rearranging the dishwasher. He had given up on my mother's seemingly haphazard loading, and he undid her "mistakes."

"Things should be done right," he muttered.

As the years passed, my father became even more obsessive. He would poke his head into my bedroom while I was studying and sniff the air to detect something rotting, perhaps an apple core. He would see schoolbooks and notes arranged around me on the floor and say, "Look at all those papers. You could burn down my house. Clean them up."

*His house.* No family house this. I finished high school and began college while living in the brick Cape Cod, but I always longed for the communal warmth that permeated my friends' homes and eluded my own.

*Did you have any childhood experience with a compulsive personality? How did it affect you?*

# MY STORY...

# Starting Over

air Lawn High School was the fourth school I attended and the second time I had to move midway through the school year. I was sixteen when school started in September 1961. I had skipped a grade, was a year ahead of my peers, and had completed two and a half years of high school in Paterson.

Roberta had been my best friend for several years, and she would be a junior at FLHS.

"Should I be a junior or a senior in the fall?" I asked her. The choice was mine to make.

"All your friends are juniors," she said. "Besides you'd have to work real hard to catch up to be a senior."

"Yeah, but I don't want to take classes over. I already took some junior classes."

"All your friends are juniors," Roberta stressed.

"Well..."

"Say yes," she urged.

"Yes," I said, and we jumped up and down together hugging and laughing. "We'll be in the same class!"

I wish the transition had been as easy as the decision. My diary heard all about it:

October, 1961

Dear Diary,
Everyone is white. There aren't any Negroes or
Puerto Ricans. No Cubans. Only white girls. Kids in
school smoke. I lost out on Honor Society, cause the
kids were already picked when I got here, and I was
about to get picked when we left. And…they are so
clique-y. All those cute little cheer leader types. At
least I have two art classes.

April, 1962

Dear Diary,
I went to Greenwich Village today on the bus and
took the subway down. Went to the art galleries.
Wish I could live there. Next time I'm going to iron
the curls out of my hair…and I'll put eye makeup on
when I get on the bus. No one to go with, but I don't
care. Their parents won't let them. Seems like I get to
do more than my friends.

May, 1962

Dear Diary,

I guess I have a real boyfriend now. And he's going to be a lifeguard at the pool this summer. He's so cute. Tomorrow we're going to take a walk in the woods near Saddle River Road, bring a picnic and a blanket…

# MY STORY...

*Did you ever have to move and transition to a new community? If so, how did you make friends? If not, did you ever welcome a newcomer to your class?*

# MY STORY...

# Leslie's Revenge

I was sixteen and Michael twelve when we had a set-to dubbed "the incident of the Coke." Having recently moved to Fair Lawn, we were sitting alone in the tiny wallpapered dinette at the round maple colonial table. Mom was in the kitchen.

We rarely got dessert, so sharing a package of crème-filled Hostess cupcakes and a Coke was a treat, but we couldn't stop quarreling long enough to enjoy the sweets. For the first time I had my own bedroom, and I accused Michael of trespassing. I knew he had taken my diary.

"I know you took it," I yelled. "I looked and I can't find it and I know you took it."

"I didn't," he said.

The arguing went on until Michael, enraged, took his cupcake and smashed it into my face. We both sat up and stared at each other, unbelieving that a tiff could come to this. I licked my lips and used my napkin to wipe the chocolate icing from my eyes. We were silent, fuming, waiting.

In slow motion I picked up the Coke bottle and dribbled the remaining ounces over his head.

"I'll kill her," he roared, and shot up like fireworks.

I ran past my mother at the kitchen sink, dashed into the pantry, and pulled the door shut. Mom ran to the door and protected me with her back against it, arms spread and one hand shielding the knob.

I heard Michael screaming, "I'll kill her. I'll kill her. Let me at her."

After prolonged effort, Mom convinced him to go upstairs and clean up, and I snuck out of the pantry to wash at the kitchen sink. Even after fifteen minutes I listened for his footsteps, still chary of leaving the safety of Mom's kitchen. Michael could be lurking in any corner to exact *his* revenge.

# MY STORY...

*Can you recall and relate the details of your sibling spats or rivalries, either humorous or potentially damaging to your relationship?*

# MY STORY...

# Two Embarrassments and a Faux Pas

**S**pring, 1958: I was a thirteen-year-old freshman at Eastside High School in Paterson, New Jersey, and mortified at the thought of speaking in front of my English class in particular, because the young teacher was good-looking and mischievous. The students' manners reflected the teacher's quirky personality. The girls were gaga and timid; the boys tittered and whispered behind cupped hands.

His outrageous hall pass was a plastic bag with a dead spider inside, and it had to be worn around the neck. I was horrified at the thought of leaving the room with that pass.

On this day the class had to read their essay assignments aloud. *Oh God, please don't call on me to read in front of the class.* Prayers ignored, I was summoned to the front of the room. I trembled in my illusory spotlight wearing my circle skirt with a hooped petticoat and two layers of crinoline underneath. My neck and face were splotchy and getting redder. In a faltering voice, I began to read my essay.

It took me a moment to hear the boys openly laughing and see them pointing at me, because I was terrified and intent on my paper.

"Ha, look at that!" Look, look, look…"

*What did I say? What did I do?*

"Psssst, look down at your skirt," said a girl in the front row.

I discovered that the circular metal band, once secured within the hem of my hooped petticoat, had come free of its casing and hung to the floor beside me. I grabbed the end and pulled it all the way out of the petticoat, snatched the dreaded spider pass from its hook above the side chalkboard, and fled to the girls' room.

It took a long time in the bathroom to recover my confidence. I blew my nose and dabbed at my tears, ensuring that I didn't mess my mascara or eye pencil, and I lingered while replacing the hoop until I heard the end-of-class bell.

When I returned to English class for my books, my teacher stood poker-faced in the front of the room with my essay in his outstretched hand. I fought my way up to him through the exiting students, grabbed the paper, and dashed to my next class, realizing too late that the spider pass was still on the girls' room sink. *Too bad.*

<hr>

**Spring, 1961:** My handsome boyfriend, a lifeguard and lettered trackman, and I had planned a day in Manhattan, because I had never been to the top of the Empire State Building. I wore my pale blue, belted cotton dress with a flared skirt that I'd bought on sale for

$8.99 at Bamberger's in Paramus. A white cardigan and low-heeled pumps set off my stylish outfit.

I'd passed the landmark numerous times on foot and seen it across the Hudson River while driving south on the Jersey side, but to go to the top, the eighty-sixth floor outdoor observation deck, with my boyfriend—that would be a treat.

After the bus from New Jersey and a subway ride, we approached the tallest building in the world and eyed the snaky line of people waiting outside. We bought our tickets for the manually operated elevator to the observation deck and joined the line.

It was a breezy, warm day, and he held my right hand while I clutched my small purse in my left, occasionally using it to smooth my windblown skirt. The wait was long, but our hand-holding, body-brushing, blushing, and grinning helped pass the time.

"Can we stop for a minute to look at the lobby and those deco elevator doors?" I asked.

After we lingered awhile and I had mentally noted the décor, we made our way into the elevator where the gloved attendant was correct in her every movement and command. Squished in the back, we continued to hold each other's sweaty hands.

When we exited the elevator onto the observation deck, I was stunned by the panorama.

"Wow! Nice, huh?" I said.

The breeze had cleared the air and we could see forever. The wall was chest high, allowing a slight lean over the edge, but there was a transparent barrier above it.

We walked the perimeter, and my boyfriend pointed out the sights that were more familiar to him than to me. We put a coin into the telescope and gawked at the nearness of the skyline.

I remember facing him one moment and then not being able to see him the next. A heavy gust of wind had blown across the floor of the brick deck and swirled upward, taking my flared skirt and crinoline with it, pressing them tight across my face. The wind held them there, exposing my legs and torso all the way to my twenty-one-inch belted waist.

With my clutch bag in one hand, I struggled to pull the skirt down, but its circular form continued to whip around my arms and chest while I tugged at the hem covering my face. When the wind died, I smoothed my skirt on all sides and peered at my boyfriend who stood gazing at me, hands in his pockets and a sympathetic smile on his face.

---

**Summer, 1962:** My four-year scholarship was at stake in today's interview at Paterson State College. A decade prior, the college had relocated from Paterson to this 250-acre hilltop campus in Wayne, having purchased former US Vice President Garret Augustus Hobart's original estate and late eighteenth-century Tudor mansion. That structure, in use as the Administration Building, is the focal point of my hapless story.

I wore high-heeled pumps, nylons, and a straight, leg-constricting skirt that summer day, because teachers, even those in training, dressed "appropriately." Unthinkable to wear even a pantsuit. In addition to primping over makeup and clothes, I wore a *fall*, a long hank of fake hair that I twisted and pinned onto my upswept hairdo. I was certain I had to appear mature to get that scholarship.

The interview was to be held on the second floor. A fieldstone pathway led around the side of the manor to the stone staircase at the rear.

Hairdo in place and skirt smoothed, I picked my way across the stone path and reached the stairs unscathed. Grateful that my spiked heels hadn't impeded me, I took each step carefully, holding myself erect, but trembling within.

So focused was I on a graceful ascent that I allowed a thin heel to be caught between two stones, and I fell forward onto one knee. In a frantic spill, I saved a total collapse onto the staircase with out-stretched palms. But, oh! My *fall* had come loose with the jerking motion, and the long hank of fake hair tumbled over my face, the end still bobby-pinned to my hairdo.

Now intent on a dignified recovery, I rose to my proudest height and, seeing no blood, began to re-pin the hairpiece when I heard a voice from below.

"You OK?" The most unwelcome words from the most attractive young man. When his blue eyes smiled, I was ready to melt.

Bruised and somewhat daunted, I smiled back and said, "Fine," but my pride prevented me from engaging him in further conversation.

The interview went well despite my flustered entrance, and although I earned the scholarship, I never met anyone else in college as handsome as the man of my thwarted opportunity.

# MY STORY...

*Describe any embarrassing moments you can recall from your teenage years. Detail the setting, the people involved, and your feelings about what happened.*

# MY STORY...

# A Jew With One Bag Packed

"**N**u? Jewish boy?"

My father asked this question about every boy I mentioned. Our Jewish identity was paramount, the only principle in our lives that held more weight than my father's dominant rule over the household.

His preoccupation was more than the result of workplace harassment, the inability to buy a home in "redlined" communities, and newsreels that brought the horrors of World War II home. It derived from an ancient and ingrained clannish response to anti-Semitism. Hanging together is what Jews have been doing for millennia.

"A Jew always has one bag packed," he would say whenever the opportunity arose.

When younger, I asked what he meant.

"We Jews have been chased from country to country, never safe from *pogroms*, expulsion, and mass slaughter. Who knows when America will turn against Jews? Best to be prepared."

I learned that his expression was figurative, but his hurt was real. He worked for Curtis Propeller during the war years, and then at another factory until his retirement. When he heard a passing coworker mutter *kike* as he frequently did, he simmered scarcely short of a boil. The full measure of his pain erupted at home.

Although the depth of my father's resentment frightened me at the time, the fear of Jewish annihilation has lingered in my consciousness ever since my teenage years.

## MY STORY...

*To what extent was your heritage important in your life? Did you ever experience bias? How was it expressed? In what ways did you band together with others of your ethnicity or religion?*

# MY STORY...

# Romance on the Job

By 4:30 p.m. on Saturday my feet hurt, but the fingers on my right hand continued their rote price-punching on the cash register at S.S. Kresge 5 & 10¢ store while my left hand moved the merchandise—a man's cotton handkerchief, a flute-edged porcelain saucer, a bottle of Jean Naté *friction pour le bain*.

"I love that rose pattern on the chinaware, don't you?" said the perfume-drenched ingénue, orange lips parted wide over protruding upper teeth.

"Yes, it's a nice pattern," I said as I glanced at the rose in the center. It reminded me of the more tedious evenings after school when I "worked the china counter" three times a week instead of this Saturday job on the cash register.

A bump on my hip from the popped-open register drawer jolted me from that dismal thought. I smiled. "That's $3.72, please."

The customer handed me a five-dollar bill that I placed in the till, and I withdrew the change by counting up from the $3.72. I counted it into her outstretched hand, bagged her purchase, and with an automatic smile, I mouthed the requisite mantra.

"Thank you for shopping at Kresge's."

"Ninety cents an hour," I reminded myself.

To pass the afternoon of performing rote tasks, I recounted the events of my lunch break. It was the highlight of my entire S.S. Kresge's week including my three evenings after school.

I held this part-time job in an era when many Cubans flocked to the New York area to escape the Castro regime, and I felt a stirring within when I thought about Arturo who had recently emigrated from Havana.

A very short yet virile Cuban, perhaps in his twenties, Arturo worked in the basement stockroom near the ladies' locker room. He was of Spanish descent with clear light skin and sparkling brown eyes, and he spoke almost no English. He wore a starched white shirt with rolled-up sleeves. The hair on his arms was thick and dark.

When I went downstairs this day to retrieve lunch money from my pocketbook I looked for him, and as I anticipated, he was waiting near the locker room door leaning on his broom handle. He brightened when he saw me. I convinced myself that I needed to practice my Spanish with him, but in truth I think that as a sixteen-year-old I was flattered by his attention, his sincerity, his charm…

"Tiene hermanas?" I asked if he had any sisters to make conversation.

"Si, tengo dos hermanas."

Yes, he had two. He sensed my need to speak slowly, perhaps enjoyed it because he focused on my face with his intense dark eyes as I tried to formulate my Spanish. A nascent smile emerged and lingered on his lips.

I can still see his heart-melting smile today, and at the time I understood that this man who diligently cleaned the basement and shelved the merchandise was well educated and had once been well-to-do. We talked for a while. Then I put my smock in the locker, got my pocketbook, and went upstairs to the lunch counter for a BLT and a Coke.

By 5:00 p.m. on Saturday, still warmed by Arturo's presence, I stood shifting from foot to foot at the register in my fashionable pumps, counting the minutes until my relief showed up and praying that my father would be on time to pick me up in the parking lot. Mom would have a footbath ready, and I could collapse into her arms, pampered and loved.

My cash register relief finally came, and I hurried to the employee locker room to get my things. On the short walk to the corner of the lot, I could think of nothing but getting my shoes off. When I saw my father's 1957 gray Oldsmobile, I hastened to get in and free my feet from the agony of pumps.

Soon I was relaxing in the club chair in our cozy living room, feet soaking in Epsom salts, and aware of Mom preparing dinner in the kitchen. Within the comfort and predictability of home I could recall my meeting with Arturo, a tiny act of risk that awakened my sensibilities. Even though I knew that nothing would come of our talks but an innocent dance of flirtation, I savored the idea of a clandestine adventure, and polished my conversational Spanish in anticipation of our next meeting.

# MY STORY...

*Have you experienced a flirtatious encounter you knew was inappropriate? How did it originate and what became of it?*

*Did you have any experience in your youth with someone who had recently immigrated? Describe it.*

*Explain an after-school job you had as a teenager and how you felt about working.*

# MY STORY...

# Rodin

"The City," as we of greater sophistication, we readers of *The New Yorker* magazine, dubbed Manhattan, lay across the George Washington Bridge, eight miles from Fair Lawn, New Jersey. Before I drove my first car, a Chevy Corvair, I took the bus and subway to visit the great museums, but mostly the "Met." I went every Sunday I could manage until I left the East Coast. In my memory, the skies were always blue, and the trees in Central Park behind the museum flaunted rich and varied greens, leaves aflutter exposing texture and light.

*Ahh!* I sighed with exhilaration as I mounted the Metropolitan Museum of Art's wide steps on Fifth Avenue. Sunday crowds, locals, and decked-out tourists milled on the steps, gaping or studying maps while their kids chased pigeons. The City's acrid fumes never dared hover over that idyllic staircase.

I'd guard my pace upon entry so as not to miss a thing. The

Egyptian tombs on the right, the Greek sarcophagi in the hall on the left, the great dome above. I held back, trying to resist the enticing staircase across from the front door that bade welcome to other awe-inspiring treasures.

Quickly, my eagerness to see the Rodin sculptures on the mezzanine outweighed the delight of the entry's panorama and impelled me to skip up the steps. There I would take time to devour the curves, the shadows, and the pathos of the greatest sculptures in my known world.

I liked to visit the cafeteria with its tables and chairs arranged around a shallow rectangular pool that had a fountain surrounded by marble statues. The eatery was especially wondrous in the off hours when I could sit unbothered, absorb the afternoon calm, and look across at the Tiffany windows in the gallery beyond.

When the afternoon faded, I retreated from my sanctuary back down the bustling steps and south on Fifth Avenue for as long as I dared wander, until the moment I knew I had to catch the subway home. Sometimes I walked as far as the Central Park Zoo on Sixty-Fourth Street or even Columbus Circle on Fifty-Ninth, lost in a fantasy about creating my own sculptural masterpiece. The wonderment of the "Met" remained an inner glow until the first hint of dusk encroached, after which I faced the reality of my home in suburbia.

# MY STORY...

What was your relationship to the arts as a young person? Did you have art or music lessons as a child? How do you feel about museums, city life?

MY STORY...

# Silence

This time it was a black rhinestone-encrusted tube of Revlon Powder Pink lipstick in a faux leather case. I didn't like pink, but it was a peace offering, and we hadn't spoken for at least three weeks. It was longer than usual, although I can't remember the particular issue or the specifics of others we fought about over the years.

Every few days my mother urged me to make up with my dad, to take the blame. Headstrong, I refused to give in. *Why should I?* He'd never admit to losing an argument, and I wouldn't relent. Given our mutual pigheadedness, my father chose silence over further discussion.

He left the room if I came in, or I wouldn't enter if he was there. He ignored me at the dinner table. I didn't go on family outings. I stayed away from home as much as possible. As part of this repetitive cycle, Harold, as I mentally called my father, would one day come home from work bearing a gift. He'd foist it on me, and grab me in a tight hug. Next he'd hold me at arm's length, look into my eyes with tears in his own, and say, "Let's forget this, honey."

The argument was never resolved, nor spoken of again. His pride wouldn't allow my having the last word. The scenario repeated itself time and again from age fifteen until I left home at nineteen in response to his goading. Even after two or more years when my mother ran interference for necessary communication, an uneasy détente with my father persisted for a decade.

Nana had set an example of using silence to deal with discord when my father was a child. During my difficult years with "Harold," Nana also imposed periods of silence on me, although her huff was usually about a perceived injury, and it trailed off some weeks after it began with a gesture or a word or two from one of us.

One day after school, I decided to wash the kitchen/dinette linoleum floor to surprise my mother when she came home from work. I was on my hands and knees on this rainy day, scrub brush in hand, pail nearby, when the back door from the porch to the dinette burst open and Nana appeared. She was about to step onto the newly washed floor with muddy boots.

"Nana, could you please sit on the couch out there to take off your rain boots? I just washed the floor."

"To a grandmother you say this?" she said. Then she marched through the newly scrubbed dinette leaving muddy tracks in her wake. Silence followed for days.

---

Another more virulent form of silence happened one afternoon when I came home from Paterson State College.

I called out to Nana, "I'm home!"

There was no answer. I wondered if she was angry and had decided not to talk to me, but I looked around anyway to see where she was.

She wasn't in the kitchen, so I went to her bedroom. She was sprawled on her lounge chair, seemingly lifeless. An upset bottle of aspirin lay on the nearby table.

"Nana, wake up," I said as I shook her. My grandmother's head lolled, and when she opened her eyes they were blank. I thought I heard her whisper, "See what happens when you disrespect a grandmother?"

I called 911 and, as instructed, I lugged her up from the chair and slung her arm across my shoulder. I paced the floor to keep her awake while waiting for the ambulance, cursing myself for being the evil person who drove Nana to do this. Yet, in a shameful corner of my mind, I wished I hadn't discovered her sprawled in that chair.

*Did your parents ever use the "silent treatment" to punish you? What other, if any, form of punishment did they administer? Can you recall specific experiences?*

*Did you ever feel guilty for your thoughts about a family member?*

# MY STORY...

# What Was I Thinking?

I smoked a delicate and highly polished briarwood pipe with a curved, ebonite stem. My father gave it to me at age seventeen when I asked if I could smoke cigarettes. He taught me how to pack Cherry Blend tobacco in pinches, take a test draw, and light the entire surface with a safety match. I doubt he thought I would actually take it up, the same as he thought I wouldn't start drinking coffee at age twelve when he said I could have some if I drank it without sugar.

Wrong on both counts.

I loved my pipe. I cradled the smooth bowl in my right hand and savored the aroma of the tobacco. It suited the arty image I was trying to portray.

My friend Roberta, on the other hand, smoked Newport menthol cigarettes from a light blue box with a Nike-like swoosh logo. Cool. She looked sophisticated. I noted that cigarettes were more portable than my beloved pipe. She could pull out a cigarette and hang it between her lips a lot faster than I could go through my pipe-smoking ritual.

"Why don't you try one of these?" she asked.

After putting her off several times, the look of the thing finally got to me. I'd be able to sit in the student lounge, buy a cup of coffee, and light up.

One time sitting in the kitchen of her flat, she lit a Newport for me and showed me how to drag.

"I can do this," I thought.

Deep inhalations, coughing, choking, turning red, getting dizzy. I experienced it all while learning to be sophisticated.

"I can't do this, Roberta."

"Sure you can. You'll get used to it."

In a week I was smoking a few cigarettes a day, some mooched, some bought. Now I could be arty in Greenwich Village with my pipe and cool on campus with cigarettes.

---

By the following summer as assistant director of a residential camp for neurologically impaired young adults, I was smoking gold-boxed Benson & Hedges. One of the teenage campers, a math autistic savant, would look around for observers, and when the coast was clear, he'd ask me, "Ya gonna have a Hedges and Bedges now?"

I'd laugh. "Not now, Jerry. I'll have one later."

He'd titter behind his hand and raise his eyebrows, thrilled to be in on a secret.

———————◼———————

In 1966 I flew on an airplane for the first time, a United Airlines DC-6. I was on my way to graduate school in Michigan.

As soon as we were in the air and I had settled down, the stewardess approached. "Would you like a drink?" she asked me.

"A Seven and Seven, please." Talk about sophistication!

She brought the drink and offered me a small box containing four Parliament cigarettes, precisely my style. I sipped and puffed, reveling in the thrill of this new adventure far from my birthplace, with no intention of ever returning home.

———————◼———————

When Roberta first taught me to smoke, I couldn't imagine buying Marlboros by the carton—three dollars and thirty-two cents when I was in graduate school. If I couldn't get a ride to the out-of-town store, I could buy them by the pack in my residence hall's vending machine—thirty-five cents.

I was that stupid. I reached for my first cigarette while still abed in the morning, inhaling and taking the dizziness for granted. Later in the cafeteria after breakfast, I had a second with my coffee. By then I was so dizzy that I had to wait before getting up from the table. No problem. I had allowed time to sit and recover from the light-headedness before going to class.

Still, I thought I was sophisticated, the cigarette hanging from my lips as Roberta's did in the old days.

When living in Berkeley, California, in the summer of 1971, I graduated to those sleek brown cigarettes, Virginia Slims. They were marketed for the elegant gown-wearing, jewel-bedecked woman. The package was enticing, the chic look irresistible.

I tried to quit about six times after that, each time the recidivist. It took the prospect of getting pregnant to finally put it behind me. Forty years nicotine free, but for the first twenty, I still craved a smoke with my coffee or a glass of wine.

Recently, I discovered my briarwood pipe and leather zip pouch with Cherry Blend tobacco in an old box of memorabilia, untouched for forty-eight years. I held the bowl in my palm, cupped my fingers around it, and remembered.

# MY STORY...

*Did you ever have to cope with any form of addiction in your youth—cigarettes, alcohol, eating disorder, drugs—either your own or that of a family member? How, if ever, was it resolved and what steps did you take to resolve it?*

*Did you ever do something risky to be defiant? How did it turn out?*

# MY STORY...

# END OF CHILDHOOD

# Breaking Point

The sandalwood fragrance of a thick brown candle permeated my bedroom and welcomed dusk. A wide array of reference books, scholarly monographs, and my three-ring, loose-leaf binder encircled me on the yellow linoleum floor. My legs were folded under me, book on my lap, and pen in hand to highlight text. The door was closed, and I was in deep concentration.

Intent on my work, I tuned out my brothers' murmurs on the other side of the wall and the occasional movements of my parents and Nana below. The stomping of my father's footsteps on the wooden stairs and the doorknob's violent twist declared an end to peace. "Harold's" face appeared in the doorway, and then he strode in.

He regarded the floor around me with a sneer. His face reddened, and the veins on his neck stiffened. He sniffed the air.

"Put out that candle. You'll burn down my house. And get all those papers off the floor. Tinder. That's what they are." These exact words remain as a scar.

"But, Dad, the candle's stable. I'm careful."

"Clean this up."

"But it's my room."

"It's my house, and if you don't like it, you can get out."

He slammed the door on his way out, and I sat immobile, shocked, and wounded.

———————■———————

After regaining my composure, I thought about what my father had said.

"This is my house, *my* house."

"Yes, *Harold*, it is your house," I thought, "and I don't belong here."

I phoned my best friend, Roberta, and told her that I would be leaving home that night. I couldn't stay with her because she had roommates, but we talked about other possibilities. I had a friend with his own apartment, and he invited me to stay with him until I could find a place to live.

Once the house was quiet that night, I packed my clothing and books, all that I might need for the immediate future, including my candle and a few art books. I owned a used black Chevy Corvair, bought with summer earnings as a camp counselor, endless nights and Saturdays at Kresge's, and babysitting for my art teacher's daughter. This valiant Chevy would carry me far from "Harold" and away from my family home.

Toward midnight I started to load the car, stealthy on the stairs, but not quiet enough. My fifteen-year-old brother, Michael, awoke and asked what was up.

I whispered, "I can't stay here anymore. I'm going to live on my own."

"Yeah," he said. "I know how it is. Wait here."

He went back into his room, and I heard him rifling around. He came out with a fistful of bills.

"Here. You'll need this."

"I can't..."

"I saved it from my Bar Mitzvah. Take it."

"From two years ago?"

"Just take it and call me."

---

Leaving my mother without a word was the hardest part of that night. Later on, separation from Mom troubled us both. I couldn't see another way out. Once a week I came for her and parked in front of the house. We went shopping or out for a meal, but I didn't see or speak to my father for over two years.

My brother was the only one who knew where I lived, and he was sworn to silence. I had found a rooming house on Broadway in Paterson, residential, but tending toward the seedy. A widowed French seamstress had converted her family home, lived downstairs, and had designated the second floor for tenants.

The home had a separate rear access via the narrow side alley. In the evenings, I parked on the street when I came home and remained in the car until no one was on the sidewalk. Then I raced through the dark, ran down the long alley, and bolted upstairs to the safety of my room.

A communal bathroom faced the stairway on the fusty-smell-ing, second-floor landing. A refrigerator stood to its right. Two bedrooms on each side opened onto the landing. My room was to the far right as I came upstairs. Two male pensioners, whom I heard in the bathroom but never saw, occupied the rooms across the hall.

A third lodger in the room next to mine took an interest in me. Esme was shaped like a curved broomstick. Her wispy gray hair was drawn into a bun at the nape of her neck. She wore one of two ancient, but clean, pale housedresses, and she shuffled in her carpet slippers.

I never saw any of the roomers leave the house, and I wondered where they got their food or what they ate. Most likely canned Spam or Chef Boy-Ar-Dee pasta warmed on a hotplate. The refrigerator was nearly empty except for my few purchases.

Esme dusted my room, made my bed, vacuumed and straight-ened. She washed the leotards and tights that I had left on a chair when I came home from evening ballet lessons. She begged to be allowed to do these things, claiming they gave purpose to her day. Accordingly, when I left in the morning I pushed my skeleton key under her door. By evening when I arrived home from school, she had pushed the key back under mine.

Each evening I noted how she had rearranged my possessions. One day my candle was on the right side of the 1930s Chippen-dale dresser with my comb and brush on the other. Another day, Esme might have moved the brown ceramic Arabia cup and saucer, a touchstone for my bridal trousseau, from my bedside table to the dresser. My leotards and tights were neatly folded on my bed. Some-times she asked about my day, and in empathy I invited her to sit beside me on the bed while I told her snippets of my life.

I had arranged to eat most dinners with Roberta and her roommates, and contributed to their food budget. I ate breakfast, an English muffin and coffee, at the corner drugstore on East Eighteenth and Broadway on my way to school. Yogurt from the hall Frigidaire was lunch. I indulged in a donut and coffee at the student lounge if I had extra money. If alone for dinner, I had a beer and some blue cheese on crackers in my room, thinking it was the best source of nourishment for the least money.

Frugality was a lesson I'd learned well. I had a full scholarship for school, including textbooks. I bought mill ends and sewed my clothes from Butterick patterns. I paid thirteen dollars a week for my room, managed my car expenses, and bought food, all with the earnings from three different jobs.

I enjoyed my lifestyle and gloried in the fact that I could live in my own room without interference. My social life was minimal aside from a few friends, but my objective was to do well in college and then go to graduate school. I spent summers directing a residential camp program for neurologically impaired young adults.

My mother anticipated my college graduation with more enthusiasm than I. To me, a bachelor's degree was a step along the way. The thrill of experiencing her daughter attend college and, what's more, graduate with honors, was an overwhelming joy to her, a child of immigrants.

She had been talking about the ceremony since early spring of my senior year, and Mom deeply wanted to host a family party in my honor following the ceremony. I had agreed to the party, because not to do it would be heartless, but I hadn't planned to invite my father to the ceremony.

"Please invite your father to your graduation," my mother asked as the time grew closer. "He misses you, and I hope you don't deprive him of this pleasure."

I relented and got tickets. I planned to meet my parents and brothers at their home in Fair Lawn and drive with them to the graduation ceremony. Nana wouldn't be coming. She was close to ninety and living in a nursing home.

On the day of the event, still in the rooming house, I was combing my hair in front of the dresser mirror when I heard a tentative knock on the door. I assumed it was Esme.

"Come in."

The door opened a crack, and from the reflection in the mirror I saw my father's head emerge, his fingers still around the side of the door. I turned, and he stepped into the room. He looked at me, scanned my surroundings, and stood dumbstruck, mouth agape, tears brimming on his lower lids. Not a word, not a movement, only tears.

After a moment, he reached into his pocket for the white, initialed handkerchief he always carried and wiped his eyes.

"I thought you weren't coming, so I begged Michael for your address."

"It's early still," I said.

We stared at each other. No movement. No words. Then he approached and grabbed me into a hug.

"I didn't know. I didn't know you were living like this. I didn't know," he said.

I accepted the hug, and he whispered, "I'm sorry."

*Where Do I Go from Here?*
https://youtu.be/~suY2sboEUk

# MY STORY...

*Was there a time in your life when you had to make a difficult decision to foster your own growth and well-being? What was the decision? Describe the circumstances that led to your making it.*

MY STORY...

# Jump-Start Your Memoir Videos

*Jump-Start Your Memoir* videos make it easier for you to write your own stories. They offer writing tips about getting started, and how to make your stories more engaging. Kick out the old *I-have-no-time* excuse and start your memoir now!

Share your accomplishment with friends and family by sending me your best 300-words-or-less story for considered inclusion on my rotating *Readers Write* website page. Email me at info@leslierupley.com.

———————◼———————

**Video 1: You Can Write That Memoir Now**
https://youtu.be/C1dTLn6FAFQ
Put aside hesitations and get inspired to begin or finish writing your memoir.

### Video 2: How Accurate is Your Memory?

https://youtu.be/noEJW7Y0hAw

Learn how you can write an authentic memoir even if you can't remember exact details of the past.

### Video 3: Purpose and Audience

https://youtu.be/iQwWLGO0keE

Consider your reasons for writing a memoir, determine who your readers will be, and set your focus.

### Video 4: A Slice of Life

https://youtu.be/QGfIClUC4eI

Decide which aspect of your life you plan to highlight and what you want your readers to learn about you.

### Video 5: Skeletons in the Closet

https://youtu.be/kSJQYEAlUmk

Give considered forethought to family secrets and dark times in your past to avoid inadvertent pain to loved ones.

### Video 6: Axe Those Tired Verbs

https://youtu.be/OBxUvHoy6Xw

Discover how to find and use powerful verbs to add vitality to your writing.

### Video 7: Hook Your Reader with Lively Dialog

https://youtu.be/1vAxNS4TfSE

Replace narrative prose with informative dialog that reflects the speaker's personality.

## Video 8: Paint Unique Characters

https://youtu.be/qSQUvu5FgEk

Use interests, sensory details, and characteristic behaviors to show each person's distinctive temperament.

## Video 9: Paint Vivid Settings

https://youtu.be/tyP4pAJPnBA

Visualize a scene in terms of its unique colors, sounds, odors, textures, and even associated taste. Make each detail capture your readers' imagination.

## Video 10: Where Do I Go from Here?

https://youtu.be/-suY2sboEUk

Stick to it. Commit to revising your stories with the regular support of other writers, online sources, and local classes.

Dear Reader,

In the introduction to this book I explained that my goal is to inspire you to write your own life story. I hope that I've succeeded in evoking your childhood memories and that you are ready to turn them into a memoir!

Since creating my stories, I've led workshops to guide others to write theirs. It's been gratifying to see participants excited to write about newly discovered memories after reading my vignettes.

If you've been similarly motivated, perhaps you can help me to reach others by leaving a review of this book on Goodreads and/or your favorite retailer.

Thanks, and many happy memories!
Leslie

# Acknowledgments

I am grateful to my husband Bill for his enduring support, to my critique partners Ann Damashino and Sheryl Ruzek, to my mentor Camille Minichino, and readers Barbara Grossman, Marilyn Friedman, Arnold Peskin, Ellen Taner, Jon Taner, Michael Taner, Jan Knight, Ruth Oxman, Terryann Satterfield, William Gottfried, Ruth Goldenberg, and Jody Sahlin.

Thanks to my editor, Nancy Silk, and to my designer, Victoria Colotta, for their patience, diligence, and expertise.

# About Leslie

L eslie Rupley is a personal historian and consultant who has written more than a dozen memoirs for her clients. While writing her childhood vignettes she realized that her experience could help others who have wanted to write their own stories. Accordingly, she expanded her memoir to provide tips for them as well as for those who have already begun their journey.

She is the author of *Beyond the Silk Mills*, a historical family saga set in Paterson, New Jersey, the one-time capital of the silk textile industry, where the former mills and Great Falls of the Passaic River that powered them inspired her writing.

Leslie lives in Walnut Creek, California, adjacent to an extensive trail system where she likes to spend her early mornings hiking. Her husband Bill, family, and friends are central to her life, but she also reads, knits, travels, and volunteers. Her remaining time is divided between writing a sequel to *Beyond the Silk Mills*, giving presentations related to her books, and teaching classes about how to begin and improve memoir writing.

Contact Leslie through her website at www.leslierupley.com.

# Stay Connected!

Contact me to comment, ask questions, or schedule workshops. I'm also available to talk at upcoming events. I always enjoy interacting with other readers!

Sign up for my Mailing list at http://eepurl.com/QFW6z

Visit my website www.leslierupley.com

Like me on Facebook at facebook.com/leslie.rupley.author

Follow me on Twitter @leslie_rupley

Follow me on Goodreads at www.goodreads.com/leslierupley

Connect with me on LinkedIn at linkedin.com/in/leslierupley

See the latest videos on my YouTube Channel
at https://www.youtube.com/c/LeslieRupley

Made in the USA
Charleston, SC
24 August 2016